A DICTIONARY

OF

ENGLISH AND WELSH SURNAMES

WITH SPECIAL AMERICAN INSTANCES

BY THE LATE

CHARLES WAREING BARDSLEY, M.A.

WORCESTER COLLEGE, OXFORD

LATE VICAR OF ULVERSTON, LANCS., AND HONORARY CANON OF CARLISLE CATHEDRAL

AUTHOR OF 'ENGLISH SURNAMES, THEIR SOURCES AND SIGNIFICATIONS'

'CURIOSITIES OF PURITAN NOMENCLATURE,' ETC.

REVISED FOR THE PRESS BY HIS WIDOW

Baltimore

GENEALOGICAL PUBLISHING CO., INC.

1980

Originally published: London, 1901
Reprinted: Genealogical Publishing Co., Inc.
Baltimore, 1967, 1968, 1980
English Publisher: Heraldry Today
London, England
Library of Congress Catalogue Card Number 67-25404
International Standard Book Number 0-8063-0022-1
Made in the United States of America

TO

WILLIAM · M^cKINLEY

PRESIDENT · OF · THE · UNITED · STATES · OF · AMERICA

THIS · DICTIONARY · OF · ENGLISH · AND · WELSH · SURNAMES

WITH · SPECIAL · AMERICAN · INSTANCES

IS · BY · EXPRESS · PERMISSION

GRATEFULLY · DEDICATED

PREFACE

BY THE LORD BISHOP OF CARLISLE

At the request of friends I have consented to write a short preface to the *Dictionary of English and Welsh Surnames*, not as possessing any technical knowledge of the subject, but because, as eldest brother of the author, it was assumed that it would be in my power to supply some biographical details which might be acceptable to many of his numerous and attached friends.

Charles Wareing Bardsley was the sixth of the seven sons of the late Canon James Bardsley and of Sarah his wife. He was born at Bank House, Burnley, in Lancashire, December 29, 1843, of which parish his father was for many years the still well-remembered curate. There can be little doubt that his early environments exercised a great influence upon his character and future pursuits. His parents were strong personalities, holding firmly the distinctive tenets of the old Evangelical school with a tendency to Puritan asceticism in the enforcement of their practical Christianity. The times in which our author's childhood was spent were stirring, and as the father possessed the confidence of his fellow townsmen, the life at the old house in which the seven brothers were brought up was an exceptionally full life. Crossing the Yorkshire moors, Burnley was not very far away from Haworth, the home of the Brontës. It was the curacy at Haworth which Mr. Bardsley had originally accepted when on the point of ordination. It was only on the day preceding his ordination at Bishopthorpe that the Archbishop of York, for some private reason of his own, refused to sanction this arrangement, and assigned to him the curacy of Keighley as a title. As Keighley however was conveniently near, the friendship between the Brontës and Mr. Bardsley was not broken, and it was to the parsonage at Haworth that Mr. Bardsley on Saturday afternoons frequently took his young wife to drink tea. When some years subsequently *Shirley* was published, the young couple read the book with keen interest, and were greatly relieved to find that they personally had not supplied any materials for the lively sketches of the three typical curates delineated in its pages. To our author and to his brothers the names of the Brontës and the associations of Haworth were very familiar.

At a somewhat later date the late Philip Gilbert Hamerton (editor of the *Portfolio*) became a school-friend of the writer of this preface. The Worsthorn Moors and the country adjoining the 'Hollins,' so graphically depicted in 'A Painter's Camp,' were traversed together; and many incidents might be recalled to illustrate the literary tastes which that precocious and brilliant youth did much to foster among his friends at Bank House.

A silent but abiding influence was the surrounding country, containing Pendle Hill and the Cliviger district, with its strange superstitions and traditions of Lancashire witches. Rich also was the neighbourhood in ancient ruins of castles and abbeys. Within the limits of a Saturday ramble were Ribchester and its Roman remains; Mytton with its marble effigies of knights in armour and its chained books. Old houses, such as Townley, Royle, Gawthorpe, lying amid lovely sylvan scenery, were open to the sons; by the kindness of a friend of their father the great works of Dr. Whitaker, the historian of Craven and of Whalley, were accessible, and the *Traditions of Lancashire* by Roby were their constant diet.

The old home—Bank House—in which the sons were brought up also exercised its spell. That the house was haunted all declared. Isolated at that time, it was after sunset a house which no one alone would willingly approach. There were cellars and even dark garrets which it required no ordinary courage to explore. When on windy moonlight nights the figures in canvas of heroic size in the great tapestry room moved to and fro, swayed by the currents of air behind the wainscot, they imprinted on the imagination of the solitary inmate impressions which fifty years and more have failed to efface from the mind of the writer [1]. As, moreover, the times were crowded with political, social, and religious controversies, in all of which his father played the local leading part, it would indeed have been strange if our author as a child in such a home and

[1] A few years ago the writer, having heard that the old home—Bank House—had fallen on evil days and had been let out as small tenements, paid a visit to Burnley to revisit the scenes of childhood and, if possible, to purchase the grand old tapestries. He was unhappily too late. 'May I see the old tapestry?' he inquired. 'It's all taken down and been made into floor-cloth,' replied the tenant; 'and there (pointing to a well trodden but featureless strip of canvas beneath the table) there's the very last bit of it.' 'But how could you do that?' said the visitor, in a tone of reproach. 'Well, you see,' was the reply, 'it was so boggartly at nights!'

in such an atmosphere, and amid such associations, had not been thereby moulded and fashioned. Excitable, highly sensitive, and yet withal dreamy and imaginative, his whole future life was intensely coloured and affected by his environment.

Upon the removal of the family to Manchester, in which city the late Canon Bardsley diligently laboured for thirty years, first as Rector of St. Philip's, Bradford Road, and latterly as Rector of the Central City Parish of St. Ann's, our author was duly sent to the Manchester Grammar School. And it was as he daily passed along Market Street on his way to the school that the names over the shops arrested his attention, and thus became the first germs of his future life study. The Cheetham Hospital adjoining the Grammar School, with its quaint rooms and ancient library, became his favourite resort, and among the black book-cases he spent all his leisure hours. Having won the school English Prize Poem he proceeded to Worcester College, Oxford, where three of his elder brothers had preceded him. Possessing much social charm with remarkable powers of composition, not only as a writer of prose and verse but also as a musician, he was in great request at college parties. His improvisations reflected every passing mood, and at times frolicsome, but mostly pathetic, they betrayed the deepest musical feeling. The dark shadows cast by insomnia and an over-vivid imagination were even then haunting him. During his first term at Oxford, oppressed by fear of darkness, he never once slept in his bed, but paced the quad, or dozed away in his armchair, the long and weary hours of night. The straitened finances of his home led him to abbreviate as much as was possible his Oxford course, and having taken his degree, he applied for admission to Holy Orders at the hands of the late Bishop Fraser of Manchester.

There are those who can still recall a somewhat unique experience in connexion with that ordination. In the early morning of the Saturday preceding his ordination, Charles Bardsley was urged to take the place of one of a cricket team by whom an important match was that day to be played on the adjoining Broughton ground. The examination was over, and his time for a few hours was his own. The Bishop was consulted, and under the circumstances his approval was obtained. Bardsley took his place, and played so successfully that he carried out his bat, winning thereby a new bat; whilst on the following morning, in the cathedral, he read the Gospel, having obtained first place in the examination. Throughout his ministry he was greatly sought after as a preacher, and as a visitor by the sick bed his ministrations were to the last singularly helpful. After a few years spent in Manchester, for the greater part at St. Ann's as curate to his father, whose health had already begun to fail, our author became Vicar of Ulverston. He had not been long vicar of that parish before the late Bishop, Dr. Harvey Goodwin, appointed him honorary canon of his cathedral of Carlisle, whilst the clergy of the new archdeaconry of Furness returned him as their proctor to the Convocation of York. When some fifteen years had thus passed, realizing that insomnia had practically disabled him from the active discharge of pastoral work, he retired with his wife and two children to Oxford. There, happily absorbed by the genius of the place, the education of his children, and the quiet prosecution of his favourite studies, he lived the latter part of his life, being very suddenly called to rest on the morning of October 30, 1898. His body was buried in Ulverston, the much-loved scene of his former ministry, and the thousands who followed him to his last resting-place felt that there was much fitness that he who among them for so many years had suffered from loss of sleep should there find that unbroken last sleep for which he had longed—

'Think of the rest to one who long has striven
'Gainst wind and tide to reach the further shore.'

Thirty years have passed since the Dictionary now launched was first laid on the stocks. It involved close research and diligent study for the greater part of the author's life. Realizing that very many years would pass before he would be justified in the publication of the Dictionary, he gave to the press some results of his studies in works which obtained from the first great reputation. Five years after leaving Oxford, in 1873, he published *English Surnames, their Sources and Significations*. This work was at once most favourably reviewed by the London *Times*, ran through several editions, and is still regarded as a standard work. In the United States it is even better known than at home, and among the greater pleasures of his life were the grateful communications and pressing invitations conveyed to him by correspondents that the author would pay a long visit to his unknown friends in America. At one time he found it necessary to set aside a day in each fortnight for correspondence with his transatlantic friends[1]. In 1879 he published the *Romance of the London*

---

[1] The author frequently expressed great admiration for the noble endeavours made by President McKinley to strengthen the ties of brotherhood among English-speaking peoples, and had declared his intention of dedicating his Dictionary to him. This wish having been made known to the President by Mr. Choate, the Minister of the United States to the Court of St. James's, Mr. McKinley very cordially assented to the request.

Directory, and in 1880, *Curiosities of Puritan Nomenclature*, works which greatly enhanced his reputation. Akin to these works were the *Memorials of St. Ann's Church, Manchester*, in 1877; *The Register of Ulverston Parish Church*, published in 1886, in combination with his friend, the Rev. L. R. Ayre, the Rural Dean of Ulverston; and also *The Chronicles of the Church and Town of Ulverston*, published independently. For several years the author's pen was also employed on works of fiction. *Brownie*, a short story, was a study drawn from the neighbourhood of the Duddon; whilst *His Grandfather's Bible* portrayed the scenery and customs of the Furness fells. Many other short sketches and tales were contributed by him to the magazine literature of the day. The materials for his first and largest work of fiction, however, entitled *John Lexley's Troubles*, a three-volume novel, were drawn mainly from the neighbourhood of Burnley. When published, many recognized, or thought that they recognized, not only the customs and localities of that district, but also some of the characters. It has already been mentioned that the family of which our author was a member was ruled on somewhat austere lines. The late Rector, the father, was beloved by all who knew him, and was oftentimes betrayed into some laxity with his own principles. Great was the delight of his sons when they beheld the good old man enjoying to the full the entertainments of the inimitable Corney Grain, whilst carefully drawing for their moral benefit a distinction between such an entertainment and a visit to a good theatre, which would have been an offence in no way to be condoned! The Puritan atmosphere of the home did not recognize the novel strictly so called. When *Now and Then*, by the late Samuel Warren was published, it was regarded not as a novel, but as a moral tale which might be profitably read aloud to the younger members of the family! Something however like a scandal ensued when it was found that, one evening, such was the interest displayed that the sons had been allowed to transgress the usual time for bed as they sat around their father and mother, who alternately took up the reading until, incredible to relate, the morning light broke in, the tale was ended, and all sought their couches at an unknown hour. The publication of *John Lexley* occasioned much perplexity. Its preparation was kept secret from the parents, and when at last a publisher had been found and the volume was favourably reviewed in the London *Daily News*, the revelation that a novel had been written and published by one of the sons could be no longer withheld—it was an anxious question as to which would prevail, Puritan prejudice or parental pride. The question was never actually decided; for whilst the good old man smiled with approval, it was with a reproving tone that he exclaimed, ' Oh, Charles, Charles! '

It was with intense sorrow that his friends learned the sad news of our author's sudden death.   Those who knew him best felt, however, that they would not have had it otherwise.   His failure of health and the non-fulfilment of his own plans and purposes were tending to sadden his closing years.   After his death there were found among his papers, in his own hand, the pathetic lines of Greg—

> ' Yes, I have failed : that golden prize
>   Of life, success—ambition's boast,
> Which dazzled once my boyish eyes,
>   I strove for, prayed for, and have lost.
>
> ' Yet I may not have lost the prize,
>   It only may not yet be won ;
> I see with dim and tearful eyes
>   The goal may still be further on.
>
> ' The star again, like morning sun,
>   May rise upon some happier shore ;
> And when a nobler race is run,
>   My Master bid me try once more.'

This *Dictionary of English and Welsh Surnames* was among the unfinished tasks, although it had absorbed the best years of the author's life.   It now goes forth to the public as the result of his widow's devotion to her husband's memory. For nearly two years she sought to decipher the microscopic writing until at length it was found possible to place the manuscripts in the hands of the Controller of the University Press.   It is possible that some errors may exist which a final revision by the author would have prevented.   Those members of the author's family who still survive him, with deep affection tender their thanks to her without whose loving toil the work had been wholly lost.

Of the value of his own work the author entertained a lowly estimate : not so the *Quarterly Review*, p. 209, 1895.   In a long and appreciative article the reviewer, although more than twenty years had elapsed since the publication of *English Surnames*, states his conviction that ' though the earliest in date of the works reviewed, Mr. Bardsley's work is in our opinion by far the most generally useful, and has the merit of being based on essentially sound principles.   We find in it the right classification.   The *preuves* given in the form of an index are taken from actual records, and the curiously apposite quotations from popular mediaeval literature enforce at every point Mr. Bardsley's conclusions.'

On January 1, 1896, the author, in closing his Introduction to this Dictionary, which he did not live to see in print, adds the following words:

' This preface is very unscientific in its arrangement. I frankly admit it, for I am not scientific. I never had the chance. The cares of a heavy parish have only allowed me minutes to jot down the results of past readings, and my occasional holidays were spent in search of proof. My MS. has been locked up for two years through illness and partial blindness. Still, the Dictionary may be useful to students. In any case, its slow preparation of twenty years has given me the one great pleasure of my life. Unhappy the man who has no hobby. I have simply been an earnest but unfortunately a flagging follower in the pursuit of the subject I love.'

The writer of this preface believes that as years pass other students will supply fresh materials and accumulate more adequate and abiding contributions to this fascinating subject, but he trusts that in the meanwhile this Dictionary will accomplish that modest object which was its author's highest aim.

JOHN W. CARLISLE.

ROSE CASTLE, CARLISLE,
April, 1901.

LIST OF REFERENCES
AND KEY TO ABBREVIATIONS

A. Hundred Rolls, 1273.
B. Calendarium Inquisitionum Post Mortem.
C. Calendarium Rotulorum Patentium in Turri Londinensi.
D. Calendarium Rotulorum Chartarum.
E. Rotuli Litterarum Clausarum in Turri Londinensi.
F. Valor Ecclesiasticus.
G. Calendarium Rotulorum Originalium.
H. Rolls of Parliament.
J. Placitorum in Dom. Cap. Westminster.
K. Testa de Neville, sive Liber Feodorum, temp. Hen. III–Edw. I.
L. Calendarium Genealogicum.
M. Writs of Parliament.
N. Munimenta Gildhallae Londoniensis.
O. Issues of the Exchequer.
P. Issue Rolls.
Q. History and Antiquities of York. (Pub. 1785.)
R. Placita de Quo Warranto, temp. Edw. I–III.
S. Guild of St. George, Norwich.
T. Excerpta e Rotulis Finium in Turri Londinensi.
V. Camden Society Publications.
    V. 1. Bury St. Edmunds Wills.
    V. 2. Dingley's History from Marble.
    V. 3. Trevelyan Papers.
    V. 4. The Camden Miscellany.
    V. 5. Obituary of Richard Smyth.
    V. 6. Diary of John Rous.
    V. 7. Liber Famelicus of Sir Jas. Whitelock.
    V. 8. Chronicon Petroburgense.
    V. 9. Proceedings against Dame Alice Kyteler.
    V. 10. Autobiography of Sir John Bramston.
    V. 11. Domesday Book of St. Paul's.
    V. 12. Ricart's Kalendar.
    V. 13. Proceedings in Kent.
    V. 14. Rutland Papers.
W. Surtees Society Publications.
    W. 1. Coldingham Priory.
    W. 2. Testamenta Eboracensia.
    W. 3. Durham Household Book.
    W. 4. Kirkby's Inquest.

W. Surtees Society Publications—*continued*.
    W. 5. Knights' Fees.
    W. 6. Nom. Villarum.
    W. 7. Illustrative Documents.
    W. 8. Priory of Finchale.
    W. 9. Fabric Rolls of York Minster : Wills and Inventories.
    W. 10. Hexham Priory.
    W. 11. Corpus Christi Guild.
    W. 12. Historiae Dunelmensis.
    W. 13. Barnes' Eccles. Proceedings.
    W. 14. Visitation of Yorkshire.
    W. 15. Feodarium Prioratus Dunelmensis.
    W. 16. Depositions from York Castle.
    W. 17. Memorials of Fountains Abbey.
    W. 18. Depositions and Eccles. Proceedings.
    W. 19. Liber Vitae.
    W. 20. Remains of Dean Granville.
X. Memorials of London (Riley).
Y. Proceedings and Ordinances : Privy Council.
Z. Calendar of Proceedings in Chancery (Elizabeth).
AA. Chetham Society Publications.
    AA. 1. Wills and Inventories, Lancashire.
    AA. 2. Three Lancashire Documents.
    AA. 3. Lancashire Chantries.
    AA. 4. Birch Chapel.
BB. Rotuli Normanniae in Turri Londinensi.
DD. Documents Illustrative of English History.
EE. Index to 'Originalia et Memoranda.'
FF. History of Norfolk (Blomefield and Parkin).
GG. Fines (Richard I).
HH. History of Hertfordshire (Clutterbuck).
MM. Rotuli Curiae Regis.
NN. Calendar and Inventories of the Treasury.
PP. History of Leicestershire (Nichols).
QQ. Register of St. James', Piccadilly.
RR. State Paper Office Publications.
    RR. 1. Patent Rolls.
    RR. 2. Compoti.
    RR. 3. Issue Rolls.
SS. History of Durham (Surtees).
TT. Calendar of State Papers (Domestic).

XX. 1. Materials for History of Reign of Henry VII.
XX. 2. RegistrumAbbatiaeJohannisWhethamstede.
XX. 3. Letters from Northern Registers.
ZZ. Calendar to Pleadings (Elizabeth).
BBB. Calendarium Genealogicum: Henry III–Edw. I. Ed. by Chas. Roberts.
DDD. Hist. and Antiquities of the County Palatine of Durham (Robert Surtees).
EEE. Petition in Parliament, 1402. Rolls of Parliament, vol. iii, p. 519.
FFF. Cartularium Abbathiae de Whiteby, Ordinis S. Benedicti (Surtees Society).
GGG. Memorials of the Church of SS. Peter and Wilfrid, Ripon, vol. i. (Surtees Society).
HHH. Sanctuarium Dunelmense et sanctuarium Beverlacense (Surtees Society).
KKK. History of Northumberland (Rev. John Hodgson).
PPP. History of Newcastle and Gateshead(Richard Welford .
QQQ. History and Antiquities of North Durham (Rev. James Raine, 1852).
RRR. The Pipe Rolls, or Sheriffs' Annual Accounts for the Counties of Cumberland, Westmoreland, and Durham during the reigns of Hen. II, Ric. I, and John.
TTT. The History of Liddesdale and the Debateable Land (Robert Bruce Armstrong. Pub. by Douglas, Edin.).
VVV. Household Books of Lord William Howard of Naworth Castle (Surtees Society).
YYY. History and Antiquities of Bristol (William Barrett, Surgeon, F.S.A.).
WWW. Chronicles of the Mayors and Sheriffs of London, 1188–1274 (Henry Thos. Riley).

C. R.—Close Rolls.
C. S. P.—Calendar of State Papers.
Cath. Ang.—Catholicon Anglicum. Ed. by S. J. H. Herrtage (Camden Society), 1882.
Cotg.—Cotgrave's French and English Dictionary, 1673.
E. E. T. S.—Early English Text Society.
E. and F. – Estates and Families of co. Cumberland (Denton).
H. E. D.—Historical English Dictionary.
L. and C. R.—Lancashire and Cheshire Record Society.
MDB.—Modern Domesday Book, 1873.
Patr. Brit. = Patronymica Britannica (M. A. Lower, 1860).
P. T. Howdenshire.—Poll Tax, Howdenshire.
P. T. Yorks.—Poll Tax, West R. of Yorkshire, 1379.
Prompt. Parv. = Promptorium Parvulorum. Ed. by Albert Way (Camden Society), 1865.
W. D. S.—Wappentagium de Strafford.

Bapt. = Baptismal.
Dim. = Diminutive.
Nick. = Nickname.
Occup. = Occupative.
Offic. = Official.
Pat. = Patronymic.

DIRECTORIES CITED.

1. *English and Welsh Post Office Directories, &c.*

Birmingham, Staffordshire, Warwickshire, Worcestershire, 1872.
Cambridge, Norfolk, and Suffolk, 1865.
Crockford's Clerical Directory, 1881–91.
Devon and Cornwall, 1873.
Durham, Northumberland, Cumberland, and Westmoreland, 1873.
Lancashire, 1873.
London Commercial and Court Directories, 1870. (When cited as London simply, the Commercial Directory is intended.)
Monmouthshire, and Chief Towns and Places in South Wales, 1871.
Kelly's Oxford Directory, 1899.
North and East Ridings of Yorkshire, with City of York, 1872.
West Riding of Yorkshire, 1867.
Return of Owners of Land, 1873, commonly known as the Modern Domesday Book, and quoted throughout as MDB.

2. *American Directories.*

Boston, U.S., 1886 (Sampson, Thurlock & Co.).
New York, 1877 (Wilson).
Philadelphia, 1885 (Jas. Gopsill & Sons).
Worcester, U.S., 1884 (Drew, Allis & Co.).

N.B. The figures attached to various towns, villages, and hamlets refer to the above Directories, and show the number of instances of surnames therein recorded as resident in those places at the date of publication.

These numbers are arranged in the same order as the different spellings of the surnames to which they are annexed, e. g.
  Abbey, Abbee, Abbe.
  London, 4, 1, 0 ; Philadelphia, 11, 0, 6.

Other works referred to :

A Lyttel Geste of Robin Hode, 16th cent.
Atkyns' (R.) History of Gloucestershire, 1712.

Bailey's English Dictionary. Edit. 1737–42.
Baines' Hist. of Lancashire. Edit. John Harland.
Bardsley and Ayre's Register of Ulverston Parish Church. Pub. by Jas. Atkinson, Ulverston, 1886.
Bardsley's (C. W.) Curiosities of Puritan Nomenclature, 1st edit., 1880. Pub. by Chatto & Windus.
—— English Surnames, 4th edit., 1889. Pub. by Chatto & Windus.

Blomefield and Parkin's History of Norfolk. 11 vols. 1805-10.
Bowditch's Suffolk Surnames, 1861.
Brand's (J.) History and Antiquities of Newcastle-on-Tyne, 1789.
Brockett's Glossary of North-Country Words, 1825.
Burn's Hist. of Parish Church Registers in England, 2nd edit., 1862.

Camden's Remains. Nicholas Okes, 1623.
Charnock's Ludus Patronymicus, 1868.
Cocke Lorelle's Bote, 16th cent.
Coucher Book of Furness Abbey. (Chetham Society.) Edited by J. C. Atkinson. 3 vols.

Dictionary of National Biography. Edited by Leslie Stephen and Sidney Lee.

Earwaker's (J. B.) History of East Cheshire, 1877.

Freeman's (E. A.) Norman Conquest of England.
Ferguson's Surnames as a Science.

Halliwell's (J. O.) Dictionary of Archaic and Provincial Words, 6th edit., 1868.
Hotten's (J. C.) Original Lists of Emigrants, 1600-1700. Pub. 1874.

Jamieson's (J.) Dictionary of the Scottish Language.

Kirby's Quest for Somerset, in which is contained the Exchequer Lay Subsidy for 1 Edw. III. (Somerset Record Society, 1889.) Edited by F. H. Dickinson, F.S.A.

Lewis' (S.) Topographical Dictionary of England. 4 vols. 5th edit., 1842.
Lower's (M. A.) Patronymica Britannica. Edit. 1860.

Madden's Privy Purse Expenses of Princess Mary, daughter of Henry VIII, afterwards Queen Mary. Edit. 1831.

Nicolas' (N. Harris) Privy Purse Expenses of Henry VIII. Edit. 1827.
—— Privy Purse Expenses of Elizabeth of York. Edit. 1830.
—— Wardrobe Accounts of Edward IV. Edit. 1830.
Nicolson (J.) and Burn's (R.) History and Antiquities of the counties of Westmoreland and Cumberland, 1777.

Ormerod's History of Cheshire.
Oxford Historical Society Publications :
    Wood's History of the City of Oxford. Edited by A. Clark, 1889.
    Register of the University of Oxford, vol. i. Edited by C. W. Boase, 1884.
    Ditto, vol. ii, pts. i, ii, iii, iv. Edited by A. Clark, 1887-89.

Piers Plowman (Pickering's edit. 1842).
Pipe Rolls, in the reign of Hen. II. Published by the Pipe Roll Society, established 1883.
Poll Tax (West Riding of Yorkshire), 1379. Published by the Yorkshire Archaeological and Topographical Association, 1882. (Always quoted as P. T. Yorks.)

Quarterly Review. Jan. 1895.

Register of the Freemen of the City of York, vol. i, 1272-1558. (Surtees Society.) Edited by Dr. Francis Collins, 1897. (Quoted as Freemen of York.)
Rudder's (S.) History of Gloucestershire, 1779.
Rylands' (J. P.) Lay Exchequer Subsidy Rolls, co. Lanc., 1332.

Skeat's (W. W.) Etymological Dictionary, 1884.
Stockdale's Annals of Cartmel, 1872.

Taylor's (Isaac) Words and Places, 1865.
Toulmin Smith's (Joshua) Memorials of Old Birmingham, 1864.
—— English Gilds (E. E. T. S.), 1870.
—— (Lucy) York Mystery Plays, 14th to 16th cents. (1885).
Tyrwhitt's (Thos.) Chaucer. Edit. 1843.

Whitaker's (T. D.) History and Antiquities of Craven, 1812.

Yonge's (Miss) History of Christian Names, 1863. (Quoted as Yonge, i, ii.)

PUBLICATIONS OF THE LANCASHIRE AND CHESHIRE RECORD SOCIETY.

Lancashire Wills proved at Richmond (1531-1760). Edited by Lieut.-Col. Fishwick.
Preston Guild Rolls (1397-1682). Edited by W. Alexander Abram.
The Register of Leyland Church (1653-1710). Edited by W. S. White.
The Registers of Prestbury Church, co. Chester (1560-1636). Edited by Jas. Croston.
Wills at Chester (1545-1720). Edited by J. P. Earwaker, F.S.A.

PUBLICATIONS OF THE HARLEIAN SOCIETY.

1. *Church Registers.*

Canterbury Cathedral (1564 onwards). Edited by Robt. Hovenden.
Kensington Parish Church (1539-1675). Edited by F. N. Macnamara and A. Story-Maskelyne.
St. Antholin, Budge Row (1538-1754) ; also St. John

Baptist on Wallbrook Island (1682–1754). Edited by J. Lemuel Chester and Geo. J. Armytage.

St. Dionis, Backchurch, London (1538–1754). Edited by J. Lemuel Chester.

St. George's Chapel, Mayfair (1740–54). Edited by Geo. J. Armytage.

St. George, Hanover Sq. (1725–1809, 2 vols.). Edited by John H. Chapman.

St. James, Clerkenwell (1551–1754). Edited by Robert Hovenden.

St. Mary, Aldermary (1558–1754). Edited by J. Lemuel Chester.

St. Michael, Cornhill (1546–1754). Edited by J. Lemuel Chester.

St. Peter, Cornhill (1538–1774, 2 vols.). Edited by G. W. G. Leveson Gower.

St. Thomas the Apostle, London (1558–1754). Edited by J. Lemuel Chester.

Stourton, co. Wilts (1570–1800). Edited by John Henry Ellis, Rector.

2. *Marriage Licences.*

1520-1828. Allegations for Marriage Licences issued by the Bishop of London. Edited by Geo. J. Armytage. Described in this work as Marriage Lic., London, i, ii.

1543–1869. Allegations for Marriage Licences issued from the Faculty Office of the Archbishop of Canterbury at London. Edited by Geo. J. Armytage. Described as Marriage Lic., Faculty Office.

1558–1699. Allegations for Marriage Licences issued by the Dean and Chapter of Westminster. Edited by Geo. J. Armytage. Described as Marriage Lic., Westminster, and sometimes as Marriage Alleg., Westminster.

1660–1694. Allegations for Marriage Licences issued by the Vicar-General of the Archbishop of Canterbury. Edited by Geo. J. Armytage. Described as Marriage Alleg., Canterbury.

LIST OF SUBSCRIBERS.

ALLEN, E. G., Bookseller, London, W.C.
ANGUS & ROBERTSON, Booksellers, Sydney, N.S.W. (2 *copies*.)
ASHER & CO., Booksellers, Berlin.
AYRE, Rev. Canon, Ulverston.

BAKER, T., Bookseller, London, W.
BARDSLEY, Rev. J. U. N., Ulverston.
BARDSLEY, Mrs. J. W., Huddersfield.
BARDSLEY, Rev. R. W., Ripon. (6 *copies*.)
BARROW-IN-FURNESS FREE PUBLIC LIBRARY.
BELL, Rev. J. B., Ulverston.
BROOKE, Sir Thomas, Bart., Huddersfield.
BRUNNER, Henry, Esq., Liverpool.
BRUNNER, Sir John, Bart., Liverpool.
BUMPUS, J. & E., Ltd., Booksellers, London, W. (2 *copies*.)
BUMPUS, J. & E., Ltd., Booksellers, London, E.C.

CARDIFF FREE PUBLIC LIBRARY.
CARLISLE, Right Rev. the Lord Bishop of. (3 *copies*.)
CARLTON CLUB, London, S.W.
CAZENOVE, C. D., & SON, Booksellers, London, W.C.
CHADWICK, S. J., Esq., Dewsbury.
CHAPMAN, Mrs., Manchester.
CHRYSTAL, R. S., Bookseller, Manchester.
CLARK, H., Esq., Croydon.
COLLINS, Dr. F., Pateley Bridge.
COLLINS, Rev. Henry, Huddersfield.
COWARD, J., Esq., Ulverston.

COWELL, Peter, Esq., Liverpool.
CROYDON PUBLIC LIBRARIES.
CYMMER WORKMEN'S LIBRARY, near Porth.

DAVIES, Rev. Prof. T. Wilton, D.D., Bangor.
DEAN, C. W., Esq., Ulverston.
DEIGHTON, BELL & CO., Booksellers, Cambridge.
DICKENSON, J., Esq., Ulverston.
DIGBY, William, Esq., C.I.E., Bromley.

EDINBURGH FREE PUBLIC LIBRARY.
ELLISON, Thomas, Esq., West Kirby.
ENYS, John D., Esq., Enys Penryn.

FRESTON, Thomas Westfaling, Esq., Prestwich.

GERISH, W. B., Esq.
GLAISHER, H. J., Bookseller, London, W.
GONVILLE AND CAIUS COLLEGE LIBRARY, Cambridge.
GOODCHILD, D., & CO., Booksellers, London, E.C.

HAINES, C. S., Esq., Ulverston.
HALES, Prof., London, N.W.
HARRASSOWITZ, Otto, Bookseller, Leipzig.
HARRISON, T., Esq., Ulverston.
HATCHARDS, Booksellers, London, W. (2 *copies*.)
HODGSON, J., Esq., J.P., Ulverston. (2 *copies*.)
HORNSBY, Miss, Ulverston.

JACKSON, R., Bookseller, Leeds. (4 *copies*.)
JAMES, Rev. Dr., Rugby.
JONES, Surgeon-General Evan, Aberdare.
JONES, E. Penllyn, Esq., Aberystwyth.

KLINCKSIECK, C., Bookseller, Paris.

LANCASTER, E. M., Esq., Worthing.
LAWS, E., Esq., J.P., F.S.A., Tenby.
LEEDS PUBLIC FREE LIBRARIES.
LEES, Rev. Samuel, West Bromwich.
LITERARY AND PHILOSOPHICAL INSTITUTION, Newcastle-on-Tyne.
LONDON LIBRARY, W.
LOW, S., MARSTON, & CO., Booksellers, London, E.C. (3 *copies*.)

MACKERETH, Mrs., Ulverston.
MACKERETH, E., Esq., Ulverston.
MACKERETH, G., Esq., Ulverston.
MCNALLY, Rev. F. G., Windermere.
MANCHESTER FREE REFERENCE LIBRARY.
MELVILLE, MULLEN, & SLADE, Booksellers, Melbourne. (3 *copies*.)
MILLER & GILL, Booksellers, London, W.C.
MORLEY, Miss, Eton College.
MORRELL, W. W., Esq., J.P., York.
MORRIS, T. E., Esq., London, E.C.

NEWINGTON, A., Esq., Croydon.

OXFORD AND CAMBRIDGE CLUB, London, S.W.

PARKER, R., Esq., Ulverston.
PATCHETT, A., Esq., Liverpool.
PIERCE, Ellis, Bookseller, Dolyddelen. (2 *copies*.)
PLATT-HIGGINS, Mrs. H., London, S.W.
POLLARD, J., Esq., Truro.
PRICHARD, Thomas, Esq., Llanerchymedd.

QUARITCH, Bernard, Bookseller, London, W. (6 *copies*.)

RATCLIFFE, Mrs., Grange-over-Sands.
REDHEAD, W., Esq., Ulverston.

RYLANDS, J. Paul, Esq., F.S.A., Birkenhead.
RYLANDS, W. H., Esq., London, W.C.

SALISBURY, Right Rev. the Lord Bishop of. (2 *copies*.)
SIMPKIN, MARSHALL, HAMILTON, KENT & CO., Ltd., Booksellers, London, E.C. (6 *copies*.)
SOTHERAN, H., & CO., Booksellers, London, W.C.
SPOTTISWOODE & CO., Ltd., Booksellers, Eton.
STECHERT, G. E., Bookseller, London, W.C. (3 *copies*.)
STEVENS, B. F., & BROWN, Booksellers, London, W.C.

THIN, James, Bookseller, Edinburgh.
THOMAS, Lieut-Col. G. T., Surbiton.
THOMPSON, Miss, Ulverston.
THOMPSON & CO., Booksellers, Belfast.
THURSHANG, Peter, Esq., Redruth.
TODD, W. H., Esq., Ulverston.
TRUSLOVE, HANSON, & COMBA, Ltd., Booksellers, London, W.
TWIETMEYER, A., Bookseller, Leipzig.

WALKER, E., Esq., Ulverston.
WELTER, H., Bookseller, Paris.
WHITHAM, S. J., Bookseller, Ulverston. (6 *copies*.)
WILLIAMS & NORGATE, Booksellers, London, W.C.
WILSON, A., Bookseller, London, E.C.
WITHAM, J. S., Esq., Ulverston.
WOODBURN, Miss, Ulverston.

YOUNG, H. E., Esq., Blundellsands.

ZAEHNSDORF, J., Esq., London, W.C. (2 *copies*.)

INTRODUCTION

——————

THE purpose of this work is to supply materials for an etymological dictionary of English and Welsh surnames. It must be understood at once that I have gone little further than an attempt to trace back our names to their original forms, to clear them from the incrustations of time, and to place each, however misleading in appearance to-day, in its own particular class. For instance, I do not give the etymology of Richard, for that has already been done by other workers, but I proceed to show that Higginson is equivalent to Dixon, by demonstrating that Hick and Dick were the *nicks*[1] of Richard in the hereditary surname period, and that Hick was lazified into Higg (just as Dicks became also Diggs); then that the diminutive of Higg became Higgin, whence the patronymics of Higgins and Higginson. Dick stuck more closely to the sharpened form and became Dickin, whence the patronymic is Dickins and Dickinson—Tillotson, son of Tillot, diminutive of Till, *nick* of Matilda. Similarly with regard to local surnames, I attempt to prove that such a directory name as Philbrick is a corruption of Fellbridge, through the modified forms of Fellbrig, Philbrigg, and the sharper Phillbrick. But I do not state, however simple it may be, the etymology of the local term Fellbridge: I have tried to get through the modifications, not to say mutilations, back to the original parent. A single other instance will suffice. The surname of Physick occurring in the London Directory is a corrupted form of Fishwick, but I do not give the etymology of that local name, simple as it seems to be: I leave that to other workers.

English surnames have been made the subject of endless guessings. Several years ago I wrote an article for a monthly Church magazine. Amongst other little items, I gave the origin of the simple occupative surname Mason, a builder. A few days later, I received an angry letter from a lady in the West Country, who stated that her name was Mason, and that she was a direct descendant of Mnason in the Acts of the Apostles, and that the family had worked their way through Phrygia and Pamphylia into Western Europe, and finally settled in the county from which she

———

[1] This contraction of the word 'nickname' is used by the author throughout this work, and is printed as he wrote it.—[A. B.]

B

addressed her letter. I at once dispatched a note of apology! Morley is commonly claimed to be from Morlaix, though the moor-ley abounds on every side. Twopeny is derived from Tupigny, in Flanders, although pence-names were quite familiar in the hereditary surname period. Fivepence, Fourpence, and Halpeny existed, and Ninepence lasted through three generations, at least, in the county of Durham. D'Aeth now takes the place of Death in our modern directories, because it was guessed by some one that it came across the 'little streak' from Aeth in Flanders. It is probably a Cambridgeshire name and comes from some little, and now forgotten, spot so called in the county. In the Hundred Rolls (1273) occurs

HUGO DE DETHE, co. Camb.
ALICIA DE DETHE, co. Camb.

Every undergraduate at Cambridge is familiar with the name to this day. In fact, talk to a very large number of people about their surname and you will find that their family came in with the Conqueror, their visiting cards laughing at them 'behind their backs.' William evidently had a very easy time of it. It is quite clear that he had only a handful of opponents to meet, and that the story of the Battle of Hastings is a gross historic fraud.

Throughout my work I have divided our surnames into the five classes I confined them to some twenty-two years ago, viz :—(1) Baptismal or Personal Names. (2) Local Surnames. (3) Official Surnames. (4) Occupative Surnames. (5) Nicknames. Practically there are only four classes, for it is often hard to distinguish between occupation and office.

After local names the largest class is baptismal names, with their endless *nicks*, *pet forms, diminutives*, &c. It may interest the reader to study my analysis of the first five letters of the alphabet in the *London Directory* (1870). I need not apologize for so many doubtful instances.

	A	B	C	D	E	Total
Local . . .	915	5093	3259	1377	716	11360
Baptismal . . .	1763	1647	1535	1935	1323	8203
Occupative . . .	37	899	1546	169	—	2651
Official . . .	139	575	949	48	26	1737
Nicknames . . .	45	2089	685	210	67	3096
(Foreign) . . .	184	569	293	419	119	1584
(Doubtful) . . .	120	850	476	193	56	1695
Total . . .	3203	11722	8743	4351	2307	30326

All the countries of Western Europe seem to have adopted the same means of securing identification, or their neighbours did it for them. Wales is the great exception. Here there is scarcely a trade name, only a few nicknames, no official surnames that I know of, just a sprinkling of local surnames, and the rest, quite 95 per cent., are baptismal names. Hence the great difficulty of identification in the Principality. Some spirited effort ought to be made by Welshmen to remedy this great defect. At present the surnames of 'gallant little Wales' defeat their own intention, namely to give individuality to the nominee.

The English natural growth of distinct branches of hereditary surnames from, say, 1250 to 1450, fortunately escaped this obstacle to identification. The five classes mentioned above have proved amply sufficient for the purpose.

One of the greatest difficulties in solving the origin of our surnames comes under the law of imitation. The parentage being forgotten, people naturally began to pronounce their names in such a way as seemed to convey a meaning. After the institution of Church Registers the clerks wrote down accordingly. Hence the pitfall into which so many stumble. Hence in co. Somerset, Greedy for Gredhay, Rainbird for Reynebaud, Trott for Troyt, Bacchus for Bakehouse, Toogood or Doogood for Thurgod, Goodyear for Goodier, Gospell for Gosbell, Physick for Fishwick, Potiphar for Pettifer, Pitchfork (co. Linc.) for Pitchforth (i.e. Pickford), Roylance for Rylands, Gudgeon for Goodson (cf. the pronunciation Hodgun for Hodgson in the North), Twentyman for Twinterman, Sisterson for Sissotson (Cecilia), Rayment for Raymond, Garment for Garmond, Forty for the old 'de la Fortheye' of co. Oxford (which still exists as Forty in the city), and a host of others. All this was perfectly natural, and to this day the provincial *sparrowgrass* remains for asparagus, and *causeway* for causey. For similar instances v. Gumboil, Popkiss, or Birdseye. Therefore, as the newspaper advertisements say, ' beware of imitations.'

Many familiar dictionary words are closely connected with surnames, which materially help to elucidate their meaning, v. Codling (apple), Cocket (coquette), or Gillott (jilt) ; but jilt has been already explained in my *English Surnames*.

Some extraordinary modifications may be mentioned. One day (1895) the driver of a tram-car on Banbury Road, Oxford, told me his name was Woosnam. I at once asked him if he came from South Lancashire. He looked somewhat astonished, but said ' yes.' 'From the neighbourhood of Bury or Rochdale ? ' I inquired. ' Rochdale,' he said. His ancestors were the familiar Wolstenholme, of that district, but he persisted that his father and mother spelt the name Woosnam, and so in some cases it is found in the Lancashire directories. In the registers of St. Mary,

Ulverston, the great Furness name of Postlethwaite is often entered Poslet. Chawner represents the occupative Chaloner; Rownson, Roanson, or Ronson represent Rowlandson or Rollinson in the Furness district of North Lancashire, and are found in the Manchester and other directories. Townson in the same division of the county stands for Tomlinson. Conclusive proof, or circumstantial evidence not absolutely proof, in these cases is forthcoming. I have only given a few instances, but many others will be found in the pages of this book. Here again the student must be warned against guessing. Only earnest reading of the published works of County Archæological Societies and Church Registers will give him the desired key to the elucidation of such curious modifications, not to say mutilations.

It may be noticed that aspirates were indifferently used—Ilbert and Heleberd were the same. Hunderhill is found for Underhill (Kirby's *Quest*, 1 Edw. III, p. 325). Hatchard now stands for Achard; Hellison is found for Ellison in the Yorkshire Poll Tax, 1379. In the Hundred Rolls of 1273, the same individual is referred to as Hippwell and Ippewell. To-day we find Hadkins and Adkins, Harnett for Arnett, Haskew and Askew, Houseley and Ouseley, Hadcock and Adcock, Hosgood and Osgood, Effingham and Heffingham, &c., running side by side.

In the surname period there seems to have been no law as regards aspirates. Many of these *h*'s are modern, but the larger number, as this dictionary will show, date from the period when surnames were becoming established. Of course it is a vice versa affair. Cf. Armitage in the directory with hermitage in the ordinary dictionary. Many old English personal names, now completely forgotten, survive in our surnames. Aldus is one such, now found as Aldus, Aldis, Aldhous, the imitative Aldhouse, Aldous, or Alldiss (v. Aldhouse). In the eastern counties it was evidently a popular font-name, especially in Norfolk:

> WILLIAM FIL ALDUSE, co. Notts, 1273. A.
> ALDUS WAVELOC, co. Camb., 1273. A.
> HUGH FIL ALDUS, co. Norf., 1273. A.

Just another instance from a large list, that of Aldrich:

> JOHN FIL ALDRECH. C.
> JOHN ALDRYCHE, bailiff of Yarmouth, 1469: FF. xi. 325.

This still lives in our directories, both in America and England, as Aldrich, and the imitative and local-looking Aldridge. From twenty to twenty-five surnames, more or less flourishing in our English and American directories, spring from the great personal name, Sagar, or Sayer. It plays havoc with the vowels; one individual, Siger de Frevile by name, is found in the Hundred Rolls (1273) as Siger, Saer, Sayer, and Seer (ii. 152, 514, 153, 523): v. Sayer for many present forms. But, as a personal name, Sayer is completely forgotten. The same remark applies to Hake and Hacon. These must suffice. A large number of examples will present themselves to those who care to consult the pages of this book; as for instance, Elvey (or Allvey), Woolrich (or Woolwright), and Kendrick (or Kenwright). A large number of names have two or three distinct origins; take Bell, for instance:

> NICHOLAS FIL BELE, co. Beds., 1273. A.
> BELLA or BELE COTTY, co. Linc., 1273. A.
> HUGH LE BEL, co. Oxf., 1273. A.
> RICHARD ATTE BELL, 1307. M.

Here are three derivations of Bell: a personal name, a nickname, and a local sign-name. Or again, Horn:

> ADAM HORN, co. Wilts, 1273. A.
> ROGER DE HORNE, co. Kent, 1273. A.
> WILLIAM ATTE HORN, co. Soms., 1 Edw. III.

Here we have first, a personal name; secondly, a local name, Horn being a parish in co. Kent; and thirdly, a sign-name.

Or once more, Gulliver. This also has three parentages: a personal, a local, and again a personal (v. Gulliver (1), (2), and (3)).

The instances of a double derivation are endless. One example will suffice. Lamb is just as often a personal name as a nickname. Lambert was a great favourite in the surname period, and its *nick* was Lamb; its diminutives being Lamb-in and Lamb-kin. Such an entry as—

> WILLIAM LE LAMBE, co. Camb., 1273. A,

represents the nickname.

The statement that surnames from female names never existed is too absurd to contradict; and the idea that such names denote illegitimacy is as utterly ridiculous to the careful student. So far as the first allegation is concerned, it is enough to point to the enormous influence such girl-names as Juliana, Constance, Isabella, Matilda, Margaret, Avice (Heloise), Emma, &c., with their many diminutives, such as Jowett, Gillott, Cust, Custance, Ibb, Ibson, Ibbott, Ibbotson, Tillott, Tillotson, Magg, Megson, Moxon, Avison (sometimes), Emmot, Emlin, Embling, Emmotson,

Emmet, and dozens of other girl-names, have had on our directories of to-day. Dennison or Tennyson, or Tennison, in nine cases out of ten are descendants of the feminine Dionise; v. Isard for a large batch. If any one will take the trouble to study the Yorkshire Poll Tax of 1379, he will be astonished to find how many children were styled after the mother's personal name while the father was living; probably because she was a stronger personality than he in the eyes of her neighbours, or because she had a dowry. In many cases, too, the child would be posthumous.

It is curious to notice apparently extinct surnames in England crop up in the U.S.A.; v. for instance, Holy Peter, now Hollopeter across the Atlantic. It seems to have long died out in the old country. So with Liard, which I can only find in New York. The same remark applies to Pallister and to Chickin. The last is found in the *Boston Directory*.

Circumstantial evidence. There are many cases where proof of the derivation is not absolute, and yet where you can scarcely hesitate to accept the evidence: v. Pim, or Pimm, or Pilson, where the origin is practically settled.

Some local and official names are to all intents and purposes the same. Hence Spence and Spencer, Panter and Pantry, Kitchen and Kitchener, Port and Porter. Take but one instance:

ROBERT LE PANTER, co. Camb., 1273. A.
JOHN DE LA PANETERIE, London, 1273. A.

Both of these occupied the position of steward of the pantry. Many instances of this double description will be found in the pages of this book. It may be argued that some of these *local* names may represent under-servants of the steward. That is possible.

Variants of family names are extraordinary in number. The Mannerings of Cheshire are said to have 137 different ways of spelling the name in their archives. I think it was Mr. Chaloner Smith who found over 400 variations of *Cushion* in old wills, &c. In Furness, North Lancs., Crewdson, Croudson, or Crowdson run together, and some of them are even now known to be connected. Dearnally and Dearnley may be seen side by side over shops; I have seen them in Higher Broughton, Manchester, eighteen years ago. Several years ago I saw Povah and Povey close together in Ellesmere, co. Salop. The Cheshire Cumberback is found in America as Counterpatch. Raleigh or Trott will furnish good instances of variety of spelling in the unsettled period of orthography. Just take Blenkin-sopp as an example: ' On April 23, 1470, Eliz. Blynkkynesoppye, of Blynkynsoppe,

widow of Thomas Blynkyensope, of Blynkkensope, received a general pardon'
(Hodgson's *Northumberland*, iii. 130). Here are four variations within two lines
written by the same hand. This will give the casual reader an idea of the
vagaries in spelling. Many of these names, like our dictionary words, attained one
settled orthography; but far more did not, as shown above. A final example:
Slater, Slatter, and Sclater, are all prospering in our directories to-day; Sclaster,
mentioned elsewhere, is extinct. We find

ADAM LE SCLATTERE, co. Oxf., 1273. A.
RICHARD LE SCLATTERE, co. Oxf., 1273. A.

Every Oxford undergraduate is familiar with Slatter, but the entries of this
surname show the natural tendency to diverge into three variants.

Of course, the further off the more likely modifications would arise, as in the
case of Counterpatch referred to above. Chisholm is an instance. In Philadelphia
this name is found as Chisom; and in Boston, although Chisholm is preserved, we
find Chisam.

It is important, where possible, to give the county wherein early extracts from
records can be found. Browning, although universal, was specially a popular
personal name in the West Country. The surname is common there. You must
look for Death in Cambridgeshire, and Daft in co. Nottingham. Jolland was
a Lincolnshire personal name; it is there you must look to-day for the surname
as well as its variants. Halliwell, in his *Provincial Dictionary*, gives us 'hext,
highest.

" The erchebischop of Canturberi
In Engelonde that is hext." '

Cf. this with

WALTER HEXTE, co. Soms., 1 Edw. III : Kirby's *Quest*, p. 186.

There are four Hexts to-day, in M.D.B. (co. Cornwall). Probably the ancestor
was the tallest in the family. Again, Halliwell furnishes us with 'halse, hazel,
co. Somerset.' In Kirby's *Quest*, quoted above, we find

RICHARD ATTE HALSE, co. Soms., 1 Edw. III, p. 181.

Thus from residence by some prominent hazel-tree we have not only surnames
representing Hazel, &c., but an early form, Halse, still preserved in the vernacular
of the county in which it arose. There are four Halses in the *London Directory*,
and two in Boston (U.S.A.). Again, take co. Durham. There are curious
surnames of local origin which found their rise in certain monastic or ecclesiastical
fabrics. Galilee is an instance.

WILLIAM DE LA GALILYE, C. R., 2 Edw. III, pt. i.
JOHN GALILEE, 1498 (*Hist. Newcastle and Gateshead*, i. 408).

No doubt this surname was attached to Durham Cathedral. It still exists in Sunderland, and has reached Liverpool, and in a modified form is found in New York. Cardinal Langley was buried in the Galilee of Durham in 1437. Now go to the Western Country. A *twitchen* was an alley or passage that went between two thoroughfares ; hence

RICHARD DE LA TWICHENE, co. Devon, 1273. A.
NICHOLAS TWYCHEENWEYE, co. Soms.: Kirby's *Quest*, p. 234.

Twitchen and Twitchin are the present form of the surname. Any reader of Anthony à Wood's *Oxford* will be familiar with this local term.

While on this subject we may notice that *h* is frequently lost in local surnames where the suffix begins with *h*: cf. Foxell for Foxhall, Greenall for Greenhall, or Blackall for Blackhall. Buckle no doubt represents Buckhill, as Windle, Windhill. Haslam is a modification of Hasleham, and Barnum is an American form of Barnham, as Chessum is an English form of Chesham. Goodenough has lost the *h* in the suffix *hough*. The most important instance of all, *ey* for *hey*, is treated of elsewhere.

In some cases the personal suffix *cock* (as in Wilcock, &c.), becomes the local suffix *cott*, and vice versa. Thus Glascott has become Glascock, Jeffcock has been turned into Jeffcott, and Grocott stares you in the face as Growcock.

In many cases English surnames are a mere translation of Norman-French names: cf. Cutbush with Talboys (i. e. Taillebois), Fairbrother for Beaufrere, Handsomebody for Gentilcorps, or Whitebread (or Whitbread) for Blanchpain. Plenty of similar instances will be found.

In an article in the *Quarterly Review*, January, 1895, a stern but kindly critic doubts the existence of surnames from sign-names of taverns, &c. I feel sure that I can satisfy him that such is the case:

THOMAS DEL HAT, co. Oxf., 1273. A.
JOHN ATTE HATTE. J.
JOHN ATTE BELLE, London. X.
RICHARD ATTE BELL, 1307. M.
HUGH ATTE COKKE. B.
WILLIAM ATTE ROBUCK, 1313. M.
GILBERT DE LA HEGLE, co. Sussex, 1273. A.
RALPH DE LE RUNCE, co. Notts, Hen. III, Edw. I. K.

With this last entry cf. Grayhorse and Whitehorse:

> WILLIAM DEL WHITHORS, Fines Roll, 2 Edw. I.
> THOMAS ATTE SWAN, Close Rolls, 2 Hen. IV, pt. ii.
> JOHN DE LA ROSE, co. Oxf., 1273. A.
> WILLIAM ATTE RAMME, Fines Roll, 14 Edw. II.

I think it is impossible to resist the evidence that many of our surnames (even when they have several parentages, as in the cases of Bell and Horn) sprang from sign-board names, and are therefore local. Most of these surnames are signs for taverns or hotels to-day: cf. Crosskeys.

At first even formal recorders, or, as we might say, registrar officers, were only too pleased to receive evidence of identity. Putting aside occupative, baptismal, and nick- names, all *local* helps were 'thankfully received.' Take the following, from a single register:

> ADAM IN THE HURNE (i. e. the corner).
> JOHN UNDERHULLE (i. e. under the hill).
> WILLIAM UPEDOUN (i. e. the upper part of the down).
> JOHN BY THE WODE (i. e. from residence thereby).
> JOHN BITHEWATER, now Bywater (from residence thereby).
> ROBERT IN THE MERCHE (i. e. from residence in the marsh).
> ALICIA IN THE DICHE (from residence by the dike).
> ROGER BENETHECLIVE (from residence under the cliff).
> LUCIA ATTE RUGEWEY (from residence on the way to the hill-ridge).
> MATILDA UPHULLE (from residence up the hill).
> JOHN BY THE MORE (from residence beside the moor).
> ROBERT BYTHEWEYE (from residence by the road side).
> ROBERT BYNETHEMOR (from residence below the moor).
> GEOFFREY BOVEWEYE (from residence above the road side).
> WALTER BYENDEBROK (from residence behind the brook).

These are all from Kirby's *Quest*, 1 Edw. III. The Hundred Rolls (1273) are just the same:

> EDWARD BY THE WODE, co. Dorset.
> ALYVA BENETHETON (i. e. below the town), co. Camb.

It is thus by incorporation we get such names as Bywater, Bythesea, Underhill, Underwood, Underdown, Attewell, Attwood, Townsend, &c.

It is interesting to observe the various meanings of *man* as a suffix:

(1) **Man**, meaning a servant, either semi-official or occupative, either for indoor or outdoor service. Our Grangemans looked after the grange; the ancestors of our Denmans attended to the pannage of the pigs (cf. Swinnart); our Bridgmans

took the toll (cf. Bridger). Ladyman and Bowerman are easily explained: take from the Yorkshire Poll Tax (1379) Ricardus Ladyman (p. 233), Johanna ye Ladimayden (p. 33), Johannes Serve-lady (p. 231), William Masterman (p. 231), William Halleman (p. 232), Cecilia del Boure (p. 154), Johannes Boureman (p. 154)—all these latter were indoor servants. Bowerman and Ladyman therefore attended 'my lady's' behests. Cf. also such names as Monkman, Priestman, or Vicarman, all servants. But we have not done; man, in the sense of servant, is conjoined with the master's personal name; hence the Yorkshire Matthewman, i.e. the servant of Matthew; Addyman, the servant of Adam (from the *nick* Addy): cf.

> Matheus de Lofthous, *firmarius*, 1379, Poll Tax, Yorks. p. 241.
> Willelmus Mathewman, ibid. p. 241.
> Magota Mathewoman, ibid. p. 241.

Here the hind and the kitchen wench take their surname from their master's personal name. Cf. again:

> Adam Symmeson, *souter* (i.e. shoemaker), 1379, P. T. Yorks. p. 25.
> Johannes serviens Ade Symmeson, ibid. p. 25.

Or take another instance:

> Adam de Wodhall: *marchaunt*, ibid. p. 25.
> Thomas serviens dicti Ade, ibid. p. 25.

This class is a fairly large one, and corrects Mr. Lower's view that Harriman was a freebooter. Hughman, and probably Human, were Hugh's servants. Even Hughesman is found in the *London Directory*; cf. Smithman, the blacksmith's assistant, or Dayman, or Daymon, the dairyman's assistant, v. Day.

(2) **Man**, a modification of *mond* in personal names: cf. Gorman for Gormund, Osman for Osmond, Rosaman for Rosamond, Wyman or Wayman for Wymond. Miss Yonge (*Christian Names*, ii. 414) has Hartmund as a personal name. I find a Herteman Hauberk in (O), showing how early the variation occurred.

As regards nicknames with an augmentive *man*, we may cite such designations as Longman, Shortman, Leishman, or Wightman. One instance seems to occur equally early. On the same page I find Nicholas Richemonde and Nicholas Richeman (1 Edw. III, Kirby's *Quest*, p. 183). I say *seems*, because it is possible that these are separate in their parentage although related.

(3) **Man**, as an augmentive suffix in personal names or nicknames. Therefore such surnames as Goldman, Tiddiman, Bateman, Richman or Rickman, Hardman, Speakman, Sweetman (commonly Swetman in the Hundred Rolls, 1273), Hickman

(except when it means the servant of Hick, i. e. Richard), Harman, Spillman (German Spielman), &c.

It may be added that there are two or three curious terminatives in *man*, which have no connexion with the word. One is Gillman or Gilman, not a dweller in a *gill*, but an imitative variant of Gillemin, or Gilmyn, a popular font-name in the surname period (v. Gilman). Another is Godliman, for Godalming:

1696-7. Married—SAMUELL CARR and ANNE HALL, of Godlÿman, co. Surrey: Reg. St. Dionis Backchurch, p. 45.

1792. Married—GEORGE WILD and MARY GODLIMAN: Reg. St. Geo. Han. Sq. i. 75.

This again is imitative. Cf. also Quarterman for the old Quatremayns.

(4) **Man** for nham in local surnames. Instances will be found scattered over the country. Indeed it is a fairly large class; cf. Parman for Parnham, Deadman for Debenham, Putman (in many cases) for Puttenham, Swetman (in some cases) for Swettenham, Highman for Highnam (a place in co. Gloucester), or Downman for Downham (in some cases). The most interesting instance, however, is Lyman for Lyneham, on account of the rapidity with which it has spread in the United States. Lyneham is a chapelry in the parish of Shipton, co. Oxford. The first instance of the change of the surname to Lyman I can find is dated 1591. A few years after, a Lyman went with the Puritan fathers to Virginia, and I was told in 1888, while at Boston, that every Lyman in the States had sprung from one individual settler. One or two of these names ending in *man* may be locative or occupative. Pullman (the poolman) may have supplied fish for his master's table, and Heathman may have been a keeper. Also Townman may have been a farm labourer. But Styleman is evidently locative (one who lived by the stile); so must be considered Hearnman (one who lived in a hearn, or corner).

R in *nicks* becomes h and d. This is of historic interest.

(1) Hence *nicks*, Hob and Dob, for Robert; whence Hobbs, Dobbs, &c.

(2) Hence *nicks*, Hodge and Dodge, for Roger; whence Hodgson, Dodgson, &c.

(3) Hence Hick[1] and Dick for Richard (the first in the surname period seemingly the most popular), whence Hickson, Dickson, &c.

These three *nicks* have given us a very large number of names. Robert, through its two *nicks*, has given us Hobbs, Hobson, sharpened into Hopps, Hopkins, Hopkinson, &c. Roger has, through its two *nicks*, given us Hodgson, Dodgson, Hodgkins, Hodgkinson, &c. Richard gave us, through its two *nicks*, scores of

---

[1] Wrongly attributed to Isaac in *English Surnames*, but corrected in the fifth edition.

surnames. Hick, as stated above, at first the favourite, gave us Hicks, Hickson, and the lazified Higg, Higgs, Higson, and the *dim.* Higgin, Higgins, Higginson, &c. From Dick we get Dicks, Dickson, Dixon, Dix, Dickinson, &c. This reference to Hick and Dick brings us to a very interesting point as regards the antiquity of nursery rhymes. The late Mr. Halliwell Phillipps would have enjoyed the confirmation of his views. From these two *nicks* we got

> '*Hick*-ory *Dick*-ory dock
> The mouse ran up the clock,
> The clock struck one, the mouse was gone,
> *Hick*-ory *Dick*-ory dock.'

As Hick disappeared almost immediately after the Reformation, this verse is stamped with the mark of age.

The same remark applies to *Humpty Dumpty.* Humphrey was a most familiar name, and gave us amongst other surnames Humphrey and Dumphry, both existing to-day. Hence, certainly long before the Reformation,

> 'Humpty Dumpty sat on a wall,
> Humpty Dumpty had a great fall;
> Not all the King's horses, nor all the King's men,
> Could put Humpty Dumpty together again.'

I once noticed in a magazine article a doubt thrown on the antiquity of *Four and Twenty Blackbirds,* on account of the line 'The King was in his Counting-house,' stating that it was a modern term. The following entry settles that matter:

NICHOLAS DEL COUNTYNGHOUSE, Issue Rolls, 4 Ric. II.

While on this subject, we must mention Bunting. It is a flourishing surname to-day. It is evidently some form of *bon-et-on*, a Norman-French expression of endearment, meaning ' good wee little one'; the final *g*, of course, being excrescent, as in Jennings, &c. Thus we have, as old as the hills, so to speak:

> 'Baby, Baby Bunting,
> Daddy's gone a-hunting,
> To get a little rabbit-skin
> To wrap the Baby Bunting in.'

The fact that Bunting was a kind of nickname is proved by the fact that four women are mentioned in the Coventry Mysteries, their names being (three of them baptismal):

'Bontyng the Brewster, and Sybyly Slynge,
Megge Merywedyr and Sabyn Sprynge.'

Cf.   ALICE BUNETUN, co. Oxf., 1273. A.
           HUGH BONTING, co. Linc., 1273. A.

In the latter case the final *g* would be an excrescence.

Y, or **a**, or **i**: intrusive for euphony. Hence Lockyer for Locker, Tawyer for Tawer, Sawyer for Sawer, Bowyer for Bower, Quarrier for Quarrer, Glasyer or Glasier for Glaser, &c.; cf. lawyer for lawer. Also we get Hard-a-way for Hardway, Green-a-way for Greenway, Ott-a-way for Ottway, Hath-a-way for Hathway, Hen-e-ry for Henry, Thack-e-ray for Thackwray, Horn-i-man for Horn-man; Nap-i-er is an historic surname for the official Naper, and even such local names as Dearnally and Dearnley go side by side.

Y and **i**. By some unwritten law, an occupative surname, and the name of the occupation itself, are discriminated. It seems to be settled that tailor is Taylor, that rider is Ryder. Similarly, a *sike* is Sykes, dike is Dykes, stile is Styles.

Here we come to a curious but natural custom. It is evident that in monosyllabic local names a genitive form was used. Brooks meant Brook's son, Dykes was Dyke's son, Sykes was Syke's son, Briggs was Brigg's son, Holmes was Holm's son, Styles was Style's son, Myers was Myer's son: cf. Jones, Williams, Tompkins, &c., a large class. The dissyllabic local class is small, the only one I remember at the moment being Borroughs or Burrows for Burrough.

Son for **ston**, thus turning a local into a baptismal surname: cf. Balderson for Balderston, Kelson for Kelston, Sherson for Sherston, Shillson for Shilston, Sprosson for Sproston, or Huddleson (Philadelphia) for Huddleston. Probably Hillson stands for Hillsdon. This list is by no means exhaustive: cf. Chilson for Childeston, Coltson for Colston, or Compson for Compston.

Sp for **th**, &c. Sturgess stands for the great personal name Thurgis, Pillsbury for Spillsbury, Pickernell for Spigurnell, and Pichfat for Spichfat. These are oddities that may be placed together. But these freaks were not uncommon: cf. Potticary and Prentice for Apothecary and Apprentice, or Cater for Achatour.

Ph for **f**, and vice versa. Cf. Physick for Fishwick, Phetteplace for Fetteplace, Philbrick for Fellbrigg (a parish in co. Norf.), Philby for Filby. On the other hand, Philcock is found as Filcock (v. Philcox), Filpot stands for Philpot, Filkin for Philkin. Again, Phillis has taken the place of Felice. Perhaps the most interesting instance in the list is that of Phillimore for Finamour, 'pure love'

(v. Finnemore, Filmore, and Phillimore, where a local origin is also given). That this charming old Norman name is parent of most of our Phillimores there can scarce be a doubt. The seeming local suffix presents no difficulty: cf. Parramore for Paramour, which when it arose meant an honest lover.

OFFICIAL AND OCCUPATIVE.

There are few variations to be mentioned under this head. The official comprises the smallest class, and occupative names the next smallest. There is no material change or modification in their form, but historically they are very interesting. Such names as Napier (with intrusive *i*), Carver, Sewer, Ewer, Chamberlain, Butler, Spencer, Page, Smallpage, &c., are with us to-day, and represent indoor offices familiar to the baronial halls of the surname period.

Of outdoor positions of official or semi-official importance we may mention such duties as those of Woodward, Pinder, Catchpole, Hunt, Falconer or Faulkner, &c. Of course, Catchpole was a nickname, but it acquired a semi-official position, like Shakespear, &c.

Son as a suffix to occupative names. This is a small but interesting class: cf. Hindson or Hinson, Herdson, Shepherdson. Even Taylorson exists in Yorkshire; I have seen the name over a shop in Ripon. I hope some member of the family will marry and have, say, nine sons, all healthy, and continue this old English surname. Tinkerson also holds a precarious existence; so does Cooperson.

Herd, as a suffix, has undergone strange experiences. The suffix itself has given us Herd, Hird, and Heard; and in compounds we get such surnames as the Yorkshire Calvert for Calveherd, Coward for Cowherd, Swinnart for Swineherd, Stoddart for Stotherd, and the old Yorkshire Oxenherd still manages to survive in Oxnard. I was delighted to see it above a shop in Newcastle-upon-Tyne at the Church Congress some years ago. Many more cases occur in this dictionary.

Monger as a suffix: cf.

> RICHARD LE FLESMONGERE (butcher), co. Bucks, 1273. A.
> THOMAS LE GARLYKMONGER, c. 1310. M.
> RALPH LE CORNMONGER. T.
> JOHN LE MELMONGERE (meal), c. 1310. M.
> DENIS LE OTEMONGER, London. X.
> WALTER LE HEYMONGERE. G.

All these are obsolete, I fear, as well as Woodmonger, &c.; but Iremonger or Ironmonger still survives.

Maker as a suffix: cf.

> WILLIAM PARCHMENTMAKER, Close Roll, 4 Henry V.
> AGNES POUCHEMAKER, co. York. W. 2.
> JOHN MONEMAKER, co. York. W. 2.
> JOHN LE CANDLEMAKERE, t. 1300. M.
> THOMAS CLOKMAKER, 1428 : Proceedings and Ordinances of the Privy Council.
> THOMAS LE AUNSEREMAKER (a scale or balance maker), London. X.

This list also could be easily added to.

Hewer as a suffix. This represents a small number, but one or two still live: cf. Woodyer for Woodhewer ('hewers of wood,' A. V.), or Stonehewer, or Fleshewer, a butcher.

> WILLIAM FLESSCHEWER, co. York. W. 2.
> JOHN FLESHEWER, *carnifex*, 1379, P. T. Yorks. p. 196.
> JOHN STONEHEWER. AA. 4.
> ROBERT LE WODEHYEWERE. H.

Smith as a suffix. The colour of the metal worked on was frequently compounded with *smith*. We find Brownsmith, Blacksmith, Greensmith, White-smith, and Redsmith, who seem severally to have worked in copper, iron, lead, tin, and gold, the last-named being in fact a goldsmith. Most of these still survive. Arrowsmith explains itself, in spite of what has been written. Billsmith and Spearsmith also require no interpretation. As regards colour-names, several examples may be mentioned :

> WILLIAM BROUNSMYTH, co. Soms., 1 Edw. III : Kirby's *Quest*, p. 107.
> SIMON BRONSMYTH, 1379, P. T. Yorks. p. 163.
> WILLIAM LE BLAKESMITH, C. R., 54 Henry III.
> RICHARD GRENSMYTHE, t. Eliz. Z.
> RICHARD LE WYTESMITH, C. R., 45 Henry III.
> JOHN RODESMITHE (Redesmith ?). D.

Oddly enough, whitesmith and blacksmith remain as occupative terms, and the others, saving one, as surnames. It is probable that Nasmith is Knifesmith; but if not it is Nailsmith, now as an occupative term, nailer. But I suspect it will be found to be Knifesmith.

Wright as a suffix. Compounds ending in *wright* are generally simple of explanation. Take such entries as:

JOHN BOTEWRIGHT, co. Norf., 1474. FF. vi. 215.
HUGH LE LIMWRYTE (a lime-burner), co. Bucks, 1273. A.
THOMAS LE GLASWRYGHTE, London. X.
JOHN CHESEWRIGHT, t. Eliz. Z.
HUGH LE SCHIPWRYTE, co. Camb., 1273. A.
WALTER WELWRYGHTE (a wheelwright), co. Essex, 1273. A.
ROBERT LE CARTWRIGHT. B.
ROBERT LE WAINWRIGHT. H.
JOHN BORDWRYGT (a carpenter), 1379, P. T. Yorks. p. 161.

We may mention also the Yorkshire Arkwright, a maker of meal-bins, shaped like a Noah's ark ; Tellwright, a manufacturer of tiles, found around Burslem ; or Slaywright, a maker of looms. Of the above, nearly all survive in our directories. But we must not be deceived by such names as Allwright, or Woolwright, or Kenwright. These are personal names; Allwright's descent is plain :

ALRICUS DE AULABY, co. York, 1273. A.
WILLIAM ALRICHT, co. Bedf., Hen. III–Edw. I. K.

For Woolwright v. Woolrich, and for Kenwright v. Kendrick.

Er as a suffix. This requires small attention : cf. Tucker, Walker, or Fuller, all in the same business :

ROGER LE TUKERE, co. Dorset, 1273. A.
GEOFFREY LE WALKERE, London, 1273. A.
ROBERT MEGSON, *walkare*, 1379, P. T. Yorks. p. 159.

Hence such occupative surnames as Parker, Tasker, Fletcher, Baker, Conder, Mawer, Mather, Kisser, Spicer, or Poulter. Kisser deserves notice, as the name still exists :

RICHARD LE KISSERE, London. X.
WALTER DE BEDEFONT, *kissere*, London. X.

The Kisser was a maker of cuishes, thigh-armour.

Ster as a suffix. At first a feminine terminative : cf. Spinster for Spinner. Hence such occupations as Rokster, Brewster, Baxter for Baker, Kempster (a wool-comber), Simister (now sempstress), Blaxter (a bleacher), Pipester (a piper), Breadmongster, all of which may be looked upon probably as avocations followed by women :

JULIANA ROKSTER, 1388. RR. 2.
MATILDA BLAKESTER, London, 1273. A.
GILIANA LE BACKSTER, co. Hunts, 1273. A.
SARA LA BREDEMONGSTERE, London. X.

ALICE PIPESTRE, Close Roll, 30 Edw. I.
AGNES KEMBESTER, 1379, P. T. Yorks., p. 219.
JOHANNA SAPER, *kemster*, 1379, P. T. Howdenshire, p. 12.

The same suffix is found in Walkster, i.e. Walker (a fuller), and Webster, both probably female employments.

JOHANNES WALKESTER, *fullo*, 1379, P. T. Yorks., p. 186.
ALICIA WRYGHT, *huswyfe*, *webster*, ibid., p. 66.

Of other examples, cf. Glaister for Glaser, Palister for Paliser, Litster (now Lister) for Litter, Slaster for Slater, Thackster or Thaxter for Thacker, or Dempster for Deemster. Palister still survives in American directories. It was an old Yorkshire term for a parker. Glaister was a glazier, and the name still lives.

ROBERTUS CLERKSON, *sclaster*, 1379, P. T. Yorks., p. 61.
AGNES SCLASTER, ibid., p. 3.

This is a Yorkshire term for a slater. Many of the above surnames flourish to-day in England and the United States.

BAPTISMAL SURNAMES.

Ing and **win** as suffix. It is curious to notice that these two suffixes go side by side, sometimes suggesting that *ing* is the parent, sometimes that *win* is, and that from a modified *in*, and excrescent *g*, it has become *ing*. The instances seem innumerable: cf. Hurlwin and Hurling or Hurlin, Hardwin and Harding, Brunwin and Bruning or Browning, Gunwin and Gunning, Goodwin and Gooding, Goldwin and Golding.

Idge as suffix for **ich**. Thus Aldrich becomes Aldridge, Eldrich becomes Eldridge, Surrich becomes Surridge, &c. These look local but are not so.

T as prefix to **a**. Hence Taggy for Aggie (Agnes), still used as a *nick* in Furness, North Lancashire; Taddy for Addy (Adam): cf. Teddy for Edward.

G after **n**, an excrescence. Hence Jenin (Littlejohn), Jening, and *gen.* Jennings; cf. Collin (Nicholas), Collins, and Collinge; Embling for Emlin or Emeline. This list could be extended to any amount.

X for **ks** and **cks**. Cf. Coxon for Cockson, Wilcoxon for Wilcockson (the son of William), Dixon for Dickson, Rixon for Rickson (Richard), Cox for Cocks, Hixon and Hix for Hickson and Hicks (Richard); cf. Baxter for Bakester (a female baker), Blaxter for Blakister (a female bleacher).

P after **m**: cf. Thompson for Thomson, Simpson for Simson (the son of

C

Simon), Hampson for Hamson (the son of Hamon).   Lampson is Lambson, i.e. Lambert's son, and is strictly only a change from *b* to *p*: cf. the local Hampton, or Southampton.

B after **m**. Cf. Embling (with excrescent *g*) for Emlin (Emeline), or Hambling for Hameline (Hamon).

D, an excrescence after **n**. Cf. ribbon and riband, and the provincial *drownded* for drowned, or *gownd* for gown. Thus Simmonds for Simmons (Simon), Hammond for Hamon, Jolland for Jollan, Walrand for Waleran, Hind for Hine, Hollingdrake for Hollingrake, Grindrod for Greenroyd, Standfield for Stanfield, Standring for Stannering. Even Somendour for Sumner existed. Rowantree is found also as Roundtree to-day, and in my *London Directory* occur three Towndrows for Townrow. Take two examples:

1603.   Buried—SUSAND CARDWELLE, St. Jas. Clerkenwell, iv. 74.

But Susan in this form has made no impression. It is different with Simon; the excrescent *d* was early in vogue:

JOHN SIMOND, co. Oxf., 1273. A.
'JOHANNES that was servant of Symond Godewyne.'—Patent Roll, 17 Ric. II, pt. 2.

Hence not merely Simmons but Simmonds. There is not the slightest evidence that Sigismund was the parent of Simond or Symond. Simon was more popular than Peter, probably because of the obnoxious Peter's pence. This objection has made a great difference to the directories of to-day.

N, a prefix to personal and local surnames with an initial vowel. Thus Nab was the *nick* of Abel, whence Nabbs; Nibb was the *nick* of Isabel; Nobbs was a variation of Hobbs, sharpened into Nopps and Hopps (Robert); cf. Noll, the *nick* of Oliver. Other instances may be furnished; Nanson for Anson. Later on Nan became Nanney and Nancy. In some cases Nelson must not be attributed to Nel (Eleanor, a most popular girl-name in the surname epoch) but to Neilson, from an equally popular Niel or Nigel. As regards Nab, we may quote the *Alchemist* (1610), where Abel, the tobacco-man, is familiarly Nab:

'Six o' thy legs more will not do it, Nab.'—Act ii. sc. 1.

Of local instances where the final *n* of 'atten' became the prefix of the name proper, we may mention Nokes, 'atten-okes'; Nash, 'atten-ash'; or Nail, 'atten-ale' (i.e. alehouse); all from residence thereby; cf. also Nalder:

PHILIP ATTENOKE, Close Roll, 3 Edw. I.
RICHARD ATTE NOKE. P.

ALICE ATTENALRE, i. e. ' at the alder-tree.'   J.
SARRA ATTENESHE.   B.
AGNES ATE NASSE, co. Oxf., 1273.   A.

Nale, and its modern imitative Nail, is an interesting relic:

' And maken him gret festes at the nale.'—Chaucer, *C. T.* 6931.

Nelmes belongs to the same category:

OSBERT ATTE ELME, co. Oxf., 1273.   A.

A or **i** turned into **in.**   Hence Pottinger for Potager, Massinger or Messinger for Messager, Clavinger for Claviger.   Pennager seems to have remained unmodified:

ROBERT CLAVYNGER (the mace-bearer).   H.
JOHN LE POTAGER (a maker of pottage, a thick soup), co. Soms., 1 Edw. III, Kirby's *Quest*, p. 272.
1762.   Married—BENJAMIN POTTINGER and ELIZ. DANCE, St. Geo. Han. Sq. i. 112.
WILLIAM LE PENNAGER (an ensign bearer).   E.

T for **d**, and vice versa.   Hence Atkins for Adkins (Adam), Atty for Addie (Adam), Tandy for Dandy, Tyson for Dyson, Tennyson for Dennison, Chantler for Chandler, Hazleteen or Hazletine for Hazledean, Prout for Proud, Thring for Dring, Henty for Hendy, Rayment for Raymond, or Dottridge for Doddridge. On the other hand we find Dandridge for Tandridge, Dibble for Tibble, Ditchburn for Titchburn, Doogood for Toogood, or Dunnicliff for Tunnicliffe.   A good instance of the disposition to interchange is found in the two entries following:

1651, Oct. 12.   Bapt.—RUTH, d. ROBERT and ELIZABETH TOOGOOD, Reg. St. Thomas the Apostle (London), p. 59.
1653, Feb. 15.   Bapt.—RALPH, s. ROBERT and ELIZABETH DOOGOOD, Reg. St. Thomas the Apostle (London), p. 59.

Ch for **j.**   Hence probably Chubb for Jubb (Job).   Hence also such an entry as Challand for Jalland:

1789.   Married—JAMES WIMBLE and MARTHA CHALLAND, St. Geo. Han. Sq. ii. 34.

Cf. Choice for Joyce.

J and **g** interchangeable.   Hence Jack and Gill, now more correctly printed Jack and Jill; Joscelyn for Goscelin, now Gosling (imitative); Jarrett for Gerard; cf. gaoler for jailer.

G and **c.**   Hence Gusterson for Custerson, Grain (imitative) for Crane, Glithcrow for Clitheroe, and vice versa.   Especially interesting is the North English Candlin for the famous old name of Gandelyn.   Grandage is found to-day for Cranidge,

Cammell (imitative) for Gammell. Even Gatcliff is entered as Catliff in P. T. Yorks., 1379, p. 63, showing how early such changes occurred. Cf. also Carbutt for Garbutt, or Camidge for Gamage.

M for **n**, when the termination of each syllable is *n*. Cf. the words random and ransom, for randon and ranson. Similarly Pensom represents Penson, Hansom is Hanson, Ransom and Ransome are Ranson (Randolph). Professor Skeat says that Hansom means Handsome. After thirty years' study I find no instance of this nickname, and it may be taken for granted that Hans (John) is the parent. We may notice here that Kingdon has become sometimes the imitative Kingdom. Amabel also became Annabel, then Hannibal, whence many curious surmises as to its origin. Passing along we may observe that Mumby is Munby, and Mumford is Mundford.

N for **m**, and vice versa. Cf. Sinkinson for Simkinson (Simon), Grinstead for Grimstead (the homestead of Grim), Sunter for Sumpter; cf. Henning and Hemming (v. Henning), vice versa; cf. Stimpson for Stinson (Stevenson), or Hempstock for Henstock. An instance may be given where Sandbach is turned into Sambach:

1677. SAMUEL CARNABY and AMY SAMBACH, Marriage Alleg. (Canterbury), p. 272.

Ce for **s**. Cf. Preece for Prees, Ellice for Ellis, Pearce for Piers, Evance for Evans, Bevance for Bevans, Hance for Hans, or Hemmence for Hemmens. Clemence for Clements may also be mentioned, although it sometimes represents the baptismal Clemens.

K for **g**, or vice versa. Cf. the present Kilbey and Gilby. A tendency to elide *c* in surnames ending in *cliff* is seen in Antliff for Antcliffe, Sutliff for Sutcliffe, Topliff for Topcliff, or Hinchliff for Hinchcliff.

N for **l**, and vice versa. A common illustration is *banister* for *baluster*. Even the old *twichen* (an alley) of the western and southern counties is found as *twichell* in the North, whence Twichell and Twichen.

W for **g** (Norman-Fr.). William for Guillaume, Warren or Waring or Wareing (excrescent *g*) for Guarin, Wye for Guy, and the *dim.* familiar Wyatt (originally Wyot) for Guyot. Also cf. Whichard for Gwichard, and Wyon (*dim.*) for Guion (Guy).

G prefixed to **w** (Welsh). Gwalter for Walter, Gwynne for Wynne, Gwatkin for Watkin, Gwelch for Welch, sharpened also into Quelch (St. Jas. Register, Clerkenwell, proves the two names to be the same); also Gwyther for Wither; Gwillam stands for William; cf. the local Quickley for Whixley.

Reversal of **r** to first syllable. Grundy for Gundry, the once famous girl-name Gundreda. I should like to know if Brodrick is not in some cases the Welsh ab-Roderick, but I have no evidence.

V for **f**, generally a West Country dialectic change. Thus Vowell for Fowell, Venn for Fenn:

> JOHN ATTE VENNE, co. Soms., 1 Edw. III, Kirby's *Quest*, p. 94.

Vowler for Fowler:

> THOMAS LE VOWELAR, co. Soms., 1 Edw. III, ibid., p. 256.

Vox for Fox:

> JOHN LE VOX, co. Soms., 1 Edw. III, ibid., p. 93.

Vry for Fry:

> STEPHEN LE VRYE, co. Soms., 1 Edw. III, ibid., p. 171.

Vrench for French:

> JOHN LE VREYNCH, co. Soms., 1 Edw. III, ibid., p. 230.

Cf. Vidler for Fidler, Vanner for Fanner, or Viveash for Fiveash.

P for **m** in female names :—

(1) Hence Margaret became the *nick* Meg, then Peg, whence Pegg, Pegson, &c. Also Margaret became *nick* Mog (Moggy is still in use in North England), hence the sharpened Mockson (Mogson), now more generally Moxon (a Yorkshire surname).

(2) Hence Martha became Matty, then Patty (except when descended from Patrick and its *nicks* in North England), Pattinson, Patterson, &c.

(3) Hence Mary became Moll and Molly, whence Poll and Polly, and resulted in such surnames as Polson, &c.

Kins (suffix) abbreviated to **iss** and **es**. Hence Perkins (Peter) became Purkiss and finally Perkes; so also Wilks for Wilkins, Danks for Dankins, Tonks for Tonkins, Dawks for Dawkins, &c.; cf. Hobbins, Hobbiss, and Hobbis, also Hollins, Holliss, Hollis (Holly).

Ou or **ow** for **o**. Cf. Poulson and Powlson for Polson (but sometimes for Paulson pronounced Powle), Howell and Powell for Hoel, Houlden for Holden, Houle for Hole, Hoult for Holt, Boulton for Bolton, Houlgate for Holgate, Houlbrook for Holbrook, Houldsworth for Holdsworth, or Houlditch for Holditch. The pretty girl's name Gold is now as a surname Gould: 'He gave me a gowlden sovereign.' Cf. *browt* for brought, or Browton-in-Furness for Broughton-in-Furness. Cf. a sentence like this: 'He *owt* to give me something off, I *bowt* it at his shop.' Hence Cowlings (with excrescent *g*) for Collins, Cowles or Coules for Coles (Nicholas). This practice may be described as a provincialism, but it has left a permanent impression on our nomenclature.

Ck and **g** (lazified forms). Cf. Fligg and Flick, Slagg and Slack, possibly Segger and Secker. In *Piers Plowman* we find Jagg for Jack. Black is found as Blag; hence Blagg, Blagden, or Blagbrough. Also cf. Brogden for Brockden.

P for **b**. Hopps is Hobbs, Hopson is Hobson, Hopkins is Hobkins, Ropkins is Robkins, and Nopps is Nobbs; Epps is Ebbs, and probably Puckle is Buckle; Plackett represents Blackett, Pullinger Bullinger, and Peverley Beverley; Pickerdike stands for the North English Bickerdike, and Peattie for Beattie has made its way into the *London Directory*. It is somewhat doubtful whether P or B was the original initial of Pickwick, an old West Country surname:

WILLIAM DE PIKEWIKE, co. Wilts, 1273. A.
WALTER DE BYKEWYK, co. Soms., 1 Edw. III, Kirby's *Quest*, p. 103.

For further references v. Pickwick; cf. purser and bursar. It is hard to tell also whether *p* or *b* is correct in Stapler and Stabler, or Stapleford and Stableford. Some will remember, after the great *Times* Trial, the play upon Pigotry and Bigotry.

A and **e** interchangeable. Gervis and Jarvis, Clerk and Clark, Perkin and Parkin, Hermitage and Armitage, &c.

Er for **in** or **en**. This was a very natural corruption; cf. Patterson for Pattinson (Patrick), Catterson for Cattinson (Catherine), Steverson for Stevenson (Stephen), Dickerson for Dickinson (Richard), Matterson for Mattinson (Martha or Matthew), Batterson for Battinson (Bartholomew), all from the *nicks* of Patrick, Catherine, Hugh, Stephen, Richard, Martha, Bartholomew, with the Norman-French dim. *in* attached (as in viol-in, &c.); turned popularly into *er*. Thus without doubt Hugh is the parent of such a name as Hutcherson (New York). These, and others, are all the result of quick or hurried pronunciation.

O and **a**. Generally North Country variations: cf. Dabbs for Dobbs, Dadd and Dadson for Dodd and Dodson; cf. also the many local Rattan Raws in the North with Southern Rotton Row.

Double diminutives in **el-ot** or **el-et**. These are found in such dictionary words as tartlet, bracelet, gauntlet, roblet, gimblet, poplet. The old *ruff*, or high collar, was styled a *partlet*:

' Jan. 1544: item from Mr. Braye ii high collar partletts, iii^s ix^d.'—Privy Purse Expenses, Princess Mary.

Hence partlet, a hen, on account of its ruffled feathers. In our modern nomenclature we find few traces of this diminutive. The *Paris Directory* has many
instances. But in old days we were very familiar with it: cf. Evelot for Eve,
Emelot for Emma, Edelot for Ede, Gibelot (now Giblett) for Gilbert, Custelot
for Custance, Richelot or Rikelot for Richard or Rikard, Sisselot for Cecilia,
Hobelot for Robert, Herbelet for Herbert (found in the *Liverpool Directory*).
Of this list several have made a marked impression on our English and American
directories: Hewlett (for Hugh or Hew), a flourishing surname in North England,
is a case in point:

> THOMAS HUGHELOT, co. Soms., 1 Edw. III, Kirby's *Quest*, p. 220.
> WALTER HUWELOT, co. Oxf., 1273. A.

Again, we retain the historic Hamlet (Shakespeare's little son was baptized Hamnet)
for Hamelot, a *dim.* of Hamon. As a baptismal name it is not dead:

> HAMLET MILOT, of Carrington, husbandman, 1587: Wills at Chester, i. 136.

Bartlett or Bartelot for Bartholomew, also still lives:

> BARTELOT GOVI, co. Hunts, 1273. A.

Eline, a *dim.* Cf. Hamlyn or Hambling for Hameline (Hamo), Emberlin or
Embling for Emeline, Hanselin for Hans, Hewling for Hughelin (Hugh), Roblin
for Robert. The excrescent *g* is strongly represented in this class.

We may notice one peculiar girl's name—Arrabella. This has puzzled even
Miss Yonge. The original name was Amabel, then Annable (in Scotland
sharpened to Annaple), whence with aspirate the surname Hanniball. Amabella
became Anabella, then Arrabella—one of those freaks hard to account for.

Double diminutives in in-ot or in-et. France has plenty of these, we have
few. The *Paris Directory* on a cursory glance furnishes us with such surnames
(at first, of course, Christian names) as Margotin (we simply kept to the one
diminutive Margot), Marioton (our Mariot), Lambinet (Lambert), Perrinot or
Perrotin (Peter), Philiponet (Philip), Jannotin (Jane), Hugonet (Hugh) whence
Huguenot, Fauconnet (Fulke). Perrinot and Perrotin (little wee Peter) simply
reverse the order of the two diminutives. The dictionary word 'marionette' in
the puppet-show owes its name to Mary (we were content with the single
diminutive Marion). So far as this class of double diminutives goes we have
only four names to show, namely, Robinet, Dobinet, Colinet, and Jannetin (this
last also reversing the order). Robinet still lives as a surname. In Spenser's
Shepherd's Calendar we find:

'Hearken, while from thy green cabinet,
The laurel song of careful Colinet.'

Colnett and Colenutt are yet alive. Jannetin also occurs (Jannet was our familiar form):

'The one's Nancy Curds, and the other Hanna Jenniting ; Ditty and Jenniting [excrescent *g*] are agreed already.'—*London's Chanticleers,* sc. xiii.

Jenniting is the apple-girl (v. Jenneting, Skeat). Dobinet existed till the middle of the fifteenth century, for we find one John Dobynette is mentioned in an inventory of goods, 1463 (*Mun. Acad., Oxon.*).

Diminutives in **ot** and **et**. These may be illustrated thus. Take Tillotson, a great Yorkshire name. Tillotson was the son of Tillot, which was the *dim.* of Till, which was the *nick* of Matilda. All the diminutives in *ot* and *et* were added to the *nick* of the name, which was always one syllable. Emmett or Emmott, or Emmetson or Emmotson, are sprung from Emma, but the *nick* being Em the *dim.* was Emmot or Emmett. Collett is the *dim.* of Col or Cole, the *nick* of Nicholas. This rule reigned supreme. I have only mentioned two instances; the directories abound with them. Thus we find Emmott or Emmett:

'Licence to the Vicar of Bradford to marry ROGER PRESTWICK and EMMOTE CROSSLEY. Bannes thrice in one day.'—1466, *Test. Ebor.* iii. 317.

Under date 1414 occurs Tyllot Thompson in the *Fabric Rolls of York Minster* (Surtees Soc.). Hence Ibbott, Ibbett, Ibbotson or Ibbetson (Isabel), Mabbott (Mabel), Dowsett or Doucett (Douce), Margott or Magot (Margaret):

THOMAS DE BALME et MAGOTA uxor ejus: *chapman,* 1379, P. T. Yorks.

Sissot was very popular (Cecilia):

' SISSOT, wife of Jak of Barsley.'—Manor of Ashton-under-Lyne (Chetham Soc.).

It is needless to proceed. Mary became Mariot, Theobalda (fem. form) became Tibbot, whence a large number of surnames:

'Work Tibet: work Annot: work Margery:
Sew Tibet: knit Annot: spin Margery.'—*Ralph Roister Doister.*

Parallel dictionary words are found in jacket, lancet, target, latchet, pocket, chariot, &c.

Diminutives in **on** or **in**. A dictionary parallel is found in viol-in, a fiddle with four strings instead of six. The *Paris Directory* has very many illustrations, this being a Norman-French diminutive. Beton represented Beatrice:

'Beton the Brewestere
  Bade him good-morrow.'—*Piers Plowman.*

Alison still survives in Scotland as the *dim.* of Alice:

'This Alison answered: Who is there
  That knocketh so?'—Chaucer, *C. T.* 3788.

Huggins or Hutchins represents a once familiar term for Hugh, Perrin for Peter, Marion for Mary, Robin or Dobbin for Robert, Colin for Nicholas, Phippin for Philip, Gibbin or Gibbon for Gilbert. This class is also a large one. An excrescent *g* was frequently appended to the surname; cf. Jennings (John), Tippings (Theobald), or Collings (Colin). The *London Directory* contains Lamming and Laming, representatives of the old Lambin, diminutive of Lambert. Lambyn Clay played before Edward at Westminster in 1306 (Chappell's *Popular Music of ye Olden Time,* i. 29). I find also

WILLELMUS LAMBYN et ALICIA uxor ejus, 1379, P. T. Yorks.

Diminutives in **kin.**

Kin came to mean a 'young one,' a child. We still speak in a diminutive sense of a lambkin, a manikin, a pipkin, a kilderkin, a jerkin, or a doitkin. Appended to baptismal names it became familiar. *A litul soth Sermun* says—

'Nor those prude yongemen
    That loveth Malekyn (Mary),
  And those prude maydenes
    That loveth Janekyn' (John).

.   .   .   .

'Masses and matins
    He kepeth they nouht,
  For Wilekyn (William) and Watekyn (Walter)
    Be in their thouht.'

The incomers from Brabant and Flanders gave a great impetus to this diminutive. They brought us Hankin (John), Lambkin (Lambert), and Bodkin (Baldwin). Of a large list I may mention Hawkins (Henry), Tompkins (Thomas), Simkin (Simon), Jenkins (John), Jeffkin (Jeffrey), Atkins, originally Adkins (Adam), Dawkins (David), Larkin (Lawrence), Dickins (Richard), and Perkins or Parkins (Peter). These are the most familiar.

Diminutives in **cock.**

The term *cock* implied pertness, especially the pertness of lusty and swaggering youth. Hence it was applied to the scullery lad, or stable-boy, or prentice:

'Come hither, Cock ; what, Cock, I say.'—*Gammer Gurton's Needle.*

We still use the term 'cock-sure.' Appended to the *nick* of boy-names we find Jeffcock (Jeffrey), Simcock (Simon), Batcock or Badcock (Bartholomew), Sandercock (Alexander), Luccock (Luke, sometimes), Maycock or Mycock (Matthew), Hitchcock or Hiscock (Hick or Hitch, i. e. Richard), Hancock or Handcock (Han, Hand, or Hans), Adcock or Atcock (Adam), Drewcock (Drew), or Palcock (Paul). Many more examples will be found in the pages of this book. *Cock* was always added to the *nick* of the baptismal name.

> 'HAMME, son of ADECOCK, held 29 acres of land ;
> MOKOCK DE LA LOWE, for 10 acres ;
> DIK, son of MOCOCK, of Breercroft, for 20 acres.'—*De Lacy Inquisition*, Chetham Soc.

So they run.

Ecclesiastical, natural, and holiday seasons have had considerable effect upon our nomenclature. Whitsunday, Pentecost (just dying out in Cornwall as a girl's baptismal name), Easter, Pash, Pask, Pace, Pacey, Midwinter, Candlemas, Noel or Nowell, Michaelmas, Christmas, and Tiffany (Epiphany), all represent old font-names, commemorating the time of the birth or baptism of the child. All but Whitsunday are existing surnames. Of the natural seasons we may mention Winter, Spring, and Summer (sometimes). Of high days we have memorials in Hockday and Hobday. Tiffany was popular, shortened frequently to Tiffen :

> THEOFANIA DE BOLEBEK, C. R., 46 Henry III.
> TEFFAN DANYLL, 1379, P. T. Yorks., p. 148.
> JOHANES HOLAND et TIFFAN uxor ejus, 1379, P. T. Yorks., p. 134.

Evidently it was a girl's name. It has left many memorials in our modern directories.

In regard to local surnames pure and simple, we have, of course, to deal with the prefix and suffix.

Taking the prefix first, the fight lay between the name of the primary settler or proprietor, and the distinctive local surroundings. Thus we get Ashton, Birkhead (now Birkett as a surname), Oakden (or Ogden), Acton, Acland, Beecham, Beechey, Hazelden, Sandford, Bradford, Oxenford, Twelvetrees, Viveash, Longton, Plumptree, Rowntree, and an enormous number of local affixes. But there is an extremely large number of local surnames prefixed with the personal name of the first settler or owner. The great name of Ulf or Wolf gives us

Ulverston, Wolferton, Wolverhampton; Wolfstan gives us Wolstenholme or Wolstencroft, Hacon gives us Haconby, Dolphin gives us Dovenby in co. Cumb., Cholmond gives us Cholmondeley, Margaret gives us Murgatroyd. In fact a huge host of surnames compounded of the occupant's personal name with the style of the dwelling, or the natural surroundings of the place, can be seen scattered over the country. Osmotherley, a place-name in cos. Lanc. and Yorks., was Osmunderley (i. e. the meadow of Osmund), sometimes written in old documents Asmunderlaw.

We find also variants of a personal name; cf. Shillingford, Killingworth, and Chillingworth. These seem to represent changes rung upon what we should now style a baptismal name; unless they represent a *family* name, as in Washington, Birmingham, &c. Hundreds of these are personal names now obsolete. Audenshaw is now a suburb of Manchester. It was once Aldwinshaw (the wood that belonged to Aldwin). Liverpool is interesting; at first it was Litherpool, and no doubt the occupier of Litherland, now a suburb of the city, was the possessor or tenant of the pool as well. Lither or Leather was a personal name, as our topography proves (cf. Leatherbarrow, Leatherhead, &c.). Take two instances as regards Liverpool, no doubt representing the same man:

RICHARD LITHERPOL, co. Lanc., Hen. III, Edw. I. K.
RICHARD DE LIVERPOL, co. Lanc., 20 Edw. I. R.

Even now Leverton exists for Letherton. But it may be asked why Litherpool became Liverpool at such an early period? The reply is simple. If you say Litherland quickly, say twelve times in a breath, with the aid of the liquid you can do it easily. Try to say Litherpool quickly twelve times in a breath and only a small percentage would escape saying Liverpool on account of the labial *p*. Thus the bird styled the liver, and emblazoned on the arms of the city, is imaginary and never existed. In a word we have yet to recognize the tremendous influence of personal names on local nomenclature.

Coming to the suffixes I shall not name many. To the general reader I advise a study of Canon Isaac Taylor's appendices to *Words and Places*. I want to point out chiefly the mutilations of such suffixes.

One of the most familiar suffixes is **ey** (sometimes **ay**). This in nineteen cases out of twenty represents *hey*, or *hay*, the *h* being elided, and meant a hedge, an enclosed place. Hay still survives in co. Norfolk for a hedge, but is dying out (Halliwell); cf. Churchey, Fotheringay, Goldingay. Of course this *ey* is to be distinguished from *ey* and *eyot*, a little islet in a stream: cf. Forty for Forthey, 'de la Fortheye,' existing in co. Oxford in 1273, and still found there in the imitative form of Forty.

White for **thwaite**, a clearing. Cf. Applewhite, Kibblewhite, Hebblewhite, &c.

Thorpe becomes **thrup, throp, trup,** or **trop.** Cf. Calthrop for Calthorp, Feltrup for Felthorp, Winthrop for Winthorp, Guntrop for Gunthorp, &c. Thrupp for Thorpe is well known to our directories.

Ham sometimes becomes **um**; rare in England, but fairly common in America: cf. Barnum for Barnham, or Holtum for Holtham.

Royd (presumably a *ridding*, a clearing) sometimes becomes **rod.** While we have Oldroyd, Murgatroyd (Margaret's clearing), &c., we have also Ormerod (Orme's clearing), Grindrod (the green clearing), with an intrusive *d*. In the *Pirates of Penzance* Murgatroyd is placed in Cornwall! It is a purely West Riding name. But poets have a recognized licence to place anybody anywhere. Cf.

JOHANNES MERGRETRODE, 1379, P. T. Yorks., p. 187.

Halgh for **hough** or **haugh**, a hill, a mound, the same as How; cf. Featherstonhalgh for Featherstonhaugh, Greenhalgh for Greenhow. Ridehalgh is a familiar name in co. Lanc.

By as a suffix is not unfrequently found as **bee**. This is not unknown in England, but is a more familiar suffix in America. Still we have a fair number of examples; cf.

1667. THOMAS LOWNES and MARY DIMBLEBEE, Marriage Alleg. (Canterbury), p. 143.
1667. Married—JOHN DAGGOT and ANN FARRABEE, St. Jas. Clerkenwell, iii. 135.
1775. WILLIAM NORRIS and SARAH APPELBEE, St. Geo. Han. Sq. i. 258.

Appelbee is still in the *London Directory.* One other instance will suffice:

1669. Married—WILLIAM CARNABEE and MARTHA COWLEY, St. Jas. Clerkenwell, iii. 160.

Carnaby is a village near York. Crossing the Atlantic in the Puritan period this form of the suffix *by* has become popular in the States. Many local suffixes describe situation. Thus:

End, as in Townsend, Woodend, from residence at the end of the town or wood; cf. Gravesend.

Side, as in Akenside or Garside, from residence by the side of the oak-trees or the garth.

Bottom or **botham**, as in Sidebotham, Higginbottom or Hickinbottom, from residence at the side of the bottom, a hollow at the foot of a hill, or from a dwelling in the hollow where Higgin (Richard) lived. As for Shufflebotham, it has been constantly asserted that it means the shaw-field-bottom. This is not true (v. Shufflebotham), but under protection of Mr. Lower, who later on changed his opinion, several who bear the name have styled themselves Shawfield; I know a clergyman who has done so. Almost all the names with *bottom* as suffix hail from the district where the three counties, Lancashire, Derby, and Chester, converge in the neighbourhood of Stockport.

Head (i.e. the upper end) becomes frequently **ett**. Aikinhead is 'the head of the oak trees,' Muirhead is 'the head of the moor,' and Birkinhead is 'the head of the birch trees,' both Aiken and Birken being adjectives as in golden. These have retained their original form, but others have not. Birkett represents 'at the birk-head,' from residence at the upper end of the birch trees. Hazlitt is Hazlehead (the head of the hazel grove). Blackett is Blackhead, if not a nick-name, then from residence at the black headland. Becket is the beck-head, from residence at the commencement of the beck: hence A'Becket (i.e. atte beck-head); and Greenett is probably from residence at the upper end of the village green. I have no proof of this last, but it looks all right. And so with many others. It is all very well to call these modifications; they are really mutilations, and require close attention.

Dale as a suffix becomes commonly **dall**. Cf. Tindall for Tindale, Tweedall for Tweedale, Dunderdall for Dunderdale, Yewdall or Udall for Yewdale, Dowdall for Dowdale, or Chippindall for Chippindale. All these are North Country variants.

How (a hill, a mound) as a suffix frequently becomes **oe** and **o**. Cf. Sholto, or Shillitoe.

Hope (a sloping hollow) as a suffix is easily obscured. Cf. Blenkinsop, Allsopp, Winship, and Nettleship. The terminations in *ship* I cannot prove, but feel sure of their parentage.

Hus or **us** for **house**, seemingly old English and not a modification. We not only have Chanonhouse (the Canon's house), Moorhouse, Wodehouse or Woodhouse, Claverhouse (? Culverhouse), Parkhouse, Taphouse, so familiar to every musical Oxford man, Pithouse, &c., but we still possess Kirkus (Kirkhouse), Loftus (Loft-house), Malthus (Malthouse), or the imitative Bacchus (Bakehouse or Backhouse, i.e. the house at the back): I suspect Bakehouse is the chief parent. I may add that the nearly extinct Pithouse (the house by the pit or hollow) may be seen at Langley, co. Bucks (1894).

Gate or **yate** must be mentioned among the suffixes. Not only have we Yates or Yeats, Yeatman or Yatman, the caretaker of the gate, but the interesting Lidgett for Lidgate, and the still more interesting West Country Lippiatt or Lipyeatt (q. v.).

Brigg (a bridge) occasionally becomes **brick**. Cf. Philbrick (a good instance) or Maybrick.

The change in suffixes ending in **all** or **ol**, to **aw** or **ow**, is curious but natural. Hence Bristow for Bristol. There is one Bristoll in the *London Directory* to twenty-four Bristows. Latimer, writing to Thomas Cromwell, speaks of the bishop of ' Gloucester and Bristow.' A farmer in the North tells you he is going ' to th' haw ' (i. e. hall). Hence Howgate for Holgate, Howroyd for Holroyd. The old Furness name of Picthall is found there to-day, and in the United States as Pickthawe and Picthow. Similarly the ancient Lancashire name, Preesall, is found now only as Presow. These are instances out of a large list.

I must hurry over some suffixes that vary. Cf. Grave, Greave, Grove: hence Snelgrove, Hargreaves. Cf. Clough and Clow or Clowe, now as surname Clowes. We find the same change in *enough* and *enow*. Cf. also *worth* and *worthy*, as in Kenworthy, Whitworth, Langworthy, and Langworth. Cf. also Craft and Croft, as in the occupative Crafter and Crofter, and the local Calcraft and Bancroft, &c. Cf. also *ford* and *forth*: Stockport was formerly Stopford or Stockforth, and Bradford in the Yorkshire Poll Tax (1379) is Bradford or Bradforth, according to the mood of the registrar. One more example must suffice here: Ley, Lea, Lee, Legh, Leigh, Legge (as in Whitelegge), as local suffixes are all variants of the same word, *ley*, a meadow.

NICKNAMES.

FISH-NAMES.

With regard to nicknames, we have to be careful. The great unwritten law of imitation once more comes in. Fish-names, so called, excepting the generic term of Fish, or Fisk, are scarcely ever what they seem, being in nine cases out of ten personal or local names. We are on safe ground when we come to bird and beast nicknames. These all represent some physical or moral characteristic that appealed at once to the popular understanding. The ruddock, or the sparrow, or the bull, or the hart, were always before people's eyes. As nicknames, they represented some quality of strength, stolidity, quickness, or song. There was nothing particularly characteristic about the fish, and they were not always to be seen. But the habits of bird and beast were always observable, and were comparable with the habits of mankind. Scarcely a single bird or beast name has escaped immortality through the aid of our nomenclature. A fierce man would be termed Wild, but often Wildbore. An agile man might be termed Lightfoot or Golightly; but others would be styled Hare, or Hart, or Stagg. A musical voice would gain for the possessor the sobriquet of Nightingale; a homely man would be called Sparrow or Ruddock, just as often Goodfellow or Goodman. It is quite different with fish-names so called. We may quote the famous chapter on 'Snakes in Iceland': 'There are no snakes in Iceland,' and say 'there are no fish-names in England.' They possessed no individuality so to speak; they led a dull and monotonous life. But in respect to Hogg, Lamb, Wildgoose, Wildbore, Fox, Woodcock, Pidgeon, Spink, Speight, Swift, Hawk, Roebuck, &c., all implied some characteristic on the part of the nominee common to the bird or the beast. Take a few instances of so-called fish-names. Spratt, like Sprott, represents the old Domesday personal name, Sprot; Salmon is the mediaeval and popular English Salamon (i.e. Solomon); Haddock is easily proved to be the same as Haydock, a parish in South Lancashire; Pike is strictly local, and Chubb is most probably a sharpened form of Jubb (i.e. Job). Turbot is the son of Turbert:

TURBERT DE WESTCOT, Pipe Roll, 2 Hen. II, p. 74.

I only furnish a single instance. Trout is the son of Troyt, a great personal name in the West Country in the surname epoch (now generally Trott). Even Plaice is Place, from residence by the place or stead, or manor, or public broadway, or courtyard:

JOHN ATTE PLACE, co. Soms., 1 Edw. III, Kirby's *Quest*, p. 258.
WILLIAM DE LA PLACE, co. Linc., 1273. A.

In fact Plaice in the *London Directory* is simply an imitative form. The law of imitation, to assert it once more, must be carefully reckoned with by the student. It is the same with Roach, which is purely imitative, being simply the 'de la Roche' of early rolls:

GILBERT DE LA ROCHE, co. Wilts, 1273. A.
1675-6. Bapt.—ELIZ., d. THOMAS ROACH, St. Dionis Backchurch, p. 121.

Gudgeon is an imitative form of Goodson or Goodison (cf. Hodgon for Hodgson, in Cumberland and North Lanc.). Keeling may represent the now nearly extinct name for a small cod, once so common on the north-east coast; but in the Hundred

Rolls (1273) it is local. Finally, Herring is, as in Harrington, a family name. The Yorkshire Bucktrout seems to be really a fish-name, and is found early :

> ROBERTUS BUKTROUT, 1379, P. T. Yorks., p. 218.

BEAST-NAMES.

We still find traces of the habit of styling people by some animal that seemed to represent their chief characteristic. Hence *vixen* for a shrewish wife ; *rascal* for a vile, mean man ; or *urchin* for a rough, mischievous boy. Without being uncomplimentary, as our Authorized Version of the Book of Revelation proves, our Bests represent Beast :

> HENRY LE BESTE, London. X.
> RICHARD LE BESTE, co. Camb., 1273. A.

Our Oliphants or Olivants (i. e. elephant) were so called from their size. From surliness the sobriquet ' le Bere ' arose, now Bear. Fierceness of temper originated ' le Wolfe,' now Wolf ; wiliness, ' le Renaud,' ' le Tod,' and ' le Fox ' ; swiftness, and other characteristics, ' le Hare,' ' le Buk ' (Buck), ' le Hart,' ' le Stagge,' &c. The badger is parent of ' le Broc ' (Brock). The farming stock gave us Bull, Vache, Bullock, Colt, Stott, Veale, Mutton, Lamb, Kidd, Hogg, Bacon, Pigg, Pork, Purcell, Grice, and so on. Camel or Cammell does not belong to this list, being but a sharpened form of the great personal name, Gamel ; and Badger is generally occupative, meaning a hawker, a dealer in corn.

BIRD-NAMES.

The generic term ' Bird ' was common, and still is:

> DAVID LE BRID, co. Oxf., 1273. A.
> HENRY LE BRID, co. Soms., 1 Edw. III, Kirby's *Quest*, p. 92.

Coming to species, falconry helped to make ' le Falcon,' ' le Kyte,' or ' le Hawk ' familiar, the originals being probably of an eagerly grasping disposition. Hence also Muskett, Buzzard, Puttock, Goshawk, Tassell, Gleed (or Glide), or Sparrow-hawk. Thus was it with other birds. A showy man was Jay, a proud man Peacock or Pocock, a man of guile Rook ; if pert, then Pye, Pyet, or Pyett ; if musical, Laverock (or Lark), Woodlark, Nightingale :

> THOMAS NIGHTEGALE, co. Glouc., 20 Edw. I. R.

Finch, Goldfinch, Spink, Goldspink, or Thrush. A young and lusty swaggerer is immortalized in Cockerell or Cock, and as a suffix (cf. Wilcock, &c.) the latter has made the word famous in English nomenclature. We still say, 'Well, old cock, how are you?' It is not necessary to go on. We have still Ruddocks, Popjays:

ROBERT POPINGEAY, 1371, co. Norf. FF.

Gulls, Storks, Crows, Doves, Speights, Pinnocks, Turtles, Swans, Ducks, Duckerells, Sheldricks, Mallards, Goss's, Woodcocks, Partridges, Pheasants, Rains:

WILLIAM LE RAIN. J.

&c., in our directories. Raven and Sparrowhawk (now Spark), however, were personal names at first (as doubtless some others). The last is as old as Domesday.

NAMES OF RELATIONSHIP.

Relationship has given us many surnames, some of which will be unrecognizable to the ordinary reader. Fairbrother represents the Norman-French Beaufrere, a brother-in-law; Fairbairn probably is equivalent to the Norman-French Beaufils (or Beaufitz), a stepson (Lower). Frearson explains itself. The Yorkshire surname Bairnfather, or Barnfather or Banfather, is the child's father, probably one with some considerable inheritance (v. Barnfather). Hitchmough or Hickmott is 'Richard's brother-in-law'; Watmough is 'Walter's brother-in-law,' and is sometimes found as Watmuff, Whatmough, and Watmore in North England. Hence also such extinct surnames as Barnmawe (the child's brother-in-law), or Elysmagh (Ellis' brother-in-law), or Hudmagh (Richard's brother-in-law), or Susannemagh (Susan's brother-in-law), or Tailliourmoghe (the tailor's brother-in-law), (v. Watmough for convincing evidence). Sisterson, a Durham and North Riding surname, must not be put in this category always. It is doubtless generally an imitative form of the old and popular Yorkshire Sissotson, 'the son of Cecilia' (v. Sissot). Again, these are only examples. It would be easy to quote such names as Uncle, Cousin or Cousins, Neave, Senior, Younger, or Widowson (sometimes). We must not include Kinsman.

TERMS OF ENDEARMENT AND FRIENDSHIP.

We still in common converse say, 'Well, old chap,' or 'My good fellow.' Hence Goodfellow, Goodbody, Goodman, Goodchild, Leifchild, Bellamy, Bonamy, Wellbeloved, Truelove, Sweetcock, Lemon or Leman, Douceamour, Parramore, Bunting. Some of these names were at first baptismal.

D

DESCRIPTIVE COMPOUNDS.

Akin to the above we constantly come across descriptive compounds; cf. John Little with Littlejohn, Bonjean (possibly now Bunyan, but that is more probably Welsh), Prettyjohn, Blithman, Younghusband, Littlehick, Micklejohn, Leishman, Gawkroger, Wightman, Merriman, Muddiman, Colfox (?). We may incidentally point out the predominance of John in names of this character. Included in this list we find such nicknames as Shakespear, Wagstaff, Breakspear, Shakelance; but not Bickerstaff, which is local. Such names as Proudfellow and Longfellow, or Freebody, explain themselves. So do Littleproud, or Sharparrow, or Bendbow (now Benbow), or Strongbow.

AGE, SIZE, SHAPE, CAPACITY.

Again we are on safe ground. We have the necessary proofs. In the surname epoch we find names that not merely described the build of the bearer, but distinguished him from somebody else with the same baptismal name. Take Little as an instance—

> JOHANNES DE BLAND et uxor, 1379: P. T. Yorks., p. 289.
> JOHANNES DE BLAND, *littill*, 1379: ibid.
> (John Bland, jun., we might almost style him.)

Again—

> JOHANNES TAILLOUR, *parws* (parvus), 1379: P. T. Yorks., p. 278.
> JOHANNES TAILLOUR, de Hyle, 1379: ibid.

Living each pair in their own small hamlet, and John being the prevailing name, they had to be identified. Thus we get familiarized with such early entries as—

> WILLIAM LE LETTLE, co. Oxf., 1273. A.
> JOHN LE LITLE, co. Berks, 1273. A.

Thus all is clear, and hence such entries as Robert le Fatte, Henry le Lene, Henry le Crask, William le Thikke, &c., occur in early rolls, and are now found in our directories as Craske, or Fatt, or Lean, or Thick, or Strong, or Long, or Short, or Longman, or Longfellow, or Ould, or Young (or Yonge), or Bigge, or Grose, or Grant (or Grand), or Grass (or Grace), or Petty, or Jeune, &c., many being Norman-French.

NICKNAMES FROM PECULIARITIES OF COMPLEXION.

A full account of these names will be found in my *English Surnames*, fourth edition, pp. 443–54. Suffice to say that we owe to nicknames a large and important list. Hence Morell, Lyard, Bayard, Favell, Burnell, Brunell, Russell, Rouse, Sor, Sorrell, Hore, White, Lilywhite, Black, Brown, Blanchflower, Brune, Grey, Grissell, Reed, Reid, Read, Swarte, Blund, Blunt, Blount, Blondin, Blundell, Dun (in most cases), Borrell, Burrell, &c. Let one or two instances suffice: the rest can be sought for in this dictionary with further information:—

> ELENA LA SORE, co. Soms., 1273. A.
> ROGER LE SOR, co. Soms., 1 Edw. III: Kirby's *Quest*, p. 258.
> WILLIAM LE DUN, co. Wilts, 1273. A.
> ROBERT LE BRUNE, c. 1300. M.
> ADAM LE HORE, co. Derby, 1273. A.

So they run, occasionally taken from the colour of the cloth they wore, as in Scarlett or Burrell (sometimes), but in general from the complexion of the hair, face, or beard. Such compounds as Nutbrown, Silverlock, Brownbeard, Flaxenhead, and Whitehead will be found in abundance. We find Anne Griselwhite mentioned in Blomefield's *History of Norfolk* (v. Index). Many of these compounds survive, many are extinct.

MENTAL AND MORAL PECULIARITIES.

This is an extremely large class. Kindly qualities are represented by Makepeace or Makejoy; social by Bland, Merry, or Gay; courteous by Curteis or Pollit; refined by Gentle, Sweet, or Hendy (or Henty); lowly by Humble or Meek; arrogance by Proud or Prout; alertness by Quick, Smart, or Snell; daring by Freak or Orped; miserliness by Pennifather; daringness again by Doughty or Bold; showiness by Gerrish; virtue by Bunn, Righteous, or Good. Bunker represents the old Bonquer; Moody and Musard testify to dreamy temperaments. But it is needless to go on. Examples will be found on every page of this work. Many forgotten expressions are recorded in our directories, as Orped or Orpwood, brave, daring, referred to above; or Crease, squeamish or particular. But there are dangers even here. We may be misled by modern spelling, Greedy (a Somersetshire name), for instance, being local, with the suffix *hey*; another illustration of imitation. Merriman, Moodiman, Slyman, Sillyman, Merryweather, Fairweather, Gladcheer, Littleproud, Proudlove, Proudfellow, or Proudfoot represent compound forms.

I have to acknowledge my deep indebtedness to Professor Skeat for a large number of M.E. instances which concern a section of names that belong to the

English dictionary as well as the English directory. I have kept his *Etymological Dictionary* constantly at my elbow. I have also used his terms 'intrusive' and 'excrescent,' not merely because they are simpler than my own, but also because these terms are needed on account of the extraordinary number of surnames in which intrusions and excrescences occur.

This preface is very unscientific in its arrangement; I frankly admit it, for I am not scientific. I never had the chance. The cares of a heavy parish have only allowed me intervals of minutes to jot down the results of past reading, and my occasional holidays were spent in search of proof. My MS. has been locked up for two years through illness and partial blindness. Still, the dictionary may be useful to students. In any case its slow preparation of twenty years has given me the one great pleasure of my life. Unhappy the man who has no hobby. I have simply been an earnest but unfortunately a flagging follower in the pursuit of the subject I love.

C. W. BARDSLEY.

Oxford, *Jan.* 1, 1896[1].

---

[1] N.B. After writing this introduction, the Author added quotations from more recent publications, e.g. *Register of the Freemen of the City of York* (Surtees Soc.).—A. B.

DICTIONARY

OF

ENGLISH AND WELSH SURNAMES

Aaron, Aarons, Aaronson.—
Bapt. 'the son of Aaron'; a Jewish
surname settled in England. I have
not met with a single English Aaron
in mediaeval times.

Jacob Aarron, 1696: Reg. St. Mary
Aldermary, London, p. 112.
London, 8, 4, 4; Philadelphia, 12, 17, 7.

Abadam.—Bapt. 'the son of
Adam' (Welsh ap- or ab-Adam);
cf. Bethell, Bloyd, Breeze, &c.

Thomas Appadam, co. Soms., 1 Edw.
III: Kirby's Quest, p. 219.
1754. Married—Richard Powney and
Eleanor Abadam: St. Geo. Chap. Mayfair, p. 280.

Abbey, Abbee, Abbe.—(1)
Local, 'at the Abbey.' from residence thereby. (2) Offic., from the
ecclesiastical title. All the evidence
is in favour of this view except in
one instance.

Henry le Abbé, co. Salop. 1273. A.
Ralph le Abbe, co. Devon, Hen. III–
Edw. I. K.
William le Abbe, co. Devon, ibid.
Robert del Abbay, 1332, co. Lanc.:
Lay Subsidy (Rylands).
William de Mikelfeld, *dictus* del Abbay,
12–13 Edw. I : Freemen of York, i. 4.
William del Abbay, *ceynturer*: ibid.
1594. George Abbey, Magd. Coll. : Reg.
Univ. Oxf. iii. 181.
1601. Richard Abby and Eliz. Hodg-
kins: Marriage Lic. (London), i. 267.
1648. Married—George Abbey and
Mary Feild: St. Jas. Clerkenwell, iii. 82.
London, 4, 1, 0; Philadelphia, 11, 0, 6.

Abbinett.—Bapt. 'the son of
Abraham,' or 'Abell,' q.v., from
the nick. Abb, with double dim.
Abb-in-et; cf. Robinet and Colinet.

Liverpool, 1.

Abbiss.—Bapt.; v. Abbs, of
which, no doubt, it is a variant.

'William Abbys, now mayor of the
Towne of Bedford,' 1534: Visitation of
Bedfordshire, 1566, p. 73.
1628. Buried—George Woodlve, from
Dan. Abiss: St. Jas. Clerkenwell, iv. 192.
—— Edward Green, from Danyell
Abbisse: ibid. p. 193.
1631. Bapt.—Eliz., d. Henrye Abbes: St.
Mary Aldermary, p. 82.
1779. James Rycroft and Elizabeth
Dianah Abbiss: St. Geo. Han. Sq. i. 303.
London, 1.

**Abbitt, Abbot, Abbott, Ab-
butson, Abbett.—**(1) Bapt. 'the
son of Abraham,' from the nick.
Abb, and dim. Abb-ot. It is all but
certain that the majority of our
Abbotts, although bearing a con-
ventual title, are thus descended.
Abraham was a favourite name in the
13th century. Abel was also popular,
and may have shared the parentage.
(2) Offic., or nickname, 'the Abbot.'

Henry Abbod, co. Oxf., 1273. A.
William Abbod, co. Oxf., ibid.
Adam Abbot, co. Hunts, ibid.
Juliana Abbot, co. Bedf., ibid.
Margareta Abbot, co. Camb., ibid.
1720. Married—Edward Sanders and
Anne Abbitt: St. Antholin, London, p.134.
London, 2, 4, 72, 0, 2; Philadelphia, 0,
6, 72, 0, 4.

Abbs, Abson, Abbison.—
Bapt. 'the son of Abraham' or
'Abel,' from nick. Abb or Abbie.
This was a familiar Norfolk surname as Abbys or Abbes. To-day
it is familiar in the same county
as Abbs.

William fil. Abi, co. Bucks, 1273. A.
Willelmus Abson, 1379: P. T. Yorks.
p. 71.

John Abbys, co. Norf., 1480: FF. vi.
445.
Thomas Abbys, co. Norf., 1536: ibid.
p. 446.
James Abbes, buried at Thetford, co.
Norf., 1555: ibid. ii. 141.
Edward Abbs, 'imbarqued in the
George' for Virginia, 1635. Hotten's
Emigrants, p. 124.
1641. Bapt.—Willm., s. Willm. Abbison:
St. Jas. Clerkenwell, i. 149.
1750. Married—William Abson and
Mary Downes: St. Geo. Chap. Mayfair,
p. 158.
MDB. (Norfolk), 3, 0, 0; London, 1, 0,
0; Liverpool, 0, 2, 0; Wakefield, 0, 1,
0; Philadelphia, 0, 0, 1.

Abdy.—Local, 'of the Abdy';
query, an old form of 'Abbey' (?).
Lower says: 'Abdy, an estate in
Yorkshire, where the family anciently resided.' This is corroborated by the following entries:—

Robert del Abdy, 1379: P. T. Yorks.
p. 17.
Johannes del Abdy, et Agnes, uxor
ejus, *taylour*: ibid.
Johannes del Abdy, et Margareta, uxor
ejus: ibid.

All these were living at Bramp-
ton-juxta-Wath. The 'del' is interesting.

1577. Edmund Abdie, London: Reg.
Univ. Oxf. vol. ii. pt. ii. p. 76.
1583. Christopher Abdye and Mary
Sentell: Marriage Lic. (London), i. 119.
1776. Married—Sir William Abdy, Bart.,
and Mary Gordon: St. Geo. Han. Sq.
i. 259.
MDB. (W. Rid. Yorkshire), 1; London,
2; Boston (U.S.), 1.

A'Becket.—Local, 'at the Beck-
head,' from residence at the head
or source of the beck; cf. Birkett,
originally Birk-head, or Birkenhead, the head of the birch-trees.
Birkett is a Cumberland surname.

Birkenhead, co. Chester, is but a variant, being the adjectival form; v. Beck. Cf. Roger a'Hulle (co. Oxf., 1273. A.), i. e. Roger at the Hill.

Wydo del Beck't, co. Linc., 20 Edw. I. R.
1801. Married—William a'Beckett and Sarah Abbott: St. Geo. Han. Sq. ii. 233. Philadelphia, 3.

Abel, Abell, Abells, Ableson, Able.—Bapt. 'the son of Abel.' Much more popular in mediaeval society than in that of the 19th century. Among the peasantry, however, Abel still receives a certain amount of attention as a font-name.

Richard Abel, co. Bucks, 1273. A.
Abel le Specer, co. Derby, ibid.
Henry Abel, co. Notts, ibid.
Allan Abel, co. Camb., ibid.
Abel le Orfeure. T.
Richard Abel, co. Soms., 1 Edw. III: Kirby's Quest, p. 201.
1578. George Abell, co. Derby: Reg. Univ. Oxf. vol. ii. pt. ii. p. 83.
1623. Richard Abelson and Ellen Brocke: Marriage Lic. (Westminster), p. 29.
1714. William Abell, patron of Brampton, co. Norf.: FF. vi. 440.
Boston (U.S.), 58, 10, 2, 0, 0; London, 7, 8, 1, 1, 0; MDB. (N. Rid. Yorkshire), Able 1.

Abethell. — Bapt. 'Ab-Ithel' (Welsh); i. e. the son of Ithel; v. Bethell, and cf. Abadam.
London, 1.

Ablett, Ablott, Abletson.— Bapt. 'the son of Abel,' from dim. Abel-ot. A feminine form occurs in the Hundred Rolls; v. infra.

Abelot (without surname), co. Camb., 1273. A.
William Abelot, co. Camb., ibid.
Abalotta de la Forde, co. Hunts, ibid.
Richard Abelote. V. 11.
William Ablot, 10 Edw. III: Freemen of York, i. 31.
'Jan. 16, 1437. Robert Rodes, of the town of Newcastle upon Tyne, conveyed a house in Gateshead to William Abletson and Agnes his wife': Brand's Hist. of Newcastle, i. 261.
1770. Rene Rogier and Hannah Ablett: St. Geo. Han. Sq. i. 194.
London, 4, 0, 0.

Ablewhite.—Local, doubtless a corruption of Applethwaite, q.v.; cf. Hebblewhite.

Ablin.—Bapt. 'the son of Abel,' from the dim. Abel-in; v. Aplin (2).
Thomas Abelyn, co. Kent, 1273. A.

Isolda Abelin, 6 Edw. I. BBB.
1685. Bapt.—John, son of Edward Ablin: St. Jas. Clerkenwell, i. 311.
1721. — Thomas, son of Francis Ablin: ibid. ii. 127.

Abraham, Abrahams, Abrahamson, Abram, Abrams, Abramson.—(1) Bapt. 'the son of Abraham.' A popular font-name in the 13th century; v. Abbot. In the Fen district especially the entries are common. The instances in the Hundred Rolls are all but entirely confined to the Fen counties. A glance at the London Directory will show that in general Abraham represents the old English stock, and Abrahams the more modern Jewish. This is proved by comparing the personal or Christian names prefixed to the instances; cf. Solomon and Salmon.

John Abraam, co. Bedf., 1273. A.
Ralph Abraham, co. Camb., ibid.
John Abraham, co. Soms., 1 Edw. III: Kirby's Quest, p. 111.
William fil. Abraham, co. Linc., 20 Edw. I. R.
Magota Abraham, 1379: P. T. Yorks. p. 299.

(2) Local, 'of Abram,' a township in the parish of Wigan, Lanc., originally written Adburgham. The Lancashire Abram and Abraham spring from this place.

Gilbert de Abram, temp. Hen. IV.
John Abraham of Abraham, temp. Hen. V: Baines' Lanc. ii. 190.
Isaac Abraham, of Liverpool, 1613: Wills at Chester, i. 128-9.
Nicholas Lucas, of Alpraham, 1598: ibid.
Robert Lythgoe, of Abram, 1578: ibid.
William Abram, parish of Sephton, 1617: ibid.
London, 24, 56, 3, 3, 0, 0; Liverpool, 11, 3, 0, 2, 0, 0; Philadelphia, 14, 21, 2, 11, 28, 1.

Abry.—Bapt. 'the son of Abrahee,' presumably a form of Abraham.

Alan fil. Abrahee, co. Linc., 1273. A.
Dyay fil. Abrahe, co. Linc., ibid.
William fil. Abbrahee, co. Linc., ibid.
1598. Edward Abrey: Reg. Univ. Oxf. i. 349.
'Alice, married to Arthure Abry, of Charnish, in com. Wilts': Visitation of Dorsetshire, 1623, p. 15.
1786. Married—Richard Lucas and Elizabeth Abrey: St. Geo. Han. Sq. i. 392.
1787. — Robert Abray and Jane Ward: ibid. p. 410.
New York, 3.

Absalom, Absalon, Absolom.—Bapt. 'the son of Absolom.' A fairly popular font-name in the 13th century, and not confined to the Jews.

'Now was ther of that chirche a parish clerk,
The which that was ycleped Absolon.
Chaucer, C. T. 3312.
Thomas Apsolon, London, 1273. A.
Absolon in le Dyche, ibid.
Thomas Absolon: Patent Roll, 19 Eliz. pt. 7.
Absolon fil. Simon. C.
William Absolon, co. Soms., 1 Edw. III: Kirby's Quest, p. 172.
George Absolon, 'bound for ye Bormodos,' 1635: Hotten's Lists of Emigrants, p. 132.
1756. Married—Clemmuell Clark and Eliz. Absalom: St. Geo. Han. Sq. i. 65.
London, 1, 1, 3; New York, 1, 1, 0.

Abson.—Bapt. 'the son of Abraham'; v. Abbs.

Aburn.—Local, 'at the burn,' corrupted to Auburn; cf. A'Becket, A'Wood, &c.

Henry Ateburn, co. Bucks, 1273. A.
Richard Atteburne, co. Kent, ibid.
1641. Francis Edmonds and Mary Aborne: Marriage Lic. (London), ii. 253.
1690. John Fishwick and Mary Aburne: Marriage Alleg. (Canterbury), p. 166.
1695. John Aburne and Ann With: Marriage Lic. (Faculty Office), p. 216.
London, 1.

Acatour, Achatour.—Official; v. Cator.

Bernard le Acatour, temp. 1300. M.
Henry le Achator. H.
Jocius le Achatur, 1273. A.
Chaucer says of the manciple who was so 'wise in buying of victuals,' that of him
'Achatours mighten take ensample.'

Achard.—Bapt. 'the son of Achard'; v. Hatchard.
London, 1; New York, 1.

Achurch.—Local; v. Atkirk.

Ackerman, Ackermann, Akerman, Akermann.—Occup. 'the Acreman': a ploughman, a husbandman, a tiller of the soil; 'both prestis and knightis mosten bicome acremen and heerdis,' 1389: Hist. Eng. Dic.

'The foules up, and song on bough,
And acremen yede to the plough.'
Lay le Freine, 176 (Halliwell).
Roger le Acreman, co. Oxf., 1273. A.
Alexander Acherman, co. Hunts, ibid.
Hugh Akerman, co. Camb., ibid.

Peter de Akerman, o. Oxf., 1273. A.
Akermann is of German birth.

1802. Married — John Sandford and Mary Ackerman: St. Geo. Han. Sq. ii. 272. London, 2, 2, 5, 0; Philadelphia, 20, 8, 3, 1.

Ackley.—Local, 'at the Ackley,' i.e. the oak-meadow. The exact equivalent of Oakley, q.v.

Ralph de Ackle, co. Oxf., 1273. A.
John de Acle, co. Oxf., ibid.
Robert de Acle, co. Bucks, ibid.
1571. Henry Acley, Ch. Ch. Coll.: Reg. Univ. Oxf. iii. 44.
1610. Henry Cannon and Mary Acly: Marriage Lic. (London), i. 322.
1769. Married — Henry Hughes and Betty Ackley: St. Geo. Han. Sq. i. 184. Boston, 1; Philadelphia, 17.

Acklom.—Local, ' of Acklam,' two parishes in co. York, one in the union of Malton, the other in the union of Stockton.

Robert de Acclom, co. York, 1273. A.
1742. Married — John Newman and Eliz. Acklom: St. Geo. Chap. Mayfair, p. 23.
1806. — John Philip Acklam and Eliz. Robinson: St. Geo. Han. Sq. ii. 353. MDB. (co. Lincoln), 1.

Ackroyd, Ecroyd, Ackeroyd, Akroyd, Akeroyd.— Local, 'of the Ackroyd,' i.e. the oak clearing; cf. Ormerod, Murgatroyd, &c. A well-known Yorkshire surname.

Richard de Akerode, co. York. W. 2.
1612. John Acroyd, co. York: Reg. Univ. Oxf. vol. ii. pt. ii. p. 328.
1618. Matthew Aickroid, co. York: ibid. p. 372.
1619–20. Samuel Akeroyd, co. York: ibid. p. 380.
1655. Buried—Mary, d. Robert Acrod: St. Thomas the Apostle (London), p. 131.
1678. John Somerscales and Susanna Aykroyd: Marriage Lic. (Westminster), p. 170.
1687. James Galliere Vareilles and Faith Aikeroyd: Marriage Alleg. (Canterbury), p. 278.
West Riding Court Dir., 28, 2, 0, 2, 6; MDB. (W. Riding), 17, 0, 1, 4, 0; Philadelphia, 8, 0, 0, 0, 0.

Acland, Ackland.—Local, ' of Acland.' 'From the situation of their ancient seat in Lankey, near Barnstaple, co. Devon, which, being in the midst of a large grove of oaks (in Saxon *ac*), obtained the name of Ac or Oakland. . . . They were settled in this place as early as the reign of Henry II.' (Lower, quoting Kimber's Baronetage.)

Richard Ackelonde, co. Soms., 1 Edw. III: Kirby's Quest, p. 247.
1609. Baldwin Aclande, co. Devon, Reg. Univ. Oxf. vol. ii. pt. ii. p. 305.
John Acklande, temp. Eliz. Z.
1641. Buried — Elizabeth Acklande, widdowe: St. Peter's, Cornhill, i. 198.
Exeter, 1, 2; MDB. (co. Devon), 3, 2; London, 4, 6; Philadelphia, 0, 2; Boston, 0, 3.

Acock, Acocks, Haucock, Haycock, Haycox.—Bapt. 'the son of Alcock,' q.v., corrupted to Accock. This took the imitative form of Haycock. At least it would appear so. If we could find any instances of Halcock representing Henry, we should then be obliged to refer the three last to that personal name.

Roger Accok et uxor, 1379: P. T. Yorks. p. 270.
1633. William Aucocke and Rebecca Richardson: Marriage Lic. (London), ii. 210.
1782. Married—George Betterton and Sarah Acock · St. Geo. Han. Sq. i. 338.
London, 1, 2, 1, 6, 1; Philadelphia, 0, 0, 0, 2, 0.

Acomb, Acome.—(1) Local, 'of Acomb,' a parish near York. (2) Local, 'of Acomb,' two townships in the union of Hexham, co. Northumberland.

Willelmus de Acom, 1379: P. T. Yorks. p. 301.
Elena Acom, 1379: ibid.
1670. Married—Henry Acum and Eliz. Blackwell: St. Jas. Clerkenwell, iii. 171.
1692. Samuel Acomb and Ann Best: Marriage Alleg. (Canterbury), p. 220.
1767. Married—Owen Scott and Mary Acombe: St. Geo. Han. Sq. i. 170.
West Riding Court Dir., 2, 0; London, 0, 3.

Acott, v. Acock; a variant; cf. Glasscock for Glasscott.

Oxford, 1.

Acre, Acres, Acker, Akers.—Local, ' of the Acre,' or Acres, from residence beside the field or fields called the Acre or Acres.

Bartholomew de Acre, or Akers, bailiff of Norwich, 1282: FF. iii. 74.
Oliver del Acre, 36 Hen. III. BBB.
Walter del Acre, ibid.
Walter del Acre, C. R., 42 Hen. III.
William del Acre, co. Essex, Hen. III-Edw. I. K.
Johannes Acrys, 1379: P. T. Yorks. p. 29.
Roger Acres, 1379: ibid. p. 291.
1691. Bapt.—John, s. Richard Acres: St. Jas. Clerkenwell, i. 340.
London, 0, 2, 1, 8; Philadelphia, 1, 0, 27, 0.

Acton.—Local, ' of Acton.' There are in England no less than sixteen parishes, hamlets, townships, &c., called Acton, i.e. the farmstead among the oaks.

John de Aketon, co. Soms., 1273. A.
Nicholas de Aketon, co. Northumb., ibid.
John de Actone, co. Soms., 1 Edw. III: Kirby's Quest, p. 188.
Drue de Acton, co. Norf., c. Hen. III: FF. ix. 111.
Johannes de Ayketon, 1379: P. T. Yorks. p. 251.
1569. Bapt. — Alexdr., son of Alexdr. Acton: St. Jas. Clerkenwell, i. 5.
1582. John Acton, co. Salop: Reg. Univ. Oxf. vol. ii. pt. ii. p. 119.
London, 6; Philadelphia, 7.

Acworth.—Local, ' of Ackworth,' a parish near Wakefield, co. York.

Ricardus de Ackeworthe, 1379: P. T. Yorks. p. 60.
Adam de Ackeworth, 1379: ibid. p. 33.
1520–30. Robert Charnock and Frances Acworth: Marriage Lic. (London), i. 7.
1589. Richard Ackworth, London: Reg. Univ. Oxf. vol. ii pt. ii. p. 172.
1600–1. Buried — Thomas Acworth: St. Donis Backchurch, p. 205.
West Riding Court Dir., 1.

Adam, Adames, Adams, Adamson.—Bapt. 'the son of Adam.' Almost the prime favourite as a font-name in the 13th century; v. Addis, Adcock, Atkins, Atkinson, Addyman, &c. Adams is remarkably well represented in the United States. A single glance at the Index to Hotten's Lists of Emigrants will suffice to show that many Adams, Addams, Adamsons, or Addamsons were among the early settlers.

John fil. Adam, co. Oxf., 1273. A.
Hugh fil. Adam, co. Oxf., ibid.
German Adam, co. Camb., ibid.
Juliana Adams, co. Hunts, ibid.
Johannes Adamson, 1379: P. T. Yorks. p. 112.
Johannes Adam, *carnifex*, 1379: ibid. p. 113.
Thomas Adamson, 1379: ibid. p. 300.
1619. Thomas Williams and Anne Addams: Marriage Lic. (London), ii. 80.
1640–1. Thomas Akmes and Eliz. Emerson: ibid. p. 256.
London, 11, 2, 180, 14; Boston, 9, 0, 363, 14.

Adamthwaite.—Local, ' of Adamthwaite ' (i. e. the clearing of Adam the first settler, probably in the 12th century), a small hamlet in Ravenstonedale, co. Westm.; v. Thwaites.

ReynoldAdaurthwaite,1541:W.Nicholls, History and Traditions of Ravenstonedale, co. Westm., p. 113.
Robert Adamthwaite, 1541 : ibid.
Richard Adamthwaite, 1541 : ibid.
1638. Bapt.—Mary, d. Thomas Adamthwaite : St. Jas. Clerkenwell, i. 139.
1665. Buried—Sibell Adamthwaite : St. Mary Aldermary, p. 186.
MDB. (co. Westm.), 2.

Adcock, Atcock.—Bapt. 'the son of Adam,' from the nick. Ade with suffix -cock (cf. Wilcock, Jeffcock, Watcock, &c.) ; v. Addis with Atcock ; cf. Atkins for Adkins.

'Hamme, son of Adecock, held 29 acres of land': De Lacy Inquisition, 1311.
Robertus Adcok, 1379: P. T. Yorks. p. 203.
Robertus Adkokson, 1379: ibid. p. 287.
William Atcok, 1379 : ibid. p. 234.
1539. Married—Thomas Smith and Katurne Adcock : St. Antholin, London, p. 1.
1673. Bapt.—Thomas, son of Thomas Adcocke : St. Jas. Clerkenwell, i. 259.
London, 12, 0 ; New York, 1, 0 ; Philadelphia, 0, 1.

Adderley, Atherly.—Local, ' of Atherley,' a parish in co. Salop, pronounced Adderley.

Henry de Addreleg, co. Salop, Hen. III-Edw. I. K.
Roger de Addeleg, co. Wilts, ibid.
1574-5. Ralph Adderley, co. Linc. : Reg. Univ. Oxf. vol. ii. pt. ii. p. 60.
1585. Ralph Adderley, co. Staff. : ibid. p. 142.
1599. Humphrey Adderley, co. Warw.: ibid. p. 235.
1686. William Cuttler and Ruth Adderley : St. Michael, Cornhill, p. 44. London, 6, 1 ; Philadelphia, 0, 2.

Addinell.—Bapt. 'the son of Adam,' from an early dim. (?) ; cf. Adnett and Adnitt, q.v.
Tadcaster, 3.

Addis, Addison, Adds, Addy, Ade, Ades, Adey, Adie, Ady, Addey, Aday, Adee.—Bapt. 'the son of Adam,' from the nick. Ad, Ade, or Addy. All are reminders of the wonderful popularity of Adam in the north of England, if not in the south ; cf. Adcock and Adkin, q.v.

Nicholas fil. Ade, 1379 : P. T. Yorks. p. 203.
Matilda Addy, 1379 : ibid.
Robertus fil. Ade, 1379 : ibid.
Alicia relicta Ade, 1379 : ibid.
Willelmus Addes, 1379 : ibid. p. 195.
Agnes fil. Ade, co. Hunts, 1273. A.
Robert Ade, co. Leic., ibid.

Emma fil Ade, co. Linc., ibid.
A common entry in the Hundred Rolls.
1574. John Addye and Eliz. Walker : Marriage Alleg. (Canterbury), p. 5.
1575. Edward Adice, co. Salop : Reg. Univ. Oxf. vol. ii. pt ii. p. 65. With the variant Adice cf. Ellice for Ellis, or Bevance for Bevans.
1580. Thomas Buller and Agnes Adye : Marriage Alleg. (Canterbury), p. 7.
1585. Henry Adis, co. Dorset : Reg. Univ. Oxf. vol. ii. pt. ii. p. 141.
1665. Henry Marsh and Leah Ady : Marriage Alleg. (Canterbury), p. 106.
1673. John Addis : ibid. p. 215.
— William Bright and Jane Adey : ibid. p. 217.
Edward Addice, 1679 : Hotten's Emigrants, p. 473.
1690. Bapt.—John, son of John and Susanah Adee : St. Dionis Backchurch, London, p. 138.
1713.—Edward. son of John Addis : St. Jas. Clerkenwell, ii. 71.
London, 8, 12, 1, 1, 2, 3, 6, 2, 1, 0, 0, 0 ; Philadelphia, 23, 8, 0, 1. 6. 0, 0, 0, 0, 0, 0, 0 ; New York, 0, 5, 0, 2, 1, 0, 0, 2, 0. 1, 1, 12.

Addyman.—Occup. 'the servant or knave of Addy,' i. e. Adam ; v. Addy and Addison. This is decidedly interesting. It is one of the chief witnesses to-day of the existence of the class of surnames to which it belongs. As a matter of course its home is in Yorkshire ; cf. Mathewman, Peterman, Perryman, Jackman, Bartleman, &c. In the following entries, although Ade (i. e. Addy) is given as the nick. of Adam, the entry is unfortunately in Latin. In English it would have read Thomas and Johannes Addyman.

Adam Symmeson, souter, 1379 : P. T. Yorks. p. 25.
Johannes servicus Ade Symmeson, 1379: ibid.
Adam de Wodhall, marchaunt, 1379 : ibid.
Thomas servicus dicti Ade, 1379 : ibid.
We are more fortunate in a further instance, where the English form is given.
Johannes Addeman, 1379 : P. T. Yorks. p. 195.
1775. Samuel Hill and Elizabeth Addeman : St. Geo. Han. Sq. i. 248.
West Riding Court Dir.. 3 ; Leeds, 2.

Ade, Adey ; v. Addis.

Adkin, Adkins, Adkinson, Atkin, Atkins, Atkinson, Atkyns, Adkisson.—Bapt. 'the son

of Adam,' from the nick. Addy, dim. Adkin, sharpened to Atkin. There is no need of course to prove this, but it is interesting to note the following : 'Adam le Fullere,' a citizen of London, is twice referred to as Adekin le Fullere (1273, Hundred Rolls, i. 426). Six centuries ago Adam probably ranked as second or third favourite among boys' names throughout England. In the north it attained a most remarkable preeminence. Four Adams are mentioned in the revenues of Conishead Priory, A. D. 1256 (West's Furness, pp. 192, 195). No fewer than six Adams figure as benefactors of Furness Abbey, circa 1290 (ibid.). The everyday form was Adekin, then Adkin, and finally Atkin (see Addison).

Geoffrey Adekyn, 10 Ric. II, co. Norf. : FF. viii. 446.
William Adekyn, co. Soms, 1 Edw. III : Kirby's Quest, p. 122.
Willelmus Adkynson, 1379 : P. T. Howdenshire, p. 16.
Edmund Adkynson, 1379 : P.T. Yorks. p. 152.
Hatkyn Benete, 1379 : ibid. p. 109.
The following come together :—
Johannes Attekyson, 1379 : P. T. Yorks. p. 238.
Alicia soror Adekynson, 1379 : ibid.
1680. Married—William Deevy and Eliz. Adkins : St. Dionis Backchurch, p. 39.
1709. Elizabeth, d. of John Adkison : St. Jas. Clerkenwell, p. 49.
1718. Married—George Handaye and Mary Adkisson : St. Michael, Cornhill, p. 60.
London : 5, 10, 0, 9, 51, 60, 1, 0 ; Philadelphia, Adkisson, 3.

Adlam, Adlum, Adman ; v. Adnam.

Adlard.—Bapt. 'the son of Adelard' or 'Athelard'; v. Allard. Adelhard was a cousin of Charlemagne, and Abbot of Corbie. (Yonge, ii. 399.)

Adelardus : Domesday.
Athelard de Barwe : Close Roll, 2 Edw. I.
Adam Adelard, co. Camb., 1273. A.
Simon fil. Aderlard, co. Linc., ibid.
'Adelard, or Alard, or Aluered Baate, chaplain of Magdalen, 1505 ': Reg. Univ. Oxf. i. 40.
John Athelard, co. Soms., 1 Edw. III : Kirby's Quest, p. 129.
1794. Married—William Tollitt and Eliz. Adlard : St. Geo. Han. Sq. ii. 120.

MDB. (Lincoln), 5; London, 4; New York, 2.

Adlin, Adling.—Bapt. 'the son of Adeline,' alias Atheline; cf. Athelard and Adlard.

William Atheline, co. Oxf., 1273. A.
Richard Athelyne, co. Camb., ibid.
Adelinus (without surname), co. Linc., ibid.
William Adelyn, co. Norf., ibid.
Henry fil Adelyne, co. Derby, ibid.
Geoffrey Adelyne, co. Camb., ibid.
1542. Buried—Richard Adlin: St. Antholin, London, p. 3.
1558. — Margaret Adlyn: St. Peter's, Cornhill, i. 113.
1572. Bapt.—Jane, d. of John Adlin: ibid. p. 14.
'Elizabeth, d. of John Adlyn, of London, draper, 1625': Visitation of London, 1634, ii. 241.

Adnam, Adlam, Adman, Adlum, Adnum.—Local, 'of Addingham.' Parishes in co. Cumberland and W. Rid. Yorkshire; cf. Swetnam and Swetman for Swettenham, or Debnam and Deadman for Debenham, or Putnam and Putman for Puttenham. Adlam is a further and natural variant; cf. *bannister* for *baluster*. With **Adnum**, cf. Barnum for Barnham.

1574-5. Robert Kychell and Anne Adman: Marriage Lic. (London), i. 63.
1768. Married—John Adlam and Ann Rode: St. Geo. Han. Sq. i. 171.
1774. — John Mason and Dorothy Adnam: ibid. i. 258.
London, 1, 3, 0, 0, 0; New York, 0, 1, 0, 3, 0; MDB. (co. Gloucester), 0, 0, 0, 1, 1.

Adnett, Adnitt, Adnet, Adnot.—Bapt. 'the son of Adam,' from the nick. Addy, dim. Add-in, second dim. Add-in-et; cf. Addinson, q.v. Adin or Addin was evidently the O.F. equivalent of Adkin, the customary English form; v. Atkins and Atkinson.

Henricus fil. Adynet, 1379: P. T. Yorks. p. 200.
Adinet del Forest, 1379: ibid.
William Addynet, co. York, 1525: W. 11, p. 201.
William Haddynytt, co. York, 1530: ibid. p. 215.
1604. Ezekiel Burbery and Anne Adnitt: Marriage Lic. (London), i. 288.
London, 1, 1, 0, 0; New York, 0, 0, 1, 1.

Adney.—Local (?).

1599. Andrew Adney, co. Salop: Reg. Univ. Oxf. vol. ii. pt. ii. p. 236.
1617-8. John Adney and Mary Steedman: Marriage Lic. (London), ii. 58.

1792. Married—Lazarus Plummer and Elinor Adney: St. Geo. Han. Sq. ii. 73. London, 2.

Adrain, Adrian, Adrinson.—Bapt. 'the son of Adrian.' The form Adrain is an old one. The sheriff, John Adrian, entered below, is recorded as John Adrain: A. i. p. 403.

John Adrien, co. Suff., 1273. A.
John Adrian, 1258, sheriff of London: WWW.
1565-6. Audrian Awdryan and Christiane Ede: Marriage Lic. (London), i. 32.
1597. Matthew Merytt and Elizabeth Adrinson: ibid. p. 241.
1628. Adrian Eyers and Ellen Woodcocke: Marriage Lic.(Westminster), p.32.
London, 1, 0, 0; Crockford, 0, 1, 0; Philadelphia, 0, 6, 0; New York (Adrain), 1.

Adshead.—Local, 'of Adshead,' some spot in the neighbourhood of Prestbury, co. Chester, whose church register teems with entries relating to the family. The surname has crossed the Atlantic.

1560. Married—John Wilkinson and Margret Adshed: Reg. Prestbury (Ches.), p. 2.
1612. Bapt. — Isabell Adshed: ibid. p. 193.
Reynold Adshed, 1558, Pott Shrigley, near Prestbury: East Ches, ii. 218.
Thomas Adeshead, 1579, of Birchincliffe: ibid. i. 18.
1731. Married—Philip Platt and Dorothy Adshad: St. Jas. Clerkenwell, iii. 258.
London, 3; Manchester, 9; Philadelphia 4.

Affleck, Afflick.—Local, ' of Auchinleck.' N.B. ' A singular contraction of the surname Auchinleck, borne by an ancient family " of that ilk " in Ayrshire. Sir Edmund Affleck, created baronet in 1782, was sixth in descent from Sir John Auchinleck, son of Gilbert A. of Auchinleck': Lower, Pat. Brit., p. 3.

1679. Bapt.—Andrew, ye son of Lt. Colonel Andrew Affleck (also spelled Aflick): St. Jas. Ch. Barbadoes; Hotten's Lists of Emigrants, pp. 497, 500.
1748. Married—William Darby and Mary Affleck: St. Geo. Han. Sq. i. 40.
1749. — Thomas Affleck and Margaret Stuart: St. Geo. Chap. Mayfair, p. 141.
Manchester, 4, 0; Philadelphia, 1, 5; New York, 6, 0.

Agar, Agars, Ager.—Bapt. ' the son of Agar,' or ' Ager.' Pro-

bably a form of Algar, a Domesday personal name, and very popular for several centuries; v. Algar.

Thomas Agar, 1544, co. York: W. 11, p. 233.
Wilfrid Agar, 1544, co. York: ibid.
1578. Buried—Joane Agar, a mayde, of fourscore years olde: St. Michael, Cornhill, p. 195.
1619. Andrew Agar: Reg. Univ. Oxf. i. 350.
1635. Married—Thomas Agar and Mary Rigley: St. Peter's, Cornhill, i. 255.
London, 9, 1, 8; Boston (U.S.), 5, 7, 0.

Agard. — Bapt.; v. Haggard. Arthur Agard, a distinguished antiquary, was descended of an old Derbyshire family. He was born in 1540, and died in 1615. He was one of the original members of the Society of Antiquaries, and was buried in Westminster Abbey. (Dict. Nat. Biog. i. 173, and Stanley's Westminster Abbey, p. 443.) Haggard is the usual form of this patronymic.

1591. Stephen Agard, co. Northampt.: Reg. Univ. Oxf. vol. ii. pt. ii. p. 184.
1634. Married—John Aggard and Mary Adderley: St. Antholin (London), p. 68.

Agasson, Agace, Aggas, Haggis.—Bapt.' the son of Agace'; a form of Agatha.

John Messor et Agacia, uxor sua, co. Camb., 1273. A.
Agacia de Gatesdon, co. Devon, ibid.
Robert fil Agacie, co. Camb., ibid.
Symon Agace, co. Hunts, ibid.
William Agaz, co. Bucks, ibid.
Simon Agasson, 1379: P. T. Yorks. p. 244.
'Agas Zibrandson, of Amsterdam,' Sept. 21, 1565: Cal. State Papers (Domestic), i. 258.
' Ralph Agas (1540-1621), a land surveyor, who rose to eminence by making maps of London. A native of Stoke-by-Nayland, in Suffolk': Dict. Nat. Biog. i. 173. This district agrees with the chief entries above.
Edward Aggas (1564-1601), bookseller and printer, son of Robert Aggas of Stoke-by-Nayland, in Suffolk: ibid. 175.
1547. Buried—Agas Larbroke: St. Dionis Backchurch, p. 181.
1578. Ralph Agas, rector of Grassenhale, co. Norf.: FF. ix. 519.
London, 0, 1, 1, 2.

Agate.—(1) Local, ' at the gate,' from residence thereby; cf. Atwood, Bywater, &c.

Adam Ategate, co. Hunts, 1273. A.
Alan Attegate, co. Camb., ibid.
Leonard Agate, temp. Eliz. Z.

(2) Bapt. 'the son of Agnes,' from the nick. Agg, dim. Agot.

Thomas Agot, 1379: P. T. Yorks. p. 69.
Johanna Agot, 1379: ibid.
John Agate, co. Soms., 1 Edw. III: Kirby's Quest, p. 135.
1768. Married—James Agate and Ann Bennett: St. Geo. Han. Sq. i. 177.
London, 2; New York, 1.

Agg, Agge.—Bapt. 'the son of Agnes,' from the nick. Agg. Aggie is still the favourite north English nick.

Alice Agge, co. Oxf., 1273. A.
Thomas Agge, co. Oxf., ibid.
William Agge, co. Linc., ibid.
1669. Philip Gurdon and Elizabeth Agge: Marriage Lic. (Westminster), ii. 169.
Boston (U.S.), 0, 1; New York, 1, 0.

Agland.—Local, a corruption of Acland, q.v. Ackland, Acland, and Agland are all found indifferently in co. Devon, the home of the name; v. Devon Directory; cf. the Lancashire Ogden for Oakden.

London, 3; Seaton (Devon), 3.

Aglionby.—Local, 'of Aglionby,' a township in the parish of Warwick, three miles from Carlisle, co. Cumb.

1583. John Aglionby, co. Cumb: Reg. Univ. Oxf. vol. ii. pt. ii. p. 132.
1619. George Aiglionbey, Oxon. doc.: ibid. p. 379.
MDB. (co. Cumb.), 4.

Aguiler, Aguylar.—Occup. 'a needler,' a maker of needles.

'A silver needle forth I drew
Out of an aguiler quaint ynow.'
Chaucer, Rom. Rose, 98.

O.F. *aguille*, a needle.

Thomas le Aguiler, co. York, 1305. M.
William le Aguiler. Q.
Lucas le Aguler, co. Camb., 1273. A.
Philadelphia (Aguylar), 2.

Aiken, Aikin, Aikens, Aikins.—Bapt. 'the son of Adam,' from the nick. Ade and dim. Adkin. The Scotch form of Atkin, q.v., was Aitkin. This was further corrupted to Aiken and Aikin.

1752. Married—Thomas Aikin and Ann Whittington: St. Geo. Chap. Mayfair, p. 226.
1771. — Henry Akin and Rebecca Adams: St. Geo. Han. Sq. i. 210.
1783. — John Aickin and Mary McDannel: ibid. p. 346.
London, 1, 3, 0, 0; Philadelphia, 18, 5, 18, 5.

Ainscough, Ainscow.—Local; v. Askew.

Ainsley, Ainslie, Annesley, Aynsley.—Local, 'of Annesley,' a parish in co. Notts, near Nottingham. But there is probably a north English local origin also. There is also Ansley, a parish in co. Warwick.

'De Reginald' de Anisleg ... in Anisleg,' Hen. III-Edw. I: K. p. 12, Notts and Derbyshire.
Johannes de Anneslegh, co. Notts, 1273. A.
John de Annesley, co. York, 20 Edw. I. R.
Johannes de Andeslay, 1379: P. T. Yorks. p. 166.
Sir Johne Ainslye, curate of Holy Island, 1544: QQQ. p. 153.
1730. Married—John Annsley and Bridget Rose: St. Geo. Chap. Mayfair, p. 320.
1751. — John Sharp and Martha Ainsley: ibid. p. 194.
London, 2, 1, 1, 1; New York, 3, 1, 1, 0.

Ainsworth.—Local, 'of Ainsworth,' a chapelry in the parish of Middleton, co. Lanc., formerly Aynesworth.

William de Aynesworth, co. Lanc., 1332: Lay Subsidy (Rylands), p. 33.
John de Aynesworth, 43 Edw. III: Baines' Lanc. i. 404.
Lawrence Ainsworth, of Pleasington, 1573: Wills at Chester (1545-1620), p. 2.
William Allen, of Ainsworth, 1588: ibid. p. 3.
Cecilia Ainsworth, of Ainsworth, widow, 1630: ibid. (1620-50), p. 2.
John Aynsworth (Linc. Coll.): Reg. Univ. Oxf. iii. 185.
London, 3; Manchester, 15; Philadelphia, 7.

Airey, Airy, Airay.—Local, 'of Airey.' I cannot find the spot, but the family arose in co. Cumberland or Westmoreland. Almost every instance can be traced back to one or other county.

'Christopher Airay (1601-70), a pioneer of English logic, was born at Clifton in Westmoreland': Dict. Nat. Biog. i. 199.
'Henry Airay (1560?-1616), a puritan divine and author, was born at Kentmere, Westmoreland, being son of William Airay, the favourite servant of Bernard Gilpin': ibid.
In the muster roll of the dependants of Walter Strickland, deputy steward of Kendal (temp. 18 Henry VI), occurs 'Edward Ayray, a byll': Nicolson and Burn, Hist. Westm. and Cumb., i. 97.
1580. Henry Ayrey, co. Westm.: Reg. Univ. Oxf. vol. ii. pt. ii. p. 91.

1681. Anthony Ayrey, of Chiping: Lancashire Wills at Richmond, ii. 10.
1783. Married—Joseph Airey, of Kendal, and Sarah Salthouse, of Ulverston: Ulverston Church Reg. ii. 427.
London, 5, 1, 0; Lancaster, 3, 0, 0; Philadelphia, 7, 1, 0.

Aiskell.—Bapt. (?) 'the son of Auskettle,'q.v. Probably a modified form. On the other hand it may be local, with the suffix -*gill*, so common to the narrow gorges of the northern counties.

1576. Henry Aisgill, co. Westm.: Reg. Univ. Oxf. vol. ii. pt. ii. p. 72.
1608. Joshua Aisgill, co. Glouc.: ibid. p. 268.

Aislaby.—Local, 'of Aislaby,' (1) a township in the parish of Eaglescliffe, co. Durh.; (2) a chapelry in the parish of Whitby, N. R. Yorks, formerly Aslakeby (v. Aslac). Hence the meaning is 'the dwelling of Aslac,' the first settler. 'Aislabie, one of the oldest names in the county of Durham, from Aislaby, a parish on the river Tees, on the banks of which the family still reside. In old documents it is written Ashlackby, and in about fifty other modes' (Lower).

Hugo de Aslaby, 1379: P. T. Yorks. p. 192.
William Aslakeby, or Aislaby, 1572: Visitation of Yorkshire, 1564, p. 3, and see note.
Katherine Aslaby, d. of Francis Aslakeby, 1557: ibid. p. 4.
1765. Charles Allanson and Elizabeth Aislabia: St. Geo. Han. Sq. i. 140.

Aitcheson, Aitchison, Acheson, Ackerson.—(1) Bapt. 'the son of Archibald' (?), from the nick. Archie, a Scotch Border favourite; *t* intrusive, as in Ritchie, from same district, q.v.

John Achesoun, 1563: Cal. State Papers relating to Scotland, edited by Thorpe, 1858, p. 190.
Archie of Gingles, 1552: Nicolson and Burn, Hist. Westm. and Cumb., i. p. lxxxii.
John Archerson, 1602: ibid. pp. cxii, cxiv.
Archie Halliday, 1602: ibid.

(2) Bapt. 'the son of Adkin,' q.v. A Border form of the great north English surname Atkinson. This is the true source of the majority of our Aitchesons, &c.

Atshison = Atkinson: Dickinson's

Glossary of the Words and Phrases of Cumberland, p. 4.

John Attechenson. XX. 1.

On Nov. 1, 1596, 28 people were drowned returning by boat from Church at Canonbie. One was buried at Kirkandrews-upon-Esk on the following day, named William Attchison, of Millrighs. This is the earlier form of the corruption, and marks the first step ': Trans. Cumb. and Westm. Ant. and Arch. Soc., vol. viii. 287.

London, 2, 6, 0, 0 ; New York, 0, 2, 3, 13 ; Philadelphia, 0, 0, 5, 8.

Aitken, Aitkin, Aitkens.— Bapt. 'the son of Adam.' The Scotch Border form of Atkin, q.v.

1744. Married—Alex. Aitkens and Jane Mecallpen : St. Geo. Han. Sq. i. 32.

1773. — William Aitken and Eliz. Shelton : ibid. p. 233.

London, 7, 0, 1 ; Crockford, 3, 0, 2 ; Philadelphia, 26, 0, 0.

Aizlewood.—Local, 'a variant of Hazlewood,' q.v.

West Rid. Court Dir., 2.

Akod.—Local, 'at the oak-head' (from residence thereby), the top or furthest reach of the oak-trees ; cf. Birk-head, now Birkett ; and v. Akenhead for further instances.

Johannes de Aykehened, 1379 : P. T. Yorks. p. 289.

West Rid. Court Dir., 14 ; Philadelphia, 1.

Akenhead. Local ; v. Akenside. Lower says, 'Akenhead : Akenside—doubtless local ; from Aiken, an early proprietor.' This latter statement is wholly incorrect.

Akenside, Akenhead, Aikenhead.—Local, 'of Akenside,' i. e. the side of the clump of oaktrees ; A.S. *acen* ; cf. Beechen, Linden, Birchen, with the adjectival suffix *-en*. The place, whether a manor or mere farmstead, is distinctly set down in the list of landed proprietors in Hodgson's Hist. of Northumberland (iv. 268). Akenside, the poet, it will be remembered, was born at Newcastle-on-Tyne in 1721. His parentage and descent, therefore, were strictly local, and his 'forbears' had wandered but a few miles from their original home ; cf. Thomas Carlyle and the city Carlisle (v. Carlisle). *-side* is a common suffix of north English local names, used in the same sense as lake-side, pit-side ;

cf. Fawcett or Garside, q.v. Also, cf. Adam de Birkinside, 1322 : E. and F., co. Cumb. p. 165.

Mark Akenside : KKK. ii. 424.

Thomas Akenhead : ibid. p. 449.

Akenhead, i. e. at the head of the oak-trees, corresponds with Birkenhead, Birkett, and Beckett, q.v.

David Akenhead, 1763 : Brand's Hist. of Newcastle, i. 559.

Johannes de Aykehenead, 1379 : P. T. Yorks. p. 289.

1769. Married—William Nedham and Eleanor Akenhead : St. Geo. Han. Sq. i. 185.

Crockford, 0, 2, 0 ; MDB. (North Rid. Yorkshire), 0, 0, 1.

Akister.—Local, 'of Acaster,' two parishes of this name near York. This surname has crossed from Yorkshire into Furness, Lancashire.

William de Acastie, *cotoler*, 1319-20 : Freemen of York. (Surt. Soc.), i. 19.

Robertus de Acastre, 1379 : P. T. Yorks. p. 4.

Johannes Acastre, 1379 : ibid. p. 296. Ulverston, 1.

Alabaster, Allblaster.—Occup. 'the Arbalester,' i. e. crossbowman ; O.F.*arbalestier* ; v. H.E.D.

'So great power oft his land, and of France le nom

With him into England, of knights, and squires,

Spearmen anote, and bowemen, and also arblasters.'

Robert of Gloucester.

' And in the kernels, here and there,

Of arblasters great plentie were.'

Chaucer, Rom. Rose, 4196.

Henry le Alblaster, c. 1300. M.

Richard le Alblaster. B.

Reginald le Arbelestre, co. Devon, 1273. A.

William le Arblaster, co. Oxf., ibid.

John le Arblaster, co. Oxf., ibid.

James Arblaster, co. Norf., 29 Hen. VI : FF. viii. 300.

Odo Arbalistar, co. Norf., temp. Stephen : ibid. xi. 142.

1565-6. Robert Eton and Margaret Aleblaster : Marriage Lic. (London), i. 33.

1624. Buried—Mr. Thomas Allyblaster, gent. : St. Peter's, Cornhill, i. 181.

London, 5, 0 ; Philadelphia, 0, 1.

Albany.—(1) Local, 'de Albini,' not the Scotch Albany. 'William de Albini attended William the Conqueror. Wace mentions him as " the butler d'Aubignie "' (Lower). Hence the Earls of Arundel.

Hugh de Albany, Earl of Arundel, temp. 1312, co. Norf. : FF. i. 504.

Godfrey Giffard, rector of Attleborough,

co. Norf., temp. Hen. III, presented by Hugh de Albany : ibid. p. 523.

Nigel de Albini, tenant in capite, co. Bucks : Domesday.

William de Albini, or D'Aubigny, pincerna regis : FF. ix. 42, 44.

William de Albania, or Albany, co. Notts, Hen. III-Edw. I. K.

Walter de Albenay, co. Linc., ibid.

(2) Bapt. 'the son of Alban,' popularly Albany. This form has survived in some districts till today.

Albany Holmes, farmer, Farnley, near Ottley : West Rid. Court Dir., p. 332.

Albany Wade, of Dothand, co. Northumberland, 1663 : KKK. iv. 314.

Albany Fertherston, of Kirkhaugh, Northumberland, 1663 : ibid. p. 319.

1626. John Hawthorne and Mary Albanie : Marriage Lic. (London), ii. 167.

Philadelphia, 4.

Albert, Allbright, Allbred, Albright.—Bapt. 'the son of Albert,' from Ethelbert or Adelbert ; German Albrecht ; v. also Allbright for further instances.

Aylbreda de Cheyny. A. ii. 463.

Aylbricht le Turner. A.

Albreda de Kanville. T.

Albred de la Haye. T.

The Albrechts of the London Dir. are all of late German immigration. Also the Albrechts of Philadelphia.

Walter Albard, co. Soms., 10 Edw. III : Kirby's Quest, p. 184.

1607. William Albright, Magd. Hall : Reg. Univ. Oxf. iii. 272.

London, 7, 0, 0, 0 ; Ulverston, 0, 1, 0, 0 ; Boston (Allbright), 1 ; Philadelphia, 24, 9, 0, 66.

Albery, Albury.—(1) Bapt. 'the son of Albray,' probably Aubrey. (2) Local, 'of Aldbury,' a parish in co. Hertfordshire, three miles from Tring ; v. Albury for other instances.

Willelmus Dyan et Albray uxor ejus, 1379 : P. T. Yorks. p. 42.

Albreda de Hill, vidua (?), 1379 : ibid.

Albray Rayson, vidua, 1379 : ibid. p. 41.

1683. Bapt.—Samuell, s. William Albury : St. Mary Aldermary, p. 109.

Albin.—Bapt. 'the son of Albin' or 'Alban': pet form Albany, q.v.

Albin le Porteur. N.

Albinus de Stapelford, co. Camb., 1273. A.

Albinus le Alblaster, C. R., 33 Edw. I.

Earlier still, in 1269, we find one

Albin de Dereby forbidden to dwell within the precincts of London city : WWW. p. 125.

For other examples see next article.

1664. Bapt.—Mary, d. Hugh Albin: St. Jas. Clerkenwell, i. 221.
1786. Married—Benign Albin and Louisa Charlier: St. Geo. Han. Sq. i. 382.
London, 2 ; Philadelphia, 1.

Albinson, Albeson, Allbeson, Albason.—Bapt. ' the son of Albin,' or ' Alban ' ; v. Albin.

Isabella fil. Albin, co. Camb., 1273. A.
John fil. Albini, co. Camb., ibid.

The following entry has probably no connexion with Alberston :

1790. Married—James Barlow and Jane Alberson: St. Geo. Han. Sq. ii. 40.

With this variant cf. Patterson for Pattinson.

Manchester, 2, 1, 1, 0 ; Philadelphia, 0, 0, 0, 1.

Albon, Albone.—Bapt. ' the son of Alban ' ; v. Allbon.

1787. Married—James Albon and Ann Pook: St. Geo. Han. Sq. i. 401.
London, 1, 1.

Albury, Albro.—Local, ' of Albury,' or ' Aldborough,' parishes in cos. Norfolk, Suffolk, York (W.R.), and York (E.R.), and Hertford ; v. Eldborough.

David de Aldebury, co. Salop, 1273. A.
Stephen de Aldebury, co. Oxf., ibid.
William de Aldebiry, co. Oxf., Hen. III–Edw. I. K.
Richard de Aldeburgh, co. Bedf., 20 Edw. I. R.
1809. Married—William Alberry and Esther Kemp: St. Geo. Han. Sq. ii. 420.
London, 2, 0 ; New York, 0, 13 ; Philadelphia, 0, 4.

Albutt, Allbutt.—Bapt. ' the son of Albot,' probably a popular form of Albrecht ; v. Albert.

John Albot, co. Devon, 1273. A.
Augustin Albot, co. Hunts, ibid.
Roger Albot, co. Bedf., ibid.
Henry Albot, rector of Rockland, co. Norf., 1350: FF. v. 486.
1751. Married—Joseph Haddock and Sarah Allbut: St. Geo. Chap. Mayfair, p. 198.
London, 1, 0 ; West Riding Court Dir., 0, 2 ; Philadelphia, 0, 1.

Alcock, Alecock, Allcock, Alcockson.—Bapt. ' the son of Allen,' from the pet form Alli-

cock or Allcock ; v. Cock, and cf. Wilcock, Jeffcock, Simcock. ' The same holds one messuage which formerly belonged to Matilda Alcoke, doghtyr.' ' The same holds one tenement which formerly belonged to Alcoke of Hynganderode': Rental of Halifax (1439), Cotton MSS. Vespasian; F. 15, Brit. Mus.

Alcok de Stonys, co. Derbys., 1273. A.
Johannes Alcokson, 1379: P. T. Yorks. p. 124.
Alcocus de Stublay, 1379: ibid. p. 202.
Willelmus Alcok, 1379: ibid. p. 152.
John Alcoc, co. Camb., 1273. A.
1578. Married—John Booth and Sicelye Allicocke : Prestbury Ch. (co. Chester), p. 63.
1585. — John Alycocke and Mawde Leighe : ibid. p. 85.
Humfry Alcokson, sup. for B.A., Oct. 10, 1552: Reg. Univ. Oxf. i. 219.
1627. Richard Hatton and Ellenor Alcocke: Marriage Lic. (London), ii. 191.

Mr. Lower says this name is a dim. of Hal, the nick. of Henry. The evidence is against this view ; v. Allkin. There is clear proof that the original form was Alycock, and that this was abbreviated to Al-cock. Allen would readily take the nick. Ally or Aly, and the suffix -cock was added as a matter of course. The important point is to remember the enormous popularity of Allen in the 13th and 14th centuries, and the absolute certainty that both nick. and pet forms would be in everyday use.

Cecilia Allicok, 1379: P. T. Yorks. p. 124.
Henry Alycock, rector of Colney, co. Norf., 1481: FF. v. 3.
'In 1493, Thomas Alicok gave 10 marks to buy a cope': ibid. iv. 128.
1692. Thomas Abbott and Frances Allicock: Marriage Lic. (London), ii. 313.
London, 9, 2, 3, 0 ; New York, 1, 0, 1, 0.

Aldam.—Local, ' of Aldham,' q.v.

Alden, Aldin, Aldine.—Bapt. ' the son of Aldwin ' ; i.e. Aylwin, with intrusive d. ' This town (Shelton, co. Norf.) in the Confessor's time belonged to Bishop Stigand, and was held of him by Aldwin, or Ailwin ': FF. v. 263. The surname was common in the 13th century, but, like every other of the numerous compounds of-win, settled

into -en, -in, and -ing ; cf. Golden, Goldin, Goulding. Audenshaw, a division of Ashton-under-Lyne, was originally Aldwinshaigh, i. e. the wood of Aldwin.

William de Aldwinshaw, 1422: Baines' Lanc. i. 440.
Adam de Aldewyneshawe, co. Lanc., 20 Edw. I: R. p. 230.
Aldwina de Blancpain, Hen. III–Edw. I. K.
William Aldyn, co. Soms., 1 Edw. III : Kirby's Quest, p. 104.
Richard Aldewyn, co. Wilts, 1273. A.
Alexander Aldeyn, co. Oxf., ibid.
Robert fil. Aldun, co. Oxf., ibid.
Reginald Aldyne, co. Norf., ibid.
Alan Aldwyne, co. Camb., ibid.
1678–9. Philip Aldwin and Susanna Weekes: Marriage Lic. (Westminster), p. 294.
London, 4, 1, 3 ; New York, 22, 0, 2.

Alder.—Local, ' at the alder-tree ' ; cf. Ash, Nash, Birch, Rowntree, &c. ; from residence thereby. The plural is found in the two entries following :—

Thomas in the Alren, co. Soms., 1 Edw. III : Kirby's Quest, p. 182.
Henry in the Alren, co. Soms., 1 Edw. III : ibid. p. 259.

' Aldren = elders ': Halliwell.

Richard atte Alre, co. Soms., 1 Edw. III : Kirby's Quest, p. 220.
John atte Alre, co. Soms., 1 Edw. III : ibid. p. 221.
Robert in the Alre, co. Soms., 1 Edw. III : ibid. p. 265.

Thus the d in Alder is excrescent.

1605. Buried — Isaacke, s. Henrie Alders: St. Jas. Clerkenwell, iv. 89.
1621. — Margrett, wife of Richard Alder: ibid. p. 154.
1743.—Eliz. Alder: St. Thomas the Apostle (London), p. 156.
London, 13 ; Philadelphia, 3.

Alderman.—Official, ' the alderman,' probably used sometimes personally ; cf. Bateman, Tiddyman, &c.

Aldermann' de Bretford, co. Sussex, 1273. A.
Jukel Alderman, Sheriff of London, 1194: WWW. p. 187.
Jacob Alderman, Sheriff of London, 1199 : ibid. p. 188.
Robert le Alderman, co. Norf., 1273. A.
Benjamin Aldermannus, co. Sussex, ibid.
Thomas Alderman, rector of St. Butolph, Norwich, 1388: FF. iv. 442.
1691. Bapt.—Thomas, son of Joseph Alderman : St. Jas. Clerkenwell, i. 341.
London, 5 ; Philadelphia, 2.

Aldersey.—Local, ' of Aldersey,' a township in the parish of Coddington, near Chester. This is settled beyond controversy by the following entries :—

Ralph Aldersey, of Chester, alderman, 1555 : Wills at Chester (1545-1620). p. 3.
Thomas Aldersey, of Middle Aldersey, Cheshire, 1588 : ibid.
Hugh Aldersey, of Aldersey, yeoman, 1635 : ibid. (1620-50). p. 3.
1588-9. John Aldersey, co. Ches.: Reg. Univ. Oxf. vol. ii. pt. ii. p. 168.
1630-1. Robert Eyre and Anne Aldersey : Marriage Lic. (London), ii. 201.
1635. Thomas Blechynden and Margaret Aldersey : ibid. p. 224.

The grandfather of Anne and Margaret Aldersey was ' John Aldersey, of Aldersey, co. Chester,' who married Anne Low, sister of Sir Thomas Low, alderman of London. Their father was Samuel Aldersey, of London, haberdasher : v. Visitation of London, 1633-4, p. 8.

Liverpool, 2 ; MDB. (Cheshire), 2.

Alderson.—Bapt. ' the son of Aldus' (v. Aldhous), a once familiar personal name. Aldus-son would soon settle down into Alderson.

1554. John Aldeson : Reg. Univ. Oxf. vol. ii. pt. ii. p. xiv.
1591. John Alderson, of London : ibid p. 183.
1620. Bapt.—Richard, son of Richard Alderson : St. Jas. Clerkenwell, i. 88.
1634. Anthony Alderson and Margaret Askell : Marriage Lic. (London), p. 216.
William Alderson, clerk, 1766 : Brand's Hist. of Newcastle-on-Tyne, i. 323.

London, 11 ; West Rid. Court Dir., 7 ; Philadelphia, 3.

Aldham, Aldam.—Local, ' of Aldham,' probably an early form of Oldham, co. Lanc., on the borders of Yorkshire. There are, however, parishes of this name in cos. Essex and Suffolk.

Adam de Aldam, 1379 : P. T. Yorks. p. 17.
Isabella de Aldam, 1379 : ibid. p. 62.
John Aldham, of Shimpling, co. Norf., 1553 : FF. i. 132.
1607. Married—Richard Aldam and Agnes Over : St. Michael, Cornhill, p. 18.
1671. Richard Kingsmill and Eunice Aldham : Marriage Lic. (Faculty Office), p. 117.
London, 2, 0 ; West Riding Court Dir., 0, 4.

Aldhouse, Aldhous, Aldis, Aldous, Aldus, Alldiss.—Bapt. ' the son of Aldus ' ; not local, as several of its corrupted forms would

seem to prove. These are simply imitative. The documentary proofs are extremely strong. Norfolk has been a long-established home for this name, both in its fontal and patronymic character.

William fil. Alduse, co. Notts, 1273. A.
Cecilia fil. Aldus, co. Oxf., ibid.
Aldus Waveloc, co. Camb., ibid.
Hugo fil. Aldus, co. Norf., ibid.
Hugo fil. Alduse, co. Norf., ibid.
Johannes Aldus, 1379 : P.T.Yorks. p. 113.
Alan Haldehous, 1379 : ibid. p. 226.
Walter Aldous, rector of Wreningham, co. Norf., 1393 : FF. v. 120.
Robert Aldhouse, rector of Narburgh, co. Norf., 1355 : ibid. vi. 165.

London, 0, 1, 4, 10, 0. 0 ; New York, 1, 2, 1, 0, 0, 0 ; Boston (U.S.), 0, 0, 0, 1, 3, 0 ; Crockford, 1, 0, 1, 1, 0, 0 ; MDB. (Suffolk), 0, 0, 0, 3, 0, 1.

Aldith, Awdith.—Bapt. ' the son of Aldith,' an early form of Edith (?).

Alditha uxor Willelmi Aufuerer, C. R., 42 Hen. III.
Adam fil. Aldith, co. Oxf., 1273. A.
William fil. Aldith, co. Wilts, ibid.
John Aldit, co. Hunts, ibid.
1588. Bapt.—Hellen, d. of Edwarde Awdeth : St. Jas. Clerkenwell, i. 20.

Aldred, Aldried.—Bapt. ' the son of Aldred.' This personal name died out soon after the surname epoch, and instances of its occurrence as a fontal name are scarce.

Aldred fil. Roger. T.
Aldred Ander, co. Camb., 1273. A.
Nicholas Alrede, co. Soms., 1 Edw. III : Kirby's Quest, p. 98.
William Alred, co. Soms., 1 Edw. III : ibid. p. 174.
1550-1. William Hawke and Magdalen Aldred : Marriage Lic. (London). i. 13.
1603. Henry Aldred, vicar of Rushall, co. Norf.: FF. v. 343.
London, 9, 0 ; Boston (U.S.), 2, 1.

Aldrich, Aldridge. — Bapt. ' the son of Alderich.' Although wearing a local guise, it is easy to see that Aldridge belongs to the baptismal class.

William Ailrich, co. Soms., 1 Edw. III : Kirby's Quest, p. 243.
John fil. Aldrech. C.
John Aldrich, co. Camb., 1273. A.
John Alrich, 1313. M.
Robertus Aldrech, 1379 : P. T. Yorks. p. 255.
John Aldryche, bailiff of Yarmouth, 1469 : FF. xi. 325.
1609-10. Peter Aldrich and Catherine Rowell : Marriage Lic. (London), i. 318.
' Robert Aldrich, or Aldridge (d. 1556), scholar and divine, was born at Burnham,

in Buckinghamshire, towards the close of the 15th century ' : Dict. Nat. Biog. i. 252.
London, 4, 43 ; Philadelphia, 13, 13.

Aldwinckle.—Local, ' of Aldwinkle,' a parish three miles from Thrapston, co. Northampton.

Henry de Audewinkle, co. Northampt., Henry III-Edw. I. K.
1648. Married—William Allwinckle and Mary King : St. Dionis Backchurch (London), p. 26.
1654. Buried—Sarah Alwincle, an auncient widd : St. Jas. Clerkenwell, iv. p. 302.
1655. — Eliz. Alwincle, an ancient wyddowe : ibid. p. 304.
London, 1.

Aldworth.—Local, ' of Aldworth,' a parish in co. Berks, near Wantage.

John Aldeworth, co. Oxf., 1273. A.
1587-8. Francis Feilde and Agnes Aldeworthe : MarriageLic.(London),i.168.
1595. John Aldworth, co. Glouc. : Reg. Univ. Oxf. vol. ii. pt. ii. p. 210.
London, 2 ; Philadelphia, 3.

Alefounder. — Official, ' the alefounder,' an inspector appointed by the Court Leet to assize and supervise the brewing of malt liquor. Another term for this office was ale-conner. A poem of James I's reign says—

' A nose he had that gan show,
What liquor he loved I trow ;
For he had before long seven years
Been of the towne the ale-conner.'

A *confirmation* by John, Abbot of Cockerham, Lancashire, 1 Ric. III, says, in regulating the price of beer, ' Yai sall gyf Ale-fwnders a fwnding galon or else a taste of ylke vessell,' &c. ; Baines' Lanc. ii. 588. This word is neither in Halliwell nor in the Hist. Eng. Dictionary ; cf. ' fondyn, or asayyn—*attempto*,' Prompt. Parv. p. 169. Way adds in a note : ' A.S. fandian, *tentare*.' Lower quotes as follows from the Norfolk Chronicle, Aug. 19, 1854 : ' At a Court Leet, or Law Day . . . of the Borough of New Buckenham, the sub-bailiff, affiers, searchers, and sealers of leather, examiners of fish and flesh, alefounders, inspectors of weights and measures, and a pinder were appointed ' : Patr. Brit. p. 5. Again Lower quotes from Three Early Metr. Rom. (Camden Soc.), p. xxxviii, as follows : 'In the records of the manor of Hale in the xvth cent. one Thomas Layet is mentioned as being fined . . . for having concealed the *founding pot* (quia concelavit le fowundynge pot), 3*d*.' Evidently the official term as well as the surname were in existence in Norfolk till a very recent period.

Mary Alfounder. PP.
Richard Alefounder. Z.
William Alefounder was rector of Birchamwell in 1374 : FF. vii. 295.
'There is a brass in East Bergholt Church to Robert Alefounder in the middle of the last century': N. and Q., June 11, 1887, p. 474.
1671. Buried—Sarah Elfounder : St. Michael, Cornhill, p. 258.
1746. — John, son of John Alefounder : ibid. p. 208.
'John Alefounder (d. 1795), portrait and miniature painter, studied at the Royal Academy, and gained a silver medal in 1782,' &c. : Dict. Nat. Biog. i. 254.
MDB. (Suffolk), 1.

Aletunner.—Occup. 'the aletunner,' one who filled *tuns* or casks with ale ; v. Turner and Tunneler.

Walter le Aletunnere, C. R., 16 Edw. I.

Alexander.—Bapt. 'the son of Alexander' ; v. Saunders. This personal name is common to all Europe, and in England was an early favourite. Stories of prodigious achievements, many of them miraculous, caused it to be immensely admired. Miss Yonge (i. 199-202) quotes Chaucer as saying—

'Alisaundres storie is commune,
That everie wight that hath discrecion
Hath herde somewhat.'
'Alysaunder, propyr name *Alexander*': Prompt. Parv.

Geoffrey fil. Alexandri, co. Oxf., 1273. A.
Alexander le Syre, co. Hunts, ibid.
Custance Alexandre, co. Camb., ibid.
Henricus Alisaundre, 1379 : P. T. Yorks. p. 189.
John Alysannder, of Attleburgh, co. Norf., 1508 : FF. i. 530.
1614-5. George Barrume and Barbara Alexander : Marriage Lic. (London), ii. 30.
1617. Bapt.—Francis, d. Peter Alexander : St. Jas. Clerkenwell, i. 79.
London, 89; Philadelphia, 201.

Alford, Alforth.—Local, 'of Alford.' Parishes in cos. Linc. and Somerset, and no doubt smaller spots in various counties, as mean-

ing 'the old ford.' For the form Alforth, v. Forth.

Robert de Aldeford, 1184: Annales Cestrienses, p. 33 (Lanc. and Ches. Rec. Soc.).
John Alforde, co. Soms., 1 Edw. III : Kirby's Quest, p. 216.
John de Aldeford, co. Hereford, 1273. A.
1634. Thomas Alford, of co. Wilts, and Bennett (i. e. Benedicta) Berisford : Marriage Lic. (London), ii. 219.
1763. Married—Thomas Ruston and Betty Alford : St. Geo. Han. Sq. i. 123.
London, 14, 1 ; Philadelphia, 10, 0 ; Boston, 5, 0.

Alfred, Allured.—Bapt. 'the son of Alfred,' or 'Alured.' This latter form is still found as a surname, although Alfred has long been the accepted orthography of the fontal name. It is curious that Alfred has so few representatives in the directories. Where Allen occupies columns, Alfred occupies lines.

Alphred Hock, co. Devon, 1273. A.
Alured de la Dene, cos. Essex and Hertf., Hen. III-Edw. I. K.
Robert Alured, co. Oxf., 1273. A.
William Alured, co. Camb., ibid.
Stephen Alfrad, co. Oxf., ibid.
Michael Alfred, co. Bucks, ibid.
Thomas Alfred, vicar of Moulton, co. Norf., 1434: FF. xi. 109.
John Alfred, co. Soms., 1 Edw. III : Kirby's Quest, p. 127.
1617. Thomas Alured and Mary Jones : Marriage Lic. (London), ii. 50.
1634. Andrew Clare and Everell Allured : ibid. p. 20.
London, 3, 1 ; Philadelphia, 2, 0.

Alfrey, Allfrey, Allfree, Alfree.—Bapt. 'the son of Alfrey,' i. e. Alfred. Alfried, Alfred, Alfrey; cf. Godfrey, Godfried, Humfrey, Humfreid : Yonge, i. pp. lxviii and lxxviii.

Elferus Tannator, co. Sussex, 1273. A.
Ricardus Alfray, 1379: P.T. Yorks. p. 9.
Thomas Alfray, 1379 : ibid.
Haldefrus fil. Hugh. Hen. III-Edw. I. K.
1666. Mickepher Alphrey and Mary Wood : Marriage Alleg. (Canterbury), p. 117.
1679. Sampson Winckworth and Mary Alfrey : ibid. p. 297.
London, 1, 3, 0, 0 ; Crockford, 0, 0, 5, 0 ; Philadelphia, 0, 0, 0, 1.

Algar, Alger, Elgar.—Bapt. 'the son of Algar,' or 'Alfgar.' In Domesday commonly found as Algar. It is also met with alone without surname attached in the Hundred Rolls, ii. 472. This sur-

name is a familiar one as Algar in co. Norfolk. It is early found there both as a personal and a surname. Algar, although forgotten now, was evidently popular in its day and generation ; cf. the place-name Algersthorp, co. Norf.

Algar le Savener, co. Camb., 1273. A.
Elena fil. Algar, co. Camb., ibid.
Ayelyine Algar, co. Camb., ibid.
John Algar, co. Oxf., ibid.
Alicia relicta Algor, co. Camb., ibid.
Eylgar de Berwe, co. Sussex, ibid.
Algar West, co. Oxf., ibid.
Walter Algar, co. Soms.: Kirby's Quest, p. 97.
Algar de Summertun, Norwich, c. 1160: FF. iii. 600.
Algar de Flegg, co. Norf., temp. Henry II : ibid. xi. 194.
Roger Algor, co. Norf., c. 1300 : ibid. iv. 285.
1767. Married—Charles Allger and Sarah Davis : St. Geo. Han. Sq. i. 70.
London, 4, 2, 4 ; MDB. (Norfolk), 5, 0, 0 ; Boston (U.S.), 0, 15, 1.

Alison, Allison.—(1) Bapt. 'the son of Alice.'

Richard fil. Alice, co. Oxf., 1273. A.
Nicholas fil. Alicie, co. Camb., ibid.
Isabel fil. Alice, co. Oxf., ibid.
John Alicesone. RR. 1.
Richard Alsesone, co. Soms., 1 Edw. III : Kirby's Quest, p. 249.

(2) Bapt. 'the son of Alice,' from the popular dim. Alison ; cf. Marion from Mary, Gibbon from Gib (i. e. Gilbert), Beaton from Beatrice, &c.

'This Alison answered: Who is there That knocketh so?'
Chaucer, C. T. 3788.
'Item.—To Symkyn, and Watkyn, and Alison Meek, servandes of John of Bolton, to ilk one of yaim, 26s. 8d.': Test. Ebor. iii. 21 (Surtees Soc.).
Alisceon de Tuxforth, co. York. W. 2.
Alison Gelyot. H.
Alison Wrangwish, co. York. W. 11.
Johannes Alysson, 1379 : P. T. Yorks. p. 106.
1590. Bapt.—Mary, d. Abraham Allyson: St. Jas. Clerkenwell, i. 23.
Thomas Alysson, rector of Melton Constable, co. Norf., 1447: FF. ix. 426.

(3) Bapt. 'the son of Allen,' corrupted from Allenson. Such a corruption was bound to take place ; cf. Pattinson and Pattison. There can be no doubt many of our Allisons are traceable to this source. For early instances, v. Allenson.

1617-8. Leonard Allensone and Christian Stavelly : Marriage Lic. (London), ii. 57.

1618. William Alleson and Eliz. Broomer: Marriage Lic. (London), ii. 60.

Allison has ramified very strongly in the United States.

London, 2, 15; West Rid. Court Dir., 0, 6; Philadelphia, 0, 86.

Alker.—Local, 'of Altcar,' a village six miles from Ormskirk, co. Lancaster. This surname is rarely found outside the county. Its origin is easily proved by the following instances :—

Margaret Alcar, of Ormskirk. *widow*, 1634 : Wills at Chester (1545-1620), p. 3.
Hector Alkar, of Ormskirk, *webster*, 1647: ibid.
William Alker, of Burscough, 1630: ibid.
Manchester, 4; Liverpool, 2; Boston (U.S.), 1.

Alkins, v. Allkins.

Allamand.—Local; v. Allman, and cf. Lallimand.

1578. Oliver Almonde, co. Oxf.: Reg. Univ. Oxf. vol. ii. pt. ii. p. 83.
1592. Roger Allmonte, or Almon: ibid. p. 192.
London, 2.

Allard, Allardson. — Bapt. 'the son of Alard,' abbreviated from Adelard; v. Adlard.

Alard le Fleminge. B.
Alard le Burser. H.
Robert Alard, 1307. M.
Ralph fil. Alard, temp. Hen. III: BBB. p. 174.
Adam Adelard, co. Camb., 1273. A.
Adelard, or Alard Baate, 1505: Reg. Univ. Oxf. i. 40.
Aluardus de Camar, Hen. III-Edw. I. K.
Alardus Flamard, ibid.
Aylard atte Stlo, co. Essex. 1273. A.
1541. Married—Robarte Walles and Eliz. Aylarde : St. Dionis Backchurch, p. 2.
'Item, the x daye paied to Alart Plymer, the jeweller, etc.' Jan. 1530 : Privy Purse Exp., Henry VIII, p. 16.
John Allardson, C. R., 32 Hen. VI.
1738. Bapt.—Ann, d. Edward Allard: St. Jas. Clerkenwell, i. 239.
London, 7, 0; Boston (U.S.), 20, 0.

Allardyce, Allardice.—Local, 'of Allardyce,' an estate in the parish of Arbuthnot, co. Kincardine, N.B.

1795. Married—James Farquhar and Helen Innes; witnesses, Alex. Allardyce and Gavin Young: St. Geo. Han. Sq. ii. 130.
London, 4, 1.

Allatt.—Bapt. 'the son of Elliot,' q.v., the dim. of Ellis.

Robert Aliot, 1273. A.
Walter Aliot, ibid.
'Alyott de Symondston held half an

oxgang of land': De Lacy Inquisition, 1311 (Cheth. Soc.).
1581. Robert Allatte, co. Linc.: Reg. Univ. Oxf. vol. ii. pt. ii. p. 99.
1587-8. William Albanie and Margaret Allatt: Marriage Lic. (London), i. 168.
London, 1.

Allaway, Ellaway.—Bapt.; v. Allvey, Alloway. This is a natural variant, the intrusive *a* being euphonic; cf. Greenaway, Hathaway, Ottaway, &c.

1608. Edward Allaway, co. Oxf.: Reg. Univ. Oxf. vol. ii. pt. ii. p. 301.
1731. Married—John Raymond and Eliz. Allaway, co. Bedf.: St. Antholin, London, p. 144.
1807. — William Lester and Maria Allaway : St. Geo. Han. Sq. ii. 374.
London, 2, 3.

Allblaster.—Occup. (v. Alabaster : an American variant.)

Allbon, Allbones.—Bapt. 'the son of Alban,' patr. Albans; v. Albinson. In the register of the parish church, Bolingbroke, Albans in the 17th century is represented by Allbones in the 19th; v. Allibone, Alban, and Albany.

John Bordett, of St. Albones, Wood Street, 1647: Reg. St. Mary Aldermary, London, p. 20.
Francis Fynimore, of St. Albones, Wood Street : Reg. St. Peter's, Cornhill, p. 248.
'Stol'n from mine host of S. Albones': Falstaff, 1 Hen. IV, iv. 2.
Willelmus Albanes, 1379 : P. T. Yorks. p. 210.
Richard Albon, co. Norf., 1273. A.
1588. Bapt.—Alban, s. Thomas Bull: St. Jas. Clerkenwell, i. 20.
Antony Albon, or Albons, sup. for B.A., Jan. 14, 1532-3 : Reg. Univ. Oxf. i. 172.
1677-8. Peter Noyes and Mary Alban : Marriage Lic. (Westminster), p. 274.
London, 2, 0; MDB. (Lincoln), 0, 2.

Allbright, Albrecht, Albert, Albertson, Albright. — Bapt. 'the son of Ailbrit'; in Domesday Ailbriht. Albrecht is a German immigrant of much later date. Allbright is English. Albert, again, is ancient and modern. For other instances, v. Albert.

Eusebi Ailbrit (also Ailbric), co. Hunts, 1273. A.
John Albert, co. Hunts, ibid.
Walter Albert, co. Oxf., ibid.
John Albertson, mayor of Yarmouth, 1688: FF. xi. 330.
Farman Alberd, bailiff of Yarmouth, 1325: ibid. p. 323.

London, 0, 6, 7, 0, 0; Philadelphia, 9, 38, 24, 52, 65.

Allbut.—Bapt.; v. Albutt.

Allcorn, Alchin, Allchin, Alchorn, Alcorn.—(1) Bapt. 'the son of Alcuin' (v. Yonge, ii. 250), corrupted to Oldcorn in north England. I have one representative in my parish (Ulverston). I place all these surnames together because it is impossible to separate them. No doubt both (2) and (1) have assimilated. In a general way Alchorn represents the local, and Alcorn the personal surname.

Richard Halchein, co. Oxf., 1273. A.
Hugh Eldcorne, co. Oxf., ibid.
Eustace Eldcorn, co. Kent, ibid.
John Alcorn, co. Essex, ibid.
Stephan Alcorn, co. Kent, ibid.

(2) Local, 'of Alchorne,' a manor in the parish of Rotherfield, co. Sussex, where the family lived in the 14th century. Some of their descendants, still resident in that parish, have, within a generation or two, corrupted their name to Allcorn (Lower).

Thomas Allcorn, 1774: Reg. Cant. Cath. p. 34.
John Alchorne, 1690: St. Mary Aldermary (London), p. 110.
Alex. Alchorne, of Southampton, married, 1695: St. Dionis Backchurch (London), p. 44.
London, 3, 1, 5, 0, 0; Boston (U.S.), 0, 0, 1, 1, 7.

Allcroft; v. Holdcroft.

Allday, Alday.—Bapt. 'the son of Aldy,' a popular form of Aldwin, or Aldred, or Aldrich, or Aldus, or some other of the once popular compounds of Ald. But the probable ancestor was Aldwin, which was early modified into Aldwy; v. Allvey.

William Aldwin, or Aldwy, co. Oxf., 1273. A.
1541. Anne, d. of Nicholas Aldy : St. Antholin (London), p. 3.
1584. John Aldaye and Anne Cowper: Marriage Lic. (London), i. 131.
London, 2, 0; Philadelphia, 0, 1.

Allen, Alleine, Alleyne, Allan, Allin, Alland.—Bapt. 'the son of Alan,' or 'Allen,' or 'Aleyn': Yonge, i. 396-7.

'Aleyne, propyr name, *Alanus*': Prompt. Parv.

Forth goth Alein, the clerk, and also John.'—Chaucer, C. T. 4015.

(The *d* in Alland is an excrescence as in Simmonds.) One of our most popular names while surnames were becoming hereditary; said to have come into England with Alan Fergéant, Count of Brittany, a companion of the Conqueror, and first Earl of Richmond, co. York. Very soon common to north England and the Scottish border.

Henry Aleyn, 1273. A.
Hugh fil. Aleyn, ibid.
Allaine Bawdyson. V. 3.
Aleyn Forman. H.
Thomas fil Alani. M.

The founder of Dulwich Coll., 1619, was Edward Allen, or Alleyne. Derivatives, Allcock, Allkins, Allnutt, and perhaps Allatt, q.v. Possibly an abbrev. of Alinot; v. Allnutt.

London, 230, 0, 2, 27, 8, 1 ; Philadelphia, 532, 0, 0, 11, 0, 0 ; Boston (U.S.), Alland 4, Allin 1.

Allenby.—Local. Doubtless a modification of Aglionby, q.v. The surname is found in Cumberland, and the full title was cumbrous.

1581. Francis Alanbye, co. Cumb.: Reg. Univ. Oxf. vol. ii. pt. ii. p. 110.
— Thomas Alanbye, co. Cumb.: ibid.
1742. Married—John Allenby and Martha Barnes: St. Geo. Chap. Mayfair, p. 18.
MDB. (co. Cumb.), 1 ; London, 1.

Allenson, Allinson, Allanson.—(1) Bapt. ' the son of Allen,' q.v.

Hugh fil. Aleyn, co. Oxf., 1273. A.
Johannes Alynson, 1379: P. T. Yorks. p. 87.
Robertus Alaynson, 1379: ibid. p. 219.
John Allevnsone. S.
William Aleynsonne. BB.
George Alonsonne. ZZ.
William Allenson, co. Norf., 1625: FF. iv. 487.
1782. Married—James Read and Agnes Alinson : St. Geo. Han. Sq. i. 331.

(2) Local, ' de Alençon,' in Normandy. Probably in some cases this is the true solution.

John de Alencon, 1 Ric. I: FF. viii. 162.
Robert de Alenson, co. Norf., 1220: ibid p. 375.
Herbert de Alenzun, sheriff of Norfolk, 25 Hen. III : ibid. vi. 123.

William de Alencon, co. Norf., 6 Ric. III : ibid. xi. 242.
William Allenson, co. Norf., 1625 : ibid. iv. 487.
London, 1, 6, 0 ; Philadelphia, 0, 1, 0 ; Boston (U.S.), 0, 0, 2.

Allerton.—Local, ' of Allerton,' a parish five miles from Knaresborough, co. York ; cf. Northallerton. Also, a township in the parish of Childwall, near Liverpool. Also, a township in the parish of Kippax, W. Rid. York.

Willelmus de Allirton, 1379 : P. T. Yorks. p. 148.
Johannes de Allerton, 1379 : ibid p. 181.
1698. Bapt.—Eliz. d. Robert Allerton : St. Jas. Clerkenwell, i. 378.
1762. Married—John Allerton and Mary Hill : St. Geo. Han. Sq. i. 109.
Boston, 1.

Alley.—(1) Local, ' of the Alley,' i. e. from residence in a narrow passage ; M.E. *aley* and *alley*. The first instance I possess is that of a foundling, found in an alley. But the name was an older one, of similar but more legitimate descent. The Hundred Rolls instances from Oxford and Cambridge seem very natural, just where we should expect alleys to be found ; v. Twitchen.

Simon de Ally, co. Lanc., Hen. III–Edw. I. K.
Walter Alleye, co. Oxf., 1273. A.
John Alley, co. Camb., ibid.
1623. Thomas Hambledon and Anne Alley : Marriage Lic. (London), ii. 131.
1706. Bapt.—Sarah Alley, a foundling : St. John Baptist, on Wallbrook (London), p. 175.
William Allee, of Litcham, co. Norf. : FF. x. 14.
1726. Married—Thomas Bougin and Jane Alley : St. Geo. Han. Sq. i. 2.

(2) Bapt. Probably in some cases Alley (a pet-name for very great favourites, Allen and Alice, q.v.) ; cf. Charlie, Teddy, &c.

London, 3 ; Boston (U.S.), 25.

Allfrey, Allfree. — Bapt. ; v. Alfrey.

Allgood, Elgood, Elegood.—Bapt. ' the son of Algod,' a forgotten personal name. Allgood, like Thoroughgood and Toogood, seems very complimentary, but it is without doubt a baptismal name, as are they. I see Lower says Algod occurs as a personal name before Domesday (Patr. Brit. p. 6).

William Algod, co. Bucks, 1273. A.
Robert Algold, co. Camb., ibid.
Ralph Algod, co. Kent, ibid.
1570. Richard Algood and Sence Dunn : Marriage Lic. (London), i. 46.
1575. James Morton and Jane Algood : Marriage Lic. (London), i. 66.
Bartholomew Algood, vicar of Wyken, co. Norf., 1679: FF. viii. 339.
John Allgoode or Algode, adm. B.A., June 30, 1449 : Reg. Univ. Oxf., vol. i. p. 4.
1786. Married—Henry Algood and Hannah Lloyd : St. Geo. Han. Sq. i. 391.
London, 2, 2, 0 : Philadelphia (U.S.A.), 0, 0, 1.

Allibone, Allibond, Alabone, Allaband, Alleborn.—Bapt.' the son of Alban,' or ' Albon ' ; v. Allbon. The *i* and *a* are intrusive for euphony, as in Greenaway, Hathaway, for Greenway and Hathway ; cf. Ottaway for Ottway. The *d* in Allibond is excrescent ; cf. provincial *gownd* for gown, and v. Simmonds.

Alibun Clipsam, co. Hunts, 1273. A.
Alibin de Wodehill, co. Wilts, Hen. III–Edw. I. K.
Luke Alibon, rector of Burgh, co. Norf., 1631 : FF. vi. 428.
Henry Allibone, 1695 : St. Peter's, Cornhill, p. 107.
Helline Allibone, 1642 : St. Mary Aldermary (London), p. 19.
William Albond, co. Soms., 2 Edw. III : Kirby's Quest, p. 225.
Job Allibon, or Allibond, fellow of Magdalen College, Oxf., 1687 : Magdalen Coll. and James II, p. 160.
1665. Buried—Samuell Allebond, stationer, of this parish : St. Dionis Backchurch (London), p. 235.
1672. Pompey Allibond and Mary Tilney : Marriage Lic. (Westminster), p. 201.

A book on the ' Cure of Consumption' is advertized by the author, Edwin W. Alabone, in the Weekly Pulpit for May 22, 1887.

Allaband and Alleborn are American variants.

London, 1, 0, 0, 0, 0 ; Philadelphia, 4, 0, 0, 2, 1.

Allingham.—Local, ' of Allingham,' a parish in co. Kent.

1792. Married—Allen Allingham and Sarah Atkins : St. Geo. Han. Sq. ii. 76.
London, 5.

Allington.—Local, ' of Allington,' parishes in cos. Dorset, Kent, Wilts, Devon, and Lincoln.

William de Allyngton, co. Soms., 1 Edw. III : Kirby's Quest, p. 171.
Peter de Alington, co. Wilts, Hen. III–Edw. I. K.

William de Alington, co. Norf., 1273. A.
1575. Bapt.—Medcalf, s. Mr. Allington:
St. Thomas the Apostle (London), p. 27.
1687. Married—Giles Allington and
Mary Lunn: St. Mary Aldermary, p. 33.
London, 1.

Allis, Alliss.—Bapt. 'the son
of Alice'; v. Alison (1).

Gocelinus fil. Alice, co. Linc., 1273. A.
Richard fil. Alise, co. Salop, ibid.
1571. George Haynes and Agnes Alles:
Marriage Lic. (London), i. 50.
1675. Bapt.—Mary, d. William Allis:
St. Jas. Clerkenwell, i. 269.
'Exuvias Antonii Allys, armigeri . . .
obiit vicesimo, nono die Octobris anno
salutis, 1709, aetatis suae, 76': St.
Nicholas, Yarmouth, see FF. xi. 394.
MDB.(Lincoln), 1, 4; Philadelphia, 1, 0.

Allison.—Bapt.; v. Alison.

**Allkins, Allchin, Alchin,
Allkin, Alkins.**—Bapt. 'the son
of Allen,' from the dim. Allikin or
Allkin; cf. Per-kin, Wat-kin, &c.
Mr. Lower suggests that it stands
for Halkin, the dim. of Henry. This
view is defeated by the fact that
Alkin has always been without the
aspirate, and has always run side
by side with its close relation
Alcock, q.v. Let it not be forgotten that Allen, as one of the
favourite personal names of the
13th and 14th centuries, must have
had its popular nick. and pet forms.
I have included Allchin and Alchin
as variants of Allkin. But v. Allcorn.

John Alkyn, 1306. M.
1617. Thomas Alkin and Mary Newman: Marriage Lic. (London), ii. 53.
1693. Married—RichardAlkin andMary
Green: St. Dionis Backchurch, p. 43.
1754. — Richard Allchin and Mary
Chandler: St. Geo. Han. Sq. i. 55.
London, 2, 5, 1, 1, 0; Philadelphia, 1,
0, 1, 0, 9.

**Allman, Almond, Allmond,
Allmen.** — Local, or nick. 'the
Alemaund,' i. e. German; cf. Fr.
Lallimond: or still more locally
'of Alemaigne,' i. e. Germany; cf.
Fr. D'Almaine. With Almond cf.
almond-furnace, i. e. a German furnace (H.E.D.); also under Almain,
'the *almond-leape*,' a German dance.

'The Almains ben ouer come,' 1314:
Guy Warw. 70 (H.E.D.).
'Forth he went into Speyne
And after into Almayne.'—ibid. 35.
'Item, the last daie (Nov. 1531) paide in

rewarde to a gentleman of Almayne':
Privy Purse Exp., Henry VIII, p. 178.
John Alaman, or Aleman, 1216: GGG.
p. 247.
Terricle Alemaund, co. Bucks, 1273. A.
Henry de Alemania, co. Notts, ibid.
Bertram de Almannia, co. Linc., ibid.
Willelmus Alman, 1379: P. T. Yorks.
p. 300.
William Alemannus. C.
John le Aleman, co. York. W. 7.
Robert Almene, co. Camb., 1273. A.
1582. Buried—Thomas Allmon: St.
Dionis Backchurch, p. 198.
Hanekin Almond, John de Almann,
varlets of Countess of Surrey, Household
Book of Queen Isabella, 1358 (Cott. MS.
Galba, E. xiv.).
Libertus Alman, rector of North Repps,
co. Norf., 1583: FF. viii. 154.
1622. Thomas Minne and Susan Al-
mond: Marriage Lic. (London), ii. 114.
London, 2, 8, 0, 0; Manchester, 3, 7, 1,
1; Philadelphia, 8, 8, 7, 0.

Allmark; v. Hallmark.
Manchester, 2.

Allnutt.—Bapt. 'the son of
Alnot' or 'Alnoth,' the A.S. Alnod.
'The Earl Warren had also two caru-
cates of land, which Alnod, a freeman,
possessed in King Edward's reign': FF.
x. 308.
'Alnoht, a freeman of Archbishop
Stigand, was lord in King Edward's
reign': ibid. viii. 25.
Rockland belonged 'to Alnoth, Godric,
Ulketel, Ulf, and William de Noers at
the Confessor's Survey': ibid. v. 483.
Earlham's Manor in Surlingham be-
longed to 'Godric the Sewer, and Alnot
the Saxon': FF. v. 469.
William Alnath, co. Wilts, 1273. A.
Cecil Aylnet, co. Oxf., ibid.
Alnot Red, co. Salop, ibid.
William Alinot, co. Bucks, ibid.
Havisia Alinet, co. Oxf., ibid.
Ailnoth Arscote, sup. for D.C.L., Nov.
10, 1513: Reg. Univ. Oxf. p. 89.
As will be seen from the above in-
stances, Alnot or Alnoth remained
in use as a personal name till the
16th century.
Cicely Alnet, temp. 1580: Visitation of
London, 1634, ii. 168.
1787. Dew Brockett and Harriot
Allnutt: St. Geo. Han. Sq. i. 406.
London, 7; Boston (U.S.), 1.

Allott, Allett, Alletson, Alot.
—Bapt. 'the son of Alot'; query,
a form of Eliot, with Eliota as
fem.; v. Elliot. In the Ulverston
Registers, co. Lanc., the forms are
Alletson, Aletson, Elatson, Elatt-
son, Elletson, Eletson, all representing the same patronymic Eliot-
son; v.Alletson in Index of Registers

of St. Mary, Ulverston. In any
case the surname, with its variants,
is of fontal origin.

Alvott de Symondston. AA. 2.
William Alotessone, co. Lanc., 1332:
Lay Subsidy (Rylands).
Alet fil. Boydini, Essex, Hen. III-
Edw. I. K.
Alota fil. Robert le Archer, co. Derby,
1273. A.
Phillip Allote, co. Hunts, ibid.
Peter Allot, co. Camb., ibid.
Adam Alot, 1379: P.T. Yorks. p. 204.
Richard Alot, 1379: ibid.
1568. Richard Allett, sup. for B.A.
Dec. 17: Reg. Univ. Oxf. i. 273.
Thomas Alot, rector of Brandeston and
Guton, co. Norf.: FF. viii. 199.
1707. Buried—Anne Alletson, a maid
to Mr. Winton: St. Mary Aldermary
(London), p. 210.
1781. Benjamin Williams and Margaret
Alletson: St. Geo. Han. Sq. i. 323.
Crockford, 4, 0, 0, 0; Philadelphia, 1,
1, 0, 1.

Alloway, Allaway.— Bapt.
'the son of Aldwy'; v. Allaway and
Allvey, where Alway is clearly identified. From Alway or Allway to
Alloway is an easy gradation; cf.
Ottaway or Greenaway for Otway and Greenway. Alloway has
ramified somewhat strongly in
America. But it arose in England.
No connexion with local Holloway; v. Allaway.

1616. Edward Hewlinge and Eliz.
Alleway: Marriage Lic. (London), ii. 43.
1780. Married—William Maslen and
Mary Allaway: St. Geo. Han. Sq. i. 311.
1786. — James Alloway and Barbara
Pittett: ibid. p. 396.
Philadelphia, 13, 0; London, 0, 2.

Allpress.—? Nick. 'the holy
priest' (?); A.S. *halig*, holy, from
hal, whole. Whatever the meaning,
the following entry refers to the
ancestor:

Thomas Alprest, co. Camb., 1273. A.

Thus -*prest* (priest) and not -*press*
is the suffix. The surname has
always had cos. Cambridge and
Hants for its habitat. There need
be no anxiety as to the want of an
h if Holy-priest be the parent. The
Hundred Rolls (1273) in scores of
cases ignore the aspirate. The
Cockney is not in it, judging by
early registers.

London, 2; MDB. (co. Hunts), 7,
(Cambridge), 1.

E

Allsop, Allsopp, Allsup, Alsop.—Local, 'of Alsop-en-le-dale,' a chapelry in the parish of Ashbourne, co. Derby. The corruption 'Allsup' is suggestive of universal pale ale! The reason why Alsop and its variants are common in the United States is because several of the name were among the earliest settlers there.

William Alsape, co. Camb., 1273. A.
Elena Alsope, co. Camb., ibid.
Thomas Alsop, 'gentleman potycary' to Hen. VIII, 1538: Privy Purse Exp., Princess Mary, p. 78, and note.
1612. John Francis and Magdalen Alsop: Marriage Lic. (London), ii. 17.
1622-3. Edward Alsopp and Anne Barker: ibid. p. 120.
1652. Bapt.—Eliz., d. Lewis Alsoppe: St. Jas. Clerkenwell, i. 180.
Joseph Alsopp (aged 14) went out to New England in the Elizabeth in 1635. Also Thomas Alsopp (aged 20). Also Robert Alsopp (aged 18). Hotten's Lists of Emigrants, pp. 58, 78, 121.
London -7, 3, 1, 8, Philade'p'iia, 1, 2, 0, 11.

Allured.—Bapt.; v. Alfred.

Allvey, Alvey, Alway, Elvey.—Bapt. 'the son of Aldwy,' a fontal or personal name long ago forgotten in England, but it lives to-day in several patronymics. Of some land in Somerton, co. Norfolk, it is said 'the Conqueror had granted this to Alwy de Tetford' (FF. xi. 197).

'Roger Bigot had a small tenure at the Survey, held by a freeman of Alwi, in King Edward's reign': FF. xi. 150.
Robert Alewi, co. Oxf., 1273. A.
Aldwy ad Fontem, co. Oxf., ibi.l.
William Aldwy, co. Oxf., ibid.
Walter Elwy, co. Oxf., ibid.
Stephen Alwy, London, ibid.
1544. Ralph Alway and Mary Bylby: Marriage Lic. (Faculty Office), p. 3.
1561-2. Thomas Alvie and Eliz. Northe: Marriage Lic. (Westminster), p. 1.
1599. Married—John Alwaye and Anne Potte: Prestbury Ch. (co. Chester), p. 142.
1681-2. John White and Susan Aylwey: Marriage Lic. (Faculty Office), p. 159.
London, 3, 4, 3, 1; Philadelphia, 0, 1, 0, 0.

Allwright, Alright. — Bapt. 'the son of Aldrich.' Mr. Lower suggests Awl-wright, a maker of awls. The origin is obvious enough. It is a mere corruption of Alderich (now Aldrich and Aldridge, q.v.), thus: Alderich, Alrick, Alwright; cf. Woolwright for Wulfric (v.

Woolrich), and Kenwright for Kendrick.

William Alricht, co. Bedf., Hen. III-Edw. I. K.
Alricus de Aulaby, co. York, 1273. A.
Richard Airich, co. Oxf., ibid.
William Alwrech, co. Camb., ibid.
Johannes Alwrich, co. Wilts, ibid.
William Ailriht, co. Camb., ibid.

A good example of the intermediate form is found in the following instances :—

1720. Married—Isaac Simpson and Eliz. Aldwright: St. Jas. Clerkenwell, iii. 244.
John Alrick, vicar of St. Peter's, Southgate, Norwich, 1593: FF. iv. 66.
1765. Married—William Allwright and Mary Clarkson: St. Geo. Han. Sq. i. 146.
London, 10, 0; Ledsham, Yorks., 1, 0; Philadelphia, 1, 0; Boston (U.S.), 0, 1.

Almond, Almonds.—Local; v. Allman.

Almsdeed. (?)

Agnes Almesdeed, 1563: Reg. Broad Chalke, co. Wilts, p. 8.

Alpe.—Nick. 'the Alpe,' i.e. a bullfinch. 'Alpe, a bryde : ficedula': Prompt. Parv. 'Alpes, fynches, and wodewales': Chaucer, R. R. 658. Alpe has existed as a surname in co. Norfolk for six centuries; cf. Finch, Sparrow, Nightingale, &c.

Thomas le Alpe, C. R., 8 Edw. III.
Matilda Alpe, co. Norf., 1273. A.
William Alpe, abbot of Langley, co. Norf., 1488 : FF. x. 150.
1579-80. Thomas Staunton and Hester Alpe: Marriage Lic. (London), i. 93.
Mary Alpe, of Burston, co. Norf., 1687 : FF. vi. 338.
1698-9. Edward Alp and Dorothy Wilson : Marriage Lic. (Faculty Office), p. 232.
MDB. (Norfolk), 1 ; London, 1.

Alstead.—Local, 'of Alstead.' I cannot find the precise locality ; but v. Halstead.

Henry de Alsted, co. Essex, 1273. A.
Roger de Alsted, co. Linc., ibid.
London, 1 ; Philadelphia, 1.

Alston, Alstone.—Local, ' of Alston,' a parish in co. Cumberland ; a chapelry in the parish of Ashburton, co. Devon ; a township in the parish of Ribchester, co. Lanc., &c. Also Alstone, a hamlet in the suburbs of Cheltenham, and a chapelry in the parish of Overbury, co. Worc.

Henry Alston, co. Camb., 1273. A.
Robert Alston, co. Camb., ibid.

Ralph de Alleston, co. Salop, Hen. III-Edw. I. K.
1624. Edward Alston and Sarah Hussey : Marriage Lic. (London), ii. 147.
1664. John Wittewronge and Clare Alstone : ibid. p. 293.
London, 11, 0 ; Philadelphia, 5, 1.

Altobasse.—Nick. Possibly from the high and low range of voice. But see legal 'alto et basso,' the submission of all differences, high and low, to an adjudicator (Bailey's Dict., 1742).

Peter Alto-basse. O.

Ambler.—Occup. 'the ambler,' one who looked after the amblers in his lord's stables ; one who taught horses to amble. Lower says 'le Ambleur, Fr., an officer of the king's stable.' Almost akin to Palfreyman, q.v. This surname has ramified strongly in Yorkshire.

'And mony fat palfray amblant' [i.e. ambling]. King Alisaunder, 3461.
'Upon an ambler esily she sat.' Chaucer, C. T. 471.

Among his other duties the ambler broke in horses, i. e. taught them to amble.

'1320. Item, pro informatione uniuspulli ad ambulandum, 11s. 6d,' i.e. for teaching a colt to amble.
Whittaker's Craven, p. 466.
Thomas le Amblur, co. York, 1273. A.
William Ambler, co. York. W. 9.
1632. Bapt.—Martha, d. Humfry Ambler: St. Jas. Clerkenwell, i. 120.
1656-7. Married — John Keys and Martha Ambler : St. Dionis Backchurch, p. 32.
London, 5 ; West Riding Court Dir., 25 ; Philadelphia, 18.

Ambrey, Amberson.—Bapt. 'the son of Amery,' q.v.; cf. Emberson and Embery from Emery. The b is intrusive, as usual after m.

Richard Amberson : Barrett, History of Bristol, index.
Robert Amberson : ibid.
Manchester, 1, 0.

Ambrose, Ambross.—Bapt. 'the son of Ambrose'; Fr. Ambroise. No doubt the fair amount of popularity obtained in England for this fontal name was due to the great St. Ambrose, Archbishop of Milan. The Church would not readily let his name be lost in obscurity (v. Yonge, Hist. Christian Names, i. 248). Ambrosi is a familiar Italian surname.

William Ambroys, co. Bedf., 1273. A.
Robert Ambros', co. Hunts, ibid.
Richard Ambrosie, co. Hunts, ibid.
Henry Ambreis, co. Oxf., ibid.
1567. Bapt.—Johane, d. William Ambrose : St. Jas. Clerkenwell, i. 4.
1641–2. Zacharie Lambert and Rachall Ambrose : Marriage Lic. (London), ii. 263.
1729. Married — Joseph Mottram and Ambrosia Ambrose : St. Geo. Han. Sq. i. 6.
London, 8, 1 ; Philadelphia, 15, 0.

Amelot.—Bapt. 'the son of Amy,' from the double dim. Amel-ot (v. Ames and Amyot) : cf. Hamelot from Hamo, or Hewel-ot from Hugh or Hew; v. Hamlet and Hewlett.

Nicholas Amelot, co. Wilts, 1273. A.
Richard fil. Amelot, co. Devon, ibid.
Amelota ad Fontem, C. R., 12 Edw. I.

Ameredith.—Bapt. 'the son of Meredith,' Ap-Meredith. Lower speaks of this name as still existing.

Hercules Ameredethe, sup. for B.C.L., Oct. 1564 : Reg. Univ. Oxf. i. 256.
1586. Lewis Ameredeth, co. Devon : Reg. Univ. Oxf. vol. ii. pt. ii. p. 148.
1588–9. Edward Amerideth, co. Devon : ibid. p. 232.

Amery, Amary, Amory, Amerson.—Bapt. 'the son of Amery' or 'Emery,' q.v. ; common to both sexes. Other variants were Americ, Almeric, and Almaric. It was decidedly popular. In the Italian dress of Amerigo it gave title to the great western continent. The United States has restored the feminine form in America, not an uncommon fontname for girls. I see in the Boston Directory, 'America Anderson, widow.' However strangely this may read, it was a common girl's name six centuries ago.

Roger Ammary, co. Bedf., 1273. A.
Americus Balistarius. E.
Johannes fil. Americ, 1379 : P. T. Yorks. p. 154.
Ameria filia Hugonis, 1379 : ibid. p. 202.
Ameria Hend Wyf, 1379 : ibid.
Americ Breton, 1306. M.
Hugh Amery. H.
Almaricus le Botiller. B.
Amery Martin, widow, 1584 : Reg. St. Peter's, Cornhill.
'Amary Clarke, widow, applies for arrears of pay due to her husband ': May 13, 1656, Cal. State Papers (Dom.).
Oswald Amerson, minister of the

Word, sup. for B.D., April 10, 1562 ': Reg. Univ. Oxf. i. 248.
1779. Married—William Ricks and Hannah Ammery : St. Geo. Han. Sq. p. 303.
1781. — Charles Wadlow and Elizabeth Amory : ibid. p. 321.
London, 11, 0, 0, 0 ; Boston (U.S.), 2, 0, 22, 0.

Ames, Amies, Amis, Amiss, Aymes.—Bapt. ' the son of Amys,' or ' the son of Amy,' with the patronymic s. ' Amye, Amy, proper name : *Amia* ': Prompt. Parv. The origin is the same. But Amice or Amys seems to have become the popular English form of the O. F. Aimée, just as Piers or Pearce came to represent the O.F. Pierre. Perhaps the Latinized forms had something to do with it. The two first entries occur close together, and probably refer to the same individual.

William fil. Amye, co. Linc., 1273. A.
William fil. Amice, co. Linc., ibid.
Adam Amys, co. Camb., ibid.
Robert Amys, co. Camb., ibid.
Amicele Noble, co. Hunts, ibid.
Hugh fil. Amicie, co. Linc., ibid.
Alice fil. Amicie, co. Suff., ibid.
John Amice, co. Oxf., ibid.

Amia, Amicia, Amise, and Amisius all occur as personal names without surnames in the Hundred Rolls, 1273.

Amis de Selves, co. Kent, Hen. III-Edw. I. K.
Amia de Rydeford, co. Linc., ibid.

The form Amiss in the London Directory is met by the entry :

'Gregory Amys, or Amisse, sup. for B.A., July 12, 1525 ': Reg. Univ. Oxf. i. 139.
Also : 1766. Thomas Amiss and Eleanor Cadman : St. Geo. Han. Sq. i. 153.

In the United States the form is all but invariably Ames. Amice or Ames continued as a girl's fontal name till the 16th century.

1540. Buried — Ameis Austin, Mr. Smith's maid : St. Antholin (London), p. 2.

The family of Ames in the Register of St. Dionis Backchurch is found as Amyes (p. 8), 1576; Ames and Ammes (p. 130), 1690 ; and Amis (p. 22), 1627. In the Register of St. Michael, Cornhill, the name is often found as Aymes :

1603. Bapt.—Daniel, son of George Aymes : p. 104.
London, 25, 4, 1, 1, 0 ; Boston (U.S.), 61, 0, 0, 0, 0 ; Philadelphia, 9, 8, 1, 0, 0.

Amflis.—Bapt. ' the son of Amflis.' This name seems to be extinct. It has long been forgotten as a fontal name, and so far I can find the surname no later than the 16th century.

Robert fil. Amflisie, co. Camb., 1273. A.
Amflis de Roldiston, co. Notts, Hen. III-Edw. I. K.
Henry Aunflis, co. Camb., 1273. A.
William Aunflis, co. Camb., ibid.
John Amfleys, co. Norf., 4 Hen. VIII : FF. x. 374.
William Amflys, mayor of Lynn Regis, 1494 : FF. viii. 533.

Amiable.—Bapt. ' the son of Amabel'; v. Annable and Hanniball.

Amabil fil. Emme. J.
Thomas Amable, co. Camb., 1273. A.
John fil. Amabilie, co. Hunts, ibid.
Edward Amiable, temp. Eliz. Z.
Joan Amiable, ibid.

Amias, Amyas.—(1) Bapt. ' the son of Amias '; v. Ames. (2) Local, ' of Amiens.'

Amias de Cotehal, co. Bucks, 1273. A.
William de Amyas, 20 Edw. I. R.
Robert de Amias, Hen. III-Edw. I. K.
Honore de Amyens, 1273. A.
Mercatores de Amias, ibid.
John Amyas, of Stotisdon, co. Salop, 1625 : Funeral Certificates (Ches. and Lanc.) p. 50.
RobertusAmias, 1379 : P. T.Yorks. p. 93.
John Amias, co. Norf., 7 Edw. VI : FF. xi. 73.
1631. Francis Amyas and Anne Athill : Marriage Lic. (London), ii. 202.
MDB. (Norfolk), 0, 1.

Amison, Amson.—Bapt. ' the son of Amice '; v. Ames.

Geoffrey fil. Amice, co. Linc., 20 Edw. I. R.
John Amysson, C.R., 7 Ric. II.
Willelmus Amyson, 1379 : P. T. Howdenshire, p. 8.
Amicia atte Weye, co. Soms., 1 Edw. III : Kirby's Quest, p. 146.

The Amsons of co. Ches. all descend from Ameson.

Hugh Ameson, co. Ches., 1537 : East Cheshire, i. 175.
1568. Married — Mathew Amson and Agnes Strettone : Prestbury Ch. (Cheshire), p. 25.
1622. — John Smale and Ellen Amesonne : ibid. p. 236.
Henry Amson, of Cotton, Cheshire, 1502 : Wills at Chester, i. 4.
Ralph Amson, of Sandbach, Cheshire, 1589 : ibid.
Manchester, 0, 1 ; MDB. (Cheshire) 0, 1 ; New York, 0, 3.

Amner.—Offic. ' the amner,'

i. e., almoner, a distributor of alms in a religious house or household. 'Was Jesu Crist ammoner?' 1300, Cursor Mundi, 15219. 'Dr Fox the Kynges Amner made an eloquent oracion in Latin': 1548, Hall, Chron. 790 (H.E.D.).

John le Aumoner, C. R., 56 Hen. III.
William le Aumoner, Fines Roll, 14 Edw. II.
Richard Aumoner, co. Hunts, 1273. A.
Alan le Aumener, co. Linc., ibid.
William Aumoner, co. Northampt., 20 Edw. I. R.
Peter Aumener, rector of Mileham, co. Norf., 1427: FF. x. p. 25.
1697. Married — John Spencer and Elizabeth Amner: St. Dionis Backchurch, London, p. 45.
1773. Richard Amner and Frances Owen: St. Geo. Han. Sq. i. 234. London, 1.

Amor, Amoore, Amore.— Local, 'at the Moor.' Abbreviated to 'A'Moor; cf. A'Beckett, Abrook, A'Wood, &c.

John Atte Mor, co. Norf., 1273. A.
Adam Ate More, co. Oxf., ibid.
Oliva Ate More, co. Oxf., ibid.
John Amour, C. R., 10 Ric. II.
'In 1528, Richard Amore, of Norwich, priest, gave 3 acres': FF. v. 108.
1766. Married—John Amor and Ann Howard: St. Geo. Han. Sq. i. 155.
1767. — William Amor and Catherine Rochet: ibid. 168.
London, 8, 2, 0; New York (Amore), 1.

Amos, Amoss.—Bapt. 'the son of Amys.' Without doubt a variant, and one more instance of the great popularity of Amice. The name of the Old Test. prophet was unknown in the 13th century. There is not a single trace of its existence. Amos, like Amias or Amyas, represents popular forms of the Norman-French Aimée, or Amys, now generally known as Amy; v. Ames. I do not suppose there were any Amos's previous to the Reformation. This variant has arisen since the Bible, in the vulgar tongue, became familiar to the people. It is simply imitative.

Thomas Amys, co. Soms., 1 Edw. III: Kirby's Quest, p. 209.
1677-8. Aaron Amos and Eliz. Potter: Marriage Alleg. (Canterbury), p. 215.

The above Aaron Amos may have been a Jew.

1767. Married — James Amos and Eleanor Jinks: St. Geo. Han. Sq. i. 163.
London, 10, 1; Philadelphia, 31, 0.

Amphlett. — Local, 'of Amfleet,' one of many local names found on the east coast of England, from Durham to Suffolk, which have -fleet for their suffix, a shallow creek. I have not yet identified the place. [Since writing the above I find my statement as to suffix confirmed, but not that relating to the locality. Mr. Lower quotes Lambarde's Dictionary: 'Amflete, Amfleot, et aliis Ampleot, a haven in France, as I gesse, near Boloigne'; v. Patr. Brit. p. 8.]

1516. Robert Amflet, mayor of Lynn Regis, co. Norf.: FF. viii. 533.
1517. William Amflete, rector of West Lexham, co. Norf.: ibid. x. 5.
1692. Bapt.—Eliz., d. Joseph Amflitt: St. Jas. Clerkenwell, i. 345.
1695. — Sarah, d. Joseph Amphleete: ibid. p. 363.
1797. Married—Edward Weigh and Mary Amphlett: St. Geo. Han. Sq. ii. 163. London, 2.

Amps.—? Bapt. 'the son of Ampe.' This has been a Cambridgeshire surname for six centuries. It is possible that it is of local origin, but there is no local prefix in my references from the Hundred Rolls, and the patronymic form Amps (cf. Williams, Jones, Wilkins, &c.) is confirmatory proof.

Richard Ampe, co. Camb., 1273. A.
Elena Ampe, co. Camb., ibid.
1567-8. William Smeethe and Joanna Ampes: Marriage Lic. (London), i. 38.
1674-5. Thomas Brace and Joane Amps, co. Camb.: Marriage Alleg. (Canterbury), p. 235.
1779. John Amps and Ann Jones: St. Geo. Han. Sq. i. 296.
Crockford, 3; MDB. (Cambridgeshire), 2.

Amyot, Amyatt.—Bapt. 'the son of Amiot,' from Amy, O.F. Amé or Aimée, dim. Ami-ot. We find Aimée in north England at an early period in the entry:

Amya del Stable, 1379: P. T. Yorks. p. 241.
Cf. also: Ammya de Wydecombe, co. Soms., 1 Edw. III: Kirby's Quest, p. 119.
William Amiot, co. Oxf., 1273. A.
Amiot de Pontefracto. DD. (v. index).
Walter fil. Amiot. GG. (v. index).
1564. James Amott: Wills at Chester, i. 4.
1612. Robert Amott, of West Derby: ibid.
1622. John Amatt, co. Essex, and Eliz. Wood: Marriage Lic. (London), ii. 117.

London, 1, 0; Crockford, 0, 1; Liverpool, 1, 0.

Ancell, Ancill, Ansell, Ansel.—(1) Bapt. 'the son of Ancel,' whence dims. Ancelot and Ancelin; v. Lancelot and Lancelin. (2) Bapt. 'the son of Anselm' (?). I merely suggest this as a possibility. No doubt the final m in Anselm might be easily dropped. But of course (1) is the true and natural solution in the majority of cases.

Ansell' de Seleden, Hen. III-Edw. I. K.
Brianus fil. Aunselli, ibid.
William Ansel, 1273. A.
Ansellus de Bray, ibid.
Aunsellus de Bray, ibid.
Ansellus de Braytem, ibid.
1545. Buried—Ansell Bonyam: St. Dionis Backchurch, p. 181.
1667. Nowell Ansell and Mary Snipe: Marriage Lic. (Westminster), p. 44.
1693. Buried—John Ansell, of Norwich: FF. iv. 239.
1727. Bapt.—Thomas, s. of Thomas Ancell: St. Jas. Clerkenwell, ii. 173.
London, 2, 1, 27, 0; Boston (U.S.), 0, 0, 2, 3.

Ancock.—Bapt. 'the son of John,' a vile variant of Hancock, q.v.; cf. the common United States surname, Arrison. It is interesting to note that Ancock is found in the county which had so close a connexion with the Flemings, who introduced Han, Hans, &c.

1619. Married—Davie Evans and Annis Ancocke: St. Peter, Cornhill, i. 250.

Annis represents Agnes; v. Annis.

MDB. (Lincoln), 3.

Anderson, Anders. — Bapt. 'the son of Andrew,' q.v. It was of course inevitable that Andrewson should become toned down to Anderson. Even Andrews has occasionally assumed the form of Anders.

Rogerus Andreweson, 1379: P. T. Yorks. p. 237.
Martin Aunderson, 1495, Yorks. W. 11.
1611. Richard Anderson and Eliz. Hawkins: Marriage Lic. (London), ii. 8.
1769. Frederick Anders and Mary Harper: St. Geo. Han. Sq. i. 185.
London, 138, 2; Boston (U.S.), 271, 1.

Anderton.—(1) Local, 'of Anderton,' a township in the parish of Standish, co. Lanc. There seems to be a second Anderton. Samuel Oldknow, of Mellor, was 'born at

Anderton, near Bolton, in Lancashire, Oct. 5, 1756, . . . and established a large muslin manufactory at Stockport in 1784': v. East Cheshire, ii. 54. Probably, however, the same place is meant. (2) Local, 'of Anderton,' a township in the parish of Great Budworth, co. Chester.

Peter Anderton, of Anderton, 2 Eliz.: Baines' Lanc. ii. 165.
William Anderton, of Little Lever, 1590: Wills at Chester (1545-1620), p. 4.
James Anderton, of Bury, 1609: ibid.
1661. Bapt.—Jane, d. Christopher Anderton: St. Jas. Clerkenwell, i. 211.
1772. Married—Thomas Anderton and Eliz. Brittan: St. Geo. Han. Sq. i. 218.
Manchester, 9; London, 2; Philadelphia, 1.

Andrew, Andrewes, Andrews.—Bapt. 'the son of Andrew'; v. Anderson. This name was very popular in the 13th century. As the name of the patron saint and knightly champion of Scotland, as title of the primatial see, no wonder that the Scotch have tried to monopolize Andrew, and no wonder that Anderson has followed Scotch emigration till Canada and the United States are flooded with it. But Andrew was very popular in its day in England, as our Andrews can testify. In any case, as an apostolic name it was bound to be popular all over Europe.

Willelmus Anderewe, 1379: P. T. Yorks. p. 219.
Robert Andreu, co. Camb., 1273. A.
Nicholas fil. Andree, co. Salop, ibid.
John Andre, co. Camb., ibid.
Henry fil. Andr', co. Oxf., ibid.
Thomas Andreu, vicar of Briston, co. Norf., 1442: FF. ix. 376.
1619. Thomas Fuller and Eliz. Andrewes: Marriage Lic. (London), ii. 74.
1623. Buried—Benjamin Andrewes, of Norwich, merchant: FF. iv. 365.
London, 26, 2, 107; Philadelphia, 18, 0, 127.

Angel, Angell.—(1) Bapt. 'the son of Angel'; in later days Angela and Angelina. For the full history of this once-popular name, v. Yonge, i. 126-7. The Puritans could not oust this name, though bitterly hated by them.

1645. Buried—Angela Boyce: Canterbury Cathedral.

1682. Bapt.—Angel, d. Sir Nicholas Butler, Knt.: St. Helen's, Bishopgate.
'Weymouth, March 20, 1625. Embarked for New England, Angell Holland, aged 21 years': Hotten's Emigrants, p. 285.

(2) Local, 'at the Angle'; v. Angle. Most probably the source of the majority of our Angels and Angells. The font-name was unknown in England, so far as I can discover, in the 13th and 14th centuries.

Robert Angel, 7 Jas. I, co. Norf.: FF. vi. 236.
1578. Michael Angell, co. Glouc.: Reg. Univ. Oxf. vol. ii. pt. ii. p. 80.
1618-9. John Angell and Anne Palmer: Marriage Lic. (London), ii. 70.
1667. Robert Mellish and Frances Angell: Marriage Alleg. (Canterbury), p. 143.
1751. Married—James Angel and Ann Lownds: St. Geo. Han. Sq. i. 46.
London, 9, 15; Philadelphia, 3, 1; Boston (U.S.), 0, 13.

Anger, Angier, Aungier.—(1) Bapt. 'the son of Aunger.' This is the probable origin of most of the variants found in modern directories.

Anger le Venator, co. Berks, Hen. III-Edw. I. K.
William fil. Aunger, co. Camb., 1273. A.
Beatrix Aunger, co. Hunts, ibid.
Peter Aunger, London, ibid.
Anger or Aunger le Rus, co. Camb., ibid.
Onger de Leycestre, co. Devon, ibid.
Robert Aunger: Kirby's Quest, p. 186.
Roger Anger, co. Soms., 20 Edw. III: ibid. p. 240.
'Angier de la Strille, a French merchant, prisoner at Dover, May 25, 1564': Rec. Office, Cal. State Papers (Domestic), i. 241.
1702. Married — Henry Anger and Anne Jones: St. Peter's, Cornhill, p. 64.

(2) Local, 'of Angers,' a city of Anjou.

Hugh de Angiers. J.
Robert Angier. XX.
Isabella Anger. H.
'A quarter of a fee in Burnham held by William Angre': FF. v. 246.
'John Angere, parson of Southacre': ibid. vi. 220.
1633. John Hercy and Mary Aungier: Marriage Lic. (London), ii. 213.
1702. George Angier and Judith Seymour: ibid. p. 328.
London, 0, 5, 1; Boston (U.S.), 0, 11, 0.

Angle.—Local, 'in the Angle,' i.e. nook, corner; from residence in some nook or corner of the road.

'Go, run, search, pry in every nook and angle of the kitchens, larders, and pastries': The Woman Hater, i. 2; v. Nangle, and cf. Herne and Wray.

Henry in the Angle, C. R., 8 Edw. I.
Alice in Angulo, co. Oxf., 1273. A.
Roger in Angulo, co. Camb., ibid.

The English portion of the Angels and Angells in the London Directory are probably from this source; v. Angel.

Elias Angel, 1379: P. T. Yorks. p. 200.
1570. Buried—Danyell Angell, son of Mr. Angell: St. Dionis Backchurch, p. 192.
1722. Married—John Angil and Eliz. Beale: St. Antholin (London), p. 137.
1744. Bapt.—Thomas, son of George Angie: St. Michael, Cornhill, p. 174.
London, 2; Boston (U.S.), 2.

Angold, Angood.—Bapt. 'the son of Angold' or 'Angod.'

Nicholas Hanegod, co. Soms., 1 Edw. III: Kirby's Quest, p. 198.
John Angod, co. Soms., 1 Edw. III: ibi i. p. 213.
Geoffrey fil. Angodi, co. Oxf., Hen. III-Edw. I. K.
Henry Angod, co. Bucks, 1273. A.
Richard Angot, co. Suff., ibid.
Stephen Angolde, vicar of Rowdham, co. Norf., 1589: FF. i. 435.
London, 2, 0; MDB. (Norfolk), 1, 0; Cambridge), 0, 5.

Anguish.—Local, 'of Angus, N.B. Although most of the instances occur in co. Norfolk, it will be seen that they are of comparatively modern date. They represent an immigration from the north. There can be no doubt about the origin. It is simply imitative, as was the custom in spelling or even pronouncing surnames.

David, Erl of Anguyshe(Angus): Visitation of Yorkshire, 1563, p. 18.
Elsabeth, Countess of Anguysh: ibid. p. 242.
'Item: to my lady Margaret Anguisshe . . . for to disporte her withall this Christmas, £6 13s. 4d.,' Dec. 1530: Privy Purse Exp., Henry VIII, p. 98.
Richard Anguish, rector of Scarning, co. Norf., 1639: FF. x. 44.
William Anguish, gent., died July 6, 1668, Norwich: ibid. iv. 305.
Thomas Anguish, of Norwich, 1633: Visitation of London, 1634, p. 227.
1749. John Anguish and Deborah Tupper: St. Geo. Han. Sq. i. 43.
'William Anguish appeared in court as defendant': Manchester Evening Mail, Feb. 15, 1888.
Leeds, '

Angwin.—Local, 'the Ange-vine,' an immigrant from Anjou. Although fairly common in mediae-val registers, this surname barely survives. It has obtained a footing, however, in the United States.

Maurice le Angevine, co. Oxf., 1273. A.
Reginald le Angevine, co. Oxf., ibid.
Geoffrey le Anngevyn. L.
Simon le Angevin. E.
Gilbertus Angevinus, Pipe Roll, 5 Hen. II.
William Angewyne, Close Roll, 14 Hen. IV.
'Osmund held it under Eustachius, and Wido Angevin after Osmond, being his nephew': FF. viii. 333.
Thomas Angewyn, lic. for M.A., June, 1511: Reg. Univ. Oxf. i. 50.
Thomas Angewyn, vicar of Witching-ham, co. Norf.: FF. viii. 311.
Mary Aungvine, 7 Hen. V, co. Norf.: ibid. ix. 109.
London, 1 ; Boston (U.S.), 1.

Anker.—Occup. 'the anker,' an anchorite or hermit; see next article.

'Sometime I am religious,
Now like an anker in an hous.'
Chaucer, R. R. 6348.

The following is imitative, the second instance probably being the name of a foundling, discovered at an inn styled 'the Anchor.'

1674-5. Bapt.—Edward, s. John An-chor: St. Dionis Backchurch (London), p. 120.
1717. Buried—Mary Anchor, a poor child: St. Michael, Cornhill, p. 165.
MDB. (Cambridge), 2; (Oxford), 3; Philadelphia, 3.

Ankerman.—Occup. 'the an-kerman,' i.e. the servant of the anker or hermit, now generally styled an anchorite; but *ancre* was the earlier form. Cf. Matthewman, Monkman, Priestman, Vikerman, Armetman (v. Armet), &c., all York-shire surnames.

'An anchor's cheer in prison be my scope.'
Hamlet, iii. 2.

William Anckerman, 1379: P. T. Yorks. p. 17.

My one London Directory in-stance deserves to be set in full :

'Frederic Ankerman, boot-maker, 77, Provost St., Hoxton.'

Probably *u* is a misreading for *n* in the following entries :

Lucia ye Aukereswoman, London, 1273: A. i. p. 413.
Lucia la Aukereswomman, London : ibid. p. 426.

Cotgrave has *ankrosse*, a female hermit.

London, 1.

Ankettle, Anketell. — Bapt. 'the son of Arnketel,' eagle caul-dron ; Arkettle, q.v., is but an-other form of the same name. Both are compounds of 'Kettle,' q.v.

Anketil le Mercer, London, 1273. A.
Peter fil. Anketill. C.
Anketill fil. Thomas. K.

The Norman form was Anskettle ; v. Oskettle.

William, son of Anschetillus, temp. 1109: Lincolnshire Survey, p. 6.
Anschetillus de Egheling : ibid. p. 25.
Robert Amketyl, co. Soms., 1 Edw. III: Kirby's Quest, p. 213.
Roger Anketyl, co. Soms., 1 Edw. III: ibid. p. 221.
John Anketill, of Shafton, obiit 1610: Visitation of London, 1634, p. 21.
Francis Anketill, of Holborne, living 1634: ibid.

I dare not say this surname is extinct in England, for I find one in Crockford ; see, however, Ans-kettle and Arkettle.

Philadelphia, 0, 4 ; Crockford, 0, 1.

Annable—Bapt. 'the son of Annable, a corruption of Amable ; v. Hanniball. This surname is well represented in the United States.

Simon Annable, vicar of Hemlington, co. Norf. 1401: FF. xi. 107.
1584. John Hallywell and Alice Ann-able, co. Suffolk: Marriage Lic. (London), i. 135.
1665. Thomas Barrow and Eliz. Ana-bell : Marriage Alleg. (Canterbury), p. 90.
1711. Married—John Daw and Mary Annable : St. Antholin (London), p. 124.
1736. Buried—Mrs. Elizabeth Annable : St. Peter's, Cornhill, p. 135.
Derby, 3 ; Boston (U.S.), 10.

Annan, Annandale.—Local, 'of Annan' or 'Annandale,' a parish and dale in co. Dumfries, through which the river Annan flows.

1702. Buried—Sarah Annand : St. An-tholin (London), p. 116.

Cf. Simmonds for Simmons, or the provincial *gownd* for gown.

London 3, 0; MDB. (Northumberland), 0, 2 ; Philadelphia, 2, 0.

Annis, Annison, Anning-son, Anness, Aningson, An-

---

nin, Anning.—(1) Bapt. 'the son of Ann,' from the dim. Annie.

'Pay me, quod he, or by the swete Seinte Anne.' Chaucer, C. T. 7193.

(2) Bapt. 'the son of Agnes,' popularly Annis, Annes, or Annas. The variant Anningson is curious, and seems founded upon some early dim. Annin, with an excrescent *g*, as in Jennings ; cf. Pattison and Pattinson. In general (2) must be looked upon as the parent of all these names. Annis was the popu-lar form of Agnes from the 14th century downwards.

'Annys: propyr name (Anneys, H., Annyce. P.)—Agnes': Prompt. Parv.
Anish Luke : Reg. St. Colomb Major, p. 39.
Annis Thring, 1606: Reg. Broad Chake, co. Wilts, p. 42.
Annise Teswell, 1623: Canterbury Cath. p. 115.
Annis Brittanie, 1625 : St. Mary Alder-mary (London), p. 15.

All these cases are feminine, and represent Agnes.

James Annyson, 1687: St. Mary Alder-mary (London), p. 109.
Isaac, s. Francis Annison, 1660: FF. iv. 265.
Maria, uxor Johannis Annyson, 1700 : ibid. p. 501.
1616-7. Peter Kinge and Mary Annys: Marriage Lic. (London), ii. 48.
London, 2, 2, 0, 0, 0, 0, 0, 0 ; MDB. (Nor-folk), 0, 3, 0, 1, 0, 0, 0 ; (Lincoln), 1, 1, 2, 0, 1, 0, 0 ; (Burnley, co. Lanc.) Anningson, 1 ; Philadelphia, 3, 0, 0, 1, 0, 2, 1.

Annore.—Bapt. 'the son of Alianore,' popularly Annore, whence later Nora, or Norah.

William Annor, co. Camb., 1273. A.
Annor (without surname), co. Bucks, ibid.
Annore Beine, co. Camb., ibid.
Annora Vidua, co. Oxf., ibid.
Annora de Aencurt, co. Notts, Hen. III-Edw. I. K.

Annott, Annotson, Annett, Annette.—Bapt. 'the son of Anne,' dim. Ann-ot ; v. Anson for many instances and fuller history. 'Annet, the common gull, so called in Northumberland': Halli-well. No doubt taken from the once popular dim. of Anne, es-pecially popular on the north-east coast of England. Annot Alyface is a character in Ralph Roister Doister, by Nicholas Udall, written about 1550. She sings :

'Work, Tibet: work, Annot: work,
  Margery:
Sew, Tibet: knit Annot: spin, Mar-
  gery:
Let us see who will win the victory.'
  Dodsley's Old English Plays, iii. 72.
'Peter Annet (1693-1769), deistical
writer, is said to have been born at
Liverpool in 1693': Dict. Nat. Biog. ii. 9.
Anota Canun, co. Oxf., 1273. A.
Johannes Anot, 1379: P.T.Yorks. p. 131.
Johannes Warnfold et Annot uxor
ejus: ibid. p. 175.
Robertus Bolt et Annot uxor ejus: ibid.
p. 175.
Annot Lund: ibid. p. 175.
Simon Annotson: ibid. p. 254.
Thomas Annotson: Pardon's Roll,
16 Ric. II.
John Annottyson, rector of Edgefield,
co. Norf., 1458: FF. ix. 388.
1707. Buried—Nicholas Anett: St. John
Baptist on Wallbrook (London), p. 196.
1717. — Richard Annett: ibid.
1781. Henry Annetts and Mary Bugg:
St. Geo. Han. Sq. i. 321.
1786. Edward Annett and Elizabeth
Parsons: ibid. p. 393.
London, 0, 0, 1, 0; New York, 0, 0, 3, 2.

Ansell.—Bapt.; v. Ancell.

Anselm.—Bapt. 'the son of
Anselm.' This personal name was
decidedly popular in its day, and
if it has no representatives in our
modern directories, the explanation
is simple: they have become incorporated with our Ansells; v. Ancell.
Anselmus fil. Anselm', co. Linc.,
1273. A.
Anselm (without surname), co. Northampt., ibid.
Anselm le Formiger, co. Kent, ibid.
Anselm de Gyse, co. Hunts, ibid.
William Anselme, 1642: Peacock's
Army List of Roundheads and Cavaliers,
p. 56.
1679. James Cotter and Mary Anselme:
Marriage Lic. (Westminster), p. 297.

**Anskettle, Askettle, Askell,
Askill, Aiskell, Askel.**—Bapt.
'the son of Anskettle,' or 'As-
kettle,' or 'Askell' (kettle as a
suffix always became kell, kill, or
kle). Anskettle (a variant of Os-
kettle, q.v.) was probably a Nor-
man introduction. For other in-
stances, v. Astell.
Robert Asketil, co. Soms., 1 Edw. III:
Kirby's Quest, p. 245.
Robert fil. Anskitiel, co. York. W. 12.
Aschetillus Bardel. Z.
Jordan Asketil, co. Suff., 1273. A.
Peter Askyl, co. Camb., ibid.
William Asketil. Q.
Askill le Fisherman. V. 8.

Simon Asketel, rector of Boyton, co.
Norf., 1361: FF. xi. 99.
Roger Asketil, rector of Randworth,
co. Norf., 1391: ibid. p. 115.
1563. Married—Ales Askell, widowe:
St. Mary Aldermary (London), p. 3.
London, 0, 0, 0, 0, 1, 0; New York
(Askel), 1.

Anson.—Bapt. 'the son of
Anne'; v. Annis and Annott.
1767. Married—Isaac Anson and Judith
Dean: St. Geo. Han. Sq. i. 161.
London, 6; Philadelphia, 10.

**Anstee, Anstey, Anstie,
Ansty, Anstice, Anstise, Anstiss.**—(1) Bapt. 'the son of Anas-
tasia,' from the nick. Anstie and An-
stice. 'Anstiss, Anstish, Anstyce, all
occur frequently as female names
in the older pages of a Devonshire
parish, where Anstice is now a
surname': Yonge, i. 250.
Anstey Mankyswyll, 1520: Reg. Univ.
Oxf. (v. index).
Anstey Hicks, 1657: Reg. St. Columb
Major, Cornwall, p. 35.
Anstice, daughter of John Nanskevell,
1602: ibid. p. 20.
Anstes Hawk, widow, buried, 1616:
ibid. p. 207.
Anstiss Symons: ibid. p. 154.
Anstis Thomas: ibid. p. 35.
Sampson Austice, married, 1709: ibid.
p. 293.
John Anstis, 1717, co. Norf.: FF. v. 317.
John Ansteye, 1623: St. Mary Alder-
mary (London), p. 15.

(2) Local, 'of Anstey' or 'Ansty.'
Parishes in diocese of Peterborough,
Sarum, St. Albans, Exeter, and
Worcester. This will concern
Anstey, Anstie, and Ansty only.
Anstice, Anstis, and Anstiss are
undoubtedly to be placed under
(1).
Roger de Anesti, co. Camb., 1273. A.
Richard de Anesty, London, ibid.
Henry Ansty, vicar of Guestwick, co.
Norf., 1386: FF. viii. 222.
1642-3. Richard Anstye and Anne
Churchey: Marriage Lic. (London), ii.
269.
1785. Married—John Anstice (co. So-
merset) and Mary Selby: St. Geo. Han.
Sq. i. 378.
London, 2, 6, 3, 1, 0, 0, 0; Crockford,
0, 3, 0, 0, 1, 0, 1; Philadelphia, 1, 0, 0, 0,
2, 3, 0; MDB. (Somerset), Anstice, 7.

Anstruther.—Local, 'of Anstruther,' in co. Fife, N.B.
'William de Candela held the barony
of Anstruther, in co. Fife, about 1153.
His grandson Henry appears to have

assumed the surname in or before 1221'
(Lower).
1690-1. Jonathan Compton and Frances
Anstruther: Marriage Alleg. (Canter-
bury), p. 172.
London, 1.

**Anthony, Antony, Antoni-
son.**—Bapt. 'the son of Antony';
the h is intrusive. 'Antony, propyr
name, Antonius': Prompt.Parv. The
name had become fairly popular in
England in the 13th century, as
having been borne by the great
hermit of the 4th century. He
was the patron saint of the swineherd, and 'as fat as a Tantony pig,'
and 'to follow like a Tantony pig,'
became proverbial expressions; v.
Yonge, i. 306; Halliwell, i. 67.
'I have behest a pygge to Saynt
Antony'; v. Prompt. Parv. p. 29,
and note by Way.
John fil. Anton', co. Linc., 1273. A.
Alice fil. Anton', co. Hunts, ibid.
Antony Stillman. H.
Agnes Antonison, temp. Eliz. Z. (v.
index).
1010. Francis Griffin and Sibill Anthonie: Marriage Lic. (London), i. 45.
1716. Married—George Brough and
Apphia Anthony: St. Michael, Cornhill,
p. 59.
London, 8, 0, 0; Philadelphia, 24, 2, 0.

Antill.—Local, 'of Ampthill.'
I owe the suggestion to Lower,
and doubt not it is correct. The
corruption was inevitable. Cf.
Amphield, or Anfield, a hamlet in
the parish of Hursley. Ampthill
is a market town seven miles from
Bedford. The surname in its corrupted form is better represented
in the United States than in England. A single glance at the
two forms below will settle any
doubts as to the true parentage of
the name.
1567. Married—John More and Joane
Antill: St. Thomas the Apostle (London),
p. 4.
1606-7. William Hames and Fidocia
Ampthill: Marriage Lic. (Westminster),
p. 15.
1670. Matthias Lodge and Frances
Anthill: ibid. p. 179.
1734. Married—John Anthill and Jone
Butt: Reg. Stourton, co. Wilts.

The second entry practically
settles any doubt.
London, 5; Manchester, 1; Philadelphia, 4.

Antioch.—Local, 'of Antioch'; cf. Veness, Janeway, &c. Probably imported as the result of the spicery trade with the East.

Godard de Antioche, Sheriff of London, 1195: WWW. pp. 187, 190.
William de Antioche, co. Soms., Hen. III-Edw. I. K.
Nicholas Antioch, 1309. M.
Robert de Antiocha. E.

I cannot discover any modern representatives.

Antliff, Antcliff, Antcliffe. —Local, ' of Arncliff,' a village and parish, W. Rid. of Yorkshire, sixteen miles north of Shipton. In local names, whose suffix is -*cliff*, there is a tendency to elide the *c*; cf. Cunliffe or Topliff for Cuncliff and Topcliff. This surname has crossed the Atlantic. No doubt the meaning is the eagle-cliff.

Thomas Arneclyff, 1379: P. T. Yorks. p. 269.
1748. Married—Luke Antcliff and Mary Tallance: St. Geo. Chap. Mayfair, p. 114.
Ulverston, 1, 0, 0; Manchester, 0, 1, 0; Boston (U.S.), 0, 0, 2.

Anton, Antoine.—Bapt. 'the son of Antony'; Fr. Antoine, Ger. Anton, M.E. Antoyn. Of course many of the United States representatives are of French and German extraction.

Robertus Antoynson, 1379: P. T. Yorks. p. 265.
Antoyn Tailliour: ibid. p. 267.
1613. Gregory Roberts and Ursula Antunn: Marriage Lic. (Westminster), p. 21.
London, 2, 0; Liverpool, 1, 0; Philadelphia, 11, 3.

Antrobus.—Local, 'of Antrobus,' a township in the parish of Great Budworth, co. Cheshire. Apart from the well-known family of that name and place, many Antrobus's may be seen in the Lanc. and Cheshire directories. They may represent junior branches of centuries ago or separate stocks. This surname has crossed the Atlantic.

1600-1. Thomas Antrobus, co. Cumb.: Reg. Univ. Oxf. vol. ii. pt. ii. p. 246.
William Antrobus, of Over Peover, 1596: Wills at Chester (1545-1620), p. 5.
Henry Antrobus, of Knutsford, 1620: ibid.
1635. Joan Antrobuss 'imbarqued in

the Planter' for New England: Hotten's Emigrants, p. 45.
1660. George Antrobus and Anna Franklin: Marriage Lic. (Westminster), p. 53.
London, 4; Manchester, 5; Philadelphia, 2.

Anvers.—Local, 'of Anvers,' i.e. Antwerp. This surname seemingly did not last long. I find no representatives during the last three centuries.

Ralph de Anvers, co. Oxf., 1273. A.
Thomas de Anvers, co. Berks, 20 Edw. I. R.

Anwyl, Anwell.—Bapt. ' the son of Anwyl.' This is a Welsh surname, and as at least ninety-five per cent. of its nomenclature is baptismal, I feel bound to place it under that class ; but I have not met with the name in early records.

1794. Married—Ellis Anwıl and Priscilla Ryder: St. Geo. Han. Sq. ii. 110.
MDB. (co. Montgomery), 2, 0; (co. Denbigh), 1, 0; (co. Flint), 1, 0: (co. Carnarvon), 1, 0; London, 1, 0; Liverpool, 1, 1; Philadelphia, 2, 0.

Anyon. — Bapt. 'the son of Eignion' or 'Enion,' a Welsh surname; v. Benyon and Eynon.

1640. John Annyon and Martha Lownds: Marriage Lic. (London), ii. 253.
1648. Married—Reginald Baxter and Martha Annion: St. Thomas the Apostle (London), p. 18.
1791. Married—David Williams and Frances Anyon: St. Geo. Han. Sq. ii. 66.
Manchester, 1.

Ape.—Nick. ' the ape.' For a reason that can be well understood this surname has not come down to modern times. ' Wilde beris and apes,' 1350 : Will. Palerne, 2298 (H.E.D.).

John le Ape, co. Oxf., 1273. A.
Alured Ape, co. Norf., ibid.

Aplin, Applin.—(1) Bapt. 'the son of Appoline.' The homily 'Against the perils of Idolatry' says, 'All diseases have their special saints as gods, the curers of them : the toothache, St. Appoline.' This was the usual English form of Appolonia, a martyr at Alexandria, who, among other tortures, had all her teeth beaten out. It was a popular girl's name, and survived the Reformation.

1593. Bapt.—Apeline, d. John Morris, clothworker: St. Peter, Cornhill.
1609. — Apoline, d. William Burton, merchant: ibid.
Appolonia Cotton. TT.
Aplin Thomas: Reg. St. Columb Major, p. 174.

(2) Bapt. 'the son of Abel,' from dim. Abelin, sharpened to Apelin ; cf. Apps for Abbs, or Epps for Ebbs.

Thomas Abelyn, co. Kent, 1273. A.

(3) Bapt. 'the son of Lyon,' a Welsh personal name, whence the patr. ap-Lyon. This undoubtedly became Applin, and represents the Applins of cos. Somerset, Hereford, and south-west England generally ; cf. Applejohn.

Ap-lln-ap-Gwyll, 1490: Hist. and Ant. of St. Davids, p. 376.
Joneda fil. Aplyon: Visitation of Glouc., 1623, p. 98.
1734. Anne, d. of Edmund Aplin: St. Jas. Clerkenwell, ii. 217.
1802. Married—Samuel Ramsey and Eliz. Aplin: St. Geo. Han. Sq. ii. 271.
London, 5, 1; MDB. (co. Somerset), 5, 0; Boston (U.S.), 3, 3; Philadelphia, 0, 2.

Apperly, Apperley.—Local, ' of Apperley.' (1) An extra-parochial district in the parish of Bywell, co. Northumberland ; (2) a hamlet in the parish of Deerhurst, co. Glouc., near Tewkesbury.

John de Apperleghe, co. Soms., 1 Edw. III : Kirby's Quest, p. 191.
William de Appert, co. Oxf., 1273. A.

The above entries seem to prove that Apperley, in co. Glouc., is the real parent.

London, 1, 0 ; Boston (U.S.), 0, 1.

Appleby, Applebee, Appelbee.—Local, 'of Appleby,' parishes in cos. Westm., Lincoln, and Leicester. Many local surnames ending in *by* are now found as *bee*, as this dictionary proves in various pages.

Geoffrey de Appelby, co. Linc., 1273. A.
John de Appleby, vicar of Tilney, co. Norf., 1372: FF. ix. 83.
Thomas de Appleby, Bishop of Carlisle, 1 Ric. II: ibid. iii. 102.
Henry de Apelby, 1367, rector of Bolton - juxta - Bowland : Whittaker's Craven, p. 131.
Johannes de Appleby, 1379 : P. T. Yorks. p. 296.

1624. William Browne and Rachel Appleby: Marriage Lic. (London), ii. 147.
1775. William Norris and Sarah Appelbee: St. Geo. Han. Sq. i. 258.
London, 20, 3, 1 ; Philadelphia, 2, 1, 0 ; Boston (U.S.), 7, 3, 0.

Appledore.—Local, ' of Appledore.' Parishes in diocs. of Canterbury and Exeter.

William atte Apeldor, co. Soms., 1 Edw. III : Kirby's Quest, p. 277.
Geoffrey Apeldore, co. Oxf., 1273. A. Salcombe (Devon), 1.

Appleford.—Local, ' of Appleford.' A chapelry in the parish of Sutton Courtney, co. Berks.

Lucia de Apelforde, co. Camb.,1273. A.
William de Appelford, co. Suff., ibid.
Pagan de Appelford, co. Berks, 20 Edw. I. R.
1630. Married—Roger Scrutton and Marie Apleford : St. Dionis Backchurch, p. 23.
1769. Benjamin Appleforde and Elizabeth Piggott : St. Geo. Han. Sq. i. 185. London, 1.

Applegarth, Applegate. — Local, ' of the Apple-garth,' *apple*, and *garth*, an enclosure ; v. Appleyard. ' Appelle-garth : *pometum* ' : Cath. Angl. This surname seems now generally found as Applegate.

Geoffrey de Appelgarth. K.
William Aplegart, co. Norf.: FF. ii. 110.
Ralph de Apelgard, co. Bucks, 1273. A.
Robert del Apelgargh, co. York, ibid.
Ralph le (de) Apelgart, co. Bucks, ibid.
Richard de Appelgart, temp. Stephen, co. Norf.: FF. v. 83.
Robert del Appelgarth, 10 Edw. II : Freemen of York, i. 16.

This last is a second entry of a name instanced above.

1769. Married—Robert Applegate and Mary Crouch : St. Geo. Han. Sq. i. 185. London, 2, 6 ; Philadelphia, 0, 32.

Appleman.—Occup. ' a seller of apples ' ; cf. ' apple-monger : *pomilius* ' : Huloet, 1552.

Nicholas Appelman : Close Roll, 16 Edw. III, pt. i.
Philadelphia, 1.

Applethwaite, Ablewhite, Applewhite.—Local, ' of Applethwaite,' a township in the parish of Windermere, co. Westmoreland. With Applewhite, cf. Hebblewhite for Hebblethwaite.

1639. Married—Thomas Applewhaite and Mary Pead : St. Dionis Backchurch, p. 24.
1646. Buried—Eliz. Applewhite : ibid. p. 225.
'1679. May the 6th. Dennis Burne, a

servant belonging to Mr. Henry Applewhite in the Ketch Prosperous for Virginia': Hotten's Lists of Emigrants, p. 352.

Appleton.—Local, ' of Appleton.' Parishes in diocs. of Norwich, Oxford, York (3), and Ripon. The meaning is obvious : *appel* or *appil*, apple, and *ton*, a town, an enclosure ; cf. Appleyard and Applegarth. Many places would naturally acquire such a title. There are townships so called in cos. Lancaster and Chester.

Thomas de Appelton, co. Oxf., 1273. A.
Wydo de Appelton, co. York, ibid.
Willelmus de Appilton, 1379 : P. T. Yorks. p. 300.
Reginald de Apulton, rector of Flitcham, co. Norf., 1369 : FF. viii. 417.
William de Appleton, rector of Titchwell, co. Norf., 1376 : ibid. x. 397.
Mabel Apulton, Norwich, 1456 : ibid. iv. 119.
1604. Christopher Appleton and Mary Lovelasse : Marriage Lic. (Westminster), p. 14.
1687. William Appelton and Mary Steele : Marriage Lic. (London), ii. 309.
London, 27 ; Philadelphia, 25.

Appletree.—(1) Local, ' at the apple-tree ' ; cf. Plumptree, Rowntree, Crabtree, &c.

(2) Local, ' of Appletree,' a hamlet in co. Northampton, seven miles from Banbury. Of course the origin is the same.

1548-9. Simon Appultre and Agnes Rudyck : Marriage Lic. (Faculty Office), p. 14.
1611-2. John Appletree and Susan Hodges : Marriage Lic. (London), ii. 11.
1730. Married—John Appletree and Ann Wytch : St. Geo. Chap. Mayfair, p. 309.
MDB. (Northampton), 1 ; (Oxford), 2 ; Philadelphia, 2.

Appleyard. — Local, ' of the Appleyard,' from *apple*, and *yard*, or *garth*, an enclosure, an orchard. ' Appullyerde, or gardeyne, or orcherde : *Pomerium* ' : Prompt. Parv. Evidently a familiar word all over the kingdom for an orchard ; cf. Applegarth.

Nicholas de Apelyerd, co. Norf., 1273. A.
Adam del Appilyerd, 1379 : P. T. Yorks. p. 194.
Magota de Appilyerd, ibid.
Alicia del Apelyerd, ibid. p. 91.
Bartholomew de Appilyerd, burgess for Norwich, 49 Edw. III : FF. iii. 101.
William de Appilyerd, bailiff of Norwich, 1386 : ibid. p. 116.
Thomas Appleyeard, temp. Eliz. ZZ. (v. Index.)

1629. Leonard Slater and Grace Apleyard : Marriage Lic. (Westminster), p. 33.
1760. Married—Jonathan Dadford and Ann Appleyard : St. Geo. Han. Sq. i. 92.
London, 8 ; West Riding Court Dir., 16 ; Boston (U.S.), 2.

Applin ; v. Aplin.

Apps.—Bapt. ' the son of Abraham,' or ' Abel,' from the nick. Abb, sharpened to App : cf. Epps for Ebbs, Hopkins for Hobkins, Hopps for Hobbs, &c. But it is only fair to suggest that App may have been the nick. for the 13th century popular name of Apsalon (Absolom). Apps would then be the patronymic. I have no evidence for this, and merely throw it out for consideration. There can be no doubt that if Apsalon be cast aside, then Apps stands for Abbs, q.v.—Since writing the above I have come across the following entry :

Thomas atte Apse, co. Soms., 1 Edw. III : Kirby's Quest, p. 174.

This, of course, is a local surname, and may share in the parentage of Apps. This would be by residence beside the apse of a church ; cf. Galilee, Porch, &c.

1658. Buried —Mary, d. Thomas Aps : St. Jas. Clerkenwell, iv. 322.
1694. Bapt.—Thomas, s. Bodwine Apps: ibid. i. 357.
1787. Married —Thomas Barker and Eliz. Apps : St. Geo. Han. Sq. i. 402. London, 8.

Arbuckle, Arbuckel.—Local, a corruption of Harbottle, q.v.; and found, like Harbottle, in the neighbourhood of that place. This surname has crossed the Atlantic, and is spreading in the United States.

Newcastle, 2, 0 ; Philadelphia, 9, 2.

Arbuthnot, Arbuthnott.—Local, ' of Arbuthnot,' ' a parish in Kincardineshire. The first of the family was Hugh de Arburbothenoth, who assumed his surname from the lands which he acquired in 1105 with the daughter of Osbert Olifard, and on which his descendants have resided for more than twenty generations ' : Lower's Pat. Brit. p. 10.

1752. Married—Robert and Ann Arbuthnot (sic): St. Geo. Chap. Mayfair, p. 219.

1752. Married—Anthony Dauvert and Mary Arbuthnot: St. Geo. Han. Sq. i. 48. London, 3, 0; Boston (U.S.), 0, 1; New York, 3, 0.

Archbell.—Bapt.; a corruption of Archibald, q.v.

West Riding Court Dir., 1; New York, 1.

Archbrag. — Nick. 'a great braggart.' Arch = chief, as in Archdeacon, Archpriest, q.v. Also cf. 'archewives': Chaucer, C. T. 9071.

Ormus Archebragge, co. Westm., 20 Edw. I. R.
Eva Archbragge, co. Westm., ibid.

Archbutt, Archbold, Archibold.—Bapt. 'the son of Archibald.' These three are simply variants; v. Archibald.

1567. Edward Brooke and Alice Archbold: Marriage Lic. (London), i. 37.
1743. Married—Anthony Stewart and Eliz. Archbould: ibid.
1772. — Elias Archbold and Bridget Dardis: St. Geo. Han. Sq. i. 223.
London, 3, 0, 0; Newcastle, 0, 2, 0; New York, 0, 5, 0; Philadelphia, 0, 1, 4.

Archdeacon, Arcedeckne.—Official, 'the archdeacon.' The name still survives, and not long ago I saw it over a hatter's shop. 'Daniel Archdeacon was recommended to the king for his services, 1610': State Papers, 1623-5, p. 545. Quite recently some members of the Archdeacon family have adopted the mediaeval Arcedekne, 'not wisely, but too well.'

William de (le?) Archdeacon, co. Norf.: FF. ix. 186.
Johannes Archedeken et uxor, 1379: P. T. Yorks. p. 145.
Thomas le Arsdekene, co. Herts, 1273. A.
Adam Ercedekne, co. Suff., ibid.
Richard l'Ercedekne. V. 9.
1751. Married—John Archdeacon and Mary Williamson: St. Geo. Chap. Mayfair, p. 199.
1786. Peter Archdeacon and Ann Clark: St. Geo. Han. Sq. i. 386.
London, 1, 0; Halifax, 1, 0; Liverpool, 2, 0; MDB. (co. Norfolk), 0, 1; Boston (U.S.), 5, 0.

Archer.—Occup. 'the archer,' a professional bowman; O.F. archier. The arbalester was a crossbowman; v. Alabaster; cf. Bowman, Bowmaker, Fletcher, Flower, &c.

Odo le Archer, co. Devon, Hen. III-Edw. I. K.
John le Archer, co. York, 20 Edw. I. R.
Richard le Archer, co. Wilts, ibid.
Thomas le Archer, co. Derby, 1273. A.

Pagan le Archier. E.
Colin le Archer, co. Heref., 45 Hen. III. BBB.
William Gilbert, rector of Ridlesworth, co. Norf., presented by Alexandrina le Archer, 1375: FF. i. 275.
1567. Married—Roberte Garnett and Alyce Archer: St. Michael, Cornhill, p. 9.
London, 52; Philadelphia, 46.

Archerson.—Bapt.; v. Aitcheson; *not* the son of the Archer.

Liverpool, 1.

Archibald.—Bapt. 'the son of Archibald.' German, Erchanbald; O.F. Archambault; Italian, Archibaldo. Miss Yonge (ii. 255) adds, 'So frequent was it (Archibald) in the houses of Campbell and Douglas, that, with its contractions of Archie and Baldie, it has become one of the most commonly used in Scotland, recalling many a fierce worthy, from old Archibald Bell-the-Cat downwards.' Archbold, Archbutt, and Archbould are modern English forms of the surname; v. Archbold, Archbutt.

Archibaldus le Flemyng, 34 Edw. I: BBB. p. 710.
Archenbald le Flemeng, Hen. III-Edw. I. K.
Roger Arkebald, co. Camb., 1273. A.
Richard Arkebolt, co. Camb., ibid.
William Ercebaud, 44 Edw. III. P.
Richard Archebold, sup. for B.D., Oct. 30, 1451: Reg. Univ. Oxf. i. 14.
1557. Married—John Archembolde and Eliz. Wylson: St. Dionis Backchurch, p. 3.

Archambault is common in Philadelphia. Twelve representatives appear in the directory. This is the result of French immigration.

London, 2; Boston (U.S.), 22.

Archpriest. — Official, 'the archpriest,' a chief priest, a vicar to a bishop, later a rural dean; v. H.E.D. The term was in use in the 17th century, for Smith, the 'silver-tongued' preacher, speaks of 'priest, or priests, or archpriests, or any such like': God's Arrow against Atheists.

Roger le Archeprest. T.
William le Ercheprestre: Fines Roll, 12 Edw. I.

Arderne, Arden, Ardron.—Local, ' of Arderne.' The present representatives in south-east Lanc. directories preserve the spellings, as Arden and Ardren are frequently

found in the records of the family. They resided at Harden Hall, near Stockport, and are reputed to have been an early branch of the Warwickshire Ardernes; v. East Cheshire, i. 161.

Heloise de Arderne, 1171: FF. viii. 342.
John de Arderne, 1220: East Cheshire, i. 462.
Peter de Arderne, 1270: ibid.
Jordan de Arderne, co. York, 1273. A.
Ralph de Ardern, co. Linc., ibid.

The *de* was dropped about 1420.

William Ardern, of Timperley, esquire, 1584: Wills at Chester (1545-1620), p. 5.
Mary Ardern, of Stockport, 1619: ibid.
John Arderne, mayor of Stockport, 1524: East Cheshire, i. 347.
1666. William Ardrene and Alice Smith: Marriage Alleg. (Canterbury), p. 114.
Manchester, 1, 1, 2; Philadelphia, 0, 1, 4.

Argent, Argentine.—Local, ' of ' or ' from Argentan,' a town in south Normandy. David de Argentomago was a tenant-in-chief under the Conqueror in cos. Bedford and Camb. His descendants were ennobled as Barons Argentine (Lower).

Richard de Argentein, co. Herts, 1273. A.
Reginald de Argente, co. Essex, ibid.
John de Argenteyn. R.
Gyles Argentyne: Visitation of Bedfordshire, 1566, p. 41.
Reginald de Argentein, co. Norf., 1265: FF. v. 91.
Giles de Argentein, co. Norf., 1281: ibid. 368.
John Argentine, minorite, sup. for B.D., Oct. 20, 1449: Reg. Univ. Oxf. i. 6.
1572. Henry Potkyn and Sicily Argentine: Marriage Lic. (London), i. 53
John Argintine, temp. 1600: Visitation of Dorsetshire, 1623, p. 98.
London, 10, 0; Philadelphia, 2, 0.

Aris, Ariss.—Local, ' of Arras,' a town in Artois famous for the manufacture of tapestry. *Not* a vulgarism for Harris.

1397. 'Draps d'Arras': Will of John of Gaunt in Nichols' Royal Wills, 156 (H.E.D.).
1536. 'Claithis of arres and tapestreis': Bellendene, Cron. Scot. ii. 56 (ibid.).
1562. 'One bede coveringe of aries worke, 8s': Richmondshire Wills, i. 161.
— 'Grant to John Bakes, arras-maker, of the office of maker and mender of the king's cloths and pieces of arras and tapestry with 12d. a day for wages': Materials for History of Reign of Henry VII, p. 259.
Robert de Arraz, London, 1273. A.
Matthew de Araz, London, ibid.

Ralph de Aras, co. Salop, 20 Edw. I. R.
Robert de Arraz. N.
Richard de Arraz, 20 Edw. I. BBB.
Thomas Arras, co. York, 1510. W. 11, p. 175.
1726. Married—Thomas Coggan and Sarah Arris : St. Geo. Han. Sq. i. 2.
1761. — Edward Aris and Mary Cockerill : ibid. p. 101.
1787. — Edward Ariss and Ann Barbere : ibid. p. 406.

The Boston Directory has an entry as follows : 'Roger S. Arras, watchman.' This is much nearer the original than the modern English variants.

London, 5, 1.

Arkettle, Arkell, Arkle, Arkless, Arkoll.—Bapt. 'the son of Arketel.' Norsk, Arnkjell, eagle cauldron ; v. Yonge, ii. 283. One more compound of Kettle (q.v.) contracted to kell, kill, or kle. 'Archill revolts against William' : Freeman, Norman Conquest, iv. 186.

Archil de Corebrigge : Pipe Roll, 5 Hen. II, pt. i.
Simon fil. Arkill. E.
Roger Arketel, co. Hunts, 1273. A.
William Arkell, co. York. W. 2.
Arkill, son of Ecgfred : Symeon of Durham (Surt. Soc.), v. index.
Alicia Arkill, 1379 : P. T. Yorks. p. 245.
Rannulf fil. Arkill, 1203 : RRR. p. 104.
Archil de Botercrame, temp. 1300 : FFF. p. 302.
1676. Edward Freeman and Ellinor Arkell : Marriage Lic. (Westminster), p. 260.
1760. William Puttman and Elizabeth Arkoll : St. Geo. Han. Sq. i. 93.
London, 0, 6, 0, 1, 2 ; Lancaster (Arkle), 3 ; New York (Arkell), 4.

Arkinstall.—Local ; v. Artingstall.

Arkmaker.—Occup. 'a maker of arks' ; v. Arkwright.

Ibota Arkmaker, 1379 : P. T. Yorks. p. 26.

Arkwright.—Occup. 'the arkwright,' a maker of arks. This article of furniture was a north English manufacture, and the surname originated there. The ark was the old-fashioned meal-chest.

'When this corn to the kniht was sold,
He did it in an arc to hold,
And opened this arc the third day.'
Tale of a Usurer.

In an inventory of household goods, dated 1559, are mentioned ' one trussin bed, with a teaster of

yealow and chamlet, one old arke, old hanggers, of wull grene and red,' &c. : Richmondshire Wills, p. 135. Twenty years earlier I find the contents of a 'mylke howse' including 'an arke, a tub, a stande, a chyrne' : ibid. p. 42. In the same book a sheep is bequeathed to one Henry Arkwright, p. 155, note.

William Arkwright, tayler, 1562 : Preston Guild Rolls, p. 30.
John Arkwright, of Broughton (Furness), 1683 : Lancashire Wills at Richmond, ii. 5.
Laurence Arkewrighte, temp. Eliz. ZZ.
Crockford, 2 ; Preston, 6 ; Philadelphia, 1.

Arlett.—Occup. for Harlot, a fellow, a servant.

'A sturdy harlot wente hem ay behind.'
Chaucer, C. T. 7336.
' He was a gentil harlot, and a kind.'
ibid. 649.

Professor Skeat connects Charlotte with this word, and refers to Arletta, the reputed mother of William I ; v. Harlot (Skeat's Dict.).

John le Harlet, co. Camb., 1273. A.
Muriel Arlot, co. Camb., ibid.
John Harlot, co. Camb., Hen. III–Edw. I. K.
1768. Married — Bartholomew Arlett and Eliz. Tellam : St. Geo. Han. Sq. i. 177.
1785. — Witham Arlott and Eliz. Thorogood : ibid. p. 379.
London, 3 ; Philadelphia, 1.

Arment, Armand.—Bapt. 'the son of Armund' ; cf. Rayment for Raymund, or Garment for Garmund. The true English form is Armine or Armyn ; Fr. Armand ; Dutch, Herman.

Armundus le Cawer, co. Linc., Hen. III–Edw. I. K.
Armand de Aspays, 1348 : FF. x. 356.
London, 1, 0 ; Philadelphia, 5, 3.

Armer, Armerer, Armour, Armor.—Occup. 'the armourer,' a maker of armour.

'Armurers and Arowsmythis,' c. 1400 : Destr. Troy, v. 1588 (H.E.D.).
'Armateur, an Armer, a provider of armes or weapons' : Cotgrave (H.E.D.).
John Armourer, mayor of Rising, co. Norf., 1343 : FF. ix. 52.
Guy le Armerer, co. Oxf., 1273. A.
Simon le Armurer. G.
Adam le Armerer, 1307. M.
Marion Armourer, co. York. W. 18.
1562-3. Buried — Syr John Armerar, parson of thys parishe : St. Dionis Backchurch, p. 186.

1640. Buried—John, sonne of Thomas Birkett, armorer : St. Peter's, Cornhill, p. 198.
London, 1, 0, 1, 0 ; Boston (U.S.), 0, 0, 3, $\frac{1}{2}$.

Arminger, Armiger.—Official, 'armiger,' an armour-bearer, a squire. This became Arminger, just as Potager became Pottinger, and Messager Messinger. Thus n is intrusive.

Radulphus Normanill and Alicia uxor ejus, armiger, 1379 : P. T. Yorks. p. 62.
Thomas Armiger. C.
Nicholas Armiger. E.
Jeffry Arminger, temp. Eliz. Z.
Robert Amiger, ibid.
Thomas Armiger, of Beaconsthorp, co. Norf., 1573 : FF. vi. 354.
1634. Edward Arminger and Alse Budsdell : Marriage Lic. (London), ii. 218.
1746. Married — Robert Armiger and Eliz. Bunbury : St. Geo. Han. Sq. i. 38.
London, 2, 0 ; Philadelphia, 0, 1.

Arminson, Armson. — Bapt. 'the son of Armand' ; v. Arment. Armandson would easily vary to Arminson, and this to Armson.

1749. Married — John Holliday and Mary Armson : St. Geo. Chapel, Mayfair, p. 156.
Preston, 2, 0 ; MDB. (Lancashire), 2, 0 ; (Salop), 0, 2.

Armistead, Armstead, Armitstead.—Local, 'at the Hermitage or hermit-stead.' M.E. eremite, a hermit, pronounced armit ; cf. Clark and Clerk, Darby and Derby, &c. This has been a Yorkshire surname for five centuries at least ; see next article.

Laurencius del Armetsted, 1379 : P. T. Yorks. p. 278.
Johannes de Armetstede, 1379 : ibid. p. 263.
William Armistead, vicar of Berwick Parva, co. Norf., 1587 : FF. x. 297.
1618. Henry Knevet and Alice Armestead : Marriage Lic. (Westminster), p. 25.
William Armystede, or Harmestede, M.A., July 4, 1527 : Reg. Univ. Oxf. i. 148.
West Rid. Court Dir., 6, 1, 1 ; London, 4, 2, 1 ; Philadelphia, 2, 0, 0 ; Boston (U.S.), 0, 6, 0.

Armit, Hermit.—Official, 'the hermit.' M.E. eremite and heremite. Pronounced also armit as in Armitage (q.v.) for Hermitage ; see last article.

John Heremite, London, 1273. A.
Gerard Heremite, co. Warw., ibid.
Silvester le Hermite, B.

Johannes Armet-man, i.e. servant of the hermit, 1379 : P. T. Yorks. p. 286 (cf. Ankerman).

William Ermyte, or Armytt, sup. for B.A., March, 1515 : Reg. Univ. Oxf. i. 94. 1768. Married — William Armat and Ann Carrington : St. Geo. Han. Sq. i. 175. London, 1, 0.

Armitage, Hermitage. — Local, ' of the Hermitage,' once pronounced *harmitage* or *armitage* in the north ; cf. Clerk and Clark, Derby and Darby, &c. ; v. Armit and Armistead. A great Lancashire and Yorkshire surname.

John Harmaytayge, co. York. W. 3. Willelmus del Ermytache, 1379 : P. T. Yorks. p. 176.

Gregory Armitage, temp. Eliz. Z. ' William Armitage, rector (of Billingford, co. Norf.), compounded for first-fruits in April, 1596 ' : FF. viii. 194. 1705-5. Married—Joseph Armitage and Mary Kedon : St. Dionis Backchurch, p. 52.

1784. — Stephen Harmitage and Sarah Benfield : St. Geo. Han. Sq. i. 361.

West Riding Court Dir.,56, 0 ; London, 12, 3 ; Philadelphia, 17, 0.

Armrod.—Local ; v. Ormerod. An American variant.

Philadelphia, 2.

Armstrong, Armstrang.— Nick. ' arm-strong ' ; cf. Strongitharm. The name of a familiar Border clan.

' Ye need not go to Liddisdale,
For when they see the blazing bale
Elliots and Armstrongs never fail.'

This surname has ramified very strongly in the States and in Canada.

William Armestrange, co. Cumb., 23 Edw. I. BBB.

Eckie Armstrong, 1615 : Household Books of Howard of Naworth Castle (Surt. Soc.), p. 444.

1627. Michael Jermyn and Frances Armestrong : Marriage Lic. (London), ii. 191.

London, 37, 0 ; Philadelphia, 275, 0.

Arnald, Arnall, Arnell.— (1) Bapt. ' the son of Arnold,' q.v. The omission of the final *d* in Arnald was perfectly natural, just as natural as to have added it if it were not there ; cf. provincial *gownd* for gown, or Simmonds for Simmons. (2) Local, ' of Arnold,' a village in the parish of Long Riston, co. York ; also 'of Arnold,' a parish in co,. Notts.

Richard de Arnall, 20 Edw. II : Freemen of York, i. 23.

John fil. Arnaldi, co. Notts, 1273. A.

Alexander fil. Ernald, co. Oxf., ibid.

Jordan Ernald, co. Oxf., ibid.

1409. Walter Arnald, rector of Thelton : FF. i. 153.

1465. John Arnald, gent., buried by the porch door ' : FF. iv. 132.

1616. Married—Richard Jaggard and Eedy Arnall : St. Antholin (London),p. 52.

London, 1, 2, 5; Boston (U.S.) (Arnal), 1.

Arne.—Bapt. ' the son of Arne,' either the nick. of Arnold (v. Arnett) or a personal name Arn (eagle), which is itself the first syllable of Arnold.

Alice Arn, wife, co. Oxf., 1273. A.

1680-1. Thomas Arne and Mary Thursfield : Marriage Lic. (London), ii. 303.

' Thomas Augustin Arne (1710-78), musical composer, son of Thomas Arne, an upholsterer, who lived in King St., Covent Garden ' : Dict. Nat. Biog. ii. 104.

Arnett, Arnet.—Bapt. ' the son of Arnold ' ; v. Arnold and Arnott. An early corruption.

Lecia Arnet, co. Camb., 1273. A.

Milisent Arnet, co. Camb., ibid.

John Arnet, co. Camb., ibid.

Arnet le Mercer, co. Oxf., ibid.

1785. Married — Charles Arnett and Mary Newton : St. Geo. Han. Sq. i. 371.

London, 6, 0; Boston (U.S.), 2, 0; Philadelphia, 7, 2.

Arnison, Armeson (?), Arnoldson.—(1) Bapt. ' the son of Arnold,' through some nick. or pet form ; v. Arnold. Armeson may be a corruption. Arnoldson, which exists to-day in the United States, would naturally become Arnison ; see next article for instances in the Hundred Rolls. (2) Bapt. ' the son of Arnys ' ; v. Harness.

1572. Married — Richard Foord and Eliz. Armeson : St. Peter, Cornhill, i. 229.

Sheffield, 2, 1, 0; Boston (U.S.), 0, 0, 1.

Arnold, Arnoll, Arnott, Arnot, Arnould.—Bapt. ' the son of Arnold ' ; Fr. Arnoud. With the corruption Arnott, cf. Archbutt for Archibald. Of course Arnold is now practically forgotten as a personal name in England. Nevertheless it was very popular in its day, and being in great favour just when fontal names were candidates for immortality as surnames, it is not to be wondered at that Arnold and its variants and corruptions are

familiar to all our directories at the close of the 19th century. I only furnish a few instances. The United States has such continental forms as Arnhold and Arnholt.

Arnald or Arnard Atte-broke, co. Essex, 1273. A.

Walter fil. Arnald, co. Linc., ibid.

Stephen Arnold, co. Kent, ibid.

John fil. Arnoldi, co. Camb., ibid.

Ayelina relicta Arnold, co. Hunts, ibid.

Warin Arnold, or Ernold, Norwich, 1486 : FF. iv. 414.

1611. John Arnold and Winifred Nelham : Marriage Lic. (London), ii. 6.

London, 80, 1, 12, 1, 1; Philadelphia, 147, 0, 2, 1, 0.

Arnulf. — Bapt. ' the son of Arnulf ' ; v. Arnolf, Yonge, ii. 282. Just as Randolph or Randulf became Randle, so Arnulf, no doubt, became Arnull, and thus was lost in Arneli and other variants of Arnold, q.v.

John fil. Ernulf, co. Camb., 1273. A.

Arnulph Grugge, co. Dorset, ibid.

Arnulf de la Cuba. co. Devon, ibid.

1766. Married—John Arnull and Eliz. Blake : St. Geo. Han. Sq. i. 158.

Aron, Arrend.—Bapt. ' the son of Aaron.' Generally of Jewish descent, but not necessarily so in all cases.

Judaeus Aron (i. e. Aron the Jew), co. York, 1273. A.

Adam Aron, vicar of Bacton, co. Norf. : 1420 : FF. xi. 21.

Jacob Aarron, 1696 : Reg. St. Mary Aldermary (London), p. 112.

Jacob Arone, 1697 : ibid.

Arone, s. of Arone Steeres, 1697: ibid. p. 204.

1654. Bapt.—Eliz., d. Thomas Aran : St. Dionis Backchurch, p. 112.

1658. Bapt.—Mary, d. Thomas Aron : ibid. p. 115.

From Aran to Arran was an easy transition.

1728. Married—William Ivie and Martha Arran : St. Geo. Han. Sq. i. 4.

This, with an excrescent *d*, became Arrend ; cf. *gownd* for gown, or Simmonds for Simmons. There can be no doubt about the fact that Arrend is Aaron in disguise.

London, 1, 1 ; Philadelphia, 2, 0.

Arrison.—Bapt. ' the son of Harry' (v. Harrison), unless Arrison be a corruption of Aaronson, which is not probable. I fear there are Cockneys in America as well as in London.

Philadelphia, 21.

Arrowsmith, Athersmith, Arsmith.—Occup. 'the arrowsmith,' a maker of iron tips, a smith. This surname is corrupted to Athersmith in Furness, North Lanc. I have two Athersmiths in my parish (Ulverston). A late occupative term. No instance in the Hundred Rolls or any other records of the 13th century, so far as my researches go. For the earliest instance given in the H.E.D. (c. 1400) v. Armer.

'Arowe-heders, maltemen, and corn mongers.'
1510. Cocke Lorelles Bote.
Henricus Breyksarth, *arusmyth*, 1379: P. T. Yorks. p. 45.
Johannes Arrowsmyth. ibid. p. 293.
Stephen Arrowsmyth. *faber*, ibid. p. 293.
Johannes Arughsmyght, ibid, p. 66.
William Arowesmythe, temp. Eliz. ZZ.
Richard Arsmith, temp. Eliz. Z.
John Arrowsmith, curate of Lynn, co. Norf., 1643: FF. viii. 504.
1748–9. Bapt. — Noble, s. Robert Arrowsmith, butcher: St. Dionis Backchurch, p. 174.
London, 8, 0, 0; MDB. (Stafford), 2, 1, 0.

Arslett, Asslett, Aslett.—Bapt. 'the son of Auncelot'; v Ancell and Lancelot. There can be little doubt about this solution, but I have no absolute proof. If Ancelot was known familiarly as Ascelot, then the rest is easy to accept.

1775. Married—Bennick Smith and Ann Aslett: St. Geo. Han. Sq. i. 259.
1777. — Edward Asslett and Rhoda Pressey: ibid. p. 274.
1781. — Thomas Smith and Mary Arslett: ibid. p. 318.
London, 1, 0, 0.

Arthur, Arthurs, Arter.—Bapt. 'the son of Arthur.' A rare font-name in the Hundred Rolls. Very common since the battle of Waterloo and the publication of Tennyson's poems.

Walter fil. Arthurii, co. Linc., 1273. A.
William Arthur, co. Essex, ibid.
Stephen Arthur, co. Wilts, ibid.
William Artur, co. Soms., ibid.
Henry Artur, co. Soms., 1 Edw. III: Kirby's Quest, p. 111.
Robert Arthur, rector of Castor, co. Norf., 1334: FF. v. 428.
1615. Robert Arthur and Margaret Ballis: Marriage Lic. (London), ii. 31.
1709. Bapt.—Benjamin Arthur, a young man about 18: St. Dionis Backchurch, p. 148.
London, 21, 2, 3 ; Boston (U.S.), 15, 0, 0.

Artingstall, Artinstall, Arstill, Arkinstall.—Local, 'of Artinstall.' I do not know the precise spot, nor can I say whether it is in Lancashire or Cheshire. The following entries will assist in the search :

1578. Bapt.—Elizabeth Artonstall, of Mottram: Prestbury Ch. (co. Chester), p. 58.
John Arstall, of Hale, 1590: Wills at Chester (1545–1620), p. 5.
William Arstall, of Ringey, parish of Bowden, 1618: ibid.
Robert Artenstall, of Hale, 1632: ibid. (1621–1650), p. 6.
Edward Arstall, of Hale, 1633: ibid.
1596. Married—William Arstall and Jane Booth : ibid. p. 132.

One thing is certain, Arstill and Artinstall represent the same name.

Manchester, 1, 1, 1, 0 ; MDB. (co. Salop), Arkinstall, 2.

Artis, Artiss, Artson.—(1) Bapt. ' the son of Arthur,' a corruption of Arthurs or Arters ; v. Arthur. The final s will thus be patronymic, as in Williams, Jones, Jennings, Wilkins, &c. (2) Local, ' of Artois.' The two first (not Artson) might easily be so derived. But I have no instances.

1619. Thomas Artice, died in Civill in Spain, and was here buried : St. Antholin (London), p. 54.
1649. Married — Sr Peter le royre Mortimer and Sarah Artson : ibid. p. 79.
1661. John Jerson and Anne Artson : Marriage Lic. (Westminster), p. 59.
London, 5, 1, 0 ; Philadelphia, 3, 0, 0.

Arundel, Arundell, Arundle.—Local, ' of Arundel,' a parish in dioc. of Chichester, co. Sussex, ten miles from Chichester.

John Arundel, co. Soms., 1 Edw. III: Kirby's Quest, p. 176.
William de Arundell, co. Salop, 1273. A.
John de Arundell, co. Cornwall, 20 Edw. I. R.
Roger de Arundel, co. Soms., ibid.
Adam de Arondel, co. Salop, Hen. III—Edw. I. R.
Gilbert de Arundell, rector of East Wrotham, co. Norf., 1321: FF. i. 467.
1612. Gregory Arundell and Eliz. Smithe: Marriage Lic. (London), ii. 13.
1765. Married—William Arundale and Ann Barnes: St. Geo. Han. Sq. i. 146.
London, 3, 5, 1 ; Philadelphia, 3, 0, 0.

Asculf. — Bapt. 'the son of Asculf.' No doubt this surname is lost in Hasell and Hazell, q.v. There are no modern representatives of the true original form. Probably some of the many Hasells and Hazells of Berkshire (a district which was familiar with the fontal name Asculf or Hascul) are to be referred to this source.

Harsculph, alias Ascurt de Cleseby, 1301. M.
Hascul de Pracres, co. Oxf., Hen. III—Edw. I. K.
Robert Ascolf, provost of Norwich, 1219: FF. iii. 58.
John Asculf, co. Bucks, 1273. A.
Roger Hasseholf, 1379: P. T. Yorks. p. 172.
Asulph Ma, co. Essex, Hen. III—Edw. I. K.

Aseltine.—Local ; v. Hasleden ; an American variant.

Boston (U.S.), 1.

Ash, Ashe, Aysh.—Local, ' at the ash,' from the original bearer's residence by a certain ash-tree ; cf. Birch, Oak, Lynde, and v. Nash. ' Esche-tre — *fraxinus* ' : Prompt. Parv. p. 143.

John de le Es, co. Norf., 1273. A.
Roger de le Es, co. Norf., ibid.
Agnes Ate Nasse, co. Oxf., ibid.
Henry de Asse, co. Warw., ibid.
Joan atte-Eshe, co. Norf., 1345: FF. v. 145.
Roger atte-Ashe, temp. Edw. II, co. Norf.: FF. ix. 505.
John at-Ash, of Bintre, co. Norf., 1349: FF. v. 205.
Robertus del Asch, 1379: P. T. Yorks. p. 102.
John atte Assh, co. Soms., 1 Edw. III: Kirby's Quest, p. 164.
1611. Bapt.—Thomas, s. Antony Ashe. St. Jas. Clerkenwell, i. 61.
1635. Married—John Drew and Eliz. Ash : St. Antholin (London), p. 69.
London, 20, 0, 0 ; Crockford, 9, 13, 0 ; Boston (U.S.), 21, 1, 0 ; MDB. (co. Devon), 6, 0, 2.

Ashburne.—Local, ' of Ashbourne,' a well-known parish in co. Derby.

Robert de Esseburne, co. Derby, 1273. A.
Henry de Essebourne, co. Derby, ibid.
Thomas de Assheburne, co. Derby, 20 Edw. I. R.
Thomas de Asheborne, rector of Colveston, co. Norf., 1351: FF. ii. 231.
1625–6. Thomas Ashborne, co. Notts, and Eliz. Watson : Marriage Lic. (London), ii. 161.
1777. Married — John Ashburn and Catherine James: St. Geo. Han. Sq. i. 282.
London, 1 ; Philadelphia, 1.

Ashburner.—Occup. 'the ashburner'; one of the oldest and most familiar names in Furness and the English Lake district. The ash-burner was a manufacturer of charcoal, to be used for the bloom-smithies of the middle ages. It is probable that the ash-burner's craft covered the process of smelting as well. The traces of ancient bloomeries are still to be found in the coppice woods that skirt the shores of Windermere, Coniston, and the Duddon estuary. Gradually the occupative term became *collier*, and ousted the other. The surname, Ashburner, however, will for ever remain a memorial of the primitive period when iron ore was smelted in the woods, whose trees supplied the fuel; see Bloomer and Collier. Instances from the Furness church registers are needless; they abound on every page.

1545. Bapt.—John Asburner: St. Mary's, Ulverston, p. 1.
William Ashburner, of Cartmell, 1696: Lancashire Wills (Richmond), p. 7.
1734. Bapt.—William, s. of Joseph Ashburner: St. Jas. Clerkenwell, ii. 216.
London, 3; Crockford, 2; Philadelphia, 7; MDB. (co. Lanc.), 17.

Ashby, Ashbee, Ashbey.—Local, 'of Ashby,' parishes in diocs. of Lincoln (4), Norwich (3), Peterborough (7). With Ashbee, cf. Applebee.

Peter de Askeby, co. Norf., 1273. A.
Gilbert de Askeby, co. Linc., ibid.
Roger de Ascheby, co. Linc., ibid.
Henry de Ascheby, co. Linc., ibid.
David de Assheby, co. Northampt., 20 Edw. I. R.
Jordan de Asscheby, 22 Edw. I. BBB.
1620. John Ashbey and Joane Watson: Marriage Lic. (London), ii. 92.
1780. Married—Charles Asbee and Eliz. Thornell: St. Geo. Han. Sq. i. 311.
London, 37, 2, 3; New York, 2, 2, 2.

Ashcroft, Ascroft, Ashcraft.—Local, 'of Ashcroft.' Seemingly a Norfolk surname. The suffix -*croft* is often found as -*craft*; cf. Meadowcroft and Meadowcraft, and v. Croft and Craft, or Crofter and Crafter. Of course the origin is simple enough, i.e. the croft or enclosure where the ash-trees grew. It is quite clear also that a Lancashire family are sprung from a place named Ashcroft in that county.

Margaret de Asecroft, co. Norf., 1273. A.
Richard Ashcroft, co. Norf., 22 Jas. I: FF. x. 206.

Humphrey Ashcroft, of Prescot, co. Lanc., 1592: Wills at Chester (1545–1620), p. 6.
Henry Ashcroft, of Preston, co. Lanc., 1602, ibid.
1684. Bapt.—Mary, d. Sara Ashcroft, widow: St. Jas. Clerkenwell, i. 308.
Manchester, 11, 0, 0; London, 3, 2, 0; Philadelphia, 3, 0, 4.

Ashdown.—(1) Local, 'of Ashdown,' a parish in dioc. of Chichester. (2) Local, 'of Ashdon,' a parish in co. Essex, three miles from Saffron Walden.

William de Assedon, London, 1273. A.
1640–1. Bartholomew Ashdowne and Mary Cuddon: Marriage Lic. (London), ii. 256.
1663. John Ashdowne and Sarah Woodgate: Marriage Alleg. (Canterbury), p. 88.
1778. Married—George Ashdon and Hannah Cope: St. Geo. Han. Sq. i. 294.
London, 10; Boston (U.S.), 3.

Ashenden.—Local, 'of Ashenden,' a parish in dioc. of Oxford, co. Bucks.

John de Essendon, co. Hertf., 1373. A.
Adam de Assenden, co. Oxf., ibid.
Robert de Assenden, co. Oxf., ibid.
1639. Humphrey Niccols and Barbara Ashenden: Marriage Lic.(London),ii. 244.
1663. Buried—Widow Assenden, a pensioner: St. Dionis Backchurch, p. 234.
1665. Married—Vallentine Ashenden and Jane Wilkins: Canterbury Cathedral, p. 60.
London, 1; Boston (U.S.), 3.

Asher.—Bapt.; v. Asser.

Ashfield.—Local, 'of Ashfield,' two parishes in co. Suffolk and a township in co. Salop.

1582. Michael Ashfilde, co. Oxf.: Reg. Univ. Oxf. vol. ii. pt. ii. p. 120.
1572. Edmund Ashfeilde, co. Bucks: ibid. p. 55.
1613. Buried—Anthony Ashfilde: St. Jas. Clerkenwell, iv. 124.
1677. Richard Ashfeild and Mary Gunning: Marriage Alleg. (Canterbury), p. 274.
MDB (co. Bedf.), 1.

Ashford, Ashforth, Ayshford.—Local,'of Ashford,'parishes in diocs. of Canterbury, Exeter, London, Southwell, and Hereford; v. Ford and Forth for the two suffixes.

John de Esseford, co. Oxf., 1273. A.
Eudo de Assheford, co. Linc., 20 Edw. I. R.
1563. Buried—William Ashforde, prentis to Roger Beawe: St. Mary Aldermary, p. 135.

1594. Thomas Aysheford, co. Devon: Reg. Univ. Oxf. vol. ii. pt. ii. p. 208.
1773. Married — Joseph Ashford and Charlotte Probert: St. Geo. Han. Sq. i. 228.
London, 15, 2, 2; New York, 0, 3, 0; MDB. (co. Devon), 7, 0, 4.

Ashley.—Local, 'of Ashley,' parishes in diocs. of Canterbury, Chester, Ely, Gloucester and Bristol, Lichfield, Peterborough, Winchester, and Oxford.

Robert de Aslegh, co. Devon, 1273. A.
Henry de Assele, co. Norf., ibid.
Walter de Asseleghe, co. Soms., ibid.
John de Asshelegh, co. Devon, Hen. III-Edw. I. K.
Robert de Asshele, co. Bedf., 20 Edw. I. R.
1617. Richard Reeve and Anne Ashley: Marriage Lic. (London), ii. 56.
1741. Married — Perret Fenton and Mary Ashley: St. Mary Aldermary, p. 51.
London, 26; Boston (U.S.), 10.

Ashlin.—Bapt.; v. Aslin.

1733. Married—William Thackeray and Abigail Ashlin: St. Michael's, Cornhill, p. 66.
1750. — Thomas Ashlin and Sarah Middleton: St. Geo. Han. Sq. i. 45.
London, 1.

Ashman.—Bapt. 'the son of Ashman'; cf. Bateman. This surname would seem at first sight to be local, representing one who lived at the ash-tree (v. Ash and Nash), but there can be little doubt that it is a personal name, and perchance the same as Assemannus in Domesday; cf. the place-names Ashmanhaugh, Ashmansworth, compounded with the name of the original tenant. Cf. the German surname Aschemann; one occurs in the New York Directory.

William Asseman, co. Suff., 1273. A.
Peter Asseman, co. Camb., ibid.
Reginald Asseman, co. Suff., ibid.
Walter Ascheman, co. Suff., ibid.
Henry Asscheman, co. Suff., ibid.
Thomas Ashman. B.
Nicholas Ashman, bailiff of Yarmouth, 1299: FF. xi. 322.
Robert Ashman, bailiff of Yarmouth, 1316: ibid.
1740. Bapt.—Hannah, d. of John Aishman: St. Jas. Clerkenwell, ii. 250.
1760. Married—John Ashman and Eliz. Skillin: St. Geo. Han. Sq. i. 99.
London,5; Boston(U.S.),4; NewYork,5.

Ashmead. — Local, 'of Ashmead,' i.e. some spot where the mead or meadow was surrounded by ash-trees. I cannot find the spot. The surname has ramified strongly in America.

Nicholas de Astmede, co. Glouc., 1273. A.
1783. Married—Benjamin Ashmead and Eliz. Clough : St. Geo. Han. Sq. i. 348.
London, 5 ; Philadelphia, 24 ; MDB. (co. Gloucester), 3.

Ashmore. — Local, ' of Ashmore,' a parish in co. Dorset, five miles from Shaftesbury.

1584-5. Robert Johanes (i.e. Jones) and Ann Ashemore : Marriage Lic. (London), i. 138.
1587-8. Married — Hugh Richardsone and Ashmore (sic) : St. Dionis Backchurch, p. 11.
1592. Buried — Ann Ashemore : St. Jas. Clerkenwell, iv. 47.
1773. Married — Thomas Hind and Sarah Ashmore : St. Geo. Han. Sq. i. 227.
London, 3 ; Philadelphia, 13

Ashton, Aston. — Local, ' of Ashton ' or ' Aston,' parishes in diocs. of Exeter, Peterborough, Bath and Wells, Sarum, Gloucester and Bristol, Chester, Liverpool, and Manchester. The meaning is simple : the *ash-town*, i. e. the enclosure with ash-trees in it ; v. Ash and Town. Naturally this would be a common place-name. With the form Aston, cf. Ascroft and Ashcroft.

Roger de Astun, co. Salop, 1273. A.
Thomas de Aston, co. Lanc., ibid.
William de Aston, co. Heref., ibid.
John de Ascheton, co. Soms., ibid.
Roger de Assheton, co. Lanc., 20 Edw. I. R.
Johannes de Aston, 1379 : P. T. Yorks. p. 278.
1618-9. William Freake and Philippa Aston : Marriage Lic. (London), i. 69.
1646. Bapt.—Peter, s. Peter Ashton : St. Jas. Clerkenwell, i. 164.
London, 41, 19 ; Boston (U.S.), 10, 4.

Ashurst, Ashhurst. — Local, ' of Ashurst.' (1) A parish in co. Kent, about four miles from Tunbridge Wells ; (2) a parish in co. Sussex, three miles from Steyning. The origin is simple, ' the Ash-hurst ' or wood ; v. Ash and Hurst. There is evidently a spot in co. Lanc. bearing this name.

Adam de Asshurst, co. Lanc., 1322 : Lay Subsidy (Rylands).
Thomas de Asshurst, co. Lanc., ibid.
1549. Married — Mihill Assherst and Christian Bowin : St. Antholin (London), p. 7.
1628. Bapt.—John, s. John Ashhurst : St. Dionis Backchurch, p. 101.

1636-7. Richard Hutton and Anne Ashhurst : Marriage Lic. (London), ii. 229.
London, 2, 2 ; Philadelphia, 0, 2.

Ashwell.—Local, ' of Ashwell.' (1) A parish in co. Hertford, about four miles from Baldock ; (2) a parish in co. Rutland, three miles from Oakham.

Richard de Aswelle, co. Suff., 1273. A.
William de Assewelle, co. Rutl., ibid.
Nichol de Asshewelle, 22 Edw. I. BBB.
Thomas Ashwell, sheriff of Norwich, 1647 : FF. ii. 398.
1627. Bapt.—Richard, s. John Ashwell : St. Jas. Clerkenwell, i. 106.
London, 11 ; New York, 2.

Ashworth.—Local, ' of Ashworth,' a chapelry in the parish of Middleton, co. Lanc., anciently Asseheworth. This small place (pop. 233 in 1861) has given birth to a surname that has become largely represented. It is familiar to every town and village in south Lancashire. Henry Ashworth (1794-1880), the friend of Cobden, was born at Birtwistle, near Bolton, a few miles from Ashworth, on Sept. 4, 1794. Caleb Ashworth, D.D. (1722-75), a celebrated dissenter, was born at Rossendale, co. Lanc. John Ashworth (1813-75), preacher, manufacturer, and author, was born at Cutgate, near Rochdale ; v. Dict. Nat. Biog. ii. 187-8. The little village has kept itself well in the remembrance of Lancashire people.

John Ashworth, of Castleton, co. Lanc., 1617 : Wills at Chester (1545-1620), p. 7.
Oliver Ashworth, of Wolfenden, co. Lanc., 1611 : ibid.
1641. Buried — Henry Ashworth, a stranger : St. Dionis Backchurch, p. 223.
1765. Married—Robert Sewell and Ann Ashworth : St. Geo. Han. Sq. i. 146.
London, 2 ; Middleton, 6 ; Manchester, 63 ; Boston (U.S.), 3.

Ask, Aske.—Local, ' of Aske.' Aske, a township in the parish of Easby, near Richmond, North Riding of Yorkshire. This surname is nearly, but not quite, obsolete.

Richard de Ask, 1369 : DDD. i, 54.
Conan d'Ask, 1391 : ibid. p. 51.
John d'Ask, 1398 : ibid. p. 55.
' Robert Aske (d. 1537), leader of the insurrection called the "Pilgrimage of Grace," was of an old Yorkshire family which took its name from Aske, in Richmondshire ' : v. Dict. Nat. Biog. ii. 189.

1602. Bapt.—Eliz., d. Robert Aske : St. Michael, Cornhill, p. 104.
1678-9. Robert Aske and Mary Bonfoy : Marriage Alleg. (Canterbury), p. 293.
1765. Married — William Barton and Dorothy Ask : St. Geo. Han. Sq. p. 141.
Sheffield, 1, 0.

Askell.—Bapt. ' the son of Askettle ' ; v. Anskettle.

Askew, Ascough, Ainscough, Ainscow.—Local, ' of Aiskew,' a township in the parish of Bedale, co. York ; v. Askey. 'Anne Askew (1521-46), protesting martyr, was the second daughter of Sir William Askew, or Ayscough, knight, who is generally stated to be of Kelsey, in Lincolnshire ' : Dict. Nat. Biog. (v. Askew). As shown above, the original form was Aiskew or Ayscough. This by an intrusive *n* became, in Lancashire, Ainscough and Ainscow. But Askew is the generally adopted form. It was natural that the surname should cross the border from Yorkshire to Lancashire.

1545. John Aiscoughe and Grisella Tuke : Marriage Lic. (Faculty Office), p. 6.
1553. Anthony Twysylton and Alice Askewe : Marriage Lic. (London), i. 14.
Margaret Askew, of Kirkbye Ireleth, North Lanc., 1570 : ibid.
1595 : Wills at Chester (1545-1620), p. 5.
John Askew, of Osmuderley, North Lanc., 1597 : Lancashire Wills at Richmond, i. 8.
1661. Edward Bedell and Barbara Ayscough : Marriage Lic. (Faculty Office), p. 55.
London, 8, 2, 0, 0 ; Manchester, 1, 0, 1, 7 ; Philadelphia, 1, 7, 0, 0.

Askey, Askie. — Local ; v. Askew. These are variants. It is perfectly natural to find Askey in co. Lincoln, where Askew was familiar for centuries.

1616. Henry Askley and Eliz. Dimmock : Marriage Lic. (London), ii. 42.
1618. Thomas Johnson and Amy Askie : ibid. p. 65.
London, 0, 1 ; MDB. (Lincoln), 2, 0 ; New York, 1, 0 ; Philadelphia, 0, 2.

Askham, Ascham.—Local, ' of Askham,' two parishes in co. York ; also Askham, a parish in co. Cumb., near Barrow-in-Furness.

Avice de Askum, co. Westm., 20 Edw. I. R.
Thomas de Askam, 1379 ; P. T. Yorks. p. 61.
' Roger Ascham (1515-68) was born

in 1515 at Kirby Wiske, near Northallerton. His family seems to have been of considerable antiquity, and to have taken its name from the villages known as East and West Askham, near York. A Roger de Askham is mentioned as an adherent of Thomas, Earl of Lancaster, in 1313 ': Dict. Nat. Biog. ii. 150.

1752. Sir Thomas Hatton and Harriott Askham: Marriage Lic.(London), ii. 346.

West Riding Court Dir., 6, 0; Philadelphia, 5, 0.

Askill.—Bapt. 'the son of Anskettle,' q.v.

Askin, Askins, Haskin, Haskins. — Bapt. 'the son of Asketin' (?), an O. F. dim. of Askettle. As Askettle became undoubtedly Askell, q.v., so Asketin probably became Askin. For further instances and remarks, v. Astell. Nevertheless, I am not quite satisfied with this solution. Like Wilkin and Wilkins from William, it would appear that Askin and Askins represent a popular nick. of some once familiar personal name.

Robert Asketin, co. Kent, 1273. A.

William Asketin, co. Kent, ibid.

1626. John Haskins and Grace Johnson: Marriage Lic. (London), ii. 168.

1774. Married—John Asking and Hannah Reedhead: St. Geo. Han. Sq. i. 239.

Crockford, 1, 1, 0, 1; London, 0, 0, 0, 3; New York, 1, 3, 3, 9.

Askwith, Asquith. — Local, ' of Askwith,' a village in the parish of Weston, near Otley, co. York. Askwith and Ashworth are the same compound, viz. *Ash* and *Worth*, q.v. Asquith is the modern popular dress.

Johannes de Askwith, 1379: P. T. Yorks. p. 260.

Hugo de Askwith: ibid. p. 238.

1579. William Askwithe and Rosina Gocianos: Marriage Lic.(London), i. 88.

1590. Michael Asquith, co. York: Reg. Univ. Oxf. vol. ii. pt. ii. p. 177.

London, 0, 0; West Riding Court Dir., 3, 9; Philadelphia, 0, 5.

Aslac, Aslachson, Hasluck, Haselock.—Bapt. 'the son of Aslak'; v. Yonge, i. 46. A well-known name in its time, of Scandinavian origin.

Thomas Aslake, co. Norf., 16 Edw. IV: FF. x. 259.

Walter Aslake, of Creke, co. Norf., 1503: ibid. p. 329.

William Aslack, co. Norf., 1531: ibid.

'The land and tenure of John, son of Aslath, of Flockthorp': ibid. iv. 557.

Aslack Lany, co. Norf., 1639: ibid. v. 394.

John Aslac, co. Suff., 1273. A.

William Haselock, co. Worc., 1601: Reg. Univ. Oxf. ii. 248.

Cf. the local Aslacton.

Reginald de Aslacton, co. Notts, 1273. A.

Richard de Aslakeby, co. York, Hen. III-Edw. I. K.

Thomas Aslakby, sup. for B.A., 1462: Reg. Univ. Oxf. i. 35.

These would signify 'the dwelling of Aslac.'

Mary, d. of Christopher Ashlock, temp. 1600; Visitation of Dorset, 1623, p. 14.

John Ashelok, sup. for B.A., May 16, 1521: Reg. Univ. Oxf. i. 119.

1624. Bapt.—Ellis, son of Robert Azlacke: St. Jas. Clerkenwell, i. 99.

The Rev. Oscar Aslachson occurs in Crockford, 1886.

London, 0, 0, 2, 0; Sheffield (Haselock), 1; Crockford, 0, 1, 3, 1.

Aslin, Ashlin, Asling, Ashling.—Bapt. 'the son of Ancel,' from the dim. Ancelin, popularly Asselin or Acelin; v. Ancell. Asselin and Ascelyne occur as personal names in the Hundred Rolls without surnames attached; v. Lancelin.

Ascelyn de Peykirk, co. Hunts, 1273. A.

Acelin Wyteknave, co. Hunts, ibid.

Richard Asselin, co. Camb., ibid.

William Asselyn, co. Camb., ibid.

Asselin (without surname), co. Northampt., ibid.

Andrew Asselyn, vicar of Northall, Middlesex, 1399: Memorials of Merton Coll. (Oxf. Hist. Soc.), p. 218.

1551. Nicholas Browne and Joanna Astlen: Marriage Lic. (London), i. 13.

The corruption to Ashlin is clearly traceable.

1557. Buried—Jone Aslyn: St. Michael, Cornhill, p. 66.

1708. — Jacob Asselin: St. John Baptist on Wallbrook, p. 106.

1725. Married—William Aslin and Eliz. Prestly: St. Geo. Han. Sq. i. 5.

1733. William Thackeray to Abigail Ashlin: St. Michael, Cornhill, p. 181.

1750. Married — Thomas Ashlyn and Sarah Middleton: St. Geo. Han. Sq. p. 45.

1782. — George Asling and Sarah Eades: ibid. p. 336.

The *g* in Asling is excrescent, as in Jennings, &c. The Cambridgeshire form is Ashling. Six centuries ago, in the same county, it was Asselin. But the change is an ordinary one.

London, 1, 1, 0, 0; MDB. (Lincoln), 0, 1, 1, 0; (Cambridge), 0, 0, 0, 1.

Aspden.—Local, ' of Aspden,' a village near Buntingford, co. Hertford. As nearly all the instances are found in Lancashire it is quite possible another locality exists, or has existed, in that county called Aspden. The origin of the word is simple; v. Dean and Aspinall.

William Aspden, of Cliviger, 1597: Wills at Chester (1545-1620), p. 7.

Robert Aspden, of Culcheth, 1607: ibid.

James Aspden, of Tockholes, 1622: ibid. (1621-50), p. 8.

London, 1; MDB. (Lancashire), 8; Manchester, 8; Philadelphia, 2.

Aspell.—Local, 'of Aspall,' a parish in co. Suffolk, one mile from Debenham.

'She gave her manors of Stonhall and Aspal, in Suffolk, which came by her mother, daughter and co-heir of Sir John de Aspal,' 1385: FF. ix. 23.

Gilbert de Aspale, co. Norf., 44 Edw. II: ibid. ii. 265.

Robert de Aspale, co. Norf., 1323: ibid. v. 73.

Thomas Aspal, rector of Francham Magna, co. Norf., 1529: ibid. ix. 499.

Probably the Lancashire Aspells represent Aspinall, q.v.: a clear instance is there given. This surname has crossed the Atlantic. Oddly enough, I find but scanty English representatives as yet.

New York, 4; Middleton (co. Lanc.), 1.

Aspenlon, Asplen, Asplin.—Bapt. 'the son of Absolom'; O.E. Aspelon. The change of *b* to *p*, and removal of *s* from after to before *p*, seem to have begun in the early decades of the 13th century. This font-name was very popular, and as a surname has existed in co. Cambridge for six centuries.

Asspelon Odierne, co. Camb., 1273. A.

Hugo fil. Asspelon, co. Camb., ibid.

Warin fil. Aspelonis, co. Camb., ibid.

Henry Aspelon, co. Oxf., ibid.

Aspelon fil. Nicholas, co. Bedf., ibid.

John Asplon, co. Hunts, ibid.

Asplon Faber, co. Hunts, ibid.

Ann Aspelin and John Aspelin : Visitation of Essex, 1541, p. 279.

Thomas Wright and Eliz. Asplyn, 1636: Marriage Lic. (London), p. 228.

Samuel Asplin, rector of Geyton-Thorp, co. Norf., 1722: FF. viii. 440.

'This morning the crew will walk over

to Mortlake, whither their boat will be taken in charge of Asplen, the University waterman': Cambridge Crew (Standard, March 15, 1887).

The first three instances above are from the county of Cambridge. It is odd to think that Asplen is unquestionably from Absolom.

London, 3, 0, 1; MDB. (co. Camb.), 0, 2, 0.

Aspinall, Aspinwall, Aspinell.—Local, 'of Aspinwall,' a property in the parish of Aughton, co. Lanc.; lit. 'the aspen-well,' i.e. the poplar-well, the well by the poplar-trees; cf. Popplewell. We still speak of 'trembling like an aspen-leaf.'

'Richard le Walais, lord of Litherland, grants by deed (temp. Hen. III) to William Pike of Aspenwelle,' &c.: Baines' Lanc. ii. 400.

'Aspinwall, or, as it is here called, Aspall Lane, was the paternal inheritance of Edward Aspinwall,' &c.: ibid. p. 404.

Gilbert de Aspenwall, co. Lanc., 1332: Lay Subsidy (Rylands).

James Aspinall, of Aspinall, 1591: Wills at Chester (1545-1620), p. 7.

Katharine Aspinwall, of Aspinwall, 1596: ibid.

Were there the slightest doubt that Aspinall is a variant of Aspinwall, the above quotations would set the question at rest for ever. The place is styled Aspinall in documents, 15 Charles I; v. Exchequer Depositions by Commission, Lancashire (Lanc. and Ches. Record Soc. V. xi. 26).

1761. Married—Solomon Franklin and Mary Aspenwall: St. Geo. Han. Sq. i. 103.
1782. — Humphrey Aspinall and Eliz. Leach: ibid. p. 340.

London, 4, 3, 0; Manchester, 10, 4, 0; Boston (U.S.), 0, 8, 2; New York, 2, 8, 0.

Asplen and Asplin; v. Aspenlon.

Asquith.—Local, 'of Askwith,' q.v.

Asser, Asher.—Bapt. 'the son of Asser.' 'Asser (says Mr. Lower), an ancient personal name, as Asserius Menevensis, the preceptor of King Alfred. Two tenants called Azor are found in Domesday': Patr. Brit. p. 13. The frequent occurrence of Asher in the United States directories is due to an influx of German Aschers, who per-

haps represent the same personal name.

Asser (without surname), canon of St. David's, 1202: Hist. and Ant. St. David's, p. 364.
John ap-Asser, canon of St. David's, 1218: ibid.
William Ascer, co. Linc., 1273. A.
Robert Asser, co. Derby, ibid.
Jordan Asser, co. Northampc., 20 Edw. I. R.
William Asser, rector of Aylmerton, co. Norf.: FF. viii. 82.
1653. Married—Bradford Bury and Eliz. Asser, of Barling, co. Essex: St. Dionis Backchurch, p. 29.
1671. John Adams and Philippa Asser, co. Herts, Marriage Alleg. (Canterbury), p. 197.
1756. Thomas Asser and Ann Coventry: St. Geo. Han. Sq. i. 61.
London, 4, 4; Philadelphia, 0, 13; New York, 0, 19.

Assman, Assmann.—Bapt.; v. Ashman.

Nichol Asseman, co. Suff., 1273. A.
New York, 1, 4.

Astell, Astle.—Bapt. 'the son of Asketel,' one of the many corruptions of this early and popular name; v. Oskell. Asketel became, of course, Askil; v. Kell. Hence the Askills below. From Askil to Astell was an easy transition. Aschetil de Ousegarth, co. York, is set down in one record variously as Aschetin, Asketin. Aschetel, and Astill; v. Index, FFF.

Anketinu de Martivall, co. Linc., 1 Edw. I. R.
Astill fil. Wlfriche, co. Oxf., 1273. A.
Astell Prepositus, co. Oxf., ibid.
William Astil, co. Oxf., ibid.
Peter Askyl, co. Camb., ibid.
Alan Askil, co. Camb., ibid.
Stephen Astel, co. Camb., ibid.
Simon Astil, co. Bucks, ibid.
Robertus Ascull, 1379: P. T. Yorks. p. 33.
Hugh Astell, rector of Aylmerton, co. Norf., 1371: FF. viii. 82.
Nicholas Astell, vicar of Stradset, co. Norf., 1450: ibid. vii. 453.

As Asketin was a familiar form (possibly diminutive) of Asketel, it is probable that Askin, Askins, and Haskins are thus derived; v. Askin.

'Item paied to Edmonde Astell, keper of Grenewiche park for thornes, &c., £3 17s. 6d.,' April 7, 1532: Privy Purse Exp., Henry VIII, p. 205.
1675. William Halfheid and Anne Astle: Marriage Alleg. (Canterbury), p. 243.

1722. Bapt.—Thomas, s. John Astill: St. Mary Aldermary (London), p. 123.
London, 2, 0; Boston (U.S.), 0, 1.

Astie.—Bapt. 'the son of Anastasia,' from the nick. Anstie (v. Anstee), abbreviated to Astie. There can be little doubt that this is the true solution. It has never been a common surname, and at present I can find representatives only in the United States. But this is not a rare occurrence.

Adam Asty, co. Kent, 1273. A.
John Asty, co. Norf., ibid.
Thomas Asty, co. Norf., 1374: FF. i. 349.
Robert Asty, rector of West Herling, co. Norf., 1410: ibid. p. 311.
1658-9. Bapt.—Francis, s. Francis Asty: St. Dionis Backchurch, p. 115.
1686. — John, s. Henry Aystie: St. Jas. Clerkenwell, i. 317.
New York, 2.

Astin, Asten, Astins.—Bapt. 'the son of Austin,' an early variant. Of course the majority of the representatives of these variants of Austin are now lost in the local surname Aston, q.v. This was inevitable, hence the scarcity of modern instances. That Astin is a variant of Austin is settled by two entries concerning the same individual; v. Aust.

Astin, or Austin Creik, co. Camb., 1273. A.
Astinus Benington, co. Linc., ibid.
Warin Astin, co. Camb., ibid.
Rogerus Astyn, 1379: P. T. Yorks. p. 63.
Johannes Aystyn, 1379: ibid. p. 295.
John Astyn, vicar of Wiggenhale, co. Norf., 1421: FF. ix. 185.
Robert Astyn, co. Norf., 1592: ibid. p. 154.

The dim. Austiline is also found.

Austelin Gournay, co. Soms., 1 Edw. III: Kirby's Quest, p. 172.
West Riding Court Dir., 1, 0, 0; London, 0, 1, 1; Boston (U.S.), 0, 1, 0; New York, 1, 11, 0.

Astle, Astell. — Local, 'of Asthill.' The suffix is commonly turned into 'le' or 'ell'; cf. Tickle for Tickhill, Buckell for Buckhill.

Richard de Asthull, 11 Edw. III: Freemen of York, i. 32.

For another origin v. Astell.

London, 0, 2; Boston (U.S.), 1, 0.

Astley.—Local, 'of Astley.' (1) A chapelry in the parish of Leigh, co. Lanc.; (2) a chapelry in the county of Salop, five miles from Shrewsbury; (3) a parish in co. Warwick, near Nuneaton; (4) a parish in co. Worcester, near Stourport. The Lancashire Astleys are all from the chapelry near Leigh in that county.

John de Astleye, co. Salop, 1273. A.
Richard de Astlegh, co. Salop, ibid.
William de Astelegh, co. Lanc., 1332: Lay Subsidy (Rylands), p. 10.
George Astley, of Heywood, co. Lanc., 1573: Wills at Chester (1545-1620), p. 8.
Margaret Astley, of Dean, co. Lanc., 1595: ibid.
1622. Richard Astley, co. Oxf., and Anne Gilborne: Marriage Lic. (Westminster), p. 28.
1762. Married—Alexander Dusser and Sarah Astley: St. Geo. Han. Sq. i. 112.
London, 4; Manchester, 6; MDB. (Lancashire), 2; Philadelphia, 2.

Aston.—(1) Local, 'of Aston' or 'Ashton,' q.v. (2) Bapt. 'the son of Astin,' q.v. That Astin became Aston is clear from three entries in the same village.

Johannes Aystyn, 1379: P. T. Yorks. p. 295.
Henricus Astyn, 1379: ibid.
Willelmus Aston, 1379: ibid.

Atcheson, Atchison. — (1) Bapt. 'the son of Adam.' (2) Bapt. 'the son of Archibald'; v. Aitcheson and Adkin.

1734. Anne, d. of John Atchison: St. Jas. Clerkenwell, i. 213.
1748. Married—Matthew Bell and Mary Atchison: St. Geo. Han. Sq. i. 41.
1783. — John Hyatt and Eliz. Atchason: ibid. p. 342.
London, 2, 5; Philadelphia, 7, 7.

Atfend.—Local, 'at the fen.' The final *d* in Atfend is excrescent; cf. *gownd* for gown, or Simmonds for Simmons, or Hamond for Hamon.

Isabella Ate Fenne, co. Oxf., 1273. A.
Henry Atefen, co. Camb., ibid.
Walter Atefen, co. Camb., ibid.
Thomas Atefen, vicar of Appleton, co. Norf., 1407: FF. viii. 332.
1678. William Atfend and Elizabeth Andrewes: Marriage Lic. (Westminster), p. 285.
1692. Francis Atfen and Ann Totthill: Marriage Alleg. (Canterbury), p. 229.

Atford.—Local, 'at the ford.'

from residence thereby; cf. Attwood, Attwell, &c.

John Ate Forde, co. Oxf., 1273. A.
Henry Ateforde, co. Oxf., ibid.
Gillian Atteford, co. Camb., ibid.
1641. Bapt.—Hannah, d. Robert Atford: St. Dionis Backchurch, p. 106.
1673. John Atford and Mary Soaper: Marriage Lic. (Westminster), p. 45.

I cannot find any modern representatives, but doubtless some exist.

Athawes.—Local, 'atte-haws,' from residence beside the haws; cf. Attwood, Attwell, Athow, &c., and v. Hawe.

William Attehawse, vicar of South Walsham, co. Norf., 1379: FF. xi. 143.
1755. Married—Thomas Boucher and Ann Athawes, of Chiswick: St. Geo. Han. Sq. i. 60.
London, 1; MDB. (co. Essex), 1.

Atherly.—Local; v. Adderley.

Atherton.—Local, 'of Atherton,' a chapelry in the parish of Leigh, co. Lanc. The Boston Directory shows that the name crossed the Atlantic some generations ago.

'Oct. 4, 1679. William Atherton, in the ship Nathaniel for Boston': Hotten's Lists of Emigrants, p. 349.
'In the reign of King John, Robert de Atherton served the office of sheriff for the county of Lancaster, and held Atherton of the Barons of Warington. His son William de Atherton held this manor by the tenth part of a Knight's fee,' &c.: Baines' Lanc. ii. 201.
Hugh de Atherton, co. Lanc., 1332: Lay Subsidy (Rylands).
Godfrey Atherton, of Bickersteth, 1597: Wills at Chester (1545-1620), p. 8.
Philip Atherton, of Atherton, 1618: ibid.
1662. Peter Shepherd and Christian Atherton: Marriage Lic. (Westminster), p. 42.
Atherton (co. Lanc.), 1; Manchester, 15; London, 9; Boston (U.S.), 20.

Athow, Attoe, Atthow, Ato. —Local, 'at the how'; v. How; cf. Attwell, Attwood, &c., for 'at the well,' 'at the wood,' &c. With the variant Attoe, cf. Hoo and Hoe, q.v.

Philip Atteho, co. Kent, 1273. A.
William Attehow, co. Norf., 14 Edw. I: FF. vii. 195.
Thomas Attehow de Methwolde, vicar of Griston, co. Norf., 1357: ibid. ii. 291.
Francis Athow, Visitation of Essex, 1541, p. 122.
Thomas Athow: ibid.

Clement Athow, rector of Bicham-well, co. Norf., 1623: FF. vii. 296.

The Lincolnshire variant Ato, although curious to look at, is perfectly plain as regards its parentage.

1694. Thomas Vincent and Dynah Athow: Marriage Alleg. (Canterbury), p. 286.
MDB. (Suffolk), 0, 1, 0, 0; (Norfolk), 0, 0, 2, 0; (Lincoln), 0, 0, 0, 1; Philadelphia, 2, 0, 0, 0.

Atkin, Atkins, Atkinson; v. Adkin.

Atkirk, Achurch.—Local, 'at the kirk' or 'church,' from residence thereby; v. Kirk and Church. Atkirk, unlike Attwood or Attwell, seems to have become extinct; but Achurch, abbreviated from Atte-Church, still exists. This, however, may represent Achurch, a township in co. Northampton.

Robert Ate Church, co. Oxf., 1273. A.
Emma Ate Cherch, co. Oxf., ibid.
Robert Atte Chyrche, co. Norf., ibid.
John Attecherch, rector of Metton, co. Norf., 1338: FF. viii. 140.
William Attechirche, co. Norf., 29 Edw. I: ibid. vii. 114.
'Agnes, wyff to Pall Atkyrke, temp. 1520': Visitation of Yorkshire, 1563, p. 164.
MDB. (Lincoln), 0, 1.

Atock, Attack, Atack, Attick.—Local, 'at the oak'; A.S. *ác*; cf. Acton, Ackworth, Ackroyd, *acorn*, &c., and v. Attwood, Attwell, &c.

Adam At the Ock, co. Salop, 1273. A.
1709. Bapt.—Eliz., d. of Thomas Atack: St. Jas. Clerkenwell, ii. 49.
1765. Married—Samuel Cooper and Christian Attack: St. Geo. Han. Sq. i. 141.
1790. — Miles Atack and Eliz. Fryer: ibid. ii. 39.
MDB. (Cambridge), 0, 1, 0, 0; West Riding Court Dir., 1, 0, 0, 0; Philadelphia, 0, 0, 2, 2.

Attenborough, Atterbury. —(1) Local, 'of Attenborough,' a parish in co. Notts. (2) Local, 'of Attleburgh,' a town in co. Norf. I have placed Attenborough and Atterbury together, as they have probably become confused in the course of centuries. In any case Atterbury represents the older Attleburgh. (3) Local, 'at the borough' or 'bury'; v. Bury.

Walter Attebure, co. Kent, 1273. A.

Alicia de Atteburwe, co. Camb., 1273. A.
Margaret de Atteburwe, co. Camb., ibid.
Richard de Atleborw, co. Camb., ibid.
Ralf de Atleburgh, temp. Edw. III, co. Norf.: FF. iv. 225.
John de Atlebergh, co. Norf., 1256: ibid. iii. 489.
John Atte-bury, 1306. M.
1661. Laurence Atterbury and Eliz. Poynter: Marriage Alleg. (Canterbury), p. 65.
1769. Married—Louis Gouyn and Eliz. Atterbury: St. Geo. Han. Sq. i. 184.
London, 10, 3; New York, 0, 9.

Atteslow. — Local, 'at the slough'; v. Slough, where manifest proof is given; cf. Attwood, Attwell, &c.

Peter Atteslo, co. Oxf., 1273. A.
William Atteslont, co Camb., ibid.
Edward Attislow, or Atslow, adm. B.A., June 26, 1555: Reg. Univ. Oxf. i. 229.
Luke Atteslowe, or Atsloe, adm. B.A., Jan. 24, 1559-60: ibid. p. 241.

Attfield.—Local, 'at the field,' from residence thereby; cf. Attwood, Attwell, v. Field.

Richard Ate Felde, co. Oxf., 1273. A.
Linot Ate Felde, co. Oxf., ibid.
John Atefelde, co. Oxf., ibid.
John Atteteld, co. Norf., 10 Hen. IV: FF. 49.
1675. John Attfeild and Elizabeth Hall: Marriage Lic. (Westminster), p. 239.
1785. Married—James Attfield and Mary Colburn: St. Geo. Han. Sq. i. 372. London, 7.

Atthill.—Local, 'at the hill,' from residence thereon; v. Hill; cf. Attwell, Attwood, &c. This surname has existed in co. Norfolk for at least five centuries.

Bateman Attehil, co. Camb., 1273. A.
Everard Attehyl, co. Camb., ibid.
Henry Attehul, co. Camb., ibid.
Gregory Attehill, rector of Ingworth, co. Norf., 1356: FF. vi. 369.
John Athill, co. Norf., 1384: ibid. vi. 501.
1558. Edward Dixson and Margaret Athill: Marriage Lic. (London), i. 18.
Crockford, 2; MDB. (co. Norfolk), 3.

Atthow; v. Athow.

Attley, Attlee, Atlay, Atlee.
—Local, 'at the lee,' from residence thereby; v. Lee; cf. Attwood and Attwell.

John Atte Lee, co. Northampt., 20 Edw. I. R.
Roger Atteleye, co. Kent, ibid.
William Attelan, co. Oxf., 1273. A.
John Attele, co. Berks, ibid.
1588. Bapt.—John, s. Francis Attley: St. Dionis Backchurch, p. 86.

1687. William Att Lee and Elizabeth Bonfoy, Marriage Lic. (Faculty Office), p. 186.
1751. Bapt. — Charles, s. Benjamin Atlee: St. Mary Aldermary, p. 131.
London, 1, 1, 0, 2; Crockford (Atlay), 2; Philadelphia (Atlee), 12.

Attmore, Atmore.—Local, 'at the moor,' from residence thereon; v. Moor.

Adam Ate Mor, co. Oxf., 1273. A.
Oliva Ate Mor, co. Oxf., ibid.
Ralph Atemor, London, ibid.
Beatrix Attemore, Norwich, 7 Ric. II: FF. viii. 270.
Simon Attemore, vicar of Crimplesham, co. Norf., 1398: ibid. vii. 314.
1748. Married—Thomas Hopes and Mary Atmore: St. Geo. Han. Sq. i. 40.
Philadelphia, 6, 12; MDB. (Norfolk), 0, 4.

Attridge, Attrich.—Local, 'at the ridge,' from residence thereby; v. Rigg or Ridge; cf. Attwood or Attwell.

Jacob Atteriche, co. Berks, 1273. A.
1777. Married—William Fowler and Jane Atridge: St. Geo. Han. Sq. i. 282.
1800. — Edward Walker and Sarah Attridge: ibid. ii. 225.
London, 2, 0; Philadelphia, 2, 0; New York, 5, 1.

Attwell, Atwell, Atwill, Attiwell, Attwill, Attewell.—Local, 'at the well,' from residence thereby; v. Wells; cf. Attwood.

Adam Ate Welle, co. Oxf., 1273. A.
John Atewelle, co. Camb., ibid.
John Atte-Well, co. Kent, 20 Edw. I. R.
Simon Atte Well, C. R., 43 Edw. III.
William Atte Well, 1313. M.
John Atwelle, ibid.
Willelmus Attewell, 1379: P. T. Yorks. p. 193.
Jeffry At-welle, rector of Erpingham, co. Norf., 1448: FF. vi. 411.
1663-4. Married—William Atwell and Mary Tyrell: St. Dionis Backchurch, p. 37.

The variant Atwill is found as early as the beginning of the 17th century.

Hugh Attwyll, parson of Cawverly, co. Devon, 1602: FF. iii. 358.
New York, 6, 4, 1, 0, 0, 0; Boston (U.S.) (Attwill), 2; London, 13, 5, 1, 0, 0, 0; Sheffield (Attiwell), 1.

Attwood, Atwood.—Local, 'at the wood,' from residence thereby; cf. Attwell, and v. Wood. Every English county has representatives of this surname.

Geoffrey Ate Wode, co. Hunts, 1273. A.
Matheus Atewode, co. Camb., ibid.
Agnes Attewode, co. Oxf., ibid.
Gilbert Atte Wode, co. Sussex, ibid.
John Attewode, co. Norf., 1391: FF. viii. 170.

William Attewood, co. Norf., 1439: ibid. 171.
1726. Married—George Atwood and Sarah Laurence: St. Mary Aldermary, p. 47.

Atwood has ramified strongly in Boston and the district.

'Philip Atwood sailed for New England in the Suzan and Ellin in 1625': Hotten's Lists of Emigrants, p. 59.
London, 13, 4; Boston (U.S.), 3, 123.

Atty.—Bapt. 'the son of Adam,' from the colloquial Addy, q.v. This was sharpened into Atty. Similarly Addison became Attison.

1624-5. Christopher Attye and Eliz. Richardson: Marriage Lic. (London), ii. 148.
1639. Bapt.—Leah, d. Thomas Atty: St. Dionis Backchurch, p. 106.
1640-1. — Mary, d. Edward Atye: ibid.
'Here lyeth the body of Richard Attyson, late pastor of Clev, who departed 7th Nov. 1659.' Cley, co. Norf.: FF. ix. 379.
1711. Married—William Attey and Frances Parr: St. Jas. Clerkenwell, iii. 233. London, 1.

Atwater, Attwater.—Local, 'at the water'; cf. Bywater, Attwood, Attwell, &c.; v. Waters. This surname, having crossed the Atlantic, is more strongly represented in New York than London.

John Atte Watere, co. Surrey, 20 Edw. I. R.
William Ate Wattere, co. Oxf., 1273 A.
John Ate Water, co. Suff., ibid.
Elias Atewater, co. Camb., ibid.
Thomas atte Watyr, C.R., 4 Hen. V.
1430. Robert atte Watre: Cal. of Wills in Court of Husting. 7. .
1605. Married—Thomas Attwater and Jane Page: St. Antholin (London), p. 43.
Crockford, 1, 0; Philadelphia, 1, 0; Boston (U.S.), 1, 0; New York, 15, 1.

Atwick.—Local, 'at the wick'; v. Wick; cf. Attwood or Attwell.

Geoffrey Attewyk, co. Essex, 1273. A.
Geoffrey Attewyche, co. Essex, ibid.
John Attewich, co. Camb., ibid.
Gervase Att-wyke, rector of Aylmerton, co. Norf., 1379: FF. viii. 82.
1779. Married—Thomas Cotton and Mary Attwick: St. Geo. Han. Sq. i. 304.
— — John Doratt and Elizabeth Atwick: ibid.

Still existing on authority of Lower (1860).

Atworth.—Local, 'of Atworth'; not a compound of 'atte' and 'worth,' but from a parish in dioc. of Sarum.

Geoffrey de Attewurth, co. Wilts, 1273. A.
William de Attewurthe, co. Wilts, ibid.

Aubin.—Bapt. 'the son of Aubin.' I presume a variant of Alban or Albin, q.v.; cf. St. Albyn for St. Alban.

Sarra Aubin, co. Hunts, 1273. A.
William Aubyn, co. Soms , ibid.
Felicia Aubyn, co. Hunts, ibid.
John Aubyn, co. Norf., 2 Edw. III: FF. viii. 461.
William Aubyn, rector of West Walton, co. Norf., 1388: ibid. ix. 141.
1699. Bapt.— Abraham Harev, s. Abraham Aubin: St. Mary Aldermary, p. 113.
London, 1; MDB. (Cambridge), 5; Boston (U.S.), 3.

Aubrey, Aubery, Aubury, Aubreyson.—Bapt. 'the son of Aubrey' (Domesday, Albericus); fem. Albreda, whence ¯Aubrey, both masc. and fem.

Aubri Bunt, co. Camb., 1273. A.
Johannes fil. Aubre, co. Oxf., ibid.
Geoffrey Aubri, co. Camb., ibid.
Richard fil. Albrici, co. Camb., ibid.
Albericus Balister. C.
Albricus le Child. T.
Ralph Aubre, rector of Antingham, co. Norf., 1305: FF. viii. 76.
Robertus Ley, Aubray uxor ejus, 1379: P. T. Yorks. p. 44.
John Aubrayson, C. R., 6 Hen. VI: FF. iii. 165.
John Aubery, or Awberry, or Aubry, sheriff of Norwich, 1460: ib'd. p. 171.
1576. Married—John Awberie and Margaret Walles: St. Mary Aldermary, p. 6.
1695. Charles Gibbon and Frideswid Aubrey: Marriage Lic. (Westminster), p. 47.
1771. Married—John Aubrey and Mary Colebrooke: St. Geo. Han. Sq. i. 206.
London, 4, 0, 1, 0; New York, 1, 1, 0, 0, (Aubry) 7.

Aucher.—Bapt. 'the son of Aucher'; v. Auger.

Auden.—Bapt. 'the son of Aldwin.' The ordinary and natural modification, v. Alden ; cf. Bawden and other forms from Baldwin.

Crockford, 3.

Audley, Audlay.—Local, ' of Audley,' a parish in dioc. Lichfield and co Stafford, formerly Aldithe-ley; Aldith no doubt being the name of the original proprietor; v. Aldith.

Eva de Audley, 45 Edw. III, co. Norf.: FF. x. 424.
Jacob de Aldithelegh, co. Salop, 1273. A.
Henry de Aldithlegh, co. Salop, ibid.
Hugo de Audeleygh, co. Staff., 20 Edw. I. R.
Nicholas de Audeley, co. Salop, ibid.

Robert Awdelye, co. Norf., 34 Hen. VIII: FF. ii. 369.
1674-5. Matthew Audley and Alice Hale: MarriageAlleg.(Canterbury),p. 238.
1780. Married—John Fardell and Ann Audley: St. Geo. Han. Sq. i. 307.
New York, 3, 1.

Audrey.—Bapt. ; v. Awdry.

Audus, Awdas.—Bapt. ' the son of Aldus,' a natural modification ; v. Aldhouse.

1799. Married—William Guntrip and Mary Audass: St. Geo. Han. Sq. ii. 195.
Sheffield, 0, 4; West Riding Court Dir., 2, 0.

Aufrere.—Occup. ' le Orfevre,' the goldsmith ; v. Offer.

Auger, Augier, Augur, Aucher.—Bapt. ' the son of Auger' or ' Aucher,' probably a French form of Oger, whence Odger, q.v. Auger and Aucher are treated as the same name in the Visitation of Essex (1541), pp. 36, 181, 211, 753.

Henry Auger, alias Henry fil. Aucher, co. Camb., 1273. A.
Auger fil. Eudon, co. Salop, ibid.
John fil. Aucheri, co. Camb., ibid.
1581. Nicholas Awger and Elizabeth Russell: Marriage Lic. (London), i. 103.
1674. Buried—Elizabeth Aucher, onely daughter of Sir Antony Aucher, Bart., co. Kent : St. Mary Aldermary (London), p. 189.
London, 1,1,1,0; Boston (U.S.), 6,0,1,0.

August.—Bapt. ' the son of Auguste.' Probably an importation from the Low Countries or France, as I find few traces of the name in England as a font-name, except in the form of Austin, q.v. The Boston (U.S.) Directory has August, Auguste, Augusta, Augustine, and Augustus among its list of surnames ; cf. German August, Fr. Auguste.

1663. Francis August, of Greenwich, and Mary Fisher : Marriage Alleg. (Canterbury), p. 93.
Francis August, 1693 : Reg. St. Mary Aldermary (London), p. 111.
1772. Married—Isaac Augustus and Rebecca Rawlings: St. Geo. Han. Sq.i.221.
London, 2; Boston (U.S.), 4.

Augustine.—Bapt. ' the son of Augustine.' Popularly known in England as Austin, q.v. Augustine is a dim. of August, q.v.

Augustin Acerisis, co. Hunts, 1273. A.
Mariota fil. Augustin, co. Hunts, ibid.
John Augustyn, co. Camb., ibid.

1596. Married—Guilbart Wylkison and Geritrude Augustin : St. Antholin, p. 38.
1613. Bapt.—Thomazin. d. John Augustine : St. Jas. Clerkenwell, i. 67.
1667-8. Nicholas Reeves and Sarah Augustin : Marriage Alleg. (Canterbury), p. 232.
London, 1 ; Boston (U.S.), 1.

Auld, Ault, Aulde.—Nick. ' the old,' a North English form ; v. Ould ; cf. Young, Yonge. The following is curious :—

1608. ' July 7, was delivered unto Christes hospitall a child that was laid at Sir William Paddie's dore, who is named Elizabeth Alde ' : St. Mary Aldermary, p. 70.
1788. Married—John Ault and Mary Williams : St. Geo. Han. Sq. ii. 16.
1805. — George Slemaker and Ann Auld : ibid. p. 333.
— — James Ault and Sarah Poucher : ibid.
London, 2, 0, 0; Manchester, 3, 2, 0; Philadelphia, 7, 2, 1.

Aust, Austen, Austin, Austing, Asten, Astin, Astins.—Bapt. ' the son of Augustine'; O.E. Austin. Very popular in the 13th century.

' Til he foundede freres
of Austynes ordre.'
Piers Plowman, 10193-4.

A whole column of Austin appears in the London Directory. The name was made common by the Austin Friars, or Black Canons, as they were often styled from their black cloaks, who were established early in the 12th century in England, and possessed of about 170 houses. Astin (q.v.), confounded often with the local Aston, was an early form.

Astin de Bennington, co. Linc., 1273. A.
Wilekin fil. Austin. C.
Austin Trim, C. R , 41 Hen. III.
Augustinus Mewhird, 1379 : P. T. Yorks. p. 286.
Willelmus Austyn-man, i. e. servant, 1379 : ibid.
John Austen, or Austyn, or Augustyne, 1538: Reg. Univ. Oxf. i. 190.
1557. Buried—Austin Clark: St. Dionis Backchurch (London).
1570. — Alice, d. of Austyn Pawmer : St. Michael, Cornhill, p. 191.
1777. Married—George Stanser and Ann Aust : St. Geo. Han. Sq. i. 273.
London, 3, 18, 89, 2, 1, 0, 1; New York, 2, 4, 94, 1, 11, 1, 0.

Auty, Awty.—Bapt. ' the son of Auty ' (?). Seemingly an early personal name. A well-known surname in co. York.

Simon Auty et Johanna uxor ejus, 1379: P. T. Yorks. p. 72.

Robertus Auty: ibid. p. 73.

Cecilia Auty: ibid.

George Autie, of Lydiate, 1596: Wills at Chester (1545-1620), p. 8.

1784. Married—John Baldwin and Eliz. Auty: St. Geo. Han. Sq. i. 363.

West Riding Court Dir., 4, 1; Boston (U.S.), 2, 0.

Aveling.—Bapt. 'the son of Aveline'; v. Eveline. The *g* in Aveling is, of course, excrescent, as in Jennings.

Avelina le Gros. J.

Avelina de Leys. J.

Avelina (without surname), co. Suff., 1273. A.

William Aveline, co. Camb., ibid.

Thomas Kyng et Avelyn uxor ejus, 1379: P. T. Yorks. p. 127.

Avelina Batayl, co. Norf., temp. 1430: FF. x. 342.

Andrew Avelyn, rector of Swanton-Morley, co. Norf., 1489: ibid. x. 57.

John Avelyn, vicar of Tibenham, co. Norf., 1503: ibid. v. 278.

Aveline is found both in the 16th and 17th centuries as a font-name.

1575. Tremor Harvye and Aveline Baldwyn · Marriage Lic. (London), i. 66.

1661-2. Samuel Temmatt and Avelin Bateman, co. Berks: Marriage Alley. (Canterbury), p. 66.

1708. Samuel Aveline and Eliz. George-Laroche: Marriage Lic. (London), ii. 337.

London, 3; Boston (U.S.), 2; MDB. (Cambridge), 7.

Avenell, Averell, Averill.—? Bapt. 'the son of Avenel' (?). Always without prefix in the Hundred Rolls, whose instances are generally in the neighbourhood of co. Camb. Mr. Lower suggests a local origin from Avenelles, in the department of Eure. This is quite possible; one thing seems quite certain, the chief modern variant is Averill or Averell. Any one who has studied the corruptions undergone by surnames will feel no surprise at this.

John Avenel, co. Camb., 1273. A.

Ralph Avenel, co. Norf., ibid.

Elena Avenel, co. Oxf., ibid.

1626. Richard Treat and Mary Averill, d. William Averell (sic): Marriage Lic. (London), ii. 178.

1664. Bapt.—Ann, d. George Averill: St. Jas. Clerkenwell, i. 221.

London, 3, 0, 0; Boston (U.S.), 0, 3, 19.

Avener.—Occup. 'the avener.' 'O.F. *avenier*, *avener*, oat-merchant. A chief officer of the stable,

who had charge of the provender for the horses' (H.E.D.).

'The aveyner shall ordeyn provande good won For the lordys horsis everychon.'

1460. Boke of Curtasye, 305.

'To John Redyng, avener, for the expenses of le palfrais, 50*l.*': Materials for History of Reign of Henry VII, p. 407.

Alan le Avener, co. Linc., 1273. A.

Walter le Avener, co. Oxf., ibid.

William le Avenare, co. Oxf., ibid.

Ralph le Avener, 1306. M.

I am afraid the surname is extinct.

Avery, Avory, Auvrey, Averson.—Bapt. 'the son of Avery'; v. Every. Avery is strongly represented in the United States, especially in Boston. This is easily accounted for. Jacob Averie (aged 33) and George Averie (aged 23) sailed for Virginia in 1635. Others of the same name followed. (v. Hotten's Lists of Emigrants, p. 121, and v. Index.)

Hugh fil. Auveray, co. Notts, 1273. A.

Ralph Averey, co. Oxf., ibid.

1541. Ralphe, son of Mr. Averson: St. Peter's, Cornhill, p. 2.

1608. Avere Thompson, co. Cumb., Queen's Coll.: Reg. Univ. Oxf. vol. ii. pt. ii. p. 301.

1609. Married—Mathewe Averson and Eliz. Phillippes: St. Michael, Cornhill, p. 19.

1621.—John Burley and Mary Avarey: Marriage Lic. (London), ii. 102.

1780.—James Avory and Lucy Christmass: St. Geo. Han. Sq. i. 315.

London, 13, 3, 1, 0; Boston (U.S.), 41, 0, 0, 0.

Aves, Avis, Avison.—Bapt. 'the son of Avis,' originally Hawisia or Hawoyse. This very soon settled into Avicia, Avice, or Avis. It was decidedly popular for several centuries, and is just coming into use again, after two hundred years of almost entire neglect. (For history of the name, v. Yonge, ii. 212.) For further instances, v. Haweis.

Eusebius Avice, co. Hunts, 1273. A.

Geoffrey fil. Avice, co. Linc., ibid.

Margaret fil. Avice, co. Camb., ibid.

Avice le Aubergere. H.

Hawisia le Gros. J.

William Avison. ZZ.

1590. Bapt.—Avis, d. Philip Cliff: Stepney Parish Church, London.

1600. — Avice, d. Thomas Bennett: Reg. St. Columb Major, Cornwall.

1601. Buried—Margery Avison: St. Peter's, Cornhill, p. 151.

1622. Samuel Avis and Eliz. Lenton: Marriage Lic. (London), i. 118.

1773. Married—George Plumley and Dorothy Avis: St. Geo. Han. Sq. i. 231.

1778. — William Aves and Mary Schooling: ibid. p. 288.

London, 5, 7, 0; Philadelphia, 0, 1, 3.

Awdrey, Awdry, Audrey.—Bapt. 'the son of Etheldreda,' popularly Awdry. St. Awdry's Fair is held on Oct. 17, at the Isle of Ely. Its St. Awdry necklaces, showy but cheap, gave rise to the term 'tawdry-lace,' whence adj. tawdry; v. Skeat.

Etheldreda le Ray, C.R., 27 Edw. III, pt. 1.

Etheldreda Plote, co. Camb., 1273. A.

Audrey Bendish, co. Norf.: FF. viii. 188.

Awdrie Butts, temp. Eliz. Z.

1567. Bapt.—Audrye Chatterton: St. Michael, Cornhill.

1579. Married—George Burton and Joane Awdry: St. Antholin (London), p. 27.

1610. Bapt.—Awdrey, d. John Cooke, butcher: St. Dionis Backchurch (London).

1624-5. Thomas White and Audrey, alias Etheldred Annie; Marriage Lic. (London), ii. 149.

Awdry Almond, 1635: Hotten's Lists of Emigrants, p. 93.

Awdie Bullinghame (fem.), 1636: St. Mary Aldermary (London), p. 18.

1737. Buried—Audry, wife of Thomas Amyas, surgeon: St. Andrew the Apostle (Norwich): FF. iv. 311.

1768. Married—Rowland Hopkins and Audery Stevens: St. Geo. Han. Sq. i. 182.

London, 0, 0, 0; Crockford, 0, 5, 0.

Awre.—Local, 'of Awre,' a parish in co. Glouc.

Robert de Awre held Awre and Box, co. Glouc., 55 Hen. III: Atkyn's Hist. Glouc., p. 122.

Walter de Awre, co. Glouc., 1 Edw. I: ibid. MDB. (co. Glouc.), 1.

Axon.—Bapt. 'the son of——' (?). This Lancashire and Cheshire surname has clearly no connexion with Axton (q.v.). It is a patronymic formed like Jaxon, Dixon, Dix, or Cox, which represent Jackson, Dickson, Dicks, or Cocks. I can but suggest that it is Atkinson, which in my part of Lancashire (Furness) is invariably pronounced Atkison or Akison; v. Atkinson.

Thomas Acson, of Knottysforth, in Cheshire, 1561: Wills at Chester (1545-1620), p. 1.

John Acson, of Leftwick, 1585: ibid.

John Ackson, of Leftwich, *yeoman*, 1641: ibid. (1621-1650), p. 1.

Thomas Axon, of Ashton-under-Lyne, *husbandman*, 1635: ibid. p. 10.

1581. Bapt.—Ellen Ackeson: Prestbury Ch. (co. Chester), p. 68.

1602. William Acson, co. Ches.: Reg. Univ. Oxf. vol. ii. pt. ii. p. 256

1616. Married—Ralph Houghton and Anna Axon : Prestbury Ch. (co. Chester), p. 210.
London, 1 ; Manchester, 4 ; Philadelphia, 1.

Axtell.—? Bapt. 'the son of Axell' (?) ; probably a variant.
Ralph Axcil, co. Soms, 1 Edw III : Kirby's Quest, p. 100.
1683. Joseph Collyer and Eliz. Axtell : Marriage Alleg. (Canterbury), p. 128.
1686. John Axstell and Mary Drew : ibid. p. 249.
1690. Married — Richard Axtill and Susanna Belt : St. Jas. Clerkenwell, iii. 209.
London, 4.

Axton, Axten, Axon.— Local, 'of Axton.' A hundred in co. Kent. Axon in the south of England seems to be but a lazy corruption. The following entries (1557-77) manifestly refer to the same family :—
1557. Married — Lawrence Axson and Margaret Tipper : St. Peter's, Cornhill, p. 15.
1561. Bapt.—Lawrence Axtoune : ibid. p. 124.
1562. Buried—Lawraunce Axton : ibid. p. 115.
1572. Bapt.—Margery, d. of Lawrence Axon : ibid. p. 223.
1577. Buried—Lawrence Axsoune, merchant taylor : ibid. p. 9.
1630. Bapt.—Everelda, d. Robert Axon : St. Jas. Clerkenwell, i. 116.
1642. — Charles, s. John Axton : ibid. i. 152.
London, 2, 2, 1 ; Manchester, 0, 0, 4 ; Philadelphia, 0, 0, 1.

Aylen, Ayling, Aylin.—Bapt. 'the son of Aylwin,' q.v. Compounds of *win* always corrupt to *in*, *en*, and *ing* ; v. Golden and Golding for Goldwin. The *g* in Ayling is, of course, excrescent ; cf. Jennings.
Ayelyne Algar, co. Camb., 1273. A.
Adam Aylyne, co. Camb., ibid.
Richard Ayline, co. Hunts, ibid.
Thomas Ailwine, co. Oxf., ibid.
1621. Bapt.—Blaize, s. Nicholas Ayleing : St. Jas. Clerkenwell, i. 90.
1769. Married — George Waldie and Ann Ayling : St. Geo. Han. Sq. i. 183.
MDB. (co. Essex), 1, 0, 1 ; London, 2, 11, 0 ; Boston (U.S.), 0, 1, 0 ; New York, 0, 2, 0.

Aylett, Ayllett, Aylott.— Bapt. 'the son of Ailet.' This is the Domesday form of the personal name (Lower). For other forms, v. Allott.
Walter Aylet, co. Camb., 1273. A.
Katerine Ayllyht, co. Camb., ibid.

John Ayllyth, co. Camb., ibid.
William Allot, co. Camb., ibid.
1628. Thomas Westbrook and Joane Aylet : Marriage Lic. (London), ii. 194.
1653. Bapt.—Charles, s. Edward Allett : St. Jas. Clerkenwell, i. 185.
1739. Married — George Turner and Eliz. Aylett : St. Dionis Backchurch, p. 67.
London, 9, 1, 4 ; Boston (U.S.), 0, 0, 1.

Ayliffe, Aylieff.—Bapt. 'the son of Ailof.' In Domesday.
Ailef de Palestu, 1176 : KKK. p. 25.
Eilaf fil. Gospatric, 1166 : ibid. p. 10.
Arnaed Fitz-Aluf, sheriff of London, 1198 : WWW.
Robertus Haylyf, 1379 : P. T. Yorks. p. 157.
Aliff White (masc.), 1648 : Reg. St. Jas. Clerkenwell, p. 171.
John Aliff, 1645 : ibid. p. 161.
Thomas Ayloffe, co. Essex, c. 1500 : FF. v. 325.
1698. Katherine, d. of Thomas Ayloffe : St. Peter's, Cornhill, ii. p. 21.
1702. Bapt.—Elizabeth, d. of Thomas Ayloffe : St. John Baptist on Wallbrook (London), p. 174.
1783. Married — William Ayliffe and Frances Weston : St. Geo. Han. Sq. i. 344.
London, 3, 1.

Aylmer, Aymer, Aymar.— Bapt. 'the son of Aylmar' or 'Ailmar.' Several instances occur in Domesday ; v. Amery. A common surname in the Hundred Rolls. It was already going out of fashion in the 13th century as a font-name, and is rarely found as such in the 14th century, but it secured hereditary honours as a surname somewhat early, and as a consequence is well represented in our directories. The *l* is usually elided in the United States, but this occurred so early as the 13th century.
Aymar Hitche, co. Hunts, 1273. A.
Adam Aylmer, co. Camb., ibid.
William Aylmar, co. Oxf., ibid.
Avice Ailmar, co. Camb., ibid.
John Aylmere, rector of Ingworth, co. Norf., 1353 : FF. vi. 368.
Thomas Ailmer, co. Soms., 1 Edw. III : Kirby's Quest, p. 129.
1616. Married — Henry Cartwrit and Ann Ailmer : St. Antholin (London), p. 52.
1607. Justinian Aylmer and Catherine Faulkner : Marriage Lic. (London), ii. 323.
London, 2, 0, 0 ; Boston (U.S.), 0, 0, 3 ; New York, 0, 0, 5 ; Philadelphia 1, 0, 0.

Aylward, Aylard. — Bapt. 'the son of Aylward' ; v. Allard.
Aylward Oldcorn. L.
Bernard Aylward, co. Wilts, 1273. A.
Beatrix Aylward, co. Bucks, ibid.
Alan Alward, co. Camb., ibid.

This last variant (common in the

Hundred Rolls) led on to Allard, q.v.
Simon fil. Aylward, co. Lanc., 20 Edw. I. R.
John Ayleward, Norwich, 1325 : FF. iv. 477.
Hamond Ayleward, vicar of Swardeston, co. Norf., 1376 : ibid. v. 52.
Nicholas Alyward, co. Soms., 1 Edw. III : Kirby's Quest, p. 179.
1691. Bapt.—William, s. William Ayleward : St. Jas. Clerkenwell, i. 343.
1705. Buried — Thomas Aylward : St. Dionis Backchurch, p. 274.
London, 2, 1 ; Boston (U.S.), 12, 0.

Aylwin, Alwin, Alwine, Alwyne.—Bapt. 'the son of Aylwin' ; v. Aylen.
Richard Alewyn, co. Wilts, Hen. III- Edw. I. K.
Alewyn (without surname), co. Norf., 1273. A.
Alwyne Tyche, co. Camb., ibid.
Robert Aylwyne, co. Camb., ibid.
Emma Aylwyne, co. Hunts, ibid.
Reginald Ailwyne, co. Camb., ibid.
Richard Aylewyn, rector of Dickleburgh, co. Norf., 1394 : FF. i. 194.
1666. Thomas Aylwyn and Mary Hunt : Marriage Alleg. (Canterbury), p. 125.
1769. Married — William Aylwin and Mary Wright : St. Geo. Han. Sq. i. 189.
London, 1, 1, 0, 0 ; Philadelphia, 0, 1, 1, 1.

Aynsley ; v. Ainsley.

Ayre, Ayer.—Official or nick. 'the heir.' It is curious to note that while Ayre is the almost universal English form (saving Eyre), Ayer is equally universal in the United States. For early and other instances, v. Ayres and Eyre.
Roger le Hayre, or Eyre, or Ayer, co. Norf., 1264 : FF. v. 310.
1583. Humphrey Mercer and Katherine Ayer : Marriage Lic. (London), i. 118.
1757. Married—Francis Lee and Ann Ayre : St. Geo. Han. Sq. i. 74.
London, 2, 0 ; Boston (U.S.), 0, 49.

Ayres, Ayars, Ayers, Ayris, Ayrs.—Nick. 'the son of the heir.' No doubt a variant of Ayre or Eyre, q.v., with the patronymic *s* suffixed, as in Jones, Simmons, Roberts, &c. Therefore literally 'the son of the heir.' My first instance seems to set the matter at rest.
John fil. Aer, co. Salop, 1273. A.
Henry Ayer, co. Linc., ibid.
'This year (1510) was Thomas Ayers, priest, of Norwich, burnt at Eccles' : FF. iii. 193.
1582. John Ayer and Alice Moyle : Marriage Lic. (London), i. 111.

1610. Hugh Jones and Eliz. Ayres: Marriage Lic. (London), p. 325.
1724. Married—Richard Ayars of St. Alpage: St. Antholin (London), p. 139.

Several families of Ayres or Aires went out to America in the 17th century, which fact accounts for its familiar recurrence in the United States; v. index, Hotten's Lists of Emigrants.

MDB. (co. Norfolk), 6, 4, 0, 1, 0; London, 25, 6, 0, 1, 1; Boston (U.S.), 7, 0, 30, 0, 0.

Ayrton.—Local, 'of Airton,' a township in the parish of Kirkby-in-Malham-Sale, near Settle, West Rid. Yorks.

Nicholaus de Ayrton, 1379: P. T. Yorks. p. 206.
Willelmus de Ayreton: ibid. p. 271.
1662. John Bond and Margery Ayrton: Marriage Alleg. (Canterbury), p. 50.
1797. Married—John Barlow and Charlotte Ayrton: St. Geo. Han. Sq. ii. 172.
1805. — William Garrott and Ellen Ayreton: ibid. p. 336.
London, 2.

Aysh, Ayshford.—Local; v. Ash and Ashford. These seem to be Devonshire variants; cf. Ric. de Ayswell (Ashwell) or Philip de Ayston (Ashton), 1273. A (index).

1627. Thomas Aysshe and Katherine Sheppard: Marriage Lic. (London), ii. 194.
1663. Thomas Sayward and Mary Gold. Alleged by Thomas Aysshe: Marriage Alleg. (Canterbury), p. 89.
1704. Robert Barker and Eliz. Aishe: Marriage Lic. (London), ii. 332.
London, 0, 2.

B

Baalham, Balam.—Local, 'of Baylham,' a parish two miles and a half from Needham, Market, co. Suffolk. The surname is evidently imitative of Baalam.

1577. Edward Ballam, co. Bucks: Reg. Univ. Oxf. vol. ii. pt. ii. p. 78.
1613. Richard Balam: ibid. p. 329.
Robert Balam, rector of Walsoken, co. Norf., 1635; FF. ix. 129.
'Juxta deponuntur Anna, uxor prima Jacobi Verdon, A. M., filia Gulielmi Balam, armigeri, 13 dic Februarii, 1684.' East Dereham, co. Norf.: ibid. x. 214.
Alexander Balam, co. Norf., 21 Eliz.: ibid. ix. 131.
1684. Anthony Balaam and Matilda Vernon: Marriage Alleg. (Canterbury), p. 175.
1731. William Tuffnell and Mary Balam: Marriage Lic. (Faculty Office), p. 252.
London, 2, 0; Philadelphia, 0, 5.

Babb, Babbs.—Bapt. 'the son of Barbara,' from the nick. Babb. Barbara was extremely popular in the 13th and 14th centuries; v. Barbot.

Walter Babbe, co. Soms., 1 Edw. III: Kirby's Quest, p. 147.
1259. Nicholas Bab: Cal. of Wills in Court of Husting.
Berthol Babbe, co. Hunts, 1273. A.
John Babbe, co. Wilts, ibid.
William Babbe, co. Oxf., ibid.
1553. Married—Richard Babh and Eliz. Tomson: Kensington Church, p. 59.
1558. — John Baldyn and Eliz. Babbs: ibid.
1596. John Babb, co. Linc.: Reg. Univ. Oxf., vol. ii. pt. ii. p. 216.
1757. Married—Walter Shropshire and Catherine Babb: St. Geo. Han. Sq. i. 73.
1765. — George Solden and Elizabeth Babbs: ibid. p. 143.
Crockford, 1, 0; London, 1, 3; Philadelphia, 12, 0.

Babbage, Babbidge, Babidge.—Local, 'of Babbage.' Probably some local name with the same prefix as Babbacombe, co. Devon, from which district the family are sprung.

1754. Buried — Edmund Babbige: St. Mary Aldermary, p. 229.
1792. Married—Benjamin Babbage and Betty Plumleigh Teape: St. Geo. Han. Sq. i. 84.
Charles Babbage (1792-1871), the inventor of calculating machines, was born near Teignmouth, in co. Devon': Dict. Nat. Biog. ii. 304.
London, 2, 2, 1; South Molton, co. Devon, 1, 0, 0; List of Farmers (Devonshire Dir.), 6, 0, 0; Boston (U.S.), 1, 5, 0.

Babelot.—Bapt. 'the son of Barbara'; v. Barbot.

Baber.—Local, 'of Baber.' Mr. Lower derives it from the Hundred of Babergh, co. Suffolk. But in the Cornwall Directory occurs a place called Baber, seemingly the same as St. Dominick. Baber is a familiar Devon and Cornwall surname.

Henry Babre, co. Camb., 1273. A.
1570. Bapt. — Alice, d. of Edward Baber: St. Jas. Clerkenwell, i. 6.
1582. Francis Baber, London: Reg. Univ. Oxf. vol. ii. pt. ii. p. 118.
1601. Married—John Baber and Jane Whitlocke: St. Michael, Cornhill, p. 17.
1608. John Baber, co. Soms.: Reg. Univ. Oxf. vol. ii. pt. ii. p. 300.
1621. Edward Baber, co. Soms.: ibid. p. 392.
1757. Married—Noah Baber and Susan Monk: St. Geo. Han. Sq. i. 73.
Crockford, 3; London, 10; New York, 1.

Babington.—Local, 'of Bab-

ington,' a parish in co. Somerset, five or six miles from Frome. Also hamlets, Great and Little Babington, near Hexham, co. Northumberland.

Hugh de Babintone, co. Derby, 1273. A.
Robert de Babington, co. Linc., ibid.
Richard de Babington Magna, co. Northumb., ibid.
William de Babynton, co. Northumb., 1340: KKK. vol. vi. p. xxxviii.
Henricus de Babbyngton, 1379: P. T. Yorks. p. 33.
1576. John Babington, co. Notts: Reg. Univ. Oxf. vol ii. pt. ii. p. 71.
1597. Henry Babington, co. Oxf.: ibid. p. 220.
'Anthony Babington (1561-86), leader of a Catholic conspiracy against Queen Elizabeth, ... descended from John de Babington ... owner of the district round Mickle and Little Babington, or Bavington, co. Northumberland': Dict. Nat. Biog. ii. 308.

The writer adds that branches of this family settled in cos. Derby and Leicester. From the latter Macaulay took his second name.

London, 3; Crockford, 10; New York, 3.

Bacheller, Bachelder.—Official, 'the bachelor'; v. Batchelar and Batchelder.

Jordan le Bachiler, co. Oxf., 1273. A.
Robert Bachelere, co. Wilts, ibid.
1583. Edmund Bachelor and Eliz. Swinson: Marriage Lic. (London), i. 126.
1600. William Bachiler, co. Worc.: Reg. Univ. Oxf. vol. ii. pt. ii. p. 243.
1610. Stephen Bachiler, co. Hants: ibid. p. 317.
Boston (U.S.), 9, 25.

Back, Backe.—(1) Local, 'at the back,' i.e. one who resided in a cottage lying behind some others.

(2) —— ? In the Eastern Counties Back seems to correspond with the German Bache.

John atte Back, co. Soms., 1 Edw. III : Kirby's Quest, p. 172.
1562-3. Richard Mothe and Beatrice Backe : Marriage Lic. (London), i. 25.
'Robert Bache, of Diss, co. Norf., husbandman,' Dec. 23, 1594 : Cal. State Papers (Domestic), iii. 569.
1754. Married — Edward Back and Alice Fowler : St. Geo. Chap. Mayfair, p. 277.
London, 10, 0 ; Philadelphia, 3, 3.

Backer.—Occup. 'the baker,' q.v. ; cf. Backhouse and Baxter.

'To . . . the backers wyffe, for v. mennes borde' : 1466, Mann. and Househ. Exp. 211 (H.E.D.).
1547. James Bacar and Hungerford (sic) : Marriage Lic. (Faculty Office), p. 11.
Edward Baccar, Aug. 20, 1591 : Cal. State Papers (Domestic), iii. 95.
London, 2 ; Philadelphia, 4.

Backhouse, Bacchus, Backus.—Local, 'at the bake-house,' from residence therein. 'Bakehowse, or bakynge house : *pistrina* :' Prompt. Parv. Halliwell mistakenly makes it a back-house, or wash-house (v. Backas, i. 130).

1502. Arnold, Chron. 93, 'Ye shal kepe noo bachous' (H.E.D.).
Willian atte Bakehous, co. Soms., 1 Edw. III : Kirby's Quest, p. 208.
Nicholas atte Bakhouse, co. Soms., ibid. p. 89.
Edmund atte Bakhus, 1307. M.
Thomas Bacchus. ZZ.

With Bacchus (imitative), cf. Kirkus (Church-house), Malthus (Malt-house), or Loftus (Loft-house).

Thomas del Bakhouse, 1379 : P. T. Yorks. p. 203.
William del Bakeus, 1379 : ibid. p. 78.
William Backhowse or Bacchus, secular chaplain, 1538 : Reg. Univ. Oxf. i. 192.
1571. George Backhouse and Ann Meryton : Marriage Lic. (London), i. 51.
1753. Bapt. — John Baccus, an adult : St. Geo. Chap. Mayfair, p. 11.
London, 8, 0, 0 ; Crockford, 1, 0, 0 ; West Riding Court Dir., 8, 2, 0 ; Philadelphia, 0, 0, 9.

Backler.—Official, 'the bachelor' ; v. Batchelor and Blackler.

Nicholas le Bakclere, C. R., 13 Edw. II.
1641. Bapt. — William, s. of George Backler : St. Thomas the Apostle (London), p. 54.
1808. Married — William Chitty and Eliz. Backler : St. Geo. Han. Sq. ii. 394.
London, 2.

Backster, Bagster, Baxter.—Occup. 'the bakester,' a baker of bread, with the feminine suffix ; originally a woman's occupation. Langland speaks of

'Baksteres and brewesteres,
And bochiers manye.'

'Baxter, bakstare, baker' : Prompt. Parv. p. 21.

Backster is one of the names in Foxe's list of Marian martyrs. The ordinances of the Guild of the Purification (Bishop's Lynn, 1367), are signed by 'Johannes Austyn, *baxter*' (English Guilds, p. 90). Capgrave says, 'In this same tyme (B. C. 205) lyved the eloquent man which hite (was called) Plautus, and for al his eloquens he was compelled for to dwell with a baxter, and grind his corne at a querne.'

Giliana le Bacster, co. Hunts, 1273. A.
John le Bakestere, co. Norf., ibid.
Elias le Baxtere, 1302. M.
Bartholomew le Bakestere. B.
Andrew le Bakester. G.
Agnes le Bakester, 1379 : P. T. Yorks. p. 197.
Cecilia Bakester, vidua, ibid. p. 42.
William Mytton, *backester*, co. York, 1430 : W. 11.
Patrick Adamson (1537-92), a Scotch prelate. 'His enemies taunted him with being a bakers son, "ane baxter's sone"' : Dict. Nat. Biog. i. 111.
Thomas Smith, *backster*, 1622 : Preston Guild Rolls, p. 73.
London, 0, 2, 56 ; New York (Backster), 1 ; Philadelphia, 0, 0, 99.

Bacon.—Nick. 'the Bacon,' a swineherd's sobriquet (?). A very common nick. in the Hundred Rolls ; cf. Pigg, Wildbore, Hogg, affording proof that Bacon may have been used of a live pig originally.

John le Bacon. T.
Cecilia Bacun, co. Norf., 1273. A.
Wymer Bacon, co. Suff., ibid.
Simon Bacon, co. Oxf., ibid.
Walterus Bacun, 1379 : P. T. Yorks. p. 101.
Thomas Bacon, 1379 : ibid. p. 34.
1546. Humphrey Luce and Ann Bacon : Marriage Lic. (London), i. 9.
1576. Matthias Bacon, London : Reg. Univ. Oxf. vol. ii. pt. ii. p. 70.
London, 63 ; Philadelphia, 78.

Badams.—Bapt. 'the son of Adam' ; Welsh, Ap-Adam, equivalent to English Adamson ; cf.

Bowen, Bevan, Bevans, Bethell, &c.

Thomas Apadam, co. Soms., 1 Edw. III : Kirby's Quest, p. 94.
John Abbadam, Bristol, 27 Edw. I. BBB.
John ap Adam, 24 Edw. I, ibid.
1597. Married — John Hunter and Mary Baddam : Kensington Ch., p. 64.
1623. Thomas Batt and Mary Baddam : Marriage Lic. (London), ii. 129.
1630. Bapt. — Phillip, s. William Baddams : St. Jas. Clerkenwell, i. 116.
Liverpool, 1.

Badcock, Batcock.—Bapt. 'the son of Bartholomew,' from nick. Bat or Bate, and suffix -cock ; v. Cock ; cf. Wilcock, Jeffcock, &c.

Geoffrey Batecok, London, 1273. A.
William Badecok, co. Camb., ibid.
Robert Batecoc, co. Oxf., ibid.
Roger Badecok, 1306. M.
Stephen Badcok, co. Soms., 1 Edw. III : Kirby's Quest, p. 88.
Badokok Jerveys, co. Soms., ibid.
1563. Buried — Vincent Badcooke : St. Peter, Cornhill, i. 117.
1609. Married — John Forwood to Briget Bedcocke : St. Thomas the Apostle (London), p. 11.
1611. — John Fell and Margerie Badcock : St. Peter, Cornhill, i. 247.
Crockford, 3, 0 ; London, 6, 1.

Baddeley, Baddiley.—Local, 'of Baddiley,' a parish in co. Chester, near Nantwich. Also 'of Badley,' a parish in co. Norfolk.

William de Badeleye, co. Essex, 1273. A.
Geoffrey de Badele, co. Suff., ibid.
Robert de Badele, co. Norf., Hen. III-Edw. I. K.
1608-9. William Badeley and Sarah Rathbone : Marriage Lic. (London), i. 310.

An unhappy corruption, of the imitative class, occurs in the following entry :—

1702. Married — James Page and Jane Badly : St. Antholin (London), p. 116.
London, 10, 2 ; Boston (U.S.), 1, 0.

Badger, Bagger.—Occup. 'the badger,' a hawker, a dealer in corn and other commodities, buying in one place to sell in another.

Thomas le Baggere, co. Oxf., 1273. A.
Robert le Bagger, co. Lanc., 1332 : Lay Subsidy (Rylands).
Willelmus Bagger, 1379 : P. T. Yorks. p. 109.
Ricardus Badger, 1379 : ibid. p. 128.
John le Baggere, C. R., 27 Edw. I.
1573. Roland Badger, co. Worc. : Reg. Univ. Oxf. vol. ii. pt. ii. p. 55.
1605. Bapt. — William, s. John Bagger : St. Thomas the Apostle (London), p. 38.

Rotherham·Dir., 4, 0; London, 7, 0; Crockford, 4, 0; West Rid. Court Dir., 7, 0; Boston (U.S.), 33, 0; New York, 3, 1.

Badkin.—Bapt. 'the son of Bartholomew,' from nick. Bate or Bat, and dim. Batkin; cf. Wilkin, Watkin, &c.; v. Badcock.

Batekyn Clericus, co. Essex, 1273. A.
Batekin Lahan, co. Essex, ibid.
1779. Married — William Allen and Hannah Battkin : St. Geo. Han. Sq. i. 298. London, 2.

Badnall; v. Bagnall.

Bagg, Bagge, Baggs, Back, Backe.—Bapt. 'the son of Bagg.' This surname occurs frequently in early rolls, and always without prefix. There seems no reason to doubt its being a Scandinavian personal name. This is confirmed by the dim. Bagelyn (cf. Hewling) and by the entry Bagekoc, where the suffix -cock occurs, which is only added to font-names; v. Introd. p. 26.

William Bage, co. Camb., 1273. A.
Henry Bagekoc, co. Camb., ibid.
Cattle (i. e. Ketel) Bagge, co. Camb., ibid.
Robert Bagge, co. Bucks, ibid.
Helias Bag', 1379: P. T. Yorks. p. 158.
Robertus Bag', 1379: ibid.
Willelmus Bag', 1379: ibid
Walter Bagg, co. Soms., 1 Edw. III: Kirby's Quest, p. 125.
William Bagelyn, co. Soms., ibid. p. 167.

In this same record we find Bagshay, i.e. 'the hedged enclosure,' belonging to Bagg.

Walter Baggesheyghe, ibid. p. 169.
London, 4, 0, 1, 12, 0; Crockford, 0, 1, 0, 4, 0; New York, 2, 0, 3, 15, 2.

Bagger.—Occup.; v. Badger.

Bagley.—(1) Local, 'of Bagley.' Bagley Wood is an extra-parochial liberty near Abingdon, co. Berks. (2) For a second parentage, v. Baguley.

Tholomeo de Baggeleyhe, co. Soms., 1 Edw. III : Kirby's Quest, p. 277.
1576. Thomas Bagley and Eliz. Hadwyn : Marriage Lic. (London), i. 72.
1581. Buried—Agnes, wife of Nicholas Bagley : St. Jas. Clerkenwell, iv. 85.
1642. — Humfry Bagly : ibid. p. 253.
London, 5; Philadelphia, 9.

Bagnall, Badnall, Bagnell.—Local, 'of Bagnall,' a chapelry in the parish of Stoke-upon-Trent, in the co. of Stafford. Badnall is

a modern corruption. Both forms are familiar in the county.

1578. Humfrey Bagnoll and Alice Hudson : Marriage Lic. (London), i. 80.
1584. Robert Bagnald, co. Staff. : Reg. Univ. Oxf. vol. ii. pt. ii. p. 139.
1597. Nicholas Bagenall, co. Carn. : ibid. p. 222.
1599. Ralph Bagnall, co. Worc. : ibid. p. 234.
1604. Married — Richard Morer and Ellen Bagnall : St. Michael, Cornhill, p. 17.
1753. — Francis Bagnell and Eliz. Dickerson : St. Geo. Chap. Mayfair, p. 237.
London, 2, 1, 0; MDB. (Stafford), 20, 3, 0; Boston (U.S.), 3, 0, 0; Philadelphia, 0, 0, 5.

Bagridge.—Local, 'of Bagridge.' The Hundred Rolls mention a place called Baggeriggestrete, co. Dorset (A. i. 102).

Walter de Baggerigg, co. Dorset, 1273. A.
Cristian Baggerig, co. Dorset, ibid.
Amice Baggerig, co. Dorset, ibid.
London, 2.

Bagshaw, Bagshawe.—Local, 'of Bagshawe.' I cannot find the spot. Probably 'the shaw of Bagg,' the first settler; v. Bagg and Shaw.

Oliver de Bogeschaghe, co. Soms., 1 Edw. III : Kirby's Quest, p. 216.
Richard de Boggeschaghe, co. Soms., ibid.
Nicholaus de Bagschaghe, 1379 : P. T. Yorks. p. 42.
Nicholas Bagshawe, temp. Eliz. Z.
Humphry Bagshawe, temp. Eliz. ZZ.
1563. Married— Richard Warren and Elenor Bagshawe : St. Thomas the Apostle (London), p. 3.
1604. Edward Bageshaw, London : Reg. Univ. Oxf. vol. ii. pt. ii. p. 278.
Sheffield, 13, 2; London, 3, 5; Philadelphia, 3, 0.

Bagster.—Occup. 'the baxter'; v. Backster.

Baguley, Bagley, Baggallay, Baggaley, Baggerley.—Local, 'of Baguley,' a township near Northenden, co. Chester. The Manchester Directory has Bagoley and Baggoley; v. Bagley.

Henry de Bageleg', cos. Salop and Staff., Hen. III–Edw. I. K.
William de Baggilegh, 1318 : Earwaker's, East Ches. ii. 156.
Hamo de Baggelegh, 1352 : ibid. ii. 234.
Johannes de Bagley, 1379 : P. T. Yorks. p. 63
William de Baggiley, mayor of Stockport, 1382: Earwaker's East Ches. i. 346.
1589-0. Thomas Baguley and Katherine Aufen : Marriage Lic. (London), i. 185.

1597. William Denby and Johane Baggalea : ibid. i. 242.
Thomas Baguley, 1622, Heaton Norris : Lanc. and Ches. Rec. Soc. xii. 152.
Manchester, 3, 2, 0, 0, 0; London, 2, 5, 4, 3, 1; Boston (U.S.), 2, 34, 0, 0, 0.

Bailey, Baillie, Baily, Baily, Bayley, Baylie, Bayly, Baylis, Bayliss, Bayles, Bayless.—Offic. 'the bailie,' i.e. bailiff. The same forms, or nearly all, may be seen in H.E.D. (v. Bailie); 'now obsolete in England, but retained in a special sense in Scotland'). O.F. bailli (13th cent.), later form of baillis (H.E.D.). Hence Baylis, Bayliss, &c.; cf. Jolly and Jolliffe.

'Artow than a bayely?' 'Ye,' quod he. —Chaucer, Freres Tale, 92 (quoted in H.E.D.).
Roger le Baillif, co. Soms., 1 Edw. III : Kirby's Quest, p. 248.
Richard le Bailiff, C. R., 7 Edw. I.
Alvered Ballivus, co. Linc., 1273. A.
Henry Baily, co. Oxf., ibid.
William Bailif, co. Oxf., ibid.
Seman le Baylif. J.
Henry le Baillie, 1307. M.
Richard le Baylif, co. Heref., Hen. III–Edw. I. K.
Adam Ballef, 1379 : P. T. Yorks. p. 197.
London, 135, 3, 1, 14, 29, 1, 5, 26, 6, 2, 1; Philadelphia, 216, 2, 0, 16, 14, 9, 2, 4, 1, 5, 0.

Bainbridge, Bambridge, Bainbrigge.—Local, 'of Bainbridge,' a township in the parish of Aysgarth, N. Rid. Yorks. This surname has spread widely, and ramified strongly.

Rogerus de Baynbryg, 1379: P. T. Yorks. p. 288.
'Christopher Bainbridge (1464 ?-1514), archbishop of York, born at Hilton, near Appleby, co. Westm.' : Dict. Nat. Biog. ii. 433.
'Thomas Bainbrigg, master of Christ's College, Camb. (1620-1646), "descended out of the North"' : ibid. p. 445.
'Reginald Baynbridge or Bainbrigg (1545-1606), schoolmaster and antiquary, born probably in Westmoreland' : ibid. p. 434.
London, 11, 1, 1; West Riding Court Dir., 2, 0, 0; Philadelphia, 17, 0, 0.

Baines, Baynes, Bains.—Local, 'of Baines,' some spot in co. York(?). Lower says 'a village near Bayeux in Normandy, probably so called from bain, a bath' (p. 16).

Henry de Bayns, co. Linc., 1273. A.
John de Bayns, co. Linc., ibid.

John de Bayns, co. Staff., Hen. III–Edw. I. K.

Suspirius de Bayons, C.R., 20 Edw. I.

Thomas de Baines, 1379 : P. T. Yorks. p. 48.

1577. Bapt. — Franunces, d. Richard Baines : St. Peter's, Cornhill, i. 18.

West Riding Court Dir., 17, 3, 0 ; London, 17, 9, 0 ; Philadelphia, 7, 0, 10 ; New York (Baynes), 1.

Baker.—Occup. 'the baker'; v. Backster and Baxter.

Walter le Baker, co. Devon, 1273. A.

William le Bakere, co. Oxf., ibid.

Alan le Baker, co. Sussex, ibid.

John le Baker, co. Soms., 1 Edw. III : Kirby's Quest, p. 219.

Roger le Baker, co. Soms., ibid. p. 220.

1555. Bapt. — Jane Baker : St. Peter, Cornhill, i. 7.

London, 272 ; Philadelphia, 420.

Balancer.—Occup. 'the balancer,' a maker of balances or weighing machines. 'Weighed in the balances,' Dan. v. 27. F. *balance*, 'a ballance, a pair of weights, or ballances,' Cotg. Cocke Lorelle's Bote includes—

'Aroweheders, maltermen, and cornemongers,

Balancers, tynne-casters, and skryveners.'

Ralph le Balancer, Liberate Roll, 15 Edw. II. He was sheriff of London in 1316.

Rauf le Balancer. M.

Radulf le Balauncer. N.

John Balauncer. G.

Ralph le Balauncer, London, 20 Edw. I. R.

Balch.—? Bapt. 'the son of Balch.' Mr. Lower suggests that this is an abbreviation of Balchin. I should rather say it was the parent ; v. Balchin.

Robert Balch, co. Soms., 1 Edw. III : Kirby's Quest, p. 252.

1604. John Balche : Reg. Univ. Oxf. i. 400.

1659. Buried—Mary, d. John Balch : St. Jas. Clerkenwell, i. 328.

London, 5 ; MDB. (co. Soms.), 4 ; Philadelphia, 3.

Balchin.—Bapt. 'the son of Baldwin,' from nick. Ball (q.v.) and suffix -*kin* ; cf. Wilkin, Tompkin, &c. Balchin is a Dutch form. Lower says the fuller form Baldechin is a German surname. We may gather from the want of early instances that this is a name more recently introduced from the continent.

1721. Bapt.—Mary, d. Richard Baulchin : St. Mary Aldermary, p. 122.

1753. Married—William Dean and Mary Balchin : St. Geo. Chap. Mayfair, p. 236.

London, 4.

Balcock.—Bapt. 'the son of Baldwin,' from the nick. Ball (q.v.) with suffix -*cock* (v. Introd. p. 26); cf. Wilcock, &c. This has become corrupted to Bawcock, an ordinary corruption; cf. Shallcross and Shawcross.

Alan Balkok, co. Hunts, 1273. A.

Geoffrey Balcok, co. York, ibid.

Johannes Balkok, 1379 : P. T. Yorks. p. 43.

Ibbot Bolkok, 1379 : ibid.

Robertus Balcok, 1379 : ibid. p. 138.

1627. Married—Richard Foge and Sara Bawcoke : St. Mary Aldermary (London), p. 16.

Still exists according to Lower.

Baldbody.—Nick. equivalent to Ballard, q.v.; cf. Freebody, Goodbody, Handsomebody, or Peabody.

Johanna Baldbody, 1379 : P. T. Howdenshire, p. 5.

Balderson, Bolderson.—Local, 'of Balderston,' q.v.; cf. Kelson for Kelston. The suffix -*ston* is frequently modified to -*son*.

London, 4, 0 ; Boston (U.S.), 1, 0 ; Manchester, 0, 3.

Balderston.—Local, 'of Balderston' or 'Balderstone,' a parish in co. Lanc., near Blackburn ; v. Balderson.

Richard de Baldreston, co. Lanc., 1332 : Lay Subsidy (Rylands).

Johannes de Baldreston, 1379 : P. T. Yorks. p. 289.

Robertus de Baldreston, 1379 : ibid.

Ric. de Baldirston, 1397 : Preston Guild Roll, p. 11.

William Balderston, 1459 : ibid. p. 12.

1591. James Balderstone and Constance Spackman : Marriage Lic.(London), i. 194.

London, 2 ; Manchester, 2 ; Philadelphia, 12.

Baldock.—Local, 'of Baldock,' a parish in co. Herts, eighteen miles from Hertford.

Robert de Baldok, co. Northampt., 20 Edw. I. R.

William de Baldak, co. Camb., ibid.

Elyas Baldek, co. Wilts, ibid.

1537. George Baldock and Agnes Hatton : Marriage Lic. (London), p. 9.

1648. Married—Nathan Baldocke and Ann Gibbons : St. Thomas the Apostle (London), p. 18.

1676. Bapt.—George, s. Samuel Baldocke : St. Mary Aldermary, p. 103.

London, 6 ; New York, 2.

Baldrey, Baldry.—Bapt. 'the son of Baldric' or 'Balderic'; v. Brodrick.

Hugo fil. Baldrici : Domesday.

Baldricus de Noneton, Hen. III–Edw. I. K.

Edward Baldri, co. Hunts, 1273. A.

Matilda Baldri, ibid.

Alicia Balrich, co. Soms., 1 Edw. III : Kirby's Quest, p. 130.

Matylda Baldry, ibid. p. 260.

1595. William Baldrye and Alice Binckes : Marriage Lic. (London), i. 223.

1665. Married—John Baldrey and Em Smith : St. Jas. Clerkenwell, iii. 125.

London, 1, 6 ; New York, 0, 1 ; Boston (U.S.), 5, 0.

Baldwin.—Bapt. 'the son of Baldwin.' As a personal name, so popular in the surname period that it has left its mark deeply indented on all our modern directories ; v. Ball, Bodden, Bawcock, &c. Baldwin occurs in Domesday. An aunt of the Conqueror married Baldwin, earl of Flanders ; and William himself espoused Matilda, daughter of the fifth Baldwin of that earldom. No wonder Flanders was called 'Baldwin's land' (Freeman's Norm. Conq. i. 601).

Stephen fil. Baldewyn, co. Camb., 1273. A.

Thomas Baldwyn, co. Oxf., ibid.

Robert Baldewyne, co. Camb., ibid.

Johannes Bawdwyn, 1379 : P. T. Yorks. p. 175.

1580. Thomas Baldwyn or Bauldwyn, co. Salop : Reg. Univ. Oxf. vol. ii. pt. ii. p. 180.

1597–8. Edward Baldwyn and Margery Draper : Marriage Lic. (London), i. 246.

London, 39 ; Philadelphia, 94.

Balestier, Ballister.—Occup. 'the arbelister,' an arbalester, or balister, a cross-bowman ; v. Banister and Alabaster.

Simon Bellyster, or Bellystre, B.A., June, 1539 : Reg. Univ. Oxf. i. 104.

Henry Balistarius, co. Berks, Hen. III–Edw. I. K.

1674. Bapt.—Ann, d. Thomas Balisster : St. Jas. Clerkenwell, i. 265.

New York, 1, 0 ; Boston (U.S.), 0, 1.

Balguy.—Nick. 'the bulgy' or 'bulky,' a stout, paunchy man ; v. Skeat (*bulge* and *bulk*); cf. Fatt, Bigg, Little, &c.

Hugh li (sic) Baylgy, co. Norf., 1273. A.

Hugh le Balgy, ibid.

Magota Balgy, 1379 : P. T. Yorks. p. 83.

Matilda Balgy, 1379 : ibid.

Dionicia Balgy, 1379 : ibid.

Cf. Geoffrey Balky, co. Linc., 1273. A.

Nicholas Balgie, or Balgee, sup. for B.A., 1866: Reg. Univ. Oxf. i. 242.
1503. Bapt. — Richard, son of John Balgay: St. Thomas the Apostle (London), p. 34.
1602. Married—John Ellis and Jane Balgay: ibid. p. 9.
London, 1; West Riding Court Dir., 1.

Balkwill.—Local, ' of Bake-well,' ? parish in co. Derby.

William (Rector de Baukwel), co. Linc., 20 Edw. I. R.
John de Bauquelle, co. Kent, ibid.
Cecilia de Baukwell, London, ibid.
Roger de Bauquell, co. Derby, ibid.
1892. Died—William Edward Balkwill: Daily Telegraph, July 14.
London, 1; New York, 1.

Ball.—(1) Bapt. ' the son of Baldwin,' from the nick. Bald. This was popularly Ball. The large number of Balls in the London Directory is accounted for by the great favour in which the name was held, and the constant influx from the Low Countries, where for a time it ruled supreme. The _d_ in some cases might be dropped later on, on account of its suggesting baldness. We find Balcock in the Hundred Rolls, -_cock_ being the suffix usually appended to the nick. of fontal names (v. Balcock). (2) Nick. ' the bald'; v. Ballard. The representatives of this sobriquet have also dropped the final _d_ to hide the truth. Amongst very many instances occur :

Custance Balde, co. Camb., 1273. A.
Richard Bald, co. Norf., ibid.
John Balle, co. Norf., ibid.
Albred Balle, co. Hunts, ibid.
John Balde, co. Soms., 1 Edw. III: Kirby's Quest, p. 115.
Isabella Balle, 1379: P. T. Yorks. p. 212.
Johannes Balde-man, i.e. John, the servant of Balde: ibid. p. 217.

From either (1) or (2) or both came a pet name given to various animals. Ball is mentioned as the name of a horse in Chaucer, as Tusser, of a sheep in the Promptorium, and of a dog in the Privy Purse Expenses of Henry VIII (Halliwell).

' Item, the 14th day (May, 1530) paied to one in rewarde for bringing home Ball the Kinges dog that was loste in the forrest of Waltham 5s.' : Privy Purse Expenses, Henry VIII, p. 43.
' Balle, schepys name ' : Prompt. Parv. p. 22.

(3) Local, ' at the Ball,' a sign-name; cf. Bell, Roebuck, &c.

John atte Balle, co. Soms., 1 Edw. III: Kirby's Quest, p. 149.
Henry atte Balle, co. Soms., 1 Edw. III: ibid. p. 258.

This sign-name has existed for centuries.

London, 64; Philadelphia, 104.

Ballard.—Nick. ' bald-headed.' The hair, or absence of it, gave us a large number of early nicknames, the majority of which still exist as surnames. Ballard seems to have been very popular for a bald-headed man; v. Ball. Professor Skeat quotes :

' And scorneden to hym saying, Stye up, ballard,' 1382 : Wyclif, 2 Kings ii. 23.
Richard Balleheved, co. Soms., 1 Edw. III: Kirby's Quest, p. 206.
Peter Ballard, co. Soms., 1 Edw. III: ibid. p. 252.
Alured Balard, co. Essex, 1273. A.
Dreu Ballard, co. Hunts, ibid.
Thomas Ballard, co. Suff., ibid.
Henry Ballard, co. Lanc., 20 Edw. I. R.
1615. Ralph Ballard, co. Oxf. : Reg. Univ. Oxf. vol. ii. pt. ii. p. 339.
1634. Married — William Mayle and Mary Ballerde : St. Mary Aldermary, p. 19.
London, 26; Philadelphia, 10.

Balleine, Ballin.—Nick. ' le Ba-lun,' i.e. the whale ; Fr. _baleine_.

Baloun (without surname), co. Leic., 1273. A.
Balun, ibid.
John le Balun, co. Heref., ibid.
Alan Balun, co. Northampt., ibid.
John le Balun. L.
London, 0, 2; Crockford, 4, 0; New York, 0, 14.

Ballinger, Ballenger.—Occup. ; v. Bullinger.

1670. Edmund Burt and Audrey Ballinger : Marriage Lic. (Westminster), p. 45.
1701. Married — Henry Kirby and Patience Ballinger: St. Peter, Cornhill, ii. 63.

Balm, Balme.—Loc. ' of Balne,' a parish near Snaith, co. York. The corruption was an early and natural one. The surname is well known in the county.
The following entries occur in the same village (Wadworth):

Johannes Balne, 1379: P. T. Yorks. p. 76.
Johannes Balm, 1379 : ibid.
Willelmus de Balne, 1379 : ibid. p. 50.
Emma de Balne, 1379: ibid. p. 46.
Thomas de Balme, 1379 : ibid. p. 39.

1745. Married—John Balm and Sarah Brewerton: St. Geo. Chap. Mayfair, p. 50.
West Riding Court Dir., 1, 5; New York, 0, 2.

Balshaw.—Local, ' of Balshaw,' some spot in the vicinity of Lathom, co. Lanc.

Adam de Balshagh, co. Lanc., 1332: Lay Subsidy (Rylands), p. 120.
John de Balshagh, co. Lanc., 1332: ibid.
1608. John Balshaw, of Snape within Scarisbrick : Wills at Chester, i. 10.
1622. William Balshaw, of Walton-le-Dale, ibid.
1628. Margaret Balshaw, of Mawdsley, spinster: ibid. ii. 11.
MDB. (co. Lanc.), 6; Liverpool, 2; Philadelphia, 1.

Bamber.—Local, ' of Bamber,' now more familiarly known as Bamber Bridge, a village three miles from Preston, co. Lanc.

1619. Robert Bamber, of Dukinfield : Wills at Chester. i. 10.
1642. Robert Bamber; Preston Guild Rolls, p. 95.
— John Bamber : ibid.
1664. Bapt.—Katharine, d. John Bomber, of Farrington : Reg. Leyland (co. Lanc.), p. 44.
1683. — William, s. Thomas Bomber, of Euxton: ibid. p. 73.
London, 2; Liverpool. 7; Manchester, 6; Boston (U.S.), 6; Philadelphia, 1.

Bambrough, Bambury.—Local, ' of Bambrough,' a parish in co. Northumberland.

Beatrix de Bamburg, co. Northumb., Hen. III-Edw. I. K.
William de Bamburgh, co. Northumb., ibid.
Anselm de Bamburg', co. Norf., 1273. A.
Robertus Janitor Castri de Bamburg, co. Northumb., ibid.
William de Bamburgh, prior of Colding-ham, 1355: QQQ. p. 380.
1524. John Fairfax and Alice Bam-borow: Marriage Lic. (London), i. 4.
1775. Married—William Bambary and Ann Goodin: St. Geo. Han. Sq. i. 252.
London, 1, 1; New York, 1, 1.

Bamfield, Bampfield, Ban-field, Banfill.—Local, ' of Bam-fyld,' some place in co. Devon or co. Somerset, whence in the latter Weston-Bamfyld, a parish six miles from Castle-Cary. As a surname Banfield is the chief variant.

1575. Ames (Amias) Banfilde, co. Devon: Reg. Univ. Oxf. vol. ii. pt. ii. p. 63.
1581. Richard Bampfild, or Bamfield, co. Devon : ibid. p. 100.
1582. Giles Bampfild, co. Devon: ibid. p. 121.
1752. Married — William Smith and

Hannah Bamfeild: St. Geo. Han. Sq. i. p. 47.

1766. Married — Sir John Saunders Sebright and Sarah Knight. Witness, Copp Warre Bampfylde: ibid. p. 154.

— — John Banfield and Betty Nunns: ibid. p. 156.

London, 1, 1, 6, 0; Exeter (Banfill), 1; MDB. (co. Devon), 0, 1, 2, 0; Boston (U.S.), 0, 0, 5, 0; Philadelphia, 0, 1, 2, 0.

Bamford, Balmforth, Bamforth, Bamfard. Local, ' of Bamford.' Bircle-cum-Bamford is a township in the parish of Middleton, near Bury, co. Lanc.

'The estate of Bamford was granted to Thomas de Bamford by Sir Adam de Bury, temp. Henry III, for his homage and services,' &c.: Baines' Lanc. i. 525.

Richard de Bamford, co. York, 1273. A.

Adam Bamforth, 1379: P. T. Yorks. p. 89.

Adam de Baumford, 1379: ibid. p. 123.

1602. William Bamford, of Bamford, parish of Bury: Wills at Chester, i. 10.

1613. James Bamford, of Hurdsfield: ibid.

1738. Henry Bamford and Eliz. Becket: St. Geo. Han. Sq. i. 22.

London, 9, 1, 0, 0; Manchester, 3, 1, 0, 0; Bury, 1, 1, 0, 0; Philadelphia, 10, 1, 2, 0; Boston (U.S.), 1, 0, 0, 1.

Bampton.—Local, ' of Bampton,' parishes in cos. Devon, Oxford, Cumberland, and Westm. A variant of the name is Banton, q.v.

Philip de Bamptone, co. Soms., 1 Edw. III: Kirby's Quest, p. 148.

Brian de Bampton, co. Oxf., Hen. III-Edw. I. K.

John de Bamton, co. Wilts, ibid.

Thomas de Bampton, co. Cumb., 20 Edw. I. R.

1785. Married—Joshua Bampton and Rebbecca Stiles: St. Geo. Han. Sq. i. 371. London, 2.

Banbury, Bambury, Bambery.—Local, ' of Banbury,' a well-known town in co. Oxford.

Thomas de Banneburi, co. Hunts, 1273. A.

Edmunde de Bannebur', co. Oxf., ibid.

William de Bannebir', co. Oxf., ibid.

1591. Edward Banberye, co. Middlesex: Reg. Univ. Oxf. vol. ii. pt. ii. p. 184.

1619. Thomas Bunburie, or Banbury, co. Kent: ibid. p. 376. But see Bunbury.

1765. Married—Joseph Powell and Mary Banbury: St. Geo. Han. Sq. i. 146.

London, 9, 1, 0; New York, 0, 0, 2.

Bancroft.—Local, ' of the bankcroft,' i. e. the enclosure on the slope. An east Cheshire name that has many representatives in the directories of south-east Lancashire; v. Bank and Croft.

1570. Buried — Jone Bancrofte, of Butley: Prestbury Ch. (co. Chester), p. 32.

1595. John Bancroft, of Macclesfield: Wills at Chester (1545-1620), p. 10.

1603. William Bancroft, of Wilmslow: ibid.

1669. Henery Banckcroft, sone of Henery Banckcroft, of Maple, bapt. April 14: Reg. Disley Church (East Cheshire), ii. 100.

1764. Married — John Bancroft and Mary Barbon Glover: St. Geo. Han. Sq. i. 136.

Manchester, 18; London, 3; Philadelphia, 30.

Banfather.—Nick.; v. Barnfather.

Banfield; v. Bamfield.

Banister, Bannister.—(1) Occup. A balister (*l* becoming *n*; cf. banisters, lit. balusters, staircase, railings), an arbalester, a crossbowman. O. F. *balestier*: 'trecenti loricati, cum balistariis et artificibus machinarum multis' (Giles, i. 57, quoted by Freeman, Hist. Norm. Conq. iv. 583); v. Alabaster. The name in various forms is found in every early list. It is sufficient to turn to the London Directory to see by the number of Bannisters the commonness of the occupation.

'Gosners, balesters, and archers': Caxton, 1489 (quoted in H.E.D.).

1557. Buried—John Corker, bailister, Ulverston (Ulverston Church).

Probably this is an instance of the curious Elizabethan custom of appending the old feminine -*ster* to names of masculine occupation. John Corker, I suspect, the bailie or bailiff of the town. But he may have been a cross-bowman.

(2) Local.

Adam de Banistre, temp. 1320: Baines' Lanc. i. 83.

This is the only entry with *de* I can find. The Testa de Neville, Hundred Rolls, and Placita de Quo Warranto have many instances, but all without prefix. It is clear however that (1) is not the only origin, judging by the character of these entries.

John Balistar', co. Norf., 1273. A. Wyot Balistarius. E. Renaud Balistarius. C.

Henry Balistar', co. Oxf., Hen. III-Edw. I. K.

Robert Balistarius, co. York, ibid.

Agnes Banastre, co. Salop, 1273. A.

Henry Banastre, co. Camb., ibid.

Thomas Banastre, co. Lanc., 20 Edw. I. R.

John Banastre, co. Berks, Hen. III-Edw. I. K.

Johannes Banastre, 1379: P. T. Yorks. p. 292.

1674. Bapt.—Anne, d. Thomas Balisster: St. Jas. Clerkenwell, i. 265.

The surname is found all over the kingdom in large numbers. It is quite possible that some of these entries represent a personal name now forgotten.

London, 12, 25; Boston (U.S.), 3, 6.

Bank, Banks, Bankes, Banke.—Local, ' at the bank,' i.e. the slope or declivity in the land. Like all other local monosyllables, it takes a final *s*, perhaps the patronymic, as in Jones, Simmonds, &c.; cf. Brooks, Styles, &c.

Nicholaus del Bancke, 1379: P. T. Yorks. p. 16.

Adam del Bank, 1379: ibid. p. 48.

Magota del Bancke, 1379: ibid. p. 202.

Richard del Bank, co. Lanc., 20 Edw. I. R.

William del Bank, co. Lanc., ibid.

1596. Simon Bancke, co. Cumb.: Reg. Univ. Oxf. vol. ii. pt. ii. p. 218.

1597. William Banks, co. Devon: ibid. p. 224.

1760. Married—John Bankes and Ann Killmister: St. Geo. Han. Sq. i. 91.

1767. — John Banks and Mary Odwell: ibid. p. 181.

London, 0, 39, 1, 0; New York, 5, 57, 0, 0; Philadelphia (Banke), 1.

Banker.—Offic.; v. Bencher.

Banknott.—Local, ' at the bank-knot,' one who resided on the *knot* or small prominence on the side of the *bank*. The name looks anachronistic, and suggests the notes issued by the Bank of England.

Robert Banknott, 30 Hen. VI: Cal. Inquis. Post Mortem.

John Banknotte, C. R., 7 Edw. IV.

Banton; v. Bampton, and cf. Banfield for Bamfield.

1656. Married—Banton and Elenor Morice: Kensington Ch., p. 75.

1757. — Josias Banton and Eliz. Price: St. Geo. Han. Sq. i. 71. London, 2.

Banwell.—Local, ' of Banwell,'

a parish in co. Soms., near Axbridge.

William de Banewell, co. Soms., 1 Edw. III : Kirby's Quest, p. 84.
Walter Banewell, co. Soms., 1 Edw. III : ibid.
John Bannwell, co. Soms., 1 Edw. III : ibid. p. 125.
1658. Bapt.—Clement, s. Job Baniwell : St. Jas. Clerkenwell, i. 200.
1694. Thomas Jepson and Margaret Banwell : Marriage Alleg. (Canterbury), p. 291.
London, 1 ; MDB. (co. Soms.), 12.

Baptist.—Bapt. 'the son of Baptiste,' Fr. I have not yet found Baptist as an English font-name before Henry VII. It never took root in England. The surname is very rare. Naturally, nearly all my instances are Johns.

1551. Bapt. Sara, d. of John Baptysse : St. Dionis Backchurch (London), p. 7.
1552. — Gresell, d. of John Baptyste : ibid.
1716. Buried—John Baptist : St. John the Baptist, Walbrook, p. 200.
1772. Married—John Baptist and Abigail Fielder : St. Geo. Han. Sq. i. 226.
1804. — Joseph Baptis and Sarah Evan : ibid. ii. 302.
London, 1 ; New York, 1.

Barbe.—Bapt. 'the son of Barbara,' from the nick. Barb, whence Babb, q.v., a Norman-French form ; v. Yonge, i. 261.

Richard Barbe, co. Soms., 1 Edw. III : Kirby's Quest, p. 249.
1795. Married—Peter Barb and Sarah Chandler : St. Geo. Han. Sq. ii. 138.
London, 1 ; Philadelphia, 2.

Barber.—Occup. 'the barber,' one who trimmed or shaved beards ; v. Barbour.

Thomas le Barbitonsor. J.
William le Barbitonsor. H.
Henry le Barbour, co. Soms., 1 Edw. III : Kirby's Quest, p. 220.
Alexander le Barbur, London, 1273. A.
Henry le Barber, co. Oxf., ibid.
Richard Barbitonsor, co. Oxf., ibid.
John le Barber, co. Camb., ibid.
Geoffrey le Barbir, co. Hunts, ibid.
1543. John Sturley and Agnes Barbor : Marriage Lic. (Faculty Office), p. 1.
London, 83 ; Philadelphia, 100.

Barberess.—Occup. 'the barberess,' a female barber. Matilda has long anticipated the lady barbers of to-day.

Matilda la Barbaresse, co. Camb., 1273. A.

Barberry, Barberie.—Bapt. 'the son of Barbara,' once popularly Barbery. Barbara was a favourite font-name in the surname period ; v. Babb, Barbot, &c.

1581. Married—William Grosse and Barbery Marbeck : St. Antholin (London), p. 28.
1609. Buried—Helline, d. Henrie Barbery : St. Jas. Clerkenwell, iv. 109.
1692. — Barberry, an old maid : Cheshunt Church Reg.
1606. — Barbery, d. Jeremiah and Barbery Bird : St. Mary Aldermary, p. 204.
1715. Married — Francis Lee and Catherine Barberry : St. Jas. Clerkenwell, iii. 238.
London, 1, 0 ; New York, 0, 1.

Barbican.—Local, 'at the barbican,' from residence thereby ; an outwork, an outwork of a fort.

William Barbican, co. Soms., 1 Edw. III : Kirby's Quest, p. 247.

Barbon, Barebone, Barebones, Barbone.—Local, (1) 'of Barbon,' a chapelry in the old parish of Kirkby Lonsdale. This originated Barbon and Barben, still existing in Furness and the district ; v. Dalton in Furness Dir. (2) Barbourne, a parish in Worcestershire. To this place we probably owe the south English Barbons, one of whom, Praisegod, was written variously Barbon, Barbone, and Barebones. A good deal of fun would have been lost to the world if a certain Parliament had been more correctly styled Barbon's Parliament. Even Barebones' Parliament is inaccurate, it should be Barebone's. 'The Long Parliament in Cromwell's time, called by derision the Rump, was headed by one Barebones, a leatherseller' (Curiosities of Literature). Here Isaac Disraeli is manifestly in error. Peck in his Desiderata Curiosa, speaking (1646) of a member of the family, styles him 'Mr. Barborne,' probably the original form, and suggesting Worcestershire as the home of the race.

John Barbon, or Barbone, 1569 : Reg. Univ. Oxf. i. 277.
John Barebone, B.A., Oxon, 1574 : ibid. vol. ii. pt. i. p. 39.
1589. Bapt. — Thomas, son of John Barbon, merchant taylor : St. Mary Aldermary, p. 63.
1690. Buried—Henry Barbon, or Barebone : St. Dionis Backchurch, p. 258.
Boston (U.S.), 0, 0, 0, 2.

Barbot, Babelot.—Bapt. 'the son of Barbara,' nick. Barb or Bab, dims. Barbot and Babelot. Diminutives in elot were not rare at the period ; cf. Hamelot from Hamo, Richelot from Richard, and Hobelot or Robelot from Robert.

Barbata, or Barbota, fil. Willelmi Garwey, temp. Hen. III. BBB. p. 166.
John Barbot, co. Camb., 1273. A.
Adam Barbot, co. York, ibid.
Nicholas Babelot, co. Camb., ibid.
Cecilia Berbotte, 1379 : P. T. Yorks. p. 15.
Betrix Barbot, 1379 : ibid. p. 27.
Barbota uxor Martini, C. R., 44 Hen. III, pt. 2.
1656. Married—Jeffery Barbet to Margaret Coife : Canterbury Cath.
1784. John Barbot and Maria Gwynn : St. Geo. Han. Sq. i. 358.
Philadelphia, 1, 0.

Barbour.—Occup. 'the barber.' As a surname a North English form, and sometimes 'of Barbour' in Scotland.

'A barbour was redi thare.' 1320, Sir Tristr. 1. lxiii. (H.E.D.)
'She clepide the barbour' : Wyclif, Judges xvi. 19.
Alice le Barbour, co. Hunts, 1273. A.
Richard le Barbour, 1302. M.
Robert le Barbour, 1307. M.
Johannes de Catton, barbour, 1379 : P. T. Yorks. p. 251.
Edmundus Barbour, 1379 : ibid.
1754. Married—Joseph Trambley and Ann Barbour : St. Geo. Chap. Mayfair, p. 271.
London, 1 ; Manchester, 4 ; New York, 20.

Barchard.—Bapt. 'a variant of Burchard' ; v. Burchett.

MDB. (co. Sussex), 2.

Barclay, Berkeley, Berkley.—Local, 'of Berkeley.' An early variant. Berkeley is a parish and market town in co. Gloucester.

Egidius de Berkeleye, co. Oxf., 1273. A.
Maurice de Berkelay, co. Soms., ibid.
Robert de Berclay, co. Northumb., 1195 : KKK. vi. 53.
Gyles de Berclay, co. Derby, Hen. III-Edw. I. K.
Seman de Berclawe, co. Camb., 1273. A.
William Bercley, co. Soms., 1 Edw. III : Kirby's Quest, p. 238.
1704. Married—Henry Barclay and Thomazine Bloome : St. Peter, Cornhill, ii. 65.
London, 29, 6, 1 ; Philadelphia, 46, 1, 2.

Barcroft.—Local, 'of Barcroft,' a property in Cliviger, co. Lanc. A family of that name lived there until 1668, being found there so early as Hen. III ; v. Baines' Lanc. (Croston's edit.), ii. 389. A rare surname in the 19th century—almost extinct, in fact.

Thomas Barcroft, of Burnley (co. Lanc.), 1571 : Wills at Chester (1545-1620), p. 11.
Henry Barcroft, of Lancashire, 1576 : ibid.
1592-3. Thomas Barcrofte, co. Worc. : Reg. Univ. Oxf. ii. pt. ii. p. 125.
1632-3. Charles Barcroft and Dorothie Crosby : Marriage Lic. (Faculty Office), p. 27.
1657. Bapt.—John, s. John Barcroft, gent. : St. Jas. Clerkenwell, i. 196.
Liverpool, 1 ; Philadelphia, 1.

Bardolph, Bardell, Bardol, Bardel.—Bapt. 'the son of Bardolf' (Yonge, ii. 404). 'Bardell : a corruption of Bardolf' (Lower). This statement is confirmed by the following entry :

Osbertus Bardolf, alias Bardol, 45 Hen. III. BBB. p. 94.

Cf. Randle or Randell for Randolph.

Dodo Barduf, co. Notts, Hen. III–Edw. I. K.
Barduphus de Cest'ton, ibid.
Uxor 'William' Bardoulf, co. Norf., 1273. A.
Roger Bardolf, co. Salop, ibid.
Henry Bardolph, co. Soms., 1 Edw. III : Kirby's Quest, p. 167.
Hugh Bardulphe, 8 Ric. I, sheriff of Westmorland : Hist. West. and Cumb. i. 27.
Edmond Bardolfe, 1572 : Visitation of Hertfordshire (Harl. Soc.), p. 26.
Edward Bardolph, 1634 : ibid. p. 2.
1668. Bapt.—Robert, s. John Bardell : St. Jas. Clerkenwell, i. 301.
1781. Married—Joseph Bardell and Mary Willioghby : St. Geo. Han. Sq. i. 326.
London, 1, 2, 0, 0 ; New York, 1, 1, 0, 1 ; Philadelphia (Bardol), 1.

Bardsley, Beardsley, Beardslee.—Local, 'of Bardsley,' a parish between Ashton and Oldham, near Manchester. But some place in the south-west district must have borne the same name, judging from references given below. All the American Bardsleys, and all the North English Bardsleys, and perhaps all the Beardsleys, hail from the Lancashire parish stated above.

Uxor William de Bardsley, de Ha, 1422 : Custom Roll and Rental of the lordship of Ashton-under-Lyne (Cheth. Soc.).

The Ha above represents the now thriving parish of Hey, close to Oldham.

1667. Samuel Bardsley, clerk, minister of Disley and Marple : Earwaker's East Cheshire, ii. 57, 98.
Robert de Berdesleghe, co. Soms., 1 Edw. III : Kirby's Quest, p. 191.
Roger de Berdesleghe : ibid.
Robert de Bardesle, co. Oxf., 1273. A.
William de Bardesley. H.
John Bardsley, of Staley, 1599 : Wills at Chester (1545-1620), p. 11.
William Bardsley, of Ashton, 1609 : ibid.
Ann Bardsley, of Greenacres, Oldham, 1617 : ibid.
London, 2, 0, 0 ; Manchester, 17, 1, 0 ; Ashton-under-Lyne, 3, 0, 0 ; New York, 3, 17, 2 ; Philadelphia, 24, 2, 1.

Bardwell.—Local, 'of Bardwell,' a parish in co. Suffolk, near Ixworth.

Nicholas Berdwell, co. Soms., 1 Edw. III : Kirby's Quest, p. 280.
1637. Married—Thomas Bagall and Margaret Bardwell : St. Jas. Clerkenwell, iii. 68.
London, 2.

Barebone.—Local ; v. Barbon.

Barefoot, Barfoot.—Nick. or Eccles. 'on naked foot,' one who went with feet bare ; a friar or pilgrim.

'Thy temple in Delphos wol I barefoot seke' : Chaucer, The F. Tale, 11390.
'Fraunceys had his brethren
Bar-fot to wenden.'
Piers P. Creed, 593-4.
'A barefoote brother ' : Rom. and Jul. v. ii. 5.
Norman Barfot, co. Linc., 1273. A.
Roger Barefot, co. Oxf., ibid.
Alan Barefot, co. Camb., ibid.
John Barfoote, 1568 : Reg. Univ. Oxf. i. 272.
Roger Barefoote, temp. 1580. Z.
1581-2. Edward Barefoote and Winifred Hildersham : Marriage Lic.(London), i. 105.
1625. Buried—Thomas Barfoote, a stranger : St. Michael, Cornhill, p. 225.
1715. Francis Barefoot : St. Peter, Cornhill, p. 71.
1717. Married—John Light and Mary Bearfoot : St. Michael, Cornhill, p. 59.
1748. — William King and Eliz. Barfoot : St. Geo. Chap. Mayfair, p. 103.
London, 2, 6 ; Oxford, 4, 5.

Bargate.—Local, 'at the Bargate.' The entrance to a city, as Temple Bar ; formed originally of posts and chain.

Jordan atte-bargate. J.
William atte Barezete, co. Soms., 1 Edw. III : Kirby's Quest, p. 199.
Jordan de la Barregate : Fines Roll, 11 Edw. I.
'The street, as well within as without

the old Gate or Bar, called Fishergate Bar, goes by the name of Fishergate ' : Hist. and Ant. of York, 1785, ii. 189.
1607. Married—Abraham Hill and Agnes Bargett : St. Mary Aldermary, p. 11.
Barrow-in-Furness, 1.

Barge, Bargeman, Bargman.—Occup. 'the barge-man.' The first entry below concerns three royal bargemen who attended the king in his journeys by water.

Petrus del Barge, *mariner*, 33 Edw. III : Freemen of York, i. 53.
John Bargeman, John Amyson, John Book, bargemen : Wardrobe Account, 48 Edw. III–1 Ric. II, 41/10.
Patricius Bargeman, 1379 : P. T. Yorks. p. 296.
George Bargeman, 1579 : Cal. State Papers (Domestic), i. 642.
1666. John Bargeman and Eliz. Dickins : Marriage Lic. (Faculty Office), p. 91.
1749. Married—Jonas Bargman and Eliz. Biggs : St. Geo. Chap. Mayfair, p. 153.
London, 1, 1, 0 ; New York, 0, 1, 0 ; Philadelphia, 1, 0, 1 ; Boston (U.S.), 0, 0, 1.

Barham.—Local, 'of Barham,' a parish in co. Hunts, six miles from Kimbolton ; also a parish in co. Kent, six miles from Canterbury ; also a parish in co. Suffolk, four miles from Ipswich.

Henry de Berham, co. Kent, 20 Edw. I. R.
Andrew de Bereham, co. Linc., 1273. A.
1564. Peter Nott and Margaret Barham : Marriage Lic. (London), i. 29.
1615. Robert Barham, co. Kent : Reg. Univ. Oxf. vol. ii. pt. ii. p. 338.
1654. Buried—John, s. John Barham : St. Jas. Clerkenwell, iv. 301.
London, 7 ; Boston (U.S.), 1.

Baring.—Bapt. 'the son of Baring' ; cf. Harding and Browning, q.v. ' The peer and the baronet descend from John Baring, of Devonshire, 18th century, son of John Baring, minister of the Lutheran church at Bremen, in Saxony' (Lower). Probably of the same parentage as Behring. True as the above may be, the same personal name was found on English soil in the surname period, and has its own descendants.

John Bering, co. Soms., 1 Edw. III : Kirby's Quest, p. 205.
Joseph Baring, Ram and Magpie, 1 Fleet Street, Bethnal Green : London Dir. 1872.
London, 2.

Barkas, Barkus.—Local, ' at the bark-house,' where the bark was stored for tanning purposes.

From residence therein or thereby; v. Barker; cf. Bacchus, Malthus, Loftus, or Lewtas.

1774. Married—George Barkas and Hannah Barnes: St. Geo. Han. Sq. i. 241. Newcastle-on-Tyne, 4, 1; Gateshead, 0, 1.

Barker, Barkmaker, Barkman.—Occup. 'the barker,' one who stripped trees of bark for the tanner. Then a preparer of bark for tanning. 'Escorceur, a barker of trees' (Cotg.). In the conversation between Edward IV and the tanner of Tamworth (Percy) it is said:

'What craftsman art thou?' said the king,
'I pray thee telle me trowe';
'I am a barker, sir, by my trade;
Now tell me, what art thou?'

In the Chester Play the barkers and tanners marched together (Ormerod's Cheshire, i. 300).

1402. 'Lego uxori Ricardi Skyrtynbek, barkar, i togam': Test. Ebor. i. 289.
Robert Barcarius, co. Linc., 1273. A.
Alan le Barkere, co. Camb., ibid.
Osbert le Barker, 1306. M.
William de York, barker, 1379: P. T. Yorks. p. 251.
Edmund Barkmaker, temp. Eliz. ZZ.
John Barkman. W. 18.
London, 111, 0, 1; Philadelphia, 96, 0, 0; New York (Barkman), 1.

Barleggs.—Local. This curious-looking name is manifestly local, the suffix being -ley, or -legh, or -legg, as in Whitelegg, q.v. I do not know the spot.

1627-7. John Dawston and Hellen Bareleggs: Marriage Lic.(London),ii. 182.
1667. Married—John Bareleggs and Eliz. Doulin: St. Jas. Clerkenwell, iii. 131.
1747. — Thomas Bearleggs and Ann Addison: St. Geo. Chap. Mayfair, p. 85. MDB. (co. Herts), 1.

Barley.—(1) Local, 'of Barlow (?), a probable variant. (2) Local, 'of Barley,' a parish in co. Herts, near Barkway. No doubt (2) is the chief parent of our southern Barleys.

William de Berele, co. Camb., 1273. A.
1565. Thomas Felde and Alice Barley: Marriage Lic. (London), i. 31.
1573. George Barley, of Overton: Wills at Chester, i. 12.
1596. Richard Barley, co. Herts: Reg. Univ. Oxf. vol. ii. pt. ii. p. 215.
1603. Married—James Barley and Eliz. Miller: St. Dionis Backchurch, p. 14.
London, 3; Philadelphia, 4; Boston (U.S.), 1.

Barlow.—Local, 'of Barlow,' near Manchester. The Lancashire Barlows spring from Barlow Hale and Barlow Moor, near Manchester. The name has ramified in an extraordinary manner. Barlow is also a parish in co. Derby, near Chesterfield, but nearly all our Barlows trace back to the neighbourhood of Manchester. The Barlows of Barlow Hale (whence William Barlow, bishop of Lincoln, born about 1550) were seated there so early as Ric. II. The first entry below probably represents Barlow, a chapelry in the parish of Brayton, West Rid. Yorks.

Johannes de Berlowe, 1379: P. T. Yorks. p. 33.
1584. Henry Barlow, co. Derby: Reg. Univ. Oxf. vol. ii. pt. ii. p. 139.
1600. John Barlow, co. Chester: ibid. p. 244.
1583. George Barlow, of Manchester, baker: Wills at Chester, i. 12.
1594. Ottiwell Barlow, of Heaton Norris: ibid.
1620. Sir Alex. Barlow, of Barlow: ibid.
1656. Married—John Barlow and Mary Tolley: St. Dionis Backchurch, p. 32.
West Riding Court Dir., 15; Manchester, 75; London, 33; Philadelphia, 47.

Barnaby, Barnabee.—Local, 'of Barnby,' q.v.; cf. Greenaway for Greenway, or Ottaway for Ottway, or Hathaway for Hathaway. No connexion with the later Barnaby used familiarly for Barnabas.

1524. Thomas Barnaby and Margaret Wallop: Marriage Lic. (London), i. 49.
1534. John Barnabe and Catherine Bonham: ibid.
1621. Eustace Barneby, or Barnaby: Reg. Univ. Oxf. vol. ii. pt. ii. p. 402.
1665. Buried—John Barnabee: St. Jas. Clerkenwell, iv. 368.
1756. Married—John Barnaby and Eliz. Tree: St. Geo. Han. Sq. i. 66.
New York, 2, 0; Boston (U.S.), 2, 2.

Barnacle.—Local, 'of Barnacle,' a hamlet in the parish of Bulkington, six miles from Coventry, co. Warwick.

Custance de Barnaucle, co. Suff., 1273. A.
Richard Barnikel: Close Roll, 18 Edw. III, pt. i.
Richard Barnakyll, 1514: Reg. Univ. Oxf. i. 91.
1545. Married—John Barnacle and Annes Chapman: St. Dionis Backchurch, p. 2.
Crockford, 3; New York, 1; Boston (U.S.), 3.

Barnard, Barnett, Barnet.—Bapt. 'the son of Bernard,' or 'Barnard.' The Cistercian monk gave a wonderful impetus in the 13th century to this name, already popular. A large number of Bernards sprang up in Furness after the Abbey came under the Bernardine rule; Bernard Gilpin's name is a case in point. The popular form was Barnet. There are more than a hundred Barnetts in the London Directory. Barnes and Barnet seem to suggest a nick. Barn and a dim. Barnett. It is quite possible that such is the case, but in general Barnes must be looked on as local, and Barnett is simply a provincial pronunciation of Barnard. Barnet is turned into a title of high degree in the following entry:

'Of Barronet Coll, for his child's lay-reston, 1s. 8d.': Churchwardens' Accounts, Gateshead, 1643.

For instances v. Bernard.

London, 71, 101, 2; Boston (U.S.), 82, 28, 1.

Barnby, Barmby.—Local, 'of Barnby,' i. e. Barnby-upon-don, near Doncaster. With Barmby, cf. Barnborough, or Barmborough, in same neighbourhood. Also cf. Bamfield and Banfield.

Richard de Barneby, co. York, 1273. A.
Henry de Barneby, co. Linc., 20 Edw. I. R.
Thomas de Barmby, 1379: P. T. Yorks. p. 65.
Thomas de Barnby, 1379: ibid. p. 241.
1584-5. Charles Barnbye, co. York: Reg. Univ. Oxf. vol. ii. pt. ii. p. 140.
1585. Francis Barnbye, co. York: ibid. p. 142.
1684. Martin Bellamy and Ann Barnby: Marriage Lic. (Faculty Office), p. 170.
West Rid. Court Dir., 1, 1; New York, 1, 0.

Barne, Barnes, Barns.—(1) Local, 'at the barn,' from residence thereby. (2) Nick. 'the bairn'; M.E. barne, a child; cf. Child and Childs. If local, Barnes takes a patronymic s like other monosyllabic local surnames; cf. Styles, Brooks, Sykes, &c.

Henry de le Berne, co. Norf., 1273. A.
Richard de la Berne, co. Kent, ibid.
William de la Berne, co. Dorset, ibid.
John atte Bern, co. Soms., 1 Edw. III: Kirby's Quest, p. 119.

Henry atte Bern, co. Soms., 1 Edw.
III : Kirby's Quest, p. 119.
William le Barne, co. York, 1273. A.
Walter le Barne, co. Linc., ibid.
Ricardus le Barne et uxor, 1379 : P. T.
Yorks. p. 144.
Thomas le Barne. T.
London, 1, 139, 6 ; Philadelphia, 0,
222, 13.

**Barnfather, Bairnfather,
Bairnsfather, Banfather.—**
Nick. ' the bairn's father,' father of
the bairn or child ; v. Barne and
Child ; cf. Priestfather, q.v. The
possessive s is unknown in these
early North English entries.

Robertus Thom-barne (i. e. Tom's
child), 1379 : P. T. Yorks. p. 155.
Johannes Wil-barne (i. e. Will's child),
1379 : ibid. p. 162.
Willelmus Barnefadir, 1379 : P. T.
Yorks. p. 209.
Johannes Barnefader, 1379 : ibid. p. 162.
Johanna Barnefadir, 1379 : ibid. p. 198.
Mary Barnfather, co. Cumb., temp.
1620 : VVV. p. 491.
1745. Married—Joseph Barnfather and
Jane Grove : St. Geo. Chap. Mayfair, p. 51.
1770. — William Barnfather and Eliz.
Carthrel : St. Geo. Han. Sq. i. 200.
1777. — James Banfather and Eliz.
Pellett : ibid. p 273.
' Mr. Bairnsfather's election to the
Directorate was confirmed, and Mr. John
Petch was re-elected auditor' : The
Yorkshire Post, Feb. 28, 1887.
West Riding Court Dir., 1, 0, 0, 0 ;
Crockford (Banfather), 3.

Barnmaw.—Nick. ' the child's
brother-in-law.' A very interesting name corroboratory of the
definition given of Watmough, q.v.;
cf. Barnfather, found also in co.
York.

William le Barnemawe, co. York,
1273. A.

Barnsley.—(1) Local, ' of
Barnsley,' a parish fourteen miles
from Sheffield, W. Rid. Yorks. (2)
Local, ' of Barnsley,' a parish in co.
Gloucester, four miles from Cirencester. Evidently (2) is the chief
parent.

1578. Walter Barnsley, co. Salop : Reg.
Univ. Oxf. vol. ii. pt. ii. p. 80.
1584. Thomas Barnesley, co. Oxf.:
ibid. p. 137.
1669. Buried—Walter Barnsley : St.
Mary Aldermary, p. 187.
1690. Henry Barnsley and Frances
Moody : Marriage Alleg. (Canterbury),
p. 156.
1767. Married—William Barnsley and
Mary Johnson : St. Geo. Han. Sq. i. 171.
London, 1 ; Philadelphia, 1.

Barnstable.—Local, ' of Barnstaple,' a port, market town, and
parish in co. Devon; v. Bastable.
MDB. (co. Soms.), 4.

Barnum.—Local, ' of Barnham,'
parishes in diocs. Ely, Chichester,
and Norwich. An American spelling. One of the earliest entries of
this name only differs by a vowel
from the transatlantic form ; cf.
Farnum, the American form of
English Farnham.

Willelmus Barnom, 1379 : P. T. Yorks.
p. 152.
Simon de Bernham, co. Norf., 1273. A.
Walter de Bernham, co. Suff., ibid.
John de Bernham, co. Kent, 20 Edw.
I. R.
Thomas de Bernham, co. Suff., ibid.
1572. Benedict Barnham, St. Alban
Hall : Reg. Univ. Oxf. vol. ii. pt. ii. p. 41.
1592. Stephen Barneham and Ann
Dawkes : Marriage Lic. (London), i.
199.
1598. Sir John Packington and Dorothy
Barnam : ibid. p. 256.
New York, 20.

Barnwell, Barnwall.—Local,
' of Barnwell,' two parishes in co.
Northampton. Barnwall is an
American variant.

William de Bernwell, vicar of Frethorp,
co. Norf., 1307 : FF. vii. 232.
John Bernevyle, co. Soms., 1 Edw. III :
Kirby's Quest, p. 200.
Robert de Barnevile, co. Soms., 1273. A.
1593-4. Robert Barnwell, St. Mary
Hall : Reg. Univ. Oxf. vol. ii. pt. ii. p. 200.
1598. Tristram Slader and Eliz.
Sparrowe. Attested by Richard Barne-
well : Marriage Lic. (London), i. 251.
1778. Married—Robert Barnewall and
Ann Hervey : St. Geo. Han. Sq. i. 289.
MDB. (Norfolk), 1, 0 ; (Suffolk), 2, 0 ;
London, 2, 0 ; New York, 0, 2 ; Phila-
delphia, 6, 0 ; Boston (U.S.), 1, 0.

Baron, Barron.—Official or
nick. 'a baron,' or a man who put
on an air of dignity such as might
become a baron. M.E. baron and
barun.

Osbert le Barun, Close Roll, 2 Edw. I.
Richard le Baron, co. Devon, 1273. A.
Geoffrey le Barun, co. Oxf., ibid.
John Barun, co. Linc., 20 Edw. I. R.
1545. John Baron and Eliz. Mathew :
Marriage Lic. (Faculty Office), p. 4.
1632. Nicholas Boemond and Susan
Barron : ibid. p. 17.
London, 6, 15 ; Philadelphia, 3, 33.

Barr, Barre.—Local, ' at the
Bar,' i. e. the entrance to the city
or town ; v. Bargate, usually made
of posts and chain.

Maurice de la Barre, co. Devon, Hen.
III-Edw. I. K.
John de la Barre, co. Staff., 20 Edw. I. A.
William atte Barre, co. Derby, ibid.
Gunilda de la Barre, co. Herts., 1273. A.
Philip de le Barre, co. Hunts, ibid.
Thomas atte Barr, co. Soms., 1 Edw.
III : Kirby's Quest, p. 150.
1765. Married—Henry Barr and Eliz.
Richardson : St. Geo. Han. Sq. i. 143.
London, 27, 1 ; Boston (U.S.), 30, 1 ;
Philadelphia, 152, 0.

Barrable. (!)

Emma Boribal, co. Oxf., 1273. A.
London, 1.

**Barrat, Barratt, Barret,
Barrett, Berrett, Berret.—**Bapt.
' the son of Berold,'the French Ber-
raud. This great surname appears
as a personal name in Domesday :
Baret, co. York.

Stephanus fil. Beroldi, Pipe Roll, 5
Hen. II.
Berard de Wattlesfeld, co. Suff.,1273. A.
Robert Berard, co. Bedf., ibid.
Agnes Barat, co. Camb., ibid.
Harvey Baret, co. Norf., ibid.
John Baret, co. Linc., ibid.
1575. Edward Barret, co. Devon, Reg.
Univ. Oxf. vol. ii. pt. ii. p. 63.
London, 9, 22, 1, 87, 1, 0 ; Philadelphia,
1, 2, 0, 160, 0, 2.

Barrell.—(1) Local, ' of Barwell,' a parish in co. Leic. and
dioc of Peterborough. Barrell is
a modification, as the following
entries show :

1688. Bapt.—Giles, son of John and
Susan Barrell : St. Jas. Clerkenwell, i. 328.
1691. — Thomas, son of John and
Susanna Barwell : ibid. p. 339.

(2) Bapt. ' the son of Barel.'
There seems to have been an early
personal name Barel, which may
share the parentage.

John Barel, co. Salop, 1273. A.
Ralph Barel, co. Suff., ibid.
William Barel, co. Soms., 1 Edw. III :
Kirby's Quest, p. 193.
1600. Robert Barrell, co. Soms.: Reg.
Univ. Oxf. vol. ii. pt. ii. p. 242.
London, 4 ; Boston (U.S.), 3.

Barringer.—Bapt. ' the son of
Beringer'; v. Berringer.

Barrington.—Local, ' of Barrington,' parishes in cos. Cambridge, Berks, Somerset, and
Gloucester.

Warin de Barenton, co. Camb., 1273. A.
Gilbert de Barenton, co. Camb., ibid.
Drogo de Barentin, co. Oxf., ibid.
William de Barentin, co. Oxf., ibid.

1575. Thomas Berington, co. Berks:
Reg. Univ. Oxf. vol. ii. pt. ii. p. 63.
1767. Married—Thomas Stephen Nocus
and Phillis Barrington: St. Geo. Han. Sq.
i. 170.
London, 5; Philadelphia, 13.

Barrow, Barrows.—Local, 'of
the barrow,' a long low hill or
mound, *gen.* barrows; cf. Bor-
roughs and Borrough.
Walter de la Barowe, C. R., 14 Edw.
III, pt. ii.
Robert de la Barwe, C. R., 3 Edw. I.
John de la Berewe, co. Worc., Hen. III-
Edw. I. K.
Richard de Barewe, co. Suff., 1273. A.
William de la Barewe, co. Essex, ibid.
John atte Barwe, co. Soms., I Edw. III:
Kirby's Quest, p. 100.
John atte Berwe, co. Soms., I E !w. III:
ibid. p. 227.
1759. Married—Thomas Barrows and
Mary Jones: St. Geo. Han. Sq. i. 83.
London, 30, 2; Philadelphia, 10, 13.

**Barrowclough, Barrowcliff,
Barraclough.**—Local, ' of the
Barrowclough'; some spot in co.
York, which I have failed to discover; v. Barrow and Clough.
Cf. Johannes de Barowchag' (i.e.
Barrowshaw), 1379 : P. T. Yorks.
p. 187.
1626-7. John Champ and Eliz. Barra-
clue : Marriage Lic. (London), ii. 183.
1690. William Heasey and Rebecca
Baroclough : Marriage Alleg. (Canterbury), p. 144.
— William Smith and Ann Barraclough : ibid. p. 138.
1765. Married—Edward Barrncliff and
Martha Whittaker : St. Geo. Han. Sq.
i. 141.
London, 0, 1, 1 ; West Rid. Court Dir.,
1, 0, 20 ; Philadelphia, 2, 0, 3.

Barry.—Local, 'of Barry.' There
can be little doubt that this was of
Norman extraction; cf. the French
Du Barry. The Irish Barrys have
made a large inroad in the Ameri-
can directories. I cannot say
whether they are of the same
parentage or not.
John de Barry, co. Soms., I Edw. III :
Kirby's Quest, p. 211.
Isabella Barri, co. Soms., I Edw. III :
ibid.
Robert Barry, co. Notts, Hen. III-
Edw. I. K.
William Barry, co. Notts, ibid.
Hugh Barry, co. Bucks, 1273. A.
Geoffrey Barri, co. Linc., ibid.
London, 36 ; Boston (U.S.), 314.

Barter.—Occup. ' the barter,'
a dealer in goods ; one who chaf-
fered, an exchanger.

Hugh le Bartur, co. Oxf., 1273. A.
1578. Adam Barter, co. Cumb.: Reg.
Univ. Oxf. vol. ii. pt. ii. p. 82.
1657. Married—Robert Porch and Eliz.
Bartor: St. Mary Aldermary, p. 27.
1747. — Richard Verrier and Betty
Bartar: St. Geo. Chap. Mayfair, p. 88.
London, 17 ; Boston (U.S.), 9.

Barth.—Bapt. ' the son of
Barth.' i. e. Bartholomew, from
nick. Barth ; v. Bate.
London, 5 ; Philadelphia, 62.

Bartholomew.—Bapt. 'the son
of Bartholomew.' A great favourite
in the surname period, as its nicks.
and dims. (Bartle and Bartlett, q.v.)
prove.
Robert Bartelmeu, co. Hunts, 1273. A.
William Bartolomeus, co. Suff., ibid.
Gilbert fil. Bartholomew, co. Camb.,
ibid.
Matilda fil. Bartholomei, co. Camb.,
ibid.
1579. John Curtys and Frances Bar-
tilmewe: Marriage Lic. (Westminster),
p. 7.
1616. Married — William Dycke, of
St. Bartlemew Exchange, and Maria
Wallis: St. Michael, Cornhill, p. 21.
1617. — Robert Turner and Suzan
Bartlemew: ibid.
London, 14 ; Philadelphia 34.

**Barthrop, Barthropp, Bar-
theropp, Bartropp, Bartrop,
Bartrap.**—Local, ' of Barthorpe,'
a hamlet in the parish of Acklam,
E. Rid. Yorks.: cf. Thrupp for
Thorp, and v. Winthorp.
1687. John Hole and Hester Bartrap:
Marriage Alleg. (Canterbury), p. 11.
1766. Married—Christopher Barthorp
and Mary Hughes: St. Geo. Han. Sq. i. 50.
MDB. (Suffolk), 1, 2, 1, 1, 0, 0 ; London,
0, 0, 0, 0, 2, 0 ; Bartrap (MDB. co. Notts), 1.

Bartle.—Bapt. ' the son of Bar-
tholomew,' from the nick. Bartle,
a form popular in north England.
For dim., v. Bartlett.
John fil. Bertol, co. Camb., 1273. A.
Bartel Frobisher, co. York. W. 9.
Bartly Bradforth, co. York. ibid.
Bartell Story, co. Northumb., 1528 :
TTT. p. xxviii.
1752. Married — Samuel Spencer and
Sarah Bartle: St. Geo. Chap. Mayfair,
p. 226.
1762.—William Baxter and Ann Bartle :
St. Geo. Han. Sq. i. 116.
London, 1 ; West Riding Court Dir., 3 ;
Philadelphia, 26.

Bartleet.—Bapt. ' the son of
Bartholomew' ; v. Bartlett.
London, 4.

Bartleman.—Occup. ' the ser

vant of Bartle,' i.e. Bartholomew.
A form of surname almost confined
to Yorkshire, where Matthewman,
Addyman, Priestman, and Vicker-
man (q.v.) arose.
Adam Batel, 1379 : P. T. Yorks. p. 196.
Simon Batelman, 1379 : ibid.
1750. Married — Thomas Scott and
Janne Bartleman: St. Geo. Chap. Mayfair,
p. 183.
1780. — David Bartleman and Mary
Brown : St. Geo. Han. Sq. i. 310.
London, 2 ; Newcastle-on-Tyne, 1 ;
Philadelphia, 2.

**Bartlett, Bartlot, Bartlott,
Bartolet, Bartolett.**—Bapt. ' the
son of Bartholomew,' from the nick.
Bartle, and dim. Bartl-ot and
Bartl-et. I subjoin a few out of
many instances in the Hundred
Rolls. The variants were numer-
ous. It is quite evident that Bart-
let or Bartlot was the popular nick.
for this then favourite Apostolic
name.
Bartelot (without surname), co. Bedf.,
1273. A.
Thomas Bartholot, co. Camb., ibid.
William Bartolot, co. Oxf., ibid.
Bartelot Govi, co. Hunts, ibid.
Alan Bartelet, co. Camb., ibid.
Richard Bartelot, co. Oxf., ibid.
Thomas Bartlot, 1379 : P. T. Yorks.
p. 106.
Robertus Bertlot, 1379 : ibid. p. 112.
1524. Thomas Barthelette and Agnes
Langwyth : Marriage Lic. (London), i. 4.
1578. Robert Bartlet, co. Dorset : Reg.
Univ. Oxf. vol. ii. pt. ii. p. 84.
1673. Buried William, s. John Bartlett :
St. Dionis Backchurch (London), p. 240.
London, 83, 10, 0, 0, 0 ; Philadelphia,
43, 0, 2, 1, 5.

Bartley.—(1) Bapt. ' the son
of Bartholomew,' from the nick.
Bartle and pet Bartl-ey; cf. Charlie,
Teddy, Bobbie, &c. Although
looking strongly local, I find no
evidence of this. We have, on the
contrary, proof that Bartley owns
Bartholomew as its parent.

Bartly Bradforth, co. York. W. 9.

This occurring in the county
where Bartle was so popular
clinches the argument; v. Bartle,
Bartlett, Bate, &c.

(2) Local, 'of Berkeley,' a variant.
1571. Francis Barteleye, co. Soms.,
I Edw. III : Reg. Univ. Oxf. vol. ii. pt. ii.
p. 50.
1591-2. Richard Barkeley, or Bartley,
co. Glouc. : ibid. p. 188.

G

In the above two entries we see evidence that the west-country surname Berkeley was sometimes modified into Bartley.

1691-2. Married—William Bartley and Eliz. Newbery: St. Dionis Backchurch, p. 43.
London, 6; Philadelphia, 24.

Barton.—(1) Local, 'of the barton,' literally the barley-croft; A.S. *bere*, barley, and *tun*, an enclosure. Afterwards 'barton' got the secondary sense of a court-yard.

William de la Berton, co. Wilts, 1273. A.
John de la Berton, co. Kent, ibid.
Reginald de la Berton, co. Glouc., ibid.

(2) Local, 'of Barton.' There are twenty-six parishes so called in Crockford. The origin is the same as (1), with this difference, that 'barton,' the single enclosure, had already grown into Barton, the hamlet or town.

Adam de Berton, co. Cumb., 20 Edw. I. R.
John de Berton, co. Kent, ibid.
Richard de Bertone, co. Hunts, ibid.
London, 57; Philadelphia, 60.

Bartram, Bartrum.—Bapt. 'the son of Bertram,' q.v.; cf. Barnard and Bernard.

Robert Bartram, co. Norf., 1273. A.
Thomas Bartram, co. Bucks, ibid.
1563. Bapt.—Frauncis and Amy Bartram: St. Jas. Clerkenwell, i. 2.
1578. Elias Martin and Bridgett Bartrom: Marriage Lic. (London), i. 81.
1585. George Bartrame, co. York: Reg. Univ. Oxf. vol. ii. pt. ii. p. 148.
London, 5, 4; Philadelphia, 11, 0.

Barwell.—Local, 'of Barwell,' a parish in co. Leic.; v. Barrell.

Ralph de Barewell, co. Wilts. 1273. A.
1603. Adam Barwell, co. Warwick: Reg. Univ. Oxf. vol. ii. pt. ii. p. 264.
1664-5. Edward Barwell and Mary Holman: Marriage Lic. (Faculty Office), p. 85.
London, 10; Philadelphia, 2.

Barwick.—Local, 'of Barwick,' parishes in cos. Norfolk, Somerset, and W. R. Yorks. A small spot in Furness furnished a local surname which has spread. I could give many instances from the Ulverston register and the Lancashire Wills at Richmond, to which I simply refer the reader.

Sampson de Berwyk, co. Wilts, 1273. A.
Philip de Berwyke, co. Wilts, ibid.

1567. Robert Debanke and Eliz. Barwyke: Marriage Lic. (Faculty Office), p. 14.
1573. George Barwyc'ke and Ellen Parkyns: Marriage Lic. (London), i. 56.
1610. Thomas Barwicke and Eliz. Pett: Marriage Lic. (London), p. 321.
London, 5; Philadelphia, 5.

Barwise, Barwis.—Local, 'of Barwise.' I cannot find the spot. But although my earliest instance comes from co. Derby, I believe the parentage of the name will be found in Cumberland. Mr. Lower says, 'An ancient name at Ilekirk, co. Cumb.'

Henry de Barweis, co. Derby, 20 Edw. I. R.
1742. Married—Joseph Barwis and Mary Fisher: St. Geo. Chap. Mayfair, p. 16.
1894. Died—John Adolphus Barwise: Daily Telegraph, Jan. 6.
MDB. (co. Cumb.), 8, 2; London, 1, 1; Philadelphia, 0, 5.

Base.—Nick. 'the base,' i. e. of low stature; v. Bass.

Geoffrey Base, co. Linc., 1273. A.
Isabella Base, 1379: P. T. Yorks. p. 193.
Thomas Base, 1379: ibid. p. 42.
1579. Antony Base and Eliz. Awdeley: Marriage Lic. (London), i. 88.
London, 2; Philadelphia, 1; New York, 1.

Basford, Bashford.—Local, 'of Barford,' a parish in co. Notts, near Nottingham. Also townships in cos. Chester and Stafford.

(Chaplain) de Baseford, co. Notts, 1273. A.
1565. Henry Basford and Joanna Newington: Marriage Lic. (London), i. 30.
1621. Samuel Basforde, co. York: Reg. Univ. Oxf. vol. ii. pt. ii. p. 398.
1695. Buried—'A child still-born to Edmond Bashford': St. Jas. Clerkenwell, iv. 56.
London, 1, 1; Philadelphia, 2, 0; Boston (U.S.), 7, 1.

Baskervill, Baskwill.—Local, 'of Bascreville,' 'now Bacqueville, in the arrondissement of Dieppe' (Lower).

Roger de Bascrevill, co. Salop, Hen. III–Edw. I. K.
Nesta de Baskervill, co. Salop, ibid.
Thomas de Baschevill, alias Baskervill, cos. Norf. and Suff., ibid.
Hugh de Baskerville, co. Salop, 1273. A.
Richard de Bascarville, 1297. M.
1590. James Baskervile, co. Glouc.: Reg. Univ. Oxf. vol. ii. pt. ii. p. 176.
1601. Humphrey Baskerville, co. Heref.: ibid. p. 249.

1623-4. Buried—Jarret Baskeuill: St. Dionis Backchurch, p. 216.
London, 1, 1; New York, 2, 0.

Baskett.—? Bapt. 'the son of Pasket.' from Pask, q.v.; dim. Pasket. This is all I can suggest. But Lower says, 'Probably Fr. Basquet, a dim. of Basque, a native of Biscay; a page or footboy, because the natives of that province were often so employed.' If I am right, the change from P to B is, as is so common in nomenclature, imitative.

William Pasket, co. Berks, 1273. A.
Adam Basket, co. Soms., 1 Edw. III: Kirby's Quest, p. 217.
1612. Thomas Basket, co. Hants: Reg. Univ. Oxf. vol. ii. pt. ii. p. 326.
1621. Robert Baskett, co. Dorset: ibid. p. 391.
1670. Richard Peesly and Margaret Baskett: Marriage Lic. (Faculty Office), p. 113.
1677. Bapt.—Mary Baskett, a foundling: St. Mary Aldermary, p. 104.
London, 3.

Basley, Bazley, Baseley.
Basely.—(1) Local, probably 'of Baslow,' a parish in co. Derby, three miles from Stoney Middleton.

(2) Local, 'of Bassaleg,' a parish in co. Monmouth, near Newport (*legge* = *lee*; cf. Lee and Legh).

(3) Bapt. 'the son of Basil,' from the pet Basily. Let me put first the following entry:

Hugh fil. Basilie, co. Notts, 1273. A.

My other instances seem strongly confirmatory:

Alan Baseli, co. Camb., ibid.
Richard Baseli, co. Oxf., ibid.
John Basely, co. Camb., ibid.
Michael Basely, co. Bucks, ibid.
John Baseley, co. Hertf., 20 Edw. I. R.
1655. Married—Edward Baseley to Alice Barton: St. Thomas the Apostle (London), p. 20.

I firmly believe (3) to be chief parent of the surname; cf. Charlie, Teddy, &c.; v. Bassil.

London, 2, 2, 1, 1; New York, 1, 4, 0, 0; Philadelphia, 3, 0, 0, 0.

Bason.—? Nick. 'the base son' (?), i. e. bastard; v. Bastard.

Willelmus Baseson, 1379: P. T. Yorks. p. 16.
1583. Robert Bason, Queen's Coll.: Reg. Univ. Oxf. vol. ii. pt. ii. p. 109.
1800. Married—William Bason and Mary Haines: St. Geo. Han. Sq. ii. 213.
London, 1.

Bass.—Nick. 'of low stature,' short and stout, corresponding to the French 'le Bas.'

Nicholas Basse, co. Soms., 1 Edw. III: Kirby's Quest, p. 271.
Hugh Basse, co. Bucks, 1273. A.
John Basse, co. Oxf., ibid.
Alicia la Bassé, co. Oxf., ibid.
1616. Married—Nicholas Basse and Hester Gore: St. Mary Aldermary, p. 13.
1646. Buried—Edward Basse, tallow chandler: St. Michael, Cornhill, p. 241.
London, 12; Philadelphia, 12.

Bassett, Basset.—(1) Nick. 'the dwarf' = O. F. basset, 'a dwarf, or very low man' (Cotgrave), a dim. of basse. (2) Local, ' de Basset,' of Norman origin. It is probable that most of the existing Bassetts can claim a local descent.

Golda Bassat, co. Camb., 1273. A.
Ela Bassett, co. Southampt., ibid.
Fulco Basset, co. Oxf ,ibid.
Ralph de Basset, co. Linc. Hen. III-Edw. I. K.
Gilbert de Basset, co. Bedf., ibid.
Hugo de Basset, co. Devon, ibid.
Simon Basset, co. Soms., 1 Edw. III: Kirby's Quest, p. 92.
1575. Edward Basset, co. Glamorgan: Reg. Univ. Oxf. vol. ii. pt. ii. p. 62.
London, 21, 1; Boston (U.S.), 44, 3.

Bassil, Bassill, Bazell. Bazelle.—Bapt. 'the son of Basil.' But more commonly a girl's name, in the form of Basilia or Basilie. It is now invariably a boy's name.

Basilia Reyngud, C. R., 23 Edw. II.
Basilia de Otteley, Hen. III-Edw. I. K.
William Basille, co. Norf., 1273. A.
Hugh fil. Basilie, co. Notts, ibid.
Robert Basil, co. York, ibid.
Basil de Borendvs, co. Suff., ibid.
1665. Married—Richard Beard and Bassilly W——: St. Jas. Clerkenwell, iii. 122.
1675. John Basnett and Eliz. Basill: Marriage Lic. (Westminster), p. 46.
London, 1, 1, 0, 0; Crockford, 0, 0, 1, 0; Philadelphia, 0, 0, 0, 1; Boston (U.S.), 0, 1, 0, 0.

Bastable.—Local, ' of Barnstaple,' a parish in co. Devon; a manifest corruption; v. Barnstable.

Ralph Barstaple, co. Soms., 1 Edw. III: Kirby's Quest, p. 215.
(Prior) de Barnestapole, co. Devon, Hen. III-Edw. I. K.

The halfway to Bastable is seen in Barstaple. The following entry and note establish this derivation:

1617. William Barstable, co. Devon. Subsc. April 11 as Barstable, and on May 30 as Bastable: Reg. Univ. Oxf. vol. ii. pt. ii. p. 362.

London, 7; Philadelphia, 1; Boston (U.S.), 2.

Bastard.—Nick. ' the Bastard,' a name proudly borne by at least one ancient English county family. ' William the Bastard' occurs in State documents as the Conqueror's surname.

Nicholas le Bastard, co. Devon, Hen. III-Edw. I. K.
William le Bastard, co. Notts, 1273. A.
Jordan Bastard, co. Bucks, ibid.
Roger Bastard, co. Northampt., 20 Edw. I. R.
Elias Bastard, 1379: P. T. Yorks. p. 292.
Thomas Bastard or Basterd, 1539: Reg. Univ. Oxf. i. 193.
1586. Thomas Bastard, co. Dorset: ibid. vol. ii. pt. ii. p. 156.
London, 5.

Baster.—Occup. ' the baster,' probably a kitchen servitor who basted the joint. ' Baster, one who bastes meat. 1525. Churchw Acc. Heybridge (Nichols, 1797), p. 181, "To she that turned the spitt, 8d.: to the Basteter, 4d. " '(H.E.D., v. Baster).

John le Bestere, co. Hunts, 1273. A.
London, 3; Philadelphia, 1.

Bastian, Basten, Bastin, Bastien, Bastion.—Bapt. ' the son of Sebastian.' In early though rare use in Cornwall and south-west England, where Spanish influence would be expected to prevail. Popularly Bastian; cf. French Bastien, which perhaps had its effect on Basten.

William, son of Sebastian Trevethan, buried 1607: Reg. St. Columb Major, p. 203.
William, son of Bastian Trevithan, bapt. 1599: ibid. p. 19.
1565-6. Bastian Bumfoy and Juliana Francke: Marriage Lic. (London), i. 32.
1603. Buried—Richard Bastian: St. Dionis Backchurch, p. 207.
1611. William Bastian or Bastin: Reg. Univ. Oxf. iii. 311.
1796. Married—Bastien Chevrey and Joanna Gale: St. Geo. Han. Sq. ii. 145.

The form Bastion occurs in Devonport Directory, co. Devon.

London, 1, 6, 5, 1, 0; List of Farmers (Devon Trades Dir.), 0, 0, 4, 0, 0; Philadelphia, 35, 0, 0, 0, 0.

Bastimer.—Occup. Perhaps for ' bastiner,' a sewer, stitcher; ' baste, to sew slightly. M. E. basten, baslyn' (Skeat); v. Way's Prompt.

Parv., note 4, p. 26; cf. Latimer for Latiner, q.v.

Hugh le Bastimer, co. Hunts, 1273. A.
Hugh le Bastimer, co. York. W. 9.

Batchelar,Batcheler,Batcheller. Batchelor, Batchelour, Batchler, Bacheller, Bachelder.—Offic. ' the bachelor,' a young knight, member of a guild, an unmarried man.

John le Bachiler, co. Oxf., 1273. A.
Nicholas le Bacheler, co. Oxf., ibid.
William le Bacheler, co. Camb., ibid.
Magg' (Margaret) Bacheler, co. Hunts, ibid.
Jordan le Bacheler. L.
Gilbert le Bacholer. E.
1621. William Batcheler, co. Oxf.: Reg. Univ. Oxf. vol. ii. pt. ii. p. 390.
1651. Thomas Funston to Cassandria Batchler: St. Mary Aldermary, p. 22.
— Abraham Ridder, batchler, to Jane Parsons, vergin: ibid.
London, 1, 1, 1, 25, 2, 1, 0, 0; Boston (US), 0, 1, 8, 5, 0, 0, 9 25.

Batchelder, Batcheldor.—Offic. ' the bachelor.' A corruption; v. Batchelar, and cf. Blackler.

1677. Walter Butler and Elizabeth Batchildar, of Chesham, Bucks: Marriage Lic. (Canterbury), p. 271.
1746. Married—William Batchelder and Ann Marshall: St. Geo. Chap. Mayfair, p. 75.
London, 2, 0; Liverpool, 0, 2; Boston (U.S.), 70, 0.

Bate, Bates, Bateson.—Bapt. ' the son of Bartholomew,' from the nick. Bate. The form Bathe below will mark the step by which Bate was reached.

Bate de Butwick, co. Linc., 1273. A.
Bate le Tackman, co. Linc., ibid.
Bathe fil. Robert, co. Linc., ibid.
Thomas Bateson, 1379: P. T. Yorks. p. 66.
Alicia Bate, wyf, 1379: ibid. p. 124.
Johannes Bateson, 1379: ibid. p. 19.
Adam Bate, 1379: ibid. p. 4.
Christopher Bateson, of Caton, co. Lanc., 1587: Lanc. Wills at Richmond, p. 23.
1615. Humphrey Bates and Joane Empson: Marriage Lic. (London), ii. 32.
1621. William Bate and Ann Hill: ibid. p. 106.
London, 8, 53, 4: West Riding Court Dir., 1, 15, 7; Philadelphia, 2, 116, 8.

Bateman, Batemanson, Batman.—Bapt. ' the son of Bateman.' Not found in Yonge's Christian Names. An old personal name. The suffix -man may be -mond or -mund; cf. Wyman, Osman, Roseaman.

Bateman de Capele, co. Suff., 1273. A.
Bateman Taye, co. Kent, ibid.
Bateman de Apletrewyk, co. York, ibid.
Cecilia Bateman, co. Hunts, ibid.
Bateman fil. Cressaunt, Close Roll, 51 Hen. III.
Willelmus Batemanson, 1379: P. T. Yorks. p. 263.
William Batmanson, 1423: DDD. ii.370.
1577. Married — Raffe Battman and Audrian Beane: St. Dionis Backchurch, p. 8.
1611-2. George Bateman and Mary Goodcole: Marriage Lic. (London), ii. 8.
1685. Married — John Bateman and Harmon Kynvin: St. Mary Aldermary, p. 33.
London, 40, 0, 0; Philadelphia, 32, 0, 1.

Bath, Bathe.—Local, 'of Bath,' the cathedral city in co. Somerset.

Job de Bath, co. Sussex, 1273. A.
John de Bathe, co. Soms., 1 Edw. III: Kirby's Quest, p. 158.
John atte Bathe, co. Soms., 1 Edw. III: ibid. p. 253.
1595. Richard Bath, co. Hants: Reg. Univ. Oxf. vol. ii. pt. ii. p. 211.
1611-2. Roger Bird and Doras Bath: Marriage Lic. (London), ii. 9.
1674. Bapt.—William, s. Joseph Bath: St. Jas. Clerkenwell, i. 263.
MDB. (co. Somerset), 8, 1; London, 15, 3; Boston (U.S.), 10, 1.

Bather.—Lower says, 'The keeper of a bath,' but without proof or reference. I look upon this as out of court; v. Batho.

1683. Married—Michaell Chapman and Elizabeth Bather: St. Michael, Cornhill, p. 43.
1752. — William Whennell and Hannah Bather: St. Geo. Chap. Mayfair, p. 216.
London, 2.

Batho, Batthew, Bather, Batha.—Local (?). This surname, with its variants, has troubled me much. Cheshire seems to have been the home of the stock. It seems probable that the Shropshire Bathers represent another variant. If local, then, like Shillito, or Shillitoe, or Shafto. &c., the original suffix would be Bat-how (v. How). But this is all I dare suggest. as I can find no spot so entitled. Bathall again suggests a local Bathall, which would become popularly Bathaw.

Richard Bathaw, of Kyddyngton, 1574: Wills at Chester, i. 15.
Aaron Bathall, of Over Alderley, 1603: ibid.
William Batha, of Dokington, in Malpas, 1610: ibid.

Adam Batho, of Cuddington, in Malpas, 1613: ibid.
Thomas Bathoe, of Larton, 1616: ibid.
1586-7. Richard Batho, Wales: Reg. Univ. Oxf. vol. ii. pt. ii. p. 157.
William Batho, rector of St. John th Baptist, Norwich, 1598: FF. iv. 288.
Ralph Bathoe, of Cuddington, gent., 1622: Earwaker's East Cheshire, i. 177.
1767. Married—Charles Brandoin and Ann Bathoe: St. Geo. Han. Sq. i. 166.
London, 1, 0, 2, 0; MDB. (co. Stafford), 0, 2, 0, 0; (co. Salop), 5, 0, 8, 0; (co. Denbigh), 0, 0, 0, 1; Boston (U.S.), 1, 0, 0, 0.

Bathurst.—Local, 'of Bathurst,' an ancient manor near Battle Abbey, co. Sussex, which was possessed by the family in the 14th century (Lower).

1604-5. George Bathurst, of London: Reg. Univ. Oxf. vol. ii. pt. ii. p. 281.
1610. Robert Bathurst, of London: ibid. p. 316.
1660. Richard Blake and Eliz. Bathurst: Marriage Lic. (Faculty Office), p. 47.
London, 3.

Batkin, Batken.—Bapt. 'the son of Bartholomew,' from the nick. Bat and suffix -kin; cf. Wilkin, Tom-kin, Wat-kin. But Batkin was evidently rare, the simple Bat or Bate being the popular form of address.

Batekin (without surname), co. Essex, 1273. A.
1779. Married — William Allen and Hannah Battkin: St. Geo. Han. Sq. i. 208.
MDB (co. Salop), 1, 0; (co. Stafford), 8, 1.

Batley.—Local, 'of Batley,' a parish in the union of Dewsbury, W. Rid. Yorkshire.

John de Bateley, co. York, 1273. A.
Isabella de Batelay, 1372: P. T. Yorks. p. 183.
1625-6. William Hampe and Ellen Batlee: Marriage Lic. (London), ii. 161.
1772. Married — John Battley and Susannah Parks: St. Geo. Han. Sq. i. 222.
London, 5; West Rid. Court Dir., 4; Philadelphia, 1.

Batling.—Bapt. 'the son of Bartholomew,' from the nick. Bate or Bat, dim. Bat-elin or Bat-ling. I fear this surname is extinct: cf. Hewling. With Batlins or Batlings, cf. Hewlings.

Thomas Batlyng, 1379: P. T. Yorks. p. 245.
Robertus Batelyng, 1379: ibid.
Johannes Battelyn, 1379: ibid. p. 21.

1705. Bapt.—Sarah, d. William Batlins: St. Jas. Clerkenwell, ii. 22.
1711. — John, s. William Batlings: ibid. 60.

Batsford.—Local, 'of Batsford,' a parish in co. Glouc., near Moreton-in-the-Marsh: or 'of Battisford,' a parish in co. Suff., near Needham Market.

William de Batesford, co. Suff., 1273. A.
Samson de Batesforde, co. Bedf., ibid.
John de Batesford, rector of Basingham, co. Norf., 1326: FF. viii. 84.
Maud de Batisford, co. Norf., 1335: ibid. ix. 480.
1766. Married—John Batsford and Ann Crook: St. Geo. Han. Sq. i. 151.
London, 5; New York, 1.

Batson.—Bapt. 'the son of Bartholomew,' from the nick. Bat; v. Batt.

1574-3. Henry Batson, co. Lanc.: Reg. Univ. Oxf. vol. ii. pt. ii. p. 61.
1593-4. Henry Batson, co. Wilts: ibid. p. 200.
1754. Married—Peter Batson and Jane Hobs: St. Geo. Chap. Mayfair, p. 270.
London, 7; Boston (U.S.), 3.

Batt, Batts.—(1) Bapt. 'the son of Bartholomew,' from the nick. Bate or Bat; v. Batson, Bate, and Batty. Batts represents the patronymic s, as in Jones, Richards, Williams.

Gilbert Batte, co. Rutland, 1273. A.
Matilda Battes, co. Camb., ibid.
Stephen Bat, co. Wilts, 20 Edw. I. R.
Clarice Batte, co. Soms., 1 Edw. III: Kirby's Quest, p. 149.
John Bate or Batt, 1570: Reg. Univ. Oxf. vol. i. p. 280.

(2) Nick. 'the bat.'

Osbert le Bat, co. Devon, Hen. III-Edw. I. K.
Reginald le Bat, co. Essex, 1273. A.
1730. Married — William Batt and Grace Wormell: St. Geo. Han. Sq. i. 7.
1786. — John Rae and Sarah Batte: ibid. i. 384.
London, 14, 2; West Riding Court Dir., 5, 0; Philadelphia, 16, 4.

Battell, Battle.—Local, 'at the battle'; M.E. bataille, i.e. battalion, guard, army, camp. 'Batalle,' an army. "Than thir twa batelles mett" ' (Halliwell).

Richard de la Batayle, co. Berks, 1273. A.
Adam de la Batayle, co. Norf., ibid.
Saer Batayle, co. Essex, ibid.
Philip de la Batayle, co. Oxf., ibid.
Richard de la Batayl, co. Glouc., 1289:

Household Exp., Bishop Swinfield (Cam. Soc.), p. 151.
1656. Bapt.—John, son of John Battell: St. Jas. Clerkenwell, i. 195.
London, 1, 3; Crockford, 0, 1; New York, 3, 6; Philadelphia, 1, 1.

Batten, Battenson, Batteson, Battinson, Battison, Battin.—Bapt. 'the son of Bartholomew,' from the nick. Bat or Bate. dim. Batt-in; cf. *viol-in*, a little viol.

Joel Batin, co. Devon, 1273. A.
Thomas Batyn, co. Soms., 1 Edw. III : Kirby's Quest, p. 91.
Batin atte Yete, co. Soms., 1 Edw. III : ibid. p. 92.
Batin Power, co. Soms., 1 Edw. III : ibid. p. 103.
Batin Walkelayn, co. Soms., 1 Edw. III : ibid. p. 121.
Bathon Mayster, co. Soms., 1 Edw. III : ibid. p. 150.
Andrew Batensonne, co. Durham,1561 : QQQ. p. 26.
John Battenson, temp. 1580. Z.
Daniel Battin, of London, *haberdasher* : 1633 : Visitation of London (1633), i. 52.
1774. Married—Joseph Battin and Eliz. Purvis : St. Geo. Han. Sq. i. 240.
1784. — William Baugham and Martha Battison : ibid. i. 357.
London, 22, 0, 1, 0, 0, 0; West Riding Court Dir., 0, 0, 0, 2, 1, 0; New York, 5, 0, 0, 0, 1, 1; Philadelphia, 3, 0, 0, 0, 5, 0.

Battersby.—Local, 'of Battersby,' a township in the parish of Ingleby Greenhow, in the North Rid. Yorks. This family name has ramified strongly, being now best represented in the Lancashire directories.

Rogerus de Bathersby, 1379: P. T. Yorks. p. 284.
1591. Henry Battersby, of Bold : Wills at Chester, i. 15.
1613. Nicholas Battersby : Reg. Univ. Oxf. vol. ii. pt. ii. p. 331.
1616. John Battersbie, of Shakerley : Wills at Chester, i. 15.
London, 6; West Riding Court Dir., 3; Manchester, 11; Philadelphia, 23.

Battershall, Battershell, Battishill, Battershill.—Local, 'of Battishill' or 'Battishall,' probably a manor or small locality in co. Devon.

William de Batteshol, co. Devon, 1273. A.
Antony Luther claims lease of Manor of Battylshall, 1582 : Rec. Office, Cal. State Papers (Domestic), ii. 83.
1691. Peter Battishill and Ann Howkey: Marriage Alleg. (Canterbury), p. 194.
Jonathan Battishill, 1738-1801, musical composer : Dict. Nat. Biog. iv. 421.

1746. Buried—Jonathan Battishill : St. Peter, Cornhill, ii. 140.
London, 1, 2, 0, 0; Plymouth, 0, 0, 0, 1 ; List of Boot and Shoe Makers' (Devon Trades Dir.), 0, 0, 1, 3; New York, 1, 0, 0, 0.

Batterson.—Bapt. 'the son of Bartholomew,' nick. Bat, dim. Batten or Battin, patr. Battinson, corrupted to Batterson ; cf. Paterson, Caterson, Custerson, Matterson, and Dickerson.

London, 1 ; New York, 6.

Batting.—Bapt. 'the son of Bartholomew'; v. Batten. The *g* is excrescent.

1565. William Battyn and Amy Rogers : Marriage Lic. (London), i. 30.
London, 1 ; Philadelphia, 2.

Battinson, Battison.—Bapt. 'the son of Bartholomew'; v. Batten. With Battison, cf. Pattison and Pattinson.

1702. Married — Thomas Batison and Eliz. Paradine : St. Peter, Cornhill, ii. 64.

Battle.—(1) Bapt. 'the son of Bartholomew,' from nick. Bartle; Bartle modified to Battle to meet Bat. In the instance below, Batelman means the 'man' or servant of Batel.

Thomas Batell', 1379: P. T. Yorks. p. 196.
Adam Batell', 1379: ibid.
Simon Batel-man, 1379 : ibid.

(2) Local ; v. Battell.

1625. Buried — Hannah, d. Thomasin Battle : St. Jas. Clerkenwell, iv. 170.
1648. Thomas Fiddes and Mary Battle: Marriage Lic. (Faculty Office), p. 39.
London, 3 ; Leeds, 1 ; New York, 6.

Batty, Battye, Battey, Battie, Battes, Batts.—Bapt. 'the son of Bartholomew,' from the nick. Batt, popularly Batty. With the patronymic *s* appended, Batty became Battys and Battes; cf. Jones, Williams, &c. Batt and Batty were favourite Yorkshire forms, and they have left their mark on its present nomenclature ; v. Batson and Battison.

Dyota Batty, 1379: P. T. Yorks. p. 181.
Thomas Batty, 1379 : ibid. p. 181.
Johannes Batty, 1379 : ibid. p. 251.
1570. Peter Pynder and Agnes Battye : Marriage Lic. (London), p. 46.
1603. John Battye, co. York : Reg. Univ. Oxf. vol. ii. pt. ii. p. 264.

1603. James Battye, co. Middlesex : ibid. p. 266.
1772. Married — Richard Battey and Betty Gerrard : St. Geo. Han. Sq. i. 217.
London, 10, 3, 0, 0, 3, 2; West Riding Court Dir., 6, 0, 1, 4, 0, 0; MDB. (West Riding, Yorks), 17, 20, 0, 1, 0, 0; New York, 2, 0, 2, 2, 0, 0; Philadelphia, 16, 1, 0, 0, 1, 4.

Baud, Baude.—Nick. 'le baud'; O.F. *baud*, joyous, gay; cf. Merry, Gay, Jolly.

Alan le Baud, co. Middlesex, Hen. III-Edw. I. K.
Geoffrey le Baud, co. Northampt., 1273. A.
Robert le Baud, co. Derby, ibid.
Johannes Baud, 1379 : P. T. Yorks. p. 86.
Richard le Baud, co. Northampt., 20 Edw. I. R.
Simon le Baud, co. Northampt., ibid.
Dominick Baude, co. Norf., temp. Hen. IV : FF. viii. 505.
'In 1543, the first cannon of cast iron that ever was made in England was cast at Buckstead, in Sussex, by Ralf Hogg and Peter Bawd': ibid. iii. 214.
1626. Bapt.—Elline, d. Jane Baud : St. Jas. Clerkenwell, i. 104.
London, 2, 0; Boston (U.S.), 0, 5.

Baudet, Baudett.—Bapt. 'the son of Baldwin,' from nick. Baud, whence the dim. Baud-et; v. Body.

Roger Baudet, co. Glouc., 1289-90: Household Exp., Bishop Swinfield (Cam. Soc.), p. 144.
New York, 1, 0 ; Philadelphia, 0, 2.

Bavent, Bavin.—Local, 'of Bavent,' a place 'four leagues north-east of Caen' (Lower). The family gave name to Eston-Bavent, co. Suffolk. Bavin and Baven are palpably variants.

Walter de Bavent, co. Linc., Hen. III-Edw. I. K.
Richard de Bavant, co. Norf., 1273. A.
Hugh de Bavent, co. Norf., ibid.
Jollan de Bavent, co. Linc., ibid.
Elizabet de Bavent, co. Norf., 20 Edw. I. R.
1614. Thomas Bavand : Reg. Univ. Oxf. vol. ii. pt. ii. p. 333.
1619. William Baven and Jane Millett : Marriage Lic. (London), ii. 79.
1626. Jonathan Head and Mary Bavin : ibid. p. 168.
London, 0, 5.

Bavirgton; v. Bevington.

Bawden, Bawdon.—Bapt. 'the son of Baldwin,' popularly Baudwin. This was gradually toned down to Baudin; v. Boden and Godin.

Baldwin or Baudwin de Rumeny, co. Worc., Hen. III-Edw. I. K.

Johanna Baudewyn, co. Camb., 1273. A. Bawden, son of John Jane, 1544: Reg. St. Columb Major, p. 3.

1547. Augustin Bawdwyn and Eliz. Wilson: Marriage Lic. (London), i. 11.

Bawden, d. of John Moyle, 1550: Reg. St. Columb Major, p. 5.

Johane Bawden, buried, 1589: ibid. p. 193.

1575. Nicholas Bawden, co. Cornwall: Reg. Univ. Oxf. vol. ii. pt. ii. p. 63.

1577. William Bawden, co. Cornwall: ibid. p. 74.

Thomas, son of Bodwine and Hanah Apps, 1694 : St. Jas. Clerkenwell, i. 357.

Bawden Maynard, English Guilds, p. 320.

London, 5, 2 ; MDB. (co. Cornwall), 5, 0 ; New York, 4, 0 ; Philadelphia, 2, 0.

Bawtree.—(1) Local, ' of Bawtry,' a small market town near Doncaster. (2) Local, ' at the Bortree' or 'Baw-tree,' i.e. the elderberry, from residence thereby ; cf. Rowntree, Birch, Nash, Nutbeam, &c. A word still in use in Furness. Elderberry wine is there ' bor-tree ' or ' bawtry-jack.' Bawtry or Bortery Stile is a farmstead in my old parish, and is found in many spellings in the Ulverston churchregister.

Coning de Bautre, co. York, 1273. A. Hugh de Bawtre, co. Notts, ibid.

Elena de Bautre, 1379: P. T. Yorks. p. 18.

Ranaldus Bawtree, co. York, 1429: W. 11, p. 245.

1604-5. Hamond Bautry, co. Linc.: Reg. Univ. Oxf. vol. ii. pt. ii. p. 280.

— Edward Bawtrey and Judith Langton : Marriage Lic. (London), i. 292.

1623-4. Richard Bawtrey and Wilmott Buffome : ibid. ii. 133.

London, 3.

Baxendale, Baxendell, Baxenden, Baxendine.—Local, ' of Baxenden' or 'Baxendale,' a locality in the district of Accrington, East Lanc. For the suffixes, v. Dean and Dale. The first named seems to have been the earliest, although both practically mean the same thing.

William de Bakestonden, co. Lanc., 1332 : Lay Subsidy (Rylands), p. 79.

John Baxenden, of Accrington, 1614: Wills at Chester, i. 15.

William Baxtenden, of Croston, 1672: ibid. iii. 23.

Thomas Baxtendine, of Bretherton, 1700 : ibid. iv. 21.

Thomas Backstendean?, of Croston, 1681 : ibid. iv. 12.

MDB. (co. Lanc.), 4, 1, 0, 0 ; Manchester, 2, 2, 0, 0 ; London, 0, 0, 1, 0 ; Boston (U.S.), 4, 0, 0, 0 ; Philadelphia, 2, 0, 0, 5.

Baxter.—Occup. ' a female baker,' a bakester ; v. Backster.

Bay.—(1) Local, ' at the bay,' i.e. bay-tree; very rare ; cf. Box, Beech, Ash, Nash, &c.

John ate Bey, co. Camb., 1273. A.

(2) Nick. ' the bay,' i.e. baycoloured or complexioned ; v. Bayard.

Walter le Bay, co. Camb., 1273. A. Nicholas le Bay, co. Bedf., ibid.

1595. Richard Cole and Mary Bay : Marriage Lic. (London), i. 227.

London, 3 ; Philadelphia, 6.

Bayard, Byard, Byatt.—(1) Local, ' of Castle Bayard,' near Grenoble. Pierre Bayard, the knight *sans peur et sans reproche*, was born here in 1476. (2) Nick. the English Bayard is, without doubt, a name of complexion, from bay, reddish brown, whence bayard, a bay horse; cf. Favel, a horse's name, and Burnel, an ass's name. 'As bold as is Bayard the blind,' i.e. a blind horse (Chaucer, C. T. 16881).

Robert Bahard, or Baiard, co. Camb., 1273. A.

Roger Bayard, co. Norf., ibid.-

Thebald le Bayard, co. Linc., ibid.

Thomas Bayard, co. Oxf., ibid.

Ricardus Bayard, 1379 : P. T. Yorks. p. 90.

Thomas Bayard, 1379 : ibid. p. 111.

Margaret Buard, co. Camb., 1273. A.

Ralph Baird, co. Northumb., 1175: KKK. vi. 22.

1665. Married—Jeames Bayarde and Elizabeth Weekes : St. Michael, Cornhill, p. 39.

1726. Bapt. — Peter Beyard : St. Antholin (London), p. 158.

London, 0, 1, 4 ; Philadelphia, 15, 8, 0

Bayldon, Bayldone.—Local, ' of Baildon,' a parish near Shipley, co. York.

Matilda de Bayldon, 1379 : P. T. Yorks. p. 199.

Ricardus Bayldon, 1379 : ibid. p. 204.

West Riding Court Dir., 8, 0 ; Boston (U.S.), 0, 1.

Baylis, Bayliss.—Nick. This surname is hard to classify, but its meaning seems obvious, viz. ' the son of the Bailey,' i.e. bailiff ; v. Bailey. Thus the final *s* is the

patronymic, as in Williams, Richards, Jones, Wilkins, &c. ; cf. Wrightson, Taylorson, Smithson, &c.

' Orate pro anima Willi. Balys ' : Blickling Church, co. Norf. : FF. vi. 407.

1767. Married — Thomas Baylis and Rachel Nereway : St. Geo. Han. Sq. i. 161.

1778. — John Parry and Eliz. Bayless : ibid. i. 284.

London, 26, 6 ; New York, 11, 2.

Bayman.—Bapt. ; v. Baynham, a corruption to which there are many parallels ; v. Deadman, Putman, Swetman. This surname is still familiar to co. Wilts, bordering on the district where Baynham arose. There cannot be a doubt as to the origin.

1658. Married — Richard Bayman to Hannah Curlinge : Canterbury Cath., p. 59.

London, 3 ; MDB. (co. Wilts), 2.

Baynard.—Bapt. ' the son of Barnard,' q.v. 'Meet me within this hour at Baynard's Castle ' (Rich. III, Act iii. sc. 5).

1550. William Curteys and Margery Baynerd : Marriage Lic. (London), i. 12.

1616. John Baynard, New Inn Hall : Reg. Univ. Oxf. vol. ii. pt. ii. p. 350.

1625. Adriel Baynard, Ball. Coll. and Magd. Hall : ibid. p. 439.

1645. John Mills and Ithamar Baynard : Marriage Lic. (London), ii. 276.

Crockford, 1 ; Philadelphia, 3.

Baynham.—Bapt. 'Ab-Eignon' (Welsh), i.e. ' the son of Eignon' or ' Ennion.' A Gloucestershire surname. Robert ap Eignon had for his son Robert Baynham, of Chorewall, in the forest of Dean. Henceforward the family were so known (vide Visitation of Gloucestershire, 1623, p. 14; Harleian Soc.). The name looks wonderfully English and local, but, as shown, is not so. Beynon, Binyon, and Benyon, q.v., are other forms ; but not Bunyan, I think.

Thomas ap Eignon, 7 Edw. III : Visitation of Glouc., 1623, p. 13.

Richard ap Eignon, 6 Ric. II : ibid.

Thomas Baynam, High Sheriff of Gloucestershire, 1476: Atkyn's Hist. Glouc., p. 40.

Alex. Baynham, High Sheriff of Gloucestershire, 1501 : ibid.

1738. Married—Richard Baynham and Frances Griffith : St. Geo. Han. Sq. i. 21.

1760. Married—John Baynom and Ann Yeates : St. Geo. Han. Sq. i. 94. London, 1 ; Crockford, 4.

Baynton.—Local, 'of Baynton' or 'Bainton' : (1) a parish in co. Northampton ; (2) a parish in co. Oxford ; (3) a tything in the parish of Edgington, co. Wilts.

John de Bayntun, *faber*, 20 Edw. II : Freemen of York, i. 23.
1661. Sir Edward Bayntun of Bremhill, Wilts, and Stuart Thynne : Marriage Alleg. (Westminster), p. 59.
1754. Married — Edward Bainton and Ann Hart : St. Geo. Chap. Mayfair, p. 275.
London, 1 ; Boston (U.S.), 5.

Bazin, Bason.—(1) Local, ' of Bashig.' (2) Nick. ; v. Bason.

Salomon de Basinge, sheriff of London, 1214 : WWW. pp. 187-190.
Adam de Basinge or Basinges, London, 1273. A.
Robert de Basinges or Basinge, London : ibid.
1583. Robert Bason, Queen's Coll. : Reg. Univ. Oxf. iii. 109.
1688. Bapt.—John Bazen, a foundline : St. Mary Aldermary, p. 109.
London, 2, 1 ; Philadelphia, 5, 0.

Bazley.—Local ; v. Basley.

Beaby.—Local, ' of Beeby '; v. Beebe.

Beach.—Local ; v. Beech.

Beacham ; v. Beauchamp.

Beadle, Beaddall, Beadell, Biddle, Beadel, Biddell.—Offic. 'the beadle,' one who executed processes or attended proclamations. The H.E.D. gives the following early dictionary forms (among others) : *lidel, beadel, beddell.*

John le Bedal, co. Soms., 1 Edw. III : Kirby's Quest, p. 188.
Alan Bedellus, co. Kent, Hen. III-Edw. I. K.
Geoffrey le Bedel, co. Kent, 1273. A.
Martin le Bedel, co. Norf., ibid.
Walter Bidellus, co. Linc, ibid.
William le Bedel, co. Linc., 20 Edw. I. R.
1578-9. Richard Bedal, co. Stafford : Reg. Univ. Oxf. vol. ii. pt. ii. p. 86.
1580-1. Richard Beedle, co. Worc. : ibid. p. 96.
1632. Bapt.—John, son of John Biddall : St. Michael, Cornhill, p. 122. The same person is entered as Beddell, p. 124, Beddelle, p. 126.
1660. Married—Marke White and Mary Biddle : St. Dionis Backchurch, p. 36.
London, 4, 0, 3, 13, 2, 3 ; New York (Bedell), 47 ; Philadelphia, 5, 0, 0, 140, 0, 0.

Beadman.—Occup. 'the beadman,' one who prays for others ; one paid to pray for the soul of his benefactor.

'Other smale mynisters, As reders and singers, Bedemen and bellringers,' 1528 : Skelton (H.E.D.).
William Bedman, co. Soms., 1 Edw. III : Kirby's Quest, p. 271.
1659. Buried—Eliza, d. John Bedman : St. Jas. Clerkenwell, iv. 328.
1793. Married — William Cullen and Catherine Beadman : St. Geo. Han. Sq. ii. 88.
London, 2.

Beake, Beak. ? I cannot discover the meaning of this surname.

Emma la Beke, co. Hunts, 1273. A.
William le Beke, co. Hunts, ibid.
Alde Beke, co. Hunts, ibid.
William le Byk, co. Oxf., ibid.
1589-90. Simon Beake, co. Kent : Reg. Univ. Oxf. ii. 175.
1609. Nicholas Wilson and Joan Beake : Marriage Lic. (London), i. 312.
1657. Bapt.—Eliz., d. Frederic Beake : St. Jas. Clerkenwell, i. 199.
London, 1, 0 ; MDB. (co. Kent), 1, 0 ; Boston (U.S.), 1, 3.

Beal, Beale, Beall.—Local, ' of Beal,' sometimes called Beal-on-the-Hill, a hamlet in north Durham, close to the sea. In Testa de Nevill it is spelt Behil, and it is recorded there that Gilbert de Behil held it of the see of Durham (QQQ. p. 203).

William Selbv, de Beall, 1631 : QQQ. Appendix, p. 156.
Thomas de Behil, 1382 : ibid. p. 203.
Laurence Beil, 1517 : ibid. p. 221.
John Bele, 1561 : ibid. p. xxxii.
Willelmus Beall, 1379 : P. T. Yorks. p. 301.
1583. Thomas Beale or Bele, co. Heref. : Reg. Univ. Oxf. vol. ii. pt. ii. p. 128.
1697. Married—John Deane and Ann Beale : St. Mary Aldermary, p. 35.
London, 14, 31, 1 ; Philadelphia, 9, 40, 3.

Beam, Beams, Beames.— Local, 'at the beam,' from residence by a prominent tree ; *beam,* wood : O.E. a tree ; cf. Nutbeam.

Osbarn Atebeame, co. Essex, 1273. A.
Robert atte Byme, co. Soms., 1 Edw. III : Kirby's Quest, p. 250.
1750. Married—Aaron Hargrave and Eliz. Beams : St. Geo. Chap. Mayfair, p. 182.
London, o, 2, 0 ; MDB. (co. Soms.), 0, 1, 0 ; Philadelphia, 26, 0, 0.

Beaman, Beament, Beamont, Beeman. — Local, ' de

Beaumont,' q.v. ; cf. Rayment for Raymond, Wyman for Wymond; Osman and Osment for Osmond. The spellings of this surname in the Reg. Univ. Oxf. vol. ii. pt. ii. are Beaman, Beament, Beamont, Beyman, Beymond, &c.

1583. Thomas Hawarde and Agnes Beyman : Marriage Lic. (London), i. 126.
1614. Richard Beamond and Eliz. Bannister : ibid. ii. 30.
1748. Married — Thomas Wright and Grace Beamont : St. Geo. Chap. Mayfair, p. 115.
1749. — Richard Daniel and Margaret Beaman : ibid. p. 142.
London, 1, 2, 1, 1 ; New York (Beament), 1 ; Boston (U.S.), 12, 0, 1, 1 ; Philadelphia, 0, 0, 0, 1.

Beamish.—Local, 'of Beamish,' a parish in co. Durham, seven miles from Gateshead. It is possible the entries below belong to some other locality.

Robert de Beaumeis, alias Beameis, co. Camb., 1273. A.
Roger de Beaumes, co. Salop, ibid.
Agnes de Beaumeys, co. Hunts, ibid.
1748. Married—John Hughes and Ann Beamis : St. Geo. Chap. Mayfair, p. 102.
London, 1 ; New York, 2 ; Crockford, 5 ; Philadelphia, 4.

Bean, Beane.—(1) Local, —— ? (2) Bapt. 'the son of Benedict,' from the nick. Ben, dim. Bennett.

Maurice de la Bene, co. Salop, 20 Edw. I. R.
Ediva Bene, co. Kent, 1273. A.
Johannes Bene, 1379 : P. T. Yorks. p. 16.
Willelmus Bene, 1379 : ibid. p. 261.

On the same page as the preceding, in the same village, occurs Willelmus Benne. If the same, the origin is simple.

Willelmus Bene, 1379 : P.T.Yorks.p.257.
Thomas Been, 1379 : ibid. p. 244.
1056. Married—Isack Beanne and Rebecke Jenner : St. Mary Aldermary, p. 26.
West Riding Court Dir., 7, 0 ; Boston (U.S.), 95, 2 ; Philadelphia, 37, 1.

Bear.—(1) Local ; v. Beer. (2) Nick. 'the bear,' one of surly temper. A common entry in early registers.

Robert le Ber, co. Kent, 1273. A.
Adam le Bere, co. Camb., ibid.
Clement le Bere, co. Oxf., ibid.
Walter le Bere, co. Oxf., ibid.
1614. Married—Fauor Beare and Catherine Powell : St. Mary Aldermary, p. 13.
1628. Hugh Beare and Dorothy Skeates : Marriage Lic. (Westminster), p. 32.
London, 6 ; Philadelphia, 9.

Bearbait, Bearbaste.—Nick. 'one who baited or basted the bear.'

'Thanne men doth the bere beyte.'
Havelok, 1838 (Skeat).

John Barbast or Barebaste, co. Glouc., 1273. A.
Geoffrey Barebast, co. Glouc., ibid.
Alexander Barebat, co. Bucks, ibid.
Thomas Barebat, co. Bucks, ibid.
John Barbast, co. Wilts, Hen. III–Edw. I. K.

Bearblock.—? Local, 'at the bearblock' (?), the block to which the bear was chained, from residence thereby.

1575. Edward Bereblocke, co. Kent: Reg. Univ. Oxf. vol. ii. pt. ii. p. 68.
1577. Henry Bereblocke, co. Kent: ibid. p. 78.
'Purchase by William Bearblocke, &c., of the reversion of certain messuages in the city of London, July 12, 1590': Cal. State Papers (Domestic), ii. 679.
1610. Antony Ramine and Susan Berblock: Marriage Lic. (London), i. 326.
1674. Buried—Daniell Bareblocke: St. Mary Aldermary, p. 189.

Charles Bearblock occurs in the Devonport Directory, co. Devon, 1873.

MDB. (co. Essex), 4.

Beard.—Nick. 'the bearded.' An early surname. Speaking of Geoffrey Martel's death, A.D. 1060, Freeman says, 'To his namesake Geoffrey, surnamed the Bearded, he left Anjou and Saintogne' (Norm. Conqest, iii. 180); v. Withibeard.

William Cum-Barba, co. Oxf., 1273. A.
Richard Cum-Barba, co. Oxf., ibid.
Hugh cum-Barba, co. Bedf., ibid.
Adam cum-Barba, 1379: P. T. Yorks. p. 238.
1622–3. Gerrard van Holbrooke and Susan Beard: Marriage Lic. (London), p. 120.
1645. Buried — Mr. Edward Bearde, grocer, in Cornhill: St. Michael, Cornhill, p. 240.
1771. Married—Richard Beard and Ann Ginder: Canterbury Cathedral, p. 96.
London, 33; Philadelphia, 28.

Beardsall.—Local, 'of Buerdsall,' a place in the parish of Rochdale, co. Lanc.

Henry Clegg, of Buerdsall, parish of Rochdale, 1607: Wills at Chester, i. 41.
James Buerdsall, of Blakley, 1610: ibid. 41.
Adam Buerdsall, of Manchester, 1546: ibid. p. 33.

Manchester, 1.

Beardsley, Beardslee; v. Bardsley.

Beare.—Local; v. Beer.

Bearward, Bearwood (?).— Occup. 'the bearward,' i. e. the keeper of a bear for exhibition of tricks; one who travels from place to place with a bear. '1399. A bereward fond a rag' (H.E.D.).

Michael le Bereward, co. Hunts, 1273. A.
1594. Buried—Margaret Barwarde: St. Michael, Cornhill, p. 206.
1609. — Robert Bearewoode, who fell doune dead in Popes Head Alley, of the plague: ibid. p. 217.

New York, 0, 1.

Beater, Bater.—Occup. 'the beater,' a wool-beater, a fuller. 'To full cloth is to felt the wool together: this is done by severe beating and pounding'; v. Full (3), (Skeat). 'Jacobus, the son of Joseph, was throwe there fro the pinacle of the temple, and after smet with a fuller's bat' (Capgrave's Chronicles, under date 30 A.D.; v. Woolbeater). 'A beter, verberator, baculator,' 1483 (Cath. Angl.).

Hugh de Ferlington, batur, 28 Edw. I: Freemen of York, i. 8.
John le Betere, co. Wilts, 1273. A.
William le Betere, C. R. 1 Edw. III: Kirby's Quest, p. 126.
John Batour, co. Soms., 1 Edw. III: ibid.
1777. Married—James Baughan and Ann Beater: St. Geo. Han. Sq. i. 272.
London, 1, 1; Crockford, 1, 0; Boston (U.S.), 0, 4.

Beaton.—Bapt. 'the son of Beatrice,' from nick. Bete and dim. Bet-on. It is found till recent days in Cornwall, that last home of decayed forms of English font-names. But its origin does not appear to have been known.

'Beton the Brewestere
Bade him good morrow.'
Piers Plowman, Pass. V.
'Bete, or Betune, propyr name, Beatrix': Prompt. Parv. p. 34.

Johannes Beton, 1379: P. T. Yorks. p. 87.
Beton de Wath: ibid. p. 100.
Beton, servant of Robert, fil. Ade, 1379: ibid. p. 88.
Betin de Friscobald. O.
John Betyn. HH.
John Beton, co. Oxf., 1273. A.
Beaten, d. of John Hoswell, 1637: Reg. St. Columb Major, p. 215.
Beaten, d. of Richard Cornishe, 1630: ibid. p. 212.
Beaten, d. of Thomas Bayley, 1629: ibid.

1694. Bapt. – Robert, son of William Beton: St. Mary Aldermary, p. 111.
London, 8; Philadelphia, 5.

Beatson, Beetson.—Bapt. 'the son of Beatrice,' nick. Bete; v. Beaton. Beatrice was, together with its nicks., a prime favourite in Yorkshire. The Poll Tax (1379) teems with it. Hence still largely represented; v. Beaton, Bettinson, and Betts.

Walter fil. Beatricie, 1273. A.
Richard Beatriceson, C. R., 11 Edw. II.
Iabelle fil. Willelmi Beteson, 1379: P. T. Yorks. p. 220.
Richard Beteson, 1494, co. York. W. 11.

These two last entries agree with Prompt. Parv. supra; v. Beaton.

1718. Married — William Grant and Elizabeth Beatson: St. Mary Aldermary, p. 44.
London, 1, 0; Sheffield, 5, 0; West Riding Court Dir., 6, 0; New York, 3, 2; Philadelphia, 5, 0.

Beattie, Beattey, Beatty.— Bapt. 'the son of Beatrice.' Beattie was the Northumbrian and Lowland Scotch form of the pet name. 'An abbreviation of the female name Beatrix' (Jamieson). The following variants of this surname are found on the Border: Baetie, Baitie, Baittie, Batie, Baty, Batye, Baytie, and Bette; v. The Debateable Land, by Robert Bruce Armstrong, p. 184.

1729. Married — William Beaty and Sarah Davis: St. Peter, Cornhill, ii. 78.
London, 11, 1, 1; Newcastle, 4, 0, 0; Philadelphia, 19, 0, 120.

Beauchamp, Beacham, Beachem, Beecham.—Local, 'of Beauchamp.' Mr. Lower mentions a Beauchamp near Avranches, and another near Havre. Its equivalent local term in England is Fairfield. Hugh de Bel-Champ, or Beauchamp (latinized in early records as 'de Bello-Campo'), obtained forty-three lordships from the Conqueror (Lower). Some of the variants may relate to some spot called Beecham (cf. Ashton), which would make them purely English, but I cannot find such a place.

John de Bello Campo, co. Soms., 1 Edw. III: Kirby's Quest, p. 187.
Thomas de Becham, co. Soms., 1 Edw. III: ibid. p. 195.

William de Bechehom, co. Oxf., 1273. A.
Roger de Bello-Campo, co. Camb., ibid.
Angareta de Bello-Campo, co. Oxf., ibid.
William de Beauchamp, co. Warw.,
Hen. III-Edw. I. K.
Roger de Beauchaumpe, co. Bedf., 20
Edw. I. R.
1600. William Beauchamp, co. Cornw.:
Reg. Univ. Oxf. vol. ii. pt. ii. p. 245.
London, 3, 2, 1, 3 ; Philadelphia, 1, 1,0,0.

Beauclerk, Beauclerc.—Nick.
'the beauclerk' (a nickname of
Henry I), 'learned clerk, good
scholar'; cf. opposite characteristic
in Manclarke, q.v.
1367. 'Henricus cognomento Beauclerk': H.E.D.
'Walker speaks satyrically of one who
bribed a Bishop's secretary to pass him
through his examination for orders, and
so "rigged he returned to Wapenham a
beauclerk"': Sufferings of the Clergy,
edited by Whittaker, p. 176.
Charles Beauclerke. PP.
1722. Lord William Beauclerk and
Charlotte Werden : Marriage Lic. (Faculty Office), p. 249.
MDB. (co. Kent), 1, 0 ; Philadelphia,
0, 1.

Beaufoy, Boffey.—Local, ' of
Beau-fd,' in the arrondissement
of Mortagne, in Normandy (Lower,
p. 22).
Ralph de Beaufow, co. Linc., 20 Edw.
I. R.
Richard de Beaufow, co. Linc., ibid.
Richard de Beaufou, co. Oxf., 1273. A.
Thomas de Beaufou, co. Linc., ibid.
Ralph Beaufey, co. Linc, ibid.
1675-6. Hercules Beaufoy and Mary
Rust : Marriage Alleg. (Westminster),
p. 250.
London, 1, 1 ; Philadelphia, 0, 1.

Beaufrere.—Nick. 'Beaufrere,'
probably an address of courtesy
like Beaupère, Bonamy, Belcher,
and Bellamy : the exact equivalent
of English ' Fairbrother,' q.v. I
doubt not *buffer,* a term of fellow-
ship still in use, is thus explained.
' Well, old buffer,' was a common
expression of greeting in my school-
days.
Walter Beaufrere, co. Northumb., 1278 :
Hodgson's Hist. Northumberland, Introduction, p. 295.
Roger Beaufrere, 1305. M.
Walter Beaufrere, 1305. M.
Walter Beaufrere, co. Soms., 1 Edw. III :
Kirby's Quest, p. 106.
John Beaufrere, C. R., 3 Edw. IV.

**Beaumont, Beaman, Bea-
ment, Beamont, Beman, Be-
mand, Bement.**—Local, 'de Bel-

mont' or 'de Beaumont.' ' Roger
de Belmont appears in Domesday
as a chief tenant in cos. Gloucester
and Dorset ' (Lower), probably a
near kinsman of the Conqueror.
' The Itin. de la Normandie gives
five places in that Province called
Beaumont' (ibid.). Nearer home
are parishes or places named Beaumont in cos. Cumb., Essex, and
Leicester (ibid.). Generally speak-
ing, the surname is of Norman extraction; v. Beaman.
Mathaeus de Bello Monte, co. Devon,
Hen. III-Edw. I. K.
Richard de Beaumund, co. Devon, 20
Edw. I. R.
Geoffrey de Beumund, co. Sou.hampt.,
1273. A.
William Beumunt, co. Oxf., ibid.
Godfrey de Beaumund, co. Northampt.,
ibid.
Richard de Bello Monte, co. Devon,
ibid.
Willelmus Beumond, 1379 : P. T. Yorks.
p. 301.
William de Bellemonte, Prepositor of
Bristol, 1240. YYY. p. 669.
1596. Francis Beaumont, co. Leic. :
Reg. Univ. Oxf. vol. ii. pt. ii. p. 218.
1622. John Beaumond, of Manchester :
Wills at Chester, ii. 18.
London, 28, 1, 2, 1, 1, 2, 1 ; New York
(Beament), 1, Boston (U.S.), 4, 12, 0, 1,
1, 0, 5.

Beaupre.—Local, ' of Beau-
preau,' a town in France. Possibly its manufactures of linen and
woollen originated the name of the
linen fabric, *beaupers* or *bewpers*
(v. H.E.D. 'beaupers '). At any
rate, the fact that the surname
existed and reached England is
corroborative, as suggesting mercantile relations.
John de Beaupre, co. Devon, 1273. A.

Beavan, Beaven, Beavins.
—Bapt. ab-Evan (Welsh), i.e. 'the
son of Evan'; v. Bevan and Bevans.
Similarly Evan and Evans are found
as Heaven and Heavens, q.v.
1676. Matthew Denis and Hannah
Beaven : Marriage Lic. (Faculty Office),
p. 137.
1752. Married—John Beavens and Eliz.
Roulatt : St. Geo. Chap. Mayfair, p. 233.
London, 10, 4, 1 ; New York, 0, 1, 0.

Beaver, Beever, Bever.—
(1) Local, ' de Beauver,' spelt in
general history ' de Beauvoir.' The
Prior of Beauver is frequently alluded to in early registers.

(Prior) de Beuver (co. Notts), or
Beauver (co. Leic.), 1273. A.
John de Beauver, co. York, ibid.
Thurstan de Beauver, co. York, ibid.
John de Beauver, co. York, Hen. III-
Edw. I. K.
1751. Bapt.—Eliz., d. William Bever :
Canterbury Cath. p. 29.

(2) Nick. 'the beaver.' a sobriquet
from the animal so called.
Adam Bever, co. Soms., 1273. A.
John le Bever. G.
Jno le Bevere. N.
1675. Edward Beaver and Ellinor
Jefferies : Marriage Alleg. (Canterbury),
p. 249.
1729. Bapt.—Eliz., d. William Bever :
St. Thomas the Apostle (London), p. 78.
London, 3, 2, 0 ; Philadelphia, 40, 0, 1 ;
New York, 10, 1, 0.

**Beavis, Beaves, Beavies,
Beauvais.**—(1) Local, 'of Beauvais,' in France. (2) Bapt. a
modification of Beavins or Bevins,
q.v.; cf. Purkiss for Perkins.
Simon de Beauveys, London, 20 Edw.
I. R.
Philip de Beauveys, London, ibid.
1557-8. Edward Beavys and Eliz.
Comes : Marriage Lic. (London), i. 18.
1601. John Grantham and Jone Bevys :
ibid. p. 266.
1606. Peter Bevis, co. Devon : Reg.
Univ. Oxf. vol. ii. pt. ii. p. 292.
1614. Charles Beavis, ibid. i. 277.
London, 15, 1, 1, 1, Boston (U.S.), 0, 0,
0, 2 ; Philadelphia, 1, 0, 0, 0.

Bebb.—Bapt. the son of Barbara,' a variant of Babb, q.v.
1611. Married—Roger Beb and Alice
Bowles : St. Michael, Cornhill, p. 20.
1741.— John Bebb and Sarah Prigg :
ibid. p. 69.
London, 1.

Beck, Becke.—Local, ' at the
beck,'from residence beside the beck,
a running stream, a small rivulet,
a word still in common use in the
North. ' Bek watyr, rendylle,
rivulus, torrens': Prompt. Parv.
Richerus del Bek, C. R., 55 Hen. III.
William en le Bec, co. York, ibid.
Ricardus del Bek', 1379 : P. T. Yorks.
p. 247.
Robert atte Bek, C. R., 19 Ric. II.
William atte Beck, temp. 1300. M.
' Robert atte Bek and Maud his wife
held lands here (Beck-Hall) in the 33rd
of Edward III' : FF. viii. 189.
1624. Alexander Shancke and Catherine
Becke : Marriage Lic. (London), ii. 140.
1759. Married—Joseph Beck and Ca-
therine Andrews : St. Geo. Han. Sq. i. 88.
London, 38, 1 ; Philadelphia, 200, 1.

Becker.—1 Bapt. ' the son of

Becker'(?). Some old personal name; cf. Beckert (German) in London Directory.

Alicia Beckar, 1379 : P. T. Yorks. p. 84.
Magota Beckar, 1379 : ibid.
1668. Married—Roger Becker and Ann Nicoles : St. Jas. Clerkenwell, iii. 164.
1761. — Ludewig Becker and Jane Toolken : St. Geo. Han. Sq. i. 101.
London, 9 ; Philadelphia, 104.

Beckett.—(1) Local, ' at the beck-head' ; v. A'Becket. (2) Bapt. ; cf. Birkett. Probably a personal name ; cf. Becker.

John Becket, co. Soms., I Edw. III : Kirby's Quest, p. 93.
Robertus Becket, 1379 : P. T. Yorks. p. 287.
1532. Robert Bekett and Elene Marshall : Marriage Lic. (London), i. 8.
1586. Thomas Jennings and Eliz. Beckett : ibid. p. 152.
1619. Richard Becket, of Ch. Ch. : Reg. Univ. Oxf. iii. 380.
London, 22 ; Philadelphia, 20.

Beckford, Bickford.— Local, ' of Beckford,' a parish in co. Gloucester, about six miles from Tewkesbury.

(Prior) de Bekeford, co. Glouc., Hen. III-Edw. I. K.
(Prior) de Bekeford, co. Glouc., 1273. A.
Adam de Beckeford, co. Glouc., ibid.
Henry de Beckeford, co. Glouc., ibid.
Alex. de Bikeford, co. Staff., ibid.
' William Beckford (1709-70), twice Lord Mayor of London. . . . The Beckfords were descended from a family long resident in Gloucestershire' : Dict. Nat. Biog. iv. 80.
1743. Married—Francis Beckford and Lady Albinia Bertie : St. Geo. Han. Sq. i. 31.
London, 2, 1 ; Boston (U.S.), 12, 45.

Beckles.—Local, ' of Beccles,' a parish in co. Suffolk.

Daniel de Beccles, Norwich, 1256 : FF. iii. 488.
Hugh de Beccles, co. Suff., 1273. A. Crockford, 2.

Beckley.—Local, ' of Beckley,' (1) a parish in co. Oxford ; (2) a parish in co. Sussex, near Rye.

Thomas de Beckelegh, co. Oxf., 1273. A.
Henry de Beckele, co. Oxf., ibid.
1622. Simon Beckley, co. Berks, and Mary Winch : Marriage Alleg. (Canterbury), p. 68.
1689. Edmund Winder and Elinor Beckley : ibid. p. 120.
1753. Married—John Beckley and Eliz. Withers : St. Geo. Chap. Mayfair, p. 258.
London, 6 ; Philadelphia, 9.

Beckman, Beckmann. — Bapt. ' the son of Beckmann '

(German). For an English example, v. Bickman.

1667. Married — John Becman and Susanna Wright : St. Jas. Clerkenwell, iii. 140.
Philadelphia, 29, 5 ; London, 0, 2.

Beckwith.—Local, ' of Beckwith,' a hamlet in the parish of Pannall, near Harrogate, co. York (cf. Askwith ; no doubt the suffix is a variant of *worth* ; v. Worth). This surname is strongly established in Boston (U.S.). ' Robert Beckwith, aged 21, went out in 1635 in the Transport, bound for Virginia ' (v. Hotten's Lists of Emigrants, p. 103).

Willelmus Bekwyt, 1379 : P. T. Yorks. p. 199.
Willelmus de Bekwyth, 1379 : ibid.
Johannes de Bekwyth, 1379 : ibid.
1562. William Beckewithe and Margaret Daye : Marriage Lic. (London), i. 24.
1572. Roger Beckwith, St. Alban Hall : Reg. Univ. Oxf. vol. ii. pt. ii. p. 41.
1754. Married—Ambrose Beckwith and Martha Smith : St. Geo. Han. Sq. i. 54.
London, 11 ; West Riding Court Dir., 5 ; Boston (U.S.), 10.

Bed.—Local, ' of the bed,' an official title : the yeoman of the bed-chamber.

Gilbert del Bed. H.
Gilbert del Bed, Close Roll, 30 Edw. I.
' To Lamberte yoman of the Bedde, viis. vid.' 1540 : Privy Purse Exp., Princess Mary, p. 86.

Beddall.—Offic. ' the beadle' ; v. Beadle.

Simon le Beddel, C. R., 56 Henry III.
1586-7. Richard Cottman and Alice Bedall : Marriage Lic. (London), i. 158.
1746. Married—Thomas Shepherd and Mary Beddall : St. Geo. Chap. Mayfair, p. 68.
London, 1 ; Philadelphia, 1 ; New York, 1.

Beddoe, Beddoes, Beddow, Bedow, Peddowe, Beddows. —Bapt. ap- or ab-Eddow. A Welsh patronymic, ' the son of Eddow' ; cf. Bevans, Bethell, Bloyd, Benyon, &c. My view is corroborated by the fact that Eddowe existed alongside Beddowe ; cf. Bithell and Ithell, Ennion and Bennion. Also as Eddowe became Eddowes, so Beddoe became Beddoes ; v. Eddowes. Although I may not have got the exact form of the personal name, there can be no doubt about

the origin as stated above. Beddoes is a double patronymic, part English, part Welsh : ab-Eddow-s. This final *s* is the same as the *s* in Williams or Jennings ; v. Bevans.

1577-8. Richard Peddowe and Johanna Green : Marriage Lic. (London), i. 78.
— Richard Love and Johanna Bedowe, widow : ibid.
1578-9. Thomas Bedo, co. Salop : Reg. Univ. Oxf. vol. ii. pt. ii. p. 85.
Edward Beddowe, of Tybroughton, co. Flint, yeoman, 1650 : Wills at Chester (1621-1650), p. 18.
Margaret Beddowe, of Hanmer, 1622 : ibid.
William Beddowe, clerk, vicar of Hanmer, 1574 : ibid. (1545-1620), p. 16.
David Eddowe, of Iscoyd, co. Flint, 1605 : ibid. p. 59.
Thomas Eddowe, of Oldcastle, 1615 : ibid.
London, 2, 0, 2, 1, 0, 0 ; Manchester, 1, 0, 0, 0, 0, 0 ; Crockford (1879), 0, 1, 0, 0, 0, 0 ; MDB. (co. Radnor), 0, 1, 0, 0, 0, 0 ; (Salop), 2, 17, 3, 0, 0, 0 ; (Pembroke), 1, 0, 0, 0, 0, 0 ; (Montgomery), 0, 4, 0, 0, 0, 0 ; New York (Beddows), 1 ; Philadelphia, 1, 0, 3, 0, 0, 0.

Bedford.—Local, ' of Bedford,' in the co. of Bedford.

John de Bedford, *taillour*, 9 Edw. III : Freemen of York, i. 30.
Jordan de Bedeford, co. Oxf., 1273. A.
Robert de Bedeford, co. Hunts, ibid.
Johannes de Bedforth, 1379 : P. T. Yorks. p. 168.
1578. Antony Bedford, co. Salop : Reg. Univ. Oxf. vol. ii. pt. ii. p. 84.
1589. John Robynson and Ann Bedford : Marriage Lic. (London), i. 180.
1707. Bapt.—Eliz., d. William Bedford : St. Jas. Clerkenwell, iii. 37.
London, 33 ; Manchester, 4 ; Philadelphia, 17.

Bedingham.—Local, ' of Bedingham,' parishes in diocs. of Norwich and Chichester. It is possible that in some instances Beadman is a corrupted form. We have parallel instances in Deadman for Debenham, and Putman for Putnam, i.e. Puttenham. Of course it would be more satisfactory to refer it to the same origin as Paternoster, and there is strong evidence for this view. The corruptions would be as follows : Bedingham, Beddenham, Bednam, Bedman, Beadman ; v. Beadman for a really satisfactory solution of that surname.

Clarice de Bedyngham, co. Norf., 1273. A.

1525-6. William Bedyngham and Elen Bolande: Marriage Lic. (London), i. 5. London, 2.

Bedward, Beddard.—Bapt. ab-Edward (Welsh) = English Edwards or Edwardson; v. Bellis for further instances. Only found on the borders of the Principality.

Richard ap Edward, of Overton, 1581: Wills at Chester (1545-1620), p. 59.
Edward ap Edward, of Knolton, 1629: ibid. (1621-1650), p. 72.

In the 18th century this had assumed the form of Bedward.

John Bedward, 1747: List of Freemen in Chester (in the Byrom Library, Chetham Library, Manchester).

From Bedward to Beddard was an easy and natural step,

1556. Edward ab-Edward, citizen of Oxford: Reg. Univ. Oxf. vol. ii. pt. i. p. 298.
1647. Married—William Bedward and Mary Hayward: St. Jas. Clerkenwell, iii. 81.
1752. — Edward Beddard and Mary Pritchard: St. Geo. Chap. Mayfair, p. 234.

The above entry is very Welsh.

Liverpool, 1, 0; London, 1, 1; MDB, (Salop), 1, 0.

Bedwin.—Local, 'of Bedwin,' two parishes, Great and Little Bedwin, in co. Wilts.

William Bedewine, co. Devon, 1273. A.
1744. Married — Cramond McDugall and Mary Bedwin: St. Geo. Chap. Mayfair, p. 40. London, 1.

Bee.—(1) Nick. 'the bee,' an industrious man, a busy woman. (2) Bapt. 'the son of Beatrice,' from the nick. Bee, still in use.

Alicia Bee, 1379: P. T. Yorks. p. 272.
Thomas Bee, 1447: cos. Northumb. and Durham: PPP. i. 315.
1587. Bapt.—William, son of Agnes Bee: St. Jas. Clerkenwell, i. 19.
1597. Edward Bee and Margery Pyke: Marriage Lic. (London), i. 245.
1745. Married — John Bee and Eliz. White: St. Geo. Han. Sq. i. 35.
London, 2; Boston (U.S.), 4.

Beebe, Beeby, Beaby, Beebee.—Local, 'of Beeby,' a village six miles from Leicester; v. Bibby.

1678. Thomas Beeby and Hannah King: Marriage Alleg. (Canterbury), p. 282.
1744. Married—James Beeby and Mary Dorman: St. Geo. Chap. Mayfair, p. 44.
1760. — James Beeby and Mary Dennis: St. Geo. Han. Sq. i. 98.

London, 2, 5, 0, 0; MDB. (co. Leicester), 0, 1, 0, 0; (co. Wilts), 0, 0, 2, 0; (co. Stafford), 0, 0, 0, 12; Philadelphia, 12, 0, 0, 0.

Beech, Beach.—Local, 'at the beech-tree'; cf. Ash, Oak, Birch, &c.

Eufemia de la Beche, co. Norf., 35 Edw. III: FF. viii. 187.
Thomas atte Beche, co. Soms., 1 Edw. III: Kirby's Quest, p. 139.
Jacob de la Beche, co. Oxf., 1273. A.
Matilda de la Beche, co. Camb., ibid.
William de la Beche, co. Oxf., ibid.
1623. Bapt.—Rebecca, d. Roger Beech: St. Jas. Clerkenwell, i. 97.
1718. Married— Thomas Beech and Rebecca Horne: St. Michael, Cornhill, p. 60.
London, 15, 16; Philadelphia, 9, 21.

Beecham; v. Beauchamp.

Beecher.—(1) Occup. I am not able to state the avocation followed by 'le Becher.' (2) Local, 'the beecher,' one who lived by some prominent beech-tree (v. Beech); cf. Bridger.

Henry le Beechur (also Becchur), co. Camb., 1273. A.
John Becher, co. Camb., ibid.
1588-9. Henry Becher, co. Hants. Reg Univ. Oxf. vol. ii. pt. ii. p. 168.
1594. William Becher, or Beecher, of London: ibid. p. 204.
1670. Married — Oliver Beecher and Sarah Wyan: St. Michael, Cornhill, p. 39.
1747. — James Beecher and Abigail Oakman: St. Geo. Chap. Mayfair, p. 82.
London, 1; Boston (U.S.), 5; New York, 12.

Beechey.—Local, 'at the Beechey,' i. e. the beech-isle, the little island covered with beech-trees. Seemingly some small islet in one of the streams or rivers in co. Oxford.—I wrote the above several years ago, but I find a second derivation, and possibly the true one in all cases:

Brownyng Bycheheye, co. Soms., 1 Edw. III: Kirby's Quest, p. 94.

This means Browning at the Beech-hey, i. e. he lived beside the beech enclosure; v. Hey, a field enclosed by beech-trees.

Thomas de la Bechey, co. Oxf., 1273. A.
1769. Married—William Beechey and Francis McLaughlin: St. Geo. Han. Sq. p. 183.
London, 2; MDB. (co. Oxford), 2; Philadelphia, 2.

Beecroft.—Local, 'at the bere-croft,' i.e. barley-croft (v. Croft); cf. Rycroft. A.S. bere, barley. Evidently a Yorkshire local surname. I find no instances in the London church registers printed by the Harleian Society. There can be no doubt about the origin of this name.

Walter de Bercroft, co. York, 1273. A.
Matilda Bercroft, co. York, ibid.
Johannes de Bercroft, 1379: P. T. Yorks. p. 182.
Willelmus de Bercroft, 1379: ibid. p. 191.
James Beecroft, 1587: Wills at Chester (1545-1620), p. 16.
Thomas Beecroft, Norwich, 1710: FF. iv. 365.
1803. Married—Robert Beecroft and Rebecca Smith: St. Geo. Han. Sq. ii. 288.
West Riding Court Dir., 4; London, 4; MDB, (West Riding Yorks), 5; Philadelphia, 9.

Beef.—Nick. 'the Beef,' beef, an ox; O.F. boef; cf. Bull, Pigg, &c.

John le Bef, co. Oxf., 1273. A.
Robert le Bef, co. Oxf., ibid.

Beeman.—Local, a corruption of Beaumont; v. Beaman.

Beer, Beere, Beare, Bear.—Local, 'at the bere,' i. e. at the byre, the farmstead, cowshed, or village; v. Words and Places, p. 157; cf. Coneybeare. Common in Devonshire place-names. The same as by in Formby, Rugby, Willoughby, &c.; cf. such places as Bere Ferrars, Bere Regis, Beer Alston, Beer Hacket, Langabeer, all in Devonshire and Dorset district.

John de Bere, co. Soms., 1 Edw. III: Kirby's Quest, p. 143.
Robert atte Bere, co. Soms., 1 Edw. III: ibid. p. 253.
William atte Byr, co. Hertf., Hen. III-Edw. I. K.
Lucy de la Bere, co. Devon: ibid.
Elyas de la Byare, co. Devon, 1273. A.
John de la Byare, co. Devon, ibid.
Reginald de Bere, co. Devon, ibid.
Richard de la Bere, co. Bedf., 20 Edw. I. R.
Robert de la Bere, co. Southampt., ibid.
John Bere, or Beere, 1534, rector of Endellion, co. Cornwall: Reg. Univ. Oxf. i. 103 and index.
1614. Married — Favor Beare and Catherine Powell: St. Mary Aldermary, p. 13.
1713. — Samuel Keymer and Sarah Beer: ibid. p. 42.

London, 12, 4, 1, 6; Plymouth, 4, 0, 2, 0; Exeter, 6, 0, 0, 0; Devonport, 4, 0, 0, 0; New York, 26, 3, 2, 15.

Beerbrewer. — Occup. 'the beer-brewer.'

'Chymney-sweepers, and costerde-mongers, Lodemen and berebrewers.'
    Cocke Lorelle's Bote.
Lambert Beerbruer, co. York. W. 11.
'Hic jacet Ricardus Lawrence filius Laurentii Berbrewer, alias Wyllyamson.' A.D. 1500: St. Simon and St. Jude (Norwich): FF. iv. 357.

Beeston, Beeson, Beesting. —Local, 'of Beeston,' a village near Leeds. With Beeson, cf. Kelson for Kelston, &c.

Radulphus de Beston, Esquier, of Beeston, 1379: P. T. Yorks. p. 192.
Willelmus de Beston, 1379: ibid. p. 201.
Johannes de Beeston, 1379: ibid. p. 206.
1579. Robert Beistone, co. York: Reg. Univ. Oxf. vol. ii. pt. ii. p. 88.
1701. Married—Ralph Beeston and Eliza Wellin: St. Jas. Clerkenwell, iii. 223.
1793. — Joseph Beeson and Eliz. Killmaster: St. Geo. Han. Sq. ii. 102.
London, 8, 0, 0; Sheffield, 1, 2, 0; West Riding Court Dir., 0, 2, 1; Philadelphia, 1, 2, 0.

Beet.—Bapt. 'the son of Beatrice,' from the nick. Bete; v. Beaton and Beatson. . Bete or Beet was a familiar nick. in Yorkshire, where Beatrice was very popular as a font-name in the 13th and 14th centuries.

Alicia Bete, doghter, 1379: P. T. Yorks. p. 233.
Johannes Bete, son, 1379: ibid. p. 13.
1687. William Beet and Rachell Sweit: Marriage Alleg. (Canterbury), p. 10.
London, 2; Sheffield, 4.

Beetson; v. Beatson and Beet.

Belcher, Belchier.—Nick. 'belsire,' grandfather, or perhaps *bel chere*, good friend; cf. Bellamy, Bowsher, and Bonamy.

'Lo, here is the belschere broght that ye bad bring': York Mystery Plays, p. 262.
'Belsyre, or belfather, faders or moders fader, *avus*': Prompt. Parv. See also Belsire (H.E.D.).
Richard Belechere, co. Glouc., 1273. A.
John Belsire, co. Kent, ibid.
Leonard Belshyre, squire bedell, Oxford, 1553: Reg. Univ. Oxf. vol. ii. pt. i. p. 288.
William Belsher, sheriff of Bristol, 1562; YYY. p. 685.

1673. Buried—Katherine Bellshar: St. Thomas the Apostle (London), p. 140.
1783. Married—Walter Belchar and Mary Ware: St. Geo. Han. Sq. i. 350.
London, 20, 2; Philadelphia, 18, 0.

Beljambe.—Nick. 'handsome legs'; cf. Foljambe.

Alexander Bele-Jambe, co. Salop, 1273.A.
Peter Belejambe, co. Wilts, ibid.
Richard Beljaumbe, c. 1315. M.

Bell.—(1) Bapt. 'the son of Bell,' i.e. Isabel; nick. Bella or Bell; v. Belson.

Bela le Barber, co. Hunts, 1273. A.
Bella or Bele Cotty, co. Linc., ibid.
Nicholas fil. Bele, co. Bedf., ibid.
Bele Scampeyn, co. Camb., ibid.

(2) Nick. 'le bel,' i.e. the beautiful.

Ralph le Bele, co. Camb., 1273. A.
Hugh le Bel, co. Oxf., ibid.
Thomas le Bel, co. Suff., ibid.
Robert le Bell, mayor of Bristol, 1239: YYY. p. 669.

(3) Local, 'at the Bell,' i.e. an inn-sign, or one who dwelt by the bell, i.e. bell-chamber.

John atte Belle. V.
Richard atte Bell, 1307. M.
John atte Belle (London). X.
Roger atte Bell, co. Soms., 1 Edw. III: Kirby's Quest, p. 81.
London, 158; Philadelphia, 324.

Bellamy, Bellamey.—Nick. a familiar expression, 'my good friend'; cf. Bonamy. A common surname in early registers.

'Feste! fy! that were a wykyd treson! Belamy, thou shal be smytt.'
    York Mystery Plays, p. 391.
'Thou bel-amy, thou pardoner,' he said.
    Chaucer, C. T. 12252.
'Belamy, fayre frynde': Prompt. Parv. p. 29.
Henry Belamy, Close Roll, 2 Edw. I.
Hugh Belami, co. Camb., 1273. A.
Roger Belamy, co. Oxf., ibid.
John Belamy, co. Soms., 1 Edw. III: Kirby's Quest, p. 233.
John Bellmy, Norwich, 1603: FF. iv. 167.
1634. Bapt.—Eliz., d. John Bellamye: St. Jas. Clerkenwell, i. 127.
1757. Married—Charles Parent and Eliz. Bellamy: St. Geo. Han. Sq. i. 71.
London, 24, 1; New York, 5, 0.

Bellard; v. Bellhird.

Bellchambers, Belchamber. —Local, 'of Belencombre,' in the arrondissement of Dieppe, in Normandy. The present forms are imitative. There is not the slightest evidence in favour of an origin akin to Bellhouse. Dr. Charnock

has unwisely permitted himself to write as follows: 'A friend assures me he knows of a William Chambers who changed his name to Bill-chambers, of which he says Bellchambers is a corruption' (Ludus Patronymicus, p. 6). 'Save me from my friends' receives a fresh consecration after this.

John de Belencumbre, co. Essex, 1273. A.
Robert de Belecumbre, co. Essex, ibid.
1654. Buried—Mary Belchamber: St. Thomas the Apostle (London), p. 130.
1677. Thomas Shelbery and Merrian Belchamber: Marriage Alleg. (Canterbury), p. 265.
1794. Married—Samuel Belchambers and Eliz. Grant: St. Geo. Han. Sq. ii. 112.
London, 2, 2; New York, 2, 0.

Bellett, Bellott, Belot.—Bapt. (?) 'the son of Isabel' (?), from the nick. Bel, dim. Bel-ot or Bel-et; v. Bell (1). The writer of the article on Hugh Bellot (1542–96), bishop of Chester (Dict. Nat. Biog. iv. 195), says, 'The Bellots were early seated in Norfolk. ...It has been suggested that the name is derived from *belette*, a weasel, or *belotte*, gentle, pretty. ... We find the name spelt in various ways: Billet, Bellott, Billett, &c.' After writing the above I find a local origin implied by two entries in Blomefield's Hist. of Norfolk. If correct, those entries are entitled to the first consideration. But I strongly suspect a double origin.

Adam Belot, co. Hunts, 1273. A.
William Belot, co. Norf., ibid.
Hervens Belet, co. Oxf., 20 Edw. I. R.
Lawrence de Belet, co. Linc., ibid.
Hervy de Belet, co. Norf., 1236: FF. v. 143.
Ingelram de Belet, co. Norf., 6 Edw. II: ibid. viii. 434.
Robert Belet, 8 Edw. II: ibid. vii. 288.
1708. Married—Charles Davis and Ann Bellot: St. Mary Aldernary, p. 38.
1758. — James Bellett and Jane Thompson: St. Geo. Han. Sq. i. 78.
London, 1, 1, 0; Crockford, 3, 0, 0; New York, 1, 0, 1.

Bellhird, Bellard.—Occup. 'a bull-herd,' a tender of bulls; A.S. *bellan*, to bellow; cf. Coward, Oxhird, Calvert, Stoddart, or Shepherd.

Simon Belhyrd, 1379: P. T. Yorks. p. 273.
Henry Bellard, 1379: ibid. p. 6.
1657. Bapt.—Henry, s. Robert Bellard: St. Jas. Clerkenwell, i. 197.

MDB. (East Rid. Yorks), 0, 1; New York, 0, 1.

Bellhouse, Bellows.—Local, 'at the Bell-house.' The bell-house or tower was frequently detached from the church; v. Bell-house (H.E.D.), early corrupted to Bellows.

Richard de Belhouse, co. Norf., 31 Edw. III : FF. vi. 16.
John de Belhouse, co. Norf., 1333 : ibid. p. 384.
Ricardus de Belhus, co. Suff., 1273. A.
Thomas de la Belhuse, co. Kent, ibid.
Johannes de Bellehous, 1379 : P. T. Yorks. p. 160.
Thomas Belhowse, C. R., 18 Ric. II.
William Dellowes, co. York, 1440. W. 2.
1590. Bapt. — Richard, s. Edward Bellowse : St. Jas. Clerkenwell, i. 23.
1771. Married—John Bellhouse and Jane Butson : St. Geo. Han. Sq. i. 209.
Crockford, 1, 0; Manchester, 4, 0; Philadelphia, 0, 8; Boston (U.S.), 0, 27.

Bellinger.— (1) Bapt. 'the son of Beranger,' a corruption. v. Berringer. (2) Occup.; v. Bullinger. The first is the more probable origin.

1563. Buried—William Dellinger : St. Peter, Cornhill, p. 118.
— Married—Thomas Bland and Rose Bellynger : ibid. p. 226.
1572-3. William Bellinger and Dorothy Ferrybye : Marriage Lic. (London), i. 55.
1620. Married—Richard Ashman and Joan Belinger : St. Peter, Cornhill, p. 250.
1658. Bapt.—Ann, d. Giles Bellinger : St. Jas. Clerkenwell, i. 201.
London, 5 ; Philadelphia, 1.

Bellingham, Billingham.— (1) Local, 'of Bellingham,' a parish in co. Northumberland. (2) Local, 'of Billingham,' a parish in co. Durham. I strongly suspect that some small spot, also called Bellingham, existed or exists in co. Norfolk, whence some of our Bellinghams and Billinghams. Mr. Lower says there is a family of Bellinghams in co. Sussex, sprung 'from Belingeham, a manor near Hastings, mentioned in Domesday' (Patr. Brit. p. 24).

William de Belingham, co. Norf., 1273. A.
Edward Billingham, co. Norf., 1546 : FF. i. 458.
Henry Bellingham, co. Norf., c. Henry V : ibid. ix. 109.
1557. Married—Cristofer Bellingham and Eliz. Scott : St. Antholin (London), p. 11.
1578. Richard Bellingam, co. Sussex : Reg. Univ. Oxf. vol. ii. pt. ii. p. 82.
1580. Henry Belingam, co. Sussex : ibid. p. 92.

1621. Grivell Gibbes and Eliz. Bellingham : Marriage Lic. (London), ii. 105.
1783. Married—Joseph Davis Baker and Martha Billingham : St. Geo. Han. Sq. i. 353.
London, 4, 1 ; MDB. (co. Norfolk), 1, 0; (co. Sussex), 4, 0; Philadelphia, 1, 1.

Bellion.— Bapt. 'the son of Enion'; Welsh Ap-Enion = Bennion, q.v.; further corrupted to Bellion; cf. *banisters* for *balusters*, staircase railings; *n* and *l* are constantly interchangeable in nomenclature.

Liverpool, 2; London, 1; New York, 1.

Bellis, Belliss, Bellys, Bellyse.—Bapt. 'the son of Ellis,' from Welsh Ap-Ellis, which became Bellis; cf. Bloyd = Ap-Lloyd. Bethell = Ap-Ithell, Beddard = Ap-Edward. Found much in Cheshire and the borders of the Principality. Also in cos. Denbigh and Flint.

Edward ap Ellis, of Royton, 1631 : Wills at Chester (1621-50), p. 73.
John ap Ellis, of Allington, 1641 : ibid.
John Bellis, 1747 : List of Freemen in Chester (in Byrom Library, Chetham Library, Manchester).
Edward Bellis, 1747 : ibid.
Griffeth lloyd ap Ellis de Yate, co. Denbigh : Visit. Glouc., 1623, p. 96.
John ap Ellis ap Griffeth, co. Denbigh : ibid.
1610. Thomas Bridge and Ursula Bellies : Marriage Lic. (London), i. 320.
1888. Married—Richard, only son of John Bellis, of Llandudno, and Judith Amelia Eaton : Manchester Courier, March 10, 1888.
MDB. (co. Ches.), 1, 0, 1, 4 ; Liverpool, 6, 0, 0, 0; March, 2, 0, 0, 0; London, 0, 1, 0, 0; Philadelphia, 8, 0, 0, 0.

Bellison, Belson.—Bapt. 'the son of Bell'; v. Bell (1) and Belson. The *i* in Bellison either represents the *a* in Bella-son, or is euphonically intrusive, as the *a* in Greenaway (for Greenway) or Ottaway (for Otway).

1556-7. Thomas Androwes and Jane Belson : Marriage Lic. (London), i. 35.
1651. Buried—William Belson : St. Jas. Clerkenwell, iv. 288.
MDB. (co. Warwick), 3, 1 ; London, 0, 2 ; Philadelphia, 0, 4.

Bellman.—Offic. 'a bell-ringer' (cf. Knowler), probably the old town-crier, or the officer who rang the hours in corporate towns.

Robertus Belleman, 1379 : P. T. Yorks. p. 123.

The first two following entries seem to suggest a second derivation :—

1600-1. Richard Bellmayne, co. Devon : Reg. Univ. Oxf. vol. ii. pt. ii. p. 322.
1621. Robert Bellmayne, co. Devon : ibid. p. 393.
1596. Buried — Zachary, s. Zachrie Bellman : St. Jas. Clerkenwell, iv. 58.
1612. — Hellin, wife of Zachary Belman : ibid. p. 122.
1752. Married—James Bellman and Ann Bennett : St. Geo. Chap. Mayfair, p. 207.
1753. Buried—Agnes, d. John Belman : Reg. of Ulverston Parish Ch. p. 275.
London, 4 ; Ulverston, 1 ; New York, 3 ; Philadelphia, 6.

Bellwether.—Nick. 'the bell-wether.' 'A very early instance of the use of this word will be found in the custumal of the manor of Brithwolton, co. Berks (Camden Soc.), where the keeper of the wethers was entitled, among his perquisites, to the belwether's fleece ("belwertheresfles"). The date is 1284-5.' (J. H. Round in Notes and Queries, Feb. 19, 1887.)

John Bellewether, 1307. M.
Stephen de le (?) Belwether. MM.

Belsham, Bellsham.—Local, 'of Belchamp,' a parish in co. Essex, three miles from Clare.

Roger de Belesham, co. Sussex, 1273. A.
1601. Jonathan Belsham, of Fulham, and Eliz. Bowles : Marriage Lic. (London), ii. 286.
London, 5, 3.

Belshaw.—Local, 'of Belshaw' or 'Balshaw.' I cannot identify the spot.

'John de Balschagh, for the service of Rochdale fee, yearly 26s. 8d.,' 1311 : Baines' Lanc. i. 483.
Johannes Belschagh, 1379 : P. T. Yorks. p. 22.
Agnes de Bolchawe, 1379 : ibid.
Adam de Bolchawe, 1379 : ibid.
1608. John Balshaw, of Snape-within-Scarisbrick : Wills at Chester, i. 10.
London, 2 ; Manchester, 4 ; Philadelphia, 7.

Belson.—Bapt. 'the son of Bell,' i. e. Isabel; v. Bell (1).

Robert fil. Bele, co. Suff., 1273. A.
1575. Thomas Belson, co. Oxf. : Reg. Univ. Oxf. vol. ii. pt. ii. p. 63.
1596. Augustine Belson, co. Oxf. : ibid. p. 216.
1707. Bapt.—Mary, d. of Willam Bellson : St. Jas. Clerkenwell, ii. 37.
1724. Married—Daniel Congey and Mary Belson : St. Mary Aldermary, p. 46.
London, 2 ; Philadelphia, 4.

Belstead.—Local, 'of Belstead,' a parish in the dioc. of Norwich and co. Suffolk. This surname is in general lost in Benstead. q.v.

Walter de Bellestede, co. Bucks, 20 Edw. I. R.
John de Belstede, co. Suff., ibid.
John de Belstede, co. Suff., 1273. A.
Robert de Belsted, co. Suff., ibid.
London, 1.

Belter. — Occup. 'a bell-founder'; v. Billiter.

'John Belleter, or Belter, secular chaplain, sup. for B.A., 20 May, 1522': Reg. Univ. Oxf. i. 125.
New York, 2.

Belton.—Local, ' of Belton,' parishes in diocs. of Norwich, Lincoln, and Peterborough. The Lincoln Beltons have strongly ramified in that county.

Hamon de Belton, co. Norf., 1257: FF. iv. 398.
John de Belton, rector of Ovington, co. Norf., 1366: ibid. ii. 296.
Henry de Belton, *pistor*, 17 Edw. II: Freemen of York, i. 22.
John de Beletun, co. Suff., 1273. A.
Gervase de Belton, co. Suff., ibid.
Nicholas de Belton, co. Suff., ibid.
William Belton, 1570: Marriage Lic. (Westminster), p. 3.
1775. Married—David Belton and Mary Nichols : St. Geo. Han. Sq. ir 251.
1782. — John Lewis and Ann Bellton: ibid. p. 331.
London, 6; MDB. (co. Lincoln), 28; New York, 6.

Beman.—(1) Occup. 'a bee-man,' a 'custos avium.' (2) Local, a corruption of Beaumont; v. Beaman. For want of proof in favour of (1) it is manifest that (2) is the chief parent. The occurrence of Beaman in Yorkshire is strongly corroborative.

Johannes Beman, 1379 :• P. T. Yorks. p. 156.
Alicia Beman, 1379 : ibid. p. 157.
1674. Bapt.—John, son of Richard Bemon : St. Jas. Clerkenwell, i. 265.
1793. Married—Thomas Ellsey and Amelia Beman : St. Geo. Han. Sq. ii. 95.
London, 2 ; New York, 3.

Bemand, Bement.—Local ; v. Beman, Beaman, and Beaumont.

1797. Married—William Bement and Mary Roberts : St. Geo. Han. Sq. ii. 167.
London, 2, 1 ; Philadelphia, 0, 6.

Bembridge.—Local, ' of Bembridge,' a chapelry in the parish of Brading, Isle of Wight. Some-

times probably a variant of Bainbridge, q.v. The following entries will show the tendency to variation :

1600. Buried—Eliz., wife of Edward Bembricke : St. Jas. Clerkenwell, iv. 67.
1637. — John Bembrigge : ibid. p. 233.
1664. — Jane Benbridge : ibid. p. 356.

These, no doubt, were all related t oone another.
London, 1.

Benbow, Benbough.—Nick. 'Bendbow,' a complimentary sobriquet for a stout archer ; cf. Stiffbow, Strongbow. Sharparrow, &c. 'Let the archer bend his bow.'—Jer. li. 3 (Auth. Version).

Roger Benbow. F.
William Bendebowe, London. X.
John Bentbow, 1440, co. York. W. 11.
Robert Benbowe, cantator Ecclesiae Christi: Reg. Univ. Oxf. vol. ii. pt i. p. 288.
'Vice-AdmiralJohn Benbow(1653-1702) was son of a tanner at Shewsbury': Dict. Nat. Biog. iv. 207.
1585. Nicholas Benbowe and Eliz. Welforde : Marriage Lic. (London), i. 142.
1607. Married—Robert Bendbowe and Jone Bowers : St. Mary Aldermary, p. 11.
1622-3.—LeonardKnightandConstance Benbowe : St. Dionis Backchurch, p. 21.
London, 6, 1.

Bence.—Bapt. ' the son of Bennett'; v. Benns; cf. Evance for Evans.

Bencher, Banker.—Offic. 'the bencher,' the 'banker.' Very early instances of some office in legal or exchequer matters, although the instances given in the H.E.D. belong to the 16th century.

Roger de Bencher, co. Oxf., 1273. A.
John le Bancker (London), 1300. M.
Robert le Banker, 1298. M.
Philadelphia, 0, 5.

Benedict. Benedictus.—Bapt. ' the son of Benedict,' more generally Bennet, q.v. One of the most popular personal names of the surname epoch, owing its favour to the Benedictines. Several of its derivatives, such as Bennet, Bennett, and Benson, are among the most familiar of English surnames.

Benedict de Pennington, co. Cumb., 1185 : RRR. p. 39.
Benedictus Willeson, 1379: P. T. Yorks. p. 232.
Benedictus Colier, 1379 : ibid. p. 233.
Reginald fil. Benedici,co.Hunts,1273. A.
Clemens fil. Benedicti, co. York, ibid.

George Benedick, co. Norf. : FF. v. 211.
London, 1, 1 ; New York, 66, 0.

Benger. ? ——
Robert Benyger, co. Soms., 1 Edw. III : Kirby's Quest, p. 185.
Manchester, 1.

Benjamin.—Bapt. ' the son of Benjamin.' Most of the instances in the London Directory are modern Jewish, but several, no doubt, represent a period when Benjamin, like Joseph, was not unpopular in England.

Caterina fil. Benjamini,co. Suff.,1273. A.
Robert Benjamin, co. Bedf., ibid.
1892. 'The wife of S. S. Benjamin, prematurely, of a son ': Daily Telegraph, Aug. 18.
London, 32.

Benn.—Bapt. ' the son of Bennet,' i.e. Benedict, from the nick. Benn; it has nothing to do with Benjamin. Benn is a familiar surname wherever the Benedictine monks had a convent. Furness Abbey, founded in the 12th century, has made Benn and Benson (q.v.) a common surname in Furness and south Cumberland.

Eborard Benne, co. Norf., 1273. A.
Robert Benne, co. Norf., ibid.
Ricardus Benne, 1379 : P. T. Yorks. p. 190.
Thomas Benne, 1379 : ibid. p. 218.
William Benne, vicar of Castor, co. Norf., 1410 : FF. xi. 211.
Peter Benne, vicar of Rowdham, co. Norf., 1430 : ibid. i. 435.
1634. Married—Anthony Beomont and Eliz. Benn : St. Thomas the Apostle (London), p. 15.
1662. Tempest Milner and Rebecca Benn : Marriage Alleg.(Canterbury),p. 78.
1771. Married—Richard Brooks and Sally Benn : St. Geo. Han. Sq. i. 205.
London, 3 ; MDB. (co. Cumb.), 9 ; Philadelphia, 10.

Bennet, Bennett.—Bapt. ' the son of Bennet,' i.e. Benedict, q.v. Bennet was the usual English form. While Furness Abbey was administrated under the Benedictine Order, Bennet was one of the commonest of baptismal names in the surrounding district (v. Benn). West, in his Hist. of Furness (pp. 188, 60, 29), records, amongst the benefactors of the Abbey and Conishead Priory, ' Benet, son of Alan,' 'Benet Penington' (1290), ' Benet de Rotington' (1256), and 'Benet, son of William' (1256).

These were all living in the immediate neighbourhood of the Abbey. Indeed, it will be found that Bennet and Benson are still common surnames in districts where the Benedictines have had foundations.

Benedict, or Benett de Hankeston, co. Camb., 1273. A.
Beneyt Mercator, co. Camb., ibid.
Nicholas Beneit, co. Oxf., ibid.
Reginald fil. Beneyt, co. Hunts., ibid.
Robert Benet, co. Soms., 1 Edw. III: Kirby's Quest, p. 89.
Joanna Benet, doghter, 1379: P. T. Yorks, p. 232.
1581. Bapt.—Thomas, s. Bennett Colwaye: St. Columb Major (Cornwall), p. 11.

The feminine Benedicta was also familiarly Bennet.

1561. Bapt.—Bennet, d. Robert Garret: St. Thomas the Apostle (London), p. 22.
1575. — Bennet, d. James Blower: ibid. p. 22.
1577-8. William Stitche and Bennett Bennett, widow: Marriage Lic. (London), i. 78.
1578. Bapt.—John, s. Thomas Bennett: St. Jas. Clerkenwell, i. 11.
London, 8, 183; New York, 18, 234.

Bennie, Benny.—Bapt. 'the son of Bennet,' i.e. Benedict, from the nick. Benn, colloquially Benny or Bennie. As a surname very rare; v. Benn and Benson.

Johannes Benny, 1379: P.T.Yorks.p.126.
1576. Arthur Leighe and Joanna Benney: Marriage Lic. (London), i. 70.
1681. Buried — Peeter Benny: St. Dionis Backchurch, p. 247.
London, 1, 0; Boston (U.S.), 2, 0.

Benning.—Bapt. 'the son of Benning'; cf. Harding, Browning, &c. Among our place-names we have Bennington, Benningbrough, and Benningholme.

Jacob Beynyn, co. Soms., 1 Edw. III: Kirby's Quest, p. 223.
John Beynyn, co. Soms., 1 Edw. III: ibid.
David Bening, co. Wilts, 1273. A.
Torald Bening, co. Norf., ibid.
1689. George Benning and Sarah Nolton: Marriage Alleg. (Canterbury), p. 116.
— Isaac Cardel Perdriel Dorgeval, captain in ye King's Troops, and Christian Bening: ibid.
London, 4; Philadelphia, 3.

Bennington.—Local, 'of Bennington,' two parishes in co. Linc., one near Boston, the other seven miles from Grantham.

Alan de Benington, co. Linc., Hen. III-Edw. I. K.

Ralph de Benington, co. Linc., ibid.
Alice de Bennington, co. Linc., 1273. A.
Astin de Benington, co. Linc., ibid.
1668. Married—Robert Hanwell and Margarett Benington: St. Jas. Clerkenwell, iii. 144.
London, 3; Philadelphia, 1.

Bennion.—Bapt.; Welsh Ap-Enion; v. Benyon.

1581. Laurence Bynion, or Benyon, or Benion, or Bygnion, co. Bucks: Reg. Univ. Oxf. vol. ii. pt. ii. pp. 50, 106.
1663. Married—Thomas Benyon and Eliz. Erland: St. Jas. Clerkenwell, iii. 113.
1687. Robert Ryder and Ann Benion: Marriage Alleg. (Canterbury), p. 4.
Liverpool, 3; Manchester, 2; New York, 1.

Bennison.—Bapt. 'the son of Bennet,' i.e. Benedict; v. Bennet. This surname in south Lancashire was at first Bennetson, but naturally settled down into Bennison.

Reginald Bennetson, of Werneth, co. Lanc., 1575: Wills at Chester (1545-1620), p. 17.
Richard Bennetson, of Romiley, 1590: ibid.
Edward Bennetson, of Stockport, 1617: ibid.

Later on this form disappears, and Bennison takes its place.

John Bennison, of Duckenfield, 1677: Wills at Chester (1660-80), p. 25.
Mary Bennison, of Gorton, 1678: ibid.
Jonathan Bennison, of Thornham, 1677: ibid.
1565. Married—William Bennetson and Katherine Cowper: Prestbury Church (co. Chester), p. 16.
1630. Buried — Ellen Bennison: ibid. p. 275.

Thus Bennison is not an extension of Benson, although the ultimate origin is the same, but an abbreviation of Bennetson.

Manchester, 4; Boston (U.S.), 6.

Benns, Bence, Bense.—Bapt. 'the son of Bennet,' from the nick. Benn; v. Benson and Benn. The patronymic Bens became Bence; cf. Ellice for Ellis, Evance for Evans. And as regards the patronymic s, cf. Jones, Williams, Richards, &c.

John Bennes, of Ipswich, rector of Bowthorp, co. Norf., 1420: FF. ii. 382.
1644. Bapt. — Elizabeth, d. Robert Bence: St. Thomas the Apostle (London), p. 55.
John Bense and Eliz. de la Hay, 1663: Marriage Alleg. (Canterbury), p. 96.
Sir Vere Vaine and Rachell Bence, 1671: ibid. p. 192.

London, 1, 0, 0; MDB. (co. Norfolk), 5, 1, 0; New York, 0, 1, 0; Boston (U.S.), 0, 0, 4.

Benson.—Bapt. 'the son of Bennet,' i.e. Benedict, from the nick. Ben or Benn. This great Benedictine name has made its mark on the modern directory in several surnames, but after Bennet, Benson occupies the first place.

Germanus Benson, 1379: P. T. Yorks. p. 232.
Thomas Benson, rector of Houghton, co. Norf., 1559: FF. vi. 133.
1570. Bapt.—William, s. John Benson: St. Antholin (London), p. 20.
1611. — Mary, d. Peter Benson: St. Michael, Cornhill, p. 109.
1617. Married — George Stokes and Agnes Benson: St. Jas. Clerkenwell, iii. 44.
London, 28; MDB. (West Rid. Yorks), 10; Manchester, 10; Philadelphia, 74.

Benstead.—Local, 'of Binstead' or 'Binsted,' parishes in cos. Sussex and Hants.

John de Benstede, co. Norf., 20 Edw. III: FF. vii. 288.
Maud de Bensted, co. Norf., 23 Edw. III: ibid. p. 504.
William de Bentestede, co. Kent, Hen. III-Edw. I. K.
1574-5. Gregory Benstede, co. Hants: Reg. Univ. Oxf. vol. ii. pt. ii. p. 61.
1606. Married — Robert Foster and Mary Benstead: St. Jas. Clerkenwell, m. 31.
1786. — Richard Didham and Frances Bensted: St. Geo. Han. Sq. ii. 394.
1787. — William Nursey and Eliz. Bensted: ibid. p. 402.
London, 3; Boston (U.S.), 1; Philadelphia, 1.

Bent, Bente.—Local, 'at the Bend' or 'Bent,' from residence thereby. Probably the bend in a river, or valley, or hillside.

Robert de la Bende, co. Salop, Hen. III-Edw. I. K.
1607. Nicholas Bent, co. Leic.: Reg. Univ. Oxf. vol. ii. pt. ii. p. 299.
1684-5. William Turton and Eliz. Bent: Marriage Lic. (London), ii. 306.
1744. Married — John Bent and Mary Oliver: St. Geo. Han. Sq. i. 33.
London, 10, 0; New York, 10, 3.

Benthall.—Local, 'of Benthall,' a parish in co. Salop, near Much Wenlock.

1610. Laurence Benthall, co. Salop: Reg. Univ. Oxf. vol. ii. pt. ii. p. 314.
1692. Buried—A male child of Walter Benthall: St. Dionis Backchurch, p. 260.
1753. Married—Thomas Benthall and Isabella Smalley: St. Geo. Chap. Mayfair, p. 264.
London, 2; Boston (U.S.), 2.

Bentham.—Local, 'of Bentham,' a parish in West Rid. Yorks, twelve miles from Settle. Most of the Benthams in the Dict. Nat. Biog. are referred back to a Yorkshire parentage.

Johannes de Bentham, 1379: P. T. Yorks. p. 289.
Ricardus de Bentham, 1379: ibid.
Thomas de Bentham, 1379: ibid.

All three were inhabitants of Bentham.

1576. Buried – Margaret, doughter of Sir Edwarde Bentaine: St. Dionis Backchurch, p. 194.
1758. Married—Matthew Bentham and Hannah Taylor: St. Geo. Han. Sq. i. 81.
London, 2; West Riding Court Dir., 3; Boston (U.S.), 2.

Bentley.—Local, 'of Bentley,' parishes in cos. Suffolk, Hants, Warwick, Derby, and Essex; also many small hamlets in various counties. In general the surname is literally Benet-legh, i.e. 'the field of Benedict,' the first occupier; v. Bennet.

John de Bentelege, co. Derby, 1273. A.
Roger de Benetleye, co. York, ibid.
William de Benetleg, co. Salop, Hen. III-Edw. I. K.
William de Bentlee, co. Salop, ibid.
Simon de Benetl', co. York, ibid.
Alicia de Benteley, 1379: P. T. Yorks. p. 300.
Richard de Benteley, co. York, 20 Edw. I. R.
William de Benetely, co. Bucks, ibid.
Ricardus de Benteley, *carpentar*, 1379: P. T. Yorks. p. 194.
1580. Edward Bentley, co. Warw.: Reg. Univ. Oxf. vol. ii. pt. ii. p. 91.
1786. Married—John Ostler and Abigail Bentley: St. Geo. Han. Sq. i. 385.
London, 29; New York, 25.

Benwell.—Local, 'of Benwell,' a township in the parish of St. John, Newcastle-on-Tyne.

1543-4. Walter Benwell and Johanna Barnes: Marriage Lic. (Faculty Office), p. 2.
1753. Married—Thomas Benwell and Margaret Alsop: St. Geo. Chap. Mayfair, p. 249.
London, 9; Boston (U.S.), 1.

Benyon, Binyon, Pinnion, Pinyon.—Bapt. Ap-Eignion, or Eignon, or Enion, i.e. 'the son of Eignion,' &c. A once popular name in the Principality. St. Einiawn was one of the early saints of the

Cymry, after whom is named a spring at Llanvareth, in Radnorshire (Yonge, ii. 161); v. Eynon and Baynham, and cf. Bevan for Ap-Evan, Bowen for Ap-Owen.

Joane Howell ap Eignion: Visit. Glouc. p. 188.
Raffe ap Eignon: ibid. p. 12.
Ennian fil. Kenewrec, 7 Hen. III: Pipe Roll, iv. 39.
David ap Eynon, 1313. M.
Meredith ap Eynon, 1322, ibid.
Rwrith ab Eynon, 23 Edw. I. BBB.
1620-1. Married—George Benyon and Alice Weste: St. Dionis Backchurch, p. 20.
1665. Bapt.—Robert, s. of Thomas Byneyon: St. Mary Aldermary, p. 101.
'Sunday Preachers, Finsbury Park Chapel—Rev. T. Enyon Davies, 6.30': Pall Mall Gazette, Saturday, June 11,1887.
London, 1, 2, 1, 1; MDB. (Denbigh Bennion, 2; (Flint) Benyon, 1; Boston (U.S.), 1, 0, 0, 0.

Beresford.—Local, 'of Beresford,' a manor and township in Astonfield, co. Stafford, possessed by the ancestors of the several noble families of this name (Lower, Patr. Brit. p. 26).

William de Boresforde, co. Soms., 1 Edw. III: Kirby's Quest, p. 233.
William de Beresford, co. Camb., 1273. A.
1612. Michael Beresford, co. Herts, Reg. Univ. Oxf. vol. ii. pt. ii. p. 327.
1647. Christopher Beresford and Mary Morgan: Marriage Lic. (Faculty Office), p. 37.
London, 8; Philadelphia, 3.

Berger, Bercher.—Occup. 'a shepherd'; Fr. *berger*. 'Bercaria or Berceria (Old Law), a sheep-pen, or sheep-fold' (Bailey's Dict. 1742). 'Bergeret, a pastoral song' (Chaucer). A statute, 37 Edw. III, c. 14 (1363), speaks of 'bovers, vachers, berchers, porchers, &c.' (v. full quotation under 'Day').

Henry le Bercher, Close Roll, 45 Hen. III.
Thomas le Bercher, co. Lanc, 20 Edw. I. R.
Dorken le Bercher, co. Camb., 1273. A.
Richard le Bercher, co. Oxf., ibid.
Ivo le Bercher, co. Camb., ibid.
Walter le Bercher, co. Soms., 1 Edw. III: Kirby's Quest, p. 148.
1753. Married—John Paul Berger and Betty Billington: St. Geo. Chap. Mayfair, p. 256.
London, 13, 0; Crockford, 2, 0; Boston (U.S.), 6, 0.

Berghman; v. Berryman.

Berkeley; v. Barclay.

Bernard, Bernardin.—Bapt. 'the son of Bernard,' dim. Bernard-in; v. Barnard.

Walter fil. Bernardi, 1214. RRR. p. 156.
William fil. Bernard, 1273. A.
Bernard Coronator, ibid.
1581. Abel Bernarde, co. Oxf.: Reg. Univ. Oxf. vol. ii. pt. ii. p. 106.
1595. Benjamin Bernarde or Barnarde, of London, ibid. p. 110.
1753. Married—Francis Bernard and Sarah Bleamire: St. Geo. Chap. Mayfair, p. 245.
London, 10, 1; New York, 36, 0.

Berner, Burner.—Occup. 'the Berner' (cf. Ventrer), one who had charge of fresh relays of dogs in hunting, a huntsman. O.F. *brenier*, *bernier*, berner; Godefroy, i. 727 A). Notes and Queries, p. 370, 1885). Special mention of the 'berner' is made in a hunting record, 5 Hen. III (Rot. Litt. Claus. i. 462; N. and Q. above). The 'yeoman-berner' is mentioned in the Parliamentary Rolls.

Richard le Berner, co. Linc., 20 Edw. I. R.
Geoffrey Berner, co. Bucks, 1273. A.
Reginald le Birner, co. Wilts, ibid.
Walter le Berner, co. Oxf., ibid.
Hugh Berner, co. Linc., ibid.
John le Brynner, Patent Roll, 20 Edw. II.

For a full account of this word and name, v. H.E.D.

Philadelphia, 10, 2.

Berney, Burney.—Local, 'of Berney,' a town in the hundred of North Greenhow, co. Norf.

Henry de Berney, co. Norf., 1268: FF. xi. 123.
Adam de Berney, co. Norf., 15 Edw. I: ibid. ix. 213.
Richard de Berney, co. Norf., 48 Edw. III: ibid. xi. 124.
Sir Thomas de Berney, of Reedham, co. Norf., 1389: ibid. 125.
Roger Burney, vicar of Holm-by-the-Sea, co. Norf., 1451: ibid. x. 334.
1591. Henry Barney, co. Norf.: Reg. Univ. Oxf. vol. ii. pt. ii. p. 184.
1759. Married — Richard Toft and Ellenor Berney: St. Geo. Han. Sq. i. 83.
1697. Bapt.—Ann, d. John Burney: St. Michael, Cornhill, p. 158.
London, 0, 5; Crockford, 1, 6; MDB. (Norfolk), 3, 0.

Berrall, Berrill.—Local, 'of Burghill,' a parish in co. Hereford, four miles from Hereford. This probably is also the source of the references to cos. Soms. and Devon.

Of the others I can say nothing, because I cannot identify the spot.

Robert de Birhulle, co. Linc., 20 Edw. I. R.
John Berhull, co. Oxf., 1273. A.
Richard de Berhulle, co. Soms., 1 Edw.
III: Kirby's Quest, p. 236.
Adam Berhull, co. Soms., 1 Edw. III: ibid.
1607-8. Tristram Berrill, co. Devon: Reg. Univ. Oxf. vol. ii. pt. ii. p. 300.
1632. Married—Thomas Deeping and Mary Berrill: St. Jas. Clerkenwell, iii. 63.
1742. — Benjamin Berrell and Agnes Hill: St. Geo. Chap. Mayfair, p. 16.
London, 2, 2; New York, 1, 1.

Berrett.—Bapt.; v. Barrat.

Berrier. —Occup. 'the berrier,' i.e. the thresher. 'Berrier, a thrasher, North.' 'Berry, to thrash corn, North.' (Halliwell.)

'iij plewmen, j berryer, and j hird,' 1573: Wills and Inv. N. C. 399 (H.E.D.).
Johannes Wacher, berier, 1379: P. T. Howdenshire, p. 30.
Johannes Beryar, laborer, 1379: ibid. p. 2.
Willelmus Beryar, laborer, 1379: ibid.
David Deryer, 1379: P. T. Yorks. p. 296.
Johannes Berier, 1379: ibid p. 232.
1585. Gregory Berrier, co. Oxf.: Reg. Univ. Oxf. vol. ii. pt. ii. p. 148.

Berringer, Berenger, Barringer.—Bapt. 'the son of Berenger.'

Berenger Gifard: Domesday.
Berenger de Todeni, ibid.
Reinerus fil. Berengarii, Pipe Roll, 5 Hen. II.
Berengarius fil. Gervase. C.
Barengaria was a fem. form familiar to English history. French, Béranger; Germ. Berangar; Span. Berenger (Yonge, ii. 275).
Berenger le Moine, co. Northampt., 1273. A.
Robert Beringer, co. Camb., ibid.
William Berenger, co. Soms., 1 Edw. III: Kirby's Quest, p. 186.
1614. William Barringer: Reg. Univ. Oxf. vol. ii. pt. ii. p. 334.
1694. Bapt.—Andrew, son of Simon Beranger: St. Antholin (London), p. 108.
London, 1, 0, 3; Philadelphia, 4, 0, 3.

Berry.—Local, 'at the Bury,' i.e. borough; v. Bury, Burrows, Burroughes, &c.

1513. John Bery, or Bury: Reg. Univ. Oxf. i. 88.
1575-6. Henry Berrie, co. Kent: ibid. vol. ii. pt. ii. p. 66.
1609. James Berrie, of the Hey, parish of Wigan: Wills at Chester, i. 18.

The Yorkshire folk have a strong propensity for quaint and humorous baptismal names. Father and son are thus described in the West Riding Directory (Stainland): John Berry, shopkeeper; Young John Berry, clogger. Young John was the son's fontal name.

London, 85; Philadelphia, 150.

Berryman, Berriman, Borrowman, Berghman.—(1) Occup. 'the bury-man,' i.e. borough-man, a man dwelling within the borough; v. Berry. (2) Possibly official from the bearer of the name occupying some position akin to a borough-reeve. As a rule a West-country name.

Robert Buryman, co. Soms., 1 Edw. III: Kirby's Quest, p. 83.
William Buryman, co. Soms., 1 Edw. III: ibid. p. 96.
1587-8. Samuel Beriman, or Berriman, co. Glouc.: Reg. Univ. Oxf. vol. ii. pt. ii. p. 162.
1615. Hugh Birriman, or Berriman, co. Soms., ibid. p. 341.
1732. Mr. John Berryman: St. Anthon (London), p. 145.
1774. Married—John Shaw and Eliz. Berriman: St. Geo. Han. Sq. i. 242.
1784. — Gerard Maley and Eliz. Berryman: ibid. p. 367.
1807. — George Richards and Margaret Borrowman: St. Geo. Han. Sq. ii. 373.
London, 6, 1, 1, 0; MDB. (co. Soms.), 2, 1, 0, 1; Philadelphia, 15, 4, 0, 0.

Bertenshaw.—Local; v. Birkinshaw.

Bertin, Bertie.—Bapt. 'the son of Bertin.' St. Bertin of France made the font-name familiar in that country, and as a French surname it occurs in the Lon. Dir. We must ascribe the English surname to the same source, although there seems strong evidence in favour of its being a pet form of Bertram, nick. Bert, dim. Bert-in. The early Bertie was evidently a popular form of Bertin.

Bertin de Boyuill, C. R. Hen. III.
1541. Bertyn Flecchar, Bury, Lanc.: Rec. Soc. Lanc. and Ches. vol. xii. p. 144.
Berton Venator, co. Glouc., 1273. A.
Bartin de Verdun, 1432: Historiae Dunelmensis (Surt. Soc.), p. lxi.
Bertram de Burgo, co. Staff., 1273. A.
Bertin de Burgo, co. Salop, ibid.

Bertram and Bertin are probably one and the same individual.

Berty Fleschar, co. Northumb., 1541. TTT. p. lii.
Compare this also with Bertyn Flecchar, above recorded, same date.
1578-9. William Dade and Lucy Bertie: Marriage Lic. (London), i. 86.
1691. Isaie Duprè and Ann Bertin: Marriage Alleg. (Canterbury, p. 205.
London, 5, 0; New York, 1, 1.

Bertram, Bertrand.—Bapt. 'the son of Bertram'; v. Bartram and Bertin.

Richard Bertram, co. Northumb., 1168: KKK. vi. 13.
Berteram le Barbur, co. Salop, 1273. A.
Bertramus de Verdun, 7 Hen. II: Pipe Roll, iv. 41.
Ricardus Bartrem, 1379: P. T. Yorks. p. 84.
Johannes Bartrem: ibid. p. 88.
1741. Married—Benjamin Bertram and Sarah Mills: St. Geo. Han. Sq. i. 27.
London, 2, 6; Philadelphia, 10, 0; New York, 13, 12.

Berwick.—Local, 'of Berwick-on-Tweed.' But v. Barwick, and cf. Derby and Darby, or Clerke and Clarke, or Perkins and Parkins.

William de Berwyk, cotoler, 18 Edw. II: Freemen of York, i. 22.
Johannes de Berwyk', 1379: P. T. Yorks, p. 252.
1616. Michael Berwicke, co. Notts: Reg. Univ. Oxf. vol. ii. pt. ii. p. 354.
1621. Samuel Berwicke, co. Notts; ibid. p. 398.
1725. Married—Isaac Dalston and Ann Berwick: St. Geo. Han. Sq. i. 1.
1745. — William Scaddan and Frances Berwick: ibid. p. 47.
West Riding Court Dir., 3; Philadelphia, 4.

Besant, Bezant, Bessant, Beasant, Bessent, Beazant, Bayzand.—Local, 'of Byzantium' (?). 'To oone he gave fyve talentis, or besauntis,' 1382, Wyclif (Matt. xxv. 15); v. H.E.D. for various instances. 'A bisaunt, bezant, or bizantine was an old coin both in gold and silver, and so called from having been minted at Byzantium. The silver bezant passed current for 2s. or thereabouts' (Pipe Rolls, vol. iii. p. 74: Pipe Roll Soc.). As almost every other coin has its representative in our nomenclature so may this. More probably, however, like Turk and Saracen, it is local, denoting an immigrant from Byzantium.

H

Robert Besant, sheriff of London, 1194: WWW.

1748. Married—John Beszant and Brittania Freeman: St. Geo. Chap. Mayfair, p. 105.

1752. — Henry Hicks and Eliz. Bessant: ibid. p. 208.

1776. Married—Robert Besant and Sarah Myers: St. Geo. Han. Sq. i. 270.

London, 3, 1, 1, 2, 1, 1, 0; MDB. (co. Glouc.) Bayzand, 1; New York, 3, 0, 1, 0, 0, 0, 0.

Best, Beste. — Nick. 'the beast,' probably not in an uncomplimentary sense; cf. *beast* in the Authorized Version of the Bible, especially in the Book of the Revelation; cf. Bull, Stott, Bullock, &c. M.E. *beste* or *best*.

'Neyther man ne best.'
Chaucer, C. T. 1978.

Richard le Beste, co. Camb., 1273. A.
William Best, co. Bucks, ibid.
Walter Best, co. Oxf., ibid.
Thomas Best, 1379: P. T. Yorks. p. 300.
Agnes Best, 1379: ibid. p. 258.
Robert Beast, or Best, sheriff of Norwich, 1495: FF. iii. 191.
1732. Married—Matthew Topham and Hannah Best: St. Geo. Han. Sq. i. 10.
London, 30, 0; West Riding Court Dir., 11, 0; Philadelphia, 34, 1.

Beswick.—(1) Local, 'of Beswick.' Lately a small hamlet, one mile and a half from Manchester, now a suburb of that city. (2) Local, 'of Beswick,' a township in the parish of Kilnwick, East Rid. Yorks. The many Beswicks of Lancashire undoubtedly hail from (1).

Thomas de Bexwik, of Manchester, 1332: Lay Subsidy (Rylands), p. 35.
Edward Beswick, of Gorton, near Manchester, 1597: Wills at Chester (1545-1620), p. 18.
Richard Beswick, of Blakeley, Manchester, 1580: ibid.
1589. Married—William Beswicke and Isabell Dosone: Prestbury Ch. (Cheshire), p. 100.
1592. Robert Beswycke and Katherine Parkyns: Marriage Lic. (London), p. 203.
Manchester, 25; London, 3; Philadelphia, 9.

Betham.—Local, 'of Beetham,' a parish in co. Westm., near Burton-in-Kendal.

Richard de Betham, co. Norf., 20 Edw. I. R.
1599. Edward Bethom, of Kendal: Lanc. Wills at Richmond, i. 31.
1622. Robert Betham: ibid.
1659. Buried—Thomas Kemton, Thomas

Betham's apprentice: St. Jas. Clerkenwell, iv. 331.
1665. Buried—Mary Bethum: ibid. p. 363.
1684. Married—Jacob Betham and Eliz. Levin: ibid. iii. 202.
London, 1; Philadelphia, 5.

Bethell, Bithell, Bethel.— Bapt.; Welsh, Ap-Ithell, 'the son of Ithell'; cf. Bevan, Bloyd, &c. Lewlyn ap Ithel, 1325. M; Evan ap Ithell. Z; Jevan ap Ithell. Z; Ann Ithell. HH; Ithell Wynn. AA. 1. Bethell is still a considerable surname in the Principality. John Bithell is found among the List of Freemen in Chester, 1747.

Stephen Bethel, co. Soms., 1 Edw. III: Kirby's Quest, p. 88.
Richard Bythell, of Chester, *innholder*, 1635: Wills at Chester (1621-50), p. 42.
1560. Nicolas Abithel, sup. for incorporation: Reg. Univ. Oxf. i. 243.
1706. Bapt.—Eliz., d. of Henry Bethel: St. Jas. Clerkenwell. ii. 29.
London, 5, 0, 0; MDB. (co. Denbigh), 0, 2, 0; (co. Chester), 2, 0, 0; Philadelphia, 4, 0, 3.

Bethune, Beaton, Betton.— Local, 'of Bethune,' in Artois. Of course Beaton has a baptismal origin also; v. Beaton. But the Scotch Beatons, of whom came the great cardinal, are probably Bethunes. The Testa de Neville mentions the 'Advocatus de" Bethun,' alias 'Betun,' alias 'Beton' (pp. 32, 36, 279).

Baldewyn de Bretonia, co. Norf., 1273. A.
Ingeram de Betoyne, London, ibid.
John de Beton, alias Betton, London, ibid.
Walter de Betonia, co. Devon, Hen. III-Edw. I. K.
Ingeram de Betun, co. Bedf., ibid.
William de Betonia, London, 20 Edw. I. R.
Laurence de Beton, London, 20 Edw. I, ibid.
Richard de Beytteyne, Lord Mayor of London, temp. Edw. II: WWW. p. 210.
1765. Married—Joseph Betton and Jane Raynor: St. Geo. Han. Sq. i. 139.
1769. — Francis Beaton and Eleanor Frale: ibid. p. 185.
London, 0, 8, 1; Crockford, 2, 0, 1; Boston (U.S.), 3, 4, 1.

Bettin, Bettinson.—Bapt. 'the son of Beatrice,' from the nick. Bete, dim. Beton; v. Beaton.

1583-4. Degory Betenson, or Bettenson, co. Cornw.: Reg. Univ. Oxf. vol. ii. pt. ii. p. 132.
1598. Thomas Bettenson, or Bettinsoonne: ibid. p. 227.

Johannes Betonson, 1379: P. T. Yorks. p. 200.
Willelmus Betonson, 1379: ibid. p. 233.
1543. Married—John Brewer and Elizabeth Bittinson: St. Peter, Cornhill, p. 221.
1582. Bapt.—Davie, son of Edward Bettine: St. Mary Aldermary, p. 60.
1661. — Ann, d. Richard Betenson: St. Jas. Clerkenwell, i. 211.
1779. Married—Charles Whitting and Mary Betinson: St. Geo. Han. Sq. i. 302.
London, 0, 2; New York, 1, 0.

Betts, Bettson, Bettison, Bett, Betson.—Bapt. 'the son of Beatrice,' from the nick. Bete or Bet; v. Beaton and Beatson. No connexion with Elizabeth. Both the nick. and the dim. occur together in Piers Plowman:

'And bade Bette cut a bough,
And beat Betoun therewith.' Pass V.

Betissa Browne, 1379: P.T.Yorks. p. 119.
Johannes Beteson, 1379: ibid. p. 39.
Gilbertus Bet, 1379: ibid. p. 44.
William Beteson, co. York. W. 2.
1581. Frances Bettes, co. Hants: Reg. Univ. Oxf. vol. ii. pt. ii. p. 108.
1590. John Betts, co. Kent, ibid. p. 176.
1696. Buried—Betson: St. Mary Aldermary, p. 204.
1743. Married—Thomas Bett and Sarah Frimley: St. Geo. Han. Sq. i. 31.
1770. — Stephen Smith and Ann Bettes: ibid. p. 202.
London, 37, 1, 0, 0, 0; Leeds, 1, 0, 1, 0, 0; Sheffield, 2, 0, 0, 0, 0; Philadelphia, 30, 0, 0, 0, 8.

Betty, Bettyes, Bettice.— Bapt. 'the son of Beatrice,' from the nick. Bet or Bett, and pet Bettie; cf. Charley or Teddie. No connexion with Elizabeth; v. Betts.

Thomas Betisson. FF.
1549. Bapt.—Tamson (Thomasine), d. John Bettie: Reg. St. Columb Major, p. 5.
1690. William Bettis and Catherine Groves: Marriage Alleg. (Canterbury), p. 150.
1697. Buried—Katherine Bettys: Canterbury Cath., p. 30.
1745. Married—Richard Betty and Hannah Curtis: St. Geo. Chap. Mayfair, p. 56.
London, 3, 3, 1; Philadelphia, 2, 0, 0.

Bevan, Bevand, Bevans, Bevens, Bevins.—Bapt. 'Ab-Evan' ('the son of Evan') = Bevan (Welsh). The *d* in Bevand is excrescent, as in Simmonds.

Rys ap Madoc ap Tudir ap Hoel ap Evan: Visit. London, 1633, i. 220.
Howel ap-Evan, c. 1300. M; Eygneun ap Yevan. D. John and

Richard Bevand are contained in the List of Freemen in Chester, 1747. Bevans is a double patronymic, part English, part Welsh = ab-Evan-s ; v. Beddoes.

Thomas Bevans, prebendary of St. David's, 1680 : Hist. and Ant. St.David's, p. 362.

1560. Married—Rycharde Bevande and Ann Kempe : St. Michael, Cornhill, p. 10 (elsewhere in same register Beavin).

1748. — John Baynham and Margaret Bevan : St. Geo. Chap. Mayfair, p. 108.

1753. — Thomas Bevans and Alice Finney : ibid. p. 267.

London, 24, 0, 1, 0, 2 ; Philadelphia, 37, 0, 16, 4, 3.

Bever; v. Beaver.

Beveridge, Beverage.— Bapt. 'the son of Beverache.' Like Aldridge (from personal name Aldrich), Beveridge has a distinctly local look about it. But the instances below make the question very doubtful. If a nick.. v. Beverage (H.E.D.). Probably a personal name.

Hugh Beverach, co. Camb., 1273. A.
Ralph Beverache, co. Camb., ibid.
Agnes Beverach, co. Camb., ibid.
Walter Beverage, co. Linc., ibid.
Thomas Beverage, co. York, ibid.
Ralph Beuerage, C. R., 2 Edw. I.

1579. Marriage Licence — Henry Buckett and Johanna Beveridge, by Bishop of London : i. 89.

— Francis Beveredge, co. Derby : Reg. Univ. Oxf. vol. ii. pt. ii. p. 222.

London, 5, 0 ; New York, 2, 1 ; Philadelphia, 6, 0.

Beverley, Beverly.—Local. 'of Beverley,' a town in the East Riding of Yorkshire.

John de Beverley, co. Northumberland, 1273. A.

Adam de Beverle, *bougher* (i.e. bowyer), 4 Edw. II : Freemen of York, i. 14.

1564-5. James Beverley, of Henley, co. Oxf., *bargeman* : Reg. Univ. Oxf. vol. ii. pt. ii. p. 13 *n*.

1674. James Beverley (co. Hunts) and Anne Duncombe : Marriage Alleg. (Canterbury), p. 236.

1778. Married—James Beverley and Mary Davey : St. Geo. Han. Sq. i. 294.

London, 6, 3 ; Boston (U.S.), 0, 6.

Bevington, Bavington.—Local, 'of Bavington.' Great and Little Bavington are townships in the parish of Bellingham, co. Northumberland.

1583. John Beavinton, or Bevinton, co. Worc. : Reg. Univ. Oxf. vol. ii. pt. ii. p. 131.

1585. Richard Bavington and Johnna

Harcourte : Marriage Lic. (London), i. 142.

1615. Richard Bevington and Mary Griffin : ibid. ii. 223.

London, 10, 0 ; Philadelphia, 0, 7.

Bewick, Bewicke.—Local, 'of Bewick.' Old and New Bewick, places in co. Northumberland. A surname still familiar on the English border. Thomas Bewick, the wood engraver, was born in the parish of Ovingham in Northumberland.

William de Bewyk, co. Wilts, 1273. A.
Robert de Bewyk, co. York, ibid.
Julian Bevyk, co. Linc., ibid.

1602-3. Edward Hunt and Sarah Bewick : Marriage Lic. (London), i. 275.

1781. Married— Thomas Bond and Margaret Bewicke: St. Geo. Han. Sq. i. 324.

London, 1, 1.

Bewsher ; v. Bowsher.

Beyer.—Occup. 'the beyer' (?). Perhaps a 'buyer,' one who purchased for the household. One instance in the London Directory, at least, is foreign.

John le Beyere, co. Hertf., 20 Edw. I. R.

Simon le Beier, co. Glouc., 1273. A.

1700. William Beyer and Eliz. Wolfe : Marriage Lic. (Faculty Office), p. 236.

London, 3 ; Philadelphia, 22.

Beynon, Baynon.—Bapt. 'Ab-Enion'; Welsh, 'the son of Enion.' One of many existing forms ; v. Baynham, Bennion, and Benyon. Two of the four clergymen in Crockford hold Welsh livings. Enion seems to have been the William or John of the Principality in the surname period.

John Beynon, sup. for B.C.L., June 22, 1507 : Reg. Univ. Oxf. p. 54.

1738. Bapt.—Thomas, son of Thomas Beynon : St. Jas. Clerkenwell, ii. 242.

Crockford, 4, 0 ; London, 5, 0 ; Liverpool, 2, 1 ; MDB. (co. Glamorgan), 8, 0 ; (co. Carmarthen), 9, 0 ; Philadelphia, 1, 1.

Bibby, Bibbey, Bibbye.— Bapt. 'the son of Bibby,' i.e. Isabella. There can be little doubt about this derivation. Bibby is a York and Lancaster surname, where Isabel was a prime favourite in the surname period. As Aggy (Agnes) became Taggy, so Ibby became Bibby. It seems clear that Bibby in Lancashire and Yorkshire has no connexion with the Leices-

tershire Beebys (v. Beebe), although some of the Beebys may now be represented by Bibby in the south of England.

Henricus Bibbe, 1397 : P. T. Yorks. p. 170.

Willelmus Bibbe, 1379 : ibid. p. 57.

Richard le fiz Bilby, C. R., 17 Edw. I.

1595. Thomas Bybie, co. Essex : Reg. Univ. Oxf. vol. ii. pt. ii. p. 211.

Nicholas Bibby, of Openshaw, co. Lanc., 1507 : Wills at Chester (1545-1620), p. 18.

Thomas Bibbie, of Pemberton, co. Lanc., 1607 : ibid. p 19.

1603. Buried—Susan, d. Adam Bibye : St. Mary Aldermary, p. 150.

— — Adam Biby, ibid.

Manchester, 9, 0, 0 ; London, 4, 1, 1 ; MDB. (West Riding), 1, 0, 0 ; Philadelphia, 5, 2, 0.

Bick.—Bapt. 'the son of Bike.' The surname is a curious one, but it seems beyond dispute to have been a personal or baptismal name at the first. Amongst the New York Bicks is found 'Gustav Bick.' I find a dim. Bikelot in A. 1273. In place-names we find Bickford, Bicham, Bicknor, and Bickley, q.v., seemingly representing the personal name of the first settler.

Richard Bikelot, co. Hunts, 1273. A.
Bike (without surname), co. Essex, ibid.
Walter Bike, co. Camb., ibid.
Bike le Clerk, co. Essex, ibid.
William Byk, co Soms., 1 Edw. III : Kirby's Quest, p. 107

1618. Thomas Bicke and Eliz. Pooley : Marriage Lic (London), ii. 66.

1652. Buried—Thomas Bick, servant to Mr. Noakes : St. Dionis Backchurch, p. 228.

London, 2 ; New York, 9.

Bickerdike, Biggadike.—Local, 'of Bicker-dike. I cannot find the spot. Evidently it means 'the dike of Bicker,' Bicker representing an early such place-names as Bickerton (in cos. Chester, York, Northumberland), Bickerston (co. Norfolk), Bickering (co. Lincoln), and Bickerstaffe (co. Lancashire). Probably Lincolnshire is the home of this surname.

Henricus Bikerdyk, 1379 : P. T. Yorks. p. 242.

1518. John Bekyrdyke : Reg. Univ. Oxf. i. 105.

1563. Buried — Margret Beckerdick : St. Mary Aldermary, p. 134.

1638. Francis Hamond and Magdalen Bicardike (co. Essex): Marriage Lic. (London), ii. 234.

1701. Nicholas Bickerdik, Norwich: FF. iv. 206.
London, 1, 0; Harrogate, 1, 0; MDB. (co. Lincoln), 0, 2.

Bickerstaff, Bickersteth, Bickerstaffe.—Local, 'of Bickerstaffe,' a village near Ormskirk, co. Lancashire; in early records spelt Bikerstat and Bykyrstath. Bickersteth is found later.

Ralph Hey, of Bickersteth, *husbandman*, 1662: Wills at Chester (1660-80), p. 128.
Adam de Bykerstaff, co. Lanc., 1289: Baines' Lanc. ii. 413.
Gilbert de Bykerstaff. J.
Robert Bickersteth, of Bickersteth, 1580: Wills at Chester (1545-1620), p. 19.
Hugh Bickerstaff, of Bickerstaff, 1600: ibid.
1752. Married—John Richards and Susanna Bickerstaff: St. Geo. Chap. Mayfair, p. 209.
MDB. (co. Lanc.), 2, 0, 2; Manchester, 1, 0, 0; London, 2, 0, 0; Crockford, 3, 6, 0.

Bickerton.—Local, 'of Bickerton,' (1) a township in the parish of Malpas, co. Chester; (2) a township in the parish of Rothbury, co. Northumberland; (3) a township in the parish of Bilton, W. Rid. Yorks. There can be no doubt that (3) is the chief parent, and then (1).

Johannes de Bikerton, *gaunter*, 25 Edw. I: Freemen of York (Surt. Soc.), i. 6.
Thomas de Bigerton, co. York, 1273. A.
Johannes de Bykerton, 1379: P. T. Yorks. p. 301.
Willelmus de Bikerton, 1379: ibid. p. 235.
John Bycharton, co. York, 1533: W. 11, p. 219.
Edmund Bickerton, of Sound, co. Ches., 1617: Wills at Chester (1545-1620), p. 19.
Humphrey Bickerton, of Wrenbury, 1594: ibid.
1592. Thomas Bickerton, co. Ches.: Reg. Univ. Oxf. vol. ii. pt. ii. p. 193.
London, 4; Manchester, 3; Philadelphia, 8.

Bickford; v. Beckford.

Bickham.—Local, 'of Bikome,' a West-country name (some small spot I cannot identify), with the suffix -*comb*; v. Bick and Combe.

Walter de Bikome, co. Soms., 1 Edw. III: Kirby's Quest, p. 245.
Godfrey de Bycombe, co. Soms., 1 Edw. III: ibid. p. 247.
1748. Married—Thomas Bickham and Susanna Jeffs: St. Geo. Chap. Mayfair, p. 106.

London, 1; MDB. (co. Soms.), 5; Philadelphia, 4.

Bickley, Bickleigh.—Local, 'of Bickleigh,' (1) a parish in co. Devon, four miles from Tiverton: (2) a parish in the same county, seven miles from Plymouth; (3) 'of Bickley,' a township in the parish of Malpas, co. Chester; v. Bick.

Henry de Bickleghe, or Bickele, co. Devon, 1273. A.
Richard de Bicalegh, co. Devon, ibid.
Huword de Bikeleg, co. Soms., Hen. III-Edw. I. K.
William de Bikelegh, co. Devon, ibid.
1575. Ralph Bicklie, co. Hants: Reg. Univ. Oxf. vol. ii. pt. ii. p. 63.
1607-8. John Bickley and Mary Brogden: Marriage Lic. (London), i. 302.
London, 4, 0; MDB. (co. Devon), 3, 1; Philadelphia, 21, 0.

Bickman.—Bapt. 'the son of Bickman,' the same as the German Beckmann; v. Beckman and Bick.

Sarra Bykeman, co. Camb., 1273. A. Philadelphia, 1.

Bickmore.—Local, 'of Bickmore.' I cannot find the spot.

John de Bykemere, co. Soms., 1 Edw. III: Kirby's Quest, p. 251.
London, 1; Boston (U.S.), 2.

Bicknell.—Local, (1) 'of Bickenhill,' a parish in co. Warwick, seven miles from Birmingham; (2) 'of Bickenhall,' otherwise called Bicknell, a parish in co. Somerset, near Taunton; v. Bignall.

William de Bigehull, co. Oxf., 1273. A.
John de Bidenhulle, co. Oxf., ibid.
William Bykenhulle, co. Soms., 1 Edw. III: Kirby's Quest, p. 105.
John de Bikenhull, co. Soms., 1 Edw. III: ibid. p. 173.
1607. Married—Richard Bicknell and Eliz. Baker: St. Dionis Backchurch, p. 46.
1726. — Benjamin Timbrell and Mary Bicknall: ibid. p. 62.
1751. Bapt.—Mary, d. of Samuel Bicknell: St. Michael, Cornhill, p. 175.
Crockford, 6; MDB. (co. Soms.), 9; London, 10; Boston (U.S.), 24.

Bickner.—Local, 'of Bicknor,' parishes in cos. Kent, Gloucester, and Monmouth; v. Bick.

(Homines) de Bykenaure, co. Soms., 1273. A.
Philadelphia, 1.

Biddell, Biddle; v. Beadle.

Biddlecombe, Biddiscombe.
—Local, 'of Bittiscombe,' a hamlet in the parish of Upton, co.

Somerset, originally Biteliscombe. The two present forms of the surname seem to be a kind of compromise.

Robert de Biteliscombe, co. Soms., 1 Edw. III: Kirby's Quest, p. 177.
Stephen de Bitelescumbe, co. Soms., 1273. A.
1747. Married—Jonathan Turner and Susanna Biddlecombe: St. Geo. Chap. Mayfair, p. 88.
1750.—Henry Biddalcomb and Mary Stringer: ibid. p. 160.
MDB. (co. Soms.) 8, 1.

Biddulph.—Local, 'of Biddulph,' a parish in co. Stafford, three miles from Congleton.

1598. Michael Biddulph, co. Staff.: Reg. Univ. Oxf. vol. ii. pt. ii. p. 228.
1605. Walter Biddulph, co. Staff.: ibid. p. 283.
1670-1. Edward Littleton and Susanne Biddulph: Marriage Alleg. (Westminster), p. 186.
1694-5. Married—Michael Bidulph and Mary Aston: St. Dionis Backchurch, p. 44.
London, 4; New York, 1.

Bidgood.—Bapt. 'the son of Bidgood,' originally Biggegod, one of a fairly large class of personal names ending in *good*; cf. Scattergood. The early form is Biggegod.

John Biggegod, co. Soms., 1 Edw. III: Kirby's Quest, p. 244.
1606. Nicholas Bidgood and Alice Howe: Marriage Lic. (Westminster), p. 15.
1621. George Bidegood, co. Somerset: Reg. Univ. Oxf. vol. ii. pt. ii. p. 398.
1798. Married—James Burrows and Ellen Bidgood: St. Geo. Han. Sq. ii. 186.
London, 3; MDB. (co. Soms.) 1; New York, 2.

Bigg, Bigge.—Nick. 'the big,' one of large, bulky proportions; cf. Little, Long, Short, &c. A familiar entry in registers of the surname epoch.

Alan Bigge, co. Camb., 1273. A.
Robert Bigge, co. Hunts, ibid.
William Bigge, co. Oxf. ibid.
1614. Richard Bigge, Marriage Lic. (London), ii. 29.
1659. Bapt.—Katherine, d. John Bigg: St. Jas. Clerkenwell, i. 206.
1752. Married—Henry Bigg (Berkshire) and Sophia Cook: St. Geo. Han. Sq. i. 47.
London, 13, 0; New York, 1, 0.

Biggadike.—Local; v. Bickerdike; cf. Biggerstaff for Bickerstaff.

Biggerstaff.—Local: v. Bickerstaff; cf. Biggadike for Bickerdike.
London, 1.

Biggin, Biggen, Biggins, Biggans.—Local, 'of Biggin,' a township in the parish of Church Fenton, co. York. No doubt other spots are so called, from *bigging*, a building, *biggins*, buildings, i.e. a stead, a habitation, a dwelling; cf. Newbiggin.

'When he come to his byggynge,
He welcomed fayr that lady vynge.'
c. 1425: Emare, 709 (H.E.D.).
'Byggynge, or beeldynge, *edificacio, structura* '1 Prompt. Parv. p. 35.
Robertus de Byggyng', 1379: P. T. Yorks. p. 237.
Ricardus Bygyng, 1379: ibid. p. 155.
'William Burrow, of Biggins': Hist. Westm. and Cumb., i. 205.
James Bigines, of Barrowheade, Furness, 1593: Lancashire Wills at Richmond, i. 32.
John Biggins, of Ulverston, Furness, 1596: ibid.
1727. Married—William Voce and Mary Diggans. St Geo Han. Sq. i. 3.
1759. — James Biggins and Jane Bond: ibid. p. 91.
London, 0, 0, 1, 0; West Riding Court Dir., 8, 1, 1, 0; Sheffield, 10, 0, 4, 0; Philadelphia, 4, 0, 2, 1.

Bigland.—Local, 'of Bigland,' an estate in the parish of Cartmell, North Lancashire. Bigland Hall is still the residence of the Biglands.

Isabell Bigland, of Bigland, in Cartmell, 1645: Lancashire Wills at Richmond, i. 32.
James Bigland, of the Grange, in Cartmell, 1623: ibid.
Henry Bigland, of Cartmell, 1634: ibid.
1738. Married — John Atkinson and Dorothy Bigland: Reg. Ulverston Ch. p. 379.
1766. — James Bigland, *husbandman*, and Mary Jackson: ibid. p. 411.
London, 2; Liverpool, 4.

Bignall, Bignell, Bignold.—Local; v. Bicknell. But Lower says, 'Bignall or Bignold, a township in co. Stafford' (Patr. Brit p. 27). The index to the register of St. Michael, Cornhill (Harl. Soc.), refers the reader from Bicknell to Bignall. So does the Reg. Univ. Oxf. (Index, vol. ii. pt. ii).

1726. Bapt. — Mary, d of Thomas Bignall: St. Michael, Cornhill, p. 169
1727. — Martha, d. of Thomas Bignell: ibid.

1733. Married—Andrew Mills and Ann Bignell: St. Antholin (London), p. 146.
London, 3, 6, 2; Philadelphia, 0, 5, 0.

Bigod, Bigot.—Nick. or offic. Roger le Bygod. A; Alina le Bigod. J; William le Bygot. A; John le Bygot. M; Gundred la Bygote, Close Roll, 5 Edw. 1. Three of these entries are of the 13th century. For the controversy on these terms, Bigod and Bigot, see Skeat's and Wedgwood's Dictionaries; also reply to Skeat by Wedgwood in the Academy, Aug. 9, 1879; see also Freeman's Norm. Conq. ii. 288. That the derisive term 'bigod' arose from the oath 'by God' seems probable. 'Pardew' (i.e. 'par Dieu') is a still existent surname with a similar origin. That it was transferred to some religious order seems equally certain (v. Wedgwood), and that through them it became a term to express religious devoteeism seems almost clear.

1750. Married—John Bigott and Grace Williams. St Geo. Chap. Mayfair, p. 159.
Philadelphia, 0, 2; New York, 0, 3.

Bilbrough, Bilberry, Dillbrough.—Local, 'of Bilborough,' a village parish near Tadcaster, co. York. Bilberry seems imitative.

Richard de Bilburgh, *molendinarius*, 1 Edw. I: Freemen of York (Surt. Soc.), i. 1.
Abraham de Bilburg (of Bilburgh), 1379: P. T. Yorks. p. 298.
Willelmus de Bilburgh, 1379: ibid. p. 301.
1567. Buried—Johane Bilbery: St. Jas. Clerkenwell, iv. 8.
1625. Buried—Widow Billbroughe, a pentioner: St. Michael, Cornhill, p. 226.
1632. — Thomas, s. John Bilborough: St. Jas. Clerkenwell, iv. 205.
1634-5. — Jane Bilbearey: St. Dionis Backchurch, p. 221.
West Riding Court Dir., 5, 0, 0; Philadelphia, 2, 0, 4.

Bilby, Bilbie, Bilbee.—Local, 'of Bilby,' a township in the parish of Blythe, co. Notts.

Robertus de Bilby, 1379: P. T. Yorks. p. 33.
Willelmus de Bilby, 1379: ibid.
1544. Ralph Alway and Mary Bylby: Marriage Lic. (Faculty Office), p. 3.
1635. Bapt.—Anne, d. Francis Bilbye: St. Jas. Clerkenwell, i. 131.

1730. Married — George Torrat and Frances Bilby: St. Geo. Chap. Mayfair, p. 318.
London, 4, 0, 0; MDB. (Somerset), 0, 3, 1.*

Bilcliffe; v. Billcliff.

Bill.—Bapt. 'the son of William.' This nick. was very uncommon; Will maintaining its hold, as Wilson, Wilkins, Wilcocks, &c., fully prove.

John Bille, co. Soms., 1 Edw. III: Kirby's Quest, p. 155.
1523. John Hall and Katherine Byll: Marriage Lic. (London), i. 3.
1567-8. William Lucas and Alice Bill: ibid. p. 39.
London, 5.

Billard.—Occup.; v. Bellbird.
Sheffield, 2; Philadelphia, 2; New York, 4.

Billcliff, Bilcliffe, Bintcliffe, Bincliff. — Local, 'of Bilcliff.' I have not identified the spot. Of course they have all one common parent; cf. *bannister* and *baluster*.

1581. Thomas Bilclif: Reg. Univ. Oxf. vol. ii. pt. ii. p. 99.
1668. Lancelot Griffin and Ann Biltcliffe: Marriage Alleg. (Westminster), p. 153.
Manchester, 1, 0, 1, 2; London, 0, 1, 0, 0; Boston (U.S.) (Billcliff), 1.

Biller.—Occup. 'the biller,' probably not a billman, i.e. one who carried a pike or halbert, but a manufacturer of the weapon.

Hugh le Biller, *peller*, 25 Edw. I: Freemen of York (Surt. Soc.), i. 6.
Henry le Billere, co. Camb., 1273. A. John Billere, co. Suff., ibid.
1666. Thomas Terrier and Mary Billier: Marriage Alleg. (Canterbury), p. 181.
London, 3; New York, 4.

Billing, Billinge, Billings.—Local, 'of Billing,' a parish in dioc. of Peterborough: also 'of Billinge,' a parish in dioc. of Liverpool. At first, no doubt, a patronymic, as proved by such placenames as Billingborough (Lincolnshire), Billingford (Norfolk), Billingham (Durham), Billinghurst, a parish in dioc. of Chichester: Billingsley, a parish in dioc. of Hereford; and Billington, a parish in dioc. of Ely.

Agnes Billyng, co. Soms., 1 Edw. III: Kirby's Quest, p. 153.

Thomas de Billinge, co. Hunts, 1273. A.

William de Billinge, co. Notts, ibid.

Adam Billing, co. Suff., ibid.

Mary de Billinge, co. Lanc., temp. Edw. I: Baines' Lanc. ii. 189.

1581. John Billings, co. Denbigh: Reg. Univ. Oxf. vol. ii. pt. ii. p. 103.

Alexander Billinge, of Billinge, 1621: Wills at Chester (1621-50), p. 22.

London, 12, 3, 5; New York, 2, 2, 24.

Billingay, Billinghay.—Local, 'of Billinghay,' a village in co. Lincoln, about nine miles from Sleaford.

Peter de Byllinggeye, co. Linc., Edw. I-Edw. III. R.

1735. Bapt.—Richard Claridge, son of Richard Billingay: St. Jas. Clerkenwell, ii. 222.

London, 1, 0; MDB. (co. Lincoln), 0, 1.

Billingham.—Local, 'of Billingham,' a parish in co. Durham, near Stockton-on-Tees.

1760. Married—William Billingham and Mary Pearce: St. Geo. Han. Sq. i. 93.

London, 1; Philadelphia, 1.

Billinghurst.—Local, 'of Billinghurst,' a parish in co. Sussex, seven miles from Horsham.

1613. Robert Billinghurste, co. Sussex: Reg. Univ. Oxf. vol. ii. pt. ii. p. 331.

1673. 'Buried—Mr. George Billinghurst in the middle of those two seats under ye Arch on ye North side of the Church': Kensington Ch. p. 144.

1778. Married—John Billinghurst and Eliz. Amey: St. Geo. Han. Sq. i. 286. London, 5.

Billingsley, Billingsly.—Local, 'of Billingsley,' a parish in co. Salop, six miles from Bridgenorth.

1581. Richard Bil'ingslie, co. Warw.: Reg. Univ. Oxf. vol. ii. pt. ii. p. 98.

1587-8. William Byllinsgley,co.Warw.: ibid. p. 162.

1593. Buried—John, s. John Billingsley: St. Jas. Clerkenwell, iv. 51.

1635. — A still-born child of William Billingslye: ibid. p. 219.

1652. — Robert Billingsly: ibid. p. 291.

London, 2, 0; Philadelphia, 0, 2.

Billington.—(1) Local, 'of Billington,' a parish in dioc. of Ely. (2) Local, 'of Billington,' a township and manor in the parish of Blackburn, co. Lancashire. The surname is well established in that county.

William de Bilington, co. Lanc., 1332: Lay Subsidy (Rylands), p. 76.

Johannes de Billyngton, 1379: P. T. Yorks. p. 284.

Adam de Billington, co. Lanc., 13 John: Baines' Lanc. ii. 85.

Antony Billington, of Wood Plumpton, yeoman, 1575: Lancashire Wills at Richmond, p. 32.

Margaret Billington, of Catforth, 1663: ibid.

Richard Billington, of Whalley, co. Lanc., 1595: Wills at Chester, i. 19.

1737. Married—Richard Billington and Eliz. Devonshire: St. Geo. Han. Sq. i. 19.

London, 6; Manchester, 6; Blackburn, 3; Boston (U.S.), 4.

Billiter.—Occup. 'a bell-founder.' An East-Anglian term. No instances appear in the Hundred Rolls (1273). 'Belleʒetare (bellyatere), campanarius': Prompt. Parv. In the Register of Wills (London), ii. 226, occurs 'William Burford, billeytere.' I forgot to look for the date of this. Stowe informs us that Billiter Lane was once known as Belʒeters Lane. This settles the origin of the surname. 'In 1349, Thomas de Baldeswell presented to the Church aforesaid as chief lord of this fee: in 1367, Adam Humphrey: and in 1385, Adam Pyk, and in 1400, Edmund Belytter, alias Belzeter' (Blomefield's Norfolk, viii. 383).

Robert le Belyetere, C. R., 7 Edw. III. pt. i.

William le Belʒetere. B.

Margaret le Billyetter, co. Norf. FF.

Edmund Belletere, co. Norf., ibid.

Robert le Bellegeter, 12 Edw. I: Freemen of York, i. 4.

Bilney.—Local, 'of Bilney,' a parish in co. Norfolk. 'Thomas Bilney, or Bylney, martyr, was member of a Norfolk family which took its name from the villages of the same designation in that county': Dict. Nat. Biog. v. 40.

Geoffrey Bylyne, co. Camb., 1273. A.

John de Bilneye, 1301. M.

William de Bilneye, co. Norf., 2 Edw. III: FF. viii. 355.

Walter de Bilney, co. Norf., 6 John: ibid. p. 446.

1627. Bapt.—Eliz., d. Edward Bilnye: St. Jas. Clerkenwell, i. 107.

Bilsborough, Bilsbrough, Billsborough, Bilsborow, Bilsborrow, Bilsbury, Bilsboro.—Local, 'of Bilsborough,' a small hamlet in the parish of Garstang, co. Lancashire.

Richard de Billisburgh, co. Lanc.: Baines' Lanc., ii. 538.

Thomas Billysborow, buried at Ribchester, 1540: Lancashire Wills at Richmond, p. 32.

Henry Bilsborrow, of Cottam, 1593: ibid.

1542. Jacobus Billysboroo: Preston Guild Rolls, p. 17.

1602. Henry Billisborowe: ibid. p. 51.

1642. Richard Bilsborowe: ibid. p. 96.

Manchester, 2, 0, 0, 0, 0, 0, 0; Preston, 0, 1, 4, 1, 0, 0, 0; Liverpool, 0, 1, 0, 0, 1, 0, 0; MDB. (West Rid. Yorks), Bilsbury, 1; New York (Bilsboro), 1.

Bilson, Billson.—Bapt. 'the son of Bell'; v. Bell (1). There is no evidence in favour of 'the son of Bill,' i.e. William. That nick. is comparatively modern. In the Modern Domesday Book (co. Warwick) there are four Bellisons, one Belson, and one Bilson, all evidently of the same stock, namely, Bellson (i.e. the son of Isabella). Bilson is an easy variant of Belson.

1561. Thomas Bilson and Margery Pussye: Marriage Lic. (London), i. 21.

1666. Thomas Bilson, of Winchester: Reg. Univ. Oxf. vol. ii. pt. ii. p. 292.

1627. Bapt.—James, s. Richard Bilson: Kensington Ch. p. 23.

1750. Married—Richard Weller and Elizabeth Bilson: St. Geo. Chap. Mayfair, p. 176.

London, 1, 0; Philadelphia, 0, 2.

Bilton.—Local, 'of Bilton,' a village parish about nine miles west of York.

Thomas de Bilton, carter, 7 Edw. II: Freemen of York, i. 15.

Adam de Bilton, 1379: P. T. Yorks. p. 293.

Johannes de Bilton, 1379: ibid.

1584. Balthazar Bucke and Ann Bylton: Marriage Lic. (London), i. 133.

West Riding Court Dir., 2; Boston (U.S.), 1.

Bimson, Bimpson.—Bapt.; a corruption of Binson, itself a corrupted form of Benson.

1727. Bapt.—Sarah, d. of William Binson: St. Jas. Clerkenwell, i. 173.

1743. Married—John Bimson and Ann Stone: St. Geo. Han. Sq. i. 29.

London, 1, 0; New York, 0, 1.

Binder.—Occup. 'the bookbinder.' This is practically settled by the Hundred Rolls, where, in the town of Oxford, Stephen Ligator, librorum, is mentioned again as Stephen Ligator. Also in the case of a William Ligator, as below; v. Bookbinder.

WilliamLigator,*libror*',Oxford,1273. A.
William Ligator, Oxford, ibid.
Simon Ligator, Oxford, ibid.
Lawrence Ligator, Cambridge, ibid.
1578-9. William Hammond and Johanna Bynder: Marriage Lic. (London), i. 84.
1595-6. Edward Byneder and Katherine Raynstropp: ibid. p. 228.
London, 2; New York, 6.

Bindloose, Bindloss, Bindlass.—Local, 'of Bindlows.' I cannot find the spot. It is clear that the suffix is *-low* (v. Lowe).

Robertus Byndlowys, 1379: P. T. Yorks. p. 256.
Johannes Byndlowys, 1379: ibid.
1582. Christopher Bindlos (co. Westm.), Queen's Coll.: Reg. Univ. Oxf. vol. ii. pt. ii. p. 123.
1666. Thomas Sutton and Grizell Bindlose: Marriage Alleg. (Canterbury), p. 170.
MDB. (co. Lanc.), o, 2, 1; London, o, 2, o; Manchester, o, 1, o.

Bingham.—Local, 'of Bingham,' a parish in dioc. of Southwell, co. Nottingham.

John de Byngham, co. Soms., 1 Edw. III: Kirby's Quest, p. 194.
Joanna de Byngham, co. Soms., 1 Edw. III: ibid. p. 207.
William de Bingham, co. Soms., 1273. A.
Geoffrey de Bingeham, co. Wilts, ibid.
Robert de Bingeham, co. Dorset, ibid.
Alicia de Byngham, 1379: P. T. Yorks. p. 40.
1567-8. Ellis Byngham and Johanna Ellis, widow: Marriage Lic. (London), i. 39.
1610. Buried—Thomas Bingam: St. Michael, Cornhill, p. 217.
1645. — Mighell Bingam: St. Mary Aldermary, p. 173.
London, 15; Philadelphia, 30.

Bingley.—Local, 'of Bingley,' a parish and market town in the West Rid. Yorks.

(Batts) de Bingelay, co. York, 1273. A.
Willelmus de Byngelay, 1379: P. T. Yorks. p. 294.
1570. Married—Rycharde Caryngton and Katharyn Byngley: St. Dionis Backchurch, p. 6.
1740. — John Richard Brinckman and Ann Bingley: St. Geo. Han. Sq. i. 24.
West Riding Court Dir., 14; London, 10; Philadelphia, 4.

Binks, Binkes.—(?) For Bilks, by change of *l* to *n*, very common in nomenclature; cf. Banister, q.v.

William Bilkys, or Bilkes, co. Linc., 1273. A.
1583. Robert Binks, or Binckes, co. York: Reg. Univ. Oxf. vol. ii. pt. ii. p. 131.
1595. William Baldrye and Alice Binckes: Marriage Lic. (London), i. 223.

1676. Bapt. — Robert, s. Andrew Binckes: St. Mary Aldermary, p. 104.
1727. Married—William Bincks and Deborah Wrench: St. Antholin (London), p. 142.
1749. — Thomas Keen and Mary Binks: St. Michael, Cornhill, p. 71.
London, 5, o; MDB. (Lincoln), 4, o; Philadelphia, o, 2.

Binney, Binnie.—Local. 'of Binnie,' an estate in the parish of Uphall, Linlithgowshire (Lower's Patr. Brit. p. 28).

Willelmus Bynny, 1379: P. T. Yorks. p. 40.
London, 1, 3; West Riding Court Dir., 4, o; Boston (U.S.), 10, o.

Binning.—Bapt. 'the son of Binning'; v. Benning, and cf. Browning and Harding.

William Bining, co. Norf., 1273, A.
John Bining, co. Norf., ibid.
1894. 'At Arkwood, Spital, Ches., the wife of T. J. Binning, of a son': Daily Telegraph, Feb. 6.
London, 3.

Binnington.—Local, 'of Binnington,' a township in the parish of Willerby, East Rid. Yorks, lit. the farmstead of Binning; v. Binning, and cf. Bennington.

1803. 'At Gledhow Terrace, South Kensington, the wife of F. W. Binnington, of a son': Daily Telegraph, Dec. 16.
MDB. (East Rid. Yorks), 4.

Binnion.—Bapt.; Welsh, Ap-Ennion; v. Bennion and Benyon.

Liverpool, 1.

Binns.—? Local. This surname has ramified most strongly in co. York.

Robert Binns, co. Linc., 1273. A.
Johannes de Bynnes, 1379: P. T. Yorks. p. 182.
Willelmus Bynne, 1379: ibid. p. 8.
Roger Byn, 1379: ibid. p. 44.
Thomas Bynne, ibid.
1780. Married—John Robinson and Hannah Binns: St. Geo. Han. Sq. i. 313.
West Riding Court Dir., 27; Halifax, 5; Philadelphia, 13.

Birbeck.—Local; v. Birkbeck.

Birch, Burch.—Local, 'at the birch,' from residence by a birch-tree (cf. Oak, Ash, Nash, &c.); v. Birks. In Lancashire, Birch generally hails from Birch, a chapelry in the parish of Middleton, near Manchester. Of course, a surname of this class is originated in a hun-

dred different places. Every directory teems with the name.

Hugh de la Byrche, co. Devon, 1273. A.
John atte Birche, temp. 1300. M.
Henry del Birches, co. Lanc., 1332: Lay Subsidy (Rylands), p. 10.
Robert del Birches, co. Lanc., 1332: ibid. p. 37.
Willelmus del Birch, 1379: P. T. Yorks. p. 293.
1571-2. Richard Byrche and Margaret Gibson: Marriage Lic. (London), i. 52.
George Birch, of Birch, 1602: Wills at Chester (1545-1620), p. 10.
Gilbert Birch, of Middleton, 1562: ibid. p. 10.
John Birch, of Manchester, *innholder*, 1592: ibid. p. 20.
London, 38, 22; Manchester, 27, 1; Philadelphia, 50, 4.

Birchall.—Local, 'of Birtles.' Odd as this may seem, it is true. For further evidence, v. Birtles.

John de Birchall de Birtles, of Gawsworth, co. Ches.: Hist. East Ches. ii. 587 *n*.
Richard Birchall, of Parr, *webster*, 1581: Wills at Chester (1545-1620), p. 20.
James Birchall, of Winwick, 1591: ibid.
Geoffrey Birchall, of Croft, in Winwick, 1614: ibid.
1778. Married — Edward Frewer and Elizabeth Birchall: St. Geo. Han. Sq. i. 289.
London, 3; Manchester, 6; MDB. (co. Lanc.), 7, Philadelphia, 15.

Birchenough.—Local, 'of the birchen-hough,' from residence thereby. Birchen is the adjective of birch, a birch-tree or trees (cf. Golden), and *hough*, like *haugh*, or *how*, means a hill or mound. Hence Birchenhough is simply the mound or hill covered with birches; cf. Goodenough. In both cases the *h* is elided.

London, 1; Boston (U.S.), 1.

Birchwood.—Local, 'at the birchwood,' from residence by a clump or grove of birch-trees; cf. Birkinshaw, an exact equivalent.

John de Birchewode, of Turton, co. Lanc., 1332: Lay Subsidy (Rylands), p. 40.
Ralph Birchwood, of Ormskirk, co. Lanc., 1608: Wills at Chester, i. 20.
Henry Birchwood, of Bostock, co. Lanc., 1616: ibid.
Liverpool, 3; Manchester, 2.

Bircumshaw.—Local; v. Birkinshaw.

Bird.—Nick. 'the bird,' perhaps from the singing propensities of the original bearer ; cf. ' He sings like a bird.' Also cf. Nightingale, Sparrow, Finch, Lark, &c.

David le Brid, co. Oxf., 1273. A.
John le Brid, co. Oxf., ibid.
Stefan Brid, co. Suff., ibid.
Geoffrey Bryd, co. Salop, ibid.
Henry le Brid, co. Soms., 1 Edw. III : Kirby's Quest, p. 92.
Johannes Bridde, 1379 : P. T. Yorks. p. 294.
1764. Married—George Bird and Ann Skinner : St. Geo. Han. Sq. i. 137.
London, 92 ; Philadelphia, 70.

Birdsall, Beardsell, Beardsall.—Local, ' of Birstall ' (?), a village parish near Dewsbury, Yorks.

Robert de Bridsall, 1379 : P. T. Yorks. p. 236.
1769. John Beardsall and Elizabeth Austin : St. Geo. Han. Sq. i. 192.
Church Fenton (Yorks), 1, 0, 0 ; West Riding Court Dir., 0, 2, 0 ; Sheffield, 0, 0, 1 ; Philadelphia, 3, 0, 0.

Birdseye, Birdsey.—Local, ' of Birdsey.' I cannot find the spot. Manifestly Birdseye is imitative. But the meaning seems clear, the ' Birdseye,' i. e. the islet or eyot in the stream frequented by birds.

1665. William Wakeling and Mary Birdsey : Marriage Alleg. (Canterbury), p. 134.
1675. Bapt. — Edward Birdsey : St. Dionis Backchurch, p. 121.
1687. Buried—Anne Birdsey : ibid.p.254.

The index under ' Birdsey ' refers the reader to ' Budsey.'

1652. Married — Francis Burgis and Eliza Budsey : St. Dionis Backchurch, p. 28.
1753. — William Birdseye and Eliz. Drane : St. Geo. Chap. Mayfair, p. 231.
London, 3, 1 ; MDB. (co. Bedford), 0, 2 ; New York, 4, 0 ; Philadelphia, 1, 0.

Birdwhistle.—Local. A somewhat pretty imitative corruption of Birtwhistle, q.v.

Manchester, 1.

Birkbeck, Birbeck.—Local, ' of Birkbeck,' so called from the *beck* or streamlet that flowed through the *birks* or birch-trees (v. Birks and Beck). A Cumberland surname. Of course, Birkbeck was too big a mouthful for ordinary and current usage, and Birbeck took its place.

Adam Byrkbeke, sup. for M.A., 16 June, 1507 : Reg. Univ. Oxf. vol. i. p. 54.
1583. Humphrey Byrkbecke (co. Westm.) Queen's Coll. : ibid. p. 127.
1600. Symond Birkebecke(co.Westm.), Queen's Coll. : ibid. p. 243.
1771. Married—Thomas Birkbeck and Susannah Evratt : St. Geo. Han. Sq. i. 213.
London, 3, 5 ; MDB. (co. Cumberland), 0, 4 ; New York, 1, 1.

Birkenhead.—Local, ' of Birkenhead,' co. Chester. The meaning is ' the head of the birch-trees ' ; cf. Aikenhead, and v. Birkett and Birkhead.

Edward Birkenhead, of Runcorn, 1607 : Wills at Chester (1545-1620), p. 20.
Richard Birchenhead, of Ashton, 1617 : ibid.
John Birkenhead, of Manley, 1620 : ibid.
' Sir John Birkenhead, or Berkenhead (1616-79), author of the *Mercurius Aulicus* and satirical poems, is said by Anthony à Wood to have been son of Randall Birkenhead, of Northwich in Cheshire ' : Dict. Nat. Biog. v. 81.
1617. Henry Birkened, co. Ches. : Reg. Univ. Oxf. vol. ii. pt. ii. p. 364.
Liverpool, 1 ; New York, 1.

Birkett, Birkhead.—Local ; North English, ' of the birk-head,' i. e. the head of the birches ; cf. Birkenhead and Beckett. The surname Haslefoot is of the same class.

Stephen Birkheade, of Borwicke, 1607 : Lanc. Wills at Richmond, i. 33.
Stephen Birket, of Warton, 1573 : ibid.
Myles Birkheade, of Winster, 1623 : ibid.
Miles Birkett, of Winster, 1646 : ibid. p. 233.
John Byrkheved, vicar of Giggleswick, in Craven, 1425 : Whittaker, p. 166.
Christopher Birkhed, vicar of Long Preston, 1636 : ibid. p. 145.
Georgius Byrkett, 1503 : HHH. p. 38.
Georgius Byrkehede, 1507 : ibid. p. 47.

The three references following concern the same person :—

Bridgitt Birkett, 1634 : St. Peter, Cornhill, p. 85.
Bridget Birkhead, 1638 : ibid. p. 197.
Bridggett Birkehead, 1653 : ibid. p. 207.
' Petition of John Birked, vicar of Christ Church, Sep. 9,' 1550 : Cal. State Papers (Domestic), i. 29.
William Byrkhed, C. R., 3 Edw. IV.
London, 16, 1 ; New York, 1, 0 ; Philadelphia, 0, 8.

Birkinshaw, Birkenshaw, Burtenshaw, Bertenshaw, Bircumshaw.—Local, ' of Birk-

enshaw,' a chapelry in the parish of Birstall, co. York. The meaning is ' the birch-wood,' *birken* being the adjective (v. Birkenhead, Akenhead, &c.). The variants are curious, but only found at a distance from their native home.

John Birchynshaw, Hen. VIII : Cal. State Papers.
Thomas Birkyschaghe, 1379 : P. T. Yorks. p. 163.
1634. Bapt.—Humphrey Birchenshaw : Prestbury Ch. (Cheshire), p. 292.
Robert Birkenshaw, 1587 : Wills at Chester, i. 21.
Ambrose Birtenshaw, of Manchester, 1584 : ibid.
Robert Birtinshaw, of Manchester, 1609 : ibid.
1782. Married — William Fligg and Isabella Burckingshaw : St. Geo. Han. Sq. p. 339.

The Standard of Oct. 12, 1886, p. 3, reports Emma Bircumshaw as appearing in court at Nottingham in a legal case. This spelling is a manifest corruption of Birkinshaw.

London, 1, 0, 3, 0, 0 ; MDB. (West Rid. Yorks), 2, 5, 0, 0, 0 ; (co. Notts), 0, 0, 0, 0, 2 ; Manchester, 0, 0, 0, 1, 0.

Birks.—Local, ' at the hirks,' from residence beside a clump of birch-trees. North English *birk*, a birch-tree ; v. Birkenhead, Birkett, Birkbeck, &c. ; and v. Birch.

Johannes del Byrkes, 1372 : P. T. Yorks. p. 215.
Cf. John del Byrches, Pardons Roll, 17 Ric. II : Reg. Univ. Oxf. iii. 267.
1607. Richard Birkes, Jesus Coll. : ibid.
1741. Married — Edward Birkes and Susanna Selby : St. Geo. Han. Sq. i. 27.
1753. — Benjamin Birks and Mary Slater : St. Geo. Chap. Mayfair, p. 239.
London, 2 ; MDB. (West Rid. Yorks), 17 ; Philadelphia, 2.

Birley.—Local, ' of Birley ' or ' Burley,' several places in co. York ; v. Burley and Burleigh.

Robert de Berlay, *mercer*, 19 Edw. II : Freemen of York, i. 23.
Johannes de Berlay, 1379 : P. T. Yorks. p. 143.
Willelmus de Birlay, *webster*, 1379 : ibid. p. 36.
Rogerus de Birlay, 1379 : ibid.
Evan Birley, *webster*, 1622 : Preston Guild Rolls, p. 88.
Manchester, 4 ; Preston, 2 ; London, 2.

Birtles.—Local, ' of Birtles,' a township in the parish of Prestbury, co. Cheshire, formerly spelt

Birchels as well as Birtles; v. Birchall.

'Cristiana, the widow of Henry de Birchels,' 17 Edw. I: East Cheshire, ii. 357.
John de Birtlis, 1324: ibid.
Ralph de Byrtheles, 6 Hen. VIII: ibid.
1563. Buried—John Birtles, of Birtles: Prestbury Church (Cheshire), p. 12.
1582. — James Byrchels, of Adlington: ibid. p. 75.
Edward Birtles, of Birtles, *yeoman*, 1595: Wills at Chester (1545-1620), p. 21.
Roger Birtles, of Birtles, parish of Prestbury, 1616: ibid.
Manchester, 4; London, 1.

Birtwhistle, Birtwistle.—

Local, 'of Birtwistle.' I cannot find the spot; cf. Entwistle. But as it is evidently in the West Rid. Yorks, it may be an early form of Briestwhistle, a hamlet in the parish of Thornhill. Birdwhistle (q.v.) is a curious imitative form.

Rob. filius Joh'is Brittwissill, 1397: Preston Guild Rolls, p. 3.
Henricus Birktwysell, *sutor*, 1379: P. T. Yorks, p. 218.
Johannes de Brytwesle, 1379: ibid. p. 284.
Ricardus de Brytwesele, 1379: ibid.
Gilbert filius Joh' of Love Clough, 1594: Wills at Chester (1545-1620), p. 21.
George Birtwistell, of Goodshaw, 1619: ibid.
1566. Anthony Birttwessel, Bras. Coll.: Reg. Univ. Oxf. vol. ii. pt. ii. p. 26.

The fact that Anthony was at Brasenose College is all but absolute proof that he came from co. Lanc.

Manchester, 1, 4; MDB. (co. York, West Rid.), 2, 1; Philadelphia, 0, 2.

Bishop, Bishopp.—

Nick. 'the bishop,' a common entry in early registers, a sobriquet readily affixed on one of ecclesiastical appearance. Nevertheless, most of our Bishops owe their title to the custom of electing a boy-bishop on St. Nicholas' Day (v. Brand, Pop. Antiq.). The ceremony was a very familiar one. Lyson quotes from the Lambeth Churchwardens' Accounts, 1523: 'For the Bishop's dynner and hys company on St. Nycolas' Day, iis. viiid.' *King* arose similarly, q.v.

John le Bissup, co. Oxf., 1273. A.
William Bisscop, co. Norf., ibid.
Henry Biscop, co. Linc., ibid.
Elvena, relicta Peter Bissop, co. Camb., ibid.
Alice Bissop, co. Oxf., ibid.

A curious proof of the existence of this popular nickname is seen in the following entry:

Bissop atte Comb, co. Soms., 1 Edw. III: Kirby's Quest, p. 182.

In the formal roll of the Preston Guild Merchant for 1602 appears the name of 'William Browne, alias Bushopp' (Preston Guild Rolls, p. 64).

James Bishop, of Warrington, 1614: Wills at Chester (1545-1620), p. 21.
1656. Married—John Golling and Eliz. Bishopp: St. Michael, Cornhill, p. 36.
1749. Bapt.—Ebenezer Busup, a foundling: ibid. p. 175.
London, 121, 5; Philadelphia, 89, 0.

Bishoprick.—

? Local. Probably the suffix is *rigg*, a ridge.

Robert Bishoprick, of Newbeggin, Richmond: North Riding Yorks. Directory, 1872.

Bispham, Biscomb.—

Local, 'of Bispham,' a village three miles from Poulton, in the Fylde district, co. Lancashire; anciently Biscopham, i.e. the bishop's dwelling (v. Baines' Hist. Lanc. ii. 507).

Averia de Bispham, co. Lanc., 1288: Baines' Hist. Lanc. ii. 507.
Henry de Bispham, co. Lanc., 1365: ibid. p. 508.
Robert de Bispham, co. Lanc., 1332: Lay Subsidy (Rylands), p. 45.
Laurence Byspham, co. Lanc., 1542: Preston Guild Rolls, p. 18.
Margaret Bispham, of Pilling, 1670: Lancashire Wills at Richmond, p. 34.
John Bispham, of Little Woolton, 1689: Wills at Chester, i. 27.
Blackburn, 1, 0; Manchester, 0, 1; Philadelphia, 16, 0.

Biss.—

Local; v. Bysh.

Bissett, Bessett, Bissatt, Biset, Bisset.—

Bapt. 'the son of Biset.' This so far tallies with Mr. Ferguson's statement that Bissett is a dim. of an old Teutonic personal name Bis. But I suspect that Biset is the full name, and not a diminutive (v. Lower's Patr. Brit. p. 29).

Biset Dapifer, co. Glouc., Edw. I. R.
Robert Biset, co. Hunts, ibid.
Maunsel Bisset, co. Worc., 1273. A.
John Besette, 1455, York. W. 11.
1602. William Bissett, co. Glamorgan: Reg. Univ. Oxf. vol. ii. pt. ii. p. 256.
1764. Married — William Bisset and Jane Mills: St. Geo. Han. Sq. i. 137.

London, 1, 1, 0, 0, 0; MDB. (W. Rid. Yorks), 0, 0, 2, 0, 0; West Rid. Court Dir., 2, 0, 0, 1, 0; Philadelphia, 11, 0, 0, 0, 2.

Blab.—

Nick. 'a tell-tale'; Simon le Blabe (Close Roll, 3 Edw. I); M.E. *blabbe*, a tell-tale. 'Blabbe, or labbe, wreyare of cownselle': Prompt. Parv.

New York, 1.

Blabber, Blaber.—

Nick. 'the blabber,' a revealer of secrets, a tell-tale; v. Blab. '1557. He was a great blabber of his tongue' (H.E.D.).

William Bluber, co. Norf., 1273. A.
Johannes Blabour, 1379: P. T. Yorks. p. 202.
1803. Married — James Brookes and Barbara Blaber: St. Geo. Han. Sq. ii. 274.
New York, 0, 1.

Blaby.—

Local, 'of Blaby,' a parish in dioc. of Peterborough and co. Leicester.

John de Blabi, co. York, 1273. A.
John de Blaby, rector of North Barsham, co. Norf., 1361: FF. vii. 51.
Thomas Blaby, rector of Woodrising, co. Norf., 1356: ibid. x. 280.
1575-6. John Blabye and Dorothy Gabbott: Marriage Lic. (London), i. 68.
1579. Tristian Blaby, co. Worc.: Reg. Univ. Oxf. vol. ii. pt. ii, p. 86.
1767. Married — Thomas Blabey and Ann Beording: St. Geo. Han. Sq. i. 167, London, 3.

Black, Blake.—

Nick. 'the black,' from the complexion; cf. Blackman, Blue, White, Hoare, Blunt, Russell, &c.

Hamo le Blake, co. Bucks, 1273. A.
Reginald le Blake, co. Camb., ibid.
Reyner le Blake, co. Norf., ibid.
Edericke le Blacke, co. Linc., ibid.
William le Blake, co. Soms., 1 Edw. III: Kirby's Quest, p. 107.
Margery la Blak, C. R., 3 Edw. II.
1783. Married—Allin Blake and Dorothy Peregrine: St. Geo. Han. Sq. i. 345.
London, 23, 69; Philadelphia, 300, 84.

Blackadar, Blackadder.—

Local, 'of Blackadder,' not far from the English border in Scotland. A river of that name also runs there.

'The lairds of Wedderburn, Blackadder, and West Nisbet,' 1545: Calendar of State Papers relating to Scotland, edited by Markham John Thorper (London: Longmans), p. 57.
Adam Blacader, prior of Coldingham, 1524: ibid. p. 19.
Patrick Blacater, 1559: ibid. p. 122.
London, 1, 0.

Blackall, Blackhall.—Local, 'of the Black-hall.' Mr. Lower says that it is a corruption of Blackwell, but this is not borne out by evidence.

Nicholas of the Blakehall, C R., Ric. II.
1702. Married — George Blackall and Martha Cornish: St. Mary Aldermary, p. 37.
1774. — Charles Burrell Massingberd and Ann Blackall : St. Geo. Han. Sq. i. 248.
London, 2, 2 ; Boston (U.S.), 2, 0 ; New York, 0, 2.

Black-ballock.—Nick.; v. Ballock (H.E.D.).

Robertus Blacballoc, co. Suff., 1273. A.

Blackbeard.—Nick. 'with the black beard.' M.E. *berd* or *berde* ; cf. Brownbeard. Blackbird is an imitative form. Blackberd occurs in Yorkshire so early as 1379. It is still to be met with there in the shape of Blackbeard.

John Blacberd, co. Oxf, 1273. A.
Richard Blacberd, co Oxf., ibid.
Johannes Blakberd, 1379 : P. T. Yorks. p. 196.
Thomas Blackberd, co. York. W. 18.
Peter Blackbeard, co. York. W. 20.
John Blackbird, co. Camb., 1612 : VVV. p. 490.
1721. Bapt. — Henry, son of Henry Blackbird : St. Jas. Clerkenwell, ii. 123.
'Mr. J. Blackbeard, of 119 Bromptonroad, applied to Mr. Biron for advice respecting the action of the Chelsea Water Company,' &c. : Standard, Sept. 21, 1888, p. 5.
Exeter, 1 ; London, 1 ; MDB. (N. Riding Yorks), 1.

Blackburn, Blackborn, Blackborne, Blackbourn, Blackburne.—Local, ' of Blackburn.' a large and thriving town in co. Lanc. There is no negro taint in Blackborn.

Willelmus de Blakburn, 1379 : P. T. Yorks. pp. 252-3.
Cristoforus de Blakeburn, 1379 : ibid.
Johannes de Blakeburn, 1379 : ibid.
John de Blakeburne, 1397 : Preston Guild Rolls, p. 4.
1593. Edward Blackburne, of Leyland, co. Lanc. : Wills at Chester, i. 21.
1605. William Blackburne, of Billington, co. Lanc. : ibid.
Manchester, 11, 0, 0, 0, 0 ; London, 20, 1, 1, 4, 2 ; Philadelphia, 41, 0, 0, 0, 9.

Blackcow, Blacow, Blackoe, Blakoe.—Local, ' of Blackhall,' co. Lanc. This looks like a nickname or sign-board name, but it is

from Black-hall, near Preston; pronounced Blackow (cf. Lindow for Lindale, Picthaw for Pickthall, &c). This name has taken the imitative form of Blackcow : William Blackcow (Proctor's Manchester Streets).

Henry Hartley, of Blacow, co. Lanc., 1615 : Wills at Chester (1545-1620), p. 85.
Margaret Blacow, of Sarnlesbury, 1611 : ibid. p. 21.
Antonius Blacoll, 1562 : Preston Guild Rolls, p. 22.
Antonius Blakecowe, 1582 : ibid. p. 24.

In this same series of records the surname is variously spelled Blacoll, Blacoe, Blackowe, Blakecowe, and Blakow ; v. Index.

Manchester, 0, 1, 0, 0 ; Preston, 0, 1, 2, 2.

Blacker.—(1) Bapt. ' the son of Blacre' (Domesday).

Ric. fil. Blacker, 12th century : FFF. p. 47.
Baldwin fil. Blacker, 12th century : ibid.
Walterus fil. Godfridi fil. Blaker, 12th century : ibid. p. 21.

(2) Occup. ' the bleacher ' ; for a feminine form, v. Blaxter.

Roger le Blackere, 1312. M.
Geoffrey le Blakere, 1313. M.
Walter le Blacker, co. Soms., 1 Edw. III : Kirby's Quest, p. 225.
Stephen le Blakar, co. Soms., 1 Edw. III : ibid. p. 263.
1605. William Blacker, co. Wilts : Reg. Univ. Oxf. vol. ii. pt. ii. p. 287.
1610. Edward Blacker, co. Wilts : ibid. p. 314.
London, 3 ; Crockford, 3 ; Boston (U.S.), 6.

Blackett, Blacket.—(1) Local, ' at the Blackhead,' the dark headland, from residence thereby ; cf. Birket and Becket, for Birkhead and Beckhead (v. Redhead). (2) Nick. ' with the black head ' ; cf. Whitehead. In any case the original form is Blackhead.

'The Blacketts of co. Northumb., trace to William de Black-heved (i.e. Blackhead), forester of Stanhope, 1350 ': Lower, Patr. Brit. p. 29.
'Mr. John Blackhead, *merchant* (of Norwich), gave 4 acres of land,' &c. : FF. iv. 222.
Michael Blacket, of Newcastle, temp. 1720 : ibid. iii. 591.
1608. Henry Blackhead, co. Herts : Reg. Univ. Oxf. vol. ii. pt. ii. p. 300.
'Dismission for Edward West, defendant, v. William Blackhead, complainant,' Dec. 1, 1591 : Cal. State Papers (Domestic), iii. 135.

1786. Married — Arthur Blackett and Mary Barlow : St. Geo. Han. Sq. i. 386.
London, 8, 0 ; MDB. (co. Northumberland), 3, 1 ; New York, 1, 0 ; Boston (U.S.), 1, 0.

Blackeyes.—? Nick. ' with the black or very dark eyes.' But it may be local ; v. my first instance and cf. Birdseye.

1625. Buried — Marke Blackseye : St. Jas. Clerkenwell, ii. 185.
1752. Married—Thomas Blackeyes and Elizabeth Bridge : Canterbury Cath., p. 92.

Blackford.—Local, ' of Blackford.' (1) a parish in co. Soms., near Wincanton ; (2) a chapelry in the parish of Wedmore, co. Soms., near Axbridge.

Robert de Blakeford, co. Soms., 1 Edw. III : Kirby's Quest, p. 123.
Adam de Blakeford, co. Soms., 1 Edw. III : ibid. p. 180.
1689. Buried—Margrett Blackford : St. Dionis Backchurch, p. 257.
1753. Married—John Baptist Blackford and Betty New Tinling : St. Geo. Chap. Mayfair, p. 244.
London, 8 ; MDB. (co. Soms.), 1 ; Philadelphia, 4.

Blackhall.—Local ; v. Blackall.

Blackham.—Local, ' of Blakenham.' Probably the same as Blakenham : two parishes, Great and Little Blakenham, near Ipswich. My instances all point to this.

Alan de Blakeham, co. Camb. 1273. A.
Richard de Blakeham, co. Suff., ibid.
Thomas de Blakeham, co. Suff., ibid.
Benedict de Blakeham, 1279. M.
1626. John Griffyn and Margaret Blackham : Marriage Lic. (London), ii. 180.
1669. Benjamin Blackham and Ellinor Preston : Marriage Alleg. (Westminster), p. 164.
MDB. (co. Suffolk), 1 ; New York, 2.

Blackistor.—Occup. 'the bleacher' ; v. Blaxter.

Blacklamb.—Nick. ' the black lamb,' the naughty, the bad ; William Blacklambe (Close Roll, 8 Edw. III). Cf. ' Ba, ba, blacksheep, have you any wool?' also ' black sheep,' for a man of exceptionally bad qualities.

Blackledge, Blackleach.—Local, ' of the Black-lake,' corrupted by imitation into Blackleach. Probably the spot mentioned in a charter (c. 1200) connected with property in Wilmslow parish. East Cheshire, from which district the name in most cases is undoubtedly sprung. 'Fulseha, Chorlegh, Pounale, and Morlegh. . . . as far as the mid stream of the Siche, which comes from the Black Lache of Shadoke mosse,' &c. Mr. Earwaker adds, 'The name Black Lache or Black Lake is now applied to a large pond on Lindow Common' (East Ches. i. 42); v. Depledge and Cartledge.

John del Blakelache, of Layland, co. Lanc. : Lay Subsidy (Rylands), p. 52.
'John Blackleech, of Laylond, co. Lanc., sonne of Nicholas Blackleech, doctor of phisick to King Henry VIII' : Visit. London, i. 76.
John Blakeleach. AA. 3.
Thomas Blakelache, ibid.
William Blacklach, of Wigan, 11 Eliz.: Lanc. and Ches. Rec. Soc. viii. 400.
1570. William Blackleach and Mary Kentish : Marriage Lic. (Westminster), p. 3.
1587. Nicholas Blackleech, co. Glouc. : Reg. Univ. Oxf. vol. ii. pt. ii. p. 160.
1601. John Blacklege, co. Soms. : ibid. p. 252.
Samuel Blacklach, mayor of Macclesfield, 1615 : East Cheshire, ii. 168.
London, 1, 0 ; Liverpool, 3, 0 ; Preston, 1, 0 ; New York, 6, 0.

Blackler.—Offic. 'the bachelor,' a surname peculiar to the West country, especially to co. Devon. The two instances below pave the way to the little eccentricity of Blackler ; v. Batchelar.

Henry Bakeler, co. Soms., 1 Edw. III : Kirby's Quest, p. 276.
Adam Bakeler, co. Soms., 1 Edw. III : ibid.
MDB. (co. Devon), 6 ; Oxford, 1.

Blackley, Blakeley, Bleackley, Bleckly, Blakely, Bleakley.—(1) Local, 'of Blackley' (usually pronounced Blakeley), a township in the old parish of Manchester. (2) Local, 'of Blakeney,' q.v. This corruption was an early one ; v. infra, and cf. Blankley for Blankney.

Adam de Blakeneye, alias Adam de Blakeleye, London, 1273. A.
William de la Blakelegh, 1301. M.
1626. Jane Blakeley, of Bury, *widow* : Wills at Chester, ii. 24.
1628. Ralph Blakeley, of Bury : ibid.

1701. Bapt.—William James, son of James and Esther Blackley : Reg. Canterbury Cath. p. 39.
London, 1, 3, 0, 1, 0, 0 ; Manchester, 3, 15, 5, 0, 2, 0 ; Philadelphia, 2, 0, 0, 1, 17, 2.

Blacklock.—Nick. 'with the black fock of hair' (cf. Silverlock, Goldlock, Lovelock) : a familiar Cumberland surname.

William Bernard, alias dictus Blaklok : Close Roll, 22 Edw. III. pt. ii.
Peter Blacloke, co. Wilts, 1273. A.
1597-8. William Blacklocke, co. Cumb.: Reg. Univ. Oxf. vol. ii. pt. ii. p. 226.
1744. Married — William James and Mary Blacklock : St. Geo. Chap. Mayfair, p. 44.
London, 3 ; MDB. (co. Cumb.), 3 ; New York, 1.

Blackman, Blakeman.—Nick. 'the blackman,' i. e. the dark-complexioned man ; cf. Black and Blacklock, White, Whiteman, and Whitman.

John Blakeman, co. Devon, Hen. III-Edw. I. K.
Henry Blacman, co. Oxford, 1273. A.
Peter Blakeman, co. Camb., ibid.
Robert Blakeman, co. Bucks, ibid.
1501. Bapt.—John, s. John Blackman : St. Jas. Clerkenwell, i. 24.
1017. Adam Blakeman, co. Staff. : Reg. Univ. Oxf. vol. ii. pt. ii. p. 361.
1767. Married—Robert Blackman and Eulina Price : St. Geo. Han. Sq. i. 181.
London, 23, 3 ; Philadelphia, 8, 2.

Blackmonster.—Local, ' of Blanchminster.' Latinized into 'De Albo Monasterio.' Killminster and Killmaster (q.v.) seem quite as repellent, and have a similar origin. Black = O.E. *blāc*, white, pale.

Thomas de Blauncmustre, co. Essex, 1273. A.
Matilda de Blancmustre, co. Middlesex : Hen. III-Edw. I. K.
William de Blancmoster, co. Essex, ibid.
Reginald de Blancnimstre, co. Oxf., ibid.
William de Albo Monasterio, co. Salop, ibid.

Lower gives the name as now existing. I have not met with it.

Blackmore, Blackmoore, Blackmur, Blakemore.—Local, 'of Blackmore.' (1) Blackmoor, parish in dioc. of Winchester ; (2) Blackmore, parish in dioc. of St. Albans. The form Blakamour seems to suggest a French nickname ; cf. Phillimore, Parramore, &c. Still, it is better to consider the *a* as

intrusive, as in Greenaway, Ottaway, Hathaway, &c.
William Blak-hommore, Norwich, 1398 : FF. iii. 114.
William de Blachomor, Norwich, 4 Ric. II : ibid. p. 117.
Margery de Blakemor, co. Soms., 1 Edw. III : Kirby's Quest, p. 244.
Richard de Blakemore, co. Oxf., 1273. A. (Prior) de Blakemore, co. Essex, ibid.
Simon Blakamour. RR. 1.
Beatrix Blakamour, London. X.
Richard Blackamore. FF.
1632. Bapt.- Ralph, s. Raph Blackmore : St. Jas. Clerkenwell, i. 121.
1745. Married—Thomas Cox and Mary Blackmore : St. Geo. Han. Sq. i. 36.
London, 23, 1, 1, 0 ; Philadelphia, 2, 0, 0, 12.

Blacksley.—Local ; v. Blakesley.

Blacksmith.—Occup.' a worker in iron.' This and Whitesmith are the only survivals of the custom of styling the different workers in metals by the colour of that on which they spent their energies ; cf. Whitesmith. Greensmith, Redsmith, Brownsmith.

William le Blakesmith, Close Roll, 54 Hen. III.
Nicholas the Blacksmith. FF.
John Blacksmythe. ZZ.
'Brydel-bytters, blackesmythes, and ferrars' . Cocke Lorelle's Bote.

Blackson.— Personal, 'the son of Black' ; cf. Brownson or Greenson. Sometimes, no doubt, a corruption of Blackstone, a local surname. But the above derivation is in general the correct one, baptismal or personal names from colours not being uncommon.

John Blakson, C. R., 17 Edw. III. pt. i. London, 0 ; Philadelphia, 9.

Blackston, Blackstone, Blakiston, Blaxton.—Local, 'of Blaxton,' a township in the parish of Finningley, West Rid. Yorks. No doubt originally Blackston or Blackstone ; cf. Buxton for Buckstone. Of William Blackstone, one of the earliest episcopal clergymen resident in New England (d. 1675), a biographer writes : ' His name was variantly spelled Blackstone, Blackston, and Blaxton' : Dict. Nat. Biog. v. 132. But it is not likely that Blaxton in co. York is the sole parent of Blackstone and its variants. Doubtless other places in South England of the same name have had their share in making up the list of surnames found in our modern directories.

Agnes Blacston, co. Camb., 1273. A.
William Blackstone, co. Bucks, 20 Edw. I. R.
Bartram Blaxton, 1539, Newcastle-on-Tyne (List of male population capable of bearing arms): PPP. vol. ii. pp. 174, 194.
1579. Marmaduke Blackston, co. Durham : Reg. Univ. Oxf. vol. ii. pt. ii. p. 87.
1625. James Blakestone, or Blackstone, and Mary Peacocke : Marriage Lic. (London), ii. 154.
1668. Married — Thomas Blaxestone and Anne Fan : St. Jas. Clerkenwell, iii. 141.
1776. Married—Hugh Cane and Dame Annabella Blakiston : St. Geo. Han. Sq. i. 268.
London, 0, 2, 0, 0 ; Crockford, 0, 0, 4, 0 ; Philadelphia, 1, 1, 11, 1.

Blackwell.—(1) Local, 'of Blackwell,' a parish in co. Derby near Alfreton. (2) Local, 'of Blackwell,' a township in the parish of Darlington, co. Durham. Other and smaller places could also be cited.

Margery de Blacwelle, co. Camb. 1273. A.
Thomas Blakewell, 1379 : P. T. Yorks. p. 256.
Margareta de Blakwell, 1379 : P. T. Howdenshire, p. 8.
1599. Richard Blackwall, co. Derby : Reg. Univ. Oxf. vol. ii. pt. ii. p. 237.
1615. John Blackwell, co. Glouc. : ibid. p. 346.
1753. Married—William Blackwell and Jemima Fowle : St. Geo. Chap. Mayfair, p. 258.
London, 24 ; Philadelphia, 12.

Blades, Blade.—? Bapt. 'the son of Blade.' An unquestionable compound personal name occurs in the case of Gilbert Bladewine, co. Norf., 1273. A ; cf. Unwin, Goodwin, &c.

Juliana Blade, co. Hunts, 1273. A.
Emma Blade, co. Hunts, ibid.
1572. Robert Blades, Glouc. Hall : Reg. Univ. Oxf. i. 380.
1575. Randall Blades, Glouc. Hall : ibid vol ii. pt. ii. p. 34.
1747. Married Thomas Brown and Jane Blade : St. Geo. Chap. Mayfair, p. 101.
London, 12, 0 ; Philadelphia, 1, 1.

Bladesmith. — Occup. 'the blade-smith,' a sword manufacurer. The 'Cuttellers, Bladesmythes, and Shethers' went together in the York Pageant (York Mystery Plays,

p. xxiii, ed. Toulmin Smith). Cocke Lorelle's Bote couples 'cutlers and bladesmythes.' 'Bladsmythe, *scindi-faber*' : Prompt. Parv.

John Bladesmyth. SS.
Thomas Bladesmith. S.
John Bladesmithe, co. York. W. 13.
John Bladsmyth, Swaffham, co. Norf. : FF. vi. 219.
Robert Raw, *blaydsmythe*, 1539, Newcastle-on-Tyne (List of male population capable of bearing arms): PPP. vol. ii. pp. 174, 194.
John Fyce, *bladsmith*, Norwich, 1489 : FF. iv. 461.

Bladon, Bladen.—Local, ' of Bladon,' a parish in Oxfordshire, near Woodstock.

Walter de Bladone, co. Oxf., 1273. A.
Agnes de Bladene, co. Oxf., ibid.
Hugh de Bladene, co. Oxf., ibid.
1659. Married — Henry Bladon, of Birmingham, and Ann Betts : St. Dionis Backchurch, p. 35.
London, 1, 0 ; Crockford, 2, 0 ; Boston (U.S.), 2, 0 ; Philadelphia, 0, 3.

Blagbrough.—Local ; v. Blakebrough.

Blagden, Blagdon.—Local, ' of Blagdon.' (1) A township in the parish of Stannington, co. Northumberland ; (2) a parish in co. Somerset, eight miles from Axbridge ; cf. Slagg and Slack.

Walter de Blakedon, co. Soms., 1 Edw. III : Kirby's Quest, p. 247.
1587. Robert Blakeden, co. Surrey : Reg. Univ. Oxf. vol. ii. pt. ii. p. 160.
1631. Bapt.—Ann, d. John Blackden : St. Michael, Cornhill, p. 121.
1688. — Sarah, d. James and Sarah Blacdon : St. Jas. Clerkenwell, ii. 325.
1689. Thomas, s. James and Sarah Blagden : ibid. ii. 332.
1697. Married –Thomas Charlton and Catherine Blagden : St. Dionis Backchurch, p. 46.
London, 2, 1 ; MDB. (co. Glouc.), 0, 1 ; Boston (U.S.), 1, 4 ; New York, 3, 0.

Blagg, Blagge.—? Nick. 'the black' (?), from the dark hair or swarthy complexion of the nominee. A variant of Black, q.v. ; cf. Slagg and Slack, Higgs and Hicks. Even Jack is found as Jagge in Piers Plowman's Vision ; cf. Blagrove for Blackgrove, or Blamire for Blackmire.

Robert Blagge, co. Norf., 10 Hen. VIII : FF. ix. 497.
John Blagg, of Macclesfield, 1617 : Wills at Chester, i. 21.
Katherine Blagg, of Bosden, parish of Cheadle, 1619 : ibid.

1784. Married — William Blagg and Eliz. Reah : St. Geo. Han. Sq. i. 362.
London, 2, 0 ; MDB. (co. Notts), 6, 0 ; Boston (U.S.), 0, 1.

Blagrove, Blagrave.—Local. ' of Blagrave,' a tithing in the parish of Lambourn, co. Berks ; lit. 'the black grove' ; v. Blagg and Grove or Grave.

1662-3. Edward Homewood and Thamor Blagrove : Marriage Alleg. (Westminster), p. 81.
1670. Bapt.—Ann, d. Edward Blagrave : St. Jas. Clerkenwell, i. 243.
1705. Married — John Blagrave and Mary Walter : St. Mary Aldermary, p. 37.
London, 1, 0 ; MDB. (co. Berks), 0, 2 ; Philadelphia, 0, 1.

Blake.—Nick. ; v. Black.

Blakebrough, Blakeborough, Blagbrough.—Local, ' of Blackborough,' a parish in co. Devon, near Cullompton. Probably some smaller spot bore this name also in co. Suffolk. The lazified variant Blagbrough is common ; v. Blagg.

Simon de Blakeberwe, co. Suff., 1273. A.
Robert de Blakeberg', co. Suff., ibid.
London, 2, 0, 0 ; Manchester, 0, 0, 1 ; Philadelphia, 0, 1, 0.

Blakemore.—Local ; v. Blackmore.

Blakeney.—Local, ' of Blakeney.' (1) A small seaport on the coast of Norfolk ; (2) a chapelry in the parish of Awre, co. Glouc.

Johannes Blaunkeney, *smyth*, 1379 : P. T. Yorks. p. 13.
Adam de Blakeneye, London, 1273. A.
Peter de Blakeneye, London, 20 Edw. I. R.
Nicholas de Blakney, co. Norf., 1392 : FF. v. 101.
Elizabeth Blakney, co. Norf., 1515 : ibid. ii. 446.
Crockford, 4 ; New York, 4.

Blakesley, Blacksley, Blakeslee.—Local, ' of Blakesley,' a parish in co. Northampton, four miles from Towcester. Blacksley is a modern variant.

'Joseph Williams Blakesley (1808-1885), dean of Lincoln, . . . was born in the City of London. . . His parents were Jeremiah George and Elizabeth Blaksley, as the name was then spelt ': Dict. Nat. Biog. v. 187.
1624. Thomas Belley and Mary Blakesley : Marriage Lic. (London), ii. 140.

1723. Married—Thomas Blakesley and Rachael Dukes: St. Michael, Cornhill, p. 62.
1775. — Samuel Blakesly and Mary Jolly: St. Geo. Han. Sq. i. 254.
London, 2, 1, 0; Boston (U.S.), 0, 0, 2.

Blamester.—Nick. 'the blamer,' with fem. suffix -*ster*; cf. Brewster, Spinster, &c.

Robert le Blaimister, co. Camb., 1273. A.

Blamire, Blamires, Blaymire.—Local, 'of the blamire,' i. e. black mire, from residence thereby. A North-country name; v. Myers.

William de la Blamire, E. and F., co. Cumb., p. 163.
1753. Married — Francis Bernard and Sarah Bleamire: St. Geo. Chap. Mayfair, p. 215.
London, 0, 1, 0; Manchester, 0, 0, 2; Ulverston, 1, 0, 0; New York, 1, 0, 0; Philadelphia, 0, 0, 1.

Blanch, Blanche.—Bapt. 'the son of Blanche.' Sometimes, no doubt, a nickname answering to English 'White.'

John Blaunche, co. Hunts, 1273. A.
Elianora Blanche, co. Camb., ibid.
Henry Blanche, co. Oxf., ibid.
Clement Blaunche, co. Warwick, 20 Edw. I. R.
John Blanche, C. R., 2 Edw. IV.
1716. Bapt.- Sarah, d. Daniel Blanch: St. Jas. Clerkenwell, ii. 95.
London, 5, 0; Philadelphia, 4, 1.

Blanchard, Blanshard, Blanchet.—Nick. 'Blanchard.' O.F. *blanchart*, whitish. A sobriquet of complexion, and probably used as a fontal name. It was used as the name for a white horse; cf. Bayard, for a bay horse.

'Vppon my stede blanchard thu ridest here.' c. 1440, Generydes (H.E.D.).
Nicholas Blaunchard, co. Lanc., 1332: Lay Subsidy (Rylands), p. 8.
Gilbert Blanchard, co. Linc., Hen. III-Edw. I. K.
William Blamchard (sic), co. Soms., 1 Edw. III: Kirby's Quest, p. 175.
William Blaunchard, co. Wilts, 1273. A.
Reginald Blaunchard, co. York, ibid.
Robert Blaunchard, co. Linc., ibid.
Willelmus Blaunchard, 1379: P. T. Yorks. p. 236.
Elena Blaunchard, 1379: ibid.
1587. Buried—Ann Blanket: Kensington Church, p. 92.

This last form is imitative, and still lives.

London, 17, 4, 1; West Riding Court Dir., 0, 1, 1; Philadelphia, 20, 0, 1.

Blanchflower, Branchflower. — Bapt. 'the son of Blanchefleur,' Angl. 'white-flower.' There is the story of 'Floriz and Blanchefleur,' E. E. Text Society (circa 1280). Lower sets down the corrupted Branchflower as still existing.

1618. George Blanchflower, co. Soms.: Reg. Univ. Oxf. vol. ii. pt. ii. p. 367.
Faith Blanchflower, temp. Eliz. Z.
George Blanchflower, of Kingston, Soms., 1625: Abstract of Somersetshire Wills, p. 21.
Thomas Blanchflower, of Gotehurst, Soms., 1659: ibid. p. 82.

From Somersetshire the surname seems to have travelled into Devonshire:

Barnabas Blanchflower, Myrtle Cottage, is set down in the Directory for Kilmington, co. Devon, 1873.
MDB. (co. Norfolk), 3, 0; (co. Devon), 1, 0.

Blanchfront. — Local, 'of Blanchfront,' from some spot in Normandy. Not a nickname, as suggested by Lower.

Johannes de Blauncefrunt, co. York, Hen. III-Edw. I. K.
Walter de Blauncefrunt, co. York, ibid.
Henry de Blancfrund, cos. Bucks and Bedf, Hen. III-Edw. I. K.
Henry Blancfront, co. Bucks, ibid.
Robert Blanfront, co. Bedf., 1273. A.
Nicholas Blaunfront, co. Bedf, ibid.
Philip Blanchfront. FF.
Joan Blaunkfront. XX. 4.
Anabel Blancfront. GG.

Blanchmains.—Nick. 'white hand,' q. v. Lower says, 'Fr. *blanches mains*, "white hands." From this peculiarity Robert de Beaumont, 3rd Earl of Leicester, received his sobriquet. It also became the hereditary surname of a family' (Patr. Brit. p. 30).

Robert Blanchmains. FF.
Humbert Blanchmains. PP.

Blanchpain.—Local, 'of Blanchpain,' of which the English translation was Whitebread and Whitbread, q. v. Some spot in Normandy. Blanchpain has a strong nickname appearance about it, but the evidence is against such a derivation.

Aldwina de Blancpain, co. Berks, Hen. III-Edw. I. K.
Roger Blancpayn, co. Camb., 1273. A.
William Blancpain, co. Camb., ibid.
Edmund Blankpayn. D.

John Blankpayn represented Cambridge in Parliament: C. R., 50 Edw. I. pt. ii.
Eugene Aram was usher, in 1744, to the Rev. Mr. Painblanc, in Piccadilly.

Bland.—Local, 'of Bland,' one of the four hamlets of which the town of Sedburgh (co. York) is comprised. It is not a complimentary nickname, but distinctly local. The name ramified strongly.

Johannes de Bland, 1379: P. T. Yorks. p. 289.
Adam de Bland, 1379: ibid.
Matilda Bland, 1379: ibid.
Wymerk de Bland, 1379: ibid. p. 246.
1753. Married — Edward Bland and Eleanor Turnbull: St. Geo. Chap. Mayfair, p. 257.
London, 25; West Riding Court Dir., 12; Philadelphia, 9.

Blankley.—Local, 'of Blankney,' a parish in dioc. of Lincoln; v. Blackley for a corresponding change of suffix -*ney* to -*ley.*

Adam de Blanckenay, co. Linc., Hen. III-Edw. I. K.
Robert de Blankeney, co. Oxf., 1273. A.
Richard de Blankeney, co. Oxf., ibid.
(Vicar) de Blaunkeneye, co. Linc., ibid.
London, 3; Philadelphia, 8.

Blanks, Blankson.—'The son of Blanch' (q. v.); a variant.

1613. Thomas Blank, or Blanck, Glouc. Hall: Reg. Univ. Oxf. iii. 324.

The following two entries manifestly concern the same couple.

1676. Married—John Crose and Eliz. Blankson: St. Antholin (London), p. 96.
— John Cross and Eliz. Blanks: Marriage Alleg. (Canterbury), p. 253.
London, 4, 0; Philadelphia, 1, 0.

Blatherwick.—Local, 'of Blatherwycke,' a parish in the dioc. of Peterborough and co. Northampton.

Simon de Blatherwyke, rector of Barton, co. Norfolk, 1314: FF. vii. 278.
1746. Married—John Blatherwick and Elinor Brearcliffe: St. Geo. Chap. Mayfair, p. 73.
1785. — Robert Foster and Ann Blatherwick: St. Geo. Han. Sq. i. 369.
London, 3.

Blaxter, Blackister, Blackistor.— Occup. 'the bleacher,' with fem. suffix -*ster*; cf. Baxter. 'Pleykstare, *candidarius*'; 'whytstare or pleykstare, *candidarius, candidaria*'; 'bleystare or wytstare (bleykester, or whytster), *candidarius'* (Prompt. Parv.). Robert Blaxter appeared as defendant in a Norfolk case at the close of the 16th century (Proceedings in Chancery, Elizabeth, i. 250). Both Blaxter and Blackistor still exist. For masculine form, v. Blacker (2).

Matilda Blakester, London, 1273. A. William le Bleckestere, co. Camb., ibid.
John le Bleckestere, co. Norf, ibid.
Richard le Bleckster, 1307, Gloucester. M.
John de (misprint for 'le') Blexter, bailiff of Norwich, 1286 : FF. iii. 74.
1608. Bapt. — Thomas, son of Henry Blaxter : Reg. Deopham, co. Norf.
Derby, 1, 0, 0 ; London, 1, 0, 0 ; MDB. (Suffolk), 0, 0, 1.

Blaze, Blazey, Blazy, Blease, Bleas, Blase.—Bapt. 'the son of Blaze.' St. Blaise was the patron saint of wool-combers, and his festival (Feb. 3) till recent days was faithfully commemorated in Yorkshire. A full-sized effigy of the bishop is carved in the principal entrance to the Bradford Exchange. As a font-name Blaise, or Blaze, just managed to survive the Reformation. Gil Blas has immortalized the name in literature ; v. Puritan Nomenclature, pp. 93, 94.

1550. Bapt. — Blaze, daughter of — Goodwinne : St Peter, Cornhill, p. 5.
1555. Married — Blase Sawlter and Collis Smith : ibid. p. 223.
1662 — Blase Whyte to Mrs. Susanna Wright, *widow* : Canterbury Cath. p. 60.
'Jan. 1537. Item, payed to Blaze for brawdering a payre of sleves for my lady's grace, xxs' : Privy Purse Expenses, Princess Mary, p. 14.
Blasius Billard : Patent Roll, 10 Hen. VII.
Blase Caryll, temp. 1600 : Visitation of London, 1634, p. 144.
1605. Bapt. — James, s. Andrew Blase : St. Jas. Clerkenwell, i. 46.
1744. Married — Joseph Tucker and Mary Bleeze : St. Geo. Han. Sq. i. 32.
London, 0, 3, 1, 1, 0, 0 ; Philadelphia, 2, 0, 0, 1, 1, 2.

Bleasdale, Blazdell, Blasdale, Blesdill.— Local, ' of Bleasdale,' a chapelry in the parish of Lancaster. The surname is still chiefly found in that district. But it has managed to cross the Atlantic, and lives in Boston in a slightly varied form.

John Bleasdale, of Inkleingreen, in Bolland, 1619 : Wills at Chester, i. 22.
Robert Bleasdall, of Bolland, 1611 : ibid.
Henry Bleasdall, of Chepin, *husbandman*, 1616 : Lancashire Wills at Richmond, i. 36.
Alice Bleasdaile, of Chipping, 1668 : ibid.
London, 1, 2, 0, 0 ; Lancaster, 5, 0, 0, 0 ; MDB. (co. Lancaster), 6, 0, 0, 0 ; Boston (U.S.), 0, 0, 1, 1.

Blencowe, Blinko.—Local, 'of Blencowe,' a township in the parish of Greystoke, co. Cumb. The corruption into Blinko, found in the London Directory, is explained by instances in London church registers.

1590. George Blincoe and Eliz. Fowler : Marriage Lic. (London), i. 188.
1618. Christopher Blencow, co. Cumb. : Reg. Univ. Oxf. vol. ii. pt. ii. p. 366.
1624. Married — George Blincoe and Mary Hickes : St. Michael, Cornhill, p. 23.
1778. Married — Thomas Blencow and Dorothy Marshall : St. Geo. Han. Sq. i. 285.
London, 2, 1 ; Oxford, 5, 0.

Blenkarn, Blenkarne, Blenkiron, Blenkhorn, Blenkhorne, Blankhorn, Blinkhorn, Blenkin.—Local, ' of Blenkarne,' a township in the parish of Kirkland, co. Cumberland. The surname has spread far, and has assumed many guises.

1576. Buried — Dennis Blinkhorne : St. Mary Aldermary, p. 140.
1666. Bapt. — John, s. John Blenkerne : St. Dionis Backchurch, p. 119.
1681-2. Joseph Pawlett and Eliz. Blinckarne : Marriage Alleg. (Canterbury), p. 87.
1777. Married — Thomas Blenkhorn and Mary Watson : St. Geo. Han. Sq. i. 277.
London, 2, 1, 1, 0, 0, 0, 0, 0 ; Crockford, 0, 1, 1, 0, 0, 0, 0, 0 ; Sheffield (Blenkhorne), 3 ; Huddersfield (Blankhorn), 1 ; West Riding Court Dir. (Blenkin), 2 ; Manchester (Blinkhorn), 3 ; New York (Blankhorn), 1 ; Philadelphia, 0, 0, 0, 0, 0, 4, 0.

Blenkinsop, Blenkensop, Blankenship, Blenkinship.— Local, ' of Blenkinsop,' a township in the parish of Haltwhistle, co. Northumberland.

Antony Blencansop, 20 Ric. II : Hodgson's Northumberland, i. 362.
Ranulf de Blenkenshope, 1240 : ibid. iii. 129.

The following spellings are curious :

' On April 23, 1470, Elizabeth Blynkkyne-soppye, of Blynkkynsoppe, widow of Thomas Blynkyensope, of Blynkkensope,' received a general pardon : Hodgson's Northumberland, iii. 130.

Why such a variety it is hard to say.

Randolf de Blekenishop, co. Northun b., Hen. III–Edw. I. K.
1572. Charles Blenckinsopp, co. Westm.: Reg. Univ. Oxf. vol. ii. pt. ii. p. 54.
1794. Married — Thomas Blinkinship and Sarah Allen : St. Geo. Han. Sq. ii. 123.
London, 4, 0, 0, 0 ; Penrith, 0, 0, 0, 4 ; Philadelphia, 0, 1, 0, 0 ; Boston (U.S.), 5, 0, 1, 0.

Blennerhassett.—Local, ' of Blennerhassett,' a township in the parish of Torpenhow, co. Cumb.

' Johannes de Hayton quondam tenuit . . . in Alderscogh, et quandam peciam terre in Blenerhayset,' 16 Ric. II : E. and F., co. Cumb. p. 174.
' Thomas Blennerhasset, of Carlisle ' : ibid. p. 83.
' Thomas Bleverhasset, appointed rector of Hardingham, co. Norf., at the age of 11, by the Pope's dispensation': FF. x. 227.
John Blenerhayset (writes) to Thomas Fayrfax, Feb. 22, 1572 : Cal. State Papers (Domestic), i. 438.
Crockford, 1 ; New York, 2.

Bletsoe, Bletso.—Local, ' of Bletsoe,' a parish in the county of Bedford, six miles from Bedford.

John de Bletsho, temp. 35 Edw. III : FF. vii. 70.
Sir John Bletso, 21 Henry VIII : ibid. ii. 442.
1587. George Bleatso and Eliz. Dudley : Marriage Lic. (London), i. 164.
1641. Bapt. — Hugh, s Nicholas Bletsor (sic) : St. Jas. Clerkenwell, i. 147.
MDB. (co. Northampton), 2, 1 ; London, 1, 0.

Blevin, Blethyn, Bliven, ? Bleything.—Bapt. ' the son of Blethyn' (Welsh). 'Meredith ap Blethyn was prince of N. Wales in the eleventh cent.' (Lower).

' At the Survey we see that King William was Lord of this manor (Mileham), but soon after Alan, son of Flaald, obtained it by the gift of William the Conqueror; also the castle of Oswaldstrey in Shropshire . . . which belonged to Meredith ap Blethyn, a Welshman or Briton ' : FF. x. 16.
Frederick Blethyn C. Hulton appears in the obituary of Manchester Guardian, June 10, 1886, descended from Blethyn de Hulton, temp. Edw. II.
Robert Blevyn, co. Norf., 1273. A.
Lewelyn ap Bledyn, 1313. M.
Nicholas Blythewin, C. R., 42 Edw. III.
' William Blethyn, bishop of Landaff,' writes to Sir Francis Walsingham,

Feb. 3, 1579: Rec. Office, Cal. State Papers (Domestic), i. 617.

1601-2. Philemon Blethin, of Llandaff: Reg. Univ. Oxf. vol. ii. pt. ii. p. 255.

James Blevin, of Croston, co. Lanc., *husbandman*, 1669: Wills at Chester (1660-80), p. 31.

Jennet Blevins, of Formby, 1677: ibid.

Richard Blevin, of North Meols (Southport), 1627: ibid. (1621-50), p. 24.

As will be seen below, the name is still represented in that district. For a sharpened form, v. Plethin.

Liverpool, 3, 0, 0, 0; Southport, 0, 1, 0, 0; Formby (co. Lanc.), 1, 0, 0, 0; Milford, 0, 1, 0, 0; New York (Bliven), 10; (Bleything), 1.

Blew, Blue.—Nick. 'the blue,' blue of complexion or dress. Cf. Black.

Walter le Bleu. E.

Robert le Bleu. E.

1581-2. Henry Blewe and Margaret Peacocke: Marriage Lic. (London), i. 107.

1700. Bapt.—Thomas, s. James Blew: St. Dionis Backchurch, p. 139.

1746. Married—Mr. Mathew Blakiston and Mrs. Mary Blew: St. Geo. Chap. Mayfair, p. 60.

1808. — Thomas Blue and Eliz. Bean: St. Geo. Han. Sq. ii. 396.

London, 1, 0; New York, 3, 5; Philadelphia, 5, 12.

Blewett, Blewitt, Bluett.—Nick. 'bluet,' one of the many nicknames of complexion. In this case probably from the dress. Fr. *bluet*, a blue woollen cloth; cf. Burrell, Burnet, Cawry-mawry, &c. 'Item, lego Gilberto Skut . . . togam meam de bluett furr': 1437. Bury Wills (H.E.D.).

Robert Bluet, co. Bucks, 20 Edw. I. R.

John Bleuit, co. Glouc., 1273. A.

Robert Bluet, co. Linc., ibid.

Walter Bluet, London, ibid.

Thomas Bloet, co. Southampton, Hen. III-Edw. I. K.

Rculandus Bloet. C.

1584. William Bluet, co. Cornwall: Reg. Univ. Oxf. vol. ii. pt. ii. p. 135.

1593. Roger Bluett, co. Devon: ibid. p. 195.

1754. Married— James Blewett and Catherine Curtiss: St. Geo. Chap. Mayfair, p. 279.

London, 1, 3, 4; Crockford, 0, 0, 7; Boston (U.S.), 2, 0, 0; Philadelphia, 0, 2, 1.

Blick.—Nick. 'the blike,' probably cognate with Blake (s.v. Black); v. Blake and Blick in H.E.D.

John le Blyk, co. Soms., 1 Edw. III: Kirby's Quest, p. 221.

Richard le Blyke, co Soms., 1 Edw. III: ibid.

1670. Leonard Clerke and Mary Blick: Marriage Lic. (Faculty Office), p. 115.

1654. Married—William Johnson and Mary Blicke: St. Peter, Cornhill, i. 259.

London, 2; Philadelphia, 2.

Blind.—Nick. 'the blind.'

Ralph le Blinde, co. Norf., 1273. A.

1544-5. Silvester Blinde and Alice Gawge: Marriage Lic. (Faculty Office), p. 3.

New York, 3; Philadelphia, 1.

Blinko.—Local; v. Blencowe.

Bliss.—Nick. 'of blithe disposition.'

John Blisse, co. Buck., 1273. A.

John Blisse, co. Cant, ibld.

1596. Bapt.—Ann, d. Richard Blisse, St. James Clerkenwell, i. 31.

London, 13; Philadelphia, 17.

Blissett, Blizard, Blizzard.

—(1) ? Nick, or personal name like Joyce, Bliss (i. e. blithe); dim. Blissot.

Blissot (no surname), co. Oxf., 1273. A.

(2) Local.

Hugh de Blesset', co. Oxf., 1273. A.

1752. Married —Joseph Blizzard and Mary Bassitt: St. Geo. Chap. Mayfair, i. 226.

London, 2, 5, 0; Philadelphia, 0, 2, 11.

Blisowench. — Nick. 'blithewench.'

Alicia Blissewenche, co. Oxf., 1273. A.

Blithe.—Nick.; v. Blyth.

Blocker.—Occup. 'the blocker,' a maker of blocks for hats, a blocker or block-hewer. Also a blocker for shoemaking. The H.E.D. quotes: '1609. Fishers, Forestallers, Regraters, Sutours, Kemesters, Bloccers' (s.v. Blocker). Hence blockhead, a duffer.

Deodatus le Blokkere, co. Norf., 1273. A.

Richard le Blockhewere. E.

Blockley.—Local, 'of Blockley,' a parish in co. Worcester, near Moreton-in-the-Marsh.

Geoffrey de Blockeleye, co. Camb, 1273. A.

Petrus de Blockeleye, 30 Edw. I: BBB. p. 634.

1806. Married—Thomas Blockley and Mary Crook: St. Geo. Han. Sq. ii. 339.

London, 5; New York, 1.

Blofield, Blofield, Blowfield.—Local, ' of Blofield,' a parish in co. Norfolk, seven miles from Norwich.

Richard de Blofield, rector of Witton, co. Norf., 1349: FF. vii. 266.

Adam de Blofield, vicar of Tunstall, co. Norf., 1377: ibid. xi. 120.

William Blofield, Norwich, 1489: ibid. iv. 461.

1596. A childe of Richarde Blofeilde, buried: Reg. St. Mary Aldermary (London). p. 148.

1613. Bapt. — Marie Blowfeild: St. Peter, Cornhill, p. 61.

London, 2, 1, 0; MDB. (Norfolk), 1, 4, 0; (co. Hunts), 0, 0, 2.

Blomfield.—Local; v. Bloomfield. London, 4.

Blondel, Blondell.—Nick.; v. Blundell.

Blood, Blud, Bloyd.—Bapt. 'the son of Lloyd,' from Ap-Lloyd; cf. Bethell, Benyon, &c. Lloyd is found as Floyd, Flood, and Flud. The patronymic became in a similar way Bloyd, Blood, and Blud. The Manchester Courier, Jan. 8, 1886, describes a trial at the Cheshire Quarter Sessions, in which a woman named Bythell (Ap-Ithell) is accused of robbing a fellmonger named Blud (Ap-Llud); cf. Bowen or Bevan (Ap-Owen or Ap-Evan).

1741. Married—John Blood and Eliz. Mann: St. Peter, Cornhill, ii 83.

1750. — Ralph Walker and Hannah Blood: St. Geo. Chap. Mayfair, p. 173.

London, 2, 0, 1; Philadelphia, 18, 0, 0.

Bloodletter. — Occup. ' the blood-letter,' a barber-surgeon. This name is now obsolete, I think, and requires no explanation. The letting of blood was a cure for all manner of complaints with our forefathers. Mr. Lower mentions a Gold le Blodleter in the records of Yarmouth as living in the 14th century (Patr. Brit. p. 31).

Thomas Blodletere, co. Oxf., 1273. A.

William Bloodletter, London. X.

John Bloodlatter, co. York. W. 12.

Hugh le Blodleter, co. Soms., 1 Edw III: Kirby's Quest, p. 280.

Bloom.—Local, ' of Brome,' a parish in the dioc. of Norwich; or ' of the broom '—a manifest corruption of Broom, q.v.—from residence near the plant so called; cf. Furse. The Norfolk Blooms are all Brooms. For further instances, v. Broom.

Henry de Brom, vicar of Great Ellingham, co. Norf., 1312: FF. i. 485.

Sir Roger de Brome, of Brome Manor, co. Norf., 1304: ibid. xi. 139.

1575. Francis Everall and Mary Blome: Marriage Lic. (London), i. 67.

1583-4. Thomas Bloome and Agnes Stempe : Marriage Lic. (London), p. 127; 1805. Married—William Bloom and Ann Young : St. Geo. Han. Sq. ii. 331. MDB. (Norfolk), 8 ; London, 5 ; Philadelphia, 23.

Bloomer, Blomer, Blumer. —Occup. 'the bloomer,' a worker at a bloomery, or bloom-smithy. The surname is found in Ulverston church register alongside Ashburner (q.v.)$_1$ while remains of ancient bloomeries are found in the woods throughout the district : '1571, March 1. Buried—Edmund Blomer, Ulverston.' Reference is repeatedly made to these blomeries in the records of Furness Abbey (West's Ant. of Furness, 1774).

Johannes Blomere, 1379 : P. T. Yorks. p. 232.
Johannes Blomer, *smyth*, 1379 : ibid. p. 81.
Johannes de Kirkeby, *blomer*, 1379 : ibid. p. 239.
William le Blomere. L.
Henry Blewmer, co. York, 1513 : W. 11, p. 181.
William Blumer, co. York, 1515 : ibid. p. 185.
1587. Geo. Blomer, co. Glouc. : Reg. Univ. Oxf. vol ii. pt. ii. p. 161.
London, 2, 1, 0 ; New York, 24, 0, 2.

Bloomfield, Blomfield, Blunderfield.—Local, 'de Blundeville,' probably Blonville, a place near Pont l'Eveque in Normandy. There can be no doubt as regards this origin so far as the Norfolk and Suffolk families of this name are concerned.

'In 1567 Thomas Blundevile, Esq., settled Blumvyle's manor, &c., on John Blumvyle, in trust for the said Thomas' : FF. v. 68.
In 1490, Richard Blomvyle, or Blundevile, Esq , had his manor and Heverlond, and died seized of them in 1603' : ibid. p. 186-7.
John de Blomevile, 1249, co. Norf. : FF. ii. 491.
William de Blundevile, 1282, co. Norf. : ibid.
William de Blumvile, co. Norf., 1273. A.
Henry Blomefield, of Fersfield, gent., 1731 : FF. i. 93.
Francis Blomefield, rector of Fersfield, 1736 : ibid. p. 101
'Here lyeth Patience, the wife of Robert King, and daughter of Thomas Blundevyle, who lived vertuously. and died religiously, Jan. 7, 1638,' Newton Ch., co. Norf. : ibid. v. 70.
1778. Samuel Blomfield to Eliz. Gould : St. Geo. Han. Sq. i. 285.

Lower, writing about Blunderfield (v. London Directory), says : 'A corruption of Blondeville. This awkward and unpromising name was borne some years ago by a farming bailiff at Bayfield Hall, co. Norfolk' (Patr. Brit. p. 32). Oddly enough he does not recognize Bloomfield as a corruption. He says, 'Bloomfield, a village in co. Worc., and probably other localities. Norfolk has long been the greatest *habitat* of the name' (ibid. p. 31). Of course Bloomfield in co. Worc. and co. Cumb. may have given rise to families of this name, but in nine cases out of ten the derivation given above will apply, and is absolutely correct of the East-Anglian representatives.

London, 11, 4, 1 ; MDB. (Suffolk), 9, 5, 0 ; Philadelphia, 3, 1, 0.

Blore, Bloor, Bloore.—(1) Local, 'of Blore,' a parish in co. Stafford. (2) Occup. 'the blower' (q.v.), a corruption. But the local origin is manifestly the one to be chiefly considered, as Blore and its variants are very familiar to Staffordshire directories, and on the Cheshire border.

1574-5. Ralph Blowre, co. Staff. : Reg. Univ. Oxf. vol. ii. pt. ii. p. 59.
1618. Ralph Bloore, of Atherton : Wills at Chester (1545-1620), p. 22.
1625. Humphrey Blore and Alice Zanckie : Marriage Lic. (London), ii. 154.
1639. Married—William Blore and Marye Poynes : St. Jas. Clerkenwell, iii. 71.
London, 3, 2, 0 ; MDB. (co. Stafford), 5, 3, 1 ; New York, 0, 2, 0.

Bloss.—Local, 'of Blois,' the well-known city in France. That the Suffolk Bloss is a variant of Blois is incontestable.

William de Blois (natural son of King Stephen) : FF. viii. 358.
Thomas Bloys, mayor of Yarmouth : ibid. xi. 326.
Prudence Blois, died 1634, Norwich : ibid. iv. 447.
The same lady is styled Prudence Bloyse : ibid. iii. 409.
Again she is styled 'Prudence Blosse, widow of Mr. Alderman Blosse,' of Norwich : ibid. p. 377.
Thomas Blosse, sheriff of Norwich, 1606 : ibid. p. 370.

Thus the conclusion is inevitable; Bloss in the 19th century is but a variant of Blois of the 12th century.
MDB. (co. Suffolk), 2 ; New York, 7.

Blossom.—Nick. 'the blossom,' i.e. the flower (cf. Flower), probably in a complimentary sense. 'Blosme, or blossum *frons*' : Prompt. Parv.

Hugh Blosme, co Suff., 1273. A.
Robert Blosme, co. Camb., ibid.
William Blosme, co. Essex, ibid.
Thomas Blossom, C. R., 20 Ric. II. pt. ii. London, 2 ; New York, 8.

Blothunt.—Occup. 'the blothunt' (v. Hunt, Boarhunt, &c.), a huntsman who exposed himself to the chief danger in attacking the wild boar, stag, or wolf (!). This instance of the word is three centuries earlier than the H.E.D. : ' In backgammon, an exposed piece or "man," liable to be taken or forfeited. . . 1598. Florio, *Caccia*, a hunting, a chasing. . . Also . . . a blot at tables' (v. Blot, *sb.²*). Perhaps the blot-hunt went after exposed animals, i. e. wild beasts that came under range of his arrow. Anyway the name is interesting to philologists.

Humfrey le Blothunte, co. Berks, 1273. A.

Blount.—Nick. 'the blonde' (v. Blunt), fair of complexion.

Blow.—? Nick. Probably a sobriquet for the then common horn-blower. Lower's suggestion is impossible. He says, 'Blow— a contraction of Bellew, Bellow, q.v. The parish in Norfolk popularly called Blo' Norton is really Norton-Bellear' (Patr. Brit. p. 31). The simple answer to this is that in 1273 the name was commonly written Blower. Blow is the name, and Blow is what has to be explained. As Blower and Blowhorn, and Hornblower and Hornblow, were then familiar sobriquets, it is quite possible that Blow was a nickname.

Henry Blowe, co. Camb., 1273. A.
Isabella Blowe, co. Oxf., ibid.
William Blowe, co. Oxf., ibid.
John Blowe, co. Soms., 1 Edw. III Kirby's Quest, p. 156.

1548-9. John Blowe and Beatrice Dawe: Marriage Lic. (London), i. 12.
1761. Married — John Puttrill and Frances Blow: St. Geo. Han. Sq. iii. 106.
London, 6; New York, 2.

Blower.—Occup. 'the blower,' probably a horn-blower; possibly an early 'bloomer,' or charcoal burner; v. Bloomer and Ashburner.

Henry le Blawer, co. Lanc., 1332: Lay Subsidy (Rylands), p. 113.
Mablia la Blouer, co. Bucks, 1273. A.
Ran' le Blowere, co. Suff., ibid.
Adam Blower, 1379: P. T. Yorks. p. 240.
William le Blowar, co. Soms., 1 Edw. III: Kirby's Quest, p. 88.
1598-9. Robert Blower, co. Oxf.: Reg. Univ. Oxf. vol. ii pt, ii. p. 233.
1643. Married — Humfreye Blowere and Elinor Wright: St. Mary Aldermary, p. 19.
London, 4; Philadelphia, 1.

Blowhorn.—Nick. 'blow-horn,' a sobriquet for a horn-blower; v. Hornblow.

Gilbert Blouhorn, co. Linc., 1273. A.
Alicia Blawhorn, 1379: P. T. Howdenshire, p. 7.
Alicia Blawhorn, *breuster*, 1379; P. T. Yorks. p. 239.

Blows, Blowes.—Local, 'of Blois,' a city in France. It has already been shown that the Suffolk Bloss is a modern variant of Blois (v. Bloss). Another variant was Blows or Blowes.

1497. John Bloys, or Blowes, rector of Shelton, co. Norf.: FF. v. 271.
Cf. William de Bloes (Blois?), co. Linc., 1273. A.
London, 1, 1.

Bloxam, Bloxham, Bloxsom, Bloxum, Bloxsome, Bloxome.
—Local, (1) 'of Bloxham,' a parish in co. Oxford: (2) a parish, Bloxham or Bloxholme, in co. Lincoln. Bloxsome is a somewhat curious variant. With Bloxum cf. American Barnum for Barnham.

William de Blocesham, co. Oxf.,1273. A.
Alexander de Bloxam, co. Oxf., ibid.
Alan de Bloxam, co. Oxf., ibid.
Geoffrey de Bloxham, co. Oxf., ibid.
Alexander de Bloxham, co. Linc., 20 Edw. I. R.
Geoffrey de Bloxholme, co. Linc., ibid.
Matilda de Bloxholme, co. Linc., ibid.
1621-2. Nicholas Bloxam, co. Glouc.: Reg. Univ. Oxf. vol. ii. pt. ii. p. 4.
1712. Married — Nathaniel Bloxham and Mary Webster: St. Jas. Clerkenwell, iii. 234.

1725. Married—Samuel Bloxham and Mary Smith: St. Geo. Han. Sq. i. 1.
1779. Mathew Bloxam, rector of Bourton-on-the-hill, co. Glouc.: Rudder's Hist. Glouc. p. 302.
London, 4, 2, 0, 0, 0, 0; MDB. (co. Glouc.), 1, 2, 0, 0, 2, 0; (co. Hereford), 0, 0, 0, 0,'0, 1; (co. Oxford), 0, 1, 0, 0, 0, 0; (co. Leicester), 0, 2, 3, 1, 0, 0; New York, 0, 1, 1, 0, 0, 0; Boston (U.S.), 0, 3, 0, 0, 0, 0.

Bloyd.—Bapt. 'Ap-Lloyd,' i. e. 'the son of Lloyd' (v. Blood). Cf. Floyd, showing the difficulty to English people of pronouncing the Ll in Lloyd.

Blubber.—Nick. 'the blubber,' i.e. the weeper, or whimperer.

William le Blubure, co. Oxf., 1273. A.
Nicholas Bluber, co. Oxf., ibid.
John de (? le) Blubure, co. Oxf., ibid.

Blue; v. Blew.

Blund.—Nick. 'the blonde,' from the complexion; v. Blunt.

Flora la Blunde, C. R., 3 Edw. I.

Blundell, Blondel, Blondell.
—Nick. 'Blondel' or 'Blundel,' the blonde, a sobriquet of complexion, 'yellow-haired.' Fr. Blond or Blund (q.v.), with terminative 'el' as in Russell and Burnell, all names of the same class. 'le Blund' was the English register form; hence Blundell is more common than Blondell. A like change is seen in other colour names found also as personal names; cf. Brown, Burnell, and Burnett.

Walter Blundel, co. Oxf., 1273. A.
Geoffrey Blondel, co. Hunts, ibid.
Geoffrey Blundel, co. Leic., Hen. III-Edw. I. K.
Nicholas Blundel, co. Lanc., 20 Edw. I. R
Robert Blundell, co. Redf., ibid.
Amicia Blondelle. FF.
Theodora Blundell, Pat. Roll, 2 Eliz. pt. 14.
Boneface Blondell, or Blundell, 1456: Reg. Univ. Oxf. i. 28.

Blondel de Nesle is reputed to have been the faithful minstrel of Richard Cœur de Lion.

Three names of complexion, Russell, Plunket, and Blundell, have made themselves conspicuous amongst English county families.

London, 21, 2, 1; Boston (U.S.), 2, 0, 1.

Blunderfield. — Local; v. Bloomfield.

Blunsum, Blunsom.—Local, 'of Bluntisham,' a parish near St. Ives, co. Huntingdon. The corruption is a very natural one.

1400. John Bluntesham, rector of Snoring Parva, co. Norf.: FF. vii. 187.

We next find the name entered Bluntsham:

1406. John Bluntsham, co. Norf.: FF. v. 353.

The last stage of modification was inevitable:

1661. Thomas Blumsome and Jane Lewgar: Marriage Lic. (London), ii. 286.
1734. Bapt.—John, s. John Blonsom: St. Thomas the Apostle (London), p. 79.
London, 2, 0; MDB. (co. Northampton), 0, 1.

Blunt, Blount.—Nick. 'the blonde,' i. e. from the fair complexion of the nominee. Originally found as le Blound or le Blund. The early entries are very numerous.

Melodia le Blount, co. Hunts, 1273. A.
Margareta le Blound, co. Camb., ibid.
Richard le Blount, co. Wilts, ibid.
Alan le Blund, co. Oxf., ibid.
Richard le Blunt, co. Wilts, ibid.
Hugo le Blund, co. Staff., 20 Edw. I. R.
Amabilla le Blunt, co. Glouc., ibid.
John le Blont, co. Soms., 1 Edw. III: Kirby's Quest, p. 214.
Johannes Blont, 1379: P. T. Yorks. p. 45.
Ricardus Blont, 1379: ibid.
Ascelina le Blund, or Blunt, co. Norf., 1272: FF. v. 498.
1767. Married—George Blount and Isabella Tinker: St. Geo. Han. Sq. i. 160.
1786. — Edmund White and Ann Blunt: ibid. p. 389.
London, 6, 6; Boston (U.S.), 10, 6.

Blyth, Blythe, Blythman, Blithe.—(1) Nick. M.E. *blithe*, gladsome, happy, a sunshiny fellow. (2) Local, 'of Blyth,' a parish in Northumb., also a parish in diocese of Southwell. This would not explain Blythman, which belongs to (1).

' My purpos was to have deyned to-day At Blythe or Dankastere.'
Robert Hode, i. 149.

William de Blithe, co. Oxf., 1273. A.
Willelmus de Blythe, 1379: P. T. Yorks p. 50.
Robert de Blythe, co. Lanc., 1332: Lay Subsidy (Rylands), p. 109.
William Blythman, co. York. W. 3.
1569. Christopher Blitheman: Reg. Univ. Oxf. i. 275.
1585. Edward Blithman, co. Durham: ibid. vol. ii. pt. ii. p. 141.
Parse Blithman, 1539, Newcastle-upon-Tyne (citizen capable of bearing arms): PPP. vol. ii. pp. 174-194.

I

(3) Bapt. 'the son of Blithe'; cf. Joyce, Lettice, &c.

Blithe de Ryseford, 1273. A.
London, 23, 6, 0, 0; Crockford (Blythman), 1; Philadelphia, 0, 12, 0, 7.

Boaler.—Occup. 'the bowler,' q.v. Seemingly a Yorkshire variant; cf. Boalter for Boulter.

West Riding Court Dir., 2; Sheffield, 2; London, 2; Philadelphia, 2.

Boalter.—Occup.; v. Boulter; cf. Boaler for Bowler.

London, 1.

Boar, Bore, Boor, Boore.—Nick. 'the boar.' M.E. *bore* and *bor*; cf. Wildbore.

Robert le Boor, Fines Roll, 14 Edw. II: Kirby's Quest. p. 237.
Richard le Bor, co. Soms., 1 Edw. III: ibid.
John le Bor, co. Wilts, 1273. A.
Reginald le Bor, co. Camb., ibid.
Richard le Bor, co. Oxf., ibid.
1616. Buried—Anne Walker, servant to Henry Boare; St. Jas. Clerkenwell, iv. 133.
1800. Married—William Bore and Eliz. Franklin: St. Geo. Han. Sq. ii. 228.
London, 1, 0, 2, 3? Philadelphia, 0, 1, 2, 0.

Board, Boards, Bord, Boord.—Local, 'at the borde' (O.F. *borde*), from residence therein. With the modern Board cf. Boardman and Boarder, both from the same parent-word. A familiar West-country surname. '*Borde,* a little house, lodging, or cottage of timber standing alone in the fields': Cotg.; cf. Fr. 'de la Borde.' Boards is the genitive, as in Styles, Brooks, Holmes, &c.

Robert Bourde, co. Soms., 1 Edw. III: Kirby's Quest, p. 228.
1597. William Taylor and Ellen Boarde: Marriage Lic. (London), i. 244.
1634. Bapt.—Thomas, s. James Boord: Kensington Ch. p. 20.
1742. Married—John Board and Eliz. King: St. Geo. Chap. Mayfair, p. 21.
MDB. (co. Soms.), 24, 1, 2, 0; London, 3, 0, 1, 1; New York, 3, 0, 2, 0.

Boardcleaner.— Occup. 'the board-cleaner' = dapifer.

Henricus de Werldlay, *bordclener,* 1379: P. T. Yorks. p. 230.
Robertus Burdeclener, 1379: ibid. p. 143.
Margareta Bordclener, 1379: ibid. p. 294.

Boarder, Border, Bordier.—Occup. 'the boarder,' a bordar, a

cottager; v. Boardman. O.F. *bordier*; Domesday, *bordarius.* One who tenanted a cottage at his lord's pleasure, rendering menial service; v. Bordar, H.E.D.

William le Border, co. Soms., 1 Edw. III: Kirby's Quest, p. 226.
1570. Married — Peter Bowrder and Francis Browne: St. Jas. Clerkenwell, iii. 4.
1647. — Thomas Mapsonne and Eliz. Bordder: St. Mary Aldermary, p. 20.
London, 1, 2, 1; Philadelphia, 0, 4, 0.

Boardman, Bordman.—Occup. 'the boardman,' a bordar, a cottager, a tenant in bondage. Found in the Latinized form *bondmannus.* A villein of the lowest rank; v. Boarder.

1588. George Bordman to Margaret Milford: St.Thomas the Apostle (London), p. 7.
1618. Thomas Bordman and Anne Phillippes: Marriage Lic. (London), ii. 59.
1619-20. Samuel Bordman, co. Lanc.: Reg. Univ. Oxf. vol. ii. pt. ii. p. 381.
1622. William Ivat and Anne Boardman: Marriage Lic. (London), p. 59.
1674. William Bordman, of Goosenargh: Lancashire Wills at Richmond, i. 38.
1755. Married—Thomas Boardman and Eliz. Ball: St. Geo. Han. Sq. i. 60.
London, 3, 0; MDB. (Norfolk), 2, 0; Philadelphia, 24, 0; Boston (U.S.), 54, 4.

Boardwright. — Occup. 'the boardwright,' a carpenter, a maker of tables and chairs, &c., probably to distinguish him from the arkwright, wainwright, wheelwright, and plow-wright. A surname long obsolete, I fear.

Johannes Bordwrygt, 1379: P. T. Yorks. p. 161.
Robertus Burdewryth, 1379: ibid. p. 156.

Boarhunt.—Occup. or official. A hunter of the wild boar, a huntsman. M.E. *hunte,* a hunter (v. Hunt); v. Blothunt.

Henry Borehunt. D.
Thomas le Borhunt (the king's huntsman): Wardrobe Account, 3 Edw. III: 33/10.

Boatman.—Occup. 'the boatman'; cf. Bargeman.

Jeffry Boteman, rector of Wood Norton, co. Norf., 1320: FF. viii. 316.
Nicholas Boteman, rector of Castor, co. Norf., 1326: ibid. xi. 211.

1566. Bapt.—Richard, s. John Botman: St. Jas. Clerkenwell, i. 3.
1654. Mr. John Boatman, upper minister, on the donation of the feoffees (Norwich): FF. iv. 189.
London, 1; Philadelphia, 1.

Boatswain.—Occup. 'the boatswain,' one who held the tiller; cf. coxswain, i. e. cogswain, from *cog,* a boat (v. Swain).

Richard le Botsweyn, 1301. M.
Edward Botswine, temp. Eliz. Z.
1782. Married—Henry Boatswain and Ann Croucher: St. Geo. Han. Sq. i. 339.

Boatvillain. — Occup. 'the boat-villain,' a boatman; cf. Boatswain, Boatman, and v. Villain. There was nothing strictly uncomplimentary about the title; v. Knave.

William Botevillein, co. Notts, 1273. A.
Richard Botevileyn, co. Bedf., ibid.
Roger Botevileyn, co. Linc., ibid.

Boatwright, Botwright, Boatright.— Occup. 'the boatwright,' a ship-carpenter, a boat-builder. *navicularius*': Prompt. Parv.

John Botewright, or Botewryth, master of Corpus Christi Coll., Camb., 1474: FF. vi. 215.
On his monument a 'third shield bears 3 boats, or barges, and a fourth has 3 wimbles, or augurs, by way of *rebus,* and in allusion to his name, Boatright, or Botewright': ibid.
1779. Married—Samuel Boatright and Ann Hiller: St. Geo. Han. Sq. i. 300.
London, 0, 2, 1; MDB. (Norfolk), 2, 1, 0; Philadelphia, 2, 0, 0.

Bobbett, Bobbet.—Bapt. 'the son of Robert,' from the nickname Bob, whence the dim. Bobbett; v. Bobbin (2). In the same way Rob was the nickname of Robert, with dim. Robet.

Robert Robet, co. Soms., 1 Edw. III: Kirby's Quest, p. 102.

Bobbett is still found in co. Soms., indeed it is the chief home of the name.

1668. Married—Thomas Evines and Eliz. Bobitt: St. Jas. Clerkenwell, iii. 140.
1742. — Samuel Sheltron and Martha Bobbet: St. Geo. Chap. Mayfair, p. 25.
1753. — Henry Webb and Eliz. Bobbett: ibid. p. 253.
London, 1, 0; MDB. (co. Soms.), 11, 0; New York, 2, 1.

Bobbin, Bobin, Bobins, Bobbins.—(1) Local (?), 'of Bobbing,' a parish near Milton, co. Kent. (2) Bapt. (?) 'the son of Robert,' from the nick. Bob,whence the dim. Bob-in, and with the ex-crescent *g* Bobing ; cf. Jennings, q.v. Possibly *bobbin*, the wooden pin on which the thread is wound, is thus derived, the custom of giv-ing such articles personal names being common (v. Jack); ' Bobine, a quil for a spinning wheele ' (Cotg.) ; cf. Robin and Robins, also from Robert.

Nicholas Bobing, co. Camb., 1273. A.
1637. Married — John Bobins and Clemens Anderton : St. Jas. Clerkenwell, iii. 69.
1688. David Bobin and Susan Chevalier : Marriage Alleg. (Canterbury), p. 63.
London, 1, 1, 0, 0 ; Philadelphia (Bob-bins), ?

Bobby.—Local, 'of Boby.' Bob is almost unknown as a nick. of Robert in the surname period. Hob was the household nick. all over the country. But v. Bobbett. Even there, however, I have scarcely any instances to record. Probably Bob came into fashion among the ' upper ten' later on, just as Jane took the place of Joan in aristo-cratic circles, when every kitchen wench was called by the latter form.

Osbert de Boby, co. Linc., Henry III–Edw. I. K.
Hugo de Bobi, co. Linc., 1273. A.
Emma de Boby, co. Linc., ibid.
Walter de Boby, co. Linc., ibid.
1786. Married — Thomas Bobby and Diana Henley : St. Geo. Han. Sq. i. 388.
London, 1.

Bock.—Nick. 'the buck,' he-goat, &c. ; v. Buck.

William Bocke, co. Soms., 1 Edw. III : Kirby's Quest, p. 231.
Richard Boke, co. Oxf., 1273. A.
Robert Bok, or Bokke, co. Hunts, ibid.
John Boc, co. Camb., ibid.
Thomas de (? le) Boc, co. Camb., ibid.
1571-2. Buried — Susan, d. William Bocke : St. Jas. Clerkenwell, iv. 13.
1583-4. Francis Bucke, co. Worc. : Reg. Univ. Oxf. vol. ii. pt. ii. p. 133.
London, 4 ; Boston (U.S.), 2 ; Phila-delphia, 13.

Bockett.—Bapt. 'the son of Bokard,' one of the many forms of Burchard ; v. Buckett. Neverthe-less, in one case the prefix *de* is

used, suggesting a local origin. For this, v. Boycott.

Isolda fil. Bochard : Denton's Estates and Families of co. Cumb., p. 102.
Peter Bokard, co. York, 20 Edw. I. R.
William Bochard, co. Linc , 1273. A.
Hugo Bochard, co. Bedf., 20 Edw. I. R.
Richard de Bochard, co. Bedf., 1273. A.
Thomas Bokett, M.A., 1452 : Reg. Univ. Oxf. i. 17.
1547. Buried—John Bokett : St. Dionis Backchurch, p. 181.
London, 3.

Bocking, Bockings.—Local, ' of Bocking,' a parish in co. Essex, near Braintree.

Reginald de Bocking, co. Hunts, 1273. A.
Walter de Bockyng, or Bockinges, co. Glouc., ibid.
Robert de Bocking, London, ibid.
London, 3, 0 ; Boston (U.S.), 1, 0 ; Philadelphia, 0, 37.

Boddington, Dodington.—Local, ' of Boddington,' parishes in cos. Glouc. and Northampton.

Robert de Bodinton, co. Bucks, 20 Edw. I. R.
1707. Married—William Strengfellow and Frances Bodington : St. Mary Aldermary, p. 38.
1739. Buried—Ann Bodington : St. John the Baptist, Wallbrook, p. 210.
1752. Married—Thomas Collyer and Eliz. Buddington : St Geo. Chap. May-fair, p. 222.
London, 6, 1 ; Manchester, 3, 0.

Boddon, Bodden.—Local, ' of Bodden.' I cannot find the spot.

Richard de Boddene, co. Soms., 1 Edw. III : Kirby's Quest, p. 228.
John de Boddene, co. Soms., 1 Edw. III : ibid.
London, 1, 0 ; Boston (U.S.), 0, 1.

Boddy ; v. Body.

Boden, Bowden.—(1) Bapt. ' the son of Baldwin,' popularly, and under French influence, Bodin and Boden (v. Bawden) ; cf. Godin for Godwin, q.v.

Bodin de Langehull, co. Oxf., 1273. A.
Boyedinus de Gaunt, co. Linc., ibid.
Bodyn de Kant (London citizen), ibid.
Walter Bodin, co. Oxf., ibid.
Dalliryver, d. Boden Moylle, 1588 : Reg. St. Columb Major, p. 15.
Richow, d. of Boden Moylle, 1591 : ibid. p. 17.
Thomas, s. of Bawden Moylle, 1595 : ibid. p. 19.
Margaret Bowden, 1600 : ibid.

(2) Local, ' of Bowden,' a parish in E. Cheshire, near Altrincham.

1581. Eliz. Bowden, of Bowden, *widow* : Wills at Chester, p. 25.
1583. Thomas Boden, co. Derby : Reg.
Univ. Oxf. vol. ii. pt. ii. p. 129.
1594. John Boden, of Childer-Thornton, *husbandman* : Wills at Chester, p. 22.
1694. Bapt —Thomas, s. of Bodwine Apps : St. Jas. Clerkenwell, i. 357.
London, 8, 35 ; Philadelphia, 4, 19.

Bodenham. — Local ; v. Bod-man.

1568. John Bodenham, Hart Hall : Reg. Univ. Oxf. vol. ii. pt. ii. p. 29.
MDB. (co. Soms.), 1.

Bodger.—Occup. ; v. Botcher.

Bodkin.—Bapt. ' the son of Baldwin,' from the nick. Baud, dim. Baudkin. A Flemish intro-duction.

Baudechon le Bocher, London, 1273. A.
Robert Bodekin, co. Oxf., ibid.
William Bodekin, co. Kent, ibid.
Andrew Bawdkyn, co. York. W. 9.
John Bodychen, 1273 : Exchequer Depositions, co. Lanc., p. 20.
1752. Married — Michael Stone and Hannah Bodkin : Canterbury Cath. p. 92.
London, 2 ; Philadelphia, 8.

Bodley, Bodilly, Bodely.—Local, ' of Budleigh.' Two parishes in dioc. of Exeter, in which district Bodilly is well known, and whence Sir Thomas Bodley, the founder of the Bodleian Library, sprung. His father was a Bodleigh, ' descended from an ancient family of Bodleigh, or Budleigh, of Dunscombe-by-Crediton' (Dict. Nat. Biog., v. 294). The origin is thus clearly apparent.

William de Bodele, London, 20 Edw. I. R.
John de Bodet, co. Camb. 1273. A.
Dennis de Buddelegh, co. Devon, 20 Edw. I. R.
1565. Bapt.—Alice, d. John Bodely : St. Thomas the Apostle (London), p. 24.
1668. Buried—Stephen Bodily : Ken-sington Ch. p. 138.
London, 3, 2, 0 ; Exeter, 3, 0, 0 ; Pen-zance, 0, 1, 0 ; Philadelphia, 4, 0, 2.

Bodman.—Local, ' of Boden-ham,' a parish in dioc. of Hereford. One of a small but distinct class of corruptions ; cf. Deadman, Putman, from Debenham, Puttenham, &c. Bodmin will suggest itself, but I find no evidence to confirm this.

1586. Married — Francis Foster and Ann Bodnam : St. Michael's, Cornhill, p. 13.
1598. Christopher Whitteridge and Margaret Bodnam : Marriage Lic. (London), i. 257.

1647. Married—Thomas Bodnam and Vrcylaye (Ursula) Watsworth: St. Dionis Backchurch, p. 2.
London, 4; New York, 1.

Body, Boddy, Bodd, Bode.—Bapt. 'the son of Baldwin,' from the nick. Baud or Bodd, familiarly Boddy. From this nick. were formed the dims. Bod-in (v. Boden), Bod-kin (q. v.), and Baud-et. It is only by realizing the enormous popularity of Baldwin that we can understand the marvellous impress it has made on hereditary nomenclature. Perhaps in some cases Body or Boddy represented the dim. Baudet, of which I furnish an instance.

William Body, co. Devon, 1273. A.
John Bodd, co. Oxf., ibid.
Richard Bodde, co. Oxf., ibid.
Thomas Bodde, co. Oxf., ibid.
John Bodde, co. Soms., 1 Edw. III: Kirby's Quest, p. 114.
Baudet le Messager, co. Glouc., 1289–1290: Household Exp., Bishop Swinfield, Cam. Soc. p. 144.
1544. Married—William Dowell and Margaret Body: St. Antholin (London), p. 4.
London, 4, 4, 0, 1; Philadelphia, 3, 5, 1, 0; New York (Bode), 23.

Bodycoat.—Local, 'of Bodicott,' a chapelry in the parish of East Adderbury, near Banbury, co. Oxford. Bodycoat is imitative.

Robert de Bodicot, co. Oxf., 1273. A.
Walter de Bodicot, co. Oxf., ibid.
1627. Humphrey Bodicot: Reg. Univ. Oxf. i. 323.
Philadelphia, 1.

Boffey.—Nick. 'good faith.'

1650. Nicholas Bonfov and Mary Shepheard: Marriage Lic. (Faculty Office), p. 45.
1655. Bapt. — Loetitia, d. Thomas Bonfoy: St. Thomas the Apostle (London), p. 60.
1793. Married—Thomas Aldridge and Ann Boffey: St. Geo. Han. Sq. ii. 105.
London, 1; Philadelphia, 1.

Boffin.—Nick. 'bonfin,' a name of endearment. Bon, good; fin, fine, delicate.

William Bonfyn, C. R., 41 Henry III.
Thomas Boffin, co. Oxf., 1273. A.
John Bofyn, co. Oxf., ibid.

The two last entries are printed Boffin and Bofyn (i.e. s not f), but I strongly suspect this is a misreading of the text. If it be so, the surname so familiar to Oxford

citizens existed in the vicinity six centuries ago.

1764. Married—James Rimes and Ann Buffin: St. Geo. Han. Sq. i. 130.
MDB. (co. Oxf.), 1; Boston (U.S.), 1.

Bofill.—Nick.; v. Bonfils.

Bogg, Boggs.—Local, 'at the bog,' from residence thereby. Boggs is genitive, as in other monosyllabic local names, such as Styles, Brooks, Sykes, Holmes, &c. Boggs therefore = Bogg's, i.e. Bogg's son; cf. Jones, Williams, Perkins, &c.

John atte Bogge, co. Soms., 1 Edw. III: Kirby's Quest, p. 146.
Robert Bogg, co. Soms., 1 Edw. III: ibid. p. 255.
Nicholas Bogges, co. Soms., 1 Edw. III: ibid. p. 256.
1637. Bapt.—Nataneel, s. John Bogges: St. Michael, Cornhill, p. 127.
London, 1, 0; Boston (U.S.), 0, 6.

Boland.—Local, 'of Bolland,' q. v.

Bold, Bolde, Bolt.—(1) Local, 'at the bold.' A.S. bold, a dwelling; cf. Danish bol, a small farm. In Lancashire, more specifically 'of Bold,' a township in the parish of Prescot. No doubt the origin is the same.

Robert de Bolde, co. Lanc., 20 Edw. I. R.
Johan de la Bolde, co. Oxf., 1273. A.
Elias de la Bolde, co. Oxf., ibid.
Robert de la Bolde, co. Oxf., ibid.
Margaret Bold, of Upton, 1572: Wills at Chester (1545–1620), p. 23.
Henry Bold, of Bold, 1603: ibid.

(2) Nick. 'the bold.'

Richard le Bolde, co. Wilts, 1273. A.
William le Bolde, co. Oxf., ibid.
Robert le Bolde. R.
Richard le Bolt, co. Oxf., 1273. A.
Robert le Bolt, co. Soms., 1 Edw. III: Kirby's Quest, p. 150.
London, 0, 0, 9; New York, 4, 1, 2; Liverpool, 6, 0, 0.

Bolden, Bolding, Boldin.—Bapt. 'the son of Baldwin,' popularly Bolder, or, with excrescent g, Bolding; cf. Golden and Golding for Goldwin, an exact parallel.

William Bolding, co. Salop, 1273. A.
1702. Married—Samuel Boldwin and Martha Paske: St. Dionis Backchurch, p. 50.
John Bolden, co. Norf., 2 Edw. VI: FF. viii. 507.
1761. Married—Thomas Flarty and Joanna Bolden: St. Geo. Han. Sq. i. 105.

1764. Married—John Coppe and Sarah Boldwing: ibid. p. 136.
London, 4, 5, 0; Philadelphia, 9, 0, 3.

Bolderson; v. Balderson.

Bolitho.—? Local. A common Cornish name, and no doubt local.

1673. John Bolitho and Ann Cox: Marriage Lic. (Faculty Office), p. 127.
Penzance, 2; Plymouth, 1.

Bolland, Boland.—Local, 'of Bolland,' Bolton-by-Bolland (or Bowland), a village parish about six miles from Clitheroe. The instances below are mostly taken from the near neighbourhood.

Robertus de Boghland, 1379: P.T. Yorks. p. 217.
Thomas de Bouland. 1379: ibid. p. 292.
Robertus de Bowland, 1379: ibid. p. 293.
Agnes de Bowland, 1379: ibid. p. 259.
Thomas Bolland, of Houston, 1593: Wills at Chester (1545–1620), p. 23.
Richard Bolland, of Ashton, 1618: ibid.
1765. Married—John Hillier and Eliz. Bolland: St. Geo. Han. Sq. i. 143.
West Riding Court Dir., 6, 0; Manchester, 1, 0; London, 0, 1; New York, 4, 25.

Bollen.—Local, 'of Boulogne'; v. Bullen.

1621. Daniel Bollen, or Boulen, co. Essex: Reg. Univ. Oxf. vol. ii. pt. ii. p. 357.
1641. Bapt.—Phebe, d. Daniel Bollen, petty canon: Canterbury Cath. p. 9.
London, 2.

Bolling, Boling. — (1) Bapt. 'the son of Bolling'; cf. Harding, Browning, &c.

William Bollyng, co. Soms., 1 Edw. III: Kirby's Quest, p. 214.

(2) Local, 'of Bowling,' q.v.

1529. Christopher Herd and Grace Bolvng: Marriage Lic. (London), i. 7.
1613. Married—Thomas Creswell and Beatrice Bollinge: St. Mary Aldermary, p. 13.
London, 0, 1.

Bollington.—Local, 'of Bollington.' (1) A township in the parish of Rosthern, co. Ches.; (2) a township in the parish of Prestbury, co. Ches. The place-name is derived from the little river Bolling, which flows through this district.

Willelmus de Bolyngton, 1379: P. T. Yorks. p. 272.
Hugh Bollington, of Buglawton, co. Ches., 1613: Wills at Chester, i. 23.
1564. Married—James Bollington and Jone Kenricke: Prestbury Ch. (co. Ches.), p. 13.

1605. Married—John Bollingeton and Jane Jacson: Prestbury Ch. (co. Cheshire), p. 167.
1766. — Daniel Mack Bain and Mary Bolington: St. Geo. Han. Sq. i. 151.
London, 1 ; Boston (U.S.), 2.

Bolsover.—Local, ' of Bolsover,' a village in co. Derby.

1755. Married—William Weaver and Eliz. Bolsover : St. Geo. Han. Sq. i. 56.
1773. — John Hayden and Jemima Bowlsover : ibid. p. 234.
MDB. (Derbys.), 3 ; (Cheshire), 1 ; Manchester, 2.

Bolster ; v. Bowlster.

Bolt ; v. Bold.

Bolter.—Occup. ; v. Boulter.

Bolton, Boulton, Bolten.—Local, ' of Bolton ' or ' Boulton,' parishes, townships, and chapelries in various counties, mostly in Lancashire, Yorkshire, Cumb., and Westm.

Michael de Boulton, co. York, 1273. A.
Thomas de Boulton, or Bolton, co. Linc., ibid.
Richard de Boulton, co. Northumb., 20 Edw. I. R.
Agnes de Bolton, 1379 : P. T. Yorks, p. 291.
1688-9. Hugh Boolton, or Boulton, co. Staff.: Reg. Univ. Oxf. vol. ii. pt. ii. p. 167.
1766. Married —George Boulton and Ann Bowker : St. Geo. Han. Sq. i. 152.
1772. — George Boulton and Sophia Morgan : ibid. p. 222.
London, 58, 20, 0 ; Philadelphia, 39, 7, 2.

Bonamy.—Nick. corresponding to English ' Goodfellow,' q.v.

William Bonamy, co. Salop, 1273. A.
Roger Bonamy, 1295. M.
1603. Buried — Frauncis, d. Jacob Bonamee : St. Jas. Clerkenwell, iv. 86.
1692-3. Louis Belain and Mary Bonamy: Marriage Alleg. (Canterbury), p. 250.

Bonaventure. — Nick. Probably a kindly wish ; cf. Goodspeed. It is found, as might well be expected, as a pursuivant's sobriquet.

' Bonne-Aventure, pursuivant of Sir Thomas Hoo' ': Wars of England in France, Hen. VI.
John Bonaventure. H.
Gist Bonaventure. J.

Bonaventura is an Italian font-name, after San Bonaventura. Probably it was transferred to England by the merchants. ' Fairaventure ' (q.v.) also existed.

Thomas Bonaventure and Henry Grand, merchants of Ireland and Wales, C. R., 17 Ric. II.
New York, 3.

Bond, Bonde.—(1) Bapt. ' the son of Bond,' v. Bonder (Yonge, Glossary). 'There are several persons called Bonde in Domesday, one of whom is somewhat contradictorily called "liber homo"' (Lower). For meaning, v. (2) below.

Bonde Brit, co. Norf., 1273. A.
' Richard Aghton v. Roger Bondesson and John Stelle,' 1352 : Croston's edit. of Baines' Lanc. i. 149.

(2) Occup. ' the bond,' a householder, a husbandman, a boor, one under the tenure styled bondage.

Emma le Bonde, co. Hunts, 1273. A.
Robert le Bonde, co. Worc., ibid.
Walter le Bond, co. Camb., ibid.
Robert le Bonde, co. Soms., 1 Edw. III : Kirby's Quest, p. 81.
John le Bonnde, co. Soms., 1 Edw. III : ibid. p. 188.
London, 64, 0 ; New York (Bonde), 2 ; Philadelphia, 96, 0.

Bondman, Bonman.—Occup. ' the bondman'; v. Bond (2). Bonman is a modified form.

William Bondman. XX. 1.
Nicholas Bondeman, co. Soms, 1 Edw. III : Kirby's Quest, p. 224.
Philadelphia, 1, 0.

Bone.—(1) Nick. ' le Bon,' corresponding to English Good.

John le Bon. O.
Durand le Bon, 1303. M.
Edward le Bone, co. Oxf., 1273. A.
John le Bone, co. Oxf., ibid.
Thomas le Bone, co. Oxf., ibid.
Roger Bone, co. Kent, 1273. A.

(2) Local.

Simon de la Bone, co. Linc., Hen. III-Edw. I. K.
London, 23 ; New York, 4.

Bonecors.—Nick. corresponding to English Goodbody.

Manellus Bonecors. E.
John Boncors, co. Soms., 1 Edw. III : Kirby's Quest, p. 244.

Bonehill, Bonhill, Bonell, Bonnell.—Local, ' of Bonehill,' a township in the parish of Tamworth, co. Stafford. The variants are well known in the county.

1585. John Bonell, co. Worc.: Reg. Univ. Oxf. vol. ii. pt. ii. p. 143.
1606. Thomas Bonnell, co. Ches.: ibid. p. 290.

Robert Bonnell, of Littleton, 1590 : Wills at Chester (1515-1620), p. 23.
1705. Married—William Faulkner and Mary Boneal: St. Jas. Clerkenwell, iii. 228.
1768. — Joseph Bonell and Mary Salter : St. Geo. Han. Sq. i. 173.
MDB. (co. Stafford), 1, 1, 1, 1 ; Manchester, 2, 0, 0, 0 ; London, 0, 0, 1, 0 ; Philadelphia, 0, 0, 0, 4.

Bonfellow. — . Nick. ' Goodfellow,' a half translation of Bon compagnon. Robert Bonefelaa (Pardon's Roll, 5 Ric. II) is a still surviving name.

' John Bonyfelowe, a scholar of Cambridge,' examined on oath, Feb. 2, 1572 : Rec. Office, Cal. State (Domestic) Papers, i. 435.
Crockford, 1.

Bonfils, Bofill.—Nick. ' Goodson,' an expression of endearment, ' My good lad ' ; cf. Bellamy and Bonifant.

' "Beaufitz," quod his fader.'
    Piers Plowman, 4819.
Hugh Beaufitz, co. Camb., 1273. A.
William Beufitz, co. Camb., ibid.
William Beaufitz, co. Warwick, Hen. III-Edw. I. K.
Richard Beaufiz, C. R., 33 Edw. III.
1618. Buried — Elizabeth Bufyll : St. Peter, Cornhill, p. 174
1710. John Beaufills : St. Antholin (London), p. 130.
1728. Married — Henry Godde and Elizabeth Beaufields : ibid. p. 142.
London, 0, 1 ; New York, 1, 0.

Bonfortune.—Bapt. or nick. ; cf. Bonaventure and Fairaventure.

William Bonefortune, sup. for B.A., Feb. 9, 1519-20 : Reg. Univ. Oxf. i. 112.

Bonham.—(1) Nick. ' le Bonhomme,' i.e. ' the goodman,' the cant name for a begging or mendicant friar (the order came into England in the 13th century). ' Bonhom, a religious man, bonhomme,' 1530 : Palsgr. (H.E.D.)

Agnes, relicta Bonhomme, co. Oxf., 1273. A.
Anketin Bonhom, co. Camb., ibid.
Humfrey Bonhome, co. Camb., ibid.
William Bonhome, co. Camb., ibid.

(2) ? Local ' of Bonham ' (?). I cannot find the spot, and strongly suspect that the ' de ' in my first instance below is a misreading of ' le ' through the fact that the surname looks local.

Maurice de Bonham, co. Somerset, 1273. A.

1597 Richard Bonham, co. Oxf.: Reg. Univ. Oxf. vol. ii. pt. ii p. 220. London, 4; Philadelphia, 5.

Boniface.—Bapt. 'Boniface,' i.e. 'well-doer'; the name of a martyr, and also a pope (Yonge, i. 384); a cant term now for the host of an inn, not from his round rubicund face, but from 'the jovial innkeeper in Farquhar's Beaux' Stratagem, 1707' (H.E.D.).

Archibald Boneface, co. Kent, 1273. A.
Ernald Boneface, co. Oxf., ibid.
Bonifacius le Clerc, co. Linc., ibid.
Bonefacius Servicus, 1228: KKK. vi. 151.
William Boneface, C. R., 44 Edw. III.
Robert Boneface. B.
Boniface atte Poule, co. Som., 1 Edw.
III: Kirby's Quest, p. 193.
Bonyface Meorys and Jackamyn Kelderley, married, 1543: St. Dionis Backchurch, London.
Boneface Blondell, sup. for B.A., 1456: Reg. Univ. Oxf. i. 28.
1606. Buried—Boniface Tatam, *vintner*, whoe dwelte in marke laine: St. Peter, Cornhill, p. 162.

Boniface of Savoy, archbishop of Canterbury (d. 1270), would give an English impetus to this name, just at the time when surnames were becoming hereditary.

London, 1; MDB. (co. Sussex), 9; Philadelphia, 2.

Bonifant, Bonnafant.—Nick. 'bon enfant,' corresponding to English Goodchild, a term of endearment; v. Bullivant.

London, 1, 0; Boston (U.S.), 0, 1.

Bonjohn.—Nick. 'Good-John.' v. Bunyan, and cf. Littlejohn, &c.

Duraund le Bon-johan, co. Linc., 1273. A.
Bonjohan (without surname), co. Linc., ibid.
John Bonjohn, London. X.

Bonken.—Nick. An expression of endearment, 'good little one'; cf. Bonfils and Bonfellow.

John Bonekyn, co. Sussex, 1273. A. London, 1.

Bonnell; v. Bonehill.

Bonner, Bonnor, Boner.—Nick. 'the debonair'; *bonair*, civil, gentle, courteous; spelt also *bonere*; v. Kyng Alisaunder, 6732, &c. (Halliwell); cf. O.F. *debonere*, *debonaire*, i.e. de bon aire. Lower remarks that 'Bishop Bonner was an excellent illustration of Horace

Smith's dictum that surnames "even go by contraries"' (Patr. Brit. p. 34). 'In sykenesse and in helthe to be boneere, and buxum in bed and at bord tyll deth us depart': Missale ad usum Eccles. Sarum (N. and Q. 1857, p. 397).

William le Bonere, co. Oxf., 1273. A.
Alice la Bonere, co. Hunts, ibid.
Walter Bonere, co. Bucks. ibid.
Johannes Boner, 1379: P. T. Yorks. p. 242.
1577. George Bonner, co. Glouc.: Reg. Univ. Oxf. vol. ii. pt. ii. p. 74.
1578. John Bonner, co. Oxf., ibid. p. 80.
London, 13, 1, 1; Philadelphia, 76, 0, 12.

Bonnet, Bonnett, Bonney, Bonny, Bonnin, Bunnett, Bonnyson.—Nick. of endearment, 'good little one,' found also as a Christian name. Bonny (comely) occurs early, and *bonye* was one form of it; v. H.E.D. But the popular pet form was Bunting, q.v.

Agnes Bonye, co. Oxf., 1273. A.
Alicia Bonye, co. Oxf., ibid.
Johannes Bonett, 1379: P. T. Yorks. p. 299.
Juliana Bonet, 1379: ibid. p. 212.
Johannes Bunnay, 1379: ibid. p. 231.
Agnes Bonny, 1379: ibid. p. 178.
Bonnetta Tyson, temp. Hen. III: Visitation of Yorks, 1563, p. 10, Harl. Soc.
1567. William Norris and Margaret Bonnyson: Marriage Lic. (London), i. 36.
1599. John Bonnytt, co. Leic.: Reg. Univ. Oxf. vol. ii. pt. ii. p. 238.
London, 3, 4, 6, 1, 5, 0, 0; Philadelphia, 2, 2, 5, 0, 2, 0, 0.

Bonsall, Bonsal, Bonsale.—Local, 'of Bonsall,' a parish in co. Derby, near Matlock.

London, 1, 0, 0; MDB. (co. Derby), 5, 0, 1; Philadelphia, 40, 5, 0.

Bonserjeant.—Nick. 'the good serjeant,' an officer of the law.

John Bonserjant, co. Oxf., 1273. A.

Bonsquier.—Nick. 'the good squire'; v. Squire.

William Bonsquier, co. Camb., 1273. A.

Bonswain.—Nick. 'the good swain'; v. Swain.

Richard Bonesweyn, co. Soms., 1 Edw.
III: Kirby's Quest, p. 107.

Bonvallet.—Nick. 'the good valet,' i.e. valet or groom.

John Bonvalet, co. Camb., 1273. A.
Richard Bonvallet, co. Oxf., ibid.

Boobbyer, Boobier, Boobyer.
—Local, 'of Bowebeare,' a place

in co. Devon, with the local suffix *-beare*, so common in that district. The modern variants are somewhat curious to look at.

1605. William Bowebeare, co. Devon: Reg. Univ. Oxf. vol. ii. pt. ii. p. 283.
1758. Married—William Warbutton and Mary Boobier: St. Geo. Han. Sq. i. 77.
1798. — James Boobbyer and Sarah Roussett: ibid. ii. 181.
London, 1, 1, 1.

Boodle, Bodle.—Official, 'the beadle.' A common form was Budel (v. Buddle), from which Boodle would easily be formed. This is more satisfactory, I think, than Lower's suggestion that it is a disguise of Bootle.

1640. Bapt.—Sara, d. Symon Bowdle: Kensington Ch. p. 32.

With this entry cf. Cowper and Cooper.

London, 4, 1; New York, 0, 1.

Bookbinder. — Occup. 'the bookbinder,' an early craft, whence a surname as old as the 13th century.

'Parchmyners and Bokebynders.'
York Mystery Plays, p. viii.
'Bokebynders and lymners.'
Cocke Lorelle's Bote.

An indenture between Oxford University and the Town, dated 1459, includes 'alle bedels . . . alle stacioners, alle bokebynders, lympners, wryters, pergemeners,' &c.: Mun. Acad. Oxon. p. 346.

Stephen Ligator, *libror*, Oxford, 1273. A.
William Ligator, *libror*, Oxford, ibid.
John Bokbyndere, London. X.
Dionisia le Bokebyndere, London, ibid.
Robert Bukebynder, co. York. W. 9.

I fear the surname is now extinct, but it lives in Binder, q.v.

Booker.—Occup. 'the butcher'; v. Bowker, of which it is a known Lancashire variant.

John Boker, co. Norf., 1273. A.
William le Bocer, co. Salop, ibid.
John Booker, of Chester, 1588: Wills at Chester (1545-1620), p. 23.

In the pedigree of Booker (London Visitation, 1633-5, vol. i. p. 87) the following variations occur: John Booker, John Boochard, and Edmund Boocher.

Nicholas Bowker, or Booker, co. Glouc., 1607: Reg. Univ. Oxf. vol. ii. pt. ii. p. 299.
'John Booker, a noted astrologer of the 17th century, was the son of John Bowker (commonly pronounced Booker), of Manchester, and was born on the 23rd of March, 1601': Baines' Lanc. i. 405.
1807. Married — Joseph Booker and Sarah Mathews: St. Geo. Han. Sq. i. 363. London, 13; Philadelphia, 6.

Bool, Boole.—Local, 'of Bole,' a parish in co. Notts, three miles from Gainsborough.

John de Bole, co. Lincoln, 1273. A. Gilbert Bole, co. Lincoln, ibid.
1577-8. James Ireland and Susanna Boole: Marriage Lic. (London), i. 79.
1690 George Bowll, co. Kent: Reg. Univ. Oxf. vol. ii. pt. ii, p. 385.
1746. Married—John Parrott and Jane Boole: St. Geo. Chap. Mayfair, p. 67.
'George Boole (1815-64), mathematician and logician, was born on Nov. 2, 1815. His father was a small tradesman in Lincoln': Dict. Nat. Biog. v. 369.
MDB. (co. Lincoln), 0, 1; London, 3, 0; Philadelphia, 0, 3.

Boon, Boone, Bown, Bowne.—(1) Local, 'de Bohun,' modified early to Bown and Boon; cf. Moon for Mohun.

John de Boon, co. Bedf., 20 Edw. I. R. Matilda Boon, co. Camb., 1273. A. Reginald Boon, co. Camb., ibid.

(2) Nick. Sometimes, no doubt, a form of Bunn and Bone (the Good).

1614. William Draper and Ellen Boone: Marriage Lic. (London), ii. 27.
1717. Michaell Boon and Ann Forcer, married: St. Michael, Cornhill, p. 59.
London, 9, 0, 7, 1; Philadelphia, 26, 29, 3, 4.

Boor, Boore; v. Boar.

Boord; v. Board.

Boorman.—Official; v. Bowerman.

Boot, Boote; v. Bott.

1584. Henry Boate, or Bote, co. Kent: Reg. Univ. Oxf. vol. ii. pt. ii. p. 138.
1590. John Boate, London, ibid. p. 178. London, 3, 1; Philadelphia, 1, 3.

Booth, Boothe.—Local, 'at the booth,' a hut, a cottage; M.E. *bothe.* The will of Thomas del Booth (1368), dwelling at Barton, near Manchester, is printed in Baines' Lancashire (edited by Croston), ii. 45. Booth, as a surname, has become strongly ramified in South Lancashire.

Rogerus del Bothe, 1379: P. T. Yorks. p. 181.
Adam del Bothe, 1379: ibid. p. 189.
Margeria del Bothe, 1379: ibid.
Odo de la Boothe, bailiff of Norwich, 1291: FF. iii. 74.
1548. Thomas Lawrence and Dionise Boothe: Marriage Lic. (London), i. 12.
Hamnet Booth, of Mouldsworth, *husbandman,* 1593: Wills at Chester, i. 23.
1716. Married — George Booth and Mary Silver: St. Mary Aldermary, p. 43.
Manchester, 88, 0; Leeds, 6, 0; London, 42, 0; Philadelphia, 102, 2.

Boothby.—Local, 'of Boothby,' two parishes in co. Linc.

Adam de Boothby, abbot of Peterborough: FF. vii. 463.
Henry Boothby, vicar of Stow-Bardolph, co. Norf., 1497: ibid. p. 447.
John de Botheby, rector of Ryton, co. Durham, 1312: DDD. ii. 264.
Thomas de Botheby, co. Linc., 1273. A.
1608. Matthew Beadle and Anne Boothby: Marriage Lic. (London), i. 306.
1784. Married—Brooke Boothby and Susanna Bristow: St. Geo. Han. Sq. i. 362.
London, 6; Philadelphia, 2.

Boothman, Bootman.—Occup. 'the boothman,' one who lived in a booth or hut (v. Booth); cf. Bridgman, Heathman, &c.

Roger Bothman, co. Hunts, 1273. A.
Henry Bootheman, temp. Eliz. ZZ.
1675. William Budge and Margarett Boothman: Marriage Alleg. (Canterbury), p. 147.
1749. Married—Christopher Boothman and Margaret Norburry: St. Geo. Chap. Mayfair, p. 156.
London, 0, 1; Manchester, 3, 0; New York, 0, 1.

Boothroyd. — Local, 'of the booth-royd'; v. Booth and Royd. A Yorkshire surname.

Ricardus de Botherod, 1379: P. T. Yorks. p. 179.
Willelmus Bowderode, 1379: ibid. p. 197.
Ricardus Butrode, 1379: ibid. p. 189.
West Riding Court Dir., 7; Philadelphia, 11.

Bootiman, Bootman, Bootyman. — Occup. 'the boothman.' Found in co. Northumberland, and no doubt the Scottish *bothie-man,* a cottager. It is a well-known surname about Newcastle-on-Tyne. Rather curiously Bonnyman and Bootiman occur together in the South Shields Directory (1885-6). 'Bothieman, equivalent to Eng. *hind,* and borrowed from the circumstance of hinds inhabiting bothies' (Jamieson). v. Boothman.

South Shields, 1, 0, 0; London, 0, 1, 0; Plymouth, 0, 0, 1; New York, 0, 1, 0.

Bootle.—Local, 'of Bootle.' (1) A parish in the suburbs of Liverpool: v. Bottle (2) for meaning; (2) an ancient town and parish in South Cumberland under the Black Combe. But (1) is the chief parent.

Matthew Bootle, co. Lanc., a servingman, 1595: Lancashire Wills at Richmond, p. 38.
Thomas Bootle, of Tatham, co. Lanc., 1598: ibid.
Thomas Bootell, co. Lanc., 1602: Preston Guild Rolls, p. 48.
William Bootell, co. Lanc., 1602: ibid.
Laurence Bootle, of Ince Blundell, 1614: Wills at Chester, i. 24.
Margaret Bootle, of Melling, 1619: ibid.
1605. Bapt. –John, s. James Bootle: St. Jas. Clerkenwell, i. 47.
London, 2; Liverpool, 3.

Bord; v. Board.

Borden.—(1) Local, 'of Borden,' a parish in co. Kent, near Sittingbourne. (2) Local, 'of Bordean,' a tithing in the parish of East Meon, near Petersfield, co. Hants.

Richard Bordon, co. Linc., 1273. A.
Robert Bordon, co. Wilts, ibid.
Richard Bordun, co. Hunts, ibid.
1750. Married — John Canewood and Ann Borden: St. Geo. Chap. Mayfair, p. 180.
Philadelphia, 31.

Border.—Occup.; v. Boarder.

Bordman; v. Boardman.

Boreham, Borham, Boram.—Local, 'of Boreham,' a parish four miles from Chelmsford, co. Essex.

Thomas de Borham, co. Suff., 1273. A.
Hernet de Borham, co. Northampton, ibid.
Harvey de Borham, co. Essex, ibid.
Robert de Borham, co. Essex, ibid.
1398. John Boram, rector of Bircham Newton, co. Norf.: FF. x. 290.
1745. Married—Samuel Boreham and Mary Phillips: St. Jas. Clerkenwell, iii. 275.
1779. — Michael Boreham and Eliz. Syme: St. Geo. Han. Sq. i. 298.
London, 10, 0, 0; MDB. (co. Essex), 6, 0, 0; (co. Suffolk), 4, 1, 1; New York, 1, 0, 0.

Borman.—Official; v. Bowerman.

Born.—Local, 'at the bourn,' from residence thereby; cf. Brook and Beck, and v. Burn.

William atte Borne, co. Soms., 1 Edw. III : Kirby's Quest, p. 109.
1560. John Borne and Margaret Paddye : Marriage Lic. (London), i. 20.
1582. Francis Bowrne, or Borne, co. Soms. : Reg. Univ. Oxf. vol. ii. pt. ii. p. 123.
1609. Buried—Angell, d. Henrie Borne: St. Jas. Clerkenwell, iv. 108.
London, 7 ; Boston (U.S.), 2.

Borough.—Local ; v. Bury.
London, 1.

Borradaile.—Local,' of Borrowdale,' a chapelry in the parish of Crosthwaite, co. Cumb., six miles from Penrith.

1547. Robert Borodall and Margaret Braryge : Marriage Lic. (London), i. 11.
1596. John Barrodall, co. Leic. : Reg. Univ. Oxf. vol. ii. pt. ii. p. 217.
1602. Edmund Slyfeld and Martha Borowdale : Marriage Lic. (London), i. 269.
1684. William Rimes and Rebecca Borradale : Marriage Lic. (Faculty Office), p. 173.
London, 3 ; Philadelphia, 1.

Borrell, Borrel, Burrell, Burrill.—(1) Nick. 'the borel,' originally a term for a kind of coarse cloth. Afterwards used adjectively for a comely man, a peasant, a countryman ; v. H.E.D., s. v. Burel (also v. Burler, ibid.). Borel was also used as a personal name.

Johanna, relicta Burel, co. Oxf., 1273. A. Burellus de Rathesnese, co. Norf., ibid. Emma Burel, co. Norf., ibid. Willelmus Burell, 1379 : P. T. Yorks. p. 234.
Johannes Borell, 1379 : ibid.
William Burel, co. Soms., 1 Edw. III : Kirby's Quest, p. 193.
1627. Bapt.—Robert, s. William Burrell : St. Jas. Clerkenwell, i. 106.

(2) Local, 'of Burrel,' a township in the parish of Bedale, North Rid. Yorks.

London, 1, 0, 22, 1 ; Philadelphia, 1, 1, 13, 2.

Borrowman. — Occup. ; v. Berryman.

Borton, Bourton.—Local, ' of Bourton' (formerly chiefly Borton), parishes, chapelries, hamlets, and tithings in cos. Berks, Bucks, Dorset, Oxford, Glouc., Soms., and Warwick.

Walter de Bourton, co. Bucks, 1273. A.
Robert de Borton, co. Dorset, ibid.
Henry de Borton, co. Norf., ibid.
Hugh de Bourtone, co. Bucks, ibid.
John de Bortone, co. Soms., 1 Edw. III : Kirby's Quest, p. 175.
Alicia de Borton, co. Staff., Hen. III– Edw. I. K.
William de Boureton, co. Devon, ibid.
1598. Buried — Joan, wife of Roger Bourton : St. Jas. Clerkenwell, iv. 63.
1683. Bapt.—Eliz., d. Lanclett Borton : ibid. i. 303.
1796. Married — William Borton and Hannah Smetham : St. Geo. Han. Sq. ii. 150.
London, 2, 7 ; Philadelphia, 5, 3.

Bosher.—Occup. 'the butcher'; M.E. *bocher*; v. Boucher and Batcher.

Richard le Bossour, co. Soms., 1 Edw. III : Kirby's Quest, p. 165.
1678. James Bosher and Mary Waring : Marriage Alleg. (Westminster), p. 290.
London, 6 ; Philadelphia, 3.

Bossum, Bossom.—Local, ' of Bosham,' a parish in co. Sussex, four miles from Chichester ; cf. Barnum for Barnham.

1594. John Hibberd and Eliz. Bosam, of Cambridge : Marriage Lic. (London), i. 218.
1743. Married—John Kent and Sarah Bossom : St. Geo. Chap. Mayfair, p. 33.
London, 0, 1 ; Oxford, 2, 12 ; Boston, 0, 4.

Bostock, Bostick.—Local, ' of Bostock,' a township in the parish of Davenham, co. Cheshire. This local surname has ramified strongly, and has wandered far.

Hugh de Bostock, co. Ches., 1423 : East Ches. i. 323.
David de Bostok, co. Ches., 1428 : ibid. i. 188.
'Philip Bostocke, of Bostocke, gent.,' 1634 : ibid. i. 178.
Arthur Bostock, of Bostock, 1560 : Wills at Chester, i. 24.
Thomas Bostock, of Chester, *brewer*, 1597 : ibid.
Ottiwell Bostock, of Warmington, 1610 : ibid.
1620. Married—William Bostock and Margrett Pilesburie : Prestbury Ch. (co. Chester), p. 227.
1674. Bapt.—Jane, d. of George Bostocke : St. Jas. Clerkenwell, i. 265.
Manchester, 7, 0 ; London, 7, 0 ; Philadelphia, 3, 14.

Boston.—Local, ' of Boston,' the well-known town in co. Lincoln.

Thomas de Botulfston, co. Suff., 1273. A.
William de Boston, prior of Beeston, co. Norf., 1314 : FF. viii. 91.

John Boston, vicar of Tottington, co. Norf., 1459 : ibid. ii. 356.
1615. Bapt.—Rebecka, d. Josias Boston: St. Michael, Cornhill, p. 112.
1786. Married — James Boston and Ann Kitchen : St. Geo. Han. Sq. i. 395.
London, 5 ; Philadelphia, 26.

Boswell, Boswall. — Local, 'de Bosville,' 'a village of 1400 inhabitants, near Yvetot, in Normandy. The family were in England in 1126, and probably from the period of the Conquest' (Lower's Patr. Brit. p. 35). This is the true parentage of Boswell, although it has such an English local look.

John de Bosevill, co. Linc., 20 Edw. I. R.
John de Bosevil, co. York, 1273. A.
Henry de Bosevil, co. Northampt., ibid.
Simon de Bosevill, co. Bedf., Hen. III– Edw. I. K.
Agnes Bosseuill, 1379 : P. T. Yorks. p. 34.
Robert de Bosewill, or Bosville, co. Norf., 1360 : FF. i. 118.
Walkeline de Boseville, co. Norf., 1199 : ibid. v. 139.
Isabell Boswel, co. Norf., 1464 : ibid. ii. 430.
William Boswell, co. Norf., 1620 : ibid. v. 222.
1752. Married—Thomas Simpson and Sarah Boswell : St. Geo. Han. Sq. i. 47.
1780. — William Ward and Julia Bosville : ibid. p. 313.
London, 10, 3 ; MDB. (co. Norfolk), 1, 0 ; Philadelphia, 0, 26.

Bosworth. — Local, ' of Bosworth,' two parishes, Husband's Bosworth and Market Bosworth, in the county of Leicester.

John de Bosworth, co. Norf., 1377 : FF. ii. 272.
Edward Bosworth, rector of Tasburgh, co. Norf., 1679 : ibid. v. 213.
1570. Bapt.—Rebecka Bosworthe : St. Jas. Clerkenwell, i. 6.
1591–2. Edmund Rionte and Margery Bosworthe : Marriage Lic. (London), i. 196.
1625. Buried—Samuell, the servant of Thomas Bosworth, *brasier*, in Gracechurch St. : St. Peter, Cornhill, p. 185.
1639. Married—William Shipley and Mary Bosworth : ibid. p. 256.
MDB. (co. Leicester), 7 ; (co. Lincoln), 5 ; London, 6 ; Philadelphia, 5.

Botcher, Bodger, Bottcher. —Occup. 'the butcher.' No connexion with *botcher* or *bodger*, a cobbler (v. Bodger, H.E.D.). M.E. *bocher*, a form of butcher.

'Brewesters, Bakers,
Bochers and Cookes.'
Piers Plowman's Vision.

Elias le Bocher, temp. 1300. M.
John le Bocher, temp. 1300. M.
William Baley, *bocher*, 1562 : Preston
Guild Rolls, p. 30.
John Schyrwod, *bocher*, co. York, 1416.
W. 11, p. 19.
Willelmus Prestman, *bocher*, 1379 :
P. T. Yorks. p. 213.
Adam Bocher, 1379 : ibid. p. 160.
Richard Bocher, 1379 : ibid.

With Bodger for Botcher, cf.
Boodger below for Butcher :

1748. Married — John Boodger and
Susanna Mason : St. Geo. Han. Sq.
i. 10.
MDB.(co.Hertford),0,1, 0 ; (co. Hunts),
0, 2, 0 ; New York (Bottcher), 2.

Botham, Bottom.—Local, ' at
the bottom,' a depression in the land,
the fall of a hillside, as in Lanca
shire dialect, ' bottom o'th moor,'
' bottom o'th hill '; cf. Birkenshaw
Bottoms, near Gomersal, co. York ;
also Bottom Brow, near Skircoat,
co. York. M.E. *botun*, *bottome*,
and *bothom*. ' Botune, or botum
(botym), *fundum* ' : Prompt. Parv.
Many compounds have found their
way into our directories, all hailing
from North-English localities ; cf.
Bottomley and Bothamley, Longbottom and Rowbotham, Sidebottom
and Sidebotham, Higginbottom
and Higginbotham, Shufflebotham,
&c., q.v.; cf. also Robertus de
Crumwelbothom, 1379 : P. T.
Yorks. p. 117.

John del Bothum, co. Lanc., 1332 : Lay
Subsidy (Rylands), p. 39.
Willelmus de Bouthom, 1379 : P. T.
Yorks. p. 187.
Laurence de Bothum, co. York,
1297. M.
1610. Married—Gilbert Bothom and
Mary Clee : St. Mary Aldermary, p. 12.
London, 1, 1 ; Boston (U.S.), 1, 0.

Botly.—Local, ' of Botley,' a
parish in co. Hants, six miles
from Southampton.

Mathew de Botheleheye, co. Soms., 1
Edw. III : Kirby's Quest, p. 259.
1661. Geo. Holland and Hannah
Botlee : Marriage Lic. (London), ii. 287.
1663. Buried—Thomas Botteley : St.
Mary Aldermary, p. 184.
London, 1.

Bott, Botte.—(1) Local, ' of
Botte.' I cannot find the spot ;
probably a variant of Booth, q.v.
v. also Bootiman.

Adam de Botte, co. Norf., 1273. A.
Walter le (? de) Botte, co. Oxf., ibid.

(2) Bapt. ' the son of Baldwin,'
from the nick. Bodd sharpened to
Bott ; cf. Botten and Botting, undoubted instances of the dim. form.

Henry Botte, co. Oxf., 1273. A.
Richard Botte, co. Salop, ibid.
Robert Botte, co. Bucks, ibid.
London, 7, 0 ; New York, 11, 1.

Botten, Botting.—Bapt. ' the
son of Bodin,' i. e. Baldwin,
sharpened to Bottin and Botting,
with the customary excrescent *g*.
An instance occurs early ; v. Boden.

Botoun le Ken, co. Hunts, 1273. A.
1731. Married — Nicholas Philps and
Eliz. Botting : St. Geo. Chap. Mayfair,
p. 322.
London, 2, 6 ; Boston (U.S.), 0, 1 ;
Philadelphia, 1, 0.

Botterill, Bottroll, Bottrill.
—Local, ' of Bottreaux.' Lower
suggests this corruption. His view
is strongly supported by the first
two entries below, which occur
close together in the Hundred
Rolls of Shropshire.

Roger de Botereus, co. Salop, 1273. A.
Reginald de Boterel, co. Salop, ibid.
William de Boterell, co. Somerset,
ibid.
1672. Bapt.—William, son of Ephraim
Botterell : St. Jas. Clerkenwell, i. 253.
London, 4, 1, 2.

Bottle.—(1) Bapt. ' the son of
Bothild.'

Botil or Botild Hod, co. Suff., 1273. A.
Margaret Botild, co. Camb., ibid.
Ralph Botild, co. Hunts, ibid.
1565. Cuthbert Bottyll, New College :
Reg. Univ. Oxf. vol. ii. pt. ii. p. 22.

(2) Local, ' at the bottle '; bottle =
a seat, a mansion ; cf. Newbottle,
Harbottle.

Richard de Botele, co. Oxf., 1273. A.
Walter de Botele, co. Oxf., ibid.
Robert atte Bothele, co. Soms., 1 Edw.
III : Kirby's Quest, p. 185.
Michel atte Bothele, co. Soms., 1 Edw.
III : ibid.

' Friend Bottle ' reads curiously
in the London Directory (1870).

1799. Bapt.—James, s. Samuel Botle, a
soldier : Canterbury Cath. p. 40.
London, 2.

Bottlemaker. — Occup. ' a
maker of bottles.' 'Myllers, carters,
and botylemakers' : Cocke Lorelle's
Bote.

Thomas Botelmaker, Close Roll, 10
Ric. II.

**Bottomley, Bothamley, Bot-
tomly.**—Local, ' of Bottomley ' or
' Bothamley,' some small spot,
probably in the W. Rid. Yorks,
which I have failed to identify.
The instance below occurs in
the township of Barkisland, in the
parish of Halifax. Bottomley now,
500 years later, is found in the
same township ; v. W. Rid. Directory.

Johannes de Bodhomlay, 1379 : P. T.
Yorks. p. 185.
Margaret Bothomley, of Deane, co.
Lanc., 1589 : Wills at Chester, i. 25.
1742. Married—Joseph Bottomley and
Ann Gant : St. Geo. Han. Sq. i. 28.
London, 9, 1, 0 ; West Rid. Court
Dir., 36, 0, 0 ; Boston (U.S.), 0, 2, 1 ;
Philadelphia, 23, 0, 0.

Botwright; v. Boatwright.

Boucher. — Occupative, ' the
butcher '; v. Bowcher, Botcher, and
Bosher.

London, 3 ; Philadelphia, 12.

Bouffler.—Nick.; v. Boutflower.

**Boughen, Bowgen, Bou-
ghan.** — ? A Norfolk surname.
I suspect it is an immigrant from
the Low Countries. I can offer no
satisfactory solution of its meaning.

George Bowgeon, sheriff of Norwich,
1574 : FF. iii. 359.
John Bowgeon, rector of West Tofts,
co. Norf., 1546 : ibid. ii. 262.
James Bowgin, vicar of Surlingham, co.
Norf., 1720 : ibid. v. 465.
1726. Married — Thomas Bougin and
Jane Alley : St. Geo. Han. Sq. i. 2.
MDB. (co. Norfolk), 2, 2, 0 ; London,
1, 0, 0 ; New York (Boughan), 1 ; Philadelphia, 1, 0, 0.

Boughey, Bowhay.—Local,
' of the Boghey,' seemingly one
who resided by the enclosed bog.
The suffix is -*hey*, a hedge, or fenced
plot of ground ; v. Hey.

Thomas Bogheye, co. Soms., 1 Edw.
III : Kirby's Quest, p. 199.
1681-2. Married — Kenelm Smith and
Ann Boughy : St. Dionis Backchurch,
p. 39.
1803. — Daniel Boughey and Eliz.
Manley : St. Geo. Han. Sq. ii. 275.
London, 2, 1 ; MDB. (co. Devon), 0, 2.

Bould; v. Bold.

London, 3 ; New York, 1.

Boultbee, Boulby, Bowlby.
—Local, ' of Boltby,' a parish in

co. York; cf. Applebee for Appleby. It appears more natural to assume that Boulby and Bowlby are modifications, but my last entry from the Hundred Rolls suggests a separate and independent origin.

Adam de Bolteby, co. York, 1273. A.
Hugh de Bolteby, co. York, ibid.
Adam de Boltby, co. York, ibid.
William de Boleby, co. Bucks, ibid.
Crockford, 4, 1, 3; Boston (U.S.), 0, 0, 3.

Boulter, Bolter, Bulter.— Occup. 'the bolter,' a sifter of meal. In the ordinances of the household of Henry VI, 1455, mention is made of the 'bakhous' (bakehouse) under thirteen officers, of whom are to be 'six gromes bulters' (Proc. Ord. Privy Council, vi. 226).

John Boltor, co. Soms., 1 Edw. III: Kirby's Quest, p. 159.
Geoffrey le Bolter, co. Berks, 1273. A.
Richard le Boltere, co. Norf., ibid.
John le Boltere, co. Hunts, ibid.
Ricardus Bultere, 1379: P. T. Yorks. p. 160.
1573-4. Ralph Daulton and Dorothy Bowlter, *widow*: Marriage Lic. (London), i. 59.
1674. Bapt. — Thomas, s. Thomas Boulter: St. Jas. Clerkenwell. i. 267.
1759. Married—Benjamin Boulter and Mary Warrick: St. Geo. Han. Sq. i. 85.
London, 11, 0, 1; New York, 0, 3, 1; Philadelphia, 6, 0, 0.

Boumphrey.—Bapt. 'the son of Humphrey,' from the Welsh 'Ap-Humphrey,' which became Pumphrey or Bumphrey (v. Pumphrey); cf. Bloyd, Bethell, Bowen, Bennion, &c.

1633. Roger Bomfrey and Susanna Ivery: Marriage Lic. (Westminster), p. 34.
'Mr. Boumphrey, general manager of the Cunard Company, advised Mr. Jesse Collings to abstain from proceeding in the steam tug' Mr. Chamberlain's arrival at Liverpool: Manchester Courier, March 12, 1888.
Liverpool, 2.

Bourn, Bourne.—Local, 'at the Burn,' q.v.

Bourse.—Local, 'at the Bourse.'
Robert atte Bourse, vicar of Briston, co. Norf., 1354 : FF. ix. 376.

Bourton ; v. Borton.

Bousfield.—Local, 'of Bousfield,' a hamlet one mile from Orton, a parish in co. Westm.

1541. Stephen Bousfell : Hist. and Traditions of Ravenstonedale, co. Westm. (W. Nicholls), p. 113.
— Reynold Bousfell : ibid.
— Henry Bousfell : ibid.
1575. Bartholomew Bousfield, or Busfell, Queen's Coll. : Reg. Univ. Oxf. vol. ii. pt. ii. p. 23, n.
1809. Married—Stephen Bousfield and Louisa Layton : St. Geo. Han. Sq. ii. 408.
London, 9; MDB. (co. Cumb.), 1; (co. Westm.), 17; New York, 1.

Boutcher. — Occupative, 'the butcher,' one of various forms; v. Butcher, Bowker, Bowsher, Bowcher.

Christopher Smythe, *bowtcher*, 1539, Newcastle-on-Tyne (List of male population capable of bearing arms) : PPP. vol. ii. pp. 174-194.
1676. George Johnson and Deborah Boutcher : Marriage Lic. (Canterbury), p. 260.
London, 2; Liverpool, 1; Philadelphia, 3.

Boutflower, Bouffler.—Nick. 'Beauflour,' comely flower; cf. Lillywhite.

James Beauflour, C. R., 10 Edw. II.
Thomas Beauflour, 1301. M.
James Beauflur, London. X.
Margaret Butflower. F.
William Beauflour. B.
Nicholas Bowtefflowre, 1539, Newcastle-on-Tyne (List of male population capable of bearing arms) : PPP. vol. ii. pp. 174-194.
Jeffery Beauflour, seneschal of Bristol, 1357 : YYY. p. 676.
John Beauflour, mayor of Bristol, 1280. ibid. p. 673.
William Boutflower, sheriff, 1702 : Brand's Newcastle-on-Tyne, i. 14.
Manchester, 2, 0; Crockford, 3, 0; London, 0, 3; New York, 0, 4.

Bovill, Bovell.—Local, 'of Boville,' now Bouville, a parish in the arrondissement of Rouen (Lower).

Warin de Bovile, co. Notts, 1273. A.
John de Boville, co. Suff., ibid.
Matthew de Bovylle, co. Surrey, 20 Edw. I. R.
Anastach' de Boyvill, co. Devon, Hen. III-Edw. I. K.
1790. Married — Thomas Bovill and Eliz. Jones : St. Geo. Han. Sq. ii. 39.
London, 6, 0; Boston (U.S.), 0, 2.

Bovingdon, Bovington.— Local, 'of Bovington,' a parish in co. Herts, near Hemel Hempstead.

Thomas Bove'don, co. Oxf., 1273. A.
1581. Richard Bovingdon, co. Bucks : Reg. Univ. Oxf. vol. ii. pt. ii. p. 110.

1774. Married — William Bovington and Eliz. Wood : St. Geo. Han. Sq. i. 241.
London, 1, 2.

Bow, Bowe.—Local, 'at the Bow,' a sign-name, from residence at an inn so called; cf. Roebuck. A likely sign in the days of archery.

Roger atte Bowe, citizen of London, C. R., 9 Edw. II.
1403. Cristina atte Bowe : Cal. of Wills in Court of Husting (2).
1579. John Bowe and Joanna Bybie : Marriage Lic. (London), i. 87.
1589. William Bow, co. Cumberland : Reg. Univ. Oxf. vol. ii. pt. ii. p. 173.
1801. Married—Richard Hartley and Lydia Bow : St. Geo. Han. Sq. ii. 249.
London, 1, 0; Boston (U.S.), 4, 12; Philadelphia, 0, 8.

Bowcher. — Occupative, 'the butcher'; v. Botcher and Boutcher. 'Bouchers, Bocheres,' York Plays, pp. xxvi, 359; 'Bowchyer, a butcher' (Halliwell).

Edward le Boucher, co. Soms., 1 Edw. III : Kirby's Quest, p. 205.
Johannes Bowcher, co. York, 1420 : W. 11, p. 21.
William Butchere, or Bowcher, 1543 : Reg. Univ. Oxf. i. 207.
1661. John Radcliffe and Judith Bowcher : Marriage Lic. (Faculty Office), p. 51.
London, 4.

Bowd.—Local, 'of Bowood.' (1) A tithing in the parish of Netherbury, co. Dorset; (2) a liberty in the parish of Calne, co. Wilts.

John Bowode, co. Soms., 1 Edw. III : Kirby's Quest, p. 195.
London, 3.

Bowditch, Bowdidge, Bowdage, Bowdich, Bowdige.— Local, 'of Bowditch,' 'an estate in Dorsetshire possessed by the family at an early period' (Lower). The name is evidently of south-western origin, and is manifestly local. With Bowdage or Bowdidge, cf. Bromage for Bromwich.

1554. Richard Bowdyche and Joanna Savage : Marriage Lic. (London), i. 15.
1769. Married—Thomas Bowditch and Hannah Fowler : St. Geo. Han. Sq. i. 180.
MDB. (Dorset), 7, 0, 0, 0, 0; (Somerset), 1, 0, 1, 1, 0; (Devon), 1, 0, 0, 0, 1; London, 3, 1, 1, 0, 0; Exeter, 0, 1, 0, 0, 0; New York (Bowditch), 2; Boston (U.S.), 31, 0, 0, 0, 0.

Bowdler, Bowdlear.—Occup. 'the bowdler,' i.e. the puddler. A steady number in the directories. 'Bowdlerized editions' has made the name famous. 'Buddle, to cleanse ore. North. "A vessel made for this purpose, like a shallow tumbrel, is called a buddle": Ray's English Words, ed. 1674, p. 116' (Halliwell). One instance below is that of a Yorkshireman, the other of a Salopian, so there can be no doubt about the origin of Bowdler; cf. 'puddle,' to work in iron, and 'puddler,' one who works iron. 'To buddle, to wash ore' (Imperial Dict., Annandale, 1882).

Richard le Boudler, co. Salop, 1273. A.
Richard le Bowdlere, co. York. W. 9.
1569. Richard Bowdeler and Agnes Yonge: Marriage Lic. (London), i. 43.
Marmaduke Bowdler, sheriff of Bristol, 1693: YYY. p. 695.
1738. Buried—Francis Bowdler: St. Michael, Cornhill, p. 294.
London, 4, 0; New York, 1, 0; Philadelphia, 1, 0; Boston (U.S.), 0, 3.

Bowoll.—Local; v. Bovill, a modification.

Henry le Bowel, co. Kent, 1273. A.
Walter de Bowell, co. Herts, ibid.
1584. Henry Skynner and Jane Bowell: Marriage Lic. (London), i. 131.
1620. George Bowll, co. Kent: Reg. Univ. Oxf. vol. ii. pt. ii. p. 385.
London, 2.

Bowen.—(1) Bapt. 'the son of Owen,' from the Welsh Ap-Owen = Bowen; cf. Bevans = Ap-Evan, Bethell = Ap-Ithell, Bloyd = Ap-Lloyd, &c. In the Visitation of London, 1634, Thomas Bowen claims descent from Thomas Bowen of Llewenny, co. Denbigh.

1487. Lewis ap-Owen, archdeacon of Cardigan: Hist. and Ant. of St. David's, p. 360.
1568. Bapt.—Daniell, son of John Abowen: St. Peter, Cornhill, i. 13.
Thomas ap-Owen, Cal. State Papers, Hen. VIII.
1582. Thomas Bowen, co. Cardigan: Reg. Univ. Oxf. vol. ii. pt. ii. p. 122.
1597. Hugh Bowen, co. Carmarthen: ibid. p. 223.
1691. Arnold Bowen, prebendary of St. David's: Hist. and Ant. of St. David's, p. 362.

(2) Local, 'de Bohun,' sometimes no doubt for Bown, q.v.

London, 27; Liverpool, 11; Philadelphia, 130.

Bower, Bowers.—(1) Local, 'of the bower,' an indoor servant, one who waited 'in my lady's chamber'; v. Bowerman. 'Bowre chambyr': Prompt. Parv.

'That chanteth thus under our boures wal.'   Chaucer, C. T. 3367.

The added s is common to these specific names. Thus the exact equivalent 'Chamber' is more generally found as Chambers; cf. Brooks and Styles for Brook and Style. Possibly it is the patronymic s, as in Perkins or Jones.

Robert Atte-bure, rector of Gunton, co. Norf., 1372: FF. viii. 123.

Perhaps the above represents Bury, q.v.

Richard atte Boure, C. R., 20 Edw. II.
John atte Beur, co. Soms., 1 Edw. III:
Kirby's Quest, p. 161.
Richard atte Bowre, 1306. M.
Agnes del Bowre, 1372: P. T. Yorks. p. 30.

(2) Occup. 'the bowyer.' The y has crept in as in lawyer, sawyer, &c. In the Order of the Procession of Occupations, Crafts, and Companies to be made on Corpus Christi Day at Norwich, 1533, the 'Fletchers, Bowers, and Turners' were placed in the second division: Blomefield's Norfolk, ii. 148.

Thomas le Bower, C. R., 7 Edw. III: pt. i.
London, 22, 14; Philadelphia, 84, 130.

Bowergroom.—Official, 'the bower-groom,' a servant who attended the room called the bower; v. Groom and Bower (1). As a servant, groom does not seem to have been confined to the male sex; v. Bowerman.

Alicia Bourgrom, co. Soms., 1 Edw. III: Kirby's Quest, p. 167.

Bowerman, Boorman, Borman, Boreman.—Official, 'the bowerman,' i.e. the servant of the bower, the male equivalent of 'bower-maiden,' an indoor servitor, a chamberlain. The corrupted forms of the surname are easily traceable; v. Burman. Below are two entries that occur side by side:

Cecilia del Boure, 1379: P. T. Yorks. p. 154.
Johannes Boureman, 1379: ibid.

This places the origin beyond dispute.

Gilbert Burman, co. Oxf., 1273. A.
Isabella Bureman, co. Essex, ibid.
William Bourman. F.
William Bowerman, or Bourman, 1506: Reg. Univ. Oxf. i. 51.
Robert Boreman, or Bourman, died 1675: Dict. Nat. Biog. v. 394.
Simon Boureman, son of James Bowreman: Visitation of London, 1633-5, vol. i. p. 92.
1632. Buried—Job Boorman, a prentice: St. Antholin (London), p. 66.
London, 2, 8, 3, 0; New York, 4, 2, 2, 0.

Bowgen; v. Boughen.

Bowker.—Occup. 'the butcher,' a North-English form. A very familiar form of the surname in co. Lancashire; v. Booker, and cf. Cowper and Cooper.

Thomas le Bouker, co. Lanc., 1379: Preston Guild Rolls, p. 5.
Thomas le Bouker, co. Lanc., 1332: Lay Subsidy (Rylands), p. 37.
Margaret Bowker, of Manchester, 1591: Wills at Chester (1545-1620), p. 25.
Arthur Bowker, of Bispham, co. Lanc., 1605: ibid.
1618. Buried—James Bowker, Prestbury Church (co. Chester), p. 221.
1629. Bapt.—Nathanyell, son of Adam Bowker: St. Jas. Clerkenwell, i. 112.
London, 5; Manchester, 30; New York, 6.

Bowland.—Local; v. Bolland.

Robertus de Boghland, 1379: P. T. Yorks. p. 217.
Rogerus Bowland, 1379: ibid.
1550. Roger Bowland and Avice Gryggesbie: Marriage Lic. (London), i. 12.
1570-1. John Bowlande and Eliz. Thene: ibid. i. 48.
London, 1; Philadelphia, 1.

Bowler.—Occup. 'the bowler,' a maker of wooden bowls and dishes. 'Bolle, vesselle: concha, luter.' 'Bolle, dysche: cantare': Prompt. Parv.

John Foune, boller, 9 Edw. III: Freemen of York, i. 30.
John le Bolur, co. Oxf., 1273. A.
Stephen le Bolur, co. Suff., ibid.
Robert le Boller, 1301. M.
Adam le Bolour, 1307. M.
Richard le Bolour, co. Lanc., 1332: Lay Subsidy (Rylands), p. 64.
1700. Bapt.—Angellet, d. of William Bowler: St. Jas. Clerkenwell, i. 385.
London, 11; Philadelphia, 10.

Bowleress.—Occup. 'the bowleress' (v. Bowler), a woman who made bowls, dishes, &c.; Juliana la Boleresse (Close Roll, 54 Hen. III). Bowlster (q.v.) also existed.

Bowling.—Local, 'of Bowling,' a chapelry near Bradford, co. York. Cf. Bolling. (2)

'Tristram Bollyng, of Bradford in co. Yorke, temp. 1580': Visitation of London, 1633-5, vol. i. p. 84.
'His grandson was Robert Bollyng, of London, "sadler and silk throwster," 1633': ibid.
1579. William Bowling and Rose Aske: Marriage Lic. (London), i. 91.
1647. Married—Robert Crosby and Mary Bowleing: St. Dionis Backchurch, p. 25.
London, 2; Boston (U.S.), 2.

Bowlster, Bolster.—Occup. 'the bowlster' (v. Bowler), a maker of bowls, dishes, &c. (with feminine terminative). Robert le Bulester (Patent Roll, 20 Edw. II); cf. Brewster, Baxter, &c.

1542. John Bolster, goldsmith, and Cristones Wolfe, married: St. Antholin (London), p. 3.
1605. Married—Henry Bolster and Joanne Hinton: Reg. Stourton, co. Wilts, p. 50.
1804. — Thomas Bolster and Mary Williams: St. Geo. Han. Sq. ii. 307.
New York, 0, 2; Boston (U.S.), 0, 18.

Bowmaker. — Occup. 'the bowmaker,' a bowyer. North English in origin. A family of the name lived in Alnwick for several centuries, and it is chiefly in Newcastle and South Northumb. that we find the surviving representatives. Fox numbers one John Bowmaker among the Marian martyrs.

Thomas Bowmaker, 1539, Newcastle-on-Tyne (List of male population capable of bearing arms): PPP. vol. ii. pp. 174-194.
Ralph Bowmaker, 1745: Blair's Hist. of Alnwick, p. 457.
George Boumaker. SS.
Robert Boumaker, co. York. W. 1.
John Bowmaykere, co. York. W. 3.

The surname still exists, I am glad to say.

Liverpool, 1.

Bowman. — (1) Occup. 'the bowman,' an archer. Mr. Lower quotes Richardson's Gathering Ode:

'Come Spearman, come Bowman,
Come Bold-hearted Truewicke,
Repel the proud foeman,
Join lion-like Bewicke.'

(2) Occup. 'a maker of bows,' a bowyer.

'To Nicholas Frost, bowman, Stephen Sedar, fletcher, Ralph the stringere... to

the aforesaid Nicholas for 500 bows, £31 8 0: to the aforesaid Stephen, 1,700 sheaves of arrows, £148 15 0': Exchequer Issues, 14 Henry IV.
John Yonger, bowman, 1539, Newcastle-on-Tyne (List of male population capable of bearing arms): PPP. vol. ii. pp. 174-194.
Robert Bowman, temp. Eliz. Z.
1570. Bapt.—Judith, d. Edmund Bowman: St. Thomas the Apostle (London), p. 25.
1581. Gabriel Bowman, co. Surrey: Reg. Univ. Oxf. vol. ii. pt. ii. p. 108.
London, 28; Philadelphia, 116.

Bown, Bowne. — Local, 'of Boun,' i.e. Bohun; v. Bowen (2).

Humfredus de Boun, co. Heref., 1273. A.
Franciscus de Boun, co. Dorset, ibid.
Milo de Boun, co. Dorset, ibid.
John de Bounn, co. Linc., ibid.

Milo de Boun, above-mentioned, occurs at p. 97, and Milo de Bohun at p. 102. The two entries, without doubt, refer to the same individual.

1579. John Bowne and Eliz. Gryffyn: Marriage Lic. (London), i. 94.
London, 7, 1; Philadelphia, 3, 4.

Bowring, Bowering.—? Bapt. 'the son of Bowring,' seemingly a personal name, like Harding and Browning. A West-country name.

Walter Bowryng, co. Soms., 1 Edw. III: Kirby's Quest, p. 194.
1807. Married—Heasma Curme and Mary Bowering: St. Geo. Han. Sq. ii. 376.
1808. John James Bowring and Mary Kelsey: ibid. p. 384.
London, 7, 0; MDB. (co. Soms.), 1, 3; (co. Devon), 4, 0.

Bowsher, Bowser, Bewsher. —(1) Occup. 'the butcher'; v. Bowcher, Botcher, &c. (2) Nick. O.F. Beau-sire,' 'fair sir,' an address of respect or courtesy; cf. Bellamy, Bonamy, Belcher. 'Beau sire ... thu spext as a fol,' c. 1300. Beket, 768 (H.E.D.); 'Thou shalle abak, bewshere,' c. 1460. Towneley Myst. 241 (ibid.).

Thomas le Bousyre, 1278. M.
Roger Beausire, co. Herefordshire, Hen. III-Edw. I. K.
1575. Henry Bowschere, Exeter Coll.: Reg. Univ. Oxf. i. 389.
1614. Bapt.—Frederick, son of Frederick Bousyr: St. Jas. Clerkenwell, i. 70.
London, 3, 2, 0; Liverpool, 0, 0, 1; Boston (U.S.), 0, 7, 0.

Bowyer.—Occup. 'the bowyer,' a maker of bows. The bowyers and fletchers (v. Fletcher) always

marched together in the trade processions. Skelton in 'The Maner of the World' says:

'So many bowyers, so many fletchers,
And so few good archers, saw I never.'
William le Boghyere, co. Sussex, 1273. A.
William le Bowiere, London, ibid.
Adam le Boghiere, c. 1310. M.
William le Bowyer. H.

With the intrusive y or i, cf. lawyer for lawer, or sawyer for sawer; v. Bower (2).

1613. Bapt. — Willyam, s. Anthony Bowyer: St. Jas. Clerkenwell, i. 68.
London, 22; Philadelphia, 4.

Box.—(1) Local, 'of Box,' a parish in co. Wilts, seven miles from Chippenham. (2) Local, 'at the box,' i.e. box-tree, from residence thereby; cf. Pine, Birch, Oak, Ash, Nash.

John de la Boxe, Close Roll, 10 Edw. III.
William atte Box, co. Soms., 1 Edw. III: Kirby's Quest, p. 152.
John atte Boxe, co. Soms., 1 Edw. III: ibid. p. 269.
Elena de la Boxe, co. Glouc., 1273. A.
Hamo Box, London, ibid.
Sampson de Boxe, co. Wilts, ibid.
Martyn Box, sheriff of London, 1283.
Henry Box, co. Norf., 1649: FF. viii. 540.
1600. Henry Box, co. Oxf.: Reg. Univ. Oxf. vol. ii. pt. ii. p. 243.
1615. Isaac Eve and Eliz. Boxe: Marriage Lic. (London), ii. 37.
1623. William Box and Charity Holmes: ibid. p. 131.
1743. Buried—Priscilla Box: St. Michael, Cornhill, p. 296.
London, 17; Philadelphia, 2; New York, 1.

Boxall, Boxell, Boxtell.— Local, 'of Boxwell,' a parish in co. Glouc., six miles from Tetbury. With Boxtell, cf. Axtell for Axell.

1575. Robert Boxall, New Coll.: Reg. Univ. Oxf. iii. 82.
1579. John Boxall, New. Coll.: ibid.

The spellings in this register are Boxald, Boxold, and Boxwell.

1750. Married — Robert Boxold and Rebecca Vanbrakill: St. Geo. Chap. Mayfair, p. 165.
1790. — Daniel Boxall and Sarah Cripps: St. Geo. Han. Sq. ii. 51.
London, 8, 2, 0; Boston (U.S.), 0, 0, 1.

Boyce, Boys, Boyse.—Local, 'del Bois,' from residence by or in a wood; cf. French Dubois, and English Wood and Attwood.

Thomas del Boyz, co. Dorset, 1273. A.
Ralph del Boys, co. Norfolk, ibid.
Henry du Boys, 1313. M.
Katerina Boyse, 1379: P. T. Yorks.
p. 149.
Richard Bosse, co. Soms., 1 Edw. III:
Kirby's Quest, p. 100.
John de Boys, rector of Fincham, co.
Norf., 1350: FF. vii. 357.
Robert de Bosco, or Boys, rector of
Fritton, co. Norf., 1300 : FF. v. 311.
1590. Bapt.—John, s. Thomas Boys:
Canterbury Cathedral, p. 1.
1594. John Bois, co. Kent: Reg. Univ.
Oxf. vol. ii. pt. ii. p. 206.
1760. Married — John Fendall and
Susanna Boyce : St. Geo. Han. Sq. i. 91.
London, 20, 12, 1; MDB. (Norfolk), 13,
0, 0; New York, 37, 0, 0; Philadelphia
(Boys), 1.

Boycott, Boykett, Bockett (?).
—(1) Local, 'of Boycott.' Lower
says, 'An estate in co. Salop still
possessed by the family' (Patr.
Brit. p. 37); v. Bockett for another
origin of that name. (2) Local, 'of
Boycutt,' an extra-parochial liberty
in co. Oxford, three miles from
Buckingham. The evidence is in
favour of this parentage.

Johannes de Boykote, co. Bucks,
1273. A.
William Boycote, co. Kent, ibid.
John de Boycote, 1302, burgess for
Leominster. M.
1781. Married—Richard Boycott and
Eliz. Malpas : St. Geo. Han. Sq. i. 329.
London, 1, 0, 3 ; Crockford, 2, 1, 2.

Boyd.—Bapt. and nick. Boidh,
an Erse name, meaning *yellow*.

'Boyd, Gael. *boidh*, fair, or yellow-
haired. A nephew of Walter, first high-
steward of Scotland, circ. 1160, was
known by this appellation, and was ancestor of the Lords Boyd, Earls of
Arran': Lower, p. 37.
'Grim, the grandson of Duff, reigned
for a short time, but was slain in battle,
in 1004, by Malcolm, and his son Boidh
was set aside, and disabled from reigning': Yonge, ii. 99.
'Boidh, Lady Macbeth's brother, was
yellow, a name surviving in the Scottish
family of Boyd': ibid. p. 101.
1741. Married—Donald Valentine and
Caler Boyd : St. Geo. Chap. Mayfair,
p. 15.
London, 26 ; Philadelphia, 300.

Boydell.—?Local, 'of Boydell' (?).
I cannot find the place.

Caterina Boydel, co. Norf., 1273. A.
1787. Married — James Boydell and
Catherine Rutland : St. Geo. Han. Sq.
i. 407.
London, 2.

Boyden.—Bapt. 'the son of
Baldwin,' popularly Bodin. Baw-
den (q.v.), and Boyden, through
Fr. Baudoin ; v. Baldwin.

Boyedin de Gaunt, 1273. A.
Thomas Boydin, ibid.
Nicholas Boydyn, ibid.
Ralph Boydin, ibid.
1565. Ralph Boydon, Ch. Ch. : Reg.
Univ. Oxf. vol. ii. pt. ii. p. 13.
1707. Married — James Hexter and
Martha Boyden : St. Geo. Han. Sq. ii. 171.
London, 5 ; New York, 4.

Boyer.—Occup. 'the bowyer'; v.
Bowyer. This form is found in the
Chester Play. Among other guilds
and companies that took part were
the 'Boyeres, Flechers, and Strin-
geres' (Ormerod's Cheshire, i. 300).
'Every boier make . . . two bowes
of elme,' 1514 : Fitzherb., Justyce
Peas (H.E.D.).

Geoffrey le Boyer. T.
Adam le Boiere. E.
William Boyer, co. Hunts, 1273. A.
1596. Bapt.—Alice, d. Thomas Boyer,
or Bowier : St. Jas. Clerkenwell, i. 31.
1608. — John, s. Edward Boyer : ibid.
i. 52.
1611. Thomas Boyer, or Bowyer, vicar
of Addingham : Whitaker's Craven,
p. 292.
1795. Married — Thomas Boyer and
Eliz. Carington : St. Geo. Han. Sq. ii. 134.
London, 4 ; Boston (U.S.), 11 ; Philadelphia, 152.

Boykett.—Local ; v. Boycott.

Boykin, Boykins.—Nick. 'the
boy-kin,' i. e. the little boy ; cf.
Wilkin, Perkin, Watkin, &c. With
the genitive Boykins, cf. Wilkins,
Perkins, Watkins, &c.

Philadelphia, 4, 1.

Boyland, Boylan.—Local, 'of
Boyland.' The place 'Boyland'
is mentioned in the Hundred Rolls,
co. Norf., vol. i. pp. 473, 476.

Richard de Boyland, co. Norf., 20 Edw.
I. R.
Thomas le Boylaund, co. Suff., ibid.
Robert de Boyland, co. Devon, 1273. A.
Ralph de Boylund, co. Norf., ibid.
1806. Married—Thomas Boyland and
Mary Wool : St. Geo. Han. Sq. ii. 247.
London, 1, 1 ; Philadelphia, 4, 17.

Braban, Brabant, Braben.
—Local, 'of Brabant,' natives of
the Duchy of Brabant. Andrew
Borde speaks of 'Flaunders, Han-
way, and Braban, which be com-

modious and plentiful contreys'
(Boke of Knowledge).

Mathew le (*sic*) Brabayn, co. Lanc.,
1332 : Lay Subsidy (Rylands), p. 111.
Gilkin de Braban, 25 Edw. I: Freemen
of York (Surtees Soc.), i. 6.
Heliseus de Brabayn, co. Linc., 1273. A.
John Braban, co. Suff., ibid.
Saher de Braban. E.
Arnald de Braban, 1307. M.
1582. Buried — Susan Brabane : St.
Dionis Backchurch, p. 197.
1742. — Robert Braben, ibid. p. 310.
1795. Married — Thomas Forty and
Sarah Brabant : St. Geo. Han. Sq. ii. 126.
London 0, 0, 1 ; Philadelphia, 0, 1, 0.

**Brabaner, Brabner, Bra-
biner.**—Local, 'the Brabaner,' i.e.
a native of the Duchy of Braban
or Brabant ; more generally 'le
Brabançon'; v. Brabazon.

Petrus Brabaner, 1379: P. T. Yorks.
p. 267.
Petrus Brabaynner, 1379: ibid. p. 222.
Johannes Brabaner, *textor*, 1379: ibid.
Adam Brabaner, 1379 : ibid. p. 239.

The name is still found in the
same county. William Brabiner is,
or was, landlord of the Three
Cranes, Doncaster (West Rid. Dir.,
1868).

Isabel Brabaner, temp. 1570. ZZ.
Robert Brabaner, ibid.
1558. Buried—Hellen, wife of Thomas
Brabynder : St. Thomas the Apostle
(London), p. 85.
London, 0, 1, 0 ; Boston (U.S.), 0, 0, 2.

Brabazon.—Local, 'le Brabançon,' a native of Braban, q.v.

Thomas Brabezon, co. York, 1273. A.
Walter Brabesun, co. Oxf., ibid.
Roger le Brabazoun, London, 20 Edw.
I. R.
William Brabazonn, co. Northampt.,
ibid.
Roger le Brabanzon, 1306. M.
Reginald le Brebanzon. H.
1601. Henry Brabazon, co. Warw. :
Reg. Univ. Oxf. vol. ii. pt. ii. p. 248.
1715. Married—Barnabas Brabazon and
Hester Knewstub: St. Michael, Cornhill,
p. 58.
London, 1 ; Crockford, 3 ; Philadel-
phia, 2.

Brace.—Local ; v. Brass.

Bracebridge. — Local, 'of
Bracebridge,' a parish in co. Linc.,
two or three miles from Lincoln.

Anketell de Bracebregg, co. Warw.,
1273. A.
John de Bracebrig', co. Linc., ibid.
Johannes de Bracebryg, 1379: P. T.
Yorks. p. 139.
1553. Thomas Brasbridge, Magd. Coll. :
Reg. Univ. Oxf. vol. ii. pt. ii. p. 6.

1754. Married—Jonathan Bracebridge and Ann Bell : St. Geo. Mayfair, p. 280. London, 3.

Bracegirdle, Bracegirdler. — Occup. 'the brace-girdler,' abbrev. to bracegirdle. It is somewhat hard to define this occupation. If it refers to 'braces,' they are an earlier institution than is generally imagined. If it be a corruption of 'breek-girdle' (Maundeville speaks of a 'breek-girdle' in his Travels, p. 50), then the difficulty is cleared up. In Memories of London (Riley) mention is made of one John le Bregerdelere, and this strengthens the latter supposition (v. Brailer). The breeches girdle would be a waistband. [In the Preston Guild Rolls, under date 1562, occurs 'William Harryson, brekemaker' (p. 29); and twenty years later 'John Sudell, breeckman' (p. 32). These may refer to brickmaking or bricklaying.]

Justinian Bracegirdle, temp. Eliz. 3.
Roger Brachegirdle, or Brachgirdle, or Brasgirdell, sup. for B.A., Dec. 3, 1556: Reg. Univ. Oxf. i. 233.
John Brachgyrdyll, or Brecchegirdle, 1544: ibid. p. 208.
Timothe Brasegirdell, 1620: St. Mary Aldermary, p. 14.
Roger Bracegirdle, of High Leigh, *yeoman*. 1649: Wills at Chester, ii. 30.
1751. John Jarman and Sarah Bracegirdle : St. Antholin (London), p. 155.
MDB. (co. Chester), 11, 0.

Bracer. — (1) Occup. 'the bracer,' i.e. the brewer. (2) Occup. 'possibly a maker of bracers,' the armguard in a suit of armour ; v. Bracer (H.E.D.). But (1) I think will be found correct ; v. Braceress.

Robert le Bracer, co. Hunts, 1273. A.
Jocius le Braciator, London, ibid.
Arnold Braciator, co. Camb., ibid.
Bartholomew le Bracer, C. R., 9 Edw. II.
Walter le Bracur, co. Camb., 1273. A.

Braceress. — Occup. 'the braceress,' i. e. the brewster ; cf. Bracer and Braceress with Brewer and Brewster.

Alicia Braciatrix, co. Oxf., 1273. A.
Clarice le Braceresse, co. Suff., ibid.
Letitia Braciatrix, co. Camb., ibid.
Emma le Braceresse. T.

Bracewell. — Local, 'of Bracewell,' a parish in co. York and dioc. Ripon.

John de Bracewell, co. Linc., 1273. A.
Willelmus de Braycewell, 1379 : P. T. Yorks. p. 138.
1610. George Brasswell and Margaret Milliter : Marriage Lic. (Westminster), p. 18.
1616. Robert Bracewell and Grace Toller : Marriage Lic. (London), ii. 43.
London, 1 ; West Riding Court Dir., 5.

Bracken, Brackin. — Local, 'of Bracken,' a township in the parish of Kilnwick, E. Rid. Yorks. This surname seems to have thrived in the United States.

1619. Henry Burbedge and Eliz. Bracken : Marriage Lic. (London), ii. 78.
1766. Married—Henry Bracken and Eliz. Hughes : St. Geo. Han. Sq. i. 154.
1782. — John Deakins and Rebecca Brackin : ibid. i. 339.
MDB. (W. Rid. Yorks), 2, 0 ; Philadelphia, 25, 5.

Brackenberry, Brackenbury, Brakenbury. — Local, ' of Brackenbury,' a parish in co. Lincoln, near Louth.

Jordan de Brakenberhe, co. Linc., Hen. III-Edw. I. K.
Robert de Bracumbergh, co. York, 20 Edw. I. R.
William de Brakenberch, co. Linc., 1273. A.
Johannes de Brakenbergh, 34 Edw. I : BBB. p. 715.
Robert de Brackenberewe, co. Linc. M.
1592. Richard Brackenbury : Reg. Univ. Oxf. i. 235.
London, 1, 1, 0 ; Crockford, 0, 4, 0 ; MDB. (co. Lincoln), 0, 20, 1.

Brackley, Brackly. — Local, 'of Brackley,' a parish in co. Northampton, twenty miles from Northampton.

Mikael de Brackele, London, 1273. A.
William de Brackely, London, ibid.
1619. Thomas Brackly : Reg. Univ. Oxf. i. 361.
1671. Married—Thomas Brackley and Sarah Turner : St. Mary Aldermary, p. 31.
1704. Robert Brackley and Eliz. Dryden : Marriage Lic. (Faculty Office), p. 246.
Boston (U.S.), 0, 1.

Braconer. — Official, 'the braconer,' a berner (v. Berner), one who held the hounds in leash (?). 'Braconier, the berner' (Halliwell). Perhaps connected with brach (Shakespeare), a hunting dog ; O.F. *brache* (Fr. *braque*), a hound.

Gilbert le Braconer, Close Roll, 28 Edw. I.
New York, 1.

Bradbeer. — Local, 'of Bradbeer,' i.e. the broad bere or byre ; v. Beer, and cf. Langabeer, the long bere. Of course a co. Devon surname.

1607. Buried — Thomas, s. Thomas Bradbere, or Bradbear : St. Jas. Clerkenwell, iv. 99.
1729. Married—Samuel Faulkner and Jane Bradbeer : St. Geo. Chap. Mayfair, p. 290.
London, 3 ; Exeter, 1.

Bradburne. — Local, 'of Bradborne,' a parish in co. Derby, five miles from Ashbourne.

1540. Richard Bradborne : Reg. Univ. Oxf. i. 285.
1573-4. John Cotton and Eliz. Bradborne : Marriage Lic. (Faculty Office), p. 16.
1662-3. Richard Morley and Anna Bradburn : ibid. p. 68.
Philadelphia, 1.

Bradbury, Bradberry. — Local, ' of Bredbury,' a township in the parish of Stockport. The name of the place is found spelt Bradbury frequently in old wills, &c. (v. instances under Brookshaw . The surname is almost universally Bradbury in the present day.

Jordan de Bredbury, co. Chester, 1270 : Earwaker's East Cheshire, ii. 40.
Adam de Bredbury, co. Chester, 1332 : ibid. p. 78.
John Bredbury, of Bredbury, 1672 : Wills at Chester (1545-1620), p. 38.
Alice Bredbury, of Moberley, 1679 : ibid.
1559-60. Henry Bradberye and Alice Lewley : Marriage Lic. (London), i. 20.
1562. Bapt.—Robert Bredbury : Prestbury Ch. (Cheshire), p. 6.
— Married—Richard Stockes and Ales Bradburye (Bredburye) : ibid. p. 7.
1664. Bapt. — Ernund, s. Edmund Bradbury : Disley Church.
MDB. (West Rid. Yorks), 25, 1 ; (co. Chester), 2, 0 ; Manchester, 24, 0 ; London, 16, 0 ; Philadelphia, 22, 2.

Bradby. — Local, ' of Bradby,' a township in the parish of Repton, co. Derby.

London, 1.

Bradden, Braddon, Braden. —Local, ' of Bradden,' a parish in co. Northampton, near Towcester.

William de Bradden, co. Northampt., 1298. M.
William de Bradene, co. Southampt., 1273. A.
1571. Edward Braddon and Ursula Stoker : Marriage Lic. (Faculty Office), p. 16.

1802. Married — William Mole and Anna Bradon : St. Geo. Han. Sq. ii. 265. London, 1, 3, 4 ; Philadelphia, 0, 1, 8.

Braddock, Briddock. — (1) Local, 'of the Bride-oak,' from residence thereby ; cf. Ash, Birch. &c. A Lanc.-Yorks. surname (v. Brideoake). Ralph Brideoake of Manchester (1613-78) became Bishop of Chichester. He was also known as Briddock, v. Dict. Nat. Biog. vi. 313. (2) Local, ' of Braddock,' a parish in Cornwall ; but I do not find any representatives.

1575. William Braddock, Corpus Christi Coll.: Reg. Univ. Oxf. i. 352.
1584. Thomas Braddock : ibid. iii. 84.
1695-6. William Hill and Frances Bradick : Marriage Lic. (London), ii, 318.
1751. Married—James Braddock and Mary Moss : St. Geo. Chap. Mayfair, i. 200.
Manchester, 3, 0 ; London, 6, 1 ; Philadelphia, 15, 0.

Bradfield.—Local, ' of Bradfield,' parishes in cos. Berks, Essex, Norfolk, and Suffolk, and smaller localities. ' At the broad field ' would naturally give birth to surnames in many parts of the country ; cf. Broadfield, Broadmeadow.

Cecile de Bradefeld, co. Suff., 1273. A.
Robert de Bradfeld, co. Suff., ibid.
Walter de Bradfeld, co. Suff., ibid.
William de Bradefel, co. Wilts, Hen. III-Edw. I. K.
Richard de Bradfelde, co. Soms., 1 Edw. III : Kirby's Quest, p. 275.
1750. Married — John Bradfield and Jane Carr : St. Geo. Chap. Mayfair, p. 159. London, 7 ; Philadelphia, 17.

Bradford.—Local, ' of Bradford,' parishes in W. Rid. Yorks, Wilts, Dorset, Soms., and Devon. Also two townships in co. Northumberland, and a township, now a suburb, of Manchester. The ' broad ford ' would naturally be familiar to many places.

Alexander de Bradeford,co. Northumb., 1107: KKK. vi. 62.
Hugh de Bradeford, co. Devon, 1273. A.
John de Bradeford, co. Wilts, ibid.
Alex. de Bradeford, co. Northumb., ibid.
Johanna Bradford, co. Soms., 1 Edw. III : Kirby's Quest, p. 225.
Johannes de Bradeford, 1379: P. T. Yorks. p. 193.
1788. Married — John Bradford and Susannah Wyberd : St. Geo. Han. Sq. ii. 7.
London, 25; Philadelphia, 44.

Bradlaugh.—Local, ' of Bradlaw.' I have not been able to identify the spot ; v. Broad and Law.

William de Bredlawe, co. Derby, 1273. A.
Robert de Bradlawe, co. Derby, ibid.
London, 1.

Bradley, Bradly, Bradlee.— Local, ' of Bradley.' Of course the local spots entitled the broad ley, i. e. broad meadow, would naturally be expected to be great. There are parishes, townships, tithings, hamlets, and chapelries of this name in cos. Berks, Ches., Devon, Leicester, Hants. Worc., Westm.. Suff., Stafford, Soms., Wilts, and W. Rid. Yorks; cf. Broadmeadow and Bradfield.

Robert de Bradeleye, co. Camb., 1273. A.
Brice de Bradeleghe, co. Soms., ibid.
William de Bradelegh, co. Devon, Hen. III-Edw. I. K.
Willelmus Brodelegh, 1379: P. T. Yorks. p. 12.
Agnes Brodelegh, 1379 : ibid.
Agnes de Bradelay, 1379: ibid. p. 200.
Richard de Bradleghe, co. Soms., 1 Edw. III : Kirby's Quest, p. 180.
Henry de Bradleye, co. Soms., 1 Edw. III : ibid. p. 203.
1749. Married—Noah Bradley and Jane Barnee : St. Geo. Chap. Mayfair, p. 139. London, 52, 6, 0 ; West Riding Court Dir., 17, 0, 0 ; Philadelphia, 332, 2, 1.

Bradnam, Bradnum, Bradman.—Local, ' of Bradenham,' a parish in the county of Norfolk ; cf. Barnum for Barnham. Bradman belongs to a somewhat large class of variants of local names ending in -enham ; cf. Deadman for Debenham, &c.

Richard de Bradenham, co. Norf., 1273. A.
Alan de Bradinham, co. Hunts, ibid.
William de Bradenham, co. Norf., 20 Edw. I. R.
Richard de Bradenham, co. Norf., 1337: FF. v. 67.
1739-40. Bapt.—Robert Bradnam : St. Dionis Backchurch, p 169.
London, 6, 0, 0 ; MDB. (Norfolk), 0, 1, 0 ; Boston (U.S.), 0, 0, 4.

Bradney.—Local, (1) ' of Bardney,' a parish in co. Lincoln, ten miles from Horncastle, sometimes called Bradney. (2) ' Of Bradney,' a place in co. Soms. belonging to

Sir Simon de Bredenie in 1346 (Lower).

Simon de Bradneghe, co. Soms., 1 Edw. III : Kirby's Quest, p. 240.
John Brodenyne, co. Soms., 1 Edw. III : ibid. p. 270.
Simon de Bardney, mayor of Bristol, 1276: YYY. p. 672.
(Abbas) de Bardeneye, co. Linc, 1273. A.
1670. Bapt.—Henrey, s. Paul Bradney : St Thomas the Apostle (London), p. 05.
London, 1 ; Philadelphia, 1.

Bradshaw. — (1) Local, ' of Bradshaw,' a village in the chapelry of Illingworth, near Halifax. Some of the Lancashire Bradshaws are sprung from Bradshaw Hall, near Wigan (v. Baines' Lanc. ii. pp. 184, 197), originally spelt Bradshaigh, but the majority from Bradshaw, an old chapelry in Bolton parish. Indeed, this last must be looked upon as the true home of four fifths of our Bradshaws.

Alan de Bradeshagh, of Radcliffe, co. Lanc., 1332 : Lay Subsidy (Rylands), p. 29.
Richard de Bradeschawe, co. Lanc., 20 Edw. I. R.
Johannes Bradeschawe, 1379 : P. T. Yorks. p. 299.
Alexander Bradshaw, of Bradshaw, parish of Bolton, 1587 : Wills at Chester, i. 26.
Richard Bradshaw, of Bolton, dyer, 1614 : ibid.
London, 23 ; West Riding Court Dir., 12 ; Manchester, 37 ; Bolton, 10 ; Philadelphia, 32.

Bradstock, Broadstock. — Local, ' of Bradenstoke.' a parish in dioc. of Salisbury. The abbreviation was an early one.

Simon de Bradestok, co. Oxf., 1273. A.
(Prior) de Bradenestock, co. Wilts, ibid.
(Prior) de Bradestok, co. Oxf., ibid.
1674. Bapt. — John, son of William Bradstock : St. Michael, Cornhill, p. 148. London, 1, 1.

Bradstreet. — Local, ' of the broad street,' i.e. the broad paved way. Evidently some spot in co. Norfolk or Suffolk.

1372. John de Bradstrete, rector of Colby, co. Norf. : FF. vi 423.
1595-6. Thomas Boldero and Ann Broadstreet : Marriage Lic. (London, i. 228.
1625. Edmund Slater and Margaret Bredstreete : ibid. ii. 153.

With this latter instance cf. Bredbury for Bradbury, q v.

1730. Married—Jonathan Bradstreet,of Ipswich, and Mary Moulton : St. Michael, Cornhill, p. 65.

1764. — Robert Garstin and Anna Eliz. Bradstreet : St. Geo. Han. Sq. i. 136. London, 1 ; Crockford, 1 ; MDB. (co. Suffolk), 2 ; Philadelphia, 8.

Bradwell.—Local, 'of Bradwell,' parishes in cos. Bucks, Suffolk, and Essex. Also townships in cos. Chester and Derby.

Richard Bradewelle, co. Soms., 1 Edw. III : Kirby's Quest, p. 272.
Hamond de Bradewell,co.Oxf.,1273. A.
Roger de Bradewelle, co. Suff., ibid.
Agnes de Braythewell, 1379: P. T. Yorks. p. 178.
Willelmus de Braythewell, 1379 : ibid. p. 17.
1593. Sampson Leycrofte and Ann Bradwell : Marriage Lic. (London), i. 211.
West Rid. Court Dir., 3 ; London, 2 ; Philadelphia, 1.

Brady.—Local, 'of the broad hey,' from residence thereby, i. e. the broad enclosure ; v. Hey. The great number of Bradys in the American directories are mostly of Irish origin.

Johannes Bradhee, 1379 : P. T. Yorks. p. 262.
1587. George Bradie and Frances Gente : Marriage Lic. (London), i. 158.
1612. Married — John Brewer and Marie (?)Bradye : St. Thomas the Apostle (London), p. 11.
1729. — James Brady and Sarah Lowing : St. Geo. Chap. Mayfair, p. 201.
West Riding Court Dir., 4 ; Sheffield, 2 ; London, 9 ; Philadelphia, 270.

Bragg, Bragger, Brager.—Nick. 'a braggart,' a boaster. 'Braggere' (Piers Plowman) ; ' Brisk, full of spirit ' (Halliwell) ; 1300, ' That maketh us so brag and bold ' (H.E.D.).

Henry Brag, co. Camb., 1273. A.
1573. Edward Bragge, of London : Reg. Univ. Oxf. vol. ii. pt. ii. p. 55.
1601. Edmund Bragge, of London : ibid. p. 252.
1795. Married—John Bragg and Mary Terry : St. Geo. Han. Sq. ii. 131.
1809. — Edward Jones and Mary Bragger : ibid. ii. 401.
London, 9, 3, 0 ; Philadelphia, 7, 0, 2.

Braham.—(1) Local, 'of Braham.' As in the case of Braim (q.v.) I cannot find the place. (2) Bapt. ' the son of Abraham.' Some Jewish Abrahams have adopted Braham.

Alan de Braham, co. Suff., 1273. A.
Richard de Braham, co. Suff., ibid.

Roger de Braham, co. Suff, ibid.
Ralph de Braham, co. Bedf., 20 Edw. I. R.
1805. Married—John Gray and Hannah Braham : St. Geo. Han. Sq. ii. 335.
London, 8 ; Philadelphia, 6.

Brailer.—Occup. ' the braeler,' a maker of cinctures or girdles, from the Old English *brayle*, from French *braie* or *braye*, i.e. breeches, whence *braiel*, a band to fasten breeches. Sailors still speak of ' brailing up sails.' Under date 1355 Mr. Riley, in his Memorials of London, gives the ' Articles and Ordinances of the Braelers.' He also has an account of the burning of some gloves and *braels* for being false in make and fashion (pp. 277 and 249).

Roger le Braeler, London, 1273. A.
Stephen le Brayeler, London. X.

Brailsford.—Local, ' of Brailsford,' a parish in co. Derby and dioc. Lichfield.

Robert de Brailisford,co. Derby,1273. A.
Henry de Braylesford, 1301, co. Derby. M.
1666. Theophilus Brailsford and Mary Oliver : Marriage Alleg. (Westminster), p. 116.
1678. Thomas Byfeld and Ann Braylesford : ibid. p. 285.
London, 3.

Braim, Braime, Braham.—Local, ' of Brame,' a local spot that I cannot discover. Braham looks like an early mutilation of Abraham, but the instances below evidently belong to a common stock ; v. Braham.

Agnes de Brame, 1379 : P. T. Yorks. p. 301.
Johannes de Brame, 1379 : ibid. p. 298.
Willelmus Brame, *barker*, 1379 : ibid. p. 259.
Nicholaus Braham, 1379 : ibid. p. 250.
1751. Married—Peter Paillon and Mary Braem : St. Geo. Chap. Mayfair, p. 201.
West Riding Court Dir., 3, 1, 1 ; Leeds, 2, 1, 0.

Brain, Braine, Brayne.—? Bapt. Possibly a form of Brand, but this is a mere guess.

Alicia Brayn, co. Camb., 1273. A.
Helena Brayn, co. Hunts ibid.
John Brayn, co. Camb., ibid.
1580. Thomas Braine and Hellen Maskall : Marriage Lic. (London), i. 96.
1751. Married — Richard Brain and Catherine Martin : St. Geo. Chap. Mayfair, p. 201.
London, 5, 5, 2 ; New York, 0, 2, 0.

Braithwaite, Braithwaite, Brathwait, Brathwaite, Breathwaite.—Local, ' of Braithwaite.' (1) A hamlet in township of Dacre, near Pateley Bridge, co. York ; (2) a hamlet in parish of Keighley, co. York ; (3) a hamlet in parish of Kirk Bramwith, near Doncaster.

Alan de Braithethwait, *hoser*, 20 Edw. II : Freemen of York, i. 23.
Geoffrey de Braytweyt, co. York, 1273. A.
Alicia Brathwayt, 1379 : P. T. Yorks. p. 243.
Willelmus de Brathwat, 1379 : ibid. p. 237.
Willelmus de Brathwayt, 1379 : ibid. p. 234.
1744. Married—Mr. Benjamin Brathwait and Mrs. Emery Coles : St. Geo. Chap. Mayfair, p. 86.
1750 — William Braithwaite and Mary Crowthers : ibid. p. 186.
London, 11, 0, 0, 0, 0 ; Boston (U.S.), 0, 0, 1, 1, 0 ; West Riding Court Dir., 12, 1, 0, 0, 0 ; Philadelphia, 0, 6, 0, 0, 3.

Bramhall, Bramall, Brammall, Brammald, Broomhall, Broomall.—Local, ' of Bramhall,' formerly also Bromale. a township in the parish of Stockport. The variants are of a natural character. The *d* in Brammald is, of course, excrescent ; cf. Simmonds for Simmons, Bryant for Bryan. The form Broomhall is a reminiscence of Bromale, as already stated, an early spelling.

Mathew de Bromale, co Ches., temp. 1150 : Earwaker's East Cheshire, ii. 9.
Ann Bickerton, of Bromall, *widow*, 1616 : Wills at Chester (1545-1620), p. 10.
Hugh Bramhall, of Hatherton, 1595 : ibid. p. 27.
Hugh Bramall, of Nether Peover, co. Ches., 1628 : ibid. (1621-50), p. 31.
Margaret Broomhall, of Little Peover, co. Ches., 1633 : ibid. p. 35.
Richard Bromall, of Birch, 1639 : ibid. p. 35.
Philip Brommall, of Knutsford, co. Ches., 1632 : Earwaker's East Ches., ii. 343.

Thus every one of the variants in our modern directories is easily accounted for.

MDB. (West Rid. Yorks.), 2, 5, 1, 2, 0, 0 ; Manchester, 1, 4, 1, 0, 4, 0 ; Philadelphia, 4, 0, 0, 0, 1, 12.

Bramley.—Local, 'of Bramley,' a chapelry and village near Leeds.

Nigel de Bramleye, co. York, 1273. A.
Willelmus de Bramley, 1379: P. T.
Yorks. p. 246.
1754. Married—Thomas Hancock and
Elizabeth Bramley : St. Geo. Chap. May-
fair, p. 280.
West Riding Court Dir., 11; New
York, 1.

Brampton.—Local, 'of Brampton,' parishes, townships, &c., in
cos. Cumb., Norf., Derby, Linc.,
Hunts, Northampton, and Suff.

Geoffrey de Bampton, co. Hunts,
1273. A.
Brian de Brampton, co. Glouc., ibid.
Alan de Bramtone, co. Camb., ibid.
William de Brampton, co. Oxf., ibid.
Adam de Brampton, co. Linc., 20 Edw.
I. R.
John de Brampton, co. Heref., Hen.
III-Edw. I. K.
William de Brampton, co. Norf., Hen.
III-Edw. I. K.
1591. Thomas Brampton and Johanna
Kynge : Marriage Lic. (London), i. 192.
London, 2 ; Philadelphia, 5.

Branch.—Local, ' of Branch,'
a hundred in co. Wilts.

Thomas Braunche, C. R., 3 Edw. I.
Benjamin Branche, co. Suff., 1273. A.
Joanna Branche, co. Soms., ibid.
Joanna de Braunche, co. Soms., ibid.
1720. Married—John Prince and Mary
Branch : St. Geo. Chap. Mayfair, p. 287.
London, 12; MDB. (co. Soms.), 2 ;
New York, 5.

Brand, Brandt.—Bapt. ' the
son of Brand' : said to be still in
use in Iceland as a fontal name.
In England it had gone out of use
before the 13th century began.

William Brand, or Brant, co. Linc.,
1273. A.
Walter Brand, or Brant, co. Linc.,
ibid.
John Brand, co. Oxf., 1273. A.
Robert Brand, co. Oxf., ibid.
Wymer Brant, co. Norf., ibid.
1796. Married—John Brand and Eliza-
beth Clubb : St. Geo. Han. Sq. ii. 157.
1802. — Thomas Brant and Abigail
Bone : ibid. ii. 257.
London, 25, 9 ; Philadelphia, 20, 51.

Brandon.—Local,' of Brandon,'
parishes in co. Norfolk; also townships in cos. Durham and Northumberland ; also a hamlet in co.
Warwick, in the parish of
Woltston.

Magota de Brandon, chapman, 1379 :
P. T. Yorks. p. 11.
1632-3. Richard Barnes and Susan Brandon : Marriage Lic. (Faculty Office),
p. 25.

1634. Married — Edward Smith and
Alice Brandon : St. Thomas the Apostle
(London), p. 15.
1791. — William Brandon and Mar-
garet Elliott : St. Geo. Han. Sq. ii. 57.
London, 12 ; New York, 16.

**Brandwin, Brangwin,
Brangwyn.**—Bapt. ' the son of
Brandwin' ; cf. Unwin, Baldwin,
Godwin, &c. ; v. Brand. Miss
Yonge says, ' Brengwain, f. Eng.-
Kelt. white bosom' : Glossary,
p. xxxvii.

Alicia Brandewyne, 1348 : Pat. Roll,
22 Edw. III.
1672. Buried — John Brangwin : St.
Dionis Backchurch, p. 239.
London, 0, 1, 1.

Branson.—(1) Bapt. ' the son
of Brand,' q.v. (2) Local, 'of
Branson,' a township in the parish
of Burton-on-Trent, co. Stafford.

Agnes Branson, 1379 : P. T. Yorks.
p. 149.
1623. Buried — John Bransoun : St.
Antholin (London), p. 57.
1708. Bapt.—Ann, d. William Brand-
son : St. Jas. Clerkenwell, ii. 42.
London, 4 ; West Rid. Court Dir.,
5 ; Philadelphia, 44.

Branston.—(1) Local, ' of Branston,' a parish in dioc. Lincoln ;
(2) 'of Branstone,' parishes in
diocs. Lichfield and Peterborough ;
(3) ' of Braunston,' a parish in dioc.
Peterborough ; (4) ' of Branxton,'
a parish in dioc. Durham.

Richard de Brandeston, co. Norf.,
1273. A.
William de Brancston, co. Northumb.,
ibid.
Hugh de Braundeston, 1282. M.
John de Brandeston, 1301. M.
1731. Married — John Branstone and
Christian May : St. Geo. Chap. Mayfair,
p. 323.
1800. — Henry Branston and Harriet
Minto : St. Geo. Han. Sq. ii. 229.
London, 3 ; Philadelphia, 6.

Brant.—Bapt. 'the son of Brand,'
or ' Brandt,' q.v. ; cf. Blund and
Blunt.

Wymer Brant, co. Norf., 1273. A.
Walter Brant, co. Linc., ibid.
1615. John Brant and Mary Marsh :
Marriage Lic. (London), ii. 33.
1750. Married—Richard Munday and
Hannah Brant : St. Antholin (London),
p. 155.
London, 4 ; Philadelphia, 16.

Branthwaite, Branwhite.—
Local, ' of Brunthwaite,' a hamlet
in the parish of Kildwick, near

Skipton, 'co. Yorks. With the
corrupted Branwhite, cf. Applewhite for Applethwaite, or Hebblewhite for Hebblethwaite.

Robert Brownthwayt, 1379 : P. T.
Yorks. p. 251.
Thomas de Braintwayt, 1379 : ibid. p. 289.
Johannes Brarntwayt, 1379 : ibid.
1418. Anora Braunthwayt : Cal. of
Wills in Court of Husting (2).
1594. William Branthwaitt : Reg. Univ.
Oxf. i. 354.
1764. Bapt.—Mary, d. Bloss Branwhite :
St. Peter, Cornhill, ii. 49.
London, 0 1 : MDB. (co. Westm.), 1,
0; Boston (U.S.), 0, 1.

Branton.—Local, ' of Branton.'
Branton, or Brampton, is a hamlet
in the parish of Cantley, West Rid.
Yorks ; v. Brampton.

Johannes Branton, 1379 : P. T. Yorks.
p. 26.
1665. Edward Husbands and Mary
Branton ; Marriage Lic. (Faculty Office),
p. 89.
London, 3 ; West Riding Court Dir.,
1 ; Philadelphia, 3.

Branwhite.—Local ; a corruption of Branthwaite, q.v.

Brasdefer.—Nick. ' iron-arm,'
or ' arm of iron,' a sobriquet for one
of great physical strength ; v. Firebrace.

Walter Brasdefer. E.
Simon Brazdefer. E.
Michael Brasdefer. BB.

Cf. Armstrong and Strongitharm.
The name seems obsolete in
England, but Pedefer has a strong
position ; v. Pettifer.

Brashier, Brassier ; v.
Braxier.

Brass, Brace.—(1) Local ; probably a form of Braose, for which
v. Bruce. (2) Local, ' of Brace,' a
parish in dioc. Hereford, co. Salop.

Nicholas de Bras, co. Bucks, 20 Edw.
I. R.
Walter Bras, co. Salop, 1273. A.
Thomas Braz, co. Soms., 1 Edw. III :
Kirby's Quest, p. 218.
Willelmus Brasse, husband, 1379 :
P. T. Howdenshire, p. 29.
Juliana Bras, vidua, 1379 : P.T. Yorks.
p. 41.
Johan Brase, 1379 : ibid. p. 43.
1581. Thomas Brase, co. Worc. : Reg.
Univ. Oxf. vol. ii. pt. ii. p. 110.
1594. John Brace, co. Worc. : ibid.
p. 205.
1607. Bapt. — Ann, d. of Antony Brass :
St. Jas. Clerkenwell, i. 372.
London, 3, 11 ; Philadelphia, 5, 4.

Brassey, Bracey, Bracy.—Local, ' of Bréci,' ! in Normandy ; cf. Vessey, undoubtedly for Vesci, a Norman local name.

Alice de Bresci, co. Camb., 1273. A.
Elias de Braci, co. Oxf., ibid.
Richard de Braci, co. Oxf., ibid.
Gilbert de Bracy, co. Bucks, ibid.
Thomas Bracve, son of Edmond Bracy, 1567: Reg. St. Dionis Backchurch, p. 80.
Edmond Bracye, son of Edmond Bracy, 1569: ibid.
Thomas Brassye, son of Edmond Brassye, 1575 : ibid. p. 82.
Izack Brassye, son of Edmond Brassye, 1578 : ibid. p. 83.
1553-4. Thomas Brassye and Anne Ober : Marriage Lic. (London), i. 14.
London, 1, 4, 0 ; Philadelphia, 0, 2, 5.

Bratton.—Local, ' of Bratton,' a chapelry in the parish of Westbury, co. Wilts.

John de Bratton, co. Soms., 1 Edw. III: Kirby's Quest, p. 248.
Emma de Bratton, co. Soms., 1 Edw. III : ibid.
Godfrey de Bratton, co. Wilts, 1273. A.
1794. Married—William Richards and Mary Bratton : St. Geo. Han. Sq. ii. 110.
London, 1 ; Philadelphia, 14.

Braun, Braund.—(1) Bapt. ' the son of Brand,' q.v. (2) Bapt. ' the son of Bryan,' q.v. With the excrescent *d*, cf. the excrescent *t* in Bryant.

1660-1. Richard Brawne and Mary Streate : Marriage Lic. (Faculty Office), p . 50.
1711. Champion Branfil and Mary Braund : ibid. p. 247.
London, 5, 6 ; Philadelphia, 15, 0.

Bray.—Local, ' of Bray,' parishes in cos. Berks and Devon.

Thomas de Bray, co. Bucks, 1273. A.
Aunsell de Bray, co. Camb., ibid.
Henry de Bray, co. Devon, ibid.
Gundreda de Bray, co. Devon, ibid.
1579. Silvester Braye, co. Oxf. : Reg. Univ. Oxf. vol. ii. pt. ii. p. 90.
1601. Oliver Braye, co. Oxf. : ibid. p. 253.
1791. Married — Thomas Bray and Elizabeth Southall : St. Geo. Han. Sq. ii. 67.
London, 28 ; Philadelphia, 22.

Braybrook.—Local, ' of Braybrooke,' a parish in co. Northampton, near Market Harborough.

Henry de Braybroc, co. Linc., 1273. A.
John de Braybrock, co. Bucks, ibid.
Robert de Braybrok, co. Bucks, ibid.
1626. John Carr and Eliz. Braybrooke : Marriage Lic. (London), ii. 172.
London, 2.

Brayer.—Occup. ' the brayer,' one who brays or pounds in a mortar.

Godfrey le Brayer, co. Oxf., 1273. A.
William le Brayer, co. Oxf., ibid.
New York, 1.

Brayshaw, Brashaw.—Local, ' of Bradshaw,' q.v.

MDB. (West Rid. Yorks.), 11, 2 ; Philadelphia, 2, 0.

Brazier, Brashier, Brasier, Brazer, Brasher.—Occup. ' the brazier,' a worker in brass. ' Brasyere, *erarius* ': Prompt. Parv. ' Pavyers, bell-makers, and brasyers ': Cocke Lorelle's Bote.

1617. Married—Peter Clarke, *brasier*, and Eliz. Cizeley : St. Michael, Cornhill, p. 21.
Reginald de Brazur, Fines Roll, 11 Edw. I.
Henry le Brazur, co. Hunts, 1273. A.
Richard le Brazur, co. Salop, ibid.
William le Brasour. N.
Robert le Brazur. G.
Thomas Brasyer, C. R., 33 Hen. VI.
1533-4. Thomas Semer and Elene Brasyer : Marriage Lic. (London), i. 9.
1574-5. Thomas Brazier, co. Salop : Reg. Univ. Oxf. vol. ii. pt. ii. p. 61.
1730. Married — William Adkins and Sarah Brasier : St. Dionis Backchurch, p. 64.
London, 7, 3, 4, 0, 0 ; Philadelphia, 4, 0, 0, 6, 0 ; New York, 3, 0, 3, 0, 3.

Breach.—Local,'of the breach,' i.e. the break in the land.

John de la Breche, co. Wilts, 1273. A.
Isaak de la Breche, co. Oxf., ibid.
Isota atte Brech, co. Soms., 1 Edw. III : Kirby's Quest, p. 137.
1802. Married — William Breach and Lucy Merritt : St. Geo. Han. Sq. ii. 259.
London, 4 ; Boston (U.S.), 3.

Breadmongster.—Occup. ' the breadmongster,' a curious feminine of breadmonger.

Sara la Bredemongstere. X.

Sara lived in London.

Breakbalk.—Nick. ; one who could win at the balk-staff, or quarter-staff ; one who could shiver his opponent's lance ; cf. Breakspear, v. Balk, *sb.* 14 (H.E.D.).

Adam Brekebalk, 1379 : P. T. Yorks. p. 298.

Breakspear, Breakspeare, Brakspear. — Nick. One of a large list of sobriquets that have become hereditary from the badge of office, or ensign of authority, or weapon carried (v. Shakespear). Like ' Bruselance ' and ' Crack-

shield,' Breakspear would be cheerfully accepted as a nickname by the successful candidate in the tournament.

Adrian Brakspere. HH.
Alexander Brakspere. MM.
William Brakespere, C. R., 3 Hen. IV. pt. ii.
Jane Breakspeare, 1653 : St. Dionis Backchurch (London), p. 29.
1665. Buried — Patience Breakspeare : St. Thomas the Apostle (London), p. 138.
Topsham (co. Devon), 0, 0, 1 ; MDB. (co. Oxford), 1, 1, 1 ; Oxford (city), 2, 0, 0.

Brear, Brears.—Local, ' at the brere,' i.e. briar-bush. M.E. *brere* :

' — sharp as brere.'
Chaucer, C. T. 9699.

Cf. Brearley and Brereton. Brear is a well-known Yorks. surname.

John in le Breres, co. Hunts, 1273. A.
Willelmus del Breres, 1379 : P. T. Yorks. p. 58.
Ricardus Brere, 1379 : ibid. p. 258.
Robertus Brere, 1379 : ibid. p. 241.
1759. Married — Robert Sharp and Sarah Brears : St. Geo. Han. Sq. i. 85.
1780. — John Betteley and Eliz. Brear : ibid. 314.
West Riding Court Dir. 7, 0 ; MDB. (co. Lincoln), 0, 2 ; (West Riding Yorks), 0, 4 ; Philadelphia, 1, 0.

Brearley, Brierley, Brierly. —Local, ' of Briarley,' a township in the parish of Felkirk, co. York.

Johannes de Brerelay, *clerk*, 13 Ric. II : Freemen of York, i. 89.
Adam de Brerelay, *wever*, 13 Ric. II : ibid. p. 105.
1752. Married—John Crother and Mary Brearley : St. Geo. Chap. Mayfair, p. 234.
London, 0, 4, 2 ; Boston (U.S.), 1, 0, 0.

Breathwaite ; v. Braithwaite.

Breedon, Breeden, Briddon, Bridden.—(1) Local, ' of Bredon,' a parish in co. Worcester, near Tewkesbury ; (2) ' of Breedon,' a parish in co. Leicester, near Ashby-de-la-Zouch.

Ralph de Bredon, co. Leic., Hen. III-Edw. I. K.
William de Bredun, co. Derby, 1273. A.
Johannes de Bredun, 1379 : P. T. Yorks. p. 28.
1603-4. Zacchaeus Breedon, co. Bucks : Reg. Univ. Oxf. vol. ii. pt. ii. p. 270.
1709. Married — Luke Breedon and Margaret Binyon : St. Jas. Clerkenwell, iii. 231.
West Riding Court Dir., 1, 1, 3, 0 ; Sheffield, 0, 0, 3, 0 ; Boston (U.S.), 0, 4, 0, 0 ; New York (Briddon), 1 ; Philadelphia (Bridden), 1.

Breese, Breeze.—Bapt. ' the son of Rees,' Welsh Ab-Rees ; cf.

Bethell, Bloyd, Benyon, Bowen, &c. Breeze is an imitative form, and is a familiar surname on the South Welsh border. Of course, Breese and Breeze are but variants of Preese or Price; v. Brice.

Robert Breese, of Poulton, co. Chester, *yeoman*, 1666 : Wills at Chester (1660-80), p. 38.
Richard Breese, of the city of Chester, 1670 : ibid.
1621. David Breese, of London (Jesus Coll.): Reg. Univ. Oxf. vol. ii. pt. ii. p. 396.
1729. Married — William Green and Eliz. Breese: St. Geo. Chap. Mayfair, p. 296.
London, 2, 2; Shrewsbury, o, 6; Boston (U.S.), 2, o; New York, 8, 2.

Brench.—A variant of Branch, q. v.

John Brench, co. Soms., 1 Edw. III : Kirby's Quest, p. 212.
Ralph Brench, co. Hunts, 1273. A. London, 1.

Brenchley.—Local, 'of Brench-ley,' a parish in co. Kent, near Lamberhurst.

1788. Married—Thomas Brenchley and Sarah Meates : St. Geo. Han. Sq. ii. 2.
London, 7 , MDB (co. Kent), 7.

Brend.—Local, 'at the brend.' ' *Brent*, steep. North' (Halliwell). A probable *subs.* 'a steep,' a de-clivitous hill; cf. Brand and Brant.

Symon del Brend, *mariner*, 12 Edw. II : Freemen of York, i. 18.
Willelmus del Brend, 1379 : P. T. Yorks. p. 51.
1571-2. Richard Osborne and Martha Brende : Marriage Lic. (London), i. 51.
London, 2.

Brennan, Brennand, Bur-nand, Brennard.—Bapt. ' the son of Brennand.' Brennard is a corruption, v. Brenhaud, infra.

Simon Brenhand, co. Camb., 1273. A.
Cecil Brenhaud, co. Notts, ibid.
Johannes Brynnehand, 1379 : P. T. Yorks. p. 200.
Robertus Brennand, 1379 : ibid. p. 245.
Adam Brennand, 1379 : ibid. p. 248.
1806. Married—Francis Brennan and Elizabeth Bartlett: St. Geo. Han. Sq. ii. 346.
London, 6, 3, 9, o; West Riding Court Dir., o, o, 2, 1; Philadelphia, 140, o, o, o.

Brenning.—Bapt. 'the son of Brenning,' seemingly a variant of Browning. The two following

entries occur together, with one other entry only intervening :

William Brennyng, co. Soms., 1 Edw. III : Kirby's Quest, p. 234.
William Brounyng, co. Soms., 1 Edw. III : ibid.
London, 1.

Brent. — Local, ' of Brent,' parishes in co. Somerset, Devon, and Suffolk.

Fulco de Brent, temp. Hen. III : FF. ii. 243.
Thomas de Brente, co. Camb., 1273. A.
Robert de Brente, co. Soms., ibid.
Faulkus de Brente, co. Essex, ibid.
Robert de Brente, co. Soms., 1 Edw. III : Kirby's Quest, p. 119.
1610. Bapt.—Susan, d. Richard Brente: St. Mary Aldermary, p. 71.
1637. Thomas Brent and Eleanor Strood : Marriage Lic. (London), i. 234.
1672. Benjamin Taynton and Judith Drent : Marriage Alleg. (Canterbury), p. 200.
London, 7; New York, 2.

Brentford.—Local, 'of Brent-ford,' a market-town in co. Middle-sex, of which it is the county town.

Philadelphia, 1.

Brereton. — Local, (1) ' of Brearton,' a village in the parish of Knaresborough, co. York; (2) ' of Brereton,' a village three miles from Sandbach, co. Chester.

William de Brerton, *carpenter*, 6 Edw. II : Freemen of York, i. 15.
Adam de Brereton, 1379 : P. T. Yorks. p. 254.
Robertus de Brereton, 1379 : ibid. p. 227.
Thomas de Brereton, 1379 : ibid p. 300.
William Brereton, of Brereton, co. Ches., 1601 : Wills at Chester, i. 28.
Amy Brereton, of Ches., 1616 : ibid.
1585. John Brereton and Margaret Kempton : Marriage Lic. (London), i. 141.
1696. Bapt. — Eliz., d. Thomas Briar-ton : St. Jas. Clerkenwell, i. 366.
London, 4; Manchester, 4; New York, 4.

Bretherton.—Local, ' of Bre-therton,' a township in the parish of Croston, co. Lancashire.

Henry de Brethirton, 1397 : Preston Guild Rolls, p. 5.
Ric. de Brethirton, 1397 : ibid. p. 6.
Thomas de Brethirton, 1415 : ibid. p. 7.
Henry Bretherton, of Croston, co. Lanc., 1612 : Wills at Chester, i. 28.
Thomas Bretherton, of Mawdesley, co. Lanc., 1610 : ibid.
1778. Married—Joseph Spooner War-ren and Amelia Bretherton : St. Geo. Han. Sq. i. 295.
London, 1 ; Manchester, 1 ; Preston, 2 ; Chorley, 1 ; New York, 1.

Brett.—Local, 'le Brit,' a native of Brittany.

Jordan le Bret, co. Northamp., Hen. III-Edw. I. K.
Eva la Brette, co. Essex, ibid.
Adam le Brett, co. Norf., temp. Edw. III : FF. ix. 234.
Ricardus le Bret, co. Hunts, 1273. A.
William le Bret, co. Soms., ibid.
Wydo le Brit, co. Devon, ibid.
Nicholas le Brett, co. Kent, ibid.
1559-60. William Brett and Johanna Hayward : Marriage Lic. (London), i. 20.
1624. Bapt.—Martha, d. George Brett : St. Jas. Clerkenwell, i. 100.
1773. Married—Abell Brett and Ann Wetton : St. Geo. Han. Sq. i. 230.
London, 36 ; Philadelphia, 14.

Breviter, Brevitor, Bretter, Brevetor.—Official, 'the breve-tour,' a private clerk, a writer of brevets for his lord ; probably ana-logous to a private secretary ; from *brevet*, dim. of brief, a letter. Still more probably one whose duty it was to note down household ex-penses, a clerk to the steward.

'At counting stuard schalle ben,
Tyll alle be *brevet* of wax so grene.
        Boke of Curtasye.
'The clerke of the kitchen shalle alle
  thynges breve.' Ibid.
'Breuetowre, *brevigerulus*': Prompt. Parv.
Peter le Brevetour, 1302. M.
Ely le Breveter. O.
Richard Brevyter. Z.

The name has never died out, although it has ever been rare. It is found in 1580 as Breviter in a Cambridge list (v. Hist. C.C.C. Camb., index). Bretter is a mani-fest corruption, and is found so spelled in the Calendar to Plead-ings (Elizabeth). Still exists : Mr. Brevitor (Standard, March 25, 1886, p. 3, col. 7).

New York, o, o, o, 1.

Brewer.—Occup. ' the brewer,' (v. Brewster). Only one or two instances occur in the Hundred Rolls.

John le Brewer, co. Soms., 1 Edw. III : Kirby's Quest, p. 231.
William le Brewere, London, 1273. A.
William le Brywer, co. Devon, ibid.
1588-9. Anthony Bruer, co. Wilts : Reg. Univ. Oxf. vol. ii. pt. ii. p. 169.
1750. Married—Charles Brewer and Pennie Mattichamp : St. Geo. Chap. Mayfair, p. 180.
London, 38 ; Philadelphia, 37.

K 2

Brewery. — Local, 'at the brewery'; v. Brewhouse.

Reynfrey de la Bruere, co. Camb., 1273. A.
Thomas de la Bruere, co. Camb., ibid.
Robert de la Bruere, co. Oxf., ibid.
Walter de la Bruario, temp. 1300. M.

Brewhouse, Brewis, Browse. —Local, 'of the brewhouse.' Mr. Lower says, 'a common corruption of Braose,' now Brieuse, in Normandy. Why not brewhouse?

Walter fil. Hugh del Breuhous, 31 Edw. I: Freemen of York, i. 9.
Hugo del Brewhouse, 1379: P. T. Yorks. p. 202.
John de Brewouse, C. R., 3 Edw. III.
1703. Married—Henry Wyley and Ann Brewhouse: St. Peter, Cornhill, ii. 64.
1739. Bapt.—Sarah, d. of Stephen Brewhouse: St. Jas. Clerkenwell, i. 245.
1760. Married—Gaetano Cozi and Ann Bruhus: St. Geo. Han. Sq. i. 94.
London, 0, 1, 2.

Brewin. — Bapt. 'the son of Brun'; v. Brown and Brune.

1595. Married—Roger Brewen and Susanna Harris: St. Michael, Cornhill, p. 15.
1609. Bapt.—Dorothee, d. Thomas Bruin: ibid. p. 108.
London, 1; Philadelphia, 2; Boston (U.S.), 1.

Brewster.—Occup. 'the brewster,' with the feminine suffix because it was probably a woman's business at first; cf. *maltster*, *spinster*, and Baxter.

Alicia de Wetmong, *breuster*, 6 Edw. II: Freemen of York, i. 14.
Matilda Clerk, *braciatrix*, 1379: P. T. Yorks. p. 300.
Thomas Breustar, 1379: ibid. p. 27.
Isabella Brewester, 1379: ibid. p. 5.
Emma la Brenstere, co. Bucks, 1273. A.
1587. Robert Brewster, co. Northampt.: Reg. Univ. Oxf. vol. ii. pt. ii. p. 161.
1749. Married—John Brewster and Rebecca Wild: St. Geo. Chap. Mayfair, p. 135.
London, 8; Philadelphia, 26.

Brian, Briant. — Bapt.; v. Bryan.

Brice, Bricot, Bryce, Bryson (?).—(1) Bapt. 'the son of Brice,' dim. Bricot. (2) Bapt. 'the son of Rice' (Welsh). from Ap or Ab-Rice; cf. Breeze for Ab-Rees, Bloyd for Ab-Lloyd, &c.; v. Breese and Price. Although, no doubt, (2) has some share in the parentage of Brice, (1) is the true source. A few instances will be sufficient evidence.

Brice fil. William, co. Linc., 1273. A.
Brice de Bradelegh, co. Soms., ibid.
John Brice, co. Camb., ibid.
Bricius de Penred, co. Cumb., Hen. III-Edw. I. K.
John Brice, co. Soms., 1 Edw. III: Kirby's Quest, p. 153.
Bricius le Daneys, co. Rutland. R.
Bricot de Brainton. MM.

As a font-name I find no trace of Brice after the Reformation, nor indeed for several generations before, but it must have been fairly popular in the hereditary surname period, judging by the strong establishment of the surname in our present directories. Bryson (possibly Brideson, now Bridson) is early met with in Henry fil. Brice (V. 8), and Barnabe Brisson (V. 4).

1753. Married—Stephen Brice and Jemima Pennell: St. Geo. Chap. Mayfair, p. 248.
1790. — Alex. Bryson and Hannah Reed: St. Geo. Han. Sq. ii. 52.
London, 10, 0, 3, 4; Philadelphia, 27, 0, 0, 27.

Brickdale.—Local, 'of the Brigdale (?),' i.e. the bridge-valley (?); cf. Philbrick for Felbridge. The suffix *-brig* often becomes *brick*; cf. Maybrick, Warbrick, &c. The simple derivation is 'the bridge that led into the dale'; v. Bridge or Brigg, and Dale.

1551. Married—John Brigdale and Joane Rokennan: St. Antholin (London), p. 9.
1610. John Brickdall: Reg. Univ. Oxf. i. 367.
London, 3.

Brickett.—(1) Bapt. 'the son of Burchard'; v. Buckett and Burchett. The corruptions are all traceable. The *r* is transferred to the first syllable, as in Brodrick for Balderick. In his Index to Marriage Licences (London) the editor refers the reader from Buckett to Brickett. (2) Local, 'at the birkhead,' i.e. from residence thereby. There is much evidence in favour of this as the true parent; v. Birkett for meaning.

George Birkhead, or Brickhead, or Brickhedd, 1599: Reg. Univ. Oxf. vol. ii. pt. iii. p. 214.
But cf. John Brykhede, C.R., 12 Hen. VI.

This is confirmatory of the following:

1583. John Bryckett, co. Northampt.: Reg. Univ. Oxf. vol. ii. pt. ii. p. 161.

The editor refers the reader to Birkhead. In this case the surname is again local.

London, 2.

Brickman. — Occup. 'the bridge-man' (v. Bridgman), of which an early form would be Brig-man; cf. Brigg. This, of course, became Brickman; cf. Hickman and Higman; v. Philbrick.

John Brickman, Pat. Roll, 3 Edw. VI, pt. ii.
1564. Married—Nicholas Brigman and Als Milmon: St. Antholin (London), p. 17.
1567. Edward Birckman: Reg. Univ. Oxf. vol. ii. pt. i. p. 300.
London, 1; Philadelphia, 1; New York, 1.

Bricknell and Bricknall.—Local; v. Brignall.

Briddon.—Local; v. Breedon.

Brideoake.—Local. This surname seems to have come from Yorkshire into Lancashire. From Manchester it reached the neighbouring town of Oldham, where it still thrives.

'Ralph Brideoake (1613–78), bishop of Salisbury, was of lowly parentage, being son of Richard Brideoake, or Briddock, of Cheetham Hill, Manchester': Dict. Nat. Biog. vi. 313.
1323. Ralph Brydock, of Gateside, a benefactor to Tyne-Bridge: Brand's Hist. of Newcastle, i. 41.
Robert Bridoke, 1334. DDD. ii. 242.
Johanna Brydok', 1379: P. T. Yorks. p. 11.
Ralph Brydok, 1403. PPP. i. 237.
Edward Bridoake, of Cheetham, Manchester, 1609: Wills at Chester (1545-1620), p. 29.
Jane Brideoak, of Cheetham: ibid. (1621-50), p. 33.
Edward Briddock, of Cheetham: ibid. (1660-80), p. 39.
Oldham, 2.

Bridge, Bridges.—(1) Local, 'at the bridge.' The variant Bridges is not a plural form. It answers to Brooks, Holmes, Styles, &c., and probably represents the genitival *s*, as in Williams, Jones, Roberts, Coles, &c. (v. Briggs). (2) Local (as regards Bridges), 'of Bruges.'

Saher de Bruges. E.
Oliver de Bruges, ibid.

The two following entries refer to the same individual :

Giles Bruges was seised of the manor of Archer-Stoke, co. Glouc., 6 Edw. IV : Atkyn's Hist. Glouc. p. 186.
Giles Brydges, died seised of the manor of Stoke-Archerds, co. Glouc., 3 Hen. VIII : ibid.

The next two entries bring us back to Bridge, of purely English introduction.

Robert atte Brugge, co. Soms., 1 Edw. III : Kirby's Quest, p. 105.
William atte Brugge, co. Soms., 1 Edw. III : ibid. p. 106.
1673-4. Buried — Ann Bridge : St. Dionis Backchurch, p. 240.
1736. Married—Samuel Calderwood and Mary Bridges : St. Geo. Han. Sq. i.18. London, 22, 22 ; New York, 10, 7.

Bridge-end. — Local, 'at the bridge-end,' from residence thereby ; v. Townsend or Woodend.

John ate Bruge-ende, co. Oxf., 1273. A.
Stephen atte Brigende. B.

Bridgeford. — Local, 'of Bridgeford.' I cannot find the spot.

Dominus de Brigeford, co. Soms., 1273. A.
1619. Buried—Agnes, wife of Thomas Bridgfort : St. Jas. Clerkenwell, iv. 146.

The preceding is another instance of change from *d* to *t*.

1792. Married—George Bridgeford and Sarah Gretton : St. Geo. Han. Sq. ii. 73. London, 1 ; Boston (U.S.), 1.

Bridger. — Local and occup. 'the bridger,' one who lived at the bridge ; cf. Bridgman. This surname belongs to the same class as Churcher, Kirker, Brooker, and Crosser. It is probable that the bridger, like the bridgeman, took toll.

Walter le Briggere, co. Soms., 1 Edw. III : Kirby's Quest, p. 173.
1582. Henry Bridger, co. Surrey : Reg. Univ. Oxf. vol. ii. pt. ii. p. 122.
1602. Samuel Bridger, co. Glouc. : ibid. p. 256.
John Bridger, temp. Eliz. Z.
1677. Henry Bridger and Elizabeth Budgen : Marriage Lic. (Canterbury), p. 270.
1803. Married—Richard Bridger and Mary Anne Whatton : St. Geo. Han. Sq. ii. 289.
London, 16 ; New York, 1 ; Philadelphia, 1.

Bridgewater. — Local, 'of Bridgewater,' a seaport and market-town in co. Somerset.

1742. Married—John Bridgwater and Ann Hartly : St. Geo. Chap. Mayfair, p. 20.
1745. Buried—Bridgwater : St. Michael, Cornhill, p. 297.
1760. Married—John Barrett and Margaret Bridgewater : St. Geo. Han. Sq. i. 97. London, 4 ; Philadelphia, 2.

Bridgman, Bridgeman. — Local and occup. 'the bridge-man,' one who resided at the bridge and took toll. Sometimes simply a resident by a bridge.

Johannes Brigeman, 1379 : P. T. Yorks. p. 18.
1582. John Bridgman, co. Glouc. : Reg. Univ. Oxf. vol. ii. pt. ii. p. 119.
— Winter Bridgman, co. Glouc. : ibid.
1646-7. James Bridgman and Prothesa Gurney : Marriage Lic. (Faculty Office), p. 33.
1796. Married—James Bridgman and Hannah Treader : St. Geo. Han. Sq. ii. 154. London, 12, 3 ; New York, 5, 3.

Brien.—Bapt. 'the son of Brien'; v. Bryan.

Brier, Briers.—Loc. ; v. Brear.

London, 1, 1 ; Philadelphia, 4, 1.

Brierley.—Local ; v. Brearley.

Brigg, Briggs.—Local, 'at the bridge,' from residence thereby ; M. E. *brigge* ; cf. Briggate, in Leeds. 'Di vggo, *pons*' : Prompt. Parv. Brigg is a well-known Yorkshire form.

Hugh ate Brugge, co. Oxf., 1273. A.
Roger ate Brugge, co. Oxf., ibid.
Amice atte Brigge, Close Roll, 8 Edw. I.
Roger del Brigge. M.
Sarra atte Brigge. B.
Juliana del Bryg, 1379 : P. T. Yorks. p. 199.
Robertus atte Brigg, 1379 : ibid. p. 23.
Ricardus atte Brygg, 1379 : ibid. p. 45.
Simon Atte-brig, vicar of Stalham, co. Norf., 1355 : FF. ix. 344.
Roger Attebrigge, rector of South Pickerham, co. Norf., 1338 : ibid. vi. 74.
1615. William Crippes and Juliana Briggs : Marriage Lic. (London), ii. 31.
West Riding Court Dir., 14, 44 ; London, 3, 49 ; Philadelphia, 1, 87.

Brighouse.—Local, 'of Brighouse,' a hamlet about five miles from Halifax, co. York.

Johannes de Brighous', 1379 : P. T. Yorks. p. 137.
1605. Robert Brighouse : Reg. Univ. Oxf. i. 356.
1636. Benjamin Brigghowsse and Anne Cowles : Marriage Lic. (London), ii. 228.
1787. Married—John Brighouse and Margaret Richards : St. Geo. Han. Sq. i. 397.
West Rid. Court Dir., 1 ; Leeds, 1 ; MDB. (West Rid. Yorks), 1.

Bright. — Bapt. 'the son of Bright.' In Domesday, 'Bricht,' co. Suffolk, is found as a suffix in Albrecht (now Albert, and as a surname Allbright), or as an affix in Brightwen (q.v.), and such early personal names as Brichtfrid, Brichtmar, Brichtric, or Brichtstar (v. Yonge's Glossary) = bright, clear, shining, flaming. John Bright's son, Mr. Albert Bright, bears twice the name his father has immortalized. As regards the style of the great Tribune's oratory, too, no title could be more fitting. So does Time bring round the changes.

Brictus le Blake, Hen. III-Edw. I. K.
Hervey Brite, co. Oxf., 1273. A.
Walter Brith, co. Bucks, ibid.
Roger Briht, co. Oxf., ibid.
William Bricht, co. Norf., ibid.
Adam Bryte, co. Soms., 1 Edw. III : Kirby's Quest, p 231.
Simon Bryght, Norwich, 1514 : FF. iv. 253.
William Bryght, prior of Peterston, co. Norf., 1393 : ibid. vii. 24.
1727. Married — Joseph Minus and Grace Bright : St. Michael, Cornhill, p. 64. London, 25 ; New York, 12.

Brighteve, Brightey?, Brighty?—Bapt. 'the son of Brighteve' ('Brichteva, fem. Nor.-Teu. bright gift': Yonge, ii. 405). The Bright eves in numerous variants dwelt for centuries in co. Norfolk, and I suspect Brightey and Brighty, in the neighbouring counties of Lincoln, Cambridge, &c., are popularized forms.

Edmund Brightyeve, or Britiff, 1467, co. Norf. : FF. ii. 379.
John Brighteve, co. Norf., 1497 : ibid. p. 581.
John Brightif, rector of Francham Magna, co. Norf., 1559 : ibid. ix. 499.
Simon Britiffe, co. Norf., 1663 : ibid. ix. 222.
Robert Brightiff, co. Norf., 1733 : ibid. p. 442.
MDB. (co. Lincoln), 0, 1, 1 ; (Hunts), 0, 0, 1 ; (Cambridge), 0, 0, 2.

Brightman. — Bapt. 'the son of Brichtman.' In Domesday, 'Brihtmanus,' co. Suffolk ; v. Bright, of which it is an augmentative, and cf. Bateman or Tiddyman.

John Brithman, co. Norf., 1273. A.
1501. William Brightman and Eliz. Irvye : Marriage Lic. (London), i. 23.
1753. Married—Daniel Kerridge and

Rebecca Brightman: St. Geo. Chap. Mayfair, p. 252.
1755. Married—James Brightman and Sarah Price: St. Geo. Han. Sq. i. 59.
London, 1; Boston (U.S.), 2.

Brightmore, Brightmoor.— Bapt. 'the son of Brichtmar' (Yonge, ii. 405). Bricmore was a learned scholar at Oxford in the 14th century (Dict. Nat. Biog. vi. 312). The name is again found at Oxford in the case of Thomas Brydmer, 1519 (Reg. Univ. Oxf. i. 110). Brightmore is the modern form; the name was always rare.

John Brithmar, co. Norf., 1273. A.
Harvey Brithnor, co. Camb., ibid.
Martin Brithnor, co. Camb., ibid.
1422. Thomas Brightmer, vicar of Thorp Market, co. Norf.: FF. viii. 174.
Adam Brithn ere, co. Norf.: ibid. p.208.
1652. John Brigtmer, co. Norf.: ibid. xi. 254.

Found as Brickmire in the 18th century:

1706. Bapt.—Sarah, d. Eleanor Brickmire: St. Jas. Clerkenwell, ii. 33.
London, 1, 0; Manchester, 1, 0; West Rid. Court Dir., 0, 1; Philadelphia, 2, 0.

Brightric.—Bapt. 'the son of Brichtric' (v. Yonge, ii. 405).

Brithric, rector of Aylesham, co. Norf., at the Conquest: FF. vi. 274.
Hardwin fil. Brichrit, co. Suff., 1273. A.

Brightwell.—Local, 'of Brightwell.' (1) A parish in co. Berks, near Wallingford; (2) also a parish in co. Suffolk, near Ipswich; v. Brittle, an evident popular variant.

Robert de Brichwell, co. Wilts, Hen. III-Edw. I. K.
Simon de Bricchtewell, co. Northampt., 1273. A.
Turstan de Brictewell, co. Oxf., ibid.
1675. Buried—Benjamin Brightwell: Kensington Ch. p. 147.
1806. Marr:ed—Edward Bailey and Hannah Brightwell: St. Geo. Han. Sq. ii. 342.
London, 2; Philadelphia, 1; Boston (U.S.), 1.

Brightwin, Brightwen. -- Bapt. 'the son of Brightwin,' or 'Bertwine' (v. Yonge, ii. 404).

Thomas Bryghtwyn, 1535: Reg. Univ. Oxf. i. 184.
1586. William Brightewyn, of London, and Johanna Tournor: Marriage Lic. (London), i. 156.
London, 1, 0; MDB. (co. Suffolk), 0, 1.

Brignall, Bricknall, Bricknell.—Local, 'of Brignall,' a

village in the North Rid. Yorks, near Greta Bridge. Brignall early gave rise to a surname, and, of course, it has occasionally changed itself into Bricknall and Bricknell. The progressive stages are easily marked, as the instances below demonstrate.

Thomas de Briggenale, 1379: P. T. Yorks. p. 228.
1664. Married—George Ogleby and Hester Brignell: St. Jas. Clerkenwell, iii. 114.
1675. Bapt.—Thomas, s. Nicolas Bricnell: ibid. i. 270.
1764. Married—William Bricknell and Winifred Profit: St. Geo. Han. Sq. i 130.
1774. — Richard Heard and Winifred Bricknall: ibid. p. 236.
London, 1, 0, 0; MDB. (co. Lincoln), 0, 1, 0; Philadelphia, 1, 0, 0.

Brigstock. — Local, ' of Brigstock,' a parish in co. Northampton, twenty-two miles fro mNorthampton.

Walter de Brigestok, co. Linc., 1273. A.
1631. John Brigstock and Francis Sutton: Marriage Lic. (Westminster), p. 33.
1663. George Brigstocke (Sussex) and Margaret Seares: Marriage Alleg. (Canterbury), p. 99.
1763. Married—William Burgin and Mary Brigstock: St. Geo. Han. Sq. i. 128.
London, 1.

Brimson.—(1) Local; probably a corruption of Brimstone: cf. Kelson for Kelston, &c. (2) Bapt. 'the son of Bryan,' a corruption of Bryanson, v. Bryan. For change of n to m, cf. Sinkinson for Simkinson, or Stimpson for Stinson, i.e. Stevenson.

Adam de Brymston, 1379: P. T. Yorks. p. 258.
1633. John Brimson, of Shevington, co. Lanc.: Wills at Chester, ii. 34.
1638. George Brimson, of Mawdsley: ibid.
1777. Married—George Curd and Ann Brimson: St. Geo. Han. Sq. p. 276.
London, 2.

Brinckman, Bringeman, Brinkman, Brinkmann.—An imported surname. Lower says, 'Brinckman; from Hanover with George I' (Patr. Brit. p. 41). In co. Lincoln this surname seems to have assumed the form of Bringeman.

1740. Married—John Richard Brinckman and Ann Bingley: St. Geo. Han. Sq. i. 24.

1778. Married—George Brinkman and Mary Richardson: ibid. p. 293.
MDB. (co. Lincoln), 1, 4, 0, 0; London, 0, 0, 4, 1; Philadelphia, 2, 0, 8, 2.

Brindle.—Local, ' of Brindle,' a village near Chorley, co. Lancaster.

James Brindle, of Chorley, *yeoman*, 1608: Wills at Chester, i. 29.
John Brindle, of Walton-le-dale, 1620: ibid.
1662. Robert Brindle: Preston Guild Rolls, p. 126.
Liverpool, 3; Chorley (co. Lanc.), 8; New York, 1; Philadelphia, 1.

Brindley.—Local, ' of Brindley,' a township in the parish of Acton, co. Chester.

1575. Edmund Brindley, of Ex. Coll.: Reg. Univ. Oxf. i. 389.
1637. John Brindley, of Macfen, parish of Malpas: Wills at Chester, ii. 34.
1642. John Brindley, of Hampton, co. Chester: ibid.
1748. Married—George Bates and Eliz. Mary Brindley: St. Geo. Chap. Mayfair, p. 112.
London, 3.

Brindsley, Brinsley.—Local, ' of Brinsley,' i.e. the meadow belonging to Brun, the first settler or proprietor. The *d* is intrusive.

Roger de Bruneslegh, 1282. M.
Gilbert de Brunneslegh, 1277, ibid.
Robert de Brunyslegh, co.Notts, 1273. A.
Gilbert de Brunyslegh, co. Notts, ibid.
1582. Gervis Brinsley, co. Notts: Reg. Univ. Oxf. vol. ii. pt. ii. p. 123.
1618. Buried—Eliz., wife of Mathew Brinsley: St. Jas. Clerkenwell, iv. 142.
London, 0, 1.

Brine.—Bapt. 'the son of Brien'; v. Bryan. The first five following belong to one family:

Thomas Bryne, 1539: Reg. Broad Chalke, co. Wilts, p. 6.
Jone Brine, 1570: ibid. p. 1.
Walter Bryne, 1638: ibid. p. 5.
Margaret Brine, 1657: ibid. p. 22.
William Bryan, 1740: ibid. p. 57.
1586. Thomas Bryn, of Kilkenny: Reg. Univ. Oxf. vol. ii. pt. ii. p. 152.
1588. Robert Bryne, co. Dorset: ibid. p. 164.
London, 4; Philadelphia, 2.

Bringhurst.—Local, 'of Bringhurst,' a parish in co. Leic., near Rockingham.

1614. Thomas Cooper and Eliz. Bringhurst: Marriage Lic. (London), ii. 29.
1748. Married—John Bringhurst and Eliz. Somerset: St. Geo. Chap. Mayfair, p. 327.
Philadelphia, 17.

Bringman, Brinkman ; v. Brinckman.

Brinkley, Brinckley.—Local, ' of Brinkley,' a parish in co. Camb., near Newmarket.

Martin de Brenkelee, co. Camb.,1273. A.
Robert de Brinkele, co. Camb., ibid.
1665. Buried—Lawrans Brinkley : St. Jas. Clerkenwell, iv. 367.
1748. Married—James Brinkley and Louise Bouquet : St. Geo. Chap. Mayfair, p. 103.
London, 1, 0 ; Philadelphia, 5, 9.

Brinklow.—Local, ' of Brinklow,' a parish in co. Warwick, near Coventry.

1743. Married—William Brinklow and Phillis Logie : St. Geo. Han. Sq. i. 30. London, 1.

Brinkworth. — Local, ' of Brinkworth,' a parish in co. Wilts, near Wotton Bassett.

1783. Married—William Addis and Sarah Brinkworth : St. Geo.Han.Sq.i.342.
London, 3 ; MDB. (co. Soms.), 3 ; (co. Wilts), 2 ; Philadelphia, 6.

Brinton.—Local, ' of Brinton,' a parish in co. Norfolk, near Holt.

Adam de Brinton, co. Oxf., 1273. A.
Thomas de Brinton, co. Hunts, ibid.
Richard de Brinton, co. Northampt., Hen. III-Edw I K.
1620. William Brinton and Johanna Griffith : Marriage Lic. (Westminster), p. 26.
1784. Married—John Brinton and Eliz. James : St. Geo. Han. Sq. i. 365.
London, 2 ; Philadelphia, 25.

Briscoe, Briscow, Brisco.—Local, ' of Brisco,' a spot close by Newbiggin, co. Cumb. (v. E. & F., c. Cumb., pp. 84-5), spelt variously Birkskeugh, Bruskowgh, and Briskow. Hence the origin is Birkshaw (the Birchwood) ; v. Birks and Shaw.

Isold de Briskow, E. & F., co. Cumb., p. 84.
William Brys(k)how, co. York, 1410. W. 11.
1586. William Briskoo, co. Cumb. : Reg. Univ. Oxf. vol. ii. pt. i. p. 155.
1592. John Briscoe, co. Herts : ibid. p. 192.
1788. Married — Edward Briscoe and Catherine Pheasy : St. Geo. Han. Sq. ii. 15.
London, 3, 0, 0 ; Philadelphia, 13, 1, 0; Boston (U.S.), 4, 0, 4.

Bristo, Bristow, Bristowe, Bristoll.—Local, ' of Bristol,' an old provincialism. Latimer, in a letter to Lord Cromwell, speaks of ' Gloucester and Bristow ' (Parker Soc. Letters to Lord Cromwell, p. 190).

John de Bristoll, co. Soms. : Kirby's Quest, p. 87.
Thomas de Bristoll, co. Soms. : ibid. p. 190.
Richard de Bristowe, co. Soms. : ibid. p. 271.
Jane Mericke, of Bristow : Visit. of London, 1634, i. 217.
Philip Grene, de Bristow : Visit. of Glouc., 1623, p. 98.
1582. Francis Bristow, co. Heref. : Reg. Univ. Oxf. vol. ii. pt. ii. p. 118.
1750. Bapt. — John James Bristol, a black man : St. Geo. Chap. Mayfair, p. 10.
London, 1, 24, 5, 1 ; Philadelphia, 0, 8, 0, 4 ; Boston (U.S.), 1, 0, 0, 1.

Brittain, Brittan, Britten, Britton, Britain, Brittin, Brittian.—(1) Local,' of Brittany.' (2) Nick. 'the Breton.' Immigrants from Brittany. A very large number occur in the Hundred Rolls of 1273.

John de Brytaygn, co. Camb., 1273. A.
Giffard le Bretun, co. Bucks, ibid.
Hugo le Bretun, co. Camb., ibid.
Roger le Bretun, co. Suff., ibid.
Alicia de Britten, 1379 : P. T. Yorks. p. 185.
Elias de Britton, 1379 : ibid.
Ricardus Britton, 1379 : ibid.
1790. Married — William Britten and Anne Keene : St. Geo. Han. Sq. ii. 52.
1796. — John Britton and Sarah Wilkins : ibid. ii. 150.
London, 7, 4, 11, 13, 3, 0, 0 ; Philadelphia, 9, 1, 1, 57, 0, 16, 2.

Brittle.—? Bapt. ' the son of Britell.' But it may be a corruption of Britwell, a parish in co. Oxford, and also a liberty so termed in the parish of Burnham,co. Bucks. This modification would be very natural ; v. Brightwell.

Richard de Brittewell, co. Oxf., 1273. A.
Eadmund de Brithwell, co. Camb., ibid.
Britellus de Ambreres, Hen. III-Edw. I. K.
1626. John Darling and Jane Britle : Marriage Lic. (London), ii. 176.
London, 3 ; Philadelphia, 1.

Brittoner,Brettoner.—Local, ' the Brittoner,' a native of Brittany ; v. Brett.

'A Bretoner, a braggere.'
            Piers P. 4105.
' He buffeted the Bretoner.'
            Ibid. 4148.
1599. Thomas Brettner and Ann Kynton : Marriage Lic. (London), i. 262.

Joel Brettoner, *linen draper*, Penistone, co. York.
MDB. (West Riding Yorks), 0, 1.

Broad.—(1) Nick. 'the broad.' i. e. the stout, the broad-shouldered. M.E. *brod*, broad.

' It was almost a spanne brode I trowe.'
          Chaucer, C. T. 155.
Cf. Broadbelt.
(2) Local, ' at the broad,' from residence thereby. Broad : a wide place ; cf. the Norfolk Broads. Oxford undergraduates still talk of ' the Broad,' for Broad Street in that city.

John le Brode. B.
Richard le Brod, temp. 1310. M.
Katerina Brode, 1379 : P. T. Yorks. p. 21.
Johannes Brode, 1379 : ibid.
Alicia Brode, co. Soms., 1 Edw. III : Kirby's Quest, p. 115.
Henry atte Brude, co. Soms., 1 Edw. III : ibid. p. 132.
Michele le Brude, co. Soms., 1 Edw. III : ibid. p. 184.
1589. John Brode, co. Worc. : Reg. Univ. Oxf. vol. ii. pt. ii. p. 172.
1803. Married—John Surman and Sarah Broad : St. Geo. Han. Sq. ii. 291.
London, 23 ; Philadelphia, 4.

Broadbelt.—Nick. 'broadbelt.' stout, with a wide waist. Found in Lanc. and Yorkshire. Sobriquets of this sort were common (v. Broadgirdle).

Joan Broydbelt, co. York. W. 2.
Robert Brodebelt, co. York. W. 17.
Adam Bradbelt, 1379 : P. T. Yorks. p. 275.
Dorothy Broadbelt, Cal. State Papers, 1562.
Thomas Brodbelt, churchwarden of Prestbury, 1820 : East Cheshire, ii. 188.
Wakefield Dir., 1 ; Philadelphia, 2.

Broadbent.—Local, ' at the broad bent,' i.e. the broad bend in the land (v. Bent). The precise spot I cannot find. It is, or was, undoubtedly in South-East Lanc., on the borders of Yorks., and probably in the parish of Saddleworth.

1570. Lawrence Bradbent, Ball. Coll. : Reg. Univ. Oxf. vol. ii. pt. iii. 84.
1590. Alice Broadbent, of Saddleworth, *spinster* : Wills at Chester, i. 29.
1630. George Broadbent, of Harrop, Saddleworth : ibid. ii. 34.
1646. James Broadbent, of 'the Green,' in Saddleworth : ibid.
Manchester, 19 ; London, 5 ; Philadelphia, 40.

Broadbotham. — Local, ' of Broadbottom,' a hamlet in the parish of Mottram-in-Longendale, co. Chester (v. Botham, Longbottom, &c.). The meaning is ' the broad hollow.'

Simon de Brodbotham (without date): East Ches. ii. 154.

1330. William de Brodebotham, ibid.

'In 1393-4, Agnes, the widow of Robert de Woley, grants to Robert de Staveley all the messuages, lands, &c., in *le Brodbotham*, which came to her as dower ': ibid.

Antony Wild, of Broadbotham, 1608 : Wills at Chester, i. 209.

Broadbridge. — Local, ' at the broad bridge.' I cannot identify the spot.

1750. Married — Thomas Edwards and Ann Broadbridge : St. Geo. Chap. Mayfair, p. 160.

London, 1 ; Boston (U.S.), 1 ; Philadelphia, 1.

Broadfield. — Local, ' at the broad field,' from residence thereby ; cf. Bradfield.

John del Brodefeld, co. Lanc., 1332 : Lay Subsidy (Rylands), p. 118.

Meurik del Brodefeld, co. Lanc., 1332 : ibid. p. 36.

1746. Married — Richard Ward and Eliz. Broadfield : St. Geo. Chap. Mayfair, p. 78.

1808. — William Henry Broadfield and Eliz. Forbes : St. Geo. Han. Sq. ii. 381.

Manchester, 1 ; Philadelphia, 1.

Broadgirdle. — Nick. for a paunchy man ; cf. Broadbelt.

William Brodgirdel, co. Notts, 1273. A.

Broadhay. — Local, ' at the broad hay,' i.e. broad hedge or enclosure ; v. Hay and Hayes.

Robert de Brodheye, co. Camb., 1273. A.

Broadhead, Brodhead. — Local, ' at the broad head,' i.e. a wide headland, from residence thereby ; cf. Birkett, Blackett, Redhead, Whitehead, &c. Some of these, doubtless, are nicknames.

Adam del Brodeheued, co. Lanc., 1332 : Lay Subsidy (Rylands), p. 113.

Alan del Brodeheued, co. Lanc., 1332 : ibid.

Walter Brodheved, co. Camb., 1273. A.

Johannes Braydhed, 1379 : P. T. Yorks. p. 121.

Edmund Broadheade, temp. Eliz. ZZ.

1572. Married — Roger Brodharde and Tymothe (sic) Porte : St. Michael, Cornhill, p. 10.

1610. Richard Broadhead, Anglesea : Reg. Univ. Oxf. vol. ii. pt. ii. p. 316.

London, 2, 0 ; Philadelphia, 5, 3 ; New York, 4, 7.

Broadhurst. — Local, ' of Broadhurst,' i.e. the broad wood (v. Hurst). The Cheshire Broadhursts spring from some small spot in the east of the county, but I have failed to discover its whereabouts.

1566. Married — Radulf Brodehurst and Eliz. Barlowe : Prestbury Ch. (co. Chester), p. 19.

1567. — John Brodehurst and Eliz. Blagge : ibid. p. 23.

1592. John Broadhurst, of Sandbach : Wills at Chester, i. 29.

1607. Richard Broadhurst, of Sutton, parish of Prestbury : ibid.

1683. Bapt. — Thomas, s. Ralph Broadhurst : St. Jas. Clerkenwell, i. 304.

1756. Married — William Broadhurst and Sarah Tagg : St. Geo. Han. Sq. i. 65.

London, 5 ; Manchester, 6 ; MDB. (co. Chester), 3 ; Philadelphia, 8.

Broadmeadow, Broadmead. — Local, ' at the broad meadow ' or ' mead,' from residence thereby ; v. Medd. Cf. Broadfield, Bradfield.

Roger atte Brodmed, co. Soms., 1 Edw. III : Kirby's Quest, p. 138.

1642. Bapt. — Marye, d. of Thomas Broadmedowe : St. Mary Aldermary, p. 88.

1724. Married — William Bradmead and Mary Mackelean : St. Michael, Cornhill, p. 63.

Manchester, 1, 0 ; MDB. (co. Soms.), 0, 4.

Broadribb. — Local ; v. Broderip.

Broadwater. — Local, ' of Broadwater,' a parish in co. Sussex, near Worthing.

(Dominus) de Brawatere, co. Sussex, 1273. A.

1590-1. Isaac Geslinge and Mary Brawdwater : Marriage Lic. (London), i. 190.

1610. Buried — Anne, wife of Thomas Bradwater : St. Thomas the Apostle (London), p. 107.

1623. — John Broadwatter : St. Mary Aldermary, p. 161.

London, 1 ; Philadelphia, 9.

Broadway. — (1) Local, ' at the Broadway,' from residence there beside ; cf. Greenway, Ridgway, &c.

(2) Local ; more particularly ' of Broadway,' parishes in cos. Dorset, Worcester, and Somerset.

Hugh del Brodweye, co. Camb., 1273. A.

John de Broadways, prepositor of Bristol, 1225 : YYY. p. 669.

Ernald de Bradeway, co. Norf., Hen. III — Edw. I. K.

Adam de Bradeweye, co. Soms., 1 Edw. III : Kirby's Quest, p. 110.

John de Bradeweye, co. Soms., 1 Edw. III : ibid.

1579. Buried — John Brodwaye : St. Michael, Cornhill, p. 198.

— — Danyell Brodwaye : ibid.

1691. Thomas Bradway, sheriff of Bristol : YYY. p. 695.

London, 3 ; New York, 7.

Broadwood. — Local, ' of the Broadwood,' from residence thereby.

Walter de Brodwode, co. Soms. A.

1563. Married — Rycharde Bradwoode and Alyce Dayle : St. Michael, Cornhill, p. 8.

London, 2.

Brocas. — Local, ' of Brocas. The two representatives in the London Directory, one a botanist, the other a fishing-tackle maker, may probably congratulate themselves in being the descendants of some junior branch of the Hereditary Masters of the Royal Buckhounds. They hailed from the district of Sault and St. Sever. For a full account, v. ' The Family of Brocas of Beaurepaire, and Roche Court ' : by Professor Montagu Burrows (Longmans, 1886). I quote two entries from the book simply to prove the local origin.

Arnald de Brokays, 1315.

John de Brocas, 1340.

1578. Pexall Broccas, co. Bucks : Reg. Univ. Oxf. vol. ii. pt. ii. p. 80.

1661. Sir William Gardiner and Jane Brocas : Marriage Lic. (Faculty Office), p. 51.

London, 2 ; New York, 1.

Brock. — (1) Nick. ' the brock,' i.e. the badger. ' Thei wenten about in brok skynnes ' : Heb. xi. 37 (Wyclif).

Robert le Brokk, co. Soms., 1 Edw. III : Kirby's Quest, p. 86.

William le Broc, co. Soms., 1 Edw. III : ibid. p. 93.

Gilbert le Brok, co. Oxf., 1273. A.

Henry le Brok, co. Devon, ibid.

Walter le Broc, co. Glouc., ibid.

(2) Local, ' at the brook' ; v. Brook.

Laurence del Broc, co. Herts, 1273. A.

Joceus de la Brok, co. Kent, ibid.

Geoffrey de la Brok, co. Kent, ibid.

William del Brok, co. Essex, ibid.

London, 23 ; Philadelphia, 28.

Brockbank. — Local ; v. Brooksbank.

Brockhill. — Local, 'of the brock-hole,' from residence thereby ; v. Brock. Of course the brock-hill, i. e. the hill frequented by brocks, may be the parent, but the evidence below seems to point to *hole* and not *hill* as the true suffix. But v. Brooksbank.

Johannes de Brokehole, 1379 : P. T. Yorks. p. 65.
Magota Brokehole, 1379 : ibid.
1742. Married—Thomas Brockell and Mary Pearse : St. Geo. Chap. Mayfair, p. 19.
1791. — William Fitz-herbert Brockholes and Mary Heneage : St. Geo. Han. Sq. ii. 62.
London, 1.

Brockhouse, Brookhouse.— Local, 'at the brook-house,' the house by the brook. More specifically 'of Brookhouse,' a hamlet in the parish of Laughton-en-le-Morthen, co. York.

William del Brokhouses, of Eccleston-cum-Heskin, co. Lanc., 1332 : Lay Subsidy (Rylands), p. 50.
Hugo de Brokehous', 1379 : P. T. Yorks. p. 87.
Alicia de Brokehouse, 1379 : ibid. p. 81.
1588. John Henley and Margaret Brockhus : Marriage Lic. (London), i. 174.
1791. Married—William Chapman and Mary Brookhouse : St. Geo. Han. Sq. ii. 57.
London, 1, 0 ; Manchester, 0, 1 ; New York, 1, 0 ; Boston (U.S.), 0, 2.

Brocklebank, Brockelbank. —Local, 'of Brocklebank,' a township in the parish of Westward, near Wigton, co. Cumb.

1576. Bapt.—Cristorfer Brockbanke : Reg. Ulverston Ch. p. 67.

This register teems with entries relating to Brockbank and Brocklebank. The surnames still abound in Cumberland and Furness.

1632. John Brockelbank, or Brockilbancke : Reg. Univ. Oxf. i. 344.
William Broclebank, rector of Southacre, co. Norf., 1725 : FF. vi. 84.
London, 1, 1 ; Manchester, 2, 0 ; MDB. (co. Cumb.), 1, 0 ; New York, 1, 0 ; Boston (U.S.), 0, 2.

Brockley.—Local, ' of Brockley,' a parish seven miles from Bury St. Edmunds, co. Suffolk.

1325. William de Brokkeley, rector of Howe, co. Norf. : FF. viii. 27.
Peter de Brokeley, co. Norf., temp. Hen. III : ibid. x. 155.

Lescelina de Brokeley, co. Norf., temp. Hen. III : ibid.
John Brocklee, rector of North Lynn, co. Norf., 1420 : ibid. viii. 540.
Philadelphia, 2.

Broderick, Brodrick.—Bapt. 'the son of Baldrick' (Yonge, ii. 210). The intrusive *r* is the *r* in the second syllable thrown back ; cf. Crewdson from Cuthbert, from the nick. Crewd or Crud, and Broderip or Brodrib (also Broadribb, Lon. Dir.) from Bawdrip, a manor near Bridgewater ; v. Baldrey.

Hugh fil. Baldrici, Domesday.
Balderic Piscenar, London, 1273. A.
Bauderic (without surname), London, ibid.
Baldric de Bosco, co. Suff., ibid.
Baldric de Taverham, co. Norf., 1327 : FF. x. 472.
Thomas Bradryk, co. York, 1510 : W. 11, p. 171.
1722. Bapt.—Charles Adams Baldrick : St. Mary Aldermary, p. 123.
London, 3, 5 ; Philadelphia, 25, 0 ; Boston (U.S.), 47, 5.

Broderip, Brodrib, Brodribb, Broadribb, Brodripp.— Local, ' of Bawdrip,' a parish near Bridgewater, co. Somerset (cf. Broderick for the intrusive *r* in the first syllable). Most of the variants are still found in co. Somerset, and are undoubtedly to be referred to Broderip.

Christopher Broadripp, co. Soms., 1610 : Abstract of Somersetshire Wills, p. 15.
Peter Brodribbe, co. Soms., 1 Edw. III : Kirby's Quest, p. 204.
1581. Thomas Brodrib, co. Soms. : Reg. Univ. Oxf. vol. ii. pt. ii. p. 105.
— William Brodrybbe, co. Soms. : ibid. p. 106.
1748. Bapt.—Charles, s. William Broderip : Canterbury Cath., p. 29.
London, 0, 1, 0, 1, 0 ; Crockford, 0, 0, 2, 0, 0 ; MDB. (co. Soms.), 1, 0, 1, 0, 1.

Brogden.—Local, 'of Brogden.' M.E. *brok*, a badger ; A.S. *broc* (v. Brock (1)) and *den* ; M.E. *dene*, a valley (v. Dean). A township in the parish of Barnoldswick, ten miles from Skipton, co. York. Other spots were probably so called. With this lazy pronunciation of Brockden, cf. Slagg for Slack, &c.

Cristiana de Boroghden (?), 1379 : P. T. Yorks. p. 207.
William Brockden, co. York, 1544 : W. 11, p. 233.
1579. Dennis Brogdon and Eliz. Galland : Marriage Lic. (London), i. 87.

1687. Richard Brockden, or Brogden, alderman of Norwich : FF. iii. 423.
1741. Ingram Brogden : Ch. Accounts, Skipton (Hist. of Skipton, p. 363).
1769. 'To George Brockden, for repairing the clock £ 11. 15s. 0d.': ibid. p. 164.
London, 4 ; West Riding Court Dir., 2 ; Philadelphia, 3.

Broker, Brooker. — Occup. 'the broker,' an agent in business transactions.

'And gart bakbityng be a brocour
To blame mennes ware.'
Piers Plowman, 2731–2.
William le Brokour, Fines Roll, 19 Edw. II.
Elena Brocker, C. R., 5 Edw. III. pt. ii.
Adam Brocker, co. Soms., 1 Edw. III : Kirby's Quest, p. 235.
1426. Nicholas Broker : Cal. of Wills in Court of Husting (2).
1798. Married—Soloman Brooker and Eliz. Hale : St. Geo. Han. Sq. ii. 191.
1807 — William Broker and Eliz. Jaquest : ibid. ii. 378.
London, 0, 12 ; Philadelphia, 0, 7.

Bromage.—Local, 'of Bromwich' (v. Bromwich) ; cf. Bowdage for Bowditch (q.v.). Proof, if needed, is furnished below :

John Bromage, patron of Bromsberrow Vicarage, co. Glouc., 1583 : Atkyn's Hist. of Gloucestershire, p. 158.

The true name of the patron was John Bromwich. Thus this variant is, at least, three centuries old.

1581. Thomas Bromidge, co. Berks : Reg. Univ. Oxf. vol. ii. pt. ii. p. 98.
1771. Married— William Bromage and Ann Willcox : St. Geo. Han. Sq. i. 212. London, 2.

Bromet, Bromhead.—Local ; v. Broomhead.

Bromfield ; v. Broomfield.

Bromley, Bromly, Bromiley.—Local, 'of Bromley.' (1) A parish in co. Kent ; (2) a township in the parish of Eccleshall, co. Stafford. Also Bromley Abbots and Bromley Bagots in co. Stafford, and Great Bromley in Essex, &c.

Thomas de Bromleh, co. Soms., 1 Edw. III : Kirby's Quest, p. 256.
Robert de Bromlegh, co. Salop, 1273. A. ibid.
Geoffrey de Bromleye, co. Stafford, ibid.
Johannes de Bromylegh, 1379 : P. T. Yorks. p. 9.
1573. Buried — Edward Bromley : St. Antholin (London), p. 23.
1587. Married—Walter Bromeley and

Joane Mouldinge: St. Jas. Clerkenwell, iii. 13.

1587. Married—Richard Bromley and Amye Mawdes: ibid.

West Riding Court Dir., 6, 0, 0; London, 19, 1, 0; MDB. (co. Stafford), 5, 0, 0; (co. Salop), 11, 0, 0; Philadelphia, 35, 0, 7.

Brommell; v. Brummell.

Bromwich.—Local, 'of Bromwich.' (1) Little Bromwich, a hamlet in the parish of Aston, co. Warwick; (2) West Bromwich, a parish in co. Stafford; (3) Castle Bromwich, a chapelry in the parish of Aston, co. Warwick (v. Bromage).

1671-2. Thomas Brumwych and Eliz. Smith: Marriage Alleg. (Canterbury), p. 68.

1748. Married — Joseph Breedon and Mary Bromwitch: St. Geo. Chap. Mayfair, p. 128.

1772. — Joseph Guningham and Eliz. Bromwich: St. Geo. Han. Sq. i. 226.

London, 2; MDB. (co. Warwick), 2; Boston (U.S.), 2.

Brook, Brooke, Brookes, Brooks.—Local, 'at the brook,' one who lived by the brook-side. Common to all parts of England, and is especially one of the great local surnames of Yorkshire. The s is customary in these short spot-names; cf. Briggs, Styles. Possibly it is the patronymic s, as in Jones, Williams, &c.; of this I cannot be sure.

Edelina del Brok, Hen. III-Edw. I. K. Robertus del Brok', ibid.
Alice de la Broke, 1273. A.
Laurence del Broc, ibid.
William atte Brouke, co. Soms., 2 Edw. III: Kirby's Quest, p. 81.
Richard atte-Brook, vicar of Horseford, co. Norf., 1419: FF. x. 436.

1604. Bapt.—Edward, s. Hugh Brooke: St. Jas. Clerkenwell, i. 44.

1616. John Thornell and Martha Brookes: Marriage Lic. (London), ii. 44.

London, 17, 28, 17, 121; Philadelphia, 22, 43, 6, 228.

Brooker; v. Broker.

Brookfield.—Local, 'at the field by the brook,' from residence thereby.

Adam del Brokefeld, of Ormskirk, co. Lanc., 1332: Lay Subsidy (Rylands), p. 110.
Gilbert del Brokefild, of Barscough, co. Lanc., 1332: ibid. p. 117.
George Brookfield, of Kingsley, yeoman, 1637: Wills at Chester, ii. 35.

Liverpool, 6; Manchester, 1; London, 2; Philadelphia, 5.

Brookhouse; v. Brockhouse.

Brooksbank, Brookbank, Brookbanks, Brookbank.—Local, 'at the brook's bank,' from residence by the bank of the brook; cf. North English Gillbanks, q.v. In some cases Brockbank may be a variant of Brocklebank, q.v. I suggest this because Brockbank runs side by side with Brocklebank in North Lancashire (Furness district), which is not far from Brocklebank in co. Cumberland. Brockbank, too, is common as a surname in the latter county. There is no reason to suppose that *brock*, a badger, has any connexion with these names; v. Brock (2).

Thomas Brokesbank', 1379: P. T. Yorks. p. 187.

1591. Married — Florence Cawdwell and Sibell Brokebanck: St. Michael, Cornhill, p. 15.

1777. John Brockbank and Louisa Maria Nicholson: St. Geo. Han. Sq. i. 273.

1779. — Christopher Smirthwaite and Eliz. Brooksbank: ibid. i. 300.

West Riding Court Dir., 7, 0, 0, 0; London, 3, 1, 2, 2: MDB. (co. Cumb.), 1, 0, 0, 5; Boston (U.S.), 0, 0, 0, 3; Philadelphia, 0, 1, 0, 0.

Brookshaw, Bruckshaw.—Local, 'of Brookshaw,' i.e. the wood by the brook, from residence thereby (v. Brook and Shaw). Some spot in East Cheshire probably, but I cannot as yet discover it. As will be seen from the entries below, the two forms of the surname have a common parent.

1574. Married — John Brookeshawe and Anne Clerke: Prestbury Ch. (co. Ches.), p. 45.

John Brookshaw, of Stockport, 1618: Wills at Chester (1545-1620), p. 30.

George Bruckshaw, of Bredbury, 1611: ibid. p. 32.

John Brookshaw, of Bredbury, 1622: Earwaker's East Cheshire, ii. 12.

Henry Bruckshaw, of Bradbury, 1670: Wills at Chester (1621-50), p. 45.

1775. Married — Thomas Bruckshaw and Ann Waterer: St. Geo. Han. Sq. i. 258.

MDB. (co. Ches.), 0, 1; Manchester, 2, 4; London, 0, 1; Philadelphia, 1, 1; Boston (U.S.), 1, 0.

Broom, Broome.—Local, 'of the broom,' from residence near

the plant so called; cf. Furse, Gorst, &c. The Norfolk Brooms have generally become corrupted to Bloom, q.v. They are generally, but not always, 'of Brome,' a parish in the dioc. of Norwich.

William de Broom, co. Norf., 1273. A.
Henry de Brom, co. Norf., ibid.
Eustace de la Brome, co. Kent, ibid.
Nicholas atte Brome, co. Soms., 1 Edw. III: Kirby's Quest, p. 146.
William atte Brome, co. Soms., 1 Edw. III: ibid. p. 260.
Willelmus del Brome, 1379: P. T. Yorks. p. 32.
Rogerus del Brome, 1379: ibid. p. 31.
Robert atte Brom, rector of Sengham, co. Norf., 1338: FF. vii. 197.
Adam de Brome, co. Norf., 1322: ibid. ix. 209.

1587. Bapt.—James, s. Henry Brome: St. Jas. Clerkenwell, i. 19.

1777. Married—John Sutton and Sarah Broome: St. Geo. Han. Sq. i. 279.

London, 23, 0; MDB. (Suffolk), 2, 0; (Essex), 1, 2; Philadelphia, 16, 8.

Brooman. — Occup. v. (1) Berryman, or (2) Bowerman. Doubtless a modification of one or the other. Nevertheless it may be baptismal, meaning 'the son of Bruman.'

Bruman le Riche, co. Oxf., 1273. A.

1749. Buried — Henry Brooman: St. Mary Aldermary, p. 228.

London, 2.

Broomfield, Bromfield.—Local, 'of Bromfield,' parishes in cos. Cumberland and Salop. Also 'of Broomfield,' parishes in cos. Somerset, Kent, and Essex. Doubtless many small spots in various counties have also helped to swell the total.

Harno de Bromfeld, co. Kent, 1273. A.
Walter Bromfeld, co. Soms., 1 Edw. III: Kirby's Quest, p. 100.
William Bromfeld, co. Soms., 1 Edw. III: ibid. p. 278.
Robert Bromfield, of Witton, 1602: Wills at Chester (1545-1620), p. 29.
Thomas Broomfield, of Stretton, 1588: ibid. p. 31.
1610. Ralph Bromseild, co. York: Reg. Univ. Oxf. vol. ii. pt. ii. p. 379.

London, 3, 3; Manchester, 1, 1; Philadelphia, 2, 1.

Broomhall.—Local; v. Bramhall.

Broomhead, Brummett, Bromhead, Bromet. — Local, 'of Broomhead,' 'an estate in Hallamshire, co. York, which passed from the family through an heiress so early as temp. Ric. II.' Courthope's Debrett, quoted by Lower (Patr. Brit. p. 42). This surname with several variants is still well known in the West Riding, and has come down through some junior or independent stock. Brummett and Bromet are very natural corruptions; cf. Birkett for Birkhead, q.v., or Beckett for Beckhead, q.v. Broomhead means the topmost reach or 'head of the broom,' from residence thereby, just as Birkett means the topmost reach or 'head of the birch-trees'; cf. Akenhead, q.v. In the same way *side* was used (v. Garside and Akenside).

1667. Married—John Broomehed and Alice Bates : St. Jas. Clerkenwell, iii. 131
1717. — George Simpson and Mary Brummett : ibid. iii. 241.
1772. — John Bromhead and Eliz. Raine : St. Geo. Han. Sq. i. 217.
1784. — William Lusty and Eliz. Brumhead : ibid. i. 356.
MDB. (West Rid. Yorks), 6, 0, 1, 2; Boston (U.S.), 0, 4, 0, 0; Philadelphia, 5, 0, 1, 0.

Brotherhood, Brotherhead. —Local, 'of the brotherhood.' One of a religious confraternity or convent. 'As for their school, it hath been maintained heretofore by a brotherhood called a *Gyld*, I trow not without some *guile'* : Latimer to Lord Cromwell, 1538 (Remains, Parker Soc. p. 403).

Nicholas Brotherhood. PP.
John Brotherhood, co. York. W. 20.
London, 1, 0; Philadelphia, 0, 3.

Brothers.—Nick. 'the brother,' *gen.* brother's.

William le Brother, co. Oxf., 1273. A.
Thomas le Bruther, co. Soms., 1 Edw. III : Kirby's Quest, p. 233.
John Brother, co. Soms., 1 Edw. III : ibid. p. 255.
1621. John Brothers and Alice Harris : Marriage Lic. (London), ii. 104.
1666. Robert Milwarde and Susanne Brother : Marriage Alleg. (Canterbury), p. 186.
London, 2; Ulverston, 1; Boston (U.S.), 6.

Brotherton.—Local, 'of Brotherton,' a parish in the rural deanery of Pontefract, co. York.

Alex. de Brotherton, co. Suff., 1273. A.
Walterus de Brotherton, 1379 : P. T. Yorks. p. 155.
Ricardus de Brotherton, 1379 : ibid.

Thomas de Brotherton, co. Norf., temp. 1340 : FF. i. 230.
1623. Michael Brotherton and Joanna Price : Marriage Lic.(Westminster), p. 29.
1792. Married — Richard Brotherton and Drusilla Pearson : St. Geo. Han. Sq. ii. 88.
London, 6; Philadelphia, 6.

Brough.—Local, 'of Brough.' Parishes, hamlets, and townships in cos. Westm., Derby, N. Rid. and E. Rid. Yorks, &c.

William de Bruggh, 1273. A. (No county mentioned.)
1566-7. Arthur Browghe and Alice Clarrys : Marriage Lic. (London), i. 35.
1684. Henry Furnis and Ann Brough : Marriage Alleg. (Canterbury), p. 181.
1744. Married—Philip Lambeth and Hannah Brough : St. Geo. Chap. Mayfair, p. 34.
1748. — John Maxwell and Margaret Brow : ibid. p. 104.
London, 4; Philadelphia, 7.

Brougham. — Local, 'of Brougham,' a parish in co. Westm., near Penrith.

William de Brouham,co. Norf.,1273. A.
1742. Married — Thomas Taylor and Dorothy Brougham : St. Geo. Chap. Mayfair, p. 30.
London, 1; Philadelphia, 1; MDB. (Westm.), 1.

Droughton.—Local, 'of Broughton.' Parishes, hamlets, chapelries, and townships in cos. Hants, Bucks, Lancs., Linc., Northampton, Oxford, Salop, Hants, Stafford, &c. Originally no doubt for Boroughtown.

Mathew de Brouehton, co. Bucks, 1273. A.
Houel de Bröton, co. Salop, ibid.
William de Broucton, co. Hunts, ibid.
John de Brouhton, co. Oxf., ibid.
1529. John Bassett and Eliz. Broughton : Marriage Lic. (London), i. 7.
1588. Buried — Margery, d. John Broughton : St. Jas. Clerkenwell, iv. 38.
1666. Christopher Broughton and Martha Temple : Marriage Lic. (Faculty Office), p. 95.
London, 9; Boston (U.S.), 6.

Brown, Browne.—(1) Bapt. 'the son of Brun' (i.e. Brown), whence also Brownson, q.v. In Domesday Brun appears as a personal name; cf. German Bruno. Brown stands sixth among the surnames of England and Wales in point of numbers.

Gamel fil. Brun, c. Hen. I : E. and F., co. Cumb., p. 49.
Brun Edrith, co. Salop, 1273. A.

Matilda relicta Brun, co. Oxf., ibid.
Brune relicta Johannis, co. Camb., ibid.
Reginald fil. Brun. MM.
Willelmus Brunson, 1379 : P. T. Yorks. p. 273.

(2) Nick. 'the brown,' a sobriquet of complexion, extremely common in all early registers.

Hugh le Brun, co. Suff., 1273. A.
Robert le Brun, co. Bucks, ibid.
Johanna la Brune, co. Oxf., ibid.
Robert Broun, co. Soms., 1 Edw. III : Kirby's Quest, p. 219.
Willelmus Broune, et uxor, 1379 : P. T. Yorks. p. 193.
London, 647, 63; Philadelphia, 1636, 20.

Brownbeard. — Nick. 'John Brownberd, son of William, a hostage from Galloway' (Letters from Northern Registers, p. 163). Janet Brownebeard was an inmate of St. Thomas' Hospital, York, Feb. 6, 1553 (Corpus Christi Guild, Surt. Soc. p. 304). The sobriquet was clearly hereditary for a time.

New York, 1.

Brownbill.—? Local. Probably an imitative corruption of some local surname at a time when the *brownbill* (the halbert of the English foot-soldier) was a familiar term.

1561. Buried—Eliz. Browmbell : Prestbury Ch. (co. Ches.), p. 5.
1565. — Joane Brownbell : ibid. p. 17.
George Brombell, of Poynton, 1573.
Nicholas Brombill, of Roby, 1608.
Lawrence Brownbell, of Poynton, 1602 : Wills at Chester (1545-1620), p. 29.
Oliver Brownbill, of Kirkby, 1614 : ibid. p. 31.

Thus it is clear that our Brownbills have no connexion with the old weapon of the English infantry. The variants in the registers of Prestbury Church (co. Ches.) are Brownbill, Brambell, Broombill, Brownbell, and Browmbell. The earliest entries (1560-80) are almost always Browmbell.

Manchester, 3; Liverpool, 2.

Brownett, Brunet, Brunett. —Bapt. 'the son of Brown,' from Brun or Brune, dim. Brunett; v. Brown.

Brunetta uxor Salomonis. T.
1676. Lewis Brunet and Dorthory Collet : Marriage Alleg. (Canterbury), p. 174.

London, 1, 0, 0; Philadelphia, 0, 5, 2; New York, 0, 1, 1.

Browning, Brunning, Brunwin.—Bapt. 'the son of Browning,' sometimes Bruning. The name was very popular.

Henry Brunwyne, co. Suff., 1273. A.
John Brunwyn, co. Suff., ibid.
Richard Brunwyn, co. Linc., ibid.
Avice Bruning, co. Camb., ibid.
John Bruning, co. Norf., ibid.
Roger Bruning, London, ibid.
Ivo Brunig, co. Hunts, ibid.
Brounyng le Fox, co. Soms., 1 Edw. I : Kirby's Quest, p. 81.
Brounyng Bycheheye, co. Soms, 1 Edw. I : ibid. p. 94.
Agnes Brownyng, 1379 : P. T. Yorks. p. 287.
1804. Married—John Garrard and Ann Brunning : St. Geo. Han. Sq. ii. p. 313.
1809. — Stephen Browning and Elizabeth Yarrow : ibid. p. 409.
London, 48, 3, 1 ; Philadelphia, 40, 0, 0.

Brownjohn. — Nick. 'brown John,' a reversal of John Brown; cf. Prettijohn, Littlejohn. John was so common as a font-name that a qualifying adjective was necessary to identify the different bearers of the name, especaily in days when all the sons in a family might be called John (v. my Curiosities of Puritan Nomenclature, p. 4). The same remark applies to Brownrobert, q.v.

'Eleanor Swetenham married to Henry Brownjohn, gent,' c. 1720 : East Cheshire, ii. 648.
1676. Nathaniel Ferebee and Sarah Brownjohn : Marriage Alleg. (Canterbury), p. 182.
London, 3 ; MDB. (co. Surrey), 1.

Brownnutt.—Nick. Probably a variant of Brownett, q.v. I do not suppose it is a reversal of the syllables in Nutbrown, q.v.

1779. Married—Richard Popple and Sarah Brownnutt : St. Geo. Han. Sq. i. 306.
1800. — William Brownnutt and Diana Williams : ibid. ii. 215.
London, 1.

Brownridge, Brownrigg.—Local, 'at the brown ridge,' from residence thereby. I cannot find the spot, but it looks North English.

1589. Buried—Helen, d. Peter Brownrigge (Browneridge) : St. Jas. Clerkenwell, iv. 39.
1639-40. — Margaret Brownerigg : ibid. iv. 241.

1643. Buried—Margaret, wife of Roger Brownerigge : ibid. iv. 259.
1784. Married—Peter Brownridge and Jane Barker : St. Geo. Han. Sq. i. 335.
London, 2, 4 ; Boston (U.S.), 0, 2.

Brownrobert, Brownrobin.—Nick. 'brown Robert' or 'brown Robin,' a mere reversal of Robert Brown ; v. Brownjohn. Brownrobin, or Brunrobyn, occurs as a surname in the archives of Yarmouth (Norfolk Arch. Soc. iv. 253). In the following instance the same individual took four successive oaths to observe the privileges of the University :

Richard Brownerobarts, citizen of Oxford, 1567 : Reg. Univ. Oxf. vol. ii. pt. ii. p. 306.
Richard Brownrobyns, citizen of Oxford. 1569 : ibid.
Richard Brownerobins, citizen of Oxford, 1570 : ibid. p. 301.
Richard Brownrobart, citizen of Oxford, 1573 : ibid. p. 302.
1567. Richard Brownroberts, or Brownrobyns : ibid. i. 410.

Brownshank.—Nick. 'Brownshank'; cf. Redshank, Shortshank, Sheepshank, &c.

Johannes Brouneshank', 1379 : P. T. Yorks. p. 53.

Brownsmith. — Occup. 'the brownsmith,' a worker in copper and brass; cf. Whitesmith, Blacksmith, Redsmith, and Greensmith. I fear this name is obsolete.

William Brownsmyth, co. Soms., 1 Edw. III : Kirby's Quest, p. 107.
Willelmus Bronesmyth, 1379 : P. T. Yorks. p. 166.
Simon Bronsmyth, 1379 : ibid. p. 163.
'Rallyn Bronsmyth, of Midelham,' 1447, co. York : QQQ. p. 242.
William Brownsmith, rector of Stiffkey, co. Norf., 1559 : FF. ix. 253.
1581. William Brownsmith, co. Essex : Reg. Univ. Oxf. vol. ii. pt. ii. p. 111.
1694. Richard Soame and Mary Brownsmith : Marriage Lic. (Faculty Office), p. 213.

Brownson.—Bapt. 'the son of Brown.'

1776. Married—Stephen Brunson and Jane Boulton : St. Geo. Han. Sq. i. 271.

For other instances, v. Brown (1).

Manchester, 3 ; New York, 2.

Brownswain. — Nick. John Brounsweyn. P. ; Thomas Brouneswayne, C. R., 13 Ric. II. pt. i.

Swain here may be Swain, a fontname, or swain, a peasant (v. Swain).

Brownsword, Brownsworth. — Local, 'of Brownsworth,' or 'Brownsward' (v. Worth). The following entry : Richard Whitswerd, C.R., 6 Edw. III, seems to prove -sward the suffix; cf. Greensward. On the other hand the register of Prestbury Church, co. Cheshire, the district in which the surname seems to have arisen, has it indifferently Brownsworth and Brownsword, and the former still exists in the neighbouring directories.

John Brownsword, master of Macclesfield Grammar School, 1561 : East Cheshire, ii. 518.
1583. Married — Randell Brownesworthe and Ellen Fernley : Reg. Prestbury Ch. p. 79.
1607. — John Brandreth and Dorothe Brownsorde : ibid. p. 176.
1622. George Newall and Eliz. Brownsworth : ibid. p. 236.
Richard Brownsword. AA. 3.
Thomas Brownesword, temp. Eliz. ZZ.
1707. Married—William Brownsword and Elizabeth Akerman : St. Dionis Backchurch, p. 54.
1726. Buried—Ellis Brownsword : St. Antholin (London), p. 158.
Liverpool, 0, 1 ; Philadelphia, 0, 3.

Browse; v. Brewhouse.

Broxholm.—Local, 'of Broxholme,' a parish in co. Lincoln, near Lincoln.

1570. Thomas Broxsam and Ann Lawghton : Marriage Lic. (London), i. 45.
1805. Married — Charles Coltes and Jane Broxholmn : St. Geo. Han. Sq. ii. 317.
London, 1.

Bruce, Browse, Brewis.—Local, 'of Braose' or 'Brause,' the castle of Braose, 'now Brieuse, two leagues from Falaise in Normandy' (Lower, p. 39). Spelt in every conceivable manner. I only furnish a few instances. Sussex, I believe, was the original home of the family.

William de Brause, co. Devon, Hen. III-Edw. I. K.
Bernard de Brus, co. Hunts, 1273. A.
Isabel de Brus, co. Essex, ibid.
Margery de Bruys, co. Oxf., ibid.
William de Breuse, co. Sussex, ibid.
Robert de Brewes, co. Linc., ibid.
William de Brewus, co. Kent, ibid.

This William is spelt in various ways, including most of the above and many others.

London, 28, 2, 1 ; Philadelphia, 50, 0, 0.

Bruckshaw.—Local; v. Brookshaw.

Brumfit, Brumfitt.—Local, 'of Broomfield,' q.v.; *field* as a suffix has been much tortured ; cf. Hatfull for Hatfield.

Henry Bromfyd : Reg. Univ. Oxf. i. 184.
London, 2, 0 ; Otley, 0, 3.

Brummell, Brommell, Brumell, Bromell.—Local, 'of Bromhill,' part of the parish of New Romney, co. Sussex ; cf. Brummett for Broomhead. There seems to have been another locality of the same name in the West country.

John Bromhulle, co. Soms., 1 Edw. III : Kirby's Quest, p. 280.
Geoffrey Bromhulle, co. Soms., 1 Edw. III : ibid.
Walter de Bromhill, co. Devon, 1273. A.
Robert de Brumel, co. Wilts, ibid.

Looking at these references we must undoubtedly seek the West country for the parentage of this local surname.

1758. Married — William Crawshaw and Sarah Brummell : St. Geo. Han. Sq. i. 82.
1796. — Daniel Weston and Hannah Brommell : ibid. ii. 145.
London, 0, 1, 0, 0 ; Philadelphia, 0, 0, 1, 2.

Brummett; v. Broomhead.

Brumpton.—Local, ' of Brumpton.' Parishes, hamlets, townships, and chapelries in cos. Salop, Kent, Middlesex, N. Rid. Yorks, and Somerset.

Peter de Brumpton, co. Derby, 1273. A.
Hugh de Brompton, co. Hunts, ibid.
Bryan de Brumpton, co. Heref., 20 Edw. I. R.
Adam de Brumpton, co. Salop, ibid.
1552. Baptised—John Brumton : Kensington Ch. p. 83.
— Bapt.—Ann, d. John Brompton : ibid. p. 3.
1768. Married — William Myers and Ann Brompton : St. Geo. Han. Sq. i. 182. London, 1.

Brumwich ; v. Bromwich.

Brumwin; v. Brunwin.

Brundish.—Local, ' of Brundish,' a parish in co. Suffolk.

Robert de Brundis, co. Essex, 1273. A.
Edmund de Brundish, rector of Castor,

co. Norf., 1349, 'buried at Brundish, in Suffolk ': FF. v. 428.
1601. Robert Brundish : Reg. Univ. Oxf. i. 355.
MDB. (Suffolk), 3.

Brundrett, Brundrit, Brundritt, Brundrette.—? Local, ' of Brundreth ' (?). A surname belonging to the Lanc.and Cheshire border. Probably the suffix is *-heath*, as in Blackheath.

1562. Married—Robert Brundreth (of Bollington) and Ales Potte : Reg. Prestbury Ch. (co. Ches.), p. 7.

Two close neighbours are thus described :

Margaret Brundreth, of Bowden, 1618 : Wills at Chester, L. and C. R. S. p. 32.
Edward Brundrett, of Bollington, 1618: ibid.

It will be seen that the Bollington Brundreths have become Brundrett.

John Brundreth, mayor of Macclesfield, 1621 : East Cheshire, ii. 465.
1757. Married—William Brundritt and Ann Rothwell : St. Geo. Han. Sq. i. 73.
Manchester, 12, 1, 1, 0 ; London, 1, 0, 0, 0 ; MDB. (co. Ches.), 2, 2, 1, 0 ; Brundrette, Boston (U.S.), 1.

Brune.—(1) Bapt. (2) Nick. ; v. Brown.

Brunel, Brunell, Brunnell.—Nick. Personal name of complexion, dim. of Fr. Brun, Eng. Brown, generally found as Burnell, q.v. Brunellus Carpenter (E.) is also entered as Burnellus.

1571. Robert Brownell and Alice Mathewe : Marriage Lic. (London), i. 49.
London, 1, 0, 1 ; New York, 0, 1, 0.

Brunet, Brunett; v. Brownett.

Brunker.—Bapt. ' the son of Brungard ' ; cf. Brynjar (Yonge, ii. 313).

Edyth Brungar, co. Soms., 1 Edw. III : Kirby's Quest, p. 239.
Adam Bryngard, co. Soms., 1 Edw. III : ibid. p. 241.
John Bryngard, co. Soms., 1 Edw. III : ibid.
Aylwin Bringert, co. Berks, Hen. III- Edw. I. K.
1603. Edward Brouncker, co. Wilts : Reg. Univ. Oxf. vol. ii. pt. ii. p. 268.
— William Brouncker, co. Wilts : ibid.
1617. Henry Brounker, co. Middlesex : ibid. p. 364.
1605. Buried—Dorothie Brunker : St. Jas. Clerkenwell, iv. 89.
London, 2 ; Philadelphia, 2.

Brunning.—Bapt. ; v. Browning.

Brunswin.—Nick. ' the Brunswine' (i. e. the brown swine), an early name for the porpoise or seal. ' *Bunswyne*, or delfyne, *foca*, *delphinus, suillus* ' : Prompt. Parv. p. 54. v. Way's note appended.

Richard Brunswin, co. Linc., 1273. A.

Brunton.—Local, 'of Brunton,' two townships in the parish of Gosforth, co. Northumberland. But no doubt often ' of Brumpton,' q.v. ; cf. Brunwin and Brumwin.

Adam de Brunton, co. Salop, 20 Edw. I. R.
1773. Married—Joseph Wheatley and Eliz. Brunton : St. Geo. Han. Sq. i. 227.
London, 11 ; Boston (U.S.), 3 ; Philadelphia, 1.

Brunwin, Brumwin.—Bapt. ' the son of Brunwin.' It is curious to note how frequently *n* and *m* are interchangeable. Brunwin is sometimes found as Brumwin. In the Modern Domesday Book for co. Essex there are four Brunwins and two Brumwins.

1801. Married—Henry Brunwin and Eliz. Hancock : St. Geo. Han. Sq. ii. 234.
London, 1, 0.

Bruselance, Brusebat. — Nick. ; cf. Breakspear, Wagstaff, Shakespear, &c.

Robert Bruselance, co. Linc., 1273. A.
John Bruselaunce, mayor of Bristol, 1229 : YYY. p. 669.
Nicholas Brusebat, co. Soms., 1 Edw. III : Kirby's Quest, p. 230.

Brushfield.—Local, ' of Brushfield,' a township in the parish of Bakewell, co. Derby.

1799. Married—Joseph Brushfield and Eliz. Taylor : St. Geo. Han. Sq. ii. 201. London, 2.

Bruton.—Local, ' the Breton,' a native of Brittany ; v. Brittain.

Elias le Brutun, co. Oxf., 1273. A.
Almaric le Brutun, co. Bucks, ibid.
John le Brutun, co. Oxf., ibid.
Richard Brutun, co. Oxf., ibid.
1616. William Bruton, co. Devon : Reg. Univ. Oxf. vol. ii. pt. ii. p. 357.
1750. Married—William Bruton and Frances Richardson : St. Geo. Han. Sq. i. 44.
London, 8 ; Philadelphia, 1 ; New York, 8.

Bryan, Bryant, Brien, Brian, Briant.—Bapt. 'the son of Bryan.' The *t* in Briant and Bryant is of course excrescent. Bryan was not an importation from Ireland, though its popularity as an English font-name is gone. It lingered in North Yorkshire, Westmoreland, and Furness till the close of the last century. 'The Bretons, who joined in the Norman Conquest, imported it to England' (Yonge, ii. 50). 'Brien was always a favourite in Brittany, and is very common as a surname with the peasantry there' (ibid.) ; v. Brine.

Wydo Bryan, co. Devon, 1273. A.
Alicia Brien, co. Camb., ibid.
Acelot Bryon, co. Camb., ibid.
Thomas fil. Brian, co. York, ibid.
Alan fil. Brian, co. York, ibid.
Brian de Brampton, co. Glouc., ibid.
William Brian, co. Soms., 1 Edw. III : Kirby's Quest, p. 207.
Colin Briant, London, 1269: WWW. p. 125.

The intermediate stage between Brian and Briant, or Bryant, is found in the following entry: '1772. Married—John Briand and Barbara Backhouse': St. George's, Hanover Square, p. 222. Cf. *riband* and *ribbon*, and Simmons and Simmonds.

London, 24, 61, 6, 2, 14 ; Philadelphia, 102, 48, 4, 6, 0.

Bryce.—Bapt. ; v. Brice.

Bryer.—Local ; v. Brear.

London, 5 ; Philadelphia, 1 ; New York, 2.

Brymer, Brimmer.—Bapt. 'the son of Brihmar,' or 'Brichtmar.' In Domesday Brihtmar, co. Suffolk ; Britmar, co. Somerset ; Brihmarus and Brumarus, co. Suffolk.

Brihmer Prepositus, Pipe Roll, 5 Hen. II.
Adam Brichmar, co. Hertf., 20 Edw. I. R.
1731. Married—John Blake and Ann Maria Brimmer : St. Antholin (London), p. 144.
1742. — Luke Brimer and Frances Kerwinn : St. Geo. Chap. Mayfair, p. 22.
1745. — Robert Brymer and Margarett Hogg : ibid. p. 25.

London, 2, 2 ; Philadelphia, o, 2.

Bryson.—Bapt. ; v. Brice.

Bubb, Bub.—Bapt. 'the son of Bubb.' Lower, quoting Ferguson, says: 'Bubba, an ancient Teutonic name.' I would, however, suggest that in some cases, like Babb (q.v.), it is a nick. of Barbara, a favourite fontal name in the surname period.

Henry Bubbe, co. Soms., 1 Edw. III : Kirby's Quest, p. 193.
Robert Bubbe, co. Soms., 1 Edw. III : ibid. p. 195.
William Bubbe, co. Wilts, 1273. A.
Simon Bubbe, co. Wilts, ibid.
Matilda Bubbe, co. Camb., ibid.
'Richard Dubbe, alias Bubbe de Horsey,' 18 Edw. I : BBB. p. 420.
1801. Married—Joseph Bubb and Martha Purkiss : St. Geo. Han. Sq. ii. 236.

London, 5, 0 ; Philadelphia, 1, 1 ; New York, 0, 3.

Buchanan.—Local, 'of Buchanan,' a parish in co. Stirling. This name has ramified strongly, and almost become English by familiarity.

1807. Married—John Buchanan and Elizabeth Richardson : St. Geo. Han. Sq. ii. 377.

London, 18 ; Philadelphia, 144.

Buck, Bucke. — Nick. 'the buck.' Two Johns in the village of Linford, co. Oxf., are set down as John Giffard le Bok and John Giffard le Hof (Placita de Quo Warranto, Edw. I. p. 86). No doubt both were sons of one Giffard, both being baptized by the same name, as was then common. The nicknames were added to secure identity (v. my Curiosities of Puritan Nomenclature, p. 4, where records of even three Johns in a family are quoted).

Roger le Buk, 1313. M.
Robertus Buk, 1379: P. T. Yorks. p. 147.
Robert Bok, co. Hunts, 1273. A.
Richard Boke, co. Oxf., ibid.
Robert de (?le) Buk, co. Essex, ibid.
Thomas Buk, co. Camb., ibid.
1572. Bapt.—Joyce, d. William Bucke: St. Jas. Clerkenwell, i. 7.
1764. Married—Benjamin Buck and Ann Taylor : St. Geo. Han. Sq. i. 130.
London, 27, 1 ; Philadelphia, 116, 0.

Buckby, Buckbee, Bugbee, Bugby.—Local, 'of Buckby,' a parish in co. Northampton, four miles from Daventry. I can find but one or two modern English representatives, but the surname

thrives across the Atlantic. With Bugbee, cf. Applebee for Appleby, and Bugden for Buckden.

William de Buckeby, or Bukeby, co. Bucks, 1273. A.
1665. William Tighe and Hannah Buckby : Marriage Alleg. (Canterbury), p. 104.
1675. William Holbeach and Jane Bugby : ibid. p. 246.
1806. Married — Joseph Baker and Sarah Bugbee : St. Geo. Han. Sq. ii. 344.
1807. — Jervoise Clark Jervoise Witcum Dancaster Bugby and Harriet Denman : ibid. p. 364.

London Court Dir., 0, 0, 0, 1 ; New York, 0, 7, 1, 0 ; Philadelphia, 5, 0, 4, 0 ; Boston (U.S.), 0, 0, 18, 0.

Buckenham.—Local, 'of Buckenham,' four parishes in co. Norfolk, viz. Old and New Buckenham, Buckenham Parva, and Buckenham Ferry.

William de Bukenham, co. Norf., 1273. A.
Ralph de Bukenham, co. Norf., ibid.
Peter de Bukenham, co. Norf., 1277: FF. i. 261.
Hugh de Bukenham, co. Norf., 1332 : ibid. p. 422.
Richard Buckenham, vicar of Quarles, co. Norf., temp. 1300: ibid. ix. 248.
Oliver Buckenham, co. Norf., 25 Eliz. : ibid. x. 14.
1786. Married—Edward Mayhew and Sarah Buckinham : St. Geo. Han. Sq. i. 385.
London, 3 ; MDB. (co. Suffolk), 1 ; New York, 3.

Buckerell. — (1) Nick. 'the buckerell,' a young buck ; cf. Cockerell and v. Buck. (2) Local, 'of Buckerell,' a parish in co. Devon, near Honiton.

Andrew Bokerell, Lord Mayor of London, 1232–7 : N. and Q. 1857, p. 197.
Peter Bokerel, co. Oxf., 1273. A.
Mathew Bokerel, London, ibid.
Robert Bokerel, co. Norf., ibid.
William Bokerell, London, ibid.

Buckeridge, Buckridge.—Local, 'at the Buckridge,' with an intrusive *e*, making three syllables ; cf. Green-a-way or Ott-a-way. I cannot find the spot, but evidently it was a ridge frequented by bucks ; v. Buck and Ridge.

1615. Anthony Buckeridge, co. Wilts : Reg. Univ. Oxf. vol. ii. pt. ii. p. 340.
1621. John Buckeridge, London : ibid. p. 400.
1747. Married—Thomas Hill and Mary Buckeridge : St. Geo. Chap. Mayfair, p. 99.
London, 5, 0 ; New York, 0, 3.

Buckett, Budgett, Bowkett.
—Bapt. 'the son of Buchard,' a form of Burchard; v. Burchett, and cf. Rickett for Ricard.

Robert Bukhard, rector of Gawsworth, Cheshire, 1383: East Cheshire, ii. 587.
Ralph Buchard, co. Oxf., 1273. A.
Walter Buchard, co. Wilts, ibid.
Godfrey Buchet, or Bucket, co. Camb., ibid.
1591–2. Matthew Buckett, co. Dorset: Reg. Univ. Oxf. vol. ii. pt. ii. p. 190.

Foreign immigration has swelled the number of our Bucketts, &c. The Visitation of London (1633–5), vol. i. p. 117, has 'Michaell Bucket borne in the dominions under the Emperor nigh Hedleborow.' His son was 'Michaell Bucket of London, made a free denison anno 14 Elizabeth.' His son Rowland Buckett was a London alderman, 1634. The origin of the surname remains the same.

London, 2, 3, 1.

Buckholt.
—Local, 'at the buck-holt,' i.e. the wood frequented by bucks; v. Buck and Holt.

Peter Atte-buckholt. J.

Buckingham.
— Local, 'of Buckingham.'

John de Bukingham, co. Oxf., 1273. A.
1648. Bapt.—George, s. John Buckingham: St. Jas. Clerkenwell, i. 171.
1773. Married—Philip Buckingham and Eliz. Coward: St. Geo. Han. Sq. i. 229.
London, 24; MDB. (co. Devon), 15; Philadelphia, 24.

Buckland.
—Local, 'of Buckland,' parishes in cos. Bucks, Gloucester, Hertford, Kent, Somerset, Surrey, &c. Originally the *laund*, or open space in the wood, where the bucks grazed; a glade, now spelled *lawn* (v. Lowndes).

Robert de Bokelond, co. Soms., 1 Edw. III: Kirby's Quest, p. 95.
Jackyn atte Boclond, C. R., 32 Edw. I.
John de Bocklonde, co. Oxf., 1273. A.
Nicholas de Bocland, co. Kent, ibid.
William de Boclond, co. Bedf., ibid.
Phillip de Boclaund, co. Herts, ibid.
John de Boclaunde, 1306. M.
1574. Bapt.—William, s. Walter Buckland: St. Jas. Clerkenwell, i. 8.
1579–80. Thomas Leadham and Cicely Buckland: Marriage Lic. (London), i. 94.
1588. Bapt. — Margery, d. Thomas Buckland: St. Jas. Clerkenwell, i. 20.
London, 20; Philadelphia, 4.

Buckle, Buckell, Buckel.
—Local, 'at the buck-hill,' from residence thereby, i.e. the rising ground frequented by bucks; cf. Buckhurst, Buckholt, &c. With the modified Buckle or Buckell, cf. Tickle or Tickell for Tickhill. Dozens, I might say hundreds, of similar instances will be found in this dictionary.

1570–1. Christopher Buckle and Alice Buntinge: Marriage Lic. (London), i. 47.
1588. Married—Robert Purie and Elizabeth Buckle: St. Mary Aldermary, p. 7.
1612. Thomas Buckle and Mary Cansfield: Marriage Lic. (London), ii. 16.
1626. John Buckell and Eliz. Whiteside: ibid. p. 167.
London, 5, 1, 1; New York, 1, 0, 0; Boston (U.S.), 1, 0, 0.

Buckler.
—Occup. 'the buckler,' a maker of buckles.

Beatrice Bokeler, 4 Edw. III: Freemen of York, i. 26.
Reginald le Bokiller, Fines Roll, 14 Edw. II.
John le Bokeler, London, 1273. A.
1572. Nicholas Buckler, St. Alban Hall: Reg. Univ. Oxf. vol. ii. pt. ii. p. 40.
Richard Bokeler, temp. Eliz. Z.
1651. Married—Hugh Edwards to Jane Buckler: St. Thomas the Apostle (London), p. 19.
1764. William Taylor and Eliz. Buckler: St. Geo. Han. Sq. i. 138.
London, 4; New York, 1; Boston (U.S.), 2.

Bucklermaker.
— Occup. 'a maker of bucklers,' i.e. shields. 'Bokelermakers, dyers, and lethersellers' (Cocke Lorelle's Bote). The 'Buklermakers' played with the 'Shethers' and Bladesmiths in the York Plays (p. xxiii).

Mathew Bucklermaker, Ludlow Ch.: Camd. Soc.

Bucklesmith.
— A manufacturer of buckles, included in the list by the author of Cocke Lorelle's Bote: 'Brydel-bytters, blacke-smyths, and ferrars; bokell-smythes, horseleches, and goldbeters.'

John le Bokelsmyth, London. X.
John Bukelsmyth, Patent Roll, 2 Hen. IV. pt. ii.

Buckley.
—Local, 'of Buckley.' (1) A parish in dioc. of St. Albans; (2) a township (Bulkeley) in co. Cheshire; v. Bulkeley. The Buckleys of cos. Lancashire and Cheshire are nearly all Bulkeleys by descent.

Christian de Bukkelegh, co. Lanc., 1332: Lay Subsidy (Rylands). p. 34.
David de Buckelay, co. York, 1273. A.
Michael de Bokele, co. Suff., ibid.
'I, Caterin Bulkley, of Chedale . . . geve and bequethe unto Sir Ric. Buckley, Kt., my nephewe, my best table clothe of diapr': ' Will of Lady Katherine Bulkeley, 1559.

In the same will Lady Katherine refers to 'Mr. Thomas Buckley, my brother' (East Cheshire, i. 206).

1589. Abraham Buckley, co. Lanc.: Reg. Univ. Oxf. vol. ii. pt. ii. p. 174.
London, 20; Manchester, 52; West Riding Court Dir., 14; Philadelphia, 166.

Buckman, Bucknam.
—Local, 'of Buckenham.' Several parishes so called in co. Norfolk; cf. Deadman, Totman, Putman, for Debenham, Tottenham, and Puttenham. Thus Buckman is one of a distinct class of local surnames where the terminative *-enham* is modified into *-man*.

Ralph de Bukenham, co. Norf., 1273. A.
William de Bukenham, co. Norf., ibid.
1619. Robert Gould and Ursula Buckman: Marriage Lic. (London), ii. 76.
1799. Married—James Buckman and Hannah Coller: St. Geo. Han. Sq. ii. 205.
London, 3, 0; Philadelphia, 21, 0; Boston (U.S.), 6, 8.

Buckmaster.
— Local, 'of Buckminster,' a parish in Leicester, not far from Melton Mowbray; cf. Killmister for Kilminster. There is a strong official appearance about the name, suggesting a 'master of the hounds,' but I find no evidence for it; the corruption is merely imitative.

Simon de Bokminstre, 1295. M.
Simon de Bukminstre, 1297, ibid.
Roger de Bukeminstre, co. Linc., Hen. III–Edw. I. K.
1618. Bapt.—James, son of James Bookemaister: St. Mary Aldermary, p. 75.
1623. John Buckmuster, settled in Virginia: Hotten's Lists of Emigrants, p. 227.
1629. Bapt.—Susan, d. William Buckmaster: St. Jas. Clerkenwell, i. 112.
1769. Married—Joseph Buckmaster and Mary Tinker: St. Geo. Han. Sq. i. 187.
London, 8; Crockford, 5; New York, 4.

Bucknall, Bucknell, Bucknill.
—Local, (1) 'of Bucknell,' a parish in co. Oxford, near Bicester; (2) 'of Bucknall,' a parish in co. Salop, twelve miles from Ludlow.

Adam de Buckenhull, co. Oxf., 1273. A.
Robert de Buckelhull, co. Oxf., ibid.
Gilbert de Bockenhull, co. Salop, ibid.

Juliana de Buckenhull, co. Oxf., 1273. A.
Madoc de Bockenhull, co. Salop, ibid.
1713. Bapt.—Edward, s. of Saml.
Buckenhill : St. Jas. Clerkenwell, ii. 73.
London, 2, 2, 1 ; Philadelphia, 0, 2, 0.

Buckskin, Buskin.—Nick. A soft leather specially prepared for leggings ; probably the sobriquet of a leather-hosier (v. Leatherhose). Hence 'Buskines, fine boots' (Florio).

Walter Bucskyn, Close Roll, 31 Edw. I.
Peter Buckeskyn. B.
Nicholas Buxskyn, temp. 1300. M.
Thomas Buckeskyn, rector of Stokesby, co. Norf., 1337 : FF. xi. 251.
'A very stout, puffy man in buckskins and Hessian boots' : Thackeray.

Buckskin inevitably tended to form Buskin, and is so represented in the directories.

London, 0, 5.

Buckson.—Local, 'of Buckston'; v. Buxton ; cf. Kelson for Kelston, &c.

Philadelphia, 2.

Buckston.—Local ; v. Buxton.

Buckthorp, Buckthought.—Local, 'of Buckthorpe,' a parish in E. Rid. Yorks, about seven miles from Pocklington. Having travelled in recent times to Land's End, it got corrupted 'by the way' into Buckthought.

Hamelin de Bugtorp, co. Notts, 1273. A.
Geoffrey de Bugetorp, co. York, Hen. III-Edw. I. K.
1806. Married—Joseph Buckthorp and Ann Bonner : St. Geo. Han. Sq. ii. 345.
London, 1, 0 ; New Quay (co. Cornwall), 0, 1 ; East Taphouse, Liskeard (co. Cornwall), 0, 1 ; St. Colomb Major, 0, 2.

Buckton, Bucktone.—Local, 'of Buckton,' a township in the parish of Bridlington, E. Rid. Yorks; also a parish in dioc. of Hereford.

Laurence de Bukton, co. Northampt., 1273. A.
Nicolas de Boketon, co. Notts, ibid.
Simon de Buctone, co. Linc., ibid.
Adam de Bucton, co. Soms., 20 Edw. I. R.
1565-6. William Bucton and Sabina Hunteman : Marriage Lic. (London), i. 32.
West Riding Court Dir., 6, 0 ; London, 2, 0 ; Philadelphia, 0, 1.

Bucktrout.—Nick. 'the male trout.' The surname still lingers well-nigh on the very spot of its birth ; cf. Trout.

Johanna Buktrowte, 1379 : P. T. Yorks. p. 180.
Robertus Buktrout, 1379 : ibid. p. 218.
1578. William Bucktrowt : Reg. Univ. Oxf. iii. 74.
1700. Bapt.—Mary, d. of Benjamin Bucktrout : St. Jas. Clerkenwell, i. 386.
Leeds Dir., 1.

Budd.—Bapt. 'the son of Bud,' or 'Bude,' a strongly established surname as the Hundred Rolls prove, some of the fontal names attached suggesting a Flemish origin. Both Budkin and Budcock, the pet forms, existed, confirming its popularity. No doubt Bud was the nick. of the universal favourite, Baldwin, to avoid the form Bawd ; cf. Bubb and Babb from Barbara.

William Budekin, co. Camb., 1273. A.
Simon Budecok, co. Norf., ibid.
Juliana Budde, co. Oxf., ibid.
Iward Bude, co. Norf., ibid.
William Budde, co. Oxf., ibid.
Simon Bud, co. Hunts, ibid.
John Budde, co. Soms., 1 Edw. III : Kirby's Quest, p. 84.
1626. Bapt.—Ellinor, d. Symon Budd : St. Jas. Clerkenwell, i. 104.
1740. Married—Christopher Budd and Prudence South : St. Geo. Han. Sq. i. 24.
London, 16 ; MDB. (co. Soms.) ; Philadelphia, 47.

Budden.—Bapt. 'the son of Budden,' i.e. Baldwin ; v. Budd.

Ermegard Budun, co. Northampt., 1273. A.
1582. John Budden (co. Dorset), Merton Coll. : Reg. Univ. Oxf. vol. ii. pt. ii. p. 123.
1597. Bapt.—Katheryne, d. Clement Budden : St. Dionis Backchurch, p. 89.
1632. Married—Simon Budden and Joane Hulberstav : Kensington Ch. p. 70.
London, 10 ; Boston (U.S.), 1.

Buddle.—Offic. 'the beadle'; M.E. *bedel* ; A.S. *býdel*. Cf. Boodle.

Lucas Budellus de Clayburne, co. Salop, 1273. A.
Eylardus le Budel, co. Oxf., 1273. A.
Reginald le Budell, co. Salop, ibid.
William le Budell, co. Soms., 1 Edw. III : Kirby's Quest, p. 234.
Robert le Budel, co. Soms., 1 Edw. III : ibid. p. 268.
1778. Married—Matthew Sooby and Grace Buddles : St. Geo. Han. Sq. i. 291.
London, 1.

Budgett. — Bapt. 'the son of Buchard'; v. Buckett.

1787. Married—John Hawkins and Sarah Budgett : St. Geo. Han. Sq. i. 404.

Bugbee and Bugby.—Local ; v. Buckby.

Bugden.—Local, 'of Buckden,' a parish in co. Huntingdon, four miles from Huntingdon, where for generations was a residence for the bishops of Lincoln. It was familiarly known as Bugden. Thomas Barlow (1607-91), bishop of Lincoln, 'resided so constantly at the episcopal palace at Buckden, near Huntingdon, and was so little seen in other parts of the diocese, that he was contemptuously styled "Bishop of Bugden," and charged with never having entered his cathedral' (Dict. Nat. Biog. iii. 227). The instances below supply ample proof of locality.

John Bukden, rector of Baldswell, co. Norf., 1419 : FF. viii. 186.
John Bugden, gent., co. Huntingdon : ibid. i. 545.
1807. Married—William Bugden and Ann Webley : St. Geo. Han. Sq. ii. 375.
London, 1.

Bugg, Bugge.—(1) ? Nick. 'the bug,' i.e. the hobgoblin, the scarecrow ; M.E. *bugge*. (2) ? Personal, 'the son of Bugge' (?). The early entries seem to prove conclusively that it is not local ; there is no local prefix to any of them. Probably (1) is the correct origin. The sobriquet would be a most natural one ; v. Bug, *sb.*, H.E.D.

Bate Bugge, co. York, 1273. A.
William Bugge, co. Oxf., ibid.
Osberne Bugge, co. Oxf., ibid.
John Bugg, co. Soms., 1 Edw. III : Kirby's Quest, p. 129.
Willelmus Bugge, 1379 : P. T. Yorks. p. 25.
Robertus Bugg', 1379 : ibid. p. 26.
Johannes Bugg', 1379 : ibid. p. 27.
Edmund Bugg, C. R., 1 Hen. IV. pt. i.
1548. Bapt.—John Bugge : St. Michael, Cornhill, p. 75.
John Bugg, March 30, 1592 : Cal. State Papers (Domestic), iii. 205.
1781. Married—Henry Annets and Mary Bugg : St. Geo. Han. Sq. i. 321.
London, 3, 0 ; New York, 0, 1.

Builder, Bulder.—Occup. 'the builder,' a mason, a waller, a builder; M.E. *bulden*, to build.

Robert Bulder, co. York, 1273. A.
Rogerus Bulder, 1379 : P. T. Yorks. p. 54.
Alicia Bulder, 1379 : ibid.
Johannes Bulder, 1379 : ibid.
New York, 0, 1.

Bulkeley, Bulkley.—Local, 'of Bulkeley,' a township in the parish of Malpas, co. Cheshire. The Manchester Directory contains fifty-two Buckleys. Most of these represent a modified form of Bulkeley; v. Buckley. I may add that the township is set down in Lewis's Topographical Dict. as ‘Buckley or Bulkeley.’

Richard de Bulkelegh, Cheadle, 1349: East Cheshire, i. 181.
William de Bulkelegh, Cheadle, 1379: ibid.
Richard de Bulkeley, Cheadle, 1454: ibid.
1587. Lancelot Bulkeley, Anglesea: Reg. Univ. Oxf. vol. ii. pt. ii. p. 160.
1597. Gabriel Bulkley, Anglesea: ibid. p. 224.
London, o, 2; Crockford, 4, 1; Philadelphia, 5, o; Boston (U.S.), 4, 2.

Bull.—Nick. ‘the bull,’ from the fierce disposition, or thickset proportions, of the original bearer of the sobriquet; cf. Pigg, Wildbore, Bullock, &c. John Bull is now the national nickname in a similar sense.

John le Bole, co. Soms., 1 Edw. III: Kirby's Quest, p. 101.
William le Bole, co. Camb., 1273. A.
Geoffrey Bolle, co. Suff., ibid.
Ralph le Bule, co. Oxf., ibid.
Robert le Bule, co. Soms., ibid.
Willelmus Bulle, 1379: P. T. Yorks. p. 193.
Elena Bull', 1379: ibid. p. 197.
1550. Robert Bull and Grace Paget: Marriage Lic. (London), i. 13.
1588. Bapt.—Alban, s. Thomas Bull: St. Jas. Clerkenwell, i. 20.
London, 81.

Bullard.—Occup. ‘a bull-herd,’ v. Bellhird; cf. Coward, Oxnard, &c., and v. Bullockherd.

Fulco Bullard, co. Kent, Hen. III-Edw. I. K.
Geoffrey Bolhard, co. Wilts, 1273. A.
Fulco Bulard, co. Kent, ibid.
1672. Jeremiah Bullard and Lucy Snowe: Marriage Alleg. (Canterbury), p. 73.
1806. Married—John Bullard and Mary Carter: St. Geo. Han. Sq. ii. 342.
London, 3; MDB. (co. Hunts), 1; Philadelphia, 6.

Bullen, Bollen, Bullene, Boleyn.—Local, ‘of Boulogne.’

‘Edmond Gray, slene at Bollen’: Visit. Yorkshire, 1563. p. 149.
Gilebert de Boolon, co. Northumb., 1168: KKK. vi. p. 13.
Pharamund de Boloynne, co. Bucks, 1273. A.
Richard de Boloygne, co. Soms., ibid.
John de Boloyne, co. Camb., ibid.

Thomas Boloyne, co. Essex, ibid.
Simon, Count of ‘Buloyne,’ co. Oxf. A.
Simon de Boleyn. FF.
Robert Buleyn, temp. 1580. Z.
1734. Married—Nicholas Bullen and Jane Carr: St. Geo. Han Sq. i. 14.
1739. — Thomas Bulline and Mary Stanfield: ibid. p. 23.
1759. — Joseph Cooper and Ann Bullin: ibid. p. 89.
London, 17, 2, 0, 0; Crockford, 4, 0, 0, 0; New York, 1, 0, 1, 0; Boston (U.S.), 2, 0, 0, 1.

Bulley, Bolley.—Local, ‘of Bulley,’ a parish in co. Glouc. A very familiar name in co. Devon.

Hugh de Bolley, co. Devon, Hen. III-Edw. I. K.
Muriel de Bolley, co. Devon, ibid.
Johannes de Bullay, 1379: P. T. Yorks. p. 139.
1699. Married—John Pitcher and Eliz. Bulley: St. Jas. Clerkenwell, iii. 221.
London, 4, 1; Exeter, 2, 0; Plymouth, 3, 0; New York, 2, 1.

Bullfinch.—Nick. ‘the bullfinch’; cf. Goldfinch and Finch. This surname seems to have deserted us and emigrated to America.

Robert Bulfinch, Close Roll, 14 Edw. III. pt. i.
1670. John Bullfinch and Mary Reeves: Marriage Alleg. (Canterbury), p. 186.
Philadelphia, 5; Boston (U.S.), 2.

Bullhead, Bullitt.—Nick. ‘the bull-head,’ a man with a bull-shaped head, or of bull-headed impetuosity; v. Bullhead and Bull-headed in H.E.D. My instances in this sense are very much earlier than those there given. With the American Bullitt, cf. Birkett for Birkhead, or Blackett for Blackhead, q.v.

John Boleheved, co. Hunts, 1273. A.
Richard Boleheved, co. Hunts, ibid.
John Bolehewed, c. 1300. M.
Adam Bulhead, 1379: P.T.Yorks. p. 236.
Philadelphia, o, 4.

Bullingbrook. — Local, ‘of Bolingbroke,’ a parish in co. Lincoln.

MDB. (co. Suffolk), 1.

Bullinger, Pullinger, Ballinger, Ballenger.—Occup. ‘le boulanger,’ the baker. Pullinger is a sharpened form.

Richard le Bulenger. E.
1564. Bapt.—(blank) d. John Bullinger: St. Thomas the Apostle (London), p. 23.
1711. Married—Abraham Bishop and Anne Ballinger: St. Peter, Cornhill, p. 69.
1769. Bapt.—John Turd and Rebecca Pullinger: St. Geo. Han. Sq. i. 186.

London, o, 1, 1, 0; Crockford, 1, 0, 0, 0; Philadelphia, 4, 18, 13, 18.

Bullitt.—Nick.; v. Bullhead.

1751. Married—John Hardcastle and Ruth Bullet: St. Geo. Chap. Mayfair, p. 192.
Philadelphia, 4.

Bullivant, Bonnivant, Bonifant, Bonnavant.—? Bapt. and nick. ‘Bon-enfant,’ Englished in some cases to Goodchild, q.v. Bullivant is the present representative form.

William Bonenfaunt, or Bonaffaunt, 1302. M.
Bonenfant Judæus (the Jew), Pipe Roll, 5 Hen. II.
Walter Bonenfant, co. Camb., 1273. A.
Bonenfant Judaus, co. Camb, ibid.
Henry Bonefant, co. Bucks, ibid.
John Bonefaunt, co. Oxf., ibid.
Robert Ballyfaunt, temp. Eliz. Z.
John Bonnyvaunt, ibid.
Phillip Bonivant, 1631: St. Dionis Backchurch (London), p. 102.
1637. Bapt.—Eliz., d. Edmond Bollifante: St. Jas. Clerkenwell, i. 135.
1674. Bapt. — Frances, d. William Bullivant: St. Thomas the Apostle (London), p. 66.
London, 7, 0, 1, 0; Boston (U.S.), 1, 0, 0, 1

Bullman, Bulman.—Occup. ‘the bull-man,’ i.e. bull-herd; v. Bullard, and cf. Coward and Cowman, Hefferman, &c.

John Boleman, co. Camb., 1273. A.
1392. Walter Bulleman, rector of Intwood, co. Norf.: FF. v. 42.
1530. Thomas Bulman, prior of Wayborn, co. Norf.: ibid. ix. 451.
1577. Thomas Wrothe and Johanna Bullman: Marriage Lic. (London), i. 78.
William Bulman. D.
1569. Buried — Ralph Bulman: St. Michael, Cornhill, p. 191.
1601. Married—Thomas Baskervile and Anne Bullman: St. Antholin (London), p. 40.
1628. Bapt.—John, s. Richard Bulman: St. Jas. Clerkenwell, i. 110.
London, 1, 3; New York, 3, 2.

Bullock.—Nick. ‘the bullock,’ affixed upon some one young, strong, and sturdy; cf. Bull, Stott, &c. A common entry in early registers.

Alan Bulloc, co. Linc., 1273. A.
Ralph Bullokke, co. Norf., ibid.
Godwin Bulloc, co. Suff., ibid
Richard Bulluc, co. Oxf., ibid.
William Bulloc, co. Oxf., ibid.
Walterus Bullok, 1379: P. T. Yorks. p. 153.
1568. Simon Bullocke, Norwich: FF. iv. 458.

L

1576. John Bullock and Amye Pollye: Marriage Lic. (London), i. 71.
1606. Married—George Pattenson and Alice Bullock: St. Dionis Backchurch, p. 15.
London, 32 ; Philadelphia, 29.

Bullockherd. — Occup. ' the bullock herd,' a tender of bullocks ; cf. Calvert, Coward, Oxnard, &c. ; v. Hird.

John le Bollochurde, co. Soms., 1 Edw. III : Kirby's Quest, p. 231.

Bullpitt.—Local, 'at the bull-pit' (?) ; cf. Cockpit and Bearblock, q.v.

1738. Married—John Bullpitt and Mary Watts: St. Antholin (London), p. 149.
1756. — Edward Willan and Mary Bullpatt : St. Geo. Han. Sq. i. 63.
1780. — William Cooke and Amy Bulpitt: ibid. p. 315.
London, 1.

Bulmer, Bullimer. — Local, ' of Bulmer,' parishes in N. Rid. Yorks and co. Essex. Doubtless the former place is the chief parent. In the latter county the surname is found sometimes in the guise of Bullimer ; cf. Greenaway for Greenway, or Ottaway for Ottway.

Walter de Bulmer, *mercer*, 1319-20: Freemen of York (Surtees Soc.), i. 19.
Richard de Bulmer, *tewer*, 1310-12: ibid. p. 14.
Bertram de Bulemer, 1143: DDD. i. 97.
John de Bulmer, co. Leic., 1273. A.
Roger de Bolemere, co. Essex, ibid.
Ansthetill de Bulmer, co. York, 20 Edw. I. R.
Walter Bolymer, co. Soms., 1 Edw. III : Kirby's Quest, p. 117.
1576. Richard Leyle and Margaret Bulmer, *widow*: Marriage Lic. (London), i. 69.
1595-6. John Beeston and Prudence Balmer: ibid. p. 228.
1656. Married—Henery Bosgrave and Mary Bullmar: St. Mary Aldermary, p. 26.
1780. — William Bulmer and Sarah Boyton: St. Geo. Han. Sq. i. 307.
York, 6, 0; London, 10, 0; MDB. (co. Essex), 0, 1; New York, 1, 0; Philadelphia, 8, 0.

Bulstrode. — Local, ' of Bulstrode,' an estate in co. Bucks (Lower's Patr. Brit. p. 45).

Preceptor Domus Milicie Templi de Bulestrode, Bucks, 1273. A.
1592. Henry Bulstrod, co. Bucks: Reg. Univ. Oxf. vol. ii. pt. ii. p. 194.
1603-4. Edward Boulstrode, co. Bucks: ibid. p. 269.
1617. Thomas Bulstrod, co. Berks: ibid. p. 365.

1675. Whitlock Bulstrode and Eliz. Dineley: Marriage Alleg. (Canterbury), p. 241.
London, 2 ; Boston (U.S.), 1.

Bulteel.—The Bulteels seem to have come into England at the close of the 16th century. The Visitation of London (1633-5), vol.i. p. 118, says: ' James Bulteel of Tourney, in Henault.' His grandson, Charles Bulteel, was living in London in 1634. The family seems to have rapidly increased, as five or six branches were settled in the south of England by the year 1670. The first instance below is interesting as marking an early settlement. Probably this family died out.

Agnes Buletel, co. Camb., 1273. A.
1673. Samuel Bulteele and Mary Jurin: Marriage Alleg. (Canterbury), p. 95.
1675. John Bulteel and Mary Woodward : Marriage Alleg. (Westminster), p. 238.
Crockford, 1 ; Manchester, 1 ; New York, 1.

Bulter.—Occup. ; v. Bolter.

Bumfrey. — Bapt. 'Ap-Humphrey' (Welsh), i.e. the son of Humphrey ; v. Boumphrey and Pumphrey.

1633. Roger Bomfrey and Susanna Ivery: Marriage Lic. (Westminster), p. 34.
Newcastle, 1.

Bumpus. — ? Nick. Lower suggests Fr. *bon pas*, good pace ; corresponding to English Lightfoot, Golightly, &c., the opposite of Malpas. This view is strongly confirmed by the first entry below:

1616. John Lloyd and Anne Bompase: Marriage Lic. (London), ii. 45.
1628. Buried—An infant daughter of Thomas Bumpas: Kensington Ch. p. 110.
1629. Bapt.—John, s. Thomas Bumpasse : p. 24.
1670. — James, son of James Bumpus: St. Jas. Clerkenwell, i. 245.
London, 7 ; Boston (U.S.), 11.

Bumstead, Bumsted, Bumpstead.—Local, ' of Bumstead,' more correctly Brumstead. The *r* was lost very early. There are parishes of Brome, Broome, and Bromeswell in co. Norf. The *broom* seems to have been a feature in the county.

Christopher Brumsteed, co. Norf., 1534: FF. ix. 327. .

Jordan de Bumstede (also Bunstede), co. Norf., 1273. A.
William de Bumstede, co. Norf., ibid.
Robert de Brumsted, co. Norf., ibid.
Edward de Brumsted, co. Norf., ibid.
Thomas de Bumpstede, bailiff of Norwich, 1380: FF. iii. 116.
1640. Bapt.—Richard, son of Elizabeth Bumsteede : St. Jas. Clerkenwell, i. 145.
London, 2, 2, 0; MDB. (co. Suff.), 0, 0, 2 ; Boston (U.S.), 8, 0, 0 ; New York, 2, 2, 0.

Bunbury.—Local, 'of Bunbury,' a parish in co. Chester, near Tarporley ; v. Banbury.

Elizabeth de Bunbery, co. Camb., 1273. A.
1473. John Bunbury, Earwaker's East Cheshire, p. 86, *n*.
1557. John Bunbury, of Chester, *merchant*: Wills at Chester, i. 33.
1585. Eliz. Bunbury, of Chester, *widow*: ibid.
1619. Thomas Bunburie, co. Kent : Reg. Univ. Oxf. vol. ii. pt. ii. p. 376.
1634. Bapt.—Daniell, son of Lawrence Bunburie: St. Jas. Clerkenwell, i. 127.
Crockford, 5.

Bunclark.—Nick. 'bon-clerk,' the learned ; cf. Beauclerk and Manclark. Bunclark still survives in the south-west of England.

Emma Bonclerk. H.
John Bonclerk. H.
MDB. (co. Devon), 2 ; Exeter, 1.

Buncombe.—Local, ' of Buncombe,' or 'Boncombe,' some spot in the West country, probably co. Soms. For suffix, v. Combe.

Richard de Bounecombe, co. Soms., 1 Edw. III : Kirby's Quest, p. 147.
MDB. (co. Soms.), 3 ; London, 2.

Bund, Bundy. — Bapt. 'the son of Bund.' The masculine Bundus is found in Domesday in cos. York, Essex, and Norfolk.

Bunde fil. Hervici, co. Norf., Hen. III-Edw. I: K. p. 284.
1741. Married — Frederic Bund and Margaret Law : St. Geo. Han. Sq. i. 27.
London, 1, 3 ; Philadelphia, 1, 5.

Bundy.—? Bapt. 'the son of Bundy' (?), i.e. Bundig. Bondig was staller under Harold, and in command at Stamford Bridge (Freeman, N. C. vol. iii. pp. 51, 361). The Yorkshire entries below may be a traditional memory ; v. Bund.

William Bondi, co. Bedf., 1273. A.
Richard Bondy, co. Bucks, ibid.
Robert Bundy, co. York, ibid.
Adam Bundy, co. York, ibid.

1663. Edward Bundee and Jane Dover: Marriage Alleg. (Canterbury), p. 89.
1801. Married — George Bundy and Sarah Brant: St. Geo. Han. Sq. ii. 242.
London, 3; Boston (U.S.), 8; Philadelphia, 5.

Bungey.—Local, 'of Bungay,' a market-town in the co. of Suffolk. A priory there gave it prominence, such institutions giving a great impetus to local surnames.

Jeffrey de Bungeye, co. Norf., temp. Edw. I: FF. iv. 225.
John de Bungey, rector of Hockwold, co. Norf., 1385: FF. ii. 186.
Remer de Bungey, sheriff of London, 1239: WWW. pp. 187-190.
Stephen de Bungheye, co. Norf., 20 Edw. I. R.
Ralph de Bungheye, co. Camb., 1273. A.
Robert de Bungeye, co. Norf., ibid.
1565. Married—John Bungey, *preacher*, and Margaret Parkes: St. Antholin (London), p. 17.
1771. — Thomas Hicks and Hannah Bungey: St. Geo. Han. Sq. i. 209.
London, 2; Philadelphia, 2.

Bunker.—?Nick. 'bon cœur' (?); cf. English Goodhart. But possibly a form of *banker*, a money-changer (v. Bank and Banker in H.E.D.) Nevertheless the familiar existence of Goodhart proves the nick. origin to be quite possible, and the instances below are somewhat corroborative.

William le Bonquer. O.
John le Boncer. B.
1584. Edward Buncker and Margaret Rowdon: Marriage Lic. (London), i. 134.
1662-3. Jeremiah Swift and Eliz. Buncker: Marriage Alleg. (Canterbury), p. 63.
1789. Married—William Bunker and Jemima Skedmore: St. Geo. Han. Sq. ii. 26.
London, 6; MDB. (co. Bucks), 3; New York, 7.

Bunn, Bunce.—(1) Nick. 'le bon,' i.e. good. Often an expression of endearment, 'good little one' (v. Bunting and Bonnet). Fr. *bon*, good, dim. *bonet*. Probably Bon or Bunn was sometimes a Christian name, as was so frequently Good, q.v.

Bonne Welle, co. Norf., 1273. A.
Rocelin le Bun, co. Wilts, ibid.
Rogerus Bonne, 1379: P. T. Yorks. p. 163.
Johannes Bunne, 1379: ibid.

(2) Local, 'de Bohun'; v. Bown.
John de Bunn, co. Sussex, 1273. A.

1618. Josias Bunn, co. Herts: Reg. Univ. Oxf. vol. ii. pt. ii. p. 372.
1788. Married—John Bunn and Mary Wallington: St. Geo. Han. Sq. ii. 16.

Bunce is for Bunns as Ellice for Ellis, Dance for Dans, or Evance for Evans.

Walter Buns, co. Oxf., 1273. A.
1671-2. John Butcher and Jane Bunce: Marriage Alleg. (Canterbury), p. 68.
1766. Married — James Howton and Martha Bunce: St. Geo. Han. Sq. i. 152.
London, 6, 9; Philadelphia, 23, 3.

Bunnell.—Local, 'of Bonehill,' co. Staff.; v. Bonehill; cf. Buckle and Buckell for Buckhill.

1608. Thomas Bunnell, co. Flint: Reg. Univ. Oxf. vol. ii. p. 300.
1609-10. Jerome Fisher and Eliz. Bunnell: Marriage Lic. (London), i. 317.
London, 1.

Bunnett; v. Bonnet.

Bunney, Bunny.—Nick. An expression of endearment. No doubt a pet form of Bunn, q.v.

1574-5. Edward Bonny, co. Sussex: Reg. Univ. Oxf. vol. ii. pt. ii. p. 59.
1588. Peter Bunney and Eliz. Stockbridge: Marriage Lic. (London). i. 169.
1601. Francis Bunny, co. Durham: Reg. Univ. Oxf. vol. ii. pt. ii. p. 253.
1612. Buried—Henery Bunny: St. Peter, Cornhill, i. 168.
London, 2, 2.

Bunting, Buntin. — Nick. 'good little pet,' a term of endearment for a little child, afterwards applied more generally. 'Bunting: a term of endearment' (Halliwell). '*Buntin*, adj., short and thick, as "a buntin brat, a plump child," Roxb.' (Jamieson). The idea here is 'a good healthy child.' Fr. *bonnetin* or *bonneton*, from *bonne*, good, with dim. *et* = bonnet (v. Bonnet or Bunnett), and second dim. *in* or *on* = bonn-et-in, or bonn-et-on. This became 'buntin,' or with excrescent *g* 'bunting' (cf. Jenin and Jenning). Many old French names are double diminutives (cf. Guillotin and Philiponet), and the practice was extended to England; cf. Col-in-et, Dob-in-et, and Rob-in-et, where the same two dims. are reversed. These, being taken from Nicholas and Robert, are male names, however. In girls' names the order seems to have been

reversed. Jannetin (afterwards in England Janneting) keeps the dims., as in Bonnetin, which probably was also used as a girl's font-name, as were Bonne and Bonnette. Four women are mentioned in the Coventry Mysteries:

'Bontyng the Brewster, and Sybyly Slynge,
Megge Mery-wedyr and Sabyn Sprynge,'

where Brewster preserves its feminine sense. Here Bonnetin has become Bonting. The name is curiously interesting as surviving in one of our favourite nursery rhymes, a strong proof of its antiquity:

'Baby, baby Bunting,
Daddy's gone a hunting,
Gone to get a rabbit skin
To wrap his baby Bunting in.'

Thus Bunn (q.v.), 'good,' is the first stage; Bonnet or Bunnett (q.v.), 'good little one.' the second; and Bunting, 'good little pet,' the third. All are well preserved in our directories.

Hugo Bonetun, co. Herts, 20 Edw. I. R.
Alice Bunetun, co. Oxf., 1273. A.
Thomas Bunetun, co. Oxf., ibid.
Hugh Bonting, co. Linc., ibid.
Henry Buntyng, co. Suff., ibid.
John Buntyng, co. Sussex, ibid.
1687. Married—Earnest Collman and Anna Maria Bonatine: St. Dionis Backchurch, p. 41.

The suffix *in* or *on* is frequently found as *oun* or *un* in early registers. Both Alison and Beton (Alice and Beatrice) are met with as Alisoun and Alisun, and Betoun and Betun. Should Bunetun prove to be local, several of my instances must be withdrawn, but they will not affect the origin of Bunting.

London, 12 (and in all town directories), 0; Philadelphia, 72, 2.

Bunyan, Bunyon.—(1) Nick. 'Bon-jean'; in English Goodjohn. (2) Bapt.; v. Benyon or Onion. I wrote a series of articles some years ago entitled the 'Romance of the London Directory,' afterwards printed in book form. I stated that Bunyan was Bonjean, and that when we talked of 'Good

John Bunyan' we simply said 'Good John' twice over. This, I believe, was incorporated in a recent life of the great dreamer. But writing more soberly now, and after more study, I feel fairly confident that Bunyan's ancestry was Welsh. The great personal name of Enion or Eignon has left a very varied number of Welsh surnames, for 'Ab-Enion,' as Benyon (q.v.) will show, played freely with the vowels. Still Bonjean is not impossible.

1624. John Olyver and Ann Bunnyon: Marriage Lic. (London), ii. 141.
1640. Robert Banyon and Margaret Baynes: ibid. p. 252.
— Married—Mathew Bunnyon and Frances Rawlyns: St. Peter, Cornhill, i. 256.
1677. Bapt.—John, son of Rowland Bannion: St. Jas. Clerkenwell, i. 276.
London, 2, 1; New York, 0, 2.

Burchett.—Bapt. 'the son of Burchard'; occurs as Burchardus, a personal name, in Domesday. In the form of Burckhardt, the surname has been imported recently from Germany; v. Buckett.

Robert Burghard, co. Suff., 1273. A.
Thomas Bargchard, co. Suff., ibid.
Warin Burchard, co. Suff., ibid.
Walter Barghbard, London, 20 Edw. I. R.
1632. Married—John Cowell and Sarah Barchett: St. Thomas the Apostle (London) p. 15.
1679. Bapt.—Elizabeth, d. of Borchard Popping: ibid. p. 68.
London, 7.

Burden, Burdon.—Local, 'of Burdon.' There are two townships of this name in co. Durham, which have given their title to a local family.

John de Bardon, cos. Notts and Derby: Hen. III–Edw. I. K.
Nicholas de Burdon, co. Wilts, 1273. A.
Lucya de Bardune, co. Devon, ibid.
Thomas Burdon, co. York, ibid.
Robertus Bardon, 1379: P. T. Yorks. p. 241.
1597. Jeffery Burden, co. Wilts: Reg. Univ. Oxf. vol. ii. pt. ii. p. 221.
1797. Married—Edward Burden and Susannah Randall: St. Geo. Han. Sq. ii. 168.
1808. — William Jackman and Sarah Bardon: ibid. p. 388.
London, 19, 7; New York, 3, 1.

Burdett, Burditt.—? Local, 'of Burdet.' Invariably without prefix,

with one exception. But this one instance is valuable. Probably, as Hugh and Robert Burdet occur in Domesday, the family hail from some spot in Normandy, and 'came in with the Conqueror.'

Nicholas Burdet, co. Linc., Hen. III–Edw. I. K.
Peter Burdet, co. Leic., ibid.
John de Burdet, Isle of 'Gerneseye,' 20 Edw. I. R.
Almeric Burdet, co. Linc., ibid.
William Burdet, co. Leic., 1273. A.
Stephen Burdet, co. Linc., ibid.
Nicholaus Burdet, *frankeleyn*, 1379: P. T. Yorks. p. 90.
Gilbertus Burdet, *faber*, 1379: ibid. p. 296.
Clement Burdett, or Burditt, 1536: Reg. Univ. Oxf. i. 185.
1788. Samuell Burditt and Rebecca Burditt: St. Geo. Han. Sq. ii. 14.
1804. Samuel Burdett and Charlotte Burdett: ibid. p. 309.
London, 5, 1; New York, 18, 0; Boston (U.S.), 13, 18.

Bureler.—Occup 'the bureler,' one who sold or manufactured *burel* cloth; v. Borrell or Burrell.

Henry le Bureler: Wardrobe Account, 49 Hen. III.—1/31.
1279. Roger de Brokesheved, *burriler*: Cal. of Wills in Court of Husting.

Burford.—Local, 'of Burford,' parishes in cos. Oxford and Salop.

William de Berford, *cordwaner*, 19 Edw. II: Freemen of York, i. 23.
William le Bereford, co. Soms., 1 Edw. III: Kirby's Quest, p. 163.
Walter le Boreforde, co. Soms., 1 Edw. III: ibid.
Hugo de Bureford, co. Salop, 1273. A.
Roger de Bureford, co. Salop, ibid.
1575. Francis Burforde, co. Worc.: Reg. Univ. Oxf. vol. ii. pt. ii. p. 68.
1796. Married—John Burford and Mary Warberton: St. Geo. Han. Sq. ii. 162.
London, 6; Boston (U.S.), 4.

Burge, Burdge.—(1) Bapt.'the son of Burge.'

Burge Attewater, co. Kent, 1273. A.

(2) Local, 'at the birch.'

John de la Burchge, co. Southampt., 1273. A.
1798. Married—James Jemmett and Elizabeth Burge: St. Geo. Han. Sq. ii. 190.
London, 17, 4; Philadelphia, 0, 2; Boston (U.S.), 4, 1.

Burger.—Occup. 'the burger,' i.e. the burgher.

Henry le Barger, London, 1273. A.
1753. Bapt.—John, son of Elizabeth Barger: St. Jas. Clerkenwell, ii. 308.
London, 3; Philadelphia, 31.

Burgess, Burges, Burgis.—Occup. 'the burgess,' i.e. the citizen; M.E. *burgeys*.

Hawise Burgeys, co. Bedf., 1273. A.
Philip Burgeis, co. Oxf., ibid.
John le Burges, co. Southampt., ibid.
Thomas Burgeys, co. Norf., ibid.
Adam Burgeys, 1379: P. T. Yorks. p. 59.
Johannes Burges, 1379: ibid.
Robert Burges, Norwich, 1519: FF. iv. 180.
1614. Married—Edward Burgis and Maud Goorde: St. Antholin (London), p. 50.
1624. Bapt.—Symon, s. Alice Burgis: St. Jas. Clerkenwell, i. 98.
London, 76, 2, 1; West Riding Court Dir., 4, 0, 0; Philadelphia, 37, 2, 0.

Burgon, Burgoyne, Burgin, Burgoin.—Local, 'de Burgoyne,' a native of Burgundy.

John de Burgoyne, co. Soms., 1273. A.
Almaric Burgoyne, co. Bedf., ibid.
John Bargoyn, co. Glouc., ibid.
Thomas Burgoyn. B.
Elizabet de Burgon, 1379: P. T. Yorks. p. 125.
Richard Burgoyne, rector of Newton, co. Norf.: FF. v. 67.
1638. Bapt.—Anne, d. John Burgin: St. Jas. Clerkenwell, i. 138.
1703. Roger Burgoyne (co. Warwick) and Constance Middleton: Marriage Lic. (London), ii. 330.
1764. Married—John Burgon and Susanna Parkin: St. Geo. Han. Sq. i. 138.
London, 0, 6, 3, 0; Crockford, 2, 1, 0, 1; Philadelphia, 0, 3, 15, 0.

Burgullian, Burling, Burlin.—? Nick. 'the Burgullian,' i.e. the boaster; it occurs in Ben Jonson's Every Man in his Humour (iv. 4): 'That rogue, that foist, that fencing Burgullian' (H.E.D.). A boaster, a braggadocio. Nevertheless the prefix is as often *de* as *le*, denoting a local origin.

William de Burgiloun, co. Norf., 41 Hen. III: FF. ix. 254.
Richard de Burguillon, co. Norf., 16 Hen. III: ibid.
Philip le Burgelun, co. Camb., 1273. A.
Hugo Burgillun, co. Hunts, ibid.
William Burgellyn, co. Norf., ibid.
William de Burgiloun, co. Linc., ibid.
William le Burguillun. L.
Geoffrey le Burgillon. T.

Perhaps corrupted to Burdline and Burline, now Burling.

1561. Bapt.—Ellin, d. Richard Burline: St. Thomas the Apostle (London), p. 23.
1562. — Elizabeth, d. Richard Burdlin: ibid. p. 22.
1563. Buried—Richard Burdlin: ibid. p. 88.
London, 0, 2, 1; Philadelphia, 0, 5, 1.

Burke, Burk. — Local, 'de Burgh,' a sharpened pronunciation. The Irish Burkes are traced to the Anglo-Norman De Burghs, one of whom settled in Ireland soon after the acquisition of that country by the English monarchs. The name Alfric de Burc, apparently of Saxon origin, appears in the Domesday of Suffolk. In the Hundred Rolls the name of the famous Hubert de Burgh, temp. King John, is sometimes written ' de Burk.'

Geoffrey de Burk, co. Hereford, Hen. III-Edw. I. K.
Walter de Burk, co. Hereford, ibid.
Hubert de Burk, co. Soms., 1273. A.
John de Burk, co. Soms., ibid.
1792. Married — James Burke and Susannah Readding : St. Geo. Han. Sq. ii. 71.
1803. — John Burk and Elizabeth Wise : ibid. p. 287.
London, 20, 1 ; Philadelphia, 228, 136.

Burleigh, Burley.—Local, ' of Burleigh ' or ' Burley,' the spellings being interchangeable. Places (including parishes, chapelries, liberties, and tithings) occur in cos. Rutland, Hants, W. Rid. Yorks, and Chester. With regard to the suffix -leigh or -ley, v. Leigh.

Nicholas Borlegh, co. Soms., 1 Edw. III : Kirby's Quest, p. 156.
John de Borleg', co. Salop, 1273. A.
Simon de Burley', co. Salop, ibid.
Hugh de Burlay, co. Berks, Hen. III-Edw. I. K.
1577. Edward Burleigh, co Wilts : Reg. Univ. Oxf. vol. ii. pt. ii. p. 75.
1578-9. Edward Burley, co. Wilts : ibid. p. 85.
1605. Henry Burlighe, co. Devon : ibid. p. 284.
London, 4, 16 ; Philadelphia, 6, 3 ; Boston (U.S.), 10, 12.

Burleson.—Local, ' of Burleston,' a parish in co. Dorset, six miles from Dorchester ; cf. Kelson for Kelston, &c. But v. Burletson or Burlinson, of which it may be a modification.

1633. Bapt.—Susan, d. Matthew Burlison : St. Thomas the Apostle (London), p. 50.
1645. Married—Thomas Haddington and Cicily Burlyson : ibid. p. 17.
Boston (U.S.), 1.

Burletson, Burlinson, Burlingson. — Bapt. ' the son of Bartholomew,' from nick. Bartle,

dim. Bartlet. In this case Bartletson has become corrupted to Burletson. The name was long confined to co. Durham and South Northumberland, but has now reached London. Burlinson, a further corruption, still remains in the Palatinate.

William Byrtletson, co. York. W. 17.
Robert Burletson, 1601 : DDD. i. 110.
Bryan Burletson, 1651 : ibid.
William Burletson. SS.
1627. Bapt.—Stephen, s. of Mathew Burlesone : St. Mary Aldermary, p. 80.
' Her Majesty and the Princess were received on alighting (at Windsor) by Mr. Burlinson, traffic manager ' : Standard, April 29, 1889.
London, 2, 0, 1 ; Sunderland, 0, 1, 0 ; New York, 2, 3, 0.

Burlingham, Burlingame.— Local, ' of Burlingham,' two parishes in co. Norf., near Acle. This surname has thrived in America, where it has assumed the form of Burlingame.

Hugh de Byrlingham, co. Norf., 1273. A.
London, 2, 0 ; Philadelphia, 0, 4 ; Boston (U.S.), 0, 7.

Burls.—Probably a form of the Cornish surname Borlase. The name reached London early.

1646. Married—John Burlace and Sarah Langcraft : St. Dionis Backchurch, p. 24.
1655. — John Blande and Sarah Burles : ibid. p. 31.
1623. Edward Burles and Mary Potter : Marriage Lic. (London), ii. 123.
London, 8 ; New York, 1.

Burman.—Offic. 'the burman,' i.e. bowerman, a chamberlain ; A.S. bur, a chamber ; v. Bowerman.

Gilbert Burman, co. Oxf., 1273. A.
Robertus Burman, 1379 : P. T. Yorks. p. 242.
1587-8. William Burman, co. Warwick : Reg. Univ. Oxf. vol. ii. pt. ii. p. 124.
1669. Married—Thomas Howard and Eliz. Burman : St. Jas. Clerkenwell, iii. 107.
1783. — William Breeze and Hannah Burman : St. Geo. Han. Sq. i. 344.
West Riding Court Dir., 4 ; London, 7 ; New York, 1.

Burmeister, Burmester.— Offic. ' the mayor,' an importation. Dutch, burgomaster ; Ger. Bürgemeister.

London, 1, 1 ; New York, 4, 3 ; Philadelphia, 2, 1.

Burn, Burne, Burns, Bourr, Bourne.—Local, ' at the burn,' i.e. stream ; M.E. burne or bourne. More especially parishes in cos. Camb., Linc., and Hants. With Burns, cf. Styles, Bridges, Holmes, Brooks, &c. Possibly the patronymic s, as in Williams, Jennings, and Jones.

John atte Bourn, C. R., 17 Edw. III. pt. i.
John de Bourne, co. Soms., 1 Edw. III : Kirby's Quest, p. 232.
William atte Borne, co. Soms., 1 Edw. III : ibid. p. 247.
John de la Burn', co. Oxf., 1273. A.
Richard de la Burne, co. Soms., ibid.
John de la Burne, co. Essex, ibid.
Robert Atte-borne, rector of Ingworth, co. Norf., 1360 : FF. vi. 368.
1618. William Bourne and Agnes Johnson : Marriage Lic. (London), ii. 67.
1754. Married — Edward Burne and Susanna Basile : St. Geo. Han. Sq. i. 53.
London, 24, 4, 9, 3, 29 ; New York, 9, 2, 425, 1, 11.

Burnaby, Burnby. — Local, ' of Burnby,' parish in dioc. York. For intrusive a, cf. Ottaway, Greenaway, Hathaway, &c.

Nicholas de Burnneby, boundour (probably for toundour), 2 Edw. II : Freemen of York, i. 17.
John de Burneby, co. Bedf., 1273. A.
1631. Richard Burneby and Tiberia Dingley : Marriage Lic. (London), ii. 201.
1742. Bapt.—Ann, daughter of John and Mary Burnby : St. Geo. Chap. Mayfair, p. 8.
London, 1, 0 ; New York, 1, 0 ; Philadelphia, 0, 2.

Burnand.—Bapt. ' the son of Brennand ' ; v. Brennan.

Burnard, Burnet, Burnett. —(1) Bapt. ' the son of Bernard,' or ' Barnard' ; cf. Barnard and Barnett. Burnard is found without surname attached in the Hundred Rolls, ii. 633.

Custance Burnard, co. Camb., 1273. A.
Richard Burnard, co. Oxf., ibid.
Robert Burnard, co. Bedf., ibid.
1546. Andrew Burnet, Jesus Coll. : Reg. Univ. Oxf. i. 410.
1729. Married — Lewis Burnett and Jane Daniel : St. Geo. Chap. Mayfair, p. 302.
1789. — Joseph Sparkhall and Ann Burnard : St. Geo. Han. Sq. ii. 25.
London, 5, 6, 27 ; Philadelphia, 0, 4, 43.

Burnell, Burnel.—Bapt. and nick. As bapt. ' the son of Burnell,' as nick. ' the Burnell,' in both cases taken from the complexion; a dim. of Fr. *brun*, i. e. Brown. In the surname period it was a popular name for the donkey.

'Dan Burnel, the asse.'
Chaucer, The Nonnes Preestes Tale.

A few lines later occurs 'Dan Russel, the fox'; v. Russell, another name of complexion. Also v. Borrell.

Burnellus Carpenter. E.
John Burnel, co. Soms., 1 Edw. III: Kirby's Quest, p. 157.
John Burnellus, co. Devon, Hen. III-Edw. I. K.
Phillip Burnell, co. Leic., 1273. A.
Hubert Burnell, co. Norf., ibid.
Geoffrey de Burnell, alias Guffy de Burnwell, co. Camb., ibid.
Hugh Burnel, co. Salop, 20 Edw. I. R.
Robert Burnell, co. Devon, ibid.
1558. Buried—Agnes Burnell, St. Peter, Cornhill, i. 113.
London, 12, 1; Philadelphia, 4, 0.

Burnet, Burnett; v. Burnard.

Burney.—Local; v. Berney. But I suspect there was a Burney in co. Soms., the *ey* or *eyot* in the *bourn*, i. e. the river; or the hey enclosing the bourn at some particular spot; v. Hey.

John de Bourneghe, co. Soms., 1 Edw. III: Kirby's Quest, p. 231.
1738. Bapt. — Thomas, s. Thomas Burny: St. Dionis Backchurch. p. 168.
London, 5; MDB. (co. Soms.), 2.

Burnley.—Local, 'of Burnley,' an important town in co. Lancaster, in the old parish of Whalley.

Thomas de Brunlay, 1379: P. T. Yorks. p. 211.
1609. John Burnley, Bras. Coll. (probably of co. Lancaster): Reg. Univ. Oxf. iii. 284.
1732. Married—John Burnley and Mary Swainston: St. Geo. Chap. Mayfair, p. 223.
London, 1; Philadelphia, 7.

Burns.—Local, 'at the burn'; v. Burn.

Burnside.—Local, 'of the burnside'; v. Burn, and cf. Garside (i. e. Garthside), Akenside (the side of the oak-wood), &c. Probably a Scottish local surname.

1751. Married — John Burnside and Sarah Button: St. Geo. Chap. Mayfair, p. 202.
Crockford, 3; London, 1; Philadelphia, 14.

Burrage, Burridge. — Bapt. 'the son of Borrich'; cf. Aldridge for Aldrich, &c.

Henry Borrich, co. Soms., 1 Edw. III: Kirby's Quest, p. 217.
1660. Buried—Susanna Burrage: St. Antholin (London), p. 87.
1709. Bapt.—George, s. George Burrish: St. Dionis Backchurch, p. 148.
1738. Buried—Ann Burridge: ibid. p. 306.
London, 5, 12; Boston (U.S.), 0, 3.

Burrell; v. Borrell.

Burrough, Burroughes, Burroughs, Burrow, Burrowes, Burrows.—Local, 'at the borough'; v. Bury. The final *s* is appended as in Brooks, Styles, Briggs. Perhaps the patronymic as in Jennings, Jones, Simonds, &c.

John atte Boroghe, co. Soms., 1 Edw. III: Kirby's Quest, p. 180.
Richard atte Boroghe, co. Soms., 1 Edw. III: ibid.
Thomas Burewe, co. Soms., 1 Edw. III: ibid. p. 218.
1742. Married — William Burroughs and Elizabeth Knight: St. Geo. Chap. Mayfair, p. 18.
1752. — Hercules Burrows and Sarah Whitehead: ibid. p. 228.
London, 8, 2, 7, 2, 6, 50; Philadelphia, 2, 0, 11, 1, 2, 42.

Burser.—Offic. 'the bursar,' a purser, a treasurer, one who bore the purse and paid the expenses (v. Purser). 'Purs, or burs, *bursa*': Prompt. Parv.

John le Burser, co. Soms., 1 Edw. III: Kirby's Quest, p. 160.
Roger le Bourcer, Stamford, 1306. M.
Adam le Burser. E.
Alard le Burser. H.
1563. Married—John Smythe and Joyce Bursor: St. Dionis Backchurch, p. 5.

Probably now lost in Purser, q.v.; cf. Pullinger for Bullinger.

Burstall.—Local, 'of Burstall.' (1) A parish in co. Suffolk, near Ipswich; (2) a parish in W. Rid. Yorks, seven miles from Leeds (spelt Birstall).

Robert de Burstal, co. Leic., 1273. A.
Magota de Burstalle, co. Suff., ibid.
Geoffrey de Burstalle, co. Suff., ibid.
Henry de Burstalle, co. Hunts, ibid.
1576. Thomas Burstall: Reg. Univ. Oxf. iii. 55.
1655. Married—William Burstall and Elizabeth Basse: St. Jas. Clerkenwell, iii. 93.
London, 1.

Burstow.—Local, 'of Burstow,' a parish in co. Surrey. No connexion with Bristowe, q.v.

John de Burstowe, 1301. M.
1573. Thomas Jourden and Marcia Burstowe: Marriage Lic. (London), i. 57. London, 1.

Burt.—(1) Local, 'of . Burt,' evidently a spot in the Eastern counties. (2) Bapt. 'the son of Burt'; possibly a variant of Bright, as in Ethelbert; v. Bright.

Thomas de Burt, co. Norf., 1273. A.
Hamo Burt, co. Norf., ibid.
Ralph Burte, co. Leic., ibid.
Roger Burt, co. Oxf., ibid.
1610. Tristram Burt, co. Dorset: Reg. Univ. Oxf. vol. ii. pt. ii. p. 315.
1749. Married—John Burt and Anne Dickins: St. Geo. Chap. Mayfair, p. 146.
London, 37; Philadelphia, 32.

Burtenshaw.—Local; v. Birkinshaw.

Burtheyn.—Offic. 'a bowerthane,' a chamberlain; cf. 'Burmayden, *ancilla*' (i. e. a chambermaid): Prompt. Parv.

William Burtheyn. G.

Burtle.—Bapt. 'the son of Bartholomew,' from the nick. Bartle (q.v.), a corruptive form; cf. Burletson. Nevertheless it may be local, as Burtle is a parish in dioc. of Bath and Wells.

Edward Burtle, *kelman*, 1539, Newcastle-on-Tyne (List of male population capable of bearing arms): PPP. vol. ii. pp. 174-94.
London, 1.

Burton. — Local, 'of Burton.' There are at least twenty-nine parishes called Burton in England (v. Crockford).

Richard de Burton, *mercator*, 5 Edw. II : Freemen of York, i. 14.
John de Burton, co. Soms., 1 Edw. III : Kirby's Quest, p. 85.
Willelmus de Burton, 1379: P. T. Yorks. p. 139.
Emma de Burton, 1379: ibid.
1754. Married — Giles Burton and Hannah Abberley: St. Geo. Chap. Mayfair, p. 271.
London, 84; Philadelphia, 112.

Burtonwood.—Local, 'of Burtonwood,' a chapelry in the parish of Warrington, co. Lanc.

Thomas Burtonwood, of Warrington, 1618: Wills at Chester (1545-1620), p. 35.
Henry Burtonwood, of Acton Grange, 1617: ibid.

1607. Married—Thomas Puttevant and Alice Burtenwood : St. Thomas the Apostle (London), p. 10.
1667. Thomas Burtenwood and Eliz. Leyton : Marriage Alleg. (Canterbury), p. 209.
1702. Married —William Burtonwood and Sarah Watts : St. Antholin (London), p. 115.
Manchester, 2 ; Philadelphia, 1.

Burwash. — Local, ' of Burwash,' a parish in dioc. of Chichester, co. Sussex, formerly Burghersh and Burghest.

William de Burwarsh, co. Kent, 20 Edw. I. R.
Robert de Burgheste, co. Sussex, 1273. A.
Henry de Burghersh, co. Notts, 20 Edw. I. R.
1678. Stephen Burwash and Eliz. Merricke: Marriage Alleg. (Canterbury), p. 228.
London, 6.

Bury, Berry.—(1) Local, 'at the borough'; v. Burrough for other forms.

William atte Bergh, co. Soms., 1 Edw. III : Kirby's Quest, p 86.
Richard atte Bury, co. Soms., 1 Edw. III : ibid. p. 106.
William atte Burgh, co. Wilts, 20 Edw. I. R.
John atte Burgh, co. Wilts, ibid.

(2) Local, 'of Bury,' with a similar but earlier origin.

Adam de la Bury, co. Oxf., 1273. A.
Richard de la Bury, co. Oxf., ibid.
Geoffrey de la Burg', co. Devon, ibid.
Richard de la Burg', co. Devon, ibid.
1646. Married —Thomas Burye and Hannah Parmenter : St. Jas. Clerkenwell, iii. 79.
1748. — Edmund Berry and Mary George : St. Geo. Chap. Mayfair, p. 122.
London, 4, 85; New York, 2, 83.

Busby, Bushby.—Local, (1) 'of Busby,' now Great Busby, a township in the parish of Stokesley, N. Riding Yorks ; (2) 'of Bushby,' a hamlet in the parish of Thurnby, four miles from Leicester.

John Busseby, co. Oxf., 1273. A.
Ricardus de Busby, 1379 : P. T. Yorks. p. 238.
Adam de Buskeby, 1379 : ibid. p. 226.
Anne Busbie, 1595: Reg. St. Dionis Backchurch (London), p. 88.
Humphrye Busbye, rector of Bexwell, co. Norf., 1556 : FF. vii. 310.
1767. Married — John Hayward and Eliz. Bushby: St. Geo. Han. Sq. i. 161.
— — Henry Smith and Elinor Busby: ibid. 169.
London, 14, 9; MDB. (North Riding Yorks), 0, 1 ; Philadelphia, 3, 2 ; New York, 4, 0.

Bush.—Local, 'at the bush'; v. Busk and Buss.

1600. Bapt. — Dorathe, d. Nicholas Bush : Kensington Ch. p. 13.
1670. Thomas Bush and Ann Chambers, alias Goodwin : Marriage Alleg. (Canterbury), p. 30.
1747. Married—Luke Bush and Isabel Fleck : St. Geo. Chap. Mayfair, p. 95.
London, 34 ; Philadelphia, 76.

Bushby ; v. Busby.

Busher ; v. Bowsher (2), and perhaps (1).

1568. William Bussher and Joanna Smithe : Marriage Lic. (London), i. 39.
1575. Henry Busher : Reg. Univ. Oxf. i. 389.
1605. Abraham Busher, of London: ibid. vol. ii. pt. ii. p. 280.
1662-3. Francis Martin and Susan Busher: Marriage Alleg. (Canterbury), p. 67.
Boston (U.S.), 2.

Busk.—Local, 'at the busk,' a bush, a thicket, from residence thereby. 'Under boske shal men weder abide' : Proverbs of Hendyng. 'Buske, or busshe, *rubus, dumus*' : Prompt. Parv. This surname has generally become Bush (q. v.) in modern times.

Hamo le Bosco, 1273. A.
Henry del Busk, ibid.
Thomas atte Busk, 1379 : P. T. Yorks. p. 110.
Agnes at Busk, 1379 : ibid.
Thomas Bosc', 1379 : ibid. p. 6.
1796. Married — Ebenezer Lankester and Hester Busk: St. Geo. Han. Sq. ii. 166.
London, 7 ; New York, 2.

Buskin ; v. Buckskin.

Buss, Busse.—Local, 'at the bush'; v. Bush and Busk.

Matilda Bus, co. Oxf., 1273. A.
Robertus Busse, co. Devon, ibid.
Adam Busse, 1379 : P. T. Yorks. p. 252.
Willelmus de Busse, 1379 : ibid. p. 250.
1771. Married — Henry Galon and Susanna Buss : St. Geo. Han. Sq. i. 213.
London, 8, 1.

Bussell, Bushell, Bushill, Buswell, Bushel.—(1) Local, 'of Bossall,' a parish in the N. Rid. Yorks. This seems to have made little impression upon the directories. (2) Bapt. 'the son of Bussell,' undoubtedly a fontal name that made itself felt throughout South England from East to West, and was not unknown in the North.

Stephan Busselman (i. e. the servant of Bussel), co. Soms., 1 Edw. III : Kirby's Quest, p. 102.
Robert Busshel, co. Soms., 1 Edw. III : ibid. p. 117.
Margareta Bosell, 1379 : P. T. Yorks. p. 31.
Johannes Bussell, 1379 : ibid.
Laurencius Bossell, 1379 : ibid.
Johanna Bossell, 1379 : ibid. p. 34.
Geoffrey Buscel, co. Norf., 1273. A.
Reginald Buscel, co. Norf., ibid.
William Bushel, co. Hunts, ibid.
John Bussel, co. Camb., ibid.
1793. Married — George Bussell and Elizabeth Spiller : St. Geo. Han. Sq. ii. 98.
1807. — John Bushell and Mary Barnfield : ibid. ii. 372.
West Rid. Court Dir., 1, 1, 0, 0, 0 ; London, 5, 8, 3, 3, 0 ; Philadelphia, 4, 6, 0, 2, 1.

Bussey.—Local, 'de Bussey,' or perchance ' of Bushey,' a parish in co. Hertford, near Watford. But there is evidence in favour of an immigration from Normandy (v. Lower, Patr. Brit. p. 47).

Amabilla de Bussehay, co. Northampton, Hen. III–Edw. I. K.
William de Bussey, co. Linc., ibid.
Lambert de Bussaye, co. Notts, 20 Edw. I R.
Hugo de Bussey, co. Linc., 1273. A.
William de Bussy, co. York, ibid.
Philip Buscy, co. Wilts, ibid.
'Sir John Bussy (d. 1399), Speaker of the House of Commons, was sheriff of Lincoln in 1379. Holinshed speaks of him as " Sir John Bushie "' : Dict. Nat. Biog. viii. 40.
Hugo de Busshy, alias Bussey, 34 Edw. I : BBB. p. 714.
1777. Married — Robert Bussey and Esther Reynolds : St. Geo. Han. Sq. i. 275.
London, 7 ; New York, 2.

Bustard.—Nick. 'the bustard,' a large bird, now as rare as the eagle in England, but familiar in the surname epoch. Nearly all the birds, large and small, are common to the directories.

John Bustard, Fines Roll, 16 Edw. II.
Robertus Bustardbank, 1379 : P. T. Yorks. p. 219.
Johannes Bustard, 1379 : ibid. p. 291.

The name lingered on, and may still exist in England.

1582. Cristofer Hudson and Elizabeth Bustard : St. Antholin (London), p. 28.
1589. Charles Bustarde, co. Oxf. : Reg. Univ. Oxf. vol. ii. pt. ii. p. 173.
1671. John Greenwood and Alice

Bustard : Marriage Alleg. (Canterbury), p. 58.
Philadelphia, 9.

Bustler.—Nick. 'the bustler,' an active but fussy man ; cf. Snell, although fussiness does not attach to that nick.

Robert le Bustlere, M.P. for co. Camb.: Close Roll, 14 Edw. III. pt. ii.
William le Bustlere, Hen. III. T.
Robert le Bustlere, Hen. III. T.

Butchart.—Bapt. 'the son of Buchard'; cf. Burchett.

Walter Buchard, co. Soms., 1 Edw. III : Kirby's Quest, p. 208.
Ralph Buchard, co. Oxf., 1273. A.
Walter Buchard, co. Wilts, ibid.
London, 2.

Butcher.—Occup. 'the butcher'; M.E. *bocher* ; O.F. *bocher*. Below are the only instances in the Hundred Rolls, and one is that of a manifest foreigner. A few years onward the name grows more familiar. For these later instances, v. Botcher and Bowker.

William le Bocer, co. Salop, 1273. A.
Baudechon le Bocher, London, ibid.
Simon le Bocher, co. Norf., ibid.
Michael le Bucher. T.
1794. Married—Jonathan Butcher and Mary Ellen Dosset : St. Geo. Han. Sq. ii. 106.
London, 56 ; Philadelphia, 57.

Butler.—(1) Occup. 'the bottler,' i.e. bottle-maker ; v. Bottlemaker. The 'pouchemakers, botellers, and capmakers' acted together in the York Plays (p. xxii). These bottles were evidently of leather. (2) Offic. 'the bottler,' i.e. butler, one who looked after the bottles. The forms of entry are endless.

'Botler schalle sett for each a messe,
A pot, a lofe, withouten distresse.'
Boke of Curtasye.
'The furst yere, my son, thou shalt be pantere, or buttilare.'
Boke of Nurture.

Katerina la Butelere, co. Norf., 1273. A.
Adam le Buteler, co. Heref., ibid.
Clement le Butiller, co. Norf., ibid.
Faukes le Buteller, co. Linc., ibid.
Richard le Botiler, co. Bucks, ibid.
William le Botilier, co. Notts, ibid.
Hugo le Botyler, co. Camb., ibid.
1635. Bapt.—Tomas Bottler, son of William Bottler : St. Michael, Cornhill, p. 125.
London, 114 ; Philadelphia, 238.

Butlin, Bucklin.—Local, 'of Buttevelyn,' some spot in Nor-

mandy. The abbreviation to Butlin is quite natural. The corruption is satisfactorily proved in Lower's Patr. Brit., Introduction, p. xxxvi. Bucklin is a modern variant.

Robert de Buttevillane, co. Norf., 1139 : FF. v. 71.
William de Buteveln, co. Norf., 1321 : ibid. ii. 302.
Thomas Botevelyn, co. Norf., 1344 : ibid. v. 72.
Roger Botevileyn, co. Linc., 1273. A.
William Botevilein, co. Bedf., ibid.
Richard Botevileyn, co. Notts, ibid.
1662. Bapt.—Mary, d. William Butlyn : St. Jas. Clerkenwell, i. 216.
1707. Bapt. — Joseph, son of John Butlin : St. Michael, Cornhill, p. 162.
1786. Married — James Bucklin and Rebecca Fowe : St. Geo. Han. Sq. i. 382.
London, 6, 1 ; MDB. (co. Suffolk), 1, 0.

Butter, Buter.—Nick. 'the butur.' 'Buture, the bittern. North' (Halliwell). 'Botor, a bustard.

"Ther was venisoun of hert and bors, Swannes, pecokes, and botors."
Arthour and Merlin, p. 116,' ibid. v. Bustard.

John le Butur, co. Camb., 1273. A.
John le Botur, co. Camb., ibid.
John Botere, co. Hunts, ibid.
1581. Richard Butter, New Coll.: Reg. Univ. Oxf. iii. 157.
1786. Married — William Torris and Frances Butter : St. Geo. Han. Sq. i. 382.
London, 5, 0 ; New York, 0, 1.

Buttercarver. — Occup. 'a butter-printer,' one who prints devices on butter. 'Avice la Butterkeruere' (*u* for *v*) (Close Roll, 1 Edw. II), to carve, to notch, to grave (Skeat's Etym. Dict. 'Carve').

Butterfield.—Local, 'of Butterfield,' some small spot, seemingly in W. Rid. Yorks. The surname has crossed the border into co. Lanc., where it is to-day familiar.

Willelmus de Botterfeld, 1379 : P. T. Yorks. p. 284.
Isabella Botterfeld, 1379 : ibid. p. 285.
1668. John Butterfeild and Elizabeth Nash : Marriage Alleg. (Westminster), p. 155.
1795. Married—Joseph Butterfield and Alice Kirk : St. Geo. Han. Sq. ii. 129.
London, 12 ; Manchester, 3 ; New York, 14.

Butterick.—Local, 'of Butterwick,' an abbreviation. Places in cos. Durham, York, and Lincoln ; cf. Fennick (i. e. Fenwick). As in the pronunciation of Warwick

and Norwich, the *w* is entirely dropped.

Elena de Butterwyk', 1379 : P. T. Yorks. p. 297.
Simon de Buterwyk, 1379 : P. T. Howdenshire, p. 2.
1700. Bapt.—Thomas, son of Thomas Butterick : St. Jas. Clerkenwell, i. 388.
1755. Married — Robert Morgan and Mary Butterwick : St. Geo. Han. Sq. i. 60.
London, 2 ; New York, 3.

Butterkid. — Nick. ' Buttertub' or 'Butter-kit'; Robert Butrekyde, 1273. A. (v. Kidder). 'Some will cutte their cake, and putte (it) into the creame, and this feast is called the creame-potte, or creamekitte' (Farming Book of Henry Best, p. 93, 1641).

Butterworth.—Local, 'of Butterworth,' an ancient division of the parish of Rochdale, co. Lanc. This surname has ramified in the most extraordinary manner. We meet with it in every village and town in Lancashire, and it has wandered into all the English colonies.

Reginald de Boterworth, temp. Hen. II : Baines' Lancashire, i. 505.
John Butterworth, of Butterworth, 1595 : Wills at Chester (1545-1620), p. 35.
Alice Butterworth, of Rochdale, 1587 : ibid.
1661. Bapt. — Margarett, d. Robert Butterworth : St. Jas. Clerkenwell, i. 211.
1766. Married — Joseph Butterworth and Jane Moss : St. Geo. Han. Sq. i. 160.
London, 9 ; Manchester, 51 ; Rochdale, 44 ; Philadelphia, 47.

Buttery.—Offic. 'at the buttery.' The keeper of the butlery, or store for liquor; 'buttery-bar' (Shakespeare); v. Skeat. Early corrupted to buttery. 'Boterye, *celarium, boteria, pincernaculum*': Prompt. Parv.

Richard of the Botery, Close Roll, 8 Hen. IV.
Bolton Abby possessed (1526) 'The Kitchine, West Larder, Paintree, Butterie Law Wrie, Backhouse, and Bruhouse'.
Whitaker's Craven, p. 401.
'To the Drawer of the Buttry, 11s.': Privy Purse Exp., Princess Mary, p. 92.
1530-1. John Buttrey and Eliz. Burnell : Marriage Lic. (London), i. 7.
1669. Bapt.—Mary, d. of John Butterye : St. Jas. Clerkenwell, i. 242.
1670. Robert Pargetter and Cassandra Buttery : Marriage Alleg. (Canterbury), p. 178.
London, 2.

Button.—Local, 'of Button,' probably, as suggested by Mr.

Lower, an early variant of Bitton, a parish in co. Glouc.

John de Buttone, co. Soms., 1 Edw. III : Kirby's Quest, p. 110.

For another John of this name, v. ibid. p. 70.

1568. Ambrose Button, co. Wilts : Reg. Univ. Oxf. vol. ii. pt. ii. p. 48.
1578-9. Henry Button, co. Wilts : ibid. p. 85.
1589. Richard Button, co. Staff. : ibid. p. 170.
1683-4. Robert Smyth and Ann Button : Marriage Lic. (Faculty Office), p. 168.
London, 18 ; Philadelphia, 12.

Buttoner.—Occup. 'the buttoner,' i. e. a maker of buttons. M.E. *boton* ; O.F. *boton*.

Reginald le Botaner, London, 1273. A.
Henry le Botoner, London, ibid.
Richard le Botyner. H.
Lawrence le Botaner. N.

Buxton, Buckston.—Local, 'of Buxton,' parishes in diocs. of Southwell and Norwich. All the early instances point to the latter as the home of the surname. All commercial activity lay in that direction. Cf. Dixon and Dickson.

Warner Buckston, co. Hunts, 1273. A.
Andreas Bucston, co. Hunts, ibid.
1669. Edward Weeks and Adry Buckston : Marriage Alleg. (Canterbury), p.22.
1745. Bapt.—Ann, d. of Wilson Buxton : St. Jas. Clerkenwell, ii. 278.
1747. — Mary Arabella, d. of Wilson Buckston : ibid. 284.
London, 10, 1 ; Boston (U.S.), 21, 0.

Buzzard.—Nick. 'the buzzard.' M.E. *busard* ; Fr. *busard*.

Eustace Busard, co. Camb., 1273. A.
Peter Busard, co. Suff., ibid.
John Busard, co. Linc., ibid.
William Buscard, co. Norf., ibid.
Andrew le Buscari (Buscard ?), co. Norf., ibid.
1672. Thomas Dearing and Eliz. Buzard : Marriage Alleg. (Canterbury), p. 72.
London, 4 ; Philadelphia, 4.

Byas, Byass.—Local, 'of the by-house' (?), i.e. the town-house ; cf. *by* as suffix in Newby, Formby, Grimsby, &c., or as affix in Byfield, Bygrave, Byfleet, &c. It is possible the by-house was used for the court that passed the local by-laws. The corruption is, if such be the case, imitative, as is customary with surnames ; cf. Loftus, Bacchus (Bakehouse), &c.

Adam de Byus, co. Linc., 1273. A.
John de Bayhus, co. Bedf., ibid.
Simon de Bayhus, co. Bedf., ibid.
Joce de Bayouse, co. Soms., 1 Edw. III : Kirby's Quest, p. 95.
'On the motion of Mr. Crewe, seconded by Mr. Byas, a resolution adopting Mr. E. Brodie Hoare as the Conservative candidate for Hampstead was passed with great enthusiasm ' : Standard, Feb. 23, 1888, p. 3.
London, 2, 3 ; Philadelphia, 1, 0.

Byatt, Byette.—Local, 'by the yate' (i.e. gate) ; v. Yates ; cf. Hyatt for Highgate.

Radulphus By-the-yate, 1379 : P. T. Yorks. p. 8.
1669-70. Richard Warner and Mary Byatt : Marriage Alleg. (Canterbury), p. 27.
1693. Thomas Wilson and Eliz. Byatt : Marriage Lic. (Faculty Office), p. 209.
London, 4, 0 ; Boston (U.S.), 0, 1.

Bye.—Local, 'at the bye,' from residence therein ; M.E. *by*, a dwelling. a village.

William in the By, co. Soms., 1 Edw. III : Kirby's Quest, p. 97.
1568. Married—Robert Bye and Susan Martin : St. Antholin (London), p. 19.
1588. Robert Bye, London : Reg. Univ. Oxf. vol. ii. pt. ii. p. 164.
1599. William Hawley and Eliz. Bye : Marriage Lic. (London), i. 261.
1621. Rice Bwy, co. Wilts : Reg. Univ. Oxf. vol. ii. pt. ii. p. 392.
London, 10 ; Philadelphia, 11.

Byers.—Local ; v. Beer.

London, 4 ; New York, 11.

Byfield.—Local, 'of Byfield,' a parish in co. Northampton, seven miles from Daventry.

John de Byfeld, co. Northampt., 1273. A.
William de Byfeld, co. Bucks, 20 Edw. I. R.
Matilda de Byfeld, co. Bucks, ibid.
1597. Nicholas Byfield, co. Warw. : Reg. Univ. Oxf. vol. ii. pt. ii. p. 219.
1616. Richard Byfield, co. Worc. : ibid. p. 349.
1741. Married — Robert Byfield and Eliz. Mole : St. Geo. Han. Sq. i. 26.
London, 6 ; Boston (U.S.), 2.

Byford.—Local, 'of Byford,' a parish seven miles from Hereford, co. Hereford.

1600. Buried — Roger Byforde : St. Jas. Clerkenwell, iv. 68.
1603. — Albon, s. Roger Byford : ibid. p. 77.
1789. Married — John Byford and Martha Baldwin : St. Geo. Han. Sq. ii. 20.
London, 10 ; Philadelphia, 1 ; Boston (U.S.), 2.

Byron, Byrom, Byrne.—(1) Local, 'of Byram,' a township in the parish of Brotherton, co. York, formerly Byrom ('Byrom,' 1379. P. T. Yorks. p. 155).

Roger de Birun, co. York, 1273. A.
Ralph de Birun, co. Linc., ibid.
Hugh de Byron, co. Notts, ibid.
Johannes de Byrom, 1379 : P. T. Yorks. p. 145.

The following three entries concern individuals in the immediate neighbourhood of Byrom :

Elena de Byrom (Byrom), 1379 : P. T. Yorks. p. 155.
Roger de Birne (Monk Fryston), 1379 : ibid. p. 154.
Thomas de Byrne (Selby), 1379 : ibid. p. 155.

(2) Local, 'of Byrom,' an estate (possibly once a manor) in the parish of Winwick, co. Lanc. All the Lancashire Byroms hail from this spot. There is clear evidence that the four following entries concern one individual :

John de Byrum, John de Byrun, John de Byrnn, John Byrn, co. Lanc., 20 Edw. I. R.

John Byrom, the Manchester Jacobite and famous epigrammatist, was a descendant.

'Henry Byrome, of Byrome, died seised of the manors of Parre and Byrome,' 1614: Baines' Lancashire, ii. 214.
John Byrom, of Byrom, in the parish of Winwick, 1593 : Wills at Chester (1545-1620), p. 35.
George Byrom, of Salford, 1558 : ibid.
1604. George Byrom, or Byrame, co. Lanc. : Reg. Univ. Oxf. vol. ii. pt. ii. p. 271.
London, 3, 0, 22 ; Liverpool, 2, 4, 21 ; Philadelphia, 8, 2, 98.

Bysh, Bysshe, Biss.—Local, 'at the bush.' A form of M.E. *busch*, a bush, a thicket, from residence thereby ; cf. Wood, Shaw, or Hurst.

William de la Buisse, co. Bedf., 20 Edw. I. R.
Walter de Buisse, co. Bedf., ibid.
Walter Bysse, co. Wilts, Magd. Hall : Reg. Univ. Oxf. vol. ii. pt. ii. p. 299.
William Byse, co. Soms., 1 Edw. III : Kirby's Quest, p. 213.
Edward Bisse, or Bysse, co. Soms., 1608 : Abstract of Somersetshire Wills, p. 7.
1627. Married—William Bissh and Jone Sharrow : St. Antholin (London), p. 62.

1653. Bapt.—Robert, son of Bartholmew Biss: St. Jas. Clerkenwell, i. 184. London, 2, 0, 1; MDB. (co. Somerset), 0, 0, 5; Philadelphia, 0, 0, 2.

Byson.—Bapt. 'the son of Bye,' probably an early and soon forgotten nick. of the then favourite Barbara (?).

Henry fil. Bye, co. Camb., 1273. A. Thomas fil. Bye, co. Camb., ibid. London, 1.

Bythesea, Bythsea.—Local,

'by the sea,' from residence on the sea-shore; cf. Sandys.

John of the Spe, 6 Ric. II: Pardon's Rolls. Thomas Bythesea, co. Soms., 1615: Abstract of Somersetshire Wills, p. 60. MDB. (Somerset), 1, 0; Wilts, 2, 1.

Bywater, Bywaters.—Local, 'by the water.' A common entry in Latin and English forms.

Mariot juxta Aquam, co. Camb., 1273. A.

John ad Aquam, co. Camb., ibid. John Bithewater, co. Soms., 1 Edw. III: Kirby's Quest, p. 109. Johannes Be the Water, 1379: P. T. Yorks. p. 180. Johanna Bythewater, 1379: ibid. p. 17. Johannes Bethewater, 1379: ibid. p. 195. 1597-8. Buried — Lawrence Bywater: St. Jas. Clerkenwell, iv. 62. 1666-7. Thomas Bywater and Mary Hunscott: Marriage Lic. (Westminster), p. 43. London, 1, 2; Crockford, 2, 0; West Riding Court Dir., 6, 0; Philadelphia, 3, 0; New York, 1, 0.

C

Cabbell, Cabell, Cable, Cabble.—Bapt. 'the son of Cabel,' one of the many variants of Cubold; v. Kibble and Cobbold.

Adam Cabel, co. Norf., Hen. III–Edw. I. K. Richard Cabel, co. Oxf., 1273. A. Benedict Cabbel, co. Soms., 1 Edw. III: Kirby's Quest, p. 197.' Henry Cabbell, co. Soms., 1 Edw. III: ibid. p. 209. Thomas Cabell, rector of Irstead, co. Norf., 1506: FF. xi. 48. 1554. Thomas Cable and Emma Woddecokk: Marriage Lic. (London), i. 15. 1640. Bapt.—Ann, d. Morris Cable: St. Jas. Clerkenwell, i. 145. 1788. Married—Samuel Kent and Kezia Cable: St. Geo. Han. Sq. ii. 16. London, 1, 1, 5, 0; New York, 0, 0, 14, 4.

Cadbury.—Local, 'of Cadbury,' two parishes in co. Somerset.

1808. Married—Mark Cadbury and Charlotte Cunningham: St. Geo. Han. Sq. ii. 397. London, 2; Philadelphia, 5.

Cadby.—Local, 'of Cadeby,' a township in the parish of Sprotborough, W. Rid. Yorks. Also parishes in the diocs. of Lincoln and Peterborough; v. Cadeson.

Ricardus de Cadby, tinctor, 1379: P. T. Yorks. p. 239. Johannes de Caudby, 1379: ibid. p. 3. Agnes de Cateby, 1379: ibid. p. 18. 1790. Married — George Cadby and Jane Springell: St. Geo. Han. Sq. ii. 48. London, 4.

Cadeson, Caddy, Cadd, Cade, Cady.—Bapt. 'the son of Cade,' an early personal name embedded in the local names Cadbury and

Cadeby (three parishes in Crockford, in diocs. of York, Peterborough, and Lincoln). With the augmentative man, Cademan or Cadman was fairly popular as a font-name so late as the 13th century; v. Cadman. Caddy was the pet form of Cade.

Margery Cade, co. Camb., 1273. William Cade, co. Linc., ibid. Adam Cadeson: C. R., 17 Edw. III, pt. ii. Matilda Cadi, 1379: P. T. Yorks. p. 273. Robertus Cadison, 1379: ibid. Johannes Cady, 1379: ibid. p. 25. William Cade, co. Soms., 1 Edw. III: Kirby's Quest, p. 153. Richard Cade, co. Soms., 1 Edw. III: ibid. 1573. Bapt.—Katherine, d. William Cade: St. Mary Aldermary, p. 57. 1602. John Cadye and Joane Tucker: Marriage Lic. (London), i. 270. London, 0, 0, 2, 2, 0; Ulverston (Caddy), 2; Boston (U.S.) (Cady), 24; Philadelphia, 0, 1, 0, 9, 3.

Cadger.—Occup. 'the cadger,' a carrier, packman.

1642. Buried—Jane Cadger, servant of Henry Coxe: St. Mary Aldermary (London), p. 172.

Cadman.—Bapt. 'the son of Cædmon.' Cadman is a North-English name. The temptation to make it occupative is great. A 'cade of herynge' is as old as the Prompt. Parv., and the cademan would seem naturally to be one who packed herring in cades, or barrels, or perhaps the cooper who made them. But the name is always found without prefix.

I think it certain that Cadman must go with Bateman and Coleman into the list of personal names. It explains Cade and Caddy as nicks. and Cadeson as a patronymic.

Walter Kademan, 1276. A. Robert Cademan. J. Thomas Cademain, 1379: P. T. Yorks. p. 208. Robertus Cadman, 1379: ibid. Ricardus Caddeman, 1379: ibid. 1752. Married—Hatton Hodgkinson and Susanna Cadman: St. Geo. Chap. Mayfair, p. 211. 1759. — Thomas Cadman and Ann Pain: St. Geo. Han. Sq. i. 89. London, 6; West Rid. Court Dir., 19; Sheffield, 14.

Cadogan.—Bapt. 'the son of Cadogan,' a Welsh name.

Cadogann ap Henry, 23 Edw. I: BBB. p. 507. Eva fil. Kadugan, co. Salop, 1273. A. Yorwor fil. Kadugan, co. Salop, ibid. Gadug' Wydhel, co. Salop, ibid. 1762. Married—John Cadogan and Esther Wale: St. Geo. Han. Sq. i. 110. London, 2; Boston (U.S.), 7.

Cadwallader, Cadwallider, Cadwalader.—Bapt. 'the son of Cadwaladyr' (Welsh); v. Yonge, ii. 94.

David ap Cadwallader, 1322. M. Kedwallader Rogers, 1598: Reg. St. Mary Aldermary (London), p. 66. 1683. Thomas Ann and Elinor Cadwallder: St. Jas. Clerkenwell, iii. 200. 1781. Married—Daniel Cadwallader and Mary Rabey: St. Geo. Han. Sq. i. 326. Liverpool, 1, 0, 0; MDB. (co. Salop), 3, 2, 0; London, 1, 0, 0; Boston (U.S.), 0, 0, 1.

Cadwell.—Local, '·of Cadwell,' a tithing in the parish of Baldwyn-Brightwell, co. Oxford.

German de Cadewelle, co. Oxf., 1273. A. Robert de Cadewelle, co. Oxf., ibid. Roger de Cadwell,co.Oxf..20 Edw.I. R. 1583. Married—William Page and Eliz. Cadwell : St. Michael, Cornhill, p. 13. 1662. John Bouden and Margaret Cadwell : Marriage Alleg. (Canterbury), p. 60.
London, 0 ; New York, 8.

Caesar.—Nick. 'the kaiser,' the emperor. Kaiser and Cayzer (q.v.) represent the early English form of the name; Caesar, generally speaking, being an immigrant. ' Julius Cesar, phisitian' to Queen Elizabeth, was a Venetian by birth. His son, Sir Julius Cesar, was Master of the Robes to James I and Charles I, and lived at Hackney, and the family ramified somewhat strongly.

'Julius Ceser Delamare, vel Seysar Delamare, docter and phisitian to Q. Eliz.' : Visit. Herts, 1572-1634, p. 133. 'At Ashton-under-Line, after a lingering illness, aged 17 months, Julius Caesar Thompson. This was the child brought into the world by the Caesarean operation at the Manchester lying-in hospital' : Gent. Mag. 1800, vol. lxx. pt. 2, p. 1293. 1581-2. Married—Julius Caesar and Dorcas Lusher : Marriage Lic. London, i. 107. 1705. Buried — Ann, d. John James Caesar : St. Antholin (London), p. 118. 1758. Married—Robert Chester and Harriet Caesar : St. Geo. Han. Sq. i. 76. London, 3 ; Philadelphia, 1.

Caffin, Caffyn. — Nick. ; v. Coffin.

Cage.—Local, 'at the cage,' from residence therein—probably some building so called, possibly for prisoners. But Halliwell has ' Cag : a stump. West.' In this case Cage = Stubbs.

John atte Cage, co. Soms., 1 Edw. III : Kirby's Quest, p. 146. 1633. Bapt.—Eliz., d. Thomas Cage : St. Antholin (London), p. 67. 1698. Married—Robert Cage and Eliz. Kilbourne : St. Dionis Backchurch, p. 47. London, 1.

Cain, Caine.—(1) Bapt. 'the son of Kane' or 'Cain,' a Manx surname ; cf. Irish O'Kane. In Manx records it is found as McKane (1408) ; MacCann (1430) ; Mac Cane (1511) ; Cain (1586) ; Cane

(1601) ; Caine (1609) ; Cayne (1610) : v. Manx Note Book, ii. 24. Mr. Caine, formerly M.P. for Barrow-in-Furness, and Mr. Hall Caine, the novelist, are both of Manx descent.

(2) Local ; v. Cane. This surname still lives in co. York, and occurs early.

Johannes Cayne, Kirkby Overblow, 1379 : P. T. Yorks. p. 233. Johannes Cayne, Knaresborough, 1379 : ibid. p. 030. 1585. Richard Cayne and Anne Porye : Marriage Lic. (London), ii. 141. 1653. Married—John Cane and Marie Wilshire : St. Michael, Cornhill, p. 31. Liverpool, 20, 4 ; Philadelphia, 50, 2.

Caines, Cains, Keynes.—Local, 'of Cahagnes,' in the department of Calvados, a village lying south-west of Caen. Early branches of the family gave title to Milton Keynes, co. Bucks ; Keynes Court, co. Wilts ; Combe Keynes, co. Dorset ; and Winkley Keynes, co. Devon (v. Lower).

John de Kaynnes, co. Bucks, 1273. A. Lucas de Kaynnes, co. Bucks, ibid. Robert de Kaynes, co. Wilts, ibid. Geoffrey de Kaynges, co. Wilts, ibid. 1756. Married—William Holford and Eliz. Caines : St. Geo. Han. Sq. i. 200. 1770. — Robert Lamb and Mary Kaines : ibid. p. 62. London, 2, 1, 0 ; Philadelphia, 2, 0, 0 ; Boston (U. S.)(Cains), 1.

Caird, Card.—Occup. ' the caird,' a gipsy, a travelling tinker. A Scotch surname.

' What means that coat ye carry on your back? Ye maun, I ween, unto the Kairds belang.' Ross, Helenore, p. 66 (Jamieson). 'This captain's true name was Forbes, but nicknamed Kaird, because when he was a boy he served a Kaird.' Spalding, i. 243 (Jamieson). 1802. Married—Henry Woodger and Eliz. Card : St. Geo. Han. Sq. ii. 268. London, 3, 4 ; Philadelphia, 1, 2.

Caitiff, Catiff.—Nick. ; M.E. caitif, a captive, a wretch ; O.F. caitif ; Lat. captivus. Probably the Catiff of the Sheffield Directory is a corruption of Catcliffe, a township in the neighbouring parish of Rotherham.

Thomas Queytyff, 1457 : Reg. Univ. Oxf. p. 31. Sheffield, 0, 1.

Cakebread.—? Nick. I cannot suggest any origin but a sobriquet for one who made cake-bread ; cf. Blanchpain or Whitebread.

1613. Married—Thomas Cakebread and Isbell Barnes : St. Peter, Cornhill, i. 248. 1632. Buried — Thomas, s. Richard Cakebread : St. Jas. Clerkenwell, iv. 205. London, 2 ; New York, 1.

Calcott, Calcut, Calcutt, Caldecott, Caulcutt, Caldecourt, Caldicott, Cawcutt, Callcott, Callcutt, Caldicot, Caldicourtt.—Local, ' of Caldecote.' Whatever this local term may mean, it is variously scattered. Of parishes alone there is a Caldecote in the diocs. of Ely, Peterborough, and Worcester ; and a Coldecott in the diocs. of Peterborough and St. Albans. Mr. Lower says there is a Caude-Côte in Normandy. He adds, ' It is a singular fact, says the Rev. John Taddy, that "wherever we have traces of a Roman road, we find hamlets in the near neighbourhood of it of the name of Caldecott. I could quote abundance of such " (Papers of the Architect. Soc. of Northampton, York, Lincoln, and Bedford, ii. 429).'

Henry de Caudecote, co. Suff., 1273. A. William de Caudecote, co. Bucks, ibid. Alexander de Caldicote, co. Camb., ibid. Albin de Caldecote, co. Hunts, ibid. Edmund de Caldicote, co. Bucks, ibid. Roger de Caldecote, co. Northumb., Hen. III–Edw. I. K. 1752. Married—Alex. Caldicutt and Ann Goodman : St. Geo. Chap. Mayfair, p. 222. 1758. Married—Thomas Parsley and Susanna Caldecott : St. Geo. Han. Sq. i. 80. 1783. — William Callcott and Ann Wheeler : ibid. p. 347. London, 6, 1, 3, 6, 1, 1, 1, 2, 0, 1, 4, 0, 0 ; MDB. (co. Camb.) Cawcutt, 2 ; Philadelphia, 0, 0, 1, 0, 0, 0, 0, 0, 0, 1, 1.

Calder.—Local, ' at the Calder,' from residence beside the Calder, one of the many rivers of that name.

Adam de Calder, 1179 : RRR. p. 24. 1711. Buried—Robert, s. John Calder : St. Dionis Backchurch, p. 280. 1798. Married — Henry Calder and Hannah Henderson : St. Geo. Han. Sq. ii. 180. London, 10 ; Boston (U.S.), 7.

Calderbank.—Local, 'of the Calder bank,' from residence on the bank of one of the rivers Calder; cf. Gillbanks, Windibank, &c.

Manchester, 1; Ulverston, 1.

Caldercourt.—Local; v. Calcott.

Calderwood.—Local, 'of Calderwood,' i.e. the wood by the Calder, q.v.

1789. Married—William Calderwood and Ann Sowersby: St. Geo. Han. Sq. ii. 29.
London, 2; Boston (U.S.), 4.

Caldicot, Caldicott, Caldicourtt.—Local; variants of Calcott.

Caldwell.—Local, 'of Caldwell,' parishes in the diocs. of Ripon and Peterborough. Probably 'the cold-well' = cold, or cald. A.S. ceald; v. Coldwell and Caudle. This surname has ramified in the most extraordinary manner in the United States. One or two early settlers must have bred a healthy family of boys, who thrived and married.

Ricardus de Coldewell, 1379: P. T. Yorks. p. 3.
Johannes de Caldewell, 1379: ibid. p. 19.
Johannes de Coldwell, 1379: ibid. p. 174.
1581. John Caldwell and Margaret Hilde: Marriage Lic. (London), i. 103.
1796. Married—John Caldwell and Margaret Mathews: St. Geo. Han. Sq. ii. 152.
Manchester, 5; London, 6; West Rid. Court Dir., 5; Philadelphia, 157.

Calf.—Nick. 'the calf'; cf. Bull, Bullock, &c.

Reginald Cauf, co. York, 1273. A.
John le Cauf, co. Linc., ibid.
Nicholas Calf, co. Glouc., ibid.
Richard Calf, c. 1300. M.
Cicilia Calff, 1379: P. T. Howdenshire, p. 6.
Nicholas Calff, secular chaplain, B.C.L. 1458: Reg. Univ. Oxf. vol. i. p. 32.
1605. Bapt.—Benjamin, s. Joyes Calf, marchant, stranger; christened in the Dutch Church: St. Dionis Backchurch, p. 92.
1738. Bapt.—Mary, d. John Calfe: St. Jas. Clerkenwell, ii. 238.
London, 1; New York, 1.

Callaway, Callway, Calloway.—Local. Not as suggested by Lower, a corruption of Galloway (though, considering the fact that C and G are so constantly interchangeable, the idea was sensi-

ble enough), but a surname derived from some small locality in co. Devon or Cornwall, which I cannot identify. The middle syllable is probably intrusive. Cf. Ottaway and Greenaway for Otway and Greenway. The suffix is, no doubt, way, a road, a path.

Walter Calewey, co. Bucks, 1273. A.
William Callewey, co. Devon, Hen. III-Edw. I. K.
Cassadra Cayllewey, co. Wilts, 20 Edw. I. K.
1524. William Caloway and Alice Cower: Marriage Lic. (London), i. 4.
1549. Bapt.—Robert, son of John Calwaie: Reg. St. Columb Major, p. 5.
1554. — Jane, d. of Thomas Calwaye: ibid. p. 7.
1683. — Phillip, son of Richard Callaway: ibid. p. 72.
1803. — Henry Callaway and Mary Selden: St. Geo. Han. Sq. ii. 275.
London, 1, 0, 0; Exeter, 1, 1, 0; Boston (U.S.), 1, 0, 1; Philadelphia, 4, 0, 3.

Callbeck.—Local, 'of Caldbeck.' An American variant; v. Colbeck.

Boston (U.S.), 3; New York, 1.

Callcott, Callcut.—Local, ' of Caldecote '; v. Calcott.

Callender, Callander.—(1) Occup. 'the calender,' one who calenders cloth, a calenderer. Cowper's 'John Gilpin' has immortalized the word. 'To calender (F. calendrier), to press, smooth, and set a gloss upon linnen, &c.; also the engine itself' (Bailey's Dict., 2-vol. edit. 1737). Orig. from cylinder, a roller.

Robert le Kalendar, C. R., 6 Edw. I.

It is possible this entry may concern some money-changer, one who kept accounts by the calendar.

'The Goldsmiths, Diers, Calanderers, and Sadlers'(order of Procession of Crafts on Corpus Christi Day (1533) from Common Hall, Norwich): FF. ii. 148.

(2) Local, 'of Callender.' Several localities in Scotland are so called in cos. Perth and Stirling.

1748. Married—John Callander and Ann Bradshaw: St. Geo. Chap. Mayfair, p. 115.
1794. — James Callender and Jane Rannie: St. Geo. Han. Sq. ii. 121.
London, 5, 0; Boston (U.S.), 13, 0; Philadelphia, 2, 1.

Callis, Calliss.—Local, 'from Calais'; v. Challis and Challice.

John de Caleys, Jersey, 20 Edw. I. R.
Robert de Calays, co. Kent, Hen. III-Edw. I. K.
Henricus de Calays, 1379: P. T. Yorks. p. 191.
Robertus Calas, 1379: ibid. p. 132.
1560. Buried—a poor starved Callis man: Reg. Allhallows, Barking, p. 69.
1603. Thomas Walker and Judith Callice: Marriage Lic. (London), i. 278.
1798. Married—Thomas Callis and Peggy Brolliat: St. Geo. Han. Sq. ii. 181.
London, 2, 0; Sheffield, 2, 1; Philadelphia, 2, 0; New York, 2, 1.

Callow.—Nick. 'the callow' (M.E. calewe), said of unfledged birds, and applied as a sobriquet; cf. Suckling. Probably it was a nickname for a bald-headed man; cf. Ballard.

John le Calewe, co. Soms., 1 Edw. III: Kirby's Quest, p. 137.
Gilbert Calwe, co. Soms., 1 Edw. III: ibid. p. 147.
Walter Calwe, co. Soms., 1 Edw. III: ibid. p. 148.
1660. Edward Barnaby and Susan Callow: Marriage Alleg. (Canterbury), p. 54.
1756. Buried—Sarah Callow: St. Peter, Cornhill, ii. 142.
London, 12; MDB. (co. Soms.), 2; Boston (U.S.), 1.

Calman.—Bapt. 'the son of Caleman,' i.e. Carloman (v. Yonge, ii. 360).

Harvens Caleman, co. Camb., 1273. A.
Roger Caleman, co. Camb., ibid.
London, 1.

Calthorp, Calthrop, Colthup.—Local, 'of Calthorpe.' (1) A parish in co. Norfolk, four miles from Aylsham; (2) 'of Cathorpe' or ' Calthorpe,' a parish in co. Leicester, four miles and a half from Lutterworth.

Radulf de Kalthorp, co. Norf., 20 Edw. I. R.
Bartholomew de Calthorp, co. Norf., 1273. A.
Gilbert de Calthorp, co. Linc., ibid.
Ranulf de Calthorp, co. Linc., ibid.
Mathew de Caltorp, co. Norf., ibid.
William de Calthorp, 14 Edw. III: FF. x. 168.
Walter de Calthorpe, 20 Edw. III: ibid.
Johannes de Colthorp', 1379: P. T. Yorks. p. 300.
Matilda de Colthorp', 1379: ibid. p. 299.
1578. Clement Calthorpe and Jane Sampson: Marriage Lic. (London), i. 80.
1615. Married—George Colthropp and Anne Evans: St. Jas. Clerkenwell, iii. 41.
London, 0, 1, 1; Crockford, 0, 4, 0.

Calverley.—Local, 'of Calverley,' a parish five miles from Bradford, W. Rid. Yorks. For a variant, v. Caverley.

Christiana de Kalverle, co. Northumb., Hen. III–Edw. I. K.
Gilbert de Calverley, co. Northumb., 1273. A.
Agnes de Calverslay, 1379: P. T. Yorks. p. 30.
Johanna de Calverley, 1379: ibid. p. 47.
1588. Married — Richarde Calverleye and Dorithie Okes: St. Michael, Cornhill, p. 14.
1785. — Joseph Calverley and Hannah Compton: St. Geo. Han. Sq. i. 370.
Crockford, 2; London, 3; West Rid. Court Dir., 4; Philadelphia, 17.

Calvert. — Occup. 'the calf-herd,' a keeper of calves. A familiar Yorkshire surname; cf. Oxnard, Coward, Stoddart, Shepherd; v. Herd.

Henry Calvehird, c. 1300. M.
John le Calvehird. H.
Warin le Calvehird, co. York. W. 4.
Johanna Calfhird, 1379: P. T. Yorks. p. 301.
Johannes Calvehyrd, 1379: ibid. p. 269.
Magota Calvehird, 1379: ibid. p. 9.
Thomas Calvert, of Cockerham, 1567: Lancashire Wills at Richmond, p. 55.
1604. Married—George Calvert and Anne Mynne: St. Peter, Cornhill, p. 244.
1719. Joseph Hall and Anne Calvert: St. Michael, Cornhill, p. 61.
London, 3; West Riding Court Dir., 25; Philadelphia, 11.

Cam, Camm.—Local, (1) 'of the Cam,' one of the rivers or streams of that name, from residence on its banks. (2) 'Of the camb,' from residence on the camb or crest of a hill, or dike. The Yorkshire Cams represent (2).

Willelmus Cambe, *constabularius*, 1379: P. T. Yorks. p. 276.
Johannes Cambe, 1379: ibid. p. 274.
Nicholaus Cambe, 1379: ibid.
Henry del Cam, co. Suff, 1275. A.
Robert de Cam, co. Oxf., ibid.
Osbert de Cam, co. Norf., 24 Hen. II: FF. ix. 523.
John de Cam, rector of Kirkby-Cane, co. Norf., 1326: ibid. viii. 34.
Thomas Cambe, of Capenwray, 1678: Lancashire Wills at Richmond, i. 55.
Jonathan Cam, of Capenwray, 1716: ibid. ii. 50.
1733. Married—Dymock Morrice and Mary Cam: St. Geo. Han. Sq. i. 12.
1771. — Edward Green and Eliz. Camb: ibid. p. 204.
London, 0, 0; Sheffield, 3, 7; West Rid. Court Dir., 2, 5; Philadelphia, 0, 4.

Camberbirch; v. Cumberbatch.

Cambray.—Local, 'of Cambray,' a city in the Netherlands. An early immigrant.

Mathew de Cambreye, co. Linc., 1273. A.
Egidius de Cambrey, London, ibid.
1664. Married—William Camray and Ann Inglefeild: St. Jas. Clerkenwell, iii. 116.
1701. — Thomas Cambray and Ruth Haynes: ibid. 223.
1798. — John Holmes and Anne Cambray: St. Geo. Han. Sq. ii. 180.
1806. — Phillipe Cambrye and Caroline Hossick: ibid. p. 355.
London, 1; Oxford, 4.

Cambridge.—Local, 'of Cambridge,' the well-known University and capital town of the county of that name.

Johannes de Cambrege, 1379: P. T. Yorks p. 119.
1729. Married—Abraham Cambridge and Millicant Tidman: St. Antholin (London), p. 143.
1760. — John Cambridge and Flora Marlow: St. Geo. Han. Sq. i. 93.
London, 3; Philadelphia, 3.

Camidge, Cammage, Gammage.—(1) Local, 'of Gamages.' It is possible, of course, that Camidge may be a corruption of Cambridge.

Godfridus de Gamages, 38 Hen. III: BBB. p. 57.
Enfemia de Gamages, 38 Hen. III: ibid.

(2) ——?

Henry le Gammage, 1273. A.
1607. Buried — A still-born son of Thomas Camage: St. Jas. Clerkenwell, iv. 100.
1769. Married—John Gamage and Mary Cooper: St. Geo. Han. Sq. i. 190.
1772. — Thomas Gammage and Eliz. Burgis: ibid. p. 223.
London, 2, 1, 1.

Cammel, Gamel.—(1) Bapt. 'the son of Gamel'; no connexion with the animal. G constantly becomes C in English nomenclature; cf. Crane for Grane, Candlin for Gandelin, &c. The first two instances occur in close juxtaposition in the same village list:

Johannes Camyll, 1379: P. T. Yorks. p. 20.
Cicilia Gamyll, 1379: ibid.

Again we find placed together:

Agnes Gamel, 1379: P. T. Yorks. p. 76.
Elizabet Gamel, 1379: ibid.
Willelmus Camel, 1379: ibid.

(2) Local, 'of Camel,' or 'Camel Queen,' a parish in co. Somerset.

Ernicius Camel, co. Heref., Hen. III–Edw. I. K.
Henry de Camel, co. Wilts, ibid.
1642. Buried—John Cammell: St. Jas. Clerkenwell, iv. 254.
1752. Married— George Camwell and Eliz. Harison: St. Geo. Chap. Mayfair, p. 222.
London, 2, 0; Philadelphia, 0, 1.

Camp.—(1) Local, 'at the camp,' i.e. field.

Felicia in Campo, co. Camb., 1273. A.
William de Campo, co. Oxf., ibid.
Johannes de Kempe, 1379: P. T. Howdenshire, p. 24.
1584. William Campe and Mary Farmer: Marriage Lic. (London), i. 130.
1699. Married — Thomas Nash and Anne Camp: St. Dionis Backchurch, p. 48.

(2) Official, 'a soldier,' a form of Kemp, q.v.

1736. Bapt.—Mary, d. John and Elizabeth Camp: St. Jas. Clerkenwell, ii. 228.
London, 13; Philadelphia, 40.

Campion.—Occup. 'le Campion,' a fighter, a contester; O.F. *champion, campion.* 'Campyon, or champyon; *athleta*' (Prompt. Parv.); v. Champion.

Beatrix le Campiun, co. Camb., 1273. A.
Custance Campyun, co. Camb., ibid.
John Campiown, co. Hunts, ibid.
Walter le Campion, co. Bucks, ibid.
Simon Campion, 1379: P. T. Yorks. p. 12.
Ricardus Campion, 1379: ibid. p. 30.
1553. Buried—Cecilie Campyon: St. Michael, Cornhill, p. 180.
1569. Henry Campion and Eliz. Lawrence: Marriage Lic. (London), i. 42.
London, 11; MDB. (co. Camb.), 2; Philadelphia, 18.

Camplin, Campling.— ? —— The suffix is manifestly the dim. *-elin* (cf. Hewling). Thus it may be of the baptismal or nickname class. If the latter, it may be a dim. of Campion, i.e. Champion, q.v. In any case William Campelin (infra) must be looked upon as the progenitor.

William Campelin, co. Norf., 1273. A.
John Camplyon, rector of Rackheath Parva, co. Norf., 1401: FF. x. 453.
1627. Buried—Margaret Camplyn, Repham, co. Norf.: ibid. viii. 247.
1679 — Titus Camplin, chymist, Norwich: ibid iv. 157.
1790. Married—William Maken and Eleanor Campelen: St. Jas. Han. Sq. ii. 35.
1791. — John Parks and Carolina Camplin: ibid. p. 62.

1797 Married—Edward Page and Mary Campling : St. Jas Clerkenwell, ii. p. 170. London, 5, 1 ; Boston (U.S.), 1, 0.

Camps.—Local, 'de Campes,' apparently some continental spot. The name now seems peculiar to the county of Cambridge.

Salomon de Campis, co. Kent, 1273. A.
William de Campes, Camb., ibid.
Henry de Campes, co. Suff., ibid.
William de Campes, co. Linc., 20 Edw. I. R.
London, 0 ; MDB. (co. Cambridge), 11 ; New York, 1.

Candleman. — Occup. ; v. Chandler.

William Candelman, C. R., 47 Hen. II.
Adam Candeleman, temp. 1300. M.

Candlemaker. — Occup. ; v. Chandler.

John le Candlemakere, temp. 1300. M.

Candlemass. — Bapt. (?) ; cf. Christmas, Middlemas, Nowell, Pask, &c., all from the season of the year in which the child was born.

Matilda Candelmes, 1379 : P. T. Yorks. p. 216.

Candlin.—Bapt, 'the son of Gandelyn.' The ballad of 'Robyn (Robin Hood) and Gandelyn' is probably as old as the reign of Edw. I (v. Encyc. Brit., 9th edit., article Robin Hood).

'Gandeleyn bent his goode bowe,
And set therein a flo.'
Robyn and Gandeleyn (A Lytell Geste of Robin Hode, ii. 38).

Gandelyn still survives in Yorkshire in the form of Candlin, where we find several instances of initial G becoming C ; cf. Cammel and Gamel.

Robertus Candelayn, 1379 : P. T. Yorks. p. 8.
Thomas Candelayn, 1379 : ibid. p. 9.
John Candelayn, 1379 : ibid.

The solitary owner of this historic name that I can discover ought to have his title set down in full. Here it is—

John Candlin, corn, hay, and straw-dealer, 187 and 189 Bright St., Sheffield (West Riding Directory, 1867).

Candy.—Local ; v. Gandy.

Cane.—(1) Local, 'of Caen,' in Normandy ; v. Cain (2).

Hugh de Caen. C.
Richard de Cane. H.
Roger de Cane, co. Linc. 1273. A.

(2) Bapt. 'the son of Cane.' 'Cane, Cana, or Canus appears in the Domesday of Sussex as a baptismal name': Lower, Patr. Brit. p. 51.

Adam Cane, co. Oxf., 1273. A.
Alicia Cane, co. Oxf., ibid.
Walter Cane, co. Hunts, ibid.

(3) Bapt. for Cain, q.v.

1747. Married—Philip Watkins and Jane Cane : St. Geo. Chap. Mayfair, p 98.
London, 6 ; Philadelphia, 4.

Cann.—Local, 'of Cann,' a parish in co. Dorset. The name is very familiar in co. Devon.

Richard de Canne, co. Oxf., 1273. A.
1678. John Cann and Eliz. Pewtner : Marriage Alleg. (Canterbury), p. 221.
1751. Married—Richard Cann and Mary Reddell : St. Geo. Chap. Mayfair, p. 205.
1765. — John Cann and Ann Stevens : St Geo. Han. Sq. i. 140.
London, 9 ; Plymouth, 4 ; Exeter, 4 ; Devon Dir. (Farmers' list), 13 ; Philadelphia, 11.

Cannon, Canon.—Official, 'the Canon' (v. Shannon) ; cf. Archdeacon, Bishop, Priest, Deacon, &c.

John le Cannon, co. Oxf., 1273. A.
William le Canon, co. Oxf., ibid.
1527. William Leghe and Alice Cannon : Marriage Lic. (London), i. 6.
1570. Bapt.—Jone. d. Jeames Cannone : St. Michael, Cornhill, p. 85.
London, 27, 0 ; Philadelphia, 130, 6.

Cant.—Local, 'of Kent,' an old pronunciation and spelling ; cf. Cantis for Kentish.

Edmund de Cant, or Kente, bailiff of Norwich. 1356 : FF. iii. 99.
1625. James Cant and Susan Dobinson : Marriage Lic. (London), ii. 155.
1751. Married—Peter Cant and Ann Richardson : St. Geo. Chap. Mayfair, p. 202.
1759. — Stephen Cant and Eliz. Hughson, St. Geo. Han. Sq. i. 83.
London, 5 ; Philadelphia, 3.

Cantis.—Local, 'the Kentish,' i. e. Kentishman ; cf. Cornwallis, and v. Kentish and Cant.

1722. Married—Valentine Cantis and Mary Cantis : Canterbury Cath. p. 75. London, 1.

Cantlay, Cantley.—Local, 'of Cantley,' (1) a parish in co. Norfolk, four miles from Acle : (2) a parish in co. York, three miles from Doncaster.

Rogerus de Cantelay, 1379 : P. T Yorks. p. 102.

1797. Married—Robert Mulcaster and Margaret Cantley, co. Cumb. : St. Geo. Han. Sq. ii. 165.
London, 1, 0 ; West Rid. Court Dir., 0, 1 ; Philadelphia, 0, 1 ; New York, 0, 1.

Cantrell, Cantrill, Cantle.—Nickname. One who rang the chanterelle. O.F. *chanterelle*, a small bell ; from *chanter*, to sing ; cf *chantrel*, a decoy partridge (Howell, quoted by Halliwell). Most of my instances hail from Yorkshire. I could have adduced others. It is there the surname is still most largely represented. With Cantrell (instead of Chantrell) cf. Candler and Chandler, Capel and Chappell, Cancellor and Chancellor.

Alice Cainterel, co. York, 1273. A.
William Chanterel, co. Northampt., ibid.
Richard Chaunterel, co. Wilts, ibid.
Martin Chanterel, co. York, ibid.
Roger Chantrel, co. Soms., 1 Edw. III : Kirby's Quest, p. 103.
Johannes Quayntorell, 1379 : P. T. Yorks. p. 28.
Johanna Quayntell, 1379 : ibid.
1569. Bapt.—John, son of John Chauntrell : St. Jas. Clerkenwell, i. 5.
1632. John Yorke and Judith Cantrell, co. Berks : Marriage Lic. (London), ii. 29.
London, 1, 1, 2 ; West Rid. Court Dir., 4, 0, 0 ; Sheffield, 0, 0, 0 ; MDB. (co. Somerset), 0, 1, 2 ; Philadelphia, 10, 0, 0.

Cantwell.—Local, 'of Kentwell.' I cannot find the spot.

Gilbert de Kentewelle, co. Suff., 1273. A.
Thomas Cantewell, C. R., 24 Hen. VI.
1743. Married—Joseph Shirley and Martha Cantwell : St. Geo. Han. Sq. i. 30.
Philadelphia, 12.

Canvaser.—Occup. 'the canvaser,' a manufacturer of canvas, hempen cloth ; M.E. *canevas*, a trisyllable in Chaucer, C. T. 12866 (Skeat).

Henry le Canevacer, temp. 1300. M.
Richard le Canvaser, ibid.

Capel, Caple, Capell, Capelle.—Local, 'at the chapel' ; Low Latin, *capella*, a sanctuary. Many chapels are so styled in England and Wales ; cf. Capel-Cynon, Capel-Dewi, Capel-Colman, and Capel-Coelbren, all in dioc. of St. David's ; Capel St. Andrew and Capel St. Mary in dioc. of Norwich ; cf. Caplin for Chaplin.

Bateman de Capele, co. Suff., 1273. A.
Andrew de Capella, co. Camb., ibid.
Maynard de Capella, co. Bucks, ibid.
Elizabeth Capell, 1696: Reg. St.
Columb Major, p. 245.
Edward Chapell, 1697: ibid.
William Caple, 1770: ibid. p. 129.
1701. Bapt. — William Capell: St.
Michael, Cornhill, p. 160.
1795. Married—Owen Myers and Mary
Capel, St. Geo. Han. Sq. ii. 139.
London, 11, 1, 2, 0; New York, 2, 0, 0,
0; Boston (U.S.), 1, 0, 1, 7.

Capgrave.—Local, 'of Capgrave,' a place in co. York. The
etymology is simple enough, 'the
shaw or little wood on the top
of the hill'; v. Cope and Grave.

Richard de Copgrave, 29 Edw. I:
Freemen of York, i. 8.
Johannes Copgrave, 1379: P. T. Yorks.
p. 92.
1621. Thomas Copgrave and Rose
Woodward: Marriage Lic. (London),
ii. 104.

Caple.—(1) Bapt. 'the son of
Cabel'; v. Cabbell, a famous West-
country surname, which has given
us Keble, &c. The h has been
sharpened in this instance to p.
(2) Local, 'at the chapel,' from
residence thereby; v. Capel.

1623-4. James Smith and Dorothy
Caple: Marriage Lic. (London), ii. 135.
MDB. (co. Somerset), 10.

Caplewood.—Local, 'of Caplewood,' probably meaning 'the
chapel-wood,' i. e. the wood beside the chapel; v. Capel.

Ricardus Capulwode, 1379: P. T.
Yorks. p. 45.
Adam Capilwode, 1379: ibid.
1613. Married—George Carter and
Katherine Caplewood: St. Jas. Clerken-
well, iii. 39.
1616. Richard Caplewood and Sarah
Peasecod: Marriage Lic. (London), ii. 42.
1617. Buried—Widow Cappellwood:
St. Dionis Backchurch, p. 214.

I do not find this name existing
to-day. Still, it probably lives.

Caplin.—Official; v. Chaplin.

Capmaker.—Occup. 'the capmaker,' a maker of caps; v. Capper.
Coke Lorelle's Bote includes,
'spynsters, carders, and cappe-
knytters.' In the York Pageant
the cap-makers are mentioned
(York Mystery Plays, p. xxii, ed.
Toulmin Smith).

Joan Chaumpeneye, *cappemakere*,
C. R., 4 Ric. II.
Thomas Capmaker. H.

Capman.—(1)Occup. 'the chapman,' q.v.; cf. Cancellor, Candler,
or Caplin, for Chancellor, Chandler,
or Chaplin.
(2) Occup. 'the capman'; v.
Capper and Capmaker.

John Capman, c. 1300. M.
James Kapman, temp. Eliz. Z.
'In memory of Mrs. Mary Chapman,
relict of Samuel Capman (sic)... 1724.'
—Thorp, near Norwich; FF. vii. 262.

Capon.—Nick. 'the capon,' a
young cock; A.S. *capun*. 'Capvne,
or capone; *gallinacius*': Prompt.
Parv. Cf. Cock, Henn, Cockerell,
&c. In East Anglia the surname
has always held its own.

Ralph Capon, co. Norf., 1273. A.
Agnes Capun, co. Norf., ibid.
Ranulph Capun, co. Linc., ibid.
Adam Capoun, co. Camb., ibid.
Thomas Capon, dean of Ipswich, 20
Hen. VIII: FF. vi. 207.
John Capon, co. Norf., 1541: ibid. x.
448.
1800. Married—Joseph Capon and Ann
Williams: St. Geo. Han. Sq. ii. 219.
London, 7; MDB. (co. Suffolk), 10;
New York, 2.

Capper.—Occup. 'the capper,'
a maker or dealer in caps. Thomas
Pendilton, capper, 1562 (Preston
Guild Rolls, p. 30). Probably made
of woollen cloth, though felt was
used. An Act of Parl., 4 Hen. VII.
c. ix, begins, 'No hatter or capper
shall felt any hat,' &c. In the
York Pageant amongst other crafts
marched the 'cap-makers'; in the
Chester Pageant the 'Cappers,
Wyerdrawers, and Pynners'; in
the Norwich Pageant the 'cappers,
hatters' (FF. ii. 148).

Symon le Cappere, co. Oxf., 1273. A.
John le Capiere, co. Oxf, ibid.
Thomas le Capiere, co. Oxf., ibid.
1581-2. Francis Capper and Eliz. Willson: Marriage Lic. (London), i. 106.
1800. Married — More Cleland and
Lydia Capper: St. Geo. Han. Sq. ii. 225.
London, 10; New York, 2; Philadelphia, 9.

**Capron, Capern, Chap-
peron, Chapron.**—Nick. Probably a sobriquet for the cowled
monks. M.E. *cape*, or cope (a
hood); O.F. *cape*, augmented into
caperon, now chaperon. The

modern sense of chaperon has no
place in nomenclature. My first
instance is interesting as describing a maker or manufacturer of
caperons.

William Caperoner, co. Soms., 1 Edw.
III: Kirby's Quest, p. 88.
Edmund Caperun, co. Norf., 1273. A.
John Caperun, Camb., ibid.
Stephen Caperun, co. Hunts, ibid.
Alice Caperun, co. Bedf., ibid.
Thomas Chaperoun. J.
Almeric Chaperon. O.
John Chaperon, co. Norf., 1400: FF.
ii. 97.
1550. Hugh Beete and Anne Capron:
Marriage Lic. (London), i. 13.
1788. Married—Robert Capron and
Mary Thomas Nixon: St. Geo. Han. Sq.
ii. 4.
London, 2, 2, 1, 0; MDB. (co. Suffolk),
1, 0, 0, 0; Philadelphia (Chapron), 2;
New York, 3, 1, 0, 0.

Capstick.—Local; v. Copestake.

**Carberry, Carbrey, Car-
bury.**—Local, 'of Carberry,' a
parish in co. Kildare, Ireland. As
this surname looks very English,
I insert it to prevent any mis-
apprehension.

1743. Philip Carbery and Mary Chester: Marriage Lic. (London), ii. 345.
1792. Married—The Right Hon. George
Evans, Baron Carbery, and Susan Watson: St. Geo. Han. Sq. ii. 82.
1806. — John Dollman and Jemima
Mary Carbery: ibid. 344.
London, 0, 0, 0; Boston (U.S.), 9, 9, 0;
Philadelphia, 23, 1, 0; New York (Car-
bury), 1.

Carbine; v. Corbyn.

Carbonel. ?
Peter Carbonel, co. Soms., 1 Edw. III:
Kirby's Quest, p. 231.
Peter Carbonel, co. Oxf., 1273. A.
Richard Carbonel, co. Salop, ibid.
Ralph Carbonel, co. Camb., ibid.
1654. Married — William Carbonnell
and Eliz. Delillors, St. Antholin (London),
p. 83.
London, 1.

Carbutt.—Bapt.; v. Garbutt,
of which it is a corruption; cf.
Cammel for Gamel, &c.

London, 2; Philadelphia, 1.

Carder.—Occup. 'the carder,'
a carder of wool, probably a female
industry; cf. Kempster.

John le Carder, 7 Edw. III: Freemen
of York, i. 27.
Robert de Coleby, *carder*, 8 Edw. III:
ibid. p. 28.

Margareta Cardar, 1379: P. T. Yorks. p. 294.
1670. Married—Willia' Johnson and Ane Carder: St. Jas. Clerkenwell, iii. 172.
1750. Bapt.—Ann, d. of Nicodemus and Ann Carder: ibid. ii. 294.
London, 3; Philadelphia, 1.

Cardew.—Local, ' of Cardew,' a manor in the old barony of Dalston, co. Cumb.

William de Carthew: E. and F., co. Cumb., p. 93.
Thomas de Karthew: ibid.
1602. Married—Robert Cardew and Ann Harte: St. Jas. Clerkenwell, iii. 26.
1694. — Jeffery Cardue and Margaret Jepsey: ibid. p. 19.
Crockford, 3.

Cardiff.—Local, ' of Cardiff.'

William de Cardiff, canon of St. David's, 1291: Hist. and Ant. St. David's, p. 364.
William de Karhurdif, co. Heref., Hen. III-Edw. I. K.
William de Kerdof, co. Wilts, ibid.
John Cardif, co. Southampt., 1273. A.
Henry Cardeyf, co. Southampt., ibid.
Ralph Cardiff, of Woolfall, parish of Audlem, 1612: Wills at Chester (1545-1620), p. 36.
1692. Married—John Cox and Mary Cardiffe: St. Jas. Clerkenwell, iii. 212.
1747. — Thomas Cardiffe and Eliz. Baker: St. Geo. Chap. Mayfair, p. 80.
Liverpool, 1.

Cardinal, Cardinall.—Nick. ' the cardinal,' the ecclesiastical dignitary; cf. Italian *cardinali*; cf. Bishop, Archdeacon, &c.

William le Cardin', co. Salop, 1273. A.
Henricus Cardynall, 1379: P. T. Yorks. p. 126.
Walter Cardinall. P.
William Cardynall, temp. Eliz. Z.
1683. Married—John Bramton and Margaret Cardinall: St. Jas. Clerkenwell, iii. 200.
1802. — John Cardinall and Jane Evans: St. Geo. Han. Sq. ii. 257.
London, 1, 0; New York, 1, 0; Boston (U.S.), 7, 0; MDB. (co. Essex), 0, 4.

Cardmaker.—Occup. ' the cardmaker,' a manufacturer of the ' card' or ' comb' used by the cloth-worker in the carding of wool and other raw material.

John Cardmaker, *minorite*, 1532: Reg. Univ. Oxf. vol. i. p. 172.
Willelmus Cardemaker, 1379: P. T. Yorks. p. 98.
Willm. Raweff, *kardmaker*, 1441: W. 11.
William Cardemaker, C.R., 3 Edw. IV. ' John Cardmaker, alias Taylor (d. 1555), martyr, was originally an Observant friar. . . . He became vicar of St. Bridget's in Fleet St., and one of the

lecturers at St. Paul's. He was brought before Bonner, May 25; 1555, and burnt alive at Smithfield, May 30': Dict. Nat. Biog. ix. 39-40.

The occupative term is found in the 17th century:

James Dewhurst, parish of Rochdale, *cardmaker*, 1637: Wills at Chester (1621-50), p. 64.

I fear the surname is obsolete.

Cardus. — Local, 'of Carruthers'; v. Carruthers.

Manchester, 1; Colne, 1.

Cardwell.—Local, ' de Cardeville.' This surname seems to be of Norman extraction. The suffix *-ville* is commonly turned into *-well*; cf. Boswell and Bosville.

William de Cardevile, co. Wilts, 1273. A.
Richard de Cardevill, co. Southampt., Hen. III-Edw. I. K.
1603. Buried—Susand Cardewell: St. Jas. Clerkenwell, iv. 74.
1612. Married—Thomas Coe and Dorath Cardwell: St. Antholin (London), p. 49.
1754. — Charles Bradley and Alice Cardwell: St. Geo. Chap. Mayfair, p. 276.
London, 3; Philadelphia, 16; MDB. (co. Oxford), 2.

Care.—Local, ' at the care,' a form of Carr, q.v., from residence thereby.

Lucas de la Care, co. Kent, 20 Edw. I. R.
1663. Buried—Robert Care: St. Jas. Clerkenwell, ii. 352.
1706. Married—John Car (or Care) and Eliz. Ariss: St. Antholin (London), p. 119.
London, 2; Philadelphia, 6.

Careless, Carless.—Nick. ' the careless,' free from anxiety and sorrow; cf. Merry, Jolly, &c.

Willelmus Careles, 1379: P. T. Yorks. p. 262.
Antony Careless, temp. 1570. Z.
1722. Married—Charles Carelesse and Rebecca Moor: St. Jas. Clerkenwell, iii. 247.
1769. — William Careless and Lydia Coles: St. Geo. Han. Sq. i. 190.
London, 3, 1; MDB. (co. Hereford), 0, 4; Philadelphia, 3, 0.

Carey, Cary.—Local, ' of Carey,' a great West-country surname. Mr. Lower, quoting Sir Bernard Burke's Landed Gentry of Great Britain and Ireland, says, ' Cary: the ancient family of Cary derives its surname from the manor of Cary, or Kari, as it is called in Domesday Book, lying

in the parish of St. Giles-on-the-Heath, near Launceston.'

John de Cary, co. Soms., 1 Edw. III: Kirby's Quest, p. 261.
Roger de Cary, co. Soms., 1273. A.
1545. Henry Carey and Ann Morgan: Marriage Lic. (Faculty Office), p. 4.
1592. Buried — John Cary: St. Jas. Clerkenwell, iv. 46.
MDB. (co. Soms.), 20, 2; London, 14, 15; Philadelphia, 116, 8.

Carle, Carleman, Karl, Karle, Carl.—Occup. ' the carle,' or ' the carleman,' a rustic, a bondman, a churl. 'Carle, or Chorle: *rusticus*. Carle, or Chorle: bondeman, or woman; *servus nativa*, *serva nativa*': Prompt. Parv. Way adds in a note, ' Anglo-Saxon *ceorl*, carlman: *rusticus*.'

Henry le Karle, co. York, 1273. A.
Ida Carle, co. Camb., ibid.
Robert Carleman, co. Camb., ibid.
Henry Carle, co. York, ibid.
Robert Karleman, co. Camb., ibid.
1438. John Carle, rector of Weeting, co. Norf.: FF. ii. 169.
1603. Buried—George Carle: St. Mary Aldermary, p. 150.
1627. Married—John Carle and Jone Weaver: St. Jas. Clerkenwell, iii. 57.
London, 1, 0, 1, 0, 0; Boston (U.S.), 6, 0, 1, 3, 7.

Carleton, Carlton.—Local, ' of Carlton.' There are at least twenty-two parishes and townships so called in England; v. Charlton and Chorlton, literally the town of Karl, or the churl.

Reginald de Karleton, co. Linc., Hen. III-Edw. I. K.
Alan de Karleton, co. Linc., 20 Edw. I. R.
John de Carleton, co. Linc., 1273. A.
Geoffrey de Karlton, co. Bedf., ibid.
Edmund de Carleton, rector of Little Poringland, co. Norf.: FF. v. 445.
Robert de Carletone, co. Soms., 1 Edw. III: Kirby's Quest, p. 129.
Anabella de Carleton, 1379: P. T. Yorks. p. 268.
Thomas de Carleton, 1379: ibid. p. 24.
Johannes de Carleton, 1379: ibid. p. 46.
1562-3. Edward Brisley and Grace Karleton: Marriage Lic. (London), i. 26.
1587. Married—Robert Harvie and Agnes Carleton: St. Jas. Clerkenwell, iii. 13.
London, 3, 0; New York, 16, 14.

Carlisle, Carlyle, Carlile, Carlill.—Local, ' of Carlisle,' the county town of Cumberland. The surname crossed the Border, the spelling undergoing slight changes. Still it is easy to see that Thomas Carlyle was born and brought up not very far from the city whence his ancestors originally sprang.

Nicholas de Carliolo, *aurifaber*, 4 Edw. II: Freemen of York, i. 13.
Thomas de Carlell, 1379: P. T. Yorks. p. 247.
Willelmus de Karleyll', *osteler*, 1379: ibid. p. 96.
Walterus de Carlhill, 1379: ibid. p. 97.
1547. Hugh Karlyle and Christian Saunders: Marriage Lic. (London), i. 11.
1586. Bapt.—Hellen, d. John Carleill: St. Jas. Clerkenwell, i. 18.
1598. Robert Jenkinson and Margaret Carleill: Marriage Lic. (London), i. 249.
1608. Richard Moorer and Bridget Carliell: ibid. p. 309.
London, 4, 1, 2, 1; West Rid. Court Dir., 5, 0, 3, 0; Philadelphia, 27, 1, 10, 0.

Carman.—Occup. 'the carman,' one who drove or let out vehicles, a carrier. The instance from Yorkshire seems to suggest this origin, as appended to the name is the occupative term *hostiler*. Shakespeare has *carman* (Measure, ii. 1). O.F. *car*, a car.

Henry Carman, co. Suff., 1273. A.
Matilda Carman, co. Norf., ibid.
Thomas Carman, *hostiler*, 1379: P. T. Yorks. p. 146.
Alicia Carman, 1379: ibid. p. 68.
John Carman, co. Norf., 1408: FF. x. 27.
1580. Christopher Plashe and Eliz. Carman: Marriage Lic. (London), i. 96.
1583. Buried—John Rychardes, a carman, who brake his neck with a fall: St. Michael, Cornhill, p. 199.
1794. Married—Hugh Bethel Simpson and Mary Carman: St. Geo. Han. Sq. ii. 119.
London, 7; MDB. (co. Suffolk), 2; (co. Camb.), 1; Philadelphia, 40.

Carn, Carne. — Local, 'of Carne.' Cornish *carn*, a rock = cairn. (1) South and West Carne are in the parish of Alternun, near Launceston; (2) Carne is a small place in the parish of St. Anthony-in-Meneage; (3) also, there is a Carne in the parish of Crowan, near Camborne, all in Cornwall. There are five Carnes in the Dict. Nat. Biog. Four were born in Cornwall.

1547–8. Richard Carne and Adriana Lynch: Marriage Lic. (Faculty Office), p. 12.
1736. Buried—Jane, wife of Thomas Carne: St. Columb Major (Cornwall), p. 267.
1746. Married—John Wilcocks and Eliz. Carn: St. Geo. Chap. Mayfair, p. 64.

London, 1, 5; Cornwall Court Dir., 0, 4; Penzance, 2, 0; Philadelphia, 1, 0.

Carnaby.—Local, 'of Carnaby,' a parish in East Rid. Yorkshire, about three miles from Bridlington.

Rogerus de Carnaby, *brasiator*, 1379: P. T. Yorks. p. 296.
Johannes Carnaby, 1379: ibid. p. 141.
1669. Married—Walter Carnaby and Martha Cooley: St. Jas. Clerkenwell, iii. 160.
— — William Carnabee and Martha Cooley: ibid.
1677. Samuel Carnaby and Amy Samback: Marriage Alleg. (Canterbury), p. 272.
London, 1; MDB. (East Rid. Yorks), 1.

Carnifex. — Occupative, 'the butcher or flesh-hewer.' Latinized in old registers into Carnifex. A very common entry.

Gocelin Carnifex, co. Hunts, 1273. A.
Berneus Carnifex, co. Camb., ibid.
Johannes Fleshewer, *carnifex*, 1379: P. T. Yorks. p. 196.

Carpenter.—Occup. 'the carpenter'; O.F. *carpentier*, a worker in wood. An extremely common entry in the Hundred Rolls.

Stephen Carpentarius, co. Devon, Hen. III-Edw. I. K.
Henricus Carpentarius, co. Lanc., 20 Edw. I. R.
John le Carpenter, co. Bedf., ibid.
Ricardus Carpentarius, co. Camb., 1273. A.
Hugh le Charpenter, co. Wilts, ibid.
Johannes Carpenter, *wryght*, 1379: P. T. Yorks. p. 33.
Willelmus Wryght, *carpenter*, 1379: ibid. p. 34.
1550. John Carpenter and Alice Segrave: Marriage Lic. (London), i. 12.
London, 54; Philadelphia, 152.

Carpmile.—Loc.; v. Cartmell.

Carr.—Local, 'at the carr' or 'kerr,' q.v. The latter is the common form of entry in the Yorkshire Poll Tax, &c. The frequency with which such entries as Robert or William del Carr, or atte Carr, or Karr, or Kerr recur in Lancashire and Yorkshire records of the 13th and 14th centuries is explained by the fact that Carr or Kerr meant a low-lying meadow. It is still so used in all the northern counties. I saw in the Clifton Arms Hotel, Blackpool, Dec. 6, 1887, a placard announcing the sale of a freehold farm near Bispham. 'All that Meadow, or Carr, containing six acres' occurred twice, and one plot of ground was called Fayles Meadow, or Deborah's Carr. In the Yorkshire Poll Tax (1379) almost every village has some one styled William or John del Kerr in it; v. Carus.

Thomas Carr, Agnes uxor ejus, 1379: P. T. Yorks. p. 43.
Willelmus att Karr, 1379: ibid. p. 44.
Johannes del Karr, 1379: ibid. p. 67.
1610. Buried—Mabell, d. John Carr: St. Jas. Clerkenwell, iv. 114.
1742. Married—James Carr and Ann Holt: St. Geo. Chap. Mayfair, p. 20.
London, 62; Philadelphia, 344.

Carradus. — Local; v. Carruthers.

Carrick.—Local, 'at the carrick,' from residence on or by the carrick, or craig, or crag; Gaelic, *carraig*, a rock. A Scotch surname. It seems at times, however, to be a French form of the above—Breton, *karrek*, a rock in the sea (v. *Crag* in Skeat's Dict.).

Richard Carrique, of Tewxbury, temp. 1580: Visitation of London, 1634, p. 140.
Martin Carrique, of London, 1634: ibid.
William Carriq, of Yateley, co. Southampton, 1657: Reg. St. Dionis Backchurch, London, p. 33.
1809. Married—John George Carrique and Jane Roche: St. Geo. Han. Sq. ii. 410.
London, 2; Philadelphia, 18.

Carrier.—Occup. 'the carrier,' a carter. This surname barely exists in England. I do not find it in leading English directories. But it has crossed the Atlantic and is found occasionally in the States.

Willelmus Cariour, *wright*, 1379: P. T. Yorks. p. 135.
Johannes Kerrear, 1379: ibid. p. 11.
Johannes Charyer, 1379: ibid. p. 12.
Richarde Cariar, 1559: Reg. St. Mary Aldermary, p. 53.
1605. Married—Leonard Chapman and Margaret Carrier: St. Jas. Clerkenwell, iii. 30.
1739. — Thomas Carrier and Eliz. Bliss: St. Geo. Han. Sq. i. 7.
The Daily Telegraph, Jan. 11, 1895, records the death of Thomas W. Carrier.
Philadelphia, 1; Boston (U.S.), 3.

Carrington.—Local, (1) 'of Carrington,' a chapelry near New Bolingbroke, co. Lincoln; (2) 'of Carrington,' a chapelry in the parish of Bowdon, co. Ches.; (3) 'of Carrington,' a village in the parish

M

of Basford, co. Notts. Both (1) and (3) have undoubtedly given birth to representatives of this surname.

1589-90. Thomas Jenkinson and Katherine Karrington: Marriage Lic. (London), i. 184.
1631. John Carrington, of Bollington: Wills at Chester (1621-50), p. 43.
1640. Thomas Carrington, of Chester: ibid.
1763. Married—John Carrington and Eliz. Ashwell: St. Geo. Han. Sq. i. 118.
London, 11; MDB. (co. Lincoln), 2; (Cheshire), 4; Philadelphia, 4.

Carrodus.—Local, 'of Carruthers,' q.v.

Carruthers, Carrudders, Cruddas, Cruddis, Cruddace, Carrodus, Carradus.—Local, 'of Carruthers,' a hamlet in the parish of Middlebie, co. Dumfries. This Border name early penetrated into Cumberland, Westm., and North Yorks, and one familiar variant is the curious surname Carrodus found in the same districts. This is proved, if proof were necessary, by such an entry as the following:

Simon Carruders, co. Northumb., temp. Edw. VI: TTT. p lxxiv.
1616-7. John Murrey and Jane Carrutherers: Marriage Lic. (Westminster), p. 23.
1622. George Caruthers and Eliz. Tilstone: Marriage Lic. (London), ii. 114.
1772. Married—Walter Carruthers and Susannah Robinson: St. Geo. Han. Sq. i. 217.
London, 6, 0, 0, 0, 0, 0, 0, 0; Newcastle, 2, 0, 1, 2, 1, 0, 0; Keighley (Carrodus), 4; Sedbergh (Carradus), 1; 'Carruthers': Philadelphia, 3; Boston (U.S.), 9.

Carsley.—Local, 'of Carsley,' some small place in the West country.

Richard de Carslegh, co. Soms., 1 Edw. III: Kirby's Quest, p. 128.
Boston (U.S.), 3.

Carson.—? Bapt. 'the son of ——?' Probably the prefix Car is a pet or popular nick. of some personal name; but I cannot suggest it. But there is one solution which would easily explain the surname, viz. Garson, i.e. Garçon, a servant (v. Gasson). C and G as initials were practically interchangeable in the nomenclature of the 13th, 14th, and 15th centuries (v. Cammel).

Alicia Careson, *wyf*, 1379: P. T. Yorks. p. 168.
London, 4; Philadelphia, 162.

Carswell, 'Casswell, Kerswell, Kerswill.—Local, (1) 'of Abbots Kerswell' (or simply Carswell), a parish a mile or two from Newton Abbot, co. Devon; (2) 'of Kings Kerswell' (or simply Carswell), a couple of miles south of Newton Abbot.

Robert de Carswell, co. Soms., 1 Edw. III: Kirby's Quest, p. 234.
Richard de Carswall, co. Devon, 1273. A. (Dominus) de Carswill, co. Devon, ibid.
William de Karswill, co. Devon, ibid.
John Careswell, *vulgo*, Caswall, Wedon; Visitation of London, 1634, p. 141.
1598. William Kerswell and Joane Warde: Marriage Lic. (London), i. 252.
Alexander Carswell, of Thorne, St. Margaret, co. Soms., 1609: Abstract of Somersetshire Wills, p. 3.
1681. Married—Thomas Godbould and Eliz. Casewell: St. Jas. Clerkenwell, iii. 190.
1757.— Stephen Fryer and Abigail Caswell: St. Geo. Han. Sq. i. 70.
London, 2, 3, 1, 2; Devon Dir. (Farmers' List), 0, 0, 5, 3; Philadelphia, 2, 0, 0, 0; New York, 1, 0, 1, 1.

Carter.—Occup. 'the carter.' *Cart* is really a dim. of *car*, hence some of the fuller forms below; cf. Charter.

Jocius Caretarius, co. Oxf., 1273. A.
Juliana le Cartere, co. Camb., ibid.
Nicholas le Carter, co. Oxf., ibid.
John le Cartere, co. Norf., ibid.
Robert le Caretter, co. Hunts, ibid.
Margaret le Careter, co. Hunts, ibid.
Ricardus Carter, 1379: P. T. Yorks. p. 5.
Thomas Bell, *carter*, 1379: ibid. p. 110.
1570. Married—Robart Carter and Margaret Byllynge: St. Dionis Backchurch, p. 6.
1574.— Richarde Carter and Cecily Ellmar: St. Jas. Clerkenwell, iii. 6.
London, 221; Philadelphia, 169.

Carteret, Cartrett.—Local, 'de Carteret,' a parish adjoining Barneville, in the arrondissement of Valognes, in Normandy. The name is found early in Jersey.

Philip de Cartaret, Jersey, 20 Edw. I. R.
John de Carteret, Jersey, ibid.
Geoffrey de Carteret, Jersey, ibid.

No doubt the name has sometimes become confused with Cartwright.

1663. Thomas Scott and Carolina de Carterett: Marriage Lic. (Canterbury), p. 91.
1670-1. Benjamin Carteret and Dorothy Lane: ibid. p. 188.

1725. Married – Edward Harvey and Mary Carteret: St. Dionis Backchurch, p. 62.
Crockford, 1, 0; Philadelphia, 1, 0; Boston (U.S.), 0, 1.

Carthew.—Local, 'of Carthew' or 'Cardew,' a spot in the parish of St. Issey, co. Cornwall; v. Gilbert's Cornwall, ii. 255. The meaning is said to be car-dew, i.e. black rock (v. Lower's Patr. Brit. p. 54). There is, however, a hamlet Carthew in the parish of Carnmenellis; also another small hamlet of the same name in the parish of Treverbyn, co. Cornwall; v. Cardew.

1548. Bapt.—Richard, son of one Cardewe: Reg. St. Columb Major (Cornwall), p. 5.
1551. — William, son of Cost Cardew: ibid. p. 6.
1594. Married—Jeffrey Cardue and Margaret Jepsey: St. Jas. Clerkenwell, iii. 19.
Thomas Carthew (1657-1704), sergeant-at-law, was eldest son of Thomas Carthew, of Cannaliggy, St. Issey, in Cornwall: Dict. Nat. Biog. ix. 219.
London, 3; Cornwall Court Dir., 1.

Cartledge, Cartlidge.—Local, 'of the Cartlach.' I cannot find the spot. No doubt it lies in South Lancashire or East Cheshire. The suffix is -*lake*, a pond, or boggy spot, constantly found as -*ledge* or -*leach* in compound local surnames; cf. Blackledge or Blackleach, and Depledge (i.e. the black pond and the deep pond), both found in the same district.

1627. Married—William Froste and Mary Cartlach: Reg. Prestbury Ch. (co. Chester), p. 261.
Eliz. Cartledge, of Betchton, *widow*, 1700: Wills at Chester (1681-1700), p. 48.
Thomas Cartlich, of Barthomley, 1671: ibid. (1660-80), p. 51.
1695. Bapt.—Hannah, d. William Cartlitch: St. Jas. Clerkenwell, i. 363.
1778. Married—James D. Kisline and Sarah Carttlage: St. Geo. Han. Sq. i. 329.
London, 3, 0; Manchester, 2, 1; Philadelphia, 10, 0.

Cartman.—Occup. 'the carter'; v. Chartman and Carter.

Manchester, 1; New York, 1.

Cartmell, Cartmel, Cartmail, Cartmale, Cartmael, Carpmile.—Local, 'of Cartmell,' a well-known town in Furness, North Lancashire. The Staffordshire variants of this surname seem to have come from North Lancashire *via* Cheshire.

Robert Cartmell, of Claughton, 1578 : Lancashire Wills at Richmond (1457-1680), p. 58.
Elizabeth Cartmall, of Claughton, 1716 : ibid. (1681-1748), p. 53.
Ann Cartmell, of Pullgarth, in Cartmell Fell, 1701 : ibid.
Thomas Cartmell, of Chester, 1648 : Wills at Chester (1621-50), p. 44.
John Cartmell, of Simondston, 1673 : ibid. (1660-80), p. 51.
London, 2, 1, 0, 0, 2, 0 ; MDB. (co. Stafford), 0, 0, 1, 1, 0, 1 ; Philadelphia (Cartmell), 1.

Carttar.—Occup. 'the carter,' a whimsical spelling ; v. Carter.

London, 2.

Cartwright.—Occup. 'the cartwright,' a maker of carts ; cf. Wainwright.

Robert le Cartwright. B.
Johannes Toppe, *cartwryght*, 1379 : P. T. Howdenshire, p. 14.
Magota Cartwryght, 1379 : P. T. Yorks. p. 7.
Henricus Wryght, *catewryght* (sic), 1379 : ibid. p. 10.
Johannes Warde, *cartwright*, 1379 : ibid. p. 11.
Johannes Percivale, *cartwright*, 1379 : ibid. p. 13.
Geoffrey Cartewirght, 1379 : ibid. p. 78.
1572-3. Richard Cartewrighte and Thomasine Baker : Marriage Lic. (London), i. 55.
1602. Married—Richard Greene and Anne Cartwright : St. Jas. Clerkenwell, iii. 26.
London, 35 ; Philadelphia, 22.

Carus, Cariss, Carass.—Local, ' of the carr-house,' i. e. the house by the carr (v. Carr or Kerr). There is no evidence in favour of the Latin *carus*, dear, beloved. It is a mere guess. Cariss and Carass seem to be Yorkshire corruptions ; cf. Loftus, Bacchus, Kirkus, &c. It is quite possible 'carr-house' may refer to the house where the car was kept. M.E. *carre* ; O.F. *car* or *char* (v. Charer, Charman, and Carman). The derivation in that case would still be local.

Richard Carous, 49 Edw. III : Hist. Westm. and Cumb., i. 37.
Thomas de Carrehuis', 1379 : P. T. Yorks. p. 48.
Johannes de Carehuis, 1379 : ibid. p. 137.
William Charus, Merton Coll., co. Westm., 1582 : Reg. Univ. Oxf. vol. ii. pt. ii. p. 119.

1601-2. Peter Carus and Ellen Lego : Marriage Lic. (London), i. 266.
1808. Married—Robert Starkey Carus and Maria Day : St. Geo. Han. Sq. ii. 394.
Crockford, 3, 0, 0 ; Pallathorp (Bolton Percy, Yorks), 0, 0, 2 ; York, 0, 1, 0.

Carver.—Official, ' the carver,' a servitor whose duty it was to carve at table. ' Item, to William Denton, carver to the Queen, £26 13s. 4d.' (1503) : Privy Purse Exp., Eliz. of York, p. 100.

Adam le Karver, co. Devon, 1273. A.
Richard le Kerver, co. Linc., ibid.
1565. Married—Steven Carver and Jayne Byllam : St. Dionis Backchurch, p. 5.
1613. Bapt.—Thomas, s. John Carvor : St. Jas. Clerkenwell, i. 68.
London, 12 ; Philadelphia, 38.

Carvill, Carvell, Carville.—Local, ' de Charville,' evidently a Norman surname, spelt Chereville or Kervile (FF. ix. 73). The following quotations from Blomefield's History of Norfolk will settle the point beyond the possibility of dispute :

Robert de Cherevill, co. Norf., 29 Hen. II : FF. vii. 82.
Roger de Cherevile, co. Norf., 10 Rich. I : ibid. ix. 73.
Walter Chervyle, rector of Bicham-Well, co. Norf., 1329 : ibid. vii. 297.
Frederic de Carvill, co. Norf. : ibid. viii. 368.
Humphrey Carvile, co. Norf., 30 Hen. VIII : ibid. p. 474.
Thomas Carvel, co. Norf., 1662 : ibid. vi. 93.
Edmund Carvill, co. Norf., 1599 : ibid. vi. 163.
1668. Married—John Carvell and Mary Rowland : St. Jas. Clerkenwell, iii. 155.
1778. — John Winbush and Esther Carvill : St. Geo. Han. Sq. i. 293.
London, 3, 4, 0 ; New York, 1, 0, 4.

Carwardine.

MDB. (co. Essex), 1.

Cary ; v. Carey.

Case, Cash.—Bapt. ; v. Cass.

Cashman, Casman.—Offic. 'a catchpoll' (v. Catcher) ; M.E. *cachen*, to catch ; O.F. *cachier*, to pursue.

Roger Cashman, 1562 : Reg. Broad Chalke, co. Wilts, p. 1.
1783. Married—Mathew Casman and Catherine Dunavan : St. Geo. Han. Sq. i. 352.
London, 2, 1 ; Philadelphia, 15, 0 ; New York (Casman), 1.

Casman ; v. Cashman.

M 2

Cass, Casson, Cash, Case.—Bapt. 'the son of Cassandra,' from the nick. Cass, a common girl's name in the 12th and 13th centuries. I only furnish a few instances :

Albric' fil.Cassandre,co.Camb.,1373. A.
Ralph fil. Cassandre, co. Camb., ibid.
Cassandre (without surname), co. Hunts, ibid.
Cassandra Metcalfe, York, 1509 : W. 11.
Casse Rumpe, co. Kent, 1273. A.
Stephen Casse, co. Soms., 1 Edw. III : Kirby's Quest, p. 165.
Johannes Case, 1379 : P. T. Yorks. p. 37.
Willelmus Casson, 1379 : ibid. p. 186.
Cassander Danyll, 1379 : ibid. p. 148.
1676. John Casse and Eliz. Bright : Marriage Lic. (Faculty Office), p. 136.
1747. Married—Daniel Cass and Eliz. Pritchard : St. Geo. Chap. Mayfair, p. 99.
London, 4, 3, 7, 12 ; West Rid. Court Dir., 10, 5, 2, 0 ; Boston (U.S.), 30, 3, 7, 20.

Castellan.—Offic. ' the castellan,' the constable of a castle. It is very probable, and almost certain, that Castleman is a corrupted form of Castellan.

Jocelin le Castlelyn, co. Sussex, 20 Edw. I. R.
John Castelyn, co. Bedf., ibid.
Thomas le Chastelain, c. 1300. M.
William Castelein co. Camb., 1273. A.
Gilbert Chasteleyn, co. Suff., ibid.
1547-8. William Hamerton and Benet Castelyn : Marriage Lic. (Faculty Office), p. 12.

Castle, Castell, Cassell.—Local, ' at the castle,' from residence thereby or therein as a servitor or keeper.

Alan de Castell, London, 1273. A.
Andrew de Castello, co. Norf., ibid.
Ranulph del Chastel, C. R., 2 Edw. I.
Robert del Chastell, co. Northumb., 1340 : KKK. p. xl.
William atte Castle, co. Soms., 1 Edw. III : Kirby's Quest, p. 134.
Thomas de Castell, 1379 : P. T. Yorks. p. 119.
Magota del Castell, 1379 : ibid. p. 179.
Roger atte Castell : Household Book of Queen Isabelle, 1358 ; Cott. MS. Galba, E. xiv.
1548. Bapt.—Katherine Castle : St. Peter, Cornhill, p. 4.
1652. Married—Richard Castle and Eliz. Newton : St. Michael, Cornhill, p. 31.
1795. — Joseph Clarke and Frances Castell : St. Geo. Han. Sq. ii. 133.
London, 30, 4, 6 ; Boston (U.S.), 6, 2, 10.

Castleman.—(1) Offic. ' the castle-man,' a servant, a keeper ; cf. Templeman, Towerman. (2)

Offic.; v. Castellan, of which Castleman is probably a corrupted form.

Ralph Castelman, co. Soms., 1 Edw. III : Kirby's Quest, p. 126.
Richard Castelman, C. R., 25 Hen. VI.
Thomas Castylman, C. R., 1-2 Philip and Mary, pt. i.
1758. Married—Henry Castleman and Dorothy Richardson : St. Geo. Han. Sq. i. 76.
1798. — William Castleman and Sarah Steptoe : ibid. ii. 193.
Philadelphia, 1.

Caston.—Local, 'of Caston,' a parish in co. Norf., three miles from Watton. A well-known family sprung from this spot and ramified strongly.

Robert de Caston, co. Norf., 1273. A.
Wydo de Caston, co. Norf., ibid.
John de Cateston, co. Norf., 30 Edw. III : FF. vii. 222.
William de Catestune, or Caston, co. Norf., 1200 : ibid. x. 245.
William Caston, co. Norf., temp. 1415 : ibid. ii. 56.
1604. Bridget Caston : Marriage Lic. (London), i. 289.
1796. Married—Matthew Coston and Mary Caste : St. Geo. Han. Sq. ii. 144.
London, 4 ; Boston (U.S.), 1.

Catcher.—Nick. 'the catcher,' a huntsman, a follower of the chase; perhaps sometimes a catchpoll (v. Catchpoll) ; M.E. *cachen*, to catch. ' Cachare or dryvare : *minator, abactor*' : Prompt. Parv.

Richard Catcher, of London, traces descent from John Cacher, 1484 : Visitation of London, 1634, p. 145.
Adam le Cacher, co. Norf., 1273. A.
Richard le Catchere, co. Norf., ibid.
William Catchare, co. Norf., temp. Edw. I : FF. vii. 306.
Hugh Catchare, co. Norf., 3 Edw. III : ibid. p. 304.
1570. Bapt.—Rycharde, s. Thomas Katcher : St. Michael, Cornhill, p. 85.
1575. John Catcher : Cal. of Wills in Court of Husting (2).
1621. Married—Thomas Haukes and Hester Catcher : St. Jas. Clerkenwell, iii. 50.

I do not find any present instances, but no doubt they exist.

Catcherell.—Offic. ' the cacherel,' a catchpoll, petty sergeant, under-bailiff, policeman. The instances in the Hundred Rolls (very many) lie almost entirely between Norfolk and Essex. 'Cacherele, a catchpole' (Halliwell). In my notebook (unfortunately without

reference) I have a couplet from an old political song :
' Nedes I must spend that I spared of yore
Ageyn this cacherele cometh.'

Hugh le Chaccherel, co. Norf., 1273. A.
Grig le Cacherel, co. Suff., ibid.
Adam le Kacherel, co. Norf., ibid.
Alexander le Cacherel, co. Norf., ibid.
Robelard Cacherellus, co. Sussex, ibid.
Thomas Cacherellus de Lodenygges, elsewhere described as the 'Cacherel de Lodene,' co. Norf., ibid.

This surname seems now lost in Catherall (q.v.), an early variant ; also in Catterall (q.v.), a local surname.

Catchpenny.—Nick. 'a catchpenny,' a man who tried to hit the popular fancy as a chapman, who had something to sell that would readily catch a penny.

N. (? Nicholas) Kachepeny, co. Soms., 1273. A.

Catchpoll, Catchpool, Catchpole.—Offic. ' the catchpoll,' one who seized people by the head ; a sheriff's officer, a bailiff ; Latinized into *cachepollus*.

' A cachepol cam forth
And cracked both their legges.'
Piers Plowman.

The weapon the catchpoll carried may still be seen in the Tower of London.

'William Cachepoll, cust. gaiole. nĩi Salop' : C. R., 55 Hen. III.
Geoffrey le Cachepol, co. Oxf., 1273. A.
Ralph le Cachepol, co. Oxf., ibid.
Hugh le Cachepol, c. 1300. M.
Michael Catchpoole, temp. Eliz. Z.
Henry Cachepole, M.P. for Hereford, C. R., 45 Edw. III.
1627. Married — Edward Bishop and Bridget Catchpoole : St. Antholin (London), p. 62.
1647. Buried—William Catchpole, servant to Mr. Humphries, victualler : St. Michael, Cornhill, p. 242.
London, 0, 4, 11.

Category.—Nick. 'one of a particular class or list.'

John Categorye, fellow of All Souls, Oxf., 1545 : Reg. Univ. Oxf. i. 222.

Cater, Cator, Caterer.—Offic. ' the cater,' a caterer, more correctly a cater, contracted from *acatour*, a buyer for a house. ' Of which achatours mighten en-semple' : Chaucer, C. T. ' Catour of a gentylmans house, *despensier* ':

Palsgrave. 'Catours, manciples, spencers, cokes' : 1459. Mun. Acad. Oxon., p. 346 ; v. Chater. The final *er* in Caterer is a needless addition, as in poulterer and upholsterer. It occurs early, as will be seen below.

William le Catur, co. Essex, 1273. A.
John le Achatur, co. Camb., ibid.
John le Catur. J.
Bernard le Acatour, c. 1300. M.
Nicholas le Catour. B.
William Katerer, co. Hunts, 1273. A.
1523. John Cater and Johanna Thrower : Marriage Lic. (London), i. 3.
1569. Married—Henry Cater and Joan Powlter : St. Jas. Clerkenwell, i. 4.
1803. — Francis John Cator and Mary Ann Humphreys : St. Geo. Han. Sq. ii. 280.
London, 12, 1, 0 ; Sheffield, 1, 0, 3 ; Philadelphia, 0, 0, 1.

Catesby.—Local, ' of Catesby,' a parish in co. Northampton.

Robert de Catesby, co. Northampt., Hen. III-Edw. I. K.
William de Cattesby, co. Northampt., ibid.

All the Catesbys mentioned in the Dict. Nat. Biog. can be ultimately referred to Northamptonshire. William Catesby (d. 1485), councillor of Richard III, of whom, and others, the couplet was written :

' The Cat, the Rat, and Lovel our dog
Rule all England under a hog,'

was son of Sir William Catesby, of Ashby St. Legers, co. Northampton.

1668. Thomas Catesby and Hope Kilcocke : Marriage Lic. (Faculty Office), p. 295.
1747. Married—Mark Catesby and Eliz. Rowland : St. Geo. Chap. Mayfair, p. 92.
London, 2.

Cathcart.—Local, ' of Cathcart,' a town in co. Renfrew.

1744. Married—Robert Cathart and Eliz. Jones : St. Geo. Chap. Mayfair, p. 35.
London, 1 ; Philadelphia, 21 ; New York, 3.

Cather.—Offic. ' the catcher.' In the same way Catcherell is found as ' le Catherel' ; v. Catherall.

Richard le Cather, co. Norf., 1273. A.
Robert le Cathere, co. Norf., ibid.

The above Richard is set down also as Richard Catherellus ; v. Catherall.

London, 1 ; Philadelphia, 2.

Catherall, Cathrall.—Offic. 'the catcherell,' q.v.; an early variant. But vide also Cattarall.

Thomas le Catherel, co. Norf., 1273. A.
Alexander Catherel, co. Norf., ibid.
Richard Catherellus, co. Norf., ibid.
1611. Buried—Jane Catheralles: St. Jas. Clerkenwell, iv. 115.
1633. — Jane Caterrall : ibid. p. 211.
1636. Edward Catherall, curate of Great Carbrook, co. Norf.: FF. ii. 338.
London, 4, 0; Manchester, 1, 0; Philadelphia, 0, 6.

Catlin, Catling, Catlyn, Catlinson, Cattlin.—Bapt. 'the son of Catherine,' from the nick. Kate or Cat, and dim. Catlin; cf. Hewelin (v. Hewling), Tomlin or Tomling. The g in Catling is excrescent, as in Jennings. A simple glance at the directory will prove that the Irish Kathleen was once a familiar English form. Catlin and Catling are common surnames in most counties. 'Item, given to Kathelyne, 7s. 6d.': Privy Purse Exp., Princess Mary (1536-7), p. 8.

Elias Katelin, co. Camb., 1273. A.
Katerina, or Kateline de Sanston, co. Hunts, ibid.
Stephen Cateline : C. R., 35 Edw. I.
Johannes Cattelynson, 1379: P. T. Yorks. p. 17.
Willelmus Cattelyn, 1379: ibid. p. 17.
Henricus Catlyn, 1379: ibid. p. 74.
Thomas Katlynson, co. York. W. 11.
Stephen Cathilyn, Patent Roll, 19 Eliz. pt. iii.
Elenore Catlynson, co. York. W. 12.
1587. John Reppingall and Elizabeth Catlyn, widow : Marriage Lic. (London), i. 164.
1788. Married—John Catlin and Susanna Hayes : St. Geo. Han. Sq. ii. 15.
1794. — William Catling and Eliz. Church : ibid. p. 109.
London, 9, 5, 1, 0, 5; Boston (U.S), 5, 0, 0, 0, 0.

Catlow, Cattlow.—Local, ' of Catlow,' some spot near Burnley or Marsden, co. Lanc.

Adam de Catlowe, of Marsden, co. Lanc., 1332 : Lay Subsidy (Rylands), p. 83.
Robert de Catlowe, of Marsden, co. Lanc., 1332 : ibid. p. 84.
John Catlow, of Handbridge, Chester, 1642 : Wills at Chester, ii. 45.
Manchester, 1, 0; Liverpool, 1, 0; Philadelphia, 0, 3.

Caton.—Local ; v. Catton.

Catsnose.—? Nick. From some imagined resemblance. Not a com-plimentary sobriquet. But perhaps after all local ; cf. Holderness, Furness, Thickness.

Agnes Kattesnese, or Kattisnese, co. Linc., 1273. A.

Catt.—Nick. ' the cat,' a sobriquet affixed on the nominee for some supposed sleekness of manner, &c. A well-known Norfolk surname : at least six centuries old in that county.

Adam le Kat. C.
Milo le Chat. E.
Elyas le Cat, co. Norf., 1273. A.
Reginald le Cat, co. Essex, ibid.
Henry le Catt, co. Norf., 14 Edw. I : FF. vii. 305.
William le Cat, co. Norf., 1275 : ibid. vi. 376.
Roger le Chat, co. Norf., temp. King John : ibid. p. 375.
1465. William Catte, rector of Edingthorp, co. Norf.: ibid. xi. 29.
William Cat, co. Soms., 1 Edw. III : Kirby's Quest, p. 143.
1678. James Catt, rector of Gresham, co. Norf., FF. viii. 129.
1692. Bapt.—Aviss, d. Thomas Catt : St. Jas. Clerkenwell, i. 344.
1803. Married—Richard Catt and Mary Stedman : St. Geo. Han. Sq. i. 295.
London, 5 ; MDB. (co. Suffolk), 5.

Cattarall, Catherall, Catterall, Cathrall, Catrell.—Local, ' of Cattarall,' a township between Preston and Garstang, co. Lanc. But v. also Catherall.

'Gilbert de la Legh, and the heir of John de Caterale, holds in demesne and service the vill of Hapton'; Knights Fees, 23 Edw. III : Baines' Lanc. ii. 693.
'In 42 Hen. III (1257-8) Richard de Caterhale . . . held, among other places, Gosenhar and Katerale': ibid. ii. 537.
Lora de Caterhale, co. Lanc., 1332 : Lay Subsidy (Rylands), p. 58.
1562. Thomas Caterall : Preston Guild Rolls, p. 26.
1593. Ellen Catterall, of Croston, co. Lanc.: Wills at Chester (1545-1620), p. 37.
Manchester, 2, 1, 4, 0, 0 ; Preston, 0, 0, 9, 0, 0 ; MDB. (co. Chester), 0, 0, 0, 1, 0; Boston (U.S.), (Catrell), 1.

Cattermole, Cattermoul, Cattermull, Catmull.—? Local, a Norfolk and Suffolk surname. I find no early traces ; perhaps an immigrant from the Low Countries.

'George Cattermole, water-colour painter (1800-68), was born at Dickleborough, near Diss, co. Norf.': Dict. Nat. Biog. ix. 322.
1802. Married—John Cathermold and Jane Ford : St. Geo. Han. Sq. ii. 256.

London, 4, 1, 1, 0; MDB. (co. Suffolk), 5, 0, 0, 0 ; (co. Essex), 0, 0, 0, 1.

Catterson.—Bapt. ' the son of Catherine,' from the dim. Catlin, q.v. Hence Cattlinson or Cattinson corrupted to Catterson ; cf. Patterson, Dickenson, or Matterson for Pattinson, Dickinson, and Mattinson.

Francis Catterson, churchwarden of Skipton, 1664 : Dawson's Hist. Skipton, p. 161.
1733. Married—John Brown and Martha Catterson : St. Geo. Han. Sq. i. 12.
London, 1.

Cattle, Cattell.—Bapt. ; v. Chettle.

1683. Thomas Gibson and Alice Cattle : Marriage Alleg. (Canterbury), p. 146.

Cattlin, Cattling. — Bapt. ' Little Katharini ' ; v. Catlin.

Catton, Caton.—Local, ' of Catton,' (1) a chapelry in the parish of Croxall, co. Derby ; (2) a parish in co. Norfolk, two miles from Norwich ; (3) a parish in East Rid. Yorks ; (4) a township in the parish of Topcliffe, N. Rid. Yorks ; (5) ' of Caton,' a chapelry in the parish of Lancaster.

Robert de Catton, or Cattune : co. Norf., 1273. A.
John Caton, co. Hunts, ibid.
John de Caton, of Lancaster, co. Lanc., 1322 : Lay Subsidy (Rylands), p. 88.
Johannes de Catton, 1379 : P. T. Yorks. p. 20.
Willelmus de Caytton, 1379 : ibid. p. 105.
1569. Married—Thomas Stevens and Agnes Catton : St. Jas. Clerkenwell, iii. 4.
1773. — William Clark and Eliz. Catton : St. Geo. Han. Sq. i. 232
London, 4, 8 ; Liverpool, 0, 5 ; West Rid. Court Dir., 2, 2 ; Boston, 0, 13.

Caudle, Cawdell, Cadle.—Local, ' of Cauldwell,' a parish in dioc. Lichfield, co. Derby. No doubt many places were so called ; v. Coldwell and Caldwell.

Cristina Caudel, co. Camb., 1273. A.
William Caudel, co. Camb., ibid.
(Prior) de Caudewelle, co. Bedf., ibid.
1587. Thomas Cawdell, yeoman, and Johanna Lowen : Marriage Lic. (London), i. 162.
1664. Bapt.—William, son of Wm. and Mary Cawdle : Reg. St. James, Clerkenwell.
1727. Married — Edward Foss and Eleanor Caudell : St. Geo. Han. Sq. i. 4.
London, 2, 2, 1.

Caughey; v. Coffee.

Caulcutt.—Local, 'of Caldecote'; v. Calcott.

Caunter.—Occup. 'the gaunter,' a glover; v. Ganter and Gaunter). The change from G to C is common in surnames; cf. Candlin and Clendening.

London, 1; MDB. (co. Devon), 12.

Caurymaury.— Nick. 'Item, presentatum quod est Johannes Caurymaury, Johannes le Fleming . . . consueti fuerunt currere cum canibus suis sine warento' (Chronicon Petroburgense, Camd. Soc., p. 138). A very coarse cloth.

'Some loke strawry,
Some cawry mawry.'
Skelton's Elynour Rumnyng.

Causton, Cawston, Cawstan.—Local, 'of Causton.' The manor of Causton in South Erpingham, co. Norfolk, is mentioned in the Hundred Rolls of 1273 (ii. 513). No doubt Causton and Caston (q.v.) have become confused, both being Norfolk surnames, but they must be carefully separated, nevertheless.

Beatrix, relict of Stephen de Causton, Edgefield, co. Norf.: FF. ix. 385.
Richer de Causton, co. Norf., 1265: ibid.
Godfrey de Causton, co. Norf., 1273. A.
William de Causton, co. Norf., ibid.
Robert Cawston, or Caston, co. Norf., 1673: FF. iv. 208.
1633. Bapt. — Thomas, s. William Cawston: St. Jas. Clerkenwell, i. 125.
1711. Buried — James Causton: St. Michael, Cornhill, p. 281.
London, 5, 3, 0; MDB. (co. Suffolk), 2, 0, 0; Philadelphia, 0, 0, 1.

Cavalier.— Offic.; v. Chevalier.

Cave.—Local, (1) 'at the cave,' from residence therein or thereby; (2) 'of Cave,' two parishes, North and South Cave, in E. Rid. Yorks.

Roger de Cave, co. Linc, 1273. A.
Robert de Cave, co. Bucks. ibid.
Willelmus del Cave, 1379: P. T. Yorks. p. 66.
Willelmus de Cave, 1379: ibid. p. 53.
1654. Married—Philip Cave, upholder, and Sarah Martin: St. Michael, Cornhill.
1692. Bapt. — John, s. John Cave, packer, St. Dionis Backchurch, p 131.
West Rid. Court Dir., 2; London, 22; MDB. (co. Lincoln), 3; Philadelphia, 16.

Cavel, Cavell, Cavill.—Local, 'of Cavil,' a township in the parish of Eastrington, E. Riding Yorks, two miles from Howden. Thence the name easily crossed over into co. Lincoln. In some cases it may be represented by some more southern locality.

Robert de Cavilla, co. Linc., 1273. A.
1353. John Cavel, rector of Sizeland, co. Norf.: FF. x. 179.
Walter Cavel, co. Soms., 1 Edw. III: Kirby's Quest, p. 110.
1546. Humfrey Cavell and Alice Nassahe: Marriage Lic. (Faculty Office), p. 7.
1793. Married — Charles Lavell and Ann Seberner Cavill: St. Geo. Han. Sq. ii. 89.
London, 1, 6, 2; MDB. (co. Lincoln), Cavill, 6; West Rid. Court Dir., 0, 0, 2; Philadelphia, 0, 0, 5.

Caverley, Caverly.—Local, 'of Calverley,' q.v.; a variant. Calverley is a parish near Bradford, Yorks.

1562. Bapt.—Edmond, s. Bryan Caverley: St. Michael, Cornhill, p. 81.

The personal name of the father would of itself suggest a Yorkshire parentage. Bryan, until the 18th century, was a great favourite in North Lancashire, and West and North Yorkshire. Of this fact I might give endless proofs. Caverly is well known in the United States. It went out early.

'Charles Caverlie, aged 17'—'imbarqued in the Mathew of London' for St. Christophers in 1635: Hotten's Lists of Emigrants, p. 81.
London, 1, 0; New York, 0, 8.

Cawcutt.—Local, 'of Caldecote'; v. Calcott, a variant.

1554-5. George Mutsett and Catherine Cawcott: Marriage Lic. (London), i. 16.
1700. Bapt.—Mary, d. Robert Cawcott: St. Jas. Clerkenwell, p. 385.

The surname is further disguised in the following entry:

1793. Married—Francis Younger and Susanna Caukett: St. Geo. Han. Sq. ii. 101.
MDB. (co. Camb.), 2.

Cawley.—Local; v. Cayley.

Cawood, Cauwood.—Local, 'of Cawood,' (1) a small town near Selby, W.Rid.Yorks; (2) a chapelry in the parish of Melling, North Lancaster.

Johannes de Cawode, 1383-4: Freemen of York, i. 81.

Johannes de Cawod', 1379: P. T. Yorks. p. 3.
Willelmus de Cawod', 1379: ibid. p. 300.
Alicia de Cawode, 1379: P. T. Howdenshire, p. 17.

This surname crossed the Atlantic, and is still found in the States.

Richard Cawood, aged 25 years, 1635: Hotten's Lists of Emigrants, p. 71.
1569. John Cawood and Agnes Keane: Marriage Lic. (London), i. 42.
1771. Married—William Cawood and Mary Jones: St. Geo. Han. Sq. i. 206.
London, 2, 0; Sheffield, 1, 4; New York, 3, 0.

Cawsey.—Local; v. Cosway.

Cawston.—Local; v. Causton.

Cawthorn, Cawthorne, Cawthron, Corthorn.—Local, 'of Cawthorne,' a village four miles from Barnsley, co. York. Corthorn is a manifest variant and is found in the district.

Gamel de Cauthorn, co. York, 1273. A.
John de Cauthorn, co. York, ibid.
Johannes de Cauthorn, 1379: P. T. Yorks. p. 124.
Johanna de Cauthorn, 1379: ibid.
'James Cawthorn (1719-61), poet, was son of Thomas Cawthorn, upholsterer, and born at Sheffield, Nov. 4, 1719': Dict. Nat. Biog. ix. 380.

Thus for 400 years the ancestry of the last-named had clung to the district of his birth.

1788. Married—Matthew Oliver and Ann Cawthorn: St. Geo. Han. Sq. ii. 10.
London, 5, 0, 0, 1; Philadelphia, 2, 1, 0, 0; West Rid. Court Dir., 0, 0, 1, 0; Sheffield, 0, 1, 1, 1.

Caxton.—Local, 'of Caxton,' a parish in co. Cambridge.

John de Caxton, co. Camb., 1273. A.
Robert de Caxton, co. Camb., ibid.
Simon de Caxton, co. Hunts, ibid.
William de Caxton, co. Northampt., ibid.

I fear the surname is extinct.

Cayley, Caley, Cawley.—Local, 'de Cailli,' from Cailli, in the arrondissement of Rouen. Hugh de Cailly, lord of Orby, co. Norfolk, was head of the family whence sprang the barony.

Osbert de Caly, co. Norf., 1273. A.
Hugh de Caly, co. Norf., ibid.
1666. John Whalley and Mary Cawley: Marriage Alleg. (Canterbury), p. 121.
London, 8, 3, 4; New York, 0, 5, 0.

Cayzer.—Nick. 'the emperor,' the Caesar, Kaiser, a title of the

Holy Roman Empire ; v. Kaiser and Caesar.

' — of Jacob a star shall spryng
That shall overcom Kasar and Kyng.'
            Townley Mysteries.
' Kynges and Knyghtes,
Kaysers and Popes.'
            Piers Plowman.

Samson le Cayser, co. Oxf., 1273. A.
Thomas le Cayser, co. Oxf., ibid.
1796. Married—Robert Cayzer and Sarah Ambridge : St. Geo. Han. Sq. ii. 147.
London, 4.

Cecil.—Bapt. ' the son of Cecil,' masc. ; or Cecile, fem. (v. Siss, Sissot, Sisselot, Sisselson, Sisson ; for the popularity of these Yorkshire variants, v. Siss). Nearly all these names represent the feminine form. Cecil seems always to have descended from the masculine form.

Richard fil. Cecille, co. Camb., 1273. A.
Cecille in the Lane, co. Oxf., 1273. A.
William Cecilie, co. Oxf., 1273. A.
Cecilia Gamyll, 1379 : P.T. Yorks. p. 20.
Cecilia fil. Roberti, 1379 : ibid.
Sissilie Linscale, co. York. W. 16.
Thomas Cecill, temp. Eliz. Z.
James Cecilia, co. Norf., 1361 : FF. vi. 521.
Sir Thomas Cecill, Knt., co. Norf., 1591 : ibid. ii. 486.
1776. Married—Henry Cecil, Esq., and Emma Vernon : St. Geo. Han. Sq. i. 265.
London, 8 ; New York, 6.

Centlivre.—Nick.; v. Hundred-pound.

Chad, Chadd.—Bapt. ' the son of Chad.'

Cedda de Alrewys, co. Stafford, 1273. A.
Henry Chadde, London, ibid.
John Chadde, London, ibid.
Henricus Ced, 1379 : P. T. Howdenshire, p. 12.
Roger Chadde, or Chede, 1518 : Reg. Univ. Oxf. i. 104.
1774. Married—William Best and Peggy Chad : St. Geo. Han. Sq. i. 236.
London, 1, 2.

Chadband.—Local, ' of Chatburn,' q.v. Nearly all Dickens' character-names are to be found in the directory ; v. Pickwick, Winkle, Snodgrass. Doubtless Chadband is a variant of Chadburn. It is found alongside Chadbourn in the Boston (U.S.) Directory.

1788. Married—John Chatband and Susannah Johnson : St. Geo. Han. Sq. ii. 5.
1802. — John Chadband and Sarah Violet : ibid. p. 271.
Boston (U.S.), 1.

Chadburn,   Chadbourne, Chadbourn.—Local, ' of Chatburn,' a township in the parish of Whalley, co. Lanc.

Johannes de Chatteburn, 1379 : P. T. Yorks. p. 256.
Henricus de Chatteburn, 1379 : ibid. p. 256.
Ricardus Chattburne, 1379 : ibid. p.268.
1636. Buried—John, s. John Chadbourne : St. Jas. Clerkenwell, iv. 225.
1660. — John Chadbourne, a poore auncient man : ibid. p. 333.
West Rid. Court Dir., 3, 0, 0 ; Sheffield, 3, 0, 0 ; Boston (U.S.), 0, 10, 38.

Chadderton, Chatterton.—(1) Local, ' of Chadderton,' a township in the parish of Oldham, co. Lancashire ; (2) ' of Catterton,' a township in the parish of Healaugh, W. Rid. Yorks.

Margaret de Chadreton, of Chaderton, co. Lanc., 1332 : Lay Subsidy (Rylands), p. 30.
'William Chaderton, or Chadderton, or Chatterton, D.D. (1540 ?-1608), bishop of Lincoln,' was born at Moston, near Chadderton : Dict. Nat. Biog. ix. 432.
Thomas Chadderton, of the Lees, Oldham, 1575 : Wills at Chester (1545-1620), p. 38.
Imyne Chatterton, of Heaton Norris, 1594 : ibid. p. 39.
Alan de Caterton, co. York, 1273. A.
Willelmus de Caterton, 1379 : P. T. Yorks. p. 248.

Although in general Chatterton must be regarded as a variant of the Lancashire Chadderton, it is almost certain that some of the Chattertons found in the Yorkshire directories are variants of Catterton, a township in the W. Riding.

1569. Robert Chaderton and Margaret Revell : Marriage Lic. (London), i. 42.
1570. John Wyllett and Margaret Chatterton, widow : ibid. p. 46.
London, 0, 7 ; Sheffield, 0, 5 ; Manchester, 4, 1 ; Philadelphia, 1, 5.

Chaddock.—Local, ' of Chaddock,' an estate in the township of Tyldesley, in the parish of Leigh, co. Lancaster. Chaddock Hall was in possession of a family of that name in the early part of the last century. Not to be confounded with Chadwick, as is done in the Index to the Preston Guild Rolls.

Daniel Chaddocke, 1682 : Preston Guild Rolls, p. 166.
Ann Chaddock, of West Leigh, spinster, 1607 : Wills at Chester (1545-1620), p. 2b.
Peter Chaddock, of Prescot, 1613 : ibid.

John Chadocke, of Chadocke, co. Lanc., 1610 : Lancashire Inquisitions, pt. ii. p. 25.
John Cheydock, of Cheydock, co. Lanc. : Wills at Chester (1621-50), p. 48.
1787. Married—James Sweetman and Ann Chadock : St. Geo. Han. Sq. i. 398.
Liverpool, 1 ; London, 1 ; Philadelphia, 1.

Chadfield.—Local. ' of Chadfield,' i.e. the field of Chad ; v. Chadd, Chadwick, &c.

1685. Charles Browne and Eliz. Chatfield : Marriage Alleg.(Canterbury), p. 199.
Manchester, 2.

Chadwick,   Chatwick.—Local, ' of Chadwick,' a hamlet in the parish of Rochdale, co. Lanc. This surname is to be met with in every town in Lancashire. It must have crossed the Atlantic at an early period, as it is strongly represented in the States directories. There is a hamlet named Chadwick in the parish of Bromsgrove, co. Worcester ; but I do not think it has made any considerable impression on nomenclature. Lancashire is the true home of the surname. Chadwick no doubt means the wick or dwelling of Chad, the original settler (v. Wick).

Nicholas de Chadwyke, temp. Edw. III : Baines' Lanc. i. 512.
Elena Chadwyk, 1379 : P. T. Yorks. p. 22.
John Holt, of Chadwick, husbandman, 1641 : Wills at Chester (1545-1620), p.113.
Ann Chadwick, of Chadwick, spinster, co. Lanc., 1636 : ibid (1621-50), p. 45.
John Chadwick, of Chadwick, gentleman, 1630 : ibid.
1669. Bapt.—Margarett, d. Edward Chadweeke : St. Jas. Clerkenwell, i. 239.
Manchester, 55, 0 ; London, 17, 0 ; Philadelphia, 40, 0 ; New York, 11, 1.

Chafen.—Nick. ; v. Coffin.

Chaffe,   Chaff. — Nick. 'le chauve,' the bald, whence dim. Chaufin ; v. Coffin.

John Chauf, co. Camb., 1273. A.
John le Cauf, co. Linc., ibid.
Reginald Cauf, co. York, ibid.
1649. Buried—Richard Chafe : St. Jas. Clerkenwell, iv. 281.
London, 2, 0 ; MDB. (co. Devon), 2, 4 ; New York, 1, 0.

Chaffinch, Chiffinch, Chiffence.—Nick. 'the chaffinch' ; cf. Spink, Goldspink, Finch, &c.

Abraham Caffinch : Proceedings in Kent (Camden Soc.), v. index.

1659. Married—John Caffinch and Ann Mason : St. Jas. Clerkenwell, iii. 102.
1683. George Saintloe and Eliz. Cheffinch : Marriage Lic. (London), ii. 305.
1684. Thomas Fryer and Eliz. Caffinch : Marriage Alleg. (Canterbury). p. 169.
MDB. (co. Wilts), 0, 0, 2.

Chaldecroft.—Local,' of Caldecote,' one of the endless variants of this surname ; v. Calcott.

London, 1.

Chalfont, Chalfant, Chalfain.—Local, ' of Chalfont,' two parishes (St. Peter and St. Giles in co. Bucks.

1570. Thomas Chalfonte and Margaret Cornewallis : Marriage Lic. (Faculty Office), p. 15.
1689. William Chaffaunt and — Tame : Marriage Alleg. (Canterbury), p. 120.
London, 2, 0, 0 ; Philadelphia, 0, 10, 0 ; New York, 0, 0, 1.

Chalk.—Local, (1) ' of Chalk,' a parish in co. Kent, near Gravesend ; (2) ' of Chalk,' the Hundred of Chalk, in co. Wilts.

William Choc, co. Salop, 1273. A.
Reginald Chock, co. Soms., 1 Edw.III : Kirby's Quest, p. 138.
1609. Alexander Chocke, co. Soms.: Reg. Univ. Oxf. vol. ii. pt. ii. 305.
1767. Married—Thomas Chalk and Eliz. Lawrence : St. Geo. Han. Sq. i. 169.
London, 10 ; MDB. (co. Wilts), 1 ; Philadelphia, 3.

Challand, Challands, Challans.—Bapt. ' the son of Jalland ' or ' Jolland,' q.v. ; a great Lincolnshire personal name in the 12th and 13th centuries. Jallands, the patronymic, became Challands, just as Jubb (q.v.) became Chubb. So also Jalland became Challand.

1789. Married—James Wimble and Martha Challand : St. Geo. Han. Sq. ii. 34.
MDB. (co. Lincoln), 0, 2, 2 ; (co. Notts), 5, 1, 0.

Challen, Chalon.—Local, ' of Chalons.' The town of Chalonssur-Marne is meant. There would be a steady immigration from the fact of its close trade relations with England (v. Chaloner).

Godfrey Challon, co. Devon, 1273. A.
Peter de Chalouns, co. Bucks, ibid.
Ralph de Chaluns, co. Wilts, ibid.
John Chalun, co. Oxf., ibid.
1796. Married — Christian Josi and Caroline Susanna Chalon : St. Geo. Han. Sq. ii. 143.
London, 4, 0 ; Philadelphia, 0, 1.

Challenger.—Nick. ' the challenger,' equivalent to Champion, q.v. I cannot help suspecting, however, that it is an imitative corruption of Chaloner, q.v. I find no early instance.

1565. Buried—Sir Thomas Challenger, Knt. : St. Jas. Clerkenwell, iv. 7.
1764. Married—William Challinger and Mary Wilks : St. Geo. Han. Sq. i. 134.
London, 4 ; Knottingley (co. York), 1 ; Philadelphia, 2.

Challis, Challice.—Local, ' of Calais ' (v. Callis) ; cf. Chatterton and Catterton, Chandler and Candler, Chancellor and Cancellor, &c. Challis was bound to become Chalice, just as Calais became Calice. Of Norwich, Blomefield in his History says : ' In 1435 the city furnished out forty men, well armed, and sent them to the defence of Calice ' : FF. iii. 146.

1779. Married—John Ealey and Eliz. Challice : St. Geo. Han. Sq. i. 302.
London, 8, 3 ; Devon Court Dir., 1, 4 ; Philadelphia, 2, 0.

Chaloner, Challenor, Challoner, Chalenor, Challiner.—Occup. ' the chaloner,' a manufacturer or seller of chalons, woollen stuffs, especially coverlets or blankets.

' In his owen chambre he made a bedde
With shetes, and with chalons fair yspredde.' Chaucer, Reve's Tale.

The term still remains in Yorkshire in the word shalloon (with which cf. Willelmus Shalunhare, 1379 : P. T. Yorks. p. 183). In the York Pageant, 1415, the Chaloners and Fullers were allowed four torches each (Hist. Ant. York, ii. 1267). The will of William Askam, dated 1390, says, ' Item, Margaretæ prenticiæ Willielmi Askams do et lego a fedir bedd, and i matras, ii shetes, and a coverlet. . . . Item, Johannæ Dagh, crisp volet and a chalon ' (Test. Ebor. i. 130, Surt. Soc.). ' And that no chalon or ray, or other chalon, shall be made, if it be not of the ancient lawful assize, ordained by the good folks of the trade ' (Ordinance of the Tapicers, Riley's London, 179). The chaloner is described as ' chaloun-

makyere ' in a Winchester Ordinance (English Gilds, p. 352). The origin of the word is simple. Like many another cloth stuff, it took its name from the town that had won celebrity by its manufacture. This was Chalons-sur-Marne, at the period in question one of the most prosperous centres of industry on the continent. How time obscures history may be seen in the fact that Mr. Lower (Patr. Brit.) gives the origin as ' boatman ' or ' fisherman ' from the old French chalun, a boat, or chalon, a net. Mr. Toulmin Smith (Old Birmingham, p. 83) records a John Phelyps, chalounere, in a charter of 1426, and styles him ' master of a ship,' and then sets to work to explain how a skipper could be found at work in the Midlands !

Jordan le Chaluner. T.
John le Chaloner. B.
Geoffrey le Chaloner, co. Essex, 1273. A.
Thomas le Chalunner, co. Camb., ibid.
Nicholas le Chalouner, co. Derby, ibid.
Elizabetha Chaloner, 1379 : P. T. Yorks. p. 25.
Ricardus Schaloner, coverlet-wever, 1379 : ibid. p. 26.
Adam Chalonar, coverlid-wefer, 1379 : ibid. p. 97.

The last two entries are very interesting, connecting as they do the name with the trade.

Thomas Spaldyng, chaloner, 1379 : P. T. Yorks. p. 156.
1616-17. Thomas Jones and Ann Challener : Marriage Lic. (London), ii. 49.
1626. Robert Barnfield and Eliz. Challiner : ibid. p. 188.
1635. William Spranger and Catherine Chaloner : ibid. p. 223.
London, 2, 1, 1, 0, 0 ; Sheffield (Challiner), 1 ; Boston (U.S.), 5, 0, 0, 2, 0.

Chamberlain, Chamberlayne, Chamberlaine, Chamberlin.—Offic. ' the chamberlain,' lit. one who had care of a chamber ; he who had charge of his lord's receipts and issues, a treasurer ; v. Chambers, where ' de la chambre,' though local in form, is practically official, and frequently meant the chamberlain.

Walter le Chamberlayn, co. Linc., 1273. A.
Martin le Chaumberleyn, co. Camb., ibid.

Geoffrey de Chamberlang, co. Wilts, Hen. III-Edw. I. K.
Ivo le Chaumberleyn, co. Warw., ibid.
Henry le Chamberlein, co. Bucks, 20. Edw. I. R.
Johannes Chaumburlayne, 1379: P. T. Yorks. p. 66.

The following eight variations occur in one register:

Colly Chamberlain: St. Peter, Cornhill, i. 123.
Anne Chamberlaine: ibid. p. 89.
William Chamberlane: ibid. p. 94.
Mary Chamberlayne: ibid. p. 90.
Elizabeth Chamberlen: ibid. p. 102.
Grace Chamberlin: ibid. p. 100.
Edward Chamberline: ibid. p. 90.
Alice Chamberlyn: ibid. p. 209.
London, 36, 5, 3, 5; Philadelphia, 37, 0, 1, 18.

Chambers.—Local, 'of the chamber.' It is somewhat curious that I cannot find any modern instance of Chamber; it is invariably Chambers; why, I do not quite see, except that the latter looks more important. Strictly speaking, Chambers is in many cases as official as Chamberlain. Both surnames arose from the exchequer room in which the revenue was paid. To pay *in cameram* was to pay into the exchequer, and the *camerarius*, or chamberlain, had the charge thereof.

Griffin delChambre, *scutifer* of Princess Isabel: Household Book of Queen Isabelle, 1358 (Cott. MS. Galba. E. xiv).
Richard atte Chambre, co. Soms., 1 Edw. III: Kirby's Quest, p. 106.
Walter de la Chaumbre, co. Linc., 1273. A.
Henry de la Chambre, co. Linc., ibid.
John of the Chaumbre, C. R., 7 Ric. II.
Robertus del Chaumbire, 1379: P. T. Yorks. p. 17.
Willelmus del Chaumbir, 1379: ibid. p. 202.
Gilbert de la Chaumbre, C. R., 25 Edw. III.
Johannes del Chaumbir, 1379: P. T. Yorks. p. 14.
Alicia Chaumbir, *maydyne*, 1379: ibid.
London, 71; West Rid. Court Dir., 28; New York, 45.

Chamen.—Bapt. 'the son of Chamond,' popularly Chaman; cf. Osman, Tesseyman, Wyman, for Osmund, Tesseymond, Wymond. Probably Chamond was an abbreviation of Charimond (v. Yonge, ii. 410).

William Chamund, co. Sussex, 1273. A.
Richard Chamun, co. Camb., ibid.

1753. Married—John Chamin and Mary Wood: St. Geo. Han. Sq. i. 50.
1762. — David Frost and Ann Chammond: ibid. p. 110.
London, 3.

Chamflower. — Local, 'de Chamflur.' There are two parishes in co. Somerset connected with the Chamflower family, viz. Huishe-Chamflower, near Taunton, and Wyke-Champflower, near Bruton (N. and Q., January 12, 1889, p. 37).

Martin de Chamflur, co. Linc., 1273. A.
Adam Chamflur, co. Dorset, ibid.
Hugo Chanflur, co. Warw., ibid.
1597. Buried—Hestar, wife of Robert Chanflowre: St. Antholin (London), p. 38.
— Robert, s. Robert Chanflowre: ibid.
1668. Married—Giles Chamflower and Sines Bert: St. Jas. Clerkenwell, i. 145.
London, o.

Chamney, Chamley, Chambley.—Local, 'le Champagnois,' an immigrant from the province of Champagne. Chamney, &c., are variants of Champney, q.v. From Yorkshire it passed into Furness, where for centuries Chamney or Chamley has been a familiar surname. Besides the original Champney, the first three following are specimens of entries in my old church-books at Ulverston:

1546. Bapt.—Isabell Chamney: Reg. Ulverston Ch. p. 2.
1547. Buried—John Chamney: ibid. p. 5.
1696. — Joyce Chamley: ibid. p. 186.
James Champney, of the parish of Ulverston, 1631: Wills at Richmond, p. 62.
James Chamney, of Ulverston, 1596: ibid.
Henry Chamley, of Dalton-in-Furness, 1672: ibid.
1565. Francis Wolman and Margaret Chamley: Marriage Lic. (London), i. 31.
1593-4. Christopher Taylor and Ann Chambly: ibid. p. 213.

In the form of Chambney this surname went out to Virginia in 1635 (v. Hotten's Lists of Emigrants, p. 113). It is found in Boston as Chamley, and at Philadelphia as Chambley. The change from *n* to *l* or vice versa is common; cf. *balusters* and *banisters*, the latter being modern.

Liverpool, o, 1, o; Ulverston, o, 1, o; Philadelphia o, o, 1; Boston (U.S.), o, 2, o.

Champain, Champagne, Champin.—Local, 'of Cham-

pagne,' an immigrant from the province of that name.

Margery de Champain, co. Norf., 1345: FF. vi. 302.
Robert de Champayne, co. Norf., 1392: ibid. i. 61.
Hugh de la Chaumpeyne, Pardons R., 6 Ric. II.
Hugh de Champayne, Hen. III-Edw. I. K.
Robert de Chaumpaigne, 1306. M.
1806. Married—John Champain and Ann Douglas: St. Geo. Han. Sq. ii. 341.
New York, o, 1, 1.

Champion.—Occup. 'the champion,' a soldier, a warrior, the winner in village sports; O.F. *champion, campion*. For further instances v. Campion.

Henry le Champiun, C. R., 56 Hen. III. p 167.
Hugo Champyon, 1379: P. T. Yorks. p. 167.
John le Champion, co. Hunts, 1273. A.
Katerina le Champioun, co. Hunts, ibid.
Edmund Campyon, or Champion, 1514: Reg. Univ. Oxf. p. 94.
1524. John Peron and Alice Champyon: Marriage Lic. (London), i. 4.
1592. Married—John Manser and Alyce Champion: St. Michael, Cornhill, p. 15.
1718. — John Champion and Eliz. Hubbard: St. Antholin (London), p. 131.
1795. — Isaac Champion and Margaret Tracy: St. Geo. Han. Sq. ii. 131.
London, 24; Philadelphia, 17.

Champlin, Chamblen.—Either a variant of Chaplin (q.v.) or of Camplin (q.v.). This is likely enough; cf.Champion and Campion, Chandler and Candler, Chancellor and Cancellor, &c. I do not find these forms in England, but only across the Atlantic.

1637. Buried—Mary, d. Michaell Chamblaine: St. Jas. Clerkenwell, iv. 231.

This entry seems to point to Chamberlain as the original form.

Boston (U.S.), 9, 3.

Champness; v. Champneys.

Champney.—Local, 'le Champagnois,' an immigrant from the province of that name (v. Champneys). For several variants of this surname, v. Chamney. In Yorkshire the surname seems to have been pronounced without the s. Perhaps, however, it was a dialectic form of Champagne. If so, the origin would still remain the same (v. Champain).

Johannes Chaumpenay, 1379: P. T. Yorks. p. 58.

Johanna Chaumpenay, 1379 : ibid.
Henricus Chaumpnay, 1379: ibid. p. 237.
1580-1. William Champney and Emma Crocksall: Marriage Lic. (London), i. 100.
1782. Married—John Platford and Eliz. Champney: St. Geo. Han. Sq. i. 329.
London, 1 ; Boston (U.S.), 16.

Champneys, Champness, Champniss.—Local, 'le Champagnois,' an immigrant from the province of Champagne ; v. Champney and Champney.

Roger le Champeneys, co. Norf., 1273. A.
John Chaumpneis, co. Linc., ibid.
Rosa Champeneys, co. Kent, 1273. A.
Bartholomew Champenais, London, ibid.
Hugh le Champneys, Hen. III–Edw. I. K.
Robert le Champeneis. E.
Stephen le Champenays. L.
1422. Thomas Champeneys, rector of Oxwick, co. Norf.: FF. ix. 508.
1693. Buried—Hanna, wife of Arthur Champneys: St. Dionis Backchurch, p. 261.
1796. Married—Rev. William Henry Champneys and Lucy Hornby: St. Geo. Han. Sq. ii. 147.
London, 4, 2, 1.

Chance.—? Bapt. 'the son of Chance' (?). It is quite possible that Chance may have been a personal name, like Bonaventure, which it exactly represented; *chance* in M.E. generally meaning a happy accident, a good mishap. It is interesting to notice that the surname is well represented in the district where I find my earliest instance :

Richard Chance, co. Warw., 20 Edw. I. R.
If it were not for the above entry we might be disposed to agree with Mr. Lower in his suggestion that Chance is a variant of Chancey (v. Chauncey). But there is not an atom of evidence so far as I know in its favour.

1747. Married—Henry Clark and Ann Chance : St. Geo. Chap. Mayfair, p. 84.
1802. — John Chance and Eliz. Allen: St. Geo. Han. Sq. ii. 269.
London, 11 ; MDB. (co. Worcester), 6 ; (co. Warwick), 1 ; Philadelphia, 22.

Chancellor, Cancellor, Chancery.—Offic. 'the chancellor,' a custodian of writings or records. The chancery (i.e. chancellery) also gave a local (practically *official*)

surname, but it is put in an abbreviated Latin form in early records, as for example :

Richard de Cancett, co. Hertf., 1273. A.
Emeric de Cancett, co. Southampt., 1273. A.

These stand for ' de Cancellaria,' i.e. the record-room. The forms of Chancellor are somewhat varied. I furnish instances from a single register :

Robert le Chaunceler, co. Camb., 1273. A.
Alan Chanceler, co. Norf., ibid.
Walter Chaunceler, co. Norf., ibid.
Robert le Caunceler, co. Bedf., ibid.
Roger le Canceler, co. Bedf., ibid.
William Cancellarius, co. Oxf., ibid.

With Chancellor and Cancellor, cf. Chandler and Candler. Since writing the above I have come across a *local* form in full :

Willelmus del Chaincery, 1379 : P. T. Yorks. p. 236. 'Serviens Edmundus Moubray, Esquier.'
1749. Married—Thomas Brooke and Eliz. Chancellor: St. Geo. Chap. Mayfair, p. 141.
London, 3, 2, 0 ; Philadelphia, 4, 0, 0.

Chandler, Chantler, Candler, Cantler.—Occup. 'the chandler': (1) a candlemaker ; (2) the official who attended to the lights in his lord's household (v. Prompt. Parv. p. 71, and Way's note). 'Candelere, *candelarius*': Prompt. Parv.

Nicholas de Malton, *candeler*, 7 Edw. II : Freemen of York, i. 15.
Johannes Thurton, *candelere*: Gild of St. George, Norwich. English Gilds.
Matilda Candeler, 1379 : P. T. Yorks. p. 25.
Robertus Knyghtman, *chaundeler*, 1379: ibid. p. 222.
John le Chanteler, C. R., 34 Hen. III.
Reginald le Chandeler, London, 1273. A.
Mathew le Candeler, London, ibid.
William Candelarius, co. Leicester, ibid.
Jordan le Chaundler. C.
John Candler, or Candeler, or Chanler, 1548: Reg. Univ. Oxf. p. 213.
1566. Married—Richard Harrison and Margrete Chanteler : Reg. Prestbury Ch. Cheshire, p. 19.
1567-8. Richard Canler and Eliz. Locke : Marriage Lic. (London), i. 38.
1628. 'Paid unto Thomas Chantler for a new clocke . . . £5. 3. 4.'—Churchwardens' Accounts, Wilmslow ; v. East Cheshire, i. 107.
London, 66, 2, 7, 0 ; Norfolk, 34, 0, 3, 0.

Chaney, Chany.—Local ; v. Cheney.

Changer.—Occup. 'the changer,' a money-changer.

Simon le Changeur, C. R., 25 Hen. III.
Symon le Changur, co. Linc., 1273. A.
Cf. John del Chaunge, 2 Edw. III : Freemen of York, i. 24.

Channon.—Offic. 'the canon' ; M.E. *chanon* ; v. Shannon. 'Chanone, *chanonicus*': Prompt. Parv.

'Nay, nay, God wot, al be he monk or frere,
Preest or chanon.'
Chaucer, C. T. 16307.
Richard Chanon, co. Soms., 1627 : Abstract of Somersetshire Wills, p. 34.
1607. Buried—Barnabie, s. John Channon: St. Jas. Clerkenwell, iv. 97.
1616. William Chanon. co. Devon : Reg. Oxf. Univ. vol. ii. pt. ii. p. 357.
London, 5 ; Philadelphia, 4.

Chanonhouse, Channelhouse, Chandlehouse, Charnelhouse.—Local, 'at the chanonhouse,' i.e. the residence of the canon ; M.E. *chanon*. This name, I believe, is obsolete in England, but still remains in the United States. A gentleman of this title was drowned in 1859 near New York. For many centuries the name was confined to Furness and the neighbouring district, and the last of the local branch died at the close of the last century. Shannon-house is now an old farm by Pennington Church, near Ulverston. Six hundred years ago it was the Chanon-house, where resided the canon of Conishead Priory, who undertook the parochial charge of the church at Pennington, then in the possession of the Augustinians. In old deeds it is written Chanonhouse and Channelhouse, and in the registers of Pennington and Ulverston both surname and place-name are found in every conceivable and inconceivable spelling, including the forbidding 'Charnel-house.'

1547. Buried—Margaret Chanonhowse: St. Mary, Ulverston, p. 5.
1642. Bapt.—Christopher, s. James Fell, of Chanonhouse: Pennington Ch., Ulverston.
1670. Buried—James Fell, of Challenhouse : ibid.
William Channelhouse, of Ulverston, 1642: Lancashire Wills at Richmond, p. 62.

Isabel Channonhouse, of Ulverston, 1613: Lancashire Wills at Richmond, p. 62.

Chanster. — Offic. or occup. Strictly the feminine of Chanter, a reciter (v. Chanter). Cf. Sanger and Sangster, q.v.

Stephen le Chanster. J.
Williametta Cantatrix. E.

Chanster could not fail to become Chancer, in which form it is found in the last century:

1789. Married—John Tatum and Barbara Chancer: St. Geo. Han. Sq. ii. 28.

Chanter. — Offic. 'the chanter,' a precentor, one who recites in song. Probably one who sang the masses in a chantry, a chantry priest. But certainly occupative sometimes. 'Chawntowre, *Cantor*': Prompt. Parv.

William le Chantur, co. Lanc., 20 Edw. I. R.
Cristiana le Chauntur, co. Camb., 1273. A.
William le Chantour, 1301. M.
Vines le Chauntur, C. R., 51 Hen. III.
William Chauntor, co. Soms., 1 Edw. III; Kirby's Quest, p. 140.
Johannes Chanter, 1379: P. T. Yorks. p. 120.
Agnes Chauntour. 1379: ibid. p. 217.
1735. Married—Edward Smart and Joyce Chanter: St. Geo. Han. Sq. i. 15.
1761. Buried—Stephen Chanter: St. Peter, Cornhill, ii. 144.
London, 21.

Chanticleer. — Nick. 'clear singer,' a familiar name for a barn-door cock. Hence, perhaps, a boaster, one who 'crows loudly.'

'A cok, highte Chaunteclere,
In all the land of crowing n'as his pere.'
Chaucer, C. T. 14854.
Roger Chaunteler, C. R., 6 Edw. III.
Thomas Chaunticler, of Attleborough, co. Norf., 1359. FF. i. 505.

If this surname descended to modern times it would probably be lost in Chantler (s.v. Chandler).

Chantler. — Occup.; v. Chandler.

Chantrey, Chantry. — Local, 'at the chantry.' The name being so rare we may readily believe that the John below was ancestor of the sculptor, Sir Francis Legatt Chantrey (1781-1841), who was the son of a carpenter living at Jordanthorpe, near Sheffield.

Johannes del Chauntre (Sprotborough), 1379: P. T. Yorks. p. 53.
1445. Henry Chantrey, vicar of East Dereham, co. Norf.: FF. x. 210.
1465. Richard Chauntrey, rector of Knapton, co. Norf.: ibid. viii. 135.
1662. Married—William Howard and Ann Chauntree: St. Jas. Clerkenwell, iii. 110.
1789. — Henry Chantree and Phoebe Woodcock: St. Geo. Han. Sq. ii. 18.
1803. — Nathaniel Chantry and Frances Dutereau: ibid. p. 277.
London, 0, 2; Goole, 0, 1; MDB. (Lincoln), 0, 4; Philadelphia, 0, 2.

Chapeler. — Occup. 'le chapeler,' a hatter; O.F. *chapel*, a hat, a head-dress, whence dim. chapelet, now chaplet. 'E qe chascun esquier porte chapel des armes son seigneur.' 'And that every esquire do bear a cap of the arms of his lord' (Stat. of Realm, i. 220).

Robert le Chapeler, co. Camb., 1273. A.
Mabil le Chapelere, co. Camb., ibid.
Theobald le Chapeler (London), ibid.
Edmund le Chapeler, c. 1300. M.

I find no modern representatives of this surname. I fear it is obsolete.

Chaperon, Capron, Chaperon. — Nick. 'a hood or bonnet'; F. *chaperon*, an augmentative form of *chape*, a hood. A common surname in the 13th and 14th centuries. It was probably the popular nickname of the cowled monks; cf. Barefoot. The chaperon of modern society, though the same word, has no place here.

'Her shapperoones, her perriwigs and tires
Are reliques which his flatt'ry much admires.'
Taylor's Workes, 1630, ii. 111.
Walter Chaperun, 1199: RRR. p. 56.
Edmund Caperun, co. Norf, 1273. A.
Sibill Caperun, co. Bedf., ibid.
William Capron, 1515: Reg. Univ. Oxf. i. 98.
Almeric Chaperon. O.
Thomas Caperoun. J.
1550. Hugh Beete and Anne Capron: Marriage Lic. (London), i. 13.
1788. Married—Robert Capron and Mary Thomas Nixon: St. Geo. Han. Sq. ii. 4.
London, 1, 3, 1; Philadelphia, 0, 0, 2; New York, 0, 3, 0.

Chaplin, Caplin, Chaplain. — Offic. 'the chaplain,' the minister of a sanctuary or inferior church. With Caplin, cf. Candler for Chand-

ler, Capell for Chapel, and Cancellor for Chancellor, &c. The Low Latin *Capellanus* is the common mode of entry.

Richard le Chapelein, co. Devon: Hen. III-Edw. I. K.
Simon Capellanus, co. Essex, 1273. A.
Richard le Chapeleyn, co. Linc., ibid.
Nicholas le Chapeleyn, co. Oxf., ibid.
Adam le Chapelayn, co. Northumberland, 20 Edw. I. R.
Johannes Chapeleyn, 1379: P. T. Yorks. p. 151.
1592. Robert Chaplyn and Alice Caterall: Marriage Lic. (London', i. 108.
1594. Henry Caplyn and Margery Unthanck: ibid. p. 216.
1628. Buried—Mary Chaplin, *widow*: St. Peter, Cornhill, i. 197.
1804. Married—George Caplin and Frances Winham: St. Geo. Han. Sq. ii. 312.
London, 29, 7, 0; Philadelphia, 1, 0, 1; Boston (U.S.), 12, 0, 0.

Chapman. — Occup. 'the chapman.' It is probable that the early chapman was stationary, and dealt in a much larger way than we are now accustomed to suppose. The travelling chapman was of a lower grade. An Act of Edward VI speaks of 'person or persones commonly called Pedler, Tynker, or Pety Chapman' (5 & 6 Edw. VI, c. 21).

Cf. Nicholaus Fleschewer, *chapman de Bees*, 1379: P. T. Yorks. p. 97.
Robertus Wulchapman, *marchand*: ibid. p. 159.
Thomas le Chapman, co. Leic., 1273. A.
Grante le Chapman, co. Devon, ibid.
Geoffrey le Chapman, c. 1300. M.
Alard le Chapman. T.
William le Chepman, co. Soms., 1 Edw. III: Kirby's Quest, p. 92.
Alicia Shepshank', *chapman*, 1379: P. T. Yorks. p. 3.
Agnes Chapman, 1379: ibid. p. 5.
Magota de Brandon, *chapman*, 1379: ibid. p. 11.
Henricus Schapman, 1379: ibid. p. 41.
1541. Bapt.—Robert Chapmanne: St. Peter, Cornhill, p. 2.
1619. — Alice, d. Gyles Chapman: St. Jas. Clerkenwell, i. 86.
London, 165; Boston (U.S.), 132.

Chappell, Chapel, Chapple, Chapell. — Local, 'at the chapel'; cf. Kirk, Church, Churchyard, &c.

Hugh de la Chapele, co. Notts, 1273. A.
Thomas de la Chapele, co. Northumberland, 20 Edw. I. R.
John atte Chapele, co. Soms., 1 Edw. III: Kirby's Quest, p. 238.
William a la Chapele, Fines Roll, 9 Edw. I.

Johannes del Chapell, 1379: P. T. Yorks. p. 191.
1671-2. William Chappell and Margaret Heeley: Marriage Lic. (Faculty Office), p. 121.
1689. Bapt. — Thomas, s. Thomas Chapell: St. Jas. Clerkenwell, i. 333.

With Chapple, cf. such an entry as—

1705. Married—William Lynford, of Whitechapple (i. e. Whitechapel), *coachman*, and Mary Jenkinson: St. Mary Aldermary (London), p. 38.
London, 35, 2, 14, 0; Philadelphia, 14, 2, 0, 2.

Chappelow, Chapplow, Chapelhow, Chaplow.—Local, 'at the chapel-how' (v. Howe). This rare surname is found in the London Directory. It has travelled from the borders of Cumberland and Westmoreland. In the former county it still exists as Chapplow, which is very misleading, suggesting *low* (v. Lowe) as the suffix.

Christopher Chappelhow, Hackthorp, 1602: Hist. Westm. and Cumb. i. 97.
Thomas Chappelhow, Hackthorp, 1602: ibid.
Thomas Chappillhow, of Underbarrow, parish of Kendal, 1608: Wills at Chester (1545-1620), p. 39.
1742. Married—Duncan Bayne and Barbara Chapplehow: St. Geo. Han. Sq. i. 28.
— — George Chapplehow and Eliz. Diment: St. Geo. Chap. Mayfair, p. 23.
London, 1, 0, 0, 0; MDB. (co. Westmoreland), 0, 0, 2, 1; (co. Cumberland), 0, 1, 0, 0.

Chard.—Local, 'of Chard,' a market-town and parish in co. Somerset.

John Chard, co. Soms., 1 Edw. III: Kirby's Quest, p. 269.
1664. Married—John Chard and Lucretia Turner: St. Jas. Clerkenwell, iii. 117.
1754. — Richard Chard and Hannah Groves: St. Geo. Han. Sq. i. 53.
MDB. (co. Soms.), 22; London, 13; Boston (U.S.), 3.

Charer, Charman.—Occup. 'the charer' or 'charman,' a driver of a *char* or *chare*, a carman; from O.F. *char*, a car. 'Chare, *currus*': Prompt. Parv. 'To Master William la Zousche, clerk of the King's great wardrobe, in money, paid to him by the hands of John le Charer, for making a certain chariot,' &c. (Issues of the Exchequer, 6 Edw. III). See also instances in Prompt. Parv. in Mr. Way's note. Capgrave

says of Helianore of France, under date 1394, 'She brought oute of Frauns xii chares ful of domicelles.' v. Carman.

Thomas le Charer, C. R., 18 Edw. I.
John le Charrer, co. Notts, 1273. A.
Richard le Charrer, c. 1300. M.
Nicholas le Charrer, co. Soms., 1 Edw. III: Kirby's Quest, p. 164.
1752. Married—John Bulley and Mary Charman: St. Geo. Chap. Mayfair, p. 220.
1809. — Francis Charman and Amy Fielder: St. Geo. Han. Sq. ii. 415.
London, 0, 3; New York, 0, 2.

Charioteer.—Occup. 'one who drove a chariot'; M.E. *charet*, the dim. of *chare*; v. Charer. 'Charyetter, *aurigarius, quadrigarius*': Prompt. Parv. ; v. Carter, which is, strictly speaking, a doublet.

Peter le Charetter, co. Camb., 1273. A.
John Charieteer, co. York. W. 2.
Thomas Charietter, temp. Eliz. ZZ.

Charity.—Local, 'of the charity.' Possibly a dispensary or 'spittle' connected with an ecclesiastical foundation.

William de la Charity. J.
John Charite, C. R., 3 Edw. I.
Ricardus Charyte, 1379: P. T. Yorks. p. 128.
Willelmus Charite, 1379: ibid. p. 141.
Thomas Charite, 1379: ibid. p. 193.
1612. Buried—Sara, d. Frederick Charitie: St. Jas. Clerkenwell, iv. 121.
1642. Married—William Charitye and Emma Last: ibid. iii. 75.

The origin as above given cannot be doubted. The baptismal Charity came far too late to obtain surnominal honours.

MDB. (co. Lincoln), 3; Philadelphia, 1.

Charles.—Bapt. 'the son of Charles'; German, Carl. 'Charlys, propyr name, *Carolus*': Prompt. Parv.

Colina Charles, co. Norf., Hen. III-Edw. I. K.
Charles (without surname), co. Kent, 1273. A.
Edward Charles, co. Suff., ibid.
William Charle, co. Norf., ibid.
Alan Charle, co. Camb., ibid.
Ida Carle, co. Camb., ibid.
Ralph Carles, co. Camb., ibid.
William Carolus, co. Norf., ibid.
1482. William Cherlys, vicar of Great Ellingham, co. Norf.: FF. i. 486.
1551. Bapt.—John Charles: St. Jas. Clerkenwell, i. 1.
1585-6. Tertullian Pyne and Mary Charles: Marriage Lic. (London), i. 145.

1621. Bapt.—Thomas, s. George and Jone Charles: St. Michael, Cornhill, p. 115.
London, 30; MDB. (co. Camb.), 4; Philadelphia, 17.

Charlesworth. — Local, 'of Charlesworth,' a hamlet in co. Derby, eight miles from Chapel-en-le-Frith. Hence well represented in Sheffield and the Yorkshire border. This surname has ramified in a remarkable manner. It seems to have reached London at a fairly early period.

Johannes de Chalesworth, 1379: P. T. Yorks. p. 81.

Crossing over into East Cheshire it is found in a curious form:

1610. Married—William Choleseworthe and Ellen Adshead: Prestbury Ch. (Cheshire), p. 186.
1571. John Pettye and Margery Charlesworth, of Stepney: Marriage Lic. (London), i. 49.
1802. — John Green and Margaret Charlesworth: St. Geo. Han. Sq. ii. 260.
London, 7; West Rid. Court Dir., 16; Sheffield, 10; MDB. (co. Derby), 8.

Charlett.—Bapt. 'the son of Charles,' from Carl or Charl, and dim. Charl-et. This came into England a second time in the 17th century as Charlet or Charlotte. Again, in the 18th century in the form of Caroline (wife of George II) it obtained a new lease of popularity. Once more, in the 19th century the lamented Princess Charlotte caused the earlier form to become immensely fashionable.

Gregory Charlett, 1512: Reg. Univ. Oxf. i. 83.
1803. Married—Anthony Charlett and Mary Green: St. Geo. Han. Sq. ii. 279.
London, 1.

Charlton.—Local, 'of Charlton.' There are nineteen parishes called Charlton in the index to Crockford; v. Carlton and Chorlton.

Richard de Churleton, co. Suff., 1273. A.
Geoffrey de Cherlton, co. Oxf., ibid.
Daniel de Cherleton, co. Kent, 20 Edw. I. R.
John de Cherelton, co. Northamp., ibid.
1588. John Charlton, of Tatton: Wills at Chester, i. 39.
1594. James Charlton, of Ashton, ibid.
Johanna Cherleton, 1379: P. T. Howdenshire, p. 27.
1654. Married—Nicholas Charleton and Sarah Abbott: St. Michael, Cornhill, p. 34.

1572. Roger Charleton and Margaret Wade: Marriage Lic. (London), i. 52. London, 20; Philadelphia, 39.

Charlwood, Charlewood.— Local, 'of Charlwood,' a parish in co. Surrey, seven miles from Reigate. John Charlewood, Charlwood, or Cherlwod (d. 1592), the stationer and printer, seems undoubtedly to have sprung from Surrey. 'Charlewood apparently came from Surrey, as on Jan. 12, 1591, we find him taking as an apprentice "Geffry Charlwood, son of Richard Charlwood, of Lye (Leigh), in the county of Surrey." Charlewood is a Surrey parish, and is not an uncommon county surname': Dict. Nat. Biog. x. 120.
1779. Married—Edward Charlwood and Betty Quarrell: St. Geo. Han. Sq. i. 305.
1800. — John Charlwood and Eliz. Billington: ibid. ii. 228.
London, 2, 0.

Charman.—Occup.; v. Charer.

Charnock.—Local, 'of Charnock'; two townships in the parish of Standish, co. Lanc., styled respectively Charnock Richard and Charnock Heath. 'Stephen Charnock (1628-80), Puritan theologian, was born in 1628, in . . . London, where his father, Richard Charnock (a relation of the Lancashire family of Charnock of Charnock), was a solicitor': Dict. Nat. Biog. x. 134.
Robert Charnock, of Charnock: Baines' Lancashire, ii. 165.
Elizabeth Charnock, of Leyland, co. Lanc., 1575: Wills at Chester (1545-1620), p. 39.
Miles Charnock, of Wigan Woodhouse, 1592: ibid.
James Charnock, of Charnock Richard, 1633: ibid. (1621-1650), p. 46.
William Charnocke, 1582: Preston Guild Rolls, p. 44.
1568. Bapt.—John, s. Nicholas Charnocke: St. Jas. Clerkenwell, i. 4.
1806. Married—James Charnock and Charlott Stacke: St. Geo. Han. Sq. ii. 341.
London, 2; Manchester, 1; MDB. (co. Lanc.), 2; Boston (U.S.), 2.

Charrington; v. Cherrington.

Charsley, Chesley.—Local, 'of Chearsley,' a village in co. Buckingham, three miles from Thame, said to be originally *Cerdicesleagh*, i.e. the lee or meadow

of Cerdic. My first instance corroborates this view. There can be no doubt that Chesley, through Chearsley, is a variant.
Robert de Cherdesle, co. Oxf., 1273. A.
1575. Married — William Chearsleye and Ellyn Edwardes: St. Michael, Cornhill, p. 11.
1809. — William Cheasley and Mary Grainger: St. Geo. Han. Sq. ii. 412.
MDB. (co. Buckingham), 5, 0; Boston (U.S.), 0, 22.

Charter.—Occup. 'the charioteer,' from O.F. *charete*, a chariot, a wagon. I suspect Carter (q.v.) has swallowed up all other forms; v. Charioteer. One of the most interesting things in the study of English nomenclature is to note the existence to-day of surnames in the same district where they arose. It is only in cos. Cambridge and Hunts that Charter is common.
Peter le Charetter, co. Camb., 1272. A.
Ralph le Charetter, co. Camb., ibid.
Simon le Chareter, co. Camb., ibid.
Lovecok Chartre, co. Soms., 1 Edw. III: Kirby's Quest, p. 117.
1600. John Charter, rector of Bale, co. Norf.: FF. ix. 358.
1675. Bapt. — John, son of Joseph Chartor: St. Jas. Clerkenwell, i. 267
1798. Married—George Charter and Eliz. Hancock: St. Geo. Han. Sq. ii. 182.
London, 1; MDB. (co. Hunts), 4; (co. Cambridge), 5; Philadelphia, 3.

Charteris, Charters, Chartres, Chartress, Chatteris.— Local, 'of Chartres,' in France. The variants are all of a very natural character.
Richard de Chartray, co. Devon, Hen. III—Edw. I. K.
Alan de Chartres, co. Hunts, 1273. A.
John de Chartres, co. Linc., ibid.
Ralph de Chartres, c. 1300. M.
Johannes Charteres, 1379: P. T. Yorks. p. 13.
1638. Married—Christopher Chattrice and Mary Bingham: St. Peter, Cornhill, p. 256.
1639. Bapt.—Joseph, s. Christopher Chatterisse, *cooke*: ibid. p. 88.
1693. Married—Richard Hawson and Martha Charterisse: St. Michael, Cornhill, p. 47.
1771. — Francis Charteris and Susan Keck: St. Geo. Han. Sq. i. 212.
1797. — William Marshall and Sarah Charters: ibid. i. 169.
London, 0,4,4,0,1; New York, 0,4,1,0,0.

Chartman.—Occup. The same as Cartman, a carter; cf. Charter for Carter.
John Chartman, rector of Sedistern,

co. Norf., 1361: Bromefield's Norfolk (v. index).

Chase.—Local, 'at the chase,' from residence in that part of the forest or park termed the chase; an open piece of ground for the herding of deer and other game; cf. Forest, Park, Lowndes. This surname has ramified strongly in the United States.
1626. Married—John Chase and Hanna Tailor: St. Jas. Clerkenwell, iii. 56.
1657. — Richard Chase and Bridgett Monday: St. Michael, Cornhill, p. 37.
1746. Richard Chase, rector of Ellingham, co. Norf.: FF. viii. 7.
London, 15; Philadelphia, 73.

Chaser.—Occup. 'the chaser,' i.e. a hunter; v. Hunter.
Brutone le Chaceour, co. Soms., 1 Edw. III: Kirby's Quest, p. 221.

Chaston.—Local, 'of Caston.' q.v. No doubt a variant, as found in the Norfolk and Suffolk counties.
MDB. (co. Suffolk), 6; London, 0.

Chater, Chaytor.—(1) Offic. 'the escheator' (?), one who inquired into escheats. After the death of a tenant an inquiry was made, and if there was failure of issue, the land escheated or lapsed to his lord. It was the same after attainder for treason or felony. Possibly Cater (q.v.), but the above is almost certainly the true derivation (v. *Cheat* in Skeat's Dictionary). (2) Offic. 'the chater,' v. Cater; cf. Candler and Chandler, &c.
Henry Escaetor, co. Oxf., 1273. A.
Ralph le Chatere, co. Warw., Hen. III—Edw. I. K.
Stephen le Chatere, co. Warw., ibid.
Thomas Chetur, *smyth*, 1379: P. T. Yorks. p. 41.
Walter le Chatur, co. Camb., 1273. A.
Agnes le Chatur, co. Camb., ibid.
1737. Married—Thomas Cheater and Sarah Blackstaff: St. Dionis Backchurch, p. 66.
1801. — John Jeans and Martha Chater: St. Geo. Han. Sq. ii. 235.
London, 8, 1; New York, 3, 1.

Chatman.—Occup. 'the chapman' (q.v.). An American variant.
New York, 4; Boston (U.S.), 2.

Chattaway.—Local, 'of Chadway.' This has become first Chadaway, then Chattaway; cf. Ottaway, Hathaway, or Greenaway for Ottway, Hathway, or Greenway. I have not discovered the spot. Of course the suffix is -*way*, a road, a path, i.e. the road leading to Chad's dwelling ; v. Chad.

1687. Bapt —Susan, d. John Chadway : St. Jas. Clerkenwell, i. 320.
1791. Married—William Chadway and Dorothy Clayton : St. Geo. Han. Sq. ii. 68.
1800. — James Davidson and Eliz. Chadaway : ibid.
London, 1 ; Philadelphia, 1.

Chatteris.—Local, 'of Chatteris,' a parish in the Isle of Ely, co. Camb. Found as Chaterich, Chateris, and Chaterus in the Hundred Rolls (1273).

Richard de Chaterus, co. Camb., 1273. A.
Sarra de Chaterus, co. Camb., ibid.
London, 1.

Chatterton.—Local ; v. Chadderton.

Chatwin.—Local ; v. Chetwynd.

Chaucer.—Occup. 'le chaucer,' a maker of cħausses, i.e. leathern breeches ; Latin, *calcearius*. Chaucer's grandfather was connected with Ipswich (v. Dict. Nat. Biog. x. 155). The surname was early found in that district.

Roger Calcwere, co. Norf., 1273. A.
Gerard le Chaucer. H.
Mary le Chaucer. N.
Ralph le Chaucer. E.
Robert le Chaucer, c. 1300. M.

Chauncey, Chauncy.—Local, 'de Chauncy.' Said to have been an estate near Amiens. The name is clearly continental, and almost certainly Norman. Among a batch of French and Walloons who went out to Virginia in 1621 are found 'Charles Chauncy, wife, and two children' (Hotten's Emigrant Lists, p. 198). Chauncy has become a popular font-name in the United States. There are four Chauncey Smiths in the New York Directory. In England Percy and Sydney, both local surnames, have undergone the same experience.

Philip de Chauncy, co. Linc., Hen. III-Edw. I. K.
William de Chaunci, or Chancy, co. Linc., 1273. A.
Humfridus de Chauncy, co. Linc., ibid.
Josep de Chauncey, co. Hunts, 20 Edw. I. R.
Thomas de Chaunċey, co. York, ibid.

1663. John Chauncey and Eliz. Taylor : Marriage Alleg. (Canterbury), p. 98.
New York, 3, 1.

Chawner.—Occup. 'the chaloner,' q.v. A known corruption.

Hugh Chawner, of Wigan, 1607 : Lancashire Inquisit. p. 79 ;
Or, Hugh Challenor, of Wigan, 1610 : ibid. p. 166 ;
Or, Hugh Challinor, of Wigan, 1612 : ibid. p. 197.
1567. Married—Randall Okes and Jone Chawnor : Reg. Prestbury Ch. (Ches.), p. 22.
1573. Abraham Wrables and Agnes Chawner : Marriage Lic. (London), i. 56.
William Chawner, vicar of Hurdsfield, near Macclesfield, 1846 : East Cheshire, ii. 454.
London, 1.

Cheales, Cheals, Cheal, Cheel.—Local, 'de Chele' or 'Cheles.' Cheal is a hamlet in the parish of Gosberton, south Linc., three miles from Donington.

Gilbert de Chele, or Cheles, or Cheyle, or Cheylle, co. Linc., 1273. A.
William de Cheyle, co. Linc., ibid.
William de Cheles, co. Salop, ibid.
Robert de Cheles, co. Salop, Hen. III-Edw. I. K.
Alex. de Cheyles, co. Salop, ibid.
1668. Edward Newcomen and Mary Cheales : Marriage Lic. (Faculty Office), p. 105.
1682. John Mellersh ˷ and Dorothy Cheale : ibid. p. 163.
Crockford, 2, 0, 0, 1 ; London, 0, 0, 0, 1.

Checker.—Occup. or offic. 'the checker,' one who checked accounts (?) ; cf. Scorer (1). More probably, however, a maker of chess-boards.

John le Cheker, co. Soms., 1 Edw. III : Kirby's Quest, p. 194.
Matthew Cheker, C. R., 8 Edw. I.
William Cheker, 1547 : TTT. p. lxxx.

Chedzoy, Chedzey, Chidzoy, Chidzey, Chedgey, Chedsey.—Local, 'of Chedzoy,' a parish near Bridgewater, co. Somerset. Chedgey in the London Directory is a very natural variant. Such surnames get more corrupted the further they wander from home.

'William Chedsey, or Cheadsey (1510?-1574), divine, was a native of Somersetshire' : Dict. Nat. Biog. x. 174.
John Chedesy, co. Soms., 1 Edw. III : Kirby's Quest, p. 101.
1778. Married—Robert Warlow and Grace Chidgey : St. Geo. Han. Sq. i. 291.
MDB. (co. Somerset), 2, 1, 1, 1, 0, 0 ; London, 1, 0, 0, 0, 1, 0 ; New York (Chedsey), 1.

Cheese.—? Nick. Probably the nickname of a cheese-factor or cheese-farmer. But I cannot speak positively ; still, cf. Pepper.

John Chese, co. Norf., 1273. A.
Hamo Chese, co. Salop, ibid.
Ricardus Chese, 1379 : P. T. Yorks. p. 270.
Thomas Chese, 1379 : ibid. p. 274.
1597. Richard Cheese and Anne Biggleskyrte : Marriage Lic. (London), i. 238.
1808. Married—William Cheese and Sarah Murray : St. Geo. Han. Sq. ii. 398.
Crockford, 3 ; London, 0.

Cheese-and-bread.—Nick. for one who was notoriously fond of bread and cheese.

Geoffrey Cheese-and-brede, co. Yorks. W. 5.

Cheesehouse.—Local, 'at the cheese-house,' the store-house for cheeses.

Adam del Cheshus, co. Camb., 1273. A.

This surname was existing in the 17th century :

1660. Married—Richard Chezus and Anne Hignett : St. Jas. Clerkenwell, iii. 103.

Cheesemaker. — Occup. 'the cheesemaker,' a maker of cheeses (v. Cheeseman). The surname does not seem to have lasted through many generations.

Robert le Chesemaker, co. Linc., 1273. A.
Thomas le Chesemaker, C. R., 17 Edw. I.

Cheeseman, Cheesman.—Occup. 'the cheeseman,' a maker or seller of cheeses ; M.E. *chese*.

John le Cheseman, co. Hunts, 1273. A.
Edward Cheseman. H.
1523. Robert Cheseman and Eliz. Wodell : Marriage Lic. (London), i. 3.
1675. Bapt.—John, s. Frances Cheseman : St. Jas. Clerkenwell, i. 268.
1704. Buried—William Cheesman : St. John Baptist on Wallbrook, p. 195.
London, 3, 11 ; New York, 0, 6.

Cheesemonger. — Occup. 'a seller of cheeses.'

Adam le Chismonger. H.
Alan le Chesmonger. L.

Cheesewright, Cheeswright, Cheeseright. — Occup. 'the cheesewright,' a maker of cheese. Wright as a suffix was generally associated with work in wood ; cf. Wheelwright, Wainwright,

Cartwright, Arkwright. In Cheese-wright we see a departure from this usage.

John Chesewright, temp. 1570. Z.
William Cheswright, ibid.
Marke Chiswright, son of Mr. Cheswright, 1609: St. Dionis Backchurch, London, p. 94.
London, 5, 2, 0; MDB. (co. Camb.), 0, 0, 1.

Cheetham, Chetham.— Local. ' of Cheetham ' or ' Chetham,' a township and suburb of Manchester. The two Chethams recorded in the Dict. Nat. Biog. x. 206-7, viz. Humphrey Chetham (1580-1653), founder of the Manchester Hospital and Library that bear his name, and James Chetham (1640-92), writer on angling, were both born within two miles of Chetham, one at Crumpsall Hall, the other at Smedley. Chetham of Chetham was a surname so early as Edward I Baines' Lanc. i. 405).

Henry Chetham, of Crumpsall (Manchester), 1603: Wills at Chester (1545-1620), p. 39.
William Chetham, of Blakeley (Manchester), 1612: ibid.
Laurence Chetham, of Stockport, 1590: ibid.
1758. Married—Joseph Cheetham and Sidwell Cornish: St. Geo. Han. Sq. i. 79.
Manchester, 43, 2; London, 4, 0; Philadelphia, 4, 0.

Chell.—Local, ' of Chell,' a township in the parish of Wolstanton, co. Stafford.

1711. Married—Arthur Gilbert and Anne Chell: St. Antholin (London), p. 124.
1768. — Richard Chell and Frances Sutton: St. Geo. Han. Sq. i. 178.
Crockford, 3; MDB. (co. Stafford), 3; New York, 1.

Chenery, Chinery, Chin-nery.—— ? I cannot help thinking this is an immigrant from the Low Countries. It is found in cos. Norfolk and Suffolk. But it might easily stand for Chinbury and be a local family surname.

Ralph de Chinebury, co. Norf., temp. 1380: FF. ii. 439.
1393. John Chenery, patron of Barton, co. Norf.: ibid. vii. 282.
1675. John Chinery, rector of Bretenham, co. Norf.: ibid. i. 443.
1682. Henry Chennery, mayor of Lynn Regis, co. Norf.: ibid. viii. 533.
1804. Married—William Mitchell and

Hester Chinnery: St. Geo. Han. Sq. ii. 315.
London, 3, 3, 3; MDB. (co. Suffolk), 2, 3, 0; Philadelphia, 1, 2, 0.

Chenevix. —— ? Mr. Lower says ' a Huguenot family settled in Ireland : one of that name was consecrated Bishop of Waterford in 1745 ' (Patr. Brit. p. 58). This was Richard Chenevix, son of Colonel Chenevix of the Guards, and grandson of the Rev. Philip Chenevix, the Protestant pastor of Limay, near Nantes, who settled in England at the time of the revocation of the Edict of Nantes (Smiles, Huguenots, p. 375). His grand-daughter and heiress, Melesina Chenevix, married—first, Colonel Ralph St. George, and secondly, Richard Trench, brother of the first Lord Ashtown in the peerage of Ireland, by whom she was mother of Richard Chenevix Trench, archbishop of Dublin (Dict. Nat. Biog. x. 184).

1726. Married—Paul Daniel Chenevix and Eliz. Deards: St. Jas. Clerkenwell, iii. 253.
Crockford (Chenevix-Trench), 2.

Cheney, Cheynoy, Cheyne, Chaney, Chany.—Local, ' de Quesnay' (?), in the canton of Montmartin, department of La Manche, Normandy (Lower).

William de Cheyney, co. Norf., 2 Hen. II : FF. x. 433.
Felicia de Cheny, co. Devon, 20 Edw. I. R.
Philip de Cheny, Guernsey, ibid.
Walter de Chenay, co. Salop, Hen. III-Edw. I. K.
Henry de Cheney, co. Camb., 1273. A.
Nicholas de Cheney, co. Camb., ibid.
William de Cheney, co. Suff., ibid.
1661. Thomas Cheney (co. Suffolk) and Eliz. Clopton: Marriage Alleg. (Canterbury), p. 59.
1663. Christopher Wilkinson and Ellen Cheyne: ibid. p. 99.
London, 3, 1, 1, 2, 1; New York, 10, 2, 1, 0, 0; Philadelphia, 3, 13, 1, 3, 0.

Cherrill.—Local, ' of Cherhill,' a parish in the dioc. of Salisbury and co. Wilts, three miles from Calne. This place was parent of an early surname.

David de Churhille, co. Devon. A.
Adam de Churhylle, co. Devon. ibid.
1788. Married—Richard Cherrill and Ann Hewitt: St. Geo. Han. Sq. ii. 13.
London, 2.

Cherrington,   Charrington.—(1) Local, ' of Cherrington,' a parish in co. Warwick, four miles from Shipston-upon-Stour ; (2) ' of Cherrington,' a township in the parish of Edgmond, in co. Salop ; (3) ' of Cherington,' a parish in co. Gloucester ; cf. Carrington and Sherrington.

William de Cherinton, co. Norf.,1273. A.
Richard de Cherinton, co. Salop, ibid.
Thomas de Cherinton, co. Salop, Hen. III-Edw. I. K.
William de Cherinton, co. Salop, ibid.
1768. Married—John Allchin and Margaret Charrinton: St. Geo. Han. Sq. i. 177.
1780. — James Winter and Ann Cherington: ibid. p. 311.
London, 4, 3; MDB. (co. Salop), 1, 0; Boston (U.S.). 10, 0.

Cherry.—Local, ' at the cherry,' from residence by a cherry-tree ; cf. Crabtree, Chestnut, Oake, Ash, Nash, &c.   M.E. *chery* or *chiri*.

William Chirie, co. Derby, 1273. A.
William Chery, C. R., 21 Hen. VI.
1569. Married—William Cherye and Alyce Foxe: St. Michael, Cornhill, p. 10.
1606. — Henrie Cherrie and Joane Fenner: St. Jas. Clerkenwell, i. 31.
Henry Cherry, 1701: Exchequer Depositions by Commission, Cheshire, p. 168.
1788. Married—John Cherry and Rebecca Holdsworth: St. Geo. Han. Sq. ii. 7.
London, 16; New York, 13.

Chesher, Cheshire, Chesshyre, Chesshire, Chesshire.—Local, ' of Cheshire' ; cf. Derbyshire, Wiltshire, &c.

Thomas de Chastirshir, C. R., 6 Edw. II.
Henricus de Chesterschyr, 1379: P. T. Yorks. p. 166.
John Cheshire, of Farrington, 1631 : Wills at Chester (1621-50), p. 47.
Alice Cheshire, of Warrington, 1615: ibid. (1545-1620), p. 39.
1609-10. Thomas Langton and Dorcas Chesshire: Marriage Lic. (London), i. 318.
London, 1, 14, 0, 0 ; Manchester, 0, 2, 1, 0; Philadelphia, 0, 2, 0, 2.

Chesley.—Local ; v. Charsley.

Chesnut.—Local ; v. Chestnut.

Chessell.—Local ; v. Chishull.

Chesser.—Local, ' of Cheshire,' q.v. ; a modern variant.

1609-10. Thomas Langton and Dorcas Chesshire : Marriage Lic. (London), i. 318.
1759. Married—John Cheser and Ann Gibs : St. Geo. Han. Sq. i. 90.

1782. Married—James Hamilton and Margaret Chessor : ibid. p. 339. Philadelphia, 1.

Chessman. — Occup. 'the cheeseman,' a dealer in cheese ; v. Cheeseman. In no way connected with the royal game of chess.

1736. Married—Absolom Robinson and Eliz. Chesman : St. Antholin (London), p. 147.
1746. — Christopher Rayner and Eliz. Chesman : St. Geo. Chap. Mayfair, p. 77.
1783. — John Burgess and Ann Chesman : St. Geo. Han. Sq. i. 342.
London, 1 ; MDB. (E. Rid. Yorks), 1 ; Philadelphia, 3 ; Boston (U.S.), 13.

Chessum, Chesson.—Local, ' of Chesham,' a natural variant ; cf. Barnum for Barnham. Chesham is a market-town and parish in co. Bucks, three miles from Amersham. Chesson is as naturally a variant of Chessum ; cf. Ransom and Ranson, Sansom and Samson, &c. The first entry following either confirms my view or denotes a different birthplace for Chesson. But cf. Cheston.

1653. Married—Thomas Creake, of Chesson, co. Harford (sic), and Eliz. Warren : St. Dionis Backchurch, p. 29.
1728. — John Chessum and Martha Howlett : St. Mary Aldermary, p. 48.
1754. — John Hunt and Mary Chessum : St. Geo. Chap. Mayfair, p. 272.
1804. — William C. Flower and Hester Chesson : St. Geo. Han. Sq. ii. 299.
London, 1,2 ; MDB. (co. Middlesex), 1,0.

Chester, Chesters.—Local, ' of Chester,' the capital town of Cheshire. Chesters is modern, and probably a kind of patronymic ; cf. Brooks, Styles, Holmes, for Brook, Style, Holme, &c. Hence Williams, Jones, &c., for Williamson, Johnson, &c.

Petrus de Cestr', co. York, 1273. A.
William de Cestre, co. Bedf., ibid.
Symon de Chestrie, co. Derby, 20 Edw. I. R.
William de Chestere, co. Soms., 1 Edw. III : Kirby's Quest, p. 272.
Elisabet de Chester, 1379 : P. T. Yorks. p. 152.
Cristiana de Chester, 1379 : ibid. p. 157.
1561-2. John Gardener and Anne Chester : Marriage Lic. (London), i. 23.
William Chester, of Newton, near Middlewich : Wills at Chester (1545-1620), p. 140.
Margaret Chester, of Coole Lane, Chester, 1623 : ibid. (1621-50), p. 47.
London, 18, 0 ; MDB. (co. Chester), 2, 6 ; Manchester, 3, 7 ; New York, 10, 0.

Chesterfield.—Local, ' of Chesterfield,' a town in co. Derby. A rare surname.

Robertus de Chesterfield, 1379 : P. T. Yorks. p. 118.
Agnes de Chasturfeld, 1379 : ibid. p. 41.
Liverpool, 1 ; Boston (U.S.), 1.

Chesterman.—Nickname, 'the Chester man,' one who hailed from Chester ; cf. Penkethman, found in the neighbourhood of Warrington. This surname is well known in the States. Adam Chesterman 'imbarqued in the Mathew of London' for St. Christophers, May 21, 1635. He was nineteen years old. Probably the present Chestermans are his descendants (v. Hotten's Lists of Emigrants, p. 81).

1772. Married—Mathew Pouncy and Hannah Chesterman : St. Geo. Han. Sq. i. 222.
1778. — George Goodwin and Hester Chesterman : ibid. p. 284.
Liverpool, 1 ; London, 3 ; Philadelphia, 5.

Chestnut, Chesnut.—Local, ' at the chestnut,' from residence by a chestnut-tree ; cf. Nash, Rowntree, Crabtree, Oake, &c. This surname, while very rare in England, has at some period crossed the Atlantic, and has now many representatives.

Philadelphia, 40, 5.

Cheston.—Local, ' of Cheshun,' a town in co. Hertford, formerly styled Cheston ; cf. Bristow for Bristol, or Stopford for Stockport. For further information, v. Notes and Queries, Nov. 8, 1890.

1565. Thomas Chestonne, New Coll. : Reg. Univ. Oxf. vol. i. pt. ii. p. 22.
1612. Buried—Richard Chestone : St. Jas. Clerkenwell, iv. 121.
1658. — Beniamyn Cheston : ibid. p. 325.
London, 3 ; Philadelphia, 5.

Chettle, Cattle, Cattell, Catell.—Bapt. ' the son of Chetel,' a weakened form of Ketel (v. Kettle). A northern mythological name. Cf. Arkettle.

Chetel Frieday, a freeman, co. Norf., 1087 : FF. viii. 51.
Cattle Bagge, co. Camb., 1273. A.
Thomas Chetill, 1379 : P. T. Yorks. p. 133.
Johannes Chetel, 1379 : ibid. p. 75.

1561. Married—Henry Chettle and Johane Talbott : St. Jas. Clerkenwell, p. 1.
Margery Chettle, of Taunton, co. Soms., 1630 : Abstract of Somersetshire Wills, p. 14.
1780. Married—William Cattell and Susanna Heakes : St. Geo. Han. Sq. i. 316.
1781. — Joseph Bridges and Hannah Chettle : ibid. p. 324.
London, 1, 8, 5, 0 ; Philadelphia, 0, 0, 13, 1 ; Boston (U.S.) (Cattle), 1.

Chetwynd, Chatwin.—Local, ' of Chetwynd,' a parish in co. Salop, near Newport.

'William Richard Chetwynd, third Viscount Chetwynd (1680 ?-1770), was the third son of John Chetwynd . . . who was younger son of Sir Walter Chetwynd of Ingestre, head of the ancient family of Chetwynd, first of Chetwynd, Shropshire, and then of Ingestre': Dict. Nat. Biog. x. 213.
John de Chedewinde, co. Salop, Hen. III–Edw. I. K.
Adam de Chetewynde, co. Salop, 1273. A.
John de Chetwind, co. Salop, ibid.

The following entries practically prove that Chatwin is a variant of Chetwynd :

Thomas Chetwen, or Chetwyn, 1511 : Reg. Univ. Oxf. i. 74.
Edward Chetwind, or ' Chetwine,' 1596 : ibid. vol. ii. pt. ii. p. 195.
William Chetwin, of West Kirby, 1607 : Wills at Chester (1545-1620), p. 40.
1754. Married—Robert Nash and Isabell Chetwynd : St. Geo. Han. Sq. i. 54.
London, 1, 4 ; Philadelphia, 0, 1.

Chevalier, Cavalier, Chevalier. — Offic. ' the chevalier,' a knight ; v. Horseman.

Thomas le Chevalier, co. Kent, Hen. III–Edw. I. K.
Jordan le Chevaler, co. Northampt., 1273. A.
Walter le Chevaler, co. Wilts, 1273. A.
Ralph Chivaler, C. R., 1 Edw. III. pt. i.
Thomas de Reresby, chivaler, 1379 : P. T. Yorks. p. 5.
1546. Thomas Cheveler, vicar of Stow, co. Norf. : FF. ii. 281.
1805. Married—William Edward Chevalier and Mary Williams : St. Geo. Han. Sq. ii. 331.
London, 5, 4, 2 ; West Rid. Court Dir., 0, 1, 0 ; Philadelphia (Chevalier), 5.

Chew.—Local, (1) ' of Chew.' Two parishes, Chew-Magna and Chew-Stoke, are situate in co. Somerset ; (2) ' de Cheux,' a village near Caen, in Normandy. This latter suggestion is Lower's (Patr.

Brit. p. 59). Of course (1) is the natural derivation of most of the representatives of this surname. It has ramified strongly in America. John Chew settled in Virginia as early as 1624 (v. Hotten's Lists of Emigrants, p. 237).

1591. Robert Chew, of Billington : Wills at Chester (1545-1620), p. 40.
1602. Married—Theodore Hanley and Jane Chewe : St. Jas. Clerkenwell, iii. 27.
1612. Roger Chew, of Mottram : Wills at Chester (1545-1620), p. 40.
1667. Thomas Chew, of Woodplumpton : Wills at Richmond, p. 64.
1766. Married—John Chew and Jane Gifford : St. Geo. Han. Sq. i. 158.
London, 4 ; Manchester, 3 ; MDB. (co. Chester), 2 ; Philadelphia, 49,

Cheyne, Cheyney.—Local ; v. Cheney.

Chichester.—Local, ' of Chichester,' a city and market-town in the co. of Sussex. This surname has crossed the Atlantic, and is well represented in the States ; rare in England.

1582. John Chechester (co. Devon), Exeter Coll. : Reg. Univ. Oxf. vol. ii. pt. ii. p. 119.
1679. Sir John Chichester, Bt., and Eliz. Bickerstaffe : Marriage Alleg. (Canterbury), p. 10.
London, 1 ; New York, 13.

Chick.—Nick. ' the chick ' ; v. Chickin.

Walter Chike, co. Oxf., 1273. A.
Thomas Chike, co. Soms., 1 Edw. III : Kirby's Quest, p. 249.
Robert Chicke, co. Soms., 1586 : Reg. Univ. Oxf. vol. ii. pt. ii. p. 153.
1601. Bapt.—Edith Chicke, reputed d. of John Loddon : Reg. Stourton, co. Wilts, p. 3.
1803. Married—Jacob Chick and Eliz. Fidler : St. Geo. Han. Sq. ii. 287.
London, 10 ; MDB. (co. Soms.), 8 ; Boston (U.S.), 36.

Chickin.— Nick. ' the chicken ' ; cf. Henn, Cock, &c. ' Cheyn, *pullus* ' : Prompt. Parv.

John Chikin, co. Camb., 1273. A.
Philip Chikin, co. Camb., ibid.
Hugh Chyken, Fines Roll, 11 Edw. I.
1650. Bapt.—Mary, d. John Chickin : St. Jas. Clerkenwell, i. 176.
' Joseph Chickin sailed for New England in 1635 ': Hotten's Lists of Emigrants, p. 285.
I fear this surname is extinct in England, but it survives in the States.
Boston (U.S.), 1.

Chidley, Chidlow. — Local, ' of Chidlow,' a township in the parish of Malpas, co. Chester.

'In memory of John Chidlow, rector of Hobbies, who died Dec. 14, 1652 '; Sizeland Ch., co. Norf.: FF. x. 180.
1803. Married—Joseph Wood and Mary Chidlaw : St. Geo. Han. Sq. ii. 275.
— — Samuel Cooper and Ann Chidlow : ibid. p. 279.
— — Thomas Chidley and Eliz. Farlow : ibid. p. 289.
London, 7, 0 ; MDB. (co. Salop), 5, 1.

Chiffence, Chiffinch.—Nick. ; see Chaffinch.

Chilcott, Chilcotte.—Local, ' of Chilcote,' a chapelry in the parish of Burton-upon-Trent, co. Derby.

Gilbert de Childecote, co. Soms., 1 Edw. III : Kirby's Quest, p. 260.
1602. John Gillett and Frances Chillcott, *widow* : Marriage Lic. (London), i. 270.
1604. Bapt.—Sarah, d. James Chilcot.
1793. Married—John Chilcot and Mary Williams: St. Geo. Han. Sq. ii. 99.
1795. — Thomas Chilcott and Sarah Crow : ibid. p. 140.
London, 5, 0 ; Philadelphia, 2, 1.

Child, Childe, Childs, Chiloe.—Nick. or offic. ' the child.' Perhaps the eldest son, the heir (v. Eyre and Ayre). Hence Childe Harold simply revives the ' Childe Waters,' ' Childe Rolands,' or ' Childe Thopas's,' of mediaeval days. It is somewhat hard to fix the sense of Child in nomenclature. It evidently means a page occasionally. In the Morte Arthure mention is made of a youth named ' Chastelayne, a chylde of the Kynges chambyre.'

William le Child, C. R., 12 Edw. I.
Godwin Child, co. Berks, Hen. III-Edw. I. K.
Brian le Child, co. Camb., 1273. A.
Walter le Child, co. Oxf., ibid.
John le Child, co. Sussex, 20 Edw. I. R.
Robertus Childe, 1379 : P. T. Yorks. p. 59.
Emma Child', 1379 : ibid. p. 59.
1639. Married—Robert Childe and Ann Leyton : St. Antholin (London), p. 72.

The form Childs and the corrupted Chiles seem to represent the patronymic *s*, as in Jones, Williams, Simmonds, &c. Lower says,' In Domesday the epithet Cild or Cilt is applied to several persons of distinction ' (Patr. Brit. p. 59).
London, 52, 2, 15, 1 ; Philadelphia, 20, 0, 51, 1.

Childerhouse.—Local, ' of the Childerhouse.' Probably a children's home or school attached to some monastery or church. It is quite clear from the evidence that the surname has sprung from Norfolk or Suffolk.

William de Childerhous, Fines Roll, 12 Edw. I.
Alex. del Childrehus, co. Norf., 1273. A.
William del Childrehus, co. Norf., ibid.
John del Childrehus, co. Suff., ibid.
Ranulf del Childrehus, co. Suff., ibid.
Bartholomew at Childerhowse, vicar of Lakenham, co. Norf.: FF. iv. 518.
Guy Childerhouse, rector of Stiffkey, co. Norf., 1413 : ibid. ix. 253.
1801. Married—Robert Childerhouse and Margaret Drury : St. Geo. Han. Sq. ii. 245.
'An inquest on the body of a man named William Childerhouse was held at Scarborough on Monday,' &c : Standard, Feb. 22, 1888.
London, 1.

Childers, Childress.—Local, —?

Isabel de Childhers, C. R., 37 Hen. III.
1665. Buried—Thomas Childers : St. Jas. Clerkenwell, iv. 364.
1746. Married—William Knight and Phillis Childres : St. Geo. Chap. Mayfair, p. 78.
Crockford, 1, 0 ; Philadelphia, 0, 1.

Childorstono ; v. Chilson.
London, 1.

Children, Childrens.—Probably some form of a personal name. Lower writes, quoting Ferguson, ' Probably the O. Germ. personal name Childeruna or Hilderuna ' (Patr. Brit. p. 59).

William Chyldren, C. R., 3 Edw. IV.
1539. Married—Symon Ponder and Dorety Children: St. Peter, Cornhill, i. 221.
1661. Richard Children and Eliz. Everest : Marriage Alleg. (Canterbury), p. 15.
1662-3. John Childron and Susan Stretfeild : ibid. p. 66.
MDB. (co. Kent), 1, 1.

Chillingworth.—A variant of Killingworth, q.v. ; cf. Church and Kirk.

Chilman, Chillman.—(1) Bapt. ' the son of Childman.' *Child,* with augmentative *man,* as in Bateman, Coleman, Tiddyman ; cf. Childebert, Childebrand, Childeric, probably all hard forms of Hild, as in Hildegard, Hildebrand, Hildebert, &c. (v. Yonge, ii. 234).

Childman (without surname), co. Camb., 1273. A.

Childmannius (without surname), co. Camb., ibid.

Nicholas Childman, co. Camb., ibid.

Eleanor Childman, uxor, co. Camb., ibid.

Mariot Childman, filia, co. Camb., ibid.

Alan Chilleman, Fines Roll, 12 Edw. I.

(2) Bapt. ' the son of Chilmond ' ; cf. Osman and Wayman for Osmund and Waymond.

William Chilemound, co. Soms., 1 Edw. III : Kirby's Quest, p. 147.

Henry Chilemounde, co. Soms., 1 Edw. III : ibid. p. 148.

John Chylemonde, co. Soms., 1 Edw. III : ibid. p. 258.

1579–80. William Hollforthe and Agnes Chilmon : Marriage Lic. (London), i. 95.

London, 1, 0 ; Crockford, 1, 0 ; Philadelphia, 0, 2.

Chilson, Childerstone.—Local, ' of Chilson,' a tithing in the parish of Charlbury, co. Oxford. This seems to have been originally Childeston.

Reginald de Childeston, co. Oxf., 1273. A.

John de Childeston, co. Oxf., ibid.

1771. Married—Martin Childerson and Mary Jackson : St. Geo. Han. Sq. i. 207.

1788. — John Witton and Ann Chillystone : ibid. ii. 15.

All the above references settle the origin of Childerstone. If Chilson is not of the same family, it must be a variant of Jilson or Gilson ; cf. Chubb for Jubb, &c.

London, 0, 1 ; Boston (U.S.), 1, 0.

Chilton.—Local, ' of Chilton.' There are many parishes in various counties of England bearing this name.

Hugh de Chilton, co. Wilts, 1273. A.

Robert de Chilton, co. Suff., 20 Edw. I. R.

Robert de Chilleton, co. Kent, Hen. III–Edw. I. K.

Chilton seems to have been introduced into America from the Kentish family.

1586–7. Bapt. — Isabell, d. James Chilton : St. Paul's, Canterbury.

1599. — Ingle, d. James Chilton : ibid.

This James Chilton was one of the Pilgrim Fathers ; v. N. and Q., March 1, 1890, p. 166.

1590. Bapt. — Priscilla, d. Edward Chilton : St. Jas. Clerkenwell, i. 23.

London, 6 ; Philadelphia, 1 ; Boston (U.S.), 1 ; New York, 1.

Chimney. — Local, ' at the chimney' ; O.F. *cheminée*.

John de la Chimyne, co. York, 21 Edw. I. R.

Ching, Chinn, Shinn.—Local, ' at the chine,' from residence thereby. A chine was a crevice or chasm ; cf. Black Gang Chine, or Shanklin Chine. In the H.E.D. are such variants as Chyne, Chynne, Chinne, or Chin (v. Chine, *sb.*[1]). The *g* in Ching is evidently an excrescence ; cf. Jennings for Jenins.

Henry de Chine, co. Camb., 1273. A.

John Chynne, co. Hunts, ibid.

1803. Married — Charles Ching and Mary Osland : St. Geo. Han. Sq. ii. 279.

1804. — Isaac Chinn and Sarah Stacey : ibid. ii. 304.

London, 2, 1, 3 ; MDB. (co. Camb.), 0, 0, 3 ; Boston (Shinn), 1.

Chipman.—Occup. ' the chapman,' q.v. A variant still common in America, and which we find in English documents of the 14th and as late as the 17th and 18th centuries.

John Chipman, co. Soms., 1 Edw. III : Kirby's Quest, p. 194.

1667. Married—William Penington and Marye Chipman : St. Jas. Clerkenwell, iii. 133.

1795. — John Hanington and Mary Chipman : St. Geo. Han. Sq. ii. 140.

Boston (U.S.), 22.

Chipp.—Local, ' at the Cheap,' i.e. the market-place, from residence therein ; cf. Cheapside and Eastcheap. Possibly, however, a personal name ; cf. the dim. Chipet :

Roger Chipet, co. Soms., 1 Edw. III : Kirby's Quest, p. 220.

This is somewhat strong evidence in favour of a fontal origin.

John Chip, co. Soms., 1 Edw. III : Kirby's Quest, p. 192.

With this cf. the Somersetshire Chisman for Cheeseman ; also cf. Chipman (q.v.) for Chepman, or Chapman, in the same county.

Oliver Chyppe, or Chepe, 1531 : Reg. Univ. Oxf. p. 164.

1620. Married — Richard Chypp and Edin Church : St. Peter, Cornhill, p. 250.

1767. — William Slaughter and Ann Chipp : St. Geo. Han. Sq. i. 160.

London, 1 ; New York, 1.

Chippendale, Chippindale, Chippindall.—Local, ' of Chippingdale,' or ' Chippendale,' the

dale in which stands the village of Chipping, on the north-eastern confines of Lancashire. An old-established family of Chippindall still has representatives in the town of Lancaster. Although the furniture-maker, Thomas Chippendale, was a native of Worcestershire, his progenitors must have ' worked down' from Lancaster. There can be no doubt about his descent. Lying on the confines of Yorkshire we find the earliest instance in that county :

Ricardus Chipyndale, 1379 : P. T. Yorks. p. 181.

1624. William Chippendall, of Gressingham : Lancashire Wills proved at Richmond, p. 65.

1649. Edward Chippendale, of Claughton, *linnen webster* : ibid.

1679. Robert Chippingdale, of Claughton : ibid.

All these dwelt in the neighbourhood of Lancaster.

London, 1, 2, 0 ; Crockford, 0, 0, 3 ; West Riding Court Dir., 0, 1, 0 ; Leeds, 1, 1, 0.

Chippin, Chipan.—Local, ' of Chipping,' anciently Chepin, a village and parish in the archdeaconry of Lancaster ; v. Chippendale.

John de Chepyn, co. Lanc., 22 Edw. III : Baines' Lanc. ii. 95.

Agnes de Chypyn, 1379 : P. T. Yorks. p. 149.

Magota Chybyn, 1379 : ibid. p. 42.

1695. Married — Thomas Chippin and Martha Gooding : St. Michael, Cornhill, p. 48.

London, 2, 0 ; New York, 0, 1.

Chisholm, Chisolm, Chisom, Chisam.—Local, ' of Chisholm.' I cannot find the spot, but -holm, the suffix, means an islet in a stream, and the affix is found in such places as Chiswick, Great and Little Chishall, &c. Lower says the prefix *chis* is *cisil*, gravel. Thus Chisholm would mean an islet with a gravel soil. The surname has been long settled in the Highlands of Scotland.

1798. Married—John Burrell and Eliz. Chisholm : St. Geo. Han. Sq. ii. 176.

London, 2, 0, 0, 0, (Chissholm), 1 ; New York, 4, 2, 0, 0 ; Boston (U.S.), 38, 0, 0, 1 ; Philadelphia (Chisom), 1.

Chishull, Chessell.—Local, ' of Chishall,' two parishes in co. Essex.

'John Chishull (d. 1280), bishop of London, was probably born in Essex, in the village of Chishall': Dict. Nat. Biog. x. 264.

He was also known as John de Chishull; v. Lewis's Top. Dict. England, i. 595. Also as John de Chisil, v. FF. vii. 62.

William de Chishill, co. Camb., 1273. A. John de Chishull, co. Camb., 20 Edw. I. R.
1582-3. Christopher Pepper and Barbara Chisshull, of Bradfield Parva, co. Essex : Marriage Lic. (London), i. 114.
1809. Married—George William Chessell and Sarah Wightman : St. Geo. Han. Sq. ii. 409.
London, 0, 1.

Chislett, Chiselett.—Local, 'of Chislet,' a parish in co. Kent, seven miles from Canterbury.

1581-2. Thomas Chislet, co. Soms.: Reg. Univ. Oxf. vol. ii. pt. ii. p. 117.
1602. William Chislett and Emma Barlow : Marriage Lic. (London), i. 271.
1639. Emnett Chislett : Cal. of Wills in Court of Husting (2).
London, 4, 0; Oxford, 1, 1.

Chisman.—Occup. 'the cheeseman' (v. Cheeseman). An old variant of the West country.

Adam le Chisman, co. Soms., 1 Edw. III : Kirby's Quest, p. 181.
Alicia Chisman, co. Soms., 1 Edw. III : ibid.
William Chisman, 1606 : St. Dionis Backchurch (London), p. 15.
1748. Married—John Rumsey and Ann Chisman : Reg. Stourton, co. Wilts, p. 56.
London, 1 ; MDB. (co. Wilts), 1.

Chisnall, Chisnell.—Local, 'of Chisnall,' now a farm-house in the township of Coppull, in the parish of Standish, co. Lanc.

'Edward Chisenhale, or Chisenhall (died 1653 ?), historian, was the eldest son of Edward Chisenhall, Esq., of Chishenhall, Lancashire': Dict. Nat. Biog. x. 259.
Edward Chisenhall, of Chisenhall, 1646 : Baines' Lanc. (Croston), p. 304.
Bryan Chisnall, 1642 : Preston Guild Rolls, p. 109.
Alice Chisnall, of Chisnall, widow, 1607 : Wills at Chester (1545-1620), p. 40.
Humphrey Chisnall, of Coppull, 1610 : ibid.
Manchester, 2, 0; Liverpool, 2, 2; London, 1, 2.

Chitterling.—Nick. 'the chitterling,' a dim. of chit, a little child; v. Chitty. 'A small child is called a chitterling in Cotton's Works, ed. 1734, p. 264' (Halliwell).

Richard Chiterling, co. Worc., 1273. A.

Chittock, Chittick.—? Nick. 'the baby-faced' (?). Probably a dim. of chit (v. Chitty and Chitterling), formed like bullock, a little bull.

Warin Chittoc, co. Hunts, 1273. A.
Roger Chittoc, co. Hunts, ibid.
1471. John Chitok, alderman of Norwich : FF. iv. 369.
1796. Married — Ellis Chittock and Phoebe Russell : St. Geo. Han. Sq. ii. 142.
1806. — John Chittock and Harriot Lyne : ibid. ii. 352.
London, 1, 1 ; Philadelphia, 0, 8.

Chitty.—Nick. 'chitty'; cf. chitty-faced, i.e. baby-faced. In Furness the small tender twigs or shoots are commonly known as chats. We still call a young and somewhat forward child a chit. Chit is strictly a young sprout; v. Chitterling. Possibly the first two instances refer to this word.

Nicholas Kitte, co.Northampt., 1273. A.
William Kitte, co. Oxf., ibid.
John Chytte, co. Soms., 1 Edw. III : Kirby's Quest, p. 208.
Agnes Chittye, temp. Eliz. Z.
John Chittie, ibid.
1587. John Maye and Isabell Chettye, relict of William Chittye; Marriage Lic. (London), ii. 166.
Mr. Henry Chitty, merchant, 1667 : St. Peter, Cornhill, p. 87.
1790. Married — Charles Chitty and Martha Laggatt : St. Geo. Han. Sq. ii. 37.
London, 8 ; Boston (U.S.), 1.

Chivell, Shovel.—Nick. Fr. cheval, a horse. There can be no doubt that Shovel is an imitative corruption.

Osbert Chevall, co. Bucks, 1273. A.
Roger Chevall, co. Bucks, ibid.
1626. William Chevall and Mary Wheeler : Marriage Lic. (London), ii. 176.
1729. Married—Daniel Chivell and Ann Dell : St. Geo. Chap. Mayfair, p. 291.
1753. — Thomas Shovell and Jane Neau : ibid. p. 257.
London, 1, 0.

Choice, Choyce.—Bapt. 'the son of Joyce,' q.v. This sharpened form is not uncommon ; cf. Chubb for Jubb, or Challand for Jalland. That this is the true derivation of Choice there can be little doubt.

Steven Choyse, 1624 : Reg. St. Mary Aldermary (London), p. 15.
1794. Married—William Choice and Catherine Garrett : St. Geo. Han. Sq. ii. 109.
London, 2, 0; MDB. (co. Leicester), 1, 1.

Cholmeley, Cholmondeley, Chumley.—Local, (1) 'of Cholmondeley,' a township in the parish of Malpas, co. Chester, pronounced Chumley ; (2) 'of Chulmleigh,' a parish in co. Devon, twenty-one miles from Exeter. It is probable that in the south of England, Cholmeley and Chumley represent the Devonshire parish.

1566-7. Thomas Cholmeley and Dorothy Bedle : Marriage Lic. (London), p. 35.
Richard Cholmondeley, of Eccleston, 1593 : Wills at Chester (1545-1620), p. 40.
1656. Bapt.—Edward, s. Henry Chomley, apothecary ; St. Dionis Backchurch, p. 113.
1666. Buried — William Chombley : ibid. p. 237.
1689. — Susanna Chumbly, widow : ibid. p. 256.
1726. Married — John Chumley and Alice Todd : St. Geo. Han. Sq. i. 2.
London, 2, 1, 1.

Chopping.—? Bapt. 'the son of Chopin,' one of the many personal names ending in ing ; v. Browning or Harding.

John Chopyn, co. Soms., 1 Edw. III : Kirby's Quest, p. 244.
1781. Married — Frederic Choppin and Susanna Sophia Bisshopp : St. Geo. Han. Sq. i. 326.
1789. — William Wilson and Ann Chopping : ibid. ii. 29.
London, 1.

Chorley.—Local, ' of Chorley,' townships in cos. Lancaster and Chester.

Bridget Chorley, of Chorley, 1595: Wills at Chester (1545-1620), p. 40.
John Chorley, of Chester, 1610 : ibid.
London, 8 ; Philadelphia, 4.

Chorlton.—Local, ' of Chorlton,' chapelries and townships in cos. Lancaster, Chester, and Stafford : v. Charlton for other early instances.

Alan de Cherleton, co. Soms., 1 Edw. III : Kirby's Quest, p. 127.
1587. Richard Chorlton, of Chorlton : Wills at Chester, i. 40.
1603. John Chorlton, of Manchester : ibid.
Manchester, 15; Philadelphia, 4.

Chown, Chowne.—Bapt. ' the son of Chun.' Probably the same as Chuon (v. Chuonmund, Yonge, ii. 417).

Chun Mervyn, co. Camb., 1273. A.
Chun Pimme, co. Camb., ibid.
Chun Pistor, co. Camb., ibid.
William Chaun, co. Linc., ibid.

Hugh Chone, co. Oxf., ibid.
Robertus Chaune, 1379 : P. T. Yorks. p. 240.

Since writing the above I have come across the following strongly corroborative evidence :

1596. Francis Chowne, or Chune, Christ Church : Reg. Univ. Oxf. vol. ii, pt. iii. p. 196.

It may be looked upon as certain that Chown and Chowne represent the old personal name Chun.

1668-9. Thomas Chowne and Eliz. Foice : Marriage Alleg. (Canterbury), p. 161.

West Riding Court Dir., 1, 0 ; London, 3, 2 ; Boston (U.S.), 1, 0.

Chrimes.—Bapt. 'the son of Grim,' v. Grimes, of which I doubt not it is a corruption. G and C constantly change places in English nomenclature ; cf. Grain and Crane, Gamel and Cammel, Gandelyn and Candlin, &c. Chrimes is found chiefly in the district where Grim was familiar. That Grim was a Cheshire personal name we know from the fact that Grimsditch is a place in that county, whence has sprung the surname. In the Modern Domesday Book (1875) we find in the same county four Chrimes and two Grimes.

Thomas Crimes, of Nether Whitley, 1616 : Wills at Chester (1545-1620), p. 47.
William Crimes, of Sandiway, 1618 : ibid.
Edward Crimes, of Kingsley, co. Ches., 1648 : ibid. (1621-50), p. 55.

Towards the close of the 17th century the spelling became Chrimes :

Robert Chrimes, of Gorstick : Wills at Chester (1681-1700), p. 53.
London, 1 ; West Rid. Court Dir., 4 ; Manchester, 2 ; Boston (U.S.), 3.

Christian.—Bapt. 'the son of Christian,' a familiar North-English font-name, though not wholly confined to the North ; generally feminine ; v. Christie and Christison. The *h* throughout all these names is intrusive.

Jordan fil. Cristine, co. Kent, 1273. A.
Agnes fil. Cristine, co. Camb., ibid.
Brice Cristian, co. Soms., ibid.
Cristina Alayne, co. Bucks, ibid.
Cristiane Lyttester, 1379 : P. T. Yorks. p. 240.
Cristiana atte Tounend, 1379 : ibid. p. 248.

1591. Hamlett Christian and Margaret Rapior : Marriage Lic. (London), i. 191.
1656. Married—Edward Christean and Eliz. Huggins : St. Peter, Cornhill, i. 261.
London, 11 ; Philadelphia, 42.

Christiandom.—Nick. William Cristendome, clerk (Close Roll, 13 Ric. II. pt. ii). A.S. *Crist*, not Latin Christ.

Thomas Kyrystendome, *cissor*, 1379 : P. T. Yorks. p. 270.

Christie, Christy, Chrystie. —(1) Bapt. 'the son of Christian,' from nick. Christie. Christie and Christy are all but invariably North English or Border surnames, Christian being a former favourite font-name in those districts. It is still a popular girl's name in the Scottish Lowlands. Formerly it was common to both sexes.

Christie Grame, 1582 : Nicolson and Burn, Hist. Westm. and Cumb., vol. i. p. xxxv.
Christie Halliday, 1602 : ibid. p. cxii.
Christie Wilkin, 1602 : ibid.

(2) Bapt. 'the son of Christopher,' from nick. Christie. Occasionally used in the Border district, but (1) more generally.

'Christopher Armstrong, alias Johnis Criste,' 1557 (i.e. Johnny's Christie—the son of John) : TTT. p. ci.
Christe Irwen, 2 Edw. VI : ibid. p. lxxvi.
London, 27, 6, 0 ; Philadelphia, 28, 76, 2.

Christison. — (1) Bapt. 'the son of Christian,' from nick. Christie, q.v.: sometimes an abbreviation of the fuller Christianson.

John fil. Cristian, co. Linc., 1273. A.
Robert fil. Cristine, c. 1300. M.
Robertus Cristianson, 1379 : P. T. Yorks. p. 110.

(2) Bapt. 'the son of Christopher,' from the nick. Christie, q.v.

Margaret Crysterson, of Hindley, *widow*, 1591 : Wills at Chester (1545-1620), p. 49.
London, 1 ; New York, 11.

Christman, Christmann, Chrisman.—Bapt. 'the son of Christman,' seemingly equivalent to Christian, once a popular personal name. I do not think Christman was ever in use at the font in England. It is a German importation. In America the surname has

obtained a firm footing. With Chrisman, cf. Chrismas for Christmas.

William Crystman, C. R., 17 Hen. VI. Philadelphia, 20, 2, 10.

Christmas, Chrismas. — Bapt. 'the son of Christmas,' so culled because born at that season ; cf. Candlemass, Nowell, Noel, Pentecost, Park, &c.

Cristemasse le Weydur, Fines Roll, 11 Edw. I.
Felicia Cristemasse, co. Hunts, 1273. A.
Geoffrey Cristesmasse, co. Essex, ibid.
Hugh Cristemasse, co. Camb., ibid.
Richard Cristemasse, 1313. M.
John Cristemesse, Close Roll, 9 Ric. II.
1626-7. Thomas Christmas and Dorothie Leesie : Marriage Lic. (London), ii. 184.
1626. Married—William Harborte and Eliz. Chrismas : St. Mary Aldermary (London), p. 15.
London, 17, 0 ; Philadelphia, 1, 0.

Christopher, Christopherson, Christoffer, Christofferson.— Bapt. 'the son of Christopher.' I have been told that all who bear the somewhat rare name of Christopherson hail from Furness, in North Lanc. Anyway it is a native, and owes its origin to the treacherous sands of Morecombe and Duddon. The legend of St. Christopher is that he found an occupation in guiding passengers across a wide stream. One night he bare unawares the child Christ, and was about to sink under an ever-increasing weight, when the Saviour said, ' Thou bearest Him who beareth the sins of the world.' No doubt there would be a shrine to the Saint for belated travellers on Chapel Isle, opposite Conishead Priory. Many a babe would be dedicated to him in gratitude for some hairbreadth escape his father had experienced. As a font-name Christopher is still extremely popular throughout Furness. Christopherson also remains :

'John Christopherson (d.1558), bishop of Chichester, was born at Ulverston, in Furness ': Dict. Nat. Biog. x. 293.

Christopher, whether as font-name or surname, is not found in the Hundred Rolls, 1273.

John Cristovirson, 1513, co. York. W. 11.
Cristoforus, et uxor ejus, *smyth*, 1379:
P. T. Yorks. p. 220.
Rogerus Cristofore, 1379 : ibid.
1545. Married — Christopher Fell and
Jenet Casson : St. Mary, Ulverston,
p. 1.
— — Lawrence Parke and Agnes
Christoferson : ibid.
1546. Buried — John Christophorson :
ibid. p. 2.
— — Christopher Scales : ibid.
Nicholas Christoferson, of Dunerdall,
1598 : Lancashire Wills at Richmond,
p. 65.
Francis Christoferson, of Coulton,
1664 : ibid.
MDB. (co. Lancaster), o, 6, o, o;
London, 6, 2, 1, o ; Boston (U.S.), 13, o,
o, 2 ; New York, 10, 1, o, o.

Christpenny. — Nick. ;   cf.
Godspenny.
Roger Cristrepeny, Close Roll, 57
Hen. III.

Christushelp.—? Nick.
William Cristushelpe, Close Roll, 39
Hen. III. pt. i.

Chrystall, Chrystall.—Local,
'of Cristall.' I cannot find the
spot, but Yorkshire seems to have
been the home of the surname,
and probably the spot itself is to be
found in that county.
Robertus de Cristall, 1379 : P. T.
Yorks. p. 240.
1790. Married — John Debenger and
Mary Crystal : St. Geo. Han. Sq. ii. 38.
MDB. (co. Surrey), o, 1 ; Philadelphia,
2, o.

Chubb. — Bapt. 'the son of
Jubb' (i.e. Job). The old form of
Job was Jubb, q.v. It was especially popular in Yorkshire, as a
reference to Poll Tax of 1379 fully
proves. There are twelve Jubbs
in the W. Rid. Court Directory
(1867). This Jubb was sharpened
into Chubb.
'William Chubbes (d. 1505), Master of
Jesus College, Cambridge (whose name
is given in the History of Framlingham
as 'Chubbis, Jubbis, Chubbs, or Jubbs),
was born at Whitby, and was educated
at Pembroke College, Cambridge, where
he took his first degree in 1465': Dict.
Nat. Biog. x. 298.

This is one more instance of
supposed fish-names not being
what they seem; cf. Salmon, Turbott, Spratt, &c.
Adam Chubbe, co. Soms., 1 Edw. III :
Kirby's Quest, p. 177.
Alicia Chubbe, co. Soms., 1 Edw. III :
ibid. p. 196.

A nearer approach to modern
Job is found in the same record :
Robert Chobbe, co. Soms., 1 Edw. III :
Kirby's Quest, p. 242.
Alicia Chobbe, co. Soms., 1 Edw. III :
ibid.
John Chubb, temp. Eliz. Z.
Isabell Chubb, ibid.
Osmund Chubbe, sup. for B.A., 1522 :
Reg. Univ. Oxf. i. 126.
John Chub, sup. for B.A., 1524-5 : ibid.
p. 137.
London, 13 ; Philadelphia, 7.

Chuffer. — Nick. 'a miser,'
Towneley Mysteries, p. 216; cf.
Pennyfather (v. Halliwell).
Simon le Chuffere, 1276. A.
Rogerus Chuffer, 1379 : P. T. Yorks.
p. 101.

Chumley.—Local ; v. Cholmeley.

Church.—Local, 'at the church'
(cf. Kirk), from residence beside
the church porch or gate; v. Kirkus.
John atte Churche, co. Soms., 1 Edw.
III : Kirby's Quest, p. 82.
Robert atte Chyrche, co. Norf.,1273. A.
Stephen Church, co. Kent, 20 Edw.
I. R.
John Atte-cherch, rector of Metton, co.
Norf., 1338 : FF. viii. 140.
William Attechirche, co. Norf., 29
Edw. I : ibid. vii. 114.
1595. Bapt.—Eliz., d. Richard Church :
St. Jas. Clerkenwell, i. 30.
1611. William Bundocke and Katherine
Churche : Marriage Lic. (London), ii. 2.
London, 42 ; Philadelphia, 16.

Churchclerk. — Official, 'the
church clerk.'
Walter le Churcheclerk, temp. 1300. M.

Churchdoor.—Local, 'at the
church door,' from residence
thereby.
Reginald atte Churchedoor, temp.
1300. M.

Churcher.—(1) Local, 'at the
churchyard,' from residence thereby. A corruption of Churchyard,
q.v. (2) Local, 'at the church-
hay,' from residence thereby (v.
Churchey), a corruption. There is
not the slightest evidence that I can
find in favour of Lower's view that
Churcher is the same as Churchman, one who had care of a church.
1514. John Churchearde (i.e. Churchyard), or Churcherd, or Chyrchar, sup.
for B.A. : Reg. Univ. Oxf. i. 92.
1750. Married — Everard Churcher

and Mary Rankin : St. Geo. Chap. Mayfair, p. 176.
1765. Married—James Charman and
Jane Churcher : St. Geo. Han. Sq. i. 140.
London, 3 ; MDB. (co. Hants), 4.

**Churches, Churchis, Chur-
chus.** — Local, 'at the church-
house,' i.e. the parsonage ; cf.
Kirkus for Kirk-house. See also
Churchouse.
1626. Laurence Churches and Ellenor
Alexander : Marriage Lic. (London),
ii. 181.
MDB. (co. Somerset), 13, 3, 1.

Churchey. — Local, 'at the
church-hay' (v. Hay), i.e. resident
within the church enclosure.
William ate Churchehaye, co. Oxf.,
1273. A.
Robert atte Churchey, co. York. W. 11.
Peter atte Churcheley, co. Soms., 1
Edw. III : Kirby's Quest, p. 106.
Richard in the Churcheye, co. Soms.,
1 Edw. III : ibid. p. 119.
1642-3. Robert Anstye and Ann
Churchey : Marriage Lic. (London),
ii. 209.

Churchgate.—Local, 'at the
church-gate,' from residence thereby—yate for gate ; cf. Yates.
Christiana atte-Chircheyate. J.
Robert atte Chirchyate, temp. 1300. M.
1338. John de Cherchegate, rector of
Shimpling, co. Norf. : FF. i. 154.

Churchill.—Loc. 'of Churchill,'
parishes in diocs. of Bath and
Wells, Glouc. and Bristol, Oxford,
and Worcester.
Richard de Churchulle, co. Soms.,
1273. A.
Nicholas de Churchhull, co. Soms., 1
Edw. III : Kirby's Quest, p. 136.
1599. Edward Goodyer and Alice
Churchill (co. Dorset): Marriage Lic.
(London), i. 262.
1751. Married — Cornelius Allen and
Ann Churchill : St. Geo. Han. Sq. i. 45.
London, 16 ; Boston (U.S), 70.

Churchman. — Official, 'the
churchman,' the custodian or
keeper of a church ; v. Kirkman for
several instances. It is interesting to notice that Churchman first
appears in Cambridgeshire. In
the neighbouring counties it still
exists.
John Churchman, co. Soms., 1 Edw.
III : Kirby's Quest, p. 83.
Walter le Chercheman, co. Camb.,
1273. A.
Ouse le Chercheman, co. Camb., ibid.
William le Chercheman, co. Camb.,
ibid.

Simon le Cherchman, temp. 1300. M.
John Chirchman, C. R., 15 Edw. III.
pt. i.
William Churcheman, co. Soms., 1 Edw.
III : Kirby's Quest, p. 270.
1373. Ralph Chercheman, rector of
Bicham-Well, co. Norf. : FF. vii. 295.
1569. John Kynge and Jane Churchman, *spinster*: Marriage Lic. (London),
i. 42.
— Robert Griffith and Dionys Churchman, *widow* : ibid. i. 43.
1790. Married — Robert Churchman
and Mary Leavens : St. Geo. Han. Sq.
ii. 42.
London, 1 ; MDB. (co. Berks), 2 ; co.
Suffolk, 2 ; Philadelphia, 8.

Churchouse.—Local, ' at the
church-house ' ; v. Kirkus.
Manchester, 1.

Churchstile.—Local, ' at the
church stile,' from residence thereby ; v. Styles.
John atte Churchestighele, temp.
1300. M.

Churchward.— Official, ' the
churchward,' a churchwarden.
Adam Kirkeward, co. York. W. 15.
London, 2 ; Devon Court Dir., 6 ;
Boston (U.S.), 1 ; New York, 1.

Churchyard.—Local, ' at the
churchyard,' one who lived in or
by the precincts of the church.
John atte Chircheyerde, Close Roll,
20 Edw. III. pt. i.
Laurence de Kirkegarth, C. R., 20
Edw. I.
Richard Chircheyerde, Patent Roll,
7 Hen. VII.
Johannes atte Cyrkarth, 1379 : P. T.
Howdenshire, p. 7.
Adam Kirkeyerde, 1379 : P. T. Yorks.
p. 190.
1603. Buried—Geo. Churchyard, slaine :
St. Jas. Clerkenwell, iv. 73.
1631. — Humpfery Churchyard, *ha-
berdasher* : St. Michael, Cornhill, p. 231.
London, 1 ; MDB. (co. Suffolk), 2.

Churley, Churly.—Local, ' of
Churley,' another form of Chorley,
q.v.
Adam Churleye, co. Soms., 1 Edw.
III : Kirby's Quest, p. 107.
London, 3, 2.

Churton.—Local, ' of Churton,'
(1) a township in the parish of
Aldford, co. Chester ; (2) a township in the parish of Farndon, co.
Chester ; (3) a parish in co.
Wilts, four miles from East Lavington.
Maria Churton, of Cholmondeley,
widow, 1628 : Wills at Chester (1621-
50), p. 48.

Thomas Churton, of Manchester, *innkeeper*, 1636 : ibid.
1744. Married — John Churton and
Ann Winslow : St. Geo. Chap. Mayfair,
p. 37.
London, 4 ; Liverpool, 3.

Chute.—Local, ' of Chute,' a
village in co. Wilts, near Ludgers-
hall.
London (Court) Dir., 1 ; Philadelphia, 4.

Circuit.— ? ——. Probably an
imitative corruption. I cannot even
suggest a derivation.
1803. Married — Joseph Circuitt and
Mary Williams : St. Geo. Han. Sq. ii. 289.
MDB. (co. Essex), 2.

Citerer.—Offic. 'a summoner'
(v. Sumner).
Richard Citerer, Close Roll, 15 Edw.
III. pt. i.

Citoler.—Occup. ' the citoler,'
a player on the dulcimer, a cithern
(gyterne, Chaucer). ' Sytolyng,
and ek harpyng,' c. 1300. K. Alis.
1043 ; v. Citole and Citoler in the
H.E.D.
Thomas Citoler, C. R., 15 Edw. III.
pt. i.
Johannes Soutolyer, 1379 : P. T. Yorks.
p. 268.

**Clabon, Clabbon, Clabburn,
Clibbon, Cliburn, Claborn,
Clibborn.**—Local, ' of Clayburn.'
I have not identified the spot.
Cliburn, a small parish six miles
from Penrith, co. Westmoreland,
may be the parent of Clibbon and
Cliburn, but as regards the others,
a South-English origin seems more
likely.
1412. Thomas Clabeyn, bailiff of Yar-
mouth : FF. xi. 324.
William Clayborne, co. Norf., 2 Edw.
VI : ibid. viii. 508.
Thomas Clayborne, mayor of Lynn
Regis, 1573 : ibid. 533.
1604. Humphrey Cleyborne and Mar-
garet Morgan : Marriage Lic. (London),
i. 292.
London, 1, 1, 1, 1, 1, 0, 0 ; MDB. (co.
Suffolk), 2, 0, 0, 0, 0, 0, 0 ; New York,
Claborn, 1, Clibborn, 1.

Clackson, Clack.—(1) Variants of Clarkson and Clerk,
q.v.; (2) Clackson is sometimes a
variant of Clackston or Claxton,
q.v.
Richard Clerkson, or Clacson, 1510 :
Reg. Univ. Oxf. i. 72.

Nevertheless the following entries
prove Clackson to be occasionally
a variant of Claxton :
1669. Bapt.—John, s. John and Elizabeth
Claxson : St. Jas. Clerkenwell, i. 241.
1675. — William, s. John and Elizabeth
Clakston : ibid. i. 267.
1774. Married—John Clack and Ann
Jeffries : St. Geo. Han. Sq. i. 237.
1778. — John Eden and Dorothy
Clackson : ibid. 286.
London, 2, 7.

Cladish.—A variant of Gladdish, q.v.; cf. Crane, Cooch,
Candlin, and Cammel, all with
initial G originally. The surname
is found in co. Kent, which is also
the home of Gladdish.
MDB. (co. Kent), 4.

Clagett, Claggitt.—? ——.
Lower says, ' Cleggett, or Claggett,
perhaps for Cleygate, a manor in
Surrey ' (Patr. Brit. p. 61). This
would be quite satisfactory if it
was known that this Cleygate
had given birth to a surname.
But I cannot find it now or at any
time in that county. There is no
doubt that Clagett, or Claggitt,
would be the natural corruption
of such a name as Cleygate.
1716. Nicholas Claggett, rector of
Bridgham St. Mary, co. Norf. : FF. i. 440.
1721. Michael Claget, rector of Pullam,
co. Norf. : ibid. v. 392.
1756. William Claggott, rector of
Mundesley, co. Norf. : ibid. viii. 143.
1809. Married — Maximilian Richard
Kymer and Mary Clagett : St. Geo. Han.
Sq. ii. 401.
London, 1, 0 ; MDB. (co. Essex), 0, 1 ;
(co. Leicester), 1, 0 ; New York, 2, 0 ;
Philadelphia, 1, 0.

Clapham.—Local, 'of Clapham,'
parishes in the diocs. of Ely, Roch-
ester, Chichester, and Ripon. The
Yorkshire Claphams have been the
most prolific. The name is mani-
festly the *ham* of Clap, or Clop ; v.
Clapp.
Alexander de Clopham, co. Kent,
1273. A.
Peter de Clopham, co. Bedf., ibid.
Reginald de Clopham, co. Bedf., ibid.
Thomas de Clapham, 1379 : P. T.
Yorks. p. 289.
1618. Married—Thomas Clapham and
Ann Price : St. Mary Aldermary, p. 13.
London, 8 ; West Rid. Court Dir., 21 ;
Philadelphia, 3.

Claphamson, Claphanson.
—This is an extremely curious

name, the genitive *son* being made a suffix to a local surname, not to a personal name as in the case of Williamson, &c. I can only recall one other instance, viz. Couplandson, which occurs in the Ulverston Church registers for two centuries, as, for instance :

1549. Bapt. — Agnes Cawplandson : Ulverston Ch. p. 8.

Claphamson has crossed the Atlantic and has become Claphanson. No doubt Norfolk was the original habitat of the family.

1597. Robert Claphamson, vicar of Hannworth, co. Norf. : FF. viii. 131.
1637. John Claphamson, rector of Castor, co. Norf. : ibid. xi. 213.
1690. Samuel Claphamson, Norwich : ibid. iv. 333.
Philadelphia, 0, 4.

Clapp, Clapson, Clapison.— —Bapt. 'the son of Clap' or 'Clop.' 'An early Danish surname. Osgod Clapa was a Danish noble at the court of Canute. From him it is supposed that Clapham, co. Surrey, where he had a country house, derives its name' (Lower, quoting Ferguson). As Mr. Lower adds, no doubt such surnames as Clapp and Clapson, and such local names as Clapton, Clapham, Clapcote, Clapperton, and Clapshaw, get their parentage from some early Clap.

Agnes Clappe, co. Oxf., 1273. A.
Henry Clappe, co. Oxf., ibid.
Thomas Clobbe, co. Camb., ibid.
John Clappe, 1514 : Reg. Univ. Oxf. i. 92.
1805. Married — William Danes and Ruth Clapp : St. Geo. Han. Sq. ii. 335.
London, 5, 1, 0; MDB. (East Rid. Yorks), 0, 0, 2; (co. Linc.), 0, 1, 0; Boston (U.S.), 100, 0, 0.

Clapton, Clapperton.—Loc. (1) 'of Clapton,' parishes in cos. Cambridge, Gloucester, Middlesex, Northampton, and Somerset; (2) 'of Clopton,' in co. Suffolk, four miles from Woodbridge. Clapperton is an amplification; cf. Greenaway and Ottoway for Greenway and Otway. The origin is plainly the *town* of Clap or Clop; v. Clapham and Clapp.

Thomas de Clopton, co. Norf., 1358 : FF. viii. 123.

Geoffrey de Cloptone, co. Soms., 1 Edw. III : Kirby's Quest, p. 141.
Juliana de Clopton, co. Camb., 1273. A.
William de Cloptone, co. Hunts, ibid.
John de Clopton, London, ibid.

Both Clapton and Clopton are found applied to the same person :

1638. Rowse Clapton, rector of Garveston, co. Norf. : FF. x. 221.
— Rouse Clopton, rector of Whinburg, co. Norf. : ibid. 273.
1682. Bapt. — William, s. William Clopton : St. Dionis Backchurch, p. 125.
1789. Married—George Clapperton and Eliz. Plant : St. Geo. Han. Sq. i. 32.
London, 4, 3; Philadelphia, 1, 0.

Clarabut.—Bapt.; v. Claringbold.

Clare.—(1) Bapt. 'the son of Clare'; cf. Sinclair.

'No, quod he, by saint Clare.'
    Chaucer, H. of F. 557.
Alan fil. Clare, co. Camb. 1273. A.
Isabella Clare, 1379 : P. T. Yorks. p. 34.
Clara Dey, 1379 : ibid. p. 90.
Clare Schepard, 1379 : ibid. p. 44.
1603. Married — John Standen and Clare Aurriance : St. Jas. Clerkenwell, iii. 27.
1775. — George Finch and Clare Fraine : St. Geo. Han. Sq. i. 258.

(2) Local, 'of Clare,' i. e. Clare Castle, in co. Suffolk. Richard de Clare (d. 1090 ?) held no less than ninety-five lordships in Suffolk, all attached to his chief lordship of Clare in the same county (Dict. Nat. Biog. x. 389). Lower, quoting Dr. Donaldson (Cambridge Essays, p. 60), says that to this family we owe the name of an English town, an Irish county, royal dukedom (Clarence), and a Cambridge college (Patr. Brit. p. 61). If by the town Clare Castle is referred to, surely this is a mistake. The family took their name from the place, not the place its name from the family.

Bogo de Clare, co. Oxf., 1273. A.
Gilbert de Clare, co. Bedf., ibid.
Richard de Clare, co. Soms., ibid.
Thomas de Clare, co. Linc., ibid.
William de Clare, co. Norf., ibid.
London, 24 ; Philadelphia, 30.

Claret.—Bapt. 'the son of Clare,' from dim. Clarot and Claret. Fr. Claire ; v. Clare.

Magota Claret, 1379 : P. T. Yorks. p. 81.

Willelmus Clarot, 1379 : ibid. p. 83.
London, 3 ; New York, 1.

Clarice, Claris, Clares.— Bapt. 'the son of Clarice.' Once popular in England as a girl-name, a French form of Clara ; v. Claridge.

'Clarice of Cokkeslane,
   And the clerk of the chirche.'
    Vision of Piers Plowman, 3113.
'Tho spak Clarice to Blauncheflour.'
Floriz and Blauncheflour, E. E. T. Soc.
Claricia la Braceresse, co. Suffolk, 1273. A.
Alan fil. Clarice, co. Camb., ibid.
John Clarice, co. Bedf., ibid.
Richard Clarisse, co. Oxf, ibid.
Claricia Crowe, co. Suffolk, ibid.
Henry Clarisse, C. R., 15 Edw. III. pt. iii.
William Claricesone, co. Soms., 1 Edw. III : Kirby's Quest, p. 90.
Clariscia de Keltemerthorp, 1379 : P. T. Yorks. p. 88.
1566-7. Arthur Browghe and Allice Clarrys : Marriage Lic. (London), i. 35.
London, 0, 1, 0 ; MDB. (co. Kent), 0, 2, 0 ; Philadelphia, 0, 0, 2.

Claridge, Clardge, Clarridge.—Bapt. 'the son of Clarice.' This derivation may be looked upon as satisfactory. Clarice was an extremely popular girl's name, and Aldridge, Surridge, &c., are formed on similar lines (v. Clarice). Since writing the above, my supposition is proved correct by two entries in the Hundred Rolls, obviously referring to the same individual :

Henry serviens Claricie, co. Camb., 1273 : A. vol. ii. p. 444.
Henry serviens Clarugge, co. Camb. : ibid. p. 438.
1788. Married—William Claridge and Louisa Careless : St. Geo. Han. Sq. ii. 14.
1793. — Robert Lees and Ann Clarriage : ibid. ii. 94.
1800. — John Inwood and Mary Ann Clarige : ibid. 214.
London, 7, 0, 0 ; MDB. (co. Oxford), 3, 1, 0 ; Boston (U.S.), 1, 0, 2 ; Philadelphia, 3, 0, 0.

Claringbold, Clarabut.— Bapt. 'the son of Clerebold' (Domesday, Clarebold, co. Suff.). This, like all other names with suffix -*bold* or -*bald*, became Clerebaud, then Clerebut or Clarabut.

Roger Clerebaud, co. Salop, 1273. A.
Clerebald le Burdel, ibid.
Willelmus fil. Clerenbald, 6 Hen. II : Whitaker's Craven, p. 296.
'Subscription to Restoration of Peterborough Cathedral, Miss Gibson, per

Mr. Clarabut': Standard, Aug. 27, 1888, p. 7.

This surname seems to have troubled the registrar:

1711. Thomas Claringbold, married: Reg. Canterbury Cath. p. 70.

1735. Elizabeth Clarabutt, married: ibid. p. 80.

1736. Elizabeth Claringbull, married: ibid. p. 81.

Probably this family are descended from William Cleribaud, co. Kent, 1273. A. Cf.—

'The following twenty-four persons were admitted masters for the Dutch— John Powells, . . . John Mynchelles, . . . Pascall Clarebote.' Norwich, 1565: FF. iii. 283.

'Mr. H. N. Claringbold was third mate of the emigrant vessel Kapunda, lost in a collision off the coast of Brazil': Manchester Guardian, Feb. 1, 1887.

'The Rev. E. B. Clarabut, B.A., licensed to St. Michael and All Angels, Walthamstow': Manchester Courier, May 17, 1888. London, 2, 0.

Claris; v. Clarice.

Clark, Clarke; v. Clerk.

Clarkson.—Nick. 'the clerk's son,' i.e. the clergyman's son. A well-known Yorkshire surname, which has spread over the North of England; cf. Wrightson, Smithson, Taylorson, Herdson, &c. Of course it was common to all the country.

Helias fil. Clerici, co. Hunts, 1273. A. Henry fil. Clerici, co. Suff., ibid. Johannes Clerke and Thomas Clerkson, father and son, 1379: P. T. Yorks. p. 273. Ricardus Clerkson, 1379: P. T. Yorks. p. 165. Willelmus Klercson, 1379: ibid. Alicia Clerkson, 1379: ibid. p. 22. 1592. John Clarkson, vicar of Burnham Overey, co. Norf.: FF. vii. 28. 1672. Bapt.—Anne, d. John Clarkeson: St. Jas. Clerkenwell, i. 254. 1793. Married—David Clarkson and Eleanor Cadday: St. Geo. Han. Sq. ii. 100. West Rid. Court Dir., 14; London, 16; Manchester, 13; Boston (U.S.), 9.

Clatworthy.—Local, 'of Clatworthy'; v. Worth and Worthy, and cf. Langworthy, Kenworthy, &c.

John Cloteworthy, co. Soms., 1 Edw. III: Kirby's Quest, p. 278. 1680. Symon Clatworthy and Ellenor Thomas: Marriage Alleg. (Canterbury), p. 129. 1683. John Brooking and Eliz. Clotworthy: ibid. p. 42. MDB. (co. Soms.), 5; New York, 3.

Claughton.—Local, 'of Claughton,' parishes in Cheshire and North Lanc. Also Claughton, a spot that gave rise to a local family in the parish of Garstang, co. Lanc. The 'village by the clough' is, no doubt, the meaning of the word, so far as relates to Claughton in North Lancashire (Baines' Lanc. ii. 610). The others will be similarly derived.

Radulphus de Claghton, 1379: P. T. Yorks. p. 274. Henry de Claghton, 1397: Preston Guild Rolls, p. 5. 1804. Married—Shem Hearnden and Peggy Claughton: St. Geo. Han. Sq. ii. 310. Crockford, 3; London, 0.

Claver; v. Cleaver.

Clavinger, Clemenger. — Official, 'the clavinger,' i.e. the mace-bearer; Latin, claviger, a clubbearer. Clavinger for Claviger follows the rule; cf. messenger for passager; v. Cleaver for history of the word. I cannot help thinking Clemenger is a corruption.

Robert Clavynger. H. Crockford, 0, 1.

Claxton.—Local, (1) 'of Claxton,' a parish in co. Norfolk; (2) 'of Claxton,' an ancient manor adjoining Greatham, co. Durham.

Roger de Claxton, co. Durham, 1272: DDD. iii. 142. Leo de Claxton, co. Durham, 1335: ibid. Keyse de Claxtune, co. Norf., 1273. A. Robert de Clakston, co. Durham, 1380: QQQ. p. 109. 1574. John Stubbes and Eliz. Claxton: Marriage Lic. (London), i. 59. 1688. Bapt.—Mary, d. Walter Clackston: St. Jas. Clerkenwell, i. 329. London, 9; Boston (U.S.), 5.

Clay.—Local, 'at the clay,' from residence by a clayey spot. The instances below are decisive in respect of this derivation.

Alicia in le Clay, co. Hunts, 1273. A. William del Cley, co. Linc., ibid. Robert del Clay, co. Linc., ibid. Henry atte Cleygh, co. Soms., 1 Edw. III: Kirby's Quest, p. 86. Agnes del Clay, 1379: P. T. Yorks. p. 20. Johannes del Clay, 1379: ibid. p. 3. Adam del Clay, 1379: P. T. Howdenshire, p. 20. 1577. Bapt.—Thomas, s. Edward Claye: St. Jas. Clerkenwell, i. 10.

1583. William Mitchell and Eliz. Claye, widow: Marriage Lic. (London), i. 121. 1592. Married — William Jones and Anne Claye, widow: St. Peter, Cornhill, p. 238. London, 21; West Rid. Court Dir., 21; MDB. (co. Lincoln), 8; New York, 13.

Clayer.—Occup. 'the clayer,' a dauber or plasterer. Cf. 'cleymanne, a dauber': Prompt. Parv. (Halliwell).

Simon le Clayere, co. Camb., 1273. A.

Claypole, Claypool, Claypoole.—Local, 'of Claypole,' a parish in co. Lincoln, five miles from Newark.

William de Claypol, co. Linc., 1273. A. Geoffrey de Cleipol, co. Linc., Hen. III-Edw. I. K. William Claypole, vicar of Wyken, co. Norf., 1388: FF. viii. 339. 1615. Married — William Cleypoole and Anne Powell: St. Jas. Clerkenwell, iii. 42. 1764. — James Beer and Ann Claypole: St. Geo. Han. Sq. i. 132. MDB. (co. Lincoln), 2, 0, 0; Philadelphia, 2, 6, 4.

Clayson, Clauson, Claussen, Claussen, Clawson.—Bapt. 'the son of Klaus,' i.e. Nicholas; German Klaus, Dutch Klasse. The name was very rare in England, where Cole and Colin ruled supreme as the nicks. of Nicholas. Doubtless the name occasionally stole over from the Low Countries.

Clays le Taburer (minstrel to the king): Wardrobe Accounts, 3 Edw. III. 33/10. Henry Clayson, C. R., Hen. IV. 1797. Married — Samuel Clayson and Jane Parker: St. Geo. Han. Sq. ii. 168. London, 2, 1, 1, 1, 0; New York, 0, 3, 0, 6, 9.

Clayton.—Local, 'of Clayton.' This would naturally be a very common place-name, and apart from small spots, farms, manors, &c., so entitled, we have parishes, hamlets, liberties, and townships in cos. Stafford (2), Sussex, York (West Riding) (4), Lancaster (3). The surname is very strongly represented in the United States.

Sewal de Claton, co. Herts, 1273. A. Hamo de Cleyton, co. Bucks, ibid. William de Cletone, co. Salop, ibid. Henry de Claytone, co. Lanc., 20 Edw. I. R. Robert de Cleyton, co. Lanc., Hen. III-Edw. I. K. Willelmus de Clayton, of Clayton, 1379: P. T. Yorks. p. 12.

Sara de Clayton, 1379 : P.T.Yorks. p. 12.
Johannes de Clayton, 1379 : ibid.
p. 149.
1570. Arthur Bourchyer and Katherine Clayton : Marriage Lic. (London), i. 45.
1641. Buried—Ann,d. Richard Cleaton: St. Peter, Cornhill, p. 198.
London, 40 ; West Rid. Court Dir., 23 ; Manchester, 32 ; Philadelphia, 101.

Clayvill, Clayville.—Local, 'de Clayville,' of French extraction. In the London Directory are found both Clavel and Clavelle, the personal names and general entry showing that they are an importation. But the surname is found at an early period in England. Mr. Lower says, 'Walter de Clavile was a tenant-in-chief in Dorset and Devon at Domesday' (Patr. Brit. p. 61).

John de Clavile or Claville, co. Devon, 20 Edw. I. R.
William de Clavyle, co. Dorset, ibid. Philadelphia, 2, 4.

Cleangrice, Cleanhog.— Nick. 'clean hog,' evidently but a half compliment ; v. Grice.

Roger Clenegris, co. Notts, 1273. A.
William Clenehog, co. Bedf., ibid.

Cleasby, Clisby, Clisbee.— —Local, 'of Cleasby,' a parish near Darlington, N. Rid. Yorks. Clisby is a variant, but like such variants is found far away from home. In its own district it is correctly Cleasby.

William de Cleseby, co. Linc., 1273. A.
Johannes de Clesbe, 1379 : P. T. Yorks. p. 79.
1587. Philip Cleysbye and Anne Wood: Marriage Lic. (London), i. 164.
1784. Married — William Clisby and Jane Clements : St. Geo. Han. Sq. i. 366.
London, 3, 9, 0 ; MDB. (North Rid. Yorks), 11, 0, 0 ; Boston (U.S.), 0, 2, 1.

Cleather.—Local, 'of Clether,' a parish seven miles from Camelford, co. Cornwall.

1604. Married — John Marriot and Katharine Cletar : St. Michael, Cornhill, p. 17.
1684-5. George Cleeter and Ann Rogers : Marriage Lic. (Faculty Office), p. 155.
London, 1 ; MDB. (co. Wilts), 2.

Cleave ; v. Clive.

Cleaver, Claver.—Offic. 'the cleaver,' i. e. mace-bearer. 'Clavia, a mace or club, as *Serjeantia Claviae* is the Serjeancy of the Mace' (Bailey). In a treaty agreed upon between the Mayor, Sheriffs, and Commonalty of Norwich in 1414, it was declared that 'the Mayor and twenty-four shall choose a common clerk, a coroner, two clavers, and eight constables ; and the sixty common council shall choose a common speaker, one coroner, two clavers, and eight constables' ; v. Bromefield's Norfolk. Without doubt Cleaver is a corruption of Claver.

Simon le Claver, co. Norf., 1273. A.
Agnes le Claver, co. Norf., 1332 : FF. iv. 405.
John le Claver, co. Norf., 1332 : ibid.
Walter le Claver, rector of All Saints, Norwich : ibid. 130.
Henry le Claver. E.
John le Clavier. BB.
John Cleaver, rector of South Creak, co. Norf., 1669 : FF. vii. 83.
William Cleaver. V. 6.
1652. Bapt.—John, s. Samuell Cleaver : St. Jas. Clerkenwell, i. 181.
1790. Married—Edward Cleaver and Sarah Dow : St. Geo. Han. Sq. ii. 40.
Crockford, 2, 0 ; London, 11, 0 ; MDB. (East Rid. Yorks), 0, 1 ; Philadelphia, 15, 2.

Clegg.—Local, 'of Clegg,' a North-English surname. No doubt a form of Clough, a break in the hillside. Almost all our Cleggs hail from Clegg, or Clegg Hall, in the parish of Rochdale.

Barnulf de Clegg (without date).
Nicholas de Clegg, 1260 : Baines' Lanc. i. 506.
Mathew de Clegg, 1260 : ibid.
Ricardus de Cleghe, 1379 : P. T. Yorks. p. 283.
Henricus de Cloghe, 1379 : ibid.
Thomas Clegg, *tanner*, co. of Middleton, co. Lanc., 1581 : Wills at Chester (1545-1620), p. 41.
Arthur Clegg, of Fieldhouse, parish of Rochdale, 1608 : ibid.
1788. Married—William Robert Clegg and Ann Thomas : St. Geo. Han. Sq. ii. 1.
London, 6 ; Manchester, 40 ; West Rid. Court Dir., 10 ; Philadelphia, 52.

Cleghorn.—Local, 'of Cleghorn,' 'a place in co. Lanark' (Lower).

1738. Married — David Cleghorn and Margaret Bentley : St. Geo. Han. Sq. i. 20.
1749. — James Cleghorn and Eliz. Pearson : St. Geo. Chap. Mayfair, p. 143.
London, 6 ; New York, 1.

Cleland, Clelland.—Personal, 'the son of Cleland,' a Scotch surname. Mr. Lower says the family were 'of that Ilk' in co. Lanark in the time of Alexander III (Patr. Brit. p. 61). The London Directory has such forms as M'Leland, M'Lellan, MacLellan, McLellan, Maclellan, and McLelland. I have inserted Cleland and Clelland here as they have an English local appearance.

1748-9. John Cleland and Jane Strudwick : Marriage Lic. (Faculty Office), p. 255.
1800. Married — More Cleland and Lydia Capper : St. Geo. Han. Sq. ii. 225.
London, 3, 0 ; Philadelphia, 1, 1 ; New York, 3, 0.

Clem, Clemie.—Bapt. 'the son of Clement,' from nick. Clem, popularly Clemie. The old song of the 'Green-gown' mentions

'Clem, Joan, and Isabel,
Sue, Alice, and bonny Nell,'

where it is obvious that Clem is feminine, representing the early Clemence.

'William Buckton, Clem Muschaunce, and others of the garrison of Berwick ' (on Tweed), 1544 : TTT. p. lx.
1608. Married — Henrie Clem and Catherine Hackerley : St. Jas. Clerkenwell, iii. 133.
London, 0, 1 ; New York, 1, 0 ; Philadelphia, 2, 0 ; Boston (U.S.), 2, 0.

Clement, Clementson, Clemans, Clemens, Clemence, Clements, Clemie, Clemitson, Clemmans, Clemments, Clemmison, Clemmits, Clemson, Clemenson.—Bapt. 'the son of Clement' or 'Clemence,' nick. Clem, dim. Clem-et, now Clemmit. Common to both sexes (cf. Constant and Constance). Clement is a rare font-name in the 19th century. It was enormously popular in the 13th. Hence as a surname itself and its variants will be immortalized in our directories.

Eustace fil. Clement, co. Oxf., 1273. A.
Hugh Clement, co. Camb., ibid.
Richard Clemence, co. Hunts, ibid.
Matthew Clemens, co. Oxf., ibid.
Peter fil. Clem', co. Salop, ibid.
Clemens Janitor, co. Norf., ibid.
Clemens filius Elenoe, 1379 : P. T. Yorks. p. 21.
Johannes Clement, 1379 : ibid. p. 76.
Petrus Clementson, 1379 : ibid. p. 296.
Robert Clement, 1468. W. 11.
Roger Clempson, temp. Eliz. Z.

Clemie Croser, 1581: Nicolson and Burn, Hist. Westm. and Cumb. i. p. xxx.
Johannes de Wode, et Clemens uxor ejus. 1379: P. T. Yorks. p. 80.
Clemence Darbishire, parish of Winwick, co. Lanc., 1596: Wills at Chester (1545-1620), p. 50.
London, 14, 2, 1, 1, 4, 49, 1, 1, 1, 1, 1, 1, 0, 0; March Dir., Clemson, 1, Clemenson, 2; Philadelphia, 44, 2, 0, 12, 1, 44, 0, 0, 0, 1, 0, 0, 3, 1.

Clemmow, Clemow, Clyma, Clymo, Clemo, Clamo.—Bapt.

'the son of Clement.' In Cornwall once popularly Clemow; cf. Cornish Pascho for Paschal.

Remfrey, son of John Clemmowe, 1544: Reg. St. Columb Major, p. 3.
Elizabeth, d. of John Clemowe, 1550: ibid. p. 5.

In other entries members of the same family are entered Clemens.

London, 0, 2, 0, 0, 0, 0; Cornwall Court Dir., 0, 0, 5, 3, 0, 0; Cornwall Dir. (Farmers' List, 1, 1, 4, 2, 0, 1, 1.

Clench, Clinch, Clynch.—

Local, 'at the clench,' a local term of which I have not discovered the origin.

John de la Clenche, co. Wilts, 1273. A.
Seman Clenche, co. Suff., ibid.
Richard Clenche, co. Suff., ibid.
1582. William Stickney and Dorothy Clenche: Marriage Lic. (London), i. 108.
1584. John Clenche, co. Norf.: FF. v. 24.
— Ambrose Clench, co. Norf.: ibid. ii. 297.
1593. Edward Hill and Margaret Clinche: Marriage Lic. (London), i. 207.
London, 2, 4, 0; Philadelphia, 0, 3, 0; Boston (U.S.), 0, 4, 1.

Clendening, Clendenning, Clendenon, Clendaniel (?).—

Local. American variants of Glendinning, q.v. The change from initial G to C has ever been common in nomenclature (v. Cammel). Clendaniel seems to be a further corruption.

Philadelphia, 2, 9, 4, 2.

Clerk, Clerke, Clark, Clarke.

—Offic. 'the clerk,' i.e. the clergyman, a clerk in holy orders. M.E. *clerk*, a priest. The surname is now almost universally Clark and Clarke, the professional form adhering to *clerk*; cf. the silent agreement between *tailor* and Taylor. If Clark and Clarke be considered

as one name, they stand ninth among the commonest surnames to be found in England.

Boniface Clericus, co. Linc., 1273. A.
Thomas le Clerk, co. Linc., ibid.
Batekyn Clericus, co. Essex, ibid.
Gilbert le Clerk. co. Oxf., ibid.
Thomas le Clerck, co. Bucks, ibid.
John le Clerck, co. Bedf., 20 Edw. I. R.
Robertus Clarke, 1379: P. T. Yorks. p. 95.
Beatrix Clerc, *wyf*, 1379: ibid. p. 58.
Henricus Clerk, 1379: ibid. p. 81.
Robertus Clerk' et Johanna uxor ejus, 1379: ibid. p. 82.
Agnes Clerk, *doghter*, 1379: ibid.p. 158.
1557. Married — Robert Clarke and Margaret Mayson: St. Dionis Backchurch, p. 3.
1583. Bapt. — Richarde, s. Rumboll Clerke: St. Jas. Clerkenwell, i. 14.
London, 3, 1, 323, 239; Boston (U.S.), 1, 1, 684, 118.

Cleve; v. Clive.

Cleveland, Cleaveland.—

Local, 'of Cleveland,' a hamlet in the parish of Ormesby, co. York.

Johannes de Clyveland, 1379: P. T. Yorks. p. 51.
Robertus de Clyveland, 1379: ibid. p. 46.
1575. Richard Cleveland and Alice Lane: Marriage Lic. (London), i. 66.
1802. Married — Thomas Vickery and Jane Cleaveland: St. Geo. Han. Sq. ii. 256.
London, 4, 0; Boston (U.S.), 20, 6.

Cleveley, Clevely, Cleverly.

—Local, 'of Cleveley,' a hamlet in the parish of Church Enstone, co. Oxf. Cleverly is a manifest variant.

John de Clyveleye, co. Oxf., 1273. A.
1611. Married— Richard Clevelley and Eliz. Adkins: St. Jas. Clerkenwell, iii. 38.
1786. — John Gutteridge and Eliz. Cleveley: St. Geo. Han. Sq. i. 390.
1787. — Charles Cleverly and Jenny Hutchins: ibid. i. 406.
London, 1, 1, 3; Philadelphia, 0, 0, 3.

Clewes.—Local; v. Clow.

Clewley, Clewlow, Clulee, Clulow, Cluley, Cluelow.—

Local, 'of Clulow,' a locality in the township of Wincle, parish of Prestbury, co. Cheshire. From Clulow Cross there is said to be a fine view over parts of Staffordshire and Cheshire. The surname has crossed the border and is well known in the former county.

1615. Married — Ralph Horderne and Anne Cluley: Reg. Prestbury Ch., co. Chester, p. 206.
1617. — Robert Millington and Ellen Cluley: ibid. p. 214.

1625. Married — John Clulo and Ann Hult: St. Mary Aldermary, p. 15.
1633. — George Davis and Bridgett Clulye: St. Jas. Clerkenwell, iii. 64.
1648. — John Paine and Eliz. Clewly: ibid. p. 82.
1727. — Thomas Cluley and Eliz. Wilks: St. Geo. Han. Sq. i. 4.
1804. John Clulow, town clerk of Macclesfield: Earwaker's East Cheshire, ii. 468.
'William Benton Clulow (1802-82), dissenting minister, was a native of Leek, Staffordshire': Dict. Nat. Biog. xi. 136.
MDB. (co. Stafford), 2, 1, 1, 4, 0, 0; London, 3, 1, 0, 0, 1, 0; Philadelphia, 1, 0, 0, 0, 5, 1.

Cleworth, Clewarth.—Local,

'of Cleworth,' some spot in South Lancashire. For the suffix, v. Worth.

Richard de Cl: worthe, of Hulton, co. Lanc., 1332: Lay Subsidy (Rylands), p. 39.
Robert Cleworth, of Astley, 1671: Wills at Chester (1660-80), p. 59.
Richard Cleworth, of Bedford, co. Lanc., 1672: ibid.
Ralph Cleeworth of Risley, co. Lanc., *husbandman*, 1730: ibid. (1721-40), p. 56.
Liverpool, 2, 0; Bolton, 1, 1; Philadelphia, 3, 0.

Clibbon, Cliburn; v. Clabon.

Clicoter.—? Nick. 'a chattering woman,' one who clickets. 'Her that will clicket' (Tusser, p. 251). 'A tatling huswife, whose clicket is ever wagging' (Cotgrave); v. Halliwell.

Magota Clicoter, 1379: P. T. Yorks. p. 45.

Cliff, Cliffe, Cleff.—Local, 'at the cliff,' a precipitous rock, a headland. M.E. *clif*, *clef*; v. Clive.

Robert de la Clif, co. York, 1273. A.
Thomas del Clif, co. Suff., ibid.
Johannes del Clife, 1379: P. T. Yorks. p. 16.
Thomas del Clyf', 1379: ibid. p. 29.
1566. Bapt.—Richard, s. Robert Cliffe: St. Jas. Clerkenwell, i. 10.
1639. John Cary and Judith Cliffe: Marriage Lic. (London), ii. 245.
London, 1, 3, 1; West Rid. Court Dir., 7, 9, 0; Boston (U.S.), 4, 3, 0.

Clifford.—Local, 'of Clifford,' parishes in diocs. of Hereford, and Glouc. and Bristol; also a township in the parish of Bramham, near Leeds, co. York.

Margaret de Clifford, co. Oxf., 1273. A.
Roger de Clifford, co. Wilts, ibid.
John de Clyfford, co. Glouc., ibid.

Johannes de Clyfford, 1379: P. T.
Yorks. p. 153.
Isabella de Clyfforth, 1379: ibid. p. 199.
1566. Bapt.—Edward, s. John Clifford:
St. Jas. Clerkenwell, i. 4.
1616. Matthias Clifford and Jane
Tibballs: Marriage Lic. (London), ii. 41.
London, 36; Sheffield, 1; Boston
(U.S.), 94.

Clifton.—Local, 'of Clifton,'
parishes in diocs. of Carlisle, Ely,
Glouc. and Bristol, Manchester, Oxford, Ripon, Southwell, York, &c.

Gilbert de Clifton, co. York, 1273. A.
Peter de Clifton, co. York, ibid.
Robert de Clifton, co. Oxf., ibid.
Richard de Clifton, co. Oxf., ibid.
Johannes de Clyfton, 1379: P. T.
Yorks. p. 50.
Willelmus de Clifton, 1379: ibid. p. 219.
1586. Buried—Eliz. Clifton: St. Peter,
Cornhill, i. 134.
1624. — Henry, s. Henry Clifton: St.
Jas. Clerkenwell, iv. 165.
London, 11; Philadelphia, 41.

Climpson.—Bapt. 'the son of
Clement,' a corruption of Clemson
(s.v. Clement). The *p* is intrusive
as in Simpson or Thompson. Clim
was an early variant of Clem, the
nick. of Clement. ' Clim, for Clement. Forby gives the name to a
kind of nursery goblin' (Halliwell).
'Then spake the good yeman Clym of
the Clough,
And swore by Mary free.'
A Lytell Geste of Robin Hode, ii. 328.
1576-7. John Clympson and Bridget
Coxwood: Marriage Lic. (London), i. 74.
1776. Married — William East and
Martha Climson: St. Geo. Han. Sq. i. 260.
1787. — Thomas Climenson and Molly
Jones: ibid. p. 409.
London, 3.

**Clinkscales, Clinkscale,
Clinkskel, Clinkskill.**—Local.
The last two only are in the London
Directory, but the others exist.
Mr. Lower, I see, has them in his
list.

Clint. — Local, 'of Clint,' a
township in the parish of Ripley,
W. Rid. Yorks. The surname
has never been common, but it
has managed to survive at least
five centuries.

Cecilia de Clynt, 1379: P. T. Yorks.
p. 210.
Alicia de Clynt, 1379: ibid.
Johannes Clynt, 1379: ibid. p. 227.
1632. William Clente and Joane Prince:
Marriage Lic. (London), ii. 208.

1783. Married — Timothy Clint and
Mary Davies: St. Geo. Han. Sq. i. 342.
London, 1; MDB. (E. R. Yorks), 1.

Clinton.—Local, ' of Glinton,'
a parish in co. Northampton, three
miles from Market Deeping. The
change from initial G to C is common in nomenclature; v. Crane,
Caunter, Candlin, Clendinning.
Mr. Lower says the Duke of Newcastle's surname is derived from
Glimpton, an estate in co. Oxford,
in early times styled and written
Clinton (v. Patr. Brit. p. 62). If
this be so, Glimpton will probably
be the parent of all.

Ivo de Clynton, co. Salop, 20 Edw. I. R.
William de Clynton, co. Derby, ibid.
Geoffrey de Clinton, co Glouc., 1273. A.
Henry de Clinton, co. York, ibid.
Thomas de Clinton, co. Bucks, ibid.
1674. John Green and Anne Clinton:
Marriage Alleg. (Canterbury), p. 228.
1683. Married—Richard Clinton and
Mary Gray: St. Jas. Clerkenwell, i. 199.
London, 4; Boston (U.S.), 27.

Clipsby.—Local, 'of Clippesby,'
a parish in co. Norfolk, three miles
from Acle.

1389. Henry Waggestaff, rector of
Clippesby, presented by Edmund de
Clipesby: FF. xi. 163.
1507. John Owdolf, rector of Clippesby,
presented by John Clippesby: ibid.
1598. Ranulph Crewe and Julian
Clipsbie (co. Norfolk): Marriage Lic.
(London), i. 252.
London, 0.

Clisbee, Clisby; v. Cleasby.

**Clithero, Clitherow, Clu-
deray.**—Local, ' of Clitheroe,' a
market-town in co. Lanc. on the
Ribble. In old English documents Clithero is written Clyde-
row. A curious relic of this is
the surname of Cluderay in the
Bradford and Leeds district.

Adam de Cliderhou, co. Lanc., 1332:
Lay Subsidy (Rylands), p. 79.
Robert de Clyderhou, co. Lanc., 1332:
ibid. p. 73.
Robert de Cliderhow, 1316, rector of
Gargrave in Craven: Whitaker, p. 231.
Johannes de Clyderowe, 1379: P. T.
Yorks. p. 112.
Johannes Cledrow, 1379: P. T. Howden-
shire, p. 13.
1545. George Colcell and Sens Clithero:
Marriage Lic. (Faculty Office), p. 5.
1661. James Clitherow and Mary
Gregory, ibid. p. 55.
London, 1, 1, 0; Bradford, 0, 0, 2;
Leeds, 0, 0, 5.

Clive, Cleeve, Cleave, Cleve.
—Local, 'at the clive.' The same
as Cliff (q.v.); M.E. *cleve* = cliff.

John atte Cliue (*u* for *v*), co. Soms.,
1 Edw. III: Kirby's Quest, p. 81.
Gilbert de la Clive, co. Devon, 1273. A.
Humfrey de la Clive, co. Wilts, ibid.
Henry de la Clyve, co. Somerset, ibid.
William atte Clive, 1301. M.
Agnes del Clife, 1379: P. T. Yorks. p. 3.
John Clyffe, or Clyve, 1510: Reg.
Univ. Oxf. i. 68.
Richard Clyve, abbot of Cirencester,
co. Glouc., 1482: Atkyns' Hist. Glouc.
p. 178.
1639. Richard Clive and Mary Alleyne:
Marriage Lic. (London), ii. 243.
1690. Alexander Cleeve and Mary
Duffield: ibid. p. 312.
London, 1, 0, 3, 1; MDB. (co. Glouc.),
0, 0, 0, 1; Boston (U.S.), 1, 0, 0, 2.

Clixby.—Local, 'of Clixby,' a
chapelry in the parish of Caistor,
co. Lincoln. Probably Clisby also
represents the name; v. Cleasby.

1688. James Hastings and Isabella
Clisbey: Marriage Lic. (Faculty Office),
p. 190.
MDB. (co. Lincoln), 5.

Close, Closs, Clos.—Local, 'at
the close'—O.F. *clos*, an enclosed
space (whence dim. *closet*)—from
residence therein. Not to be confounded with Clowes, which has
a different origin.

Johannes del Clos, 1379: P. T. Yorks.
p. 254.
Willelmus del Clos, 1379: ibid.
1545. Bapt.—John Close: St. Dionis
Backchurch, p. 181.

The following entry is curious:

1697. Bapt.—Picken Close, a foundling
att Picken's Coffee house dore: St. Jas.
Clerkenwell, i. 373.
London, 2, 1, 0; Sheffield, 3, 0, 0;
West Rid. Court Dir., 2, 0, 0; New
York, 18, 1, 2.

Clothier.—Occup. 'the clothier,'
a cloth-weaver or a dealer in cloth,
a draper.

' As clotheres kemben hir wolle.'
Piers P. 5631.
Cf. Robert Clothman, C. R., 2 Edw. IV.
1626. Nicholas Clothyer and Anne
Nelson: Marriage Lic. (London), ii. 171.
1582. Buried — Mary Clothyer: St.
Dionis Backchurch, p. 197.
London, 6; MDB. (co. Somerset), 9;
Philadelphia, 39.

Cloud.—Local, 'at the cloud,'
from residence thereby; 'cloude, a
clod' (Ritson, quoted by Halliwell).

Probably my instance infra refers to some prominent mound of earth.

Robert atte Cloude, co. Soms., 1 Edw. III : Kirby's Quest, p. 137.

Richard Clode, co. Soms., 1 Edw. III : ibid. p. 191.

1751. Married—Thomas Granbum and Rachael Cloud : St. Geo. Chap. Mayfair, p. 204.

1770. — George Boxall and Elinor Cloud : St. Geo. Han. Sq. i. 196.

London, 1 ; Philadelphia, 23.

Clough, Cluff.—Local, 'at the clough,' from residence thereby. A clough is a breach in the hillside, a ravine between hills. 'Boggart Hole Clough' is well known to Manchester people ; v. Clow.

'Had we the keys, said Clim oſ the Clough,
Ryght wel then shoulde we spede.'
A Lytell Geste of Robin Hode, ii. 329.

Alicia del Clogh, co. Lanc., 1332 : Lay Subsidy (Rylands), p. 86.

Robert del Clogh, co. Lanc., 1332 : ibid. p. 50.

Thomas del Clogh, 1379 : P. T. Yorks. p. 68.

Henricus de Cloghe, 1376 : ibid. p. 42.

1688. Buried—Mary Clough, grand-niece to Dr. Meriton : St. Michael, Cornhill, p. 271.

1690. Bapt. — William, s. Thomas Clugh : St. Jas. Clerkenwell, i. 339.

London, 2, 2 ; West Rid. Court Dir., 34, 0 ; Philadelphia, 2, 14.

Clow, Clowe, Clowes, Clewes, Clews. — Local, 'at the clough,' q.v. North Eng. *clow* ; cf. *enough* and *enow*. With the patronymic Clowes, cf. Brooks for Brook, Sykes for Syke, Holmes for Holme, Styles for Style, &c. No doubt it is the genitival form, as in Williams, Jones, Jennings, &c. M.E. *clow*, or *clough*. 'Sende him to seche in clif and clow': Cursor Mundi, Trin. MS., l. 17590 (v. Clough, Skeat's Dict.).

Willelmus de Clowe, 1379 : P. T. Yorks. p. 181.

Edward Clowes, of Northwich, *husbandman*, 1649 : Wills at Chester (1621-50), p. 50.

Richard Clowes, of Whiteley, *yeoman*, 1645 : ibid.

1595. William Gregory and Joan Clowes : Marriage Lic. (London), i. 222.

1725. Married — James Finch and Diana Clews : St. Geo. Han. Sq. i. 1.

London, 2, 0, 7, 0, 0 ; MDB. (co. Chester), 0, 0, 3, 1, 0 ; (co. Derbyshire), 0, 0, 2, 1, 1 ; Boston (U.S.), 1, 0, 0, 1, 3.

Clubb.—? Local. A curious name, seemingly of Cheshire origin.

Farndon, near Chester, seems to have been the habitat of the family.

Hugh Clubb, of Farndon, 1588 : Wills at Chester (1545-1620), p. 42.

John Clubb, of Holt, 1607 : ibid.

Francis Clubbe, of Farndon, 1695 : ibid. (1681-1700), p. 55.

John Clubbe, of Worthenbury, 1689 : ibid. p. 56.

1803. Married — Thomas Club and Mary Sophia Merle : St. Geo. Han. Sq. ii. 273.

London, 1 ; Manchester, 2 ; Liverpool, 1 ; Philadelphia, 1.

Cluelow, Clulee, Cluley, Clulow ; v. Clewley.

Clutterbuck. — This family settled in England from the Low Countries at the time of the Duke of Alva's persecution of the Protestants. In 1586 Thomas Cloerterbooke was sheriff of Gloucester, and from that county the existing gentry families of Clutterbuck spring (Lower's Patr. Brit. p. 63).

1585. Thomas Clutterbooke and Joanna Allen : Marriage Lic. (London), i. 141.

Jasper Cluterbuck, alderman of Gloucester, 1659 : Atkyns' Hist. Glouc. p. 99.

1654. Married — Joseph Clutterbuck and Ann Gulliford : St. Mary Aldermary, p. 24.

London, 7 ; MDB. (co. Glouc.), 20 ; New York, 1.

Clutton, Clutten.—Local, ' of Clutton,' a township in the parish of Farndon, co. Chester ; also a parish in co. Somerset. The Cheshire township is the chief parent. The variant Clutten is three centuries old.

Thomas Clutton, of Nantwich, 1575 : Wills at Chester (1545-1620), p. 42.

John Clutten, of Carden, 1595 : ibid.

Thomas Clutton, of Eaton Green, 1689 : ibid. (1681-1700), p. 56.

Urian Clutton, co. Chester, 25 Hen. VIII (1533) : Earwaker's East Cheshire, ii. 86 *n.*

Owen Clutton, co. Chester : ibid.

1793. Married—Joseph Francis Fearon and Jane Clutton : St. Geo. Han. Sq. ii. 96.

London, 6, 1 ; Manchester, 1, 0 ; MDB. (co. Lancaster), 1, 0.

Coachman ; v. Couchman.

Philadelphia, 2.

Coad, Coode. — ? Local. A Cornish surname. Both forms are found in records of the same family.

1658. Bapt.—Richard, son of Robert Code : Reg. St. Columb Major (Cornwall), p. 54.

1660. — Mary, d. of Robert Coode : ibid. p. 55.

1662. — William, son of Robert Coade : ibid p. 56.

1672-3. Thomas Coode and Eliz. Wicks : Marriage Alleg. (Canterbury), p. 87.

London, 2, 5 ; Cornwall Court Dir., 1, 6.

Coate, Coates, Coats.—Local, (1) 'at the cote' or 'cotes,' i.e. cottages ; (2) ' of Cotes,' a township in the parish of Eccleshall, co. Stafford ; also a hamlet in the parish of Prestwold, co. Leicester.

Egidius de Cotes, co. Norf., 1273. A.

Robert de Cotes, co. Bucks, ibid.

Geoffrey de Cotes, co. Linc., ibid.

Ralph atte Cote, co. Soms., 1 Edw. III : Kirby's Quest, p. 108.

Thomas del Cotes, 1379 : P. T. Yorks. p. 47.

Johannes del Cotes, 1379 : ibid. p. 14.

Henricus del Cote, 1379 : ibid. p. 214.

Willelmus atte Cotes, 1379 : P. T. Howdenshire, p. 17.

1561. Buried—Joane Coates : St. Peter, Cornhill, i. 114.

1563. — John Cotes : ibid. p. 117.

1625. William Turner and Susanna Coates : Marriage Lic. (London), ii. 158.

London, 1, 26, 3 ; West Rid. Court Dir., 0, 20, 0 ; Philadelphia, 1, 83, 7.

Cobb, Cobbe, Cobson, Copson. — Bapt. ' the son of Jacob,' from nick. Cob or Cop ; v. Coppin.

Cobbus Faber, 10 Hen. II, Pipe Roll, p. 25.

Richard Cobbe, co. Camb., 1279. A.

Robert Cobbe, co. Oxf., ibid.

Thomas Cobson, 1379 : P. T. Yorks. p. 191.

1675. Married—William Cobson and Jane Pritchett : St. Jas. Clerkenwell, p. 181.

With Copson for Cobson, cf. Hopkins for Hobkins.

1651. Bapt.—Eliz., d. Emanuell Cobson : St. Jas. Clerkenwell, i. 177.

1665-6. Buried—Amey Cobb, *widow* : St. Dionis Backchurch, p. 237.

1788. Married — George Cobb and Frances Letchford : St. Geo. Han. Sq. ii. 8.

London, 20, 0, 0, 1 ; Atherstone (co. Warwick), Copson, 1 ; MDB. (co. Warwick), Copson, 3 ; New York, 28, 1, 0, 0.

Cobbett.—(1) Bapt. ' the son of Jacob,' from the nick. Cob, dim. Cobb-et ; v. Cubitt and Coppin. (2) Bapt. ' the son of Cuthbert,' pronounced Cowbet in cos. York and Durham. Probably the North-English Cobbetts are thus derived.

Cf. Nicholas Cowbeytson, co. York. W. 9.

But (1) must be looked upon as the true general derivation.

1745. Married—Antony Montel and Sarah Cobbett : St. Geo. Chap. Mayfair, p. 50.
1770. —Thomas Warr and Jane Cobbett : St. Geo. Han. Sq. i. 303.
London, 10 ; New York, 1 ; Boston (U.S.), 1.

Cobbin, Cobbing.—Bapt. 'the son of Jacob,' from the nick. Cob, dim Cobb-in or Cobb-on ; cf. Col-in from Nicholas, Rob-in from Robert, or Gibb-on from Gilbert. But Coppin (q.v.) was the sharpened form.

Ralph Cobin, co. Essex, 1273. A.
William Cobon, co. Camb., ibid.
1773. Married—John Cobbin and Ann Brass : St. Geo. Han. Sq. i. 227.
London, 1, 1 ; Philadelphia, 3, 0.

Cobblodick, Cuppleditch.—Local, ' of Cobbledyke.' This has no reference to a dike made of cobble-stones, but to the name of the proprietor ; v. Cobbold and Kibble, where Kibel is shown to be a familiar Lincolnshire personal name.

Roger de Cubbeldik, 1313, co. Linc. M.
Alan de Cubbeldyk, 1323, ibid.
John Cobeldyke, C. R., 1 Hen. IV. pt. i.
Johannes de Cupeldik, co. Linc., 1273. A.
John de Culbeldyke, co. Linc., Edw. I. R.
1593. 'George Coppledicke, or Coppuldike, elected principal of Bernard's Inn ' : N. and Q., March 12, 1887, p. 203.

The name still exists as Cobbledick, but I have no instance at hand.

'Warrant to acquit Edward Copledick,' April 26, 1594 : Cal. State Papers (Domestic), iii. 489.
Derby, 0, 3.

Cobbler.—Occup. 'the cobbler,' an early occupative term, as is proved by my instances. *Cobclere* occurs in Piers Plowman. The surname has been extinct for some generations back, I imagine.

Robert le Cobeler, co. Bucks, 1273. A.
Ricardus Cobler, 1379 : P. T. Howdenshire, p. 7.

Willelmus Cobbeler, 1379 : P. T. Yorks. p. 46.
London, 0.

Cobbold, Corbold, Corbould, Cubill, Cobell, Cobel, Cubel.—Bapt. 'the son of Cobbold,' found in Domesday as Cubold. With an initial K (v. Kibble) the surname assumed many guises. The instances both under Kibble and below are confined (saving co. Oxf.) to the South-Eastern counties. These settled into the forms with C as initial. Towards the West from co. Oxford K became the initial. I am speaking, of course, generally.

Simon Cubaud, co. Suff., 1273. A.
Hamo Cubald, co. Norf., ibid.
William Cubbel, co. Camb., ibid.
Robert Cubbel, co. Oxf., ibid.
Thomas Cobald, bailiff of Yarmouth, 1353 : FF. xi. 323.
1649. Bapt.—Frideswide, d. William Corbould : St. Jas. Clerkenwell, i. 174.
1800. Married—John Cobble and Maria Green : St. Geo. Han. Sq. ii. 224.
London, 2, 1, 3, 0, 2, 0, 0 ; MDB. (Suffolk), 0, 0, 0, 0, 0, 0, 0 ; (Norfolk) Cubill, 1 ; New York (Cobel), 2 ; Philadelphia (Cubel), 1.

Cobcroft.—Local, ' at the cobcroft,' i.e. the field or enclosure on the cob (v. Cobden). A Yorkshire surname.

Thurstan Cobcroft, co. York. W. 11.
'George Cobcrafte embarked in the Thomas for Virginia, 1635 ' : Hotten's Lists of Emigrants, p. 85.

Cobden.—Local, ' of Copedene.' I cannot find the spot, but it must have been in co. York. The derivation is simple ; v. Cope and Dean, and also Cobcroft and Copestake.

Alan Copdane, co. York. W. 11.
Geoffrey le Coppden, c. 1307. M.
John Copedenne. A.
John Copedenne, co. Oxf., 1273. A.
Ralph Copdaine, 1690 : St. Peter, Cornhill, ii. 102.
1687. John Naishe and Ann Cobden : Marriage Alleg. (Canterbury), p. 288.
Philadelphia, 1.

Cobelot. — Bapt. 'the son of Jacob,' from the nick. Cob, dim. Cob-elot ; cf. Hewlett.

John Cobelot, co. Suff., 1273. A.

Cobham, Cobbam. — Local, ' of Cobham,' parishes in cos. Kent

and Surrey. The surname seems to claim the Kent parish for its parent.

John de Cobeham, co. Kent, 1273. A.
Reginald de Cobeham, co. Kent, ibid.
William de Cobbeham, co. Hants, Hen. III—Edw. I. K.
1577. Edward Cobham and Mary Hornebie : Marriage Lic. (London), i. 78.
1609. Married — William Tyre and Mary Cobhame : St. Jas. Clerkenwell, iii. 35.
1745. — Luke Cobham and Mary Rogers : St. Geo. Han. Sq. i. 35.
'John de Cobham, third Lord Cobham (d. 1408), was son of John de Cobham, Constable of Rochester Castle ' : Dict. Nat. Biog. xi. 155.
'Thomas de Cobham, bishop of Worcester (d. 1327), was a member of the well-known Kentish family of Cobham ' : ibid. xi. 157.
London, 2, 1 ; Boston (U.S.), 1, 0.

Cock.—(1) Nick. 'the cock,' from the pertness or swagger of the bearer ; cf. Henn, Fowl, &c.

John le Cok, co. Soms., 1 Edw. III : Kirby's Quest, p. 171.
Henry le Cok, co. Soms., 1 Edw. III : ibid. p. 180.
William le Kok, C. R., 3 Edw. I.
Thomas Cokk, 1379 : P. T. Yorks. p. 125.

(2) Local, ' at the Cock,' a sign-name.

John a Kok, C. R., 9 Edw. I.

Cf. Attwood, A'Becket, &c. As I have shown in my Preface, there are many sign-names.

1606. Married — Joseph Cock and Hannah Sprott : St. Mary Aldermary, p. 11.
London, 16 ; Philadelphia, 2 ; New York, 3.

Cockayne.—Local, 'of Cokayne,' the Utopia of early English fable :

'Fur in sea, bi west Spaygne,
Is a lond ihote Cockaygne.'

Whether or not the name of th's legendary region was afterwards transferred to London as the centre of luxury and ease, resulting in the London *cockney*, seems not to be decided ; v. Cocking, in explanation of the large number of Cockaynes in co. York.

Nicholas de Cokayne, co. Sussex, 1273. A.
Alan de Cokayne, co. Sussex, ibid.
Richard de Cokayne, co. Essex, ibid.
1660-1. Scipio Cokayn and Eliz. Hope : Marriage Lic. (Faculty Office), p. 50.

1671. Daniel Thorne and Eliz. Cockayne: Marriage Lic. (Faculty Office), p. 120. London, 1 ; Sheffield, 14.

Cockcroft, Cockroft, Crowcroft.—Local, ' of Carcroft,' a hamlet in the parish of Owston, W. Rid. Yorks. The corruptions were inevitable; Crowcroft is found in the Doncaster Directory, and Carcroft is in the Doncaster rural deanery.

Thomas de Carrecroft, 1379 : P. T. Yorks. p. 47.
1764. Married—John Normanton and Ann Cockcroft : St. Geo. Han. Sq. i. 136. West Rid. Court Dir., 3, 11, 1 ; London, 0, 2, 0 ; Doncaster, 0, 0, 2 ; Philadelphia, 2, 4, 0.

Cocker.—Occup. 'the cocker,' i.e. cockfighter (?). ' Cokker ' in this sense occurs in the Towneley Mysteries :

' These dysars, and these hullars, These cokkers, and these bullars.'
Simon le Cockere, co. Oxf., 1273. A.
John le Cochere, co. Sussex, ibid.
Adam Coker, co. Essex, ibid.
William le Kokere, co. Soms., ibid.
John le Coker, c. 1300. M.
Willelmus Coker, Ebota uxor ejus, smyth, 1379 : P. T. Yorks. p. 44.
London, 4 ; Philadelphia, 11.

Cockerell, Cockerill, Cockrill, Cockrell, Cockrille.—Nick. 'the cockerel'; M.E. cokerel, a little cock. 'Cokerelle: gallus' (Prompt. Parv.).

Geoffrey Cokerell, co. Norf., 1273. A.
John Cokerel, co. York, ibid.
Reginald Kokerel, co. Camb., ibid.
Matilda Cokrell, 1379 : P. T. Yorks. p. 145.
Elias Cokrell, 1379 : ibid. p. 209.
Alicia Cokerell, 1379 : ibid. p. 248.
1530. Clement Cokerell and Margaret Edmonds : Marriage Lic. (London), i. 7.
London, 11, 2, 3, 3, 0 ; West Rid. Court Dir., 0, 0, 0, 1, 0, 0; MDB. (co. Suffolk), 1, 0, 1, 3, 0 ; New York, 0, 2, 1, 1, 1.

Cockerham, Cockram, Cockrem, Cockeram. — ? Local, ' of Cockerham' (?), a parish between Lancaster and Garstang; in Domesday spelt Cocreham. It lies on the little river Cocker. Nevertheless, I cannot find the existence of this surname in Lancashire. Thus the probability is that all the above are mere variants of the Irish Corkeran or Corkran ; cf. Ransom and Ranson, Sansum and Samson, &c. The interchange of civilities be-

tween *n* and *m* is as common in nomenclature as in the dictionary. A comparison between the following entries from one London register will have its weight on the thoughtful reader :

1789. Married—Samuel Cockram and Rebekah Smith : St. Geo. Han. Sq. ii. 23.
1799. — Michael Corkran and Sophia Abell : ibid. p. 204.
1807. — Francis Lonsdale and Eliz. Cockran : ibid. p. 363.

Such a sequence of entries is not easily got over.
Crockford, 1, 1, 1, 0 ; London, 0, 1, 1, 0 ; MDB. (Dorset), 1, 0, 0, 3.

Cocket. — Nick. 'little cock,' from Cock, and dim. Cock-et, a little strutting fellow ; cf. coquette, and v. Cock. My first extract is probably one of the earliest instances yet found of coquette.

Agatha le Couket, co. Soms., 1 Edw. III : Kirby's Quest, p. 189.
Nicholas Coket, co. Soms., 1 Edw. III : ibid. p. 206.
Hugh Coket, co. Bucks, 1273. A.
John Coket, co. Bucks, ibid.
1668. John Cockett and Ann Flexmer : Marriage Lic. (Faculty Office), p. 104.
1765. Married—Thomas Cockett and Sarah Silverthorne : St. Geo. Han. Sq. i. 150.

Cockey.—Local, ' of Cochagh,' a West-country name (v. Haigh). There is Cockey, a hamlet near Bury, co. Lanc., but it seems to bear no relation to the existing surname.

Alice de Cochagh, co. Soms., 1 Edw. III : Kirby's Quest, p. 149.
John de Cocheye, co. Soms., 1 Edw. III: ibid. p. 191.
1747. Married—Peter Cockey and Jane Porter : St. Geo. Chap. Mayfair, p. 88.
MDB. (co. Soms.), 2 ; New York, 4.

Cockhead.—Nick. 'Cockhead,' one who strutted with head up, consequentially. Nevertheless, it is possible it is local, one of the terminatives in *head*; v. Head, Akenhead, Birkett, Blackett, &c.
Simon Cochoved, C. R., 17 Edw. III, pt. ii.
Willelmus Kokheved, 1379 : P. T. Yorks. p. 272.
1784. Married—Joseph Cockhead and Mary Okell : St. Geo. Han. Sq. i. 306. London, 3.

Cocking, Cockin. — Local, ' of Coken,' a hamlet on the Wear,

co. Durham, which early gave rise to a surname. The large number of Cockaynes in co. York would seem to prove that there has been some confusion between the two names ; v. Cockayne and Cogan.

Gilbert de Cokun, co. Northumberland, 20 Edw. I. R.
John de Coken, vicar of Billingham, 1391 : DDD. iii. 146.
Alice de Coken, 1319 : ibid. i. 206.
Petronilla de Cokyn, temp. 1350 : ibid. 205.
John Cokin, co. Notts, 1273. A.
John Cokyn, co. Derby, 20 Edw. I. R.
1669. Married—William Cockin and Eliz. Barnerd : St. Jas. Clerkenwell, iii. 156.
1806. — Joseph Cocking and Catherine Eliz. Jordan : St. Geo. Han. Sq. ii. 348. London, 6, 0 ; West Rid. Court Dir., 6, 4 ; Philadelphia, 0, 1.

Cockle, Coghill, Cockhill, Cogill, Coggill. — Local, ' of Cockhill.' Some spot in the West Rid. Yorkshire. The West Riding directories seem alone to have preserved the correct form. Several of these forms may be corruptions of the Yorkshire Cowgill, q.v. There seems to be a spot in co. Somerset bearing this name.

Elizabetha de Cokhill, 1379 : P. T. Yorks. p. 182.
Johannes de Cokhill, 1379 : ibid.
Mathew de Cokhull, co. Soms., 1 Edw. III : Kirby's Quest, p. 133.
John Cokhull, co. Soms., 1 Edw. III : ibid.
1692. Bapt. — Joseph, s. Edward Coggill : St. Jas. Clerkenwell, i. 347.
1802. Married—Charles William Doyle and Sophia Cramer; witness, John Coghill : St. Geo. Han. Sq. ii. 257.
London, 10, 2, 0, 0, 0 ; West Rid. Court Dir., 0, 0, 0, 1, 1, 0 ; Sheffield (Coghill), 1 ; Leeds (Coggill), 1 ; New York (Coggill), 4.

Cockler.—Occup. 'a cockler,' a gatherer of cockles; M.E. cokeles. Roger le Cokhelere (Close Roll, 4 Edw. I). The word is still in use on the English north-west coast.

Cockman, Cookman.—Occup. (1) 'the cookman,' i.e. either the cook himself, with augmentative *man*, as in husbandman, merchantman, &c., or the cook's assistant ; cf. Kitchener and Kitchenman. Lower permits himself to write ' Cockman, a cockfighter '; v. Cook, and cf. Matthewman, Addyman, Ladyman, &c.

William Cokeman, co. Soms., 1 Edw. III : Kirby's Quest. p. 260.
John Cukeman, C. R., 45 Hen. III.
William Cokeman. J.
John Cookman, co. York. W. 9.
1796. Married—Joseph Cockman and Eliz. Skinner : St. Geo. Han. Sq. ii. 150.
1800. — Joseph Roberts and Harriot Cookman : ibid. p. 220.
London, 6, 2 ; MDB. (E. Rid. Yorks), 0, 1 ; Philadelphia, 0, 6.

Cockrill; see Cockerell.

Cocks, Cockson, Cox, Coxe, Coxen, Coxon, Coxson.—Personal. 'Cock,' a term of familiarity. There are over two columns of Coxes in London Dir. The history of the name is interesting, and every stage can be proved conclusively. The natural pertness of boys, so like the habits of the strutting barn-door fowl, caused *cock* to be used much in the sense of our 'Well, old Cock, how are you!' There was an affinity between the boy in the scullery and the cock in the yard : both swaggered, and both could crow. In the Nun's Priest's Tale of Chaucer it is said of Chanticleer,

'Nothing ne list him thanne for to crow,
But cried anon cok, cok, and up he sterte.'

Thus 'cock' became the general sobriquet of a sharp and forward lad. The farm-lad, the scullion, or the apprentice was ever 'Cock' by itself, or if attached to his Christian name, Jeff-cock, or Will-cock, or Bat-cock, or Han-cock. Thus we have the story of Cocke Lorelle, and the old nursery rhyme begins :

'Who killed Cock Robin?'

Again, in Gammer Gurton's Needle (1566) the boy is simply 'Cock':

'My gammer is so out of course,
And frantic all at once,
That Cock, our boy, and I, poor wench,
Have felt it on our bones.'

Sometimes the font-name was forgotten in the term, hence such entries as 'Item, to Cok, my servant, xxs' (Will of Roger Thornton, 1429 : PPP. i. 283); 'Cok ffenwyk' and 'Cok Crissop'

(Patent Roll, 13 and 14 Hen. VII). 'Coc le Afeyte' was forbidden to live in London, 1269 (WWW. p. 125). The patronymic of this was Cocks or Cockson.

Coc de Slepe, co. Salop, 1273. A.
Edward Cockson. Z.
John Cockson. EE.
Cok' Carnifer, 1379 : P. T. Yorks. p. 98.

These have become modernly Cox. Coxe, Coxon. and Coxen (cf. Wilcoxon for Wilcockson, Dix and Dixon for Dicks and Dickson, Rix and Rixon for Ricks and Rickson, also cox-comb). One or two instances will suffice :

Thomas Kokson, 1379 : P. T. Yorks. p. 272.
Cok Wighame, co. Northumberland, 1404 : TTI. p. 187.
Robert Cockson, or Cokson, or Coxson, or Coxon, sup. for B.A., Jan. 1555-6 : Reg. Univ. Oxf. i. 231.
'Walter Cocks or Cox, chaplain, sup. for B.C.L., 20 April, 1515 : ibid. p. 95.
John Cockis, or Coxe, allowed to determine Mich. term, 1546 : ibid. p. 213.

How popular Cock was, Cox and Coxe are sufficient proof. There are over 1000 Coxes in London commercial centres alone, counting five to a family For compounds of Cock (v. above), such as Simcock and Simcox, Laycock, Pidcock, Mycock, Jeffcock, &c., see these names in their proper places. It is clear that *cock* became, like *kin*, a pet desinence ; and in the class of names I have just mentioned, must to all intents and purposes be considered as such. Certain sobriquets of a more or less depreciative character were similarly formed. Dawcock (i.e. Jack-daw) was an empty-headed noodle. In Appius and Virginia (1563) Mansipula says (Act i. sc. 1) :

'My lady's great business belike is at an end :
When you, goodman dawcock, lust for to wend.'

An earlier form of

'Pillicock, Pillicock sate on a hill,
If he's not gone he sits there still,'

will be found in King Lear. A lobcock was a lubberly fellow. 'Baligant, an unweldie lubber, great lobcock' (Cotgrave). In 'Wily Beguiled' Will Cricket says to Churms, 'Why, since you were

bombasted that your lubberly legs would not carry your lobcock body.' Meacock and nescock were effeminate fellows. In 'Wit without Money,' Valentine says, 'For then you are meacocks, fools, and miserable.' 'And shall I then, a mecocke, or a milkesop?' Greene's Gwydonius, 1593 ; cf. Sweetcock (q.v.).

Swetecoka de Hornden, C.R., 16 Edw. I.
London, 24, 0, 227, 2, 3, 3, 0 ; Philadelphia (Coxson), 2 ; New York, 8, 0, 150, 3, 0, 1, 0.

Cockshall, Cockshaw. — Local, 'at the Cockshaw,' from residence thereby ; cf. Shallcross and Shawcross ; v. Shaw.

Symon de Cokschaghe, 1379 : P. T. Yorks. p. 127.
1703. Married — Jonathan Cockshaw and Jane Mary Norgrove : St. Geo. Han. Sq. ii. 97.
London, 1, 0 ; New York, 0, 1.

Cockshott, Cockshot, Cockshoot, Cockshutt, Cotshott.— Local, 'of Cockshut,' a chapelry in the parish of Ellesmere, co. Salop. But there is strong evidence of the existence of another place of the same name in co. Lancashire or the W. Rid. of Yorks. Cotshott is an American variant.

Edmund Cockshott, 1662 : Preston Guild Rolls, p. 127.
Alice Cockshutt, of Padiham, *widow*, 1630 : Wills at Chester (1621-50), p. 51.
Edward Cockshutt, of Walton-le-dale, 1628 : ibid.
1704. Married — Thomas Cockshott and Eliz. Mason : St. Geo. Han. Sq. ii. 122.
West Rid. Court Dir., 9, 0, 0, 0, 0 ; London, 2, 0, 0, 0, 0 ; Manchester, 1, 1, 4, 0, 0 ; MDB. (co. Lancaster), 0, 0, 1, 3, 0 ; Philadelphia, 1, 0, 0, 0, 2.

Cockspur.—Nick. 'cock-spur,' a sobriquet as old as the days of cock-fighting (v. Cocker). Nevertheless, it is curious that this surname should have lingered on into the 18th century. The sobriquet would be readily affixed upon a man of a combative and belligerent mood, especially a fire-eater or swashbuckler.

Alice Cokespore, Fines Roll, 11 Edw. I.
Robertus Cokspour, 1379 : P. T. Yorks. p. 162.
1741. Bapt. — Lambert, s. Henry Cockspur : St. Jas. Clerkenwell, i. 254.

Codd, Code.—Bapt. 'the son of Cuthbert,' from nick. Cudde (v. Codling). If this be true, as I suspect it is, it will be yet one more instance of a fish-name not being what it seems to be; cf. Chubb, Salmon, Spratt, Turbott. All the same, this may be an exception.

Henry Cod, co. Oxf., 1273. A.
Ricardus Code, 1379 : P. T. Yorks. p. 6.
Thomas Codde, Norwich, 1558 : FF. iv. 97.
1586. David Codd and Margaret Asheley : Marriage Lic. (London), i. 156.
1765. Married — James Benson and Eleanor Cod : St. Geo. Han. Sq. i. 147.
1777. — Emery Codd and Mary Carley : ibid. p. 274.
London, 5, 0 ; MDB. (co. Suffolk), 1, 0 ; Boston (U.S.), 0, 2 ; Philadelphia, 0, 2.

Coddington, Codington.— Local, 'of Coddington,' (1) a parish in county Notts, two miles from Newark ; (2) a parish in co. Hereford, three miles from Ledbury ; (3) a parish in co. Chester, two miles from Handley.

William de Codynton, London, 20 Edw. I. R.
John de Codyngton, London, 20 Edw. I : ibid.
Harvey de Codinton, co. Essex, 1273. A.
'William Coddington (1601-78), governor of Rhode Island, New England, a native of Lincolnshire' : Dict. Nat. Biog. xi. 203.

The last-named would probably spring from the Nottinghamshire Coddington.

Jane Coddington, of Frodsham, *widow*, 1640 : Wills at Chester (1621-50), p. 51.
Robert Coddington, of Chester, *tanner*, 1635 : ibid.

These, no doubt, represent the Cheshire parish. It is this family that has crossed the borders into Lancashire.

1614. Bapt.—Agnes, d. William Coddington : St. Jas. Clerkenwell, i. 71.
Manchester, 1, 0 ; London, 1, 0 ; MDB. (co. Chester), 1, 0 ; (co. Lincoln), 1, 0 ; New York, 19, 2.

Codling, Cudling, Codlin.— (1) Bapt. 'the son of Cuthbert' (?), from Cudbert ; nick. Cud, dim. Cudling or Codling ; cf. Hewling, from Hew (Hugh).

Adam Cudelyne, 1379 : P. T. Yorks. p. 252.
Robert Codelyng, 1379 : P. T. Yorks. ibid.
Robert Codling, co. Linc., 1273. A.

William Codling, co. Linc., ibid.
Adam Codelyng, 1379 : P. T. Yorks. p. 5.

(2) Nick. ; v. Quodling.

1772. Married—John Codling and Eliz. Keates : St. Geo. Han. Sq. i. 222.
London, 2, 0, 0 ; York, 0, 0, 1.

Codner, Codnor. — Occup. 'the cordwainer,' of which Cordiner and Codner are variants ; v. Cordiner.

Robert Codner, bailiff of Bristol, 1346 : Barrett's Hist. of Bristol.
1642. Bapt.—Allyce, d. James Codner : St. Jas. Clerkenwell, i. 151.
Kingskerswell (Devon), 3, 0 ; London, 4, 0 ; MDB. (Devon), 6, 1.

Codrington.—Local, ' of Codrington,' a tithing in the parish of Wapley, three miles from Chipping Sodbury, co. Glouc.

'Sir Edward Codrington (1770-1851), admiral, came of the old family of Codrington, of Dodington, co. Glouc.': Dict. Nat. Biog. xi. 204.
'Robert Codrington (d. 1665), author, born "of an ancient and genteel family in Gloucestershire"': ibid. xi. 209.
1686. John Courthope and Rachaell Codrington : Marriage Lic. (Faculty Office), p. 180.
1797. Married—Joseph Lyons Walrond and Caroline Codrington : St. Geo. Han. Sq. ii. 175.
London, 1.

Coe.—Nick. ' the coe,' i.e. the jackdaw ; A.S. *ceo, cornix.* ' Coo, byrde or schowhe ; Koo, byrde or schowghe ; *monedula, nodula* ' (Prompt. Parv.). ' Koo, a byrde ' (Palsg.). Mr. Way quotes in a note :

— ' the churlysshe chowgh,
The route, and the kowgh :—
At this *placebo,*
We may not well forego
The countrynge of the coe.'
Skelton's Philip Sparrow.

Hence no doubt ' Coe, an odd old fellow. Norf.' (Halliwell); an old jackdaw, as we might say.

Beatrix le Coe, co. Norf., 1273. A.
William le Koo, co. Camb., ibid.
Ricardus Koo, 1379 : P. T. Yorks. p. 38.

It is interesting to note that the Prompt. Parv. references, the quotation from Halliwell, and one of my Hundred Roll instances, are all from co. Norfolk. Again we find :

Jeffry Coo, of Ashill, co. Norf., 1458 : FF. ii. 349.

William Coe, of Ashill, co. Norf., 1526 : ibid. p. 354.

Thus Coo and Coe were identical. Coe is still a familiar Norfolk surname.

London, 21 ; MDB. (co. Suffolk), 4 ; Boston (U.S.), 23.

Coffee, Coffey, Caughey.— Bapt. 'O'Coffey,' an Irish patronymic. Coffee, of course, is imitative. Biddy in the instance below speaks for her own nationality. It is said that the original form of O'Coffey was O'Cobhthaidh. Dr. Charnock says that Murragh O'Cobhthaidh was bishop of Derry and Raphoe, temp. 1173 (v. Ludus Patronymicus, p. 18). Both of the modern forms are naturally found at Liverpool, which numbers so many Irish among its population.

1704. Married—Thomas Coffee and Winifred Hillman : St. Jas. Clerkenwell, iii. 227.
1803. — William Jakins and Bidey (Biddy) Coffee : St. Geo. Han. Sq. ii. 279.
London, 3, 3, 1 ; Liverpool, 2, 2, 1 ; New York, 21, 48, 2.

Coffer, Cofferer.—(1) Official, ' the cofferer,' one who had charge of a coffer, a treasurer. (2) Occup. ' the cofferer,' a maker of coffers. In the Trevelyan Papers (Camden Soc.) we find ' Item, to Edmund Peckham, coferer of the King's House, for the expenses, and charges,' &c. This concerns (1). Again we read of :

' Pype-makers, wodemongers, and orgyn-makers,
Coferers, carde-makers, and carvers.'
Cocke Lorelle's Bote.

This concerns (2).

William le Coffare, co. Soms., 1 Edw. III : Kirby's Quest, p. 112.
Saloman le Coffrer, Fines Roll, 14 Edw. II.
John le Coffrir, London, 1273. A.
Godfrey le Coffrer, London, ibid.
Richard le Coffrer, London, 20 Edw. I. R.
1278. Godfrey le Coffrer : Cal. of Wills in Court of Husting.

I find no modern instance of the surname.

Coffin, Caffin, Caffyn, Chafen, Chaffine.—Nick. ' the bald.' A mere variation of Caffin, the earliest form being Chaufin, which would readily become Coffin and Caffin. This form seems to have taken root in the south-western counties of England. Edward Coffin, the Jesuit, was born at Exeter, 1571 (Dict. Nat. Biog. xi. 215). Several Devonshire families bear the name; cf. Fr. *chauve*, bald (v. Chaffe), and Calvin, from Latin *calvus*. Probably Chaufin was a dim.

'*Calvus* protests for foes he doth not care:
For why? They cannot take from him *one hair.*'
Satyrical Epigrams, 1619.

Henry Coffyn, co. Soms., 1 Edw. III : Kirby's Quest, p. 99.
Richard Chaufin, co. Notts, 1273. A.
Robert Coffyn, co. Linc, ibid.
William Coffyn, co. Devon, ibid.
Thomas Chafyn, 1505: Reg. Univ. Oxf. i. 40.
1788. Married—Robert Gilbert and Mary Coffen : St. Geo. Han. Sq. ii. 10.
— — Thomas Coffin and Agatha Waterman ; ibid. p. 16.
1794. — John Chaffin and Isabella Blandell ; ibid. p. 117.

In France the enthusiastic devotion of Nicholas Chauvin I gave rise to the term Chauvinism. Chaufin was the Hundred Roll form ; v. supra.

London, 5, 2, 1, 1, 0 ; MDB. (co. Devon), 1, 0, 0, 0, 0 ; New York, 45, 0, 0, 0, 1.

Cogan, Coggan, Coggen, Cogin, Coggin, Coggon.— Local, 'of Cogan,' a parish in dioc. of Llandaff, which gave birth to an early surname. As regards the forms found in cos. York and Lincoln, it is probable they are but variants of Coken (v. Cocking).

Richard Cogan, co. Soms., 1 Edw. III: Kirby's Quest, p. 87.
John de Cogan, co. Somerset, 1273. A.
John de Cogan, co. Devon, ibid.

From this it is clear that the south-west forms of the surname are derived from the Llandaff parish. To Somerset and Devon was not a long journey.

1605. Richard Browne and Hellen Coggen: St. Jas. Clerkenwell, ii. 30.
1716. John Coggain and Sarah Fetchew: ibid. p. 239.
1723. Joseph Cogin and Jone Sellway : ibid. p. 248.

1789. Married—Thomas Coggin and Eliz. Tillcock : St. Geo. Han. Sq. ii. 24.
1809. — William Shickle and Eliz. Cogan : ibid. p. 410.
MDB. (co. Somerset), 1, 5, 1, 1, 0, 0 ; (co. Lincoln), 0, 3, 0, 0, 1, 2 ; London, 3, 2, 0, 0, 0, 0 ; Boston (U.S.), 25, 2, 0, 0, 5, 0.

Cogger, Cogman, Coger.— Occup. 'the cogger' or 'cogman,' the master of a cog-boat (cf. cock-boat and cockswain). 'Cogboote : *scafa*' (Prompt. Parv.); 'hevy hulkis, grete coggis'; v. Way's Prompt. Parv. p. 252, *n*. 5.

' And found Jason and Hercules also, That in a cogge to lond were ygo.'
Chaucer, Legend of Good Women.

Henry Cogger. P.
1621. George Cogger and Alice Nash : Marriage Lic. (Westminster), p. 27.
1628. William Gurnett and Freezwyth Coger : ibid. p. 33.
'William Middleton, of this town (Castor, co. Norfolk), blacksmith, by will dated Jan. 20, 1647 . . . gave to the poor 3s. 4d. a year . . . and tied all his house and ground . . . for payment thereof, which are now in the possession of Benjamin Cogman': FF. v. 430.

Norfolk has given us several of these names ; v. Bargeman, Boatman, &c. Probably Cockman has absorbed this name, of which I see six in the London Directory. As shown above, cockboat and cockswain have undergone the same change.

New York, 2, 0, 2.

Coghill.—Local ; v. Cockle.

Coglin. — Bapt. 'the son of Cockelin,' from Cock (q.v.), used personally ; dim. Cockelin. The customary laziness brought this down to Coglin.

Agnes Cokelin, co. Camb., 1273. A.
Imania Cokelin, co. Camb., ibid.
London, 1.

Cogswell, Coxwell.—Local, ' of Coggeshall,' a parish in the dioc. of St. Albans. Wherever a monastery was founded it drew together a community, and this in the surname period was likely to foster a local nomenclature. The early Coggeshalls by corruption became Cogswell and Coxwell. There need be no hesitation in accepting this origin. It is absolutely certain. The surname is still confined to a limited radius of the

place, which was of considerable importance.

(Abbas) de Cogeshalle, co. Essex, 1273. A.
Roger de Cogeshall, co. Essex, ibid.
Reginald Cokkeshale, co. Kent, ibid.
Ralph de Coggeshal, co. Essex, Hen. III-Edw. I. K.
Maria de Coggeshale, co. Norf., 20 Edw. I. R.
1681. Married—John Cogeswell and Ann Pare : St. Jas. Clerkenwell, iii. 227.
London, 6, 1 ; New York, 8, 0.

Coifer, Coifster.—Occup. 'the coifer' or 'coifster,' a maker of caps or cowls, probably knitted. Coifster has the fem. suffix.

Nicholas le Coifstere, Close Roll, 16 Edw. III. pt. i.
Emma la Coyfere, co. Oxf., 1273. A.
Dionysia la Coyfere, co. Oxf., ibid.
Ralph le Coifier. E.
Peter Coyfer, C. R., 32 Hen. III.

As a surname Coifer would soon be lost in Coffer, q.v. The French Coiffier is in the London Directory (1870).

Coiner.—Occup. 'the coiner' ; cf. Minter. v. Cuner.

William le Coiner, co. Soms., 1 Edw. III : Kirby's Quest, p. 197.

Coish, Coysh.—Bapt ' the son of Coise.'

Agnes fil. Coise, co. Camb., 1273. A.

The spelling, as will be seen below, was retained till the close of the 16th century :

Rafe, son of Nicholas Quoise, 1564 : Reg. St. Mary Aldermary (London), p. 55.
William, son of Nicholas Quoise, 1565: ibid. p. 55.
Anthonie, son of Nicholas Coise, 1577 : ibid. p. 59.
Alice, d. of Margret Coys, 1563 : ibid. p. 135.
Mary, wife of Richard Coysh, 1672 : ibid. p. 188.
London, 3, 2.

Coke.—Occup. 'the cook' (v. Cook).

Roger le Coke, c. 1300. M.
Alexander Coke, co. Camb., 1273. A.
William Coke, co. Norf., ibid.
Magota Coke, 1379: P. T. Yorks. p. 4.
Alicia Cok', 1379 : ibid.
1807. Married — Richard Smith and Eliz. Coke : St. Geo. Han. Sq. ii. 361.
London, 1 ; Boston (U.S.), 1.

Coker.—Local, 'of Coker,' two parishes in co. Somerset.

John de Coker, co. Soms., 1 Edw. III Kirby's Quest, p. 192.

William de Coker, co. Soms., 1 Edw.
III: Kirby's Quest, p. 243.
Thomas Coker, co. Somerset, 1273. A.
Adam Coker, co. Essex, ibid.
1650. Bapt.—Sarah, d. Walter Coker:
St. Dionis Backchurch, p. 110.
1791. Married — Thomas Coker and
Eliz. Long: St. Geo. Han. Sq. ii. 62.
London, 7; Boston (U.S.), 2.

Colbeck, Coulbeck, Colebeck.
— Local. 'of Caldbeck.' A
parish in co. Cumb. With Coulbeck, cf. Colson and Coulson, Colt
and Coult, &c.; v. Callbeck.

1787. Married—Thomas Walford and
Mary Coleback: St. Geo. Han. Sq. i. 408.
1790. — John Colbeck and Sarah
Richardson: ibid. ii. 44.
1798. Buried—Thomas Coalbeck,
shoemaker: Reg. St. Mary, Ulverston,
p. 622.
1806. Married—James Webster and
Tabitha Colback: St. Geo. Han. Sq.
ii. 347.
London, 2, 0, 1; MDB. (co. Lincoln),
0, 5, 0.

Colbert, Colbertson.—Bapt.
'the son of Colbert,' found as a
personal name in Domesday, co.
Devon; cf. Coleswain, Colegrim,
Colbran.

Leeds, 1, 0; London, 2, 0; Philadelphia,
15, 1.

Colbran, Colborn, Colborne, Colbourn, Colbourne, Colbrain, Colbron, Colebourne, Colburn.
—(1) Bapt. 'the son of
Colbrand,' found as a personal
name in Domesday, co. Devon;
cf. Coleswain and Colegrim. The
variants Colborn, Colbourn, &c.,
were inevitable.

Malger Colebrond, co. Sussex, 1273. A.

As Colbran the surname is still
to be found in that county.

Robert Colbern, co. Soms., 1 Edw. III:
Kirby's Quest, p. 84.
William Colebrond, co. Soms., 1 Edw.
III: ibid. p. 230.
Ricardus Collebround, 1379: P. T.
Yorks. p. 67.
Margareta Colbrand, 1379: ibid. p. 140.
1631. Bapt.—William, s. Thomas Col-
borne; St. Jas. Clerkenwell, i. 119.
1642. — James Colbran: St. Antholin
(London), p. 75.
1677. — Laud, s. John Colebron: St.
Jas. Clerkenwell, i. 277.

(2) Local, 'of Colbourne,' a township in the parish of Catterick, N.
Rid. Yorks. But I find no representatives in Yorkshire of any family of

that name. The true origin of all
the forms is (1). Since writing
the above I find this view corroborated by Mr. Earwaker in his
East Cheshire, ii. 131. He records
that William Coulborn was vicar of
Mottram-in-Longdendale in 1695.
He adds in a note, 'he may perhaps
be identified with a "William Col-
bron" who matriculated at Oxford
from Wadham College, 26th March,
1686.'

London, 1, 1, 2, 1, 2, 0, 0, 0, 0; MDB.
(co. Kent), Colbrain, 1; (co. Sussex),
Colbran, 1; New York, 0, 0, 1, 0, 0, 0,
1, 1, 1.

Colby, Coleby.—Local, 'of
Colby' or 'Coleby.' Colby is a
parish in dioc. Norwich, and Coleby a parish in dioc. Lincoln. No
doubt from Cole (q.v.), the first
resident.

William de Colebi, co. Westm., 1176:
RRR. p. 161.
William de Colleby, co. Linc., 1273. A.
(Dominus) de Coleby, co. Linc., ibid.
William de Coleby, co. Oxf., ibid.
John de Coleby, co. Norf., 20 Edw. I. R.
Willelmus de Colby, 1379: P. T. Yorks.
p. 126.
William de Colby, rector of Wilby,
co. Suff., 1331: FF. v. 389.
John de Colby, rector of Pulham, co.
Norf., 1331: ibid.
1695. Married—Joseph Colebey and
Eliz. Luckock: St. Jas. Clerkenwell,
iii. 216.
London, 2, 2; Philadelphia, 5, 0.

Colchester, Colchesters.—
Local, 'of Colchester.' It seems
to be a very scarce surname.

1652. Married — Richard Colchester
and Eliz. Kensey: St. Michael, Cornhill,
p. 31.
1894. Henry Sparrowe Colchester:
Daily Telegraph, Aug. 4, 1894.
London, 1, 1; New York, 1, 0; Boston
(U.S.), 1, 0.

Colchin.—Bapt. 'the son of
Nicholas,' from the nick. Cole or
Col, and with pet suffix Col-kin;
cf. Wilkin, Dickin, Watkin, Simpkin, &c. This is easily proved by
the first two entries following:

John Colkyn, co. Kent, 20 Edw. I. R.
Hamo Colekyn, co. Kent, Hen. III-
Edw. I. K.
1768. Married—Thomas Colchin and
Ann Jacobs: St. Geo. Han. Sq. i. 184.
1796. Joseph Colchin and Mary Marshall: ibid. ii. 148.

Colclough, Colecrough.—
Local, 'of Colclough,' 'an estate
in Staffordshire, in which county
the family resided, temp. Edw. III':
Lower's Patr. Brit. p. 65. Cole-
crough, found in the same county,
is a manifest variant.

1678. Adam Colclough and Mary
Blagge: Marriage Alleg. (Canterbury),
p. 289.
1758. Married—John Colclough and
Abigail Shelley: St. Geo. Han. Sq. i. 74.
London, 1, 0; MDB. (co. Stafford),
5, 1.

Coldwell, Couldwell, Coald-
well.—Local, 'of Coldwell' (v.
Caldwell), a township in the union
of Bellingham, co. Northumberland.
Also of Colwell, a township in the
union of Hexham, same county.

Johannes de Coldwell, 1379: P. T.
Yorks. p. 174.
Thomas de Coldwele, 1379: ibid.
1561-2. Giles Hodgkinson and Eliz.
Coldewell: Marriage Lic. (London), i. 23.
1572. John Colwell and Margaret
Boseley: Marriage Lic. (Westminster),
p. 4.
1661. John Inians and Mary Coldwell:
Marriage Alleg. (Canterbury), p. 12.
London, 3, 0, 0; West Rid. Court Dir.,
4, 2, 0; Boston (U.S.), 5, 0, 2.

Cole, Coles.—Bapt. 'the son of
Nicholas,' from nick. Cole, whence
the dim. Col-in. Coles is the patronymic or genitive form; cf. Williams, Jenkins, Jones, &c.

'Havell, and Harvy Hafter,
Jack Travell, and Cole Crafter.'
Skelton, Why come ye nat to Courte.

This nick. of Nicholas has made
an extraordinary impression upon
English nomenclature (v. Colly,
Collins, &c.).

Rand' fil. Cole, co. York, temp. 13th
century: FFF. p. 47.
Johannes Cole, 1379: P. T. Yorks.
p. 92.
Elias Cole, 1379: ibid.
1588. Married—Bazill Beconn and Anne
Coale: St. Michael, Cornhill, p. 14.
1665. — Thomas Coles and Honour
Birde: ibid. p. 39.
London, 176, 47; Philadelphia, 108, 32.

Colebrook.—Local, 'of Cole-
brook.' (1) Colebrook, a parish in
dioc. Oxf.; (2) a manor in co.
Devon. The latter spot is spelt
Colbrok, Colbroke, and Colebroke,
in the Hundred Rolls (i. 67–71).

Henry de Colbrok, co. Devon, 1273. A.
1575. Buried—Eliz. Colbrocke : St. Jas.
Clerkenwell, iv. 17.
1638. Bapt.—Mary, d. Thomas Colebrooke : ibid. i. 140.
1773. Married — Thomas Colebrook
and Eliz. Harris: St. Geo. Han. Sq. i. 234.
London, 3.

Colegrim.—Bapt. 'the son of
Colegrim.' In Domesday found as
Colegrim, co. York; cf. Coleswain
and Culbran, q.v.

Reginald Colegrim, co. Notts, 1273. A.
Hugh Colegrim, co. Oxf., ibid.

Coleman, Colman. — Bapt.
'the son of Coleman,' the German
form of Columba (Yonge, i. 388).
Nov. 1 with Germans is St. Colman's Day. But it is not a later
immigration, for Coleman or Cole-
mannus is a Domesday personal
name. It is purely English (v.
Coulman, a variant).

Robert fil. Colman, 22 Hen. II : Westm.
and Cumb. i. 27
Robert fil. Coleman, 1176: RRR p. 160.
Coleman le Hen, co. Suff., 1273. A.
Editha Colman, co. Oxf., ibid
Martin Coleman, London, ibid.
Matilda Colman, 1379 : P. T. Yorks.
p. 203.
1551. Married—Thomas Tanfelde and
Margarett Colman : St. Michael, Corn-
hill, p. 6.
1595. Bapt.—Johane, d. George Cole-
man : St. Jas. Clerkenwell, i. 29.
London, 69, 10; Philadelphia, 161, 8.

Coleridge, Coldridge, Coul-
ridge, Colridge. — Local, ' of
Coleridge,' a parish in dioc. of
Exeter.

Crispianus de Colrigge, co. Devon,
1273. A.
Richard de Colrugge, co. Berks, ibid.
London, 3, 0, 0, 0; Teignmouth, 2, 0,
0, 0; Devon Dir. (Farmers' List), 0, 2,
0, 0; Exeter (Couldridge), 1; Newton
Abbot, 0, 1, 0, 0; North Bovey (Colridge),
4; Philadelphia, 0, 1, 0, 0.

Colesweyn.—Bapt. ' the son of
Colswegen.' In Domesday found
as Colsuan, co. Camb. ' Coles-
wegen and Ivo—that is doubtless
Ivo Taillebois—are spoken of as
uncles of a nephew of the Countess
Lucy ' (Freeman, N. C. iii. 779); v.
Swain.

Stephen Colesweyn, co. Hunts, 1273. A.
William Colsueyn, co. Wilts, ibid.
John Colswayn, co. Soms., 1 Edw. III :
Kirby's Quest, p. 212.

Colfox, Colfax, Colefax, Co-
lyfox. — Nick. 'the colfox,' a
crafty fellow; lit. 'coal-fox, a fox
with black marks '; cf. Stelfox.

' A col-fox, ful of sleigh iniquitee.'
    Chaucer, C. T. 15221.
Ricardus Colvox, co. Salop, 1273. A.
Thomas Colfox, 1511 : Reg. Univ. Oxf.
i. 76.
1550. Buried — Annes Coolefox : St.
Peter, Cornhill, i. 110.
' Mr. Colefax met Lord Randolph
Churchill on the Bradford railway plat-
form' : Yorkshire Post, Oct. 27, 1886.
MDB. (co. Dorset), 2, 0, 0, 1 : Pudsey
(Colefax), 1 ; New York (Colfax), 3

Colkin. — Bapt. ' the son of
Nicholas,' from nick. Col, and dim.
Col-kin ; cf. Watkin, Simpkin, &c.

John Colkyn, co. Kent, 20 Edw. I. R.
Hamo Colekyn, co. Kent, Hen. III-
Edw. I. K.

Collard.—Bapt. 'the son of
Collard,' an early personal name
with Col for prefix (cf. Colbert,
Colegrim, Coleman). Found in co.
Gloucester as a personal name, it
still remains there as a surname.

Colard Hariel, co. Glouc., 1273. A.
1595-6. Nicholas Collard and Margaret
Listney : Marriage Lic. (London), i. 229
1769. Married—Henry Collard and
Eliz. Raynard : St. Geo. Han. Sq. i. 189.
London, 7; MDB. (co. Glouc.), 2 ;
New York, 4.

Collarmaker. — Occup. Per-
haps a maker of horse-collars.

Willelmus Colermaker, 1379 : P. T.
Yorks. p. 74.

Collect.—? Bapt. 'the son of
Nicholas,' from the nick. Col, and
dim. Col-et or Colette. Found as
Colecta in the 14th century. For
quotation from Prompt. Parv., v.
Collett. I believe the surname is
extinct, but it lasted till the close of
the 16th century, and is imitative.

Osbert Collecte, co. Norf., 1273. A.
Colecta de Rughschawe, 1379 : P. T.
Yorks. p. 125.
1596. Buried—Richard Collect, Mr.
Raymentes man : St. Peter, Cornhill, i. 145.

Colledge, College.—Local, ' at
the college' (?), from residence in
or near some collegiate foundation.
I have no actual proof.

John Colledge, of Colne, clothworker,
1639 : Wills at Chester (1621-50), p. 51.
1578. Buried—Gregory Collage, servant
to Antony Kellyngham : St. Dionis Backchurch, p. 195.

1670. Married—Henry Collidge and
Allice Wright : St. Jas. Clerkenwell, iii.171.
London, 1, 0 ; MDB. (co. Derby), 1, 0 ;
Manchester, 2, 0; Philadelphia, 0, 1 ;
Boston (U.S.), 0, 1.

Coller, Collar.—Occup. ' the
coller,' i. e. collier. This was an
early form. The following first two
instances occur on the same page of
the Yorkshire Poll Tax ; cf. Lawyer
for Lawer, Sawyer for Sawer, &c.

Magota Colyer, 1379 : P. T. Yorks. p. 6.
Johannes Coller, 1379 : ibid.
1803. Married—John Coller and Esther
Peas : St. Geo. Han. Sq. ii. 295.
1806. — George Collar and Sarah
Eaging : ibid. ii. 348.
London, 1, 1 ; Philadelphia, 3, 17,

Collett, Collette.—Bapt. ' the
son of Nicholas,' from nick. Col or
Cole, dim. Col-et, often used for
a girl's name, and Latinized into
Colecta or Coleta. This form lingered on till the 16th century, as
the following entry will show :

1523. Robert Sweten and Coleta Got-
fery : Marriage Lic. (London), i. 3.
' Colette, propyr name (Collet, P).
Colecta ' : Prompt. Parv. p. 87. See
Collect.

' Kytt Cakeler, and Colett Crane,
Gylle Fetyse, and Fayr Jane.'
    Coventry Mysteries.
Colett de Sautre, co. Hunts, 1273. A.
Walter Colet, co. Salop, ibid.
Dyonisia Colet, co. Oxf., ibid.
Coleta Elot, 1379 : P. T. Yorks. p. 154.
Henricus Tayllour, et Collette uxor
ejus, 1379 : ibid. p. 127.
Johannes Colet, 1379 : ibid. p. 135.
' John Colet (1467?-1519), dean of St.
Paul's, and founder of St. Paul's Schools,
was probably born in the parish of St.
Antholin, London, where his family
resided ' : Dict. Nat. Biog. i. 321.

This preserves the earlier form.

1495. ' Collet Smyth, wife of Henry
Smyth, was buried before St. Catherine's
image.' Norwich : FF. iv. 404.
London, 17, 1 ; Boston (U.S.), 5, 0.

Colley, Collie.—Bapt. ' the son
of Nicholas,' from nick. Coll, and
dim. Colley ; v. Colly and Colls.

' Ran Colle our dogge, and Talbot, and
    Gerlond ' : Chaucer, C. T. 15389.

All these are font-names (v. Talbot and Garland). One can scarce
help asking the question, that since
talbot has come to denominate a
particular species of dog, and is
taken from the personal name Talbot, why should not colley, another
name for a particular species, be

O 2

taken from Colley, the once familiar substitute for Nicholas? At any rate Chaucer places them together.

Johannes Colly, 1379 : P. T. Yorks. p.88.
Willelmus Colley, 1379 : ibid. p. 17.
1561. Roger Colley and Ellen Anderson: Marriage Lic. (London), i. 22.
1778. Married—John Collie and Mary Hodgson : St. Geo. Han. Sq. i. 291.
London, 8, 2 ; Boston (U.S.), 8, 1.

Collier, Collyer, Collyear.—

Occup. 'the collier,' i.e. a charcoal-burner. '1598, Jan. 8. Buried, a daughter of a collier at Blawith' (Registers, Ulverston). An Act of Parliament (Elizabeth) is entitled, 'An Act that timber shall not be felled to make *coals* for the burning of iron.' The Psalmist speaks of 'coals of juniper.' Collier is the term still used throughout Furness and along the Duddon for a charcoal burner. The fuel was used in the bloom-smithies. See Ashburner and Bloomer.

Adam Colier, 1379 : P. T. Yorks. p. 233.
Benedictus Colier, 1379 : ibid.
John le Collier. C.
Henry le Colyer, co. Bucks, 1273. A.
Robert le Coliere, co. Bedf., ibid.
Thomas le Colier, co. Hunts, ibid.
1570. Zachary Collyer and Alice Hawkyns: Marriage Lic. (London), i. 47.
London, 42, 22, 1 ; New York, 25, 7, 0.

Collin, Collins, Collinson, Colling, Collings, Collinge.—

Bapt. 'the son of Nicholas,' from nick. Coll or Cole, dim. Col-in (cf. Rob-in, Jen-in, &c.). The *g* in Colling and Collings is excrescent (cf. Jennings). Through careless pronunciation, Collings has become Collinge. v. Cole.

Colinus de Newill, co. Linc., 1273. A.
William fil. Colini, co. York, ibid.
Alan Colin, co. Norf., ibid.
John fil. Colini, co. Suff., ibid.
John Colyngs, co. Soms., 1 Edw. III : Kirby's Quest, p. 169.
Johannes Colinson, 1379 : P. T. Yorks. p. 74.
Johannes Colynson, 1379 : ibid. p. 239.
Colin serviens Johann' Vest, 1379 : ibid. p. 88.
Colina Charles, co. Norf., Hen. III– Edw. I. K.
1585. William Inman and Katherine Collyn : Marriage Lic. (London), i. 141.
1682. Married — Jacob Marsh and Mabella Collins : St. Michael, Cornhill, p. 43.
London, 4, 178, 12, 4, 18, 1 ; New York, 13, 425, 0, 1, 1, 1.

Collingham.—

Local, 'of Collingham,' a parish in the W. Rid. Yorks, near Wetherby.

Johannes de Colyngham, 1379 : P. T. Yorks. p. 22.
Thomas de. Colyngham, 1379 : ibid. p. 223.
1613. Married—Thomas Smith and Marie Collingham : St. Michael, Cornhill, p. 20.
Sheffield, 1 ; Keighley, 1.

Collingwood.—

Local, 'of Collingwood.' This is a Northumberland surname, and it has flourished there for centuries. No doubt the spot so called is in that county, but I have not discovered it.

'Lord Collingwood (1750–1810) was born in Newcastle-on-Tyne, Sept. 26, 1750' : Dict. Nat. Biog. xi. 357.
'Roger Collingwood (fl. 1513), mathematician, wrote under the name of Carbo-in-ligno!' ibid. p. 362.
Robert Collingwoode, co. Durham, 1542 : QQQ. p. xx.
Edward Collingwood, co. Linc., 1589 : Reg. Univ. Oxf. vol. ii. pt. ii. p 175.
1690. Bapt. — Thomas, s. Thomas Collinwood : St. Jas. Clerkenwell, i. 337.
1764. Married—Edward Collingwood and Mary Hurnby : St. Geo. Han. Sq. i. 129.
London, 14 ; MDB. (co. Northumberland), 5 ; Boston (U.S.), 4.

Collis, Collison, Colliss, Collisson.—

Bapt. 'the son of Nicholas,' from nick. Col, dim. Colly, patronymic Collys, now Collis, Collison of course being the fuller form (v. Colly). Nevertheless as Pattinson becomes Pattison, so Collinson might become Collison (v. Collin). The origin remains the same.

1574. Thomas Collys and Johanna Chapman : Marriage Lic. (London), i. 60.
1640. Married — Rafe Collesson and Margere Knight : St. Michael, Cornhill, p. 28.
London, 14, 9, 2, 2 ; Sheffield, 2, 0, 2, 0 ; Philadelphia, 10, 1, 0, 5 ; New York, 2, 2, 0, 0.

Collishaw ; v. Cowlishaw.

Colls, Colles.—

Bapt. 'the son of Nicholas,' from nick. Coll, Col, or Cole (v. Cole), patronymic Colls.

Alan Colle, co. Linc., 1273. A.
Adam Colle, co. Hunts, ibid.
Sweyn Colle, co. Wilts, 20 Edw. I. R.
Cf. Johannes Colson, 1379 : P. T. Yorks. p. 168.
Anabilla Coll, 1379 : ibid. p. 174.
Colle Badyer, 1379 : ibid. p. 282.

1777. Married—Joseph Colles and Esther Copithorn : St. Geo. Han. Sq. ii. 274.
1796. — Joseph Clark and Ann Colls : ibid. p. 60.
'Yesterday, a defence was entered by Mr. P. Coll, Crown Solicitor (Ireland),' &c. : Daily Telegraph, Dec. 8, 1887, p. 5.
London, 8, 0 ; Crockford, 0, 2 ; New York, 0, 3.

Collumbell, Collambell.—

Bapt. 'the son of Columbell'; v. Columbine, of which it seems to be a kind of diminutive.

John Columbel, co. Camb., 1273. A.
Thomas Columbell, of Manchester, 1623 : Wills at Chester (1621–50), p. 51.
1763. Married—David Collumbell and Eliz. Clarke : St. Geo. Han. Sq. i. 124.
1801. — Nathaniel Collumbell and Amelia Bentley : ibid. p. 238.
Derby, 6, 0 ; London, 0, 1.

Colly, Collie, Colley.—

Bapt. 'the son of Nicholas,' from nick. Col and Cole, dim. Colley, q.v. This form of Nicholas was extremely popular in Yorkshire, judging by the Poll Tax. I furnish but a few instances.

Adam Coly, 1379 : P. T. Yorks. p. 12.
Agnes Coly, 1379 : ibid.
Rogerus Coly, 1379 : ibid.
Willelmus Colly, 1379 : ibid. p. 17.
1561. Roger Colley and Ellen Anderson : Marriage Lic. (London), i. 22.
London, 8, 2, 0 ; Boston (U.S.), 0, 1, 9.

Colnett, Colenutt, Collinette.—

Bapt. 'the son of Nicholas,' from nick. Col, and double dim. Col-in-et. Double diminutives are rare in England, common in France ; cf. Dobinet and Robinet.

'Hearken awhile from thy green cabinet, The laurel song of careful Colinet.'
Spenser's Shepherd's Calendar.

Elsewhere in the poem it is Colin.

Colinet de la Mare : Wars of England in France (Henry VI), v. index.
Colinet de Grandchamp : ibid.

Collinette, a French importation, occurs in the London Directory (1884).

1696. Married—Hussey Collnett and Eliz. Swan : St. Michael, Cornhill, p. 49.
London, 1, 0, 0 ; Leeds, 0, 1, 0.

Colpitts.—

Local, 'of the coalpits,' found, as would naturally be expected, in Newcastle and neighbourhood.

1576–7. Nicholas Collpotts and Katherine Tatham : Marriage Lic. (London), i. 74.

John Colepitts, *hoastman*, 1729 (epitaph, St. Nicholas, Newcastle-on-Tyne): Braund's Newcastle, i. 385.
George Colpits, of Killingworth, 1763: ibid. i. 509.
Newcastle, 1.

Colson.—Bapt. 'the son of Nicholas,' from nick. Col or Cole, popularly Colley.

Johannes Collesson, 1379: P. T. Yorks. p. 21.
Johannes Colleson, 1379: ibid. p. 57.
Isabel Colson, 1495, co. York. W. 11, p. 161.
John Cowlson, 1512: ibid. p. 179
1563. Buried—Goodwife Colson: St. Jas. Clerkenwell, iv. 5.
1579. Richard Richardson and Eliz. Colson: Marriage Lic. (London), i. 88.
London, 7; New York, 3.

Colston, Coulston, Coulstone.—Local, (1) 'of Colston,' a parish in co. Notts. The surname early crept into co. York. (2) 'of Coulston,' a parish in co. Wilts, eight miles from Devizes. Edward Colston, merchant and philanthropist, was born at Bristol, 1636 (Dict. Nat. Biog. xi. 406). The surname, with variants, still exists in cos. Wilts, Gloucester, and Somerset.

John de Colston, co. Notts,20 Edw.I. R.
William Colstan, co. York, 1273. A.
Johannes Colstane, 1379: P. T. Yorks. p. 151.
1575. William Starte and Judith Coldestone: Marriage Lic. (London),i.65.
1797. Married—Thomas Colston and Susannah Bowra: St. Geo. Han.Sq.ii.173.
5, 0, 0; (Wilts), 1, 0, 0; (co. Glouc.), 2, 1, 1; Philadelphia, 5, 1, 0.

Colt.—Nick. 'the colt'; cf. Bull, Cow, Stagg, Buck, &c. For a variant, v. Coult. The sobriquet would readily be affixed on one of frisky, springy action.

'He was al coltish, ful of ragerie.'
Chaucer, C. T. 9721.
Reginald le Colt, co. Salop, 1273. A.
William le Colt, co. Wilts, ibid.
Ranulph Colt, co. Norf., ibid.
Ricardus Colte, 1379: P. T. Yorks. p. 81.
Thomas Colt, 1379: ibid. p. 83.
Henry le Colt, co. Lanc., 1332: Lay Subsidy (Rylands), p. 23.
1572-3. Richard Colte and Frances Dennys: Marriage Lic. (London), i. 55.
1609. Nicholas Colte, rector of Shimpling, co. Norf.: FF. i. 155.
London, 3; Philadelphia, 2.

Coltart.—Occup. 'the coltherd'; v. Coulthard.

Coltman, Coultman.—Occup. 'the coltman,' a colt-herd (v. Coulthard); cf. Cowman, Bulman, Hefferman.

Geoffrey Coltman, 1313. M.
Richard Coltman, 1494, co. York. W. 11.
1703. Married—Thomas Coultman and Margaret Davis: St. Michael, Cornhill, p. 52.
1759. — Nathaniel Coltman and Eliz. Taylor: St. Geo. Han. Sq. i. 90.
London, 6, 1; MDB. (co. Lincoln), 5, 2; Boston (U.S.), 4, 0.

Colton.—Local, 'of Colton,' parishes in cos. Norfolk and Stafford; also a township in the parish of Bolton Percy, West Rid. Yorks. Often confounded with Coulton, q.v.

John de Coleton, co. Devon, 1273. A.
Henry de Colton, co. Stafford, 20 Edw. I. R.
Willelmus de Colton, 1379: P. T. Yorks. p. 215.
Johannes de Colton, 1379: ibid.
Nicholas de Coltone, co. Soms., 1 Edw. III: Kirby's Quest, p. 167.
Thomas de Coltone, co. Soms., 1 Edw. III: ibid.
1656. Married—Firman Holton and Anne Colton: St. Dionis Backchurch,p. 32.
London, 2; Sheffield, 5; Boston (U.S.), 24.

Coltson.—(1) Bapt. a variant of Colson, q.v. (2) Local, a variant of Colston, q.v.

1564. Buried—Thomas Coltson: St. Dionis Backchurch, p. 189.
London, 2.

Columbine, Cullumbine, Cullabine.—Bapt. 'the son of Columbine,' 'dove-like' (Yonge, i. 387). Columbina le Noreis (Rot. Claus., 14 Hen. III). The surname is found at Barnsley, Yorks, as Collumbine, and at Sheffield as Cullabine.

1625. William Collenbine and Parnell Webb: Marriage Lic. (London), ii. 158.
1739. Peter Colombine, Norwich: FF. iii. 452.
1740. Married—Adam Colonbine and Mary Nicholson: St. Mary, Ulverston, ii. 379.
1757. Paul Columbine, rector of Thurlton, co. Norf.: FF. viii. 61.
London, 1, 0, 0; Barnsley, 0, 1, 0; Sheffield, 0, 0, 1.

Colville, Colvile, Colvill, Colwell, Colwill. — Local, 'of Colville.' Lower says, 'There are three places in Normandy called Colleville. . . . From which of these came William de Colvile of Yorkshire, and Gilbert de Collavilla of Suffolk, mentioned in Domesday, is not yet ascertained' (Patr. Brit. p. 66). With Colwell and Colwill, cf. Boswell for Bosville. There is a township named Colwell in the parish of Chollerton, co. Northumberland. But the above is the more probable origin.

Roger de Colevil, co. Norf., 1273. A.
Walter de Colevile, co. Linc., ibid.
Philip de Colevill, co. Linc., ibid.
Roger de Colewell, co. Glouc., ibid.
John de Colvele, co. Camb., ibid.
Philip de Colwil, co. Camb., ibid.
Johannes Colvill, et Magota uxor ejus, *taillour*, 1379: P. T. Yorks. p. 67.
Peter Colewille, co. Soms., 1 Edw. III: Kirby's Quest, p. 144.
John Colwelle, co. Soms., 1 Edw. III: ibid. p. 182.
1642. John Colwell and Mary Chancy: Marriage Lic. (London), ii. 265.
1739. Married—John Edwards and Hannah Colvill: St. Michael, Cornhill, p. 68.
London, 1, 1, 2, 2, 2; New York, 4, 0. 2, 33, 0; Boston (U.S.), 5, 0, 0, 7, 1.

Colvin, Colven.—Bapt. 'the son of Colvin.' 'Colvin or Colvinus was a Devonshire tenant-in-chief, and held his lands in the reign of Edward the Confessor, and at the making of Domesday' (Lower's Patr. Brit. p. 65). Coffin, which is still found in co. Devon as a surname (v. Coffin), is in many cases but a variant.

1733. Married—Thomas Brewer and Jane Colvin: St. Jas. Clerkenwell, iii. 261.
London, 2, 1; Philadelphia, 5, 0.

Colwell, Colwill; v. Colville.

Combe, Combes, Combs.—Local, 'at the comb,' i.e. the cell or hollow in the hillside. An enormous number of local compounds are based on this word, probably because, being sheltered, habitations were made there. Celtic, *cwm*, a hollow. Probably, however, the instances below refer to the A.S. *camb*, the crest of a hill. Combs and Combes have taken *s* as a suffix, as with many other one-syllabled local surnames; cf. Styles, Brooks, Briggs, Holmes, &c.

John in le Coumbe, co. Soms , 1 Edw.
III : Kirby's Quest, p. 79.
Gilbert ate Cumbe, co Oxf., 1273. A.
John ate Cumbe, co. Oxf, ibid.
Roger de la Cumbe, co. Oxf., ibid.
Henry de la Cumbe, co. Soms., ibid.
John de la Coumbe, co. Glouc., 1289:
Household Exp., Ric. de Swinfield, Camd.
Soc., p. lxxxv.
Robertus Combe, 1379 : P. T. Yorks,
p. 5.
Radulphus de Combe, 1379 : ibid. p. 6.
Edmund de la Comb, co. Norf., 16
Edw. I : FF, vii. 347.
1522. William Combes and Eliz.
Walsyngham : Marriage Lic. (London),
i. 2.
1573. John Combe and Sicily Palfre-
man : ibid. p. 56.
London, 3, 2, 5 ; Philadelphia, 1, 4, 16.

Comber, Comer, Cumber.—
Occup. 'the comber,' i.e. the wool-
comber ; cf. Kempster. The early
importance of this occupation was
bound to create and preserve this
surname. Comer drops the b : usually
after m the same letter is intrusive ;
but there is no accounting for the
freaks of popular nomenclature.

Richard le Cumbere, co. Camb.,1273. A.
John le Cumbur, co. Oxf., ibid.
Walter le Comber. E.
1662. Married—Toby Comer and Sarah
Parker : St. Peter, Cornhill, i. 263.
1792. — Thomas Comber, *clerk*, and
Eliz. Coote : St. Geo. Han. Sq. ii. 78.
London, 4. 4. 5 ; Philadelphia, 13, 3, 0.

Comberbach, Comberbirch.
—Local ; v. Cumberbatch.

**Comfort, Comford, Com-
port, Comeford. —** Local, ' of
Comport.' Mr. F. A. Crisp, in one
of his collections of pedigrees,
clearly shows that the family of
Comport was frequently known
as Comfort. Nevertheless, Comfort is found so early as the Hundred Rolls of 1273. Therefore in
some cases it may be a nickname.
But the local derivation is preferable.

Richard Cumfort, co. Oxf., 1273. A.
William Cumfort, *grocer*, C. R., 14
Hen. VI.

Mr. Crisp (Fragmenta Genea-
logica, v. 1) has 'Edward Comport, alias Comford, of Chiselhurst,
co. Kent.' His son was 'Richard
Comport, alias Comfort, of Chiselhurst.' It is curious to observe
that in the Modern Domesday
Book (1875) the county of Kent is

represented by one Comfort and
four Comports. Hence it is certain
that Comfort is in many cases an
imitative variant of Comport, or
Comford, a local surname.

1665. Married—Abraham Comefort and
Kathern Mitchell : St. Jas. Clerkenwell,
iii. 122.
1794. — Edward Edwards and Jane
Comport : St. Geo. Han. Sq. ii. 121.
London, 8, 0, 0, 0 ; MDB. (co. Kent),
1, 0, 4, 0 ; Philadelphia, 24, 2, 0, 4.

Commander.—Offic. 'the commander'; cf. commodore. I was
surprised, on referring to the London Directory, to find the surname
still in existence.

William le Cummandur, or Comandur,
co. Soms., 1273. A.
Randolph Comander, of Preston, 1701 :
Lancashire Wills at Richmond, p. 64.
Ralph Commander, of Preston, 1744 :
ibid.
1603. Buried—James Comaunder : St.
Jas. Clerkenwell, iv. 82.
1663. Charles Fleetwood, of Feltwell,
co. Norf. and Dame Mary Hartoppe, of
Newington, co. Middlesex ; alleged by
Hercules Commander, of St. Faith's,
London, gent. : Marriage Lic. (Faculty
Office), p. 76.
London, 2.

Complin.—Nick. (?). I cannot
explain this surname, saving from
compline, the last service of the
day :

' Lo whilke a complin is ymell hem alle.'
Chaucer, C. T. 4169.

The chaplain might get the
sobriquet through some forgotten
incident.

Katherin Complin, 1690 : St. Peter,
Cornhill, ii. 103.
1640. Henry Complyn. vicar of
Witchingham. co. Norf. : FF. viii. 307.
1668. Philip Complin and Alice Purdue :
Marriage Lic. (Faculty Office), p. 1.
London, 1 ; co. Hants, 3.

Comport ; v. Comfort.

Compson.—Local, ' of Compston.' I do not for a moment
suppose this is of baptismal origin,
or that the final *son* is the patronymic as in Wilson, Thomson,
&c. There is no personal name
Com or Comp, nor any pet form
of any personal name so formed.
No doubt it is a local surname
which has dropped the *t*. I cannot
discover the locality, however ; cf.
Kelson for Kelston. This class is
a fairly large one.

London, 1 ; MDB. (co. Stafford), 2 ;
Philadelphia, 1.

Compton.—Local, ' of Compton,' parishes in cos. Berks, Hants,
Surrey, Sussex, Wilts, Dorset,
Gloucester, Somerset, &c. Many
smaller spots bear the name in
various counties.

Edith de Compton, co. Soms., 1 Edw.
III : Kirby's Quest, p. 128.
Nicholas de Compton, co. Linc.,1273. A.
Richard de Comton, co. Camb., ibid.
Bartholomew de Compton, co. Wilts,
20 Edw. I. R.
Robert de Compton, co. Linc.. ibid.
Odo de Compton, co. Southampton,
Hen. III–Edw. I. K.
1610. Bapt.—Mary, d. John Compton :
St. Jas. Clerkenwell, i. 60.
1698. Married—William Compton and
Eliz. Hatton: St. Dionis Backchurch, p.47.
London, 16 ; Philadelphia, 14.

**Comyn, Comyns, Commin,
Comins, Cumin, Cumings,
Cummin, Cumming, Cum-
mings, Cummins.—**? Local, ' de
Comines' (?). This is the customary Norman derivation. I find no
positive evidence in favour of the
view. William Cumine, Lord Chancellor of Scotland, temp. David I,
is said to have laid the foundation of what became one of the
most influential houses in Scotland
(Lower's Patr. Brit.). Whatever
be the origin, all the forms here
given are variants of the surname
Comyn.

Admund le Comyn, co. Norf., 14 Edw.
II : FF. ix. 435.
Florentina Comin, co. Oxf., 1273. A.
Peter Comyn, co. Wilts, ibid.
Stephen Comyng, co. Essex, ibid.
Thomas Comyn, co. Glouc., ibid.
Alexander Comyn, co. Oxf., 20 Edw.
I. R.
David Comyn, co. Northumb., Hen.
III–Edw. I. K.
William Cumyn, co. Wilts, ibid.
1642. Bapt.—Sarah, d. Christopher
Cummins : St. Jas. Clerkenwell, i. 153.
1698. Robert Comins and Mary Henley :
Marriage Lic. (London), ii. 323.
1708. John Comyns and Eliz. Court-
hope : ibid. p. 337.
1764. Married—Thomas Hendy and
Mary Comming : St. Geo. Han. Sq. i. 131.
London, 3, 1, 1, 1, 1, 4, 2, 20, 8, 16 ;
New York, 1, 0, 0. 3, 0, 2, 0, 25, 124, 20.

**Conan, Conant, Connant,
Connand, Conning, Connon.**
—Bapt. 'the son of Conan,' an
early legendary name (v. Yonge,

ii. 82). No doubt more modern representatives of this name would be found in our directories had not Conan as a surname got confused with the more ecclesiastical Cannon or Canon. The final *t* and *d* in Conant and Conand are, of course, excrescences.

Conon Bardoul was ninth Abbot of Furness (circa 1185): West's Antiquities of Furness, p. 84.
Conan de Kirketun, co. Linc., Hen. III-Edw. I. K.
Conan le Mire, Hen. III. T.
Conan Piscator, co. Linc., 1273. A.
Petronilla fil. Conayn, co. Linc., ibid.
William Conayn, co. Linc., ibid.
Henry fil. Conani, co. York, ibid.
Robert Connand et uxor ejus, 1379: P. T. Yorks. p. 233.
Adam Conand, 1379: P. T. Howdenshire, p. 22.
Conon d'Ask, co. York, 1391: DDD. i. 51.
'Robert Beste, chaplain to chantry, St. John Gateshead, on the presentation of the patron, Conane Barton, Esq , 1496': Brand's Hist. Newcastle-on-Tyne, i. 492.

As a personal name Conan lingered on till the close of the 15th century. It is also interesting to notice that in the two counties (York and Lincoln) where we find the personal name was once in use we see the surname flourishing to-day.

Cunan Metcalfe, 1501: PPP. p. 3.
1788. Married — Michael Conon and Mary Ann Budd : St. Geo. Han. Sq. ii. 15.

Conning was an inevitable variation :

1775. Married—John Coning and Mary Freer: St. Geo. Han. Sq. i. 251.
1806. — Thomas Conning and Maria Adey : ibid. ii. 357.
MDB. (co. Lincoln), 0, 3, 1, 0, 0, 0; New York, 1, 14, 0, 0, 0, 0; MDB. (North Rid. Yorks), Conning, 2; Dewsbury (co. York), Connon, 1.

Conder.—Occup. 'the conder,' one who signals to boats from a height the direction taken by shoals of herring or pilchards ; from *con*, to con, to observe closely. For intrusive *d*, cf. Pinner and Pinder, ribbon and riband, Simmons and Simmonds. 'Conders (of a ship), those who *cond* or give direction to the steersman for guiding or governing of a ship' (Bailey, 1737). An Act, 1 James I, c. xxiii, says, 'persons called Balcors, Huors,

Condors, Directors, or Guidors, at the fishing tymes . . . have used to watch and attend upon the high hilles and grounde near adjoining to the sea coast . . . for the givinge notice to the fishermen.'

1658. Bapt.—Francis, sonne of Francis Condor: Canterbury Cathedral, p. 11.
1714. Married—Samuel Conder and Esther Carpenter : St. Mary Aldermary, p. 42.
London, 2 ; MDB. (West Rid. Yorks), 4.

Conelly.—Local, ' of Conely,' not Irish, but English, with termination in *ley* ; cf. Coneybeare in the same district. Conelly probably means the meadow frequented by coneys, i. e. rabbits.

Henry Conely, co. Soms., 1 Edw. III :
Kirby's Quest, p. 237.
John Conely, co. Soms., 1 Edw. III : ibid.
London, 7 ; New York, 2.

Coney.—Nick. 'the coney,' i.e. rabbit ; cf. Hare. 'Cony, *cuniculus*' (Prompt. Parv.).

Griffin Cony, co. Hereford, Hen. III-Edw. I. K.
Richard Conni, co. Salop, 1273. A.
John Conay, co. Hunts, ibid.
Henry Coney, of Ditton, 1592 ; Wills at Chester (1545-1620), p. 43.
Grace Coney, of Halsall, *widow*, 1595 : ibid.
1585. Bapt.—Sara, d. Thomas Cony : St. Jas. Clerkenwell, i. 17.
1794. Married—Samuel Coney and Eliz. Mills : St. Geo. Han. Sq. ii. 109.
London, 5 ; Philadelphia, 2.

Coneybeare, Coneybeer, Conibear, Connabear, Connibear, Connibeer, Conybear, Conibeer.—Local, ' of Collibear,' a hamlet in the parish of Tawstock, co. Devon. The change from *l* to *n* is common ; cf. *bannister* and *baluster*. This is a familiar Devonshire name. The suffix is very common in local names in that district ; cf. Phillimore and Finamore.

1690. John Conybeare and Grace Wilcocks : Marriage Lic. (Faculty Office), p. 197.
1757. Married—Richard Colliber and Ann Vitty : St. Geo. Han. Sq. i. 69.
Devon County Dir. (Farmers' List), 1, 1, 1, 1, 1, 2, 1, 0 ; London (Conibeer), 1.

Congreve, Congreave.—Local, ' of Congreave.' I cannot find the spot ; cf. M.E. *coni*, a rabbit ; M.E. *grave*, probably a woodland

avenue, graved, or cut out of the forest (v. Greaves).

'William Congreve (1670-1729), the dramatist, was born at Bardsey, near Leeds. The family had long been settled at Stretton, co. Stafford': Dict. Nat. Biog. xii. 6.
Mark Conigrave, or Cunygrave, 1556 : Reg. Univ. Oxf. i. 233.
1667. John Congrave and Eliz. Orton : Marriage Alleg. (Canterbury), p. 216.
1789. Married—Thomas Congreve and Mary Oades : St. Geo. Han. Sq. ii. 17.
London, 2, 0 ; MDB. (co. Stafford), 0, 1 ; New York, 3, 0.

Coning.— Bapt. 'the son of Conan,' sometimes Conayn and Coning ; v. Conan.

Nicholas fil. Coning, 1273. A.
Michael Conning. W. 20.
Peter Conyng. P.
Nicholas Conyng. H.

Coningham.—(1) Local, ' of Coningham,' a parish in the dioc. of St. Albans. To be carefully distinguished from Cunningham, q.v.

Robert de Coningham, London, 1273. A.

(2) Local, ' of Conisholme,' a parish in dioc. of Lincoln, formerly Coningholm as well as Conisholm.

Alan de Coningholm, co. Linc., 1273. A.
Alan de Coningesholm, co. Linc., 20 Edw. I. R.

Coningholm is several times the surname of this same Alan in the Hundred Rolls. In a general way (1) must be looked upon as the home of the Coninghams of to-day.

1781. Married—Thomas Coningham and Ann Seager : St. Geo. Han. Sq. i. 326. London, 5.

Coningsby, Conisbee, Collisbe, Conigsby.—Local, ' of Coningsby,' a parish in co. Lincoln, eight miles from Horncastle. Conisbee is a manifest variant. In the neighbouring county of Notts, Conisbee has become Collisbe ; cf. *bannister* and *baluster*, *n* for *l* or *l* for *n* being common in nomenclature.

Christopher Conynsby, co. Norf. : FF. ix. 156.
Amphelicia Conynsby, co. Norf., temp. Hen. VII : ibid. ii. 180.
John Conysby, co. Norf., 36 Hen. VIII : ibid. viii. 329.
1563. Buried—Humphreye Conysbye : St. Michael, Cornhill, p. 187.

1586. Married—William Tynmarke and Bennet Conesby: St. Jas. Clerkenwell, iii. 12.

Thus it is clear that Conisbee is a variant at least 350 years old ; cf. Applebee for Appleby.

London, 2, 2, 0, 0; MDB. (co. Notts), 0, 0, 1, 0 ; Philadelphia, 0, 0, 0, 1.

Conner ; v. Cuner.

Connington.—Local, 'of Connington,' parishes in cos. Camb. and Hunts. My first instance shows that there is or was a Connington in co. York.

William de Conyngton in Cravene, 12 Edw. III : Freemen of York, i. 33.
Robert de Conyton, co. Camb., 1273. A.
Robert de Conintone, co. Bedf., ibid.
William de Coniton, co. Camb., ibid.
John de Conitone, co. Hunts, ibid.

Connop.—Local, 'of Conhope,' a township in the parish of Aymestrey, co. Hereford, four miles from Pembridge. The surname is still distinctly a Herefordshire one.

1776. Married—Joseph Eeles and Sarah Connop: St. Geo. Han. Sq. i. 268.
London, 1 ; MDB. (co. Hereford), 7.

Conquerant, Conqueror, Conquestor.—Nick. 'the conqueror,' one who was champion in wrestling, &c. ; cf. Campion or Champion.

Robert Conqueraunt, co. Oxf., 1273. A.
William Conqueror, London, ibid.
William Conquestor, co. Wilts, ibid.

Conquest. — ? Local, 'de la Conquest' (?), from residence on some estate won by fighting. I can suggest no other derivation (v. Conquerant). Lower says, 'Houghton-Conquest, co. Bedford, derives its suffix from the family who were possessors of it before 1298' (Patr. Brit. p. 67). Conquest is still a Bedfordshire surname.

John Conquest, co. Bedf., 20 Edw. I. R.
Alicia Conquest, co. Bedf., ibid.
1630. Robert Remmington and Catharine Conquest : Marriage Lic. (London), ii. 200.
1724. Married—John Conquest and Mary Rivington : St. Jas. Clerkenwell, iii. 250.
London, 5; MDB. (co. Bedford), 1 ; Philadelphia, 4.

Considine, Cossentine.—Bapt. 'the son of Constantine,' corrupted through Cossentine; cf. Consterdine. In Cornwall and Devon, where both forms are known, Constantine was a favourite fontname in the past, as the registers of St. Columb Major fully prove.

Cornwall Dir. (Farmers' List), 0, 3 ; New York, 8, 0.

Constable.—Offic. 'the constable,' a peace-officer. O.F. *conestable.*

'And comaunded a constable.'
                              Piers P. 1278.
Margareta Constabille, 1379 : P. T. Yorks. p. 105.
Ricardus Constabularius, 1379 : ibid. p. 79.
John le Conestable. B.
Robert le Conestable. G.
Jordan Constabul', co. Northumb., 1273. A.
Clemens le Conestable, co. Norf., ibid.
William Constable, co. Kent, ibid.
1617. Married—Robert Constable and Jane Record : St. Jas. Clerkenwell, iii. 44.
1639-40. Marmaduke Constable and Anne Davies : Marriage Lic. (London), ii. 247.
London, 12 ; Philadelphia, 8.

Constance.—(1) Bapt. 'the son of Constantine,' popularly Constan. With the patronymic *s* this became Constans, and then Constance ; v. Costain. (2) Bapt. 'the son of Constance,' popularly Custance, q.v. Constance was often a boy's name.

1568. Bapt.—Constance, s. William Frenshe : St. Jas. Clerkenwell, i. 4.
1629. 'Petition of Captain Constance Ferrar for losses at Cape Bretun' : Cal. State Papers (Colonial).
1665. 'Communication from Constance Pley to the Commissioners in relation to the arrival of a convoy' : ibid. (Home).
1792. Married—George Medley and Eliz. Constance: St. Geo. Han. Sq. ii. 84. London, 3.

Constantine.—(1) Bapt. 'the son of Constantine' ; M.E. Constantyn. The name was decidedly popular, and as a surname is found also in the forms of Consterdine, Cossentine, and Considine, q.v. Costain (q.v.) was the nick. form.

'Shul fynden a Keye of Costantyns cofres' : Piers P. 6254-5.
Johanna Constantine, co. Kent, 1273. A.
Nicholas Costentin, co. Hunts, ibid.
Geoffrey Costentin, co. Bedf., 20 Edw. I. R.
Constantinus Walker, 1379 : P. T. Yorks. p. 147.
Johannes Costantyn, 1379 : ibid. p. 240.

(2) Local, 'of Constantine,' a village and parish near Falmouth, co. Cornwall.

Thomas de Costantin, co. Salop, 1273. A.
Roger de Costantyn, co. Salop, ibid.
1702. Bapt.—' John Constantine, whose mother fell in labour in the street ': St. Michael, Cornhill, p. 160.
London, 3; Sheffield, 5; West Rid. Court Dir., 5 ; New York, 6.

Consterdine.—Bapt. 'the son of Constantine.' Consterdine is found in cos. Lancashire and Yorkshire, where Constantine or Costantine was chiefly popularized. I do not think there can be any question on the subject. Consterdine must be regarded as a variant of Constantine.

Manchester, 2 ; Philadelphia, 3.

Converse.—Nick. 'the convert,' one who had become an adherent of the Church, one who had submitted to Church ordinances.

Roger le Convers, co. Glouc., 1273. A.
Richard Conversus, co. York, ibid.
John le Convers, co. Norf., ibid.
Dionise le Convers, co. Camb., ibid.
1635-6. Joseph Mann, gent., of Sudbury, Suffolk, and Mary Essex, of East Merse, co. Essex . . . John Convers, of Pelden, attests consent of Richard Essex, his brother-in-law : Marriage Lic. (London), ii. 225.
1691. Robert Brissenden and Livewell Convers : Marriage Alleg. (Canterbury), p. 192.
Boston (U.S.), 27.

Conway.—Local, 'of Conway,' one of the few Welsh towns that have originated a surname. In the United States this name has ramified in a most extraordinary manner. Aron Conway was settled in Virginia in 1623 (Hotten's Lists of Emigrants, p. 179). The forms of the name in Hotten's Lists are Conaway, Conoway, and Conway (v. index) ; cf. Greenaway and Ottaway for Greenway and Otway.

1561. Bapt.—John, s. Rowland Connyway : St. Jas. Clerkenwell, i. 1.
1584. Married—John Conaway and Catherine Bramgan : St. Jas. Clerkenwell, iii. 11.
1612. Thomas Conway and Barbara Burt : Marriage Lic. (London), ii. 13.
1625. John Connaway and Grace Temperance (sic) : ibid. p. 156.
1629. Bapt.—Eliz., d. John Conoway : St. Michael, Cornhill, p. 120.
London, 21 ; Philadelphia, 210.

Conyers. — Local, 'de Coigniers.' Lower says that 'Roger de Coigniers came into England about the end of the reign of William the Conqueror, to whom the Bishop of Durham gave the constableship of Durham. The family gave the suffix to Howton Coigniers, co. York' (Patr. Brit. p. 68).

Adam le (sic) Conyers, co. Suff., 1273. A.
Robert le (sic) Conyers, co. Suff., 20 Edw. I. R.
1693. Married—John Barrett and Sarah Coniers : St. Jas. Clerkenwell, iii. 213.
1799. — John Barker and Caroline Conyers : St. Geo. Han. Sq. ii. 197.
London, 3 ; Philadelphia, 8.

Cooch. — A manifest variant of Gooch, q.v. ; cf. Candlin, Cammel, and Crane (2).

London, 1 ; MDB. (co. Hunts), 2 ; Boston (U.S.), 1.

Coode ; v. Coad.

Cook, Cooke. — Occup. 'the cook,' one who baked pies, &c., for sale.

'Brewesters, Bakers, Bochers, and Cookes.'　　　　Piers Plowman.
'Drovers, cokes, and pulters,
Yermongers, pybakers, and waferers.'
　　　　Cocke Lorelle's Bote.

The Corpus Christi Play (York) styles them 'Cukes'; the Norwich Play includes them among the 'Vintners, Brewers, Hostlers, and Inkeapers.' An ordinance passed 2 Ric. II styles them Cooks and Pastelers (v. my English Surnames, 3rd edit. p. 365). Coke (q.v.) is an early form. Every early register teems with the name.

John Cocus, co. Norf., 1273. A.
Alexander Cocus, co. York, ibid.
Emma Coca, co. Camb., ibid.
Matthew Cocus, co. Oxf., ibid.
Roger le Cok, temp. 1300. M.
1611. Bapt.—Rachael, d. John Cooke : St. Dionis Backchurch, p. 94.
1631-2. Married—Edmund Shoard and Dorothee Cooke : ibid. p. 23.
London, 193, 89 ; Boston (U.S.), 273, 29.

Cooker. — (1) Local ; v. Coker. (2) Occup. ; v. Cocker. This variant is now only found in the States, but it is preserved in English registers. The more likely origin is (1).

1797. Married—Samuel Cooker and Eliz. Lipscombe : St. Geo. Han. Sq. ii. 174.
Philadelphia, 10.

Cookman. — Occup. ; v. Cockman.

Cooks. — Occup. 'the son of the cook'; v. Cook and Cookson ; cf. Wills and Wilson, Sims and Simson, Watts and Watson, &c. It is not often an occupative name takes the patronymic as if it were a personal name, but sometimes such is the case ; cf. Taylorson, Clarkson, Widdowson ; v. next article.

1589. William Cookes and Ann Jennets : Marriage Lic. (London), i. 183.
1809. Married—William Cookes and Mary Cheetham : St. Geo. Han. Sq. ii. 420.
London, 1 ; Boston (U.S.), 1.

Cookson, Cuckson. — Nick. 'the cook's son'; cf. Taylorson, Wrightson, Smithson, Clarkson. It seems absolutely impossible to distinguish between Cookson and Cockson (or Coxon), they have been so inextricably mixed for centuries (v. Cocks). Cuckson is a Yorkshire variant of Cookson. It is interesting to note that 'Cukes' is the style given to the Cooks' Company in the York Pageant (1415) ; v. my English Surnames, 3rd edit. p. 416.

William fil. Coci, co. Norf., 1273. A.
Robert fil. Coci, co. Suff., ibid.
Thomas Cokson, 1379 : P. T. Yorks. p. 275.
Henry Cukeson, 1457, co. York. W. 11.
1577. Bapt.—Anne Cukeson : St. Jas. Clerkenwell, i. 10.
1735. Married—Thomas Cookson and Margaret Robinson : St. Geo. Han. Sq. i. 16.
London, 9, 0 ; New York, 1, 1 ; Sheffield, 0, 2.

Coombe, Coombes, Coombs, Coomes. — Local ; v. Combe and Combes, of which they are variants.

1789. Married—Benjamin Coomes and Eliz. Hayward : St. Geo. Han. Sq. ii. 27.
1794. — Samuel Coombs and Jane Ann Vanderkeer : ibid. p. 112.
1798. — Thomas Coombe and Ann Lowe : ibid. p. 191.
1800. John Coombes and Mary Curtis : ibid. p. 216.
London, 4, 19, 17, 1 ; Boston (U.S.), 0, 3, 35, 1.

Coomber, Comber. — Occup. 'the comber'; v. Comber, a variant ; cf. Coombe for Combe.

1765. Married—Caleb Coomber and Isabella Swafford : St. Geo. Han. Sq. i. 150.

1792. Married—John Ball and Mary Coomer : ibid. ii. 75.
London, 6, 0 ; New York, 0, 1.

Coope, Coop. — Local, 'at the cope'; v. Cope.

1569-70. Buried—Eliz. Coupe : St. Jas. Clerkenwell, iv. 10.
1588. Bapt.—John, s. Edwarde Coope : ibid. i. 20.
1657. Married—Mathew Coope and Rachaell Tall : Reg. Canterbury Cath., p. 58.
1765. — John Chadwick and Susanna Coope : St. Geo. Han. Sq. i. 143.
London, 1, 0 ; Philadelphia, 1, 2.

Cooper, Couper. — Occup. 'the cooper,' a maker of tubs, casks, &c. ; v. Cowper. A common and early trade-name leaving many descendants.

Alan le Cupere, co. Camb., 1273. A.
Henry le Cupper, co. Notts, ibid.
Richard le Cupare, co. Oxf., ibid.
Jordan le Cupere, co. Oxf., ibid.
Willelmus Couper, 1379 : P. T. Yorks. p. 5.
Willelmus Milner, couper, 1379 : ibid. p. 14.
Robert Cupper, bailiff of Yarmouth, 1425 : FF. xi. 324.
1607. Married—William Cooper and Winifred Cope : St. Michael, Cornhill, p. 18.
London, 275, 4 ; New York, 213, 0.

Cooperson. — Occup. 'the son of the cooper'; cf. Taylorson, Wrightson, Smithson.

The Rev. Timothy Cooperson was vicar of Broughton-in-Furness, 1749-77 : Register of Broughton Church.

Cope. — Local, 'at the cope,' from residence at the summit, or cope of the hill, or eminence ; cf. Copestake and Copeland, and v. Copp.

1574. Buried—Joane Cope : St. Antholin (London), p. 23.
1612. Bapt.—Mary, d. John Cope : St. Jas. Clerkenwell, i. 64.
London, 27 ; Philadelphia, 86.

Copeland, Copland, Coupland. — Local, 'of Coupland,' a township in the parish of Kirk Newton, co. Northumberland. With Copland, cf. Copp. I believe a large tract of country in Cumberland also bore this name. The forms of the surname in the Ulverston registers are Copeland, Coupland, Cowpland, Cawpland, and Capeland. I suspect they represent the Cumberland locality. John de

Coupland was the hero of the battle of Neville's Cross in 1346. He took David Bruce prisoner. No doubt he represented the Northumberland township.

David de Coupelond, co. Northumb., 20 Edw. I. R.

Johannes de Coupeland', 1379 : P. T. Yorks. p. 47.

1611. Married—William Cawpland and Jeneta Colton : St. Mary, Ulverston, p.111.

1617. Henry Cowpland or Copeland, of Hornby : Lancashire Wills at Richmond, p. 78.

1619. Bapt.—James, s. James Copland : St. Jas. Clerkenwell, i. 84.

London, 15, 6, 5 ; Boston (U.S.), 49, 0, 0 ; Philadelphia, 30, 0, 3.

Copestake, Copestick, Copstick, Capstick, Capstack.—Local, ' at the copstake,' the post on the top of the round hill or mound ; *cob* or *cop*, a summit. ' Cop, a mound, a bank, a heap. North' (Halliwell) ; cf. copingstone. The name is North English, and has undergone several corruptions, of which Capstick is the commonest ; cf. Cape and Cope, Roper and Raper.

Johannes Copstake, 1379 : P. T. Yorks. p. 288.

Robertus Cowpstake, 1379 : ibid.

Ingrene Caupstake, 1379 : ibid.

John Cobstake, circa 1440, co. York. W. 2.

Thomas Capstack, vicar of Ash, 1783 : DDD. ii. 337.

Edward Capstack, 1791, vicar of Gill, Barnoldswick.

1729. Married—John Capstack and Eliz. Haynes : St. Geo. Chap. Mayfair, p. 297.

1749.—William Copestick and Dorothy Hewit : ibid. p. 149.

1800.—George Copestick and Sophia Findlow : St. Geo. Han. Sq. ii. 219.

London, 1, 2, 0, 0, 0 ; Manchester, 1, 0, 0, 1, 0 ; Preston, 0, 1, 2, 2, 0 ; Halifax (Capstack), 1 ; Sedbergh, 0, 0, 7, 0, 0 ; New York (Copestick), 1 ; Philadelphia, 0, 5, 0, 1, 0.

Copinger, Coppinger.— ? I cannot get at the derivation of this surname. Mr. Lower's suggestion is ridiculous : ' The more probable derivation is from *coppin*, which Halliwell defines as "a piece of yarn taken from the spindle." A Coppinger was then, perhaps, in mediaeval times, one who had the care of yarn, or who produced it' (!!!) : Patr. Brit. p. 68.

Adam Copinger, 1643 : Reg. St. Dionis Backchurch, London, p. 107.

Henry Copinger, co. Norf., 1573 : FF. i. 460.

1580. Edward Becher and Frances Coppinger, *widow* : Marriage Lic. (London), i. 97.

1661. Buried—Fraunces, d. Gideon Coppinger : St. Jas. Clerkenwell, iv. 339. London, 1, 2 ; Philadelphia, 0, 3.

Copleston, Coplestone, Copplestone.—Local, ' of Coplestone,' a hamlet in the parish of Colebrook, co. Devon.

Hugo de Copleaston, co. Devon, 1273. A.

1577. John Coplestone and Alice Wood : Marriage Lic. (London), i. 75.

Lewis Coplestone, co. Devon, 1607 ; Oriel Coll. : Reg. Univ. Oxf. vol. ii. pt. ii. p. 294.

1662. Buried—Winifride, d. Sir John Copplestone : St. Jas. Clerkenwell, iv. 346. London, 0, 1, 0 ; Crockford, 6, 0, 0 ; Devon Dir. (Farmers' List), 0, 1, 3.

Copley.—Local, ' of Copley,' a hamlet in the township of Skircoat, in the parish of Halifax. Sir Godfrey Copley (d. 1709), founder of the Copley medal, was a Yorkshireman. The portrait-painter, John Singleton Copley, father of Lord Lyndhurst, came of a Yorkshire family who had settled in Ireland in 1661 (v. Dict. Nat. Biog. xii. 177).

Robertus de Coplay, 1379 : P. T. Yorks. p. 282.

Johannes de Copelay, 1379 : ibid. p. 6.

Willelmus de Coppelay, 1379 : ibid. p.54.

Lionel Coppeley, C. R., 21 Hen. VI.

1792. Married—Robert Montagu and Mary Eliz. Copley (of Bath) : St. Geo. Han. Sq. ii. 76.

London, 9 ; West Rid. Court Dir., 8 ; Sheffield, 13 ; New York, 5.

Copner.—Nick. ' the copener,' i.e. a lover, a sweetheart ; cf. Drury or Drewry. ' *Copiner*, a lover, A.S.' (Halliwell). The surname still exists in co. Devon, where it can be traced back for six centuries.

Richard le Copenere, co. Devon, Hen. III–Edw. I. K.

Richard le Copener, co. Devon, 1273. A. William Capenor, co. Soms., 1 Edw. III : Kirby's Quest, p. 238.

1613. Married — John Cobnor and Catherine Jenkins : St. Jas. Clerkenwell, iii. 39.

1726. — Andrew Downes and Mary Copner : St. Geo. Han. Sq. i. 3. London, 1 ; MDB. (co. Devon), 1 ; Barnstaple, 1 ; Ilfracombe, 1.

Copp.— Local, ' at the copp,' from residence at the top or *cop* of the hill, or eminence. ' Coppe :

top of an hey thyng ; *cacumen*' (Prompt. Parv.). Way adds an important note (q.v.), and quotes the Wickliffite version of Luke iv. 29, 'And they ledden him to the coppe of the hil . . . to cast him down' ; cf. Mow Copp, a parish in East Cheshire.

1331. John de la Coppe, co. Norf. : FF. ix. 471.

Richard de la Coppe, rector of Oxburgh, 4 Edw. III : ibid. vi. 190.

Roger Coppe, co. Dorset, 1273. A.

Richard Coppe, co. Soms., 1 Edw. III : Kirby's Quest, p. 175.

1753. Married—John Rider and Eliz. Copp : St. Geo. Chap. Mayfair, p. 241. London, 4 ; New York, 3.

Copped, Coppard.—Nick. ' the copped,' i.e. with the high-peaked hat. ' Long coates and copped caps ' (Sandys' Travels, p. 47). ' High copt hats, and feathers flaunt a flaunt ' (Gascoigne, p. 216). ' A little coppyd hill ' (Fabyan, i. 123). ' Copt Hall, more properly Copped Hall, was a name popularly given to houses conspicuous for a high-pitched peaked roof' ; cf. Copthall Court, Throgmorton St., London ; Copthall, Epping, &c. I gather the above from Mr. Venable's letter to N. and Q., Oct. 23, 1886, pp. 334-5 ; v. Copestake.

Henry Copehude, co. Soms., 1 Edw. III : Kirby's Quest, p. 206.

Robert Copehode, co. Soms., 1 Edw. III : ibid. p. 207.

Hugo le Coppede, co. Leicester, 1273. A. John le Copede, 1307. M. London, 0, 3 ; MDB. (co. Sussex), 0, 7.

Coppendale. — Local ; seemingly a variant of Chippendale, q.v.

1786. Married—John Dalby and Mary Coppendale : St. Geo. Han. Sq. i. 392. London, 2.

Copper.—Occup. ' the cooper.' Other forms are Cowper and Couper, q.v. The first two following names are entered together :

William le Coupper, 24 Edw. I : Freemen of York (Surtees Soc.), i. 6.

John de Kendale, *copper*, 24 Edw. I : ibid.

John le Coppar, of Bradleghe, co. Soms., 1 Edw. III : Kirby's Quest, p. 231.

John le Coppare, of Lottesham, co. Soms., 1 Edw. III : ibid.

Robert le Copper, C. R., 45 Edw. III.

1747. Married—William Copper and

Hannah Maples: St. Geo. Chap. Mayfair, p. 86.
London, 1; Philadelphia, 1.

Copperbeard.—Nick. 'with the copper-coloured beard'; v. Brownbeard, Blackbeard, &c.

Robert Coperberd. N. (v. index).

Copperwheat. — Local, ' of Cowperthwaite'; v. Cowperthwait, a variant. Almost all the surnames ending in *thwaite* hail from North England, especially from cos. Cumberland and Westmoreland, and the Furness portion of Lancashire. This suffix has ever been too big a mouthful in the south; cf. Applewhite for Applethwaite, or Hebblewhite for Hebblethwaite.

1591. Married—William Copperthert and Magdalen Furnes: St. Jas. Clerkenwell, iii. 16.
1597-8. Beve Cooperthwaite and Margaret Crooke: Marriage Lic. (London), i. 246.
1667. Married—Walter Cowperthwaite and Isabell Townson: St. Mary, Ulverston, i. 150.
Edward Cowperthwaite, of Cartmell, 1647: Lancashire Wills at Richmond, p. 78.
Henry Cowperthwayte, of Cartmell, 1673: ibid.
1762. Married — James Denney and Sarah Cowperthwaite: St. Mary, Ulverston, ii. 405.
1767. — John Stanley and Martha Copperthite: St. Geo. Han. Sq. i. 181.
1770. — Edward Elliott and Sarah Copperthwite: ibid. p. 200.
London, 1.

Coppin, Coppen, Copping, Coppins, Coppens.—Bapt. 'the son of Copin,' i.e. Jacob. An early French equivalent of Italian Coppo, the nick. of Jacob, dim. Coppin; cf. Rob-in, Col-in, &c. The *g* in Copping is, of course, an excrescence; cf. Jenning for Jenin.

Copin, or Copyn, or Jacob de Troye, London, 1273. A.
Hervens Copin, co. Camb., ibid.
Ivo Copin, co. Camb., ibid.
Alexander Copping, co. Norf., ibid.
Richard Copping, co. Hunts, ibid.
Cf. Jacop de Painton, co. Linc., ibid.
Richard Coppyng, co. Soms., 1 Edw. III: Kirby's Quest, p. 228.
Johannes Copyn, *flecher*, 1379: P. T. Yorks. p. 155.
Robert Coppin, rector of Hethel, co. Norf., 1468: FF. v. 109.
'John Coppin, or Copping (died 1582), Brownist, was an inhabitant of Bury St. Edmunds': Dict. Nat. Biog. xii. 191.

This is the district where the name was popular; v. instances above.

London, 8, 6, 12, 2, 0; New York, 1, 0, 1, 0, 0; Boston (U.S.), 0, 0, 1, 2, 1.

Coppinger; v. Copinger.

Copple, Coppell, Coppel.—Local, 'of Coppull,' a township and parish near Chorley, co. Lanc.

Henry de Cophull, of Ormskirk, co. Lanc., 1332: Lay Subsidy (Rylands), p. 109.
John de Cophull, of Coppehull, co. Lanc., 1332: ibid. p. 49.
Elizabeth Taylor, of Coppul, *widow*, 1503: Wills at Chester (1545-1620), p. 188.
Richard Copple, of Aintree, parish of Sephton, 1606: ibid. p. 44.
Paul Copple, of Kirkdale, 1607: ibid.
Edward Standanought, of Copple, 1619: ibid. p. 181.
Liverpool, 1, 1, 1; Manchester, 0, 1, 0; New York, 0, 1, 2.

Coppock, Coppack, Coppak, Coppick, Coppuck.—? Local, ' of Coppock' (?), probably some small estate in East Cheshire. The surname with its variants is confined to that district and South Lancashire. Thomas Coppock, the Jacobite and pretended Bishop of Carlisle, who was drawn, hanged, and quartered in that city in 1746, was a native of Manchester; while James Coppock (1798-1857), the famous electioneering agent, and one of the founders of the London Reform Club, was born at Stockport (v. Dict. Nat. Biog. xii. 193).

Thomas Coboke, 1379: P. T. Yorks. p. 177.
William Coppock, of Mollington, *tailor*, 1597: Wills at Chester (1545-1620), p. 44.
Jane Coppock, of Nether Peover, 1603: ibid.

In a deed concerning some rights and privileges belonging to a ferry in the township of Northenden, dated 1539, one of the witnesses is Geoffrey Coppock (East Cheshire, i. 268).

1759. Married—William Coppack and Margaret Dewick: St. Geo. Han. Sq. i. 85.

This surname has crossed the Atlantic.

Manchester, 5, 1, 1, 0, 0; London, 1, 0, 0, 1, 0; Philadelphia, 2, 0, 0, 0, 4.

Copson.—Bapt.; v. Cobb.

Corbett, Corbitt, Corbet.—? Local. Said to be of Norman extraction. Lower says (quoting Courthope's Debrett), 'Corbet, a noble Norman, came into England with the Conqueror, and from his son Roger Corbet descended the baronial house, as well as the families of the name now existing' (Patr. Brit. p. 68).

Peter Corbet, co. Devon, 1273. A.
Alianor Corbet, co. Bucks, ibid.
Felicia Corbet, co. Hunts, ibid.

There are many other entries relating to the family in the above register.

Nicholas Corbet, co. Northampt., 20 Edw. I. R.
Richard Corbit, co. Warwick, Hen. III-Edw. I. K.
1581. Married—Francis Quicke and Marie Corbite: St. Dionis Backchurch, p. 9.
1599. — Richard Lee and Anne Corbett: St. Michael, Cornhill, p. 16.
London, 27, 1, 0; Boston (U.S.), 71, 0, 1.

Corbin, Corbyn.—Local, 'of Corbin.' I cannot identify the place. Evidently a West-country surname.

Petrus de Corbyn, co. Devon, Hen. III-Edw. I. K.
Philip Corbin, co. Devon, ibid.
Walter Corbin, co. Soms., 1273. A.
Ralph Corbin, co. Oxf., ibid.
William Corbyn, co. Soms., 1 Edw. III: Kirby's Quest, p. 111.
1700. Married—Simon Corbin and Jane Bendall: St. Dionis Backchurch, p. 49.
1717. — Christopher Bond and Rachell Corbin: St. Michael, Cornhill, p. 59.
1808. — Garrard Corbyn and Harriet Dowding: St. Geo. Han. Sq. ii. 394.
London, 0, 2; MDB. (co. Dorset), 1, 0; Philadelphia, 13, 2.

Corbishley.—Local. A place in the parish of Wilmslow, co. Cheshire, mentioned circa 1200 (v. infra), 'together with the hamlets of Styhale, Curbichelegh, and Northcliffe' (Earwaker's East Cheshire, i. 42). 'From this place a family named Curbishley, resident in this township for many generations, derived their name' (ibid. p. 138).

Adam de Curbicheley, c. 1300: Earwaker's East Chesh. i. 138.
Hugh Curbythly, of Stiall, 1527: ibid.
Arthur Curbishley, of Styall, *yeoman*, 1598: ibid.
1751. Married—James Corbishley and Jane Bradshaw: St. Jas. Clerkenwell, iii. 283.
London, 1; Manchester, 1.

Corbold, -bould ; v. Cobbold.

Corbridge, Corbidge.—Local, 'of Corbridge,' a parish in the union of Hexham, co. Northumberland.

Henry de Corbrig, *mercator*, 4 Edw. II : Freemen of York, i. 14.
Sheffield, 1, 1 ; Doncaster, 1, 0.

Corby.—Local, 'of Corby,' parishes in cos. Lincoln and Northampton.

Alan de Corby, co. Linc., 1273. A.
Henry de Corby, co. Leic., ibid.
Osbert de Coraby, co. Linc., ibid.
1591. Married—Thomas Corby and Friswede Rich : St. Jas. Clerkenwell, iii. 15.
1757. — Thomas Corby and Ann Sparrow : St. Geo. Han. Sq. i. 68.
London, 10 ; New York, 4.

Corbyn, Carbine, Corbin.—(1) Local, 'of Corbyn,' probably a Norman locality. (2) Bapt. 'the son of Corbin.' Unquestionably there are two origins.

Milo de Corbyn, co. Devon, Hen. III-Edw. I. K.
Petrus Corbyn, co. Devon, ibid.
Walter Corbyn, co. Soms., 1273. A.
Margery Corbin, co. Camb., ibid.
Ralph Corbin, co. Oxf., ibid.
'Robert, son of Corbun, had a grant of a lordship.' 'Corbun also had the grant of 10 acres of land ': FF. x. 168.
'Robert, son of Corbutio, or Fitz-Corbun, held it ': ibid. v. 189.
(Corbution, or Corbon, occurs : ibid. viii. 65.)
1616. Married—John Baker and Margarett Corbin : St. Jas. Clerkenwell, iii.43.
London, 2, 2, 0 ; Crockford, 1, 0, 0 ; Philadelphia, 2, 0, 13.

Cordeaux, Cordukes, Cordeux, Corduke.—! Local.

1779. Married—Matthew Cordeux and Susanna Dodd : St. Geo. Han. Sq. i. 306.
York, 1, 2, 0, 0 ; London, 1, 0, 2, 0 ; New York, 0, 0, 0, 1.

Corderoy, Cordery, Cordrey, Cordaroy, Corderey.—Local, 'of the Ropery.' While there is every temptation to fall in with Mr. Lower's statement that Corderoy is 'Cœur-du-roi, *king-hearted*,' there is no evidence to support it. In fact the name is local, I presume, the French *corderie*, a rope-walk ; cf. Pommery and Pomeroy, or Cowderoy and Cowdery.

John de la Corderie, 21 Edw. I : BBB. p. 465.

Peter de Corderoy, 1297. M.
Emma Querderay, 1379 : P. T. Yorks. p. 128.
John Corderoy, 1440. W. 11.
John Cordrey, 1531 : Reg. Univ. Oxf. i. 165.
William Corderoy, married, 1719-20 : St. Dionis Backchurch, London.
1577. Married—William Wytlye and Anne Cordrye : St.Michael, Cornhill, p. 11.
1692. Buried—Philip, s. Philip Corderoy: ibid. p. 273.
London, 5, 2, 5, 1, 0 ; Philadelphia, 0, 5, 1, 0, 1.

Cordiner, Cordner, Codner.—Occup. 'the cordwainer,' i.e. shoemaker, one who made shoes of Cordovan leather. 'Sowtare, or cordewaner (cordynare), *sutor, alutarius* ': Prompt. Parv.

Alan le Cordewaner, London, 1273. A.
Stephen le Corduwaner, co. Norf., ibid.
Hugh le Cordewener, co. Camb., p. 194.
Durant le Cordwaner, 1295. M.
1503. 'Item, to Rutte, the Quene's cordener, for shoys and buskyns, &c. ': Privy P. Exp., Elizabeth of York, p. 85.
'Item, received of John Bent, and John Davies, cordiner, for one pew, 2 shillings ': Churchwardens' Expenses, Ludlow, p. 184 (Camden Soc.).
Robert Browne, *cordoner*, 1539 : PPP. ii. 174.
Richard Cordoner, 1539 : ibid.
Richard Kyrkus, *cordoner*, 1539 : ibid. p. 194.

As an occupative term 'cordwainer' is only just dying out. Both 'souter' and 'cordwainer' occur in the following entry :

Robertus Souter, *cordewenar*, 1379 : P. T. Yorks. p. 41.
Robert Horneclyf, *cordyner*, 1543 : Freemen of York, i. 264.
London, 0, 0, 4 ; Philadelphia, 0, 2, 0.

Cordingley, Cordingly.—Local, 'of Cordonley.' I have not discovered the precise spot, but we may fairly assume that it was some small estate situated in the West Riding of Yorkshire. The instance below from the Poll Tax (1379) occurs at Bowling, near Bradford.

Ricardus de Cordonlay, 1379 : P. T. Yorks. p. 185.
1795. Married—Jacob Bateman and Mary Cordingley : St. Geo. Han. Sq. ii. 133.
1803. — Hubert Bushby and Ann Cordingley : ibid. p. 290.
West Rid. Court Dir., 4, 0 ; Philadelphia, 4, 2.

Cordwin, Corden, Cording, Cordin.—Local, 'the Cordovan,' an emigrant from Cordova, in

Spain ; v. Cordiner. It is very probable that Corden and Cording (with excrescent *g*) are variants. 'His shoon of Cordewane,' Chaucer, Sire Thopas.

Lambert Cordewan, co. Oxf., 1273. A.
1588. Married—William Corden and Jone Malyn : St. Peter, Cornhill, i. 237.
1612. Henry Cordywen and Alice Tuckwell : Marriage Lic. (London), ii. 13.
1796. Married—John Hammond and Martha Cordwin : St. Geo. Han. Sq. ii. 145.
London, 0, 2, 2, 0 ; New York, 0, 0, 0, 1.

Corker.—Occup. 'the calker,' one who calked tubs. 'The ancients of Gebal, and the wise men thereof, were in thee thy calkers,' Ezekiel xxvii. 9 (marginal note, 'stoppers of chinks'). Corker is a North-English surname, and found for centuries in Furness and Yorkshire alongside Cooper and Tubman. The only Corker in the Dict. Nat. Biog. (xii. 217), viz. James Corker (1636-1715), Benedictine monk, was a native of Yorkshire.

1549. Buried — John Corker : Reg. St. Mary, Ulverston, p. 9.
1584. Sibel Corker, of Ulverstone : Wills at Richmond, p. 73.
1629. Married — John Watkins and Margery Corker : St. Antholin (London), p. 63.
1705. Bapt.—Anne, d. of John Corker : Reg. St. Mary, Ulverston, p. 291.
1722. Margaret Corker, Bark-house Bank, Colton : Lancashire Wills at Richmond, p. 66.
1808. John Burt and Martha Corker : St. Geo. Han. Sq. ii. 397.
West Rid. Court Dir., 1 ; Sheffield, 4 ; Boston (U.S.), 2 ; New York, 1.

Cornall, Corney, Cornell.—Local, 'of Cornall.' Some small estate in the Fylde district, co. Lanc., to be distinguished from the South-English Cornell, q.v. That the Lancashire surname Corney is a variant of Cornall is beyond dispute ; cf. Presoe for Presall. The Carter family are described as ' of Stainall' (1723), 'of Stana' (1719), and Stanoe (1690) ; v. Lancashire Wills at Richmond, ii. 51.

John Cornall, of Cornall, 1672 : Lancashire Wills at Richmond, i. 73.
Henry Carter, of Cornoe, 1661 : ibid. p. 56.
Adam Corney, of Rosaker, 1666: ibid. p. 73.

Richard Corney, of Greenall, 1571: Lancashire Wills at Richmond, i. 73.
Richard Cornah, of Greenall, 1737: Lancashire Wills at Richmond, ii. 66.
John Cornall, of Greenall, 1692: ibid.
Laurence Cornoe, of Greenalgh, 1668: ibid.
Henry Cornall, of Rossiker, parish of Kirkham, 1721: ibid.
Rowland Cornah, of Rosaker, 1736: ibid.

Thus Cornall, Cornah, Cornoe, and Corney are all variants of one name, the locality seeming to lie in or adjacent to the parish of Kirkham. Even Greenall mentioned above is found as Greenoe.

Ellen Cornall, of Greenoe, 1681: Lancashire Wills at Richmond, ii. 66.
Liverpool, 2, 3, 0; Preston, 1, 0, 0; Kirkham, 0, 0, 1; Philadelphia, 0, 8, 45.

Cornelius.—Bapt. 'the son of Cornelius.' This is not an English surname. At least I find no trace of the font-name on English soil in the 12th, 13th, and 14th centuries, the period when font-names were being turned into permanent surnames. Cornelius and Cornelia became very popular in the Low Countries through the fact that relics of the martyred Pope Cornelius were placed in the Chapter of Rosnay, in Flanders (v. Yonge, i. 314). The actress, Theresa Cornelys (1723–97) took the name from Cornelis de Rigerboos, a gentleman at Amsterdam (Dict. Nat. Biog. xii. 223). Lucas Cornelisz (1495–1552 ?), historical painter, was son of Cornelis Engelbrechtsen, of Leyden (ibid. p. 222). It is true John Cornelius (1557–94), the Jesuit, was born at Bodmin, co. Cornwall, but his parents were Irish (ibid. p. 222), and Cornelius (pet Corney) has been a popular font-name in the Emerald Isle for many centuries.

1571. Bapt.—Jeames Corneye, son of Cornelius, a stranger: St. Michael, Cornhill, p. 85.
1575. Married—Peter Boney and Christian Cornelis: ibid. p. 11.
London, 5; Philadelphia, 16.

Cornell.—(1) Local, ' of Cornhill,' a part of London. As regards the derivation of the Lancashire Cornells, v. Cornall.

Stephen de Cornhell, or Cornhille, or Cornhull, or Cornill (London). 1273. A.
Reginald de Cornhull, co. Kent, ibid.
Robert de Cornhull, sheriff of London, 1245: WWW. pp. 187, 190.
1582. Buried—Margaret Cornhill: Reg. St. Antholin (London), p. 28.

(2) Local, ' of Cornwall.'
Roysa de Cornewell, co. Oxf., 1273. A.

(3) ? Bapt. 'the son of Cornwel' (?).
Matilda Corunel, co. Camb., 1273. A.
Robert Corunel, co. Camb., ibid.
1707. Married—John Palmer and Sarah Cornall: St. Michael, Cornhill, p. 54.
London, 14; Philadelphia, 48.

Corner.—There are three distinct origins of this surname: (1) a local, (2) an official, (3) an occupative origin.

(1) Local, ' of the corner,' cf. Hearne and Wray.
John de la Cornere, co. Suff., 1273. A.
William de la Cornere, co. Bucks, ibid.
John atte Cornere, co. Soms., 1 Edw. III: Kirby's Quest, p. 85.
Robert atte Cornere, 1307. M.
Rand Corner, 1379: P. T. Yorks. p. 163.

(2) Official, ' the coroner,' corrupted to ' corner.'
Geoffrey Coronator, co. Suff., 1273. A.
Henry le Corouner, co. Suff., ibid.
John le Coroner, 1303. M.
Richard Crowner, C. R., 25 Hen. VI.

(3) Occup. 'the corner,' i.e. a player on the horn, Fr. corne. Cornet, the dim., is still a familiar instrument.
Johanna la Cornore, co. Oxf., 1273. A.
John le Corner, co. Derby, ibid.
William le Corner, London, ibid.
'Wiard le Corner, John le Harper, Roger le Trumper, and Thomas le Vielour were the King's Minstrels ': Wardrobe Account, 3 Edw. III. 33/10.
London, 9; New York, 11; Philadelphia, 5.

Corney.—(1) Bapt. 'the son of Cornelius,' q.v., popularly Corney.
(2) Local, ' of Corney,' a parish near Bootle, co. Cumberland. The suffix seems to be -hey or -hay, q.v.
Robert de Cornay, co. Lanc., 1332: Lay Subsidy (Rylands), p. 95.
Roger de Cornay, co. Lanc., 1332: ibid. p. 91.
1546. William Holland and Florence Cornye: Marriage Lic. (London), i. 9.
1745. Married—John Corney and Eliz. Geary: St. Geo. Han. Sq. i. 36.
London, 5; Liverpool, 3; Philadelphia, 8.

Cornforth, Cornford.—Local, ' of Cornforth,' a township in the

parish of Bishop's Middleham, co. Durham. Bradford is found entered as Bradforth in the Yorkshire Poll Tax (1379); v. Ford and Forth.

1798. Married — Isaac Titlow and Eleanor Cornforth: St. Geo. Han. Sq. ii. 181.
1809. — David Cornford and Sarah Howes: ibid. p. 418.
London, 2, 3.

Cornish.—Local, ' the Cornish,' a Cornish man. A corruption or abbreviation of Cornwallis, q.v. Also cf. Kentish and Devonish. We do not expect to find Cornish in Cornwall, but in Devonshire. Coming over the border the stranger would be called Cornish from the county he had left. Hence Cornish is rare in Cornwall and common in Devonshire. We may safely conclude that when we find Cornish in Cornwall the bearer has returned to the county whence his ancestors sprang.
William Cornish. D.
Margery Cornish. H.
Walter Corneys, co. Soms., 1 Edw. III: Kirby's Quest, p. 153.
1554. Thomas Corneyshe and Eliz. Byshopp: Marriage Lic. (London), i. 15.
1584. Bapt.—Elizabeth, d. of James Cornish: St. Columb Major (Cornwall), p. 12.
London, 27; MDB. (co. Devon), 31; (Cornwall), 2; Boston (U.S.), 14.

Cornmonger. — Occup. ' the cornmonger.' This surname, I fear, is obsolete; cf. Mealmonger, Haymonger, and Oatmonger.
Walter le Cornmanger, C.R., 10 Edw. I.
Hugh le Cornmonger, co. Oxf., 1273. A.
Ralph le Cornmonger. T.
Henry le Cornmongere, temp. 1300. M.
Geoffrey Cornmanger, co. Soms., 1 Edw. III: Kirby's Quest, p. 100.

Cornthwaite. — Local, ' of Cornthwaite,' one of the many North-English local surnames with suffix -thwaite (v. Thwaites). It is found in the North Lonsdale and Furness district of Lancashire.

Richard Cornethwet, of Silverdale, 1610: Lancashire Wills at Richmond, p. 73.
Robert Cornethwaitt, of Caton, 1636: ibid.
John Cornethwait, of Burton, 1664: ibid.
1692. Married—Thomas Fell and Julia Cornthwait: St. Mary, Ulverston, i. 195.

1786. Bapt.—John. s. Thomas Cornthwaite: St. Mary, Ulverston, ii. 508. Liverpool, 1.

Cornwall, Cornwell.—Local,
from co. Cornwall; cf. Kent, Lancashire, Derbyshire, &c. v. Cornish.

Hugo de Cornub', co. Devon, 1273. A.
Roger de Cornub', co. Berks, ibid.
Hugh Cornwell, co. Oxf., ibid.
Geoffrey de Cornwayle. B.
Wauter de Cornwaile, 1313. M.
Robert Cornwal, co. Soms., 1 Edw. III: Kirby's Quest, p. 170.
1565. Edward Herne and Joanna Cornewell: Marriage Lic. (London), i. 31.
1571. John Cornewall and Katherine Leake: ibid. 50.
1587. Married — Richard Davis and Mari Cornwell: St. Dionis Backchurch, p. 11.
London, 1, 22; Philadelphia, 3, 14.

Cornwallis. — Local, 'the
Cornwaleys,' i.e. the Cornishman; cf. 'Wallace' (Ingleram le Waleys: B.), a Welshman.

Thomas le Cornwaleys, co. Norf., 1273. A.
Beatrix Cornwaleys, co. Norf., ibid.
Philip le Cornwaleys. L. \
Walter le Cornwaleys. X.
Hugh le Cornwalche, co. Soms., 1 Edw. III: Kirby's Quest, p. 210.
Thomas Cornwalleis, co. Norf., 1564: FF. ii. 276.
1596. William Sandes and Eliz. Cornwallis: Marriage Lic. (London), i. 235.
1753. Married—Hon. Edward Cornwallis and Hon. Mary Townshend: St. Geo. Han. Sq. i. 49.
London (Court Dir.), 1.

Corpe, Corp.—Local, 'of Corp.'
I have not discovered the spot.

Stephen de Corp, co. Linc., 1273. A.
Simon Corp, London, 20 Edw. I. R.
John Corp, co. Soms., 1 Edw. III: Kirby's Quest, p. 231.
1744. Married—Harry Corp and Ann ——: St. Geo. Chap. Mayfair, p. 42.
1801. — Richard Corpe and Frances Cottrell: St. Geo. Han. Sq. ii. 239.
London, 5, 1; MDB. (co. Soms.), 1, 2.

Corry, Corrie, Cory, Curry, Currie, Currey.—Local, 'at the
corrie.' Such at least seems to be the origin of this well-known Scotch surname. It is introduced here simply because it looks English, and is found in one variant or another in every considerable English town. Sir Walter Scott, in his Lady of the Lake, has

'Fleet foot in the corrie,'

and a footnote explains thus: 'Corrie or Cori, the hollow side of the hill where game usually lies.'
1742. Married — John Goddard and Margaret Curry: St. Geo. Chap. Mayfair, p. 26.
1749. Thomas Thompson and Ann Corrie: ibid. p. 134.
London, 9, 8, 7, 14, 18, 7; Philadelphia, 18, 3, 2, 146, 21, 10.

Corsellis.—? Local. A Dutch
importation.

'Lucas Corsellis, son of Lucas Corsellis, christ⁴ at the Dutch Church, 1611': Reg. St. Dionis Backchurch (London), p. 95.
1606. Buried—Eliz., d. Michaell Corsellis: ibid. p. 94.
1611-2. Bapt.—Lucas Corsellis: ibid. p. 209.
London, 1.

Corser, Corsar; v. Cosser.

Cort.—Local, 'at the court,' an
enclosure, a mansion (v. Court); M.E. cort.

Richard le Cort, co. Oxf., 1273. A.

This, no doubt, ought to be 'de la Cort.' The error is common in early registers.

1583. Stephen Swan and Eliz. Corte: Marriage Lic. (London), i. 117.
1722. Married—John Cort and Margaret King: St. Jas. Clerkenwell, iii. 247.
London, 1; Crockford, 1; New York, 5.

Corthorn; v. Cawthorn.

Cortis.—Nick.; v. Curtis.

1551-2. Bapt.—Susanna Corteys, d. William Corteys: St. Dionis Backchurch, p. 75.
London, 1; New York, 2.

Cosgrove, Cosgrave, Cosgriff. — Local, 'of Cosgrove,' a
parish in co. Northampton.

Crockford, 0, 2, 0; London, 1, 0, 0; Manchester, 4, 0, 0; Liverpool, 4, 1, 2; New York, 67, 0, 3.

Cosser, Corser, Corsar. —
(1) Occup. 'the corviser,' i.e. the shoemaker. These are modifications. 'William Smyth, corviser, 1397' (Preston Guild Rolls, p. 10). A curious feminine form is to be met with in the directory for the Chester Pageant, wherein it is ordered that the 'Corvesters and Shoemakers' do march together (Ormerod's Cheshire, p. 301). 'And that the corveses bye ther lether in the scid yeld halle'

(Ordinances of Worcester, English Gilds, p. 371). 'Porters, fesycyens, and corsers' (Cocke Lorelle's Bote).

Ralph le Coreviser, co. Oxf., 1273. A.
Henry le Coreveser, co. Hunts, ibid.
William le Coreviser, co. Salop, ibid.
Cristina Corveiser, co. Hunts, ibid.

(2) Occup. 'the corser,' a dealer in horses. The king's corser was an officer who acted as king's agent in purchasing horses. 'Johannes Martyr, corsere,' occurs in an old Oxford record, dated 1451 (Mun. Acad. Oxon. p. 616). 'Corsoure of horse, mango': Prompt. Parv. p. 94. Horman says, 'Corsers of horses (mangones) by false menys make them loke fresshe'; v. Way's note as above. The Hundred Rolls (1273) have no instance of the surname, while of (1) the instances are many.

William de Morpath, cosour, 9 & 10 Edw. III : Freemen of York, i. 29.
Jakemin de Gracia, corsour, 9 & 10 Edw. III : ibid. p. 30.
Durand le Corveser. M.
1578. Bapt. — John, s. John Corser, clothworker: St. Peter, Cornhill, i. 19.
1580. — Katharine, d. John Corzer, clothworker: ibid. p. 22.
London, 4, 0, 1; Crockford, 0, 1, 0; Boston (U.S.), 0, 1, 0.

Cost, Coste.—Bapt. 'the son
of Constantine,' from nick. Cost; cf. Cust, the nick. of Custance. Constantine was a popular fontname in Cornwall; v. Considine.

Richard fil. Coste, Hen. III-Edw. I. K.
William, son of Cost Cardew, 1551: Reg. St. Columb Major, p. 6.
Cost Batte, and Emblem his wiffe, 1582: ibid. p. 141.
London, 2, 4; Philadelphia, 2, 0.

Costabadie; v. Custobodie.

Costain, Costin, Costen, Coston.—Bapt. 'the son of Constantine' (familiarly Costantine), from nick. Costain or Costin. This nick. lasted till the 17th century.

1586. Married — Constantine Maude and Isabella Hartley: Reg. Keighley, Yorks (N. and Q., July 3, 1886).
1617. Buried—The wife of Costaine Maude: ibid.
1583. Bapt. — Judith, d. of Costane Mawd: Reg. Halifax, Yorks.
1597. Buried—Antony, son of Costan Robinson: ibid.
1600. — Costanus Maud: ibid.

Costin Radger, co. Suff., 1273. A.
Isabella Costin, co. Suff., ibid.
Costin de Ecĕa, co. Suff., ibid.
John Costyn, mayor of Lynn, co. Norf., temp. Hen. III : FF. viii. 492.
Richard Costyn, co. Soms., 1 Edw. III : Kirby's Quest, p. 119.
Willelmus Costyn, 1379 : P. T. Yorks. p. 206.
Robertus Costyn, 1379 : ibid.
Johannes Costyneson, 1379 : ibid. p. 207.
William Costantyn (1314), or Costyn (1311), or Constantyn (1322), returned as burgess for Bedford in 1305. M.
'Patricius Constyne (1537-92), afterwards known as Patrick Adamson, a distinguished Scotch prelate, wrote his name variously Consteane, Conston, Constant, and Constantine. About the year 1576 he adopted the name of Adamson, and his adversaries did not fail to twit him on the change.
" Twyse his surnaime hes mensuorne :
To be called Cōsteine he tho' (thought) schame :
He tūke up Cōstantine to name
.   .   .   .
Now Doctor Adamsone at last." '
Dict. Nat. Biog. i. 112.
'The West Derby Board of Guardians met yesterday . . . present, among others, Dr. Costine': Liverpool Mercury, July 28, 1887.
1637. Buried—Frances Coston, *widow* : St. Peter, Cornhill, i. 197.
London, 1, 2, 1, 0 ; Philadelphia, 0, , 4, 1.

Costello, Costelloe, Coatollow.—Local, 'of Costello,' i. e. the barony of Costello, co. Mayo, Ireland. Dudley Costello, the journalist, although born in Sussex, was son of James Francis Costello, born in the barony of Costello (v. Dict. Nat. Biog. xii. 276). It seems strange that Philadelphia should possess (if we average five to a family) over 500 Costellos, and London be so poorly represented in its directory.
London, 3, 1, 1 ; Crockford, 3, 0, 0 (all in Irish benefices) ; Philadelphia, 117, 0, 0.

Coster, Costar. — ? Nick. ; 'round-headed,' like a costard or apple. Undoubtedly Costard with the final *d* elided. The name without prefix is found in all early registers. Costermonger is similarly for costard-monger. The name is found in widely separated districts, as the following instances will show.
'George Costard, astronomical writer (1710-82), was born at Shrewsbury': Dict. Nat. Biog. xii. 274.

Reginald Costard, co. Glouc., 1273. A.
Emma Costard, co. Oxf., ibid.
Richard Costard, co. Camb., ibid.
John Costard, co. Linc , 20 Edw. I. R.
Margery Costard, co. Linc., ibid.
Thomas Costard, 1379 : P. T. Yorks. p. 115.
1790. Married—James Costar and Eliz. Spreckleson : St. Geo. Han. Sq. ii. 51.
1792. — James Coster and Eliz. Keep : ibid. p. 88.
London, 13, 1 ; Philadelphia, 9, 0.

Cosway, Cossey, Causey, Cawsey.—Local, 'at the causeway,' more correctly, causey, a paved way. In Prompt. Parv. spelt *cawcewey* from the Fr. *chaussée*. A 'causey' runs over a moss in my old parish at Ulverston. It is as old as the register (1542). The surname, however, seems peculiar to co. Devon.
'Richard Cosway, painter (1740-1801), was born at Tiverton, co. Devon': Dict. Nat. Biog. xii. 279.
Nathaniel Causey and Thomas Causey, settlers in Virginia, 1623 : Hotten's Lists of Emigrants, pp. 171, 181.
Robert de Chauci, co. Wilts, 1273. A.
John de Chausy, co. Glouc., ibid.
Geoffrey de Chauseya, or Chausi, or Chausie, co. Oxf., Hen. III-Edw. I. K.
1715. Bapt.—Catesby, s. James Causey : St. Michael, Cornhill, p. 165.
1795. Married—John Palmer and Susannah Cawsey : St. Geo. Han. Sq. ii. 140.
1809. — James Cosway and Sarah Willson : ibid. p. 407.
London, 1, 2, 0, 0 ; Devon Dir. (Farmers' List), 2, 0, 1, 8 ; MDB. (co. Devon), 5, 0, 0, 4.

Cotgrave. — Local, 'of Cotgrave,' a parish in co. Notts. The Cheshire Cotgraves seem to be derived from an estate in that county. Lower says, 'Thomas, one of the grandsons of the great William Belward, Lord of Malpas, held the lands of Cotgrave, and from them assumed the surname de Cotgrave' (Patr. Brit. p. 71) ; v. Greaves.
Robert de Cotegrave, co. Notts, 1273. A.
Ralph Cotgreave, of Christleton, 1588: Wills at Chester (1545-1620), p. 44.
George Cotgrave, 1612 : ibid.
William Cotgreave, of Chester, 1620 : ibid.
Jane Cotgreave, of Warrington, 1684 : ibid. (1681-1700), p. 60.
I do not find any modern instances, but it would be dangerous to say the surname is extinct.

Cotsford.—Local, 'of Cottisford,' a parish in dioc. of Oxford.
Richard de Cotesford, 22 Hen. II : Westm. and Cumb. i. 27.
Robert de Cotesford, co. Oxf., 1273. A.
Richard de Cotesford, co. Norf.. ibid.
1567-8. John Cosforde and —— Harpar : Marriage Lic. (London), i. 38.
1593. James Wingfeilde and Margery Cotesforde : ibid. p. 208.
London, 2.

Cotshott. — An Americanism for Cockshott, q.v.

Cottam, Cottom.—Local, ' of Cottam,' lit. Cote-ham. Parishes in diocs. of York and Southwell ; also a hamlet near Preston, whence the Lancashire Cottams. ' John Haydok de Cotom' (Preston Guild Rolls, p. 8); 'Cuthbert Cottam' (ibid. p. 160). There are also parishes styled Cotham in diocs. of Southwell, and Glouc. and Bristol. This latter is nearer the original form.
John de Cotum, co. Northumb., 1273. A.
Richard de Cotum, co. Notts, ibid.
Gilbert de Coteham, co. Camb., ibid.
Henry de Coteham, co. Camb., ibid.
Richard Cottam, of Overstanden, co. Lanc., 1621 : Wills at Chester (1621-50), p. 53.
1667. Married—Edward Wallgrave and Eliz. Cottum : St. Jas. Clerkenwell, iii. 148.
London, 7, 0 ; Manchester, 4, 0 ; Preston, 3, 1 ; Boston (U.S.), 5, 0.

Cotter, Cotman, Cottman, Cottwife.—Occup. 'the cotter,' one who held in absolute villenage ; servile tenants, who were mere chattels of their lord, being alike in person and goods at the disposal of their superior. They are Latinized as Cotmanni and Cottarii in Domesday, and elsewhere as Cotterelli (v. Pipe Rolls, P. R. Soc. iii. 78). Beatrix Cotewife may have been a widow, holding as tenant after the husband's decease.
William le Cotiere, co. Oxf., 1273. A.
John fil Cotman, co. Northumb., ibid.
Thomas fil. Cotman, co. Northumb., ibid.
Richard Coteman, co. Oxf., ibid.
John Coteman, co. Camb., ibid.
Beatrix Cotewif, co. Hunts, ibid.
Simon le Cotere. FF.
1663. Samuel Cottman and Eliz. Osburne : Marriage Alleg. (Canterbury), p. 113.
London, 7, 0, 1, 0 ; Preston (Cotman) 1 ; Philadelphia, 35, 1, 14, 0 ; Boston (U.S.), 104, 0, 1, 0 ; New York, 30, 0, 4, 0.

Cotterell, Cotterill, Cottrell, Cottrill.— Occup. 'the cotterel.' 'Coterelle, *tugurinus*': Prompt. Parv. The cotterel was an inferior tenant, probably holding in absolute villenage; cf. Cotman, Boardman, &c.; v. Cotter.

Stephan Coterel, co. Soms., 1 Edw. III: Kirby's Quest, p. 234.
Walter Coterel, co. Soms., 1 Edw. III: ibid. p. 235.
Richard Coterell, co. Devon, 1273. A.
Alice Coterel, co. Camb., ibid.
Henry Coterel, co. Bedf., ibid.
William Coterel, 1303. M.
1662. Richard Cotterell and Mary Fennihowse: Marriage Alleg. (Canterbury), p. 61.
1662-3. Henry Cottrill and Eliz. Minne: ibid. p. 73.
London, 7, 2, 24, 1; New York, 4, 3, 14, 0; Philadelphia, 3, 0, 4, 5.

Cottingham.—Local, 'of Cottingham.' (1) A parish near Hull, E. Rid. Yorks; (2) a parish in co. Northampton, two miles from Rockingham. 'George Cottingham, aged twenty years, sailed for Virginia in 1635' (v. Hotten's Lists of Emigrants, p. 114). The surname has become well established in the States.

Robertus de Cotyngham, 1379: P. T. Howdenshire, p. 23.
1547. Edmund Bragge and Eliz. Cotingham: Marriage Lic. (London), i. 10.
— Roger Wollowes and Christian Cottyngham: ibid. p. 11.
1791. Married — Thomas Cottingham and Catherine Cox: St. Geo. Han. Sq. ii. 58.
London, 2; MDB. (co. Lincoln), 2; Philadelphia, 6.

Cottle.—Local, 'of Cottle,' an extra-parochial liberty in the hundred of Bradford, co. Wilts, originally Cothull.; v. Hull. Poor Cottle, the bookseller, and would-be writer, was thus pilloried by Byron in his English Bards and Scotch Reviewers:

'O Amos Cottle! Phoebus! What a name
To fill the speaking trump of future fame!
O Amos Cottle! for a moment think
What meagre profits spring from pen and ink.'

Elyas Cotel, co. Wilts, 1273. A.
Roger Cotel, co. Oxf., ibid.
Robert Cothulle, co. Soms., 1 Edw. III: Kirby's Quest, p. 206.
John de Cothulle, co. Soms., 1 Edw. III: ibid. p. 207.

1605. Married—George Cottle and Eliz. Goodall: St. Jas. Clerkenwell, iii. 30.
1803. — William Cottel and Mary Drake: St. Geo. Han. Sq. ii. 285.
MDB. (co. Wilts), 3; (co. Somerset) 4; London, 2; Boston (U.S.), 20.

Cotton, Cottone.—Local, 'of Cotton.' There are parishes in diocs. of Norwich and Lichfield of this name, but several places not arrived at parochial honours are so called. The diocs. of Ely and Peterborough also have each a parish styled Coton, of which instances are given below.

Robert de Cottone, co. Camb., 1273. A.
Richard de Cottoune, co. Camb., ibid.
William de Coton, Pardons Roll, 15 Ric. II.
Ralph de Cotun, co. Northumb., 1273. A.
Richard de Cotton, co. Norf., ibid.
1573-4. Married—John Cotton and Eliz. Bradborne: Marriage Lic. (Faculty Office), p. 16.
London, 40, 0; Boston (U.S.), 42, 1.

Coucher.—Occup. 'a coucher,' a tapiser, one who made cushions, carpets, hangings, &c. The Tapisers and Couchers went together in the York Play, 1415 (York Mystery Plays, p. xxiii). Possibly allied to cushion, the latter being a diminutive. But see 'Couch' (Skeat), to lay down, to set, to arrange, O.F. *coucher*; and cf. 'Couche, to lay, to place, frequently applied technically to artists' work:

"Alle of palle werke fyne
Cowchide with newyne." (Halliwell.)
1526. 'Item, one cowcher, or carpett for a longe table, 56s. 8d.': (Inventory, Skipton Castle) Whitaker's Craven, p. 400.
John le Cochere, co. Sussex, 1273. A.
William Coucher, co. York. W. 2.
William Cawood, *cowcher*, co. York, 1431. W. 11.
Robert Bell, *cowcher*, co. York, 1442: ibid.
1544. Buried—Mary Cocher: St. Peter, Cornhill, p. 107.
1758. Married—John Cowcher and Ann Nicholes: St. Geo. Han. Sq. i. 79.
1760. — Charles Cowcher and Mary Horn: ibid. p. 92.

Couchman. — Occup. 'the couchman.' This would seem to be our modern coachman. 'Aug. 4, 1640. Dorothy Coachman, d. Tilney Coachman, buried' (Smith's Obituary, p. 17). This Tilney is recorded elsewhere as 'Tilney Couchman.'

John Coacheman, temp. Eliz. E.
Richard Coachman, ibid.
William Cowcheman. EE.
1669. Married—William Ryman and Allise Couchman: St. Jas. Clerkenwell, iii. 159.
1764. — Henry Couchman and Susanna Barnes: St. Geo. Han. Sq. i. 139.
London, 8; New York, 1.

Coulbeck.—Local; v. Colbeck.

Couldwell. — Local; v. Coldwell.

Leeds, 1.

Coull, Coules, Cowell, Cowle, Cowles. — (1) Bapt. 'the son of Nicholas,' from nick. Cole, provincially Coul (v. Coulson and Coulling). Cole and Coles (q.v.) are the general forms. (2) Local, 'of Couhill' or 'Cowhill,' some small spot in or near Blackburn, co. Lanc.

John de Couhill, of Rishton, co. Lanc., 1332: Lay Subsidy (Rylands), p. 82.
John de Coule, of Blackburn, co. Lanc., 1332: ibid. p. 83.
1582. Married — Thomas Woodcrafte and Margaret Cowell: St. Michael, Cornhill, p. 13.
1636. Benjamin Brighouse and Anne Cowles, widow of Richard Cole (sic): Marriage Lic. (London), ii. 228.
1809. Married — Joseph Coules and Lucy Bedford: St. Geo. Han. Sq. ii. 405.
London, 2, 2, 12, 1, 5; Philadelphia, 0, 0, 14, 0, 2.

Coulling, Couling, Cowling, Cowlin. — (1) Bapt. 'the son of Nicholas,' from nick. Coll or Cole, and dim. Coll-in or Colin (v. Collins). An early provincialism has turned all the surnames from Coll or Cole into Coul or Cowl; v. Coulson and Coull, and cf. Coulton for Colton, Coupe for Cope, Coulthard for Colthird, &c. The final *g* is an excrescence, as in Jennings, &c. (2) Bapt. 'the son of Couling,' one of many personal names terminating in *ing*; cf. Browning or Harding. This must be considered the chief parent of the South-English Coulings, &c.; v. Culling for other instances.

Richard Couling, co. Soms., 1 Edw. III: Kirby's Quest, p. 149.
William Coulyng, co. Soms., 1 Edw. III: ibid. p. 209.
London, 1, 3, 3, 3; West Rid. Court Dir., 0, 0, 2, 0; Swinefleet, W. Rid.

Yorks, o, o, 3, o; Boston (U.S.) (Cowling), 3.

Coulman.—Bapt. 'the son of Coleman,' q.v., a variant; cf. Coull, Couling, Coulson, &c.

1809. Married—William Coulman and Susannah Glover: St. Geo. Han. Sq. ii. 407.
MDB. (co. Lincoln), 2; London, 1.

Coulson. — Bapt. 'the son of Nicholas,' from nick. Cole, pronounced Coul (v. Coulling). Colson (q.v.) is the usual form. In some cases possibly a corruption of Colston, a local surname, q.v.

1666. John Hampstead and Isabelle Coulson: Marriage Alleg. (Canterbury), p. 181.
1805. Married — John Coulson and Bethiah Treacher: St. Geo. Han. Sq. ii. 336.
London, 151; West Rid. Court Dir., 6; MDB. (co. Lincoln), 7; Philadelphia, 4.

Coulston, Coulstone.—Local; v. Colston.

Coult.—Nick. 'the colt,' q.v.; cf. Coulthard.

1589. John Colte, or Coult, co. Hereford: Reg. Univ. Oxf. vol. ii pt. ii. p. 174.
1796. Married — Richard Coult and Hester Morgan: St. Geo. Han. Sq. ii. 149.
MDB (co. Lincoln), 3.

Coulthard, Coulthart, Coultate, Coltart, Cottell.—Occup. 'the colt-herd,' a keeper of colts; cf. Coultman for Coltman, Coult for Colt. Also cf. Calvert, Oxnard, Stothard, Coward, &c., all with suffix *-herd*, a herdsman; v. Herd.

Johannes Coltehird, 1379: P. T. Yorks. p. 107.
John Colthirde, co. York. W. 9.
Davy Cowthird, co. York. W. 18.
Bartholomew Colthyrd, 2 Hen. IV: E. and F., co. Cumb., p. 176.
1759. Married—Richard Coultart and Eliz. Hammond: St. Geo. Han. Sq. i. 91.
1780. — Thomas Watson and Dorothea Coulthard: ibid. p. 313.
London, 3, 1, 0, 0, 0; West Rid. Court Dir., 0, 1, 0, 0; MDB. (co. Lancashire), 0, 0, 0, 2, 0; Philadelphia, 1, 0, 0, 0, 1.

Coulton.—Local, 'of Coulton,' a parish in High Furness, North Lancashire, which early originated a surname. Often confounded with Colton, q.v.

Richard Coulton, of Kirkby Ireleth, Furness, 1595: Lancashire Wills at Richmond, p. 75.
Isabel Coulton, of Soutergate, Ulverston, 1615: ibid.

1746. Married—William Coulton and Mary Alcock: St. Geo. Chap. Mayfair, p. 61.
London, 2; MDB. (Furness, North Lancashire), 5; Philadelphia, 3.

Coumbe.—Local; v. Combe, of which it is a variant.

London, 3; Philadelphia, 1.

Councillor, Councellor, Counseller, Counsellor. — Official, 'the councillor.' M.E. *counceller*, a legal or official adviser. Oddly enough, this surname is now scarcely known in England. It has found a home, however, across the seas.

Roger Kynciller, C. R., 9 Edw. I.
Philadelphia, 1, 1, 1, 3; Whalley (co. Lanc.), o, o, o, 1.

Counsell, Counsel. — (?) It would be easy to hazard guesses over this name, but I forbear.

William Counsayl, co. Soms., 1 Edw. III: Kirby's Quest, p. 169.
Roger Consayl, co. Soms., 1 Edw. III: ibid. p. 218.
1609. Married—Henrie Councell and Wynifritt Clarke: St. Jas. Clerkenwell, iii. 35.
1742. — William Counsell and Mary Parsons: St. Geo. Chap. Mayfair, p. 24.
London, 2, 9; Philadelphia, o, 1.

Count, Countess.—Official or nick. 'the count,' 'the countess.' O.F. *conte*, or *comte*, a count, an earl. 'Comte a count, an earle' (Cotg.). Countess is naturally found more frequently in early rolls because Earl was the English equivalent of Count; v. Earl.

John le Cunte. E.
William le Comte, Close Roll, 51 Hen. III.
Alicia Contesse, co. Oxf., 1273. A.
Judetha Comitissa, co. Hunts, ibid.
Livina Comitissa, co. Camb., ibid.
Henry fil. Comitis, co. Devon, ibid.
Reiner de (sic) Counte, co. Norf., 35 Hen. III: FF. x. 66.
'In 1293, Henry, son of Henry le Counte of Norwich, formerly one of the butlers to Henry I, gave them a house in Pottergate': ibid. iv. 247.
Simon le Counte, co. Norf., 34 Hen. III: ibid. viii. 441.
1769. Married—John Count and Anne Cossens: St. Geo. Han. Sq. i. 187.
1802. — Louis Comtess and Mary Rogers: ibid. p. 258.
London, 1, 0; MDB. (co. Essex), 1, 0; New York, 2, 0.

Counterpatch. — Local, 'of Comberbach' (v. Cumberbatch).

This curious variant is given on the authority of Mr. Bowditch. 'In the London Morning Herald of June 24, 1859, are mentioned suits of Messrs. Hemsworth, Counterpatch, and Bedborough': Suffolk Surnames, p. 316.

Countinghouse. — Local, 'of the counting-house,' a chamberlain or treasurer. 'Cowntinge hows, *computoria*': Prompt. Parv. The name suggests the early origin of the nursery rhyme:

'The king was in his counting-house.'
Nicholas del Countynghouse; Issue Rolls, 4 Ric. II.

Countryman. — Nick. 'the countryman,' out of the country, a peasant, a boor.

John Contreman, co. Camb., 1273. A.
Cf. 1586. Buried—Eliz. Clifton, d. of William Clifton, *cuntryman*: St. Peter, Cornhill, p. 134.

There are three entries of a similar character on the same page.

Philadelphia, 1.

Coup, Coupe.—Local, 'at the cope,' a North-English variant (v. Cope); cf. Coupland and Copeland.

1569. Buried—Eliz. Coupe: St. Jas. Clerkenwell, iv. 10.
Isabella Cowpe, of Manchester, *widow*, 1620: Wills at Chester (1545-1620), p. 45.
John Cowpe, of Walton-le-dale, 1602: ibid.
Manchester, 1, 6; New York, 5, 2; Philadelphia, 1, 0.

Courage, Courridge.—Local. No doubt in general an imitative form of Kerridge, q.v. In any case the suffix may be set down as *-ridge*. Mr. Lower suggests a more modern origin for one branch. 'A family of this name (Courage) settled here after the Revocation of the Edict of Nantes': Patr. Brit. p. 72.

Augustin de Courig', co. Devon, Hen. III–Edw. I. K.
London, 6, 1.

Court, Courtman. — Local, 'at the court,' an enclosed space, a large mansion, a tribunal. O.F. *cort*, *curt*.

John de la Curte, co. Essex, 1273. A.
Adam Curtman, co. Camb., ibid.

Augustin de la Curt, Guernsey, 20 Edw. I. R.
Mathew de la Curt, Guernsey, ibid.
John atte Court, C. R., 18 Ric. II.
1653. Married—William Court and Mary Court: St. Dionis Backchurch, p. 29.
1678. Bapt.—Ane, d. Thomas Court: St. Jas. Clerkenwell, i. 280.
1701. Married—Thomas Courtman and Sara Lloyd: St. Dionis Backchurch, p. 50.
London, 18, 0; New York, 3, 0.

Courthope, Coathupe. — Local, 'of Courthope.' Mr. Lower says Courthope 'first occurs in a Subsidy Roll at Wadhurst, co. Sussex, in exactly its present form, temp. Edw. I. The real source of the name appears to be the estate of Curthope, in Lamberhurst, in that county, which Theobald, archbishop of Canterbury in the 12th century, gave to the Abbey of Leeds' (v. Hasted, v. 308).
1592. John Courtopp, *yeoman*, and Anne Tyler: Marriage Lic. (London), i. 201.
1628-9. Francis Courthop and Anne Hastlin: ibid. ii. 195.
1632. John Courthopp and Anne Speed: ibid. ii. 207.
1681. Married—Brian Courthope and Eliz. Hamond: St. Jas. Clerkenwell, iii. 190.
London, 1, 0; Manchester, 0, 1; MDB. (co. Sussex), 1, 0.

Courtney, Courtenay. — Local, 'de Courtenay,' in the Isle of France; a great Devonshire family.
Hugo de Courteney, co. Devon. 1273. A.
John de Curtenay, co. Soms., ibid.
Henry de Curteneye, co. Soms., ibid.
Hugh de Courteneye, co. Bedf., 20 Edw. I. R.
Egelina de Curtenay, co. Oxf., Hen. III-Edw. I. K.
Robert de Courteneya, co. Devon, ibid.
Alienora de Courtenaye, co. Soms., 1 Edw. III: Kirby's Quest, p. 245.
Johannes Courtenay, 1379: P. T. Yorks. p. 117.
Ricardus Courteney, 1379: ibid.
1563. Married—George Fynche and Anne Courtney: St. Michael, Cornhill, p. 8.
1586.— William Cortney and Dorothie Maddoxe: St. Jas. Clerkenwell, iii. 12.
1792.— George Courtenay and Catherine Stapelton: St. Geo. Han. Sq. ii. 80.
London, 11, 0; Philadelphia, 45, 5.

Cousen, Cousens, Cousins, Couzens, Cousin, Cussons, Cussen, Cossins, Cossin.—

Nick. 'the cousin,' a kinsman or near relative; M.E. *cosin*. The final *s* is patronymic, as in Jenkins, Williams, Jones, &c. The Yorkshire directories are still well supplied with instances, but so are many other county directories. Such entries as the following are common:
Henricus Parsoncosyn, 1379: P. T. Yorks. p. 91.
Johannes Vikercosyn, 1379: ibid. p. 226.
Robert Frere-cosyn, 1379: ibid. p. 155.
Johannes Cosyn, *drapour*, 1379: ibid. p. 57.
Ricardus Cosyn, 1379: ibid. p. 58.
Alicia Cosyn, 1379: ibid.
Richard le Cusyn, co. Bedf., 1273. A.
William le Cusyn, co. Bedf., ibid.
John le Cosyn. G.
Thomas le Cozun. E.
Of the three Cosins in the Dict. Nat. Biog., Edmund Cosin, or Cosyn, Vice-chancellor of Cambridge University (fl. 1558), was a native of co. Bedford; the great John Cosin, bishop of Durham, (born 1594), was a native of Norwich; and the civil lawyer, Richard Cosin (1549?-1597), was born at Hartlepool.
London, 0, 7, 16, 3, 1, 0, 1, 3, 0; West Rid. Court Dir., 5, 1, 2, 1, 1, 1, 0, 0, 0; New York, 1, 0, 6, 1, 1, 0, 3, 1, 1.

Coutts, Coots, Couts.—?
1588. Buried—William Cootes: St. Dionis Backchurch, p. 132.
1693. Bapt.—James, s. Thomas Coutts: ibid. p. 200.
Jennett Coutts, 1774: St. Peter, Cornhill, ii. 54.
London, 5, 3, 0; Philadelphia, 2, 2, 0; New York, 1, 0, 1.

Cove.—Local, 'of Cove.' North Cove and South Cove are two parishes in co. Suffolk. The surname arose in that district.
Sir Thomas de Cove, co. Norf., 1330: FF. x. 189.
Sir John de Cove, co. Norf., 9 Edw. II: ibid. p. 185.
Ralph de Cove, co. Stafford, 1273. A.
Robert de Cove, co. Norf., 20 Edw. I. R.
1793. Married—Jeremiah Biggs and Eliz. Cove: St. Geo. Han. Sq. ii. 94.
London, 3.

Covell, Covelle, Covill.—Local, 'of Colville,' q.v.; a corruption.
'John Covel, Covell, or Colvill (1638-1722), Master of Christ's College, Cambridge, was born at Horningsheath, Suffolk,' &c.: Dict. Nat. Biog. xii. 355.

1610. Thomas Covell and Martha Pecocke: Marriage Lic. (London), p. 320.
1664. Thomas Covell and Judith Blagge: Marriage Lic. (Faculty Office), p. 81.
London, 2, 0, 0; Boston (U.S.), 18, 3, 4.

Coveney, Coveny.—Local, 'of Coveney,' a parish six miles from Ely, in co. Cambridge.
Thomas Coveney, or Covenney, 1548: Reg. Univ. Oxf. i. 213.
John Coveney, co. Kent, Magd. Hall, 1586: ibid. vol. ii. pt. ii. p. 151.
1624-5. Edward Crowe and Eliz. Coveney: Marriage Lic. (London), ii. 149.
London, 3, 1; Boston (U.S.), 12, 16.

Coventry.—Local, 'of Coventry,' in the county of Warwick.
Thomas de Coventre, co. Oxf., 1273. A.
William de Covingtre, co. Oxf., ibid.
Walter de Coventre, co. Linc., Hen. III-Edw. I. K.
Alexander de Coventre, co. Warwick, 20 Edw. I. R.
Johannes de Coventre, 1379: P. T. Yorks. p. 105.
1575. Married—William Bright and Hellen Coventrie: St. Jas. Clerkenwell, iii. 6.
John Coventrie, of West Kirby, co. Lanc., 1604: Wills at Chester (1545-1620), p. 45.
1801. Married—George Coventry and Mary Allen: St. Geo. Han. Sq. ii. 239.
London, 14; Philadelphia, 1.

Cover, Cuverer.—Occup. 'le cuver,' the cooper, a maker of coops; Fr. *cuve*. The suffix in Cuverer is reduplicated; cf. Poulter-er.
Adam le Cuver, co. Camb., 1273. A.
Michael le Cuver, co. Camb., ibid.
Walter le Cuver. O.
Richard le Cuverer, co. Camb., 1273. A.
Adam le Covreur, c. 1300. M.
1787. Married—Charles Cover and Eliz. Snow: St. Geo. Han. Sq. i. 402.
London, 4, 0; Philadelphia, 1, 0.

Coverdale, Coverdill.—Local, 'of Coverdale,' in Richmondshire, co. York. 'Miles Coverdale, translator of the Bible, was born in 1488, "patria Eboracensis," says his friend and contemporary Bale (Scriptores, 1557-9, p. 721), and Whitaker assumes the surname to have been taken from the district of his birth, Cover-dale, in what is called Richmondshire, in the North Riding (Hist. Richmondshire, i. 16, 107)'; v. Dict. Nat. Biog. xii. 364. There need be no hesitation in accepting this view.

Johannes Coverdale, 1379: P. T. Yorks. p. 239.
1625. Married—Francis Coverdall and Debbora —— : St. Jas. Clerkenwell, iii. 54.
1809. — Thomas Coverdale and Sarah Milles: St. Geo. Han. Sq. ii. 408.
Ripon, 1, 0; West Rid. Court Dir., 1, 0; London, 7, 0; Philadelphia, 6, 1.

Coverley, Coverly.—Local, 'of Coveley'; cf. Cleverly for Cleveley, q.v.

Malger de Covele, co. Bucks, 1273. A.
Bartholomew de Covele, co. Bucks, ibid.
1669. Married—Francis Coverley and Jane Luxfell: St. Jas. Clerkenwell, iii. 158.
London, 1, 1; Boston (U.S.), 0, 6.

Covert.—Local, 'at the covert,' a wood full of thickets, a hiding-place for deer, &c. A surname taken from residence thereby.

Roger de Covert, co. Sussex, 20 Edw. I. R.
William le (sic) Covert, co. Sussex, Hen. III–Edw. I. K.
1527-8. John Coverd and Margaret Bayly: Marriage Lic. (London), i. 6.
1627. William Brokett and Emme Covert, co. Surrey: ibid. ii. 189.
1665. Married—Launcelott Peckworth and Frauncis Covert: St. Jas. Clerkenwell, iii. 118.
London, 0; Philadelphia, 7.

Cow, Cowe.—Nick. 'the cow'; cf. Bull, Bullock, &c.

William le Cue, 3 Edw. II: Freemen of York, i. 12.
Ralph le Cue, 15 Edw. II: ibid. p. 20.
Maurice le Cu, co. Soms., 1 Edw. III: Kirby's Quest, p. 115.
Thomas le Cu, 1273. A.
Ralph le Cou, c. 1300. M.
Robert le Ku, C. R., 37 Hen. III.
Willelmus Cou, 1379: P. T. Yorks. p. 233.
1806. Married—Richard Jennings and Ann Cowe: St. Geo. Han. Sq. ii. 347.
Boston (U.S.), 0, 1.

Coward, Cowart. — Occup. 'the cow-herd,' a great North-English surname. In the Furness district of Lancashire it contends with the Tysons, Atkinsons, and Ashburners for the front place. v. Herd.

1618. Buried—Archie, the cowhird of Goswick: Reg. Holy Island. QQQ. p. 151.
William le Kukerde, co. Camb., 1273. A.
John Kuhirde, co. Hunts, ibid.
John le Kuhyrde, co. Cumb., 20 Edw. I. R.
Richard le Kuhyrde, co. Cumb., ibid.
Cecilia Cowehird, *laborer*, 1379: P. T. Yorks. p. 219.

Robertus Cowehyrde, 1379: ibid. p. 167.
Henry le Couhirde, Rot. Fines, 3 Edw.II.
John Coward, or Cowhird, of Ulverston, 1622: Lancashire Wills at Richmond, p. 75.
Rowland Cowherd, or Cowhert, or Coward, of Kirkby Ireleth, 1637: ibid. p.77.
Hellen Cowart, of Out Rawcliffe, 1663: ibid. p. 76.

Cowherd, the original form, still exists (v. Cowherd). This surname is well represented across the Atlantic. 'Samuel Coward owned land in Barbadoes in 1679' (v. Hotten's Lists of Emigrants, p. 461).

London, 7, 1; MDB. (co. Lancaster), 17, 0; Philadelphia, 29, 0.

Cowderoy, Cowdery, Couldery.—Local, 'of the hazel copse'; F. *coudraie*, a filbert orchard. There can be no doubt that in some particular instances some of the names set under Corderoy should be also set under Cowderoy, the surnames founded on the two having become inextricably united; v. Corderoy.

John de Coudray, 1273. A.
William de Coudraye, 1307. M.
Peter de Coudray. R.
1618. Buried — Francis, s Andrewe Cowdrye: St. Thomas the Apostle, p. 110.
1619. — Andrewe Cowdrie: ibid. p. 111.
London, 6, 1, 1; New York, 0, 1, 6.

Cowgill.—Local, 'of Cowgill,' a hamlet in the parish of Sedbergh, W. Rid. Yorks. Probably Colgill is the original form. The instances below are found in the neighbourhood of Settle.

Johannes de Colgyll, 1379: P. T. Yorks. p. 269.
Alicia de Colgyll, 1379: ibid.
Manchester, 3; West Rid. Court Dir., 7; Philadelphia, 5.

Cowherd.—Occup. 'the cowherd'; v. Coward for instances. Cowherd is almost extinct, but Coward is very strongly represented in North-English directories. The form Cowherd, unmutilated, is preserved in William Cowherd, the founder of the sect of Cowherdites, as they were familiarly styled. He was born at Carnforth, Lancashire, in 1763, the district where Coward is one of the best-known surnames.

John Cowherd, rector of Heringby, co. Norf., 1435: FF. xi. 225.
MDB. (co. Lancaster), 1.

Cowley.—Local, 'of Cowley,' parishes in cos. Gloucester, Middlesex, and Oxford.

Roger de Couele, co. Oxf. 1273. A.
Alex. de Coueleye, co. Oxf., ibid.
1622. Buried—Saray, d. Walter Cowley: St. Jas. Clerkenwell, iv. 156.
1656. — John, s. James Cowly: ibid. p. 309.
London, 14; Oxford, 7; Boston (U.S. 3; Philadelphia, 6.

Cowlishaw, Coulshaw, Collishaw, Cowlinshaw. — Local, 'of Cowlishaw,' a hamlet in the township of Crompton, in the parish of Prestwich, co. Lanc. This surname has crossed over the border into Yorkshire, and is strong there. It is Americanized into Cowlinshaw.

Manchester. 2, 0, 0, 0; London, 0, 2, 0, 0; Sheffield, 6, 0, 0, 0; MDB. (co. Notts), 1, 0, 4, 0; Boston (U.S.) (Cowlinshaw), 1.

Cowman.—Occup. 'the cowman,' one who looked after the cows; v. Coward and Cowherd.

John Cowman, C. R., 7 Edw. IV.
1760. Married—William Cowman and Rachael Taylor: St. Geo. Han. Sq. i. 93.
Manchester, 1; New York, 2.

Cowmedon.—Local.

1754. Married—Thomas Cunningham and Ann Cowmedon: St. Geo. Chap. Mayfair, p. 276.

Cowper.—Occup. 'the cooper'; v. Cooper. 'Cowpare, *cuparius*': Prompt. Parv. p. 99. A statute of Elizabeth's reign includes such artisans as 'lynnen-weavers, turners, cowpers, millers, earthen-potters' (5 Eliz. c. iv. 23).

Ricardus Turner, *cawper*, 1379: P. T. Yorks. p. 41.
Johannes Turnour, *cowper*, 1379: ibid.
Johannes Cowper, *glover*, 1379: ibid.
Johannes Couper, *coupar*, 1379: ibid. p. 97.

The poet 'Cowper pronounced his name as Cooper' (Dict. Nat. Biog. xii. 401). It seems odd that this information should be necessary, but to this day people almost invariably speak of Cow-per.

1592. Buried—Eliz., d. William Cowper: St. Jas. Clerkenwell, iv. 46.
London, 7; Philadelphia, 2.

Cowperthwait, Cowperthwaite. — Local, 'of Cowperthwaite,' one of the many local names ending in -*thwaite* common to cos. Cumb. and Westm. and the Furness district of North Lanc. Cowperthwaite, no doubt, means the cooper's enclosure (v. Thwaites and Cowper). For instances, v. Copperwheat.

Manchester, 1, 0; Philadelphia, 7, 3.

Cox, Coxon. — Bapt. ; v. Cocks.

Coxhead. — Probably local, *head* being a common suffix to placenames ; cf. Birkenhead and Akenhead, q.v. Nevertheless it may be a nickname, *cockshead*, on account of some fancied resemblance.

1635. John Winter and Martha Cockshead: Marriage Alleg. (Canterbury), p. 213.
1697. Bapt.—John, s. Thomas Cockshead: St. Jas. Clerkenwell, i. 370.
1798. Married—Thomas Coxhead and Isabel Atkinson: St. Geo. Han. Sq. ii. 177.
— George Coxhead and Mary Williams: ibid. ii. 185.

This surname went to America at an early period :
'John Coxshedd, aged 14, sailed for Virginia in the Paul, July 6, 1635 ': Hotten's Lists of Emigrants. Philadelphia, 2.

Coy. — Local, 'of Quy,' a chapelry in the parish of Stow, co. Cambridge. Formerly Quoy.

Felice de Quoye, co. Camb., 1273. A.
Walkelin de Queye, co. Camb., ibid.
Ralph de Quoye, co. Camb., ibid.
1636. Bapt.—Mabell, d. John Coye: St. Jas. Clerkenwell, i. 134.
1747. Married—William Gardiner and Mary Coy: St. Mary Aldermary, p. 51.
MDB. (co. Camb.), 2 ; Philadelphia, 3.

Crabb, Crabbe. —? Local, 'at the crab-tree.' The objection to a local origin is that no prefix 'de la' or 'atte' is to be found in the early instances. Still, it is not easy to suggest any other interpretation; cf. Birch, Ash, Lynde, Oake, Crabtree, Plumptre, and Rowntree. Crabbetre, *acerbus, macianus* ': Prompt. Parv.

Henry Crabbe, co. Camb., 1273. A.
Robert Crabbe, co. Soms., ibid.
Richard Crabbe, co. Norf., ibid.
Matilda Crab, 1379: P. T. Yorks. p. 95.
Johannes Crabbe, 1379: ibid. p. 85.

Henry Crabbe, co. Soms., 1 Edw. III : Kirby's Quest, p. 196. '
London, 18, 4 ; Philadelphia, 1, 0 ; New York, 0, 1.

Crabtree. — Local, 'at the crab-tree' (v. Crabb), from residence thereby. This is a great Yorkshire surname ; cf. Rowntree, Plumptre, Oake, Chestnut, Ash, Nash, &c. It is odd to think that by dwelling beside a particular crab-tree, the descendants of a particular pair should so increase that a perceptibly large number of people in the county of York should now be familiarly known by the name. The name, too, has crossed the ocean. Where was that particular crab-tree in the county of York ?

John Crabtre, co. York. W. 16.
William Crabtree, co. York. ibid.
'Edward Crabbtree emigrated to Virginia in 1635 ': Hotten's Lists of Emigrants, p. 129.
1563. Bapt.—Agnes Crabtree: St. Jas. Clerkenwell, i. 2.
1662. — Sarah, d. Samuell Crabtree: St. Michael, Cornhill, p. 143.
London, 3 ; West Riding Court Dir., 17 ; Leeds, 6 ; Sheffield, 3 ; Halifax, 8 ; Philadelphia, 12.

Crace. — Crace is entered as a single personal name in the Hundred Rolls (ii. 28). Probably, however, it was a nickname ; v. Crass.

London, 3.

Crackenthorpe, Crakanthorpe. — Local, 'of Crackenthorp,' a manor, co. Westmoreland.

William de Crickenthorp', co. Westm., 20 Edw. I. R.
William de Crakenethorp, co. Westm., ibid.
Deborah Crackanthorp', of Lancaster, 1746 : Lancashire Wills at Richmond, p. 72.

The following is a curious corruption :
1695. Buried—William Crackinthought: St. Mary Aldermary (London), p. 203.

Still earlier we find in the same register :
1559. Buried—Thomas Cockingthorp, *merchant-taylor*: St. Mary Aldermary (London), p. 133.
MDB. (co. Lincoln), 0, 1 ; (co. Westmoreland), 0, 1.

Cracknall, Cracknell. —? Local or nickname. A curious feature about English nomenclature is the number of surnames which seem inseparably connected with breadbaking. I do not refer to occupative names like Baxter, Baker, Waferer, &c., or local names like Backhouse or Bacchus (q.v.). I speak of what seem to be nicknames taken from the loaf itself ; cf. Simnel, Blanchpain, and Whitebread. Yet Blanchpain is local, and Whitebread, or Whitbread, may be a mere translation (v. Blanchpain). A cracknel is a kind of crisp biscuit. 'Crakenelle, brede, *crepetullus, fraginellus* ': Prompt. Parv. Nevertheless the surname may be local, with suffix -*hall* or -*hill*.

1579. Married—Lyonell Craknell and Johane Downe: St. Michael, Cornhill, p. 12.
1756. — Samuel Cracknell and Eliz. Wright: St. Geo. Han. Sq. i. 61.
London, 1, 13 ; Boston (U.S.), 0, 1.

Crackshield. — Nick. (v. Breakspear). Thomas Crackyshield was rector of North Creak, co. Norf., in 1412 (FF. vii. 77).

Crackstring. — Nick. One who drew his bowstring too tense ; one of a large list of sobriquets from archery.

Ricardus Crakestryng, 1379 : P. T. Yorks. p. 91.

Cracroft, Crayeroft. — Local, 'of Cracroft.' 'The family were lords of the manor of Cracroft, co. Lincoln, in 1284': Lower (quoting Burke's Landed Gentry). With the form Cracraft *infra*, cf. Craft for Croft, and Meadowcraft for Meadowcroft. This surname has crossed the Atlantic as Craycroft.

1638-9. John Cracroft and Magdalen Hambleton: Marriage Lic. (London), ii. 240.
1725. John Radley and Ann Cracraft : Marriage Lic. (Faculty Office), p. 251.
1751. Bapt.—Mary, d. William Cracraft : St. Dionis Backchurch, p. 175.
London, 1, 0 ; MDB. (co. Lincoln), 2, 0 ; Philadelphia, 0, 4.

Craddock, Cradock, Cradick, Craddick. — Bapt. 'the son of Caradoc,' a Welsh personal name.

David Craddock, co. Soms., 1 Edw. III : Kirby's Quest, p. 90.
Robert Craddoc, co. Soms., 1 Edw. III : ibid. p. 93.

Cradock ap Howell ap Grono : Visit. Glouc. (Harl. Soc.), p. 114.
'Philip Cradock, Chancellor of St. David's,1417': Hist. and Ant. St. David's, p. 365.
'Sir John Francis Caradoc, Lord Howden (1762–1839), general, changed his name from Cradock to Caradoc in 1820. He was the only son of John Cradock, archbishop of Dublin': Dict. Nat. Biog. ix. 27.
London, 9, 2, 1, 0 ; Manchester, 4, 0, 0, 1 ; Philadelphia, 3, 2, 0, 0 ; New York, 3, 1, 0, 1.

Crafford.—Local, 'of Crawford,' a variant ; v. Crawford, Crofford, and Crowfoot.
1582. Nicholas Crafforde and Dorothy Mustchampe : Marriage Lic. (London), i. 109.
1620. Bapt.—Susan, d. John Craforth : St. Jas. Clerkenwell, i. 86.
1689. — Eliz., d. William Craford : ibid. p. 330.
London, 4.

Craft.—Local, 'at the croft,' a northern form of Croft, q.v. ; cf. Crapper for Cropper, Cracraft and Meadowcraft for Cracroft and Meadowcroft.
Roger de Crafte, co. Bedford, Hen. III–Edw. I. K.
1620. Bapt. — Robart, s. Christopher Craft : St. Jas. Clerkenwell, i. 86.
1786. Married — Edward Craft and Betty Hunt : St. Geo. Han. Sq. i. 386.
London, 4 ; New York, 27.

Crafter.—Occup. 'the crafter,' one who occupied a small farm ; a northern form of Crofter ; v. Craft.
London, 8.

Cragg, Craggs.—Local, 'at the crag' or 'crags,' from residence thereby.
Adam del Crag, co. Lanc., 1332 : Lay Subsidy (Rylands), p. 88.
Robert del Crag, co. Lanc., 1332 : ibid. p. 61.
1582. Francis Puckeringe and Blanche Cragge : Marriage Lic. (London), i. 111.
1592-3. John Cragges and Eliz. Connylowe : ibid. i. 205.
London, 3, 1 ; Boston (U.S.), 3, 0 ; Philadelphia (Cragge), 1.

Craig, Craigg, Craige.—Loc. (1) 'at the craig,' i.e. crag, from residence thereby. More specifically (2) 'of Craig,' a name given to several parishes and villages in Scotland. Both (1) and (2) are Scotch.
1748. Married—Alex. Craigg and Eliz. Johnson : St. Geo. Chap. Mayfair, p. 121.
London, 20, 0, 0 ; Boston (U.S.), 54, 0, 1 ; Philadelphia, 245, 1, 13.

Craigh.—Local ; a variant of Craig, q.v.
Liverpool, 1 ; Philadelphia, 1.

Craighead.—Local, 'of Craighead,' a place in the parish of Dailly, co. Ayr (Lower) ; several other places in N.B. also bear the same name ; lit. the head of the craig (v. Craig). Head is a common suffix to place-names ; cf. Akenhead and Birkenhead.
Boston (U.S.), 1 ; Philadelphia, 5.

Craighill, Craghill.—Local, 'of Craighill.' Several places in Scotland bear this name ; lit. the rocky mound ; v. Craig and Carrick.
Baltimore, 1, 0 ; Liverpool, 0, 1.

Craigie, Craggy.—Local, 'of Craigie,' parishes in cos. Ayr, Perth, and Linlithgow.
1767. Married—John Harding and Ann Craggy : St. Geo. Han. Sq. i. 171.
London, 1, 1 ; Boston (U.S.), 5, 0.

Craigmyle, Creagmile.—Local, 'of Craigmill,' a village in the parish of Logie (Lower) ; lit. the mill by the craig (v. Craig and Carrick).
1640. John Craigmyll and Ann Price : Marriage Lic. (London), ii. 251.
London, 1, 0 ; Philadelphia, 0, 8.

Craik, Crake, Creek, Creak.—Local, (1) 'of the creek'; M.E. creke, North-Eng. crake and craik, a bend, an inlet, a cove ; cf. Crake-valley, near Ulverston ; (2) 'of Craike,' a parish in co. Durham, three miles from Easingwold. Probably the origin is the same.
Ralph Crake, co. York, 1273. A.
Philippus de Crayk', 1379 : P. T. Yorks. p. 101.
Elena Crayke, 1379 : ibid. p. 53.
1653. Married — Thomas Creak, co. Harford (sic) and Eliz. Warren : St. Dionis Backchurch, p. 29.
1788. Married—William Appleby and Eliz. Creek : St. Geo. Han. Sq. ii. 16.
1791. — William Staines and Mary Crake : ibid. p. 61.
London, 2, 3, 1, 1 ; Philadelphia, 1, 0, 0, 0 ; Boston (U.S.), 1, 0, 0, 0.

Cramer.—Occup. ; v. Creamer.

Cranbrook.—Local, 'of Cranbrook,' a market-town and parish in Kent.
1793. Married — William Cranbrook and Eliz. Glover : St. Geo. Han. Sq. ii. 98.
London Court Dir., 1.

Crandidge.—Nick. ; a corruption of 'Grandage,' q.v.
Pontefract Dir., 1.

Crane.—(1) Nick. 'the crane'; cf. Stork, Gull, &c. (2) Bapt. 'the son of Grane.' The initial was early changed from G to C : cf. Candlin and Cammel for Gandelyn and Gamell. Grane was a common personal name in co. York in the 13th and 14th centuries ; v. Grain. .
John le Cran, co. Soms., 1 Edw. III : Kirby's Quest, p. 98.
Thomas le Cran, co. Soms., 1 Edw. III : ibid. p. 252.
Johannes Crane, Alicia uxor ejus, 1379 : P. T. Yorks. p. 27.
Elisot Grane, 1379 : ibid.
John Crane de Cranebrok, C. R., 16 Ric. II.
Stephanus Crane, 1379 : P. T. Yorks. p. 34.
Dionisia Cranne, vidua, 1379 : ibid. p. 41.
John Crane, 1536 : Reg. Univ. Oxf. i. 185.
1789. Married—William Durrant and Mary Crane : St. Geo. Han. Sq. ii. 27.
London, 31 ; Philadelphia, 32.

Cranefield, Cranfield.—Local, 'of Cranfield,' a parish in co. Bedford, seven miles from Ampt hill.
Philippa de Cranefeld, co. Oxf., Hen. III–Edw. I. K.
Alexander de Crannefeld, co. Hunts, 1273. A.
1606. Bapt.—Eliz., d. John Cranfeild : St. Jas. Clerkenwell, i. 47.
1611. Married—Thomas Cranfeild and Eliz. Bathe : St. Dionis Backchurch, p. 17.
1624. — William Grave and Grace Cranfeilde : St. Michael, Cornhill, p. 24.
London, 2, 2.

Cranford.—Local, 'of Cranford,' a parish in co. Northampton, four miles from Kettering.
John de Cranniford, co. Northampton, Hen. III–Edw. I. K.
Ralph de Craneford, co. Northampton, ibid.
Geoffrey de Cranford, co. Devon, 1273. A.
John de Cranford, co. Leicester, ibid.
Richard de Cranford, co. Bucks, ibid.
1607. Bapt.—Jane, d. Cuthbert Cranford : St. Jas. Clerkenwell, i. 47.
1654. Married—Henry Smith and Eliz. Cranford : St. Michael, Cornhill, p. 34.
New York, 1.

Cranitch.—An American form of Crandidge, q.v. The modern variants of this great early surname are a curious study.

1578. Married—Thomas Cranedge and Eliz. Hudson: St. Thomas the Apostle (London), p. 6.
1707. John Cranidge and Eliz. Tibbis: Marriage Lic. (London), ii. 336.
Boston (U.S.), 3 ; New York, 3.

Crank.—Local, ' of Crank.' I cannot find the spot in North Lancashire. But there is a place in Rainford, co. Lanc., called Crank, which has given name to Crank Station. Crank Hall and Crank Farm are still properties there.

'James Cranke (1746?-1826), artist, was born at Urswick-in-Furness about 1746. It is supposed that he studied in London, in the studio of his uncle, James Cranke (1717-80), and afterwards settled at Warrington as a portrait-painter': Dict. Nat. Biog. xiii. 17.
Henry Cranke, of Little Urswicke, 1662: Lancashire Wills at Richmond, i. 79.
Nicholas Cranke, of Urswicke, 1692: ibid. ii. 73.
William Crank, of Ulverston, 1734: ibid.

There are numerous entries of this name in the Ulverston registers :

1748. Bapt.—Frances, d. John Crank, of Ulverston: St. Mary, Ulverston, ii. 340.
1751. Buried—Mary, d. John Crank, of Ulverston : ibid. i. 272.
Ulverston, 1 ; Urswick, 2 ; London, 1 ; Philadelphia, 1.

Crankshaw, Cronshaw, Crownshaw, Cranshaw. — Local, ' of Cronkshaw,' the twisting or winding shaw, i.e. wood. Cronkshaw seems to have lain in the parish of Rochdale or Bury, co. Lanc. Cronshaw and Cranshaw are variants of the surname, and Crankshaw is the more correct modern representative. This form is well represented across the Atlantic.

Ellen Cronkshaw, of Musbury, 1618: Wills at Chester (1545-1620), p. 48.
John Cronkshaw, of Hunterholme in Pendle, 1617: ibid.
William Cronkshaw, of Musbury, 1624: ibid. (1621-50), p. 57.
Thomas Holt, of Cronkshaw, 1642: ibid. p. 113.

That Cronshaw is a variant is easily proved.

Cf. Francis Bould, of Cronshawe, 1613: Lancashire Inquisitions, p. 254.

Francis Bold, of Graynshey [G for C], 1588 : Wills at Chester (1545-1620), p. 23.
James Cronshaw, *farmer*, Cronshaw Fold, Musbury : Kelly's Lancashire Dir., 1873, p. 1584.
Manchester, 4, 3, 0, 0 ; Sheffield, 0, 0, 1, 0 ; Bolton (Lanc. , 1, 0, 0, 3 ; Philadelphia, 15, 2, 0, 0.

Cranley.—Local, ' of Cranley,' a parish in co. Surrey, eight miles from Guildford.

Avice de Cranele, co. Bedf., 1273. A.
1667. Bapt.—John, s. John Cranley : St. Jas. Clerkenwell, i. 232.
1790. Married—John Reddy and Sarah Cranley : St. Geo. Han. Sq. ii. 50.
London, 1 ; New York, 1.

Cranmer, Cranmore.—Local, ' of Cranemere.' I see no reason to doubt Lower's statement, ' anciently Cranemere, the hillside of a low swampy country at Long Melford, co. Suffolk ' (Patr. Brit. p. 74). Although Archbishop Cranmer was born in co. Notts, there is no reason to suppose his surname belongs to the soil of that country. Besides, Cranemere mentioned above gave rise to a surname :

Hugh de Cranemere, co. Linc., 1273. A.
Roger de Cranemere, co. Herts, ibid.
William Cranemere, rector of Bawsey, co. Norf., 1414 : FF. viii. 346.

The last-named is again referred to as follows :

William Cranmere, rector of Hillington, co. Norf., 1412 : FF. viii. 467.

This may be looked upon as absolutely conclusive.

1679. Married — John Cranmer, co. Surrey, and Dorothy Gilbert : St. Dionis Backchurch, p. 30.
1734. — Isaac Cranmer and Margaret White : ibid. p. 64.

I fear the surname is almost obsolete in England. It is found, however, in the United States directories.

Philadelphia, 6, 1 ; Liverpool, 1, 0.

Cranswick.—Local, ' of Cranswick.' I have not identified the hamlet, but doubtless it is in Yorkshire.

William de Crauncewyk, *mercer*, 12 Edw. II : Freemen of York, i. 18.
John de Crauncewyk, co. York, 1273. A.
Isabella de Crauncewyk, 1379 : P. T. Yorks. p. 301.
London, 1 ; Sheffield, 1 ; West Rid. Court Dir., 4.

Cranwell.—Local, ' of Cranwell,' a parish in co. Lincoln, four miles from Sleaford.

Adam de Cranewell, co. Linc., 1273. A.
Robert de Cranewell, co. Linc., ibid.
Richard de Cranewell, co. Kent, ibid.
1545. Bapt.—Mark, s. Jasper Cranwell : St. Dionis Backchurch, p. 73.
1646. Married—Fitzhugh Cranwell and Sindonye Fowles : St. Jas. Clerkenwell, iii. 79.
1801. — Robert Cranwell and Eliz. Dina Horniman : St. Geo. Han. Sq. ii. 249.
London, 3 ; Boston (U.S.), 1.

Crapper.—Occup.; v. Cropper.

Craske.—Nick. ' the crask,' i.e. the fat, the lusty. ' Craske, fryke of fatte ' (Prompt. Parv.). ' Crask. fat, lusty, in good health and spirits, hearty ' (Halliwell). A Norfolk surname.

Walter le Crask, vicar of Netesherd, co. Norf., 1314 : FF. xi. 50.
William Craske, co. Suff., 1273. A.
Adam Crask, vicar of Lesyate, co. Norf., 1380 : FF. viii. 340.
Hamond Crask, of Norwich, 1642 : ibid. iii. 383.
Thomas Craske, common councilman, of Norwich, 1742 : ibid. iii. 452.
1789. Married — Simon Craske and Rose Rickwood : St. Geo. Han. Sq. ii. 27.
MDB. (co. Norfolk), 3 ; New York, 2.

Crass.—Nick. ' the crass,' i.e. fat or lusty ; v. Craske.

William Crassus, co. Wilts, 1273. A.
Richard le Cras, co. Oxf., ibid.
William le Cras, co. Camb., ibid.
Thomas le Craas, co. Soms., 1 Edw. III : Kirby's Quest, p. 131.
(Theo)bald le Cras, co. Soms., 1 Edw. III : ibid.
Stephen Crassus. J.
William Cras, 1379 : P. T. Howdenshire, p. 22.
1698. Bapt.—John, s. Samuell Crass : St. Jas. Clerkenwell, i. 377.

Crassweller; v. Crosweller.

Crast; v. Crust.

Craswell. — Local; v. Crosswell and Crosweller.

Craven. — Local, ' of Craven,' i.e. the district of Craven in W. Rid. Yorks. The surname has for centuries been very strongly represented in Yorkshire, especially in the West Riding.

Paulinus de Cravene, 12 Edw. I : Freemen of York, i. 3.
Agnes de Craven, 1379 : P. T. Yorks. p. 175.
Johannes de Craven, 1379 : ibid. p. 140.
Roger de Crauen, 1379 : ibid. p. 229.
Robert de Craven, rector of Bolton-

juxta-Bowland, 1304 : Whitaker's Craven, p. 131.
1619. Bapt.—John, s. Richard Cravon : St. Michael, Cornhill, p. 114.
1669. Married—Ezekyell Craven and Mary Browne : St. Jas. Clerkenwell, iii. 169.

This surname early crossed the Atlantic, and has ramified strongly in the States.

Thomas Craven, aged 17 years, 'imbarqued' for Virginia in 1635. Still earlier in 1626, Richard Craven received 150 acres by patent : Hotten's Lists of Emigrants, pp. 112, 272.
London, 17 ; West Rid. Court Dir., 42 ; Philadelphia, 64.

Crawcour.—Local, ' de Crevecœur.' This ancient baronial surname still survives in the London Directory. The modern form closely resembles some of the mediaeval variants.

Alexander de Crevequer, co. Linc., 1273. A.
Hamo de Crevequer, co. Bedf., ibid.
Robert de Crewquer, co. Bucks, ibid.
Cecilia le (sic) Creuker, co. Linc., ibid.
Lewin Crawcour & Co., upholsterers : London Directory.
Morris Crawcour, inkstand and ruler maker : ibid.
London, 2.

Crawford, Crauford, Craufurd, Crawforth. — Local, ' of Crawford,' a parish in Lanarkshire, also several smaller places in North Britain. ' Sir Reginald de Craufurd, sheriff of Ayrshire in 1296, seems to have been the common ancestor of many branches of the family' (Lower's Patr. Brit. p. 74). The variants of this surname are extremely numerous, among which are Crowfoot, Crafford, Croffit ; v. Crofford.

Nicholas de Crauford, co. Soms., 1273. A.
Robert de Crauford, co. Oxf., ibid.
1685. Bapt.—Anne, d. John Crawford : St. Jas. Clerkenwell, i. 314.
1744. Buried — A. Crawford : St. Thomas the Apostle (London), p. 156.
London, 31, 1, 2, 1 ; Philadelphia, 253, 0, 0, 0.

Crawley.—Local, 'of Crawley,' townships and parishes in cos. Northumb., Oxford, Hants, Sussex, &c.

Dñs. Alan de Craule, co. Oxf., 1273. A.
London, 24 ; Boston (U.S.), 11.

Crawshaw, Crawshay.—Local, ' of Crawshaw,' now called

Crawshaw-booth, a hamlet in the parish of Whalley, co. Lanc.
Adam de Crawschawe, 1379 : P. T. Yorks. p. 287.
Juliana de Crawshaw, 1379 : ibid. p. 85.
Thomas Crawshaw, of New Hall Hey, 1602 : Wills at Chester (1545-1620), p. 46.
1758. Married — William Crawshaw and Emma Brummell : St. Geo. Han. Sq. i. 82
1760. — Thomas Hill and Susanna Crawshay : ibid. i. 97.
London, 1, 3 ; West Rid. Court Dir., 12, 0 ; Manchester, 8, 0 ; Philadelphia, 4, 0.

Craycroft.—An American variant of Cracroft, q.v.

Crayford.—Local, ' of Crawford,' q.v., one of many variants ; v. Crawford and Crofford.
Liverpool, 1.

Creamer, Cramer. — Occup. ' the creamer,' i.e. huckster, or pedlar. ' Of the above there are —2 cadgers (fish carriers), 2 creamers, persons who go through the parish . . . and buy butter, hens, eggs, &c., mostly for the Dundee market' : P. Kirkden, Forfars. Statist. Acc. ii. 508 (Jamieson). Hence creamerie, cramery, merchandise, goods usually sold by a pedlar.

'With my cramery gif ye list mell.'
Lyndsay, S. P. R. ii. 94.

A crame was a pedlar's pack. 'Ane pedder is called an marchand, or creamer, qhua bearis ane pack or creame vpon his back' (Skene, Verb. Sign.). All my quotations are from Jamieson, who shows that cream, craim, and crame also denoted a market booth or stall, and a cramer or creamer was the occupant.

1675. Married — William Rolfe and Eliz. Creamer : St. Michael, Cornhill, p. 40.
1 07. — Edward Sankey and Fanny Cramer : St. Geo. Han. Sq. ii. 371.
London, 3, 4 ; Philadelphia, 40, 25.

Crease, Crees, Creese. — Nick. ' the creeze,' a West-country surname. ' Creeze, squeamish. West' (Halliwell) ; a fastidious man, particular, nice.

William Crees, co. Soms., 1 Edw. III : Kirby's Quest, pp. 116, 118.
Clement Crees, co. Soms., 1 Edw. III : ibid.
Robert Crees, co. Soms., 1 Edw. III : ibid.

1793. Married — Thomas Crees and Sarah Stephens : St. Geo. Han. Sq. ii. 90.
— — John Payne and Ann Crees : ibid. ii. 105.
MDB. (co. Soms.), 9, 6, 1 ; London, 2, 0, 1 ; Philadelphia, 6, 8, 0.

Creasey, Creasy, Creassey, Cressey, Cressy. — Local, ' de Cressy.' No doubt Crecy in Picardy, the scene of the famous battle. The surname in several forms is strongly represented now in Lincoln, Norfolk, and Suffolk.

Alexander de Cressi, co. Linc., 1273. A.
Hugh de Cressy, co. Kent, ibid.
William de Cressy, co. York, ibid.
Johannes de Cressy, 1379 : P. T. Yorks. p. 271.
Willelmus Cressy, 1379 : ibid. p. 3.
Isabella Cressy, 1379 : ibid. p. 154.
Roger de Cressi, co. Norf., 24 Hen. III : FF. xi. 217.
Stephen de Cressi, co. Norf., 50 Hen. III : ibid. xi. 219.
Peter Cressy, bailiff of Yarmouth, 1341 : ibid. xi. 323.
MDB. (Lincoln), 13, 0, 0, 3, 0 ; (Norfolk), 2, 0, 0, 2, 0 ; London, 4, 2, 0, 1, 1 ; Barnsley (Creasey), 1 ; West Rid. Court Dir. (Creassey), 1 ; Bradford (Cressey, 1 ; New York (Creasy), 3 ; Philadelphia (Cressey), 4.

Creech.—Local ; v. Cridge.

Creed. —(1) Local, ' of Creed,' a parish in co. Cornwall. (a) Bapt. ' the son of Creed.' Crede is manifestly a personal name in the Hundred Rolls in districts far removed from Cornwall. It occurs in every case without a prefix, in itself an argument in favour of a fontal origin. No doubt it means creed, i.e. belief, answering to faith, so familiar as a girl's name later on.

Henry Crede, vicar of Horning, co. Norf., 1381 : FF. xi. 56.
John Creyde, co. Soms., 1 Edw. III : Kirby's Quest, p. 80.
Alan Crede, co. Suff., 1273. A.
Mabilia Crede, co. Camb., ibid.
Roger Crede, co. Hunts, ibid.
1577. Anthony Creede, co. Herts, and Johanna King, widow : Marriage Lic. (London), i. 76.
1665. Married — William Creed and Margery Nein : St. Jas. Clerkenwell, iii. 121.
1731. — Charles Creed and Mary Gilbert : St. Geo. Han. Sq. i. 9.
London, 7 ; MDB. (co. Norfolk), 1 ; Philadelphia, 2.

Creek.—Local ; v. Craik.

Crees, Creese. — Nick. ; v. Crease.

Creighton; v. Crichton.

Crespin. — Bapt. 'the son of Crispin,' q.v. This variant is found very early in co. Devon, where Crispin is still a familiar surname.

Richard Crespin, co. Devon, 1273. A.
Robert Crespin, co. Devon, ibid.
Nicholas Crespyn, co. Devon, ibid.
Margery Cressebyn, co. Dorset, ibid.
M. Crespin is witness to a marriage, July 8, 1794 : St. Geo. Han. Sq. ii. 115.
London, 1 ; Philadelphia, 2.

Cressey, Cressy. — Local ; v. Creasey.

Cresson. — Bapt. for Gresson ; v. Grayson. An American variant. The change from initial G to C is very common in English nomenclature ; v. Candlin, Crane, Clendening, &c.

Philadelphia, 22.

Cresswell, Creswell. — Local, 'of Cresswell.' Two parishes bear this name, one in co. Northumberland, the other in co. Stafford.

Thomas de Cressewell, co. Staff., Hen. III–Edw. I. K.
Henry de Creswell, co. Staff., 20 Edw. I. R.
Robert Cressewyle, co. Derby, 1273. A.
Ricardus Cresuill, 1379 : P. T. Yorks. p. 27.
Emmot Creswyll, 1379 : ibid. p. 45.
John Cresswell, co. York, 1591–2 : Reg. Univ. Oxf. vol. ii. pt. ii. p. 188.
1615. Bapt. — Parnell, d. John Creswell : St. Jas. Clerkenwell, i. 72.
London, 12, 2 ; Sheffield, 1, 0 ; West Rid. Court Dir., 3, 0 ; Philadelphia, 10, 8.

Crest. — Local, 'at the crest,' the summit of the hill.

Rogerus del Crest, 1379 : P. T. Yorks. p. 106.
Johannes del Crest, 1379 : ibid.

Creswick. — Local, ' of Creswick,' a hamlet in the parish of Ecclesfield, near Sheffield.

Johannes de Cressewik', 1379 : P. T. Yorks. p. 40.
Johannes de Croswik', 1379 : ibid. p. 41.
1679. Francis Creswicke and Mary Ridges : Marriage Lic. (Faculty Office), p. 146.
1800. Married — Abram Tyzack Rawlinson and Eliza Eudocia Albenia Creswicke : St. Geo. Han. Sq. ii. 225.
London, 3 ; Sheffield, 4 ; West Rid. Court Dir., 3.

Crew, Crewe. — Local, ' of Crew,' a township in the parish of

---

Farndon, co. Chester, now a large and thriving town since it became the centre of so much railway activity.

Robert Crewe, of Wallasey, 1608 : Wills at Chester (1545–1620), p. 47.
Thomas Crewe, of Holt, 1613 : ibid.
Elizabeth Crew, of Houghton, 1690 : ibid. (1681–1700), p. 63.
Urian Crewe, of Tushingham, *yeoman*, 1697 : ibid.
1611. Bapt. — Roger, s. Helen Crewe : St. Jas. Clerkenwell, i. 62.
1654. — Ann, d. Isaac Crewe : ibid. p. 188.
London, 9, 2 ; MDB. (co. Chester), 0, 2 ; (co. Stafford), 0, 4 ; Philadelphia, 7, 1.

Crewdson,   Crowdson, Croudson. — Bapt. 'the son of Cudbert,' i.e. Cuthbert, from the nick. Cruddy. Doubtless the original nick. was Cuddy. But when the donkey became familiarly so called, Cruddy took its place. Crewdson and its variants are chiefly found in Furness and the neighbouring districts.

Thomas Crudd', 1379 : P. T. Yorks. pp. 123, 129.
Ricardus Crudde, 1379 : ibid.
Johannes Crudde, 1379 : ibid.
1545. Married — Leonard Ormundie and Agnes Crowdson : St. Mary, Ulverston, i. 1.
1546. Buried — Jenet Crowdson : ibid. p. 3.
1589. Agnes Crewdson, of Dalton : Lancashire Wills at Richmond, p. 79.
1592. John Croudson, of Kirkby Ireleth : ibid. p. 84.
1676. Roland Crowdson, of Torver : ibid.

Two of the oldest churches in Furness (Aldingham and Kirkby Ireleth) are dedicated to St. Cuthbert. This would make the fontal name very popular. As regards the great saint's connexion with the district, v. Miracles of St. Cuthbert (Surtees Soc.).

MDB. (Lancashire), 2, 4, 0 ; Ulverston, 7, 0, 0.

Crichton, Creighton, Craighton, Crighton. — Local, ' of Crichton,' an old estate and castle in co. Edinburgh.

'Crichton ! though now thy miry court
But pens the lazy steer and sheep.'
                                        Marmion.

' Sir Alexander Crichton (1763–1856), physician, was born at Edinburgh ' : Dict. Nat. Biog. xiii. 58.

' James Crichton, surnamed the Admirable (1560–85 ?), was born probably at Eliock, Dumfriesshire. He signed himself Creichton ' : ibid. p. 63.
' William Crichton, or Creighton (fl. 1615), Jesuit, was a native of Scotland ' : ibid. p. 93.
' Robert Creighton, or Crichton (1593–1672), bishop of Bath and Wells, was born at Dunkeld, Perthshire ' : ibid. p. 69.

It is thus clear that although there is Creighton, a township in the parish of Uttoxeter, co. Stafford, the various forms all represent one surname, and that is the Scotch Crichton.

London, 4, 3, 0, 0 ; Boston (U.S.), 1, 15, 0, 0 ; New York (Crighton), 1 ; Philadelphia, 0, 44, 2, 0.

Crick. — Local, ' of Crick,' a parish in dioc. of Peterborough. Probably from A.S. *crecca*, a creek. i.e. a bend, nook, corner. Skeat quotes (v. Creek) Cricklade (Creccagelád) in Wiltshire, and Creccanford, now Crayford, in Kent.

Bartholomew de Crekke, co. Suff., 1273. A.
Jacobus de Crakke, co. Suff., ibid.
Matilda de Crec, co. Camb., ibid.
Bartholomew de Crec, co. Norf., Hen. III–Edw. I. K.
James de Creke, co. Norf., temp. Hen. III : FF. xi. 252.
London, 9 ; MDB. (Norfolk), 1 ; (Suffolk), 1 ; Boston (U.S.), 1.

Crickmer. — Local, ' of Crakemore' (a combination of ' Crake' and ' Moor ') ; v. Craik. I do not know the spot.

Cecilia Crakemore, 1379 : P. T. Yorks. p. 133.
1793. Married — James Crickmer and Sarah Janaway : St. Geo. Han. Sq. ii. 95.
1803. — Thomas Raynham and Sarah Crickmore : ibid. p. 293.
London, 3.

Cridge, Creech. — (1) Local. Probably ' of Crick,' a hamlet in the parish of Caerwent, in co. Monmouth. These surnames are undoubtedly of West-country parentage ; cf. Kirk and Church, or Bridge and Bridge. (2) Local, ' of Crich,' a parish in co. Derby, near Alfreton.

Peter de Cryche, co. Soms., 1 Edw. III : Kirby's Quest, p. 274.
Robert de Criche, co. Notts, 1273. A.
1665. Buried — Jane Creech : St. Jas. Clerkenwell, iv. 367.

MDB. (co. Soms.), 2, 1 ; Boston (U.S.), 4, 0 ; New York, 1, 0.

Cripps, Crips. — (1) Nick. ' the crisp,' i.e. the curly ; v. Crisp; cf. the provincial *waps* for wasp.

' As writeth John in the Apocalips,
Her heer that oundie was and crips.'
Chaucer, House of Fame, iii. 296.

Henry le Cripse, co. Soms., 1 Edw. III : Kirby's Quest, p. 97.
Adam le Cripse, co. Soms., 1 Edw. III : ibid. p. 204.
Adam le Creps, co. Oxf., 1273. A.

(2) Bapt. ' the son of Crispin,' from the nick. Crisp or Crips.

Reginald Crips, co. Kent, 1273. A.
Walter Crips, co. Hunts, ibid.
Morice Crips, co. Oxf., ibid.

For an incidental proof that Crisp and Crips were nicks. of the same name, v. Scripps.

1744. Married—Joseph Lakin and Mary Cripps : St. Geo. Han. Sq. i. 31.
1759. — John Crips and Frances Faulkner : ibid. i. 90.
London, 18, 2 ; MDB. (co. Oxford), 2, 0 ; Philadelphia, 23, 0.

Crisp, Crispe.—(1) Nick. ' the crisp,' i.e. with the curly hair ; v. Cripps (1). ' Crisping-pins,' Isa. iii. 22. ' Cryspyng eyrene' : Cath. Ang. ' Cryspe, as here (hair), or other lyke' : Prompt. Parv.

' And yet also of our prentis Jankin,
For his crispe here, shining as gold so fin.' Chaucer, C. T. 5886.

Robert le Crespe, co. Oxf., 1273. A.
Thomas le Crespe, co. Soms., ibid.
Gilbert le Crispe, co. Oxf., ibid.
Reginald le Crispe. J.
Richard Cryspe, C. R., 8 Ric. II.

(2) Bapt. ' the son of Crispin,' from the nick. Crisp; v. Cripps (2).

1523. Thomas Cryspe and Anne Staleham : Marriage Lic. (London), i. 3.
1603. Married — Hatton Crispe and Joane Fenton : St. Jas. Clerkenwell, iii.28.
1788. — John Robson and Mary Crisp : St. Geo. Han. Sq. ii. 12.
London, 27, 2 ; Boston (U.S.), 5, 0.

Crispin, Crispen, Crispenn, Crispinn.—Bapt. ' the son of Crispian,' more generally Crispin ; v. Crisp (2) and Cripps (2) ; cf. Crespin, a common Devonshire variant.

Milo fil. Crispini, co. Oxf., 20 Edw. I. R.
William Crispin, co. Wilts, ibid.
Peter Crispin, co. Norf., 34 Hen. III : FF. ii. 155.

Richer Crispyng, of Norwich, 1392 : ibid. iv. 387.
John Crispyng, of Norwich, 1423 : ibid. iv. 31.
William fil. Crispian, co. Oxf., 1273. A.
Robert Crispien, co. Camb., ibid.
Crispianus de Colrigge, co. Devon, ibid.
Crispian de Columbers, co. Linc., ibid.
Richard Crispine, co. Oxf., ibid.
Robert Crisping, co. Linc., ibid.
1632-3. Ephraim Crispin and Martha Bond, *widow* : Marriage Lic. (Westminster), 34.
1721. Married—John Bedwell and Jane Crispen : St. Dionis Backchurch, p. 60.
London, 2, 0, 0, 0 ; MDB. (co. Suffolk), 1, 0, 0, 0 ; (co. Devon), 5, 0, 0, 0 ; Philadelphia, 10, 2, 2, 1.

Critchlow, Critchley.—Loc. ' of Critchlow,' or ' Chritchlow,' some small spot in co. Lancashire, probably in the neighbourhood of Chorley. I have failed to discover it. The surname has ramified in a remarkable manner.

Richard Crichlow, of Leyland, 1587 : Wills at Chester (1545-1620), p. 47.
John Crichlowe, of Croxton, 1593 : ibid.
Thomas Chrichlowe, of Leyland, 1606 : ibid. p. 40.

The same individual is thus referred to in the first two entries :

Edmund Crichlow, 1662 : Preston Guild Rolls, p. 143.
Edmund Critchley, 1682 : ibid. p. 183.
Anne Chrichlaw, of Ashtonbank, 1672 : Lancashire Wills at Richmond, p. 65.
William Critchley, of Lea, 1673 : ibid. p. 79.
1804. Married — Joseph Critchley and Eliz. Parker : St. Geo. Han. Sq. ii. 307.
London, 0, 2 ; Manchester, 4, 9 ; Philadelphia, 1, 2.

Croasdale, -dell, -dill ; v. Crossdale.

Crocker, Croker, Croaker.—Occup. ' the crocker,' a potter, a maker of crocks, a once familiar name for the occupation, used by Wyclif in place of our ' potter's vessel' (Ps. ii. 9). From M.E. *crokke*, an earthen pitcher : ' There is also white clay, and red for to make of crokkes, and steenes (stone-jars), and other vessels' (John de Trevisa, 1387). A well-known Devonshire surname.

Adam le Crockar, C. R., 31 Edw. I.
John le Crochere, co. Devon, Hen. III-Edw. I. K.
Simon le Crockere, co. Oxf., 1273. A.
William Crockare, co. Oxf., ibid.
John le Crokere, 1301. M.

Roger le Crocker, co. Soms., 1 Edw. III : Kirby's Quest, p. 174.
John le Crokker, co. Soms., 1 Edw. III : ibid. p. 135.
1580. William Croker and Margaret Horsey : Marriage Lic. (London), i. 98.
1746. Married—Pasco Croker and Sarah Russell : St. Mary Aldermary, p. 51.
1779. — John Crocker and Ann Clare : St. Geo. Han. Sq. i. 392.

This surname has ramified in a truly marvellous manner in the United States. But it went out with the early settlers.

' Richard Crocker, a child, living in Virginia, 1623 ' : Hotten's Lists of Emigrants, p. 81.
' Henry Crocker came to Virginia in the Abigail, 1620 ' : ibid. p. 221.

About the same time came another Henry Croker, in the Marigold. Jone, his wife, joined him later on, sailing in the Swan ; v. Hotten, p. 237. If these were fruitful and multiplied in the first generation, the present large number is readily accounted for.

London, 32, 6, 0 ; MDB. (co. Devon), 13, 4, 0 ; New York, 29, 10, 0 ; Boston (U.S.), 102, 0, 0.

Crockett, Crockitt, Crocket.—Local. The origin is undoubtedly local, but I cannot discover the precise spot.

William de Cruket, co. Southampton, 20 Edw. I. R.
Avicia de Cruket, co. Dorset, Hen. III-Edw. I. K.
Thomas de Cruket, co. Dorset, ibid.
1647. Married—James Hatter and Jone Crockett : St. Jas. Clerkenwell, iii. 82.
London, 6, 1, 1 ; Boston (U.S.), 36, 0, 0.

Crockford.—Local, ' of Crockford,' seemingly some small locality in co. Oxford.

Walter de Crukeford, co. Oxf., 1273. A.
1687. William Welles and Joane Crockford : Marriage Alleg. (Canterbury), p. 298.
1690. Married—Joseph Crockford and Dorcas Dring : St. Jas. Clerkenwell, iii. 207.
London, 2 ; Boston (U.S.), 1 ; Philadelphia, 1.

Crocombe.—Local, ' of Crowcombe,' a parish in co. Somerset, ten miles from Taunton.

Gilbert de Crokum, co. Northumberland, 20 Edw. I. R.
Geoffrey de Crocumbe, co. Warwick, Hen. III-Edw. I. K.

Geoffrey de Crewecumb, co. Devon, Hen. III–Edw. I. K.
MDB. (co. Devon), 5.

Crofford, Croford, Croffet, Croffut, Crofut, Crofoot, Croffit.—Local, 'of Crawford,' q.v. The usual English variant is Crowfoot, q.v. The forms here given are all peculiar to the United States.

New York, 1, 1, 1, 1, 8, 0, 0; Boston (U.S.), 1, 0, 0, 0, 1, 1, 1.

Croft. — Local, (1) 'at the croft,' a small farm, a field, an enclosure. Hence such local names as Meadowcroft, Littlecroft, &c.; v. Craft.

'Thanne shaltow come by a croft.'
Piers P. 3650.

(2) Local, 'of Croft,' parishes in cos. Hereford, Leicester, Lincoln, and York.

Johannes del Croft, 1379 : P. T. Yorks. p. 222.
Willelmus del Croft, 1379 : ibid. p. 111.
Ricardus de Crofte, 1379 : ibid. p. 20.
Walter in the Crofte, co. Soms., 1 Edw. III : Kirby's Quest, p. 263.
Thomas in le Croft, Fines Roll, 14 Edw. II.
Roger de Crofte, co. Salop, 1273. A. William de Croft, co. York, ibid.
1669. Bapt.—Hanna, d. George Croft : St. Jas. Clerkenwell, i. 243.
London, 18; Philadelphia, 15.

Crofton.—Local, 'of Crofton,' (1) a township in parish of Thursby, co. Camb.; (2) a hamlet in parish of Orpington, co. Kent; (3) a township in parish of Diddlebury, co. Salop; (4) a chapelry in parish of Titchfield, co. Hants; (5) a parish in W. Rid. Yorks, four miles from Wakefield. Naturally many places would be called Crofton ; v. Croft.

Richard de Crofton, co. Bucks, 1273. A.
Robert de Crofton, co. Bucks, ibid.
Henry de Crofton, co. Northumberland, 20 Edw. I. R.
Jordan de Crofton, co. Northumberland, ibid.
Hugo de Crofton, co. Wilts, Hen. III–Edw. I. K.
Robertus de Croftone, 1379 : P. T. Yorks. p. 66.
Agnes de Crofton, 1379 : ibid. p. 17.
Thomas de Crofton, 1379 : ibid. p. 24.
1541. Bapt. — Richard Crofton : St. Peter, Cornhill, i. 2.
1548. — John Crofton : St. Michael, Cornhill, p. 75.

London, 3 ; Manchester, 1 ; Philadelphia, 6.

Crompton, Crumpton.—Loc. 'of Crompton,' a township in the parish of Oldham, co. Lanc. This surname has ramified strongly throughout Lancashire, and is well known in the States.

Hugh de Crompton, co. Lanc., 30 Hen. 1 : Baines' Lanc. i. 467.
Edward Crompton, of Crompton, 1587: Wills at Chester (1545-1620), p. 47.
John Crompton, of Dean, 1554 : ibid.
Richard Crompton, of Radcliffe, 1612 : ibid.
1781. Married — John Crompton and Ruth Baxter : St. Geo. Han. Sq. ii. 327.
London, 4, 2 ; Manchester, 29, 0 ; Philadelphia, 18, 1.

Cromwell.—Local, 'of Cromwell,' a parish in co. Notts, dioc. of Lincoln. One of my instances below reminds me more forcibly of the Cavaliers' toast, 'Wash this crumb well down.' No doubt Cromwell was more generally pronounced Crumwell then than now. Spellings mislead, as is so remarkably proved in the case of Cowper, even now popularly called Cow-per instead of Coop-er; cf. again Raleigh, which was evidently pronounced Rawley (v. Cowper and Raleigh). Cromwell is now a commoner surname in the United States than in England.

Ralph de Crumwell, co. Glouc., 1273. A.
Henry de Crommevile, co. Kent, ibid.
Johannes de Crumbwelle, 32 Edw. I : BBB. p. 670.
Idonia de Croumbwelle, co. Derby, 20 Edw. I. R.
Ralph de Cromwell, co. Norf., 1385 : FF. viii. 389.
1779. Married—Robert Lowe and Mary Cromwell : St. Geo. Han. Sq. i. 298.
Crockford, 1 ; Boston (U.S.), 3 ; Philadelphia, 17.

Cronshaw, Crownshaw.—Local, 'of Cronkshaw'; v. Crankshaw.

Crook, Crooke, Crookes, Crooks.—Local, 'of Crook,' (1) a hamlet in the parish of Shevington, co. Lanc.

William del Crok, co. Lanc., 1332 : Lay Subsidy (Rylands), p. 48.
George Crooke, of Newborough, 1590 : Wills at Chester (1545-1620), p. 48.
John Crooke, of Fence-in-Pendle, 1590: ibid.

(2) A hamlet near Kendal, co. Westm. The surname is still found in the neighbourhood. The Yorkshire instances below seem to point to some place or places in the West Riding. Probably both Crook and Crookes are related to *creek*, a bend in a valley, or a cove in a bay.

John de Cruk, co. Soms., 1 Edw. III : Kirby's Quest, p. 214.
Johannes de Cruke, 1379 : P. T. Yorks. p. 143.
Thomas de Crokes, 1379 : ibid. p. 42.
Johanna de Crekes (sic), 1379 : ibid.
1615. Bapt.—Helen, d. Arthur Crooks: St. Jas. Clerkenwell, i. 73.
1620. — Thomas, s. Thomas Crooke : ibid. p. 89.
West Rid. Court Dir., 5, 0, 12, 0 ; Boston (U.S.), 8, 3, 0, 10 ; Manchester, 9, 0, 2, 1.

Crookbone. — Nick. 'crookbone,' i.e. deformed ; cf. Crookshank.

Thomas Crokebayn, 1379 : P. T. Yorks. p. 216.
Willelmus Crukebayn, 1379 : ibid. p. 153.
Johannes Crukeban', 1379 : ibid.

Crooked.—Nick.'crook-backed.'
Cicely Crokede, Close Roll, 1 Edw. II.

Crookshank, Cruikshank, Cruickshank, Crookshanks.—Nick. 'with the crooked shanks,' a bow-legged man. A Scotch surname ; cf. Sheepshanks.

'John Crookshanks (1708-95), captain in the navy ': Dict. Nat. Biog. xiii. 206.
'William Cumberland Cruikshank (1745-1800), anatomist, was born in Edinburgh ': ibid. 260.
'Isaac Cruikshank (1756?-1811 ?), caricaturist, was son of a lowlander, living at one time in Leith. He was father of the famous George Cruikshank ': ibid.258.

This evidence and the prevailing form Cruikshank clearly testify that the surname is of Scotch extraction.

1745. Married — Gavin Crookshanks and Isabella Cassie : St. Geo. Chap. Mayfair, p. 57.
1748. — John Bonney and Mary Cruckshanks : ibid. p. 125.
London, 0, 1, 4, 0 ; Philadelphia, 4, 3, 0, 0.

Cropper, Crapper.—Occup. 'the cropper,' a mower, a sickler, a field-labourer. With Crapper, cf. Crafter for Crofter, Meadowcraft for Meadowcroft, &c.

'Roger the Cropper for his tenement, and whole service, the present 8*d*, the farm 15s': Custom Roll, Manor of Ashton-under-Lyne, Cheth. Soc.

Willelmus Crapper, 1379 : P. T. Yorks. p. 197.

Hawen Cropure, 1379 : ibid. p. 162.

Matilda Crapper, 1379 : ibid. p. 9.

Gilbert Cropper, of Whiston, *husbandman*, 1591 : Wills at Chester (1545-1620), p. 48.

1655. Married—Edward Cropper and Joan Pearce : St. Jas. Clerkenwell, iii. 93.

London, 3, 3 ; West Rid. Court Dir., 0, 2 ; Boston (U.S.), 2, 0.

Crosbie, Crosby, Crossby.—

Local, 'of Crosby,' townships in cos. Cumberland, Lincoln, N. Rid. Yorks, Lancaster, and Cumberland.

Geoffrey de Crosseby, co. Linc., 1273. A.

Thomas de Crosby, 1379 : P. T. Yorks. p. 34.

Robertus de Crosseby, 1379 : ibid. p. 294.

Walterus de Crosseby, 1379 : ibid. p. 223.

1603. Hugh Russitor and Anne Crosby : Marriage Lic. (London), i. 278.

With the following, cf. Applebee for Appleby, q.v.

1669. Bapt. — William, s. Thomas Crossbee : St. Jas. Clerkenwell, i. 242.

1806. Married — Henry Otway Brand and Pyne Crosbie (co. Bedf.) : St. Geo. Han. Sq. ii. 351.

1807. — Samuel Crosbey and Susanna Postens : ibid. ii. 367.

London, 3, 0 ; West Rid. Court Dir., 0, 3, 1 ; Manchester, 1, 7, 1 ; MDB. (co. Lincoln), 0, 13, 0 ; Philadelphia, 0, 31, 0 ; Boston (U.S.), 4, 180, 0.

Crosier, Crozier.—Offic. 'the

crosier,' one who carried the bishop's cross or pastoral staff. 'Crocere, *crociarius*, *crucifer*' : Prompt. Parv. 'A croser, *cruciferarius*, *crucifer*' : Cath. Ang. Way, commenting on this word, quotes concerning the martyrdom of St. Thomas of Canterbury, ' one Syr Edward Gryme, that was his croyser, put forthe his arme with the crosse to bere of the stroke' : Legenda Aur. (v. the full note, Prompt. Parv. p. 104).

Simon le Croyser, temp. 1300. M.

Mabel le Croyser. G.

William Croyser. G.

Cristiana Croiser, 1379 : P. T. Yorks. p. 191.

Johannes Croser, 1379 : ibid. p. 202.

John Crosier, co. Norf., 6 Hen. V : FF. ix. 310.

William Crosier, co. Norf., 46 Edw. III : ibid. vi. 191.

1775. Married—Laurence Neilson and Esther Crozer : St. Geo. Han. Sq. i. 255.

1787. — Samuel Burrows and Alice Crozier : ibid. p. 409.

London, 3, 5 ; Philadelphia, 2, 25.

Crosland, Crossland.—Local,

'of Crosland,'now South Crosland, near Meltham, W. Rid. Yorks.

Ricardus de Crosseland, living in North Crosseland, 1379 : P. T. Yorks. p. 176.

Thomas de Cosseland (for Crossland), living in Crosselandfosse, 1397 : ibid. p. 177.

Willelmus de Crossland, 1379 : ibid. p. 183.

1720. Buried — William Crossland, *victualler* : St. Dionis Backchurch, p. 290.

London, 3, 2 ; West Rid. Court Dir., 23, 9 ; Boston (U.S.), 0, 1 ; Philadelphia, 5, 4.

Crosley ; v. Crossley.

Cross, Crosse.—Local, 'at the

cross,' one who dwelt by or near the roadside or market-cross ; v. Crouch.

Jordan ad Crucem, co. Bucks, 1273. A.

Humfrey de Cruce, co. Oxf., ibid.

Conan ad Crucem, co. Linc., ibid.

John atte Cross, 1302. M.

Johannes del Crosse, 1379 : P.T. Yorks. p. 195.

Johanna del Crosse, 1379 : ibid. p. 169.

Roger del Cros, co. Northumberland, 20 Edw. I. R.

John de la Croix, co. Berks, ibid.

Sampson atte Croice, co. Soms., 1 Edw. III : Kirby's Quest, p. 109.

Andreas de la Croys, 1379 : P. T. Yorks. p. 224.

Thomas atte-cross, rector of Bexwell, co. Norf. : FF. vii. 309.

1585. Bapt.—John, s. Richard Crosse : St. Jas. Clerkenwell, i. 16.

London, 71, 8 ; Philadelphia, 52, 0 ; Boston (U.S.), 76, 4

Crossbowmaker.—Occup. 'a

maker of crossbows'; cf. Bowmaker.

Laurence Crossebowemaker, C. R., 28 Hen. VI.

Crossdale, Croasdell, Croasdill, Crosdale, Croasdale.—Lo-

cal, 'of Crosdale.' I have not identified the spot. Crossing over the border from Yorkshire the name found a home in Furness, North Lanc., where it still exists in several forms. In the United States it has occasionally become Croasdill. As Croasdale it is strongly represented in the Philadelphia Directory. That

Yorkshire is the home of the surname there can be no doubt.

Johannes de Crosdale, 1379 : P. T. Yorks. p. 282.

Robert Croasdale, of Elmeredge, in Chippin, 1737 : Lancashire Wills at Richmond, p. 73.

1762. Married — Henry Croasdell, of Coulton, *barber*, and Isabel Hurst : St. Mary, Ulverston, ii. 405.

Manchester, 1, 0, 0, 0, 0 ; London, 0, 2, 0, 0, 0 ; Philadelphia, 1, 0, 3, 1, 21.

Crosser, Croser.—Offic. ' the

crosier,' q.v. This is the most natural and obvious origin, although it may mean one who dwelt by the village or roadside cross ; cf. Bridger, Churcher, &c.

1769. Married—Daniel Green and Mary Crosher : St. Geo. Han. Sq. i. 190.

New York, 0, 1.

Crossfield. — Local, 'at the

cross-field,' i.e. the field that lay crosswise. Possibly because a cross was in it ; v. Cross and Crouch. A North Lancashire surname.

John Crowchefylde, C. R., 8 Edw. IV.

William Crosfeild, of Poulton,*husband-man*, 1618 : Lancashire Wills at Richmond, p. 82.

John Crosfelld, of Cartmel, 1635 : ibid.

Richard Crossfield, of Poulton, 1669 : ibid.

1597. Bapt. — Edward, s. Edward Crosfield : St. Mary, Ulverston, i. 87.

1655. Married — Thomas Lawe and Mary Crosfeild : St. Jas. Clerkenwell, iii. 94.

Manchester, 1.

Crosskell, Croskill.—Local,

'of Crossgill.' I cannot find the spot. The surname is rare and confined to North Lancashire. Nevertheless it has crossed the Atlantic.

Robert Croskyll (buried at Lancaster), 1541 : Lancashire Wills at Richmond, p. 82.

Richard Croskell, of Ellel, 1661 : ibid.

James Crosgill, of Ellel, 1680 : ibid.

Anne Crossgill, of Ellel,1664 : ibid. p. 83.

William Crosskell, of Ellel, 1619 : ibid.

Lancaster, 1, 0 ; Ellel (co. Lanc.), 1, 0 ; Boston (U.S.), 0, 1.

Crosskeys. — Local, 'at the

Cross Keys,' a sign-name ; cf. Roebuck, Whitehorse, &c. This was a well-known ecclesiastical symbol at a time when the power of the keys was a familiar dogma. Probably it would swing on some roadside inn hard by a bishop's palace or other ecclesiastical foundation ; v. Hist. of Signboards. The surname still exists.

1610. Married—Thomas Croskeves and Dorathe Smith : St. Michael, Cornhill, p.19.

Crossley, Crosley.—Local, 'of Crossley.' This is a great West Riding surname, and is found there five centuries ago, but I have not discovered the precise spot that gave birth to it.

Johannes de Crosselay, 1379 : P. T. Yorks. p. 9.
Willelmus de Crosselay, 1379 : ibid.

The same record (p. 189) registers the following inhabitants of Stansfield (Halifax), where the surname is now so strong—Isabella Groslee, Elena Crossle, Thomas Grosseleys, Johannes Grosles. The change of initial from C to G and vice versa is common ; cf. Crandidge for Grandage, also a Yorkshire instance.

West Rid. Court Dir., 45, 0 ; London Dir., 20, 4 ; Philadelphia, 26, 4.

Crossman.—Local, 'the crossman,' one who dwelt by the cross. For early instances, v. Crotchman.

Nicholas Crousman, co. Soms., 1 Edw. III : Kirby's Quest, p. 90.
Philip Crosman, co. Soms., 1 Edw. III : ibid. p. 236.
Thomas Crosman, co. Soms., 1 Edw. III : ibid. p. 246.
1578. Buried — Stephen Crosseman : Kensington Reg. p. 89.
London, 2 ; Philadelphia, 2.

Crosswell, Craswell, Croswell.—Local, 'at the cross-well,' from residence thereby ; v. Crosweller.

1669. Married — John Crosswell and Lydia Gregory : St. Jas. Clerkenwell, iii. 169.
London, 1, 0, 0 ; Boston (U.S.), 0, 1, 5.

Crosthwaite, Crossthwaite, Crosswhite.—Local, 'of Crosthwaite,' a parish in co. Cumb., also a chapelry in co. Westm.; v. Thwaites. As usual, the suffix -thwaite has become -white ; cf. Applewhite, Hebblewhite, &c.

John de Crostweyt, co. Norf., 1273. A.
Gawin Crostwat, cistercian, 1534 : Reg. Univ. Oxf. i. 181.
Richard Crosthwaite, of Kirkby Kendall, 1729 : Lancashire Wills at Richmond, p. 75.
1721. Bapt.—James, s. of Mr. Crosthwaite : St. Mary, Ulverston, ii. 309.

London, 2, 0, 0 ; Liverpool, 4, 1, 0 ; Preston, 0, 2, 2 ; Boston (U.S.), 0, 0, 1 ; Philadelphia, 12, 0, 0.

Croston, Croxton, Croxon, Croxson.—Local, 'of Croston,' formerly Croxton, a parish near Chorley, co. Lanc. ; spelt Croxton (1201), Crokeston (1204) ; v. Baines' Lanc. ii. 114-5.

'Thomas Croxton, or Croston (co. Ches. 1603–63 ?), a colonel in the Parliamentary army': Dict. Nat. Biog. xiii. 248.
1621. Geffry Croxton, of Manchester, gentleman : Wills at Chester (1621–50), p. 58.
1636. George Croston, of Bury, gentleman : ibid.
Manchester, 2, 2, 0, 0 ; Liverpool, 2, 2, 0, 0 ; London, 1, 0, 2, 1 ; Philadelphia, 0, 2, 0, 0.

Crosweller, Crassweller.—Local, 'the cross-weller,' one who resided by the cross-well. Mr. Lower writes, 'In the middle ages, when many wells were deemed sacred, crosses were often erected near them, to denote their sanctity. A resident near such a spot would readily acquire the surname of "atte Cross-well," which would afterwards modify itself to Crossweller' (Patr. Brit. p. 76). There can be no doubt that Crosweller means one who dwelt beside the cross-well ; cf. Bridger, Crosser, Bridgman, Crossman, &c. With the variant Crassweller, cf. Craswell for Crosswell.

1554. William Carewe and Joanna Cresweller : Marriage Lic. (London), i. 15.
1700. Married — James Hales and Catherine Craswell : St. Jas. Clerkenwell, iii. 222.
1805. — James Crassweller and Eliz. Bleach : St. Geo. Han. Sq. ii. 324.
London, 2, 2.

Crotch.—Local, 'at the cross'; v. Crouch. This variant seems to have belonged to the southeastern counties.

'William Crotch (1775-1847), composer, born in Green's Lane, St. George Colgate, Norwich, was youngest son of Michael Crotch, a carpenter': Dict. Nat. Biog. xiii. 230.
William atte-croch, co. Camb., 1273. A.
John Croch, of Cornbury, co. Herts, 10 James I : FF. ix. 133.
1581. Christopher Crotch, vicar of Hunstanton, co. Norf.: ibid. x. 327.
London, 1.

Crotchman. — Local, 'the crotchman,' one who lived by the

crouch or cross, formed like Kirkman and Bridgman ; v. Crossman, and cf. Crotch with Cross.

Richard Crocheman, co. Camb., 1273. A.
Cassandra Crocheman, ibid.
William Crocheman, C. R., 16 Ric. II. New York, 1.

Crothers. — Local, 'of Carruthers,' one of the endless variants of Carruthers, q.v. An Americanized form.

Philadelphia, 27.

Crouch.—Local, 'at the cross,' i.e. the roadside or market-cross, once so familiar a sight at the intersection of the great country thoroughfares, or in the chartered market-steads. Crouch still lingers in our 'crutched' or 'crouched friars.' Langland describes a pilgrim as having 'many a crouch' embroidered 'on his cloke.' Blomefield says of an old Norwich church, 'St. Crowche's was dedicated in honour of the Invention of the Holy Cross, but is now totally demolished; the churchyard is still surrounded with common lanes or passages': FF. iv. 299.

John atte Crouche, co. Soms., 1 Edw. III : Kirby's Quest, p. 213.
John atte Cruche, 1273. A.
Matilda atte Crouche. B.
Millesenta Cruche, co. Norf., 1273. A.
Robert Cruche, co. Norf., ibid.
Nicholas atte Crouche, C. R., 2 Ric. II.
Stephen atte Crouche, vicar of Wigenhale, St. Mary's, co. Norf., 1358 : FF. ix. 182.
London, 21 ; Philadelphia, 12.

Croucher, Crutcher.—Local, 'the croucher,' one who lived by the crouch (q.v.) or cross. This name may be set beside Kirker and Bridger, and names of that class ; cf. Crotchman, q.v. Croucher, of course, is to Crosser or Crotcher what Crotchman is to Crossman.

William Crowcher, C. R., 30 Hen. VI.
John le Crocher. K.
John Crowcher, rector of Feltwell, co. Norf., 1430 : FF. ii. 198.
1754. Married — Joseph Henley and Mary Croucher : St. Geo. Han. Sq. i. 51.
1786. — Stephen Leighton and Sarah Croutcher : ibid. ii. 385.
London, 5, 3 ; Boston (U.S.), 4, 0.

Crouchhouse.—Local, 'at the crouch-house,' i.e. the house by the cross ; v. Crouch.

William atte Crouchhouse, C. R., 27 Edw. III.

Crouchley.—Local, a variant of Critchlow, q.v. The number of the variations of this Lancashire surname is very large; v. Crutchley.

Margaret Crouchley, of Burtonwood, 1591: Wills at Chester (1545-1620), p. 48.
Ralph Croutchley, of Cronton, 1623: ibid. (1621-50), p. 58.
1604. Married — Cuthbert Crowchley and Marie Martin: St. Jas. Clerkenwell, iii. 28.
Manchester, 1.

Crow, Crowe.—Nick. 'the crow,' from some fancied resemblance; cf. Rook, Nightingale, Sparrow, Raven, &c.

Ralph Crawe, co. Norf., 1273. A.
Geoffrey Crowe, co. Norf., ibid.
John Crawe, co. Suff., ibid.
Walrann Crowe, co. Suff., ibid.
William Croe, co. Suff., ibid.
Hugh Crowe, co. Soms., 1 Edw. III: Kirby's Quest, p. 130.
Adam Croe, 1379: P. T. Yorks. p. 88.
1431 William Crawe, vicar of Wigenhale, St. Peter's, co. Norf.; FF. ix. 185.
Philip Crowe, co. Norf., 1307: ibid. ii 366.
1717. Buried — Richard Crowe, co. Norf.: ibid. i. 404.
1794. Married—John Crowe and Christian Doddo: St. Geo. Han. Sq. ii. 112.
London, 15, 8; MDB. (co. Suffolk), 3, 4; (Norfolk), 2, 14; Philadelphia, 15, 17.

Crowder, Crowther.—Occup. 'the crowder' or 'crowther,' a professional player on the crowd at fair or wedding feast. '*Giga*, a fiddle, a croud, a kit, a violin' (Florio); cf. Fiddler, Piper.

'The pipe, the tabor, and the trembling crowd.' Spenser, Fairy Queen.

'But his eldre sone was in the feeld, and whanne he cam and neighede to the hous he herde a symfonye and a crowde': (Wycliffe) Luke xv. 25.

Richard le Cruder, co. Kent, 1273. A.
Katerina Crowder, 1379: P. T. Yorks. p. 144.
Johanna Crouder, 1379: ibid. p. 237.
Thomas le Crouder, co. York. W. 2.
'The *Inquisition post mortem* of Robert de Davenport (1436) was taken before John de Legh, Escheator (1437), by the oaths of John Pygot, Robert del Dounes, ... William le Crouther,' &c.: Hist. East Cheshire, i. 424.
1625. Bapt. — Nathaniell, s. Danyell Crowder: St. Jas. Clerkenwell, i. 101.
London, 3, 7; Philadelphia, 8, 30.

Crowdson; v. Crewdson.

Crowell.—Local, 'of Crowell,' a parish in co. Oxford, five miles from Tetsworth. It is an extraordinary fact, that while my London Directory is without a representative, the Boston Directory has nearly a hundred.

Geoffrey de Crowelle, co. Oxf., 1273. A.
Gilbert de Crowele, co. Oxf., ibid.
Thomas de Crowelle, co. Oxf., ibid.
Deonisia de Crawel, co. Bedf., ibid.
London, 0; Boston (U.S.), 97; Philadelphia, 10.

Crower.—Nick. 'the crower'; for a fanciful origin v. Lower's Patr. Brit. p. 77. No doubt it was a sobriquet affixed on one of boastful tendencies, one who could sound his own trumpet.

Henry le Crower, co. Kent, 1273. A.
John le Crowere, co. Norf., ibid.

Crowfoot, Crowfort, Crofoot, Crofut.—Local, 'of Crawford,' an imitative corruption. Crowfort marks the intermediate stage when he writes; 'Crowfoot. This name may be local, ... but it is more probably derived from some peculiarity of gait on the part of the original bearer. "To strut like a crow in a gutter" is a proverbial phrase': Patr. Brit. p. 77. For many American variants, v. Crofford.

1736. Henry Crowefoot, co. Norf.: FF. i. 98.
1796. Married—William Crowfoot, or Crawford, and Eleanor Wallace: St. Geo. Han. Sq. ii. 142.
London, 1, 1, 0, 0; MDB. (co. Suffolk), 1, 2, 0, 0; (Norfolk), 2, 0, 0, 0; Boston (U.S.), 0, 0, 2, 1.

Crowhurst.—Local, 'of Crowhurst,' (1) a parish in co. Surrey, four miles from Godstone; (2) a parish in co. Sussex, three miles from Battle.

Walter de Croherst, co. Sussex, 1273. A.
1777. Married — William Ansell and Mary Crowhurst: St. Geo. Han. Sq. i. 282.
London, 11; Boston (U.S.), 1.

Crowle, Curle, Crowl, Curl.—Local, 'of Crowle,' a parish in co. Lincoln. Curle seems to have been an early corruption.

Robert de Croule, co. Worc., 1273. A.
Walter de Cryl, co. Soms., 1 Edw. III: Kirby's Quest, p. 214.

Thomas de Curle, 1379: P. T. Yorks. p. 279.
Johannes de Crull', 1379: ibid. p. 153.
Thomas de Crull', 1379: ibid. p. 154.
Henricus Curle, 1379: ibid. p. 29.
Richard de Crowell, or Richard de Crol, co. Linc., 1273. A.
London, 1, 1, 0, 0; Leeds, 1, 0, 0, 0; Philadelphia, 0, 0, 3, 5.

Crowley.—Local, 'of Crowley,' a township in the parish of Great Budworth, co. Chester. But this cannot be the parent of the extraordinary number of Crowleys in the States. In the Boston list are 22 Michaels, 19 Patricks, 39 Timothys, 17 Dennises, 17 Corneliuses, and 33 Daniels. Thus it is clear that the vast majority of the American Crowleys are of Irish descent; cf. Crawley.

John Crowley, of Northwich, 1680: Wills at Chester (1660-80), p. 69.
1615. Bapt. — Winifred, d. Richard Crowley: St. Jas. Clerkenwell, i. 74.
1796. Married—John Grubb Crowley and Rebecca Ragless: St. Geo. Han. Sq. ii. 154.
London, 7; Boston (U.S.), 249.

Crowther; v. Crowder.

Crowthers.—Local; a variant of Carruthers, q.v. No connexion with Crowther.

1796. Married—George Crowders and Eliz. Winter: St. Geo. Han. Sq. ii. 150.
London, 1; Philadelphia, 4.

Croxton, Croxon, Croxson.—Local, 'of Croxton,' parishes and hamlets in cos. Cambridge, Lincoln, Chester, Norfolk, Leicester, and Stafford. The corrupted forms are of an ordinary character, and there is no baptismal name to suggest a different origin; cf. Johnson and Johnstone.

Elena de Croxstone, co. Hunts, 1273. A.
Sarra de Croxtone, co. Camb., ibid.
Richard de Croxtone, co. Northumb., ibid.
Abbas de Crokeston, or Croxton, co. Leic., ibid.
1605. Married—William Johnson and Frances Crockson: St. Jas. Clerkenwell, iii. 129.
1667. — Robert Harwood and Ellin Croxson: ibid. p. 134.
1669. — John Croxston and Jane Garnum: ibid. p. 156.
London, 0, 2, 1; Crockford, 1, 0, 0; Philadelphia, 3, 0, 0; New York, 0, 1, 0.

Cruddas, Cruddis, Cruddace.—Local, 'of Carruthers,' corruptions of Carrodus, which is again a corruption of Carruthers. q.v. All the forms are North English.

1888. Married—T. T. M. Austin to Bertha M. Cruddas, of Warden, co. Northumb. : Standard, Jan. 14, 1888.

Cruikshank.—Nick.; v. Crookshank.

Crummack, Crummock, Cromack.—Local, 'of Crumbok,' some spot in the W. Riding of Yorks that I cannot identify. It is manifest that Crumbok would become Crummock in the course of a few generations.

'Robert Hartley Cromek (1770–1812), engraver, was born at Hull': Dict. Nat. Biog. xiii. 144.

Undoubtedly this is a variant of Crumbok, only diversified slightly from Cromack, one of the present existing forms.

Johannes de Crumbok, 1379 : P. T. Yorks. p. 266.
Robert Crumbok, 1379 : ibid.
Willelmus Pece de Crombak, 1379 : ibid. p. 286.

This latter was so registered to distinguish him from another William Pece in the same village (Austwick). We may reasonably presume the locality was in the immediate neighbourhood.

William Crumbocke, de Clarkehill, *freeholder*, 1600 : (A List of Freeholders in Lancashire) Lanc. and Ches. Record Soc. xii. 235.
Ellen Crombok, of Clarkehill, in Whalley, *widow*, 1649 : Wills at Chester (1621–50), p. 56.
Manchester, 1, 0, 0 ; West Rid. Court Dir., 0, 0, 1 ; York, 1, 0, 0 ; Boston (U.S.), 0, 0, 2.

Crump.—Nick. 'the crump,' i.e. the crooked. 'Crumpt, or crookt : Nomenclator, p. 44' (Halliwell). The surname is well known in the United States. Bridget Crompe emigrated to Virginia in 1635, and Thomas Crompe was already settled there in 1624 (v. Hotten's Lists of Emigrants, pp. 117, 227).

Richard le Crumppe, co. Salop, 1273. A.
Constancia Crompe, co. Oxf., ibid.
Hugh le Crumpe. T.
1564. Thomas Crompe and Eliz. Bover : Marriage Lic. (London), i. 29.
1674. Bapt.—Mary, d. George Crumpe : St. Jas. Clerkenwell, i. 264.

1789. Married—Joseph Crump and Jane Mason : St. Geo. Han. Sq. ii. 19.
London, 18 ; Philadelphia, 8 ; Boston (U.S.), 5.

Cruse, Crews, Crewes.—(1) Nick. 'the cruse,' i.e. the merry ; cf. Merry, Jolly, Joyce, Merryweather, &c. '*Crous*, merry, brisk, lively ; *cruse* or *crous*, saucy, malapert': Kennett, MS. Lansd. 1033.

'Aȝeyn hem was he kene and crous.' Cursor Mundi. (Halliwell.)
Nicholas le Cruse, co. Bedf., 1273. A.
Henry Cruse, co. Bedf., ibid.

(2) Local. A Cornish surname. All the forms are found in the same register.

1637. Bapt.—Edward, son of William Cruse : St. Columb Major, Cornwall, p. 41.
1652. — Arthur, son of William Crews : ibid. p. 51.
1656. — Eliz., d. of William Crewse : ibid. p. 53.
1668. — William, son of Edward Crewes : ibid. p. 62.
London, 9, 3, 0 ; Truro, 0, 0, 2 ; Philadelphia, 3, 0, 0.

Cruso.—Local. Evidently a Flemish name. In the Dict. Nat. Biog. we are informed how it came to pass that 'Robinson Crusoe' got its title. Timothy Cruso (probably related to Timothy Cruso infra) was a Presbyterian minister, born about 1656. His family resided at Newington Green, Middlesex. Studying at Newington Green Academy, he had for a fellow-student Daniel Defoe, 'who immortalized his surname by the Adventures, published in 1719' (xiii. p. 264).

'Antony Cruso, of Howne Coat in Flanders, father of John Cruso of Norwich, father of Timothy Cruso of London, living 1634 ': Visitation of London, 1634, i. 209.
Aquila Crusoe, common councillor, Norwich, 1687 : FF. iii. 423.
1692. Francis Cruso, *clerke*, and Mrs. Anne Mobberley, both of the parish of St. James, Westminster : St. Mary Aldermary (London), p. 34.
John Cruso, prebendary of St. David's, 1667 : Hist. and Ant. St. David's, p. 367. Crockford, 1.

Crust, Crast. — ? Local, ' of Crust ' (?). I suggest a local origin because of two instances infra. But the surname is found so widely scattered in the 13th century that I feel sure in many cases it is a

personal name, probably a nick. of Christian or Christopher. Both were favourites at the time.

Geoffrey de Crusta, co. Hereford, 1273. A.
Stephen Cruste, co. York, ibid.
John Crust, co. Essex, ibid.
Amicia Cruste, co. Oxf., ibid.
Roger Cruste, co. Suff., ibid.

Lincolnshire seems to be the chief habitat of the surname in the 19th century. Since writing the above I am led to ask the question, Is it not local, and a form of Cross ?

Philip de Crast, co. Soms., 1 Edw. III : Kirby's Quest, p. 157.
Thomas atte Crost, co. Soms. : ibid. p. 179.
Roger atte Crost, co. Soms. : ibid. p. 181.
1668. Married—Robert Crust (or Crast) and Eliz. Smith : St. Jas. Clerkenwell, iii. 153.
MDB. (co. Lincoln), 8, 0 ; London, 0, 1.

Crutcher.—Local ; v. Croucher.

Crutchley, Crutchloe. — Local ; v. Critchlow, of which these are variants.

1763. Married—Oliver Ball and Ann Crutchley : St. Geo. Han. Sq. i. 125.
London, 2, 1 ; Philadelphia, 3, 0.

Cruthers.—Local, ' of Carruthers,' q.v. An American variant ; v. Crothers.

Philadelphia, 4.

Cryer.—Official, ' the crier,' one who announced the mandate of bench and council ; one who raised the 'hue and cry'; the common crier.

Philip le Criour. E.
Wat le Crever. G.
Edward le Creiour. N.
Johanna Cryour, 1379 : P. T. Yorks. p. 46.
Alicia Crioure, 1379 : ibid. p. 47.
1590. Bapt. — Ferdinando, s. John Cryer : St. Jas. Clerkenwell, i. 23.
1788. Married — Clement Cryer and Frances Cryer : St. Geo. Han. Sq. ii. 14.
London, 1 ; Sheffield, 4 ; Ashton-under-Lyne, 1 ; Philadelphia, 3.

Cubill ; v. Cobbold.

Cubit, Cubitt, Cupit, Cupitt.—Bapt. ' the son of Jacob,' from nick. Cob and dim. Cob-et ; v. Cobb and Coppin. This derivation is all but settled by the earliest form found in Norfolk of this essentially Norfolk surname ; v. Cobbett.

Geoffrey Cobet, co. Norf., 1273. A.
Roger Cobet, co. Norf., ibid.

The nick. Cobb and the dim. Copping are found among the bailiffs of Norwich (1378-95): FF. iii. 116. The change from *o* to *u* is eccentric, but so are an endless number of corruptions in this dictionary. The above is strongly confirmed by the fact that Collier is Cullyer, and Colley or Colly is Culley, in co. Norfolk (q.v.). Probably the dialectic sound of *o* was *u* in this district.

Benedict Cubitt, bailiff of Yarmouth, 1566: FF. xi. 328.
1739. Married—Benjamin Barber and Barbara Cubitt : St. Geo. Han. Sq. i. 22.
1756. — Thomas Cubitt and Mary Gray : ibid. p. 61.
MDB. (Norfolk), 1, 18, 0, 0; London, 1, 15, 2, 0 ; Philadelphia, 2, 0, 0, 5.

Cubley.—Local, ' of Cubley,' a parish in co. Derby, six miles from Ashbourne.

Johannes de Coubelay, *souiter*, 1379 : P. T. Yorks. p. 83.
London, 2 ; Sheffield, 2 ; West Rid. Court Dir., 1.

Cuckold.—Nick. 'the cuckold,' i.e. a man with a false and untrue wife. The surname did not last long ; Cuckoo fared better.

Cecilia Cokwald, 1379 : P. T. Yorks. p. 172.

Cuckoo.—Nick. 'the cuckoo'; M.E. *coccou, cukkow*; v. Cuckold. This surname still exists.

John Cucku, co. Kent, 1273. A.
John Coccow, C. R., 51 Edw. III.
William Cuckow, rector of Thurning, co. Norf., 1434 : FF. viii. 282.
Thomas Cuckowe. V. 13.
Stephen Cuckoo. FF.
1656. Buried—John, s. Daniel Cucko : Reg. Canterbury Cathedral, p. 120.
1659. Bapt. — Thomas, ye sonn of Thomas Cucku' : ibid. p. 121.
MDB. (co. Kent), 1.

Cuckson.—Nick. ; v. Cookson.

New York, 1.

Cudd, Cuddy.—Bapt. 'the son of Cuthbert' ; nick. from Cud and Cuddy. Hence in the North 'cuddy,' a donkey ; v. Crewdson.

John Cudson, co. York. W. 15.
Cuddie Taylor, 1587 : Nicolson and

Burn, Hist. Westmoreland and Cumb., vol. i. p. xxxiii.
Cuddy, servant of Paite, 1587 : ibid.
Cudde Grahame, co. Northumb., 1541 : TTT. p. xlix.
Cudde Robson, co. Northumb., 1541 : ibid.
1548. Bapt.—John, s. William Cud : Reg. Kensington, p. 2.
1725. Married — Peter Nichols and Clementia Cudde: St. Mary Aldermary, p. 47.
London, 2, 0 ; Philadelphia, 0, 5.

Cuerden.—Local, 'of Cuerden,' a township in the parish of Leyland, co. Lancs.

'Richard Kuerden, M.D., physician and antiquary, was the son of Gilbert Kuerden, of Kuerden, near Preston, and born about 1620' : Baines' Lanc. ii. 143.
Eliz. Cuerden, of Cuerden, 1601 : Wills at Chester (1545-1620), p. 49.
John Cuerden, of Cuerden, 1604 : ibid.
Thomas Cuerden, of Walton-en-le-Dale, 1608 : ibid.
Preston, 4 ; Philadelphia (Cuerten ?), 3.

Cullen, Cullin.—Local, ' of Cologne'; cf. Bullen for Boulogne.

John de Coloigne, co. Norf., 1344 : FF. v. 368.
1660 1. Peter Cullen and Jane Croke : Marriage Lic. (London), ii. 282.
1795. Married—John Cullen and Mary O'Neill : St. Geo. Han. Sq. ii. 133.
London, 11, 0 ; Philadelphia, 0, 10.

Culley, Cully.—Bapt. 'the son of Nicholas'; v. Colley. This is a Norfolk form, where *o* seems commonly to have become *u*; cf. Cubitt for Cobbett, and Cullyer for Collier.

Thomas Culley, sheriff of Norwich, 1559 : FF. iii. 358.
Joshua Culley, or Cully, mayor of Norwich, 1606 : ibid. p. 370.
MDB. (Norfolk), 3, 0 ; London, 6, 2 ; Boston (U.S.), 3, 4.

Culling.—Bapt. 'the son of Culling,' one of many personal names ending in *-ing*; cf. Browning or Harding, and v. Coulling. The place-name Cullingford evidently means Culling's ford, just as Cullingworth means the worth or farm of Culling ; v. Coulling (2) for other instances.

William Culling, co. Soms., 1 Edw. III : Kirby's Quest, p. 154.
Adam Culling, co. Soms., 1 Edw. III : ibid.
Alan Culling, co. Camb., 1273. A.
1661. Giles Lytcott and Sarah Culling : Marriage Lic. (Faculty Office), p. 55.
London, 1 ; New York, 1.

Cullingford, Culliford.—(1) Local, 'of Cullingford' or 'Gulliford.' Gulliford is a hundred in co. Dorset, probably at first Cullingford ; v. Culling. (2) Local, 'of Colyford,' a hamlet in the parish of Colyton, co. Devon.

London, 3, 2.

Cullum, Culham.—Local, ' of Culham,' a parish in co. Oxford. A purely English name ; it has nothing to do with Mac-cullum.

Ranulf de Colham, co. Salop, 1273. A.
William Culhame, or Colham, or Culme, 1570 : Reg. Univ. Oxf. i. 278.
1595-6. John Cullum and Jane Price : Marriage Lic. (London), i. 229.
1669. Married—Beccaman Turner and Abygall Cullum: St. Jas. Clerkenwell, iii. 167.
1779. — Philip Culham and Mary Bailey : St. Geo. Han. Sq. i. 305.
London, 10, 1 ; New York, 2, 0.

Cully.—Local ; v. Kewley.

Cullyer, Culyer.—Occup. 'the collier,' a Norfolk form; cf. Cubitt for Cobbett in the same county ; v. Collier.

John, son of John Cullyer, Marlingford, co. Norf., 1640 : FF. ii. 458.
1610. Joseph Eliot and Eliz. Cullier : Marriage Lic. (London), l. 327.
London, 0, 2 ; MDB. (Norfolk), 1, 1 ; New York, 0, 4.

Culpeck.—Local, 'of Killpeck,' a parish in co. Hereford, eight miles from Hereford.

Hugh de Kylpek, co. Glouc., Hen. III-Edw. I. K.
John de Kylpec, co. Hereford, ibid.
London, 3.

Culshaw, Kilshaw.—Local, 'of Culcheth,' a township in the parish of Winwick, co. Lanc. The Culcheths of Burscough spelt their name variously as Culcheth, Culshaw, and Kilshaw. 'The place is called Kilsha by the common people ': Baines' Lanc. ii. 218.

Henry de Culchet, co. Lanc., 1201 : Baines' Lanc. ii. 197.
Gilbert de Kulchet : ibid. ii. 210.
William Kilshaw, of Burscough, 1617 : Wills at Chester (1545-1620), p. 115.
Geoffrey Culcheth, of Hindley, 1585 : ibid. p. 49.
Thomas Culcheth, of Leigh, 1611 : ibid.
John Kilshaw, of Burscough, 1619 : ibid. p. 115.
Edward Culshaw (Culcheth), of Burscough, 1641 : ibid. (1621-50), p. 58.
John Culcheth, of Culcheth, parish of Winwick, 1640 : ibid.

William Culcheth, or Culshaw, of Burscough, 1665: ibid. (1660-80), p. 70.
MDB. (co. Lanc.), 11, 2; Burscough (Lanc.), 2, 0; Boston (U.S.), 1, 0.

Culver.—Nick. 'the culver,' i.e. culver, a dove. The final *d* and *t* in the instances below seem excrescent; cf. Pidgeon, Dove, and the local Culverhouse, i.e. dove-cote.

William Culvere, or Culvert, co. Heref., 1273. A.
John Culvard, or Culverd, or Culvert, co. Oxf., ibid.
William Culverd, co. Oxf., ibid.
1690-1. Percivall Hartt and Elisha (? Eliza) Culver: Marriage Lic. (Faculty Office), p. 199.
London, 7; Philadelphia, 4.

Culverhouse.—Local, 'at the culver-house,' i.e. the dove-cote; v. Culver. Pigeon-houses were attached to all large establishments; many of them still exist. An interesting article by Chancellor Ferguson on the importance of pigeons in the early *cuisine* may be seen in the Transactions Cumb. and West. Ant. and Arch. Soc. (vol. ix. pt. ii. pp. 412-434), where are several sketches of old culver-houses. It is very probable that the Sçotch Claverhouse is a corruption.

Henry atte Colverhouse, co. Soms., 1 Edw. III: Kirby's Quest, p. 95.
Roger atte Colverhous, co. Soms., 1 Edw. III: ibid. p. 124.
Matthew de Columbariis, co. Wilts, 1273. A.
(?) Avicia de Columbiers, co Wilts, ibid.
1582. John Culverhouse (co. Essex) and Joan Kalladaye: Marriage Lic. (London), i. 111.
1653. Bapt. — Thomas, son of John Cullverous: St. Jas. Clerkenwell, i. 183.
Elsewhere Culverous, Culverus (ibid. pp. 179, 206).
London, 3; MDB. (co. Wilts), 1.

Culverwell.—Local, ' of the culver-well,' probably the well which was frequented by doves; v. Culver and Culverhouse.

1619. Married—Daniell Ball and Proteza Culverwell: St. Peter, Cornhill, i. 250.
1646. Buried — Thomas Culverwell: St. Mary Aldermary, p. 174.
London, 7; Boston (U.S.), 1; New York, 1.

Cumber.—Occup.; v. Comber.

Cumberbatch, Comberbirch, Comberbach, Cumberpatch, Camberbirch, Cumber-

beach, Cumberbirch.—Local, ' of Comberbach,' a township in the parish of Great Budworth, co. Chester. The modern variants of the surname are many and curious; v. Counterpatch.

Roger Comberbach, of Wych Malbank, 1603: Wills at Chester (1545-1620), p. 43.
Richard Cumberbach, of Congleton, 1633: ibid. (1621-50), p. 58.
1739. Married—Francis Durham and Mary Cumberbach: St. Geo. Han. Sq. i. 23.
1795. — John Cumberpatch and Eliz. Sones: ibid. ii. 140.
London (Cumberbatch), 1; Manchester, 0, 0, 0, 0, 0, 1, 1; MDB. (co. Chester), 0, 1, 0, 0, 1, 0, 0; (co. Northampton), 0, 0, 0, 1, 0, 0, 0; (co. Stafford), 0, 0, 0, 2, 0, 0, 0, 0.

Cumberland.—Local, 'of Cumberland,' the well-known county; cf. Derbyshire, Lancashire, &c.

1670. Richard Cumberland and Ann Quinsey: Marriage Lic. (London), ii. 297.
1703. Married—John Cumberland and Hannah Bennett: St. Dionis Backchurch, p. 51.
London, 3; New York, 2.

Cummin, Cumming, Cummings, Cummins, &c.; v. Comyn.

Cundall, Cundell.—Local, 'of Cundall,' a parish in the dioc. of Ripon.

Willelmus de Cundall', 1379: P. T. Yorks. p. 298.
1623. Nicholas Cundill and Frances Evans: Marriage Lic. (London), ii. 125.
— Cecil Parrie and Eliz. Condall, d. Clement Cundall: Marriage Lic. (Westminster), p. 30.
London, 6, 1; Leeds, 3, 0; Boston (U.S.), 1, 0.

Cunditt, Cundy, Cundey.—Local, 'of the conduit,' by the aqueduct, or drain, or sewer. Cundy is the familiar Yorkshire form; v. Cundy, in Brockett's Glossary. 'Cundy, a sewer, a conduit: North' (Halliwell). 'Cundyte, of watyr, *aqueductus*': Prompt. Parv.

Reginald del Conduyt, C. R., 16 Edw. III. pt. ii.
Thomas Cundy, 1379: P. T. Yorks. p. 14.
Peter Cundi, co. Camb., 1273. A.
Felice Cundit, co. Camb., ibid.
William de Kundy, co. Hants, Hen. III-Edw. I. K.
1792. Married—William Cunditt and Mary Rock: St. Geo. Han. Sq. ii. 74.
London, 1, 7, 0; West Riding Court

Dir., 0, 1, 1; Philadelphia, 0, 1, 1; Boston (U.S.), 0, 3, 0.

Cuner, Conner.—Occup. ' the cuner,' i.e. the coiner of money; cf. Monier. Skeat says, 'O.F. *coin*, a wedge, stamp on a coin. . . . Latin *cuneus*, a wedge.' Probably some of our Conners, as distinct from Connor, are thus descended.

Norman le Cuner, co. Camb., 1273. A.
Nicholas le Cuner, co. Oxf., ibid.
Sampson le Cunerer, co. Bedf., ibid.
Henry Cunator, co. Hunts, ibid.
London, 0, 4; Philadelphia, 0, 14.

Cunliffe, Cuncliffe, Condlyffe, Cundiff.—Local, ' of Cundcliff,' now Cunliffe Hill, in the township of Billington, near Blackburn, Lanc. *Cliff* is undoubtedly the suffix; cf. Topliff for Topcliff.

Robert de Cundeclif, or Cunteclif, co. York, 1273. A.
Adam de Cunliffe, 1317-8: Baines' Lanc. ii. 31.
Christabel Cunliffe, of Altham, *widow*, 1595: Wills at Chester (1545-1620), p. 49.
Thomas Dewhirst, of Cunliffe in Rishton, *husbandman*, 1648: ibid. (1621-50), p. 65.
William Clayton de Cunliffe, 1642: Preston Guild Rolls, p. 109.
Ellis Cunliffe, 1642: ibid.
Nicholas Cundliffe, 1662: ibid. p. 156.
Nicholas Cunliffe, co. Lanc., 1606: Reg. Univ. Oxf. vol. ii. pt. ii. p. 291.
1809. Married — Foster Cunliffe, of Wrexham, and Hon. Emma Crew: St. Geo. Han. Sq. iii. 406.
London, 7, 0, 0, 0; Manchester, 13, 1, 0, 1; MDB. (co. Ches.), 2, 0, 1, 2; Philadelphia, 7, 1, 0, 0.

Cunningham, Cuningham, Cunnynghame.—Local, ' of Cunningham,' a district in North Ayrshire, containing a large number of parishes.

1592. Buried—Thomas Conningham: St. Michael, Cornhill, p. 204.
1711. Married—Robert Hammond and Eliz. Cunningham: ibid. p. 56.
London, 26, 1, 0; West Rid. Court Dir., 1, 0, 1; Philadelphia, 316, 0, 0.

Cuppage.—Offic. 'the cuppage,' a cup-bearer, one of the many household officers who waited at the feast; akin to Sewer, Ewer, Napier (q.v.). Cuppage, though rare, still exists; cf. Smallpage and Littlepage.

John Cupage. AA. 3.

Cuppleditch.—Local; v. Cobbledick.

Curle.—Local; v. Crowle.

Curr.—Nick. 'the cur'; M.E. *curre*, a dog. Possibly, however, the Curr of the London Directory is a misspelling for Kerr, q.v.

John le Curre, co. L1nc., 1273. A.
1676. John Curre and Ann Nicholas: Marriage Alleg. (Canterbury), p. 256.
1752. Married—Joseph Bird and Eliz. Curr: St. Geo. Chap. Mayfair, p. 212.
London, 1; New York, 2.

Currer, Currier, Curryer.—Occup. 'the currier,' a leather-dresser.

Adam le Corur, C. R., 9 Edw. I.
Maurice le Couraour, 21-2 Edw. I: Freemen of York (Surt. Soc.), i. 5.
Simon Currour, 1379: P. T. Yorks. p. 224.
Johanna Corour, 1379: ibid. p. 37.
1656. Richard Summerell and Alice Currier: St. Michael, Cornhill, p. 36.
1661. Richard Currier and Catherine Shreeve: Marriage Lic. (London), ii. 285.
'John Bonar (1722-61) married (1746) Christian Currier, of Edinburgh': Dict. Nat. Biog. v. 336.
Philadelphia, 0, 7, 0; London, 0, 0, 7.

Currey, Currie, Curry; v. Corry.

Curson.—Local; v. Curzon.

Curteis, Curtice, Curties, Curtis, Curtiss, Curtius.—Nick. 'the courteous,' one of courtly manners; M.E. *curteys* and *corteys*; O.F. *curteis*. A popular surname from the 13th century downwards. It was perfectly natural that a sobriquet of this complimentary character should be retained where possible. 'Curteyse, *urbanus*': Prompt. Parv.

Richard Courteys, co. Northumberland, Hen. III-Edw. I. K.
Robert Courteys, co. Soms., 1 Edw. III: Kirby's Quest, p. 105.
William le Curteis, co. Camb., 1273. A.
Walter Curteys, co. Oxf., ibid.
Osbert le Curteys, co. Essex, ibid.
Henry Corteys, co. Devon, ibid.
Richard le Corteys, co. Oxf., ibid.
Adam Curtase, 1379: P. T. Yorks. p. 202.
Johannes Curtas, 1379: ibid. p. 204.
1550. William Curteys and Margery Baynerd: Marriage Lic. (London), i. 12.
1569. Bapt.—Eliz., d. Thomas Curtys: St. Jas. Clerkenwell, i. 5.
1718. Married — James Curtis and Priscilla Brathwaite: St. Michael, Cornhill, p. 60.
London, 1, 1, 1, 88, 2, 1; Boston (U.S.), Curtice, 4; New York, 0, 0, 0, 110, 14, 0.

Curtepy.—Nick. for one remarkable for the cut of his cloak or gaberdine; M.E. *courtepy*, a short cloak.
'Ful thredbare was his overest courtepy.' Chaucer, C. T. 292.
Richard Curtepie, 1273. A.
William Cortepy, ibid.

Curthose.—Nick. (?); v. Shorthose.
Robert Curthose, 1273. A.

Curtmantle.—Nick. for one remarkable for the cut, &c., of his courtepy, or cloak; v. Curtepy.
Henry Curtmantel. PP.

Curtvalour.—Nick. for one whose courage was short-lived, a pot boaster.
Richard Curtevalur, co. Bedf., 1273. A.

Curtwallet.—Nick. for one who carried a small bag; or, metaphorically, one who was needy.
Martin Curtwallet, co. Oxf., 1273. A.

Curwen, Curwin.—Local, 'of Culwen,' a lordship in Galloway, Scotland. It is said that the alteration to Curwen took place about the reign of Henry VI. The family early settled in the neighbourhood of Workington, co. Cumb.
Patric de Culwen, 35 Edw. I: Westm. and Cumb. i. 90-91.
Gilbert de Culwen, 17 Edw. I: ibid.
Gilbert de Culwen, 3 Edw. II: E. and F., co. Cumb., p. 171.
William de Culwen, 19 Ric. II: ibid. p. 172.
Robertus Curwen, 1379: P. T. Yorks. p. 223.
London, 3, 0; Philadelphia, 1, 1.

Curzon, Curson.—Local. 'Geraldine de Curzon came into England with the Conqueror. His descendants were in Derbyshire, temp. Henry I, and Curzon, Lord Scarsdale, is "of Scarsdale" in that county' (Lower).
Richard de Curzoun, co. Derby, 20 Edw. I. R.
Henry de Curzoun, co. Derby, ibid.
Thomas de Curzon, co. Northampt., ibid.
Agnes Curson, 1379: P. T. Yorks. p. 18.
Sibilla Curson, 1379: ibid. p. 22.
London, 2, 2; New York, 1, 1.

Cushen, Cushing, Cushion, Cushin.—Bapt. 'the son of Custance,' from nick. Cuss, dim.

Cussin; cf. *viol*, dim. *violin*; also Jean, dim. Jennin, and, with excrescent *g*, Jenning; also Pierre, dim. Perrin, now Perring; also Nicholas, nick. Col, dim. Colin, now Collins and Colling.
Johannes Cussyng, 1379: P. T. Yorks. p. 161.
London, 3, 3, 2, 0; New York (Cushin), 2; Boston (U.S.), 0, 152, 0, 0.

Cussons, Cussans, Cousins, Couzens, Cousens, Cosens.—Bapt. In many cases a natural corruption of Custance, one of the most popular of girl-names. But see Cousen and Cousin, which in the singular number generally have a different origin, though here again, perhaps, it is sometimes Cuss-in (v. Cushen). This is a case where, two distinct sources being proved, absolute certainty as to which was the actual origin is impossible.
Ricardus Cusson (=the son of Cus, i.e. Custance), 1379: P. T. Yorks. p. 7.
Johannes Cusson, 1379: ibid. p. 29.
1571. Married—Thomas Coossyne and Dorothy Holforde: St. Michael, Cornhill, p. 10.
1577. Buried — Pawle Standyshe, servant to Thomas Cosin: ibid. p. 105.
Askham Bryan, Yorks (Cussans), 1; West Rid. Court Dir., 1, 0, 2, 1, 1, 0; Manchester (Cousins), 1; London, 0, 0, 16, 3, 5, 0; London Court Dir. (Cozens), 1; New York, 0, 0, 6, 1, 0, 0.

Cust, Cuss.—Bapt. 'the son of Custance,' usually Custance (q.v.), from nick. Cust or Cuss; cf. 'Cuskin, a drinking-cup, "a cup, a cuskin": Nomenclator, p. 232' (Halliwell). Cup-names were commonly taken from the girls who handed them; v. Jug in Skeat's Etym. Dict.
Cust de Clementhorp, 10 Edw. III: Freemen of York, i. 30.
Custe Newman, 1273. A.
Robert fil. Cust, ibid.
Custe Alver, ibid.
Cus nepta Johannis Frost, co. Camb., ibid.
Cuss Balla, co. Hunts, ibid.
Matilda Custe, *doghter*, 1379: P. T. Yorks. p. 102.
1701. Bapt.—John, s. Thomas Cust, *cutler*: St. Dionis Backchurch, p. 140.
London, 2, 2; Crockford, 3, 0.

Custance, Custerson.—Bapt. 'the son of Coustance.' The popular form was Custance.

Q

'But Hermegild loved Custance as hire lif,
And Custance hath so long sojourned ther.'   Chaucer, C. T. 4956-7.

To-day as surnames both Custance and Custerson (i. e. Custance-son) are familiar to Cambridgeshire. Custance as a personal name was a favourite in that county in the 13th century. For Custerson, cf. Matterson, Paterson, and Catterson, from Mattinson, Pattinson, and Cattinson.

Constance, or Custance de Byerne, co. Notts, 1273. A.
John Custaunce, co. Camb., ibid.
Henry fil. Custance, co. Camb., ibid.
Custance Burnard, co. Camb., ibid.
Custance de Bergh, 1379 : P. T. Yorks. p. 60.
Adam Custanson, 1379 : ibid.

The last two instances entered together are probably mother and son.

Willelmus Custeson, 1379 : P.T. Yorks. p. 192.
Custans serviens Petri atte Milne, 1379: ibid. p. 41.
Petronilla Custaunce, 1379: ibid. p. 103.
1629. Married — Henry Custance and Maria Godbeare : St. Michael, Cornhill, p. 26.
1801. — Robert Custance and Eliz. Smith : St. Geo. Han. Sq. ii. 238.
London, 4, 2 ; MDB. (co. Cambridge), 3, 2 ; Boston (U.S.), 1, 0.

Custlot.—Bapt. 'the son of Custance,' i.e. Coustance, from nick. Cust (q.v.), and dim. Custelot ; cf. Hewlett = Hugh-elot.

Elena Custlot, 1379 : P. T. Yorks. p. 222.
Alicia Custlot, 1379 : ibid.

Custobodie, Curtobodie, Costabadie, Costobadie. — I can make nothing out of this curious surname. I find it in the form of Crestobody in the last century ; in co. Northampton it is found as Curtobodie. I suspect it is a Scotch local name.

1776. Married—Samuel Chapman and Arabella Crestobody: St. Geo. Han. Sq. i. 272.
London Court Dir., 0, 0, 0, 1 ; MDB. (co. Lincoln), 1, 0, 0, 0 ; (co. Northampton), 0, 1, 0, 0 ; (North Rid. Yorks), 0, 0, 2, 0.

Cutbill.—Bapt. 'the son of Cutbold.' This is the only satisfactory solution I can offer.

Nicholas Cotebold, co. Soms., 1 Edw. III : Kirby's Quest, p. 147.

Walter Cotebold, co. Soms., 1 Edw. III : ibid. p. 151.
London, 1.

Cutbush.—Local. Like so many other old French names, a translation into English. It is simply Talboys anglicized ; O.F. *taillebois*, i. e. cut wood, probably a *ridding* ; cf. Fairbrother for Beaufrere, or Handsomebody for Gentilcorps. Many similar instances will be found in this dictionary.

1752. Married—Thomas Cutbush and Mary Gibbs: St. Geo. Chap. Mayfair, p. 214.
London, 5.

Cuthbert, Cuthbertson.—Bapt. 'the son of Cuthbert.' As might be expected, these surnames are found chiefly in the north of England, as are other forms, such as Crewdson and Crowdson.

William Cudbriht, co. Camb., 1273. A.
Johannes Cuthbrid, 1379 : P. T. Yorks. p. 140.
1771. Married — Ridley Cuthbertson and Ann Maria Dickson : St. Geo. Han. Sq. i. 210.
West Rid. Court Dir., 2, 1 ; London, 10, 11 ; Philadelphia, 21, 2.

Cutlack.—Bapt. 'the son of Guthlac,' sharpened into Cuthlack; v. Goodlake. It is interesting to notice that the surname still clings to the county where it is found six centuries ago. The change from initial G to C is common in nomenclature ; v. Caunter.

John Gudloc, co. Camb., 1273. A.
1556. Guthlac Cordall, rector of Colteshall, co. Norf. : FF. vii. 310.
London, 1 ; MDB. (co. Cambridge), 4 ; (Suffolk), 1 ; (Hunts), 1.

Cutler.—Occup. 'the cutler,' a maker of knives, &c. A curiously common entry, whether as surname or trade-name, in Yorkshire Poll Tax, 1379. From its frequency I should have expected a larger number of Cutlers in the present directories of that county.

Saleman le Cotiler, London, 1273. A.
Matilda la Cutiller, co. Linc., ibid.
Ricardus Hyngham, *cotteler*, 1379 : P. T. Yorks. p. 10.
Willelmus Cottelar, 1379 : ibid. p. 39.
Thomas Hank, of Handsworth, *coteler*, 1319: ibid. p. 45.
Johannes Cotelar, of Handsworth, *bakester* : ibid.

The last two names are placed together. The modern form was arrived at in good time :

1637. Married — William Cutler unto Marye Nortone : St. Mary Aldermary (London), p. 18.
London, 21 ; Sheffield, 2 ; New York, 16.

Cutt, Cutts, Cutson.—Bapt. 'the son of Cuthbert,' from the nick. Cutt. These surnames are found chiefly in the district where St. Cuthbert had made his great name a household word.

'Now Cut and Bause !
Breng forth the clubbes and staves.'
A Lytell Geste of Robin Hode, ii. 56.

The first instance is in Latin form :

Cutus de Lincoln, co. Linc., 1273. A.
Radulphus Cutte, 1379 : P. T. Yorks. p. 9.
Willelmus Cutte, 1319 : ibid. p. 1.
Johannes Cuttesone, 1379 : ibid. p. 15.
William Cutt, alias Cuttes, son of Robert Cuttes, of Sheffield, 1610 : Visitation of London, 1633, i. 213.
1546. John Strangwayes and Gertrude Cutson : Marriage Lic. (London), i. 9.
London, 1, 3, 0 ; Sheffield, 0, 8, 0 ; New York, 0, 2, 0.

Cuttance.—Bapt. 'the son of Custance,' q.v. ; a corruption.

'Mr. Povey, myself, and Captain Cuttance': Pepys' Diary, 1662, p. 122, Chandos edition.
London, 1.

Cutter.—Occup. 'the cutter,' i.e. cloth-cutter. This was Latinized as Cissor :

Walter Cyssor, 1273. A.
Hugh Cissor, c. 1300. M.
Thomas Taylour, *cissour*, 1379 : P. T. Yorks. p. 100.

In this last instance probably the surname and trade-name are closely connected ; v. Chaloner for two similar instances.

Adam Cutter, 1379 : P. T. Yorks. p. 92.
Robert Foster, *cutter*, 1643 : St. Mary Aldermary (London), p. 89.
1610. Buried—Christopher Cutter : St. Jas. Clerkenwell, iv. 114.
London, 2 ; Philadelphia, 10 ; Boston (U.S.), 90.

Cutwolf.—Bapt. 'the son of Cuthwolf'; cf. Cuthbert and Cuthwolf with Ethelbert and Ethelwolf.

Robertus Cutwolf, 1379 : P. T. Yorks. p. 233.
Thomas Cutwolf, 1379 : ibid.
Emma Cutwolf, 1379 : ibid. p. 230.
Robert Cutwolf, C. R., 19 Hen. VI.

D

Dabbs, Dabb.—Bapt. ' the son of Robert,' from the nick. Dob, pronounced Dab in the North ; cf. Rab for Rob (v. Dobb). Similarly the double diminutive Dob-in-et is found as Dabinet (v. Dobinet). In my old parish registers (Ulverston) Johnson is frequently spelt Janson, especially during the 17th and 18th centuries.

1520-1. Henry Dabbe and Eliz. Hopper: Marriage Lic. (London), i. 1.
1571. Buried—Elizabeth Dabbes, servant to Mr. Harveye: St. Dionis Backchurch, p. 192.
1672. Married—Steven Miles and Saray Dab: St. Jas. Clerkenwell, iii. 176.
London, 4, 0; Philadelphia, 4, 0; MDB. (co. Lincoln), 0, 1.

Dabney.—Local; v. Daubeney.

Dace.—Local, ' of Dayce.' I do not know where the place is situated.

Avery de Dayce, co. Camb., 1273. A.
1803. Married—George Dace and Sarah Harrington: St. Geo. Han. Sq. ii. 286.
MDB. (co. Essex), 3; Philadelphia, 2.

Dack.—? ——. A curious Norfolk surname. It is found in that county in the 13th century, and still remains there.

Alexander Dacke, co. Norfolk, 1273. A.
Simon Dack, rector of Brampton, co. Norf., 1404 : FF. vi. 439.
Roger Dack, of Heydon, co. Norf., 1404 : ibid.
1653. Married — Edward Dack and Rebecca Holden : St. Dionis Backchurch, p. 29.
MDB. (co. Norfolk), 2 ; New York, 2.

Dacre.—Local, ' of Dacre,' a hamlet eleven miles south-east from Ripon, co. York ; also Dacre, a village near Penrith.

Ranulph de Dacre, co. Cumb., 20 Edw. I. R.
Cecilia de Dacre, 1479: P. T. Yorks. p. 253.
1662-2. Married — John Bryan and Honor Dacre : Marriage Alleg. (Canterbury), p. 84.
1668. Married — Franses Stene and Martha Dacre : St. Jas. Clerkenwell, iii. 146.
Manchester, 1.

Dadd, Dadds, Dadson.—Bapt. ' the son of Dod,' a variant of Dodd, Dodds, and Dodson, q.v. For further information, v. Dabbs and Dadswell.

1705. Married — Richard Dade and Hanah Wilkinson: St. Jas. Clerkenwell, iii. 227.

The Daily Telegraph (Jan. 27, 1893) records the death of Mary Campbell Dadson.

London, 3, 1, 0 ; Boston (U.S.), 3, 0, 0.

Dadswell—Local, ' of Dowdeswell,' q.v., a variant ; cf. Dabbs for Dobbs, or Dadds for Dodds.

London, 1.

Daft, Daff.—Nick. ' daft ' and 'daff,' probably allied to 'deaf,' dull of hearing. Also a foolish sort of fellow, ' daffe, or he that spekythe not yn tyme' : Prompt. Parv. p. 111.
'I shal be halden a daffe, or a cocknay.'
Chaucer, C. T., 4016.
' Beth not bedaffed for your innocence.'
Ibid. 9067.

A Daft might have played in the Notts County Eleven in 1273 as well as 1886. The only instance occurring in the Hundred Rolls is there, probably the progenitor.

William Daft, co. Notts, 1273. A.
Lefeke Daffe, co. Notts, ibid.
Robert Daft, Fines Roll, 11 Edw. I.
Roger Daffe, co. Soms., 1 Edw. III :
Kirby's Quest, p. 196.
1664. Bapt.—Sarah, d. Richard Daft : St. Jas. Clerkenwell, i. 221.
London, 2, 0 ; MDB. (co. Notts), 5, 0 ; (co. Kent), 0, 1.

Dagg, Daggett.—Bapt. ' the son of Dag'; Icel. dagr = day. The dim. seems to have been Daggett in England, but Daggett is a Yorkshire surname, and as such may be but a corruption of Tagg, q.v.; cf. Tennyson for Dennison.

Georgius Dag, tapytour, 32 Hen. III : Freemen of York, i. 260.
1605. Thomas Robbins and Eliz. Dagge: Marriage Lic. (London), i. 297.
1667. Married—John Daggot and Ane Farrabee : St. Jas. Clerkenwell, iii. 135.
London, 3, 0 ; Leeds, 0, 1 ; Hartlington, Yorks, 0, 1 ; Boston (U.S.), 0, 26.

Dagnall, Dagnell.—Local, ' of Dagnall,' a parish in the dioc. of Oxford.

Ivo de Dagenhale, co. Bucks, 1273. A.
Henry de Dagenhale, co. Camb., ibid.
William de Dagenhale, co. Camb., ibid.
1783. Married—Samuell Dagnall and Martha Weatherley : St. Geo. Han. Sq. i. 347.
London, 3, 0 ; New York, 0, 1.

Dagworthy.—Local, ' of Dagworthy,' a hamlet in the parish of Old Newton, co. Suffolk; cf. Langworthy and Kenworthy for Langworth and Kenworth.

John de Dagworth, co. Norf., 1257 : FF. ii. 466.
Nicholas de Dagworth, co. Norf., 1400 : ibid. vi. 385.
Osbert de Dageworth, co. Norf., Hen. III-Edw. I. K.
John de Dagworth, co. Suff., 1273. A.
John de Daggeworth, London, 20 Edw. I. R.
London, 1.

Daily, Dailey.—Variants of the great Irish surname Daly. Of course Daily is imitative.

1805. Married—John Tunnacliff and Harriot Daily : St. Geo. Han. Sq. ii. 322.
London, 1, 1 ; Philadelphia, 34, 43.

Dain, Daines, Dains.—Local, ' at the Dene' (v. Dean and Dane), from residence therein.

Richard de la Dane, co. Kent, 1273. A.
Walter atte Dane, co. Kent. ibid.
Robert de la Dane, co. Kent, ibid.
Agnes del Daine, 1379 : P. T. Yorks. p. 110.
1799. Married—John Daines and Jane Ellis: St. Geo. Han. Sq. i. 208.
London, 5, 1, 0 ; Philadelphia, 0, 1, 1.

Daingerfield.—Local ; v. Dangerfield.

Daintree.—Local, ' of Daventry ' (?), a parish in co. Northampton. The suffix in the modern variant Daintree is imitative of tree, as in Plumptree, Crabtree, Rowntree, or Peartree.

Robert de Davintre, rector of Stratton, Norfolk, 1317 : FF. v. 197.
Richard Dawntre, rector of Intwood, co. Norf., 1482 : ibid. 42.
Simon de Daventre, co. Northampton, 20 Edw. I. R.

John de Davyntre, co. Hunts, 1273. A.
Johannes Dauentry, 1379 : P. T. Yorks.
p. 105.
1640. Bapt.—Elizabeth, d. John Daintrey : St. Thomas the Apostle (London),
p. 54.
1771. Married—William Daintree and
Eliz. Cook : St. Geo. Han. Sq. i. 216.
London, 3.

Dainty.—? Local, 'of Daventry (?),' an imitative variant of
Daintree, q.v. I see no other solution, as there is no trace of a nickname Dainty, i.e. nice, particular,
delicate.

1584. Robert Davntye and Margery
Trever: Marriage Lic. (London), i. 134.
1593-4. Roger Dayntie, *tailor*, and
Joane Barton : ibid. p. 212.
London, 2 ; Philadelphia, 6.

Daisy, Daisey.—Nick. ' the
daisy'; M.E. *dayesye*, i.e. the eye
of the day. Mr. Lower suggests
a local origin. He writes, ' Possibly
from the ancient barony of Aisié
(D'Aisié), in the arrondissement of
Pont Audemer, in Normandy'
(Patr. Brit. p. 80). He furnishes
no evidence. My first instance
practically settles the matter.

Robert Dayeseye, co. Hunts, 1273. A.
Roger Daisye. V. 9.
New York, 1, 1 : Philadelphia, o, 5.

Dakin, Dakins, Daykin, Deykin.—Bapt. ' the son of David,'
from nick. Daw, and dim. Daw-kin ;
cf. Wilkin, Watkin, &c. The original
nick. seems to have been pronounced
Day rather than Daw ; v. Dawkins.

Daykenus (without surname), co. Rutland, 1273. A.

The three names following occur
on the same page :

Dakyn de Idsford, 1379 : P. T. Yorks.
p. 283.
Johannes Dawkyn. 1379 : ibid.
Henricus Daykyn, 1379 : ibid.
1547-8. Thomas Hide and Agnes
Dakyn : Marriage Lic. (London), i. 11.
1793. Married — Robert Minson and
Ann Dakins : St. Geo. Han. Sq. ii. 98.
1804. — Paul Daykin and Eliz. Shabiey:
ibid. p. 308.
London (1884), 7, 1, 1, 1 ; Boston (U.S.),
13, 0, 0, 0.

Dalby, Dalbey.—Local, ' of
Dalby,' (1) a parish in N. Rid.Yorks;
(2) a parish in co. Lincoln, near to
Spilsby ; also three parishes in co.
Leicester. Dalbey is an American
variant of the surname, but it existed

in the mother-country in the 17th
century.

Willelmus de Dalby, *osteler*, 1379 :
P. T. Yorks. p. 47.
Matilda Dalby, 1379 : ibid. p. 207.
1569. Robert Whaley and Anne
Dalbye : Marriage Lic. (London), i. 44.
1604. Married—Edward Dalbey and
Saint Yonge : St. Jas. Clerkenwell, iii. 28.
West Rid. Court Dir., 5, o ; London,
11, 9; Philadelphia, 4, 7.

Dale.—Local, 'at the dale,'
from residence therein. Dale is
a common suffix in place-names ;
cf. Dunderdale, Tyndale, Martindale, Tweedall, &c.

Ralph de la Dale, co. Suff., 1273. A.
Thomas de la Dale, co. Suff., ibid.
Richard del Dale, co. Lanc., 1332 :
Lay Subsidy (Rylands), p. 17.
Thomas del Dale, 1379 : P. T. Yorks. p. 9.
Robertus del Dale, 1379 : ibid.
Willelmus at Dale, 1379 : ibid. p. 45.
Johannes at Dale, 1379 : ibid.
1545. Married—Water (Walter) Mar lar
and Mary Dale : St. Antholin (London),
p. 5.
1567. — Thomas Dale and Christyan
Hobkyns : St. Dionis Backchurch, p. 6.
London, 46 ; New York, 26.

Dallah.—Local, 'of Dalla,' now
Dalla Gill, a parish ten miles from
Ripon. The place is thus included :
' Misese, Lungle, Skeldon, Dala,
Sweton, Dalehouses, et Nidderdale'
(Poll Tax, 1379, p. 237).

Ricardus de Dala, 1379 : P. T. Yorks.
p. 238.
Manchester, 2.

Dallaway, Dalloway.—Local,
' of the dale-way ' ; *a* comes in
intrusively, as in Hathaway, Ottaway, Greenaway. M.E. *wey*, a way.

John Dalwey, co. Linc., 1273. A.
1666. Married—Richard Dallaway and
Mary Mandering : St. Jas. Clerkenwell,
iii. 124.
1798. — Isaac Wiltshear and Sarah
Dalloway: St. Geo. Han. Sq. ii. 184.
London, 1, o ; MDB. (co. Worcester),
1, 3.

Dalling, Dallin, Dallyng.—
Local, ' of Dalling,' a parish in co.
Norfolk, sometimes called Field
Dalling.

Phillip de Dalling, co. Norf., 10 John :
FF. ix. 219.
Eustace de Dalling, co. Norf., 6 Edw.
II : ibid.
Peter de Dallyng, co. Norf., 1291 : ibid.
iv. 440.
Roger Dallyng, vicar of Brooke, co.
Norf., 1409 : ibid. x. 108.

Symon de Dallinge, or Dallinghe, co.
Norf., 1273. A.
1744. Married—John Dalling and Eliz.
Richardson : St. Geo. Han. Sq. i. 34.
London, 1, 1, 1 ; Philadelphia, 2, 0, 0 ;
Boston (U.S.), 0, 1, 0.

Dallman, Dalman. — Local,
' the daleman,' one who resided in
a dale ; v. Dollman. Not to be
confused with D'Almaine.

Robertus Dalman, 1379 : P. T. Yorks.
p. 58.
Cf. Johannes de Dall, 1379 : ibid. p. 254.
London, 2, 1 ; New York, o, 1.

Dalphin.—Bapt. ; v. Dolphin.

Dalrymple.—Local, ' of Dalrymple,' lands situated in Ayrshire,
spelt in early records Dalrumpill
or Dalrumpyl. The ancestors of
the earls of Stair took their surname therefrom.

1707. Married—John Dalrimple and
Elenor Campbell : St. Peter, Cornhill,
ii. 67.
London, 4 ; Philadelphia, 6.

Dalston.—Local, ' of Dalston,'
a parish in co. Cumberland, four
miles and a half from Carlisle.

(Homines) de Daleston, co. Cumb.,
20 Edw. I. R.
1725. Married—Isaac Dalston and Ann
Berwick : St. Geo. Han. Sq. i. 1.
London, 1.

Dalton. — Local, ' of Dalton,'
parishes in cos. Lancs., Durham, and
Yorks (E. Rid.); townships in cos.
Lancs., Northumberland, Yorks
(N. Rid. and W. Rid.), and Durham.
Meaning ' the town in the dale.'
This place-name is chiefly found in
the hilly districts of North England.

Henry de Dalton, co. Northumb.,
1273. A.
William de Dalton, co. Northumb., ibid.
Richard de Dalton, London, 20 Edw.
I. R.
Johannes de Dalton, 1379 : P. T. Yorks.
p. 26.
Willelmus de Dalton, 1379 : ibid. p. 51.
1554. Bapt.—Elizabeth Daltonne : St.
Peter, Cornhill, i. 6.
1557. — Ellen Dalton : ibid. p. 7.
1639. Married—Jeremye Daunaye and
Katherine Daulton : St. Jas. Clerkenwell,
iii. 71.
London, 35 ; Philadelphia, 46.

Daltree, Daltry.—Local ; v.
Dawtrey.

Damant, Dammant, Damont.—? Local. I do not know
the origin of this name.

Thomas Damant, co. Norf., 1731: FF. vi. 292.

1803. Married—Thomas Whight and Ann Damant: St. Geo. Han. Sq. ii. 283.

London, 2, 0, 0; MDB. (co. Norfolk), 1, 1, 0; (co. Suffolk), 0, 0, 1; Boston (U.S.), 1, 0, 0.

Damm, Dam.—Local, 'at the dam,' from residence beside the mill-dam, &c.

Petrus dil Dam, co. Norf., 1273. A. Robertus de Dam', 1379: P. T. Yorks. p. 174.

Johannes de Dam', 1379: ibid. John atte Dam, vicar of Necton, co. Norf., 1409: FF. vi. 54. Robert Atte-dam de Wrotham, vicar of Griston, co. Norf., 1361: ibid. ii. 291.

1679. Bapt.—George, s. Thomas Dam and Fillis, his wife: St. Thomas the Apostle (London), p. 69.

Anne Damme, of Chipping, 1663: Lancashire Wills at Richmond (1457–1680), p. 86.

London, 3, 0; New York, 20, 1; Boston (U.S.), 5, 4.

Dampier, Damper.—Local, 'de Dampiere,' (1) a place near Dieppe; (2) a place in the department of Orne; both in Normandy (Lower).

Richard de Damper, co. Linc., 1273. A London Court Dir., 1, 0; MDB. (West Rid. Yorks), 1, 0; (co. Kent), 0, 2; (co. Southampton), 3, 0.

Damry, Dammery.—Local, 'de Amory,' a Norman local surname.

Roger de Amory, co. Bucks, 1273. A. Richard Ammary, co. Bedf., ibid. Robert Dammori, co. Oxf., ibid. Roger Damori, co. Oxf., ibid. Roger Damary, co. Norf., 1322: FF. x. 294.

1669. Married—Edward Yorke and Ellin Damery: St. Jas. Clerkenwell, iii. 162.

London, 1, 0; Philadelphia, 0, 1.

Damsell.—Nick. 'the damsel'; O.F. *damoisel*, a young squire or page. The later *damoiseau* is found in Lond. Dir. as a French surname.

Simon Damsell, co. Bucks, 1273. A. Johannes Damysell', 1379: P. T. Yorks. p. 13.

Robertus Damysell', 1379: ibid. p. 116. Lawrence Damysell, co. York. W. 2.

1567. Philip Watkins and Anne Damesell: Marriage Lic. (London), i. 36.

1700. Thomas Tidde and Mary Elliott; consent attested by Joseph Damsell, uncle of said Mary Elliott: Marriage Lic. (Faculty Office), p. 237.

1709. Buried—William Damsell: St. John Baptist on Wallbrook, p. 197. Liverpool Court Dir., 1.

Danby.—Local, 'of Danby,' two parishes in co. York.

Simon de Danby, co. Linc., Hen. III–Edw. I. K.

1565. John Danbye and Johanna Farr, *widow*: Marriage Lic. (London), i. 31.

1765. Married—Francis Danby and Mary Kendall: St. Geo. Han. Sq. i. 147.

London, 4; Leeds, 4; Philadelphia, 9.

Dancaster.—Local, 'of Doncaster,' an early form.

John de Danecastre, London, 1273. A. 1450. William Dancastre, rector of Walcot, co. Norf.: FF. ix. 351.

1577. Buried — Margarett, wife of Thomas Danckester: St. Michael, Cornhill, p. 194.

1593. — Robert Fox, servant with Mr. Dancaster: St. Peter, Cornhill, i. 142.

London, 1.

Dance.—Bapt. 'the son of Daniel,' from the nick. Dan, whence the patronymic Dans, sharpened to Dance; cf. Evance for Evans.

Amicia Daunce, 1379: P. T. Yorks. p. 127.

Thomas Danse, 1379: ibid. p. 14. Willelmus Daunse, 1379: ibid. p. 84.

1722. Married—Giles Dance and Sarah Brett: St. Antholin (London), p. 136.

London, 7; Philadelphia, 2.

Dancer, Danser.—Occup. 'the dancer,' a professional dancer at fair, festival, and wedding; cf. Hopper, Crowder, &c.

Hervey le Dansur, co. Norf., 1273. A. Ralph Danser, co. Glouc., ibid. William le Dauncer, co. Soms., 1 Edw. III: Kirby's Quest, p. 180.

Johannes Daunser, 1379: P. T. Yorks. p. 156.

1709. Married — John Jackson and Eleanor Dancer: St. Jas. Clerkenwell, iii. 231.

London, 4, 0; Philadelphia, 2, 2; MDB. (co. Salop), 0, 1.

Dancey, Dancy, Dansie, Dauncey.—Local, 'of Dauntsey,' a parish in dioc. of Gloucester and Bristol—natural and inevitable corruptions.

Peter de Dauntesy, co. Berks, 1273. A. Richard de Dauntesye, co. Wilts, ibid.

1539. Married—William Bower and Johane Dauncy: St. Antholin (London), p. 1.

1542. Buried—Mistriss Dancy, wife of Alderman Dancy: ibid. p. 3.

1696. Married — Thomas Dansie to Sarah Dansie: ibid. p. 110.

London, 1, 2, 1, 0; New York, 0, 3, 0, 0; MDB. (co. Gloucester), 3, 0, 0, 1.

Dancocks.—Bapt. 'the son of Daniel,' from nick. Dan, and suffix -*cock*. The patronymic would be Dancocks = Dancocks' son; cf. Wilcocks or Wilcox, and v. Cocks.

John Dancock. G.

1668. Married—Philip Dancockes and Anne Spicer: St. Jas. Clerkenwell, iii. 151. London, 2.

Dandelion.—Nick. 'tooth of lion'; F. *dent-de-lion*; cf. Quodling.

Hugh Daundalyn, Close Roll, 32 Edw. I. William Daundelynn. B. Robert Daundelin, co. Southampton, 20 Edw. I. R.

A family named Dandelyon long existed in the Isle of Thanet (v. Lower's Patr. Brit.).

1410. John Daundelyon: Cal. of Wills in Court of Husting (2). New York, 1.

Dando, Dandoe.— ?——. Mr. Lower writes, 'A corruption of D'Anlo. Ashton Dando, a tithing in the parish of Ashton, was formerly called Ashton D'Anlo' (Patr. Brit. p. 81). This statement scarcely tallies with the instances furnished below, belonging as they do to the 13th century and to the same district. I am strongly inclined to believe that Dando was a Scandinavian personal name. Toke, in the third instance, strengthens this view.

Alexander Dando, co. Somerset, 1273. A. Fulco Dando, co. Somerset, ibid. Toke Dando, co. Somerset, ibid.

1803. Married — Gabriel Dando and Mary Wiles: St. Geo. Han. Sq. ii. 281.

London, 9, 0; New York, 1, 1.

Dandridge.—Local, 'of Tandridge,' a parish in dioc. of Winchester. For change of T to D, v. Tennyson and Dandy.

1687-8. Henry Price and Ann Dandridge: Marriage Alleg. (Canterbury), p. 52.

1779. Married—William Laws and Susanna Dandrage: St. Geo. Han. Sq. i. 305.

London, 3; New York, 2.

Dandy, Dandison.—Bapt. 'the son of Andrew,' from nick. (Scotch) Dandy; v. Tandy. This nick. was an early one, and once as much English as Scotch.

Dandi (without surname), co. Linc., 1273. A.
Richard Dande, co. Hunts, ibid.
Dandy (without surname), co. Linc., 20 Edw. I. R.
Willelmus Dandy, et uxor ejus, 1379: P. T. Yorks. p. 251.
Thomas Dandisone, co. Lanc., 1332: Lay Subsidy (Rylands). p. 25.
'Andro Elwand, callit Dand of Bag-hed,' 1541: TTT. p. xlviii.
Dande Elwald, 1515: ibid. p. 205.
Dand Pringill, 1516: QQQ. p. ix.
Dand Ellot, 1586: ibid. p. xxxviii.
Dande Eleot, 1586: ibid.
1742-3. Bapt.—Ann, d. John Dandy: St. Dionis Backchurch, p. 170.
MDB. (West Rid. Yorks), o, 1.

Dane, Danes.—Local, ' at the dane' or 'dean' (v. Dain and Dean), from residence therein. Nothing to do with Denmark and the Danes. Danes is probably the patronymic, as in Holmes, Styles, Williams, Jones, &c.

John de la Dane, C. R., 32 Edw. I.
William de la Dane, co. Kent, 1273. A.
Willelmus Danes, 1379: P. T. Yorks. p. 215.
1804. Married—Samuel Dane and Eliz. Wallis: St. Geo. Han. Sq. ii. 300.
1805. — William Danes and Ruth Clapp: ibid. p. 335.
London, 5, 3; Boston (U.S.), 23, 0.

Dangerfield, Daingerfield.—Local, ' D'Angerville.' Five places in Normandy still bear the name of Angerville (Lower's Patr. Brit. p. 82). I see no reason to doubt this derivation. The French terminative -ville occasionally becomes -field in English nomenclature; cf. Turbyfield for Turberville. ' William de Angerville, anno 1200, had a writ of right against Robert de Angerville, for Angerville advowson: Rot. Normanniae in Turri Lond. 2 John; Madox, Hist. Excheq. p. 360' (quoted in FF. i. 297).

Benedict de Angerville, temp. Hen. II: FF. i. 296.
1659. Married — Foulke Dangerfeild and Ruth Coutchmund: St. Dionis Back-church, p. 35.
1784. — Thomas Dangerfield and Mary Anne Lapidge: St. Geo. Han. Sq. i. 358.
London, 9, 1; Philadelphia, 2, 1.

Dangerous.—Nick. ' the dangerous,' one who has power to harm.

William Daungerous, Close Roll, 13 Edw. III. pt. ii.
Gerard Daungerus, co. Linc., 1273. A.

Daniel, Daniell, Daniels, Dannell. — Bapt. ' the son of Daniel.' A popular personal name in the 13th century; v. Dann, Danks, and Dannett.

Alicia Daniel, co. Glouc., Hen. III-Edw. I. K.
Simon Danyel, co. Soms., 1 Edw. III: Kirby's Quest, p. 90.
Beatrix Danyell', 1379: P. T. Yorks. p. 69.
Robertus Danyell', 1379: ibid. p. 19.
Thomas Daniell, 1379: ibid. p. 40.
Oliva Danyl, 1379: ibid. p. 148.
Teffan Danyll, 1379: ibid.
1689-90. Buried—Sarah Daniel: St. Dionis Backchurch, p. 257.
London, 27, 14, 27, 3; Philadelphia, 21, 0, 56, 0.

Danish.—Local, ' the Dane'; cf. English, Irish, Welsh, Norris, Cornwallis, Kentish, and London-ish, q.v. This national surname is now completely lost in Dennis, q.v.

Roger le Daneis, co. Camb., 1273. A.
Henry le Daneys, co. Devon, Hen. III-Edw. I. K.
John le Daneys, co. Camb., ibid.
Roger le Deneys, co. Camb., 20 Edw. I. R.
Symon le Deneys, co. Suff., ibid.
Joel de Deneys, co. Devon, 1273. A.
Robert le Deneys, co. Soms., 1 Edw. III: Kirby's Quest, p. 102.

Danks. — Bapt. ' the son of Daniel,' from nick. Dan, and dim. Dankin, whence patronymic Dankins. Dankins has fared like every other surname with suffix -kins—in process of time it has got reduced to -kys and -ks; cf. Perks from Perkins, Dawks from Dawkins, Wilks from Wilkins, Tonks from Tonkins, &c.

Gunnild' Danekin, co. Glouc., Hen. III-Edw. I. K.
Adam Dankyn, co. Soms., 1 Edw. III: Kirby's Quest, p. 120.
Richard Dankyn, co. Soms., 1 Edw. III: ibid.
1572. Thomas Danks, rector of Heden-ham, co. Norf.: FF. x. 145.
1800. Married—Charles Hasketh and Mary Danks: St. Geo. Han. Sq. ii. 213.
1805. — Daniel Ayres and Sarah Danks: ibid. p. 323.
London, 6; Boston (U.S.), 1.

Dann, Danson.—Bapt. ' the son of Daniel,' from nick. Dan. For several centuries Danson has been a familiar South Cumberland and Furness surname. It is found in the neighbourhood of Millom.

The London Directory is not represented.

1552. Married—William Danson and Jenet Myers: St. Mary, Ulverston, p. 18.
1553. Bapt.—Agnes Danson: ibid. p. 20.
Christopher Danson, of Ulverston, 1636: Lancashire Wills at Richmond (1457-1680), p. 86.
1624. Married — Walter White and Mary Dannsonn: St. Antholin (London), p. 58.
1693. Francis Dann and Jane Newman: Marriage Lic. (Faculty Office), p. 210.
London, 6, 0; Manchester, 1, 2; Liverpool, 0, 6; Boston (U.S.), 4, 0.

Dannett, Dannatt, Dannot.—Bapt. ' the son of Daniel,' from nick. Dan, dim. Dann-et; cf. Hewet for Hugh, or Willett for William, i. e. Will-et. These diminutives are simply inexhaustible.

Cristiana Danet, co. Norf., 1273. A.
William Danet, co. Northampt., 20 Edw. I. R.
John Dannet, of Chester, baker, 1593: Wills at Chester (1545-1620), p. 50.
Thomas Dannott, of Chester, 1612: ibid.
1666. James Stephens and Elizabeth Dannett, of Stowell, co. Glouc.: Marriage Lic. (Faculty Office), p. 95.
MDB. (co. Lincoln), 1, 10, 0; Philadelphia, 1, 2, 0; Boston (U.S.), 0, 0, 1.

Danvers.—Local, ' D'Anvers,' of Antwerp.

Ralph de Anvers, co. Oxf., 1273. A.
Robert de Anvers, co. Berks, Hen. III-Edw. I. K.
Thomas de Anvers, co. Berks, 20 Edw. I. R.
1660. Samuel Danvers and Abigail Arnold: Marriage Alleg. (Canterbury), p. 53.
1662. Charles D'Anvers and Hannah Brayne: ibid. p. 78.
1710-11. Richard Sheppard and Anne Danvers: St. Dionis Backchurch (London), p. 55.
London, 3; Philadelphia, 2.

Dapifer.—Offic. ' a sewer'; v. Sewer.

Henry Dapifer, 1273. A.
Sewall Dapifer. J.

Darby, Derby. — Local, ' of Derby,' the capital of the county of that name. With the two spellings, cf. Clerk and Clark, Parkins and Perkins, &c. The ' race for the Darby' is now almost universal, but in my part of the world (North Lancashire) it is as often as not the ' Derby.' Cf.

' Mirabile Pecci; or the none-such wonder of the Peak in Darby shire.' Lond. 1669.

Robert de Derby, co. Lanc., 1332 :
Lay Subsidy (Rylands), p. 9.
William de Dereby, co. Derby, Hen.
III-Edw. I. K.
Robertus de Derby, 1379 : P. T. Yorks.
p. 137.
Johannes Derby, 1379 : ibid. p. 28.
Nicholaus de Derby, 1379 : ibid. p. 48.
1733. Married—Thomas Walthall and
Sarah Darby : St. Geo. Han. Sq. i. 11.
London, 19, 4 ; Philadelphia, 11, 5.

**Darbyshire, Darbishire,
Derbyshire,Derbyzier.**—Local,
'ot Derbyshire'; cf. Willsher, Chesshire, Kentish, Cornish, &c. As
might be expected, we find a good
number of instances in such a large
neighbouring centre as Manchester.
The American variant Derbyzier is
a curious one.

Adam de Derbyshire, co. Lanc., 1332 :
Lay Subsidy (Ryfands), p. 49.
Robert de Derbyshire, co. Lanc., 1332 :
ibid. p. 50.
Idonia Darbyschyre, 1379 : P. T.
Yorks. p. 282.
John Darbishire, of Bold, 1591 : Wills
at Chester (1545-1620), p. 50.
John Derbyshire, of Worsley, 1592 :
ibid, p. 53.
Manchester, 10, 1, 12, 0 ; London, 3, 2,
0, 0 ; Philadelphia, 0, 0, 17, 1.

Darcy, D'Arcy, Darcey.—
Local, 'de Arcy.' Norman de
Areci was a tenant-in-chief in co.
Lincoln, temp. William I. The
surname is Norman.

Osbert de Arcy, co. Linc., 1273. A.
Roger de Arci, co. Linc., ibid.
Thomas Darcy, co. Linc., ibid.
Norman Darcy, co. Linc., ibid.
Norman Darci, co. Linc., Hen. III-
Edw. I. K.
Henry Darci, co. Linc., ibid.
1525. Robert Darsey and Johanna
Bassett : Marriage Lic. (London), i. 4.
1610. Married—Sir George Trencher,
Knt., and Mrs. Penellopey Darsey :
St. Jas. Clerkenwell, iii. 36.
1795. — John Darcy and Eliz. Minifee :
St. Geo. Han. Sq. ii. 131.
London, 2, 3, 0 ; Boston (U.S.), 0, 7, 0 ;
Philadelphia, 3, 2, 1.

Dare.—?——. I have no solution of this name to offer.

Roger Dare, co. Soms., 1 Edw. III :
Kirby's Quest, p. 130.
William Dare, co. Soms., 1 Edw. III :
ibid.
Richard le Dare, co. Soms., 1 Edw. III :
ibid. p. 199.
Robert le Dare, co. Soms., 1 Edw. III :
ibid. p. 200.
Gilbert Dare, co. Bedf., 1273. A.
1771. Buried — Hannah Dare : St.
Peter, Cornhill, ii. 148.
London, 8 ; Philadelphia, 14.

Dark, Darke. — ? Local,
D'Arques, from Arques, now a
bourg and castle four miles from
Dieppe. Probably the De Arcis
of Domesday (v. Lower). Nevertheless it is far more natural to
consider it a nickname from the
dark complexion of the bearer,
and add it to the already formidable
list of colour-names ; cf. Brown,
White, &c. M.E. derk, dark.

John Derke, co. Norf., 1273. A.
John Derk, co. Camb., ibid.
Thomas Derk, rector of Burnham
Westgate, co. Norf., 1344 : FF. vii. 30.
Nicholas Darke, 1534 : Reg. Univ.
Oxf. i. 181.
1579. John Darke and Margaret Eppe :
Marriage Lic. (London), i. 90.
1789. Married—John Obee and Char-
lotte Dark : St. Geo. Han. Sq. ii. 29.

Looking at the above references
it must be clear that mine is the
only satisfactory derivation.
London, 8, 6 ; New York, 1, 3.

Darkin, Dearkeen.—Bapt. 'the
son of Darkin,' i.e. Dearkin, 'dear
little one'; cf. Dearman and Darling. Derkin is found as a single
personal name in the Hundred
Rolls. In the same register Darling is found as Derling; cf. Lovekin.

Derkin (without surname), co. Camb.,
1273. A.
Ralph Derkin, co. Camb., ibid.
Derkin fil. Derkini de Lacre, 38 Hen.
III : BBB. p. 58.
Dorkin le Bercher, co. Camb., 1273. A.
Willelmus Derkyn, et Alicia uxor ejus :
P. T. Yorks. p. 65.
Robertus Derkyn, 1379 : ibid. p. 89.
Henricus Derkyn, 1379 : ibid. p. 122.
1750. Bapt.—John, s. Joseph Dorkin :
St. Jas. Clerkenwell, ii. 296.
London, 3, 1 ; New York, 1, 0.

Darley.—Local, ' of Darley,' (1)
a parish in co. Derby, three miles
from Matlock ; (2) a township in
the parish of Hampsthwaite, W.
Rid. Yorks.

John de Derleye, co. Yorks, 1273. A.
Richard de Derleye, co. Derby, ibid.
Robert de Derleg, co. Derby, ibid.
Agnes de Derlay, 1379 : P. T. Yorks.
p. 245.
Nicholaus de Derlegh', 1379 : ibid.
p. 177.
Beatrix de Derlay, 1379 : ibid. p. 2.
1587-8. Henry Blather and Clasia
Darley : Marriage Lic. (London), i. 166.
1689. Married—John Rhodes and Mary
Darley : St. Michael, Cornhill, p. 45.

1774. Married — George Darley and
Mary Harber : St. Geo. Han. Sq. i. 239.
London, 6 ; Sheffield, 6 ; Philadelphia,2.

Darling, Dorling.—Nick. 'the
darling,' a term of endearment ; cf.
Sweetlove, Douceamour, &c.

Ralph Durlyng, co. Soms., 1 Edw.
III : Kirby's Quest, p. 123.
Ricardus Derlyng, 1379 : P. T. Yorks.
p. 24.
Adam Derlyng. 1379 : ibid. p. 146.
Johannes Derlyng, 1379 : ibid. p. 11.
Adam Darlyng, 1379 : ibid. p. 215.
Henry Derlyng, Rot. Clause, 22 Ric.
II. pt. ii.
1583-4. Married— Antony Facet and
Jane Darline : St. Dionis Backchurch,
p. 10.
1657. — John Layton and Eliz. Darling :
ibid. p. 33.
1793. — James Darling and Mary
Brown : St. Geo. Han. Sq. ii. 88.
London, 11, 4 ; Sheffield, 5, 0 ; Boston
(U.S.), 70, 0.

Darlington.—Local, ' of Darlington,' a well-known town in co.
Durham.

1694. Married — Thomas Darlington
and Barbara Taylor : St. Jas. Clerkenwell, iv. 215.
1790. — Jonathan Birkinshaw and
Catherine Darlington : St. Geo. Han. Sq.
ii. 52.
London, 3 ; New York, 4.

Darnell.—Local, ' of Darnall,'
a chapelry in the parish of Sheffield,
W. Rid. Yorks.

Robert Darnel, co. Norf., Hen. III-
Edw. I. K.
Agnes Darnel, co. Suff., 1273. A.
Henry Darnel, co. Camb., ibid.
William Darnel, co. Hunts, ibid.
Thomas Darnal, 1379 : P. T. Yorks.
p. 45.
Roger Dernele, 1379 : ibid. p. 205.
1740. Married—William Carr and Jane
Darnell : St. Geo. Han. Sq. i. 26.
1744. — Robert Bryan and Hannah
Darnel : St. Jas. Clerkenwell, iii. 275.
1785. — James Thornton and Mary
Darnall : St. Geo. Han. Sq. i. 374.
London, 6 ; Crockford, 7 ; Phila-
delphia, 12.

**Darrell, Darell, Dayrell,
Dayrrell.**— ?——.

Adam Dayrel, co. Oxf., Hen. III-Edw.
I. K.
Henry Dayrel, co. Bucks, 1273. A.
Ralph Dayrel, co. Bucks, ibid.
Isabella Darel, co. York, ibid.
Gilbert Dayrel, co. Linc., ibid.
1663. Henry Darell and Mary Legg :
Marriage Alleg. (Canterbury), p. 98.
Crockford, 1, 0, 0, 0 ; London Court
Dir., 1, 1, 1, 1 ; Boston (U.S.), 1 0 0,0 ;
New York, 5, 0, 0, 0.

Darrington.—Local, 'of Darrington,' a parish in W. Rid. Yorks, three miles from Pontefract. The surname would easily cross the border into co. Lincoln.

Robert de Derington, co. Linc., 1273. A.
Walter de Derington, co. Linc., ibid.
John de Dirington, co. Linc., Hen. III-Edw. I. K.
Robertus de Daryngton, 1379 : P. T. Yorks. p. 95.
John de Deryngton, *horner*, 6 Edw. II : Freemen of York, i. 14.
1778. Married — Richard Lewry and Ann Darrington : St. Geo. Han. Sq. i. 284.
London, 2 ; Philadelphia, 1.

Darwen, Darwin, Darwent.—(1) Local, 'of Darwen.' Over and Lower Darwen are towns in the ancient parish of Blackburn, co. Lanc., so called because located on the small stream the Darwen, a variation of the common river-name Derwent. Both towns and rivulet are so spelt in early documents ; for instances, v. Baines' Lanc. ii. 81-3. The Sheffield Darwins and Darwents are doubtless of Derwent, q.v.

Robertus Darwent, 1379 : P. T. Yorks. p. 164.
Henricus Darwent, *walker*, 1379 : P. T. Yorks. p. 274.

(2) Bapt. 'the son of Derewin,' found in Domesday as Derewen.

Derewyn (without surname), co. Oxf., 1273. A.
1678. Thomas Hird and Anne Darrwin : Marriage Alleg. (Canterbury), p. 288.
Manchester, 1, 0, 1 ; London, 0, 2, 0 ; Sheffield, 0, 4, 5 ; New York, 0, 1, 0 ; Philadelphia, 1, 0, 0.

Daubeney, Daubeny, Daubney, D'Aubney. — Local, 'de Aubigny,' a spot in Normandy (v. Taylor's Rom. de Rou, p. 220). 'William de Albini attended William the Conqueror at the Conquest. Wace mentions him as the "butler D'Aubignie"' (ibid. p. 221). Lower has a good article on the name (Patr. Brit. p. 5). In some of the instances infra the *de* is practically duplicated.

William de Aubeni, co. Notts, 1273. A.
William de Daubeney, co. Bucks, ibid.
John Daubini, co. Linc., ibid.
Hugh de Aubeny, co. Norf., ibid.
Ordnell de Daubeny, cos. Warw. and Leic., Hen. III-Edw. I. K.

William de Aubeny, co. Linc., ibid.
Ascelina Daubeny, co. Bedf., 20 Edw. I. R.
1540. Married—Olyver Dawbney and Anne Forde : St. Dionis Backchurch (London), p. 1.
MDB. (co. Glouc.), 3, 0, 3, 0 ; Boston (Daubeny), 13 ; London, 0, 1, 3, 1 ; Crockford, 1, 5, 1, 0.

Dauber, Dawber, Dorber.—Occup. 'the dauber,' a plasterer. 'And one built up a wall, and, lo, others daubed it with untempered mortar' : Ezek. xiii. 10.

'The Mayor of Attringham, and the Mayor of Dover,
The one's a thatcher, the other a dauber.'
Grose's P. Dict. (v. Craven Dialect).

The surname is by no means extinct.

Willelmus Dauber, 1379 : P. T. Yorks. p. 44.
Johannes Doweber, 1379 : ibid. p. 49.
Johannes Douber, 1379 : ibid. p. 56.
Ralph Dowber, of Little Crosby, 1617 : Wills at Chester (1545-1620), p. 55.
William Dowber, of West Derby, 1614 : ibid.
New York, 1, 0, 0 ; Liverpool, 0, 1, 0 ; MDB. (co. Lincoln), 0, 8, 0 ; Manchester, 0, 0, 1.

Daughtrey.—Local ; v. Dawtrey.

Dauncey.—Local ; v. Dancey.

Daunt.—Probably for Davenant.

Matilda Daunt, 1379 : P. T. Yorks. p. 33.
William Davenant, alias Dannent, and Elizabeth Holmes, 1632 : Marriage Lic. (Faculty Office), p. 29.
1612. Buried — Ann Daunt : Reg. Stourton (co. Wilts), p. 65.
London, 1 ; Crockford, 5 ; New York, 2.

Davenport, Devenport, Devonport.—Local, 'of Davenport,' a township in the parish of Astbury, East Cheshire. The surname has ramified in a remarkable manner. The variants recorded above seem to be confined to the immediate district within which the township is situated.

Orm de Davenport, co. Ches., 1166 : Earwaker's East Cheshire, ii. 379.
Ralph de Davenport, co. Ches., 1415 : ibid. ii. 381.
John Davenport, of Henbury, 1555 : Wills at Chester (1545-1620), p. 51.
Ralph Davenport, of Prestbury, 1574 : ibid.
1593. Buried—Richarde Davemporte : Reg.PrestburyChurch(co. Chester), p.120.
1594. Bapt. — Thomas Davemporte : ibid. p. 121.

Manchester, 23, 4, 1 ; London, 18, 0, 0 ; Philadelphia, 61, 0, 0.

David, Davidson.—Bapt. 'the son of David.' The more popular patronymic was Davis or Davies from the nick. Davy.

Dauid (*u* for *v*) Walschman, 1379 : P. T. Yorks. p. 26.
David, et Alicia uxor ejus, 1379 : ibid. p. 41.
Dauyd Bene, 1379 : ibid. p 276.
1578. Maurice David and Sarah Ivatt : Marriage Lic. (London), i. 52.
London, 7, 36 ; Boston (U.S.), 9, 60.

Davidge, Davage.—Bapt. 'the son of David,' a corruption of Davids.

Richard Davydge, 1591 : Cal. State Papers (Domestic), iii. 6.
George Davidge, Norwich, 1704 : FF. iv. 282.
1717. Married—Thomas Davidge and Frances Bedford : St. Dionis Backchurch, p. 59.
London, 4, 2 ; Boston (U.S.), 2, 0.

Davie, Davies, Davis, Davison, Davy.—Bapt. 'the son of David,' nick. Davy.

Henry Davy, co. Soms., 1 Edw. III : Kirby's Quest, p. 114.
Richard Davy, co. Suff., 1273. A.
William Davy, co. Oxf., ibid.
Johannes Dauyson (*u* for *v*), 1379 : P. T. Yorks. p. 20.
Alicia Dauy, 1379 : ibid. p. 103.
Johannes Dauyman (i.e. the servant of Davy), 1379 : ibid. p. 173.
Matilda Dauy, *doghter*, 1379 : ibid. p. 261.
Davie Grame,1602: Nicolson and Burn, Hist. Westm. and Cumb., vol. i. p. cxiv.
Davie, his son, 1602 : ibid.
Davie Bankhead, 1602 : ibid.
1526. John Davyson and Eliz. Bella : Marriage Lic. (London), i. 5.
1579. Buried—Davy up Bevan, sonne of Bevan up Davy; Mr. Smithes' man, 30 years : St. Peter, Cornhill, i. 127.
London, 7, 230, 361, 31, 24 ; Philadelphia, 2, 40, 932, 32, 3.

Davitt. — Bapt. 'the son of David.' This variant is now generally found in Ireland and among the Irish in the United States, but it was a familiar English form in the 13th century.

Davit de Wudebregg, co. Norf., 1273. A.
Isabel uxor Davit, co. Camb., ibid.
Godfrey Davit, co. Oxf., ibid.
Davit Burre, co. Camb., ibid.
Philadelphia, 3.

Daw, Dawe, Dawes, Daws.—Bapt. 'the son of David,' from the nick. Daw; v. Dawson and Dawkins.

'And Daw the dykere deye for hunger.'
Piers P. 4461-2.
Ralph Dawe, co. Soms., 1 Edw. III:
Kirby's Quest, p. 87.
Daw le Pestour. H.
Dawe le Falconer. DD.
Johannes Dawe, 1379 : P. T. Yorks.
p. 155.
Daue Codelyng, *faber*, 1379 : ibid.
p. 263.
Lovekin Dawes, co. Oxf., 1273. A.
Richard fil. Dawe, co. Bucks, ibid.
Dawe Robson, co. York, 1473. W. 11.
1593. Married — Thomas Dawes and
Bennett Jeoffrey: St. Jas. Clerkenwell,
iii. 17.
1711. — John Daw and Mary Annable :
St. Antholin (London), p. 124.
1788. — George Dawe and Mary Hart :
St. Geo. Han. Sq. ii. 6.
London, 15, 7, 26, 8 ; New York, 8, 0,
6, 0.

**Dawbarn, Dawbin, Daw-
born.**—Bapt. 'the bairn of Daw,'
exactly equivalent to Dawson.
Such entries are common in old
Yorkshire records ; v. Barnfather.
Cf. Robertus Thombarne, 1379 : P. T.
Yorks. p. 155.
Johannes Wilbarne, 1379 : ibid.
Adam Gibbarne (i.e. Adam, the barn
of Gib [Gilbert]), 1379 : ibid. p. 215.
1578. Robert Dawborne and Susanna
Treves : Marriage Lic. (London), i. 83.
1644. Married — Thomas Dawborne
and Deborah Thomson : St. Dionis Back-
church, p. 24.
London (1884), 4, 1, 1.

Dawber.—Occup. ; v. Dauber.

**Dawkins, Dawkens, Dawkes,
Dawks.**—Bapt. 'the son of David,'
from nick. Daw, dim. Daw-kin.
With the abbreviated forms, cf.
Perkins, Perkes, and Perks ; also
Wilkins, Wilkes, and Wilks.
Dorken le Bercher, co. Camb., 1273. A.
Johannes Dawkyn, 1379 : P. T. Yorks.
p. 89.
Robertus Dorkyn, 1379 : ibid. p. 283.
John Dawkyns. F.
1677. Married—William Daukines and
Ledia Smith: St. Jas. Clerkenwell, ii. 184.
1721. — John Dawkins and Ann Ellis :
St. Antholin (London), p. 136.
London, 11, 1, 3, 0 ; Boston (U.S.), 2,
0, 0, 0.

Dawson, Dowson.—Bapt. 'the
son of David,' from the nick. Daw
or Dow ; v. Daw. The earlier
nick. would seem to have been
Daud, then Daw or Dow. The
following are entered together,
and are evidently members of one
family :

Magota Daudwyfe, 1379 : P. T. Yorks.
p. 272.
Matilda Daudoghter, 1379 : ibid.
Again, we find four entries in
close conjunction :
Beatrix Daudewyf, 1379 : P. T. Yorks.
p. 218.
Johannes Dauson, 1379 : ibid.
Robertus Dauson, 1379 : ibid.
Johanna Dowedoghter, 1379 : ibid.
Osbarn Daweson, 1379 : ibid. p. 23.
Walterus Daweson, 1379 : ibid. p. 59.
In the same village occur, among
a few inhabitants :
Robertus Doweson, 1379 : P. T. Yorks.
p. 116.
Willelmus Daweson, 1379 : ibid.
London, 73, 4 ; New York, 40, 0.

**Dawtrey, Daughtry, Dal-
tree, Daltry, Daltrey.**—Local,
'of Dawtrey.' Mr. Lower writes
as follows : 'Hawtrey, Haultrey.
The family were in Sussex in
Norman times. . . . The name was
derived from their residence on a
high bank or shore. Norman-Fr.
haulte-rive, and hence the latinization *De Alta Ripa*, often modified
to Dealtry and Dawtrey, while
Hawtrey and Haultrey are closer
adhesions to the primitive form'
(Patr. Brit. p. 151). He further
adds that Hauterive is in the
arrondissement of Alençon in Normandy.
Robert de Alta Ripa, co. York, 1273. A.
Thomas de Alta Ripa, co. York, ibid.
Elena de Dautry, 1379 : P. T. Yorks.
p. 29.
Nicholaus Dautry, 1379 : ibid.
Thomas Dawtre, 1379 : ibid. p. 151.
Johanna Dautre, 1379 : ibid. p. 195.
1617. Married — Anthony Cobbe and
Christyan Dawtrye : St. Jas. Clerken-
well, iii. 44.
MDB. (North Rid. Yorks) 0, 0, 1, 0, 0 ;
Halifax, 1, 0, 0, 0, 0 ; Crockford (Daltry),
2 ; Leeds, 2, 0, 0, 0, 0 ; West Rid. Yorks
Court Dir., 0, 1, 0, 0, 0 ; London, 0, 1, 0,
0, 3 ; Philadelphia (Daltry), 1.

Day, Dey.—Occup. 'the deye'
or 'day,' a maid, a dairy-maid,
whence 'dairy' (v. Dairy, Skeat's
Etym. Dict.).
'She was as it were a maner dey.'
Chaucer, C. T. 14852.
The word is still in use in some
of the midland and southern coun-
ties, as well as in Scotland. Early
entries of the name are common :
Cecilia le Day. J.
Richilda la Deye, Close Roll, 4 Edw. I.

A feminine suffix is met with
in—
Emma le Deyster, Close Roll, 5 Edw. I.
That the male sex in course of
time were called 'deys' seems clear.
In a Statute, 37 Edw. III (1363),
we find enumerated ' cow-herds,
shepherds, swine-herds, deyes, and
all other keepers of live stock'
(vachers, berchers, porchers, deyes,
et tous autres gardeinz des bestes) ;
v. Way's Prompt. Parv. p. 116 for
an interesting note.
1492, 'William Bayly, my dey' :
Will of Hadley, in Somerset House
(H.E.D.).
Willelmus Dey, 1379 : P. T. Yorks. p. 12.
Ricardus Dey, 1379 : ibid. p. 3.
Thomas le Dey, 1379 : ibid. p. 27.
Stephen le Dagh. T.
Thomas le Day. M.
There are two columns of Day
in the London Directory, but as
Day and Daw, and Daycock and
Dawcock, are forms from David
(q.v.), these are not all descended
from the occupative term.
London, 150, 2 ; New York, 125, 11.

Daycock, Doacock. — Bapt.
'the son of David,' from nick. Day
or Daw and suffix -*cock* (v. Cock) ;
cf. Wilcock, Jeffcock, Simcock.
With the variant Deacock, cf. Deakin for Dakin or Daykin, and Meacock for Maycock.
1684. Buried—Peter Decock, *a stranger* : St. Dionis Backchurch (London),
p. 251.
London, 1, 2.

Daykin.—Bapt. ; v. Dakin.

Dayman (1), **Daymon.** —
Occup. 'the dayman,' a dairyman
(v. Day) ; probably the suffix -*man*
is a mere augmentative as in
Husbandman. Otherwise it means
the day's man, i.e. the servant of
the keeper of a dairy; cf. Priestman,
Matthewman, Addyman, Dentshman, &c. Mr. Lower, quoting
Burke's Landed Gentry, says, 'A
known corruption of Dinan.' This
is quite inadmissible.
Johannes Dayman, 1379 : P. T. Yorks.
p. 301.
1767. Married — David Powell and
Sarah Dayman : St. Geo. Han. Sq. i. 171.
London, 2, 0 ; Philadelphia, 0, 4.

Dayman (2), **Dayment, Day-mond, Daymont, Damon.**— Bapt. 'the son of Dymond'; v. Diamond. The name is undoubtedly sometimes baptismal. Raymond has passed through all the same forms save the last, which is a mere poetical imitation. For instances, v. Diamond.

London, 2, 1, 1, 1, 1.

Dayrell; v. Darrell.

Daystar. — Nick. 'the day-star.'

Robert Daysterre, 1273. A.

Deacock.—Bapt. 'the son of David'; v. Daycock.

Deacon.—Offic. 'the deacon,' one of the lower order of the clergy; cf. Archdeacon, Priest, &c. v. also Deakin (2).

William le Dekne, C. R., 39 Hen. III.
John le Dekne, C. R., 25 Edw. I.
Gile Deacon, co. Norf., 1273. A.
Richard le Dekene, co. Norf., ibid.
Adam le Dekene, co. Suff., ibid.
Peter le Dekne, co. Camb., ibid.
Simon Dekene, co. Soms., 1 Edw. III: Kirby's Quest, p. 98.
1628. Married—Richard Deacon and Jone Stokes: St. Jas. Clerkenwell, iii. 59.
London, 34; Philadelphia, 54.

Deadman.—Local; v. Deben-ham.

Deaf.—Nick. 'the deaf'; M.E. *deef, def, defe* (Skeat).

Adam Def, C. R., 18 Edw. I.
1738. Married—Lewis Mackfarson and Jane Deafe: St. Geo. Han. Sq. i. 20.

Deakin, Deaken.—(1) Bapt. 'the son of David,' a variant of Dakin (q.v.); cf. Deacock for Day-cock, or Meacock for Maycock. (2) Offic. 'the deacon' (q.v.). Probably sometimes confused with this surname.

Peter Deakin, of Barrow, *yeoman*, 1638: Wills at Chester (1621-50), p. 63.
Thomas Deakin, of Wimbolds Trafford, *husbandman*, 1640: ibid.
1802. Married — Samuel Deakin and Ann Smith: St. Geo. Han. Sq. ii. 262.
London, 6, 0; Manchester, 12, 1; New York, 2, 0.

Deal.—Local; v. Dole.

Dean, Deane, Deen. — (1) Local, 'at the dean,' from residence therein; M.E. *dene,* a valley. Often

found as a suffix in local names, as in Todmorden, Rottingdean.

Thomas de la Dene, co. Herts, 1273. A.
Jacob de la Dene, co. Kent, ibid.
Johanna del Dene, 1379: P. T. Yorks. p. 89.
Willelmus del Dene, 1379: ibid. p. 83.
Johannes de Denne, 1379: ibid. p. 234.

(2) Offic. 'the dean.'

Robert le Deen, co. Camb., 1273. A.
John le Dean, co. Soms., 1 Edw. III: Kirby's Quest, p. 81.
London, 91, 23, 0; New York, 93, 21, 2.

Dear, Deare, Deer, Deere.— Nick. (1) 'the dear,' precious, beloved; cf. Darling. (2) 'the deer'; cf. Stagg, Buck, Roe, Doe, Roe-buck.

Robert le Dere, co. Oxf., 1273. A.
Ralph le Dere, co. Oxf., ibid.
Lawrence le Dere, c. 1300. M.
William le Deer, co. Soms., 1 Edw. III: Kirby's Quest, p. 204.
Thurstan Dere, 1459: Preston Guild Rolls, p. 15.
1776. Married—John Dear and Carus (sic) Rochford: St. Geo. Han. Sq. i. 261.
London, 14, 1, 4, 3; Philadelphia, 5, 0, 1, 1.

Dearden, Durden.—Local, 'of Dearden,' or 'Duerden,' or 'Durden.' The precise spot seems to be Dearden, near Edenfield, Bury, co. Lanc. The surname clung for a long time to the immediate district, as will be seen from the subjoined references:

George Durden, of Loveclough, 1640: Wills at Chester, p. 69.
Robert Durden, of Whitefield, 1646: ibid.
Edward Duerden, of Castleton, 1631: ibid.
Elizabeth Dearden, of Middleton, 1630: ibid. p. 63.
Thomas Dearden was rector of Bury, 1599: Baines' Lanc. i. 517.
Manchester, 10, 1; Philadelphia, 9, 0.

Dearing.—Bapt.; v. Dering.

Dearlove.—Nick. An expression of affection; cf. Sweetlove, True-love, Douceamour, &c. Found as a surname in Yorkshire five centuries ago, it has always been represented there from that time downwards.

Johannes Derlof', 1379: P. T. Yorks. p. 247.
1633. Henry Benson and Elizabeth Dearlove, of Knaresboro', co. York: Marriage Lic. (Faculty Office), p. 30.

1779. Married—Robert Lily and Anne Dearlove: St. Geo. Han. Sq. i. 303.
1798. — Richard Darlove and Margaret Harkus: ibid. ii. 183.
London, 1; Scotton (co. York), 1; Leeds, 1; MDB. (West Rid. Yorks), 2; (co. Berks), 4.

Dearman.—Bapt. 'the son of Dereman.' In Domesday Dere-man and Derman; an expression of affection, beloved, precious; cf. Sweetman, Darling, Dearlove, &c.

Dereman de Bure, 1185: RRR. p. 39.
William fil. Derman, 1195: ibid. p. 79.
William Dereman, co. Essex, 1273. A.
Johannes Derman, 1379: P. T. Yorks. p. 119.
1773. Married—Edward Dearman and Ann Deacon: St. Geo. Han. Sq. i. 229.
London, 3; West Rid. Court Dir., 2; New York, 1.

Dearnaley, Dearnaly, Dearn-ley, Dearnly, Dennerley, Den-nerly.—Local, 'of Dearnley,' in the parish of Rochdale, now a separate ecclesiastical district. The variants of the surname are many, but marked by easy and natural gradations.

1677. Richard Dearneley, of Manchester: Earwaker's East Cheshire, ii. 138.
Manchester, 1, 1, 1, 1, 2, 1; London (Dennerley), 1; Philadelphia (Dearnley), 7.

Dearsley.— Local. I cannot find the place; probably some small spot in co. Cambridge or Norfolk.

Alan de Dersle, co. Camb., 1273. A.
John de Deresle, co. Camb., ibid.
1596. Thomas Deerslye, *clerk*, and Eliz. Nichollson: Marriage Lic.(London), i. 234.
1673. John Dersley, sheriff of Norwich: FF. iii. 420.
London, 3; MDB. (co. Suffolk), 1; (co. Norfolk), 1.

Death, Däeth.—Local, 'of Dethe,' a spot I have failed to discover. 'Aeth is a place in Flanders, and the family of Death, or D'Aeth, of Knowlton, baronets, are asserted to have come from that locality. See Burke's Ext. Baronetage': Lower, p. 85. The day of judgement will revise Burke, or, at least, ask for proof. On the strength of that statement Death is now occasionally found as Däeth. Old Cambridge men will remember the firm of Death and Dyson, which latter name they unkindly pronounced Dy-soon. It is interesting to note that the earliest instance I can find of the name is registered in that county.

Hugo de Dethe, co. Camb., 1273. A.
Alicia de Dethe, co. Camb., ibid.
1598. Married—John Death and Hellen Hickes: St. Jas. Clerkenwell, p. 21.
Anthonie Death, 1591: St. Mary Aldermary (London), p. 8.
'The body of Serjeant-Major Death was found in the Ribble, at Preston, Jan. 7': Standard, Jan. 8, 1887.
London, 9, 1; MDB. (co. Cambridge), 1, 0.

Debell.—Bapt.; v. Dibble.

Debenham, Debnam, Deadman, Dedman, Debman.—Local, 'of Debenham,' a parish in dioc. of Norwich. It is absolutely certain that Deadman is a variant. The steps of corruption were as follows: Debenham, Debnam, Deadnam, and Deadman. It is one more case of imitation, for which there is such a strange tendency in nomenclature. Hundreds of examples may be found in this dictionary. Lower has, 'Deadman, a *known* corruption of Debenham.' I did not see this till the above was written; cf. Putnam for Puttenham, Twyman for Twineham, Buckman for Buckenham, Totman for Tottenham.

John de Debenham, co. Hunts, 1273. A.
1688-9. Buried—Martha Harris, sister to Samuel Deadman: St. Dionis Backchurch, p. 256.
1706. — Samuel Debnam: ibid. p. 275.
No doubt the same individual is here referred to.

1669. Buried — Edward, s. Richard Debnam: St. Michael, Cornhill, p. 257.
1783. Married — Rice Deadnam and Mary Shawbridge: St. Geo. Han. Sq. i. 342.
1799. Bapt — James, son of James Dedman, a soldier: Canterbury Cath. p. 40.
London, 10, 6, 1, 2, 0; Philadelphia, 0, 0, 0, 0, 2.

Debonnaire.—Nick. 'the debonair'; Fr. *débonnaire*; v. Bonner.

Philip le Debeneyre, co. Linc., 1273. A.
1754. Married—John Debonnair, co. Middlesex, to Ann Tennant: St. Dionis Backchurch (London), p. 70.
1762. — Nicholas F. T. Winch and Susannah Debonnaire: St. Geo. Han. Sq. i. 113.
London, 1.

Dedman.—Local; v. Debenham.

Dee.—Local, 'by the Dee,' from residence on the banks of the river Dee. A Cheshire surname; cf. Yeo.

1572. David Dee: Reg. Univ. Oxf. vol. ii. pt. iii. p. 22.
1577. David Dee, A.M., and Marcia Roper: Marriage Lic. (London), i. 79.
William Dee, of Worthenbury, 1608: Wills at Chester (1545-1620), p. 52.
Richard Dee, of Worthenbury, 1608: ibid.
Randle Dee, of Bronnington, 1614: ibid.
1792. Married—Richard Dee and Mary Newman: St. Geo. Han. Sq. ii. 78.
London, 7; Manchester, 2; Boston (U.S.), 17.

Deeble.—Bapt.; v. Dibble.

Deed, Deedes, Deede.—? Bapt. 'the son of Dede' (?). Of this the patronymic would be Dedes, as in the case of Williams, Jones, Dickins, &c. Such placenames as Dedmore, Dedham, Dedworth, and Deddington point to an early personal name Ded or Dede; cf. Didsbury, now practically a suburb of Manchester.

Johannes Dede, *talour*, 1379: P. T. Yorks, p. 156.
Johannes Dede, et uxor, 1379: ibid. p. 167.
Johannes Dede, 1379. ibid. p. 207.
1604. Abraham Deede, *weaver*, and Sarah Edwards: Marriage Lic. (London), i. 287.
London (1884), 5, 2, 0; Boston (U.S.), 2, 1, 1.

Deeker.—Occup. 'the dicker' (q.v.), a variant; cf. Decks.

London, 1.

Deeks.—Bapt. 'the son of Richard,' a variant of Dicks (v. Dick). So we find Deeke for Dick:

1741. Married—Robert Deeke and Ann Hooper: St. Geo. Han. Sq. i. 27.

So also Deekins for Dickins:—

1728. Married—William Sartorius and Eliz. Deekins: St. Geo. Han. Sq. i. 5.
1767. — Thomas Deeks and Judah Terrell: ibid. p. 161.
London, 9; New York, 2.

Deemer, Demer.—Offic. 'the deemer,' a judge, one who pronounced the verdict or doom; v. Dempster. When we say, 'I deem so,' we mean 'I judge so.' 'Demar (or domesman, P.), *Iudicator* (*Index*, P.)': Prompt. Parv. p. 118.

Simon le Demer: Calendarium Inquisitionum Post Mortem (v. index).

1807. Married—William Demer and Eliz. Moore: St. Geo. Han. Sq. ii. 369.
London, 1, 0; Philadelphia, 10, 4.

Deer, Deere.—Nick.; v. Dear.

Deering.—Bapt.; v. Dering.

Defoe.—'Daniel De Foe was born in London, 1661, and was the son of James Foe, a butcher. The prefix *De* was not added to the family name of Foe by our author until he had reached manhood': Chambers' Encyc. iii. 467. This is proved by the accompanying entries. Foe is not English, and no doubt Daniel added the *De* through pride and family tradition of a continental origin.

1685. Buried—Jane Fenn, servant to Mr. Foe: St. Michael, Cornhill, p. 269.
1688. — Mary Foe, d. Daniell Foe: ibid. p. 270.
— — John Foe, son of John Foe: ibid. p. 271.
1720. — Tufley, son of Nathaniel Defoe and Mary his wife: ibid. p. 285.

Deighton, Dighton.—Local, 'of Deighton,' (1) a chapelry in the parish of Northallerton, N. Rid. Yorks; (2) a township in the parish of Escrick, E. Rid. Yorks; (3) Kirk Deighton, a parish in W. Rid. Yorks.

Robert de Dighton, *pistor*, 3 Edw. III: Freemen of York, i. 25.
Petrus de Dighton, *faber*, 1379: P. T. Yorks. p. 224.
Margareta de Dighton, *vidua*, 1379: ibid.
Johannes de Dyghton, 1379: ibid. p. 169.
1717. Married — Gabriel Cooper and Eliz. Dighton: St. Jas. Clerkenwell, iii. 240.
1803. — James Cadenhead and Joanna Deighton: St. Geo. Han. Sq. ii. 294.
MDB. (West Rid. Yorks), 4, 0; London, 6, 2; Philadelphia, 6, 2.

Delamare, Delamere, Delmar.—Local, 'de la mere,' at the mere, from residence beside a lake; M.E. *mere*, a pool; cf. Ellesmere. Thus similarly rose the great name of 'de la Pole.'

John de la Mere, co. Oxf., 1273. A.
Pagan de la Mere, co. Oxf., ibid.
Henricus del Mere, 1379: P. T. Yorks. p. 210.
Robertus del Mere, 1379: ibid.
1675. Married — John Delamare and Susanna Reffrey: St. Jas. Clerkenwell, iii. 182.

1717. Married—John Dennis and Mary de la Mare : St.Antholin (London), p. 130. London, 2, 1, 3 ; New York, 2, 0, 3.

Delf, Delve, Delves, Delph.— Local, 'of the delf,' a deep place dug out, or one so naturally formed as to seem artificially made. '*Delf,* a quarry of stone or coal ; a deep ditch or drain. A.S.' '*Delve,* a ditch or dell (Spenser). Also a quarry' (Halliwell). Cf. Delph, a village in the parish of Saddleworth, co. Yorks. 'Delph is a large and important village situated in a deep and narrow valley' : W. Rid. Dir. (1867), p. 710.

Peter de Delve, co. Bedf., 1273. A.
John de Delves, co. Ches., 1390 : East Cheshire, i. 172.
Thomas Delves, of Nantwich, co. Ches., 1649 : Wills at Chester, p. 64.
John Ridealgh, of the Delves, co. Lanc., *yeoman,* 1566 : ibid. p. 160.
London, 1, 1, 2, 0 ; Liverpool, 1, 1, 0, 0 ; New York (Delph), 1.

Delicate, Dellicate.— ?——.
Thomas Delicate,*bedale* : MDB. (North Rid. Yorks, 1875).
London, 0, 1.

Dell.—Local, 'at the dell' (a variant of Dale, q.v.), from residence therein.

1651. Married—Israell Dell and Eliz. Wildblood : St. Jas. Clerkenwell, iii. 87.
1777. — Harden Dell and Eliz. Chamberlain : St. Geo. Han. Sq. i. 279.
London, 19 ; New York, 7.

Dellow.—Local. Mr. Lower says, 'Fr. De l'Eau; the same as Waters' (Patr. Brit. p. 86). This is an unfortunate statement. Waters is almost invariably baptismal, meaning 'the son of Walter' (v. Waters), and there is no evidence in favour of the French origin. But it is clearly local.

William Dellowe, co. Wilts, 1273. A.
William Delhou, co. Oxf., ibid.
Walter Delho, co. Herts, ibid.
1600. Married—John Delloe and Eliz. Raynoldes : St. Jas. Clerkenwell, iii. 24.
1757. — George Dellow and Mary Brown : St. Geo. Han. Sq. i. 74.
London, 3 ; Philadelphia, 2.

Delver.—Occup. 'the delver,' one who digs or delves. '*Delvere,* a digger. A.S.' (Halliwell).
John le Delver, Close Roll, 29 Edw. I.

Demer.—Offic. ; v. Deemer.

Dempsey, Dimpsey, Dinsey, Dempsy, Demsey.—An Irish surname, of the origin of which I know nothing. I have placed it here because it looks so like an English local surname.
1745. Buried—Jane Dempsey : St. Mary Aldermary, p. 226.
1797. Married—John Morris and Ann Dimpsey : St. Geo. Han. Sq. ii. 165.
1800. — William Day and Catherine Dimsey : ibid. p. 218.
London, 6, 0, 1, 0, 0 ; New York, 76, 0, 0, 2, 3.

Dempster.—Offic. 'the deemster,' one who pronounced the doom, a judge ; still an official title in the Isle of Man. Strictly speaking, the suffix is feminine, as in Brewster, Baxter, or Webster. The masculine form existed ; v. Deemer.
Christopher Dempster. Q.
Liverpool, 3 ; Philadelphia, 12.

Denby, Denbigh, Denbeigh.—Local, 'of Denby,' a village near Penistone, co. Yorks.
John de Denby, rector of Hempstead, co. Norf., 1347 : FF. ix. 311.
Johannes de Denby, *smyth,* 1379 : P. T. Yorks. p. 90.
Ricardus de Denby : ibid.
Robertus de Denby : ibid. p. 56.
Eva de Denby : ibid. p. 194.
Michael Denbigh, or Denby, 1596 : FF. x. 44 and i. 209.
1609. Bapt.—John, s. Robert Denbeigh : St. Jas. Clerkenwell, i. 57.
1797. Married — William Denby and Sarah Abel : St. Geo. Han. Sq. ii. 165.
West Rid. Court Dir., 12, 5, 0 ; London, 2, 1, 1 ; New York, 4, 0, 0.

Denford.—Local, 'of Denford,' parishes in the diocs. of Peterborough and Oxford.
Roger de Deneford, co. Northampt., Hen. III-Edw. I. K.
Walter de Deneford, co. Northampt., ibid.
Sarra de Denford, co. Northampt., 20 Edw. I. R.
London, 2.

Denham.—Local, 'of Denham,' parishes in diocs. of Ely, Oxford, London, and Norwich.
Jeffrey de Denham, rector of Titleshale, co. Norf., 1360 : FF. x. 68.
William de Denham, co. Norf., 1292 : ibid. iv. 386.
John de Denham, co. Soms., 1 Edw. III : Kirby's Quest, p. 160.
Oliver de Denham, co. Cornwall, 1273. A.
Possibly the last two instances refer to Dinham, q.v.

1586-7. Anthony Denham and Eliz. Blanke, *widow* : Marriage Lic. (London), i. 157.
1640. Buried—Richard Denham, *innholder* : St. Peter, Cornhill, p. 198.
London, 11 ; Philadelphia, 3.

Denis, Denison.—Bapt. ; v. Dennis.

Denley.—Local, 'of Denley.' I cannot find the spot.
Robert de Denlegh, co. Devon, Hen. III-Edw. I. K.
1808. Married—William Denley and Mary Ottley : St. Geo. Han. Sq. ii. 382. London, 2.

Denman.—Local, 'the denman, one who lived in a dean.; a swineherd (?) ; v. Denyer. In the same village dwelt—
Thomas de Denne, 1379 : P. T. Yorks. p. 235.
Richard de Denne, 1379 : ibid.
Adam Denman, 1379 : ibid.
1618. Bapt.—John, s. Richard Denman : St. Peter, Cornhill, i. 67.
1807. Married — James Denman and Jane Mills : St. Geo. Han. Sq. ii. 367.
West Rid. Court Dir., 1 ; London, 9 ; New York, 6.

Denmark.—Local, 'of Denmark,' no doubt from the country of that name ; a recent immigrant.
1808. Married—Robert Denmark and Mary Bosworth : St. Geo. Han. Sq. ii. 388.
London, 1 ; New York, 1 ; Philadelphia, 1.

Denn, Denne.—Local, 'at the den,' i.e. dean, from residence therein ; v. Dean, Dain, and Dane.
Matilda de la Denn, co. Devon, 1273. A.
Baldewin de la Denne, co. Kent, ibid.
Walterus Denne, 1379 : P. T. Yorks. p. 153.
Cecilia de Deñ, 1379 : ibid. p. 189.
Anota del Deñ, 1379 : ibid. p. 190.
Ricardus Denne, 1379 : ibid. p. 202.
1771. Married—Thomas Messer and Eliz. Denn : St. Geo. Han. Sq. i. 215.
London, 1, 7 ; Philadelphia, 9, 0.

Dennerley.—Local ; v. Dearnaley.

Dennett, Dennit.—Bapt. 'the son of Dennis,' dim. Dennet ; v. Dennis. It is feminine in Piers Plowman :

'Save Jagge the jogelour,
And Jonette of the stuwes,
And Danyel the dees pleyere,
And Denote the baude.' 3936-40.
Alicia Denet, co. Bedf., 1273. A.
Robert Dynot, co. Oxf., ibid.

1675. Married—Christopher Dynett and Mary Vandermersch: St. Dionis Backchurch, p. 38.

1731. — Samuel Dennitt and Lueza Sheakle: St. Antholin (London), p. 144.

1773. — Thomas Moss and Eleanor Dennett: St. Geo. Han. Sq. i. 229.

— — Thomas Matches and Mary Dennett: ibid. p. 235.

London, 3, 0; Philadelphia, 0, 1.

Dennington, Denington.—Local, 'of Dinnington.' (1) Dennington, a parish in co. Suffolk; (2) Dinnington, a parish in W. Rid. Yorks, seven miles from Worksop.

Johanna de Denyngton, 1379: P. T. Yorks. p. 9.

Under the heading 'Villata de Dynnyngton' (i. e. Dinnington) occurs:

Robertus de Denyngton, 1379: P. T. Yorks. p. 68.

1771. Married—Sampson Marks and Hannah Dennington: St. Geo. Han. Sq. i. 216.

London (1884), 4, 4; Philadelphia, 3, 0.

Dennis, Dennison, Denniss, Denis, Denison, Dennisson.—(1) Bapt. 'the son of Dennis.' Both Denis and Denise, masculine and feminine forms, were in common use. Crossing over from France, this font-name was for a while exceedingly popular, especially in Yorkshire and the North, and has left its mark in such familiar surnames as Dyson, Denny, Dennett, Dyatt, Dyett, and Dye, apart from the list here given. Tenison or Tennyson is also a variant, q.v. The feminine Dennise lingered on in South-West England till the close of last century.

Richard fil. Dionise, co. Norf., 1273. A.

Michael fil. Dionisie, co. Camb., ibid.

Robert Denysson, 1379: P. T. Yorks. p. 273.

Adam Denyson, 1379: ibid. p. 268.

Denes Lister, co. York. W. 9.

Richard Dionys, 1307. M.

John Denyson, co. York. W. 13.

1472. Simon Denyse, Norwich: FF. iv. 261.

Denneyse Fowler, temp. Eliz. Z.

1713. Buried—Dennis Powell, *widow*: Reg. Broad Chalke, co. Wilts, p. 54.

— — Dennis, wife of Alex. King: ibid.

1785. Married—Joseph Lovering and Eliz. Denneys: St. Geo. Han. Sq. i. 369.

(2) Local, 'le Deneys,' i. e. the Danish; v. Danish.

London, 35, 7, 2, 2, 3, 0; New York, 42, 24, 0, 7, 16, 1.

Denny, Dennys.—Bapt. 'the son of Dennis,' from the pet form Denny; v. Dennis. One family of Denny is found in co. Cumberland and the Furness district of North Lancashire. Their origin is easily made out by putting together a few entries from Lord William Howard's Household Books (Naworth Castle).

Dennis Bell, 1612: VVV. p. 490.

Dennis Livock, 1612: ibid. p. 491.

Dennis Potter, 1612: ibid.

Dennie Underwoode, 1640: ibid. p. 503.

Margaret Dennie, 1633: ibid. p. 500.

The above will give some idea of the once great popularity of the font-name.

Johannes Denny, 1379: P. T. Yorks. p. 209.

Johannes Denny, 1379: ibid. p. 65.

Agnes Denisse, 1379: ibid. p. 73.

1572. John Dennye and Joanna Hylton: Marriage Lic. (London), i. 54.

1774. Married — Henry Denny and Sarah Aldridge: St. Geo. Han. Sq. i. 247.

London, 18, 1; Philadelphia, 27, 0.

Densham, Densem, Densumbe.—Local, ' of Denscombe.' I cannot find the spot, but it is one of the many place-names in co. Devon and the district of South-West England, with the suffix -*combe*. The name is known at Exeter as Densumbe, which is the halfway house between Denscombe and Densham.

1769. Married — Samuel Broad and Sarah Denscombe: St. Geo. Han. Sq. i. 191.

Exeter, 5, 0, 1; London, 4, 0, 0; MDB. (co. Devon), 6, 2, 0.

Denston, Densten.—Local, ' of Denston,' (1) a township in the parish of Alveton, co. Stafford; (2) a parish in co. Suffolk.

William de Denston, rector of Strumpshaw, co. Norf., 1349: FF. vii. 257.

Clement Denston, Norwich, 1429: ibid. iii. 360.

London, 2, 0; Philadelphia, 0, 2.

Dent.—Local, ' of Dent,' a township in the parish of Sedbergh, W. Rid. Yorks. This surname has ramified in a remarkable manner. As Dent lies on the immediate borders of Westmoreland, we need not be surprised to find the surname so familiarly known in that county.

Johannes de Dente, *textor*, 1379: P. T. Yorks. p. 188.

Thomas de Dent, 1379: ibid.

Emma de Dent, 1379: ibid. p. 265.

John Dent, of Warton, 1678: Lancashire Wills at Richmond, i. 89.

1576-7. Edmund Dente and Margaret Woorrall: Marriage Lic. (London), i. 73.

1682. Married—Tobias Dent and Edeth Parsones: St. Jas. Clerkenwell, iii. 196.

London, 28; West Rid. Court Dir., 6; MDB. (North Rid. Yorks), 23; (co. Westmoreland), 19; Philadelphia, 11.

Dent-de-fer.—Nick. O. F. 'irontooth'; cf. Bras-de-fer and Pedefer.

Robert Dent-de-fer. E.

Denton.—Local, ' of Denton.' The Yorkshire Dentons (a large colony) hail from Denton, a township in the parish of Otley. Other Dentons spring from parishes so named in the diocs. of Canterbury, Ely, Durham, Chichester, Lincoln, Manchester, Norwich, Peterborough, and Carlisle. Of course it means the ' town in the dean or forest.'

Hamo de Denton, co. Norf., 1273. A.

Warin de Dentone, co. Hunts, ibid.

Johannes de Denton, 1379: P. T. Yorks. p. 105.

Matilda de Denton, 1379: ibid. p. 214.

Alan de Denton, co. Linc., Hen. III-Edw. I. K.

Nigel de Denton, co. Linc., ibid.

1547. Denton and Elizabeth Griffith: Marriage Lic. (London), i. 10.

1626. Married—William Baw and Eliz. Denton: St. Jas. Clerkenwell, iii. 56.

London, 16; West Rid. Court Dir., 21; New York, 8.

Dentshman.—Occup. 'Dennis' man,' i.e. the servant of Dennis. One more of the many Yorkshire names of this class that have survived the wear of time; v. Matthewman, Jackman, &c. My last instance absolutely settles the derivation of this strange-looking name.

Robertus Dyonysman, 1379: P. T. Yorks. p. 139.

Willelmus Dynysman, 1379: ibid. p.155.

Ricardus Dynysman, 1379: ibid.

Alicia Denseman, 1379: ibid. p. 61.

Leeds, 1.

Denver, Denvir.—Local, ' of Denver,' a parish in co. Norfolk, one mile from Downham Market.

Egelina de Denver, co. Norf., 41 Hen. III: FF. ix. 110.

Walter de Denver, co. Norf., 41 Hen. III: ibid.

William de Denver, lord of Denver, co. Norf.: ibid. vii. 130.

Ebrad de la Denver, temp. Ric. I, co. Norf.: FF. ii. 325.

Walter de Denever, co. Norf., 1273. A.

William de Denevere, co. Norf., ibid.

Liverpool, o, 2 ; Philadelphia, 5, 1.

Denyer.—Local, 'the denyer,' one who lived in the dean or den ; v. Dean and Dain ; cf. Bridger, Crosser, &c. The *y* is intrusive (for euphony), as in *lawyer, sawyer,* and *bowyer.*

Matilda Denyer, 1379 : P. T. Yorks. p. 126.

Willelmus Dayner, 1379 : ibid. p. 136.

Alicia Deynour, 1379 : ibid.

1610. Thomas Denne and Dorothy Tanfeild : Marriage Lic. (London), i. 323.

1766. Married — James Denyer and Martha Robinson : St. Geo. Han. Sq. i. 151.

London, 9.

Depledge, Dapledge.—Local, 'at the deep lake.' An East-Cheshire name, found in the registers of Mottram-in-Longdendale parish church as Deplache. This reminds us of Blackleach (v. Blackledge) in the same district. The origin is *deep lake.* Halliwell has 'Lache,' a bog (Yorkshire); *leach,* a lake or large pool (Lancashire). In the will of Thomas del Booth, 1368, the testator leaves 30s. to make a causeway near 'le Poll' (the pool), and 'Urb-lache' and 'le Bar-lache,' two boggy places so named ; v. Baines' Lanc. (Croston's edit.), ii. 45.

Thomas Deplach, of Newton, co. Ches., 1647 : Wills at Chester (1620–50), p. 64.

Ralph Deplich, of Newton, 1681 : ibid. (1681–1700), p. 72.

West Rid. Court Dir., 3, o ; Liverpool, 2, o ; Manchester, o, 1.

Derby.—Local ; v. Darby.

Derbyshire.—Local ; v. Darbyshire.

Derham.—Local, ' of Dereham,' two parishes (East and West Dereham) in co. Norfolk.

Robert de Derham, co. Norf., 1273. A.

John de Dereham, co. Norf., 3 Hen. III : FF. vii. 85.

Hawise de Dereham, co. Norf., ibid.

Geoffrey de Derham, co. Suffolk, 11 Edw. III : ibid. ix. 106.

1556. Baldwin Derham, rector of Mundford, co. Norf., ibid. ii. 247.

1589. Robert Dereham and Sarah Fringe, *widow* : Marriage Lic. (London), i. 182.

1778. Married—William Derham and Margaret Martin : St. Geo. Han. Sq. i. 293.

London, 4 ; New York, 5.

Dering, Deering, Dearing.—Bapt. 'the son of Dering.' Lower, quoting Hasted's Kent, mentions a Deringus de Morinis whose baptismal name descended to his children as their surname in the 12th century. There is a Kentish tenant in Domesday named Derinc fil. Sired. I suspect it is the early Derewin (v. Darwen) ; cf. Goulding for Goldwin.

Ricardus Deryng', *souter,* 1379 : P. T. Yorks. p. 95.

1651. Bapt.—Ann, d. John Deering : St. Jas. Clerkenwell, i. 178.

1661.— Anthony, s. of Mr. Henry Deearinge : Canterbury Cath. p. 12.

1755. Married—Edward Dering and Selina Furnese : St. Geo. Han. Sq. i. 57.

1796.— William Henry Jones and Mary Dearing : ibid. ii. 143.

London, 1, 4, 3 ; Philadelphia, 2, o, 2.

Derrick, Dirrick.—Bapt. 'the son of Theodoric,' nick. Derrick ; v. Terry. The German form is Dietrich, the Dutch Dirk (Yonge, ii. 337.) Most of our Derricks and Dirricks have come from the Low Countries. This form never became strictly indigenous. Dederic was the first Anglicized form.

Dedericus Campe, C. R., 3 Edw. IV.

Dederic Johnson, C. R., 4 Edw. IV.

1545–6. Richard Baker and Mary Deryke, of Petney, co. Norf. : Marriage Lic. (Faculty Office).

1560. Buried—Barnicke Dericke, servant with John Draper : St. Antholin (London), p. 13.

London, 3, 1 ; Philadelphia, 6, o.

Derwent.—Local, ' of Derwent,' a chapelry in the parish of Hathersage, co. Derby. This will explain the Sheffield Darwins, but the instance below will represent Darwen (q.v.) in co. Lanc.

William de Derwent, co. Lanc., 1332 : Lay Subsidy (Rylands), p. 76.

Manchester, 1 ; Philadelphia, 1.

Derwentwater. — Local, ' of Derwentwater.'

John de Derewentwatre, co. Cumb., 31 Edw. I : BBB. p. 639.

Henry de Derewentwater, 1302. M.

Thomas de Derwentwater. L.

1753. Married—Ashby Mickleborough and Hannah Derwentwater : St. Geo. Chap. Mayfair, p. 263.

Desborough, Disbrow—Local, ' of Desborough,' a parish in co. Northampton, six miles from Kettering. The American variant Disbrow is somewhat strongly represented in New York. The intermediate form Desbrow is found in English registers.

1703. Married—Robert Desbrow and Ellinor Sharrard : St. Dionis Backchurch, p. 51.

1722. — Richard Desborough and Bridgett Woodland : St. Jas. Clerkenwell, iii. 247.

1770. — Thomas Stirrup and Frances Desbrough : St. Geo. Han. Sq. i. 197.

1789. — Edward Disbrowe and Charlotte Hobart : ibid. ii. 24.

London, 2, o ; New York, o, 20.

Desert.—(1) Nick. 'the deserted, the abandoned one,' probably an adjective rather than a substantive.

Roger le Desert, Close Roll, 28 Hen. III.

(2) Local, ' of the waste,' the wild, the desert place.

William del Desert, Close Roll, 20 Edw. I.

1747. Married—Andrew Desert and Hannah Taylor : St. Geo. Chap. Mayfair, p. 101.

Dethick. — Local, ' of Dethwick,' a parish in the dioc. of Southwell, co. Derby.

Robert Dethec, co. Notts, Hen. III–Edw. I. K.

Geoffrey de Detheke, co. Derby, 1273. A.

1632–3. Thomas Bassett and Mary Dethicke: Marriage Lic. (Faculty Office), p. 28.

Manchester, 1.

Deuce.—Bapt. ' the son of Douce'; v. Dowse. This curious corruption is found at Stanley-cum-Wrenthorpe, near Wakefield (v. W. Rid. Directory).

Devenish.—Local, 'the Devonish,' i.e. a Devon man ; cf. Kentish and Cornish, Cornwallis, Londonish, &c.

Walter le Deveneys, co. Devon, Hen. III–Edw. I. K.

Johanna le Devenisshe, co. Soms., 1 Edw. III : Kirby's Quest, p. 86.

Nichol le Devenys, 1313. M.

Reginald le Deveneys, co. Suff.,1273. A.

Sabina le Deveneyse, co. Oxf., ibid.

Henry Devoniensi, co. Dorset, ibid.

Robert Devenysh, rector of Little Moulton, co. Norf., 1408 : FF. v. 208.

1663. Married—John Devenish and

Dorothy Bowles: St. Jas. Clerkenwell, iii. 112.
1806. — Benjamin Devonish and Eliz. Court: St. Geo. Han. Sq. ii. 358, London, 3.

Devenport.—Local; v. Davenport.

Deverell, Deverall.—Local, 'of Deverill,' a parish in co. Wilts.

Geoffrey Deverel, co. Soms., 1 Edw. III: Kirby's Quest. p. 91.
Flyas de Deverel, co. Wilts, Hen. III–Edw. I. K.
Alice de Diveryll, co. Oxf., 1273. A.
Eustace de Deverel, co. Wilts, 1273. A.
(*Persona*) de Deverel, co. Wilts, ibid.
Johannes Deverell, *bawer* (i.e. bowyer), 1379: P. T. Yorks. p. 99.
1590–1. Robert Deverell, *husbandman*, and Alice Richardson: Marriage Lic. (London), i. 190.
1782. Married—Henry Deverill and Mary Stevenson: St. Geo. Han. Sq. i. 340.
— — Thomas Griswood and Dorothy Deverill: ibid.
London, 7, 2; New York 2, 0; Philadelphia, 5, 0.

Devil, Deville.—(1) Local, 'de Eyville.'

Nicholas de Eyvil, co. Notts, 1273. A.
John de Eyville, co. Notts, ibid.
Robert de Eyvill, co. Oxf., Hen. III–Edw. I. K.
Goscelin de Eyville, c 1300. M.
Thomas Deyville, co. Notts, 20 Edw. I. R.

(2) Nick. 'the Devil.'

Roger le Diable. J.
Osbert Diabolus. J.

Possibly a pleasantry on the local form. The following curious entry occurs in the registers of St. Peter, Cornhill, i. 121:

1571. Burying of Jeames the Devill Ducheman.
London, 0, 1; New York, 0, 2.

Devonshire. — Local, 'of Devonshire'; cf. Kent, Wiltshire, Darbyshire, Cheshire, &c.

1582. William Gryffyn and Agnes Devonshier: Marriage Lic. (London), i. 111.
1805. Married—Abraham Devonshire and Margaret Godlee Wilson: St. Geo. Han. Sq. ii. 337.
London, 1; Philadelphia, 5.

Dewdney, Doudney, Dowdney.—Local, 'of Dowdney.' I cannot find the spot.

1797. Married—Samuel Dowdney and Ann North: St. Geo. Han. Sq. ii. 166.
London, 4, 3, 0; MDB. (co. Somerset), 0, 0, 2; New York, 1, 1, 1.

Dewey, Dewy, Dewing.—Bapt. 'the son of Dewin,' popularly Dewy. The Domesday form of this personal name was Derewin, one of the endless compounds of -*win*; cf. Unwin, Goldwin, Baldwin, &c. The *g* in Dewing is excrescent, as in Golding, Jennings, &c.

Willelmus Dewyn, 1379: P. T. Yorks. p. 12.
Beatrix Dewyn, 1379: ibid. p. 28.
Ricardus Dewy, 1379: ibid. p. 49.
Thomas Dewy, 1379: ibid. p. 76.
Johannes Dewy, 1379: ibid. p. 107.
1640. William Couley and Sarah Clarke (consent of her uncle, Richard Dewyn): Marriage Lic. (London), ii. 253.
1776. Married—Robert Dewey and Ann Sutton: St. Geo. Han. Sq. i. 266.
London, 3, 1, 1; Philadelphia, 7, 0, 1.

Dewhurst, Dewhirst, Dewherst.—Local, 'of Dewhurst.' A Lancashire surname, but I have not found the exact spot, although the first two instances bring us near to it. For the terminative, v. Hurst or Hirst.

Adam del Dewyhirst, co. Lanc., 1332: Lay Subsidy (Rylands), p. 84.
Roger de Dewyhirst, co. Lanc., 1332: ibid. p. 78.

The former of these lived within the bounds of Wilpshire-cum-Dinkley, the latter in Livesey.

Ellen Dewhurst, of Spotland, co. Lanc., 1592: Wills at Chester (1545–1620), p. 53.
Robert Dewhurst, of Rivington, co. Lanc., 1588: ibid.
1788. Married—John Boyle and Agnes Dewhurst: St. Geo. Han. Sq. ii. 4.
London, 2, 2, 0; Manchester, 11, 1, 0; Philadelphia, 3, 1, 0; New York, 2, 1, 1.

Dewsbury, Duesberry, Duesbury.—Local, 'of Dewsbury,' a town in W. Rid. Yorks.

Willelmus de Deusbiry, 1379: P. T. Yorks. p. 191.
Alicia Dewesbiry, 1379: ibid. p. 60.
Robertus de Dewesbiry, 1379: ibid. p. 29.
Thomas Dewsbury, of Chester, 1614: Wills at Chester (1545–1620), p. 53.
Ann Dewsbury, of Aston, 1590: ibid.
1793. Married—Clement Dewsbury and Sarah Foley: St. Geo. Han. Sq. ii. 105.
London, 2, 0, 0; Philadelphia, 1, 0, 0; Manchester, 0, 1, 1.

Dewsnap.—Local, 'of Dewsnap.' Probably the terminative is the local *knap*, a hill; v. Knapp. The spot itself was somewhere in East Cheshire, either in or near

the parish of Cheadle. The Inquisition *post mortem* of Geoffrey de Chedle says, 'Inq. p. m. taken the Wednesday after the feast of St. Barnabas, 22 Edw. I (1294) . . . by the oaths of William Danyers, John de Boudon (Bowdon), Richard de Deusnape, Thomas de Carinton, Robert de Aston,' &c. All the names belong to the district; v. East Cheshire, i. 171.

Richard de Dewsnap, 1369 (Mottram): East Ches. ii. 157.
Thomas Dewsnap, 1637 (Mottram): ibid. 128.
1796. Married—Robert Dewsnap and Sarah Williams: St. Geo. Han. Sq. ii. 153.
West Rid. Court Dir., 5; London, 3; Manchester, 3; New York, 2.

Dexter.—Occup. 'the dighester,' i.e. a dyster or dyer. There are six Dexters to one Dyster in the London Directory, yet we should expect a larger number of the latter if it alone represented the old and familiar *dighester*. For further instances, v. Dyster. There can be little doubt about the accuracy of this derivation.

Robert le Dighestre. D.
1604. Married—Edward Dexter and Eliz. Benbo: St. Michael, Cornhill, p. 17.
1609–10. George Dexter and Ann Abell: Marriage Lic. (London), i. 317.
London, 6; West Rid. Court Dir., 2; Philadelphia, 9.

Dey.—Occup.; v. Day.

D'Eyncourt.—Local. 'Walter de Aincurth, or D'Eyncourt, came over with William the Conqueror, and received from him several lordships in the shires of Northampton, Derby, Nottingham, York, and Lincoln' (Lower, quoting Kelham's Domesday).

John de Deyncourt, co. Linc., 1273. A.
Eadmund Deyncurt, co. Linc., ibid.
Eadmund de Eyncurt, co. Northampt., ibid.
Oliver de Eyncurt, co. Northampt., ibid.
Ralph de Eyncurt, co. Notts, ibid.
1546. Richard Dune and Anne Dencorte: Marriage Lic. (Faculty Office), p. 7.
London, 1.

Diable, Dible.—(1) Bapt.; v Dibble. (2) Nick. 'the Devil.'

Osbert Diabolus. C.
Roger le Diable. J.

1616. Married—John Jaimes and Ann Dible : St. Michael, Cornhill, p. 21.
1628. — Rafe Rothwell and Sara Diball : St. Mary Aldermary, p. 16.
London, 1, 1 ; Philadelphia, 0, 1.

Dialogue.—? Local. A curious imitation of some local (?) surname.

Philadelphia, 4.

Diamond, Dymond, Dimond, Diment, Diament, Dimon.—Bapt. 'the son of Dymond.' In America this surname with its variants is strongly represented. The variation *-ment* for the suffix *-mond* is common; cf. Garment for Garmond, or Rayment for Raymond, or Osment for Osmond. Diamond is an imitative corruption. For another derivation of Diment, Dimon, and Dimond, v. Diment.

Deamande de Pisingge, co. Kent, 1273. A.
Willelmus Dymond', 1379 : P. T. Yorks. p. 91.
Robertus Dymond', 1379 : ibid.
1614. William Awstripp and Lucy Diamond : Marriage Lic. (London), i. 29.
1758. Married—Edward Spice and Mary Diman : St. Geo. Han. Sq. i. 82.
London, 3, 2, 8, 2, 0, 0 ; Philadelphia, 65, 0, 8, 0, 2, 5.

Dibb, Dibbs, Dibson.—(1) Bapt. 'the son of Theobald,' from the nick. Tebb or Tibb, changed to Dibb, of which the patronymic is Dibbs ; v. Dibble. (2) Bapt. 'the son of Isabella,' from the nick. Tibb (v. Tebb) with a similar change of initial. Dibb is a common surname in Yorkshire, where Isabella and its nick. Tibb were especially familiar five centuries ago.

1621. Thomas Dibb and Ursula Wyld : Marriage Lic. (London), ii. 102.
1796. Married—Richard Dibson and Jane Tomling : St. Geo. Han. Sq. ii. 142.
London, 2, 2, 0 ; W. Rid. (Yorks) Court Dir., 5, 0, 0 ; New York, 0, 2, 0.

Dibben.—Local, 'of Deepden'; cf. Dibble and Dibden.

1750. Married—James Dibon and Frances Crebessac : St. Geo. Chap. Mayfair, p. 174.
1809. — James Dibben and Eliz. Milton : St. Geo. Han. Sq. ii. 420.
London, 7 ; New York, 1.

Dibble, Dipple, Deeble, Daybell, Debold, Debell, Dible,

Diable.—Bapt. 'the son of Theobald,' from the nick. Tibble, which became also Tipple, q. v. A lazy pronunciation changed these to Dibble and Dipple. Interchanges between D and T were very common. For several instances v. Tennyson (originally Dennyson). There can be no doubt about this derivation. So early as the Hundred Rolls we find :

Ralph Dibald, co. York, 1273. A.

An unmistakeable variant of Tibald, the popular form of Theobald. Miss Yonge has the order thus : Theobald, Tybalt, Tibble, Dibble (Hist. Christian Names, ii. 338). The Netherlands form is Dippolt.

William Dibel, London, 1273. A.
1611. Margaret Dybald, killed at Norwich : FF. iii. 364.
1720. Buried—Sarah Deble, servant to Mr. Eddowes : St. Michael, Cornhill, p. 290.
1761. Married—John Dipple and Sarah Wincote : St. Geo. Han. Sq. i. 102.
1788. Bapt.—John Schleicher and Hannah Dibble : ibid. ii. 2.
1792. John Dible and Sarah Cross : ibid. p. 77.
London, 3, 5, 1, 0, 0, 0, 1, 1 ; Sheffield (Debell), 2 ; Boston (U.S.), 1, 0, 0, 0, 1, 0, 0, 0 ; New York, 3, 2, 0, 0, 0, 0, 0, 0.

Dibdale.—Local, 'of the deep dale.' I cannot identify the spot. The derivation is manifest.

Rogerus de Depedale, 1379 : P. T. Yorks. p. 247.
Johannes Depdale, 1379 : ibid. p. 210.
1588. Married—James Stanborough and Joane Dibdall : St. Jas. Clerkenwell, iii. 13.
1632. — John Wood and Isabell Dibdale : ibid. p. 63.

Dibden, Dibdin.—Local. (1) 'of Depden,' a parish in co. Suffolk, eight miles from Bury St. Edmunds ; (2) 'of Dibden,' a parish in co. Hants, three miles from Southampton, anciently Depedene, literally 'the deep valley.'

Randolph de Depeden, co. Oxf., 1273. A.
Richard Depeden, C. R., 20 Ric. II. pt. i.
Ricardus Depeden, 1379 : P. T. Yorks. p. 292.
Geoffrey de Depeden, co. Norf., c. 1150 : FF. ix. 7.
John Debden. XX. 1.
London, 0, 2.

Dicas.—Local ; v. Dykehouse.

Dicconet.—Bapt. 'the son of Dicconet,' from Richard, a double French diminutive ; cf. Rob-in-et and Col-in-et.

Willelmus Dyconet, 1379 : P. T. Yorks. p. 181.

Dicey.—Local; v. Dixey.

Dick, Dickson, Dixon, Dicks, Dix.—Bapt. 'the son of Richard,' from the nick. Dick, which ran a severe race for popularity with Hick (q.v.), and finally monopolized the public favour. With Dixon and Dix, cf. Rixon and Rix of the same parentage. Nix and Nixon are also parallel cases.

William Dycks : Visit. of Yorks (1563), p. 105.
William Dix, il id.
Thomas Dykkes, rector of Bodney, co. Norf., 1421 : FF. vi. 18.
William Dykk, rector of Godwick, 1420 : ibid. ix. 510.
Willelmus Dycson, 1379 : P. T. Yorks. p. 194.
Rogerus Dikson, 1379 : ibid. p. 84.
1557. Bapt.—John Dyxonne, St. Peter, Cornhill, i. 7.
1569-70. William Dixsonne and Judith Madewell : Marriage Lic. (London), i. 45.
1668. Married—Robert Dickes and Eliz. Sanders : St. Jas. Clerkenwell, iii. 140.
1669. — Edward Biges and Mary Dicke : ibid. p. 157.
London, 13, 25, 94, 6, 11 ; Philadelphia, 57, 91, 82, 3, 23.

Dickason, Dickeson.—Bapt. A corruption of Dickinson ; v. Dickens. Cf. Pattison or Patteson for Pattinson.

1686. Bapt.—Susanna, d. Eliz. Dickason : St. John the Baptist, Walbrook, p. 169.
1692. — Danniel, s. Eliz. Dickeson : ibid. p. 171.

Evidently the same mother.

1801. Married—Abraham Dickeson and Esther Hawkins: St. Geo. Han. Sq. ii. 238.
London, 2, 0 ; New York, 0, 1.

Dickens, Dickenson, Dickins, Dickinson, Dicconson, Dickons.—Bapt. 'the son of Diccon'—not Dickin, for which there is no evidence. The parent, of course, is Richard. The nicks. of names beginning with R seem to have taken the initial D ; cf. Dodge for Roger, Dob for Robert, and Dumphrey for Humphrey. But our Dickins really represents the French form Diquon or Digon ;

and Diggon or Diccon as a popular name for Richard lasted till recent times. All early instances are French in form. There is no Dickin in the Hundred Rolls. Even Dick is rare ; Hick, or Higg, or Hitch being the first popular English nicks. of Richard ; v. Hick, Higgin, and Hitchcock.

'"One of the messengers of Eleanor, countess of Montfort, in 1265, was called Diquon": Blaauw's Barons' Wars.

"Jockey of Norfolk, be not too bold,
  For Dickon thy master is bought and sold."
(King Richard III, Act v. Scene 3.)' :
             Lower, p. 89.
'Gog's souls, Diccon, Gib our cat had eat the bacon, too.'
        Gammer Gurton's Needle.

It is certain that nearly all our Dickinses and Dickinsons, Dickenses and Dickensons, &c., are mere assimilations to the English suffix in -kin, as there is no single trace that an English form existed. The French form got naturalized. In North Lancashire the French form lingered on till the close of the 16th century.

Cicely Diconson, of Broughton, 1572 : Lancashire Wills at Richmond (1457-1680), p. 93.
Margery Dickonson, of Burton, 1599 : ibid. p. 92.
Thomas Dicconson, of Dalton, 1596 : ibid. p. 90.
Richard Digon, London, 1273. A.
Roger Digun, co. Wilts, ibid.
Alice Dikun, co. Oxf., ibid.
Alicia Dycon mayden, 1379 : P. T. Yorks. p. 200.
Ricardus Dicon, 1379 : ibid. p. 14.
Willelmus Diconson, 1379 : ibid. p. 32.
Matilda Dicon-wyf, webester, 1379 : ibid. p. 58.
Robertus Dikkonson, 1379 : ibid. p. 81.
Johannes Decunson, 1379 : ibid. p. 86.
1600. Buried—An infant son of Daniell Diconsonne : St. Antholin (London). p. 40.
London, 5, 6, 12, 47, 0, 0 ; MDB. (co. Notts), Dickons, 3 ; Philadelphia, 6, 1, 0, 89, 0, 0.

Dicker.—Occup. 'the diker,' a hedger or ditcher. Ditcher is but a weakened pronunciation of Dicker ; cf. ditch and dike (v. Ditch, Skeat's Dict.).

Richard le Diker, co. Soms., 1 Edw. III : Kirby's Quest, p. 257.
Ricardus Diker, 1379 : P. T. Yorks. p. 4.
Robertus Tomson, diker, 1379 : ibid. p. 86.

Johannes Dyker, 1379 : ibid. p. 10.
Adam Wynk, diker, 1379 : ibid. p. 30.
Willelmus de Thornholm, dyker, 1379 : ibid. p. 121.
1647. Married — James Maley and Abitha Dicher : St. Dionis Backchurch, p. 25.
1780. — John Dicker and Charlotte Farmer : St. Geo. Han. Sq. iii. 307.
London, 14 ; Philadelphia, 2 ; New York, 3.

Dickerson.—Bapt. 'the son of Richard,' a corruption of Dickenson, q.v. ; and cf. Patterson, Catterson, Matterson, from Pattinson, Cattinson, and Mattinson. Dickerson has crossed the Atlantic, and is in a flourishing state in the city of New York.

1748. Married—Samuel Jones and Lucy Dickerson : St. Jas. Clerkenwell, iii. 279.
1785. Francis Noble and Sarah Dickerson : St. Geo. Han. Sq. i. 377.
London, 3 ; New York, 23.

Dickery.—Bapt. 'the son of Digory,' a sharpened form. Evidently an old-established Cornish personal name. Miss Yonge says it is a romantic name found in an old metrical tale of a knight called D'egaré (Christian Names, ii. 482).

1617. Michael Oldisworth and Susan Poyntz, with consent of her mother, Jane Dickerie, alias Pointz, wife of Mr. Dickerie : Marriage Lic. (London), ii. 50.
Degory, son of Degory and Pentecost Keast, 1712 : Reg. St. Columb Major, p. 253.
1753. Married—Peter Dickery and Eliz. McCaughan : St. Geo. Chap. Mayfair, p. 255.
London, 1 ; Philadelphia, 22.

Dickman, Digman.—Occup. ' Dick's man, the servant of Dick,' not the same as Dyker, or Dicker, a maker of dikes, a ditcher, but of the same class as Vicarman, Addiman, Bartleman, or Matthewman, q.v. Ricardus and Thomas Dykman below are found in a list of the householders of Staveley, amongst whom are also Willelmus Mathewman and Magota Mathewoman. Nevertheless, v. Dykeman.

Alicia Dikman, 1379 : P. T. Yorks. p. 160.
Willelmus Dykman, 1379 : ibid. p. 143.
Ricardus Dykman, 1379 : ibid. p. 241.
Thomas Dikman, 1379 : ibid.
Johannes Dykman, 1379 : ibid. p. 214.
Robertus serviens Ricardi, 1379 : ibid. p. 200.

Amicia serviens Ricardi, 1379 : ibid.
Adam Richardman, 1379 : ibid. p. 216.
Thomas Richardman, 1379 : ibid. p. 223.
Ricardus Richardman, 1379 : ibid.

These men would unquestionably be called Dickman in common parlance among their fellows.

1596. Married—John Lufton and Joane Dickman : St. Dionis Backchurch (London), p. 12.
1798. — Jonathan Dodd and Mary Dickman : St. Geo. Han. Sq. ii. 183.
London (1884), 2, 1 ; New York, 2, 0.

Dicks.—Bapt. ; v. Dick.

Dicksee.—Local ; v. Dixey.

Digance, Diggens, Diggins, Digginson, Diggons. — Bapt. All forms of Dickins and Dickinson. As early as 1273 Digun or Digon was in common use. For early instances, v. Dickens.

1574. Thomas Digons, or Diggons, or Dyggons : Reg. Univ. Oxf. vol. ii. pt. iii. p. 47.
John Digginson, temp. Eliz. Z.
Agnes Digeson, ibid.
1722. Married—Robert Anderson and Lidia Diggins : St. Michael, Cornhill, p. 62.
1795. — William Diggens and Eleanor W. Livingston : St. Geo. Han. Sq. ii. 123.
London (1884), 1, 2, 1, 0, 0 ; New York, 0, 0, 2, 0, 1.

Digby.—Local, 'of Digby.' A parish in co. Lincoln.

Alice de Digneby, co. Linc., 1273. A.
Robert de Digeby, cos. Warw. and Leic., Hen. III–Edw. I. K.
Anna de Diggby, cos. Warw. and Leic., ibid.
Henry de Diggeby, co. Linc., 20 Edw. I. R.
1660. Married—John Digby and Susan Almond : St. Jas. Clerkenwell, iii. 106.
London, 13 ; New York, 1.

Diggles, Diggle.—Local, ' of Diggle,' once a farmstead, scarcely a hamlet, in the parish of Saddleworth, on the Yorkshire border of South Lancashire. Whilst this seems to be the undoubted parent of the name in co. Lanc., there is a trace of another family of Diggles in the West country, possibly of baptismal origin.

Richard Diggle, of Manchester, linen-webster, 1637 : Wills at Chester, p. 66.
William Diggel, co. Soms., 1 Edw. III : Kirby's Quest, p. 170.
1696. Samuel Diggle and Elizabeth Cley : Marriage Lic. (Faculty Office), p. 221.

London, 1, 0; Manchester, 3, 4; Philadelphia, 2, 2.

Diggs, Digges.—Bapt. 'the son of Richard,' from nick. Dick, whence patronymic Dicks and Dix. This, influenced by the French Digon or Digun (English Diccon, whence Dicconson), became Diggs or Digges; cf. Diggins (v. Digance) and Diglin (q v.), which can scarcely be styled corruptions. They are Anglicized French forms. The English equivalents are Dickins and Dicklin.

Henry Dygge, co. Soms., 1 Edw. III : Kirby's Quest, p. 208.
1666. John Castilon and Margaret Diggs : Marriage Alleg. (Canterbury), p. 128.
1669. Edmand Lawrence and Mary Diggs : Marriage Lic. (Faculty Office), p. 107.
London, 1, 0; Crockford, 0, 2; Philadelphia, 5, 0.

Dight.—? Bapt. 'the son of Dight' (?). Probably a personal name. It is still familiar to co. Somerset.

Thomas Dighte, co. 'Soms., 1 Edw. III : Kirby's Quest, p. 107.
1588. Bapt.—Isabel, d. John Dight : St. Mary Aldermary, p. 62.
1806. Married—John Dight and Margaret Colquhoun : St. Geo. Han. Sq. ii. 354.
London, 1; MDB. (co. Soms.), 3; Philadelphia, 2.

Dighton.—Local; v. Deighton.

Diglin.—Bapt. 'the son of Richard,' from nick. Dick, and dim. Dicklin, which occurs as early as the Hundred Rolls; cf. Jacklin, Nickling, Hewling, &c., from John, Nicholas, and Hugh. Diglin is a lazified form; cf. Jagge in Piers Plowman for Jack.

Dikelin (without surname), co. Norf., 1273. A.
1615. William Jefferey and Lomley Diglin : Marriage Lic. (London), ii. 32.

Dignum, Dignam.—Occup. The same as Digman by change in order of letters (v. Dickman); cf. Deadman for Debnam, Putman for Putnam, Swetman for Swetnam, &c.

1766. Married — Thomas Shaw and Bridget Dignam : St. Geo. Han. Sq. i. 158.
1786. — Peter Carroll and Margaret Dignum : ibid. p. 386.

London (1884), 1, 0; Lanc. Court Dir. (1887), 1, 1.

Dilcock. — Bapt. No doubt Dilcock, like Wilcock, Simcock, &c., belongs to the personal class. It represents some early name with the suffix -cock appended (v. Cocks). It is found in Yorkshire in the 14th century, and remains there to-day. Probably it is Dilkcock (v. Dilke and Dilks), but I dare not do more than suggest it.

Adam Dilkoc, 1379 : P. T. Yorks. p. 109.
Thomas Dylkok, 1379 : ibid. p. 110.
Emot Dilkok, 1379 : ibid.
London, 1; MDB. (West Rid. Yorks), 1.

Dilke, Dilks, Dilkes.—Bapt. 'the son of Dilk,' probably a name of Dutch origin; v. Dilcock.

Nicholas Dilkes, co. Camb., 1273. A.
1624. Married—Thomas Dilkes and Eliz. Bonham : St. Jas. Clerkenwell, iii. 53.
1690. William Dilke, rector of Bixley, co. Norfolk : FF. v. 450.
1801. — William Dilke and Sophia Smith : St. Geo. Han. Sq. ii. 245.
London, 0, 1, 2; Boston (U.S.), 0, 1, 0.

Dill. — ? Bapt. 'the son of Dill' (?). This solution seems highly probable; cf. Dillwyn, Dilworth, &c. The name still flourishes in co. Somerset.

Geoffrey Dylle, co. Soms., 1 Edw. III : Kirby's Quest, p. 116.
Alan Dille, co. Camb., 1273. A.
Robert Dille, co. Bucks, ibid.
1637. Married—Joseph Dill and Faith Staples : St. Jas. Clerkenwell, iii. 68.
London, 1; MDB. (co. Soms.), 2; Philadelphia, 26.

Dillwyn, Dilling. — ? Bapt. 'the son of Dylewin' (?). But it may be local. There is a Dilwyn, a parish in the dioc. of Hereford. If baptismal, then it is natural to find the variant Dilling. Almost all the personal names ending in -win become -ing by corruptive influences. Thus, for instance, Golding or Goulding represents the personal name Goldwin.

Philip Dylewyne, co. Norf., 1273. A.
Mariot Dylewyne, co. Norf., ibid.
Henricus Dyllyng, 1379 : P. T. Yorks. p. 92.
1615. Married — John Spender and Anne Dylwyne : St. Jas. Clerkenwell, iii. 41.
London, 1, 1; New York, 0, 1; Philadelphia, 0, 1.

Dilworth, Dillworth.—Local, 'of Dilworth,' a township on the brow of Longridge Fell, in the parish of Ribchester, co. Lanc.; spelt Dylleword in a record of 1292 (v. Baines' Lanc. ii. 110).

William de Dilleworth, of Ribchester, co. Lanc., 1332 : Lay Subsidy (Rylands), p. 87.
Robertus de Dilworth, 1379 : P. T. Yorks. p. 32.
Ellen Dilworth, of Broughton, 1586 : Lancashire Wills at Richmond (1457–1680), p. 93.
William Dilworth, of Ribchester, 1672 : ibid.
Ewan Dilworth, 1562 : Preston Guild Rolls, p. 29.
1790. Married — John Dilworth and Catherine Harrison : St. Geo. Han. Sq. ii. 44.
Manchester, 1, 0; London, 3, 0; Philadelphia, 5, 1.

Dimbleby, Dimblebee.—Local, 'of Dembleby,' a parish in co. Lincoln, six miles from Folkingham. With Dimblebee, cf. Applebee for Appleby, q.v.

William de Dembeby (sic), co. Lincoln, Hen. III-Edw. I. K.
1667. Thomas Lownes and Mary Dimblebee : Marriage Alleg. (Canterbury), p. 143.
1691. Solomon Dimbleby and Eliz. Stebbing : ibid. p. 200.
1805. Married—Peter Boddy and Eliz. Dimbleby : St. Geo. Han. Sq. ii. 320.
London, 1, 0; MDB. (co. Leicester), 0, 5.

Dimcock.—? Bapt. 'the son of Diamond' (?), q.v., from nick. Dime, and suffix -cock (v. Cocks); cf. Wilcock, Simcock, &c.

Robert Dymecock, co. Wilts, 1273. A.

Diment, Dimond, Dimman, Dimont. — Local, 'of Dinant' (q.v.). That these are variants of Dinant scarcely admits of a doubt. Found in Devonshire and the south-west of England, they have come directly across from Brittany. Mr. Lower includes Dyamond among these variants. No doubt a certain amount of confusion exists between the variants of the personal name Dymond and the variants of the local name Dinant; v. Diamond.

1660. Married—John Dimond and Eliz. Weuer : St. Mary Aldermary, p. 29.
1685. John Tylley and Dorathy Dimont, alias Diamond: Marriage Alleg. (Canterbury), p. 218.

1758. Married — Edward Spice and Mary Diman : St. Geo. Han. Sq. i. 82.
MDB. (co. Devon), 2, 3, 0, 0 ; (co. Somerset), 1, 0, 1, 1 ; London, 2, 8, 0, 0 ; Philadelphia, 0, 8, 0, 0.

Dimes.—Bapt. 'the son of Diamond,' q.v., from nick. Dime ; cf. Dimcock. Corroborative evidence in favour of this view is found in the fact that in the county of York, where Diamond or Dymond was a favourite name, we find the patronymic Dimeson.

Ricardus Dimeson, 1379 : P. T. Yorks. p. 142.
1700. Married — Charles Vale and Sarah Dymes : St. Antholin (London), p. 114.
London (1884), 4 ; New York, 1.

Dimmock, Dymock, Dymoke, Dimmick, Dimick, Dimock.—Local, 'of Dymock,' a parish in co. Gloucester. Mr. Lower quotes with deserved ridicule an absurd statement from Burke's Landed Gentry, that this family (Dymock) claims descent from Tudor Trevor, lord of Whittington, in Shropshire, from whom sprang David ap Madoc, commonly called Dai, whence the gradual corruptions Dai-madoc, Damoc, Dymoc, Dymock.

1557. Buried — Anne, wife of John Dymmocke : St. Dionis Backchurch (London), p. 184.
1594. Giles Dimmock, vicar of Duntsbourn Abbotts : Atkyns' Hist. Gloucestershire, p. 213.
1746-7. Bapt.—Jane, d. Lewis Dymoke : St. Dionis Backchurch (London), p. 173.
London, 4, 0, 1, 2, 0 ; MDB. (co. Glouc.), Dimmock, 1 ; Boston (U.S.), 2, 0, 0, 2, 8, 8.

Dimond ; v. Diamond.

Dimsdale, Dinsdale, Dingsdale.—Local, 'of Dinsdale,' a parish in co. Durham ; also a township in co. York.

John de Dimedale, co. Norf., Hen. III-Edw. I. K.
1589. John Dimesdale and Eliz. Price : Marriage Lic. (London), i. 177.
1630. Bapt. — Katherine, d. George Dymsdall : St. Jas. Clerkenwell, i. 116.
1801. Married—John Doyle and Sarah Margaret Dinsdale : St. Geo. Han. Sq. ii. 236.
London, 4, 3, 0 ; Bolton, 0, 0, 1 ; Liverpool, 3, 1, 0.

Dinant.—Local, 'of Dinant,' a town in Brittany.

Geoffrey de Dinant, co. Somerset, Hen. III-Edw. I. K.
Hawise de Dinant, co. Berks, ibid.
Oliver Dinaunt, co. Linc., 1273. A.
Rolaund Dinaunt, co. Dorset, ibid.
London, 1 ; New York, 2.

Dineley.—Local, 'of Dyneley,' seemingly some spot in the W. Rid. of Yorks.

Margareta de Dynlay, 1379 : P. T. Yorks. p. 186.
Ustas' Dynelay, 1379 : ibid. p. 211.
'John de Dyneley holds the fourth part of one Knight's fee in Downum (Downham) of the said Duke,' Knights' Fees, 23 Edw. III : Baines' Lanc. ii. 694.
1803. Married — Thomas Liley and Charlotte Dineley : St. Geo. Han. Sq. ii. 274.
Manchester, 1 ; London, 1.

Dingle.—? Local. It is difficult to arrive at a derivation. There is no local prefix to the Hundred Roll instances. Under ordinary circumstances it would be natural to suggest 'at the dingle,' the little dell, from residence therein.

William Dynghale, 1379 : P. T. Yorks. p. 190.
William Dingel, co. Hunts, 1273. A.
Henry Dinggel, co. Camb., ibid.
Helewise Dinggel, co. Camb., ibid.
1807. Married—John Dingle and Sarah Drake : St. Geo. Han. Sq. ii. 361.
London, 6 ; Oxford, 7 ; Philadelphia, 5.

Dingley.—Local, 'of Dingley,' a parish in co. Northampton, about three miles from Market Harborough.

Roger de Dingeley, co. Norf., 1330 : FF. ii. 376.
1586. Miles Okeley and Dorothy Dyngley (co. Bucks) : Marriage Lic. (London), i. 158.
1598-9. Rufus Rogers and Eliz. Dingley (co. Southampton) : ibid. p. 260.
1754. Married—Abel Beck and Sarah Dingley : St. Jas. Clerkenwell, iii. 285.
London, 6 ; Boston (U.S.), 6.

Dingwall, Dingwell.—Local, 'of Dingwall,' a parish in co. Ross, N.B.

1789. Married — James Ramsey and Catherine Dingwall : St. Geo. Han. Sq. ii. 24.
London, 5, 1 ; New York, 2, 0.

Dinham.—Local, 'of Dinham,' a hamlet in co. Monmouth, five miles from Chepstow.

William Dynham, co. Soms., 1 Edw. III : Kirby's Quest, p. 156.
Oliver de Dynham, co. Devon, 1273. A.
Robert de Dyneham, co. Devon, ibid.

1602. John Dinham (co. Oxford) and Eliz. Dormer : Marriage Lic. (London), i. 269.
London, 2.

Dinnis.—Bapt. ; v. Dennis. A variant.

MDB. (co. Devon), 3.

Dipple.—Bapt. ; v. Dibble.

Diprose.—Local, 'de Préaux.' Lower says, 'A corruption of De Préaux. There are in Normandy seven places called Préaux, two of which are St. Michel de Préaux and Notre Dame de Préaux': Patr. Brit. p. 90.

1769. Married—John Diprose and Eliz. Henning : St. Geo. Han. Sq. i. 188.
London, 4.

Disbrow.—Local, 'of Desborough' (q.v.) ; an American variant.

Disher.—Occup. 'the disher,' one who made dishes, &c., in pewter. This name evidently passed over to America with the Puritans.

John le Discher. O.
Robert le Dishere, London. X.
Margaret le Disheresse, 1273. A.
Walter le Dissher, co. Soms., 1 Edw. III : Kirby's Quest, p. 126.
1608. Richard Disher and Lucy Kemis : Marriage Lic. (London), i. 309.
1693-4. Hector Moore and Eliz. Disher : Marriage Alleg. (Canterbury), p. 283.
Philadelphia, 2.

Dishman.—Occup. 'the ditchman,' the same as Dykeman, q.v. In the same way we have both Dicker and Ditcher ; cf. Kirk and Church.

MDB. (co. Lincoln), 2.

Disley.—Local, 'of Disley,' a township in the parish of Stockport.

Jordan de Distelegh, 1273 : East Ches. ii. 85.
John de Distelegh, 1308 : ibid.
1782. Married—Elias Disley and Mary Caton : St. Geo. Han. Sq. i. 337.
Liverpool, 4 ; London, 1.

Dismore.—Local, 'of Dismore.' I cannot find the spot.

1691. Married—Thomas Nickins and Ann Dismore : St. Jas. Clerkenwell, iii. 209.
1720. — Richard Dismore and Mary Bembridge : St. Mary Aldermary, p. 44.
London, 2.

Disney.—Local, for ‘de Isney.’ The family gave name to Norton Disney, co. Lincoln; they are said to have come from Isigné, near Bayeux, famous now for its butter.

Johannes de Iseny, co. Linc., 1273. A.
Nigel de Iseny, co. Linc., ibid.
Adam de Isny, co. Linc., ibid.
William Diseney, co. Linc., Hen. III-Edw. I. K.
Adam de Dysny, co. Linc., 20 Edw. I. R.
1713. Married—Nicolas Calton and Elizabeth Disney, of Bleshly, co. Bucks: St. Michael, Cornhill, p. 57.
London, 1; Crockford, 3; Philadelphia, 5.

Diss, Dyce.—Local, ‘of Diss,’ a parish in co. Norfolk, originally Dice. Blomefield heads his history of the Hundred of Diss, ‘Dice, now Diss’: FF. i. 2. v. also Dixey.

William de Disse, co. Essex, 1273. A.
William de Diss, rector of Denton, co. Norf., 1317: FF. v. 411.
Richard de Dysse, rector of Chatgrave, co. Norf., 1350: ibid. x. 126.
Thomas Dysse, vicar of Necton, co. Norf., 1546: ibid. vi. 55.
1664. Bapt.—Diana, d. Aaron Dyes: St. Jas. Clerkenwell, i. 222.
London, 1, 0; MDB. (Suffolk), 1, 0; Crockford, 0, 1; Philadelphia, 0, 2; Boston (U.S.), 0, 1.

Ditch.—Local, ‘at the ditch,’ from residence thereby; v. Dyke and Dykes.

Absolon in le Dyche, co. Camb., 1273. A.
Alicia in the Diche, co. Soms., 1 Edw. III: Kirby's Quest, p. 104.
Richard atte Dyche, C. R., 35 Edw. I.
Richard atte Dich, C. R., 23 Edw. III. pt. i.
1723. Married—Daniel Dyche and Mary Ramsden: St. Peter, Cornhill, i. 75.

The name Ditch belongs to the same class as Towns-end, Wood-end, Street-end, West-end.

Cf. John de Dichende, 20 Edw. I. R. New York, 1.

Ditchburn.—(1) Local, a variant of Tichborne, q.v.; cf. Tennyson for Dennison, &c. (2) Local, ‘of Ditchburn,’ a small township in the parish of Ellingham, co. Northumberland.

1546. Buried—John Decheborn: St. Peter, Cornhill, p. 108.
1776. Married—Jean Rihoy and Susannah Ditchborn: St. Geo. Han. Sq. i. 270.
London, 1.

Ditchfield.—Local, ‘at the ditch-field,’ i.e. the field by the dike or ditch. A Lancashire surname, evidently derived from some small spot in or near the parish of Prescot.

John de Dychefield (of Ditton), co. Lanc., 1332: Lay Subsidy (Rylands), p. 13.
William Ditchfield, of Ditton, 1567: Wills at Chester (1545-1620), p. 54.
John Ditchfield, of Ditton, 1582: ibid.
Margaret Ditchfield, of Sutton, widow, 1594: ibid.
John Ditchfield, of Prescot, 1603: ibid.
1669. John Ditchfeild and Mary Griffith: Marriage Lic. (Westminster), p. 44.
London, 0; Manchester, 6; Liverpool, 2.

Ditchman.—Occup.; v. Dykeman.

Ditton.—Local, ‘of Ditton,’ parishes in the diocs. of Canterbury, Liverpool, Rochester, and Hereford.

John de Ditton, co. Lanc., 1332: Lay Subsidy (Rylands), p. 13.
William de Dittone, co. Soms., 1 Edw. III: Kirby's Quest, p. 188.
Nicholas de Dytton, co. Sussex, 1273. A.
John de Ditton, co. Camb., ibid.
1786. Married—John Diton and Mary Bocquois: St. Geo. Han. Sq. i. 389.
London, 2; Philadelphia, 1.

Dive, Dives.—Local, ‘de Dive,’ probably some spot in Normandy. That both forms of the name are local is manifest; thus while Lazarus in the directories is what it seems to be, it is not so with Dives. Lower says there is a village called Dives in the department of Calvados, in Normandy.

Guido de Dive, co. Oxf., Hen. III-Edw. I. K.
William de Dive, co. Northampt., ibid.
Hugo de Diva, co. Northampt., ibid.

That Dives represents the same name is conclusively shown by the following two entries, which relate to the same individual:

William de Dyve, co. Oxf., Hen. III-Edw. I. K.
William de Dyves, co. Oxf., ibid.
1641. Bapt.—Thomas, son of Simon Dives: St. Dionis Backchurch (London), p. 106.
1642. Buried—Joane, d. Richard Dive: St. Thomas the Apostle (London), p. 123.
London, 2, 2.

Diver.— ? Occupative, ‘the diver’ (?). I cannot suggest any other derivation. It is interesting to notice that Diver is still a familiar surname in co. Cambridge; it is found there six centuries ago.

Gunnilda Divere, co. Camb., 1273. A.
Alanus Diverus, co. Oxf., ibid.
1742. William Diver, for a year's rent of part of the Great Garden, Norwich: FF. iv. 452.
London, 2; Philadelphia, 11; MDB. (co. Camb.), 4.

Dix, Dixon.—Bapt. ‘the son of Richard,’ from nick. Dick. whence patronymic Dicks, spelt Dix; v. Dick.

Dixey, Dixie, Dicey, Dicksee.—Local, ‘of Disce’; no connexion with Dick or Richard. Most certainly a form of Dyce (v. Diss), and local. The instances below point to a close relationship with Dyce. Disce is a hundred in co. Norfolk according to the same record (FF.); v. also A. i. 472.

Miles de Disce, rector of Haylesdon, co. Norf., 1329: FF. x. 431.
John Dixy, vicar of Keteringham, co. Norf., 1562: ibid. v. 90.
Lawrence Dixi, co. Camb., 1273. A.
Sabina Dixi, co. Camb., ibid.
Hugo Discy, co. Camb., ibid.
Robert Discy, co. Hunts, ibid.
Alicia Dixi, 1379: P. T. Yorks. p. 204.
1694. Bapt.—George, s. Benjamin Dixcy: St. Jas. Clerkenwell, i. 359.
1700. — Eliz., d. John Dixey: ibid. p. 386.

These references are quite conclusive, and more could be furnished.

London, 7, 2, 3, 2; Philadelphia, 19, 1, 0, 0.

Doane.—Local. An American variant of Done (q.v.), but found in England in the sixteenth century.

1591. Buried—Elizabethe Doane, d. Richard Doane: St. Michael, Cornhill, p. 203.

Probably this form went over with the Puritans.

Dobb, Dobbs, Dobby, Dobson.—Bapt. ‘the son of Robert,’ from nick. Dob. As will be seen (v. Hobb), Robert gave title to ghosts and haunting spirits. Hence the familiar hobs and dobbies. A ghost is a dobby in Furness. ‘Dobby, a fool, a silly old man; also, a kind of spirit' (Halliwell).

Dobbe de Laungel', co. Oxf., 1273. A.
William Dobbe, co. Norf., ibid.
Robert Dobes, co. Oxf., ibid.
Johanna Dobbewyf (i. e. the wife of Dob), 1379: P. T. Yorks. p. 221.
Isabella Dobson, 1379: ibid. p. 22.
Robertus Dobsone, 1379: ibid. p. 67.
Ricardus Dobman (i. e. the servant of Dob), 1379: ibid. p. 103.
Agnes Dob, *doghter*, 1379: ibid. p. 131.

'Abraham Dobby, miller,' appears in the W. Rid. Yorks Directory as resident in Bishop Thornton.

London, 2, 7, 3, 22; New York, o, 10, o, 15.

Dobbin, Dobbing, Dobbings, Dobbyn, Dobbyns, Dobinson, Dobbins.—Bapt. 'the son of Robert,' from nick. Dob, dim. Dob-in; cf. Rob and Rob-in. Dobbin, from being a pet name for a horse, became a specific term for an old and jaded horse. Of course the *g* in Dobbing and Dobbings is an excrescence, as in Jennings, Hewlings, &c.

Matilda Dobin, co. Oxf., 1273. A.
John Dobyn, co. Camb., ibid.
Robert Dobyn, co. Soms., 1 Edw. III: Kirby's Quest, p. 118.
Willelmus Dobyn, 1379: P. T. Howden-shire, p. 18.
Johannes Dobynson, 1379: P. T. Yorks. p. 299.
1593. Thomas Dobbinson and Eliz. Smithe: Marriage Lic. (London), i. 207.
1602. John Dobbyn and Joane Diglett: ibid. p. 271.
1610. Samuel Loveday and Agnes Dobins: ibid. p. 324.
1725. Married — Thomas Dobbinson and Mary Chandler: St. Geo. Han. Sq. i. 1.
London, 5, 1, 2, 1, 1, 0, 0; York (Dobinson), 1; Carlisle (Dobinson), 1; New York (Dobbin), 7, (Dobbins), 13.

Dobell, Doble; v. Doubble.

Dobie, Dobbie.—Bapt. 'the son of Robert,' from nick. Dob. North Eng. *dobbie* or *dobby*; Scotch, *dobie*; v. Dobb.

John Doby, co. Linc., 1273. A.
1630. Married—Edmund Dobye and Ann Parsley: St. Jas. Clerkenwell, iii. 61.
1682. — Thomas Woodard and Alice Dobbey: ibid. p. 197.
1765. — John Bayley and Mary Doby: St. Geo. Han. Sq. i. 144.
London, 1, o; Boston (U.S.), 1, 2.

Dobinet.—Bapt. 'the son of Robert,' from nick. Dob, and double dim. Dob-in-et; cf. Colinet and Robinet.

John Dobynette, 1463: Mun. Acad. Oxon.
1809. Married—Enos Stower and Ann Dabinett: St. Geo. Han. Sq. ii. 419.

The Rev. T. Burn, of Wiscanton, informs me that the surname now exists in the neighbourhood of Wiscanton, co. Somerset.

Doblin.—Bapt. 'the son of Robert,' from the nick. Dob (v. Dobb), and the dim. Dob-elin. In the same way we find Hob-elin formed from Hob, the other nick. of Robert; v. Hoblyn. For a familiar instance of this dim. v. Hewling.

Emma Doblyn, 1379: P.T. Yorks. p. 290.
Boston (U.S.), 3.

Dobson.—Bapt. ; v. Dobb.

Docker.—Local, 'of Docker,' a township in co. Westmorland, four miles from Kendal.

Elizabeth Dockar, 1579: Lancashire Wills at Richmond, i. 95.
William Docker, 1587: ibid.
1564. Bapt. — Robert, s. Thomas Docker: St. Jas. Clerkenwell, i. 3.
1565. Buried — Robert, s. William Docker: ibid, iv. 6.
MDB. (co. Westmorland), 5; London, 3; Philadelphia, 4.

Docking.—Local, 'of Docking,' a parish in co. Norfolk, eleven miles from Rougham.

John de Docking, London, 1273. A.
Hervey de Dokking, co. Norf., 6 Hen. III: FF. viii. 333.
Ralph de Docking, co. Norf., 2 Edw. II: ibid. vii. 115.
William Docking, co. Norf., 1415: ibid. vi. 42.
1803. Married — John Docking and Eliz. Hinson: St. Geo. Han. Sq. ii. 287.
London, 1; MDB. (co. Norfolk), 1.

Dockreay, Dockree, Docwra, Dockray, Dockery, Dockrey.—Local, 'of Dockwray,' a hamlet in Matterdale, co. Cumb. As regards the suffix *-wray*, v. Wray, and cf. Thackeray.

Robert Dokcra, C. R., 6 Edw. IV.
Isabel Dockraye, or Dockeray, 1560: Lanc. Wills at Richmond, i. 95.
1697. Buried — Dorathy Dockeray: Reg. Ulverston, i. 187.
Robert Dokeraa: Visit. of Yorks, 1563, p. 181.

Another curious spelling is found in the following entry:

1764. Married—Edward Harrison and Mary Dockeary: St. Geo. Han. Sq. i. 129.

MDB. (co. Cumberland), Dockray, 1; London, 1, 2, 3, o, o, o; Manchester, o, o, o, 3, o, o; Boston (U.S.), o, o, o, 3, 1, o; New York (Dorkrey), 1.

Docksey.—Local; v. Doxey.

Dod, Dodd, Dodds, Dods, Dodson, Dodshon, Dodshun.—(1) Bapt. 'the son of Dod.' In Domesday, Dodo, co. Wilts; also Alwinus Dodesone, co. Herts.

Brihtric, son of Dodda: Freeman's Norman Conquest, v. 760.
Doda Tatte: Close Roll, 42 Hen. III.
Walter Dodde, co. Soms., 1 Edw. III: Kirby's Quest, p. 99.
Benedict Dod, co. Northampt., 1273. A.
Peter Dod, co. Oxf., ibid.
Richard Dod, co. Camb., ibid.
William Dod, co. Salop, ibid.
Magota Dodson, 1379: P. T. Yorks. p. 10.
Johannes Dod, 1379: ibid. p. 19.

(2) Bapt. 'the son of David,' popularly Daud (?).

Daud Jonson, 1379: P. T. Yorks. p. 224.
William Daudson, 1379: ibid. p 235.
Elias Daudson, 1379: ibid. p. 276.
Willelmus Daud, 1379: ibid. p. 63.
Johannes Daudson, 1379: ibid.
Willelmus Daud, 1379: P. T. Howden-shire, p. 1.
Daud de Setel, *hosier*, 5 Edw. I: Freemen of York, i. 82.

It is quite possible these belong to (1), but I have a strong impression that David was so styled.

London, 1, 31, 7, 1, 7, 1 (1884), 1; New York, 1, 37, 4, o, 2, o, o.

Doddemeade, Doddimead, Dodamead. — Local, 'of Dodmead,' seemingly some small spot called Dod-mead,' i. e. the meadow belonging to Dod, q.v.

1781. Married—Robert Dodimead and Eliz. Harmon: St. Geo. Han. Sq. i. 318.
1805. — Samson Strike and Eliz. Dod-mead: ibid. ii. 333.
1807. William Dodimead and Margaret Wagstaffe: ibid. ii. 372.
London, 1, o, o; MDB. (co. Somerset), o, 1, o; Philadelphia, o, o, 2.

Dodding.—Bapt. 'the son of Dodding.' In Domesday found as Dodingus, co. Middlesex, and Doding, co. Bucks. This surname lasted in the neighbourhood of Kendal till the last century. The Doddings lived at Conishead Priory, near Ulverston, till the heiress-general married John Braddyll; cf. Browning and Harding. Personal names ending in *-ing* were common.

Thomas Dodyng, co. Soms., 1 Edw. III : Kirby's Quest, p. 183.

John Doding, co. Soms., 1273. A.

Edmond Dodding, 1596 : Lancashire Wills at Richmond (1457-1680), p. 95.

James Doddinge, of Burton-in-Kendal, 1597 : ibid.

Sarah Dodding, of Connyshcad, 1679 : ibid.

1693. Bapt.—Betteris, d. Miles Dodding, of Cunishead : Reg. St. Mary, Ulverston, p. 93.

Liverpool, 1.

Doddington, Dodington.—
Local, 'of Doddington,' parishes in cos. Cambridge, Kent, Lincoln, Northumberland, and Northampton ; also a township in co. Chester.

William de Dodington, co. Linc., Hen. III-Edw. I. K.

Robert de Dodinton, cos. Salop and Staff., ibid.

Erneus de Dodington, co. Linc., 1273. A.

Symon de Dodingtun, co. Kent, ibid.

Osbert de Dodinton, co. Linc., ibid.

1605. Bapt.—William, s. Christopher Doddington : St. Jas. Clerkenwell, i. 45.

MDB. (co. Somerset), o, 2 ; (Dorset), 1, o.

Doddridge, Dudderidge, Dodridge, Dottridge, Dutteridge.—Local, 'of Dodridge,' some spot in co. Devon or the southwest country.

Richard de Doderige, co. Devon, 1273. A.

William de Doderegge, co. Devon, 20 Edw. I. R.

1577. John Dodridge : Reg. Univ. Oxf. vol. ii. pt. iii. p. 66.

1508. John Dawdridge and Katherine Riddlesden : Marriage Lic. (London), i. 255.

John Dodridge, Knt., co. Norf., 1620: FF. iii. 367.

1779. Married — John Dodridge and Hannah Farmer : St. Geb. Han. Sq. i. 299.

Devon Court Dir., o, o, 2, o, o ; Plymouth, 1, o, o, o, o ; London, o, o, o, 1, o ; MDB. (co. Soms.), o, 2, o, o, o ; (co. Devon), 1, o, o, o, o ; (co. Salop), o, o, o, o, 1.

Dodge, Dodgson, Dodgin, Dodging, Dodgon, Dodgshon, Dodgshun.—(1) Bapt. 'the son of Dod' (q.v.), whence the patronymic Dodds and Dodson, pronounced Dodge and Dodgson ; cf. Davidge for Davids. (2) Bapt. 'the son of Roger,' from nick. Dodge ; v. Hodge. Dodgson and Hodgson are still pronounced

Dodgin and Hodgin in North Lancashire.

Henry Doggesone, co. Lanc., 1332 : Lay Subsidy (Rylands), p. 38.

Willelmus Dogeson, 1379 : P. T. Yorks. p. 300.

Helena Dogeson, 1379 : ibid. p. 74.

Ricardus Dogman, i. e. the servant of Dodge : ibid. p. 79.

Willelmus Dogeman : ibid. p. 291.

Robertus Doggeman : ibid.

John Doggeson, 1397 : Preston Guild Rolls, p. 3.

1740. Married—Thomas Dodshon and Hannah Hinton : St. Jas. Clerkenwell, iii. 269.

London, 6, 2, o, 1, o, o, o ; Wigan (Dodgin), 1 ; Burnley, o, o, o, o, 1, 1, o ; Leeds (Dodgshun), 2 ; Philadelphia, 12, 4, o, o, o, o, o.

Dodging.—Bapt. 'the son of Dodge,' from the dim. Dodgin ; cf. Colin for Nicholas. The final g is excrescent as in Jennings. Thus the surname is-explained ; v. Dodge.

Dodgyn de Sourhulle, co. Soms., 1 Edw. III : Kirby's Quest, p. 181.

London, 1.

Dodman.—(1) Bapt. 'the son of Dodeman,' probably Dode or Dodde, with augmentative -man ; cf. Bateman, Coleman, Tiddyman, and v. Dod.

Henry Dodeman, co. Wilts, 1273. A.

William Dodeman, co. Hunts, ibid.

Peter Dodeman, co. Kent, ibid.

John Dodman, co. Norf. FF.

(2) Occup. 'the servant of Dod' (v. Dod) ; cf. Matthewman.

Robertus Daudman, 1379 : P. T. Yorks. p. 243.

London, 2.

Dodwell.—Local, 'of Dodwell.' I cannot find the spot.

1695. Francis Broderwick and Henrietta Dodwell : Marriage Lic. (Faculty Office), p. 217.

1767. Married—George Sture and Jane Dodwell : St. Geo. Han. Sq. i. 179.

London, 4 ; Philadelphia, 2.

Dodworth, Dodsworth.—Local, 'of Dodworth,' a township in the parish of Silkstone, near Barnsley, co. York. As a surname the more usual form is Dodsworth, i.e. Dods' farmstead.

Walterus de Dodworth', 1379 : P. T. Yorks. p. 70.

Willelmus de Dodword, 1379 : ibid. p. 87.

1772. Married—Robert Dodsworth and Mary Naylor : St. Geo. Han. Sq. i. 221.

York, o, 5 ; London, o, 1 ; West Riding Court Dir., 1, 4 ; New York, 4, 1.

Doe.—Nick. 'the doe,' the female of the buck ; cf. Buck, Stagg, Roe, Roebuck, &c.

John le Do, co. Soms., 1 Edw. III : Kirby's Quest, p. 195.

Matilda la Do, co. Soms., 1 Edw. III : ibid. p. 221.

William le Do, co. Oxf., 1273. A.

John le Do, co. Camb., ibid.

Walter Do, co. Devon, Hen. III-Edw. I. K.

1729. Married—Benjamin Doe and Jane Shackledge : St. Geo. Han. Sq. i. 6.

London, 5 ; Oxford, 2 ; New York, 3.

Doggett, Dugget, Dugood, Duguid, Doogood, Docket, Doget.—Bapt. 'the son of Doget.' By its universal distribution (without prefix) this is manifestly a personal name. It is equally manifest that it is not one of the common diminutives in -et, as it would not be invariably so entered in the formal records below. I have no doubt it is the Domesday Thurgod, found early as Toged, now Toogood. In the same way Doget became Dogood.

Cf. Hugo Toged, 1379 : P. T. Yorks. p. 74.

Johannes Doget, 1379 : ibid. p. 41.

John Doget, co. York, Hen. III-Edw. I. K.

Alicia Doget, co. Camb., 1273. A.

John Doget, co. Oxf., ibid.

John Doget, London, ibid.

John Doget, co. Soms., 1 Edw. III : Kirby's Quest, p. 108.

William Doget, co. Soms., 1 Edw. III : ibid. p. 141.

1557. Married — John Burchall and Katherine Doegood : St. Peter, Cornhill, i. 223.

1657. — Benjamin Spooner and Agnes Doged : ibid. p. 261.

Thus Dogood and Toogood are from the same parent ; v. Thurgood. Since writing the above I have come across the following entries :

1651. Bapt. — Ruth, d. Robert and Elizabeth Toogood : St. Thomas the Apostle (London), p. 59.

1653. — Ralph, s. Robert and Elizabeth Doogood : ibid.

1577. Buryed—Nicholas, sonne of John Docket : St. Peter, Cornhill, i. 125.

London, 10, 2, 1, 1, o, o, o ; Philadelphia (Doggett), 5 ; New York (Doget), 1.

Doig, Doidge.—Bapt. 'the son of Doig' or 'Doidge.' These surnames, familiar to cos. Lancashire and Yorkshire, are not to be confounded with Dodge and Dodgson. I saw Doidge over a shop window in Blackpool on November 17, 1887.

Ricardus Doegeson, 1379 : P. T. Yorks. p. 253.
Elienora Doegeson, 1379 : ibid.
Alicia Doege-wyf, 1379 : ibid. p. 219.
Willelmus Doegeson, 1379 : ibid. p. 247.
Johannes Doegeman (i. e. the servant of Doege), 1379 : ibid. p. 253.
Ricardus Doeggson, 1379 : ibid. p. 266.
1755. Married—John Macfarquhar and Maria Doig : St. Geo. Han. Sq. i. 56.
1771. — John Doidge and Elizabeth Parent : ibid. i. 211.
London, 2, 3 ; New York, 2, 0.

Dolby, Dolbey.—Bapt. 'the son of Dolbe.' It would seem as if Dolby was but a variant of the local Dalby (q.v.), but that is entered as Daleby, whereas Dolbe is found both as font-name and surname side by side with Dolby.

Dolbe del Hulwerk, co. Oxf., 1273. A.
Thomas Dolbe, co. Oxf., ibid.
Walter Dolbe, co. Bucks, ibid.
1716. Married — John Whenham and Mary Dolby : St. Jas. Clerkenwell, iii. 239.
1744. — John Dolby and Mary Francis : St. Geo. Chap. Mayfair, p. 38.
London, 6, 0 ; New York, 0, 2 ; Philadelphia, 6, 9.

Dole, Deal, Deale.—Local, ' of the dole,' i. e. the dole, deal, or portion, a division of land. ' Dole, a share or portion. Also to set out or allot . . . a boundary mark, either a post or a mound of earth (East). . . . A piece of heath or common off which only one person has a right to cut fuel (Norf.)' : Halliwell ; v. Dowle and Dowler ; cf. Dole Bank, a hamlet in the parish of Bishop Thornton, W. Rid. Yorks.

William de la Dole, co. Camb., 1273. A.
Thomas atte Dela, de Fodeston, rector of Foston, co. Norf., 1361 : FF. vii. 365.
John atte Dole, vicar of Wigenhale, co. Norf., 1374 : ibid. ix. 172.
1602. Bapt.—William, s. Thomas Dole : St. Jas. Clerkenwell, i. 41.
1671. — Frances, d. John Deale : ibid. p. 253.
London, 3, 3, 0 ; New York, 2, 5, 2.

Dollar, Doller. — Local, ' of Doller.' I have not discovered the

spot. Of course the modern form Dollar is imitative of the familiar coin.

Laurence de Doller, co. Devon, 1273. A.
Ralph Doller, co. Norf., ibid.
1671. Bapt. — Margarett, d. William Dolor : St. Jas. Clerkenwell, i. 248.
1684. — Eliz., d. Joseph Doller : ibid. i. 306.
1808. Married—John Talbot and Ann Dollar : St. Geo. Han. Sq. ii. 392.
London, 2, 0 ; New York, 0, 1.

Dolley.—Local ; v. Doyle. A variant.

John Doly, co. Soms., 1 Edw. III : Kirby's Quest, p. 166.
1729. Buried—John Dolly : Canterbury Cathedral, p. 138.
1744. Married—Peter Harris and Ann Dolly : St. Geo. Chap. Mayfair, p. 44.
Oxford, 5.

Dolling, Dollen.—Bapt. 'the son of Dolling' ; v. Browning or Harding. Dolling is one of many personal names ending in -ing ; cf. Downing. Dollen is a variant for which co. Somerset is responsible.

Thomas Dollyng, co. Soms., 1 Edw. III : Kirby's Quest, p. 96.
John Dolling, co. Soms., 1 Edw. III : ibid. p. 130.
Richard Dollyng, co. Soms., 1 Edw. III : p. 213.
1597-8. Daniel Dollinge and Ellen Harrison : Marriage Lic. (London), i. 247.
1617. Gilbert Knapp and Joan Dollin : ibid. ii. 55.
1639. Daniel Gookin and Mary Dolling : ibid. ii. 246.
London, 4, 0 ; Philadelphia, 3, 0 ; MDB. (co. Soms.), 1, 2.

Dollman, Dolman.—(1) Local, ' the dolman.' I suspect equivalent to Dale and Dallman, q.v. In the Yorkshire Poll Tax we find on p. 234, 'Adam Denman and Johannes de Den' (one who resided in the den or dean) ; also ' Johannes Dolman and Johanna de Dale ' (one who resided in the dale). (2) Local, ' the doleman,' one who resided at the dole or landmark ; v. Dole, Dowle, and Dowler.

Nicholas Doleman, co. Soms., 1 Edw. III : Kirby's Quest, p. 188.
Richard Doleman, co. Oxf., 1273. A.
Alice Dolman, temp. Eliz. Z.
1760. Married—James Moorhouse and Hannah Doleman : St. Geo. Han. Sq. i. 92.
London, 5, 4 ; Philadelphia, 0, 5 ; Boston (U.S.), 2, 0.

Dolphin, Dalphin.—Bapt.'the son of Dolphin' (Domesday, Dolfin) : Yonge, i. 156–7. Popular in France ; cf. Dauphin. For corrupted forms, v. Duffin ; cf. Dovenby, co. Cumb., a corruption of Dolphinby, and Dolphinholme, near Lancaster, both beyond doubt styled from the personal name of the early resident.

Dolfinus de Kirkeby, 21 Ric. II : Furness Coucher Book, i. 188.
Eva fil. Dolphine. J.
Johannes Dolfyn, 1379 : P. T. Yorks. p. 27.
Adam Dolfynson, 1379 : ibid. p. 284.
Annes Dolphyn, 1541 : Reg. St. Dionis Backchurch, p. 72.
John Dolfyn, co. York. W. 2.
William Dolfin, co. Suff., 1273. A.
Cf. Adam de Dolfynby, co. Cumb., 20 Edw. I. R.
1579. Buried — William Dowlphin, 90 yeares old : St. Peter, Cornhill, i. 127.
1606-7. Rowland Dolphenne, co. Worc. : Reg. Univ. Oxf. vol. ii. pt. ii. p. 293.
London, 1, 1 ; Crockford, 3, 0 ; Liverpool, 2, 0 ; Ribchester. 3, 0 ; Philadelphia, 6, 0.

Dombell.—Local ; v. Dumbell.

Domesday. — ? Local. Probably Lower is right in explaining this as local, ' from one of the many religious establishments to which the name of Maison-Dieu, *Domus-Dei*, or God's House, was given.'

Richard Domysday, rector of Fincnam co. Norf., 1434 : FF. vii. 362.
Richard Domesdaye, rector of Caldecote, co. Norf., 1435 : ibid. vi. 60.
Thomas Dumpysday, vicar of Wiggenhall (St. Mary Magdalen), 1399 : ibid. ix. 172.

Dominey, Dominy, Dominick.—Bapt. 'the son of Dominic' ; both masculine and feminine, Dominicus and Dominica ; in Spain, Domingo. For history of the name and saints so called, v. Yonge, i. 445. Dominey was the pet form. It has always been rare in England.

Dominicus de Buketon, Fines Roll, 19 Edw. II.
Domenyk Euan, C. R., 34 Hen. VI.
1576. Buried—Dennys Dominicus : St. Jas. Clerkenwell, iv. 18.
1615. Dominicke, wife Joannis Street, co. Wilts : Reg. Broad Chalke, p. 43.
1550. Buried—Mr. Domynyke, *prest* : St. Dionis Backchurch (London), p. 183.
1702. Married—Benjamin Domine to Mary Johnson : St. Michael, Cornhill, p. 51.

1796. Married—William Alcock and Fanny Dominy: St. Geo. nan. Sq. ii. 153. London, 1, 1, 0; New York, 0, 0, 15.

Domville, Donville.—Local; v. Dumville.

Donald, Donalds, Donaldson.—Bapt. 'the son of Donald.' The Scotch patronymic is Macdonald, but in the Lowlands and on the Border the more English form was Donalds and Donaldson.

Donaldus de Heselrigg, 35 Edw. III: Hodgson's Northumberland, iv. 80.
Donaldus Palfreman, 1379: P. T. Yorks. p. 76.
Johannes Danald, 1379: ibid. p. 267.
London, 8, 1, 19; New York, 15, 2, 53.

Doncaster.—Local, 'of Doncaster,' a well-known town in co. York. For a variant of the surname, v. Dancaster.

Ralph de Doncastre, co. York, 1273. A.
Andrew de Doncaster, *tewer*, 4 Edw. II: Freemen of York, i. 13.

For the occupation 'tewer,' v. Tuer.

Adam de Donecastre, 1379: P. T. Yorks. p. 65.
Ricardus de Donecastre, 1379: ibid. p. 24.
Johannes Doncastre, 1379: ibid. p. 45.
1407. William Doncastre, chaplain of Carrow, co. Norf.: FF. iv. 526.
1765. Married—John Hinge and Eliz. Doncaster: St. Geo. Han. Sq. i. 448.
London, 3; West Rid. (Yorks) Court Dir., 5.

Done, Doane, Doan.—Local, 'at the down,' from residence on the slope of the hill; v. Donne, Downe, or Downes. A variant peculiar to co. Chester, and found in the district. Doane has become the established American form.

Richard Done, of Chester, *ironmonger*, 1579: Wills at Chester (1545-1620), p. 55.
Catherine Done, of Manchester, 1608: ibid.
John Done, of Utkinton, co. Chester, *husbandman*, 1638: ibid. (1621-50), p. 67.
Thomas Done, of Warrington, *gentleman*, 1648: ibid.
1634. Married—Hugh Done and Ellen Fryer: St. Jas. Clerkenwell, iii. 65.
MDB. (co. Chester), 11, 0, 0; Manchester, 2, 0, 0; Boston (U.S.), 0, 29, 0; New York, 3, 18, 1.

Donkin, Dunkin.—Bapt. 'the son of Duncan,' a modification (imitative) towards such diminu-

tives as Wilkin, Tomkin, Watkin, &c.

'Sir Rufane Shaw Donkin (1773-1841), surveyor general of the Ordnance, belonged to a respectable Northumbrian family, said to be of Scotch descent, and originally named Duncan': Dict. Nat. Biog. xv. 218.
William fil. Donkani, co. Cumb., 20 Edw. I. R.
Alnon Donykyn, co. Soms., 1 Edw. III: Kirby's Quest, p. 96.
Richard Donykyn, co. Soms., 1 Edw. III: ibid.
1633. Thomas Cater to Elizabeth Dunkin: Canterbury Cathedral, p. 56.
1660. George Dunkin to Eliz. Lewis: St. Dionis Backchurch (London), p. 36.
London, 5, 6; New York, 0, 8; Boston (U.S.), 1, 0.

Donne, Donn, Don.—Local, 'at the down,' from residence on the slope of the hill; v. Downe.

Gilbert de la Donne, co. Essex, 1273. A.
Robert de la Donne, co. Kent, ibid.
Nicholas Donn, co. Oxf., ibid.
John Donne, rector of Matlask, co. Norf., 1386: FF. viii. 137.
Thomas Donne, of Holt-Market, co. Norf., 1685: ibid. iv. 333.
1645. Married—Edward Francis and Jahell Donn: St. Jas. Clerkenwell, iii. 78.
London, 5, 0, 0; New York, 1, 4, 0; Manchester, 0, 0, 2.

Donnett.—Bapt. 'the son of Donatus' or 'Donata'(Latin, *given*). The English form seems to have been Donnet; cf. *donet*, a primer, or grammar, by Donatus, 1466. 'Fore a donet for master George, 12d.': Sir John Howard's Household Book. 'Donet, *Donatus*': Prompt. Parv. p. 126.

'Donatus, prior of Windham, granted to Allan ... 5 acres of the demeans of Windham Convent': FF. ii. 516.
1594. Christopher Hamden and Elizabeth Donatt: Marriage Lic. (London), i. 215.
1637. Buried — Donnett Maddocke: Reg. St. Columb Major, p. 214.
1638. — Donet Duncomb: ibid. p. 215.
London, 1; Boston (U.S.), 1.

Doodson, Dootson.—Bapt. 'the son of Dod,' corruptions of Dodson (v. Dod).

Isabella Doodson, of Farnworth, 1634: Wills at Chester, p. 67.
John Doodson, of Kearsley, 1627: ibid. Manchester, 1, 1; Bolton, 2, 0; Philadelphia, 0, 2.

Dopson.—Bapt. 'the son of Robert,' from nick. Dob; a corruption of Dobson; cf. Hopps and Hopson for Hobbs and Hobson.

1770. Married—John Smith and Mary Dopson: St. Geo. Han. Sq. i. 196.
1797. — John Dopson, or Dobson, and Eliz. James: ibid. ii. 165.
London, 1.

Dorber.—Occup.; v. Dauber.

Dorchester.—Local, 'of Dorchester, (1) a borough and market-town in co. Dorset; (2) a parish in co. Oxford, four miles from Wallingford.

Agatha de Dorkcestre, co. Oxf., 1273. A.
Richard de Dorkcestre, co. Oxf., ibid.
Thomas de Dorchestre, co. Soms., 1 Edw. III: Kirby's Quest, p. 272.
John Dorchestre, co. Soms., 1 Edw. III: ibid. p. 277.
1622. Married—William Sherman and Alice Dorchester: St. Mary Aldermary, p. 15.
1777. — Andrew Symington and Mary Dorchester: St. Geo. Han. Sq. i. 276.
Boston (U.S.), 4.

Dore.—Local, 'of Dore,' a chapelry, co. Derby, and a parish, co. Hereford.

Thomas Dore, co. Bedf., 1273. A.
(Abbas) de Dore, co. Hereford, ibid.
Thomas de Dore, 1379: P. T. Yorks. p. 67.
1747. Married—Moses Dore and Rebeccah Rideant: St. Antholin (London), p. 154.
London, 11; New York, 12.

Dorey, Doree.—Local, 'of Dory.' I cannot identify the place.

Geoffrey de Dory, co. Linc., Hen. III: Edw. I. K.
John Dory, co. Linc., 1273. A.
Fulco Dory, co. Linc., ibid.
London, 3, 2; Philadelphia, 7, 0.

Dorling.— Nick.; v. Darling.

Dorman, Durman.—Offic. 'the doorman'; v. Dorward.

Nicholas Doreman. O.
1637. Married — John Dorman and Eliz. Hatton: St. Antholin (London), p. 71.
London, 2, 0; MDB. (co. Soms.), 0, 3; New York, 11, 0.

Dormer, Dormar.—? Local. I cannot find any earlier record of this surname than the references in the Yorkshire Poll Tax. These point to a local origin, -*mire* being a common suffix to North English local names; cf. Blamire, and v. Myers.

Willelmus Dormire, 1379: P. T. Yorks. p. 68.
Agnes Dormire, 1379: ibid.

1573-4. William Hawtrye and Joan Dormer: Marriage Lic. (London), i. 59.
1620. Married — John Wise and Thomasine Dormer: St. Dionis Backchurch, p. 20.
1809. — William Hodgson and Sarah Dormer: St. Geo. Han. Sq. ii. 409.
London, 9, 1; Philadelphia, 11, 0.

Dorrance.—An American variant of Durrans, q.v.

Dorset, Dorsett.—Local, 'of Dorset'; cf. Devon, Derbyshire, Cheshire, &c. Probably sometimes confounded with Dowsett, q.v.

Geoffrey de Dorsete, co. Soms., 1 Edw. III: Kirby's Quest, p. 87.
1545. Francis Dorcett and Anne Hopper: Marriage Lic. (Faculty Office), p. 4.
1572. Robert Dorset: Reg. Univ. Oxf. vol. ii. pt. ii. p. 23.
1748. Married—Robert Day and Susanna Dorset: St. Geo. Han. Sq. i. 41.
London, 2, 3; New York, 0, 6.

Dorturer, Dotterer.—Offic. 'the dorturer,' i.e. an attendant of the dortour, dorter, or dorture, a dormitory; Fr. *dortoir*, a sleeping chamber. 'Dortowre, *dortorium*': Prompt. Parv. 'Dorter, dortoir, dorture, the common room where all the Friars of one Convent sleep a' nights': Bailey's Dict., 1742. In the Monastical Church of Durham (1593), 'the chambre where he (the cellarer) dyd lye was in the dorter': p. 83. Heywood says:

'The tongue is assigned of wordes to be sorter;
The mouth is assigned to be the tongue's dorter.'

I suspect the 'Dorturer' of our rolls was an official in the household of the king or noble; one who looked to the sleeping accommodation.

William le Dortorer, Close Roll, 3 Edw. II.
Robert le Dorturer. B.
William le Dorturer. DD.
Cf. Robert de Wederhale, *del dortur*, 7 Edw. III: Freemen of York, i. 27.
Philadelphia, 0, 5.

Dorward, Durward, Dorwart.—Offic. 'the door-ward'; M.E. *dore*. This surname in the form of Durward has been immortalized by Walter Scott's Quentin Durward. v. Durknave.

'Alan Durward (or Alanus Ostiarius, Hostiarius, le Usher), justiciar of Scotland (d. 1268), was the son of Thomas Ostiarius. . . . Durward makes his first appear-

ance as Alan "Ostiarius domini Regis Scocie":' Dict. Nat. Biog. xvi. 266.
Geoffrey le Doreward, co. Essex, 1273. A.
Richard Doreward, co. Essex, ibid.
Elias Dorewarde. B.
Isabel Dorewarde. H.
John Durward. B.
London, 1, 0, 0; Philadelphia, 0, 1, 5.

Dosier, Dossor.—Occup. 'the dosier.' Perhaps a manufacturer of dosers, i.e. tapestry hangings (v. Doser, Halliwell).

Richard le Dosyere, co. Oxf., 1273. A.
Robert le Dosier, co. Oxf., ibid.
Walter le Dosier, co. Oxf., ibid.
Gilbert le Dosser, co. Essex, ibid.
John Dawson. EE.
East Rid. Yorks (Hutton Cranswick), 0, 1.

Dosset.—? Local. A corruption of Dorset, q.v. If not this, it must be baptismal, and be a corruption of Dowsett (q.v.), which seems the more natural interpretation.

1575. Thomas Dossett and Alice Abraham: Marriage Lic. (London), i. 65.
1769. Married—Thomas Dossett and Mary Brackney: St. Geo. Han. Sq. i. 187.
London, 2; Philadelphia, 2.

Dottridge.—Local; v. Doddridge, of which it is a manifest corruption.

Doubble, Doubell, Double, Dobell, Doble.—? Bapt. 'the son of Dobel,' one of the many personal names ending in *el*. The genitive Dobels is strongly confirmatory of this view; cf. Williams, Jones, Tompkins, &c.

Hamo Dubel, co. Norf., 1273. A.
William Dubel, or Dobel, or de Dobil, co. Norf., ibid.
James Dobell, of Bungeye, rector of Markshall, co. Norf., 1300: FF. v. 48.
Edmund Double, co. Norf., 41 Eliz.: ibid. viii. 272.
David Dobel, co. Soms., 1 Edw. III: Kirby's Quest, p. 170.
Alicia Dobeles, co. Soms., 1 Edw. III: ibid.
1809. Married—William Double and Sarah Dainton: St. Geo. Han. Sq. ii. 410.
London, 6, 2, 5, 9, 6; Boston (U.S.), 0, 0, 2, 0, 2.

Doubleday.—?Nick. 'Dubledent,' i.e. double-tooth. This surname, which troubled Mr. Lower sorely, and over which I myself have spent many a miserable ten minutes, is probably as explained above; cf. Dent-de-fer, Dandelion, and Duredent, i.e. hard-tooth.

Johannes Dubledent, co. Essex: Pipe Roll, 10 Hen. II. p. 36.
1625. Married — Edward Foxley and Judith Doubleday: St. Antholin (London), p. 59.
London, 3; New York, 9.

Doublet. — Nick. 'doublet,' from the wearer's custom of using that garment; cf. Curthose, &c.

John Doublet, Close Roll, 7 Ric. II. London, 1.

Douce. — Bapt. 'the son of Douce'; v. Dowse.

1758. Married—John Douse and Ann Smith: St. Geo. Han. Sq. i. 82.
1761. — Simon Peirce and Sarah Douse: ibid. p. 100.
London, 2.

Douceamour.—Nick. of endearment; v. Sweetlove. Cf. Paramor, Finnemore, Phillimore.

Robert Douceamour, Close Roll, 8 Edw. IV.
Felicia Duzamour: Domesday, St. Paul's, Camden Soc.

Doucedame. — Nick. 'sweet lady.' Cf. Douceamour.

Roger Ducedame, London, 1273. A.

Doughty.—Nick. 'the doughty,' i.e. the strong, the valiant; M.E. *duhti* and *dohti*.

John Dughti, de Strensall, *carnifex*, 8 Edw. II: Freemen of York, i. 16.
Johanna Doughti, 1379: P. T. Yorks. p. 133.
Johannes Doughty, *taylour*, 1379: ibid. p. 165.
Adam Doughty, 1379: ibid. p. 103.
Robertus Dughty, 1379: P. T. Howdenshire, p. 12.
Johannes Dughti, 1379: ibid.
1632. Bapt.—John, s. Richard Dowtye: St. Jas. Clerkenwell, i. 121.
Edward Doughtie, of Stockport, *clerk*, 1616: Wills at Chester (1545-1620), p. 55.
1806. Married—Daniel Doughty and Ann Gray: St. Geo. Han. Sq. ii. 348.
London, 22; Boston (U.S.), 5.

Doulman, Dowlman.—Variants of Dollman, q.v.; cf. Coulson for Colson, Coules for Coles, &c.

MDB. (co. Lincoln), 1, 2.

Douthart, Douthwaite. — Local; v. Dowthwaite.

Dove.—Nick. 'the dove,' a sobriquet affixed on account of the gentle character of the original bearer; cf. Pidgeon, Woodcock, Nightingale, &c. Hawk would be a nickname representing the opposite characteristic.

Richard le Duv, c. 1300. M.
Nicholas le Duv, ibid.
Richard Dove, co. Norf., 20 Edw. I. R.
1759. Married—Joseph Drew and Mary Dove: St. Geo. Han. Sq. i. 84.
London, 14; Philadelphia, 7.

Dover.—Local, 'of Dover,' one of the cinque ports, situated in co. Kent.

Richard de Dovere, co. Bedf., 20 Edw. I. R.
Godwinus de Dovre. C.
Fuker de Dovre, co. Linc., Hen. III-Edw. I. K.
Hugo de Dovre, co. Wilts, ibid.
John de Dovere, co. Hunts, 1273. A.
1668. Bapt.—Saray, d. Franses Dover: St. Jas. Clerkenwell, i. 236.
1793. Married—James Dover and Millicent Frost: St. Geo. Han. Sq. ii. 89.
London, 5; Philadelphia, 9.

Dow, Dowe.—Bapt. 'the son of David,' from nick. Daw or Dow; v. Dawson for many instances.

Agnes Dowe, 1379: P. T. Yorks. p. 58.
Hugo Dowe, 1379: ibid. p. 191.
Alicia Dowe, 1379: ibid.
Adam Dowe-man, i. e. the servant of Dow, 1379: ibid. p. 202.
1573-4. William Dowe and Ellenor Ellyott: Marriage Lic. (London), i. 59.
London, 8, 0; New York, 18, 1.

Dowbiggin, Dowbekin.—Local, 'of Dowbiggin,' a hamlet in the parish of Sedbergh, W. Rid. Yorks.

Johannes de Dowfbyggyng, 1379: P. T. Yorks. p. 289.
Robertus de Dowfebyging, 1379: ibid.
Christopher Dowbikine, of Tatham, 1613: LancashireWills at Richmond, i. 97.
John Dowbiggin, of Tatham, 1678: ibid.

For the probable origin of this name, v. Duff.

Liverpool, 1, 0; Bolton, 0, 1.

Dowdall, Dowdle, Dowdell.—Local, 'of Dowdale,' seemingly a Yorkshire place-name.

Nicholaus de Dodale, 1379: P. T. Yorks. p. 117.
Johannes de Dowedale, 1379: ibid.
Willelmus de Dowedale, 1379: ibid.
Willelmus Doudale, 1379: ibid. p. 84.
1773. Married — James Dowdell and Mary Morris: St. Geo. Han. Sq. i. 235.
1775. — James Vicary and Grace Dowdle: ibid. p. 252.
1801. Henry Kusder and Jane Dowdall: ibid. ii. 242.
London, 1, 1, 0; Liverpool, 3, 0, 0; New York, 2, 0, 7.

Dowdeswell, Dowderswell.—Local, 'of Dowdeswell,' a parish in co. Gloucester, four miles from Cheltenham.

William de Doudeswell, co. Oxf., 1273. A.
Robert de Doudeswell, co. Glouc., ibid.
1682. William Dowdeswell, of Aston, co. Glouc., and Eliz. Gibbard: Marriage Lic. (Faculty Office), p. 160.
1778. Married—William Weller Pepys and Eliz. Dowdeswell: St. Geo. Han. Sq. i. 278.
London, 2, 0; MDB. (co. Glouc.), 10, 1; New York, 1, 0.

Dowell.—Local, 'at the dowl'; v. Dowle. A variant. 'John Dowle' was High Sheriff of Gloucestershire in 1624. His father was 'James Dowel,' a wealthy Bristol merchant; v. Atkyns, Hist. Gloucestershire, pp. 40, 110. The variation is a very natural one.

London, 6; MDB. (Gloucestershire), 1; Philadelphia, 2.

Dowland, Douland, Dowlind.—Local, 'of Dowland,' a parish in co. Devon. The Yorkshire instance seems to imply another Dowland in that county, especially as the surname is fairly familiar in the North.

Willelmus de Dowland,-1379: P. T. Yorks. p. 268.
1626. Robert Dowland and Jane Smalley: Marriage Lic.(London), ii. 177.
1794. Married—Thomas Feeny and Mary Dowland: St. Geo. Han. Sq. ii. 120.
MDB. (co. Wilts), 1, 0, 0; (co. Somerset), 0, 1, 1; Manchester, 1, 0, 0; MDB. (Lincoln), 1, 0, 0.

Dowle, Dowler.—Local, 'at the dowl,' or 'the dowler,' one who lived at the dowl; v. Dole. 'Dole, merke, *meta, tramaricia*': Prompt. Parv. Way has an important note on this. 'Forby gives this word as still used in Norfolk, the mark being often a low post, called a dool-post. . . . Bishop Kennet states that landmarks, or boundary stones, are in some parts of Kent called "dowle-stones," and explains *dole*, or *doul*, as signifying "a bulk, or green narrow slip of ground left unplowed in arable land." . . . Queen Elizabeth in her Injunctions, 1559, directs that at the customary perambulations on the Rogation Days, the

admonition shall be given, "cursed be he which translateth the boundes and dolles of his neighbor."' It is thus made clear that *dowle* was a form of *dole*, or *doll* (a partition). Thomas at the dowle, or William Dowler, meant one who resided on such a strip of ground, or by such a landmark. An instance in co. Cambridge is given under Dole, q.v.

Hugo de Doole, co. Surrey, Hen. III-Edw. I. K.

With Dowler, cf. Downer, Bridger, Churcher, &c.

1762. Married — John Stevens and Sarah Dowle: St. Geo. Han. Sq. i. 115.
1769. — George Dowler and Margery Lee: ibid. p. 187.
London, 3, 1; Philadelphia, 1, 5; New York, 1, 1.

Dowlman ; v. Doulman.

Dowman. — (1) Local, 'of Downham,' abbreviated from Downman; v. Downman and Downham. (2) Occup. 'Dow's man,' i. e. the servant of Dow, or Daw (David); v. Dow and Dowson (2), and cf. Matthewman, Priestman, &c. This class of surnames is chiefly found in Yorkshire.

Adam Doweman, 1379: P. T. Yorks. p. 202.
William Dawman, 1379: ibid. p. 249.
1570. Robert Dowman and Ellen Towres: Marriage Lic. (London), i. 45.
1774. Married—Charles Dowman and Sarah Thompson: St. Geo. Han. Sq. i. 242.
Crockford, 1.

Downe, Downes, Down, Downs.—Local, 'of the Downs,' i. e. the sloping declivity, from residence thereby.

Gilbert de la Donne, co. Essex, 1273. A.
Matilda de la Don, co. Devon, ibid.
Henry de la Dune, co. Sussex, ibid.
Sibil atte Doune, co. Soms., 1 Edw. III: Kirby's Quest, p. 128.
John atte Doune, co. Soms., 1 Edw. III: ibid.
May Downe, 1379: P. T. Yorks. p. 130.
Johannes Downe, 1379: ibid.
Willelmus de Doynes, 1379: ibid. 213.

The following occur in the list of Mayors of Macclesfield :

Reginald del Downes, 1407: East Cheshire, ii. 464.
Reginald del Downes, 1445: ibid.

Peter Downes, Esq., 1779: ibid. p. 467.
Edward Downes, Esq., 1810: ibid.
1703. Married — Thomas Pollet and Misericordia Down: St. Antholin (London), p. 116.
London, 1, 22, 14, 11; Philadelphia, 0, 17, 5, 58.

Downer.—Local, 'the downer,' one who resided on the down (v. Downe); cf. Bridger, &c.
1683. William Downer and Barbara Greene: Marriage. Alleg. (Canterbury), p. 150.
1727. Married — Simon Hinton and Eliz. Downer, Great Marlow, Bucks: St. Geo. Han. Sq. i. 4.
London, 2; Philadelphia, 4.

Downham.—Local, 'of Downham,' parishes in cos. Cambridge, Essex, Lancaster, Norfolk, and Suffolk.
Clemence de Dunham, co. Camb., 1273. A.
Robert de Dunham, co. Norf., ibid.
John de Dunham, co. Linc., ibid.
Stephen de Dunham, co. Suff., ibid.
Roger Dounham, co. Soms., 1 Edw. III: Kirby's Quest, p. 199.
Willelmus de Downom, 1379: P. T. Yorks. p. 264.
Johannes Downom, 1379: ibid. p. 215.
Johannes de Donnom, 1379: ibid. p. 218.
1802. Married—Robert Downham and Margaret Renton: St. Geo. Han. Sq. ii. 257.
London, 4.

Downing.—Bapt.; v. Dunning.

Downman, Dunman.—(1) Local, 'the Down-man,' one who resided on the down (v. Downe); cf. Bridgman, Dallman, &c.
John Dunman, co. Oxf., 1273. A.
William Dunman, co. Oxf., ibid.

(2) Local, 'of Downham' (q.v.), corrupted to Downman; cf. Putman, Deadman, Sweetman, &c.
Robert Downnam, or Doneman, or Downeman, B.A., 1579: Reg. Univ. Oxf. vol. ii. pt. iii. p. 87.
'William Downham, whose name is sometimes spelt Downame and Downman (1505-77), bishop of Chester, was born in Norfolk in 1505': Dict. Nat. Biog. xv. 397.
1796. Married—Thomas Dunman and Ann Melsom: St. Geo. Han. Sq. ii. 143.
London, 1, 1; Crockford, 3, 0.

Downton.—Local, 'of Downton,' (1) a parish in co. Wilts, six miles from Salisbury; (2) a parish in co. Hereford, three miles from Leintwardine.
Isabella de Dunton, co. Salop, 1233. A.
Jordan de Dontone, co. Oxf., ibid.

1632. Bapt. — Bridgett, d. Thomas Downton: St. Jas. Clerkenwell, i. 120.
1730. Married—William Cartwright and Jane Downton: St. Geo. Chap. Mayfair, p. 315.
London, 5; Crockford, 4.

Dowsabell.—Bapt. 'the son of Dowsabell,' the same as Dulcibella.
William Dassabele, co. Soms., 1 Edw. III: Kirby's Quest, p. 266.
Dowsabell Cobbe, co. Norf. FF.
Dowzable Mill, temp. Eliz. Z.
Dussabell Caplyn, ibid.
Thomas Duszabell, c. 1300. M.

Dowse, Dows, Dowson.— Bapt. 'the son of Douce' (sweet). A French introduction, a girl's name, v. Dowson.
Duce Mercatrix, 1273. A.
Douce de Moster, ibid.
William Douce, 1313. M.
Matilda Douce-douther (the daughter of Douce), 1379: P. T. Yorks. p. 83.
Ricardus Schepherd: Douse, mater ejus, 1379: ibid. p. 91.
John fil. Douse, co. York. W. 5.
John Dowsson, temp. Eliz. Z.
1807. Married — Thomas Townsend and Sarah Jemima Dowse: St. Geo. Han. Sq. ii. 370.
1808. — James Dows and Ann Wickenden: ibid. p. 381.
— — William Dowson and Eliz. Morgan: ibid. p. 386.
London, 7, 1, 4; New York, 0, 4, 0; Philadelphia (Dowson), 1; Boston (U.S.) (Dowse), 7.

Dowsett.—Bapt. 'the son of Douce,' dim. Douset or Dousot.
Walter fil. Dussote, 1273. A.
John Doucett. PP.
1675-6. John Dowsett and Amy Clerk: Marriage Lic. (Faculty Office), p. 136.
1789. Married—Thomas Stinton and Mary Dowset: St. Geo. Han. Sq. ii. 30.
London, 7; Boston (U.S.), 1; New York, 1.

Dowsing.—Bapt. 'the son of Douce,' dim. Dousin, now Dowsing, with excrescent g as in Jennings, i.e. Jenin-s; v. Dowse.
Jordan Dousing, co. Linc., 1273. A.
Richard Dusing, co. Norf., ibid.
Johannes Dousyng, 1379: P. T. Yorks. p. 166.
1669. Married—Nicholas Doussin and Eliz. Coleman: St. Jas. Clerkenwell, iii. 159.
1796. — Thomas Dowsing and Ann Dakin: St. Geo. Han. Sq. ii. 148.
London, 2.

Dowson.—(1) Bapt. 'the son of Douce,' q.v. The evidence is in favour of this being the chief parent.

Richard Doucesone, co. Soms., 1 Edw. III: Kirby's Quest, p. 125.
Johannes Douceson, 1379: P. T. Howdenshire, p. 20.
Emmota Douceson, 1379: ibid.
John fil. Douse. W. 5.
John Dowsson. Z.

(2) Bapt. 'the son of David,' nick. Daw and Dow; v. Dow.
Beatrix Daude-wyf, 1379: P. T. Yorks. p. 218.
Johannes Dauson, 1379: ibid.
Johanna Dowe-doghter, 1379: ibid.
Ricardus Dauson, 1379: ibid.
Adam Dowe-man, 1379: ibid. p. 202.
Agnes Dyconwyfdowson, i.e. the wife of Dycon, son of Dow, 1379: ibid. p. 226.
London, 4; Philadelphia, 1.

Dowthwaite, Douthwaite, Douthwait, Douthart, Douthert, Douthirt.—Local, 'of Dowthwaite,' some small spot on the borders of North Lancashire and the West Riding, but I cannot identify it. This surname has crossed the Atlantic and has undergone several natural corruptive changes. The suffix -thwaite (v. Thwaites) seems curiously susceptible to corruption (v. Hebblewhite). In my old church register (Ulverston) Postlethwaite is occasionally found as Poslett.
Robertus de Dowthwayt, 1379: P. T. Yorks. p. 248.
1572. Richard Ayleward and Joanna Duffwheate: Marriage Lic. (London), i. 52.
John Dowthwayte, of Cappen, Capenburrow, 1667: Lancashire Wills at Richmond, i. 97.
Thomas Dowthwayte, of Newton, 1662: ibid.
1714. Married—Barnard Dowthwaite and Mary Chandler: St. Dionis Backchurch, p. 57.
1733. Bapt.—Robert, s. John Dowthwait, of Kendal: St. Mary, Ulverston, ii. 321.
Sheffield, 0, 2, 0, 0, 0, 0; Liverpool, 1, 0, 1, 0, 0, 0; London, 1, 0, 0, 0, 0, 0; Philadelphia, 0, 0, 0, 2, 3, 2.

Doxey, Doxsey, Docksey.— Local, 'of Docksey.' I have not discovered the spot. It seems to mean the islet in the stream where the docks grew plentifully. The surname has always been a rare one, but it is found at an early period.
Hugh de Dokesey, cos. Salop and Staff., Hen. III-Edw. I. K.
Robert de Dockesey, co. Wilts, 1273. A.

1582. Married — John Sandes and Wynnifrid Dockeysaye: Ulverston Church, i. 79.

1592. Bapt. — Marie Dockesye, alias Turner: Prestbury Church, E. Cheshire.

1739. Married — Thomas Doxey and Mary Fell: St. Geo. Han. Sq. i. 23.

London, 0, 1, 0; Manchester, 3, 0, 0; Lanc. Court Dir., 1, 0, 1; Philadelphia, 2, 0, 0.

Doyle, D'Oyle, Doyley. — Local, 'de Oilgi,' or 'de Ouilli,' in Normandy. Lower says, 'Doyle, one of the commonest of Irish surnames, and presumed to be of Anglo-Norman origin.' This is confirmed by a large number of English instances. A fair proportion of the Doyles of our directories have never had any connexion with Ireland. Probably it is the same as D'Oyley. Lower adds, · Robert de Oilgi was a tenant-in-chief in many counties, and Wido de Oilgi in co. Oxf. (Domesday).' 'It was probably from Ouilli-le-Bassett, in the canton of Falaise, written in the 11th century Oillei, the family originated': Patr. Brit. p. 94. v. Dolley.

Robert Doilli, co. Oxf., Hen. III-Edw. I. K.

Richard de Oyli, co. Oxf., ibid.

Henry Doilly, co. Oxf., ibid.

Matilda de Oylly, co. Dorset, 1273. A.

Dominus de Doyli, co. Oxf., ibid.

Henry de Oyly, or de Oylly, or Oyli, or Doyli, or Doylly, or Doyly, or Doyl, co. Oxf., ibid.

John de Oyly, co. Stafford, 20 Edw. I. R.

Juliana Doyle, 1379: P. T. Yorks. p. 20.

Johannes Doyle, et Alicia uxor ejus, 1379: ibid. p. 28.

Katerina Doylle, 1379: ibid. p. 56.

1643. Buried—Francis Doyley: St. Peter, Cornhill, i. 200.

London, 9, 2, 1; New York, 258, 0, 0.

Drabble, Drabel.—Bapt. 'the son of Drabel' (?). Probably a baptismal name, but another origin must obviously be suggested, that of *drabble*, a slattern; cf. Drabble-tail. 'Draplyd (drablyd, K.), *paludosus*': Prompt. Parv. p. 129.

Willelmus Drabill', 1379: P. T. Yorks. p. 199.

Ricardus Dobrell', 1379: ibid.

Robertus Drabill', 1379: ibid. p. 85.

Harvey Drabil, co. Camb., 1273. A.

Geoffrey Drabel, or Drapol, co. Camb., ibid.

Matthew Drabel, co. Warw., ibid.

1782. Married—William North and Martha Drabble: St. Geo. Han. Sq. i. 333.

1797. — Thomas Hotchkiss and Mary Drabble: ibid. ii. 166.

West Rid. Court Dir., 6, 0; London, 2, 0; Philadelphia, 0, 1.

Drage.—? ——

John Dragge, co. Soms., 1 Edw. III: Kirby's Quest, p. 101.

1667. Married—Thomas Dradge and Eliz. Ginces: St. Jas. Clerkenwell: iii. 131.

1740. — Thomas Pacey and Alice Drage: ibid. p. 269. London, 6.

Dragon.—Nick. 'the dragon,' a winged serpent; M.E. *dragun*; Fr. *dragon*.

Walter le Dragon, or Dragun, co. Linc., 1273. A.

William le Dragon, co. Linc., ibid.

Thomas Dragon: Fines Roll, 8 Ric. II.

Robert Dragon, C. R., 24 Edw. III. pt. ii.

William Dragoun, 1281: Royal Letters, No. 1854.

This surname seems to have become extinct. I cannot find any modern instances.

Drain.—Local, 'at the drain,' from residence thereby. In several cases the Philadelphia directory spells the name Drahn, implying in those instances a continental origin.

John atte Drene, co. Soms., 1 Edw. III: Kirby's Quest, p. 116.

London, 6; Philadelphia, 9.

Drake.—Nick. 'the drake'; cf. Duck, Goose (but not Gosling, q.v.), Wildgoose, &c.

Richard le Drake, co. Lanc., 1332: Lay Subsidy (Rylands), p. 39.

Adam le Drake. B.

Martin le Drake. E.

Seman Drake, co. Camb., 1273. A.

Stephen Drake, co. Soms., 1 Edw. III: Kirby's Quest, p. 117.

Ricardus Drake, et Magota uxor ejus, 1379: P. T. Yorks. p. 57.

Johannes Drac, 1379: ibid. p. 193.

1645. Married — Thomas Martin and Sarah Drake: St. Dionis Backchurch, p. 24.

London, 33; Philadelphia, 43.

Drakeford.—Local, 'of Drakeford.' I have not found the spot.

1602. William Drakeford, of Congleton, co. Ches.: Earwaker's Hist. East Cheshire, ii. 241, n.

1617. John Drakeford, of Withington,

co. Lanc. 1617: Wills at Chester (1545-1620), p. 56.

1753. Married—Joseph Drakford and Sina Hughs: St. Geo. Han. Sq. i. 50.

1790. — Thomas Drakeford and Eliz. Evans: ibid. ii. 42.

London, 3; Liverpool, 1.

Drakes.—Local; v. Drax.

Dranfield, Dransfield; v. Dronsfield.

Draper, Drapper, Dreaper. —Occup. 'the draper,' a dealer in cloth.

Henry le Draper, co. Lanc., 1332: Lay Subsidy (Rylands), p. 51.

Roger le Draper, co. Wilts, 1273. A.

Auwred le Draper, co. Camb., ibid.

Roger le Drapere, co. Soms., 1 Edw. III: Kirby's Quest, p. 225.

Rogerus de Croshawe, *drapour*, 1379: P. T. Yorks. p. 4.

Johannes Drapour, *drapour*, 1379: ibid. p. 117.

1642. Buried—Mr. William Claxston, a *drapper*: St. Mary Aldermary (London), p. 172.

London, 33, 2, 1; Crockford, 6, 0, 3; Philadelphia, 21, 0, 0.

Drawbridge. — Local, 'at the draw-bridge,' from residence thereby.

1748. Married—John Drawbridge and Mary Watts: St. Geo. Han. Sq. i. 41.

London, 2; Liverpool, 1.

Drawespe.—Nick. A mongrel form of English Drawsword; q.v.; Fr. *épée*, sword.

Thomas Drawespe, co. Oxf., 1273. A.

William Drauespe, co. Hunts, ibid.

Drawsword.—Nick. A cant term for an over-zealous official; cf. Catchpoll, Shakespear, Wagstaff, &c. One of a large class. M.E. *swerd*.

Henry Draweswerd, co. Camb., 1273. A.

Maurice Draughswerd, 1313. M.

Thomas Drawsweryd, 1487, co. York. W. 11.

Thomas Drawswerd, vicar of Thrickby, co. Norf., 1492: FF. xi. 254.

I fear the surname is extinct.

Drax, Drakes. — Local, 'of Drax,' a valley near Selby, co. York.

Prior de Drax, co. York, 1273. A.

Alanus de Drax, 1379: P. T. Yorks. p. 39.

Robertus de Drax, 1379: ibid. p. 83.

1662. Hugh Frankland and Mary Drax: Marriage Lic. (Faculty Office), p. 63.

— Married — Hugh Fraunclyn and Mary Draxe: St. Jas. Clerkenwell, iii. 109.

1665-6. Henry Drakes and Catherine Marshall: Marriage Lic. (Faculty Office), p. 90.
MDB. (co. Lincoln), 1, 2.

Draycott.—Local, 'of Draycot.' parishes in dioc. Glouc. and Bristol, Salisbury, Lichfield, and Bath and Wells.

John de Draycote, co. Somerset, 1273. A.
Richard de Draycote, co. Oxf., ibid.
Adam de Dracote, co. Soms., 1 Edw. III : Kirby's Quest, p. 104.
Richard de Draycot, cos. Salop and Staff., Hen. III–Edw. I. K.
Alan de Dreycote, co. Wilts, ibid.
William de Draicote, rector of Sutton, co. Norf., 1346 : FF. ix. 347.
1504. Married—Thomas Dracott and Susan Buggins : St. Jas. Clerkenwell, iii. 19.
1789. — Robert Moggridge and Ann Draycott : St. Geo. Han. Sq. ii. 17.
London, 1.

Drayson.—Bapt. 'the son of Drew,' q.v. This is found sometimes as Dreye in the Hundred Rolls in. co. Camb.

Hugh Droye, co. Camb., 1273. A.
Stephen Dreye, co. Camb., ibid.
MDB. (co. Northampton), 2 ; London, 3.

Drayton.—Local, ' of Drayton.' There are no less than sixteen parishes in the same set down in Crockford : in dioceses of Bath and Wells, Norwich, Oxford, Peterborough, Lichfield, Southwell, London, and Ely.

Matilda de Drayton, co. Camb., 1273. A.
Beatrix de Draytone, co. Hunts, ibid.
Simon de Drayton, co. Warw., Hen. III–Edw. I. K.
Johannes de Drayton, 1379 : P. T. Yorks. p. 126.
Willelmus de Draghton, 1379 : ibid. p. 270.
Robertus de Draghton, 1379 : ibid.
Richard de Drayton, bailiff of Yarmouth, 1284 : FF. xi. 322.
1576. Married—William Drayton and Margaret Topley : St. Jas. Clerkenwell, iii. 7.
London, 5 ; Philadelphia, 9.

Draywater. — Nick. ' Drawwater,' the sobriquet of a waterman, a drawer of water ; v. Waterman, Waterleader.

Richard Drawater, co. Bucks, 1273. A.
1623. Married—Richard Lussell and Anne Drawater : St. Jas. Clerkenwell, iii. 52.
1624. Buried—Ann Drawater, sister to John Piggot's wife : St. Peter, Cornhill, i. 182.
1656. — Mathew Drawater, stacioner : St. Thomas the Apostle (London), p. 131. London, 1.

Draywoman. — Occup. ' the dray-woman,' the feminine of drayman.

Joan Dreywooman : Privy Seal Bills, Nov. 16, 1565 (7 Eliz.).

Dreaper.—Occup. ; v. Draper.

Dresser.—Occup. ' the dresser.' Probably a gardener, a dresser of plants.

Raphe Dresser, temp. Eliz. Z.
John Dresser, co. York. W. 16.
London, 4.

Drew, Drewe, Drews, Druce, Drewes.—Bapt. ' the son of Drew,' or ' Dru' (Drogo in Domesday). Dru de Baladon introduced it, a follower of the Conqueror (Yonge, ii. 465). Sir Drew Drury was keeper of Mary of Scotland. An illegitimate son of Charlemagne bore it, so probably it is Frankish. Drew enjoyed a fair share of public favour, but only took one diminutive, Druett or Drewett, q.v. Drew has nothing to do with Andrew. In the year 1400 Drew Barentyn, twice Lord Mayor of London, came before the Council, asking to have his name Drew set down in the list of those who possessed the freedom of the city, the scribe having entered it as Andrew (Riley's Memorials of London, p. 554). Drew, as a fontal name, survived the Reformation.

1583. Buried—Drew, sonne of Nicholas Hewet : St. Peter, Cornhill, i. 23.
1620. Married—Drue Simonds and Eliz. Willington : St. Dionis Backchurch, p. 20.
William fil. Drogonis, co. Linc., 1273. A.
Eborard Dru, co. Camb., ibid.
Isouda Drewe, co. Hunts, ibid.
Gilbert Dreu, co. Oxf., ibid.
Johannes Drewe, 1379 : P. T. Yorks. p. 62.
Robertus Drue, 1379 : ibid. p. 73.
Richard Drue, or Drew, bailiff of Norwich, 1392 : FF. iii. 116.
1527. John Drewes and Dame Eliz. Verney : Marriage Lic. (London), i. 6.

Druce is a modern but inevitable variant of Drews ; cf. Ellice for Ellis, or Evance for Evans, but v. Druce (2).

1803. Married—James Druce and Sarah Dutton : St. Geo. Han. Sq. ii. 276.
London, 57, 1, 0, 23, 0 ; New York, 47, 0, 1, 0, 1.

Drewery, Drewry ; v. Drury.

Drewett, Drewet, Druitt.—Bapt. ' the son of Drew,' or ' Dru,' of which personal name the dim. was Drewett, or Druett ; v. Drew.

Druettus Malerbe, co. Northampt., 1273. A.

This landowner is elsewhere entered as Drogo Malerbe, which settles any doubts, if such existed, as to the relationship between Druett and Dru.

Druett de Pratello, co. Oxf., 1273. A.
Hugh Druet, co. Soms., 1 Edw. III : Kirby's Quest, p. 207.
1583. Thomas Ryckner and Dorothy Drewett : Marriage Lic. (London), i. 121.
1788. Married—Josiah Ebborn and Mary Drewett : St. Geo. Han. Sq. ii. 2.
— — John Drewitt and Ann Lancaster : ibid. p. 8.
1792. — Thomas Druitt and Ann Lemon : ibid. p. 71.
London, 7, 1, 8 ; New York, 1, 0, 0.

Driffield. Driffill.—Local, ' of Driffield,' (1) two parishes in E. Rid. Yorks ; (2) a parish in co. Glouc., four miles from Cirencester. The variant Driffield is a common corruption of -field as a suffix in place-words ; cf. Duffill for Duffield.

Thomas de Driffeld, co. Oxf., 1273. A.
Hugh de Driffeud (sic). co. York, ibid.
Johannes de Dryffeld, 1379 : P. T. Yorks. p. 22.
1669. Married—Rauley Rattford and Hester Driffeild : St. Jas. Clerkenwell, iii. 165.
West Rid. Court Dir., 1, 0 ; MDB. (co. Lincoln), 2, 6 ; New York, 0, 1.

Dring. Thring.—Occup. ' the dreng.' Halliwell says, ' Drenges, a class of men who held a rank between a baron and a thayn.' Sir Henry Ellis in his Introduction to Domesday says, ' The *drenchs* or *drenghs* were of the description of allodial tenants, and from the few entries in which they occur, it certainly appears that the allotments of territory which they possessed were held as manors.' Whatever the title implied, one thing is certain, it became a surname, and flourishes in the 19th century.

William Dreng, co. Soms., 1 Edw. III : Kirby's Quest, p. 95.

'Dreng de Trocchelai,'1161: KKK. vi. 6.
William fil. Patrick Dring, 1219 : ibid.
p. 121.
Robertus Dring, 1379 : P. T. Yorks.
p. 12.
John Dreng, co. York, 1273. A.
1690. Married—Joseph Crockford and
Dorcas Dring: St. Jas. Clerkenwell,iii.207.
1779. — Robert Dring and Sarah
Gardiner : St. Geo. Han. Sq. i. 302.
London, 6, 3 ; Boston (U.S.), 1, 0 ;
MDB. (co Lincoln), 12, 1.

**Drinkale, Drinkhall, Drink-
hill, Drinkall.**—Nick. for one
who loved the ale-cup. It is as
natural a sobriquet as Drinkwater.
But it may be local, of course, with
suffix *-hale* or *-hall* ; v. Hale.

Elewan Drynkhale, co. Norf., 1273. A.
Thomas Drinkale, 1379 : P. T. Yorks.
p. 153.
Willelmus Drinkale, 1379 : ibid. p. 193.
George Drinckhall, of Mannor, parish
of Dalton, 1690 : Lancashire Wills at
Richmond (1681-1748), p. 90.
Ralph Drinckhall, of Russeland in
Furness Fells, 1690 : ibid.
Liverpool, 0, 1, 0, 0 ; MDB. (co. Notts),
0, 0, 1, 1.

Drinkdregs.—Nick. for an old
toper, one who drained his cup to
the last drop.

Geoffrey Dringkedregges. V. 8.

Drinker.—Nick. 'the'drinker,'
a tippler, a toper.

Walter le Drinkere, Close Roll, 25
Edw. I.
William Drynker, Patent Roll, 19 Eliz.
pt. vi.
1684. Married—Richard Drinker and
Elianor Bryhtll : Reg. Canterbury Cath.
p. 62.
Philadelphia, 1 ; New York, 4.

Drinkwater.—? Nick. There is
no evidence, so far as I am aware,
to support Camden's statement that
Drinkwater is a corruption of Derwentwater, q.v. The name is found
in the 13th century in its simple
form, and no doubt was the sobriquet of some early teetotalers ;
cf. Drunkard, Sober.

John Drinkewater, co. Salop, 1273. A.
Richard Drynkewatere, 1309. M.
1586. Married—Hamlett Drinkwater
and Anne Tyndall : St. Jas. Clerkenwell,
iii. 12.
1652. Bapt.—Francis, s. Francis Drinkwater : St. Dionis Backchurch, p. 111.
London, 7 ; Manchester, 16 ; Philadelphia, 6.

Driver.—Occup. 'the driver.'
A surname that would naturally be
perpetuated ; cf. Carter, Wagner,

Cartman, Charter, Carrier, Packer,
&c.

William le Dryver, co. Lanc., 1332 :
Lay Subsidy (Rylands), p. 85.
John le Drivere, c. 1300. M.
Richard le Drivere, ibid.
Johannes Dryver, 1379 : P. T. Yorks.
p. 267.
Cf. fem. Alicia le Driveres, co. Camb.,
1273. A.
Cf. Hunter and Huntress.

1563. Married—John Dryver and Alice
Edwardes : St. Jas. Clerkenwell, iii. 2.
1667. — Richard Driver and Judey
Hinsman : ibid. p. 131.
London, 18 ; Sheffield, 5 ; Manchester,
11 ; Philadelphia, 22.

**Dronsfield, Dransfield,
Dranfield, Drowsfield.** —
Local, ' of Dronfield,' a parish six
miles from Sheffield. Dronsfield is
probably the more correct form,
while Drowsfield is a palpable
variant.

Edmundus de Drounesfeld, 1379 : P. T.
Yorks. p. 101.
Oldham, 9, 1, 0, 0 ; Manchester, 0, 1, 1, 1.

Druce.—(1) Bapt. ' the son of
Drew,' q.v. The same as Drews ;
cf. Ellis and Ellice, Avis and Avice,
Danns and Dance (from Daniel).

(2) Local, ' of Dreux.'

John le Droys, co. Wilts, Hen. III-
Edw. I. K.
William le Droys, or *de* Droys, co.
Wilts, ibid.
Elyas le Drueys, co. Bucks, 1273. A.
Geoffrey le Drueys, co. Wilts, ibid.
Stephen Drueys, co. Wilts, ibid.
Robert Druves, or Druys, or Droys, or
Dreys, or *de* Drywes, co. Wilts, 20 Edw.
I. R.

No doubt all these are local and
hail from Dreux, in Brittany. This
is confirmed by the fact that Herman
de Dreuues was a tenant-in-chief in
co. Hereford, in Domesday ; cf. the
common entry *le* Bruce for *de* Bruce.

London, 23 ; Boston (U.S.), 1.

Druitt.—Bapt. ; v. Drewett.

Drummer.—Local, ' of Dummer,' q.v. ; an imitative corruption.
The suggestion, ' one who, in military exercises, beats the drum,' is
very doubtful (v. Lower's Patr.
Brit. p. 95).

1752. Married—James Drummer and
Mary Stiles : St. Geo. Chap. Mayfair,
p. 215.
1804. — John Drummer and Lucy
Scoltock : St. Geo. Han. Sq. ii. 303.
New York, 1 ; Philadelphia, 1.

Drummond.—Local, ' of Drymen,' co. Stirling, N.B. This
surname, although Scotch, is so
familiar in England that I append
Mr. Lower's statement. ' Drummond : " the noble house of Drummond " says Collins, " derived from
Malcolm Beg (i.e. 'low,' or short "),
who flourished under Alexander
II, and being possessed of the lands
of Drymen, co. Stirling, took that
surname, which in after times varied
to Drummond " (Peerage, edit. 1768,
v. 77). The name is found spelt
in eighteen different ways (Ulster
Journal Arch. No. 20). Of these,
Drumyn, Drummane, and Dromond
are the principal:' Patr. Brit. p. 95.
Hence it is clear that the final *d* is
excrescent, as in Simmonds, &c.

London, 11 ; New York, 29.

Drunkard.—Nick. ' the drunkard' ; cf. Sober, Drinkwater, &c.
Naturally this surname has not
been perpetuated.

Maurice Druncard, co. Devon, 1273. A.

Drury, Drewery, Drewry.
—Nick. ' a lover, a sweetheart,
a darling' ; O.F. *druerie*.

' Or beare the name of Druerie.'
Chaucer, R. of R. 5964.

The virgin is described as 'Cristes
drurie' in Arthour and Merlin
(Halliwell).

' It is as dereworthe (precious) a drury
As deere God hymselven.'
Vision of Piers Plowman, 633.

Cf. Paramor, Lover, Douceamour, Finnemore, &c.

Alice Druerie, co. Hunts, 1273. A.
Nigel Drury, co. York, ibid.
Thomas Drory, 1379 : P. T. Yorks.
p. 21.
Willelmus Drory, 1379 : ibid.
Johannes Drury, 1379 : ibid. p. 240.
1629. Married—Thomas Errington and
Jone Drewrye : St. Jas. Clerkenwell,
iii. 61.
1662. — Francis Drury and Eliz.
Terry : ibid. p. 109.
London, 15, 1, 1 ; West Rid. Court
Dir., 6, 0, 0 ; Sheffield, 6, 0, 0 ; Leeds,
1, 1, 0 ; New York, 5, 0, 1.

**Drysdale, Drysdall, Drys-
dell.**—Local, ' of Dryfesdale,' a
parish in co. Dumfries.

1801. Married—William Drysdale and
Harriot Mills : St. Geo. Han. Sq. ii. 243.
London, 8, 1, 0 ; New York, 3, 0, 1.

Dubber.—Occup. 'the dubber,' a flipperer, a furbisher of old garments. Probably, when in earlier use, a decorator of dress, one who embellished with gold lace, &c. The company of the Dubbers joined the procession of the York Pageant (v. York Mystery Plays, p. xxvi). Halliwell suggests they were trimmers or binders of books. Bishop Latimer, speaking of another bishop, says, 'There stood by him a dubber, one Doctor Dubber, he dubbed him by-and-by, and said,' &c. (Second Sermon before Edward VI.)

Hugh de Croft, *dubber*, 13 Edw. II : Freemen of York, i. 18.
Hugo Wystow, *douber*, 1379 : P. T. Yorks. p. 156.
Robert le Dubber, C. R., 28 Edw. I.
Jordan le Dubbere. B.
Stephen le Dubbere, c. 1300. M.
Payn le Dubbour. N.
Adam Dubbere, co. Soms., 1 Edw. III : Kirby's Quest, p. 81.
'One messuage, 1 garden, . . . 2 acres of pasture in Dalton (Wigan parish, co. Lanc.), now in the tenures of Richard Dowber and John Crosse,' &c. (1605) : Lancashire Inquisitions, pt. i. p. 31.
1610. Bapt.—Avis, d. Henry Dubber. St. Jas. Clerkenwell, i. 60.

Dubbs.—Local, 'at the dub.' 'Dub, a small pool of water, a piece of deep and smooth water in a rapid river. North Eng.' (Halliwell).

'Spared neither dub nor mire.'
Robin Hood, i. 106.
Adam del Dobbes, 1379 : P. T. Yorks. p. 284.
London, 1 ; Boston (U.S.), 1.

Duck.—There are three distinct origins of Duck—(1) Nick. 'the duck'; cf. Drake. (2) Nick 'the Duke,' q.v.; O.F. *duc*; M.E. *duk*. (3) Bapt. 'the son of Marmaduke,' from nick. Duke; v. Duke, Dukes, and Duckett. For several important instances, v. Duke.

John le Duk, co. Soms., 1 Edw. III : Kirby's Quest, p. 135.
Adam Doke, 1379 : P. T. Yorks. p. 282.
1577-8. Richard Fearne and Margery Ducke : Marriage Lic. (London), i. 78.
1731. Bapt.—Anne, d. Henry Duck : St. Mary Aldermary, p. 125.
London, 10 ; New York, 3.

Duckett, Duckitt, Ducket, Duckit.—Bapt. 'the son of Marmaduke,' from nick. Duke, diminutive Duket. Camden says, 'Mar-

maduc, a name usual in the North' (Remains, p. 71); v. Duke and Dukes.

Richard Duket, co. Linc., Hen. III–Edw. I. K.
Dulcia Duket, 1273. A.
Doket Flasby, 1379 : P. T. Yorks. p. 274.
Adam Doket, 1379 : ibid. p. 20.
Johannes Doket, 1379 : ibid. p. 274.
Willelmus Dokette, 1379 : ibid. p. 47.

The full name is spelt Marmeduke in the same record ; v. p. 265. This decides the question, if any doubt could exist.

Alan Doke-son, 1379 : Preston Guild Rolls, p. 3.

We find a horse called by this name in the Household Books of Lord William Howard of Naworth Castle (Surt. Soc.):

1621. 'Shoing (shoeing) Gray Ducket, 4d.,' ibid. p. 196.
London, 2, 2, 0, 0 ; Crockford (Ducket); 2 ; Preston (Duckett), 5 ; West Rid. Court Dir., 0, 2, 0, 2 ; Philadelphia, 18, 0, 0, 0.

Duckinfield.—Local, 'of Dukinfield,' a township and chapelry in the parish of Stockport.

Hamo de Dokenfeld, 1294 : East Cheshire, ii. 156.
Richard de Dokenfeld, 1299 : ibid.
John de Dokenfeld, 1359 : ibid. p. 9.
Edmund Duckenfield, of Taunton, 1599 : Wills at Chester (1545-1620), p. 56.
Alice Dukenfield, of Taunton, parish of Ashton-under-Lyne, 1616 : ibid.
MDB. (West Rid. Yorks), 1 ; Philadelphia, 1.

Duckmanton.—Local, 'of Duckmanton,' a parish in co. Derby, four miles from Chesterfield. The surname has crossed over the borders into co. Notts, and is well known there.

MDB. (co. Notts), 7.

Duckworth.—Local, 'of Duckworth,' an estate in Oswaldtwistle, a township in the parish of Whalley, co. Lanc.

'In the reign of Edward III (1327-77) Richard de Radcliffe held two carucates of land in Oswaldtwisle and Duckworth, at that time called Dokeward': Baines' Lanc. ii. 53.
Henricus de Dukeworth, 1379 : P. T. Yorks. p. 64.
Johannes Dukeworth, 1379 : ibid.
Manchester, 16 ; London, 8 ; New York, 6.

Dudderidge.—Local ; v. Doddridge.

Dudgeon, Dudson. — Bapt. Merely variants of Dodgson or Dodson (v. Dodge). That Dodson had become Dudson fairly early we have proof :

1656. Married—Simon Dudson and Sarah Chalenor : St. Thomas the Apostle (London), p. 20.

There need not be the slightest hesitation in accepting this origin ; cf. Gudgeon for Goodson.

James Doodeson, of Kersley, parish of Dean, 1609 : Wills of Chester (1545-1620), p. 55.
1806. Married—James Dudgeon and Margaret Donald : St. Geo. Han. Sq. ii. 343.
London (1884), 4, 0 ; Ripon, 2, 0 ; Philadelphia, 3, 0.

Dudleston.—Local, 'of Dudleston,' a chapelry in the parish of Ellesmere, co. Salop.

MDB. (co. Salop), 2.

Dudley. — Local, 'of Dudley,' an important town in co. Worcester.

Perceval de Duddelegh, Hen. III–Edw. I : K. p. 93.
Willelmus Dudely, 1379 : P. T. Yorks. p. 5.
Isolda Doudely, 1379 : ibid.
Johannes Dudly, 1379 : ibid.
Magota Duddely, 1379 ; ibid. p. 33.
1549. Buried — John Dudleye : St. Michael, Cornhill, p. 179.
1789. Married—William Dudley and Mary Foster : St. Geo. Han. Sq. ii. 29.
London, 18 ; Philadelphia, 20.

Dudman.—Bapt. 'the son of Dodeman'; v. Dodman (1); cf. Bateman, Tiddyman, &c.

Simon Dudeman. D.
Ralph Deudeman, 1307. M.
Obbe Dudeman. E.
Johannes Dudeman, 1379 : P. T. Yorks. p. 143.
Thomas Dudeman, 1379 : ibid.
1563. Buried — John Doodman : St. Peter, Cornhill, i. 116.
1795. Married—Henry Solomon and Susannah Dudman : St. Geo. Han. Sq. ii. 136.
London, 4.

Duesberry, Duesbury. — Local, 'of Dewsbury,' q.v.

Duff. — ? Bapt. 'the son of Douf' (?) ; cf. Scotch Macduff.

Robertus Douff, et uxor ejus, 1379 : P. T. Yorks. p. 246.
Johannes Douf, et Johanna uxor ejus, 1379 : ibid. p. 121.
Robertus Dowfe, et Alicia uxor ejus, 1379 : ibid. p. 112.

Willelmus Douf, et Magota uxor ejus, 1379: ibid. p. 113.
Cf. Cristiana Dewfebygyng, 1379: ibid. p. 286.
Robertus de Doufebygyng, 1379: ibid. p. 289.
Johannes de Dowfbygyng, 1379: ibid. i.e. the bigging or building of Douf, now Dowbiggin, q.v.; cf. Newbiggin. All this seems to point to the existence of a personal name Douf or Duff. I doubt not it is the Macduff of North Britain.

London, 15; Philadelphia, 56.

Duffield, Duffell, Duffill, Duffit, Duffitt.—Local, 'of Duffield,' a parish in co. Derby; also two townships in co. York. The usual corruptions of the suffix -field have taken place in this surname; cf. Brumfit for Broomfield, or Hatfull for Hatfield.

Richard de Duffeld, co. Linc., Hen. III-Edw. I. K.
John de Duffeld, co. Derby, 1273. A.
Johannes de Dulfeld', 1379: P. T. Yorks. p. 158.
Johannes de Duffeld, 1379: ibid. p. 117.
1556-7. Married—John Duffell and Jone Ynglyshe: St. Dionis Backchurch, p. 3.
1586. — Henry Sukar and Sarah Duffild: St. Antholin (Londen), p. 32.
1722. — John Duffell and Elizabeth Barker: ibid. p. 137.
1791. — John Duffill and Mary Pertes: St. Geo. Han. Sq. ii. 66.
London, 14, 3, 1, 0, 0; York, 1, 0, 1, 1; 1; Philadelphia (Duffield), 28.

Duffin, Duffyn, Duffan.—Bapt. 'the son of Dolphin,' popularly Doven and Duffen. There need be no hesitation in accepting this origin. The personal name was common, and a corrupted form was inevitable; v. Dolphin.

Willelmus Duffane, 1379: P. T. Yorks. p. 133.
Nicholaus Duffane, 1379: ibid.
Since writing the above I find the point practically settled by the Lancashire Inquisitions (Lancashire and Cheshire Record Soc.). A comparison of Ribchester names (1606) on p. 60, and Ribchester names (1609) on p. 148, will serve to show that Robert Dolphin in the one case, and Robert Dewfine in the other, were one and the same person. There are several Dolphins in the present directory for Ribchester.

1759. Married—William Bruce and Margaret Duffin: St. Geo. Han. Sq. i. 4.
London (1884), 5, 1, 0; Manchester, 0, 1, 0; Philadelphia, 8, 0, 0.

Duffus.—(1) Local, 'of Duffus,' a parish in Morayshire, Scotland. (2) Local, 'at the duff-hus,' i.e. dove-house, where pigeons were bred. The same individual is thus referred to:

Robert del Dyffehus, co. Suff., 1273. A.
Robert del Duffhus, co. Suff., ibid.
Robert Dufhus, co. Suff., ibid.
1742. Married—Hugh Corner and Mary Duffis: St. Geo. Chap. Mayfair, p. 23.

Dugdale, Dugdill, Dugdall.—Local, 'of Dugdale,' some small dale on the borders of Lancashire and Yorkshire. Sir William Dugdale, the celebrated antiquary, sprang from the borough of Clitheroe (Baines' Lancashire, ii. 16).

Agnes Doghdale, 1379: P. T. Yorks. p. 283.
John Dugdale, of Chatburn, 1596: Wills at Chester (1545-1620), p. 57.
Nicholas Dugdale, of Clitheroe, 1612: ibid.
1741. Married—William Dugdale and Deborah Martin: St. Geo. Han. Sq. i. 26.
London, 2, 0, 0; Manchester, 2, 0, 0; Liverpool, 3, 0, 0; MDB. (West Rid. Yorks), 1, 1, 0; (co. Devon), 0, 0, 2; Philadelphia, 2, 0, 0.

Duggan, Duggin.—Bapt. 'the son of Richard,' from French Digon. In England this became Diggon and Diccon (v. Dickens); in Wales tricks were played with the vowels. Hence such entries as:

1577. Buryed—Doggon Jones, sonne of Evan Jones: St. Peter, Cornhill, i. 125.

Thus Spenser begins one of his pastorals:

'Diggon Davie, I bid her " good day," Or Diggon her is, or I missay.'

Certainly, however, tricks were played with the vowels in England also, and it is not necessary to suppose that all our Duggins and Duggans are Welsh.

London, 3, 2; Boston (U.S.), 40, 0.

Dugget, Dugood, Duguid.—Bapt.; v. Doggett.

Duke.—(1) Bapt. 'the son of Marmaduke,' from nick. Duke; v. Dukes. (2) Offic. or nick. 'the Duke,' i.e. the leader.

John le Duc, co. Soms., 1 Edw. III: Kirby's Quest, p. 83.
Robert le Duc, co. Oxf., Hen. III-Edw. I. K.
Roger le Duc, co. Oxf., ibid.
William le Duc, C. R., 3 Edw. I.
Johannes Duke, 1379: P. T. Yorks. p. 176.
1567. William Joyse and Mary Duke: Marriage Lic. (London), i. 36.
1643. Married — Thomas Duke and Marye Picke: St. Mary Aldermary, p. 19.
London, 15; New York, 21.

Dukes, Dukeson.—Bapt. 'the son of Marmaduke,' from the nick. Duke; v. Duckett.

1634. 'To Duke Shillito, owing him for trimming my Lord, £1 2s.': Household Books at Bolton Abbey (Hist. of Skipton, p. 97).

Still a Yorkshire font-name; cf. Duke Redmayne, Stirton, Skipton, in W. Rid. Dir. Probably in modern Yorkshire fondness for 'Earl,' 'Marquis,' &c., as Christian names was started by the idea that Duke belonged to the same category.

Johannes Dokeson, 1397: Preston Guild Rolls, p. 8.
Robert Dukeson, co. Lanc. Z.
Richard Duck, or Dooke, or Doke, 1510: Reg. Univ. Oxf. i. 72.
'This first edition of the Scintillula contained twelve sets of commendatory poems, noticeably, one by Isaac Walton, and another by Dr. R. Dukeson in Latin': Life of Dr. Fuller, by J. E. Bailey, p. 503.

A note, ibid. p. 246, speaks of him as Dr. Duckson, rector of St. Clement Danes, in 1634. This is the form of his name generally used by Church historians.

Thomas Duckesson, of Houghton, James Duckeson, Harry Duckeson: (List of Recusants in 1586) Croston's edit. of Baines' Lancashire, i. 240.
'One Duckson, an old priest, continueth in Samlesburye by common report': ibid.
1656.Married—Thomas Mason and Ann Dukson: St. Mary Aldermary, p. 25.
Evan Duckeson, of Brindle, co. Lanc., 1693: Wills at Chester (1681-1700), p. 76.
London, 8, 0; Philadelphia, 12, 0.

Dumbell, Dumbill, Dumble, Dombell.—Local. A variant of Domville (q.v.), a great Cheshire surname. There is not the shadow of a doubt about this derivation.

Cf. James Domvile, 1521: Earwaker's Hist. of East Cheshire, i. 295.
James Dowmbill, 1522: ibid. p. 296.
Peter Dombell, of Newton in Maker-

field, *milner*, 1639: Wills at Chester (1621-50), p. 67.

Elizabeth Dombell, 1568: ibid. (1545-1620), p. 55.

Hannah Dumbell, of Newton-in-Makerfield, 1669: ibid. (1660-80), p. 82.

Richard Dumbell, of Newton, 1674: ibid.

Liverpool, 3, 1, 0, 1; Philadelphia, 2, 0, 0, 0; New York, 0, 0, 1, 0.

Dumbelton, Dumbleton.—Local, 'of Dumbleton,' a parish in co. Gloucester, six miles from Evesham. Probably 'the town of Dumbold,' from the name of the first settler.

Thomas de Dumbilton, co. Bucks, 1273. A.

Odo de Dumbleton, co. Glouc., ibid.

1795. Married—John Dumbleton and Sarah Buckler: St. Geo. Han. Sq. ii. 133.

1796. — James Dumbulton and Eliz. Wells: ibid. p. 157.

London, 1, 5; Philadelphia, 1, 0.

Dummer, Dumper.—Local, 'of Dummer,' a parish in co. Hants, four miles from Basingstoke. No doubt the Hampshire Dumper is a variant. First it would be Dumber, then Dumper.

John de Dummer, co. Soms., 1273. A.

Henry de Dummere, co. Soms., ibid.

1802. Married—William Burns and Ann Dummer: St. Geo. Han. Sq. ii. 267.

London, 2, 0; MDB. (co. Southampton), 1, 4; Philadelphia, 1, 0; Boston (U.S.), 1, 0.

Dumphrey, Dumphries, Dumphry.—Bapt. 'the son of Humphrey,' a nick. form, probably as old as—

'Humpty-Dumpty sat on a wall, Humpty-Dumpty had a great fall.'

which unmistakably refers to Humphrey; cf. Hodgson and Dodgson, both from Roger; also Hobson and Dobson, both from Robert.

'Mr. Dumphrey, a working man, will second the resolution': Standard, May 14, 1886.

'Mr. Dumphries, the churchwarden (St. Mary Magdalen, Bermondsey), said the hissing occurred at the mention of the Queen and Royal Family, and also at the Eighth Commandment': Standard, Feb. 9, 1887.

The following entry reminds us of Dumfriesshire, but it need not trouble us, I imagine. It is probably imitative.

1721. Bapt.—James Dumfrise, a native of East India, a servant to Sir John Brown: St. Michael, Cornhill, p. 167.

Possibly a Scotchman gave him the name of his native county.

New York (Dumphry), 1.

Dumphy.—A variant of Dumphrey; v. Dunphy.

Dumville, Dunville, Domville, Donville.—Local, 'de Donville,' 'in the arrondissement of Lisieux,' in Normandy, anciently written Dumoville, as in a papal bull of 1210' (Lower, quoting from the Itin. de la Normandie). A family settled very early in co. Chester. v. Dumbell.

Hugo de Donvile, or Donvil, co. Salop, 1273. A.

Gilbert Domville, of Lymm, esquire, 1607: Wills at Chester (1545-1620), p. 55.

William Domville, of Lymm, 1625: ibid. (1621-50), p. 67.

William Domvile, of Middleton, *gentleman*, 1647: ibid.

London, 2, 1, 1, 1; Manchester, 2, 0, 0, 0.

Dunbabin, Dunbobbin, Dunbobin. — ? —. A curious East Cheshire surname. I cannot suggest any satisfactory derivation.

Ralph Dunbabin, of Warrington, 1598: Wills at Chester (1545-1620), p. 57.

Anthony Dunbabin, of Warrington, *woollen-draper*, 1597: ibid.

Robert Dunbabin, of Runcorn, 1639: ibid. (1621-50), p. 69.

William Dunbabin, of Frodsham, 1630: ibid.

Warrington, 0, 2, 1; Manchester, 3, 0, 0.

Dunbar.—Local, 'of Dunbar.' A Scotch surname.

Philippus Donbar, 1379: P. T. Yorks. p. 100.

London, 8; Philadelphia, 36.

Duncalf, Duncalfe, Duncuft. —Local, 'at the dun-croft'; cf. Metcalfe. I only suggest this as a guess, as a proved solution of the surname is beyond my reading. The Duncalfs of Foxwist, co. Cheshire, are found with that name so early as 1306. The name constantly occurs in Cheshire records.

Thomas Duncalf, of Foxwist, 1396: Earwaker's Hist. of East Ches. ii. 258.

Thomas Duncalf, of Foxwist, 1566: ibid.

Richard Duncalf, of the Meyre, 1584: Wills at Chester (1545-1620), p. 57.

Ralph Duncalf, of Rostherne, 1604: ibid.

John Duncalf, 1622: Salford, vol. xii. p. 148, Lanc. and Ches. Rec. Soc.

1696. Married—Simon Duncalfe and

Ann Rogerson: St. Antholin (London), p. 110.

Manchester, 2, 1, 2; London, 0, 2, 0; New York, 1, 0, 0.

Duncan, Duncanson.—Bapt. 'the son of Duncan.' A Scotch surname.

Duncann' de Lascell', co. Bedf., Hen. III–Edw. I. K.

Willelmus Dunkan, 1379: P. T. Yorks. p. 234.

London, 30, 1; New York, 80, 2.

Dunch.—Nick. 'the dunch,' i.e. deaf. '*Dunch*, deaf, dull, "deafe, or hard of hearing" (1582). . . . A dunch passage, a blind, dark passage': Halliwell. Cf. Daff and Daft.

Stephen Dunche, co. Camb., 1273. A.

William Dunche, vicar of Santon, co. Norf., 1490: FF. ii. 158.

Robert Dunch, rector of East Bilney, co. Norf., 1409: ibid. ix. 462.

1598. William Dunche, of Wyttenham, Berks, and Mary Cromwell, of Hichinbrooke, co. Hunts: Marriage Lic. (Westminster), p. 12.

1785. Married—James Dunch and Judith Sykes: St. Geo. Han. Sq. i. 375.

London, 2.

Duncombe, Duncum, Duncomb.—Local, 'of Duncombe.' I have not identified the spot.

1598. Francis Duncombe and Temperance Rudd: Marriage Lic. (London), i. 248.

1752. Married—Christopher Crowe and Barbara Duncombe: St. Geo. Han. Sq. i. 47.

1803. — Edward Duncumb and Hester Cade: ibid. ii. 281.

London, 10, 2, 0; New York, 0, 0, 2.

Dunderdale, Dundendale.—Local, 'of Dunnerdale,' a township in the parish of Kirkby Ireleth, Furness, embracing the valley of the Duddon as far as Seathwaite; cf. Tyndale, Tweedale, Teasdale, &c.

Robert Dunderdale, of Hathornthwaite, 1677: Lancashire Wills at Richmond, i. 98.

John Dunderdall, of Chipping, 1666: ibid.

Nicholas Dawson, of Bow Hall, in Dunnerdale, 1726: ibid. ii. 81.

1809. Married—James Murr and Isabella Dunderdell: St. Geo. Han. Sq. ii. 415.

London, 2, 0; Manchester, 2, 1; Preston, 6, 0; Philadelphia, 4, 0.

Dunham.—Local, 'of Dunham.' two parishes, Great and Little

Dunham, in co. Norfolk; also Dunham-on-Trent in the dioc. of Southwell.

Joel de Dunham, co. Linc., Hen. III–Edw. I. K.
Reginald de Dunham, co. Norf., ibid. London, 8; New York, 74.

Dunkerley, Dunkerly, Dunkley, Dunckley, Duncklee, Dunklee. —Local, ' of Dunkerley.' I cannot find the spot, but it is a surname belonging to co. Lancs. The variants are many. It is possible that Dinkley, a township in the parish of Blackburn, is the parent; indeed I may say that it is all but certain.

Roger de Dynkedlegh, of Wilpshire cum Dinkley, co. Lanc., 1332: Lay Subsidy (Rylands), p. 84.

This entry practically proves the parentage suggested above.

Robert Dunkerley, of Crompstall, husbandman, 1588: Wills at Chester (1545–1620), p. 57.
Manchester (Dunkerley), 7; Oldham (Dunkerley), 13; London, 0, 1, 14, 3, 0, 0; Philadelphia, 6, 0, 1, 6, 1, 0; Boston (U.S.) (Dunklee), 10.

Dunkerton. —Local, ' of Dunkerton,' a parish in co. Somerset, five miles from Bath.

Nicholas de Donkerton, co. Soms., 1 Edw. III : Kirby's Quest, p. 87.
1615. Married—Willyam Dunkerton and Sara Goebye: St. Jas. Clerkenwell, iii. 41.
MDB. (co. Somerset), 5.

Dunkin, Dunkinson. —Bapt. 'the son of Duncan,' q.v. No doubt imitative of the common English suffix -kin, as in Wilkin, Wilkinson, Tompkin, Tompkinson, &c. ; cf. Donkin.

1598. Richard Bromlye and Mary Dunkyn : Marriage Lic. (London), i. 253.
1660. Married—George Dunkin and Eliz. Lewis: St. Dionis Backchurch, p. 36.
1772. — John Dunkin and Eliz. Hooper: St. Geo. Han. Sq. i. 221.
London, 6, 3; New York, 8, 2.

Dunlop, Dunlap. —Local, ' of Dunlop.' 'Traced to the year 1260, when Dom. Gulielmus de Dunlop was lord of Dunlop, in Ayrshire, an estate still in the possession of the family' (Lower's Patr. Brit. p. 97). This Scotch surname in the form of Dunlap swarms in the United States. A Mr. Dunlop at

a dinner party, where puns on names were the subject of conversation, said, ' No pun could be made on his name.' ' Oh, yes, sir,' said a guest; ' lop off the last syllable, and it is done.' Although not an English surname, I have entered it in this dictionary as many Scotch names have become so familiarized on English soil that the fact that they are immigrants is well-nigh forgotten by many.

Robert Denlopp, of Edinburgh, in Scotland, 1619 : Wills at Chester (1545–1620), p. 52.
London, 6, 0 ; Philadelphia, 5, 112.

Dunn, Dun, Dunne. — (1) Local, ' at the dun'; M.E. dun, a hill ; v. Downe.

Thomas de la Dune, Close Roll, 2 Edw. I.
Gilbert atte Dune, co. Essex, 1273. A.
Gilbert de la Dune, or Dunne, co. Essex, ibid.
Henry de la Dun, co. Devon, Hen. III–Edw. I. K.

(2) Nick. 'the dun,' a dull brown, a name given from the complexion of the bearer. ' Dunne of hewe': Rom. of Rose, 1213.

Simon le Dun, co. Derby, Hen. III–Edw. I. K.
William le Dunne, co. Devon, 1273. A.
Robert le Dun, co. Norf., ibid.
William le Dun. B.
1597. Married—Richard Whitbey and Janne Dunne: St. Jas. Clerkenwell, iii. 20.
London, 83, 1, 0; New York, 316, 2, 52.

Dunnage. —Local, ' of Dunwich,' a parish in the dioc. of Norwich ; cf. Aldridge for Aldrich.

Nicholaus de Duneswich, co. Norf., Hen. III–Edw. I. K.
Roger de Dunwich, rector of Sidestrand, co. Norf., 1333 : FF. viii. 170.
Walter de Dunwich, rector of Brinton, co. Norf., 1354 : ibid. ix. 370.
1800. Married—Thomas Dunage and Eliz. Rowland: St. Geo. Han. Sq. ii. 420. London, 4.

Dunnicliff, Dunnicliffe.— Local. A variant of Tunnicliffe, q.v.; cf. Tennyson or Tennison for Dennison.

1800. Married—William Coutts and Mary Duneclift : St. Geo. Han. Sq. ii. 221. Oldham, 0, 1 ; Philadelphia, 2, 0.

Dunning, Downing. —Bapt. 'the son of Dunning.' Dunnig and Dunnigs (i.e. Dunning) occur

as personal names in the Hundred Rolls, 1273 ; cf. Browning and Harding. Bruning is frequently found for Browning.

John Dounynne, co. Soms., 1 Edw. III : Kirby's Quest, p. 90.
John Dunnyng, co. Soms., 1 Edw. III : ibid. p. 245.
Johannes Dunnyng, 1379 : P. T. Yorks. p. 37.
Alicia Downyng, 1379 : ibid.
Johannes Downnyng, 1379 : ibid. p. 39.
Hervey Dunning, co. Camb., 1273. A.
Richard Duning, co. Oxf., ibid.
John Dunning, or Downing, sheriff of Norwich, 1432 : FF. iii. 163.
1768. Married — John Dunning and Martha Cole : St. Geo. Han. Sq. i. 180.
London, 22, 20; New York, 31, 42.

Dunnington. —Local, ' of Dunnington,' (1) a township in E. Rid. Yorks ; (2) a parish four miles from York; (3) 'of Donington,' a parish in Lincolnshire; (4) ' of Donnington,' a hamlet near Newbury, Berks.

John de Dunington, co. Oxf., 1273. A.
Johannes de Donington, ibid.
Thomas de Dunington, co. Oxf., ibid.
Walter de Donington, co. Linc., ibid.
Gilbert de Duningtun, co. Linc., ibid.
Oliver de Dunington, co. Linc., ibid.
1530. John Parmynter and Margaret Dunnyngton : Marriage Lic. (London), i. 7.
MDB. (West Rid. Yorks), 2.

Dunphy, Dumphy, Dunphie. —Bapt. 'the son of Dunphy,' i.e. Humphrey ; v. Dumphrey. The change from m to n is common, and vice versa ; cf. Sinkinson for Simkinson, and Ransom for Ranson.

London, 2, 0, 0 ; London Court Dir., 1, 0, 1 ; Philadelphia, 5, 7, 0.

Dunsford. —Local, ' of Dunsforth,' a township in the parish of Aldborough, W. Rid. Yorks; v. Ford and Forth.

John de Dunnysford, co. Bucks, 1273. A.
Johanna de Dunysford, webster, 1379 : P. T. Yorks. p. 135.
Willelmus de Dunforth, webster, 1379 : ibid. p. 97.
1805. Married—John Warren and Ann Dunsford : St. Geo. Han. Sq. ii. 333.
London, 1 ; Philadelphia, 1.

Dunstan, Dunston, Dunstone. —(1) Bapt. 'the son of Dunstan.' One of this name was Abbot of Glastonbury and Archbishop of Canterbury.

Thomas Dunstan, co. Kent, 1273. A.
Dunstan de Berstede, co. Kent, ibid.
Mabil fil. Dunstani, co. Suff., ibid.
Han Donestan, 1379 : P. T. Yorks. p. 299.

(2) Local, 'of Dunston,' parishes in the diocs. of Lincoln, Southwell, Norwich, Oxford, and Durham. The first two are represented in the first two instances below :

Hugh de Dunston, co. Linc., Hen. III–Edw. I. K.
William de Dunston, co. Notts, ibid.
William de Donstone, co. Derby, 1273. A.
1578. John Dunstane and Eliz. Bagley : Marriage Lic. (London), i. 82.
1593. Richard Rymes and Anne Dunston, co. Staff. : ibid. p. 208.
1601. Richard Dunstone and Sarah Wall : ibid. p. 265.
London, 2, 1, 1 ; Crockford, 2, 0, 0 ; Boston (U.S.), 1, 0, 0 ; New York, 1, 2, 0.

Dunster.—Local, ' of Dunster,' a parish in co. Somerset.

Richard de Dunsterre, co. Soms., 1 Edw. III : Kirby's Quest, p. 278.
1603. Buried—Margaret Dunster : St. Jas. Clerkenwell, iv. 82.
1748. Married—William Dunster and Mary Bell : St. Geo. Chap. Mayfair, p. 126.
London, 7 ; Crockford, 1 ; New York, 2.

Dunsterville.—Local, ' de Dunstanville '

Rosia de Dunstanewyll, co. Camb., 1273. A.
Walter de Dunstanevile, co. Camb., ibid.
Walter de Dunstavile, co. Wilts, ibid.
1583. Married—Thomas Lucas and Eliz. Dunstarvilde : St. Dionis Backchurch, p. 10.
William Dunsterfield, of Raby, 1617 : Wills at Chester (1545–1620), p. 57.
John Dunsterville, of Raby, parish of Neston, 1634 : ibid. (1621–50), p. 69.
Lucy Dunsterville, of Denwall, *widow*, 1650 : ibid.
Boston (U.S.), 1.

Dunton.—Local, ' of Dunton,' parishes in the diocs. of Ely, Norwich, Oxford, Peterborough, and St. Albans.

Gilbert de Dunton, co. Norf., Hen. III–Edw. I. K.
John de Dunton, co. Linc., ibid.
Isabella de Dunton, co. Salop, 1273. A.
Jordan de Duntone, co. Oxf., ibid.
1593. Thomas Dunton (co. Essex) and Letitia Trott : Marriage Lic. (London), i. 207.
1807. Married—John Weller and Mary Dunton : St. Geo. Han. Sq. ii. 373.
London, 2 ; New York, 5.

Durand, Durant, Durrant, Durran.—Bapt. ' the son of Durand,' or ' Durant.' ' Durand, co. Hants ' : Domesday. v. Durrans.

John fil. Doraunt de Moreby, 5 Edw. II : Freemen of York, i. 14.

Roger fil. Durandi, temp. 1230 : GGG. p. 199.
Durand le Bonjohan, 1273. A.
Henry fil. Durant, ibid.
Durant le Cordwaner, 1295. M.
Ivo Duraunt, 1273. A.
Willelmus Durant, *matras maker*, 1379 : P. T. Howdenshire, p. 28.
Johannes Dorand, 1379 : P. T. Yorks. p. 118.
Hugo Doraunt, 1379 : ibid. p. 214.
1589. Married—Philip Durrant and Eliz. Goodwyn : St. Jas. Clerkenwell, iii. 14.
London, 3, 7, 1, 21 ; Philadelphia, 9, 3, 0, 0.

Duredent, Durden (?).—Nick. ' Duredent,' i.e. hard tooth ; cf. Doubleday, Dent-de-fer, and Dandelion. Durden may be local, as a corruption of Dearden, but it is far more natural to consider it a corrupted form of the nickname ; the evidence is all in favour of this view.

Philip Duredent, co. Bucks, 1273. A.
Roger Duredent, or Durdent, co. Derby, ibid.
1577. Thomas Durden, or Durdant, or Durdent : Reg. Univ. Oxf. vol. ii. pt. ii. p. 68.
1637. Married—Nicholas Durdent and Eliz. Wyett : St. Jas. Clerkenwell, iii. 68.
1719. — Robert Durdant and Sara Lee : ibid. p. 243.
1792. — William Metyard and Sarah Durden : St. Geo. Han. Sq. ii. 75.
London, 0, 0.

Durham.—Local, ' of Durham,' the capital of the county of that name.

Walter de Durham, London, 1273. A.
William de Dureham, London, ibid.
John de Durame, co. Essex, ibid.
1695-6. Married—George White and Jane Durham : St. Dionis Backchurch, p. 44.
London, 14 ; Philadelphia, 26.

Durknave.—Offic. ' the doorknave,' i.e. the porter, from *dur*, door, and *knave*, a servant ; v. Dorward.

' Robertus de Leiburne attornat Robertum Normand et Johannem Durknave ad deliberandum Willelmo Scharp de Furnes seisinam de manerio suo,' &c., 13th cent. (?) : Furness Coucher Book, i. 40.

Durman.—Offic. ' the doorman ' ; v. Dorman, Dorward, and Durknave.

Durnford.—Local, ' of Durnford,' a parish in co. Wilts, two miles from Amesbury.

Richard de Durneford, co. Wilts, 1273. A.
Richard de Derneford, co. Wilts, Hen. III–Edw. I. K.
William de Durneford, co. Wilts, ibid.
James de Dernford, rector of Berningham, Northwood, co. Norf., 1340 : FF. viii. 96.
1808. Married—William Durnford and Meliscent Abbott : St. Geo. Han. Sq. ii. 395.
London, 5.

Durrans, Dorrance.- Bapt. ' the son of Durand ' (q.v.), a corruption of the patronymic Durands by omission of the *d*.

1676. Married—Gabriel Durance and Isabel Tecis : St. Jas. Clerkenwell, iii. 182.
1788. — William Durance and Eliz. Fowles : St. Geo. Han. Sq. ii. 14.
London (1884), 2, 0 ; Philadelphia, 0, 4.

Durrant ; v. Durand.

Durward.—Offic. ; v. Dorward.

Dury, Durie.—Local.   Mr. Lower says, ' Durie, an estate in the parish of Scoonie, co. Fife.' ' The laird of Durie ' (Cal. State Papers relating to Scotland, edited by M. J. Thorpe. London : Longmans, p. 309) complains in 1570 of the capture of one of his servants.

Andrew Dury, abbot of Melrose, 1524 : Cal. State Papers relating to Scotland, p. 20.
Henry Durye, 1571 : ibid. p. 327.
Peter Durye, 1571 : ibid.

Lower separates Dury from Durie. ' Dury. The "braes of Dury" are in the parish of Fowlis-Wester, in the centre of Perthshire.' The name in any case is Scotch, and local.

1780. Married—John Dury and Jean Telfer : St. Geo. Han. Sq. i. 311.
London, 2, 1.

Dutch.—Local, ' the Dutch,' a Dutchman ; cf. English.

Walter de Deusshe, C. R., 30 Edw. I.
1789. Married — Edward Dutch and Sarah Priseman : St. Geo. Han. Sq. ii. 21.
1799. — William Dutch and Eliz. Hunt : ibid. p. 209.
MDB. (co. Lancaster), 2 ; New York, 4.

Dutchman.—Local, ' the Dutchman ' ; cf. Welshman.

Michael Ducheman, C. R., 16 Ric. II.
Flour Ducheman, alias Flour Chapell, of London, *jeweller*, C. R., 16 Hen. VI.
Rotherham, Yorks, 1 ; MDB. (co. Norfolk), 1.

S 2

Dutson, Dutt.—Bapt. 'the son of Dionisia,' from nick. Dye, dim. Dyot, and patronymic Dyotson; v. Dyet and Dyerson.

London, 1, 1; Philadelphia, 0, 4.

Dutton.—Local, 'of Dutton,' a township in the parish of Ribchester, co. Lancs. A family of Duttons arose here very early, and their ramifications have spread over the whole of Lancashire and the W. Rid. of Yorkshire.

Henry de Dutton, of Bispham, co Lanc., 1332: Lay Subsidy (Rylands), p. 72.
Richard, son of Ughtred de Dutton, and William de Dutton, grant lands in Dutton to Henry de Clayton': Baines' Lanc. ii. 110.
William Dutton, 1415: Preston Guild Rolls, p. 8.
1579. Thomas Dutton and Judith Jennings: Marriage Lic. (London), i. 89.
Manchester, 18; London, 13; New York, 13.

Duxbury, Duxbarry, Dukesbury.—Local, 'of Duxbury,' a township in the parish of Standish, co. Lancs.

1632. Bapt.—Raph, s. James Duxbury: St. Jas. Clerkenwell, i. 121.
Ann Duxbury, of Woodhouse, 1639: Wills at Chester (1621-50), p. 70.
Henry Duxbury, of Tottleworth, 1629: ibid.
Henry Duxbury, 1642: Preston Guild Rolls, p. 110.
Manchester, 5, 1, 0; New York, 2, 0, 0; Philadelphia, 4, 0, 1.

Dwarber.—Occup. 'the dauber,' q.v. This corruption is analogous to those of Dwight, Dwyer, and Dwerrihouse, q.v.

London (1884), 1.

Dwerrihouse, Dwerryhouse.—Local, ' at the dwyer-house' (v. Dwyer), from residence thereby. The name Dwerrihouse is found, like Dwyer, chiefly in cos. Lancs. and Yorks, where we should expect it.

William de Dwerihouse, of Wrightington, co. Lanc., 1332: Lay Subsidy (Rylands), p. 51.
Henry Dwarrihouse, of Halewood, 1623: Wills at Chester, p. 70.
William Dwarryhouse, of West Derby, 1647: ibid.
1782. Married—John Dwerrihouse and Susanna Oldfield: St. Geo. Han. Sq. i 337.
London, 1, 0; Liverpool, 0, 1.

Dwight.—? Bapt. 'the son of Dionisia' (?). This name has caused much trouble. Mr. Lower suggests a corruption of Thwaite. A much simpler origin would be that it is a corruption of the once common Dyot (v. Dyet and Dyson), the pet name of Dionisia; cf. Dwarber for Dauber, Dwyer for Dyer, and note the following entry:
Magota Duyott', 1379: P. T. Yorks. p. 271.
The usual form in this register of names is Dyot and Diot; v. Dight.
The following are contained in the register of St. Peter, Cornhill, i. 86:
1634. Bapt. — Elizabeth, d. William Dwoit, *tallow-chandler*.
1635. — Marye, d. William Dweyght, *tallow-chandler*.
The above is strong evidence in favour of my view.
William Dwyte, Mayor of Thetford, 1511: FF. ii. 56.
1767. Married—James Clough and Jane Dwight: St. Geo. Han. Sq. i. 168.
London, 1; Philadelphia, 6.

Dwyer.—(1) Occup. 'the dyer'; v. Dyer. Evidently an early provincialism; cf. Dwerrihouse for Dwyerhouse, and Dwight for Dyot (?). (2) Bapt. for O'Dwyer, an Irish surname. This is the true origin of nine-tenths of the instances in all our English directories; cf. Connor and O'Connor, Connell and O'Connell, &c.

1764. Married — Thomas Young and Susanna Dwyer: St. Geo. Han. Sq. i. 135.
1888. Died—Kate O'Dwyer: New York Tribune, June 11, 1888.
London, 2; West Rid. Court Dir., 1; York, 2; Liverpool, 4; New York, 150.

Dyce.—Local; v. Diss.

Dye.—Bapt. 'the son of Dionisia,' from the nick. Dye, whence dim. Dyet (q.v.) and patronymic Dyson (q.v.).

Robertus Dy, 1379: P. T. Yorks. p. 143.
Willelmus Dei (sic), 1379: ibid. p. 193.
1803. Married—Robert Dye and Eliz. Treby: St. Geo. Han. Sq. ii. 276.
1806. — Richard Dye and Ann Read: ibid. p. 340.
London, 6; Philadelphia, 9.

Dyer.—Occup. 'the dyer'; M.E. *deyen*, to dye.

'An haberdasher, and a carpenter,
A webbe, a deyer, and a tapiser.'
Chaucer, C. T. 363-4.

v. Dyster, Lister, Tucker, Walker, Fuller, &c.

John Dyar, co. Soms., 1 Edw. III: Kirby's Quest, p. 235.
John le Deyere, co. Oxf., 1273. A.
Geoffrey le Deghere. G.
Nicholas le Deighere. M.
Richard le Dyghar, co. Soms., 1 Edw. III: Kirby's Quest, p. 104.
John le Dyghar, co. Soms., 1 Edw. III: ibid.
Ricardus Dier, 1379: P. T. Yorks. p. 185.
Richard le Dyer, of Kiderminster, rector of Fincham, co. Norf., 1333: FF. vii. 357.
1625. Buried—Phillip Dier, *cordwainer*: St. Dionis Backchurch, p. 217.
London, 58; New York, 32.

Dyerson, Dyason.—Bapt. 'the son of Dionisia,' a modification of Dyotson (v. Dyet); cf. Ibberson and Ibeson, modified forms of Ibbotson, an exact parallel, as both surnames are of Yorkshire origin; v. Dyson.

Adam Diotson, 1379: P. T. Yorks. p. 179.
1623. Henry Dyason and Priscilla Carter: Marriage Lic. (London), i. 129.
London (1884), 1, 0; London Court Dir., 0, 1; New York, 1, 0.

Dyet, Dyett, Dyot, Dyott, Dyte, Dight.—Bapt. 'the son of Dionisia,' from nick. Dy and dim. Dy-ot. A tremendous favourite in Yorkshire in the surname epoch. Every Yorkshire record contains instances; v. Dye and Dyson. Dyte and Dight are more recent corruptions.

Diot Mason, 1379: P. T. Yorks. p. 124.
Diot de Wodehous, 1379: ibid. p. 110.
Willelmus Wege, et Diot uxor ejus, 1379: ibid. p. 75.
Johannes Chetel, et Diot uxor ejus, 1379: ibid.
Robertus Diot, et Mariona uxor ejus, 1379: ibid.
1622. William Mullett and Alice Dyatt: Marriage Lic. (London), i. 111.
1784. Married—Joseph Dyett and Mary Mack: St. Geo. Han. Sq. i. 363.
London, 1, 1, 0, 0, 2, 3; Manchester, 1887 (Dyott), 1; Philadelphia (Dyott), 7; New York (Dight), 1.

Dyke, Dykes, Dike.—Local, 'of the dike or dikes,' i.e. banks, trenches.

Robert del Dykes, co. Cumb., 31 Edw. I. BBB. p. 639.
Adam del Dike, 1379: P. T. Yorks. p. 75,

Nicholaus del Dyk, 1379: P. T. Yorks. p. 101.
William del Diks, 2 Hen. IV: E. and F., co. Cumb., p. 176.
William del Dykes, 16 Ric. II: ibid. p. 174.
London, 14, 4, 4; New York, 1, 3, 4.

Dykehouse, Dicas. — Local, 'at the dike-house,' i.e. the house by the dike.

Johannes Dykehouse, 1379: P. T. Yorks. p. 211.
Johannes Dicas, *barkar*, 1379: ibid. p. 136.
John Dicas, or Dicus, of Handbridge, Chester, 1631: Wills at Chester, ii. 65.
1688-9. Buried—Mr. Humphrey Dicas: Canterbury Cath. p. 128.
London (1884), 1, 0.

Dykoman, Ditchman. — Occup. 'the dikeman,' a hedger or ditcher.

William Dikemon, co. Lanc., 1332: Lay Subsidy (Rylands), p. 64.
Thomas Dikeman, co. Norf., 3 Hen. IV: FF. ix. 234.

Richard Dikeman, co. Norf., 24 Hen. III: ibid. vi. 29.
John Dikeman, co. Norf., 20 Edw. III: ibid.
Manchester, 0, 1; Philadelphia, 1, 0.

Dymoke.—Local; v. Dimmock.

Dyson.—Bapt. 'the son of Dionisia,' from the nick. Dy or Dye, whence the patronymic Dyson. Almost all our Dysons hail from Yorkshire, where the font-name had a popularity second only to those of Matilda and Isabel. Of course Dionisius, the masculine form, was not unknown, and for a time Denny and Dennis were the common property of both sexes; v. Dye, Dyet, and Dennis, for other forms. I only furnish two or three instances from the Poll Tax (1379); but they abound.

Johannes Dison, 1379: P. T. Yorks. p. 18.

Johannes Dison, 1379: ibid. p. 124.
Dionisia uxor Thome Dison, 1379: ibid. p. 19.
1688. Married—Thomas Dyeson and Elizabeth Cox: St. Peter, Cornhill, ii. 58.
London, 9; West Rid. Court Dir., 45; Manchester, 16; New York, 4.

Dyster.—Occup. 'the dyster,' a dyer; cf. Lister. In the Corpus Christi Procession (Coventry, 1444), there walked among other crafts, the 'Gurdilers, Taylours, Walkers, Shermen, Deysters, Drapers, and Mercers' (Sharp's Coventry Mysteries, p. 160).

Robert le Dighestere. G.
Walter le Dighestere, ibid.
Thomas Dyster. B.
1767. Bapt.—John, s. John and Jane Dyster: St. Peter, Cornhill, ii. 51.
London (1884), 2.

Dyte.—Bapt.; v Dyet. For a different solution, v. Dight.

London, 3.

E

Eaddy, Eady, Eadie.—Bapt. 'the son of Ede,' from the pet Edie or Eddie. For fuller statement and many instances, v. Eddie.

1779. Married—James Eady and Charlotte Agar: St. Geo. Han. Sq. i. 298.
London, 1, 2, 2; New York, 0, 0, 11.

Eade, Eades.—Bapt. 'the son of Ede'; v. Eddie. Eades and Eade are modern variants of Edes and Ede, q.v.

1670. Bapt.—Robert, s. Robert Eades: St. Jas. Clerkenwell, i. 243.
1687. — Mary, d. John Edes: ibid. p. 323.
1773. Married—James Eade and Abigail Chamberlain: St. Geo. Han. Sq. i. 234.
1775. — Thomas Eades and Barbara Jane Morey: ibid. p. 255.
London, 11, 5; Boston (U.S.), 0, 1.

Eaden.—Bapt.; v. Eden.

Eadie.—Bapt.; v. Eddie.

Eadon.—Bapt.; v. Eden.

Eagle, Eagles.—(1) Nick. 'the eagle'; cf. Hawk, Sparrowhawk, Heron, &c. (2) ? Local, 'at the Eagle,' a sign-name; cf. Roebuck.

William Egle, co. Camb., 1273. A.
Custance Egle, co. Camb., ibid.

Gilbert de la Hegle, co. Sussex, 1273. A.
1594. Thomas Leese and Katherine Eagles: Marriage Lic. (London), i. 216.
1612. Bapt.—Anne, d. William Eagle: St. Jas. Clerkenwell, i. 71.
1777. Married—Joseph Eagle and Eliz. Johnson: St. Geo. Han. Sq. i. 281.
1780. — Daniel Miller and Anna Maria Eagles: ibid. p. 314.
London, 8, 8; New York, 11, 2.

Eagleston; variant of Eggleston.

Oxford, 9.

Eagleton.—Local; v. Eggleton.

Eagling.—Bapt.; v. Eglon.

Eakin, Eakins.—Bapt.; v. Ekin.

Ealand.—Local; v. Eland, of which it is a variant.

Eales, Elles, Eells, Eeles.—Bapt. 'the son of Elye'; O.F. for English Ellis. The genitive or patronymic form would be Elyes, thus differing slightly from the English Ellis. But v. Ellis, where instances of the French form will be found. I only suggest this; I have no actual proof.

Elye de Bleynnaker, C, R., 36 Hen. III.
1680. Married—John Kinghain and Saray Eeles: St. Jas. Clerkenwell, iii. 187.
1789. Married—John Eales and Mary Morton: St. Geo. Han. Sq. ii. 26.
1807. — William Eells and Sarah Grapham: ibid. p. 376.
London, 4, 2, 0, 3; Boston (U.S.), 0, 5, 4, 4.

Eames, Emes.—(1) Bapt. 'the son of Emma,' from the nick. Em or Emm; v. Emms. This seems to be the most satisfactory solution. The Norfolk Emms is also found in the form of Emes.

Mary Emes, wife of Edmund Hudson, *draper*, died August 18, 1608: FF. viii. 362.

(2) Local, 'at the elms,' from residence thereby; v. Elms (1). By some provincialism this became Ealmes. After that Eames was unavoidable.

1567-8. Thomas Ealmes and Catharine Lambarte: Marriage Lic. (London), i. 38.
1606. Married—Danyell Emes and Eliz. Lakins: St. Jas. Clerkenwell, iii. 31.
1732. — Rev. Charles Wragg and Catherine Emes: St. Mary Aldermary, p. 49.
London, 7, 2; New York, 10, 2.

Eardley.—Local, ' of Eardley,' probably one of the parishes now known as Ardley (dioc. Oxford), Ardeley (dioc. St. Albans), and Ardleigh (ibid.). Lower says, ' Eardley, a township in Staffordshire.'

Ralph de Erdeleye, co. Camb., 1273. A.
Walter de Erdele, co. Hunts, ibid.
London, 5 ; New York, 1.

Earl, Earle, Earll.—Offic. or nick. ' the earl'; cf. Count, Baron, &c.

Thomas le Yurl, Pat. Roll, 4 Edw. III. pt. ii.
Geoffrey le Erle, Fines Roll, 10 Edw. I.
Roger le Erle, co. Camb., 1273. A.
Walter le Erle, co. Soms., 1 Edw. III:
Kirby's Quest, p. 113.
Henry le Erl, co. Soms., 1 Edw. III:
ibid. p. 201.
Robertus Erle, 1379 : P. T. Yorks.
p. 160.
Thomas Erlle, 1379 : ibid. p. 89.
1650. Bapt.—Mary, d. Everard Earle:
St. Jas. Clerkenwell, i. 174.
1705. — Sarah, d. William Earle : St.
Mary Aldermary, p. 117.
London, 16, 19, 1 ; New York, 20, 40, 2.

Earlam, Earlem.—Local ; v. Erlam.

Earley, Early.—Local, ' of Earley,' a parish in dioc. Oxford. Lower says, ' A liberty in the parish of Sonning, co. Berks.' The form Early without the e in the second syllable is, of course, imitative, and indeed the entry :

Nicholas le Urrly, co. Norf., 1273. A.

suggests in some instances a nickname for one who ' caught the worm' in good time. But viewed generally the name must, without hesitation, be placed in the local class of surnames.

Clemens de Erleghe, co. Soms., 1273. A.
Philip de Erlee, co. Soms., ibid.
Warin de Erlegh, co. Soms., ibid.
1580. Married—Thomas Early and Agnes Odium : St. Jas. Clerkenwell, iii. 8.
London, 1, 14 ; New York, 10, 37.

Earnshaw, Ernshaw.—Local; v. Hernshaw.

Earp.— ? —— I cannot suggest any derivation of this name.

1561. William Erpe and Eliz. Brett:
Marriage Lic. (London), i. 22.
1809. Married—William Kendrick and Mary Erpe: St. Geo. Han. Sq. ii. 405.
London, 2 ; Manchester, 6 ; New York, 2.

Earwaker, Earwicker.—Local, ' of Erewaker.' I cannot find the place.

Simon de Erewaker, C. R., 39 Hen. III. pt. i.
Adam Edwaker, co. Oxf., 1273. A.
Thomas Edwaker, co. Oxf., ibid.
1662. Married—Thomas Aylett and Jane Arwaker: St. Thomas the Apostle (London), p. 21.
Manchester, 1, 0; London, 1, 1 ; New York, 0, 2.

Eason, Esson.—Bapt. ' the son of Ede ' or ' Eade '; v. Eddie. A corruption of Eadison.

1627. Married—Thomas Eason and Hester Grove: St. Jas. Clerkenwell, iii. 57.
1669. — John Hadon and Eliz. Eson:
ibid. p. 166.
London, 6, 1 ; New York, 6, 0.

East, Easte.—Local, ' at the east'; from residence at the east end of the town or village. Cf. West, North, and South.

Robert del Est, co. Camb., 1273. A.
Richard Est, co. Linc., ibid.
Geoffrey Est, co. Oxf., ibid.
Cf. Emma ate Estend, co. Oxf., ibid.
Hugh ate Estend, co. Oxf., ibid.

This of course implies residence at the east end. The ' West End ' has long been familiar to us.

London, 20, 0; Philadelphia, 3, 0;
Boston (U.S.), 0, 1.

Eastburn.—Local, ' of Eastburn': (1) in the township of Kirkburn, E. Rid. Yorks ; (2) ' of Eastburn,' in the parish of Kildwick, W. Rid. Yorks.

Bradford, 2 ; York, 1 ; Hull, 1 ; Philadelphia, 30.

Eastcott.—Local, ' of Eastcott,' a tithing in the parish of Urchfont, co. Wilts.

Richard de Estcott, co. Wilts, 1273. A.
Hugh de Estcote, co. Camb., ibid.
London, 1.

Eastend.—Local, ' at the east end '; v. East.

Emma ate Estend, co. Oxf., 1273. A.
Hugh ate Estend, co. Oxf., ibid.
Adam in Estend, co. Oxf., ibid.

Easter.—Local, ' of Easter,' two parishes (Good Easter and High Easter) in co. Essex.

London, 1 ; MDB. (co. Essex), 3 ; co. Norfolk), 3 ; Boston (U.S.), 3.

Easterbrook, Esterbrooke, Esterbrook, Estabrook, Esta-
brooks.—Local, ' of Eastbrook.' I have not found the spot. The intrusive a in Estabrooks or Estabrook is euphonic, as in Ottaway, Greenaway, &c. The next stage was Easterbrook. Cf. John atte Esterford (Kirby's Quest, p. 260).

John le (? de) Eastbrook, co. Soms., 1 Edw. III: Kirby's Quest, p. 224.
1658. Married—Richard Dalton and Frances Easterbrooke: St. Dionis Backchurch, p. 34.
1772. — William Phillips and Jane Eastabrook: St. Geo. Han. Sq. i. 226.
London, 2, 1, 0, 0, 0 ; Boston (U.S.), 6, 0, 1, 33, 4.

Easterby.—Local, ' of Eastby,' a township in the parish of Skipton, W. Rid. Yorks. At first for euphony the surname would be pronounced Eastaby, then Easterby ; cf. Ottaway and Greenaway for Ottway and Greenway ; also cf. Patterson for Pattison.

MDB. (North Rid. Yorks), 2 ; (West Rid. Yorks), 1.

Easterday. — Bapt. ' son of Easterday'; v. Christmas, Pentecost, Nowell, Whitsuntide, &c.

Philadelphia, 4.

Easterling, Isterling.—(1) Local, ' the Easterling'; (2) ' of Estherlinge,' some spot in co. Norf. that I cannot identify.

(Homines) de Estherlinge, co. Norf., 1273. A.
Walter de Eastherling, co. Norf., c. 1300: FF. i. 319.
Ralph de Eastherling, co. Norf., c. 1300: ibid.
London, 1, 0; Liverpool, 0, 1.

Eastgate.—Local, ' of Eastgate,' a hamlet in the parish of Stanhope, co. Durham. But no doubt many small spots would be so termed.

Andreas de Estgate, co. Norf., 1273. A.
Geoffrey de Estgate, co. Linc., ibid.
Martin de Estgate, co. Norf., ibid.
London, 2.

Eastham.—Local, ' of Eastham,' a parish in co. Chester, nine miles from Chester : the Lancashire Easthams are sprung from this parish. Also a parish in co. Worcester.

Alice Eastham, of Walton (co. Lanc.), 1602: Wills at Chester (1545-1620), p. 58.
Adam Eastham, of Walton-le-dale, 1611 : ibid.

Humphrey de Eastham, 1265, co. Norf.: FF. vii. 190.
Manchester, 4; Liverpool, 5; Preston, 5; Boston (U.S.), 2.

Eastman, Eastmond.—Bapt. 'the son of Estmund'; -mund becomes by corruption -man; cf. Osman, Wyman, &c. It would seem as if Eastman should be of the same class as Westerman, q.v.; but there is no evidence of this. All the proofs are in favour of Estmund.

John Estmond, co. Soms., 1 Edw. III : Kirby's Quest, p. 108.
Geoffrey Estmund, co. Camb., 1273. A.
Cecil Estmond, co. Camb, ibid.
Hugh Estmund, co. Camb., ibid.
John Estmond, co. Camb., ibid.
John Estmond, of Gressenhall, co. Norf., 1604: FF. ix. 517.
1692. Married—Rowland Porter and Sarah Easeman: St. Jas. Clerkenwell, iii. 210.
1748. — Daniel Eastmond and Hannah Overton: St. Geo. Han. Sq. i. 40.
1754. — John Tinson and Eliz. Eastman: ibid. p. 51.
London, 8, 0; New York, 14, 1.

Easton. Local, 'of Easton,' parishes in cos. Hunts, Norfolk, Northampton, Hants, Suffolk, Wilts, Essex, Somerset, and Leicester. Also hamlets in various counties; cf. Weston, Norton, Sutton, and many others.

Philip atte Estone, co. Soms., 1 Edw. III : Kirby's Quest, p. 230.
Alan de Eston, co. Oxf., 1273. A.
Ranulph de Eston, co. Hunts, ibid.
Geoffrey de Eston, co. Norf., ibid.
John de Eston, co. York, 20 Edw. I. R.
Walter de Eston, vicar of Tyrington, co. Norf., c. 1460: FF. ix. 97.
1572. Married—John Steedman and Alice Easton : St. Jas. Clerkenwell, iii. 5.
1738. — John Easton and Mary Head: St. Michael, Cornhill, p. 68.
London, 13 ; New York, 14.

Easttey, Eastty, Easty.—Local. These are manifestly variants of some local surname. Probably for Eastry, a parish in co. Kent, three miles from Sandwich.

London, 1, 2, 1.

Eastwell.—Local, 'of Eastwell,' a parish in co. Kent, three miles from Ashford.

?Richard de Estvelde, co. Kent, 1273. A.
London, 1.

Eastwood.—Local, 'of Eastwood,' a hamlet in the parish of Keighley, co. York. This surname has increased almost into a clan or colony. Doubtless, however, many other spots would be so termed. But Eastwood must be considered a Yorkshire surname for all that.

Jacob de Estwode, co. Suff., 1273. A.
Walter de Estwode, co. Bedf., ibid.
John de Estwode, co. Kent, ibid.
Rogerus de Estwode, 1379: P. T. Yorks. p. 189.
Johannes de Estwode, 1379 : ibid.
Johannes de Estwode, et Sibota uxor ejus, 1379: ibid. p. 19.
London, 3 ; West Rid. Court Dir., 37 ; Philadelphia, 29.

Eatock.—Local ; v. Eatough.

Eaton.—Local, 'of Eaton.' There are townships so termed in cos. Berks, Cheshire, Derby (4), and Salop; parishes in cos. Derby, Notts, Salop, Hereford, Bedford, Stafford, Berks, &c. The place-name and surname are now all but invariably spelt Eaton.

Peter de Eton, co. Hunts, 1273. A.
Brian de Eton, co. Wilts, ibid.
Robert de Etone, co. Berks, 20 Edw I. R.
Walter de Eton, co. Heref., Hen. III–Edw. I. K.
1563. Married—Thomas Eaton and Katherine Brown : St. Jas. Clerkenwell, iii. 2.
1588. — Harry Eton and Judithe Wylkynson: St. Michael, Cornhill, p. 14.
1669. — Thomas Bennitt and Margarett Eton : St. Jas. Clerkenwell, iii. 166.
1710. — John Eaton and Anne Eaton : St. Michael, Cornhill, p. 55.
London, 30; Manchester, 15; New York, 37.

Eatough, Eatock, Eattock.—Local, 'of Ethough,' evidently some small spot with hough as the suffix.

Oliver Ethoughe, of Altham, 1585: Wills at Chester (1545-1620), p. 61.
Richard Etough, of Huncote, 1624 : ibid. (1621-50), p. 74.
Henry Etough, vicar of Lakenham, co. Norf., 1728: FF. iv. 518.
Preston, 1, 0, 0; Manchester, 0, 2, 0; Philadelphia, 0, 0, 1.

Eatwell.—Local, 'of Etwall' (q.v.), a parish in co. Derby. An imitative variant.

London, 4.

Eavenson.—Bapt. 'the son of Eve.' One English form of the

patronymic was Eaveson, q.v. This across the Atlantic seems to have become first Eavison, then Eavenson ; cf. Pattison and Pattinson. Of course it may be but a variant of Evanson.

Philadelphia, 10.

Eaves.—(1) Bapt. 'the son of Eve,' q.v. (2) Local, 'of Eaves,' a hamlet in the parish of St. Michael-on-Wyre, co. Lancaster. All the Lancashire Eaves must be looked upon as sprung from this spot.

Thomas Eaves, of Fullwood, husbandman, 1641: Lancashire Wills at Richmond (1457-1680), p. 99.
Richard Eives, of Fishwicke, glover, 1599: ibid. p. 102.
Robert Eaves, of Houghwick, Penwortham, 1612: Wills at Chester (1545-1620), p. 58.
Richard Eyres, 1542. Preston Guild Rolls, p. 17.
Thomas Eyres, de Fyshwyk, 1542: ibid. p. 19.
London, 1; Manchester, 8; Preston, 4; New York, 2.

Eaveson.—Bapt. 'the son of Eve,' q.v.

Ebbetts, Ebbutt, Ebbets, Ebbett, Ebbitt.—Bapt. 'the son of Isabelle,' from nick. Ibb, dim. Ibbot, sometimes Ebbot. This would readily occur, as Elizabeth and Isabella are in reality the same name, and ran side by side in a race for popularity.

Thomas Gaylyour, et Ebbot sa femme, 1379: P. T. Yorks. p. 43.
Johan Tynete, et Ibbot sa femme, 1379: ibid. p. 4.
Ibbot Bolkok, 1379: ibid.
Ebota Stry, 1379: ibid.
Ebbett, d. of Sampson Morcambe, 1601: Reg. St. Columb Major, p. 20.
Ibbett, d. of Richard Sprey, 1579: ibid. p. 10.
Ebbot, d. of Walter Coryton, 1633: ibid. p. 213.
Alice Ebotson (cf. Ibbotson), co. York. W. 2.
London, 1, 2, 0, 0, 0; New York, 0, 0, 6, 0, 2; Boston (U.S.), 0, 0, 0, 2, 0.

Ebbs, Epps, Eppson, Epperson, Epp.—Bapt. 'the son of Ebb.' The name has no connexion with Ebba, sister of St. Oswald and founder of Coldingham Priory. Ebb, the parent of our Ebbs and Epps, was the nick. of Isabella, so popular in its day. Isabella took two nicks. Ibb and Ebb, and two dims. Ibbot and Ebbot (v. Ebbetts). There is no difficulty, of course, about Epps ; cf. Mapps and Mapson for Mabbs and Mabson, Hopps for Hobbs, and Hopkins for Hobkins. Eppison below is manifestly Ebbeson. With the variant Epperson, cf. Patterson for Pattison.

Henry Ebison, alias Ibbotson, co. York. TT.

Thomas Ebson, 1379 : P. T. Yorks. p. 154.

John Ebbes, 1505, Norwich : FF. iv. 497.

1547-8. Richard Longman and Agnes Ebbes : Marriage Lic. (London), i. 11.

Thomas Eppes, mayor of New Romney, 1584 : Cal. State Papers (Domestic), iii. 167.

1607. Married—Edward Powell and Eliza Ebbes : St. Jas. Clerkenwell, iii. 32.

1660. — George Granger and Eliza Eppison : ibid. p. 103.

1667. — William Badham and Elizabeth Ebbe : ibid. p. 131.

1681. — Thomas Goodwin and Mary Ebeson : ibid. p. 193.

London, 3, 3, 0, 0, 0 ; MDB. (co. Notts), 0, 0, 0, 1, 0 ; New York, 1, 0, 0, 0, 4.

Ebison.—Bapt. 'the son of Isabella,' from nick. Ibbie or Ebbie ; cf. Ebbs and Ebbetts, and v. Ibbinson and Ebbs.

1681. Married — William Hore and Issabell Ebbyson : St. Jas. Clerkenwell, iii. 193.

London (1884), 1.

Ebsworth.—Local, 'of Ebsworth.' For suffix, v. Worth ; for prefix we must not go to Ebbs (q.v.), but to a more ancient personal name, Ebba. One Ebba was sister of St. Oswald ; cf. the place-names, Ebbs-Fleet, Ebchester, Ebbesborne-Wake, Ebbsmore, Epworth, &c. These have no connexion with Isabel.

1683. Married—Robert Plaskett and Mary Ebsworth : St. Jas. Clerkenwell, iii. 201.

1770. — Thomas Ebesworth and Eliz. Robotham : St. Geo. Han. Sq. i. 201.

London, 6 ; New York, 1.

Eccles, Eckles.—Local, 'of Eccles': (1) an ancient parish near Manchester, now a suburb of the city; (2) a parish in co. Norfolk, near Stalham. Both places became parents of the surname.

Adam de Ecclis, of Heaton with Halliwell, co. Lanc., 1332 : Lay Subsidy (Rylands), p. 36.

Robert de Ecclis, of Pilkington, co. Lanc., 1332 : ibid.

Richard Eccles, co. Camb., 1273. A.

Robert de Eccles, co. Norf.: FF. viii. 342.

John de Eccles, co. Norf., 59 (sic) Edw. III : ibid. vi. 172.

Johannes Eclus, 1379 : P. T. Yorks. p. 83.

Humphrey Eccles, of Dean, 1603 : Wills at Chester (1545-1620), p. 58.

Thomas Eccles, of the Hough, husbandman, 1641 : ibid. (1621-50), p. 71.

London, 6, 0 ; Manchester, 10, 0 ; Philadelphia, 17, 3.

Eccleshall, Eckersall, Eckershall, Eckershell.—Local, 'of Eccleshill': (1) a township in the parish of Bradford, W. Rid. Yorks ; (2) a township in the parish of Blackburn, co. Lancaster; (3) 'of Eccleshall,' a parish in co. Stafford, seven miles from Stafford.

Robert de Eccleshale, co. Warwick, Hen. III-Edw. I. K.

Agnes Ecgleshill, 1379 : P. T. Yorks. p. 208.

Richard de Ecceleshull, co. Lanc., 1332 : Lay Subsidy (Rylands), p. 58.

1601. Married—John Shorre and Joane Eccesole : St. Jas. Clerkenwell, iii. 25.

1792. — Joseph Eccleshall and Ann Selway: St. Geo. Han. Sq. ii. 78.

Manchester, 1, 1, 1, 1.

Eccleston, Ecclestone. — Local, 'of Eccleston': (1) a parish in co. Chester, three miles from Chester ; (2) a parish in co. Lancaster, five miles from Chorley ; also three townships in co. Lancaster.

Robert de Eccleston, co. Lanc., 20 Edw. I. R.

Henry de Eccliston, of Newton-le-Willows, co. Lanc., 1332 : Lay Subsidy (Rylands), p. 11.

Richard Eccleston, of Eccleston, parish of Croston, co. Lanc., 1618 : Wills at Chester (1545-1620), p. 38.

Henry Eccleston, of Wrightington, 1593 : ibid.

Edward Eccleston, of Eccleston, 1623 : ibid. (1621-50), p. 71.

John Eccleston, of Chester, yeoman, 1640 : ibid.

1598. Bapt. — Margaret, d. Richard Eccleston : St. Michael, Cornhill, p. 101.

1650-1. — Theodore, s. Richard Eccleston, merchant: St. Dionis Backchurch, p. 111.

New York, 2, 0 ; Liverpool, 2, 0 ; MDB. (co. Stafford), 0, 1.

Eckersley.—Local, 'of Ecclesley' (?), corrupted to Eckersley (?). Hence it may be compared with such other place-names as Eccle-

sall, Ecclesfield, Eccleshall, Eccleshill, Eccleston, and Eccleswell. The surname is common to Lancashire and Yorkshire.

Henry de Ecclesleye, co. York, 20 Edw. I. R.

Johanna de Ecclesleye, co. York, ibid.

Jane Eckersley, of Bedford, spinster, co. Lanc., 1603 : Wills at Chester (1545-1620), p. 58.

Thomas Eckersley, of Middle Hulton, 1603 : ibid.

Roger Eckersley, of Bedford, parish of Leigh, 1648 : ibid. (1621-50), p. 71.

London, 1 ; Manchester, 8 ; W. Rid. Yorks Court Dir., 2 ; Philadelphia, 4.

Eckhard, Eckert, Eckett.—Bapt. 'the son of Echard.' The surname lasted for many centuries in co. Norfolk, and probably still exists there. With the corrupted Eckett, cf. Richard, Rickard, and Rickett.

Adam Ecard, co. Norf., 1273. A.

1515. William Echard, rector of Cley, co. Norf.: FF. vi. 42.

1537. Thomas Echard, bailiff of Yarmouth, co. Norf. : ibid. vi. 327.

1544. Married—Thomas Echarde and Eliz. Tood : St. Dionis Backchurch, p. 2.

1695. John Eacharde, rector of Wreningham, co. Norf.: FF. v. 121.

London, 0, 3, 0 ; Manchester, 1, 0, 0 ; Crockford, 0, 0, 1 ; Philadelphia, 1, 76, 0.

Ecroyd.—Local ; v. Ackroyd, of which it is a variant ; a° well-known Yorkshire surname.

London, 2 ; Manchester, 2 ; West Rid. Court Dir., 2 ; Philadelphia, 1.

Eddie, Eddis, Edds, Eddison, Eddy, Ede, Edes, Edgson, Edie, Edis, Eade, Eades, Eadie, Eady, Eaddy, Edison, Edeson.—Bapt. 'the son of Ede' or 'Edde,' pet form Eddy or Eady. Although this feminine font-name is now obsolete, it has made a most remarkable impression on our English directories. It lingered into the 17th century as a personal name. Every imaginable variant of the surname is found. No doubt the name was occasionally a nick. of Edward or Edmund, but the above derivation must be looked upon as absolutely decisive in the case of the great majority. I have furnished a large number of instances in order that the reader may note how familiar this girl's name was. Edgson (q.v.) is a variant of Eddison.

Eda, uxor Ricardi Gretword, C. R., 39 Hen. III. pt. i.
Edde (without surname), co. Norf., 1273. A.
Edde fil. Hugh, co. Hunts, ibid.
William fil. Ede, co. Suff., ibid.
Robert fil. Ede, co. Hunts, ibid.
William Ede, co. Norf., ibid.
Johannes Edeson, 1379: P. T. Yorks. p. 134.
Adam Edson, 1379: ibid. p. 55.
Edda mater Johannis, 1379: ibid. p. 84.
1533. Richard Fyddes and Johanna Edley: Marriage Lic. (London), i. 8.
Edie Waugh, 1602: Nicolson and Burn, Hist. Westm. and Cumb., vol. i. p. cxiii.
Thomas Andrew and Edye Cowdall, married, temp. 1545: Visitation of London, 1634, p. 17.
Herbert Eedes, or Edes, 1606: Reg. Univ. Oxf., vol. ii. pt. ii. p. 291.
1541. Bapt.—Eede,d.William Lymbott. St. Dionis Backchurch, p. 72.
1606. George Eades, co. Norf.: FF. ii. 240.
1610. Married—Edde Bunham (feminine): Reg. Elmham, co. Norf.
1616. — Richard Taggard and Eedy Arnall: St. Antholin (London), p. 52.
1621. — Andrew Stucke and Edey Kege: St. Mary Aldermary (London), p. 14.
1632. Edmund Eade, rector of Ovington, co. Norf.: FF. ii. 297.
London, 1, 2, 2, 1, 1, 10, 3, 4, 7, 1, 11, 5, 7, 2, 1, 0, 0; MDB. (co. Notts) (Eddison), 2; New York (Edeson), 1; Philadelphia, 2, 4, 0, 0, 16, 0, 1, 0, 0, 3, 0, 0, 2, 0, 0, 1, 0; Boston (U.S.) (Edds), 1.

Eddiman.—Occup.'Eddy-man,' i.e. the servant of Eddy (v. Eddie); cf. Matthewman, Perryman, Addyman, Jackman, &c.

1390. Robert Edyman, prebend of Norwich Cathedral: FF. iv. 173.
1507. Thomas Edeman, prebend of Norwich Cathedral: ibid.

Eddington; v. Edington.

Eddis, Eddison.—Bapt. 'the son of Ede.' For fuller statement and many instances, v. Eddie and Edis.

1758. Married—Edward Eddes and Eleanor Pocket: St. Geo. Han. Sq. i. 79.
London, 2, 1; Philadelphia, 4, 0.

Eddowes, Eddowis.—Bapt. 'the son of Eddow' (Welsh); v. Beddoe, where the evidence is very strong. Beddoes is also found answering to Eddowes.

Elizabeth Eddowe, of Chester, *widow*, 1632: Wills at Chester (1621-50), p. 71.

Sarah Eddowe, of Edge, co. Chester, *spinster*, 1640: ibid.
Randle Eddowes, of Stockton, co. Chester, *gent*, 1625: ibid.
Ann Eddowes, of Plumbley, *widow*, 1641: ibid.
1733. Married—Francis Eddowes and Eliz. Lewis: St. Geo. Han. Sq. i. 12.
London, 1, 0; Manchester, 1, 0; MDB. (co. Chester), 1, 1; Philadelphia, 4, 0.

Ede, Edes.—Bapt. 'the son of Ede'; v. Eddie for fuller statement and many instances.

Symon fil. Ede, co. Hunts, 1273. A.
1565-6. Audrian Awdryan and Christiane Dda: Marriage Lic. (London), i. 32.
1603. Thomas Edes and Margery Bishop: ibid. p. 280.
1803. Married — William Ede and Eliz. Holdaway: St. Geo. Han. Sq. ii. 280.
London, 10, 3: Boston (U.S.), 0, 14.

Edelot.—Bapt. 'the son of Ede' (q.v.), from double dim. Ed-el-ot; cf. Hewlett, Custlot, &c.

Edelota la Daye, co. Soms., 1 Edw. III: Kirby's Quest, p. 96.

Eden, Eaden, Eddon, Eadon.—Bapt. 'the son of Ede,' from dim. Edon; v. Eade. If this be not satisfactory there is only one other solution, viz. Idonia. If this were sometimes called Edonia we might expect the form Edon as well as Iddon, which we know to represent Idonia.—— Since writing the above I have found an instance:

Edonia Turnour, Agnes uxor, 1379: P. T. Yorks. p. 130.

Unfortunately this appears to be a masculine name.

Nicholas fil. Edon, co. Norf., 1273. A.
Roger fil. Edon, co. Norf., ibid.
Nel fil. Edine, co. Oxf., ibid.
Henry Edon, co. Oxf., ibid.
Johan Mountenay, et Edden sa femme, *fleshewer*, 1379: P. T. Yorks. p. 43.
Robertus Busby, et Eden uxor ejus, *smyth*, 1379: ibid. p. 101.
Johannes Slipar, et Edan uxor ejus, 1379: ibid. p. 109.

Looking at all these instances carefully, I suspect that they are all diminutives of the then popular girl's name Ede.

1660. Married — Henrie Sadde and Parnell Eaden: St. Jas. Clerkenwell, iii. 24.
London, 8, 1, 2, 1; Philadelphia, 4, 0,0,0.

Edensor.—Local, 'of Edensor'; v. Ensor.

Edes; v. Ede and Eddie.

Edgar. — Bapt. 'the son of Edgar.'

William Edger (sic), co. Soms., 1 Edw. III: Kirby's Quest, p. 136.
London, 11; Philadelphia, 42.

Edge.—(1) Local, 'at the edge,' from residence thereby; M.E. *egge*. ' *Slaw*, or dul of egge (dul of wyt), *obtusus*': Prompt. Parv. (2) Local. More specifically ' of Edge,' a township in the parish of Pontesbury, co. Salop.

Robert atte Egge, co. Soms., 1 Edw. III: Kirby's Quest, p. 136.
Is (? Isabel) atte Egge, co. Soms., 1 Edw. III: ibid. p. 137.
John de Egge, co. Salop, 1273. A.
Agnes del Egge, 1379: P. T. Yorks. p. 171.
Henry del Egge, of Withington, co. Lanc., 1332: Lay Subsidy (Rylands), p. 34.
John del Egge, of Reddish, co. Lanc., 1332: ibid. p. 32.

Therefore the Lancashire Edges probably hailed from Alderley Edge.

1617. Married — Henry Rappitt and Isabel Edge: St. Jas. Clerkenwell, iii. 44.
London, 4; Manchester, 14; Philadelphia, 10.

Edgecombe, Edgecomb, Edgcombe.—Local, 'of Edgecombe,' an estate in the parish of Milton Abbot, co. Devon. The earldom springs from the same property.

William de Egghacombe, co. Devon, 1273. A.
London, 5, 0, 0; MDB. (co. Devon), 1, 1; Boston (U.S.), 8, 0, 0.

Edgerley, Edgerly.—Local, ' of Edgerley,' a township in the parish of Aldford, co. Chester; cf. Adgarley, a township in the parish of Urswick, North Lancashire.

Manchester, 1, 0; Liverpool, 1, 0; Boston (U.S.), 1, 20.

Edgerton.—Local; v. Egerton.

Edgeworth.—Local, 'of Edgeworth': (1) a parish in co. Glouc., six miles from Cirencester; (2) a township in co. Lancaster, five miles from Bolton. For meaning, v. Edge and Worth.

Peter de Eggeworth, co. Glouc., Hen. III–Edw. I. K.

Hugh de Eggeworthe, of Turton, co. Lanc., 1332: Lay Subsidy (Rylands), p. 40.

Roger de Eggeworthe, of Edgeworth, co. Lanc., 1332: ibid.

John Egewurthe, 1519: Reg. Univ. Oxf. i. 117.

Richard Edgworth, of Orford, 1603: Wills at Chester (1545-1620), p. 59.

1615. Married—Thomas Mostrope and Katherine Edgwoorth: St. Jas. Clerkenwell, iii. 41.

1689. — Richard Merick and Mary Edsworth: St. Dionis Backchurch, p. 42.

1702. — Thomas Lee and Sarah Edgeworth: St. Michael, Cornhill, p. 51.

This surname seems to have become somewhat rare in England, but lives in America.

Boston (U.S.), 4 ; Crockford, 2.

Edghill, Edgell.—Local, ' of Edghill,' (1) a chapelry in the parish of Walton-on-the-Hill, Liverpool ; (2) a township in co. Stafford, three miles from Lichfield.

London, 4, 2 ; Philadelphia, 0, 3.

Edgington, Edginton. — Local, ' of Edgington,' probably a form of Eggington (q.v.) ; cf. Egg and Edge, Brigg and Bridge.

London, 6, 1 ; Oxford, 3, 5.

Edgley.—Local, ' of Edgley,' a hamlet in the parish of Stockport, co. Chester. No doubt many other small spots are so called.

Richard Edgley, of Marbury, 1593: Wills at Chester (1545-1620), p. 59.

Humphrey Edgley, of Nantwich, 1617: ibid.

London, 9 ; Manchester, 1.

Edgson.—Bapt. ' the son of Ede' ; patronymic Eddison or Eadson, whence variant Edgson ; cf. Gudgeon for Goodison, Dodgson for Dodson. For fuller statement and more instances, v. Eddie.

1640. Married — John Edgeson and Mary Beedler (Needler ?): St. Dionis Backchurch, p. 24.

1789. — Christopher Eadson and Martha Smith : St. Geo. Han. Sq. ii. 27.

1790. — John Banks and Mary Eadson : ibid. 47.

1808. — Thomas Brand and Hannah Edgson : ibid. 396.

London, 4.

Edington, Eddington. — Local, ' of Edington,' (1) a town-

ship in the parish of Mitford, co. Northumberland ; (2) a township in the parish of Moorlinch,. co. Somerset ; (3) a parish in co. Wilts, near Westbury.

Gilbert de Edyngton, co. Soms., 1 Edw. III : Kirby's Quest, p. 142.

London, 4, 4 ; MDB. (co. Soms.), 0, 2 ; Philadelphia, 2, 0.

Edis, Edison.—Bapt. ' the son of Ede.' For fuller statement and instances of Edison, v. Eddie.

1744. Married — Thomas Eddis and Cherry Odell : St. Jas. Clerkenwell, iii. 274.

1791. — Ambrose Clerk and Eliz. Edeson : St. Geo. Han. Sq. ii. 53.

London, 6, 0 ; Philadelphia, 3, 2.

Edkins.—Bapt. ' the son of Edward,' from the nick. Eddie and dim. Ede-kin ; cf. Wilkin, Tompkin, Jenkin, &c. From the instances given below it will be seen that for five centuries at least the surname has lingered on in Oxfordshire and Berkshire. The final s in Edkins is genitival, as in Wilkins and Simpkins.

Edekin Gomey, co. Oxf., 1273. A.

John Edekin, co. Oxf., ibid.

Elena Edkynes, co. Soms., 1 Edw. III : Kirby's Quest, p. 210.

1800. Married—Charles F. de Coetlogon and Emily Edkins, co. Berks : St. Geo. Han. Sq. id. 215.

1804. — Thomas Edkins and Susanna Bourne : ibid. p. 305.

London Court Dir., 3 ; Philadelphia, 2.

Edlestone.—Local, ' of Edleston.'

Manchester, 1.

Edlett.—Bapt. ' the son of Eade,' from dim. Edelot.

Edelota Darby, co. Oxf., 1273. A.

Ydelot Binytheton, co. Devon : Hen. III–Edw. I. K.

1584. Daniel Edlett and Anne Blackwell : Marriage Lic. (Westminster), p. 9.

Edlin, Edling.—Bapt. ' the son of Edeline' or 'Adeline'; v. Adlin.

Edilena Aylefe, co. Camb., 1273. A.

Robert fil. Edeline, co. Hunts, ibid.

John Edelyne, co. Camb., ibid.

Reginald Edelyne, co. Camb., ibid.

Edelina del Brok. K.

Ediline fil. Nicholai Coci : Cal. and Inventories of the Treasury.

Henricus Edlyn, 1379 : P. T. Yorks. p. 129.

Henricus Edelyn, 1379 : ibid. p. 63.

1607. Michael Edlin, co. Hants, Lincoln Coll.: Reg. Univ. Oxf. vol. ii. pt. ii. p. 299.

1669. Married—Henry Edlin and Mary Edlin : St. Jas. Clerkenwell, iii. 162.

1714. Buried—Anna, wife of Col. Edmond Edlyne : St. Michael, Cornhill, p. 283.

1796. Married—John Edlin and Sarah Seabrook : St. Geo. Han. Sq. ii. 151.

London, 5, 1 ; Boston (U.S.), 0, 1.

Edlington.—Local, ' of Edlington,' (1) a parish in co. Lincoln, near Horncastle ; (2) a parish in co. York, five miles from Doncaster.

MDB. (co. Lincoln), 3.

Edmund, Edmunds, Edmundson, Edmand, Edmands, Edmans, Edmonds, Edmondson, Edmonson.—Bapt. ' the son of Edmund.' In North Lancashire Edmundson or Edmondson has been a familiar surname for centuries.

Simon fil. Edmundi, co. Norf., 1273. A.

Thomas fil. Edmundi, co. Kent, ibid.

Thomas Edmund, London, 20 Edw. I. R.

William Edmund, co. Bedf., ibid.

Edmund fil. Osmund, co. Berks, Hen. III–Edw. I. K.

Johannes Edmund, 1379 : P. T. Yorks. p. 125.

Edmundus del Grange, 1379: ibid. p. 39.

Robertus Edmondson, taylour, 1379 : p. 130.

Johannes Edmondson, 1379: ibid. p. 173.

Margaret Edmondson, of Catton, 1577: Lanc. Wills at Richmond, i. 101.

Leonard Edmondson, of Melling, 1582: ibid.

1809. Married—Thomas Edmands and Mary Brown : St. Geo. Han. Sq. ii. 410.

London, 0, 10, 1, 1, 2, 2, 51, 1, 0 ; Manchester (Edmundson), 5; (Edmondson), 13 ; (Edmonson), 2 ; New York, 2, 4, 1, 1, 3, 0, 13, 3, 0.

Edney.—Bapt. ' the son of Idonia,' popularly Edonia and Edeney, a favourite girl's name in the 13th and 14th centuries ; v. Iddison and Iddon.

Edonia Roy, 1379 : P. T. Yorks. p. 31.

Ideny, wife of Edw. Stannowe, 1644 : Reg. Beetley, Norf.

1577. William Edney and Eliz. Burlacie : Marriage Lic. (London), i. 75.

1784. Married—Edward Edney and Sarah Hill : St. Geo. Han. Sq. i. 365.

London, 9 ; Oxford, 2 ; New York, 1.

Edolph.—Bapt. 'the son of Edolph.' Mr. Lower writes, 'an ancient personal name, written in the Saxon Chronicle Eadulph. The same as Adolphus' (Patr. Brit. p. 101). No doubt this is true.

Henry Edolf, co. Soms., 1 Edw. III : Kirby's Quest, p. 144.
William Edolf, co. Soms., 1 Edw. III : ibid.

Edred.—Bapt. 'the son of Edred.'

Hugh Edred, co. Hunts, 1273. A.
John Edred, co. Oxf., ibid.

Edridge, Edrich.—Bapt. 'the son of Edrich' or 'Edric'; cf. Richard and Rickard, and v. Aldridge for Aldrich. The name seems to have been popular between Lincoln and Norfolk.

John Edrich, co. Soms., 1 Edw. III : Kirby's Quest, p. 134.
Roger Edrich, co. Soms., 1 Edw. III : ibid. p. 241.
Edericke le Blacke, co. Linc., 1273. A.
Edrich le Blacke, co. Linc., ibid.

No doubt the last two entries refer to the same individual.

Edrich (without surname), co. Norf., 1273. A
Nicholas Edrych, co. Oxf., ibid.
Andrew fil. Edrich, co. Camb., ibid.
Roger Edryk, rector of St. Matthew the Apostle (Norwich), 1328: FF. iv. 375.
John Ederych, vicar of Halvergate, co. Norf., 1426: ibid. xi. 105.
1668. Married—William Edridge and Anne Prince: St. Jas. Clerkenwell, iii. 141.
London, 6, 0; MDB. (Norfolk), 1, 2.

Edson.—Bapt. 'son of Ede'; v. Eddie.

New York, 8 ; Philadelphia, 9.

Edward, Edwards, Edwardson, Edwardes.—Bapt. 'the son of Edward.' It is a curious thing to note that while our Richardsons, Williamsons, and Harrisons can be numbered by thousands, Edwardson has always been a very rare surname. The shorter Edwards has monopolized everything. Yet Williams, Richards, and Harris have not been put down by their longer brethren.

William Edward, co. Soms., 1 Edw. III : Kirby's Quest, p. 102.
Adam Edward, 1379: P. T. Yorks. p. 103.
Willelmus Edward, taylour, 1379 : ibid. p. 15.
Ricardus Edward, 1379 : ibid. p. 24.

John Edwardson, of Bold, 1594: Wills at Chester (1545-1620), p. 59.
Roger Edwardson, of Kenyon, 1624 : ibid. (1621-50), p. 73.
1415. Robert Edward : Cal. of Wills in Court of Husting (2).
1600. Married—Richard Edwardson and Eliz. Harford : St. Jas. Clerkenwell, iii. 41.
London, 2, 321, 0, 0; Liverpool (Edwardson), 5; Philadelphia, 6, 197, 0, 1.

Edwin, Edwins.—Bapt. 'the son of Edwin,' a much rarer fontname in the surname epoch than might have been expected. For obvious reasons Edward was the favourite.

Robert Edwine, co. Hunts, 1273. A.
Agnes Edwine, co. Oxf., ibid.
Simon Edwyne, co. Camb., ibid.
Christina Edwyne, co. Soms., 1 Edw. III : Kirby's Quest, p. 98.
William Edwyne, co. Soms., 1 Edw. III : ibid.
1540. Bapt.—Luce Edwinne : St. Peter, Cornhill, i. 2.
1546. Buried—Leonard Edwyn : ibid. p. 108.
1578. — John, s. John Edwyn, plague : St. Michael, Cornhill, p. 195.
London, 1, 1 ; New York, 2, 0.

Edzard.—Evidently a foreign importation, unless it be a variant of Ezard, q.v.

1730. Bapt. Anna Maria, d. Gustavus Jacob and Astrea Edzard : St. Mary Aldermary, p. 125.
London, 1.

Eede, Edes.—Bapt. 'the son of Ede'; v. Eddie.

1541. Bapt. — Eede, d. of William Lymbott : Reg. St. Dionis Backchurch, London, p. 72.
London, 2, 1.

Egerton, Edgerton.—Local, of Egerton,' (1) a township in the parish of Malpas, co. Cheshire ; (2) a parish in co. Kent, thirteen miles from Maidstone.

1554. Ralph Egerton, of Christleton : Wills at Chester, i. 60.
1614. John Egerton of Tatton : ibid.
London, 3, 0 ; New York, 3, 3.

Egg.—? Local. Probably 'at the egg,' from residence thereby. Egg seems to be a hard form of Edge, q.v. ; cf. Bridge and Brigg.

London, 5; Philadelphia, 1.

Eggett. — ? ——

London, 4.

Eggington, Egginton. — Local, (1) 'of Eggington,' a cha-

pelry in the parish of Leighton Buzzard, co. Bedf. ; (2) 'of Egginton,' a parish in co. Derby, near Burton.

Liverpool, 1, 0 ; New York, 0, 2.

Eggins.—Bapt. A variant of Eakins or Ekins, v. Ekin ; cf. Higgins for Hickins.

London, 2.

Eggleston, Egleston.—Local. (1) ' of Egglestone,' a chapelry in the parish of Middleton-in-Teesdale, co. Durham ; (2) 'of Eggleston Abbey,' in the parish of Rokeby, union of Teesdale, N. Rid, Yorks. Probably in some cases a lazified form of Eccleston, q.v. ; cf. Slagg for Slack, &c.

1581. Christopher Day and Margery Eggleston: Marriage Lic. (London), i. 104.
1603. Buried—John Eggleston : St. Jas. Clerkenwell, iv. 85.
1623. — Edward Egglestone : ibid. 161.

The large number of Egglestons or Eglestons in America is probably explained by the following item :

'1635. Richard Eggleston sailed for Virginia from the Port of London'. Hotten's Lists of Emigrants, p 102.

Doubtless all were related to one another.

East Rid. Yorkshire, 1, 0 ; New York, 3, 11; Boston (U.S.), 17, 0; Philadelphia, 7, 0.

Eggleton, Egleton, Egalton, Eagleton.—Local, 'of Egleton,' (1) a chapelry in the parish of Oakham, co. Rutland ; (2) a township in the parish of Bishops Frome, co. Hereford.

Simon de Egilton, co. Rutland, 1273. A.
1758. Married—John Eagelton and Esther Atlee : St. Geo. Han. Sq. i. 82.
1779. — John Egleton and Hannah Dean : ibid. p. 306.
London, 3, 3, 1, 4; Philadelphia, 8, 0, 0, 3.

Eglington, Eglinton.—Local, ' of Eglinton,' a village near Greenock, in Scotland.

New York, 2, 1; London, 1, 1.

Eglon, Eglin, Eagling, Eggling.—Bapt. 'the son of Egelin.' It is interesting to notice that the surname still flourishes in the district where the fontal name was familiar. The final *g* is excrescent, as in Jennings, q.v.

Egelina de Denver: co. Norf., 41 Hen. III: FF. ix. 110.
1274. Dionisia Egeline: Cal. of Wills i. Court of Husting.
Hegelina Burdan, co. Bedf., Hen. III-Edw. I. K.
Engelina Burdan, co. Bedf., ibid.
Egelina de Curtenay, co. Berks, ibid.
William Egelin, co. Suff., 1273. A.
Roger Egolyn, co. Soms., 1 Edw. III: Kirby's Quest, p. 156.
1787. Married—John Eagling and Mary Palmer: St. Geo. Han. Sq. i. 402.
London, 1, 0, 2, 0; Haverthwaite, near Ulverston, 0, 1, 0, 0; MDB. (Norfolk), 0, 0, 3, 0; Philadelphia, 0, 0, 0, 3.

Eightshillings. — Nick. ; cf. Ninepence, Fourpence, Centlivre, Thousandpounds.

1666. Jeremiah Eightshillings, of St. Leonard, Shoreditch, *tallow chandler, bachelor*, and Susanna Angier, alias Angell, of Stepney, Middlesex: Marriage Lic. (Harl. Soc.) v. p. xxiii.
1691. Buried—Jeremiah Eightshillings: Reg. St. Leonard's, Shoreditch.

Ekin, Ekins, Eakin, Eakins, Ekyns.—Bapt. 'the son of Ekin,' but what this is the pet name for I have not discovered. It evidently belongs to the same class as Watkin, Wil-kin, Tomp-kin, &c., which gave us the genitive forms of Watkins, Wilkins, Tompkins, &c. The only explanation I can suggest is that Ekin is a modification of Edkin (v. Edkins).

1598. Thomas Marrott and Mary Eakyn: Marriage Lic. (London), i. 255.
1693. Bapt.—Gyles, s. Gyles Ekyns: St. Jas. Clerkenwell, i. 351.
1721. Married—Samuel Ekin and Eliz. Brown: ibid. p. 245.
1730. Samuel Eakins, sheriff of Norwich: FF. iii. 449.
1792. — Jeremiah Ekins and Ann Rea: St. Geo. Han. Sq. ii. 80.
London, 0, 4, 0, 0, 1; New York, 0, 0, 5, 4, 0.

Elam.—Local, 'of Elham,' a parish in co. Kent, eleven miles from Canterbury. Probably originally Elmham.

Helewis de Eleam, co. Linc., 20 Edw. I. R.
Henry de Ellham, London, 1273. A.
Walter de Elmham, co. Suff., ibid.
London, 9; West Rid. Court Dir., 2; Boston (U.S.), 1.

Eland, Ealand.—Local, 'of Eland,' an ancient village near Halifax, co. York. This surname has made little impression upon the directories.

Willelmus de Elland, 1379: P. T. Yorks. p. 48.
Thomas de Eland, *taylour*, 1379: ibid. p. 166.
Johannes de Eland, 1379: ibid. p. 193.
West Rid. Court Dir., 1, 0; MDB. (co. Lincoln), 1, 4; Boston (U.S.), 2, 0.

Elcock, Elcox. — Bapt. 'the son of Ellis,' from nick. Ell, with popular suffix -*cock* (v. Cocks), as in Wilcock, Simcock, &c.; v. Ellis. The earliest instance below has the aspirate before it. All the forms of Ellis are occasionally thus entered in the Hundred Rolls, Helie being about as common as Elie. With Elcox, cf. Cox for Cocks, or Wilcox for Wilcocks.

Roger Hellecok, co. Glouc., 1273. A.
Hellecok, —, co. Bucks, ibid.

This last entry is misprinted Hellebok.

Johannes Elkoc, et Emmot uxor ejus, *taylour*, 1379: P. T. Yorks. p. 89.
Willelmus Elkoc: ibid. p. 90.
Ricardus Elcok: ibid. p. 173.
1620. Married—Thomas Owenton and Eliz. Elcocke: St. Jas. Clerkenwell, iii. 48.
William Elcock, of Leighton, 1595: Wills at Chester (1545-1620), p. 60.
London, 3, 0; Manchester, 3, 0; New York, 1, 2; Philadelphia, 3, 0.

Elcombe, Elcum.—Local; v. Ellacombe.

Eldborough.—Local, 'of Aldborough'; v. Albury. With Elbro in the instances below, cf. the New York variant of Albro.

1768. Married—Jacob Elborough and Mary Smith: St. Geo. Han. Sq. i. 172.
1776. — Robert Elbrow and Ann Smith: ibid. p. 270.
1805. — John Gibbs and Hannah Elbro: ibid. ii. 321.
1809. — Joseph Monk and Ann Elbora: ibid. p. 400.
London, 1.

Elder.—Nick. 'the elder.' The usual form in the Yorkshire Poll Tax is Senior, and this has become one of the strongly established surnames of that county.

Ricardus ye Elder, 1379: P. T. Yorks. p. 214.

1648. Married—Thomas Elder and Jone Gibbs: St. Jas. Clerkenwell, iii. 82.
London, 9; Philadelphia, 44.

Elderkin, Elderking.—Bapt. 'the son of Elder,' from personal name Elder, with suffix -*kin*, as in Wilkin, Tompkin, &c. Probably of Flemish extraction.

MDB. (co. Lincoln), 0, 1; New York, 1, 0; Philadelphia, 2, 0.

Eldershaw.—Local, 'at the elder-shaw,' from residence beside a small shaw or wood of elders; v. Ellershaw.

1618. Buried—William Eldershaw: St. Michael, Cornhill, p. 221.
1791. Married—Thomas Eldershire and Martha Hawgood: St. Geo. Han. Sq. ii. 55.
1796. — John Eldershaw and Jane Campbell: p. 148.
Liverpool, 1.

Eldred.—Bapt. 'the son of Eldred,' the same as Aldred, q.v.

1569-70. William Fynche and Anne Eldreade, *widow*: Marriage Lic. (London), i. 44.
1669. Married—Mathew Stevens and Ann Eldrid: St. Jas. Clerkenwell, iii. 161.
1793. — Newlyn Peter Shawyer and Sarah Eldred: St. Geo. Han. Sq. ii. 105.
MDB. (Suffolk), 2; (co. Hunts), 3; New York, 7.

Eldridge, Eldredge.—Bapt. 'the son of Alderich'; v. Aldrich.

1597-8. Otwell Eldridge and Anne Itree: Marriage Lic. (London), i. 245.
1692. Married—John Eldridge and Sarah Clay: St. Jas. Clerkenwell, iii. 211.
London, 17, 0; New York, 32, 10.

Elener, Elnor.—Bapt. 'the son of Eleanor,' found as Alianora, Heleanora, &c., in mediaeval registers.

Hugh fil. Elyenor, co. Bedf., 1273. A.
Robert Elyenore, co. Linc., ibid.
Alicia Alianor, Guernsey, 20 Edw. I. R.
Alianori Bushe. EE.
Joseph Alianore, M.P. for Colchester, C. R., 13 Edw. III. pt. i.
Johannes Eliner, 1379: P. T. Yorks. p. 126.
John Elynor, rector of Ingworth, co. Norf., 1447: FF. vi. 368.
Bartholomew Ellnor, 1633: Visitation of London, i. 254.
1801. Married—George Frederic Hipp and Ann Elnor: St. Geo. Han. Sq. ii. 232.
Sheffield, 1, 0; London, 0, 2.

Eley; v. Ely.

Elfick; v. Elphick.

Elgar.—Bapt. 'the son of Algar,' q.v. (for a variant v. Ilgar, under which are some early instances).

1627. Married—George Harrison and Jone Elger: St. Jas. Clerkenwell, iii. 57.
1648. — Thomas Elgar and Eliz. George: ibid. p. 82.
London, 4; New York, 2.

Elgee, Elgie, Elgey, Elgy.—Bapt. 'the son of Elgar' (?), seemingly a pet form of this early personal name; v. Algar. The pet name for Algernon has long been Algie.

1783. Married—William Elgie and Eliz. Doratt: St. Geo. Han. Sq. i. 349.
London, 1, 2, 0, 0; MDB. (North Rid., Yorks), 0, 1, 1, 1.

Elgood.—Bapt.; v. Allgood.

Eling.—Local, 'of Eling,' a parish in the New Forest, five miles from Southampton.

Ichenard Eling, co. Worc., Hen. III-Edw. I, K.
1795. Married—Thomas Keell and Frances Eling: St. Geo. Han. Sq ii. 100.
London, 1; New York, 2.

Eliot, Eliott.—Bapt. 'the son of Elliot,' q.v.

London, 1, 1; New York, 4, 4.

Elkin, Elkins.—Bapt. 'the son of Elkin,' from Elie (Elias), dim. Elekin (three syllables), abbreviated to Elkin; v. Ellis. Elekin is found as a single personal name without surname in the Hundred Rolls as given below. Also as Elekyn in the *Munimenta Gildhallae Londoniensis.*

Elekin (without surname), co. Oxf., 1273. A.
Robert Elkyn. X.
1520. Richard Elkyn and Johanna Carter: Marriage Lic. (London), i. 7.
1605. Married—William Macham and Marie Elkin: St. Jas. Clerkenwell, iii. 30.
London, 3, 7; New York, 10, 2.

Elkington, Elkinton.—Local, ' of Elkington,' (1) a parish in co. Northampton, three miles from Welford; (2) two parishes, North and South Elkington, in co. Lincoln, near Louth.

John de Elkincton, co. Lincoln, 1273. A.
1700. Married—John Crick and Joyce Elkington: St. Jas. Clerkenwell, iii. 223.
1807. — Coleman Gill and Mary Elkington: St. Geo. Han. Sq. ii. 369.
London, 8, 0; Philadelphia, 1, 20.

Ell, Elson.—Bapt. 'the son of Elen,' from the nick. Ell, the foundation of the dim. Elot or Ellot.

Cf. Ricardus Elson, 1379: P. T. Yorks. p. 156.

Here, as in other cases, Elson must be distinguished from Ellison, although both forms are now confounded together.

1579. Lewis Frewellyn and Jane Ellson: Marriage Lic. (London), i. 90.
1594. Married—William Elson and Alice Duglas: St. Jas. Clerkenwell, iii. 18.
1793. — James Ell and Ann Hughes: St. Geo. Han. Sq. ii. 97.
London, 6, 3; New York, 2, 2.

Ellaby; v. Ellerby.

Ellacombe, Elcombe, Elcum, Ellicombe.—Local, 'of Ellacombe,' a place under the Haldon hills, co. Devon, where the 'de Ellacombes' were resident in 1306 (Lower's Patr. Brit. p. 103).

London, 0, 1, 1, 2; Crockford, 1, 0, 2, 0; MDB. (co. Glouc.), 3, 0, 0, 1.

Ellard. — Bapt. 'the son of Eylard,' doubtless a form of Aylward, q.v.; frequently found as Allard.

Eylard, fil. Nicholas, co. Oxf., 1273. A.
Robert Elward, co. Suff., ibid.
Roger Elward, rector of Swanton Novers, co. Norf., 1532: FF. ix. 444.
London, 2; New York, 5.

Ellary.—Local; v. Elleray.

Ellaway; v. Allaway, a variant.

Ellen, Elen, Elin, Eline, Ellin.—Bapt. 'the son of Ellen,' i.e. Ellen or Eleanora, a favourite girl's name in the surname period, sometimes found as Alianora.

Agnes Eleyne, Fines Roll, 11 Edw. I: Kirby's Quest, p. 133.
William Elyn, co. Soms., 1 Edw. III: ibid.
William fil. Elinne, co. Norf., 1273. A.
Henry fil. Elene, co. Linc., ibid.
Hugh fil. Elyenor', co. Bedf., ibid.
David fil. Elene, co. Camb., ibid.
Margaret fil. Eline, co. Suff., ibid.

Willelmus Elyne, 1379: P. T. Yorks. p. 135.
Margareta Helyn, 1379: ibid. p. 124.
Johannes Helyn, 1379: ibid.
1669. Married—John Payne and Hanna Ellin: St. Jas. Clerkenwell, iii. 161.
1791. — Thomas Ellen and Ann Cadby: St. Geo. Han. Sq. ii. 65.
London, 8, 2, 1, 0, 0; New York, 0, 0, 0, 1, 2.

Elleray, Ellery, Ellary.—Local, 'at the eller-ey,' i.e. the islet in the stream on which the ellers or alders grew; or 'at the eller-hay,' i.e. the eller enclosure (v. Hay). A North Lancashire surname. I have no distinct proof of either derivation. One more derivation may be suggested, that of ellerhow (v. How). One spot in Furness is so called, and the surname is clearly of Furnessian parentage. Ellerhow would readily vary into Ellery.

1664. Agnes Elleric, of Ellell: Lancashire Wills at Richmond (1457-1680), p. 102.
1737. William Ellerey, of Hawkshead: ibid. (1681-1748), p. 93.
1772. Married—William Smith and Martha Ellery: St. Geo. Han. Sq. i. 220.
1758. Bapt.—Margaret, d. James Ellerey: Ulverston Church, p. 353.

The variants in the last-named register are Elleray, Ellery, and Ellerah.

London, 0, 1, 0; Manchester, 1, 0, 0; Lancaster, 1, 0, 0; Liverpool, 0, 0, 1; New York, 0, 9, 0.

Ellerbeck.—Local, 'of Ellerbeck,' a township in the parish of Osmotherley, N. Rid. Yorks. The surname passed over the border and was found in North Lancashire comparatively early. The meaning is 'the streamlet by the ellers,' i.e. alder-trees; v. Beck. Of course the name is North English.

Alan de Ellerbek, co. York, 1273. A.
Henricus de Ellerbek, 1379: P. T. Yorks. p. 257.
Matilda de Ellerbek, 1379: ibid.
Elena de Ellerbek, 1379: ibid. p. 229.
John de Ellerbec', co. Lanc., 1332; Lay Subsidy (Rylands), p. 118.
Richard de Ellerbek, co. Lanc., 1332: ibid. p. 109.
1669. Married—Robert Hudson and Eliz. Ellerbec: St. Jas. Clerkenwell, iii. 166.
1785. — Archibald Little and Jane Ellerbeck: St. Geo. Han. Sq. i. 369.

The following instance is interesting:

1551. Buried—Rychard Elderbeke: St. Dionis Backchurch, p. 183.
Liverpool, 2; Ulverston, 1; Manchester, 2; MDB. (West Rid. Yorks), 2.

Ellerby, Ellaby.—Local, 'of Ellerby,' (1) a township in the parish of Swine, E. Rid. Yorks; (2) a township in the parish of Lythe, N. Rid. Yorks. The variant Ellaby seems to be a fairly old one. The meaning is 'the dwelling by the alder-trees.'

1620. Married—Richard Ellabye and Katherine Pellam: St. Jas. Clerkenwell, iii. 48.
1719. — Robert Cox and Mary Ellaby: St. Antholin (London), p. 132.
MDB. (North Rid. Yorks), 5, 0; Sheffield, 0, 1.

Ellerker.—Local, 'of Ellerker,' i.e. the low-lying ground on which the ellers grew; more specifically, a township in the parish of Brantingham, E. Rid. Yorks.

John de Ellerker, *taillour*: 8 Edw. II: Freemen of York, i. 16.
1593. Buried—William Ellerker, out of Mr. Woodroofe's howse: St. Mary Aldermary, p. 146.
1678. Bapt.—Frances, d. Francis Eliker: St. Jas. Clerkenwell, i. 282.
1679-80. Richard Furnis and Mary Ellerker, d. of John Ellerker, of Doncaster, co. York: Marriage Lic. (Faculty Office), p. 149.
1752. Married—Richard Townsend and Mary Elleker: St. Geo. Chap. Mayfair, p. 213.
MDB. (North Rid. Yorks), 2; Ulverston, 1; MDB. (East Rid. Yorks), 3.

Ellershaw.—Local, 'at the eller-shaw,' from residence beside a coppice of ellers, i.e. alder-trees; cf. Eldershaw, and v. Shaw. Many local names have this prefix, as Ellerbeck, Ellerton, Ellerby. Ellershaw is a Yorkshire surname. That county is still its chief habitat.

Thomas de Ellerschawe, 1379: P. T. Yorks. p. 289.
Thomas Ellerschawe, of Tatham, 1631: Lanc. Wills at Richmond (1457-1680), p. 102.
Ellen Ellershaw, of Green, parish of Tatham, 1666: ibid.

From other sources I gather that Ellershaw hails from the neighbourhood of Tatham.

Liverpool, 1; West Rid. Court Dir., 5; Philadelphia, 1.

Ellerton.—Local, 'of Ellerton,' (1) a parish in E. Rid. Yorks; (2) two townships in N. Rid. Yorks. The lit. meaning is 'the dwelling by the alder-trees'; cf. Ashton.

(Prior) de Ellerton, co. York, 1273. A.
John de' Ellerton, *tannour*, 28 Edw. I: Freemen of York, i. 7.
Agnes de Ellerton, 1379: P. T. Yorks. p. 32.
Johannes de Ellyrton, 1379: ibid. p. 148.
1749. Married—Thomas Whitehead and Mary Ellerton: St. Geo. Chapel, Mayfair, p. 139.
London, 2; West Rid. Court Dir., 6.

Ellesmere, Elsmere, Elsmore, Elsmoor. — Local, ' of Ellesmore,' a parish in co. Salop.

1616. Married—David Elsmore and Phillip Gowen: St. Jas. Clerkenwell, iii. 43.
1779. — Joseph Jerome and Eliz. Elsmore: St. Geo. Han. Sq. i. 303.
London, 0, 1, 0, 0; MDB. (co. Salop), 1, 0, 0, 0; (co. Stafford), 0, 0, 4, 1.

Ellett, Elletson.—Bapt.; v. Ellot for full statement and many instances.

1770. Married—Richard Ellet and Mary Hayman: St. Geo. Han. Sq. i. 196.
— — Roger Hope Elletson and Anna Eliza Gamon: ibid.
London, 2, 0; MDB. (West Rid. Yorks), 0, 1; Philadelphia, 1, 0.

Ellice.—Bapt. 'the son of Ellis' (q.v.); cf. *whence, hence, thence,* from whennes, hennes, thennes, and thens; also Pierce for Piers: 'Sir Pierce or Piers Butler, eighth earl of Ormonde and first earl of Ossory, died 1539' (Dict. Nat. Biog. viii. 72).

Cecilia Elice, co. Camb., 1273. A.
Duce Elice, co. Oxf., ibid.
Ellice Cowper, temp. Eliz. Z.
Ellice Apprice, ibid.
Ellice Price, co. Merioneth, 1607: Reg. Univ. Oxf. vol. ii. pt. ii. p. 299.
1805. Married—Edward Ellice and Lady Hannah Althea Bettesworth: St. Geo. Han. Sq. ii. 417.
London, 1.

Ellicombe.—Local; v. Ellacombe.

Ellicot, Ellicott.—Local, 'of Elcote.' Not to be confounded with Ellisot, q.v. I made this mistake in my English Surnames. I cannot find the place. It is told of Dean Elliot, whose superior was

Bishop Ellicott, that he was wont to say humorously that he was the bishop without the *c*, as good a pun as nomenclature ever boasted. The *i* in Ellicot is intrusive for euphony's sake; cf. Greenaway for Greenway, or Hathaway for Hathway.

Robert de Elcote, co. Wilts, 1273. A.
1628. Married—Silvester Price and Eliz. Ellcott: St. Peter, Cornhill, i. 252.
1799. — James Powell and Ann Ellacott: St. Geo. Han. Sq. ii. 199.
1800. — Edmund Ellecot and Sarah Tant: ibid. p. 221.
London, 0, 1; Crockford, 0, 1; New York, 0, 3.

Elliff, Ealiff.—Bapt. 'the son of Aylof'; v. Iliffe and Ayliffe.

London, 1. 0; MDB. (co. Surrey), 2, 0; New York, 0, 1.

Ellingham.—Local, 'of Ellingham,' parishes in diocs. Durham, Norwich (2), and Winchester.

Ralph de Elingham, cellarer of Hoxne Priory, Norwich, 1272: FF. iii. 612.
William de Elingham, co. Camb., 1273. A.
Ralph of Elyngham, rector of Great Ellingham, co. Norf., 1362: FF. i. 485.
Walter de Elyngham. rector of West Lynn, co. Norf., 1329: ibid. viii. 535.
1690. Married—William Ellingham and Christian Doe: St. Jas. Clerkenwell, iii. 208.
London, 2; Boston (U.S.), 1.

Ellingthorpe, Ellinthorp, Ellinthorpe.—Local, ' of Ellinthorpe,' a hamlet in the parish of Aldborough, N. Rid. Yorks.

MDB. (co. Lancaster), 1, 0, 0; Bradford, 0, 1, 0; MDB. (West Rid. Yorks), 0, 0, 1.

Ellington.—Local, 'of Ellington,' (1) a parish in co. Huntingdon; (2) a township in the parish of Woodhorn, co. Northumberland; (3) a township in the parish of Masham, N. Rid. Yorks.

John de Ellington, co. Linc., 1273. A.
Geoffrey de Ellinton, co. Glouc., ibid.
Henry de Elington, co. Oxf., ibid.
John de Elington, co. Northumb., ibid.
Ricardus de Elyngton, 1379: P. T. Yorks. p. 234.
1640. Married—Paull Wright and Ann Ellington: St. Peter, Cornhill, i. 257.
London, 2; Philadelphia, 2.

Elliot, Elliott, Eliot, Eliott.—Bapt. 'the son of Elias'; O.F.

Elye (Eng. Elias), dim. Elyot. One reason why Elliott is so largely represented in our directories is that it has absorbed nearly all our Elletts or Ellots, who are descended from Ellen ; v. Ellot.

Elyot ad Cap' Ville, co. Camb., 1273. A.
Henry Elyot, co. Bucks, ibid.
Thomas Elyot, co. Camb., ibid.
Eliottus de Balliol. E.
Richard Eliot, 1307. M.
Adam Elyotson, 1379 ; P. T. Yorks. p. 241.
Thomas Elyott, rector of Dickleburgh, co. Norf., 1303 : FF. i. 194.
1607. Married—Thomas Eliot and Margaret Waite : St. Michael, Cornhill, p. 18.
London, 13, 116, 1, 1 ; New York, 22, 104, 2, 4.

Ellis, Ellison.—Bapt. ' the son of Ellis ' ; O.E. Elis or Elys (Elias). Ellison may originate from the English form—thus Elis, Elis-son ; or from the O.F. form, thus Elie, Elie-son. Instances of both are given below, but the Hundred Rolls abound with the name in all counties. This name was wonderfully popularized throughout Western Europe by the Crusaders. ' Elyce, propyr name (Ely, K., P.), *Helias* ' : Prompt. Parv.

Elis Kneyt, co. Bucks, 1273. A.
Henry fil. Elis, co. Camb., ibid.
Agnes uxor Elys, co. Camb., ibid.
Simon fil. Elys, co. Bedf., ibid.
Nicholas fil. Elye, co. Camb., ibid.
Roger fil. Elye, co. Salop, ibid.
Robert Elleson, 1379 : P. T. Yorks. p. 156.
Adam Elisson, 1379 : ibid. p. 195.
Stephanus Elisson, *smyth*, 1379 : ibid. p. 3.
Alicia Elys, *wyf*, 1379 : ibid. p. 33.
Elys Burton, 1379 : ibid. p. 121.

In some cases, no doubt, Ellison is Elen-son.

Cf. Johannes Elynson, 1379 : P. T. Yorks. p. 207.
Johannes Elynson, 1379 : ibid. p. 208.
Alicia serviens Elene, 1379 : ibid. p. 209.
Elena Mott, 1379 : ibid.

Elene was wonderfully popular at the period. Elynson, of necessity, would become Ellison. The diminutives of the two names underwent the same confusion (v. Elliot and Ellot). I may add that Ellis was

still a familiar font-name in the 16th century :
Ellis Pigot, Didsbury, Manchester, 1597 : Wills at Chester, i. 152.
Ellis Pollard, Great Harwood, 1587 : ibid. p. 153.
1548. Ellis Pollard and Johanna Chapman : Marriage Lic. (London), i. 11.
London, 161, 22 ; Philadelphia, 188, 27.

Ellisot.—Bapt. ' the son of Ellisot,' from Ellis (q.v.), dim. Ellisot. A once very common pet name, which, strangely enough, has left no such mark on the directory as might have been expected. It was generally a girl's name, and a great favourite in Yorkshire in the 14th century.

Elisote, co. Camb., 1273. A.
Ellisote Dispenser (fem.), co. Camb., ibid.
Thomas Taylour et Elisot' uxor ejus, 1379 : P. T. Yorks. p. 111.
Elissota Scote, 1379 : ibid. p. 109.
Adam Storure et Elissot' uxor ejus, 1379 : ibid.
Elisota Domicella. W. 2.
Ellsot Bustard. ibid.

Elliston ; v. Elston.

Ellithorne.—Local, ' at the eller-thorn,' i.e. the thorn-bushes by the ellers, or alder-trees. A North-English name. Probably the surname arose in the near neighbourhood of Ulverston. A portion of that town is called the Ellers, but the alder-trees have disappeared and the stream has become a drain, and is covered. The name in the Ulverston Ch. Register is found as Elithorn, Elithorne, Elinthorne, Ellithorn, &c.

1599. Bapt.—Edward, s. John Elithorn : Reg. St. Mary, Ulverston, i. 89.
— Jane, d. John Elithorn : ibid. p. 90.

This register has very many entries of this surname.

1563. Buried—William Elithorne : St. Michael, Cornhill, p. 186.
1679. Edward Ellethorne, Lancaster : Lancashire Wills at Richmond, i. 102.
Manchester, 1 ; Ulverston (1893), 2.

Ellot, Ellett, Elletson.—Bapt. ' the son of Ellot,' a female name, probably a dim. of Ellen, commonly found as Elene. Helot reminds us of Helen. Many of our Elliots no

doubt owe their parentage to this name rather than Elias. The change from Ellot to Elliot would readily occur ; v. Ellett.

Elota Bryan, 1379 : P. T. Yorks. p. 144.
Ellota de Ingleton, 1379 : ibid. p. 289.
Johannes fil. Ellote, 1379 : ibid. p. 290.
Johannes Helot', *barker*, 1379 : ibid. p. 28.
Thomas Ellot and Richard Ellet, 1379 : ibid. p. 36 (in close juxtaposition).
Peter de Balefeld, et Elot, sa femme, 1379 : ibid. p. 43-45.
Johannes Ellotson, 1379 : ibid.
Ebot Elot, 1379 : ibid.
Henricus Helot, 1379 : ibid.
Cf. Willelmus Hely,a (for Elena), 1379 : ibid. p. 62.
1617. Married—Richard Aill and Ann Ellett : St. Jas. Clerkenwell, iii. 44.
London, 0, 2, 0 ; MDB. (West Rid. Yorks), 0, 0, 1.

Ellsworth. — Local ; v. Elsworth.

Ellwood, Elwood.—(1) Bapt. ' the son of Aylward,' q.v. The variant Elward occurs in the 13th century.

Robert Elward, co. Suff., 1273. A.
1603-4. William Elward and Alice Godfrey : Marriage Lic. (London), i. 284.

(2) Local, ' of Ellwood ' (?) I cannot find the spot.

1609. George Ellwood and Thomasine Orgall : Marriage Lic. (London), i. 315.
1668. Married—James Ellwood and Eliz. Wall : St. Jas. Clerkenwell, iii. 143.

Should no place-name Elwood exist, then our Elwoods and Ellwoods are mere local imitations, and really represent Elward, that is, they are of baptismal origin.

London, 7, 2 ; New York, 2, 5.

Elmer, Elmar.—Bapt. ' the son of Elmer,' i.e. Aylmer, q.v. To be carefully distinguished from Elmore, q.v.

Eylmer, fil. Sirich, co. Suff., 1273. A.
John Eylmer, co. Oxf., ibid.
Elmericus de Besye, co. Suff., ibid.
Walter Elmer, co. Soms., 1 Edw. III : Kirby's Quest, p. 166.
' Item, gevin to maistres Elmer, &c., xs,' 1537 : Privy Purse Exp., Princess Mary, p. 28.
' Item, geven to Maistres Aelmer, &c., vs.,' 1537-8 : ibid. p. 53.
1574. Married—Richarde Carter and Cecily Ellmar : St. Jas. Clerkenwell, iii. 6.

1804. — John Elmer and Ann Gillam: St. Geo. Han. Sq. ii. 303.
London, 7, 0 ; Philadelphia, 7, 1.

Elmhurst.—Local, ' of the elm-wood '; M.E. *elm,* Icel. *almr,* Dan. *alm* ; for suffix, v. Hurst.
Alicia de Elmerst, 1379 : P. T. Yorks. p. 80.
Robertus de Aylmeherst, 1379 : ibid. p. 82.
Philadelphia, 1.

Elmore.—Local, ' of Elmore,' (1) a hamlet in co. Dorset, half a mile from Shaftesbury ; (2) a parish in co. Gloucester, six miles from Gloucester. This surname must be distinguished from Elmer, although no doubt they have been confused. The index to the registers of St. James, Clerkenwell, puts Ellmar and Elmer under the heading of Elmore. This is a great mistake.
1733. Married—Thomas Pitman and Mary Elmore : St. Jas. Clerkenwell, iii. 261.
London, 1 ; New York, 7.

Elms, Elmes.—(1) Local, ' at the elms,' from residence beside a clump of elm-trees, or some single elm in a prominent position ; cf. Birch, Ash, Oak, &c.
John atte Elme, co. Soms., 1 Edw. III : Kirby's Quest, p. 90.
William atte Elme, co. Soms., 1 Edw. III : ibid. p. 167.
Osbert atte Elme, co. Oxf., 1273. A.
(2) Local, ' of Elm,' (*a*) a parish in co. Somerset ; (*b*) a parish in co. Cambridge.
Benedict de Elme, co. Soms., 1273. A.
Nicholas de Elme, prior of Wormegay, co. Norf., 1302 : FF. vii. 500.
London, 7, 7 ; New York, 2, 0 ; Philadelphia, 2, 6.

Elmslie,Emsley,Hemsley.—Local, ' of Helmsley,' a market-town in N. Rid. Yorks.
1796. Married—John Elmsley and Mary Hallowell : St. Geo. Han. Sq. ii. 151.
1804. — William Harris and Esbell Elmsley : ibid. p. 308.
MDB. (West Rid. Yorks), 0, 10, 1 ; London, 6, 0, 6 ; Manchester, 0, 2, 0 ; New York, 1, 0, 0.

Elnor.—Bapt. ; v. Elener.

Elouis.—Bapt., i.e. Heloise ; v. Elwes.
Crockford, 1.

Elphick, Elphic, Elphicke, Elfick.—Bapt. ' the son of Ælfech.' Mr. Lower says, ' Ælfech occurs in Domesday as having been a sub-tenant in Sussex, temp. Edward the Confessor, and not long previously (1006) St. Elphegus or Alphage was archbishop of Canterbury' (Patr. Brit. p. 103). This derivation seems natural.
1580-1. John Aynscombe and Susanna Elfecke, *widow*: Marriage Lic.(London), i. 99.
Margaret Elphick, of Prescot, 1649: Wills at Chester (1621-50), p. 71.
Robert Elphicke, 1656 : St. Dionis Backchurch (London), p. 113.
1667. Married—John Ellthicke and Mary Atkins : St. Jas. Clerkenwell, iii. 136.
London, 2, 0, 0, 2 ; MDB. (co. Essex), 0, 1, 1, 0.

Elsam, Elsom.—(1) Bapt. ' the son of Elselm,' probably a variant of Anselm.
Robert Elselm, co. Kent, 1273. A.
Ralph Elselm, co. Kent, ibid.
Richard Elsem, co. Kent, ibid.
(2) Local, ' of Elsham,' a parish in co. Lincoln, five miles from Glandford Bridge.
Hugh de Elsam, co. Linc., 1273. A.
1665. Married—Alexander Cooper and Eliz. Elsam : St. Jas. Clerkenwell, iii. 119.
1787. — George Jones and Priscilla Elsom : St. Geo. Han. Sq. i. 409.
London, 2, 2 ; MDB. (co. Lincoln), 0, 1 ; Manchester, 1, 1.

Else.—? Bapt. ' the son of Ellis ' (?), a variant of Ellis, q.v.
David Elyse, co. Flint, 1635 : Wills at Chester (1621-50), p. 73.
1762. Married—Nathaniel Elkins and Isabella Els : St. Geo. Han. Sq. i. 115.
1785. — William Else and Margaret Saul : ibid. p. 368.
London, 1 ; Philadelphia, 3.

Elsmere, Elsmore, Elsmoor.—Local ; v. Ellesmere.

Elson.—Bapt. ; v. Ell.

Elstob.—Local, ' of Elstob,' a township in the parish of Stainton, co. Durham.
London, 2.

Elston, Ellston, Elliston.—(1) Bapt. ' the son of Elstan,' an early personal name ; cf. Dunstan.

Elstan de Bac, temp. Hen. II, co. Norf.: FF. xi. 66.
Henry Elstan, co. Oxf., 1273. Á.
(2) Local, ' of Elston,' (*a*) a township in the parish of Preston, co. Lanc. ; (*b*) a parish in co. Notts.
Ellen Elston, of Ribleton, *widow*, 1587: Lancashire Wills at Richmond (1457-1680), p. 102.
Anne Elston, of Preston, 1673 : ibid.
George Elston, of Lytham, 1662 : ibid.

A family of Elstons sprung from Elston in Preston parish has been resident in Heyhouses, Lytham, for several centuries.
Richard Elston, of Heyhouses, Litham, 1633 : Lancashire Wills at Richmond (1457-1680), p. 102.
1765. Married—William Elston and Christian Harcourt : St. Geo. Han. Sq. i. 147.
London, 9, 1, 5 ; Lytham (Heyhouses), Elston, 1 ; New York, 4, 0, 0.

Elsworth, Ellsworth.—Local, ' of Elsworth,' a parish in co. Cambridge, near Caxton.
Thomas de Ellesworth, co. Camb., 20 Edw. I. R.
Albin de Ellesworthe, co. Camb., 1273. A.
Sanson de Ellesworth, co. Camb., ibid.
Robert de Elesworde, co. Camb., ibid.
1668. Married—Robert Elesworth and Anne Singellton : St. Jas. Clerkenwell, iii. 147.
London, 2, 1 ; Boston (U.S.), 0, 16.

Eltaft, Eltoft.—Local, ' of the elm-toft ' ; v. Toft.
Johannes de Eltoft, 1379 : P. T. Yorks. p. 205.
West Rid. Court Dir., 1, 0 ; Manchester, 0, 1.

Elvey, Elvy.—Bapt. ; v. Allvey.
1668. Married—Richard Valance and Margarett Elvey : St. Jas. Clerkenwell, iii. 155.
London, 1, 1 ; Philadelphia, 0, 1.

Elvin, Elvins.—Bapt. ' the son of Aylwin ' ; v. Elwin, and cf. Elves for Elwes.
1755. Married—Emery Puttick and Elvin (or Elwin) : St. Geo. Han. Sq. i. 59.
London, 5, 1 ; New York, 1, 0 ; Philadelphia, 0, 2.

Elwes, Elves.—Bapt. ' the son of Heloise ' (Yonge, ii. 390), a popular English name in its day, generally found as Helewise or Helwys. Elwes in the London Visitation (1634) traces from Helwis, vel Helwish (i. 256).

William de Lancaster, Baron of Kendal (temp. Hen. II), 'married Helwise de Studevill, and by her had issue Helwise, his daughter, and heir': West's Ant. of Furness, p. 29.

That Elwes and Elves now represent the name there can be no doubt.

Helevisa Swalwe, 1273. A.
Elwisia de Cream, ibid.
Helewys de Cream, ibid.
Elewis Hervi, co. Camb., ibid.
Johannes Helwys, 1379: P. T. Yorks. p. 295.
Nicholaus Helwys, *firmarius*, 1379: ibid.
Robertus Helwys, 1379: ibid. p. 15.
London, 2, 5; Crockford, 4, 0.

Elwin, Elwyn.—Bapt. 'the son of Aylwin' (q.v.); cf. Elvin, a variant. The instances are all from East Anglia, where this personal name seems to have been exceedingly popular.

Bartholomew fil. Elewan, co. Norf, 1273. A.
Elewan Drynkale, co. Norf., ibid.
Elwyn le Heyward, co. Norf., ibid.
William Elwin, co. Suff., ibid.
Geoffrey Elwyne, co. Norf., ibid.
Elwinus de Parrok, co. Kent, 20 Edw. I. R.
1532–3. Stephen Jonson and Agnes Elwyn: Marriage Lic. (London), i. 8.
London, 4, 1; Crockford, 6, 2; Boston (U.S.), 1, 0.

Elwood; v. Ellwood.

Elworthy, Ellworthy. — Local, 'of Elworthy,' a parish in co. Somerset, six miles from Wiveliscombe.

London, 7, 1; MDB. (co. Somerset), 5, 0.

Ely, Eley.—(1) Bapt. 'the son of Elie' or 'Ely.' For many instances v. Ellis.

John fil. Elie, co. Linc., 20 Edw. I. R.
Reginald fil. Elye, co. Linc., 1273. A.
Gilbert Elye, co. Kent, ibid.

(2) Local, 'of Ely,' the capital of the Fen district.

Nicholas de Ely, bailiff of Norwich, 1227: FF. iii. 58.
Michael de Ely, co. Norf., 1273. A.
John de Ely, co. Norf., ibid.
Alan de Ely, rector of Blickling, co. Norf.: FF. xi. 145.

1560. Married—Robarte Barrington and Jone Elye: St. Dionis Backchurch, p. 4.
1619. — Daniel Bennett and Mary Eeley: ibid. p. 19.
London, 4, 7; MDB. (Suffolk), 1, 0; (Cambridge), 1, 0; New York, 61, 3.

Embelin, Emblen, Emblin, Embling, Emblem.—Bapt. 'the son of Emelin,' popularly Emlin and (with intrusive *b*) Emblin. Emblem is an imitative corruption.

John fil. Emelyne, co. Soms., 20 Edw. I. R.
Willelmus Emelyn, 1379: P. T. Yorks, p. 109.
Emelina la Petyte, C. R., 12 Edw. II.
1439. John Emelyn, rector of Witchingham, co. Norf.: FF. viii. 310.
1602 Bapt.—Edward, s. William Emlin : St Jas, Clerkenwell, i. 40.

The baptismal name with the intrusive *b* is found in several registers :

Emblen, d. of Thomas Horkie, 1585: Reg. St. Columb Major, Cornwall, p. 13.
Emblen, d. of John Jerman, 1586: ibid.
1639–40. John Hobson and Emblen Hornett: Marriage Lic. (Westminster), p. 38.

The following represents a further corruption :

1665. Married—John, s. Isaac and Imblin Miller: St. Jas. Clerkenwell, i. 226.
London, 1, 2, 2, 1, 1; Manchester (Emblem), 2; Oxford (Embling), 2; New York (Emblin), 1.

Emberley.—Local, 'of Embley,' a tithing in the parish of East Wellow, co. Hants.

1691. Married—Edward Watts and Mary Embley: St. Jas. Clerkenwell, iii. 209.
MDB. (co. Hants), 1.

Emberson.—Bapt. 'the son of Emery'; v. Emerson. The *b* in Emberson is, of course, intrusive.

London, 3; New York, 2.

Embery, Embrey, Embree, Embury.—Bapt. 'the son of Emery,' q.v. The *b* is intrusive; cf. Embelin.

1667. Married—John Embree and Mary Odaway : St. Jas. Clerkenwell, iii. 139.
1780. — Benjamin Embry and Sarah Butcher: St. Geo. Han. Sq. ii. 31.
London, 1, 0, 0, 0; MDB. (co. Salop), 0, 1, 0, 0; New York, 0, 0, 6, 4.

Embleton.—Local, 'of Embleton,' (1) a parish in co. Northumberland; (2) a chapelry in co.

Durham, parish of Sedgefield; (3) a chapelry in co. Cumberland, parish of Brigham.

London, 8.

Emelot.—Bapt. 'the son of Emma,' from the nick. Em, and double dim. Em-el-ot; cf. Hewlett for Hew-el-ot; v. Hewlett.

Emelot (without surname). J.
Elena Emelot, co. Hunts, 1273. A.
Robert Emelot, co. Hunts, ibid.
1619. Bapt.—Mary, d. — Emlitt : St. Jas. Clerkenwell, i. 84.

Emeny, Emney, Emmoney, Emmens, Emanson, Eminson, Emons.—Bapt. 'the son of Imayne' (not in Miss Yonge's Glossary). Once a popular girl's name, now passed into oblivion.

Imanta de Monte Alto, 20 Edw. I. R.
Emoni Turbend, co. York, 1273. A.
Ymanya de Thuyt, co. Norf., ibid.
Johannes Ymanie, co. Kent, ibid.
Golda Ymaine, co. Camb., ibid.
Imanie Spurngold, co. Camb., ibid.
Emayn de Ireby, 1379: P. T. Yorks. p. 225.
Imayne de Nesfeld, 1379: ibid. p. 239.
Johannes Nemyny, 1379: ibid. p. 32.

This last is manifestly a nick. form ; cf Nibbs, Nopps, Nabbs, &c.

Imyne Chatterton, of Heaton Norris, *widow*, 1594: Wills at Chester (1545–1620), p. 39.
'Pardon to Robert Emanson, *yeoman*, of Berwick, for piracy,' June 8, 1594: Cal. State Papers (Domestic), iii. 515.
1610. Married—Emonie Thurston (masculine) : Elmham Ch., co. Norfolk.
1675. Buried—Emmynie Burgess: Great Fransham Ch., co. Norfolk.
1707. Married—William Best and Frances Immynes: St. Michael, Cornhill, p. 54.
1717. — William Emmins and Eliz. House: St. Jas. Clerkenwell, iii. 240.
1782. — Samuel Love and Jane Imons: St. Geo. Han. Sq. i. 339.
1783. — Joseph Grey and Ann Emens: ibid. p. 353.
1792. — Thomas Emans and Mary Ann Blandford : ibid. ii. 73.

The latest instance I have noticed of Emeny as a baptismal name is the following :

1777. Married—Emeny Codd and Mary Carley: St. Geo. Han. Sq. i. 274.
London, 4, 0, 0, 3, 0, 1, 1; MDB. (co. Berks), Emeny, 1; (co. Notts), Emmons, 1.

Emerick, Emerich.—Bapt. 'the son of Emeric'; v. Emery and Amery.

Emeric de Beaill, co. Norf., 1273. A.
Emericus de Sacy. B.
Emericus de Bosco. C.
1807. Married—John Emmerich and
Mary Green: St. Geo. Han. Sq. ii. 375.
London, 1, 0; New York, 2, 4.

Emerson.—Bapt. 'the son of
Emery,' q.v.; more generally
Amery; v. Empson.

Richard Emryson, co. York. W. 12.
John fil. Emerici, c. 1300. M.
William Emeryson, co. York. W. 8.
Richard Emerson, co. York. W. 2.
1529. William Emerson and Mary
Newce: Marriage Lic. (London), i. 7.
London, 16; Philadelphia, 26.

Emerton.—Local, 'of Emberton,' a parish in co. Bucks.

Nicholas de Emberton, co. Bucks,
Hen. III–Edw. I. K.
1569. Henry Edmente and Joan Emerton: Marriage Lic. (London), i. 42.
1688. Bapt.—William, s. Richard Emerton: St. Jas. Clerkenwell, i. 328.
London, 4; Boston (U.S.), 2.

Emery.—Bapt. 'the son of
Emery' or 'Amery,' q.v. Emery
lingered on to the close of the
18th century as a girl's or boy's
name.

1602. Married—Emerye Tilney and
Eliz. Hart: St. Mary Aldermary, p. 10.
1669. — Edmund Baker and Easter
Emerye: St. Jas. Clerkenwell, iii. 162.
1785. — George Bye and Emery Lane:
St. Geo. Han. Sq. i. 381.
London, 17; Philadelphia, 66.

Emes; v. Eames.

Emley, Embley, Emely.—
Local, 'of Emley' or 'Elmley,'
a parish near Wakefield. There
are also two parishes in co. Worcester, viz. Elmley Lovett and
Elmley Castle.

Albred de Elmeleie, co. Oxf., 1273. A.
Peter de Elmeleie, co. Oxf., ibid.
John de Emelay, 1318. M.
Magot de Emley, of Doncaster, 1379:
P. T. Yorks. p. 46.
Willelmus de Emley, of Doncaster,
1379: ibid.
1691. Married—Edward Watts and
Mary Embley: St. Jas. Clerkenwell, iii.
209.
MDB. (West Rid. Yorks), 0, 2, 0;
Newcastle, 1, 0, 0; Sheffield, 0, 1, 0;
Manchester, 1, 1, 0; Philadelphia, 5, 0, 1.

**Emmott, Emmotson, Em-
met, Emmets, Emmett, Emott,
Emmitt.**—Bapt. 'the son of Em-

ma,' from nick. Emm, dim. Emm-ot
or Emm-et. A very favourite form
of the name in Yorkshire, but
popular all over the country. It
is found in burial registers in Furness till the year 1790 as a Christian
name.

1433. 'Dispensation from Selow for
Richard de Akerode and Emmotte de
Greenwood to marry, they being related
in the fourth degree. Issued from Rome
by Jordan, Bishop of Alba,' &c.: Test.
Ebor. iii. 317.
Emmot de Kibar, co. Soms., 1 Edw.
III: Kirby's Quest, p. 149.
Emmote Kneyt, co. Bucks, 1273. A.
Emmete de Fur', co. Camb., ibid.
Emmot Rokelar, 1379: P. T. Yorks.
p. 46.
Johannes Emmotsone, 1379: ibid.
p. 133.
Emmota serviens Johannis, 1379: ibid.
p. 269.
Adam Emotson, 1379: ibid. p. 37.
Emmet Chapman, co. York. W. 9.
Emmetta Catton, London. X.
Emmot Plummer, co. York. W. 2.
1579. Edmund Ball and Emott Burton:
Marriage Lic. (London), i. 91.
1613. Bapt.—Marie, d. Thomas Em-
met: St. Michael, Cornhill, p. 111.
1710. Married—George Emmott and
Mary Harding: St. Jas. Clerkenwell, iii.
232.
London, 2, 0, 1, 1, 9, 0, 0; New York,
0, 0, 19, 0, 5, 3, 0; Philadelphia (Emmott), 2; MDB. (West Rid. Yorks),
Emmitt, 1.

Emms, Emps.—Bapt. 'the son
of Emma,' from the nick. Emm,
whence the dim. Emm-ot, q.v.
Also cf. Emps with Empson for
Em-son with intrusive p.

Robert Em, of Stody, co. Norf., 4 Edw.
III: FF. ix. 439.
Richard Eme, co. Soms., 1 Edw. III:
Kirby's Quest, p. 175.
1554. Edmund Emmes, rector of
Hasingham, co. Norf.: FF. vii. 234.
1592. Married—Henry Smyth and
Emme Unquier: St. Jas. Clerkenwell,
iii. 16.
1622. Nicholas Emms, sheriff of Norwich: ibid. iii. 371.
1631. Buried—Em White, an ancient
mayd: St. Mary Aldermary, p. 166.

A Puritan Christian name appears in the following:

'Here lieth the body of Preserved, the
daughter of Thomas Preserved Emms,
who departed this life in the 18th year of
her age, on the 17th of November, 1712.'
Yarmouth Church: FF. xi. 393.
1807. Married—Thomas Emms and
Martha Allen: St. Geo. Han. Sq. ii. 370.
London, 8, 0; New York, 0, 1.

Emperor.—Nick. 'the emperor'; cf. King, Bishop, and the
French Lempriere, now a settled
resident in England.

Richard le Emperer. G.
1685. Robert Emperor, *common councilman*, Norwich: FF. iii. 423.
1735. Buried—William Emperor, of
Norwich: ibid. iv. 297.
1805. Married—John Emperor and Ann
Berry: St. Geo. Han. Sq. ii. 326.

Empsall; v. Hemshall.

Empson.—(1) Bapt. 'the son
of Emery,' whence Emerson, corrupted to Emson, and with intrusive
p to Empson. This is proved by
the following entries relating to
one and the same man:

Richard Emryson, 1490: Scriba Regis-
tri Domini Prioris Dunelm. (HHH. p. 16.)
Richard Emerson, 1491: ibid.
Richard Empson, 1495: ibid.

(2) Bapt. 'the son of Emma,'
from the nick. Em or Emm, whence
Emson, and with intrusive p Empson. This, no doubt, is the more
general origin.

Johannes Emson, 1379: P. T. Yorks.
p. 185.
Johannes Emmeson, 1379: ibid. p. 127.
Rogerus Emson, 1379: ibid. p. 41.
Robertus Emmeson, 1379: ibid. p. 60.
John Emyson, vicar of Great Carbrook,
co. Norf., 1522: FF. ii. 338.
William Empson, co. Norf., 1507: ibid.
iv. 257.
1808. Married—Edward Empson and
Helen Steel: St. Geo. Han. Sq. ii. 394.
London, 6; West Rid. Court Dir., 3.

**Endacott, Endecott, Endi-
cott.**—Local, 'of Endacott' (?), a
spot in co. Devon which I cannot
find.

London, 0, 1, 0; MDB. (co. Devon), 8,
0, 0; Devon Dir. (Farmers' List), 9, 0, 1;
Philadelphia, 0, 0, 5.

Enefer, Enever, Ennever.—
Bapt. Probably a *g*-less pronunciation of the once popular Gwenever,
whence the Cornish Jenifer, q.v.

1631. Buried—Eliz. Enniver, *a servant*:
St. Mary Aldermary, p. 167.
1741. — John Ennever: St. Michael,
Cornhill, p. 295.
London, 3, 4, 1; MDB. (co. Suffolk), 2,
0, 0; New York, 0, 0, 7.

Engall.—Bapt. 'the son of
Engal' or 'Ingle'; v. Ingle; cf.
German Engel, recently imported
into the London directories.

London, 4.

Engeldew, Engeldow, Engledow ; v. Ingledew.

1787. Married—Charles Park Engledow and Jane Bright: St. Geo. Han. Sq. i. 406.
London, 0, 1, 0; Crockford, 0, 0, 1.

Engilard.—Bapt. 'the son of Engilard.'

Engilardus fil. Ralph, co. Salop, 1273. A.
Richard fil. Engilar, co. Salop, ibid.
William Iggelard, co. Sussex, ibid.
Isabel Ingelard, co. Bedf., ibid.
London, 2.

Engineer.—Occup. 'the engineer'; v. Jenner.

England.—Local, ' of the Ingland,' either Inge's land, i.e. the land of Inge, a personal name (v. Yonge, ii. 248), or, more probably. the ing-land, i.e. the meadow-land by the stream. 'Ing, a meadow, generally one lying near a river. North' (Hallewill); v. Ing. Nothing to do with England as national territory. But surnames, as shown in hundreds of instances in this dictionary, inevitably tend to imitation.

Alicia de Ingeland, 1379: P. T. Yorks. p. 225.
Isabella Ingeland', 1379: ibid. p. 186.
Willelmus Ingland', 1379: ibid. p. 193.
Robertus Ingland, 1379: ibid.
1668. Married—Joseph Ingland and Anne Smith: St. Jas. Clerkenwell, iii. 141.
London, 17; Philadelphia, 24.

Englebert.—Bapt. 'the son of Englebert'; v. Yonge, ii. 249. The American instances are a German importation.

Engelbert Blund. E.
Philadelphia, 6.

Englefield.—Local, ' of Englefield,' a parish in co. Berks, six miles from Reading.

William de Engelfeld, co. Devon, 1273. A.
William de Englefeld, co. Kent, ibid.
John de Engelfeld, co. Oxf., ibid.
Thomas de Englefeld, co. Oxf., ibid.
London Court Dir., 3.

English.—Local, 'the English,' no doubt the Scotch Inglis anglicized, as English in England would be an unlikely sobriquet ; v. Inglis.

William le Englich, co. Soms., 1 Edw. III: Kirby's Quest, p. 230.

As le Frenssh is so common in this register it is quite possible that in some cases a feeling of opposition gave rise to a nickname ; a game of French and English at an early date. But the Scotch Inglis is no doubt the chief parent.

1668. Married—Richard Inglish and Eliz. Macland: St. Jas. Clerkenwell, iii. 146.
London, 19; Philadelphia, 110.

Enion.—Bapt. ; v. Eynon.

Ennever.—Bapt. ; v. Enefer.

Enright.— ? —— An Irish surname found frequently in the United States. It is placed here as the second syllable looks like the English suffix -wright, as in Arkwright, Cartwright, Wainwright, &c., with which, however, it has no connexion.

1805. Married—Patrick Enright and Catherine Eagon: St. Geo. Han. Sq. ii. 334.
London, 1 ; Liverpool, 1 ; New York, 20 ; Philadelphia, 11.

Ensor, Edensor.—Local, ' of Edensor,' a parish in co. Derby, two miles from Bakewell. Always pronounced Ensor.

Richard de Edenesore, co. Camb., 1273. A.
1604. Daniel Ensor and Eliz. Wymple: Marriage Lic. (London), i. 286.
1796. Married—John Ensor and Amphillis Mapes: St. Geo. Han. Sq. ii. 152.
London, 2, 0; MDB. (co. Somerset), 1, 0; (co. Stafford), 1, 1; (co. Derby), 1, 2.

Ensworth.—Local, ' of Ainsworth,' most probably a variant of the well-established Lancashire surname Ainsworth, q.v. In any case Ensworth has become absorbed in the county by Ainsworth.

William Eansworth, corporal, co. Ches., 1651: East Cheshire, ii. 68.
John Ensworth, of Robie, co. Lanc., 1671: Wills at Chester (1660-80), p. 89.
William Ensworth, of Hulme, co. Lanc., 1672: ibid.
Nicholas Ensworth, of Heswall, yeoman, 1664: ibid.
London, 1 ; Boston (U.S.), 3.

Entwisle, Entwistle, Entwhistle.—Local, ' of Entwistle,' a township in the parish of Bolton, co. Lancaster.

Robert de Hennetwisle, co. Lanc., temp. John: Baines' Lanc. i. 576.

Giles Entwistle, of Entwistle, 1582 : Wills at Chester (1545-1620), p. 61.
Robert Entwistle, of the Foxholes, 1574 : ibid.
Thomas Entwistle, of Entwistle, 1620 : ibid.
1622. Johannes Enwhisley: Preston Guild Rolls, p. 90.
London, 1, 8, 0; Manchester, 6, 8, 1 ; Entwistle, 0, 1, 0 ; New York, 2, 5, 0.

Envious. -Nick. 'the envious.' I do not think this surname has survived. It seems to have sprung up in co. Norfolk.

Hamo le Enveyse, co. Norf., 1273. A.
Geoffrey le Envyse, co. Norf., ibid.
William le Enuyse (u for n), co. Herts, ibid.
Silvester le Enueyse (u for v), co. Hunts, ibid.
William l'Enveyse, temp. Hen. III, co. Norf.: FF. x. 163.

Epperson, Epps, Eppson.—Bapt. ' the son of Ebb'; v. Ebbs.

Erlam, Earlem, Earlam.—Local, ' of Irlam,' a hamlet in the township of Barton-on-Irwell, near Manchester ; v. Irlam.

George Erlam, of Erlam, husbandman, 1637 ; Wills at Chester (1621-50), p. 74.
Thomas Erlam, of Eccles, innkeeper, 1646. ibid
Thomas Erlam, of Erlam, husbandman, 1647: ibid.
MDB. (co. Chester), 2, 0, 3; Manchester, 0, 1, 1.

Ervin, Erwin. — Local ; v. Irving.

Escombe, Escolme, Escome, Eskholme.—Local, 'of Escombe,' a chapelry near Bishop Auckland, co. Durham. As regards the Lancashire forms, it would seem as if they were sprung from some spot called Eskholm, i.e. the little island in the Esk (v. Holmes). Eskdale in co. Cumberland would thus be the birthplace of this surname.

Roger de Estcumbe, London, 1273. A.
Thomas Escholme, of Ellel, 1608 : Lancashire Wills at Richmond (1457 1680), p. 103.
John Escome, of Pilling, 1611 : ibid.
Roger Escome, of Forton, 1661 : ibid.
London, 3, 0, 0, 0; Preston, 0, 0, 1, 0; MDB. (co. Lancaster), 0, 2, 0, 0; Rotherham, 0, 0, 0, 3.

Escreet, Escritt.—Local, ' of Eskrigg.' I doubt not these are mere corruptions of Eskrigg, being found not far from the district in which that surname took its rise. The instances given under Eskrigge, q.v., strongly confirm this view.

MDB. (East Rid. Yorks), 1, 1.

Esh.—(1) Local, 'of Esh' or 'Ash,' a chapelry in the parish of Lanchester, five miles from Durham. (2) Local, 'at the esh,' from residence beside some particular and familiar ash-tree. 'Esche, tre, *fractinus*' (*fraxinus*, P.) : Prompt. Parv. p. 143.

1337. John de Fraxino, alias Atte Eshe, co. Norf.: FF. ix. 476.
1345. Roger atte Eshe, co. Norf.: ibid. v. 145.
1453. Richard Esh, rector of Morley, co. Norf.: ibid. ii. 480.
MDB. (East Rid. Yorks), 3.

Eshelby, Exelby.—Local, 'of Exe by,' a township in the parish of Burneston, N. Rid. Yorks, near Bedale. I think there can be little doubt that Eshelby is a variant of Exe by. It runs side by side with Exelby in the very district in which the two surnames arose. My second instance below is confirmatory, supplying as it does an intermediate pronunciation.

William de Askelby, *mercer*, 15 Edw. III: Freemen of York, i. 35.
1577. Edmond Bainham and Ellen Eselbee: Marriage Lic. (London), i. 77.
1594. Henry Hankin and Jane Excelbie: ibid. p. 215.
1799. Married—John Eshelby and Sarah Adcock: St. Geo. Han. Sq. ii. 197.
MDB. (West Rid. Yorks), 1, 4; (North Rid. Yorks), 2, 1; London, 2, 0.

Eskholme.—Local; v. Escombe, where it will be seen that two surnames of separate origin have become confused together.

Eskrigge.—Local, 'of Eskrigg,' a chapelry in the parish of Lancaster, co. Lanc. For two curious variants, v. Escreet.

Thomas Eskarigge, of Over Kellet, 1569: Lancashire Wills at Richmond (1457-1680), p. 102.
Roger Aiskrigge, of Over Kellet, 1592: ibid.
Anne Esricke, of Escricke, 1624: ibid.
Robert Eskrigg, of Eskrigg, 1670: ibid.
1562. Peter Estgrigge and Catherine Kellie: Marriage Lic. (London), i. 23.
1583. Bapt.—Mathewe Eskrigg: St. Mary, Ulverston, p. 80.

1596. Buried—Thomas Eskrige: ibid. p. 114.
Liverpool, 2; MDB. (co. Chester), 2.

Esmond.—Bapt. 'the son of Estmund'; v. Eastman.
London, 1; New York, 2.

Essex.—Local, 'of Essex'; cf. Derbyshire, Devonshire, Cheshire, &c.

Henry de Essex, co. Suff., Hen. III–Edw. I. K.
Roger de Essex, co. Essex, 1273. A.
Ralph de Essex, co. Glouc., ibid.
Wolmer de Essex, London, ibid.
Walter de Essex, co. Herts, 20 Edw. I. R.
Johannes de Esex, 1379: P. T. Howdenshire, p. 22.
1553-4. John Essex and —— Barbor, *widow*: Marriage Lic. (London), i. 14.
1710. Bapt.—Frances, d. John Essex, *music master*: St. Dionis Backchurch, p. 149.
London, 6; Philadelphia, 8.

Estabrook, Esterbrook.—Local; v. Easterbrook.

Estcourt.—Local, 'of Eastcourt,' a tithing in the parish of Crudwell, co. Wilts.
London, 1; Crockford, 2; MDB. (East Rid. Yorks), 1; Boston (U.S.), 2.

Estridge.—Local, 'of Estridge.'
William de Esteryge, co. Wilts, 1273. A.
Crockford, 1.

Etchells, Etchell. — Local, 'of Etchells,' an old manor and township in the parish of Stockport, co. Ches. Many entries relating to this family will be found in the register of Marple Church, Cheshire. Amongst the owners of land in Marple in 1662 was George Etchells (v. East Cheshire, ii. 53, *n*.).

1561. Buried—Ellen Ecchuls: Reg. Prestbury Ch. (co. Ches.), p. 6.
1570. Married—Robert Proudlove and Emme Etchuls: ibid. p. 30.
William Etchells, of Lymm, co. Chester, 1613: Wills at Chester (1545-1620), p. 61.
Richard Etchells, of Pott Shrigley, 1604: ibid.
Manchester, 6, 3; MDB. (co. Chester), 3, 0; Philadelphia, 2, 2.

Eteson, Ettson.—Bapt. 'the son of Ede'; v. Eddie, of which these are sharpened variants; cf. Tennyson for Dennison. Also v. Etty.

'Two youths named Eteson and Wignall were drowned yesterday afternoon

on the river Ribble at Preston by the upsetting of a boat': Liverpool Mercury, April 23, 1889.
West Rid. Court Dir., 3, 0; New York, 0, 1.

Etheredge, Etheridge, Etheridge, Etridge.—Local, 'of Etheridge' or 'Ethridge.' I cannot find the spot.

1773. Married—George Etheredge and Ann Lowder: St. Geo. Han. Sq. i. 230.
1786. — Thomas Etheridge and Ann Fairbrother: ibid. p. 383.
— — Mark Walton and Catherine Ethridge: ibid. p. 386.
London, 1, 5, 1, 1; Philadelphia, 0, 1, 0, 0; New York (Ethridge), 1.

Etherington, Ethrington, &c.—Local; v. Hetherington.
London, 5, 0; Preston, 0, 1; Boston (U.S.), 2, 0.

Etty.—Bapt. 'the son of Eddie,' a sharpened form of the surname Eddie, q.v.; cf. Eteson for Eddison.
London, 1; Philadelphia, 1.

Etwall, Ettwell.—Local, 'of Etwall,' a parish in co. Derby, six miles from the county town; v. Eatwell.

Robert de Etewalle, co. Derby, 1273. A.
Henry Etwell, C. R., 20 Edw. IV.
London, 0, 1; MDB. (co. Hants), 3, 0.

Eustace, Ewstace, Eustes, Eustis.—Bapt. 'the son of Eustace,' St. Eustachius (Yonge, i. 209-10).

Eustace le Chaloner, C. R., 32 Edw. I.
Adam fil. Eustace, co. Camb., 1273. A.
Henry fil. Ewstace, co. Hunts, ibid.
Richard Eustace, co. Camb., ibid.
William fil. Eustachii, co. Norf., 20 Edw. I. R.
Lucia Eustasy, co. Soms., 1 Edw. III: Kirby's Quest, p. 131.
Robert Ewstace, 1513: Reg. Univ. Oxf. i. 85.

There are some curious spellings of this name :

1747. Married—George Cook and Mary Eustiss: St. Geo. Han. Sq. i. 38.
1779. — John Ewstes and Mary Hobbs: ibid. p. 299.
London, 6, 1, 0, 0; New York, 12, 0, 1, 1.

Evance.—Bapt. 'the son of Evan'; v. Evans; cf. Ellice and Avice for Ellis and Avis. Latimer spells it Evance. 'Right Honourable, *salutem*. And, Sir, as I perceive, by this bearer, Mr. Evance,' &c. (Letters to Lord Cromwell, Aug. 1538, Parker Soc., p. 399).

1630. Buried—John, son of William Evance : St. Michael, Cornhill, p. 231.
1788. Married—James Yates and Jane Evance : St. Geo. Han. Sq. ii. 3.

Evans, Evanson.—Bapt. 'the son of Evan,' a Welsh personal name.

Howell ap Yevan. H.
David ap Evan. Z.
Joane Howell ap Evan Sais : Visit. Glouc. (Harl. Soc.), p. 180.

The first form of the name seems to have been Jevon, then Yevan, lastly and permanently, Evan ; v. Jevon.

Philadelphia, 472, 4 ; MDB. (co. Carmarthen), 188, 0.

Eve, Eves, Evison, Eaves, Eaveson. — Bapt. 'the son of Eve.' Adam was the favourite boy's name throughout the north of England in the 13th century. Eve was not so popular, yet it took firm ground. The form Eaves is generally of local origin (v Eaves), but not always, as Eaveson clearly shows.

Eva Textrix, co. York, 1273. A.
John fil. Eve, co. Camb., ibid.
Reginald fil. Eve, co. Bedf., ibid.
Cecilia fil. Evœ. T.
Eva le Warre. A.
Eva Chapman, 1379 : P. T. Yorks. p. 3.
1568. Married—Pawle Osterlynge and Agnes Eve : St. Jas. Clerkenwell, iii. 4.
1573-4. John Evyson and Isabell Smithe : Marriage Lic. (London), i. 59.
1575. Robert Mannoppe and Johanna Eve : ibid. p. 67.
London, 8, 5, 3, 1, 0 ; Manchester (Eaveson), 2 ; Philadelphia, 2, 2, 2, 1, 0.

Eveleigh. — Local, 'of Eveleigh.' I have not been able to find the spot.

London, 2.

Eveling, Evelyn, Eveline.—Bapt. ' the son of Aveline ' ; v. Aveling.

London, 1, 0, 0 ; Crockford, 0, 2, 0 ; Philadelphia, 0, 0, 1.

Evelot.—Bapt. ' the son of Eve ' (q.v.), from the double dim. Eve-el-ot ; cf. Hewlett.

John Evelot, co. Soms., 1 Edw. III : Kirby's Quest, p. 158.
Evelot Wascel, co. Soms., 1 Edw. III : ibid. p. 199.

John Evelote, co. Soms., 1 Edw. III : ibid. p. 226.

Evenden.—Local, ' of Evenden,' evidently a Kentish surname, although I have not identified the spot. The Hundred Roll instances manifestly refer to the place.

Gunnora de Ethinden, co. Kent, 1273. A.
Richard de Ethindenn, co. Kent, ibid.
1755. Married—Edward Evenden and Mary Sparrow : St. Geo. Han. Sq. i. 57.
1782. — James Evenden and Sarah Collett : ibid. p. 329.
London, 4, 0 ; MDB. (co. Kent), 4, 2.

Evenett —Bapt. ' the son of Eve,' from the double dim. Ev-in-et ; cf. Rob-in-et, Col-in-et, Dob-in-et. Evenett exists at Church Coniston, North Lanc. (v. Ulverston Advertiser, July 1, 1886).

Everard, Evered, Everett, Everitt, Everit. — Bapt. ' the son of Everard ' (Yonge, ii. 272-3). Everett and Everitt are natural modifications.

Fulco fil. Everardi, co. Linc., 20 Edw. I. R.
Nicholas fil. Everardi, co. Camb., 1273. A.
Alan Everard, co. Oxf., ibid.
Everard de la Mer, C. R., 13 Edw. I.
Johannes Everard, 1379 : P. T. Yorks. p. 301.

The step between Everard and Everett or Everitt was Evered. The final _d_ was then sharpened into _t_.

1527. Thomas Jeffes and Margery Evered : Marriage Lic. (London), i. 6.
1619. Bapt.—Everitt, s. George Saunders : St. Jas. Clerkenwell, i. 85.
1666. Married—Edward Everet and Ann Walcock : ibid. iii. 125.
London, 6, 3, 24, 8, 0 ; New York, 2, 0, 29, 5, 7.

Everingham. — Local, ' of Everingham,' a parish in the E. Rid. Yorks, five miles from Market Weighton.

Adam de Everingham, co. Notts, 1273. A.
1672. Bapt.—Mary, d. Robert Everingham : St. Jas. Clerkenwell, i. 253.
London, 2.

Eversden.—Local, ' of Eversden,' two parishes (Great and Little Eversden) near Caxton, co. Cambridge.

Lucia de Everisdon, co. Camb., 1273. A.
John de Everesdone, ibid.

William de Eversdone, ibid.
London, 1.

Eversley.—Local, ' of Eversley,' a parish in Hants, three miles from Hartford Bridge.

John de Eversle, co. Kent, 1273. A.
Walter de Eversle, co. Kent, ibid.
London Court Dir., 1.

Everson, Every.—Bapt. ' the son of Everard,' q.v.

Nicholas Everardsonne. BB.
Peter Everadsonne, ibid.
Fulco fil. Everardi. R.

Perhaps some of our Eversons are from the abbreviated form of Everard, viz. Every.

1667. Married—Mathew Everson and Bridgitt Lasey : St. Jas. Clerkenwell, iii. 130.
London, 8, 2 ; Philadelphia, 2, 0 ; New York, 7, 3.

Evetts, Evitt, Evott.—Bapt. ' the son of Eve,' dim. Evot or Evet. This dim. was especially popular in cos. York and Durham. William de Kyrkby (A.D. 1391) bequeathed articles to ' Evœ uxori Johannis Parvyng.' Further on in his will he speaks of the aforementioned ' Evotam ' (Test. Ebor. i. 145-6, Surtees Soc.).

Evota de Durham. X.
Evota de Bolthorp, 1379 : P. T. Howdenshire, p. 21.
Evota Butty, 1379 : ibid. p. 11.
Evota de Stanley, co. York. W. 2.
William Evote. X.
1691. Buried—Joseph Evatt : St. Mary Aldermary, p. 201.
1717. Married—ArnoldEvetts and Sarah Antram : St. Jas. Clerkenwell, iii. 240.
1789. — James Evett and Mary Humphrys : St. Geo. Han. Sq. ii. 24.
London, 1, 2, 0 ; New York, 0, 0, 1 ; Philadelphia, 0, 1, 0.

Evilchild.—Nick. ; cf. Goodchild.

Alan Evilchild, co. Camb., 1273. A.

Evington.—Local, ' of Evington,' a parish near Leicester, in the county of that name.

Manchester, 1.

Evinson. —Bapt. ; v. Evans. An American variant of Evanson.

Boston (U.S.), 1.

Ewart, Youart, Ewert.—(1) Occup. ' the ewe-herd,' one who tended ewes ; cf. Calvert, Coward, Oxnard, Shepherd, &c.

This is no mere guess, as may be easily seen from my instances. The name is found in the district where we should expect to see it.

Matilda Yowherd, 1379 : P. T. Yorks. p. 266.
Thomas Yowhyrd, 1379 : ibid. p. 264.
Johannes Ewehird, 1379 : ibid. p. 22.

The next stage in spelling was Eward; cf. Coward :

John Eward, of Burton, 1646 : Lanc. Wills at Richmond (1457-1680), p. 103.
Jane Eward, of Burton-in-Kendal, 1678 : ibid.

This became Ewart ; cf. Calvert.

(2) Local, ' of Ewart,' a township in the parish of Doddington, co. Northumberland. The Scotch border Ewarts sprang from this place, and are well represented in English directories.

Miss Youart advertises her School in the Ulverston News, Jan. 23, 1886.
London, 6, 0, 0 ; New York, 3, 0, 3.

Ewbank, Ewebank, Eubank.— Local, ' of the yew-bank.' from residence on the bank where the yew-trees grew (v. Ewes) ; cf. Windibank, Gillbanks, Calderbank, Fairbank, &c.

George Ewbanke, or Ubancke, of Holmscales, in the parish of Burton, 1636 : Lanc. Wills at Richmond (1457-1680), p. 103.
1587. Thomas Ubancke and Rose Baker : Marriage Lic. (London), i. 160.
1805. Married—William Ubank and Sarah Bouch : St. Mary, Ulverston, ii. 453.
MDB. (W. Rid. Yorks), 2, 1, 0 ; London, 3, 0, 0 ; New York, 0, 0, 1.

Ewen, Ewing, Ewan, Ewings, Ewins.—Bapt. ' the son of Ewan.' Not always Scotch, as the font-name was popular in North England. Probably cognate with the Welsh Evan. The g in Ewing and Ewings is, of course, excrescent, as in Jennings.

Ewanus Byrches, 1562 : Preston Guild Rolls, p. 28.
Ewanus Burye, 1562 : ibid. p. 29.
Ewanus Barwick, 1562 : ibid.
Ewanus Dilworth, 1562 : ibid.
Ewanus Kellett, 1562 : ibid.
Manchester, 4, 3, 1, 0, 0 ; London, 6, 3, 0, 1, 3 ; Philadelphia, 3, 79, 3, 0, 0.

Ewer.—Offic. ' the ewer,' an officer of the ewery (v. Ewery). one who ministered at the table

of his lord, and carried water round for the guests ; v. Napier.

Brian le Ewer. E.
Richard le Ewere. H.
William le Ewer. T.
1565. Married—Robert Ewer and Alyce Worrall : St. Michael, Cornhill, p. 9.
1592. Francis Ewer, co. Herts, yeoman, and Johanna Siblee : Marriage Lic. London), i. 199.
1665. Married—Jacob Ewer and Joane Banbury : St. Mary Aldermary, p. 31.
1710. — William Lovett and Sarah Ewer : St. Jas. Clerkenwell, iii. 232.
London, 6 ; Boston (U.S.), 7.

Ewery.—Local, ' of the ewery,' equivalent to ' le ewer' (v. preceding article), an officer of the ewery, one who superintended the scullery, either in a religious or a baronial house. He also looked after the basins in which guests washed their hands before, during, and after meals. The absence of forks would make such attendance welcome.

1503. ' Item, to Thewry, xxs' : Privy Purse Exp. Eliz. of York, p. 90.
Ricardus del Ewry, 1379 : P. T. Yorks. p. 204.
Johannes del Ewry, 1379 : ibid. p. 214.

Ewes, Ewe.— Local, ' at the yew-trees,' or singly ' at the yew-tree' ; M.E. ew.

' Maple, thorn, beche, hazel, ew, whipultre.' Chaucer, C. T. 2925.

The surname is doubtless lost in Hughes.

Jordan del Ewe, co. Wilts, 1273. A.
John del Ewe, co. Salop, ibid.
Johannes del Ewes, et Agnes uxor ejus, 1379 : P. T. Yorks. p. 61.
Johannes del Ewes, et Sara uxor ejus, walker, 1379 : ibid.
1684. Bapt.—Richard, son of Richard and Mary Ewe : St. Jas. Clerkenwell, i. 309.
Philadelphia, 0, 4.

Exall, Excell. — Local, ' of Exhall,' two parishes in co. Warwick. The variant Excell is clearly imitative of the dictionary word excel, to surpass. Endless similar imitations are scattered throughout this book. v. Axtell.

1701. Married—Richard Exall and Eliz Bushbey : St. Jas. Clerkenwell, iii. 224.
1796. — Samuel Willington and Esther Excell : St. Geo. Han. Sq. ii. 156.
1808. — Aam (Adam ?) Francis Laijmond and Ann Excell : ibid. p. 379.
London, 1, 2.

Excuser.—Offic. ' the excuser.' one who took up causes and freed from charges (?).

Peter le Escuzer. H.

Exton.—Local, ' of Exton.' (1) a parish in co. Rutland, five miles from Oakham ; (2) a parish in co. Somerset, four miles from Dulverton ; (3) a parish in Hants. fifteen miles from Alton. The last seems to be the parent of the surnames.

Alexander de Exton, co. Devon, 1273. A.
Nicholas de Extone, co. Wilts, 20 Edw. I. R.
Gervase de Exton, co. Devon, Hen. III-Edw. I. K.
William de Exton, co. Devon, ibid.
Richard de Extone, co. Soms., 1 Edw. III : Kirby's Quest, p. 178.
1770. Married—William Berry and Amya Exton : St. Geo. Han. Sq. i. 96.
London, 1.

Ey, Eye.—Local. ' of Eye,' (1 : a parish in co. Suffolk ; (2) a parish in co. Northampton ; (3) a parish in co. Hereford.

Stephen de Eye, co. York, 1273. A.
Ernald de Ey, co. Norf., ibid.
Agnes de Eye, co. Camb., ibid.
Peter atte Eye, co. Norf., 11 Edw. III : FF. viii. 286.
London, 1, 0 ; New York, 3, 0 ; Philadelphia, 0, 1.

Eyles.— ?

John Eyle, co. Soms., 1 Edw. III : Kirby's Quest, p. 102.
London, 5 ; Oxford, 3.

Eynon, Enion.— Bapt. ' the son of Eignion ' or ' Enion,' a Welsh surname ; v. Benyon for history and further instances.

William ap-Eynon, 1384 : Hist. and Ant. St. David's, p. 369.
Morgan ap-Eynon, 1384 : ibid. p. 369.
Morgan ap-Eineon, archdeacon of Brecon, 1389 : ibid. p. 360.
Thomas Eynon, archdeacon of Brecon. 1758 : ibid. p. 360.
Manchester, 0, 1 ; Liverpool, 1, 0 : MDB. (co. Carmarthen), 3, 0 ; Philadelphia, 6, 0.

Eyre, Ayre.—Offic. or nick. ' the heir'; M.E. heyre, eyr, or eyre ; O.F. heir, the h, of course, being silent.

Henry le Eyer, co. Oxf., 1273. A.
Adam le Eyr, co. Camb., ibid.
William le Eyre, co. Camb., ibid.
London, 20, 2 ; Philadelphia, 32, 1.

Eyton.—Local, ' of Eyton,' (1) a parish in co. Hereford ; (2) a township in the parish of Alberbury, co. Salop ; (3) a chapelry in the parish of Wroxeter, co. Salop.

Roger de Eyton, co. Salop, 1273. A.
William de Eyton, co. Salop, Hen. III-Edw. I. K.
Peter de Eyton, co. Salop, 20 Edw. I. R.

Thomas Eyton, rector of North Lynn, 1451 : FF. viii. 540.
1660. Married—Kendricke Eyton and Jane Ellis : St. Jas. Clerkenwell, iii. 106.
Kendrick Eyton, of Eyton, 1602 : Wills at Chester (1545-1620), p. 62.
William Eyton, of Chester, *nailor*, 1584 : ibid.
London, 4 ; MDB. (co. Salop', 4.

Ezard.—Bapt. ' the son of Izod,' i.e. Isolda. The number of variants

of the famous old personal name Isolda is remarkably large ; v. Isard for a fuller statement. Yorkshire is the chief habitat of all the variants.

1596. Henry Dunmore and Eliz. Ezarde, widow of Edward Esarde : Marriage Lic. (London), i. 236.
MDB. (E. Rid. Yorks), 1 ; Leeds, 1 ; Manchester, 2.

F

Faber. — Occup. A wright. The name has been assumed through being habitually set down by some clerkly pen in Latin as ' Faber' instead of 'Wright.' The first three following occur on the same page :
Adam Marshall, *faber*, 1379 . P. T. Yorks. p. 300.
Robertus fil. fabri, 1379 : ibid.
Robertus Faber et uxor ejus, 1379 : ibid.
Adam le Fabir, co. Norf., 1273. A.
Allan Faber, co. Linc., ibid.
Edward Faber, co. Soms., 1 Edw. III : Kirby's Quest, p. 95.
London, 6 ; New York, 31.

Fabian.—Bapt. ' the son of Fabian.' The name was familiar, as is evidenced by 'Also Fabian Flatterer and Cicely Claterer,' in 'Cocke Lorelle's Bote.' It is found in the Reformation period :
1553. Married—Fabyan Wythers and Alyce Machyn : St. Michael, Cornhill.

In 1593 (Aug. 10) the same record registers the burial of Roberte Fabyan and Anne Fabian, brother and sister. They died in the plague (p. 204).

1582. Bapt. — Joyce, d. of Fabyan Banester : St. Jas. Clerkenwell, i. 13.
William Fabyane, curate of Hilton Chapel, Monk-Wearmouth, 1506 : DDD. ii. 39.
1526. Robert Fabyan and Marion Violett : Marriage Lic. (London), i. 5.
— Alexander Bell and Eliz. Fabene : ibid.
London, 1 ; New York, 8.

Fagg, Fagge.—Bapt. ' the son of Fag.'
Robert Fag, co. Soms., 1 Edw. III : Kirby's Quest, p. 279.
Jahanna Fag, co. Soms., 1273. A.

Peter Fag, co. Oxf., ibid.
London, 4, 1.

Faggetter.—Occup. One who made up fagots into bundles. Fr. *fagoteur*, a fagot maker, Cotgr. A family of Faggetters have been settled for a considerable time at Lower Heyford, co. Oxf.

1896. Married— Robert Edwin Newell and Mary, d. Charles Faggetter, of Pirbright, Surrey : Oxford Times, April 18, 1896.

Fair.—Local.
John de Fayre, C. R., 29 Edw. I.
London, 6 ; Boston (U.S.), 4 ; Philadelphia, 16.

Fairbairn, Fairbairns. — Nick. 'fair child,' a native of co. York, where *bairn* is found in several surnames ; cf. Barnfather.

Robertus Thom-barne (i.e. Tom's child), 1379 : P. T. Yorks. p. 155.
Johannes Wil-barne (i.e. Will's child), 1379 : ibid.

The instances prove the origin ; cf. Fairchild. Not to be confounded with Fairburn, q.v.

Johannes Fayrebarne, 1379 : ibid. p. 214.
Willelmus Fairebarn, 1379 : ibid. p. 236.
Robertus Fayrebarne, 1379 : ibid. p. 150.
London, 4, 4.

Fairbank, Fairbanks, Firbank. — Local, (1) 'at the fairbank,' i.e. the yellow bank, from residence thereby ; cf. Windybank, Ewbank, &c., and v. Bank ; (2) ' of Firbank,' a township in the parish of Kirkby Lonsdale, co. Westm. The surname is still to be found in the district.

Robert Firebancke, of Wennington, parish of Mellinge, 1638 : Lancashire Wills at Richmond, ii. 109.
1803. Married—William Fairbanks and Frances Freer : St. Geo. Han. Sq. ii. 288.
London, 2, 2, 0 ; New York, 2, 12, 0 ; MDB. (co. Monmouth), 0, 0, 1 ; (co. Westmoreland), 0, 0, 1.

Fairbeard.—Nick. 'with the fair beard' ; cf. Fairfax, Brownbeard, Blackbeard, &c.
Thomas Fayrebeard, licence to sell ale in city of Oxford, 1590 : Reg. Univ. Oxf. vol. ii. pt. 1 p. 425.
Stephen Fairebeard, citizen of Oxford, 1620 : ibid. p. 312.

The curate of St. James', Clerkenwell, in 1722 was Mr. Fairbeard. His name is appended to many weddings ; v. Marriages at St. Jas. Clerkenwell, iii. 246, 247.

1748. Married — Daniel Lovett and Sarah Fairbeard : St. Jas. Clerkenwell, iii. 280.

Fairbrass. — Nick. ; v. Firebrace.

Fairbrother. Farebrother. Farbrother.—Nick. A brother-in-law, a direct translation of the French Beaufrere or Bonfrere ; cf. Fairchild with Beaufitz.

' There till Mr. Fairebrother come to call us out to my father's to supper.' Pepys' Diary, 1660, p. 45.
Walter Beaufrere, c. 1300. M.
Roger Beaufrere, ibid.
Adam Bonfrere, 1379 : P. T. Yorks. p. 179.
1624. Married—Saywell Wright and Margrett Fayrebrother : St. Jas. Clerkenwell, iii. 53.
1733. Bapt.—Rebecca, d. John Fairbrother : St. Michael, Cornhill, p. 171.
London, 1, 8, 2 ; Crockford, 2, 3, 2 ; New York, 4, 0, 0.

Fairburn.—Local, ' of Fairburn,' a village near Ledsham, Leeds. Not to be confounded with Fairbairn, q.v., although both must be considerably mixed, especially as the two surnames arose in the same county.

Margaret de Fareburn, co. Kent, 1273. A.
London, 3 ; West Rid. Court Dir., 6 ; Leeds, 2.

Fairchild.—Nick. ' fair child,' an exact equivalent, or translation of O.F. *beau-fitz*, an expression of endearment, or courtesy, ' fayre chylde, *ephebus, epheba* ' : Prompt. Parv. Way adds in a note, ' afterwards used only to signify a son-in-law.'

'Beau-fitz, quod his fader.'
Piers Plowman, l. 4819.

v. North-English Fairbairn, and cf. Fairbrother with Beaufrere.

Margaret Fairechilde, C. R., 9 Ric. II.
Robert Fairchilde, ibid. 34 Hen. III.
Adam Fayrchild, co. Oxf., 1273. A.
Ralph Fayrchild, co. Camb., ibid.
John Fairohild, co. Soms., 1 Edw. III :
Kirby's Quest, p. 85.
John Fairchild, bailiff of Norwich, 1354 :
FF. iii. 99.
London, 3 ; Philadelphia, 5.

Fairclough, Faircloth.—Local, ' of the fair clough.' Faircloth is a curious corruption. But this is a poor attempt at disguising the origin of a surname as compared with the name of the learned Calvinist, Dr. Featly, vicar of Lambeth, much lauded by Fuller and A. Wood, who died in 1645. He is only known to fame as Dr. Featly, but he was born Fairclough, as all biographical notices show, ad ex. ' Life of Thomas Fuller ' (J. E. Bailey), p. 494. This alone will remind the reader of some of the difficulties we have to contend with. In the second entry below we see how still further the name was distorted.

1583. John Fairclough, of Upholland :
Wills at Chester (1545-1620), p. 62.
1655. Married—Mr. Samuell Fear Cloth, minister of Houghton Conquest, and Mrs. Frances Folter, of Ketton in Suffolke, by Justyce Bacon : St. Peter, Cornhill, i. 260.
1669. Married—Allfabell Farcloe and Anne Cabell : St. Jas. Clerkenwell, iii. 165.
John Fayreclogh, C. R., 8 Hen. IV.

1700. Bapt.—Sarah, d. of Joseph Faircloth : St. Jas. Clerkenwell, p. 4.
London (1884), 3, 4 ; New York, 3, 0.

Fairfax.—Nick. ' with the fair fax,' i.e. the fair hair; cf. Fairhair.
'A syde head and a fare fax.'
Towneley Mysteries.
Thomas Fayrfax, c. 1300. M.
Ricardus Farefax, 1379 : P. T. Howdenshire, p. 6.
Willelmus Fayrfax, 1379 : P. T. Yorks. p. 292.
1587. Thomas Barbor and Johanna Fayerfaxe : Marriage Lic. (London), i. 166.
1642. Married — Thomas Price and Katherine Fearfax : St. Peter, Cornhill, i. 257.
1781. Married—John Fairfax and Phœbe Elborn : St. Geo. Han. Sq. i. 327.
MDB. (co. Lincoln), 1 ; (East Rid. Yorks), 1 ; (West Rid. Yorks), 1 ; Crockford, 1 ; Philadelphia, 1.

Fairfield.—Local, ' of Fairfield,' parishes and chapelries in cos. Lancaster, Derby, Somerset, &c.
London, 1 ; Boston (U.S.), 18.

Fairhair.—Nick. ' with the fair hair ' ; cf. Fairfax.
Richard Bryan, *dicti* ffairher, C.R., 1 Edw. III. pt. i.
Peter Fairher, co. Soms., 1 Edw. III :
Kirby's Quest, p. 281.
John Fairhere, C. R., 30 Edw. III.
Anota Fairehare, 1379 : P. T. Yorks. p. 228.
'1522. To Mr. William Farehaire, Doctor of Laws ' : Letters of Fraternity, Durham Priory, p. 119, Surtees Soc.
Edward Fayreheire, circa 1560. Z.

This surname has probably been absorbed by Farrar.

Fairhead.—Nick. ' with the fair head ' ; cf. Fairfax, Fairhair, Whitehead.
John Fayrhed, Pardon R., 6 Ric. II.
1469. Juliana Fairhed : Cal. of Wills in Court of Husting (2).
1587. Peter Butcher and Agnes Fayerhed (co. Essex) : Marriage Lic. (London), i. 162.
MDB. (co. Essex), 3.

Fairholme, Fairham.—Local, ' at the fair holm ' (v. Holmes and Home). Probably Fairham is a variant ; v. Ham (2).
Ricardus Fairhome, 1379 : P. T. Yorks. p. 59.
Johannes Fayrhome, 1379 : ibid. p. 91.
London (1884), 1, 0 ; Rochdale, 0, 1.

Fairleigh, Fairley, Fairlie, Farley.—Local, ' of Fairleigh ' or ' Fairley,' (1) a parish in co. Soms., seven miles from Bath; (2) a parish in co. Hants, near Basingstoke;

(3) also ' of Farley,' parishes in cos. Kent and Surrey, and chapelries and townships in cos. Stafford and Wilts.
Adam Farlegh, co. Soms., 1 Edw. III :
Kirby's Quest, p. 271.
Jacob de Farlegh, co. Wilts, 1273. A.
Hugh de Farleye, co. Suff., ibid.
London, 0, 1, 2, 11 ; Philadelphia, 1, 2, 0, 94.

Fairman.—Bapt. ; v. Firmin.

Fairmaner, Faremaners, Fairminer.— ? Local. Mr. Lower says, ' most likely a translation of the French *Beau Manoir*, the ' fair manor ' : Patr. Brit., p. 108.
London, 1, 0, 1 ; West Rid. Court Dir., 0, 1, 0 ; Sheffield Dir., 1, 0, 0.

Fairweather, Fayerweather.—Nick. A colloquial expression for a happy, sunshiny fellow; v. Merryweather.
John Fayrweder, co. Camb. 1273. A.
Hugh Fairweder, co. Linc., ibid.
Alexander Fairewedre, C. R., 16 Edw. III. pt. ii.
Juliana Fayerweder, 1379 : P. T. Howdenshire, p. 17.
Valentine Fairewether, C. R., 1-2 Philip and Mary, pt. viii.
1683. Married—Peter Farewether and Mercy Blunt : St. Jas. Clerkenwell, iii. 199.
1783. — John Fairweather and Sarah Axtel : St. Geo. Han. Sq. i. 344.
London, 9, 0 ; New York, 1, 2 ; Boston (U.S.), 5, 0.

Faithfull, Faithful.—Nick. ' the faithful.' Soon after the Reformation Faithful became a baptismal name, rivalling Thankful among the Puritans. It is still in use in cos. Devon and Cornwall.
'Faithful Teate, minister at Sudbury, Suffolk ' : Sibbes' Works, I. xxvi, ed. Nichol, 1862.
1640. Bapt.—Benjamin, son of Faithful Bishop : St. Columb Major, p. 170.
1713. Buried—Mary, d. Faithfull and Joan Cock : ibid. p. 253.

In the Cornwall Directory I find at Newquay, in the parish of St. Columb Major, the name of 'Faithful Veal, shoemaker.' Thus for 250 years this title has been fontal in that ancient parish. As seen above it was applied to both sexes. Bunyan gave the name to the martyr of Vanity Fair :
'Sing, Faithful, sing, and let thy name survive,
For though they killed thee, thou art yet alive.'

This is strictly true even from a directory point of view.

London, 5, 1 ; New York, 1, 0.

Fakes, Feggs.—Bapt. 'the son of Fulk,' which has a great many variants ; v. Folk and Fulke.

Fakes de Breaute. E.
Willelmus Feygs, 1379 : P. T. Yorks. p. 44.

Falcon, Falken.—Nick. 'the falcon.' It would be a capital sobriquet for a pursuivant.

Faulcon Pursevaunt. XX. 1.
Richard Faucon, co. Soms., 1 Edw. III : Kirby's Quest, p. 214.

It is possible the name may be baptismal ; v. Fulchon.

New York, 0, 1.

Falconer, Falkner, Faulkner.—Occup. and offic. 'the falconer,' the keeper of his lord's or lady's falcon.

Richard le Fauconer, co. Hunts, 1273 A.
Walter le Fauconer, co Hunts, ibid.
John le Fauconer, co. Soms., 1 Edw. III : Kirby's Quest, p. 214.
John Fauconner, co. Soms., 1 Edw. III : ibid. p. 269.
Geoffrey Fauconer, 1379 : P. T. Yorks. p. 53.
London, 5, 4, 42 ; Boston (U.S.), 3, 0, 51 ; Philadelphia, 0, 7, 47.

Falder, Faulder. — Occup. 'the falder,' a herd, a shepherd, one who tended cattle ; A.S. *fald*, a fold. A well-known North-English surname, especially familiar to co. Cumberland; cf. Crofter or Crafter, q.v.

Rob of the Fald, 1581 : Nicolson and Burn, Hist. Westm. and Cumb., i. p. xxxvi.
Rob Grame of the Fald, 1581 : ibid.
Manchester, 0, 2 ; MDB. (co. Cumberland), 7, 6.

Falk, Faulkes, Falke.—Bapt. 'the son of Fulk,' one of very many forms ; v. Folk and Fulke.

Edmund Falkes. H.
Johannes Falke, et Albreda uxor ejus, 1379 : P. T. Yorks. p. 42.
Ricardus Falke, Alice sa femme, 1379 : ibid. p. 3.
New York, 57, 0, 4.

Falkland.—Local, 'of Falkland.'

Walter de Folkelonde, co. Soms., 1 Edw. III : Kirby's Quest, p. 162.

Falkner ; v. Falconer.

Fall.—Local, 'at the fall,' i.e. waterfall, or local declivity, from residence thereby.

Edmund del Fal, co. Linc., 1273. A.
Richard del Fal, co. Linc., ibid.
William de la Falle, co. Glouc., ibid.
London, 2 ; New York, 4.

Fallowfield.—Local, 'of Fallowfield,' a parish near Manchester. Of course some other Fallowfield may have given birth to the surname.

Thomas ffalowefeld, Close Roll, 7 Hen. IV.
Christopher Falowfelde, Principal of Edmund Hall, 1505 : Reg. Univ. Oxf. i. 293.
Richard Fallowfeild, co. Camb., 1588 : ibid. vol. ii. pt. ii. p. 167.
1745. Bapt.—John, son of Mr. Fallowfield, of Ulverstone : St. Mary, Ulverston, ii. 337.
1779. Married — Bryan Marshall and Louisa Fallofield : St. Geo. Han. Sq. i. 299.
London, 1 ; Philadelphia, 1.

Fallows.—Local, 'of the fallows,' i.e. the fallow lands ; v. Falwes (Halliwell).

William de la Faleys, co. Wilts, 20 Edw. I. R.
Elyas de la Faleise, co. Sussex, Hen. III-Edw. I. K.
Ralph de la Faleyse, co. Hants, ibid.
Diot de Falus, 1379 : P. T. Yorks. p. 89.
Thomas de Falus, 1379 : ibid.
Thomas del Falghes, co. Ches., 1376 : East Ches. ii. 50 n.
Thomas ffaloghys, co. Ches., 1487 : ibid. i. 243.
1563. Married—Rendull Fallowes and Anne Liversuche : Reg. Prestbury, East Ches. p. 11.
1602. Bapt.—Margery Fallowes : ibid. p. 153.
London, 3 ; Manchester, 8 ; Philadelphia, 5.

Falshaw, Fallshaw.—Local, 'of Fulshaw,' a manor in the parish of Wilmslow, East Cheshire.

Matthew de Fulscha, c. 1200 : East Cheshire, i. 42.
Willelmus Faldschawe, 1379 : P. T. Yorks. p. 287.
Manchester, 2, 9 ; London, 0, 2.

Falstaff, Falstoffe, Fastolfe.—Bapt. 'the son of Fastolf,' one of the endless terminatives in -*ulf* (Yonge, ii. 414). 'A great Norfolk family, one of whose members Shakespeare is supposed to have caricatured in his immortal Sir John Falstaff. . . . It appears from Domesday that a Fastolf held one church in the borough of Stamford, co. Linc., freely from the King': Lower, Patr. Brit. p. 108.

Huceus fil. Frostolfi, 21 Ric. II : Furness Coucher Book, i. 188.
Nicholas Fastolf, co. Bedf., 20 Edw. I. R.
Alexander Fastolf, bailiff of Yarmouth, 1280 : FF. xi. 322.
Thomas Fastolf, bailiff of Yarmouth, 1305 : ibid.

Fanbrother.—Local, 'of Fanrother,' a township in the parish of Hebburn, co. Northumberland. The surname got into co. Chester, and has there become Fanbrother.

1502-3. Robert Fenrother, Prestbury, co. Chester : Earwaker's East Cheshire, ii. 513.
MDB. (co. Ches.), 1.

Fancourt.—Local, 'of Fancourt.'

Gerard de Fanecourt, co. Linc., 1273. A.
London, 4 ; Philadelphia, 1.

Fanne.—Local, 'at the fan,' i.e. threshing-floor ; v. Fanner and Vann.

William atte Fanne. R.
Margery Fanne, temp. Eliz. Z.

Fanner.—Occup. 'the fanner,' i.e. the winnower. 'Winnowed with the shovel and with the fan': Isa. xxx. 24 (Auth. Vers.) ; F. *van*. Hence also Vanner, q.v.

'Barbers, bokebynders, and lymners, Repers, faners, and horners.'
    Cocke Lorelle's Bote.
Walter le Fannere. X.
Simon le Fannere. X.
John Fanner, co. Wilts, 1562 : Reg. Broad Chalke, p. 1.
London, 2 ; New York, 1.

Faraday, Farraday, Fereday.—Occup. 'a travelling merchant' or 'chapman': a translation of *journey* (which in Chaucer's time meant a day's journey) ; M.E. *faren*, to travel ; cf. *thoroughfare*, *welfare*, and *farewell* ; v. Sojourner.

Liverpool, 2, 0, 0 ; Manchester, 0, 1, 0 ; London, 3, 0, 3 ; Philadelphia, 0, 5, 0.

Farewell, Farwell.—Local, 'of Farewell,' a parish in co. Stafford, two miles from Lichfield.

Richard Farewel, co. Suff., 1273. A.
Thomas Farewel, co. Suff., ibid.
1796. Married—Samuel New and Eliz. Farwell : St. Geo. Han. Sq. ii. 149.

1797. Married — Isaac Snoxell and Mary Farewell : ibid. ii. 165.
London, 0, 1 ; MDB. (co. Stafford), 0, 1 ; New York, 2, 1 ; Boston (U.S.), 0, 42.

Farley ; v. Fairleigh.

Farman ; v. Firmin.

Farmer.—Occup. 'the farmer,' one who cultivated a farm.

Johannes Spenser, *firmarius* j Manerii, 1379 : P. T. Yorks. p. 10.
Ricardus de Wenteworth, *firmarius* unius Graunge, 1379 : ibid.
Johannes del Grange, *fermour* del Grange : ibid. p. 30.
Thomas Fermour, *husband*, 1379 : P. T. Howdenshire, p. 24.
Robertus Ryvyll, *fermer*, 1379 : P. T. Yorks. p. 142.
Robertus Friston, *farmer* de Parsonage, 1372 : ibid. 160.
1575. John Farmer and Eliz. Randall : Marriage Lic. (London), i. 66.
1722. Married — Francis Farmer and Mary Willson : St. Mary Aldermary, p. 45.
London, 42 ; New York, 34.

Farmery, Firmery.—Local, 'at the fermery,' i.e. infirmary, hospital. O.F. *enfermerie.* ' Fermerye, *infirmaria, infirmitorium* ' : Prompt. Parv. With the modern Farmery, cf. Clerk and Clark, Perkin and Parkin, &c.; v. Spittle.

John atte Fermery, co. Soms., 1 Edw. III : Kirby's Quest, p. 225.
Raulyn de la Fermerie, 1306. M.
Idonia de la Fermerie. B.
John le (sic) Fermery. H.
1592-3. Edward Lister and Anne Farmarie : Marriage Lic. (London), i. 205.
1796. Married — George Farmery and Sarah Wybrow : St. Geo. Han. Sq. ii. 154.
Leeds, 1, 0 ; MDB. (co. Lincoln), 1, 0 ; New York, 1, 1.

Farndon.—Local, 'of Farndon,' a parish in co. Ches.
London, 1.

Farnell, Farnhill, Farnill, Fernell.—(1) Local, 'of Fernhill,' probably the small estate so-called in Nether Alderley, East Cheshire. (2) Local, 'of Farnhill,' a township in the parish of Kildwick, W. Rid. Yorks, spelt Farnhill in the Yorkshire Poll Tax, 1379, p. 267. The surnames of which these two places were the parents seem to have been inextricably mixed. How easily corruptions arise is proved by the first two following entries :

Edmund Greave, of Fernhill, in Spotland, 1608 : Wills at Chester (1545-1620), p. 75.
John Greave, of Fernell, 1613 : ibid.
John Fernall, of Chester, *baker*, 1606 : ibid. (1545-1620), p. 63.
Francis Fearnall, of Chester, 1679 : ibid. (1660-80), p. 92.
Ann Fernall, Prestbury, co. Ches., 1775 : Earwaker's East Cheshire, ii. 204.
1777. Married — James Farnell and Susanna Chapman : St. Geo. Han. Sq. i. 280.

Many rising slopes would bear this name.

John de Farnhull, co. Wilts, 1273. A.
Nicholas de Farnhull, co. Wilts, ibid.
West Riding (Yorks) Court Dir., 1, 1, 1, 1 ; MDB. (West Riding Yorks), 1, 4, 0, 1 ; Manchester, 2, 0, 0, 0 ; London, 2, 0, 0, 0 ; MDB. (co. Stafford), 1, 0, 0, 0.

Farnham.—Local, 'of Farnham,' a parish and market-town in Surrey, ten miles from Guildford.

John de Farnam, *carnifex*, 17 Edw. II : Freemen of York, i. 22.

Here the *h* is elided, as in Barnum, &c.

1665. Edward Farnham and Katherine Higgons : Marriage Lic. (Faculty Office), p. 89.
1666. Bapt. — Susanna, d. John Farnam : St. Jas. Clerkenwell, i. 228.
London, 8 ; Boston (U.S.), 34.

Farningham.—Local,'of Farningham,' a parish in co. Kent.
Ralph de Ferningham, co. Kent,1273. A.

Farnley.—Local, 'of Farnley'; v. Fearnley.
Johannes de Farnelay, 1379 : P. T. Yorks. p. 131.
London (1884), 2 ; Philadelphia, 2.

Farnum.—Local,'of Farnham,' an American corruption ; cf. Barnum for Barnham.

' John Singleton Copley, Lord Lyndhurst (1772-1863), was son of John Singleton Copley, and his wife Mary Farnum Clarke, born in Boston, U.S. : ' Dict. Nat. Biog. xii. 182.
Philadelphia, 10.

Farran, Farrance, Farrand, Farrant, Farrants, Farren, Farrent, Farrin.—Bapt. ; v. Farrimond.

Henry Ferant, co. Oxf., 1273. A.
Walter Ferrant, co. Camb., ibid.
Benedict Feraunt, co. Norf., ibid.
Ferentus Balistarius, co. Hants, Hen. III–Edw. I. K.
London, 1, 2, 2, 13, 1, 5, 1, 3 ; Philadelphia, 6, 0, 8, 1, 0, 36, 1, 0.

Farrar, Farrer.—Occup. 'a maker of horse-shoes '; O.F. *ferrer*, to shoe horses (v. Ferrer), now a farrier in an altered sense. For form Farrer, in place of Ferrer, cf. Clark and Clerk, Darby and Derby, *parson* and *person*, also *farrier*, the occupative term. Once a great Yorkshire trade-name, now a great Yorkshire surname.

Thomas le Ferrur, C. R., 3 Edw. I.
Willelmus Ferour, *ferour*, 1379 : P. T. Yorks. p. 156.
Johannes Crayk, *ferour*, 1379 : ibid.
Hugo Farrour, 1379 : ibid. p. 40.
Thomas Farrour, 1379 : ibid. p. 41.
William de Wistow, *ferrour*, 3 Edw. II : Freemen of York, i. 12.
London, 6, 8 ; West Riding Court Dir., 32, 10 ; Philadelphia, 5, 6.

Farrimond.—Bapt. 'the son of Faramond.' 'Faramond ; Pharamond, an ancient Teutonic personal name' (Lower, Patr. Brit. p. 109). 'Travellers again had their name from *fara*, the modern German *fahren*, and the scarcely disused English to *fare*, meaning to journey. The most noted instance is Faramund, who, in the guise of Pharamond, is placed at the head of the long-haired Frankish dynasty' (Yonge, ii. 432); cf. Osman for Osmond, or Wyman for Wymond.

Faremanne (without surname), 1169 : RRR. p. 13.
Fareman Alberd, 1325. M.
Johannes fil. Fareman, 1316. M.
Edward Farman, co. Soms., 1 Edw. III : Kirby's Quest, p. 127.
Upholland, near Wigan, 1 ; Manchester, 1.

Farrington.—Local, ' of Farrington,' a township in the parish of Penwortham, co. Lancaster. No doubt in many cases a variant of Farringdon, but the Lancashire Farringtons are derived as stated above.

Roger Faryndon, co. Soms., 1 Edw. III : Kirby's Quest, p. 257.
Johannes de Feryngton, 1379 : P. T. Yorks. p. 56.
John Farington, of Farington, 1595 : Wills at Chester (1545-1620), p. 62.
Roger Farington, of Farington, 1608 : ibid.
1793. Married — William Dance and Mary Farrinton : St. Geo. Han. Sq. ii. 88.
London, 7 ; Manchester, 4 ; Liverpool, 5 ; Philadelphia, 22.

Farthing.—(1) Local or nick-name.

Geoffrey Ferthing, 1273. A.
William Ferthing, 1306. M.
Richard Ferthing, C. R., 18 Edw I.
Robertus Farthing, 1379 : P. T. Yorks.
p. 89.

(2) Local, 'of Faringdon,' a parish in co. Berks.

Thomas Fartheyn, 1311. M.
Thomas Fardeyn, 1320. M.
Thomas Farendyn, 1323. M.

The three entries above refer to one individual.

London, 6 ; Oxford, 1 ; Philadelphia, 4.

Farwell.—Local ; v. Farewell.

Fassett.—Local, ' of Forcett ' ; v. Fawcett.

1627. Married—Samuell Fassett, *preacher*, and Eliz. Shaw : St. Peter, Cornhill, p. 252.
1775. — Edward Fassett and Isabella Jackson : St. Geo. Han. Sq. i. 254.
London, 2 ; Philadelphia, 12.

Fathers.—Nick. ' the father.' The s is patronymic as in Williams, Jones, Tompkins, &c. It is curious to notice that three counties close to one another supply my early instances ; cf. the Yorkshire Barnfather.

Arnald le Fader, co. Wilts, 1273. A.
Richard le Fader, co. Oxf., ibid.
Robert Fader, co. Soms., 1 Edw III : Kirby's Quest, p. 265.
1786. Married — George Woods and Ann Fathers : St. Geo. Han. Sq. i. 390.
London, 1 ; Oxford, 5.

Fatt.—Nick. ' the fat,' a corpulent person. An early sobriquet ; cf. Bigg, Little, Thick, &c.

Robert le Fatte, co. Soms., 1 Edw. III : Kirby's Quest, p. 246.
Michel le Fatte, co. Soms., 1 Edw. III : ibid. p. 249.

Cf. John Fatman in the same record, p. 251.

William le Fatte, 1307. M.
1588. John Fatt, *yeoman*, and Anne Weaver : Marriage Lic. (London), i. 169.
London, 3 ; New York, 2.

Faulkner ; v. Falconer.

Faux.—Bapt. ' the son of Fawke,' a variant of Fulke, q.v. The genitive was thus Fawkes, and this naturally became Faux ; cf. Baxter, Cox, Wilcox, &c. ; v. Fawkes.

Nel Faukes, co. Camb., 1273. A.
William Faukes, co. Norf., ibid.

Geoffrey Faukes, co. Hunts, ibid.
John Faux. H.

Fawcett, Fozard.—Local, ' of Forcett,' a chapelry in the parish of Gilling, N. Rid. Yorks. The surname has ramified in the most surprising manner. Fozard is a curious, but not unnatural corruption (cf. Gozzard for Gooseherd). It is found in the district where Fawcett arose.

Adam de Fawsyde, 1379 : P. T. Yorks. p. 288.
Willelmus Fawoyde, 1379 : ibid.
Adam de Fawesyde, 1379 : ibid.
1607. Bapt. — Eliz., d. John Forsett, *taylor* : St. Dionis Backchurch, p. 93.
John Faucet, of Over Kellet, 1537 : Lancashire Wills at Richmond (1457-1680), p. 105.
Richard Fawcet, of Over Kellet, 1602 : ibid.
1723. Married—John Fawcett and Mary Chater : St. Mary Aldermary, p. 46.
London, 14, 0 ; Leeds, 10, 0 ; West Rid. Court Dir., 29, 0 ; MDB. (West Rid. Yorks), 36, 0 ; West Ardsley (near Wakefield), 0, 2 ; Philadelphia, 8, 0.

Fawkes.—Bapt. ' the son of Fawke ' or ' Fawkes ' (v. Fulke, Faux, and Fowke), one of very many variants. It was still in use as a font-name in the 17th century.

Faukesius de Brente, 1273. A.
Faukes le Buteller, ibid.
Willelmus Faukes, 1379 : P. T. Yorks. p. 220.
Robertus Fawkes, 1379 : ibid. p. 213.
Fauke de Glamorgan. E.
1612. Married — Fawke Marrow and Isabell Jackway : St. Jas. Clerkenwell, iii. 39.
London, 4 ; Philadelphia, 3.

Fawson, Faxon.—Bapt. ' the son of Fawke ' ; v. Fawkes.

1675. Buried — Thomas Fawson : St. Mary Aldermary (London), p. 189.
1734. Bapt. — Thomas, son of John Fasson : St. Jas. Clerkenwell, i. 217.
London, 1, 1 ; Boston (U.S.), 0, 33 ; Philadelphia, 0, 3.

Fayerman.—Bapt. ; v. Firmin.

Fayerweather. — Nick. ; v. Fairweather.

Fazackerley, Fazakerley, Phizackerley.—Local, ' of Fazakerley,' a township in the parish of Walton-on-the-hill, near Liverpool. The variant Phizackerley is found only, I believe, in the Furness district of North Lancashire.

Roger Fazakerley of Fazakerley, 1394 : Baines' Lanc. ii. 290.
Nicholas Fazakerley, de Walton, 1600 : Lanc. and Cheshire Rec. Soc. xii. 239.
Robert Fazacreley, of West Derby, *gent.*, 1631 : ibid. xii. 213.
Robert Middleton, of Fazakerley, 1582 : Wills at Chester (1545-1620), p. 136.
Judith Fazakerley, of Walton, 1647 : ibid. (1621-50), p. 76.
1792. Buried—Lawrence Phezackerley, *mariner* : St. Mary, Ulverston, ii. 615.
Liverpool, 9, 0, 0 ; Manchester, 3, 1, 0 ; Ulverston, 0, 0, 2.

Fear, Feare.—Nick. ' the fere,' the proud, the fierce, the bold (A. N.).

' And of Burgayne dewke Loyere,
He was a bolde man, and a fere.'
Halliwell.
' And of hys sone, that good squyere,
Whyll he was ' hole and fere.' ibid.
Kirby's Quest, p. 134.
Robert le Fere, co. Soms., 1 Edw. III : ibid.
London, 3, 1.

Fearman.—Bapt. ; v. Firmin.

Fearnehough ; v. Fernihough.

Fearnhead.—Local, ' of Fearnhead,' a township in the parish of Warrington, co. Lancs.

Grace Fearnhead, of Fearnhead, 1613 : Wills at Chester (1545-1620), p. 63.
Peter Fearnhead, of High Leigh, 1596 : ibid.
Richard Fearnhead, of Fearnhead, co. Lancs., *yeoman*, 1604 : ibid.
Manchester, 1 ; London, 1 ; New York, 1.

Fearnley, Fernley, Ferneley.—Local, ' of Farnley,' near Leeds, spelt Fernelay in the Poll Tax, 1379 ; v. Farnley.

Johannes de Fernelay, living at ' Fernelay,' 1379 : P. T. Yorks. p. 191.
Johannes de Fernelee, 1379 : ibid. p. 181.
Margeria de Fernelee, 1379 : ibid. p. 181.
Johanna de Ferenlowe, 1379 : ibid. p. 4.
London, 3, 2, 0 ; Manchester, 1, 2, 2 ; West Rid. Court Dir., 8, 1, 1 ; Philadelphia, 0, 7, 0.

Fearnside, Fearnsides, Fearnside.—Local, ' of Fearnside,' probably some spot adjacent to Fearnhead, q.v. The suffixes -*head* and -*side* are common in local names ; cf. Akenhead and Akenside, places close together, both the parents of surnames ; also cf. Garthside, from residence at the side of the garth or orchard (s.v. Garside).

1595. Robert Farnside, of Worsley, parish of Eccles: Wills at Chester (1545-1620), p. 62.
1615. Henry Ferneside, of Thurston: ibid. p. 63.
Liverpool, 0, 0, 1; MDB. (co. Lancaster), 0, 0, 4; West Rid. (Yorks), 2, 2, 0.

Fearon.—Occup. 'the feron,' probably a smith. The feminine form, infra, presents no difficulty, as strong men's work is found frequently represented in the Hundred Rolls, &c. The name is derived by M. de Greville (v. Lower's Patr. Brit.) from some kindred word to farrier, O.F. *ferrer*, to shoe a horse; v. Ferrer.

Alan de Feron, London, 1273. A.
Stephen le Feron, London, ibid.
Henry le Feron, London, ibid.
Margery le Feron. B.
London, 6; Philadelphia, 18.

Featherston, Featherstone, Fetherston.—Local, 'of Featherston,' a parish in co. York.

Petrus de Fetherstan, 1379: P. T. Yorks. p. 25.
Simon de Fetherston, 1379: ibid. p. 30.
London, 1, 11, 0; Philadelphia, 1, 3, 2; New York, 5, 0, 1.

Featherstonhaugh. — Local, 'of Fetherstonhaugh,' a manor said to be in co. Northumberland. One of our longest surnames; v. Featherston.

1749. William Featherstonehalgh, master of St. Mary's Hospital, Newcastle-on-Tyne: Brand's Hist. of Newcastle, i. 85.
London, 1; Crockford, 1.

Feavearyear, Feaviour.— ?——. A curious surname peculiar to Norfolk and Suffolk.

'In 1622 it (i.e. Street Hall) was conveyed to Talbot Pepys, Esq., and Richard Feveryere, gent.': FF. vi. 99.
MDB. (Suffolk), 2, 0; (Norfolk), 1, 1.

Feggs.—Bapt.; v. Fakes.

Felbridge.—Local, 'of Felbrigge,' a parish in co. Norfolk.

Thomas de Felebrig, co. Northumb., 1273. A.
Matilda de Felbrigge, co. Norf., ibid.
Philadelphia, 1.

Feld.—Local; v. Field.

Felgate, Folgate.—(1) Local, 'at the fold-gate,' from residence at the entrance of the fold or enclosure; probably the sheepfold.

(2) Local, 'at the fall-gate.' 'Fallgate, a gate across a public road. Norfolk' (Halliwell). Probably this is the true derivation, as my instances seem to prove. No doubt a wooden bar that rose and fell across the road.

Peter de la Falgate, co. Norf., 1273. A.
Eliseus de Falgate, co. Norf., ibid.
Richard de Faldgate, co. Norf., ibid.
John de Faldgate, co. Norf., ibid.
Robert Atte-faldgate, rector of Repham, co. Norf., 1356: FF. viii. 245.
John Atte-faldgate, rector of Fishley, co. Norf., 1354: ibid. xi. 103.
Thomas Faldyate: Pardon's Roll, 5 Ric. II.
John atte Foldyate. J.
Thomas Atte Falgate, rector of Denver, co. Norf., 1395: FF. vii. 319.
1635. William Stephens and Blanche Fellgate: Marriage Lic. (London), ii. 222.
1770. Married — Robert Falgate and Eliz. White: St. Geo. Han. Sq. i. 196.
London, 6, 1; MDB. (Suffolk), 4, 0.

Felix.—Bapt. 'the son of Felix'; as often as not a female name; v. Phillis. The first two entries following refer to the same individual:

Felix de Kanoto, Hen. III-Edw. I: K. p. 58.
Felicia de Kaneto, ibid. p. 59.
Felice Holeg, co. Soms., 1 Edw. III: Kirby's Quest, p. 143.
Johannes Sorowles, et Felix uxor, 1379: P. T. Yorks. p. 131.
London, 2; New York, 10.

Fell.—Local, 'at the fell,' from residence on or near the fell; 'by frith and fell,' a common phrase in early poetry; a fell was a hill or moor open and unenclosed. Sheep that graze on such scanty pastures are called fell-sheep in Furness. So ramified is the surname Fell in Furness that in the register in the parish church of Ulverston (1542-1813) there are not less than 2,500 entries concerning the family or families, the entries concerning John Fell alone numbering over 200.

' Moyses wente up on that felle
Fourty dayes there gon dwelle.'
Cursor Mundi (Halliwell).
1545. Married — Thomas Fell and Margaret Wright: St. Mary, Ulverston, p. 1.
1563. Brian Fell, of Pennington, Furness: Lancashire Wills at Richmond (1457-1680), p. 106.
1565. Christopher Fell, of Ulverston, ibid.
London, 16; Ulverston, 8; Philadelphia, 67.

Fellows, Fellowes.—Nick. 'the fellow,' a comrade, à companion, or simply a body, a sociable man; cf. Goodfellow, Goodbody, Longfellow, &c. Fellows is the genitive.

John Felagh, co. Soms., 1 Edw. III: Kirby's Quest, p. 135.
London, 10, 2.

Felon, Fellon.—Nick. ' the felon,' a treacherous person; M.E. *felun*, O.F. *felon*.

Henry de Felun, co. Hunts, 1273. A.

This surname seems to have lasted till the close of the 17th century in England, and still exists in America.

1671. Bapt. — Joseph, son of Joseph and Tabytha Fellon: St. Jas. Clerkenwell, i. 252.
New York, 0, 1; Philadelphia, 0, 1.

Felstead.—Local, 'of Felstead,' a parish in the dioc. of St. Albans, co. Essex, four miles from Great Dunmow.

William de Feltested, co. Essex, 1273. A.
Thomas Felstead, bailiff of Yarmouth, 1649: FF. xi. 329.
1692. Married — Francis Cruso and Anne Mobberley, by licence, by Mr. Thomas Felsted: St. Mary Aldermary, p. 34.
1723. Married — Adam Felsted and Mary Pratt: St. Michael, Cornhill, p. 62.
London, 5.

Felter.—Occup. 'a felt manufacturer,' a cloth of matted wool used in making hats, &c. ' Feelte or qwylte: *filtrum*': Prompt. Parv.

Henry le Felter, Close Rolls, 1 Edw. I.
New York, 17; Philadelphia, 3.

Feltham.—Local, 'of Feltham,' a parish in co. Middlesex, four miles from Hounslow.

1798. Married — John Turner and Susannah Feltham: St. Geo. Han. Sq. ii. 182.
London, 1.

Felthorpe, Feltrup.—Local, 'of Felthorpe,' a parish in co. Norfolk, seven miles from Norwich. The variant Feltrup is of the ordinary character; cf. Calthrop for Calthorpe, and v. Thorp.

John de Felethorp, co. Norf., 1273. A.
Thomas de Felethorp, co. Norf., 1358: FF. iii. 603.

Peter de Felthorp, rector of Congham, co. Norf., 1343 : ibid. viii. 388.
MDB. (co. Norfolk), 1, 0; Sheffield, 0, 2.

Felton.—Local, 'of Felton,' parishes in cos. Hereford, Northumberland, and Salop.

John de Feltone, co. Notts, 20 Edw.I. R.
William de Feltone, co. Northumb., ibid.
William de Felton, rector of St. Mary Magdalen, Warham, co. Norf., 1349 : FF. ix. 266.
Johannes de Felton, 1379 : P. T. Yorks p. 138.
1578-9. Edward Felton and Eliz. Crockett : Marriage Lic. (London), i. 86.
1669. Married — Thomas Felton and Jane Smith : St. Jas. Clerkenwell. iii. 165.
London, 13 ; New York, 11 ; Philadelphia, 34.

Feltrup.—Local ; v. Felthorpe.

Feltwell.—Local, ' of Feltwell,' a parish in co. Norfolk, six miles from Brandon.

Hugo de Feltewelle, co. Norf., 1273. A.
Jeffrey de Feltwell, co. Norf. : FF. ix. 140.
John Feltwell, Norwich, 1460 : ibid. iv. 404.
1528-9. Thomas Leghe and Eliz. Feltwell : Marriage Lic. (London), i. 6.
Philadelphia, 5.

Fender.—Offic. or nick. An abbreviation of ' defender.' One who defends or wards off, a likely name for a hayward ; cf. ' fender,' a fireplace guard ; also 'fence' and 'defence.'

Roger atte Fendour, Close Roll, 9 Edw. II.
London, 1 ; New York, 1 ; Philadelphia, 5.

Fenemore ; v. Finnemore.

Fenn, Fen.—Local, ' at the fen.' The instances are chiefly from the Fen country. For a West-English variant, v. Venn.

Isabella ate Fenne, co. Oxf., 1273. A.
Robert de la Fenne, co. Soms., ibid.
John atte Fen, bailiff of Yarmouth, 1377 : FF. xi. 324.
Thomas Fenn, bailiff of Yarmouth, 1453 : ibid. p. 235.
Roger atte Fenne, co. Soms., 1 Edw. III : Kirby's Quest, p. 107.
John atte Fene, Close Rolls, 14 Edw. III. pt. i.
Julian atte Fen : Household Book of Queen Isabelle, 1358, Cott. MS., Galba E. xiv.
Walter atte Fenne, C. R., 1 Edw. II.
Thomas de Fenne, C. R., 2 Edw. I.
1617. Maurice Fenn and Lucy Beomont : Marriage Lic. (London), ii. 52.

1725. Married — Samuel Fenn and Sarah Phipps : St. Mary Aldermary, p. 47.
London, 22, 0; MDB. (co. Camb.), 4, 1 ; (Norfolk), 6, 0 ; Philadelphia, 8, 0.

Fennell.—Local, ' at the vennel' ; v. Vennel, and cf. Venn and Fenn, Vanner and Fanner.

Fennemore, Fennimore.— Local ; variants of Finnemore.

Oxford, 1, 1.

Fenner.—Occup. ; v. Venner.

Fenney, Fenny.—Local, ' of Fenay,' now Fenaybridge, in the township of Lepton and parish of Kirkheaton, near Huddersfield, W. Rid. Yorks. Not to be confounded with the Scotch Finney.

Thomas de Fenay, 1379 : P. T. Yorks. p. 119.
Adam de Feny, 1379 : ibid. p. 177.
Willelmus de Feney, 1379 : ibid. p. 176.
Sibilla de Feney, 1379 : ibid. p. 179.
1597-8. William Fenney and Catherine Forman : Marriage Lic. (London), i. 246.
1807. Married—William Fenney and Charlotte Gordon : St. Geo. Han. Sq. ii. 367.
W. R. Yorks Court Dir., 2, 0; London, 1, 0 ; Liverpool, 0, 1 ; Boston (U.S.), 0, 1.

Fenreve.—Offic. ' the fen-reve,' a guardian of the Fens.

Adam Fenreve, co. Hunts, 1273. A.
Symon Fenreue, co. Hunts, ibid.

Fenton.—Local, ' of Fenton,' (1) a township near Carlisle, co. Cumb. ; (2) a chapelry in the parish of Beckingham, co. Lincoln ; (3) a hamlet in the parish of Kettlethorpe, co. Lincoln ; (4) a hamlet in the parish of Wooler, co. Northumb.

Gilbert de Fenton, co. York, 1273. A.
Robert de Fenton, co. Linc., ibid.
Thomas de Fenton, co. Devon, ibid.
Henry de Fenton, co. Linc., Hen. III-Edw. I. K.
John de Fenton, co. Devon, ibid.
Ralph de Fenton, rector of Warham, co. Norf., 1358 : FF. ix. 265.
Ricardus de Fenton, 1379 : P. T. Yorks. p. 130.
Johannes de Fenton, 1379 : ibid. p. 54.
Robertus de Fenton, 1379 : ibid. p. 94.
1741. Married — Perret Fenton and Mary Ashley : St. Mary Aldermary, p. 51.
1807. — William Fenton and Eliz. Beal : St. Geo. Han. Sq. ii. 363.
London, 24 ; Boston (U.S.), 28.

Fenwick.—Local, ' of Fenwick,' (1) a township in the parish of Stamfordham, co. Northumberland; (2) a township in the parish of Campsall, W. Rid. Yorks.

Thomas a Fenyk, of Lytell Harle : Visit. Yorks., 1563, p. 284.
Johannes de Fenwyk', et Avicia uxor ejus, marchant debeses, 1379 : P. T. Yorks. p. 113.
West Rid. Court Dir., 2 ; London, 8 ; MDB. (co. Northumberland), 14 ; Philadelphia, 1 ; Boston (U.S.), 2.

Fereday.—Occup. ; v. Faraday.

Ferguson, Fergusson, Farguson, Fargusson, Fargie, Fergie.—Bapt. ' the son of Fergus ' (Scotch) ; v. Yonge, ii. 55. The name crept over the border into Cumberland and Northumberland ; nick. Fergie or Fargie.

Gilbert fil. Fergusi, 1182 : RRR. p. 30.
Fergie of Meadopp, 1586-7 : Nicolson and Burn, Hist. Westm. and Cumb., pp. xxxiv-vi.
Fargus Grame, 1602 : ibid. p. cxiv.
William Fargy, 1654 : Hist. of Alnwick, by G. Tate, p. 79.
Peter Fergesoun, 1547 : TTT. p. lxxx.
London, 31, 9, 1, 1, 0, 0 ; Philadelphia, 226, 8, 0, 0, 0, 0 ; Boston (U.S.), 98, 0, 0, 0, 0, 0.

Fermor.—Occup. ' the farmer '; v. Farmer.

Robertus del Halle, fermer, 1379 : P. T. Yorks. p. 206.
London, 1.

Fernell.—Local ; v. Farnell.

Fernihough, Fernyhough, Fearnehough, Fernhough, Ferneyhough.—Local, ' of the fern-halgh,' i.e. the mound, or hill covered with ferns ; v. Halgh and Hough, and cf. Greenhalgh and Greenhough. The spot must evidently be looked for in co. Stafford, on the Cheshire side.

Richard de la Fernyhalgh, co. Staff. : Pardon's Roll, 6 Ric. II.
William Fernihaugh, merchant, v. Daniel Danvers, sugar-baker, co. Lanc., 1693 : Exchequer Depositions, p. 83.
Thomas Fernihaugh v. Henry Bradshaw, co. Ches., 1669 : ibid. p. 136.
John Fearnihough, of Doddington, co. Ches., yeoman: Wills at Chester(1621-50), p. 76.
John Fernyhough, co. Ches., 1672 : Earwaker's East Cheshire, ii. 645.
MDB. (co. Stafford), 1, 3, 0, 0, 7 ; Manchester, 2, 1, 0, 0, 0 ; London, 0, 1, 0, 0, 0 ; Liverpool, 1, 1, 0, 0, 0 ; MDB. (co. Ches.), 1, 2, 0, 1, 0 ; Sheffield, 0, 0, 4, 0, 0.

Ferrabee, Ferraby, Ferebee.—Local, ' of Ferriby.' North and South Ferriby are parishes in cos.

York and Lincoln. With Ferrabee cf. Applebee for Appleby.

William de Feriby, dean of Cranwich, co. Norf., 1388 : FF. ii. 228.
John Fereby, alias Verby, founded a Grammar School at Campden, co. Glouc. in 1487 : Rudder's Hist. Glouc. p. 324.
1675. Married—Nathaniell Feribee and Eliz. Sommers : St. Mary Aldermary, p. 32.
1787. — John Price and Harriot Ferraby : St. Geo. Han. Sq. iii. 401.
MDB. (co. Glouc.), 2, 0, 0 ; (co. Lincoln), 0, 2, 0 ; London, 0, 1, 1 ; Philadelphia, 0, 0, 1.

Ferrand, Farrand, Farrant.
—(1) Local. From some place of the name in Normandy. Ferrand is still found about Skipton, where for several centuries the Ferrand family were Wardens of the castle.

John Feraunt, co. Soms., 1 Edw. III : Kirby's Quest, p. 83.
Hugo de Feraunt. 1334, vicar of Carlton-in-Craven : Whitaker, Hist. Craven, p. 226.

(2) Bapt. ; v. Farran.

London, 0, 1, 13 ; West Rid. Court Dir., 3, 4, 0 ; New York, 0, 2, 2.

Ferrer, Ferrier.—Occup. 'the farrier,' a maker of horse-shoes ; O.F. ferrer, to shoe horses ; spelt 'ferrour' in Fabyan's Chronicle. Fr. fer, iron ; Lat. ferrum, iron ; cf. Pettifer, Brasdefer, Firebrace ; v. Farrar.

Roger le Ferur, co. Dorset, 1273. A.
Thomas le Ferour. co. Soms., 1 Edw. III : Kirby's Quest, p. 101.
Johannes de Helistones, ferror, 1379 : P. T. Yorks. p. 183.
Johannes Ferour, ferour, ibid. p. 151.
William Ferour, ferour, ibid. p. 156.

The halfway house to Farrar is seen in the following :

1617. Bapt.—Jeane, d. William Ferrar : St. Michael, Cornhill, p. 113.
1735. Married—Ivory Ferrar and Eliz. Powell : St. Dionis Backchurch, p. 66.
London, 1, 5 ; West Rid. Court Dir., 0, 1 ; MDB. (Lincoln), 1, 0 ; New York 3, 4.

Ferreter.—Occup. 'the ferreter.' Probably a dealer in, or manufacturer of, ferret, i.e. silk tape.

Walter le Furettour, Close Rolls, 12 Edw. II.

Ferriman,   Farriman. — Occup. 'the ferryman,' one who conveys people over a river.

Johannes Wryght, faryman, 1379 : P. T. Howdenshire, p. 7.

Thomas Feryman, 1379 : P. T. Yorks. p. 153.
John Faryman, C. R., 12 Hen. IV.
Nicholas Feryman, 1379 : P. T. Howdenshire, p. 18.
Johannes Feryman, 1379 : P. T. Yorks. p. 63.
Johannes de Walcote, feryman, 1379 : ibid. p. 105.
Robertus Toure, feryman, 1379 : ibid.

In the village of Armin occur

Johannes Moram, feryman, 1379 : P. T. Yorks. p. 121.
Adam Feriman, 1379 : ibid.
London, 3, 1.

Ferry, Ferrie, Ferrey.—
Local, 'at the ferry.' Probably the bearer of the name resided at the ferry in order to carry on his business as a ferryman ; v. Ferriman.

Roger de Ferye, co. Yorks, 1273. A.
William de Ferie. co. Yorks, ibid.
Johannes de Fery, 1379 : P. T. Yorks. p. 100.
Johannes del Fery, 1379 : ibid. p. 22.
London 0, 1, 1 ; West Rid. Court Dir., 0, 1, 0 ; Philadelphia, 48, 0, 0.

Fettiplace, Fetiplace.—? Local. The present American form is Phetteplace, q.v.

Adam Feteplace, co. Oxf., 1273. A.
Walter Feteplece, co. Oxf., ibid.
Edward Fetiplace, B.A., 1546 : Reg. Univ. Oxf. p. 212.
1663. John Collins and Anne Fettiplace, co. Berks : Marriage Alleg. (Canterbury), p. 93.
1671-2. William Nutley and Catherine Fettiplace : Marriage Lic. (Westminster), p. 45.

Fewster.—Occup. 'the fewster,' a maker of saddle-trees.

Robertus de Cathale, fufster, 1277-8 : Freemen of York (Surt. Soc.), i. 3.
Geoffrey le Fufster, 1283 : ibid. p. 4.
Nicholas le Fuster, Close Roll, 21 Edw. III. pt. ii.
Ricardus Fuystour, 1379 : P. T. Yorks. p. 241.
Ralph le Fuster. M.
Robert Fuster. F.
Willelmus Fystour, 1379 : P. T. Yorks. p. 254.
William Fewster, master of Endowed School, Braithwaite, Dacre : West Rid. Dir., 1867.
Christopher Fewster, curate of Stockton, 1599 : DDD. iii. 187.

An interesting name, now found as Fewster. 'The Sellers(Saddlers), Verrours, and Fuystours went together in the York Pageant' (York Mystery Plays, p. xxvi, ed. Toulmin Smith) ; in the Chester Play 'the

Saddlers and Fusters' (Ormerod's Cheshire, i. 300) ; and in Cocke Lorelle's Bote the 'Bladesmythes, fosters, and sadelers.' Thus saddlers and fusters went always together. In his Memorials of London Mr. Riley mentions a 'Welsh Polyfuyster'(p. xxii). Strictly speaking, a fuster was a joiner, one who made the wooden framework of the saddle-tree. No doubt related to O.F. fust, a staff, stake, stock, stump, trunk, or log (v. Fust (1), Skeat). Lat. fustis. Our fusty and fustiness are of similar origin. The spelling 'foster' in Cocke Lorelle's Bote suggests that some of our Fosters are so derived ; v. Foster.

London (1891), 4 ; Knottingley, Yorks, 2 ; Acomb, near York, 1 ; Philadelphia, 1.

Fewterer, Fewter, Vewter.
—Occup. 'the fewterer,' a dog-holder, the man who held the dogs in leash. 'Fewterer, in hunting or coursing, the man who held the dogs in slips, or couples, and loosed them' (Halliwell). 'Vewter, a keeper of hounds' (ibid.). I quoted two lines in my English Surnames (third edition, p. 236), but unfortunately did not give the reference :

'The vewtrer two cast of brede he tase,
Two lesshe of greyhounds if that he has.'

Walter le Feuterer co. Hants. 1273. A.
Geoffrey le Wewterer, co. Norf., ibid.
John le Vautrer, co. Essex, ibid.
Godfrey le Futur: co. Oxf., ibid.
Simon le Futur, co. Suff., ibid.
Fulcher le Fewtrer, co. Norf. FF.
Richard Vewtrer, C. R., 3 Hen. VI.
1667. Mark Barrington and Eliz. Fetter : Marriage Lic. (Canterbury), p. 141.
1731. Bapt.—Robert, son of Jonathan Vautier : St. Peter, Cornhill, ii. 37.
London (Futter), 1 ; (Futcher), 1 ; Philadelphia (Futcher), 2.

Fickett, Ficket.—Nick. 'the fitchet,' i.e. polecat (v. Fitchett), of which this is merely a harder form.

Henry Fiket, co. Suff., 1273. A.
Stephen Fiket, co. Suff., ibid.
1668. Philip Dayrell and Elizabeth Fickett : Marriage Alleg. (Canterbury), p. 160.
New York, 0, 1 ; Boston (U.S.), 5, 0.

Fickling.—Bapt. 'the son of Fulk,' dim. Fulkelin or Fuckling, whence Fickling ; cf. Hewling for Hewelin, and v. Hicklin. Fulk

was extremely popular, and was dressed in every possible form.

William Fukkelyn, co. Suff., 1273. A. London, 4.

Fickus.—Bapt.'the son of Figg,' q.v. Fick and Fickins seem sharpened forms of Figg and Figgins.

William Fyke, co. Norf., 1273. A. London (1884), 3.

Fiddey, Fiddy; v. Friswid.

Fiddyment.—Bapt. 'the son of Frethemund' (?). There can be little question about this. The suffix -*mond* or -*mund* becomes commonly corrupted to -*ment*; cf Rayment and Garment for Raymond and Garmund. The form Friddement would soon lend itself to Fiddyment.

Thomas Frethemund, co. Kent, 1273. A. 1470. Thomas Fydyan, or Fvdymont. rector of Shelton, co. Norf.: FF. v. 271. London, 1.

Fidge.—Nick. 'the fitch,' i.e. polecat ; v. Fitch (2). In the same way Fitchett became Fidgett, q.v.

Richard Fige, co. Oxf., 1273. A. 1653. Married—Phillipp Wheeler and Priscilla Fidge : St. Dionis Backchurch (London), p. 29. London, 1.

Fidgeon, Fidgen.—Bapt. 'the son of Vivian.' Vivian was found in many forms ; v. Phythian.

Roger Fidian, co. Camb., 1273. A. Alexander Fichion, co. Camb., ibid. Henry Fithion, co. Camb., ibid.

Fichion is clearly the ancestor of Fidgeon and Fidgen.

1747. Married—William Oldham and Lucy Fidgeon : St. Geo. Han. Sq. i. 38. London, 0, 1.

Fidgett.—Nick. 'the fitchet,' i.e. polecat ; v. Fitchett (s.v. Fitch, 2); a manifest imitative corruption ; cf. Fidge and Fitch.

1658. Married—Thomas Fidgitt and Mary Smith : St. Dionis Backchurch, p.34. Oxford, 1.

Fidler, Fitler, Fiddler.—Occup. 'the fiddler,' a player on the fiddle ; v. Vidler. Fitler is a sharpened form of the surname, peculiar to the United States.

Johannes Fydeler, 1379: P.T.Yorks.p.79. Stephanus Fythelar, 1379 : ibid. p. 126. Alicia Fithyller, 1379 : ibid. p. 96. London, 3, 0, 0 ; Oxford, 3, 0, 0 ; Philadelphia, 14, 14, 1.

Field.—Local, 'at the field,' from residence in or by a field.

Thomas atte Felde, 1301. M. William de la Felde, co. Glouc., 20 Edw. I. R. John de la Felde. co. Heref., ibid. Linot ate Feld, co. Oxf., 1273. A. William a la Feld, co. Oxf., ibid. John in the Feld, co Soms., 1 Edw. III: Kirby's Quest, p. 103. Stephan atte Feld, co. Soms., 1 Edw. III : ibid. p. 164. London, 122, 0 ; New York, 76, 3.

Fielddrake.—Nick. 'the little bustard '; cf. *field-duck.*

Ricardus Feldrak', 1379: P. T. Yorks, p. 123.

Fielden.—Local, ' of Fielden'; a well-known Lancashire surname.

1574. Roger Fielden, vicar of Leigh, co. Lanc. : Wills at Chester, i. 64. 1502. James Fielden. of the parish of Rochdale, co. Lanc. : ibid. West Rid. Court Dir., 6; Manchester, 6.

Fielder.—Occup. 'the fielder,' a farm labourer.

London, 12 ; New York, 10.

Fieldhouse.—Local, 'at the field-house'; cf. Moorhouse, Loftus, &c. Many spots would naturally acquire this title. An instance below existed in the parish of Rochdale.

Randulphus Feldhowses, 1379 : P. T. Yorks. p. 289. Johannes de Feldhouse, 1379 : ibid. p. 185. John Feeldhouse emigrated to Virginia in 1634 : Hotten's Lists of Emigrants, p. 36. 1600. Married—Thomas Wood and Joane Feilduse : St. Jas. Clerkenwell, iii. 24. Arthur Clegg, of Fieldhouse, parish of Rochdale, 1608 : Wills at Chester (1545-1620), p. 41. London, 4 ; Leeds, 5 ; Boston (U.S.), 1; Philadelphia, 1.

Fieldsend.—Local, 'at the field-end,' i.e. at the end of the field ; cf. Townsend, Overend, Woodend, &c.

Johannes de Feldehend, 1379 : P. T. Yorks. p. 190.

With this, cf. Townshend. The *h* in both cases is intrusive. On the next page (191) occurs Thomas atte Tounehend.

Sheffield Dir., 6.

Fife.—Local ; v. Fyfe.

Figg, Figge, Figgess, Figgiss, Figgins, Figgs, Fig.—

Bapt. 'the son of Vig.' Vig, found also as Wig; v. Wigg. 'Wigg or Vig (War), is found in the genealogy of Odin ' (Yonge, ii. 409). Both forms lasted long enough to become incorporated into our hereditary nomenclature ; but they must have lapsed at an early period. Compound forms, such as Vig-brand. Vig-fus, Vig-hard, Vig-laf, and Vig-leik, were all in use, one or two still existing in Scandinavia. With the change from initial V to F and vice versa. cf. Venn and Fenn, Vowler and Fowler, Venner and Fenner, &c. , v. Figgin.

William Fig, co. Camb., 1273. A. Richard Fige, co. Oxf., ibid. 1 Henry VIII. 'To Figge, the taborer, 6d ': Churchwarden's Book, Kingston-on-Thames, Brand's Pop. Ant. i. 147. London, 7, 1, 1, 1, 2, 0, 1 ; New York, 0, 6, 0, 0, 0, 0, 0 ; Philadelphia (Fig), 1 ; (Figgins), 3.

Figgin.—Bapt. 'the son of Figg,' with dim. Figg-in. With Figg and Figgin, cf. Wigg and Wiggin. For further information. v. Figg. Figgiss and Figgess are modifications of Figgins, just as Perkiss and Perkes are modified forms of Perkins.

Filbert, Philbert, Philibert. —Bapt. 'the son of Philibert.' St. Philibert's day was Aug. 22 (old style). Professor Skeat shows the probability of the *filbert* being called after the saint, the nutting season then commencing, and quotes 'The Philibert that loves the vale' (Peacham's Emblems, ed. 1612). See Yonge's Christian Names, ii. 231. The American Philiberts are chiefly of French origin.

Fulbert Pedifer, London. **X.** Oto Fulbryght, and Emmota, his mother, Close Rolls, 24 Hen. VI. Robert Filberd, C. R., 6 Edw. IV. Philadelphia, 11, 0, 6.

Filby, Filbee, Filbey.—Local, ' of Filby,' a parish in co. Norfolk. With Filbee, cf. Applebee for Appleby.

Ralph de Fileby, co. Norf., 1280 : FF. xi. 217. Robert de Fileby, co. Norf., 1315: ibid. Roger de Fileby, co. Norf., 1273. A.

Nicholas de Fyleby, rector of Burgh, co. Norf.: FF. xi. 155.
1325. Richard de Phileby, rector of Stokesby, co. Norf.: ibid. p. 250.
1768. Married—William Fillbey and Mary Morris: St. Geo. Han. Sq. i. 178.
London, 7, 1, 0; MDB. (Norfolk), 2, 0, 0; New York, 2, 0, 1.

Filcock.—Bapt. 'the son of Philip,' from the nick. Phil, and pet Philcock; cf. Wilcock, Simcock, &c. In the same way Philkin became Filkin, q.v.

Richard Filcock, of Cholmeston, co. Ches., *yeoman*, 1663 : Wills at Chester (1660–80), p. 93.
Thomas Filcock, of Nantwich, 1677 : ibid.
MDB. (co. Ches.), 1; (co. Stafford), 1.

Fildes, Files.—Local, ' of the Fylde,' a well-known surname in co. Lanc., doubtless arising from the Fylde district. The final *s* is probably genitive as in Sykes, Brooks, Milnes, Holmes, Knowles, &c.

1594. Alice Fyldes, parish of Eccles, *widow*: Wills at Chester, i. 69.
1604. Thomas Fyldes, of Pendlebury: ibid.
1619. Thomas Fyldes, of Manton : ibid.
London, 2, 0; Manchester, 17, 1; Philadelphia, 1, 0.

Filiol.—Nick. ' filiol,' a godson ; cf. F. *filleul*, a godson. Lower says, '*filiolus regis* occurs in the laws of Ina and of Henry I, and the Confessor makes grants *filiolo suo*, to his godson, or adopted son'; v. Ellis, Introd. Domesday.

Edmund Filiol, co. Wilts. 1273. A.
John Fillolle, co. Bucks, ibid.
Richard Fillol, co. Essex, ibid.

I think Filiol is obsolete as a surname; v. Godson (2).

Filkin, Filkins.—Bapt. ' the son of Philip,' from nick. Phil and suffix *-kin* ; cf. Wilkin, Watkin, Tompkin, &c. With Filkin, cf. Filcock, q.v.

John Fylkyn, of Tatenhall, co. Ches., 1549 : East Cheshire, ii. 10.
Philip Filkyn, co. Ches., 1453 : ibid. p. 89.
Jane Fylkin, of Stapleford, *spinster*, 1583 : Wills at Chester (1545–1620), p. 69.
Thomas Filkin, of the Spittle, Boughton, *yeoman* : ibid. (1621–50), p. 76.
Liverpool, 2, 0 ; New York, 0, 4 ; MDB. (co. Cornwall), 0, 1.

Filliter.—Occup. 'the filleter,' a maker of frontlets or fillets for ladies. 'Fylette, *philacterium*': Prompt. Parv. p. 160.

'Hire fillet brode of silk, and set full hye.'   Chaucer, C. T. 3243.

Way says, 'Johanna domina de Roos bequeaths in 1394, "unam longam filetam de rosis de per', &c."': Test. Ebor. i. 203. The surname has just managed to survive.

Ricardus le Feloter, 1379 : P. T. Yorks. p. 282.
West Rid. Court Dir., 1 ; Crockford, 1.

Fillman, Fileman.—(1)Occup. ' the servant of Phill,' i.e. Philip ; cf. Matthewman, Addyman, Jackman, Ladyman, &c.

Robertus Philipman, 1379 : P. T. Yorks. p. 208.

(2) Bapt. ' the son of Philomena.'

Philomena Sturdi, co. Hunts, 1273. A.

(1) is the most probable solution—in fact we may consider it demonstrated.

London, 1, 2 ; Philadelphia, 10, 0.

Fillpot.—Bapt. ' the son of Philip,' from dim. Philipot, whence Philpot and the imitative Fillpot ; v. Filkin and Philcox.

Roger Fylpot. FF.
John Filpot. F.
Anne Fillpott, 1668 : St. Jas. Clerkenwell (Harl. Soc.), i. 236.
Alicia Filyp, 1379: P. T. Yorks. p. 162.
Henricus Filip, 1379 : ibid.
1585. Buried—A woman that died in Filpott lane : St. Dionis Backchurch, p. 199.
1661. — Anne Heward, a lodger in Fillpott lane : ibid. p. 233.
London, 1.

Finch.—Nick. 'the finch.' M.E. *finch* (v. Spink) ; cf. Goldfinch and Goldspink.

Philip Fynch, co. Soms., 1 Edw. III: Kirby's Quest, p. 271.
Thomas Finch, co. Camb., 1273. A.
Agnes Finche, 1379 : P. T. Yorks. p. 58.
Thomas Fynche, 1379 : ibid. p. 57.
Johannes Fynche, 1379 : ibid. p. 182.
London, 42 ; Philadelphia, 14.

Fincham.—Local, ' of Fincham,' a parish in co. Norfolk.

Nigellus de Fincham, co. Norf., temp. William II : FF. vii. 349.
William de Fincham, co. Norf., 52 Hen. III : ibid.

Thomas de Fincham, co. Norf., 22 Edw. III : ibid.
Thomas Fincham, of Fincham, co. Norf., 1550 : ibid.
John de Fincham, co. Norf., 1273. A.
Walter de Fincham, co. Norf., ibid.
MDB. (Suffolk), 8 ; (Norfolk), 1 ; London, 9 ; Philadelphia, 1.

Findlater.—Local, ' of Findlater,' a locality in the parish of Fordyce, Banffshire ; cf. Linklater.
London, 3.

Findsilver.—Nick. Probably. for ' fine-silver,' i.e. pure, unalloyed. M.E. and O.F. *fin*, perfect.

Hugh Findesilver, co. Camb., 1273. A.
John Findesilver, co. Camb., ibid.

Finegod.—Bapt. ' the son of Finegod.'

Fineket Freman, co. Camb., 1273. A.
Amary Finegod, co. Bedf., ibid.
Robert Finegod, co. Bedf., ibid.

Finian.—Bapt. ' the son of Finian.'

Phinian de Roghale, co. Salop, 1273. A.
John Finian, co. Oxf., ibid.

Finn, Finney, Finnie.—(1) Bapt. 'the son of Phin.' In Domesday ' Phin,' cos. Essex and Suffolk. Finney seems to be simply the diminutive. (2) Nick. ' the fine,' the exquisite, the delicate, the refined.

Robert le Fyne, co. Soms., 1 Edw. III: Kirby's Quest, p. 270.
Katherine Fin, co. Hunts, 1273. A.
Maggot Fin, co. Hunts, ibid.
Thomas Fin, co. Suff., ibid.
Thomas Fyn, *chapman*, 1379 : P. T. Howdenshire, p. 10.
Roger Fyne, 1379 : ibid.
Isabella Fynne, 1379 : P. T. Yorks. p. 24.
Nycholas Fynn, 1604 : DDD. iii. 413.
Robertus Fyn, 1307. M.
London, 1, 14, 0 ; Manchester, 3, 3, 0 ; Crockford, 1, 1, 0 ; Philadelphia, 60, 19, 2.

Finnemore, Finnimore, Fenimore, Fenemore, Fynmore, Fenomore.—(1) Local, ' of Finmere,' a parish in co. Oxford, eight miles from Bicester.

Gilbert de Fenamore, co. Wilts, 1273. A.

(2) Bapt. ' the son of Finamour,' i.e. pure love, perfect love ; cf. Douceamour, Paramor, &c.

'Tho spak Clarice to Blancheflour
Wordes ful of fin amour.'
Floriz and Blancheflour, E. E. Text Soc.

As in many other surnames *n* has become *l*, and thus Finnemore has turned itself into Phillimore, q.v.

John Finamur, C. R., 56 Hen. III.
Hugh Finamur, co. Norf., 1273. A.
Dulcia Fynamour, Wardrobe Accounts, Edw. I.
John Fynamour, C. R., 3 Hen. IV. pt. i.
John Fynamore, sup. for B.A., 1539: Reg. Univ. Oxf vol. i. 194.
1597. Married — John Fynnemor and Anne Flynter : St. Michael, Cornhill, p. 16.
1673-4. Buried—John, son of William Finmore : St. Paul's, Covent Garden.
1737-8. — Frances Eliz., d. Henry Fynmore : ibid.
London, 1, 1, 0, 3, 0, 0 ; Philadelphia, 0, 0, 11, 3, 0, 6.

Firebrace, Fairbrass, Farbrace. — Nick. ' iron-arm' ; cf. Armstrong, Strongitharm, Brasdefer ; v. Pettifer. Perhaps a legendary name. Professor Skeat, in his Etym. Dict. (s.v. *Biestings*), alludes to the ' Romance of Ferumbras.'

Robert Ferebraz, C. R., 48 Hen. III.
Robert Ferbras, co. Bucks, 1273. A.
Henry Ferebraz, co. Oxf., ibid.
John Ferbraz, co. Bucks, ibid.
1678. Bapt. — Sarah, d. Henry Fierbrasse : St. Mary, Aldermary (London), p. 104.
1680. — Mary, d. Henry Fyerbras : ibid. p. 105.
MDB. (co. Kent), 0, 1, 4.

Firmin, Farman, Fairman, Fearman, Fayerman, Firman, Fireman.—Bapt. ' the son of Firmin,' ' Farman,' or ' Ferman.' In Domesday Farman and Farmannus. The great home of this name and all its varied forms was Norfolk. From hence it extended as Firmin into Essex. In these districts the surname is still common. It is curious to note that the form Fayerman still exists.

Adam fil. Phareman, Fines Roll, 7 Ric. I-16 John.
John Faverman, co. Norf., 1273. A.
Richard Fayrman, co. Norf., ibid.
Walter Fayrman, vicar of Lakenham, co. Norf., 1369 : FF. iv. 518.
Farman Alberd, bailiff of Yarmouth, 1325 : ibid. xi. 323.

This same individual is found as Fairman Alberd, 1306 (M.).

John fil. Fermin de Amyas, 9 Edw. II : Freemen of York, i. 16.

Firmin Capell, co. Camb., 1273. A.
Firman de Lavenham, co. Norf., 1324 : FF. vi. 104.
Robertus Fermyn, *skynnar*, 1379 : P. T. Yorks. p. 99.
Firmine Rookwood, 1552, co. Norf. : FF. xi. 113.
1545. Buried — Fyrmyn Adams : St. Dionis Backchurch, p. 181.
1576. — Francis Farman : ibid. p. 194.
1597. Bapt.—John, son of Mr. Fairman, *mercer* : St. Mary Aldermary, p. 66.
Baker : Marriage Lic. (London), ii. 84.
MDB. (Suffolk), 0, 4, 1, 0, 0, 1, 0 ; (Norfolk), 0, 4, 0, 1, 1, 0, 0 ; (Essex), Firmin, 1 ; (co. Monmouth), Fireman, 1 ; London (Firmin, 9 ; Philadelphia, 0, 0, 17, 0, 0, 5, 0.

Firminger. —Occupative. ' the cheesewright' ; O.F. *fromageur* ; cf. Pottinger and Messinger for Potager and Messager.

William le Formager, London, 1273. A.
Robert Formagier, co. Linc., ibid.
Godfrey le Furmager, London, ibid.
Ely le Furmager. O.
Andrew Firminger, temp. Eliz. Z.
John Farmynger, ibid.
1802. Married — Mathew Takes and Sarah Firminger : St. Geo. Han. Sq. ii. 264.
London, 3.

Firstling.—Nick. ' the firstling,' the first child ; cf. Suckling.

Bartholomew Frestlyng, Close Roll, 25 Edw. III.
William Firstling. FF.

Firth.—Local, ' at the firth' ; v. Frith.

Johannes del Firth, 1379 : P. T. Yorks. p. 189.
Johannes Firthe, 1379 : ibid. p. 6.
Willelmus del Firthe, 1379 : ibid. p. 56.
London, 7 ; Philadelphia, 50.

Firtree.—Local, ' at the fir-tree' ; cf. Crabtree, Plumptre, Rowntree, &c.

William del Fertre, co. Suff., 1273. A.

Fish, Fishe.—Nick. ' the fish.'

John le Fysche. Q.
Robert le Fissh, co. Soms., 1 Edw. III : Kirby's Quest, p. 125.
Philip le Fissh, co. Soms., 1 Edw. III : ibid. p. 127.
Radulphus Fysche, 1379 : P. T. Yorks. p. 6.
Ricardus Fisch', 1379 : ibid. p. 97.
London, 15, 1 ; Philadelphia, 40, 0.

Fisher.—Occup. ' the fisher,' one who obtained his living by fishing.

Robert 'le Fyscer, co. Bucks, 1273. A.
Margery le Fischere, co. Hunts, ibid.
Ibota Fischher, 1379 : P. T. Yorks. p. 81.
Alicia Fyssher, 1379 : ibid. p. 9.
Willelmus Drory, *fysher*, 1379 : ibid. p. 21.
Hugo Fysseher, 1379 : ibid. p. 158.
Walter Fissher, *piscator*, 1379 : ibid. p. 230.
London, 190 ; Philadelphia, 532.

Fishlock.—Local, ' at the fishlake,' from residence thereby. This seems to be a Yorkshire surname.

Juliana Fysshelake, 1379 : P. T. Howdenshire, p. 21.
Matilda de Fishelake, 1379 : P. T. Yorks. p. 14.
Isabella de Fyshelak', 1379 : ibid. p. 49.
London, 2.

Fishman.—Occup. ' the fishman,' a fisher.

1461. Andrew Fishman, rector of Beeston, co. Norf. : FF. x. 405.
New York, 1.

Fishmonger. — Occup. ' the fishmonger,' a rare term.

Johannes de Bollay, *fyshemanger*, 1379 : P. T. Yorks. p. 50.
William Fyshmonger. F.

Fishpool.—Local, ' at the fishpool' ; cf. Fishlock.

Julian atte ffispole, Close Roll, 29 Edw. I.

Fishwick.—Local, ' of Fishwick,' a township in the parish of Preston, co. Lanc. ; v. Physick.

1415. Agnes de Fysschewyk : Preston Guild Rolls, p. 8.
1582. John Meate, de Fysshewicke : ibid. p. 43.
— John Fysshewick : ibid. p. 45.
1606. Anthony Fishwick, of Preston : Wills at Chester, i. 65.
1612. John Fishwick, of Withnell : ibid.
Manchester, 4 ; Preston, 3.

Fisk, Fiske.—Nick. ' the fish.' Icelandic, *fiskr* ; Danish, *fish* (Skeat).

New York, 24, 10 ; London, 4, 0.

Fison.—Bapt. ; v. Fyson.

Fitch (1), Ffitch. (1)— Nick. ' the son,' a corruption of Fitz, or Fiz. The old spelling is generally Fiz. The spelling with *t* was an attempt to preserve the old sound of N.F. *s* (v. Skeat). Fitz-Gerald or Fitz-William sounds well enough, but Fitz suggested the inevitable vulgarism of Fitts (v.

infra), so Fitch began to rule the directory. For a second origin, v. Fitch (2).

Gilbert Fiz, co. Camb., 1273. A.
Walter Fiz, co. Bedf., ibid.
William Fiz, co. Soms., ibid.
Cf. Robert Fiz-Payn, co. Northampt., 20 Edw. I. R.
1670-1. Married — Thomas Fitts and Mary Date: Marriage Alleg. (Canterbury). p. 186.
1695. — Thomas Fitch and Mary Limpany: St. Antholin (London), p. 109.
London, 35, 2 ; New York, 54, 0.

Fitch (2), **Fitchett, Ffitch** (2). —Nick. 'the fitch' or 'fitchet,' i.e. the polecat; v. Fitchew. O.F. *fissau*, 'a fitch or fulmart': Cotg. 'Fitchet, a polecat; also called fitch, fitcher, fitchew,' &c. (Halliwell). 'Fichet, a stoat: Salop' (ibid.). Both forms were in early use as a surname. For another meaning for Fitch, v. Fitch (1).

William Fitche, co. Norf., 1273. A.
Roger Fichet, co. Camb., ibid.
Crispiana Fichet, co. Suff., ibid.
Richard Fichet, co. Devon, 20 Edw. I. R.
Henry Fychet, co. Soms., 1 Edw. III:
Kirby's Quest, p. 118.
John Fichet, co. Soms., 1 Edw. III:
ibid. p. 146.
Ricarda Fychet, C. R., 19 Ric. II.
1691. Married—Thomas Fitchett and Elisebeth Soundes : St. Jas. Clerkenwell, iii. 191.
London, 35, 3, 2 ; Oxford, 0, 4, 0 ; New York, 54, 1, 0.

Fitchew.—Nick. 'the fitchew,' i.e. polecat (Polecat was also a surname, q.v.) ; spelt *fitchew* in King Lear, iv. 6. 124 (Skeat) ; a corruption of O.F. *fissau* (ibid.) ; v. Fitch (2) and Fitchett.

1615. Bapt. — Elizabeth, d. Richarde Fitchoe: St. Thomas the Apostle (London), p. 42.
1742. Married — Richard Milson and Ann Fitchaw: St. Jas. Clerkenwell, iii. 272.
London, 2.

Fithian.—Bapt. 'the son of Vivian,' an American variant; v. Phythian.

New York, 3 ; Philadelphia, 18.

Fitkin.—Bapt. 'the son of —— (?).' Probably of Dutch origin, although so early found in the form of Fiddekyn on English soil. Fiddy would be the pet form of one of the many German personal names

prefixed with Fred. Perhaps for Frederic ; cf. Watkin, Wilkin, &c.

Thomas Fiddekyn, Fines Roll, 8 Edw. I.
Thomas Fidekyn, co. Bucks, 20 Edw. I. R.

The second stage was Fidkin :

1595. Married—Ellis Martin and Hellen Fidkin : St. Jas. Clerkenwell, iii. 19.
1772. — Edward Davis and Ann Fidkin : St. Geo. Han. Sq. i. 226.

The third and last stage, Fitkin, was inevitable, and is the present form.

London, 4.

Fitler.—Occup. 'the fiddler,' a sharpened form of Fidler, q.v.

Fitter.—Occup. 'the fitter,' a joiner, a carpenter, one who joined or fitted separate parts together ; a common occupative term in the 19th century for one who puts separate portions of machinery together. The early fitter probably worked in wood. Indeed, the name may be looked upon as a synonym of joiner.

Geoffrey le Fittere, co. Camb., 1273. A.
Robert le Fittere, co. Camb., ibid.
1548. Buried — Hellen Fytter : St. Michael, Cornhill, p. 178.
1661. Married — William Fitter and Jane Trott : ibid. p. 38.
1748. Bapt.—Samuel, s. Jaspar Fitter : St. Mary Aldermary, p. 131.
London, 6 ; New York, 5.

Fitzcharles.—Bapt. 'the son of Charles.'

William Fitzcharles, *pedlar* : New York Directory.
New York, 1.

Fitzgerald.—Bapt. 'the son of Gerald.'

London, 18 ; Philadelphia, 207.

Fitzgibbon, Fitzgibbons.—Bapt. 'the son of Gilbert' ; v. Gibbon. With the genitive *s* in Fitzgibbons, cf. Williams, Gibbons, Jones, Watkins, &c.

London, 4, 0 ; Philadelphia, 4, 6.

Fitzharris.—Bapt. 'the son of Henry' ; v. Harries.

Philadelphia, 1, ; New York, 5.

Fitzhenry.—Bapt. 'the son of Henry.'

Philadelphia, 3 ; Liverpool, 3.

Fitzherbert.—Bapt. 'the son of Herbert.'

Fitzhugh.—Bapt. 'the son of Hugh,' exactly equivalent to Howson, Hewson, or Welsh Pugh-ap-Hugh.

Philadelphia, 3.

Fitzjames.—Bapt. 'the son of James.'

London Court Dir., 1.

Fitzjohn.—Bapt. 'the son of John,' the exact equivalent of Johnson, or 'Simon, son of Jonas,' or Welsh Upjohn.

William Fitz-John, co. Norf., 15 Edw. I : FF. vii. 242.
Sir Robert Fitz-John, of Ashwellthorp, co. Norf., 1383 : ibid. v. 118.
1766. Married — Thomas Lyon and Lucy Fitzjohn : St. Geo. Han. Sq. i. 159.
1781. — George Hodson and Eliz. Fitzjohn : ibid. i. 319.
MDB. (co. Cambridge), 3 ; London, 1.

Fitzmaurice, Fitzmorris.—Bapt. 'the son of Maurice.'

London, 5, 0 ; Philadelphia, 8, 2.

Fitzpatrick.—Bapt. 'the son of Patrick.'

London, 4 ; Philadelphia, 207.

Fitzroy.—Nick. 'the king's son.'

London Court Dir., 6 ; Philadelphia, 2.

Fitzsimmons, Fitzsimons, Fitzsimon.—Bapt. 'the son of Simon.'

Richard Fitz-Symond, co. Norf., 1419 : FF. iv. 87.
Philadelphia, 30, 4, 0 ; Manchester, 1, 0, 0 ; Liverpool, 0, 4, 1 ; MDB. (co. Cumberland), 0, 3, 0.

Fitzwater.—Bapt. 'the son of Walter' ; v. Walter and Waters.

London, 1 ; Philadelphia, 2.

Fitzwilliam.—Bapt. 'the son of William.'

Johannes fitz William, *chivaler*, et Elizabetha uxor ejus, 1379 : P. T. Yorks. p. 52.
Edmundus fitz William, *armiger*, 1379 : ibid. p. 53.
Boston (U.S.), 2.

Fiveash.—Local, 'at the five ash trees' ; cf. Twelvetrees and F. *quatrefages* ; v. Vivash.

London, 1.

Fivefeet.—Nick.

John ffyvefeet, Close Roll, 12 Hen. IV.

Fivepenny.—Nick.; cf. Four-pence.

John Fivepeni, co. Oxf., 1273. A.

Flack.—Local, 'at the flack,' i.e. flag, whence our flagstone, a term formerly employed to describe turf as well as stone; cf. Slack and Slagg.

Robert del Flac, co. Kent, 1273. A.
Dorothy Flack, co. Norf., 1715: FF. viii. 390.
London, 32; Boston (U.S.) 7; Philadelphia, 5.

Fladgate.—Local, 'at the flood-gate,' the door or gate of the mill-race; 'flode-gate of a mylle, *sino glociiorium*' (Prompt. Parv.).

Walter atte Flodgate, co. Soms., 1 Edw. III: Kirby's Quest, p. 274.
William Fludgate, C. R., 6 Hen. IV.
'Margaret, d. John Durham, ... late wife of Alan Heyngham, of ... in Norfolk, released to Ralph Somerton ... all her right in Begviles manor, and in a marsh, called Floodgates ... in the 5th Henry IV': FF. xi. 195.
London, 3.

Flamank.—? ——. A Cornish surname.

1595. Buried—Roger Flamacke, gent: Reg. St. Columb Major, p. 195.

The editor adds, 'fourth son of John Flamank, second son of Richard Flamock.'

London, 1.

Flanders.—Local, 'of Flanders,' an immigrant from the Low Countries, a well-known Cambridgeshire surname. It is curious to note that a 'de Flanders' was settled there in the 13th century. Probably he was the progenitor of all the Flanders in the county. On the other hand, the 'de Flandres' of Yorkshire have left no descendants, unless the surname was changed to Fleming, q.v.

Jacobus de Flandres, co. Camb., 1273. A.
Thomas Flandres, co. Soms., 1 Edw. III: Kirby's Quest, p. 256.
Robertus del Flaunderes, 1379: P. T. Yorks. p. 110.
Johannes de Flaundres, 1379: ibid. p. 165.
Johannes de Flaundre, 1379: ibid.
1809. Married—William Bateman and Ann Flanders: St. Geo. Han. Sq. ii. 407.
London, 4; MDB. (co. Cambridge), 11; New York, 10.

Flanner, Flawner, Flawn.—Occup. 'the flawner,' a custard-maker, a seller of flawns, a kind of pancake. O.F. *flaon*, a custard. 'Flawne, mete; *flamicia*' (Prompt. Parv.). 'A flawne, *opacum*' (Cath. Ang.). Caxton says, in the Boke for Travellers, 'of mylke and of egges, men make flawnes (*flans*).' Mr. Way adds (v. note, p. 164, Prompt. Parv.) 'recipes for making flawnes will be found in the Forme of Cury.'

Proverb, 'As flat as a flawn.' Kennett.

The surname was common, and ultimately settled down into Flanner.

William le Flaoner, London, 1273. A.
William le Flaoner. B.
Roger le Flaoner, London, 1307. X.
John Flawner, London. X.
Adam le Flauner, *cocus*, 12 Edw. II: Freemen of York, i. 18.
John Flauner entered C C.C. Camb., in 1649: Hist. C.C.C. Camb.
In 1641 John Flanner was rector of Kilverstone: FF. i. 546.

Flatman.—Occup. 'the flat-man,' a Norfolk and Suffolk surname, where boat-names are common; cf. Bargeman, Cockman, &c. Fleet now means a collection of boats. A.S. *fleót*, a ship.

Henry Floteman, 1551, co. Norf.: FF. vii. 377.
1669. Married—Robert Flattman and Agrippina Branseley: St. Jas. Clerkenwell, iii. 157.
MDB. (Suffolk), 6; London, 2.

Flatt.—Local, 'at the flat,' from residence thereon. This derivation is all the more probable because the habitat of the name is co. Norfolk.

MDB. (co. Norfolk), 9; Philadelphia, 1.

Flaxenhead.—Nick. 'with the flaxen hair,' fair-haired; cf. Fairfax.

Richard Flaxennehed, co. Camb., 1273. A.

Flaxman, Flexman.—Occup. 'the flaxman,' a dresser of flax. M.E. *flax*; A.S. *fleax* (Skeat).

William Flexman, co. Hunts, 1273. A.
Ralph le Flexman, co. Glouc., 20 Edw. I. R.
John Flexmon, co. Glouc., ibid.
William Bancroft, *flaxman*, 1582: Preston Guild Rolls, p. 35.

William Bancroft, *flax-seller*, 1562: ibid. p. 28.
Ralph Lever, of Chorley, *flaxman*, 1663: Wills at Chester (1660–80), p. 168.
1706. Bapt.—Jeremiah, son of Clousley Flaxman, and Annavick, his wife: St. Michael, Cornhill, p. 162.
London, 4, 3.

Flaxwife.—Occup. 'the flax-wife,' a spinner of flax; v. Flax-man.

Cristina la Flexwyfe, London. X.

Fleck; v. **Flick.**

Fleeman.—? ——. A variant of Freeman or Fleming, more probably the former.

MDB. (co. Lincoln), 1; New York, 1.

Fleet.—Local, 'at the fleet,' or 'of Fleet,' parishes in diocs. Lincoln, Salisbury, and Winchester; from 'fleet,' a creek, a bay. Hence Fleet Street, by the old Fleet Ditch; cf. Herringfleet, Fleetwood, Northfleet, &c.; v. Prompt. Parv. p. 166, and Way's note thereon, who quotes Fladbury, formerly Fleotbury, and Twining Fleet on the Avon, among other place-names.

John de Flete, co. Linc., 1273. A.
Richard de Flet, co. Linc., ibid.
Laurence de Flete, co. Linc., 20 Edw. I. R.
Fulco de Flete, rector of West Lynn, co. Norf., 1349: FF. viii. 535.
1579–80. Married—Thomas Fleete and Elsabeth Emerton: St. Dionis Backchurch, p. 9.
1580. Edward Clerke and Bridget Fleet: Marriage Lic. (London), i. 100.
London, 7; New York, 7.

Fleetwood.—Local, 'of Fleet-wood,' a town and seaport in co. Lancaster. From an inconsiderable hamlet Fleetwood has become an important seaboard town. The surname arose in the days of its obscurity.

Elizabeth Fleetwood, of Rossall, *widow*, 1624: Lancashire Wills at Richmond (1457–1680), p. 112.
Richard Fleetwood, of Preston, 1668: ibid.
William Fleetwood, of Kirby, 1607; Wills at Chester (1545–1620), p. 65.
John Fleetwood, of Knowsley, *yeoman*, 1635: ibid. (1621–50), p. 78.
1676. Buried—Eliz. Fleetwood, servant to Mr. Simonds: St. Michael, Cornhill, p. 262.
1802. Married—Henry S. Craufurd and

U 2

Sophia Fletewood: St. Geo. Han. Sq. ii. 265.
London, 3 : MDB. (co. Lancaster), 7 ; Oxford, 4 ; Philadelphia, 2.

Flegg.—Local, 'of Flegg.' East and West Flegg are hundreds in the county of Norfolk.

Algar de Flegg, co. Norf., temp. Hen. II : FF. xi. 194.
Henry de Flegg, co. Norf., temp. Ric. I: ibid.
John de Flegg, co. Norf., temp. Hen. III : ibid. viii. 84.
William de Flegg, co. Norf., 53 Hen. III : ibid.
John Flegg, Bokenham Ferry, co. Norf., 7 Hen. VIII : ibid. vii. 213.
London, 3 ; MDB. (Norfolk), 2.

Fleming, Flemming.—Local, 'the Fleming,' one who came from Flanders.

John le Flemeng, co. Linc., 1273. A.
Walter le Flemmeng, co. Linc., ibid.
Richard le Flemyng, co. Devon, ibid.
William Flemmyng, co. Soms., 1 Edw. III : Kirby's Quest, p. 89.
London, 35, 1.

Flesher.—Occup. 'the flesher,' a butcher. To be carefully distinguished from Fletcher, although the two names have got mixed. A butcher is still a flesher in Scotland, and the 'flesh-market' is not unknown in the North of England, where 'meat' and 'flesh' have still separate meanings.

Miles Flesher. V. 5.
Robert Flesher, co. York. W. 2.
Adam Flescher, 1379: P. T. Yorks. p. 29.
Johannes Flescher, 1379 : ibid. p. 5.
Boston (U.S.), 1.

Fleshhewer.—Occup. 'a carnifex,' a slaughter-man, a man who cuts up the carcases of cattle for the shambles ; cf. *stone-hewer*, *wood-hewer*, *block-hewer*. The name was early lost in Flesher, i.e. butcher, and not in Fletcher ; v. Flesher ; cf. Fleshmonger.

Robert Fleshewer, Pardon Rolls, 6 Ric. II.
Peter le Flesshewere, C. R., 30 Edw. III.
William Flesschewer, co. York. W. 2.
John Fleshewer. H.
Willelmus de Rypon, *flesshewer*, 1379 : P. T. Yorks. p. 252.
Johannes de Staynlay, *flesshewer*, 1379 : ibid.
Willelmus del Clay, *flesshewer*, 1379 : ibid. p. 3.
Johannes Fleshewer, *bocher*, 1379 : ibid. p. 14.
Agnes Flesschewer, 1379 : ibid. p. 81.

An attempt to rescue this surname from absorption into Flesher is found so late as the 16th century.

William Fleshware, of Chester, *weaver*, 1577 : Wills at Chester (1545-1620), p. 65.

Fleshmonger. — Occup. 'the fleshmonger,' a seller of flesh-meat, a butcher. Cocke Lorelle's Bote comprises, among others—

'Woolemen, vynterers, and flesshe-mongers.'

The Pardoner in the same poem thus begins his role :

'Here is first Cocke Lorelles the knyght,
And Symkyn Emery, mayntenaunce agavnz ryght,
With Slyngthryfte Fleshemonger.'

'Also, the usage of fleshe-mongeres ys swych, that everych fleshemongere.' &c. (Usages of Winchester, English Gilds, p. 354). William Fleshmonger, D.C.L., was Dean of Chichester in 1528 (Hist. Oxford, Ackerman, p. 154).

Richard le Flesmongere, co. Bucks, 1273. A.
William le Flesmongere, co. Bucks, ibid.
Eudo le Fleshmongere, c. 1300. M.
William Fleshemongere. F.

Fletcher. — Occup. 'the fletcher,' a maker of arrows. The pattern-makers petitioned the Commons in 1464 to have restored to them the use of the 'Tymber called aspe,' lately the monopoly of arrow manufacturers, 'So that the Flecchers thorough the Reame (realm) may sell their arrows at more esy price' (Rot. Parl., Edw. IV).

'Paied to Guilliam the kinge's flletcher for arowes for my lorde of Richemonde xxs.' : Privy Purse Expenses, Henry VIII, p. 40.
1542. 'Payd to the fletcher for fether-ynge of a shaffe of shayffe arroys, &c., 20d.' : QQQ. p. 296.

In the old Guilds we find the Bowyers and Fletchers invariably walking together (v. Bowyer).

Ralph le Fleccher, co. Linc., 1273. A.
Nicholas le Flecher, co. Linc., ibid.
Adam le Flecher, co. Northampt., ibid.
Henry le Fletcher, ibid.
Robert le Fleccher. E.
Adam le Fletcher. S.
Robertus Fleger, 1379 : P. T. Yorks. p. 120.

Johannes Fleccher, 1379 : ibid. p. 37.
Stephanus Fletcher, 1379 : ibid. p. 42.
Johannes Copyn, *flecher*, 1379 : ibid. p. 155.
1619. George Duyre, *fletcher*, and Sibell Michaelwright : Marriage Lic. (London), ii. 78.
London, 101 ; Philadelphia, 84.

Flewellin, Flewelling. — Bapt. 'son of Llewellyn '; cf. Floyd with Lloyd ; v. Llewellyn.

Oxford, o, 1 ; New York, 3, o.

Flewitt, Flewett.— ? ——. I cannot suggest any derivation of this surname. I do not think it is English, and being found first in London may be an immigration from the Low Countries.

1558. Bapt.—Richard Flewet : St. Peter, Cornhill, i. 8.
1561. — Jane, d. William Fluett : ibid. p. 80.
1571-2. Owen Evans and Margaret Flewett : Marriage Lic. (London), i. 51.
1762. Married—Thomas Sheppard and Catherine Fluitt : St. Geo. Han. Sq. i. 112.
London, 1, 0 ; Crockford, o, 1.

Flick, Fleck. — Nick. 'the spotted,' streaked, dappled (?).

'A flecked pie.' Chaucer, C. T. 9722.
William le Flik, C. R., 3 Edw. I.
Peter Fleke, co. Soms., 1 Edw. III : Kirby's Quest, p. 186.
William Fleke, co. Soms., 1 Edw. III : ibid.
London, 1, 9 ; Philadelphia, 26, 28.

Flinders.—Local, 'of Flanders,' q.v. A corruption.

London (1884), 2.

Flint, Flindt.—Bapt.'the son of Flint.' 'In Domesday we have in Suffolk an Alwin Flint ' (Lower, Patr. Brit. p. 117). Mr. Lower further says, ' Our Anglo-Saxon ancestors had a subordinate deity whom they named Flint, and whose idol was an actual flint-stone of large size. The name of the god would readily become the appellation of a man ' (ibid.). The compound Flinthard, manifestly an early personal name, is found in the Hundred Rolls.

Jacobus Flinthard, co. Warw., 1273. A.
John Flinchard, co. Essex, ibid.
John Flint, or Fleynt, co. Bucks, ibid.
Sivardus Flynt, 21 Ric. II : Furness Coucher Book, i. 188.
Willelmus Flynt, *walker*, 1379 : P. T. Yorks. p. 101.

Flint is a common surname in the

Poll Tax of 1379 (Yorks). I only furnish one instance. The name is scattered hither and thither without prefix. There can be no doubt it was a personal name. Steel (q.v.) enjoyed a similar popularity; cf. the German Flindt.

London (1884), 27, 2; Philadelphia, 16, 1.

Flitcroft, Flitcraft.—Local, 'of Flitcroft.' Some spot in South Lancashire. For the suffix, v. Craft or Croft.

1587. George Flitcroft, of Kenyon, parish of Winwick: Wills at Chester (1545-1620), p. 66.
1602. Peter Flitcroft, of Kenyon: ibid.
1628. Bapt.—Richard, s. Richard Fleetcraft: St. Jas. Clerkenwell, i. 107.
Manchester, 1, 0; Bolton, 9, 0; Philadelphia, 0, 2.

Flockton.—Local, 'of Flockton,' a township in the parish of Thornhill, near Wakefield, Yorks.

Johannes de Flogton: P. T. Yorks. p. 24.
Robertus de Flocketon: ibid. p. 53.
Johannes de Froketon: ibid.
London, 1; Philadelphia, 1.

Flood.—(1) Bapt. Welsh Floyd or Flood=Lloyd; v. Floyd.
(2) Local, 'at the flood,' from residence at the point in the river where the water is apt to flood. The Norfolk Floods are manifestly so sprung.

John de la Flode, co. Hants, 1273. A.
Nicholas de la Flod, or Flode, co. Wilts, 20 Edw. I. R.
Robert Flode, rector of Downham, co. Norf., 1412: FF. vii. 342.
John Flod, or Flud, vicar of Sporle, co. Norf., 1516: ibid. vi. 120.
George Flood, preacher, Norwich, 1595: ibid. iv. 188.
London, 10; MDB. (co. Norfolk), 7; New York, 86.

Florence, Florance. — (1) Bapt. 'the son of Florence.' Not a modern girl's name; frequently found in the 13th and 14th centuries.

John Florence, co. Bedf., 1273. A.
Florence de Coye, co. Camb., ibid.
Florence de Lisle, co. York, 3 Edw. II.
Florence de Wygeton, C. R., 14 Edw. II.
Florence, wife of Richard Malyns: ibid. 1 Ric. II. pt. i.
Florence Gorges: ibid. 3 Hen. V.

(2) Local, 'of Florence,' in Italy.
John de Florence, co. Norf., 20 Edw. I. R.

William Florence, Close Roll, 7 Edw. III. pt. i.
Gam'ia de Florence, co. York, 1273. A.
Bartholomew de Florence, co. York, ibid.

There are allusions to the Mercatores de Florence, or Marchandz de Florence (cos. Lincoln and Northampton), in the same record.

1579. Garrett Florence and Catherine Pomfrett: Marriage Lic. (London), i. 91.
1651. Married—Thomas Bourn and Mary Florance: St. Jas. Clerkenwell, iii. 86.
London, 5, 0; Philadelphia, 7, 1.

Floris. — Bapt. 'the son of Florence,' q.v. An abbreviation.

Flory, Florey; v. Flurry.

Flower. — (1) Occup. 'the flower,' an archer, one who shot a flo, or arrow. The latter was a later word.

'His bowe he bent, and set therein a flo.'
Chaucer, Manciple's Tale.
John le Floer, co. Devon, 1273. A.
William Floere, co. Devon, ibid.
Nicholas le Flouer. J.
Reginald le Flower. B.

(2) Bapt. 'the son of Flower,' a natural personal name; cf. Rose. The following instance is strongly corroborative:

William Floureson, co. Soms., 1 Edw. III: Kirby's Quest, p. 141.
Johanna Floure, 1379: P. T. Yorks. p. 104.
Matilda Flowr, 1379: ibid. p. 215.
1567. Bapt. — Elizabeth, d. Edwarde Flower: St. Mary Aldermary, p. 137.
1573. Thomas Flowre and Jane Hardinge: Marriage Lic. (London), i. 57.
London, 20; Philadelphia, 2.

Flowerday.—Nick. or local. A Norfolk surname, probably introduced from the Low Countries.

John Floure-dieu, co. Norf., 1541: FF. v. 28.

Cf. Ingledew and Engeldew.

John Flowerdew, of Hetherset, co. Norf., 1549: FF. iii. 222-3.
'Commission of rebellion to John Flowerdew, Feb. 12, 1592': Cal. State Papers (Domestic), iii. 182.
William Flowerdew, rector of Ashby, co. Norf., 1606: FF. x. 95.
1555-6. Roger Mychell and Helen Flowerdewe: Marriage Lic. (London), i. 17.
1577. Married — Richard Fryar and Thomassin Flowerdewe: Reg. Deopham, co. Norfolk.

1685. Married — John Roll and Anne Flowerdew: St. Dionis Backchurch (London).
London, 2; MDB. (Norfolk), 4.

Floyd, Flude, Flood.—Bapt. Welsh Lloyd. The English attempt at pronouncing this name could get no further than Floyd, Flood, &c.; cf. Blood and Bloyd.

'I am a gentylman and come of Brutus' blood;
My name is Ap-Ryce, Ap-Davy, Ap-Flood.'
Andrew Borde's Boke of Knowledge.

Cf. Flewellin and Llewellyn.

'Thomas Lloyd, or Floyd, sup. for B.C.L., 31 May, 1510': Reg. Univ. Oxf. i. 69.
Thomas Lloide, or Floide, 1569: ibid. i. 274.
David Lloyde, or Floyd, 1570: ibid. i. 278.

This surname is not uncommon in cos. Chester and Lanc., and on the border of the Principality.

Richard Flood, co. Salop, temp. 1580: Visitation of London, 1634, ii. 279.
Roger Fowke and Katherine Floodd (in margin, 'Lloyd'), widow: Marriage Lic. (Westminster), p. 18.
1675. Charles Hutchinson and the Lady Mary Lloyd, alias Floyd: Marriage Alley, (Canterbury), p. 243.
1771. Married — William Flude and Mary Doubtfire: St. Geo. Han. Sq. i. 205.
London, 13, 3, 10; New York, 27, 0, 89.

Flurry, Flory, Flury, Florey. —(1) Bapt. 'the son of Florence,' from the nick. Flory; v. Florence.
(2) Local, 'de Flury,' seemingly a Norman surname. The local derivation is manifestly the true one in regard to the majority of these forms.

Flory Oliver (fem.), co. Salop, 1273. A.
Agnes Flury, co. Linc., ibid.
John Flury, co. Linc., ibid.
Egidius de Flory, co. Soms., 20 Edw. I. R.
Peter Flury, co. Glouc., ibid.
Robert de Flury, co. Linc., Hen. III-Edw. I. K.
1402. Richard de Flory, rector of Little Wreningham, co. Norf.: FF. v. 115.
1568-9. Philip Florye and Catherine Bexewell: Marriage Lic. (London), i. 41.
1589-90. William Howson and Joane Florey, co. Hants: ibid. i. 184.
1729. Married—James Flory and Eliz. Marriott: St. Dionis Backchurch, p. 63.
1809. — Daniel Willis and Mary Ann Florey: St. Geo. Han. Sq. ii. 402.
London, 1, 0, 0, 0; Crockford, 0, 1, 0, 0; Philadelphia, 0, 0, 3, 0; MDB. (co. Norfolk), 0, 0, 0, 2.

Flutter.—Occup. 'the fluter,' one who played the musical pipe or flute; O.F. *flaute*; cf. Harper, &c.

'There mightest thou see these flutours, Minstrales, and eke jogelours.'
Chaucer, R. of R. 763-4.
Alanus Floyter, 1379 : P. T. Yorks. p. 282.
Henricus Floyter, 1379 : ibid. p. 274.
Nicholas le Floutere. B.
London, 1.

Flyor, Flier.—Nick. (?).

Alan le Flier, C. R., 17 Edw. I.
Richard Flyar, of Utoxeter, co. Stafford, temp. 1570 : Visitation of London, 1633, i. 281.
New York, 0, 1.

Foakes. — Bapt. 'the son of Fulk,' one of very many variants ; v. Fulke and Fooks. Foakes is a corruption of the intermediate form Folkes ; v. Folk. The final *s* is patronymic ; cf. Jones, Williams, Jennings, &c.

Foke Odell. H.
Ralph Foke, co. Oxf., 1273. A.
1796. Married — Thomas Foakes and Alice Pailthorpe : St. Geo. Han. Sq. ii.158.
London, 1.

Foale, Foall.—Nick. 'the foal'; M.E. *fole*, a foal. Almost all animal names are to be found in our directories of to-day. ' *Fole*, yonge horse, *pullus* ' : Prompt. Parv.

Reginald Fole, co. Hunts, 1273. A.
Henry Fole, rector of Hackford, co. Norf., 1352 : FF. ii. 497.
MDB. (co. Devon), 3, 0 ; London, 1, 0 ; Philadelphia, 0, 1.

Foden, Fowden.—Local, 'of Foden,' now Foden Bank, in the township of Sutton, parish of Prestbury, co. Cheshire. This surname is well represented in Cheshire and Lancashire.

1563. Married — Phillip Fowden and Katherine Broke : Prestbury Church, co. Ches.. p. 11.
1568. — Hugh Fowdon, or Foden, and Margery Stubbs : ibid. p. 25.
1592. Robert Fowden, of Warford : Wills at Chester (1545-1620), p. 67.
1613. John Foden, of Sutton, co. Ches. : ibid. p. 68.
London, 3, 0 ; Manchester, 11, 2 ; MDB. (co. Chester), 8, 3.

Foe ; v. Defoe.

Fogg.—? ——. A well-known Lancashire surname. I can only suggest a local origin. Lower states that it is an ancient Kentish family

(Patr. Brit. p. 117). Across the Atlantic this surname has ramified very strongly.

1509. Thomas Fogg, co. Norf.: FF. v. 499.
1592. Robert Fogg, of Radcliffe, *yeoman* : Wills at Chester (1545-1620), pp. 66-7.
1599. Married—William Norwood and Anne Fogg : St. Jas. Clerkenwell, iii. 23.
1610. Annie Fogg, of Darcy Lever : Wills at Chester (1545-1620), p. 66.
1615. Thurston Fogg, Blackburn : ibid. p. 67.
London, 4 ; Manchester, 2 ; MDB. (co. Lancaster), 7 ; Boston (U.S.), 59.

Fold, Folds.—Local, ' at the fold,' from residence thereby ; v. Foulds.

John atte Fold, co. Soms., 1 Edw. III :
Kirby's Quest, p. 151.
Philadelphia, 0, 1 ; New York, 2, 0.

Foley, Fooley.—An Irish surname. The New York Directory contains 227 Foleys (which are prefixed among other Irish fontal names), 7 Cornelius's, 2 Dennis's, 1 Dominick, 19 Michaels, and 22 Patricks. Mr. Lower, quoting Collins, says that ' The family of Foley have been of ancient standing in co. Worcester and some adjoining counties.' This would suggest a local English origin, of which no proof is offered. Foley must be looked upon as an Irish surname, and h:nce has no place in this dictionary.

London, 0, 0 ; Manchester, 5, 0 ; Liverpool, 6, 0 ; New York, 227, 1.

Folgate.—Local, ' at the foldgate,' from residence thereby ; v. Felgate.

William atte Fulghyate, C. R., 20 Edw. I.
John atte Foldyate. J.
Thomas Faldyate, Pardons Roll, 5 Ric. II.
London, 1.

Folger.—Bapt. 'the son of Fulcher,' q.v. An American variant.

New York, 7.

Foljambe, Fuljambe, Fulljames, Fuljames.—Nick. One of a few descriptive French names compounded with *-jambe*, i.e. leg ; cf. Beljambe, 'handsome leg.' ' Edward Longshanks was Edward "avez les long jaumbes"' (v. Lower on'Foljambe'). Shanks was

the English form; cf. Sheepshanks, Pyshank, &c. Foljambe seems to be 'fool-legged.' Almost all the names compounded with *-shank* and *-jambe* are of an unkindly or satirical character. Lower says, ' Sir Thomas Foljambe was bailiff of the High Peak, co. Derby, in 1272.'

Thomas Folejambe, co. Derby, 1273. A.
Robert Folejambe, co. Derby, ibid.
Geoffrey Fulgeam, Visitation of Yorks, 1563, p. 128.
1533. John Fulgeam, rector of Clery, co. Norf. : FF. vi. 43.
1596. Bapt.—Odelia, d. Hercules Foljambe : St. Jas. Clerkenwell, i. 31.
1774. Married—Francis Farrand Foljambe and Mary Arabella Thornhagh : St. Geo. Han. Sq. i. 242.
MDB. (co. Glouc.), 0, 0, 3, 1 ; London, 0, 0, 1, 0 ; West Rid. Court Dir., 1, 0, 0, 0 ; Boston (U.S.), 1, 0, 0, 0.

Folk, Folkes, Folks, Folke.—Bapt. 'the son of Fulk.' Every possible guise of this popular name is found ; v. Falk, Fulke, and Foakes.

Folke de Monte Pinzini, cos. Essex and Herts, Hen. III–Edw. I. K.
Folkes (without surname), co. Camb., 1273. A.
John Folke, co. Camb., ibid.
Matilda Folkis, co. Bucks, ibid.
Folc, or Fulco, fil.Warin, co. Glouc., 20 Edw. I. R.
1574. Robert Folkes and Elizabeth Grave: Marriage Lic. (London), i. 61.
1782. Married — Robert Beverley and Eliz. Folks : St. Geo. Han. Sq. i. 337.
London, 1, 2, 2, 0 ; New York, 4, 1, 1, 2.

Folkard.—Bapt. ; v. Fulcher.

Follenfant. — Nick. ; ' Fr. "foolish child," probably a term of endearment': Lower, Patr. Brit. p. 117.

Hugh Folenfaunt, co. Notts, 1273. A.
Ingram Folensfaunt, co. York, ibid.
London, 1.

Follett, Follitt, Ffolliott.—Nick. ; Fr. *follet*, frolicsome, wanton, gay. ' Folett, *fatuellus, stolidus, follus* ' : Prompt. Parv. Lower says, ' Folliot, &c. . . . The surname has become historical from Gilbert Foliot, bishop of Hereford, the staunch defender of Henry II ' (Patr. Brit. p. 118).

Nicholas Folet, co. Kent, 1273. A.
Sampson Folyot, co. Wilts, ibid.
Jordon Folyot, co. Suff., ibid.
Margery Folyet, 1301. M.
Robert Follit, co. Soms., 1 Edw. III
Kirby's Quest, p. 275.

Ricardus Folyot, 1379 : P. T. Yorks. p. 26.
London, 3, 5, 0 ; Crockford (Ffolliott), 1 ; Boston (U.S.), 11, 0, 0.

Followfast.—Nick. Probably the sobriquet of a pursuivant ; cf. Golightly, Lightfoot, &c.

Gudytha Foloufast, 1379 : P. T. Yorks. p. 246.
Willelmus Foloufast, 1379 : ibid.

Folly, Folley.—Local, 'at the folly.' 'Any ridiculous building not answering its intended purpose' (Halliwell). Many counties have spots so called. But Lower notices a use of Folly different from this. It seems to have meant a fragile, temporary structure. He connects it with N.F. *foillie*. In the Rom. de Rou (l. 10136) we read

'mult veient loges e foillies'—

which M. Pluquet explains as 'baraques faites avec des branches d'arbre.' Mr. Lower refers to N. and Q., Nov. 1856 (p. 349). Looking at his reference I find C. W. Bingham drew attention to the above quoted line.

Henry de la Folye, co. Wilts, 1273. A.
Roger de la Folye, co. Wilts, ibid.
Richard de la Folye, co. Wilts, ibid.
London, 0, 2 ; New York, 1, 0 ; Philadelphia, 0, 3.

Folsom.—Local. An American variant of Foulsham, q.v.

Fon, Fone.—Offic. 'the fon,' a professional fool; cf. *fond* = foolish.

'Alein, by God thou is a fonne.' Chaucer, C. T. 4087.
Petrus Fonne, co. Notts, 20 Edw. I. R.
Peter le ffoon, Close Roll, 4 Edw. III.
Willelmus Fones, 1379 : P. T. Yorks. p. 41.
1548. Married — Henrye Fones and Alyce Gylpyn : St. Michael, Cornhill, p. 5.
1761. — Joseph Middleton and Catherine Fones : St. Geo. Han. Sq. i. 104.
1781. — John Nicholas and Mary Fone : ibid. i. 319.
Derby, 0, 2 ; Philadelphia, 1, 0 ; Boston (U.S.), 0, 4.

Fooks.—Bapt. 'the son of Fulk.' One of almost interminable corruptions of Fulk, from the patronymic Fulkes or Foulkes, frequently found as Fowkes. The last stage of change was Fooks. The great popularity of Fulk amongst all classes must be realized in studying the mutations of fortune experienced by this baptismal name. So late as the 17th century Fulk is found as a fontal-name in the form of Fook.

1611. Fooke Edmonds and Anne Smithe : Marriage Lic. (London), i. 6.
1618. Married — Thomas Fookes and Agnes Turner : St. Michael, Cornhill, p. 22.
1682. Buried — Henry Fookes, in the churchyard : St. Peter, Cornhill, i. 96.
London (1884), 8 ; Philadelphia, 2.

Fool, Foll.—Nick. or offic. 'a fool, a jester' ; O.F. *fol*, M.E. *fol*. No surprise need be felt at its absence from modern directories ; v. Follett.

Baldwin le Folle, co. Camb., 1273. A.
John le Folle, co. Sussex, ibid.
Peter le Folle, co. Wilts, ibid.
Alexander le Fol. C.
Johannes Stultus. DD.
Robertus Foll', 1379 : P. T. Yorks. p. 31.
Magister Johannes Fool : Wardrobe Account, 44-5 Edw. III, 40/3.
Richard Foole, of Livesey, 1575 : Wills at Chester (1545-1620), p. 67.
Margaret Foole, 1597, ibid.
New York, 0, 1 ; Philadelphia, 0, 2.

Foord.—Local. A variant of Ford, q.v.

London, 8 ; MDB. (co. Kent), 6 ; New York, 1.

Foot, Foote, Foott.—(1) Local, 'at the foot'—of the hill, slope, &c. Of the same class as Head (q.v.): *-head*, *-side*, and *-foot*, are common terminals of local surnames ; cf. Hazlett (Hazlehead) and Hazlefoot, Akenhead and Akenside. (2) Bapt. 'the son of Fot.' This has more evidence in its favour than (1). Among the under-tenants of Domesday we find Ernui Fot in co. Cheshire, and Godwin Fot in co. Kent. Out of very many instances in the Hundred Rolls (1273) not one has a local prefix. That Fot or Foot was a personal name before it became a surname I cannot doubt.

Matilda Fot, co. Linc., 1273. A.
Walter Fot, co. Norf., ibid.
Geoffrey Fot, co. Camb., ibid.
Johannes Fote, 1379 : P. T. Yorks. p. 15.
1647. Bapt.—Mary, d. Thomas Foote : St. Jas. Clerkenwell, i. 167.
London, 20, 3, 1 ; Philadelphia, 2, 30, 0.

Footman.—Occup. 'the footman.' An early term for a foot-soldier, as distinguished from a horseman ; v. Horsman. 'Fotmann, or he that goythe on foote, *pedester*' : Prompt. Parv.

London, 2 ; Philadelphia, 1.

Forbes.—Local, 'of Forbes.' a town and barony in co. Aberdeen. 'The family possessed that lordship as early as temp. William the Lion, and were seated at Pitscottie in the same shire in 1476' (Lower, quoting Debrett).

1550. James Forbesse and Ellen Vauser : Marriage Lic. (London), i. 13.
London, 35 ; New York, 50.

Ford, Forde.—Local, 'at the ford.' Probably the original bearer occupied an official or occupative position in maintaining a way ; v. Forth. At any rate a ford would attract a settlement in its close neighbourhood. Hence the familiarity of the surname. Hence, too, so many place-names with suffix *-ford* or *-forth*.

Richard de la Forde, co. Norf., 1273. A.
William de la Forde, co. Kent, ibid.
Peter ate Ford, 1313. M.
David de la Forde, co. Soms., 1 Edw. III : Kirby's Quest, p. 89.
William atte fflourde, Close Roll, 23 Edw. III. pt. ii.
Stephen atte Forde, C. R., 45 Edw. III.
1620. Married — Henry Feekes and Alyce Foorde : St. Jas. Clerkenwell, iii. 48.
Hugh Ford, of Scholes in Wigan, *coverlet-weaver*, 1661 : Wills at Chester (1660-80), p. 96.
London, 119, 3 ; New York, 132, 4.

Fordham.—Local, ' of Fordham': (1) a parish in co. Cambridge ; (2) a parish in co. Essex, six miles from Colchester ; (3) a parish in co. Norfolk, near Downham Market.

Richard de Fordham, co. Essex, 1273. A.
Andrew de Fordham, rector of Griston, co. Norf., 1213 : FF. ii. 291.
Henry de Fordham, rector of Wood-Norton, co. Norf., 1344 : ibid. viii. 316.
London, 17 ; MDB. (co. Norfolk). 3 ; (co. Essex), 8 ; (co. Camb.), 18 ; New York, 6.

Forge.—Local, 'at the forge,' from residence thereby. Probably the blacksmith himself.

John de la Forge, C. R., 2 Edw. I.
Agnes Forge, 1379 : P. T. Yorks. p. 22.
Cecilia Forge, 1379 : ibid. p. 68.
New York, 2.

Forlorn.—Nick. An outcast, a woebegone man.

Henry Forlone, Pardons Roll, 8 Ric. II.

Forman, Foreman, Formon.—Bapt. 'the son of Forman.' One of the many varieties of the once common Farman or Firmin, q.v. This surname has nothing to do with the occupative term 'foreman' or 'gaffer.'

Willelmus Forman, 1379 : P. T. Yorks. p. 8.
Ricardus Forman, 1379 : ibid. p. 8.
Johannes Forman, 1379 : ibid. p. 39.
Robertus Formain, 1379 : ibid. p. 162.
Roger Forman, rector of Boughton, co. Norf., 1544 : FF. vii. 302.
London (1884), 7, 14, 1 ; New York, 18, 7, 0.

Forrest.—Local, 'at the forest,' from residence therein or thereby.

Johannes del Forest, 1379 : P. T. Yorks. p. 301.
Thomas de Forest, 1379 : ibid. p. 169.
Adinet del Forest, 1379 : ibid. p. 200.
London, 16 ; New York, 16.

Forrester, Forster. — Offic. 'the forester,' a custodian of the extended woods, a keeper. Forster is a modification.

Petrus Forestarius, co. Bucks, 1273. A.
Jordan le Forester, co. Berks, ibid.
Nicholas le Forester, co. Linc., ibid.
Gilbertus Forester, 1379 : P. T. Yorks. p. 145.
Radulphus Forester, 1379 : ibid. p. 11.
Willelmus Forster, 1379 : ibid. p. 75.
Roger Forster, 1379 : ibid. p. 90.
London, 6, 51 ; New York, 20, 36.

Forsdick, Forsdike, Fossdick, Fossick, Fosdick.—Local, 'of Fosdyke,' a parish in co. Lincoln ; v. also Fosdick for an apparently different parentage.

John de Focedik, co. Linc., 1273. A.
London, 2, 1, 2, 1, 0 ; New York, 0, 0, 0, 0, 4.

Fort, Forte.—Nick. 'strong, powerful'; O.F. *fort*, strong. Fort occurs in this sense in Kyng Alisaunder (l. 7710). There would be many a laugh at the expense of Sampson le Fort in the village where he lived ; v. infra.

William le Fort, or Forte, co. Linc., 1273. A.
Sampson le Fort, co. Bedf., ibid.
Adam le Fort, co. Camb., ibid.
Lucia Fort, 1379 : P. T. Yorks. p. 38.
Richard Fort, co. Soms., 1 Edw. III : Kirby's Quest, p. 101.

John le Fort, co. Soms., 1 Edw. III : ibid. p. 208.
1604. Bapt.—Anne, d. Robert Forte : St. Jas. Clerkenwell, i. 43.
London, 4, 0 ; Philadelphia, 20, 2.

Forth.—Local, 'at the forth,' i.e. ford ; v. Ford. Bradford in co. Yorks is 'Bradeforth' in the 1379 Poll Tax, p. 190 ; cf. Spofforth and Spofford, Clifford and Clifforth, in the same record.

Reginald de la Forthe, co. Suff., 1273. A.
Hugh del Forth, 1319 : DDD. i. 206.
William Atte-forth, de Bergh, rector of North-Burlingham, co. Norf., 1337 : FF. vii. 224.
John Atte-forth, co. Norf., 16 Edw. III : ibid. viii. 330.
Agnes Atte-forth, co. Norf., 48 Edw. III : ibid. xi. 19.
Willelmus Forthe, 1379 : P. T. Yorks. p. 14.
1633-4. Robert Vesey and Anne Forth : Marriage Lic. (London), ii. 216.
1703. Married — Joseph Forth, of Newinton, in Surrey, and Hannah Cox : St. Mary Aldermary, p. 37.
London, 2 ; New York, 1.

Fortnam, Fortnum.—? Local, 'of Frettenham' (?), a parish in co. Norfolk. The surname on the face of it is local with suffix -*ham*, just as Barnum stands for Barnham, or Swetnam for Swetenham. Nevertheless the surname belongs to co. Oxford, and its ancestor is manifestly

Nicholas Fortanon, co. Oxf., 1273. A.

Cf. Ransom for Ranson, or Hanson for Hanson. This suggests some different derivation.

1792. Married — John Fortnam and Eliz. Deykes : St. Geo. Han. Sq. ii. 72.
London, 2, 1 ; MDB. (co. Oxford), 0, 4 ; Philadelphia, 0, 2.

Forty.—Local, 'at the forth-ey,' i.e. the islet in the ford- or forth-hey, an enclosure by the ford ; v. Hey. It has nothing to do with numerals. The instances below are decisive. The original bearers of the name dwelt on some little island or holm in a river or stream, or in an enclosure by the riverside. Mr. Lower says, 'Forty is used by the Scotch poet Douglas in the sense of brave ; Fr. *fort*. Hence Forty and Fortyman probably refer to the courage of their original owners.' This solution is quite beside the

mark. The interpretation is as given above.

Adam de la Fortheye, co. Oxf., 1273. A.
Roger de la Fortheye, co. Oxf., ibid.
William de la Fortheye, co. Oxf., ibid.
Richer atte Forty, co. Hunts, ibid.
'Sir Julius Benedict, the eminent musician (1804-85), married for his second wife Mary Comber Fortey': Dict. Nat. Biog. iv. 217.
London, 3 ; MDB. (co. Hereford), 3 ; Oxford, 4.

Forward, Forwood.— Bapt. 'the son of Forward.' The same individual is thus referred to :

Bartholomew Forreward, co. Camb., 1273. A.
Bartholomew Forward, co. Camb., ibid.
1600. Peter Forwardson, rector of All Saints, Warham, co. Norf. : FF. ix. 265.
London, 4, 3 ; New York, 1, 3.

Fosdick.—Local, 'at the fox-dike,' from residence thereby : a dike frequented by foxes ; v. Dyke and Fox. But v. Forsdick.

Thomas Foxdich, co. Soms., 1 Edw. III : Kirby's Quest, p. 280.
London, 2.

Foskett, Fosgate, Fosket.—Local, 'of Foxcote.' There can be little doubt about this interpretation. The surname is a familiar one, and the entries concerning Foxcote are plentiful. It was a likely corruption. Probably Foscot (originally Foxcote?), a parish in co. Bucks, is the home of most of our Fosketts ; see an instance from co. Bucks, below.

Robert de Foxkote, co. Bucks, 1273. A.
Ralph de Foxcot, co. Essex, ibid.
Roger de Foxcot, co. Salop, Hen. III-Edw. I. K.
Henry de Foxcote, co. Hants, 20 Edw. I. K.
1781. Married—Richard Foskett and Eliz. Wyatt : St. Geo. Han. Sq. i. 326.
London, 12, 0, 0 ; Boston (U.S.), 1, 4, 0 ; New York (Fosket), 2.

Foss, Fosse.—Local, 'at the foss or force,' a waterfall ; cf. Wilberforce, once Wilberfoss. A small spot in Rutland, near Ulverton, is called Foss Forge, where there is a fine waterfall. Airey Force is familiar to tourists in the Lake district.

Richard atte Fosse, C. R., 1 Edw. II.
Johannes Fosse, 1379 : P. T. Yorks. p. 192.
Willelmus de Fosse, 1379 : ibid. p. 196.
Richard de Fosse, co. Soms., 1 Edw. III : Kirby's Quest, p. 226.

Margery atte Fosse, co. Soms., 1 Edw. III : Kirby's Quest, p. 227.
Robert atte Fosse, co. Soms., 1 Edw. III : ibid. p. 240.
London (1884), 3, 1 ; New York, 10, 0.

Foster.—Occup. 'the forester.' An early abbreviation; v. Forrester.

'Now priest, now clerke, now fostere.'
Chaucer, Rom. Rose, 6329.
Benedictus Foster, 1379 : P. T. Yorks. p. 83.
Dionicia Foster, 1379 : ibid. p. 86.
The same individual is thus referred to :
Robert Foster, *cutter*, 1643 : Reg. St. Mary Aldermary (London), p. 89.
Robert Forster, *cutter*, 1644 : ibid.
London, 108 ; New York, 200.

Fotherby.—Local, 'of Fotherby,' a parish in co. Lincoln, three miles from Louth ; v. Fothergill.
London, 2.

Fothergill.—Local, 'of Fothergill.' Some small spot in North England in or near the parish of Ravenstonedale, co. Westmoreland, which I cannot identify ; cf. Cowgill, Gillbanks, Gaskell, Wintersgill, and v. Gill (2). No doubt Fother is an old Scandinavian personal name ; cf. the place-names Fotherby, Fotheringham, Fotherley, Fotheringay, &c. Thus Fothergill means the *gill* where Fother settled (v. Gill), Fotherby means the *by* or dwelling where Fother lived, Fotheringham means the *ham* or homestead of the family of Fother, Fotheringay means the *hay* or enclosure of the family of Fother, and Fotherley means the *ley* or meadow of the family of Fother. That Matterstang Forest and Ravenstonedale are the homes of this name there cannot be the shadow of a doubt.

1541. Miles Fothergill : W. Nicholls, Hist. and Traditions of Ravenstonedale, pp. 112, 113.
Jenkyn Futhergill : ibid.
Martin Futhergill : ibid.
1553-4. John Fodergyll and Jane Feltys : Marriage Lic. (London), p. 14.
'The School in the parish of Ravenstonedale was endowed in 1668 by Thomas Fothergill, B.D., Master of St. John's College, Camb., who was born at Brounber in the same parish ' : Burn and Nicolson's Hist. of Cumb. and Westm., i. 524.

1785. Married—John Martin and Mary Fothergill : St. Geo. Han. Sq. i. 370.
London, 4 ; Manchester, 4 ; Boston (U.S.), 2.

Fotheringham, Fotheringhame.—Local, ' of Fotheringham.' ' A place in the parish of Inverarity, co. Forfar' (Lower) ; v. Fothergill.
1761. Married — William Hooper and Mary Fotheringham : St. Geo. Han. Sq. i. 105.
1781. — William Fothringham and Mary Clark : ibid. p. 321.
London, 2, 0 ; New York, 0, 3.

Foulds, Fould.—Local, 'at the fold,' an enclosure for sheep or cattle. Foulds takes a patronymic *s* like such other one-syllabled local surnames as Holmes, Styles, or Brooks ; cf. Williams, Jones, or Watkins, in baptismal surnames. Foulds is a Lancashire surname, so that we need not be surprised at the pronunciation.—Since writing the above I find Folds to be a hamlet in the ancient parish of Bolton, co. Lancashire. This probably is the habitat, and if so, then Folds must be looked upon as a plural form including several enclosures.

1584. James Foulds, of Trawdon : Wills at Chester (1545-1620), p. 68.
1599. Robert Foulds, of Colne : ibid.
1675. John Foulds, of Clayton-in-le-Moores : ibid. (1660-80), p. 98.
1677. Richard Foulds of Hargreham Eaves : ibid.
1779. Married — George Parsons and Mary Foulds : St. Geo. Han. i. 299.
Manchester, 3, 0 ; Liverpool, 1, 0 ; Philadelphia, 6, 0 ; MDB. (co. Lancaster), 2, 1.

Foulfish (?).—Nick.; cf. Rottenherring.
Robert Fulgheffish, Close Roll, 13 Edw. I.

Foulger.—Bapt. ; v. Fulcher, of which it is a corruption.

Foulkes, Foulke, Foulk.—Bapt. 'the son of Fulk'; v. Fowke, Folk, and Fulke.
Foulk Aldersey, of Chester, *alderman*, 1608 : Wills at Chester (1545-1620), p. 2.
Fowlke Grevill, c. Eliz. Z.
1583. Bapt.—Foulke, son of Cristofer Walton : St. Jas. Clerkenwell, i. 15.
London, 7, 0, 0 ; New York, 3, 8, 2.

Foulsham, Foulsom, Folsom.—Local, ' of Foulsham,' a parish in co. Norfolk. With Foulsom or Folsom, cf. Newsom and Newsham. This surname in the form of Folsom has widely extended its ramifications in the United States.
Ernald de Folsham, co. Norf., 1273. A.
Nicholas de Folsham, co. Suff., 20 Edw. I. R.
Elias de Folsham, rector of Bokenham-Ferry, co. Norf., 1349 : FF. vii. 215.
Simon Folsham, bailiff of Yarmouth, 1446 : ibid. xi. 325.
Thomas Foulsham, rector of Clippsby, co. Norf., 1490 : ibid. xi. 163.
1568. Peter Smithe and Emma Folsam : Marriage Lic. (London), i. 40.

This last entry proves, if proof were needed, the parentage of the American Folsoms.

MDB. (Norfolk), 2, 0, 0 ; London, 2, 1, 0 ; Boston (U.S.), 1, 0, 87.

Foundling.—Nick. 'the foundling,' a deserted child ; M.E. *fundeling* and *fundling* (v. Skeat).
Hugo Fundling, co. Camb., 1273. A.

Fountain, Fountaine, Founteen.—Local, ' at the fountain,' from residence thereby.
Adam de la Funteyne, co. Norf., 41 Hen. III : FF. viii. 271.
Richard a la Funteyne, Close Roll, 55 Hen. III.
Geoffrey de la Fontayne, London, 1273. A.
William Fonteyn, co. Soms., 1 Edw. III : Kirby's Quest, p. 261.
1570. Buried — Anne Fowntane : St. Dionis Backchurch, p. 192.
1587-8. Edward Foote and Susan Fownteyne, co. Herts : Marriage Lic. (London), i. 166.
1592. Married — John Geoffrey and Joane Fowntayne : St. Jas. Clerkenwell, iii. 16.
London, 11, 1, 0 ; Boston (U.S.), 2, 0, 0 ; Philadelphia, 11, 0, 1.

Fouracre, Fouracres.—Local, ' at the four-acre,' from residence in a field or enclosure styled the Fouracre ; a Somersetshire surname.
William Fourakre, co. Soms., 1 Edw. III : Kirby's Quest, p. 146.
John Foweraker, co. Soms., 1605 : Reg. Univ. Oxf. vol. ii. pt. ii. p. 284.
1799. Married — John Fouracres and Martha Bower : St. Geo. Han. Sq. ii. 210.
— — John Foster and Ann Foreacker : ibid. ii. 205.
London, 0, 2 ; MDB. (co. Somerset), 3, 0 ; Philadelphia, 6, 0.

Fourniss.—Local ; v. Furness.
London (1884), 1.

Fourpence, Fourpenny.— Nick. It is hard to know how such sobriquets arose; cf. Nine-pence, Hundredpound, Centlivre, Fivepenny, &c.

Rober:us Forpens, 1379 : P. T. Yorks. p. 301.
Thomas Fourpeni, co. York. W. 9..

Fowden.—Local; v. Foden.

Fowell.—Nick. ; v. Fowl.

Fower.—Occup. 'the fower,' a sweeper, a cleaner, a scourer. 'Fowar or clensare, *mundator*, *purgator*': Prompt. Parv. Mr. Way adds, 'the appellation Fowar occurs as a surname in the Issue Rolls of the Exch. 44 Edw. III, "William Fowar, falconer."' '*Escureur*, a scowrer, cleanser, feyer' (Cotgr.).

Roger le Fower, co. Hunts, 1273. A.

Of the Middle-row in Norwich Blomefield writes :

'Four of the houses in this row were built by Robert Tannys, and settled in 1527, on the city " yeerly, and holly to be expended upon, aboute, and towardys the charges of a common cart, or carts for the carriage awey of the filthy matter comyng of the makyng clene, *fowing*, and swepyng of the stretys "' : FF. iv. 234.

Fowke, Fowkes.—Bapt. ' the son of Fulk.' One more of the almost endless forms of Fulke (q.v.). Fowke became a surname in the 13th century, and lingered on as a baptismal name till the 17th century.

Fowke de Coudrey, co. Bucks, 1273. A.
Mabil Fouke, co. Hunts, ibid.
Thomas Fouke, co. Oxf., ibid.
Richard Fouke, co. Soms., 1 Edw. III : Kirby's Quest, p. 127.
Johannes Fowke, 1379 : P. T. Yorks. p. 158.
Fulk, or Fowke Owen, 1567 : Reg. Univ. Oxf. i. 268.
1603. Buried—Richard Fowke, servant to Nicholas Colquitt : St. Mary Alder-mary (London), p. 151.
1606. — Mr. Fowke Drake, parson of Fyfeilde : Reg. Broad Chalke, co. Wilts, p. 42.
Fowke Dutton, of Chester, *draper*, 1558 : Wills at Chester (1545-1620), p. 57.
London, 3, 2 ; Philadelphia, 0, 1.

Fowl, Fowle, Fowell.—Nick. ' the fowl'; cf. Bird ; v. Fuggle.

William le Foule, co. Essex, 1273. A.
John Fonell, co. Oxf., ibid.
Richard le Foel, co. Oxf., ibid.

William Foghel, co. Soms., 1 Edw. III : Kirby's Quest, p. 83.
Eustace Foghel, co. Soms., 1 Edw. III : ibid. p. 242.
Johanna Foughle, 1376 : P. T. Yorks. p. 25.
1578. Married—Edmonde Fawsett and Eliz. Fowle : St. Michael, Cornhill, p. 12.
London, 1, 6, 2 ; Boston (U.S.), 0, 44, 0 ; New York (Fowell), 1.

Fowler.—Occup. 'the fowler,' a hunter of birds. It is somewhat strange that Fox follows Fowler in our directories!

John the Foeglere, co. Wilts, 1273. A.
William le Foggheler, co. Soms., 1 Edw III : Kirby's Quest, p. 8.
Henry le Fogheler, co. Soms., 1 Edw. III : ibid. p. 2.
Ricardus Foghler, 1379 : P.T.Yorks. p. 7.
Rogerus Foghler, 1379 : ibid. p. 59.
London (1884), 81 ; New York, 120.

Fowlherd, Fullard.—Occup. ' the fowl-herd,' one who tended poultry (?) ; cf. Rookherd, Swan-herd ; v. Herd.

Johannes Foylhird, 1379 : P. T. Yorks. p. 217.
London, 0, 1.

Fox.—Nick. ' the fox,' one of somewhat sly and cunning disposi-tion : not intended to be actually un-complimentary, or the name would not have been so frequently and willingly accepted. We still speak of a man as ' foxing,' or being ' foxy.' The Yorkshire Poll Tax has a very large number of in-stances.

John Fox, co. York, 1273. A.
Richard Fox, co. Norf., ibid.
Matilda Fox, *doghter*, 1379 : P. T. Yorks. p. 6.
Robertus Fox, 1379 : ibid. p. 10.
Johannes Fox, *smyth*, 1379 : ibid. p. 27.
1576. Married — Thomas Hyndy and Agnes Foxe : St. Dionis Backchurch, p. 8.
London (1884), 139 ; New York, 258.

Foxcroft.—Local, ' of the fox-croft,' from residence in an en-closure so called ; v. Croft. Judging by the entries furnished below there can be no doubt that the surname arose in the neighbour-hood of Bentham, on the Yorkshire border of North Lancashire.

Johannes de Fowscroft, 1379 : P. T. Yorks. p. 289.
Thomas Fowscroft, of parish of Caton, 1551 : Lancashire Wills at Richmond (1457-1680). p. 114.
George Fouxcrofte, of Littledale in Caton, 1599 : ibid.

John Foxcrofte, of Littledale in Caton, 1642 : ibid. p. 115.
1605. Miles Corney and Mary Fox-crofte, co. Camb. : Marriage Lic. (London), i. 295.
1616. Buried — John, s. Mr. Richard Foxcrofte, *gent*, born in Cambridge : St. Michael, Cornhill, p. 220.
1668. Married—William Goodman and Anne Foxcraft : St. Jas. Clerkenwell, iii. 144.
London, 2 ; Manchester, 2 ; MDB. (West Rid. Yorks), 2 ; Boston (U.S.), 4.

Foxhall, Foxall, Foxell.— Local, ' of Foxhall,' a parish in co. Suffolk, four miles from Ipswich.

FF. i. 545.
1561. John Foxall and Sibell Whippe : Marriage Lic. (London), i. 22.
1654. Buried—William Foxhall, *wea-ver* : St. Michael, Cornhill, p. 246.
1757. Married—Thomas Foxhall and Eliz. Morton : St. Geo. Han. Sq. i. 69.
1768. — Thomas Foxall and Eliz. Humphreys : ibid. p. 173.
London, 1, 4, 1.

Foxholes. — Local, ' of Fox-holes,' a parish in E. Rid. Yorks, seven miles from Sledmere.

Robert de Foxoles, co. York, 1273. A.
Richard de Foxoles, co. York, ibid.
John Foxholes, *minorite*, sup. for B.D., 1451 : Reg. Univ. Oxf. i. 14.

Foxley, Foxlee.—Local, ' of Foxley,' (1) a parish in co. Norfolk, three miles from North Elmham ; (2) a parish in co. Wilts, three miles from Malmesbury. The former place seems to be the parent.

1334. Richard de Foxele, vicar of Horning, co. Norf. : FF. xi. 56.
1392. John de Foxle, co. Norf. : ibid. ix. 387.
Thomas de Foxley, co. Norf., 9 Ric. II : ibid. viii. 283.
1595. Bapt. — Richarde, s. Alexander Foxley : St. Michael, Cornhill, p. 99.
1622. — Anna, d. Alexander Foxley : St. Jas. Clerkenwell, i. 93.
1726. Married — Thomas Foxley and Eliz. Horne : St. Michael, Cornhill, p. 63.
London, 2, 1 ; Philadelphia, 1, 0.

Foxton, Foxon, Foxten.— Local, ' of Foxton,' a parish in co. Cambridge, six miles from Cam-bridge ; (2) a parish in co. Leicester, three miles from Market-Har-borough ; (3) a township in the parish of Sedgefield, co. Durham. The variant Foxon arose through lazy pronunciation.

Richard de Foxstune, co. Suffolk, 1273. A.

John de Foxton, co. Camb., ibid.
Simon de Foxton, rector of Middle
Harling, co. Norf., 1308 : FF. i. 315.
Thomas Foxtone, rector of Hintlesham,
co. Norf., 1316 : ibid. iii. 631.
1665. Married — William Foxson and
Jane Lee : St. Jas. Clerkenwell, iii. 118.
1669. — James Foxon and Eliz. Overin :
ibid. iii. 160.
1690. Bapt. — Thomas, s. Thomas
Foxen : ibid. i. 336.
London, 0, 2, 0 ; MDB. (West Riding
Yorks), 2, 0, 0 ; New York, 0, 0, 1.

Foxwell.—Local, 'of Foxwell.'
I cannot find the spot.
1580. Married — Ellis Foxwell and
Jane Russell, *widdowe* : St. Mary Alder-
mary, p. 6.
1599. — Lewes Foxwell and Susan
Coleman : St. Jas. Clerkenwell, iii. 22.
London, 4 ; Philadelphia, 1.

Foy, Foye.—? Bapt. 'the son
of Faith' ; M.E. *fey* ; O.F. *foi* (v.
Skeat).
Willelmus Foye, 1379 : P. T. Yorks. p. 6.
Magota Foy, 1379 : ibid. p. 80.
Johannes Faythe, 1379 : ibid. p. 129.
London, 6, 0 ; Philadelphia, 45, 2.

Frampton.—Local, 'of Framp-
ton,' parishes in diocs. Lincoln,
Salisbury, and Glouc. and Bristol.
Thomas de Frampton, or Franton, co.
Linc., 1273. A.
William de Frampton, co. Linc., ibid.
1638. Married — John Framtone and
Dorothy Crosse : St. Mary Aldermary,
p. 18.
1720. Bapt.—John, s. Cristofer Framp
ton : ibid. p. 122.
London, 14 ; Boston (U.S.), 3.

France. — (1) Local, ' from
France ' ; cf. Kent, Somerset, &c.
Herman de Francia. C.
Jenyn de Fraunce, 1379 : P. T. Yorks.
p. 139.
Johannes de Fraunce, 1379 : ibid. p. 209.
Janyn de Fraunce, 1379 : ibid. p. 192.

(2) Bapt. ' the son of Francis,'
from nick. France, or Fraunce.
Fraunce, son of Richard Hawke, 1589 :
Reg. St. Columb Major, p. 15.
Helyn, d. of John Fraunce, 1543 : ibid.
p. 2.
Fraunce, son of William Phillep, 1546 :
ibid. p. 4.
Fraunce, son of Richard Fysher, 1550 :
ibid. p. 6.
London, 13 ; Philadelphia, 24.

Francis, Frances, Francies.
—(1) Local, ' le Fraunceys,' a
Frenchman. The terminal Eys =
ish, as in Kentish, Cornish, Welsh,
&c. There need be no astonish-
ment at the large number of

Francis's in our directories. Every
13th and 14th century record has
instances.
Richard le Fraunceys. A.
Gilbert le Franceys. B.
Henry le Franceis. C.
Adam Fraunceys, 1379 : P. T. Yorks.
p. 5.
Johannes Frawnes, 1379 : ibid. p. 82.

(2) Bapt. ' the son of Francis.'
London (1884), 101, 3, 1 ; Philadelphia,
62, 0, 0.

**Francom, Frankham, Fran-
combe, Frankcomb, Frankum.**
—Offic. ' le Franchomme,' a freeman (v. Freeman) ; *b* is excrescent
in Francomb ; cf. Hampson, Thompson.
Henry le Franchomme, co. Hunts,
1273. A.
Reginald le Fraunchomme, co. Hunts,
ibid.
Andrew Franchom, co. Northampton,
ibid.
Hugh le Fraunchumme, co. Linc., ibid.
Robert Frankhome. G.
William Francombe, c. Eliz. Z.
1572. Thomas Maryott and Agnes
Franckham : Marriage Lic. (London), i. 52.
1733. Married—William Bartlett and
Sarah Franckomb : St. Jas. Clerkenwell,
iii. 261.
1736. — William White and Eliz.
Frankham : St. Geo. Han. Sq. i. 18.
London, 1, 3, 0, 1, 1 ; Oxford (Fran-
combe), 5.

Franey.—? Bapt. ' the son of
Frances ' (?), from nick. Franny,
later Fanny ; cf. Charley, Teddie,
Willy, &c.
1597. Buried—Franny Brine, co. Wilts :
Reg. Broad Chalke, p. 41.
Crockford, 1 ; New York, 1.

Frank, Franke.—Offic. ' the
frank,' i. e. free ; O.F. *franc*.
Walter le Franke, co. Wilts, 1273. A.
William le Fraunk, Close Roll, 8 Edw.I.
William le Fraunk, co. Soms., 1 Edw.
III : Kirby's Quest, p. 216.
Fulco le Frank. E.
Robertus Franke, *franklan*, 1379 :
P. T. Yorks. p. 195.
London (1884), 20, 0 ; Philadelphia,
133, 8.

Frankish, Franks.—Local.
A form of Frances, i. e. French.
Robertus Frankys, 1379 : P. T. Yorks.
p. 22.
Willelmus Frankys, 1379 : ibid. p. 61.
Ricardus Frankissheman, 1379 : ibid.
p. 243.
Ric. Frankys, or Frankysshe, 1522 :
Reg. Univ. Oxf. i. 129.
1681. Bapt.—John, s. John and Avis
Frankes : St. Jas. Clerkenwell, i. 294.

1758. Married — Jervis Franks and
Margaret Barber : St. Geo. Han. Sq. i. 75.
London, 2, 28 ; Philadelphia, 3, 36.

**Franklin, Frankling,
Francklyn, Franklen,
Francklin.**—Occup. ' the frank-
lin,' a freeholder ; M.E. *frankelein*.
The *g* in Frankling is, of course,
an excrescence ; cf. Jennings.
Robert le Fraunkelyn, co. Bucks,
1273. A.
Simon le Fraunkeleyn, co. Berks, ibid.
William le Fraunkelayn, co. Dorset,
Hen. III–Edw. I. K.
Richard le Fraunkelyn, co. Warw., ibid.
William Fronkeleyn, co. Soms., 1 Edw.
III : Kirby's Quest, p. 205.
Willelmus Sampson, *fraunkeleyn*,
1379 : P. T. Yorks. p. 293.
1561. Married—Thomas Franclyn and
Frideswide Watwood : St. Michael, Cornhill, p. 8.
1581. Bapt.—Hellen, d. James Franck-
len : St. Jas. Clerkenwell, i. 12.
1582. — Peter, s. James Francklyn :
ibid. p. 13.
London, 60, 1, 1, 1, 0 ; New York, 69,
0, 1, 1, 0 ; MDB. (co. Lincoln), Francklin, 2.

Fransham.—Local, ' of Fran-
sham,' a parish in co. Norfolk ; to
be carefully distinguished from
Francom (q.v.) and its many forms.
William de Fransham, co. Norf.,
1273. A.
John de Fransham, co. Norf., 52 Hen.
III : FF. viii. 383.
Gilbert de Fransham, co. Norf., 1334 :
ibid. ix. 499.
MDB. (Norfolk), 1.

Fraward.—? Nick. ' perverse,
froward.'
Magota Fraward, 1379 : P. T. Yorks.
p. 196.
Adam Fraward, 1379 : ibid.

Fray, Fraye.—Bapt. ' the son
of Fray.' This name is generally
found in compounds, as in Godfrey,
Frederick, Wilfred, &c. ; v. Yonge,
ii. 190.
Fray Punsard, co. Oxf., 1273. A.
London, 1, 1 ; New York, 2, 0.

Frean, Frayne, Frame.—
Nick. ' the frem,' or ' fren,' i.e.
the stranger. ' *Frem*, strange,
foreign, unknown ' : Halliwell.
' *Frenne*, a stranger, an aliene,
a forraine, a frenne. Florio, p. 19 '
(Halliwell) ; cf. Strange.
Robert le Freyne, co. Bucks, 1273. A.
William le Freyne, co. Bucks, ibid.
Stephen le Fren, co. Somerset, ibid.
William le Freyner, co. Linc., ibid.

Robertus Frayn, 1379 : P. T. Yorks. p. 105.
London, 1, 2, 1 ; Philadelphia, 0, 1, 32.

Frear ; v. Frere.

Frearson.—Nick. 'the son of the friar' ; v. Frere. This York-shire surname crossed the borders into North Lancashire, and is found chiefly in Furness.

Cf. Robertus Frer, *cosyn*, 1379 : P. T. p. 155.
Thomas Frereson, *smyth*, 1379 : ibid. p. 10.
Willelmus Frerson, 1379 : ibid. p. 211.
John Freerson, of Grysedaill, 1588 : Lancashire Wills at Richmond (1457-1680), p. 116.
William Frearson, of Hawkshead, 1596 : ibid.
John Frearson, of Grisdall, 1646 : ibid.
1682. Buried—David Phreason, of Flan : St. Mary, Ulverston, p. 170.
1690. — Agnes, d. Robert Frearson, of Flan : ibid. p. 180.
London, 1 ; Broughton-in-Furness, 3 ; MDB. (co. Lancaster), 2 ; Sheffield, 2.

Frederick, Fredericks.—Bapt. 'the son of Frederick.' An extremely rare font-name in England in the 13th and 14th centuries. Both instances are on the East coast, closely connected with the Low Countries, which is significant.

Fretheric Swym, co. Linc., 1273. A.
Walter Fretheryk, co. Suff., ibid.
Crockford, 1, 0 ; London, 0, 1 ; New York, 27, 30.

Free.—Nick. 'the free' ; v. Fry.

Walter le Free, co. Wilts, 1273. A.
John le Free, co. Soms., 1 Edw III : Kirby's Quest, p. 86.
London, 4.

Freeborn, Freeborne, Free-burn.—Bapt. 'the son of Frebern.' In Domesday we find it thus : 'Friebernus,' cos. Essex and Suffolk. The present general form Freeborn is imitative of the diction-ary word *free-born*. But there is no relationship. In the United States, however, Freeborn has become a familiar font-name :

Freeborn G. Luckey, *lawyer* : New York Directory (1878).
Freeborn G. Smith, *pianos* : ibid.
Robert Frebern, 1172 : KKK. vi. 20.
Agnes Frebern, co. Camb., 1273. A.
Walter Frebern, co. Bedford, ibid.
William Frebern, co. Suffolk, ibid.
Thomas Frebern, co. Soms., 1 Edw. III : Kirby's Quest, p. 252.

Richard Frebern, rector of Thorp-Abbots, co. Norf., 1324 : FF. v. 325.
1574. Thomas Somerfelde and Eliz. Frebarne : Marriage Lic. (London), i. 62.
1585. Thomas Nutt and Frances Fre-borne, co. Essex : ibid. p. 144.
1753. Married — David Munro and Henrietta Freebairn : St. Geo. Han. Sq. i. 50.
1756. — John Freeborn and Mary Earle : ibid. p. 61.
London, 2, 0, 0 ; Manchester, 1, 0, 0 ; New York, 10, 1, 2.

Freeland.—(1) Bapt. 'the son of Freeland' ; cf. Rowland. Frelond occurs in every early record with-out prefix. It was, I imagine, in many instances, a personal or font name. (2) Local, ' of Free-land,' a parish in the dioc. of Oxford.

Aymer, son of Walter Frelund, co. Norf., 1198 : FF. ii. 463.
Matilda Frelond, co. Camb., 1273. A.
Hugh Frelond, co. Oxf., ibid.
John Frelond, co. Norf., 20 Edw. I. R.
Richard Frylende, C. R., 28 Edw. III.
Robertus Freland, 1379 : P. T. Yorks. p. 207.
Willelmus Freland, 1379 : ibid. p. 203.
1590-1. Thomas Frelande and Lucy Wilkyns : Marriage Lic. (London), i. 190.
1595-6. Humphrey Freeland and Agnes Style : ibid. p. 227.
1705. Married—Peter Freeland and Elenor Levingstone : St. Michael, Corn-hill, p. 53.
London, 4 ; New York, 9 ; Philadel-phia, 20.

Freeman.—(1) Occup. ' the freeman,' one who is not a serf, one with peculiar privileges.

John le Freman, co. Hunts, 1273. A.
Geoffrey le Freman, co. Bucks, ibid.
Richard Freman, co. Lincoln, 20 Edw. I. R.
Robertus Freman, 1379 : P. T. Yorks. p. 63.

(2) Bapt. 'the son of Fremond.' Germ. Freimund, Fr. Fremont. Terminatives in *-mund* or *-mond* become *-man* by corruption ; cf. Osman, Wyman, Tesseyman, &c. Of course (1) must be looked upon as the chief parent.

Fremund de Erdington, co. Salop, 1273. A.
Arnold Fromont, co. Camb., ibid.
Robert Fromund, co. Oxf., ibid.
Fremund Inge, co. Bedford, 20 Edw. I. R.
Jordan fil. Fromund : DDD. i. 2.
1627. Married — John Morse and Dorathy Freeman : St. Michael, Cornhill, p. 25.

1630. Bapt.—Isabel, d. Symon Free-man, *clothworker* : St. Peter, Cornhill, p. 82.
London, 110 ; New York, 104.

Freemantle, Fremantle. — Local, 'of Freemantle,' a parish in the dioc. of Winchester, near Southampton.

Nigel de Freymauntel, Close Roll, 32 Hen. III.
Richard de Fremantell, c. 1300. M.
Hugh de Frigido-Mantello. E.
1737. Buried—John Freemantle, from Salisbury : St. Michael, Cornhill, p. 293.
1784. Married — Thomas Wells and Sarah Bridget Fremantle : St. Geo. Han. Sq. i. 367.
London Court Dir., 1, 2 ; Crockford, 1, 2 ; Boston (U.S.), 1, 0.

Frembald.—Bapt. ' the son of Frembald,' a compound of Frith and Bald.

Frimbaldus (without surname), co. Suff., 1273. A.
Thomas Frembald, co. Bedf., 20 Edw. I. R.
Nicholas Frembaud, co. Bedf., ibid.
Frethebaldus (without surname), 21 Ric. II : Furness Coucher Book, i. 188.

Fremont, Fremunt.—Bapt. 'the son of Fremund' ; v. Free-man (2).

New York, 2, 1.

French.—Local, ' the French,' an incomer from France.

Symon le Frensch, co. Wilts, 1273. A.
William le ffrenssh, C. R., 33 Edw. I.
Eborard le Frenshe. G.
Walter le Frensshe, co. Soms., 1 Edw. III : Kirby's Quest, p. 86.
1564. Thomas Frenche and Cicilie Sysley, *widow* : Marriage Lic. (London), i. 29.
London (1884), 91 ; New York, 99.

Frenchbaker. — Occup. ' the French baker' ; perhaps a maker of French rolls !

Richard Frenshbaker. D.

Frenchman. — Local, ' the Frenchman' ; cf. Dutchman.

Gyllame Freynsman. W. 3.
Robertus Franchman, 1379 : P. T. Yorks. p. 231.
Ricardus Frankissheman, 1379 : ibid. p. 243.
John ffrensshman, Close Roll, 8 Hen. IV.
1583. John Frenchman and Johanna Sexbye : Marriage Lic. (London), i. 123.
New York, 1.

Frend ; v. Friend.

Frere, Frear, Freer.—Offic. ' the friar' ; v. Fryer, one of a religious brotherhood.

Benedictus le Frere, co. Camb., 1273. A.
John le Frere, co. Norf., ibid.
Walter le Frere, co. Essex, Hen. III-
Edw. I. K.
Cecylia le Frere, co. Soms., 1 Edw. III :
Kirby's Quest, p. 231.
Magota Frere, 1379 : P. T. Yorks. p. 48.
Isabella Frere, 1379 : ibid. p. 22.
Philip Fryer or Freear, 1519 : Reg.
Univ. Oxf. i. 109.
1540. Married — Mavnerd Frere and
Margaret Tonsoune : St. Peter, Cornhill,
i. 221.
1558. Anthony Eton and Eliz. Freer :
Marriage Lic. (London), i. 18.
1773. Married—James Jacob and Sarah
Frear : St. Geo. Han. Sq. i. 232.
London, 6, 0, 0 ; Manchester, 0, 1, 0 ;
Liverpool, 0, 1, 1 ; New York, 1, 1, 3.

Frereman. — ? Occup. 'the
friar's man-servant' ; cf. Priestman, **Monkman**, Matthewman,
Ladyman, &c. Probably it means
the man, i.e. the servant, of the
friar.

Richard Frereman, C. R., 45 Edw. III.

Freshfish. — Nick. A fish-
hawker's sobriquet ; cf. Freshherring.

John Freshfisch. H.
Robert Freshfissh. X

Freshherring. — Nick. Probably, like Peascod and Goodherring, the sobriquet of the street
hawker who cried his goods.

Margaret Fressheharyng. X.

Freshney.—Local, 'of Friskney,' a parish in co. Lincoln. I do
not state this positively, but I
presume it is so.

'Graland de Longo Campo ten' di'
feod' . . . in Freskenay et alibi' : K.
p. 308.
Hugh de Freskenaye, co. Linc., Hen.
III-Edw. I. K.
Alice de Fresken', co. Linc., ibid.
Ralph de Friskeneye, rector of North
Lynn, co. Norf., 1376 : FF. viii. 540.
Simon Friskney, vicar of Whitwell, co.
Norf., 1441 : ibid. p. 295.
1799. Married — John Freshney and
Ann Heritage : St. Geo. Han. Sq. ii. 209.
Crockford, 1 ; New York, 4.

Freshwater. — Local ; possibly ' of Freshwater,' a parish in co.
Hants, near Yarmouth (I. of W.).
But more probably from some small
spot so called in some other county,
as I find no traces of the surname
in Hampshire or Devonshire.

John Freshwater, rector of Little
Thorp, co. Norf., 1371 : FF. i. 137.

1759. Married — Thomas King and
Mary Freshwater : St. Geo. Han. Sq. i. 86.
London, 7.

Freston.—Local, ' of Freston,'
a parish in co. Suffolk, four miles
from Ipswich.

William de Freston, co. Linc., Hen.
III-Edw. I. K.
Thomas de Freston, co. Suffolk, 20
Edw. I. R.
MDB. (co. Norfolk), 1.

Frewen, Frewin, Frewing.
—Bapt. 'the son of Frewen.' The
Domesday forms are Frauuinus
(co. Devon), Freowinus (co. Suffolk), Freuuinus (co. Essex), and
Frauuin (co. Sussex). The last
instance reminds us that there
have been Frewens in Sussex since
Domesday.

William Frewyn, co. Sussex, 1273. A.
Ralph Frewyne, co. Oxf., ibid.
William Frewyne, co. Soms., 1 Edw.
III : Kirby's Quest, p. 207.
Frowynus de Ispringrode : Wardrobe
Roll, 8–9 Edw. III. v. 36/3.
Johannes Frewyne, 1311. M.
1588. Bapt.—Accepted, sonne of John
Frewen : Reg. Northlam, co. Sussex.
1591. — Thankful, sonne of John
Frewen : ibid.

The above ' Accepted ' lived to
become Archbishop of York.

London, 1, 4, 1 ; MDB. (co. Sussex),
3, 1, 0 ; New York, 1, 0, 0 ; Philadelphia,
3, 0, 0.

Frick.— ?

Walter Freke, co. Soms., 1 Edw. III :
Kirby's Quest, p. 132.
London, 1.

Friday.—Nick. or personal ;
cf. Saturday. Probably given in
some such way as Robinson Crusoe's
man Friday got his sobriquet. It
is impossible now to know how
this surname arose, whether or
not because born on that day (cf.
Nowell, Pentecost, Christmas, &c.).
At any rate it does not seem to be
a corruption of something else, as
in the case of the local Munday.
The old Friday superstition may
have something to do with it.

Simon Fridey, co. Linc., 1273. A.
Adam Friday, co. Oxf., ibid.
Nicholas Friday, co. Bedf. ibid.
Ralph Friday, C. R., 21 Edw. III. pt. ii.
Richard Friday, C. R., 13 Hen. IV.
1784. Married—Richard Wright and
Hannah Friday : St. Geo. Han. Sq. i. 356.
MDB. (co. Kent), 7 ; London, 1 ; New
York, 2 ; Philadelphia, 6.

Friend, Frend. — Nick. 'the
friend.' M.E. *frend.*

John le Frend, Close Roll, 6 Edw. II.
Geoffrey le Frend, co. Soms., 1 Edw.
III ; Kirby's Quest, p. 82.
Robert le Frend, co. Soms., 1 Edw. III :
ibid. p. 92.
Walter le Frend, co. Soms., 1 Edw. III :
ibid. p. 251.
Alicia Frende, 1379 : P. T. Yorks. p. 37.
Willelmus Frynd', 1379 : ibid. p. 71.
London, 2, 2 ; New York (Frend), 1 ;
Philadelphia, 24, 0.

Fripp, Tripp, Trippe, Thripp.
—Local, 'at the thorp,' i.e. a
village. Alone or in compounds
thorp has run through many corruptions ; cf. Westrop, Westrup,
Thrupp, Throp, &c., but the following are the oddest :

Thomas Thripp, co. Wilts, 1580 : Reg.
Broad Chalke, p. 2.
Thomas, son of John Phripp, co. Wilts.
1607 : ibid. p. 42.
Elizabeth Phripp, co. Wilts, 1607 : ibid.
p. 42.
1674. Buried—Ursula Fripp, co. Wilts :
ibid. p. 49.
1739. Married—James Mort and Eliz.
Tripp : St. Jas. Clerkenwell, iii. 268.
London, 4, 13, 0, 1 ; New York, 3, 9, 3, 0.

**Frisby, Frisbee, Frisbie,
Frisbey.**—Local, 'of Frisby,' a
chapelry in co. Leicester ; cf.
Applebee and Filbee, for Appleby
and Filby.

John de Friseby, co. Leicester, 1273. A.
Simon de Friseby, co. Lincoln, ibid.
Robertus de Frysby, 1379 : P. T.
Yorks. p. 75.
William de Frisseby, rector of Filby,
co. Norf., 1412 : FF. xi. 218.
1605. Thomas Wells and Anne Frisby :
Marriage Lic. (London), i. 298.
1725. Married—John Whikes Frisbey
and Mary Mason : St. Geo. Han. Sq. i. 1.
London, 13, 3, 0, 0 ; MDB. (Leicester),
6, 0, 0, 0 ; Philadelphia, 18, 0, 6, 1.

Frisdick, Frostick.—Local,
'of Frosdyke,' some spot apparently
in co. Norfolk. The variant Frostick
is curious.

Robert Frosdit, or Frosdike, rector of
Tacolneston, co. Norf., 1540 : FF. v. 170.
James Frosdyke, co. Norfolk, 1574 :
ibid. ii. 523.
1801. Married — Thomas Clark and
Hermon Frostick : St. Geo. Han. Sq.
ii. 231.
1803. — William Frosdick and Mary
Eaton : ibid. p. 294.
London, 0, 2 ; MDB. (co. Norfolk), 3, 0.

**Friswid, Fiddy, Fiddey,
Fiddes.**—Bapt. 'the son of Frideswide.' For the story of this English

saint, v. Yonge, ii. 196; see also Green, Hist. Eng. People, i. 339. Miss Yonge suggests Fiddy as the nick. form. The font-name was familiar up to the Reformation.

1553. Bapt. — Fridaysweede, d. of Mr. Southworth: St. Antholin, Bridge Row (London).
1561. Married—Thomas Franclyn and Fryswyde Watwood: St. Michael, Cornhill.

Frith, Firth.—Local, 'at the frith' or 'firth,' q.v., a bay, an estuary, a wide valley, as in Chapelle-Frith, co. Derbyshire.

Richard de la Fryth, co. Norf., 1273. A.
John atte Frithe. FF.
William atte Frith, Fines Roll, 9 Edw. I.
Thomas atte Fryth, 1379: P. T. Yorks. p. 45.

Both Firth and Frith are familiar patronymics, but the dictionary use is confined to the poets.
'Both in the tufty frith, and in the mossy fell.'
Drayton, Polyolbion, Song 17.
London, 19, 7; Philadelphia, 2, 53.

Frithesant.—Bapt. 'the son of Frethesantha' (Yonge, ii. 196). I do not know that this has become in any form a surname. I have set it here in case such should be the fact, because it seems well to unearth a forgotten font-name, and because it helps to explain the now historic name Inglesant, q.v.

Frethesence mater Reginaldi, co. Camb., 1273. A.
Frethesaunt Paynel, co. York, Hen. III–Edw. I. K.
Adam fil. Freyesent, co. York, 13th century: FFF. p. 18.
William fil. Freyesent, co. York: ibid.
Thomas Frysund, co. Berks, Hen. III–Edw. I. K.

Frobisher; v. Furber.

Frodsham.—Local, 'of Frodsham,' a market-town and parish in co. Ches., ten miles from Chester. The surname seems to have travelled early to London.

1548. Edward Frodesham, of Elton: East Cheshire, ii. 534.
1595. Robert Frodsome and Anne Smythe: Marriage Lic. (London), i. 225.
Margaret Frodsham, of Eccleston, 1606: Wills at Chester (1545-1620), p. 69.
John Frodsham, of Elton, 1610: ibid.
1763. Married — Peter Fradsom and Mary Lambourne: St. Geo. Han Sq. i. 118.
London, 4; MDB. (co. Chester), 1.

Froggatt, Froggitt, Frog-

gett. — Local, 'of Froggatt,' a township in co. Derby, on the border of Yorkshire, near Sheffield. This surname has spread widely.

London, 2, 1, 0; MDB. (Derbys.), 8, 0, 0; Sheffield, 11, 0, 1; Philadelphia, 1, 0, 0.

Froom.—Local, 'of Frome' or 'Froome,' parishes in cos. Soms. and Hereford.

Walter de Frome, co. Oxf., 1273. A.
Reginald de Frome, co. Soms., 1 Edw. III: Kirby's Quest, p. 208.
William de Frome, co. Soms., 1 Edw. III: ibid. p. 129.
John Frome, co. Soms., 1 Edw. III: ibid. p. 158.
London, 7.

Frost.—Personal or bapt. 'the son of Frost,' evidently a Scandinavian personal name, answering later on to the fontal names Christmas, Nowell, or Midwinter. Winter (q.v.) we know was a personal name. To the same class belongs Snow, a great favourite, of Scandinavian parentage.

Henry Frost, co. Norf., 1273. A.
Robert Frost, co. Linc., ibid.
John Frost, C. R., 18 Edw. I.
Johannes Froste, 1379: P. T. Howdenshire, p. 12.
Dionisius Frost, 1379: P.T.Yorks. p. 75.
London, 80; Philadelphia, 40.

Frostick; v. Frisdick, a manifest corruption.

Froud, Froude, Frowde, Frude.—? Bapt. 'the son of Froud' (?). This name has troubled me much. There is not a trace of it in the Hundred Rolls and other contemporary records, so far as my researches have gone. Mr. Lower, however, has an important note upon it. 'The epithet frode, wise, was applied to more than one eminent Northman' (v. Laing's Chronicle of the Sea Kings of Norway, i. 26, 29). In Domesday we find a Frodo, described as '*frater Abbatis* (Bury St. Edmunds), and he had a son Gilbert, called *filius Frodonis*.' This is a satisfactory statement as far as it goes. I wish I could light upon some intermediate links.

London, 7, 3, 1, 0; New York, 1, 1, 0, 1.

Fruin. — Bapt.; variant of Frewen.

Oxford, 2.

Fruiter.—Occup. 'the fruiterer,' a dealer in fruit. M.E. *fruit, frut.*

Gilbert le Fruter, London, 1273. A.
Ralph le Fruter, London, ibid.
Philip le Fruter, de London, 11 Edw. III : Freemen of York, i. 32.

Fry, Frye.—Nick. 'the fry,' i.e. the free. 'The child that was so fry. Rembrun, p. 424' (Halliwell). The surname Fry, therefore, has no doubt a double origin, in some cases meaning 'free' in a civil sense (v. Freeman), in others free, that is, frank, in disposition. Elizabeth Fry, 'the female Howard,' as she was called, possessed the right name.

Thomas le Frye, co. Wilts, 1273. A.
Geoffrey le Frye, co. Wilts, ibid.
Thomas le Frie, C. R., 14 Edw. I.
Roger le Frye, co. Wilts, 20 Edw. I. R.
John le Frye, co. Southampton, Hen. III–Edw. I. K.
William le Frye, co. Soms., 1 Edw. III : Kirby's Quest, p. 95.
1595. Bapt.—Dorothie, d. of Robert Frye : St. Jas. Clerkenwell, i. 29.
London, 52, 0 ; New York, 17, 7.

Fryer. — Offic. 'the friar'; v. Frere.

Henricus Friere, *souter*, 1379 : P. T. Yorks. p. 164.
1549. Edward Fryer, *brewer*: Reg. Univ. Oxf. ii. pt. i. p. 330.
London, 25 ; New York, 11.

Fryman.—Occup. 'the freeman' (q.v.); cf. Fry for 'free.'

MDB. (co. Kent), 1.

Fuggle.—Nick. 'the fowl'; A.S. *fugol*, Icel. *fugl.* But I would suggest that this surname is the result of immigration from the Low Countries, and is the Dutch Vogel, easily enough corrupted into Fuggle. The etymology remains the same; v. Fowl and Vowell.

London, 1 ; MDB. (Kent), 4.

Fulbrook; v. Fullbrook.

Fulcher, Fullcher, Fulker, Folkard, Futcher, Foulger, Folger.—Bapt. 'the son of Folker' or 'Fulker.' This name is in Camden's small list. 'Fulcher (Sax.), "lord of people"' (Rem. p. 62). For history of Folker, one of the champions of Burgundy, 'the mighty fiddler of Alsace,' v. Yonge, ii. 329–30. The English form was more generally Fulke, q.v. Miss Yonge is wrong in saying Fulk 'never took root in England,' as the article 'Fulke' will show. Folkard was both a German and Danish form.

Fulchard, provost of Thetford, co. Norf., 1140: FF. ii. 141.
Fulcher de Carlton, 1150: Whitaker's Craven, p. 222.

Whitaker quotes also an old charter, 'Ego, Fulcerus filius Herberti de Carlton dedi, &c.'

Walter Fulcher, co. Linc., 1273. A.
William Fucher, co. Hunts, ibid.
John Folkard, co. Bucks, ibid.
Fuker de Dovre, Hen. III Edw. I, K.
Warin Fucher, ibid.
Johannes Fowcher, 1379: P. T. Yorks. p. 193.
Margaret Fowcher. D.
1611. Married — Edward Fowcher and Ann Harris: St. Jas. Clerkenwell, iii. 38.
1651-5. — Giles Fulcher and Jane Lacey: St. Dionis Backchurch, p. 30.
1789. — John Fitch and Eliz. Foulger: St. Geo. Han. Sq. ii. 22.
1801. — John Futcher and Ann Weston: ibid. p. 245.
1806. — William Folkard and Mary Ann Duncombe: ibid. p. 338.
London, 8, 1, 2, 7, 1, 6, 0; New York, 1, 0, 0, 1, 0, 0, 7.

Fulchon.—Bapt. 'the son of Fulchon,' the dim. of Fulcher, Fulker, Fulke, q.v.

Ralph fil. Fulchon, 1273. A.
Faulcon Pursevaunt. XX. 1.

Fulford, Fullford, Fulforth.
—Local, 'of Fulford,' parishes in the diocs. of York and Lichfield, and a tithing in the union of Crediton, co. Devon. The North-English Fulfords probably hail from the parish of Fulford, E. Rid. Yorks.

William de Foleford, co. Devon, 1273. A.

There seems to have been also a Southfulford in co. Soms., in which dwelt the two individuals named below :

Thomas de Fuleford, co. Soms., 1 Edw. III: Kirby's Quest, p. 150.
Walter de Fuleford, co. Soms., 1 Edw. III: ibid.
London, 7, 2, 1; Philadelphia, 0, 1, 1.

Fulham, Fullam.—Local, 'of Fulham,' a parish in Middlesex.

1651. Buried — John Fulham, St. Michael, Cornhill, ii. 244.
1750. Married — John Fulham and Mary Byrne: St. Geo. Chap. Mayfair, p. 164.
1799. — William Pither and Eleanor Fullam: St. Geo. Han. Sq. i. 206.
Boston (U.S.), 1, 0; New York, 5, 5.

Fuljambe.—Nick.; v. Foljambe.
West Riding Court Dir., 1.

Fulke, Fulkes.—Bapt. 'the son of Fulk'; v. Folk. A personal name now almost forgotten, although it has left an impress on hereditary nomenclature that can never be effaced. Both as fontname and as patronymic it went through every variety of dress, and almost disguise. Enough to say that all our endless Fulkes, Foulkes, Fakes, Faux, Fawkes, Faulks, Fowkes, Folkes, Foakes, were thus originated; for instances see under these several names. Historically Fulke has given us two miscreants: the favourite of John outlawed by Henry III, and the sanguinary hero of November 5. For diminutives of Fulke, see Fulchon.

Fulke Paynel, co. Devon, 1273. A.
Walter fil. Fulc', co. Bedf., ibid.
Fulco fil. Fulconis, co. Camb., ibid.
Fulke le Taverner. B.
London, 0, 1.

Fullalove, Fullilove.—Nick. 'full-of-love,' a direct translation of Plainamour, translations of this kind being common; v. Smallwriter, Fairbrother, Fairchild, &c.

1433. Roger Full-of-Love, of Quydenham, resigned vicarage of Tottington, co. Norf.: FF. ii. 356.
1462. Ralph Full-of-Love, rector of West Lynn, co. Norf.: ibid. viii. 536.
London, 1, 3.

Fullbaron.—Offic.' a full baron'; cf. Halfknight.

Rogerus Fulbaron, 1379: P. T. Yorks. p ?1.

Fullbrook, Fulbrook.—Local, 'of Fulbrook,' a parish in the dioc. of Oxford.

Gilbert de Fullebroke, co. Oxf., 1273. A.
Robert de Fulebroke, co. Suff., ibid.
Walter de Folebroc, co. Bucks., ibid.
John Fulbrook, C. R., 9 Hen. IV.
London, 2, 2; Oxford, 0, 1.

Fuller.—Occup. 'the fuller.' the cloth-bleacher or felter; v. Skeat (Full); also the article on Fuller, Walker, and Tucker in my English Surnames (5th ed.), p. 324.

Gilbert le Fuller, co. Hertf., 1273. A.
Ambrose le Fullur, co. Salop, ibid.
London, 75; Philadelphia, 57.

Fulljames —Nick. A curious corruption of Foljambe, q.v.
London, 1.

Fullwood, Fulwood.—Local, (1) 'of Fulwood,' a township in the parish of Lancaster, co. Lancs.; (2) 'of Fulwood,' an ecclesiastical district in the parish of Sheffield, W. Rid. Yorks. This seems to have been the habitat of the family.

Hugo de Folewode, taylour, 1379: P. T. Yorks. p. 22.
Ricardus de Folewod, 1379: ibid. p. 59.
Hugo de Fulewode, 1379: ibid. p. 66.
London, 3, 0; MDB. (W.R. Yorks), 0, 1.

Fulton.—Local, 'of Fulton,' 'an extinct border village in co. Roxburgh' (Lower).

John de Fultone, co. Camb, 1273. A.
Robert de Fultone, ibid.
London, 8; New York, 35.

Funk.—Nick. 'the funk,' cross, peevish. 'Funk, cross, ill-tempered. Oxon' (Halliwell). Oxfordshire is sufficiently near to Somersetshire to explain the following entry :

John le Funke, co. Soms., 1 Edw. III: Kirby's Quest, p. 99.
London, 3.

Furber, Furbisher, Frobisher, Furburshaw.—Occup. 'the furber' or 'furbisher.' A furbisher or scourer of armour and metals generally, found also as 'furbearer.' 'Thomas Fetherston, furbearer, A.D. 1586': Memorials of Old Birmingham, Toulmin Smith, p. 88. Frobisher is the most prominent modern form of the surname. The 'Smiths, Forbers, and Pewterers went together in the Chester Play, inaugurated 1339' (Ormerod's Cheshire, i. 300). 'Foorbyschowre, eruginator' (Prompt. Parv.). 'Frobischer, a furbisher: explained by urigenator in Nominale MS.' (Halliwell). The American Furburshaw seems to be a corruption of Furbisher.

John le Furber. E.
Alan le Fourbour. G.
Thomas le Furbisur, 1303. M.
Thomas Fourbour, 1379: P. T. Yorks. p. 161.
Matilda Forbuschour, 1379: ibid. p.163.
Anabilla Fourbour, 1379: ibid. p. 251.
John Forbysher, or Frobusher, or Frobysher, sup. for B.A., 1520: Reg. Univ. Oxf. i. 115.
1588. Bapt. — Martha, d. Erisia Furbussher: St. Jas. Clerkenwell, i. 20.
1791. Married—John Furber and Anne Mihill: St. Geo. Han. Sq. ii. 53.
London, 5, 0, 0, 0; New York, 5, 0 1, 1; West Rid. Court Dir. (Frobisher), 4.

Furby.—Local, 'of Ferriby'; v. Ferrabee. A modern variant.

1763. Married — John Winstanley and Eliz. Furby: St. Geo. Han. Sq. i. 126.
London, 1; Oxford, 3; New York, 1; Philadelphia, 1.

Furneaux.—Local, 'of Furneaux,' a Norman name, possibly from Furneau-sur-Baise, near Falaise, or Furneaux-sur-Vire, near St. Lo (v. Lower).

Robert de Furneus, co. Notts, 1273. A.
Isabella de Furneus, ibid.
Simon de Forneaux, co. Soms., 1 Edw. III: Kirby's Quest, p. 242.
Willelmus de Furneux, 1379: P. T. Yorks. p. 49.
London, 2; Crockford, 4; Boston(U.S.),2.

Furner.—Occup. 'the furner,' i.e. baker; Fr. *fournier*. '*Furnour*, a baker (Latin). See Ord. and Reg. pp. 70, 232. Still in use in Kent' (Halliwell). '*Furner*, a malkin for an oven. Lincoln' (ibid.).

William le Furneur, co. Camb., 1273. A.
Henry le Furner, C. R., 17 Edw. I.
William le Fourner, 6 Edw. III: Freemen of York, i. 27.
London, 2; New York, 2.

Furness, Furnice, Furniss, Furnas.—Local, 'of Furness,' the portion separated by the Morecambe estuary from the rest of Lancashire. It underlies cos. Cumberland and Westmoreland.

Reyner de Furneys, co. Linc., 1273. A.
Michael de Fournes, 21 Ric. II: Furness Coucher Book, i. 188.
Sibilla de Fournays, 1379: P. T. Yorks. p. 199.
Johannes de Fournays, 1379: ibid.p.186.
Thomas Furneys, 1379: ibid. p. 13.
1586-7. Buried—Annes Furnes, *widow*: St. Dionis Backchurch, p. 199.
1729. Married — John St. John and Eliz. Furnese: St. Geo. Han. Sq. i. 6.
1784.—Thomas Turbitt and Ann Furniss, ibid. p. 362.
London, 11, 1, 5, 0; MDB. (co. Westmoreland), 1, 0, 0, 4; Philadelphia, 17, 0, 2, 0.

Furnival, Furnivall.—Local, 'Fourneville,' in the neighbourhood of Honfleur, Normandy.

Gerard de Furnivall, co. Linc., 1273. A.
Thomas de Furnivall, co. York, ibid.
Thomas Furnyuall, *chivaler*, 1379: P. T. Yorks. p. 31.
Johanna Furnyuall, 1379: ibid.
London, 1, 3; Philadelphia, 2, 0.

Fursan.—Local, 'at the furze,' from residence thereby; cf. Gorst. 'Furzen, furze': Tusser, p. 189.

Matilda atte Fursan, co. Soms., 1 Edw. III: Kirby's Quest, p. 177.

Furse, Furze.—Local, 'at the furze,' i.e. the gorse, from residence thereby; cf. Gorst.

John de la Furse, co. Devon, 1273. A.
Robert de la Furse, ibid.
London (1884), 6, 4; Philadelphia, 0, 2; New York, 1, 0.

Fyfe, Fyffe, Fife.—Local, 'from Fife,' i.e. Fifeshire; cf. Devonshire, Kent, Somerset, &c.

London (1884), 4, 2, 4; New York, 3, 2, 2; Philadelphia, 1, 1, 7.

Fysh.—Nick.; v. Fish.

Fyson, Fison.—Bapt. 'the son of Fye.' It is difficult to explain the origin of this surname, so familiar to co. Cambridge, but probably Fye was the nick. of Felicia, a very popular girl's name in the surname period.

MDB. (co. Camb.), 15, 5; London, 2, 1.

G

Gaball, Gabell, Gable, Gabriel, Gableson, Gabrielson, Gabel.—Bapt. 'the son of Gabriel,' popularly Gabel. Rare in early registers.

Gabriel Attelond, co. Kent, 1273. A.
Gabel Brenn, co. Norf., ibid.
Thomas Gabriell, 1379: P. T. Yorks. p. 186.

A feminine Gabriela existed, also found as Gabella.

1539. Bapt. — Gabella, d. of Robert Tans: St. Peter, Cornhill, i. 1.
London, 1, 1, 5, 11, 0, 0, 0; Liverpool, 0, 0, 1, 3, 1, 2, 0; New York, 0, 0, 4, 18, 0, 2, 7.

Gabb.—Bapt. 'the son of Gabriel,' from nick. Gab; v. Gaball.

William Gabbe, Close Roll, 20 Ric. II. pt. ii.
Cf. Thomas Gab-Nave (i. e. Thomas, the servant of Gab), 1379: P. T. Yorks. p. 13.
London, 5; New York, 1; Philadelphia, 1.

Gabber, Gabler, Gaber.—Nick. 'the gabber,' a liar, a talkative, gossiping, untruthful man. We can readily understand why this surname has not come down to our modern directories. To gabble, and a gabbler, are frequentatives of this word; M.E. *gabben*, to talk idly.

Stephen le Gabbere, co. Oxf., 1273. A.
Gerard le Gabur, co. Suff., ibid.
John Gaber, co. Soms., 1 Edw. III: Kirby's Quest, p. 209.
William Gabbere, C. R., 3 Hen. IV. pt. ii.
Liverpool (1887), 0, 1, 0; New York, 0, 7, 1.

Gabbett, Gabbott, Gabbotts, Gabits, Gabbatt.—Bapt. 'the son of Gabriel,' from nick. Gab, and dim. Gabb-ot or Gabb-et.

John Gabbett, of Middleton, co. Lanc.: Wills at Chester (1545-1620), p. 09.
John Gabbott, of Broomicroft, co. Lanc.: ibid.
London, 1, 0, 0, 0, 0; Crockford, 2, 1,

0, 0, 0; Manchester (1887), 0, 2, 1, 1, 0; New York (Gabbatt), 1.

Gadd.—? Bapt. 'the son of Gad' (?).

John Gad, co. Soms., 1 Edw. III: Kirby's Quest, p. 108.
Mathew Gad, co. Soms., 1 Edw. III: ibid. p. 254.
Thomas Gedde, 1379: P. T. Yorks. p. 62.
1717. Bapt.—William, s. James Gad: St. Jas. Clerkenwell, ii. 97.
1734. Married—William Duncaffe and Margaret Gadson: ibid. iii. 262.

Gadson above is probably a corruption of Gadsden, otherwise it would settle the question.

London, 5; MDB. (co. Soms.), 4; Philadelphia, 4.

Gadsby.—Local, 'of Gaddesby,' a chapelry six miles from Melton Mowbray, co. Leicester.

1752. Married — William Gozna and Eliz. Gadsby: St. Geo. Han. Sq. i. 47.
London, 5; Philadelphia, 9.

Gadsden, Gadsdon.—Local, 'of Gaddesden.' Great and Little Gaddesden are parishes in co. Herts, near to Hemel Hempstead.

Audufus de Gatesden, co. Bedf.,1273. A.
Agace de Gatesdon, co. Devon, ibid.
Richard de Gatisdene, co. Bucks, ibid.
John de Gattsdene, co. Norf., ibid.
William de Gatesden. M.
John de Gatesden, co. Norf. FF.
1692. Bapt.— Johnson Holman, s. John Gadsdon : St. Jas. Clerkenwell, i. 349.
London, 7, 3 ; Philadelphia, 2, 0.

Gaffer.—Nick. 'grandfather'; cf. 'gammer,' for grandmother. Gaffer became a familiar term of address, similar to our 'Well, old chap, how are you?' As time went on a gaffer was a foreman.

Jacobus Gafare, 1379 : P. T. Howden shire, p. 4.
Willelmus Gafer, 1379 : P. T. Yorks. p. 234.

Gainer, Gainor.— Bapt. ; v. Gaynar.

Gainsborough. — Local, 'of Gainsborough,' a parish in co. Lincoln.

1714. Bapt. Robert, s. Matthias Gainsborough : St. Peter, Cornhill, ii. 29.
MDB. (co. Lincoln), 2.

Gaitskell.—Local. A variant of Gaskell (q.v.), more correctly Gaisgill.

Elizabeth Gateskell, of Dalton, 1623 : Lancashire Wills at Richmond, i. 121.
Mary Gaitskell, of Dalton, 1646 : ibid. p. 117.
Robert Gaitskell, of Little Urswick, 1645 : ibid.

The descendants of this family still live in the neighbourhood, but in the name of Gaskell.

West Rid. Court Dir., 1 ; London, 2.

Gale.—Local, 'at the gaol,' from residence thereby. 'Gayles, gaols' (Halliwell).

Johanna del Gaylle, 1379 : P. T. Yorks. p. 295.
Agnes del Gaylle, 1379 : ibid. p. 142.
Johannes del Gayle, 1379 : ibid.
Willelmus Gayle, 1379 : ibid.
1696. Married—Edward Fewtrill and Martha Gale : St. Mary Aldermary (London), p. 35.
London, 45 ; Boston (U.S.), 36.

Galer, Gayler, Gaylor. — Offic. 'the gaoler,' a turnkey.

Adam le Gaoler, co. Norf., 1273. A.
Richard le Gayeler, co. Oxf., ibid.
John le Gaylur, co. Bedf., ibid.

Thomas Gaylyour, Ebbot sa femme, 1379 : P. T. Yorks. p. 43.
London, 4, 7, 1 ; New York, 0, 7, 0.

Gales.—Local, 'the Welshman,' from Wales ; v. Wallace.

Thomas le Galeis. E.
Henry le Galeys. R.

A regulation concerning the sale of wool in the reign of Edward III speaks of' MerchantzEngleis,Galeis, ou Irreis': Stat. of Realm, i. 334.

Ricardus Galeys, 1379 : P. T. Yorks. p. 253.
London, 2 ; Boston (U.S.), 3.

Galesmith.—?

Robert le Galesmith, 1251, bailiff of Newcastle : PPP. vol. ii.

Galilee, Galley.—Local, 'of the galilee,' a surname of exceptional interest which has barely survived. The galilee of our cathedrals is founded no doubt on the phrase, 'Galilee of the Gentiles' (Matt. iv. 15). It was a porch or chapel attached to a church and used as a penitentiary, and even as a mortuary. A galilee exists at Lincoln, Ely, and Durham cathedrals. At times they seem to have been set apart for women, who were restricted within certain limits. My first instance is general ; all the others no doubt owe their origin to the galilee in Durham Cathedral. I was quite delighted, in a visit to Tynemouth, to find the name still existing in the neighbourhood of Newcastle. Galley, as will be seen below, is a corruption. Probably the founder was verger of the galilee, or dwelt under the shadow.

William de la Galilye, C. R., 11 Edw III. pt. i.
'Cardinal Langley was buried in the Galilee at Durham,' 1437 : Hist. Newcastle and Gateshead, i. 337.
Bishop Neville 'requested with his dying breath to be buried in the Galilee, near the tomb of the Venerable Bede,' 1457 : ibid. i. 337.
John Galilee, 1498 : Hist. Newcastle and Gateshead, i. 408.
Dominus John Galilee, 1502, Chantry-priest of St. Nicholas, Newcastle : ibid. ii. 10.
James Galilee, 1535 : ibid. ii. 145.
Robert Galilee, cantarist in chantry at Gateshead Ch., 1535 : ibid. ii. 145.
John Gallale, tanner, 1539 : ibid. ii. 187.
Robert Galilee, of Lintz Green, wheelwright, 1539 : ibid. ii. 165.

'I forgive John Galley, 40s.' 'I forgive Robert Galley, 30s,' 1551. (This last item is from a will quoted by the editor, who identifies these two names as members of the Galilee family : ibid. ii. 280.) A friend of mine had an acquaintance with a Galilee in Newcastle, a retired sea-captain, who was living in 1886.

Sunderland Dir. (Gallilee), 1, (Galley) 2 ; Liverpool, 1, 0 ; New York, 0, 2.

Gall, Galle.—Bapt. 'the son of Galle.' Lower says, 'An ancient personal name. Two saints Galle occur in the Roman Calendar, one of whom was a Scotch abbot' (Patr. Brit. p. 124). Miss Yonge says, 'Col or Gall was the name of a companion of St. Columbanus. . . . His name of St. Gall is still attached to the great monastery near the Lake of Constance'(Hist. Christian Names, ii. 76).

Peter Galle, co. Linc., 1273. A.
Hugh Galle, co. Salop, ibid.
Sibilla Galle, co. Suff., ibid.
Philip Galle, co. Linc., 20 Edw. I. R.
1550. Buried — Julyan Gawle : St. Michael, Cornhill, p. 179.
1758. Married David Gall and Ann Risbridger : St. Geo. Han. Sq. i. 82.
London, 3, 0 ; MDB. (Lincoln), 1, 0 ; Boston (U.S.), 1, 1 ; New York, 6, 1.

Galland.—(1) Bapt. ; v. Golland and Jolland. (2) Nick. ; v. Gallant. A possible modification, but (1) is the probable origin, being a Lincolnshire surname.

Gallant.—Nick. 'the gallant.'

Thomas Galaunt, co. Suff., 1273. A.
London, 1 ; Boston (U.S.), 6 ; New York, 2.

Gallard, Gaylard, Gaylord, Gillard.—(1) Nick. 'the gaillard,' the gay, the joyous, the bold. The spelling of the surname has gradually, yet naturally, settled down into Gillard, although other variants occur.

'Gaillard he was, as goldfinch in the shawe.' Chaucer, The Cook's Tale.
John Gayllard, co. Camb., 1273. A.
William Gallard, co. Oxf., ibid.
John Galard, co. Oxf., ibid.
Margery Gaylard, co. Soms., 1 Edw. III : Kirby's Quest, p. 209.
Sabina Gaylard. H.
Nicholas Gaylard. T.

(2) Bapt. 'the son of Gaillard,'

X

a girl's name ; cf. Joyce and Hillary.

Gaillarda Blome, Close Roll, 5 Edw. II.
Gaylarde uxor Arnaldi de Puribus, Close Roll, 39 Hen. III. pt. iv.
1667. Bernard Galard and Joane March : Marriage Alleg. (Canterbury), p. 138.
1673. William Archbould and Mary Gillart : ibid. p. 214.
1676-7. Joshua Gallard and Anne Wakefield : p. 263.
London, 1, 1, 0, 8 ; New York (Gaylord), 7.

Gallatly.—Nick.; v. Golightly.

Gallaway, Galloway, Gallwey, Galway.—Local, 'from Galloway,' the south-eastern portion of Scotland. Crossing the border the name is soon found in co. Northumberland, thence it came into Yorkshire. In Lancashire and the West Riding the name is now very familiar. The early forms seem to have included Gallowaie, Galaway, Galeway, Galewey, and Galway.

Alan de Galeweya, cos. York and Oxf., 1273. A.
Robert Galewey, co. Oxf., ibid.
Adam de Gallowaie, 1306, bailiff of Newcastle : Hist. Newcastle and Gateshead (List of Bailiffs), vol. ii.
Adam Galway, 1326 : ibid. i. 64.
Richard Galloway, 1343, mayor of Newcastle : ibid. i. 117.
Robertus de Galway, 1379 : P. T. Yorks. p. 72.
Johannes de Galway, 1379 : ibid.
John de Galeway, 1378, rector of Meldon : Hodgson's Northumberland, ii. 8.
Richard Galway, 1367 : ibid. p. 5.
Thomas Galway, *firmarius*, 1379 : P. T. Yorks. p. 223.
London, 5, 9, 1, 1 ; Galloway : Manchester, 10 ; West Riding, 4 ; New York, 5, 7, 0, 11.

Gallon, Gallyon, Gellion.—Bapt. 'the son of Juliana,' more popularly Gillian. A single glance at the Hundred Rolls, where all manner of forms, all over the kingdom, are found, practically sets the matter at rest. The font-name was enormously popular even before 'Jack and Jill' made the nick. so familiar ; v. Gill. Galyena occurs without surname in co. Suffolk in 1273 (A. ii. 193).

Gillian Cook, co. Kent, 1273. A.
Gilian de la Mill, co. Soms., ibid.
Robert Galian, co. Oxf., ibid.
Fulco Galyon, co. Camb., ibid.

Roger Gulyan, co. Camb., ibid.
William Gillion, co. Hunts, ibid.
Richard Galon, co. Soms., 1 Edw. III : Kirby's Quest, p. 250.
William Galoun, co. Soms., 1 Edw. III : ibid. p. 79.
1771. Married — Henry Galon and Susanna Buss : St. Geo. Han. Sq. i. 213.

It is just possible, however, that as Walter (Gualter) took the dim. form Walon (v. Wallen), so Gualter would become Gualon ; cf. Guarin and Wareing, Garner and Warner, Guillaume and William, with their corresponding dims. Gillott and Willott, Gallon and Gallyon, would readily be formed in this way.

London, 0, 1, 1 ; West Rid. Court Dir., 1, 0, 0.

Galpin, Galpen.—Bapt. 'the son of Galopin.' My first instance is found in the Hundred Rolls for co. Oxford, and the name is at the present day well known to the residents of the city as Galpin.

Nicholas Galopin, co. Oxf., 1273. A.
Richard Galopyn, co. Soms., 1 Edw. III : Kirby's Quest, p. 236.

Mr. Lower's statement that Galpin is a corruption of the Scotch MacAlpin is utterly out of the question.

London, 5, 0 ; Oxford, 5, 0 ; New York, 2, 2.

Galsworthy.—Local ; v. Goldsworthy.

Galt, Gault.—Nick. 'the galt'; O.E. *galt*, a boar pig ; cf. Pigg, Wildbore, Hogg, &c. 'Galt, a boar pig (North) ; a gallte, *nefrendus*: Nominale MS.' (Halliwell). 'Gresse growene as a galte': Morte Arthure MS. Lincoln, F. 65 (ibid.). 'Galte (or gylte) swyne, *nefrendus*': Prompt. Parv. And v. *galt*, Jamieson's Dict.

Gilbert Galt, co. Norf., 1273. A.
Liverpool, 1, 0 ; Manchester, 0, 2 ; New York, 2, 5.

Galway, Gallway ; v. Gallaway.

Gamage, Gammage, Camidge.—Local, 'de Gamage,' or 'Gamages,' or 'Camages.' The variant Camidge need present no difficulty, as C and G were constantly interchangeable, as this dictionary incontestably proves ;

cf. Grain and Crane, Grandage and Crandidge, &c. I cannot identify the spot ; probably it is continental.

William de Gamages, co. Glouc., 1273. A.
Henry de Gamage, or Gamages, co. Oxf., ibid.
Alicia Gamage, co. Oxf., ibid.
Philip de Camiges, co. Wilts. ibid.
1541. Married—Roger Gammadge and Eliz. Fisher : St. Antholin (London), p. 2.
1769. — John Gamage and Mary Cooper : ibid. i. 190.
1772. — Thomas Gammage and Eliz. Burgis : ibid. i. 223.
London, 3, 1, 3 ; New York, 1, 1, 0.

Gamble, Gambles, Gammell, Cammell, Gammel.—Bapt. 'the son of Gamel,' a once popular but now forgotten North-English personal name (v. Freeman, Norm. Conq. ii. 477). It is compounded with many local names. The modern accepted surname form is Gamble and Gambles, the *b* being intrusive after *m*, as in Gambling, q.v. Cammell is without question the same name.

Walter fil. Gamel, 6 Hen. II : Whitaker's Craven, p. 296.
Gamel de Sandford, 32 Hen. II : Nicolson and Burn, Hist. Westm. and Cumb., i. 428.
Gamel de Clifton, 1197 : RRR. p. 176.
Gamel de Penred, 1190 : ibid. p. 56.
Huttred fil. Gamelli, co. Northumb., 1273. A.
Allan fil. Gamel, co. Salop, ibid.
Gamal Dele, C. R., 3 Edw. I.
Adam Gamal, C. R., ibid.
Adam fil. Gamel : West's Ant. of Furness, p. 190.
Gamele de Pennington : ibid. p. 2.
Elena Gamyll, 1379 : P. T. Yorks. p. 197.
Henricus Gamyll, 1379 : ibid. p. 8.
Johannes Camyll, 1379 : ibid. p. 2.
Johannes Gamolson, 1379 : ibid. p. 42.

Cf. the local Gambswell (i.e. Gamel's well), in the parish of Ulverston ; also Gamblesby in co. Cumb.

John Gamble and Anne Beck, 1673 : Marriage Alleg. (Canterbury), p. 217.
London, 12, 0, 2, 2, 0 ; MDB. (Lincoln), Gambles, 1 ; West Rid. Court Dir., 9, 1, 1, 2, 0 ; Boston (U.S.), Gammells, 6 ; Philadelphia, 92, 0, 1, 0, 1.

Gambling, Gamlin, Gamlen.—Bapt. 'the son of Gamel,' from the dim. Gamelin ; with intrusive *b*, Gamblin, and with excrescent *g*, Gambling ; cf. Jennings for Jennins, or Gamble for Gamel (v. Gamble).

Odo fil. Gamelini, Domesday.
Robert Gamelyn, co. Hunts, 1273. A.
Reginald Gamelyn, co. Hunts, ibid.
Ralph Gamelin, co. Hunts, ibid.
Thomas Gymelyn, 1379 : P. T. Yorks. p. 61.
1625-6. John Browne and Margaret
Gamblin : Marriage Alleg. (Canterbury),
p. 31.
1666. John Gamlin and Frances Hoare:
ibid. p. 118.
1737-8. Buried — Samuel Gambling :
St. Dionis Backchurch, p. 306.

John Gambling appeared in a
police case at Bradford, co. York,
Jan. 3, 1889 (Manchester Courier,
Jan. 4, 1889).
London, 0, 1, 1 ; MDB. (Suffolk), 1,
0, 0; New York, 2, 0, 0.

Game.—Local, 'at the game.'
'Game, a rabbit warren' (Halliwell).
John de la Gayme, co. Oxf., 1273. A.
Alicia del Gamme, 1379 : P. T. Yorks.
p. 124.
Agnes del Gamme, 1379 : ibid.
1750. Married—John Game and Mary
Nunn : St. Geo. Han. Sq. i. 43.
London, 9.

Gamman, Gammon, Gamon.
—Nick. Mr. Lower thinks these
names are representative of an old
personal name, but my first instance
disproves this suggestion. It seems
to suggest some one fond of sport.
At any rate, v. game (Skeat); cf.
backgammon (ibid.).
John le Gamone, or le Gamene, co.
Southampton, 1273. A.
William Gamen, co. Suff., ibid.
Geoffrey Gamon, co. Oxf., ibid.
Richard Gamen, co. Norf., ibid.
1588. Married — Robert Jones and
Joane Gammon : St. Jas. Clerkenwell,
iii. 13.
1767. — Richard Gammon and Mary
Burch : St. Geo. Han. Sq. i. 164.
1772. — Richard Gamon and Grace
Jeffreys : ibid. p. 216.
London, 3, 6, 0; New York, 0, 3, 0;
Philadelphia (Gamon), 1.

Gammell, Gammel.—Bapt.
'the son of Gamel'; v. Gamble;
cf. Cammel.
Philadelphia, 1, 1.

Gander, Gandar.—Nick. 'the
gander'; M.E. gandre; cf. Goose,
Goss, Wildgoose, Graygoose, &c.
Roger Gandre, co. Suff., 1273. A.
Abraham le Gendre, Close Roll, 2
Edw. I.
Thomas Gandre, London. X.
Reginald le Gandre, co. Soms., 1 Edw.
III : Kirby's Quest, p. 211.
1624. Reginald Gander and Mary
Sherman : Marriage Lic. (London), ii. 149.

1781. Married—William Bartholomew
and Rachel Gander : St. Geo. Han. Sq.
i. 327.
London, 4, 1 ; New York, 3, 1 ; Philadelphia, 0, 1.

Gandy, Candy.—Local, ' of
Gandow' (?). I cannot find the
spot, and I cannot come to any
nearer solution than this.
Johannes Gandawe, 1379 : P. T. Yorks.
p. 39.
Thomas Gandowe, 1379 : ibid. p. 47.
London, 5, 2 ; Philadelphia, 9, 12.

Gane.—? Bapt. 'the son of
Gane' (?). There is a parish in
co. Hereford, near Monmouth,
named Ganerew. The surname
evidently belongs to the West
country; cf. gane fish, a hornbeak
(Halliwell).
Nicholas Gain, co. Suff., 1273. A.
Robert Gane, co. Soms., 1 Edw. III :
Kirby's Quest, p. 206.
John Gane, co. Soms., 1 Edw. III :
ibid. p. 227.
London, 6 ; MDB. (co. Soms.), 9.

Gannaway.—Local, ' of Genoa,'
early varied into Janaway and
Janeway, q.v.
1783. Married—George Gannaway and
Eliz. Macan : St. Geo. Han. Sq. i. 343.
London, 5.

Gannock. — Local, 'at the
ganock,' seemingly from residence
at an inn or hostel. As tavern gave
us Taverner, the keeper of a tavern,
so ganock gave us Ganocker, the
keeper of a ganock. The Proclamation of the Mayor of Norwich
on coming into office set forth
'that all Brewsters and Gannokers
selle a gallon of ale, of the best,'
&c., A.D. 1424 (FF. ii. 100). 'Gan-
neker (ganokyr), ganearia' (Prompt.
Parv.). 'Gannok, standard, ensign'
(Halliwell). ' Gannoker, an innkeeper' (ibid.). Hence the local
surname, 'at the ganock.'
Thomas atte Ganock, co. Norf., 20
Edw. III : FF. vii. 195.

Gant.—(1) Nick. 'the gaunt';
v. Gaunt.
Warin le Gant, co. Camb., 1273. A.
Hugh le Gant, co. Oxf., ibid.
(2) Local, ' of Ghent' ; v. Gaunt.
Gilbert de Gant. J.
Reginald de Gante. E.
Stephen de Gant, co. Northampton,
1273. A.
Robert de Gant, co. Linc., ibid.
Gilbert de Gant, co. Linc., ibid.

For modern instances, v. Gaunt.
(3) Nick. 'the gannet'; M. E.
(contraction) gante; the sea-fowl
so termed. 'Gante, byrde, bistarda' :
Prompt. Parv.
Nicholas Ganet, co. Oxf., 1273. A.
Robert Ganet, co. Oxf., ibid.
Lucas Ganet, co. Devon, ibid.
London, 4 ; New York, 2.

Ganter, Gaunter, Gunter.—
(1) Occup. ' the ganter,' a glover ;
O.F. gant, a glove ; v. Gantlett.
Geoffrey le Ganter, co. Camb., 1273. A.
Adam le Ganter, co. Oxf., ibid.
Adam de Quixlay, gaunter, 27 Edw. I :
Freemen of York (Surt. Soc.), i. 7.
John le Gaunter. N.
Stephen le Gaunter, temp. 1310. M.
Richard le Gaunter, 11 Edw. II : Free-
men of York, i. 17.
(2) Bapt. ' the son of Gunther,'
q.v.
London, 4, 0, 2 ; New York, 6, 0, 1.

Gantlett, Gauntlett.—Local,
' at the gauntlet.' Probably a sign-
name—cf. Roebuck, Whitehorse,
&c.—otherwise a nickname. The
gantlet was an iron glove; O.F.
gantelet, ' a gantlet, or arming glove'
(Skeat, gauntlet). A double dim.
of 'gant,' a glove, gant-el-et; cf.
Hew-el-ot, now Hewlet ; Rich-el-
ot from Richard, Hob-el-ot from
Hob, Robert, &c.
Henry Gauntelett, temp. Eliz. Z.
Roger Gauntlett, temp. Eliz. Z.
1641. Philip Gantlett and Joanne
Avery : Marriage Lic. (Westminster),
p. 40.
1678. Hugh Gauntlett and Anne
Chaytor : Marriage Alleg. (Canterbury), p. 295.
London, 3, 2.

Gapp.—Local, ' at the gap,' i.e.
the breach in the hillside, &c.
'Gap of a walle, intervallum' :
Prompt. Parv.
'Right as the hunter in the regne of Trace,
That stondeth at a gappe with a spere.'
Chaucer, C. T. 1639.
Savatus del Gap, co. Norf, 1273. A.
Robert ate Gappe, co. Hunts, ibid.
William atte Gapp, C. R., 16 Edw.
III. pt. i.
Alan Atte-gap, de Burgh, rector of
Haylesdon, co. Norf., 1335 : FF. x. 431.
Simon atte Gappe, bailiff of Yar-
mouth, 1377 : ibid. xi. 324.
Alexander atte Gappe, bailiff of Yar-
mouth, 1419 : ibid.

As will be seen below, this surname is still familiar to co. Norfolk.

X 2

1716. Bapt.—Thomas, s. William Gape: St. Antholin (London), p. 129.
London, 4 ; MDB. (Norfolk), 2.

Garbett, Garbutt, Garbott. —Bapt. 'the son of Gerbold,' or Gerbaud; cf. Arnold and Arnaud (v. Yonge's Christian Names, ii. 327-8). There can be no doubt about this interpretation. Among the benefactors of Conishead Priory in the 12th century was one 'Roger de Cayres, (who) gave two acres and three roods of land . . . and all his land in Marle-riding, a toft and messuage, which Gerbot once held, in Haverbrec' (West's Ant. of Furness, p. 191).

Robert Gerbot, co. Salop, 1273. A.
William Garbode, or Garbolde, co. Norf., ibid.
Gilbert Gerebod, co. Oxf., ibid.
Gerbald le Escald, co. Linc., ibid.
Adam Gerebaud, co. Hunts, ibid.
Cf. John de Gerberdestone (i. e. Gerberd's farm), co. Soms., 1 Edw. III: Kirby's Quest, p. 260.
Milo Gerbod, co. Northampton, Hen. III–Edw. I. K.
Alicia Gerbot, co. Salop, 34 Edw. I : BBB. p. 707.
John Gerbed, or Gerbot, co. Cumb., 28 Edw. I : ibid. p. 581.
William Garbott, co. York. W. 11.
Gerbod de Escals : Pipe Roll, 10 Hen. II. p. 15.
1757. Roger Garbutt and Ann Elsley : St. Geo. Han. Sq. i. 410.
1759. Phillipp Garbett and Mary Pritchard : ibid. i. 89.
London, 2, 4, 0 ; New York, 1, 2, 1.

Gard, Garde.—Offic. 'the guard,' cognate with Ward, q.v.

Cf. Robert le Garder (co. Oxf., 1273. A.) with Warder.
John le Gard, co. Camb., 1273. A.
Symon Gard, co. Oxf., ibid.
Rogerus Garde, 1379 : P. T. Yorks. p. 101.
1787. Married—John Gard and Eliz. Bray : St. Geo. Han. Sq. i. 410.
London, 2, 0 ; Philadelphia, 5, 5.

Garden, Gardyne.—Local, 'at the garden,' from residence thereby ; cf. Orchard, Appleyard, &c.

William del Gardin', co. Oxf., 1273. A.
Thomas del Gardyn, C. R., 20 Edw. I.
William del Gardyne, C. R., 3 Hen. V.
John Garden, or Gardyn, 1545 : Reg. Univ. Oxf. i. 211.
Thomas del Gardin, co. Kent, Hen. III–Edw. I. K.
1606. Married — Robert Mathewsone and Margaret Garden : St. Jas. Clerkenwell, iii. 31.
London, 4, 1 ; New York, 4, 0.

Gardiner, Gardner, Gardener, Gairdner.—Occup. 'the gardener.' As might be expected, a familiar entry in every mediaeval record. The large number of representatives in the London Directory indirectly proves the popularity of the avocation.

Geoffrey le Gardiner, co. Oxf., 1273. A.
Richard le Gardiner, co. Camb., ibid.
Ralph le Gardener, co. Hunts, ibid.
William le Gardiner, or Gardener, co. Linc., ibid.
William Gardinar, co. Lanc., Hen. III–Edw. I. K.
Gilbert de Iikeley, *ga(r)thener*, 9 Edw. III : Freemen of York, i. 29.
William le Gardener, C. R., 8 Edw. I.
Thomas Gardiner, 1379 : P. T. Yorks. p. 208.
Thomas Garchiner, 1379 : ibid. p. 107.
London, 43, 103, 6, 1 ; Philadelphia, 90, 115, 9, 0.

Gare, Gear, Geare.—Local, 'at the gare' (?), from residence thereby. Latterly the popular variants seem to have been Gear and Geare through a form Gayer.

Stephen de la Gare, co. Kent, 1273. A.
Lucas atte Gare, co. Kent, 20 Edw. I. R.
Lucas de la Gare, co. Kent, ibid.
Allen Atte-gar, vicar of Elmham, co. Norf., 1356 : FF. ix. 493.
1568. Married—Hercules Gooderyn and Eliz. Gayre : St. Mary Aldermary (London), p. 4.
1715. Archibald Hutchinson and Mary Gayer : Marriage Lic. (London), ii. 339.
1771. Married — John Gear and Ann Bamford : St. Geo. Han. Sq. i. 215.
London, 3, 5, 1 ; Philadelphia, 0, 8, 0.

Garford, Garforth, Garfitt. —Local, 'of Garforth,' a parish seven miles east of Leeds, co. York ; v. Forth and Ford.

Robert de Gerford, co. York, 1273. A.
Johannes de Garforth, 1379 : P. T. Yorks. p. 195.
Johanna de Garforth, 1379 : ibid.
Agnes de Gerforth, 1379 : ibid. p. 198.
Johannes de Gerforth, of Gerforth, ibid. p. 216.
London, 1, 0, 0 ; West Riding Court Dir., 0, 4, 2 ; Sheffield, 0, 0, 3 ; Philadelphia (Garforth), 5.

Gargory.—Bapt. 'the son of Gregory,' a corrupted form ; cf. Garland for Graland. Dickens' Joe Gargery, in Great Expectations, was evidently taken, nominally speaking, from real life ; cf. Pickwick, Snodgrass, &c.

Birmingham (1884), 1.

Gargrave. — Local, 'of Gargrave,' W. Rid. Yorks.

Johanna de Gayregraue (*u* for *v*), 1379 : P. T. Yorks. p. 217.
Johannes de Gayregraue, *ffrankeleyn* : ibid.
Willelmus de Gayregraue, *textor* : ibid.
The two last-named persons lived at 'Gayregraue.'

Garland, Garlant.—(1) Bapt. 'the son of Graland,' probably the Breton Gradlon (v. Yonge, ii. 88). It is found as a dog's name :

'Ran Colle our dogge, and Talbot, and Gerlond.' Chaucer, C.T. 15389.

Graland soon became Garland.

Graland de Runchamp, Hen. III–Edw. I. K.
Graland de St. Leodegario : ibid.
Graland de Longo Campo : ibid.
John Garlande, 1379 : P. T. Yorks. p. 127.
Thomas Gerland, 1379 : ibid. p. 224.

(2) Local.

Gilbert de Garlande, C. R., 28 Edw. I.
William le (? de) Garlaunde, C. R., 3 Edw. I.
London, 20, 3 ; Boston (U.S.), 39, 0.

Garlick, Garlic.—Nick. 'a garlick-monger' (q.v.), or a peasant; one who smelt of garlick. But the first solution is probably the correct one ; v. Peppercorn, where a spicer is so called in 1379. Nothing could be more natural than such a sobriquet. Lancashire and Yorkshire were strongly represented by this name ; they are so still.

Robert Garlec, co. Camb., 1273. A.
Margareta Garlek, 1379 : P. T. Yorks. p. 26.
Henry Garlycke, Patent Roll, 1 Eliz., pt. ix.
William Garleke, of Poulton, 1560 : Lancashire Wills at Richmond, p. 119.
Jane Garlic, of Thornton, 1661 : ibid.
London, 7, 0 ; Manchester, 4, 0 ; Preston, 1, 0 ; West Rid. Court Dir., 5, 0 ; New York, 6, 1 ; Philadelphia, 4, 2.

Garlicker.—Occup. 'the garlicker,' a dealer in garlick.

Willelmus Garleker, 1379 : P. T. Yorks. p. 73.
Willelmus Garlekar, *chapman*, 1379 : ibid. p. 94.

Garlickmonger.—Occup. 'the garlick-monger,' a dealer in garlick. This helps to the explanation of Garlick, q.v.

John Garlekemongere. B.
Henry le Garlekemongere, temp. 1310. M.
Thomas le Garlykmonger : ibid.

Garman, Garmeson.—Bapt. 'the son of Garmond'; v. Garment. Cf. Osman, Wyman, and Roseaman, from Osmond, Wymond, and Rosamund.

Germundus de Hodenhull, Hen. III-Edw. I: K. p. 89.
London, 4, 2; Philadelphia, 23, 0.

Garment.—Bapt. 'the son of Garmond,' or 'Gardmund' (Yonge, ii. 241); v. Grimond. Cf. Raiment and Rayment, from Raymond; v. Rayment.

London, 1; Boston (U.S.), 1.

Garner, Garnar, Gerner.—(1) Bapt. 'the son of Garnier'; O.E. Warner (Yonge, ii. 412); v. Warner (2), and cf. Gwilliam and William. Garnier was the once popular French form of the name. It has nothing to do with a granary, as suggested by Lower.

Stephen Gerner, co. Linc., 1273. A.
Gerner de Lancaster, Fines Roll, 11 Edw. I.
Johannes Carner, 1379: P.T. Yorks. p. 161.
1609. Buried — Marie Garner, St. Michael, Cornhill, p. 217.
1713. Buried — Ashton Garner, St. Mary Aldermary (London), p. 213.

(2) Occup. 'the gardener,' firstly corrupted to Gardner, secondly to Garner. As regards most of the North-English Garners there can be no doubt about this solution. It can be proved beyond question.

Christopher Gardiner, or Garner, 1584: Lancashire Wills at Richmond, p. 117.
John Gardiner, or Garner, of Aldingham, 1584: ibid.
Christopher Garner, of Much Urswicke, 1575: ibid. p. 120.

A further instance will sufficiently prove my point. It concerns the stock mentioned above.

1706. Bapt.—Eliz., d. of Mathew Gardner: Reg. Ulverston Ch., p. 291
1709. Bapt. — Margrat, d. of Matthew Garner, ibid. p. 294.
London, 23, 3, 3; Manchester, 17, 0, 0; Philadelphia, 20, 0, 9.

Garnet, Garnett.—Bapt. 'the son of Garnet,' if such a personal name existed, but more probably 'the son of Guarin' (?). Although I have no absolute proof to adduce, I cannot hesitate to assert that this is the O.F. Guarinot (a diminutive in ot of the very popular Guarin),

just as Warnett is Warinot (a diminutive in ot of Warin), the English dress of the same name (v. Wareing and Warinot). Assuredly it is a font-name, or the pet form of a font-name. An inspeximus of the charter of the manor of Ulverton, 10 Henry IV, is witnessed among others by 'Garnet our Forester' (West's Ant. of Furness, p. 34).

Vivianus Gernet, 30 Hen. III: BBB. p. 11.
Rog. Gernet, co. Essex, 1073. A.
William Gernet, co. Notts, Hen. III-Edw. I. K.
Willelmus Garnett, 1379: P.T. Yorks. p. 128.
Johanna Garnet, 1379: ibid. p. 125.
1591. Married — Nicholas Boughe and Agnes Garnet, St. Mary Aldermary (London), p. 8.
London, 0, 6; Philadelphia, 1, 6.

Garneys, Garnies, Garness, Garniss. — ? Bapt. 'the son of Garneys'(?). I cannot find any prefix, and am forced to the conclusion that, like Harness, it is sprung from a personal name. This surname has been settled in Norfolk and Suffolk for six centuries. But the early scattered instances strongly presuppose a fontal origin.

Roger Garneys, co. Suff., 1273. A.
John Gerneys, co. Southampton, ibid.
John Gerneys, co. Linc., ibid.
Thomas Garnys, 1379: P.T. Yorks. p. 167.
Robert Garnys, 1379: ibid.
Robert Garneys, 1384, co. Norf.: FF. v. 291.
Ralph Garneys, 1446, co. Norf.: ibid. v. 292.
Nicholas Garnish, 1599, co. Norf.: ibid. v. 293.
London, 0, 0, 1, 0; MDB. (Suffolk), 3, 1, 0, 0; Manchester (Garniss), 1; New York (Garniss), 2.

Garnham. — (?) Bapt. Not local, as its appearance would so naturally suggest, but the modernly accepted form of the old surname Gernon. For a similar instance, cf. Baynham, an exact parallel. There is no discoverable spot called Garnham, and the fact that such a formerly familiar surname as Gernon has no present representatives, save in one or two rare instances, goes to prove that it still exists in another shape. I have no

doubt about this solution. For early instances, v. Garnon. In the following instance there is no change saving m for n; cf. Ransom for Ranson, or Sansom for Sanson.

1669. Married — John Croxston and Jane Garnum: St. Jas. Clerkenwell, iii. 156.
Cf. 1782. — James Garnon and Eliz. Sherlock: St. Geo. Han. Sq. i. 340.
London, 11.

Garnon, Gernon.— (?) ——. Lower, &c., says it is 'de Gernon,' from some undiscoverable spot in Normandy. There is no local prefix to the many entries in the Hundred Rolls or the Testa de Neville; v. Garnham.

Robert le Gernoun, co. Hunts, 1273. A.
Hugh le Gernoun, co. Hunts, ibid.
John Gernun, co. Oxf., ibid.
William Gernon, co. Derby, ibid.
Gilbert Gernun, co. Wilts, Hen. III-Edw. I. K.
Roger Gernon, co. Wilts, ibid.
Crockford, 1, 0.

Garrard, Gerard, Garratt, Garrett, Garrad, Garritt, Garrod, Garrood, Garrud, Garrott, Garret.—Bapt. 'the son of Gerard'; O.F. Garret, Germ. Gerhard; v. Jarratt. Adding together all the forms under J and G, Gerard is truly remarkable for the number of its variants. In Ireland Gerard and Gerald have become confused, and Fitz-Garrett and Fitz-Gerald are said to be representatives of the same name and family (v. Yonge, ii. 326). It is possible the same confusion existed in England. In any case Gerard is distinct in origin from Gerald.

Johannes Gerard, 1379: P.T. Yorks. p. 56.
Thomas Gerard, 1379: ibid. p. 142.
Gyrerd Tolus, 1379: ibid. p. 242.
Adam Garet, co. Soms., 1 Edw. III: Kirby's Quest, p. 204.
'To Garrett Jonson, for shoes, xs. xd.'
'To Garratt Jonson, for shoes, iiis.': Hous. Exp., Princess Eliz. (Cam. Soc.), pp. 16, 18.
Garret Hawkinson. Z.
Thomas Garard, or Garrarde, or Garrett, 1511: Reg. Univ. Oxf. i. 104.
1678. Buried — Garit Pender: Reg. Cheadle Ch., Cheshire.
'Here lyeth the body of Garrat Cocke, gentleman.' Epitaph, 1637: Brand's Hist. of Newcastle-on-Tyne, i. 384.
'Petition of Elizabeth Fitz-garrat,' 1583: Cal. State Papers (Domestic), ii. 125.
Garret Fitz-garret, 1586: ibid. ii. 344.

London, 17, 5, 13, 41, 8, 2, 18, 2, 0, 0, 0; New York, 2, 14, 2, 15, 0, 1, 0, 0, 2, 2, 0; Philadelphia, 0, 1, 1, 130, 0, 0, 0, 0, 0, 0, 0; Boston (U.S.) (Garrood), 2.

Garraway.—Local, 'of Garway,' a parish in co. Hereford, seven miles from Monmouth; but v. Gore. With Garraway, cf Greenaway for Greenway, and Ottaway for Otway.

John Garewy, co. Glouc., 20 Edw. I. R.
1682. Buried — William Garaway, St. Peter, Cornhill, ii. 97.
1754. Married — James Costidell and Eliz. Garway, St. Geo. Han. Sq. i. 52.
London, 2; Boston (U.S.), 2.

Garretson, Garrison, Garrettson.—Bapt. 'the son of Gerard' (v. Garrard), popularly Garret. In some cases it may represent Garriston, from the place of that name, co. York, as suggested by Lower; but all evidence is in favour of my view, which is a simple and natural one.

John Garredsone. Z.
Andrew Garretson. TT.
1639. William Farrington and Ruth Garrison, Marriage Lic. (Westminster), p. 38.
Philadelphia, 12, 51, 3.

Garside, Gartside, Garthside.—Local, 'at the garth-side,' i.e. living at the side of the garth, the yard or orchard.

Cf. Richard atte Garthend, 1379 : P.T. Yorks. p. 245.

This surname first dropped the *h*, secondly the *t*, and is now almost universally Garside. 'In the reign of Edward I lived Sir Baldwin Teutonicus, . . . who granted to Sir Robert de Holland, in free marriage with Joan, his daughter, all his lands in Butterworth, the Cleggs, Garthside, Akedene, Holynworth, and Halght in Rochdale' (Baines' Lancashire, i. 505). I believe Garthside lay in Crompton, between Rochdale and Oldham. The surname arose there, and still lives in the district. An article in an Oldham newspaper in 1879, which I have misplaced, entitled 'Old Homesteads,' quoted an entry relating to

Robert de Garcesside, 6 Edw. III.
Alice Garside, of Oldham, *widow*, 1597: Wills at Chester (1545-1620), p. 70.

John Gartside, of Saddleworth, 1597: ibid.
Thomas Gartside, of Deanshaw, *husbandman*, 1593: ibid.
'James Gartsyde, for xxⁱⁱ in goods, xs.' (Spotland) Subsidy Roll, 1541, Salford Hundred: Lanc. and Ches. Rec. Soc. xii. 146.

Oddly enough, the full form still exists in Liverpool. I had thought it long extinct. Probably it is a modern restoration.

London, 3, 0, 0; Manchester, 21, 4, 0; Liverpool (Garthside), 1; New York, 3, 0, 0; Philadelphia, 2, 3, 0.

Garstang.—Local, 'of Garstang,' a market-town and parish in North Lancashire.

John de Gairestang', 1379: P.T. Yorks. p. 145.
Rogerus de Gerstan', 1379: ibid. p. 234.
Willelmus de Garston,1379: ibid. p. 257.
William Garstange, 1582: Preston Guild Rolls, p. 44.
Thomas Garstange, 1642: ibid. p. 98.
Andrew Garstang, of Leyland, 1616: Wills at Chester (1545-1620), p. 70.
William Garstang, of Lostock, 1610: ibid.
West Rid. Court Dir., 2; Manchester, 2; Blackburn, 3; Preston, 1.

Garth, Garthe.—Local, 'of the garth,' i.e. the yard, the enclosure. In Yorkshire Garth has occasionally become Gath, q.v. Cf. Garside.

Beatrice del Garthe, 1379 : P. T. Howdenshire, p. 10.
Willelmus del Garth', 1379: P.T.Yorks. p. 225.
London, 2, 0; West Rid. Court Dir., 1, 0; New York, 3, 1.

Garton.—Local, 'of Garton,' two parishes in E. Rid. Yorks, one in Holderness, the other near Great Driffield.

Willelmus de Garton, 1379: P. T. Yorks. p. 295.
Thomas de Garton, *drapour*, et Magota uxor ejus: ibid. p. 97.
London, 7; New York, 1; Philadelphia, 30.

Gascoigne, Gascoine, Gascoyen, Gascoyne.—Local, 'from Gascony,' a Gascoyen; v. Gaskin.

'And reed wyn of Gascoigne.'
Piers P. 455.
William de Gasconia, co. Bucks, Hen. III-Edw. I. K.
Geoffrey Gascoyne, co. Norf., 1273. A.
Peter Gascoyng, co. Devon, ibid.
Philip le Gascoyne. T.
Jacob Gascoigne. B.
Johannes Gascoigne, 1379: P. T. Yorks. p. 295.

1624. Bapt. — Dorothye, d. George Gascoigne, St. Jas. Clerkenwell, i. 98.
1696. John Gascoyne and Sarah Johnson: Marriage Lic. (London), ii. 319.
London, 0, 3, 1, 5; New York, 2, 2, 0, 2.

Gaselee.—Local, 'of Gazeley,' a parish in co. Suffolk, five miles from Newmarket.

Alexander de Gasele, co. Norf., 1273. A.
Andrew de Gasele, co. Norf., ibid.
1630. Married — Thomas Gasleye and Marye Turnor: St. Mary Aldermary (London), p. 17.
1669. John Paynell (co. Norf.) and Catherine Gasley, of Norwich: Marriage Alleg. (Canterbury), p. 167.
London, 3.

Gasgarth, Gaskarth.—Local, 'of Gatesgarth,' a hamlet at the foot of Buttermere, co. Cumb.; cf. Gaskell and Gaitskell.

Thomas Gaskirth, of Ulverston, 1616 : Lancashire Wills at Richmond, i. 121.
Margaret Gatescarthe, of Ulverston, 1609: ibid.
John Gaskarth, of Carke, 1739: ibid. ii. 111.

So late as the present century it is found in Ulverston under the form of Gaskett.

1807. Married — Robert Dalzell, of Ulverston, *shoemaker*, and Ann Gaskett, of Kendal: Ulverston Ch., p. 457.
Liverpool, 1, 1.

Gaskell, Gaskill, Gaskall.—Local, 'of Gaisgill,' a hamlet two miles from Tebay, co. Westmoreland. A compound of *gill*, a narrow ravine (v. Gill); cf. Wintersgill, and v. Gaitskell. The hamlet of Gaisgill being on the Yorkshire border, it is easy to see why the surname is found in the Poll Tax (1379) for W. Rid. Yorks.

Alicia de Gasegill', 1379 : P. T. Yorks. p. 236.
Agnes de Gasegyll', 1379 : ibid. p. 241.
Johannes Gaysegill', 1379 : ibid. p. 250.
Robertus Gays-gill', 1379 : ibid. p. 256.
Katerina de Gasegyl', 1379 : ibid. p. 269.
Cf. Jacobus de Gasegill, of 'Rymyngton,' 1379 : P. T. Yorks. p. 270.
Johannes de Holgill, of 'Rymynton,' 1379 : ibid.
Johannes de Hawesgile, of 'Rymyngton,' 1379 : ibid.
John Gaysgill, co. Lanc., C. R., 12 Hen. IV.
Edward Gaskell, 1560: Lancashire Wills at Richmond, i. 121.
Richard Gaytscalle, of Dalton, 1595: ibid.
Robert Gateskell, of Dalton, 1616: ibid.

London, 2, 0, 0 ; Manchester, 8, 2, 0 ; West Rid. Court Dir., 2, 0, 2 ; New York, 2, 1, 0.

Gaskin, Gasking, Gaskoin, Gasquoine.—Local, 'of Gascony.' A native of Gascony, a Gascon ; v. Gascoigne.

Philip de Gascon', co. Salop, 1273. A.
William Gascon. B.
Robert Gaskyn. F.
Johannes Gascône, 1379 : P. T. Yorks. p. 213.
1599. Married – Richarde Gaskynne and Jane Cooke : St. Michael, Cornhill, p. 16.
1623. — Thomas Gaskin and Judith Clifford : Marriage Lic. (London), ii. 129.
London, 5, 1, 1, 1 ; Boston (U.S.), (Gaskin), 6.

Gasson, Gashion.—(1) Bapt. 'the son of Cass' (q.v.) for Casson. C and G were constantly taking one another's places ; cf. Cammel for Gammel. (2) Occup. 'the Garçon,' i.e. lad, page, attendant ; v. Carson.

'Ther sone was a prowde garson,
Men hym clepyd Syr Befown.'
MS. Cantab. Ff. ii. 38, f. 15 (Halliwell).
Richard le Garzun, C. R., 4 Edw. I
John Garcon le Persone, C. R., 7 Edw. I.

Probably (2) represents the true origin. Gashion is a curious but not unique corruption ; cf. Gration for Grayson.

1773. Married—William Richards and Sarah Gasson, St. Geo. Han. Sq. i. 229.
London, 3, 2 ; New York, 1, 1.

Gaston.—Local, ' of Gascony,' an early corrupted form of Gaskin or Gaskon. The same individual is thus referred to :

William de Gasconia, co. Bucks.
Hen. III-Edw. I. K.
William de Gaston, co. Bucks, ibid.

Probably again referred to as :

William de Gaston, co. Kent, 1273. A.
1757. Married —William Gaston and Sarah Gibbs: St. Geo. Han. Sq. i. 72.
London, 2 ; Philadelphia, 4.

Gatacre, Gateacre.—Local, 'of Gatacre,' an estate in co. Salop (v. Lower's Patr. Brit. p. 125). The surname still clings to that county.

John de Gatacre, co. Salop, 1273. A.
Stephen de Gatacre, co. Salop, ibid.
1660. Charles Gataker and Sarah Wharton : Marriage Lic. (Canterbury), ii. 48.
MDB. (Salop), 2, 0 ; London Court Dir., 0, 1.

Gatcliff, Gatliff, Gatecliff.—Local, ' of Catcliffe,' in the parish of Rotherham, co. Yorks. For Gatliff, cf. Topliff for Topcliff.

Adam de Catteclyf, 1379 : P. T. Yorks. p. 63.
1763. Married—Charles Gatecliffe and Eliz. Crofard : St. Geo. Han. Sq. i. 128.
London, 0, 1, 0 ; Manchester Dir., 3, 0, 0 ; West Rid. Court Dir., 0, 1, 1.

Gatcomb.—Local, ' of Gatcomb,' a parish three miles from Newport, Isle of Wight.

Matilda de Gatecumb, co. Sussex, 1273. A.
William de Gatecumbe, co. Bucks, 20 Edw. I. R.
1585-6. Henry Gatcombe and Alice Sweethable: Marriage Lic. (London), i. 147.
Boston (U.S.), 3.

Gate, Gates.—(1) Local,'at the gate' (v. Yates), from residence thereby.

John atte Gate : Close Roll, 16 Edw. III. pt. ii.
Silvester atte Gates, rector of Brinton, co. Norf., 1354 : FF. ix. 370.
Thomas de Gayte, 1379 : P. T. Yorks. p. 107.
Johannes atte Gate, 1379 : ibid. p. 244.
Robertus de Gate, 1379 : ibid. p. 288.
Custancia del Gates, 1379 : ibid. p. 49.

(2) Offic. ; O.F. waite, gaite, a guard, a watcher, a sentinel. Hence the Christmas waits. 'Wayte, a spye. Wayte, waker (i.e. watcher)': Prompt. Parv. Cf. 'lying in wait.'

Hugh le Geyt : co. Oxf., 1273. A.
Adam le Gayt. B.
Robert le Gait. M.
Johannes Gayte, 1379 : P. T. Yorks. p. 21.
London, 2, 11 ; Philadelphia, 0, 25.

Gatehouse, Gatus.—Local, 'at the gate-house,' of the monastery, church, &c. With Gatus, cf. Loftus or Bacchus, for Lofthouse and Backhouse.

Cf. John Fox, of Gatehouse, in Ellel, 1678 : Lanc. Wills at Richmond, p. 115.
1774. Married — George Allen and Margaret Gatehouse : St. Geo. Han. Sq. i. 246.
London, 3, 0.

Gater.—Occup. ; cognate with M.E. waitere, a watchman ; cf. Gate (2), and Wait and Wayte. Nothing to do with Gate-er, one who dwelt by a gate, as suggested by Mr. Lower (Patr. Brit. p. 126).

Michael le Geytere, co. Hunts, 1273. A.
1762. Married—John Gater and Mary Whalle : St. Geo. Han. Sq. i. 114.
1779. — Robert Barker and Mary Gater : ibid. 302.
London, 2.

Gath.—Local, 'at the garth,' a modification peculiar to co. York ; v. Garth.

Halifax, 3 ; Sheffield, 1 ; Philadelphia, 1.

Gathergood. — ? —. Probably a fontal name with god, gaud, or gold as suffix ; cf. Garbett, Thoroughgood, &c. Gathergood looks as if it were the opposite of Scattergood, which was undoubtedly a baptismal name.

MDB. (Norfolk), 5.

Gatley, Gately.—Local, ' of Gateley,' a parish in Norfolk, near Fakenham.

Johannes de Gaythele, 1379 : P. T. Yorks. p. 13.
Philadelphia, 4, 4.

Gatlin, Gatling.—Bapt. 'the son of Gertrude' (?). Clearly, from the instances given, the diminutive of some fontal-name. As Gertrude has given us the pet Gatty, so Gatelin would be the double dim. ; cf. Catelin for Kate, now Catlin and Catling (q.v.), an exactly analogous case. The surname crossed the Atlantic, and gave us there the Gatling-gun. It is quite possible that Gatlin or Gatling is Catlin or Catling ; cf. Cammel and Gammel.

Geoffrey Gatelin, co. Wilts, 1273. A.
Johanna Gatelyn, co. Wilts, ibid.
New York, 1, 2.

Gattey, Gatty, Gattie.—Bapt. 'the son of Gertrude,' from nick. Gatty. It is curious to note that the registrars of the 16th and 17th centuries found as much difficulty in spelling Gertrude as Ursula. The latter bothered them completely. I have seen it written Oursley twice. At first I could not understand it as a girl's name.

1618. Married—Henry Parkehurst and Gartwrite Wetherall, St. Antholin (London), p. 53.
Garthred Good, 1666 : Reg. Broad Chalke, co. Wilts.
Gartrude, wife of Marke Lawrie, 1698 : Reg. St. Columb Major, p. 245.
Deborah Gatty, widow, 1730 : ibid. p. 264.

William Gattey, 1728 : Reg. St. Columb Major, p. 263.
1782. Married — William Gattie and Ann Stead : St. Geo. Han. Sq. i. 339.
London, 2, 0, 1 ; Crockford, 0, 3, 0.

Gatton.—Local, ' of Gatton,' a parish in co. Surrey.

Hamo de Gattune, co. Kent, 1273. A.
Robert de Gatton, co. Sussex : Hen. III-Edw. I. K.
John de Gatton, co. Notts : ibid.
Alicia de Gatton, 1379 : P. T. Yorks. p. 142.
1591. Thomas Gill and Eliz. Gatton, co. Essex : Marriage Lic. (London), i. 195.
1669. Francis Gatton, co. Essex, and Susanna Smith : Marriage Alleg. (Canterbury), p. 173.

Gatward.—Occup. ' the gateward,' a porter, a keeper of the gate ; an official at a monastery, church, or hall. This surname still lives in the county in which it arose.

William le Gateward, co. Essex, 1273. A.
1778. Married — James Gatward and Mary Rudling : St. Geo. Han. Sq. i. 284.
MDB. (co. Essex), 4.

Gauger, Gager, Gaiger.—Offic. ' the gauger,' an inspector of casks, &c., from gauge or gage, to measure.

' Item, that all wines, red and white, which shall come unto the said realm shall be well and lawfully gauged by the King's gaugers, or their deputies ' (bien et loialment gaugez par le gaujeour le Roi, ou son depute) : Stat. of Realm, i. 331.
William Gauger : Close Roll, 15 Edw. III. pt. ii.
Alexander le Gauger. N.
Henry le Gaugeour. N.
Alan Gauger, c. 1300. M
Ulverston, 1, 0, 0 ; London (1887), 0, 1, 2 ; Philadelphia, 2, 1, 0.

Gaunt, Gant.—(1) Nick. ' the gaunt,' thin, slender ; cf. Bigg, Little, Thick, &c.

Hugh le Gant, co. Oxf., 1273. A.
John le Gant, co. Oxf., ibid.
Gilbert le Gaunt, co. Camb., ibid.
Robert le Gaunt, co. Linc., ibid.
Thomas le Gaunt, co. Soms., 1 Edw. III : Kirby's Quest, p. 104.

(2) Local, ' of Ghent.' Shakespeare has several puns on 'gaunt,' in which both interpretations are involved ; v. Gant.

Henry de Gaunt, co. Soms., 1273. A.
Maurice de Gaunt, co. Soms., ibid.
Simon le Gaunt, temp. 1300. M.
Willelmus Gaunte, 1379 : P. T. Yorks. p. 172.
Petrus de Gaunt. 1379 : ibid.
1538. Richard Good and Alice Gaunt : Marriage Lic. (London), i. 9.

1646. Bapt.—George, s. George Gaunt : St. Jas. Clerkenwell, i. 164.
1711. Married — Edward Loder and Eliz. Gant : St. Michael, Cornhill, p. 56.
London, 3, 4 ; Philadelphia, 2, 4.

Gauntlett ; v. Gantlett.

Gavelocker.—Occup. ' a maker of gaveloks,' i.e. spears or javelins.
' The term is still used in the North for an iron crow or lever ' (Halliwell).

Richard Gavelakere, co. Soms., 1 Edw. III : Kirby's Quest, p. 112.

Gawen, Gavin.—Bapt. ' the son of Gawen.' Sir Gawaine was the hero of the battle with the giant Rhyence :

' That Gawain with his olde curtesie.'
Chaucer, The Squire's Tale.

Miss Yonge says, ' His name, whether as Gawain or Gavin, was popular in England and Scotland in the Middle Ages ' (v. Hist. Christian Names, ii. 138-9). In North Lancashire Gawen was still a familiar font-name in the 17th century.

Goselena fil. Gawyne, co. Camb., 1273. A.
Peter Gowyn, 1379 : P. T. Yorks. p. 28.
Emma Gawyn, 1379 : ibid. p. 48.
1530-1. Gawin Carew and Anne Shelston : Marriage Lic. (London), i. 8.
1609-10. — William Gawin : St. Dionis Backchurch (London), p. 94.
Gaven Richardson, 1631 : QQQ. p. 155.
1653. Bapt. — Gawne Gilpin : Reg. Ulverston Ch. i. 127.
Gawen Lowther, of Harthwaite Bank, 1669 : Lancashire Wills at Richmond, p. 186.
1680-1. Buried—An, wife of Gawen Stephenson : ibid. p. 169.
1687. Bapt.—Christopher, son of Gawen Stephenson : ibid. p. 35.
1706. Bapt.—Susanna Maria, d. John Gawin : St. Jas. Clerkenwell, ii. 28.
1776. Married — Thomas Colly and Catherine Gaven : St. Geo. Han. Sq. i. 261.
London, 0, 2 ; Philadelphia, 0, 22.

Gawkroger, Gawkrodger.—Nick. ' awkward Roger.' A Yorkshire name that has ramified strongly, and is found in every local directory. 'Gawk, a simpleton' (Skeat). The adjective was in use early in Yorks. But I cannot find the surname in question in the Poll Tax, 1379.

Adam Gawke, 1379 : P. T. Yorks. p. 265.
Robertus Goukeman, 1379 : ibid. p. 246.

Thomas Goykeman, co. York, .c. 1460. W. 11.

An April fool is an April gowk in Yorkshire :

' On the first of April
Hunt the gowk another mile.'
Dawson's Hist. of Skipton, p. 375.

If the origin be as stated it is a curious instance of a surname, largely represented, arising out of some single forgotten incident ; cf. Prettijohn, Littlejohn.

Halifax Dir., 4, 1 ; West Rid. Court Dir., 7, 1 ; London (1887), 1, 2.

Gay, Gaye.—Nick. ' the gay,' the light-spirited ; cf. Jolly, Jolliff, Merry, &c.

Adam le Gay, co. Oxf., 1273. A.
Robert le Gay, co. Oxf., ibid.
William Gay, co. Soms., 1 Edw. III : Kirby's Quest, p. 127.
London, 27, 1.

Gaylard, Gaylord ; v. Gallard.

Gayler, Gaylor.—Offic. ; v. Galer.

Gayles ; v. Gales.

Gaynar, Gaynor, Gainer, Gayner, Gainor.—Bapt. ' the son of Gwenivere.' 'Gaynore, Queen Gweniver' (Halliwell). This origin seems indisputable. Yet I lack any further evidence. At the same time it must be recollected that all, or nearly all, of the other names of the Arthurian story are well represented in our modern directories.

London, 1, 1, 0, 0, 0 ; MDB. (co. Glouc.), 0, 0, 4, 4, 0 ; Philadelphia, 0, 10, 0, 2, 2.

Gayton.—Local, ' of Gayton' : (1) a township in co. Chester ; (2) a parish in co. Norfolk ; (3) a parish in co. Northampton ; (4) a parish in co. Stafford ; (5) two parishes in co. Lincoln ; v. Gatton.

Ralph de Gayton, co. Linc., 1273. A.
Richard de Gayton, ibid.
London, 5 ; Philadelphia, 1.

Gaywood.—Local, ' of Gaywood,' a parish in co. Norfolk, near Lynn Regis.

Robert de Geywode, London, 1273. A.
London, 1.

Gaze.—Bapt. ' the son of Gaze.' ' Mr. Ferguson refers it to an old German personal name Gaiso' (Lower). My first instance confirms this view.

Gazo de Calido Monte,co.York, 1273. A.
Nigel Gase, co. Linc., ibid.

But cf.

Andrew le Gays, co. Bedf., Hen. III-Edw. I. K.
London, 6 ; New York, 2.

Gear, Geare.—Local ; v. Gare.

Geary, Gery, Garry, Gerry.—Bapt. 'the son of Gerl.' A personal name as old as Domesday. Uxor Geri was a tenant-in-chief in co. Gloucester. Lower gives both Gery and Geri as Domesday forms. Both occur frequently in the Hundred Rolls.

Richard Jery, co. Hunts, 1273. A.
John Gery, co. Bedf., ibid.
Nicholas Gery, co. Hunts, ibid.
Dionise Geri, co. Oxf., ibid.
Walter Geri, co. Camb., ibid.
1521. Thomas Jary, vicar of Binham, co. Norf.: FF. ix. 212.
1645. Married — John Barnes and Dorithy Geary : St. Dionis Backchurch (London), p. 24.
1646. — John Gerey and Eliz. Sabin : St. Peter, Cornhill, i. 257.
1745. — John Corney and Eliz. Geary : St. Geo. Han. Sq. i. 36.
London, 14, 1, 0, 0 ; York, 0, 0, 2, 0 ; New York, 46, 1, 24, 7.

Geck, Gecke.—Nick.; an object of scorn, a simpleton. A.S. *geac*, a cuckoo, a silly fellow.

'The most notorious geck.'
Twelfth Night, v. 1.
'And to become the geck and scorn O' th' other's villany.'
Cymbeline, v. 4.
Gilbert Gekke, co. Oxf., 1273. A.
Henry le Gekke, ibid.
Henry le Geke, ibid.
London, 2, 0 ; Philadelphia, 2, 1.

Gedge, Giggs. — Local, ' of Gegges,' a spot seemingly in the parish of Filby, co. Norfolk. The surname is strictly a Norfolk one, and has existed there for many centuries.

'Matthew de Salle granted Gegges part in trust to William de Frisseby, rector of Filby, 1412, and Edmund Norman, son of John, died lord in 1444 ' : FF. xi. 218.
Isabel Gegges, co. Norf., 1402 : FF. xi. 218.
John Geggs, co. Norf., 10 Hen. VI: ibid. ix. 205.
Richard Geggh, co. Norf., 1448: ibid. ii. 234.

Richard Gegge, of Saham, co. Norf., 1367: ibid. 269.
Willelmus Gegge, 1370: P. T. Yorks. p. 61.
'Here resteth expectinge the second cominge of our Saviour Jesus Christ, the Body of Margaret Gedge, wife of Robert Gedge . . . buried the 24th of July, 1619. . . . Also John Gedge, father of the said Robert, was buried 24 Nov. 1621, aged 87' : FF. v. 415.

It is thus clear that Gegges or Giggs (it is also found in this latter form in the History of the county) became Gedge between 1450 and 1600. The form Geggh above (1448) seems to point to the departure.

London, 7, 1 ; MDB. (Norfolk), 9, 0.

Gedling.—Local, ' of Gedling,' a parish three miles and a half from Nottingham.

Hugh de Gedling, co. Notts, 1273. A.
1676. Married — Thomas Dove and Eliz. Gidling : St. Michael, Cornhill, p. 41.
London, 1.

Gedney.—Local ; v. Gidney.

Gee.—Local, ' of Gee,' now Gee Cross, a prosperous village in the parish of Stockport. That all our Gees hail from this spot admits of no doubt. The local registers teem with them. A glance at the index to Earwaker's East Cheshire will show that they had early spread themselves out into the surrounding country. The surname has ramified strongly.

Dicon Gee, Stockport Parish, 1494 : East Cheshire, ii. 10.
1562. Marriage — Thomas Gee and Anne Lowe : Reg. Prestbury, co. Ches., p. 8.
— Buried—John Gee : ibid. p. 9.

The name frequently occurs in the last-named register.

1590. Buried — Uxor Jo'his Gee de Godley Hall: Reg. Mottram in Longendale, co. Ches.
Manchester, 17 ; London, 23 ; Philadelphia, 19.

Geeves. — Bapt. ' the son of Geve.' No doubt a form of Geff, the nick. of Geoffrey. In the instances below Gyveson is now found as Jephson and Jepson, q.v. The latter is the Lancashire form. The Manchester Directory has eight Jepsons. The final *s* in Geeves is

genitive, as in Williams, Jones, Dickins, &c. ; v. Jeffs.

William fil. Geve, co. York, 1273. A.
Richard Geves, co. Oxf., ibid.
Thomas fil. Henry Gyveson : Preston Guild Rolls, p. 2.
Francis fil. Thome Gyveson, ibid. p. 6. London, 3.

Geffkins.—Bapt. ' the son of Geoffrey,' from the nick. Geff and dim. Geff-kin ; cf. Wilkins, Watkins, &c.

Mr. J. T. Geffkins, playing for Hampshire v. Sussex, at Brighton, July 22, 1889, made 8 runs: v. London Papers, July 23, 1889.

Gelbart.—Bapt. ; v. Gilbart.

Geldard, Geldart, Gelder, Gelderd, Geldert.—Occup. ' the geld-herd,' a herdsman (*geld* and *herd*). A great patronymic in South Cumberland and Furness. To this day cows and ewes are advertized as *geld* cows and *geld* ewes, i.e. not with young (v. Towneley Mysteries, p. 75). The geld-herd and cow-herd (v. Coward) have left two of the oldest and most strongly ramified names in the Lake District ; v. Herd for list of derivatives.

'Item. pro geldherdo, pro tripherdo' : v. Tripper : Whitaker's Craven, 1317, p. 465.

The editor adds, ' Geldherds are elsewhere called " pastores sterilium animalium," hence the modern surname Geldert.'

Petrus Geldhird, 1379 : P. T. Yorks. p. 238.
Ricardus Geldhird, ibid.
Ricardus Geldhyrd, ibid. p. 287.
Jenet Geldert, of Gleaston, 1595 : Lancashire Wills at Richmond, p. 122.
Anne Geldard, of Ulverston, 1641 : ibid.
George Geldart,of Ulverston, 1661 : ibid.
West Riding Court Dir., 2, 2, 7, 1, 1 ; New York (Gelder), 1, Boston (Geldert), 5.

Gelding.—Bapt. Another form of Golding or Goulding (v. Golden).

Geldanus de Twykeburgh, co. Devon. Hen. III-Edw. I. K.
Geldanus de Uppehill, co. Devon, ibid. London, 1.

Gell.—Bapt. ' the son of Gell.' A form of Gill (q.v.), the nick. of Juliana, or Gillian, as it was more familiarly known.

Gelle Winter, co. Camb., 1273. A.
Emma Gele, co. Suff., ibid.
Thomas Gele, 1379 : P. T. Yorks. p. 301. London, 2 ; New York, 2.

Gellatly.—Nick.; v. Golightly.

Gellion.—Bapt.; v. Gallon.

Gem, Gems, Gemson.—Bapt. 'the son of James,' popularly Jim and Jem, or Gem; cf. Jill and Gill. From the absence of pet forms of James it is probable that the 14th century only saw anything like a familiar use of this name. Indeed James was very rare — only a student of nomenclature knows how rare. James has bequeathed us few surnames. Its confusion with John through Jack has, no doubt, had much to do with this. The other leading Apostolic names have left rich legacies in our directories.

William fil. Gemme, co. York, 1318. M.
Richard fil. Gimme, co. Lanc., 20 Edw. III. R.
William fll. Gimme, ibid.
Robertus Gemson, 1379: P. T. Yorks. p. 160.
Hugo Gimme, 1379: ibid. p. 163.
Ricardus Gemme, 1379: ibid. p. 152.
Johannes Gemmys, 1379: ibid. p. 214.
Agnes Jemme, 1379: ibid. p. 150.
Thomas Gem, 1379: ibid. p. 15.

Cf. the dims. Gemmett and Jemmett:

1618. Andrew Weekes and Mary Gemmett: Marriage Lic. (London), ii. 61.
London, 1, 1, 1; Crockford, 3, 0, 0; Preston, 0, 0, 2; Boston (U.S.), 0, 2, 0.

Genet.—? Bapt. 'the son of Genet,' i.e. Janet or Jeannette; v. Jennett.

Janeta Barker, co. Camb., 1273. A.
'Item, Genett Bowman, 10s.' 'Item, Genett Pepper, 8s.' 1579. Wages paid by 'Dame Thomasyne ladye Thornburgh': Hist. Cumb. and Westm. (Nicolson and Burn), i. 119.
London, 2; New York, 6.

Genever.—Bapt. 'the son of Guinevere'; v. Jenifer.
Crockford, 1; Birmingham (1884), 1; New York, 1.

Genner.—Occup.; v. Jenner.
1634. Buried.—Ellen Barnet, servant to Mr. Gennere: St. Michael, Cornhill, p. 233.

The editor identifies the above as Mr. Arthur Jenner.

London, 1.

Gentilcorps; v. Handsomebody.

Gentilhomme.—Nick.'gentleman,'well-bred,polished; v. Gentleman.

Thomas Gentilhomme. H.

Gentle, Gentil, Jentle.—Nick. 'the gentle.' Originally one who was not a Christian; later, one of polished, well-bred manners, 'genteel.' Then, again, one of gentle, benign character.

William le Gentil, co. York, 1273. A.
Robert le Gentill, or Gentyl, co. Wilts, ibid.
John le Gentyl, co. Soms., 1 Edw. III: Kirby's Quest, p. 94.
William le Gentil: Patent Roll, 4 Edw. III. pt. ii.
Agnes Gentildoghter, 1379: P. T. Yorks. p. 24.
Johannes Gentill', 1379: ibid. p. 61.
Robertus Pedifer, *gentil'*, 1370: ibid. p. 277.
1555. Christning of Mathew Jentyll: St. Peter, Cornhill, i. 7.
London, 4, 1, 1; New York, 4, 2, 1.

Gentleman.—Nick.'thegentleman'; v. Gentle; cf. Fr. Gentilhomme, q.v.

Robert Gentilman, co. Bedf., 1273. A.
Nicholas Gentilman, co. Bedf., ibid.
Johannes Gentilman, 1379: P.T. Yorks. p. 243.
John Gentulman, C. R., 20 Ric. II. pt. i.
William Gentilman. V. 11.
1663. Samuel Gentleman and Sarah Hudson: Marriage Lic. (London), ii. 42.
1762. Married — John Gentleman and Mary Allin: St. Geo. Han. Sq. i. 108.
New York, 2; Boston (U.S.), 1.

Gentry.—? Local. I fail to discover any information about this name.
London, 11; Philadelphia, 12.

Geoffrey.—Bapt. 'the son of Geoffrey.' By a curious freak this name is scarcely ever found surnominally in this form; v. Jeffery, and cf. Gerard and Jerard. The harder form of Godfrey, however, retains the earlier initial. The name occurs in Domesday, and gradually forged its way to the forefront of frequency. No doubt Godfrey or Geoffrey of Lorraine, of crusading renown, had much to do with its West-European popularity. The forms (always with G) are endless in the Hundred Rolls.

John fil. Geffrei, co. Hunts, 1273. A.
Warin Geffrey, co. Camb., ibid.
Simon Geffray, co. Oxf., ibid.
Galfridus de la Grange, co. Bucks, ibid.
Galfridus fil. Galfridi, co. Oxf., ibid.

George, Georgeson. — Bapt.

'the son of George.' A somewhat rare name in early mediaeval records. Quite modern in popularity, in spite of the many Georges in the London Directory. The fuller patronymic Georgeson has always been excessively rare. St. George of England ought to have impressed his name more deeply upon our directories.

Georgius de Furnell, cos. Notts and Derby, Hen. III–Edw. I. K.
Robert Gorge, co. Oxf., 1273. A.
William Gorge, co. Camb., ibid.
Jeorgius Clericus, co. Linc., ibid.
Georgius Williamson, 1379: P. T. Yorks. p. 243.
1563. Buried—Georgeson (sic) servant to Mr. William Hall: St. Michael, Cornhill, p. 188.
1604. James Georgeson, of Speke: Wills at Chester (1545-1620), p. 71.
1623. Married—Samuell Wilkinson and Anne George: St. Peter, Cornhill, i. 188.
1624. William Mason and Dorothy Georgeson: Marriage Lic. (London), ii. 147.
London, 72, 0; Manchester (1887), 17, 1; New York, 38, 0.

Gerald.—Bapt. 'the son of Gerald'; v. Garrard.
London, 1.

Gerard, Gerrard; v. Garrard.
London, 5, 4; Oxford, 1, 0.

Gerish, Gerrish, Gerras, Gerres. — Nick. garish,' i. e. showy, resplendent, staring.
'And pay no worship to the garish sun.'
Romeo and Juliet, iii. 2.

The earliest instances of the surname are connected with co. Oxford.

William le Geriss, co. Oxf., 1273. A.
John le Gerisse, co. Oxf., ibid.
Umfrey le Gerische, co. Oxf., ibid.
Cristina Gerygge, co. Soms., 1 Edw. III
Kirby's Quest, p. 267.
1787. Married — William Sharpe and Letitia Gerrish: St. Geo. Han. Sq. p. 402.
London, 1, 2, 1, 1; New York, 1, 1, 0, 0; Boston (U.S.), Gerrish, 32.

German, Germon, Germain. —Bapt. 'the son of German.' No doubt a personal name taken or given from the country; cf. Norman. For one or two variants of the surname, v. Jarman.

Germanus de Hode, Hen. III–Edw. I: K. p. 178.
Johannes Germayne, co. Southampton, 1273. A.
Simon Germeyn, co. Oxf., ibid.
John Germyn, co. Northampt., 20 Edw. I. R.
Germanus Hay, co. York, ibid.

Germanus Benson, 1379: P. T. Yorks. p. 232.

Germanus Gardyner, 1379: ibid. p. 159.

1646. Bapt.—John, s. William and Jone German: St. Jas. Clerkenwell, i. 166.

1672. — John, s. William and Grace Jermane: ibid. p. 257.

London, 5, 0, 3; Crockford, 0, 4, 0; Philadelphia, 14, 0, 0.

Gerner.—Bapt. ; v. Garner.

Gerring.—Bapt. 'the son of Guarin.' The usual English form of which was Warren or Warin ; v. Wareing. The final g is an crescent, as in Jennings.

Geryn Burnel, co. Salop, Hen. III-Edw. I. K.

Richard Geryn, co. Camb., 1273. A. Hubert Gerin, co. Bedf., ibid.

Thomas Garyn, co. Camb.. ibid.

John Geryn, co. Kent, 20 Edw. I. R.

Constance Geryn, co. Soms., 1 Edw. III: Kirby's Quest, p. 115.

1745. Married — John Gerring and Martha Dounton: St. Geo. Han. Sq. i. 35.

Oxford, 1 ; Philadelphia, 2.

Gerrish.—Nick. ; v. Gerish.

Gervas, Gervis.—Bapt. 'the son of Gervase' ; v. Jarvis.

London (1887), 1, 2.

Gery.—Bapt. ; v. Geary.

Gethin, Gething, Getting, Gethen.—Bapt. 'the son of Gethin.' No doubt Welsh, and it is almost equally certain that Gittens is the same name with the genitival s suffixed. Hence probably a personal name ; v. Gittens. The final g in Gething is excrescent.

Ellis Gethin, co. Denbigh, matric. Oxford, 1578: Reg. Univ. Oxf. vol. ii. pt. ii. p. 83.

Maurice Gethin, co. Denbigh, matric. Oxford, 1578: ibid.

Roger Gethin, co. Salop, Bras. Coll., 1578: ibid. p. 81.

Humphrey Gethen, of Worthenbury, 1633: Wills at Chester (1621–50), p. 85.

Lilly Gethin, of Worthenbury, 1633: ibid.

1793. Married.—William Morgan and Margaret Gethyn: St. Geo. Han. Sq. ii. 96.

1798. — George Dryden and Eliz. Gethin: ibid. p. 184.

— — James Brechin and Alice Gething: ibid. p. 187.

London, 0, 3, 2, 0; MDB. (Glamorgan), 0, 3, 0, 0; (Montgomery), 1, 0, 0, 0 ; (co. Salop), 0, 0, 0, 1.

Geves, Geveson, Gyves, Jeeves.—Bapt. 'the son of Geve.' An early North-English form of

Geff, which has survived the wear and tear of time in a patronymic form. The nick. of Geoffrey, q.v. In this case Gyveson (infra) merely stands for Jephson.

William fil. Geve, co. York, 1273. A. Adam fil. Willfridd Gyveson : Preston Guild Rolls, p. 6.

Francis fil. Thome Gyveson: ibid. p. 7.

1610. Nicholas Geeves and Margaret Harbord: Marriage Lic. (Westminster), p. 19.

Leeds, 1, 0, 0, 2; West Riding Court Dir., 1, 0, 0, 41 Manchester, 0, 0, 1, 0; Boston (U.S.), Jeeves, 1.

Gibb, Gibbs, Gibbe, Gibbes, Gibson, Gibby.—Bapt. 'the son of Gilbert,' from nick. Gib ; v. Gilbert.

'How Gyb, good morne : wheder goys thou ?
The Nativity. Towneley Mysteries.

As Tib was the name for a female cat, so was Gib for a male, but the distinction was gradually forgotten:

'Now, master, as I am true wag,
I will be neither late, nor lag,
But go and come with gossips cheer,
Ere Gib, our cat, can lick her ear.'
Peele's Edward I.

'For right no more than Gibbe, our cat,
That awaiteth mice and rattes to killen.'
Rom. of Rose.

'For who that's but a queen, fair, sober, wise,
Would from a paddock, from a bat, a gib,
Such dear concernings hide?'
Hamlet, iii. 4.

Hence such opprobrious epithets as 'flibber-gib,' or 'flitter-gibbet,' found in Latimer, Burton, and, later, Walter Scott. Gib was also applied to a young gosling (v. Halliwell).

Adam Gibbe, 1311. M.

Perseval Gybson, co. York, W. 11.

Robert Gybbyson, co. York, ibid.

Johannes Gybbson, 1379: P. T. Yorks. p. 90.

Willelmus Gybson, 1379: ibid. p. 208.

Alicia Gybson, 1379: ibid. p. 144.

Cecilia Gib-wyf, 1379: ibid. p. 28.

Custancia Gibwyf, 1379: ibid. p. 111.

Thomas Gybbys. XX. 1.

Robert Gybbys. FF.

A notorious rascal named Gybby Selby is mentioned in the Calendar of State Papers for 1562.

Johannes Gyb, 1379: P. T. Yorks. p. 148.

Thomas Gyb-man (the servant of Gib), 1379: ibid.

London, 11, 84, 0, 1, 72, 0; Liverpool (1887), Gibby, 1 ; Boston (U.S.), Gibby, 3; Philadelphia, 21, 76, 0, 0, 228, 0.

Gibbard, Gibberd. — Bapt. 'the son of Gilbert' (q.v.), popularly Gibbert, Gibberd, or Gibbard. The first order of variation is found in the following entries :

Henry Gilbard, co. Norf., 1273. A.

John Gilbard, co. Norf., ibid.

John Gilbard, co. Camb., ibid.

William Gilberd, co. Glouc., 20 Edw. I. R.

The second variation was inevitable :

1720. Bapt.—Eliz., d. Timothy Gibbard : St. Jas. Clerkenwell, p. 190.

1778. Married. — John Gibbard and Ann Eedy : St. Geo. Han. Sq. p. 289.

London, 4, 1.

Gibbens, Gibbin, Gibbins, Gibbings.—Bapt. 'the son of Gilbert,' from nick. Gib, dim. Gibb-on or Gibb-in ; cf. Rob-in, Col-in, &c. The g in Gibbings is excrescent ; cf. Jennings ; v. Gibbon. Instances from a single register show some curious spellings :

1541. Bapt. — Ellen Gybbinnes : St. Peter, Cornhill, i. 2.

1544.— Joane Gibbynnes : ibid. p. 3.

1549. Buried—John Gybbens. ibid. p 109.

1617. Bapt.—Katherine Gybbins : ibid. p. 66.

London, 1, 1, 17, 7 ; New York, 2, 1, 5, 1 ; Philadelphia, 3, 0, 2, 0.

Gibbon, Gibbons, Gibbon-son.—Bapt. 'the son of Gilbert,' from nick. Gibb, dim. Gibb-on ; cf. Alison and Marion from Alice and Mary. 'Gybonn or Gylberde, propyr name, Gilbertus' : Prompt. Parv. It proves the great popularity of Gibbon that it should precede Gilbert in the glossary quoted ; v. Gilbert. Gybon Waller is a character in one of the Towneley Mysteries.

John Giboun, 1307. M.

Robert Gybbon, 1307. H.

Gibun de Mortemer, temp. Edw. II : GGG. p. 268.

Nicholas Gybonson, 1379: P. T. Yorks. p. 292.

Roger Gibonson, 1379: ibid. p. 158.

Robertus Gybonson, 1379: ibid. p. 248.

Gibon Otes, 1439: Rental of Halifax. Cotton MSS. Vespasian, F. 15, Brit. Mus.

John Gibbonson. F.

1597. Married—Nicholas Gibbons and Ellen Chambers: St. Mary Aldermary (London), p. 9.

John Gibbinson, 1579: Lancashire Wills at Richmond, p. 122.
Margaret Gibbonson, 1623: ibid.
London, 9, 38, 0; Philadelphia, 9, 73, 0.

Giblett. — Bapt. 'the son of Gilbert,' from nick. Gib, dim. Gib-elot; cf. Hewlett from Hew (Hugh); v. Gilbert.

Dera Gibelot, co. Camb., 1273. A.
John Gibbelote, co. York. W. 2.
Henry Gybelot, co. Soms., 1 Edw. III: Kirby's Quest, p. 206.
Matilda Giblot, 1579: P. T. Yorks. p. 144.
William Giblet, 1557: Reg. Univ. Oxf. i. 234.
1675. Married — William Giblet and Jone Cawdrey: St. Jas. Clerkenwell, iii. 182.
1766. — John Giblet and Eliz. Montagu: St. Geo. Han. Sq. i. 154.
London, 2; MDB. (co. Soms.), 9; New York, 1.

Giblin, Gibling. — Bapt. 'the son of Gilbert,' from nick. Gib, dim. Gib-liñ. The g is excrescent in Gibling; cf. Hewling for Hewlin, q.v. Although I find no early instances there can be no doubt about the origin of this name.

London, 2, 1; New York, 10, 0.

Gidden, Giddens, Giddings, Gittens, Gittins, Gittings. — Local, (1) 'of Gidding,' or (2) 'Gedding.' (1) A parish near Stilton, co. Hunts; (2) a parish near Stowmarket, co. Suffolk. The final s in Giddens and Giddings probably represents the ge and gge (pronounced like *hinge*) found in the entries below:

Nicholas de Gedding, co. Essex, Hen. III–Edw. I. K.
John de Geddingge, co. Suff., 1273. A.
Geoffrey de Geddinge. co. Suff., ibid.
Richard de Geddingge, co. Hunts, ibid.
Henry de Geddinge, co. Hunts, 20 Edw. I. R.
1666. Married — Peeter Clyne and Elliner Gittinges: St. Jas. Clerkenwell, iii. 146.

The preceding item is entered in the index as Giddings.

1702. Married — Richard Gunning and Mary Giddings: St. Dionis Backchurch, p. 51.
1744. Bapt. — James, son of John Gidden: St. Jas. Clerkenwell, ii. 270.
London, 1, 1, 2, 2, 4, 0; New York, 0, 1, 6, 1, 0, 1.

Giddy. — (1) Nick. 'the giddy.' (2) Local, 'of Gidde.'
Nicholas de Gidd, co. Hunts, 1273. A.

Ralph Gydye, co. Soms., 1 Edw. III: Kirby's Quest, p. 214.
John Gydye, co. Soms., 1 Edw. III: ibid.
London, 2.

Gideon. — Bapt. 'the son of Gideon.' But as I find no early instance it is perhaps of Jewish descent and later importation.
Robert Gideon, 1679: Reg. St. Mary Aldermary (London). p. 105.
London, 3; Philadelphia, 11.

Gidney, Gedney. — Local, 'of Gedney,' a parish near Wisbech, co. Lincoln. This surname has become corrupted to Kidney, q.v.
Hervey de Gedeney, co. Linc., 1273. A.
1689. Married — John Seayre and Dorcas Gedney: St. Michael, Cornhill, p. 46.
1751. Bapt. — Ann, d. Caleb Gedney: St. Jas. Clerkenwell, ii. 299.
London, 5, 0; MDB. (Norfolk), 0, 2; New York, 3, 19.

Giffard, Gifford. — Bapt. 'the son of Giffard.'
Giffard le Bretun, 1273. A.
Giffard Piscator, ibid.
Gyffard Reynold, co. Bucks, ibid.
Gifford Wyting, co. Soms., ibid.
Giffard de Lucerna, 20 Edw. I. R.
Johanna Juffard, 1379: P. T. Yorks. p. 54.
Johannes Juffard, 1379: ibid. p. 37.
Henry Giffard, co. Soms., 1 Edw. III: Kirby's Quest, p. 101.
London, 5, 14; New York, 0, 25.

Giffen, Giffin. — Bapt. 'the son of Geoffrey,' from the nick. Giff, and dim. Giff-on; cf. Alison, Marion, and Guyon, from Alice, Mary, and Guy. I have but one early instance, but it is a very satisfactory one; cf. Gifkins.
Willelmus Gyffon, 1379: P. T. Yorks. p. 180.
1640. Buried — Grace Giffen, kild by a fall: St. Mary Aldermary (London), p. 171.
London, 1, 2; New York, 2, 8.

Gifkins. — Bapt. 'the son of Geoffrey,' from nick. Giff, with suffix -kin, as in Watkin, Wilkin, &c.; cf. Jeffkins. The Standard, Jan. 27, 1887. says, concerning a town's meeting at Chatham to commemorate the Queen's Jubilee, 'It was influentially attended, and was presided over by the High Constable, Mr. H. J. Gifkins.'
Robertus Gyffe, 1379: P. T. Yorks. p. 156.

Gigger. — Occup; v. Jigger.

Giggler. — ? Nick. 'the giggler (?).' But perhaps a form of Juggler.
Robert le Gigelere, co. Camb., 1273. A.

Gilbart, Gelbart. — Bapt. 'the son of Gilbert' (q.v.); cf. Robart for Robert, or Hubbard for Hubert.
London, 2, 0; Oxford, 0, 1.

Gilbert, Gilbertson. — Bapt. 'the son of Gilbert'; Old Frank Giselbert. That at least twenty surnames, more or less familiar, are founded upon 'Gilbert,' need cause little surprise. It seemed to exercise a fascination over our ancestors. The Gilbertines were an English order, founded in the 12th century by St. Gilbert, who was born at Sempringham, co. Lincoln. There were numerous convents of this order at the time of the suppression. The name was naturally popular. The nick. was Gib, the chief dim. 'on'; hence Gibbon. The different corruptions of Gibbon are given in their place. Diminutives in 'let' and 'ling' give us our Gibletts and Giblings (Lond. Dir.). Gilpin was formed from Gilb-in (v. Gilpin), and was peculiar to the North of England.
Isolda fil. Gilberti, 1273. A.
Robert Gilbertus, ibid.
Eustace fil. Gilebert, ibid.
Nicholas Gilberdson, 1379: P. T. Howdenshire, p. 31.
Johannes Gilberd, 1379: P. T. Yorks. p. 1.
London, 75, 3; Philadelphia, 192, 1; New York (Gilbertson), 4.

Gilby, Gilbee, Gilbey, Gillbee, Gillbey. — (1) Local, 'of Gilby,' a hamlet in the parish of Pilham, co. Lincoln. (2) Local, 'of Kilby,' a parish in co. Leicester, six miles from Leicester. It seems certain that this is one solution: v. Kilbey. (3) Bapt. 'the son of Gilbert,' from the pet Gilbie; cf. Charley, Teddie, &c. The following entry confirms this strongly:
John Gilbeson, co. Soms., 1 Edw. III: Kirby's Quest, p. 142.
1571. Richard Gilbye, or Kelby, co. Linc.: Reg. Univ. Oxf. vol. ii. pt. ii. p. 51.
1619. Robert Kilbie,co. Leic.,ibid.p.374.
1794. Married — John Gilby and Mary Jecklins: St. Geo. Han. Sq. ii. 121.

London, 8, 0, 3, 1, 1 ; West Rid. Court Dir., 0, 1, 0, 0, 0 ; New York (Gilby), 1.

Gilder.—Occup. 'the gilder.'

Ralph le Gelder. X.
London, 3 ; Oxford, 4 ; New York, 4.

Gildersleve, Gildersleeve, Gildeslieve. — Nick. 'with sleeves braided with gold.' M.E. *gilden*, A.S. *gyldan*, to gild. Gilder is a corruption of Gilden, as the instances below will show. It is curious that the name should still survive. The surname arose in co. Norfolk.

Roger Gyldenesleve, co. Norf., 1273. A.
John Gildensleve, Fellow of College of the Holy Cross, Atteburgh, co. Norf., 1421: FF. i. 540.
Robert Gyldensleve, C. R., 15 Hen. VI.
John Gildensleve, rector of Little Cressingham, co. Norf., 1588: FF. vi. 111.

In the form of Gildersleeve this surname has reached the United States. The American Journal of Philology was edited, 1880–4, by Basil L. Gildersleeve (v. Quaritch's Catalogue, No. 80, p. 8). The large list of Gildersleeves in the New York Directory seems to point to an early settlement in the new country.

London, 2, 0, 0 ; New York, 0, 28, 1.

Gildhouse. — Local, 'at the gild-house,' the same as Gild-hall, the place where the trade or craft-gild met.

'Wel semed eche of hem a fayre burgeis,
To sitten in a gild halle on the deis.'
Chaucer, C. T. 372.
William de Gildhous, Close Roll, 18 Edw. III. pt. i. (v. Green, Hist. Eng. People, i. 222).
George Gildus, of Maghull, 1638: Wills at Chester (1621–50), p. 85.
Richard Gildus, of Maghull, 1638: ibid.

With the above cf. Loftus and Saltus for Lofthouse and Salt-house.

Giles.—Bapt. 'the son of Giles,' a curious familiar form for Egidius. It is very difficult to find a Giles in the 13th and 14th centuries registers, as it is all but invariably entered Egidius. Whether or no Giles was originally a contraction of Egidius, or a substitute for it, it is hard to say. The two seem to have nothing in common. I cannot but think that as Gill was

familiar for Julia, so Giles at first represented Julius (v. Yonge, i. 188, for an interesting paragraph on the subject). We must remember that exactly the same accident has befallen Jack as representing John, as it does in England, yet, more correctly, James.

Egidius, or Gilius Gowsell, co. Linc., 1273. A.
Jordan fil. Egidii, co. Linc., ibid.
Osbert fil. Egidii, co. Linc., ibid.
1564. Married — Nicholas Giles and Christian Newell : St Mary Aldermary, p. 4.
1576. — Edwarde Giles and Agnes Herne : ibid. p. 6.
London, 56 ; New York, 25.

Gilkins, Gilkes, Gilks, Gilkin.—Bapt. 'the son of William' or 'Guillaume,' from the nick. Gill, and dim. Gil-kin. Possibly from Gill or Jill (v. Gill), but *-kin* was rarely added to girls' names, Malkin (Mary) being almost the only exception. Gilkes and Gilks are modifications of Gilkins, just as Perkes and Perks are of Perkins, or Dawkes and Dawks of Dawkins. And further, just as Guillaume gave us Gilkin, so William gave us Wilkin ; and similarly, just as William gave us Wilcock, so Gilcock once represented Guillaume.

Cecilia Gilkoc, co. Hunts, 1273. A.
Gilkinus de Braban, 25 Edw. I : Freemen of York (Surt. Soc.), i. 6.
1753. Married — Samuel Watters and Eleanor Gilks : St. Geo. Chap. Mayfair, p. 247.
London, 0, 3, 4, 0 ; New York (Gilkin), 1.

Gill.—(1) Bapt. 'the son of Gill.' Either Gill, nick. of William (Guillaume), or Gill or Jill, the nick. of Juliana. Both were in use for a time, but the latter finally ruled supreme, and Will quickly became the nick. of the other ; v. Gillson.

Richard fil. Gille, co. Camb., 1273. A.
Gille Hulle, co. Camb., ibid.
Roger Gille, co. Oxf., ibid.
Magota Gil-doghter, 1379 : P. T. Yorks. p. 209.
Elizabethe Gylle-doghter, 1379 : ibid. p. 261.
Robert Gille, 1379 : ibid. p. 11.

(2) Local, 'at the gill' or 'ghyll,' a deep glen or ravine.

Johannes del Gill, 1379 : P. T. Yorks. p. 295.
Magota del Gylle, 1379 : ibid. p. 212.

1609. Married — John Gill and Eliz. Norman : St. Mary Aldermary (London), p. 11.
London, 73 ; Philadelphia, 132.

Gillam, Gilliam, Gillham.—Bapt. 'the son of William,' an early form of Guillaume.

Petrus Gillam, 1379 : P. T. Yorks. p. 10.
Willelmus Giliam, 1379 : ibid. p. 267.
Giliaum Spyser, 1379 : ibid. p. 89.
Ricardus Gillumman, i.e. the servant of Gillum : ibid. p. 258.
Gillam Treasorer, C. R., 1–2 Philip and Mary, pt. iv.

For modern instances, v. Gillham.

Manchester, (1887), 2, 0, 0 ; London (1887), 5, 1, 8 ; Philadelphia, 11, 7, 2 ; New York, 0, 9, 3.

Gillard.—Nick. ; v. Gallard.

Gillbanks, Gilbanks.—Local, 'of Gillbanks.' There is a hamlet in co. Cumb. so called, but every village near a *gill* has its gill-banks. I had one in my old parish of Ulverston. Of course, the surname is North English.

1788. Married — Isaac Gillbanks, of Kirkby Ireleth, and Isabella Newby, of Ulverston : St. Mary, Ulverston, ii. 432.
West Rid. Court Dir., 0, 1 ; London, 2, 0 ; Liverpool, 3, 0.

Gillbard.—Bapt. 'the son of Gilbert' (q.v.) ; v. Gibbard.

Henry Gilbard, co. Norf., 1273. A.
John Gilbard, co. Norf., ibid.
William Gilberd, co. Wilts, ibid.
Launceston, 2.

Gillett ; v. Gillott.

Gillham, Gilliam, Gillam, Gilliams. — Bapt. 'the son of William' ; v. Gwilliam or Gwillim. Although Gillham looks local, there is no reason for doubting its connexion with William. For earlier instances, v. Gillam.

1605. Bapt. — William, s. Richard Gyllam : St. Jas. Clerkenwell, p. 46.
1773. Married — Samuel Gillham and Martha Allen : St. Geo. Han. Sq. i. 227.
1770. — John Gilliam and Ann Turner : ibid. p. 301.
London, 3, 2, 2, 0 ; New York, 3, 0, 0, 0 ; Philadelphia, 2, 7, 10, 6.

Gillibrand, Gellibrand. — Local, 'of Gelybrand.' Although settled in England at an early period, this seems to be a Scotch surname. It has a firm footing in

Lancashire. Preston was its first centre.

Henry Gilibrond, 1313. M.
John Gilibrond, 1313. M.
Laurence de Gelybrand, or Jelibrand, 1360: The Exchequer Rolls of Scotland, ii. 52.
Richard Gelybrond, *shereman*, 1562: Preston Guild Rolls, p. 30.
1577. Married—John Smyth and Margery Gellybrand: St. Jas. Clerkenwell, i. 7.
Jacobus Gilibrond, 1602: ibid. p. 62.
James Gellibrand, of Preston, *feltmaker*, 1615: Lancashire Wills at Richmond, p. 122.
Ellen Gillibrand, of Blackburn, 1617: Wills at Chester (1545-1670), pp. 72, 111.
Isabella Jollibrand, of Lathom, 1610: ibid. p. 14.
Hugh Jollibrand, of Lathom, 1608: ibid.
London, o, 1; Manchester, 5, 0; Blackburn, 4, 0; Chorley (Lanc.), 2, 0; Preston, 1, 0; Philadelphia, 2, 0.

Gilling, Gillings, Jillings.—Local, 'of Gilling.' There are two Gillings, both townships, in co. York, one near Richmond, the other near Helmsley. But the instances below suggest localities further south. As in several other cases of local names ending in *-ing*, the *g* being sometimes pronounced soft (as in *singe*) has caused Gilling to become Gillings; cf. Billinge or Billings for Billing.

Adam de Gilling, co. Kent, 1273. A.
Simon Gilling, co. Camb., ibid.
Seer de Gilling, co. Hunts, ibid.
Thomas Gillyng, co. Soms., 1 Edw. III : Kirby's Quest, p. 148.
Thomas de Gillyng, co. Salop, 20 Edw. I. R.

But I find a Yorkshire instance:

Robert de Gillyng, 13 Edw. I : Freemen of York, i. 4.
1609. Married—Edward Lawman and Mary Gillinge: St. Jas. Clerkenwell, iii. 35.
1698. — William Taylor and Ann Gilling: St. Antholin (London), p. 112.
London, 1, 3, 2; Boston (U.S.), 1, 1, 0.

Gillingham.—Local, 'of Gillingham': (1) a parish in co. Norfolk, near Beccles; (2) a parish in co. Dorset, near Shaftesbury; (3) a parish in co. Kent, near Chatham.

Gild' de Gillingham, co. Dorset, 1273. A.
Robert de Gyllingham, co. Norf., ibid.
Hugh de Gillingham, co. Kent, 20 Edw. I. R.
Robert de Gillingham, co. Norf., ibid.
Richard de Gillingham, co. Soms., 1 Edw. III : Kirby's Quest, p. 215.
1771. Married—William Lawrance and

Betty Gillingham: St. Geo. Han. Sq. i. 214.
London, 4; Philadelphia, 56; Boston (U.S.), 4.

Gillman; v. Gilman.

Gillon. — Bapt. 'the son of Giles,' from the dim. Gillon; cf. Mari-on, Gibb-on, &c. Cf. the many references to Egidius (Giles) de Argentein and Gilon de Argentein in the Hundred Rolls, where it is evident the allusions are to one and the same person.

London, 1; New York, 16.

Gillott, Gillett.—It is important to observe at the outset that these two well-established surnames have two distinct origins, one masculine, the other feminine, both of the baptismal or personal class. I will deal with the masculine first. (1) Bapt. 'the son of William,' from the N.Fr. Guille (English Will), and dim. Guill-ot (English Willott or Willett). This made only a slight impression on English nomenclature, the desire to keep it distinct from Gilot, the nick. and dim. of Juliana (v. Gillott, 2), causing Williamot, shortened to Wilmot, to predominate. In France the *double* diminutive Guillotin will be for ever remembered as the surname of the doctor who invented the murderous instrument that bears his name; cf. Gillotyn Hansake, 20 Hen. VI: Wars of English in France, Henry VI, vol. ii. p. 531.

In the Hundred Rolls we find Gilcock for Wilcock. I proceed to furnish a few instances of the masculine use:

Gwillotus Clerk. C.
Guillot le Balister. E.
Gilot le Heanberger, London. X.
Guillot des Robes, Wardrobe Roll, 4 Edw. III.
Gelot Webester et Johanna uxor ejus, 1379: P. T. Yorks. p. 50.
Johannes Gillotson: ibid. p. 227.

(2) Bapt. 'the son of Juliana,' popularly Gilliam, nick. Jill or Gill, dim. Gillot.

'*Husband.*   Alle the day long
Thus it fell to my lott, Gylle, I had sich grace.
Wife. It were a fowlle blott to be hanged for the case.

Husband. I have skapyd, Jelott, oft as hard a glase.'
Towneley Mysteries, p. 106.

This quotation disposes of all doubts on the subject, did they exist. Oddly enough, it gives the initial G in one case and J in the other. In one of the old metrical sermons it is said :

'Robin will Gilot
Leden to the nale,
And sitten there togedres
And tellen ther tale.'
See my English Surnames, 3rd edit. p. 74.

It was through the inconstancy of Gilot we got our dictionary word *jilt*. I now proceed to furnish instances of the feminine use :

Thomas Taylour et Gillot uxor ejus, 1379: P. T. Yorks. p. 120.
Robertus Lyster et Gillot' uxor ejus, 1379: ibid. p. 125.
Gillote Fox, 1379: ibid.
Johannes G'lotson, 1379: ibid. p. 91.
Willelmus Gilliote, 1379: ibid. 156.
Johannes Undyrhyll et Gyllot' uxor ejus, 1372: ibid. p. 125.
Willelmus Geliot, 1379: ibid. p. 262.
Johannes Gylyott', 1379: ibid. p. 218.

These will suffice.

London, 5, 30; Philadelphia, 8, 2.

Gillow.—Bapt. 'the son of Gillow'; no doubt the same as Gillott (1), q.v. Another attempt to distinguish the masculine Gillot from the feminine Gillot or Gilot. The name passed over the borders of Yorkshire into Lancashire.

Gilow serviens (i.e. the servant of) Johannis, 1379: P. T. Yorks. p. 154.
Gylaw et Agnes uxor ejus, 1379: ibid. p. 89.
Willelmus Gyllow, 1379: ibid. p. 140.
Ricardus Gillowe, 1379: ibid. p. 14.
Willelmus Gylowe, 1379: ibid. p. 256.
1662. Richard Gillow, of Brining: Lancashire Wills at Richmond, i. 124.
1664. Richard Gillow, of Winmerley: ibid.
1729. Thomas Gillow, of Winmarleigh : ibid. ii. 114.
London, 1; Lancaster, 1.

Gillsland, Gilleland.—Local, 'of Gilsland,' co. Northumberland.

Johanna Gillesland, 1379: P. T. Yorks. p. 183.
1614. John Leveridge and Rosamund Guilsland : Marriage Lic. (London), ii. 26.
Philadelphia, 6, 1.

Gillson, Gillison, Gilson.—Bapt. 'the son of Juliana,' from the nick. Gill or Jill. Occasionally it may mean 'the son of Giles,' but there is little evidence. The proofs in favour of Jill are conclusive; v. Gill (1) and Gillott (2).

Alan fil. Gille, co. Linc., 1273. A.
William fil. Gille, co. Linc., ibid.
John Gille, London, ibid.
Johannes Gilleson, 1379: P.T.Yorks. p.8.
Johannes Gilson, 1379: ibid. p. 13.
Hugo Gilleson, 1379: ibid. p. 49.
Johannes Gilleson, 1379: ibid. p. 69.
Johannes Gylesson, 1379: ibid. p. 270.
1687. Married — Thomas Gilson and Mary Cittle: St. Michael, Cornhill, p. 45.
London, 1, 0, 11; Philadelphia, 0, 0, 17; Boston (U.S.), Cillison, 1.

Gilman, Gillman. — Bapt. 'the son of Gilmyn.' Through French Guillaume we at length attained William. In the meanwhile the Low Countries brought us Gillemin or Willemin, which we finally retained with the G prefix.

John Wylemin, co. Bucks, 1273. A.
William Wylemyn, co. Camb., ibid.
John Wylemyn, London, ibid.
Anketius fil. Gilmyn, co. Camb., ibid.
Walter Gilmin, co. Oxf., ibid.
John Gylemyn, co. Bucks, ibid.
Gylemyn Coc', co. Kent, ibid.
Richard Gilemyn, 1311. M.
Cristopher Gylemyn, co. Soms., 1 Edw. III: Kirby's Quest, p. 212.
Waldeof fil. Gilmyn: E. and F., co. Cumb., p. 41.
Gilmyn serviens Rogeri Fulbaron, 1379: P.T. Yorks. p. 231.
Johannes Gylmyne, 1379: ibid.
1546. John Carter and Gylmen Haverd: Marriage Lic. (Faculty Office), p. 8.
London, 3, 4; Philadelphia, 14, 2.

Gilmichael. — Bapt. 'the son of Gilliemichael.' 'Gillmichael was common, and turned into Gilmichel. The influence of the great Keltic mission at Lindisfarn, on the north of England, is visible as late as the Norman Conquest, for Domesday Book shows four northern proprietors, called respectively Ghilemicel, Ghilander, Ghillepetair, and Ghilebrid' (Yonge, ii. 115); cf. Malcolm.

Cillemighel Adam, co. Lanc., Hen. III-Edw. 1. K.
Gilimghal de Merton, 21 Richard II: Furness Coucher Book, i. 188.

Gilmore, Gilmour, Gillmor, Gillmore. — (1) Local, 'of Gillmoor,' a hamlet in the parish of Bishop Thornton, co. Yorks. (2) Bapt. 'the son of Gilmoir,' Scotch (Gilmory or Gilmoir, 'servant of

Mary': Yonge, ii. 115); cf. Gilmichael.

Gilamor fil. Gilandi, c. 1100: E. and F., co. Cumb., p. 143.
Gilamor, 'his cousin,' ibid.
London, 2, 7, 0, 0; West Riding Court Dir., 0, 1, 1, 0; Crockford, 3, 0, 2, 2; Philadelphia, 66, 32, 0, 4.

Gilpin. — Bapt. 'the son of Gilbert' (?), from the dim. Gilb-in; cf. Gibb-on, Mari-on, &c. Gilpin is a well-known patronymic in Furness and Westmoreland. Edwin Gilpin of Kentmere was father of Bernard Gilpin, the Apostle of the North, born in 1517. The solution seems satisfactory. Rob-ert, Lamb-ert, and Gilb-ert took the pet forms of Rob-in, Lamb-in, and Gilb-in. The two latter, by a natural law, have become Lampin and Gilpin.

Gilbert Gylpin. H.
1548. Married — Henry Fones and Alyce Gylpyn: St. Michael, Cornhill, p. 5.
Richard Gillpin, of Aldingham, 1614: Lancashire Wills at Richmond, p. 124.
Roger Gilping, of Littledalle, 1666: ibid.

A curious corruption of Gilpin occurs in the following entry:

1689. Married — Phillip Hartley and Ann Giltpenn: St. Jas. Clerkenwell, p. 205.
London, 1; West Riding Court Dir., 2; Ulverston, 1; Philadelphia, 30.

Gilyard. — Nick.; v. Gallard.

West Riding Court Dir., 1.

Gimingham. — Local, 'of Gimingham,' a parish near North Walsham, co. Norfolk.

John de Gymingham, co. Norf., 1273. A.
Reyner de Gymingham, co. Norf., ibid.
London, 1.

Gimson. — Bapt. 'the son of Jim'; v. Gem.

London, 2; MDB. (co. Camb.), 3.

Gingell. — Local, 'of Gingdale,' some spot in co. Wilts or Gloucester. I have not identified the place, but Gingell is thus originated. The surname is still closely connected with the district in which it arose. As Charles Dickens got Pickwick from the neighbourhood of Bath, it is possible that Alfred Jingle came from the same quarter.

Michael de Gingedale, co. Wilts, 1273. A.
1762. Married — Richard Saltunstall

and Betty Gingell: St. Geo. Han. Sq. i. 114.
London, 2; MDB. (co. Glouc.), 5; (Wilts), 1.

Ginger. — Nick. Probably in allusion to the occupation of the bearer, a spicer; cf. Pepper, Mustard, Peascod, Freshherring, &c. Richard Peppercorn was a spicer, 1379; v. Peppercorn. It may have reference, of course, to some moral characteristic. M.E. gingivere, O.F. gengibre.

Godfrey Gyngivre, 1313. M.
Agnes Gyngyvere, London. X.
London, 0; New York, 1.

Gipp, Gipps, Gipson, Gypson. — Bapt. 'the son of Gilbert,' from nick. Gibb, sharpened to Gipp; cf. Hopps for Hobbs, or Hopson for Hobson; v. Gibb and Gilbert. While this appears to be the natural solution, it must not be forgotten that Geoffrey gave us Jephson, that its early nick. was Gef, and that Gep may have been another nick. familiar to the period.

Johannes Gepson, 1379: P. T. Yorks. p. 7.
Johannes Gepson, 1379: ibid. p. 64.
Robertus Jepson, 1379: p. 109.
Thomas Gepson, 1379: p. 115.
Cf. Alicia Geppe-dohter, 1397: ibid. p. 237.
Agnes Gef-doghter, 1379: ibid. p. 27.
Alicia Gef-doghter, 1379: ibid. p. 124.
Alicia Gefray-wyf, 1379: ibid.

The last two are entered together, evidently mother and daughter.

London Court Dir., 0, 1, 0, 0; Philadelphia, 2, 0, 1, 0.

Girardot. — Bapt. 'the son of Gerard,' dim. Girard-ot. A French name, an immigration. Lower says it came in after the revocation of the Edict of Nantes.

London, 1; Crockford, 1; New York, 1.

Girdler. — Occup. 'the girdler,' a maker of waistbands or belts. A girdler's gild seems to have existed in all the larger towns. The 'girdellers' formed part of the procession (1415) in the York Pageant. At Norwich, in 1533, they walked with the coverlet-weavers and darnick-weavers (Blomefield, Norfolk, ii. 148); at Chester, with the poynters, card-makers, and hatters (Ormerod's

Cheshire, i. 300). Cocke Lorelle's Bote includes 'gyrdelers, forborers, and webbers.'

Adam le Gurdlere, co. Bucks, 1273. A.
Geoffrey le Gurdler, co. Bucks, ibid.
William Gurdeler, co. Oxf., ibid.
Ralph le Gurdeler, Close Roll, 35 Edw. I.
Robert le Girdlere, c. 1300. M.
Gilbert le Haxby, *girdeler*, 21 Edw. I : Freemen of York, i. 5.
Henricus Girdelar, 1379 : P. T. Yorks. p. 159.
London, 3 ; Philadelphia, 1 ; Boston (U.S.), 2.

Girdlestone.—Local, 'of Gridleston,' some spot seemingly in co. Somerset. In fact this is all but certain, as Gridel and Grideliston occur together in a roll of that county.

Robert Gridel, co. Soms., 1 Edw. III : Kirby's Quest, p. 177.
Geoffrey de Grideliston, co. Soms., ibid.

Thus the meaning of the surname is 'the town (i.e. farm) of Gridel'; v. Town.

1698-9. Married — Henry Gurdelston (co. Norf.), and Joannah Busbey : St. Dionis Backchurch (London), p. 47.
London, 4 ; Crockford, 4.

Gisborne, Gisbourne, Gisburn, Gisborn.—Local, 'of Gisburne,' a parish seven miles from Clitheroe, co. York.

Thomas de Gysburn, 1379 : P. T. Yorks. p. 285.
Willelmus de Gisburn,1397: ibid. p. 272.
London, 3, 2, 0, 0 ; West Rid. Court Dir., 0, 0, 3, 0 ; Liverpool, 1, 0, 0, 0 ; Philadelphia (Gisborn), 1.

Gishard.—Occup. 'the gooseherd'; v. Gozzard.

Giskin.—Bapt. Probably Flemish.

Gyskynde la Chambre, Patent Roll, 17 Ric. II. pt. ii.

Gislingham.—Local, 'of Gislingham,' a parish in co. Suffolk, five miles from Eye. The spellings are many and curious in early registers. I have selected the more remarkable.

Robert de Gyssislyngham, co. Norf., 1273. A.
William de Giselingham, co. Suff., ibid.
William de Gyselyngham, co. Kent, 20 Edw. I. R.
1770. Married—George Fain and Ann Gislinham : St. Geo. Han. Sq. i. 198.
London, 1.

Gissing.—Local, 'of Gissing,' a parish in co. Norfolk, four miles from Diss.

Adam de Gissing, co. Norf., 1273. A.
Stephen de Gissinge, co. Norf., ibid.
London, 3.

Gittens, Gittins.—(1) Bapt. 'the son of Gethin' (?), a Welsh name ; v. Gethin. I have no absolute proof of the above derivation, but as Gethin and Gittens with their variants run side by side in Wales and the English border counties, there can be little doubt as to the reasonableness of the idea. (2) Local ; v. Gidden. This does not concern the Welsh surname with its variants. The following proves that Gethin was pronounced Gittin :

Richard Gittin, of Malpas, 1603 : Wills at Chester (1545-1620), p. 72.

The following was evidently a Welsh marriage :

1629. John Pughe and Eliz. Gittins : Marriage Lic. (London), ii. 195.
Jane Gittens, of Lea, 1672 : Wills at Chester (1621-80), p. 104.

Thus Gethin or Gittin is to Gittins or Gittens as Evan is to Evans, or William to Williams.

London, 2, 4 ; MDB. (Salop), 4, 6 ; (Flintshire), 0, 1 ; (Denbigh), 0, 1 ; (Radnor), 0, 1 ; New York, 1, 0.

Gladding, Glading. — Bapt. 'the son of Gladwin,' modified to Gladding. The *g* is excrescent (v. Gladwin) ; cf. Golding for Goldwin, and probably Harding for Hardwin.

London, 6, 1 ; Philadelphia, 1, 26 ; New York, 2, 0.

Gladman.—Bapt. 'the son of Gladman' ; cf. Gladwin. Probably a personal name ; cf. Bateman, Tiddiman, &c. The suffix *-man* seems rather an augmentative than a corruption of *-mond* or *-mund*, although Gladmond seems a natural solution. In any case it is almost certain that the name was personal at first, and was either Gladman or Gladmond.

1666. John Gladman and Eliz. Shepheard : Marriage Lic.(Westminster), p.43.
1747. Bapt.—Emila, d. William Gladman : St. Peter, Cornhill, ii. 44.
London, 4.

Gladstone, Gledstanes.—Lo-

cal, 'of the Gledstanes.' A Scotch surname. The final *s* was dropped in quite modern times. Probably the stones or rocks frequented by the gledes, or kites ; v. Glede.

William de Gledstanys, co. York. W. 1.
Johannes Gledstanis de Wynitonhaw, 1497 : TTT. p. xvi.
Andrew Gledstanis, 1497 : ibid.
1547. 'Item, to Thonne Gledstanis and Archebald Banker, quhilkes of befoir war payit to the xv day of July instante, etc., xxviiis' : TTT. p. lxxxiii.
Philp Gledstanis, 1541 : TTT. p. 211.
1668. George Gleadstone (York) and Mary Capper : Marriage Alleg. (Canterbury), p. 162.
London, 6, 1 ; New York, 2, 0.

Gladwin.—Bapt. 'the son of Gladwin,' one of the endless personal names with *-win* as suffix ; cf. Baldwin, Unwin, Godwin, &c.

Walter Gladewyne, co. Camb., 1273. A.
Roger Gladewine, co. Camb., ibid.
Radulphus fil. Gladewini. J.
1672. Bapt.—Katherine, d. William Gladwin : St. Mary Aldermary, p. 102.
London, 4 ; Oxford, 1 ; New York, 3.

Glaisher.—Occup. 'the glazier'; v. Glazer.

Emanewell Runwell, *glasher*, 1642 : Reg. St. Mary Aldermary (London), p. 88.
London, 2.

Glaister.—Occup. 'the glazier,' with termination in *ster*; cf. Slaster for Slater, Blaxter for Bleacher, &c.

London, 1 ; Manchester, 1 ; Bolton, 1 ; Boston (U.S.), 1.

Glaisyer.—Occup. 'the glazier'; v. Glazer.

West Rid. Court Dir., 1.

Glasbrook, Glassbrooke.—Local ; v. Glazebrook.

Oxford, 1, 1.

Glascock.—Local; v.Glasscock.

London, 1.

Glaser, Glasier.—Occup. 'the glazier'; v. Glazer.

London, 2, 1 ; New York, 24, 0.

Glasscock, Glasscott, Glascott.—Local, 'of Glascote.' A manifest corruption of Glascote, a township in the parish of Tamworth, co. Warwick. The Irish family of Glasscott claim extraction from the Glascocks of High Estre, co. Essex (Lower).

'To my father's, where Charles Glascocke was overjoyed to see how things are now' : Pepys' Diary, 1659, p. 11.

John Glasecok, C. R., 32 Hen. VI.
London, 3, 0, 0; New York (Glascott), 1.

Glasswright. — Occup. 'the glasswright,' a maker of glass. *Glasen* in the instances below is strictly the adj.; cf. gold-en, lin-en, wooll-en. The author of the History of Newcastle and Gateshead, curiously enough, describes one of his local worthies under date 1351 as Henry Glassen Wright (p. 138). Three names would have astonished the said Henry's contemporaries not a little.

Walterus Glassenwryght, 1379: P. T. Yorks. p. 51.
Robertus de Spalding, *glasenwryght*, 1379: ibid. p. 48.
Walter Glasenwryght. W. 15.
Nicholas le Glaswryght, London. X.
Thomas le Glaswryghte, London, ibid.

Glaysher.—Occup. 'the glazier'; v. Glazer; cf. Glaisher.

London, 3.

Glazebrook, Glassbrooke.—Local, 'of Glassbrock,' originally Glasenbrook, i.e. the stream with a glassy appearance. With the adjective *glasen*, cf. gold-en, lind-en (strictly the lind, or linden tree), &c.; see a similar instance under Glasswright.

Elena de Glasenbroke, 1379: P. T. Yorks. p. 263.
1675-6. Bapt.—Mary, d. Robert Glasebrooke: St. Dionis Backchurch, p. 121.
London, 8, 0; Liverpool (1887), 3, 0; Oxford, 0, 1.

Glazer, Glazier.—Occup. 'the glazier.' The different forms of this name in the London Directory are Glaisher, Glaser, Glasier, Glaysher, Glazer, and Glazier. Other surnames from the manufacture of glass are Glasswright (q.v.) and Glassman. The *i* in Glazier is equivalent to the *y* in Bowyer and Sawyer, and the *h* in Glaisher is the result of careless treatment of the extra syllable.

Adam Glasere, 1379: P. T. Yorks. p. 49.
Robert Glazier, temp. 1560. Z.
London, 1, 1; New York, 1, 1; Philadelphia, 0, 24.

Gleadowe.—Local, 'of Gledhow,' a hamlet two or three miles from Leeds; v. How (2) and Glede.

The meaning is 'the how frequented by kites.'

Allexander de Gledow, 1379: P. T. Yorks. p. 126.
Henricus de Gledehow, 1379: ibid. London, 1.

Glede, Glide, Glyde, Gleed. —Nick. 'the glede,' a species of kite. 'And the glede, and the kite, and the vulture after his kind': Deut. xiv. 13. A.S. *glida*, a kite.

John Glide, co. Camb., 1273. A.
Henry le Glide, c. 1300. M.
Adam le Glide, ibid.
Simon Glide. B.
William le Glede, C. R., 14 Edw. II.
William Glide, co. Soms., 1 Edw. III: Kirby's Quest, p. 151.
Symon Glede, 1379: P. T. Yorks. p. 67.
1632. Married—Thomas Milton and Mary Glide : St. Jas. Clerkenwell, iii. 64.
West Rid. Court Dir., 0, 0, 1, 0; London, 0, 0, 0, 1; MDB. (co. Soms.), 0, 0, 8, 0.

Gledhill, Gleadhill, Gledhall, Gleadall.—Local, 'of Gledhill,' a well-known Yorkshire surname. I have not identified the spot so termed. It will, I doubt not, be found in the West Riding. Probably it means 'the hill frequented by gledes'; v. Glede, and cf. Gladstone and Gleadowe.

Ricardus de Gledhill, 1379: P. T. Yorks. p. 185.
Thomas de Gledhill, 1379: ibid.
West Rid. Court Dir., 13, 2, 1, 2; London, 4, 0, 0, 0; New York, 3, 0, 0, 0.

Glendenning, Glendinning, Glendening, Glendining, Glindinning. — Local, 'of Glendinning,' an ancient estate at Westerkirk, co. Dumfries (Lower). This surname, with its variants, is steadily penetrating England, but I believe the immigration began in comparatively recent times.

Adam de Glendonwyn, 1286: The Debateable Land, by R. Bruce Armstrong, pp. 158-61.
Simon de Glendoning, 1398: ibid.
John de Glendonewyne, 1479: ibid.
1772. Married—Frederick Glendining and Rebecca Brown: St. Geo. Han. Sq. i. 222.
West Rid. Court Dir., 1, 5, 0, 0, 0; London, 0, 0, 1, 1, 0; Liverpool, 1, 2, 0, 0, 1; Philadelphia, 8, 2, 6, 0, 0.

Glenman.—?

John le Glenman, Rot. Fin., 7 Edw. I.

Glew.—Nick. 'one of joyous

disposition,' glee; M.E. *glee*, also *gleu* and *glew*: Havelok, 2332; A.S. *gleow*, *gliw* (v. Skeat and Halliwell).

Agnes Glewe, co. Hunts, 1273. A.
Roger Glewe, co. Hunts, ibid.
Johannes Glugh, 1379: P. T. Yorks. p. 66.
Thomas Glwe, 1379: ibid.
Ricardus Glew, 1379: ibid. p. 35.
London, 3; Leeds, 1; New York, 2.

Glitheroe.—Local, 'of Clitheroe,' co. Lanc.; v. Clithero.

Liverpool, 1.

Glossop, Glassup.—Local, 'of Glossop,' a parish in the High Peak of Derbyshire, on the Lanc. border.

1605. Married—John Sumner and Ann Glossop: Reg. Prestbury, Ches., p. 172.
1682. Clifford Glossopp, de Hatton Carden, London : Preston Guild Rolls, p. 186.
1768. Married — Simeon Smith and Ann Glassap: St. Geo. Han. Sq. i. 173.
London, 2, 0; Manchester, 3, 0; Liverpool, 1, 1; West Rid. Court Dir., 4, 0; Philadelphia, 2, 0.

Glover.—Occup. 'the glover.' Entries of this name are rare in the earlier registers, 'le Gaunter' being the general form; v. Gauter.

Richard le Glovere, co. Bedf., 1273. A.
Cristiana la Glovere. H.
Johannes Cowper, *glouer* (*u* for *v*), 1379: P. T. Yorks. p. 41.
Elias Glouer, et Magota uxor ejus, Doncaster: ibid. p. 46.
Thomas Glouer, et Sibilla uxor ejus, Doncaster: ibid.
Hugo Glouer, *glouer*, Ripon : ibid. p. 251.
1685. Married—William Baker and Eliz. Glover: St. Michael, Cornhill, p. 44.
London, 48 ; Crockford, 11 ; West Rid. Court Dir., 17 ; New York, 45.

Glyde; v. Glede.

Gobbett.—Bapt. 'the son of Godbold,' q.v. This is the natural solution. At the same time the surname looks like a diminutive. Gabbett and Gabbott are diminutives of Gabriel, from the nick. Gabb. If Gabb was provincially pronounced Gobb, we should have to refer Gobbett to Gabriel. Nevertheless Godbold seems the natural parent. The first instance below almost settles the point; cf. Arnold for Arnaud, and Arnett for Arnott, an exact parallel; also Garbett for Gerbold.

Y

John Gobaud, co. Hunts, 1273. A.
John Gobet, co. Soms., 1 Edw. III:
Kirby's Quest, p. 175.
Elizota Gobett, 1379: P. T. Yorks.
p. 238.
Agnes Gobet, 1379: ibid. p. 33.
Ricardus Gobet, 1379: ibid. p. 54.
Johannes Gobet, 1370: ibid. p. 213.
Alderman George Gobbet, sometime
sheriff of this city, Nov. 7, 1723,' Norwich:
FF. iv. 314.
London, 3.

Gobby, Gobey.—Bapt. 'the
son of Gobey,' probably a nick. or
pet form of Godbold, q.v. In any
case the surname is of personal
origin. The 17th and 18th century
forms were as various as it was
possible to make them. I append
a few instances from one register
in London.

Nigel Gobey, co. Norf., 1273. A.
Richard Gobey, co. Norf., ibid.
1615. Married—Willyam Dunkerton
and Sara Goebye: St. Jas. Clerkenwell,
iii. 41.
1665. — Ritchard Gobee and Mary
Ward: ibid. p. 123.
1666. — William Bate and Marget
Gobye: ibid. p. 125.
1705. — Edward Watson and Jane
Gobbey: ibid. p. 228.
London, 5, 1.

Godard, Godart.—Bapt. 'the
son of Godard'; v. Goddard.

**Godbehere, Goodbehere,
Godber.** — Bapt. 'the son of
Godber,' which perhaps is an
abbreviation of Godbert. That the
surname is taken from the cry
'God be here' is absurd. Of
course the spelling has become
imitative, which has itself helped
to suggest such an origin. Lower
says, 'I have met with it as a surname in Sussex, temp. Hen. III.'

John Godbehere, C. R., 34 Hen. VI.
1588. Bapt.—John, son of Richard
Godbehere: St. Jas. Clerkenwell, i. 20.
Richard Godbeare, temp. Eliz. Z.
John Godbehere, 1628: St. Mary
Aldermary (London), p. 165.
John Goodbeere, of Deane parish, co.
Lanc: Wills at Chester (1545-1620), p. 73.
London, 0, 1, 0; Derby, 1, 0, 0; Man-
chester (1887), 4, 2, 1.

Godbold, Godbolt, Gobbett.
—Bapt. 'the son of Godbold' (not
in Yonge). 'Occurs in Domesday
as a previous A.S. *tenant*' (Lower).

Godebold (without surname). J.
Godebold de Writel, Hen. III–Edw. I:
K. p. 270.

Richard Godbold, co. Norf., 8 Eliz.:
FF. vii. 427.
Thomas Godbould, co. Norf., 15 Jas. I:
ibid. x. 43.
1681. Married—Thomas Godbould and
Eliz. Casewell: St. Jas. Clerkenwell,
iii. 190.
London, 5, 2, 3; Boston (U.S.), 6, 0, 0.

Goddard, Godart, Godard.
—(1) Bapt. 'the son of Godard.'
This personal name obtained a
strong footing in England, and
has left a large number of descendants. It corresponds to the German
Gotthard (v. Yonge, ii. 176).

Godard de Thurton, co. Norf., 1273. A.
Simon Goddard, London, ibid.
John fil. Godard, co. Camb., ibid.
Peter Godard, co. Norf., 20 Edw. I. R.
Goddard Freebodye, temp. Eliz. Z.

(2) Nick. 'the good herd'; cf.
Goodgroom, Goodknave, &c.

Symon Godhird, 1379: P.T. Yorks.p.207.
Alicia Goderd, 1379: ibid. p. 191.

It is doubtful whether this
sobriquet had much influence on
(1), which is the true parent of our
Goddards.

1716. Bapt.—Joseph, s. Joseph Godard:
St. Michael, Cornhill, p. 165.
London, 47, 2, 0; New York, 18, 0, 2;
Boston (U.S.), 50, 0, 0.

Godden, Godding.—Bapt.; v.
Godwin.

Godfrey, Godfree, Godfreed.
—Bapt. 'the son of Godfrey'; v.
Geoffrey. Godfrey of Lorraine,
the famous Crusader, made this
personal name as familiar as did
Cœur de Lion his own. But Richard
was an Englishman, and Godfrey
was not. Therefore in this country,
at least, Richard obtained the
superiority. But coming at the
epoch of hereditary surnames both
have wielded an enormous influence
upon nomenclature.

'And sire Godefray Go-wel.'
Piers. P. 5196.
Henricus fil. Godefridi, 7 Hen. II:
Pipe Roll, iv. 57.
Peter fil. Godfrey, co. Norf., 1273. A.
Alan Godefray, co. Kent, ibid.
'Willelmus Godefray, 1379: P.T. Yorks.
p. 124.
1614. Bapt.—Eliz., d. Stephen Godfrye:
St. Mary Aldermary (London), p. 73.
London, 31, 3, 1; Philadelphia, 45, 0, 0.

Godinot.—Bapt. 'the son of
Godwin,' from O.F. Godin, dim.
Godinot. 'Henry Godynot (Close

Roll, 23 Edw. III. pt. ii), feminine
Godinette' (Yonge, ii. 175); v.
Woodnott.

Godkin.—Bapt. 'the son of
Godfrey' (?), from Godkin, a dim.
Probably this form was directly
imported from the Low Countries.

Godekin de Coufeld, London, 1273. A.
Godekin de Cusa, London, ibid.
Derby, 1; Preston, 1; New York, 2.

Godlee, Godley, Godly.—
Local, ' of Godley,' a township in
the parish of Mottram-in-Longdendale, Cheshire.

Robert de Godelegh, 1294: East
Cheshire, ii. 156.
Henry de Godelegh, 1299: ibid.
William de Godelegh, 1349: ibid. p. 154.
Gilbert de Godelegh, 1349: ibid.
Hamelinus de Godelee, 35 Edw. I:
BBB. p. 743.
Willelmus de Godlay, 1379: P. T.
Yorks. p. 193.
Cecilia de Godelay, 1379: ibid.
1775. Married—John Shead and Mar-
garet Godly: St. Geo. Han. Sq. i. 257.
London, 2, 2, 0; Manchester, 0, 1, 0;
Philadelphia, 0, 5, 0.

Godly is found as a Puritan font-
name, but it has nothing to do
with the origin of the surname.
It came too late to influence anything but Christian names, and
soon became unfashionable in that
category.

1639. Edward Burton and Godley
Neale: Marriage Lic.(Westminster), p. 38.

It is found still earlier:

1579. Bapt. — Godlye, d. Richard
Fauterell: Warbleton, Sussex.
1611. Bapt.—Godly, d. Henry Gray.
Joane Standmer and Godly Gotherd,
sureties: South Berstead, Sussex.

I could furnish other instances
(vide my Curiosities of Puritan
Nomenclature, pp. 152-3).

Godliman.—Local, 'of Godalming,' co. Surrey, formerly, and
still popularly, so called. Lower
has Godliman as an existing surname in his Patr. Brit. Doubtless
he had met with it in the neighbouring county of Sussex, where
he spent so many years of his life.

'Jone Inwood, of Goddlemen, in co. Surrey': Visitation of London, 1633-5, p. 162.
1696-7. Married—Samuell Carr and
Anne Hall, of Godlyman, co. Surrey: St.
Dionis Backchurch, p. 45.
1792. Married—George Wild and Mary
Godliman: St. Geo. Han. Sq. i. 75.

Godling.—Bapt. 'the son of Good,' q.v., from the dim. Godelin ; cf. Hewling.

Godelena Deye, Close Roll, 30 Edw. I.
Godlena atte Heglond, Patent Roll, 4 Edw. III. pt. ii.

Godman.—Bapt. 'the son of Godmund.' Of course Godman may be a variant of Goodman, q.v. In fact the instances are strongly in favour of that solution. Still Godmund existed, and this would inevitably become Godman ; cf. Osman for Osmund, and Wyman for Wymond.

Ricardus Godmund, co. Suff., 1273. A.
Godman le (de la ?) Grene, co. Norf., ibid.
Martin Godman, co. Essex, ibid.
Lucas Godman, co. Norf., ibid.
1671. Richard Sell and Mary Godman : Marriage Alleg. (Canterbury), p. 194.
London, 1 ; Philadelphia, 1.

Godolphin.—Local, ' of Godolphin,' a hamlet in the parish of Breage, five miles from Helston, co. Cornwall, anciently written Godolcan or Godolghan. ' John de Godolphin is said to have possessed the manor at the time of the Conquest ' (Lower, quoting Gilbert's Cornwall, i. 520).

1669. Francis Godolphin (co. Wilts) and Eliz. Mordaunt : Marriage Alleg. (Canterbury), p. 167.
London, 1.

Godrich, Goodrich, Goodrick, Goodridge.—(1) Bapt. ' the son of Godric.' So common as to make Godric and Godiva the Jack and Jill of their day ; v. Goodeve.

Walter Goderiche, co. Bedf., 1273. A.
William Godriche, co. Oxf., ibid.
Stephen Godrich, co. Suff., ibid.
Ambrosius fil. Godrige, co. Camb., ibid.
Robert fil. Godric. J.
William Godrick. H.
Godric, abbot of Winchcombe : Freeman, Norman Conquest, iv. 177.
Godric, sheriff of Berkshire : ibid. p. 38.
Henry Godrych, co. Soms., 1 Edw. III : Kirby's Quest, p. 125.
Robertus Goderik, 1379 : P. T. Yorks. p. 260.

With Goodridge, cf. Aldridge for Alderich.

(2) Local, ' of Goodrich ' ; v. Gutteridge (2).

London, 3, 3, 3, 6 ; Philadelphia, 0, 10, 0, 0.

Godsall, Godsell.—(1) Local, ' of Godshill,' a parish in the Isle of Wight, near Newport.

Hugo de Gaddeshull, co. Southampt., Hen. III–Edw. I. K.

(2) Bapt. 'the son of Godsol.' Lower quotes Mr. Ferguson, who says that Godesilus was an early Burgundian king. One thing is certain, the majority of our Godsells and Godsalls are of personal, or, as we should now say, of baptismal origin.

Amice Godsol, co. Camb., 1273. A.
Cecilia Godsol, co. Camb., ibid.
Augustin Godsoule, co. Hunts, ibid.
Basilia Godsowele, co. Norf., ibid.
Radulphus Godsale, Millour, 1379 P. T. Yorks. p. 115.
London, 0, 0, 7 ; Philadelphia, 0, 1.

Godsalve, Godsave, Godsiffe.—Nick. ' on God's half,' i.e. on the side of God, possibly a Crusading name, otherwise a religious title relating to some perpetual vow. It is recorded that Agnes, the sister of Thomas à Becket, married a member of an old city family, Theobald Agodshalf (in Latin, ex parte Dei), who was baron of Hulles or Helles in Ireland (Historic Towns, edited by E. A. Freeman). Again, it might have been part of a property made over to a monastery or church.

Henry à Godeshalve, co. Camb., 1273. A.
Cf. Walter Goduspart, co. Soms., 1 Edw. III : Kirby's Quest, p. 202.
William de Godeshalve, C. R., 15 Edw. III. pt. ii.
' Item, geven to the nurce and mydwife of Maistres Goddeshalf, my ladies grace being godmother to his childe,' 1536 : Privy Purse Exp., Princess Mary, p. 19.
Thomas Godsalfe. W. 9.
Barbara Godsalve. FF.
1647. Bapt.—Charles, son of John Godsalve : Reg. St. Michael, Cornhill, p. 135.
Thomas Godshalff, or Godsalve, of Warton, 1588 : Lancashire Wills at Richmond, pp. 124–5.
Rowland Godshalfe, of Newton, 1650 : ibid.
Bryan Godsallffe, of Berwick, 1607 : ibid.

From these forms Godsiffe naturally came into existence.

Liverpool (Godsiffe), 1.

Godsfold.—Local, ' of Godesfold.' Probably without any religious significance, simply meaning the fold or enclosure of Gode or Good, a personal name ; v. Good.

John de Godesfold, C. R., 16 Edw. III. pt. ii.

Godsknight. — Nick. ' God's servant.'

John Goddesknyght, C. R., 5 Edw. II.

Godson.—(1) Bapt. 'the son of Gode' or ' Good.' A common fontal name (v. Good and Goodison), found also as Gott, probably a Flemish form.

Cf. Gotte le Mazoun, co. Hunts, 1273. A.
Ralph fil. Godde, co. Warw., ibid.
Thomas fil. Gode, co. Camb., ibid.
Walter fil. Gode, co. Suff., ibid.
Willelmus Gotson, 1379 : P. T. Yorks. p. 234.

(2) Nick. ' the godson,' i.e. the spiritual relation. It is curious to note that Godson and Godmother are found in the Hundred Rolls. Had Godson belonged to (1) it would have been set down as ' fil. Gode.' Understood as a sponsorial title it was necessary to enter it in full.

William Godeson, co. Camb., 1273. A.
William Godmoder, co. Camb., ibid.
Richard Godsone, co. Camb., ibid.
1388. William Godeson : Cal. of Wills in the Court of Husting (2).
Richard Fitz-Dieu, marchant, 12 Edw. III : Freemen of York, i. 33.
Cf. Agnes Goddoghter, 1379 : P. T. Yorks. p. 55.
London, 4 ; Philadelphia, 1, New York, 1.

Godspenny. — Nick. ' earnestmoney.' ' A God's pennie, an earnest penny ' : Florio, p. 39.

Thomas Godespeny, Close Roll, 3 Edw. III.

Godwin, Godden, Godding, Godin, Goding, Godon.—Bapt. ' the son of Godwin ' ; v. Goodwin. The common suffix -win was corrupted to -in and -ing apart from French forms ; cf. Gunning for Gunwin, Bodden or Boddin for Baldwin. Thus the g is excrescent. It is manifest, however, that most of the instances below are French forms. v. Golden.

Godin de Bech, co. Camb., 1273. A.
Godun le Bere, co. Camb., ibid.
Roger Godin, co. Camb, ibid.
William Godin, co. Oxf., ibid.
John fil. Godini, co. Hunts, ibid.
Alice Goding, co. Camb., ibid.
Alice Godson, co. Oxf., ibid.
Gaudinus de Albo Monast'io, Hen III. K.
Gaudinus de Aseby, co. Linc., 20 Edw. I. R.
London, 26, 7, 1, 1, 2, 0 ; New York, 15, 1, 0, 0, 1 ; Philadelphia, 22, 0, 1, 0, 0, 0.

Goff, Goffe.—Nick. 'the gough,' i.e. the red-complexioned. A Welsh nickname, taken from the complexion of the face or hair; v. Gough.

Roger Goffe, co. Camb., 1273. A.
Jevan Gogh, co. Camb., 1325. M.
'Another time, he, and Pinchbacke, and Dr. Goffe, now a religious man:' Pepys' Diary, 1666, p. 325.

This was Dr. Gough, clerk of the Queen's Closet and her Assistant Confessor.

London, 16, 1 ; New York, 18, 1.

Goffee, Guffey.—? Bapt. ' the son of Govy (?).' This curious surname in the London Directory would seem to defy elucidation, and yet we have evidence of its established position in the 13th century in the neighbourhood of co. Hunts. I furnish a few instances.

Bartelot Govi, co. Hunts, 1273. A.
Augustin Govi, co. Hunts, ibid.
Eusebius Govy, co. Hunts, ibid.
Thomas Govy, co. Hunts, ibid.
1665. Married — George Guffie and Christibala Baizley : St. Jas. Clerkenwell, iii. 117.
London, 1, 0 ; Philadelphia, 0, 1.

Goggin, Gogin.—Bapt. ' the son of Goggin.' The O.F. nick. for Margaret was Gogo (Yonge, ii. 266–7). The popular dim. would be Gogin. The entries of this form in the Hundred Rolls are so many that it was evidently very familiar. The final g, of course, is excrescent, as in Jenning for Jenin. 'James Goggin, head gamekeeper to Mr. Crosbie, Ardfert Abbey, . . . was surprised to find his house in the possession of a gang of moon-lighters' (Standard, Monday, Dec. 20, 1886). I only suggest the above as the entry Gogwine seems to denote one of the innumerable font-names with the suffix -win ; cf. Baldwin, Aylwin, Unwin, &c. (cf. Golden for Goldwin).

Michael Goggyng, co. Camb., 1273. A.
Herveus Goging, co. Camb., ibid.
Agnes Gogwine, co. Bucks, ibid.
Alice Gogun, co. Oxf., ibid.
London, 1, 0 ; Boston, 0, 8.

Gold, Gould, Goold.—Bapt. ' the son of Gold.' All from A.S. gold, metaphorically precious ; later on Precious itself became a font-name and then a surname (v. Precious). For intrusive u in Gould, cf. Gouldfinch and Gould-smith (Lond. Dir.). Golde and Goldus (1086, Domesday) are personal names.

Adam Gold, 1273. A.
Golda Imayn, ibid.
Golda Bassat, co. Camb., ibid.
Golda de Rosa, co. Kent, Hen. III– Edw. I. K.
Willelmus Golde, 1379 : P.T.Yorks.p.28
Ricardus Gold', 1379 : ibid. p. 277.
1396. Golda Barnby : Cal. of Wills in the Court of Husting (2).

Gold is also found as a nickname, where Gold is equivalent to golden, i.e. of a bright deep yellow complexion.

Adam le Gold, C. R., 21 Edw. III. pt. ii.
London, 9, 49, 7 ; Philadelphia, 21, 52, 3.

Goldbeater.—Occup. 'the gold-beater' ; cf. Leadbeater.

Robert le Goldbeter, co. Glouc., 1273. A.
Julian le Goldbeter, C. R., 49 Hen. III.
Bartholomew le Goldbetter. C.
1467. 'Thomas Goldbeter, buried by Katharine his wife ; he was a glazier, but gentleman of coat armour.' St. Peter per Mountergate, Norwich : FF. iv. 94.

Golden, Golding, Goulden, Goulding, Goolden, Gooling.—(1) Bapt. ' the son of Goldwin,' q.v. For change of suffix -win into -en, -in, and -ing, v. Godwin and Goggin. It was quite general before the close of the 13th century. But again French influences are traceable in some of the instances below.

Golding Palmarius, co. Kent, 1273. A.
Hilde Golden, co. Camb., ibid.
Nicholas Goldin, co. Oxf., ibid.
Thomas Goldine, co. Oxf., ibid.
Hugo Golding, co. Suff., ibid.
Willelmus Goldyng, 1379 : P. T. Yorks. p. 228.
Robertus Goldyng, pelliparius, 1379 : ibid. p. 222.
Isabella Goldyng, 1379 : P. T. Howden-shire, p. 26.

The family of Golden, Broad Chalke, co. Wilts, are entered Golding in 1563 ; Goulden, 1707 ; and Golden, 1672 (Reg. Broad Chalke, pp. 1, 24, 70).

(2) Nick. ' the golden,' probably from the complexion of the hair ; cf. Goldenlock.

Henry le Gulden, 1316. M.
Henry le Gilden, 1325. M.

Roger le Gildene, co. Soms., 1 Edw. III :
Kirby's Quest, p. 222.
London, 0, 34, 5, 9, 2, 1 ; West Rid.
Court Dir. (Golden), 2 ; Philadelphia, 70, 0, 0, 4, 0, 0.

Goldenlock.—Nick. 'with the golden lock' ; cf. Silverlock.

Walter Guldeloc, co. Oxf., 1273. A.
Geoffrey Gildeneloc, co. Norf., ibid.
Gildeneloc Cachellus (i.e. the Catch-pole), so styled to distinguish him from his neighbour Stuward Cachellus, co. Norf., 1273. A. i. 439.

Goldfinch.—Nick. 'the gold-finch.'

Agnes Goldfinche, co. Oxf., 1273. A.
William Goldfynch. B.
Ricardus Goldfynch, 1379 : P. T. Yorks. p. 72.
John Goldfynche, C. R., 13 Hen. IV.
1649. Ambrose Starke married Mary Goldfinch : Reg. Canterbury Cath. p. 57.

The marriage of Lavinia Maria Goldfinch was announced in the Standard, May 12, 1887.

Mr. R. Goldfinch, of Herne Bay, has discovered the fossilized remains of a northern elephant projecting from the clay close by the beach. (Manchester Courier, Feb. 29, 1888.)

London, 1.

Goldhawk.—Nick. 'the gold-hawk.'

John Goldhauk : Close Roll, 2 Hen. IV. pt. i.
London, 1.

Golding.—Bapt. ; v. Golden.

Goldingay, Goldinjay, Good-enday, Goldinger.—Local, ' of Goldinghay,' i.e. the hay or enclosure of Golding the proprietor. I have not found the spot (v. Hay and Golden) ; cf. Billingay.

1647. Married—Nathaniell Browne and Grace Gouldinghaye : St. Jas. Clerken-well, iii. 81.
Birmingham (1884), 2, 1, 0, 0 ; Manchester (1887), 0, 0, 1, 1.

Goldingham.—Local, ' of Gold-ingham.'

William de Goldingham, co. Suff., 1273. A.
John de Goldyngham, co. Suff., 20 Edw. I. R.
Alan de Goldingham, co. Norf., ibid.
1629. Married — James Gouldingham and Elline Sessyons : St. Jas. Clerken-well, iii. 60.
1663. — Stephen Goldingham and Mar-garett Reading : ibid. p. 114.
Crockford, 2.

Goldington.—Local, ' of Goldington,' a parish in co. Bedford, two miles from Bedford.

Peter de Goldington, co. Bucks, Hen. III-Edw. I. K.
Alvredus de Goldingtone, co. Camb., 1273. A.
Roger de Goldyngton, co. Bedf., 20 Edw. I. R.
William de Goldingtone, co. Kent, ibid.
1631. Married—Francys Gouldington and Ann Boyfield: St. Jas. Clerkenwell, iii. 62.
1675 — Thomas Goldington, of Harrow-the-Hill, and Margaret Toothaore: St. Michael, Cornhill, p. 41.

Goldman.—Bapt. 'the son of Goldman,' compounded of the personal name Gold and the augmentative *man*; cf. Bateman, Tiddiman.

1626. Robert Gouldman and Catherine Newton: Marriage Lic. (London), ii. 185.
1649. Michaell Evans and Joyce Gouldman: St. Dionis Backchurch, p. 26.
London, 1; Boston (U.S.), 11; Philadelphia, 23.

Goldney.—Local, ' of Goldney.' I cannot find the spot. The suffix is evidently -*hey* or -*hegh*; v. Hey and Haig.

Thomas Gildenegh, co. Soms., 1 Edw. III: Kirby's Quest, p. 116.
William Gildenegh, co. Soms., 1 Edw. III: ibid.
Richard Gyldeneghe, co. Soms., 1 Edw. III: ibid. p. 217.
London, 2.

Goldring.—Bapt. 'the son of Goldring.' Evidently some early personal name with Gold for prefix; cf. Goldwin.

John Goldring', co. Camb., 1273. A.
Richard Goldring', co. Camb., ibid.
Edmund Goldrun, co. Wilts, ibid.
William Goldryng, co. Soms., 1 Edw. III: Kirby's Quest, p. 136.
Henry Goldryng, co. Soms., 1 Edw. III: ibid.
1398. John Goldryng: Cal. of Wills in Court of Husting (2).
1786. Married — Zachariah Goldring (co. Surrey) and Eliz. Smith: St. Geo. Han. Sq. i. 386.
London, 3.

Goldsbrough, Goldsbury, Goldsbro', Goldsberry.—Local, ' of Goldsborough,' a parish near Knaresborough, W. Rid. Yorks; lit. ' the borough of Gold,' the proprietor; v. Gold and Burrough.

1675. Edwin Griffin and Anne Goldesborough: Marriage Alleg. (Canterbury), p. 244.
1695. Married — Christopher Gouldsbrough and Sibbel Lewis: St. Jas. Clerkenwell, iii. 216.
1734. Buried—Sarah, wife of Captain William Goldsborough: St. Dionis Backchurch (London), p. 303.
London, 0, 1, 1, 0; West Riding Court Dir., 1, 0, 0, 0; Philadelphia, 10, 0, 0, 2.

Goldsmith.—Occup. ' the goldsmith,' generally Latinized in Norman-Fr. registers.

Geoffrey Aurifaber, co. Salop, 1273. A.
Walter Aurifaber, co. Oxf., ibid.
Richard le Goldsmythe, co. Soms., 1 Edw. III: Kirby's Quest, p. 205.
Thomas Goldsmyth', *goldsmyth*, of Wakefield, 1379: P. T. Yorks. p. 160.
Johannes fil. Galfridi, *goldsmych*: ibid. p. 71.
Hugo Goldsmyth', ibid.
Agnes Goldsmyche, ibid. p. 73.
London, 26; Philadelphia, 55.

Goldson; v. Gouldstone.

Goldspink.—Nick. ' the goldfinch.' ' Spink, the chaffinch. Var. dial.': Halliwell. v. Spink.
London, 1.

Goldsworthy, Golsworthy, Galsworthy.—Local, ' of Goldsworth ' or ' Goldsworthy,' lit. ' the *worth* of Gold,' i.e. the estate of Gold, the first settler; v. Gold and Worth. I cannot discover the spot: cf. Kenworthy and Langworthy for Kenworth and Langworth.

London, 5, 1, 0; MDB. (Bucks), 1, 0, 0; Devon Farmers' Dir., 0, 0, 1.

Goldthorp, Goldthorpe.—Local, ' of Goldthorp,' i.e. the *thorp* of Gold, the proprietor; v. Gold and Thorp. A Yorkshire surname.
West Riding Court Dir., 7, 1; Philadelphia, 2, 2.

Goldwin.—Bapt. 'the son of Goldwin.' For French and corrupted forms, v. Golden. Goldwin is a Domesday personal name, and became a favourite. It is one of the endless compounds with -*win* as suffix; cf. Unwin, Goodwin, Baldwin, &c.

William Goldwyn', co. Northumberland, 1273. A.
Richard Goldwyne, co. Sussex, ibid.
Joldewin fil. Savarici, Pipe Roll, 5 Hen. II.
Richard Joldewyne, 20 Edw. I. R.

Magota Goldewyn, 1379: P. T. Yorks. p. 53.
Thomas Goldwyne, C. R., 45 Edw. III.
Gilbert Gyldewyne, C. R., 12 Hen. IV.
Gilbert Golewyne, co. Soms., 1 Edw. III: Kirby's Quest, p. 103.
1730. Married — Goldwin Piner and Hannah Beley: St. Geo. Han. Sq. i. 327.
1781.— John Goldwin and Eliz. Robinson: ibid.
London, 1; New York, 1.

Goldwyer.—? Bapt. ' the son of Goldwire ' (?). One of the many compounds of Gold, q.v.

Thomas Goldwire, C. R., 45 Edw. III.
Petition of Jane Gouldwyer, 'a pore afflyctted creator ': Cal. State Papers (Domestic), 1580, l. 703.
' John Goldwire was ejected from the vicarage of Arundel, co. Sussex in 1662 ': N. and Q., Aug. 13, 1887.
London, 1.

Golightly, Gellatly, Galletly.—? Nick. ' go lightly.' A sobriquet for a messenger, a pursuivant, herald, harbinger (?); cf. Lightfoot, Hobbletrot, &c. A North-English surname. Possibly the name is local as ending in -*ly* (? ley). Nevertheless it was extremely common for pursuivants to have nicknames of this kind.

Roger Galichtley, 1313. M.
James Golyghtlye, co. York. W. 9.
' Rect of William Golightly, 10s.' 1622: VVV. p. 157.
Henry Golightly, 1654: Hist. of Alnwick, p. 79.
1648. Bapt. — James, s. James Gallantly, St. Peter, Cornhill, i. 91.
1649. — Henry, s. James Gallatley: ibid. p. 94.
London, 0, 3, 2; Crockford, 3, 0, 0.

Golland.—Bapt.; v. Jolland; cf. Goslin and Joslin.

Gomersall, Gomersal.—Local, ' of Gomersal ' (Great and Little), two villages in the parish of Birstall, near Dewsbury, co. York.

Hugo de Gomersall, 1379: P. T. Yorks. p. 207.
Willelmus de Gomersall (of Gomersall), 1379: ibid. p. 185.
London, 3, 0; West Rid. Court Dir., 1, 1; Philadelphia, 2, 0.

Gomm, Gomme, Gumm.—Bapt. ' the son of Gom,' a long-forgotten personal name.

Matilda fil. Gume, co. Camb., 1273. A.
Richard Gom, co. Camb., ibid.
John Gom, co. Camb., ibid.
Radulpho Gomo, co. Soms., 1 Edw. III: Kirby's Quest, p. 167.
London, 10, 3, 1; Philadelphia, 1, 0, 0.

Gooch, Gutch. Goodge, Goudge, Gudge.—Bapt. 'the son of Guch.' This personal name, probably used by both sexes, has escaped the vigilant eye of Miss Yonge; but it was well established for a time, and has left many descendants. In Yorkshire the surname seems to have settled down into Gutch, in Norfolk into Gooch; and Goodge, Goudge, Gudge, and Gouge are other and more general variants. In Wales we meet with Gouch or Goch in the 14th century. Dr. William Gouge, born 1575, was a learned Puritan, whose commentary on the Hebrews is still consulted. The *d* in Goodge, &c., is intrusive, but it is found so early as 1379; v. infra.

John fil. Guche, co. Salop, 1273. A.
Roger Guch, co. Wilts, ibid.
Gilbert Goche, co. Norf., ibid.
John Goche, co. Camb., ibid.
Evan ap-Gouch, 1313. M.
Lewlyn ap-Ithel Goch, 1325. M.
Johannes Thorpe, *frankeleyn*, et Gudche uxor ejus, 1379: P. T. Yorks. p. 160.
Goch Delyn, 1384: Hist. Ant. St. David's, p. 373.
Goch Morydych, ibid.
1572. Married—John Robertes and Ioan Goudgeson: St. Mary Aldermary (London), p. 5.
1590. Bapt.—Ellen, d. Robert Gooche, merchant of Yarmouth: St. Peter, Cornhill, p. 36.
1626. Mathew Goche and Cicely Rockwood: Marriage Lic. (London), p. 184.
1630. Margaret, fil. John Gouch, co. Norf.: FF. ix. 207.
1665. Thomas Gwydatt and Anne Googe: Marriage Lic.(Westminster),p.43.
1668. Married—John Goodge and Anne Nichols: St. Jas. Clerkenwell, iii. 146.
London, 21, 3, 0, 10, 1; York (Gutch), 2; West Riding Court Dir., 1; Philadelphia, 2, 0, 0, 0, 0; MDB. (Norfolk), Gooch, 8.

Good, Goode.—(1) Nick. 'the good,' corresponding to French *le bon*.

Richard le Gode, co. Soms., 1 Edw. III: Kirby's Quest, p. 195.

(2) Bapt. 'the son of Gode.' This is the source of most of our Goods; cf. Goodwin and Godwin as compounds.

Goda Herrt, 1273. A.
William fil. Gode, ibid.
Goda Poggel, ibid.
Norman fil. Gode, ibid.

Goda de Castre, ibid.
Gode de Scorham, temp. 1300: FFF. p. 124.
Hawen Cropure et Gude uxor ejus, 1379: P. T. Yorks. p. 162.
Goda de Berewyk, Hen. III–Edw. I: K. p. 155.
Hugo Gud', 1379: P. T. Yorks. p. 175.
Cecilia Gud', 1379: ibid.
Robertus Godde and Elena uxor ejus: ibid. p. 26.
Willelmus Gude: ibid. p. 63.
1402. Goda Pope: Cal. of Wills in Court of Husting (2).
1770. Married — Bartholomew Goode and Mary Caporn: St. Geo. Han. Sq. i. 200.
1805. — Abraham Good and Eliz. Turner: ibid. ii. 337.
London, 26, 26; Philadelphia, 48, 3.

Goodair.—Bapt. 'the son of Gudhir' (Yonge, ii. 173); v. Goodier.

Eva Godayr, 1379: P. T. Yorks. p. 160.
London, 2; Manchester, 2; Preston, 4.

Goodale, Goodall.—Local, ' of Goldale,' now Gowdall, a township in the parish of Snaith, co. York, formerly Goldale.

Villa de Goldale, 1379: P. T. Yorks. p. 132.

This surname has ramified and spread in a remarkable manner.

Johannes Godhale, 1379: P. T. Yorks. p. 6.
Ricardus de Goldall, 1379: ibid. p. 139.
Johannes Godhall, 1379: ibid. p. 118.
Agnes Godhall, 1379: P. T. Howdenshire, p. 32.
Johannes Gudhall, 1379: ibid. p. 29.
1635. Married — Thomas Goodall and Alice Fluen: St. Jas. Clerkenwell, iii. 66.
London, 4, 13; West Riding Court Dir., 0, 20; Boston (U.S.), 16, 1; Philadelphia, 2, 16.

Goodanew; v. Goodenough, of which it is a variant; cf. *enough* and the provincial *enow*.

'Charles Goodanew, *news agent*, 42, Vauxhall St.': Plymouth Dir. 1873.

Goodbarne, Goodban, Goodbun. — Nick. 'the good bairn'; M.E. *barn*, a child. A North-English form of the more general Goodchild, q.v.

Thomas Godbarne, Fines Roll, 11 Edw. I.
Robertus Gudbarn, 1379: P. T. Yorks. p. 102.
Willelmus Gudbarn, 1379: ibid. p. 256.
Isolda Godebarn, 1379: ibid.
London, 0, 2, 1; Tadcaster, 1, 0, 0; West Rid. Court Dir., 1, 0, 0.

Goodbehere.—?Bapt.; v. Godbehere.

Goodbody.—Nick. Possibly a free translation of the French Beaucorps as Handsomebody is of Gentilcorps. But there is no reason why it should not be of native growth. · He's a good soul,' ' He's a kind body,' are still in popular use; cf. *busybody*, an early compound.

Alicia Godbodi, 1273. A.
1721. Bapt.—Jacob, s. Thomas Gibbody: St. Jas. Clerkenwell, ii. 130.
London, 5; New York, 3.

Goodbrand.—Bapt. 'the son of Goodbrand,' lit. good sword or God's sword.

Walter Godisbrond, 1273. A.
London, 2.

Goodchap.—Nick. Looks colloquial and familiar. ' Good cheap.' extremely cheap. It answers to *bon marché* in Cotgrave. In Douce's Collection is a fragment of an early book printed by Caxton, who promises to sell it ' good chepe' (Halliwell). Probably a hawker's cry; v. Peascod.

Ricardus Godchep, co. Camb., 1273. A.
William Godchep, co. Suff., ibid.
Jordan Godchep, London, 20 Edw.I. R.
Lower adds, ' The corresponding family name Goed Koop is found in Holland': Patr. Brit. p. 133.
London, 1.

Goodchild.—Nick. 'the good child'; cf. Goodbarne.

Johanna Godechylde, 1379: P. T. Yorks. p. 167.
London, 16; Philadelphia, 11.

Gooddie, Gooddy, Gooday, Goodhay, Goody, Goodey.—(1) Bapt. 'the son of Goday,' an early personal name, one of the many compounds of *god* or *good*; cf. Godwin and Goodwin. (2) Bapt. 'the son of Gode,' a favourite girl's name in the 13th and 14th centuries. No doubt this would be popularly ' Goody '; cf. ' Goody Two Shoes.' v. Good (2).

William Gody, co. Soms., 1 Edw. III: Kirby's Quest, p. 112.
Henricus Goday, 1379: P. T. Yorks. p. 285.
Willelmus Goday, 1379: ibid. p. 220.
Willelmus Goday, senior, 1379: ibid.

1617. William Goodday and Anne Smith: Marriage Lic. (London), ii. 50.
1626. Thomas Goody and Susan Read: ibid. p. 177.
London (1884), 0, 3, 0, 0, 4, 9; Manchester, 4, 1, 1, 1, 0, 0; New York (Goodey), 2.

Goodenough.—? Local. Probably from Godin (v. Godinot), the name of the first settler, and *hough, haugh,* or *how,* a hill, a mound. Oddly enough, we have the opposite seeming characteristic in Badenough, which is proved to be local by the entry 'Seignor de Badenough' (19 Edw. I): Furness Coucher, p. 178, Cheth. Soc. This entry occurs several times.

Geoffrey Godynogh, co. Kent, 1273. A.
Radulphus Godenogh, 1379: P. T. Yorks. p. 118.
Johannes Godynogh, 1379: ibid.
Robertus Gudynegh, 1379: ibid. p. 114.
1667. Richard Goodenough and Sarah Harrison: Marriage Alleg. (Canterbury), p. 137.
London, 2; New York, 9.

Goodered.—Bapt. ; v. Goodred.
London, 1.

Gooderson.—Bapt. ; v. Goodison, cf. Patterson for Pattison.
London, 2; New York, 3.

Goodes.—Bapt. ; v. Goodus.

Goodeve.—Bapt. 'the son of Godiva' (Yonge, ii. 176). A common name in Domesday. Godric and Godiva were the Jack and Jill of their period. The Norman nobles derisively styled Henry I and his Queen by these two names. Professor Freeman, quoting William of Malmesbury, says, 'Norman insolence mocked at the English king and his English lady under the English names of Godric and Godgifu' (v. 170). This personal name lasted till the 17th century.

John Godyf, co. Oxf., 1273. A.
Godefe de Okerige, co. Norf., ibid.
Walter Godhyve, co. Soms., 1 Edw. III: Kirby's Quest, p. 195.
Henry Godhyve, co. Soms., 1 Edw. III: ibid. p. 91.
William Godeth, 1379: P. T. Yorks. p. 142.
Gudytha Foloufast, 1379: ibid. p. 246.
Goditha Bybbesworth, C. R., 7 Edw. IV.
Goodeth, wife of John Seymour, 1597: Abstract of Somersetshire Wills, p. 24.
1608. Bapt.—Goodife, d. John Whetton: Jas St. Clerkenwell, i. 55.

1661. Bapt.—William, s. John and Goodeth Hampton: St. Jas. Clerkenwell, i. 212.
London, 3; Bristol, 4; New York, 2.

Goodfellow.—Nick. 'the good fellow,' a good companion, an honest mate ; cf. Goodfriend.

'Ne no knyght ne no squyer
That wolde be a good felawe.'
A Lytell Geste of Robin Hode.
Roger Godfelawe, co. Essex, 1273. A.
William Godefelawe, C. R., 1 Hen. V.
Thomas Godfelewe. H.

Cf. Truefellow, Longfellow, Stringfellow, &c.
London, 7; Philadelphia, 29.

Goodfriend.—Nick. 'the good friend'; cf. Goodchild, Goodfellow.

Cf. Robertus Gudefeir, 1379: P. T. Yorks. p. 121.
Willelmus Godefere, 1379: ibid. p. 112.

Fere, in the North Country and Scotland, means 'a friend, companion.'
Philadelphia, 1; New York, 2.

Goodgame.—Nick. ; v. Goodgroom.
MDB. (co. Oxford), 1.

Goodge.—Bapt. 'the son of Guch'; v. Gooch.

Goodger.—Bapt. 'the son of Godeyer'; v. Goodier. A corruption of Goodier, just as Woodger is of Woodier or Woodyer; cf. Gudgeon for Goodison.

1785. Married—William Goodger and Mary Siver (or Siven): St. Geo. Han. Sq. i. 372.
— James Goodjer and Eliz. Feast: ibid. p. 380.
London, 2; Oxford, 2.

Goodgroom, Goodgame, Goodram, Gooderham, Goodrem, Goodrum.—Nick. 'the good groom'; M.E. *grom.* A common entry in the Hundred Rolls. If the reader will repeat to himself Goodgroom several times he will see, in default of a local origin, that Gooderham was an inevitable corruption. This view is strongly sustained by the fact that there are no Goodgrooms in our directories, which for so popular a nickname would be curious if no corruptions existed.

Symon Godegrom, co. Sussex, 1273. A.
Robert le Godegrom, co. Hunts, ibid.
John Godgrom. H.

Robert Godgrom, co. Soms., 1 Edw. III: Kirby's Quest, p. 158.
John le Godegrom, co. Soms., 1 Edw. III: ibid. p. 212.
1529-30. Richard Goodgame and Elinor Blacton: Marriage Lic. (London), i. 7.
1623. John Weekes and Eliz. Goodgame: ibid. ii. 132.
1701. Bapt.—Anne, d. of William Goodgrome: St. Dionis Backchurch, p. 140.
London, 0, 0, 0, 2, 1, 0; MDB. (Norfolk), 0, 0, 0, 2, 0, 2; (co. Oxford), Goodgame, 1.

Goodhart, Goodheart.—(1) Nick. 'good heart,' the kindhearted; M.E. *herte,* heart; cf. Bunker. Allied to such names as Cœur de Lion, Trueman, Goodfellow, &c.

Alexander Godherte. E.
Walter Godherte, ibid.

(2) Bapt. 'the son of Godard' (?), possibly in some cases an imitative corruption; v. Goddard. The following first two entries are manifestly variants of Godard:

Richard Godart, co. Bucks, Hen. III-Edw. I. K.
Adam Godart, co. Camb., 1273. A.
1658. Married—John Lyon and Lucey Goodhart: St. Jas. Clerkenwell, iii. 100.
London, 5, 1; New York, 6, 4.

Goodherring.—Nick. Probably a fish-hawker who cried 'good herring' in the streets; cf. Peascod and Freshherring. This surname seems to have lingered on in the form of Gooderin.

Adam Godharing, 1273. A.
1568. Married—Hercules Gooderyn and Eliz. Gayre: St. Mary Aldermary (London), p. 4.

Goodhew, Goodhugh, Goodhue.—Nick. 'good Hugh.' A common spelling of Hugh was Hew, found in parish registers till the close of last century. Hence also Goodhew. One of a class of compounds made out of the favourite font-names of the time; cf. Goodrobert, Prettyjohn, Meiklejohn, and the French Bonjean. Goodhue is the chief American form. 'Nicholas Goodhue went out to Virginia in the ship James in 1635' (Hotten's Lists of Emigrants, p. 108).

John Godhug', co. Essex, 1273. A.
Hugh Godhewe, 1307. M.
William Godhugh, 1305. M.
London, 4, 3, 0; New York, 1, 0, 3.

Goodhind.— Nick. 'the good hind,' i.e. the good *hine*, the good servant. Exactly equivalent to Goodknave and Goodgroom, q.v.; v. Hind and Hine.

Johannes Godehyue et uxor ejus, *webster*, 1379: P. T. Yorks, p. 220.

No doubt this is a misreading for Godehyne.

Taunton (co. Somerset), (1884), 1.

Goodier, Goodger, Goodyear, Goodyer, Goodear. — Bapt. ' the son of Gudhir' or 'Gudvar' (Yonge, ii. 173, 175). Englished to Godeyer. Goodyear is the favourite modern form, as was likely, being imitative. Another variant is Goodair, q.v.

Cest' Godyer, co. Hunts, 1273. A.
John Godeyer, C. R., 10 Ric. II.
Willelmus Goddeyere, 1379: P. T. Yorks. p. 197.
Simon Godeyere, *smyth*, 1379: ibid. p. 29.
Willelmus Godeyere, 1379: ibid.
1613. John Appleston and Susan Goodier: Marriage Lic. (London), ii. 23.
1626-7. Edward Burford and Anne Goodyeare: ibid. p. 184.

The Liverpool Directory has Goodere. Cf.

1636. Thomas Goodere and Mary Bartlett: Marriage Lic. (London), ii. 228.
London, 0, 2, 5, 2, 0; Manchester, 11, 0, 2, 0, 1; West Rid. Court Dir. (Goodyear), 2; New York (Goodyear), 8; Boston (U.S.) (Goodyer), 1.

Gooding, Goodden, Goodinge, Goodings, Goodin.—(1) Bapt. ' the son of Goodwin,' q.v. From the form Godwin (q.v.) just the same variants have issued. The suffix -*win*, even when not the French *in*, commonly became in, en, and *ing*. (2) Bapt. 'the son of Gooding'; cf. Harding, Browning, &c.

London, 10, 1, 1, 1, 0; Boston (U.S.), 10, 0, 0, 0, 1.

Goodison, Goodisson, Gooderson, Goodson.—Bapt. (1) 'the son of Godith' (v. Goodeve), or (2) 'the son of Goodier' (v. Goodair), or (3) 'the son of Gode' (v. Good). Probably all are now mixed up.

John Godithson, Pardons Roll, 17 Ric. II.
William Godythson, 1379: P. T. Yorks. p. 244.
Gudytha Foloufast, 1379: ibid. p. 247.
Johannes Godyeson, 1379: ibid. p. 87.

Ricardus Godeson, 1379: ibid. p. 45.
Margareta Gudson, *wyf*, 1379: ibid. p. 114.
William Godeson, co. Camb., 1273. A.
Richard Godsone, co. Camb., ibid.
Willelmus Godeth, 1379: P. T. Yorks. p. 142.
Robertus Guditson, 1379: ibid. p. 144.
London, 1, 1, 2, 0; West Rid. Court Dir., 5, 0, 0, 0; Stannington (co. York), 2, 0, 0, 0; Leeds, 3, 0, 0, 0; Liverpool (1887), (Goodson), 2; Philadelphia, 0, 0, 0, 1.

Goodjohn.—Nick. 'good John,' a direct translation of the early imported Bonjean; cf. Smallwriter, Whitbread, &c. Possibly for Goodison; v. Gudgcon.

MDB. (co. Cambridge), 2.

Goodknave.—Nick. 'the good knave,' i.e. good servant; M.E. *knave*, a lad or servant. ' Knave, or ladde, *garcio*': Prompt. Parv.
' All had hire lever han borne a knave child.' Chaucer, C. T. 8320.
Henry Godknave, co. Camb., 1273. A.
William Godknave, co. Bucks, ibid.
Geoffrey Godeknave, co. Oxf., ibid.
Gilbert Godknave. B.
William Goodknave. D.
Cf. Johannes Jakkesknave, 1379: P. T. Yorks. p. 268.
Thomas Wyllknave, 1379: ibid. p. 269.
Thomas Gabknave, 1379: ibid. p. 13.

Goodknave would sound odd in the 19th century. I do not find any modern instances of the surname.

Goodlad.—Nick. 'the good lad,' i.e. good servant; v. Goodknave. Almost all my instances refer to county York.

Robertus Godelad', 1379: P. T. Yorks. p. 45.
Johannes Godeladd', 1379: ibid. p. 128.
Ricardus Gudlad', 1379: ibid. p. 152.
Thomas Gudelade, 1379: ibid. p. 299.
Willelmus Guddeladde, 1379: ibid.
London, 1.

Goodlake.—Bapt. ' the son of Gudleik' (Yonge, ii. 174, 318), or more probably the A.S. Guthlac : v. Cutlack.
1550. Thomas, son of Goodluke Coote: Reg. St. Dionis Backchurch (London), p. 75.
1552. Edward, son of Goodluke Cotte: ibid. p. 203.
1596. Mr. Goodluck Cott: ibid.
This was probably a Dutch family.
London, 2; Oxford, 1.

Goodlamb.—Nick. 'the good lamb'; cf. Whitelam.

William Godlomb, co. Norf., 1273. A.
James Godlambe, C. R., 9 Edw. II.
Aykys (fem.) Godlomb, co. Norf., ibid.

Goodland.—(1) ? Bapt. 'the son of Jodland' or 'Godland'; v. Golland and Jolland. (2) Local, 'of Godland.'
Richard fil. Jodlani, 1273. A.
Hugo Godland, ibid.
Henricus de Godland, 1379: P. T. Yorks. p. 184.
London, 3; New York, 1.

Goodlass.—? Local. It is odd that we should have both Goodlad and Goodlass in our directories.
Liverpool (1887), 1.

Goodliffe, Goodliff.—Bapt. 'the son of Godeleva,' a form of Godiva (Yonge, ii. 176). St. Godeleva of Terouenne was murdered in 1070.
Godeliva la Ferrur, temp. Hen. III. T.
London, 1, 0; New York, 3, 2.

Goodman, Godman, Gudeman.—(1) Bapt. ' the son of Godmund,' corrupted to Goodman; cf. Osman, Wyman, Roseaman, &c., from Osmund, Wymond, Rosamund, &c.
Richard Godmund, co. Suff., 1273. A.
Godman Brū, co. Norf., ibid.
Alan fil. Godemanni, co. Camb., ibid.
Godman Omet, co. Soms., 1 Edw. III : Kirby's Quest, p. 245.
Godman le Glaggere. J.
Herbert fil. Godman. C.
(2) Occup. Equivalent to householder, the goodman as opposed to goodwife; cf. husband and housewife. 'The goodman of the house': Matt. xx. 11. ' The goodman is not at home': Prov. vii. 19. See Husband.
Muriel Godeman, co. Camb., 1273. A.
Henry le Godman, co. Camb., ibid.
Willelmus Gudeman, 1376: P. T. Yorks. p. 177.
Johannes Godeman, 1379: ibid. p. 219.
Willelmus Godeman, 1379: ibid. p. 118.
John Godeman, C. R., 18 Ric. II.
'Will Grame, goodman of Medop,' 1602: Nicolson and Burn, Hist. Westm. and Cumb., vol. i. p. cxiv.
1654. Buried—Charles, s. Charles Goodman: St. Michael, Cornhill, p. 246.
London, 39, 1, 0; Philadelphia, 96, 1, 1.

Goodred, Goodered.—Bapt. ' the son of Godred,' possibly a variant of Godard; v. Goddard.
Robert Godred, co. Linc., 20 Edw. I. R.
Dominus Godred, co. Linc., 1273. A.
Isabel Godrid, co. Camb., ibid.

John Godred, co. Camb., 1273. A.
William Godrad, co. Wilts, 20 Edw. I. R.
Robert Goodred, 1379: P. T. Yorks.
p. 289.

As a baptismal name Goodred seems to have lingered on in Lincolnshire till the 16th century.

'Anthony Gilby, Elizabeth his wife, and Goddred their sonne' were admitted into the 'Englishe Churche and Congregation at Geneva,' Oct. 13, 1555. Gilby was born in Lincolnshire, and fled on the accession of Mary: v. Burn's Hist. Parish Registers (1862), p. 275.
1690. Married—Matthias Goodred and Eliz. Taylor; St. Jas. Clerkenwell, iii. 208.

London, 1, 1.

Goodrich, Goodrick, Goodridge.—Bapt.; v. Godrich.

Goodrobert. — Nick. 'good Robert'; cf. Bonjean, Prettijohn, Goodhew.

Robert Goderobert. P.

Goodshipman. — Nick. 'the able seaman'; v. Shipman.

John Godeshipman, C. R., 44 Edw. III.

Goodsmith.—Nick. 'the good smith,' probably referring to his abilities at the forge, not to his moral character.

Robert Godesmith, 1468. W. 11.

Goodson.—Bapt.; v. Goodison.

Goodspeed.—Nick.; lit. 'good success,' as a sobriquet applied to a fortunate man.

Robert Godspeede, C. R., 9 Hen. IV.
John Godespede, C. R., 19 Ric. II.
Ralph Godisped. A.

Probably a direct translation of Bonaventure, q.v.

Philadelphia, 1; Boston (U.S.), 16, New York, 3.

Goodswain.—Nick. 'the good swain,' equivalent to Goodfellow, q.v.

Henry Godesweyn, 1273. A.
John Godesweyn, co. Hunts, ibid.
Roger Godesweyn, c. 1300. M.
Roger Godesweyn, Pardon Roll, 6 Ric. II.
John Godeswayne was Fellow of Exeter College, 1436: Reg. Univ. Oxf. i. 22.

Goodus, Goodes (?). — Bapt. 'the son of Godhus' or 'Godus'; cf. Aldus or Aldhouse. This personal name seems to have been popular in Yorkshire.

Roger Godhus, co. Hunts, 1273. A.
Hugh Godhos, co. Bucks, ibid.

Ricardus Wryght et Agnes uxor ejus, 1379: P. T. Yorks. p. 54.
Gudus filia ejus, 1379: ibid.
Johannes Godus et Cecilia uxor ejus, 1379: ibid. p. 68.
Ricardus Perkynson et Gudus uxor ejus, 1379: ibid. p. 20.
Thomas Gudus, 1379: ibid. p. 21.
Godus Tholyn, wyf, 1379: ibid.
1618. Henry Ruggesby and Mary Goodes: Marriage Lic. (London), ii. 65.
London, 0, 5; Philadelphia, 0, 3.

Goodwin, Godwin, Goodwyn.—Bapt. 'the son of Godwin' (Yonge, ii. 175); v. Godwin. The Goodwin Sands received its title from Godwin, Earl of Wessex, to whom the land belonged.

Godwin Lambesune, Hen. III–Edw. I. K.
Lucas fil. Godwin, co. Camb., 1273. A.
Alice fil. Godewine, co. Oxf., ibid.
Hugh fil. Godewin, co. Salop, ibid.
William fil. Godewyni, co. Norf., ibid.
John Godwin, co. Oxf., ibid.
William Godewyn, co. Linc., ibid.
Godewin Gonelord, co. Kent, 20 Edw. I. R.
Godwin Pescodde. FF.
Willelmus Godewyn, 1379: P. T. Yorks. p. 221.
Johannes Godewyn, 1379: ibid.
William Godewyn or Goodwyn, 1448: Reg. Univ. Oxf. i. 2.
1567. Bapt.—John, s. John Goodwyn: St. Jas. Clerkenwell, i. 4.
London, 7, 26, 1; Philadelphia, 86, 22, 0.

Goody.—Bapt.; v. Gooddie.

Goodyer.—Bapt.; v. Goodier.

Googe. — Bapt. 'the son of Guch'; v. Gooch.

Goold. — Bapt. 'the son of Gold,' q.v.

Goolden, Goolding.—Bapt.; v. Golden.

Goose, Goos.—(1) Nick. 'the goose'; v. Goss (1). (2) Bapt. 'the son of Goce'; v. Goss (2). Goose has been a familiar surname in Norfolk for six centuries, and I give that family a separate article because I believe they have no connexion with the nickname, but are of baptismal origin. Just as our Goslings represent the old personal name Gocelin, so Goose in Norfolk represents its parent, the old personal name Goce. Hence also the Norfolk Gooches; v. Gooch.

Joose de Ram, Norwich, 1571: FF. iii. 288.

John Goose, of Lawick, *husbandman*, 1598: Lancashire Wills at Richmond, p. 125.
Thomas Goose, of Winmerley, 1585: ibid.
MDB. (Norfolk), 4, 0; Philadelphia, 0, 6.

Gooseman, Goosman. — Occup. 'the gooseman,' a gooseherd, a tender of geese; cf. Swanherd.

Great Grimsby (1884), 1, 0; Boston (U.S.), 0, 1.

Goosetree, Goostry, Goostrey. — Local, 'of Goostrey,' a village in Cheshire, near Holmes Chapel.

William de Goostree, 1339: East Ches. ii. 646.
Cicely de Goostree, 1339: ibid.
Manchester (1887), 1, 0, 0; Birmingham (1884), 0, 1, 0; Boston (U.S.), (Goostrey), 2.

Gorbold.—Bapt. 'the son of Gerbold' (Yonge, ii. 328); v. Garbett.

William Gorebald, co. Camb., 1273. A.
London, 2.

Gore, Goreway.—Local, 'at the gore,' 'at the gore-way.' I confine myself to the local meaning of the word. As a local term Bailey says, 'Gore, a small narrow slip of land.' Skeat says, 'Gore, a triangular piece let into a garment, a triangular slip of land.' Halliwell says, 'Gore, a small narrow slip of ground' (quoting Kennett, Gloss. p. 80). Evidently a gore was a piece of land in shape of the gore of a garment; v. Skeat, Gore (2). A gore is a three-cornered slip of cloth let in a slit to widen the girth of a garment.

'A barm-cloth, as white as morwe milk,
Upon her lendes, ful of many a gore.'
Chaucer, The Miller's T. 3237.

William ad le Gorewege, co. Camb., 1273. A.
Alan atte Gore, co. Essex, ibid.
William de Gora, co. Wilts, ibid.
Thomas de la Gore, co. Suff., 20 Edw. I. R.
Simon atte Gore, co. Soms., 1 Edw. III: Kirby's Quest, p. 84.
Adam Gorwege, co. Soms., 1 Edw. III: ibid. p. 106.
1614-5. Richard Gorwaye and Jane Wright: Marriage Lic. (London), ii. 30.
1619. Thomas Pegrim and Mary Gore: ibid. p. 76.
Cf. Adam Grengore (i.e. the green gore), 1379: P. T. Yorks. p. 275.
London, 14, 0; Philadelphia, 12, 0.

Gorham.—Local, 'of Gorham.'

William de Gorham, co. Oxf., 1273. A.
Hugh de Gorham, co. Linc., ibid.

With the following, cf. American Barnum for Barnham:

1642. Bapt.—Mary, d. John Gorum, *butcher*: St. Peter, Cornhill, i. 89.
London, 3; MDB. (Hunts), 1; Philadelphia, 6.

Goring, Gorringe. — Local, 'of Goring,' parishes in diocs. of Chichester and Oxford. Mr. Lower, writing of a county with which he was so familiar, says, ' Gorringe and Gorring, both Sussex surnames, and doubtless modifications of the ancient local name Goring in that county. As in the case of Hardinge, the *g* in the latter of these two forms has been improperly softened, and the pronunciation is Gorrinje' (Patr. Brit. p. 134).

Priorissa de Goringe, co. Oxf., 1273. A.
Philip Goring, co. Wilts, ibid.
1622. Bapt.—Hester, d. Richard Goringe: St. Jas. Clerkenwell, i. 95.
1667. Herbert Hay and Margaret Goring, of Lewes: Marriage Alleg. (Canterbury), p. 135.
London, 5, 5; New York, 3, 0.

Gorman.—Bapt. 'the son of Gormund'; cf. Osman and Wyman from Osmund and Wymond. Perhaps related to the Irish Gorman and O'Gorman. Lower says,' *Gormund* is an old Scotticism from the French *gourmand*, an enormous eater, a glutton.' This is not a happy solution, as the surname is not a Scotch one.

William Gormund, co. Wilts, 1273. A.
London, 5; New York, 130.

Gorringe.—Local; v. Goring.

Gorst, Gorse.—Local, 'at the gorse'; cf. Furse, q.v. Corrupted into Gorst. Thus the *t* in Gorst is excrescent. The surname is chiefly found in cos. Lanc. and Ches.

'Ralph Gorse, or Gorst, B.A., second master of Chester Grammar School, 1640; master of Winwick Grammar School, co. Lanc., 1666; master of Prestbury Grammar School, co. Ches., 1667': v. Earwaker's East Ches. ii. 519.
His nephew was Thomas Gorst.
Cf. William Newton-de-Gorses, 1609, Wilmslow: ibid. i. 105.
William de Gorz, cos. Warw. and Leic., Hen. III–Edw. I. K.

Johannes Garsce, 1379: P. T. Yorks. p. 68.
Liverpool, 5, 2; Manchester, 1, 0; London, 2, 0.

Gorstidge, Gorstige, Gorstice, Gossage, Gorstage, Gorsuch.—Local, ' of Gorsuch,' a spot in the parish of Ormskirk, co. Lanc. The many variants are curious but natural. The *t* is intrusive; cf. the Lancashire surname Gorse and Gorst, which represents one and the same name.

James Gorsuch, of Gorsuch, Scarisbrick, *gent*, 1615: Wills at Chester (1545-1620), p. 74.
James Gorsuch, of Ormskirk, 1605: ibid.
Ellen Gorsuch, of Knowsley, *widow*, 1575: ibid.
Henry Gorsage, of Kirkdale, 1579: ibid.
Peter Sant, of Gorstich, 1609: ibid.
Henry Gorstich, of West Derby, Liverpool, 1669: ibid. (1660–80), p. 106.
Edward Gorsuche, 1602: Preston Guild Rolls, p. 62.
Jacobus Gorsuch de Gorsuch, *gent*, 1642: ibid. p. 112.
Liverpool, 1, 1, 1, 1, 0, 0; Southport (Gorstage), 1; London (Gorsuch), 3.

Gorsuch.—Local; v. Gorstidge.

Gorwill.—Local, 'at the gorewell'; v. Gore.

Walter de Gorewell, co. Essex, 1273. A.
London, 1; New York, 1.

Gosbell.—Bapt.; v. Gospell.

Goshawk. — Nick. 'the goshawk,' literally goose-hawk (v. Skeat). But perhaps for Gosschalk (q.v.), which form of Gottschalk occurs in the London Directory. In such a case it would be imitative.

William Goshawke, rector of Bawsey, co. Norf., 1540: FF. viii. 346.
North Creake (co. Norfolk), 3; MDB. (Suffolk), 1.

Goslett.—Bapt. 'the son of Goce,' from double dim. Gocelet or Gocelot, of which I cannot find an early instance; cf. Roblett (Robelot) from Rob, Robert, or Hewlett (Hewelot) from Hew, i.e. Hugh; v. Joyce and Goss (2).

Charles Gostlett: Visit. Glouc. (1623), p. 67.
1773. Married—Arthur Goslet and Martha Kemp: St. Geo. Han. Sq. i. 228. London, 2.

Goslin, Gosline, Gosling, Goslings, Gossling, Gostling.—Bapt. 'the son of Goce' or ' Josse,' from dim. Gocelin or Josselin. In Gosling the *g* is excrescent; cf. Rawling, Tomling, Jennings, &c.; v. Goss (2) and Joslin.

Goslinus Dapifer, temp. 1109: Lincolnshire Survey, p. 6.
Gilbert, son of Gocelin: ibid. p. 2.
Goselina fil.Gawyne,co.Camb.,1273. A.
Symon Goseling, co. Norf., ibid.
Gauselin Johannes, 20 Edw. I. R.
Matilda fil. Gocelini, 20 Edw. I: BBB. p. 755.
Goslinus Dayvill, 1379: P. T. Yorks. p. 33.
Robert Geslyng, 1379: ibid. p. 43.
'John Gostlin, Master of Gonville and Caius Coll., Camb.' (1566?-1626): Dict. Nat. Biog. xxii. 265.
John Gostling (d. 1733), *chorister*: ibid.
London, 4, 0, 19, 1, 0, 5; Philadelphia, 2, 5, 2, 0, 4, 0.

Gospatrick.—Bapt. 'the son of Gospatrick.'

Gospatric fil. Mapbennoc, 1159: RRR. p. 2.
Waldeni' fil. Gospatricii, 1185: ibid. p. 40.
Gospatric fil. Raven, 1177: KKK. p. 26.
Eilaf fil. Gospatric, 1166: ibid. p. 10.
Gospatrick fil. Ormi, 21 Ric. II: Furness Coucher Book, i. 188.

Gospell, Gosbell.—Bapt. 'the son of Godesbal,' an imitative corruption.

Hugh Godesbal, co. Oxf., 1273. A.
Katherine Gosebolle, co. Hunts, ibid.

After five centuries the descendants of the above are found in the same district.

1736. Married—Gilbert Seabrook and Mary Gosbell, co. Bucks: St. Geo. Han. Sq. i. 17.

Gospell still exists. I have seen it, but forgot to note my instance down.

London, 0, 1.

Goss, Gosse.—(1) Nick. 'the goose'; M.E. *gos*; cf. Duck, Drake, Wildgoose, &c.

1502. 'Item, delivered to John Goose, my Lord of Yorkes fole (fool) in reward, 12*d*': Privy Purse Exp., Elizabeth of York, p. 2.
Isabel le Gous, co. Camb., 1273. A.
Walter le Gows, co. Camb., ibid.
Michael le Goys, co. Soms., ibid.
Richard le Gos, C. R., 36 Hen. III.
John le Goos, 1313 M.
Richard le Goos, co. Soms., 1 Edw. III: Kirby's Quest, p. 136.

Cicilia Gous, 1379: P. T. Yorks, p. 44.
Johannes Gosse, 1379: ibid. p. 117.
1538. Elyzabeth Goose, d. of Robarte Goose: St. Dionis Backchurch (London), p. 71.

A curious conjunction of names is found in the first of the following entries:

1549. Married—Nicholas Ferret and Agnes Goose: St. Dionis Backchurch (London), p. 2.
'Thomas Goose was executed at Garstang, co. Lanc., Feb. 14, 1716, for joining the Scotch insurgents in 1715': Baines' Lanc. ii. 533.

Although Wildgoose still exists, our Gooses (I may not say Geese) have now stuck to Goss as a preferable form.

(2) Bapt. 'the son of Goce,' whence dim. Gocelin or Josselin; v. Goose (2) and Goslin. Although the diminutive has quite overshadowed the root-name, it was decidedly popular in its day. For full account, v. Joyce. In a hamlet containing fourteen householders there are found the two following names:

Simon Joce, co. Soms., 1 Edw. III: Kirby's Quest, p. 207.
William Goose, co. Soms., 1 Edw. III: ibid.

Cf. the hard and soft g in Gocelin and Goslin.

London, 7, 0; Crockford, 2, 2; Philadelphia, 6, 2.

Gossage; v. Gorstidge.

Gosschalk, Gottchalk, Gottschalck. — Bapt. 'the son of Gottschalk.' Though a modern German immigrant surname, it was very early introduced into England as a font-name by the Flemings; it scarcely can be said, however, to have taken root.

Godescallus (without surname), co. Salop, 1273. A.
William Godescalk, co. Oxf., ibid.
Godeskalke de Estlaund, co. Linc., ibid.
Godefry fil. Godescallus. C.
Godeskalcus Armorer, co. York. W. 2.
London, 1, 0, 0; Manchester, 0, 1, 1; Philadelphia, 0, 0, 4.

Gosset, Gossett.—Bapt. 'the son of Goce' or 'Josse,' from dim. Gocet or Josset; v. Joyce.

Isabella Josset, co. Camb., 1273. A.
Robert Josset, co. Camb., ibid.
London, 1, 0; Philadelphia, 0, 2.

Gossip.—Nick. 'the gossip' or 'godsib,' lit. god-relative, a sponsor in baptism (v. Skeat). Crony is a later meaning.

Willelmus Gossyp, 1379: P. T. Yorks. p. 20.
Emma Gosyp, 1379: ibid. p. 21.
Isabella Gossyp, 1379: ibid.
West Rid. Court Dir., 2; Doncaster, 1.

Gostling.—Bapt.; v. Goslin. The t is intrusive.

Gothard, Goddard, Godart.—Occup. 'the goatherd; A.S. gat and herd, as in cowherd, shepherd; v. Herd. Gothard in Yorkshire is undoubtedly the descendant of some old goatherd who took his surname from the occupation.

'Burning of Goddesbrigg, 3000 kine and oxen, 4000 sheep and gate,' 1587: Nicolson and Burn, Hist. Westm. and Cumb., i. p. xxxvi.
Symon Godhird, 1379: P. T. Yorks. p. 207.
Johannes Gaytbyrd, 1379: ibid. p. 273.
John Godherd, co. York, 1470. W. 11.
Robert Gaytherd, co. York, 1472, ibid.
Roland Gateard, co. York. W. 9.
Robert Gatherd, co. York, ibid.

Of course Goddard (q.v.) has a different origin from the above, but none the less is it certain that in some cases Gothard has assimilated itself thereto.

London. 2, 48, 2; Sheffield, 1, 7, 0; Huddersfield, 1, 1, 0; Philadelphia, 2, 21, 0.

Gotobed.—Bapt. 'the son of Godbert.' This surname must unquestionably be referred back to Godebert (Yonge, ii. 177), though after a time the name has itself suggested a jeu d'esprit.
The following instances will suffice for evidence:

Roger Godberd, co. Notts, 1273. A.
John Gotebedde, co. Camb., ibid.
Roger Godeberd. J.
Henry Gotobed, temp. 1580. Z.

Johannes Gotobedde (RR. 1) seems to mark the divergence into a pleasantry. Mr. Lower quotes 'Robert Gotobedd, Winchelsea, 20 Edw. I. Juliana Gotobedde, ibid.' A mere nickname would not be found all over the country. It appears certain that Godebert is the root of all.

1621. Ann Gotobed: Cal. of Wills in Court of Husting (2).

1760. Married—Charles Godbed and Penelope Cooper: St. Geo. Han. Sq. i. 94.
London, 2; Manchester, 1; MDB. (Cambridge), 7.

Gott.—Local, 'at the gott,' a drain or water-channel. A wellknown Yorkshire name. In Craven dialect and in Hallamshire a gote or goyt denotes a water-channel from a mill-dam; cf. Gutter; v. Skeat on gut and Way's Prompt. Parv. p. 205; cf. the Yorkshire Sykes.

John de la Gote, 3 Edw. III: Freemen of York, i. 25.
Johannes del Gote, 1379: P. T. Yorks. p. 6.
Magota del Gote, 1379: ibid. p. 7.
Johanna atte Gotte, 1379: P. T. Howdenshire, p. 5.
Robertus atte Gotte, 1379: ibid.
London, 1; West Rid. Court Dir., 11; New York, 4.

Gottchalk, Gottschalck; v. Gosschalk.

Goudge.—Bapt. 'the son of Guch'; v. Gooch.

Gough. — Nick. (Welsh) 'the red-complexioned'; v. Goff. One of the very few nicknames that can be found in Welsh directories.

Robert Gogh, co. Soms., 1 Edw. III: Kirby's Quest, p. 237.
London, 23; Philadelphia, 13.

Goulborn, Goulburn, Gouldbourne, Gouldburn. — Local, 'of Golborne,' a small township in the parish of Winwick, co. Lanc.

'In the reign of Henry III, Thomas de Goldebur' held of the King the third part of the fee of one Knight; and William, the son of Hamo, held three bovates in Goldburn of the gift of Augustine, father of the said Thomas': Baines' Lanc. ii. 212.
Manchester, 2, 1, 1, 1.

Gould.—Bapt.; v. Gold.

Gouldstone, Goulstone, Gulson, Goulson, Goldson, Goulston.—Personal, 'the son of Goldstan.' Although these surnames look local, it is very doubtful whether such be the case. I cannot find any spot so called, and all early instances are without the prefix de or de la. On the other hand, Goldstan would be a likely personal name; cf. Wulfstan and Goldwin.

Hugh Goldston, co. Bedf., 1273. A.
Michael Goldston, co. Bedf., ibid.

Ralph Goldston, co. Bedf., 1273. A.
Geoffrey Goldston, co. Bucks, Hen.
III-Edw. I. K.
William Goldstan, co. Linc., 20 Edw.
I. R.
Johannes Gulderson, 1379: P. T. Yorks.
p. 148.
1670. Lancelot Addison and Jane
Gouldston (or Gulston): Marriage Alleg.
(Canterbury), p. 179.
1761. Married—Henry Goldstone and
Frances Ford: St. Geo. Han. Sq. i. 100.
1764. — Samuel Godson and Hannah
Cordery: ibid. p. 128.
London, 6, 4, 3, 0, 0, 0; Liverpool
(1887), 0, 0, 0, 1, 1, 0; Boston (U.S.),
(Goulston), 6.

Goundrey; v. Gundry.

Gourder, Gourdmaker. —
Occup. 'the gourder,' one who
carried liquor in a vessel called
a gourd, perhaps so called from
its shape (Halliwell).

'To the Manciple he toke the gourd
again.'   Chaucer, C. T. 17031.
Martin le Gourdmaker, 11 Edw. III:
Freemen of York, i. 32.
Philip de Turnay, gourder, 3 Edw.
III: ibid. p. 25.

Although not a surname, this
last entry may interest the student.

Gow. — Occup. 'the smith'
(Gaelic).

London, 7; New York, 3.

Goward.—? Local. Probably,
as suggested by Lower, a corrupted
form of Gower (q.v.) with an excrescent d; cf. Simmonds for Simmons. Nevertheless it may be a
personal name, and mean 'the
son of Goward,' i. e. Godward.
This is strongly corroborated by
the existence of Goward in the
Hundred Rolls of 1273 A. D.

Wydo Goward, co. Norf., 1273. A.
1613. Married—Robert Godward and
Susan Remnant: St. Dionis Backchurch
(London), p. 18.
1666. — Ritchard Biggs and Mary
Goward: St. Jas. Clerkenwell, iii. 127.
London, 3; Boston (U.S.), 5.

Gower. — Local, a variant of
Gore, q.v.; cf. Power.

David Gower, co. Soms., 1 Edw. III:
Kirby's Quest, p. 89.
London, 21; Boston (U.S.), 1.

Gozzard, Gishard.—Occup.
'the gooseherd,' a tender of geese.
One of many compounds of herd;
cf. Coward, Calvert, and Stoddart.

Gooseherd was a Yorkshire surname, and still remains there as
Gozzard and Gishard. These solu-
tions are absolutely certain.

Joan Gushyrde, co. York. W. 11.
Agnes Gusehyrd, co. York, ibid.
John Gooshewed, co. York. W. 19.
London, 1, 0; Leeds, 1, 0; Rotherham,
0, 1.

Grace, Gras, Grass.—(1) Nick.
'le gras,' the fat, the lusty. Common to every early register. The
personal name Grace came far too
late to affect surnames. Nevertheless cf. Gracio de Frese, C. R.,
1 Edw. II.

Ascelin le Gras, co. Norf., Hen. III-
Edw. I. K.
Roger Grassus, co. Linc., ibid.
Roger le Gras, co. Wilts, 1273. A.
Alan le Gras, co. York, ibid.
Hugh le Gras, co. Linc., ibid.
Richard le Gras, co. Berks, 20 Edw. I. R.
Amabel le Gras, c. 1300. M.
Thomas Gras fil. Johannis Pomeray,
Pardons Roll, 12 Ric. II.

(2) Local, 'at the grass,' from
residence thereby.

William atte Grase, co. Soms., 1 Edw.
III: Kirby's Quest, p. 110.
1548. Married—Roberte Dowethe and
Eliz. Grace: St. Michael, Cornhill, p. 5.
1574. Bapt.—Margery, d. Thomas
Grace: St. Jas. Clerkenwell, i. 8.
1744. Married—Thomas Grace and
Mary Hotchkis: St. Geo. Han. Sq. i. 33.
London, 12, 1, 0; Philadelphia, 60, 1, 0.

Gradwell, Graddell.—Local,
'of Gradwell' or 'Gradwells,' now
a farm in the township of Ulnes-
Walton, in the parish of Croston,
co. Lanc. The surname has spread
in the surrounding district.

Richard Gradell, 1542: Preston Guild
Rolls, p. 15.
John Gradell, clericus, 1562: ibid. p. 21.
Edward Graddell, 1622: ibid. p. 68.
Thomas Gradwell, 1642: ibid. p. 130.
Richard Gradell, of Preston, 1550:
Lancashire Wills at Richmond, p. 125.
Roger Graddell, of Wood Plumpton,
1680: ibid.
Manchester, 6, 0; Preston, 3, 0; Liver-
pool, 2, 0; Philadelphia, 2, 0.

Grafton.—Local, 'of Grafton,'
parishes in diocs. of Peterborough,
Worcester, Hereford, and Salisbury. The Yorkshire instances below concern Marton-cum-Grafton,
a parish three miles from Borough-
bridge, in the liberty of Knaresborough.

William de Grafton, 2 Edw. II: Free-
men of York, i. 12.
Robertus de Grafton, 1379: P. T.
Yorks. p. 243.
Alicia de Grafton, 1379: ibid. p. 295.
London, 6; Philadelphia, 2.

Grain. — Bapt. 'the son of
Grain.' In spite of the local entry
below, this name must have a personal origin. There are nearly a
dozen Graynesons in the Yorkshire
Poll Tax. I only give a few instances. The forms Graynewife
and Grayneman, too, strongly cor-
roborate this view; v. Crane (2).

Willelmus de Grayne, 1379: P. T.
Yorks. p. 156.
Walterus Grayne, 1379: ibid.
Thomas Grayne, 1379: ibid. p. 4.
Johannes Grayneson, 1379: ibid. p. 32.
Ricardus Grayneson, 1379: ibid. p. 122.
Robertus Grayneson, 1379: ibid.
Willelmus Grayne, husband, 1379:
P. T. Howdenshire, p. 23.
Alanus Grayne, brewster, 1379: ibid.
p. 24.
Cf. Alicia Graynewyfe (i. e. the wife of
Grayne), 1379: P. T. Yorks, p. 123.
Willelmus Grayne-man (i. e. the servant
of Grayne), 1379: ibid. p. 241.
Thomas Grayne-barn (i. e. the child of
Grayne), 1379: ibid. p. 291.
London, 4; Oxford, 4; Philadelphia, 1.

Graindorge. — (1) Local, 'de
Grandorge,' a Norman name
which settled, among other places,
in Craven, co. York. This surname in various guises still lives
in the West Riding; v. Grandage.
(2) Nick. 'a barley-corn'; cf. English
'John Barleycorn'; v. Lower,
Patr. Brit. pp. 18 and 136.

William Graindeorge, 1127: Furness
Coucher Book, i. 25.
William Greindeorge, co. York, 1273. A.
William Greyndeorge, C. R., 7 Edw. I.
Johannes Greyndorge, 33 Edw. I:
BBB. p. 696.

A curious corruption is found in
the following :

Mergareta Dangorge, 1379: P. T.
Yorks. p. 39.

Almost as curious is the modern
Yorkshire form of Crandige :

George Crandidge: Pontefract Dir.

But Grandage (q.v.) is the modern
form.

Grainge.—Local; v. Grange.

Grainger.—Occup.; v. Granger.

Grammer.—Occup. 'the grammer,' a teacher of grammar, a grammarian.

William Gramery, co. Wilts, 1273. A.
Andrew le Gramayre, co. York, ibid.
William Grammaticus. J.
Richard le Gramayre. G.
William le Gramary, M.P. for co. Ebor., C. R., 20 Edw. III. pt. ii.
Johanna Gramary, 1379: P. T. Yorks. p. 153.
1647. Bapt.—Eliz., d. Jonathan Grammer: St. Jas. Clerkenwell, i. 167.
1648. — John, s. Jonathan Grammar: ibid. p. 171.
London, 4; New York, 2.

Grandage, Grandridge. —
(1) Local. The name occurs early in co. York, and is still found there as Grandage and Crandidge; v. Graindorge. (2) Nick.; v. Graindorge (2).

Nicholas Grandage, *armatus*, 1379: P. T. Yorks. p. 274.
Thomas Grandage, 1379: ibid.
Robertus Grandage, 1379: ibid.
Christopher Grandorge, 1631, vicar of Broughton in Craven.
West Rid. Court Dir., 3, 0; Dewsbury, 0, 1.

Grandison. — Local? It is thought that this surname came from the Netherlands (v. Lower).

Otto de Grandisono, co. Cardigan, Edw. I. R.
William de Grandisono, co. Glouc., ibid.
Boston (U.S.), 1.

Grange, Grainge.—Local, 'at the grange'; O.F. *grange*, a granary, or barn for corn. 'Johannes attes Prions, et Alicia uxor ejus, fermour del graunge': 1379, P. T. Yorks. p. 71.

Johannes del Grange, 1379: P. T. Yorks. p. 30.
Simon del Graunge, 1379: ibid. p. 19.
Alicia del Graunge, 1379: ibid. p. 21.
Gregorius del Grange, 1379: ibid. p. 39.
London, 3, 1; Oxford, 0, 2; Philadelphia, 5, 0.

Grangeman. — Occup. 'the grangeman,' the same as Granger, q.v.

Willelmus Grangman, 1379: P. T. Yorks. p. 227.

Granger, Grainger.—Occup. · the granger,' one who kept a grange or granary, a farmer; v. Grange.

Johannes Graunger, 1379: P.T. Yorks. p. 288.

Willelmus Graungere, 1379: ibid. p. 66.
Henricus Graunger, 1379: P. T. Howdenshire, p. 24.
Thomas Graynger. F.
London, 8, 10; West Rid. Court Dir., 6, 1; New York, 21, 4.

Grant.—(1) Nick. 'le grand,' great, large. A sobriquet for one of big and broad proportions, a giant in size. This surname has ramified very strongly in Scotland.

Gregory le Grant, co. Camb., 1273. A.
John le Graunt, co. Oxf., ibid.
Richard le Graunt, co. Wilts, ibid.
Hamo le Graunt, co. York, ibid.
William le Graunt, co. Berks, Hen III—Edw. I. K.
Ralph le Grant, co. Wilts, ibid.
Thomas Graunte, 1379: P. T. Yorks. p. 119.
1575. Married—Patricke Graunt and Jane Belgrave: St. Dionis Backchurch (London), p. 8.
1648. — Samuell Grant and Sara Hower: St. Peter, Cornhill, i. 258.

(2) Nick. 'the son of Grant.' No doubt the origin is the same. Either affixed to a very plump baby (!), or a sobriquet given later on to a very big boy, which sobriquet gradually ousted his baptismal name. School nicknames even now last for a lifetime.

Roger fil. Grant, co. Salop, 1273. A.
Grant le Chapman, co. Devon, ibid.
London, 71; Philadelphia, 108.

Grantham.—Local, ' of Grantham,' a town in co. Lincoln.

1544. Married—John Grantam and Katheryn Bennet: St. Dionis Backchurch (London), p. 2.
London, 7; Philadelphia, 1.

Granvill, Granville.—Local; v. Grenville.

Gras, Grass. — Nick. 'fat, lusty '; v. Grace.

Gration.—Bapt. A variant of Grayson, q.v. This curious but natural corruption is found in Yorkshire, one of the great homes of Grayson. It stands for Grayshon, the *h* being intrusive, as in Townshend for Townsend, Hodshon for Hodgson, &c.

Cf. Margaret Hodshon, of Little Urswick, 1660: Lancashire Wills at Richmond, p. 153.
Robert Hodshon, of Hawkshead, 1646: ibid.
It only remains to prove that the form Grayshon existed. It is even

now in the Leeds and Pudsey directories, the very district where Grayson is so common, and where Gration has established itself.

Bradford, 2; Leeds, 1.

Grave, Graves. — (1) Local, ' of the grave' (v. Greaves); the earlier form of Greave or Grove. (2) Offic. 'the graff'; v. Graveston.

Edith de la Grava, co. Oxf., 1273. A.
Henry de la Grave, co. Oxf., ibid.
Hugh de la Grave, co. Soms., ibid.
John de la Grave, co. Wilts, ibid.
Geoffrey de la Grave, co. Glouc., Hen. III—Edw. I. K.
Sibilla de la Grave, co. Glouc., 20 Edw. I. R.
Robert atte Grave, c. 1300. M.
Johannes Graue (*u* for *v*), 1379: P. T. Yorks. p. 282.
Adam Grayf, 1379: P. T. Yorks. p. 121.
Johanna Grayf, 1379: ibid. p. 9.
Robertus Grayff, 1379: ibid.
1600. Edmund Grave and Dorothy Smith: Marriage Lic. (Westminster), p. 13.
1607. Married—John Johnson and Rose Graves: St. Jas. Clerkenwell, iii. 32.
London, 7, 33; Manchester, 4, 2; New York, 1, 35.

Graver.—Occup. ' the graver,' i.e. a digger, a diker. In Furness the following conversation might occur :

'What's ta bin doing !'
'I've bin graving pe-at' (digging peat).
'How's ta done?'
'I've grovin six carts.'

Willelmus Grauer (*u* for *v*), 1379: P. T. Yorks. p. 65.
Walter Grauer (*u* for *v*), 1379: ibid. p. 207.
Henricus Grauer (*u* for *v*), 1379: ibid. p. 246.
London, 1; Philadelphia, 29.

Graveson.—Nick.; v. Grayson.

London (1887), 1; Bolton, 1.

Graveston, Grayston.—Bapt. 'the son of the greeve'; v. Grayson. Corruptions of Graveson. Proof, if needed, may be found in the Guild Rolls of Preston; v. Index, where Graysoun, Grayveson, and Grayveston represent the same patronymic.

Manchester, 1, 0; Preston, 0, 1.

Gray, Grey. — (1) Nick. 'the grey,' from the complexion of the hair; cf. Russell, Brown, White, Black, &c. (2) Local, 'de Grey.' I do not know the spot, but (1) is the chief parent.

Robert de Gray, co. Oxf., 1273. A.
John le Gray, co. Camb., ibid.
Eva de Grey, co. Soms., ibid.
Peter le Gray, *irenmanger*, 13 Edw.
II : Freemen of York, i. 18.
1523. William Knevett and Katharine
Grey : Marriage Lic. (London), i. 3.
London, 123, 21 ; Philadelphia, 228, 24.

Graygoose.—Nick. 'the graygoose'; cf. the simpler 'Goss,' a
common entry in the Hundred
Rolls (1273), or Wildgoose.

'Thomas Drywood, *gent*, of Stifford,
Essex, and Mary Graygoose, of St. An-
drews, in Hertford, widow of William
Graygoose, *yeoman*,' 1623 : Marriage
Lic. (London), ii. 126.
1639. Henry Graygoose and Elizabeth
Hobley : Marriage Lic. (Westminster),
p. 38.

Grayhorse.—? Local, 'at the
Gray Horse' (?), probably a sign-
name. Alexander Grayhorse, Prior
of Trentham, Patent Roll, 2
Hen. VII. pt. i. Cf. Whitehorse,
Roebuck.

Grayshon.—Nick.; v. Gration.

**Grayson, Gresson, Greeson,
Grierson, Grearson, Grason.**—
Nick. 'the son of the reeve'; A.S.
gerefa. Yorkshire is the true early
home of this name. It is quite
possible that Gregson (from Gregory) may have become modified
to Gresson in some few cases.
Geoffrey, also, may make its claim
felt. But, in general, we are bound
to assume, judging by the evidence
given below, that Grayson and his
confrères are descendants of the
old English *greeve*; cf. Wrightson,
Taylorson, Herdson, Hindson, &c.
v. Grave (2).

Alicia Grayfdoghter, 1379: P.T. Yorks.
p. 188.
Willelmus Grayf, 1379 : ibid.
Johannes Grayfson, 1379 : ibid. p. 186.
Agnes Grayfwyf, 1379 : ibid. p. 197.
Thomas Grayfson, 1379 : ibid.
Emma Grefeson, 1379 : ibid. p. 234.
Thomas Grayfson, 1379 : ibid. p. 35.
Thomas Grayfson, 1379 : ibid. p. 193.
Johannes Graueson (*u* for *v*), 1379 : ibid.
p. 279.
Johannes Graue (*u* for *v*), 1379 : ibid.
p. 283.
Mary Grayson, co. York. W. 16.
Cuthbert Greyson (or Greveson), 1516 :
Reg. Univ. Oxf. i. 98.
John Graveson, of Warton, 1565: Lan-
cashire Wills at Richmond, p. 126.
Gervas Graveson, of Yealand Stors,
1593 : ibid.

George Grayson, of Salwicke, 1639:
ibid.
John Greason, of Lancaster, 1637:
ibid.
Parnell Greyson, of Salwick, 1668:
ibid. p. 130.

All these names manifestly belong
to one stock, and settle the matter,
if any controversy existed. For
two corrupted forms, v. Grayshon
and Gration.

Sheffield (Grayson), 12 ; West Rid.
Court Dir. (Grayson), 8 ; Liverpool
(1887), 8, 1, 1, 7, 1, 0; Dewsbury (Grason),
1 ; Philadelphia (Grayson), 6.

Grazier.—Occup. 'the grazier,'
a rare term ; I only find it once.

William le Grasiere, co. Bucks, 1273. A.

Great.—Nick. 'the great,' large,
big ; cf. Grant.

Henry le Grete, co. Bucks, 1273. A.
Peter le Grete, co. Salop, ibid.

Greathead, Greated.—Nick.
'great head,' probably a translation
of French *Grosseteste*, q.v.

Agnes Gretheved, co. Linc., Edw. I-
II. R.
Peter Gretheued, C. R., 17 Edw. III.
pt. i.
Thomas Gretehed. H.
Hugo Grethed, 1379: P. T. Yorks.
p. 206.
Willelmus Gretehed, 1379: ibid. p. 198.
1619. Marmaduke Greathead and
Katherine Dorrell : Marriage Lic. (Lon-
don), p. 81.
1755. Married—Thomas Greathead and
Ann Spray : St. Geo. Han. Sq. i. 58.
London, 1, 1.

**Greatorex, Great-Rex, Great-
rex, Greatorix.**—(1) Local, 'at
the great ridge'; v. Rigg and
Ridge. (2) Local, 'at the great
rake or rakes.' 'Rake, a rut, crack,
or crevice. North' (Halliwell). In
Furness and co. Cumb. it seems
to have been a sheep-track up the
fells. But of this I cannot speak
positively. I had both Rake and Out-
rake as localities in my late parish
(Ulverston). Probably Raikes
owes its origin to one of these many
places. Thus Greatorex seems
to be either 'of the great ridge'
or 'of the great rakes,' from residence thereby. If the former, then
ridge has been sharpened into *rex*.

1582. Augustine Brandon and Eliz.
Greatracks, of Westham, co. Essex :
Marriage Lic. (London), i. 110.
1647. Married—Samuel Gratrix and

Jane Wingfield : St. Jas. Clerkenwell,
iii. 81.
1659. Married—John Greatrake and
Ursula Whitaker : ibid. p. 101.
1697. — James Berry and Rebecca
Greatrick : ibid. p. 217.
London, 10, 1, 1, 0 ; Manchester, 6, 0,
0, 1 ; Philadelphia, 1, 0, 2, 0.

Greaves, Greeves. — Local,
'at the greave' or 'greaves.' For
variants and many instances, v.
Grave and Graver. Equivalent to
Grove, q.v. Originally a glade
or lane cut through the trees in
the forest; from English verb *grave*,
to cut ; A.S. *graf*, a grove.

'For so raythely thay rusche with
roselde speris,
That the raskaille was rade, and rane
to the grefes.'
Morte Arthure, MS. Lincoln,
F. 83 (Halliwell).

Fairfax speaks of the
'Wind in holts and shady greaves.'
Agnes de Greues (*u* for *v*), 1379 : P. T.
Yorks. p. 267.
1610. Bapt.—May, d. John Greaues,
pewterer : St. Dionis Backchurch (Lon-
don), p. 94.
London, 25, 4 ; Manchester, 19, 0 ;
Philadelphia, 29, 6.

Gredley.—Local, 'of Gredley.'
Adam Gredle, co. Lanc., Hen. III-
Edw. I. K.
Robert de Gredle, co. Oxf., 1273. A.
Thomas Gredley, co. Notts, ibid.
Hawys de Gredley, co. Suff., 20 Edw.
I. R.
London, 2.

Greedy.—Local, ' of Gredhey.'
Greedy is an imitative dress. As
regards the suffix, v. Hey. The
name is evidently a West-country
one.

Robert Gredheye, co. Soms., 1 Edw.
III : Kirby's Quest, p. 244.
MDB. (co. Somerset), 2.

Greely, Greeley.—Local, 'of
Greeley.' I cannot find the spot.
From the evidence below it would
seem that the meaning is 'the grey
meadow'; v. Ley; cf. Whiteley
and Blackley.

Thomas de Greyley, co. Rutland,
1273. A.
Albricus de Greyleye, co. Rutland,
ibid.
Robert de Greyle, co. Camb., ibid.
Robert Greyleg, co. Soms., 1 Edw. III :
Kirby's Quest, p. 248.
London, 1, 0 ; New York, 2, 6.

Green, Greene.—Local, 'at
the green,' from residence thereby.

A grassy plat used by the village as common. As every village had its green, it is not surprising that our modern directories teem with the name.

Deonisia ate Grene, 1273. A.
Warin de la Grene, ibid.
Robert de la Grene, C. R., 3 Edw. I.
Petrus de Grene, 1379: P. T. Yorks. p. 10.
Adam del Grene, 1379: ibid. p. 16.
Willelmus del Grene, 1379: ibid. p. 55.
London, 340, 10; New York, 265, 111.

Greenacre. — Local, 'of the green acre' or 'green acres'; -acre is not an uncommon suffix to local names. Greenacre means the green field.

Ric. de Grenacres, 6 Edw. III: Oldham Guardian, 'Old Homesteads.'
Arthur Grenachar, 1564: Reg. Univ. Oxf. i. 254.
Alexander Grenacres, 1564: ibid. p. 255. London, 5.

Greenall. — Local; v. Greenhalgh, of which it is a corruption.

1688. Mr. John Greenball (Greenhalgh), of Brandlesom, and Mrs. Anne Tatton, of Withinshawe: Reg. Northenden, co. Ches., East Ches. i. 304.

Greenaway, Greenway. — Local, 'at the green way' or 'road'; a intrusive for euphony; cf. Otway and Ottaway. No doubt many spots would be styled the green way, but probably the place denoted in the following has given birth to many of this name: 'John Bridgeman (1577-1652), bishop of Chester, was born at Exeter. His grandfather . . . had, with other issue, two sons, Michael the eldest, . . . and Thomas, of Greenway, Devonshire': Dict. Nat. Biog. vi. 317. This is probably Greenway, in the parish of Churston Ferrers.

Robert Grenewey, co. Oxf., 1273. A.
John Grenewey, co. Soms., 1 Edw. III: Kirby's Quest, p. 81.
John atte Grenewey, co. Soms., 1 Edw. III: ibid. p. 107.
Thomas Greenewaie, 1567: Reg. Univ. Oxf. i. 266.
Thomas Greenway, of Oswaldtwistle, 1618: Wills at Chester (1545-1620), p. 76.
1643. Married—Robert Hyron and Eliz. Grinnoway: St. Peter, Cornhill, i. 257.
London, 6, 0; Plymouth, 0, 2; MDB. (Devonshire), 1, 2; Oxford, 7, 0; New York, 2, 0; Philadelphia, 0, 1.

Greenbank. — Local, 'at the green bank,' a common term for small verdant slopes. There is a Greenbank in my old parish (Ulverston) overlooking the church, now covered with houses; cf. Windebank.

1642. Married—William Grover and Alice Greenbanke: St. Peter, Cornhill, i. 257.
1661. John Greenbancke (Worcester) and Martha Hanson: Marriage Lic. (London), ii. 283.
Nicholas Greenbancke, of Caton, 1595: Lancashire Wills at Richmond, p. 107
Alice Greenbancke, of Caton, 1641: ibid.
London, 1; Manchester, 1; Philadelphia, 4.

Greenett. — Local; v. Greenhead.

Greenfield, Greenfeld. — Local, 'at the green field'; cf. Grenfell.

Willelmus Grenefeld', 1379: P. T. Yorks. p. 208.
Elena Grenefeld', 1379: ibid. p. 209.
Birmingham (1884), 3, 0; New York, 11, 2.

Greengarth. — Local, 'at the green garth'; v. Garth.

Henricus Grenegarth, 1379: P. T. Yorks. p. 214.

Greengrass. — Local, 'at the green grass'; cf. Greenfield. I find no early instances.

1623. Married—William Arkinstall and Bridget Greenegrasse: St. Antholin (London), p. 57.
1657.—Thomas Greenegrasse and Eliz. Burton: St. Dionis Backchurch (London), p. 33.

Greenhalgh, Greenhough, Greenhow, Greenough, Greenow, Greenup, Greenhaulgh. — Local, 'of Greenhalgh,' a township in the parish of Kirkham, co. Lanc. Also 'of Greenhalgh,' now Greenhalgh Castle, in Garstang parish, co. Lanc. (spelt Greenhaugh; v. Baines' Lanc. ii. 534). With Greenhough and Greenow, cf. enough and enow: halgh = haugh.

Cf. Gilbert del Whithalgh, 1397: Preston Guild Rolls, p. 4.
Arthur Greenhalgh, of Heap, 1576: Wills at Chester (1545-1620), p. 76.
Thomas Greenhalgh, of Ashton in Winnick, 1584: ibid.
Robert Greenhough, of Great Sankey, 1613: ibid.

James Greenalgh, of Cornerow, 1672: Lancashire Wills at Richmond, p. 128.
Agnes Greeneoff, of Dalton, 1635: ibid.
Richard Greenope, of Dalton, 1590: ibid. p. 129.
William Greenup, of Colton, 1661: ibid.

A single glance at these wills will show a common origin and stock. Members of the same family are thus entered in the neighbouring register of Ulverston a century later:

1791. Bapt.—William, s. Joseph Greenhow, of Southwaite; Reg. Ulverston Ch., ii. 519.
1810. Buried—Anne, d. John Greenhough: ibid. p. 639.

Thus every variant is found in entries relating to one stock.

1699. Married—Robert Greenenough and Philadelphia Starr: St. Michael, Cornhill, p. 50.
1785. David Greenough, vicar of Gill, Barnoldswick: Whitaker's Craven, p. 86.
London, 1, 1, 3, 2, 1, 0, 0; Manchester, 14, 6, 3, 2, 0, 3, 0; MDB. (co. Lanc.), 8, 1, 0, 1, 0, 1, 1; Philadelphia, 7, 0, 0, 2, 0, 0, 0.

Greenham. — Local, 'of Greenham,' a chapelry in the parish of Thatcham, co. Berks.

Ralph de Greneham, co. Suff., 1273. A.
Ralph de Grenham, co. Suff., 20 Edw. I. R.
London, 1.

Greenhead, Greenett. — Local, 'at the green head,' i.e. the green promontory. As Greenhead became Greenett so Blackhead became Blackett; cf. also Birkett and Hazlitt.

Willelmus Grenehude, 1379: P. T. Yorks. p. 143.
Henricus Grenehode, barkar, 1379: ibid. p. 159.
Johannes Grenehode, 1379: ibid. p. 167.

Greenhill. — Local, 'at the green hill,' or more specifically 'of Greenhill': (1) a liberty in the wapentake of Corringham, co. Lincoln; (2) a hamlet in the parish of Harrow, co. Middlesex. But many small spots would be called the green hill, and the surnames may have arisen in half a dozen localities.

John de Grenhull, co. Bedf., 1273. A.
John de Grenhull, co. Soms., 1 Edw. III: Kirby's Quest, p. 137.

Robertus de Grenhill', 1379: P. T. Yorks. p. 73.
Thomas de Grenehill', 1379 : ibid. p. 19.
Johannes de Grenehill', 1379: ibid. p. 142.
1750 Married—George Sayer and Mary Greenhill : St. Geo. Han. Sq. i. 44.
Birmingham (1884), 6 ; London, 12.

Greenhorn.—Nick. Still existing. A young simpleton, one who is like a young animal whose horns are only just sprouting.

Christopher Greynhorne, co. York. W. 15.
'Greynhorne as name of an ox occurs in Towneley Mysteries, p. 8': Halliwell.
London, 1 ; Manchester (1887), 1.

Greenhouse.—Local, 'at the green-house,' from residence thereby or therein.

William de Grenhous, co. Camb., 1273. A.
London, 1 ; Philadelphia, 3.

Greening, Greenig. — Bapt. 'the son of Greening' ; cf. Browning or Harding.

Robert Grenyg, co. Norf., 1273. A.
London, 7, 0 ; Philadelphia, 0, 9.

Greenleaf.—? Nick. 'Greenleaf, a character in the pageants of Robin Hood' (Lower). No doubt the same as Greenman, q.v. Nevertheless, the surname seems to be local, i.e. Green-cliff ; cf. Antliff for Antcliff, and Topliff for Topcliffe.

Johannes de Grenelef et Lora uxor ejus, *spicer*, 1379: P. T. Yorks p. 15
Elen Grenelef, co. Soms., 1 Edw. III : Kirby's Quest, p. 222.

This name through early emigration has become strong in America.

'William Greenlefe sailed from Gravesend in 1635 for St. Christopher's': Hotten's Lists of Emigrants, p. 128.
Robert Greenleafe went so early as 1610, and settled at 'Charles Cittie in Virginia'—married, and left children: ibid. p. 204.
New York, 11.

Greenman, Greeneman.—Nick. 'the green man,' signifying a savage. Strutt describes the greenmen of old shows as 'whimsically attired and disguised with droll masks, having large staves or clubs headed with cases of crackers.' The term is still retained in the sign of 'The Greenman and Still' in Oxford Street and other places (Halliwell) ; cf. Greenleaf. These

men, attired in green leaves, were ever an accompaniment in public pageants. The Lord Mayor's Show used to engage their services. 'Then cam 2 grett wodyn with 2 grett clubes all in grene': Machyn's Diary, Oct. 29, 1553. 'On the x of Julee met her (Queen Elizabeth) in the Forest, as she came from hunting, one clad like a savage man all in ivie': Nicholl's Progresses of Queen Elizabeth, i. 494. As with King, q.v., Greenman or Greenleaf became the popular sobriquet of the man who represented the character, and passed on to his children. But see further History of Signboards, pp. 366-7. In spite of all this it is probable that Greenman was the cant name at a still earlier period for a forester, who was always dressed in 'Lincoln' or 'Kendal green,' as all our ballads relate ; v. History of Signboards, pp. 367-8.
New York, 3, 1 ; Philadelphia, 16, 0.

Greenoak. — Local, 'at the green oak'; cf. Greentree.

Cecilia de Greneake, 1379: P. T. Howdenshire, p. 9.
Johannes Grenak, 1379: P. T. Yorks. p. 205.
Ricardus Greneake, 1379 : ibid. p. 291.
1641. Buried—Sarah Greenick, pitt in ye East yard : St. Peter, Cornhill, i. 198.
London, 1.

Greenrod, Greenroyd. — Local ; v. Grindrod.

Greenslade, Grinslade. — Local, ' of the green slade,' a spot in co. Devon ; v. Slade.

'Robertus de Greneslade tenet in Greneslade iii p'tem,' co. Devon. K.
Antony Greneslade, temp. Eliz. Z.
'Oct. 27, at Poltimore Church, G. G. Hick to Bessie Greenslade, Stoke Canon': Standard, Oct. 30, 1886.
London, 1, 3.

Greensmith. — Occup. 'the greensmith,' probably a worker in lead or laten.

Henry Greensmith, temp. Eliz. Z.
Richard Grensmythe, ibid.
Edward Greensmith, co. Norf. FF.
Cf. Blacksmith, a worker in iron, Brownsmith in copper and brass, Whitesmith in tin, and Redsmith in gold. It is only in our direc-

tories, however, that traces of all these sobriquets exist, Blacksmith and Whitesmith alone remaining as occupative titles. Greensmith may be seen over a hosier's shop in Southport, Lancashire ; v. Brownsmith, Redsmith, &c.

Richard Grenesmith, 1611 : Reg. St. Mary Aldermary, p. 155.
1768. Married—John Greensmith and Martha Weaver : St. Geo. Han. Sq. i. 178.
Harrogate, 2 ; Philadelphia, 6.

Greenstreet.—Local, 'at the green street.'

Johanna de Grenestrate, co. Camb., 1273. A.
1669. Symon Greenstreete and Mary Treswallen : Marriage Alleg. (Canterbury), p. 166.
London, 3 ; Crockford, 5.

Greentree. — Local, 'at the green tree'; cf. Rowntree, Crabtree, Langtree, &c.

1762. Married—William Greentree and Hannah Turner : St. Geo. Han. Sq. i. 108.
Philadelphia, 1.

Greenway. — Local, 'at the green way,' by augmentation more usually Greenaway, q.v.

London, 3 ; Boston (U.S.), 1.

Greenwebb. — Occup. 'the green-webb,' a weaver of green cloth ; cf. Greensmith, a worker in lead or laten. John Grenewebbe, co. Salop (Pardon's Roll, 6 Ric. II) ; cf. 'Kendal green,' a favourite cloth colour for foresters, woodwards, &c.

Greenwood.—Local, 'at the green-wood,' a well-known Yorkshire name. Of course other spots might give rise to the surname. But it is absolutely certain that some small spot between Huddersfield and Slaithwaite has given birth to the Greenwoods, who have ramified so marvellously in that county.

Johannes de Grenewode et Agnes uxor ejus, *ffarmour* de Graunge (Huddersfield), 1379: P. T. Yorks. p. 179.
Johanna de Grenewod', 1379: ibid. p. 180.
Ricardus de Grenewode, 1379 : ibid.
1539. Married—John Leame and Alice Greenwood : St. Peter, Cornhill, i. 221.
London, 30 ; West Rid. Court Dir., 63 ; Philadelphia, 76.

Greg, Gregg, Gregson. — Bapt. 'the son of Gregory,' from nick. Greg. For some reason or other Gregory was very popular as a font-name in cos. Yorkshire and Lanc. in the 13th and 14th centuries. In North Lancashire, as a result, Gregson became almost a colonial surname. Preston seems to have been the leading centre.

Simon fil. Greg, 1273. A.
Robert Grege, ibid.
Johannes Gregge, 1379: P. T. Howden-shire, pp. 9-10.
Willelmus Gregge, 1379: ibid.
Johannes Gregson, 1379: P. T. Yorks. p. 286.
Henricus Gregson, 1379: ibid.
Hugo Gregson, 1379: ibid. p. 198.
Johanna Greg-doghter, 1379: ibid. p. 290.
Thomas Gregson, of Plumpton, 1540: Lancashire Wills at Richmond, p. 130.
Richard Gregson, of Ingolhead, 1587: ibid.
Robert Gregson, of Preston, 1607: ibid.
Cristopher Gregson, 1542: Preston Guild Rolls, p. 16.
London, 1, 7, 4; Preston, 0, 0, 14; Manchester, 2, 1, 3; New York, 1, 2, 5; Boston (U.S.) (Gregson), 1.

Grogory.— Bapt. 'the son of Gregory.' This fontal name is now rarely used, but our directories prove a widespread popularity in the 13th and 14th centuries; v. Greg, Greig, Grigg, Gregson, &c. 'In the West it was borne (the name Gregory) by that greatest and best of papal watchmen to whom the English Church looks back as the original awakener of her faith' (Yonge, i. 255).

'Ac Gregory was a good man.'
Piers P. 4625.

No wonder it won great favour in pre-Reformation days, for apart from the great Pope Gregory, a succession of Gregorys sat on the papal chair.

Gregory Grimbawd, co. Oxf., 1273. A.
Elyas fil. Gregor', co. Camb., ibid.
Peter Gregory, co. Bedf., ibid.
Richard fil. Gregorii, co. Bucks, ibid.
Gregorius othe Castell, C. R., 9 Ric. II.
Gregory Bodsankorthe, C. R., 10 Ric. II.

I only furnish a few instances. The Hundred Rolls prove a general liking for the name, and thousands of people to-day owe their surnames to the then reigning feeling in its favour.

London, 66; Philadelphia, 66.

Greig.— Bapt. 'the son of Gregory,' from nick. Greg, q.v. Greig is the Scotch form, but it was not always so.

Robert Greyg, co. Soms., 1 Edw. III: Kirby's Quest, p. 268.
London, 21; New York, 9.

Grenfell.—Local, 'at the green fell'; v. Fell, a great North-English name. The evidence is not in favour of its being a variant of Grenville. In some cases, however, it may be.

Hugo de Grenfell, 1379: P. T. Yorks. p. 273.
Ricardus de Grenfell, 1379: ibid. p. 278.
London, 1.

Grenville, Granvell, Granville.—Local, 'of Grenville,' doubtless the same as Granville, a familiar seaport of Lower Normandy. The Grenvilles of Wootton, co. Bucks, descend from Richard de Grenville, who came in with the Conqueror in the train of Walter Giffard, Earl of Longueville and Buckingham; v. Lower's Patr. Brit. p. 138. I subjoin a few spellings from the Hundred Rolls:

Thomas de Grenwille, co. Oxf., 1273. A.
Richard de Grenville, co. Oxf., ibid.
William de Grenville, co. Oxf., ibid.
Adam de Greynevile, co. Wilts, ibid.
Eustace de Greynville, co. Bucks, ibid.
1666. Richard Grenvill (co. Bucks) and Elianore Temple: Marriage Alleg. (Canterbury), p. 115.
1676. Robert Maur and Eliz. Greinvile: ibid. p. 256.
London, 1, 1, 4; Philadelphia, 0, 0, 6.

Gresson.—Nick.; v. Grayson.

Gresty, Gristy, Grestey.—Local, 'of Gresty,' a township in the parish of Wybunbury, co. Chester.

1604. Randle Grastie, of Warford: Wills at Chester (1545-1620), p. 74.
1624. Elizabeth Lownes, of Grestie, co. Ches.: ibid. (1621-50), p. 144.
1639. Humphrey Greste, of Farnworth: ibid. p. 91.
1648. Henry Grastye, of Warford, co. Ches.: ibid. p. 88.

Later on the surname assumed new variants:

1692. Elizabeth Greastie, of Macclesfield, widow: Wills at Chester (1681-1700).
1696. Joseph Greasty, of Great Warford, gentleman: ibid.

From Greasty the last change took place, viz. to Gresty, and that,

with its own variants, is the form found in the district directories.

Manchester, 9, 2, 0; MDB. (co. Chester), 3, 0, 1; Philadelphia, 1, 0, 0.

Greswold.—Local, 'of the greswold,' i.e. the wold whereon the gris or grice fed; v. Grice.

George Greswold, or Gryswolde, or Grysold, 1533: Reg. Univ. Oxf. i. 176.
London, 2; Philadelphia, 2.

Greville, Grevile, Grevel.—Local, 'of Greville' Lower (Patr. Brit. p. 138) quotes as follows: 'Greville, a parish at the extremity of the isthmus of La Hogue, in Normandy, is supposed to have given name to the Lord of Greville who accompanied the Conqueror; but this is uncertain as there were three distinct fiefs which gave to their possessors the title of Sire de Greville' (M. de Gerville in Mem. Soc. Ant. Norm., 1825).

John de Greville, co. Wilts, 1273. A.
'This family was founded by the wool trade in the 14th cent. by William Grevel, "the flower of the wool-merchants in the whole realm of England," who died, and was buried at Campden, co. Glouc., in 1401': Shirley's Noble and Gentle Men.
1672-3. Henry Grevill and Eliz. Baker: Marriage Alleg. (Canterbury), p. 213.
London, 4, 0, 0; MDB. (co. Glouc.), 0, 1, 0; New York, 2, 0, 1.

Grew, Grewe.—? Nick. 'the grew.' 'Grew, a greyhound. North' (Halliwell). It is worth noticing, however, that my instances are from Yorkshire. Henry III in 1250 spent his Christmas at York. In the expenditure for that visit appears the provision of '7000 fowls, 1750 partridges, 125 swans, 115 'grues' (an unknown bird), 125 peacocks, 290 pheasants,' &c.; v. Miss Holt's paper in Christmas number of The Fireside, 1887, p. 15. As every other bird in the list is a familiar surname to-day, there is no reason why the 'grue' should not be the same.

Johannes Grewe, 1379: P. T. Yorks. p. 48.
Johanna Grewe, 1379: ibid. p. 129.
Agnes Grewe, 1379: ibid. p. 130.
London, 1, 0; Philadelphia, 12, 1.

Grexon.—Bapt. 'the son of Greg' (q.v.); cf. Gregson, of which

Z

it is a sharpened form ; cf. Baxter and Bagster for Bakester.

Derby, 1.

Greygroom.—Nick. from the colour of hair or clothes.

Robert Greygrom, Fines Roll, 1 Edw. III.

Greylock.—Nick. 'with the grey lock,' a common kind of sòbriquet in the surname period ; cf. Silverlock, Lovelock, Blacklock, &c. ; M.E. *lok*. But in some cases these are personal names ; cf. Havelock or Horlock.

William Greylake, co. Soms., 1 Edw. III: Kirby's Quest, p. 115.
Peter Greylake, co. Soms., 1 Edw. III: ibid. p. 117.
Margery Greylake, co. Soms., 1 Edw. III : ibid. p. 119.
John Greylok, vicar of Kempston, co. Norf., 1396 : FF. ix. 525.

Greyshank. — Nick. 'greyshanked,' with legs dressed in grey.

Gilbert Greyschanke, co. Kent, 1273. A.

Greystock.—Local, ' of Greystock,' a parish eleven miles from Penrith, co. Cumb.

William Graystok, 1542: Preston Guild Rolls, p. 17.
Thomas Graistock, of Garstang, 1561: Lancashire Wills at Richmond, p. 126.
Parnwell Graystocke, of Preston, 1670: ibid.
Henry Graystock, of Ribchester, 1673 : ibid.
1739. Bapt.—Margaret, d. Thomas Graystock : Reg. Ulverston Ch. p. 329. Manchester, 1.

Gribble, Grimble, Grimball.—Bapt. 'the son of Grimbald,' a once familiar personal name in England. Gribble is the modern accepted surnominal form, although the more correct Grimble exists. Grimbald, a Saxon saint, was a monk of St. Omer, but placed at Oxford by King Alfred. Amongst the benefactors of Conishead Priory, in Furness, was ' Jordan, fil. Hugh, fil. Grimbald' (West's Ant. of Furness, p. 191). Grimbald of Plessis joined a rebellion against Duke William (Freeman's Norm. Conq. ii. 244).

Grimbaldus Aurifaber, co. Wilts: Domesday.
Grimbald or Grinbaud Pancefot, co. Glouc., 1273. A.
Gregory Grimbawd, co. Oxf., ibid.

Warin Grimboll, co. Suff., ibid.
Mabilia Grymbald, or Grymbaud, co. Linc., 30 Edw. I : BBB. p. 622.
Matilda Grymbard, 1379: P. T. Yorks. p. 5.
Adam Grymbald, *wryght*, 1379: ibid. p. 30.
John Grimbald, co. Linc., Hen. III-Edw. I. K.
Robert Grimbaud, co. Northampton: ibid.
1585. Bapt.—Eliz., d. William Grymbolde: St. Michael, Cornhill, p. 93.
1586. — Anne, d. William Grymbolde: ibid. p. 94.
1625. Buried.—Thomas Gribble: St. Dionis Backchurch (London), p. 218.
London, 7, 2, 0 ; MDB. (Lincoln), 0, 3, 0 ; New York, 1, 0, 2.

Grice. — Nick. 'the grice,' 'a young pig.

'Gris: porcel ': Reliq. Antiq. ii. 79 (Halliwell).
'Gryce, swyne or pygge—*porcellus* ': Prompt Parv. p. 211.
'A grise, *porcellus*: a swyne ': Cath. Ang.
'Goode gees and grys ': Piers Plowman, l. 450.

Cf. Pigg, Hogg, Bacon, Purcell.

John le Gris, co. Norf., 1273. A.
Nicholas le Gris, or Grice, bailiff of Norwich, 1259: FF. iii. 59.
Thomas le Gris, 1313. M.
Adam Gris, 1379 : P. T. Yorks. p. 160.
Johannes Gryse, 1379: ibid. p. 27.
London, 11 ; MDB. (Norfolk), 3 ; Philadelphia, 13.

Grierson ; v. Grayson.

Grieve. — Offic. ' the greve '; v. Grayson.

Liverpool (1887), 4 ; Philadelphia, 7.

Griffin.—Bapt. (Welsh), 'the son of Griffin' or 'Griffith,' the name of many Welsh princes (Yonge, i. 353-4).

Griffin ap Oweyn. R.
Tuder fil. Griffini, 12 Edw. I: BBB. p. 348.
Griffin Parpoynt, C. R., 5 Edw. III. pt. ii.
Robertus Gryffyn, 1379 : P. T. Yorks. p. 152.
John Gryffyn, 1379: ibid. p. 141.
Gryfyn or Gryffyth Leyson, 1524: Reg. Univ. Oxf. i. 135.
1564. Bapt.—John, son of Griffyn Hall: St. Jas. Clerkenwell, i. 3.
1584. — Fraunces, son of Griffyn Jones (in the paper register, as distinct from the vellum, it is Griffith): ibid. p. 16.
London, 56 ; Philadelphia, 140.

Griffinhoofe.—' This German name was introduced into England by one of the physicians of George

I ' (Lower, p. 139). But the name is found earlier.

1574. Buried—Abraham Gryffyn-Hoffe, son of William Gryffyn Hoffe, *stranger* : St. Dionis Backchurch (London), p. 193. Crockford, 2.

Griffith, Griffiths. —, Bapt. (Welsh). A variant of Griffin, q.v.

John ap Griffith, of Bangor, 1585: Wills at Chester (1545-1620), p. 77.
Edward ap Griffith, of Halewood, 1581: ibid.
London, 32, 96 ; Philadelphia, 150, 51.

Grigg, Griggs, Grigs, Grigson.—Bapt. 'the son of Gregory,' from the nick. Greg or Grig ; v. Greg.

'Grigge rapit, dum *Davie* strepit, comes est quibus *Hobbe*': Gower.

Speaking generally, and judging by registers, Grigg was popular in the south, and Gregg in the north.

Grigge (without surname), co. Suff., 1273. A.
Richard fil. Grigge, co. Camb., ibid.
Grigge le Fulur, co. Camb., ibid.
Serle Grigg, co. Camb., ibid.
John Grigg, co. Soms., 1 Edw. III: Kirby's Quest, p. 114.
Ricardus Grygge, 1415: Preston Guild Rolls, p. 7.
1625. Nicholas Broadhurst and Joane Grigson: Marriage Lic. (London), ii. 155.
1626. Robert Grigges and Agnes Parkes: ibid. p. 166.
1633-4. Richard Peacocke and Rechard Grigg: ibid. p. 215.
London, 14,8,1,2 ; Philadelphia, 13,9,0,0.

Grim, Grimes.—Bapt. 'the son of Grim.' The *s* is genitive = Grim's son. Grim was common in the 13th century ; cf. place-names Grimston, Grimstead, and Grimscote in the Hundred Rolls. Also cf. Grimoldby, Grimshaw, or Grimsditch ; v. Grimbert and Grimkettle.

Peter fil. Grim, Pipe Roll, 6 Hen. II.
Alan Grime, co. Camb., 1273. A.
Robert Grim, co. Hunts, ibid.
Warin Grim, co. Camb., ibid.
Henry Grym, co. Soms., 1 Edw. III : Kirby's Quest, p. 231.
' Grym de Stanlegh holdeth Stanley, as of ancient tenure, in the name of forestry (*circa* 1300)': East Cheshire, ii. 3.
Johannes Gryme, 1379: P. T. Yorks. p. 111.
Ricardus Gryme, 1379: ibid.
Willelmus Gryme, 1379: ibid. p. 245.
Ellen Gryme, of Bury, *widow*, 1575: Wills at Chester (1545-1620), p. 78.
London, 0, 8 ; West Rid. Court Dir., 2, 0 ; Philadelphia,35, 30 ; New York, 26,1.

Grimball, -ble; v. Gribble.

Grimbert. — Bapt. 'the son of Grimbert' or 'Grimbard'; v. Yonge, ii. 189. One of the compounds of Grim, q.v.

Matilda Grymbard, 1379: P. T. Yorks. p. 5.

Grimbly; v. Grimoldby.

Grimes; v. Grim.

Grimkettle, Grimkil.—Bapt. 'the son of Grimketel' (Yonge, ii. 189). A compound of Kettle, q.v. Cf. Arkettle.

Grinchetyl. O.
Grimkettle. FF.
Mathew Paris, under date 1047, says of the Bishopric of Selsey: 'Defuncto Grinketel, Selesiensi pontifice, Hecca regis capellanus successit.'

In compounds Kettle usually became Kill and Kell. Hence the following entry:

Stephen Grimekil, 20 Edw. I. R.

Grimmit, Grimett, Grimmet.—Bapt. 'the son of Grimhild' (v. Yonge, ii. 189). The first stage of corruption would be Crimhilt, next Grimilt, and then finally Grimmit. So early as the 14th century we find Grymyd running side by side with Grymyld:

Johannes Grymyd', 1379: P. T. Yorks. p. 148.
Johannes Grymyld', 1379: ibid. p. 127.
1555. Married—John Saunders and Eliz. Grymholde: St. Dionis Backchurch, p. 3.
1771. — George Grimmett and Mary Reeve : St. Geo. Han. Sq. i. 211.
— — John Page Crayden and Ann Grimmett : ibid. p. 214.
Manchester (1887), 1, 0, 0; Birmingham, 1, 4, 2.

Grimoldby, Grimbleby, Grimbly.—Local. 'of Grimoldby,' a parish in Linc., five miles from Louth. 'Alanus de Linc' tenuit in capite . . . 4 bovat' in Grimelbi' (K. p. 339, Hen. III). The surname in its correct form still lives in co. Lincoln, but, like many another surname, fares badly as it gets further from home. Probably the meaning is 'the by (i.e. the dwelling) of Grimwald'; v. Yonge, ii. 189.

Gilbert de Grimmolby, co. Linc., 1273. A.
Mariota de Grimmolby, co. Linc., ibid.
John de Grimoldeby, co. Linc., Hen. III–Edw. I. K.
Walterus de Grimoldeby, co. Linc. Hen. III–Edw. I. K.

London, 0, 1, 1; MDB. (Lincoln), 3, 0, 0; Oxford, 0, 0, 2.

Grimond, Grimmond, Garment—Bapt. 'the son of Gardmond' (Yonge, ii. 241); v. Garment.

Edmund Gurmund, co. Norf., 1273. A.
John Germund, co. Soms., ibid.
Thomas Germund, co. Soms., ibid.
Thomas Germunt, co. Leic., Hen. III–Edw. I. K.
London, 1, 2, 1; New York, 3, 0, 1.

Grimsditch. — Local, 'of Grim's dike,' i.e. the dike of Grim, a Cheshire surname. There is a Grimesdike, a hamlet in the parish of Barwick-in-Elmet near Leeds, co. York ; but a Grimsditch in the Hundred of Bucklow, co. Ches., seems to have given rise to this surname ; v. Grim and Grimes for the personal name.

Peter Grymesdiche, 1474: East Cheshire, ii. 381 n.
Hugh Grymesdich of Grimesdich, co. Ches.: Visit. Herts, 1572, p. 17.
John Grimsditche, of Grimsdiche: Compositions for Knighthood, Cheshire, 1631 (1545-1620), p. 206.
John Grimsditch, co. Ches., 1674: Exchequer Depositions (1545-1620), p. 138.
Thomas Grimsditch, M.P. for Macclesfield, 1837 : East Cheshire, ii. 485.
Liverpool (1887), 2.

Grimshaw.—Local, 'of Grimshaw,' some woody place in South Lancashire, called no doubt after its earliest possessor, Grim (q.v.). This surname is very common in cos. Lanc. and York.

Adam de Grymeshawe, (Tottington) co. Lanc., 20 Edw. I. R.
Thomas Sagar, of Grimshaw, 1618: Will at Chester (1545-1620), p. 168.
Alice Grimshaw, of Great Harwood, 1579 : ibid. p. 77.
Richard Grimshaw, of Clayton-on-the-Moors, 1575: ibid.
Nicholas Grymeshawe, 1622 : Preston Guild Rolls, p. 79.
London, 5 ; Manchester, 24; Philadelphia, 4.

Grimson.—(1) Bapt. 'the son of Grim,' an early personal or font name ; v. Grim.

Cecilia Grymeson, 1379: P. T. Yorks. p. 233.
Ellen Grimyson, of Teales, widow, 1616: Lanc. Wills at Richmond, p. 130.

(2) Local, 'of Grimston,' co. York; v. Grimston.

New York, 1.

Grimsteed.—Local, 'of Grimstead,' a parish in co. Wilts, i.e.

the homestead of Grim, the first settler or proprietor ; v. Grim.

Peter de Grymstede, co. Soms., 1 Edw. III : Kirby's Quest, p. 212.
MDB. (co. Soms.), 4.

Grimston, Grimstone. — Local, 'of Grimston' or 'Grimstone.' There are three townships named Grimston in co. York, also a parish near York city. Also two parishes named Grimstone, one in co. Linc., the other in co. Norfolk. The northern localities seem to have originated the surname.

Adam de Grinneston, co. York, 1273. A.
William de Grinneston, co. York, ibid.
Godfrey de Grimeston, co. Oxf., ibid.
Johannes de Grymeston, 1379 : P. T. Yorks. p. 210.
Thomas de Grymston, 1379 : ibid. p. 132.
William de Grimeston, 16 Edw. II : Freemen of York, i. 20.
1626. Bapt.—Harbot Kell (sic), the sonne of Sir Henrey Grimston, and the lady Margeritt his wif: St. Michael, Cornhill, p. 118.
London, 1, 0 ; Crockford, 2, 0 ; West Rid. Court Dir., 5, 0 ; Philadelphia, 0, 2.

Grimwade, Grimwood. — (1) ! Bapt. 'the son of Grimwald' (?); v. Yonge, ii. 189. (2) Local, 'of Grimwood,' i.e. Grim's wood ; cf. Grimshaw, i.e. Grim's shaw.

London, 3, 9.

Grinder, Grinter (?), Grenter (?).—Occup. 'the grinder.' Very rare.

John Grynder, C. R., 16 Ric. II.
John Grinder, High Sheriff of Gloucester, 1405 : Atkyns' Hist. Glouc. p. 39.
'Joan, the widow of Richard Grinder, died endowed with Rodley,' 24 Hen. VI: Rudder's Hist. Glouc. p. 793.
MDB. (co. Somerset), 0, 1, 1 ; New York, 0, 1, 0.

Grindlay, Grindley.—Local, 'of Grindley,' a township in the parish of Malpas, co. Ches.

1569. Bapt.—Thomas Gryndley, Mottram : Reg. Prestbury (Cheshire), p. 27.
1576. Buried—Margaret Gryndley, Mottram, ibid. p. 54.
London, 2, 1; Manchester, 1, 2 ; Boston (U.S.), 0, 5.

Grindle, Grindell, Grindall. — Local, 'of Grindall,' a chapelry in the parish of Bridlington, E. Rid. Yorks.

Roger de Grendale, co. Hunts, 1273. A.
Walter de Grendale, co. York, ibid.

1617. Married — Phillip Hatton and Mary Grindall: St. Jas. Clerkenwell, i. 44.
1630. Bapt.—Judyth, d. William Grindall : ibid. p. 114.
Crockford, 2, 0, 0 ; Liverpool, 0, 1, 0 ; New York, 4, 0, 1.

Grindon.—Local, 'of Grindon' or 'Grendon,' townships or parishes in cos. Durham, Stafford, Northampton, Warwick, Hereford, and Buckingham.

Robert de Grendon', co. Salop, 1273. A.
Geoffrey de Grendon', co. Oxf., ibid.
John de Grendon', co. Derby, ibid.
Peter de Grendon, co. Northampton, Hen. III–Edw. I. K.
Robert de Grendon, co. Warwick, ibid.
Warin de Grendon, co. Hereford, 20 Edw. I. R.
John de Grendon, 1379 : P. T. Yorks. p. 298.
1749. Bapt.—Thomas, s. Daniel Grendon : St. Peter, Cornhill, i. 44.
Manchester, 1.

Grindrod, Greenrod, Greenroyd.—Local, 'of the green road' or 'the green royd' ; v. Royd, and cf. Ormerod, Murgatroyd, &c. Grindrod is the usual modern form, in which the *d* is intrusive. An old will marks the place where the Greenroyd lay :

William Riding, of Grindrod, in Hundersfield, 1626 : Wills at Chester (1621–50), p. 184.

Hundersfield is the eastern division of the parish of Rochdale, co. Lanc.

Rychard Grenerowde, 1541 : Subsidy R., Salford Hundred, vol. xii. p. 145 (Rec. Soc., Lanc. and Ches.).
James Greenrodd, of Manchester, 1617 : Wills at Chester (1545–1620), p. 76.
Richard Greenrode, of Inchfield in Rochdale, 1623 : ibid. (1621–50), p. 90.
Richard Greenroad, of Broadinge, 1671 : ibid. (1660–80), p. 109.
London, 0, 1, 0 ; Rochdale, 7, 0, 0 ; Manchester, 5, 0, 0 ; Bolton, 2, 0, 0 ; Halifax (Greenroyd), 1 ; Philadelphia, 12, 0, 0.

Grinold.—? Bapt. 'Grimwald' (Yonge, ii. 189).

Willelmus Gronell, 1379 : P. T. Yorks. p. 286.
West Rid. Court Dir., 1 ; Sheffield, 1.

Grinslade ; v. Greenslade.

Grinstead, Grinsted.—Local, 'of Grimstead' ; *m* has become *n* ; cf. Sinkinson for Simkinson, Tonkin for Tomkin, &c. ; v. Grim. There are two parishes called Grimstead in the dioc. of Salisbury.

John de Grimstede, co. Wilts, 1273. A.
William de Grinnstede, co. Wilts, ibid.
London, 0, 1 ; Crockford, 1, 0.

Gripper.—Occup. 'the graper,' a maker of grapes. ' *Graip, Grape.* A dung-fork, a three-pronged fork' (Jamieson). 'A grape, *ubi forke, tridens*' : Cath. Ang.

'Two gads of yerne viiis, ... a graype, 2 yerne forks ' : Wills and Inventories of the Northern Counties (Surtees Soc.), ii. 171.
1292. Peter le Graper, burgess of Newcastle-on-Tyne : Brand's Hist. of Newcastle, i. 41.
Richard le Graper. H.
Agnes Graper. B.
London, 3.

Grisewood.—Local, ' of Grisewood,' a wood frequented by grice ; v. Grice, and cf. Greswold.

John Gryswood. W. 11.
London, 1.

Gristy.—Local ; v. Gresty.

Gritten, Gritton.—(1) Local, ' of Gretton,' a chapelry in the parish of Winchcombe, co. Glouc. ; (2) ' of Gretton,' a parish near Rockingham, co. Northampton.

Nicholas de Gretton, co. Glouc., 1273. A.
Thomas de Gretton, co. Glouc., ibid.
Adam de Gretton, co. Camb., ibid.
1665. Richard Squire and Mary Gretton : Marriage Alleg. (Canterbury), p. 106.
1672. Charles Colman and Eliz. Gritton : ibid. p. 206.
London, 3, 2 ; New York, 1, 0.

Grocock, -cott, Groocock, -cott ; v. Growcock.

Groom, Groome. — Occup. 'the groom,' i.e. the servant ; cf. Goodgroom.

Robert le Grom, co. Camb., 1273. A.
Seman le Grom, co. Suff., ibid.
Johannes Grom, 1379 : P. T. Yorks. p. 104.
Robertus Grome, 1379 : ibid. p. 113.
Adrian Grom, C. R., 17 Hen. VI.
London, 32, 1 ; Philadelphia, 28, 9.

Gros, Grose, Gross, Grosse, Groce.—Nick. 'the gross,' large, fat, heavy ; cf. French Grosjean, equivalent to Scotch Micklejohn ; v. Grace.

Almaricus Grossus, co. Oxf., 1273. A.
Jordan le Gros, co. Bedf., ibid.
John le Gros, co. Oxf., ibid.
Roger le Gros, co. Norf., 20 Edw. I.
1673. Married—Charles Groce and Eliz. Swollowe : St. Jas. Clerkenwell, iii. 177.
1678–9. John Manley and Anne Grosse : Marriage Alleg. (Canterbury), p. 291.
London, 1, 10, 11, 5, 0 ; Philadelphia, 3, 7, 200, 3, 2.

Groser.—Occup. ' the grocer,' an engrosser, a wholesale dealer, as distinct from regrater, a retail dealer (Liber Albus, Riley, p. 547). Almost too late to get into the directory, as 'spicer' was the earlier term ; v. Spicer. It was not till 1617 that the Grocers' became an independent Company. ' John Guter, grossarius,' 1310 (Riley's Memorials of London). In 1363 a statute of Edward III speaks of ' Merchauntz nomely Grossers,' because they 'engrossent totes maners des merchandises vendables.' The following is early and curious : ' Laurence de Beton, Hugo le Fourbor, *Walter le Grorst Spicer*, John de Preston,' &c. These names occur in a list of London tradesmen (Edw. II, R. p. 458).

London, 2.

Grossetete. — Nick. ' grosseteste.' The English form was ' Greathead,' q.v., still existing. Robert Grosseteste, elected bishop of Lincoln in 1235, was born at Stradbrook, co. Suff.

Richard Groceteste, co. Salop, 1273. A.
Peter Grossetest, co. York. W. 4.
Robert Groteste, London. X.
London, 1.

Grosvenor.—Offic. 'le grosveneur,' the head hunter. It is said that the family descend from an uncle of Rollo, the founder of Normandy, and that the first settler in England was Gilbert le Grosvenor, nephew of Hugh Lupus, earl of Chester, himself nephew of the Conqueror ; v. Lower's Patr. Brit. p. 140.

Robert le Grovenur. J.
Robert le Grosvenur. T.
1663. Samuel Sommers, *girdler*, and Sarah Grosvenor : Marriage Alleg. (Canterbury), p. 98.
1667–8. Thomas Alsopp and Mary Grossevenure : ibid. p. 147.
London, 11 ; New York, 6.

Grote. — ? ——. Probably for Great (q.v.) the big, the tall.

William Grote, co. Bedf., 1273. A.
Henry Grote, co. Soms., 1 Edw. III : Kirby's Quest, p. 240.
London, 1.

Grove, Groves.—Local, 'at the grove,' a clump of trees, originally a woodland avenue cut out from the forest ; v. Grave and Greaves.

Hawysa atte Grove, co. Soms., 1 Edw.
III : Kirby's Quest, p. 116.
Stephen atte Grove, co. Soms., 1 Edw.
III : Kirby's Quest, p. 120.
Thomas atte Grove, co. Soms., 1 Edw.
III : ibid. p. 251.
Willelmus del Grove, 1379: P. T.
Yorks. p. 35.
1668. Married—George Groves and
Dorothy Waterson : St. Jas. Clerkenwell,
iii. 144.
1699. Bapt.—Anne, d. Samuel Grove,
tillit painter : St. Dionis Backchurch
(London), p. 138.
London, 31, 36 ; Philadelphia, 24, 54.

**Growcock, Grocock, Gro-
cott, Groocott, Groocock.—**
? Local. The suffix *-cock* and *-cott*
got confused from the days of the
Hundred Rolls (1273) ; *-cock* would
denote in general a baptismal origin,
as in Wilcock ; *-cot* or *-cott* a local
origin, as in Westcot. There is no
baptismal name that would be likely
to originate the surname. It is
most probably local, but I cannot
identify the spot ; cf. Glasscock for
Glascott.

1759. Married—Henry Grocock and
Jane Elliott : St. Geo. Han. Sq. i. 88.
1765. — Benjamin Growcock and
Frances Thridgould : ibid. p. 140.
1767. — John Stokes and Ann Groocock : ibid. p. 163.
1782. — Thomas Carel and Sarah
Growcot : ibid. p. 339.
Manchester (1887), 1, 3, 3, 0, 0 ; Liverpool (1887), Groocott, 1 ; New York
(Groocock), 3.

Grubb, Grubbe, Grub. —
? Personal, 'the son of Grub' (?).
Burke's Landed Gentry says, 'The
family of Grubbe, spelt in the old
registers Grube or Groube, migrated
from Germany about the year 1430,
after the Hussite persecutions, and
subsequently settled at Eastwell, in
the parish of Potterne, co. Wilts,
where they have ever since remained.' As will be seen below,
the name occurs two centuries
earlier on English soil without the
assistance of a foreign persecution
to make it respectable.

John Grubbe, co. Norf., 1273. A.
Alan Grubbe, co. Camb., ibid. p. 107.
Johannes Grubb', 1379: P. T. Yorks.
p. 106.
Johannes Grubbe, 1379: ibid. p. 5. Also
again on pp. 9, 10.
1596. Bapt.—Jane, d. Thomas Grubbe :
St. Jas. Clerkenwell, i. 31.
London, 8, 1, 0 ; Philadelphia, 62, 0, 0 ;
New York (Grub), 6.

Grubber.—Occup. 'the grubber.' The general idea seems to
be one who used spade or axe
on the turf or close to the roots of
trees. 'Grubbare in the erthe, or
other thynggys ; *fossor*' : Prompt.
Parv. The following entry is one
amongst many containing names
of monastery servants whose surnames represented the offices they
severally fulfilled :

1344. 'To John Grubber, for covering
the grange, and the long stable, 16*d*':
Accounts of Holy Island Monastery
(QQQ. p. 87).

Possibly the roof of both grange
and stables was composed of sods,
or of wood obtained by grubbing
trees.

Ricardus Grubber, 1379: P. T. Yorks.
p. 16.
Johannes Grubber, 1379: ibid.
Agnes Grubber, 1379: p. 93.
Johannes Grobbar, 1379: ibid. p. 82.
Thomas Grubber, 1379: ibid. p. 93.

I dare not say that Grubber is
obsolete as a surname, but I have
not come across it.

Grundulf.—Bapt. 'the son of
Grundulf,' one of the many compounds of Ulf.

Henricus Grundelf, 1379: P. T. Yorks.
p. 273.
Adam Grundulf, 1379: ibid.
Ricardus Grundolff, 1379: ibid. p. 288.
Willelmus Grundolf, 1379: ibid. p. 290.

Grundy.—Bapt. 'the son of
Gundry,' q.v. This variant (with
which cf. Brodrick for Baldrick)
strongly ramified in South Lancashire, and has extended itself in
every direction. It is said that
Bury is the home of this particular
stock.

James Grundy, of Rumworth, 1579:
Wills at Chester, (1545-1620), p. 77.
John Grundy, of Astley, parish of
Leigh, 1587: ibid.
Peter Grundy, of Farnworth, 1618: ibid.
'Roger Grundie, in goods, £iii. viiis.'
(Rumworth) : Subsidy Roll, 1622 (Lanc.
and Ches. Rec. Soc. xii. 160).
Manchester, 28; London, 3; Phila-
delphia, 11.

Guarin, Guerin.—Bapt. 'the
son of Guarin'; v. Warin or Wareing, and Warren (2).

Guarinus de Chauncy.   E.
Guarinus Banastre.   C.
Ivo fil. Guarin, ibid.
Philadelphia, 0, 5.

Gubbin, Gubbins. — Local,
'de Gobion,' seemingly of Norman
local origin, registered early as
Gubin and Gubyun. Gubbin looks
strangely like the diminutive of
some forgotten personal name, but
all the evidence is strongly in
favour of the above solution. Gubbins seems to be a modern innova-
tion. Gubbin was the 18th century
form.

John Gobion, London, 1273. A.
Jocens Gubyun or Gobyun, co. Sussex,
ibid.
Thomas Gubin, co. Oxf., ibid.
Reginald Gobiun, co. Bedf., ibid.
Richard de Gobyun, co. Linc., 20 Edw.
I. R.
Thomas Gobyon, co. Notts, ibid.
1775. Married—John Gubbin and Eliz.
Scott : St. Geo. Han. Sq. i. 257.
Crockford, 0, 2 ; Philadelphia, 0, 2.

Gubby ; v. Guppy.

Gudge. — Bapt. 'the son of
Guch'; v. Gooch.

Gudgeon, Gudgen. — Bapt.
A modification of Goodison, q.v.
Although not exactly analogous,
Hodgson and Dodgson are invariably pronounced to this day in the
North as Hodgun and Dodgun ; cf.
Woodger for Woodyer. Especially
notice Dudgeon (London Dir., 4)
for Dodgson. Gudgeon travelled
out of Yorkshire some generations
ago through the Skipton district
into Furness, where it is a well-
known surname. It is corroborative of my view that Gudgeon is
found in the very county (Yorks)
where Goodison was so early and
so strongly established. v. Good-
john.

1632. Buried—Ann Goodgion, of Skip-
tonn, who in her lifetime had been mid-
wife to 920 children : Reg. Skipton
Church.
William Gudgion, *vintner*, 1655 : Rent
Roll of Skipton (Dawson's Skipton,
p. 199).
London, 3, 1 ; Manchester (1887), 4, 0 ;
Philadelphia, 0, 1.

Guest.—(1) Nick. 'the guest,'
the received stranger ; M.E. *gest*.
An early form was *gist*.

'The lighte of grace that gastely giste.'
(Halliwell.)

Roger Gest, co. Wilts, 1273. A.
Adam le Gest, Fines Roll, 11 Edw. I.
Laurence le Gist, co. Soms., 1 Edw.
III : Kirby's Quest, p. 104.

Rogerus Gest, 1379 : P. T. Yorks. p. 88.
Robertus Gest, 1379 : ibid. p. 92.

(2) Local.

Gilbert de Geyste, co Norf., 1273. A.
1604. Buried—Lettis Gest, servant with
Mr. Thomas Blande : St. Mary Aldermary, p. 152.
London, 12 ; Philadelphia, 18.

Guffey ; v. Goffee.

Guichard, Whichcord (?),
Gichard. — Bapt. 'the son of
Guichard'; v. Whiskard for other
variants. Whichcord can hardly
fail to be a variant.

Wichard de Grosse, co. Linc., 1273. A.
Gwychardus Charron, 1315 : DDD. i.
74.
Guichard de Charron, 1431 : ibid. p. 19.
John Gychard, 1340 : KKK. vol. vi.
p. xxxix.
London, 1, 1, 0 ; West Rid. Court Dir.,
0, 0, 1.

Guille. Guillet.—Bapt. 'the
son of Guillaume,' from nick. Guille,
corresponding to our familiar Will ;
v. Gillott for a fuller history. These
and other forms, like Guillaume, are
of modern French importation.

London, 3, 2 ; New York, 2, 0.

Guinness. — Local, probably
'of Guines.'

Baldwin de Ginnes. C.
Radulph de Ginnes, ibid.

But Mr. Lower says, 'A modern
corruption of the old Irish Ma-
gennis' (Patr. Brit. p. 140).

London, 2 ; New York, 1 ; Boston
(U.S.), 2.

Guion, Guyon.—Bapt. 'the
son of Guy,' from the dim. Guyon ;
cf. Mari-on, Gibb-on, &c. The great
popularity of the other dim. Guiot
(v. Wyatt) made Guion rare. But
there are three Wyons in the
London Directory, and Guyon
itself is not extinct.

'Olyvere Guyon, a jakett of blue, and
murreye cloth': Wardrobe Accounts,
Edw. IV, 1480, p. 164.

With the following entries, cf.
Marian for Marion :

John Guiun, co. Westm., 1273. A.
Nicholas Gyan, co. Soms., 1 Edw. III :
Kirby's Quest, p. 101.
Cristina Gyan, co. Soms., 1 Edw. III :
ibid.
William Gyon, 1379 : P. T. Yorks.
p. 287.
Crockford, 0, 3 ; Sheffield, 3, 0 ; Phila-
delphia, 5, 3.

Guise.—(1) Local, 'of Guise,'
the district so called in the east
of France. (2) Bapt. 'the son of
Guy,' whence Guys ; cf. Williams,
Jones, &c.

Anselm de Gyse, co. Hunts, 1273. A.
John de Gyse, co. Berks, Hen. III-
Edw. I. K.
John de Gyse, co. Bedf., 20 Edw. I. R.
William de Gyse, co. Norf., ibid.
1675. Thomas Alderne and Ellinor
Guise : Marriage Alleg. (Canterbury),
p. 245.
1691. Bapt.—John, s. John Guyes : St.
Jas. Clerkenwell, i. 340.
London, 1 ; Oxford, 3 ; Philadelphia, 4.

Gull.—(1) Bapt. 'the son of
Gull,' equivalent to Gill (Jill), being
a more correct nick. of Juliana.

Robert Gulle, co. Linc., 1273. A.
Richard Gulle, co. Linc., ibid.
Johannes Gulle, 1379 : P. T. Yorks.
p. 14.
Magota Gulle, 1379 : ibid.

(2) Nick. 'the gull,' the sea-
bird so called.

Clement le Gul, co. Oxf., 1273. A.
Richard le Gul, co. Oxf., ibid.
Thomas Gul, co. Camb., ibid.
London, 2.

Gulliver, Gulliford. — (1)
Bapt. 'the son of Gulfer.' 'Gulfer
of Villerai' made peace and submitted to William (Freeman's Norm.
Conq. iv. 640). Probably the
Scandinavian Gunnolfr by change
of l for n, a common habit (v. Yonge,
ii. 317).

Richard Gulavere, co. Northampt.,
Hen. III-Edw. I. K.
Roger Gulafre, co. Oxf., ibid.
John Golafre, co. Oxf., 1273. A.
Henry Gulafre, co. Norf., ibid.
Peter Golafre, co. Camb., ibid.
Thomas Gulafre, co. Glouc., 20 Edw.
I. R.
Godfrey Golofre, co. Soms., 1 Edw. III:
Kirby's Quest, p. 100.

(2) Local, 'of Guildford,' or perhaps 'Guldeford,' dioc. of Chichester. Lower says, 'Gulliver occurs
in London Dir. in juxtaposition with
Gulliford, suggesting a common
origin.' A correspondent of N.
and Q. says, 'The names of Gulliver
and Gulliford are quite common
in parts of Somerset, about Kilmington, Stourton, and Brewham,
and I have frequently seen them
spelt both ways' (N. and Q., 2 Ser.
iii. 422). These surmises are correct, as the following entries prove :

Walter Guillefer, 1633 : St. Peter,
Cornhill, i. 84.
Walter Gullifer, 1654 : ibid. p. 208.
Henry Gulliford, 1670 : ibid. ii. 89.
Henry Gullifer, 1671 : ibid.
Walter Gulliford, 1672 : ibid.

Lawton Gilliver was Pope's
bookseller, and it has been suggested that Swift had a grudge
against him. Hence Lemuel Gulliver, the initials being the same.
Of course Gilliver is but another
corruption of the same name. Cf.
Telfer and Telford.

1779. Married—Walter Gullifer (co.
Essex) and Mary A. Crosby : St. Geo.
Han. Sq. i. 303.

(3) ? Bapt. 'the son of Guinevere' (?), one of endless instances
of the change of n into l, or vice
versa ; cf. Phillimore for Finnemore,
bannister for *baluster.* Hence 'Gilliver—a wanton wench' (Halliwell),
a memory of the character of the
queen, who was

'Bad when little, worse when great.'

London, 4, 2 ; Boston (U.S.), 1, 1.

Gully.—(1) Local, 'at the gully,'
from residence by or in a narrow
channel or gully ; seemingly a West-
country name. (2) Local, 'of Goleheye.' For suffix, v. Hey.

Robert de Goleheye, co. Soms., 1 Edw.
III : Kirby's Quest, p. 246.
John Gulye, co. Soms., 1 Edw. III :
ibid. p. 105.
London, 1.

Gulson ; v. Gouldstone.

Gumboil.—Bapt. 'Grimbold.'
This curious corruption is instanced
as existing both by Lower and
Ferguson. I have not met with
it. The Testa de Neville supplies
the origin in its different forms of
Grimbold :

John Grimbald, Hen. III-Edw. I. K.
Richard Grimbaud, ibid.
Robert Grumbaud, ibid.
Robert Gumbaud, ibid.

As *-bald* or *-bold* is the correct
suffix, the last would be Gumbold,
which would easily lead by the law
of imitation to Gumboil. Gumbrell
(London Directory) looks as if it
belonged to this stock.

(Gumbrell), London, 1 ; Philadelphia, 1.

Gumbrell.—Bapt. ; v. Gumboil.

Gumm.—Bapt. ; v. Gomm.

Gummer.—Bapt. 'the son of Gomer'; cf. Gomersall, a parish in the W. Rid. of Yorks.

Cumer (G for C?) de Gaunkevill, co. Linc., Hen. III–Edw. I. K.
Gom'us (i. e. Gomerus) de Riston, 1273. A.
Simon Gomer, co. York, ibid.
Stephen Gumer, co. Leic., ibid.
Robert Gomar, co. Hunts, ibid.
London, 2; Boston (U.S.), 1.

Gunby, Gunbie.—Local, 'of Gunby,' two parishes in co. Lincoln, one near Spilsby, the other near Colsterworth. The meaning is the *by* or dwelling of Gunn; v. Guntrip.

Thomas de Gunneby, cos. York and Linc., 20 Edw. I. R.
1542. Married—John Gunby and Eliz. Parett: St. Dionis Backchurch (London), p. 2.
London, 2, 1.

Gundolf.—Bapt. 'the son of Gundolf'; cf. Randolph.

William Gundolf, co. Soms., 1 Edw. III: Kirby's Quest, p. 94.

Gundry, Grundy, Goundry, Gunderson.—Bapt. 'the son of Gundred' or 'Gundry,' a once common, but now forgotten fontname, but it has immortalized itself in Mrs. Grundy.

Gundrea, mater Rogeri de Moubraie, 1138, called by Young the historian of Whitby, 'Gundrey Mowbray': FFF. p. 516.
Gundreda Giffard, 28 Edw. I: BBB. p. 581.
Gundred Basingham, temp. Edw. I: Visitation of Yorkshire (1563), p. 361 (Harl. Soc.).
Gundred la Bygote, C. R., 5 Edw. I.
Gundrada, daughter of Gerbod and Matilda: Freeman, Norm. Conq. iii. 86.
William of Lancaster, first baron of Kendal, married Gundred, countess of Warwick: West's Ant. of Furness, p. 29.

Grundy seems gradually to have ousted Gundry, although both exist as surnames. The process of change from Gundry to Grundy is shown in the following entry from the Plymouth Directory, 1873:

'William Grundry, dining rooms, 112, Union St.'

where an *r* is introduced into the first syllable before the *r* in the second has been yet deposed. It is curious to note that in North Durham, where Gundrey was well

known six centuries ago, the surname of Goundry is common. I soon found five in the neighbourhood of Gosforth in August, 1886. Still more interesting was it to find Gunderson in North Shields, an evident patronymic founded on the name.

Gundr' filia Fulco Paynel, 1273. A.
1775. Married—Nathaniel Gundry and Julia Maria Palmer: St. Geo. Han. Sq. i. 253.
London, 4, 3, 1, 0; Manchester, 0, 28, 0, 0; Philadelphia, 2, 0, 0, 0.

Gunn, Gunson, Gunns, Gunnis.—Bapt. 'the son of Gawen,' popularly Gunn. Gunson is well known in the Furness district of North Lanc., and Gawen was till recently a font-name there; v. Gawen.

Matilda fil. Gunne, co. Camb., 1273. A.
William Gunne, co. Suff., ibid.
Nicholas Gunne, co. Hunts, ibid.
Bartholomew Gunson, sup. for B.A., 1514: Reg. Univ. Oxf. i. 91.
Robert Gunson, of Haverthwaite, 1575: Lancashire Wills at Richmond, p. 131.
Roger Gunson, vicar of Fincham, co. Norf., 1587: FF. vii 358.
James Gunson, of Tatham, 1595: ibid.
London, 14, 0, 0, 2; Lancashire Court Dir., 1, 4, 0, 0; MDB. (Norfolk), 1, 0, 2, 0; (Suffolk), 3, 0, 0, 0; Philadelphia, 38, 7, 0, 5.

Gunnell.—Bapt. 'the son of Gunnilda,' popularly Gunnell; v. Quennell.

Gunnilda Diverc, 1273. A.
Gonnilda de Depe, ibid.
William fil. Gunnilde, ibid.
Alan Gunnyld, ibid.
Stephen fil. Gunnild', ibid.
Gonnild de Coleford, co. Soms., 1 Edw. III: Kirby's Quest, p. 166.
Gunild Hoperis, co. Soms., 1 Edw. III: ibid. p. 145.
Gunell' de Caudlouby, Hen. III–Edw. I. K.
Gunnilda Reyngud, C. R., 23 Edw. I.
1565. Thomas Gunnell and Anne Butler: St. Dionis Backchurch (London), p. 5.
1730.— Thomas Bunney and Ann Gunnell: St. Geo. Han. Sq. i. 7.
London, 3; New York, 1.

Gunner.—Bapt. 'the son of Gunner.' The forms in Domesday are many. In co. Hereford, Gunner; in Berks, Gunnere; in Essex, Gunnerus; in Cheshire, Gunnor; in Devon, Gonnar. The form in Miss Yonge's Glossary is Gunnar (Christian Names, ii. 315).

Gunnora de la More, Hen. III–Edw. I. K.
Mathew fil. Gunnar, 35 Edw. I: BBB. p. 39.
Guner Wygle. H.
Willelmus Gonnor', 1379: P. T. Yorks. p. 43.
Michael Gonnar (in charge of artillery!), Issue Roll, 11 Edw. IV.
London, 7; New York, 2.

Gunnery.—Bapt. 'the son of Gundry,' q.v. The variation is a natural one; cf. Hendry and Henery for Henry.
Crockford, 1.

Gunning.—Bapt. 'the son of Gunwyn,' one of the many northern names with prefix *Gun*; v. Gundry, Gunner, Gunnell, Gunther, Gunter, &c. For corruption into Gunning, cf. Ayling from Aylwin. The *g* is excrescent, as in Jennings, &c.

Gundewyn de Nethergate, co. Suff., 1273. A.
Gerald Gundwyn, co. Suff., ibid.
Gerard Gunwyn, co. Suff., ibid.
Willelmus Gunwyn, 1379: P. T. Yorks. p. 79.

The last two entries relate to the same individual.

1752. George William, earl of Coventry, and Maria Gunning: St. Geo. Han. Sq. i. 47.
London, 6; New York, 20.

Gunson.—Bapt. 'the son of Gunn,' q.v.

Gunther, Gunter.—Bapt. 'the son of Gunter.' Lower says that both Gonther and Gunter appear as tenants in Domesday; v. Gunther, Yonge, ii. 315.

Walter Guntard, co. Norf., 1273. A.
John Gunter, co. Oxf., ibid.
Adam Gunter, 1319: PPP. i. 49.
Gunter fil. Herbert: Pipe Roll, 11 Hen. II. p. 41.
'Mr. William Gunther, Central Works, Oldham, exhibits four turbines' (Manchester Exhibition): Manchester Courier, July 25, 1887.
London, 3, 2; Philadelphia, 14, 1.

Gunton.—Local, 'of Gunton,' parishes in cos. Norfolk and Suffolk. This surname is still a representative name in co. Norfolk. The meaning is 'the town' or 'enclosure' of Gunn; v. Town and Gunn, and cf. Guntrip.

'In 1243, Matthew de Gunton, and Isabel, his wife, had a release for 20s. per ann. of their portion of titles in Castre ' : FF. xi. 204.

Geoffrey de Gunneton, co. Suff., 1273. A. Adam de Guntone, co. Norf., ibid.

Henry de Gunton, cos. Warw. and Leic., Hen. III–Edw. I. K.

Murdac de Gunton, cos. Warw. and Leic., ibid.

John de Gunton, vicar of Tunstal, co. Norf., 1361 : FF. xi. 120.

London, 8 ; MDB. (Norfolk), 10 ; (Suffolk), 1 ; New York, 1.

Guntrip. — Local, 'of Gunthorpe,' a modification ; cf. Thripp or Thrupp for Thorp. (1) A parish in co. Norf. ; (2) a hamlet in the parish of Paston, co. Northampton ; (3) a township in the parish of Lowdham, co. Notts ; (4) a hamlet in the parish of Belton, co. Rutland. In all cases meaning the ' thorp of Gunn,' the name of the original settler ; v. Gunn and Gunson, and cf. the place-names, Gunton, Gunby, and Gunthwaite, &c.

Bartholomew de Gunthorp, London, 20 Edw. I. R.

Robert de Gunthorp, London, ibid.

1623. William Gunthropp and Katherine Gibbons : Marriage Lic. (London), ii. 121.

1698. Married—George Houlroyd and Martha Gunthrupp : St. Dionis Backchurch (London), p. 47.

1780. — Peter Truck and Eleanor Gunthorpe : St. Geo. Han. Sq. i. 312.

Crockford, 1.

Guppy, Gubby (?). — Local, 'of Gopheye,' some spot in the West country. The suffix is -hey, a hedge or enclosure ; v. Hey.

Nicholas Gopheye, co. Soms., 1 Edw. III : Kirby's Quest, p. 141.

Cf. also Mabilla de Gopeworthy, co. Soms., 1 Edw. III : ibid. p. 148.

1412. Robert Guppeye : Cal. of Wills in Court of Husting (2).

1608. Bapt.—Margaret, d. John Gooppie : St. Jas. Clerkenwell, i. 54.

London, 2, 2 ; Exeter, 1, 0 ; MDB. (co. Soms.), 4, 0 ; Philadelphia, 2, 0.

Gurdon, Gurden.—Local, 'de Gourdon.' ' This family came into England with the Conqueror from Gourdon, on the borders of Perigord ' (B. L. G., quoted by Lower).

Amwina de Gurdon, co. Southampton, Hen. III–Edw. I. K.

Adam de Gurdune, co. Southampton, ibid.

Bartholomew Gurdun, co. Norf., 1273. A.

Thomas Gurdun, co. Oxf., ibid.

Roger Gurdon, co. Camb., ibid.

Adam Gurdon, co. Soms., 1 Edw. III : Kirby's Quest, p. 127.

1674. Bapt.—Deborah, d. John Gurdon, *merchant* : St. Dionis Backchurch (London), p. 120.

1784. Married—Henry Gurden and Eleanor Hall : St. Geo. Han. Sq. i, 358.

London (1893), 3, 1 ; Oxford, 0, 6.

Gurney, Gurnay, Gurnee.— Local, ' of Gournai,' probably Gournai-en-Brai, in the arrondissement of Neufchatel. We are told that there were two Hugh de Gournays at the battle of Hastings.

'li viel Hue de Gornai
Ensemble o li sa gent de Brai.'
Roman de Rou (quoted by Lower).

The two Hughs received grants of land in Norfolk, in which county the name is still strong.

Milesenta fil. Hugh de Gorney, co. Bedf., 1273. A.

John de Gurnay, co. Norf., ibid.

Anselm de Gurney, co. Glouc., ibid.

Robert de Gurnay, co. Wilts, Hen. III–Edw. I. K.

John de Gorney, co. Soms., 1 Edw. III : Kirby's Quest, p. 158.

Robert Gournay, rector of Hethel, co. Norf., 1438 : FF. v. 109.

London, 41, 0, 0 ; MDB. (Norfolk), 13, 0, 0 ; New York, 10, 0, 6 ; Philadelphia, 13, 1, 0.

Gusterson. — Bapt. 'the son of Custance,' a corruption of Custerson (v. Custance).

London, 2.

Gutch. — Bapt. ' the son of Guch '; v. Gooch.

Gutlack. — Bapt. 'the son of Guthlac'; v. Goodlake.

London, 1.

Gutter.—Local, 'at the gutter,' from residence thereby ; M.E. *gotere.* v. Gott.

John de la Gotere, Fines Roll, 15 Edw. II.

Andrew de la Gotere, C. R., 32 Edw. I. Philadelphia, 1.

Gutteridge, Guttridge.—(1) Bapt. ' the son of Godrich,' q.v. (2) Local, ' of Goodrich ' or ' Gotheridge,' a parish in co. Hereford.

' Jonathan Swift
Had the gift
By fatherige, motherige,
And by brotherige,
To come from Gotherige :
But now is spoiled clean,
And an Irish dean.'

(Pope's lines on ' Swift's Ancestors,' Globe edit. of Pope's Works, p. 497.) Swift set up a monument to his grandfather in the church at Goodrich.

Thomas de Goderigge, co. Wilts, 1273. A.

1693. Benjamin Browne and Deliverance Gutteridge : Marriage Lic. (Canterbury), p. 210.

Deliverance was an occasional Puritan personal name ; see my Curiosities of Puritan Nomenclature, pp. 169–70.

London, 7, 3 ; Philadelphia, 3, 0.

Guy.—Bapt. ' the son of Guy.' It appears to have prevailed in France very early as Guy, Guies, Guyon, and the feminine Guiette ' (Yonge, ii. 31). The English dims. were Wyot and Wyon ; v. Wyatt. In the days of gunpowder plot and Guy Fawkes the name lost caste, and as a fontal title has never recovered itself.

John fil. Gwydonis, co. Oxf., 1273. A.

Robert Gy, co. Camb., ibid.

Guy de Boys. H.

Imbert fil. Guidonis. T.

1573. Bapt.—Jane Gwye : St. Jas. Clerkenwell, i. 7.

1597. — William, s. Richarde Guy : ibid. p. 32.

1666. Nathaniel Ponder and Mary Guy : Marriage Alleg. (Canterbury), p. 124.

London, 21 ; Philadelphia, 24.

Guyatt. — Bapt. ' the son of Guy,' from dim. Guy-ot ; v. Wyatt. This form has maintained an independent position from the first, although Wyatt is the almost universal English dress ; cf. Gwilliam and William.

Johannes Gyott, *faber*, 1379 : P. T. Yorks. p. 247.

Aleyn Gyott. H.

William Wyett, or Wyat, or Wiotte, or Gwyett, sup. for B.A., 1564 : Reg. Univ. Oxf. i. 251.

1743. Married—John Gyot and Mary Hoskins : St. Geo. Han. Sq. i. 31.

1753. — William Guyat and Mary Bradford : ibid. p. 50.

1757. — Thomas Gyett and Ann Thompson : ibid. p. 68.

London, 1.

Guyon. — Bapt. ' the son of Guy '; v. Guion.

Gwatkin.—Bapt. ' the son of Walter ' (Gualter), from nick. Wat and dim. Wat-kin. Gwatkin, like

Gwillim, is a Welsh form, but adheres more closely to the original ; cf. the following entries :

1640. Buried—Katherine, d. Gwalter Oake : St. Antholin (London), p. 73.
1688. Married—Gualter Langley and Jane Scrivener : St. Jas. Clerkenwell, iii. 205.
London, 1 ; Boston (U.S.), 1.

Gwilliam, Gwillim. — Bapt. 'the son of William,' a Welsh form ; cf. Gwatkin.

John ap-Gwilym, Chancellor of St. David's, 1351 : Hist. and Ant. St. David's, p. 365.
Guilim ap Griffith, 1450 : East Ches. i. 181.
R. V. A. Gwillim, 1763 : ibid. ii. 301.
1609. Bapt.—Bridgitt, d. Richard Guillame : St. Jas. Clerkenwell, i. 56.
1615. Married—Richard Guilyams and Ruth Odill, St, Michael, Cornhill, p. 21.

1764. Married—Gwyllym Bissell and Eliz. Rooke : St. Geo. Han. Sq. i. 137.
Manchester, 1, 0 ; London, 1, 5 ; Philadelphia, 2, 0 ; Boston (U.S.), 0, 2.

Gwinn, Gwyn, Gwynn, Gwynne, Gwin. — Nick. ' the white ' (Welsh), probably from the complexion ; cf. English White.

Lewis Gwyn, archdeacon of Cardigan, 1568 : Hist. and Ant. St. David's, p. 360.
London, 1, 2, 6, 4, 0 ; Philadelphia, 4, 0, 7, 0, 3.

Gwyther.—Bapt. ' the son of Wither ' ; v. Wither and Withers. Welsh form Gwyther ; cf. Gwalter and Gwilliam for Walter and William.

London, 2.

Gye.—Bapt. ' the son of Guy,' q.v. A variant.

London, 3 ; Philadelphia, 1.

Gylby.—Local ; v. Gilbey, of which it is a variant.

London, 1.

Gyles.—Bapt. ' the son of Giles,' q.v. A variant.

1548.—Christning of Anne Gyles : St. Peter, Cornhill, i. 4.
London, 3.

Gynn, Gynne. — Probably variants or corruptions of Gwynn or Gwynne ; v. Gwinn.

1668. Married—Thomas Gin and Issabell Andrewes : St. Jas. Clerkenwell, iii. 145.
London, 1, 1.

Gyot.—Bapt. 'the son of Guyot'; v. Wyatt.

Henry Gyot, co. Soms., 1 Edw. III : Kirby's Quest, p. 225.

H

Habgood, Hopgood.— Bapt. 'the son of Habgood.' One of the numerous terminatives in -good ; cf. Thoroughgood, Scattergood, Osgood, &c.

1670. Francis Rickards and Sibbell Hopgood : Marriage Lic. (Faculty Office), p. 114.
London, 3, 4 ; MDB. (co. Berks), 2, 0 ; (co. Glouc.), 4, 0 ; Boston (U.S.), 0, 1.

Hablot.— Bapt. 'the son of Herbilot ' or ' Hebelot.' Probably a dim. of Herbert.

Richard Herbelette, C. R., 1 Hen. IV. pt. i.
Cf. Hewlett, Roblett, Emelot, Giblett, &c.

Hack.—(1) Bapt. ' the son of Hake,' q.v. This great Scandinavian personal name has made a mark on our local nomenclature, as will be seen further on.

Henry Hak, co. Linc., 1273. A.
William Hack, co. Soms., 1 Edw. III : Kirby's Quest, p. 253.

(2) Local, ' at the hatch,' from residence beside a half-door, still called a hatch. ' Hack, a half-door, a hatch, co. Norfolk' (Halliwell).

Geoffrey de la Hak, co. Devon, Hen. III–Edw. I. K.

Cf. Kirk and Church, Hackman and Hatchman, &c.

London, 9 ; New York, 10.

Hacker.—Bapt. ' the son of Hacgard'; v. Haggard and Haggar or Hagger ; cf. Jagge, in Piers Plowman, for Jack. Slagg and Slack, Haggett and Hackett, go side by side in the same way.

William Hakkere, C. R., 12 Hen. IV.
London, 9 ; Philadelphia, 14.

Hackett, Haggitt, Haggett. —Bapt. ' the son of Hake,' from dim. Haket. There can be no doubt about this origin. Though forgotten now Hake, Haket, and Hacon were very familiar in the surname period. Hake still survives in co. York as Haggitt (cf. Hick and Higg), more generally Hackett. As with Hack, Hake, and Hacon, the instances naturally are found towards the East coast ; v. Hake.

Mabil Haket, co. Linc., 1273. A.
Ralph Haket, co. Bucks, ibid.
Robert Haket, London, ibid.
Thomas Haket, 1379 : P. T.Yorks. p. 13.
Johanna Haket, 1379 : ibid. p. 18.
Rolland Haket, co. Linc., Hen. III– Edw. I. K.
John Haget, co. Soms., 1 Edw. III : Kirby's Quest, p. 210.

Roger Haket, co. Linc., ibid.
1586. Bapt.— Ralphe, s. Richard Hackett : St. Jas. Clerkenwell, i. 17.
1767. Married — Thomas Hackit and Ann Fitzwalter : St. Geo. Han. Sq. i. 164.
1802. — William Haggett and Sarah Shepherd : ibid. ii. 270.
London, 9, 0, 1 ; Leeds, 0, 1, 0 ; West Rid. Court Dir., 0, 1, 0 ; New York, 56, 0, 0.

Hackford, Hackforth.—(1) Local, ' of Hackford,' two parishes in co. Norfolk. No doubt the meaning is 'the ford of Hake,' a great personal name ; v. Hake and Hack (1). (2) Local, ' of Hackforth,' a township in the parish of Hornby, N. Rid. Yorks. I do not think this has any representative in the directories. Both Hackford and Hackforth are, I suspect, of the same Norfolk parentage ; v. Ford and Forth.

Nicholas de Hacford, bailiff of Norwich, 1263 : FF. iii. 59.
Matilda de Hakeford, co. Norf., 1273. A.
Ranulph de Hakeford, co. Norf., ibid.
Adam de Hacford, co. Norf., ibid.
Thomas de Hakeford, co. Norf., 20 Edw. I. R.
1591. Bapt. — Warner, s. Nicholas Hackford : St. Jas. Clerkenwell, i. 25.
1631. — Eliz., d. John Hackforth : ibid. i. 119.
London, 1, 1 ; MDB. (co. Linc.), 1, 0 ; Philadelphia, 1, 0.

Hacking, Hackin.—Local, 'of Hacking,' now Hacking Hall, a place in the township of Billington, in the parish of Blackburn, co. Lancs. A family 'de Hacking' arose there early. The surname has ramified strongly, but has wandered little, there being only one representative in the London Directory. I cannot find it on American soil.

William de Hacking, 1328, Billington: Baines' Lancashire, ii. 86.
1582. Hugh Hackyng, *carpenter*: Preston Guild Rolls, p. 46.
1602. Robertus Hackinge, filius Hugonis: ibid. p. 48.
1675. William Hacking, of Rainhill: Wills at Chester (1660-80), p. 111.
Manchester, 10, 1; Blackburn, 10, 0; London, 1, 0.

Hackland; v. Acland; a variant.
New York, 1.

Hacklittle.—Nick. for a lazy woodcutter.

Walter Hakelutel, co. Salop, 1273. A.

Hackman, Hatchman.—(1) Bapt. 'the son of Hakeman,' an augmentative of Hake, q.v.; cf. Bateman, Tiddiman, Hickman, &c. (2) Bapt. 'the son of Hagmund.' All terminatives in *-mund* or *-mond* become *-man*; cf. Wayman and Osman for Wymond and Osmund.

Thomas Hakeman, co. Norf., 1273. A.
John Haghmund, co. Kent, ibid.
William Haghmund, co. Kent, ibid.
Alan Hagheman, co. Southampton, ibid.
Rotelin Hakeman, co. Soms., 1 Edw III: Kirby's Quest, p. 119.
Richard Hatcheman, C. R., 1 Mary, pt. vi.
1648. Buried—Henry Hatchman, servant to Mr. Kelke, *pewterer*: St. Michael, Cornhill, p. 242.
London, 2, 7; New York, 6, 0; Boston (U.S.), 0, 1.

Hackney.—Local, 'of Hackney,' a parish in co. Middlesex, in the London district. Probably 'the *hay* (enclosure) of Hacon'; v. Hacon.

Benedict de Hakeneye, London, 1273. A.
Robert de Hakeneye, London, ibid.
Adam de Hakenay, 1379: P. T. Yorks. p. 176.
London, 5; Philadelphia, 14.

Hackshall.—Local, 'of Hackensall,' a hamlet in the parish of Lancaster. A family of Hacken-shaw or Hackensall was early located there. For origin of the local name, v. Hacon, and cf. *Shall-cross* and *Shawcross*.

'In the reign of Ric. I, Geoffrey the Bowman, ancestor of the Sherburnes, was lord of Hackensall . . . and Robert de Hacinesho paid 10 marks in 3 John (1201), for confirmation of his charter': Baines' Lanc. ii. 541.
'In 48 Hen. III, John de Hacunsho held Hacunesho, Persho, and Hamelton': ibid.
John de Haconshowe, 1379: Preston Guild Rolls, p. 1.
John de Hacschawe, 1379: ibid. p. 5.
London, 2.

Hackwell, Hakewill.—Local, 'of Hackwell,' i.e. the well of Hake; v. Hack (1) and Hake.

Roger de Hakewell, co. Essex, 1273. A.
London, 1, 0; Crockford, 0, 1.

Hackworth.—Local, (1) 'of Hackworth,' i.e. the *worth* or farmstead of Hake; v. Hack (1), Hake, and Worth. (2) 'of Ackworth,' of which in the North it seems to be an aspirated variant; v. Acworth.

Peter de Hakeworth, co. Devon, 1273. A.
John de Hakeworth, co. Devon, Hen. III-Edw. I. K.
London, 1; Crockford, 1; MDB. (co. Durham), 1.

Hacon.— Bapt. 'the son of Hacon' (allied to Hake, q.v.). In Domesday the forms are Hacon, co. Herts; Hacun, cos. Wilts and Notts. Lower writes, 'Hacon: a family so surnamed reside at Swaffham, co. Norfolk, and are doubtless of Norse extraction. Hacon the Good and Hacon the Broad-shouldered occur among the kings of Norway.' Why the Norfolk Hacons should be of 'Norse extraction' because the font-name Hacon was popular in England in the 12th and 13th centuries is not easy to see. Still more unfortunate is the writer in a further remark: 'In the Hundred Rolls for Suffolk we find mentioned one Semannus Hacon, "Hacon the Sailor," *which looks sufficiently Norwegian*'! This is to put the cart before the horse with a vengeance, for Semannus is the font-name and Hacon the surname. As a font-name Semannus is simply the Latinized Seman, still surviving in the surname Seaman, q.v. But this 'Norse extraction' is no better nor worse than a hundred conjectures in print at this moment. Cf. Haconby, a parish in co. Linc. Mr. Freeman (Norman Conquest, iii. 219) writes, under date 1052, 'According to another account, Godwine, on his reconciliation with Eadward, gave hostages to the king for his good behaviour in the persons of his youngest son Wulfnoth and his grandson Hakon, the son of Swegen.'

Hugh fil. Hacun, 1178: KKK. vi. 29.
Wibert fil. Hacun, 1188: RRR. p. 61.
Richard fil. Akun, 1192: ibid. p. 50.
Semannus Hacon, co. Suff., 1273. A.
William fil. Haconis, co. Linc., ibid.
Richard Hakun, co. Linc., ibid.
Johannes Hacun, 1379: P. T. Yorks. p. 107.
John Hakon, bailiff of Yarmouth, 1395: FF. xi. 324.
William Hacon, vicar of Tunstal, co. Norf., 1384: ibid. xi. 120.
MDB. (Norfolk), 2; (co. Cumberland), 1.

Hadcock.—Bapt. 'the son of Adam'; v. Adcock, of which it is a variant; cf. Hadkins, Hadkinson, and Haddy, all from Adam, and standing for Adkins, Adkinson, and Addy.

Johannes Hadcok', 1379: P. T. Yorks. p. 114.
Johannes Adcok', junior, 1379: ibid.
Boston (U.S.), 1; Philadelphia, 1.

Haddan, Hadden, Haddon.—Local, 'of Haddon,' parishes in diocs. of Ely and Peterborough.

Robert de Hadden, co. Oxf., 1273. A.
Agnes de Hadden', co. Oxf., ibid.
Jordan de Haddone, co. Hunts, ibid.
Cristina de Haddon, co. Oxf., 20 Edw I. R.
John de Haddon', co. Glouc., ibid.
Ricardus de Hadden', 1379: P. T. Yorks. p. 16.
London, 3, 5, 4; MDB. (co. Camb.), 0, 2, 1; Philadelphia, 0, 6, 8.

Haddelsey.—Local, 'of Haddelsey,' a chapelry and township in the parish of Birkin, W. Rid. Yorks, five miles from Selby.

Willelmus de Hathelsay, *lyster*, of Selby, 1379: P. T. Yorks. p. 155.
Johannes Hathelsay: ibid. p. 156.
Juliana de Hatelsay: ibid. p. 139.
MDB. (co. Lincoln), 1.

Haddock.— Local, 'of Haydock,' co. Lanc., q.v. It is a well-known fact that Haddock is an imitative variant of Haydock.

Margaret Haydock, of Eaves, 1663: Lanc. Wills at Richmond, p. 142.
Robert Haydock, of Eaves, 1671: ibid.
Ellen Haddock, of Eaves, 1679: ibid. p. 132.
Robert Haddocke, of Eaves, 1669: ibid.
Richard Haddock, of Turton, co. Lanc., 1679: Wills at Chester (1660-80), p. 111.
James Haddock, of Samlesbury, co. Lanc., 1678: ibid.
John Haydock, of Turton, co. Lanc., 1666: ibid. p. 124.
George Haydock, of Samlesbury, co. Lanc., 1672: ibid.
Bolton (Lanc.), 6; Liverpool, 4; Manchester, 1; London, 8; New York, 11.

Haddow; v. Hadow.

Haddy. — Bapt. 'the son of Adam'; v. Addy, of which it is a variant; cf. Hadkinson and Hadkins for Adkinson and Adkins, both representing the dim. of Adam. In the same way we find Hoddy for Oddy. These unexpected aspirates are found at an early period.

John Haddy, co. Bedf., 1273. A.
Alicia Haddi, co. Camb., ibid.
1808. Married — Thomas Lacy and Mary Haddey : St. Geo. Han. Sq. ii. 383. Philadelphia, 2.

Haden; v. Haydon.

Hadfield. — Local, 'of Hadfield,' a parish in co. Derby. This surname has ramified itself in a most marvellous fashion in Lancashire and Yorkshire, having crossed its boundaries into both counties evidently at an early period. Yet London has only one representative.

Sheffield, 17; London, 1; Manchester, 33; Philadelphia, 11.

Hadkinson, Hadkins, Hadkiss. — Bapt. 'the son of Adam,' for Adkinson and Adkins, q.v. All terminatives in -kiss are a modification of -kins; cf. Popkiss. Hadkiss is therefore manifestly Hadkins; cf. Hoddy for Oddy.

London, 0, 1, 2; Manchester, 2, 0, 0.

Hadland. — Local; v. Headland.

Hadley. — Local, 'of Hadley' or 'Hadleigh.' In cos. Essex and Suffolk I find two parishes of Hadleigh, and in co. Middlesex a parish Hadley.

Robertus de Hadleya, co. Suff., 1273. A.
Nicholas de Haddileg', co. Salop, ibid.
John de Hadlee, London, ibid.
London, 11; MDB. (co. Glouc.), 3; New York, 17.

Hadlow. — Local, 'of Hadlow,' a parish in co. Kent. As in many other cases where -low (v. Low) is lost in -ley (v. Ley), Hadlow has evidently been lost in Hadley.

John de Hadlo, co. Kent, 1273. A.
Nicholas de Hadlo, co. Kent, ibid.
London, 1; MDB. (co. Kent), 3.

Hadnutt. — Local; v. Hoddinott.

Hadow, Haddow. — Local.

London, 2, 0; MDB. (co. Bedford), 3, 0; (co. Cambridge), 0, 2.

Hadskis, Hadkiss. — Bapt. 'the son of Adam.' A corruption of Hadkins (q.v.), which is Adkins (q.v.) with an aspirate prefixed; cf. Hotchkiss for Hodgkins. or Popkiss for Hopkins. Hadskis is a curious-looking name, but the derivation is simple enough.

Manchester, 2, 0; London, 0, 2.

Hadwen, -win; v. Hardwin.

Haffenden. — Local, 'of Haffenden,' some spot in co. Kent or Sussex that I cannot discover. The name has existed for many generations at Heathfield in the latter county (v. Lower).

MDB. (co. Sussex), 3; London, 1.

Hagan, Hagon. — Bapt. ' the son of Hagan.' In Domesday Hagon is found in such cases as Hagana, Hagane, and Haganus, all in Norfolk. For history of the name, v. Yonge, ii. 319-20. Possibly Hagan and Hacon (q.v.) are closely related. The Emperor of Germany's new ironclad (1895) is Hagen, after the famous giant of the Nibelungen Saga.

Robert Hakene, co. Norf., 1273. A.
William Hakene, co. Norf., ibid.
London, 1, 1; Boston (U.S.), 23, 0.

Hagell. — Bapt. 'the son of Haghel.' One of the many personal names with suffix -el.

William Haghel, co. Soms., 1 Edw. III : Kirby's Quest, p. 165.
Gilbert Haghel, co. Soms., 1 Edw. III : ibid. p. 244.
London, 3.

Hagenild, Hahnel(?), Hannel(?). — Bapt. 'the son of Hagenild.'

Hagenild' de Bedewill, co. Norf., Hen. III-Edw. I. K.
Thomas Haenild, co. Suff., 1273. A.
Haenyld (without surname), co. Suff., ibid.
London, 0, 1, 1; Boston (U.S.), 0, 2, 0.

Hagg. — Local, 'at the haw'; v. Haig or Hague, of which it is a variant.

Gilbert de Hagha, co. Linc, 1273. A.
Thomas Hag, 1379 : P. T. Yorks. p. 87.
Willelmus Hag, 1379 : ibid.
London, 1; MDB. (co. Cumberland), 2; Philadelphia, 1; New York, 1.

Haggard, Agard. — Bapt. 'the son of Hachard' or 'Hacgard'; v. Hatchard.

Ivo Hacgard, co. Suffolk, 1273. A.
Ralph Hacgard, co. Suffolk, ibid.
John Hacgard, co. Suffolk, ibid.
London, 2, 0; Philadelphia, 0, 2.

Haggas, Haggis, Hagges. — Bapt. 'the son of Agace'; v. Agasson and Aggas. Aspirates come and go as they like in early registers. There cannot be the shadow of a doubt about this derivation. My first instance settles the point.

Emma Hagase, 1379: P. T. Yorks. p. 269.
1563. Buried — John Haggas, prentis to John Bowthe, merchant-tayler: St. Mary Aldermary, p. 135.
Keighley, 4, 0, 0; West Rid. (Yorks) Court Dir., 3, 0, 0; London, 0, 2, 0; Philadelphia, 1, 0, 1.

Hagger, Haggar. — Bapt. 'the son of Hacgard.' The final d has been dropped; v. Haggard; cf. Haggerston, i.e. the town or farm of Hagger.

MDB. (co. Essex), 1, 1; London, 12, 0; Boston (U.S.), 1, 0.

Haggerstone. — Local, 'of Haggerston,' a parish in co. Middlesex.

MDB. (co. Cambridge), 1.

Haggett, Haggatt. — Bapt. 'the son of Hackett,' q.v.

MDB. (co. Glouc.), 1, 1; London, 1, 0; New York, 1, 0.

Hagyard. — Bapt. 'the son of Hacgard.' A variant found in co. York; v. Haggard.

Bridlington Quay, East Rid. Yorks, 2.

Haiden.—Local, 'of Haydon,' q.v.

MDB. (co. Glouc.), 2.

Haig, Haigh, Hague.—Local, 'at the haw,' i.e. the hedged field or enclosure; A.S. *haga*, an enclosure; Du. *haag*, a hedge; whence Gravenhage, i.e. the count's garden, the place called by us 'the Hague' (v. Skeat, *haw*). In Yorkshire and Lancashire the same spelling has been adopted as one of the forms of Haig. The spread of Haigh in Yorkshire has been something extraordinary; but it had many representatives to start with.

Gilbert del Hagh', 1379 : P. T. Yorks. p. 50.
Robertus del Hagh', 1379 : ibid. p. 131.
Ricardus del Hagh', 1379 : ibid. p. 179.
Robert atte Haghe, co. Norf. : FF. x. 283.
Richard atte Haghe, co. Norf. : ibid. ii. 461.
Roger atte Heygh, co. Soms., 1 Edw. III : Kirby's Quest, p. 111.
Thomas Haghe, of the parish of Rochdale, 1604 : Wills at Chester (1545-1620), p. 78.
Piers Haigh, of Lymm, 1603 : ibid.
James Hague, son of James Hague, 1692 : ibid. (1681-1700), p. 104.
Manchester, 0, 15, 14 ; West Rid. Court Dir., 1, 64, 10 ; New York, 7, 9, 9.

Hail, Haile.—Local ; v. Hale.

Hailes.—Local ; v. Hales.

Hailstone.—Local, 'of Hailstone,' perhaps for Hallystone, a parish in co. Northumberland.

Johannes de Helistones, 1379 : P. T. Yorks. p. 183.
Ricardus de Helistones, 1379 : ibid.
1583. Married—Morgaine Hubble and Tomison (Thomasine) Halestone : St. Antholin (London), p. 30.
London, 1 ; MDB. (co. Cambridge), 1 ; (co. Essex), 1.

Hain, Haine, Haines, Hains, Hayn, Hayne, Haynes, Heynes.—(1) Bapt. 'the son of Haine,' genitive Haines. That the origin is fontal admits of no doubt. Cf. Hainsworth or Ainsworth, i.e. the farmstead of Hain, the proprietor or tenant ; v. Worth. Some of my instances may be related to Hans ; v. Hanson.

Thomas fil. Hayene, co. Norf., 1273. A.
Ralph Hayne, co. Soms., 1 Edw. III : Kirby's Quest, p. 180.

William Hayne, co. Soms., 1 Edw. III : ibid.
Walter Heynes, co. Soms., 1 Edw. III : ibid. p. 235.
Ade Heynes, co. Soms., 1 Edw. III : ibid.

Cf. Danish Heynssen :
'Heynssen and Martienssen, commission agents': Manchester Directory.

The following entries are interesting :

Johannes Hauneson, 1379 : P. T. Yorks. p. 187.
Adam Hauneson, 1379 : ibid. p. 179.
Johannes Hayne, 1379 : ibid. p. 184.
Robertus Haynson, 1379 : ibid. p. 121.
Thomas Hane, 1379 : ibid. p. 300.
Alice Heynes, co. Soms., 1 Edw. III : Kirby's Quest, p. 160.

(2) Local, 'of Haynes,' a parish in the dioc. of Ely.

1581. Married—Percival Archboll and Susan Heynes : St. Mary Aldermary, p. 7.
London, 2, 2, 27, 4, 2, 10, 69, 1 ; New York, 1, 0, 38, 0, 4, 4, 31, 0.

Hainsworth. — Local, ' of Hainsworth,' i.e. the farm or *worth* of Hain, the first settler ; v. Hain and Worth. Probably a variant of Ainsworth, q.v.

MDB. (co. Cambridge), 1 ; Philadelphia, 1.

Hairby.—Local, 'of Hareby,' a parish in co. Lincoln, four miles from Spilsby.

MDB. (co. Lincoln), 2.

Hairmonger. — Occup. ' the hairmonger,' one who bought hair for cushions, bolsters, &c. ; M.E. *her*, hair.

Robert le Hyrmonger, co. Oxf., 1273. A.
Hugh le Hermonger, co. Hunts, ibid.

Hairproud.—Nick. for some mediaeval Absolom.

Richard le Herprute, co. Wilts, 1273. A.

Hairster.—Occup. ' the hairster,' a dealer in horsehair, for saddles, couches, &c. The Hayresters duly appeared in the Corpus Christi Play, York, 1415 (v. my English Surnames, p. 417). Hayresters, workers in horsehair (v. L. Toulmin Smith's York Mystery Plays, and see an interesting footnote at p. xxv). The occupative term as a surname seems to have lasted till the reign of Henry VII.

John Hayster, *goldsmyth*, 7 Hen. VII : Freemen of York, i. 216.
Roger de Beverlay, *hairster*, 28 Edw. I : ibid. p. 8.

Hake.—Bapt. 'the son of Hake,' A great Scandinavian name that has made its mark on the local nomenclature of the Eastern counties ; v. Hackett, Hack, and Hacon. Naturally the instances are upon the East coast.

Aaron fil. Hake, 56 Hen. III : BBB. p. 158.
Hake fil. Pyctavini, co. Linc., 1273. A.
Hacca fil. Pictavini, co. Linc., ibid.

The last two entries refer to the same individual.

Peter fil. Hake, co. Linc., 1273. A.
Haco le Muner, co. Suff., ibid.
Hako Strek, co. Suff., ibid.
London, 2 ; Crockford, 3 ; New York, 7.

Hakewill ; v. Hackwell.

Haldane, Haldean, Halden.—Bapt. ' the son of Haldane' (Yonge, ii. 432). Haldanus, co. Essex ; Halden, co. Cheshire ; Haldene, co. Yorks (Domesday).

Waldief fil. Haldeni, Pipe Roll, 5 Hen. II.
Haldenus Presbiter, ibid.
Halden de Chillum, 1171 : RRR. p. 19.
Haldin de Stalham, co. York, 1273. A.
Haldanus Minister, co. Norf., ibid.
Robert Haldeyn, co. Suff., ibid.
John Haldeyn, co. Suff., ibid.

In the Hundred Rolls the personal name (not surname) appears as Haldanus, Haldeyn, Haldeynus, and Haldoyn, all in co. Norfolk.

1747. Married—Morris Flood and Ann Haldin : St. Geo. Han. Sq. i. 38.
London, 2, 0, 2 ; New York, 1, 0, 2.

Haldenby.—Local, ' of Haldenby,' a township in the parish of Adlingfleet, W. Rid. Yorks. Of course the meaning is the *by* or dwelling of Haldane, the first settler ; v. Haldane.

Robertus de Haldanby, 1379 : P. T. Yorks. p. 104.
West Rid. (Yorks) Court Dir., 1 ; Hull, 2.

Hale, Haile, Hail.—Local, 'at the hale,' i.e. Hall (q.v.), from residence there, either as proprietor or servant.

Richard de la Hale, co. Oxf., 1273. A.
Walter en le Hale, co. Sussex, ibid.
Robert in the Hale, Close Roll, 2 Edw. I.
John atte Hale, co. Soms., 1 Edw. III : Kirby's Quest, p. 161.
Warin in the Hale, Pardons Roll, 9 Ric. II.
Edward Atte-hale, co. Norf., 11 Hen. IV : FF. vii. 49.

1617. William Hale and Anne Lydyat: Marriage Lic. (London), ii. 56. London, 60, 2, 0; MDB. (co. Glouc.), 23, 5, 3; New York, 52, 0, 0; Boston (U.S.) (Hail), 1.

Hales, Hailes. — Local, ' of Hales': (1) a parish in co. Stafford; (2) a parish in co. Norfolk; (3) a parish (Hales Owen) in co. Worcester.

Alexander de Hales, co. Norf., 1245: FF. viii. 21.
Ralph de Hales, co. York, 20 Edw. I. R.
Richard de Hales, co. Salop, 1273. A.
Robert de Hales, co. Wilts, ibid.
Matilda de Hales, co. Norf., ibid.
Thomas de Hales, 1379: P. T. Yorks. p. 128.
1575. Charles Hales and Eliz. Fysshe: Marriage Lic. (London), i. 66.
1662. Bapt.—Isabell, d. Henry Hales: St. Jas. Clerkenwell, i. 216.
1805. Married — James Hailes and Marie Donaldson: St. Geo. Han. Sq. ii. 320.
London, 24, 3; Philadelphia, 10, 0.

Halestrap.—Local, ' of Halesthorp.'

MDB. (co. Herts), 2.

Halewood.— Local, ' of Halewood,' a township in the parish of Childwall, co. Lanc.

Richard Hallwood, of Much Woolton, 1603: Wills at Chester (1545-1620), p. 79.
William Hallwood, of Gatacre, within Little Woolton, 1623: ibid. (1621-50), p. 93.
MDB. (co. Lanc.), 3; Liverpool, 1.

Haley.—Local, ' of Hailey,' a parish in the dioc. of Oxford. Also ' of Haighley,' a parish in the dioc. of Norwich. The Haleys of co. York are a different stock, but I cannot identify the locality whence they are sprung.

Petrus Haley, co. Oxf., 1273. A.
Johannes de Haylay, 1379: P. T. Yorks. p. 220.
Willelmus Haylay, 1379: ibid.
London, 9; West Rid. Court Dir., 11; Philadelphia, 87.

Halfacre.—Local, ' at the Halfacre,' from residence on a piece of land so termed; v. next article. Possibly Halfnaked was an early imitative corruption; v. Halfnaked. One of M. Pasteur's cures from threatened hydrophobia was Walter Halfacre, a London gentleman (v. Standard, March 3, 1886).

1801. Married—Henry Halfacre and Ann Brown: St. Geo. Han. Sq. ii. 234.
1805. — Joshua Halfacker and Frances Smith: ibid. p. 322.
MDB. (co. Southampton), 2; MDB. (co. Berks), 1; Oxford, 2.

Halfhide.—Local, ' at the Halfhide,' from residence on a piece of land so termed because it was half a hide by measurement; v. Hyde.

1640. Buried — Mary Halfehide: St. Antholin (London), p. 74.
London, 4.

Halfknight, Halfnight. — Offic. ' the half knight,' one not in full knighthood.

Geoffrey Halveknit, co. Oxf., 1273. A.
Nicholas Halve Knycht, co. Wilts, ibid.
Clement Halfknyth, Fines Roll, 9 Edw. I.
Alianora Halfknyght, Close Roll, 12 Hen. IV.

That the surname existed till the present generation is proved by the fact that several years ago I saw it stated in a newspaper as a curious coincidence that in a northern town two houses, closely adjacent, were occupied, one by Mr. Doubleday, the other by Mr. Halfnight. Unfortunately I did not make a note of it.

Sunderland, 0, 1.

Halfnaked.—Local, ' of Halfnaked.' Lower says, ' Walter de Halfenaked lived in Sussex in 1314.' The manorial estate from which he derived his name is now called Halnaker. It is near Goodwood': Patr. Brit. p. 143. Probably Halfacre (q.v.) is a descendant.

Adam de Halfenaked. H.
Adam de Halnaked, c. 1315. M.

Halford, Holford. — Local, ' of Halford,' a chapelry in the parish of Bromfield, co. Salop; also a parish in co. Warwick, four miles from Shipston. The probable meaning is the hall-ford, the ford by the hall. For a second derivation of Holford, v. Holdford.

Robert de Haleford, co. Warw., Hen. III-Edw. I. K.
William de Halford, co. Devon, 1273. A.
William de Holeford, co. Oxf., ibid.
1531. Robert Halford and Catherine Molson: Marriage Lic. (London), i. 8.
1695. Married—Thomas Halford and Mary Bacon: St. Michael, Cornhill, p. 48.
1706. Thomas Holford (or Hallford)

and Anne Ottoway: Marriage Lic. (London), ii. 335.
London, 18, 4; MDB. (co. Cambridge), 2, 0; Boston (U.S.), 1, 0; Philadelphia, 5, 0.

Halfpeny, Halfpenny, Hapenny.—? Local. This surname seems to belong to the nickname class; v. Fivepenny, Ninepence, Twentypence, &c. But probably it is of local parentage.

Robert de Apenny. C.
William Halpeni, co. Oxf., 1273. A.
Richard Halpeny, co. Oxf., ibid.
Walter Halpeni, co. Devon, ibid.
Juliana Halpeny, co. Soms., 1 Edw. III. Kirby's Quest, p, 101.
Robert Halpeny, co. Soms., 1 Edw. III. ibid. p. 266.
Johannes Halepeny, theker (i. e. thatcher), 1379: P. T. Yorks. p. 282.
1598. Married — William Chatterton and Agnes Halfepeny: St. Thomas the Apostle (London), p. 9.
1729. — Thomas Wright and Lydia Halpenny: St. Peter, Cornhill, ii. 79.
London, 0, 2, 0; Shrewsbury, 0, 1, 0; Philadelphia, 0, 8, 0; Boston (U.S.), Hapenny, 2.

Halgh.—Local, ' at the halgh,' from residence thereby = Haugh (q.v.), a mound, a little hill; cf. Greenhalgh and Ridehalgh; v. Hough and Houghton.

Elias del Halgh, co. Northumb., 20 Edw. I. R.
Andrew de Halgh, co. Lanc., ibid.
Emma del Halgh, 1379: P. T. Yorks. p. 47.
Johannes de Halgh', 1379: ibid. p 74.
1546. George Halche and Emma Dey: Marriage Lic. (London), i. 9.

Haliburton; v. Halliburton.

Haliday; v. Halliday.

Halifax, Hallifax.—Local, ' of Halifax,' a well-known town in the W. Rid. Yorks.

Johannes Halyfax, laborer, 1379: P. T. Yorks. p. 210.
Margreta Halyfax. laborer, 1379: ibid.
1779. Married — John Hallifax and Letitia Arnold: St. Geo. Han. Sq. i. 301.
London, 0, 1; Awkley (near Doncaster), 1, 0; Oxford, 1, 0.

Hall. — Local, ' at the hall.' This has, of course, produced separate stocks all over the country, and every local directory teems with the name; v. Hale. The *hall* was almost as familiar as the *green*. It seems to have been a kind of superior and more pretentious dwelling, but not ' the Hall,' as understood in the present day.

Roger de la Halle, co. Camb., 1273. A.
Walter de la Halle, co. Salop, ibid.
William atte Halle, C. R., 16 Edw. III.
pt. ii.
Willelmus atte Hall', 1379: P. T. Yorks.
p. 24.
Isabella at ye Halle, ibid. p. 145.
Thomas del Hall, c. Hen. IV: E. and
F., co. Cumb., p. 140.
London, 281 ; New York, 360.

Hallam, Hallum.—Local, ' of
Hallam,' i.e. Upper Hallam, a
scattered township in the old parish
of Sheffield ; cf. Hallamshire (v.
Hampshire).

Willelmus de Hallom, 1379: P. T.
Yorks. p. 36.
Elena de Hallum, 1379 : ibid. p. 74.
1588-9. Thomas Hallom, *cordwainer*,
and Bridget Michell : Marriage Lic.
(London), i. 175.
1735. Married—William Hallam and
Jane Griffin : St. Geo. Han. Sq. i. 16.
1767. — Thomas Hallum and Eliz.
Bingham : ibid. p. 179.
MDB. (co. Derby), 16, 0 ; (co. Essex),
0, 1 ; West Rid. Court Dir., 6, 0 ; Sheffield,
15, 0 ; New York, 1, 0.

Hallett.—Local, ' of the hallhead,' i.e. the head of the hall ;
cf. Akenhead, Birkenhead, Hollingshead, i.e. the head of the
oaks, birches, and hollies. Birkenhead, or Birkhead, is now written
Birkett, q.v. Also cf. Blackett for
Blackhead.

1691. Bapt.—Nathaniell, son of Nathaniell Hallhead : St. Michael, Cornhill,
p. 155.
London, 23 ; New York, 16.

Halley.—Local, ' of Halley.'
I cannot find the spot. Derbyshire
seems to be the home of the Hal-
leys. Other references to the
county might have been given.

William de Hallee, co. Glouc., 1273. A.
John de Hally, co. Derby, ibid.
William de Hally, co. Derby, ibid.
John Hally, co. Derby, ibid.
1550. Bapt. — Eliz. Hallaye : St.
Michael, Cornhill, p. 75.
1790. Married—Timothy Halley and
Catherine Winnell : St. Geo. Han. Sq.
ii. 42.
London, 4 ; New York, 8.

Hallgarth, Halgarth.—Local,
' of Hallgarth,' a township in the
parish of Pittington, co. Durham.

MDB. (co. Lincoln), 3, 0 ; Sheffield, 0, 1.

**Halliburton, Halleburton,
Haliburton.**—Local.

MDB. (co. Lanc.), 1, 1, 2.

**Halliday, Haliday, Holli-
day.**—Bapt. ' the son of Haliday,'
a name given to a child born on a
holy day ; cf. Hobday. Hockaday,
Pentecost, Christmas, Whitsunday,
&c. A.S. *hálig*, holy.

'And hold wel thyn haliday
Heighe til even.'
Piers Plowman, 3664.
Richard Haliday, co. Bucks, 1273. A.
Gerard Haliday, co. Suff., ibid.
Alan Halyday. H.
Willelmus Haliday, 1379 : P. T. Yorks.
p. 137.
Johannes Halyday, 1379 : ibid. p. 150.
Adam Halyday, 1379 : ibid. p. 40.
John Haliday, C. R., 37 Hen. III.
1578. Leonard Hallidaye and Anne
Wincoll : Marriage Lic. (London), i. 80.
1583. Thomas Wallys and Alice Holli-
daye : ibid. 119.
1645. Married — John Holyday and
Alice Case : Canterburv Cath. p. 57.
London, 8, 1, 11 ; West Rid. Court
Dir., 8, 0, 6 ; Philadelphia, 10, 0, 13.

**Halliwell, Hollywell, Hol-
lowell, Holliwell.**—(1) Local,
' of Halliwell,' a township in the
parish of Dean, co. Lanc. ; (2) ' of
Hollowell,' a parish in the dioc.
of Peterborough. The former of
these two places has made Halliwell a familiar surname in South
Lancashire. Many small spots
styled the Holywell must also
have contributed to swell the list
of surnames.

Adam de Holewell, co. Norf., 1273. A.
Simon de Holewell, co. Bedf., ibid.
John de Holowell, co. Bucks, ibid.
Godfrey de Haliwell, London, ibid.
Richard de Holewell, co. Hunts, ibid.
John of Halewelle, of Halliwell, Dean,
co. Lanc., 1288 : Baines' Lanc. i. 543.
John de Holewell, co. Soms., 1 Edw.
III : Kirby's Quest, p. 86.
Edith de atte Holywelle, co. Soms., 1
Edw. III : ibid. p. 197.
William de Halegewelle, co. Devon,
Hen. III-Edw. I. K.

Probably this last entry represents the A.S. *hálig*, holy, pure ;
later on found as *hali* or *holi*. Pure
and healthy springs would, no
doubt, all over the country take a
name after the character of the
water, being *whole* or *whole*-some—
not necessarily sacred or *holy*, as
the word is now understood.

London, 1, 1, 0, 0 ; Manchester, 8, 0, 0,
0 ; Philadelphia, 6, 0, 103, 0.

Hallmark. — Nick. ' half a
mark,' from the coin ; cf. Nine-

pence, Twelvepence, Hundredpound, Thousandpound, &c. Ninepence nearly succeeded in becoming
a permanent surname. Halfmark
in Hallmark has really done so.
With the corrupted Hallmark, cf.
our *ha'penny*, which goes even
further in the way of corruption.

Robert Alfmarck, co. Hunts, 1273. A.
Johannes Half-mark, 1379 : P. T.
Yorks. p. 77.
Emma Halmark', Sheffield, 1379 : P. T.
Yorks. p. 42.
1388. John Halfmark : Cal. of Wills
·in the Court of Husting (2).
Manchester, 1 ; Liverpool, 1 ; Preston,
1 ; MDB. (co. Chester), 1.

Hallows, Hallowes.— ?

MDB. (co. Derby), 4, 2.

Hallsworth.—Local ; v. Holdsworth. It is hard to say whether
it belongs to Haldsworth or Halesworth, to Yorkshire or Suffolk.

1565. William Hallesworthe : Reg.
Univ. Oxf. ii. 14.
1794. Married—John Clark and Jane
Hallsworth : St. Geo. Han. Sq. ii. 108.
Crockford, 1 ; Philadelphia, 1.

Hallward.—Bapt. ' the son of
Aylward,' q.v. It is quite possible
the origin may be ascribed to some
' keeper of a hall,' as Mr. Lower
suggests, but there is no evidence.
The derivation given above is the
natural one. This dictionary shows
that aspirates are of no account in
nomenclature. It is probably an
imitative corruption of Aylward.

Johannes Halward, 1379 : P. T. Yorks.
p. 161.
1784. Married—Rev. John Hallward
and Mary Lambard : St. Geo. Han. Sq.
ii. 364.
MDB. (co. Kent), 1 ; Crockford, 2.

**Hallworth, Halwarth, Halls-
worth.**—Local, ' of Hallworth.'
I cannot find the spot. With
Hallsworth for Hallworth, cf.
Holdsworth for Holdworth, or
Huddersfield for the earlier Hud-
dersfield. I feel very certain that
Hallworth and Hallsworth are
mere variants of Holdsworth (q.v.),
a recognized Yorkshire surname.

Johannes de Halworth, 1379 : P. T.
Yorks. p. 254.
1794. Married—John Clark and Jane
Hallsworth : St. Geo. Han. Sq. ii. 108.
London, 1, 0, 0 ; New York, 0, 1, 0 ;
Philadelphia, 1, 0, 1.

Halman.—Occup. 'the hall-man,' i.e. the servant at the hall; v. Ladyman, Bowerman.

Willelmus Halleman, 1379: P. T. Yorks. p. 232.
Roger Halman, 1379: ibid.
Johannes Halman, 1379: ibid. p. 59.
1619. William Hallman and Joane Hobbes: Marriage Lic. (London), i 74.
London, 1; New York, 1.

Halmshaw; v. Hampshire.

Halpin, Hallpin, Halpen.—Bapt 'the son of Harpin,' q.v. No doubt a variant. This form is strongly represented in the United States.

1779. Married—John Halpin and Sarah Strode: St. Geo. Han. Sq. i. 306.
London, 1, 0, 0; West Rid. (Yorks) Court Dir., 1, 0, 0; Liverpool, 2, 0, 0; Philadelphia, 30, 0, 7.

Halsall.—Local, 'of Halsall,' a parish in co. Lanc., three miles from Ormskirk.

Gilbert de Halsale, co. Lanc., 20 Edw. I. R.
Alan de Halsale, co. Lanc., ibid.
Richard Halsall, co. Lanc., 1586: Reg. Univ. Oxf. ii. 150.
Henry Halsall, of Halsall, 1574: Wills at Chester (1545-1620), p. 79.
Ann Halsall, of Halsall, *widow*, 1589: ibid.
Cuthbert Halsall, of Hallsall, 1619: ibid.
1622. Mark Quested and Eliz. Halsall, *widow*: Marriage Lic. (London), ii. 110.
1803. Married — Ralph Halsall and Amey Fenton: St. Geo. Han. Sq. ii. 288.
Liverpool, 3; Ormskirk, 1; Manchester, 2; London, 2; New York, 1; Philadelphia, 3.

Halse.—Local, 'at the halse,' from residence thereby. 'Halse, the hazel tree. Co. Somerset' (Halliwell).

Richard atte Halse, co. Soms., 1 Edw. III: Kirby's Quest, p. 181.
John de Halse, co. Soms., 1 Edw. III: ibid. p. 191.
John de Halse, co. Soms., 1 Edw. III: ibid. p. 277.
London, 4; Boston (U.S.), 2.

Halsey.—(1) Local, 'of Hallsley.' Although this is the undoubted origin of the name I cannot find the spot. Nothing can be more unsatisfactory (speaking etymologically, not genealogically) than Mr. Lower's quotation from Burke's Landed Gentry, that 'the founder of this family was William Hawse, alias Chamber, to whom Henry VIII

granted the rectory and patronage of Great Gaddesden, co. Herts, where, under the name of Halsey, the family have ever since resided': Patr. Brit. p. 144.

1564-5. John Haulsley, Trin. Coll. Oxf.: Reg. Univ. Oxf. ii. 24.

In this register Halsey, Haulsee, Hallcé, and Haulsley are placed under the same heading (v. Index, pt. iv). (2) Local, 'at the halse-hey,' i.e. the enclosure of hazel-trees, from residence thereby; v. Halse and Hey.

1565. Married — Robert Halsay and Bridget Dawson: St. Mary Aldermary, p. 4.
1620. Whorwood Shadwell and Eliz. Halsey, *widow*: Marriage Lic. (London), ii. 91.
1741. Married—John Halsey and Mary Lowndes: St. Geo. Han. Sq. i. 27.
London, 11; MDB. (co. Kent), 1; (co. Hertford), 1; (co. Soms.), 1; Philadelphia, 3.

Halstead, Halsted. — (1) Local, 'at the hall-stead,' from residence thereby or therein; v. Hall and Stead. (2) Local, 'of Halstead,' two parishes, one in co. Essex and the other in co. Kent. Also a township is so called in the parish of Tilton, co. Leicester. (1) supplies the derivation of this place-word. Nearly all our Halsteads hail from Yorkshire, from a spot I cannot discover.

Adam Hallestede, *webester*, 1379: P.T. Yorks. p. 96.
Ricardus Hallestedes, *osteler*, 1379: ibid. p. 47.
1587. John Halsteede, *goldsmith*, and Anne Lea: Marriage Lic. (London), i. 164.
1618. Richard Halsted, co. York: Reg. Univ. Oxf. ii. 371.
1684. Bapt.—Mary, d. Charles Halsteed: St. Jas. Clerkenwell, i. 308.
London, 1, 5; Manchester, 1, 1; West Rid. Court Dir., 6, 1; Philadelphia, 16, 0.

Halton.—Local, 'of Halton,' parishes or chapelries in cos. Leicester, Chester, Buckingham, Northumberland, Lincoln (3), York (3), &c.

John de Halton, co. York, 1273. A.
Richard de Halton, co. Linc., ibid.
Simon de Halton, co. Salop, ibid.
Robert de Halton, co. Suffolk, 20 Edw. I. R.
Adam de Halton, 1379: P. T. Yorks. p. 193.

Emma de Halton, 1379: ibid.
Johannes de Halton, 1379: ibid. p. 206.
1565-6. Robert Halton and Joanna Drayner: Marriage Lic. (London), i. 32.
1791. Married—John Haughton James and Mary Halton: St. Geo. Han. Sq. ii. 54.
London, 4; New York, 2.

Ham.—(1) Bapt. 'the son of Hamo,' from nick. Hamme; v. Hamlet and Hammond.

Johannes Hamme, 1379: P. T. Yorks. p. 44.

(2) Local, 'of the ham'; A.S. *ham*, a home, a dwelling. Also 'of Ham,' parishes in the diocs. of Canterbury, Salisbury, Rochester, &c. The original meaning is the same.

Robert de la Hamme, co. Sussex, 1273. A.
John de Hamme, co. Wilts, ibid.
William de Ham, co. Camb., ibid.
Alice de Hamme, co. Soms., 1 Edw. III: Kirby's Quest, p. 186.
John atte Ham, co. Soms., 1 Edw. III: ibid. p. 162.
Martin atte Ham, co. Soms., 1 Edw. III: ibid.
Juliana in le Hame, co. Soms., 1 Edw. III: ibid. p. 171.
1699. Bapt. — Jonathan, s. Jonathan Ham: St. Jas. Clerkenwell, i 281.
London, 6; Oxford, 2; New York, 10.

Hambidge; v. Hambridge.

Hamblet, Hamblett.—Bapt. 'the son of Hamon,' from the double dim. Ham-el-ot, whence Hamlet, and with intrusive *b* Hamblet; v. Hammon, Hamlet, and Hamlin; cf. Hewlett for Hew-el-ot (little Hugh).

Hamlet Ashton, of Glazebrook, 1594: Wills at Chester (1545-1620), p. 6.
Hamblett Ashton, 1622: Preston Guild Rolls, p. 79.
Hamlett Assheton, of Glasbrooke, 1642: ibid. p. 106.

The instances from the Ashton family settle the matter if any doubt existed. Therefore Hamblet or Hamblett is a variant of Hamlet, q.v.

1609. Married—Nathaniell Man and Sara Hamblett: St. Dionis Backchurch, p. 17.
1613. Dionisius Smithe and Rebecca Hamblett: Marriage Lic. (London), ii. 21.
Manchester, 1, 0; MDB. (co. Chester), 1, 0; New York, 1, 0; Boston (U.S.), 0, 2.

Hambleton, Hambelton.—Local, 'of Hamilton,' or 'Hambleton,' or 'Hambledon'; v. Hamerton and Hamilton. The *b* is intrusive.

London, 4, 2; New York, 1, 0.

Hamblin, -bling; v. Hamlin.

Hambly; v. Hamley.

Hambridge, Hambidge. — Local, 'of Hambridge.' I do not know where this place is. Hambidge is a manifest variant.

1583. Anthony Hambridge and Margaret Temple : Marriage Lic. (London), i. 117.
1802. Married — George Hambridge and Mary White : St. Geo. Han. Sq. ii. 269.
London,2,2; Oxford,0,2; New York,0,1.

Hambro, Hambrow.—Local, 'of Hanbury'; variants of Hanbury or Handborough, q.v. The change from *n* to *m* and vice versa is common; cf. Henning and Hemming. I do not think that Hamburgh is the parent; all the evidence is to the contrary.

Nicholas de Hamberegh, co. Kent, 1273. A.
Richard de Hambyr', co. Oxf., ibid.
John de Hamberegh, co. Kent, ibid.
John de Hambury, co. Derby, 20 Edw. I. R.
1574. Married—George Stondes and Joyce Hambre : St. Mary Aldermary, p. 5.

Richard de Hambyr' mentioned above lived in co. Oxford, where lies the parish of Handborough. Carefully compare this with the Oxfordshire instances under Hanbury. I doubt not my statement is correct. Handborough would readily become Hambro or Hambrow.

London, 2, 1; Boston (U.S.), 12, 0.

Hambrook.— Local, 'of Hambrook,' a chapelry in the parish of Winterbourne, co. Gloucester, six miles from Bristol.

MDB. (co. Kent), 1; London, 1; New York, 2.

Hamburger.—Local,'the Hamburger,' a native of Hamburg. This is not in all cases a newly imported surname. It occurs in the 13th century.

Reginald le Hamberger, London, 1273. A.
London, 3; New York, 32.

Hamell, Hamel, Hamil, Hamill. — Bapt. 'the son of

Hamel'; cf. the local Hamilton, 'the town of Hamil' (v. Town). From the same root as Hamo; v. Hammon and Hamlin.

Isabella Hamell, 1379 : P. T. Yorks. p. 301.
1784. Married—John Ward and Fanny Hamill : St. Geo. Han. Sq. i. 359.
London, 0, 1, 0, 0; Crockford, 0, 1, 0, 0; Ulverston, 1, 0, 0, 0; Philadelphia, 13, 5, 2, 37.

Hamer.—Local, 'of Hamer,' a village in the parish of Rochdale, co. Lanc. This surname has spread throughout the surrounding district.

John de Heymer, c. Edw. IV : Baines' Lanc. i. 507.
Thurston de Heymer, 1574 : ibid.
1590. Samuel Hamer, Bras. Coll. : Reg. Univ. Oxf. ii. 180.
1596. James Hamer and Constance Churche : Marriage Lic. (London), i. 233.
Edmund Hamer, of Hamer, parish of Rochdale, 1597 : Wills at Chester (1545-1620), p. 80.
Henry Haymer, 1572 : ibid.
Francis Hamer, of the parish of Bury, 1610 : ibid.
Manchester,13; London,6; NewYork,3.

Hamersly; v. Hammersley.

Hamerton, Hammerton.— Local, 'of Hamerton,' probably the same as Hambleton, a township in the parish of Brayton,near Selby, co. York. The variant is a natural one. 'Near Sutton in Wincle township is a small farm, now known as Hammerton, but formerly called Hammelton, Hambleton, or Hamilton': Earwaker's East Cheshire, ii. 449.

Geoffrey de Hamertone, co. Hunts, 1273. A.
Johannes de Hamyrton, 1379 : P. T. Yorks. p. 156.
Johannes de Hamerton, 1379 : ibid.
1547-8. William Hamerton and Benet Castelyn : Marriage Lic. (Faculty Office), p. 12.
1616. Bapt. — Jerome, s. Thomas Hammerton : St. Jas. Clerkenwell, i. 74.
1803. Married — Thomas Hammerton and Ann Nicholl : St. Geo. Han. Sq. ii. 280.
West Riding Court Dir., 2, 3; London, 1, 3; Philadelphia, 1, 0.

Hamil, Hamill; v. Hamell.

Hamilton.—Local, 'of Hamilton.' Although there are several Hambledons (diocs. Peterborough, Oxford, and Winchester) and one

Hambleton (dioc. Manchester), not to mention smaller spots (v. Hambleton), the Scottish Hamiltons are traced to Hambledon, a manor in co. Bucks (v. Lower, Patr. Brit. p. 144). It is probable that the English Hamiltons are sprung from a dozen different sources. There is a Hambleton, a township in the parish of Brayton, near Selby, co. York. v. Hamell.

William de Hameledene, co. Bucks, 1273. A.
Robert de Hameledene, co. Oxf., ibid.
Alexander de Hameldone,co.Bucks,ibid.
Thomas de Hameldene, co. Glouc., ibid.
Richard de Hameleden, co. Surrey : Hen. III-Edw. I. K.
Robert (parson of the church at) Hameldon, co. Surrey : 20 Edw. I. R.
London, 61.

Hamlet, Hamlett. — Bapt. 'the son of Hamon,' from nick. Ham, and double dim. Ham-el-ot. Later on it assumed the settled form of Hamlet; its rivals were Hamnet and Hamlin, q.v. As a font-name Hamon has nearly disappeared, although Hamlet and Hamnet are still retained in a few old-established families. The Masseys of co./Chester have retained this name for centuries. The forms in the Visitation of Cheshire, 1580 (Harl. Soc., pp. 170-5) are Hamon de Massy, 23 Edw.III; Hamond Massy, temp. Hen.IV; Hamlett Massy, 1566; and Hamnett Massy (p. 124). The De Lacy Inquisition, 1311, has 'The wife of Richard, son of Hamelot.' Both Hamlet and Hamnet were commonly used in the last century as font-names, although their relation as diminutives of Hamon was quite forgotten. Hamlet Winstanley, the painter, was born at Warrington in the year 1700. In Kent's London Directory for 1736 several Hamnets are found as font-names. I furnished an instance in Notes and Queries some years ago of the same person being known as Hamnet or Hamlet. It was in the case of one of the Massyes of Cheshire. Shakespeare's little son was alike Hamnet or Hamlet, after his godfather Hamnet Sadler. A good instance occurs in

Privy Purse Expenses, Elizabeth of York (pp. 21 and 63):

Nov. 13, 1502. Item: the same day to Hamlet Clegge, for money by him layed out ... iiis. iiiid.

June 13, 1502. Item: the same day to Hampnet Clegge, for money by him delivered to the Quene, vis. viiid.

Besides the familiar Hammond the following surnames are undoubtedly sprung from Hamon and its diminutives: Hammett, Hammonds, Hamond, Hamlet, Hamlyn (all from Crockford's Cler. Dir.), Hammatt, Hamlin, Hamling, Hamblet, Hamblin, Hambling, Hampson, Ham, and Hams (all from Lond. Dir.). That Hamo was known as Ham is proved by 'Hamme, son of Adcock, held twenty-nine acres of land': De Lacy Inquisition, 1311.

Hamlet Ashton. AA. 1.
Richard fil. Hamelot. AA. 2.
Hamelet de la Burste. NN.
Hamlet Milot, of Carrington, *husbandman*, 1587: Wills at Chester (1545-1620), p. 136.
1604-5. Thomas Hamlett, co. Hants: Reg. Univ. Oxf. ii. 279.
Ellen Hamlett, of Roby, co. Lane., 1685: Wills at Chester (1681-1700), p. 107.
1791. Married — Thomas Hamlet and Eliz. Clark: St.Geo. Han. Sq. ii. 58.
Manchester, 4, 1; MDB. (co. Chester), 2, 0; Boston (U.S.), 2, 3.

Hamley, Hambly.—Local, 'of Hamley.' I cannot find the spot.

1737. Married — Peter Hambly and Agnes Jenkinson: St. Geo. Han. Sq. i. 19.
1788. Married — Rev. Thomas Hambly (of Widford, Herts) and Ann Hallett: ibid. ii. 10.
MDB. (co. Cornwall), 1,11; London, 1, 0.

Hamlin, Hamling, Hamlyn, Hamblin, Hambling.—Bapt. 'the son of Hamo' or (Fr.) Hamon, from dim. Hamelin (v. Hammon); cf. Hewling for Hewelin (Hugh). The *g* in Hamling and Hambling is, of course, excrescent, and the *b* in Hamblin and Hambling is equally, of course, intrusive.

Hamelin de Humpton, Hen. III.-Edw. I. K.
William Hamelin, co. Linc., 1273. A.
Walter Hamline, co. Linc., ibid.
Hamelin de Godelee, 35 Edw. I: BBB. p. 743.
Osbert Hamelyn, 1306. M.
Hamelyn de Trap. H.
Hamalin Prepositus. C.
Hamelin (without surname), co. Camb., ibid.

Robertus Hamelyn, 1379: P. T. Yorks. p. 297.
Thomas Hamelyn, 1379: ibid. p. 221.
1618. Bapt. — Margaret, d. Thomas Hamlin: St. Jas. Clerkenwell, i. 82.
1799. Married. — John Bean and Ann Hamblen: St. Geo. Han. Sq. ii. 199.
London, 3, 1, 2, 1, 3; Philadelphia, 7, 0, 2, 2, 1.

Hamman, Hammand.—Bapt. 'the son of Hamon'; v. Hammon.
London, 1, 0; MDB. (co. Cambridge), 0, 1; Oxford, 1, 0.

Hammence.—Bapt. A variant of Hammonds or Hammons, q.v.; cf. Evance for Evans, but v. Hemmence.
MDB. (co. Cambridge), 2.

Hammersley, Hamersly.—Local, 'of Hamersley,' a locality probably to be found in co. Stafford.
1610. Walter Hamersley, co. Staff.: Reg. Univ. Oxf. ii. 365.
1617. William Hamersly, co. Staff.: ibid. p. 310.
1801. Married.—John Ryan and Mary Hammersley: St. Geo. Han. Sq. ii. 245.
MDB. (co. Stafford), 7, 0; London, 5, 0; Manchester, 2, 0; Philadelphia, 0, 7.

Hammersmith, Hamersmith.—Local, 'of Hammersmith,' a parish in co. Middlesex, near London. I find no trace of the surname in England.
Philadelphia, 1, 0; New York, 1, 1.

Hammerton; v. Hamerton.

Hammett, Hammatt, Hammitt.—Bapt. 'the son of Hamon,' modified forms of Hamnett, q.v.
1581. Hammett Penketman and Izabell Browne: Marriage Lic. (London), i. 103.
1595. Thomas Streete and Margaret Hammatt: ibid. p. 226.
1761. Married — James Lymans and Eliz. Hammett: St. Geo. Han. Sq. i. 102.
London, 3, 1, 0; Manchester, 1, 0, 0; New York 2, 0, 2; Philadelphia, 7, 0, 5.

Hammon, Hammond, Hamondson.—Bapt. 'the son of Hamon' or, with excrescent *d* (as in Simond), Hamond. A very popular font-name in its day, now all but entirely forgotten. Nevertheless its diminutives, Hamelot, Hamonet, and Hameline, survived till the 18th century as font-names, the parent having lapsed into oblivion; v. Hamlet, Hamnett, and Hamlin. For Hamondson, v. Hampson, in which form it finally settled down.

Hamund Brande, Sheriff of London, 1203: Riley's Chronicles of the Mayors and Sheriffs of London, p. 187.
Hamund le Mester, co. Hunts, 1273. A.
Hamo, or Hammund de Cursun, co. Salop, ibid.
Adelina fil. Hamund, co. Hunts, ibid.
Alan Hamund, co. Oxf., ibid.
William fil. Hammund, co. Linc., ibid.
Hammond Chyckwell, Lord Mayor of London, 1319: N. and Q., 1857, p. 197.
Hamond Cobeler. H.
John Fitz-hamond (=Fitz-Aymon). D.
Hammond Hansart, 1556: Reg. Univ. Oxf. p. 231.
1648. Bapt.—Abraham, son of George Hammon: St. Dionis Backchurch, p.109.
London, 7, 101, 0; Manchester, 0, 7, 0.

Hammons, Hammonds.—Bapt. 'the son of Hamon'; the *d* is excrescent and the *s* patronymic; v. Hammon.
Crockford, 0, 1; Boston (U.S.), 1, 0.

Hamner; v. Hanmer.

Hamnett, Hamonet.—Bapt. 'the son of Hamon,' from dim. Hamon-et; v. Hammon. This soon became Hamnet. The rival dim. of Hamnet was Hamlet (Hamelot), and frequently both forms are ascribed to the same individual, but they must be kept distinct, v. Hamlot. Hamnet as a font-name existed till the last century. It was extremely popular in Cheshire for many centuries. As a surname it is naturally found in that district, the Hamonet of the London Directory representing a Frenchman, a teacher of music.

1522-3. Hamnet Shawe and Eliz. Shypman: Marriage Lic. (London), p. 3.
'Hamynet Harrington, gentleman usher,' 1526: Letters and Papers (Foreign and Domestic), Hen. VIII.
Hamnet Burgess, 1619: Wills at Chester, p. 33.
Hamnett Warburton, 1631: Lanc. and Ches. Rec. Soc. xii. 206.
1643. Buried — Hamnet Hide, from Mr. Hollingsworth's: St. Antholin (London), p. 76.
1729. Married — John Creighton and Eliz. Hamnet: St. Peter, Cornhill, ii. 79.
London, 0, 1; Manchester, 3, 0.

Hampden.—Local, 'of Hampden,' a parish (divided into Great and Little) in co. Bucks. The famous John Hampden, although born in London, was the son of William Hampden, of Hampden, co. Bucks.

Alexander de Hamden, co. Bucks: Hen. III-Edw. I. K.

A a

Alexander de Hamden,co. Oxf., 1273. A.
Alexander de Hampeden, co. Bucks, ibid.

1581. Thomas Hamdenne, co. Northampton: Reg. Univ. Oxf. ii. 99.
1591-2. Jerome Horsey and Eliz. Hampden, daughter of Griffin Hampden, late of Hampden, co. Bucks, Esq.: Marriage Lic. (London), i. 195.
London, 1 ; Crockford, 3.

Hamper.—Offic. ' the hanaper.' The corruption was all but inevitable. A hanaper was a kind of basket in which to store documents, &c. Hence the Hanaper Office, and the familiar hamper (v. English Surnames, 4th edit., p. 388). The hanaper seems to have had charge of the stored-up indentures, &c. ' Hanypere or hamper, *canistrum* ': Prompt. Parv.

Geoffrey le Hanaper, co. Camb.,1273. A.
John Hanaper, co. Hunts, ibid.
William Henyper,co. Soms., 1 Edw. III: Kirby's Quest, p. 232.
London, 2.

Hampermaker. — Occup. ' a maker of hampers or hanapers,' a basket-maker ; v. Hamper.

William Hampermaker. H.
Walter Hampermaker. RR. 3.

Hampshire, Hampsheir, Hamsher, Hamshar, Hampshaw, Halmshaw, Hamshaw. —(1) Local, ' of Hallamshire,' easily and naturally corrupted to Hampshire. There can be no doubt about the Yorkshire Hampshires ; they are descended from Hallamshire folk. Nine-tenths of our Hampshires = Hallamshire. The order is Hallomshire, Halmshire, Hamshire, and (with customary intrusive *p* after *m*, as in Simpson or Thompson) Hampshire. The intermediate link is found in Halmshaw, to be seen in the West Rid. Court Directory.

Thomas de Hallomshire, 1379 : P. T. Yorks. p. 32.
Henricus de Hallomshire, 1379 : ibid. p. 2.
Thomas Halomschire, 1379 : ibid. p. 186.
Robertus Hallomshire,1379 : ibid.p.294.

(2) Local, ' of Hampshire ' ; cf. Wiltshire, Devonshire, &c.

London, 1, 1, 2, 1, 0, 0, 0 ; Wakefield (Hampshire), 2 ; Leeds (Hampshire), 2 ; Sheffield (Hampshire), 3 ; Wakefield (Hampshaw),1 ; Sheffield,(Hampshaw), 1; West Riding Court Dir. (Halmshaw, 1);

Liversedge (Halmshaw), 2 ; Balne, Yorks (Hampshaw), 1.

Hampson.—Bapt. ' the son of Hamon' or, with excrescent *d*, 'Hamond'; v. Hammon. Sometimes Hampson (the *p* is intrusive, as in Simpson or Thompson) is a corruption of Hamondson. Occasionally it may be direct from the nick. Hamme ; v. Ham. The Manchester and South Lancashire directories conclusively prove, by the large number of Hampsons they contain, how locally popular was Hamond in the 14th and 15th centuries as a font-name. For an extended proof of this, v. Hamlet.

Robertus Hameson, 1379 : P. T. Yorks. p. 76.
Hamo fil. Hamonis. C.
William Hamnerson, temp. Eliz. ZZ.
John Hamson. V. 5.
Alice Hamundson, co. York. W. 2.
John Hawmundson, co. York. W. 11.
1551. Married — William Pyncheback and Jone Hamson : St. Michael, Cornhill, p. 6.
1553. Bapt. — Alice Hampsonne : St. Peter, Cornhill, i. 6.
London, 4 ; Manchester, 36 ; Philadelphia, 19.

Hampton.—Local, ' of Hampton.' There are at least thirteen parishes of this name in England, representing the diocs. of Worcester, London, Hereford, Oxford, Exeter, and Lichfield.

John de Hampton, co. Som., 1273. A.
William de Hamptone, co. Hunts, ibid.
Nicholas de Hampton, co. Wilts, ibid.
Philip de Hampton, co. Camb., ibid.
Geoffrey de Hampton, co. Linc., ibid.
1575. John Hampton and Eliz. Laymere : Marriage Lic. (London), i. 67.
1661. Bapt.—William, s. John Hampton : St. Jas. Clerkenwell, i. 212.
London, 12 ; Philadelphia, 39.

Hanbrook.—Local ; v. Hambrook, of which it is a variant ; cf. Ransom for Ranson.

MDB. (co. Kent.), 1.

Hanbury, Handbury, Hanberry, Hanbrey, Handburry. —Local, (1) ' of Hanbury,' (*a*) a parish in co. Stafford, seven miles from Burton ; (*b*) a parish in co. Worcester, four miles from Droitwich ; (2) ' of Handborough,' a parish in co. Oxford, three miles from Woodstock. The chief variants of the surname are found in the United States.

Walter de Haneber', or Haneberowe, co. Oxf., 1273. A.
Robert de Haneberge, co. Oxf., ibid.
Richard de Hanburgh, co. Northampt., 20 Edw. I. K.
Alex. de Haneburgo, co. Staff.: Hen. III-Edw. I. K.
John de Haneber', co. Oxf., ibid.
Thomas de Haneberwe, co. Soms., 1 Edw. III : Kirby's Quest, p. 226.
John de Haneberwe, co. Soms. : ibid.
Phillip de Handbury, rector of Wells, co. Norf., 1327 : FF. ix. 285.
1558. William Hanbury and Alice Ferryman, *widow* : Marriage Lic. (London), i. 19.
1592. Francis Hanburye, co. Middlesex : Reg. Univ. Oxf. pt. ii. p. 191.
London, 13, 0, 0, 0, 0 ; MDB. (co. Cambridge), 0, 1, 0, 0, 0 ; (co. Bucks), 2, 0, 0, 0, 0 ; New York, 2, 0, 1, 1, 1.

Hanby, Handby.—Local, ' of Hanby,' a hamlet in the parish of Lavington, co. Lincoln. The *d* in Handby is intrusive ; cf. Handcock or Handbury. Also cf. Simmonds for Simmons.

Roger de Hanby, co. Linc., 20 Edw. I. R.
1582. Thomas Hanbye and Isabell Wayte : Marriage Lic. (London), i. 112.
1769. Married — William Dand and Jane Hanby : St. Geo. Han. Sq. i. 184.
MDB. (co. Derby), 1, 1 ; London, 0, 1.

Hance ; v. Hands.

Hancock, Handcock, Hancocks, Hancox.—Bapt. ' the son of John,' from Han, and suffix *-cock* (v. Hankin); cf. Wilcock, Wilcox, Jeffcock, Simcock, and Simcox ; v. Cocks or Cox. The *d* in Handcock is, of course, intrusive. Hancock was more popular than Hankin, and is found in the Hundred Rolls (1273). I do not find any instance of Hankin in those registers.

Hanecock Birunc, co. York, 1273. A.
Warynus Hancock, 1379 : P. T. Yorks. p. 204.
Agnes Hankok-wyf, 1379 : ibid. p. 283.
Robert Hancock, 1379 : ibid. p. 82.
Willelmus Hancok', 1379 : ibid. p. 45.
1619. Richard Tirrell and Katherine Hancoxe : Marriage Lic. (London), ii. 83.
1651. Married — John Steele, *batchler*, and Abigell Hannkock, *vergen*: St. Mary Aldermary, p. 22.
1762. George Handcock and Eleanor Jackson : St. Geo. Han. Sq. i. 110.
London, 49, 0, 1, 1 ; West Riding Court Dir., 7, 1, 0, 0 ; Boston (U.S.), 40, 1, 0, 0.

Hand, Hands, Hance.—Bapt. ' the son of John,' from the Dutch imported Han or Hans. The *d* is excrescent, as in Simmonds for Simmons; v. Hancock, Hankin, and Hanson. With Hance, cf. Evance for Evans or Ellice for Ellis.

'Haunce the Luter, iis. *vid.*': Privy Purse Exp., Princess Mary, p. 104.
Hans Berner. O.
Hans Doubler, ibid.
Hanse et uxor ejus, 1379 : P. T. Yorks. p. 231.
Matilda Han-wyfe, 1379 : ibid. p. 16.
Thomas Hand', 1379 : ibid. p. 65.
Laurence Hande, 1379 : ibid.
1521. John Hance and Johan Audley : Marriage Lic. (London), i 7.
1588. Bartholomew Hands and Barbara Kittson : ibid. p. 172.
1594. John Hind and Joane Simons : ibid. p. 213.
London, 14, 8, 3 ; Philadelphia, 82, 1, 32.

Handbury; v. Hanbury.

Handby; v. Hanby.

Handcock; v. Hancock.

Handforth, Handford, Hanford.—Local, ' of Handforth,' a township in the parish of Cheadle, co. Chester, formerly Honford or Hondford. For suffix, v. Forth or Ford.

John de Honford, i.e. Handforth, 1370 : Earwaker's Hist. East Cheshire, I. 249.
Thomas de Honford, 1398 : ibid.
Richard Handforth, of Godley, 1598 : Wills at Chester (1545–1620), p. 81.
Hugh Handford, of Marton, *tailor*, 1638 : ibid. (1621–50), p. 95.
Nicholas Handforth, of Godley, parish of Mottram, 1635 : ibid.
1565. Married.—Robert Honforde and Katherine Kyrke : Reg. Prestbury Ch. (co. Ches.), p. 10.
1598. John Hanforth and Joane Cheyney : Marriage Lic. (London), i. 250.
1784. Married. — Jacob Stannard and Harriot Handford : St. Geo. Han. Sq. i. 355.
Manchester, 5, 3, 0 ; MDB. (co. Chester), 1, 4, 0 ; London, 0, 7, 0 ; Philadelphia, 7, 3, 6.

Handley.—Local ; v. Hanley.

Handsaker, Handshaker.—Local, ' of Handsacre,' a parish in co. Stafford, near Rugeley. This surname looks as if it were the sobriquet of some demonstrative welcomer of his friends, but the spelling and pronunciation are simply imitative.

William Hondeshakere, 1302. M.
Elizabeth Hondesacre, C. R., 18 Hen. VI.
1623. Rowland Powell and Bridget Handsaker : Marriage Lic. (London), ii. 133.

1656. Buried — Joane Hansaker, *a pensioner* : St. Michael, Cornhill, p. 248.
MDB. (co. Stafford), 1, 0.

Handsomebody.—Nick. This name somewhat startled the public when it figured in the newspapers a few years ago in a list of honours. No doubt a rough translation of the old Gentilcorps.

William Gentilcorps. M.
Richard Gentylcors. X.

Handson; v. Hanson; cf. Handcock for Hancock.

MDB. (co. Cornwall), 1 ; (co. Lincoln),4.

Handy.—Nick. 'the handy,' the expert, the ready, the attentive ; v. Hendy, a M.E. form of the same word.

Robert Handy, C. R., 16 Edw. III. pt. i.
1792. Married — William Handy and Mary Goode : St. Geo. Han. Sq. ii. 84.
1793. — Thomas Handy and Sarah Hodges : ibid. p. 102.
London, 1 ; Oxford, 1 ; New York, 22.

Handybody. — Nick. ' the handy body,' the ready, the useful ; v. Handy and Hendy, and cf. Goodbody.

Nicholas Hendibody, co. Soms., 1 Edw. III : Kirby's Quest, p. 189.

Hane.—Nick. 'the hen' (?), cf. A.S. *hana*, a cock, of which *hen* is the feminine.

Alicia le Hane, co. Bucks, 1273. A.

Hanger.—Local,'at the hanger,' from residence beside some sloping grounds so termed ; cf. Shelfhanger, a parish in co. Norwich ; Hanging Heaton, a parish in W. Rid. Yorks ; Hanging Ditch, in Manchester ; and the various Heaning Woods, Heaning Banks, &c., in Furness and co. Cumberland.

' It is divided into a sheep-down, the high wood, and a long hanging wood called the Hanger ' : White's Hist. Selborne, Letter i.
Richard atte Hanger, C. R., 6 Hen. IV.
1630. Married — John Hanger and Ellin Smyth : St. Jas. Clerkenwell, iii. 62.
1643. George Buller and Mary Hanger : Marriage Lic. (London), ii. 269.
1717–8. Right Hon. Henry, Lord Colerane and Alice Hanger : Marriage Lic. (London), ii. 340.
Oxford, 1 ; New York, 1 ; Philadelphia, 1.

Hanham, Hannam, Hannum.—Local, ' of Hanham,' a hamlet in the parish of Britton, co.

Gloucester, five miles from Bristol. With the American variant Hannum, cf. Barnum for Barnham.

Thomas de Hanam, co. Soms., 1273. A.
Roger de Hanam, co. Soms., 1 Edw. III : Kirby's Quest, p. 270.
1587–8. John Hannam, co. Dorset : Reg. Univ. Oxf. ii. 163.
1589. John Hannam and Eliz. Incente, *widow* : Marriage Lic. (London), i. 180.
1594. Married — Henry Hannam and Marg. Huberden : St. Jas. Clerkenwell, iii. 18.
1795. Married — James Hannam and Martha Patty : St. Geo. Han. Sq. ii. 129.
MDB. (co. Dorset), 4, 3, 0 ; London, 1, 7, 0 ; Philadelphia, 0, 0, 17.

Hanker.—Occup. ' the anchorite' ; M.E. *ancre*, a hermit. The aspirate is common in the early registers.

John le Hanekere, co. Oxf., 1273. A.
Adam Hanekare, co. Oxf., ibid.
1703. Buried — John Peter Hanker, *merchant* : St. Dionis Backchurch, p. 271.
Philadelphia, 1.

Hankey.—? Bapt. ' the son of John' (?). Probably a modification of Hankin, as suggested by Lower (v. Patr. Brit. p. 149) ; v. Hankin. All the same a spot must be looked for in co. Chester, styled Hankey, which may have given birth to a local surname.

1533. John Hanky, of Churton : Earwaker's East Cheshire, ii. 86 n.
1562. Hugh Hankey, of Churton : Wills at Chester (1545–1620), p. 81.
1610. Robert Hankey, of Darnell : ibid.
1761. Married — John Cholmley and Anne Hankey : St. Geo. Han. Sq. i. 102.
MDB. (co. Kent), 2 ; Philadelphia, 1.

Hankin, Hanking, Hankins, Hankinson.—Bapt. ' the son of John,' from dim. Johan-kin = Harkin or Jankin ; v. Hanson. The English form was Jankin or Jenkin, but Hankin, introduced from the Low Countries, gradually naturalized itself, though it never became actually English. ' Hankin Booby was a common name for a clown ' : Chappell's English Songs, i. 73.

' Thus for her love and loss poor Hankin dies,
His amorous soul down flies.'
Musarum Deliciae, 1655.
' Hanekin Almond, varlet of the Countess of Surrey' : Household Book of Queen Isabelle, 1358 ; Cot. MS. Galba. E. xiv.
Alex. Henekyng, co. Soms., 1 Edw. III : Kirby's Quest, p. 272.

Hanekin de Fine. E.
Hanekyn Jocelyn. N.
Hankyn Maynwaryng. H.
Randolph Hankynson, temp. Eliz. ZZ.
Garret Hankinson, temp. Eliz. Z.
1761. Married — Thomas Hankin and Margaret Wilkinson : St. Geo. Han. Sq. i. 105.
1782. — Thomas Hankins and Rebecca Hillier : ibid. p. 339.
1787. — George Hankinson and Mary Smith : ibid. p. 402.
London,7,2,7,0 ; Philadelphia, 0, 0, 6, 9.

Hanks.— Bapt. 'the son of John'; v. Hankin and Hanson.
(1) A corruption of Hankins ; cf. Perks from Perkins, Dawks from Dawkins, Hawks from Hawkins, &c. (2) Hanka or Hanke was an early Low Country pet-name for John (v. Yonge's Glossary). Introduced into England the patronymic would be Hanks. In either case the origin is practically the same. We find it early on the south-east coast, where we should naturally expect it to appear.
Roger Hanke, co. Norf., 1273. A.
1564. Bapt.—Eliz. Hanckes, borne in the feildes : St. Jas. Clerkenwell, i. 2.
1585. — William, s. Richard Hanckes : ibid. p. 17.
1789. Married — William Hanks and Lucy Edwards : St. Geo. Han. Sq. ii. 18.
London, 7 ; Oxford, 4 ; New York, 5.

Hanley, Handley, Handly.—Local, (1) 'of Hanley,' parishes in cos. Stafford, Worcester, and Lincoln ; (2) 'of Handley,' parishes in cos. Chester and Dorset.
Tristram de Hanle, co. Suff., 1273. A.
William de Hanleye, co. Salop, ibid.
Warin de Hannelaye, co. Linc., ibid.
Robertus de Hannelay, 1379 : P. T. Yorks. p. 6.
Peter de Hanlav, 1379 : ibid. p. 48.
Willelmus de Hanlay, 1379 : ibid. p. 174.
1605. Thomas Hanley and Hester Gosson ; Marriage Lic. (London), i. 296.
1611. Robert Handley, of Manchester : Wills at Chester (1545-1620), p. 81.
1619. John Handleighe, co. Dorset : Reg. Univ. Oxf. ii. 377.
Manchester, 11, 2, 0 ; London, 9, 2, 0 ; New York, 82, 9, 2.

Hanman, Handman.—Local, 'of Hanham' (q.v.), in co. Glouc. At first sight it would seem to mean 'the servant of Hand' (q.v.): cf. Addiman, Matthewman, Priestman, &c. But the evidence is in favour of a local origin ; cf. Sweatman for Swettenham, Deadman for

Debenham, Godliman for Godalming, &c.
1609. John Handman, co. Glouc. (found in 1613 as Hanman): Reg. Univ. Oxf. ii. 306, iii. 319.
MDB. (co. Glouc.), 2, 1.

Hanmer, Hamner.—Local, 'of Hanmer,' a parish in the dioc. of St. Asaph. The change from Hanmer to Hamner (an American form) is found as early as the 16th century in England.
William Jenkin, of Hanmer, 1568 : Wills at Chester (1545-1620), p. 109.
Lewis Hamner (sic), co. Salop, 1575 : Reg. Univ. Oxf. pt. ii. p. 62.
Edward Hanmer, of Seswick, co. Denbigh, 1598: Wills at Chester (1545-1620), p. 81.
Anthony Hanmer, of Bellfield, parish of Hanmer, 1615 : ibid.
1766. Married — Humphrey Hanmer and Catherine Newton : St. Geo. Han. Sq. i. 153.
London, 10 ; Manchester, 4, 0 ; Liverpool, 4, 0 ; MDB. (co. Denbigh), 2, 0 ; Boston (U.S.), 1, 2 ; Philadelphia, 0, 1.

Hanmore.—Local, 'of Hanmer' (q.v.), a variant which now seems confined to the United States.
1624. Bapt.—Anne, d. Thomas Hanmore : St. Jas. Clerkenwell, i. 98.
1697. — Ann, d. Robert Hanmore : ibid. p. 274.
New York, 1 ; Philadelphia, 1.

Hannah, Hanna.—Local, 'of Hannah,' a parish in co. Lincoln, three miles from Alford. I believe, however, a large number of Hannas and Hannahs are of Scotch descent, probably variants of the local surname Hannay.
1622. Robert Hanna and Jane Styward : Marriage Lic. (London), ii. 110.
1677. Bapt.—John, s. John Hanna : St. Jas. Clerkenwell, i. 277.
MDB. (co. Lincoln), 1, 0 ; London, 4, 1 ; New York, 8, 30 ; Philadelphia, 10, 78.

Hannam; v. Hanham.

Hannen, Hannan.—Probably a variant of Hanham (q.v.), being found in the same county.
MDB. (co. Dorset), 1, 0 ; (co. Wilts), 1, 0 ; London, 1, 1.

Hanniball, Honeyball, Honeybell, Honiball, Honniball, Annable.—(1) Bapt. 'the son of Annable,' 'that perplexing name, Annabella,' as Miss Yonge styles it (Hist. Christian Names, ii. 283).

There is no difficulty about it. Originally it was Amable or Amabel, but very soon became Annabel, whence the Scottish Annaple and Annabella. From this was formed Arabella ; cf. Harry from Henry. The Hundred Rolls give the true and earliest forms ; v. Annable.
Amabilia (without surname), co. Bucks, 1273.. A.
John fil. Amabilie, co. Hunts, ibid.
John Amable co. Camb., ibid.
Amabilla de Amet, co. Linc., Hen. III—Edw. I. K.
Amabil, or Amable, or Amiable de Bydun, co. Bedf., ibid.

The next stage, as above stated, was a change from *m* to *n*.
Richard Anabilla, C. R., 9 Ric. II.
John Anable, C. R., 22 Edw. III. pt. i.
Peter fil. Annabel, 1311. M.
Johan Brase, et Anabul sa femme, 1379 : P. T. Yorks. p. 43.
Anabilla de Harpham, co. York. W. 2.

The final stage was to aspirate the initial vowel, so common a practice in names, as shown over and over again in this dictionary (v. Hodson). We may look upon the surname Hanniball therefore as imitative of the famous Hannibal of our school-days.

(2) Bapt. 'the son of Hannibal.' Unquestionably in some cases Hanniball and its variants must be looked upon as derived from the historical name. We find it as early as the 13th century :
Mathew Hanybal, C.R., 39 Hen. III. pt. i.

It was also introduced into England from Italy by spicemerchants and money-lenders :
Peter Haniballus, civis Romanus. C.

Speaking generally, however, I doubt not the Hanniballs, &c., of our London and other English directories are but imitative, and are in reality derived from the once very familiar girl's name Annable. I may add that Arabella, the Scotch variant of Annabella, was early anticipated by the following entry :
Arable de Meyhamme, co. Kent, Hen. III–Edw. I. K.

I append a few instances from modern registers :
Thomas Hannyball, 1513 : Reg. Univ. Oxf. i. 88.

1805. Married — William Green and Margaret Hanniball : St. Geo. Han. Sq. ii. 328.

— — John Clarke and Eliz. Honneyball : ibid. p. 331.

London, 0, 4, 1, 1, 2, 0 ; Boston (U.S.), Annable, 9.

Hanning. — Local, 'of Hanham' ; v. Hanham, Hannen, and Hanman.

MDB. (co. Glouc.), 1.

Hannington.—Local, 'of Hannington,' parishes in cos. Northampton, Wilts, and Hants.

Adam de Hanington, co. Westm., 20 Edw. III. R.

1627. Thomas Gladwin and Frances Hannington : Marriage Lic. (London), ii. 188.

1794. Married—Samuel Hanington and Grace Elford : St. Geo. Han. Sq. ii. 118.

London, 2 ; New York, 1 ; Boston (U.S.), 1.

Hannum; v. Hanham.

Hanrott.—Bapt.'the son of Henry,' from dim. Henriot ; v. Harriot.

Hansard, Hassard, Hazard. —Local, 'the Hansard,' a merchant of one of the Hanse towns, a member of the Hanseatic league. Lower, following Ferguson, says it is a personal name. This is quite possible, but so far as I am aware neither offers any evidence. My instances are from the East coast, which strongly suggests a Hanseatic origin. Luke Hansard, the founder of the Parliamentary Hansard, was born in Norwich in 1752 (Chambers' Encyc. v. 232). As will be seen below, his ancestors were 'in the same county five centuries earlier. Hassard and Hazard are perhaps modifications ; but v. Hassard.

Gilbert Haunsard, co. Linc., 1273. A.
John Haunsard, co. Norf., ibid.
John Hasard, co. York, ibid.
John Haunsard, co. Northampton, Hen. III-Edw. I. K.
Gilbert Haunsard, co. Linc., 20 Edw. I. R.
William Hasard, C. R., 36 Hen. III.
Alan de Haunsard, taverner, 4 Edw. II : Freemen of York, i. 13.
1624-5. Edward Hassard and Eliz. French : Marriage Lic. (London), ii. 151.
1631. John Hansard and Afra Nevinson : ibid. p. 204.

London, 3, 2, 4 ; New York, 0, 3, 30.

Hanscomb, Handscomb, Hanscom, Hanscome.—Local,

'of Hanscomb.' I cannot find the spot. In the United States this surname has ramified strongly as Hanscom. Of course the suffix is -comb ; v. Combe.

1618. Robert Hanscombe and Sarah Fells : Marriage Lic. (London), ii. 65.

1652. Married—William Hanscom and Mary Tennant : St. Jas. Clerkenwell, iii. 88.

1668. — Thomas Wale and Anne Hanscome : ibid. p. 148.

London, 3, 0, 0, 0 ; MDB. (co. Bucks), 0, 2, 0, 0 ; Boston (U.S.), 0, 0, 35, 1.

Hanselin.—Bapt. 'the son of John,' from Dutch nick. Hans, and dim. Hans-elin ; cf. Hewling.

Johannes Hanselyn, junr., et Agnes uxor ejus, 1379 : P. T. Yorks. p. 107.
Johannes Hanselyn, senr., et Beatrix uxor ejus, mercer, 1379 : ibid.
Willelmus Hanselyn et Matilda uxor ejus : ibid. p. 106.

Probably u is a misreading for n in the following :

Hugo Haucelin, or Hauselin, co. Linc., 1273. A.
Ralph Haucelin, co. Linc., ibid.

Hanslip. — Local, 'of Hanslope,' a parish in dioc. of Oxford, co Bucks. With Hamslape (intra) cf. Hanbrook for Hambrook.

Emma de Hamslape, co. Northampton, Hen. III-Edw. I. K.
William de Hamslape, co. Bucks, 1273. A.
John de Hameslapp, co. Bucks, ibid.

London, 2.

Hansom.—Bapt. 'the son of Hans ' (v. Hanson) ; n frequently becomes m in patronymics where the first syllable ends in n ; cf. Ransom for Ranson, Sansom for Sanson, &c. Professor Skeat (v. Hansom), referring to the cab so-called, says, 'An abbreviation for "Hansom's patent safety cab."' From the name of the inventor.' When he goes on to say, 'Hansom is no doubt the same as handsome, in which the d is frequently dropped. Many surnames are nicknames,' he is unfortunate. I have never discovered any trace of Handsome as a nickname. The above is the natural and correct origin.

1668. Married — John Hansum and Mary Jepson : St. Jas. Clerkenwell, iii. 146.

1772. Married—John Hansom and Mary Abben : St. Geo. Han. Sq. i. 223.
Barnoldswick, near Shipton (Yorks), 1 ; New York, 4.

Hanson.—Bapt. 'the son of John,' from the Dutch introduced Han or Hans ; v. Hankin. There are few traces of the name in the Hundred Rolls of 1273. The large business done between the English and Low Countries in the 14th century, however, made the foreign forms familiar, especially in counties like Yorkshire.

William Hanneson, Pat. Roll, 4 Edw. III. pt. ii.
Richard Hanson, co. York. W. 2.
Matilda Hanwyfe, 1379 : P. T. Yorks. p. 26.
Adam Hanneson, 1379 : ibid.
Robertus Hanson, 1379 : ibid. p. 187.
Willelmus Hanson, 1379 : ibid. p. 45.
Johanna Hanson, wyf, 1379 : ibid. p. 36.
Johannes Hanneson, ibid. p. 211.
William Hanneson, 1379 : Preston Guild Rolls, p. 2.
1641. Bapt.—Jane, d. Thomas Handsonne : St. Peter, Cornhill, i. 89.

London, 21.

Harber, Harbar, Harbour. —Occup. 'the harbourer,' one who shelters or harbours people, one who provides lodging ; cf. O.F. herberge, 'a lodging, a house, a harbour,' Cotg. ; cf. Harbinger.

Geoffrey Herbour, co. Camb., 1273. A.
John Herbour, co. Camb., ibid.
William le Herber. E.
Richard le Hareber. N.
1656. Buried — Anne Harber, servant with Mr. Kelke : St. Michael, Cornhill, p. 248.
1785. Married—Thomas Shaw and Ann Harbour : St. Geo. Han. Sq. i. 373.

London, 2, 1, 2 ; Philadelphia, 1, 0, 0.

Harbage; v. Harbridge.

Harberd, Harbert, Harbord, Harbourd. — Bapt. 'the son of Herbert.' These are modifications rather than corruptions ; cf. Hubbard and Hubert, Harman and Herman, Perkins and Parkins.

Henry Herberd, co. Bedf., 1273. A.
Walter Herberd, co. Oxf, ibid.
Adam Herbard, co. Soms., 1 Edw. III : Kirby's Quest, p. 180.

A via media is found in the following entry :

William Harborte unto Mistress Eliz. Chrismas, 1626 : St. Mary Aldermary (London), p. 15.
1624. Bapt. — John, s. Edward Harbort : St. Jas. Clerkenwell, i. 100.

1637. Bapt.—Anne, d. Isaac Harbert: St. Jas. Clerkenwell, i. 135.

1762. Married — William Curby and Jane Harbeart, or Herbert : St. Geo. Han. Sq. i. 115.

1783. — George Armytage, *bart.*, and Mary Harbord, d. Sir Harbord Harbord: ibid. p. 350.

London, 1, 0, 3, 0 ; Liverpool, 0, 0, 3, 1 ; MDB. (co. Cornwall), 0, 1, 0, 0 ; Philadelphia (Harbert), 6.

Harbidge ; v. Harbridge.

Harbin, -son ; v. Harbison.

Harbinger, Harberger. — Offic. ' one who goes before his lord to secure lodging ' (whence a forerunner) ; M.E. *herbergeour* ; O.F. *herberger*, to harbour, to lodge ; O.F. *herberge*, a lodging (v. Harber). Halliwell has a quotation in the above sense from Hall, Henry VIII, f. 36, on Harbegiers.

' By herbergeours that wenten him beforn.' Chaucer, C. T. 5417.

Wolsey, in 1526, leaving London, had ' his harbingers passing before to provide lodging for his train ' : Cavendish, i. 87. Presents on New Year's Day, ' The Harbingers,' xvs.' 1542-3 : Privy Purse Exp., Princess Mary, p. 103, and see note.

William le Harbeiour. B. Boston (U.S.), 0, 1.

Harbison, Harbeson, Harbin, Harbinson.—Bapt. 'the son of Harberd,' q.v. (i.e. Herbert). The Daily Telegraph (June 30, 1894) announced the marriage of the Rev. W. Harbinson. Hence Harbison and Harbeson are mere modifications of Harbinson, Harbin being the dim. of Harberd ; cf. Huskinson and Huskison, Pattinson and Patteson or Pattison.

London, 1, 0, 1, 0 ; Philadelphia, 30, 5, 0, 0.

Harborow, Harbrow, Harbroe.—Local, ' of Harborough,' two parishes, one in co. Leic. the other in co. Warwick.

Adam Hareborgh, co. Soms., 1 Edw. III : Kirby's Quest, p. 108. MDB. (co. Surrey), 0, 1, 1 ; London, 3, 0, 1.

Harbottle.—Local, ' of Harbottle,' a township in the parish of Hallystone, co. Northumberland.

Richard de Herbotell, 17 Edw. II : Freemen of York, i. 22.

1537. Ralph Harbotell and Cristina Warren : Marriage Lic. (London), i. 9. London, 3.

Harbour, Harbor.—Occup. ; v. Harber.

MDB. (co. Southampton), 2, 1.

Harbridge, Harbidge, Harbage. — Local, ' of Harbridge,' a chapelry in the parish of Ringwood, co. Southampton.

MDB. (co. Chester), 5, 0, 0 ; (co. Warwick), 1, 2, 3 ; London, 1, 0, 0 ; Philadelphia, 1, 4, 0.

Harcourt.—Local, ' of Harcourt.' 'A town and ancient château, now in ruins, near Brionne in Normandy, which gave title to the French Ducs de Harcourt ' (Lower, Patr. Brit. p. 147). It is somewhat curious to note that Harcourt has seldom travelled beyond the lines of patrician life. It is seldom found in the tradesman's directory. It is not so with our Nevilles, Howards, Sinclairs, Mortimers, Pierpoints, Braybrooks, &c. (v. Lower, ibid.)

Ivo de Harecurt : Pipe Roll, 11 Hen. II. p. 84.

London, 4 ; Boston (U.S.), 1.

Hardaker, Hardiker, Hardacre.—Local, ' of Hardacre.' I cannot find the spot or spots so called. Co. York must be looked upon as the chief centre ; cf. Halfacre or Fouracre.

John de Hordacre, co. Soms., 1 Edw. III : Kirby's Quest, p. 252. Willelmus Hardaker, 1379 : P. T. Yorks. p. 284. Nicholaus Hardacre, 1379 : ibid. p. 276. 1778. Married—Thomas Hardaker and Frances Lindley : St. Geo. Han. Sq. i. 288. London, 1, 0, 0 ; Manchester, 2, 1, 0 ; West Riding (Yorks) Court Dir., 4, 0, 2.

Hardaway.—Local, ' at the hard way,' i.e. the hard road, from residence thereby. The middle *a* is intrusive for euphony ; cf. Green-a-way, Ott-a-way, Hath-a-way, &c.

The Daily Telegraph, April 3, 1894, announces the death at Brentford of George Hardaway.

London, 1.

Hardcastle.—Local, ' of Harden Castle ' (?). Mr. Lower writes, ' Must be, I think, a contraction of

Harden Castle, the ancient residence of the Scotts of Harden, and a fine specimen to this day of a border fortress, in Roxburghshire ' (Patr. Brit. p. 147). This is quite possible. It is found in cos. Northumberland and Durham. I am strongly inclined to this view, but evidence is lacking, so far as my reading goes.

1586. Francis Garladay, *sadler*, and Ellen Harcastell : Marriage Lic. (London), i. 150.

1621. Thomas Hartcastle and Katherine Grace : ibid. ii. 103.

1737. Married—Robert Hardcastle and Jane Stabels : St. Geo. Han. Sq. i. 18. Newcastle, 1 ; Durham, 1 ; Stockton-on-Tees, 1 ; Northumberland Court Dir., 3 ; London, 8 ; New York, 5.

Hardekin.—Bapt. 'the son of Hardy,' from the dim. Harde-kin ; cf. Wil-kin, Wat-kin, or Tomp-kin; v. Hardy and Hardman.

Hardekin de Hailesle, co. Essex, Hen. III-Edw. I. K. Hardekin (without surname), co. Essex, 1273. A.

William Hardeken, co. Norf., ibid. John Hardekyn, co. Norf., ibid. John Hardekin, co. Bedf., ibid.

I fear the surname is extinct, saving it be in Harkin. It would be strange if a surname seemingly so securely settled in several counties should have no descendants.

Harden.—Local, ' of Harden,' a hamlet in the parish of Bingley, W. Rid. Yorks. Other small spots may have been so called. No doubt many of this name are now found as Harding, q.v.

Ricardus de Hareden, co. Wilts, 1273. A. Henry de Hardene, co. Northumb., 20 Edw. I. R. William de Hardene, co. Sussex, ibid. Willelmus de Hardeyn, 1379 : P. T. Yorks. p. 283. Adam de Hardeyn, 1379 : ibid. 1577-8. James Harden and Jane Cotton : Marriage Lic. (London), i. 78. 1671. Bapt.—Saray, d. William Harden : St. Jas. Clerkenwell, i. 252. London, 6 ; New York, 15.

Harderne ; v. Arderne.

MDB. (co. Chester), 2.

Hardfish.—Bapt. 'the son of Hardyfish,' probably a Scandinavian personal name, as it is found in cos. York and Norfolk; v. Hardy.

Clemensia Hardfysche, 1379: P. T. Yorks. p. 100.
Richard Hardfysshe, rector of Rockland Tofts, co. Norf., 1466: FF. i. 474.
John Hardyfish, rector of Reedham, co. Norf., 1460: ibid. xi. 131.

Hardhead.—Nick, 'the hardheaded man.'

Willelmus Hardhede, 1379: P. T. Yorks. p. 125.

Hardiker; v. Hardaker.

Hardiman; v. Hardman.

Hardiment, Hardyment.—Bapt. 'the son of Hardimund'; cf. Hardfish, and v. Hardy. The suffix -mond or -mund is frequently found modified into -ment; cf. Garment or Rayment.

MDB. (co. Norfolk), 5, 1.

Harding, Hardinge.—Bapt. 'the son of Harding.' Two columns of Hardings in the London Directory testify to the position once occupied by this name at the font; v. Hardwin.

Hugh Harding, co. Camb., 1273. A.
Nicol Harding, co. Oxf., ibid.
Robert fil. Harding. E.
Maurice fil. Harding. E.
Nicholas fil. Hardinge: Pipe Roll, 6 Henry II. p. 59.
Johannes Hardyng', 1379: P. T. Yorks. p. 140.
Thomas Hardyng', 1379: ibid.
London, 105, 3.

Hardingham. — Local, 'of Hardingham,' a parish in co. Norfolk, near Hingham. Literally 'the ham (homestead) of Harding'; v. Harding. Probably the Somerset instance represents another birthplace of this name.

Cf. John de Hardingtone, co. Soms., 1 Edw. III: Kirby's Quest, p. 160.
London, 5; MDB. (co. Lincoln), 1.

Hardisty, Hardesty, Hardistry.—Local, 'of Hardolfsty,' i.e. the *sty* of Hardolf, Hardolf being the personal name (one of the endless compounds of Ulf) of the original settler; cf. Thorpinsty Hall, Cartmel, in Furness, which means the *sty* of Thorpin, now the surname Turpin. A sty was 'a pen, enclosure, cabin,' generally for cattle, poultry, or swine, hence

pig-sty. The Hardistys hail from the parish of Fewston, seven miles from Otley. The name is still familiar there, and Hardisty Hill is a spot there. The Hardistys (chiefly farmers) have probably not moved from their home for six centuries.

Johannes de Hardolfsty, 1379: P. T. Yorks. p. 246.
Stephanus de Hardolfsty, 1379: ibid.

These instances come from Timble Great (Villa de Tymble), a village in the parish of Fewston. The little stock has ramified well. Many of our largest represented surnames hail from a single pair located in a small spot. A large family of boys, who marry, and beget boys, soon sets the ball rolling.

1687. Married—Benjamin Oakeley and Grace Hardistey: St. Michael, Cornhill, p. 45.
Fewston, 4, 0, 0; West Riding Court Dir., 7, 0, 0; London, 2, 0, 0; Sheffield, 0, 2, 0; Manchester, 3, 0, 2.

Hardman, Hardiman, Hardeman.—(1) Occup. 'the servant of Hardy,' not to be confounded with Hartman, q.v. The following occur as householders of Tadcaster in 1379 (P. T. Yorks. p. 151):

Willelmus Hardy, *marchaunt.*
Thomas Hardy, *hostiler.*
Henricus Hardyman.
Radulfus Hardyman.
Matilda serviens Hardy.
Ricardus Hardyman.

It is quite clear from the above that the Hardys were the masters and the Hardymans the servants. Thus the latter belong to the same class as Matthewman, Ladyman, Vickerman, Jackman, &c., q.v. The surname lived as Hardyman till the 16th century. 'John Hardyman, prebend of Chester, 1563' (Ormerod's Cheshire, i. 223). Every town in Yorkshire has one or two Hardmans in its directory, which is the settled modern form.

1575. Buried — John Hardyman: St. Michael, Cornhill, p. 193.
West Riding Court Dir., 3, 0, 0; London, 2, 1, 0; Manchester, 16, 0, 1; MDB. (co. Bucks), 0, 2, 0.

Hardmeat.—Local, 'of Hardmead,' a parish in co. Bucks.

William Hardmete, co. Linc., 1273. A.
1674. Thomas Hardmett and Sarah Blackerby: Marriage Lic. (Canterbury), p. 228.
Hull, 1.

Hardress.—Local,'of Hardres,' two parishes near Canterbury, co. Kent.

Gunnora de Hardres, co. Kent, 1273. A.
Robert de Hardres, co. Kent, ibid.
1676. Buried — Hester, d. Sir Richard Hardres, *baronett*: St. Dionis Backchurch, p. 242.
1695. Bapt.—John, son of Mr. Edmund Hardresse: Canterbury Cath. p. 20.

Hardstaff.—Nick. applied to a tipstaff or catchpoll; cf. Shakespear, Wagstaff, &c. Probably the original Hardstaff used his symbol of office freely.

MDB. (co. Derby), 2.

Hardwick, Hardwicke. — Local, 'of Hardwick.' (1) A very small hamlet in the parish of Astoncum-Aughton, co. York; (2) East Hardwick, a township and village in the old parish of Pontefract, co. York; (3) West Hardwick, a hamlet in the parish of Wragby, co. York. Also other spots in co. Derby, &c.

Robert de Herdewyk, Camb. and Hunts, Hen. III–Edw. I. K.
Henry de Herdewyk, Camb. and Hunts, ibid.
Ermina de Herdwych, co. Camb., 1273. A.
Alicia de Hardwyk, 1379: P. T. Yorks. p. 40.
Agnes de Herdewik, 1379: ibid. p. 16.
Robertus de Hardewyk, 1379: ibid.
1609. James Williams and Anne Hardwicke: Marriage Lic. (London), i. 316.
1621. Humphreye Hardwicke, co. Worc.: Reg. Univ. Oxf. 397.
London, 18, 3; West Rid. Court Dir., 10, 1; Boston (U.S.), 13, 0; MDB. (co. Derby), 9, 0.

Hardwin, Hadwin, Hadwen.—Bapt. 'the son of Hardwin'; O.F. Hardouin. Hardvinus de Scalers (Domesday).

Hardwin fil. Brichrith, co. Suff., 1273. A.
Godwin fil. Hardwini, co. Norf., ibid.
Philip Hardwyn, co. Norf., ibid.
London, 0, 0, 6; West Rid. Court Dir., 0, 1, 2.

Hardy. — Nick. 'the hardy'; also a personal name with same meaning. That Hardy was a personal name occasionally is proved by evidence under Hardman and Hardekin. Whether baptized or only nicknamed Hardy, the sobriquet was naturally an acceptable one, and no wonder our modern directories bear witness to its popularity. Hardy is several times mentioned as the name of the page to the huntsman to Bishop Swinfield, 1289-90. He bore no other title (Household Exp., Ric. de Swinfield, Cam. Soc., pp. 136, 142, &c.).

Thomas Hardi, 1273. A.
Richard Hardy, 1307. M.
Thomas Hardy, 1379: P. T. Yorks. p. 204.
London, 53; Sheffield, 18; West Rid. Court Dir., 24.

Hardycors. — Nick. 'one of hardy frame'; a mongrel word, half English, half French; cf. Handsomebody or Gentilcorps.

Robertus Hardycors, 1379: P. T. Yorks. p. 292.
Simon Hardcorse. F.

Hardyment; v. Hardiment.

Hare.—Nick. 'the hare,' probably affixed on some one fleet of foot. Naturally looked upon as a complimentary sobriquet, and retained in the family; cf. Lightfoot.

Hugh le Hare, co. Oxf., 1273. A.
Richard le Hare, co. Hunts, ibid.
Robert le Hare, C. R., 20 Edw. III. pt. i.
Johannes Hare, 1379: P.T. Yorks. p. 48.
Willelmus Hare, 1379: ibid. p. 119.
London, 24.

Harfield.—Local, 'of Harfield,' a parish in Middlesex, four miles from Uxbridge.

London, 4; New York, 13.

Harford.—Local; v. Hereford.

Hargate, Hargitt.—Local, 'of Hardgate,' a hamlet in the parish of Bishop Thornton, co. York. There can be no doubt about the derivation of this name.

Johannes Hardgate, 1379: P.T. Yorks. p. 172.
Alicia Hardgat, 1379: ibid.
Johannes Hardgat, 1379: ibid. p. 171.
1616. Edmund Hargett: Reg. Univ. Oxf. iii. 343.
1746. Married—Thomas Hargate and Mary Reynolds: St. Jas. Clerkenwell, iii. 277.
London, o, 1; Sheffield, 2, 1; West Rid. Court Dir., o, 1.

Hargood.—Bapt. 'the son of Haringod.' This, as can be seen from the evidence below, became Heregod, finally Hargood. The suffix -god is common; cf. Godwin or Goodwin, Scattergood and Thoroughgood or Toogood. For the prefix, v. Herring. With Heregod and Hargood, cf. Clerk and Clark, or Herman and Harman.

William Harongaud, co. Suff., 1273. A.
William Heregod, co. Kent, ibid.
John Heringod, co. Kent, ibid.
Stephen Heringod, co. Kent, ibid.
Walter Herigaud, co. Soms., 1 Edw. III : Kirby's Quest, p. 216.
'1613. Robart Harrigad for a carvell, 1s.': Brand's Newcastle, ii. 343.
London, 2.

Hargrave, Hargraves, Hargreave, Hargreaves, Hargreves, Hargrove, Hargroves. —Local, 'of Hargrave,' parishes in diocs. Chester, Ely, Peterborough; grave = grove. Probably the hare-grove (v. grove, Skeat). The Hargreaves of Lancashire probably spring from Hargrave, co. Chester.

John de Haregrave, co. Bucks, 1273. A.
John de Hargreve. C.
William de Haregreve, 1296: East Cheshire, ii. 607.
Richard de Haregreve, 1296: ibid.
Henry Hargrevys, 1486, co. York. W. 11.
Ambrose Hargreves, or Hargrave, Bras. Coll., 1586 (co. York): Reg. Univ. Oxf. vol. ii. pt. ii. p. 151.
London, 5, 2, 0, 6, 0, 1, 2; Manchester, 4, 4, 3, 39, 1, 0, 0; MDB. (co. Lanc.), Hargreaves, 51.

Harker.—? Occup. Mr. Lower says, 'A corruption of Harcourt.' This seems unsatisfactory. But I can offer nothing better myself. Still I suspect it has some reference to hunting, and may be the sobriquet of the huntsman himself.

MDB. (co. Derby), 4; London, 9.

Harkness, Hartness.—Local, 'of Harkness.' I cannot find the place; cf. Furness, Holderness, &c.

MDB. (co. Cumb.), 1, 3; London, 3, 0.

Harland.—Local, 'of Harland.' Evidently an East Riding name, but I cannot discover the spot.

MDB. (East Rid. Yorks), 7; New York, 6.

Harley.—Local, 'of Harley,' a parish in co. Salop, near Much Wenlock. But doubtless several smaller spots bear this name.

Henry de Herley, co. Berks, 1273. A.
Clemens de Herleghe, co. Soms., ibid.
Adam de Herleg, co. Soms., Hen. III–Edw. I. K.
Matilda Herlay, 1379: P. T. Yorks. p. 189.
Willelmus Herlay, 1379: ibid.
1646. Bapt. — Susanna, d. Nicholas Harlye: St. Jas. Clerkenwell, i. 164.
1743. Married — John Harley and Magdalen Lenoir: St. Mary Aldermary, p. 51.
London, 17; Philadelphia, 57.

Harling.—Bapt. 'the son of Harlwin,' modified to Harling, with excrescent g; v. Golding for Goldwin. Almost every compound in -win is now found as -ing.

Herlewinus (without surname), co. Norf., 1273. A.
Henry Herlewine, co. Kent, ibid.
Thomas Herlewine, co. Linc., ibid.
John Herlewyn, co. Bucks, ibid.
Stephen Harlwyn, co. Soms., 1 Edw. III : Kirby's Quest, p. 138.

In the course of another century Herlwin began to assume its present character :

Agnes Herlyng', 1379: P. T. Yorks. p. 287.
West Riding Court Dir., 1; Ripley, 1; London, 7.

Harlot; v. Arlett.

Harlow.—Local, 'of Harlow,' a parish in co. Essex, twenty-three miles from London.

Richard de Herlawe, co. Essex, 1273. A.
Nicholas de Herlawe, co. Northampton, ibid.
1599. Thomas Harlowe, co. Middlesex: Reg. Univ. Oxf. ii. 239.
1601. John Harlowe, of Enfield, co. Middlesex, and Agnes Searle, co. Essex: Marriage Lic. (London), i. 265.
1647. Bapt.—Alyce, d. John Harlow: St. Jas. Clerkenwell, i. 168.
1795. Married—William Harlow and Jane Gossett : St. Geo. Han. Sq. ii. 128.
London, 6; Philadelphia, 5.

Harman, Harman, Hermon, Hermanson.—Bapt. 'the son of Herman.' As early as Domesday found as Hermannus; cf. the German Hermann. With Harman, cf. Clark and Clerk, Parkins and Perkins, &c.

Nicholas Herman, co. Suffolk, 1273. A.
Cecilia Hereman, co. Hunts, ibid.
Herman de Boys, Issue Roll, 44 Edw. III.
Walter Herman, ibid.

Herman de Francia. C.
Herman de Alemannia. G.
Alan Herman, 1293. M.
Walter Hermanson, Issues of the Exchequer, see Index.
Thomas Herman, 1379 : P. T. Yorks. p. 252.
Ricardus Harman, 1379 : ibid. p. 50.
John Urmynson, co. York. W. 11.
Harman Clynke, 1549 : Reg. Univ. Oxf. i. 8.
Harman Arnold, 1535 : ibid. p. 183.
London, 22, 2, 1, 0.

Harmar, Harmer.—Bapt. 'the son of Herimar' (Yonge, ii. 408). Occurs in Domesday as Hermerus among the tenants-in-chief in Norfolk.

Hermer de Bekeswell, Hen. III–Edw. I : K. p. 293.
Robert fil. Hermer. C.
Johannes Hermer, 1379 : P.T. Howdenshire, p. 12.
Ricardus Hermer, 1379 : P. T. Yorks. p. 143.
Hopkins Harmar. Z.
1649. Bapt.—Edward, s. Josua Harmer : St. Jas. Clerkenwell, i. 173.
1804. Married—Benjamin Harmer and Bridget Graniell : St. Geo. Han. Sq. ii. 309.
London, 2, 13 ; Sheffield, 2, 0 ; Philadelphia, 0, 72.

Harmsworth. — Local, 'of Harmondsworth,' a parish in co. Middlesex.

London, 1 ; MDB.(co. Southampton), 2.

Harness, Harneis, Harnish.—Bapt. 'the son of Harnes' or 'Hernes.' No doubt a compound of *arn* (eagle), as in Arnold, and cognate with Ernest. A well-known Lincolnshire surname to-day, and found there six centuries ago.

Robert fil. Hernis', co. Linc. 1273. A.
John fil. Hernici, co. Linc., ibid.
Roger Herneys, co. Norf., ibid.
John Harneys, co. Camb., ibid.
Herne' de Stano, co. Suff., ibid.
Robert Arnys, 1379 : P. T. Yorks. p. 214.
Robertus Arnis, 1379 : ibid.
Johanna Ernys, 1379 : ibid. p. 173.
Robert Hernays, 1379 : ibid. p. 296.
Ernis de Hamwell, co. Linc., Hen. III–Edw. I. K.
Philip Harneys, C. R., 47 Hen. III.

With the American form Harnish, cf. German Harnisch, of which four occur in the Philadelphia Directory.

London, 1, 0, 0 ; Leeds, 1, 0, 0 ; MDB. (Lincolnshire), 6, 1, 0 ; Boston (U.S.), 0, 0, 1.

Harnett ; v. Arnett ; cf. Hives for Ives, &c.

MDB. (co. Kent), 6.

Harold, Harrold, Harrod.
(1) Bapt. 'the son of Harold.' This personal name was far less common than might have been expected. It never attained any actual popularity, and was scarcely in use when Richard, Robert, Roger, &c., were rising into a position that through the aid of hereditary surnames has made them immortal.

(2) Local ; v. Harrold (2).

Agnes Harald, co. Oxf., 1273. A.
John Harald, co. Wilts, ibid.
Reginald Haralt, co. Oxf., ibid.
Roger Harold, co. Bucks, ibid.
Gilbert fil. Harold. J.
Harold fil. Roberti. J.
Robertus Harald', 1379 : P. T. Yorks. p. 297.
Stephen Harald', 1379 : ibid.
1551. Married—Thomas Harralde and Julyan Hyde : St. Michael, Cornhill, p. 6.
London, 1, 6, 4.

Harp.—Local, 'at the Harp,' a sign-name ; v. Roebuck. Harp, like many other of our surnames, is found in America in abundance, but is hard to find in England.

Florencia atte Harpe, co. Soms., 1 Edw. III : Kirby's Quest, p. 207.
Roger atte Harp, co. Soms., 1 Edw. III : ibid.
John Cook, called atte Harpe, 1388 : Cal. of Wills in the Court of Husting (2).
John atte Harpe, C. R., 7 Hen. V.
1764. Married — Thomas Morris and Eliz. Harp : St. Geo. Han. Sq. i. 128.
Philadelphia, 7.

Harper, Harpur.—Occup. 'the harper,' one who made his living by playing at fair and festival ; cf. Fidler, Tabor, Crowther, Piper, &c. Sometimes these names represent an official position, being musical performers in the pay of royalty or the greater lords. 'Harpowre, *citharista*' : Prompt. Parv. p. 228.

Henry le Harpur, co. Camb., 1273. A.
Ralph le Harpur, co. Oxf., ibid.
Nicholas le Harpur, co. Camb., ibid.
Adam le Harper, co. Soms., 1 Edw. III : Kirby's Quest, p. 126.
Thomas le Harpour, co. Soms., 1 Edw. III : ibid. p. 131.
Isabella Herpour, 1379 : P. T. Yorks. p. 7.
Willelmus Harper, 1379 : ibid. p. 190.
Rogerus Harper, 1379 : ibid. p. 282.

1748. Married—Sir Lister Holte and Mary Harpur : St. Geo. Han. Sq. i. 28.
London, 56, 0 ; MDB. (co. Bedford), 1, 1 ; Boston (U.S.), 30, 0.

Harpham.—Local, 'of Harpham,' a parish in E. Rid. Yorks, near Great Driffield.

Thomas de Harpam, 1379 : P. T. Yorks. p. 107.
MDB. (co. Lincoln), 6 ; West Rid. (Yorks) Court Dir., 1.

Harpin.—Bapt. 'the son of Harpin,' probably from Harfinn ; cf. Turpin from Thorfinn. It is found as a personal name in the Hundred Rolls, i. 360 (co. Norfolk).

Thomas Harpyn, co. Norf., 1273. A.
' Adam Harpin was faulconer to Bishop Swinfield in 1289-90 ' : Household Exp., Ric. de Swinfield, Cam. Soc. p. 15.
Henricus Harpyn, 1379 : P. T. Yorks. p. 208.
Magota Harpyn, 1379 : ibid.
Johanna Harpyn, 1379 : ibid.
1714. Bapt. — Mary, d. of Francis Arpin : St. Jas. Clerkenwell, ii. 77.
1739. — Ann, d. of John Harpin : ibid. p. 246.
MDB. (co. Derby), 1 ; West Rid. Court Dir., 1 ; Thurstonland, co. York, 1.

Harpley.—Local, 'of Harpley,' a parish in co. Norfolk, four miles from Rougham.

MDB. (co. Middlesex), 1.

Harraden, Harradine, Haridine, Harradence, Harridine, Horoden.—Local, 'of Harrowden,' places in cos. Northampton and Bedford.

John de Harewedon, co. Northampton, 20 Edw. I. R.
London, 3, 3, 0, 0, 0, 0 ; MDB. (co. Camb.), 0, 0, 1, 0, 0, 0 ; (co. Hertford), 0, 0, 0, 1, 0, 0 ; (co. Lincoln), Horoden, 1 ; (co. Hunts), 0, 1, 0, 0, 2, 0.

Harrier, Harrer.—Offic. 'the harrier' (?), the master of the harriers, hounds for hare-hunting.

John le Hariare, Close Roll, 10 Edw. III.
Thomassinus, valet of Nicholas le Herier, Close Roll, 4 Edw. I.
Philadelphia, 0, 5.

Harries, Harris, Harrison, Hurrisson.—Bapt. 'the son of Harry,' this being the English attempt at pronouncing the French Henri. Thus Harry is not a nick. of Henry, but the English representative form. Hence our endless Harrisons, not Henrysons. All our kings were popularly known as Harry in their own times. The practice of styling them Henry is quite modern. The feminine Henrietta dates only from the Stuart period, while Harriot or Harriet was in use early enough to become a surname. One or two Henriots occur, but they are quite exceptional. The many columns of Harrises and Harrisons in our directories testify to the great popularity of the name six and seven centuries ago. The first Harry was born on English ground, and for that reason was more favourably regarded than the Conqueror's elder sons (v. Freeman's Norm. Conq. iv. 228.) It is interesting to note that Hanry was a common early form of entry, being a kind of half-stage between Fr. Henri and Eng. Harry.

Hanry Carpenter, co. Oxf., 1273. A.
John Hanry, co. Bucks, ibid.
Henry, or Hanry le Notte, co. Warwick: Henry III–Edw. I. K.
Henry, or Hanry de Rokeley, co. Warwick: ibid.
Reginald Herryerson. FF.
1510. John Harris, or Harries: Reg. Univ. Oxf. i. 73.
1547-8. Edward Broke and Anne Harrys: Marriage Lic. (London), i. 11.
London, 3, 356, 264, 3; Liverpool (Harrisson), 2.

Harriman, Harryman. — Occup. 'the servant of Harry'; cf. Matthewman, Addyman, Periman, &c. Mr. Lower says, 'One who harried, a freebooter.' It is curious that I chiefly find the name in co. Cumb., where the Scotch raids were so common in former times. Nevertheless, the origin given above is the natural one, and it belongs to a class that has made a distinct mark upon nomenclature. In the first two instances given below we must remember that the pronunciation of Henry would be much as if spoken in French, Harry being not a pet form of Henry, but a spelling assimilated to the sound.

Ricardus Henryman, 1379: P.T. Yorks. p. 279.
Willelmus Henriman, 1379: ibid. p. 155.
Mary Harriman, 1632: St. Dionis Backchurch, p. 103.

1794. Married — John Harriman and Eliz. Tobey: St. Geo. Han. Sq. ii. 118.
1807. — William Harryman and Sarah Steade: ibid. p. 366.
Workington, 1, 0 (Dir. 1829); MDB. (co. Cumberland), 3, 3; (co. Derby), 6, 0; New York, 12, 0.

Harrington. — Local, 'of Harrington,' a town in co. Cumberland.

Ricardus de Heryngton, 1379: P.T. Yorks. p. 250.
London, 16; Philadelphia, 55.

Harriot, Henriot, Hanrott. — Bapt. 'the son of Harry' or 'Henry,' from the dim. Harri-ot or Henri-ot. As a pet-name for a boy Harriot had become forgotten. Its present popularity it owes to Henrietta Maria, who restored it to life, this time in favour of the girls. From the Caroline period Harriet has held her own. Harriot and Henriot as surnames, however, take us back to the Plantagenets.

Walter Henriot, co. Soms., 1 Edw. III: Kirby's Quest, p. 201.
Heriot Heringflet, co. Norf. FF.
Thomas Haryette. G.
William Haryott, ibid.
Alicia Henriot, co. York. W. 2.
Robert Henriot, co. York, ibid.
1550. Married — Gryffyn Mathewe and Jone Harryot: St. Michael, Cornhill, p. 6.
1570. Bapt. — Katerin, d. William Harriot: St. Antholin (London), p. 20.
1591. Robert Holman and Anne Harriott: Marriage Lic. (London), p. 194.
London, 0, 0, 2.

Harrobin; v. Horobin.

Harrod; v. Harold.

Harrold. — (1) Bapt. 'the son of Harold,' q.v. (2) Local, 'of Harrold,' a market-town and parish eight miles from Bedford.
MDB. (co. Leic.), 5.

Harrop, Harrup. — Local, 'of Harrop,' a spot in South Lancashire or East Cheshire that I cannot find. This name is chiefly found in the parish of Prestbury, co. Ches. (v. Reg. Prestbury). The meaning seems to be 'the hare-hope'; cf. Haslop, Blenkinsopp, &c.

1560. Buried — James Harrop: Reg. Prestbury (co. Ches.), p. 3.
1563. — Ann Harrop: ibid. p. 12.
1590. Thomas Harrop, of Adlington: Wills at Chester, i. 84.
1592. Oliver Harrop, of Quirk, in Saddleworth: ibid.

Manchester, 21, 0; London, 4, 0; MDB. (co. Bucks), 0, 1.

Harrower. — Occup. 'the harrower,' i.e. a tiller of land.

Geoffrey le Harewere, co. Norf., 1273. A.
Johannes Harower, 1379: P. T. Yorks. p. 261.
New York, 2; Philadelphia, 1.

Harrowsmith; v. Arrowsmith. Probably not a maker of harrows; but v. Harrower.
MDB. (co. Lincoln), 1.

Harsant, Harsent. — ?
MDB. (co. Suffolk), 2, 1; London, 4, 0.

Harse. — ? Local.
? Cristina de Harsy, 1 Edw. III: Kirby's Quest, p. 142.
MDB. (co. Soms.), 5; Oxford, 8.

Harslett, Harslet. — ? Local, 'at the hare-slade' (?), i.e. a slade frequented by hares. This is more probable than might seem at a first glance; v. Hare and Slade.

Robert de Hareslad, co. Soms., 1 Edw. III: Kirby's Quest, p. 166.
London, 1, 1.

Harsley. — Local, 'of Harsley.' East and West Harsley (one a parish, the other a township) are in the N. Rid. Yorks.
MDB. (co. Lincoln), 5.

Hart, Harte. — Nick. 'the hart'; cf. Stagg, Roe, Roebuck, Buck, &c., evidently popular as a sobriquet.

John le Hert, co. Kent, 1273. A.
Isabella le Hert. co. Camb., ibid.
Richard le Hert, c. 1300. M.
Richard le Hert, co. Soms., 1 Edw. III: Kirby's Quest, p. 96.
Johannes Hert, 1379: P. T. Yorks. p. 38.
Agnes Hert, 1379: ibid.
Thomas le Hert, or Hart, bailiff of Norwich; 1390: FF. iii. 116.
1578. John Harte and Johanna Kirbye: Marriage Lic. (London), i. 83.
1599. Bapt. — Agnes, d. Henrie Hart: St. Jas. Clerkenwell, i. 35.
London, 150, 0; Sheffield, 2, 0; New York, 277, 2.

Hartcliffe. — Local, 'of Hartcliff.' Some spot in the W. Rid. Yorks. I have failed to discover it.

Adam de Hertclif', 1379: P.T. Yorks. p. 35.

The above was resident in Bradfield, W. Rid. Yorks.

Thomas de Hartclyffe (of Kimberworth): P. T. Yorks. p. 67.
Manchester, 1.

Harting.—Local, 'of Harting,' a parish in dioc. of Chichester, co. Sussex.

John de Herting, co. Essex, 1273. A. London, 3.

Hartland.—Local, 'of Hartland,' a parish in dioc. ot Exeter, co. Devon.

Abbas de Hertilaund, co. Devon, 1273. A.
London, 5; MDB. (co. Glouc.), 11.

Hartle.—Local, 'of Harthill,' (1) a parish in the W. Rid. Yorks, eight miles from Worksop; (2) a township in the parish of Bakewell, co. Derby.

Robert de Herthul, co. Derby, 1273. A.
Robert de Herthill, co. Derby, ibid.
Ricardus de Herthil, co. Derby, Hen. III–Edw. I. K.
Edmundus de Herthille, of Harthill, 1379: P. T. Yorks. p. 14.
Willelmus de Herthille, 1379: ibid.p.33.
1603. Francis Hartill and Anne Staunge: Marriage Lic. (London), i. 279.
1770. Married — Daniell Hartill and Mary Johnson: St. Geo. Han. Sq. i. 197.
Sheffield, 1; Manchester, 1; MDB. (co. Derby), 3.

Hartley.—Local, 'of Hartley,' parishes in diocs. of Rochester and Winchester, and hamlets in various places. Also smaller spots, in some cases now forgotten.

Ricardus de Hertlay, 1379: P. T. Yorks. p. 10.
Willelmus de Hertelay, 1379: ibid.

The above lived in the parish of Ecclesfield, W. Rid. Yorks. The surname has ramified in an extraordinary manner in the West Riding. The parentage in all probability will have to be sought for in Ecclesfield parish or the immediate neighbourhood.

Brian de Hertheley, co. Linc., 1273. A.
Richard de Hertleye, co. Salop, ibid.
1623. Christopher Hills and Eliz. Hartley, of Stepney: Marriage Lic. (London), ii. 121.
West Rid. (Yorks) Court Dir., 62; London, 28; Boston (U.S.), 19.

Hartman.—Bapt. 'the son of Hartmund' (Yonge, ii. 414). The suffix -mond or -mund becomes -man; cf. Osman, Wyman, Sickman, &c.; cf. the German Hartmann.

Hetteman Hauberk. O.
London, 1.

Hartness. — Local, 'of Harkness,' q.v. A corruption.
Liverpool, 2; New York, 1.

Hartnup, Hartnupp.—? Local.
MDB. (co. Kent), 2, 2.

Harton.—Local, 'of Harton.' There is a parish of this name in the dioc. of Durham, but probably the entries below concern some smaller place more south.

John de Harton, cos. Bedf. and Bucks, Hen. III–Edw. I. K.
Hugh de Hartone, co. Camb., 1273. A. London, 2.

Hartopp, Hartup.—? Local.
MDB. (co. Leic.), 3, 0 ; London, 0, 1.

Hartridge.—Local, 'of Hartridge.'
Richard de Herterngge, co. Berks, Hen. III–Edw. I. K.
London, 6; MDB. (co. Kent), 4.

Hartshorn, Hartshorne.—Local, 'of Hartshorne,' a parish in the dioc. of Lichfield and co. Derbyshire. Perhaps a piece of land originally so termed from its resemblance to a hart's horn; cf. Langhorn.

Henry de Hertishorn, co. Derby, Hen. III–Edw. I. K.
Richard de Hertishorn, co. Derby, ibid.
Alice Hertishorn, Fines Roll, 10 Edw.IV.
London, 7, 3; MDB. (co. Derby), 1, 0.

Hartwell. — Local, 'of Hartwell,' parishes in the diocs. of Oxford and Peterborough.

Decennarius de Hertwell, co. Northampton, 1273. A.
Agatha de Hertwell, co. Bucks, ibid.
Robert de Hertwell, co. Bucks, ibid.
London, 3; Oxford, 4.

Hartwright.—Occup.; a corruption of Arkwright, q.v. The half-stage towards this form is met in the following entry:

1610. Buried — Hughe Arthewryght: Reg. Prestbury, co. Ches., p. 187.

But an earlier instance occurs:

George Hartewright, 1455. W. 11.

This is found in the very district in which the surname Arkwright arose.

Manchester, 1; London, 1; Liverpool, 1; MDB. (co. Glouc.), 1.

Harverson, Harveson.—Bapt. 'the son of Harvey,' q.v.
London, 4, 0; Philadelphia, 0, 1.

Harvey, Harvie.—Bapt. 'the son of Harvey.' This great personal name had not become so rare in the 12th and 13th centuries that it could escape surnominal honours. On the contrary, it is still found as a fairly familiar personal name up to the beginning of the 14th century. No modern directory, whether in England or the United States, is without representatives of the surname, and in this manner it has secured immortality. The last two centuries has seen the practice made popular of using surnames for baptismal names. Thus the late Bishop of Carlisle was Harvey Goodwin, although for several centuries Harvey has been obsolete as a personal name.

Harvey Dunnyng, co. Camb., 1273. A.
Warin Hervi, co. Camb., ibid.
Robert fil. Hervei, co. Linc., ibid.
Herveus le Gos, co. Linc., ibid.
Harveus Belet, co. Oxf., 20 Edw. I. R.
London, 142, 4.

Harwar.—?
MDB. (co. Chester), 4; London, 2.

Harward.—Bapt. 'the son of Herward.' No doubt often confused with Harwood; v. Howard (2).

Robert Herward, co. Norf., 1273. A.
Beatrice Hereward, co. Camb., ibid.
Richard Herward, co. Camb., ibid.
Hereward de Hale, co. Northampt., Hen. III–Edw. I. K.
John Hereward, co. Soms., 1 Edw. III: Kirby's Quest, p. 160.
Randolph Hereward, co. Soms.: ibid. p. 269.
Willelmus Herwarde, 1379: P.T.Yorks. p. 33.
Agnes Harward', 1379: ibid. p. 160.
1568. William Harwarde and Alice Canell, or Cavell: Marriage Lic. (London), i. 40.
1574–5. Edmund Harwarde, of London, Reg. Univ. Oxf. ii. 60.
1785. Married — Charles Harward, Dean of Chichester, and Louisa Yonge : St. Geo. Han. Sq. i. 380.
London, 2; MDB. (co. Derby), 1.

Harwood. — (1) Local, 'of Harewood,' a village and parish about eight miles north of Leeds. Also of Harwood, a township in the parish of Bolton, co. Lanc. (2) Bapt. 'the son of Harward,' q.v. There can be no doubt but that these two names have become inextricably mixed.

Alicia Harewode, co. Soms.,1 Edw. III:
Kirby's Quest, p. 246.

Nicholas de Harewod: ibid. p. 259.

Robertus de Harwodde, 1379: P. T.
Yorks. p. 300.

Adam de Harwode, 1379: ibid. p. 199.

William de Harwode, of Harwode,
1379: ibid. p. 213.

Manchester, 9; London, 30; West Riding Court Dir., 5; Sheffield, 4; Leeds, 2.

Haselden, -dine; v. Hasleden.

Haseler, Hasler, Haysler.—
Occup.; v. Hastiler.

London, 1, 1, 1.

Haselgrove.—Local, 'at the hazel-grove.'

MDB. (co. Bedford), 1.

Hasell.—Local, 'at the hazel-tree'; v. Hazell (1).

London, 2.

Haselock.—Bapt.; v. Aslac.

Haske.—Nick. ' harsh, bitter';
M.E. *haske*. '*Harske*, or *haske*, as sundry frutys': Prompt. Parv.

Thomas le Haske, C. R., 4 Edw. II.

Haskett.—Bapt. 'the son of Hasculf' (?); v. Asculf.

Hascoit Musard: Early Hist. Oxford, Parker, p. 384.

Harsculph, or Ascurt de Cleasby, 1301. M.

Haskew; v. Askew, of which it is a variant.

MDB. (co. Derby), 1.

Haskill.—Bapt.; v. Askell.

MDB. (co. Monmouth), 1.

Haskins.—Bapt.; v. Hadskis.

London, 3.

Haslam, Haslem, Hasleham, Haselam.—Local, 'of Haslam,' i.e. Hazel-ham. One of the many place-names with Hazel as prefix; cf. Haslop for Hazelhope (?).

West Riding Court Dir., 5, 1, 0, 0; London, 7, 0, 0, 1; Manchester, 7, 0, 1, 0.

Hasleden, Haselden, Haseldine, Haseltine, Heaselden, Hazeldine, Hazzledine.—Local, 'of the hazel-dean'; M.E. *dene*, a vale. Many spots would bear this name.

William de Haseldene, co. Soms., 1 Edw. III: Kirby's Quest, p. 94.

Adam Haseldene, co. Soms.: ibid. p. 238.

Adam de Haseldene, co. Soms.: ibid. p. 251.

Willelmus de Hesledeyn, 1379: P. T. Yorks. p. 289.

Jeppe de Hesilden, 1379: ibid. p. 271.

An American variant in the form of Aseltine is found in the Boston Directory.

London, 4, 4, 1, 2, 0, 3, 1; Manchester (Heaselden), 1; Philadelphia (Hasseltine), 6.

Haslehurst, Haslehust.—Local, 'at the hazel-hurst' (v. Hurst), equivalent to Hazlegrove or Hazlewood, q.v.

London, 2, 2; West Riding Court Dir., 2, 0.

Haslewood.—Local; v. Hazlewood.

Haslop, Haslip, Heslop, Hyslop, Huslop.—Local, 'at the hazel-hope'; v. Hope. I have no doubt as to this origin, but possess no proof to offer.

London, 3, 2, 1, 0, 0; MDB. (co. Cumberland), 0, 0, 3, 1, 1.

Hasluck.—Bapt. 'the son of Aslac,' q.v.

Hassall.—Local, 'of Hassall,' a township in the parish of Sandbach, co. Chester.

London, 2; MDB. (co. Chester), 11; Philadelphia, 2.

Hassard, Hasset, Hazard.—
Bapt. 'the son of Hasard.' This personal name has left descendants enough to fill a niche in our directories.

Haseud Sulny, co. Somerset, 1273. A.

Thomas Hasard, co. Wilts, ibid.

Geoffrey Hassot, co. Camb., ibid.

John Hasard, co. York, ibid.

1634. Buried — Constance Hasarde, Canterbury Cathedral, p. 117.

London, 2, 2, 4; Crockford, 2, 0, 1.

Hassell.—Local, (1) 'of Hassell,' some spot in co. Oxford. (2) 'at the hazel,' from residence beside some particular hazel-tree; cf. Crabtree, Ash, Birch, &c.; v. Halse, where proof will be found; also v. Hazell.

'Persona de Hassell tenet de feod' Pet' fil. Oliveri, &c.,' co. Oxf., 1273. A.

John de Hassell, co. Oxf., ibid.

Oliver de Hassell, co. Oxf., ibid.

London, 12; Philadelphia, 4.

Hastead, Haystead, Hasted.—
Local.

MDB. (co. Norfolk), 1, 1, 0; London, 0, 0, 1.

Haster, Hester.—(1) Occup. Probably the old 'Hayrester' or

'Hairster.' Halliwell says, 'Hayre, a garment made of goat's hair. Hayrester, a maker of hayres.' 'Hayresters, workers in horsehair (?)' (York Mysteries, Toulmin-Smith). Cecile in the Second Nunne's Tale was thus dressed:

'Under hire robe of gold, that set ful faire,
Had next her flesh, yclad hire in an haire.'

Again:

'Ne she was gay, fresh, ne joliffe,
But seemed to be full ententife
To goode workes, and to faire,
And thereto she had on an haire.'
Rom. of. Rose.

The hair garment was seemingly worn for mortification of the flesh by nuns and other religious persons. In the York Mysteries the 'Turnours, Hayresters, and Bollers' (i. e. Bowlers, makers of bowls) went together. Therefore the hairster may have also occupied himself in hair-stuffing of couches and saddles; a kind of upholsterer in fact, since the other two were undoubtedly engaged in wood-work.

(2) Occup.; v. Hastiler. O.F. *hasteur*, a hastiler, one who superintended the roasts.

London, 0, 6; Philadelphia, 0, 2.

Hastiler, Hastler, Haseler, Hasler, Haysler.—Occup. 'the hastiler,' i. e. a turn-broach, a kitchen servitor.

Philip le Haster. A.

John Haster. W. 9.

Thurstan le Hastiler. E.

William Hastiler. M.

'Hastlere, that rostythe mete, *assator, assarius*': Prompt. Parv. Mr. Way, in a valuable note, has several references to the 'hastator' and 'hastalarius' and compares the French *hasteur*. He adds, 'Humphrey de Bohun, Earl of Essex, among the household servants mentioned in his will, 1361, as "potager, ferour, barber, ewer," mentions "Will. de Barton, hastiler"' (Royal Wills, p. 52). Among the domestic officers of the Earl of Northumberland, 1511, was a 'yoman cooke... who doith hourly attend in the kitching at the haistry for roisting of meat' (Ant. Rep. iv. 244). In Lancashire the hastener is the tin screen for preserving and reflecting the heat when the roast is on the spit. The origin seems plain: 'Haste, a spit or broach' (Cotgrave). Lat. *hasta*, a lance, a pike. The modern forms of the surname are Haster, Hastiler, Hastler, Haseler, Hasler, and Haysler, all being somewhat rare.

London, 0, 0, 1, 4, 1; Philadelphia (Hassler), 9.

Hastin, Hasting, Hastings. —(1) Bapt. 'the son of Hasting' (v. Yonge, ii. 384); cf. Browning, Harding, &c.

Hasting Moyse, co. Suff., 1273. A.
William Hastinge, co. Oxf., ibid.

(2) Local, ' of Hastings,' in co. Sussex, the principal of the Cinque ports.

Henry de Hastinge, co. Bedf., 1273. A.
Richard Hastings, co. Camb., ibid.

The entry above may belong to (1).

Henry de Hastinges, co. Northampt., ibid.
1668. Married — Thomas Hastings and Eliz. Martin : St. Jas. Clerkenwell, iii. 143.
1799. — Maurice Lenthall and Mary Hastings : St. Geo. Han. Sq. ii. 206.
London, 2, 0, 20 ; Philadelphia, 0, 0, 36.

Haswell, Hastwell.—Local, ' of Haswell,' a parish in co. Durham. Possibly some other locality bears the same name.

Stephen de Hassewell, co. Oxf., Hen. III–Edw. I. K.
Helia de Haswelle, co. Camb., 1273. A.
1795. Married — William Masterman and Margaret Haswell : St. Geo. Han. Sq. ii. 135.
1804. — John Hastwell and Dinah Goodes: ibid. p. 304.
Sunderland, 6, 0 ; London, 7, 1 ; New York, 2, 0.

Hatch. — (1) Local, 'at the hatch'; v. Hack (2).

Richard de la Hacche, co. Wilts, 1273. A.
Agnes apud Hache, co. Oxf., ibid.
John atte Hache, co. Oxf., ibid.

(2) Bapt. 'the son of Hache'; v. Hack (1). The harder form Hake (q.v.) was more general.

Hache de la Hacche, co. Linc., 1273. A.
Hacca fil. Pictavini, co. Linc., ibid.
Thomas Hach, co. Soms., 1 Edw. III : Kirby's Quest, p. 132.
1620. Bapt.—George,s Richard Hatch: St. Jas. Clerkenwell, i. 147.
1622. Ralph Roades, *joyner*, and Grace Hatch, *widow* : Marriage Lic. (London), ii. 111.
London, 21 ; Philadelphia, 18.

Hatchard, Hatchett, Hatchette.—Bapt. 'the son of Achard.' With Hatchett, cf. Birkett for Birkhead, or Blackett for Blackhead. This corruption is common.

Henry Achard, co. Hunts, 1273. A.
Richard Achard, co. York, ibid.
Achard de Ramisby : Pipe Roll, 11 Hen. II. p. 59.
Achard le Fevre, Hen. III. T.
Isabella Achard, 27 Edw. I : BBB. p. 570.
Johannes Hachet, 1379 : P. T. Yorks. p. 53.
Margareta Hachet, 1379 : ibid. p. 49.
Robertus Achard, 1379 : ibid. p 134.

As this dictionary proves, the aspirate was commonly added to names beginning with a vowel ; cf. Hodson (2), Hoddy, or Hanniball (1).

1574. Bapt. — William, s. William Hatchett : St. Jas. Clerkenwell. i. 254.
1787. Married — Thomas Hatchard and Jane Smither : St. Geo. Han. Sq. i. 405.
London, 8, 6, 0 ; New York, 0, 0, 1.

Hatchman ; v. Hackman.

Hatechrist. — Nick. This objectionable sobriquet has now disappeared from the directories.

William Hatecrist, co. Bedf., Hen. III–Edw. I. M.
William Hatecrist, co. York. W. 4.

Hatfield, Hatfull—Local, (1) ' of Hatfield,' an extensive village parish seven miles north-east from Doncaster. Hatfull in the London Directory is a curious-looking corruption. (2) ' of Hatfield,' parishes in cos. Hereford and Hertford.

William de Hatfield, co. Essex, 1273. A.
Agnes de Hatfield, co. Camb., ibid.
Johannes de Haytefeld', 1379 : P. T. Yorks. p. 39.
1606. Buried — Frances, d. Joshua Hatfeild (sic) : St. Mary Aldermary, p. 204.
Sheffield, 5, 0 ; London, 15, 2 ; West Riding Court Dir., 8, 0 ; Boston (U.S.), 12, 0.

Hathaway.—Local, ' of Hathway,' i.e. the heathway. The middle *a* is intrusive, as in Greenaway, Ottaway, &c.

Willelmus de Haythewy, 1379 : P. T. Yorks. p. 227.
1582. Richard Hathewaye and Annie Maddox : Marriage Lic. (London), i. 112.
1621. Francis Hathway : Reg. Univ. Oxf. ii. 400.
George Hathwaye, 1633 : St. Mary Aldermary, p. 17.

1734. Married — George Hathaway and Annie Phipps: St. Jas. Clerkenwell, i. 262.
London, 5 ; Philadelphia, 12.

Hatherton.—Local, ' of Hatherton,' a township in the parish of Wybunbury, co. Chester.

MDB. (co. Chester), 2.

Hathornthwaite.—Local ; v. Haythornthwaite.

Hatmaker.—Occup. 'the hatmaker'; cf. Hatter and Hatt.

William Hatmaker. H.
Sibill Hatmaker : Pat. Roll, 3 Edw. VI. pt. ii.

Hatt.—Local, 'at the Hat,' a signname, practically equivalent to hatter.

Thomas del Hat, co. Oxf., 1273. A.
Henry Hat, co. Wilts, ibid.
William Hat, co. Norf., ibid.
John atte Hatte. J.
John Hatt, of Leckampstead, co. Berks: Visitation of London, 1635, i. 364.
John Hatt, attorney in Guildhall, 1634 : ibid.
London, 3 ; Oxford, 4.

Hatter.—Occup. 'the hatter,' a manufacturer, a dealer in hats.

Henry le Hatter, co. Hunts, 1273. A.
William le Hattere, co. Oxf., ibid.
Alexander le Hattere, Close Roll, 16 Edw. III. pt. i.
Robert le Hattare, 1301. M.
Edward le Hattere, co. Soms., 1 Edw. III : Kirby's Quest, p. 276.
Robertus Hatter, 1379 : P. T. Yorks. p. 46.
Robertus Hatter, 1379 : ibid. p. 121.
1618. William Pearcie and Frances Hatter, of East Tilbury, co. Essex : Marriage Lic. (London), ii. 61.
I do not find any living representatives of this name in England.

New York, 3.

Hattersley, Hatterslay. — Local, ' of Hattersley,' a township in the parish of Mottram-in-Longdendale, co. Chester.

Willelmus de Hatyrlay, 1379 : P. T. Yorks. p. 92.
Amicia Hattirslay, 1379 : ibid.
1799. Married — George Hattersley and Harriot Langford : St. Geo. Han. Sq. ii. 195.
Manchester, 6, 0 ; MDB. (co. Cambridge), 1, 0 ; London, 1, 1.

Hauberger.—Occup. 'the hauberger,' a maker of hauberks, the coat of ringed metal. Habergeon is a diminutive.

' Sche me fond palfrey and sted,
Helme, haberion, and odour wed.'
Halliwell.

John le Hauberger, Close Roll, 12 Edw. II.
Gilbert le Hauberger. B.
John le Haubergere. N.
Roger le Haubergom, 12 Edw. II : Freemen of York, i. 18.

Haugh.—Local, 'at the haugh,' from residence thereby. 'Haugh means a mound, equivalent to *how*, in Silver How, Howgill, Fox How, places in the Lake district' (v. Isaac Taylor's Words and Places, p. 477); v. Halgh, and cf. Haughton and Halghton (s.v. Houghton).

MDB. (co. Cumberland), 2.

Haughton.—Local; v. Houghton.

Hautboys.—Local; O.F. *haut-bois*. In original sense of a 'high wood,' a 'hautboy being a *wooden* instrument of a high tone' (Skeat); cf. Boyce.

Adam de Hautboys, C. R., 29 Edw. III.

Hauxwell.—Local, 'of Hawks-well.' Many small farmsteads are called Hawkswell. I had one in my old parish (Ulverston), the birthplace of Judge Fell, the friend of Bradshaw the regicide and the husband of the lady who afterwards married George Fox the Quaker. Derived either from the *bird* or the personal name, probably the latter, as there is strong evidence of the popularity of this name ; cf. Sparrowhawk, at first a personal name, and v. Hauk, Yonge, ii. 283.

John de Haukewell, co. Suff., 1273. A.
Peter de Haukeswell, co. Kent, Hen. III-Edw. I. K.
London, 1.

Havelock.—Bapt. 'the son of Havlok.' An early personal name. The Havelocks seem to have sprung from co. Durham. 'Geoffrey Gaimar's metrical romance, called Le Lai d'Havelok le Danois, records the valorous doings of a great Danish chieftain' (Lower's Patr. Brit. p. 150). It has always been a rare surname in England, although now immortalized.

John Havelok, C. R., 7 Edw. IV.
MDB. (co. Durham), 1 ; South Shields, 1 ; Sunderland, 2.

Haven.—Local, 'at the haven,' from residence thereby.

William del Havene, co. Linc., Edw. I. R.
William atte Havene, co. Essex, 1273. A.
William de la Havene, co. Linc., ibid.
London, 1 ; New York, 7.

Havercake. — Nick. ' haver-cake,' i.e. oatcake.

Matilda Havercake, co. Norf., 1273. A.

Havergal.—Local, 'of Haver-gill.' I cannot find the particular spot ; cf. such other local surnames with suffix -*gill* as Gaskell, Win-tersgill, Fothergill, &c. Somewhat resembling this name is

Thomas de Howbergill, 1379 : P. T. Yorks. p. 216.

But whether or no it is the original parent I cannot say. If Howber-gill became popularly Habbergill, then Havergal would be all but inevitable.

George Heuergell, 1700 : Reg. St. Mary Aldermary, London, p. 114.
George Havergill, 1700 : ibid.
Crockford, 2.

Haverson.—Bapt. 'the son of Harvey.' Harveyson corrupted to Harverson (q.v.), and again to Haverson.

London, 1.

Haviland.—Local, ' of Havi-land.' I cannot find the spot, and I cannot accept Mr. Lower's solution.

MDB. (co. Sussex), 1 ; Philadelphia, 16.

Havill, Hovell.—Local, ' de Hautville.' Probably some spot in Normandy. It is found in every conceivable form in early registers, Hautville, Hauvile, Hauvill, Hau-ville, Hauvyle, Havele, Havell, Havile, Havill, and Haville being the commonest. The modern Hovell unfortunately suggests a mean dwelling. It is occasionally Latinized, as *Alta Villa*.

'In 1196 Sir Ralph de Havile was lord of Erlham, by Norwich. He was a younger brother of Humphrey de Havile, de Alta Villa, or Hautville' : FF. vii. 139.
Thomas de Havile, co. Norf., 1266 : ibid. p. 140.
Henry de Hauville, co. Norf., 1273. A.
John de Havill, co. Norf., 1318 : ibid.
1589-90. John Dawes and Agnes Havell : Marriage Lic. (London), i. 185.
1626-7. Hoogan Hovell, *grocer*, and

Mary Haregrave : Marriage Lic. (London), ii. 182.
1804. Married — Thomas Hovell and Eliz. Furnace : St. Geo. Han. Sq. ii. 316.
London, 3, 1 ; Philadelphia, 0, 2.

Hawcroft.—Local. A York-shire surname, therefore probably a corruption of Havercroft (oat-field). A township in the parish of Felkirk, W. Rid. Yorks; cf. Rycroft (rye-field), Barcroft (barley-field), Bancroft (bean-field). But v. Haycraft.

Walterus Hauercroft, 1379 : P. T. Yorks. p. 84.
Adam de Hauercroft, 1379 : ibid. p. 111.
West Riding Court Dir., 3 ; Manches-ter, 1.

Hawe, Hawes (1), Haws.—Local, 'at the haw,' i.e. garth, yard, or enclosure; v. Hay and Haig.

' And eke ther was a polkat in his hawe.'
Chaucer, C. T. 12789.

Cf. a *haw-haw*, also such local surnames as Haworth, Hawley, Hawthorn. &c. For a second origin of Hawes, v. next article.

Alan del Hawes, co. Camb., 1273. A.
John de la Hawe, co. Hunts, ibid.
Peter in le Hawe, co. Kent, ibid.
Maurice atte-Hawe, rector of Frethorp, co Norf., 1349 : FF. vii. 232.
William atte-Hawe, rector of Newton, co. Norf., 1362 : ibid. v. 67.
Thomas del Hawe, 1379 : P. T. Yorks. p. 210.
London, 0, 31, 2.

Hawes (2), Haweis, Hawis-son.—Bapt. 'the son of Hawys,' whence Avice; v. Aves. Hawys occurs as a personal name, without surname, in co. Camb., in the Hundred Rolls (1273), ii. 444.

Reginald fil. Hawise, co. Camb., 1273. A.
Richard Hawyse, co. Oxf., ibid.
Hawis de Stanweye, co. Norf., ibid.
Hawis de Bolron, co. Lanc., 1332 : Lay Subsidy (Ryland), p. 93.
Hawis de Quency, co. Linc., Hen. III-Edw. I. K.
Hawis de Ripon, 19 Edw. II : Free-men of York, i. 23.
William Hawys, co. Soms., 1 Edw. III: Kirby's Quest, p. 180.
Johannes Hawys, 1379 : P. T. Yorks. p. 38.
Richard Hawisson, mayor of Stock-port, 1378 : Hist. East Cheshire, i. 464.
London, 31, 0, 0 ; Crockford, 2, 2, 0.

Hawgood. — Bapt. ; v. Har-good.
London, 3.

Hawk, Hawke.—Nick. 'the hawk,' a sobriquet affixed to one of a fierce, or wild, or cruel disposition ; cf. Eagle, Falcon, Heron, &c. No doubt, too, Hawk, like Sparrow-hawk (q.v.), was a personal name, or, as we should now say, a baptismal name as well as a nickname ; v. Hauxwell.

Jocelin de Hawke, co. Linc., 1273. A.

Probably this is a misreading for 'le Hawke.'

Thomas Hauke, 1379 : P. T. Yorks. p. 218.
Thomas Hauke, *coteler*, 1379 : ibid. p. 45.
Adam Hawke, 1379 : ibid. p. 203.
Johannes Hawke, 1379 : ibid.
1577. Buried—John Hawke : St. Mary Aldermary, p. 140.
1601–2. Edmund Hawke, *skinner*, and Avice Bishop : Marriage Lic. (London), i. 267.
London, 0, 4 ; New York, 5, 2.

Hawken.—Bapt. 'the son of Henry' ; v. Hawkin, of which it is a Cornish variant.

MIIB, (co. Cornwall), 12.

Hawker.—Occup. 'the hawker,' one who hawked goods from place to place. On the origin of the word, and its connexion with Huckster, v. Skeat. Hucker as well as Huckster (q.v.) existed as surnames in the 13th century.

John le Haueker, co. Wilts, 1273. A.
Hugh le Haukere, co. Camb., ibid.
Alice la Haukere, Fines Roll, 11 Edw. I.
Robert le Haukere, C. R., 16 Edw. I.
John le Haukere, c. 1300. M.
Simon le Hauckere, M.
London, 12 ; Philadelphia, 1.

Hawkes ; v. next article.

Hawkin, Hawking, Hawkings, Hawkins, Hawkes, Hawks.—Bapt. 'the son of Henry' or 'Harry,' from the nick. Hal, dim. Halkin, popularly Hawkin ; cf. Shallcross and Shawcross, *faw* for fall, *haw* for hall, in various dialects. Mary and Harry formed their nicks. and diminutives on the same lines, as thus : Mary, Mal. Malkin, Mawkin ; Harry, Hal, Halkin, Hawkin ; v. Malkin.

'Shal noon heraud ne harpour
Have a fairer garnement
Than Haukyn the actif man.'
Piers Plowman.
Haukyn Ferers. O.
Haukyn Mayne. H.

Haukyn de Hauville. R.
Haukyn Talbotman, 1379 : P. T. Yorks. p. 285.
Henricus Hawkynne, 1379 : ibid. p. 166.
Johannes Haukyn, 1379 : ibid. p. 98.

The *g* in Hawking is excrescent, as in Jennings or Colling. Hawkins is reduced to Hawkes and Hawks, as are Perkins, Dawkins, Jenkins, and Judkins to Perkes, Dawks, Jenks, and Juckes or Jukes.

'William Hawkvs, or Hawkyns, B.A., Oct. 1539 ': Reg. Univ. Oxf. i. 195.
London, 0, 2, 6, 95, 24, 1 ; MDB. (co. Cornwall), 1, 1, 1, 5, 1, 0.

Hawkrigg, Hawkridge.—Local, ' of Hawkrigg' or ' Hawkridge,' a parish in co. Somerset. Several places would easily get such a name.

MDB. (co. Cumberland), 1, 0 ; (co. Lanc.), 5, 0 ; (co. Notts), 0, 1.

Hawksford, Hawkesford. —Local, ' of Hawksford.' I cannot find the spot.

MDB. (co. Salop), 1, 0 ; (co. Warwick), 0, 1.

Hawkshaw.—Local, ' of Hawkshaw.' I cannot find the locality ; v. Hawk.

Peter Hawkshaw, of Hambleton, 1707: Lancashire Wills at Richmond, ii. 129.
Edward Hawkshawe, of Preston, 1718: ibid.
MDB. (co. Sussex), 1.

Hawksley, Hawksly.—Local, ' of Horkesley,' two parishes (Great and Little) in the dioc. of St. Albans.

Robert de Horkesle, or Robert de Horkele, co. Suff., 1273. A.
Robert de Horkesle, co. Essex, ibid.
Walter de Horkeleye, co. Norf., Hen. III–Edw. I. K.
London, 8, 0 ; MDB. (co. Derby), 1, 1.

Hawkswood. — Local, ' of Hawkswood.' I cannot find the spot.

MDB. (co. Warwick), 1.

Hawksworth.—Local, (1) ' of Hawksworth,' a parish in co. Notts, eight miles from Newark. (2) ' of Hawkswith,' a township in the parish of Arncliffe, W. Rid. Yorks. No doubt originally Hawksworth ; cf. Askwith in the same county.

Johannes de Haukesworth, *wright*, 1379 : P. T. Yorks. p. 35.
Willelmus de Haukesworth, *wright*, 1379 : ibid.

Anabilla de Hewkesworth, *vidua*, 1379 : ibid. p. 219.
1587. John Juneslarde and Margaret Hawkesworth : Marriage Lic. (London), i. 161.
1801. Married — John Bruckner and Sophia Hawksworth : St. Geo. Han. Sq. ii. 243.
West Riding Court Dir., 10 ; MDB. (co. Derby), 4 ; London, 1 ; Philadelphia, 2.

Hawley.—Local, ' of Hawley.'
London, 7 ; MDB. (co. Kent), 4 ; Philadelphia, 18.

Haworth, Heworth.—Local, ' of Haworth,' a village near Keighley, co. York, whose vicarage is famous as the former residence of Charlotte Brontë, her father being the vicar. Not to be confounded with Howorth, though no doubt the names have become mixed.

Alicia de Haworth, 1379 : P. T. Yorks. p. 11.
Johannes Haueworth, 1379 : ibid. p. 194.
Johannes de Haworth, 1379 : ibid. p. 200.
Otes de Haworth', 1379 : ibid. p. 188.
1594. John Haworthe, co. Lanc.: Reg. Univ. Oxf. vol. ii. pt. ii. p. 202.
London, 4, 0 ; West Riding Court Dir., 6, 0 ; Thorpe Audlin (near Pontefract), 0, 1 ; Boston (U.S.), 3, 0.

Hawthorn, Hawthorne. — Local, ' at the hawthorn,' from residence by some prominent haw thorn tree. Perhaps Horethorn has a share in the parentage.

Galfridus Hackthorn, co. Hunts, 1273. A.
John atte Horethorne, co. Soms., 1 Edw. III : Kirby's Quest, p. 279.
Sabina atte-horethorn. T.
Adrian Hauthorne, 1551 : Reg. Univ. Oxf. i. 218.
Gilbert Hawthorn, co. Soms., 1589–9 : ibid. vol. ii. pt. ii. p. 168.
1597. Married — Walter Hawthorne and Alice Dyer : St. Jas. Clerkenwell, iii. 21.
1626. John Hawthorne, co. Berks, and Mary Albanie : Marriage Lic. (London), ii. 167.
1793. Married — John Hawthorn and Mary King : St. Geo. Han. Sq. ii. 93.
London, 10, 1 ; Boston (U.S.), 0, 9.

Hawxhurst. — Local, ' of Hawkshurst.' Probably for Hawkhurst, a parish in co. Sussex ; cf. Holdsworth for Holdworth, &c.
Philadelphia, 1.

Haxby.—Local, ' of Haxby,' a parish four miles from York.
Johannes de Haxby, *mercer*, 1 Edw. I : Freemen of York (Surt. Soc.), i. 1.

Gilbertus de Haxby, *girdeler*, 21–2
Edw. I : Freemen of York (Surt. Soc.),
i. 5.
1602–3. Thomas Haxbye and Jane
Spence : Marriage Lic. (London), i. 274.
Leeds, 1 ; MDB. (N. Rid. Yorks), 2 ;
(co. Lincoln), 3.

Haxcell, Haxell.—(1) Local,
probably 'of Hawkeswell,' a parish
in co. Essex, near Rochford. (2)
Local, 'of Haxhill.' I cannot find
the spot. But Kirby's Quest seems
to prove that the suffix is -*hill*, not
-*well*. v. Axtell.

John de Haukewell, co. Suff., 1273. A.
Peter de Haukeswell, co. Kent, Hen.
III-Edw. I. K.
1404. John Haukeswell, Shaveling,
rector of Wilbv, co. Norf. : FF. i. 366.
William de Haxhulle, co. Soms., 1 Edw.
III : Kirby's Quest, p. 187.
1712. Married — George Rossbey and
Mary Haxwell : St. Jas. Clerkenwell, iii.
235.
1762. — George Hawxwell and Hannah
Ockford : St. Geo. Han. Sq. i. 115.
MDB. (co. Essex), 1, 0 ; London, 0, 2.

Hay, Haye, Hayes.—Local,
'at the hay,' i.e. the haw or hedge,
an enclosure ; cf. Hayward or
Haward, a hedge-ward ; v. Haig
and Hawe. The popular form in
the North of England was Haig,
Haigh, and Hague.

'But right so as these holtes, and these
hayes,
That have in winter dead been and
dry.' Chaucer, Troilus.
Eborard de li Heys. co. Norf., 1273. A.
John del Heys, co. Norf., ibid.
Nicholaa de la Hay, co. Linc., ibid.
Robert in the Hay, Close Roll, 18
Ric. II.
Ricardus del Haye, 1379 : P. T. Yorks.
p. 178.
Petrus del Hay, 1379 : ibid. p. 124.
Cecilia de la Hay, co. Soms., 1 Edw. III :
Kirby's Quest, p. 111.
William atte Haye. J.
London, 31, 1, 40 ; West Rid. Court
Dir., 6, 0, 6.

Haybiddel, Haybittel.—Offic.
'the hay-beadle,' a hayward or
keeper, from *hay*, a hedge, an
enclosure, and *beadle*, a bailiff ;
v. Hayward. 'This surname is
peculiar to cos. Surrey, Sussex,
and Kent, where it has flourished
for centuries. It may still be found
in the neighbourhood of Reigate'
(v. Lower's Patr. Brit., and Sussex
Arch. Coll. v. 261). The 16th century form was Heybetyll.

1692. Bapt. — Elizabeth, d. Thomas
Habetell : St. Jas. Clerkenwell, i. 345.
1694. Bapt.—Thomas, s. Thomas Hay-
betle : ibid. p. 357.
1711. Married—Thomas Kempton and
Eliz. Haybetel, ibid. iii. 236.

Haycock, -cox ; v. Hedgcock.

Haycraft, Haycroft.—Local,
'at the hay-croft,' from residence
therein ; v. Hay and Croft or
Craft.

Hugo de la Heycroft, co. Oxf., 1273. A.
William a la Heycrofte, co. Oxf., ibid.
Robert de Heycrofte, co. Oxf., ibid.
Johannes Haycroft, 1379 : P. T. Yorks.
p. 195.
1578. Edward Haycroft or Heycroft :
Reg. Univ. Oxf. vol. ii. pt. iii. p. 72.
1620. Tristram Heycroft and Mary
Horner : Marriage Lic. (London), ii. 94.
1809. Married — John Haycraft and
Ann Jordan : St. Geo. Han. Sq. ii. 413.
London, 3, 1 ; Manchester, 1, 2 ; Phila-
delphia, 0, 1 ; Oxford, 0, 2.

Haydock. — Local, 'of Haydock,' a manor in the parish of
Winwick, co. Lanc. For a well-
established corruption, v. Haddock.

Henry de Haydok, co. Lanc., 20 Edw.
I. R.
Gilbert de Eydock, or Haidoc, 23
Edw. III : Baines' Lanc. ii. 213.
Gilbert de Haydock, 1330 : ibid. p. 206.
John de Haydok, 1379 : Preston Guild
Rolls, p. 3.
Manchester, 2 ; Liverpool, 2 ; New
York, 9.

**Haydon, Hayden, Heydon.
Haydan, Haden.** — Local, ' of
Haydon,' parishes in cos. Dorset
and Essex ; also a chapelry in the
parish of Warden, co. Northumberland.

Richard de Haydon, or Heydon, co.
York, 1273. A.
John de Haydon, co. Soms., ibid.
Agnes de Heydone, co. Oxf., ibid.
Thomas de Heydon, co. Bucks, 20 Edw.
I. R.
Philip de Haghdon, co. Soms., 1 Edw.
III : Kirby's Quest, p. 134.
1574. Francis Haydon or Heydon :
Reg. Univ. Oxf. vol. ii. pt. iii. p. 42.
1586. Benjamin Heiden, ibid. i. 204.
1651. Married — Edward Sanderford
and Anne Heydon : St. Mary Aldermary,
p. 22.
1656. Bapt. — Joseph, s. Thomas and
Sara Hayden : St. Jas. Clerkenwell, i.
195.
1658. — Jane, d. Thomas and Sara
Haydon : ibid. p. 201.
London, 12, 6, 1, 0, 6 ; New York, 4, 60,
2, 1, 6.

Hayhurst.—Local, ' of Hay-

hurst,' some spot in north-east
Lancashire, in or near the parish
of Ribchester, where the name has
existed for centuries. The origin
of the word is simple ; v. Hay and
Hurst, and cf. Haywood, which is
a synonym.

Lawrence Hayhurst, of Ribchester,
1571 : Lancashire Wills at Richmond, i.
143.
John Hayhurst, of Ribchester, 1672 : ibid.
Eliz. Hayhurst, of Dutton, 1675 : ibid.
Jane Hayhurst, of Preston, 1677 : ibid.
Henry Hayhurst, of Dilworth, 1664 :
ibid.
MDB. (co. Chester), 2 ; Preston, 4 ; Man-
chester, 6 ; London, 1 ; Philadelphia, 6.

Hayland.—Local, ' at the hayland,' i.e. the enclosed land (v.
Hay), from residence thereby.

Johannes de Hayland, co. Linc., 1273.
A.
Johannes del Haland, 1379 : P.T.Yorks.
p. 156.
MDB. (co. Lincoln), 1.

Haylard, Aylard.—Bapt. ; v.
Allard.

1647. Thomas Lewes and Frances
Highlord : Marriage Lic. (Faculty Office),
p. 35.
London, 1, 1.

Haylett, Haylock.—Bapt. ' the
son of Heylot.' It is interesting
to notice that Haylock runs side
by side with Haylett in the several
counties where alone the latter
now flourishes as a surname, and
where as a personal name it is
first found. I cannot but consider
it a corrupted form. Blomefield
has an instance in Norwich, viz. :

Nicholas Heylakke, 1621 : FF. iv. 480.
Heylot (without surname), co. Camb.,
1273. A.
Emma Heylot, co. Hunts, ibid.
Robert Heylot, co. Bedf., ibid.
Nicholas Heylot, rector of Thurne, co.
Norf., 1356 : FF. iv. 179.
Daniel Heylet, rector of St. Michael at
Pleas, Norwich, 1612 : ibid. iv. 327.
William Heylett, vicar of Hevingham,
co. Norf., 1658 : ibid. vi. 380.
MDB. (Norfolk), 6, 1 ; (Essex), 1, 1 ;
(Cambridge), 0, 9 ; London, 1, 9.

Hayley.—Local, ' of Hayley.'
Seemingly some spot in co. Yorks.

Johannes de Heylelee, 1379 : P.T.Yorks.
p. 186.
Willelmus Haylay, 1379 : ibid. p. 220.
1802. Married — Edward Hayley and
Ann Abbott : St. Geo. Han. Sq. ii. 253.
West Rid. (Yorks) Court Dir., 1 ;
London, 2.

Hayling, Haylings. — Bapt. 'the son of Heilin'; v. Heylin. The _g_ is excrescent.

Haylock. — Bapt.; v. Haylett.

Hayman, Heyman. — (1) ? Offic. 'the hayman' (?), equivalent to Hayward or Heyward, q.v. (2) Bapt. 'the son of Hamon' or 'Hammon,' q.v. The _d_ in Hammond is excrescent. There can be little doubt that almost all our Haymans are descended from the once very popular personal name of Hamon. The corruption is purely imitative; for instance, we find a bailiff of Yarmouth, who occupied the office in two separate years, entered as follows :

1450. Haman Pulham : FF. xi. 325.
1454. Hamon Pulham : ibid.

In 1445, also, he is entered Haman; in 1459, Hamon; and in 1465, Haman. There can be no hesitation in accepting this derivation.

1636. Francis Spicer, _cordwainer_, and Eliz. Heyman : Marriage Lic. (London), ii. 226.
1682. Married — Peetur Heyman and Mary Browne : St. Jas. Clerkenwell, iii. 195.
London, 9, 0; New York, 15, 47.

Haymes. — Bapt. 'the son of Haym' or 'Hayms.' Probably a corruption of Hayn or Hayns; v. Hain, and cf. Hemming and Henning.

Hayms Wauter, prior of Blackburgh, co. Norf., c. 1180 : FF. ix. 32.
Adam Haym, co. Dorset, 1273. A.
Richard Haym, co. Oxf., ibid.
London, 2.

Hayne, Haynes; v. Hain.

Haysler; v. Hastiler.

Haysom. — Local; v. Heysham.

Haystead; v. Hastead.

Hayter. — Local, 'of Haytor,' a hundred in co. Devon.

John Haytour, co. Soms., 1 Edw. III : Kirby's Quest, p. 169.
John Haytour, co. Soms., 1 Edw. III : p. 178.
1687. Bapt. — Elizabeth, d. John Heyter : Reg. Stourton, co. Wilts, p. 18.
1706. — John, son of Hugh Heyter : ibid. p. 21.
1726. — John, son of William Heytor : ibid. p. 25.
London, 11.

Haythornthwaite, Hathornthwaite. — Local, 'of Hawthornthwaite.' A North-English name; v. Thwaites.

MDB. (co. Lanc.), 4, 2.

Hayton. — Local, 'of Hayton' : (1) a parish in co. Cumberland, eight miles from Carlisle ; (2) a township in the parish of Aspatria, co. Cumberland ; (3) a parish in co. Notts, three miles from East Retford.

MDB. (co. Cumberland), 23; London, 6; Philadelphia, 1.

Hayward, Haward. — (1) Offic. 'the hayward,' a keeper of cattle, literally 'hedge-watcher'; v. Hay or Hey. There were two kinds of Haywards : the hayward of the town or village, who kept the common cattle from straying or trespassing ; and the hayward of the lord of the manor, or religious house. See Way's note, Prompt. Parv. p. 234.

'To the hayward of Portham Poolmead, . . . or of all the hay meadows near Gloucester.' Diss. of Glouc. Abbey, 31 Hen. VIII : Rudder's Glouc. pp. 140-1.
'Hayward. A keeper of the common herd of cattle of a town ' : Bailey's Dict.

(2) Bapt. 'the son of Haward.' For instances and proof, v. Howard.

Adam le Hayward, co. Devon, 1273. A.
Roger le Hayward, co. Bucks, ibid.
Alicia le Hayward, co. Hunts, ibid.
Robert le Heyward, co. Soms., 20 Edw. I. R.
Nicholas le Hayward, c. 1300. M.
Robertus Hayward, 1379 : P. T. Yorks. p. 151.
Magota Hayward, 1379 : ibid.
1598. Thomas Michaell and Audrey Hayward : Marriage Lic. (London), i. 255.
1615. Bapt. — Thomas, s. Richard Hayward : St. Jas. Clerkenwell, i. 73.
1619. — Michaell, s. Richard Haward : ibid. p. 85.
1622. — John, s. Richard Hayward : ibid. p. 94.
London, 74, 11; New York, 35, 0; Philadelphia, 18, 0.

Haywood. — Local; v. Heywood.

Hazard; v. Hassard.

Hazeldine, Hazzledine. — Local, 'of the hazel-dean'; v. Hasleden, of which these are variants.

Hazell, Hazle, Hazel. — Local, (1) 'at the hazel,' i.e. the hazel-tree, from residence thereby ; (2) 'of Hessle,' a township in the parish of Wragby, co. Yorks.

Cristiana de Hesill, 1379 : P. T. Yorks. p. 110.
Willelmus de Hesill', 1379 : ibid. p. 111.
Thomas Hesell, 1379 : ibid. p. 75.
1788. Married — Joseph Hazle and Martha Toms : St. Geo. Han. Sq. ii. 10.
1805. — John Hazell and Sarah Gurney : ibid. p. 323.
London, 18, 3, 0; MDB. (co. Berks), 3, 0, 2.

Hazlegrove, Hesslegrave. — Local, 'at the hazel grove,' from residence thereby ; v. Greaves.

London, 1, 0; West Riding Court Dir., 0, 1.

Hazlehurst. — Local, 'at the hazel hurst,' i.e. the hazel wood ; v. Hurst and Hazlewood.

MDB. (co. Chester), 6.

Hazlewood, Haslewood, Heselwood, Haselwood. — Local, 'of Hazlewood,' parishes in diocs. Southwell and Norwich. Also Hazlewood, a township in the parish of Skipton, Yorks ; and Hazlewood, a township in the parish of Tadcaster, Yorks.

Ricardus de Hesilwode, 1379 : P. T. Yorks. p. 145.
Robertus de Heselwode, 1379 : ibid. p. 140.
John Hesilwode, 1379 : ibid. p. 142.
1553. Married — John Hasylwood and Katheryne Weste : St. Michael, Cornhill, p. 6.
West Rid. Court Dir., 4, 0, 0, 1; London, 3, 2, 0, 0; York (Heselwood), 2.

Hazlitt, Hazlet, Hazlett, Haslet, Haslett. — Local, 'at the hazel head,' i.e. one who dwelt at the head of the hazel wood ; cf. Akenhead (the head of the oaks) and Birkenhead (the head of the birks or birches). By corruption Birkenhead or Birkhead became Birkett, just as Beckhead (at the head of the beck, the stream) became Becket. In a similar way Hazelhead narrowed itself into Haslet, &c. Hazlehead is a hamlet in the parish of Thurlstone, W. Rid. Yorks; cf. Haselfoot (i.e. one who dwelt at the foot of the hazel wood), London Directory. — Three years after writing the above I came across:

1582. Roger Haslehead, rector of Croglin, co. Cumb.: Jefferson's Hist. of Leath Ward, p. 102.
London, 4, 2, 0, 0, 0; Philadelphia (U.S.), 3, 6, 41, 2, 13.

Heacock; v. Heathcoat or Heathcock, of which it is an abbreviation. Similarly Heathfield has become Heafield.

1630. Married—Anthonie Hartley and Margery Heacocke: St. Jas. Clerkenwell, iii. 61.
1788. — John Stephenson and Eleanor Heacock: St. Geo. Han. Sq. ii. 10.
London, 1; Philadelphia, 10.

Head.—Local, 'at the head,' from residence at the *head* of the wood, valley, stream, &c.; cf. Birkett for Birkhead (i.e. at the head of the birks or birches). *Head* is often found as a suffix in this sense; cf. Akenhead, Birkenhead, Muirhead; possibly sometimes a sign-name; v. Harp and Roebuck.

Thomas del Heved, co. Notts, 1273.
Willelmus del Heued, 1379: P. T.Yorks. p. 233.
Cecilia del Heued, 1376: ibid.-p. 228.
London, 41; MDB. (co. Cumberland), 9; Philadelphia, 5.

Headham.—Local, 'of Headham,' a township in the parish of Gainford, co. Durham.

MDB. (co. Cumberland), 1; (co. Durham), 2; Crockford, 3.

Heading, Hedding, Hedden, Headen, Headon.—Local, 'of Headon' or 'Hedon,' parishes in diocs. Southwell and York.

Gerard de Hedon, co. Notts, 1273. A.
Symon de Hedon, co. Notts, ibid.
Nicholas de Hedon', co. Camb., ibid.
Willelmus de Hedon, 1379: P.T.Yorks. p. 118.
London, 0, 0, 0, 2, 3; MDB. (co. Bedford), 1, 1, 0, 0, 0; (co. Berks), 2, 0, 3, 0, 0.

Headington. — Local, ' of Headington,' a parish in co. Oxford, half a mile from the University city.

Sibel de Hedindon, co. Oxf., 1273. A.
William de Hedindon, co. Oxf., ibid.
Nicholas de Hedinton, co. Berks, Hen. III-Edw. I. K.
Osbert de Hedindon, co. Berks, ibid.
Johannes de Hedyngton, 1379: P. T. Yorks. p. 73.
Thomas Heddington, 1579: Reg. Univ. Oxf. iii. 79.

1753. Married—John Headington and Eliz. Cummings: St. Geo. Han. Sq. i. 49.
London, 1; MDB. (co. Berks), 3.

Headland, Hadland.—Local, 'of the headland,' from residence thereon.

John del Havedland, co. Suffolk, 1273. A.
London, 6, 5; MDB. (co. Dorset), 1, 0.

Headley, Hedley, Headly.—Local, 'of Headley' or 'Hedley,' parishes in the dioc. of Winchester. The entries below seem to relate to another spot:

Alan de Hedleg', co. Salop, 1273. A.
Nicholas de Heddeleg', co. Salop, ibid.
Cecilia de Hedlegh, co. Staff., 20 Edw. I. R.
Willelmus de Hedlay, 1379: P.T.Yorks. p. 147.
Margareta de Hedelay, 1379: ibid. p. 150.
1598. John Hedlye and Agnes Daye: Marriage Lic. (London), i. 254.
London, 1, 4, 0; MDB. (co. Cambridge), 4, 0, 6.

Headman.—? Occup. 'the head man' (?), i.e. the gaffer, the master; v. Master and Masterson.

1614. John Hedman: Reg. Univ. Oxf. vol. ii. pt. ii. p. 333.
1690. Bapt. — Caleb, son of Philip Headman: St. Michael, Cornhill, p. 155.
London, 1.

Headon.—Local; v. Heading.

Heafield; v. Heathfield, of which, no doubt, it is an abbreviation; cf. Heacock for Heathcock.

London, 1.

Heal, Heale, Heales.—Local, 'at the hele,' from residence thereby. Hele seems to be a variant of Hill.

John in the Hele, co. Soms., 1 Edw. III: Kirby's Quest, p. 109.
Edith atte Hele, co. Soms., 1 Edw. III: ibid. p. 110.
William in the Hele, co. Soms., 1 Edw. III: ibid. p. 121.
Edith in le Hele, co. Soms., 1 Edw. III: ibid.

I could give many more instances from the same record. One thing is certain, the West country is the chief habitat of the surname. The MDB., co. Soms., proves that Mr. Lower mentions a Sir Roger de la Heale, co. Devon, temp.

Hen. III (Patr. Brit. p. 153); v. Heald for a North-English variant.

London, 4, 1, 6; MDB. (co. Soms.), 11, 2, 0; New York, 6, 0, 0.

Heald.—(1) Local, 'at the hele' (q.v.). Here *d* is an excrescence; cf. Neild for Neil. Both Heald and Neild are familiar to South Lanc.

1582. Married—Hughe Grene and Anne Heylde: Reg. Prestbury, co. Ches., p. 75.
1586. Buried—Rychard Heale, or Hull: ibid. p. 92.
1603. Robert Heald, of Bury: Wills at Chester, i. 88.
1610. John Heald, of Astley: ibid.
London, 3; Manchester, 10; Philadelphia, 15.

Healey, Heeley, Healy, Heely.—(1) Local, 'of Healey,' a township in the parish of Masham, N. Rid. Yorks. Also 'of Heley,' a chapelry in the parish of Rochdale, co. Lanc. Also Heeley, a parish two miles from Sheffield.

Adam de Helegh, c. 1280, co. Ches.: East Ches. i. 44.
Thomas del Hulegh, 1326: ibid. i. 170.
Thomas del Heghlegh, 1363: ibid. p.196.
William Hellye, of Macclesfield, 1579: ibid. p. 18.
1566. Buried—uxor Jacobi Heyleye: Reg. Prestbury, co. Ches., p. 21.
1577. — Anne Healye: ibid. p. 57.
1599. — Margaret Healeye: ibid.p. 144.
Johannes de Helay, 1379: P. T. Yorks. p. 183.
Ricardus Helagh, 1379: ibid. p. 291.

(2) Bapt. 'the son of Helye,' i.e. Ellis; v. Heelis and Ely or Eley.

William fil. Helye, co. Bucks, 1273. A.
Henry fil. Helye, co. Bucks, ibid.
Philip de Heleye, co. Norf., ibid.
Alicia de Heghlegh, 1379: P.T. Yorks. p. 93.
Johannes de Helay, 1379: ibid. p. 4.
George Helie, co. Linc., 1574: Reg. Univ. Oxf. ii. 58.
Stephen Heely, co. Kent, 1600: ibid. p. 240.
1602. Married—Robert Wilkins and Joane Healey: St. Jas. Clerkenwell, iii. 26.
1669. Cresswell Hunt and Mary Hely: Marriage Lic. (Faculty Office), p. 108.
Manchester, 11, 0, 0, 0; West Rid. Court Dir., 5, 2, 0, 0; London, 8, 0, 6, 1.

Heap, Heape.—Local, ' of Heap,' a township in the parish of Bury, near Manchester. This surname has many representatives in co. Lanc., and has safely crossed the Atlantic. A charter (temp. 10

Hen. III) concerning a gift of land in this district is signed by Adam de Bire, Roger de Midelton, and Robert de Hep; v. Baines' Lanc. i. 524.

Edmund Fenton, of Heap, 1574; Wills at Chester (1545–1620), p. 63.
Richard Heap, of Rawtenstall, 1618: ibid. p. 89.
John Heap, of Broadroad, parish of Bury, 1638: ibid. (1621–50), p. 103.
Richard Henpe, of Failsworth, 1621: ibid.
Manchester, 11, 2; London, 6, 0; Philadelphia, 9, 0; New York, 1, 1.

Heard.—Occup.; v. Herd.

Hearle; v. Earl.

MDB. (co. Cornwall), 7.

Hearn, Hearne, Hurn, Hurne, Hern, Herne.—(1) Local, 'in the herne' (i.e. nook or corner), from residence therein.

'Lurking in hernes, and in lanes blinde.'
     Chaucer, C. T. 16026.
'In hernes (i. e. corners and out-of-way places in the house), xiiis. iiiid.; item x sylver spones, xxiiis. iiijd.': Richmondshire Wills, p. 41.
Henry en le Hurne, co. Bucks, 1273. A.
Adam in the Hurne, co. Oxf., ibid.
Thomas ate Hurne, co. Oxf., ibid.
Robert in the Herne, C. R., 12 Edw. III. pt. ii.
William atte Hurne, C. R., 15 Edw. III. pt. iii.
Reginald in the hurne, C. R., 21 Edw. III. pt. ii.
Thomas in the Hyrne, 1379: P. T. Yorks. p. 175.

(2) Nick. 'the hern' or 'heron'; v. Heron.

Henry le Herne, co. Norf., 1273. A.
1525. Giles Hern and Cecilia More: Marriage Lic. (London), i. 4.
1686. Bapt.—Eliner, d. John Herne: St. Jas. Clerkenwell, i. 320.
1773. Married—William Crossland and Mary Hurne: St. Geo. Han. Sq. i. 235.
London, 20, 5, 4, 0, 1, 0; Philadelphia, 16, 0, 2, 0, 10, 1.

Hearnman.—Local, 'one who lived in a herne'; v. Hearn.

Roger Hurneman, co. Soms., 1 Edw. III: Kirby's Quest, p. 245.

Hearnshaw; v. Hernshaw.

Hearsey; v. Hersee.

Hearsnip.—Local.

MDB. (co. Lanc.), 1.

Hearthband. — Nick. ' the hearth-band,' probably synonymous with husband, lit. 'a house-

holder.' 'Herthe, where fyre ys made': Prompt. Parv.
William Hertheband, C. R., 16 Edw. III. pt. i.
John Hertheband, C. R., 12 Ric. II.

Heartsease.—Nick. 'comfort-bestowing,' the name of the pansy. A term of endearment; cf. Sweet-love, Phillimore, &c.
Johannes Hartsese, 1379: P. T. Yorks. p. 69.

Heaselden; v. Hasleden.

Heasman. — Occup. Possibly 'the heysman,' one who looked after the heys, a keeper; v. Hayman and Hayward. Also v. Hey.
London, 3; MDB. (co. Sussex), 4.

Heath.—Local, 'at the heath,' from residence upon the heath; cf. Moor, Moss, Myers, &c.
John de la Hethe, co. Wilts, 1273. A.
William atte Hethe, co. Oxf., ibid.
Adam atte Hethe, co. Soms., 1 Edw. III: Kirby's Quest, p. 89.
John atte Hethe, co. Soms., 1 Edw. III: ibid. p. 108.
Robert del Heth', 1379: P. T. Yorks. p. 175.
Adam del Heyth, C. R., 16 Edw. III. pt. ii.
Ralph atte Heythe, rector of Rockland Tofts, co. Norf., 1398: FF. i. 475.
Waryn Atte-Heyth, co. Norf., 1398: ibid. ix. 218.
Thomas Atte-Hethe, rector of Ringstead Parva, co. Norf., 1376: ibid. x. 347.
1577. Married—Robert Chambers and Helen Heathe: St. Mary Aldermary, p. 6.
1585. Bapt.—Fraunces, d. John Heath: St. Jas. Clerkenwell, i. 17.
London, 82; New York, 42.

Heathcoat, Heathcote, Heathcock. — Local, 'at the heath-cote,' the exact locality unknown. As usual (v. Glasscock) the suffixes -cote or -cot and -cock are inextricably confused, -cock being as often used for -cote as not, even in 13th century records. Wilcock (q.v.) is found as Wilcot in the same roll that contains the first instance below; v. Coate and Cocks for the difference in meaning. It is just possible however that Heath-cock was a nickname, as the black-cock sometimes goes by that name. In that case there is no connexion between Heathcote and Heathcock.
Walter Hathecok, co. Essex, 1273. A.
1600. Bapt. — Margeret, d. George Heathcock: St. Dionis Backchurch, p. 90.

1609. George Simon and Alice Heathcott: Marriage Lic. (London), i. 313.
1710. Married—Michael Heathcote and Mary Coxon: St. Jas. Clerkenwell, iii. 243.
London, 1, 2, 0; Crockford, 0, 10, 0; Liverpool, 0, 1, 1; New York, 0, 1, 0.

Heathen.—Nick. 'the heathen, a pagan, an unbeliever.
Walter le Hethene, Close Roll, 43 Hen. III.

Heather.—(1) Local, 'the heather,' one who lived on the heath, q.v. The little moorland shrub is called heath-er because it is an 'inhabitant of the heath' (Skeat). (2) Local, 'of Heather,' a parish in co. Leicester, four miles from Ashby-de-la-Zouch. This must be looked upon as the true derivation.
1633. Married—John Heather and Eliz. Armet: St. Mary Aldermary, p. 17.
1695. Bapt.—John, s. Izban Heather: St. Jas. Clerkenwell, i. 363.
1788. Married—William Heather and Hannah Dine: St. Geo. Han. Sq. ii. 6.
London, 17; Philadelphia, 3.

Heathfield.—Local, 'of Heath-field,' a parish in co. Sussex, nine miles from Uckfield; also a parish in co. Somerset, five miles from Taunton.
Walter de Hethfeld, co. Norf., 1265: FF. viii. 370.
Lynot de Hethefeld, co. Oxf., 1273. A.
Livesa de Hethfeld, co. Oxf., ibid.
Thomas Hethfeld, co. Soms., 1 Edw. III: Kirby's Quest, p. 236.
1662. Thomas Heathfield (co. Surrey) and Alice Cuddington: Marriage Lic. (Faculty Office), p. 66.
London, 2; Boston (U.S.), 5.

Heathman.—Local, 'the heath-man,' one who dwelt on the heath, probably the keeper; v. Heather, Heath, &c., and cf. Bridgman, Milman, &c.
MDB. (co. Cornwall), 1.

Heatley.—Local, 'of Heathley.' I cannot find the spot.
Johannes de Hethele, 1379: P. T. Yorks. p. 80.
Johanna Hethele, 1379: ibid. p. 83.
Robertus de Hetlegh, 1379: ibid. p. 84.
London, 3; New York, 1.

Heaton.—Local, 'of Heaton.' (1) A village and chapelry in the ancient parish of Bradford, Yorks. (2) There is a little nest of Heatons in close neighbourhood to Manchester, which has made the name very familiar to the directories of South Lancashire and East Cheshire.

'Hugh de Worthyngton and John de Heton hold of the said John half of one Knight's fee in Worthyngton and Heton-under-Horwich.' Knights' Fees, 23 Edw. III : Baines' Lanc. ii. 695.
Anilla de Heton, Pat. R., 20 Edw. II.
Radulfus de Heton, 1379 : P. T. Yorks. p. 78.
Alicia de Heton, 1379 : ibid. p. 192.
Ricardus de Heton, 1379 : ibid. p. 193.

This last-named person is set down as living in Heton-in-Bradford-dale.

Manchester, 18 ; London, 6 ; West Rid. Court Dir., 10.

Heaven, Heavens. — Bapt. 'the son of Evan.' An imitative corruption ; cf. Beavan for ab-Evan, usually Bevan or Beavans for Bevans. Heaven is generally found on the Welsh border.

Bristol, 13, 1 ; London, 1, 2.

Heaver.—Local, 'of Heaver.'
MDB. (co. Sussex), 5 ; London, 2,

Heaviside.—Local.
MDB. (co. Durham), 4 ; Ulverston, 2.

Hebard, Hebbard, Hebbert, Hebert.—Bapt. 'the son of Hubert'; v. Hibbard and Hubert. The forms Hubert has taken are astonishingly large. Hubbard is, however, the favourite (v. Hubert).

Henry Heberd, 1273. A.
Reginald Heberd, ibid.
Adam Hebert, ibid.
Nicholas Hebert, ibid.
London, 2, 2, 1, 1 ; Crockford (Hebert), 3.

Hebb, Hebson, Hebbes.—Bapt. 'the son of Hebert' (v. Hebard), from nick. Hebb. It is curious how surnames die out. Even two centuries ago Hebson was well represented in Lancashire and Yorkshire. I cannot find any descendant.

Herberdus Hebbe, co. Hunts, 1273. A.
Alicia Hebbe, 1379 : P. T. Yorks. p. 157.
Ricardus Hebson, 1379 : ibid. p. 242.
Thomas Hebson, of Whittington. co. Lanc., 1613 : Lancashire Wills at Richmond, i. 144.
William Hebson, of Poulton, co. Lanc., 1679 : ibid.
1611. Married—Henrie Greene and Allice Hebb : St. Thomas the Apostle (London), p. 11.
William Hebson, 1682 : Preston Guild Rolls, p. 169.

Thomas Hebson, 1682 : ibid.
Crockford, 1, 0, 0 ; MDB. (co. Bedford), 0, 0, 1.

Hebblethwaite, Heblethwaite, Heblethwaite, Heblewhite, Hebblethwait.—Local, 'of Heblethwaite.' The piece of country styled Heblethwaite is within three miles of Sedburgh, on the Yorkshire and Westmoreland border. With Hebblewhite, cf. Applewhite for Applethwaite.

Agnes de Hebletwayt, of Sedburgh, West Rid. Yorks, 1379 : P. T. Yorks. p. 289.
Richard Hebletwayt, of Sedburgh, West Rid. Yorks, 1379 : ibid.
John Heblethwett, of Carneforth, co. Lanc., 1595 : Lancashire Wills at Richmond, i. 144.
Robert Heblethwaite, vicar of Mellinge, 1647 : ibid.

These and other records in the same register concern people within a few miles of Sedburgh.

1580. William Hebblethwayte, Mag. Hall : Reg, Univ. Oxf. vol. ii. pt. ii. 91.
1605. Buried — Mary Heblethwayte, widdowe : St. Mary Aldermary, p. 152.
MDB. (co. Chester), 1, 0, 0, 0, 0 ; Manchester, 0, 1, 0, 0, 0 ; Liverpool, 0, 0, 1, 1, 0 ; Boston (U.S.), 0, 0, 0, 0, 1 ; Philadelphia, 1, 0, 0, 0, 0.

Hebden, Hebding.—Local, 'of Hebden,' a township in the parish of Linton, eleven miles from Skipton, W. Rid. Yorks.

Dionisius de Hebdeyn, tyngtor (living in Hebden), 1370 : P. T. Yorks. p. 266.
Adam de Hebden, salter, 1 Edw. II : Freemen of York, i. 11.
MDB. (co. Lanc.), 3, 0 ; West Riding Court Dir., 8, 0 ; Skipton, 1, 0 ; Philadelphia, 3, 6.

Heberden.—Bapt. 'the son of Hubert,' from dim. Hibberdine ; v. Hebard and Hubbardine.

John Heberden, or Hyberdyn, or Hubbardyn, sup. for B.A., Dec. 1529 : Reg. Univ. Oxf. i. 148.

An 18th century sixain on three famous London doctors ran :

'You should send, if aught should ail ye,
For Willis, Heberden, or Baillie :
All exceeding skilful men,
Baillie, Willis, Heberden ;
Uncertain which most sure to kill is
Baillie, Heberden, or Willis.'
London, 1.

Hebgin.—?
MDB. (co. Norfolk), 2.

Hebson.—Bapt. ; v. Hebb.

Hedden, -ing; v. Heading.

Hedgcock, Heycock, Haycock, Haycox. — Nick. 'the hedge-cock.' One of many names received from birds ; v. Haw, Hay, Hey, all variants of the same word hedge. Haycox (= Haycocks) is the genitive form ; cf. Cox for Cocks, Wilcox for Wilcocks.

Robertus Heghcok', et uxor ejus, 1379 : P. T. Yorks. p. 114.
1581. Francis Heycock : Reg. Univ. Oxf. ii. 108.
1584-5. Thomas Baspoole and Agnes Haycockes : Marriage Lic. (London), i. 136.
Hester Hedgcock, 1709 : Reg. Canterbury Cath. p. 69.
1710. Married — William Selby and Sarah Hedgecock : St. Antholin (London), p. 123.
Richard Hedgecock, 1726 : ibid. p. 76.
1800. Married—William Haycock and Catherine Rogers : St. Geo. Han. Sq. ii. 218.
London, 1, 1, 6, 1 ; West Rid. Court Dir., 0, 1, 0, 0 ; Liverpool. 2, 0, 1, 0 ; MDB. (co. Kent), 2, 0, 0, 0 ; Philadelphia, 0, 0, 2, 0.

Hedge, Hedges.—Local, 'at the hedge,' from residence thereby.

John de la Hegge, co. Kent, 1273. A.
Walter de la Hegge, London, ibid.
Edith atte Hegge, co. Soms., 1 Edw. III : Kirby's Quest, p. 169.
William atte Hegge, C. R., 26 Edw. III.
London, 2, 16 ; Oxford, 0, 27 ; New York, 1, 10.

Hedgehog.—Nick. 'the hedgehog'; cf. Pigg, Hogg, Wildbore, &c. I have only once met with this curious surname.

1618-9. Dominick Vanoutwick and Barbara Hedghogg, widow of John Hedghogg : Marriage Lic. (London), ii. 70.

Hedgeman. — Occup. 'the hedgeman,' a hedger, one who made fences.

MDB. (co. Kent), 1.

Hedglands, Highland, Highlands, Hayland, Hedgeland.—Local, (1) 'at the hedge-lands,' or (2) 'at the highlands.' But probably (2) is an imitative variant ; v. Hedgcock for somewhat similar changes.

Wulford atte Heghelonde, co. Kent, 1273. A.
Thomas de Heyelonde, co. Sussex, ibid.
1587. Abraham Hylande and Joyce Butcher : Marriage Lic. (London), p. 164.

1787. Married—John Morrison and Mary Hedgeland : St. Geo. Han. Sq. i. 403.
London, 2, 1, 1, 1, 0 ; MDB. (co. Cornwall), Hedgeland, 1.

Hedgley. — (1) Local, 'of Hedgeley,' a township in the parish of Eglingham, co. Northumberland. (2) Local, 'of Hedgerley,' a parish in co. Bucks, three miles from Beaconsfield.
MDB. (co. Essex), 1.

Hedingham.—? Local, 'of Hedingham,' two parishes in co. Essex (Castle Hedingham and Sible Hedingham).
London, 1.

Hedkins ; v. Edkins ; cf. Hatchard and Achard, or Haskew and Askew.
MDB. (co. Warwick), 1.

Hedley ; v. Headley.

Heeley, Heely ; v. Healey.

Heolis, Hellis, Heelas, Healas, Healass.—Bapt. 'the son of Helys,' i.e. Ellis, q.v. The first of these two forms has always had a fair number of representatives in cos. Lanc. and York.
Hugh fil. Helys, co. Hunts, 1273. A.
Robert fil. Helys, co. Hunts, ibid.
Agnes Helys, co. Oxf., ibid.
Cissot serviens Thome Helys, 1379 : P. T. Yorks. p. 175.
1554. Buried — Thomas Heelys, a porter : St. Peter, Cornhill, i. 111.
1679. — George Heellis, who was kild with a gunn : Reg. Skipton-in-Craven.
London, 2, 3, 0, 0, 0 ; West Rid. Court Dir., 2, 0, 0, 0, 0 ; Manchester, 3, 0, 0, 0, 0 ; MDB. (co. Berks), 0, 0, 3, 0, 0 ; (East Rid. Yorks), 0, 0, 0, 1, 1.

Heffer, Hepher.—Nick. 'the heifer'; cf. Bull, Stott, Palfrey.
MDB. (co. Cambridge), 4, 2 ; London, 5, 1.

Heffill, Heffell.—Local; probably a modified form of Haffield. The suffix -*feld* occasionally becomes -*fell*; cf. Hatfull for Hatfield, q.v.
Richard de Haffeld, co. Hunts, 1273. A.
London, 2, 1 ; MDB. (co. Norfolk), 1, 0 ; Crockford, 1, 0.

Heffingham ; v. Effingham ; cf. Hatchard and Achard.
London, 1.

Heigham, Higham.—Local, 'of Heigham,' a parish in co. Norfolk, seven miles from Acle.

Also 'of Higham,' parishes in cos. Kent, Bedford, Suffolk, Leicester, and Northampton, besides many other smaller localities ; v. Higham.
Ralph de Hegham, co. Norf., 1273. A.
Thomas de Hegham or Heyham, co. Kent, ibid.
Robert de Heyham, co. Suff., ibid.
MDB. (co. Suffolk), 5, 2 ; London, 2, 9.

Heighway, Highway.—Local, (1) 'of Highway,' a parish in co. Wilts, four miles from Calne ; (2) 'at the highway,' from residence on the high-road ; M.E. *heigh weye*, Piers Plowman, B. x. 155 (v. High, Skeat).
Richard de Heyweye, co. Wilts, 20 Edw. I. R.
Richard Highwey, C. R., 24 Hen. VI.
1619-20. William Highway and Anne Selman : Marriage Lic. (Westminster), p. 26.

In later times this surname was occasionally given to foundlings, but this does not affect the position of the origin as given above.
1648. Bapt.—William Highway, filius populi : St. Jas. Clerkenwell, i. 169
London, ?, 0 ; MDB. (co. Salop), 6, 0 ; (co. Stafford), 2, 0.

Heir ; v. Eyre. (v. Skeat).
Roger le Heir, C. R., 13 Edw. III. pt. iii.

Hele.—Local, 'at the hele'; v. Heal.
London, 1 ; Carlisle, 1 ; Philadelphia, 3.

Hellaby.—Local, 'of Hellaby,' a township in the parish of Stainton, W. Rid. Yorks.
MDB. (co. Warwick), 1.

Hellen, Hellin, Helling, Hellings.—(1) Bapt. 'the son of Hellen,' with excrescent *g* Helling and Hellings ; cf. Jennings, or Hewling and Hewlings.
Johannes Helyn, 1379 : P. T. Yorks.
Margareta Helyn, 1379 : ibid.
(2) Local.
John de Helyne, co. Wilts, 1273. A.
MDB. (co. Essex), 1, 1, 0, 0 ; London, 0, 0, 2, 1.

Hellersden ; v. Hillersdon.

Helliar, Hellier, Hellyar, Hellyer, Helyear ; v. Hillier.

Hellis.—Bapt. 'the son of Ellis'; v. Heelis. Aspirates are

of no account in early nomenclature. Ellison is found as Hellison in 1379.
Johannes Helysson, 1379 : P. T. Yorks. p. 277.
1789. Married — John Mason and Frances Hellis : St. Geo. Han. Sq. ii. 28.
London, 3.

Helm, Helme.—(1) Local, 'at the elm'; cf. Ash, Oak, Birch, &c. The aspirate is no obstacle to this view ; v. Hellis, &c., and cf. Empsall and Hempsall, or Elmsley and Helmsley. (2) Bapt. 'the son of Helm.' Although Miss Yonge has Helmar in her Glossary, and Helmsley would seem to be 'the meadow of Helm,' still I have not found a single trace of a personal name Helm in old records. I consider (1) to be the solution.
MDB. (co. Hereford), 2, 1.

Helpringham. — Local, 'of Helpringham, a parish in co. Lincoln, seven miles from Sleaford.
MDB. (co. Lincoln), 1.

Helps, Help.—?
MDB. (co. Glouc.), 4, 1.

Helsdon.—Local, 'of Hellesdon,' a parish in co. Norfolk.
Reginald de Hildesdon, co. Oxf., 1273. A.
Robert de Hildisdone, co. Bucks, ibid.
London, 4.

Helsham.—Local, 'of Hildersham,' a parish in the dioc. of Ely.
William Helsam, co. Hunts, 1273. A.
Talebot de Hildesham, co. Suff., 20 Edw. I. R.
London, 2.

Hemans, Hemmens.—Bapt. 'the son of Emeny.' This forgotten font-name found as Emayn and Imania, like all other names beginning with a vowel, early took an *h* to it. It was very popular along the East coast (v. Emeny), and existed as a Christian name till the close of the 17th century in Norfolk. The *s* in Hemans is, of course, the patronymic, as in Jones. Emeny was a favourite in Yorkshire, where the nick. Nemeny existed, so we cannot be surprised to find Hemmens as a surname in the same county.
Heman Grelin, co. Suff., 1273. A.

Hemin' uxor B'car, co. Camb., 1273. A.
1646. Married — John Heamans and
Mary Peyhen : St. Dionis Backchurch,
p. 25.
1764. — Thomas Conner and Elizabeth
Hemans : St. Geo. Han. Sq. i. 132.
London, 1, 1 ; York, 0, 1 ; New York,
1, 0.

Hembery, Hembrow, Hem-bry, Hembergh, Hembury.—
Local, 'of Hembury,' now Broad-hembury, a parish in North Devon,
near Honiton. This surname has
been somewhat prolific of variants,
but all are of the customary type ;
cf. Harborow.
John de Hembury, co. Soms., 1 Edw.
III : Kirby's Quest, p. 274.
John Hembure, co. Soms., 1 Edw. III :
ibid. p. 277.
1804. Married—Samuel Hembury and
Eliz. Darley : St. Geo. Han. Sq. ii. 298.
1807. — John Cadding Hemberow and
Martha Wallis : ibid. p. 369.
MDB. (co. Soms.), 1, 10, 4, 1, 4 ; Lon-don, 2, 1, 1, 1, 0.

Heming, Hemings.—Bapt. ;
v. Hemming.
London, 1, 1.

Hemingbrough, Hem-brough.—Local, 'of Heming-brough,' a parish near Selby,
E. Rid. Yorks.
MDB. (co. Lincoln), 1, 1.

Hemington.—Local, 'of Hem-ington,' parishes in the diocs. of
Peterborough, Exeter, and Bath
and Wells. Also ' of Hemingston,'
a parish in the dioc. of Norwich.
Reginald de Hemington, co. Norf.,
1273. A.
John de Hemyngton, co. Hunts, ibid.
London, 2.

Hemingway, Hemming-way, Hemmaway, Heminway.
—Local, 'of Hemingway,' i.e. the
road that led to Heming's house ;
v. Hemming (cf. Hemingfield, a
village near Wombwell, co. York).
Representatives of this name will
be met with in nearly every town
and village in the West Riding.
I have not discovered the precise
spot. Two of the individuals re-ferred to infra lived in Southow-ram.
Thomas Emyngway, 1379 : P. T. Yorks.
p. 192.
Willelmus Hemyngway, 1379 : ibid.
p. 187.
Johannes Hemyngway, 1379 : ibid.

1790. Married — Henry Fletcher and
Elinor Hemingway : St. Geo. Han. Sq.
ii. 39.
1800. — Thomas Heminway and Eliz.
Ashley : ibid. p. 213.
West Riding Court Dir., 10, 3, 0, 0 ;
MDB. (co. Cambridge), 0, 0, 1, 0 ; New
York, 3, 1, 0, 3.

Hemmence, Hemmans, Himmens.—Bapt. ; v. Immins
and Hemans.
MDB. (co. Cambridge), 1, 0, 0 ; (co.
Lincoln), 0, 1, 0 ; (co. Southampton),
0, 0, 1.

Hemming, Hemmings. —
Bapt. 'the son of Hemming.'
'Hemming, a Danish personal
name' (Lower). The Hundred
Rolls prove the name to have
become well established in the
13th century ; cf. the local Hem-ingborough in the dioc. of York,
Hemingby (Lincoln), Hemingford
Grey (Ely), Hemminghall (Norwich),
Hemingston (ibid.), Hemington
(Exeter, Bath and Wells, Peter-borough') ; v. Henning.
Henry Hemmeng, co. Suff., 1273. A.
John Hemming, co. Oxf., ibid.
John Hemmyng, co. Kent, ibid.
Robertus Hemmyng, 1379 : P. T. Yorks.
p. 41.
1574. Buried—Jane, d. Thomas Hem-mynges : St. Dionis Backchurch, p. 193.
1579-80. Married — Thomas Prestone
and Elsabeth Hemmyng : ibid. p. 9.
London, 15, 7 ; Philadelphia, 12, 1.

Hempstead, Hemstead.—
Local, ' of Hempstead,' a parish in
co. Norfolk.
Reginald de Henestede, co. Norf.,
1273. A.
Ranulf de Hemsted, co. Norf., ibid.
John de Hemsted, co. Norf., ibid.
Hamo de Hemstede, co. Norf., Hen.
III–Edw. I. K.
London, 1, 1 ; MDB. (co. Berks), 0, 2.

Hempstock ; v. Henstock.

Hemshall, Empsall, Hemp-sall, Hemsoll. — Local, 'of
Helmeshall,' some spot in the
W. Rid. Yorks ; cf. Emsley for
Helmsley in the same district.
With Hemsoll, cf. Plimsoll. The
_p_ is intrusive.
Johannes de Helmeshall, 1379 : P. T.
Yorks. p. 115.
1755. Married — John Hempsall and
Sarah Booth : St. Geo. Han. Sq. i. 57.
Sheffield, 0, 0, 2, 1 ; London, 1, 0, 0, 0 ;
West Rid. (Yorks) Court Dir., 0, 2, 0, 0.

Hemsley.—Local, 'of Helms-ley' ; v. Elmslie.
MDB. (co. Kent), 6 ; Philadelphia, 2.

Hemsworth, Himsworth.—
Local, ' of Hemsworth,' a parish in
W. Rid. Yorks, six miles from
Pontefract.
London, 1, 0 ; West Rid. (Yorks)
Court Dir., 2, 1 ; MDB. (co. Norfolk),
1, 0 ; Sheffield, 3, 0.

Henbrey.—Local, 'of Hen-bury.'
London, 2 ; MDB. (co. Sussex), 2.

Hender.—?
MDB. (co. Cornwall), 5.

Henderson ; v. Hendry.

Hendrick, Hendricks.—
Bapt. 'the son of Henry'; Dutch
Hendrik. Modern immigration has
added Hendriks and Henriques
to the London Dir., but Hendrick
and Hendricks represent a much
earlier importation from the Low
Countries. The _d_ is intrusive, as
in our own Hendry for Henry.
John Hendrich, co. Camb., 1273. A.
William Heneriche, co. Oxf., ibid.
John Henricks, son of Henry Henrix,
of Antwerpe, in Brabant, temp. 1600 :
Visitation of London, 1633, i. 376.
London, 2, 0 ; Philadelphia, 7, 62.

Hendry, Hendrie, Hender-son.—Bapt. 'the son of Henry.'
The _d_ is intrusive. Hendry is still
a common provincialism for Henry.
In Wales this was the ordinary
form, as is proved by the surnames
Appendrick and Pendry, q.v. ; cf.
ribbon and _riband_, Simmons and
Simmonds. The border clan of
Henderson are found as Hendir-sonne, Henresoun, Henryesson,
and Hendersonne in documents of
the 16th and 17th centuries (v. The
Debateable Land, by R. Bruce
Armstrong, p. 182).
Thomas Hendeson, 1379 : P. T. Yorks.
p. 202.
'Jesu, have mercy on the sawl of
Hendry Anderson, A. M., sometime
Mayor of this town,' 1562 : Brand's
Hist. of Newcastle-on-Tyne, i. 281.
1601. Buried—Mr. Hendereye Jay : St.
Antholin (London), p. 41.
1695. Isaac Bourdon and Mary Hen-dery : Marriage Lic. (Faculty Office),
p. 215.
Hendere Hewitt ; v. Proceedings in
Kent, 1640 : Camden Soc.
London, 5, 0, 81 ; Liverpool, 4, 1, 25.

Hendy, Hendiman, Henty, Hendey.—Nick. 'the hendy,' the courteous, the polite. Henty is a sharpened form.

'*Hende*: gentle, polite. "Hende he was, and mylde of mode." *Hendy*: "And he is curteys and hendy " ': Halliwell.

> 'Sire, ye should be hendy
> And curteis.' Chaucer, C. T.

Thomas le Hendy, co. Norf. FF.
John le Hendy, co. Norf., ibid.
Robert le Hendy, co. Norf., 1273. A.
William Hendeman, co. Hunts, ibid,
William Hendeman, 1307. M.
Margareta uxor Johannis Hende, 1379: P. T. Yorks. p. 170.
John Hende was Lord Mayor of London, 1391.
London, 3, 0, 3, 0; York (Hendey), 1.

Heneage.—Local, 'of Heneage.' Mr. Lower says, 'Sir Robert de Heneage was in Lincolnshire temp. William Rufus. I find no locality so called ' (Patr. Brit. p. 154).

1546-7. Andrew Byllysbye and Margaret Henneage; Marriage Lic. (Faculty Office), p. 9.
1791. Married — William Fitzherbert Brockholes and Mary Heneage: St. Geo. Han. Sq. ii. 62.
MDB. (co. Hertford), 1.

Henery.—Bapt. 'the son of Henry.' An old as well as modern vulgarism for Henry. For another variant, v. Hendry. Henery, as will be seen by evidence below, is common to many counties.

Thomas Henery, co. Kent, 1273. A.
1621. Buried—Henery Fletcher: Annals of Cartmel, p. 556.
Joane uxor Henery Naylor: Visit. Glouc., 1623, p. 189.
1656. Married — Henery Jepson and Jennett Smith : ibid. p. 558.
1748. Bapt.—Henery, s. John Hurdle : Reg. Stourton, Wilts, p. 31.
London, 3.

Henfrey.—Bapt. 'the son of Henfrey,' a form of Humphry which is found in many early guises. The change from *m* to *n* is common in surnames ; cf. Annable for Amabel (v. Hanniball). Also cf. Ransom for Ranson, and Hansom for Hanson.

William Honfrey, co. Soms., 1 Edw. III : Kirby's Quest, p. 145.
Aunfray (without surname), co. Oxf., 1273. A.
Richard Aunfrey, co. Bucks, ibid.
John Aunfrey, co. Oxf., ibid.

Andrew fil. Aunfrey, co. Sussex, ibid.
Walter fil. Hunfidi, co. Camb., ibid.
With which cf.
Robert Aumfrey, co. Hunts, 1273. A.
Martin Aumfrey, co. Oxf., ibid.
'Mr. A. G. Henfrey made 16 for Northamptonshire v. Lancashire at cricket, July 15, 1887 ' : Standard, July 16, 1887.
1746. Married—William Henfrey and Hannah Walker : St. Geo. Han. Sq. i. 37. London, 1.

Henley, Henly, Hendley.—Local, 'of Henley,' parishes in the diocs. of Oxford, Norwich, and Worcester.

Philipp de Heneleg', co. Salop, 1273. A.
John de Heneleye, co. Warw., ibid.
William de Henle, co. Salop, Hen. III-Edw. I. K.
John de Heneleghe, co. Soms., 1 Edw. III : Kirby's Quest, p. 230.
Willelmus de Henley, 1379 : P. T. Yorks. p. 276.
London, 10, 2, 0 ; MDB. (co. Wilts), 1, 5, 1.

Henn.—(1) Nick. 'the hen,' perhaps affixed on account of the homeliness of the bearer, or because he was 'henpecked'; cf. Cock, Drake, Wildgoose, &c.

Coleman le Hen, co. Suff., 1273. A.
Thomas le Hen, co. Suff., ibid.
Roger le Hen, co. Soms., 1 Edw. III : Kirby's Quest, p. 100.
Thomas le Hen, C. R., 4 Edw. II.

(2) Bapt. 'the son of Hen.'

John fil. Hen, co. Notts, 1273. A.
Henna, the wife of Aron, co. York, ibid.
1559. Married—George Holt and Agnes Henn : St. Thomas the Apostle (London), p. 3.
London, 3.

Henniker, Hennicker.—? Perhaps a modern importation. Mr. Lower says, 'The ancestors of Lord Henniker were a mercantile family from Germany, who settled in London early in the 18th century ' (Patr. Brit. p. 154).

MDB. (co. Essex), 3, 0 ; (co. Glouc.), 0, 1 ; London, 1, 0.

Henning, Hennings, Henningsen.—Bapt. 'the son of Henning' or 'Hemming.' This change of letters was common (v. Sinkinson for Simkinson), and three instances occur in the Hundred Rolls, where in one case the same individual is thus described :

Reginald de Hemington, co. Norf., 1273. A.
Reginald de Henington, co. Norf., ibid.
In the other :
Roger de Hemingthon, co. Norf., 1273. A.
Roger de Heningthon, co. Norf., ibid.
In a third :
Nicholas de Hemingford, co. Camb., 1273. A.
Nicholas de Henningford, co. Camb., ibid.
Henning de Bigefrid, co. Berks, ibid.
Thomas Hennyng, or Hemyng, sheriff of Norwich, 1498 : FF. iii. 191.
Henningsen is, of course, foreign.
London, 4, 3, 1.

Henriot.—Bapt. ; v. Harriot.

Henry, Henryson. — Bapt. 'the son of Henry'; v. Harries. Henryson is extremely rare, the early change into Henderson having become alike popular and permanent.

Jordan fil. Henr', co. Northumb., 20 Edw. I. R.
Thomas Henryes, co. Soms., 1 Edw. III : Kirby's Quest, p. 82.
Thomas Henrysone, C. R., 50 Edw. III. pt. i.
Willelmus Henryson, 1379 : P. T. Yorks. p. 153.
Willelmus Henrison, junior, 1379 : ibid.
London, 32, 0.

Henshaw, Henshall, Hensher. — Local, 'of Henshaw.' A place in the parish of Prestbury, co. Chester. In the church register the name is spelt indifferently Henshall and Henshaw ; v. Henn and Shaw ; cf. Shallcross and Shawcross.

Richard de Henneshagh, 1365 : East Ches. ii. 527.
Edward Henshawe, of Henshawe, 1579 : East Ches. i. 18.
The editor adds in a footnote, 'near Siddington, in Prestbury Parish.'
John Kershawe, of Henshawe, 1541 : Lanc. and Ches. Rec. Soc. xii. 145.
1560. Married — Rauf Crowder and Agnes Henshawe : Reg. Prestbury, co. Ches., p. 2.
1570. Buried—Sysley Henshall (Henshawe) : ibid. p. 32.
Jeremy Henshall, Manchester, 1701 : Lanc. and Ches. Rec. Soc. xi. 99.
Agnes de Hensalle, 1379 : P. T. Yorks. p. 157.
Dionisius de Hensale, 1379 : ibid.
This last name is Hensall, a

township in the parish of Snaith, co. York, whence Henzell, found in the directory for Seaham Harbour, co. Durham.

Manchester, 10, 5, 0 ; London, 10, 1, 2 ; MDB. (co. Chester), 1, 12, 0.

Hensley.—Local, 'of Hensley.'

London, 2 ; MDB. (co. Cambridge), 2.

Hensman, Hinxman, Hincksman, Hinksman, Hinckesman, Hinchman.— Offic. 'the henchman,' a horseman (not haunch-man, v. Skeat), a groom, from A.S. *hengest*, a horse. An Act passed in 1463 to restrain excess in apparel makes an exception in favour of 'Hensmen, Heroldes, Purceyvantes, Swerdeberers, as Maires, Messagers, and Minstrelles' (Stat. Realm, ii. 402). 'Item, the same daye paied to the yoman of the henxman for ther lodging at ii tymes at Westm., xiis' (1532) : Privy Purse Expenses, Henry VIII, p. 209. Throughout these entries the hinxman was 'a page of honor' ; v. note by Sir Harris Nicolas, editor of above, p. 370 ; cf. Palfreyman.

William Henxman, C. R., 1 Hen. V.
1674. Buried—Thomas Hinchman, son of Thomas Henchman (sic) : St. Dionis Backchurch, p. 240.
London, 3, 0, 1, 1, 0, 0 ; MDB. (co. Salop), 0, 0, 0, 0, 2, 0 ; New York (Hinchman), 4.

Henson.—Bapt. 'the son of Heyn.' From this Heynson or Henson was formed. Not a modification of Henryson. v. Hain.

Hugh Balle Heynesone (i. e. Hugh Balle, the son of Heyne), C. R., 32 Edw. I.
Willelmus Henson', sen., *spicer*, 1379 : P. T. Yorks. p. 108.
Willelmus Henson', jun., *taylour*, 1379 : ibid.
1682. Married — Robert Henson and Eliz. Hall : St. Jas. Clerkenwell, iii. 198.
1735. — Philip Henson and Eliz. Shevin : St. Geo. Han. Sq. i. 16.
London, 9 ; West Rid. Court Dir., 2 ; Sheffield, 1 ; Philadelphia, 27.

Henstock, Hempstock, Hemstock. — Local, 'of Hinstock,' a parish in co. Salop, five miles from Newport.

MDB. (co. Derby), 4, 0, 0 ; (co. Lincoln), 0, 2, 0 ; (Notts), 0, 0, 1.

Henton.—Local, 'of Henton,'

a liberty in the parish of Chinnor, co. Oxford, near Thame. There are three parishes in cos. Wilts and Somerset called Hinton (q.v.), and it is very probable that one of them at least is represented in my examples.

William de Henton, co. Oxf., 1273. A.
Alex. de Henton, co. Soms., ibid.
Hugh de Hentone, co. Soms., 1 Edw. III : Kirby's Quest, p. 136.
Walter de Hentone, co. Soms., 1 Edw. III : ibid. p. 205.
London, 3 ; Oxford, 1.

Henty.—Nick. ; v. Hendy, of which it is a sharpened form.

Henwood.—Local, 'of Henwood.' There is a tithing of this name in the parish of Cumnor, co. Berks.

MDB. (co. Cornwall), 26 ; London, 10 ; Oxford, 2.

Hepburn.—Local.

MDB. (co. Bucks), 1.

Hepher.—Nick. ; v. Heffer.

Heppenstall, Heptonstall, Heptinstall, Hippenstiel, Hippensteel.—Local, 'of Heptonstall,' a township in the old parish of Halifax, W. Rid. Yorks.

West Rid. Court Dir., 5, 2, 0, 0, 0 ; Sheffield, 3, 0, 1, 0, 0 ; Philadelphia, 0, 0, 0, 2, 2.

Hepton.—Local, 'of Hebden,' q.v. A Yorkshire variant. The change from *b* to *p* is early found.

Robertus de Hepdeyne, 1379 : P. T. Yorks. p. 259.
Johannes de Hebden, 1379 : ibid.
Willelmus de Hebden, 1379 : ibid.

All three were resident in the village of Markington. The change from suffix -*den* to -*ton* is common ; cf. Huntington and Huntingdon. Although these two surnames represent different places they have become inextricably mixed.

Leeds, 4.

Hepworth.—Local, 'of Hepworth,' a township in the old parish of Kirkburton, near Huddersfield.

Clic' de Hepworth, 1379 : P. T. Yorks. p. 80.
Johannes de Hepworth, 1379 : ibid. p. 179.
Thomas de Hepworth, 1379 : ibid. p. 32.
1577-8. Henry Skydmore and Kathe-

rine Hepworthe : Marriage Lic. (London), i. 168.
1794. Married—James Hepworth and Sarah Rook : St. Geo. Han. Sq. ii. 116.
London, 4 ; West Rid. Court Dir., 14 ; New York, 3.

Herapath.—Local.

1791. Married—Simon Herapath and Eliz. Franey : St. Geo. Han. Sq. ii. 61.
MDB. (co. Kent), 2 ; London, 3.

Herbelet.—Bapt. 'the son of Herbert,' from dim. Herbelot ; cf. Hamlet for Hamelot, from Hamond ; or Hewlet for Hewelot, from Hugh or Hew.

Richard Herbelette, Close Roll, 1 Hen. IV. pt. i.
Liverpool, 1.

Herberer.—?

Edmund Heyberer, C. R., 12 Ric. II.

Herbert, Herbertson, Herbison.—Bapt. 'the son of Herbert.' 'St. Haribert was archbishop of Cologne about the year 1000, and at that time the name became extremely common among the French nobility. A Norman settler had brought it to England even in the time of Edward the Confessor' (Yonge's Christian Names, ii. 407). It was a popular and fashionable personal name throughout England in the 12th and 13th centuries. Hence it obtained surnominal honours in the form of Herbertson. Herbison is a corrupted form of Herbertson.

Thomas Herebert, Hen. III–Edw. I. K.
Emma Hereberd, ibid.
Herbertus de Hereford, ibid.
Gilbert Herebert or Hereberd, co. Camb., 1273. A.
Richard fil. Herebert, co. Salop, ibid.
1768. Married—John Herbertson and Ann Bettridge : St. Geo. Han. Sq. i. 182.
1799. — James Herbertson and Sarah Fitch : ibid. ii. 196.
London, 56, 0, 0 ; New York, 52, 0, 2.

Herd, Heard, Hird, Hurd. —Occup. 'the herd,' i.e. the cattle-tender, found in compounds like Shepherd, Calvert (calve-herd), Coward, Oxenherd. M.E. *herde*, in Piers Plowman *hurde*. Heard is one of the instances among hundreds of the great imitative tendency in spelling surnames.

Robert le Hirde, co. Suff., 1273. A.
Richard le Herde, co. Camb., ibid.
David le Hyrde, co. Norf., ibid.

William le Hurde, co. Soms., 1 Edw. III: Kirby's Quest, p. 220.

The entries are very common in the Yorkshire Poll Tax:

Alanus Hyrd', 1379: P. T. Yorks. p. 268.
Nicholaus Hyrd', 1379: ibid.
Johannes Hird', 1379: ibid. p. 254.
London, 1, 19, 7, 2.

Herdman, Herdsman, Hurdman.—Occup. 'the herdsman,' a guardian of cattle.

Margery Herdman, co. Berks, 1273. A.
Martin Herdman, co. Kent, ibid.
Henry le Herdeman, Close Roll, 6 Edw. I.
William le Herdeman, 25 Edw. I: BBB. p. 542.
John Herdman, co. Soms., 1 Edw. III: Kirby's Quest, p. 140.
Mawde Hurdman, c. 1300. M.
Christopher Hurdsman, co. York. W. 16.
1524. John Hurdman and Anne Naysshe: Marriage Lic. (London), i. 3.
London, 0, 1, 1; MDB. (co. Durham), 2, 0, 0; (co. Lincoln), 0, 0, 3.

Herdson, Hirdson, Heardson.—Nick. 'the son of the herd,' i.e. herdsman; v. Herd; cf. Hindson and Hinson or Hineson. At one time the family had strongly ramified in North Lancashire, now scarcely any representatives exist.

1569. Thomas Herdeson and Katherine Whitehorne: Marriage Lic. (London), i. 42.
John Herdson, of Lytham, 1671: Lancashire Wills at Richmond, i. 145.
Jenetta Heardson, of Lytham, 1666: ibid. p. 143.
Isabel Hirdson, of Ulverston, 1597: ibid. p. 148.
Francis Heirdson, of Newton, 1621: ibid. p. 144.

Hereford, Herford, Harford.—Local, 'of Hereford,' sometimes 'of Hertford.' The surnames representing the two towns seem to have early got confused.

Warin de Hereford, co. Camb., 1273. A.
Roger de Herford, co. Hunts, ibid.
Walter de Herford, co. Camb., ibid.
Simon de Hereford, co. Linc., 20 Edw. I. R.
Margery Herford, co. Soms., 1 Edw. III: Kirby's Quest, p. 171.
John de Hareford, co. Soms., 1 Edw. III: ibid. p. 262.
1766. Married—Christopher Foss and Anna Hereford: St. Geo. Han. Sq. i. 152.
London, 1, 2, 6; MDB. (co. Hereford), 3, 0, 0.

Heriot, Heriott.—(1) Local,

'of Heriot,' a parish in the county of Edinburgh. (2) Bapt. 'the son of Henry,' from dim. Henriot, which became Heriot just as Henry became Harry; v. Harries and Harriot.

1764. Married — Thomas Heriot and Mary Moody: St. Geo. Han. Sq. i. 134.
London, 1, 1.

Heritage. — Local, 'of the heritage,' from residence on a spot or property so called. A local surname of this character would easily arise. I know a spot near Oldham, co. Lanc., which from time immemorial has gone by the name of 'Dowry,' taking its title no doubt under similar circumstances. The first instance below should have been entered John de la Heritage.

John Erytage, co. Hunts, 1273. A.
John Heritage, co. Oxf., ibid.
Richard Herytage, 1519: Reg. Univ. Oxf. i. 109.
1558. Thomas Snowden and Alice Heritage: Marriage Lic. (London), i. 18.
Ralph Heritage, of Dukenfield, 1578: Wills at Chester, i. 90.
1809. Married —Benjamin Murry and Catherine Herritage: St. Geo. Han. Sq. ii. 409.
London, 8; Oxford, 4; New York, 1; Philadelphia, 20.

Herlwin, Hurlin, Hurling.—Bapt. 'the son of Herlwin.' All the early terminatives in -win became -in and -ing; v. Godwin and Urlwin.

Herlewin or Harlewin, Abbas de Becco, co. Linc., 1273. A.
Thomas Herlewin, co. Oxf., ibid.
Henry Herlewine, co. Kent, ibid.
Herlewin (without surname), co. Norf., ibid.
Herlewin de Raundes, co. Northampt., 20 Edw. I. R.
London, 0, 1, 0; Boston (U.S.), 0, 1, 1.

Herman, Hermon. — Bapt. 'the son of Herman'; v. Harman.

Hermit.—Occup. 'the hermit'; v. Armit.

William Hermyte, C. R., 8 Edw. III.

Hermitage. — Local, 'at the hermitage,' from residence at a place so called; v. Armitage.

1633. Bapt. — Isaack, s. Henry Hermitage: St. Jas. Clerkenwell, i. 220.
1802. Married — Richard Farington and Eliz. Hermitage: St. Geo. Han. Sq. ii. 272.
London, 3; Boston (U.S.), 2.

Hern, Herne; v. Hearn and Heron.

Hernshaw, Earnshaw, Hearnshaw, Ernshaw. — (1) Nick. 'the hernshaw,' a young heron. Heronsew is still used in co. Cumberland in the same sense. (2) Local, 'at the heronshaw,' a heronry, from residence beside the same. Cotgrave has O.F. haironniere, 'a heron's neast, or ayrie; a herneshaw, or shaw of wood wherein herons breed' (v. heronshaw, Skeat). Probably Henshaw (q.v.) is a variant of Hernshaw.

Johannes Hernchagh, 1379: P. T. Yorks. p. 174.
1631. Laurence Earnshaw, of Hollingworth: Wills at Chester (1621-50), p. 70.
1800. Married — Thomas Dunkle and Eliz. Earnshaw: St. Geo. Han. Sq. ii. 215.
Manchester, 0, 5, 1, 1; London, 0, 4, 0, 0; West Riding (Yorks) Court Dir., 1, 16, 3, 0.

Heron, Herron.—Nick. 'the heron'; cf. Crane, Stork, Hawk, &c. For early examples, v. Hearn (2).

Ricardus Heron, 1379: P. T. Yorks. p. 82.
Emma Herun, 1379: ibid.
Agnes Herun, 1379: ibid. p. 88.
1546. Nicholas Heron and Alice Bassett: Marriage Lic. (London), i. 10.
1695. Edward Heron and Mary Gee: ibid. ii. 316.
London, 5, 1; New York, 8, 1.

Herrewyn.—Bapt. 'the son of Helwin.' A manifest corruption; v. Herlwin.

John Herelwyn, co. Bucks, 1273. A.
London, 1.

Herring, Hering, Herrin.—Bapt. 'the son of Haring' (Yonge, ii. 406). There can be no doubt about the parentage of our Herrings. It will be observed that the prefix le is never found in these early records, suggesting that the surname is not (at least in the majority of cases) a nickname taken from the fish. They are generally found inland also. It is quite certain, too, from such local names as Harrington, Herrington, Herringham, Herringshaw, Herringswell, and Herringstone, that the personal title was of very early use. It may be regarded that most of our Herrings are of fontal origin.

John Hareng, co. Bedf., 1273. A.
Alan Haring, co. Camb., ibid.
Nigel Haring, co. Camb., ibid.
Robert Herin, co. Camb., ibid.
Roger Hering, co. Oxf., ibid.
Reymund Heryng, 1307. M.
Alice Haryng, C. R., 32 Hen. III.
1729. Married — John Herring and Mary Bennet: St. Geo. Han. Sq. i. 6.
1748. — William Hering and Sarah Russell : ibid. p. 40.
London, 22, 3, 0; Philadelphia, 33, 22, 3.

Herringbreeder.—Occup.'the herring-breeder.' Oysters we know may run short. A similar fear seems to have originated this name. It is a curious sobriquet.

Symon Haryngbredere, London, 1273. A.

Herringham.—Local, 'of Herringham.' I cannot find the spot. It means the ham or homestead of Herring, the possessor; v. Herring, Herringshaw, &c.

MDB. (Notts), 1.

Herringshaw. — Local, 'of Herringshaw,' some spot in co. Lincoln. The derivation is obvious, the shaw or wood that belonged to Haring or Herring, the tenant; v. Herring.

MDB. (co. Lincoln), 5.

Herrington.—Local, 'of Herrington,' literally 'the town of Haring,' the first settler; v. Herring and Harrington. Herrington is a double township in the parish of Houghton-le-Spring, co. Durham.

London, 1 ; Philadelphia, 3.

Hersee, Hersey, Hearsey.—Local, 'de Herci.' I cannot find the place ; probably in Normandy. Mr. Lower says, 'Malveysin de Hercy was Constable of the honour of Tykhill, co. York, temp. Hen. III': Patr. Brit. p. 155.

Richard de Hercy, co. Norf., 1273. A.
Robert Herci, co. Norf., ibid.
John de Hercy, cos. Warw. and Leic., Hen. III-Edw. I. K.
Hugh de Hercy, co. Notts, 20 Edw. I. R.
1597-8. John Hercy or Hersey, co. Middlesex : Reg. Univ. Oxf. pt. ii. p. 225.
1600. Married—Clement Hearsey and Eliz. Gyatt: St. Jas. Clerkenwell, iii. 24.

1765. Married — Thomas Hersey and Jane Jackson : St. Geo. Han. Sq. i. 139.
London, 3, 3, 2 ; Philadelphia, o, 1, o ; Boston (U.S.), 2, 67, 3.

Heseltine. — Local, 'at the hazel-dean' ; v. Hasleden.

London, 4.

Hesket, Heskett.—(1) Local, 'of Hesketh.' The surname is frequently spelt Hesket ; v. Hesketh.

'He and his wife gave their inheritance to Sir William Heskayte ': Baines' Lanc. ii. 115.

In the Preston Guild Rolls the name is spelt variously Hesketh and Heskett (v. Index, p. 225). (2) Local, 'of Heskett,' a parish in co. Cumberland. This, of course, is the parent of the Cumberland Heskets and Hesketts.

MDB. (co. Cumberland), 2, 4.

Hesketh.—Local, 'of Hesketh,' a parish once attached to the parish of Croston, co. Lanc.

William de Eskeyth, co. Lanc., 20 Edw. I. R.
1415. Nicholas de Hesketh : Preston Guild Rolls, p. 8.
— Thomas fil. Nich. Hesketh : ibid. p. 10.
1544. Thomas Hesketh and Alice Holcroft : Marriage Lic. (Faculty Office), p. 3.
1592. Thomas Hesketh, of Bickerstaff : Wills at Chester (1545-1620), p. 90.
London, 4 ; Manchester, 9 ; MDB. (co. Chester), 9 ; Philadelphia, 3.

Heskin.—Local, 'of Heskin,' a township in the parish of Eccleston, near Chorley, co. Lanc. Wrightington is also a township in the same parish.

1584. Married — John Heskyn and Margery Hollys : St. Jas. Clerkenwell, iii. 10.
Hugh Heskin, of Heskin, 1618 : Wills at Chester (1545-1620), p. 90.
Roger Heskin, of Wrightington, 1582 : ibid.
William Heskyne, of Coppull, *butcher*, 1646 : ibid. (1621-50), p. 105.
Alice Walell, of Heskyn, *widow*, 1638 : ibid. p. 225.
Liverpool, 1 ; Preston, 1.

Heslop.—Local ; v. Haslop.

Hesmondhalgh. — Local, ' of Hesmondhalgh,' some spot in or near Ribchester, co. Lanc. The derivation is simple — the halgh of Esmond or Osmond, the first settler.

For meaning of suffix, v. Halgh and Haugh, and cf. Greenhalgh, Ridehalgh, or Featherstonhaugh.

John Hesmondhalgh, of Clayton-le-dale, 1608 : Wills at Chester (1545-1620), p. 90.
MDB. (co. Lanc.), 1 ; Ribchester, 5.

Hessey.—Local, 'of Hessay,' a village and township in the parish of Moor Monkton, co. York.

John de Hesey, co. Camb., 1273. A.
Henry Hesee, co. Salop, ibid.
Sewal de Hessay, 21-2 Edw. I : Freemen of York (Surt. Soc.), i. 5.
Willelmus de Hessay, 1379: P. T. Yorks. p. 149.
Robertus de Hessay, 1379 : ibid.
Nicholaus de Hessay, of Hessay, 1379 : ibid. p. 294.
London, 1 ; Crockford, 2 ; West Rid. Court Dir., 3.

Hester, Easter.—Local, ' of the Ester ' or ' Estre.' Not from Hester or Esther, a scriptural name which I have not yet met with at the requisite period. 'Estre, court, street, town (A.N.).

" So long he lived in that estre,
That for hys name he hight Tuncestre."

Estres, the inward parts of a building, chambers, walks, passages in a garden (A.N.); v. Will. and Werw. p. 64 ' (Halliwell).

'The estres of the grisly place.'
Chaucer, C.T. 1973.
Robert de le Estre, co. Suff., 1273. A.
Robert del Ester, co. Camb., ibid.
William del Estre, co. Devon, Hen. III-Edw. I. K.

Hester and Easter seem to be modern imitative garbs of the word.

London, 6, 1 ; Boston (U.S.), 5, 3.

Hetherington. — Local, ' of Hetherington.'

MDB. (co. Cumberland), 35 ; London, 7 ; Philadelphia, 24.

Hethorn ; v. Hawthorn, of which it is a variant.

MDB. (co. Chester), 1.

Hew, Hews, Hewes, Hewson, Hewison.—Bapt. 'the son of Hugh '; M.E. Hew ; v. Hugh. 'Howe, Hewe, propyr name, *Hugo*': Prompt. Parv.

Hew Herison, co. Norf. FF.
John Hewissone, temp. Eliz. Z.
Hewe Hare, ibid.
Hewe Whithede, ibid.
'Item, paid to Hewe Watson, for a

bawdrike to the first belle, 10d.' : Ludlow, Churchwardens' Accounts, Camden Soc.
Johannes Hueson, 1379: P. T. Yorks, p. 148.
London, 0, 1, 4, 5, 0 ; York (Hewison), 3.

Heward.—(1) Bapt., and (2) Offic. ; v. Howard and Harward.
London, 2 ; Sheffield, 3.

Hewartson, Hewertson.— Bapt. 'the son of Hugh.' No doubt a corruption of the great Yorkshire surname Hewetson ; v. Hewett. It would cross into Furness and Cumberland, where it is still well known. I do not think it has any connexion with the Scotch Ewart.
1800. Jennet Hewartson: Annals of Cartmel, p. 304.
Lancaster, 0, 1.

Hewby.—Local ; v. Hubie.

Hewer.—Occup. 'the hewer'; cf. Woodhewer, Stonehewer, Fleshhewer, Blockhewer, 'hewers of wood' (Auth. Version). As a general term Hewer will no doubt represent either a wood or stone cutter.
Ralph le Heuer. B.
Benedict le Huwere, co. Camb., 1273. A.
Walter le Howere, co. Kent, ibid.
London, 4 ; MDB. (co. Hereford), 2.

Hewett, Hewetson, Hewitson, Hewitt.—Bapt. 'the son of Hugh' ; M.E. Hugh, How, and Hew, dim. Hughet and Hewet ; v. Hew ; cf. Howett, Howitt, and Howetson.
Robert Hughet, 1313. M.
Gilbert Huet, co. Soms., 1 Edw. III : Kirby's Quest, p. 228.
W—— Hughet, co. Soms., 1 Edw. III : ibid. p. 279.
Agnes Huet-wyf, 1379: P. T. Yorks. p. 220.
Ricardus Huetson, 1379: ibid. p. 199.
Willelmus Howetson, 1379: ibid. p. 117.
John Hewette. H.
John Huetson, co. York. W. 12.
William Heuetson, co. York. W. 8.
Elizabeth Hewetson, temp. Eliz. Z.
1520-1. Thomas Hughet and Margaret Harford : Marriage Lic. (London), i. 1.
'John Hewit, alias Huet, of Newcastle, goldsmith, by his will, dated Sept. 9, 1738, bequeathed,' &c. : Brand's Hist. of Newcastle-upon-Tyne, i. 275.
London, 25, 9, 1, 51.

Hewgill.—Local ; v. Hugill.

Hewish.—Local ; v. Huish.

Hewison.—Bapt. ; v. Hew.

Hewlett, Hewlitt, Hughlett.—Bapt. 'the son of Hugh' ; M.E. Hew and Hugh, double dim. Hugh-el-lot or Hew-el-ot ; cf. such dictionary words as *streamlet* or *partlet*, and such directory names as Bartlett or Hamlet. v. Hew.
William Huwelot, co. Hunts, 1273. A.
Walter Huwelot, co. Oxf., ibid.
Walter Hughelot, co. Kent, ibid.
John Huelot, co. Camb., ibid.
William Hughlot, 1313. M.
Thomas Hughelot, co. Soms., 1 Edw. III : Kirby's Quest, p. 220.
Johannes Hughlot, 1379 : P. T. Yorks. p. 125.
1692. Bapt. — Daniell, s. Thomas Hewlett : St. Jas. Clerkenwell, i. 347.
London, 13, 1, 0 ; New York, 11, 0, 0 ; Philadelphia, 7, 0, 3.

Hewling, Hewlings, Hughlings.—Bapt. 'the son of Hugh' ; M.E. Hew or Hugh, dim. Hewlin or Hugelin, and with excrescent g Hewling ; cf. Jennings ; v. Hew. An interesting story is told of Hugolin, chamberlain to Edward the Confessor, by the late Dean Stanley in his Westminster Abbey, p. 15. For American forms, v. Hullin.
Hueline de Uggeshale, co. Norf., temp. William II : FF. i. 117.
Hugelin, alias Huelin Sampe, co. Linc., 1273. A.
Nicholas fil. Hugline, co. Linc., ibid.
Henry Hulin, co. Norf., ibid.
Warin Huline, co. Camb., ibid.
Alexander fil. Hugelin, co. Camb., ibid.
Simon Huweline, co. Camb., ibid.
William Huweline, co. Camb., ibid.
Hugelina Coyne : Patent Roll, 2 Hen. IV. pt. ii.
Johannes Huelyn, 1379 : P. T. Yorks. p. 140.
Alanus Hoghlyn, 1379 : ibid. p. 38.
1627. Bapt.—Marie, d. Edward Huelin: St. Dionis Backchurch, p. 101.
1778. Married—John Whitt and Eliz. Hewling : St. Geo. Han. Sq. i. 292.
London, 0, 2, 0 ; West Rid. Court Dir., 0, 0, 1.

Heworth.—Local ; v. Haworth.

Hewson.—Bapt. ; v. Hew.

Hewster, Hustter.—Occup. 'the hewster,' i.e. Hewer (q.v.), with fem. suffix -ster; cf. Slaster, Walkster, Webster, &c. In the Chester Play the procession was joined by the Company of the Hewsters.
Richard le Hewster, sheriff of Cheshire, 1382 : Ormerod's Cheshire, i. 302.
1545. Buried—Richard Houster : St. Peter, Cornhill, i. 107.

1561. William Hewster, citizen of Oxford : Reg. Univ. Oxf. vol. ii. pt. i. p. 299.
1569-70. Married—Nycholas Bottome and Mary Hewistere : St. Dionis Backchurch, p. 6.
1674. Bapt.—John, s. John Hewster : St. Thomas the Apostle (London), p. 66.
MDB. (co. Durham), 0, 1.

Hext. — Nick. 'the highest' ; A.S. hext, 'highest.'
'The erchebischop of Canturberi, In Engelelonde that is hext.'
Halliwell.
Probably, as a surname, the tallest man in the particular community in which he dwelt.
Nicholas Exte, co. Soms., 1 Edw. III : Kirby's Quest, p. 186.
Walter Hexte, co. Soms., 1 Edw. III : ibid.
1614. Ames Hext : Reg. Univ. Oxf. vol. ii. pt. ii. p. 333.
1626. Thomas Burrough and Anne Hext, of Little Bursted, co. Essex : Marriage Lic. (London), ii. 171.
MDB. (co. Cornwall), 4.

Hextall.—?
MDB. (co. Leic.), 3 ; London, 1.

Hexter.—? Local, 'of Exeter' (?). I cannot suggest any other origin, and Mr. Lower has preceded me in the suggestion. There would be nothing extraordinary in this derivation, as the aspirate comes and goes at pleasure in English surnames, as this dictionary fully proves. It would be strange if Exeter was not represented in our directories. It can only be represented by Hexter, as Exeter does not exist as a surname.
John de Excestre, co. Wilts, 1273. A.
1797. Married — James Hexter and Martha Boyden : St. Geo. Han. Sq. ii. 171.
The strongest proof of the above derivation is that Hexter is a familiar Devonshire surname.
Exeter, 5 ; London, 2 ; New York, 5.

Hey, Heys, Heyes.—Local, 'at the hey,' a hedge or enclosure, from residence thereby ; v. Hay.
William de la Heye, co. Camb., 1273. A.
Simon atte Heye, co. Oxf., ibid.
Willelmus del Heye, 1379 : P. T. Yorks. p. 28.
Ricardus del Hey, 1379 : ibid. p. 285.
Henry Hey and Eliz. Ellsworth, 1598 : Marriage Lic. (London), i. 252.

John Hey, *joyner*, and Eliz. Burfeild: Marriage Lic. (London), ii. 28. Manchester, 2, 6, 1 ; West Rid. Court Dir., 13, 0, 0 ; New York, 4, 0, 0.

Heybourn, Heybourne, Heyburn.—Local, 'of Heybourn,' the streamlet that flowed by the hedge. Mr. Lower, writing on Hepburn, says, 'From the lands of Hebburne, Hayborne, or Hepburne, co. Durham, near the mouth of the Tyne.' But other spots would also bear the name; v. Hey and Burn.

MDB. (co. Bucks), 1, 1, 0; New York, 1, 0, 3.

Heycock; v. Hedgcock.

Heydon; v. Haydon.

Heyen.—Local, 'at the heyen,' i.e. hedges, from residence thereby. This term is evidently the plural of *hey*, a hedge, an enclosure ; cf. *alren* for elders (v. Alder). Possibly some of our Hayns and Haynes are so derived.

William atte Heyene, co. Soms., 1 Edw. III : Kirby's Quest, p. 140.

Heyer.—Nick. 'thè heir'; v. Eyre and Ayre. The American directory instances, by the Christian names prefixed, seem in most cases to be of German parentage.

Richard le Heyer, co. Glouc., 1273. A. John le Heyer, co. Oxf., ibid. London, 2 ; New York, 7.

Heygate, Heygatt. — Local, 'at the hey-gate,' from residence thereby ; v. Hey and Gate.

MDB. (co. Derby), 2, 0; (co. Hert.), 0, 1.

Heyhoe.—Local.

MDB. (co. Norfolk), 3.

Heylin, Heylyn, Hayling, Haylings. — Bapt. 'the son of Heilin.' Possibly a variant of Aylwin, q.v. The aspirate need give no trouble, as this dictionary fully demonstrates. Of course the *g* in Hayling and Haylings is excrescent ; cf. Jennings.

Philip fil. Heilin, co. Salop, 1273. A. Robert fil. Heilin, co. Salop, ibid. B'ucha uxor Heilini, co. Salop, ibid. 1544. Buried—Anne Heylyn : St. Peter, Cornhill, i. 107. 1628. Thomas Haylin and Susan Wilkinson : Marriage Lic. (London), ii. 152. 1678. Married — Edward Hylin and Mary Dun : St. Michael, Cornhill, p. 41. London, 1, 1, 1, 1.

Heyman; v. Hayman.

Heysham, Haysom.—Local, 'of Heysham,' a parish on the coast of Morecambe Bay, co. Lanc. (Hessam in Domesday).

'A branch of the Hessams, or Heyshams, retained the local appellation long after the family had ceased to have any connexion with the parish (Heysham). William and Robert Heysham were born in Lancaster, and, going to London, became eminent merchants there, and both served in several parliaments in the reigns of Queen Anne and George I ': Baines' Lanc. ii. 593.

London, 1, 0 ; Crockford, 0, 1 ; MDB. (co. Cumberland), 4, 0; Philadelphia, 1, 0.

Heywood, Haywood.—Local, 'of Heywood,' a town in the old parish of Bury, South Lancashire.

'The estate of Heywood was granted by Sir Adam de Bury to Peter de Heywood, who was living in 4 Edw. I ': Baines' Lanc. i. 525.

Adam de Hauewode, C. R., 42 Hen. III. Ricardus de Heywode, 1379 : P. T. Yorks. p. 19. Dorothy Heywood, of Heywood, *spinster*, 1607: Wills at Chester (1545-1620), p. 92. Richard Heywood, of Hill House, Rochdale, 1590 : ibid. Manchester, 37, 3 ; London, 10, 14 ; New York, 11, 4.

Hiam.—Local, 'of Higham,' q.v. Also v. Heigham.

London, 5 ; MDB. (co. Glouc.), 3.

Hiatt; v. Hyett.

Hibbard, Hibbart, Hibberd, Hibbert, Hibbit, Hibbitt, Hibbett, Hibbits, Hibbitts, Hibberson.—(1) Bapt. 'the son of Herbert' or 'Hubert'; cf. Hobart, Hubert, Hebard. Doubtless in some cases all the forms in Hibbard are thus described, although the change from *e* and *u* to *i* is abrupt. (2) Bapt. 'the son of Isabella,' from nick. Ibb, and dim. Ibbet ; v. Ibbett and Ibbetson. The enormous popularity of Isabella in Yorkshire gave us a ring of changes upon it in the North of England, and amongst others (with an aspirate) Hibbot and Hebot. These gradually assimilated themselves to the surnominal forms rung upon Herbert ; cf. Hibberson with Ibberson, Hibbitt with Ibbitt, Hibbit with Ibbit, Hibbett with Ibbett, q.v.; also cf. Ibberson and Hibbard. I think the comparison is

conclusive. At the same period aspirates were indifferently used ; cf. Hoddy for Oddy, Hemmens for Emmens (v. Hemans), &c. That the aspirate was used for nicks. of Isabella is proved by such entries as :

Johannes Frere, et Hibbot uxor ejus, 1379 : P. T. Yorks. p. 120. Johannes atte Baris, et Hebot uxor ejus, 1379 : ibid.

The usual form in this roll is Ibbot. The same person is probably alluded to in the following first two entries :

1580. Thomas Hibbott, co. Worc., Bras. Coll. : Reg. Univ. Oxf. ii. 94. 1584. Thomas Hibbotts, Bras. Coll. : ibid. iii. 120. 1591. James Hibbert, *barbitonser*, and Mary Heydon : Marriage Lic. (London), i. 193. 1625. Richard Hibberd and Ursula Wells : ibid. ii. 157. 1665. Nathaniel Hibbert, of Werneth, *husbandman* : Wills at Chester (1660-80), p. 130. 1678. Richard Hibbott, of Alpram : ibid. 1770. Married — Samuel Sprang and Mary Hibbet : St. Geo. Han. Sq. i. 194. 1786. — Thomas Hibbard and Mary Parker : ibid. p. 391. 1794. — John Scott and Mary Hibbarts : ibid. ii. 163.

This, as in Hibbotts supra, is the patronymic *s*, as in Jones, Williams. Watkins, &c. Hence the American Hibbits or Hibbitts.

1808. Married — Richard Darvin and Diana Hibbart : ibid. p. 385.

It is quite clear that the two derivatives (1) and (2) are correct. It is equally clear that the representatives of both have become inextricably mixed in our modern directories.

West Riding Court Dir., 2, 0, 2, 11, 0, 0, 0, 0, 0, 1 ; York (Hibbett), 1 ; MDB. (co. Essex), Hibbitt, 1 ; London, 3, 1, 6, 6, 2, 3, 0, 0, 0, 0 ; Sheffield, 2, 0, 8, 10, 0, 0, 0, 0, 0, 1 ; Philadelphia, 7, 0, 10, 6, 0, 0, 0, 0, 2, 1.

Hibberdine.—Bapt. ; v. Heberden.

London, 1.

Hibbert; v. Hibbard.

Hibbins.—Bapt. 'the son of Hubert,' popularly Hibbert, from nick. Hibb, dim. Hibbin, patr. Hibbins ; v. Hubert.

1560. Buried — Thomas Hebins : St. Mary Aldermary (London), p. 133. 1573. Married — Peter Hibbins, *goldsmith*, and Margret Overton : ibid. p. 5.

1685. Henry Hibbins and Lucretia Barrow : Marriage Lic. (Canterbury), p. 179.
1744. Married — James Hendrie and Eliz. Hibbins : St. Geo. Han. Sq. i. 32. London, 1.

Hibbitt(s ; v. Hibbard.

Hibbs, Hibson.—(1) Bapt.' the son of Isabella,' from nick. Ibb, with an aspirate ; cf. Ibeson (West Riding Court Dir.) ; v. Hibbard (2), where the subject is discussed. (2) Bapt. 'the son of Hubert,' popularly Hibbert, whence the nick. Hibb, and patr. Hibbs or Hibson.

John Hibson, co. York, 1442. W. 11.
Richard Hebson, co. York, 1442. ibid.
1762. Married—Samuel Smith and Ann Hibbs : St. Geo. Han. Sq. i. 115.
London, 2, 0 ; Philadelphia, 43, 0.

Hibling.—Bapt. ' the son of Hubert,' from the nick. Hibb and dim. Hibelin, with an excrescent g ; cf. Hewling.

MDB. (co. Cambridge), 1.

Hichens, Hichisson.—Bapt. ' the son of Richard,' from the nick. Hitch ; v. Hitchen.

London, 3, 2.

Hick, Hicks, Hickes, Hickey, Hickie, Hickson.—Bapt. 'the son of Richard,' from the nick. Hick or Higg, whence Higgs, and the dims. Higgin, Higgins, and Higginsons ; v. Higgin. The pet form of Hick was Hickey. That Hick was popular is clear.

' Hikke the hackney-man
And Hugh the nedlere.'
Piers Plowman.

' Bat-que Gibbe simul, Hykke venire subent.'
Gower.

That Hick was the nick. of Richard, for a time rivalling Dick, is clearly manifest. Roger, Robert, and Richard, the then popular boys' names in R, produced three nicks. in D, viz. Dodge, Dob, and Dick. They also produced three nicks. in H, viz. Hodge, Hob, and Hick ; cf.

' Humpty-Dumpty sat on a wall,
Humpty-Dumpty had a great fall.'
Or, again :
' Hickery-Dickery-Dock,
The mouse ran up the clock ' :
where are clear reminiscences of Humphrey and Richard. Thus

useful are these old nursery rimes for etymological purposes. If it be objected that Hick is hard and Richard soft, the same objection applies to Dick, the fact being that Rickard is not an uncommon entry. Besides, Hick had a softened variant in Hitch, whence our Hichins, Hichinsons, Hitches, Hitchinsons, Hitchmoughs, Hitchins, and Hitchings ; v. Hitchen. In the after-race for popularity Dick won at a canter, and while Hick is forgotten, Dick holds his own.

Hikke de Sauteby, co. York, 1273. A.
Johanna Hickson, 1379 : P. T. Yorks. p. 119.
Henricus Hikson, 1379 : ibid. p. 244.
Willelmus Hykson, 1379 : ibid. p. 264.
Adam Hyk, 1379 : ibid. p. 154.
Robertus Hicson, 1379 : ibid. p. 222.
1656. Buried — William Hix, taylor : St. Michael, Cornhill, p. 248.

With Hix, cf. Nix, Cox, &c.

London, 2, 59, 3, 4, 2, 6.

Hickcox ; v. Hickok.

Hickford. — Local, ' of Hickford,' some spot in co. Salop. Sir Robert Atkyns, in his Ancient and Present State of Gloucestershire, says (p. 109) that ' The Higfords were of an ancient family in co. Salop, originally styled Hugford.' About the reign of James I the surname was turned into Higford : this, of course, has now become Hickford ; cf. Higg and Hick, Slagg and Slack, &c.

Edith de Hicford, co. Oxf., 1273. A.

This entry seems to prove that Hickford was a known form of the name six centuries ago.

MDB. (co. Salop), 1.

Hickin, Hickins.—Bapt. ' the son of Richard,' from the nick. Hick, and dim. Hickin, exactly corresponding to Dick and Dickin. For full history, v. Hick. Hickin is very rare, the popular variant being Higgin, q.v. Hickin, however, is more correct.

Hekyn de Wath, 1379 : P. T. Yorks. p. 70.
Alicia Hykyn, 1379 : ibid. p. 139.
1583. John Hickyns, haberdasher, and Eliz. Sheffeilde : Marriage Lic. (London), i. 120.
1666. Married — Even Tomas and Susannah Hickins : St. Jas. Clerkenwell, iii. 123.

1739. Married — Porter Hickin and Mary Horton : St. Geo. Han. Sq. i. 23.
Manchester, 1, 0 ; London, 1, 0 ; New York, 1, 0.

Hickinbotham, -bottom ; v. Higginbotham.

Hicklin, Hickling. — Local, ' of Hickling.' (1) A parish in co. Norfolk, three miles from Stalham ; (2) a parish in co. Notts, eight miles from Melton Mowbray.

Brian de Hikeling, co. Norf., 1273. A.
Thomas de Hikeling, co. Norf., ibid.
Henry de Hikelyng, co. Notts, 20 Edw. I. R.
Nicholas de Hickling, prebend of Norwich Cathedral, 1334 : FF. iv. 172.
Adam de Hickling, prebend of Norwich Cathedral, 1364 : ibid. p. 173.
1806. Married—William Hickling and Mary Vause : St. Geo. Han. Sq. ii. 345.
London, 2, 3 ; Barnsley, 0, 1 ; Philadelphia, 0, 6.

Hickman. Higman.—(1) Bapt. ' the son of Hickman'; cf. Bateman or Tiddeman. Lower says, 'The pedigree of the extinct baronet family Hickman, of Gainsborough, is traced to Robert Fitz-Hickman, lord of the manors of Bloxham and Wickham, co. Oxford, 56 Hen. III. Hence the name must have been originally a baptismal appellation.' Higman is the result of laziness in pronunciation.

Hukeman de Moricebi, 1196 : RRR. p. 80.
Walter Hikeman, co. Oxf., 1273. A.

(2) Occup. ' the servant of Hick,' q.v. ; cf. Addyman, Matthewman, Jackman, Bartleman, and Hitchman, which is but a weakened variation. For a good illustration of this, v. Hitchman.

1691. Bapt.—Eliz., d. Edward Hickman : St. Jas. Clerkenwell, i. 342.
1697. Married—Daniell Hickman and Ann Pope : St. Michael, Cornhill, p. 49.
London, 21, 1 ; Philadelphia, 61, 5.

Hickmott.—? Nick. A variant of Hitchmough (?), q.v.

1548. John Hychmoughe, or Hychmoght : Reg. Univ. Oxf. i. 215.
1564. Married—John Taylor and Jone Hyckmote : St. Michael, Cornhill, p. 9.
1567. Anthony Hickmoate and Rose Milles : Marriage Lic. (Faculty Office), p. 14.
1585. Bapt. — Fraunces, s. Edward Hickmot, sadler : St. Peter, Cornhill, i. 28.
London, 1.

Hickok, Hickcox.—Bapt. 'the son of Richard,' from the nick. Hick (q.v.), and the augmentative Hickcock; cf. Wilcock, Wilcox, Jeffcock, and Cox; v. Cocks. Of course Hickcox stands for Hickcocks, the final s being the genitive form, as in Jones, Williams, &c. For further instances, v. Hitchcock, a weakened form.

Hikoc (without surname), co. Hunts, 1273. A.
'Nicholas de Mulsewrthe and Hikoc and Ric. Curteys and Alic' Derlewele, tenant,' &c.: A. ii. 615.
1392. Hekoc del Pantre: Cal. of Wills in the Court of Husting (2).
1615. Married — Henry Maning and Eliz. Hickcocke: St. Mary Aldermary, p. 13.
1617. John Stanforth and Eliz. Hickoxe: Marriage Lic. (London), ii. 54.
1640. William Williams and Margaret Hicocke: ibid. p. 254.
1775. Married — James Edwards and Sarah Hiccock: St. Geo. Han. Sq. i. 250.
New York, 9, 0; Boston (U.S.), 1, 1.

Hicks, Hickson; v. Hick.

Hiddleston; v. Huddlestone. A variant.

MDB. (co. Cambridge), 1.

Hide; v. Hyde.

Hieatt, Hiett; v. Hyett.

Higbee, Higbie, Higby.—Local, 'of Higby.' I cannot find the spot; cf. Applebee.

1702. Married — Richard Higbey, of Bushey, co. Hertford, and Eliz. Cooke: St. Michael, Cornhill, p. 51.
London, 1, 0, 0; Philadelphia, 16, 3, 2.

Higdon.—? Bapt. 'the son of Higdon' (?). So the evidence seems to prove; but it has a very local appearance.

John Hikedun, co. Worc., 1273. A.
Higdon de Slynesby, et uxor ejûs, ad valorem militis, 1379: P. T. Yorks. p. 239.
1640. John Higdon and Joane Durden: Marriage Lic. (London), ii. 252.
1749. Married — Daniel Higden and Margaret Clifton: St. Geo. Han. Sq. i. 42.
London, 3; MDB. (co. Dorset), 1.

Higg, Higgs, Higson.—Bapt. 'the son of Richard,' from the nick. Higg, a lazy pronunciation of Hick. All the evidence required will be found under Hick and Higgin, q.v. Higson is the general variant of Hickson in South Lancashire. Higg, like Higgin, is found at an early period.

Hugh Higge, co. Lincoln, 1273. A.
Richard Higge, co. Lincoln, ibid.
1585. Elizabeth Higson, of Brereton Wills at Chester (1545-1620), p. 93.
1614. Gawen Higson, of Swinehead: ibid.
1808. Married — Daniel Higgs and Phoebe Littleford: St. Geo. Han. Sq. ii. 386.
London, 1, 31, 0; Manchester, 0, 2, 14; Philadelphia, 0, 6, 0.

Higgate.—Local, 'of Highgate'; v. Hyett.

Philadelphia, 4.

Higgin, Higgins, Higginson, Higgens, Higgons, Higgon.—Bapt. 'the son of Richard,' from the nick. Hick, which became Higg, and the dim. Hickin, which became Higgin; cf. Diggs and Dix, Wiggins and Wickins, Higginbotham and Hickinbotham, or Slagg and Slack; v. Hick for full history, and Hickin for further evidence. The parent of Higgin, and all its descendants, is indisputably Hickin, the dim. of Hick, which means that Richard is the ancestor of all. I stated in my English Surnames (1875) that Isaac was the parent, giving my reasons. But I was altogether wrong, and I take this opportunity of apologizing for what at best was only a guess. -For a brief time Hickin and Higgin ran alongside, but the lazier Higgin speedily won, and now as a surname Hickin is very rare.

Hekyn de Wath, 1379: P. T. Yorks. p. 70.
Hygyn de Bowland, 1379: ibid. p. 255.
Alan Hygginson, or Hickynsone, 1552: Reg. Univ. Oxf. i. 219.
1580. Married—John Ball, clothworker, and Sisley Higgenson: St. Mary Aldermary, p 6.
1588. Leonard Hyggyn, or Higune, of Estmotherlie: Lanc. Wills at Richmond, i. 163.
1677. George Wheeler and Grace Higgons: Marriage Lic. (Canterbury), p. 270.
London, 2, 36, 1, 4, 1, 0; Manchester, 4, 17, 5, 0, 0, 0; MDB. (co. Pembroke), Higgon, 1.

Higginbotham, Higginbottom, Hickinbotham, Hickinbottom, Hickenbotham, Higenbotam.—Local, 'of the Higginbottom,' a small spot, now, I believe, obsolete titularly, in the neighbourhood of Marple and Macclesfield, in East Cheshire.

The meaning, no doubt, is the bottom, or hollow depression in the land, where Higgin or Hickin resided; v. Higgin, Hickin, and Higg. In Mr. Earwaker's Hist. East Cheshire appear the names of John Rowbothome, John Sidebothome, and Ottiwell Heginbothome, as owners of land in 1672 (ii. 53 n.). There is no doubt this is the district where several of our most familiar surnames with suffix -bottom arose; v. Shufflebottom, Sidebottom, Longbottom, and Rowbottom; also v. Botham.

John Hyggynbothom, 1563: Reg. Prestbury Church, co. Ches., p. 11.
Nicholas Hichinbothome, of Marple, gent., 1579: Earwaker's East Cheshire, i. 18.
Alice Higginbotham, of Marple, 1595: Lanc. and Ches. Record Soc. ii. 93.
1762. Married — Joseph Higenbotom and Sarah Bacon: St. Geo. Han. Sq. i. 110.
London, 1, 3, 5, 0, 0, 0; Manchester, 10, 6, 0, 0, 0, 0; New York, 1, 1, 0, 1, 0, 1.

Higgon(s; v. Higgin.

Higgott.—Bapt. 'the son of Richard,' from the nick. Hick (commonly pronounced Higg), and dim. Higgot; cf. Emmott, Marriott, Elliot, &c.

MDB. (co. Derby), 2.

High.—Nick. 'the high,' i.e. tall, the distinguished; M.E. hey. Cf. Hext.

Robert le Heye, co. Bucks, 1273. A.
Robert le Hey, 1301. M.
1567-8. Robert Hye and Ellen Maller: Marriage Lic. (London), i. 38.
1585. William Sharpe and Cecily Highe, widow: ibid. p. 139.
1804. Married—Peter High and Jane Loxley: St. Geo. Han. Sq. ii. 299.
London, 3; Philadelphia, 11.

Higham. — Local, 'of the Hegham,' i.e. the enclosed dwelling, a spot in East Cheshire that gave rise to a surname now very familiar to the directories of the surrounding district. Also parishes in the diocs. of Norwich, Peterborough, and Rochester, which no doubt have contributed to the list in South England; v. Hey and Ham, also cf. Heigham.

Robertus de Hegham, 1379: P. T. Yorks. p. 24.

John del Heghome, 1401, co. Ches.: East Ches. i. 50 *n.*
John de Hegheme, 1408 : ibid. i. 114.
John Higham, 1445 : ibid. ii. 17.
Rauf Hegham, 1481 : ibid. i. 159.
William Higham, 1648 : ibid. ii. 24.
Manchester, 17 ; London, 9.

Highland, Highlands, Hyland, Hiland.—Local ; v. Hedglands ; cf. Higham.

Philadelphia (Hiland), 4 ; New York, 4, 1, 0, 0.

Highman.—Local, ' of Highnam,' a hamlet in the parish of Churcham, co. Glouc. Of course the surname became Highman; cf. Swetman, Deadman, Putman, for Swetenham, Debenham, Putenham.

MDB. (co. Glouc.), 1.

Highmoor.—Local, ' at the high moor,' from residence thereon.

1804. Married—Joseph Jellicoe and Charlotte Leigh ; witness Anthony Highmore : St. Geo. Han. Sq. ii. 302.
MDB. (co. Cumberland), 2.

Highway; v. Heighway.

Highwood.—Local.

MDB. (co. Kent), 2 ; London, 2.

Higman.—(1) Bapt ' the son of Hickman.' q.v. (2) Occup. ' the servant of Hick' ; v. Hickman (2) ; cf. Higg for Hick, or Higgin for Hickin.

London, 1 ; MDB. (co. Cornwall), 1.

Hignett.—Bapt. ' the son of Richard,' from nick. Higg, double dim. Higg-in-et; cf. Col-in-et, Rob-in-et. Dob-in-et, &c. Found in cos. Cheshire and Lanc. The single diminutives were extremely popular in the same district ; v. Higgin.

Ralph Hignett, 1559 : Wills at Chester, ii. 93.
Hugh Hignett, of Ashton, 1619 : ibid.
MDB. (co. Chester), 8 ; Liverpool, 9.

Higson.—Bapt. ; v. Higg.

Hilbert.—Bapt. ' the son of Ilbert,' q.v. The aspirate is commonly found in these early personal names; cf. Hoddy, Hanniball, Hosken, &c.

MDB. (co. Lincoln), 1 ; Philadelphia, 7.

Hild.—Bapt. ' the son of Hilda ' (v. Yonge, ii. 234-7). Found in such compounds as Hildebrand, Hildebert, Hildeman (v. Hillmer), Hildegar (v. Hilger), and in such

place-names as Hildesley (v. Hildersley) or Hillersdon, once Hildesdon or Hilderston, all denoting tenancy by Hild or Hilda.

Thomas fil. Hillde, co. Linc., 1273. A.
Walter Hilde, co. Oxf., ibid.
London, 1.

Hildebrand, Hildebrandt.—Bapt. ' the son of Hildebrand.' A fairly familiar English fontal name in the surname period ; v. Hild.

(Dominus) Hildebrandus, co. Camb., 1273. A.
Gilbert Hildbrond, co. Soms., 1 Edw. III : Kirby's Quest, p. 273.
Gregory Hildebrand, co. Linc., ibid.
MDB. (co. Wilts), 1, 0 ; London, 1, 1.

Hilder, Helder.—(1) Nick. ' the hilder,' i. e. the elder; cf. Senior, Younger, &c. ' Hilder, the elder, co. Norf.' (Halliwell).' The aspirate is a matter of no moment as the Hundred Rolls (1273) put an initial *h* just as the registrar pleased. (2) But Mr. Lower, after quoting Halliwell, adds, ' But the Supp. to Aelfric's Vocab. says, " *hyldere*, lictor, vel vergifer," i. e. an usher or macebearer (Wright's Vocab. p 60).'

London, 7, 0 ; MDB. (co. Kent), 4, 0 ; Philadelphia, 0, 1.

Hildersley.—Local, ' of Hildersley.' ' Hildersley, a tithing in co. Glouc.' (Lower).

—— de Hyldest, co. Glouc., 1273. A.

The personal name is not given, either because the page is undecipherable or torn. Thus Hildersley, more correctly Hildesley, means ' the meadow of Hilde ' ; v. Hild.

London, 6.

Hilditch, Hildick.—Local, ' of the hill-dike ' ; v. Dyke, and cf. Cobbledick for Cobbledike. Hilditch is a variant of Hildike, as ditch is of dike. The spot so named would seem to be on the border-land between Cheshire and Staffordshire.

1590. Randle Hilditch, of Alsager : Wills at Chester (1545-1620) p. 93.
1634. Alice Hilditch. of Battesley, co. Chester : ibid. (1621-50), p. 107.
1749. Married—Daniel Baker and Mary Hildick : St. Mary Aldermary, p. 52.
1786. — Thomas Hilditch and Ellinor Williams: St. Geo. Han. Sq. i. 387.

London, 4, 0 ; MDB. (co. Essex), 1, 0 ; (co. Chester), 2, 0 ; (co. Stafford), 2, 2 ; New York, 0, 1.

Hildred, Hildreth. — Bapt. ' the son of Hildred ' (v. Yonge. ii. 237). Another compound of Hild, q.v.

1784. Married — Alex. Patterson and Mary Hilldrad : St. Geo. Han. Sq. i. 307.
1789. — John Woodcock and Eliz. Hildreth : ibid. ii. 25.
London, 0, 3 ; MDB. (co. Lincoln), 9, 0.

Hildsmith.—Occup. Probably a hiltsmith, one who made sword-hilts.

William Hyldsmyth, co. Camb., 1273. A.

Hildyard; v. Hillyard.

Hiles. — Local, ' at the hill,' from residence thereon, genitive Hiles ; cf. Hills for Hill. Thus also Styles, Holmes, Brooks, Mills, &c.

Hugh atte Hile, co. Soms., 1 Edw. III : Kirby's Quest, p. 216.
Robert atte Hyle, co. Soms., 1 Edw. III : ibid.
Felicia atte Hile, co. Soms., 1 Edw. III : ibid.
Manchester Court Dir., 3 ; Oxford, 4 ; Philadelphia, 8.

Hilger, Hilgers.—Bapt. ' the son of Hildegar,' one of the many compounds of Hild, q.v. (v. Yonge, ii. 235).

Julian Hildegar, co. Hunts, 1273. A.
William Hildegar, co. Hunts, ibid.
Emma Hilgar, co. Oxf., ibid.
Philadelphia, 1, 1.

Hilhouse, Hillhouse.—Local, ' at the hill-house,' i.e. the house on the hill ; cf. Moorhouse, Fieldhouse. With Hellus (infra), cf. Loftus for Lofthouse, or Malthus for Malthouse ; v. Backhouse.

Nicholas del Hellus, co. Bucks, 1273. A.
1597-8. Richard Pallmer, *husbandman*, and Grace Hellhouse, widow of Robert Hellhouse, *carpenter*, of Purley, co. Essex : Marriage Lic. (London), i. 248.
1795. Married —Thomas Dykes and Ann Hillhouse : St. Geo. Han. Sq. ii. 137.
London, 4, 0 ; MDB. (co. Suffolk), 0, 1 ; New York, 0, 3 ; Philadelphia, 0, 1.

Hill.—Local, ' at the hill,' from residence thereon. There is no necessity to explain why our directories teem with Hills. As every village required its smith, and thus made Smith our great national occupative surname, so almost every small district had its rising ground called ' the hill,' the resident thereon taking his surname from it.

Alan del Hil, co. Essex, 1273. A.
Walter de la Hille, co. Devon, ibid.
Henry de la Hille, co. Devon, Hen. III-
Edw. I. K.
Thomas del Hill, 1379: P. T. Yorks.
p. 202.
Robertus del Hill', *laborer*, 1379: ibid.
p. 219.
1580. Bapt. — Thomas, s. Rycharde
Hill: St. Jas. Clerkenwell, i. 12.
London, 277; New York, 201.

Hillam.—Local, ' of Hillam,' a
township in the parish of Monk
Fryston, W. Rid. Yorks.

1745. Married — John Hillam and
Eleanor Rolt : St. Geo. Han. Sq. i. 35.
1786. — Anthony Hillam, of Great
Billing, co. Northampt., and Susannah
Rudkin : ibid. i. 387.
Hull, 2.

Hillard; v. Hillyard.

Hillary, Hillery.—Bapt. 'the
son of Hilary,' made popular by St.
Hilary of Poitiers ; Fr. S. Hilaire.
Familiarized to us by Hilary Term,
from 13th (Camb.) and 14th (Oxf.)
Jan. to Friday and Saturday before
Palm Sunday.   St. Helier, Jersey,
represents another saint.

Hillary Constabularius, co. York,
1273. A.
Hillaria la Waleyse, co. Hunts, ibid.
Illaria Purcel. T.
John Hyllary, co. Soms., 1 Edw. III :
Kirby's Quest, p. 194.
Hillary le Clerkes, co. Soms., 1 Edw.
III : ibid. p. 208.

As a font-name common to the
close of the 16th century.

Johannes Hillary, 1379: P. T. Yorks. p. 13.
1547. Married — Hillary Finch and
Jane Whyte : St. Dionis Backchurch
(London).
1593. Bapt.—Hillary, sonne of Hillary
Turner, *draper* : St. Peter, Cornhill.
1781. Married — George Hillary and
Isabella Battin : St. Geo. Han. Sq. i. 321.
London, 1, 2 ; New York, 0, 4.

Hiller.—(1) Occup. 'the hiller'
or 'hillyer,' a roofer, a tiler, a
slater (v. Hillier) ; cf. *lawer* and
lawyer, *sawer* and *sawyer*, *bower*
and *bowyer*.   A Yorkshire form.
The American directories contain
a much larger number of Hillers
than the English, but most of them
are of German extraction.   Their
derivation is not within the compass of my work.   (2) Bapt. ' the
son of Hillary,' from a nick. Hillar.

Hillar Howell, co. Soms., 1 Edw. III :
Kirby's Quest, p. 233.
Alicia Hillour, 1379 : P. T. Yorks. p. 161.

Cf. Harpour, Drapour, Taylour,
in the same register for Harper,
Draper, Taylor.

1548. John Hyller and Katherine Hall :
Marriage Lic. (Faculty Office), p. 13.
1601. Maurice Hiller, co. Wilts : Reg.
Univ. Oxf. ii. 250.
1661. Joseph Hiller, of Watford, Herts,
yeoman, and Alice Phelps: Marriage
Lic. (London), ii. 285.
1672. Bapt. — Dorothy, d. William
Hiller : St. Jas. Clerkenwell, i. 253.
Sheffield, 5 ; West Rid. Court Dir., 2 ;
London, 4 ; New York, 15.

**Hillersdon, Hillsden, Hel-
lersden.**—Local, ' of Hillesden,'
a parish four miles from Buckingham, co. Bucks; v. Hillson for
a variant.

Reginald de Hildesdon, co. Oxf.,
1273. A.
Robert de Hildisdon, co. Bucks, ibid.
1619. Richard Hillersdon, co. Devon
(Ex. Coll.) : Reg. Univ. Oxf. pt. ii. p. 379.
1725. Married — Dennis Farrer and
Eliz. Hillersdon : St. Michael, Cornhill,
p. 63.
MDB. (co. Bucks), 1, 1, 0 ; (co. Essex),
0, 0, 1.

Hillhouse; v. Hilhouse.

**Hillier, Hillyer, Hellier,
Hellyer, Helliar, Hellyar,
Helyear.**—Occup. 'the hellier,'
i.e. a roofer, a tiler, a thatcher, a
slater, &c.   Of the Tartars Sir John
Maundeville says, 'The helyngt̄ of
their houses, and . . . the dores
ben alle of wode.'   'Also, that non
Tylers called hillyers of the cite . . .
compelle ne charge ne make no
tyler straunger . . . to serve at his
rule and assignement,' &c.   (The
Ordinances of Worcester, English
Gilds, p. 398.)

Robert le Heliere, co. Kent, 1273. A.
Michael le Helier, co. Soms., 1 Edw.
III : Kirby's Quest, p. 103.
William le Heliere, co. Soms., 1 Edw.
III : ibid. p. 121.
Robert le Hillier, C. R., 21 Edw. III.
pt. ii.
Thomas Hellier, temp. Eliz. Z.
London, 17, 4, 5, 2, 0, 0, 0 ; MDB. (co.
Dorset), 0, 0, 2, 6, 2, 1, 2.

Hillman, Hilman. — Local,
' the hillman,' one who dwelt on the
hill; cf. Bridgman, Heathman, &c. ;
v. Hill and Hull (2).   Nevertheless we must not forget that Hillman
may stand in some cases for Hilde-
mand or Hildemund, and thus be
of baptismal origin.

William Huleman, co. Hunts, 1273. A.
William Heleman, co. Devon, ibid.
1586-7. Edmund Herenden and Ellen
Hullman : Marriage Lic. (London), i. 159.
London, 8, 0 ;   MDB. (co. Hereford),
0, 1 ; (co. Sussex), 8, 1.

Hillmer, Hilmer.—Bapt. 'the
son of Hildemar '; v. Hild. Hildemar as a personal name occurs in
co. Hunts, 1273 (A. ii. p. 595).
In the same year it is found also
as a surname.

Henry Hildemar, co. Camb., 1273. A.
Nicholas Hildemar, co. Hunts, ibid.
Thomas Hildemar, co. Camb., ibid.
London, 1, 1.

Hills.—Local, ' at the hill,' q.v.
Hills is not a plural form ; it is the
genitive of Hill, as in Jones, Williams, &c.   This is common in
monosyllabic local surnames ; cf.
Brooks, Stubbs, Holmes, Knowles,
or Styles.

1570. Married—John Hylls and Joyce
Wodned : St. Michael, Cornhill, p. 10.
1575. Barnabas Hills and Katherine
Lecke : Marriage Lic. (London), i. 67.
1789. Married—George Hills and Sarah
Flanner : St. Geo. Han. Sq. ii. 29.
London, 34 ; New York, 20.

Hillsden.—Local ; v. Hillersdon.

Hillson, Hilson.—Local ; v.
Hillersdon and Hillsden.   A common variant in local surnames
ending in *-ston* or *-sdon*; cf. Kelson,
Hinkson, &c.   Hilson is found in
co. Hunts, in the neighbourhood
of Hillersdon.

1798. Married — Benjamin Page and
Ann Hillsdon : St. Geo. Han. Sq. ii. 187.
London, 0, 6 ; MDB. (co. Hunts), 0, 1 ;
Boston (U.S.), 1, 0.

Hillstead.—Local, ' at the hillstead,' from residence at some
farm-house or homestead on the
hill.

1789. Married—George Meadows and
Sarah Hillstead : St. Geo. Han. Sq. ii. 25.
1792. — Richard Hillstead and Mary
Irwin : ibid. p. 74.
London, 3.

**Hillyard, Hilleard, Hilliard,
Hillard, Hildyard, Hilyard.**—
(1) Local, ' at the hill-garth ' or
' hill-yard.'   Not to be confounded
with Hillier, q.v.

Thomas Hillard, co. Soms., 1 Edw.
III : Kirby's Quest, p. 131.

Robert de Hildgard, co. York, 1273. A.
Robert de Hildyard, co. York, ibid.
Robert Hiliard, co. York, ibid.
Robert Hildeyerd, co. York, ibid.

These four entries represent, no doubt, the same individual.

(2) Bapt. 'the son of Hildegard' or 'Hildeward'; v. Hild. Also v. Yonge, ii. 235. 'Hildyard, formerly Hildheard, an ancient personal name. The family are said to have sprung from Robert Hildheard, of Normanby, co. York, in the year 1109.' So says Lower, quoting Burke's Landed Gentry. This family, however, as shown above, is of local origin. But I have found several entries that settle the point that in some cases these names are of baptismal origin.

Julian Hildegar, co. Hunts, 1273. A.
Hildiardus Bel. J.
Hilward de Broughton, 1409: West, Antiquities of Furness, p. 37.
Robert Helleyerd, C. R., 4 Hen. V.
London, 4, 1, 1, 2, 0, 0; MDB. (Dorset), 0, 0, 0, 0, 1, 1; Philadelphia, 4, 0, 12, 4, 0, 6.

Hilson.—Local; v. Hillson.

Hilton.—Local, 'of Hilton,' i.e. the hill-town; v. Hulton. Parishes and townships in cos. Derby, Dorset, Durham, Hunts, Stafford, N. Rid. Yorks, &c.

Richard de Hilton', co. Camb., 1273. A.
Adam de Hiltone, co. Hunts, ibid.
Symon de Hyltone, co. Hunts, ibid.
Johannes de Hilton, 1379: P.T. Yorks. p. 196.
London, 11; Manchester, 29.

Himmens; v. Hemmence.

Himsworth; v. Hemsworth.

Hinchcliffe, Hinchliff, Hinchliffe, Hinscliffe, Hinchcliff.—Local, 'of Hinchcliff,' now Hinchliff Mill, a spot in the township of Austonley, close to Holmforth, W. Rid. Yorks. The c in cliff is generally lost, as in Topliff. There are two Hinchliffs and two Hinchliffes in the township of Austonley (v. West Riding Court Dir.). It is astonishing how sedentary some families are; v. Hardisty for a similar instance.

Johannes de Hyncheclyff', 1379: P.T. Yorks. p. 174.
Willelmus de Hynchecliff', 1379: ibid.
Ricardus de Hynchecliff', 1379: ibid.

These were resident in Holm-

firth. Their parentage is therefore undeniable.

1728. Married—Joseph Hinckliffe and Eliz. Mantle: St. Geo. Han. Sq. i. 5.
London, 0, 6, 0, 0, 0; Manchester, 1, 1, 8, 0, 0; West Rid. Court Dir., 4, 5, 17, 2, 0; Philadelphia, 9, 1, 4, 0, 1.

Hinchman; v. Hensman.

Hinckley.—Local; v. Inkley.

Hincks, Hinks.—Bapt. 'the son of Hinche' or 'Hink.'

Matilda Hinche, co. Linc., 1273. A.

Hence such place-names as Hinckley, Hinksey, or Hinchcliff.

MDB. (co. Leic.), 1, 1; London, 3, 4.

Hincksman; v. Hensman.

Hind, Hinde.—Occup. 'the hind,' a peasant, labourer; v. Hine.

London, 9, 3.

Hinderwell.—Local. ' of Hinderwell,' a parish in N. Rid. Yorks, nine miles from Whitby.

London, 2.

Hindhaugh, Hindhough.—Local, ' of Hindhaugh,' some spot in co. York which I cannot identify. The suffix is -haugh or -halgh, a mound; cf. Featherstonhaugh, Greenhalgh and Ridehalgh; v. Haugh and Halgh.

Robertus de Hyndagh', 1379: P.T. Yorks. p. 72.
Robertus Hyndaglh', 1379: ibid. p. 73. Both resident in Tickhill, W. Rid. Yorks. The spot must be sought for in the immediate district.

Newcastle, 2, 0; New York, 1, 2.

Hindle.—Local, ' of Hindle.' The d seems to be intrusive; cf. Simmonds for Simmons.

Ricardus de Hunhill, 1379: P.T. Yorks. p. 137.
Thomas Hunhill, 1379: ibid.
West Rid. Court Dir., 7.

Hindley.—Local, 'of Hindley.' (1) A township in the parish of Wigan, co. Lanc.; (2) two townships in the parish of Felkirk, W. Rid. Yorks, styled Cold Hiendley and South Hiendley, but formerly spelt Hyndelay. The Yorkshire instances refer to these.

' Adam de Hindele held two bovates in Hindele of ancient feofment,' temp. Hen. II: Baines' Lanc. ii. 190.

Margareta de Hyndelay, 1379: P.T. Yorks. p. 24.
Roger de Hyndelay, 1379: ibid. p. 5.
Matilda de Hyndelay, 1379: ibid.
Simon Hindley, of Wigan, nailor, 1591: Wills at Chester (1545–1620), p. 95.
Jennet Hindley, of Aspull, Wigan, 1613: ibid.
Manchester, 11; London, 4; New York, 3.

Hindmarsh, Hindmarch.—Local, 'of Hindmarch,' North England. I cannot find the spot.

MDB. (co. Durham), 1, 2.

Hindson.—Nick. 'the son of the hind'; v. Hind; cf. Hineson and Hinson (q.v.), representatives of an earlier form.

Liverpool, 1; MDB. (co. Cumberland), 9.

Hine, Hyne.—Occup. ' the hine,' now hind, a peasant. The d is excrescent. M.E. hine; A.S. hina, a servant; v. Hind.
' Ther n'as bailliff, ne herde, ne other hine.' Chaucer, C. T. 604.
Robert le Hine, co. Suff., 1273. A.
John le Hyne, co. Oxf., ibid.
Stephen le Hine, 1313. M.
William le Hyne, co. Soms., 1 Edw. III : Kirby's Quest, p. 218.
Ricardus Hynne, 1379: P.T. Yorks. p. 177.
Cecilia Hyne, 1379: ibid. p. 172.
1631. Bapt.—Paul, son of Humiliation Hyne: Reg. St. Dionis Backchurch (London), p. 102.
1636. — Rebecca, d. of Humiliation Hinde: ibid. p. 104.
1669. Bapt.—John, s. Morgan Hyne: St. Jas. Clerkenwell, i. 241.
London, 14, 1; Oxford, 11, 0; New York, 13, 0.

Hineman.—(1) Occup. 'the hineman,' i.e. a herdsman; v. Hine. (2) An American variant of the German Heinemann.

Boston (U.S.), 3.

Hinge.—Local; v. Ing.

MDB. (co. Kent), 1; London, 3.

Hingley; v. Inkley.

MDB. (co. Stafford), 3; (co. Worc.), 11.

Hingston, Hinkston, Hinkson.—Local, 'of Hinxton,' a parish in co. Cambridge, nine miles from Cambridge. It is almost certain that the American Hinkson is a modified form.

Walter de Hinxston, co. Camb., 1273. A.
1785. Married — Philip Hingston and Ann Saint John : St. Geo. Han. Sq. i. 376.
1796. — Thomas Hingston and Phillis Burgess: ibid. ii. 147.
London, 3, 0, 0; Philadelphia, 0, 1, 8.

Hinkin, Hinkins.—Bapt. 'the son of John' (?). Probably variants of Hankin and Hankins, q.v.

1787. Married — Joseph Hinkins and Jane Davies : St. Geo. Han. Sq. i. 409. Manchester, 0, 2 ; MDB. (co. Cambridge), 2, 1 ; London, 0, 1.

Hinkley ; v. Inkley.

Hinks ; v. Hincks.

Hinksman ; v. Hensman.

Hinkson, -ston ; v. Hingston.

Hinshelwood, Hinshillwood.—Local, 'of Hinshelwood.' I cannot find the spot.

MDB. (co. Lanc.), 1, 0 ; Manchester, 2, 0 ; Philadelphia, 0, 2.

Hinson, Hineson.—Nick. 'the son of the hine,' now hind, with excrescent d (v. Hine) ; cf. Clarkson, Wrightson, Smithson, and Hindson.

Henry Hynson, 1379 : P. T. Yorks. p. 291.
Thomas Hyneson, *ploghwryght,* 1379 : ibid. p. 292.
Ellen Hyneson, co. York. W. 9.
Thomas Hynson, temp. Eliz. Z.
1617. Buried — Phillip Hinson : St. Dionis Backchurch (London), p. 214.
1673. Bapt. — John, s. John Hinson : St. Jas. Clerkenwell, i. 258.
Manchester, 1, 0 ; London, 1, 0 ; Liverpool, 0, 2 ; Philadelphia, 9, 0.

Hinton.—Local, 'of Hinton.' Parishes in the diocs. of Salisbury, Winchester, Oxford, Peterborough, and Bath and Wells.

Thomas de Hynton, co. Oxf., Hen. III-Edw. I. K.
Lucia de Hineton, co. Berks, ibid.
Matilda de Hinton, co. Middlesex, ibid.
John de Hinton, co. Camb., 1273. A.
Roger de Hinton, co. Dorset, ibid.
1544. Buried—Griphet Hyntonne : St. Peter, Cornhill, i. 107.
London, 27 ; Oxford, 7 ; Philadelphia, 6.

Hipkin, Hipkins, Hipps, Hipkiss.—Bapt. 'the son of Hibbert' (?), from nick. Hib and dim. Hib-kin, sharpened to Hip and Hipkin ; cf. Hoppe and Hobbs, or Hopkin, &c. The East-coast instances seem to point to the Low Countries as the home of this name. Hubert or Hobart was a familiar fontal name in co. Norfolk in the surname period.

Hyppe (without surname), co. Norf., 1273. A.
John Hyppe, co. Norf., ibid.
Lecia Hippe, co. Suff., ibid.

1646. Married—Steven Hipps and Ann Allin : St. Dionis Backchurch (London), p. 25.
London, 0, 3, 0, 0 ; Sheffield, 0, 0, 1, 0 ; MDB. (Norfolk), 2, 0, 0, 0 ; (co. Southampton), 3, 0, 0, 0 ; (co. Stafford), 0, 10, 0, 2.

Hippensteel, Hippenstiel ; v. Heppenstall.

Hipsley, Hippisley, Hippesley.—Local, 'of Ipsley,' a parish in co. Warwick, six miles from Alcester ; cf. Hipwell for Ipwell.

(Hōies) de Ippesleye, co. Warwick, 20 Edw. I. R.
1624. George Hippisley and Thomazen Syas : Marriage Lic. (London), ii. 138.
John Hippsley sailed for St. Christophers in 1635: Hotten's Lists of Emigrants, p. 135.
1679. Bapt.—John, s. John Ipsley, St. George, Barbadoes : ibid. p. 466.
1792. Married — John Hippesley and Sarah Taylor : St. Geo. Han. Sq. ii. 79.
Crockford, 0, 2, 0 ; Boston (U.S.), 0, 2, 0 ; MDB. (co. Wilts), 0, 1, 0 ; (East Rid. Yorks), 2, 0, 0.

Hipwell.—Local ; probably 'of Hipswell,' a chapelry of Catterick, N. Rid. Yorks.

Thomas de Ippewell, co. Oxf., 1273. A.
Johannes de Hypeswelle, 1379 : P. T. Yorks. p. 128.
1805. Married — Thomas Farnes and Mary Hipswell : St. Geo. Han. Sq. ii. 329.
W. Rid. (Yorks) Court Dir., 1 ; London, 1 ; MDB. (co. Bedford), 2.

Hird.—Occup. ; v. Herd.

Hirdson.—Nick. ; v. Herdson.

Hiron, Hirons, Hiorns.— ? Bapt. ; v. Irons.

MDB. (co. Warwick), 2, 3, 1 ; Oxford, 1, 1, 1.

Hirst.—Local ; v. Hurst.

Hiscock, -cocks, -coke, -cott, -cox ; v. Hitchcock.

Hissey.—Local. A variant of Hussey (q.v.), found in the same part of the country side by side ; cf. Hill for Hull.

MDB. (co. Berks), 3.

Histed ; v. Isted.

Hitch, Hytche.—Bapt. 'the son of Richard,' from the nick. Hich ; v. Hitchcock and Hitchmough. The harder-sounded Hick (q.v.) was more popular and has left deeper impressions on our directories.

Geoffrey fil. Hiche, co. Camb., 1273. A.
Walter Hicch, co. Hunts, ibid.
Ricardus Hiche, 1379 : P. T. Yorks. p. 28.
Willelmus Hiche, 1379 : ibid. p. 57.

1581. Thomas Hitche and Katherine Annion : Marriage Lic. (London), i. 104.
1674. Bapt.—Susanna, d. John Hitch : St. Jas. Clerkenwell, i. 263.
1807. Married — Caleb Hitch and Sarah Waller : St. Geo. Han. Sq. ii. 374.
London, 2, 1 : MDB. (co. Hunts), 1, 0 ; New York, 4, 0.

Hitchcock, Hitchcox, Hiscock, Hiscocks, Hiscoke, Hiscott, Hiscox.—Bapt. 'the son of Richard,' from nick. Hich (Hitch) or Hick. The initial R seems to have commonly nicked into H ; cf. Hodge for Roger, and Hob for Robert. For suffix -cock, v. Cocks. The harder form Hickcock (v. Hick) is found in the Hundred Rolls.

'Item, Nicholas de Mulseworthe, et Hikoc, et Ricardus Curteys tenent una virgat,' &c., co. Hunts, 1273 : A. ii. 615.

As seen below, the hard form lasted till the 17th century.

Hichecok Bedell, co. York, 1273. A.
Willelmus Higecok, 1379 : P. T. Howdenshire, p. 32.
Thomas Huchecok, co. Soms., 1 Edw. III : Kirby's Quest, p. 272.
Higecok de Trent, London. X.
William Hychcok, co. York. W. 3.
1553-4. Roger Watts and Agnes Hytchecooks : Marriage Lic. (London), p. 15.
1597. Alice Hiccock, of Stanney : Wills at Chester, p. 92.
1636. Bapt. — Nicolas Hekkox, s. Abraham Heskcok (i.e. Hitchcock) : St. Michael, Cornhill, p. 126.
1657. Married — John Great and Eliz. Hiccockes : St. Dionis Backchurch, p. 33.
1662. Bapt. — Richard, s. Thomas Hickocke : St. Peter, Cornhill, i. 101.
1705. Married — John Hichcock and Hannah Crowley : St. Dionis Backchurch, p. 52.
London, 25, 1, 5, 3, 2, 1, 2.

Hitchen, Hitchin, Hitching, Hitchings, Hitchins, Hitchinson.—Bapt. 'the son of Richard,' from the nick. Hitch (v. Hitchcock), dim. Hitch-in ; not to be confounded with Hutchins (q.v.) and Hutchinson. The g in Hitching and Hitchings is, of course, an excrescence ; cf. Jennings for Jenins, itself also a dim. (Jen-in) like Hitchin.

William Hychyns. F.
David Henchenesson. FF.
John Hitchinson, 1607 : Reg. St. Mary Aldermary, p. 153.
1623. Married — Richard Hitchinson to Anne Booth : Reg. Prestbury, co. Ches., p. 242.
London, 1, 2, 3, 2, 6, 1 ; MDB. (co. Chester), Hitchen, 11.

Hitchman.—Occup. 'the servant of Hitch' (Richard); v. Hitch; cf. Matthewman or Addyman, and v. Hickman.

William Hichman, co. Oxf., 1273. A. William Hikeman, co. Oxf., ibid.

No doubt these two entries concern the same individual, proving the identity of Hitchman and Hickman, if proof were necessary.

1774. Married — Edward Banks and Jane Hitchman : St. Geo. Han. Sq. i. 242. London, 0 ; MDB. (co. Warwick), 4 ; Oxford, 6 ; New York, 4.

Hitchmough.—Nick. ' Richard's brother-in-law '; v. Hitch (Richard) and Watmough, where the suffix is fully dealt with (v. Hickmott for a good instance).

Robert Hichmughe, or Hytchmoughe, co. Lanc., 1584 : Bras. Coll. : Reg. Univ. Oxf. vol. ii. pt. ii. p. 136.
Thomas Hitchmough, of Liverpool, 1591 : Wills at Chester (1545–1620), p. 95.
Robert Hitchmough, of Hale-bank, 1592 : ibid.
Edward Hitchmough, 1 Geo. I : List of Papists, Baines' Lanc. ii. 607.
Manchester, 2 ; Garston (Lanc.), 3.

Hives.—Bapt. ; v. Ive(s.

MDB. (co. Bucks), 1.

Hix.—Bapt. ' the son of Richard,' a variant of Hick, q.v. ; v. Hixson ; cf. Dixon for Dickson, or Dix for Dicks, from the same personal name Richard.

1633. Humphrey Bedingfield and Abigail Hixe : Marriage Lic. (Faculty Office), p. 32.
1653. Bapt. — James, s. William Hix : St. Michael, Cornhill, p. 139.
MDB. (co. Dorset), 1 ; Boston (U.S.), 1.

Hixson, Hixon.—Bapt. ' the son of Richard '; for Hickson, of which both are variants, v. Hick ; cf. Dixon, Rixon, Moxon, and Coxon for Dickson, Rickson, Mockson, and Cockson.

1572. John Hixson and Eliz. Raynolds : Marriage Lic. (Westminster), p. 4.
1777. Married — Jeremiah Lock and Susanna Hixson : St. Geo. Han. Sq. i. 277.
1784. — George Mold and Mary Hixon : ibid. p. 355.
Manchester, 1, 0 ; London, 0, 1 ; MDB. (co. Kent), 0, 1 ; Boston (U.S.), 3, 8.

Hizzard.—Bapt. ; v. Izzard, of which it is a variant. Thus Hizzard is the old personal name Isolda.

Such are the fluctuations of fortune in nomenclature.

Hoad.—Local ; v. Hoath.

MDB. (co. Warwick), 1.

Hoadley.—Local, ' of Hoathley.' East and West Hoathley are parishes in co. Sussex. Of the truth of this derivation there can be no doubt.

1616. Thomas Hodely, co. Sussex (Queen's Coll.) : Reg. Univ. Oxf. vol. ii. pt. ii. p. 356.
1705. Samuel Hoadly, Master of the Free School, Norwich : FF. iv. 9.
1798. Married—William Hoadley and Catherine Rhodes : St. Geo. Han. Sq. ii. 191.
MDB. (co. Sussex), 2 ; London, 1 ; New York, 4.

Hoar, Hoare, Hore.—Nick. ' the hoar,' i.e. the white, the greyish white; probably from complexion of the hair ; cf. Fairfax, Grey, White, Black.

> ' Ac olde men and hore
> That help-lees ben of strengthe.'
> Piers Plowman, 4682–3.

Very common in the Hundred Rolls, as for instance :

Adam le Hore, co. Derby, 1273. A.
John le Horre, co. Norf., ibid.
Alicia la Hore, co. Oxf., ibid.
Richard le Hore, co. Soms., 1 Edw. III : Kirby's Quest, p. 84.
London, 3, 55, 6 ; New York, 5, 8, 4.

Hoarder.—Nick. ' the hoarder,' the miser, one who hoarded up all he could scrape together ; M.E. *hord* (v. Skeat).

Richard le Horder, co. Soms., 1 Edw. III : Kirby's Quest, p. 99.
William le Horder, co. Soms., 1 Edw. III : ibid. p. 226.

Hoath, Hoad.—Local, ' of Hoath,' a parish in co. Kent, six miles from Canterbury. With Hoad, cf. Hoadley for Hoathley.

MDB. (co. Sussex), 1, 2 ; London, 0, 3.

Hobart.—Bapt. ' the son of Hubert.' An early variant ; v. Hubert.

William Hoberd, 1379 : P. T. Yorks. p. 18.

With the above cf.

1759. Married — James Hobbard and Amelia Graves : St. Geo. Han. Sq. i. 83.

The Visitation of Essex (1541) gives the surname of the family of Huberd indiscriminately as Huberd,

Hobert, Hubert, and Hobart (v. Index, pp. 804–5). Memorials of a family spelt indifferently Hubbard or Hobart are (or were) to be found in Little Plumstead Church. co. Norfolk (FF. vii. 247–8).

1615. Miles Hobart, of London : Reg. Univ. Oxf. ii. 340.
London, 3 ; New York, 21.

Hobbins, Hobbiss, Hobbis.—Bapt. ' the son of Robert,' from nick. Hob, and dim. Hobb-in ; cf. Cob-in from Nicholas, or Rob-in from Robert. Hobbiss or Hobbis is a modification ; cf. Hollis and Holliss for Hollins.

Hobbyn (without surname), co. Norf.: Index to Blomefield's Norfolk.
1779. Married — Thomas Hobbis and Eliz. Gilder : St. Geo. Han. Sq. i. 303.
MDB. (co. Warwick), 2, 0, 0 ; London, 1, 1, 0 ; Crockford, 2, 0, 0 ; Garston (co. Lanc.), 0, 0, 3.

Hobbletrot.—Nick. (?) ; cf. Trotter.

Willelmus Hobiltrotte, 1379 : P. T. Yorks. p. 140.
Cristiana Hobiltrotte, 1379 : ibid.

Hobbs, Hobson, Hobbes.—Bapt. ' the son of Robert,' from the nick. Hob, patronymic Hobbs and Hobson. Naturally these surnames have left many descendants. For variants, v. Hoppe. Owing to its popularity Hob became the everyday term for a country clown.

Agnes Hobbis, co. Hunts, 1273. A.
John Hobbe, co. Oxf., ibid.
John Hobbes, co. Soms., 1 Edw. III : Kirby's Quest, p. 114.
William Hobbeson, co. Soms., 1 Edw. III : ibid. p. 261.
Willelmus Hobbes, 1379 : P. T. Yorks. p. 27.
Petrus Hobbeson, 1379 : ibid. p. 103.
Willelmus Hobbeson, 1379 : ibid.
Robertus Hobson, 1379 : ibid. p. 44.
Obbe Dudeman. E.
Hob fil. Ralph. DD.
Hobbe the Werewede. C.
1569. Married — John Hobs and Avis Gore : St. Mary Aldermary, p. 4.
London, 61, 14, 2 ; Boston (U.S.), 64,8,0.

Hobby.—(1) Local, ' of Hoby,' a parish in co. Leicester. (2) Bapt. ' the son of Robert,' from the nick. Hob, and pet Hobby or Hobbie. The local derivation is the more probable one. Hoby is found as Hobby in the following entry :

'The Right Hon. Charles, Earl of Manchester, bachelor . . . and the Hon. Dodington Grevill, spinster, about seventeen, her parents dead, and she at the disposal of Thomas Hobby, Esq., her father-in-law, who consents.' Feb. 19, 1690-1 : Marriage Lic. (Faculty Office), p. 199.

The said Thomas was of the Hoby family.

1574. Edward Hobbie, co. Berks: Reg. Univ. Oxf. vol. ii. pt. ii. p. 57.
1614-5. Married — Richard Hobby and Sara Bathe : St. Dionis Backchurch, p. 18.
1803. — John Hanson and Sarah Hoby: St. Geo. Han. Sq. ii. 290.
MDB. (co. Hereford), 3 ; London, 1 ; New York, 13.

Hobcroft, Hopcraft, Hobcraft, Hopcroft.—Local, ' of Hobcroft,' i.e. the enclosure of Hob (Robert), the first occupier. Hopcraft is a variant ; cf. Hopps for Hobbs, and v. Craft.

1798. Married — Thomas Hopcraft and Susanna Perren : St. Geo. Han. Sq. ii. 192.
London, 1, 0, 1, 0 ; MDB. (co. Bucks), 0, 3, 0, 0 ; Oxford (Hopcroft), 5 ; New York, 0, 1, 0, 2.

Hobday.—Bapt. ' the son of Hobday,' the same as Hockaday (q.v.), one of the many fontal names taken from feasts and festivals.

' Spent on the wyves that gadyred money on Hob Monday, 10d.,' 1496 : Churchwardens' Accounts, St. Mary at Hill, London (Brand's Pop. Ant. i. 113).
' Gathered by the women on Hob Monday, 13s. 4d.,' 1497 : ibid.
London, 2.

Hobelot.—Bapt. ' the son of Robert,' from nick. Hob and dim. Hob-elot ; cf. Hewlett from Hughelot.

Constance Hobelot, co. Camb., 1273. A.

Hobgen.— ?

MDB. (co. Sussex), 5.

Hobhouse, Hoppus.—Local.

MDB. (co. Cornwall), 1, 0 ; London, 1, 0 ; Oxford, 2, 0.

Hobler.—Official, ' the hobler.' The hobler held tenure of his lands by maintenance of a hobby, or nag, which was to be used in the lord's service. He was a light horseman.

' As well hobellers as archers.' Paston Letters (ed. 1841), ii. 154.
It is somewhat curious to read of a Hobler being a *walker*, but of

course that refers to his occupation ; v. Walker, and cf. Ambler.
Adam Hobler, *walker* : P. T. Yorks. p. 222.
Adam Hobler, 1379 : ibid. p. 239.
Alicia Hobeler, 1379 : ibid. p. 246.
This surname seems to be almost extinct.

New York, 1.

Hoblyn.—Bapt. ' the son of Robert,' from the nick. Hob and dim. Hob-elin ; cf. Roblin or Hewling, from Robert and Hugh or Hew.

Thomas Hoblyn, co. Cornwall, Queen's College, 1607 : Reg. Univ. Oxf. vol. ii. pt. ii. p. 299.
London, 1 ; MDB. (co. Cornwall), 8.

Hobman.—(1) Occup. ' the servant of Hob,' i.e. Robert ; cf. Matthewman, Jackman, Dickman, Hickman, &c. (2) Official, ' the hobman,' probably for hobbyman, one who looked to or rode a hobby, a small horse ; O.F. *hobin* ; cf. Palfreyman. ' For x hobyes, and palfreys ' (Wardrobe Account, Edw. IV, p. 153). Hence ' to ride a hobby.'

Willelmus Hobman, 1379 : P. T. Yorks. p. 180.
Ricardus serviens Roberti de Nesfeld : ibid.
Robertus serviens Roberti de Nesfeld, 1379 : ibid. p. 239.
Immediately above these two last are entered Johannes serviens Johannis and Ricardus serviens Johannis Leke, whence our Jackmans. In formal records it is only occasionally we find registered such an everyday phrase as Jackman and Hobman, although the above would no doubt be so called ; cf. Vickerman and Ladyman. Also note:

Johannes Robertman, 1379 : P. T. Yorks. p. 207.
1649. Buried—John Hobman: v. Index Smith's Obituary, Cam. Soc.
1690. — Jane, d. James Hobman: St. Mary Aldermary, p. 200.
London, 1 ; MDB. (co. Surrey), 1 ; Boston (U.S.), 1.

Hobson.—Bapt. ; v. Hobbs.

Hoby.—Local, ' of Hoby ' ; v. Hobby.

London, 3.

Hockaday, Hockerday.—Bapt. ' the son of Hockday.' An

ecclesiastical festival commencing the fifteenth day after Easter, styled Hokeday or Hocktide. The feast ceased to be observed after the Reformation (v. Brand's Pop. Ant. i. 107-13). The child would be so named from being born or baptized during this festival ; cf. Christmas, Pask, Nowell, Pentecost, Whitsunday, &c. Pentecost is still a baptismal name in co. Cornwall, or was up to the beginning of the present century. The *a* in Hockaday is intrusive ; cf. Greena-way, Ott-a-way, &c.

John Hockeday, temp. Eliz. Z.
London, 1, 1 ; MDB. (co. Cornwall), 1, 0.

Hockenhull, Hocknell. — Local, ' of Hockenhull,' a township in the parish of Tarvin, near Tarporley, co. Ches.

Hamo Hokenhull, 25 Hen. VIII : East Cheshire, ii. 86 *n.*
Richard Hocknell, 2 Eliz. : ibid p. 166.
Thomas Hockenhull, of Hockenhull Platt, 1577 : ibid. p. 412.
1577. Married — Thomas Hockenell and Margearye Davemporte : Prestbury Register (co. Ches.), p. 56.
Ellen Hocknell, of Crowton, 1597: Wills at Chester, p. 96.
John Hockenhull, of Hockenhull, 1606: ibid.
1731. Buried — Zenobia, wife of John Hockenhull : St. Michael, Cornhill, p. 291.
Manchester, 2, 0 ; Liverpool, 1, 0 ; London, 0, 1.

Hockin, Hocken, Hocking, Hockings.—Bapt. ' the son of Henry,' from nick. Hal, dim. Halkin, more commonly Hawkin. This again has been corrupted to Hockin, and with excrescent g to Hocking. The genitive form is Hockings ; cf. Jennings for Jenins. Hawkins, Hockin, and Hocking are familiar Cornish variants of Hawkin, q.v.

1591. Married—Fraunces Hocken and Margret Todhunter : St. Mary Aldermary, p. 8.
London, 7, 2, 5, 3 ; MDB. (co. Cornwall), 23, 2, 11, 0.

Hockley, Hockly.—Local, ' of Hockley,' a parish in the dioc. of St. Albans, co. Essex.

William de Hokkele, co. Hunts, 1273. A.
Thomas de Hokkeleghe, co. Soms., 1 Edw. III : Kirby's Quest, p. 189.
1593-4. Richard Powle and Anne Hockley, *widow* : Marriage Lic. (London), i. 213.

1606. Married — John Hockley and Eliz. Tytton : St. Jas. Clerkenwell, iii. 30.
1797. — John Hockley and Jane Brees: St. Geo. Han. Sq. ii. 172.
London, 14, 2 ; Philadelphia, 3, 0.

Hocombe. — (1) Local, ' of Hockham,' a parish in co. Norfolk.
(2) Local. A corruption of Holcomb, q.v.

(Dominus) de Hocham, co. Norf., 1273. A.
1349. Benedict de Hocham, vicar of Topcroft, co. Norf. : FF. v. 189.
Adam de Ockeham, co. Norf., temp. 1250: ibid. i. 466.
Edmund de Hockham, co. Norf., 24 Hen. III : ibid. vi. 97.
1766. Married — Richard Hockham and Mary Miles: St. Geo. Han. Sq. i. 152.
London, 1.

Hoctree.—Local, ' at the oak-tree ' (?) ; cf. Plumptree, Crabtree, Rowntree, &c. I have no proof.

MDB. (co. Surrey), 2.

Hodder.—Local, ' of Hodder.' I cannot find the spot. It is evident that it must be looked for in York-shire.

Johannes de Hoder', 1379 : P. T. Yorks. p. 262.
Anabilla de Hedre, 1379 : ibid. p. 283.
Isabella de Hedre, 1379 : ibid.
1763. Married — Henry Beaton and Mary Hodder : St. Geo. Han. Sq. i. 120.
Sheffield, 1 ; Oxford, 1 ; Philadelphia, 5.

Hoddinott, Hadnutt. — Lo-cal, ' of Hodnet,' a parish in the dioc. of Lichfield, co. Salop.

William de Hodenet, or Hodinet, or Hodynet, co. Salop, 20 Edw. I. R.
Odo de Hodenot, co. Salop, Hen. III-Edw. I. K.
Baldwin de Hodenet,co. Salop, 1273. A.
1787. Bapt. — John, son of John Hoddinot, Reg. Stourton, co. Wilts, p. 43.
London, 1, 1.

Hoddy.—Bapt. ' the son of Oddy ' (q.v.). The aspirate is common in early registers to names beginning with a vowel ; cf. Han-niball (1) or Hodson (2).

Johannes Hode, i.e. Hoddy, 1379 : P. T. Yorks. p. 99.
Robertus Hode, 1379 : ibid. p. 161.
London, 3.

Hodge, Hodges, Hodgson.—Bapt. ' the son of Roger,' from nick. Hodge. The d is intrusive, as in Rodgers. I only discover one early instance with the d in it.

Alice Hogges, co. Soms., 1 Edw. III :
Kirby's Quest, p. 128.
Johannes Hodgeson, 1379 : P. T. Yorks. p. 111.
Thomas Hogge, 1379 : ibid. p. 171.
Johannes Hoggeson, 1379: ibid. p. 39.
William Hoggeson, C. R., 4 Hen. IV. pt. i.
John Hoggeson, co. Norf. F.
Richard Hoddgessone. H.
Ebbota Hoggese, 1379 : P. T. Yorks. p. 44.
Ricardus Hoge, servant, 1379 : ibid. p. 11.
Johanna Roger, servant, 1379 : ibid.

The last two are entered toge-ther. In replying to the registrar's question, the woman had respect-fully said she was the servant of Roger, the man more familiarly that he was the servant of Hodge.

Hogge de Hedle, Pat. R., 14 Hen. VII. London, 22, 54, 50 ; Manchester, 6, 5, 18.

Hodgett, Hodgetts.—Bapt. ' the son of Roger,' from nick. Hodge, and dim. Hodg-et ; cf. Emmott, Drewett, Marriott, El-liott, &c.

1577. Richard Ivatt and Agnes Hod-gett : Marriage Lic. (London), i. 76.
London, 1, 0 ; Liverpool, 0, 2 ; MDB. (co. Stafford), 0, 6 ; (co. Worc.), 1, 7.

Hodgin, Hodgins, Hodg-ings.—Bapt. ' the son of Roger,' from nick. Hodge and dim. Hodg-in ; cf. Col-in, Collins, Col-lings, from Nicholas. The final g in Hodgings is excrescent, as in Jennings or Collings.

Manchester (Hodgin), 3 ; (Hodgings), 1 ; London (Hodgins), 2.

Hodgkin, Hodgkins, Hodg-kinson, Hodgkiss, Hodgskin.—Bapt. ' the son of Roger,' from nick. Hodge, and suffix -kin = Hodg-kin (v. kin, Skeat). Genitive form Hodgkins ; cf. Williams, Wilkins, Jones, &c. With Hodgkiss (a cor-ruption of Hodgkins), cf. Hotch-kiss, Popkiss, or Purkiss.

John Hogekyn. H.
Charles Hodgskines, temp. Eliz. Z.
John Hoddeskynson, temp. Eliz. ZZ.
1562. John Hodgkin and Isanna Truxton: Marriage Lic. (London), i. 23.
1601-2. Richard Abby and Eliz. Hodg-kins, widow : ibid. i. 267.
1656-7. Married—William Parker and Eliz. Hodgskins: St. Dionis Backchurch, p. 33.
London, 0, 4, 18, 2, 1 ; Oxford (Hodg-kins), 4 ; Philadelphia (Hodgkin), 2.

Hodgman.—Occup. ' Hodge's man,' i.e. the servant of Hodge (q.v.) ; cf. Ladyman, Matthewman, Addyman, Priestman, Vickerman, &c. Although seemingly extinct in England, the surname has crossed the Atlantic.

John Hogeman, co. Soms., 1 Edw. Kirby's Quest, p. 241.
New York, 5 ; Philadelphia, 1.

Hodgshon.—Bapt. ' the son of Roger,' a variant of Hodgson (v. Hodge). This form is very commonly found in old wills, paro-chial documents, &c., in Cumber-land, Northumberland, Westmore-land, and North Lancashire ; cf. Townshend for Townsend.

1591. James Hodgshon, of Cark : Lanc. Wills at Richmond, i. 150.
1611. Cuthbert Hodgshon, parish of Haukeshead : ibid.
1616. John Hodgshon, of Caton : ibid.

In the register of St. Mary, Ulverston, the name is spelt in-differently Hodgson and Hodg-shon; v. Index published by James Atkinson, Ulverston.

MDB. (co. Durham), 2.

Hodgson.—Bapt. ; v. Hodge.

Hodkinson, Hodkison, Hod-skinson.—Bapt. ' the son of Roger,' modifications of Hodgkin-son, q.v. ; cf. Hodson for Hodgson. With Hodkison, cf. Pattison for Pattinson.

1626. Ellen Hodkinson, of Salwick, widow : Lanc. Wills at Richmond, i. 153.
1661. Richard Hodskinson, of Tar-niker : ibid.
1695. Michael Hodskinson,of Sowerby: ibid. ii. 138.
1710. Richard Hodkinson, of Hamble-ton : ibid.
Manchester, 6, 1, 0 ; Liverpool, 1, 0, 1.

Hodsden, Hodsdon.—Local, ' of Hoddesdon,' a market-town in the parish of Great Amwell, in co. Hertford.

Hubert de Hodeston,co. Bucks, 1273. A.
1589. Married — George Smythe and Joane Hodgdon : St. Mary Aldermary, p. 8.
1614. John Hodsdon : Reg. Univ. Oxf. vol. ii. pt. ii. 333.
1616. Bapt. —Sara, d. John Hodsden : St. Jas. Clerkenwell, i. 74.
MDB. (co. Bucks), 1, 0 ; London, 0, 2 ; Boston (U.S.), 0, 16 ; New York, 1, 0.

Hodson.—(1) Bapt. ' the son of Roger,' from the nick. Hodge, whence Hodgson, abbreviated to Hodson; cf. Dodson, from Dodgson; v. Hodkinson. (2) Bapt. 'the son of Odo,' from the nick. Oddy, sometimes Hoddy (q.v.), whence Odson or Hodson. There can be no doubt that Odo is the parent of many of our Hodsons. In Yorkshire it was for two centuries one of the most popular font-names for boys. The aspirate presents no difficulty.

Willelmus Hodson, 1379: P. T. Yorks. p. 267.
Robertus Odeson, 1379: ibid. p. 81.
Alicia Odson-wyf, 1379: ibid. p. 80.
Johannes Odson, 1379: ibid. p. 79.
London, 15.

Hoe.—Local, 'at the ho,' probably a form of Hoo, q.v.

Hoff.—Local; v. Huff.

MDB. (co. Lincoln), 1; New York, 24.

Hogard.—Occup.; v. Hoggard.

Hogarth; v. Hoggarth.

Hogben.—? Local. I have no solution to offer. Mr. Lower writes, 'Probably a pigstye, from *hog*, and *bin*, a crib, a hutch. This Kentish surname was probably applied in the first instance to a swineherd' (Patr. Brit. p. 160). According to this suggestion the origin of Hogben is local, 'at the hog-bin.' This, of course, is very unsatisfactory. No evidence is advanced. I cannot help thinking it is an immigrant from the Low Countries. I find no early trace of it.

1786. Married — Samuel Ardron and Mary Bellamy Hogben: St. Geo. Han. Sq. i. 391.
1807. — John Francis Bonnet and Frances Hogben: ibid. ii. 366.
MDB. (co. Kent), 18; London, 1.

Hogg, Hogge.—(1) Bapt. 'the son of Roger,' from nick. Hodge or Hogg; cf. Mag and Madge, from Margaret. (2) Nick. 'the hog'; cf. Pigg, Grice, Wildbore, Bacon, &c.

Alice le Hog, co. Oxf., 1273. A.
Philip le Hog, co. Kent, ibid.
Peter Hog, co. York, ibid.
Nicholas Hogg, co. Soms., 1 Edw. III: Kirby's Quest, p. 123.
Oliver le Hogg: ibid. p. 200.

(3) Local, 'at the Hog,' a sign-name; cf. Roebuck (2).

Richard del Hog, 1313. M.

1698. Married—Thomas Kneaton and Jane Hogg: St. Mary Aldermary, p. 35.
London, 50, 0; MDB. (co. Bedford), 2, 2; Boston (U.S.), 10, 1.

Hoggard, Hoggart, Hogard, Hoggett, Hoggitt.—Occup. 'the hog-herd,' a swineherd; cf. Swinnart, Calvert, Coward, or Stoddart.

Nicholas Hogherde. F.
Margaret Hoggard. F.
Willelmus Hoghyrd, 1379: P. T. Yorks. p. 269.
John Hogerd, co. York. W. 11.
William Hoghearde, 1640: VVV. p. 502.
1627. Bapt. — Thomas, s. Henry Hogget: St. Dionis Backchurch, p. 101.
— — Frances, d. Henry Hogged: ibid.
1765. Married — James Hoggard and Anna Maria Jacques: St.Geo. Han. Sq. i. 145.
MDB. (North Rid. Yorks), 3, 4, 0, 1, 2; Leeds (Hoggard), 2; London, 0, 0, 2, 4, 0; Beeston, Leeds (Hoggard), 1.

Hoggarth, Hogarth.—Occup. 'the hog-herd'; cf. Coward, Stoddart, Calvert, Swinnart. It is said that Hogarth the painter's name was originally Hoggart. Of course Hog-garth, i.e. 'at the hog-yard' or 'hog-garth,' would be a very natural local surname, but I do not find it; v. Hoggard for instances.

MDB. (co. Cumberland), 1, 2; (co. Westmoreland), 3, 4; London, 1, 0; West Rid. Court Dir., 0, 1.

Hoggins, Hogins.—Bapt. 'the son of Roger,' from the nick. Hodge, sometimes Hogg. dim. Hogg-in; cf. Huggins from Hugh, or Higgins from Richard.

London, 1, 0; New York, 0, 1.

Hoghton.—Local, 'of Hoghton,' a chapelry in the parish of Leyland, five miles from Preston, co. Lanc.; v. Houghton.

Johannes de Hoghton, 1379: P. T. Yorks. p. 34.
Sir Richard Hoghton, of Hoghton, baronet, 1635: Wills at Chester (1621-50), p. 110.
London, 2.

Hoglamb.—Nick. 'the hog-lamb'; M.E. *lomb*, a lamb. The term 'hog-lamb' is still applied to a sheep of about one year old. It is interesting to notice that this surname is connected with co. Lincoln, where at this moment Weatherhog (q.v.) is a familiar cognomen.

Hugo Hoggelomb, co. Linc., Hen. III–Edw. I. K.

Hogman, Hogmon. — (1) Occup. 'the hogman,' a swineherd: cf. Bullman, Cowman, &c. (2) Occup. 'Hodgeman,' i.e. the servant of Hodge; cf. Matthewman, Addiman, Ladyman, or Hickman.

John Hogeman, co. Camb., 1273. A.
Johanna Hoggeman, 1379: P.T. Yorks. p. 80.
1640. Nicholas Hodgman: v. Index to Proceedings in Kent, Cam. Soc.
1743. Married—Mathew Hogman and Susanna Pay: Canterbury Cathedral, p. 85.
'Frederick Hogmon, *blacksmith*.' Fenwick, near Doncaster: West Riding Directory.

Hogsflesh.—Nick. This is a Sussex surname, and was very familiar at one time in Worthing and the surrounding district. A local jingle says:

'Worthing is a pretty place,
And if I'm not mistaken,
If you can't get butcher's meat,
There's Hogsflesh and Bacon.'

Charles Lamb chose the name Hogsflesh as the groundwork of his little comedy, 'Mr. H——.' Pigsflesh occurs as early as 1300.

Margery Hoggesflesh, temp. Eliz. Z.
William Hoggesflesh, ibid.
MDB. (co. Berks), 2; (co. Southampt.), 1; (co. Surrey), 1.

Holbeck, Holbech, Holbeche.—Local, 'of Holbeach,' a town in co. Lincoln, formerly Holbeck or Holbeche.

Everard de Holebech or Holebeck, co. Linc., 1273. A.
Hugh de Hollebeche, co. Linc., ibid.
Thomas de Holebeck, co. Linc., ibid.
Agnes de Holebeck, cos. Notts and Derby: Hen. III–Edw. I. K.
Adam de Holebeche, co. Linc., 20 Edw. I. R.
Johanna de Holbek, 1379: P.T. Yorks. p. 215.
1631. Barnabas Holbech and Mary Oldfield: Marriage Lic. (London), ii. 202.
1638. Alexander Chute and Eliz. Holbeck: ibid. p. 236.
London, 1, 0, 0; MDB. (co. Warwick), 0, 2, 3.

Holberry, Holborow, Holbrow, Holborrow.—Local, 'of Aldbury' (?), a parish in the dioc. of St. Albans. The aspirate presents no difficulty.

John de Holebury, co. Bedf., 1273. A.
Hugh Holdebury, co. Bucks, ibid.
London, 1, 1, 3, 0; MDB. (co. Wilts), 0, 2, 1, 2.

Holberton.—Local, ' of Holberton,' a parish in co. Devon, four miles from Modbury.

MDB. (co. Devon), 4; (co. Middlesex), 3.

Holborn, Holbourn, Holburn.—Local, ' of Holborn,' one of the divisions of London.

MDB. (co. Lincoln), 1, 2, 0; London, 1, 0, 1.

Holborow, -borrow, -brow.—Local; v. Holberry.

MDB. (co. Glouc.), 9, 7.

Holbrook, Holebrook, Hullbrook. Local, ' of Holbrook.' (1) A parish in co. Suffolk, six miles from Ipswich; (2) a parish in co. Derby, five miles from Derby. Both places seem to have given rise to a surname. Evidently there is a locality called Holbrook in the West country. Holbrook has ramified very strongly in the Puritan settlements of America.

William de Holebrok, co. Linc., 1273. A.
Richard de Holebrokke, co. Suff., ibid.
Roger de Holebrokke, co. Notts, ibid.
Isota Holebrok, co. Soms., 1 Edw. III : Kirby's Quest, p. 140.
Henry de Holebroc, co. Devon, Hen. III–Edw. I. K.
William Holbroke, 1379 : P. T. Yorks. p. 79.
In 1635 Thomas Holbrooke, ' of Broadway,' aged 34, with his wife, two sons, and a daughter, embarked for New England (v. Hotten's Lists of Emigrants, p. 285).
1622. Randall Holbrooke and Anne Green, *widow* : Marriage Lic. (London), ii. 118.
London, 11, 1, 0; MDB. (West Riding Yorks), 0, 0, 1; Boston (U.S.), 78, 0, 0.

Holcomb, Holcombe.—Local, ' of Holcombe,' parishes in cos. Somerset, Devon, and Lancaster. Also a tithing in the parish of Newington, co. Oxford.

Henry de Holecoumbe, co. Devon, Hen. III–Edw. I. K.
John de Holecumbe, co. Soms., 1273. A.
Geoffrey de Holecumb, co. Oxf., ibid.
Simon de Holecumb, co. Oxf., ibid.
Ralph de Holecumb, co. Soms., 1 Edw. III : Kirby's Quest, p. 142.
1574. Edward Holcum, co. Soms. (Trin. Coll.) : Reg. Univ. Oxf. vol. ii. pt. ii. p. 57.
1808. Married — George Carpenter and Mary Holcomb : St. Geo. Han. Sq. ii. 393.
London, 1, 6; New York, 6, 1.

Holdam, Holdum.—Local, ' of Holdham,' probably some spot called Oldham or Aldham, i.e. the old stead. The aspirate presents no difficulty; v. Holberry.

Walter Aldham, co. Suff., 1273. A.
MDB. (co. Bucks), 1, 1.

Holdaway, Holdway.—Local. Probably ' at the old way,' from residence thereby. The aspirate presents no difficulty; cf. Holdam and Holberry. Local surnames with suffix -*way*, a road, are common in cos. Devon and Somerset. The intrusive *u* in Holdaway is for euphony; cf. Ottaway, Greenaway, Hathaway, &c.

MDB. (co. Southampton), 2, 4.

Holdcroft, Allcraft, Holecroft, Holdcraft.—Local, ' of Holcroft,' probably the croft in the hole or hollow; v. Croft or Craft, and Hole. Of course the *d* in Holdcroft and Holdcraft is excrescent; cf. Simmonds for Simmons, or *riband* for ribbon.

Johannes de Holcroft, 1379 : P. T. Yorks. p. 192.
1560. Bapt. — John, s. Richard Holcroft : St. Jas. Clerkenwell, i. 5.
1660. Married—George Holcroft and Eliz. Cannady : St. Jas. Clerkenwell, iii. 106.
1668. — George Holdcraft and Eliz. Courtney : ibid. 147.
1693. William Waterhouse and Susan Holcraft : ibid. iii. 212.
London, 0, 1, 0, 0; New York, 1, 1, 0, 0; Philadelphia, 0, 0, 4, 7.

Holden, Holding, Houlden, Howlden, Houlding.—Local, ' of Holden.' This surname has spread all over the English-speaking world. Holden was an estate in the parish of Haslingden, co. Lanc. A family of that name early sprang from the place. The *g* in Holding and Houlding is excrescent, as in Jennings, q.v. With Houlden or Howlden, cf. Houldsworth for Holdsworth, or Coules for Coles.

Robert de Holden, co. Lanc., 56 Hen. III : Baines' Lanc. ii. 49.
Magota de Holdene, 1379 : P. T. Yorks. p. 135.
Oliver Holden, of Haslingden, co. Linc., 1588 : Wills at Chester (1545-1620), p. 97.
Adam Holden, of Spotland, co. Lanc., 1596 : ibid.

Catherine Holden, of Holden, 1685 : ibid. (1681-1700), p. 128.
Ralph Holden de Holden, 1642 : Preston Guild Rolls, p. 114.
London, 18, 7, 1, 0, 1; Manchester, 32, 2, 0, 0, 0; Sheffield (Howlden), 4; Preston, 12, 1, 0, 0, 0; Philadelphia, 78, 0, 0, 0, 0.

Holder.—Occup. 'the holder,' probably an earlier form of ' up-holder,' originally an auctioneer. one who held up goods for sale. Upholsterer has a different meaning now, but it is an augmentative of the feminine 'up-holster,' founded on ' up-holder.'

Robert le Holdere, co. Glouc., 1273. A.
Robert le Holdere, co. Norf., ibid.
Robert le Holdere, co. Camb., ibid.

I suspect these are different people.

London, 18; Boston (U.S.), 8.

Holderness, Holdernesse.—Local, ' of Holderness,' a district in East Yorkshire.

'Lordings, ther is in Yorkshire, as I gesse,
A mersh contree ycalled Holdernesse.'
Chaucer, C. T. 7293.
Robert de Holderness, 17 Edw. II : Freemen of York, i. 22.
Rogerus de Holdernesse, 1379 : P. T. Yorks. p. 115.
Johannes de Heldernes, 1379. ibid. p. 107.
1797. Married — William Holderness and Jane Widdows : St. Geo. Han. Sq. ii. 160.
London, 7, 2; Boston (U.S.), 1, 0; Philadelphia, 1, 0.

Holdford, Holdforth, Holford, Holforth.—Local, ' of Holdford,' a parish in co. Somerset, ten miles from Bridgewater. For a second derivation of Holford, v. Halford. With regard to the suffix -*ford* or -*forth*, v. Ford or Forth.

John de Holeford, co. Soms., 1 Edw. III : Kirby's Quest, p. 164.

This entry suggests that Holdford was originally Holeford, i.e. the ford in the hollow; v. Hole. In such a case the *d* is intrusive.

1579-80. William Hollforthe, *skinner*, and Agnes Chilmon : Marriage Lic. (London), i. 95.
1783. Married — William Luvark and Mary Holdford; St. Geo. Han. Sq. i. 352.
London, 1, 0, 4, 10; MDB. (co. Lincoln), 0, 1, 0, 0; (co. Wilts), 0, 0, 1, 0; (West Rid. Yorks), 0, 1, 0, 1.

Holdgate; v. Holgate.

Holditch, Houlditch, Holdich.—Local, 'of Holdich.' A family of this name was settled in co. Norfolk for many centuries. I cannot find the spot.

Gilbert de Holdiche, co. Norf., 9 Edw. II : FF. vi. 29.
Richard Holdich, co. Norf., 29 Edw. III : ibid.
Richard Holeditch, co. Norf., 15 Edw. IV : ibid. viii. 443.
1767. Married — Jeffry Holdich, co. Essex, and Ann Showell : St. Geo. Han. Sq. i. 165.
1787. — Paul Morgand and Eliz. Holditch : ibid. p. 399.
1792. — Edward Houlditch and Anne Bisshoppe : ibid. ii. 84.
MDB. (co. Devon), 3, 1, 0; (co. Lincoln), 0, 0, 2 ; (co. Suffolk), 0, 0, 1 ; New York, 0, 0, 1.

Holdroyd ; v. Holroyd.

Holdway ; v. Holdaway.

Holdsworth, Houldsworth, Wholesworth, Holesworth.—(1) Local, 'of Halesworth,' a parish in co. Suffolk, early pronounced Haldsworth. (2) Local, 'of Haldsworth,' a spot in co. York which I have not identified. One thing is certain, the Lancashire and York-shireHoldsworths orHouldsworths are sprung from a family represented in the following entries :

John de Haldeworth, co. York, 1273. A.
Johannes Haldeworthe, of Leathley, 1379 : P. T. Yorks. p. 221.
, Ricardus de Haldeworthe, of Southowram, 1379 : ibid. p. 187.
Johannes de Haleworth', sutor, 1379 : ibid.

Of the Suffolk surname the following are instances :

1374. Adam de Halesworth, prior, Norwich : FF. iv. 339.
1495. Richard Haldysworth, rector of Ridlesworth, co. Norf. : ibid. i. 275.
1613. Robert Haldesworth, rector of Great Wrotham, co. Norf. : ibid. p. 467.

Of the Yorkshire surname the following are instances :

1593-4. Joshua Houldsworth, co. York : Reg. Univ. Oxf. vol. ii. pt. i. p. 198.
1595. Robert Haulsworth, or Holdsworth, co. York : ibid. p. 211.
1596. Henry Hauldesworth, co. York: ibid. p. 215.
1602. Michael Haldsworth, co. York : ibid. p. 259.

Thus the changes from Haldeworth or Haldsworth in the 13th century to Holdsworth or Houldsworth in the 19th are clearly marked at every stage.

London, 16. 0, 0, 0; Beverley, East Rid. Yorks (Holesworth), 1 ; Manchester, 5, 2, 0, 0; West Rid. Court Dir., 35, 0, 0, 0; Philadelphia, 12, 0, 1, 0.

Hole.—Local, 'at the hole,' the cavity, the hollow, from residence therein or thereby; cf. Hoyle and Holl, both of which are variants of the same name.

Richard de la Hole, co. Oxf., 1273. A.
Roger atte Hole, co. Soms., 1 Edw. III : Kirby's Quest, p. 122.
Isabella del Hole, 1379 : P. T. Yorks p. 35.
Rogerus del Hole, 1379 : ibid. p. 181.
Willelmus in le Hole, 1379 : ibid. p. 40.
Johanna in the Hole, 1379 : ibid. p. 37.
Walter atte Hole, C.R., 21 Edw.III.pt.ii.
1626. John Hole and Anne Wheeler : Marriage Lic. (London), ii. 171.
1806. Married—John Hole and Sarah Andrews : St. Geo. Han. Sq. ii. 343.
London, 7 ; MDB. (co. Devon), 41.

Holeyman ; v. Hollyman.

Holford ; v. Halford, Holdford.

Holgate, Howgate, Houlgate, Holdgate.—(1) Local, 'of Holdgate,' a parish in the dioc. of Hereford. But the North-English Holgates are manifestly from some spot nearer home. Such was Holgate or Holdgate, a township in the suburbs of York. With Howgate, cf. Holroyd and Howroyd.

William de Holgate, or Holdegate, or Holegate, co. Linc., 1273. A.
Walter de Hollegate, co. Linc., ibid.
Alicia Haldegate, 1379 : P. T. Yorks. p. 141.
Nicholaus Holgate, 1379 : ibid. p. 188.
'Willelmus Holgate, resident in 'Acom' cum Holgate,' 1379 : ibid. p. 299.

(2) Local, 'atte hallgate,' from residence thereby.

Nicholas atte Halleghet, co. Soms., 1 Edw. III : Kirby's Quest, p. 229.
Thomas atte Halle-yat, 11 Edw. III : Freemen of York, i. 32.
London, 6, 1, 0, 1 ; West Rid. Court Dir., 11, 4, 0, 1 ; York (Houlgate), 3.

Holifield.—Local.

MDB. (co. Oxford), 1.

Holker.—Local, 'of Holker,' two townships, Upper and Lower Holker, in the parish of Cartmel, North Lancashire.

1587. Nicholas Holker, of Oswaldtwistle, husbandman : Wills at Chester, i. 97.
1593. Eliz. Holker, of Monton, parish of Eccles : ibid.

1617. Ellen Holker, of Eccles : ibid.
MDB. (co. Lanc.), 1 ; Manchester, 1.

Holkum.—Local, 'of Holkham.' a parish in co. Norfolk.

Bertram de Holkham, co. Norf., 12 Hen. III : FF. ix. 233.
Peter de Holkham, co. Norfolk, 12 Hen. III : ibid.
MDB. (co. Kent), 1.

Holl.—(1) Local, 'at the hole '; M.E. hol, the hollow, the cave ; cf. Hoyle, a familiar Lancashire surname and a variant of Hole. The two undermentioned persons were residents in Sheffield :

Thomas atte Holl', 1379 : P. T. Yorks. p. 44.
Alicia in le Hoyle, 1379 : ibid.

The local connexion is incontestable.

(2) Bapt. 'the son of Hoel ' ; v. Powell.

Jestyn ap Owen ap Holl: Visit. Glouc., Harl. Soc., p. 113.
Margaret Holl ap Rees ap Towdor : ibid. p. 114.

Of course (1) must be regarded as the true parent of the present surname.

London, 3 ; Manchester, 1.

Holland.—(1) Local, 'of Holland,' a settler in England from Holland. This is rare.

William de Holond, co. Oxf., 1273. A.
Ricardus de Holand', 1379 : P. T. Yorks. p. 6.
Johannes de Holand', 1379 : ibid.

(2) Local, 'of Holland.' In general the surname takes its rise from the two Hollands in co. Lanc., viz. Down Holland, a township in the parish of Halsall, and Up Holland, a township in the parish of Wigan. Among the townspeople of strictly indigenous growth who were on the roll of the Preston Guild Merchant (A.D. 1397) appears ' Robert de Holand' (Preston Guild Rolls, p. 1).

'Thomas de Lathom, chevalier, Robert de Holand, chevalier . . . hold of John de Ware, one knight's fee' (in Childwall, Turton, &c.): Knights' Fees, 23 Edw. III, Baines' Lanc. ii. 694.
'Holand, a priory of Blake Monkes, a ii miles from Wigan' : Leland.

In Lancashire this surname has ramified marvellously, and has spread all over the world.

Thomas Holland, of Downholland, 1592: Wills at Chester (1545-1620), p. 98.
Richard Holland, of Downholland, 1608 : ibid.
John Holland, of Upholland (Wigan), 1619 : ibid.
Henry Holland, co. Lanc., 1600 : Reg. Univ. Oxf. II. 242.
Richard Holland, co. Lanc., 1615 : ibid. p. 343.
Manchester, 42 ; Liverpool, 19 ; London, 81 ; Boston (U.S.), 129.

Hollander.—Local. An immigrant from Holland.

Gerald Holonder, C. R., 12 Hen. IV. Boston (U.S.), 7.

Hollely.—Local, 'at the holly-ley,' from residence thereby, i.e. the meadow filled with holly-bushes ; v. Ley.

1750. Married — John Hollely and Sarah Duckett : St. Geo. Han. Sq. i. 43. Sheffield, 2 ; London, 1.

Hollick.—Local, 'of Holwick,' a township in the parish of Ronaldkirk, N. Rid. Yorks ; cf. Physick for Fishwick, and also cf. the pronunciation of Warwick or Norwich. MDB. (co. Warwick), 5.

Holliday ; v. Halliday.

Hollidge.—Local, doubtless 'of the hollin-hedge.' This would first become Hollyhedge, then Hollidge ; v. Hollins.

Ricardus de Holhaghe, 1379: P. T. Yorks. p. 89.
Johannes Holynghege, 1379 : ibid. p. 172.
1763. Married — Samuel Hollidge and Mary Warrington : St. Geo. Han. Sq. i. 121. London, 3.

Hollier ; v. Hollyer.

Hollingdale.—Local, 'of the dale where the hollies grow' ; v. Hollins and Hollingworth (2).

London, 2 ; Philadelphia, 1.

Hollingrake, Hollingdrake.—Local, 'of the hollin-rigg,' the ridge where the hollies grow. A farm in Ulverston near the back of a low-lying ridge of hills is called the Rake. Perhaps a confusion of Hollinlake.

Willelmus Holylake, 1379 : P.T. Yorks. p. 218.

In any case *d* is intrusive.

Hepstonstall, near Halifax, 2, 0 ; MDB. (co. Lanc.), 0, 1 ; (West Rid. Yorks), 0, 2.

Hollings ; v. Hollins.

Hollingshead, Hollinshead.—Local, 'of the hollins head,' i.e. one who dwelt at the head of the hollin-bushes ; cf. Akenhead (the head of the oaks), Birkenhead, or Birkett ▬ Birkhead (the head of the birches). A resident by the side of the oaks gave us Akenside, q.v.: *-head* and *-side* are common suffixes to local names of this class. The form Holinshead was made early immortal by the Chronicler. East Cheshire has given birth to a large number of Hollingsheads from some immediate locality of that name. v. Hollins.

John del Holynshede, 1408 : East Ches. ii. 335 *n.*
Hugh Hollinshead, of Bosley, *yeoman*, 1541 : ibid. p. 616.
1560. Married — Peeter Carter and Isabel Hollinshed : Reg. Prestbury, co. Ches., p. 3.
1561. Bapt. — Edwarde Hollynshed : ibid. p. 2.
John Holyncet, 1467 : ibid. p. 52.
1644. Married — William Hollinshead and Sarah Louch : St. Thomas the Apostle (London), p. 17.
Manchester, 1, 0 ; Liverpool, 0, 2 ; London, 1, 0 ; New York, 2, 2.

Hollingsworth ; v. Hollingworth.

Hollington.—Local, ' of Hollington,' (1) a parish in co. Sussex ; (2) a village in the parish of Checkley, co. Stafford ; (3) a township in the parish of Longford, co. Derby.

Thomas de Holindon, co. Oxf., 1273. A. London, 4 ; MDB. (co. Kent), 1.

Hollingworth, Hollingsworth, Hollinworth, Hollinsworth.—Local, 'of Hollingworth,' (1) a township in the parish of Mottram-in-Longdendale, co. Ches.; (2) a chapelry in the dioc. of Chester, lit. 'the farm amid the holly-bushes'; M.E. *holin, holyn*, now holly ; v. Hollins and Worth.

Johannes de Holynworth, 1379 : P. T. Yorks. p. 4.
Rogerus Holymworth, 1379 : ibid. p. 37.
John de Holynworth, of Disley, co. Ches., 1438 : East Cheshire, ii. 86.
John de Holynworth, 1325 : ibid. p. 142.
1560. Married — John Hollinworth and Margaret Smyth : Reg. Prestbury, co. Ches., p. 2.
London, 2, 11, 0, 1 ; Manchester, 5, 3, 1, 0 ; New York, 0, 10, 0, 0.

Hollinpriest. — Local (?). I cannot find the spot.

MDB. (co. Chester), 2.

Hollins, Hollings, Holling.—Local, 'at the hollins,' i.e. the holly-bushes, from residence thereby ; M.E. *holin* and *holyn*. The *g* in Hollings and Holling is excrescent ; cf. Jennings.

Willelmus del Holyns, 1379 : P. T. Yorks. p. 184.
Alicia del Holyns, 1379 : ibid.
Johannes Holyn, 1379 : ibid. p. 157.
Johannes Holyns, 1379 : ibid. p. 88.
Johannes del Holyns, 1379 : ibid. p. 200.
1524-5. John Hollyns and Margaret Clerke, *widow* : Marriage Lic. (London), i. 4.
1577. Thomas Hollinges and Mary Curwen : ibid. p. 75.
1619. Bapt.—Eliz., d. Roger Hollings : St. Jas. Clerkenwell, i. 84.
London, 3, 5, 0 ; Manchester, 5, 0, 0 ; New York, 0, 3, 3.

Hollis, Holliss.—Local, 'at the hollins,' from residence beside some holly-bushes ; v. Hollins. The corrupted form Hollis or Holliss is not an exceptional case ; cf. Purkiss for Perkins, Popkiss for Popkins, or Hotchkiss for Hotchkins.

London, 30, 1.

Hollow.—Local, 'in the hollow,' from residence in a hollow or basin-like spot ; cf. Hole, Hoyle, or Holl ; M.E. *holwe* (Chaucer).

Peter in le Halwye, co. Camb., 1273. A.
Roger in le Halwye, co. Camb., ibid.

Holloway, Hollway.—Local, 'of the hollow way' or 'holy way.'

Johannes de Holeweye, co. Wilts, 1273. A.
William de Holeweye, co. Warw., ibid.
William Holeweye, co. Soms., 1 Edw. III : Kirby's Quest, p. 81.
1581. Michael Baynes and Sibill Holloway : Marriage Lic. (London), i. 103.
London, 42, 6.

Hollowell ; v. Halliwell.

Hollyer, Hollier.—(1) Bapt. 'the son of Oliver,' from the modified Ollier, q.v. Aspirates present no difficulty, as will be seen from a perusal of letter 'H.' (2) Local, 'the hollyer,' one who dwelt by the holly-bushes ; cf. Bridger or Holmer. Of course Hillier (q.v.) may be the parent.

London, 2, 1 ; MDB. (co. Kent), 1, 0 ; (co. Leic.), 0, 2.

Hollyman, Holleyman, Holman, Holeyman, Holliman. Holloman, Holyman.—(1)Nick. 'the holy man,' i. e. the priest, the friar. With Hollyman, cf. Hollywell, or *hollyhock* and *holiday*. The shorter Holman must be referred to M.E. *hool* or *hol*, holy without 'the suffix -*y*. (2) Local, 'the holly-man,' the man who dwelt by the holly-bushes; cf. Bridgman, Heathman, &c.; v. Hollyer. But (1) is manifestly the chief parent.

Walter Halloman, co. Linc., 1273. A.
William Holyman, co. Linc., ibid.
John Holman, co. Kent, ibid.
Johannes Halman, *flessher*, 1379: P. T. Yorks. p. 121.
Adam Holman, *marchaunt*, 1379: ibid. p. 97.
Thomas Halman, 1379: ibid. p. 297.
Robert Halyman, co. York. W. 15.
Digorie Holman, temp. Eliz. Z.
Richard Hollyman, ibid.
1531. 'To Robert Halyman, of Newcastle, *yeoman*, the next vacation of the free chapel of St. Catherine': Brand's Hist. of Newcastle-on-Tyne, i. 27.
1582. Lionel Holyman, Magd. Hall (of London): Reg. Univ. Oxf. vol. ii. pt. ii. p. 119.
1628. Married—Anthony Allin and Mary Holliman : St. Michael, Cornhill, p. 25.
London, 6, 1, 22, 1, 1, 1, 1.

Hollywell.—Local; v. Halliwell.

Holm, Holme, Holmes, Holms, Home, Homes.—Local, 'at the holm,' from residence upon a' holm, an islet in, or a flat land beside, a river. The word as a placename is common all over England. In my old parish (Ulverston, North Lanc.) is an Appletree-holm in the river Crake. 'Holm, place besydone a water; *hulmus*': Prompt. Parv. The word is sometimes found spelt *home* or *holms*. 'Homes, probably *holms*, which signified originally river-islands' (Kennett).

Goscelin de Holme, co. Suff., 1273. A.
John in le Holmp (sic), co. Camb., ibid.
Robert del Holm, co. York, 20 Edw. I. R.
Thomas del Holme, 1379: P. T. Yorks. p. 217.
Adam del Holme, 1379: ibid. p. 198.
Johannes del Holme, 1379: ibid.
Adam atte Home, C. R., 14 Edw. III. pt. ii.
1574. Robert Cooke and Johanna Homes, of Isleworth: Marriage Lic. (London), i. 62.

1615. Bapt.—Alice, d. Thomas Holmes : St. Jas. Clerkenwell, i. 72.
London, 0, 3, 117, 2, 3, 5.

Holman.—Nick.; v. Hollyman.

Holmer, Homer.—(1) Local, 'the holmer,' one who lived on a holm or home (v. Holm); cf. Bridger, Fielder, or Churcher. (2) Occup. 'the heaumer,' a maker of helms or helmets; O.F. *healme*, *heaume*. 'Lord, how hasteley the souldyoures buckled their healmes': Hall, Ric. III, fol. 32 b.

Manekyn le Heaumere. H.
Alan le Heumer, 16 Edw. II : Freemen of York, i. 21-33.
John Tournay, *heumer*, 12 Edw. III: ibid.

(3) Local, 'of Holmer,' a parish two miles from Hereford.

Peter de Homere, co. Soms., 1 Edw. III : Kirby's Quest, p. 216.
John de Homere, co. Soms., 1 Edw. III : ibid. p. 222.
1704. Married—Thomas Homer and Anne Sprigmore: St. Antholin (London), p. 117.
London, 3, 8; MDB. (co. Stafford), 0, 11.

Holmes, Holms ; v. Home.

Holroyd, Howroyd, Holdroyd.—Local, ' of Holroyd,' probably the hollow clearing; v. Holl ; cf. Holgate and Howgate.

Galfridus de Holrode, 1379: P. T. Yorks. p. 184.
London, 7, 1, 0; Bradford, 12, 2, 0; MDB. (West Rid. Yorks), 36, 0, 1.

Holt.—Local, 'at the holt,' from residence thereby; a wood, a grove, a shaw.

' Now they hye to the holte.'
Morte Arthure (Halliwell).
Henry de la Holte, co. Worc., 1273. A.
William del Holt, co. York, ibid.
William atte Holte, co. Soms., 1 Edw. III : Kirby's Quest, p. 230.
Walter atte Holte, co. Soms., 1 Edw. III : ibid. p. 231.
London, 42.

Holtby.—Local, ' of Holtby,' a parish five miles from York. The derivation seems manifest, i.e. the *by* (dwelling) in the holt (wood) ; v. Holt.

William de Holteby, co. York, Edw. I. R.
John de Holteby, *potter*, 11 Edw. II : Freemen of York, i. 17.
MDB. (co. Lincoln), 4; (East Rid. Yorks), 11.

Holtham, Holtum.—Local, ' of Holtham,' i.e. the homestead by the holt or wood ; v. Ham and Holt. The variant Holtum reminds us of the American Barnum for Barnham.

John de Holtham, co. Linc., 1273. A.
MDB. (co. Warwick), 0, 2 ; London, 1, 0.

Holton.—Local, ' of Holton,' i.e. the town or farmstead by the holt or wood (v. Town and Holt); parishes in cos. Lincoln, Oxford, Somerset, and Suffolk ; v. Houlton for a variant.

London, 11 ; Oxford, 4 ; New York, 41.

Holtorp.—Local,' of Holthorp,' i.e. the thorp by the holt or wood (v. Holt and Thorp), some small spot in co. Lincoln which I do not find.

Matilda de Holthorp, co. Linc., Edw. I-Edw. III. R.
William de Holthorp, co. Linc., ibid.
London, 2.

Holway ; v. Holloway. A variant.

MDB. (co. Devon), 2.

Holyday.—Bapt. ; v. Halliday.

MDB. (North Rid. Yorks), 1.

Holyfather.—Nick. 'the holy father'; probably affixed to the bearer on account of his austerely religious habits ; cf. Holypeter.

Richard Holifader, co. Soms., 1 Edw. III : Kirby's Quest, p. 103.

Holyland.—Local, ' at the holly-land,' i.e. the holly-lawn, the old *laund*, a clear green space in the wood; v. Land and Laund. Holyland is, of course, like a hundred other surnames, imitative.

Thomas Holilond, co. Hunts, 1273. A.
1564. Married—John Lute and Margaret Hollylande : St. Michael, Cornhill, p. 8.
1574.—Davye Hollelande and Judethe Allen : ibid. p. 11.
1605. Ralph Browne and Ann Holliland : Marriage Lic. (London), i. 298.
London, 2 ; MDB. (co. Leic.), 2.

Holyoake, Holyoak.—Local, 'at the holly-oak.' Mr. Lower says this is from residence by some oak-tree to which sanctity was attached, and asserts, without furnishing instances, that in early charters

it is Latinized as 'de sacra quercu.'
The origin seems to be simply
residence by the holly-oak, now
generally holm-oak ('Holme or
holy, *ulmus, hussus*': Prompt.
Parv.), so called from the resemblance of its leaf to the holly; cf.
Rowntree, Crabtree, Ash, Nash,
Oake, Nokes, &c.

1687. Married — Thomas Holyoake
and Hannah Sanders: St. Michael, Cornhill, p. 45.
1697. — Samuell Smith to Mercy
Hallioake: St. Antholin (London), p. 112.
London, 3, 0; MDB. (co. Bedford), 0, 1;
(co. Leic.), 4, 3.

Holypeter, Hollopeter. —
Nick. 'Holy Peter'; cf. Holyfather. Thus we have such sobriquets as Littlejohn, Micklejohn,
&c. It is curious to find the pre-
sence in America of a surname
apparently extinct in England.
But this is constantly occurring.

William Halupetir, co. Hunts, 1273. A.
Philadelphia, 0, 2.

Holywaterclerk.—Offic. 'the
holy water clerk.'

Hugh Hali-watere-clerk, 1313. M.

Homan.—Occup. 'the man of
How,' i.e. the servant of Hugh,
dialectically How; v. Howson;
cf. Matthewman, Addyman, Bartleman, Hobman, Dickman, Harriman, &c.

William fil. Howman, co. Hunts,
1273. A.
John Huweman, co. Oxf., ibid.
John Human, co. Camb., ibid.
1653. Married—John Homan, *caster-
maker*, and Anne Frier: St. Michael,
Cornhill, p. 31.
London, 3; New York, 16.

Home, Homes. — Local; v.
Holm.

Homer; v. Holmer.

Homersham. — Local, 'of
Homersham.' I cannot find the
spot.

MDB. (co. Kent), 6; London, 1.

Homewood.—Local, 'of Holm-
wood' or 'Homewood'; v. Holm
and Holmes. I cannot find the
locality.

MDB. (co. Kent), 8; London, 9.

Homfray.—Bapt. 'the son of
Humphrey,' q.v. The variants of
this name are very numerous.

MDB. (co. Essex), 1.

Hone.—Local, 'at the hone,'
from residence thereby. A.S. *hán*,
a stone, rock; frequently applied
to a stone serving as a landmark
(v. H.E.D., *hone*, sb.'). Evidently
a West-country name.

Agnes Hone, co. Oxf., 1273. A.
Thomas Hone, co. Oxf., ibid.
— (personal name is torn off) de la
Hone: Kirby's Quest, p. 279
London, 9; Oxford, 1.

Honey, Hony.—Nick. Probably a title of endearment; cf.
Honeylove, Sweet, Sweetlove, &c.

Richard Honey, co. Camb., 1273. A.
Alicia Hony, co. Camb., ibid.
1771. Married — Savill Godfrey and
Amy Honey: St. Geo. Han. Sq. i. 205.
1776. — Henry Harding and Mary
Hony: ibid. p. 268.
MDB. (co. Cornwall), 5, 1; London,
9, 0; Oxford, 4, 0; Boston (U.S.), 2, 0.

Honeyball.—Bapt. 'the son of
Hannibal,' q.v. A curious variant.

London, 1; MDB. (co. Kent), 1.

**Honeybourne, Honeyborn,
Honeybun, Honeybunn,
Honeyborne, Hunnybun,
Honeybone.** — Local, (1) 'of
Honeybourne,' a parish in co.
Gloucester, near Evesham. (2)
'of Honeybourne,' a parish in co.
Worcester, also near Evesham.
Mr. Lower has also 'Hunnybum,'
'a ludicrous corruption'; but I have
not come across it. Hunnybun
exists, however.

London, 1, 1, 1, 1, 0, 0, 0; MDB. (co.
Glouc.), 0, 0, 0, 0, 2, 0, 0; (co. Hunts),
Hunnybun, 1; (co. Middlesex), Honey-
bone, 1.

Honeyfield.—Local,'of Honeyfield.' A West-country name, but
I cannot find the spot.

MDB. (co. Dorset), 4; (co. Glouc.), 1.

Honeylicker.—Nick. A curious
sobriquet for one who was fond of
licking honey.

Hugh le Honylikkere, co. Soms., 1
Edw. III: Kirby's Quest, p. 197.
John Honylikkere, co. Soms., 1 Edw.
III: ibid.

Honeylove.—Nick. A term of
endearment; cf. Sweetlove, Leifchild, Lovelock, Lovekin, &c.

Mary Honilove, 1647: St. Dionis Backchurch (London), p. 109.
1672. Samuel Poynter and Sarah
Honnylove: Marriage Lic. (Canterbury),
p. 212.

Honeyman, Honyman. —
Occup. 'the honey-man,' a bee-man
(v. Beman); M.E. *hony*.

John Honeman, co. Camb., 1273. A.
Thomas Honeman, co. Suff., ibid.
Osbert Honiman, co. Oxf., ibid.
Robert Honiman, co. Staff., 1581:
Reg. Univ. Oxf. vol. ii. pt. ii. p. 101.
1664. Edward Honeyman and Mary
Cox: Marriage Lic. (Westminster), p. 45.
London, 2, 1; MDB. (co. Salop), 0, 2.

Honeysett.—? Local.

London, 2; MDB. (co. Sussex), 2.

**Honeywell, Honeywill,
Honnywill.**—Local, 'of Honeywell.' I cannot find the spot.

MDB. (co. Devon), 1, 2, 0; (co. Glouc.),
0, 0, 1.

Honeywood, Honywood.—
Local, 'of Honeywood.' I fail to
identify the place.

MDB. (co. Sussex), 0, 2; London, 1, 0.

Honniball; v. Hanniball.

MDB. (co. Somerset), 2.

Hoo, Hoe.—Local, 'of the
hoo,' said to mean a 'spit of land';
cf. the Hundred of Hoo, between
the Thames and Medway. Possibly
in some cases a form of the local
How, q.v.

John del Hoo, co. Bucks, 1273. A.
Margaret del Hoo, co. Bucks, ibid.
Hugh de la Ho, co. Oxf., ibid.
Reginald de la Ho, co. Wilts, ibid.
Matilda de la Ho, co. Bedf., ibid.
Lettice Atte-Hooe, co. Norf., 9 Edw. II:
FF. ii. 229.
John de Hoo, temp. Hen. III: ibid.
John Atte-hoe, vicar of Erlham, co.
Norf., 1447: ibid. iv. 513.
John Atte-hoo, vicar of Brisley, co.
Norf., 1453: ibid. ix. 470.
Walter de Hoo, co. Soms., 1 Edw. III:
Kirby's Quest, p. 178.
1776. Married — John Hoe and Jane
Chamberlain: St. Geo. Han. Sq. i. 269.
London, 0, 3; New York, 0, 11.

Hood. — Bapt. 'the son of
Richard,' from the nick. Hud or
Hood, as suggested by the writer
of the article 'Robin Hood,' Encyc.
Brit. (vol. xx. p. 606, edit. 1886).

But Hud is not a nick. of Odo, as he asserts, following Lower (Patr. Brit. ; v. Hood), but of Richard. For proofs, v. Hudd. The entries of Hud are endless in old rolls and records. It must not be forgotten that 'A Lytell Geste of Robin Hode' spells it thus, which is not far from Hud in sound.

Matilda Hud-doghter, 1379 : P. T. Yorks. p. 221.
Emma Hud-wyf, 1379 : ibid. p. 218.
Johannes Hud-son, 1379 : ibid. p. 216.
John Hod, co. Soms., 1 Edw. III : Kirby's Quest, p. 133.
London, 36.

Hoof.—Local ; v. Hough.

MDB. (co. Southampton), 1.

Hook, Hooke.—Local, 'at the hook,' from residence in the bend or sudden turn of a lane or valley ; cf. Hooker (2). 'Hoke, a nook or corner. Kennett' (quoted by Halliwell) ; cf. Horn (3).

Reginald de le Hoke, co. Wilts, 1273. A.
Walter del Hoke, co. Glouc., ibid.
Love del Hok, co. Oxf., ibid.
Robert de Hok, co. Soms., 1 Edw. III : Kirby's Quest, p. 118.
Richard atte Hoke, co. Soms., 1 Edw. III : ibid. p. 181.
Robert atte Houk, co. Soms., 1 Edw. III : p. 225.
Margareta del Hoke, *webester*, 1379 : P. T. Yorks. p. 125.
Alexander de Hok', 1379 : ibid.
Willelmus de Hok', 1379 : ibid. p. 113.
1576. Anthony Hooke and Mary Kember : Marriage Lic. (London), i. 71.
1795. Married — Thomas Hook and Mary Evans : St. Geo. Han. Sq. ii. 137.
London, 14, 18 ; New York, 8, 1.

Hooker. — (1) Occup. 'the hooker,' a maker of hooks. There can be scarcely a doubt that this is the chief origin of the name, but there is a curious lack of references. (2) Local, 'the hooker,' one who lived by a hook in the land ; v. Hook ; cf. Bridger, Heather, Churcher, &c.

Robert le Hoker, co. Kent, 1273. A.
Hugh Hoker, co. Norf., ibid.
William le Hoker, c. 1315. M.
John Hoker, London. X.
London, 16.

Hookham.—Local, 'of Hockham,' a parish in co. Norf.

Robertus de Hokeham, co. Norf., temp. Edw. I. K.
London, 4 ; Oxford, 3,

Hoole.—Local, 'of Hoole,' a parish in co. Lanc., seven miles from Preston ; also a township in the parish of Plemonstall, co. Ches.

'Hoole gave name to a family as early as King John, for we find Walter de Hole among the inquisitors of the Wapentake of Leylandesir' in that reign' : Baines' Lanc. ii. 120.
Richard Hoole, of Great Layton, 1587 : Lancashire Wills at Richmond, i. 146.
James Hoole, of Tonge, 1587 : Wills at Chester (1545-1620), p. 100.
Robert Hoole, of Bebbington, 1610: ibid.
1662. George Hoole : Preston Guild Rolls, p. 147.
Manchester, 2 ; Preston, 5 ; London, 5 ; New York, 5.

Hooley, Hooly.—Local, 'of Howley.' I cannot find the spot. It seems certain that this is a Lancashire, Yorkshire, or Cheshire surname, and the locality must be looked for there. For derivation, v. How (2) and Ley.

John Hooley, of Dukenfield, 1613 : Wills at Chester (1545-1620), p. 100.
Robert Hooley, of Bebbington, 1610 : ibid.
Hugh Hooley, of Houghend, parish of Manchester, 1611 : ibid.
Jane Hooley, of Adlington, 1617 : ibid.
Miles Howley, of Adlington, 1668 : ibid. (1660-80), p. 143.
William Howley, of Duckenfield, 1676 : ibid.
1790. Married — Francis Genet and Eliz. Hooley : St. Geo. Han. Sq. ii. 35.
Manchester, 6, 0 ; Liverpool, 2, 0 ; London, 1, 0 ; New York, 2, 1 ; Philadelphia, 11, 0.

Hooper.—Occup. 'the hooper,' a maker of hoops for barrels. 'Hoope, hope, vesselle byndynge; *cuneus, circulus*' : Prompt. Parv.

Alexander le Hopere,co.Devon,1273. A.
Andrew le Hopere, c. 1315. M.
Ralph le Hopere, Fines Roll, 57 Hen.III.
John le Hopere, co. Soms., 1 Edw. III : Kirby's Quest, p. 103.
Walter Hoper, or Howper, sub. for B.A., April, 1515 : Reg. Univ. Oxf. i. 95.

Cf. Cooper and Cowper.

London, 75.

Hooson, Huson.—Bapt. 'the son of Hugh'; M.E. Hew and How. A variant of Hewson (v. Hew).

Robertus Huson, 1379 : P. T. Yorks. p. 175.
Thomas Usson, *barker*, 1379 : ibid. p. 176.
Willelmus Hueson, 1379 : ibid. p. 139.
1648. Married — William Huson and Grace Phillipps : St. Dionis Backchurch, p. 26.

1693. John Huson and Catherine Slaughter : Marriage Lic. (Faculty Office), p. 211.
Manchester, 5, 0 ; London, 0, 1 ; MDB. (co. Derby), 0, 1.

Hopcraft, -croft.—Local ; v. Hobcroft.

Hope, Hopes.—Local, (1) 'at the hope,' from residence thereby : a sloping hollow between two hills was called a 'hope.' (2) Parishes so called (probably with a similar origin) in cos. York, Derby, Kent, and Hereford. As a suffix we find *hope* in such place-names as Stanhope or Harrop ; as an affix in Hopcroft, Hopton, Hopley, or Hopwood.

Roger de la Hope, co. Hereford, 1273. A.
Richard de Hope, co. Salop, ibid.
John atte Hope, co. Soms., 1 Edw. III : Kirby's Quest, p. 135.
Walter atte Hope, co. Soms., 1 Edw. III : ibid.
Edith atte Hope, co. Soms., 1 Edw. III : ibid. p. 234.
Alicia de Hope, 1379 : P. T. Yorks. p. 201.
David atte Hope. O.
1590. Fulk Hope-Joyner and Eliz. Hopkyn : Marriage Lic. (London). i. 190.
1678. Bapt.—May, d. John Hope : St. Jas. Clerkenwell, i. 281.
London, 21, 1 ; West Rid. Court Dir., 7, 3 ; Philadelphia, 46, 0.

Hopewell.—Local, 'at the hope-well,' that is, the well or spring by the hope ; v. Hope. The Puritan font-name Hopewell came too late to influence surnames, but. failing evidence in favour of a local origin, it might be an early nickname for one of a hopeful disposition. Nevertheless, although I find no trace of the surname in Derbyshire, it must be remembered that Hopewell is a liberty in the parish of Sawley in that county.

Hopewel Foxe, co. Glouc., 1662 : v. my Curiosities of Puritan Nomenclature, p. 160.
Hopewell Voicings, Tetbury, 1720 : ibid.
London, 3 ; Philadelphia, 1.

Hopewood ; v. Hopwood.

Hopgood.—Bapt.; v. Habgood.

Hopkin, Hopkins, Hopkinson.—Bapt. 'the son of Robert,' from nick. Hob or Hobbe, and dim. Hob-kin ; cf. Watkin, Wilkin, or

Tompkin. Hopkin is a sharpened form. v. Hoppe, &c.

Nicholas Hobekyn, co. Camb., 1273. A. Roger Hobekyn, co. Camb., ibid. Hobbekin, of Windsor, co. Glouc., 1289: Household Exp., Ric. de Swinfield, Cam. Soc. p. 145. Alicia Hobkynnes, co. Soms., 1 Edw. III : Kirby's Quest, p. 214. Agnes Hobkyn-wyf, 1379 : P. T. Yorks. p. 34.
Rogerus Hobson, 1379 : ibid. p. 35. Alicia Hob-doghter, 1379 : ibid. p. 36. 1664. Walter Hobekyne, or Hopkin, of Warton : Lancashire Wills at Richmond, p. 148. 1567. Married — Thomas Dale and Christyan Hobkyns : St. Dionis Backchurch, p. 6. 1570. Buried — John Hopkynnes : St. Peter, Cornhill, i. 121. 1616. Married — Ephraim Hopkinson and Alice Harris : ibid. p. 249. 1626. Anthony Hobkin, or Hopkin, of Warton : Lancashire Wills at Richmond, p. 148.
London, 3, 74, 17.

Hopley.—Local, ' of Hopley.' There is Hopley's Green, a township in the parish of Almeley, co. Hereford, but I suspect we must seek for the place further north. Co. Chester seems to be the home of the family. The meaning is ' the meadow in the hope'; v. Hope and Ley.

1615. William Hopley, of Malpas, co. Ches. : Wills at Chester, i. 101. 1662. Randle Hopley, of Overton, co. Ches., *yeoman* : ibid. ii. 140. 1672. William Hopley, of Boulsworth, co. Ches., ibid.
MDB. (co. Chester), 4 ; London, 3.

Hoppe, Hopps, Hops, Hopson.—Bapt. ' the son of Robert,' from the nick. Hob or Hobbe. Insert *b*'s for all the *p*'s in this list, and the origin is manifest; v. Hobbs and Hobson, and cf. Hopkins and Hopkinson.

London, 4, 2, 1, 4.

Hopper.—Occup. ' the hopper,' i.e. dancer at fair and festival.

'Why hop ye so, ye high hills?'
     Psa. lxviii. 16 (P.B.V.).
Richard le Hopper, co. Oxf., 1273. A. Gerard le Hopper, co. Suff., ibid. Reginald le Hopper, co. Camb., ibid. Elena Hopper, 1379 : P. T. Yorks. p. 136.
London, 7.

Hoppus ; v. Hobhouse.

Hopton.—Local, ' of Hopton,' parishes in diocs. Ripon, Norwich,

and Hereford, lit. ' the town in the hope' ; v. Hope.

Osbert de Hopeton, co. Suff., 1273. A. Nicholas Hopetun, co. Camb., ibid. Ricardus de Hopetone, co. Norf., ibid. Johannes de Hopton, 1379 : P. T. Yorks. p. 222. Willelmus de Hopton, 1379 : ibid. Adam de Hopton, 1379 : ibid. p. 169. 1594. Bapt.—Francis, s. John Hopton : St. Jas. Clerkenwell, i. 29. 1790. Married — Robert Hopton and Ann Gilbert : St. Geo. Han. Sq. ii. 42.
London, 9 ; West Rid. Court Dir., 1 ; New York, 3.

Hopwood, Hopowood. — Local, ' of Hopwood,' a township in the parish of Middleton, near Manchester. A family of this name, still represented, has resided here for many centuries.

Adam de Hopwood, 1359 : Baines' Lancashire, i. 479. Willelmus Hopwood' et uxor, 1379 : P. T. Yorks. p. 205. John Hopwood, of Middleton, 1587 : Wills at Chester (1545-1620), p. 101. James Hopwood, of Hopwood, 1615 : ibid.

Through younger branches in the distant past, or separate and more homely stocks, this surname has ramified strongly in South Lancashire.

Manchester, 17, 0 ; London, 12, 0 ; Philadelphia, 4, 1.

Horberry.—Local, ' of Horbury,' a chapelry in the parish of Wakefield, W. Rid. Yorks. With Horberry, cf. Berry for Bury.

John de Horbiry, co. York, 1273. John de Horbiry, co. Bedf., 20 Edw. I. R. Elizabet de Horbiry, co. Bedf., ibid. 1335. William de Horbury, rector of Ashill, co. Norf. : FF. ii. 349. Robert Horbery, *tayllour*, 1379 : P. T. Yorks. p. 96. Johannes de Horbyry, 1379 : ibid. p. 202. 1634. Married—Richard Horberie and Mabell Linaker : St. Jas. Clerkenwell, iii. 66.
MDB. (co. Lincoln), 4.

Hordern, Horden.—(1) Bapt. ' the son of Hodierne.'

Robert fil. Hodierne, 1196 : KKK. vi. 58. Asspelon Odierne, co. Camb., 1273. A. Thomas Hodierne, or Hodyerne, co. Camb., ibid. Ricardus Hordane, 1379 : P. T. Yorks. p. 126. Henricus Hordane, 1379 : ibid. p. 126.

Lower quotes, ' Hodyerne Elys,' from the ' Nonar. Inq. (co. Sussex) p. 396.'

(2) Local, ' of Horderne,' a manor in the township of Rainow, in the parish of Prestbury, co. Ches. All the Hordernes of this and neighbouring districts hail from this spot.

John de Horderne, co. Ches., 1273 : East Ches. ii. 526 *n*. Edmund Hordron, 1460 : ibid. p. 2. Johannes Horderon, 1379 : P. T. Yorks. p. 37.
Ricardus Hordane, 1379 : ibid. p. 126. 1563. Married—Hughe Horderon and Mary Oldfeild : Reg. Prestbury, co. Ches., p. 11. 1564. — Edwarde Hatton and Margaret Hordrone : ibid. p. 14. William Hordern, of Congleton, 1595 : Wills at Chester (1545-1620), p. 101. Hugh Hordern, of Macclesfield, 1604 : ibid.
London, 1, 0 ; Manchester, 2, 0 ; Crockford, 2, 1 ; MDB. (co. Ches.), 2, 0.

Hore.—Nick. ; v. Hoar.

Horley.—Local, ' of Horley,' (1) a parish in co. Oxford, four miles from Banbury ; (2) a parish in co. Surrey, six miles from Reigate.

Walter de Horley, co. Bedf., 1273. A. Phillip de Horligge, co. Norf., ibid. 1782. Married — Richard Horley (co. Surrey) and Mary Steer : St. Geo. Han. Sq. i. 334.
London, 8 ; MDB. (co. Bedford), 3.

Horlock, Horlick.—(1) Nick. ' with the hoar-lock,' i.e. a white lock of hair ; cf. Silverlock, Greylock, Blacklock, &c. (2) Bapt. ' the son of Horlok'; cf. Havelock, Aslac, &c.

Henry Horlok, co. Soms., 1 Edw. III : Kirby's Quest, p. 118.
MDB. (co. Glouc.), 1, 4 ; London, 1, 1.

Horn, Horne.—(1) Bapt. ' the son of Horn.' Beyond a doubt a personal name. Lower says, ' One Alwin Horne held lands in Middlesex and Herts before the making of Domesday. Horn is a personal name of great antiquity, and is borne by the hero of a celebrated old English and French romance. For his history, see Wright's Essays, i. 3.' The instances in surname form are many.

Adam Horn, co. Wilts, 1273. A.
Henry Horn, co. Northampt., ibid.
Walter Horn, co. Oxf., ibid.
Johannes Horne, 1379: P. T. Yorks.
p. 17.

(2) Local, 'of Horne,' a parish
in co. Kent.

Roger de Horne, co. Kent, 1273. A.

(3) Local, ' at the Horn,' a sign-
name; cf. Roebuck, Whitehorse,
&c.

William atte Horn, co. Soms., 1 Edw.
III : Kirby's Quest, p. 155.
Thomas atte Horne, co. Soms., 1 Edw.
III : ibid. p. 257.

At the same time Horn in these
two cases may represent a piece of
ground shaped like a horn, and
therefore so styled; cf. Hook.

William Horne, of London, and Jane
Alisunder, *widow* : Marriage Lic. (Lon-
don), i. 29.
London, 17, 38; Oxford, 15, 5.

**Hornblower, Hornblow,
Horniblow.**—Occup. 'the horn-
blower,' sometimes abbreviated to
hornblow, whence the variant
Horniblow. ' Cornicen, horn-
blawere': Wright's Vocab. p. 73.

1608. Roger Horneblower and Mary
Poulton : Marriage Lic. (London), p. 305.
1626. Bapt. — Edmund, s. Richard
Hornblow : St. Jas. Clerkenwell, i. 104.
1805. Married — George Horniblow
and Ann Curtis : St. Geo. Han. Sq.
ii. 335.
London, 2, 1, 0; MDB. (co. Glouc.),
1, 0, 0; (co. Oxford), 0, 0, 1; Boston
(U.S.), 3, 0, 0.

Hornbuckle.— ? Local. This
looks uncommonly like a nickname,
but I cannot help thinking it is an
imitative corruption of Harbottle,
q.v. It is found in cos. Lincoln
and Norfolk. In 1581 John Harbottle was bailiff of Yarmouth (v.
FF. xi. 328). Additional evidence
in favour of this view is found in
the fact that Arbuckle is one of the
familiar surnames in Northumberland, where Harbottle lies; v.
Arbuckle.

John Hornbuckle. PP.
1633. Bapt.—Anne, d. William Hornebuckle : St. Peter, Cornhill, p. 84.
1673. — William Hornebuckle, *parish
clerk* : St. Jas. Clerkenwell, i. 260.
1806. Married — Richard Hornbuckle
and Hannah Milton : St. Geo. Han. Sq.
ii. 349.
MDB. (Lincoln), 2; (Norfolk), 1;
(Berks), 1; (co. Leic.), 2; New York, 2.

Hornby, Hornsby. — Local,
' of Hornby,' parishes in cos. Lanc.
and York, probably from Horn,
the name of the settler; v. Horn.
As the knowledge of place-names
increases, it will be made more
and more clear how large a proportion of them are styled after
the personal name of the first
resident. Hornsby stands to
Hornby as Huddersfield to Hud-
derfield (the earliest spelling), or
Holdsworth to Holdworth.

Johannes de Horneby, 1379: P. T.
Yorks. p. 268.
Agnes de Horneby, 1379 : ibid. p. 103.
Jenet Horneby, of Woodplumpton,
1638 : Lancashire Wills at Richmond,
i. 156.
Henry Hornbie, of Kirkham, 1662 :
ibid.
William Hornby, of Eccleston, 1668 :
ibid.
London, 2, 7; Manchester, 8, 0 : Shef-
field, 4, 0; New York, 4, 0; Boston
(U.S.), 0, 1.

Horncastle.—Local, ' of Horncastle,' a market-town and parish
in co. Lincoln.

William de Hornecastre, co. Lincoln,
1273. A.
Ralph Hornecastell, co. Norf., ibid.
Walter Horncastell', 1379 : P. T.
Yorks. p. 74.
Johanna de Hornecastill', 1379 : ibid.
p. 104.
1741. Married—John Horncastle and
Eliz. Warren : St. Michael, Cornhill, p. 69.
London, 2; West Rid. Court Dir., 1;
Sheffield, 1; MDB. (co. Cumberland), 1.

Horner. — (1) Occup. ' the
horner,' one who manufactured
horn into cups, &c. (2) Occup.
' the horner,' a horn-blower; cf.
Corner (3). Only one instance
occurs in the Hundred Rolls, where
Corner is the usual form.

Matilda le Hornere, co. Hunts, 1273. A.
Richard le Horner, 1303. M.
John le Horner. B.
Johannes Horner, 1379 : P. T. Yorks.
p. 129.
Ricardus Hornar, 1379 : ibid. p. 44.
Johannes Forester, *horner*, 1383-4 :
Freemen of York, i. 81.
1565. Bapt.—Thomas, s. John Horner :
St. Jas. Clerkenwell, i. 3.
1594. Giles Peacock and Eliz. Horner :
Marriage Lic. (London), i. 220.
London, 27; West Rid. (Yorks) Court
Dir., 11; Philadelphia, 82.

Horniblow; v. Hornblower.

Hornigold; v. Hornyhold.

Horniman.—Occup. 'the horn-
man,' a horn-blower. The intrusive
i is euphonic, as *a* in Green-a-way,
Ott-a-way, &c.

London, 1.

Hornsby.—Local, 'of Hornsby,'
i. e. dwelling of Horn; v. Hornby.

London, 7.

Hornsey.—(1) Local, 'a parish
in the E. Rid. Yorks, seventeen
miles from Hull; (2) ' of Hornsey,'
a parish in co. Middlesex, six miles
from London.

London, 2; MDB. (East Rid. Yorks), 1.

Hornshaw.—' Local, 'of Hornshaw,' either the crooked shaw
or Horn's shaw; v. Horn and Shaw.

MDB. (East Rid. Yorks), 2.

**Hornyhold, Hornyold, Hor-
nigold.**—Local, ' of Horninghold,'
a parish in co. Leicester, four miles
from Uppingham. Mr. Lower
writes : 'Hornyold. The first recorded ancestor is John de Hornyold, temp. Edw. III. Local place
unknown' (Patr. Brit. p. 163). Of
course it is Horninghold in Leicestershire, the settlement of the
family of Horn (v. Horn); cf. the
place-names Horningsea, Horning-
low, Horningsham, Horningsheath,
or Horningtoft.

1680-1. Thomas Horniold and Dorothy
Fitzherbert, *widow* : Marriage Lic.
(Faculty Office), p. 154.
1709. Married — Henry Garrett and
Susanna Horningold : St. Mary Alder-
mary, p. 39.
'In this vault lieth Mr. Henry Hornin-
gold, May 26, 1726, 35.' Independents'
Meeting House, Norwich : FF. iv. 463.
MDB. (co. Worc.), 1, 1, 0; (co. Nor-
folk), 0, 0, 1.

Horobin, Harrobin.—Local,
' of Horobin.' I believe this is a
small spot in the parish of Taxal,
co. Derby. The following entries
clearly prove that Horobin and
Harrobin are one and the same
name :

John Horabin, of Westhoughton, 1591 :
Wills at Chester (1545-1620), p. 101.
Thomas Horabin, of Bolton, 1612 : ibid.
Richard Horrobin, of Bolton, 1633 :
ibid. (1621-50), p. 115.
William Horrobin, of Little Bolton,
1633 : ibid.
1696. Bapt. — Katherine, d. Thomas
Harrabin : St. Jas. Clerkenwell, ii. 193.

1790. Married — John Horrabin and Sarah Bromfield: St. Geo. Han. Sq. ii. 48.

It will be seen that the Bolton Horobins first became Horrobin, and then Harrobin, as they exist to-day.

Bolton (co. Lanc.), 0, 2, MDB. (co. Derby), 4, 0; (co. Stafford), 11, 0.

Horoden; v. Harraden.

Horridge.—Local, ' of Horwich,' a chapelry in the parish of Dean, co. Lanc. A well known variant.

Nicholas de Horwich, 1397: Preston Guild Rolls, p. 5.
James Horridge, of Over Darwen, 1608: Wills at Chester, i 101.
James Horwich, of Over Darwen, 1632: ibid. ii. 115.
Anthony Horridge, 1613: Reg. Univ. Oxf. vol. ii. pt. ii. p. 330.
'Messuage in Horrage, alias Horwich, lately in the possession of Thomas Urmstone,' 1675: Exchequer Depositions, co. Lanc., p. 51.
Manchester, 3; Bolton, 1; Philadelphia, 2.

Horrocks, Horrox, Horrex.—Local, ' of Horrocks,' probably the spot known as Horrocksford Hall, in the parish of Clitheroe, co. Lanc. The tendency of surnames to corrupt as they get further from their native home is shown in Horrox and Horrex (London Dir.), which are unknown in Lancashire; cf. Dixon and Dickson.

William Horrocks, of Rumworth, co. Lanc., 1584: Wills at Chester (1545-1620), p. 101.
Peter Horrocks, of Turton, co. Lanc., 1596: ibid.
James Horrocks, of Horwich, co. Lanc., 1604: ibid.
1775. Married—William Horrex and Ann Parsonson: St. Geo. Han. Sq. i. 258.
London, 2, 1, 2; Manchester, 28, 0, 0; Philadelphia, 25, 0, 0.

Horscraft, Horscroft. — Local, ' at the horse-croft'—nothing to do with furriery; v. Craft, Meadowcraft, Haycraft, &c. Possibly in some cases a corruption of house-croft, 'the field beside the house.' This name occurs early:

Johannes de Huscroft, 1379: P. T. Yorks. p. 106.

But ' horse-croft,' the enclosure for horses, is the true parent.

John de Horscrofte, co. Essex, 1273. A.

Elsewhere in the same record he is found as John de Hoscroft (v. p. 138), hence Oscroft, q.v.

'Richard, son of Drogo, of St. Edmunds, gave the monks of Castle Acre a yearly rent of 10s., to be paid out of the estate of Richard de Horse-croft, his villein ': FF. ii. 355.
London, 1, 0; MDB (co. Sussex), 0, 1.

Horsefield; v. Horsfield.

Horsegood.— Bapt.; v. Hosegood.

Horseman, Horsman. — Occup. or official, ' the horseman,' either a mounted soldier or a keeper or breeder of horses; cf. Hobler and Palfreyman.

Agnes le Horseman, co. Bucks, 1273. A.
Robert le Horsman, co. Oxf., ibid.
Walter Horsman, co. Hunts, ibid.
Henry le Horsman, C. R., 10 Edw. I.
William Horssemanne, 1640: VVV. p. 502.
1589. Married — John Horseman and Agnes Ward: St. Jas. Clerkenwell, iii. 14.
1593. Buried — Abraham Horsman, plague: St. Michael, Cornhill, p. 204.
London, 2, 2; Acomb (York), 1, 0; Oxford, 1, 2; New York, 1, 2; Boston (U.S.), 0, 3.

Horsemonger.—Occup. ' the horsemonger,' a dealer in horses.

Leo le Horsmongere, co. Camb., 1273. A.

Horsepool, Horspool. — Local, ' of Horsepool,' a township in the parish of Thornton, co. Leicester.

1562. Simon Horsepole and Eliz. Smithe: Marriage Lic. (London), i. 23.
1602. Married — William Horspoole and Marie Washington: St. Jas. Clerkenwell, p. 25.
1786. Married — John Horspool and Sarah Chamberlain: St. Geo. Han. Sq. i. 396.
MDB. (co. Norfolk), 1, 1; Oxford, 0, 1.

Horsey.—Local, ' of Horsey-next-the-Sea,' a parish in co. Norfolk.

1269. Thomas de Horseye, bailiff of Yarmouth: FF. xi. 322.
Alicia de Horsey, co. Norf., 1273. A.
Mathew de Horseye, co. Norf., ibid.
John de Horsy, co. Soms., 1 Edw. III:
Kirby's Quest, p. 140.
John de Horsy, co. Soms, 1 Edw. III: ibid. p. 182.
1622. Thomas Tavell, husbandman, and Margaret Horsey: Marriage Lic. (London). ii. 114.
1676. Buried — Robert Horsey: St. Mary Aldermary, p. 190.
London, 12; Philadelphia, 3.

Horsfall.—Local, ' at the horsfall,' probably the hoarse fall, the loud, harsh cataract; M.E. *hors*, *horse*, *hoarse*. But cf. Yorks. dial. *Hose, Horse*, a deep vale between two mountains (Hutton, Tour to Caves), and *fall*, a valley, ' hanger ' (Lucas, Nidderdale). The surname has spread far and wide in cos. York and Lancaster. The spot itself seems to have lain in the old parish of Halifax.

Ricardus del Horesfall (Stansfield), 1379; P. T. Yorks. p. 189.
Johannes Horsfall, 1379: ibid.
1661. Ellen Horsfall, of Lancaster: Lancashire Wills at Richmond, i. 157.
1796. Married—Thomas Horsfall and Ann Newman: St. Geo. Han. Sq. ii. 144.
London, 2; MDB. (North Rid. Yorks), 7; West Rid. Court Dir., 32; New York, 4.

Horsfield, Horsefield. — Local, ' at the horse-field,' an enclosure for horses. The parentage is clearly North English, but I cannot find the spot. It will probably be found in Yorkshire, as I find no Lancashire records. Cf. Horscraft.

1596. Bapt. — Dorothie, d William Horsefold: St. Jas. Clerkenwell, i. 31.
1795. Married—Richard Thornton and Eliz. Horsefield: St. Geo. Han. Sq. ii. 132.
Manchester, 8, 2; MDB. (West Rid. Yorks), 6, 3; London, 3, 0; Philadelphia, 1, 0.

Horsford.—Local, ' of Horsford,' a parish in co. Norfolk, four miles from Norwich. But ' the horse ford ' would naturally be a common place-name, and several spots may have given birth to the surname. The surname in the North of England springs from Horsforth, a chapelry in the parish of Guiseley, near Leeds; v. Ford and Forth.

Johannes de Horsford, 1379: P. T. Yorks. p. 146.
Robertus de Horseforth, of Horseforth, 1379: ibid. p. 202.
Alicia de Horseforth, of Horseforth, 1379: ibid.
Robertus de Horsford, 1379: ibid. p. 223.
James de Horsford, clerk, co. Norf.: FF. ii. 272.
William de Horsford, burgess in Parliament for Norwich, 4 Edw. III: ibid. iii. 100.
1682-3. Ridley Horsford and Mary Roe: Marriage Lic. (London), ii. 304.
MDB. (co. Cornwall), 3; London, 5.

Horsington.—Local, 'of Horsington,' parishes in diocs. Lincoln, and Bath and Wells. The former seems to have originated the surname.

Jollan de Horsinton, co. Linc., Hen. III-Edw. I. K.
Gerald de Horsington, co. Linc., ibid.
Gilbert de Horsington, co. Linc., 1273. A.
Henry de Horssington, co. Linc., ibid.
1671. Bapt.—Jessper, s. Jessper Horseington: St. Jas. Clerkenwell, i. 249.
1792. Married — John Lorraine and Eliz. Horsington: St. Geo. Han. Sq. ii. 86.
London, 2.

Horsley.—Local, 'of Horsley,' parishes in diocs. of Glouc. and Bristol, Southwell, Winchester, and Newcastle - on - Tyne (cos. Derby, Surrey, Northumberland, and Gloucester).

Robertus de Horslegh, co. Staff., 20 Edw. I. R.
Lucas Horselie, co. Soms., 1 Edw. III: Kirby's Quest, p. 156.
1546. Thomas Horseley and Margaret Whytewell: Marriage Lic. (London), i. 9.
1791. Married — John Horsley and Mary Burton: St. Geo. Han. Sq. ii. 53.
London, 17; Boston (U.S.), 1.

Horsman; v. Horseman.

Horsnail, Horsnaill, Horsnell. — ? Local. I give this up; but I feel sure it is of local origin. Mr. Ferguson's idea, that it may refer to one who was as swift-footed as a horse,' connecting it, I presume, with *snel* (v. Snell), quick, active, is not good enough.

1639. Francis Rolfe and Margaret Horsnell : Marriage Lic. (London), ii. 246.
1644. Audrey, wife of George Horsnell, co. Norf.: FF. x. 444.
1650. Bapt. — John, son of Thomas Horsenell: St. Dionis Backchurch, p. 110.
William Horssnaile, 1700: St. Jas. Clerkenwell, p. 388.
1804. Married—William Horsnaile, co. Berks, and Eliz. Wilson: St. Geo. Han. Sq. ii. 299.
London, 0, 1, 1; MDB.(co. Essex), 2,0,0.

Horspool; v. Horsepool.

Horstead. — Local, ' of Horstead,' parishes in diocs. Chichester and Norwich (cos. Norfolk and Sussex).

John de Horstede, co. Essex, 1273. A.
Nicholas de Horstede, co. Norf., ibid.
William de Horstede, co. Middlesex, Hen. III-Edw. I. K.

John de Horstead, co. Norf., 15 Edw. II : FF. x. 445.
Gerard de Horstede, rector of Wheatacre, co. Norf., 1325: ibid. viii. 65.
Ralph de Horstede, co. Soms., 1 Edw. III : Kirby's Quest, p. 216.
1786. Married — Thomas Nicholson and Eliz. Horstead : St. Geo. Han. Sq. i. 384.
London, 1.

Horswell, Horswill.—Local, ' of Horsewell,' a West-country surname. I cannot find the spot. With the variant Horswill, cf. Kerswill for Kerswell in the same district.

William Horsewell, 1514: Reg. Univ. Oxf. i. 92.
London, 1, 0; Plymouth, 1, 3.

Horton.—Local, 'of Horton': (1) a township in the parish of Bradford, Yorks; (2) a township in the parish of Gisburn. Yorks; (3) Horton-in-Ribblesdale, near Settle, co. Yorks. This surname has strongly ramified in the United States. From the earlier entries it would seem that some other spots similarly styled, parents of surnames, existed in South England.

Thomas de Horton, co. Devon, 1273. A.
William de Horton, co. Kent, ibid.
Adam de Horton, co. Camb., ibid.
Emma de Horton, 1379: P. T. Yorks. p. 287.
Dionisia de Horton, 1379: ibid. p. 190.

The latter was a resident in Bradford.

1583-4. Roger Horton and Margery Singer : Marriage Lic. (London), i. 127.
1680. Married — John Horton and Sarah Houghton : St. Michael, Cornhill, p. 42.
West Riding Court Dir., 12; New York, 71.

Horwood.—Local, ' of Horwood,' parishes (Great and Little Horwood) in co. Bucks; also a parish so named in co. Devon. I find but one representative in United States directories.

William de Horwode, co. Kent, 1273. A.
Alex. de Horewod, co. Bucks, ibid.
Richard de Horewod, co. Bucks, ibid.
John de Horewode, co. Northampton, 20 Edw. I. R.
1572. William Wallys and Eliz. Horwood : Marriage Lic. (London), i. 54.
1633. Married — Isaac Harbor and Cicelye Horwood : St. Jas. Clerkenwell, iii. 56.
London, 20; MDB. (co. Bucks), 6; (co. Devon), 1; New York, 1.

Hose.—(1) Local, 'at the house,' a retainer or servant at the house or hall ; a variant of House, q.v. ; cf. Hall.

Geoffrey de la Hose, co. Wilts, Hen. III-Edw. I. K.
Richard de la Hose, co. Northampton, ibid.

(2) Local, 'of Hose,' a parish in co. Leicester, seven miles from Melton Mowbray.

Hugh de Hose, co. Staff., Hen. III-Edw. I. K.
Alan Hose, co. Norf., 1273. A.
1799. Married—Charles Hose and Sarah Grimsdale : St. Geo. Han. Sq. ii. 209.

Mr. Lower says (Patr. Brit. p. 163), 'Hose, the garment.' This does not help much to the derivation of the name.

London, 3 ; New York, 3.

Hosegood, Hosgood, Horsegood.—Bapt. 'the son of Osgod'; v. Osgood. The aspirate got into these names very early; cf. Hoddy for Oddy, and such an entry as this :

Rogerus Hosbarne (Osborne), 1379 : P. T. Yorks. p. 108.

or earlier :

Alice Hosebern, co. Camb., 1273. A.

Hosegood and Hosgood are very familiar names in the South-west of England.

Walter Hosgod, co. Oxf., 1273. A.
Robert Hosegod, co. Wilts, ibid.
London, 3, 0, 0 ; Devon Trade Directory (Farmers), 5, 1, 0 ; Devon Court Dir., 1, 0, 1.

Hosford.—Local, 'of Horsford,' q.v. A variant.

London, 2 ; New York, 5.

Hosier, Hozier.—Occup. 'the hosier,' a manufacturer of hose, gaiters, coverings for the legs. Originally Hoser, the *i* creeping in for euphony ; cf. *lawyer* and *bowyer* for *lawer* and *bower*.

William de Kekby, *hoser* : Freemen of York, i. 15.
William de Snayth, *hosier* : ibid.
Cristian le Hosyer, C. R., 32 Edw. I.
Philip le Hosier, c. 1300. M.
Lawrence Hosyer. H.
Thomas Hosyer, 1379 : P. T. Yorks. p. 252.
1579. Married—Steven Howssyer and Agnes Webbe: St. Dionis Backchurch (London), p. 9.
London, 3, 0 ; Oxford, 5, 0.

Hosken, Hoskin, Hosking, Hoskins.—(1) Bapt. 'the son of Osmund,' or 'Osgood,' or 'Osberne.' There can be little doubt about this derivation. The aspirate is commonly found in names beginning with vowels ; cf. Hoddy for Oddy, or Hosgood for Osgood, or Hodson for Odson. This being settled the rest is easy. Oskin must be a dim. like Wilkin or Watkin, and the only question is, Was it a dim. of Osmund, Osgood, or Osberne? The *g* in Hosking is excrescent.

Osekin (without surname), London, 1273. A.
Robert Osekin, London, ibid.

(2) ? Bapt. 'the son of Roger,' from nick. Hodge, dim. Hodgekin, corruptly pronounced Hotchkin, then Hoskin, with excrescent *g* Hosking. I merely suggest this as a possibility. All evidence is in favour of (1).

London, 2, 1, 12, 14 ; MDB. (co. Cornwall), 7, 17, 9, 0.

Hotchkin, Hotchkiss.—Bapt. 'the son of Roger,' from nick. Hodge, dim. Hodgekin, patronymic Hodgekins, corruptly Hotchkiss ; cf. Popkiss, Purkiss, &c. For instances of the more correct forms, v. Hodgkin.

1677. Bapt.—Martha, d. Thomas Hotchkis : St. Jas. Clerkenwell, i. 278.
1690. Buried—Hannah Hotchkis : St. Antholin's, Budge Row, London, p. 106.
1799. Married—James Hotchkiss and Eliz. Lovell : St. Geo. Han. Sq. ii. 206.
1809. — Lambert Hotchkin and Hannah Mill : ibid. p. 406.
London, 2, 2 ; MDB. (co. Hertford), 0, 1 ; (co. Salop), 0, 3.

Hoth.—Local, 'at the hoth,' i.e. heath. 'Hoth, a heath. Launfal, 250' (Halliwell). Cf. *hoth*, gorse or furze (Parish, Sussex Dialect). v. Heath.

John del Hoth, co. Norf., 1273. A.
Richard del Hoth, co. Norf., ibid.

Hotham.—Local, 'of Hotham,' a parish in E. Rid. Yorks.

Robert de Hothum, co. York, 1273. A.
John de Hotham, bishop of Ely, 19 Edw. I : FF. ii. 213.
Johannes de Hothum, 1379 : P. T. Yorks. p. 53.
1765. Married — Rev. John Hotham and Susanna Mackworth : St. Geo. Han. Sq. i. 142.
MDB. (co. Kent), 2 ; (E. Rid. Yorks), 5.

Hothersall.—Local, ' of Hothersall,' a township in the parish of Ribchester, co. Lanc., near Preston.

Thomas de Hudresale, temp. Edw. III : Baines' Hist. Lanc. ii. 107.
Alice Hoddersale, of Ribchester, 1560 : Lancashire Wills at Richmond, i. 149.
Robert Hothersall, of Hothersall, *husbandman*, 1587 : ibid. p. 157.
John Hothersall, of Alston, *yeoman*, 1589 : ibid.
George Hothersall, of Grimsargh, 1665 : ibid.
1571. George Huthersall and Eliz. Thomas, *widow* Marriage Lic. (London), i. 49.
William Hothersall, of Grimsargh, co. Lancaster, *husbandman*, 1661 : Wills at Chester (1660-80), p. 141.
Preston, 5 ; Boston (U.S.), 1 ; Philadelphia, 1.

Houchen, Houchin.—Bapt. 'the son of Hugh,' from the dim. Hugchon and Huchon, by and by Hutchin. For instances, v. Hutchins ; cf. Gibbon from Gilbert (i.e. nick. Gibb, dim. Gibbon) ; v. Gibbens.

London, 1, 5.

Hough, Houfe.—Local, ' of the hough.' The same word as *haugh* or *how*, a hill, a mound (v. How). 'A hollow or dell. North' (Halliwell). There is a hamlet called Hough-end in the parish of Bramley, near Leeds. Houfe is a curious corruption, but not unlike the instance below (v. also Huff). Of the Cheshire and South Lancashire Houghs nearly all hail from Hough, now called 'the hough,' a portion of the parish of Wilmslow, co. Ches.

Willelmus de Huff, 1379 : P. T. Yorks. p. 194.
1564. Married—William Houghe and Ales Ayneswoorthe : Prestbury Ch. (co. Ches.), p. 13.
1618. Henry Hough, of the Hough, parish of Wilmslow : Wills at Chester (1545-1620), p. 101.
1660. Married—John Huff and Mary Richman : St. Dionis Backchurch, p. 36.
West Rid. Court Dir., 4, 0 ; Sheffield, 3, 1 ; Manchester, 8, 0 ; MDB. (co. Chester), 8, 0.

Houghton, Haughton, Howton.—Local, 'of Haughton,' or 'Halghton,' but found in a variety of forms ; cf. Greenhalgh or Ridehalgh, both North-English sur-

names, variants of which are Greenough and Riddeough. We also find Featherstonhalgh for Featherstonhaugh. There are endless towns, villages, hamlets, and small localities bearing the name of Haughton or Houghton in England ; v. Halgh and Haugh.

John de Haleghton, co. York, 1273. A.
Alexander de Houhton, co. Camb., ibid.
Richard de Howton, co. Linc., Hen. III-Edw. I. K.
William de Halghton, co. Northumberland, 20 Edw. I. R.
Matilda de Halghton, huswyf, *webster*, 1379 : P. T. Yorks. p. 62.
Willelmus de Halghton, 1379 : P. T. Yorks. p. 103.
Thomas Houghton, of Houghton, 1621 : Wills at Chester (1621-50), p. 116.
Ellen Houghton, of Houghton, *widow*, 1647 : ibid.
London, 36, 3, 1.

Houlbrook ; v. Holbrook, of which it is a variant.

MDB. (West Rid. Yorks), 1.

Houlden, -ing ; v. Holden.

Houlditch ; v. Holditch.

Houldsworth ; v. Holdsworth.

Houle, Houl.—Local, 'at the hole,' from residence in some steep cavity ; v. Hole, Holl, Hoyle ; cf. Hoult for Holt, Cowles for Coles (v. Coull), Houlgate for Holgate, Houldsworth for Holdsworth, &c.

Willelmus Houle, 1379 : P. T. Yorks. p. 45.

In the same village (Handsworth) were resident Henry att Hoyle and Thomas att Hoyle.

1791. Married—Peter Houl and Eliz. Lancaster : St. Geo. Han. Sq. ii. 59.
London, 3, 1 ; Boston (U.S.), 1, 0.

Houlgate ; v. Holgate, of which it is a variant.

MDB. (co. Derby), 1.

Houlgrave, Houlgreave.—Local, ' of Youlgrave,' a parish in co. Derby, three miles from Bakewell.

Henry Hulgreave, of Halewood, 1607 : Wills at Chester (1545-1620), p. 103.
Ellen Hulgreave, of Halewood, 1613 : ibid.
MDB. (co. Lanc.), 2, 1.

Hoult.—Local, 'at the holt,' from residence thereby ; v. Holt. For similar instances, v. Houle.

1625. John Hoult, of Turton: Wills at Chester (1621-50), p. 117.
1630. Ralph Hoult, of Timperley: ibid.
1794. Married—John Turner and Mary Hoult: St. Geo. Han. Sq. ii. 112. Sheffield, 3.

Houlton.—A variant of Holton, q.v.; cf. Hoult for Holt.
London, 2.

Houndsfield, Hounsfield.— Local, 'of Hounsfield.' I cannot identify the spot.
MDB. (co. Derby), 2, 2; (West. Rid. Yorks), 1, 5.

Hounslow.—Local, 'of Hounslow,' a parish in co. Middlesex, nine miles from London.
MDB. (co. Berks), 1; London, 3; Oxford, 14.

House, Howse.—Local, 'at the house,' from residence in some large hall or mansion as servant or retainer; possibly it might represent the proprietor himself.
Geoffrey de la House, co. Hunts, 1273. A.
William de la House, co. Hunts, ibid.
Richard de la Huse, co. Bucks, ibid.
Jacob Huse, co. Soms., 1 Edw. III: Kirby's Quest, p. 79.
London, 15, 8.

Housecarl.—Offic. 'the housecarl.' A soldier, one of a paid military force originally organized by Cnut (Canute): Freeman, N.C. i. 440; also see his Appendix, KKK.
Alexander Huskarle, Hen. III–Edw. I. 'K.
Thomas Huskarle, ibid.
Thomas Huscarl, co. Oxf., 1273. A.
Thomas Huscarll, C. R., 14 Edw. III. pt. i.

Household.—Local, 'of the household,' an indoor servant.
MDB. (co. Cambridge), 3; (co. Suffolk), 2; Philadelphia, 1.

Householder, Housekeeper.—Occup. 'the householder,' 'the housekeeper.' I find no trace of these names on English soil. I cannot but think they are of American origin.
Philadelphia, 6, 7.

Houseley, Housley.—Local, 'of Houseley,' a spot in the W. Rid. Yorks which I cannot find. Probably it will be found in the parish of Ecclesfield. v. Ouseley.
Johannes de Houselay, *marchant de besties*, 1379: P. T. Yorks. p. 9.

Isabella de Houselay, 1379: ibid. Sheffield, 0, 2; West Riding Court Dir., 1, 2; London, 0, 3.

Houseman, Housman.—Occup. 'the houseman,' the indoor manservant; cf. Bowerman, Castleman, Housecarl. This surname, early found in co. York, 'crossed the border and settled in the neighbourhood of Lancaster. A well-known vicar of Lancaster bore this name at the beginning of the century. Two hundred years earlier the name occurs in local wills; v. infra. I find no representatives in the district now.
Johannes Howsman, 1379: P. T. Yorks. p. 276.
1572. Francis Husseman and Anne Browne: Marriage Lic. (London), p. 53.
1604. Leonard Howsman, of Warton: Lancashire Wills at Richmond, p. 158.
1622. James Houseman, of Lancaster, *glover*: ibid.
1630. Anthony Howseman, of Warton: ibid.
London, 3, 0; Crockford, 1, 2; Rigley (co. York), 3, 0.

Housewife.—Occup. 'the housewife,' a female occupier or householder; v. Husband.
Rose Husewif, co. Camb., 1273. A.
Richard Husewif, Close Roll, 30 Edw. I.
John Hosewyf. G.
Beatrix de Herlyngton, huswyf, *webster*, 1379: P. T. Yorks. p. 64.

Housin; v. Howson.

Houston.—Local, 'of Houston.' Mr. Lower writes, 'The ancient knightly family so called originally bore the name of Paduinan from a place in co. Lanark. In the 12th cent. Hugh de P. acquired the lands of Kilpeter, and built a residence there, to which he gave the name of Hugh's Town, now Houston, co. Renfrew. His descendants of that ilk borrowed their surname from it' (Patr. Brit. p. 164). Like many another Scotch name, it is well represented in the United States.
1808. Married—Thomas Houston and Eliz. Ladd: St. Geo. Han. Sq. ii. 390.
London, 5; New York, 34.

Hovell; v. Havill.

Hovenden.—Local, 'of Hovenden.' I cannot find the spot.

Alan de Hoveden, co. York, 1273. A.
London, 2.

How, Howe, Howes, Hows, Howse.—(1) Bapt. 'the son of Hugh'; How, in South England. 'Howe, Hewe, propyr name, *Hugo*': Prompt. Parv. (2) Local, 'of the howes.' How, a hill, a mound; cf. Silver How and Fox How in the Lake district of England.
'Lands in the Howes, which he had from his mother Alice del Howes' (ext. deed of grant by John de Levens), temp. Edw. I: Hist. Westm. and Cumb. i. 89.
Roger del Howes, co. Camb., 1273. A.
Richard del Howes, co. Camb., ibid.
Letitia atte How, 1313. M.
John de la How, co. Norf. FF.
London, 19, 52, 28, 4, 8.

Howard. — There are two distinct origins of the surname Howard, one official, the other baptismal; one representing the once familiar office of Hayward (q.v.), the other representing the still earlier personal name Hereward. Both of these names, totally distinct in origin, had a determined bias towards the form Howard, and in time reached it. The *hog-ward* theory needs no arguments to refute it. But I may say in passing that our Hoggarts are the natural descendants of the hogherd, for that and not hog-ward was his name. I will first deal with the official name. (1) Official, 'the hayward,' i.e. the custodian of the fences, from *hay* or *haw*, a hedge, and *ward*, a guardian.
Elwin le Heyvard, co. Norf., 1273. A.
Alice le Heyward, co. Hunts, ibid.
Geoffrey le Hayward, co. Camb., ibid.
Piers le Hawarde. H.
'Thomas Hawarde, and his brother Henry Haiwarde,' 1568: Reg. Univ. Oxf. i. 269.
William Heyward or Howard, sheriff of Norwich, 1657: FF. iii. 402.
'Edward Howard, or Heyward's gift to this parish is £3 per annum, given to the poor in bread,' 1663. St. Swithin's Ch., Norwich: ibid. iv. 256.

It is clear that if Hayward was also pronounced Haward, the further step to Howard would be inevitable. I do not think, however, that more than a small proportion of our Howards are thus sprung, as Hayward became the settled form in nomenclature and is so found in all our directories. (2) Bapt. 'the son of Heward.' The different stages of this personal name seem to have been Hereward, Harward, Haward or Heward, and Howard. It is commonly found in the 12th, 13th, and 14th centuries, and had become a surname when the Hundred Rolls were compiled. Most of our Howards are unquestionable descendants of the personal name.

Hewardus dil Per, co. Suff., 1273. A.
Hewerard Ban, co. Camb., ibid.
Heward de Horewelle, co. Camb., ibid.
Hewerad Samar, co. Camb., ibid.
John Hewerard, co. Camb., ibid.
Heward Morpeth, rector of Skeyton, co. Norf., 1554 : FF. vi. 363.
Adam fil. Heward. J.
William Howard. J.
John Fitz-howard, co. York. W. 2.
Roger Harwarde, or Hawerde, 1539 : Reg. Univ. Oxf. i. 193.
'Item, to Heyward Skynner, cs.' 1503 : Privy Purse Exp., Eliz. of York, p. 100.

The evidence given above is absolutely conclusive. Hewerard was the same as Heward, and Heward as Howard. The case of Heyward Skynner is curious, as it has got confounded with the occupative or official Hayward. It is interesting to notice that the 'Norfolk Howards' are found as Haward, one more link of importance.

'Item, to my Lord Haward, cxx¹,' 1503 : Privy Purse Exp., Eliz. of York, p. 99.

Another connexion seems to be found in the following :

1565-6. Henry Hawarde, Esq., son of Sir Thomas Hawarde, Viscount Bindon, and Frances Mewtys : Marriage Lic. (London), i. 32.

A note says, 'Succeeded in 1582 as Viscount Howard, of Bindon.' I leave to genealogists the task of deciding whether the Duke of Norfolk's name belongs to (1) or (2). I should say (2), and make him a direct descendant of Hereward the Wake. I dare say his Grace would offer no objections. It is the double origin, of course, that has made Howard so familiar a surname throughout England.
London, 141.

Howarth, Howorth.—Local, 'of Howarth,' an estate in the parish of Rochdale, co. Lanc. Howorth and Haworth (q.v.) are inextricably mixed.

'Todmorden, with a great waste, is held of William de Haworth,' temp. Edw. III : Baines' Lanc. i. 483.
Randal Howarth, of Spotland, parish of Rochdale, 1532 : ibid. p. 511.
Ann Howarth, of Crawshaw Booth, co. Lanc., 1616 : Wills at Chester (1545-1620), p. 102.
George Howarth, of Bury, co. Lanc., 1609 : ibid.
Dennis Haworth, of Crawshaw Booth, 1620 : ibid. (1621-50), p. 101.
Robert Haworth, of Haworth, 1639 : ibid. p. 102.
Manchester, 50, 5 ; London, 2, 0 ; Philadelphia, 27, 0.

Howchin.—Bapt. 'the son of Hugh,' from dim. Huchon ; v. Houchen and Hutchins.

Isabella Huchon, doghter, 1379 : P. T. Yorks. p. 157.
London, 1.

Howcroft.—Local. Perhaps for Havercroft, but more probably ' of Howcroft,' just as it stands, i.e. the croft on the how ; v. How and Croft.

Adam de Hauercroft, 1379 : P. T. Yorks. p. 111.
Manchester, 3.

Howden.—Local, 'of Howden,' a market-town and parish in E. Rid. Yorks, twenty miles from York.

Stephen de Houden, co. York, 1273. A.
Johannes de Houden, 1379 : P. T. Yorks. p. 48.
Johannes de Howden, 1379 : ibid. p. 128.
1608. Bapt.—Jane, d. Rowland Howden : St. Jas. Clerkenwell, i. 52.
1779. Married — James Lorimer and Jean Howdon : St. Geo. Han. Sq. i. 296.
MDB. (co. Lincoln), 3 ; London, 2 ; New York, 2.

Howe ; v. How.

Howel, Howell, Howels, Howells.—Bapt. 'the son of Hoel,' Welsh ; v. Powell. Howells is the genitive form ; cf. Jones, Hughes, Williams, &c.

Hoel fil. Oeni, 7 Hen. II : Pipe Roll, iv. 22.
Howel le Waleys, 1313. M.
Howel ap David, 1313. M.
Hoel fil. Philip. C.
William ap Howell ap Rice : Visit. Glouc., Harl. Soc., p. 179.
Hyllar Howell, co. Soms., 1 Edw. III : Kirby's Quest, p. 233.

London, 1, 62, 2, 2 ; MDB. (co. Carmarthen), 0, 20, 0, 28.

Howes ; v. How.

Howett, Howitt, Howetson.—Bapt. 'the son of Hugh,' from dim. Hugh-et, or Hew-et, or How-et ; v. How and Hewett.

Matilda Howet, 1379 : P. T. Yorks. p. 106.
Johanna Howet, 1379 : ibid.
Adam Howot, 1379 : ibid. p. 82.
Robertus Howetson, 1379 : ibid. p. 33.
Dionisia Howet, doghter, 1379 : ibid.
Willelmus Howetson, 1379 : ibid. p. 117.
Diota Hoet, 1379 : ibid. p. 202.
Johanna Hoet, 1379 : ibid.
1641. Otho Procter and Suzan Howett : Marriage Lic. (London), ii. 261.
1767. Married — Jordan Steele and Catherine Howitson : St. Geo. Han. Sq. i. 169.
London, 2, 6, 0 ; West Rid. Court Dir., 0, 3, 0.

Howgate.—Local ; v. Holgate, and cf. Howroyd with Holroyd, q.v.

MDB. (West Rid. Yorks), 4.

Howgego.—?

MDB. (co. Essex), 1 ; (co. Suffolk), 1 ; London, 1.

Howkins.—Bapt. Probably a variant of Hawkins, v. Hawkin ; cf. Howett for Hewett.

MDB. (co. Bedford), 4.

Howland.—Local. Possibly ' of Hoyland ' (q.v.), a parish in W. Rid. Yorks.

MDB. (co. Bucks), 4 ; London, 6.

Howlden ; v. Holden.

Howlett, Howlet.—Bapt. 'the son of Hugh,' from How or Hew (M.E. forms), and double dim. How-el-ot or Hew-el-ot ; v. How and Hewlett ; cf. Howett and Hewett.

Johannes Houlot et uxor ejus, 1379 : P. T. Yorks. p. 291.
Adam Howlot et Agnes uxor, 1379 : ibid. p. 112.
Roger fil. Hulot, co. York. W. 8.
William Houghlot. O.
Houlot de Ranchestre. AA. 4.
John Howlett. F.
Humphrey Howlett, temp. Eliz. Z.

The following two instances are noteworthy, proving that Howlett and Hewlett are the same. Of course the proof was not needed.

1673. Bapt.—Alice, d. Thomas and Dorothy Howlett : St. Thomas the Apostle (London), p. 66.

1674. — Anne, d. Thomas and Dorothy Hewlett: St. Thomas the Apostle (London), p. 66.
1684. — John, s. John Howlett: St. Jas. Clerkenwell, i. 294.
London, 16, 0; Oxford, 1, 1; New York, 7, 0; Philadelphia, 8, 1.

Howley.—Local, 'of Howley'; v. Hooley.

Johannes de Houlay, 1379: P. T. Yorks. p. 170.
Liverpool, 2; New York, 2.

Howling.—Bapt. 'the son of Hugh,' from the variant How (v. How and Howson), and dim. Howelin. The final *g* is an excrescence, as in Hewling.
London, 2.

Howman.—(1) Occup. 'Hughman,' i.e. the servant of Hugh; cf. Matthewman, Addyman, Priestman, Vickerman, &c. How was a common variant of Hugh; v. Howson. (2) Local, 'the howman,' one who resided on the how; v. How (2), and cf. Heathman, Bridgman, &c.
Gilbert Houman, co. Hunts, 1273. A.
Henry Houman, co. Hunts, ibid.
MDB. (co. Essex), 2; (co. Glouc.), 2

Howorth; v. Howarth.

Howroyd; v. Holroyd.

Howsam.—Local, 'of Howsham,' a township in the parish of Scrayingham, E. Rid. Yorks.
MDB. (co. Lincoln), 2.

Howse; v. House and How.

Howson, Howsin, Housin, Howsan.—Bapt. 'the son of Hugh'; v. Howlett. The form How for Hugh seems to have been familiar to the South. 'Howe or Huwe (*v* for *u*), propyr name, Hugo': Prompt. Parv.
Henricus Howesson, 1379: P. T. Yorks. p. 173.
Carolus Howson. F.
Simon Howissone, rector of Attleburgh, co. Norf., 1374: FF. i. 524.
John Howesson, rector of Scoulton, co. Norf., 1381: ibid. ii. 344.
MDB. (co. Cumberland), 5, 0, 0, 0; (co. Lincoln), 3, 0, 2, 1; London, 3, 0, 0, 0; West Rid. Court Dir., 5, 2, 0, 0.

Howton; v. Houghton.

Richard de Houton, co. Hunts, 1273. A.
Robert de Houton, co. Hunts, ibid.
London, 1.

Hoy, Hoye.—Local, 'at the hoy,' from residence thereby. Probably a provincial form of How, q.v.; cf. Hoyle for Hole.
Adam del Hoy, 1379: P. T. Yorks. p. 149.
Hugo del Hoy, 1379: ibid. p. 147.
Robertus del Hoye, *carnifex*, 1379: ibid. p. 205.
1645. Bapt.—William, s. Christopher Hoye: St. Jas. Clerkenwell, i. 163.
1802. Married — William Hoy and Dorothy Leplatneir: St. Geo. Han. Sq. ii. 252.
London, 6, 2; New York, 13, 7.

Hoyland.—Local,'of Hoyland,' parishes in co. York; cf. also Holland-Fen, in co. Linc. No doubt Holland and Hoyland are now inextricably mixed up; v. Holland; cf. Hoyle and Hole.
John de Hoyloind, co. Linc., 1273. A.
William de Hoylaund, co. Linc., ibid.
Ralph de Hoyland, co. Linc., ibid.
John de Hoyland, co. Norf., 20 Edw. I: FF. ix. 86.
Johannes Holand et Teffan uxor ejus, 1379: P. T. Yorks. p. 163.
London, 2; West Rid. Court Dir., 13; New York, 1.

Hoyle, Hoyles.—Local, 'at the hole'; N. Eng. *hoyle*. In Yorks and Lancashire *hole* is still dialectically *hoyle*. Any one who lived in a round hollow or pit would be Thomas or Ralph in the Hoyle.
Thomas de Hoyle, C. R., 34 Hen. III.
Alicia in le Hoyle, 1379: P.T.Yorks. p. 42.
Alicia del Hoyle, 1379: ibid. p. 110.
Willelmus de Hoyles, 1379: ibid. p. 21.
1590. Edward Hoyle, of Haslingden, co. Lanc.: Wills at Chester (1545-1620), p. 103.
1613. John Hoyle, of Spotland, co. Lanc.: ibid.
1763. Married — Robert Hoyle and Anne Holmes: St. Geo. Han. Sq. i. 127.
London, 3, 0; Manchester Dir., 14, 1; New York, 5, 0; West Riding (Yorks) Court Dir., 15, 0.

Hozier.—Occup. 'the hosier'; v. Hosier.

Hubbard; v. Hubert.

Hubbardine.—Bapt. 'the son of Hubbard' (Hubert), from dim. Hubbardin; v. Heberden. There is a strong letter of Bishop Latimer's to one Hubbardine or Hubbardin, an opponent of the Reformation (Latimer's Remains, Parker Soc. pp. 319-20). Now often spelt Hibberdine and Heberden; cf. Hubbard, Hebard, and Hibbard.

Hubbersty, Hubberstey, Hubersty. — Local, 'of Hubbersty.' I have not identified the spot. It seems to be in North Lancashire. Of course the root is *sty*, as in Thorpinsty Hall in the same district; v. Turpin. As Thorpinsty took its name from the original proprietor Thorfin, so Hubbersty will represent the original proprietor Hubert.
Thomas Hubbersteigh, of Liverpool, 1609: Wills at Chester (1545-1620), p. 103.
Thomas Hubberstie, of Flookburghe, in Cartmell, 1615: Lancashire Wills at Richmond, i. 159.
Nathan Hubberstye, of Yealond Conyers, 1709: ibid. ii. 144.
William Hubberstee, 1664: Exchequer Depositions, co. Lanc., p. 39.
1789. Married — John Hubbersty and Sarah Franklin: St. Geo. Han. Sq. ii. 31.
MDB. (co. Lanc.), 3, 1, 2; Crockford, 1, 0, 0; London, 1, 1, 0.

Hubert, Hubbard, Hubbert, Hubberd, Hobart.—Bapt. 'the son of Hubert' (St. Hubert, patron of hunters; v. Yonge, ii. 302). Once very popular as Hubbard and Hubberd. 'Old Mother Hubbard' may have represented a feminine form. There were sure to have been plenty of Hubertas who would be Hubbard in common life.
Hubertus de Vall, Pipe Roll, 5 Hen. II.
Hubertus Monetarius, Pipe Poll, 5 Hen. II.
Osbert Houbard, co. Soms., Edw. III: Kirby's Quest, p. 227.
Hubert le Priur, Close Roll, 54 Hen. III.
Hubert Blakewhit, C. R., 23 Edw. III. pt. ii.
Petrus Hubard, 1379: P. T. Yorks. p. 153.
Alicia Hubard, 1379: ibid. p. 154.
Isabella Hoberd, 1379: ibid. p. 18.
1559. Married — John Tonnstall and Jane Hubbarde, or Hubberte: St. Michael, Cornhill, p. 7.
London, 2, 36, 3, 1, 3.

Hubie, Huby, Hewby, Hubey:— Local, 'of Hewby,' a hamlet in the parish of Harewood, co. Yorks. Probably it means the *by* or dwelling of Hew, i.e. Hugh; v. Hew and Hewett.
Robertus Huby, *drapour*, 1379: P. T. Yorks. p. 214.
Magota de Huby, 1379: ibid. p. 214.
Alicia de Huby, 1379: ibid.

These names are found in Shadwell in the immediate neighbourhood of Harewood.

1608. William Hubbie and Margaret Reade: Marriage Lic. (London), i. 303. Sheffield, 1, 0, 0, 0 ; London, 0, 1, 1, 0 ; MDB. (co. Bucks), 0, 0, 0, 1.

Hucker.—Occup. 'the hucker,' a hawker or pedlar, the early masculine of Huckster, q.v.

William le Huckere, c. 1300. M. John le Hukker, co. Soms., 1 Edw. III : Kirby's Quest, p. 190. , New York, 2.

Huckett.—Bapt. 'the son of Hugh,' from the dim. Huggett, sharpened to Huckett (v. Huggett) ; cf. Hicks for Higgs, Diggs for Dicks or Dix, and Huckin for Huggin.

London, 5.

Huckin, Hukin, Hukins, Huckins, Huckings. — Bapt. 'the son of Hugh,' from dim. Hugh-kin (v. Huggins); cf. Wilkin, Tomkin, &c. The g in Huckings is excrescent, as in Jennings, Hewlings, &c. These names have all but entirely been lost in Huggin and Huggins (q.v.). The parentage is the same ; cf. Hickson and Higson, Hickins and Higgins, &c.

Hughkin Byston. A.A. 1. Willelmus Huckyn, 1379 : P. T. Yorks. p. 152. 1643. Married — Edmund Saare and Anne Hukin : Canterbury Cath. p. 56. London, 1, 0, 0, 0, 0 ; Sheffield, 0, 1, 1, 0, 0 ; MDB. (co. Derby), 0, 1, 0, 0, 0 ; Oxford, 0, 0, 0, 0, 1 ; Philadelphia, 0, 0, 0, 1, 0 ; New York, 0, 0, 0, 1, 1.

Huckle, Huckel. — ? —— Perhaps a corruption of Hucknall, q.v.

London, 1, 1 ; MDB. (co. Camb.), 4, 0.

Hucknall.—Local, 'of Hucknall.' The parish of Hucknall Torkard lies in co. Notts, six miles from Nottingham.

Hamo de Hukenelle, co. Suff., 1273. A. Walter de Hukenill, co. Linc., 20 Edw. I. R. MDB. (co. Leic.), 5.

Huckster, Huxter.—Occup. 'the huckster' or pedlar, lit. the fem. of Hucker (q.v.) ; v. Hawker.

Peter le Hukstere, 1313. M. MDB. (co. Dorset), 0, 1.

Hudd, Huddy, Hudson.— Bapt. 'the son of Richard,' a strange North-English nick. of Richard, taken from the second syllable. In the Close Roll, 20 Edw. III, part i, occurs amongst several Lancashire names 'Matthew de Sutheworth dictus Maykyn,' and 'Ricardus dictus Hudde de Walkden.' In both cases the familiar and everyday form of Christian name is added. In Gower's Latin verses on Wat Tyler's insurrection all the nick. forms of the common names of day are introduced—Wat, Tom, Sim, Bat, Gib, Hick, Col, Bob, Will, Grig, Davie, Hob, Larkin, Jud, Jib, Jack, and Hud :

'Hudde ferit, quem Judde terit, dum Tibbe juvatur, Jacke domosque viros vellit, en ense necat.'

It is manifest that Richard must be included, as being about the fourth name in the list of frequency. In place of Dick, Hud is recorded ; cf. also Ricardus de Knapton and Cristiana Hud-wyf, 1379 : P. T. Yorks. p. 294. That the form was familiar Hudde de Knaresborough (E.), Hudde Garcio de Stabulo (DD.), Richard Huddeson (H.), and John Hudeson (W. 2), prove. All these entries are found in the North.

Hudde (without surname), co. Oxf., 1273. A. William Hudde, co. Camb., ibid. Johannes Hudson, 1379 : P. T. Yorks. p. 135. Willelmus Hudde, 1379 : ibid. p. 89. Thomas Hudde, co. Soms., 1 Edw. III : Kirby's Quest, p. 131. Johannes Hudeson, 1379 : P. T. Yorks. p. 32. Adam Huddeson, 1379 : ibid. p. 171. Agnes Hud-wyf, 1379 : ibid. p. 79. 1545. William Huddy and Bridget Smyth : Marriage Lic.(Faculty Office), p.5. 1547. Bapt. — Jane Hudsonne : St. Peter, Cornhill, i. 3. London, 1, 1, 74 ; Manchester, 0, 0, 21 ; MDB. (co. Glouc.), 2, 1, 0.

Huddart, Huddert, Huthart.—Local ; probably variants of Huthwaite. In the Ulverston registers Poslett stands for Postlethwaite, and as a suffix -thwaite is taken liberties with in every manner in that district and cos. Cumb. and Westm. ; cf. Applewhite for Applethwaite.

MDB. (co. Cumberland), 5, 1, 1.

Huddle.— ? ——. Cf. Huddlestone.

Willelmus Hodell'.1379:P.T.Yorks.p.38. West Rid. Court Dir., 1.

Huddlestone, Huddleston, Hudderston, Huddleson. — Local, 'of Huddleston,' a part-township in the parish of Sherburn. W. Rid. Yorks. The Huddlestons of Millom Castle, co. Cumb., were very early established in that place.

John de Hodeleston, co. Cumb., 20 Edw. I. R. Willelmus de Hodilston, 1379 : P. T. Yorks. p. 216. William Hudleston, parish of Whittington, 1587 : Lancashire Wills at Richmond, i. 159. Thomas Huddleston, of Newbarnes, Dalton-in-Furness, 1623 : ibid. 1711. Married—John Huddleston and Eliz. Hely : St. Jas. Clerkenwell, iii. 234. Sheffield, 2, 0, 0, 0 ; MDB. (co. Cambridge), 2, 1, 1, 0 ; (co. Cumberland), 1, 2, 0, 0 ; Philadelphia, 0, 0, 0, 2.

Hudling.—Bapt. 'the son of Richard,' from nick. Hud (v. Hudd), and dim. Hud-elin ; cf. Hewling for Hugelin from Hugh.

Jordan Hudelin, co. Bedf., 1273. A. Agnes Hudelyn,1379 : P. T. Yorks. p.34.

Hudsmith.—Occup. 'the hudsmith.' I cannot suggest a solution. Perhaps a maker of huds or hobs ; Hudstone, the hobstone. North (Halliwell). The word, used in connexion with a fireplace, is alluded to by Best, in his Rural Economy of Yorkshire (1641): 'They take the stickes and sette them up on ende, slanttinge against the hudde ; and keep a good fire under them.'

Edmund Hudsmyth, 1582 : Preston Guild Rolls, p. 46. William Hudsmyth, 1582 : ibid. Ralph Hudsmyth, 1582 : ibid.

Hudson ; v. Hudd.

Huet, Huett.—Bapt. 'the son of Hugh,' from the dim. Hughet or Hewet.

1599. Charles Huett and Mary Barnham : Marriage Lic. (London), i. 261. Humphrey Huett, of Wybunbury,1605 : Wills at Chester (1545-1620), p. 103. Ann Huet, of Haslington, 1660 : ibid. (1660-80), p. 144. Catherine Huett, of Doddleston, 1680 : ibid.

Cf. Huetson for Hewetson.

1805. Married—John Huetson and Ann Swinnerton : St. Geo. Han. Sq. ii. 324. Manchester, 1, 0 ; Philadelphia, 3, 4.

Huey. — Bapt. 'the son of Hugh,' from the pet form Hughey; cf. Charley and Teddy for Charles and Edward. Hew was as familiar a form as Hugh (v. Hew). This surname has ramified strongly in Philadelphia. It is rare in England.

1588. William Hughie and Anne Keynsham: Marriage Lic. (London), i. 174.
1796. Married — William Bray and Sarah Hewey: St. Geo. Han. Sq. ii. 152. London, 1; Philadelphia, 20.

Huff. — Local, 'at the hough' (q.v.), from residence thereby, provincially pronounced *huff*; cf. *enough* and *enow*, or the pronunciation of Waff for the North-English Waugh; cf. Muff for Mough.

1605. Married — John Huffe and Johane Barrowe: St. Jas. Clerkenwell, iii. 30.
1803. — Thomas Huff and Mary Ann Hall: St. Geo. Han. Sq. ii. 278.
MDB. (co. Glouc.), 2; Manchester, 1; Philadelphia, 33.

Huggett. — Bapt. 'the son of Hugh,' from the dim. Hughet, modified to Huggett, though generally to Hewett (q.v.).
London, 6.

Huggins, Hugginson, Huggons. — Bapt. 'the son of Hugh,' dim. Hug-in or Hug-on; cf. Col-in, Jen-in (now Jenning), Lambin, &c.; also cf. Gibbins and Gibbons from Gilbert. 'Hugyn held of the same Earl an ox gang of land' (De Lacy Inquisition, Cheth. Soc. p. 6). The French fondness for double diminutives gave them the famous name Huguenot(Hug-in-ot), so that we must trace that religious sect to an *individual*, if we would get at its origin.

Hugyn. AA. 2.
William Hugginson, co. Norf. FF.
Mary Huggison, co. York. W. 16.
Willelmus Hugune, 1379: P. T. Yorks. p. 114.
Hugo Hugune et Alicia uxor ejus, 1379: ibid. p. 116.
Ricardus Hugune et Petronilla uxor ejus, 1379: ibid.
Lawrencius Hogon-man (i. e. the servant of Hogon), 1379: ibid. p. 287.
1561. John Russell and Johanna Huggens: Marriage Lic. (London), i. 21.
1707. William Huggonson, of Priest Hutton: Lancashire Wills at Richmond, ii. 145.

1790. Married — Samuel Huggins and Sarah Henwood: St. Geo. Han. Sq. ii. 47.
London, 16, 0, 0; Selby (Yorks), Huggons, 1.

Hugh, Hughes. — Bapt. 'the son of Hugh.' It would be impossible to overrate the influence of Hugh (M.E. Hew in North, How in South) on our English nomenclature. Thousands of people owe their nominal existence to it. It had pet and diminutive forms of every guise, as in Hewett and Howitt, Hewlett and Howlett, Hewling and Howling, Huggin and Huckin, Houchin and Howchin, Hutchins and Hutchinson, and many others. Hugh had an early start, for it is found in considerable strength in Domesday. St. Hugh of Cluny, St. Hugh of Grenoble, St. Hugh, Bishop of Lincoln, above all, the infant martyr, St. Hugh of Lincoln, said to have been crucified by the Jews about 1250, all gave impetus to the use of it. It became popular in Wales, and Hughes and Pugh (ap-Hugh) were the result.

Edde fil. Hugh, 1273. A.
Richard Hewes. F.
Richard Hewes. Z.
John Hughe, co. Soms., 1 Edw. III : Kirby's Quest, p. 91.
London, 0, 174.

Hughesman, Hugman. — Occup. 'Hugh's man,' i.e. the servant of Hugh, one of a large class of surnames; cf. Addyman, Matthewman; v. Howman and Human.

John Huweman, co. Oxf., 1273. A.
Cf. Robert Huwechild, i. e. Robert, the child of Hugh, co. Camb., on the same page (index).
Johannes Hewman, 1379: P. T. Yorks. p. 148.
Laurentius Hogon-man, 1379: ibid. p. 287.
With Hogon, cf. Huggins, q.v.
London, 1, 1.

Hughff. — Local, 'at the hough'; v. Huff.
MDB. (co. Durham), 2.

Hughitt. — Bapt. 'the son of Hugh,' from the popular dim. Hugh-et; v. Hewett or Hewitt, Howett, Huett.

1520-1. Thomas Hughet and Margaret Harford: Marriage Lic. (London), i. 1.
Philadelphia, 2.

Hughlett. — Bapt. 'the son of Hugh,' from the early dim. Hughelot; v. Hewlett.

Hughson. — Bapt. 'the son of Hugh'; v. Hew. The English form is now all but universally Hewson; cf. Hewlett and Hughlett.

Johannes Hughson', 1379: P. T. Yorks. p. 295.
Nicholas Hughson', 1379: ibid.
Ann Hughson, of Liverpool, *widow*, 1583: Wills at Chester (1545-1620), p. 103.
John Hughson, of Dutton, co. Chester, 1616: ibid.
Richard Hughson, of Kingsley, co. Ches., 1616: ibid.
1598. Edward Walker and Ciceley Hughson: Marriage Lic. (London), i. 250.
1759. Married — Stephen Cant and Eliz. Hughson: St. Geo. Han. Sq. i. 83.
New York, 5.

Hugill, Hewgill, Hughill. — Local, (1) 'of Hugill,' a chapelry in the parish of Kendal, co. Westm.; (2) 'of Howgill,' a chapelry in the parish of Sedbergh, W. Rid. Yorks.

Matilda de Hogyll, Sedburgh, 1379: P. T. Yorks. p. 289.
1607. Married — Christopher Swainson and Eliz. Howgill: St. Mary, Ulverston, p. 110.
1610. Thomas Howgill, co. Yorks: Reg. Univ. Oxf. vol. ii. pt. ii. p. 316.
1662. Robertus Hugell: Preston Guild Rolls, p. 132.
Robert Hugill, of Preston, 1683: Lancashire Wills at Richmond, ii. 145.
Thomas Hugill, of Preston, 1698: ibid.
MDB. (co. Middlesex), 1, 0, 0; (co. Westmoreland), 0, 3, 0; (East Rid. Yorks), 2, 0, 0; (North Rid. Yorks), 8, 0, 1.

Huish, Huyshe, Hewish. — Local, 'of Huish,' a parish in dioc. Exeter. Devonshire has parishes of Huish, North Huish, South Huish, and a place named Melhuish, whence the surname. It seems to be a local term peculiar to the district. Huish as a parish is spelt Hewis (Hundred Rolls, i. 83, A.D. 1273).

John de Hiwyssh, co. Soms., 1 Edw. III: Kirby's Quest, p. 246.
Richard de Hewysh, co. Cornwall, 20 Edw. I. R.
Richard de Hewis', co. Wilts, ibid.
1568. Thomas Hewish, co. Devon: Reg. Univ. Oxf. vol. ii. pt. ii. p. 48.
1611. Bapt. — James, s. Thomas Hewish: St. Jas. Clerkenwell, i. 62.
1659-60. Married — George Broderwick and Mary Huish: St. Dionis Backchurch, p. 35.
1800. — Low Westwood and Maria Joanne Huish: St. Geo. Han. Sq. ii. 218.

London, 2, 0, 1 ; Devon Court Dir., 1, 2, 0.

Hukin, Hukins.—Bapt. ; v. Huckin. A natural variant.

London, 1, 1.

Hulbert, Hulburd, Hulburt.
—Bapt. 'the son of Albrecht' or 'Ulbricht' (Yonge, ii. 396), earlier forms of Albert. Hulburt is the popular American form. The aspirate presents no difficulty, as this dictionary fully shows.

William Hulberte, or Howlbarte, 1530: Reg. Univ. Oxf. i. 163.
MDB. (co. Wilts), 11, 0, 0; London, 12, 1, 0; Philadelphia, 3, 0, 6.

Hulings, Hulin.—Bapt. ; v. Hullin.

Hull, Hulle.—(1) Local, 'of Hull,' an important seaport town in E. Rid. Yorks.

Elena de Hull', 1379: P. T. Yorks. p. 46.
Robertus Hull', 1379 : ibid. p. 216.

(2) Local, 'at the hull,' i.e. hill.

'Upon the hulles hyhe
Of Othrin and Olympe also,
And eke of three hulles mo
She fond and gadreth herbes sweet.'
            Gower.
'By dales and by hulles.' Piers P. 5451.
Elyas de la Hulle, co. Wilts, 1273. A.
Gunnilda de la Hull, co. Oxf., ibid.
Roger a' Hull, co. Oxf., ibid.
Leticia atte Hulle, co. Soms., 1 Edw. III : Kirby's Quest, p. 91.
Richard of the Hull, Close Roll, 16 Edw. III. pt. ii.
Nicholas atte Hulle. B.
Jordan de la Hulle. J
London, 21, 0; Manchester, 9, 0; New York, 54, 2.

Hullbrook; v. Holbrook.

Hullett.—Bapt. 'the son of Hugh,' from double dim. How-el-ot, whence also Hewlett and Howlett (q.v.).

Roger fil. Hulot, co. York. W. 8.
John Hulot, co. Linc. 1273. A.
Thomas Hulet, 1379 : P. T. Yorks. p. 121.
1730-1. Buried—Robert Hulett, late kinsman to Mr. Good : St. Dionis Backchurch, p. 300.
London, 1.

Hulley. — Local, 'of Hughley,' i.e. the meadow that belonged to Hugh, or where Hugh lived. In Lewis's Top. Dict. it is said, 'Hughley, a parish in co. Salop.
. . . The parish derives its name

from Hugh de Le, who was proprietor of the manor in the 12th century' (ii. 529). Some small spot in the W. Rid. Yorks may also have been so called ; v. Lee, Lea, Legh, or Leigh.

Henricus de Hughleghe, 1379 : P. T. Yorks. p. 69.
Sheffield, 2 ; West Rid. Court Dir., 2 ; Manchester, 2.

Hullin, Hullings, Hulings, Hulin, Huling.—Bapt. 'the son of Hugh,' from dim. Hugolin (v. Hewling or Hewlings, where many and conclusive instances are given). Hullin and Hullings are the American forms, the _g_ being excrescent, as in Jennings.

'After waiting two months, Mr. Holroyd at length obtained employment with the respectable firm of merchants, Messrs. Hullin and Woodruff. Mr. Hullin was president of the Bank of Louisiana' : Life of Abraham Holroyd, poet and antiquary, Old Yorkshire, ii. p. 232.

Huling lingered on in England till the beginning of the 18th cent.

1708. Buried—Mary Huling, cousin of Elias Jenklins. St. Dionis Backchurch, p. 276.
MDB. (co. Glouc.), 0, 0, 0, 6, 1 ; Philadelphia, 2, 1, 16, 0, 0.

Hullock; v. Ullock.

MDB. (co. Cumberland), 2 ; (co. Westmoreland), 1.

Hulme ; v. Hume.

Hulse, Hulls (?).—Local, 'of Hulse,' a township in the parish of Great Budworth, co. Chester.

1473. Thomas Hulse, co. Ches. : East Cheshire, ii. 86 _n._
1581. Robert Hulse, co. Ches. : Reg. Univ. Oxf. vol. ii. pt. ii. p. 110.
1600. William Hulse, of Poole, _husbandman_ : Wills at Chester (1545-1620), p. 104.
1616. William Hulse, parish of Sandbach : ibid.
— George Hulse, of Wheelock (Sandbach parish) : ibid.
1805. Married—Thomas Hulse and Mary Pammenter : St. Geo. Han. Sq. ii. 320.
MDB. (co. Chester), 10, 0; London, 2, 2 ; Philadelphia, 4, 0.

Hulton.—Local, 'of Hulton.' Three townships in the parish of Dean, co. Lanc., whence the Lancashire Hultons. Hulton = Hilton or Hill-town ; cf. Hull and Hill.

'William Hulton, alias Hilton, of Hilton Parke (now Hulton Park), co. Lanc. ' : London Visitation, 1635, p. 400.
Jarpord de Hulton, 1199-1200 : Baines' Lanc. i. 534.
Richard de Hulton, 1311 : ibid.
Manchester, 9 ; Philadelphia, 2.

Human.—Occup. 'Hugh-man,' i.e. the servant of Hugh ; cf. Matthewman, Addyman, Priestman, Vickerman, &c. ; v. Howman and Hughesman. It is interesting to note that Human is found in the Hundred Rolls for co. Cambridge (1273), and still flourishes there.

John Human, co. Camb., 1273. A.
John Hugman, co. Soms., 1 Edw. III : Kirby's Quest, p. 184.
MDB. (co. Cambridge), 8 ; Boston (U.S.), 1.

Humberston, Humberstone. Hummerstone. Local, (1) 'of Humberston,' a parish in co. Lincoln, four miles from Great Grimsby ; (2) 'of Humberstone,' a parish in co. Leicester, three miles from Leicester.

MDB. (co. Lincoln), 2, 3, 0 ; (co. Cambridge), 0, 1, 0 ; (co. Essex), 0, 0, 1 ; London, 0, 4, 0.

Humbert. Bapt 'the son of Humbert' (Yonge, ii. 296).

Hunbertus le Pugeis, co. Bucks, 1273. A.
London, 4.

Humble.—Local, 'of Humble.' 'Humble. Though looking like a moral characteristic, this appellation is doubtless derived from the manor of West Humble, in the parish of Mickleham, co. Surrey' (Lower). Whether this spot be the true parent or not, I cannot say, but I suspect Lower is quite correct in assigning a local origin.

William de Humbill, co. Worc., Hen. III-Edw. I. K.
1529-30. William Humble and Eliz. Hope : Marriage Lic. (London), i. 7.
London, 1 ; MDB. (co. Chester), 2 ; Newcastle, 8.

Humby.—Local, 'of Humby.' Great Humby is a chapelry in the parish of Sowerby, co. Lincoln ; Little Humby is a hamlet in the parish of Ropsley, co. Lincoln.

MDB. (co. Dorset), 4 ; London, 4.

Hume, Humes, Hulme, Hulmes, Hum. — Local, 'of

Hulme.' There are several townships so called in cos. Lanc. and Ches., the meaning is the same as Holm, q.v., and cf. Home and Hume: in both cases the *l* is elided.

Ralph de la Hume, co. Norf., 1273. A.
Henry Hulme, of Stockport, 1610: Wills at Chester (1545-1620), p. 103.
London, 17, 1, 9, 0, 1; Manchester, 4, 1, 34, 2, 0; Oxford (Hum), 1.

Humfress, Humfrey.—Bapt. 'the son of Humphrey'; patr. Humphreys (v. Humphery).

London, 2, 3.

Humpage.—? ——. Can it be a corruption of Humfress (q.v.)? Otherwise I think it must be the 'home-page,' the indoor servant; cf. Housecarl, Littlepage, Smallpage, Bowerman, Ladyman, &c.

MDB. (co. Glouc.), 1; London, 1; Manchester, 1.

Humpherson.—Bapt. 'the son of Humphrey.' A variant of Humphreyson.

1763. Married—John Higgins and Eliz. Humpherson : St. Geo. Han. Sq. i. 122.
London, 1; MDB. (co. Worc.), 1.

Humphery, Humphrey, Humphreys, Humphreyson, Humphries, Humphris, Humphriss, Humphry, Humphrys.—Bapt. 'the son of Humphrey.' The spelling of this name varied much; more frequently than not there was no aspirate. Sometimes also it is set down as Unfrey, but the interchange of courtesies between *n* and *m* is common in nomenclature; cf. Ransom for Ranson or, more correctly, Randson.

John Hunfray, co. Oxf., 1273. A.
Henry fil. Umfridi, co. Oxf., ibid.
Peter Umfry, co. Oxf., ibid.
Umfrey le Gerische, co. Oxf., ibid.
Richard Umfrey, co. Oxf., ibid.
Thomas Howmfra, 1379 : P. T. Yorks. p. 138.
Humfridus de Bassingbourn. C.
John Humphreson, parish of Winwick, *yeoman*, 1663 : Wills at Chester (1660-80), p. 145.
London, 6, 22, 54, 1, 1, 14, 4, 1, 9, 7.

Hundleby, Hondleby.—Local, 'of Hundleby,' a parish in co. Lincoln, one mile from Spilsby.

MDB. (co. Lincoln), 2, 1.

Hundley.—Local; v. Huntley.

Hundred, Hundredth, Hundreder.—(1) Local, 'at the hundred,' i.e. the county division; M.E. *hundreth*. (2) Offic. 'the bailiff of the hundred.'

Geoffrey le Hundreder, C.R., 45 Hen. III.
Helyas le Hunderd, co. Hunts, 1273. A.
Geoffrey atte Hundrethe, Close Roll, 7 Edw. II.

'The hundred is a subdivision of a county, so called either because each old hundred or ten tithings found 100 fidejussores of the King's Peace, or else because it found 100 able men for war.' All persons fit to serve on juries 'were called Hundredors (hundredarii). Hundredor was sometimes applied to the bailiff of a hundred. Each hundred had its independent court' (Introd. to Pipe Rolls, p. 84, P.R.S.).

Hundredpound.—Nick. Probably a direct translation of the French Centlivre. William Hundredpound was mayor of Lynn Regis, in Norfolk, in the year 1417 (v. Index, Blomefield's Norfolk). And now comes a curious coincidence, if it be not something more. Susanna Centlivre, the dramatic author who died in 1723, was brought up at Lynn Regis (v. Dict. Nat. Biog.). It is true that her husband, Joseph Centlivre, was cook-in-chief to Queen Anne, and it was some years after her public appearance that she married him. Still it seems possible that she may have met him in childhood in the neighbourhood of Lynn Regis, and that Hundredpound had been restored by the descendants of the old mayor into French again. The name of Centlivre survived. Cf. Whitbread for Blanchpain, Handsomebody for Gentilcors, &c.

Grace Centlivre, co. Surrey (v. Index to Hist. and Ant. Surrey).
Joseph Centlivre, co. Surrey, ibid.

Hunnybun; v. Honeybourne.

Hunsley.—Local, 'of Hunsley,' a township in the parish of Rowley, E. Rid. Yorks.

MDB. (East Rid. Yorks), 1.

Hunsworth.—Local; v. Unsworth.

Philadelphia, 8.

Hunt, Hunte.—Occup. and offic. 'the hunt,' a huntsman; M.E. *hunte*, a hunter (this latter being a later form). This is proved incidentally by the fact that there are four columns of Hunt in the London Directory to one of Hunter.

'A halpeny the hunte takes on the day
For every hound the sothe to say.'
Old Poem.
'With hunte and horne, and houndes him beside.' Chaucer, C. T. 1680.
Alice le Hunte, co. Oxf., 1273. A.
Thomas le Hunte, co. Camb., ibid.

The entries are very numerous in this register, embracing many counties.

Gilbert le Hunte, 1302. M.
John le Hunt. B.
Robert le Hunte, co. Soms., 1 Edw. III : Kirby's Quest, p. 85.
Robert le Honte, co. Soms., 1 Edw. III : ibid. p. 111.
London, 209, 0.

Huntbach.—Local, 'of Huntbach.' I cannot find the place : cf. Sandbach, Comberbach, &c., all in co. Chester or the immediate district.

Manchester, 1; MDB. (co. Chester), 2.

Hunter.—Occup. or offic. 'the hunter.' The earlier form is *hunte*; v. Hunt. While Hunt is very common I can only find one Hunter in the Hundred Rolls (1273). It became popular soon after, however, as our directories clearly prove.

Adam le Huntere, Close Roll, 52 Hen. III.
Nicholas Hunter, co. York, 1273. A.
Thomas le Hunter, c. 1300. M.
London, 60.

Huntingford. — Local, 'of Huntingford,' a tithing in the parish of Wotton-under-Edge, co. Gloucester.

MDB. (co. Surrey), 2.

Huntington, Huntingdon.—Local, (1) 'of Huntingdon'; (2) 'of Huntington,' parishes in cos. Hereford and York. There can be little doubt that some of our Huntingtons are sprung from

Huntingdon, the sharpened form being more popular.

Adam de Huntindon, London, 1273. A.
Alan de Huntingdon, co. Linc., ibid.
Robert de Huntingdone, co. Hunts. ibid.
Agnes de Huntingdone, co. Camb., ibid.
Peter Wodfoghel de Huntington, 1319–20): Freemen of York (Surt. Soc.) i. 19.
Johannes de Huntyngton, 1379: P. T. Yorks. p. 244.
Thomas de Huntyngton, 1379: ibid. p. 49.
1619. James Jones and Bridget Huntingdon : Marriage Lic. (London). ii. 78.
1780. Married — Leonard Huntington and Margareta Clark : St. Geo. Han. Sq. ii. 30.
1795. — William Northey and Mary Huptington : ibid. p. 133.
London, 0, 6; Manchester, 0, 4; Sheffield, 1, 0; New York, 27, 2.

Huntley, Hundley, Huntly.

—Local, 'of Huntley,' a parish in co. Gloucester, seven miles from Gloucester.

London, 10, 2, 0; MDB. (co. Worc.), 0, 2, 0; (co. Wilts), 6, 0, 0; Philadelphia, 12, 0, 3.

Hunton, Huntoon.—Local,

'of Hunton,' (1) a parish in co. Kent, near Maidstone; (2) a chapelry in the parish of Brompton-Patrick, near Richmond, N. Rid. Yorks; (3) a parish in co. Hants. Both Yorkshire and Hampshire are represented in our directories, especially Yorkshire.

Roger Hunton, 1379: P. T. Yorks. p. 265.
1585. Richard Hunton, co. Wilts: Reg. Univ. Oxf. ii. 141.
1610. William Hunton, co. Wilts: ibid. p. 310.
1616. William Hunton (co. Wilts) and Eliz. Jaie: Marriage Lic. (London), ii. 42.
MDB. (North Rid. Yorks), 4, 0; Devon Court Dir., 1, 0; London, 3, 0; New York, 1, 4.

Huntress, Huntriss.—? Occup.

'the huntress' (?). Seemingly a feminine of Hunter. A Latinized form occurs in the surname period.

Agnes Venatrix, co. Hunts, 1273. A.
West Rid. Court Dir., 1, 1; Doncaster, 0, 1.

Huntsman.—(1) Occup. 'the

hunt-man,' from hunt, a hunter, and the augmentative man; cf. merchant-man or husband-man. (2) Occup. 'the hunt-man,' i.e. the man (=servant) of the hunt, the

servant of the hunter; v. Hunt; cf. Matthewman, Vickerman, Priestman, Addyman, &c. Huntman was gradually assimilated to the familiar dictionary form huntsman.

Walter Hunteman, co. Camb., 1273. A.
Simon Huntman, 1379: P. T. Yorks. p. 282.
Joan Huntman. C.
Cf. Willelmus Hunter, 1379: P. T. Yorks. p. 273.
Thomas Hunter-man, 1379: ibid.

i. e. Thomas was the servant of William Hunter.

1565–6. William Bucton and Sabina Hunteman (of Ingarstone): Marriage Lic. (London), i. 32.
1650. Bapt. — Richard, s. Richard Huntsman : St. Jas. Clerkenwell, i. 176.
London, 6; MDB. (co. Lincoln), 5.

Hunwick.—Local, 'of Hun-

wick,' a township in the parish of St. Andrew, Auckland, co. Durham.

MDB. (co. Essex), 1.

Hurd.—Occup.; v. Herd.

Hurditch.— Local, 'of Hurd-

wich,' the dwelling or farmstead of the 'herd,' a keeper of cattle. It is clear from my references that -wick or -wich and not -ditch is the suffix; cf. the pronunciation of Norwich; v. Wick. Evidently a West-country name. It may be observed that Hurd, and not Herd, is found in co. Somerset; v. Herd.

John Hurdich, co. Soms., 1 Edw. III: Kirby's Quest, pp. 236–7.
Roger Hurdich, co. Soms., 1 Edw. III: ibid.
William Hurdwyche, co. Soms., 1 Edw. III: ibid.
MDB. (co. Soms.), 2.

Hurdman.—Occup.; v. Herd-

man, and cf. Hurd for Herd.

Hurlbatt, Hurlbutt, Hurl-

bert.—(1) Nick. 'a hurl-bat,' one who has shown powers in the old game of hurling. For full account, v. Strutt's Sports and Pastimes, pp. 98–9. The bat for hurling was called a 'clubbe' or 'hurle-batte' (p. 99). Probably, also, a familiar sobriquet of a cloth-beater or woolbeater; v. Beater. (2) Bapt. 'the son of Hurlbert.'

Robert Hurlebat. X.
John Hurlebat, C. R., 24 Edw. III. pt. i.
Robert Hurlebat, 15 Ric. III : v. N. and Q., Jan. 24, 1857, p. 75.

Thomas Hurlebatte, 15 Ric. III : ibid.
John Hurlebatt, circa 1570. Z.

W. H. Hurlbert figures in a correspondence with Mr. Chamberlain (Manchester Evening Mail, May 14. 1886).

Manchester Dir. (Hurlbutt), 1.

Hurle.—Local; v. Hurrell.

Hurley, Hurly.—Local, 'of

Hurley,' a parish in co. Berks. near Maidenhead. This surname is very strongly represented in the New York Directory, but as Dennis. Michael, Cornelius, Patrick, and other popular Irish personal names are generally found as the prefix, it is hardly necessary to state that a large number of the instances are of Hibernian origin. Their derivation, therefore, must be sought for in that country.

Randolph de Hurlegh, co. Soms., Hen. III–Edw. I. K.
(Prior) de Hurleye, co. Oxf., 1273. A.
(Prior) de Hurle, co. Berks, ibid.
John de Hurlee, prior of Windham, co. Norf., 1317: FF. ii. 519.
1670. Bapt.—Mary, d. Henrye Hurley : St Jas. Clerkenwell, i. 246.
1771. Married—John Hurley and Helen Fladgate : St. Geo. Han. Sq. i. 224.
London, 12, 0; New York, 101, 4.

Hurlin.—Bapt.; v. Hurlwin;

cf. Urlwin and Herrewyn.

Hurlstone.—Local, 'of Hurl-

ston,' a township in the parish of Acton, co. Chester.

Henry Hurleston, co. Ches., 14 Edw. IV : East Ches. ii. 115.
John Hurleston, of Hurleston, co. Lanc., 1566: Visit. Bedford, 1566, p. 177.
Richard Hurleston, of Hurleston, co. Lanc., 1566: ibid.
1593. Margaret Hurleston, of Manchester, widow: Wills at Chester, i. 105.
1612. William Hurleston, of Chester : ibid.
London, 3.

Hurman.—Bapt.; v. Herman

(s.v. Harman); cf. Hurd and Hurdman for Herd and Herdman.

MDB. (co. Somerset), 18.

Hurn, Hurne.—Local; v.

Hearn.

Hurrell, Hurle.—Bapt. 'the

son of Hurel.' This personal name is found from Somersetshire to Cambridgeshire, but I can discover no traces of it north of the Trent.

John Hurel, co. Oxf., 1273. A.
Richard Hurel, co. Camb., ibid.
Roger Hurel, co. Berks, ibid.
John Hurle, co. Oxf., ibid.
Stephen Hurel, co. Soms., 1 Edw. III:
Kirby's Quest, p. 140.
Henry Hurel, co. Soms., 1 Edw. III:
ibid. p. 271.
London, 5, 3; MDB. (co. Soms.), 0, 1.

Hurren, Hurran.—Local; v.
Hearn. A modern variant.

London, 9, 1.

Hurry; v. Urry.

Willelmus Hure, 1379: P. T. Yorks.
p. 105.
MDB. (co. Cambridge), 3.

Hursley.—Local, 'of Hursley,'
a parish in the dioc. of Winchester,
co. Hants, near Winchester.

William de Hurslee, co. Wilts, 1273. A.
London, 1.

Hurst, Hirst.—Local, 'at the
hurst,' a wood, a thicket. This
surname has ramified in the most
remarkable manner in the West
Riding of Yorkshire, Hirst being
the favoured form. In compound
names, generally attached to words
denoting a particular kind of 'tree ;
cf. Hazlehurst, Ashurst, Lyndhurst,
and Elmhurst.

Robert de la Hurste, Hen. III–Edw.
I. K.
Ivo de Hirst, co. Hunts, 1273. A.
Richard de Hirst, co. Hunts, ibid.
John atte Hurst, 1302. M.
William de la Hurst. B.
Agnes del Hyrst, 1379: P.T.Yorks. p. 96.
Willelmus del Herst, 1379: ibid. p. 80.
Adam del Hyrst, 1379: ibid. p. 169.
Willelmus del Hirst, 1379: ibid. p. 131.
1614. Bapt.—John, s. Robert Hirst:
St. Jas. Clerkenwell, i. 71.
1617.— Mary, d. Robert Hurst: ibid.
p. 77.
London, 28, 4; West Rid. Court Dir.,
11, 94.

Hursthouse.—Local, 'at the
hurst-house,' from residence in
a cottage by the hurst, i.e. wood ;
v. Hurst ; cf. Woodhouse.

MDB. (co. Derby), 1.

Hurt, Hurtt.—Nick. Probably
a form of Hart, q.v. ; A.S. *heort*.

Amicia le Hurt, co. Oxf., 1273. A.
Thomas le Hurt, co. Oxf., ibid.
Hugh le Hurt, co. Oxf., ibid.
London, 2, 0 ; Philadelphia, 2, 3.

Husband,Husbands.—Occup.
'the husband,' a householder, an
occupier, the head of a family ; cf.

Housewife. 'Husbonde, husbond
of gouernaunce, *paterfamilias*':
Prompt. Parv. Possibly the final *s*
in Husbands is the patronymic or
genitive, as in Jones, Williams, &c.

Walter le Husebond, co. Camb.,
1273. A.
Robertus Foghler, et Cecilia uxor ejus,
husband, *webster*, 1379: P. T. Yorks.
p. 63.
Matilda de Halghton, huswyf, *webster*,
1379: ibid. p. 62.
Willelmus Frankys et Isabella uxor
ejus, husband, *smyth*: ibid.
John Husebonde, co. Soms., 1 Edw.
III : Kirby's Quest, p. 115.
William Husebond, co. Soms., 1 Edw.
III : ibid.
1728. Married—William Phillips and
Hannah Husband : St. Geo. Han. Sq.
i. 5.
1742. Buried — James Husbands: St.
Dionis Backchurch, p. 310.
London, 0, 1 ; Manchester, 2, 0 ;
Ripon, 1, 0 ; Philadelphia, 8, 4.

Huscroft. — Local, 'of the
house-croft' (v. Croft) ; v. Oscroft,
which is probably a variant.

Cisot de Hustcroft, 1379 : P. T. Yorks.
p. 120.
Johanna Huscreft, 1379 : ibid.
Hugo de Huscroft, 1379 : ibid.
Wakefield, 1 ; MDB. (West Riding,
Yorks), 1.

Huskinson, Huskisson.—
Bapt. 'the son of Hugh.' Variants
of Hutchinson ; v. Hutchins ; cf.
Hiscock for Hitchcock. The Daily
Telegraph, July 8, 1893, announces
the death of Mary Huskinson.

MDB. (co. Lincoln), 0, 1.

Huson.—Bapt. ; v. Hooson.

**Hussey, Husey, Huzzey,
Huzza.**—Local, 'of Hussey.'
Probably Heussé in the department of La Manche. This surname
is strongly represented in South-
west England.

Geoffrey Husey, co. Wilts, 1273. A.
Reginald Husey, co. Wilts, ibid.
Hugo de Hussey, co. Rutl., 20 Edw.
I. R.
Elizabeth Hussey, 1538 : Reg. Broad
Chalke, co. Wilts, p. 6.
Henricus Huszey, 1542 : ibid.
1663. John Evans and Judith Husee:
Marriage Lic. (Canterbury), p. 90.
London, 18, 1, 0, 0 ; Devon Court Dir.,
5, 0, 0, 0 ; MDB. (co. Berks), 2, 0, 1, 0 ;
(co. Glouc.), 2, 0, 0, 1.

Hustler, Husler.—Occup.'the
hostiler,' i.e. the innkeeper ; v.

Ostler. The early instances are
found chiefly in Yorkshire.

Robert le Hostler, co. Norf., 1273. A.
Johannes Martin, *hostiler*, 1379 : P. T.
Yorks. p. 156.
Thomas Husteler, 1379 : ibid.
Robertus Husteler, 1379 : ibid. p. 276.
William Hustler, 1665, vicar of Ilkley :
Whitaker's Hist. of Craven, p. 270.
1700. Thomas Peirse and Anne Hustler
(Acklam, co. York): Marriage Lic.
(Faculty Office), p. 236.
London, 2, 0 ; Manchester, 1, 0 ; Shef-
field, 0, 3 ; MDB. (co. Suffolk), 4, 0 ;
(North Rid. Yorks), 3, 0.

Hustter; v. Hewster.

Hustwick.—Local, 'of Hurst-
wick,' a township in the parish of
Wragby, W. Rid. Yorks.

MDB. (North Rid. Yorks), 2.

Hutcherson.—Bapt. 'the son
of Hugh,' from the dim. Hutchin.
Hutcherson is a variant of Hutchinson (v. Hutchins). In the same
way Pattinson is frequently found in
the guise of Patterson; cf. Catterson for Cattinson.

New York, 2.

**Hutchins,   Hutchings,
Hutchinson,   Hutcheson,
Hutchison.**—Bapt. 'the son of
Hugh,' from the dim. Huchon or
Huchin (later Hutchin); cf. Marion
for Mary, or Robin for Robert.
Chiefly North English; v.Houchen
and Howchin. 'Huchone, Hugo,
nomen proprium viri': Cath. Ang.
The *g* in Hutchings is excrescent ;
cf. Jennings. Hutcheson and
Hutchison are modifications of
Hutchinson ; cf. Pattison for Pat-
tinson, or Purkiss for Perkins.

John Huchoun, co. Soms., 1 Edw. III :
Kirby's Quest, p. 221.
Isabella Huchon, *doghter*, 1379 : P. T.
Yorks. p. 119.
Willelmus Huchon,*son*,1379: ibid. p.172.
Isota Huchonson, 1379 : ibid. p. 210.
Willelmus Hugchonson, 1379 : ibid.
p. 136.
Agnes filia Hugonis, 1379 : ibid.

The last two are placed together,
no doubt brother and sister.

Mathew Huchonson, 1379 : P. T. How-
denshire, p. 16.
Johannes Huchesson, co. York. W. 19.
Hutchin Graham, of Peretree, 1586 :
Nicolson and Burn's Hist. Westm. and
Cumb., vol. i. p. xxxiv.
London, 16, 19, 42, 2, 8; MDB. (co.
Westmoreland) (Hutchinson), 21.

Huthart; see Huddart.

Huthwaite, Huthwait. — Local, 'of Huthwaite,' some spot in co. Cumberland, or the district of Furness, N. Lanc., possibly for Heathwaite, a township in the parish of Kirkby-Ireleth, Furness, N. Lanc.

Richard Higgin, of Houthwaite, Furness, 1607 : Lancashire Wills at Richmond, i. 147.
MDB. (co. Hereford), 1, 0 ; Barrow-in-Furness, 1, 0 ; Boston (U.S.), 0, 1.

Hutson. — Bapt. 'the son of Richard'; cf. Hudson, of which it is a corrupted form ; v. Hudd.

1548. Bapt. — William Hutsoune : St. Peter, Cornhill, i. 4.
1746. Married — Thomas Hutson and Eliz. Pettitt : Canterbury Cath. p. 88.
London, 2 ; MDB. (co. Lincoln), 3.

Hutton. — Local, 'of Hutton.' There are twenty-nine parishes or townships in England named Hutton mentioned in Lewis' Topographical Dictionary.

Andrew de Hotton, co. Southampton, Hen. III-Edw. I. K.
Thomas de Hoton, co. Linc., 1273. A. John de Hoton, co. Northumberland, ibid.
Adam de Hoton, co. Cumb., 20 Edw. I. R.
William de Hoton, drapour, 1379 : P. T. Yorks. p. 69.
Ricardus de Hoton, 1379 : ibid. p. 102.
Alexander de Hoton, faber, 1379 : ibid. p. 301.
1572. John Hutton and Jane Flynte, widow : Marriage Lic. (London), i. 53.
1735. Bapt. — Thomas, s. Thomas Hutton : St. Mary Aldermary, p. 127.
West Riding Court Dir., 13 ; London, 31 ; Philadelphia, 65.

Huxford. — Local, 'of Huxford.'
MDB. (co. Devon), 2.

Huxham. — Local, 'of Huxham, a parish in co. Devon, four miles from Exeter.
MDB. (co. Devon), 7.

Huxley. — Local, 'of Huxley,' a township in the parish of Waverton, co. Chester.

'This Inq. P. M. was taken at Chester, on the Tuesday next after the Feast of Trinity, 4 Hen. VIII, by the oath of Richard Gerard, . . . Hugh Tilston, of Huxley, Nicholas Huxley, John Walton, of Sutton, and Robert Cotgreve, junr' : East Cheshire, ii. 528.
1546. Bapt. — Toby Huckslie : St. Peter, Cornhill, i. 3.
1578. Margaret Huxley, of Nantwich : Wills at Chester, i. 106.
1602. Richard Huxley, of Duddon : ibid.
London, 6 ; MDB. (co. Chester), 2.

Huxtable. — Local, 'of Huxtable'; cf. Barnstable in the same district. Staple (q.v.) is undoubtedly the suffix.
MDB. (co. Devon), 19.

Huxter. — Occup. ; v. Huckster.

Huyshe. — Local ; v. Huish.

Huyton. — Local, 'of Huyton,' a parish in co. Lanc., seven miles from Liverpool.

James Huyton, of West Derby (co. Lanc.), 1595 : Wills at Chester (1545-1620), p. 106.
Robert Huyton, of parish of Wigan, 1594 : ibid.
MDB. (co. Lanc.), 1 ; Manchester, 1.

Huzzay, Huzzey ; v. Hussey.

Hyatt. — Local ; v. Hyett.

Hyde, Hide. — Local, 'at the hide,' from residence thereby. Hide, a measure of land of about 120 acres ; A.S. hīd. Numberless spots are so styled. There are not less than six parishes in Crockford's Clerical Directory.

John de la Hyde, co. Oxf., 1273. A. Richard de la Hyde, co. Wilts, ibid.
Adam atte Hyde, c. 1300. M. Gilbert de la Hyde. J.
1527-8. Thomas Spenser and Agnes Hide : Marriage Lic. (London), p. 6.
London, 41, 1 ; Manchester, 18, 0.

Hyett, Hieatt, Hyatt, Highett, Highatt, Hiett, Hiatt. — (1) Local, 'of High-gate,' corrupted to Hy-yate, and finally Hyett ; cf. Yates for Gates. Probably Highgate in London is referred to, as the instances are mostly found in that locality. Cornhill (v. Cornell (1)) we know was parent of an early surname. (2) Local, 'at the haigh-gate,' the gate or yate into the enclosure, from residence thereby ; v. Haig.

John atte Hagheyate, co Soms., 1 Edw. III : Kirby's Quest, p. 205.
1583. Thomas Hiegat, co. Middlesex : Reg. Univ. Oxf. vol. ii. pt. ii. p. 127.
1590. Richard Seyman and Eliz. Hyegate : Marriage Lic. (London), i. 189.
1608. Buried — Eliz. Hyeat, servant to Mr. Moore : St. Dionis Backchurch, p. 210.
1630. — A child of John Hiyates' : St. Antholin (London), p. 64.
1651-2. Married — William Hyott and Anne Hatchman : St. Dionis Backchurch, p. 28.
1718. Married — John Hiott and Isabella Barnes : St. Peter, Cornhill, ii. 72.
1751. — Edward Hyatt and Martha Fuller : St. Michael, Cornhill, p. 72.

In the same register spelt Hyatt in 1650 and Hyet in 1653,

London, 5, 1, 5, 0, 1, 0, 0 ; MDB. (co. Glouc.), 9, 0, 6, 0, 0, 0, 0 ; Maryport (co Cumb.) (Highett), 1 ; (co. Oxford), 0, 2, 2, 0, 0, 1, 1.

Hyland ; v. Highland.
MDB. (co. Sussex), 1.

Hynard. — ? Bapt. 'son of Inard ' (?) ; v. Inward.
MDB. (co. Suffolk), 2.

Hyne. — Occup. 'the hind'; v. Hine.

Hyslop ; v. Haslop.

Hythe. — Local, 'at the hythe ': a form of Hyde, q.v.

Eustace de la Hythe, co. Camb., 1273. A. Walter de la Hythe, co. Camb., ibid.

I

Ibb, Ibbs, Ibson, Ibeson, Ibbison. — Bapt. 'the son of Isabel,' from the nick. Ibb. Although common to England, Yorkshire is the great centre of these forms, where Isabelle was the rival of Matilda in the surname period. Ibson becomes Ibison or Ibeson, just as Greenway becomes Greenaway; v. Ebbs. The diminutive forms, however, have made the greatest impress on our directories; v. Ibbett.

Johannes Ibson, 1379: P.T.Yorks. p. 293.
Thomas Ibson, 1379: ibid. p. 111.
1640. Married—William Ibison and Eliz. Pickring: St. Jas. Clerkenwell, iii. 73.
1800. — Robert Giles Ibbs and Mary Mathews: St. Geo. Han. Sq. ii. 212.
London, 0, 2, 0, 0, 1; West Rid. Court Dir., 0, 0, 0, 1, 0; Leeds (Ibbison), 1; Huddersfield (Ibeson), 2; New York (Ibsen), 1.

Ibberson, Ipperson.—Bapt. 'the son of Isabel,' modifications or corruptions of Ibbotson (v. Ibbett). This is easily proved by instances, although none are needed. Ipperson is a sharpened form; cf. Epps for Ebbs.

George Ibberson, parish of Garstang, 1748: Lanc. Wills at Richmond, ii. 147.
1753. Married—John Iberson and Frances Stapleton: St. Geo. Chap. Mayfair, p. 245.
1765. — Andrew Rohl and Olive Ibberson: St. Geo. Han. Sq. i. 145.
The following entries concern Roger Ibbotson's children:
1611. Bapt.—Margaret, d. Roger Ipperson: St. Jas. Clerkenwell, i. 63.
1614. — Barnaby, d. Roger Ibbatson: ibid. p. 70.
1620. — Prudence, d. Roger Ipperson: ibid. p. 89.
West Rid. Court Dir., 4, 0; MDB. (co. Hunts), 3, 0; New York, 1, 0.

Ibbett, Ibbetson, Ibbitt, Ibitson, Ibbot, Ibbotson.—Bapt. 'the son of Isabel,' from the nick. Ibb and dim. Ibb-ot or Ibb-et. From Yorkshire down to Cornwall this was the favourite nurse-name of Isabel. But Yorkshire has the honour of originating several lead-

ing representatives of this list. Ibbotson is found in every village and town. I could furnish shoals of instances of Ibbot or Ebbot (v. Ebbetts) as girls' names in that county, but must be content with a few.

Johannes Ibotteson, 1379: P. T. Yorks. p. 218.
Ibot Baker, 1379: ibid. p. 27.
Ibota Waferer, 1379: ibid. p. 26.
Robertus Ibbotson, 1379: ibid. p. 67.
Matilda Ibot, *doghter*, 1379: ibid. p. 172.
Willelmus Kene, et Ibota uxor ejus, 1379: ibid. p. 197.
Ibbota fil. Adoe, co. York. W. 2.
Ibote Babyngton, temp. Eliz. Z.

In Cornwall, the last home of pre-Reformation diminutives, Ibot or Ebot was used as a font-name till the end of the 17th century.

1579. Bapt.—Ibbett, d. Richard Sprey: St. Columb Major, p. 10.
London, 3, 8, 0, 0, 0, 2; West Rid. Farmers' Dir. (Ibbitson), 4; West Rid. Court Dir., 0, 3, 0, 0, 0, 17; Sheffield (Ibbitt), 4; Philadelphia, 0, 2, 0, 0, 0, 2.

Ibbinson, Ibinson. —-Bapt. 'the son of Isabel,' from the nick. Ibb and dim. Ibb-in; cf. *violin* from *viol* or Colin from Col, the nick. of Nicholas; or Robin from Rob, the nick. of Robert.

1642. Bapt.—Allyce, d. William Ibbinson: St. Jas. Clerkenwell, i. 153.
1780. Married—Richard Ibbinson and Betty Munden: St. Geo. Han. Sq. i. 317.
MDB. (co. Lancaster), 0, 1.

Ibbison, Ibbs, Ibeson, Ibson; v. Ibb.

Ibbot, Ibbotson; v. Ibbett.

Ichenard, Ignard, Inard; v. Inward.

Icke, Ick, Ickes.—Bapt. 'the son of Richard,' from the nick. Hick, q.v. The surname seems to have lost its aspirate. With Ickes, cf. Hicks.

MDB. (co. Stafford), 2, 0, 0; (co. Sussex), 0, 1, 0; Philadelphia, 0, 0, 0.

Iddison, Iddeson, Ideson, Ide.—Bapt. 'the son of Idonia,' from the nick. Ide or Idde, whence Iddeson. Sometimes, no doubt,

a corruption of Idonson (v. Iddon), of which I have supplied several instances below. The root origin is the same in either case.

William Ide, co. Camb., 1273. A.
Agnes Ydd-maydon (i. e. the maid of Idd), 1379: P. T. Yorks. p. 132.
Ricardus Ideson, 1379: ibid. p. 197.
Thomas Idonson, 1379: ibid. p. 55.
Willelmus Idoynson, 1379: ibid. p. 292.
1599. Anthony Ide and Margaret Sorrell: Marriage Lic. (London), i. 262.
Idde Peadie, *widow*, 1665: Reg. St. Mary Aldermary (London), p. 185.
Manchester (Iddison), 1; Burnley (Ideson), 1; Lanc. Court Dir. (1887), 0, 1, 1, 0; Boston (U.S.) (Ide), 18.

Iddols.— ?——. Possibly baptismal from some forgotten personal name. In that case Iddols is the genitive; cf. Jones, Williams, &c.

1620. Richard Vawcill and Frances Iddoll: Marriage Lic. (London), ii. 86.
MDB. (co. Wilts), 2.

Iddon, Idone.—(1) Bapt. 'the son of Idonia,' once an extremely common font-name in Yorkshire. The nick. of this was Idon; for instances, v. Iddison.

William Idony, London, 1273. A.
John fil. Idonee, co. Norf., 20 Edw. I. R.
Idone Strangman, co. Soms., 1 Edw. III: Kirby's Quest, p. 159.
Idonia Gabun, 1379: P. T. Yorks. p. 6.
Idonia Snatchberd, 1379: ibid. p. 132.
Idonia Mollyng, 1379: ibid.
1585. John Balsey and Eliz. Iden: Marriage Lic. (London), i. 143.
Ulverston, 1, 0; Lanc. Court. Dir. (1887), 3, 0; Boston (U.S.), 0, 1.

Ide.—Bapt.; v. Iddison.

MDB. (co. Sussex), 2; Philadelphia, 5.

Idiens.— ?——. I cannot suggest any derivation.

MDB. (co. Stafford), 3.

Idle, Idell.—Local, 'of Idle,' a township and village in the parish of Calverley, W. Rid. Yorks. It is curious to note that while the United States have rejected Idle, and retained the more accurate Idell, they have got a surname Idler, q.v.

Matilda de Ydell, 1379: P. T. Yorks. p. 100.

Johannes de Idill, 1379: P. T. Yorks.
p. 101.
  Willelmus de Idill, 1379: ibid.
  1549. Bapt.—Edward Idle: St. Peter,
Cornhill, p. 4.
  1600. William Idill, or Idle, co. York,
Reg. Univ. Oxf. vol. ii. pt. ii. p. 241.
  1647. Bapt—Charles, s. Christopher
Idle: St. Jas. Clerkenwell, i. 167.
  1719-20. John Idell and Ann Washington: Marriage Lic. (Faculty Office).
p. 249.
  London, 3, 0; Leeds, 2, 0; Philadelphia,
0, 18.

Idler, Ideler.— ? —. I have
no suggestion to offer concerning
the derivation of this American
surname. I do not think it is a
nickname. Probably a variant of
Adler, of which there are eleven
instances in the Boston and twenty-
six in the Philadelphia Directory.
This Adler is almost certainly the
German Adelgar.

  Philadelphia, 7, 0.

Ifold, Ifould, Ifill. — Local,
' of Ifield,' parishes in cos. Kent
and Sussex. With the corrupted
Ifill, cf. Hatfull for Hatfield, q.v.

  1793. Married—William Ifold and
Hannah Lane: St. Geo. Han. Sq. ii. 90.
  1795.—John Ifold and Susanna Maling:
ibid. p. 129.
  London, 1, 0, 0; MDB. (co. Berks), 0,
1, 0; Philadelphia, 0, 0, 6.

Iggulden, Iggalden, Igglesden.—Local, ' of Ingleden,' i.e.
the dene or dean (valley) of Ingle,
the first settler. I cannot find the
place. v. Ingold and Ingle.

  Robert de Incledene, co. Devon, 1273. A.

  Cf. Inkersole for Ingersoll, q.v.
That this is the parent there cannot be the slightest doubt.

  1692. John Incledon and Anne Wynvard: Marriage Lic. (Faculty Office),
p. 204.
  1745. Married—Peter Postlethwaite and
Anne Iggalden: Canterbury Cathedral,
p. 88.
  London, 3, 0, 1; MDB. (co. Bedford),
0, 1, 0; (co. Kent), 2, 0, 1.

Ikin.—Local, ' of Ikin,' a parish
in co. Suffolk, five miles from
Orford.

  1583. Richard Iken and Elizabeth
Stone: Marriage Lic. (London), i. 122.
  1792. Married—John Ikin and Sarah
Walker: St. Geo. Han. Sq. ii. 77.
  London, 4; MDB. (co. Chester), 1;
New York, 1.

Ilbert. — Bapt. ' the son of
Ilbert,' a somewhat rare personal
name found in the 12th and 13th
centuries. It managed, however,
to secure surnominal honours, and
thus lives on in our directories,
though I fear it is obsolete as a
fontal name.

  Ilbert le Moneyer, 5 Hen. II, Pipe Rolls, i.
  Ilbert le Cementer. GG.
  Ilbert de Hereford. DD.
  Robert Ilberd, co. Oxf., 1273. A.
  John Hilberd, co. Soms., 1 Edw. III:
Kirby's Quest, p. 109.
  London Court Dir., 2; MDB. (co.
Devon), 4.

Ilderton.—Local, ' of Ilderton,'
a parish in co. Northumberland,
four miles from Wooler.

  Walter de Ildirton, 1397: Preston Guild
Rolls, p. 5.
  London, 1.

Iles.—Local; v. Isles.

Ilgar, Ilger.—Bapt. ' the son
of Hildegar.' The first modification
was Hilger, then Ilger. I fear
the surname is obsolete in this
form, but it survives in Elgar, q.v.

  Emma Hilger, co. Oxf., 1273. A.
I. K.
  John Ilger, co. Norf., Hen. III–Edw.
I. K.
  1547-8. John Ule and Catherine Ilgar:
Marriage Lic. (London), i. 11.

Iliff, Iliffe.—Bapt. ' the son of
Ailof'; v. Ayliffe.

  1622. William Charsley and Frances
Ilive: Marriage Lic. (London), ii. 118.
  1640. Bapt.—William, s. John Iliff: St.
Jas. Clerkenwell, i. 144.
  1687. — Katherine, d. Richard Ilive:
St. Peter, Cornhill, ii. 13.
  1791. Married—Anthony Iliff and Mary
Holt: St. Geo. Han. Sq. ii. 65.
  London, 3, 3; MDB. (co. Leicester), 0,
3; Philadelphia, 1, 2.

Illedge, Illich.—Local. I cannot find the spot, but I doubt not
it is in Cheshire, and that the
suffix is -lache, a lake; cf. Depledge,
Blackledge; v. Lach.

  1620. Married—William Hyde and
Cassandra Illidge: St. Jas. Clerkenwell,
iii. 49.
  1632. Richard Illedge, of Chorlton:
Wills at Chester (1621-50), p. 120..
  1635. Henry Illedge, of the Hough, co.
Chester, tailor: ibid.
  1698. George Illidge, of Nantwich,
joiner: ibid. (1681-1700), p. 142.
  MDB. (co. Kent), 1, 0; Boston (U.S.),
0, 1.

Illing.—(1) Bapt. ' the son of
Aylwin,' q.v. We similarly find

Iliff (q.v.) for Ailof. The g, if the
derivation be true, is excrescent, as
in Jennings, Hewling, &c.

  Walter Illing, co. Leic., 1273. A.

  (2) Local. ' of Illing.' I cannot
find the spot.

  Robert de Ylinge, co. Kent, 1273. A.
  1592. Buried—Henry Illen: St. Jas.
Clerkenwell, iv. 44.
  1750. Married—Samuel Harrison and
Martha Illing: St. Geo. Chap. Mayfair,
p. 179.
  MDB. (co. Bucks), 3.

Illingworth, Illingsworth.—
Local, ' of Illingworth,' a chapelry
in the parish of Halifax, W. Rid.
Yorks. The American form is
generally Illingsworth. No doubt
the form Ingleworth is the correct
one, implying not the ' worth' or
farmstead in some local ingle or
nook, but the ' worth' or farmstead
of Ingle the original settler; a
Scandinavian personal name; v.
Ingle.

  Hugo de Ingelworth, 1379: P. T. Yorks.
p. 168.
  Agnes de Elyngworth, 1379: ibid.
p. 186.
  Johannes de Ilkyngworth, 1379: ibid.
p. 184.
  1585. John Illingworthe and Alice Justice: Marriage Lic. (London), i. 144.
  1790. Married—John Illingsworth and
Sarah Howes: St. Geo. Han. Sq. ii. 43.
  1808. — William Illingworth and Hannah Vaughan: ibid. p. 390.
  London, 3, 0; Leeds, 10, 0; Sheffield,
7, 0; Liverpool, 0, 1; Halifax, 6, 0; New
York, 3, 0; Boston (U.S.), 0, 2; Philadelphia, 0, 7.

Illsley, Ilsley.—Local, ' of Ilsley,' two parishes in co. Berks, nine
miles from Newbury. This surname is spreading rapidly in the
United States.

  1581. Thomas Ilsley, co. Berks: Reg.
Univ. Oxf. vol. ii. pt. ii. p. 101.
  1733. John Ilsley and Margaret Owen:
Marriage Lic. (Faculty Office). p. 252.
  1793. Married—William Penny and
Catherine Illsley: St. Geo. Han. Sq.
ii. 90.
  — Henry Strowbridge and Teresia
Ilsley: ibid. p. 102.
  MDB. (co. Leicester), 2, 0; London, 0,
2; Oxford, 1, 0; Boston (U.S.), 0, 20.

Ilott.—(1) Local (?), ' at the
islet,' from residence thereon; v.
Isles. (2) Bapt.; v. Aylett, and
cf. Iliff and Illing. This second
derivation is the most probable.

William Ilot, co. Suff., 1273. A.
1612. Buried—A child still-born to
William Ilett: St. Jas.Clerkenwell, iv. 121.
1620. Bapt.—William, s. Thomas Ilott:
ibid. i. 87.
1798. Married—John Bird and Ann
Ilett: St. Geo. Han. Sq. ii. 178.
London, 1; MDB. (co. Hertford), 1;
(co. Kent), 2; Oxford, 1.

Ilsley.—Local; v. Illsley.

Image.— ?——. I can offer no
satisfactory explanation. It is
evidently imitative.
1563. Buried—Richarde Image: St.
Jas. Clerkenwell, iv. 4.
MDB. (co. Suffolk), 2.

Imbert. — Bapt. 'the son of
Isambert'; O.F. Ysambar, con-
tracted in Germany to Isabert, in
England to Imbert (Yonge, ii. 293).
Imbert de Monte Ferandi, C. R., 51
Hen. III.
Henry Isemberd,co.Southampt.,1273.A.
Ralph Isembere, co. Southampt., ibid.
Hugh Ymberd, co. Bucks, ibid.
Imbert de Salinis. B.
Isembert Burrellus. C.
Imbertus de Rakinton, Hen. III-Edw.
I. K.
Imbertus Pugeys, ibid.
Imbert Jacyn, Fines Roll, 11 Edw. I.
Imbert Blaunk, C. R., 6 Edw. fl.

In the London Directory this
great old name is represented by one
solitary tobacconist. Mrs. Caroline
Imbert ought to sell the finest old
'Virginian.
1753. Married—Abraham Jeval and
Mary Imbert: St. Geo. Chap. Mayfair,
p. 264.
London, 1; Crockford, 1; Boston
(U.S.), 1.

Imeson; v. Imm.

Imfrey.— Bapt. 'the, son of
Humphrey.' This personal name
appears in endless guises in medi-
aeval registers; v. Henfrey.
Richard Umfrey, co. Norf., 1273. A.
William fil. Umfri, co. Essex, ibid.
Robert Umfrey, co. Linc., ibid.
MDB. (co. Somerset), 1.

**Imm, Imms, Im, Imeson,
Ims, Immison, Impson.**—Bapt.
'the son of Emma,' from the nick.
Em changed to Im. Thus Imeson
is but a variant of Empson, q.v.,
Im or Imm of Emm or Emme,
and Ims or Imms of Emms, q.v.
There cannot be a doubt about this
derivation; cf. Ibbett and Ebbetts
or Izard and Ezard. With the

American Impson, cf. Thompson or
Simpson.
1574. Married—William Kelsea and
Isabell Imme: St. Dionis Backchurch, p. 7.
1742. — John Imeson and Sarah Read:
St. Geo. Chap. Mayfair, p. 29.
1794.— Josiah Wheeler and Frances
Imeson : St. Geo. Han. Sq. ii. 109.
1802. — George Imms and Eliz. Wilson: ibid. p. 259.
London, 0, 0, 1, 1, 3, 0, 0; MDB. (co.
Glouc.), 1, 0, 0, 0, 0, 0, 0; (co. Hereford),
0, 4, 0, 0, 0, 0, 0; (North Rid. Yorks), 0,
0, 0, 4, 0, 0, 0; Sheffield (Immison), 1;
New York (Impson), 2.

Immins, Immings. — Bapt.
'the son of Imayne'; v. Emeny.
An interesting relic of an old and
forgotten personal name. Immins
is the genitive form; cf. Jennings,
Williams, &c. The g in Immings
as in Jennings is an excrescence.
1658. Buried—William Immings: St.
Jas. Clerkenwell, iv. 325
1662. George Imminge and Mary
Smith : Marriage Alleg. (Canterbury),
p. 53.
1666. George Inings and Mary Low:
ibid. p. 191.
1690. Jeremy Immyns and Susanna
Welles : ibid. p. 176.
1707. Married — William Best and
Frances Immynes: St. Michael, Cornhill,
p. 54.
MDB. (co. Leicester), 1, 0.

Impett. — Bapt. (?), 'the son
of Imbert,' q.v. The corruption
would easily occur. The first
variant would be Impert, then
Impet or Impit. In the same way
Epps stands for Ebbs.
1695. Buried—Ann Impitt, widdow:
Canterbury Cathedral, p. 76.
1724. Married—William Impit and
Martha Coleman : ibid. p. 130.
1780. — John Impet and Mary Franklin: St. Geo. Han. Sq. ii. 23.
MDB. (co. Kent), 2.

Impey. — Local, 'of Impey.'
Mr. Lower says, 'This name is or
has been numerous in cos. Bucks,
Surrey, and Essex, in which last
county stands Impey Hall' (Patr.
Brit. p. 168). I doubt not this is
the true spot.
1639. Married—Thomas Impaye and
Martha Goddard: St. Jas. Clerkenwell,
iii. 71.
1699-1700. Richard Awsiter and Martha
Impey: Marriage Lic. (Faculty Office),
p. 235.
1793. Married—George Lovibond and
Martha Impey : St. Geo. Han. Sq. ii. 91.
MDB. (co. Essex), 2; London, 2;
Oxford, 1.

**Imray, Imrie, Imeary, Im-
brie.**—Bapt. 'the son of Amery'
or 'Emery,' q.v. As is commonly
the case in surnames, I has become the initial in place of E;
cf. Ebbot and Ibbott. Emms and
Imms. Empson and Imeson, Ebbs
and Ibbs. The b in Imbrie is intrusive; cf. Emblin for Emlin.
1749. Married — David Imbrie and
Frances Atkins : St. Geo. Chap. Mayfair,
p. 149.
London, 3, 1, 0, 0; MDB. (co. Durham),
0, 0, 1, 0; Philadelphia, 0, 1, 0, 0.

Ince.—Local, 'of Ince,' (1) a
parish eight miles from Chester;
(2) a township in the parish of
Wigan, co. Lanc.
Hugh Ince, co. Ches., 1575: Reg. Univ.
Oxf. vol. ii. pt. ii. p. 65.
James Ince, of Ince, parish of Wigan,
1608: Wills at Chester (1545-1620), p. 106.
Randle Ince, of Chester, shoemaker,
1609: ibid.
1667. Married—John Ince and Catherine
Derritt : St. Jas. Clerkenwell, iii. 240.
1672-3. John Ince and Anne Cheyney :
Marriage Alleg. (Canterbury), p. 211.
London, 7; Wigan, 1; MDB. (co.
Chester), 2; Boston (U.S.), 1.

Inch.—Local, 'of Inch' or 'of
the Inch,' a Scottish surname.
Several parishes, &c., so called are
in that country. Inch signifies island,
or level ground contiguous to a
river (Lower's Patr. Brit. p. 168);
cf. Inch Island (Taylor's Words
and Places, second edit. p. 213).
1563. Buried—Elyn Ynch, prentice with
Mr. Franke: St. Dionis Backchurch, p.187.
1665. Married—John Inch and Eliz.
Cannon : St. Jas. Clerkenwell, iii. 121.
1668. — Thomas Inch and Rebecca
Heter : ibid. p. 140.
London, 1; MDB. (co. Cornwall), 4;
Philadelphia, 2.

**Inchbald, Inchbold, Inch-
board.**—Bapt. 'the son of Ingebald,' no doubt one of the many
compounds of Inge, as in Ingram,
Ingold, &c.; cf. Archibald, Baldwin.
Willelmus Ingebald, 1379: P. T. Yorks.
p. 230.
Emma Inchebald, 1379: ibid. p. 249.
Johannes Hynchebald,1379: ibid. p. 236.
Thomas Hinchebald', 1379: ibid. p. 242.

Inchboard is a curious corruption
(imitative like most corruptions)
found in the Manchester Directory,
1887.

London, 1, 0, 0; West Rid. Court Dir., 0, 2, 0.

Inchliffe. — Local; v. Hinchcliffe.

MDB. (co. Worcester), 1.

Inckle, Inkle. — Bapt.; v. Ingle, a variant; cf. Inkersoll for Ingersoll, q.v.

1731. Bapt.—Elizabeth, d. William Inkell: St. Jas. Clerkenwell, ii. 195.
London Court Dir., 1, 0; Philadelphia, 0, 1.

Ind. — Probably local, 'atten-end,' from residence at the end of a row of cottages, or the end of the road, whence Nind, q.v.; cf. Nash, Noakes, &c. If this be true, which is likely, then *end* must have been popularly pronounced Ind, which is not improbable; cf. Nangle for 'atten-angle,' one who lived in the corner of the road or buildings. The following seems to have got an aspirate; but this is very common at the period:

1310. John Atte-hinde, rector of Burnham Ulp, Norf.: FF. vii. 32.
1667. Bapt.—Thomas, s. Thomas Inde: St. Jas. Clerkenwell, i. 232.
1750. Married—Thomas Ind and Ann Dock: St. Geo. Chap. Mayfair, p. 162.
MDB. (co. Essex), 2; (co. Glouc.), 2; (co. Wilts), 4; Oxford, 2.

Indor, Indoe, Inder.— ?——. Of this surname with its variants I can make nothing.

MDB. (co. Somerset), 4, 2, 0; (co. Hants), 0, 0, 1

Ineson. — Bapt. 'the son of Idonia,' a favourite Yorkshire font-name in 13th and 14th centuries. There were two nicks., one Ide from the first syllable, the other Ine from the second syllable, one giving us Iddison (q.v.), the other Ineson.

Idonia Wryght, 1379: P. T. Yorks. p. 55.
Johannes Ineson: *wryght*, 1379: ibid.
Adam Ineson, 1379: ibid.
Thomas Idonson, 1379: ibid.
Johannes Ine, 1379: ibid. p. 5.
Johannes Ineson, 1379: ibid. p. 23.
Rogerus Ine, 1379: ibid. p. 186.
Willelmus Ineson, 1379: ibid. p. 187.
1751. Married—Mathew Insone and Eliz. Stevens: St. Geo. Chap. Mayfair, p. 199.
York, 2; Leeds, 1; Blackpool, 1; Boston (U.S.), 1.

Inett. — Bapt. 'the son of Idonia'; v. Ineson, from the nick. Ine and dim. In-ot; cf. Emmett or Emmott, Marriott, &c.

Inot atte Mor, co. Soms., 1 Edw. III: Kirby's Quest. p. 148.
MDB. (co. Stafford), --

Infant. — Nick. 'the infant'; cf. Child, Ayre, and Eyre.

William le Enfant, co. Salop, 1273. A.
John le Enfaunt, co. Oxf., ibid.

Ing, Inge, Ings, Indge. — (1) Local, ' of the ing.' 'Ing, a meadow, generally one lying low near a river. North' (Halliwell); cf. Ingmire Hall, situated by the Lune at Sedbergh. (2) Bapt. 'the son of Inge' (v. Yonge, ii. 248). Image, son of Harald, was King of Norway in the 12th century. Compounded with Ing were such personal names as Ingram, Inger, Ingle, and Ingold, q.v.

John Inge, co. Oxf., 1273. A.
William Inge, co. Hunts, ibid.
Roger fil. Inge, co. Northumb., 20 Edw. I. R.
Robert Inge, rector of Salthouse, co. Norf., 1327: FF. ix. 431.

There cannot be the shadow of a doubt that (2) is the chief parent of Ing, Inge, Ings, and Indge, all being variants of the personal name Ing, found as a prefix to such Scandinavian personal names as Ingram, Ingle, Ingulf, or Ingvar (English Inger).

1753. Married—Mark Ing and Sarah Falkener: St. Geo. Chap. Mayfair, p. 252.
1801. — William Lewis Ings and Mary Sheering: St. Geo. Han. Sq. ii. 249.
1807. — Thomas Ing and Jane Longman: ibid. p. 372.
London, 2, 1, 3, 2; New York, 2, 0, 0, 0.

Ingall.—Bapt.; v. Ingle.

Ingalton. — Local, ' of Ingleton,' i.e. the town of Ingold, popularly Ingle; v. Ingle and Ingleton.

MDB. (co. Bucks), 2.

Ingamells.—Local, ' of Ingoldmells,' a parish in co. Lincoln, five miles from Burgh. Of course it was impossible for the name to be conversationally so pronounced. It was too much trouble. Thus it has become Ingamells. It is still closely attached as a surname to the county. In the following entry it is curiously

corrupted to Ingarnells, or perhaps it is misprinted.

1798. Married—Thomas Ingarnells and Hannah Hooper: St. Geo. Han. Sq. ii. 277.
MDB. (co. Lincoln), 12; London, 2.

Inge; v. Ing.

Inger, Ingerson.—Bapt. 'the son of Ingvar,' a Scandinavian personal name founded on the root Ing, q.v.; cf. the local surname Ingerthorp, i.e. the thorp of Inger. the name of the first settler. As a fontal name Inger is found at the close of the 15th century.

Roger Inger, co. Wilts, 1273. A.
Ingre Jonson, co. York, 1472. W. 11.
John Ingerson, 1560: Lancashire Wills at Richmond, i. 324.
Thomas Ingerson, 1558: ibid.
1589. Henry Humfry and Ellen Inger: Marriage Lic. (London), i. 180.
1670. Bapt.—Jone, d. Thomas Inger: Kensington Ch. p. 52.
London, 2, 0; Manchester, 2, 0; Boston (U.S.). 0, 2.

Ingerfield, Ingarfield. — Local, ' of Ingerfield,' literally the ' field of Inger,' the first settler. I do not know the spot; v. Inger. No doubt sometimes the ' field of Ingle '; v. Ingle. The name Inglefield would be sure to become Ingerfield in popular parlance; v. Inglefield. Cf. Ingerthorpe.

1432. John Inglefield, co. Norf.: FF. vi. 385.
'Alice her sister and coheir, married Philip de Inglefield, of Inglefield, in Berkshire,' temp. 1407: ibid.
William Inckerfelde, 1524: Reg. Univ. Oxf. i. 132.
London, 0, 2.

Ingerooll, Ingersaul, Inkersoll, Inkersole. — Local, ' of Ingersaul,' i.e. the saule or sale of Inger; v. Inger and Sale or Saul (2). Similarly we find in the London Directory Plimsoll and Plimsaul, where the same suffix occurs. Where the spot is I cannot say. Sale, a hall (Fr. *salle*), is commonly found in the 12th, 13th, and 14th century registers. With the sharpened form Inkersoll, cf. Inkerfield for Ingerfield (q.v.).

John Inkersall, co. Sussex, 1607: ibid. vol. ii. pt. ii. p. 295.
1536-7. Richard Joland and Agnes Inkersall: Marriage Lic. (London), p. 9.
1588-9. Thomas Inkersall and Johanna Lockey: Marriage Lic. (London), p. 176.

1661. Married—Henry Ingersoll and Mary Worrell: St. Jas. Clerkenwell, iii. 108.
1675-6. John Chittwell and Mary Inger-soule: Marriage Alleg.(Canterbury), p.159.
MDB. (co. Cornwall, 0, 1, 0, 0; (co. Middlesex), 1, 0, 0, 0; (co. Essex), 0, 0, 0, 2; (co. Derby), 0, 0, 1, 0; Philadelphia, 12, 0, 0, 0.

Ingerthorpe.—(1) Local, 'of Ingerthorpe,' a township in the parish and liberty of Ripon, Yorks. Literally the 'thorp of Inger,' the first proprietor; v. Ingerfield.
Thomas de Ingrethorp, 1379: P. T. Yorks. p. 257.

(2) Local, 'of Inglethorp,' modified into Ingerthorp. Literally the 'thorp of Ingle,' or 'Ingold,' or 'Inghild.' This spot was evidently in co. Norfolk.
John de Inghaldistorp, co. Norf., 1273. A.
Thomas de Ingaldsthorp, co. Norf., temp. John: ibid. ix. 84.
Edmund de Inglethorp, co. Norf., 15 Edw. I: FF. vi. 27.
Thomas de Ingelthorp, co. Kent, 20 Edw. I. R.
Ivetta de Inglethorp, co. Norf., 33 Edw. I: FF. vi. 27.
1661. Thomas Barnes and Eliz. Inglethorpe: Marriage Lic. (London), ii. 289.
MDB. (co. Warwick), 1.

Ingham.—Local, 'of Ingham.' (1) A parish in co. Lincoln, eight miles from Lincoln; (2) a parish in co. Norfolk, near Stalham; (3) a parish in co. Suffolk, four miles from Bury St. Edmunds. Literally the 'homestead of Ing,' the original settler; v. Ing (2). Doubtless many smaller spots would be so termed. The surname has ramified strongly in Yorkshire.
John de Ingham, co. Norf., 1273. A.
Nicholas de Ingham, co. Norf., ibid.
Oliver de Ingeham, co. Wilts, ibid.
1626. Bapt.—Thomas, sonne of Mr. Thomas Ingham, esquire: Canterbury Cathedral, p. 5.
1629. John Ingam and Dorothy Bowen: Marriage Lic. (Westminster), p. 33.

Probably the following is an imitative corruption:
1680. Bapt. — Cristopher Income, s. Bartholomew and Elisebeth Incum: St. Jas. Clerkenwell, i. 288.
London, 5; West Rid. Court Dir., 35; Philadelphia, 17.

Ingilby; v. Ingleby.

Ingle, Ingall, Ingleson. — Bapt. 'the son of Ingle' or 'Engel'; cf. the local Ingleton and Ingleby, from the name of the founder of the settlement; v. Ingold.
Emma Ingel, co. Hunts, 1273. A.
Geoffrey Ingal, co. Hunts, ibid.
Alicia Ingle, 1379: P. T. Yorks. p. 75.
Johannes Ingill, 1379: ibid. p. 63.
Robertus Ingill, 1379: ibid.
Willelmus Ingill, 1379: ibid. p. 38.
Agnes Ingilson, 1379: ibid. p. 32.
1651-2. Married—William Ingall and Eliz. Palmer: St. Dionis Backchurch, p. 28.
1656. Bapt.—Margaret, d. William Ingoll: St. Peter, Cornhill, i. 97.
1657. — William, s. William Ingle: St. Jas. Clerkenwell, i. 200.
London, 12, 0, 0; MDB. (co. Suffolk), 1, 2, 0; (West Rid. Yorks), 4, 0, 1; West Rid. Court Dir., 1,1,1; Philadelphia, 5,1,1.

Inglebright.—Bapt. 'the son of Inglebert.'
Robert Ingelberd, or Ingelbert, co. Linc., 1273. A.
1574. Bapt.—John, s. John Inggulbirth: St. Dionis Backchurch, p. 82.
1609. John Browning and Mary Ingleburt, widow: Marriage Lic. (London), i. 316.
'Here lie the bodies of Elizabeth and Susan, all the daughters of Thomas and Mary Inglebright—Susan died Jan.1,1702, aged one year—Elizabeth died Sept. 25, 1717, aged 19.' Thomas Inglebright, the father, was a grocer in Watlington, co. Norf.: FF. vii. 484.
1701. William Doiley and Martha Englebeard: Marriage Lic. (London), ii. 326.

Ingleby, Ingilby.—Local, 'of Ingleby,' a parish in N. Rid. Yorks. Also several townships in cos. Derby, Lincoln, and Yorks. Literally 'the dwelling of Ingle,' q.v.
Gilbert de Ingelby, taillour, 11 Edw. II: Freemen of York, i. 17.
Thomas de Ingleby, Rector of Houghton, co. Norf., 1361: FF. vi. 132.
Thomas de Ingleby, 1379: P. T. Yorks. p. 235.
1566. Francis Ingliby (sic), Bras. Coll.: Reg. Univ. Oxf. i. 26.
George Winter married Jane, d. of Sir William Ingleby of Ripley, co. York. Thomas Winter sonn and heir, 1594. Visitation of Worcestershire, 1569, p. 128.
1636. Miles Richardson and Mary Inglebee, widow: Marriage Lic.(London), ii. 229.
London, 1, 0; West Rid. Court Dir.,9, 6.

Ingledew, Engeldow, Engledew.—Bapt. 'the son of Ingledew'(?), one of the many compounds of Ingle, q.v. It is found half-latinized in the Hundred Rolls in the entry:
Henry Angel-Dei, co. Linc., 1273. A.
John Angel-Dei, co. Linc., ibid.

This I take to be but a play upon the word, as is common in such Latin entries. Otherwise it would be equivalent to the German Gott-schalk, i.e. God's servant. As a surname it has made a safe and secure position for itself in English directories.
1588. John Ingledewe and Elinor Stanney: Marriage Lic. (London), i. 172.
1693. John Ingledew (co. York) and Eliz. Smalbone: Marriage Lic. (Faculty Office), p. 207.
London, 7, 1, 0.

Ingledon.—Local. A variant of Ingleton, q.v.
Liverpool, 1.

Inglefield.—Local. 'of Inglefield,' i.e. the field of Ingle, the first settler; v. Ingle. I have not found the spot; v. Ingerfield.
William de Engelfeld, co. Kent, 1273. A.
John de Engelfeld, co. Oxf., ibid.
1624. Bapt.—Anne, d. Robert Inglefeild: St. Jas. Clerkenwell, i. 98.
1732. Married—Samuel Inglefield and Margaret Ridout: St. Geo. Han. Sq. i. 10.
Manchester, 1.

Inglesant, Inglesent.—?Bapt. 'the son of Inglesant,' probably one of the many personal names compounded of Ing and Ingle; cf. Johanna Ketelsang (1379, P. T. Yorks, p. 237), an obvious compound of Kettle, q.v.
Johannes Inglesant, 1379: P. T. Yorks. p. 245.
Willelmus Ingelsant, 1379: ibid.
Dom. Stephen Yngelsant, 1518: W. 11, p. 192.

Mr. J. Paul Rylands writes to me:
'In the Poll Book for the election of a Knight of the Shire for co. Leicester, January, 1775, the names of John Inglesant and Samuel Inglesant, of Sileby, occur as freeholders.'

The following entry suggests a local origin. I met with it after writing the above:
John de Englsayn, co. Camb. 1273. A.
Manchester (1887), 0, 1; MDB. (co. Leicester), 2, 0; London Court Dir., 0, 1.

Ingleson; v. Ingle.

Ingleton.—Local, 'of Ingleton,' a chapelry in the parish of Bentham, W. Rid. Yorks, near the Lancashire border. Literally 'the town of Ingle,' from the personal name of the first settler; v. Ingle.

Ellota de Ingleton, of Bentham, near Ingleton, 1379 : P. T. Yorks. p. 289.
Robertus de Ingleton, of Bentham, near Ingleton, 1379 : ibid.

The surname was to be found in the district in the 17th century.

John Ingleton, of the parish of Warton, 1608 : Lancashire Wills at Richmond (1457-1680), p. 163.
Robert Ingleton, of the parish of Warton, 1614 : ibid.

I fear the surname is extinct, but I dare not be positive, as I generally find an instance after making such an assertion. It occurs at the close of last century.

1731. Married—John Ingleton and Eliz. Garvis : St. Geo. Han. Sq. i. 9.
1798.—William Halliday and Susannah Ingleton : ibid. ii. 182.

Inglett, Inglet.—Bapt. 'the son of Ingel,' from the dim. Ingel-ot; v. Ingle. Judging by the instances below it would seem as if, amid variations of the spelling of the surname, William had been retained in the family as the traditional personal name.

William Ingelot, co. Oxf., 1273. A
William Hingelot, co. Norf., ibid.
Richard Yngelot (sic), co. Soms., 1 Edw. III : Kirby's Quest, p. 228.
1540. Robert Inglot, rector of Bodham, co. Norf. : FF. ix. 369.
'Here William Inglott, organist, doth rest,
Whose art in musick this Cathedral blest.'
Norwich Cathedral, 1621 : FF. iv. 29.
1652. Bapt.—Eliz., d. William Inglott, free of the Wine Coopers: St. Peter, Cornhill, i. 94.
1671. — Mary, d. William Inglett: St. Jas. Clerkenwell, i. 281.
MDB. (co. Camb.), 1, 0 ; (co. Hunts), 0, 1.

Inglewood.—Local, ' of Inglewood.' Literally, the 'wood of Ingle,' the first settler ; v. Ingle. I have not found the precise spot.

1417. John Ingelwode, vicar of Claxton, co. Norf., FF. x. 117.
Philadelphia, 1.

Ingley ; v. Inkley. A variant.

1704. Alexander Petty and Susanna Ingley: Marriage Lic. (London), ii. 332.
London, 1.

Inglis, Inglish, Ingliss.—Local,' the English,' i.e. the Englishman, a name originating in the Lowlands. A State document relating to a serious raid across the border in 1541, speaks of the attacking party as gathering 'to the number of fifty-two Inglismen' (TTT. p. lii). Again, reference is made to 'Andro Frostar, Ady Frostar, Johne Frostar, Inglismen' (ibid. p. liii); v. English.

Walter Ingeleys, co. Oxf., 1273. A.
Idonea la Engleys. J.
Roger Ingleys, c. 1300. M.
Johannes Inglays, 1379 : P. T. Yorks. p. 243.
1668. Married—Richard Inglish and Eliz. Macland: St. Jas. Clerkenwell, iii. 146.
1795. — John Hays and Sarah Inglish: St. Geo. Han. Sq. ii. 136.
London, 14, 1, 0 ; MDB. (co. Suffolk), 0, 0, 1 ; Philadelphia, 3, 0, 0.

Inglishby ; v. Ingoldby.

Ingman.—Occup. 'the servant of Ingram'; cf. Bartleman, Dickman, Addyman, &c.; v. Matthewman. Had it not been for the instances from the Yorkshire Poll Tax, I should have unhesitatingly put it down as ' the servant of Ing,' q.v. Perhaps that is the truer derivation.

Johannes Ingraman, 1379: P. T. Yorks. p. 33.
Robertus Ingram, *servant*, 1379: ibid. p. 56.
1444. Thomas Ingman, vicar of Dersingham, co. Norf. : FF. viii. 400.
1464. John Ingman, vicar of Kilverstone, co. Norf. : ibid. i. 546.
1763. Married—William Ingman and Hannah Knight : St. Geo. Han. Sq. i. 117.
Lanc. Court Dir. (1887), 1.

Ingold. — Bapt. 'the son of Ingold.' One of many personal names founded upon the root Ing (v. Yonge, ii. 248); cf. the local Ingoldsby, Ingoldsthorpe, or Ingoldmels, proving how familiar a name it was among the early settlers. Probably Ingle (q.v.) and Ingall were variants.

Edmund Ingold, co. Suff., 1273. A.
Cecilia de (?) Ingolde, co. Hunts, ibid.
1562. Married—John Abowen and Jane Inggould: St. Peter, Cornhill, i. 225.
1634. — Caleb Ingold and Eliz. Powell: St. Mary Aldermary, p. 17.
1645. Richard Curtis and Ann·Ingole: Marriage Lic. (London), i. 293.
London, 2 ; MDB. (co. Lincoln), 1 ; New York, 2.

Ingoldby, Ingoldsby, Inglishby.—Local, ' of Ingoldsby,' a parish in co. Lincoln. Lit. the ' by or dwelling of Ingold,' the first settler ; v. Ingold. The same individual is thus referred to on the same page:

Roger de Ingoldeby, co. Linc., 1273. A. (i. 387.)
Roger de Ingoldesby, co. Linc., ibid.

Thus Ingoldby and Ingoldsby are the same.

Thomas de Ingoldebi, co. Hunts, 1273. A.
1581. Anthony Ingoldsbye, co. Bucks: Reg. Univ. Oxf. vol. ii. pt. ii. p. 103.
1605. Richard Ingoldsby, co. Bucks: ibid. p. 279.
1678-9. Richard Ingoldsby (co. Bucks) and Mary Collmore : Marriage Lic. (Faculty Office), p. 145.
1691. William Ingoldsby and Theophila Lucey : Marriage Alleg. (Canterbury), p. 197.
London, 2, 0, 0 ; MDB. (co. Hunts), 0, 1, 6 ; (co. Lincoln), 2, 1, 0 ; Philadelphia, 0, 1, 1 ; Boston (U.S.), 0, 2, 0.

Ingott.—Bapt. ' the son of Ingold,' a modification of Ingold (q.v.); cf. Tibbott for Theobald. Ingot occurs early.

John Ingot, co. Soms., 1 Edw. III : Kirby's Quest, p. 218.
MDB. (co. Chester), 1.

Ingram, Ingraham.—Bapt. 'the son of Ingram ' or Ingelram, one of the many compounds of which Ingle or Engle is the prefix.

' Ingelram the first, count of Ponthieu ' : Freeman's Norman Conquest, iii. 135.

One of these Ingelrams of Ponthieu married the Conqueror's sister Adelaide. By-and-by Ingeram or Ingram became the recognized form.

Engeram Betencurt. E.
Ingeramus de Holtot, co. Northumb., Hen. III-Edw. I. K.
Ingelram (without surname), co. Camb., 1273. A.
Sibil Ingelram, co. Hunts, ibid.
Ingeram de Betoyne, co. Hunts, ibid.
Peter Ingeram, co. Wilts, ibid.
John Ingeram, co. York, ibid.
Ingeramus (without surname), co. Bucks, ibid.
William Engram, co. Soms., 1 Edw. III : Kirby's Quest, p. 254.
Ingram Carter, *wryght*, 1379 . 1. Yorks, p. 33.
Willelmus Ingram, 1379: ibid. p. 35.
Ingelramus de Gren, 1379: ibid. p. 74.
Willelmus Ingramson, *smyth*, 1379: ibid. p. 130.

The temptation to make this surname look like one of local origin was too great to be resisted :

1618. Buried—Thomas Ingerham, *cloth-*

worker, in the Liberary: St. Peter, Corn-hill, i. 174.

In America this form has settled down into Ingraham.

London, 29, 0; Philadelphia, 61, 11.

Ingrey. — Bapt. 'the son of Ingelry.' Ingrey is a modification; cf. Ingram for Ingelram.

Robert Ingelry, co. Hunts, 1273. A.
1633. Thomas Hallowell and Deborah Ingrey: Marriage Lic. (London), ii. 212.
1638. Married—Mark Lingwood and Thomazin Ingrey: St. Jas. Clerkenwell, iii. 69.
MDB. (co. Bedford), 3; (co. Camb.), 1.

Ings; v. Ing.

Ingulf.—Bapt. 'the son of In-gulf' (Yonge, ii. 248). A secretary of William the Conqueror bore this name.

John Ingulf', co. Camb., 1273. A.
Thomas Ingulf', co. Camb., ibid.

Inions. — Bapt. 'the son of Eineon,' one of the many variants of the great Welsh personal name Enion or Eynon; v. Benyon. Inions is the genitive form; cf. Jones, Watkins, Williams.

'Eineon (fl. 1093), Welsh prince, and warrior, son of Collwyn, played a great part in the famous legend of the Conquest of Glamorgan by the Normans': Dict. Nat. Biog. xvii. 167.

The surname is, as might be ex-pected, found chiefly on the Welsh border. But it is not common, Enion, Eynon, &c., being the modern surnominal forms. Onions (q.v.) is an imitative variant of the same name.

1593. Buried—Joane, d. William Ineon, of the plague: St. Michael, Cornhill, p. 204.
1621-2. Hugh Inniones (*upholder*) and Gillian Pearson: Marriage Lic. (Lon-don), ii. 108.
MDB. (co. Salop), 2.

Inkersole, -soll; v. Ingersoll.

Inkle; v. Inckle.

Inkley, Inckley, Incley, Hinkley, Hinckley.—Local, 'of Hinckley,' a parish in co. Warwick, but partly in co. Leicester. In surnames it is quite common to find an aspirate lost or added, but es-pecially lost. In its more correct form the surname has ramified strongly in the United States.

1557. Married—Robert Hynckeley and Tomasyn Emerye: St. Michael, Corn-hill, p. 7.
1605. Bapt.—Eliz., d. Michael Hinch-ley: St. Jas. Clerkenwell, i. 45.
1638. — George, s. George Incely: ibid. p. 140.
1643. — Thomas, s. George Inclye: ibid. p. 154.
1789. Married—James Hinckley and Eliz. Stanbrook: St. Geo. Han. Sq. ii. 16.
London, 1, 0, 0, 2, 1; MDB. (co. Lin-coln), 4, 0, 0, 0, 1; (co. Northampton), 0, 1, 2, 0, 0; Boston (U.S.), 0, 0, 0, 53, 16.

Inkpen.—Local, 'of Inkpen,' a parish near Hungerford, in Berk-shire. Literally, the '*pen*,' or en-closure of *Inge*,' the first settler; v. Ing, and cf. Penfold.

Nicholas de Ingepenne, co. Berks, Hen. III-Edw. I. K.
William de Ingepenne, co. Berks, ibid.
Richard de Ingepenne, co. Bucks, 1273. A.
John Glasyere de Inkpenne, C. R., 1 Hen. IV. pt. ii.
William Inkpenne, temp. 1490, co. Norf.: FF. ii. 62.
1750.' Married—James Inkpen and Sarah Hayes: St. Geo. Chap. Mayfair, p. 161.

In my last reference the name returns to its original form:

1790. Married—Thomas Ingpen and Harriet Lockyer: St. Geo. Han. Sq. ii. 52.
London, 1.

Inman.—Occup. 'the inn-man,' a lodging-house keeper. Later on the terms innholder and innkeeper took its place. Inman, however, attained surnominal honours, and thus is amply avenged. M.E. *in*; '*in*, hospicium': Prompt. Parv. A synonymous surname is Oastler from Hosteler. Inman has existed in Furness, North Lancashire, for centuries, and still flourishes.

Willelmus Indmon, 1379: P. T. Yorks. p. 85.
Willelmus Inman, 1379: ibid. p. 287.
Margaret Inman, of Broughton-in-Fur-ness, 1507: Lancashire Wills at Richmond (1457-1680), p. 164.
1502. Bapt.—Annes (Agnes), d. John Inman: St. Peter, Cornhill, i. 10.
1607. Married—Edward Inman and Margaret Broughe: St. Jas. Clerkenwell, i. 32.
London, 9; Sheffield, 2; Philadelphia, 9; Boston (U.S.), 1.

Innes, Inns, Innis.—Local, 'of Innes,' an estate in the parish of Urquhart, co. Moray. The first possessor who assumed the name

was Walter de Innes, who died in the reign of King Alexander II (Lower's Patr. Brit. p. 169). Innes seems to be an abbreviation.

1704-5. James Assheton and Eliz. Innes: Marriage Lic. (London), ii. 333.
1790. Married—William Innes and Mary Cook: St. Geo. Han. Sq. ii. 45.
1809. — Robert Inns and Sarah Lewis: ibid. p. 418.
London, 10, 2, 0; Oxford, 11, 0, 0; Boston (U.S.), 4, 0, 12.

Innocent.—Bapt. 'the son of Innocent.' No doubt originally connected with Childermas, or Holy Innocents' Day; cf. Christmas, Midwinter, Nowell, all names given at the font, commemorative of the particular season wherein the child was born or baptized.

John Innocent, Issue Roll, 44 Edw. III.
Maud Innocent, C. R., 4 Hen. IV. pt. i.
John Incent, 1505: Reg. Univ. Oxf. i. 42.
1541. Buried—Edward Innocent: St. Peter, Cornhill, i. 105.
1589. John Hannam and Eliz. Incente, *widow*, of East Ham, co. Essex: Mar-riage Lic. (London), i. 180.
1621. Married—Symond Innocent and Isabell Askewe: St. Jas. Clerkenwell, iii. 50.

Innocent is still a font-name on the Continent; cf. 'Innocent Marizi, picture-frame manufacturer,' Lon-don Dir., 1874.

London, 3; Sheffield, 8; MDB. (co. Derby), 2.

Inns.—?——. Perhaps a modi-fication of Innes, q.v. But v. Ince.

1698. William Legatt and Rebecca Inns: Marriage Lic. (London), ii. 323.
MDB. (co. Bucks), 3.

Inskip, Inskipp, Inskeep.—Local, 'of Inskip,' a manor in the parish of St. Michael le Wyre, co. Lanc., in Domesday spelt Inscip.

1622. John Inskippe: Preston Guild Rolls, p. 79.
1631. John Inskip, of Garstang, *clerk*: Lancashire Wills at Richmond (1457-1680), p. 164.
1753. Buried—Thomasina Inskept, *a pensioner*: St. Dionis Backchurch (Lon-don), p. 318.
1803. Married — James Elphick and Maria Inskip: St. Geo. Han. Sq. ii. 295.
Manchester, 1, 0, 0; London, 0, 1, 0; MDB. (co. Stafford), 4, 0, 0; Phila-delphia, 2, 1, 1.

Insley, Inslee.—Local, perhaps a corruption of Illsley, q.v.

1764. Married—Thomas Insley and Sarah Hawkins: St. Geo. Han. Sq. i. 131. MDB. (co. Warwick), 3, 0; New York, 2, 9.

Instance.—?——. I can make nothing of this.

MDB. (co. Essex), 1.

Instone, Inston.—Local, 'of Ingston' (?). I cannot find the spot.

1742. Married—Francis Instone and Betty Abley: St. Geo. Chap. Mayfair, p. 23. MDB. (co. Salop), 4, 0; (co. Worcester), 3, 1.

Inward, Inwards.—Bapt. 'the son of Inard,' probably a softened form of Ichenard; gen. Inwards.

Ithenard, or Ingnard, or Ignard fil. Stephen, co. Berks: Hen. III-Edw. I. K. Stephen fil. Ynardi, co. Berks: ibid. Ichenard de Crunge, co. Worc.: ibid. Hynard de Aumeruge, co. Hereford: ibid.

The first three following seem closely connected:

Ichenard Eling, co. Worc., Hen. III-Edw. I. K. Ynard de Elinrugge, co. Worc., ibid. Ythenard de Elrug, co. Berks, ibid. 1684. Buried—Richard, s. John Inward: St. Dionis Backchurch (London), p. 250. 1685. — Sarah Inward, d. Richard Inwood (sic), *lodger*: ibid. p. 127. — Thomas Cooper and Mary Innard: Marriage Alleg. (Canterbury), p. 219. London, 1, 3; MDB. (co. Essex), 1, 0.

Inwood.—Local, 'of Inwood.' I cannot find the spot. Seemingly a West-country name.

Thomas de Inwode, co. Soms., 1 Edw. III: Kirby's Quest, p. 233. Adam Inwod, co. Soms., 1 Edw. III: ibid. p. 235. 1662-3. John Inwood and Annabella Halie: Marriage Lic. (Faculty Office), p. 69. 1748. Married—John Inwood and Sarah Anderson: St. Geo. Chap. Mayfair, p. 108. London, 6; Boston (U.S.), 2.

Ion, Ionn.—Bapt. 'the son of John.' I presume this is so, but have no proof to offer.

Richard Ion, co. Camb., 1273. A. 1752. Married—William Ion and Eliz. Wilson: Reg. St. Mary, Ulverston, p. 385. 1789. — John Ion and Eliz. Jones: St. Geo. Han. Sq. ii. 31. London, 3, 1; MDB. (co. Cumberland), 2, 0.

Irby.—Local, 'of Irby,' now Irby-upon-Humber, a parish in co.

Lincoln. Also 'of Ireby,' a parish in co. Cumberland.

Margaret de Ireby, co. Lincoln, Hen. III-Edw. I. K. William de Irreby, co. York, 1273. A. 1561. William Brightman and Eliz. Irbye: Marriage Lic. (London), i. 23. 1703-4. Anthony Irby and Mary Flint: ibid. ii. 331. 1785. Married—Rev. Charles Harwood and Louisa Young, witness William Henry Irby: St. Geo. Han. Sq. i. 380. MDB. (co. Norfolk), 1.

Iredale, Iredell, Irdale.—Local, 'of Airedale,' i.e. the valley of the river Aire, Yorks; ct. other North-English surnames such as Tweedale, Tindal, Lonsdale, Teasdale, &c.

1753. Married—Matthew Iredale and Eliz. Roberts: St. Geo. Chap. Mayfair, p. 264. MDB. (co. Cumberland), 8, 0, 0; (West Rid. Yorks), 4, 0, 0; London, 3, 0, 0; Liverpool, 0, 0, 1; Philadelphia, 0, 4, 0.

Ireland.—Local, 'of Ireland,' an immigrant from the Emerald Isle; cf. Holland, Scott, Inglis, Welsh, Dutchman, &c.

Simon de Irlande, co. Oxf., 1273. A. Geoffrey Irlond, co. Soms., 1 Edw. III: Kirby's Quest, p. 184. Thomas de Ireland, 1379: P. T. Yorks. p. 176. Johannes de Yrland, 1379: ibid. p. 173. Margereta Ireland, 1379: ibid. p. 92. Walterus Irland, 1379: ibid. p. 160. 1598. Married—George Ireland and Sarah Baker: St. Dionis Backchurch (London), p. 13. 1669. Bapt.—Thomas, s. Andrew Ireland: St. Jas. Clerkenwell, i. 241. London, 19; Boston (U.S.), 20.

Iremonger; v. Ironmonger.

Ireson.—? Bapt. I have no suggestion to offer.

1670. Thomas Ireson (co. Northampt.) and Bridget Morris: Marriage Alleg. (Canterbury), p. 177. 1752. Married—Simon Ireson and Sarah Merritt: St. Geo. Chap. Mayfair, p. 218. 1799. — William Ireson and Sarah Liversage: St. Geo. Han. Sq. ii. 195. MDB. (co. Northampton), 2; Oxford, 1; Boston (U S.), 7.

Ireton.—Local; v. Irton.

Irish.—Nick. 'the Irish,' an Irishman; v. Ireland.

Richard le Irishe, co. Salop, 1273. A. Henry le Ireys, temp. 1300. M. John le Irreys. H. Philip le Iryssh, co. Soms., 1 Edw. III: Kirby's Quest, p. 100.

Johannes Yrisshe, 1379: P. T. Yorks. p. 227. Thomas Irysshe, 1379: ibid. p. 300. Ricardus Irys, 1379: ibid. p. 56. Thomas Irissh, Pardons Roll, 6 Ric. II. 1582. Freeman Iryshe: Reg. Univ. Oxf. vol. ii. pt. ii. p. 122. 1677. Bapt.—Edward, s. Peter Irish: St. Jas. Clerkenwell, i. 278. London, 6; MDB. (co. Devon), 6; Boston (U.S.), 7.

Irishman.—Nick. 'the Irishman.' Cf. Dutchman, Welshman, &c.

'One tenement in the tenure of Edward Newton; one tenement in the tenure of Edward Irishman: one tenement' &c. (of Lynn Regis, co. Norf., 2 Edw. VI): FF. viii. 507.

Irlam.—Local, 'of Irlam.' This locality near Manchester generally goes by the name of 'Irlam o'th Heights.'

John Erlam, of Cadishead, 1590: Wills at Chester (1545-1620), p. 61. Alexander Irlam, of Irlam, 1595: ibid. p. 107. Thomas Irlam, of Pendlebury, 1601: ibid. 1743. Married—Nathaniel Irlam and Ann Ralph: St. Geo. Chap. Mayfair, p. 33. MDB. (co. Chester), 2; Manchester, 10.

Ironfoot.—Nick. 'iron foot'; cf. Pedifer, of which this is probably a translation.

Peter Yrenefot, co. Camb., 1273. A.

Ironman.—Occup. 'the ironman,' i.e. ironmonger, q.v.

London, 1; MDB. (co. Leicester), 1.

Ironmonger, Iremonger.—Occup. 'the ironmonger'; v. Iremonger.

John le Irmongere, co. Oxf., 1273. A. John Irinmongere, co. Hunts, ibid. Richard Irinmonger, co. Bucks, ibid. Daniel le Irmongere, c. 1300. M. William le Irremongere, ibid. 1582. William Horsell and Katherine Iremonger: Marriage Lic. (London), i. 109. 1617. Married—Henry Holden and Joane Ironmonger: St. Jas. Clerkenwell, iii. 45. 1666. — Richard Warner and Elinor Iremonger: ibid. p. 126. MDB. (co. Derby), 1, 0; (co. Leicester), 1, 0; (co. Notts), 1, 0; (co. Hunts), 0, 4.

Irons, Iron.—?

1668. John Irons and Eliz. Hall: Marriage Lic. (Faculty Office), p. 104. 1741. Bapt.—Thomas, s. John Irons: St. Geo. Chap. Mayfair, p. 3. MDB. (co. Bedford), 4, 0; London, 6, 2; Philadelphia, 16, 0.

Ironside, Ironsides.—? Nick. 'the iron-side,' a sobriquet for some strong, thick-ribbed man. History is familiar with Cromwell's Ironsides. But it must not be forgotten that Durham is a large centre of the haematite industry, and that -*side* is a common local suffix in that district (v. Akenside). Therefore it might well be that Iron-side simply meant 'at the side of the iron lode,' or ' pit.'

John Irenside, *mercer*, 8 Edw. III: Freemen of York, i. 29.
1577. Ralph Ironsyde, co. Durham: Reg. Univ. Oxf. vol. ii. pt. ii. p. 77.
1604. Gilbert Ironside, co. Glouc.: ibid. p. 274.
Gilbert Ironside, 1661, bishop of Bristol: Crockford's Clerical Directory, p. xxxviii.
1685-6. William Pawlett and Martha Ironside: Marriage Alleg. (Canterbury), p. 224.
London, 2, 0; Sheffield, 3, 0; MDB. (co. Durham), 1, 0; (co. Glouc.), 0, 1.

Irton, Ireton.—Local, (1) 'of Irton,' a parish in co. Cumberland; also a township in the parish of Seamer, N. Rid. Yorks; (2) 'of Ireton,' a parish in co. Derby, near Wirksworth.

William de Irton, co. York, 1273. A.
Stephen de Irtone, co. Derby, ibid.
Thomas de Irton, co. Camb., 20 Edw. I. R.
1619. Richard Irton, co. Wilts: Reg. Univ. Oxf. vol. ii. pt. ii. p. 379.
1662. Robert Ireton: Preston Guild Rolls, p. 147.
1662. Edward Nelthorp and Mary Sleigh, d. Mrs. Ireton: Marriage Alleg. (Canterbury), p. 76.
Philadelphia, 0, 4.

Irving, Irvin, Irvine, Irwin, Urwin, Urwen, Erwin, Ervin.—Local, (1) 'of Irvine,' a parish in Ayrshire; (2) 'of Irving,' a parish in Dumfriesshire. That all these variants come of one or two stocks is incontestable. Mr. Robert Brúce Armstrong in his book, The Debateable Land (p. 185), finds the following variations of this bordername: Irving, Erwing, Erwyn, Irrwin, Irrwing, Irveyn, Irwynn, and Urwen. The last is a well-known form of the surname in Northumberland. This is the only variant without representation in my copy of the London Directory. It is not often that a surname is

found with three different initial letters.

Cristofer Urwen, of Boneshawe, co. Northumb., 1547: Armstrong's Debateable Land, Appendix, p. lxxiv.
Cuthbert Urwen, of Robbegate, co. Northumb., 1547: ibid.
1752. Married—Thomas Davis and Thomasine Urwin: St.Geo. Han. Sq. ii.223.
1759. — Thomas Reading and Isabella Irwing: ibid. i. 48.
1762. — Joseph Irving and Marcy Scott: ibid. p. 188.
1763. — Laurence Irvine and Lydia K. Chamberlayne: ibid. p. 116.
1769. — William Irwin and Mary Dalton: ibid. p. 84.
1800. — Gardiner Greene and Eliz. Clarke,witness George Erving: ibid p.126.
London, 10, 4, 6, 9, 2, 0, 2, 1; Newcastle (Urwin), 6; MDB. (Northumberland), 0, 0, 0, 2, 2, 0, 0, 0; Philadelphia, 12, 76, 25, 118, 0, 0, 36, 47.

Irwin.—Local; v. Irving.

Isaac, Isaacs, Isaacson, Isacke.—Bapt. 'the son of Isaac.' A well-known personal name in the surname period, but no more confined to the Jews than Adam or Abel. Hundreds of English people bear one or other of these surnames in whose veins there flows not a single drop of Jewish blood.

Walter Isak, co. Soms., 1 Edw. III: Kirby's Quest, p. 254.
Isak de Draytone, co. Soms., 1 Edw. III: ibid. p. 173.
Johannes Isakson, 1379: P. T. Yorks. p. 246.
Robert fil. Isaac, co. Linc., 1273. A.
Isaac Judæus (the Jew), co. York, ibid.
Johannes Isaak, co. Norf., ibid.
John Ysac, co. Oxf., ibid.
William Isaak, C. R., 25 Hen. VI.
1618. John Isick and Ursula Lawes, or Lawson: Marriage Lic. (London), ii. 67.

There is nothing Jewish in the following entry:

1745. Bapt.—Thomas, son of Thomas and Barbara Isaac: St. Jas. Clerkenwell, ii. 275.
1790. Married—Richard Isaacs and Mary Peters: St. Geo. Han. Sq. ii. 43.
1808. — John Foster and Caroline Isaacson: ibid. p. 394.
London, 17, 68, 8, 1; Boston (U.S.), 10, 19, 7, 0.

Isaard.—Bapt.; v. Isard.
MDB. (co. Kent), 1.

Isabell, Isbell.—Bapt. 'the son of Isabel,' a very popular font-name in its day; v. Ibbett and Ibbetson. Isabells is the genitive form; cf. Jones, Williams, Jennings, &c.

Walter Ysabelle, co. Oxf., 1273. A.
John Isabell, co. Norf., ibid.
Walter fil. Isabell, co. Linc., ibid.
William Isabel, co. Soms., 1 Edw. III: Kirby's Quest, p. 79.
Ricardus Deyne et Isabella uxor ejus, 1379: P. T. Yorks. p. 3.
Matilda Isebell, 1379: ibid. p. 120.
Johannes Issebell, 1379: ibid. p. 163.
Johannes Isbell, 1379: ibid.
1523. William Isabelles, rector of St. Augustine, Norwich: FF. iv. 477.
1617. Married—Thomas Brickell and Ann Isbell: St. Antholin (London), p. 52.
Thomas Issable, 1711: Reg. St. Columb Major, p. 253.
Crockford (1880), 1, 0; Boston (U.S.), 0, 1.

Isard, Isitt, Issard, Issott, Izard, Izat, Izod, Izzard, Izatson, Isaard, Issitt, Isett.—(1) Bapt. 'the son of Izod,' or 'Ysolt,' or 'Isolda.' This batch of surnames was given up in despair by Mr. Lower. I, myself, in my English Surnames, got astray in ascribing them to Isabel. Their origin is a very simple one, as given above; the fact being that Isolde was a very popular girl's name at the surname period. Ysolt is, of course, one of the names connected with Arthur's Court, coming in the episode of Tristan. It was very popular in Yorkshire and Cornwall, in the latter of which counties I find it a font-name within the last hundred years, in the forms of Isot and Izot. For other variants, v. Ezard and Izard.

Isolda Longespe, co. Hunts, 1273. A.
Richard fil. Isolda, co. Linc., ibid.
Roger fil. Isolde, co. Hunts, ibid.
Isota Holebrook, co. Soms., 1 Edw. III: Kirby's Quest, p. 140.
Matilda fil. Isolde, 1379: P. T. Yorks. p. 18.
Johannes Isaude, 1379: ibid. p. 144.
Johannes Isot, 1379: ibid. p. 186.
Johannes Isote, 1379: ibid. p. 197.
Margareta Isod, 1379: ibid. p. 151.
Isota Sekker, 1379: ibid. p. 219.
Isota Layth, 1379: ibid. p. 185.
Isotte Symes, temp. Eliz. Z.
Izott Barn, ibid.
Ezotta Hall, co. York. W. 11.
John Issot, co. York. W. 16.
Sarah Issot, co. York. W. 15.
1576. Bapt.—Isott, d. Richard Moylle: St. Columb Major (Cornwall), p. 9.
1588. Married—John Thomas and Anne Issolde: St. Jas. Clerkenwell, iii. 13.
1612. Isylte Darwin, *widow*, of Walton-le-dale, co. Lanc.: Wills at Chester (1545-1620), p. 50.
Izett Reynolds, together with three

other little children, was drowned in a boat accident at Aughrim, Ireland, May 12, 1891: Manchester Examiner and Times, May 13, 1891.

For other modern instances, v. Izard.

1625-6. Thomas Hebblethwaite and Joane Isard: Marriage Lic. (London), ii. 161.
Philadelphia (Isard), 9.

Isblower.—Occup. 'the iron-blower,' an ironfounder; v. Isemonger.

Thomas le Ysblower, Fines Roll, 11 Edw. I.

Iselton.—Local, ' of Iseldean.' I cannot find the spot.

Martin de Iseldene, London, 1273. A. London, 1.

Isemonger, Iseminger. — Occup. 'the ironmonger.' A.S. *iren* and *isen*, iron; cf. **Isengard**, Isenhard, Isenbrand, i.e. iron-defence, iron-firm, and iron-sword: Yonge, vol. i. p. lxxx, Glossary.

Richard Ismonger, c. 1300. M.
Edward Esemonger, Patent Roll, 15 Edw. IV. pt. i.
Isebel le Isemongere. G.
Agnes la Ismongere, London. X.
1801. Married—Francis Easter and Sarah Izemonger: St. Geo. Han. Sq. ii. 238.
1808. — Thomas Riley and Mary Isemunger: ibid. p. 386.
MDB. (co. Sussex), 1, 0; London, 1, 0; Philadelphia, 0, 9.

Isgar.—Bapt. 'the son of Isgar.' This surname still flourishes in the West country. Miss Yonge says (ii. 293) the meaning is 'iron-spear.'

John Isgare, co. Soms., 1 Edw. III : Kirby's Quest, p. 265.
1666. Philip Packer and Sarah Isgar: Marriage Lic. (Faculty Office), p. 96.
1695. Bapt.—James, s. William Isgar : St. Jas. Clerkenwell, i. 362.
1697. — John, s. William Isgar: ibid. p. 371.
MDB. (co. Somerset), 4.

Isham, Isom.—Local, ' of Isham,' a parish in co. Northampton, three miles from Kettering. The corrupted Isom is a natural one.

Henry de Isham, co. Northampt., Hen. III-Edw. I. K.
1416. John Isham, prior of Windham, co. Norf. : FF. ii. 519.
1582. Buried—Grace, d. Robert Isam : St. Michael, Cornhill, p. 198.
1590. Thomas Stacye and Agnes Isam

(of Lincoln): Marriage Lic. (London), i. 187.
1621-2. Edward Isham, co. Linc. : Reg. Univ. Oxf. vol. ii. pt. ii. p. 404.
1625. Married—Edward Isum and Eliz. Morryer: St. Jas. Clerkenwell, iii. 54.
1807. — Thomas Isom and Charlotte Harris: St. Geo. Han. Sq. ii. 372.
Crockford, 2, 0; London, 1, 1 ; Philadelphia, 1, 1 ; Boston (U.S.), 4, 0.

Isherwood.—Local, ' of Isherwood.' I cannot find the spot. It is a Lancashire surname, originally Usherwood, i.e. the wood of the usher, the door-keeper. The word usher has now a very confined sense. It was a most familiar term in the surname period ; v. Usherwood.

John Usherwood, of Brindhill, 1585 : Wills at Chester (1545-1620), p. 197.
Arthur Isherwood, of Great Leven, *yeoman*, 1594 : ibid. p. 107.
James Isherwood, of Whalley, 1605 : ibid.
1800. Married—Thomas Isherwood (of Leigh, co. Lanc.) and Ann Barlow: St. Geo. Han. Sq. ii. 219.
London, 4; Manchester, 11; Liverpool, 6; Preston, 4 ; Philadelphia, 6.

Isitt, Iositt, Tsett.—Bapt. ' the son of Isolt' ; for history and early instances, v. Isard.

1802. Married—Thomas Isatt and Anna Foret: St. Geo. Han. Sq. ii. 268.
'On the 22nd inst. at Adelaide Road, N.W., Frederic Thomas Isitt, aged 65' : Daily Telegraph, Nov. 2, 1887.
London, 2, 0, 0; MDB. (co. Suffolk), 0, 2, 0; Philadelphia, 2, 0, 3.

Isles, Isle, Iles.—Local, ' at the isle,' from residence on some little island on a river, or by the seashore. As a rule, monosyllabic local surnames take a final *s*; cf. Stubbs, Styles, Brooks, Holmes, &c. Probably it is the genitive form, as in Williams, Jones, Wilkins, &c.; M.E. *ile*, an isle ; O.F. *isle*.

John del Ile, co. Oxf., 1273. A.
Baldwin del Ille, or de Insula, co. Oxf., ibid.
Malves del Ile, co. Norf.; FF. i. 301.
Thomas Iles, Ch. Ch., Oxf.: Reg. Univ. Oxf. vol. ii. pt. ii. p. 277.
1579. Nicholas Iles and Mary Jacques: Marriage Lic. (London), i. 87.
1678. Charles Carter and Susanne Isles: Marriage Alleg. (Canterbury), p. 285.
London, 1, 0, 0; MDB. (co. Berks), 1, 0, 0 ; (co. Lincoln), 0, 4, 0 ; (co. Gloucester), 0, 0, 6 ; Philadelphia, 5, 0, 4.

Isley.—Local, ' of Isley,' a chapelry in the parish of Kegworth, co. Leicester.

1569. James Peckham and Anne Isley, of Chart, near Sutton Valence: Marriage Lic. (Faculty Office), p. 15.
1607. Martin Barneham and Unam Isley : Marriage Lic. (Westminster), p. 16.
1729. Married—Robert Barrett and Ann Isley: St. Geo. Chap. Mayfair, p. 289.
MDB. (co. Hunts), 1 ; Philadelphia, 1.

Islip, Islop.—Local, ' of Islip.' (1) a parish in co. Northampton, near Thrapston ; (2) a parish in co. Oxford, seven miles from the University city.

Gilbert de Ythslep, co. Oxf., 1273. A.
Gilbert Islep, co. Hunts, ibid.
Walter de Islep, rector of Gresham, co. Norf., 1305 : FF. viii. 128.
William de Islep, rector of Foxley, co. Norf., 1360 : ibid. p. 212.
' One tenement in the tenure of Beatrice Isloppe,' Lynn Regis, co. Norf., 2 Edw. VI : ibid. p. 507.
1781. Married—Thomas Lucas and Mary Islip: St. Geo. Han. Sq. i. 323.
MDB. (co. Bedford), 2, 0 ; (co. Camb.), 1, 0 ; (co. Rutland), 2, 0 ; London Court Dir., 0, 1 ; Philadelphia, 1, 0.

Ismay.—Bapt. ' the son of Ismay,' a somewhat rare girl's name found in the 13th century. It managed to become a surname, and still lives.

Ysemay Vidua, co. Oxf., 1273. A.
Isemay Egleberd (fem.), co. Oxf., ibid.
Roger fil. Ysmay, co. Linc., ibid.
Isamaya Hibernica. DD.
1753. Married—John Ismay and Catherine Joad: St. Geo. Chap. Mayfair, p. 262.
1802. Buried—Ann Ismay, in the cloyster yard: Canterbury Cathedral, p. 154.
London, 1 ; MDB. (co. Kent), 1 ; (co. Cumberland), 2 ; New York, 1.

Isom.—Local ; v. Isham.

Ison, Izon, Izen.— (1) Bapt. ' the son of Isan,' probably a Welsh personal name as it is found associated with Floyd. Also modern instances are found in Liverpool, where the Welsh population is so large. (2) Local, ' of Isham,' q.v., a corruption of Isom ; cf. Ransom and Ranson.

Isan Floyd, 1569 : Reg. Univ. Oxf. i. 275.
1617-8. Thomas Browne and Margaret Ison : Marriage Lic. (London), ii. 57.
1624. John Skip and Margaret Isans : ibid. p. 140.
1788. Married—Thomas Ison and Hannah Jack son: St. Geo. Han. Sq. ii. 3.

1793. Married—William Field and Mary Izon: St. Geo. Han. Sq. ii. 93.
London, 1, 0, 0; Liverpool, 2, 0, 0; MDB. (co. Leicester), 1, 0, 0; (co. Warwick), 1, 2, 0; New York (Izen), 1.

Issard, Issott.—Bapt. 'the son of Isolt;' for history and early instances, v. Isard and Izard.

1625-6. Thomas Hebblethwaite and Joane Isard, *widow*: Marriage Lic. (London), ii. 161.
1690. Married—Edmund Issard and Bridget Arnold: St. Jas. Clerkenwell, iii. 208.
Lancashire Court Dir. (1887), 1, 0; Leeds, 0, 1.

Isted, Histed.—Local, probably 'of Irstead,' a parish in co. Norfolk, twelve miles from Norwich.

1621. Thomas Isted, co. Devon: Reg. Univ. Oxf. vol. ii. pt. ii. p. 390.
1631. Richard Isted and Anne Goodwin: Marriage Lic. (London), ii. 203.
1703. Thomas Isted and Anne Rose: Marriage Lic. (Faculty Office), p. 246.
London, 1, 1; MDB. (co. Northampton), 1, 0; (co. Sussex), 3, 0; Oxford, 0, 1; New York, 2, 0.

Isterling.—Local; v. Easterling, a variant.
Liverpool, 1.

Isworth.—Local, 'of Ixworth,' a parish in co. Suffolk, seven miles from Bury St. Edmunds.

1315. William de Ixworth, vicar of Little Melton: FF. v. 9.
1360. John de Ixworth, rector of Threxton, co. Norf.: ibid. ii. 362.
London, 1.

Ithell.—Bapt. 'the son of Ithel'; v. Bethell. A Welsh personal name.

Ithell Wynne. AA. 1.
Thomas Ithell, rector of Emneth, co. Norf., 1573: FF. viii. 409.
John Ithell, of Kelsall, 1612: Wills at Chester (1545-1620), p. 107.
1589-90. Hugh Ithell and Parnell Bowlton: Marriage Lic. (London), i. 185.
1623. Jonah Faunce and Dorothy Ithell, *widow*: ibid. ii. 127.
MDB. (co. Chester), 1; Philadelphia, 1.

Ivall, Ival.—Bapt. 'the son of Ivel.' I can only furnish one instance.

Ivel Faber, co. Devon, Hen. III-Edw. I. K.
London, 2, 0; Philadelphia, 0, 1.

Ivatt, Ivatts, Ivetts.—Bapt. 'the son of Ivo' or 'Ive,' dim. Ivote. Ivette, or Ivetta (v. Ive). Ivo de

Usegate was bailiff of York in 1271. A few years after we find the Church of Askam-Richard, close to the city, given by William de Archis, and Ivetta, his wife, to the Nunnery of Monkton. In 1729 Alicia Iveson was buried in St. Martin's, Micklegate. Thus in the one city we have memorials of the male, female, and hereditary use of this once famous font-name (v. History and Antiquities of York. Printed by A. Ward, 1785).

Ivote le Bolure, co. Camb., 1273. A.
John fil. Ivette, co. Hunts, ibid.
Thomas fil. Ivettoe. E.
Ivetta de Inglethorpe, co. Norf., 33 Edw. I: FF. vi. 27.
Margaret Ivot, co. Norf., 1449: ibid. i. 195.
1579. Thomas Ivatts and Johanna Stodder: Marriage Lic. (London), i. 92.
1617. Anthony Younge and Lydia Ivatt: ibid. ii. 54.
1622. William Ivat and Anne Boardman: ibid. p. 111.
London, 0, 1, 0; Crockford, 1, 0, 0; MDB. (co. Camb.), 18, 0, 0.

Ive, Ives, Iveson, Ivison.—Bapt. 'the son of Ivo' or 'Ive.' Miss Yonge has an interesting account of this name (ii. 249-50). Probably connected with Ives, the saint who gave the title to St. Ives in co. Huntingdon (who, legend says, was a Persian bishop, and set up a hermitage on that spot), and Iva, similarly commemorated at St. Ives in co. Cornwall. The great Ivo de Taillebois reminds us of the Norman equivalent, St. Ives of Brittany; and St. Ivo de Chartres, imprisoned for his opposition to the adultery of Philip I, gave a natural impetus to the popularity of the name. v. Ivatt.

Walter fil. Ive, co. Salop, 1273. A.
William fil. Ive, co. Cornw., ibid.
Ive Hook, co. Hunts, ibid.
Ivo fil. Warin, 1306. M.
Aimeric fil. Yvo. C.
Antony Iveson, co. York. W. 11.
William Iveson, co. York. W. 2.
Adam Iveson, 1379: P. T. Yorks. p. 264.
Yvo Milner, 1379: ibid. p. 258.
Yvo Pape, 1379: ibid. p. 268.
1592. Anthony Iveson, rector of Hayneford, co. Norf.: FF. x. 424.
1620. Benjamin Emmens and Rose Ives: Marriage Lic. (London), ii. 88.
London, 3, 19, 2, 1; New York, 0, 33, 0, 4.

Ivens, Ivinson.—(1) Bapt. 'the son of Ivo' or 'Ive,' q.v. An early French form was Yvon or Ivone (Yonge, ii. 250), but it was popularized also in England.

Ivo, or Iwein Titneshove, cos. Staff. and Salop, Hen. III-Edw. I. K.
Ivo Pantulf, or Yvonus Pantulf, cos. Staff. and Salop, ibid.
Peter fil. Ivone, co. Camb., 1273. A.
Nicholas fil. Ivone, co. Salop, ibid.
William fil. Yvone, co. Hunts, ibid.
Ivone Beaudontz, co. Soms., 1 Edw. III: Kirby's Quest, p. 176.
Ivone Pyonye, co. Soms., 1 Edw. III: ibid.

(2) Bapt. 'the son of Evan,' from an early form Ivan.

David ap Ivan. XX. 1.
Ivon ap Howell: v. Visitation of Worcestershire, 1569, p. 78.
Meredith ap Ivan ap Robert: Visitation of London, 1635, p. 354.
'Miss Evans, or Ivins, to adopt the pronunciation most in vogue with her circle of acquaintances': Sketches by Boz, ch. iv.
1691. Married—Robert Iveans and Eliz. Bennill: St. Jas. Clerkenwell, iii. 210.
1692. Bapt.—Susanna, d. Robert Ivens: St. Michael, Cornhill, p. 156.
1788. Married—Samuel Howse and Ann Ivinges: St. Geo. Han. Sq. ii. 11.

With this variant, cf. Jennings for Jenins.
Crockford, 4, 0; MDB. (co. Cumberland), 0, 3; Philadelphia, 5, 0.

Ivers, Iverson; v. Ivor.

Ives, Iveson; v. Ive.

Ivetts; v. Ivatt.

Ivey, Ivie, Ivy.—Bapt. 'the son of Ive,' from the pet-form Ivie or Ivey; cf. Charley and Charlie. v. Ive.

1595. Married—Marke Ivy and Mary Green: St. Jas. Clerkenwell, iii. 19.
1641. William Ivie and Flora Bingley: Marriage Lic. (London), ii. 257.
1808. Benjamin Ellis and Eliz. Ivey: St. Geo. Han. Sq. ii. 400.
London, 5, 0, 0; MDB. (co. Cornwall), 3, 0, 0; Lanc. Court Dir., 0, 0, 2; New York, 5, 1, 0; Philadelphia, 1, 0, 2.

Ivimey, Ivimy, Ivamy, Ivermee.—?——. I cannot suggest any satisfactory derivation. Mr. Lower writes, 'There was a favourite character in the old Christmas games called Ivy, whose antagonist was Holly: and the frolics of the *Holly-boy* and the *Ivy-girl* were maintained in Kent (on St. Valentine's Day) till towards the close of the 18th century (Gent. Mag. 1779). See the Song of the "Holly and Ivy" quoted in Hone's Mysteries, p. 94, where Ivy is made to be of the feminine gender :

"Holly and his mery men, they dawnsyn and they syng:
Ivy and hur maydyns, they wepen and they wryng."

The singular name Ivymey, Ivimey, signifying *Ivy-maiden*, Mr. Ferguson thinks, may be from this source.' This view is not impossible. The surname King has generally so risen (v. King and Kingman); cf. the nick.

Martin le Yungemey, co. Sussex, 1273. A.

i.e. the young maiden.

1765. Married—Giles Ivemie and Jane Harris: St. Geo. Han. Sq. i. 148.
1778. — Thomas Ivimey and Eliz.Times: ibid. p. 184.
1788. — John Davis and Ann Ivemey: ibid. ii. 11.
London, 5, 2, 0, 1 ; MDB. (co. Dorset), 0, 0, 1, 0; (co. Cornwall), 1, 0, 0, 0.

Ivor, Ivers, Iversen, Iverson.—Bapt. 'the son of Ivar'; seemingly another form of Ivo or Ive. Still in use in Denmark, and has crossed the waters in patronymic guise as Iversen (v. London Directory). My references are Welsh, and if further proof was needed of the cosmopolitan use of the name, the Irish and Scotch MacIver and MacIvor would supply the deficiency. v. Ive.

Llewelyn ap Ivor, 1321. M.
William ap Ivor, 1322. M.
1565. Bapt.—Tovall Iver's child, an Irishman, named Roger: St. Antholin (London), p. 18.

1739. Married—John Iverson and Anne Couchman: Canterbury Cathedral, p. 83.
Probably this is a variant of Iveson (v. Ive).
London, 1, 2, 2, 0; Boston (U.S.) (Iverson), 3.

Ivory, Ivery.—(1) Local, 'of Ivery.' The family de Ivery were descended from Rodolph, half-brother to Richard the First, Duke of Normandy, who for killing a monstrous boar, while hunting with the Duke, was rewarded with the Castle of Ivery, on the river l'Evre, and from thence entitled Comes de Iberio (Dunkin's Oxfordshire, i. 22). Lower adds to the above, ' John de Ivery obtained the manor of Ambrosden, co. Oxon, in 1077, and Hugh de Ivri occurs as its lord in Domesday Book.' It is believed the name so originated is obsolete.

1391. William Yvory: Cal. of Wills in the Court of Husting (2).

(2) Bapt. 'the son of Ivor,' popularly Ivory; v. Ivor. ' Ireland had a St. Ivor or Ivory, who was considered to have prayed away from Fernegenall the *mures majores qui vulgariter Rati vocantur* so completely that none ever survived there again ; but whether he was named by Dane or Kelt does not appear. At any rate, St. Ivory was deemed good to invoke against rats' (Yonge, ii. 249-50).

Ivory Malet, temp. 1270. DD.

The above instance seems to have anticipated croquet by half a dozen centuries. It reminds me of such combinations as Savage Bear, More Fortune, River Jordan, Christmas Day, or Pine Coffin. Christmas Day appeared in 1884 at a trial in

Lancaster (v. my English Surnames, 5th edit. pp. 508-9).
(3) Bapt. ' the son of Every ' (v. Everson). In some cases the familiar surname Every has assumed the imitative form of Ivory (cf. Ivens for Evans). The same individual is referred to as —
Mr. Iverye, 1583 : Reg. Univ. Oxf. vol. ii. pt. i. p. 106.
Mr. Every, 1592 : ibid. p. 230.
Mr. Everie, 1594 : ibid. p. 254.
Mr. Evorie, 1594 : ibid. p. 317.
Mr. Ivory, 1598 : ibid. p. 320.
1611 Roger Bomfrey and Susanna Ivery: Marriage Lic. (London), ii. 34.
1663. Buried—Anne Ivory, a kinds-woman of Mr. Thos. Honeylove, *haberdasher*: St. Dionis Backchurch p. 234.
1668-9. Married—Edmund Clofe and Mary Iverey: St.Jas. Clerkenwell, iii. 154.

I suspect (3) is the chief parent of Ivory.
London, 3, 0; MDB. (co. Essex), 2, 0 ; Philadelphia, 2, 0; New York, 2, 2; Boston (U.S.), 4, 0.

Ivy; v. Ivey.

Izard, Izzard, Izod, Izat, Izatson, Izatt.—Bapt. ' the son of Isolt '; for history and early instances, v. Isard.

1661. Married—Richard Stack and Miriam Izard: Marriage Alleg. (Canterbury), p. 63.
1666. — George Liddell and Rachael Izatt: ibid. p. 119.
1668. — Henry Izod and Anne Bartlett: ibid. p. 152.
1670. — Thomas Izzard and Eliz. Fesson : St. Jas. Clerkenwell, iii. 171.
London, 4, 5, 4, 0, 0, 0; Crockford, 3, 0, 0, 1, 0, 0; MDB. (co. Glouc.) (Izod), 2 ; Oxford (Izzard), 3 ; Boston (U.S.) (Izatt), 1 ; Philadelphia, (Izard), 1.

Lower has Izatson in his Patr. Brit. p. 170. I have not yet met with an instance. He suggests that it is a corruption of Isaacson. I doubt not it must be placed here.

Izen, Izon; v. Ison.

J

Jack, Jackes, Jacks, Jacke.— Bapt. 'the son of John,' from nick. Jack; v. Jakes. It seems probable that for a short period after Jack was becoming the nick. for John, robbing James of the distinction, Jakes with an *s* answered for Jacques or Jacobus, and Jake or Jack without an *s* for John.

John le Warner, *or* Jacke le Warner, co. Norf., 1273. A. i. 441-2.
John de Bondec', *or* Jakke de Bondec, co. Bucks, ibid. ii. 344.
Jacobus Amadur, *or* Jakes Amadur, co. Linc., ibid. i. 357, 353, 385, 396.
1753. Married—William Jack and Eliz. Davison : St. Geo. Chap. Mayfair, p. 252.
1788. — John Tobias and Eliz. Jacks : St. Geo. Han. Sq. ii. 2.
London, 9, 2, 3, 0 ; New York, 7, 1, 2, 1.

Jackaman.—A variant of Jackman, q.v. ; cf. Jackaway.

MBD (co. Suffolk), 1.

Jackaway, Jackways, Jakeway.—Bapt. 'the son of Jacques,' variants of the French Jacques. First it would become Jackway, then Jackaway ; cf. Greenaway for Greenway, or Hathaway for Hathway.

1613. Married—Fawke Marrow and Isabell Jackway : St. Jas. Clerkenwell, p. 39.
1614. — Robert Jaquey and Margery Paine : ibid. p. 40.
These instances are conclusive.
Philadelphia, 6, 0, 0 ; MBD. (co. Soms.), 0, 1, 1.

Jackett, Jacquette. — Bapt. 'the son of Jack,' from dim. Jacket ; cf. O.F. Jaquette, a girl's name. The dictionary 'jacket' has probably a similar origin, being the dim. of O.F. *jaque*, a jack or coat of mail, which Ducange assigns to the Jacquerie, or revolt of the peasantry nicknamed Jacques Bonhomme, A.D. 1358 ; v. Skeat.

John Jaket, C. R., 1 Hen. V.
1411. Roger Jaket : Cal. of Wills in Court of Husting (2).
1680. Married—Thomas Stringfeild and Deboray Jacket : St. Jas. Clerkenwell, iii. 180.
1753. — John Nash and Ann Jackett : St. Geo. Chap. Mayfair, p. 263.

1788. — William Jackett and Susannah Norman : St. Geo. Han. Sq. ii. 16.
1808. — Thomas Jacquet and Mary Hanell : ibid. p. 392.
— — Robert Jaquet and Sarah Springford : ibid. p. 381.
Philadelphia, 0, 2 ; MDB. (co. Cornwall), 1, 0.

Jackling, Jacklings, Jacklin.—Bapt. 'the son of Jacqueline,' a. name probably introduced from Flanders. It lingered as a fontname till the Reformation : ' 1598, March 15, Buried Jacolyn Backley, widow' (St. Dionis Backchurch, London). The final *g* is excrescent as in Jennings. And the final *s* in Jacklings is the patronymic as in Williams or Jennings.

Jakoline le Blonde, temp. Hen. III : E. & F., co. Cumb., p. 102.
Johannes Jakolini, co. Camb., 1273. A.
Jakelina Vanne, C. R., 2 Edw. II.
Thomas de (sic) Jaclyn, 1379 : P. T. Yorks. p. 112.
Petrus Jaclyn, 1379 : ibid. p. 228.
1749. Married — James Walker and Mary Jackling : St. Geo. Han. Sq. i. 42.
1794. — John Pearce and Mary Jacklin : ibid. ii. 117.
London, 1, 1, 0 ; MDB. (co. Camb.), 0, 0, 1 ; (co. Lincoln), 0, 0, 13.

Jackman.—Occup. 'the man of Jack,' i.e. the servant of Jack ; cf. Addyman, Peterman, Matthewman. I find no evidence that Jackman was a man who wore a *jack*, as suggested by Mr. Lower ; cf. Jakeman. The following are entered together :

Johannes de Clyfford, 1379 : P. T. Yorks. p. 153.
Robertus Jakman, 1379 : ibid.
Johannes Dycson, 1379 : ibid.
Thomas Jak-son, 1379 : ibid.
Johannes Jak-man, 1379 : ibid.
Cf. Elias Joneman, 1379 : ibid. p. 149.
Johannes Joneman, 1379 : ibid. p. 181.
Willelmus Joneman, 1379 : ibid. p. 209.
Thomas Jonman, 1379 : ibid. p. 213.
Cf. also, Willelmus Jakknave (i.e. Jack's knave, the servant of Jack), 1379 : ibid. p. 267.
Robertus Jakman, 1379 : ibid.
1545. William Jackman and Ann Woodford : Marriage Lic. (Faculty Office), p. 5.
1564. Edward Jackman and Anne Style : Marriage Lic. (London), i. 27.
London, 9 ; Oxford, 4 ; Boston (U.S.), 4.

Jackson.—Bapt. 'the son of John,' from the popular nick. Jake or Jack, q.v. Instances are unneeded, but I furnish a few.

Robert fil. Jake, co. Camb., 1273. A.
Henricus fil. Jake, co. Camb., ibid.
Johannes Jakson, 1379 : P. T. Yorks. p. 301.
Willelmus Jacson, 1379 : ibid. p. 8.
Robertus Jackeson, 1379 : ibid. p. 23.
Willelmus Jakeson, 1379 : ibid. p. 32.
1547. Bapt.—John, s. Thomas Jacson : Kensington Ch. p. 2.
1582. Married — Steven Roodes and Marget Jakson : ibid. p. 62.
London, 260 ; New York, 344.

Jacob, Jacoby, Jacobson, Jacobs.—Bapt. 'the son of Jacob.' Although the personal names prefixed to these surnames in the London Directory generally denote a Jewish origin, it is not so in all cases. There are Jacobs and Jacobsons of purely English descent. The same remark applies to Jacob and possibly to Jacoby. The last was well established as a personal name in the 13th century.

Thomas Jacoby, co. Camb., 1273. A.
William Jacob, co. Camb., ibid.
William fil. Jacobi, co. Kent, ibid.
Jacobus de Broxton, 1379 : P. T. Yorks. p. 112.
Alicia fil. dicti Jacoby, 1379 : ibid. p. 6.
Johannes fil. Jacoby, 1379 : ibid. p. 7.
Jacobus fil. Ricardi, 1379 : ibid.
1598. Edward Woorall and Mary Jacobson : Marriage Lic. (London), i. 248.
1789. Married—Bryan Sergeant and Avis Jacobs : St. Geo. Han. Sq. ii. 34.
London, 19, 6, 14, 82 ; Philadelphia, 20, 85, 3, 142.

Jacomb.—? Local, ' of Jacomb.' I cannot find the spot. Probably a West-country name, where the suffix is, and was, so common : v. Combe.

1676. Bapt. — Thomas, s. William Jacomb : St. Mary Aldermary, p. 103.
1677. Thomas Jacomb, D.D., and Amy Forth, *widow* : Marriage Alleg. (Canterbury), p. 265.
1724. Married—Henry Jacomb and Frances Hinde : St. Michael, Cornhill, p. 63.
London, 5.

Jacox.—Bapt. ; v. Jeacock.

Jadis.—Bapt. 'the son of Jadis.' The history of this personal name is quite unknown to me. I do not find it mentioned in any work on the subject.

Jadis de Hangerhale, co.Camb., 1273. A.
Richard fil. Jadis, co. Camb., ibid.
Richard Jado, co. Camb., ibid.
William Jado, co. Camb., ibid.
1785. Married—Charles Skyrme and Isabella Jane Jadis: St. Geo. Han. Sq.i.381. Philadelphia, 1.

Jaffray.—Bapt. 'the son of Geoffrey,' a popular pronunciation.

1653. Married—Robert Jeffery and Mary Moxham : Reg. Broad Chalke, co. Wilts, p. 71.
1659. Bapt.—Mary, d. Robert Jaffery : ibid. p. 68.
1753. Married—Taylor Ansell and Sophia Jaffray : St. Geo. Chap. Mayfair, p. 258.
London, 2 ; Philadelphia, 1.

Jaggard.—Bapt. 'the son of Jaggard'; cf. the French Jacquard.

William Jagard, co. Camb., 1273. A.
1609. John Jaggard and Anne Chapman : Marriage Lic. (London), ii. 314.
1601. Richard Jaggard, co. Middlesex : Reg. Univ. Oxf. vol. ii. pt. ii. p. 391.
1702. John Jaggard, curate of St. Nicholas, Lynn : FF. viii. 504.
1729. Married—John Tobias Jaccard and Christian Moody : St. Geo. Han. Sq. i. 6.
1781. — Samuel Jaggard and Eliz. Abell : ibid. p. 328.
London, 1 ; MDB. (co. Suffolk), 1 ; (co. Warwick), 2 ; Philadelphia, 7.

Jagger, Jaggar.—Occup. 'the jagger,' one who works draught-horses for hire (Halliwell). Only found in Yorkshire. Probably from the personal name Jack (O.E. Jagg), and related to Jockey, i.e. one who rides horses for hire ; v. Jack. Cf. 'Jagge the jogelour,' Piers Plowman's Vision, Pass. Sext. 3935.

Thomas Jager, 1379: P. T. Yorks. p. 93.
Johannes Jagher, 1379 : ibid. p. 185.
1625. Married—Anthony Callis and Susan Jagger : St. Jas. Clerkenwell, iii. 55.
1652. — James Jaggar and Phillis Richardson : St. Dionis Backchurch, p. 29.
1660. Richard Pibus and Eliz. Jagger, widow, Marriage Alleg. (Canterbury), p. 51.
1803. Married—Thomas Jagger and Isabella Appleton : St. Geo. Han. Sq.ii.294.
West Rid. Court Dir., 1, 1 ; Flockton (West Rid. Yorks), 4, 0 ; Fixby (West Rid. Yorks), 1, 0 ; Philadelphia, 9, 0.

Jaggs.—Bapt. ' the son of Jack,' from the lazy pronunciation Jagg. 'Jagge the jogelour,' Piers Plowman. v. Jagger and Jiggens. Jaggs is the genitive form ; cf. Jones, Williams, Tompkins, &c.

MDB. (co. Essex), 1 ; New York, 1.

Jago.—Bapt. 'the son of James,' from the Spanish Iago, which must have crossed over into Cornwall at some early period. The surname is fairly well established in that county, cf. Bastian for Sebastian, a fontal name familiar to the same shire.

Thomas Jagoe, 1583 : Reg. St. Columb Major, p. 141.
Oliver Jagoe, 1617 : ibid. p. 208.
1608. Married—John Jago and Margaret Griffin : Kensington Ch. p. 65.
1754. — Thomas Jago and Margaret Deane : St. Geo. Chap. Mayfair, p. 273.
1809. — Thomas William Jago and Jane Bridges : St. Geo. Han. Sq. ii. 406.
London, 2 ; Philadelphia, 1.

Jaine; v. Jane.

Jakeman, Jakerman.—Occup. 'jakesman,' i.e. the servant of Jake, i.e. Jack ; v. Jackman. Jackerman is a corruption. The first stage would be Jake-a-man, as in Green-a-way and Hath-a-way ; cf. Jackaman.

1692. Charles Jakeman and Sarah Waldoe : Marriage Alleg. (Canterbury), p. 222.
1714. Bapt.—Margaret, d. Nicholas Jakeman : St. John the Baptist, Wallbrook, p. 178.
1799. Married—John Jakeman and Catherine Baker : St. Geo. Han. Sq. ii. 56.
London, 2, 0 ; Tadcaster, 1, 0 ; Tadcaster East, 1, 0 ; MDB. (co. Worc.), 4, 1 ; Philadelphia, 2, 0.

Jakes, Jaques. — Bapt. 'the son of John,' from the nick. Jack or Jake, but when found as a Christian name Jakes stood for Jaques = James. It is curious to notice that Jakes has been avoided for some generations, Jacks or Jacques being the popular forms. The local *jakes* (a house of office) has caused the objection.

Agnes Jakkes, 1273. A.
Jake Heriet, ibid.
Robert fil. Jake, ibid.
Richard Jakes, co. Soms., 1 Edw. III : Kirby's Quest, p. 198.
Ricardus Jakes, 1379: P. T. Yorks. p. 61.

Robertus Jakes, 1379: ibid. p. 103.
Robertus Jak', 1379 : ibid. p. 104.
Johanna Jacke-wyf, 1379 : ibid. p. 111.
Johannes Jake, 1379 : ibid.
1618. Married—William Carter and Abigall Jaques : St. Dionis Backchurch, p. 19.
1636. Bapt.—John, s. Thomas Jakes : St. Peter, Cornhill, i. 87.
London, 0, 17 ; MDB. (co. Lincoln), 1, 7 ; Philadelphia, 0, 1.

Jakeway; v. Jackaway.

Jakins. — Bapt. 'the son of John,' either a corruption of Jankin, or more directly from Jack-kin.

Jakynus atte Boclond, C. R., 34 Edw. I.
1803. Married—William Jakins and Bidey Coffee : St. Geo. Han. Sq. ii. 279.
London, 2 ; MDB. (co. Camb.), 1.

Jalland.—Bapt. ; v. Jolland.

Jamaison, Jamason.—Bapt. Variants of Jamicson; v. James.

New York, 1, 1.

Jamaway.—A corruption of Janaway, q.v.

MDB. (co. Warwick), 1.

Jamblin.—Bapt. 'the son of Gamelin'; v. Gambling, of which it is a variant; cf. Joslin and Goslin.

MDB. (co. Cambridge), 1.

James, Jameson, Jamieson, Jamison, Jamson.—Bapt. 'the son of James.' The purely English Jamison and its variants are almost entirely confined to North England, and indeed the great majority are of Lowland Scottish descent. On the other hand, James as a surname is as often South English as North, which accounts for the multitude of its modern representatives. It is particularly strong in the West country.

James or Jacobus Audithleg', co. Salop, 1273. A.
Walter James, co. Soms., 1 Edw. III : Kirby's Quest, p. 122.
Jacobus Maldeson, 1379 : P. T. Yorks. p. 216.
Willelmus Jamessson, (sic) 1379 : ibid.
Johannes Jamesman (i.e. the servant of James), 1379 : ibid. p. 146.
Alicia James, *doghter*, 1379 : ibid. p. 225.
Henricus Jamsman, 1379 : ibid. p. 272.
Johannes James, 1379 : ibid. p. 300.
1566-7. Robert Mowlde and Alice James : Marriage Lic. (London), i. 35.
1769. Married—William Jamison and Mary Smith : St. Geo. Han. Sq. i. 186.
— — Thomas Jameson, of Alnwick, and Ann Wilson : ibid. p. 193.

London, 187, 25, 5, 2, 2; MDB. (co. Soms.) (James), 45; Philadelphia, 180, 17, 12, 68, 0.

Janaway, Janeway, Janna-way, Gannaway, Janway, January, Jennaway.—Local, ' of Genoa ' ; cf. Lombard. The Genoese traded much with England, both in silks and spices.

'The Janneys comyne in sondre wyses, Into this londe wyth dyverse merchaun-dysses': Libel on English Policy.

January is a curious imitative corruption.

Benedict de Janua. E.
William de Janua, co. Kent, 1273. A.
1670. Buried—Jeremiah Jenowaye: St. Michael, Cornhill, p. 257.
1715. Bapt.—Sarah, d. Richard Janna-way: St. Jas. Clerkenwell, ii. 84.
1717. — Thomas, son of Thomas Jane-way: St. Antholin (London), p. 130.

Another curious imitative corruption is found in a London register.

1787. Married—John Nibbs and Sarah Johnaway: St. Geo. Han. Sq. i. 398.
London, 1, 3, 1, 5, 1, 1, 0; MDB. (co. Berks) (Jennaway), 1; Philadelphia (Jane-way), 2.

Jane, Jayne, Janes, Janson, Jannings, Jankin, Jaine, Jaynes, Jans, Janse.— Bapt. ' the son of Jan,' i.e. John. Hence also Jannings for Jennings, or Jankin for Jenkin. In the North there was a strong tendency towards Jan. Johnson is entered as Janson from 1545 to 1700 in the church registers at Ulverston ; cf. Tamplin for Tomlin.

Janne le Lordig, co. Oxf., 1273. A.
Walter Jankin, co. Hunts, ibid.
Robert Janes, co. Soms., 1 Edw. III : Kirby's Quest, p. 117.
William Janes, co. Soms., 1 Edw. III : ibid. p. 190.
William, son of John Jane, 1548 : Reg. St. Columb Major, p. 5.
John, son of William Jane, 1605 : ibid. p. 22.
1539. Bapt.—Gabella, d. Robert Jans: St. Peter, Cornhill, i. 1.
1540. — Emme, d. Robert Jance : ibid. p. 2.
1555. — John Janes : ibid. p. 7.
1606. Buried—a servant of William Jannsonne, vintner : ibid. p. 162.
Thomas Jan, Janne, or Jane, bishop of Norwich, 1499 : FF. iii. 543.
1438. Roger Janneson, vicar of Shern-bourne, co. Norf. : ibid. x. 361.
1471. John Jannys, of Norwich : ibid. v. 350.

Later on this became Janes :

1716. Elizabeth Janes, spinster, co. Norf. : FF. viii. 339.
1805. Married—John Jaynes and Mary Cutts: St. Geo. Han. Sq. ii. 330.
London, 3, 0, 10, 5, 1, 0, 0, 0, 0, 0; MDB. (co. Gloucester), 2, 2, 0, 0, 0, 0, 0, 1, 0, 0; Boston (U.S.) (Jans), 1; (Janse), 4 ; Philadelphia, 2, 9, 5, 5, 0, 0, 0, 1, 0, 0.

Janet, Jannett.—Bapt. ' the son of Jan,' from dim. Jan-et or Janot ; cf. Emmett or Emmott, the dim. of Emm, i.e. Emma. Probably at first masculine as well as feminine.

Henry Janot, co. Soms., 1 Edw. III : Kirby's Quest, p. 250.
1781. Married—James Peter Janet and Mary Liddle : St. Geo. Han. Sq. i. 320.
London, 1, 0 ; Boston (U.S.), 0, 1.

Janion, Jenions, Jannance.—Bapt. ' the son of Janion ' (i.e. John), a Welsh variant of English Jenin ; v. Jennings.

John Janion, of Lower Bebington, 1587:.Wills at Chester (1545-1620), p. 109.
Thomas Janion, of Great Saughall, 1591 : ibid.
Ellen Janion, of Chester, 1611 : ibid.
John Jennyon, of Christleton, 1687 : ibid. (1681-1700), p. 141.
Robert Janyon, of Liverpool, ship-wright, 1698 : ibid.
Liverpool, 2, 1, 0 ; Manchester, 1, 0, 1 ; London, 1, 0, 0.

Janney.—Bapt. ' the son of John '; v. Jenney, Jannings, Jane.

' At Macclesfield, the Monday next after the feast of the Exaltation of the Holy Cross, 9 Hen. IV (1408) before Richard de Manley, escheator, by the oaths of Robert de Huyde, Nicholas de Davenport, . . . John Janny, William Wilot,'&c.: Hist. East Cheshire, ii. 157.
1566. Married—Randelle Jannye and Alice Wilkeson : Prestbury Ch. (co. Ches.), p. 19.
1570. Bapt.—Edward Jannye : ibid.p.29.
1758. Married—John Janney and Mary Hart : St. Geo. Han. Sq. i. 82.
1778. — William Gelson and Sarah Janney : ibid. p. 292.
MDB. (co. Lincoln), 7 ; Philadelphia, 25.

Jannings, Janning.—Bapt. 'the son of John,' a variant of Jen-nings (q.v.), from the O.F. Jenin, the dim. of Jean ; v. Jane.

1346. Nicholas Janing, rector of Spar-ham, co. Norf. : FF. viii. 260.
London, 1, 0 ; MDB. (co. Suffolk), 3, 0.

Jans(e, Janson ; v. Jane.

Jaques.—Bapt. ; v. Jakes.

Jardine, Jarden.—Local, ' at the garden,' from residence thereby. An old Scottish form ; v. Garden or Gardyne.

1725. Thomas Jardin and Eliz. Washington : Marriage Lic. (Faculty Office), p. 250.
1759. Married—Andrew Gray and Jane Jardine : St. Geo. Han. Sq. i. 86.
London, 2, 0 ; MDB. (co. Suffolk), 2, 0 ; (co. Surrey), 0, 1 ; Manchester, 3, 0 ; Boston (U.S.), 2, 0 ; Philadelphia, 6, 24.

Jarman, Jarmain, Jermyn, Jermin, Jerman.—Bapt. ' the son of German,' q.v. ; cf. Jeffrey and Geoffrey, Joscelyn and Goslin, Jarratt and Garrard.

John Germyn, 20 Edw. I. R.
Jerman Bradbone, 1634 : Visitation of London (1633-5), i. 97.
John Jermin, 1647 : St. Jas. Clerken-well, i. 168.
Margarett Jerman, 1670 : ibid. p. 244.
1623. Margaret Jarman, of Upholland : Wills at Chester (1621-50), p. 123.
1665. Peter Arrowsmith and Rose Jer-myn : Marriage Alleg. (Canterbury), p. 106.
1673. Joseph Day and Hannah Jerman : ibid. p. 216.
1750. Married—Harvey Combe and Christian Jarman : St. Peter, Cornhill, ii. 86.
London, 5, 1, 4, 1, 0 ; Philadelphia, 5, 0, 0, 1, 5.

Jarratt, Jarred, Jarrett, Jarritt, Jarrad, Jerrette.—Bapt. ' the son of Gerard '; v. Garrard. This form does not seem older than the Reformation.

Jarret Blithman, Newcastle, 1539 : PPP. ii. 174-94.
Jarrard Gore, temp. Eliz. Z.
Jarat Nycholson, co. York. W. 9.
Elizabeth, d. of Jarrett Dashwood, gent, and Anna-Maria his wife, Jan. 18, 1741, aged 7 weeks, St. Gregory, Nor-wich : FF. iv. 279.
1688. Buried—William, son of Thomas Jarrad : St. John the Baptist on Wall-brook, p. 189.
1728. Bapt.—John, son of John Jerratt : ibid. p. 158.
1778. Married — Jarrett Juson and Hannah Hickman : St. Geo. Han. Sq. i. 293.
London, 1, 2, 7, 1, 0, 0 ; MDB. (co. Lincoln) (Jarrad), 1 ; Philadelphia (Jar-rett), 16 ; New York (Jerrette), 1.

Jarrold.—Bapt. ' the son of Gerald ' (q.v.) ; a variant.

MDB. (co. Suffolk), 3.

Jarrom ; v. Jerome.

Jarvis, Jervis, Jervois.— Bapt. 'the son of Gervase.' The initial *g* ruled supreme at first, but *j* in the end almost entirely monopolized the position. Gervas (q.v.), however, still exists.

John fil. Gervacii, co. Camb., 1273. A.
William fil. Gervasii, co. Hunts, ibid.
Stephen Gerveis, co. Camb., ibid.
Henry Gerveys, co. Norf., ibid.
Geruasius, et uxor, 1379: P. T. Yorks. p. 152.
Johannes Jerwas, 1379: ibid. p. 110.
1560. Bapt.—Eliz. d. Edmond Jervice: St. Michael, Cornhill, p. 79.
1662. Richard Chandler and Winifred Jervoise: Marriage Alleg. (Canterbury), p. 77.
1729. Bapt. — Jervoice, son of John Finch: St. Peter, Cornhill, ii. 36.
London, 67, 6, 0; Crockford, 6, 6, 1; Philadelphia, 34, 1, 0; New York, 45, 3, 1.

Jasper. — Bapt. 'the son of Jasper'; Fr. Gaspard. Very rare in England as a surname. I have not found any early instances, but it was at one time common as a Christian name.

Jasper Cranwell, 1545: Reg. St. Dionis Backchurch, p. 73.
1647. Bapt. — Jesper, son of Jesper Loward: St. Jas. Clerkenwell, i. 169.
1672. — Mary, d. John Jessper: ibid. p. 254.
1689. Buried—Margarett Jesper: St. Mary Aldermary, p. 200.
London, 1; MDB. (co. Cornwall), 4; Boston (U.S.), 4.

Jauncey.—Local, a variant of Chauncey, q.v.; cf. Chubb for Jubb.

1784. Married — Robert Digby and Eleanor Jauncey: St. Geo. Han. Sq. i. 363.
1795. — John Scott and Ann Jancey: ibid. ii. 127.
1808. — George Green and Eliz. Jancey: ibid. p. 381.
London, 1; MDB. (co. Hereford), 2; co. Worc.), 3; New York, 1.

Javens, Javan.—Bapt. 'the son of Javin'; v. Jevon. Javens is a genitive form; cf. Williams, Jones, &c.

Adam Javin, co. Camb., 1273. A.
1703. Buried—Sarah Rutter, a lodger at Mr. Javin's: St. Mary Aldermary, p. 208.
MDB. (co. Lincoln), 4, 0; London, 1, 1.

Jay, Jaye.—(1) Nick. 'the jay,' a chatterer, a gaily-dressed person. (2) Local, ' of Jay,' a township in the parish of Leintwardine, co. Hereford.

John le Jay, 1313. M.
Thomas le Jay, Fines R., 20 Edw. II.

William le Jay, co. Soms., 1 Edw. III: Kirby's Quest, p. 102.
Richard Jay, C. R., 32 Hen. VI.
Thomas Jaye, 1511: Reg. Univ. Oxf. i. 77.
1630. Married—Thomas Smith and Eliz. Jaye: Kensington Ch. p. 70.
1722. Bapt.—Thomas, s. William Jay: St. Jas. Clerkenwell, ii. 33.
London, 19, 3; MDB. (co. Hereford), 7, 0; Philadelphia, 1, 0; Boston (U.S.), 1, 0.

Jayne(s; v. Jane.

Jaycocks, -cox; v. Jeacock.

Jeacock, Jeacocke. Jacox, Jecock, Jaycocks, Jaycox.— Bapt. 'the son of John,' from the nick. Jack and suffix -*cock*. Jack-cock was soon abbreviated to Jacock, and this became corrupted into Jeacock. The patronymic Jacocks, of course, became Jacox; cf. Wilcock and Wilcox, and v. Cocks. Jancock is found early:

1397. Richard Jancock: Cal. of Wills in Court of Husting (2).
1669. Married—Edward Endell and Margarett Jeccockes: St. Jas. Clerkenwell, iii. 158.
1700. — Caleb Jacock and Eliz. Thornhill: ibid. p. 222.
1712. — James Sharplers and Eliz. Jeacock; ibid. p. 235.
London, 1, 3, 0, 0, 0, 0; Crockford, 0, 0, 1, 0, 0, 0; Manchester, 9, 0, 0, 1, 0, 0; New York, 0, 0, 0, 0, 1, 2.

Jeakins, Jeakes.—Bapt. 'the son of John,' from the nick. Jack, and dim. Jack-kin. In the same way we derive Jeacock (q.v.) from Jack-cock; cf. Wilcock and Wilkin. Just as Dawkins became corrupted to Dawkes, and Perkins to Perkes, and Wilkins to Wilkes, so Jeakins became corrupted to Jeakes.

1772. Married—John Jakins and Mary Pettis: St. Geo. Han. Sq. i. 223.
1806. — Robert Jeakins and Eliz. Winsall: ibid. ii. 352.
London, 3, 1.

Jealous.—? ——. Probably nothing to do with the quality *jealous*, but an imitative corruption of some baptismal name.

1603. Bapt.—George, s. William Jellis: St. Jas. Clerkenwell, i. 41.
1783. Married—Henry Gillies and Mary Downing: St. Geo. Han. Sq. i. 344.
MDB. (co. Camb.), 2; (co. Lincoln), 4.

Jean(s, Jeanes; v. Jeens.

Jeavons.—Bapt.; v. Jevon.

Jebb, Jebson.—Bapt. 'the son of Geoffrey,' from nick. Gepp or

Jepp; v. Jephson = Jepps and Jepson. A lazy pronunciation; cf. Slagg and Slack, &c.

1642. Buried—Sarath Jebson, Mr. Pecke his servant: St. Mary Aldermary, p. 172.
1710. Married—Edward Thompson and Eliz. Jebb: St. Michael, Cornhill, p. 60.
1735. — Rev. John Jebb and Ann Gansel: St. Geo. Han. Sq. i. 15.
London, 2, 0; MDB. (North Rid. Yorks), 0, 1; Philadelphia, 3, 0.

Jeckell, -kills, -kyl(l; v. Jekyll.

Jecks.—Bapt. 'the son of John': v. Jex.

Jee.—Local, a variant of Gee, q.v.

1563. Buried—Johane, d. Thomas Jee: St. Jas. Clerkenwell, iv. 3.
1797. Married—William Jee and Eleanor Farrell: St. Geo. Han. Sq. ii. 163.
1803. — John Jee and Margaret Brunt: ibid. p. 292.
London, 3; MDB. (co. Leicester), 2; New York, 1.

Jeens, Jeans, Jean, Jeanes, Jeynes, Jeynson, Jeannes.— Bapt. 'the son of John.' To the influence of the O.F. dim. Jenin we owe our English Jennings (q.v.). To the influence of Jean we owe the variants of Jones here given; v. Jane and Jones.

Alan fil. Jene, co. Linc., 1273. A.
1595. Married—John Johnson and Jone Geynson: Prestbury Ch. (co. Ches.), p. 126.
1663. Thomas Lovell and Mary Jeenes: Marriage Alleg. (Canterbury), p. 90.
1667. Thomas Jeynson, vicar of Prestbury, co. Ches.: Wills at Chester (1660-80), p. 152.
1801. Married—Robert Jeanes and Eliz. Jones: St. Geo. Han. Sq. ii. 233.
— — John Jeans and Martha Chater: ibid. p. 235.
London, 1, 4, 1, 2, 1, 0, 0; Philadelphia, 0, 0, 0, 9, 0, 0, 1; New York (Jeens), 2.

Jeeves, Jeves.—Bapt. 'the son of Geoffrey,' from nick. Jeff, patronymic Jeffs. The Yorkshire Poll Tax contains endless references to Jeff, or Geff, or Gep; v. Gipp and Jeffs and Jephson. No wonder therefore that corrupted forms have come down to us; v. Geeves, where the Yorkshire instances will be found clearly explained.

Thomas Jeve, co. Soms., 1 Edw. III: Kirby's Quest, p. 264.
1570. William Jeffes, of Gray's Inn: Marriage Lic. (Westminster), p. 3.

1578. James Jeve and Catherin Cowarne: Marriage Lic. (London), i. 80.
1671. John Jeffs and Eliz. Elliston: Marriage Alleg. (Canterbury), p. 197.
London, 2, 2; Sheffield, 3, 0; West Rid. Court Dir., 4, 0.

Jeff; v. Jeffs.

Jeffcock, Jeffcoat, Jephcott, Jeffcott. — Bapt. 'the son of Jeffrey' or 'Geoffrey,' q.v., from the nick. Jeff, with suffix -*cock*; v. Cock. With the corrupted Jephcott, cf. Glasscock for Glascott, a kind of reverse parallel.

Reginald Geffecok, C. R., 1 Hen. V.
John Jeffcocke, temp. Eliz. Z.
1616. Married—Thomas Merrett and Agnes Jefcott: St. Mary Aldermary, p.13.
1713. — John Hall and Mary Jephcott: St. Dionis Backchurch (London), p. 56.
London, o, 2, 2, 0; MDB. (West Rid. Yorks), 2, 0, 0, 0; Philadelphia, 0, 0, 0, 1; New York (Jeffcott), 4.

Jefferson, Jeffreson.—Bapt. 'the son of Geoffrey,' q.v.; cf. Jarratt, Gerald, &c.

1545. Buried—Agnes Giffersonne: St. Antholin (London), p. 5.
1747. — Sarah Jefferson: St. Mary Aldermary, p. 227.
London, 8, 1; Philadelphia, 22, 0.

Jeffery, Jefferay, Jefferey, Jefferies, Jefferis, Jefferiss, Jefferys, Jeffree, Jeffrey, Jeffreys, Jeffries, Jeffryes, Jeffrie, Jeffry.—Bapt. 'the son of Geoffrey,' q.v. The various forms cited and the numbers of their representatives furnish some sort of idea of the enormous popularity of this now old-fashioned font-name in the 13th and 14th centuries. To give more than one or two modern references would be superfluous.

Rogerus Jeffray, 1379: P. T. Yorks. p. 198.
1613-4. Married—Thomas Cook and Alice Gowen, alias Jefferey: St. Dionis Backchurch (London), p. 18.
1635. Buried—Captayne William Jefferyes: St. Jas. Clerkenwell, iv. 217.
1636. — John, s. William Jefferie: ibid. p. 220.
— — Roberte Jefferies: ibid.
1664. — Richard Jeoffries: ibid. p. 355.
London, 32, 1, 1, 6, 2, 4, 14, 1, 8, 7, 14, 7, 0, 0; Philadelphia, 1, 0, 0, 5, 17, 0, 5, 0, 12, 3, 56, 0, 1, 1.

Jeffkins, Jeffkyns. — Bapt. 'the son of Geoffrey,' from the nick. Jeff, and dim. Jeff-kin; cf. Watkin, Wilkin, &c. Jeffkins is

the genitive form, as in Watkins, Wilkins, &c.

1792. Married—Thomas Jeffkins and Mary Wilson: St. Geo. Han. Sq. ii. 76.
1804. — William Neighbour and Eliz. Jefkins: ibid. p. 305.
London, 1, 0; MDB. (co. Surrey), 1, 1.

Jefford, Jeffords.—Bapt. 'the son of Giffard,' q.v.; cf. Gervase and Jarvis, Gannaway and Jannaway.

1639. Andrew Jefford and Mary Steevens: Marriage Lic. (Westminster), p. 38.
1720. Buried—John Jafford: St. Mary Aldermary, p. 216.
1755. Married—John Jefford and Sarah Gatfield: St. Geo. Han. Sq. i. 59.
. London, 2, 0; Philadelphia, 2, 3.

Jeffreson; v. Jefferson.

Jeffrey(s, -ries; v. Jeffery.

Jeffs, Jeffes, Jeff.—Bapt. 'the son of Geoffrey,' q.v. The old nick. was Gef or Geff, but J is almost invariably the initial of the surname formed from it; v. Jeeves.

Alan.fil. Gef, co. Linc., 1273. A.
Alicia Gef-doghter, 1379: P. T. Yorks. p. 124.
Alicia Gefray-wyf, 1379: ibid.
1527. Thomas Jeffes and Margery Evered: Marriage Lic. (London), i. 6.
1635. Thomas Hollbacke and Eliz. Jeffes: Marriage Lic. (Westminster), p. 35.
London, 5, 0, 0; MDB. (co. Suffolk), 1, 3, 0; (North Rid. Yorks), 0, 0, 1; Boston (U.S.), 1, 0, 0.

Jeggins, Jeggs; v. Jiggens.

Jekyll, Jeckell, Jeckyll, Jeckyl, Jeckills, Jickles, Jeckel.—Bapt. 'the son of Jukel' or 'Gikel.' Although the personal name soon died out, the surname formed from it struggled into existence and still lives. Jeckills is the genitive form (as in Williams, Jones, &c.), and of this Jickles is a manifest variant.

Jukel Alderman, sheriff of London, 1194: WWW. p. 187.
'Gikel de Smithetun gave to Saint Cuthbert one carucate,' temp. 1200: DDD. iii. 288.
Johannes Jukel, co. Bucks, 1273. A.
Richard Gikell, co. Linc., ibid.
Nicholas Gikel, *carnifex*, 3 Edw. III: Freemen of York, i. 25.
Johannes Jekyll, temp. 1400: Hist. Dunelmensis (Surt. Soc.), cccviii.
1670. John Catesby and Eliz. Jekyll (co. Essex): Marriage Alleg. (Canterbury), p. 178.
1739. Married—Robert Jeckell and Mary Rogers: St. Geo. Han. Sq. i. 23.

London, 1, 1, 1, 0, 0, 0, 0; MDB. (co. Camb.) (Jeckyl), 1; (co. Lincoln) (Jeckills), 1; (Jickles), 1; New York (Jeckel), 1.

Jelbart.—' The son of Gilbert, q.v.; a Cornish variant.

1782. Married—Laurence Collins and Mary Jelbeart: St. Geo. Han. Sq. i. 340.
MDB. (co. Cornwall), 4.

Jellet, Gellett. — Bapt. 'the son of Julian,' popularly Gillian, whence dim. Juliet, popularly Geliet, whence *jilt*, a wanton, a flirt; v. Julian.

Robertus Gelietson, 1379: P. T. Yorks. p. 286.
Adam Gelietson, 1379: ibid.
Robertus Geliot, 1379: ibid.
1618. Bapt.—Anne, d. Andrew Jellit: St. Jas. Clerkenwell, i. 81.
1668. Thomas Powell and Dorothy Jellett: Marriage Alleg. (Canterbury), p. 239.
1833. Married—George Gillett and Mary Ann Goodwin: Canterbury Cathedral, p. 104.
Crockford, 3, 0; London, 0, 1; Philadelphia, 5, 0.

Jelley, Jelly.—(1) Bapt. A corruption of Jenney, q.v. In the same way Jennison became Jellison, q.v. (2) Bapt. 'the son of Juliana,' from the nick. Jill ('Jack and Jill') turned into the pet Jilly or Jelly; cf. Jelyan for Gillian:

1570. Married—Myles Jelyan and Agnes Smythe: St. Jas. Clerkenwell, i. 4.

Or Jelson for Gilson or Jilson:

1661. Married—Benedict Jelson and Ann Merrill: St. Jas. Clerkenwell, p. 108.

Hence the shorter form Jill became Jell, Jelley, or Jelly.

1562.—John Gellye (co. Herts) and Katherine Fallys: Marriage Lic. (London), i. 24.
1610. Married—William Jelley and Iland Crosse: St. Jas. Clerkenwell, iii. 36.
1748. — John Jelley and Joyce Whitehead: St. Geo. Han. Sq. i. 41.
1784. — John Jelly and Rachel McDuggull: ibid. p. 360.
London, 8, 0; Manchester, 0, 1; Boston (U.S.), 2, 3.

Jellicoe, Jellico, Jellicorse.— ? Nick. The old nickname Gentilcors naturally arises to one's mind. This would popularly become Jellicour or Jellicorse. In the United States this name has assumed the form of Jericho, q.v. It will be seen that Jellicorse still exists, and

Jellicour existed so late as the 17th century.

William Gentilcorps, 1301. M.
Richard Gentylcors, London. X.
James Jelicoe, of Whitchurch, co. Salop, *yeoman*, 1648: Wills at Chester (1621–50), p. 123.
Mark Jellicour, of Handbridge, 1678: ibid. (1660–80), p. 151.
John Jolycoe, of Great Barrow, *black-smith*, 1667: ibid. p. 155.
1644. Bapt.—William, s. William Jellico: St. Jas. Clerkenwell, i. 159.

It is almost certain that Hand-somebody is a translation of Gentil-cors. ‘Thy fayre body so gentyl’ (Robert of Gloucester, p. 205), i.e. graceful, noble, *genteel*.

Crockford, 2, 0, 1; Liverpool, 0, 1, 0; Manchester, 0, 0, 1; London, 1, 0, 0.

Jellison, Jellerson. — (1) Bapt. ; v. Jennison ; cf. *bannister* for *baluster*. Although now only found, I believe, in America, it was an English corruption, finding its way, no doubt, with the Pilgrim Fathers. (2) Bapt. A variant of Jillson, q.v.

1592. Richard Gelyson and Mary Hope: Marriage Lic (London), i. 203.
1593. Bapt.—Luce, d. William Jellyson, or Gennysson: St. Jas. Clerkenwell, i. 27.
1621. — Henry, s. Robart Jellison: ibid. p. 92.
1663. Married—John Gillison and Susanna Parker: St. Mary Aldermary, p. 30.
1665. Bapt.—Thomas, s. John Jellison and Susanna, his wife: ibid. p. 101.

This conclusively proves that Jellison is sometimes ‘the son of Gill,’ the nick of Jullana, whence we get Gillson and Jillson, q.v., Jellison being a variant.

Boston (U.S.), 9, 2.

Jemison; v. Jimpson.

Jemmett.—Bapt. ‘the son of James,’ from nick. Jem and dim. Jemm-et; cf. Emmett (little Emma), Hewett (little Hugh), &c. Although the derivation is certain I have not discovered an early instance.

1657. Married—William Banes, *car-man*, and Marye Jemmett: St. Michael, Cornhill, p. 32.
1661. Samuel Jemmatt (co. Berks) and Avelin Bateman: Marriage Alleg. (Canterbury), p. 66.
1712. Married—Thomas Bishop and Mary Jemmett: St. Mary Aldermary, p. 41.
London, 2; MDB. (co. Kent), 2.

Jenckes; v. Jinks or Jinkins.
Boston (U.S.), 1.

Jenifer. — Bapt. ‘the son of Guinevere,’ one of Arthur’s wives. Still in use in Cornwall as Jenifer or Jennifer (v. Yonge, ii. 132) ; v. Genever, which is the more correct form. Also v. Juniper.

Jenefer, d. of Thomas Bosowarne, 1554: Reg. St. Columb Major, p. 7.
Jenniphret Norton, *widdow*, 1623: ibid. p. 210.
1623. John Foster, Stepney, and Jene-fer Foster, of St. Mary Woolnoth: Marriage Lic. (London), ii. 196.
‘Comes Captain Jenifer to me, a great servant of my Lord Sandwiches,’ 1666–7: Pepys’ Diary, Chandos edit., p. 371.
Jennifer, d. of John Stephens, 1770: Reg. St. Columb Major, p. 285.
1661. Married—Walter Jeniver and Jane Wright: St. Jas. Clerkenwell, iii. 107.
Boston (U.S.), 1.

Jenions.—Bapt. ; v. Janion.

Jenkin, Jenking, Jenkins, Jenkinson, Jenkyns. — Bapt. ‘the son of John,’ from dim. Jen-kin ; cf. Wilkin, Watkin, Tompkin, Simpkin, &c. The *g* in Jenking is excrescent, as in Jennings. The tendency at first was to Jon-kin, but the influence of the N. French Jenin was too strong ; v. Jennings.

Adam Janekyn, co. Soms., 1 Edw. III: Kirby’s Quest, p. 183.
Johannes Wayte, et Agnes uxor ejus, 1379 : P. T. Yorks. p. 59.
Johannes serviens ejus, 1379 : ibid.
Robertus Jonkinson, 1379 : ibid.

The last three entries occur together.

Alicia Jonkyn, 1379: P. T. Yorks. p. 104.
Johanna Jonkyn-wyf, 1379: ibid. p. 123.
Johannes Jonkynson, 1379: ibid.
Jenkin Vaughan, prebendary of St. David’s, 1621 : Hist. and Ant. St. David’s, p. 361.
1602. Ralph Jenkinson, alias Johnson, of Longton : Wills at Chester (1545–1620), p. 109.
London, 4, 1, 74, 15, 1; Philadelphia, 0, 0, 140, 13, 0.

Jenks; v. Jinks or Jinkins.
London, 2; Boston (U.S.), 29.

Jennaway; v. Janaway.

Jenner.—Occup. ‘the engineer,’ a military officer who worked the catapult, &c. As *engine* became shortened to *gin* or *ginne*, so Engi-ner became Ginner ; v. my English Surnames, 5th edit. p. 229.

Waldinus Ingeniator, co. Linc.: Domesday.
Richard le Engynur, C. R., 18 Edw. I.
Hugh le Ginnur, co. Oxf., 1273. A.
William le Engynur, co. Suff., ibid.
Richard le Enginur. B.
Ernulf le Enginnur. E.
William le Genour, 1306. M.
1598. Robert Pascall and Gresagon Jeynor: Marriage Lic. (London), i. 254.
1608. Bapt.—John, the son of Henrye Jenoure, *marchant*: St. Peter, Cornhill, i. 58.
1781. Married—Samuel Jenner and Catherine Roberts: St. Geo. Han. Sq. i. 324.
London, 13 ; Philadelphia, 11.

Jennett, Jennette, Jinnett.—Bapt. ‘the son of John’ or ‘Joan,’ from dim. Jennet. It is as likely to be masculine as feminine ; v. Janet.

1589. William Cookes and Ann, d. Humphrey Jennetts: Marriage Lic. (London), i. 183.
1615. Bapt.—Robert, s. James Jennettes: St. Peter, Cornhill, i. 63.
1762. Married—Richard Jennet and Mary Colclough: St. Geo. Han. Sq. i. 113.
London, 1, 1, 0 ; Philadelphia, 1, 0, 1.

Jenney.—(1) Bapt. ‘the son of John.’ For instances, v. Jennison. (2) Local, ‘de Gyney,’ or ‘Gisnei,’ or ‘Gisney,’ no doubt from Guisnes, near Calais.

Roger de Gisnei, or Gisney, 9 Ric. I, co. Norf. : FF. x. 452.
1250. Ingelram de Gisnei, or Gyney, co. Norf. : ibid. iv. 454.
James Gyney, co. Norf., 1395 : ibid. ix. 308.

Later on, and after the prefix was dropped, the orthography was changed to Jenney.

John Jenney, of Intwood, sheriff of Norwich, 1486: FF. iii. 191.
Roger Jeney, co. Norf., 20 Edw. III : ibid. xi. 75.
Suckling Jenny, co. Norf., 1691: ibid. viii. 237.
1565. Married—William Dowdall and Joane Jenny: St. Jas. Clerkenwell, iii. 3.
London, 1 ; Boston (U.S.), 13.

Jenningham; v. Jerningham.

Jennings, Jenyns, Jennens.—Bapt. ‘the son of John ’; O.F. Jehan; O.E. Jan; dim. Jan-in ; cf. Col-in, Rob-in, &c. Jan or Jehan left us Jan-et and Jan-son. Jan-in (through influence of later Jean) became Jenin, with excrescent *g* Jenning, and with patronymic *s* Jennings.

'Item, to Janyn Marcazin, mynstrelle, 66s. 8d.': Privy Purse Exp., Elizabeth of York, p. 100.

Janyn le Breton, co. Lanc., 1332: Lay Subsidy (Rylands), p. 120.

Janyn de Gynes, 1379: P. T. Yorks. p. 240.

Janyn serviens Johannes warde, 1379: ibid.

Ienyn de Fraunce, 1379: ibid. p. 139.

Jane, d. of Stephen Jenyn, 1548: Reg. St. Columb Major, p. 5.

John Genens, or Jenens, citizen of Oxford, 1573: Reg. Univ. Oxf. vol. ii. pt. i. pp. 302-3.

Francis Jenance, or Jennens, or Jenens: ibid. pp. 303-4.

Thomas Jennyns, co. Norf., 13 Eliz.: FF. viii. 432.

1571. Buried—Jeames Jennynges: St. Peter, Cornhill, i. 121.

1610. Ralph Jenyngs, of Chester: Wills at Chester (1545-1620), p. 109.

London, 91, 0, 0; MDB. (co. Camb.), 4, 2, 0; Philadelphia, 90, 0, 3.

Jennison, Jenney, Jenny.—Bapt. 'the son of John,' from O.F. Jean, dim. Jenin; v. Jennings. The feminine Jenny was probably not in use at this time. It is almost certain that it was a masculine form at first and a modification of Jenin, just as Colly was of Colin.

Alan fil. Jene, co. Linc., 1273. A.

John Jenysyn. F.

Ioan Geneson, co. York. W. 11.

Willelmus Gyneson, 1379: P. T. Yorks. p. 77.

Ricardus Gene, 1379: ibid. p. 78.

Thomas Genne, 1379: ibid. p. 82.

Agnes Gine, 1379: ibid. p. 86.

Agar Genyson, 1546: St. Dionis Backchurch (London), p. 2.

Robert Jennison, *merchant*, 1668. Tomb, St. Nicholas, Newcastle-on-Tyne: Brand's Hist. of Newcastle, i. 281.

1666. John Jenney and Mary Reading: Marriage Alleg. (Canterbury), p. 128.

Manchester, 2, 0, 0; Boston (U.S.), 9, 13, 1; Philadelphia, 2, 0, 2.

Jentle. — Nick. 'the gentle'; v. Gentle.

1555. Bapt.—Mathew Jentyll: St. Peter, Cornhill, i. 7.

1577. Buried — Raphe Jentle: St. Michael, Cornhill, p. 195.

1591-2. Edmund Jentill and Johanna Hussey: Marriage Lic. (London), i. 195. London, 1; New York, 1.

Jephcott.—Bapt.; v. Jeffcock, a corruption.

Jephson, Jepps, Jepson.—Bapt. 'the son of Geoffrey,' from nick. Geff or Gepp; v. Gipp for

several instances. South Lancashire is a well-known habitat of Jepson.

Thomas Gepson, 1379: P. T. Yorks. p. 123.

Jeppe de Hesilden, 1379: ibid. p. 271.

Johannes Jepson, 1379: ibid. p. 86.

Nicholas Jepson, of Mostyn, 1595: Wills at Chester (1545-1620), p. 109.

Robert Jepson, of Oldfield, Manchester, 1614: ibid.

1603. Bapt.—William, s. Robert Jeppes: St. Jas. Clerkenwell, i. 41.

London, 3, 3, 6; Manchester, 0, 0, 8; Boston (U.S.), 0, 0, 12.

Jeremy. — Bapt. 'the son of Jeremy,' i.e. Jeremiah; M.E. Jeremy.

Jeremy de Caxton, co. Norf., 1239: FF. iii. 46.

1638. Married—Gilbert Jeremi and Eliz. Raulinges: St. Michael, Cornhill, p. 28. London, 3; Philadelphia, 1.

Jericho.—An imitative corruption of Jellicoe, q.v.

Philadelphia, 2.

Jerman, Jermin; v. Jarman.

Jermy, Jermey. — Bapt. 'the son of Jermin.' At first sight this name would seem to be Jeremy, q.v., but Blomefield in his History of Norfolk, to which county the Jermys belong, says positively that Jermin is the true parent; v. Jarman. This is likely to be true, as Jermyn has been for centuries a Norfolk patronymic.

Sir John Germyn, or Jermy, *knight*, temp. 1300, co. Norf.: FF. v. 386.

Robert Jermye, of Norwich, 1533: ibid. i. 382.

Thomas Jarmy, co. Norf., 1652: ibid. v. 387.

In opposition to the above cf.

Jeremye Gooch, 1617, co. Norf.: FF. iv. 248.

Jermey Gooch, 1652, co. Norf.: ibid. p. 321.

Perhaps the explanation is that surnames were then beginning to be fashionable as fontal names, and Jermey being thus used was miswritten or confused with Jeremy.

1658. Married—Thomas Knowles and Eliz. Jermy: St. Jas. Clerkenwell, iii. 101.

1666. Francis Jermy and Ann Wilsford: Marriage Lic. (Faculty Office), p. 92.

MDB. (co. Norfolk), 4, 0; London, 0, 1.

Jermyn; v. Jarman.

Jerringham, Jernegan, Jenringham. — Bapt. 'the son of Gernegan.' The second *n* is excrescent; cf. Pottinger and Messinger for Potager and Messager. In some documents bearing the seal of Queen Elizabeth (1572), concerning the town of Yarmouth, Sir Henry Jerningham, knight, is set down as 'Sir Henry Jernegam' not less than three times; v. FF. xi. 288-91. Blomefield says, 'That Jernegan was anciently a Christian name is very true, as numerous records prove. In 1195, there was a fine levied of lands in Edricheston, in Warwickshire, between Reginald de Claverdon and Gernagan his brother, and about this time it was a common name in France, as we find from Lobineau, in his History of Britain (i. 105), where Jernegon de Pontchasteau and some others of the name are mentioned' (FF. ii. 411).

Jernegan Fitz-Hugh, 1180, co. Norf.: FF. ii. 411.

Walter Gernegan, co. Suff., 1273. A.

William Gernegon, co. Norf., ibid.

1675. Francis Jernegan (co. Norf.) and Anna Blount: Marriage Alleg. (Canterbury), p. 243.

1767. Married—William Jerfiingham and Frances Dillon: St. Geo. Han. Sq. i. 166.

MDB. (co. Devon), 0, 0, 1; Boston (U.S.), 0, 5, 0.

Jerome, Jerram, Jerrems, Jarrom. — Bapt. 'the son of Jerome.' I do not find any early English instances. It must have been a rare name in this country. Miss Yonge writes, 'The spear raven, Gerramn, is the old English Jerram that has become lost in Jerome' (Hist. Christian Names, ii. 328). I cannot discover any trace of an old English name Jerram as distinct from Jerome. Jerrems is the genitive form, as in Jones, Williams, &c.

1614. John Watson and Eliz. Jerome: Marriage Lic. (Westminster), p. 21.

1729. Married—Joseph Jerram and Ann Elgar: St. Geo. Chap. Mayfair, p. 286.

1748. — Stephen Jerom and Mary Callard: ibid. p. 124.

1770. — John Fisher and Eliz. Jerrom: St. Geo. Han. Sq. i. 196.

Jermyn; v. Jarman.

1779. Married — Joseph Jerome and Eliz. Elsmore: St. Geo. Han. Sq. i. 303. London, 2, 1, 0, 0; Philadelphia, 3, 3, 0, 0; MDB. (co. Lincoln), 0, 1, 1, 0; (co. Leicester) (Jarrom), 2.

Jervis,-vois.—Bapt. ;v. Jarvis.

Jessmaker.—Occup. 'a maker of *jesses*,' the straps of silk or leather by which the hawk was held.

Robert le Jesemaker, co. Linc., 1273. A.

Jesson. — Bapt. 'the son of Geoffrey,' from nick. Geff, whence Geffson, which gradually assumed the form of Gesson, then Jesson; cf. Joslin and Goslin.

Willelmus Gesson, 1379: P. T. Yorks. p. 18.
1628. Married—Henry Jesson and Amy Munden: St. Michael, Cornhill, p. 25.
1661. John Jesson and Anne Artson: Marriage Lic. (Canterbury), p. 59.
1790. Married—Thomas Jesson and Ann Green: St. Geo. Han. Sq. ii. 41.
London, 3; Philadelphia, 3; MDB. (co. Leicester), 2.

Jessop, Jessup, Jessopp, Jessupp. — Bapt. 'the son of Joseph'; O.E. Josep. Any doubt on the subject is settled by the subjoined references from the York Poll Tax:

Willelmus Josop, 1379: P. T. Yorks. p. 170.
Johannes Jesop, 1379: ibid.
Richard fil. Josep, co. Camb., 1273. A.
Adam Josep, c. 1300. M.
Josep le Taverner. J.

No doubt the pronunciation was influenced by the Lombardic merchants and Italian Jews. Jessop is simply Giuseppe Anglicized, 'Isaac of York' could have told us something about it.

1612. William Newsam and Eliz. Jesopp: Marriage Alleg. (Canterbury), p. 20.
1663. William Jesup (co. Linc.) and Eliz. Woolby: ibid. p. 90.
1746. Married—Thomas Jessapp and Ann Hill: St. Geo. Chap. Mayfair, p. 80.
London, 9, 10, 0, 0; MDB. (co. Essex), 1, 0, 1, 1; West Rid. Court Dir., 12, 0, 0, 0; Crockford, 0, 0, 2, 0; Philadelphia, 0, 6, 0, 0; Boston (U.S.), 4, 1, 0, 0.

Jester. — Occup. 'the jester,' the professional fool or jester in attendance on the king or baron; v. Fool.

1665. Married—Thomas Straford and Sarah Jester: St. Jas. Clerkenwell, i. 121.
1666. Bapt.—Eliz., d. Christopher Jester: ibid. p. 230.

1802. Married—George Groom and Lydia Jester: St. Geo. Han. Sq. ii. 257.
Coventry, 1; Philadelphia, 16.

Jeune.—Nick. 'le jeune,' i.e. the young; v. Young and Jung.

Agnes le Jevene, co. Oxf., 1273. A.
William le Jeuene, London, ibid.
Bartholomew le Jevene, co. Bedf., ibid.
Bartholomew le Jouene, C. R., 36 Hen. III.
London, 2.

Jeves.—Bapt. ; v. Jeeves.
London, 2.

Jevon, Jevons, Jeavons.—Bapt. (Welsh) 'the son of Jevan' or 'Yevan' or 'Evan'; v. Evans. Jevan appears in the list of early archbishops of St. David's; v. Crockford (1891), p. xxxvii.

Heine fil. Yevan, co. Salop, 1273. A.
John ap Howell ap Jevan: Visit. of Gloucestershire (Harl. Soc.), p. 179.
Howell ap Yevan. H.
Jevan ap Rees. G.
Jevan ap Adam, 1327. M.
Javin Coke, 1384: Hist. and Ant. St. David's, p. 369.
1594. Hopkin ap Jevan, co. Glamorgan: Reg. Univ. Oxf. vol. ii. pt. ii. p. 207.
1600. Jevan, or Evan Thomas, co. Glamorgan: ibid. p. 243.
1658. Buried—Ann, wife of Thomas Jevon: St. Thomas the Apostle (London), p. 132.
Liverpool, 0, 4, 0; Dalton-in-Furness, 0, 0, 1; Lanc. Court Dir., 0, 1, 2; MDB. (co. Stafford), 4, 1, 3; New York (Jevons), 1.

Jew.—Nick. 'the Jew,' a common entry in mediaeval registers; v. Jewson.

John le Gyw, C. R., 28 Hen. III.
Thomas le Jeu, co. Notts, 1273. A.
Mosse le Jen, co. Northampt. 20 Edw. I. R.
Mirabilla Judaeus. C.
1557. Richard Jewe: Cal. of Wills in Court of Husting (2).

The editor seems doubtful of the name in the following entry:

1582. Buried—Thomas Renoldes, servant to Mr. Jew (?): St. Antholin (London), p. 29.

Jewell, Jewelson.—Bapt. 'the son of Joel'; O.E. Juel and Jewel. v. Joel; cf. Job and Jubb, Jordan and Jurden, &c.

Warin fil. Juelis, co. Devon, Hen. III-Edw. I. K.
Juel de Stanhuse, co. Devon, ibid.
Juel de Buketon, co. Devon, ibid.
Jordan fil. Juel, 25 Edw. I: BBB. p. 543.
Jordan fil. Jowell, 25 Edw. I: ibid.

William Juel, co. Soms., 1 Edw. III: Kirby's Quest, p. 202.
John Juell, C. R., 18 Ric. II.
John Jowell, sheriff of Norwich, 1486: FF. iii. 191.
Robert Jewelson, of Skipton, Yorks, 1741: Dawson's Hist. of Skipton, p. 363.

A curious mixture of the old form and the new is found in the following entries:

1615. Buried—Elizabeth, d. Joell Jewell: St. Columb Major, p. 207.
1639. — Senobie, widow of Joell Juell: ibid. p. 216.
London, 20, 0; Philadelphia, 10, 0.

Jewett, Jewitt.—Bapt. 'the son of Juliana,' from the dim. Juliet, popularly, in North England, Juet; v. Jowett.

William Juet, co. Hunts, 1273. A.
1629. Bapt.—Gabriel, s. John Jeuett: St. Jas. Clerkenwell, i. 111.
1778. Married—James Jewett and Eliz. Clarke: St. Geo. Han. Sq. i. 292.
London, 1, 1; MDB. (West Rid. Yorks), 0, 3; Philadelphia, 7, 2.

Jewison.—Bapt. A corruption of Jewelson, a Yorkshire surname, where Jewell was the form for Joel; v. Jewelson (s.v. Jewell).

West Rid. Court Dir., 3; MDB. (East Rid. Yorks), 2.

Jewkes; v. Jukes.

Jewsbury.—(1) Local, 'at the jewsbury,' i.e. the district or part of a town set apart for the residence of Jews; v. Jury. The surname is North English, and not found in the London Directory. The York Pageant (1417) was arranged to play at certain points of the city, amongst others 'at the end of Jubir-gate' (query Jewbury-gate): York Mystery Plays, p. xxxiii, ed. Toulmin Smith. (2) Local, 'of Dewsbury,' a town in W. Rid. Yorks. Probably a corruption, as suggested by Mr. Lower. This view is strengthened by the fact that the surname seems confined to Lancashire and Yorkshire.

MDB. (West Rid. Yorks), 1; Manchester, 3.

Jewson, Juson.—Nick. 'the Jew's son' (?). Nevertheless, the instance below seems to refute this statement since Peter would not be used as a personal name by a strict Jew. With the variant

Juson, cf. Jury for Jewry; v. Jewison for a second and different origin.

Peter fil. Gewe, co. Linc., 1273. A.
1600. Thomas Fewson, or Jewson, co. Bucks: Reg. Univ. Oxf. vol. ii. pt. ii. p. 240.
1745. Married — Samuel Cobley and Eliz. Jewson: St. Geo. Chap. Mayfair, p. 55.
1778. — Jarrett Juson and Hannah Hickman: St. Geo. Han. Sq. i. 293.
London, 3, 1.

Jex, Jecks.—Bapt. 'the son of Jacques'; v. Jakes.

Agnes Jakkes, co. Hunts, 1273. A.
1384. Jeffery Jeckkes, rector of St. Peter, Norwich: FF. iv. 330.
1475. George Jekkes, rector of South Pickenham, co. Norf.: ibid. vi. 74.
The Vicarage of Corpesty, co. Norf., was sold by Heydon (temp. Elizabeth) to Thomas Jecks and John Shakle, and by them to the Bacons, and in 1611 William Bacon separated,' &c.: ibid.

Thomas Jecks is again referred to:

1589. Thomas Jex presented to rectory of Irmingland, co. Norf.: FF. vi. 322.

Cf. Cox for Cocks, Dix for Dicks, Dixon for Dickson.

1783. Married—William Raker and Ann Jex: St. Geo. Han. Sq. i. 350.
London, 3, 1; New York, 3, 3.

Jeynes, Jeynson; v. Jeens.

Jibb.—(1) Bapt.; v. Jebb. (2) Bapt. 'the son of Gilbert,' from the nick. Gib; v. Gibb, and cf. Goslin and Joslin.

MDB. (co. Lincoln), 1.

Jickles; v. Jekyll.

Jiffard. — Bapt. 'the son of Giffard,' q.v.

Johannes Juffard, 1379: P. T. Yorks. p. 37.
Johanna Juffard, 1379: ibid. p. 54.

Jiggens, Jeggins, Jeggs, Jegen.—Bapt. 'the son of Jegg,' whence the dim. Jeggon. Jiggens or Jeggins is the genitive, as in Jennings, Jones, Williams, &c. There can be little doubt that the original name was Jackson (i.e. little Jack), which became Jaggin or Jeggin. Jack is found as Jagg in early rolls, and is so styled by the author of Piers Plowman. The surname Jeggins seems to have arisen in co. Essex, where Jeggins, Jeggs, and Jaggs are still to be met with.

In 1590 John Jeggon, son of Robert Jeggon, of Coggeshall, co. Essex, was appointed Warden of Bennet College (now Corpus Christi), Cambridge. He was a strict disciplinarian. He fined the undergraduates for some offence and with the mulct whitened the college hall.—On one of the screens a young fellow wrote:—
'Doctor John Jeggon, of Bennet College, Master,
Broke the Scholars' heads, and gave the Hall plaister.'
The Doctor, seeing it as he passed by, subscribed extempore:
'Knew I but the wag, that writ this in a bravery,
I'd commend him for his wit, but whip him for his knavery': FF. iii. 562.
Claricia Jagun, co. Norf., 1273. A.
1613. John Jeggon, Bishop of Norwich: FF. vi. 443.
1621. Robert Jegon, of Norwich: ibid.
'Mr. William Jeg gave a small piece of land in this parish' (East Dereham): ibid. x. 218.
1667. Thomas Walker and Arabella Jiggons: Marriage Alleg. (Canterbury), p. 132.
1673. Thomas Bland and Anne Jegon, widow: ibid. p. 220.
London, 1, 0, 0, 0; London Court Dir., 0, 1, 0, 0: MDB. (co. Essex), 0, 2, 1, 0; Philadelphia (Jegen), 1.

Jigger.—Occup. 'the jigger,' a player on the gige or gigue, a musical instrument; hence jig, a dance. Italian giga, a fiddle; cf. Crowder or Crowther, and Fiddler. This surname lasted till the 16th century. I suspect it is now extinct.

John le Gigur, co. Oxf., 1273. A.
Walter le Gigur, co. Oxf., ibid.
Alexander le Gigur. T.
Bigelot le Gigur. DD.
John Gygour, co. Soms., 1 Edw. III: Kirby's Quest, p. 227.
1544. Buried—Anne Giger: St. Peter, Cornhill, i. 107.

Jillings.—Local; v. Gilling(s.

Jillson. — Bapt. 'the son of Juliana,' from the nick. Jill, which is the usual English form, although Jill was more common than Gill; v. Gillson and Jellison.

1603. Buried—Richard Smyth, servant to Richard Jellson: St. Jas. Clerkenwell, iv. 84.
1626. — William, s. Benedict Jilson: ibid. p. 187.
1661. — William, s. William Jelson: ibid. p. 339.
Philadelphia, 2.

Jimpson, Jimison, Jemison.—Bapt. 'the son of James,' from the nick. Jim. The p is in-

trusive, as in Simpson and Thompson.

William Gimmison, co. York. W. 20.
1808. Married—John Handley and Eliz. Jimerson: St. Geo. Han. Sq. ii. 389.
Manchester, 1, 0, 0; Philadelphia, 0, 3, 3.

Jinkins, Jinks.—Bapt. 'the son of John,' from dim. Jenkin, whence Jinkin, the patronymic of which was Jinkins. This passed through the usual stages of modifications into Jinks, and was turned into Ginx in the story of 'Ginx's Baby,' which created a certain sensation a few years ago; cf. Dawks, Wilks, Perks, Tonks, &c., from Dawkins, Wilkins, Perkins, Tonkins, &c.; cf. Jinckson for Jenkinson in the following:

1577-8. James Nicolls and Johanna Jinckson: Marriage Lic. (Westminster), p. 6.
1603. Buried—Mr. Bernard Jynkes, parson of this parish: St. Dionis Backchurch (London), p. 207.
1606. Married—Robert Lymbarr and Amye Jenckes: ibid. p. 15.
1658-9. — Robert Jenkes and Grace Halsey: ibid. p. 34.
1666. Francis Jenkes and Sarah Wallwin: Marriage Alleg. (Canterbury), p. 116.
1670. Bapt.—Francis, son of Francis Jinckes: St. Michael, Cornhill, p. 146.
London, 1, 2.

Joachim.—Bapt. 'the son of Joachim.' Modern immigration has helped to preserve the surname.

Richard Joachim, co. Camb., 1273. A.
Nicholas Jochim, co. Camb., ibid.
London, 2; Philadelphia, 1; New York, 3.

Job, Jobson, Jobe.—Bapt. 'the son of Job'; v. Jupp, Chubb, Jobling, &c. Job was a favourite personal name in the hereditary surname period, and in consequence has left many descendants. No doubt the Mystery Plays had much to do with its popularity.

William Jobba, co. Oxf., 1273. A.
Elyas Jobbe, co. Suff., ibid.
John fil. Job, co. Camb., ibid.
Nicholas Jobbe, vicar of Swerdeston, co. Norf., 1318: FF. v. 52.
1567. Married—Thomas Jackson and Eliz. Jobson: St. Dionis Backchurch (London), p. 6.
1589. Bapt.—Katherine, d. Michael Jobson: St. Jas. Clerkenwell, i. 22.
1672. Thomas Clithero and Jane Job: Marriage Alleg. (Canterbury), p. 206.
London, 6, 6, 0; Philadelphia, 1, 2, 1.

Jobbins.—Bapt. 'the son of Job,' from the dim. Jobbin ; cf. Col-in, Rob-in, &c. The final *s* is the genitive form, as in Jennings, Williams, &c.

1623. Married—John Jobbins and Susan Wetherley : St. Jas. Clerkenwell, iii. 53.
1704. Bapt.—Elizabeth, d. Isaac Jobbins : St. Michael, Cornhill, p. 161.
London, 3 ; MDB. (co. Wilts), 1 ; Philadelphia, 3.

Jobling. — Bapt. 'the son of Job,' from dim. Jobelin ; cf. Hewling ; v. Joplin and Jupling. Jobelin seems to suggest the origin of Jobelin, a stupid man. ' Jobelin, a sot, a fool' (Cole's Eng. Dict., 1684). 'Joblin, a stupid boy. Somerset' (Halliwell). ' As patient as Job' is even now not used complimentarily. Job's patience has even seemed to imply want of energy, and the term would easily become a nickname for lethargy, but was not easily distinguished from sheer stupidity ; v. Joppe, Joppus, and Joppa, Prompt. Parv., where Joppe may be Job. Jobling may therefore belong to the nickname class without affecting the origin given above.

1738. Bapt.—Jane, d. Henry Jobling : St. Jas. Clerkenwell, ii. 241.
1788. Married—Charles Turner and Susanna Joblin : St. Geo. Han. Sq. ii. 14.
1809. — Isaac Watts and Margaret Jobling : ibid. p. 415.
Crockford, 3 ; Manchester, 1 ; Boston (U.S.), 2.

Jobson ; v. Job.

Joce, Jose. — Bapt. 'the son of Goce' ; v. Joyce. A well-known West-country surname, but formerly generally familiar as a personal name.

Geoffrey Jose, co. Hunts, 1273. A.
Nicholas Jose, co. Hunts, ibid.
Philip Joce, co. Norf., temp. Edw. II : FF. vii. 288.
William Joce. co. Soms., 1 Edw. III : Kirby's Quest, p. 199.
John Joce, co. Soms., 1 Edw. III : ibid.
Joceo de Bayouse, co. Soms., 1 Edw. III : ibid. p. 95.
John Joce, co. Norf., 50 Edw. III : FF. vii. 289.
Thomas Jose, 1379 : P. T. Yorks. p. 266.
1752. Married—Thomas Joce and Sarah Massa : St. Geo. Chap. Mayfair, p. 214.
MDB. (co. Devon), 6, 0 ; (co. Cornwall), 0, 14 ; New York, 0, 2.

Joel, Joell.—Bapt. ' the son of Joel' or ' Johel,' a fairly favourite name in the 13th and 14th centuries ; v. Jewell.

Joel de Stok, C. R., 47 Hen. III.
Joelus de Bosco, Hen. III–Edw. I. K.
William Joel, co. Hunts, 1273. A.
Joel le Warrener. H.
Johel Thenkersman, C. R., 1 Edw. II.
Joel de Bukyngton, C. R., 15 Ric. II.
1723. Married—John Joel and Eliz. Hippeth : St. Mary Aldermary, p. 46.
1789. — William Gibb and Mary Joel : St. Geo. Han. Sq. ii. 31.
London, 7, 0 ; West Rid. Court Dir., 8, 1 ; Sheffield, 2, 0 ; New York, 6, 0.

John.—Bapt. ' the son of John,' a Welsh surname. John was never an English surname. Johnson monopolized the honours.

Edward ap-John, archdeacon of Caermarthen, 1509 : Hist. and Ant. St. David's, p. 360.
Robert ap-Edward John, of Bangor, 1599 : Wills at Chester (1545–1620), p. 109.
William ap-Thomas John, of Pulford, 1606 : ibid.
Edward ap-John, of Hanmer, *laborer*, 1584 : ibid.
1666. Married—Robert Ralt and Charity John : St. Jas. Clerkenwell, iii. 129.
1751. — Thomas John and Joanna Russell : St. Geo. Chap. Mayfair, p. 204.
London, 2 ; Liverpool, 3 ; MDB. (co. Pembroke), 25 ; New York, 23.

Johns, Johnson, Johnes.—Bapt. ' the son of John,' originally pronounced and spelt Jone ; v. Jones. It will be well to give a fairly large number of instances.

Robert Johns, co. Soms., 1 Edw. III : Kirby's Quest, p. 126.
Johannes Webster, 1379 : P. T. Yorks. p. 187.
Willelmus Joneson, 1379 : ibid.
Willelmus Johnson, 1379 : ibid. p. 221.
Robertus Johanson, 1379 : ibid. p. 36.
Juliana Jonesson, *webster*, 1379 : ibid. p. 161.
Ricardus Joneson, 1379 : ibid. p. 2.
Robertus Jonson, 1379 : ibid. 187.
Lewis Johns, prebendary of St. David's, 1486 : Hist. and Ant. St. David's, p. 361.

The following represents one of the earliest Puritan Christian names :

1583. Bapt.—Evangeliste, s. Evangeliste Johnson : St. Michael, Cornhill, p. 92.
1600. Lewis Johnes, co. Monmouth : Reg. Univ. Oxf. vol. ii. pt. ii. p. 244.
— William Johnes, co. Montgomery : ibid. p. 245.
London 21, 343, 1 ; New York, 16, 680, 4.

Joice.—Bapt. ; v. Joyce.

MDB. (co. Essex), 1 ; Boston (U.S.), 1 ; New York, 2.

Joiner, Joyner.—Occup. ' the joiner,' rare. Probably *joiner* as an occupative term came into use somewhat later than *carpenter*. The surname seems barely to have maintained an existence, while Carpenter and Wright are represented by thousands.

' Carpenters, coupers, and joyners.'
Cocke Lorelle's Bote.

Hugh le Joignour. G.
Alan le Jovgnour. N.
Richard Joynere, 1564 : Reg. Univ. Oxf. i. 254.
1566. Stephen Wyseman and Mary Joyner : Marriage Lic. (London), i. 34.
1743. Married—Thomas Joiner and Mary Walters : St. Dionis Backchurch, p. 68.
1767. — Francis Willince and Ann Joyner : St. Geo. Han. Sq. i. 162.
London, 1, 8 ; Boston (U.S.), 4, 0.

Jolin, Joline.—Bapt. ' the son of Jolin' or ' Jollan' ; v. Jolland.

Jolin de Dunholme, co. Hunts. 1273. A.
Henry fil. Jolani, co. Hunts. ibid.
1649. Married—Samuel Jollins and Anne Mosely : St. Jas. Clerkenwell, iii 81.
1738. Buried—E. Jollins : St. Thomas the Apostle (London), p. 154.
London, 1, 0 ; Philadelphia, 0, 4.

Joll ; see Jull.

Jolland, Golland, Galland, Jollands, Jollans, Jalland.—Bapt. ' the son of Jollan,' possibly, as stated by Camden, a corruption of Julian. The *d* in Jolland is excrescent ; cf. *riband*, Simmond, and Hammond, for *ribbon*, Simon, and Hamon. The font-name is almost entirely found in co. Lincoln, where also the surname seems to have originated. It is interesting to notice that Lincolnshire is still the chief habitat of all the various forms. With the initial G, cf. Gill and Jill, Garrett and Jarratt, Gosling and Joscelyn. The final *s* in Jollands and Jollans is the patronymic, as in Williams, Jennings, &c.

Jollan de Hamby, co. Linc., Hen. III Edw. I. K.
Jollanus de Heyling, co. Linc., ibid.
Jodlanus de Nevill, co. Linc., ibid.
Jollan de Hemby, co. Linc., ibid.
Gilbert fil. Jolani, co. Linc., 1273. A.
William fil. Jollani, co. Linc., ibid.

F f

Robert Jollayn, co. Linc., 1273. A.
Ricardus Joland, 1379: P. T. Yorks.
p. 8.
Katerina Golland, 1479, York: W. 11,
p. 106.
1536-7. Richard Joland and Agnes Inkersall: Marriage Lic. (London), i. 9.
1698. Married—William Joland and
Anne Gurney: St. Dionis Backchurch,
p. 47.
London, 1, 1, 2, 0, 0, 1; MDB. (co.
Lincoln), 1, 4, 2, 1, 1, 0; (East Rid.
Yorks) (Jalland), 2; Philadelphia (Galland), 2.

Jolliff, Jolliffe, Joliffe. —
Nick. 'the jolif,' i.e. the festive,
sportive ; O.F. *jolif*, the earlier
form of jolly ; cf. *bailiff* and *bailey.*.

'Forth he goth, jolif and amorous.'
      Chaucer, C. T. 3355.
John Jolyf, co. Hunts, 1273. A.
Henry Jolyffe, c. 1300. M.
Robertus Jolyf, 1379: P. T. Yorks.
p. 208.
Alicia Jolyff, 1379 : ibid. p. 270.
John Jolyf, C. R., 1 Hen. IV. pt. i.
1670. William Hawkins and Edith
Joliffe (of Dorchester): Marriage Alleg.
(Canterbury), p. 179.
Liverpool, 0, 1, 0; MDB. (co. Kent),
0, 1, 1; (co. Worcester), 0, 0, 1; New
York (Joliffe), 1.

Jolly, Jolley, Joly, Jollie.—
Nick. 'the jolly,' merry, gay, festive;
v. Jolliff. Prof. Skeat connects
it with Yule ; Icel. *jol.* The following entries referring to the
same individual are interesting :

Johannes Yoly, 1379: P. T. Yorks.
p. 265.
Agnes, serviens Joly Johan, 1379: ibid.
p. 226.

Hence the double forms Little
and Little-john in our directories.
In the latter case the font-name
becomes permanently incorporated
with the nickname. Jolly-john
might as easily have been perpetuated. Note, however, Y and J in
the instance given ; v. Joy for
similar instance.

William Golye, 1273. A.
Henricus Joly, 1379: P. T. Yorks.
p. 142.
Ricardus Jolyman, 1379: ibid. p. 119.
Willelmus Jolyman, 1379: ibid. p. 16.
Johannes Jolyman, 1379: ibid. p. 32.

With these instances, cf. Merriman and Merry.

1715. Buried—Theodorius Joley, servant to Mr. Philips, the barber: St.
Michael, Cornhill, p. 283.
London, 12, 1, 0, 0; Philadelphia, 12,
8, 5, 3.

Jollypace. — Nick. With the
merry step, lively gait; M.E.
pas ; cf. Golightly, Lightfoot.

Henry Jolypas, C. R., 17 Ric. II.
'And forth we riden a litel more than
pas.'   Chaucer, C. T. 825.

Jonas. — Bapt. 'the son of
Jonas.' Generally of Jewish de-
scent, but in early use as an
English font-name.

Jonas de Powis, Pipe Roll, 11 Hen. II.
1548-9. Richard Jonas (? Jones) and
Joanna Smyth: Marriage Lic. (Faculty
Office), p. 14.
1736. Bapt.—Ann, d. William Jonas :
St. Jas. Clerkenwell, ii. 226.
London, 13; Philadelphia, 7.

Jones, Joneson.—Bapt. 'the
son of John (?), or 'Johan,' or
'Jone,' as at first written and pronounced, both masculine and feminine. In the 13th and 14th centuries Johan stood for both Johannes and Johanna. This being
awkward, the masculine took the
form of John (Jon), the feminine
of Joan (Jone). But it is quite
clear from evidence that for a time
the sound Jone represented both.
In the Poll Tax, 1379, co. Yorks
(p. 43), we find for instance :

Johan Chapman et Lesot sa femme.
Johan servant de dit Johan.
Henri de Nortburne et Johan sa femme.
Robert Geslyng et Johan sa femme.
Johan Quenyld.
Matilda Jones, co. Hunts, 1273. A.
Walter fil. Jone, co. Hunts, ibid.
Ralph Jones-man, C. R., 30 Edw. I.
Walter Jones, co. Soms., 1 Edw. III:
Kirby's Quest, p. 231.
Ricardus Jone-son, 1379: P. T. Yorks.
p. 104.
Alicia Jone-doghter, 1379: ibid.
Johanna Jone-wyf, 1379: ibid. p. 23.
Jane Joneson, of Audlem, *widow*, 1594:
Wills at Chester (L. and C. R. S.), p. 111.
Jane Joneson, of Marton, *widow*, 1605:
ibid.

Joneson has become absorbed
by Johnson. Indeed, Joynson is
the only variant that remains.

London, about 650, 0; Philadelphia,
1262, 0.

Jonet, Jonetson.—Bapt. 'the
son of John' (?) ; M.E. Jone, dim.
Jonet. Probably for a time Jonet
was masculine as well as feminine.
But Janet (q.v.) won the day.

Johannes Jonetson, 1379: P. T. Yorks.
p. 18.
Willelmus Jonet, 1379 : ibid. p. 88.

Johannes Jonet, 1379 : ibid. p. 91.
William Jonetson, C. R., 9 Ric. II.

Jonson. — Bapt. 'the son of
John,' for Johnson, but quite as
early a form; cf. Jones. I often
wonder how 'Poems by Benjamin
Johnson' would read. But 'rare
Ben's' name is several times spelt
Johnson by his friends.

Magota Jon-wyf, 1379: P. T. Yorks.
p. 86.
Margareta Jon-dowtter, 1379: ibid.
p. 88.
Thomas Jon-son-Dycon-son, 1379: ibid.
p. 240.
1527. Rawlyns and Johanna Jonson :
Marriage Lic. (London), i. 6.
1556. Christning of Ellen Jonsonne: St.
Peter, Cornhill, i. 7.
Christopher Jonson, or Johnson, 1557:
Reg. Univ. Oxf. i. 234.
London, 1 ; New York, 6.

Joplin, Jopling.—Bapt. 'the
son of Job,' from dim. Joblin ; v.
Jobling. In Jopling the final *g*
is excrescent, as in Jennings ; cf.
Hamlin and Hamling from Hamo,
and Tomlin or Tomling from Tom
(Thomas). The change from *b* to
p is common ; cf. Hoblin and Hop-
lin, Hobson and Hopson, Hobbs
and Hopps, Robson and Ropson,
all from Robert. Also cf. Jopson
for Jobson.

1712. Married—John Hague and Han-
nah Joplin: St. Geo. Chap. Mayfair,
p. 28.
1763. — John Taylor and Eliz. Jopling :
St. Geo. Han. Sq. i. 120.
1804. — Robert Haines and Sarah
Joplin: ibid. ii. 313.
MDB. (co. Camb.), 1, 0; Lancashire
Court Dir., 1, 1; Manchester, 0, 1;
Liverpool, 1, 0.

Jopson. — Bapt. 'the son of
Job'; v. Job, Jupp, and Joplin.
Jopson was an early sharpened
form of Jobson.

Johannes Jopson, 1379: P. T. Yorks.
p. 289.
1579. Thomas Jopson, co. York: Reg.
Univ. Oxf. vol. ii. pt. ii. p. 89.
1597-8. Francis Jopson, or Jobson, co.
Westm.: ibid. p. 226.
Liverpool, 2.

**Jordan, Jordanson, Jordi-
son, Jordeson, Jorden, Jordon.**—Bapt. 'the son of Jordan.'
This great personal name, that has
made such a strong impression
on English and West European
nomenclature, received its impetus,

like Ellis (Elias), John, and Baptist, from the Crusades. Flasks of Jordan water, we know, were brought home to be used for fontal purposes. John the Baptist was the second Elias, and the baptizer of Jesus Christ. Naturally Jordan was added to the list, and became popular throughout Western Europe. Only a trained student of nomenclature can know what a favourite it became in England. Every register has its muster of instances. Judd was the nick. (whence Judd, Judde, and Judson, q.v.), and Judkin the dim. after the prevailing fashion that gave us Watkin, or Wilkin, or Simpkin, or Tompkin (whence Judkins toned down to Juckins, Juggins, Juckes, and Jukes, q.v.). Dean Stanley says, 'The name of the river has in Italy and Spain, by a natural association, been turned into a common Christian name for children at the hour of baptism, which served to connect them with it' (Sinai and Palestine, p. 333). The late dean did not seem aware that the practice was equally common in England.

Roger fil. Jurdan, co. Camb., 1273. A.
Robert fil. Jordan, co. Oxf., ibid.
Jordan atte Mull, temp. 1300. M.
Matilda relicta Jordani, 1379: P. T. Yorks. p. 210.
Jordanus Thorneton, 1379: ibid. p. 211.
Thomas Jordanson: Three Lancashire Documents (Cheth. Soc.), p. 51.

Jordy or Jurdy is early found as the nick. of Jordan:

Bartholomew Jurde, co. Camb., 1273. A.
Henry Jurde, co. Hunts, ibid.
Jurdi (without surname), co. Suff., ibid.
James Jurdeson. GG.
1763. Married—Francis Nelson and Rachel Jurdison: St. Geo. Han. Sq. i. 118.
London, 65, 0, 2, 1, 0, 0; Philadelphia, 183, 0, 0, 0, 8, 5.

Jose; v. Joce.

Joseph, Josephs.—Bapt. 'the son of Joseph'; v. Jessop. Many of the modern directory Josephs are of Jewish extraction, but there are also a fair number of Josephs who have a purely English descent.

Galian' relict Joseph, co. Oxf., 1273. A.
Thomas Joseph, co. Soms., 1 Edw. III:
Kirby's Quest, p. 89.
Edith Josep, co. Soms., 1 Edw. III: ibid. p. 95.
1577. John Joseph, co. Kent: Reg. Univ. Oxf. vol. ii. pt. ii. p. 74.
1754. Married—Anthony Joseph and Mary Thomas: St. Geo. Chap. Mayfair, p. 276.
1799.—John Gough and Jane Josephs: St. Geo. Han. Sq. ii. 198.
1803.—William Burrell and Amelia Joseph: ibid. p. 278.
London, 39, 5; New York, 56, 11.

Joslin, Joselin, Josolyne, Josselin, Josslyn, Joscelyne, Josling, Joslyn, Josline.—Bapt. 'the son of Josse' or 'Goce,' dim. Josselin or Gocelin; v. Joyce. The g in Josling is excrescent; cf. Jennings, Rawling, Hewling, &c.

Thomas Jocelyn, co. Essex, 1273. A.
Jocelinus de Braggrowe, co. Devon, ibid.
Stephen Jocelin, co. Warw., Hen. III-Edw. I. K.
1548. John Heron and Jane Joslyn: Marriage Lic. (Faculty Office), p. 13.
1590. Thomas Josselyn and Dorothy Scott (excommunication removed): Marriage Lic. (London), i. 188.
John Joslinge and Joanna Humfrye: ibid. p. 191.
1672. Robert Sawyer and Mary Joscelyn: Marriage Alleg. (Canterbury), p. 80.
London, 4, 1, 1, 1, 1, 0, 0, 0, 0; Crockford (Joscelyne and Josling), 2, 1; Philadelphia, (Joslin) 8, (Joslyn) 1, (Josline) 1.

Joule, Joul, Jowle, Joules.—Bapt. 'the son of Joel.' This was popularly styled Jowel. In course of time this became a monosyllable, and is now commonly found in Derbyshire as Joule or Jowle. The patronymic or genitive form is Joules; cf. Jones, Williams, Simpkins, &c. For instances of Jowel, v. Jewell.

1643. Married—Robert Jole and Eliz. Dennis: St. Antholin (London), p. 76.
1650.—Augustine Jowles and Dorothy Ridley: St. Jas. Clerkenwell, iii. 85.
1662. Henry Jowles and Rebecca Alleyn: Marriage Alleg. (Canterbury), p. 75.
1762. Married—George Joules and Margaret Potter: St. Geo. Han. Sq. i. 113.
1767.—John Stent and Sophia Joules: ibid. p. 164.
MDB. (co. Derby), 4, 2, 1, 0; Philadelphia, 2, 0, 0, 0.

Jourdan, Jourden.—Bapt. 'the son of Jordan,' q.v.

William Jurdan, co. Oxf., 1273. A.
Magot Jurdan, vidua, 1379: P. T. Yorks. p. 42.
Isabella Jurdan, 1379: ibid. p. 99.
1573. Thomas Jourden and Marcia Burstowe: Marriage Lic. (London), i. 57.
1585-6. Thomas Shereman and Secile Jourden: ibid. p. 144.
London, 2, 0; Boston (U.S.), 0, 1.

Jowett, Jowitt.—Bapt. 'the son of Juliet.' A New England corruption. There can be, I suspect, no controversy on the origin of these names. Julian or Gillian early took to itself a dim. Juliet or Gilot. The more correct Juliet would, of necessity, almost become Juwet in Yorkshire and the north of England generally; v. Jewett. Of course this modification was not wholly northern.

Robert Jouet, co. Soms., 1 Edw. III: Kirby's Quest, p. 207.
Johannes Juwett, 1379: P. T. Yorks. p. 249.
Robertus Jowet, 1379: ibid. p. 105.
Adam Jowete, 1379: ibid. p. 185.
Johannes Jowete, 1379: ibid.
Willelmus Jowet, 1379: ibid. p. 195.
1539. Married—Richard Juet and Katherine Averell: St. Peter, Cornhill, i. 221.
London, 1, 1; West Rid. Court Dir., 23, 5; New York, 0, 2; Philadelphia, 2, 0.

Joy.—Nick. for one of joyous disposition. Perhaps baptismal; cf. Joyce. The dim. Joyet is found in the case of Richard Joyet, co. Camb. (1273. A.) Joy is a common entry in early registers.

Elena Joye, co. Hunts, 1273. A.
Simon Joye, co. Camb., ibid.
John Joye, co. Oxf. ibid.
Martin Joye, co. Soms., 1 Edw. III: Kirby's Quest, p. 206.
Robertus Yoy, 1379: P. T. Yorks p. 289.
Robertus Yoy, junior, 1379: ibid.
Willelmus Joye, 1379: ibid. p. 3.

With Yoy, cf. Yoly for Jolly.

1472. Godfrey Joye, alderman of Norwich, died: FF. iv. 213.
1593. Henry Joye and Eliz. Fisher: Marriage Lic. (London), i. 208.
London, 11; Philadelphia, 14.

Joyce, Joycey, Joysey, Jowsey.—Bapt. 'the son of Josse' or 'Goce.' Cognate in origin with joy and joyous; Latin gaudere. Rendered popular by St. Josse the hermit, who refused the sovereignty of Brittany (v. Yonge, i.

396). Nearly forgotten as it is, this name was parent of the dim. Jocelyn, and thus secured immortality through its offspring. From the first there was in England a choice of initials, G or J. If G, then the name was pronounced hard as in *gospel*, if J, soft as in *gentile*. Thus it is that we have Gosling and Joscelyn in our directories, while both are the same name. The early entries of Josse or Goce are numerous, the diminutives at first being rare. Such are some of the registrations:

Goce Fitz-peter, sheriff of London, 1211: WWW. pp. 187-90.
Goce le Pesur, sheriff, 1218: ibid.
Goce le Juvene, sheriff, 1220: ibid.
Josse Sephurd, 1273. A.
Alexander Joce, ibid.
John fil. Jocey, ibid.
Reginald fil. Jocei, ibid.
Nicholas Jose, ibid.
Manasseh fil. Jossy, ibid.
Goceus Gothel, Hen. III–Edw. I. K.
Robert fil. Jocei, 20 Edw. I. R.
1618. William Hercules and Jane Jowsey: Marriage Lic. (Westminster), p. 24.

The name became distinctly popular, and many diminutives arose, Josselin and Gocelin being the chief. For instances, v. Goslin and Joslin. Gosset and Goslett (q.v.) added themselves to the list. The parent form Josse became Jocey, as already seen, and through French influence (cf. *rejoice* and *joy*) Joyce and Joycey. This last is common in Durham and the Newcastle district; v. Newcastle Directory.

William Joysey, 1561, Tweedmouth: QQQ. p. 25.
'John Moorhead, clerk, against William Joysee in a ple of trespas,' 1614: ibid. p. 243.

It needs only to add that Joyce became a favourite girl's name, though some of the early instances may be masculine.

Joyce Faukes. H.
Joyce Tibetot, ibid.
Joice Frankline, co. York. W. 9.
1563. Buried—Joyce, wife of Thomas Armstrong: St. Dionis Backchurch (London), p. 187.

I find that the name Joyce occurs once as a nickname, equivalent to joyous:

Richard le Joyce. J.
London, 30, 1, 4, 0; Sunderland (Jowsey), 1; Philadelphia, 76, 0, 10, 0.

Joyner.—Occup.; v. Joiner.

Joynson, Joynes.—Bapt. 'the son of John'; v. Johns. This form has existed in Cheshire for several centuries. It was a compromise between Johnson and Joneson; v. Jones. The latter is found in Cheshire at an early period:

'William le Crouther, William le Baron, Robert de Bookynton, Henry Jonesson of Werford,' &c.: Hist. East Ches. i. 424.
Robert Joynson, of Eaton, co. Ches., 1582: Wills at Chester (1545-1620), p. 111.
John Joynson, of Eaton, co. Ches., 1613: ibid.
1619. Arthur Joynson, of Waverton: Hist. East Ches. ii. 146.

Of course Welsh influence had much to do with these Cheshire variants of Johnson.

Sheffield, 0, 2; Manchester, 6, 0; London, 0, 2; MDB. (co. Chester), 6, 0; Philadelphia, 0, 2.

Jubb, Jupp, Juppe.—Bapt. 'the son of Job.' Jubb was, generally speaking, the North-English, Jupp or Joppe the South-English form. This probably explains *jubbe*, a drinking vessel, i.e. a Job's comforter.

'With bred and chese, and good ale in a jubbe.' Chaucer, C. T. 3628.

Jack and Jug (Joan) were both similarly employed; *jug* still exists. v. Jupp.

Elyas Jubbe, co. Suff., 1273. A.
Warin Jubbe, co. York, ibid.
Johannes Jubbe, 1379: P. T. Yorks. p. 104.
Ricardus Jubbe, 1379: ibid.
Ales Jubbe, temp. 1495, co. York: Visitation of Yorkshire (Harl. Soc.), p. 57.
1502-3. Martin Jubb and Ursula Smith: Marriage Lic. (London), i. 205.
1864. Married—Gartland and Selina Fanny Jubb: Canterbury Cathedral, p. 108.
West Rid. Court Dir., 13, 0, 0; London, 0, 13, 0; Boston (U.S.) (Jubb), 1; New York (Juppe), 1.

Juckins, Jukinson. — (1) Bapt. 'the son of Jordan,' from the nick. Judd, and dim. Judkin. The patronymic Judkins was modified into Juckins; v. Jukes and Juggins.

I have only seen one instance of Jukinson.

1641. Married—Ralfe Jukinson and An Lane: Canterbury Cathedral.

(2) Bapt. Possibly a Flemish name, from a nick. Jo (Joseph?), and dim. Jokin.

William Jokin, co. Suff., 1273. A.
John Jowkin, 1379: P. T. Yorks. p. 295.

In spite of these two entries I cannot but think that the extremely popular font-name Jordan with its nick. Judd is the parent. Judkins was bound to become Juckins and Jukinson or Juckinson.

Judd, Judde, Jude.—Bapt. 'the son of Jordan,' from nick. Jud, but possibly an early form of Jude. The former is much more probable as Jordan (q.v.) was one of the favourite names of the surname era. Jurdi occurs as a single name (A. ii. 198), also Jurdy (A. ii. 148), which are obviously nicks. of Jordan. Henry Jurde and Bartholomew Jurde occur in the same register. These would readily become popularized into Juddy. In the account of Wat Tyler's insurrection Gower says:

'*Hudde* ferit, quem *Judde* terit, dum Tibbe juvatur.'

Henry Judde, co. Camb., 1273. A.
Aaron Judde, co. Linc., ibid.
Alicia Jude-doghter, 1379: P. T. Yorks. p. 172.
Johannes Juddeman (i. e. the servant of Judde), 1379: ibid. p. 93.
Johannes Judd', 1379: ibid. p. 165.
John Jude, 1585: Reg. St. Columb Major, p. 142.
John Judde, 1593: ibid. p. 143.
1774. Married—John Jude and Betty Harman: St. Geo. Han. Sq. i. 243.
London, 31, 0, 4; New York, 24, 0, 1.

Judge.—? Offic. 'the judge'; cf. Justice. So far I have come across no early instances, and suspect it is generally Judds corrupted (i.e. the son of Jordan); v. Judd and Judkins. In this case Judge would be imitative.

1575. William Judges and Agnes Okendale: Marriage Lic. (London), i. 66.
1616. Richard Judge, co. Montgom.: Reg. Univ. Oxf. vol. ii. pt. ii. p. 348.
1675. Matthew Wright and Mary Judge: Marriage Alleg. (Canterbury), p. 245.
1746. Married—Simon Norcut and

Sarah Judge: St. Geo. Chap. Mayfair, p. 80.

London, 13; New York, 32.

Judkins, Judkin.—Bapt. 'the son of Jordan,' from nick. Jud, dim. Judkin; v. Jukes, which is a modification.

1648, Buried—Thomas Judkins, servant to Mr. Thomas Lucis: St. Dionis Backchurch, p. 39.
1668. James Taylor and Grace Judkin: Marriage Lic. (Faculty Office), p. 103.
1677. Married—Edward James and Jane Judkin: St. Dionis Backchurch, p. 776.
1778. — George Gundrey and Eliz. Mary Judkins: St. Geo. Han. Sq. i. 291.
London, 5, 0; MDB. (co. Warwick), 0, 1; Boston (U.S.), 15, 0.

Judson. — Bapt. 'the son of Jordan,' from nick. Jud; v. Judd.

Ricardus Judson, 1379: P. T. Yorks. p. 71.
Willelmus Judson, 1379: ibid. p. 203.
Thomas Judson, 1379: ibid. p. 90.
Johannes Jodson, 1379: ibid. p. 108.
Agnes Jod-doghter, 1379: ibid. p. 263.
William Juddeson, Pardons Roll, 15 Ric. II.
1574. Buried—Briget, d. John Judson: St. Peter, Cornhill, i. 123.
1594. Bapt.—Dority, d. Robert Judson: St. Antholin (London), p. 37.
London, 2; Philadelphia, 25.

Juggins, Juggings. — Bapt. 'the son of Jordan,' from the nick. Judd, whence the dim. Jud-kin, whence Judkins. This became modified to Juckins, and this to Juggins. The g in Juggings is excrescent, as in Jennings, Collinge, &c.; cf. Slack and Slagg. The surname is somewhat rare. v. Judkins.

1650. Married—Thomas Juggins and Alice Wentworth: St. Jas. Clerkenwell, iii. 85.
1651. Buried—John, s. John Juggin: ibid. iv. 286.
1793. Married — Edmund Hall and Mary Juggins: St. Geo. Han. Sq. ii. 89.

An amusing leading article on the case of Mrs. Juggings occurs in the Daily Telegraph, Nov. 5, 1889.

London, 1, 0; Oxford, 4, 0; Boston (U.S.), 1, 0.

Jugler.—Occup. 'the juggler.'

Robert Jugler, C. R., 21 Ric. II. pt. i.
Richard Juggolir: Kirby's Quest, p. 273.
Henricus Juglore, 1379: P. T. Yorks. p. 284.

Jugson; v. Juxon.

Jukes, Jewks, Juckes, Jewkes. — Bapt. 'the son of Jordan,' from nick. Judd, and dim. Jud-kin. With a patronymic s (as in Williams) this became Judkins, by-and-by corrupted into Judkiss, Juckiss, and finally Jukes, &c.; cf. Hawkins, Hawkiss, Hawkes from Henry, or Perkins, Perkiss, Perkes from Peter; v. Dawkins. Also v. Juckins, Judkins.

1570–1. Thomas Jeux and Ellen Johnson: Marriage Lic. (London), i. 48.
1588. George Jucks, co. Salop, Reg. Univ. Oxf. vol. ii. pt. ii. p. 164.
1594. Simon Juckes, London: ibid. p. 205.
1615. Francis Juckes, co. Salop: ibid. p. 337.
1621. Bapt.—James, s. Thomas Jucks: St. Jas. Clerkenwell, i. 90.
1630. Richard Jucks and Eliz. Taunton: Marriage Lic. (Westminster), p. 38.
1768. Married—Joel Jukes and Mary Garlick: St. Geo. Han. Sq. i. 175.
London, 5, 0, 0, 0; Liverpool, 0, 0, 1, 0; Boston (U.S.), 1, 0, 0, 1.

Julian, Julien, Julyan, Julyans.—Bapt. 'the son of Juliana,' from the martyr of that name, beheaded at Nicomedia under Galerius (Yonge, i. 320). Popular at an early period, both in the Low Countries and in Normandy. It attained such favour in England that Jack and Jill took the place of Godric and Godgivu as representatives of the sexes. The ordinary form was Julyan and Gillian, in which latter shape it reached the 16th century.

1573. Married—John Carrington and Gillyan Lovelakei: St. Dionis Backchurch, p. 7.
1586. Bapt.—Gillian, d. Thomas Jones, grocer: St. Peter, Cornhill, i. 30.

Earlier instances are easily obtainable:

'Jelyan Joly at signe of the Bokeler.'
Cocke Lorelle's Bote.

Gillian Coc, co. Camb., 1273. A.
Robert Gilion, co. Camb., ibid.
Hugh fil. Juliane, co. Oxf., ibid.
Peter fil. Juliane, co. Hunts, ibid.
Roger Juliane, co. Camb., ibid.
Geoffrey Julyan, C. R., 17 Edw. III. pt. i.
Alanus Alscy, et Juliana uxor ejus, 1329: P. T. Yorks. p. 7.
1574. William Bragdon and Bennet Julyans: Marriage Lic. (London), i. 61.
1591. Bapt.—Robert, s. Miles Julyon: St. Jas. Clerkenwell, i. 25.

1774. Married—James Julian and Eliz. Yandley: St. Geo. Han. Sq. i. 243.
1793. — Jean Jullien and Edith Hunt: ibid. ii. 101.

The nick. of Julian, as will have been understood above, was Jill or Gill.

'I am careful to see thee carelesse, Jylle.
I am woful to see thee wytlesse, Wyll.'
Heywood's Epigrams.

'Sir, for Jak nor for Gille
Wille I turne my face.'
Towneley Mysteries, Noah.

Richard fil. Gille, co. Camb., 1273. A.
Gille Hull, co. Camb., ibid.

This nick. gave birth to Gill and Gillson, q.v. The dim. was Juliet, a name later on to be made familiar for ever. This was ordinarily corrupted into or modified into Juet, Jewett, or Jowett, q.v.

Juetta fil. William. T.
Roger fil. Jowette. ibid.
William fil. Juet, co. Camb., 1273. A.
Jowet Barton, co. York. W. 11.

Hence our various Jewitts, Jewetts, and Jowitts, also our Jewitsons, Jowetsons, Jewisons, and Jewsons.

Christopher Jewitson. Z.

Besides Juliet there was the corresponding form Gillot or Gillet. In one of the old Metrical Sermons it is said:

'Robin will Gilot
Leden to the nale,
And sitten there togedres,
And tellen their tale.'
Gillot Carel. (BB.)

But our Gilletts and Gillotts must as a rule be referred to William; v. Gillott. From Juliet or Gilot we got 'Jill.' Constant association with Jack made it a cant term for an inconstant girl:

'All shall be well, Jack shall have Gill;
Nay, nay, Gill is wedded to Will.'

Shakespeare has a similar slighting allusion, flirt-gill (Romeo, ii. 4); flirt-gillian (Beaumont and Fletcher, The Chances, iii. 1). 'A jillet brak his heart at last': Burns, On a Scotch Bard. Another instance of the disrepute of Julian lies in the local 'Julian Bowers' or 'Gelyan Bowers,' a name for the old-fashioned mazes or labyrinths formed by hedges. To find Jillian seated laughing in the centre was the gallant's difficulty. Correspondents in N. and Q. (1855, pp. 65, 132, 193) ascribed them to the Roman period and the Emperor Julian or Julus, son of Aeneas, and quote Virgil, Aen. v. 1. A Julian Bower is noticed in Stukeley's Itinerarium Curiosum, p. 91. Several of the above observations will be found elsewhere, but I thought it better, with a fontal name that has made such a deep impression on our nomenclature, to give a somewhat complete statement.

London, 5, 2, 1, 0 ; New York, 8, 5, 0, 0.

Jull, Joll.—Bapt. 'the son of Julian' (q.v.), from the nick. Jill, or more correctly Jull. A Cornish name.

John Jolle, 1549: Reg. St. Columb Major, p. 5.
Richard Julle, 1575 : ibid. p. 9.
John Joulle, 1579 : ibid. p. 140.
Joane Jule, 1585 : ibid. p. 142.
1704. Married—Robert Jull and Sarah Stone : Canterbury Cathedral, p. 67.
1802.—William Warner and Harriot Jull : St. Geo. Han. Sq. ii. 250.
London, 4, 0 ; Boston (U.S.), 0, 1.

Jump.—Local, 'of Jump,' probably the hamlet of Jump in the parish of Wombwell, co. Yorks.

William Jump, of Hesketh, 1612 : Wills at Chester (1545-1620), p. 112.
Robert Jump, of North Meols, 1614 : ibid.
1569. Married—John Willyams and Margery Jumpe : St. Jas. Clerkenwell, iii. 4.
1688-9. Thomas Jump and Eliz. Martendale : Marriage Alleg. (Canterbury), p. 93.
London, 1 ; Liverpool, 5 ; Crockford, 2 ; Philadelphia, 5.

Jung, Junge, June.—Nick. ' the young'; Fr. ' le Jeune.' With an excrescent *g* ; cf. Jennings.

Matilda Jun, co. Camb., 1273. A.
Johannes le Junge, co. Camb., ibid.
Robert le Jevene, co. Wilts, ibid.
Simon le Jevene, co. Oxf., ibid.
London, 4, 0, 0 ; New York, 44, 5, 3.

Junior. — Nick. 'the junior,' the younger of two men bearing the same name ; cf. Senior. It was a very common thing for two or three brothers to bear the name of John. This necessitated some mark of distinction ; v. my Curiosities of Puritan Nomenclature, p. 4.

Robert Junior, co. Linc., 1273. A.
'John le Senior, *priest*, and John le Junior ': FF. v. 384.

These were brothers.

1752. Married—Lewis Brunet and Jeane Junier : St. Geo. Chap. Mayfair, p. 213.
London, 1 ; Philadelphia, 8.

Juniper, Junifer.—Bapt. 'the son of Gwenever' or 'Guinevere'; v. Jenifer. Another name of King Arthur's court. Lancelot was her lover. In Cornwall it has been a font-name for hundreds of years in the several forms of Juniper, Jenifer, and Jennefair. It was still common in the 17th and 18th centuries.

1691. Bapt.—Junipher, d. of Edward Rickard : St. Colomb Major, co. Cornwall.
1692. — Junipher, d. of Robert Dunkin : ibid.
1700. — Jenifer, d. of Richard Janes: ibid.
1701. — Jenifer, d. of Matthew Battrell : ibid.

The surname has been made familiar by Mr. Juniper of the Sussex county cricket eleven. It is in the London Directory. (v. Miss Yonge, Christian Names, ii. 132, for the story of Gwenever.)

1753. Married—John Juniper and Eliz. Keckerman : St. Geo. Chap. Mayfair, p. 239.
London, 1, 0 ; MDB. (co. Worcester), 0, 1 ; (co. Norf.), 3, 0 ; Boston (U.S.), 1, 0.

Jupiter.—Bapt. No doubt an imitative corruption of Juniper, q.v.

1798. Married—William Jupiter and Catherine Davis: St. Geo. Han. Sq. ii. 187.
Jane Jupiter, *tailoress*, 1 Shawmut Terrace : Boston (U.S.).

Jupp, Juppe.—Bapt. 'the son of Job'; M.E. Joppe. The story of Job told in the religious plays would make the name very popular; v. Jopson and Joplin ; v. also Jubb and Chubb. With Jupp, cf. Ropps for Robbs, or Hopps for Hobbs.

Joppe (without surname), co. Bedf., 1273. A.
Thomas Jop, co. Oxf., ibid.
John Joppe, co. Hunts, ibid.
Henry Joppe, co. Wilts, ibid.
John Joppe, co. Soms., 1 Edw. III : Kirby's Quest, p. 257.
1618. Bapt. — Elizabeth, d. Thomas Juppe : St. Dionis Backchurch, p. 97.
1676-7. William Hampton and Judith

Evans, alleged by Benjamin Jupp : Marriage Alleg. (Canterbury), p. 185.
London, 13, 0 ; New York, 0, 1.

Jurden, Jurdon.—Bapt. 'the son of Jordan,' q.v.

Jurdana de Cantok, co. Soms., 1 Edw. III : Kirby's Quest, p. 261.
William Jurdan, co. Soms., 1 Edw. III : ibid.
1582-3. Married—William Shearland and Katherine Jurdenne : St. Dionis Backchurch, p. 10.
1669. — Humfrey Jurden and Allice Andrew : St. Jas. Clerkenwell, iii. 166.
1670. — John Jurden and Mary Hurbin : ibid. 170.
Boston (U.S.), 1, 0 ; Philadelphia, 0, 1.

Jury.—Local, ' of the Jewry,' that part of a town which was set apart for the Jewish population; v. Jewsbury.

'Ther was in Asie, in a gret citee, Amonges Cristen folk a Jewerie.'
Chaucer, C. T. (beginning of Prioress' Tale).
'And I am juge of all Jury' (i.e. Judea): York Mystery Plays, p. 130, l. 127.

Cf. Jewry in London.

John Jewrie : Pat. Roll, 19 Eliz. pt. xii.
1670. Married—John Jury and Allice Tealor : St. Jas. Clerkenwell, iii. 171.
1840. — William Bennett and Mary Jury : St. Geo. Han. Sq. ii. 306.
London, 3 ; Boston (U.S.), 3.

Juson; v. Jewson.

Just. — Nick. 'the just,' the righteous, the fair-dealing ; cf. Righteous. I have not found any early instances, and to-day the name is rare.

1764. Married—Adam Just and Margaret Burkit : St. Geo. Han. Sq. i. 134.
London, 1 ; Manchester, 1 ; Grange-over-Sands (N. Lanc.), 2 ; Philadelphia, 1 ; Boston (U.S.), 1.

Justan; v. Justin.

Justice, Justis. — Offic. ' the justice,' a judge. A feminine form occurs twice in the Hundred Rolls.

'Joseph was justice Egipte to loke.'
Piers P. 4825-6.
Eva la Justice, co. Norf., 1273. A.
John le Justice, co. Oxf., ibid.
Henry Justis, co. Bucks, ibid.
Robert le Justise. E.
Johanna Justys, 1379 : P. T. Yorks. p. 60.
Robertus Justys, *wryght*, 1379 : ibid.
Johannes Justys, 1379 : ibid.
1571. John Justice, London : Reg. Univ. Oxf. vol. ii. pt. ii. p. 51.
1636. William Justice and Mary Hooker : Marriage Lic. (London), i. 226.
London, 3, 0 ; MDB. (co. Salop), 4, 0 ; Boston (U.S.), 6, 1.

Justicer.—Offic. 'the justice,' augmented into Justicer.

'Come, sit thou here, most learned justicer': K. Lear, Act iii. sc. vi.
'A perfect patterne of an upright justicer': Holinshed, Hist. of Scotland, p. 63, quoted by Halliwell.
Michael Justicer, C.R., 5 Hen. IV. pt. ii.

Justin, Justyne, Justan, Juston.—Bapt. 'the son of Justin.' In spite of St. Justina and Justin Martyr, Justin was little used in England, but it was popular in Wales. 'Yestin was one of the many old Roman names that lingered on long among the Welsh' (Yonge, i. 398).

Jestyn ap Owen, ap Holl : Visit. Glouc. (Harl. Soc.) p. 113.
Justian Hill : ibid. p. 30.
Jenetta fil. Nevan, ap-Lyon ap-Jestin :' ibid. p. 98.
London, 0, 1, 0, 0; Liverpool, 0, 0, 1, 0; Oxford, 1, 0, 0, 0; Philadelphia, 2, 2, 0, 1.

Jutson, Jutsum.—Bapt. 'the son of Jordan,' from nick. Jud, whence the patronymic Judson, sharpened to Jutson. The change from the final *n* to *m* in Jutsum is not uncommon; cf. Ransom for Ranson, Milsum for Milson, and v. Sanson and Sansom.

1777. Married—Richard Jutson and Eliz. Young : Canterbury Cathedral, p.97.
London, 1, 3.

Juxon, Jugson.—Bapt. 'the son of Jordan,' from nick. Jud. A corruption of Judson; cf. Jutson; also cf. Coxon for Cockson.

1583-4. Thomas Juxon and Eliz. Ireland : Marriage Lic. (London), i. 126.
1614. Buried—A stillborn of Albion Jugsonn : St. Antholin (London), p. 50.

With the above entry, cf. Juggins for Judkins.

1545. John Jugson : Cal. of Wills in Court of Husting (2).
1619. Married—Arthur Juxon and Anne Saunders : St. Thomas the Apostle (London), p. 18.
1665.—William Juxson and Eliz. Tymson : St. Michael, Cornhill, p. 39.

K

Kable.—Bapt. ; v. Cabbell and Kibble.

London, 1 ; Philadelphia, 1.

Kain, Kane, Kayne.—(1) Bapt.; v. Cain. (2) Local, ' of Caen' in Normandy.

Roger de Kana, co. Linc., 1273. A.
John Kane, co. Bedf., ibid.
William de Kan, co. Essex, Hen. III-Edw. I. K.
Lucia Cayne, 1379 : P. T. Yorks. p. 242.
'Nicholas Bever from a gimnasium at Kane in Normandy, sup. for B.D. June 15, 1506': Reg. Univ. Oxf. i. 46.
1618, Bapt. — Benjamin, s. Robert Kaine : St. Michael, Cornhill, p. 213.
1751. Married — Charles Kain and Judith Jones : St. Geo. Chap. Mayfair, p. 195.
1752. — Francis Kane and Ann Wilcocks : ibid. p. 217.
London, 6, 2, 0 ; MDB. (co. Lanc.), 0, 1, 1 ; Philadelphia, 32, 325, 1.

Kaines, Kains.—Local, ' of Kaynes' or 'Keynes.' I cannot identify the place, probably Norman.

Robert de Kaynes, co. Northampton, 1273. A.
Robert de Kaynes, or Keynes, co. Wilts, 20 Edw. I. R.
Hawysia (Avice) de Kaynes, co. Northampton, ibid.
Roger de Kaynes, co. Devon, ibid.
1572. Humphrey Keynes, St. Alban Hall : Reg. Univ. Oxf. vol. ii. pt. ii. p. 40.
— James Keynes, St. Alban Hall : ibid.

1749. Married — John Boaz and Ann Kaines : St. Geo. Chap. Mayfair, p. 132.
1770. — Robert Lamb and Mary Kaines : St. Geo. Han. Sq. i. 200.
Philadelphia, 0, 1.

Kaiser, Kazer, Keyser, Kezar, Kezor, Keyzor.—Nick. 'the emperor'; v. Cayzer and Caesar; cf. Lemprière. Some of the American instances, especially those in New York, are of German extraction, and merely modern importations.

Robert le Keser, co. Kent, Edw. I-Edw. III. R.
Lambert Keser, co. Kent, ibid.
1663. Thomas Keysar and Rachael Ward : Marriage Alleg. (Canterbury), p. 99.
1670. John Keyser and Alice Pike : ibid. p. 40.
1672. George Kezar and Eliz. Oldom : ibid. p. 78.
1739. Married—Adam Keiser and Mary Milborn : St. Geo. Chap. Mayfair, p. 13.
London, 3, 0, 3, 0, 0, 1 ; Boston (U.S.), 5, 1, 7, 4, 3, 0 ; New York (Keyser), 37.

Karl, Karle ; v. Carle.

Karslake, Kearslake, Kerslake.—Local, ' of Karslake.'

1586. John Kerslake, or Kersleck, co. Cornwall : Reg. Univ. Oxf. vol. ii. pt. ii. p. 156.
1677-8. John Kerslake and Mary Larcomb : Marriage Alleg. (Canterbury), p. 213.

London, 5, 0, 6 ; Warwick, 0, 1, 0 ; Philadelphia, 0, 0, 2.

Kay, Kaye.—(1) Local, ' at the quay,' from residence thereby.

'Et de 5s. de firma unius tenementi jacen' in le *Kaysyd* (i.e. Kay-side) in tenura Johannis Blakeston,' 30 Hen. VIII : Brand's Hist. of Newcastle-on-Tyne, i. 408.
John del Kai, sheriff of London, 1201 : WWW. p. 187.
Jordan Kay, 1273. A.
Robertus Cay, 1379 : P. T. Yorks. p. 242.
Alanus Kay, 1379 : ibid. p. 47.
Johanna Caa, 1379 : ibid. p. 119.
Willelmus Ka, 1379 : ibid. p. 118.
Thomas Key, or Cay, master of University College, Oxford, died 1572 : Oxford Hist. Soc. viii. 183.
1557-8. Robert Kaye and Lucy Barbur : Marriage Lic. (London), i. 18.
1674. Bapt.—Mary, d. Arthur Key : Canterbury Cathedral, p. 15.
1700. Married—Thomas Kay and Eliz. Cotton : St. Dionis Backchurch, p. 49.

A clergyman named Kaye once said in my hearing that his surname might be spelt with one, two, three, or four letters, as it pleased the scribe, viz. K, Ka, Kay, Kaye.

London, 26, 5 ; New York, 13, 2.

Kayne.—Bapt.; v. Kain.

Keal, Keel, Keele, Keale.—
Local, ' of Keal.' East and West
Keal are parishes in co. Lincoln.

Robert de Kele, co. Linc., 1273. A.
William de Kele, co. Linc., ibid.
1579. Sebastian Keele, co. Bucks:
Reg. Univ. Oxf. vol. ii. pt. ii. p. 87.
1598. Robert Keale, co. Essex, and
Eliz. Smythe : Marriage Lic. (London),
i. 253.
1602-3. William Austen and Katherine
Keale, *widow* : ibid. i. 274.
1604. Bapt.—Henrie, s. Thomas Keele:
St. Jas. Clerkenwell, i. 45.
1618. — Jeffrey, s. William Keale:
ibid. i. 82.
London, 0, 1, 3, 0 ; MDB. (co. Lincoln),
6, 1, 0, 0 ; New York, 3, 0, 1, 1.

Kean, Keen, Keene, Keane, Kene.—
(1) Nick. ' the keen,' the
sharp, the quick, the eager. (2)
Local, ' of St. Keyne,' a parish in
co. Cornwall, near Liskeard, from
St. Kayne, or Keyne, a saint of
the 5th century. The nick. is
undoubtedly the chief parent; cf.
Quick, Snell, Sharp, &c.

Hugh le Kene, co. Oxf., 1273. A.
Reginald le Kene, co. Bucks, ibid.
William le Kene, co. Bucks, ibid.
Simon de Kyne, co. York, Edw. I-
Edw. III. R.
Thomas Kene, co. Soms., 1 Edw. III:
Kirby's Quest, p. 109.
Gilbertus Kene, 1379 : P. T. Yorks. p. 17.
Willelmus Kene, *wryght*, 1379 : ibid.
p. 19.
Robertus Kene, 1379 : ibid. p. 25.
1587. William Kine, co. Dorset (=
Keyne) : Reg. Univ. Oxf. vol. ii. pt. ii.
p. 159.
1598. Married—Richarde Fludde and
Hester Keane : St. Michael, Cornhill,
p. 16.
1617. — John Keene and Katherine
Andrews : ibid. p. 21.
1681. Buried — Thomas Keyne: ibid.
p. 265.
London, 21, 35, 20, 0, 0 ; New York,
13, 4, 6, 21, 2.

Kearsey.—Local, ' of Kersey,'
q.v. ; cf. Karsley for Kearsley,
Kearshaw for Kershaw.

Richard de Karsy, co. Worc., Hen.
III-Edw. I. K.
London, 3 ; MDB. (co. Wilts), 1.

Kearshaw ; v. Kershaw. A
North-Yorkshire variant.

Middlesborough, 1.

Kearslake ; v. Karslake.

Kearsley, Keasley.—Local,
' of Kearsley,' a township in the
parish of Dean, co. Lanc.

Richard Kersley, of Westhoughton,
1604 : Wills at Chester, i. 114.
Roger Kersley, of Westhoughton, 1620:
ibid.
1610. John Kersly, Glouc. Hall : Reg.
Univ. Oxf. i. 402.
1618-9. John Karsley and Elmina
Barton : Marriage Lic. (London), ii. 70.
1673. Philip Burton and Eliz. Kearsly :
Marriage Alleg. (Westminster), p. 221.
London, 2, 2 ; Manchester, 6, 0.

Kearton.—Local, ' of Kirton,'
a North-Yorkshire variant ; v.
Kirton. In the same district Kearshaw is found for Kershaw.

MDB. (North Rid. Yorks), 5.

Keasbey, Kisbee, Kisby, Kisbey.—
Local, ' of Keisby,' a
hamlet in the parish of Lavington,
co. Linc.

(Dominus) de Kiseby, co. Linc., 1273. A.
1574-5. Robert Kisbie, co. Berks : Reg.
Univ. Oxf. vol. ii. pt. ii. p. 61.
1581. Paul Kysbie, co. Berks: ibid.
p. 111.
MDB. (co. Linc.), Kisby, 1 ; (co. Hunts),
0, 1, 3, 0 ; (co. Lancaster), Kisbey, 2 ;
Philadelphia (Keasby), 3 ; London (Kisbee), 1.

Keast.— ? ——. A Cornish
name.

MDB. (co. Cornwall), 4 ; London, 3.

Keat, Keate, Keates, Keats.
—Bapt. ' the son of Kett,' but
whether Kett represents a nick. of
Catherine, or, like Kit, of Christopher, I cannot say. The forms
are found all over England, confirming a baptismal derivation. The
variants given in the Oxford
Registers are : Keete, Keighte,
Keit, Ket, Keyt, Kight, Kighte,
Kite, Kitte, and Kyte. Several
of these are variants of Kite, q.v.
Keats or Keates is the genitive, as
in Williams, Jones, &c.

William Ket, co. Norf., 1273. A.
1575. Jerome Kighte, co. Oxf. : Reg.
Univ. Oxf. vol. ii. pt. ii. p. 68.
1581. Thomas Keate, or Keighte : ibid.
p. 113.
1589. Edward Keat, co. Berks : ibid.
p. 173.
1789. Married — Jeremiah James and
Ann Keate : St. Geo. Han. Sq. ii. 34.
1791. — James Watts and Hannah
Keates : ibid. p. 53.
1795. — Richard Keats and Mary
Widdison: ibid. p. 125.
1803. Joseph Hyde and Frances Keet :
ibid. p. 293.
London, 2, 1, 7, 3 ; Philadelphia
(Keates), 2.

Keatch, Keech, Keach, Ketch, Keitch, Kedge.—Nick.
' Kedge,' brisk, active. It occurs
as *Kygge* or *Kydge*=jocundus, in
Prompt. Parv. p. 274. Hence we
need not be surprised to find the
home of the surname to be in
co. Norfolk and the neighbouring
shires. ' *Kedge*, brisk, budge, hale,
lively. Suff.': Ray and Moor (v.
Wray's note on Kygge in Prompt.
Parv.).

Peter Kech, co. Norf., 1273. A.
Emma Kech, co. Camb., ibid.
Adam Kyg, co. Bucks, ibid.
John Keche, co. Soms., 1 Edw. III :
Kirby's Quest, p. 100.
1430. John Keche, rector of Erping-
ham, co. Norf. : FF. vi. 411.

On a brass plate in the ancient
church of St. Helen's, Norwich,
could be read :

' Hic jacet corpus Dni. Edmundi
Keche, presbyteri ': FF. iv. 379.
1620. Henry Keitch and Magdalen
Chambers : Marriage Lic. (London),
ii. 95.
1621. Married — Andrew Stucke and
Edey Kege: St. Mary Aldermary, p. 14.
1673. John Keech and Mary Rutland :
Marriage Alleg. (Canterbury), p. 226.
London, 1, 1, 0, 0, 0, 2 ; Crockford
(Keitch), 1 ; Boston (U.S.) (Keach), 7 ;
Philadelphia (Keech), 6.

Keatley.—Local. Either a vari-
ant of Kettley or Keighley, q.v.

1752. Married—William Keetly and
Eliz. Sayers : St. Geo. Chap. Mayfair,
p. 215.
Birmingham, 1 ; New York, 1 ; Boston
(U.S.), 1.

Keable, Kebbel, Keble, &c.
—Bapt. ; v. Kibble.

Keddington.—Local, (1) ' of
Keddington,' a parish in co. Lincoln,
near Louth ; (2) ' of Kedington,'
a parish in co. Suffolk, on the
border of Essex.

John de Kediton, co. Essex, 1273. A.
Godfrey de Kediton, co. Camb., ibid.
1582. Henry Keddington, rector of
Bergh-Apton, co. Norf. : FF. x. 100.
MDB. (co. Suffolk), 2.

Kedge, Keech ; v. Keatch.

Keedwell, Kidwell.— ? Bapt.
' the son of Kedwell ' ; seemingly
a Welsh personal name, possibly
an abbreviation of Cadwallador, or
Cadwallon (v. Yonge, ii. 94). There

is a parish of Kidwelly in the dioc. of St. David's.

1589. Roger Kidwall: St. Mary Aldermary, p. 8.
1598. Bapt.—Kedwallader, son of Kedwell Rogers: ibid. p. 65.
1747. Married—John Saxon and Catherine Kidwell: St. Geo. Han. Sq. i. 30.
London, 1, 1 ; MDB. (co. Glouc.), 4, 0 ; (co. Somerset), 2, 0 ; (co. Monmouth), 1, 1 ; Philadelphia, 0, 2.

Keefe, Keeff, Keeffe.—? Local.

1797. Married — William Hearn and Margaret Keefe: St. Geo. Han. Sq. ll. 175.
1800. — Michael Shine and Margaret Keif: ibid. p. 210.
1806. — John Keeffe and Sarah Shaw: ibid. p. 344.
London, 3, 1, 1 ; Philadelphia, 30, 0, 2.

Keel, Keele ; v. Keal.

Keeler, Keelar.—Occup. 'the keeler,' a bargeman, one who navigated a keel. Brockett has quotations in 1378 and 1440 (p. 244). The surname is found on the East coast, just where one would expect it.

1750. Married — Thomas Keeler and Jane Plaw: St. Geo. Chap. Mayfair, p. 183
1799. — Alexander Keeler and Jean Duncan: St. Geo. Han. Sq. ii. 208.
West Rid. Court Dir., 1, 0 ; Sheffield, 1, 0 ; London, 3, 0 ; MDB. (co. Kent), 6, 1 ; Philadelphia, 26, 0.

Keeley, Kealey, Keely.—Local, 'of Keighley,' q.v. The variants of this name are many. From the epitaphs in the churchyard of Keighley it is clear that the place was often pronounced Keeley in the last century.

1563. Buried—Martha Keely: St. Peter, Cornhill, i. 116.
1689. Bapt. — Anne, d. of William Kealy: St. Jas. Clerkenwell, i. 332.
1747. Married — Thomas Brislet and Ann Keeley: St. Geo. Chap. Mayfair, p. 87.
1793. — Martin Kealey and Hester Curren: St. Geo. Han. Sq. ii. 92.
1794. — Charles Bullock and Ann Keely: ibid. p. 123.
London, 4, 1, 0 ; Philadelphia, 22, 1, 53.

Keeling, Keelinge, Keiling, Keelin.—(1) Nick. 'the keeling,' i.e. a special small cod ; Icel. *keila*, a kind of small cod. On visiting the North-east coast in the summer of 1886, I failed to find the word in use, yet both word and name were there for centuries.

'Item, 189 Kelinges and codlinges,

&c., £16 13s. 7d.' 1350, Account of Holy Island Monastery : QQQ. p. 99.
John Kelynge, master of Greatham Hospital, 1463 : DDD. (Durham), iii. 136.
Henry Keling, rector of Houghton-le-Spring, 1482 : ibid. i. 156.

(2) Local, 'of Keelin.' I suspect the Staffordshire, Cheshire, and Lancashire Keelings are of local origin. But I cannot find the spot. The final *g* is in this case an excrescence, as in Jennings, Hewlings, &c.

' In 56 Hen. III (1272), Henry de Lacy granted for his service all that land which William of Keelin and William his son formerly held, and which reverted to the grantor by the felony of William de Keelin ': Baines' Lanc. (Croston's edit.), ii. 404.
Walter de Kelin, co. Hunts, 1273. A. Osbert Kelyng, co. Hunts, ibid.
1526. William Kelyng and Anne Lacy : Marriage Lic. (London), i. 5.
1582. Daniel Keeling, co. Oxf. : Reg. Univ. Oxf. vol. ii. pt. ii. p. 119.
1645. Nathaniel Waterhouse and Eliz. Kelinge : Marriage Lic. (London), ii. 276.
1661. Edward Keling and Alice Cave : ibid. p. 284.
London, 12, 0, 0, 0 ; MDB. (co. Stafford), 11, 1, 1, 0 ; Philadelphia, 1, 0, 0, 1.

Keen, Keene ; v. Kean.

Keenlyside, Kinleyside.—Local, probably 'of Kinneyside,' a township in the parish of St. Bees, co. Cumberland. A purely North-English surname.
Sunderland, 2, 0 ; MDB. (co. Durham), 1, 1.

Keep.—Local, 'at the keep,' the donjon or stronghold of a castle.
William atte Kep, C. R., 18 Edw. I.
Roger Kep, co. Soms., 1 Edw. III : Kirby's Quest, p. 163.
Richard atte Kippe, co. Soms., 1 Edw. III : ibid. p. 168.
1617. Henry Keepe, co. Berks : Reg. Univ. Oxf. vol. ii. pt. ii. p. 365.
1643. Buried—Mr. Cristever Keape, a stranger : St. Michael, Cornhill.
1661. Bapt. —Peter, s. Peter Keepe : St. Jas. Clerkenwell, p. 210.
1743. Married — Thomas Nelson and Joanna Keep : St. Geo. Han. Sq. i. 30.
London, 8 ; New York, 12.

Keeper.—Offic. 'the keeper,' a woodward, also the keeper of any stronghold ; v. Keep. 'The keeper of the prison' (Acts xvi. 27).
'John Keeper, or Woodward, of Buckholt-wood : Rudde's Gloucestershire, pp. 140-1.

William Kepere, co. Hunts, 1273. A.
John Keeper, temp. Eliz. Z.
1567. John Keper: Reg. Univ. Oxf. ii. 268.
1568. John Keeper, or Keper, or Kepar, Hart Hall : ibid. vol. ii. pt. ii. p. 39.
Johannes Kauper, 1379 : P. T. Yorks. p. 87.

Keetley.—Local. A variant of Kettley or Keighley, q.v.
Birmingham, 1.

Keeton ; v. Ketton.

Keevil.—Local, 'of Keevil,' a parish in co. Wilts, four miles from Trowbridge.
1620. Bapt.—Jaine, d. Henry Kevill : St. Jas. Clerkenwell, i. 87.
London, 2 ; New York, 1.

Keighley, Keeley, Kealey, Keithley, Keightley, Keightly.—Local, 'of Keighley,' a well-known town in the W. Rid. Yorks. Many of these variants are to be seen in the epitaphs of the parish churchyard of Keighley. For other variants, v. Kightley.

Henry Kighele, co. Lanc., Edw. I-Edw. III. R.
Johannes de Kyghelay, 1379 : P. T. Yorks. p. 199.
William de Kigheley, 1397 : Preston Guild Rolls, p. 6.
1576. John Kighlye, co. Linc. : Reg. Univ. Oxf. vol. ii. pt. ii. p. 72.
1583. Philip Kyghley, or Kygleye, co. Worc. : ibid. p. 127.
1612. Robert Keigley, of the Whitelee, in Goosnargh : Wills at Chester, i. 112.
1662. Joseph Dey and Margaret Keighley : Marriage Alleg. (Canterbury), p. 69.
1676. Holmer Lunne and Elizabeth Kightly : ibid. p. 260.
London, 6, 4, 1, 0, 0, 0 ; West Rid. Court Dir., 10, 0, 0, 2, 0, 0 ; Kendal (Keightley), 1.

Keitch ; v. Keatch.

Keith.—Local, 'of Keith,' an estate in the parish of Humble, co. Haddington. Mr. Lower adds that several parishes and places in Scotland bear this name.

1582. Robert Keathe, co. York : Reg. Univ. Oxf. vol. ii. pt. ii. p. 119.
1675. John Keith and Ann Sweeting : Marriage Alleg. (Canterbury), p. 147.
London, 13 ; Philadelphia, 24.

Keithley ; v. Keighley.

Kekewick, Kekewich, Kekwick.—Local, 'of Kekewick,' co. Chester. Spelt Kekewicke and

Kekewike in the Accounts of Norton Abbey (v. Lanc. and Ches. Records, i. 103–4). The name passed into Cornwall several centuries ago.

Peter Kykewhych, 1518: Reg. Univ. Oxf. i. 105.
1574–5. Gregory Keckwiche, co. Cornwall: Reg. Univ. Oxf. vol. ii. pt. ii. p. 81.
John Keakwich, of Aughton, *yeoman*, 1650: Wills at Chester (1621–50), p. 127.
John Keyquick, Liverpool, 1677: ibid. (1660–80), p. 72.
Robert Darwell, of Keckquick, co. Chester, *husbandman*: ibid. (1660–80), p. 159.
1622. Peter Rawson and Ellen Kewquitt: Marriage Lic. (London), ii. 110.
Cumberland Court Dir., o, o, 1; London, o, 1, o; MDB. (co. Cornwall), 1, o, o.

Kelby.—Local; v. Kilbey.

Kelcey.—Local; v. Kelsey.

Keld, Kell.—Local, 'at the keld,' from residence thereby. 'Keld, a well (Craven dialect), smooth reaches of water in a rough stream' (Halliwell). A common term in Yorks, Westm., and Cumb. for a well or spring. Icel. Kelda, *palus* (Brockett). The *d* seems to have been entirely disconnected from the name in Yorkshire.

Willelmus atte Keld, 1379: P. T. Yorks. p. 242.
Johannes atte Keld, 1379: ibid. p. 3.
Dionisius del Kell, 1379: ibid. p. 22.
Rogerus Kell, 1379: ibid. p. 123.
Thomas atte Keld, 1379: ibid. p. 255.
William del Keld, 1396: FFF. p. 566.
Cf. Johannes de Kelfeld (i.e. the wellfield), 1379: P. T. Yorks. p. 16.
1739. Married—Lancelot Kell and Jane Wilsby: St. Dionis Backchurch, p. 67.
London, o, 5; West Rid. Court Dir., o, 5; Philadelphia, o, 2.

Kelham, Kellam.—Local, 'of Kelham,' a parish in co. Notts, two miles from Newark.

Walter de Kelome, co. Notts, 1273. A.
Peter de Kelum, co. Notts, Hen. III-Edw. I. K.
1696. Married — Christopher Kelham and Grace Bennett: St. Michael, Cornhill, p. 48.
1700. — John Kelham and Sarah West: ibid. p. 50.
1763. — Joseph Kelham and Sarah Flower: St. Geo. Han. Sq. i. 125.
London, 1, o; MDB. (co. Northampton), o, 1; (co. Notts), 2, o; New York, o, 2.

Kelk.—Local, 'of Kelke.' 'The estate of Kelke, co. Linc., was owned by a family so designated from it. There are also two townships in Yorkshire called Kelk' (Lower, Patr. Brit. p. 176). Great and Little Kelk, the townships referred to, are about five miles from Great Driffield, E. Rid. Yorks.

Walter Kelke, co. Norf., 1273. A.
1656. Thomas Kelke and Anne Milton (publication): St. Michael, Cornhill, p. 36.
1731. Married—John Kelke and Alice Tompson: St. Geo. Han. Sq. i. 8.
1754. — John Tomlinson and Eliz. Kelk: St. Geo. Chap. Mayfair, p. 268.
London, 3; Crockford, 2; Sheffield, 2; New York, 1.

Kell.—Local; v. Keld.

Kellaway, Kelleway.—Local, 'of Kellaways,' a parish in co. Wilts, near Chippenham. It seems to have been known in earlier times as Kellaway, not Kellaways. With Kelloway, cf. Solloway in the same district.

Elyas de Kaylewey, co. Wilts, Hen. III-Edw. I. K.
1592. Richard Keyllwaye, co. Soms.: Reg. Univ. Oxf. vol. ii. pt. ii. p. 191.
1598. Francis Kellway, co. Devon: ibid. p. 228.
1599. Bapt.—Henrie, s. Henrie Kellway: St. Jas. Clerkenwell, i. 35.
1604. Ralph Kellway, co. Soms.: Reg. Univ. Oxf. vol. ii. pt. ii. p. 274.
1612. Thomas Kelloway, of Bettefield, parish of Hanmer: Wills at Chester (1545–1620), p. 112.
1639. John Starkey and Susan Kellaway: Marriage Lic. (London), ii. 244.
— Thomas Pate and Winifred Kellaway: ibid. p. 246.
1754. Married—William Kelloway and Ann Arnold: Reg. Stourton, Wilts, p. 57.
London, 5, o; MDB. (co. Hants), 1, 5; Sheffield, o, 1; Boston (U.S.), o, 1.

Keller.—(1) Local, 'of Keller.' I cannot find the spot. Perhaps from the Low Countries. (2) Occup. 'the keller,' probably a kilner. 'A furnace or kell': Cleaveland, p. 40. 'A kiln, as lime kell. South' (Halliwell).

Elias de Keller, London, 20 Edw. I. R.
John Keller, 1379: P. T. Yorks. p. 235.
Symon le Keller, de London, 16 Edw. II: Freemen of York, i. 20.
1686. Godfrey Keller and Eliz. Savery: Marriage Alleg. (Canterbury), p. 236.
1716. Married — Richard Keller and Sarah Neal: St. Jas. Clerkenwell, iii. 239.
London, 4; Boston (U.S.), 1.

Kellett, Kellet.—Local, ' of Kellett,' a village near Carnforth. North Lanc. This surname still holds its place in Furness and the district round the village.

Orme de Kellet (de Lonesdale), co. Lanc., 20 Edw. I. R.
Johannes Kelett, 1379: P. T. Yorks. p. 253.
1557. Married — Edward Kellet and Anne Fell: St. Mary, Ulverston, p. 20.
1575. George Turner and Isabel Kellett: Marriage Lic. (London), i. 66.
1562. Ewan Kellett, *mylner*: Preston Guild Rolls, p. 29.
1589. John Kellatt, of Cartmell: Lancashire Wills at Richmond (1457–1680), p. 172.
1604. Hugh Kellett, of the High, Cartmell: ibid.
London, 1, o; Manchester, 6, o; Lanc. Court Dir., 8, 2; Philadelphia, 3, 1.

Kellington.—Local, ' of Kellington,' a parish in W. Rid. Yorks.

1681–2. Job Kellington and Rachael Wyld: Marriage Alleg (Canterbury, p. 87.
1714. Bapt.—Sarah, d. William Kellington: St. Jas. Clerkenwell, ii. 79.
1736. Buried—Joseph Kellington: St. Michael, Cornhill, p. 293.
Hull, 2.

Kellow, Kellough.—Local, ' of Kelloe,' a parish in co. Durham, six miles from Durham.

Patrick de Kellawe, co. York, Edw. I-Edw. III. R.
William de Kellawe, co. Linc., ibid.
1612–3. John Kellowe, *poulter*, and Mary Presson: Marriage Lic. (London), ii. 18.
1616. Bapt.—Susan, d. John Kellowe: St. Jas. Clerkenwell, i. 75.
1640. Samuel Kello and Mary Emelie: Marriage Lic. (London), ii. 254.
1789. Married—Job Dowsing and Jane Kellow: St. Geo. Han. Sq. ii. 17.
London, 3, o; Boston (U.S.), o, 2.

Kelsall, Kelsey, Kilshall, Kilshaw, Kelsell, Kelsow.—Local, ' of Kelsall,' a township in the parish of Tarvin, co. Chester. For a second derivation of Kelsey, v. Kelsey. The Lancashire Kelseys, however, must be referred to Kelsall in Cheshire.

Reginald de Keleshalle, co. Camb., 1273. A.
Roger de Keleshelle, co. Camb., ibid.
Johannes Kelesall, 1379: P. T. Yorks. p. 75.
1561. Buried—John Kelsow (Kelsall): Reg. Prestbury, co. Ches., p. 5.
— Married—James Kelsow and Blaunch Broke: ibid. p. 4.
1570. Bapt.—Elizabeth Kelsall: ibid. p. 30.

The name is also spelt Kilshaw in the same register.

Manchester, 7, 5, 0, 0, 0, 0; Lanc. Court Dir., 10, 2, 1, 1, 0, 0; Philadelphia, 1, 10, 0, 0, 2, 0; New York (Kelsey), 16; (Kelsow), 1.

Kelsey, Kelcey.—Local, 'of Kelsey,' two parishes, North and South Kelsey, in co. Lincoln.

Brice de Keleseye, co. Linc., 1273. A.
Peter de Keleseve, co. Linc., ibid.
1550. Bapt.—Elisabeth Kelsaye: St. Michael, Cornhill, p. 76.
1552. Married—William Keltredge and Agnes Kelsaye: ibid. p. 6.
1574. — William Kelsea and Isabell Imme: St. Dionis Backchurch, p. 7.
1795. — Thomas Kelsey and Maria Thomas: St. Geo. Han. Sq. ii. 123.
MDB. (co. Kent), 7, 6; (co. Lincoln), 32, 0; London, 21, 0; Boston (U.S.), 15, 0.

Kelston, Kelson.—Local, 'of Kelston,' a parish in co. Somerset, four miles from Bath. Many local surnames ending in -ston become -son.

1687-8. John Kelson and Eliz. Clark: Marriage Alleg. (Canterbury), p. 52.
London, 0, 3; MDB. (co. Somerset), 1,3

Kemball, Kemble. — Local, 'of Kemble,' a village and parish near Cirencester, co. Wilts. Not to be confounded with Kimbell, although that must have been occasionally done.

1657. Married—John Kemball and Jane Jones: St. Jas. Clerkenwell, iii. 99.
1680. John Kemball and Grace Grey: Marriage Alleg. (Canterbury), p. 45.
1736. Married—James Kemble and Judith Davies: St. Geo. Han. Sq. i. 18.
1742. — George Kemble and Eliz. Pool: St. Geo. Chap. Mayfair, p. 23.
London, 1, 4; Crockford, 0, 3; MDB. (co. Suffolk), 4, 0; Philadelphia, 0, 32.

Kember, Kimber.—(1)Occup. 'the comber,' a wool-comber; cf. Kembester, now Kempster, a female wool-comber. (2) Local, 'of Kimber.' South Kimber in co. Cornwall. The first is the more probable origin; v. Kemper.

1617. John Neave and Thomasine Kember: Marriage Lic. (London), ii. 56.
1770. Married—Thomas Kimber and Alice Hastings: St. Geo. Han. Sq. ii. 301.
— — George Mansfield and Eliz. Kember: ibid. p. 304.
London, 1, 10; Devon Dir. (Farmers' List), 0, 1; New York, 0, 6.

Kemble.—Local; v. Kemball.

Kemme, Kemm, Kem. — Local, 'at the keme.' 'Kemb,' a stronghold. North England' (Halliwell).

Katherine dil. Keme, co. Suff., 1273. A.
Adam Keme, co. Camb., ibid.
Antec' de Kembe, co. Linc., ibid.
Agnes Kemme,1379: P. T. Yorks. p. 105.
Thomas Keme, 1379: ibid. p. 114.
1602. Married—John Kemme and Sara Potter: St. Dionis Backchurch, p. 14.
1626-7. Edmund Beane and Hannah Keme: Marriage Lic. (London), ii. 184.
London (1887), 2, 0, 0; Crockford, 2, 0, 0; MDB. (co. Wilts), 3, 0, 0; Philadelphia, 0, 1, 1.

Kemmis, Kimmis, Kemish, Kimmish.—Local, 'of Kemeys,' two parishes in co. Monmouth. 'The Baronets, created 1642, extinct 1735, claimed to be of the noble house of Camois. . . . The family were early settlers in Wales, where as lords of Camaes and St. Dogmaels in Pembrokeshire they exercised authority little short of 'regal' (Lower, quoting Burke's Ext. Barts.).

Arthur Kemys (co. Somerset), Queen's Coll., 1586: Reg. Univ. Oxf. vol. ii. pt. ii. p. 151.
William Kemys of the Began: Visit. Glouc., 1623, p. 98.
Jevan ap Moris Kemys: ibid.
1553-4. Christopher Nappe and Eliz. Kemyes: Marriage Lic. (London), i. 14.
1570. Married—Richard Foster and Ellyn Kemyshe: St. Dionis Backchurch, p. 6.
1608. — Henrie Callis and Frannces Kemish: St. Michael, Cornhill, p. 19.
1637. Walter Kemis and Anne Pascall: Marriage Lic. (London), i. 230.
London, 1, 1, 0, 0; Crockford, 0, 1, 0, 0; MDB. (co. Wilts), 0, 0, 1, 0; (co. Hants), 0, 0, 4, 1.

Kemp, Kempe, Kempson.—Offic. or occup. 'the kemp,' a knight, a soldier, a champion.

'Then it is time for mee to speake,
Of Kern Knightes and Kempes greate.'
                        Guy and Colbrand.
' Here is Kempis full Kene to the Kyng for to care ': York Mystery Plays, p. 291, l. 521.
Alan Kempe, co. Suff., 1273. A.
William Kemp, co. Oxf., ibid.
Ricardus Kempe,1379: P.T.Yorks.p. 28.
Johannes Kempe, 1379: ibid. p. 47.
1775. Married—John Dixon and Ann Kempe: St. Geo. Han. Sq. i. 254.
London, 51, 1, 3; Philadelphia, 26, 1, 0.

Kemper.—Occup. 'the kember,' a wool-comber; v. Kempster, with its feminine terminative as in

spinster, ' Brewster, &c. This seems to be an American variant; v. Kember.

Philadelphia, 10.

Kemplay.—Local, 'of Kempley,' a parish in co. Gloucester.

1800. Married—Robert Carlisle and Ursula Kempley: St. Geo. Han. Sq. ii. 224.
Beverley (E. R. Yorks), 2; London, 1.

Kempson, Kempston. — (1) Nick. 'the kemp's son'; v. Kemp; cf. Wrightson, Smithson, Hindson, &c. (2) Local, 'of Kempston,' parishes in cos. Bedford and Norfolk. The suffix -ston frequently became son; cf. Kelson for Kelston.

Richard Kemson, 1379: P. T. Yorks. p. 291.
1661-2. Nicholas Kempsone and Hester Busby: Marriage Alleg. (Canterbury), i. 21.
1683-4. Nicholas Kempson and Eliz. Best: ibid. ii. 156.
1729. Married—William Lyley and Mary Kempson: St. Geo. Chap. Mayfair, p. 308.
London, 3, 0; Birmingham, 3, 0; Boston (U.S.), 0, 1.

Kempster, Kemster.—Occup. ' the kembster,' a wool-comber. 'Kempstare, pectrix': Prompt. Parv. Originally a feminine occupation; cf. spinster. Johanna la Kempster (X). Margery la Kembestere (Close Roll, 18 Edw. I). A prayer to the Commons in 1464, respecting the importations of foreign goods, mentions ' the makers of wollen cloth within this Reame (Realm) as Wevers, Fullers, Dyers, Kempsters, Carders, and Spinners' (Rot. Parl. Edw. IV). Cf. 'unkempt locks.'

'Hir brighte heer was kempt, untressed all.' Chaucer, C. T. 2289 (Skeat's ed.).
Peter Cambestre, co. Camb., 1273. A.
Agnes Kembester, 1379: P.T. Yorks. p. 219.
Johanna Saper, kemster, 1379: P. T. Howdenshire, p. 12.
Robertus Kembster, 1379: ibid. p. 8.
1684. William Watts and Eliz. Kempster : Marriage Alleg. (Canterbury), p. 165.
1747. Married—Richard Kempstar and Susanna Chips: St. Geo. Chap. Mayfair, p. 99.
1791. — Joseph Wright and Eliz. Kempster: St. Geo. Han. Sq. ii. 68.

1806. Married—Isaac Olive and Mary Kempester : St. Geo. Han. Sq. ii. 355.
London, 5, 0 ; MDB. (co. Salop), 6, 0 ; Birmingham, 2, 0 ; New York, 1, 0 ; Boston (U.S.), 1, 0.

Kempthorne, Kimpthorne. —Local, 'of Kempthorne.' This family name was derived from Kempthorne, an estate in the parish of Beer-Ferris, co. Devon ; v. C. S. Gilbert's Cornwall (quoted by Lower).

1585. Bapt.—John, s. George Kempthorne : St. Jas. Clerkenwell, i. 17.
1602-3. Richard Kempthorne, co. Cornw. : Reg. Univ. Oxf. vol. ii. pt. ii. p. 263.
Crockford, 4, 0 ; MDB. (co. Cornwall), 1, 1.

Kempton.—Local, 'of Kimpton' (q.v.), probably a variant.

1599. Bapt. — Robarte, s. William Kempton : St. Antholin (London), p. 39.
1707. Married — James Calcott and Mary Kempton : St. Peter, Cornhill, ii. 67.
1720. Bapt.—Eliz., d : William Kempton : St. Dionis Backchurch, p. 290.
1749. Married—John Kempton and Mary Turner : St. Geo. Chap. Mayfair, p. 149.
London, 9 : Philadelphia, 10.

Kench ; v. Kinch.

Kendal, Kendall, Kendell, Kendle, Kendel. — Local, 'of Kendal,' co. Westm. The manufacture of 'Kendal green' made this town early famous, and of necessity caused the surname to be common. The result is that it is familiar to every directory in the English-speaking world. The river *Kent*, I need not say, still flows through the *dale*. The surname is frequently met with in all the adjacent villages and towns of the Furness district of North Lancashire.

Johannes de Kendall, 1379 : P. T. Yorks. p. 268.
Thomas de Kendale, 1379 : ibid. p. 99.
Edmundus de Kendall, 1379 : ibid. p. 200.
Johannes de Kendall, *webster*, 1379 : ibid. p. 206.
John Kendall, of Aldyngham, 1571 : Lancashire Wills at Richmond (1457-1680), p. 173.
Roger Kendoll, of Ulverston, 1582 : ibid.
Elizabeth Kendall, of Clitheroe, *widow*, 1593 : Wills at Chester (1545-1620), p. 113.
London, 0, 32, 1, 1, 0 ; Manchester, 6, 4, 0, 0, 0 ; New York, 0, 31, 0, 0, 1.

Kenderdine.—(?)
MDB. (co. Stafford), 4 ; New York, 13.

Kendrew.— ? Bapt. A corruption of Kendrick, q.v.
1744. Married—Samuel Barratt and Susanna Kendra : St. Geo. Chap. Mayfair, p. 41.
1747. — Thomas Evans and Mary Kendrey : ibid. p. 86.
1785. — Robert Kendrew and Harriot Garbutt : St. Geo. Han. Sq. i. 369.
London, 1 ; Liverpool, 1.

Kendrick, Kenrick, Kenrack, Kenwright, Kenwrick. —Bapt. 'the son of Kenwrec.' Domesday Kenricus and Kenric. It is the still earlier Cynric, one of which name defeated the Welsh at Salisbury (Freeman, N.C. i. 319). With Kenwright (which seems to imply an occupation ; cf. Cartwright, Arkwright), cf. Allwright for Aldrich.

Nicolas Kenewrek, co. Soms., 1 Edw. III : Kirby's Quest, p. 90.
Kenwrec fil. Maddoc, 7 Hen. II : Pipe Roll, iv. 39.
Ennian fil. Kenewrec, 7 Hen. II : ibid.
Hugo fil. Kenewrec, 7 Hen. II : ibid.
David ab-Kenewrek, Wardrobe Roll, 14-15 Edw. I–III. 3/23.
Davyd Kenrycke, 1565 : Reg. St. Dionis Backchurch (London), p. 79.
Richard Kendrick, of Rape, 1593 : Wills at Chester (1545-1620), p. 113.
Kendrick Eyton, of Eyton, 1602 : ibid. p. 61.
Kenrick Evans, of Chester, alderman, 1613 : ibid. p. 62.
1601. David Kendrighe and Eliz. Overton : Marriage Lic. (London), i. 264.
1666. Bapt.—John, son of Rise Kendricke : St. Jas. Clerkenwell, i. 229.
Lanc. Court Dir., 3, 3, 1, 2, 0 ; Liverpool, 4, 3, 0, 0, 0 ; London, 12, 2, 0, 0, 0 ; MDB. (co. Worcester), 9, 0, 0, 0, 1 ; Philadelphia (Kendrick), 27.

Keningale.—Local, 'of Kenninghall,' a parish in co. Norfolk, three miles from East Harling.
1451. John de Kenninghale, Norwich : FF. iv. 420.
Dr. John Kenninghall, Norwich, temp. Hen. V : ibid. p. 349.
London, 2.

Keniston, Kenniston, Kennison, Kennerson.—Variants of Kynaston, q.v. The American forms of Kennison and Kennerson seem to suggest a baptismal derivation. But such is not the case. There are dozens of parallel instances in this dictionary. The

suffix *-ston* or *-stone* is frequently corrupted to *-son*. The instances below show how the ball of corruption was set rolling ; cf. Kelson for Kelston.

1592. Buried — Francis Kennystone : St. Michael, Cornhill, p. 203.
1598. — William Kennyston, *upholder*, ibid. p. 209.
1641. Marmaduke Dollman and Margaret Kennaston : Marriage Lic. (London), ii. 258.
London, 2, 0, 0, 0 ; Boston (U.S.), 3, 8, 7, 1.

Kenn. — (1) Nick. 'le ken,' from N.F. *ken* ; O.F. *chien*, a dog, whence *kennel*, a place for dogs ; v. Kennet. Both (1) and (2) represent another instance of a name that seems to be nearly defunct.

Walter le Ken, co. Oxf., 1273. A.
Eborard le Ken, co. Camb., ibid.
Thomas le Chene, co. Norf., ibid.
Geoffrey le Ken. B.
Reginald le Chien, C. R., 24 Edw. I.

(2) Local, 'of Kenn,' a parish in co. Somerset, ten miles from Axbridge.

John de Ken, co. Soms., 1 Edw. III : Kirby's Quest, p. 113.
Walter de Ken, co. Soms., 1 Edw. III : ibid.
1670-1. John Kenn and Mary Bland : Marriage Alleg. (Canterbury), p. 50.
1753. Married — Richard Kenn+ and Rachael Jackson : St. Geo. Chap. Mayfair, p. 266.
New York, 1.

Kennard ; v. Kenward.

Kennell, Kennel.—Local, 'of Kenell.' I cannot find the spot, but evidently it is in the West country.

John de Kenell, co. Hereford, Hen. III–Edw. I.
1601. Richard Keynell, co. Dorset : Reg. Univ. Oxf. vol. ii. pt. ii. p. 247.
1607. Buried—Eliz., d. Thomas Kennell : St. Jas. Clerkenwell, iv. 98.
1774. Married — John Kennell and Martha Church : St. Geo. Han. Sq. i. 240.
London, 2, 0 ; Philadelphia, 0, 2 ; New York, 4, 7.

Kennerley.—Local, 'of Kennerleigh,' a parish in co. Devon, five miles from Crediton.

1661. Married—John Kennaley and Margaret Hill : St. Jas. Clerkenwell, iii. 106.
1746. — Henvill Anderson and Ann Kennerly : St. Geo. Chap. Mayfair, p. 65.
1798. — John Stevenson and Mary Kennerley : St. Geo. Han. Sq. ii. 189.
Birmingham, 2.

Kennet, Kennett.—(1) Nick. 'le kenet.' N.F. *kenet*; M.E. *kenet*, a little dog, a dim. of *ken* (v. Kenn). 'Kenet, hownde, *caniculus*': Prompt. Parv. 'Kenettys, teroures, butchers houndes, dunghyll dogges': Dame Julyan Berner's Doctryne, quoted by Way. 'A kenit; *caniculus*': Cath. Ang. (2) Local, 'of Kennett,' a parish in co. Camb., five miles from Newmarket. Also East and West Kennett, parishes in co. Wilts.

Peter de Kenet, co. Norf., 1237: FF. i. 349.
Nicholas de Kenet, co. Kent, Hen. III-Edw. I. K.
Thomas de Kenete, co. Berks, ibid.
Peter de Kenet, co. Wilts, 1273. A.
William de Kenet, co. Camb., ibid.
1586. William Kennett and Barbara Eglesfield: Marriage Lic. (London), i. 152.
1596. Richard Clark and Susan Kennett (co. Essex): ibid. p. 229.
1789. Married—Peircy Kennett and Catherine Carty: St. Geo. Han. Sq. ii. 29.

It is manifest that (2) is the chief parent.

London, 3, 16; Philadelphia, 0, 4.

Kennicott.—Local, 'of Kencott,' a parish in co. Oxford, five miles from Burford. With the intrusive *i* in Kennicott, cf. the *a* in Ottaway, Greenaway, and Hathaway.

MDB. (co. Durham), 2.

Kenninton, Kennington.— Local, 'of Kennington,' (1) a parish in co. Kent, two miles from Ashford; (2) a district in the parish of Lambeth, London; (3) a parish in co. Berks, two miles from Oxford.

Ivo de Kenington, co. Suff., 1273. A.
Thomas de Kenington, co. Suff., ibid.
Walter de Keninton, co. Oxf., ibid.
1795. Married—Richard Woodington and Ann Kenington: St. Geo. Han. Sq. ii. 127.
· 1802. — John Kenington and Frances Jenkins: ibid. p. 257.
London, 1, 0; MDB. (co. Lincoln), 0, 6; New York, 0, 1; Boston (U.S.), 0 3.

Kennison, Kenniston, &c.; v. Keniston.

Kenrack, -rick; v. Kendrick.

Kensall, Kensal, Kensel, Kensil, Kensill. — Local, 'of Kensal,' now familiarly known as Kensal Green, co. Middlesex.

John de Keneshal, or Keneshale, co. Norf., 1273. A.
1591. William Kensall: Reg. Univ. Oxf. i. 338.
1624. John Kensall: ibid. p. 339.
London (Kensall), 1; Philadelphia, 0, 1, 4, 21, 5.

Kensington.—Local, 'of Kensington,' a parish in co. Middlesex. This surname seems to have crossed the Atlantic and made its home there.

Reginald de Kensington, co. Norf., 1273. A.
(Persona) de Kensinton, co. Middlesex, 20 Edw. I. R.
1791. Married—James Kensington and Hannah Bues: St. Geo. Han. Sq. ii. 66.
Philadelphia, 9.

Kent.—Local, 'of Kent'; cf. Derbyshire, Cornish, Cheshire, &c., and v. Kentish. The Kentish people seem to have possessed strong migratory tendencies, de Kent being a common entry in early registers. Hence the numbers in modern directories.

Robert de Kent, co. Norf., 1273. A.
Gilbert de Kent, co. Linc., ibid.
Richard de Kent, co. Hereford, Hen. III-Edw. I. K.
Benedict de Kent, co. Bedf., 20 Edw. I. R.
Johannes de Kent, *smyth*, 1379: P. T. Yorks. p. 17.
Johannes Kent et Ibbota uxor ejus, 1379: ibid. p. 44.
Thomas de Kent, 1379: ibid. p. 160.
1607. John Kent, co. Wilts: Reg. Univ. Oxf. vol. ii. pt. ii. p. 295.
1623. Richard Kent and Awdrie Twyneowe: Marriage Lic. (London), ii. 121.
London, 64; West Rid. Court Dir., 5; Boston (U.S.), 56.

Kentish.—Local, 'the Kentish,' a man of Kent; cf. Devonish, Cornish, or Cornwallis.

Ricardus Kenteys (co. Kent), Hen. III-Edw. I. K.
William de (le?) Kenteys, ibid.
Richard le Kenteys, co. Hants, 1273. A.
Robert le Kenteys, co. Camb., ibid.
William le Kenteys. E.
1582. Thomas Fuller and Alice Kentishe (of St. Albans, Herts): Marriage Lic. (London), i. 108.
1777. Married — Ross Kentish and Maria Read: St. Geo. Han. Sq. i. 277.
London, 6; New York, 1.

Kenward, Kennard.—Bapt. 'the son of Kenward,' a Domesday personal name.

'Keneward, a freeman of King Edward, held Duntesborne,' Domesday: v. Atkyns' Hist. Glouc. p. 213.

Ralph Keneward, co. Kent, 1273. A.
Ricardus filius Kenardi, Fines Roll, 10 Edw. I.
1751. Married—David Kennard and Jesse Cummins: St. Geo. Chap. Mayfair, p. 192.
1809. — Richard Kennard and Frances Hamlin: St. Geo. Han. Sq. ii. 408.
1858. Bapt.—Mary Jane, d. Geo. Kenward: Canterbury Cath. p. 50.
London, 2, 15; Philadelphia, 0, 21; Boston (U.S.), 1, 19.

Kenworthy.—Local, 'of Kenworthy,' a manor in East Cheshire; cf. Langworthy for Langworth or Longworth; v. Worth.

Roger de Kenworthey, co. Ches., 1276: East Ches. p. 22.
William de Kenworthey, co. Ches., 1389: ibid. p. 196.
Robert de Tatton, of Kenworthey, 1370: ibid. i. 307.
James Kenworthy, of Saddleworth, 1588: Wills at Chester (1545-1620), p. 113.
Richard Kenworthy, of Saddleworth, 1616: ibid.
Manchester, 7; West Rid. Court Dir., 8; Philadelphia, 8.

Kenwrick; v. Kendrick.

Kenwright.—Bapt. 'the son of Kenwrec'; v. Kendrick. Woolright and Allwright are similarly corrupted from Woolrich and Aldrich.

Manchester, 1; Liverpool, 1; MDB. (co. Lanc.), 1.

Kenyon, Kenion, Kennion. —Local, 'of Kenyon,' a township in the parish of Winwick, co. Lanc.

Jordan de Kenyon, 25 Edw. I: Baines' Lanc. ii. 211.
Adam Kenyon, de Kenyon, 1358: ibid.
1562. Jacobus Kenyon, *shoemaker*: Preston Guild Rolls, p. 30.
Katherine Kenion, of Altham, *widow*, 1594: Wills at Chester (1545-1620), p. 113.
Elizabeth Kenyon, of Warrington, 1596: ibid.
William Kenion, of Manchester, 1608: Lancashire Inquisitions, p. 115.
Manchester, 25, 0, 0; London, 6, 0, 0; New York, 7, 0, 0; West Rid. (Yorks) Court Dir., 7, 2, 1.

Kerbey, Kerby; v. Kirkby.

Kerchiefwasher. — Occup. 'a washer of kerchiefs'; M.E. *covenchef*, a cloth used for a head covering. As a favourite decoration of the ladies of the period it would require a special 'stiffener.' Although it could not live it is a surname of some antiquarian interest as descriptive of the times.

Isabella Kierchiefwassher, 1379 : P. T. Yorks. p. 237.

Kerford, Kerfoot, Kerfut.—Local, ' of Kerford.' I cannot identify the spot, and have only one early instance. Kerfoot is, of course, a corruption. Lancashire and Yorkshire are manifestly the district within which the place must be found.

Ricardus de Kerfforth, 1379 : P. T. Yorks. p. 79.
1572. Buried—Margarette Kyrfote, of Bollington : Reg. Prestbury, co. Ches., p. 39.
1583. John Kirfoote, or Kyerfoote, co. Ches.: Reg. Univ. Oxf. vol. ii. pt. ii. p. 131.
John Kerford, 1661, Wrexham : Exchequer Depositions (co. Lanc.), p. 35.
Thomas Kirfoote, 1664, Lancaster: ibid. p. 41.
1688. Nathan Kerfoot and Bridgett Gaton : Marriage Alleg. (Canterbury), p. 88.
1741. Married—Samuel Kerfoot and Eliz. Jones: St. Geo. Chap. Mayfair, p. 15. Manchester, 1, 2, 0 ; Boston (U.S.), 0, 0, 1.

Kernel, Kernell.—Local, ' at the kernel,' i.e. battlement. One more instance of a surname, seeming to have died out in England, being found only on American soil.

' The maydene, whitt as lely-floure,
Laye in a kirnelle of a towre.'
MS. Lincoln A. i. 17, f. 107 (Halliwell).
Robert del Kerneyle, co. Hunts, 1273. A.
Robert de la Kirnele, co. Hunts, 20 Edw. I. R.
New York, 0, 1 ; Philadelphia, 0, 2.

Kerr, Ker.—Local, ' at the kerr,' a low-lying meadow, from residence thereby ; v. Carr.

John del Ker, co. Notts, Edw. I–Edw. III. R.
John del Kar, co. Lanc., ibid.
Henricus del Kerre, *webester*, 1379 : P. T. Yorks. p. 26.
Johannes del Kerre, 1379 : ibid. p. 9.
Roger del Kerre, 1379 : ibid. p. 35.
Petrus in the Kare, 1379 : ibid. p. 42.
Willelmus atte Karr, 1379 : ibid. p. 44.
Johannes del Karr, 1379 : ibid. p. 67.
John in the Kerr, C. R., 21 Ric. II. pt. i. London, 27, 1 ; Philadelphia, 55, 3.

Kerrey, Kerry, Kery.—Local, ' of Kerrey,' a parish in co. Montgomery.

1616. Richard Kerie, co. Salop : Reg. Univ. Oxf. vol. ii. pt. ii. p. 254.
1620-1. William Kery, or Kerry, co. Salop: ibid. p. 385.

1590. Buried—Fayth Kerye : Kensington Parish Ch. p. 93.
1594. Ould father Kerrey buryed his daughter, Eliz. Kerry : ibid. p. 94.
— Ould father Kerye buryed an other of his daughters : ibid.
1599. Married—Henry Egleton and Agnes Kerry : ibid. p. 64.
London, 1, 0, 0 ; Oxford, 0, 3, 0 ; Boston (U.S.), 0, 1, 1.

Kerridge, Kerrich. — Local, ' of Kerridge,' an elevated locality in the parish of Prestbury, co. Cheshire. Alfred Gatley, the sculptor, was born at Kerridge in 1816. Lower, under Courage, has ' Currage, a manor in the parish of Cheveley, co. Bucks.' The latter place seems to be the chief parent of the name.

Thomas Kerridge, London, 1631 : FF. i. 166.
Mary Carreige, 1631 : Reg. St. Dionis Backchurch (London), p. 102.
Susanna Carriage, d. of Thomas Kerridge, 1632 : ibid. p. 103.
Hester Kerridge, 1633 : ibid.
John Kerrich, rector of Banham, co. Norf., 1735 : ibid. i. 353.
Samuel Kerrish, vicar of Dersingham, co. Norf., 1761 : ibid. viii. 400.
1753. Married—Daniel Kerridge and Rebecca Brightman : St. Geo. Chap. Mayfair, p. 252.
London, 6, 0 ; MDB. (Norfolk), 4, 2 ; (Suffolk), 5, 1 ; Manchester, 2, 0.

Kerrison.—Local, ' of Kerdeston,' a parish in co. Norfolk, near Reepham. There is no escape, so far as I can see, from this conclusion. Otherwise, one of the earliest and commonest of Norfolk names has left no descendant. On the other hand, where else has the great Norfolk name of Kerrison sprung ? It is not a baptismal surname. Finally, Kerdeston would readily become Keriston, and then Kerrison. Personally I have not a doubt about this derivation ; cf. Kelson for Kelston.

Roger de Kerdeston, co. Norf., 1273. A.
William de Kerdeston, co. Norf., 20 Hen. III : FF. x. 112.
Leonard Kerdeston, co. Norf., 9 Ric. II: ibid. p. 114.
Thomas Kerdeston, co. Norf., 1446: ibid.

The histories of Norfolk teem with these entries. If the reader will repeat Kerdeston six times over to himself he will see how easily the corruption would arise.

Robert Karrison, of Milton Green, co. Chester, 1620 : Wills at Chester, i. 212.
Hugh Kerrison, of Dodleston, 1640 : ibid. ii. 129.
1802. Married—James Kerrison and Eliz. Pearce : St. Geo. Han. Sq. ii. 272.
London, 3 ; MDB. (co. Norfolk), 11 ; Boston (U.S.), 1 ; New York, 1.

Kerry ; v. Kerrey.

Kersey.—Local, ' of Kersey,' a parish in co. Suffolk, near Hadleigh.

Selvestre de Kereseye, co. Suff.,1273. A.
Robert de Kersy, co. Soms., 1 Edw. III : Kirby's Quest, p. 185.
1715. Married — John Kersey and Rebecca Taylor : St. Jas. Clerkenwell, iii. 239.
1745. Buried — Juliana Kersey, Mr. Hare's mother : St. Michael, Cornhill, p. 297.
1786. Married—Thomas Kersey and Nancy Larkin : St. Geo. Han. Sq. i. 393.
MDB. (co. Suffolk), 11 ; London, 6 ; Philadelphia, 2.

Kershaw, Kershow.—Local, ' of Kirkshaw,' in the parish of Rochdale, co. Lanc. For the loss of *k*, cf. Kirby for Kirkby. ' Lands in Kirkshaw, Little Wardle . . . and Spotland' (Lanc. and Cheshire Records, pt. ii. p. 330). The surname that has sprung therefrom has ramified in an extraordinary manner, and is known in all English-speaking countries.

Matthew de Kyrkshagh, co. Lanc., 1281 : Baines' Hist. Lancashire (Croston's edit.), pt. xxxi. p. 69.
Geoffrey del Kyrkeshagh, of Rochdale 1390 : ibid.
John de Kyrkshagh, or Kershaw, of Townhouses, in Rochdale, 1424 : ibid.
Edward Kershaw, of Upper Townhouse, 1572 : Wills at Chester (1545-1620), p. 114.
Edward Kershaw, of Townhouse, 1617 : ibid.

From this period the surname is invariably found as Kershaw. The meaning, of course, is the shaw or wood by the church. I find two instances of the earlier form in the first two following entries :

Agnes Kirkeschagh, 1379 : P. T. Yorks. p. 189.
1630. Bapt.—Thomas Kirkshawe : Reg. Prestbury, co. Ches., p. 273.
1752. Married—Charles Kershaw and Eliz. Sooby : St. Geo. Chap. Mayfair, p. 228.
Rochdale, 27, 0 ; Manchester, 40, 0 ; West Rid. Court Dir., 32, 0 ; London, 14, 0 ; Philadelphia, 51, 5.

Kerslake ; v. Karslake.

Kerswell, Kerswill.—Local, 'of Kerswell.' There are two parishes of this name, both in co. Devon, viz. Abbots Kerswell and Kings Kerswell; v. Carswell.

William de Kareswalle, co. Salop, 1273. A.
1598. William Kerswell and Joane Warde : Marriage Lic. (London), i. 252.
1621. John Kerswell : Reg Univ. Oxf. vol. ii. pt. ii. p. 401.
1681 9. Thomas Stone and Sarah Karswell : Marriage Alleg. (Canterbury), p. 120.
London, 1, 2 ; New York, 1, 1.

Kerton ; v. Kirton.

Kerwin.—Local ; v. Curwen. Originally Culwen, a lordship in Galloway, Scotland.

1571. Married — Androe Kerwyn and Margaret Swarhande : St. Michael, Cornhill, p. 10.
1621-2.—Richard Dowdswell and Barbara Keruin : St. Dionis Backchurch, p. 20.
1679. — Henry Kerwin and Ann Barlow : St. Mary Aldermary, p 32.
London, 1 ; Philadelphia, 6.

Kestell, Kestle, Kessell, Kessel.—Local, 'of Kestell,' in the parish of Egloshayle, co. Cornwall. A family of this name was settled there from the time of King John till about the year 1737 (C. S. Gilbert's Cornwall).

1602-3. Walter Kestell, co. Cornwall : Reg. Univ. Oxf. vol. ii. pt. ii. p. 263.
1619. John Kestell, or Kestle, co. Cornwall : ibid. p. 376.
1700. Married — James Kessall and Hannah Maud : St. Dionis Backchurch, p. 49.
Devon Court Dir., 1, 0, 0, 0 ; London, 0, 0, 0, 1 ; MDB. (co. Cornwall), 0, 4, 2, 0 ; Cornwall Dir. (Farmers' List), 0, 2, 1, 1 ; New York (Kessel), 3 ; Boston (U.S.), 0, 1, 0, 1.

Kesterton.—Local, ' of Kesterton.' I have not found the spot.

Birmingham, 5 ; London, 1.

Kesteven.—Local, ' of Kesteven.' Lower says, ' A division of co. Lincoln.' I doubt not this is true, as nearly all the early local references belong to that county.

(Coronator) de Kestevene, co. Linc, 1273. A.
(Coronator) de Ketstevene, co. Linc , ibid.

Alexander de Kestevene, co. Northumb., 1273. A.
Johannes de Kesteven, 1379 : P. T. Yorks. p. 63.
Hugo Kesteven, 1379 : ibid. p. 91.
Adam de Ketsteven, 6 Edw. III : Freemen of York, i. 26.
London, 2 ; West Rid. Court Dir., 1 ; MDB. (co. Notts), 1.

Keswick, Kissick.—Local, 'of Keswick,' the town so called at the head of Derwentwater ; also a parish in co. Norfolk, and a township in W. Rid. Yorks. With Kissick, cf. Physick for Fishwick.

Ralf Kesewic, co. Nort., 1378 : FF. iv. 180.
Johannes de Kesswyk, 1379 : P. T. Yorks. p. 100.
Johannes de Keswyk, 1379 : ibid. p. 208.
Philadelphia, 0, 9.

Ketch ; v. Keatch.

Ketelbern.—Bapt. 'the son of Ketelbern'; cf. Osborn, and v. Kettle. Alongside the first of my instances we find Ketelbert de Kelesholt ; probably a relative. As usual, these names of Norse derivation are found on the East coast.

Ketelbron de Keles, co. Linc., Hen. III–Edw. I. K.
Roger Ketilbern, co. Suff., 1273. A.
1641. Buried — Marye Ketilbourne : St. Jas. Clerkenwell, iv. 247.

Kettering, Ketring.—Local, ' of Kettering,' a market-town and parish in co. Northampton.

Robert de Keteringe, co. Camb., 1273. A.
Richard Ketering, co. Northampt., 20 Edw. I. R.
1382. Roger Ketering, rector of Burnham Ulp, co. Norf. : FF. vii. 32.

It is interesting to notice how frequently a surname that seems to have died out in England is found across the Atlantic.

Philadelphia, 3, 1.

Keteringham, Kitteringham.—Local, ' of Keteringham,' a parish in co. Norfolk.

Agnes de Keteringham, co. Norf., 1273. A.
Thomas de Keteringham, co. Norf., 1342 : FF. v. 97.
William de Keteringham, co. Norf., 40 Edw. III : ibid. vi. 40.
Birmingham, 1, 0 ; MDB. (co. Norfolk), 6, 2.

Kettle, Kettell, Kettelle.—Bapt. 'the son of Kettle.' Ketel, Ketil, Cytel, or Chetel, the sacrificial cauldron of northern mytho-

logy. A large number of surnames are founded on Kettle and its compounds ; v. Chettle, Oskettle, Arkettle, Grimkettle, Steinkettle, Wulfkettle ; also their abbreviations, such as Kell and Chell, Oskell, Arkell, Thurkle, &c.

Ketil, son of Tostig : Freeman, Norm. Conq. iii. 375.
The father of William of Lancaster, baron of Kendel, was Gilbert, the son of Ketel, the son of Eldred, the son of Ivo de Taillebois (of Domesday): West's Ant. of Furness, p. 28.
' Alan, son of Ketell, gave one-half of Kinemund.' Revenues of the Priory of Conishead : ibid. p. 193.
Emma fil. Ketel, co. Camb., 1273. A.
Kettle le Mercer, co. Camb., ibid.
Revner Ketel, co. Norf., ibid.
Robert fil. Ketell. J.
Willelmus Ketyll, 1379 : P. T. Yorks. p. 128.
Thomas Ketill, 1379 : ibid. p. 153.
1582-3. Edmund Kettle, or Kettell, co. Worc., Reg. Univ. Oxf. vol. ii. pt. ii. p. 125.
1583. Christopher Kettell, co. Hertf.: ibid. p. 131.
1612. Robert Vincent and Alice Kettle : Marriage Lic. (London), ii. 12.
1700. Bapt. — Deborah, d. Henry Kettle : St. Jas. Clerkenwell, i. 387.

For variants, v. Chettle.

London, 13, 0, 0 ; Boston (U.S.), 2, 6, 5.

Kettleborrow, Kettleborough.—Local, ' of Kettleburgh,' a parish in co. Suffolk, near Framlingham. For derivation, v. Kettle and Burrough.

William de Ketelbergh', co. York, 1273. A.
John de Ketelbergh', co. Norf, ibid.
1317. Steven de Kettleburgh, rector of Fincham, co. Norf.: FF. vii. 361.
1347. John de Kettlebury, rector of West Walton, co. Norf.: ibid. ix. 141.
1630. Married — Daniel Callis and Hellin Kettleboorow : St. Antholin (London), p. 64.
1682-3. Joseph Tullie and Ann Kettleborough : Marriage Alleg. (Canterbury), p. 124.
MDB. (co. Leicester), 1, 0 ; (co. Lincoln), 0, 2.

Kettleby.—Local, 'of Kettleby,' a hamlet in the parish of Wrawby, co. Lincoln ; the by or dwelling of Kettle, the first settler.

1589. John Kettlebie, co. Worc.: Reg. Univ. Oxf. vol. ii. pt. ii. p. 169.
1604. Thomas Ketilby, co. Worc.: ibid. p. 271.
1652. George Kettleby and Eliz. Kinaston : St. Antholin (London), p. 81.

1688. Arthur Lowe and Susanna Kettleby : Marriage Alleg. (Canterbury), p. 90.
1693. Ralph Ketelbey and Mary Freeman : ibid. p. 266.
1704. Harrington Kettilby and Margaret Beverly : Marriage Lic. (London), ii. 332.

Kettlewell.—Local, 'of Kettlewell' (i.e. the well of Kettle (q.v.), the first settler), a market-town and parish in W. Rid. Yorks, fifteen miles from Skipton.

Stephen de Ketelwelle, co. York : Edw. I-Edw. III. R.
John Ketelwel, 1379 : P. T. Yorks p. 238.
Alessander Katelwell, co. York. W. 11.
1583. Richard Kettlewell and Fortune Rydall : Marriage Lic. (London), i. 125.
1676. William Beresford and Ann Kettlewell : Marriage Lic. (Westminster), p. 259.
London, 4 ; West Rid. Court Dir., 11 ; Boston (U.S.), 1 ; New York, 1.

Kettlewood.—Local, 'of Kettlewood' (i.e. the wood of Kettle (q.v.), the original proprietor), some small spot in E. Rid. Yorks. One member of the family of Kettlewood seems to have reached London more than three centuries ago.

1551-2. Married — Thomas Francke and Elyn Ketellwoode : St. Dionis Backchurch, p. 3.
1586. John Kettlewood, of London, grocer, and Eliz. Penny : Marriage Lic. (London), i. 156.
MDB. (East Rid. Yorks), 3.

Kettley, Kitley.—Local, 'of Ketley,' a chapelry in the parish of Wellington, co. Salop.

1561. Married—Richard Wilch'm and Eliz. Kitly : St. Thomas the Apostle (London), p. 3.
1573. Henry Roe and Susanna Keteley : Marriage Lic. (London), i. 58.

Possibly the above is a variant of Keighley, q.v.

1742. Bapt. — William, s. Ambrose Kitely : St. Jas. Clerkenwell, ii. 261.
1781. Married—George Thornton and Amey Ketly : St. Geo. Han. Sq. i. 321.
London, 1, 1.

Ketton, Keeton, Kitton.—Local, 'of Ketton,' (1) a township in the parish of Lamplugh, co. Cumberland ; (2) a parish in co. Rutland, near Stamford.

Johannes de Keton, 1379 : P. T. Yorks. p. 63.
Henry de Ketton, 1379 : ibid. p. 237.

1506. Thomas Keton, rector of Langale and Kirksted, co. Norf. : FF. x. 165.
1805. Married — Thomas Keeton and Ann Fuller : St. Geo. Han. Sq. ii. 331.
Lanc. Court Dir., 2, 0, 0 ; MDB. (co. Norfolk), 2, 0, 1 ; London, 0, 1, 0.

Kevan, Kevin.—Bapt. 'the son of Kevin' (Yonge, ii. 108), evidently a Welsh name.

Kavan ap Howell, 20 Edw. I. R.
London, 2, 0 ; Philadelphia, 0, 3.

Kew.—(1) Occup. 'the cook.'

Nicholas le Keu, co. Notts, 1273. A.
Walter le Keu, co. Oxf., ibid.

The same individual is thus described :

William le Keu, 1301. M.
William Cocus, 1302. M.
William le Keu, or Cocus, 1306. M.

(2) Local, 'of Kew,' the well-known parish in the dioc. of Rochester.

1688. Thomas Palfrey and Mary Kew : Marriage Alleg. (Canterbury), p. 79.
1809. Married—John Kew and Flora Sharman : St. Geo. Han. Sq. ii. 416.
London, 4.

Kewell, Kevell.—Local, 'of Kewell,' seemingly some small spot in co. Somerset with the local suffix -well.

John Kewel, co. Oxf., 1273. A.

This name seems sometimes to have been registered Kevell.

William de Kiwell, co. Soms., 1 Edw. III : Kirby's Quest, p. 159.
1598. George Rewitt, co. Warwick : Reg. Univ. Oxf. vol. ii. pt. ii. p. 227.

In a footnote the editor says that this last name is indistinct. It might be Rewill, or Revell, or Kevel.

1620. Bapt. — Janie, d. Henry Kevill : St. Jas. Clerkenwell, i. 87.
1751. Married — William Garrett and Eliz. Kevell : St. Geo. Chap. Mayfair, p. 193.
London, 2, 0 ; Philadelphia, 0, 1.

Kewley, Cully.—Local, 'of Quilli,' near Falaise, Normandy.

Hughe de Cuilly, 1313. M.
Hugo de Cully, 1314. M.
Roger de Cuilly, 1315. M.
Roger de Kuly. 1318. M.
Roger de Kuylly, 1322. M.

The Isle of Man Kewleys are said to be a mere variant of Kelly, the great Manx patronymic. It is a question I am not able to decide.

1777. Married — William Kewley and Joyce Verty : St. Geo. Han. Sq. i. 274.
Crockford, 9, 0 ; London, 0, 2 ; Philadelphia, 0, 8.

Keymer, Keymar.—Local, 'of Keymer,' a parish in the dioc. of Chichester, co. Sussex.

1601. Richard Kemer, co. Kent : Reg. Univ. Oxf. vol. ii. pt. ii. p. 247.
Richard Kemeyre, 1604 : St. Dionis Backchurch, London, p. 15.
1713. Married — Samuel Keymer and Sarah Beer : St. Mary Aldermary, p. 42.
1793. Married — Francis Keymer and Anne Gilman : St. Geo. Han. Sq. ii. 93.
London, 4, 0 ; New York, 1, 1.

Keyser, Keyzor, Kezar, Kezor.—Nick. ; v. Kaiser.

Keyworth.—Local, 'of Keyworth,' a parish in co. Notts, seven miles from Nottingham.

1590. Buried—Tobie Keworth, servant to Mr. John Hodgkins : St. Mary Aldermary, p. 145.
1786. Married—George Cheshire and Catherine Keyworth : St. Geo. Han. Sq. i. 386.
MDB. (co. Notts), 10 ; London, 4 ; New York, 2.

Kibble, Keable, Kebbel, Kebbell, Kebble, Keeble, Keble, Kibel.—Bapt. 'the son of Kibble,' i.e. Cubold. A strong confirmation of the view that Kibble was an old personal name is the existence of such local names as Kibblethwaite, Kibbleworth, Kibblestone, Cobbledick, q.v. The absence of prefixes in the instances below is additional evidence. I doubt not it is the Domesday Cubold, and therefore a mere variant of Cobbold, q.v.

Michael Kibbel, co. Hunts, 1273. A.
William Kibbel, co. Camb., ibid.
Thomas Kibel, co. Linc., ibid.
Reginald Kibel, co. Linc., ibid.
Stephen Cubbel, co. Oxf., ibid.
1525. George Kebyll and Katharine Terell : Marriage Lic. (London), i. 5.
1686. Bapt. — John, s. John Keeble : St. Jas. Clerkenwell, i. 320.
1607. Thomas Keble, co. Suff., and Mary Tirrell : Marriage Lic. (Westminster), p. 15.

The variants of this surname have simply run riot in our registers, especially in modern times. I append a few from one record :

1804. Married — Thomas Keable and Millicent Shepherd : St. Geo. Han. Sq. ii. 303.

1806. Married—John Kibble and Ann Mary Lockley: St. Geo. Han. Sq. ii. 346.
— — Henry Strong and Eliz. Kebble: ibid. p. 341.
1807. — Richard Keeble and Mary Whiting: ibid. p. 366.
1809. — John Kebbell and Sarah Parsons: ibid. p. 414.
London, 5, 3, 3, 1, 3, 10, 0, 0; Crockford (Keble), 3; New York (Kibel), 2; Boston (U.S.), Kibble, 5.

Kibblewhite.—Local, 'of Kibblethwaite'; cf. Applewhite for Applethwaite. The prefix represents the personal name of the settler. The meaning is, 'the thwaite (clearing) of Kibble'; v. Kibble and Thwaite. I cannot find the spot.

1575. Michael Kiblewhite, of London: Reg. Univ. Oxf. vol. ii. pt. ii. p. 68.
1560. Bapt. — Michael, s. John Keblewhite: St. Mary Aldermary (London), p. 53.
1597. Married — Roger Gwine and Joane Kebelwhite: ibid. p. 6.
1678. Bapt. — Eliz., d. Edward Kiblwhite: Marriage Alleg. (Canterbury), p. 16.
1684. — Ann, d. Edward Kiblewhite: ibid. p. 18.
1895. Married—Abraham Boxall and Sarah Kibblewhite: St. Geo. Han. Sq. ii. 322.
London, 2.

Kibby, Kibbee, Kibbe.—Local, 'of Kirkby,' a variant of Kirby; v. Kirkby. With Kibbee, cf. Applebee for Appleby.

Birmingham, 7, 0, 0; Boston (U.S.), 0, 1, 0; Philadelphia, 5, 0, 2.

Kidd.—Nick. 'the kid,' a man of a frisky disposition; cf. Doe, Roe, Buck, Roebuck, &c.

Reginald Kyd, co. Oxf., 1273. A.
Ricardus Kyd, 1379: P. T. Yorks. p. 226.
Thomas Kydde, 1379: ibid. p. 222.
Willelmus Kydde, 1379: ibid. p. 209.
1611. Anthony Kydde and Julian Percy: Marriage Lic. (London), ii. 4.
1631-2. Archibald Kyd and Sara Butler: ibid. p. 204.
1799. Married — William Kidd and Christian Willson: St. Geo. Han. Sq. ii. 202.
London, 20; Philadelphia, 33.

Kidder.—Occup. 'the kidder,' i.e. a huckster. 'Kiddier, a huckster.' East' (Halliwell). An Act of Edward VI speaks of 'the buying of anye corne, fyshe, butter, or cheese by any such Badger, Lader, Kyddier, or Carrier as shal be assigned and allowed to that office'

(5 and 6 Edw. VI, c. 14). A confirmation of this Act by Elizabeth alters Kyddier to Kydder. The name is frequently found in the Poll Tax, 1379, W. Rid. Yorks., several instances being given below.

William le Kydere, 25 Edw. I: BBB. p. 542.
Johannes Kyder, 1379: P. T. Yorks. p. 18.
Johannes Kydder, 1379: ibid. p. 58.
Johannes Kydder, 1379: ibid. p. 155.
Richard Kydder, temp. Eliz. Z.
1580. John Kydder and Christian Morgan. Marriage Lic. (London), i. 96.
1635-6. Buried — Richard, s. Richard Kidder: St. Jas. Clerkenwell, iv. 219.
1790. Married — John Kidder and Phoebe Ross: St. Geo. Han. Sq. ii. 40.
London, 1; Philadelphia, 1; Boston (U.S.), 34.

Kiddle, Kiddall, Kidall, Kiddell.—(1) Local, 'of Kiddal,' a hamlet in the parish of Barwick-in-Elmet, seven miles from Leeds. (2) ? Bapt. 'the son of Kedwall'; v. Keedwell. If this be correct it would explain the large number of Kiddles in cos. Gloucester and Somerset, as Kidwell would readily become Kiddle.

Thomas de Kidale, 1379: P. T. Yorks. p. 227.
Beatrix de Kydhall, 1379: ibid. p. 224.
Walterus de Kydhall, 1379: ibid.
1606. John Sedgewicke and Petronella Kiddall: Marriage Lic. (Westminster), p. 15.
1718. Married — Thomas Kiddle and Mary Maidman: Reg. Stourton, co. Wilts.
1802. — Jonathan Lock and Susanna Kiddell: St. Geo. Han. Sq. ii. 264.
London, 3, 0, 0, 1; MDB. (co. Somerset), 18, 0, 0, 0; (co. Norfolk), 5, 0, 2, 0; New York, 1, 0, 0, 0.

Kidgell.—? Bapt. 'the son of Kiggel.' It is curious to find the surname still lingering in co. Somerset.

Matilda Kiggel, co. Hunts, 1273. A.
Robert Kiggel, co. Soms., 1 Edw. III: Kirby's Quest, p. 178.
MDB. (co. Soms.), 1.

Kidman.—(1) Occup. 'the kidman,' a man who looked after young goats; cf. Cowman, Gooseman, Bullman, &c. (2) Bapt. 'the son of Kideman'; probably a variant of Cadman, q.v. This must be accepted as the chief parent.

Alan Kydeman, co. Norf., 1273. A.
Walter Kademan ,co. Soms., ibid.

Guy Kidman, C. R., 4 Edw. IV.
Alfric, son of Kideman, co. Norf.: FF. vii. 145.
1735. Charles Kidman, rector of Banham, co. Norf.: ibid. i. 353.
1743. Buried — Bathsheba, wife of the Rev. Brewer Kidman: St. Michael, Cornhill, p. 296.
1744. Married — John Parkinson and Sarah Kidman: St. Geo. Han. Sq. i. 33.
London, 3; MDB. (co. Hunts), 5.

Kidner.—Local, 'of Kitenare,' some estate or manor in co. Somerset that I am unable to identify. The modification of the name into Kidner is a natural one.

William de Kitenare, co. Soms., 1 Edw. II: Kirby's Quest, p. 192.
William Kytenor, co. Soms., ibid. p. 142.

The surname is well represented in the county in the 19th century. A member of the family seems to have travelled into Yorkshire at an early period:

Adam Kitener, 1379: P. T. Yorks. p. 165.
London, 2; MDB. (co. Somerset), 8; Boston (U.S.), 1.

Kidney.—Local. An imitative corruption of Gidney, q.v. A good example of the principle laid down in this dictionary; cf. Kilby and Gilbey.

1593. Buried — John Kidney, or Kydney: St. Jas. Clerkenwell, iv. 52.
1665. Married — Thomas Kidney and Mary Vellis: ibid. iii. 118.

Private Kidney (co. Lanc.) scored high in the first stage of the Queen's Prize at Wimbledon, July 10, 1888 (v. Daily Papers).

London, 1; Philadelphia, 6.

Kidson.—Bapt.; v. Kitson.

Kidwell; v. Keedwell.

Kifford, Kefford. — ? Local, 'of Guildford'; possibly an old pronunciation. But perhaps a sharpened form of Giffard, q.v.; v. Kidney.

George Guldeford, or Gilford, or Kifforde, 1556: Reg. Univ. Oxf. i. 232.
1623-4. John Kifford and Alice Butcher: Marriage Lic. (London), ii. 134.
1744. Married — Thomas Kefford and Mary Bunyan: St. Geo. Chap. Mayfair, p. 35.
London, 1, 3.

Kift.—Nick. 'the kift,' i.e. the ungainly, the awkward. 'Kift, awkward, clumsy. West' (Halli-well).

John Kyft, co. Soms., 1 Edw. III: Kirby's Quest, p. 80.

We find similar nicknames, such as Snell (q.v.) and Crees, in the same register; v. Crease.

1616. Edward Kyfte, co. Glouc.: Reg. Univ. Oxf. vol. ii. pt. ii. p. 352.
1674. Joseph Smart and Mary Herbert, alleged by Richard Kiff: Marriage Alleg. (Canterbury), p. 124.
1675. Henry Hinton and Eliz. Corbett, alleged by Richard Kift: ibid. p. 152.
1703. Married — Joseph Lester and Eliz. Kift: St.Dionis Backchurch, p. 51.
MDB. (co. Soms.), 1; Philadelphia, 3.

Kightley, Kightly.—Local, 'of Keighley,' q.v. The variants of this old surname are many.

1574. George Kyghtelye and Grisill Crayforde: Marriage Lic. (London), i. 63.
1808. Married—Samuel Kightely and Mary Costelow: St. Geo. Han. Sq. ii. 389.
London, 1, 1.

Kilbey, Kilby, Killby, Kilbee, Kelby.—Local, (1) 'of Kilby,' a parish in co. Leicester; (2) 'of Kelby,' a parish in co. Lincoln. The latter seems to be the chief parent. Probably Gilbey, Gillbee, Gilby, &c., are in many cases but variants.

Richard de Kelby, co. Linc., 1273. A.
William de Keleby, co. Linc., ibid.
Roger de Kelleby, co. Linc., ibid.
William de Kyleby, co. Leic.: Hen. III-Edw. I. K.
1351. William de Keleby, rector of Kelling, co. Norf.: FF. ix. 406.
Roger de Kileby, co. Norf.: ibid. viii. 465.
1712. Died—Anchor Kilby, sub-sacrist, co. Norwich: ibid. iv. 24.
1797. Married — Richard Kilbey and Eliz. Coffee: St. Geo. Han. Sq. ii. 172.
London, 4, 5, 3, 0, 0; Philadelphia, 0, 0, 0, 0, 3; New York (Kilby), 2; Oxford (Kilbee), 2.

Kilbrick.—Local, 'of Kelbrook,' a chapelry in the parish of Thornton, W.R. Yorks, near Colne.

1704. John Kelbreck, of Hambleton: Lancashire Wills at Richmond (1681-1748), p. 155.
MDB. (co. Lanc.), 1.

Kilburn, Kilbourn, Kilborn, Kilbourne, Kilborne.—Local, 'of Kilburn,' (1) a hamlet, partly in the parish of Hampstead, co. Middlesex; (2) a parish in N. Rid. Yorks, seven miles from

Thirsk; (3) a township in the parish of Horsley, co. Derby.

Ralph de Kylburn, co. Derby, 1273. A.
1587. Married—Richard Kylborne and Alice Sackfelde: St. Michael, Cornhill, p. 14.
1626. — Isaac Kilbourne and Mary Fayrefax: St. Jas. Clerkenwell, iii. 56.
1746. — William Killbourn and Ann Killbourn: St. Geo. Chap. Mayfair, p. 75.
1807. — John Kilbourn and Mary Ann Jennings: St. Geo. Han. Sq. ii. 370.
London, 2, 1, 0, 0, 0; MDB. (co. Warwick), 0, 0, 1, 0, 0; New York, 3, 0, 0, 5, 1; Philadelphia, 7, 0, 0, 0, 0.

Kilford. — Local, 'of Guildford' (?). This is highly probable; cf. Kisby and Gisby, Kilbey and Gilbey, &c.

1556. George Kilforde: Reg. Univ. Oxf. vol. ii. pt. ii. p. xiv.

The following seems to be a curious variant:

1550. William Cocks and Margaret Kyllyfedd: Marriage Lic. (London), p. 13. London, 1.

Kilham, Killam.—Local, 'of Kilham,' a parish in E. Rid. Yorks, near Great Driffield; also a township in the parish of Kirk-Newton, co. Northumberland.

John de Kyllum, co. York, Hen. III-Edw. I. K.
1709. Married — Richard Marsh and Jane Kilham: Canterbury Cath. p. 69.
1845. — Marmaduke Kelham and Julia Ann Christie: ibid. p. 106.
MDB. (co. Sussex), 1, 0; (West Rid. Yorks), 1, 0; London, 0, 1; Philadelphia, 0, 2.

Killbull, Killbullock, Killhare, Killhog.—Nicknames for a pig-sticker or slaughter-man. Prof. Skeat says *kill* was originally to *strike*, to deaden with a blow. Thus Killbull and Killbullock meet the case exactly; M.E. *culle*, kill.

Reginald Cullebel (-bol?), co. Oxf., 1273. A.
Henry Cullebulloc, co. Bedf., ibid.
William Cullehar', co. Oxf., ibid.
William Cullehog', co. Oxf., ibid.

Killer.—(1) Occup. 'the kilner,' q.v.; a variant; cf. Keller (2). But v. Killbull. Perhaps it means a slaughterer or pig-sticker. (2) Local, 'of Keller'; v. Keller (1).

MDB. (co. Derby), 3; New York, 1.

Killhare, -hog; v. Killbull.

Killick; v. Killwick.

Killigrew.—Local, 'of Killigrew.' Mr. Lower says, 'In charters, *Cheligrevus*, a manor in the parish of St. Erme, co. Cornwall, where this celebrated family resided from an early date down to the reign of Richard II': Patr. Brit. p. 179.

1590. Robert Killegrew, co. Hants: Reg. Univ. Oxf. vol. ii. pt. ii. p. 181.
1615. Henry Killygrew, co. Cornwall: ibid. p. 336.
1722. Married—Charles Killigrew and Eliz. Vaughan: St. Antholin (London), p. 136.
1743. Bapt. — Thomas, s. Thomas Killigrew: St. Michael, Cornhill, p. 173. Boston (U.S.), 4.

Killingback, Killingbeck.—Local, 'of Killingbeck.' I do not know the spot.

Mr. Killeingbeck, curate of St. Nicholas Chapel, Lynn, co. Norfolk, 1682: FF. viii. 504.
1688. Richard Baines and Francis Killingbeck: Marriage Alleg. (Canterbury), p. 54.
1722. Bapt. — Thomas, s. William Killingbeck: St. Jas. Clerkenwell, ii. 134. London, 2, 0; Philadelphia, 0, 1.

Killingsworth, Killingworth, Chillingworth, Chillingsworth.—Local, 'of Killingworth,' a township in the parish of Long Benton, co. Northumberland. Possibly another spot so called may have existed in co. Norfolk. Of course Shillingsworth is an imitative corruption of Chillingsworth. With Chillingworth, cf. Church and Kirk.

Adam de Kellyngworthe, co. Norf., 1273. A.
1388. Thomas de Killingworth, vicar of Windham, co. Norf.: FF. ii. 508.
1561. Richard Killingworth, co. Norf.: ibid. p. 244.
1576. John Kyllingworthe and Alice Smithe, *widow*: Marriage Lic. (London), i. 71.
1616. John Killingworth, of London: Reg. Univ. Oxf. vol. ii. pt. ii. p. 353.
1713. Married — John Shillingsworth and Isabella Boyce: St. Jas. Clerkenwell, iii. 235.
London, 1, 0, 3, 0; MDB. (co. Norfolk), 0, 1, 0, 0; Philadelphia, 0, 0, 0, 2.

Killmaster; v. Kilminster.

Killwick, Killick, Killik.—Local, 'of Kildwick,' a parish in W. Rid. Yorks. With Killick, an inevitable variant, cf. Physic for Fishwick.

1601. Buried — John Kylleck : St. Dionis Backchurch, p. 205.
1662. John Killicke and Isabel Covell: Marriage Alleg. (Canterbury), p. 57.
1745. Married—William Killick and Diana Bateman : St. Geo. Chap. Mayfair, p. 45.
1789. — George Samples and Amy Killick : St. Geo. Han. Sq. ii. 25.
London, 2, 7, 1.

Kilminster, Killmaster, Killmister.—Local, ' of Kilminster,' near Wick, Scotland (Lower). The suffix -minster generally corrupts to -master or -mister ; cf. Buckmaster and Kittermaster.

1753. Married — William Kilmaster, alias Bradley, and Betty Povey : St. Geo. Chap. Mayfair, p. 247.
1760. — John Bankes and Ann Killmister : St. Geo. Han. Sq. i. 91.
1793. — Joseph Beeson and Eliz. Killmaster : ibid. ii. 102.
London, 1, 0, 0 ; MDB. (co. Oxf.), 0, 1, 0 ; (co. Glouc.), 2, 0, 2 ; (co. Stafford), 0, 0, 1.

Kilner.—Occup. ' the kilner,' a limeburner, one who superintended a kiln. Kilner has been for many centuries a Furness (North Lanc.) surname, but it seems to have nearly died out. I could furnish scores of entries from the Ulverston register. The name survived in the town till some thirty years ago.

1545. Bapt.—Elizabeth Kilner: St. Mary Ulverston, p. 1.
1546. Buried — Esabell Kilner : ibid. p. 3.
1560. Bapt.—Anthonie Kilner : ibid. p. 37.
1587. Thomas Kilner, of Aldingham : Lancashire Wills at Richmond, i. 174.
1598. John Lendall and Margaret Kilner : Marriage Lic. (London), i. 248.
1626. James Killner, of Ulverston : Lancashire Wills at Richmond, i. 174.
1732. Married—Nathaniel Killner and Sarah Bishop: St. Geo. Han. Sq. i. 10.
London, 4 ; Manchester, 1 ; Boston (U.S.), 2.

Kilpack, Kilpeck.—Local, ' of Kilpeck,' a parish in co. Hereford.

Hugh de Kilpec, co. Salop, Hen. III Edw. I. K.
1583. Married — John Kilbecke and Cecily Masterson : St. Jas. Clerkenwell, iii. 10.
London, 1, 0 ; Crockford, 1, 1 ; Oxford, 1, 0.

Kilpin.—Local, ' of Kilpin,' a township in the parish of Howden, E. Rid. Yorks.

1594. Richard Kilpin : Reg. Univ. Oxf. vol. ii. pt. ii. p. 204.
1603. Robert Kilpin, co. Bucks: ibid. p. 267.
1690. Bapt.—Sarah, d. William Killpin: St. Jas. Clerkenwell, i. 338.
1720. Married—Benjamin Kilpin and Susanna Butler : St. Mary Aldermary, p. 45.
London, 3.

Kilsby.—Local, ' of Kilsby,' a parish in co. Northampton, six miles from Daventry.

1678-9. William Killsbe and Ann Whiting: Marriage Alleg. (Canterbury), p. 223.
1732. Married — John Killsbey and Sarah Dyer: St. Jas. Clerkenwell, iii. 260.
1744. — Edward Kilsby and Ann Meridith : St. Geo. Chap. Mayfair, p. 34.
London, 4.

Kilshaw.—Local ; v. Culshaw. A corruption of Culcheth. For a second derivation, v. Kelsall.

1570. Married — Wyliam Kylshaye and Sarah Sturlay : St. Dionis Backchurch, p. 6.
1617. William Kilshaw, of Burscough : Wills at Chester, i. 115.
1619. John Kilshaw, of Burscough: ibid.
1622. John Kilshawe : Preston Guild Rolls, p. 67.
1688. Buried — Margaret, d. Edw. Kilshaw: Reg. Leyland, co. Lanc. p. 247.
MDB. (co. Chester), 1.

Kilvington.—Local, ' of Kilvington,' (1) a parish in co. Notts, seven miles from Newark ; (2) a parish in N. Rid. Yorks, near Thirsk.

1733. Buried—Eliz. Kilvington : St. Mary Aldermary, p. 222.
1736. — Thomas Kilvington : ibid. p. 223.
1763. Married—Joseph Shout and Eliz. Kilvington : St. Geo. Han. Sq. i. 120.
Hull, 1 ; MDB. (North Rid. Yorks), 5 ; Manchester, 1.

Kimball, Kimble, Kimbel. —Local, ' of Kimble '; v. Kimbell. Familiar American forms.

1654-5. Married — Henry Finch and Margrett Kimball : St. Dionis Backchurch, p. 30.
1729. — William Kimbal and Joanna Pickett : St. Geo. Chap. Mayfair, p. 298.
1751. — Albin Hadon and Eliz. Kimble: ibid. p. 199.
1754. — Timothy Honnor and Mary Kimbell : ibid. p. 269.
Philadelphia, 24, 14, 3.

Kimbell, Kimble.—Local, ' of Kimble.' Great and Little Kimble are parishes in co. Bucks, near

Wendover, and should be carefully distinguished from Kemble (v. Kemball), although at times, no doubt, they have become confused. For other variants, v. Kimball.

Richard de Kinebelle, co. Bucks, 1273. A.
John de Kinebelle, co. Oxf., ibid.
Nicholas Kymbell, co. Norf., 3 Hen. IV : FF. ix. 430.
1718. Married—John Phillibrown and Mary Kimbell : St. Michael, Cornhill, p. 60.
1775. — John Kimbell and Eliz. Plumb: St. Geo. Han. Sq. i. 250.
MDB. (co. Warwick), 4, 0 ; London, 0, 1.

Kimber ; v. Kember.

Kimberley, Kimberly.— Local, ' of Kimberley,' a parish in co. Norfolk.

Eustace de Kimberle, co. Norf., 1308 : FF. iv. 442.
Hugh de Kymberly, burgess of Great Yarmouth, 17 Edw. III : ibid. viii. 30.
1571. Robert Kymberlie and Rose Ive : Marriage Lic. (London), i. 50.
1611. Bapt.—John, s. William Kemberley : St. Jas. Clerkenwell, i. 63.
Birmingham, 10, 0 ; London, 5, 0 ; MDB. (co. Warwick), 2, 0 ; New York, 0, 3.

Kime, Kyme. — Local, ' of Kyme.' South Kyme is a parish in co. Lincoln, eight miles from Tattershall ; North Kyme is a township in the same parish.

Philip de Kyme, co. Linc., 1273. A.
Rosa de Kyme, co. Linc., ibid.
William de Kyma, co. Linc., ibid.
Lucia de Kyme, co. York, 20 Edw. I. R.
Symon de Kyme, co. Linc., Hen. III– Edw. I. K.
1638. Robert Lloyd and Eliz. Kyme : Marriage Lic. (London), iii. 237.
1641. Nightingale Kyme and Eliz. Pigeon : ibid. p. 199.
MDB. (co. Lincoln), 7, 1.

Kimmis(h ; v. Kemmish.

Kimpthorne ; v. Kempthorne.

Kimpton.—Local, ' of Kimpton,' (1) a parish in co. Hertford ; (2) a parish in co. Hants, five miles from Andover.

Thomas de Kymynton, co. Soms., 1 Edw. III : Kirby's Quest, p. 80.
1674. John Kimpton and Sarah Pease: Marriage Alleg. (Westminster), p. 228.
1682. Thomas Kimpton and Eliz. ——: Marriage Alleg. (Canterbury), p. 93.
London, 19 ; New York, 2.

Kinch, Kinnish, Kench.— Bapt. A Manx surname, corresponding to the Irish McGuiness and Gaelic McGinnis. The Manx forms are McInesh, 1511; Kynnishe, 1601; Kinnish, 1626; Kennish, 1732 (v. Manx Note Book, ii. 65).

Donold Kynyshe, 1601: The Manx Note Book, i. 61.

1685. Richard Kinch and Martha Sheppard: Marriage Alleg. (Canterbury), p. 207.

1731. Bapt.—Ann, d. Nathaniel Kinch: St. John Baptist on Wallbrook, p. 183.

Liverpool, 0, 2, 0; Manchester, 2, 0, 0; Birmingham, 0, 0, 1; New York, 3, 0, 0; Oxford, 1, 0, 1.

Kindell.—Local, 'of Kendall.' One of several variants.

London, 2; Boston (U.S.), 1.

Kinder, Kynder, Kender.— Local, 'of Kinder,' a hamlet in the parish of Glossop, co. Derby, near Chapel-en-le-Frith.

Philota de Kender, co. Derby, 1273. A.

1576. Married—John Kynder and Ales Holme: Reg. Prestbury (co. Ches.), p. 53.

1581. John Kinder, or Kynder, co. Linc.: Reg. Univ. Oxf. vol. ii. pt. ii. p. 102.

1752. Married — John Kinder and Martha Attersoll: St. Geo. Chap. Mayfair, p. 219.

1793. — William Kinder and Catherine Butcher: St. Geo. Han. Sq. ii. 94.

1800. — William Kinder and Mary Stokes: ibid. p. 219.

London, 2, 0, 0; MDB. (co. Derby), 3, 0, 0; (co. Lanc.), 1, 1, 0; Birmingham, 3, 0, 1; Boston (U.S.), 3, 0, 1.

Kindersley.—(1) Local, 'of Kinnersley,' q.v. The *d* is intrusive; cf. *riband* for *ribbon*, or Simmonds for Simmons. (2) Local, 'of Kingsley.' There is evidence in favour of this view. Kingsley became Kinsley, as we know. This with the intrusive *d* would become Kindsley. The intrusive *r* also presents no difficulty; cf. Patterson for Patteson, &c.

1597. Thomas Kindesley, or Kingsley, London: Reg. Univ. Oxf. vol. ii. pt. ii. p. 220.

— William Kindesley, London: ibid.

1618. Thomas Kyndesley. of Warrington: Wills at Chester, i. 116.

As this name occurs in the vicinity of Kingsley it helps to support the above suggestion (v. Kinsley for further confirmation).

1613. Married—Robert Kindersly and Mary Auston: St. Antholin (London), p. 49.

MDB. (co. Dorset), 1.

Kindon; v. Kingdon.

King.—Offic. 'the king.' There are four columns of Kings in the London Directory. An explanation is manifestly needed. Our Kings are of no royal descent; nor yet is the title always a mere nickname, like Caesar, Kaiser, Emperor (q.v.), from the royal bearing or appearance of the original nominee. The entries are in this direct and plain fashion:—Hamond le King. A. Robert le Kynge. G. Saher le King. H. The Hundred Rolls (1273) also furnish a William Littleking. There is also a Roger Wyteking. K. Stature and dress will account for these. The fact is the progenitors of our Kings acted in that capacity in the numerous festival and mock ceremonials of mediaeval times. At Epiphany-tide the Magi ('Kings of the East') were represented in every village.

> 'Thy mummeries, thy twelfe-tide kings
> And queens, thy Christmas revellings.'
> Herrick.

Besides the king and queen enthroned on May-day (who would maintain their regal title through the year, at least), there was the familiar 'King of Misrule,' whom every great nobleman possessed. In the manor of Ashton-under-Lyne (1422) we find 'Hobbe the King,' and a festival to be held there is under the supervision of 'Margaret, widow of Hobbe the King, Hobbe Adamson, Jenkin of the Wood,' &c. (v. Three Lancashire Documents, Cheth. Soc.). One more quotation will suffice:

> 'We, Adam Backhous and Harry Nycol, hath made account for the Kenggam (King-game) that same tyme don William Kempe, *Kenge*, and Joan Whytebrede, *Quen*, and all costs deducted, £4 5s. 0d.': Churchwarden's Accounts, Kingston-upon-Thames (Lysons).

'Queen' also existed as a surname, q.v. That King should be so largely represented now simply proves that every town and village had its festival, and that the 'King' was proud of his title; so were his children. Thus it became hereditary; v. Kingsman and Kingson.

John le Kyng, co. Norf., 1273. A. Walter le Kyng, co. Camb., ibid. Willelmus Kyng', 1379: P. T. Yorks. p. 35.

1611-2. William Kinge and Elliner White: Marriage Lic. (London), ii. 9.

London, 355; Philadelphia, 360.

Kingaby.—Local, 'of Kingerby,' a parish in co. Lincoln, five miles from Market Rasen.

1794. Married—James Kingaby and Ann Andrews: St. Geo. Han. Sq. ii. 106. London, 2.

Kingcombe, Kingcome, Kingscomb.—Local, 'of Kingcombe,' a tithing in the parish of Toller Porcorum, near Beaminster, co. Dorset.

1789. Married — John Nicholas and Bridget Kingcome: St. Geo. Han. Sq. ii. 19.

Bristol, 1, 3, 0; London, 1, 0, 0; MDB. (co. Devon), 0, 2, 1.

Kingdon, Kingdom, Kindon.—Local, 'of Kingdon,' or more probably 'Kingsdon,' a parish in co. Somerset, near Somerton. Kingdom is an imitative corruption; cf. Hansom for Hanson, or Ransom for Ranson. With Kindon, cf. Kinsley for Kingsley, or Kinsman for Kingsman. No doubt, as intimated in the index to the two registers, the two following entries concern the same couple:

1709. Married — Henry Kindon and Eliz. Plucknet: St. Antholin (London); p. 122.

1710. Bapt.—Eliz., d. Henry and Eliz. Kingdom: St. John Baptist on Wallbrook, p. 176.

Thus Kindon and Kingdom are variants of Kingdon.

1752. Married — Bryan Connor and Mary Kingdon: St. Geo. Chap. Mayfair, p. 217.

Bristol, 3, 2, 0; London, 6, 0, 1; Tenby, 0, 1, 0; MDB. (co. Devon), 20, 2, 0; Philadelphia, 1, 0, 2; Boston (U.S.), 3, 0, 0.

Kingett, Kinggett. — Nick. 'the kinget' or 'kinglet,' a dim. of King. In the same way we have the two dims. of Hew (Hugh), viz. Hewett and Hewlett. v. King.

Johannes Kinglot, 1379: P. T. Yorks. p. 156.

London, 2, 2.

Kingham.—Local, 'of King-ham,' a parish in co. Oxford, four miles from Chipping Norton.

1721. Buried — Mary Kinghom: St. Thomas the Apostle (London), p. 149.
1749. Married — Edward Ralph and Mary Kingham: St. Geo. Chap. Mayfair, p. 146.
1774. — Edward Wench and Mary Kingham: St. Geo. Han. Sq. i. 239.
London, 3; MDB. (co. Oxford), 1.

Kinglake.—Local, 'of King-lake.' I cannot find the spot. Assuredly a West-country name.

1608. William Kinglacke, co. Soms.: Reg. Univ. Oxf. vol. ii. pt. ii. p. 302. MDB. (co. Somerset), 12.

Kingman; v. Kingsman.

Kingsbury.—Local, 'of Kings-bury,' (1) a parish in co. Middle-sex ; (2) a parish in co. Warwick ; (3) a parish in co. Somerset.

Adam de Kinggesbire,co.Linc.,1273. A.
Philip de Kingesbire, co. Dorset, Hen. III-Edw. I. K.
1603. Married — John Stacye and Katheryn Kyngssberie: Reg. Stourton, co. Wilts, p. 50.
1791. — John Gibbs and Mary Kings-bury : St. Geo. Han. Sq. ii. 61
London, 8; Birmingham, 1 ; Philadel-phia, 4.

Kingscomb; v. Kingcombe.

Kingscote, Kingscott.—Local, 'of Kingscote,' a parish in co. Gloucester, eight miles from Stroud.

William Kingescott, of Kingescott, co. Glouc.: Visitation of Gloucester (1623), p. 99.
Troyolus Kingescott, co. Glouc, 1623 : ibid. p. 100.
1663. Bapt.—John, s. John Kingscot : Reg. Cowley, co. Glouc.
1722. Married — Nicholas Kingscote and Margaret Merrett: Reg. Stone, co. Glouc.
London, 1, 0 ; MDB. (co. Gloucester), 1, 1.

Kingsey.—Local, 'of Kingsey,' a parish in co. Bucks, two miles from Thame. The suffix is -hay, as in Fotheringhay ; v. Hay.

John de Kyngeshaye, co. Suff., 1273. A.
William de Kyngeshaye, co. Suff., ibid.
1710. Married — Peter Kingsey and Ann Amler : St.Antholin (London), p. 123.
1764. Married — Evan Kingsey and Mary Platts: St. Geo. Han. Sq. i. 136.

Kingsford.—Local, 'of Kings-ford,' a hamlet in the parish of

Wolverley, near Kidderminster, co. Worcester. Other spots would naturally bear this title.

Avicia de Kyngesford, co. Worc., Hen. III-Edw. I. K.
Henry de Kyngesford, co. Devon, 1273. A.
John de Kingsford, co. Norf., 1372: FF. vii. 51.
1746. Married — William Lott and Eliz. Kingsford: Canterbury Cath. p. 88.
1751. — John Kingsford and Eliz. Rose : ibid. p. 92.
London, 9 ; New York, 3.

Kingsland.—Local, 'of Kings-land': (1) a parish in co. Hereford, four miles from Leominster ; (2) a chapelry in the parish of Islington, co. Middlesex. Other spots would naturally bear this name.

Mathew de Kyngeslond, co. Kent, 1273. A.
1596. Bapt.—Robert, s. James Kings-land : St. Jas. Clerkenwell, p. 31.
1708. Married — John Kingsland and Jane Minge: Canterbury Cath. p. 68.
1711. — Thomas Kingsland and Eliz. Worham : ibid. p. 70.
MDB. (co. Kent), 5 ; New York, 26.

Kingsley.—Local, 'of Kings-ley.' (1) A township in the parish of Frodsham, co. Cheshire. Although Kingsley is somewhat scarce to-day in Cheshire and South Lan-cashire, it must not be forgotten that its variants Kinsley and Kindersley (q.v.) are familiar there. (2) A parish in co. Southampton, near Alton. (3) A parish in co. Stafford, near Cheadle.

Adam de Kyngeslegh : East Cheshire, ii. 161.
William Rutter, of Kyngesleye, 7 Hen. VIII: ibid. p. 86 n.
1588. Edmund Kingsley, of Wigan: Wills at Chester, i. 115.
1620. John Kingsley, of Haigh : ibid.
1803. Married — John Kingsley and Peggy Barber : St. Geo. Han. Sq. ii. 289.
London, 2 ; Manchester, 1 ; Philadel-phia, 10.

Kingsman, Kinsman, King-man. — (1) Official, 'the king's man,' i.e. servant, a royal servitor. Probably also one who looked after royal property, a steward, a wood-ward, &c. (2) Occup. 'the king's man,' or assistant in the many festivities in which the king was personated ; v. King.

William Kingman, co. Soms., 1 Edw. III : Kirby's Quest, p. 130.

Thomas Kyngesman, Close Roll, 19 Ric. II.
Richard Kyngesman, 1273. A.
Ralph Kyngesman, 1311. M.
Alanus Kyngesman, 1379 : P. T. Yorks. p. 134.
1611. Robert Kingman, co. Soms. : Reg. Univ. Oxf. vol. ii. pt. ii. p. 325.

There is no trace of Kinsman being what it seems to imply ; cf. Kinsley for Kingsley. It is an imitative corruption of Kingsman, the said corruption being as old as the reign of Elizabeth.

John Kynnesman. ZZ.
Leonard Kinsman, Z.

Since writing the above I find Simon Kynnesman, C. R., 9 Hen. VI.

Nevertheless this earlier date does not militate against the view I hold. For conclusive evidence, v. Kinsman. An analogous instance is met with in Kinsley (q.v.), a corruption of Kingsley through an intermediate form Kindsley. Thus, too, we find Kindsman as a similar intermediate step.

1639. Bapt.—Owen, s. Richard Kins-man : St. Jas. Clerkenwell, p. 143.
1656. — Mary, d. Reuben Kindsman : St. Dionis Backchurch, p. 114.
1659. Married—William Hopkins and Sarah Kindsman : ibid. p. 34.

But the earlier forms of entry are after this fashion :

1533. Jeffrey Kingsman, rector of Sutton, co. Norf.: FF. ix. 348.
1573. Myles Kyngesman and Johanna Walker : Marriage Lic. (London), p. 58.

We may take it that the cor-ruptions began at the beginning of the reign of Henry VI, when, the original meaning being for-gotten, the possessors of the name took up the *significative* form of Kinsman.

London, 0, 2, 0 ; New York, 1, 0, 6 ; Boston (U.S.), 0, 0, 13, 39.

Kingsmill. — Local, 'at the king's mill,' a mill held of the king by the miller. One of these was in co. Hants.

Hugo de la Kingesmille, co. Southamp-ton, 1273. A.
Peter de Kingesmill, co. Wilts, ibid.
1574. Richard Kyngsmyll and Eliz. Stonehouse : Marriage Lic. (London), i. 61.
1582. Francis Kingsmell, co. South-ampton: Reg. Univ. Oxf. vol. ii. pt. ii. p. 123.

1585. John Kingsmill, co. Norf.: FF. vii. 188.

1610. Robert Spatman and Amy Kingesmeale: Marriage Lic. (London), p. 325.

1684. Col. Heneage Finch and Anne Kingsmell: Reg. Univ. Oxf. vol. ii. pt. ii. p. 305.

London, 2; Crockford, 3; Philadelphia, 1.

Kingsnorth.—Local, 'of Kingsnorth,' a parish in co. Kent, three miles from Ashford.

1732. Married—Charles Coombs and Margaret Kingsnorth: St. Geo. Han. Sq. i. 9.

1762. — Thomas Kingsnorth and Mary Howard: ibid. p. 112.

London, 1; MDB. (co. Kent), 6.

Kingson, Kinson.—Nick.' the king's son,' i.e. the son of the man who acted as king in the local festivals (v. King). It is impossible to entirely separate Kingson and Kingston: many of the latter, no doubt, started life as Kingson.

Reginald Kyngesone, co. Hunts, 1273. A.

Simon Kyngeson, 1307. M.

The first three of the following entries occur together:

Johannes Kyng, *hosteler*, 1379: P. T. Yorks. p. 270.

Johannes Kyngson, 1379: ibid.

Thomas Kyngson, 1379: ibid.

Thomas Kyngeson, 1379: ibid. p. 177.

Cf. Johanna Kyng', *doghter*, 1379: ibid. p. 175.

This is sufficient evidence of the derivation given above.

1585-6. Richard Kingson, *laborer*, and Margaret Wood: Marriage Lic. (London), i. 146.

1753. Married — James Millson and Ann Kingson: St. Geo. Chap. Mayfair, p. 239.

MDB. (co. Devon), 0, 1; Birmingham, 0, 1.

Kingston, Kingstone.—Local, (1) 'of Kingston,' parishes in cos. Cambridge, Devon, Somerset (2), Southampton, Sussex (2), Berks, Wilts, E. Rid. Yorks, &c.; (2) 'of Kingstone,' parishes in cos. Kent, Stafford, and Hereford.

Peter de Kyngeston, London, 1273. A.

Robert de Kingeston, co. Glouc., ibid.

Cristina de Kyngeston, co. Camb., ibid.

Lenote de Kyngeston, co. Sussex, ibid.

William de Kyngeston, co. Wilts, ibid.

Amicia de Kyngeston, co. Oxf., ibid.

John de Kyngeston, co. Soms., 1 Edw. III: Kirby's Quest, p. 85.

1578-9. Edward Kingeston and Barbara Plellowe: Marriage Lic. (London), p. 85.

1618. Edmund Kingstone, co. Glouc.: Reg. Univ. Oxf. vol. ii. pt. ii. p. 368.

1788. Married—Thomas Kingston and Ann Johnson: St. Geo. Han. Sq. ii. 14.

1806. — John Robertson and Jane Kingstone: ibid. p. 345.

London, 11, 1; MDB. (co. Somerset), 0, 2; Philadelphia, 20, 0.

Kingswell, Kingwell, Kingwill.—Local, 'at the king's well,' from residence thereby. The surname evidently hails from Hampshire, whence also Kingsmill comes. Indeed the two names are confounded in one instance.

1581. Ferdinando Kingswell, Hants: Reg. Univ. Oxf. vol. ii. pt. ii. p. 105.

A footnote to this entry records that in Matriculation he was returned as Ferdinando Kingsmell (v. Kingsmill).

1597. Buried—Harrye Kyngewell: St. Michael, Cornhill, p. 208.

1602. Edward Kingswelle, Hants: Reg. Univ. Oxf. vol. ii. pt. ii. p. 256.

1604. Richard Kingeswell, or Kinswell, Hants: ibid. p. 277.

1607. Richard Kingswell, Hants: ibid. p. 298.

London, 1, 4, 1; MDB. (co. Devon), 0, 3, 2.

Kington, Kinton.—Local, 'of Kington.' parishes in cos. Hunts, Warwick, Wilts, Worcester, and Dorset. With the variant Kinton, cf. Kinsley for Kingsley, or Kinsman for Kingsman.

Stephen de Kington, co. Norf., 1273. A.

Robert de Kington, co. Oxf., ibid.

1586. John Kynton and Margery Pemerton: Marriage Lic. (London), i. 153.

1752. Married — Weackham Kington and Sarah Armistmie (sic) Stead: St. Geo. Chap. Mayfair, p. 231.

London, 2, 0.

Kingwell, Kingwill.—Local; v. Kingswell.

Kinleyside; v. Keenlyside.

Kinmond, Kinman, Kynman.—Bapt. 'the son of Kinmond.' All personal names with suffix *-mond* corrupt to *-man*; cf. Osman, Wyman, Wayman, Tesseyman, &c.

1620. Married — Edward Kennyman and Mary Quince: St. Dionis Backchurch (London), p. 20.

1623-4. William Kynman and Joane Fowler: Marriage Lic. (London), ii. 134.

1711. Bapt. — Elizabeth, d. Francis Kinman: St. Jas. Clerkenwell, ii. 63.

1753. Married—Hill Burton and Eliz. Kinnimond: St. Peter, Cornhill, ii. 86.

London, 0, 1, 0; MDB. (co. Lincoln), 0, 0, 3; Sunderland, 1, 0, 0.

Kinnard.—Bapt.; v. Kenward. An American variant.

Philadelphia, 6.

Kinnersley, Kinnersly, Kinseley, Kynnersley.—Local, 'of Kinnersley,' a parish in co. Salop, five miles from Wellington; also a parish in co. Hereford, four miles from Weobley. v. Kindersley, and cf. Kinsley.

Hugh de Kinardeslegh, co. Hereford, Hen. III-Edw. I. K.

Richard de Kinardesle, co. Hereford, ibid.

Thus the name means the field of Kenward, the original settler or proprietor; v. Kenward.

1576. Nicholas Kinnersley, co. Linc.: Reg. Univ. Oxf. vol. ii. pt. ii. p. 72.

1581. Buried – Dorothye Kynnerseleye: Reg. Prestbury, co. Ches., p. 72.

1597. Married—Henry Kinnerslie and Margery Butler: St. Mary Aldermary, p. 9.

1676. Thomas Kinnersley and Mary London: Marriage Lic. (Canterbury), p. 259.

MDB. (co. Stafford), 2, 2, 0, 0; (co. Worcester), 0, 0, 0, 1; London, 0, 0, 1, 0; Birmingham, 0, 0, 0, 1; New York (Kinnersley), 1.

Kinnish; v. Kinch.

Kinsey.—Local, (1) 'of Kilnsea,' a parish in E. Rid. Yorks; (2) 'of Kilnsay,' a hamlet in the parish of Burnsall, W. Rid. Yorks; (3) 'of Kingsley'(?). I cannot help coming to the conclusion that Kinsey in cos. Ches. and Lanc. is a variant of Kingsley. The *g* was lost in Kinsley, q.v., and the *l* in Kinsey. I doubt not that in the South of England most of our Kinseys are modifications of Kingsey (q.v.); cf. Kinsman for Kingsman, or Kinsley for Kingsley.

1471. William Kynnesay, vicar of Hitcham, co. Norf.: FF. x. 311.

1586. William Chinseie, or Kinssee, co. Ches.: Reg. Univ. Oxf. vol. ii. pt. ii. p. 154.

1592. Married — Thomas Joneson and Eliz. Kynseye: Reg. Prestbury, co. Ches., p. 114.

1602. John Kynsey, co. Ches.: Reg. Univ. Oxf. vol. ii. pt. ii. p. 258.

1608. Married — John Kinsey and Dorithie Byrtles: Reg. Prestbury, co. Ches., p. 179.
1729. — Charles Kinsey and Kerthrine Rever: St. Antholin (London), p. 143.
London, 8; Philadelphia, 21; MDB. (co. Ches.), 4.

Kinsley, Kinsly, Kinseley, Kinzley.—Local. ' of Kingsley,' q.v. This name is found in the Cheshire and Lancashire neighbourhood of Kingsley. No doubt a variant. In the Index to the Wills at Chester (v. infra) the two names are treated as the same. A parallel case is met with in Kinsman for Kingsman, q.v. We even find the intermediate form of Kindsman. Under the one heading Kingsley, the Index to the Reg. Univ. Oxf. gives the following variants: Kindesley, Kingesley, Kinsley, and Kyngysley. The *d* in the instances below is therefore merely intrusive. v. Kindersley.
Adam Kindsley, of Charnock Richard, 1627: Wills at Chester (1621-50), p. 130.
John Kindeley, of Duxbury, *husbandman*, 1639: ibid.
Robert Kindsley, of the City of London, 1699: ibid. (1681-1700), p. 148.
1662. Thomas Kindsley: Preston Guild Rolls, p. 157.
1800. Married—William Carroll and Mary Kinsley: St. Geo. Han. Sq. ii. 230.
Liverpool, 3, 0, 0, 0; Manchester, 1, 0, 0, 0; MDB. (co. Chester), 0, 1, 0, 0; Philadelphia, 31, 0, 0, 3; London, 0, 0, 1, 0.

Kinsman.—Occup.; v. Kingsman. All the evidence is in favour of this derivation. For a parallel case, v. Kinsley for Kingsley. For further evidence, v. Kingsman.
1588-9. George Kinesman, co. Northampton: Reg. Univ. Oxf. vol. ii. pt. ii. p. 168.

The two following entries settle the question:
1674. Bapt.—Deborah, d. Herold and Deborah Kingsman: St. Michael, Cornhill, p. 148.
1676. — Eliz., d. Herold and Deborah Kinsman: ibid. p. 149.
Boston (U.S.), 14; Philadelphia, 2.

Kinson; v. Kingson.

Kinton; v. Kington.

Kipling, Kepling, Kippling. —Local, ' of Kiplin,' a township in

the parish of Catterick, N. Rid. Yorks. The final *g* is excrescent, as in Jennings. &c.
1756. Married—Samuel Platt and Eliz. Kippling: St. Geo. Han. Sq. i. 60.
London, 4, 0, 0; MDB. (N.Rid. Yorks), 6, 0, 0; Stockton-on-Tees, 0, 1, 0; New York, 3, 0, 0; Philadelphia (Kippling), 1.

Kippax.—Local, ' of Kippax,' a village eight miles east of Leeds.
Adam Kypas, 1379: P. T. Yorks. p. 95.
Johannes de Kypax, 1379: ibid. p. 205.
Johanna Kepas, 1379: ibid. p. 18.
Johannes de Kepax, 1379: ibid. p. 82.

With the forms Kypax and Kypas, cf. Lomax and Lomas in the neighbouring county of Lancaster.
1749. Married—Paul Bowns and Mary Kippax: St. Geo. Chap. Mayfair, p. 157.
1751. Buried—John, s. Thomas Kippax: St. Michael, Cornhill, p. 209.
1754. Bapt.—Mary, d. Thomas Kippax: ibid. p. 176.
Lanc. Court Dir. (1887), 8.

Kipping, Kippen. — ? Bapt. ' the son of Kiping' (?). The surname occurs frequently, but always without prefix, in the Hundred Rolls. Still, it may be local; cf. Browning and Harding, both personal names.
Ralph Kiping, co. Norf., 1273. A.
Henry Kipping, co. Camb., ibid.
Adam Kyping, co. Oxf., ibid.
Alexander Kippinge, co. Hertford, 20 Edw. I. R.
Robert Kipping, co. Soms., 1 Edw. III: Kirby's Quest, p. 138.
1591-2. Herman Kyppinge, or Kyppyn, and Faith Etheridge: Marriage Lic. (London), i. 196.
1795. Married — James Kipping and Dinah Offin: St. Geo. Han. Sq. ii. 129.
London, 6, 1.

Kipps, Kipp.—? Bapt. Probably a corruption of Gipp, q.v.; cf. Gilbey and Kilbey.
1752. Married—John Foord and Jane Kipps: St. Geo. Chap. Mayfair, p. 207.
1805. — Thomas Kipps and Jemima Irwin: St. Geo. Han. Sq. ii. 321.
London, 4, 0; Philadelphia, 0, 6.

Kirby; v. Kirkby.

Kirk, Kirke.—Local, ' at the kirk,' from residence beside the church; v. Church.
William atte Kirke, C. R., 19 Ric. II.
Robert atte Kirke. J.

Robertus del Kirke, 1379: P. T. Yorks. p. 183.
Johannes de Kirke, 1379: ibid. p. 57.

A curious intermediate form between Kirk and Church is found in the Hundred Rolls.
John de la Chirke, co. Linc., 1273. A.
1547. Married — Guylberte Johnson and Jawbyn Kyrke: St. Michael, Cornhill, p. 5.
1742. — Alex. Kirk and Eliz. Hunter: St. Geo. Chap. Mayfair, p. 30.
London, 19, 2; Philadelphia, 174, 2.

Kirkaldy, Kirkaldie, Kirkcaldie.—Local, ' of Kirkcaldy,' a royal burgh and parish in co. Fife. A modern importation into England.
London, 5, 2, 1.

Kirkbank. — Local, ' at the kirk bank,' from residence on the side of the slope on which the church was built; cf. Kirkup and Chappelow.
MDB. (co. Kent), 2; London, 3.

Kirkbride, Kirkbright.
Local, ' of Kirkbride,' a parish in co. Cumb., about six miles from Wigton.
Richard de Kirkebride co. Cumb., 20 Edw. I. R.
1742. Married — George Holride and Katherine Kirkbride: St. Geo. Chap. Mayfair, p. 18.
Philadelphia, 11, 0; MDB. (co. Westm.), 2, 0; Lofthouse (co. Yorks), 0, 4; West Riding Court Dir., 1, 0.

Kirkby, Kirby, Kerbey, Kerby. — Local, ' of Kirkby.' Parishes and hamlets too numerous for particular mention, chiefly in the North of England and in the counties along the East coast. Just as Kirkby became Kirby, so Kirkton became Kirton, q.v.
Adam de Kyrkeby, co. York, 1273. A.
Alex. de Kyrkeby, co. Linc., ibid.
Thomas de Kirkeby, co. Norf., ibid.
John de Kyrkeby, co. Westm., 20 Edw. I. R.
Roger de Kyrkeby, co. Hunts, ibid.
Alan de Kirkeby, co. Linc., ibid.
Johannes de Kirkeby, 1379: P. T. Yorks. p. 50.
1594. John Kerbie and Eliz. Bendowe: Marriage Lic. (London), i. 216.
1806. Married—George Kerbey and Ann Woodford: St. Geo. Han. Sq. ii. 339.
London, 4, 36, 2, 6; Philadelphia, 0, 46, 1, 1.

Kirker; v. Churcher.
Boston (U.S.), 5.

Kirkham. — Local, 'of Kirkham,' a parish in co. Lanc. This parish is one of the largest in the county, comprising about 130 square miles, or 41,736 statute acres. Naturally such an area gave birth to a local surname, and although no great family of Kirkham can be recorded, the name made its way among the less important classes. To-day it is a familiar cognomen throughout the country, America, and the Colonies.

Walter de Kirkham, co. Northumb., Edw. I–Edw. III. R.
Adam de Kirkham, 1379: P. T. Yorks. p. 30.
Agnes de Kyrkham, 1379: ibid. p. 300.
Johannes Kyrkam, 1376: ibid. p. 79.
1575. John Kirkham, co. Surrey: Reg. Univ. Oxf. vol. ii. pt. ii. p. 65.
1582. William Kirkeham and Eliz. Smith, *widow*: Marriage Lic. (London), p. 111.
1597-8. Robert Kyrkham, or Kirkham, co. Middlesex: Reg. Univ.~Oxf. vol. ii. pt. ii. p. 225.
London, 5; Manchester, 14; New York, 7.

Kirkland, Kirtland, Kɜrtland, Keartland. — Local, 'of Kirkland,'(1) a parish in co. Cumberland; (2) a township in the parish of Torpenhow, co. Cumb.; (3) a township in the parish of Garstang, co. Lanc.; (4) a township in the parish of Kendal, co. Westm. Kirtland is a manifest corruption.

(Homines) de Kyrkelaund, co. Cumb., 20 Edw. I. R.
Hugh de Churchlond, co. Soms., 1 Edw. III: Kirby's Quest, p. 163.
1585. Henry Woode and Johanna Kirkelande (co. Derby): Marriage Lic. (London), i. 142.
1586. David Jones and Anne Kyrtland, widow of Henry Kirtland: ibid. i. 150.
1790. Married — Andrew Milne and Catherine Kirkland: St. Geo. Han. Sq. ii. 45.
1797. — James Kirkland and Eliz. Brown: ibid. p. 160.
London, 5, 2, 1, 1; Philadelphia, 5, 0, 2, 0.

Kirkley, Kirley, Kirly. — Local, 'of Kirkley,' (1) a township in the parish of Ponteland, co. Northumberland; (2) a parish in

co. Suffolk, near Lowestoft. With the variants Kirley and Kirly, cf. Kirby for Kirkby.
1232. Richard de Kirkely, vicar of Buxton, co. Norf.: FF. vi. 441.
William de Kirkely, prior of Norwich: ibid. iv. 444.
Abraham de Kirkele, co. Suff., 1273. A.
Thomas de Kirkele, co. Suff., ibid.
1639. Robert Kirkley and Mary Penny: Marriage Lic. (Westminster), p. 39.
1686-7. Charles Kirly and Eliz. Hunter: Marriage Alleg. (Canterbury), p. 272.
1745. Married — Thomas Kirkly and Sarah Page: St. Geo. Chap. Mayfair, p. 54.
Manchester, 4, 0, 0; London, 0, 1, 3; Boston (U.S.), 1, 0, 0.

Kirkman. — Offic. 'the kirkman,' the keeper or guardian of the church; v. Churchman.
Roger le Kyrkeman, co. Linc., 1273. A.
Symon Kirkeman, co. Suff., ibid.
Alan Kyrkeman, co. Norf., ibid.
Gilbertus Kyrkman, 1379: P. T. Yorks. p. 26.
Johannes Kyrkman, 1379: ibid.
Ricardus Kirkeman, 1379: ibid. p. 64.
1597. Charles Kyrckman, co. Linc.: Reg. Univ. Oxf. vol. ii. pt. ii. p. 224.
1609. William Kynder and Anne Kirkeman: Marriage Lic. (London), i. 316.
London, 10; Philadelphia, 5.

Kirkness. — Local, 'of Kirkness,' a headland in~ Shetland. The following entry is thoroughly Scotch:
1753. Married — John Isbister and Jennet Kirkness: St. Geo. Chap. Mayfair, p. 256. London, 1.

Kirkpatrick.—Local, 'of Kirkpatrick,' parishes in cos. Dumfries and Kirkcudbright; the church dedicated to St. Patrick. Cf. Marychurch, Kirkbride, &c.
1687-8. Thomas Kirkpatrick and Mary Turner: Marriage Lic. (London), ii. 309.
1747. Married—David Cockburn and Agnes Kirkpatrick: St. Geo. Chap. Mayfair, p. 90.
1803. — Guthrie Kirkpatrick and Mary Green: St. Geo. Han. Sq. ii. 294.
London, 2; MDB. (East Rid. Yorks), 3; Philadelphia, 80.

Kirkshaw; v. Kershaw.
Worcestershire Court Dir., 1.

Kirkup.—Local, 'at the kirk hope,' i.e. the hope on which the church stands; v. Kirk and Hope; cf. Greenup (s. v. Greenhalgh), Trollope, &c.
1754. Married—George Morwick and Sarah Kirkup: St. Geo. Han. Sq. i. 54.
1786. — William Davis and Mary Kirkup: ibid. i. 386.

London, 1; MDB. (co. Durham), 3; Newcastle, 2; New York, 1; Boston (U.S.), 1.

Kirkus, Churchouse.—Local. 'of the kirkus,' i.e. kirk-house or parsonage, but afterwards applied to the inn by the church gate, where at weddings, christenings, or funerals 'refreshments' might be had. There is a 'kirkus' by the church at Ulpha, beyond Broughton-in-Furness. Kirkus as a surname of course dates from the earlier meaning, and may be set beside Parsonage, Monkhouse, Vickridge, &c.
John Kyrkhuse and Richert Kyrkus occur as men capable and fit to bear arms in Newcastle-upon-Tyne, 1539: PPP. ii. 181.
1552. Married—Humfrey Kyrkys and Beatrixe Thomson: St. Dionis Backchurch, p. 3.
'To John Milburn of Kirkehous for tith,' 1617: VVV. p. 99.
Henry Kirkhouse was Master of Trinity House, Newcastle-on-Tyne, for the year 1662: Brand's Newcastle, ii. 337.
Manchester, 1, 1; Hull, 5, 0.

Kirkwood. — Local, 'at the kirk wood,' from residence in the wood beside the church.
1699-1700. Married — John Kirkwood and Bridget Heath: St. Dionis Backchurch, p. 48.
1751. — William Kirkwood and Mary Lotan: St. Geo. Chap. Mayfair, p. 198.
1775. — Thomas Kirkwood and Catherine Wright: St. Geo. Han. Sq. i. 258.
London, 1; Philadelphia, 7.

Kirland.—Local, 'of Kirkland,' q.v. Just as Kirkby has become Kirby, so Kirkland has become Kirland.
Philadelphia, 3.

Kirley, Kirly; v. Kirkley.

Kirshaw.—Local. A variant of Kershaw, q.v.
1716. Bapt. — Catherine, d. Edmund Kirshaw: St. Mary Aldermary, p. 121.
1754. Married — Kirshaw and Mary Bellamy: St. Geo. Chap. Mayfair, p. 270.
MDB. (co. Warwick), 2.

Kirsopp, Kirsop.—Local. A Northumberland local name with the suffix *-hope* (v. Hope); cf. Blenkinsopp in the same county; v. Kirkup, of which it may be a variant, the more probably as both belong to the same district.
1791. Married—John Lee and Sarah Kirsop: St. Geo. Han. Sq. ii. 60.
Liverpool, 2, 0; Newcastle, 0, 3.

Kirtland.—Local, 'of Kirkland,' q.v.

New York, 4.

Kirtley.—Local, 'of Kirkley,' a township in the parish of Ponteland, ten miles from Newcastle, co. Northumberland. A corruption; cf. Kirtland for Kirkland.

Sunderland, 3; Newcastle, 1.

Kirton, Kerton.—Local, 'of Kirton,' (1) a parish in co. Lincoln, near Boston; (2) a parish in co. Suffolk, nine miles from Ipswich; (3) also Kirton-in-Lindsey, co. Lincoln, eighteen miles from Lincoln. All three seem to be modifications of Kirkton; cf. Kirby for Kirkby.

Alicia de Kirketon, co. Norf., Edw. I-Edw. III. R.
Alex. de Kirketon, co. Linc., ibid.
Simon de Kirketon, co. Linc., ibid.
Sir John de Kirton, co. Norf., 33 Edw. III: FF. ix. 107.
Robert Kyrton, co. Norf., 13 Edw. IV: ibid. xi. 208.
1576. Henry Kyrton and Eliz. Canler: Marriage Lic. (London), I. 72.
1591 2. William Kirton, co. Northampton: Reg. Univ. Oxf. vol. ii. pt. ii. p. 188.
1622. Bapt.—Amy, d. William Kertone, dwelling in the backe lann: St. Mary Aldermary, p. 77.
London, 4, 3; MDB. (co. Lincoln), 5, 1; New York, 1, 0.

Kisbee, Kisbey, Kisby.—Local; v. Keasbey.

Kislingbury.—Local, 'of Kislingbury,' a parish in co. Northampton.

1651. Bapt.—Sarah, d. Edward Kislingberry: St. Thomas the Apostle (London), p. 60.
1653. Buried—Ann, d. Edward Kislingbery: ibid. p. 129.
MDB. (co. Berks), 1.

Kiss.—?——. Probably some early personal name; of kin to the German Kisch, instances of which are in the London Dir.

1455. Thomas Kysse, balliff of Yarmouth: FF. xi. 325.
1573. Married—Lawrence Kyshe and Bridgett Phillipson: St. Jas. Clerkenwell, iii. 5.
1765. — William Woodward and Sarah Kish: St. Geo. Han. Sq. i. 146.
London, 1; New York, 1.

Kisser.—Occup. 'the kisser,' a maker of cuishes, thigh-armour.

F. *cuisse*, the thigh; O.F. *cuissaux*. 'Cuisses, armour for the thighs': Cotgrave.

'And no son of a great lord, that is to say, of an earl or baron, shall have other armour than mufflers and cuishes'—(' ne seit arme fors de mustilers e de quisers'): Stat. of Realm, i. 231.

Walter de Bedefont, *kissere*, London. X.
Richard le Kissere, ibid.
1750. Married—Edward Kishere and Sibell Clipsham: St. Geo. Chap. Mayfair, p. 169.
1738. Married—Benjamin Kishere and Rachel Bonufold: St. Geo. Han. Sq. i. 21.
1754. — William Burton and Mary Kisher: St. Geo. Han. Sq. i. 55.
London, 1.

Kissick; v. Keswick.

Kitcat, Kitcatt. —? Local. Probably an imitative corruption of some local name ending in *-cott*; cf. Westcott, Kingscott, Caldecott.

London, 1, 0; MDB. (co. Dorset), 0, 1; (co. Glouc.), 1, 0.

Kitchen, Kitchin, Kitching.—Local, 'at the kitchen,' equivalent to Kitchingman, q.v. The *g* in Kitching is, of course, excrescent, as in Jennings and a hundred other surnames.

Henry atte Kychene, temp. 1300. M.
Richard del Kechin. H.
Nicholas de la Kechyn: Patent Roll, 17 Ric. II. pt. ii.
Johannes del Kechyn, 1379: P. T. Yorks. p. 21.
Johannes del Kychyn, 1379: ibid. p. 142.
Thomas del Kichyn, 1379: ibid. p. 188.
1578. James Kytchen, of London: Reg. Univ. Oxf. vol. ii. pt. ii. p. 81.
1616. Abel Kitchen, of Bristol: ibid. p. 356.
London (1874), 9, 6, 8; West Rid. Court Dir., 4, 2, 5; Philadelphia, 27, 2, 0; New York, 10, 0, 10.

Kitchener, Kitchiner.—Occup. 'the kitchener,' equivalent to Kitchingman (q.v.), and v. Kitchen.

'John Silvester, *kychynner*,' a member of the dissolved Abbey of Hayles, co. Glouc.: Rudder's Hist. Glouc. p. 487.
Adam Kitener (?), 1379: P. T. Yorks. p. 165.
1569. Married—Edward Kychener and Mary Pyers: Marriage Lic. (London), p. 43.
1618. Thomas Kechener, co. Devon: Reg. Univ. Oxf. vol. ii. pt. ii. p. 371.
1716. Married—John Kitchenner and Eliz. Hare: St. Jas. Clerkenwell, ii. 239.
London (1874), 2, 3.

Kitchingman, Kitchingham, Kitchenman. — Occup. 'the kitchen-man,' a scullion, a cook. The corrupted Kitchingham is more common in the reverse case; cf. Deadman and Swetman for Debenham and Swetenham.

Willelmus Kychynman, 1379: P. T. Yorks. p. 203.
Johannes Kychynman, 1379: ibid.
Beatrix Kychynman, 1379: ibid. p. 204.
Hugo Kychynman, 1379: ibid. p. 206.

Four Kychynmans occur also on p. 209, resident in the village of 'Colyngham.' The surname is common in Yorkshire records.

1661. Willoughby West and Ester Kitchingman: Marriage Lic. (Canterbury), p. 61.
1666. Thomas Kitchinman and Anne Browne: ibid. p. 123.
London (1874), 2, 1, 0; West Rid. Court Dir., 3, 0, 0; Leeds (Kitchenman), 1; Philadelphia, 0, 0, 21.

Kite. — Nick. 'the kite,' a sobriquet for one of wild, voracious habits; cf. Hawk, Falcon, Sparrow-hawk.

Hugo Kyte, 1379: P. T. Yorks. p. 213.
John Kyte, rector of Wolferton, co. Norf., 1507: FF. ix. 196.
1739. Married — Edward Kite and Phebe Jefferys: St. Antholin (London), p. 150.
1783. — John Kite and Jane Lever: St. Geo. Han. Sq. i. 345.
1790. — Henry Kyte and Jane Sullivan: ibid. ii. 42.
London, 9; Philadelphia, 33.

Kitewild.—Nick. 'wild as a kite' (?); v. Kite.

Jordanus Kitewilde, co. Bucks, 1273. A.

Kitley; v. Kettley.

Kitson, Kidson. — (1) Bapt. 'the son of Christopher,' from nick. Kit, patr. Kitson. (2) Bapt. 'the son of Katherine,' from nick. Kit. This nick. lasted in the North till the 16th century. I had several in my own registers at Ulverston. We still use the pet Kitty.

Johannes Lund et Kit uxor ejus, 1379: P. T. Yorks. p. 175.
Thomas Ketson, 1379: ibid. p. 170.
Johannes Kytson, 1379: ibid. p. 211.
Alicia Kytson, 1379: P. T. Howdenshire, p. 7.
1579. John Kytson, co. Salop: Reg. Univ. Oxf. vol. ii. pt. ii. p. 86.
1581. Robert Kitson, co. York: ibid. p. 98.
1585. Richard Kitson, or Kidson, co. York: Reg. Univ. Oxf. vol. ii. pt. ii. p. 148.

1590. John Kitson, co. Glouc. : Reg. Univ. Oxf. vol. ii. pt. ii. p. 178.

1746. Married — Richard Wynn and Mary Kitson : St. Geo. Chap. Mayfair, p. 70.

1752. — Thomas Kidson and Mary Bell : ibid. p. 208.

London, 7, 2 ; West Rid. Court Dir., 7, 1 ; Lanc. Court Dir. (Kidson), 4 ; Leeds, 2, 2 ; New York, 5, 1.

Kitt, Kitts.—Bapt. 'the son of Christopher,' from the nick. Kit ; v. Kitson.

Nicholas Kitte, co. Northampton, 1273. A.

William Kitte, co. Camb., ibid.

Osbert Kyt, co. Soms., 1 Edw. III : Kirby's Quest, p. 155.

1621. Buried — Jone Kitts : St. Jas. Clerkenwell, iv. 154.

1667-8. Henry Kitt and Mary Long : Marriage Alleg. (Canterbury), p. 233.

1669. Married — Thomas Rolley and Jane Kitte : St. Jas. Clerkenwell, iii. 169.

Plymouth, 3, 1 ; Boston (U.S.), 0, 4.

Kitten.—Nick. 'the kitten' ; cf. Catt.

William Kytene, co. Oxf., 1273. A.

But cf.

Johanna de Ketyne, 1379 : P. T. Yorks. p. 167.

Nevertheless this *de* may be a misreading of the text, and ought to be *lc*.

Philadelphia, 3.

Kitteringham ; v. Ketteringham.

Kittermaster. — Local, 'of Kidderminster' ; cf. Buckmaster and Killmaster. Lower, quoting Burke's Landed Gentry, shows that the Kittermasters of Meriden, co. Warwick, spelt their name Kydermister in 1543, Kydermaster in 1568, and Kittermaster in 1649 (Patr. Brit. p. 181).

Richard Kidderminster, abbot of Winchcombe, 1498 : Dict. Nat. Biog. (Colet), xi. 323.

1594. John Keedomister, or Keederminster, co. Bucks : Reg. Univ. Oxf. vol. ii. pt. ii. p. 201.

1597. Robert Kederminster, or Kiderminster, co. Bucks : ibid. p. 219.

1663. William Kittermaster and Margaret Harland : Marriage Lic. (Faculty Office), p. 74.

1693. Jonathan Seyton and Hester Kittermaster (co. Warw.) : Marriage Alleg. (Canterbury), p. 257.

F. J. Kittermaster, of Shrewsbury School, has taken an open Scholarship at King's Coll., Cambridge ' : Manchester Courier, Dec. 31, 1887.

Crockford, 1 ; MDB. (co. Warwick), 2.

Kittle. — Bapt. 'the son of Kettle ' (q.v.).

' Robert Ketyll, or Kyttell, sup. for B.A., April, 1513 ' : Reg. Univ. Oxf. i. 86.

1608. Buried—an abortive, the sonne of Francis Scotte, the sonne-in-law to Edward Kittle, dwellinge in Cornhill : St. Peter, Cornhill, i. 163.

1676. Richard Small and — Kittle : Marriage Alleg. (Canterbury), p. 180.

London, 1 ; New York, 10.

Kitto, Kittoe, Kittow.—? Local. A Cornish surname.

John Kittowe and Elizabeth Bland, 1543 : Marriage Lic. (Faculty Office), p. 1.

Tamson (i. e. Thomasine) Kyttowe, 1581 : Reg. St. Columb Major, p. 141.

John, son of Joane Kettoe, 1604 : ibid. p. 201.

James Kettowe, or Kittowe (co. Somerset), Queen's Coll., 1608 : Reg. Univ. Oxf. vol. ii. pt. ii. p. 301.

London, 3, 1, 0 ; Cornwall Dir. (Farmers), 3, 0, 11 ; MDB. (co. Cornwall), 2, 0, 8.

Kitton ; v. Ketton and Kitten, of either which it may be a modification.

Kitts ; v. Kitt.

Knabwell. — Local, 'at the knap-well,' i.e. the well at the hilltop ; v. Knap.

Robert de Cnapwell, 1273. A. John de Cnabwelle, ibid.

Knaggs.—Local, 'at the knaggs' or 'knagg,' from residence thereby. A Yorkshire surname, as might be expected. 'Knag, the rugged top of a hill. North' (Halliwell). 'Knaggs, pointed rocks, or rugged tops of hills ' (Brockett).

1620-1. Thomas Reekes and Joane Knagges : Marriage Lic. (London), ii. 96.

1637. Buried — Prina, d. William Knagge : St. Jas. Clerkenwell, iv. 231.

1665. — Alice Knagg : ibid. iv. 365.

London, 3 ; Hull, 3 ; MDB. (N. Rid. Yorks), 6 ; New York, 1.

Knapman.—Local, 'the knapman,' the man on the knap or hilltop, from residence thereon (v. Knapp) ; cf. Bridgman, &c. A well-known Devonshire surname.

James Knapman. Z.

William Knapman. ZZ.

1601. James Knapman, co. Devon : Reg. Univ. Oxf. vol. ii. pt. ii. p. 246.

1607-8. John Knapman, co. Devon, Exeter Coll. : ibid. p. 300.

1648. Married—Richard Hill and Eliz. Knapman : St. Michael, Cornhill, p. 30.

1799. — William Knapman and Susanna Davis : St. Geo. Han. Sq. ii. 211.

London, 3 ; Plymouth, 4 ; MDB. (co. Devon), 14.

Knapp.—Local, 'at the knap,' a summit, a hilltop, from residence thereon. ' Some high knap or tuft of a mountaine' : Holland, trans. of Pliny, bk. xi. c. 10 (v. Skeat on Knop). 'Knap, a hillocke, or knap of a hill' : Cotgrave. Cf. *knop* (Exod. xxv. 31), the earlier form of *knob*, a round protuberance. So *knab* or *nab* for *knap*. ' Nab, the summit of an eminence. North' (Halliwell). v. Knabwell.

John Cnape, co. Camb., 1273. A.

John Knapp, co. Bucks, ibid.

Capella de la Cnappe. DD.

Margaret atte Cnappe, co. Soms., 1 Edw. III : Kirby's Quest, p. 206.

Johannes Knape, 1379 : P. T. Yorks. p. 15.

Johannes Knaype, 1379 : ibid. p. 200.

1553-4. Christopher Nappe and Eliz. Kemyes : Marriage Lic. (London), i. 14.

1681. Bapt.—Robert, s. Robert Knapp : St. Jas. Clerkenwell, i. 206.

London, 9 ; Philadelphia, 52.

Knapper.—Local, 'the knapper,' i.e. the man on the hilltop ; cf. Bridger, and v. Knapp.

William Knapper. G.

1710. Married—Isaac Beckett and Ann Knaper : St. Jas. Clerkenwell, iii. 232.

1730. — John Gray and Jane Knopper : St. Geo. Chap. Mayfair, p. 319.

New York, 1 ; Philadelphia, 1.

Knapton, Napton. — Local, ' of Knapton,' i.e. the town on the knap, (1) a township in the parish of Acomb, W. Rid. Yorks ; (2) a township in the parish of Wintringham, E. Rid. Yorks ; (3) a parish in co. Norfolk, three miles from North Walsham ; v. Knapp and Town.

Estrilda de Knapeton, co. Norf., 1273. A.

Thomas de Cnapeton, co. Suff., ibid.

Adam de Knapeton, of Norwich, 1292 : ibid. iv. 386.

William Knapton, co. York. W. 16.

Elisabet de Knapton, 1379 : P. T. Yorks. p. 212.

Thomas Knapton, 1379 : ibid. p. 125.

Clement de Knapton, co. Norf., 1386 : FF. iv. 122.

1586. Albinus Knapton, co. Wilts : Reg. Univ. Oxf. vol. ii. pt. ii. p. 157.

1759. Married—John Nickelson and Mary Knapton : St. Geo. Han. Sq. i. 85

1790. Married—Bartholomew Napton and Susanna Hine: Reg. Univ. Oxf. vol. ii. pt. ii. p. 47.

London, 0, 1; Boston (U.S.), 6, 0.

Knatchbull.—I cannot classify this singular surname. Mr. Lower says (quoting Shirley's Noble and Gentle Men), 'The first recorded ancestor of the family is John Knatchbull, who had lands in the parish of Lymne, co. Kent, in the reign of Edward III, and there some of the name remained down to the time of Charles I. The main branch were at Mersham-Hatch, in the same county, by purchase temp. Henry VI, and there the present baronet yet resides' (Patr. Brit. p. 181).

1592. Buried — Thomas, s. Richard Nashbull, of Madehatche, co. Kent: St. Michael, Cornhill, p. 204.

1613. Married — George Knatchbull and Jone Gilbarde: Canterbury Cath. p. 55.

1667. Richard Sheafe and Mary Knatchbull, of Cranbrook, co. Kent: Marriage Lic. (Faculty Office), p. 98.

1734. Married — Edward Hearst, of New Sarum, and Alicia Knatchbull, of Mersham, co. Kent: St. Geo. Han. Sq. i.13.

London, 1; MDB. (co. Kent), 4.

Knave.—Occup. 'the knave,' i.e. a servant, a lad; v. Goodknave.

Adam le Cnave, co. Soms., 1 Edw. III: Kirby's Quest, p. 259.

Kneebone.—? Local. A Cornish name.

Jane, d. of Grace Kneebone, 1585: Reg. St. Columb Major, p. 13.

Anthony Kneebone, of Gwenapp, 1753: ibid. p. 112.

1681. Married—William Holmes and Mary Kneebone: St. Jas. Clerkenwell, iii. 190.

1692. Amor Steffe and Susan Kneebone: Marriage Alleg. (Canterbury), p. 232.

1796. Married—William Pummis and Margery Kneebone: St. Geo. Han. Sq. ii. 148.

London, 2; MDB. (co. Cornwall), 2; Cornwall Dir. (Farmers' List), 6.

Kneedler.—Occup.; v. Needler.

Philadelphia, 21.

Kneeshaw.—Local, 'of Kneesall,' a parish in co. Notts, four miles from Ollerton. As is common in such names, the suffix has -aw instead of -all; cf. Shallcross and Shawcross, Lindall and Lindow,

Preesall and Presow, Picthall and Picthaw.

(Ballivus) de Kneshale, co. Notts, 1273. A.

Richard de Knewshale, rector of Beetley, co. Norf., 1341: FF. ix. 467.

Ricardus Knesall, 1379: P. T. Yorks. p. 210.

Lanc. Court Dir. (1887), 1; Liverpool, 2; Philadelphia, 1.

Knell, Knill.—Local, 'of Knill,' a parish in co. Hereford, three miles from Kingston.

Henry de Knell, co. Bedf., Hen. III-Edw. I. K.

Gille de Knille, co. Camb., 1273, A.

Robert de Knille, co. Camb., ibid.

John atte Knyle, co. Soms.: Kirby's Quest, p. 184.

1571-2. John Knell and Margaret Barrell: Marriage Lic. (London), i. 51.

1600. John Knell, co. Kent: Reg. Univ. Oxf. vol. ii. pt. ii. p. 240.

1656. Married —James Knell and Eliz. Berry: Canterbury Cath. p. 58.

London, 4, 6; Crockford, 1, 0; MDB. (co. Hereford), 0, 5; New York, 6, 0.

Kneller.—Occup. 'the kneller,' a bellringer; v. Knowler (1). The surname is English in spite of Sir Godfrey Kneller. Mr. Lower says it was formerly common in East Sussex (Patr. Brit. p. 181). But I cannot for one moment accept the local derivation he suggests.

London, 1; Philadelphia, 3.

Kneresboro. — Local, 'of Knaresborough,' a market-town in the W. Rid. Yorks. The surname seems almost extinct.

Stephen de Knaresburg', co. York, 1273. A.

Thomas de Knaresburg', co. York, ibid.

1583. Thomas Knaresboroughe and Margarett Wytter: Marriage Lic. (London), i. 121.

Philadelphia, 1.

Knevitt, Knyvett. — Local, 'de Knyvet.' I cannot find the place.

Mathew de Knyvet, co. Notts, 1273. A.

Geoffrey Knyfet, co. Camb., ibid.

Thomas Knyvet, co. Essex, ibid.

John de Knevet, co. Norf., temp. 1430: FF. i. 378.

1523. William Knevett, of the Household of our Lord the King, and Katherine Grey: Marriage Lic. (London), p. 3.

Nathaniel Knevet, co. Norf., 1633: FF. xi. 167.

1571. Henry Knevet, London: Reg. Univ. Oxf. vol. ii. pt. ii. p. 51.

1789. Married—Thomas Knevit and Easter Hart: St. Geo. Han. Sq. ii. 19.

London, 1, 1.

Knewstub, Knewstubb.—Local, 'of Knewstubb,' a spot in or near the parish of Ravenstonedale, co. Westm. The suffix is -stubb; v. Stubbs.

Thomas Knewstupp, his wife, and 2 children: Hist. and Traditions of Mallerstang Forest, co. Westm., W. Nicholls, p. 95.

John Knewstupp and his mother: ibid. p. 97.

John Knewstupp and 2 children: ibid.

1696. Buried—Ann Knewstub: St. Michael, Cornhill, p. 275.

1698. — Mary Knewstub: ibid. p. 276.

1734. William Knewstub: Hist. and Traditions of Ravenstonedale, co. Westm., W. Nicholls, p. 116.

— Anthony Knewstub: ibid. p. 117.

London, 1, 1.

Knibb, Knibbs.—Bapt. 'the son of Isabel,' from the nick. Ibb. This became popularly Nib or Nibb, whence the patronymic Nibbs (q.v.). Knibb and Knibbs are variants of Nibbs; cf. Nobbs.

1604-5. William Knebb and Susan Awsten: Marriage Lic. (London), i. 294.

1734. Married — Isaac Knibbs (co. Northampton), and Eliz. Hawkins: St. Antholin (London), p. 146.

1795. — John Colbeck and Susanna Knibb: St. Geo. Han. Sq. ii. 139.

1803. — Henry Knibs and Sarah Rook: ibid. p. 292.

London, 3, 1; Manchester, 1, 1; Birmingham, 3, 1; Boston (U.S.), 0, 1.

Knifesmith, Neasmith, Nasmith.—Occup. 'the knifesmith,' a maker of knives; cf. Cutler. It has been stated as beyond need of evidence that Nasmith and Neasmith are corrupted forms of Nailsmith, a maker of nails. The instances furnished below seem to point strongly in favour of knifesmith. For the other theory I have found no evidence.

1594. Married — Roberte Knysmithe and Eliz. Weekes: St. Michael, Cornhill, p. 15.

1595. Bapt. — Eliz., d. Robert Knysmythe: ibid. p. 99.

The earlier and complete form is found in the Valor Ecclesiasticus, viz. Henry Knyfesmythe (F.). I forgot to note date and page (v. Index). But it will be seen at once by any candid observer that, failing evidence to the contrary,

Neasmith and Nasmith are corruptions of the old Knifesmith. Besides, Nailer (v. Naylar) was the accepted occupative term for a maker of nails.

London, o, 1, 1.

Knifton, Knyfton. — Local, 'of Kniveton,' a parish in co. Derby, near Ashbourn.

John de Knyveton, co. Derby, 20 Edw. I. R.
1605. Gilbert Knyveton : Reg. Univ. Oxf. i. 237.
1630. Married—Thomas Knifton and Katherine Swetna : Reg. Prestbury, co. Ches., p. 274.
Charles Knifton, of Raby, 1685 : Wills at Chester (1681-1700), p. 149.
1788. Married — William Bowerman and Eliz. Knifton : St. Geo. Han. Sq. ii. 4.
London, 1, 0 ; MDB. (co. Somerset), 0, 1.

Knight.—Official, 'the knight,' a man-at-arms, a military follower ; A.S. *cniht*, a servant.

John le Cnitht, co. Suff., 1273. A.
Gilbert le Knyt, co. Camb., ibid.
Roger le Knith, co. Oxf., ibid.
Ellis le Knyght, co. Wilts, ibid.

Other forms in the same registers are Knicht, Knyght, Knict, Kneyt, Knigt, Kniht, Knyth, and Knit.

Roger le Knyt, C. R., 3 Edw. I.
Johannes Knyght', 1379 : P. T. Yorks. p. 21.
Willelmus Kneyte, 1379 : ibid. p. 27.
Thomas Knycht, 1379 : ibid. p. 28.
Willelmus Knygth, 1379 : ibid. p. 76.
1599. Married—Thomas Burves and Jone Knight : St. Antholin (London), p. 40.

A curious Puritan Christian name is seen in the following :

1638. Bapt.—John, s. of Know-God Knight : St. Jas. Clerkenwell, p. 140.

I fear his enemies would pronounce it No-Good !

London, 151 ; Philadelphia, 152.

Knightley, Knightly.—Local, 'of Knightley,' a township in the parish of Gnosall, co. Stafford. The variant Knightly is imitative.

Robert de Knyghstelce, co. Staff., Edw. I.-Edw. III. R.
Robert de Knyghistele, co. Staff., ibid.
1574. Edward Knightlie, co. Northampton : Reg. Univ. Oxf. vol. ii. pt.ii.p.58.
1597-8. Seymour Knightley, co. Northampton : ibid. p. 225.
1698. Thomas Knightley (co. Northampton), and Sarah Mitford : Marriage Lic. (London), ii. 324.

1808. Married—James Knightley and Eliz. Bennett : St. Geo. Han. Sq. ii. 391.
London, 2, 2 ; New York, 1, 0.

Knighton.—Local, 'of Knighton.' (1) West Knighton, a parish in co. Dorset, four miles from Dorchester ; (2) a chapelry in the parish of Lindridge, co. Worcester ; (3) a chapelry in the parish of St. Margaret, Leicester.

Thomas de Knyghton, 1379 : P. T. Yorks. p. 147.
1544. John Alen and Margaret Knyghton : Marriage Lic. (Faculty Office), p. 3.
1583-4. George Knighton and Susan White : Marriage Lic. (London), i. 127.
1688. John Knighton and Eliz. de Champner : Marriage Alleg. (Canterbury), p. 89.
London (1884), 4 ; New York, 3.

Knightson.—Nick. 'the son of the knight' ; cf. Wrightson, Taylorson, Smithson, or Hindson.

Alicia fil. Ricardi Knyghtson, 1379 : P. T. Yorks. p. 217.
1721. Married—William Fareley and Eliz. Knightson : St. Jas. Clerkenwell, iii. 245.

Knill.—Local ; v. Knell.

Knipe.—Local, 'at the knap' (v. Knapp) ; a variant. This North-English surname existed for several centuries in Cartmel parish, North Lancashire. Though it died out there it made its way into the surrounding district. It must be considered a Furness surname.

1597. Elizabeth Knype, of Warton : Lancashire Wills at Richmond (1457-1680), p. 178.
— William Knype, of Cartmel : Stockdale's Annals of Cartmel, p. 34.
1601. Bapt.—Marie, d. Isaac Knypp : St. Mary, Ulverston, p. 91.
1612. Jenkin Knype, of Hawkshead : Lancashire Wills at Richmond (1457-1680), p. 178.
1661. William Knipe, of Grysdale : ibid.
Agnes Knipe, of Town-end, *widow*, 1698 : Wills at Chester (1681-1700), p. 149.
London, 3 ; Liverpool, 1 ; New York, 8.

Knock.—(1) Local, 'atten-oak,' from residence beside some specially prominent oak-tree. The surname at first was Noke or Nock (v. Noakes). Then by imitation it became Knock. (2) Local, 'at the knock,' a hill, a knoll ; Celtic and Gaelic, *cnoc*, 'collis' (Lower).

Tenentes de la Knocke, co. Kent, 1273. A.
1717. Married — Robert Knock and Sarah Keete : Canterbury Cath. p. 73.
1788. — Robert Pattle and Charlotte Knocke : St. Geo. Han. Sq. ii. 7.
1797. — William Taylor and Caroline Knocke : ibid. p. 171.
London, 3 ; Boston (U.S.), 2.

Knocker.—? Local. Like Knowler (2), one who dwelt on a knoll, Knocker may mean one who dwelt on a knock (v. Knock). I cannot suggest any other derivation. But in favour of it is the fact that both Knock and Knocker are Kentish names. This will seem fairly strong evidence to some.

1685. Bapt. — Friswith, d. George Knocker ; St. Antholin (London), p. 102.
1693. Buried — Richard, s. George Knocker : St. John Baptist on Wallbrook, p. 191.
1726. Married—Jacob Thompson and Eliz. Knocker : St. Michael, Cornhill, p. 63.
MDB. (co. Kent), 4 ; New York, 1.

Knoll, Knollys, Knowles, Knolles.—Local, 'at the knoll,' from residence thereon ; M.E. *knol*, a hill, a summit. The final *s* in Knowles, Knollys, &c., may be patronymic, as in Brooks, Styles. Holmes, &c., corresponding to Jones, Williams, &c., in surnames of the baptismal class.

Roger de la Cnolle, co. Devon, 1273. A.
John Cnolle, co. Dorset, ibid.
Robert de la Cnolle, co. Sussex, ibid.
John atte Knolle. B.
Cecilia de Knolle, 1379 : P. T. Yorks. p. 123.
Johannes Knoll', 1379 : ibid. p. 160.
Thomas de Knoll', 1379 : ibid. p. 276.
Robert de Knollys, 1397 : Preston Guild Rolls, p. 6.
1583. Bapt. — Eliz., d. William Knowlles : St. Jas. Clerkenwell, i. 15.
1598-9. Married—Robert Knowels and Mary Wryght : St. Dionis Backchurch, p. 14.
London, 1, 1, 40, 0 ; Philadelphia, 11, 0, 81, 1.

Knoller, Knollman ; v. Knowler.

Philadelphia, 1, 1.

Knollys.—Local ; v. Knoll.

Knope, Knopp, Knop. — Local, 'at the knop,' from residence thereon ; v. Knapp and Knipe.

1771. Married—John Greenfield and Betty Knopp : St. Geo. Han. Sq. i. 212.
London, 1, 0, 0 ; Philadelphia, 0, 4, 3.

Knott, Knotts.—(1) Local, 'at the knot,' the summit of a rocky hill, from residence thereon; cf. Knapp, Knaggs, and Knoll, all of similar origin. (2) Bapt. 'the son of Cnut' (Canute). (3) Nick.; v. Nott.

Richard Knotte, London, 1273. A. Peter Cnotte, co. Salop, ibid. Robertus Knotte, 1379: P. T. Yorks. p. 46.
Ricardus Notte, 1379: ibid. p. 70.
Isabella Notte, 1379: ibid. p. 71.
Thomas Knot, 1379: ibid. p. 224.
1662. Married—James Rokeby and Judith Knott: St. Dionis Backchurch, p. 37.
London, 20, 3; Philadelphia, 21, 0.

Knowell, Knoell.—Bapt. 'the son of Nowell'; v. Nowell and Knowlson.

1655. Married — John Knouell and Abigal Straley: St. Dionis Backchurch, p. 31.
MDB. (co. Somerset), 1, 0; Philadelphia, 0, 4.

Knowlden; v. Knowlton.

Knowler, Knowlman.—(1) Occup. 'the knowler' or 'knowlman,' a bellringer, a chimer; v. Ringer, Bellringer. (2) Local, 'one who dwelt on a knoll'; v. Knoll and Knocker.

'Carillonneur, a chymer, or knowler of bels': Cotgrave's Dict. 1611.
'Where bells have knolled to church': As You Like It, ii. 7. 114.
1616. Buried—Wilmore Knowleman, servant to Mr. Norman Paynter: St. Peter, Cornhill, i. 172.
— John Knowler, co. Kent: Reg. Univ. Oxf. vol. ii. pt. ii. p. 348.
1618. Richard Knoller, co. Kent: ibid. p. 375.
1691. Married—George Knowler and Bridget Foucke: St. Dionis Backchurch, p. 42.
1743. Bapt.—Ann, d. John Knowler, recorder of this city: Canterbury Cath. p. 28.
1770. Married—Henry, Lord Digby and Mary Knowler: St. Geo. Han. Sq. i. 202.
1805. — William Knowler and Hannah Butcher: ibid. ii. 317.
London, 3, 2; MDB. (co. Devon), 0, 3; New York, 0, 1.

Knowles, Knowlys.—Local; v. Knoll.

Walter atte Cnolle, co. Soms., 1 Edw. III: Kirby's Quest, p. 232.
Roger de Knolle, co. Soms., 1 Edw. III: ibid. p. 245.
New York, 27, 0.

Knowlman; v. Knowler.

Knowlson.—(1) Bapt. 'the son of Olive' or 'Oliver,' from the nick. Noll, patronymic Nollson; cf. Towler for Toller, or Toulson for Tolson, or Coulson for Colson. (2) Bapt. 'the son of Nowell' or Noel'; v. Noel.

Alexander Nouelson, Pardons Roll, 6 Ric. II.

Of these two derivations the last must be accepted as the more probable, as possessing evidence. But it must not be forgotten that the first is in strict accordance with rule; cf. Nibbs, Nobbs, Nabbs, Nopps, &c. In either case the initial *K* is imitative of the local Knowles, q.v.

1757. Married—Richard Nowlson and Margaret Wilcocks: St. Geo. Han. Sq. i. 71.
York, 4; London, 1; MDB. (N. Rid. Yorks), 5.

Knowlton, Knowlden.—Local, 'of Knowlton,' a parish in co. Kent. There seems to be little doubt that Knowlden is a lazily pronounced variant. Knowlton has flourished for some time in the United States. Various small spots would naturally bear the name; v. Knowles and Town.

Richard de Knolton, co. Soms., 1 Edw. III: Kirby's Quest, p. 253.

The two following Kentish entries are strongly conclusive of the view that Knowlden is a variant of Knowlton:

1658. Married—Thomas Godfrey and Anne Knowlden: Canterbury Cath. p. 59.
1665. — John Smyth and Mary Knolden: ibid. p. 60.
1776. — William Knowlton and Mary Howse: St. Geo. Han. Sq. i. 261.
1799. — Francis Knowlton and Sarah Widley: ibid. ii. 196.
London, 0, 4; Worcester (U.S.), 20, 0; New York, 19, 0.

Knowsley.—Local, 'of Knowsley,' a township in the parish of Huyton, co. Lanc., three miles from Prescot.

1570. Bapt. — William, s. Robert Knowesley: St. Jas. Clerkenwell, i. 6.
1585. Thomas Steere and Isabell Knowsley, d. William Knowsley, late of Denbigh, in Wales: Marriage Lic. (London), i. 142.

1586-7. 'Henry Knowsley, or Knousley, co. Denbigh: Reg. Univ. Oxf. vol. ii. pt. ii. p. 157.
James Knowsley, of the city of Chester, 1689: Wills at Chester (1681-1700), p. 150.
Plymouth, 2; Exeter, 1.

Knox. — Local, 'of Knocks,' from residence on the lands of Knocks or Knox, co. Renfrew. The Knoxes were of that ilk at an early period, and sometimes wrote themselves of Ranfurly, whence the family of Knox, earls of Ranfurly in Ireland. The great Reformer was of this family (Lower's Patr. Brit. p. 182).

London, 18; Boston (U.S.), 44.

Knyfton; v. Knifton.

Knyvett; v. Knevitt.

Kohn.—Offic. 'the cohen' or priest (Hebrew). A German immigrant.

London, 3; Philadelphia, 45.

Kortright. — ?

Worcestershire Court Dir., 1; New York, 1.

Kramer, Kramar, Kreamer, Kreemer, Kremer.—Occup.; v. Creamer.

London, 1, 0, 0, 0, 0; Philadelphia, 98, 9, 16, 1, 9.

Kripps, Krips; v. Cripps. These are American variants.

Philadelphia, 3, 8.

Kyffin.— ? Bapt. 'the son of Kyffin' (?), seemingly a Welsh personal name, perhaps a variant of Griffin.

1586. Lewis Kyffin, co. Denbigh: Reg. Univ. Oxf. vol. ii. pt. ii. p. 153.
1590. John Kyffin, co. Salop: ibid. p. 178.
1620. Cadwalader Kyffin, Hart-Hall: ibid. i. 293.
1622. Bapt.—Annis, d. Robart Kiffen: St. Jas. Clerkenwell, i. 93.
1639. William Marsh and Anne Kiffin: Marriage Lic. (London), ii. 243.
London, 1; MDB. (co. Denbigh), 5; (co. Carnarvon), 4; Philadelphia, 1; Liverpool, 1.

Kyme; v. Kime.

Kynaston, Kynston, Keniston.—Local 'of Kynaston.' I

cannot find the spot; but it is a Shropshire surname.

Richard de Kynestan, co. Notts, Hen. III-Edw. I. K.
1610. Buried—Anne Byrtles, of Byrtles. A footnote says, 'daughter of Roger Kynaston, of Lightwick, co. Salop': Reg. Prestbury, co. Ches., p. 187.

1510. Bapt. — Thomas, s. Thomas Kynaston : St. Peter, Cornhill, i. 22.
1583. — William, s. Thomas Kynaston : ibid. p. 26.
Charles Kynston, *tripe dresser*, 94, Hill Street, Birmingham : Birmingham Directory (1872).
MDB. (co. Surrey), 2, 0, 0; (co. Salop), 7, 0, 0; London, 4, 0, 2.

Kynder ; v. Kinder.

Kynman ; v. Kinmond.

Kynnersley ; v. Kinnersley.

Kyte.—Nick.; v. Kite.

Oxford, 1 ; Boston (U.S.), 3.

L

Labern, Laborn.—Local ; v. Layburn.

Labourer. — Occup. ' the labourer'; cf. Workman, Tasker, &c. I do not think this surname now exists, but it reached the 16th century. v. Labrey.

Avicia Laborer, 1379 : P. T. Yorks. p. 219.
Isabel Laberer, c. 1560. ZZ.
Robert Laborer, ibid.
1618. William Laborer, London : Reg. Univ. Oxf. vol. ii. pt. ii. p. 369.

Labrey, Labbree, Labrie.—Occup. ' the labourer,' q.v. I suspect this is the true origin of this curious surname. Indeed, the following three entries seem conclusive on the point :

Thomas Laborer, Over Burrow, 1599 : Lancashire Wills at Richmond (1457-1680), p. 179.
John Labray, of Burton in Kendall, 1645 : ibid.
Thomas Labrey, of Burton, 1665 : ibid.

The following, too, shows the half-stage :

William Laboura, of Brows in Midleton, 1710 : ibid. (1681-1748), p. 161.

Thus the several stages would be : Laborer, Labberer, Labbere, Labrey, or Labbree ;. v. Labourer, for earlier instances.

Manchester, 2, 0, 0 ; Philadelphia, 0, 3, 0 ; New York, 3, 0, 1.

Lach, Lache.—Local, ' at the lache,' from residence beside a lache or lake. No doubt Lache as a surname is lost in Leach, and has materially helped to swell the large list in the Lancashire and Cheshire directories. In proof of this, v. Blackleach, i.e. ' the black lache or lake.'

Henry del Lach, Preston, 1397: Preston Guild Rolls, p. 6.
Richard Lach, *husbandman*, Preston, 1642 : ibid. p. 100.
Thomas Lache, of Great Harwood, *woollen-weaver*, 1590 : Wills at Chester (1545-1620), p. 116.
Edward Lache, of Facit, co. Lanc., 1603 : ibid.
George Lach, of Bretton, co. Flint, 1630 : ibid. (1621-50), p. 132.
New York, 3, 0 ; Philadelphia, 2, 0.

Lack.—Local, ' at the lake,' from residence thereby ; a variant ; cf. the French Du Lac, and v. Lach and Lake.

William Lack, co. Soms., 1 Edw. III : Kirby's Quest, p. 223.
William Lack, jun., co. Soms., 1 Edw. III : ibid.
1682. Samuel Holleway and Ann Lacke : Marriage Alleg. (Canterbury), p. 113.
1800. Married—John Lack and Frances Moss Parry : St. Geo. Han. Sq. ii. 220.
1807. — Thomas Lack and Eliz. Yeatman : ibid. p. 376.
London, 13 ; Philadelphia, 2 ; New York, 4.

Lackey, Lackie. —? ——. Mr. Lower says, ' A personal attendant, a footman.' I do not think there is any connexion, but I cannot suggest another derivation.

1750. Married—John Lackie and Rebecca Baxter : St. Geo. Chap. Mayfair, p. 180.
London, 1, 0 ; Philadelphia, 20, 1.

Lacklove.—Nick. ' lack love.' a cold, phlegmatic man, the opposite of ' full love.'

Simon Lakelove, co. Bedf., 1273. A.

Lacy, Lacey, Lassey, Lassy. —Local, ' de Laci,' from some place of that name in Normandy. Ilbert de Laci (Domesday). The surname has spread widely, and has representatives in every grade of

society. The variants Lassey and Lassy are met by early forms of a similar character.

Gilbert de Lascy, co. Salop, 1273. A. Walter de Laci, co. Salop, ibid.
Robertus Lascy, 1379 : P. T. Yorks. p. 124.
Isabella Lassy, 1379 : ibid.
1571. Peter Lacye and Hester Shawe : Marriage Lic. (London), i. 48.
1761. Married—Thomas Lasey and Mary Vipoint : St. Geo. Han. Sq. i. 107.
London, 16, 17, 0, 0 ; MDB. (West Rid. Yorks), 7, 0, 4, 0 ; Philadelphia, 19, 34, 0, 1.

Ladbrook, Ladbrooke. — Local, ' of Ladbroke,' a parish on the road from Oxford to Coventry, co. Warwick.

Juliana de Lathebroc, co. Oxf., 1273. A.
Henry de Lodbroc, co. Warw., ibid.
1618. Robert Ladbrooke, co. Warw. Reg. Univ. Oxf. vol. ii. pt. ii. p. 368.
1627. Married—Cristofer Martyn and Margret Lagbrooke (sic) : St. Jas. Clerkenwell, iii. 58.
1662. Buried—Thomas Ladbroke, servant to Mr. Savage Barrell, *hosier* : St. Dionis Backchurch, p. 234.
London, 3, 0 ; MDB. (co. Warwick), 0, 1.

Ladbury. — Local, ' of Lathbury,' q.v.

Ladd.—Offic. ' the lad,' i.e. the servant, the young servitor, the page.

Roger Ladde, co. Hunts, 1273. A.
Thomas Ladde, co. Camb., ibid.
John le Ladde, 1322. M.
John le Ladde, C. R., 8 Edw. III.
1587. William Callaway and Joane Lad, *widow* : Marriage Lic. (London), i. 101.
1688. Bapt.—James, son of John Ladd : St. Jas. Clerkenwell, i. 329.
London, 5 ; New York, 15.

Laddington.—Local. A variant of Loddington or Luddington, q.v.
MDB. (co. Northampton), 1.

Lade.—Local, 'at the lade' or 'lathe,' equivalent to Barnes; v. Barne (1). 'Lathe, a barn. North England' (Halliwell). 'Berne, or lathe' (Prompt. Parv.). 'Grangia, lathe, or grange' (Ortus). 'Lathe, *apotheca, horreum*' (Cath. Ang.); v. Leathes.

'Why ne had thou put the capel in the lathe?' Chaucer, The Reeve's Tale.
John de la Lade, co. Lanc., 1273. A.
Richard de la Lade, C. R., 28 Edw. I.
Edmund de la Layde, C. R., 17 Edw. I.
Thomas atte Lathe, C. R., 16 Ric. II.
Hugh de la Lade, Fines Roll, 11 Edw. I.
1729. Buried—Thomas Lade: Canterbury Cathedral, p. 138.
London, 1.

Ladychapman. — Occup. A curious compound; v. Chapman.

William Ladychapman, C. R., 25 Edw. III.

Ladyman.—Occup. 'the lady's man,' i.e. the servant of the lady, i.e. the baron's or squire's wife; cf. Matthewman, Addyman, Priestman, Vickerman. The origin is easily settled by a comparison of the first batch of entries, all but one being recorded in close juxtaposition.

Ricardus Ledyman, 1379: P. T. Yorks. p. 233.
Johanna ye Laydimayden, 1379: ibid. p. 33.
Johannes Serve-ledy, 1379: ibid. p. 231.
Willelmus Masterman, 1379: ibid.
Willelmus Halle-man, 1379: ibid. p. 232.
Alan Ladyman, temp. Edw. II: GGG. p. 286.
1581. John Ladyman and Margarett Collsell · Marriage Lic. (London), i. 102.
1700. Bapt.—Dianah, d. Charles Ladyman: St. Jas. Clerkenwell, i. 389.
1787. Married—Thomas Ladyman and Ann Ludlow: St. Geo. Han. Sq. i. 403. Liverpool, 2.

Laidler, Laddler. — Local. Variants of the Scotch Laidlaw.

1752. Married—James Sams and Jane Ladler: St. Geo. Chap. Mayfair, p. 218.
MDB. (co. Northumberland), 3, 0; (co. Cumberland), 0, 1; New York, 1, 0.

Laird.—Occup. or offic. 'the lord'; v. Lord. A Scotch form; cf. Layard.

1781. Married—John Laird and Eliz. Monk: St. Geo. Han. Sq. i. 318.
1782. — John Laierd and Catherine Jones: ibid. p. 331.
London, 3; New York, 17.

Lait, Layt, Laight.—Local, 'at the lathe' or 'barn' (v. Lade); cf. Leathes.

Thomas atte Lathe, C. R., 16 Ric. II.
Sibota at Layte, 1379: P. T. Yorks. p. 161.
1746. Married—John Russell and Ann Laight: St. Geo. Chap. Mayfair, p. 73.
London, 2, 1, 0; New York, 0, 0, 3.

Laithwaite; v. Lewthwaite.

Lake.—Local, 'at the lake,' from residence thereby; v. Lach and Lack.

William atte Lake, co. Oxf., 1273. A.
William de la Lake, co. Salop, ibid.
William de la Lake, Fines Roll, 11 Edw. I.
Philip atte Lake, co. Soms., 1 Edw. III: Kirby's Quest, p. 257.
William of the Lake, Pardons Roll, 6 Ric. II.
Arthur Lake, co. Southampt., 1588: Reg. Univ. Oxf. vol. ii. pt. ii. p. 165.
1620. Bapt.—Anne, d. Francis Lake: St. Jas. Clerkenwell, i. 87.
London, 33; New York, 23.

Lakeman. — (1) Local, 'of Lakenham,' a parish in co. Norfolk. This corruption is one of many of a similar character; cf. Buckman for Buckenham, Putman for Putnam (Puttenham), Swetman for Swetnam (Swetenham), Deadman for Debnam (Debenham), &c. Lower's suggestion that it means the lake man, the man who lived by the lake, is not supported by any proof. (2) ? Bapt. 'the son of Lacman,' an old personal name. Lacman assisted Duke Richard of Normandy against Odo of Chartres (Freeman, Norm. Conq. i. 456). Lacman was king of Man, 1075–1093 (ibid. ii. 632). A Scandinavian name corresponding to Engl. Lawman. But I can find no corroborative evidence in the rolls of the 12th, 13th, and 14th centuries.

Reginald de Lakeham, co. Norf., 1273. A.
Geoffrey de Lakenham, co. Herts, 20 Edw. I. R.
Simon de Lakenham, vicar of Tibenham, co. Norf., 1394: FF. v. 278.
William Lakenham, rector of South Rungton, co. Norf., 1511: ibid. vii. 402.

For another probable variant of Lakenham, v. Larkman.

London, 3; New York, 1; Boston (U.S.), 11.

Lamacraft.—Local, 'of Lambcroft,' a hamlet in the parish of Kelsterne, co. Lincoln. For suffix -*craft* instead of -*croft*, v. Craft and Crafter. There is one drawback to this derivation. Devonshire seems to be the home of the name. Probably there is or was a Lambcroft in that country. The second *a* is intrusive; cf. Ottaway and Greenaway for Ottway and Greenway.

1647. Bapt.—Mary, d. Michael Lamcroft: St. Jas. Clerkenwell, i. 167.
1648. — Christopher, s. Michael Lamecraft: ibid. p. 169.
London, 1; MDB. (co. Devon), 1; Upton Pyne (Devon), 2; Exeter, 1.

Lamb, Lambe.—(1) Nick. 'the lamb'; cf. Bull, Bullock, Fox. Affixed to one of a mild, inoffensive character.

William le Lambe, co. Camb., 1273. A.
Richard le Lam', co. Northampt., ibid.
Ingrida Lomb, co. Hunts, ibid.

(2) Bapt. 'the son of Lambert,' from Lamb the nick., whence such diminutives as Lamb-in and Lambkin (q.v.) were found.

1558. William Justyce and Jane Lambe: Marriage Lic. (London), i. 19.
1665. Buried—Ann Lam, servant to Mr. Clark: St. Dionis Backchurch, p. 236.
London, 57, 4; New York, 60, 0; Philadelphia, 76, 1.

Lambard, Lambarde.—Bapt. 'the son of Lambert,' q.v. It might be thought that this was a corrupted form of Lombard (q.v.), a native of Lombardy, but the evidence is entirely in favour of the personal name Lambert; cf. Hibbard for Hibbert. For a second origin, v. Lambert (1), and cf. Coward for Cowherd.

Hugo Lambard, co. York, 1273. A.

Lambert Godfrey, a local justice, thus describes himself:

'Lambarde Godfrey, 1654, Maidstone, co. Kent': Burn's History of Parish Registers, p. 168.
1581. Anthony Lambarte, *silk weaver*, and Awdrie Stone: Marriage Lic. (London), p. 102.
1596. William Lambard, co. Bucks: Reg. Univ. Oxf. vol. ii. pt. ii. p. 216.
1764. Married—William Lambart and Ann Batty: St. Geo. Han. Sq. i. 138.

1784. Married—John Hallward and Mary Lambard: St. Geo. Han. Sq. i. 364. London, 1, 0; MDB. (co. Kent), 1, 2; New York, 1, 0.

Lambelet. — Bapt. 'the son of Lambert,' from the nick. Lamb (q.v.), and dim. Lambelot; cf. Hewlett and Ablett for Hughelot and Abelot.

1772. Married—John Lambelet and Sarah Starbuck: St. Geo. Han. Sq. i. 223.
New York, 1.

Lambert. — (1) Occup. 'the lamb-herd'; cf. Calvert, Coward, Stoddart, Swinnart, and Shepherd; v. Hind. Most unquestionably many of our Lamberts represent the occupation of lamb-herd. The Yorkshire Calverts all stand for the old occupative calveherd.

Johannes le Lambehirde, 1310: Whitaker's Craven, p. 462.
John Lambherde, C. R., 5 Edw. IV.
Johannes Lamberd, 1379: P. T. Yorks. p. 272.
Thomas Lambhyrd, 1379: ibid.

The two last named are set down together.

Willelmus Lamhird, 1379: P. T. Yorks. p. 183.
Barbara Lamheard, 1596: St. Dionis Backchurch (London), p. 89.

(2) Bapt. 'the son of Lambert.'
Lambert Suet, C. R., 36 Hen. III.
Adam fil. Lamberti, co. Linc., 1273. A.
Roger Lamberd, co. Norf., ibid.
Stephen Lambert, co. Oxf., ibid.
William Lambryt, co. Hunts, ibid.
London, 77; New York, 66.

Lambertson, Lamberson.— Bapt. 'the son of Lambert.' I am not certain whether or not this surname still exists in England.

John Lambertson, son of Nicholas Lambertson, 1603, co. Lanc.: Exchequer Depositions, L. & C. R. S. p. 11.

The above lived at Warton, Lancaster. A century later we find the name, slightly abbreviated, in a neighbouring parish:

Thomas Lamberson, of Bolton-le-Sands, 1715: Lancashire Wills at Richmond (1681–1748), p. 162.
John Lambertson, of Warton, 1647: Lancashire Wills at Richmond (1457–1680), p. 180.
Agnes Lambertson, of Bolton-le-Sands, 1661: ibid.
George Lamberson, of Warton, 1637: ibid.

1559. Buried—Richard Lamerson: St. Peter, Cornhill, i. 114.
New York, 1, 4.

Lambeth, Lamberth, Lambirth.—Local, 'of Lambeth,' a parish in co. Surrey.

Richard de Lambeth, citizen of London, 5 Edw. III: FF. x. 10.
1786. Married—Thomas Lamberth and Esther Hagar: St. Geo. Han. Sq. i. 394.
1789. — William Ward and Abigail Lambeth: ibid. ii. 18.
1796. — William Gray and Mary Lambeth: ibid. p. 158.
London, 2, 2, 0; Boston (U.S.), 0, 0, 3.

Lambin, Lampin, Lamin, Laming, Lammin, Lamming, Lamping. — Bapt. 'the son of Lambert,' from the nick. Lamb and dim. Lamb-in; cf. viol-in, Rob-in, Col-in. The g in Laming, &c., is excrescent (cf. Jennings), and the p for b in Lampin is a common exchange; cf. Lampson and Lampett.

Lambyn Clay played before the King at Westminster, at the great festival in 1306 (Popular Music of the Olden Time, Chappell, i. 29). The Flemish Lambert had a great influence on English nomenclature for a time, nearly as great, in fact, as Baldwin.

John Lambyn, co. Camb., 1273. A.
Henry Lambin, London, 20 Edw. I. R.
Edmund Lambin, London, ibid.
William Lambyn, 1379: P. T. Yorks. p. 48.

Later the b has been dropped, and Laming or Lamming are the usual forms, especially in co. Lincoln, where Lambert (owing to Flemish immigration) was exceedingly common in the surname period. As an interesting proof of this, v. Lammiman.

1683. Married—Roger Laming and Rachel Ball: St. Michael, Cornhill, p. 43.
London, 1, 0, 0, 6, 1, 1, 1; MDB. (Lincoln), 0, 0, 0, 8, 3, 6, 0; Boston (U.S.) (Laming), 3.

Lambkin, Lampkin, Lambking, Lamkin.—Bapt. 'the son of Lambert,' from the nick. Lamb and dim. Lamb-kin. A Flemish introduction, no doubt; cf. Wilkin, Simpkin, &c. The g in Lambking is an excrescence, as in Jennings.

Lambekin de Lamburne, London, 1273. A.

Lambekin de Carsell, London, ibid.
Lamkynus de Braban, 1379: P. T. Yorks. p. 250.
Lambekyn fil. Eli. C.
Lamkyn Loker. O.
Lambekin Taborer: Wardrobe Account, 48 Edw. III–1 Ric. II. 41/10.
1608–9. William Money and Christian Lamkin: Marriage Lic. (London), i. 311.
1643. Married—Henry Palmer and Eleanor Lamkin: St. Dionis Backchurch, p. 24.
Philadelphia, 0, 0, 1, 0; Boston (U.S.), 0, 0, 0, 4.

Lambole, Lamboll, Lamble.—Local, 'of Lampole.' I do not know where the locality is. Of course the suffix is -pole = pool.

John Lampole, co. Norf., 1366: FF. vii. 242.

The final d in the following name is an excrescence:

1610. John Lambold, co. Berks: Reg. Univ. Oxf. vol. ii. pt. ii. p. 317.
1797. Married—Richard Lamble and Mary Weston: St. Geo. Han. Sq. ii. 163.
1807. — James Bush and Rebecca Lambole: ibid. p. 369.
London, 1, 1, 1.

Lamborn, Lambourn, Lambourne.—Local, 'of Lambourn,' (1) a parish in co. Berks, near Hungerford; (2) a parish in co. Essex, near Romford (for suffix, v. Burn).

William de Lamburne, co. Suff., 1273. A.
Alicia de Lamburne, co. Oxf., ibid.
Lambekin de Lamburne, London, ibid.
John de Lamborne, co. Soms., 1 Edw. III: Kirby's Quest, p. 85.
1525–6. John Lamburn and Alice —— (blank): Marriage Lic. (London), i. 5.
1583. William Vincent and Anne Lamborne (co. Bucks): ibid. p. 125.
1663. Henry Goddard and Margaret Lamburne: Marriage Alleg. (Canterbury), p. 87.
London, 1, 1, 0; MDB. (co. Bucks), 0, 2, 1; (co. Oxford), 2, 0, 1; Philadelphia, 2, 0, 0.

Lambshead, Lamzead. — ? Local. 'A Scottish local surname' (Lower). This may be so, but all my directory examples are from cos. Devon and Cornwall; cf. Sheepshead. Lamzead is a curious variant.

Agnes Lambesheved, co. Hunts, 1273. A.
Ilsington (co. Devon), 4, 0; MDB. (co. Devon), 4, 1.

Lambson, Lampson, Lamson.—Bapt. 'the son of Lambert,' from Lamb, the popular nick. of Lambert; v. Lambertson.

Godwin Lambesune, co. Berks, Hen. III-Edw. I. K.
Johannes Lambeson, 1379: P. T. Yorks. p. 253.
Ricardus Lambeson, 1379: ibid.
Thomas Lamson, C. R., 4 Edw. IV.
William Lampson, temp. Eliz. ZZ.
Edward Lamson. FF.
1626. Married—Clement Lamson and Francis Spinke: St. Michael, Cornhill, p. 24.
1680. Buried—Thomas Lambson, *mariner*: St. Dionis Backchurch, p. 256.
1770. Married—George Lamson and Catherine Lovett: St. Geo. Han. Sq. i. 202.
London, 2, 1, 1; Boston (U.S.), 0, 1, 32.

Lambton, Lampton.—Local, 'of Lambton,' a township in the parish of Chester-le-Street, co. Durham.

1461. William Lambton, master of Balliol College: Reg. Univ. Oxf. i. 26.
1663. Ralph Marshall and Isabell Lambton: Marriage Lic. (Faculty Office), p. 75.
1732. Married—Edward Lambton and Harriet Santlow: St. Jas. Clerkenwell, iii. 260.
MDB. (North Rid. Yorks), 1, 0; (co. Durham), 0, 1.

Lamerton.—Local, 'of Lamerton,' a parish in co. Devon, three miles from Tavistock.

MDB. (co. Cornwall), 2; London, 1.

Lamin, Laming; v. Lambin.

Lamkin; v. Lambkin.

Lammas.—Local, 'of Lammas,' a parish in dioc. of Norwich. Not from the season or festival of Lammas, as is the case with Christmas, Nowell, Pentecost, and Whitsunday, q.v. The first three instances probably concern the same individual.

Richard de Lammesse, London, 1273. A.
Richard Lammasse, co. Camb., ibid.
Richard de Lamnesse, co. Camb., ibid.
Richard de Lammesse, prior of Austin Friars, Norwich, 1367: FF. iv. 91.
Thomas Lammas, co. Norf.: FF.
Daniel Lammas, 1620: St. Mary Aldermary, p. 14.
1642. Married—John Lamas and Sara Donaldson: St. Jas. Clerkenwell, i. 75.
London, 2; Oxford, 3; MDB. (Norfolk), 1.

Lammiman, Lamminam, Lamyman. — Occup. 'the man of Lammin,' i.e. Lambert's servant.

All these forms are peculiar to co. Lincoln, where Lammin, Lamin, and Lamming are also common; cf. Matthewman, Addyman, Ladyman, &c. This class of surname is largely represented in our directories. Lambert, swelled by Flemish immigration, was a very familiar fontal name in the Eastern Counties; v. Lambin.

1542. Buried—Maye Lamymam (sic): St. Peter, Cornhill, i. 106.
MDB. (Lincoln), 3, 1, 8.

Lammin(g; v. Lambin.

Lampard, Lampert. — (1) Bapt. 'the son of Lambert,' q.v. (2) Local, 'of Lamport,' q.v.

1620. Richard Crolley and Eliz. Lampert: Marriage Lic. (London), p. 94.
1683. John Lampard and Ann Cockquerell: Marriage Alleg. (Canterbury), p. 146.
1745. Bapt.—John, s. Thomas Lampard: Reg. Stourton, co. Wilts, p. 30.
1770. — Edward, s. Thomas Lampard: ibid. p. 37.
London, 4, 1; Boston (U.S.), 5, 0.

Lampet, Lampitt. — Local, 'de Lampet.' I cannot find the spot. Probably it lies in Normandy.

1356. William de Lampet: FF. v. 328.
1444. Ralph Lampet, bailiff of Yarmouth: ibid. xi. 325.
'To Julian Lampit, recluse at Carhoe, 10s.,' Will of Sir Thomas Erpingham, 1427: ibid. iv. 39.
1621. William Lampit, co. Worc.: Reg. Univ. Oxf. vol. ii. pt. ii. p. 400.
The Vicar of Ulverston, William Lampett, was one of the dispossessed ministers in 1662. Probably the last entry refers to the same individual.
Leamington, 1, 0; MDB. (co. Essex), 1, 0; (co. Worc.), 0, 3.

Lampin(g.—Bapt.; v. Lambin.

Lampkin; v. Lambkin.

Lamplough, Lamplugh. — Local, 'of Lamplugh,' a parish in co. Cumberland.

Robert de Lamplugh, temp. Hen. II: E. and F. (co. Cumb.), p. 29.
Adam de Lamplugh, temp. Hen. John: ibid.
Johannes de Lamplogh, co. Cumb., 1319. M.
George Lamplugh, or Lampleughe, co. Cumb., 1588: Reg. Univ. Oxf. vol. ii. pt. ii. p. 164.
1655-6. Married—Thomas Lamplugh and Katherine Meuerell: St. Dionis Backchurch, p. 31.

London, 4, 1; MDB. (East Rid. Yorks), 10, 8; Philadelphia, 0, 3.

Lamport, Lampert.—Local, (1) 'of Lamport,' a parish in dioc. of Peterborough; (2) 'of Landport,' a parish in dioc. of Winchester. Lower adds, 'An estate now called Landport at Lewes, Sussex, had owners called Lamport, temp. Edward III.' One instance below agrees with this statement.

Richard de Lamport, co. Wilts, 1273. A.
Walter Lamport, co. Sussex, ibid.
1799. Married—Joseph Hughes and Eliz. Lamport: St. Geo. Han. Sq. ii. 33.
London, 1, 1; MDB. (co. Surrey), 2, 0; New York, 2, 4.

Lamprey, Lampray.—Local, 'of Lamprey,' evidently a Devonshire name. No more a fish-name than is Salmon, or Chubb, or Spratt, or Herring. The same individual is thus referred to:

William de Lanteprey, co. Devon, 1273. A.
William Lampreye, co. Devon, ibid.
Simon de Lampree, co. Devon, Hen. III-Edw. I. K.
Devon Court Dir., 1, 0; MDB. (co. Warwick), 0, 1; Boston (U.S.), 11, 0.

Lampson, Lamson.—Bapt.; v. Lambson.

Lamyman; v. Lammiman.

Lancashire. — Local, 'from Lancashire'; cf. Wiltshire, Derbyshire, &c. Oddly enough we often find these county names well represented in the very shires which the bearers had left to seek their fortunes. The explanation is, these wanderers did not go far, probably over the border only, into the next county, and their sons or grandsons were likely to return, bearing the surname that had been given to them in the place of their brief sojourn.

1604. Robert Lancashire, of Syddall: Wills at Chester (1545-1620), p. 117.
1625. James Lancashire, of Blakeley: ibid. (1621-50), p. 132.
1693. Bapt.—Ellen, d. Robert Lankishire: St. Antholin (London), p. 108.
London, 1; Manchester, 9.

Lancaster, Lankester. — Local, 'of Lancaster,' the well-known county town of Lancashire.

Willelmus de Lancastre, 1379: P. T. Yorks. p. 99.

1454. Robert Lankester, B.C.L.: Reg. Univ. Oxf. i. 22.

1568-9. Walter Lancaster and Magdalen Shinghleton, *widow*: Marriage Lic. (London), i. 41.

Four varieties of spelling occur in the following three entries relating to one and the same family. The clerk started well, but fell off:

1598. Married—Christofer Lancaster and Mary Cripps: St. Antholin(London), p. 39.

1600. Bapt.—Robart, s. Cristifer Lanckister: ibid. p. 40.

1602.— Ane Lankkester, d. Creatofer Lankester: ibid. p. 41.

London, 21, 5; New York, 8, 0.

Lance. — Bapt. 'the son of Lancelot,' from nick. Lance (v. Yonge, ii. 120), not from Lawrence. The nick. form is found for centuries on the Anglo-Scottish border, where Lancelot was one of the favourite font-names. The same individual is described under both guises in the two following entries:

Lancelot Hodshon, 1663: KKK. iv. 299.

Lance Hodgshon, 1663: ibid.

Mabil Lance, co. Oxf., 1273. A.

Johanna Lance, co. Oxf., ibid.

Lance Car, 1516: QQQ. p. ix.

Lance Newton, 1663: KKK. iv. 286.

1692. Bapt.—Mary, d. Richard Lance: St. Jas. Clerkenwell, p. 345.

London, 8; New York, 1; Philadelphia, 17.

Lancelin.—Bapt. 'the son of Ancell'; O.F. L'ancell; dims. Lancel-in and Lancel-ot. v. Ancell and Aslin.

'Ivo, the Chaplain and his homagers, and the homage of Master Anseline, and Hubert de Shimpling,' 1266: FF. i. 208.

Lancelyn de Pira, co. Essex, 1273. A.

John Lancelin, co. Oxf., ibid.

William Lancelyn, co. Hunts, ibid.

Henry Launcelyn, co. Linc., ibid.

Roger Lanseleyene, Fines Roll, 12 Edw. I.

Aunselen de Gise, *miles*, 7 Edw. II: v. Pedigree of Gyse, Visitation of Gloucestershire, 1623, p. 72.

Beauma, *uxor.* Aunselin, 7 Edw. II: ibid.

'The oath of John Launcelyn was taken at Chester concerning the property of Margaret de Arderne, Sept. 29, 1423': East Cheshire, i. 323.

Jane Lancellen, of Neston, *widow*, 1605: Wills at Chester (1545-1620), p. 117.

Lancelot, Launcelotte. — Bapt. 'the son of Lancelot.' Very

common in Cumberland and N. England generally for many centuries. The nick. was Lance, q.v. For further information, v. Lancelin.

Acelot Bryon, co. Camb., 1273. A.

Acelota Palmer, co. Hunts, ibid.

Lanslot Colynson, 1509: Reg. Univ. Oxf. i. 65.

Lancilot Colynson, co. York, 1513. W. 11.

Lancelot Hethe, 1548: St. Dionis Backchurch, p. 74.

Lancelot Hutton, 1640: VVV. p. 502.

Lancelot Crow, 1612: ibid. p. 491.

1568. Bapt. — William, s. Fryseley Launcelott: St. Michael, Cornhill, p. 84.

John Lancelott, of Neston, 1618: Wills at Chester (1545-1620), p. 117.

Hugh Lancelott, of Little Neston, *husbandman*: ibid. (1660-80), p. 162.

London, 2, 0; MDB. (co. Chester), 0, 1.

Lanchester.—Local, 'of Lanchester,' a parish in co. Durham.

Roger de Lancastre, co. Northumb., 1273. A.

1750. Married—James Pickernell and Eliz. Lanchester: St. Geo. Chap. Mayfair, p. 182.

1790. — James Lancaster and Mary Dorrington: St. Geo. Han. Sq. ii. 35.

MDB. (co. Suff.), 2; London, 2.

Land.—Local, 'at the land,' from residence beside the *launde* or land, the open wood; v. Landman, and Lund or Lowndes. The modern word is *lawn*.

William de la Lande, co. Oxf., 1273. A.

Jacob de la Lande, co. Warwick, 20 Edw. I. R.

Richard de la Lande. B.

William atte Land, c. 1300. M.

1579. Married — Richard Land and Eliz. Fuller: St. Jas. Clerkenwell, iii. 8.

1651. — Hugh Joanes and Susan Land: St. Peter, Cornhill, i. 258.

1741. Buried—James Land: Reg. Stourton, co. Wilts, p. 78.

London, 9; New York, 2; Philadelphia, 31.

Lander, Landor. — Occup. 'the lavender'; early contracted to Launder, q.v., and later on to Lander or (as in the poet's case) Landor.

1592. Buried—Thomas Lander: St. Antholin (London), p. 35.

1688. Bapt.—Ann, d. Edward Lander: St. Jas. Clerkenwell, i. 325.

1710. — Mary, d. Ephraim Lander: St. Michael, Cornhill, p. 166.

London, 7, 0; MDB. (co. Stafford), 6, 5; New York, 19, 0.

Landless. — Local. In the Modern Domesday Book for co. Lancaster occurs 'Ralph Landless,

Blackpool, 25 acres, 2 roods, 2 perches.' This has a very contradictory look, but no doubt the surname is of local origin, the suffix being -*lees*; v. Lees.

MDB. (co. Lancaster), 1; Manchester, 1; Philadelphia, 3.

Landman.—Occup. 'the landman,' one who looked after the *launde* or open wood, especially the beasts of chase that found covert around; v. Land, Lund, &c.

Richard le Landman, c. 1300. M.

1609. Richard Landeman and Martha Darby: Marriage Lic. (London), i. 316.

1623. John Landman, living in Virginia: Hotten's Lists of Emigrants, p. 172.

New York, 6; Philadelphia, 1.

Landor.—Occup.; v. Lander.

Landry.—Local; v. Laundry.

Lane. — Local, 'at the lane,' from residence therein; v. Lone. Naturally this surname is well represented in our directories all over the country.

William atte Lane, C. R., 48 Hen. III.

Robert de la Lane, co. Devon, 1273. A.

Cecil in the Lane, co. Oxf., ibid.

Emma a la Lane, co. Oxf., ibid.

Jurdan atte Lane, co. Soms., 1 Edw. III: Kirby's Quest, p. 257.

1575. John Lane and Johanna Noxe: Marriage Lic. (London), i. 66.

1580. William Lane, co. Berks: Reg. Univ. Oxf. vol. ii. pt. ii. p. 94.

London, 81; New York, 150.

Laner, Lanyer.—Occup. 'the laner,' a wool-merchant, a wool-comber. Fr. *lainier*, a wool-stapler, a wool-sorter. With Lanyer, cf. Sawyer or Bowyer.

Bartholomew le Laner, co. Hunts, 1273. A.

Symon le Laner, co. Hunts, ibid.

William Lannator, co. Wilts, ibid.

Ivo le Laner, C. R., 19 Edw. I.

Richard Lanour, co. Soms., 1 Edw. III: Kirby's Quest, p. 131.

Walter de (? le) Laner, 2 Edw. III: Freemen of York, i. 24.

John le Laner. T.

1567. Evan Forges and Joanna Lanyer: Marriage Lic. (London), i. 36.

1645. Buried — Æmilia Laneire: St. Jas. Clerkenwell, iv. 263.

Lang, Lange.—Nick. 'the lang,' i.e. the long, the tall. Hence such nicks. as Langbachelor, and such local surnames as Langabeer, Langdale, Langford, Langham, Langley, Langmead, Langridge, Langston, or Langton, q.v.; cf. Strang for Strong.

Hamo le Lang, c. 1300. M.
John le Lange. L.
Richard le Lange, co. Soms., 1 Edw.
III : Kirby's Quest, p. 266.
Ricardus Lang, 1379: P. T. Yorks.
p. 36.
1639. Buried—'Ellis Lange, brought
home from Tyborne' (!): St. Jas. Clerkenwell, iv. 238.
1665. — Sarah Lang: ibid. p. 367.
London, 19, 7; New York, 162, 63.

Langabeer.—Local, 'of Langabeer.' 'In this neighbourhood
(Lidford, co. Devon) we find Langabeer, Beardon, Beer Alston, Beer
Ferrers' (Taylor's Words and
Places, p. 179). The meaning of
this place-word is the long byre,
the long dwelling, or farm; cf.
Scotch *byre*, a stall, Icelandic *boer*,
a farmstead. The *a* is intrusive for
the sake of euphony; cf. Greenaway, Ottaway, or Hathaway.
London, 1.

Langbachelor. — Nick. 'the
long bachelor.' The instance below is amusing, with its intrusive
a; cf. Greenaway for Greenway;
v. Bacheller.
William le Langabacheler, co. Soms.,
1 Edw. III : Kirby's Quest, p. 180.

Langcake. — ? Nick. ; cf.
Blanchpain, Whitbread, Cakebread, &c. Seemingly a N. England
name.
1750. Married—Thomas Langcake and
Mary Wilkinson: St. Geo. Chap. Mayfair,
p. 169.
1784. — James Wyer and Sarah Langcake, of Greenwich: St. Geo. Han. Sq.
i. 364.
London, 1; MDB. (co. Cumb.), 4;
New York, 1; Boston (U.S.), 1.

Langdale, Langdell.—Local,
'of Langdale,' a parish in co. Westmoreland.
Robert de Langedale, co. Westmoreland, 20 Edw. I. R.
Alban Langdale, 1554 : Reg. Univ.
Oxf. i. 224.
1673. Married—Edward Langdale and
Eliz. Landoys: St. Michael, Cornhill,
p. 40.
London, 4, 1; Philadelphia, 1, 1.

Langdon. — Local, 'of Langdon.' Parishes in cos. Kent and
Essex. The Kent Langdon is
divided into East and West Langdon.
Bartholomew de Langedon, co. Essex,
1273. A.

Cecil de Langedon, co. Kent, ibid.
William de Langedone, co. Essex, ibid.
John de Langedone, co. Soms., 1 Edw.
III : Kirby's Quest, p. 177.
1587. Robert Langdon and Alice
Garsshe, *widow*: Marriage Lic. (London), i. 161.
1791. Married — Ann Langdon: St. Geo. Han. Sq. ii. 60.
London, 9; New York, 16.

Langfit.—Local, 'of Langford.'
A corruption.
William de Langfit, co. Northumb., 20
Edw. I. R.
1586. William Dickenson, *damasker*,
and Eliz. Langfitt, relict of Peter Langfitt, *cordwainer*: Marriage Lic. (London),
i. 152.

Langford.—Local, 'of Langford' (i.e. the long ford). Eight
parishes are so called in various
counties.
Nigel de Langeford, co. Derby, 1273. A.
John de Langeford, co. Essex, ibid.
Beatrice de Langeford, co. Oxf., ibid.
John de Langeford, co. Wilts, ibid.
1309. Thomas de Langeford, vicar of
Swaffham, co. Norf. : FF. vi. 224.
Ralph de Langeford, co. Soms., 1 Edw.
III; Kirby's Quest, p. 85.
John Langforde, co. Oxf, 1581 : Reg.
Univ. Oxf. vol. ii. pt. ii. p. 110.
1609. William Langford and Margaret
Deux : Marriage Lic. (London), i. 316.
1718. Married—John Langford and
Susanna Barton: St. Dionis Backchurch,
p. 59.
London, 16; Boston (U.S.), 8.

Langham, Lanham.—Local,
'of Langham.' Parishes in diocs.
Ely, Peterborough, St. Albans, and
Norwich.
William de Langham, co. Suff., 1273. A.
Henry de Longeham, co. Linc., ibid.
Dionis de Langham, co. Norf., ibid.
1575-6. Henry Langham and Jane
Northroffe, *widow*, Marriage Lic. (London), p. 68.
1621. Edward Langham, co. Northampt.:
Reg. Univ. Oxf. vol. ii. pt. ii. p. 389.
1647-8. Married — Thomas Langham
and Sarah Turgis : St. Dionis Backchurch, p. 25.
London, 7, 3; Oxford, 3, 1; New York,
3, 0.

Langhorn. — ? Local. At first
sight this might seem to be a nick.
for a huntsman, &c., from the
length of the horn he carried; cf.
Shakespear, Wagstaff, &c. Probably, however, it is local, from
some piece of land so called from
its shape. Then the surname would
originally be 'at the lang horn,'
from residence thereby; cf. Harts-

horn, which is local. Also v.
Horn.
1581. William Langhorne, co. Cumb. :
Reg. Univ. Oxf. vol. ii. pt. ii. p. 102.
1648. Christopher Conyers and Eliz.
Langhorne, of Putney : Marriage Lic.
(Faculty Office), p. 40.
1795. Married—Samuel Langhorn and
Mary Jones: St. Geo. Han. Sq. ii. 129.
London, 3; Philadelphia, 1; New
York, 1.

Langland.—Local, 'of Langland.' I cannot find the spot.
Hugh de Langelonde, co. Soms., 1
Edw. III : Kirby's Quest, p. 249.
London, 1.

Langley.—Local, 'of Langley.'
Parishes in diocs. Canterbury,
Norwich, Worcester, and Bath and
Wells.
Thomas de Langeleye, co. Oxf., 1273. A.
Peter de Langlege, co. Wilts, ibid.
Ralph de Langleye, co. Wilts, ibid.
Geoffrey Langleg, C. R., 8 Edw. I.
Richard de Langela, co. Soms., 1 Edw.
III : Kirby's Quest, p. 259.
1538-9. Married—Petter Skreven and
Alys Langlee : St. Dionis Backchurch,
p. 1.
1581. William Price and Dorothy
Langley, *widow*: Marriage Lic. (London),
i. 102.
— Thomas Langley, co. Salop: Reg.
Univ. Oxf. vol. vii. pt. ii. p. 100.
London, 28; Boston (U.S.), 32.

Langman.—Nick. 'the long
man'; v. Shortman; cf. Longfellow, Long, and Longman.
William Langman, co. Soms., 1 Edw.
III : Kirby's Quest, p. 82.
William Langeman, C. R., 7 Ric. II.
1729. Married—Gamaliel Maud and
Alice Langman: St. Jas. Clerkenwell,
iii. 256.
London, 3; MDB. (co. Devon), 1;
New York, 1; Philadelphia, 3.

**Langmead, Langmaid,
Longmate.** — Local, 'of Langmead,' i.e. the long meadow.
Langmaid shows the usual later
tendency to an imitative corruption. Seemingly a Devonshire
surname, judging by the directories.
And yet it is clear that there was
another Langmead in the Eastern
counties. Longmate is a palpable
corruption. Cf. Broadmeadow.
Geoffrey de Longo Prato, co. Camb.,
1273. A.
John de Longo Prato, co. Camb., ibid.
Richard Langemede, co. Soms., 1
Edw. III : Kirby's Quest, p. 240.
Hugh Langemede, co. Soms., 1 Edw.
III : ibid. p. 241.

1802. Married—James Longmate and Eliz. Callender: St. Geo. Han. Sq. ii. 270.
1808. — James Langmead and Maria Brien: ibid. p. 392.
London, 4, 0, 0; Devon Court Dir., 4, 1, 0; MDB. (co. Lincoln), 0, 0, 2; Boston (U.S.), 0, 4, 0.

Langridge, Langrish, Langrick.—Local, (1) 'of Langridge,' a parish in co. Somerset, near Bath; (2) 'of Langrish,' a tithing in the parish of Petersfield, co. Hants. These separate surnames are now inextricably mixed. With Langrick, cf. Longrigg; v. Longridge.

Stephen de Langerigg', co. Kent, 1273. A.
Robert de Langerich, co. Herts, 20 Edw. I. R.
Walter de Langereche, co. Kent, Hen. III–Edw. I. K.
William Langerugg, co. Soms., 1 Edw. III : Kirby's Quest, p. 272.
1519. Richard Langrysh, or Langrige: Reg. Univ. Oxf. i. 112.
1585. Roger Langrishe, co. Hants: ibid. vol. ii. pt. ii. p. 144.
— Robert Langrishe, co. Hants: ibid. vol. ii. pt. ii. p. 145.
1765. Married—Thomas Langrish and Sarah Cole: St. Geo. Han. Sq. i. 147.
1775. — Joseph Porter and Jane Langridge : ibid. p. 257.
London, 9, 1, 0; MDB. (East Rid. Yorks), 0, 0, 1; New York, 2, 0, 0.

Langstaff; v. Longstaff.

Langston, Langstone, Lankston.—Local, ' of Langstone,' a parish in co. Monmouth, near Newport.

1564. Thomas Langstone and Eliz. Baughe, widow : Marriage Lic. (London), i. 29.
1745. Bapt.—Daniel, s. Benjamin Langstone : St. Jas. Clerkenwell, ii. 276.
London, 5, 0, 1; MDB. (co. Hereford), 2, 1, 0.

Langstroth, Langstrath, Langstreth, Longstreeth, Longstreth.—Local, 'of the lang strother,' i.e. the long marsh; v. Strother, a North-English and Border name. The last syllable seems to have been dropped in modern times.

Richard Langstrothyr, sup. for B.C.L., 1448 : Reg. Univ. Oxf. i. 1.
William Langstrother, 1450 : ibid.
John Langstreth, of Forsbancke, parish of Tatham, 1676: Lancashire Wills at Richmond (1457-1680), p. 180.
'Private Langstroth, of the Canadian team, was a winner of £15 in the shooting for the Queen's Prize at Wimbledon, July 19, 1887': Standard, July 20, 1887.

London (Longstreeth), 2; MDB. (co. Lancaster), 1, 0, 1, 0, 0; Philadelphia (Longstreth), 27; New York, 5, 1, 1, 0, 0.

Langton.—Local, 'of Langton.' There are at least eight parishes in England so termed, two in co. York, three in co. Lincoln.

Geoffrey de Langeton, co. Linc., 1273. A.
William de Langeton, co. Linc., ibid.
Robertus de Langeton, 1379 : P. T. Yorks. p. 222.
1576. John Lancton, co. Linc. : Reg. Univ. Oxf. vol. ii. pt. ii. p. 71.
Ellen Langton, of Caton, 1595 : Lancashire Wills at Richmond (1457-1680), p. 180.
John Langton, of Preston, 1680 : ibid.
1598. Thomas Langton and Mary Stockmeade : Marriage Lic. (London), i. 251.
London, 23; Manchester, 5; MDB. (co. Lincoln), 7; New York, 5.

Langtree, Langtry. — (1) Local, ' of Langtree,' a parish in co. Devon, eight miles from Bideford, in the Hundred of Shebbear. It is spelt Langetrewe in the Hundred Rolls (i. 78) of 1273.

Agnes Langtree, 1538: Reg. Broad Chalke, co. Wilts, p. 6.
Thomas Lantree, 1548 : ibid. p. 7.

(2) Local, ' of Langtree,' a township in the parish of Standish, four miles from Wigan, co. Lanc.

Richard Langtree, of Langtree, 1596 : Wills at Chester (1545-1620), p. 117.
Edward Langtree, of Langtree, 1624 : ibid. (1621-1650), p. 133.
Manchester, 1, 0; Crockford, 0, 2; Boston (U.S.), 0, 5; New York, 1, 0.

Langworth, Langworthy.—Local, 'of Langworth'; v. Worth; cf. Kenworthy, Whitworth, &c. Probably the name may be referred to Upper Langwith, a parish in co. Derby; cf. Askwith for Askworth.

William de Langwathe, co. Linc., 1273. A.
John Langworthe, co. Worc., 1576 : Reg. Univ. Oxf. vol. ii. pt. ii. p. 71.
1524. Thomas Barthelett and Agnes Langwyth : Marriage Lic. (London), i. 4.
1762. Married—Arthur Langworth and Sarah Buckoke : St. Geo. Han. Sq. i. 116.
1803. — Peter Flinn and Sarah Langworthy : ibid. ii. 286.
London, 2, 3; MDB. (co. Devon), 0, 10; Boston (U.S.), 0, 2; New York, 0, 3.

Lanham; v. Langham.

Lankasheer.—Local, ' of Lancashire,' a variant; v. Lancashire.

1808. Married—John Lankshear and Margaret Pearson : St. Geo. Han. Sq. ii. 381. MDB. (co. Somerset), 1.

Lankester.—Local, ' of Lancaster,' q.v.

Lansdell, Lansdale.—Local, 'of Lonsdale,' q.v. The instances below conclusively prove that Lansdell and Lansdale are mere variants of Lonsdale, and originated in North Lancashire.

William Landysdale, or Londysdall, 1511 : Reg. Univ. Oxon. i. 75.
Richard Lonsdale, of Booths, 1595 : Wills at Chester (1545-1620), pp. 117-118.
Thomas Lonsdale, of Simonstone, 1591 : ibid.
Richard Lansdale, of the Booths, 1588 : ibid.
Robert Lansdale, of Simonstone, 1598 : ibid.
1571. Alexander Rigbye and Margaret Landesdale : Marriage Lic.(London),i. 48.
1577-8. Thomas Golde and Margaret Lansdall : ibid. p. 79.
1665. Buried—John, s. of John Landsdall, barber : St. Dionis Backchurch, p. 236.
London, 3, 1; Philadelphia, 0, 4.

Lansdown, Lansdowne. — Local, ' of Lansdowne,' a level tract of country in the neighbourhood of Bath. A battle was fought here in 1643 between Charles I and the Parliamentary forces.

Jacob de Launtesdoune, co. Soms., 1 Edw. III : Kirby's Quest. p. 86.
1753. Married—John Lansdown and Betty Phillot : St. Geo. Chap. Mayfair, p. 235.
1795. — John Lansdown and Catherine Shury : St. Geo. Han. Sq. ii. 140.
London, 2, 1.

Lanyer.—Occup. ' the lanyer '; v. Laner.

Lapage.—Occup. ' a law-page '; v. Lappage.

Lapish.—Offic. ' a law-page '; v. Lappage.

Lappage, Lapage, Lapish, Lapide.—Offic. ' the law-page.' Probably an apparitor or summoner, a servant of the law. Not 'le Page,' the evidence being contrary. Lapish and Lapide are somewhat curious variants.

Johannes Lawpage, 1379 : P. T. Yorks. p. 289.
Agnes Lawpage, co. York. W. 2.
Christopher Lawpage. FF.
1778. Married—Samuel Lapidge and Sarah Lowe : St. Geo. Han. Sq. i. 290.
1787. — Peter Reynolds and Susanna Lappage : ibid. p. 399.

London (Lappage), 1; West Rid. Court Dir., 1, 2, 2, 0; Thorne, near Doncaster (Lapidge), 1; New York (Lapage), 1.

Lappin, Lapping, Lappine. —Bapt. 'the son of Lapin.' Probably, however, a contraction of Lampin or Lambin, q.v., the pet name of Lambert. The *g* in Lapping is an excrescence, as in Jennings.

Lapinus Roger, M.P. for Canterbury, C. R., 8 Edw. III.
Thomas Lapyn, C. R., 18 Ric. II.
Makinus Lappyng. XX. 1.
1749. Married—James Merchant and Susanna Lapine: St. Geo. Chap. Mayfair, p. 143.
London, 1, 1, 0; New York, 5, 0, 2.

Lapworth.—Local, 'of Lapworth,' a parish in co. Warwick, near Henley-in-Arden.

1562. Michael Lappworthe: Reg. Univ. Oxf. i. 248.
1588–9. Edward Lapworth, co. Warwick: ibid. vol. ii. pt. ii. p. 168.
1744. Married—Francis Lapworth and Eliz. Loder: St. Jas. Clerkenwell, i. 275.
London, 4; MDB. (co. Warwick), 1; Philadelphia, 1; Boston (U.S.), 1.

Larder.—Local, 'of the larder,' an official who superintended the larder or place for the reception of lard. O.F. *lardier*, 'a tub to keep bacon in' (Cotgrave). 'Lardery, a larder; v. Ord. and Reg. p. 21: *lardarium*, a lardyr-hows. Nominale MS.' (Halliwell). v. Lardner.

William del Larder, C. R., 37 Hen. III.
John Larder: Privy Seal Bills, Nov. 1–16, 1559, 1 Eliz.
1616. John Larder, co. Dorset: Reg. Univ. Oxf. vol. ii. pt. ii. p. 357.
London, 1; MDB. (co. Lincoln), 7.

Lardner, Lardiner, Lardnar. —Offic. and occup. 'the lardiner,' a bacon-salter, a steward of the larder. Lard, the melted fat of swine; 'larde of flesche' (Prompt. Parv.). Lardiner, the officer who superintended, as well indoors as out of doors, the supply of pig-stock.

'David le Lardiner holds one serjeantry, and he is keeper of the gaol of the Forest, and Seizer of the Cattle which are taken for the King's debts': Hist. and Ant. of the City of York, vol. iii. (York, 1785.)
'The fleshours' sale serve the burgessis all the time . . . in preparing of their flesh, and in laying in of their lardner.'—The Lawes and Constitutions of Burghs in the Regiam Majestatim, p. 243, Edin-

burgh, 1774: quoted by Brand, Pop. Ant. i. 220, edit. 1841.
Ywon the Lardaner, co. Glouc., 1289: Household Exp. Ric. de Swinfield, Camd. Soc. p. 168.
Thomas le Lardiner, c. 1300. M.
Philip le Lardiner. B.
Hugh le Lardiner. L.
1693–4. John Lardner and Hannah Moore: Marriage Lic. (Faculty Office), p. 210.
1701. Bapt.—Edward, s. John Lardner, *apothecary*: St. Dionis Backchurch, p. 140.
London, 3, 0, 0; New York, 1, 0, 0; Philadelphia, 4, 0, 1.

Large.—Nick. 'the large,' the big, the bulky; cf. Small, Bigg, Little, Fatt, Lean, &c.

Robert le Large, co. Oxf., 1273. A.
William le Large, co. Essex, ibid.
Andrew le Large, C. R., 6 Edw. I.
Thomas le Large, co. Soms., 1 Edw. III: Kirby's Quest, p. 209.
1595. Thomas Large, co. Sussex: Reg. Univ. Oxf. vol. ii. pt. ii. p. 210.
1630. Bapt.—Ruth, d. Thomas Large: St. Jas. Clerkenwell, i. 116.
1647–8. Dudley Avery and Jane Large: Marriage Lic. (Faculty Office), p. 38.
1787. Married—John Large and Mary Rawlings: St. Geo. Han. Sq. i. 403.
London, 10; New York, 2.

Larimer; v. Lorimer.

Lark, Larke.—Nick. 'the lark,' one who sang 'like a lark'; cf. Nightingale. Bird-names were very popular, as our directories prove; v. Finch, Spinks, Jay, Goldfinch, &c. Lark is a contraction of O.E. *laverock* (v. Laverack).

Hamo Larke, co. Norf., 1273. A.
William le Lerk, C. R., 7 Edw. I.
1545. Buried—Cecyly Lavoroke: St. Dionis Backchurch, p. 181.
Nicholas Larke, co. Linc., 1584: Reg. Univ. Oxf. vol. ii. pt. ii. p. 140.
1679. Bapt.—Ane, d. Robert Larke: St. Jas. Clerkenwell, i. 285.
London, 6, 2; New York, 0, 1; Philadelphia, 4, 1.

Larkin, Larking.—Bapt. 'the son of Lawrance,' pronounced Larance, whence the nick. Larry, dim. Lar-kin; cf. Wil-kin. The *g* is, of course, excrescent. Although I have not much direct evidence, there can be no doubt about the origin.

Larance Kyllum: Visit. Yorks, 1563, p. 178.
Larance Hamerton: ibid. p. 153.
Larance Hamerkine, 1623: St. Mary Aldermary, p. 15.

1546. Thomas Larkyng and Clare Sanders: Marriage Lic. (Faculty Office), p. 8.
1620. Bapt.—Joane, d. Thomas Larkings: St. Jas. Clerkenwell, i. 87.
1684. Buried—Eliz. Larkin, servant to Mr. James Bayly: St. Dionis Backchurch, p. 251.
London, 10, 5; Philadelphia, 40, 0.

Larkman.—Local, 'of Lakenham,' a parish in co. Norfolk. The local surname became unquestionably Lakeman, q.v. As Larkman is a Norfolk and Suffolk surname, we may suppose that it is the result of a local pronunciation with long *ā*; Lahkman would soon become Larkman. I doubt not this is the true derivation; cf. Swetman for Swetenham, or Deadman for Debenham.

William Lacknam, 1524: Reg. Univ. Oxf. i. 135.
London, 4; MDB. (co. Norfolk), 3; (co. Suffolk), 1.

Larnder; v. Launder.

Larrett, Larritt.—Bapt. 'the son of Lora,' or 'Laura,' or 'Laurencia'; dim. Lorett or Laurett. 'It was the Provençal Lora de Sades, so long beloved of Petrarch, who so made this one of the favourite romantic and poetical names, above all, in France, where it is Laure, Lauretta, Loulon' (Yonge, i. 368). But possibly Larrett or Larrit is a dim. of Larry, the nick. of Laurence. Still the origin would be the same.

Laurencia, comitissa de Leycestre, Hen. III-Edw. I. K. p. 236.
Loretta, com' de Leycestre, ibid. p. 166.
Lauretta de Wyum, ibid. p. 328.
Lora de Scaccario, 1273. A.
Lora de Herthill, 1379: P. T. Yorks. p. 14–15.
Lora Mawer, 1379: ibid.
Lora de Grenelef, 1379: ibid.
Lora Soker, 1379: ibid.
1577. Edward Larratt and Katherine Wheelor: Marriage Lic. (London), i. 75.
London, 1, 2.

Lasbury.—Local, 'of Lasborough,' a parish in co. Gloucester, near Tetbury.

London, 1.

Lascelles, Lassells, Lascell, Lassell, Lasselle, Lasell, Laselle.—Local, 'de Lascelles.' Mr. Lower says 'la Lacelle is a place in the arrondissement of Alençon in Normandy' (Patr. Brit. p. 187).

William de Lassell, co. Linc., Hen. III-Edw. I. K.

Alan de Lascelle, co. Northampt., 1273. A.

William de Lasceles, co. York, ibid.

Roger de Lascelles, co. York, ibid.

1574. Francis Lassells, co. Richmond: Reg. Univ. Oxf. vol. ii. pt. ii. p. 57.

1665. Cuthbert Wytham and Lucy Lassell: Marriage Alleg. (Canterbury), p. 142.

London, 5, 0, 0, 0, 0, 0, 0; Crockford, 5, 0, 0, 0, 0, 0, 0; New York, 1, 0, 3, 0, 0, 3, 1; Boston (U.S.), 0, 0, 0, 4, 2, 0, 0.

Lasham, Lassham, Lassam. —Local, ' of Lasham,' a parish in co. Southampton.

Richard de Lasham, co. Suff., 1273. A.

A single register will suffice to give instances of the variants.

1800. Married—Thomas List and Sarah Lasham: St. Geo. Han. Sq. ii. 215.

1808. — Michael Lassam and Eliz. White: ibid. p. 394.

1809. — Henry Lassham and Eliz. Hill: ibid. p. 412.

London, 1, 1, 2.

Lassey.—Local; v. Lacy.

Latchford, Letchford. — Local, ' of Latchford,' a chapelry in the parish of Grappenhall, co. Chester. Also a hamlet in the parish of Great Haseley, co. Oxford. It is quite possible that Latchford and Letchford represent two different places ; v. Letchford.

1609. Nicholas Latchford, of Pinnington: Wills at Chester (1545-1620), p. 118.

1666. Married—Edward Blacford and Margett Litchford: St. Jas. Clerkenwell, iii. 130.

1679. John Lachford, of Macclesfield: Wills at Chester (1660-80), p. 161.

1788. Married — George Cobb and Frances Letchford: St. Geo. Han. Sq. ii. 9.

1806. — George Tweedle and Ann Latchford: ibid. p. 358.

London, 4, 3; Manchester, 0, 1; Philadelphia, 0, 4.

Latham, Leatham, Lathom, Laytham, Leethem, Leathem, Leetham, Lethem.—Local, ' of Lathom,' a chapelry in the parish of Ormskirk, co. Lanc. The surname has ramified very strongly and spread far and wide, probably from *lade* or *lathe*, a barn. A distinguished family took their name from this place. In Yorkshire this

surname took the form of Leatham and Leathom, unless it had a separate local origin. But the meaning is the same (v. Leathes), as *leath* is found to be a Yorkshire form of *lade* or *lathe* mentioned above ; literally, therefore, ' the barn-house.'

Henry de Latham, co. Soms., 1 Edw. III : Kirby's Quest, p. 169.

Johannes de Lethom, 1379: P. T. Yorks. p. 241.

Thomas de Lathom, co. Lanc., 1382 : Baines' Lancashire, ii. 414.

1605-6. Edward Lathom, co. Lanc. : Reg. Univ. Oxf. vol. ii. pt. ii. p. 288.

1616. John Lathom, or Latham, co. Lanc. : ibid. p. 353.

London, 21, 0, 0, 0, 0, 0, 0, 0; Manchester, 9, 0, 0, 1, 0, 0, 0, 0; West Rid. Court Dir., 3, 8, 0, 0, 1, 0, 0, 0; Hull, 1, 0, 0, 0, 0, 0, 3, 1; New York, 21, 0, 0, 0, 0, 2, 0, 0; Philadelphia, 13, 1, 0, 0, 0, 3, 0, 1.

Lathbury, Ladbury.—Local, ' of Lathbury,' a parish in co. Bucks, near Newport Pagnell. Ladbury may be for Ledbury ; but the prefix seems to be *lade* or *lathe*, a barn ; v. Lade.

(Domina) de Lathbiry, co. Bucks, 1273. A.

John de Lathebyr, co. Bucks, ibid.

1578. Francis Lathburye, co. Derby: Reg. Univ. Oxf. vol. ii. pt. ii. p. 80.

1579. Ralph Barton and Rose Lathburie: Marriage Lic. (London), i. 92.

1609. Bapt.—Marie, d. Isak Lathburie: St. Michael, Cornhill, p. 108.

1745. Married—Edward Ladbury and Frances Dale: Canterbury Cathedral, p. 88.

London, 3, 3; Philadelphia, 4, 0.

Lathom ; v. Lathom.

Lathrop, Lathrope.—Local, ' of Lowthorp,' q.v.

Latimer, Lattimer, Lattimore. — Occup. ' the latimer,' an interpreter ; lit. a speaker of Latin. O.F. *Latinier*. ' Latonere, or he that usythe Latyn speche ' (Prompt. Parv. p. 289) ; v. Way's note. ' Sir John Maundevile, speaking of the routes to the Holy Land, says of the one by way of Babylon, "And alle weys fynden men Latyneres to go with hem in the contrees . . . in to tyme that men conne the langage"': Voiage, p. 71. An old poem says :

'Lyare was mi latymer,
Sloth and sleep mi bedyner.'
Wright's Lyric Poetry, p. 49.

Hugo Latinarius, 1086 : Domesday.

William le Latiner. G.

Warin le Latymer. B.

Nicholas le Latimer. M.

Alan le Latimer, co. Suff., 1273. A.

Symon le Latimer, co. Suff., ibid.

William Latymere, 1513: Reg. Univ. Oxf. i. 89.

1586. John Hollowaie and Johanna Latimer : Marriage Lic. (London), i. 151.

For a second derivation, v. Latoner.

London, 5, 1, 0; Crockford, 1, 0, 0; MDB. (co. Warwick), 0, 0, 1; Philadelphia, 19, 3, 4.

Latoner, Latner. — Occup. ' the latoner,' one who worked in laton or latten, probably a mixture of lead with brass or copper. M.E. *laton*.

' He had a crois of laton, ful of stones.'
Chaucer, C. T. 701.

As a surname inextricably mixed with Latiner or Latimer, an interpreter. Thus Latimer has two distinct origins ; v. Latimer.

Thomas le Latoner, temp. 1300. M.

Nicholas Musket, *latoner*, 3 Edw. II : Freemen of York, i. 12.

Richard le Latonere. V. 9.

Robertus Latoner, 1379: P. T. Yorks. p. 39.

Richard Latoner, bailiff of Yarmouth, 1341 : FF. xi. 323.

1579. Edward Latner, co. Glouc. : Reg. Univ. Oxf. vol. ii. pt. ii. p. 89.

1583. Oswold Greated and Dorcas Moncke, *widow*, relict of John Moncke, *latten-founder* : Marriage Lic. (London), i. 125.

New York, 0, 2.

La Touche. — Local, ' de la Touche.' David Digues de la Touche, a Huguenot, settled in Ireland after the revocation of the Edict of Nantes. He was a scion of the noble house of Blesois, who held considerable lands between Blois and Orleans (Lower, quoting Burke's Landed Gentry).

Crockford, 4 ; Oxford, 1.

Launcelotte. — Bapt. ; v. Lancelot.

Laund.—Local, ' at the laund '; v. Land and Lund.

Gernes de la Launde, co. Warw.: Hen. III-Edw. I. K.

John de la Launde, co. Linc. : ibid.

Robert de la Laund, co. Essex, 1273. A.

Nicholas atte-Launde, co. Norf., 1401 : FF. v. 6.

1585-6. Richard Westemyll and Dorothy Launde : Marriage Lic. (London), i. 148.

Launder, Lavender, Larnder.—Occup. 'the lavender,' a washerwoman or a washerman. '*Buandière*, launderer': Hollyband's Dictionarie, 1593. 'Lauender, wassher, or lawndere, *lotrix*': Prompt. Parv. Mr. Way in a note quotes Caxton (Boke for Travellers), 'Beatrice the lauendre shall come hethir after diner, so gyve her the lynnen clothis.'

'Envy is lavender of the Court alway.'
Legend of Good Women.

Beatrice Ap Rice, laundress to Princess Mary (daughter of Henry VIII), is always set down as 'Mistress Launder':

'Item, paid for 2lb. of starche for Mts. Launder, viii*d*.': Privy Purse Expenses, Princess Mary, p. 160.
1530. 'Item, paied to the lawnder that wasshith the children of the kinges pryvat chambre, 48*s*. 4*d*.': ibid. Henry VIII. p. 75.
Alice la Lavander, co. Bedf., 1273. A.
Cecilia la Lavender, co. Camb., ibid.
Peter le Lavender, co. Camb., ibid.
1538. William Launder: Reg. Univ. Oxf. i. 192.
Isabel la Lavendre. E.
1752. Married—Richard Morris and Ann Lavender: St. Geo. Han. Sq. i. 47.
London, i, 4, 1 ; Boston (U.S.), 1, 5, 0.

Laundry, Landry. — Local, 'of the laundry'; v. Launder, the officer who superintended the washing department ; cf. Wardrop (at the wardrobe) and Wardroper (the wardrober). Practically the local form is the same as the official. This surname has crossed the Atlantic and flourishes in the States, although all but extinct in England.

Alice atte Lauendre, C. R., 3 Edw. I.
Robert de la Lavendrye, Fines Roll, 11 Edw. I.

The first two following names occur together :

William le Lavender, co. Soms., 1 Edw. III : Kirby's Quest, p. 205.
Roger atte Louendrye, co. Soms., 1 Edw. III : ibid.
1773. Married—John Bidwell and Jane Landry : St. Geo. Han. Sq. i. 233.
Boston (U.S.), 7, 19.

Laundy. — Local, 'of the laundry'; v. Laundry. A corruption.

1790. Married—Edward Moggridge and Sarah Laundy: St. Geo. Han. Sq. ii. 43.
London, 3.

Laurence. — Bapt. ; v. Lawrance.

Laurie. — Bapt. 'the son of Lawrence'; v. Lowric.

Lavender; v. Launder.

Laverack, Laverick, Lavrick, Loverock. — Nick. 'the laverock' or 'lavrock,' i.e. the lark, probably because the bearer was a good blithe singer, or of bright and cheery habits; cf. Nightingale, Finch, Goldfinch, &c. ; v. Lark.

Richard Laverock, co. Notts, 1273. A.
Willelmus Lauerok, 1379: P. T. Yorks. p. 277.
1759. Married—Grey Elliott and Mary Laverik: St. Geo. Han. Sq. i. 89.
1764. — John Laverick and Ann Weston: ibid. p. 133.
Hull, 4, 1, 1, 0 ; Stourbridge (co. Worc.), 0, 0, 0, 1.

Lavington.—Local, 'of Lavington,' a parish in co. Lincoln, four miles from Folkingham ; also two parishes (East and West Lavington) in co. Wilts.

Hugh de Lavinton, co. Linc.: Hen. III—Edw. I. K.
Ralph de Lavinton, co. Linc.: ibid.
Reginald de Lavinton, co. Wilts, 1273. A.
William de Lavinton, co. Wilts, ibid.
Hugh de Lavington, rector of Bircham Magna, co. Norf., 1310: FF. x. 293.
Robert de Levyngton, co. Soms., 1 Edw. III: Kirby's Quest, p. 272.
1669. Married—Edward Top and Anne Lavinton: St. Jas. Clerkenwell, iii. 167.
London, 4.

Law, Lawe, Lawes. — (1) Local, 'at the low,' i.e. hill; v. Low. The seeming plural form Lawes represents the common tendency to tack on an *s* in monosyllabic local surnames; cf. Styles, Oakes, Brooks, Sykes, Dykes, &c. Probably the patronymic *s*, as in Williams, Jones, &c. ; v. Brook. (2) Bapt. 'the son of Lawrence,' from the nick. Law. For instances, v. Lawson. The final *s* in Lawes will here represent the patronymic, as in Jones, Williams, Jennings, &c.

William de la Lawe, co. Northumb., 1273. A.

Ralph de la Law, or Lowe, co. Salop : ibid.
Robertus del Lawe, 1379 : P. T. Yorks. p. 210.
Johannes de la Law, 1379: ibid. p. 140.
1527-8. John Brewer and Agnes Lawes : Marriage Lic. (London), i. 6.
1591. John Lawe, *yeoman*, and Eliz. Manfeilde : ibid. p. 191.
London, 36, 0, 7 ; West Rid. Court Dir., 21, 1, 0 ; New York, 30, 1, 2.

Lawday.—? Bapt. 'the son of Loveday' (?), q.v. A corruption.
London, 1.

Lawford.—Local, 'of Lawford,' parishes in cos. Essex and Warwick.

1682. Married—Edward Golding and Mary Lawford: St. Michael, Cornhill, p. 43.
1710. Buried—Anne Lauford: Reg. Stourton, co. Wilts.
London, 12 ; Boston (U.S.), 3.

Lawless.—Nick. 'the lawless,' uncontrolled, unrestrained ; M.E. *laweles*, lawless.

Hugo Laghlese, 1314. M.
John Laweles, C. R., 19 Ric. II.
John Laweles, C. R., 1 Hen. IV. pt. i.
1619. Francis Godingham and Alice Lawlesse : Marriage Lic. (London), i. 79.
1746. Married—William Coolley and Ann Lawless: St. Geo. Chap. Mayfair, p. 74.
London, 3 ; Philadelphia, 16.

Lawley.—Local, 'of Lawley.' I cannot find the spot.

1595-6. George Lawley, co. Salop : Reg. Univ. Oxf. vol. ii. pt. ii. p. 213.
1652. Bapt.—John, s. William and Sibbell Lawly : St. Jas. Clerkenwell, i. 179.
1698. Robert Palmer and Hester Lawley : Marriage Lic. (Faculty Office), p. 229.
MDB. (co. Salop), 3 ; London, 7 ; Philadelphia, 6.

Lawman.—Offic. 'the lawman,' i.e. the lawyer, 'the man of law,' as Chaucer would say.

Ranulf Lawman, co. Hunts, 1273. A.
Peter Laweman, co. Camb., ibid.
Thomas Laweman, co. Oxf., ibid.
Willelmus Lawghman, 1379 : P. T. Yorks. p. 273.
1607. Married — Edward Lawman, *girdler*, and Fraunces Keuall : St. Michael, Cornhill, p. 18.
London, 3.

Lawrance, Lawrence, Laurance, Laurence, Lawrenson.—Bapt. 'the son of Laurence.' This saint 'of universal popularity' has made a deep impression upon our nomenclature; v. Law (2), Lawson, Lowrie, Laurie, Larkin, Larrett, &c.

Gilbert Laueronce, co. Camb., 1273. A.
John fil. Laurence, co. Linc., ibid.
Simon fil. Laurencii, London, 20 Edw.
I. R.
Nicholas Lawranson, of Poynton, co. Ches., 1584: Wills at Chester (1545-1620), p. 119.
James Lawranson, of Maghull, 1613: ibid.
Josiah Lawrenson, of Frodsham: ibid. (1681-1700), p. 152.

Memorials to members of one and the same family represent the name as follows:

Mary, wife of John Laurence, 1736: FF. iv. 133.
Ester, wife of John Lawrence, 1796: ibid.
Mary, d. of John and Ester Laurance, 1727: ibid.
London, 13, 126, 1, 12, 0; Liverpool, 0, 15, 0, 1, 8; New York, 5, 37, 0, 10, 0.

Lawrey, Lawrie, Lawry.—Bapt. 'the son of Lawrence'; v. Lowrie.

Lawson.—Bapt. 'the son of Laurence' or 'Lawrence,' from the nick. Law; v. Law (2).

Willelmus Lauson, 1379: P. T. Yorks. p. 146.
Law Robynson, 1379: ibid. p. 255.
Henricus Laweson, 1379: ibid. p. 135.
Agnes Law-wyf, 1379: ibid. p. 291.
1554. James Castelys and Eliz. Lawson: Marriage Lic. (London), i. 15.
1576. William Lauson, co. Lanc.: Reg. Univ. Oxf. vol. ii. pt. ii. p. 72.
1664. Bapt.—Jone, d. Randall Lawson: St. Jas. Clerkenwell, i. 222.
London, 46; West Rid. Court Dir., 16; New York, 66.

Lawton.—Local, 'of Lawton,' a parish in co. Ches., now Church-Lawton, but simply Lawton in earlier records; v. Earwaker's East Cheshire, ii. 207, 239. In South England probably sometimes confused with Laughton.

1575. Thomas Lawton, co. Ches.: Reg. Univ. Oxf. vol. ii. pt. ii. p. 67.
Mr. Lawton, parson of Lawton, 1620: Lanc. and Ches. Rec. Soc., p. 51.
Thomas Lawton, 1634: Earwaker's East Ches. ii. 211.
Thomas Lawton, of Lawton, 1595: Wills at Chester (1545-1620), p. 119.
John Lawton, of Church Lawton, co. Ches., 1607: ibid.
Randle Lawton, of Chester, 1604: ibid.
1587. Christopher Walker, *bricklayer*, and Anne Lawton: Marriage Lic. (London), i. 160.

Manchester, 29; London, 11; New York, 23.

Lawyer.—Occup.'the lawyer'; v. Lawman, and cf. Sawyer and Bowyer.

New York, 3; Philadelphia, 3.

Lax, Laxe.—? Local, 'at the lake,' from residence thereby. The chief home of this surname is co. Somerset, where we find Lack (i.e. Lake) at an early period. A.S. *lac* (Skeat); Fr. *lac*, a lake. Hence a surname Lack, and with the final *s* (cf. Holmes, Styles, Brooks, Sykes, &c.) Lacks. This by and by would become Lax; cf. Dix Rix, Wix, Wilcoxon, for Dicks, Ricks, Wicks, Wilcockson. This seems to me a simple solution.

1729. Married—Joseph Lax, of Whitby, co. York, and Anne Dodd: St. Geo. Chap. Mayfair, p. 295.
MDB. (co. Soms.), 8, 0; Philadelphia, 1, 0; New York, 6, 1.

Laxton.—Local, 'of Laxton.' (1) Laxton or Lexington, a parish in co. Notts; (2) Laxton, a parish in co. Northampton.

Henry de Laxington, co. Linc., 1273. A.
Robert de Laxinton, co. Linc., ibid.
Simon de Laxton, co. Norf., 1361: FF. v. 33.
1542. Married—Thomas Eswell and Annes Laxtonne: St. Peter, Cornhill, i. 221.
1578-9. Morgan Laxton and Margaret Smithe, *widow*: Marriage Lic. (London), i. 84.
1680. Martin Laxton and Eliz. Jones: Marriage Lic. (Faculty Office), p. 153.
1799. Married—William Robert Laxton and Phoebe Parker: St. Geo. Han. Sq. ii. 209.
London, 8.

Lay.—Local, 'at the lay,' from residence thereby; v. Lee.

John de la Lay, co. Linc., 1273. A.
John du Lay, co. Hunts, ibid.
John du Lay, co. Bedf., 20 Edw. I. R.
1615. Married—Olyver Laye and Eliz. Wildictott: St. Jas. Clerkenwell, iii. 41.
1770.— Benjamin Lay and Winifred Robinson: St. Geo. Han. Sq. i. 197.
London, 5; Oxford, 5; New York, 11.

Layard. — ? Occup. or ? offic. ; probably 'the lord.' A variant of Scottish Laird, q.v.

1743. Daniel Peter Layard and Susanna Henrietta Boysragon: Marriage Lic. (London), ii. 345.
Crockford, 2.

Layburn, Layborn, Laybourn, Laborn, Labern.—Local, (1) 'of Leyburn,' a parish in the N. Rid. Yorks; (2) 'of Leybourn,' a parish in co. Kent.

William de Leybourne, co. Kent, 1273. A.
Roger de Leyburne, co. Hunts, ibid.
Henry de Leyburne, co. Kent, 20 Edw. I. R.
Thomas de Layburn, 1379: P. T. Yorks. p. 209.
1618. Married—William Myllarde and Thomyzin Labourne: St. Michael, Cornhill, p. 21.
1781.— Matthew Gilpatrick and Margt. Laybourn: St. Geo. Han. Sq. i. 320.
London, 0, 3, 1, 1, 2; New York, 2, 0, 1, 0, 0.

Laycock.—Local, 'of Laycock,' now a suburb of the town of Keighley, W. Rid. Yorks, one of the five manors into which that town was divided.

Johanna Lakkoc, 1379: P. T. Yorks. p. 197.
Johannes de Laccok, 1379: ibid. p. 263.
Thomas de Lacokke, 1379: ibid.
1630. Married—John Painter and Dorothy Laycock: St. Peter, Cornhill, i. 253.
— — William Bartlemew and Ann Laycock: St. Antholin, London, p. 64.
London, 3; West Rid. Court Dir., 24; Philadelphia, 12.

Layer.—Occup. 'the layer,' i.e. a stone layer (Latinized into *cubatores*), one who sets the stones in building, a waller. ' Layere, or werkare wythe stone and mortere, *cementarius*' : Prompt. Parv. p. 294, and v. Way's note thereon. Probably the term was familiar to co. Norfolk, as the above quotation suggests, for Layer has been a Norfolk surname for many centuries. In the contract for building Fotheringay Church, 1425, the chief mason undertakes neither to 'set mo nor fewer freemasons, rogh setters, ne leyers' upon the work but as appointed (Dugdale, Mon. iii. 164).

George Layer, of Bury, co. Suff., 1429: FF. vi. 354.
William Layer, sheriff of Norwich, 1526; mayor, 1537: ibid.
'Here resteth the body of Mary, daughter of Christopher Layer, citizen and alderman of Norwich, who deceased the 9th of October, 1602': ibid. p. 357.
Mary Layer, 1710, Boughton, Norfolk: ibid.
1661. Francis Layre, of Hanningham,

co. Norf., and Eliz. Bowle: Marriage Alleg. (Canterbury), p. 64.
New York, 3; Philadelphia, 21.

Layland, Leyland, Leeland, Leland.—Local, 'at the lay land.' Two parishes in co. Lanc. bear the name of Layland or Leyland. A valuable note by Way in the Prompt. Parv. (p. 285) on the word 'lay, londe not telyd,' explains the meaning. Amongst other authorities he quotes 'laylande; terre nouvellement labouree' (Palsgrave); 'a leylande, frisca terra' (Cath. Ang.); 'selio, a lee lande' (Ortus). Thus Layland means fallow or unploughed land. For the connexion of lay with lea and lee, v. Lee.

Johannes Leyland, 1379: P. T. Yorks. p. 161.
Ellis Leyland, of Nether Wyersdale, 1679: Lancashire Wills at Richmond (1457-1680), p. 182.
Thomas Lealand, of Nether Wyersdaile, 1670: ibid.
1688. Bapt.—William, son of Richard Layland: St. Jas. Clerkenwell, i. 329.
London, 6, 1, 0, 0; West Rid. Court Dir., 1, 2, 0, 0; MDB. (co Warwick), 0, 0, 1, 0; New York, 0, 0, 0, 17.

Layman. — ? ——. Mr. Lower thinks this is a personal name, and the same as Layamon, who transcribed the Roman de Brut. I would suggest that it is only a variation of Lawman, q.v.—or perhaps of Leman, q.v.

'Here lyeth the body of Habbakuk Layman, surgeon, who departed this life the 5th day of April, An. Dom. 1699,' Kenninghall, co. Norf.: FF. i. 223.
London, 2; Philadelphia, 7; New York, 4.

Laytham; v. Latham.

Layton.—Local, 'of Layton.' East and West Layton, two townships in N. Rid. Yorks; also a township in the parish of Bispham, co. Lanc. Doubtless many small spots are so called; cf. Leighton.

Richard de Layton, co. Cumb., 20 Edw. I. R.
1581. Thomas Laitone, co. York: Reg. Univ. Oxf. vol. ii. pt. ii. p. 96.
1626. Thomas Heylen and Anne Layton, widow: Marriage Lic. (London), ii. 167.
— Bapt.—Ann, d. William Layton: St. Jas. Clerkenwell, i. 103.
1657.— Mary, d. Richard Laighton: ibid. p. 108.
London, 18; Philadelphia, 20.

Lazenby, Lazonby.—Local, 'of Lazonby,' a village in co. Cumberland. But the Yorkshire Lazenbys hail from Lazenby, a manor in the parish of Kirk Leatham, co. York.

Ricardus Lasynbi, 1379: P. T. Yorks. p. 285.
Willelmus de Lethom, 1379: ibid.
William Laysynby, C. R., Ric. II. pt. ii.
1632. Bapt.—Benjamine, s. Richard Lazenby: St. Antholin (London), p. 66.
1696. Buried—Robert Lasinby, rector of St. Antholin: ibid. p. 110.
1701. Bapt.—Mary, d. William Lasingby, haberdasher of hats: St. Dionis Backchurch, p. 140.
London, 2, 0; West Rid. Court Dir., 2, 0; Manchester, 0, 2; Boston (U.S.), 1, 0; Philadelphia, 2, 0.

Lea, Leah.—Local, 'at the lea'; v. Lee. Leah is unquestionably a variant. It is not Jewish, but purely English. The intermediate stage was Leay.

William de la Lea, co. Oxf., 1273. A.
John atte Lea, 1301. M.
Richard Lea, of the Lea, co. Ches., 1563: Wills at Chester (1545-1620), p. 119.
Robert Lea, of Sutton, 1588: ibid.
1682. Bapt.—Henry, s. William Leay: St. Jas. Clerkenwell, i. 300.
1799. Married—John Leah and Eliz. Barker: St. Geo. Han. Sq. ii. 197.
London, 29, 3; Manchester, 11, 4; MDB. (co. Chester), 16, 1; New York, 4, 0.

Leach, Leech, Leachman.—
(1) Occup. 'the leech,' a physician; M.E. leche. 'Leche, medicus': Prompt. Parv.

'The divel made a reve for to preche, Or of a souter a shipman, or a leche.' Chaucer, C. T. 3902.

'Harpemakers, leches, and upholsters, Porters, fesycyens, and corsers.' Cocke Lorelle's Bote.

With Leachman, cf. merchantman, Priestman, &c.

Edmund le Leche, co. Oxf., 1273. A.
William le Leche, co. Oxf., ibid.
Robert le Leche, 1307. M.
John le Leche. X.
Robertus Leche, taverner, 1379: P. T. Yorks. p. 161.

(2) Local, 'at the lache,' i.e. the lake. In co. Lancaster Leach has absorbed Lache (q.v.), which explains the commonness of that surname in that shire.

London, 47, 11, 1; Oxford, 8, 6, 0; New York, 33, 15, 0.

Leacroft.—Local, 'of Leacroft,' a township in the parish of Cannock, co. Stafford.

1576. Bapt.—Robert, s. Robert Lecroft: armorer: St. Peter, Cornhill, i. 18.
1593. Buried—Margery, ignoti cognominis, Mr. Lecrafte's mayd, of the plague: ibid. p. 141.
1607. Bapt.—Richard Leycraft, s. Sampson Leycrafte: ibid. p. 57.
1614. Married—Daniel Barker and Mary Leacrofte: ibid. p. 248.
Crockford, 1.

Leadbeater, Leadbetter, Leadbitter, Tidbetter, Liberty(?).—Occup. 'the lead-beater'; cf. Goldbeater. It is probable that Liberty is a corruption, the intermediate form being Libiter. The following entry strongly confirms this view:

1669. Married—John Bayley and Saray Libiter: St. Jas. Clerkenwell, i. 156.
Gonnilda le Ledbetere, co. Bucks, 1273. A.
Ricardus Ledebatter, 1379: P. T. Yorks. p. 193.
Robertus Ledebeter, 1379: ibid. p. 20.
1561-2. John Leadbeater and Christiana Andrewes: Marriage Lic. (London), i. 23.
1788. — John Winkfield and Margaret Leadbitter: St. Geo. Han. Sq. ii. 1.
1792. — William Leadbetter and Eliz. Miller: ibid. p. 72.
London, 3, 2, 1, 0, 1; Manchester, 2, 2, 0, 0, 0; Crockford, 0, 0, 1, 0, 1; New York, 2, 2, 0, 0, 0; Boston (U.S.) (Liberty), 1.

Leader.—Occup. 'the leader,' a carrier, a carter. Farmers still lead hay in the North, as for instance in my old parish (Ulverston). 'Lede wythe a carte, caruco': Prompt. Parv. Mr. Way quotes from the Liber Niger Regis, Edw. IV, an ordinance commanding that no seller of wheat for the use of the King's house 'be compelled to lede or carrye his wheete' more than ten miles at his own cost. Waterleaders for water-carriers was the old familiar term for the occupation; v. Waterleader; cf. Loder or Loader, q.v.

1519. Richard Ledar, rector of Fouldon, co. Norf.: FF. vi. 34.
1601. Bapt.—Alexander, s. Henrie Leeder: St. Jas. Clerkenwell, i. 38.
1654. Thomas Leader, co. Norf.: FF. vi. 35.
1688. George Leader and Mary Newnam: Marriage Alleg. (Canterbury), p. 91.

1771. Married—James Leader and Jane Gardner : St. Geo. Han. Sq. i. 205. London, 6 ; Philadelphia, 1.

Leadley.—Local ; v. Leathley.

Leadman.—Occup., probably a water-leader ; v. Leader and Loadman. A.S. *ladman*, a carrier.

1618. Married—Thomas Leadman, of St. Gyles, Creplegate, and Marie Smythe : St. Michael, Cornhill, p. 21.
1633. William Ledman and Ellen Burrowes : Marriage Lic. (London), p. 212. Philadelphia, 2.

Leaf, Leefe, Lief, Leafe.— Nick. 'the lief,' i.e. dear ; v. Leifchild. The dim. *lief-kin*, a term of endearment, occurs in Palsgrave's Acolastus, 1540 ; v. *leefekyn*, Halliwell's Dict.

Pagan Lef, co. Norf., 1273. A.
Alice le Lef, co. Camb., ibid.
Lone the Lef, co. Hunts, ibid.
Nicholas Leve, co. Soms., 1 Edw. III : Kirby's Quest, p. 123.
Lucia le Lyf, co. Soms., 1 Edw. III : ibid. p. 140.
1677. Married—Richard Owen and Susanna Leefe : St. Michael, Cornhill, p. 41.
1754. — James Leaf and Eliz. Clarke : St. Geo. Chap. Mayfair, 277.
London, 4, 2, 0, 0 ; MDB. (North Rid. Yorks), 0, 1, 2, 1.

Leah.—Local ; v. Lea, of which it is a manifest variant.

Leak, Leake, Leek. — Local, 'of Leek,' a parish in dioc. of Lichfield ; also 'of Leake,' parishes in diocs. of York, Lincoln, and Southwell.

John de Lek, co. Linc., 1273. A.
Roger de Leke, co. Linc., ibid.
Teobald de Lek, co. Linc., ibid.
John de Leek, co. Notts, 20 Edw. I. R.
1595. Thomas Leeke, co. Northampt. : Reg. Univ. Oxf. vol. ii. pt. ii. p. 211.
— Bapt.—John, s. Arthur Leake, *merchant-tailor* : St. Peter, Cornhill, i. 42.
London, 1, 10, 1 ; New York, 3, 4, 2.

Leaman ; v. Leman.

Lean.—Nick. ' the lean,' a spare man ; cf. Large, Small, Bigg, Little, Lyte, &c. Thus Lean is the opposite of Fatt, q.v.

Walter Lene, co. York, 1273. A.
Roland le Lene, co. Bucks, ibid.
Henry le Lene, co. Soms., 1 Edw. III : Kirby's Quest, p. 278.
1605. Matilda Leene, of Chester, *widow* : Wills at Chester, i. 120.
1797. Married—Thomas Joyner and Eliz. Lane, or Leane : St. Geo. Han. Sq. ii. 171.

1800. Married—Guy Waterman and Henrietta Lean : ibid. p. 218.
MDB. (co. Soms.), 4 ; Boston (U.S.), 2.

Lear, Leer.—Local, ' de Leyre,' probably Lire, in the arrondissement of Evreux in Normandy.

William de Leyre, Leic., 1273. A.
William de Leyre, London, 20 Edw. I. R.
1602. Buried—Thomas, s. of Christofer Leere : St. Mary Aldermary, p. 150.
1647. Married — Vincent Lear and Anne Carter : St. Thomas the Apostle, London, p. 18.
1722. Bapt.—Mary, d. James Leeer : St. Jas. Clerkenwell, ii. 134.
London, 3, 3 ; Crockford, 3, 0 ; New York, 4, 0 ; Philadelphia, 13, 1.

Learoyd.—Local, ' of the learoyd,' from *lee*, *lea*, *legh*, or *leigh*, a meadow, and *royd*, a ridding ; v. Royd.

Alicia Legh-rode, 1379 : P. T. Yorks. (Sowerby), p. 195.
Richard Leyrod, of Manchester, *clerk* : Wills at Chester (1621-50), p. 139.
West Rid. Court Dir., 12 ; Boston (U.S.), 3.

Leason. — Bapt. ' the son of Lettice ' ; v. Leeson.

Leatham.—Local ; v. Latham.

Leather, Leathers. — Bapt. 'the son of Leather.' Although I have scarcely any instances, there can be no doubt of the origin of names prefixed with Leather. Leather was a personal name. 'One *Lethar* was a bishop in the days of Æthelbert. Cod. D.pl. 981 '(Lower, Patr. Brit. p. 190). Hence such localities as Letheringham and Letheringsett, and such local surnames as Leatherdale, Leatherby, Leatherhead, or Leatherbarrow. Leatherwine occurs as a single name (without surname), co. Camb. 1273. A. (vol. ii. p. 493). With this cf. Bald-win, Un-win, &c. ; v. Liverpool.

1582. Buried—Alyce Lether, daughter of William, of the plague : St. Michael, Cornhill, p. 197.
1623. Peter Leather and Sarah Bainam : Marriage Lic. (London), ii. 127.
1633. Married—Nathaniel Carter and Ann Leather : St. Antholin (London), p. 67.
1663. Samuel Pine and Sarah Leather : Marriage Alleg. (Canterbury), p. 87.
London, 5, 1 ; New York, 1, 0 ; Oxford, 1, 0.

Leatherbarrow, Leatherberry, Leatherbury, Letherbury.—Local, ' of Leatherbarrow ' ; v. Leather and Barrow. One Leatherbarrow is a hill by Windermere Lake.

1581. Nicholas Letherborow, co. Warw. : Reg. Univ. Oxf. vol. ii. pt. ii. p. 107.
1582. Anthony Leatherbarrow, of Aughton : Wills at Chester, i. 120.
1600. Married—Edward Leatherborow, of Coventry, and Cibell Pywell : St. Peter, Cornhill, i. 241.
1618. Cicely Leatherbarrow, of Wigan : Wills at Chester, i. 120.
1661-2. John Booth and Mary Letherbarrow : Marriage Alleg. (Canterbury), p. 23.
London, 1, 0, 0, 0 ; Philadelphia, 0, 3, 14, 3.

Leatherby, Letherby, Leatherbee. — Local, ' of Letherby.' I do not know where the place is ; v. Leather.

London, 1, 1, 0 ; Boston (U.S.), 0, 0, 12.

Leatherdale. — Local, ' of Leatherdale,' a parish in dioc. Ripon, co. York. v. Leather.

London, 2.

Leatherhead. — Local, ' of Leatherhead ' or ' Letherhead,' a parish in dioc. of Winchester, co. Surrey. Lower says, 'formerly Lederede.' v. Leather.

John de Leddred, co. Soms., 1273. A.
Richard Leddred, co. Soms., ibid.
John de Ledrede, co. Wilts, 20 Edw. I. R.
1733. Married—Thomas Leatherhead and Eliz. Upshot : St. Geo. Han. Sq. i. 12.

Leatherhose.—Nickname for one who wore or sold buskins ; cf. Shorthose.

John Letherhose, co. Oxf., 1273. A.
Richard Letherhose, co. Glouc., 20 Edw. I. R.

Leatherman, Letherman.— Occup. 'the leatherman,' a dealer in leather. Possibly the man or servant of Leather ; v. Leather and Matthewman.

Adam Letherman, C. R., 12 Edw. III. pt. iii.
Philadelphia, 6, 1.

Leathes, Leathe, Leath.— Local, ' of the lathes,' i.e. the barns, the grange ; v. Lade. The surname has arisen in several localities.

' Lathes is a hamlet next unto Warnpool, and was so called of a grange or farm which the Lord of Whitrigg had there. Of that place the family of the Lathes took their name . . . until Adam Leathes, now owner of the demesne thereof, sold the tenements and residue of the hamlet to the inhabitants. . . It was given by Robert, the son of Robert de Dunbretton, to his kinsman Henry, whose posterity were thereupon called *de le Leaths*'; E. and F., co. Cumb., p. 76.

Appended is a quotation :

' Robertus filius Roberti dedit Leathes Henrico fratri suo, Hen. III ' : Gilpin.

Thomas atte Lathe, rector of Stokesby, co. Norf., 1356 : FF. xi. 051.

Johannes del Lethe, 1379 : P. T. Yorks. p. 50.

A family of Leathes sprung up in co. Norfolk, and is still represented.

' The manor house was lately called the Lathes, it stands a little distance from Pokethorp Street.' Pokethorp Manor, Norwich : FF. iv. 428.

Again, we read of the same manor :

' John Corbet (4 Edw. VI), had a lease of the Cellerie's, or St. Leonard's meadow, containing six acres, lying between the river and street, the *Lathes* close, and fold-course, and liberty of shak . . . in the manor house and yard, and all thereon built, called the Lathe-yard ' : ibid. iv. 429.

The origin of the Norfolk Leathes is thus distinctly apparent.

Stanley Leaths, rector of Matlask, Norfolk, 1741 : ibid. viii. 137.

' Thomas Atte-lathe married first Alice, daughter and heir of Sir William Wisham, and Margaret his wife, and in her right presented as lord to the church of Elingham Parva, in Norfolk, in 1468 ' : ibid. vii. 449.

Gilbert del **Lathes**, 25 Edw. I : Freemen of York, i. 6.

London, 1, 0, 2 ; Crockford, 2, 0, 0 ; York, 0, 1, 0 ; MDB. (Norfolk), 3, 0, 0 ; New York, 0, 0, 1 ; Boston (U.S.), 0, 1, 0.

Leathley, Leadley. — Local, ' of Leathley,' a parish in the W. Rid. Yorks, i.e. ' the meadow by the barn ' ; v. Lade and Leathes.

1579-80. Henry Leathelye and Fortune Hallywell : Marriage Lic. (London), p. 94.

London, 1, 0 ; Leeds, 3, 1 ; MDB. (North Rid. Yorks), 0, 6 ; Philadelphia, 0, 1.

Leavenbread.—Nick. Probably Isabel was so familiarly entitled because she baked this sort of bread ; cf. Blanchpain, Whitbread, Cakebread, &c.

Isabella Leuanbrede, 1379 : P. T. Yorks. p. 199.

Leaver, Lever. — Local, ' of Lever,' q.v. Although the variant Leaver is not now very common in South Lanc., it formerly was frequently found in that district.

1621. Robert Leaver, of Darcey Lever : Wills at Chester, ii. 135.

1635. James Leaver, of Darcey Lever : ibid.

1647. Roger Leaver, of Bolton : ibid.

Here the true spelling of the locality is preserved, while the surname originated by that same locality has changed its orthography.

London, 15, 8 ; Manchester, 2, 14 ; New York, 0, 2.

Leaversuch.—Local ; v. Liversage, of which it is a variant.

MDB. (co. Essex), 1.

Leche.—Occup. ; v. Leach.

1552. John Leche, of Carden, co. Ches.: Wills at Chester. i. 120.

1605. James Leche, of Lower Place, in Castleton : ibid.

Liverpool, 1.

Lechmere. — Local, ' of Lechmore,' probably some moor in the vicinity of Lechlade, a parish twenty-eight miles from Gloucester. The surname seems to have arisen in that district.

1587-8. Richard Lechmore, or Lichmoore, co. Heref.: Reg. Univ. Oxf. vol. ii. pt. ii. p. 162.

1599. Edmund Leachmore, or Lechemoore, or Lechmoor, co. Heref.: ibid. p. 233.

1679. Sandys Lechmere and Joan Holmes : Marriage Lic. (Faculty Office), p. 148.

1677. Thomas Lechmere and Jane Blagrave : Marriage Alleg. (Canterbury), p. 273.

MDB. (co. Hereford), 1 ; Crockford, 1.

Leck. — Local, ' of Leck,' a township in the parish of Tunstall, near Lancaster.

Johannes de Lek, 1379 : P. T. Yorks. p. 199.

Willelmus de Lek, 1379 : ibid.

1575. Barnabas Hills and Catherine Lecke : Marriage Lic. (London), i. 67.

1587-8. Anthony Lecke, co. Herts, and Mary Knagge : ibid. p. 167.

Ulverston, 1 ; New York, 2 ; Philadelphia, 1.

Ledgar(d, Ledger ; v. Legard.

Ledsham, Ledson. — Local, ' of Ledsham,' a parish in W. Rid. Yorks, six miles from Pontefract.

Ledson is a corrupted form ; v. Lettsom and Lett.

1540. Buried—Thomas Ledsam : St. Dionis Backchurch (London), p. 178.

1582. Thomas Ledsum, co. Ches.: Reg. Univ. Oxf. vol. ii. pt. ii. p. 123.

1606. Buried—Jane, d. Cuthbert Ledsome : St. Jas. Clerkenwell, iv. 95.

— George Ledsham, of Inner Temple, London : Wills at Chester, i. 120.

1809. Married—Charles Hope and Sarah Ledson : St. Geo. Han. Sq. ii. 401.

Melling, near Liverpool, 0, 3 ; MDB. (co. Ches.), 1, 0.

Lee.—Local, ' at the lea,' from *ley, legh, lea,* or *lay,* a meadow, a grassy plain. The local names with which this word is incorporated as affix or suffix are innumerable ; cf. Leighton, Chudleigh, Eckersley, Leyburn, &c. Of itself, also, it represents countless spots styled Lee, Lees, Leigh, Lea, Leece (a village in Furness), &c. The local surnames built upon it are equally numerous, comprising (without adducing compound forms) Lee, Lees, Leese, Leece, Legg, Legge, Legh, Leigh, Ley, Lay, and Lea, all of which see under their respective heads.

Henry de la Lee, co. Camb., 1273. A Richard de la Lee, co. Wilts, ibid. John de la Lee. J. Roger de la Lee. B. Johannes del Lee, 1379 : P. T. Yorks. p. 155.

1550-1. John Lee and Agnes Masset : Marriage Lic. (London), i. 13.

1565. Bapt.—Anne, d. Henry Lee : St. Jas. Clerkenwell, p. 3.

London, 191 ; New York, 258.

Leece.—(1) Local, ' at the lees,' v. Lees ; cf. Ellice for Ellis, or Avice for Avis. (2) Local, ' of Leece,' a hamlet near Ulverston, in the Furness district of North Lancashire. The derivation is the same as (1). Leece is still found as a surname in Ulverston and the neighbourhood. It is commonly met with in the Ulverston Church registers.

1546. Buried—Eliz. Leece : St. Mary, Ulverston, p. 3.

1561. Bapt.—Brian Liese : ibid. p. 38.

1593. Jenet Leece, of Coulton, Furness : Lancashire Wills at Richmond (1457-1680), p. 183.

1597. William Leice, of Bardsey, Furness : ibid.

Ulverston, 1.

Leech.—Occup. ; v. Leach.

Leedham, Leedam, Leedom.—Local, 'of Lathom'; v. Latham. One familiar form of Lathom is Leatham or Leetham, and of this Leedham, Leedam, and the American Leedom are variants. It is astonishing how many variants of Lathom are to be found scattered over the world.

Hull, 1, 0, 0; MDB. (co. Stafford), 5, 0, 0; Philadelphia, 0, 0, 28; Boston (U.S.), 1, 0, 0.

Leeds.—Local, 'of Leeds,' the well-known town in the W. Rid. of Yorks.

1565. Buried—Elizabethe Leedes, alias Grove: St. Michael, Cornhill, p. 188.
1575. Edward Leedes, co. Sussex: Reg. Univ. Oxf. vol. ii. pt. ii. p. 65.
1609. Thomas Leedes, co. Sussex: ibid. p. 305.
1647-8. Charles Leeds, of Biddenden, Kent, and Sarah Taylor: Marriage Lic. (Faculty Office), p. 38.
Crockford, 1; New York, 17.

Leek.—Local; v. Leak.

Leeland.—Local; v. Layland.

Leeman, Leemon; v. Leman.

Leeming. — (1) Local, 'of Leeming,' a village near Bedale, co. York. (2) Personal, 'the son of Leming' (v. Halliwell, and Prompt. Parv. pp. 295-6). In the Towneley Mysteries Leming is a horse's name, from its bright, flashing colour.

'Say, Malle and Stott, wille ye not go? Lemynge, Morelle, White-horne, io.'

The editor (Preface, p. xii) says that Leming as a cow's name occurs in the will of a West Riding yeoman. That Leming was a personal name and became a surname seems indubitable.

Stephen Leming, co. Oxf., 1273. A.
William Leming, co. Oxf., ibid.
Stephen de Leminge, co. Kent, ibid.
Johannes Lemyng, 1379: P. T. Yorks. p. 5.
Isolda Lemyng, 1379: ibid.
Willelmus Lemyng, *sutor*, 1379: ibid. p. 277.
1545. Buried—Urseley (Ursula) Lemynge: St. Dionis Backchurch, p. 180.
1645. William Leming (Essex) and Ellen Rolt: Marriage Lic. (London), ii. 276.
London, 2; West Rid. Court Dir., 7; Philadelphia, 2.

Leeper, Leaper.—Nick. 'the leper,' a variant; v. Lepper. The

fact that Leper or Lepper is now nearly extinct shows a tendency to throw it off as objectionable. Hence, probably, the deceptive-looking Leeper.

1567. Thomas Leper, of Over Kellet: Lancashire Wills at Richmond (1457-1680), p. 182.
1598-9. John Leaper and Florence Dawson: Marriage Lic. (London), i. 259.
1611. Robert Leaper, of Over Kellet: Lancashire Wills at Richmond (1457-1680), p. 182.
1746. Married—William Leapper and Ann Manning: St. Geo. Chap. Mayfair, p. 72.
London, 2, 0; New York, 1, 0; Philadelphia, 5, 0; Oxford, 0, 1.

Leer.—Local; v. Lear.

Lees, Leese, Leighs.—Local, 'at the lees' (v. Lee), from residence thereby. Also 'of Lees,' a hamlet in the parish of Ashton-under-Lyne. This has originated a large number of the South Lancashire Lees.

Roger de Lees, co. Norf., 1273. A.
John de Lees, co. Norf., ibid.
Avelina de Leys. J.
William de Leghes, ibid.
1577. William Sulham and Anne Lease, *widow*: Marriage Lic. (London), i. 76.
1582. Robert Leese, of Ashton-under-Lyne: Wills at Chester, i. 121.
1593. Edward Leese, of Ashton-under-Lyne: ibid.
1687. Bapt.—Richard, son of Richard Leighs: St. Jas. Clerkenwell, i. 323.
London, 12, 4, 0; Manchester, 47, 1, 0; MDB. (co. Stafford), 18, 10, 0; New York, 13, 0, 0.

Leeson, Leason.—(1) Bapt. A corruption of Levison, v. Lewis. I am told that the Levison-Gowers call themselves the Lesson-Gowers. (2) Bapt. 'the son of Lece,' i.e. Lettice. Lecia and Lece seem to have been popular forms.

Lecia de Eltesle, co. Camb., 1273. A.
Robert fil. Lece, co. Camb., ibid.
Lecia Arnet, co. Camb., ibid.
Johannes Lesson, 1379: P. T. Yorks. p. 79.
Gryfyn Leyson, 1524: Reg. Univ. Oxf. i. 135.
1625. Joseph Willmor and Sarah Leason: Marriage Lic. (London), ii. 154.
1666. Francis Bromley and Frances Leeson: Marriage Alleg. (Canterbury), p. 197.
London, 5, 3; Liverpool, 2, 0; New York, 2, 1.

Leete.—Bapt. 'the son of Lettice,' from the nick. Lete; v. Lett.

We find a dim. Letelin also existing at the hereditary surname period.

Walter Letelin, co. Norf., 1273. A.

Cf. Hewelin, i.e. little Hew (v. Hewling).

Letia (without surname), co. Camb., 1273. A.
Nicholas fil. Lete, co. Bedf., ibid.
Roger Lete, co. Oxf., ibid.
Walter Lete, co. Suff., ibid.
1745. Married—Thomas Leett and Rebecca Wittaker: St. Geo. Chap. Mayfair, p. 54.
1778. — Edward Griffiss and Mary Leet: St. Geo. Han. Sq. i. 284.
London, 9; New York, 3.

Leetham, -them; v. Latham.

Leftwich. — Local, 'of Leftwich,' a township in the parish of Davenham, co. Chester.

Johannes Lethewyche, 1379: P. T. Yorks. p. 54.
1602. John Leftwich, of Leftwich, co. Ches.: Wills at Chester, i. 121.
1641. William Leftwich, of Northwich, *gentleman*: ibid. ii. 136.
1647. Ellen Leftwich, of Weaverham, *widow*: ibid.
1751. Married—James Pritchard and Mary Leftwich: St. Geo. Chap. Mayfair, p. 196.
London, 8.

Legard, Ledgard, Ledger, Ledgar, Ledgerson.—Bapt. 'the son of Leger.' I find no evidence in favour of Lower's statement that the origin is 'le garde,' the guard or keeper. The final *d* is a common excrescence. St. Leger was a canonized priest of Chalons, the French form being Leguire (Yonge, ii. 430). With the intrusive *d* in Ledger, cf. Rodger for Roger.

Leggard de Aula, co. Camb., 1273. A.
Lyger de la Frache, co. Oxf., ibid.
Adam Leger', co. Camb., ibid.
Andrew fil. Legg', co. Camb., ibid.
Thomas Leggard, co. Norf., ibid.
Johannes Leggard, *hostiler*, Bradforth (Bradford), 1379: P. T. Yorks. p. 190.
Willelmus Lyggard, 1379: ibid.
1584. John Legerde and Alice Alsopp, *widow*: Marriage Lic. (London), i. 132.
1595-6. Christopher Roffie and Catharine Leger, *widow*: ibid. p. 227.
1746. Bapt.—Eliz., d. John Ledgerson: St. Jas. Clerkenwell, ii. 281.
London, 0, 1, 7, 1, 0; West Rid. Court Dir., 0, 5, 1, 0, 0; MDB. (co. Stafford) (Ledgerson), 1; Leeds (Ledgard), 1; Sheffield (Ledger), 5; Philadelphia (Ledger), 8.

Legerton.—Local, 'of Leger-ton.'

Hugh de Legerton, co. Notts, 1273. A. London, 1.

Legg, Legge.—(1) Local, 'at the leigh' or 'legh' (v. Lee); cf. Whitelegge and Whiteley.

John de Leg, co. Oxf., 1273. A.
Pagan de la Leg, co. Wilts, Hen. III-Edw. I. K.
Avice de Leg, co. Salop, ibid.

(2) Bapt. 'the son of Legg,' a personal name of the history of which I know nothing. Perhaps a nick. of Legard, q.v.

Andrew fil. Legge, co. Camb., 1273. A.
Nicholas Legge, co. Hunts, ibid.
Roger Legge, co. Soms., ibid.
John Legge, co. Soms., 1 Edw. III: Kirby's Quest, p. 260.
William Legge, co. Hunts, 1581: Reg. Univ. Oxf. vol. i. pt. ii. p. 100.
1630. Bapt.—Robert, s. John Legge: Reg. Stourton (co. Wilts), p. 7.
1770. Married—William Legg and Ann Cawdron: St. Geo. Han. Sq. i. 200.
London, 19, 4; New York, 1, 1; Philadelphia, 6, 1.

Leggatt, Leggett, Loggitt, Loggott, Loggate, Leggat.—(1) Local, 'at the lidgate' (q.v.), an inevitable corruption; 'atte Lidgate' or 'Lidyate' was one of our commonest entries, and must have left many representatives. (2) Offic. 'the legate,' an ambassador, a commissioner; M.E. *legate, legat*; O.F. *legat*.

Geoffrey le Legat, co. Devon, 1273. A.
Robert Legat, co. Camb., ibid.
Thomas Legat, co. Norf., ibid.
Ricardus Leget, 1379: P. T. Yorks. p. 268.
1585. Married—Richard Colfe and Elsabeth Legget: St. Dionis Backchurch, p. 10.
1770. — Henry Legitt and Catherine Eagan: St. Geo. Han. Sq. i. 198.
London, 0, 8, 16, 1, 2, 0; MDB. (co. Lincoln), 0, 1, 2, 21, 1, 0; New York, 3, 36, 0, 0, 0, 6.

Legh, Leigh.—Local, 'at the legh'; v. Lee. The reason why Leigh has so much larger a representation in the Manchester Directory than that of London lies in the fact that Leigh, a parish in South Lanc., early gave rise to a family name that has very strongly ramified. Of course the origin of the name is the same. The *i* in

Leigh was inserted in more recent times.

Pagan a la Legh, co. Wilts, 1273. A.
Richard de la Legh, co. Oxf., ibid.
Johel de Legh, co. Devon, ibid.
Avelina de la Legh, co. Surrey, 20 Edw. I. R.

An old Cheshire family still preserve the old form Legh.

1580. Thomas Legh, of Atherton: Wills at Chester, i. 121.
1617. Jane Leigh, of High Leigh, *widow*: ibid.
1636. William Legh, of Bolton, *linen-draper*: ibid. ii. 137.
London, 0, 17; Manchester, 0, 44; New York, 0, 6.

Leicester; v. Lester.

Leifchild, Liefchild.—Nick. 'lief child,' i.e. dear child (v. Leaf); *lief*, dear, still exists in 'I had as lief'; cf. Darling.

William Lefchild, C. R., 3 Edw. I.
William Levechilde, C. R., 13 Hen. IV.
Cf. Cecilia Levebarne, 1379: P. T. Yorks. p. 141.
1606. Bapt.—Henry, s. Henry Lift-child: St. Jas. Clerkenwell, p. 367.
1763. Married—John Church and Martha Leafchild: St. Geo. Han. Sq. i. 120, London, 1, 1.

Leigh, 1.—Local; v. Legh.

Leighton.—Local, 'of Leighton,' parishes in cos. Hunts, Salop, and Bedford. Also two townships in co. Ches., in the parishes of Nantwich and Neston; v. Layton, Lee, and Legh.

Henry de Leyton, co. Bucks, 1273. A.
Roger de Leyton, co. Hunts, ibid.
Clement de Leyton, co. Hunts, ibid.
Adam de Leytun, co. Salop, Hen. III-Edw. I. K.
1601. Robert Leighton, co. Salop: Reg. Univ. Oxf. vol. ii. pt. ii. p. 253.
1750. Married—Thomas Leighton and Mary Ann Tash: St. Geo. Chap. Mayfair, p. 182.
London, 15; Philadelphia, 10.

Leishman, Lishman.—Nick. 'leish' or 'lish,' nimble, strong, active, stout, alert, lithe. A North-English term.

'Wha's like my Johnny,
Sae leish, sae blithe, sae bonny?'
The New Keel Row (v. Brockett).

Cf. Blythman, Merriman, Strongman.

1783. Married—Joseph Lishman, *husbandman*, and Betty Macartney, *widow*: St. Mary, Ulverston, p. 427.

1785. Married—Robert Lishman and Jane Park: ibid. p. 429.
1806. — Stephen Hagan and Frances Leisman: St. Geo. Han. Sq. ii. 349.
1809. — Henry Hawkins and Mary Lisseman: ibid. p. 410.
London, 2, 0; West Rid. Court Dir., 0, 1; New York, 2, 0.

Leitch, Leitche.—Local and occup.; v. Leach. This is probably a Scottish variant.

London, 2, 0; Liverpool, 4, 1; New York, 6, 0.

Leland; v. Layland.

Leman, Lemmon, Lemon, Leeman, Leemon, Leaman, Limon.—Bapt. 'the son of Leman,' a corruption of Liefman. No doubt in some instances employed as a nickname, meaning dear one, sweetheart; cf. Leifchild.

'And hail that madyn, my lemman.'
Towneley Mysteries.

But its use as seen below compels us to place it mainly in the category of fontal names. The forms in the London Directory show little change. It was a familiar joke some few years ago to say that there were two Lemons in the House of Commons and only one Peel.

Leman Brū, co. Norf., 1273. A.
Alan fil. Leman, co. Camb., ibid.
Eldred Leman, co. Suff., ibid.
Thomas Leiman, co. Oxf., ibid.
William Lemon, of Preston, 1642: Wills at Chester (1621-50), p. 138.
1672. James Wynstanley and Eliz. Leman: Marriage Alleg. (Canterbury), p. 83.
1746. Married—William Lemon and Mary Newman: St. Geo. Chap. Mayfair, p. 66.

The following has an excrescent *d*, as in Simmonds or Hammond:

1752. Married—John Lemond and Dorcas Massey: St. Geo. Chap. Mayfair, p. 214.
1790. — John Newton and Lucy Lemmon: St. Geo. Han. Sq. ii. 45.
London, 4, 4, 15, 2, 0, 0; MDB. (co. Lincoln) (Limon), 3; (East Rid. Yorks) (Leaman), 1; Plymouth (Leaman), 2; New York, 7, 2, 5, 2, 1, 0.

Lemprière.—Nick. 'the emperor'; cf. King, Caesar, &c.

'In the Chartuleries of the Abbaye de la Trinitè, at Caen, this patronymic goes through the various gradations of Imperator, L'Empereur, Lemprere, Lempreur, to Lempriere': Lower, Patr. Brit. p. 192.

1580-1. Hugh Lamprier, of Jersey: Reg. Univ. Oxf. vol. ii. pt. ii. p. 96.
1610. Philip Lempriere, of Jersey: ibid. p. 314.
1725. Married—James Lemprier and Sarah Atkinson: St. Mary Aldermary (London), p. 47.
London, 1; MDB. (co. Surrey), 1; New York, 1.

Lenecock.—Bapt. 'the son of Leonard,' from the nick. Lenny and the suffix -*cock* (v. Cock, and cf. Wilcock, Simcock, &c.); v. Leney.
Robertus Lenecok, 1379: P. T. Yorks. p. 102.
Ricardus Lenecok, 1379: ibid.
Margareta Lenecok, 1379: ibid.

Leney, Lenney, Lenny.— Bapt. 'the son of Leonard,' from the nick. Lenny.
Lenne Textor, co. Camb., 1273. A.
Osbert fil. Lene, co. Suff., ibid.
William Leny, co. Worc., ibid.
1786. Married — George White and Eliz. Lenny: St. Geo. Han. Sq. i. 382.
London, 2, 2, 2; Philadelphia, 0, 4, 8.

Lennard; v. Leonard.

Lent. — ? Bapt. 'the son of Lent' (?), from the ecclesiastical season; cf. Nowell, Midwinter, Christmas, Pentecost, Pask, &c.
William Lent, co. Oxf., 1273. A.
1675. Bapt.—John Hengoe, s. Hengoe Lentt: St. Thomas the Apostle, p. 67.

The two following entries may bear on the season:
Willelmus Lenten, 1379: P. T. Yorks. p. 30.
Johannes Lentyn, 1379: ibid. p. 257.
London, 2; New York, 29.

Lenthall, Lentell.—Local, ' of Leinthall': (1) Earls Leinthall, a chapelry in the parish of Aymestrey, co. Hereford; (2) Leinthall-Starkes, a parish in co. Hereford.
1377. Roger de Leynthale, rector of Mundham, co. Norf.: FF. x. 171.
1575. William Lentall, co. Hereford: Reg. Univ. Oxf. vol. ii. p. 65.
1611. Robert Leynthall, co. Oxf.: ibid. p. 324.
1609. Bapt.—William, s. William Lentall: St. Jas. Clerkenwell, i. 238.
1799. Married—Maurice Lenthall and Mary Hastings: St. Geo. Han. Sq. ii. 206.
London, 1, 1; Boston (U.S.), 0, 1.

Lenton.—Local, ' of Lenton,' a parish in co. Notts, near Nottingham.
Clemence de Lentone, co. Hunts, 1273. A.

Simon de Lenton, co. Derby, 20 Edw. I. R.
1579. William Buckley and Eliz. Lenton: Marriage Lic. (London), i. 92.
1613. Bapt.—William, s. John Lenton: St. Jas. Clerkenwell, i. 67.
London, 2; Philadelphia, 1.

Leo.—Bapt. 'the son of Leo.' Seemingly in the hereditary surname period a Jewish personal name.
Leo le Horsmongere, co. Camb., 1273. A.
Jacobus fil. Leonis, co. Linc., ibid.
Judeus Leo, co. Linc., ibid.
London, 3; New York, 5.

Leonard, Leonards, Lennard, Lenard.—Bapt. 'the son of Leonard.' For history of the name, v. Miss Yonge's Christian Names, i. 180. St. Leonard was a popular saint both in England and in France.
William Leonard, co. Hunts, 1273. A.
1546. James Leonard and Alice Barber: Marriage Lic. (Faculty Office), p. 8.
1606. Sampson Lennard, co. Norf.: FF. vi. 302.
1650. John Lennard and Jane Binding, *widow*: Marriage Lic. (Faculty Office), p. 45.
1791. Married—George Leonard and Eleanor Martin: St. Geo. Han. Sq. ii. 65.
London, 14, 1, 4, 1; Philadelphia, 134, 1, 6, 0.

Leopard, Lepard, Leppard, Lippard.—Nick. 'the leopard'; cf. Bull, Fox, &c.
John Lyppard, co. Norf., 1273. A.
Reginald Leopard, C. R., 28 Edw. I.
John Lepard. H.
1738. Married—Thomas Rogers and Eliz. Leopard (co. Surrey): St. Antholin (London), p. 149.
1790. — Richard Leopard and Sarah Wheeler: St. Geo. Han. Sq. ii. 38.
1794. — James Evans and Ann Lippard: ibid. ii. 117.
London, 0, 5, 2, 2; MDB. (co. Sussex), 1, 0, 6, 0; Middlesborough (Leopard), 2; New York (Leopard), 1.

Lepper.—Nick. ' the leper.' It has been said that leprosy was brought into Europe by the Crusaders. There were several spitals or hospitals for lepers in England. In the *Assisa de Foresta*, assigned by Manwood to 6 Edw. I, it is enacted that if any beast of chase be found wounded or dead, ' *caro mittatur ad domum leprosi, si qua prope fuerit*.' ' Lepyr, or lepre, man or woman or beeste, *leprosus*.

Lepyr, or lepre, sekenesse, *lepra*': Prompt. Parv., and see Way's note thereon.
Geoffrey le Lepere, co. Oxf., 1273. A.
Walter le Lepere, co. Bucks, ibid.
Robert Leper, co. Linc., ibid.
William le Lepar, C. R., 13 Edw. I.
Cf. Magister et Fratres Hospital' Sci. Jacobi Leprosi, London: A. i. 420.
Alicia Lepar, 1379: P. T. Yorks. p. 154.
1558. Buried—Thomas Leper, *bowyer*: St. Mary Aldermary, p. 133.
1576. John Hunte and Joyce Leper, *widow*: Marriage Lic. (London), i. 72.
West Rid. Court Dir., 1; New York, 2; Philadelphia, 6.

Leppington.—Local, ' of Leppington,' a chapelry in the parish of Scrayingham, E. Rid. Yorks.
1634. Bapt.—Marie, d. Roberte Lepington: St. Jas. Clerkenwell, i. 130.
1680-1. Lemuell Leppington and Sarah Allen: Marriage Alleg. (Canterbury), p. 50.
MDB. (West Rid. Yorks), 1.

Lermit. — Occup. 'l'hermite,' the hermit; cf. Armitage.
Dennis Lermitt, or Lermyt, of Norwich, 1621: FF. iii. 365.
Crockford, 1.

Lescombe.—Local, ' of Lescomb.' One of the many placenames ending in -*comb*, so frequently to be met with in the West country (v. Combe).
Thomas de Lescomb, co. Soms., 1 Edw. III: Kirby's Quest, p. 138.
London, 1.

Lesingham.—Local, ' of Lessingham,' a parish in co. Norfolk, near Stalham.
1674. Thomas Lessingham and Sarah Francklin: Marriage Alleg. (Canterbury), p. 113.
1676. Henry Lesingham and Dinah Penny: ibid. p. 174.
1713. Married—Samuel Lesingham and Mary Miller: St. Mary Aldermary, p. 42. London, 1.

Lester, Leicester, Leycester. —Local, ' of Leicester,' the well-known capital of the county of that name.
Ongar de Leycestre, co. Devon, 1273. A.
Sandre de Leycestre, London, ibid.
Robert de Lestre, co. Camb., ibid.
Henry de Laycestre, *specer* (i.e. *spicer*), 6 Edw. II: Freemen of York, i. 15.
1578. Ralph Lester, co. Ches.: Reg. Univ. Oxf. vol. ii. pt. ii. p. 80.

1604-5. Thomas Leycester, or Lester, co. Essex: ibid. p. 279.
London, 24, 1, 1; Crockford, 10, 3, 0; MDB. (co. Chester), 0, 0, 2; New York, 31, 1, 0.

L'Estrange. — Nickname, 'le Estrange,' the stranger; v. Strange, the recognized English form.

Alex. le Estraunge, co. Norf., 1273. A.
Roger le Estrange, co. Linc., ibid.
Roger Extraneus, co. Bedf., ibid.
Roger le Extrange, co. Bedf., ibid.
1546-7. Nicholas Lestrange and Catharine Men: Marriage Lic. (Faculty Office), p. 9.
1661. Alex. Scott and Ann Lestrange: ibid. p. 55.
Crockford, 2; New York, 6.

Lesturgeon, Lestourgeon. — Nick. 'the sturgeon,' q.v. Evidently a French importation.

1746. Married—Peter Lesturgeon and Mary Hide: St. Geo. Chap. Mayfair, p. 69.
1768. — Aaron Lestourgeon and Caroline Douxsaint: St. Geo. Han. Sq. i. 178.
1772. — Isaac Lesturgeon and Ann Wragg: ibid. p. 225.

Letchford.—Local, ' of Lechford,' possibly Leckford, a parish in co. Southampton. But v. Latchford.

Alex. de Lecheford, co. Oxf., 1273. A.
Philip de Lecheford, co. Oxf., ibid.
Walter de Lecheford, co. Oxf., ibid.
1592. Married—William Marten and Isabel Lechforde: St. Mary Aldermary, p. 8.
1616. Arthur Knight and Eliz. Lechford: Marriage Lic. (London), ii. 45.
Oxford, 1; Philadelphia, 4.

Letchworth. — Local, ' of Letchworth,' a parish in co. Hertford, near Hitchin.

Urban de Lecheworth, co. Essex, Hen. III-Edw. I. K.
1579. Giles Holden and Ellen Lechworthe: Marriage Lic. (London), i. 89.
London, 1; Philadelphia, 3.

Lethbridge.—Local, ' of Lethbridge.' Like Mr. Lower (Patr. Brit. p. 193), I cannot find the spot. It is evidently a Devonshire surname, and no doubt the locality is or was in that county.

1615. Anthony Lethbridge, co. Devon, gentleman: Reg. Univ. Oxf. vol. ii. pt. ii. p. 339.
1803. Married—Thomas Buckler Lethbridge and Ann Goddard: St. Geo. Han. Sq. ii. 280.
London, 4; Plymouth, 9; MDB. (co. Devon), 11; New York, 3; Boston (U.S.), 3.

Letherby; v. Leatherby.

Letheridge.—Bapt. ; v. Leveridge, of which this is an American variant. Cf. Leverton for Letherton.

Boston (U.S.), 1.

Leton; v. Letton.

Lett, Letts, Lettson, Lettsom, Letson.—Bapt. 'the son of Lettice' (Latin, laetitia, gladness). As a girl's name Lettice was very popular in its day. It is now rare. It suffered at the Reformation, and still more so in the Puritan era, not being a Bible name, and implying hilarity. Lett was the nick., Letts and Lettson being the patronymics. Lettsom is occasionally a corrupted form of Lettson (cf. Ransom for Ranson, or Hansom for Hanson), but in general it is local (v. Lettsom). It is said that a well-known doctor of the last century used to sign his prescriptions 'I. Lettsom,' whence the following:
'When any patient calls in haste,
I physics, bleeds, and sweats 'em;
If after that they choose to die,
Why, what care I?
    I Lettsom.'

Nicholas fil. Lete, co. Bedf., 1273. A.
John fil. Lettice, co. Camb., ibid.
Warin Lettice, co. Suff., ibid.
Lettice Kygelpeny, C. R., 28 Edw. I.
John Lettesone, c. 1300. M.
Johannes Leteson, 1379: P. T. Yorks. p. 211.
Willelmus Letis, 1379: ibid. p. 130.
Alicia Letis, 1379: ibid.
1683. Bapt.—Ann, d. Ralph Lett: St. Jas. Clerkenwell, i. 301.
1782. Married—Richard Hammonds and Ann Lettes: St. Geo. Han. Sq. i. 332.
London, 2, 8, 0, 0, 0; New York, 2, 1, 0, 0, 8.

Lettice.—Bapt. 'the son of Lettice' ; v. Lett for further information and earlier instances.

John Lettice. PP.
1568. George Bell and Judith Lettice: Marriage Lic. (London), i. 39.
1647. Buried—William, s. George Lettice: St. Jas. Clerkenwell, iv. 274.

Letton, Letten, Leton.—Local, ' of Letton,' a parish in co. Norfolk, one mile from Shipdham.

Simon de Leton, or Letton, co. Norf., 1273. A.
1337. William de Letton, rector of Buckenham Parva, co. Norf.: FF. ii. 269.
'John, son of Richard de Letton, for 4 marks and a gold ring, gave lands in Heringeshae,' &c. : ibid. x. 48.

1808. Married—William Little and Mary Letten: St. Geo. Han. Sq. ii. 390.
London, 1, 1, 0; New York, 0, 0, 1.

Lettsom. — Local, ' of Ledsham.' Although Lettsom is undoubtedly baptismal in some cases (v. Lett), it is as unquestionably local in others. Ledsham is a parish six miles north from Pontefract. Lettsom is a sharpened form.

Robertus de Ledesam, 1379: P. T. Yorks. p. 154.
Johannes de Ledsam, 1379: ibid. p. 145.
1570. Henry Ledsham: Reg. Univ. Oxf. I. 277.
1602-3. Hugh Rymell and Anne Ledsam, widow: Marriage Lic. (London), p. 276.
1603. Thomas Ledsham and Eliz. Danvers: ibid. p. 279.
1775. Married—Joseph Webb and Eliz. Letsome: St. Geo. Han. Sq. i. 249.

Lever. — Local, ' of Lever.' Great Lever is a township in the parish of Middleton, co. Lanc. Little Lever is a chapelry in the parish of Bolton, co. Lanc.

Alexander Lever, of Burnley, 1560: Wills at Chester (1545-1620), p. 122.
Richard Lever, of Little Lever, 1588: ibid.
Margaret Lever, of Lever, 1603: ibid.
Mary Lever, of Bolton-in-le-Moors, widow, 1668: ibid. (1660-80), p. 168.
1587. James Tanner and Cicely Leaver (co. Essex): Marriage Lic.(London), i.161.
Robertus Leyver, 1602: Preston Guild Rolls, p. 65.
Manchester, 14; London, 8; New York, 2.

Leverett. — ? Nickname, 'the leveret(?),' a young hare; v. Hare.

William Leverit, co. Oxf., 1273. A.
Agnes Leverit, co. Oxf., ibid.
1577-8. William Leverett and Juda Cole: Marriage Lic. (London), p. 78.
1601. Bapt.—Anthonie, son of Godfrey Leveritt: St. Jas. Clerkenwell, i. 39.
1625. Married—Thomas Leueritt and Ann Nicholls: ibid. iii. 55.
1702. — Roger Leveret and Hanah Speak: ibid. p. 225.
London, 1; Manchester, 2; Oxford, 3; New York, 2.

Leveridge, Leverick, Leverich.—Bapt. 'the son of Leofric' ; cf. Aldridge for Aldrich. Many surnames ending in -ridge seem to be of local origin ; yet they merely represent the -rich or -rick, that is, the suffix of so many early personal names. Coleridge is local, Leveridge is personal.

Mariota Leverich, co. Hunts, 1273. A.

Henry Leverige, co. Camb., 1273. A.
Robert Leverikke, co. Linc., ibid.
Roger Lefrich, co. Salop, ibid.
Richard Leverich, co. Soms., 1 Edw.
III : Kirby's Quest, p. 153.
1587. John Leveridge, co. Northampt.:
Reg. Univ. Oxf. vol. ii. pt. ii. p. 161.
1613. Bapt.—Charles, s. John Lyve-
ridge: St. Jas. Clerkenwell, i. 67.
1733. Buried—Joshua Leverick: St.
Dionis Backchurch, p. 302.
1778. Married—William Levridge and
Eliz. Turner: St. Geo. Han. Sq. i. 294.
London, 2, 0, 0; New York, 6, 0, 11.

Leversha.—Local, ' of Levi-
shagh,' a manor in the parish of
Buxton, co. Norfolk.

Halfred de Leveshagh, co. Norf.,
c. 1200: FF. vi. 445.
Henry de Leveshagh, co. Norf., c. 1260:
ibid.
William de Leveshaye, co. Norf., 20
Edw. I. R.
London, 1.

Leverton.—Local, ' of Leverton,' parishes in cos. Notts and
Lincoln. Also found as Letherton,
proving its origin, viz. ' the town of
Lether,' its first settler; cf. Liverpool for Litherpool; v. Litherland.

William de Letherton, co. Linc.,
1273. A.
William de Levertone, co. Linc., ibid.
Henry de Leverton, co. Linc., ibid.
Thomas de Leverton, co. Linc., 20
Edw. I. R.
1572. Bapt.—Jane, d. John Leverton:
St. Mary Aldermary, London, p. 57.
1578. Walter Hunt and Eliz. Leverton:
Marriage Lic. (London), i. 82.
London, 6; MDB. (co. Lincoln), 4;
Philadelphia, 1.

**Levett, Levet, Levette, Le-
vitt.**—(?) Local, ' of Livet.' Mr.
Lower says, 'From one of the places
in Normandy called Livet. The
Itin. de la Normandie mentions no
less than eight of these' (Patr.
Brit. p. 194). This derivation
seems probable.

William Levett, co. Linc., 1273. A.
Eustacius de Livet, co. York, Hen. III-
Edw. I. K.
1537. John Shelley and Johanna Levet:
Marriage Lic. (London), i. 9.
John Leavett, or Levet, co. Sussex,
1590: Reg. Univ. Oxf. vol. ii. p. 176.
Thomas Levite, or Levet, co. York,
1610: ibid. p. 318.
1694. Richard Levett and Ann Sweet-
apple: Marriage Lic. (London), ii. 316.
London, 8, 1, 1, 0; New York, 3, 1, 0, 1.

Levin(son; v. Lewin.

Levison.—Bapt. ' the son of
Lewis,' q.v. Also v. Leeson.

Roger Leveson, co. Oxf., 1273. A.
William Leveson, co. Oxf., ibid.

The Levisons in the New York
Directory are mostly of Jewish
parentage, 'the son of Levi,' as
is shown by the personal names
appended.

London, 1; New York, 14.

Lew, Lewe.—Local, ' at the
lew,' i.e. lee, a sheltered place
(v. *lee*, Skeat, who says the word
lee is Scandinavian); cf. Lewthwaite, a local Cumberland surname, i.e. sheltered meadow.
Professor Skeat adds, 'The true
English word is *lew*,' and quotes
its provincial use from Halliwell.

Alicia ate Lewe, co. Hunts, 1273. A.
John de Lewe, co. Salop, ibid.
1614. Married—Robert Lew and Prudence Greene: St. Jas. Clerkenwell, iii. 41.
1749.— Mark Demonther and and Sarah
Lew: St. Geo. Chap. Mayfair, p. 137.
New York, 0, 1; Boston (U.S.), 3, 0.

Lewd.—Nick. ' the lewd,' i.e.
the ignorant, untaught, one of the
laity, a layman. 'Lered and lewed,'
i.e. clergy and laity (v. Piers Plowman, Bk. iv. 11).

William le Lewed, c. 1300. M.
Robert le Lewed, ibid.
Robert le Lewede, C.R., 5 Edw. III. pt.i.
Roger Lude, co. Soms., 1 Edw. III :
Kirby's Quest, p. 184.
Nicholas Lude, co. Soms., 1 Edw. III :
ibid.

Lewes.—Local, ' of Lewes,' a
market-town in co. Sussex. The
surname is almost entirely lost in
Lewis (q.v.), that name also being
found in the form of Lewes.

John de Lewes, co. Oxf., 1273. A.
1555. Thomas Lewes and Alice Poole:
Marriage Lic. (London), i. 16.
1577. Thomas Lewes, co. Monmouth :
Reg. Univ. Oxf. vol. ii. pt. ii. p. 75.
— Lewes Hewes, co. Glamorgan : ibid.
1580. William Lewes, London: ibid.p.92.
Crockford, 1.

**Lewin, Levin, Levine, Le-
vene, Levinson, Levenson,
Lewinson.**—Bapt. ' the son of
Leofwin,' from the popular form
Lewin or Levin. Of one Leofwine,
a Warwickshire thegn, Professor
Freeman quotes, 'Leuuinus emit
ab Alwino fratre suo,' and again,
' Hanc terram dixit Leuuinus se
tenere de Vlstano Episcopo ' (Hist.
Norm. Conq. v. 785).

Leofwin, son of Hugh, temp. Ric. I :
Freeman, Norm. Conq. v. 894.
Leofwin, son of Godwin, temp. Ric. I :
ibid. iii. 361.

This Leofwin was in command
at Stamford Bridge.

Robert Lefwyne, co. Oxf., 1273. A.
Cecilia Leffeyne, co. Hunts, ibid.
Nicholas Leffeyne, co. Hunts, ibid.
William Lewine, co. Norf., ibid.
Henry Lewyn, co. Northumb., ibid.

The above references very clearly
mark the stages by which Lewin
was reached.

Lewin Scani, co. Bedf., 20 Edw. I. R.
Henry Lewyn, burgess of Newcastle-
on-Tyne, 1292: Brand's Hist. of Newcastle, i. 41.
1626. Bapt.—Barbary, d. Levin Wel-
den: St. Michael, Cornhill, p. 118.
1674. Buried—A child of Charles and
Levine Hornsby: St. Thomas the Apostle
(London), p. 140.
London, 18, 1, 1, 2, 1, 0, 0; New York,
16, 20, 10, 2, 7, 7, 5.

Lewington, Lewinton. —
Local, ' of Levington,' a parish in
co. Suffolk, five miles from Ipswich ;
cf. Lewin and Levin in the preceding article.

1662-3. John Hill and Sarah Lewington: Marriage Alleg. (Canterbury),
p. 84.
1749. Married—John Lewington and
Mary Crowhurst: St. Geo. Chap. Mayfair, p. 147.
1765.— Samuel Lewington and Jemima
Paice: St. Geo. Han. Sq. i. 139.
London, 3, 2.

Lewis, Lewison, Levison.—
Bapt. ' the son of Louis' or 'Lewis '
(for the history of this personal
name read an interesting account
in Yonge, ii. 387-9). Miss Yonge
thinks Lewis is used by the Welsh
as an Anglicanism of Llewelyn.
This view is confirmed by the following entry:

Llewelyn ap-Madoc, alias Lewis Rede,
archdeacon of Brecon, 1437 : Hist. and
Ant. St. David's, p. 360.
John Levesone, co. Soms., 1 Edw. III :
Kirby's Quest, p. 110.
Lewis ap-Owen, archdeacon of Car-
digan, 1487 : Hist. and Ant. St. David's,
p. 361.
Lewis ap-Rhys, prebendary of St.
David's, 1502 : ibid. p. 361.
William Lewison, archdeacon of Caer-
marthen, 1554 : ibid. p. 360.
1521. William Lewys and Alice Mason :
Marriage Lic. (London), i. 2.
1586. Humphrey Smith and Ursula
Lewson, alias Levison : ibid. p. 150.
London, 220, 1, 1; New York, 344, 2, 14.

Lewknor, Luckner.—Local, 'of Lewknor,' a parish in co. Oxf. I am informed that this surname still exists in Sussex.

Geoffrey de Leweknore, co. Oxf., 1273. A.
Alina de Leuekenore, co. Bucks, ibid.
Roger de Leukenore, co. Sussex, 20 Edw. I. R.
1568. Mathew Machell and Mary Lewckenare: Marriage Lic. (London), i. 39.
1625. Edward Lewkner and Sarah Richardson: ibid. ii. 151.
Boston (U.S.), 0, 1

Lewtas.—Local. I cannot find the spot. It is essentially a Lancashire name.

George Lewtus, of Out Rawcliffe, 1675: Lancashire Wills at Richmond (1457-1680), p. 183.
Manchester, 2; Lancaster, 1; MDB. (co. Lancaster), 4.

Lewthwaite, Laithwaite.—Local, 'of Lewthwaite,' some spot in co. Cumberland, or Furness, North Lancashire, with the familiar suffix -thwaite (v. Thwaite); probably a corruption of Leathwaite (v. Lea); cf.

1670. William Bisbrowne, of Leathwayte, Furness: Lancashire Wills at Richmond (1457-1680), p. 34.
Cf. Lucraft for Leacraft; v. Leacroft.
1546. Buried—George Lewteth (Lewthwaite): St. Mary, Ulverston, p. 3.
1553. Married—John Greene and Agnes Lewteth: ibid. p. 21.
1670. — George Fell and Helenar Leauthet: ibid. p. 151.
1650. James Lewthwaite, of Bardsey, parish of Urswick: Lancashire Wills at Richmond (1457-1680), p. 183.
1697. John Lewthwaite, of Lancaster: ibid. (1681-1748), p. 166.
1750. Married—Joseph Speck and Eliz. Leathwait: St. Michael, Cornhill, p. 72.
1792. — John Lewthwaite and Mary Tweedie: St. Geo. Han. Sq. ii. 84.
London, 2, 0; MDB. (co. Cumberland), 5, 0; Manchester, 1, 1.

Lewty. — ? Local. I cannot find any definite information about this North Lancashire surname.

Leonard Lewtie, of Much Plumpton, 1608: Lancashire Wills at Richmond (1457-1680), p. 183.
Edmund Lewtie, of Lea, 1673: ibid.
John Lewtye, of Plumpton Magna, 1676: ibid. p. 184.
London, 1; MDB. (co. Lancaster), 1; Preston, 2.

Ley.—Local, 'at the lea' or 'legh' (q.v.), from residence thereby.

William de Ley, co. Hunts, 1273. A.
John de Leya, co. Oxf., ibid.
Philip de la Ley, co. Northumb., 20 Edw. I. R.
1546. Thomas Dodsworth and Eliz. Ley, widow: Marriage Lic. (Faculty Office), p. 8.
1593. Married—Robart Leymine and Katharine Ley: St. Dionis Backchurch, p. 12.
1699. Bapt.—Mary, d. Robert Ley: St. Jas. Clerkenwell, i. 382.
London, 8; New York, 10.

Leycester.—Local, 'of Leicester'; v. Lester. Leycester is the oldest form.

Leyland.—Local; v. Layland.

Leyson, Lewson, Leyshon.—Bapt. 'the son of Lewis,' a Welsh surname. The h in Leyshon is intrusive, as in Dodgshon or Hodgshon; v. Lewis.

1453. Lewis Leyson: Reg. Univ. Oxf. i. 20.
1454. Robert Lewson: ibid. p. 24.
1524. Gryffyth Leyson: ibid. p. 135.
Ystrad Rhondda (South Wales), 0, 0, 1; Llantrissant, 0, 0, 1.

Liard.—Nick.; v. Lyard.

Libbe, Libby, Libbie, Libbey, Libbis.—Bapt. 'the son of Isabel,' from the nicks. Ibb and Libb, popularly Libby or Libbie. The variants of this surname are very well represented in the United States. The present nursery name is still Libby; for Elizabeth and Isabel are the same name, and are interchangeable in mediaeval records.

William Lybbe, chaplain, 1506: Reg. Univ. Oxf. i. 45.
John Libb, co. Oxf.: ibid. vol. ii. pt. ii. p. 149.
London, 0, 2, 0, 0, 2; Boston (U.S.), 1, 86, 4, 26, 0.

Liberty.— (?) Occup. Probably a corruption of Leadbeater, q.v. But Mr. Lower thinks it must be considered local. Then it would be 'of the liberty,' from residence in some early franchised district so called. There is a village called Liberty in co. Fife.

1669. Married—John Bayley and Saray Libiter: St. Jas. Clerkenwell, iii. 156.

This looks like a halfway house between Leadbeater, q.v., or Lidbetter, and Liberty.

London, 1; Crockford, 1; Boston (U.S.), 1; Worcester (U.S.), 5.

Libtrot; v. Liptrott.

Licence; v. Lysons, an imitative variant.

Lickbarrow; v. Litchbarrow.

Lickfold, Lickfeld.—Local, 'of Lickfold,' a place near Petworth, co. Sussex (Lower).

MDB. (co. Sussex), 2, 0; London, 4, 0; Philadelphia, 0, 3.

Lickorish; v. Liquorish.

Lidbetter.—Occup.; v. Leadbeater.

Crockford, 1.

Liddell, Liddle, Liddall, Liddel.—Local, 'of the Liddel,' a river in Roxburghshire. The surname settled in Newcastle at an early period; v. Lower, Patr. Brit. p. 194.

1586. George Gardener and Mary Lyddall: Marriage Lic. (London), i. 154.
1680. Bapt.—Mary, d. William Lydall: St. Dionis Backchurch, p. 154.
1752. Married—William Goodchild and Mary Liddell: St. Geo. Chap. Mayfair, p. 220.
1775. — John Claxton and Mary Liddle, St. Geo. Han. Sq. i. 258.
MDB. (co. Cumberland), 5, 1, 0, 0; (co. Northumberland), 5, 0, 0, 1; London, 6, 6, 1, 0; New York, 5, 2, 0, 0.

Liddington, Lidington. —Local, 'of Liddington': (1) a parish in co. Rutland, near Uppingham; (2) a parish in co. Wilts, near Swindon.

Robert de Liddinton, co. Oxf., Hen. III-Edw. I. K.
(Tenentes) Lidinton, co. Rutland, 1273. A.
Fulco de Lydinton, co. Oxf., ibid.
Thomas de Ledintone, co. Soms., 1 Edw. III: Kirby's Quest, p. 203.
1603. Bapt.—Eliz., d. Thomas Liddington, armorer: St. Peter, Cornhill, i. 53.
1795. Married—Thomas Bullivant and Susannah Liddington: St. Geo. Han. Sq. ii. 134.
MDB. (co. Northampton), 1, 2.

Liddon.—Local, 'of Lydden,' a parish in co. Kent, near Dover. Probably this is the true parent; but there may have been a spot bearing this name in the West country.

John de Lyddone, co. Soms., 1 Edw. III: Kirby's Quest, p. 177.

Adam de Lyddone, co. Soms., 1 Edw. III: Kirby's Quest, p. 177.
1543-4. John White and Johanna Lydden, of Whittsam, co. Kent: Marriage Lic. (Faculty Office), p. 2.
1800. Married—William Lyddon and Bessey Goldsmith: St. Geo. Han. Sq. ii. 224.
London, 3; New York, 1.

Lidgate, Lidgett, Liggett, Ligate, Ligget, Lydiate, Liddiatt.—Local, 'at the lidgate,' from residence thereby, a common local term in old records. Lidgate, a gateway, an entrance, perhaps a covered way (v. Skeat on *lid*). As a child I played on a spot called Lidgate, near Waterhead, Oldham. 'John Dodds dwellynge at Lodgayte at the signe of the spayd': *Liber Bursarii Eccles. Dunelmensis*, Surt. Soc. Bishop Hotham in 1320 gave for alms 'tenementum vocatum Lythgates': *Hist. Elien. Ang. Sacra.* p. 643.

Robert atte Lidegate, C. R., 14 Edw. I.
Walter atte Lideyate. H.
Matilda atte Lydeyate, 1379: P. T. Yorks. p. 119.
Robertus atte Lytheyate, 1379: ibid. p. 122.
Johannes Robert-man atte Lythgat, 1379: ibid. p. 123.

For the suffix *-yate*, v. Yate.

1591. Thomas Lidiot, co. Oxf.: Reg. Univ. Oxf. vol. ii. pt. ii. p. 187.
1602. John Death and Mary Lidiatt: Marriage Lic. (London), i. 269.
1627. Married—Edward Underwood and Dorothy Lidyate: St. Jas. Clerkenwell, iii. 58.

Ludgate is found as well as Lidgate; cf. Ludgater in next article.

1784. Married—Thomas Harper and Rebecca Ludgate: St.Geo. Han.Sq. i. 365.

Hence the local Ludgate, London.

Manchester (Liggett), 1; London (Lidgett), 1; Liverpool (Lidgate), 1; MDB. (co. Chester) (Lydiate), 1; (co. Salop) (Ligget), 1; (co. Derby) (Ligate), 1; (co. Glouc.) (Liddiatt), 2; New York (Lidgate), 1.

Lidgater, Ludgater.—Local, 'the lidgater,' one who resided at a lidgate (q.v.). This surname incidentally proves the former familiarity of the local term *lidgate*; v. Bridger.

1738. Married—William Ludgater and Ann Langstaff: St. Geo. Han. Sq. i. 21. Crockford, 0, 2.

Lidington ; v. Liddington.

Lidlington.—Local, 'of Lidlington,' a parish in co. Bedf., near Ampthill.
London, 1.

Lidster.—Occup. 'the litster,' a dyer. The later and almost universal form was Lister, q.v. Lidster is naturally found in Yorkshire, the great home of the litsters, both as regards occupation and name.

Hull, 2; Sheffield, 3; West Rid. Court Dir., 1; MDB. (co. Lincoln), 1.

Lidstone.—Local, 'of Lidstone,' a hamlet in the parish of Church Enstone, co. Oxf.
London, 2; Philadelphia, 2.

Lief ; v. Leaf.

Liefchild ; v. Leifchild.

Liefqueen. — Nick. 'dear quean.' M.E. *lef*, dear; and M.E. *quene*, a woman, a quean, a strumpet. But probably here simply 'dear woman,' a title of endearment like Bellamy; cf. Leifchild.

Edith Lefquene, 1273. A.
Johannes Lefquen, ibid.

Ligget(t ; v. Lidgate.

Light.—Nick. 'the little,' a variant of Lyte; cf. Lightman, a later variant of Lyteman (i.e. Littleman); v. Lyte. It is quite possible that Light might refer to the light tread of the original bearer of the sobriquet, but I find no evidence.

1586. William Bellamye and Hester Lighte: Marriage Lic. (London), i. 150.
1626. Married—Thomas Broughe and Ann Light: St. Michael, Cornhill, p. 24.
London, 7; MDB. (Hants), 8.

Lightbody.—Nick. for one of light weight, nimble and agile.
London, 1; New York, 4.

Lightbourn, Lightbourne, Lightbound, Lightbown, Lightbowne.—Local, 'of Lightbourn.' Probably there are several spots so called in co. Lancashire. A suburb of my old parish (Ulverston, North Lancashire) is called Lightburne, the beck or burn flowing alongside (v. Burn). With the corrupted Lightbound, cf. Simmonds for Simmons, or *riband* for *ribbon*. The *d*, of course, is an excrescence. That Lightbown and

Lightbowne are variants of Lightbourn is proved below, although proof is not needed. There is no representative of any of the forms in my London Directory (1870). It is well confined to co. Lancashire.

Roger Lightborn, of Caton, 1593: Lancashire Wills at Richmond (1457-1680), p. 184.
Robert Lightbourne, of Eccles, 1598: Wills at Chester (1545-1620), p. 123.
William Lightbourne, of Bolton-le-Moors, 1614: ibid.

In the next generation the name is written Lightbowne:

James Lightbowne, of Manchester, 1621: Wills at Chester (1621-50), p. 139.
Alexander Lightbowne, of Eccles, 1638: ibid.

In Ulverston, Lightburn is a name over a shop in close proximity to the suburb Lightburne.

1781. Bapt.—Ann, d. George Lightburn: St. Mary, Ulverston, p. 498.
MDB. (co. Lancaster), 1, 1, 1, 0, 0; Manchester, 0, 1, 0, 1, 2; Liverpool (Lightbound), 4; New York (Lightbourn), 1.

Lightfoot.—Nick. 'light foot,' from the light springy tread of the bearer; cf. Golightly and Pettifer; also Lithefoot, below.

William Lightfot, co. Camb., 1273. A.
Henry Lithfot, co. Oxf., ibid.
Robert Lightfot, 1301. M.
Willelmus Lightfote, 1379: P. T. Yorks. p. 239.
1571. Randall Smythe and Mary Lightfoot,*widow*: Marriage Lic.(London),i. 49.
London, 8; Crockford, 8; New York, 1.

Lightoller, Lightowler, Lightowlers.—Local, 'of Lightowlers,' an estate in the parish of Stockport.

John Lightowlers, of Withnell, co. Lanc., 1606-7: Lancashire Inquisitions, pt. i. p. 74.
Robert Lightowler, of Wyndybank, 1620: Wills at Chester, i. 123.
James Chadwick, of Lightowlers, parish of Stockport, 1621: ibid. ii. 45.
Edmund Lightowler, of Castleton, 1623: ibid. p. 139.
1624. Bapt.—John, s. Thomas Lightollors: St. Jas. Clerkenwell, i. 98.
1631. Married—Thomas Godfrey and Ann Lightellers: ibid. iii. 62.
Chorley (co. Lanc.), 1, 0, 0; North Bierley (Yorks), 0, 3, 5; New York, 0, 3, 0.

Liley, Lilie ; v. Lilly.

Lill.—Local, 'of Lille,' i.e. the French town of that name.

Robert de Lill, co. Oxf., Hen. III-Edw. I. K.

William de Lille, co. Oxf., 1273. A.

Robert de Lille, co. Oxf., ibid.

1734. Married—William Lill and Eliz. Randal: St. Geo. Han. Sq. i. 13.

London, 4; MDB. (co. Lincoln), 10; Boston (U.S.), 2.

Lillicrap, Lillicrapp, Lilly-crap, Lillycrop.—Local. This curious surname is found in cos. Devon and Cornwall. I cannot suggest a derivation, but no doubt it is the name of some locality.

Plymouth, 6, 0, 0, 0; London, 0, 1, 0, 0; MDB. (co. Cornwall), 0, 0, 2, 1.

Lillingston.—Local, ' of Lillingstone,' two parishes, one in co. Bucks, the other in co. Oxf.

1689. Marmaduke Constable and Eliz. Lillingstone: Marriage Alleg. (Canterbury), p. 123.

Oxford, 1.

Lillington.—Local, ' of Lillington': (1) a parish in co. Dorset, near Sherborne; (2) a parish in co. Warwick, near Leamington.

1616. John Lillington: Reg. Univ. Oxf. i. 360.

1691. Nathaniel Huthnance and Susanna Lillington: Marriage Alleg. (Canterbury), p. 196.

1806. Married—Thomas Barnett and Susanna Lillington: St. Geo. Han. Sq. ii. 214.

Lilly, Lilley, Lillie, Liley, Lillee, Lilie.—(1) Bapt. ' the son of Lily.' The dim. Lilion (now Lilian) must have been in early use, as it is found as a surname in the Hundred Rolls ; cf. Marion for Mary, now Marian.

Geoffrey Lilion, co. Bedf., 1273. A.

(2) Local, ' of Lilley,' a parish in co. Hertf., four miles from Luton. (3) Local, ' of Lilly,' a hamlet in the parish of Catmore, co. Berks. My two first instances occur in the neighbourhood.

Nicholas Lilie, co. Oxf., 1273. A.

William Lilie, co. Oxf., ibid.

Beatrix Lyly, 1379: P. T. Yorks. p. 214.

Robert Lyllye, 1546: Reg. Univ. Oxf. i. 213.

1564. Gilbert Lyllye and Joanna Matthewe, widow: Marriage Lic. (London), i. 30.

1571. John Lyllie, co. Kent: Reg. Univ. Oxf. vol. ii. pt. ii. p. 51.

1605. Bapt.—William, s. Raphe Lylly: St. Jas. Clerkenwell, i. 45.

London, 8, 16, 5, 2, 0, 0; MDB. (co. Lincoln), 1, 8, 0, 0, 1, 0; New York, 14, 7, 5, 0, 0, 2.

Lillyman, Lilleyman, Lilleman, Lilliman.—Occup. ' the servant of Lilly,' q.v. One more instance of a fairly large class of surnames compounded of -man (i.e. servant) as suffix to the baptismal name of the master. The most conspicuous instances are Matthewman, Addyman, and Perryman, q.v. Although not entirely confined to that county, Yorkshire must be looked upon as the home of this batch of surnames.

Ricardus Lilyman, 1379: P. T. Yorks. p. 72.

Johannes Lelman, 1379: ibid. p. 75.

Thomas Lelyman, 1379: ibid. p. 63.

1752. Married—James Lillyman and Ann Pugh: St. Geo. Chap. Mayfair, p. 232.

Sheffield, 1, 1, 0, 0; Swinton (near Rotherham), 0, 0, 1, 0; MDB. (co. Lincoln), 0, 0, 0, 1; Boston (U.S.) (Lillyman), 2.

Lillywhite.—Nick. ' the lily-white,' one whose complexion was white as a lily. One of endless surnames of a similar class ; v. White, Reid, Black, Russell, Burnell, &c.

1664. Married—Thomas Lilliwhite and Rebecca Benbrigg: St. Jas. Clerkenwell, iii. 116.

1723. William Washington and Sarah Lillywhite, widow: Marriage Lic. (Faculty Office), p. 250.

1788. Married—Emery Mussett and Mary Lillywhite: St. Geo. Han. Sq. ii. 12.

1796. — Charles Hensley and Lucy Lillewhite : ibid. p. 157.

London, 4.

Lilter.—Occup. ' the lilter,' a player on an instrument, a singer.

Roger le Lilter, co. Hunts, 1273. A.

Lilwall.—Local, ' of Lilwall,' a township in the parish of Kington, co. Hunts.

1783. Married—John Wolf and Eliz. Lillwell: St. Geo. Han. Sq. i. 342.

London, 1.

Limbert, Limbird. — Bapt. ' the son of Lambert ' (?). This corruption is found in co. Norfolk three centuries ago. This county being adjacent to the Low Countries we naturally expect to see Lambert and its corruptions familiar there.

Stephen Lymbert, died Oct. 10, 1580. Norwich: FF. iv. 61.

1785. Married—John Limbird and Ann Elborn : St. Geo. Han. Sq. i. 375.

London, 1, 2 ; New York, 5, 0.

Limbrey.—Local, ' of Limbury.' a hamlet in the parish of Luton. co. Bedf.

1605. John Lymberie, co. Soms.: Reg. Univ. Oxf. vol. ii. pt. ii. p. 284.

1666. William Limbery and Sarah Swanley: Marriage Alleg. (Canterbury), p. 188.

1686. James Field and Eliz. Limbrey : ibid. p. 230.

London, 1.

Limbrick, Limrick. — (1) Local, ' of Lambrigg' (?), a township in the parish of Kendal, co. Westm. The suffix -brigg (bridge) often becomes brick; cf. Philbrick and Maybrick. (2) Local ' of Limerick ' (?), with an intrusive b after m, as is so common. The surname would first become Limrick, then Lim-b-rick. I have an impression that if there are any low-lying hills about Limber in co. Linc. the origin is Limberigg, i.e. Limberidge, one who lived on the ridge thereby; cf. Coleridge, &c.

1564-5. James Limbericke: Reg. Univ. Oxf. vol. ii. pt. ii. p. 24.

— Thomas Limbericke: ibid.

1667. Married — Thomas Wall and Mary Lemericke: St. Jas. Clerkenwell, iii. 137.

1748. — Thomas Limberick and Eliz. Chamberlain: St. Geo. Chap. Mayfair, p. 114.

London, 1, 0 ; Liverpool, 0, 1 ; New York, 0, 1 ; Boston (U.S.), 0, 1.

Limburg, Limberg.—Local, ' of Limburg.' But more probably ' of Limber,' a parish and a hamlet (Magna and Parva) in co. Linc. Mr. Lower writes these as Limbergh.

Johannes de Lymbergh', 1379: P. T. Yorks. p. 113.

Robertus de Lymburgh', 1379: ibid.

London, 1, 0 ; New York, 1, 0 ; Boston (U.S.), 0, 1.

Limeburner. — Occup. ' the limeburner.' It is never safe to say a surname is extinct. Limeburner was in existence at the latter end of last century; cf. Limewright. Since writing the above I find the surname has crossed the Atlantic, and is in a fairly flourishing condition.

John le Lymberner, Rot. Fines, 7 Edw. I.

Robert le Lymbrennere, C. R., 13 Edw. II.
1760. Married—Benjamin Limeburner and Sarah Wilkshire: St. Geo. Han. Sq. i. 94.
Philadelphia, 4.

Limehirst.—Local, 'at the limehurst,' from residence beside a wood of lime-trees; v. Hirst.

Johannes del Lymehirst, 1379: P. T. Yorks. p. 35.

Limes.—Local, ' at the limes,' more correctly 'lines,' i.e. the linden-trees, from residence beside some particular lime-tree or trees; v. Limehirst.

Hugo del Lymbe, 1379: P. T. Yorks. p. 179.
1708. Married—John Limb and Mary West: St. Antholin (London), p. 121.
London, 1.

Limewright. — Occup. 'the limewright,' a limeburner. M.E. *lym*, lime.

Hugh de Limwryte, co. Bucks, 1273. A.

Limiter.—Offic. 'the limiter,' i.e. a friar licensed to beg within certain prescribed limits; cf. Fryer, Monk, &c.

1581. George Limiter, or Lymiter, co. Kent: Reg. Univ. Oxf. vol. ii. pt. ii. p. 103.
Mary, d. of George Limiter of Canterbury: Visitation of Glouc., 1623, p. 166.
Turning, however, to the Canterbury register, I find:
1712. Buried—Peter Lemastre: Reg. Canterbury Cathedral, p. 314.
which the register of affidavits spells Lematre. So it may be but a French name Anglicized. There are six Lemaitres in the London Dir.

Limmer.—(1) Local, ' of Limber' (?). Limber Magna is a parish, and Limber Parva a hamlet, in co. Lincoln, near Caistor. Limmer is probably a variant, but v. Limner. (2) Occup. 'the limer,' a limeburner; v. Limewright and Limeburner. Limer would naturally settle down into Limmer.

Thomas de Limer, bailiff of Norwich, 1245: FF. iii. 58.
William de Lymar, co. Northampt., 1273. A.
John de Limer, co. Hunts, ibid.
Agnes Limer, co. Hunts, ibid.
Adam Lymer, co. Camb., ibid.
1620-1. Robert Limber and Jane Roberts: Marriage Lic. (London), ii. 96.

1627. Married—Thomas Limer and Bridget Wilkinsone: St. Mary Aldermary, p. 16.
1776. — Stephen Limmer and Eliz. Deewes: St. Geo. Han. Sq. i. 263.
There can be little doubt that both (1) and (2) share the parentage of Limmer.

London, 2; New York, 3.

Limner, Limmer, Lomer, Lommer.—Occup. 'the limner,' an illuminator of books, missals, &c. (v. Limmer for a different origin.)
'Parchemente makers, skynners and plowers,
Barbers, boke-bynders, and lyminers.'
Cocke Lorelle's Bote.
Nicholas Cotes, *lummer*, 1421, York. W. 11.
' *Lymnyd*, as bookys, *elucidatus*; lymnore, *elucidator, miniographus*': Prompt. Parv. It is natural to find Oxford and Cambridge represented in the Hundred Rolls, as seen below. In the *Mun. Acad. Oxon.*, p. 550, we find a quarrel settled between 'John Conaley, lymner,' and John Godsend, 'stationarius.' It is arranged that the former shall occupy himself 'liminando bene et fideliter suos libros.'

Thomas Liminor, co. Camb., 1273. A.
Ralph Illuminator, co. Oxf., ibid.
John de Gippeswyk, *lomenoure*, 14 Edw. III: Freemen of York, i. 34.
Henry Lumynour, C. R., 15 Ric. II.
Thomas Lumpner, 1470, York. W. 11.
Godfrey le Lomynour. T.

Limner lingered on till the 18th century, and perhaps is not yet defunct.
'John Limner, of Chevington, and Eliz. Sibbes, of this town, were married August 22nd, 1700': Sibbes' Works, i. cxlii.
1767. Married—Donald McDonald and Sarah Lomer: St. Geo. Han. Sq. i. 167.
1787. — William Collin and Prudence Limmer: ibid. p. 407.
There need be no hesitation in accepting these as modern forms of this old and interesting occupative name. It is found, as already seen, as Lummer (with the *n* dropped) in Yorkshire in the 15th century. The following is unmistakable:
1562. Buried—William, son of Harry Lomner: St. Dionis Backchurch, p. 78.
1374. Henry Lumnor, or Liminour, or Lomynour, or Lumnour, or Luminour: FF. iv. 185, iv. 180, iii. 113, ii. 398, v. 56.

London, 0, 2, 2, 0; MDB. (co. Suffolk), 0, 2, 0, 0; Boston (U.S.), 0, 1, 0, 1.

Limon; v. Leman.

Limrick; v. Limbrick.

Linacre, Linaker, Lineker, Linneker.—Local, ' of Linacre,' a township in the parish of Walton-on-the-hill, co. Lancaster. One of many local terms with -*acre* as suffix; cf. Stirzaker, Whittaker.

Peter de Linacre, co. Camb., 1273. A.
Mabilia de Linacre, co. Camb., ibid.
1573. Robert Pepper and Agnes Lynecar: Marriage Lic. (London), i. 58.
Thomas Linaker, of Chester, 1602: Wills at Chester (1545-1620), p. 124.
Robert Linaker, of Great Meols, 1613: ibid.
John Lynacre, of Stourton, parish of Bebbington, 1614: ibid. p. 128.
Elizabeth Johnson, of Linacre, *widow*, 1616: ibid. p. 110.
1809. Married—Michael Edward Jacob and Catherine Liniker: St. Geo. Han. Sq. ii. 411.
Liverpool, 4, 2, 0, 0; MDB. (co. Ches.), 0, 1, 0, 0; (West Rid. Yorks), 0, 0, 1, 0; Sheffield (Linneker), 1.

Lincey; v. Lindsey.

Linck, Lincke; v. Link.

Lincoln.—Local, ' of Lincoln,' the cathedral city of the shire of that name. The surname has ramified strongly in the United States.

Robert de Linccolne, co. Notts, 1273. A.
Richard de Linccolne, co. Hunts, ibid.
Hugh de Lyncoln, *piscator*, 3 Edw. II: Freemen of York, i. 12.
Daniel de Lyncoln, 1324. M.
Adam de Lincoln, 1379: P. T. Yorks. p. 206.
William Lincoln, 1537: Reg. Univ. Oxf. i. 189.
1753. Sibella Lincon, carried to be buried at Epping, Essex: St. Dionis Backchurch, p. 319.
London, 15; Boston (U.S.), 149.

Lind, Lynde, Lynd.—Local, ' at the lind,' i.e. the linden-tree, modernly, the lime-tree. *Lind* is the true subs., and *linden*, like woollen or golden, is the adj. (Skeat). Lind is the root of many local names, such as Lyndhurst, Lindley, Lindale, and Lindow, q.v.

Henry de la Lynde. B.
Robert ate Lynde, temp. 1300. M.
Thomas de la Lynde, co. Soms., 1 Edw. III: Kirby's Quest, p. 197.
1596. Humphrey Linde, of London: Reg. Univ. Oxf. vol. ii. pt. ii. p. 218.

1800. Married—Peter Snowdon and Harriot Linde: St. Geo. Han. Sq. ii. 222. London, 3, 1, 0; New York, 0, 8, 1.

Lindale, Lindall, Lindell, Lyndall.—Local, 'of Lindall'; v. Lindow.

London, 0, 0, 0, 1; Philadelphia, 1, 0, 1, 9.

Lindley, Linley.—Local, 'of Lindley,' a parish in the outskirts of Huddersfield, co. Yorks. Smaller spots will, no doubt, be so called; v. Lind.

Robert de Linleye, co. Bedf., 1273. A.
Augustin Lynleye, co. Soms., 1 Edw. III: Kirby's Quest, p. 94.
1594. Arthur Lindley, co. York: Reg. Univ. Oxf. vol. ii. pt. ii. p. 207.
1670. John Lindeley and Anne Wilson: Marriage Lic. (Faculty Office), p. 116.
London, 5, 5; West Rid. Court Dir., 4, 11; New York, 4, 1.

Lindow, Lindo.—Local, 'of Lindall,' in Furness, North Lancashire, a hamlet two miles from Ulverston. This became Lindaw, and then Lindow. Thus in the same district Presow (as a surname) represents the older Precsall, and Picthaw stands for Picthall. Lindow has crossed the Duddon into Cumberland.

1546. Bapt.—Elesabeth Lindoe: Reg. Ulverston Ch., p. 2.
— — Kataran Lindoe: ibid.
George Lindo, or Lyndoe, of Urswick, 1592: Lancashire Wills at Richmond, p. 184.
Margaret Lindowe, of Ulverston, 1598: ibid.
James Lindall, of Ulverston, Furness, 1661: ibid.
Elizabeth Lindaw, of Aradfoot, Ulverston, 1662: ibid.
London, 1, 4; MDB. (co. Cumberland), 2, 0; Ulverston, 1, 0; New York, 0, 5.

Lindraper.—Occup. 'the linen-draper.' Linen, like woollen, is an adjective; the subs. is *lin*. God made 'ffor to cover us and clethe us also lyne, and wolle, and lethire' (Mirror of St. Edmund, E.E.T.S., p. 21). Cocke Lorelle's Bote includes 'lyne-webbers' and 'lyne-drapers'; v. Liner.

Ino le Lyngedraper, C. R., 52 Hen. III.
William le Lyndraper. G.
Wymund le Lyngedraper, co. Oxf., 1273. A.
Elias le Lyndraper, temp. 1300. M.
William le Lynged(r)aper, 7 Edw. II: Freemen of York, i. 15.

Lindsey, Lindsay, Linsey, Linzee, Lincey. — Local, 'of Lindsey.' Lindsey, a parish in co. Suffolk; no doubt it means the 'linden-isle.' Probably other spots are so called. A division of co. Lincoln is still called the 'Parts of Lindsey.' The instances below are widely separated, and point to more than one spot so called.

Walter de Lyndesay, 56 Hen. III: Nicolson and Burn's Hist. Westm. and Cumb., i. 35.
Thomas de Lyndesey, co. Derby, 1273. A.
Henry de Lindeseye, co. Kent, ibid.
Robert de Lindesay, co. Notts, ibid.
William de Lyndeseye, co. Northampt., 20 Edw. I. R.
William de Lyndesaie, 11 Edw. I: Nicolson and Burn's Hist. Westm. and Cumb., i. 35.
Willelmus de Lyndesay, 1379: P. T. Yorks. p. 273.
Jacobus de Lyndesay, 1379: ibid. p. 164.
1546. Ralph Brooke and Eliz. Lynseye: Marriage Lic. (London), i. 9.
1793. Married—William Ball and Margaret Lindsey: St. Geo. Han. Sq. ii. 99.
London, 14, 17, 2, 0, 0; MDB. (co. Berks.) 0, 0, 0, 1, 0; Crockford (Lincey), 1; Philadelphia; 19, 124, 2, 0, 0.

Line, Lyne.—Local, 'at the lane' (?), from residence therein. Probably one of the many dialectic forms of the word *lane*.

Thomas in ye Lyen, 1379: P. T. Yorks. pp. 140-1.
Willelmus in ye Lyne, 1379: ibid.
Johannes del Lyen, 1379: ibid.
1582. Buried—William Lyne, sonne of John Lyne; he dyed of ye plague, yers 29: St. Peter, Cornhill, i. 129.
1606. Richard Lyne, co. Hants: Reg. Univ. Oxf. vol. ii. pt. ii. p. 289.
London, 11, 4; New York, 0, 1: Boston (U.S.), 2, 0.

Lineaweaver. — Occup.; v. Linwebb.

Lineker.—Local; v. Linacre.

Liner, Lyner.—Occup. 'the liner,' a flax-dresser; v. Lindraper.

Richard de Wymondham, *lyner*, 9 Edw. III: Freemen of York, i. 29.
1668. Married—Thomas Lynear and Saray Browne: St. Jas. Clerkenwell, iii. 160.

With Lynear, cf. Bowyer, *lawyer*, &c., the *e* being for euphony as the *y* in Bowyer.

Philadelphia, 1, 0; New York, 0, 1.

Linford, Linforth. — Local, 'of Linford,' two parishes (Great and Little Linford) in co. Bucks. The suffix *-forth* = ford (v. Forth).

Roger de Lynford, co. Bucks, 1273. A.
1591. William Osborne and Parnell Lyndeforde: Marriage Lic. (London), i. 194.
1670. Bapt.—John, s. John Linford: Kensington Ch. p. 53.
London, 4, 2; New York, 1, 0.

Ling, Linge.—(1) Local, 'at the ling,' one who resided on the heath or ling; cf. Heath, Gorst, Furse. 'Lynge of the hethe (lynge, or hethe)': Prompt. Parv. Mr. Way in a note easily proves that ling was a common term for heath. He adds, 'Skinner gives ling as the common appellation of heath in Lincolnshire.' (2) Local, 'of Ling,' a parish in co. Somerset, six miles from Bridgewater. Both Ling and Linge are familiar surnames in the county. Probably the origin is the same.

Henry atte Lyng, co. Norf., 52 Hen. III; FF. x. 117.
John de Ling, co. Norf., 1273. A.
Roger de Lyng, bailiff of Norwich, 1370: FF. iii. 100.
1379. Married—James Bland, *draper*, and Ellen Ling, *widow*: St. Mary Aldermary, p. 6.
Henry and John Linge were resident in Virginia, in 1623: Hotten's Lists of Emigrants, p. 72.
1661. Buried—Ann Ling: St. Antholin (London), p. 88.
London, 13, 0; MDB. (Norfolk), 6, 0; (Somerset), 13, 1; Boston (U.S.), 5, 0.

Lingard, Linguard.—Occup. 'the ling-ward' (?) or 'ling-guard' (?). I can only suggest this solution. The great Catholic historian was of Lincolnshire parentage. Canon Tierney, after stating this fact, says, 'The family name, with the accent on the first syllable, is still common in the district. (Claxby), which, within the memory of persons yet alive, was a wild expanse covered with furze and *ling*' (Lingard's Hist. of Eng. i. 2, edit. 1854). Lancashire and Cheshire have been familiar with the surname for at least five centuries; cf. Woodward, and v. Ling.

Robert Lyngard, de Preston, co. Lanc., 1415: Preston Guild Rolls, p. 10.

1566. Married—Lawrence (blank) and Dorythye Lyngarde, *widow*: St. Michael, Cornhill, p. 9.

Thomas Lingard, of Eccles, *butcher*, 1569: Wills at Chester (1545-1620), p. 124.

John Lingard, of Middlewich, 1595: ibid.

Laurence Lingart, of Fullwood: Lancashire Wills at Richmond (1457-1748), p. 185.

London, 4, 0; Manchester, 8, 0; MDB. (co. Lincoln), 3, 1; Philadelphia, 3, 0.

Lingen, Lingain.—Local, 'of Lingen,' a parish in co. Hereford; v. Lingham.

John de Lyngayne, co. Salop, 1273. A.
1586-7. John Lingen, of Gloucester Hall: Reg. Univ. Oxf. vol. ii. pt. ii. p. 157.
1698. Married—John Lingen and Sarah Muddiclip: St. Michael, Cornhill, p. 49.
MDB. (co. Hereford), 1, 0; (co. Worc.), 1, 0; Boston (U.S.), 0, 1.

Linger.—Local, 'of Lingure.' Probably of Norman extraction. It is interesting to note that the early Oxfordshire Lingures are still to be met with in the neighbouring county of Buckingham.

Robert de Linguire, co. Berks, Hen. III-Edw. I. K.
Henry de Lingure, co. Oxf., ibid.
Alice de Lyngure, co. Oxf., 1273. A.
1609. Buried—Jane, d. Nicholas Lingar: St. Jas. Clerkenwell, iv. 106.
1628. — Joyce Linger: ibid. p. 193.
1632. — Ursula Linger: Canterbury Cath. p. 117.
MDB. (co. Bucks), 2; New York, 1; Philadelphia, 1.

Lingham.—Local, 'of Lingen,' a parish in co. Hereford. Mr. Lower says, 'Lingham, a known corruption of Langham.' I think this must be a mistake. The evidence is distinctly in favour of the derivation given above; v. Lingen.

Leonard Lyngham, or Lyngam, 1541: Reg. Univ. Oxf. i. 200.
Richard Lingam, or Lingen, from Stoke Edyth in co. Hereford, 1542: ibid. pp. 204, 313.
1650. Married—Edmund Lingham and Margarett Jackson: St. Dionis Backchurch, p. 27.
London, 1; Crockford, 3; MDB. (co. Worc.), 1; New York, 2.

Lingwood.—Local, 'of Lingwood,' a parish in co. Norfolk.

John de Lyngwood, of Norwich, 1294: FF. iv. 386.
William de Lingwood, co. Norf., 9 Edw. II: ibid. vii. 237.

1568. Buried—Rowlande, s. John Lyngwood: St. Michael, Cornhill, p. 189.
Thomas Lyngwoode, rector of Ovington, co. Norf., 1601: FF. ii. 296.
London, 1; MDB. (co. Essex), 1; (co. Suffolk), 3.

Link, Linke, Linck, Lincke.
—Local, 'atte ling,' a variant; v. Ling. Way in his note to *lynge* in the Prompt. Parv. (p. 305) quotes, 'In Wiltshire nere Shaftesbery is an heth that growth ful of that (Junipere femel) and of lynk, and the lynk is heyere than that,' &c. Nevertheless, this surname may be a variant of Lynch, q.v.

1594. William Lincke (or Linke), co. Oxf.: Reg. Univ. Oxf. vol. ii. pt. ii. p. 202.
1781. Married—Charles Howse and Mary Link: St. Geo. Han. Sq. i. 325.
London, 3, 0, 0, 0; New York, 23, 4, 6, 3.

Linklater, Linkletter. — Local. A Shetland name; cf. Findlater.

London, 2, 0; Boston (U.S.), 0, 3.

Linneker; v. Linacre.

Linley.—Local; v. Lindley.

Linnell.—Bapt. 'the son of Lionel,' which is proved below to have become popularly Lynell or Linel.

Leonel de Anvers. H.
Lunell Wodeward, co. Essex, 1273. A.
Reginald Linel, co. Linc., ibid.
1513. Richard Lyonell: Reg. Univ. Oxf. i. 87.
1577. Richard Lynell and Margery Awsten, of Kensington: Marriage Lic. (London), i. 76.
1579. John Barnefeilde and Margery Lyonell, *widow*, of Kensington: ibid.

Probably Margery is the same person in both instances. This is very strong evidence in favour of my view.

1612. Married—Henry Lynnell and Margaret Rothley: St. Dionis Backchurch, p. 18.
1620. — Robert Spriggins and Ann Linnell: St. Jas. Clerkenwell, iii. 48.
London, 1; MDB. (co. Northampton), 13; Boston (U.S.), 23.

Linnett, Linnet.—Bapt. 'the son of Linot,' which, no doubt, is the dim. of some familiar girl's name. Now we turn Caroline into the nick. Lina, which would become Linot with the dim. suffix. But Caroline was unknown in the sur-

name epoch. Probably it was for Elenot, a dim. of Elen or Ellen. It must be remembered that Eleanora was a most popular girl's name at the period, and must have had its nicks. and dims.

Lenote de Kyngeston, co. Soms., 1273. A.
Linota atte Feld, ibid.
Linota the Widow, ibid.
Lyna de Stoford, co. Soms., 1 Edw. III: Kirby's Quest, p. 145.
Beatrix Linot, 1379: P. T. Yorks. p. 41.
Willelmus Lynot, 1379: ibid. p. 43.
1550-1. Thomas Bond and Ellen Lynnett: Marriage Lic. (London), i. 13.
1753. Married—Jasper Linnet and Ann Redman: St. Geo. Chap. Mayfair, p. 240.
London, 2, 0; MDB. (co. Northampton), 1, 0; Boston (U.S.), 1, 1.

Linsey.—Local; v. Lindsey.

Linstead.—Local, 'of Linstead, a parish in co. Kent. Also two parishes (Magna and Parva Linstead) in co. Suffolk.

Richard de Lindested, co. Kent, 1273. A.
John de Linstede, parson of Cawston, 1370: FF. v. 381.
Thomas de Linstead, of Norwich, 1676: ibid. iv. 311.
1804. Married—John Widdison and Eliza Linstead: St. Geo. Han. Sq. ii. 315.
London, 2; Oxford, 1.

Linthwaite.—Local, 'of Linthwaite,' a chapelry in the parish of Almondbury, W. Rid. Yorkshire, four miles from Huddersfield.

Roger de Lingthweyt, co. Norf., 1273. A.

The above entry may represent some other spot.

Willelmus de Lyntthewayt, 1379: P. T. Yorks. p. 181.
1606. Edmund Linthwaite, of Saddleworth: Wills at Chester (1545-1620), p. 124.
1619. Buried—Alice, wife of James Lynthweight, *merchant-talor*: St. Peter, Cornhill, i. 175.
1675. James Linthwitt, of Knare: Wills at Chester (1660-80), p. 169.
London, 1; Crockford, 1.

Linton, Lynton.—Local, 'of Linton,' parishes in cos. Cambridge, Devon, Hereford, Kent, and York (W. Rid.). Also townships in cos. Derby, Hereford, York (W. and N. Rid.).

William de Lynton, co. Worc., Hen. III-Edw. I. K.
Richard de Linton, London, 1273. A.
Robert de Lynton, co. Camb., ibid.

Hugh de Linton, co. York, 20 Edw. I. R.

Laurencius de Lynton (of Linton), 1379 : P. T. Yorks. p. 269.

1545-6. Robert Lynton and Katherine Johnson : Marriage Lic. (Faculty Office), p. 6.

1686. Bapt.—William, s. Thomas Linton · St. Jas. Clerkenwell, i. 317.

1719. Married—John James and Margaret Linton : St. Dionis Backchurch, p. 59.

London. 7, 0 ; Manchester, 1, 1 ; Philadelphia, 31, 0.

Lintott.—Local, ' de Lintot,' ' a place in the department of Seine Inferieure, Normandy, another in the arrondissement of Havre. The family were in Shropshire in the 12th century ' (Lower's Patr. Brit. p. 196).

Ralph de Lintot, co. Essex, 1273. A.

1722. Married—Joshua Lyntott and Mary Habersham : St. Jas. Clerkenwell, i. 247.

1789. — Thomas Bonnett and Eliz. Lintott : St. Geo. Han. Sq. ii. 32.

London, 7 ; Philadelphia, 4.

Linwebb, Lineaweaver.—Occup. ' a linen webster.'

Alina la Lynwebbe, C. R., 6 Edw. II.

Linen is literally the adjective of *lin*, as woollen is of *wool* ; cf. *lin-seed*. ' Lyne-webbers,' Cocke Lorelle's Bote : v. Lindraper. The surname survives in the United States as Lineaweaver.

Philadelphia, 0, 3.

Lippard.—Nick. ; v. Leopard.

Lippett, Lippiatt.—Local ; v. Lipyeatt.

Lippincott, Lippencott.—Local, ' of Luffincott,' a parish in co. Devon, seven miles from Holsworthy. Mr. Lower says, ' The baronets (extinct 1829) traced their family into Devonshire in the 16th century, and there is little doubt that the name was originally Luffincott, from a parish in that county so called ' (Patr. Brit. p. 196.) The surname is now very rare in England, but it has ramified in the most extraordinary fashion in the United States. I see no reason to doubt Mr. Lower's derivation. Everything points to a Devonshire habitat.

John Lippencott, co. Cornwall, 1585 : Reg. Univ. Oxf. vol. ii. pt. ii. p. 143.

Arthur Lippincot, co. Devon, 1594 : ibid. p. 205.

1777. Married—Eli Lippencott and Sarah Richards : St. Geo. Han. Sq. i. 279.

MDB. (co. Gloucester), 1, 1 ; New York (Lippencott), 2 ; Philadelphia, 120, 0.

Lipscomb, Lipscombe, Lipscoumb.—Local, ' of Lipscomb.' I cannot find the spot. Possibly a variant of Liscombe, a hamlet in the parish of Soulbury, co. Bucks.

1673. William Lipscomb and Frances Gundey : Marriage Alleg. (Canterbury), p. 97.

1788. Married—William Lipscomb and Frances Longhurst : St. Geo. Han. Sq. ii. 4.

1792. — Samuel Sutcham and Susan Lipscombe : ibid. p. 70.

London, 2, 4, 1 ; Philadelphia, 1, 0, 0.

Liptrott, Liptrot, Libtrot.—? Local, ' of Liptrott ' (?). I cannot find the spot. It is a well-established Lancashire surname. Mr. Lower, quoting Ferguson, says, ' It corresponds with a German name Liebetrut ' (Patr. Brit. p. 196). In this case it would probably be a personal name.

Richard Liptrot, of Lowton, 1601 : Wills at Chester (1545-1620), p. 124.

Jane Liptrott, of Haulgh, parish of Bolton, 1617 : ibid.

John Liptrott, of Lawton, co. Lanc., *yeoman*, 1647 : ibid. (1621-50), p. 140.

Alexander Liptrott, of Chorley, *yeoman*, 1649 : ibid.

1612. Bapt.—Ann, d. William Liptrod : St. Jas. Clerkenwell, i. 64.

1749. Married—Ralph Dell and Alice Liptrot : St. Geo. Chap. Mayfair, p. 139.

Bolton (co. Lanc.), 2, 0, 0 ; Manchester, 0, 1, 1 ; London, 0, 1, 0.

Lipyeatt, Lippett, Lippiatt.—Local, ' at the loop-gate,' from residence thereby. Either the gate (or yate) at the bend of the road, or the gate through a hole in the wall ; cf. loop-hole (v. *loop*, Skeat). This compound local term occurs frequently in West-country records. It gave birth to a hamlet Lypeat, in the parish of Kilmersdon, co. Soms.

Robert de Luppegate, co. Wilts, 1273. A.

John atte Lupeyate, co. Soms., 1 Edw. III : Kirby's Quest, p. 204.

Thomas atte Lupeyate, co. Soms., 1 Edw. III : ibid. p. 94.

Editha atte Lupeyate, co. Soms., 1 Edw. III : ibid. p. 97.

1450. Philip Lepegate, or Lypgate : Reg. Univ. Oxf. i. 10.

1460. Mr. Philip Lepeyate, rector of Salle, co. Norf. : FF. viii. 274.

1619. William Lipyeatt, co. Wilts : Reg. Univ. Oxf. vol. ii. pt. ii. p. 374.

1648. Bapt.—William, s. William Lippiat : St. Jas. Clerkenwell, i. 169.

1686-7. Thomas Hatchett and Eliz. Lippyatt (co. Wilts) : Marriage Lic. (Faculty Office), p. 183.

1734. Married—William Lipyeat and Mary Jefferys : St. Antholin (London), p. 146.

The following entry mentions a Lypiat in co. Glouc. :

1749. Married—Charles Cox, of Lypiat, co. Glouc., and Eliz. Westley, of Kemble, co. Wilts : St. Geo. Han. Sq. i. 41.

London, 0, 1, 0 ; MDB. (co. Devon), 1, 0, 0 ; (co. Somerset), 0, 0, 2.

Liquorish, Lickorish, Lickrish.—Nick. ' the liquorish,' also lickerish, one dainty, or nice in his palate ; one inclined to be greedy or gluttonous.

' To fulfill all thy lickerous talent.'
Chaucer, C. T. 12473.

' A proud peevish flirt, a liquorish, prodigal quean ' : Burton's Anat. Melanc. (Introduction, p. 64).

1637. Bapt.—Ann, d. John Licorishe · St. Jas. Clerkenwell, i. 136.

1652. — William, s. John Licorish : ibid. p. 180.

1654. Buried—Eliz., d. John Licoris : ibid. iv. 301.

London, 2, 0, 0 ; MDB. (co. Northampton), 1, 0, 0 ; London Court Dir., 0, 1, 1.

Liscomb, Liscombe, Liscom.—Local, ' of Liscombe,' a hamlet in the parish of Soulbury, co. Bucks. In some instances, no doubt, a variant of Luscombe, q.v. (v. also Lipscomb.)

1623. William Michell and Jane Liscombe : Marriage Lic. (London), ii. 128.

New York, 5, 1, 0 ; Boston (U.S.), 1, 0, 4.

Lishman.—Nick. ; v. Leishman.

Lisle, Lyle.—Local, ' at the isle,' from residence thereon. In Crockford ' de Lisle.'

Robert del Ile, 1 Edw. III : KKK. iv. 83.

Richard del Isle, 1323 : ibid. v. 303.

John Lisle, 1338 : PPP. p. 102.

Robertus del Ile, 1379 : P. T. Yorks. p. 156.

1744. Married—Nicholas Lyle and Eliz. Davenport : St. Geo. Chap. Mayfair, p. 40.

1747. — Davie Lisle and Jane Harrison : ibid. p. 95.

London, 1, 3 ; Crockford, 2, 2 ; New York, 1, 7.

Lister, Litster, Lyster.—
Occup. 'the litster,' a dyer. Both
trade-name and surname, founded
on the trade-name, existed in Yorkshire for centuries. To-day it is
one of the largest represented
surnames in the shire. 'Lystare,
clothe dyynge (or lytaster of clothe
dyynge, s. lytstar, P.), *tinctor*':
Prompt. Parv. '*Tinctor*, a lyster':
Ortus. 'A littester, *tinctor, tinc-
trix*': Cath. Ang. A chantry in the
church of All Saints, York, was
erected in the 15th century by
'Adam del Bank, littester' (Hist.
and Ant. of York, ii. 269). Not
found in the Hundred Rolls, 1273.

Hugh le Litster, co. Notts, 20 Edw.I. R.
Andrew le Litster, 1301. M.
Joane Lyttestere, C.R., 20 Ric. II. pt. i.
Cristiana Lyttester, *lyster*, 1379 : P. T.
Yorks. p. 249.
Robert le Lyster, 1397 : Preston Guild
Rolls, p. 1.
Nycholas le Lystere. G.

Lower says the Norfolk rebellion
in 1381 was called Lister's rebellion, because headed by John
Lister, or Littester, a dyer of
Norwich (Patr. Brit. p. 196); v.
also Way's note to *lystare* in Prompt.
Parv., p. 307.

1547. Married—Thomas Lyster and
Mary Pugborne : St. Dionis Backchurch,
p. 2.
London, 20, 0, 0 ; West Rid. Court
Dir., 41, 0, 0 ; MDB. (co. Cumb.), 0, 3, 0;
Oxford (Lyster), 1.

Liston, Listone, Lyston.—
Local, 'of Liston,' a parish in co.
Essex, near Sudbury.

Godfrey de Liston, co. Essex, Hen. III-
Edw. I. K.
Thomas de Liston, co. Essex, 1273. A.
Geoffrey de Lyston, co. Camb., ibid.
Johannes de Liston, co. Essex, 31
Edw. I : BBB. p. 641.
1668. Married—Arthur Martin and
Mary Lisston : St. Jas. Clerkenwell, iii. 153.
New York, 2, 0, 1 ; Philadelphia, 1, 1, 0.

Litchbarrow, Lickbarrow.
—Local, (1) 'of Litchborough,' a
parish in co. Northampton, near
Towcester ; (2) 'at the Lichbarrow'
(i.e. the mound of the dead); cf.
Litchfield, lich-gate, and lich-wake
(Chaucer). A.S. *lic*, a corpse.

Thomas de Lichesbarue, Hen. III-
Edw. I : K. p. 36.
In connexion with this entry

the place *Lichesbar* occurs in the
Hundred of Falewesle, co. Northampton.

William Lechebarowe, C. R., 42 Edw.
III.
Thomas Lychebarowe, C.R., 6 Hen. IV.
John Lychbarow, 1451 : Reg. Univ.
Oxf. i. 15.
1601.William Lickbarrowe, co.Westm.:
ibid. vol. ii. pt. ii. p. 253.
1647. Thomas Lickbarrow : Lancashire
Wills at Richmond, i. 184.
1686. Eliz. Lickbarrow, of Inskipp :
ibid. ii. 167.
1709. Jane Lickbarrow, of Langdale :
ibid.
1795. Buried—John Lickbarrow, of
Ulverston : Reg. St. Mary, Ulverston,
North Lanc. p. 618.

Litchfield.—Local, 'of Lichfield,' a city in co. Stafford.

1450. Richard Lychfeld : Reg. Univ.
Oxf. i. 10.
1594. Thomas Fowler and Anne Liche-
feild, *widow* : Marriage Lic. (London),
i. 219.
1663. Married—Henry Cookman and
Eliz. Litchfeild : St. Jas. Clerkenwell,
p. 112.
London, 9 ; Boston (U.S.), 61.

Litherland.—Local, 'of Litherland,' a township in the parish of
Sefton, near Liverpool. Liverpool
itself was originally Litherpool.

Richard Litherpol, Hen. III-Edw. I. K.
William de Litherland, co. Lanc., ibid.

Thus Liverpool and Litherland
are derived from the name of
the original settler, viz. Lither or
Leter ; cf. Leverton for Letherton.

William Litherland, of Whiston, 1582 :
Wills at Chester, (1545-1620), p. 124.
James Litherland, of West Derby
(Liverpool), 1609 : ibid.
1513. Robert Lytherlond, or Leder-
land : Reg. Univ. Oxf. i. 87.
1572. Titus Wystocke and Susanna
Letherland, co. Essex : Marriage Lic.
(London), i. 53.
1646. Buried—Eliz. Leatherland, *a
servant* : St. Dionis Backchurch, p. 225.
Liverpool, 5 ; Manchester, 4.

Lithgoe, Lithgow; v. Lythgoe.

Litster.—Occup. ; v. Lister.

**Little, Littell, Lytle, Litel,
Lytell, Lyttle.—**Nick. 'the little';
cf. Bigg, Small, and Long. Sometimes affixed as a sobriquet on the
least of two bearing the same
name.

Johannes de Bland, et uxor, 1379 : P. T.
Yorks. p. 289.
Johannes de Bland, littill, 1379 : ibid.
Johannes Tailliour, parws (i. e. parvus),
1379 : ibid. p. 278.
Johannes Tailliour, de Hyle, 1379 : ibid.
William le Letle, co. Oxf., 1273. A.
Wiscard Litil, co. Hunts, ibid.
John le Litle, co. Berks, ibid.
Julian Litel, co. Camb., ibid.
1544-5. Simon Bedell and Margaret
Litell, *widow* : Marriage Lic. (Faculty
Office), p. 4.
1619. Bapt.—John, s. Davye Little :
St. Jas. Clerkenwell, p. 85.
London, 45, 3, 0, 0, 0, 0 ; Liverpool,
23, 0, 2, 0, 0, 0 ; New York, 86, 19, 0, 1, 1, 1.

Littleboy, Littleboys.—Possibly a nickname, 'little boy';
synonymous with Littlepage and
Smallpage (q.v.), but more probably local, *-boy* or *-boys* representing the common suffix *-bois*,
a wood ; cf. Mortiboy or Worboise.
In this case it is doubtless the
French Lillebois Anglicized and
made imitative.

1603. John Wood and Sarah Littleboy,
widow of John Littleboy, of Rochester :
Marriage Lic. (London), i. 285.
William Littleboys, of Over Peover,
gent, 1625 : Wills at Chester (1621-50),
p. 140.
1687. Bapt.—Hanna, d. Henry Little-
boye : St. Jas. Clerkenwell, i. 323.
1688. Married—Joshua Taylor and
Grace Litleby : St. Peter, Cornhill, ii. 58.
London, 1, 1 ; Philadelphia, 2, 0.

Littlebury.—Local, ' of Littlebury,' a parish in co. Essex, near
Saffron Walden.

Martin de Littlebury, temp. Hen. III :
FF. ix. 168.
Laurence de Lytlebory, co. Camb.,
1273. A.
John de Lytlebury, co Hunts, ibid.
1605-6. Philip Littlebury, co. Linc. :
Reg. Univ. Oxf. vol. ii. pt. ii. p. 287.
1693-4. John Littlebury and Susanna
Dodsworth : MarriageAlleg.(Canterbury),
p. 284.
London, 1.

Littlechild.—Nick. 'the little
child'; cf. Fairchild, Leifchild,
Child, &c.

London, 1.

Littlecot.—Local,'of Littlecot,'
a chapelry in the parish of Chilton
Foliatt, co. Wilts ; also ' of Little-
cote,' a hamlet in the parish of
Stewkley, co. Bucks.

Adam de Litlecote, co. Wilts, Hen. III-
Edw. I. K.
Symon de Lutlecote, co. Wilts, 1273. A.

Philip de Luttelcot, co. Wilts, 1273. A.
Robert de Luttlecot, co. Bucks, ibid.
1550. John Cowper and Alice Litlecote:
Marriage Lic. (London), i. 12.

Littledale.—Local, 'of Littledale,' a hamlet in the parish of Lancaster, co. Lanc.

1605. John Littledale, of Ronray (?): Wills at Chester, i. 124.
London, 1; Liverpool, 3; MDB. (co. Ches.), 3.

Littlefair. — ? Nick. 'little fellow'; cf. Playfair, little playmate, from the North Country *fere*, a companion, a mate.

Farewell, my doughter Kateryne, late the *fere* to Prynce Artour, late my chyld so dere': Halliwell.
Thomas Lytlefayr, or Litlefere, co. Durham, 1585: Reg. Univ. Oxf. vol. ii. pt. ii. p. 142.
MDB. (co. Durham), 1; (North Rid. Yorks), 9.

Littlefield.—Local, 'of Littlefield,' one of the hundreds of Kent (Lower). Of course many small enclosures would be called the 'little field.'

1610. Thomas Littlefeild, or Lyttlefeld, co. Hants: Reg. Univ. Oxf. vol. ii. pt. ii. p. 317.
1684. Thomas Littlefeild and Sarah Allen: Marriage Alleg. (Canterbury), p. 183.
1751. Married—John Littlefield and Mary Tempest: St. Geo. Chap. Mayfair, p. 197.
London, 3; Boston (U.S.), 114.

Littlehale. — Local, 'at the little hale,' i.e. at the little hall (v. Hale), from residence therein or thereby. The final *s* in Littlehales is too common in local surnames to need explanation; cf. Williams, Styles, &c.

1557. Bapt.—Thomas Lyttellhaylle, son of George Lyttyllhayle: St. Dionis Backchurch, p. 77.
1558-9. Married—George Lytilhale and Eliz. Wryght: ibid. p. 4.
1618. Richard Wilkinson and Joane Littleale: Marriage Lic. (London), ii. 64.
1679-80. Edward Pawlett and Hannah Littlehayles: Marriage Lic. (Faculty Office), p. 149.
1778. Married—John Cole and Martha Littlehales: St. Geo. Han. Sq. i. 289. Boston (U.S.), 4.

Littlehick.—Nickname, 'little Richard,' from the nick. Hick, q.v.; cf. Littlejohn.

Richard Litelhikke, C. R., 9 Ric. II.

Littlejohn, Littlejohns. — Nick. 'little John,' equivalent to John Little. A mere reversal of order between baptismal name and surname; cf. Fr. Petit-jean.

Richard fil. Parvi-Johannis, co. Camb., 1273. A.
Parvus Johannes, 1379: P. T. Yorks. p. 224.
Pety Jon et uxor, 1379: ibid. p. 283.
'Y met hem bot at Wentbreg, seyde Lytyll John': Robin Hood, i. 83.
Nicholas Peti John, C. R., 35 Hen. VI.
1607-8. Hugh Littlejohn, co. Devon, St. Mary Hall: Reg. Univ. Oxf. vol. ii. pt. ii. p. 300.
1766. Married—Robert Littlejohns and Eliz. Whiting: St. Geo. Han. Sq. i. 158.
London, 8, 1; MDB. (co. Devon), 0, 3; New York, 4, 0; Boston (U.S.), 5, 0.

Littlemore.—Local, 'of Littlemore,' a liberty in the parish of St. Mary the Virgin, partly in Bullingdon, partly in Oxford, two miles and a half from Oxford. Probably many spots would be similarly entitled. There is one in Cheshire.

(Priorissa de Lytlemore, co. Oxf., 1273. A.
1609. George Littlemore, of Chester; Wills at Chester, i. 124.
1650. Thomas Littlemore, of Littlemore, co. Ches., *gent*: ibid. ii. 140.
1748. Married—Samuel Littlemoore and Ann Cantrell: St. Geo. Chap. Mayfair, p. 105.
London, 2; MDB. (co. Ches.), 3.

Littlepage.—Nick. 'the little page,' a young or small servitor; v. Smallpage.

Lawrence Litilpage, C. R., 1 Hen. V.
1681. Nicholas Awnsham and Ann Littlepage: Marriage Alleg.(Canterbury), p. 82.
1703. Robert Littlepage, co. Oxf., and Martha Smith: Marriage Lic. (Faculty Office), p. 245.
1762. Married—Joseph Littlepage and Phillis Burrell: St. Geo. Han. Sq. i. 109.

Littleproud.—Nick. 'the little proud.' Although this surname lasted at least four centuries and made a gallant effort to survive, it is, I fear, extinct; cf. Smallpride.

Matilda Lytillprowd, 1379: P. T. Yorks. p. 125.
Robertus Lyttylproud, 1379: ibid. p. 95.
Reginald Littleprowe, Mayor of Norwich, 1532: FF. iii. 219.

Of the appointment to the seventh prebend in Norwich Cathedral we read:

'1536. Stephen Prewet, presented by Elizabeth Littleproud by grant from the Bishop': FF. iv. 173.
'1619. Mr. John Littleproud, a young man, lately in priest's orders, for the help of his living, being but a grammar scholar, was buried Nov. 1' (at Attleburgh): ibid. i. 535.
1701. Married—Robert Littleproud and Frances Avery: St. Jas. Clerkenwell, iii. 223.

Littler.—Local, 'of Littleover,' a village in co. Derby. The name crept over the border into Cheshire, and remained firmly fixed there; cf. the pronunciation Peevor for Peover, a parish in co. Chester.

John de Littelore, 1401: East Ches. ii. 9.
Richard Lytler, 1582: ibid. p. 382.
Ralph Litlor, 1602: ibid. p. 241.
1588. Married—Geffray Mottershed and Jone Lytler: Reg. Prestbury, Ches., p. 97.
Thomas Litler, of Eddisbury, 1576: Wills at Chester (1545-1620), p. 124.
John Littler, of Chester, *alderman*, 1619: ibid.
1623-4. Buried—Robert Littleler, servant of Gilbert Allam: St. Dionis Backchurch, p. 216.
1660. Married—Richard Littler and Ann Knight: St. Jas. Clerkenwell, iii. 105.
1796. Married—Edmund Littler and Eliz. Henman: St. Geo. Han. Sq. ii. 150.
London, 1; Manchester, 3; MDB. (co. Chester), 5; Philadelphia, 2.

Littleswain.—Nick. 'the little swain'; v. Swain.

Philip Litsweyn, co. Oxf., 1273. A.

Littleton.—Local, 'of Littleton,' parishes and townships in cos. Chester, Dorset, Middlesex, Somerset, Hants, Wilts, Worcester, and Gloucester.

Michael de Lutelton, co. Wilts, 1273. A.
Henry de Lutleton, co. Soms., 1 Edw. III: Kirby's Quest, p. 85.
Francis Littleton, co. Staff., 1575: Reg. Univ. Oxf. vol. ii. pt. ii. p. 65.
John Littleton, co. Worc., 1576: ibid. p. 71.
1590. John Litleton and Mereall Bromley: Marriage Lic. (London), i. 189.
1751. Married—Joseph Littleton and Sarah Bury: St. Geo. Chap. Mayfair, p. 194.
London, 1; Boston (U.S.), 1.

Littlewood.—Local, 'of Littlewood,' a well-established West Riding surname, in which division of the county of York it first arose. The precise spot was seemingly in the neighbourhood of Holmfirth.

Johannes de Litylwode, 1379: P. T. Yorks. p. 174.

Willelmus de Litilwode, 1379: P. T. Yorks.

1576-7. German Fryer and Alice Littlewood: Marriage Lic. (London), i. 74.

1664. Bapt.—Ann, d. Robert Littlewood: St. Jas. Clerkenwell, i. 222.

1754. Married—Joseph Littlewood and Joyce Sharp: St. Geo. Chap. Mayfair, p. 275.

London, 8; West Rid. Court Dir., 10; Sheffield, 8; Philadelphia, 13.

Littleworth, Littlewort. — Local, ' of Littleworth,' i.e. at the little worth or farm. This surname has been corrupted into Littlework and Littlewort. Littleworth is an ecclesiastical district in the union of Faringdon, co. Berks.

1591. Edmund Littleworke, co. Berks, *pleb.*: Reg. Univ. Oxf. vol. ii. pt. ii. p. 187.

1665. William Litleworck and Sarah Edwards: Marriage Alleg.(Canterbury), p. 142.

London, 1, 1.

Litton. — Local, ' of Litton, parishes in cos. Somerset and Dorset; also townships in cos. Hereford and York (W. Rid.), and also a hamlet in the parish of Tideswell, co. Derby.

Hugh de Litton,co.Northampt.,1273. A.

Symon de Litton, co. Suff., ibid.

Alicia de Lytton, 1379: P. T. Yorks. p. 273.

1583. William Litton and Eliz. Myles, *widow*: Marriage Lic. (London), i. 125.

1607. Married—Edward Litton and Eliz. Friarson: St. Michael, Cornhill, p.18. London, 2.

Lively, Liveley. — Local (?). Mr. Lower says, ' From natural disposition.' This may be so. More probably we must look for a local origin with the common suffix *-ley*, as in Morley or Ripley.

1543. Buried—Robarte Lyvely: St. Dionis Backchurch, p. 179.

1549. Married—Robarte Kynge and Alys Lyveley: ibid. p. 2.

London, 1, 0; Philadelphia, 0, 2; New York, 2, 0.

Livens; v. Living.

Livermore.—Local, ' of Livermere,' two parishes, Great and Little Livermere, in co. Suffolk, about six miles from Bury St. Edmunds. From Suffolk the surname wandered into Essex, where it is still familiar as Livermore ; cf. Whitmore for Whittemore.

1239. Agnes Livermere, co. Norf.: FF. vi. 150.

William de Lyvremere co.Suff.,1273. A.

1349. William de Lyvermere, rector of Croxton, co. Norf., FF. ii. 154.

1668. Married—Richard Renoles and Eliz. Livermore : St. Jas. Clerkenwell, iii. 151.

1675-6. John Livermore, co. Essex, and Eliz. Peirson : Marriage Alleg. (Canterbury), p. 251.

London, 7; MDB. (co. Essex), 7; Boston (U.S.), 26.

Liverpool.—Local, ' of Liverpool,' a city in co. Lancaster. I fear the surname is extinct in England. For the derivation of the name, v. Litherland. Probably the same Lither who owned the ' land ' owned the ' pool ' also.

Richard de Liverpol, co. Lanc., 20 Edw. I. R.

Richard Litherpol,co. Lanc., Hen. III-Edw. I. K.

John de Lyverpole, 19 Edw. II : Baines' Lancashire, ii. 295.

Adam de Liverpool, temp. Edw. III: ibid. p. 296.

Edward Liverpool, of Stoke, *blacksmith*, 1633 : Wills at Chester (1621-50), p. 140.

Boston (U.S.), 1.

Liversage, Liversedge, Liversidge, Liverseege. — Local, ' of Liversedge,' a township in the parish of Birstall, nine miles from Leeds. But there seems to have been a place of this name also in the West country.

Ralph Leversedge, co. Soms., 1583-4 : Reg. Univ. Oxf. vol. ii. pt ii. p. 133.

Thomas Leversage, co. Ches., 1607 : ibid. p. 297.

Roger Liversage, of Woolston, 1582 : Wills at Chester (1545-1620), p. 124.

William Liversage, of Wheelock, 1613 : ibid.

1573. Bapt.—John Jeffreys, alias Leversedg: Reg. Stourton, co. Wilts, p. 1.

1690. Married—John Trimboy and Eliz. Leversage : ibid. p. 53.

London, 0, 0, 1, 0 ; Liverpool, 1 2, 1, 0 ; MDB. (West Rid. Yorks), 0, 4, 3, 0 ; Manchester, 0, 0, 0, 1.

Livesey, Livesley, Livezey, Livezley, Livzley, Livzey. —Local, ' of Livesey,' a township in the parish of Blackburn, co. Lanc. Livesley is a corruption. By a curious freak the American variants in all cases turn s into z. The surname has established itself strongly in the United States.

' Livesey gave name to a family, the owners of Livesey Hall, ... who became extinct early in this century, and of whom

James Levesey in 2 Edw. VI held Levesey as a manor ' : Baines' Lanc. ii. 80.

1578. William Sherlocke and Ellen Livesey, *widow* : Marriage Lic.(London)¸ p. 83.

George Livesey, of Blackburn, 1592 : Wills at Chester (1545-1620), p. 125.

James Livesey, of Livesey, 1619 : ibid.

Roger Livesey, of Darwen (nr. Blackburn), 1620 : ibid.

London, 2, 0, 0, 0, 0, 0 ; Manchester, 14, 3, 0, 0, 0, 0 ; Philadelphia, 0, 0, 30, 2, 1, 2 ; New York (Livesey), 4.

Living, Liveing, Livens, Levinson, Livings.—Bapt. ' the son of Liven,' probably like Lewin (q.v.), a variant of Leofwin, the intermediate form being Liffin. Mr. Lower says, ' An Anglo-Saxon personal name. There was a Living, archbishop of Canterbury, and another Living, bishop of Worcester' (Patr. Brit. p. 197). The final *g* is excrescent.

William fil. Lyfyne, co. Bedf., 1273. A.

Richard Lyfyne, co. Camb., ibid.

Richard Livesone, co. Camb., ibid.

Adam Livene, co. Camb., ibid.

Roger Livene, co. Camb., ibid.

1579-80. Jeffry Lyvinge and Eliz. Pattenson : Marriage Lic. (London), i. 94.

1591. Timothy Levinge, co. Warw. : Reg. Univ. Oxf. vol. ii. pt. ii. p. 183.

1593. Bapt. — Leven, d. Lambrighte Vandelo, a stranger (elsewhere described as a Dutchman): St. Michael, Cornhill, p. 205.

1715. Married—John Living and Eliz. Millett : ibid. p. 58.

1791. — William Fitch and Mary Livens : St. Geo. Han. Sq. ii. 63.

1806. — Joseph Sparrow and Ann Living : ibid. p. 338.

London, 2, 2, 3, 1, 0 ; NewYork (Livings), 1 ; Boston (U.S.) (Living), 2.

Livingstone, Livingston.—Local, ' of Livingstone,' a parish in co. Linlithgow.

1789. Married—Alex. Cowie and Sarah Livingston : St. Geo. Han. Sq. ii. 29.

London, 1, 5 ; Boston (U.S.), 4, 25.

Llewellin, Llewellyn, Llewellen, Llewallen. — Bapt. ' the son of Llewellyn' (Welsh). The double *l* in Welsh has always been a stumbling-block to the English ; cf. Floyd for Lloyd. An instance of the difficulty occurs in the Wills at Chester (1545-1620), Lanc. and Ches. Rec. Soc :

Richard Thwellin, of Holt, 1618 : p. 192.

1715. Married—Richard Luellyn and Eliz. Bromwich: St. Peter, Cornhill, ii. 71.

1776. Married—William Gaunt and Mary Lewelling: St. Geo. Han. Sq. i. 268. London, 1, 7, 0, 0 ; Philadelphia, 2, 1, 13, 3 ; Boston (U.S.) (Lewellyn), 2.

Lloyd. — Bapt. 'the son of Lloyd,' a Welsh personal name; v. Floyd and Bloyd. This surname is known over the whole English-speaking world.

1577. Jenkin Lloyde, co. Montgomery : Reg. Univ. Oxf. vol. ii. pt. ii. p. 74.
1579. Francis Lloyde, co. Carnarvon : ibid. p. 90.
1585. Griffith Lloid, co. Radnor : ibid. p. 143.
1559. Richard Lloyd, of Chester : Wills at Chester, i. 125.
1610. Robert Lloyd, of Chester : ibid. London, 144 ; Philadelphia, 118.

Load. — Local, 'at the lode,' from residence thereby. ' Lode, a leaning wall. Glouc.' (Halliwell). It is interesting to notice that the name is early found in the neighbouring county of Somerset.

Robert atte Lode, co. Soms., 1 Edw. III : Kirby's Quest, p. 106.
1753. Married—William Load, co. Worc., and Eliz. Read : St. Geo. Chap. Mayfair, p. 261.
1760. — Thomas Load and Sarah Squibb : St. Geo. Han. Sq. i. 184.
London, 1.

Loader, Loder, Lodder.— Occup. ' the loader,' i.e. a carrier. M.E. lode, a burthen ; ' loders, carriers' (Halliwell) ; v. Leader.

Emma la Lodere, co. Oxf., 1273. A.
Agnes Lodere, co. Oxf., ibid.
Robert Loder, 1537 : Reg. Univ. Oxf., i. 188.
1559-60. William Loder and Agnes Mychell : Marriage Lic. (London), i. 20.
1781. Married—Thomas Loader and Margaret Atkins : St. Geo. Han. Sq. i. 323.
London, 14, 4, 2 ; New York, 2, 7, 0.

Loadman, Loadsman. — Occup. 'the loadman,' a carrier ; v. Loader, Leadman, or Leader. ' Lodysmanne, vector, lator, vehicularius' : Prompt. Parv. p. 310. Mr. Way adds as a note, 'The lodesman seems to be here the carrier ; Anglo-Saxon ladman, ductor.'

1792. Married—Richard Loadman and Eliz. Kane : St. Geo. Han. Sq. ii. 86.
1801. — Thomas Anstead and Henrietta Loadsman : ibid. p. 240.
John Loadman, farmer, Crate house, Crakehall : North Rid. Yorks Dir., 1872.
East Rid. Yorks Dir. (Farmers' List), 5.

Loadstar. — Nick. 'the lodestar' or 'load-star,' i.e. pole-star. The star that leads.

'And after was she made the lodesterre.'
Chaucer, The Knight's Tale.
James Lodsterre, co. Kent, 1273. A.

Lobb, Lob.—Nick. 'the lobb,' a loutish country bumpkin, a clownish rustic. 'A blunt countrie lob' (Stanihurst, p. 17). In Somersetshire the last person in a race is called the lob (Halliwell) ; cf. lobcock, a lubber. ' Baligaut, an unwelde lubber, great lob cocke' (Cotgrave) ; cf. the Somersetshire Crease and Kift ; cf. looby.

Adam Lobbe, co. Norf., 1273. A.
Richard Lobbe, co. Soms., 1 Edw. III : Kirby's Quest, p. 150.
1752. Married—Peter Lobb and Catherine Stranger : St. Geo. Chap. Mayfair, p. 223.
1799. — Thomas Guymerl and Eliza Lobb : St. Geo. Han. Sq. ii. 210.
London, 5, 0 ; New York, 1, 2 ; Philadelphia, 10, 0.

Lobley.—Local, ' of Lobley.' I cannot find the spot. Evidently Lancashire is its habitat.

1560. William Lobley and Margaret Allen : Marriage Lic. (London), i. 97.
Roger Lobley, of Worston, 1621 : Wills at Chester (1621-50), p. 141.
Adam Lobley, of Woodall, co. York, 1665 : ibid. (1660-80), p. 171.
London, 1 ; Liverpool, 2 ; MDB. (co. Lancaster), 3 ; New York, 2 ; Philadelphia, 5.

Lock, Locke.—Local, ' at the lock,' from residence thereby. A hatch or wicket. The English surname is not to be confounded with Gaelic loch, a lake ; v. Prompt. Parv. ; M.E. loke, a door-fastener.

Robert atte Waterlok, C. R., 45 Hen. III.
Geoffrey Loc, or Lock, co. Suff., 1273. A.
William Lock, co. Oxf., ibid.
Richard atte Loke, Fines Roll, 18 Edw. II.
John Loke, co. Soms., 1 Edw. III : Kirby's Quest, p. 261.
1577. Zachary Locke, London : Reg. Univ. Oxf. vol. ii. pt. ii. p. 76.
London, 42, 11 ; Philadelphia, 10, 12.

Locker.—Occup. ' the locker' or 'locksmith' ; v. Lockyear.

1605. Henry Locker and Eliz. Herd : Marriage Lic. (London), i. 295.
1608. Thurstan Locker, of Manchester : Wills at Chester, i. 125.
London, 2 ; Philadelphia, 10.

Locket, Lockett. — ? Bapt. Not a corruption of Lockhart, as suggested by Lower. It is found as simple Loket in the 13th century. It seems to be the dim. of some personal name ; cf. Emmett for Emma.

Eudo Loket, co. Norf., 1273. A.
Johannes Loket, 1379 : P. T. Yorks. p. 172.
1574-5. William Locket, co. Soms. : Reg. Univ. Oxf. vol. ii. pt. ii. p. 62.
1601. Giles Lockett, co. Dorset : ibid. p. 252.
London, 3, 3 ; Manchester, 0, 7 ; New York, 0, 2.

Lockington. — Local, ' of Lockington,' (1) a parish in co. Leicester, seven miles from Loughborough ; (2) a parish in E. Rid. Yorks, six miles from Beverley.

Ralph de Loketon, co. York, Hen. III-Edw. I. K.
Geoffrey de Lukinton, co. Wilts, ibid.
Robert de Lokinton, co. York, 1273. A.
William de Lokinton, co. York, ibid.
Roger de Lokynton, co. Soms., 20 Edw. I. R.
1648. Bapt.—John, s. Richard Lockington : St. Jas. Clerkenwell, i. 169.
1678. Thomas Ladd and Amy Lockington : Marriage Alleg. (Canterbury), p. 288.
1721. Buried—Stephen Lockington : St. Antholin (London), p. 134.
London, 5 ; Philadelphia, 1.

Lockley.—Local, ' of Lockerley' (?), a parish in co. Southampton, six miles from Romsey.

1549. Married—John Lockly and Ellen Oliver : St. Peter, Cornhill, i. 222.
1580. Roger Lockley and Alice Berrye, widow, Marriage Lic. (London), i. 96.
1793. Married—John James Ashley and Charlotte Sophia Lockley : St. Geo. Han. Sq. ii. 103.
London, 4.

Locksley.—Local, ' of Locksley' ; v. Loxley.
Oxford, 1.

Locksmith.—Occup. ' the locksmith.' ' Loksmyne, serefaber' (Prompt. Parv.). Locksmith, I fear, is obsolete ; but v. Lockyear, which has a vigorous existence.

Robert Locsmyth, co. Hunts, 1273. A.
William Loksmyth, c. 1300. M.
Roger Locksmyth, vicar of Wighton, co. Norf., 1384 : FF. ix. 208.
William Loksmyth, C. R., 6 Hen. VI.
1605. William Locksmith, co. Glouc. : Reg. Univ. Oxf. vol. ii. pt. ii. p. 287.
— Married—William Locksmith and Katharine Markham : St. Michael, Cornhill, p. 18.

1620. Anthony Locksmith, co. Surrey, and Susan Rogers: Marriage Lic. (London), ii. 93.

Lockton.—Local, 'of Lockton,' a chapelry in the parish of Middleton, N. Rid. Yorks.

Hugh de Loketon, co. York, Hen. III-Edw. I. K.
Ralph de Loketon, co. York, ibid.
1648. John Lockton, co. Linc., and Mary Fairfax: Marriage Lic. (Faculty Office), p. 40.
1729. Married—Richard Hawkins and Ann Lockton: St. Geo. Han. Sq. i. 6. London, 1.

Lockwood.—Local, 'of Lockwood,' a village in the ancient parish of Almondbury, W. Rid. Yorks. This local surname has ramified strongly and spread widely.

Willelmus de Lokewod, 1379: P. T. Yorks. p. 177.
Thomas de Lockewod, 1379: ibid. p. 178.
1575. Married—Roberte Clayton and Elizabethe Lockwood: St. Michael, Cornhill, p. 11.
1621-2. John Lockwood and Joane Padnowl: Marriage Lic. (London), ii. 108.
1626. John Watkyns and Margaret Lokewood: ibid. p. 169.
London, 24; West Rid. Court Dir., 31; New York, 110.

Lockyear, Lockyer, Locker.—Occup. 'the lockyer,' the locksmith; M.E. *loke*, a lock. More correctly lock-er, but *y* has intruded, as in *sawyer, lawyer, bowyer* for saw-er, law-er, bow-er.

Henry le Lockier, London, 1273. A.
Nicholas le Lokyere, co. Soms., 1 Edw. III: Kirby's Quest, p. 211.
Lucas le Lokier, co. Soms., 1 Edw. III: ibid. p. 273.
Robert Harward, *loker*, 1443: Mun. Acad. Oxon. p. 535.
1608. Married—Abraham Bateman and Ursula Lockyer: St. Michael, Cornhill, p. 19.
1735.—James Sanger and Joan Lockier: Reg. Stourton, co. Wilts, p. 55.

It is interesting to notice that while Lockyer has predominated over Locksmith in our personal nomenclature, yet locksmith has nearly ousted lockyer as an occupative term.

London, 1, 15, 2; New York, 0, 4, 0; Philadelphia, 0, 10, 3.

Lodder, Loder; v. Loader.

Lodge.—Local, 'at the lodge,' a small cottage, a place to rest in.

M.E. *logge*. 'Logge, or lytylle house': Prompt. Parv. p. 311.

Roger de la Logge, C. R., 32 Edw. I.
William atte Logg, co. Soms, 1 Edw. III: Kirby's Quest, p. 195.
Johannes del Loge, 1379: P. T. Yorks. p. 283.
Thomas Lodge, or Loge, 1520: Reg. Univ. Oxf. i. 113.
1575. Bapt.—Jane, d. Robert Lodge: St. Jas. Clerkenwell, i. 9.
1577. Miles Lodge, co. York: Reg. Univ. Oxf. vol. ii. pt. ii. p. 78.
London, 19; New York, 4.

Loe.—Local, 'at the low,' from residence thereon; v. Low; cf. Hoe, sometimes a variant of How.

1598. Humphrey Lowe, or Loe, co. Ches.: Reg. Univ. Oxf. vol. ii. pt. ii. p. 229.
1621. William Loe, co. Warw.: ibid. p. 390.
1657. Buried—Emery Loe: St. Jas. Clerkenwell, iv. 315.
1788. Married—Francis Loe and Charlotte Goodman: St. Geo. Han. Sq. ii. 11. London, 2.

Loft, Lofts.—Local, 'at the loft,' an attic, a garret, a room in the roof; cf. Lodge. The final *s* in Lofts is common to all monosyllabic local names (cf. Holmes, Lowndes, Brooks), and in fact is the genitive, as in Williams, Tompkins, Jones, &c. v. Loftus.

Alenus atte Loft, co. Hunts, 1273. A.
Angnes ad le Loft, co. Hunts, ibid.
Walter ad le Loft, co. Hunts, ibid.
1669. Married—William Loft and Mary Morgan: St. Jas. Clerkenwell, iii. 171.
1738. — Stephen Hasser and Anne Loft: St. Dionis Backchurch, p. 66.
1753. — Stephen Loftes and Mary Cox: St. Geo. Chap. Mayfair, p. 247.
London, 2, 7; Crockford, 2, 0; New York, 1, 1.

Loftus, Lofthouse. — Local, 'at the loft-house,' a house with an attic or cock-loft above it. This is a Yorkshire surname and several places are so termed. The chief are Lofthouse, a village three miles north of Wakefield, and Lofthouse, a village in the parish of Kirkby Malzeard.

Robert de Lofthus, C. R., 28 Edw. I.
Richard Lofthouse, co. York. W. 16.
John Loftous, co. York, ibid.
Robertus Lofthouse, 1379: P. T. Yorks. p. 193.
John de Lofthouse, C. R., 17 Ric. II.
1593-4. William Loftous, co. York: Reg. Univ. Oxf. vol. ii. pt. ii. p. 200.
1667. Arthur Bostock and Catherine

Loftus: Marriage Alleg. (Westminster), p. 135.
London, 4, 0; Sheffield, 0, 2; Leeds, 6, 2; New York, 17, 0; Philadelphia, 34, 4.

Logsdon; v. Longsdon. An unmistakable variant.

Lomas, Lomax.—Local, ' of Lomax,' a small spot in the parish of Bury, co. Lanc. I do not know whether it can still be identified, but it has given birth to a family name that has ramified itself in a wonderful manner.

Christopher Lomax, of Bury, 1590: Wills at Chester (1545-1620), p. 125.
Jeffery Lomax, of Heap, 1590: ibid.
Laurence Smethurst, of Lomax, parish of Bury, 1624: ibid. (1621-50), p. 201.
Edmund Smethurst, of Lomax, parish of Bury, *yeoman*, 1638: ibid.
Oliver Lumas, 1602: Preston Guild Rolls, p. 63.
Oliver Lumax, 1622: ibid. p. 70.
Richard Lumas-jur', 1602: ibid. p. 63.
Richard Lumax-jur', 1622: ibid. p. 70.

The double instances given above prove, if proof were needed, that Lomax and Lomas are one and the same name.

Manchester, 31, 18; London, 7, 10; New York, 3, 4.

Lomb; v. Lumb.

Lombard, Lumbard.—Nick. 'the Lombard,' one who came from Lombardy. One or two of the names recorded below are evidently Jewish.

Jacob le Lumberd. E.
Jacobina la Lumbard, London. X.
Denteyt Lumbardus, London, 1273. A.
Richard Lomberd, co. Kent, ibid.
John Lumbard, co. Oxf., ibid.
Michael le Lumbard, C. R., 12 Edw. I.
Marcus le Lumbard, C.R., 20 Edw. I.
Nicholas Lombard, or Lumbarde, 1567: Reg. Univ. Oxf. i. 267.
1657. Married—Hugh Lumbard and Jane Tayler: St. Jas. Clerkenwell, iii. 99.

Lombard Street, London, took its name from being the district in which the Italian merchants resided. It will be seen that several of the instances above hail from the metropolis.

London, 1, 0; New York, 7, 2.

Lombardy.—Local, ' of Lombardy'; v. Lombard.

New York, 1.

Lomer.—Occup.; v. Limner.

Lond; v. Lund.

Londesborough; v. Lowndesbrough.

London.—Local, 'of London'; v. Londonish.

Jordan de London, co. Berks, Hen. III–Edw. I. K.
Haginus de London, co. Northumb., 1273. A.
Gilbert de Londonia, co. Salop, ibid.
William de London, co. Wilts, 20 Edw. I. R.
Osbert du Londone, co. Soms., 1 Edw. III: Kirby's Quest, p. 261.
1570. John Harker and Susan London: Marriage Lic. (Faculty Office), p. 15.
1730. Married—Edward London and Eliz. Phillips: St. Dionis Backchurch, p. 64.
London, 21; New York, 18.

Londoner, Londner.—Nick. 'the Londoner,' one who hailed from London.

William Londoner, alias Tinsley, 1564: Visitation of Yorkshire, p. 324.
'Sir Henry Tinsloo (Tinsley), *knight*, whose Auncetors were called Londoner, alias Gresbroke,' 1564: ibid. p. 325.
New York, 1, 2.

Londonish.—Local, 'of London'; cf. Spanish, Kentish, Cornish, Devenish, Norris, &c. 'Londonoys' (Chaucer), a Londoner, one, as we now say, born within sound of Bow Bells. a cockney.

Ralph le Lundreys. T.
Richard Londoneys, co. Camb., 1273. A.
William Londeneys, co. Hunts, ibid.
William Londonissh, temp. 1300. M.

Lone.—Local, 'at the lone,' i.e. lane; v. Lane (M.E. *lane* and *lone*), from residence thereby.

Ralph de la Lone, co. Norf., 1273. A.
Beatrix Lone, co. Hunts, ibid.
1590. Edward Lone (co. Essex) and Margaret Hepcott: Marriage Lic. (London), i. 186.
1719. Bapt.—Ann, d. William Lone: St. Michael, Cornhill, p. 166.
London, 1.

Long.—Nick. 'the long,' from the stature of the original bearer; cf. Longfellow and Longman; cf. also Short, &c.

Henry le Longe, co. Bucks, 1273. A.
John le Longe, co. Hunts, ibid.
Walter le Longe, co. Salop, ibid.
Johanna Long', 1379: P. T. Yorks. p. 130.
1536-7. Thomas Bolton and Mary Long: Marriage Lic. (London), i. 9.
London, 75; New York, 124.

Longacre, Longaker.—Local, 'at the long-acre,' from residence at a field so called; cf. Fouracre.

Philadelphia, 13, 18.

Longbotham, Longbottam, Longbottom. — Local, 'at the long bottom,' i.e. the long hollow; v. Bottom, and cf. Ramshotham, Higginbottom, and especially Broadbotham.

Thomas Langbotehom, 1379: P. T. Yorks. p. 187.
Ricardus Longbotehom, 1379: ibid.
1557. Thomas Longbottom, rector of Ashwell Thorp, co. Norf.: FF. v. 163.
1603-4. Richard Longbothom, co. York: Reg. Univ. Oxf. vol. ii. pt. ii. p. 270.
1612. John Longbothome and Margery Hutchins: Marriage Lic. (London), ii. 18.
1685. Bapt.—Anne, d. Samuel Longbotham: St. Jas. Clerkenwell, i. 314.
1705. Married—John Langbotham and Margaret Newman: St. Mary Aldermary, p. 38.
London, 1, 0, 0; Manchester, 4, 0, 0; Philadelphia, 0, 0, 6.

Longcroft. — Local. 'of the long croft,' i.e. the long field or enclosure (v. Croft), from residence thereby.

Stephen de la Lungecrofte, co. Wilts, 1273. A.
1646. Married—John Burlace and Sarah Longcraft: St. Dionis Backchurch, p. 25.
London, 1.

Longden.—Local, 'of Longdon' or 'Longden,' parishes in the diocs. of Hereford, Lichfield, and Worcester.

Robert de Longedon, co. Salop, 1273. A.
Roger de Longedon, co. Salop, ibid.
1577. William Longdon, co. Soms.: Reg. Univ. Oxf. vol. ii. pt. ii. p. 75.
1599-1600. George Longden, co. Derby: ibid. p. 239.
London, 5.

Longfellow.—Nick. 'the long fellow'; cf. Goodfellow, Bonfellow, Stringfellow, &c. This surname is only found in records and registers of co. York. The American poet was the descendant of a Yorkshire family.

Peter Langfellay, co. York. W. 11.
Elizabeth Longfellow, co. York. W. 16.
Margery Langfellow, 1491, co. York. W. 11.
Henry Emmott, alias Longfellow, 1590 (Reg. Skipton Ch.): Dawson's Hist. of Skipton, p. 207.

1645. Bapt. — William, s. of William Longfellow: Reg. Skipton Ch.
New York, 1; Boston (U.S.), 18.

Longhurst.—Local, 'of Longhurst' (v. Hurst), a township in the parish of Bothal, near Morpeth. co. Northumb. But other and smaller localities would probably bear this name.

John de Langehirst, co. Hertf., 1273. A.
Walter de Langhurst, co. Sussex, 20 Edw. I. R.
1690. John Underhill and Elliner Longhurst: Marriage Alleg. (Canterbury), p. 145.
1791. Married—John Longhurst and Sarah Killick: St. Geo. Han. Sq. ii. 53.
London, 13; New York, 1.

Longley.—Local, 'of Longley,' a hamlet in the parish of Ecclesfield, near Sheffield (cf. Langley), from *long*, long, and *ley* or *lee*, a meadow; v. Lee.

Thomas de Longlegh, 1379: P. T. Yorks. p. 169.
Willelmus Longlegh, 1379: ibid.
1565. Married—Robart Longly and Ellen Watkinson: St. Antholin (London), p. 17.
1697. — Benjamin Longly and Ruth Tadhunter: Canterbury Cath. p. 65.
1761. — John Longlee and Sarah Saunders: St. Geo. Han. Sq. i. 107.
London, 13; West Rid. Court Dir., 11; Sheffield, 2; Philadelphia, 19.

Longman. — Nick. 'the long man'; cf. Longfellow, Long, Lang, Short, &c.

1547-8. Richard Longman and Agnes Ebbes: Marriage Lic. (London), i. 11.
1758. Married—Lambert Howard and Eliz. Longman: St. Geo. Han. Sq. i. 82.
1788. — James Longman and Anne Sawer: ibid. ii. 3.
London, 14; New York, 6.

Longmate.—Local; v. Langmead.

1802. Married—James Longmate and Eliz. Callender: St. Geo. Han. Sq. ii. 270.

Longmire.—Local, 'of Longmire,' a well-known Westmoreland surname, whence *-mire* is a common suffix to local place-names; cf. Blamire.

1632. Thomas Longmyre, of Claughton: Lancashire Wills at Richmond, i. 186.
1698. Dorothy Longmire, alias Jackson, of Torver: ibid. ii. 168.
1738. Buried—John, s. William Longmire: St. Mary, Ulverston, p. 261.
MDB. (co. Cumberland), 1; (co. Westmoreland), 10; New York, 4.

Longridge, Longrigg. — Local, 'of Langrigg,' a township in the parish of Bromfield, co. Cumberland. The surname derived from this place is now generally spelt Longridge (v. Langridge) and Longrigg.

Margaret Langrige, of the parish of Burton, 1598: Lancashire Wills at Richmond (1457-1680), p. 180.
1805. Married—John Gooch and Ann Longridge: St. Geo. Han. Sq. ii. 339.
London, 1, 0; MDB. (co. Cumberland), 0, 7; New York, 0, 1; Philadelphia, 1, 0.

Longsdon, Logsdon.—Local, 'of Longstone'; v. Longson. There can be no doubt that Logsdon is Longsdon with the *n* elided. It is equally evident that both Longsdon and Logsdon are not variants of Longden, which would give a senseless signification to the name. We may safely presume that Longstone became Longsdon, and then Logsdon. It is pleasant to have a view of this kind corroborated after making the statement. Since writing the above I find Longsdon to be a familiar Derbyshire surname, and not unknown in the immediate neighbourhood of Longstone.

1617. Bapt.—Anne, d. John Logsdon: St. Jas. Clerkenwell, i. 78.
London, 2, 2; MDB. (co. Derby), 2, 0.

Longson. — Local, 'of Longstone.' Great Longstone is a chapelry three miles from Bakewell, co. Derby. Little Longstone is a hamlet almost equidistant from the same town. Many names ending in *-son* are local, the *t* in the suffix *-stone* being elided. It is just possible that Longson is an abbreviation of Lawrenson (the son of Lawrence), a surname peculiar to Lancashire. To many this will seem the more probable derivation. To one or the other Longson must be referred. Nevertheless the fact that Longson is a Derbyshire name is strong evidence in favour of my first view.

Ulverston, 2; Manchester, 2; MDB. (co. Derby), 1.

Longstaff, Longstaffe, Langstaff. — Nick. The sobriquet of some sergeant, bailiff, catchpoll, or other officer of the law. Nicknames from the weapon or badge of office were very common; cf. Shakespear, Wagstaff, and *tipstaff*.

William Longstaf, co. Norf., 1273. A.
William Longstaff, co. Norf., 20 Edw. III: FF. ii. 264.
1660. Married—John Longstaffe and Eliz. Blowe: St. Jas. Clerkenwell, i. 105.
1748. — William Pricklowe and Barbara Longstaff: St. Geo. Han. Sq. i. 40.
London, 3, 1, 1; MDB. (North Rid. Yorks), 7, 0, 0; New York, 1, 0, 0.

Longstreeth. — Local; v. Langstroth.

Longtoft.—Local, 'of Langtoft,' a parish in co. Lincoln, near Market Deeping.

Godfrey de Langetot, 24 Hen. III: FF. viii. 199.
Ralph de Langetot, co. Wilts, Hen. III-Edw. I. K.
John de Langetoft, co. Hunts, 1273. A.
Richard Langetot, co. Oxf., ibid.
MDB. (North Rid. Yorks), 1.

Longton.—Local, 'of Longton,' a chapelry in the parish of Penwortham, co. Lanc., five miles from Preston; cf. Langton.

Evan Longton, of Ormskirk, 1597: Wills at Chester (1545-1620), p. 126.
William Longton, 1602: Preston Guild Rolls, p. 53.
Jacob Longton, *glover*, 1642: ibid. p. 101.
Katherin Longton, of Wyersdale, *widow*, 1617: Lancashire Wills at Richmond (1457-1680), p. 186.
Liverpool, 5; Preston, 1.

Longworth, Longworthy.—Local, 'of Longworth,' a township in the parish of Bolton, co. Lancaster. With Longworthy, cf. Langworthy or Kenworthy, the suffix *-worth* (v. Worth) frequently becoming *worthy*.

1572. Peter Sturer and Isabel Longeworthe: Marriage Lic. (London), i. 53.
Ralph Longworth, of Edgworth, near Bolton, *tailor*, 1587: Wills at Chester (1545-1620), p. 126.
George Longworth, of Bolton, 1596: ibid.
Alice Longworth, of Longworth, 1612: ibid.
1621. John Longworth, co. Northampt.: Reg. Univ. Oxf. vol. ii. pt. ii. p. 391.
London, 1, 1; Manchester, 14, 1; New York, 3, 0.

Lonsbrough ; v. Lowndesbrough.

Lonsdale, Londsdale. — Local, 'of Lonesdale,' the vale of the Lune ; cf. Tyndale, Tweedale, Dunderdale ; v. Lansdell and Lancaster.

Thomas de Londesdale, 1379: P. T. Yorks. p. 268.
Willelmus de Londesdale, 1379: ibid.
John Lonsdale, of Pendle, 1592: Wills at Chester (1545-1620), p. 126.
William Lonsdall, of Newton, 1674: Lancashire Wills at Richmond, i. 186.
1757. Married—Christopher Lonsdale and Eliz. Reeve: St. Geo. Han. Sq. i. 69.
London, 10, 0; Manchester, 4, 0; MDB. (co. Kent), 1, 1; New York, 4, 0.

Look, Looke.—Bapt. 'the son of Luke'; v. Luke. This variant is found in co. Somerset.

1747. Married—John Look and Ann Whitcombe: St. Geo. Chap. Mayfair, p. 95.
MDB. (co. Somerset), 6, 0; New York, 2, 2; Boston (U.S.), 7, 0.

Looker, Luker.—Occup. 'the looker,' i.e. watcher, a herdsman. '*Looker*, a shepherd or herdsman. South' (Halliwell). 'Looker. In the south of England a herdsman, especially in marshy districts ; a man who superintends cattle and drives them to higher ground in case of sudden floods' (Lower, Patr. Brit. p. 199).

1582. William Lookar, co. Hants: Reg. Univ. Oxf. vol. ii. pt. ii. p. 123.
1649. Robert Looker, of Chester: Wills at Chester, ii. 142.
1686. Married—Francis Looker and Katherine Stronte: St. Michael, Cornhill, p. 45.
1795. — Thomas Looker and Sarah Nocks: St. Geo. Han. Sq. ii. 129.
London, 5, 6; MDB. (co. Surrey), 2, 2; Boston (U.S.), 1, 5.

Loose.—(1) Local, 'of Loose,' a parish in co. Kent, near Maidstone. (2) Bapt. 'the son of Lewis.' An imitative variant.

Edward Lewse, co. Glamorgan, 1577: Reg. Univ. Oxf. vol. ii. pt. ii. p. 75.
London, 2; Philadelphia, 8.

Loosemore.—Local; v. Luxmoore.

Loraine, Lorraine. — Local, 'of Lorraine'; v. Loring.

1680. Married—Samson Lorane and Rose Dutton: St. Jas. Clerkenwell, iii. 189.
1692. William Loraine and Ann Smith: Marriage Alleg. (Canterbury), p. 216.
Crockford, 1, 0; Philadelphia, 3, 1.

Lord.—Offic. 'the lord,' the master, the head of the household; v. Master and Masterman.

Robert le Loverd, co. Oxf., 1273. A.
William le Loverd, co. Notts, ibid.
Roger le Lord, co. Camb., ibid.
Walter le Lord, co. Hunts, ibid.
Richard le Lord, fil. Margarete le Lord, C. R., 9 Ric. II.
1642. Bapt.—Judith, d. Richard and Avis Lord: St. Jas. Clerkenwell, i. 150.
1647. — Jesper, son of Jesper Loward: ibid. p. 169.
London, 23; Manchester, 30; New York, 68.

Lorey; v. Lowrie.

Loriman; v. Lurryman.

Lorimer, Lorymer, Larimer, Lorrimer. — Occup. 'the lorimer,' a maker of horses' bits, &c.; ' *laremar*, that maketh byttes, *esperonnier*' (Palsgrave); O.F. *lorimier*, later *lormier* (Skeat). It will be seen, however, that Lormar occurs in the 13th century, also Lorimar, the more correct form.

Gervase Lorimarius, or Sadler, bailiff of Norwich, 1239: FF. iii. 58.
Adam le Lorimer, co. Salop, 1273. A.
Richard le Lorimer, co. Essex, ibid.
Thomas Lormar, co. Essex, ibid.
William Lorinar, co. Oxf., ibid.
Alan le Lorymer. T.
Thomas le Lorymer, 1313. M.
Thomas Loremar, 1379: P. T. Yorks. p. 99.
1503. 'Item, to Symond Warde of London, *lorymere*, for v DD bittes, lxxs.': Privy Purse Exp., Elizabeth of York, p. 97.
1643. Married—Richard Lorrimore and Ann Smyth: St. Mary Aldermary, p. 19.
1779. — James Lorimer and Jean Howden: St. Geo. Han. Sq. i. 296.
London, 2, 2, 0, 0; Boston (U.S.), 4, 0, 1, 2.

Loring, Lorin. — Local, 'of Lorraine,' formerly a French province.

Peter le Loring, co. Bedf., 1273. A.
John le Loreng, co. Oxf., ibid.
Alice Loring, co. Soms., 1 Edw. III: Kirby's Quest, p. 131.
Emma Loring, co. Soms., 1 Edw. III, ibid.
Sir Roger Lorynge, 1566: Visitation of Bedfordshire, p. 13.
1636. Married—William Loringe and Margret Turnore: St. Mary Aldermary, p. 18.
Crockford, 1, 0; London, 0, 1; New York, 6, 0.

Lorriman.—Occup. ' Lorry's man,' i.e. the servant of Lawrence;

---

cf. Matthewman, Sandeman, Addiman, &c., and v. Lowrie.

West Rid. Court Dir., 2.

Lory.—Bapt. ' the son of Lawrence '; v. Lowrie.

Lott.—Bapt. 'the son of Lott.' All my instances are from the South-Eastern counties. Probably an immigrant from the Low Countries. As Abraham was common, it seems natural that Lot should be the same. The story, as an attractive one, would be familiar to the peasantry. The leading personages of the Old Testament as well as the New were utilized at the font.

Richard fil. Lote, co. Camb., 1273. A.
Robert Lote, co. Camb., ibid.
Walter Lotte, co. Camb., ibid.
William Lot, co. Suff., ibid.
John Lotte, co. Norf., ibid.
1608. Jeoffrey Farrant and Mary Lott: Marriage Lic. (Westminster), p. 16.
1626. Henry Lott and Joane Hill: Marriage Lic. (London), ii. 180.
London, 6; MDB. (Suffolk), 7; New York, 6.

Loudan, -don; v. Lowden.

Lound, Lounds; v. Lund.

Louth.—Local, ' of Louth,' a well-known town in co. Lincoln.

Robert de Luda, co. York, Hen. III–Edw. I. K.
John de Luda, co. Linc., 1273. A.
Richard de Luda, co. Linc., ibid.
Eva Louth, co. Soms., 1 Edw. III: Kirby's Quest, p. 97.
1616. Buried—William Lowth: St. Jas. Clerkenwell, iv. 137.
1674. Henry Champante and Sarah Lowth: Marriage Lic. (Westminster), p. 231.
East Rid. Court Dir., 1; MDB. (co. Lincoln), 1; Philadelphia, 4.

Love.—(1) Bapt. ' the son of Love.' That this was a fontal name the dims. Love-cock and Love-kin (q.v.) amply prove.

Love del Hok, co. Oxf., 1273. A.
1610. Bapt. Love Hewlett: Reg. Burgh, Norfolk.
1631–2. Buried—Love Ballard: Reg. Berwick, Sussex.
1662. Bapt.—Love Appletree: Reg. Banbury.

There is no reason to suppose that this name was introduced by the Puritan party. That it was favoured by them there can be no doubt.

---

(2) Nick. ' the love,' the dear one, or, as suggested by Mr. Lower, some English modification of the French ' le loup,' the wolf.

Alan le Love, co. Camb., 1273. A.
Walter Love, co. Camb., ibid.
1581. Nathaniel Love, co. Wilts: Reg. Univ. Oxf. vol. ii. pt. ii. p. 112.
London, 25; Philadelphia, 76.

Loveband; v. Lovibond.

MDB. (co. Devon), 4.

Lovecock.—Bapt. 'the son of Love' (q.v.), with suffix -*cock* (v. Cock); cf. Wilcock, Adcock, Dadcock.

Roger Lovecock. B.
Matthew Lovecok, co. Oxf., 1273. A.
Henry Lovecok, co. Essex, ibid.
John Lovecok, co. Soms., 1 Edw. III: Kirby's Quest, p. 90.
Lovecok de Murifield, co. Soms., 1 Edw. III: ibid. p. 174.
Lovecok le Carter, co. Soms., 1 Edw. III: ibid.

The gen. Lovecocks also occurs; cf. Wilcocks.

Robert Lovecoks, co. Soms., 1 Edw. III: ibid. p. 91.

Loveday.—Bapt. ' the son of Loveday.' Of the same class as Christmas, Pentecost, Nowell, &c. The font-name lingered on as Lowdy in Cornwall, the last refuge of many old English favourites, till the 18th century, and is not yet extinct. ' John Lovdesman ' (John, the servant of Loveday) occurs in the Hundred Rolls, 1273, in co. Norfolk (i. 439). The word occurs in Piers Plowman:

'I kan holde love-dayes
And here a reve's rekenyns.'

Halliwell says: 'A day appointed for settlement of differences by arbitration.'

'But helle is fulle of suche discorde,
That ther may be no loveday.'
Gower MS. Soc. Ant. 134, f. 37.

Walter Loveday, co. Camb., 1273. A.
Richard Loveday, co. Hunts, ibid.
Ralph Loveday, co. Camb., 1313. M.
Hugo Lofdey, 1379: P. T. Yorks. p. 8.
Lovdie, d. Thomas Jenkin, 1578: Reg. St. Columb Major, p. 11.
Lowdye Trelogan, 1601: ibid. p. 20.
Lowdy, d. William Trekeene, 1622: ibid. p. 210.
Loveday, wife of Thomas Vivian, 1768: ibid. p. 284.

The Devon County Directory has 'Mrs. Loveday Budd, miller,' resident in the parish of Dolton.

London, 7; New York, 1.

Lovejoy. — Nick. A pretty sobriquet ; cf. Makeblithe. Just the surname to be handed down. No fear of any male member of the family trying to get rid of it.

1578. William Randeson and Johanna Lovejoye, *widow*: Marriage Lic. (London), i. 83.

1669. Buried—Robert Lovejoy, a carpenter, killed by a fall of a piece of timber: St. Michael, Cornhill, p. 257.

1685. Bapt.—Eliz., d. John Lovejoy: St. Jas. Clerkenwell, i. 314.

1689. — John, s. John Lovjoy: St. Antholin (London), p. 105.

1756. Married—Samuel Lovejoy and Sarah Wagger: St. Geo. Han. Sq. i. 66.

London, 6; New York, 14.

Lovekin, Luffkin, Lufkin, Lufkins.—Bapt. 'the son of Love' (q.v.), from the dim. Lovekin. This has now almost universally settled down into Lufkin; cf. Watkin for Walter, or Tompkin for Thomas. From Shropshire Lovekin came northwards into Cheshire, and as Lufkin is now in the Manchester Directory.

Lovekin Dawes, co. Oxf., 1273. A.
Robert Luvekyn, co. Oxf., ibid.
Lovekyn Piscator, co. Salop, ibid.
Lovekyn Stukepenne, co. Kent, ibid.
Richard Lovekvn, 1313. M.
Margery Lovekyn, co. Soms., 1 Edw. III : Kirby's Quest, p. 111.

1546. John Osborne and Philipa Lufkyne, *widow*, of the King's Household: Marriage Lic. (Faculty Office), p. 7.

Mathew Lovekin, of Wiston, 1647: Wills at Chester (1621–50), p. 142.

Randle Lovekin, of Wibunbury, 1691 : ibid. (1681–1700), p. 162.

'Maistres Lovekyn to give in almes, 10s.,' 1542-3 : Privy Purse Expenses, Princess Mary, p. 99.

'Maistres Luffkyn to give in almes, 10s.', 1543: ibid. p. 114.

This conclusively proves Luffkin or Lufkin and Lovekin to be one and the same name.

London, 0, 0, 1, 1 ; Manchester (Lufkin), 1 ; MDB. (co. Salop), 1, 0, 0, 0 ; (co. Essex), 0, 0, 4, 0 ; Philadelphia, 2, 0, 1, 0.

Lovelace, Loveless. — Nick. ' the loveless ' (?).

Albricus Loveles, co. Suff., 1273. A.
Sarra Loveles, co. Hunts, ibid.

1587. Robert Lovelisse, co. Berks: Reg. Univ. Oxf. vol. ii. pt. ii. p. 160.

1734. Married—Thomas Grinaway and Sarah Loveless : St. Geo. Han. Sq. i. 13.

1754. — Joseph Lovelace and Eliz. Owen : ibid. p. 51.

London, 3, 3 ; Philadelphia, 1, 3.

Lovelady.—Local(?). A curious name, but doubtless a mutilation of some local surname ; cf. Toplady.

Ann Lovelady, of Sephton, 1679 : Wills at Chester (1660-80), p. 172.

MDB. (co. Lancaster), 1 ; Liverpool, 7.

Lovell.—(1) Bapt. ' the son of Lovel,' probably a dim. of Love, q.v.

Lovel le Clerc, co. Essex, 1273. A.
Lovel (without surname), co. Suff., ibid.

(2) Nick. 'the lovel,' i.e. the little wolf. ' It is a derivative of the Lat. *lupus*, wolf, thus : Lupus, Loup, Lupellus, Louvel, Lovel ': Lower's Patr. Brit. p. 200. Lovel was, like Talbot, a dog's name. 'William Collingborne, executed in 1484, wrote as follows of the favourites of Edward III (Catesby, Ratcliffe, and Lovel) :

"The Ratte, the Catte, and Lovell, our dogge,
Rule all England under the Hogge."'

(Lower, ibid. p. 200). It is curious to notice that Wolf was used both as fontal name and nickname at the same period; v. Wolff, and also Lowell.

Baldewin Lovel, co. Devon, Hen. III–Edw. I. K.
Caterina Lovel, co. Oxf., 1273. A.
1576. John Lovel, co. Soms.: Reg. Univ. Oxf. vol. ii. pt. ii. p. 71.
1762. Married—William Lovell and Eliz. Dalton : St. Geo. Han. Sq. i. 110.

London, 27 ; Philadelphia, 10.

Lovelock. — Nick. 'with the lovelock,' i.e. pendant curls, &c.; cf. Silverlock, Blacklock, &c.; v. Lovelocker. The early *lovelock* was as familiar as the later *chignon*. A prominent lovelock would give the wearer the sobriquet.

'Why should thy sweete love-locke hang dangling downe,
Kissing thy girdle-stud with falling pride?'
The Affectionate Shepheard, 1594.

John Lovelok. J.

1611-2. Thomas Ricards and Joane Lovelacke : Marriage Lic. (London), p. 10.

1625-6. George Windor and Anne Lovelock : ibid. p. 160.

1770. Married—John Smith and Mary Lovelock : St. Geo. Han. Sq. i. 198.

London, 5; MDB. (co. Berks), 4 ; New York, 1.

Lovelocker.—Occup. Seemingly a lovelocker, one who made up lovelocks, perhaps with false hair, analogous to the later perukemaker ; v. Lovelock.

Walter le Loveloker, Oxford, 1273. A.

Did he cater for the 'Varsity dandies of the period ?

Lovelot. — Bapt. From Love (q.v.), and dim. Love-elot ; cf. Hewlett, &c. The following reference distinctly proves the popularity of Love as a font-name. Lovelock (q.v.) is additional evidence.

Lovelota Gemmete, co. Soms., 1 Edw. III : Kirby's Quest, p. 220.
Adam Lovelot, co. Soms., 1 Edw. III : ibid. p. 234.

Lovely, Lovelee.—Nick. ' the lovely.'

William Louelyk, C. R., 35 Edw. I.
1772. Married—John Tamberlin and Ann Lovely : St. Geo. Han. Sq. i. 224.
Crockford, 2, 0 ; MDB. (co. Lincoln), 0, 1 ; New York, 4, 0 ; Philadelphia, 2, 0.

Lover.—Nick. 'the lover' ; cf. Paramor, Phillimore, &c.

William le Lovere, co. Norf., 1273. A.

I believe it has been generally thought that ' lovyer' was a modern vulgarism ; seemingly it is not so.

John le Lovyere, co. Soms., 1 Edw. III : Kirby's Quest, p. 179.
Walter le Loveyere, co. Soms., 1 Edw. III : ibid.
1762. Married—William Lover and Margaret Hornsby: St. Geo. Han. Sq. i. 114.

New York, 2.

Loveredge, Loveridge. — Bapt. ' the son of Loverich'; cf. Aldridge for Aldrich.

William Loverich, co. Oxf., 1273. A.
Robert Loverik, co. Linc., ibid.
1666. Henry Clarke and Grace Loveridge : Marriage Lic. (Westminster), p. 115.
1805. Married—Aaron Loveridge and Mary Gattfield : St. Geo. Han. Sq. ii. 319.

London, 1, 4 ; Philadelphia, 0, 2.

Loverock; v. Laverack.

Lovett, Lovitt.—? Bapt. 'the son of Love' (q.v.), from the dim. Lov-et; cf. Emmott, &c. As Love became Lovell (q.v.), so also it became Lovet. 'Little wolf' seems to be the meaning; v. Love.

Thomas Lovet, co. Northampt., 1273. A.
Henry Lovet, co. Devon, ibid.
Willelmus Louott, 1379: P. T. Yorks. p. 240.
1583. William Lovett, co. Staff.; Reg. Univ. Oxf. vol. ii. pt. ii. p. 131.
1668. Bapt.—Mary, d. William Louett: St. Michael, Cornhill, p. 146.
1800. Married—Charles Wheeler and Eliz. Lovitt: St. Geo. Han. Sq. ii. 229.
London, 7, 1; New York, 10, 2.

Lovibond, Loveband. — Nick. (?). Probably a sobriquet of a playfully satirical character affixed to one who was a slave or bond to love; v. Bond. But it may have been a personal name, for Love-bond would make a pretty child's name; cf. Love, Lovekin, Lovecock, Loveday. Also cf. Lovelot (Kirby's Quest, p. 234).

Nicholas Loveband, co. Norf., 20 Edw. I. R.
Thomas Lovehybonde, co. Soms., 1 Edw. III: Kirby's Quest, p. 231.
William Lovybonde, co. Soms., 1 Edw. III: ibid. p. 250.
1608. Edward Lovibond, Isle of Wight: Reg. Univ. Oxf. vol. ii. pt. ii. p. 301.
1698. Henry Lovibond and Anne Collins: Marriage Lic. (Faculty Office), p. 230.
1702. Thomas Thorpe and Anne Lovibond: ibid. p. 244.
1784. Married—John Edmonds and Theodosia Jane Loverbond: St. Geo. Han. Sq. i. 360.
London, 2, 1; New York, 2, 0.

Loving.—Local, 'of Lovaine,' a well-known city in the Netherlands. The final g is, of course, excrescent, as in Jennings and a host of names, the corruption being imitative. The instances below fully prove my statement.

Godfrey de Luvayn, co. Bedf., Hen. III–Edw. I. K.
Mathew Lovein, co. Glouc., ibid.
Muriel de Lovayn, co. Suff., 1273. A.
Mathew de Lovayne, co. Suff., ibid.
John Loveyn, co. Norf., 1365: FF. v. 186.
Ellen Loveyn, co. Norf., 1365: ibid.
1608. William Lovinge, of Newport, Isle of Wight: Marriage Lic. (London), i. 305.

1623. Bapt.—Mary, d. Stephen Loven: St. Jas. Clerkenwell, i. 96.
1703. Married—Thomas Loveing and Eliz. Rothwell: St. Dionis Backchurch, p. 51.
London, 1; Philadelphia, 1.

Low, Lowe.—Local, 'at the low,' i.e. the hill; A.S. *hlaw* or *hlœw*, a hill; v. Law (1).

Ralph de la Lowe, co. Salop, 1273. A.
Hugh de la Lowe, co. Heref., ibid.
Crist. atte Lowe, co. Soms., 1 Edw. III—Kirby's Quest, p. 256.

The following occur in the list of mayors of Macclesfield:

Thomas del Lowe, 1430: East Ches. ii. 464.
Thomas Lowe, 1448: ibid.
George Lowe, 1607: ibid. p. 465.
London, 33, 46; New York, 41, 45.

Lowcock.—Bapt. 'the son of Lawrence,' from the nick. Law or Low (v. Lowson), and suffix *-cock*; cf. Wilcock, and v. Cock.

Alicia Lowcok', 1379: P. T. Yorks. p. 205.
Willelmus Loucok', 1379: p. 134.
1767. Married—Thomas Park and Deborah Lowcock: St. Geo. Han. Sq. ii. 169.
Manchester, 2; Sheffield, 1.

Lowden, Loudan, Louden, Loudon. — Local. Probably 'of Loudson,' a parish in co. Ayr. The surname has crossed the border and is well known in co. Cumb.

1716. William Lowden, of Kirkham: Lancashire Wills at Richmond, ii. 169.
1753. Married — Thomas Dalby and Sarah Lowden: St. Geo. Chap. Mayfair, p. 265.
London, 6, 1, 0, 0: MDB. (co. Cumb.), 1, 0, 0, 0; Boston (U.S.), 8, 0, 1, 12.

Lowder; v. Lowther.

Lowell.—Nick. and bapt. There is not the shadow of a doubt that Lowell is a variant of Lovell. For a conclusive proof a Cambridgeshire Lovel is found with his name spelt both ways in the Hundred Rolls.

Fulco Lovel, co. Camb., 1273. A.
Fulco Lawol, co. Camb., ibid.
1531. Thomas Lovell, or Lowell, or Louwell: Reg. Univ. Oxf. i. 164.
1655. Married—Peter Hentton and Jenne Louell: St. Mary Aldermary, p. 24.
1745. — Charles Tarr and Elioner Lowell: St. Geo. Chap. Mayfair, p. 55.
London, 1; New York, 4.

Lowman. — (1) Occup. 'the servant of Low,' i.e. Lawrence; v. Lowson. This class of occupa-

tive names is somewhat large; v. Matthewman, Addyman, &c. (2) Local, 'the low-man,' one who lived on the low (v. Low); cf. Denman, Berryman, &c.

1587. Francis Lowman, co. Devon: Reg. Univ. Oxf. vol. ii. pt. ii. p. 159.
1664-5. John Huett and Faith Lowman (co. Hants): Marriage Lic. (Faculty Office), p. 86.
1673. Married—John Lowman and Frances Knowles: St. Peter, Cornhill, ii. 55.
1688. Buried—Frances Loman, in the North Isle: ibid. p. 101
London, 3, New York, 1; Boston (U.S.), 1.

Lowndes, Lownds; v. Lund.

Lowndesbrough, Lowndsbrough, Lowndsborough, Lonsbrough, Londesborough, Lownsbury, Lounsberry, Lounsbery, Lounsbury. — Local, 'of Londesborough,' a parish in E. Rid. Yorks, two miles and a half from Market Weighton.

MDB. (North Rid. Yorks), 1, 0, 0, 0, 0, 0, 0, 0, 0; Hull, 0, 1, 0, 0, 0, 0, 0, 0, 0; New Malton, 0, 0, 1, 0, 0, 0, 0, 0, 0; Fridaythorpe, York, 0, 0, 0, 1, 0, 0, 0, 0; Scarborough, 0, 0, 0, 0, 1, 0, 0, 0, 0; Philadelphia, 0, 0, 0, 0, 0, 6, 2, 1, 2.

Lowrie, Lowry, Laurie, Lawry, Lawrey, Lawrie, Lory, Lorey.—Bapt. 'the son of Lawrence.' In the Lowlands and on the Borders, popularly Lowrie or Laurie, whence the many NorthEnglish and Scottish variations of this name. The English sobriquet of the fox was Reynard, q.v. In Scotland Lawrence stood sponsor to the animal.

'Whilk slee Tod Lowrie hads without his mow.'
Ramsay's Poems, ii. 143.
'He said; and round the courtiers all and each
Applauded Lawrie for his winsome speech.' ibid. p. 500.

Hence 'Lowrie-like,' having the crafty look of a fox. The full name Lawrence was also applied to the fox, proving that Lowry and Lawry are the true offspring of the name.

'Lawrence the actis and the proceis wrait.'
Bannatyne Poems, p. 112, st. 4.

All my quotations are from Jamieson.

K k

1677. Buried—Mary Lowery: St. Dionis Backchurch, p. 243.
1742. Married—Edward Lowry and Sarah Gilbert: St. Geo. Chap. Mayfair, p. 20.
1784. — Hugh Laurie and Frances Storie: St. Geo. Han. Sq. i. 362.
London, 1, 8, 8, 1, 1, 10, 0, 0; MDB. (co. Cornwall), Lory, 7; New York, 4, 18, 2, 0, 0, 4, 2, 8.

Lowson.—Bapt. 'the son of Lawrence,' from the nick. Law or Low; cf. Lowrie for Laurie, and v. Lawson. Lawson is a familiar Cumberland surname.

1616. Henry Lowson, co. Cumb.: Reg. Univ. Oxf. vol. ii. pt. ii. p. 351.
1753. Married—John Baxter and Ann Lowson: St. Geo. Chap. Mayfair, p. 256.
London, 2; Boston (U.S.), 1.

Lowther, Lowder. — Local, ' of Lowther,' a parish in co. Cumb. In the Household Books of Lord William Howard of Naworth Castle (Surt. Soc.) the name is spelt variously as Lowther, Louther, Lowder, and Louder.

Robertus de Louther, 1310, co. Westm. M.
Hugo de Louthre, 1319, co. Cumb., ibid.
Ann Lowder, 1622, co. Cumb.: VVV. p. 495.

Sir John Lowther, of White-haven, had two daughters baptized in London at the church of St. Martin's-in-the-Fields. They are thus entered:

1664. Bapt.—Catherine, d. of Sir John Lowder, *knight*: Transactions Cumb. and Westm. Ant. and Arch. Soc. pt. ii. vol. ix. p. 341.
1667. — Jane, d. of Sir John Lowther: ibid.
1606(?). Rowland Lowder, of Staveley, in Cartmell: Lancashire Wills at Richmond, i. 186.
1670. Rowland Lowther, of Stayley, in Cartmell: ibid.
1796. Married—Anthony Jackson, *husbandman*, and Betty Lowther: St. Mary, Ulverston, p. 442.
London, 4, 1; Crockford, 2, 1; MDB. (co. Cumb.), 13, 0; New York, 8, 0; Philadelphia, 5, 8.

Lowthian, Lothian, Lowthin, Lowthing. — Local, ' of Lothian,' a Scottish surname that has crept across the Border. Lothian is a district on the south side of the Forth, including the

counties of Haddington, Edinburgh, and Linlithgow.

Ranulph de Louthiane, co. Northumb., 1273. A.
1791. Married—Robert Lowthian and Mary Bodimeade: St. Geo. Han. Sq. ii. 69.
Manchester, 2, 0, 1, 1; MDB. (co. Cumb.), 8, 0, 0, 0; Boston (U.S.), 0, 2, 0, 0; New York, 1, 2, 0, 0.

Lowthorpe, Lathrop, Lathrope, Lowthrop.—Local, ' of Lowthorp,' a parish in the E. Rid. Yorks, near Great Driffield. My first entry clearly proves that the American Lathrop is but a variant; cf. Winthrop for Winthorp, and v. Thrupp.

1602. John Lowthroppe, or Lawthrop, co. York: Reg. Univ. Oxf. vol. ii. pt. ii. p. 259.
1608. Bapt.—John, s. Robert Leythorpe: St. Jas. Clerkenwell, i. 55.
1610. — Robert, s. Robert Laytharopp: ibid. p. 59.
1740. Married—Robert Lathropp and Ann Tomkins: St. Geo. Han. Sq. i. 25.

These four entries supply, as will be seen, a complete chain of evidence.

London, 1, 0, 0, 0; Hull, 2, 0, 0, 0; East Rid. Court Dir., 0, 0, 0, 1; Philadelphia, 0, 6, 1, 0.

Loxham.—Local, ' of Loxham.' I have not found the spot. A Lancashire surname.

William Loxham, of Longton, *butcher*, 1622: Preston Guild Rolls, p. 89.
Robert Loxum, of Preston, 1675: Lancashire Wills at Richmond (1457-1680), p. 186.
Thomas Loxam, of Preston, 1677: ibid.
Eliz. Loxham, of Preston, 1733: ibid. (1681-1748), p. 169.
Edward Loxham, of Kirkham, 1737: ibid.
Preston, 2; Barrow-in-Furness, 1.

Loxley.—Local, ' of Loxley,' a liberty in the parish of Uttoxeter, co. Stafford; also a parish in co. Warwick, near Stratford.

Richard de Lokesley, *taillour*, 14 Edw. III: Freemen of York, i. 34.
Thomas de Lokeslay, 1379: P. T. Yorks. p. 35.
1740. Bapt.—Edward. s. Abraham Loxley: St. Geo. Chap. Mayfair, p. 1.
1767. Married—William Davis and Grace Loxley: St. Geo. Han. Sq. i. 167.
London, 1; MDB. (co. Glouc.), 3; Oxford, 2; Philadelphia, 1.

Luard.— ? ——. ' At the Revocation of the Edict of Nantes, 1685, Robert Abraham Luard came from Caen in Normandy and settled in London, *a quo* the Luards of Lincolnshire and Essex ': Lower's Patr. Brit. p. 201.

1754. Married—Peter Robert Luard and Jane Burryan: St. Geo. Chap. Mayfair, p. 273.
London, 1; MDB. (co. Essex), 5; (co. Lincoln), 2.

Lubbock.—Local, ' of Lübeck,' on the Trave, near Hamburg.

Robert de Lubyck, co. Linc., 1273. A.
Bernard de Lubic, co. York, ibid.
Hildebrand de Lubek. J.
Hellbrand de Lubeck, co. Norf., 14 Edw. I: FF. ix. 363.
1686. Bapt.—Anne, d. Herman Lewbeck: St. Jas. Clerkenwell, i. 319.
Richard Lubbock, sheriff of Norwich, 1714: FF. iii. 436.
William Lubbock, rector of Lammas, co. Norf., 1738: ibid. vi. 294.
London, 4; MDB. (co. Lincoln), 1.

Lucas. — Bapt. 'the son of Luke.' A single glance at the London Directory will suffice to show that Lucas, not Luke, was the early English form.

' And al that Marc hath y-maad,
Mathew, Johan, and Lucas.'
Piers Plowman, 3498-9.
Lucas Cacherellus, co. Norf., 1273. A.
Lucas Bercator, co. Camb., ibid.
John Lucas, co. Soms., 1 Edw. III: Kirby's Quest, p. 261.
Willelmus Lucas, 1379: P. T. Howdenshire, p. 23.
Thomas fil. Lucas, co. York. W. 15.
1561. Richard Lucas and Alice Pumfrett: Marriage Lic. (London), i. 22.
London, 83; New York, 27.

Luccock, Lucock, Lowcock.—(1) Bapt. 'the son of Luke'; with suffix -*cock*, Lukecock, popularly Luccock; v. Cock. (2) Bapt. 'the son of Lawrence,' a variant of Lowcock, q.v.

Robert Lukok, *bocher*, 13 Edw. III: Freemen of York, i. 33.
1681. Married—William Luccocke and Eliz. Wright: St. Jas. Clerkenwell, iii. 194.
1752. — John Moris and Sarah Luckock: St. Geo. Chap. Mayfair, p. 232.
1794. — John Lucock and Ann Dawson: St. Geo. Han. Sq. ii. 109.
London, 1, 3, 3.

Luck, Lucke, Luckie, Luckey.—(1) Bapt. 'the son of

Luke,' popularly Luck and Luckie on the Scottish border.

1624. Married—Sir Samuell Lucke and Eliz. Freeman: St. Michael, Cornhill, p. 24.

1627. Bapt.—Samvell, s. Sir Samvell Luke: ibid. p. 119.

'Lucke Moffett, for one howse, 4*d*,' 1631: QQQ. p. 155.

Hence diminutives Luckett and Luckin, q.v.

(2) Local, 'of Luke,' probably Liege in the Netherlands, with which province and city we were closely related by commercial ties. Andrew Borde says in his Boke of Knowledge, 'The lond of Lewke is a pleasant countre, the chiefe towne is the cytie of Lewke. The speche is base Doche' (quoted by Lower).

Theobald de Luke, co. York, 1273. A.
Reynen de Luke, co. York, ibid.
William Lucke, co. Camb., ibid.
John de Luke, 1317. M.
1733. Married—Richard Luckie and Jane Warden: St. Geo. Han. Sq. i. 12.
1756. — Thomas Luck and Jane Featherston: ibid. p. 64.
London, 12, 0, 3, 0; New York, 8, 3, 1, 7.

Luckett.—Bapt. 'the son of Luke,' from dim. Luke-et, popularly Lucket (v. Luck); cf. Emmott from Emma, or Collett from Cole (Nicholas).

Matilda Luket, co. York, 1418: W. 11, p. 20.
Walter Luket, co. York, 1418: ibid.
1629. Buried—George, s. Richard Luckett: St. Jas. Clerkenwell, iv. 196.
1802. Married—George Luckett and Rosanna Taylor: St. Geo. Han. Sq. ii. 264.
London, 2; Oxford, 2.

Luckin. Lucking, Lukeing, Lukyn, Luckings, Lucken, Luken, Lukens. — Bapt. 'the son of Luke,' from dim. Luke-in; with excrescent *g* Lukeing, and with patronymic *s* Lukeings, popularly Luckin, Lucking, and Luckings; v. Luck.

Jane Luckin. FF.
1548. Martin Pugson and Joanna Luckynes: Marriage Lic. (Faculty Office), p. 13.
1587. John Luckyn and Anne Sampford: Marriage Lic. (London), i. 162.
1591. Walter Lukyn, co. Essex: Reg. Univ. Oxf. vol. ii. pt. ii. p. 186.

1609. Buried—Martha Lukin, servant to the Lady Denney: St. Antholin (London), p. 47.
London, 2, 3, 1, 2, 1, 0, 0, 0; New York, 0, 2, 0, 0, 0, 1, 1, 1.

Luckman, Lukeman. — Occup. 'the man of Luke,' i.e. servant. In the North popularly Luck, q.v. This is a surname of a distinct class; v. Matthewman, Ladyman, or Addyman, and cf. Lowman.

1683. Married—John Lucman and Suzanna Bennett. St. Jas. Clerkenwell, iii. 199.
London, 1, 1; Philadelphia, 3, 0.

Luckner; v. Lewknor.

Lucombe. — Local, 'of Luccombe,' a parish in co. Somerset; also written Luckham.

Geoffrey de Luccombe, co. Soms., 1 Edw. III: Kirby's Quest, p. 246.
1752. Married—Richard Shepperd and Eliz. Luckham: St. Geo. Chap. Mayfair, p. 221.
1756. — Thomas Marchant and Sarah Luckham: St. Geo. Han. Sq. i. 87.
London, 3.

Lucraft, Luckcraft, Luckratt, Loucraft.—Local, 'of Leacroft,' a township in the parish of Cannock, co. Stafford. The suffix -*croft* is frequently found as -*craft*; v. Craft. A novel published several years ago by Messrs. Besant and Rice, entitled The Case of Mr. Lucraft, has helped to give prominence to this surname. There can be little doubt that all the above forms are variants of Leycraft or Leacroft. Of course smaller spots than Leacroft in Staffordshire may have originated the surname, as the term *leacroft* would be a common place-word; v. Lea and Croft.

Francis Leycrofte, or Leighcrofte, London, 1584: Reg. Univ. Oxf. vol. ii. pt. ii. p. 134.
1601. Buried—Sara, d. Samson Lecraft, *armorer*: St. Peter, Cornhill, i. 151.
1607. Bapt.—Richard, s. Sampson Leycrafte, *brasier*: ibid. p. 57.
1608. Buried — Samson Leycrofte, *brasier*: ibid. p. 163.
London, 2, 0, 0, 0; MDB. (co. Devon), 0, 1, 3, 0; Plymouth, 0, 0, 1, 0; Boston (U.S.), 0, 0, 0, 1.

Lucy, Lucey.—(1) Local, 'de Luci.' Luci is a parish in the

arrondissement of Neufchâtel, in Normandy. The Lucys of our modern directories represent two totally different derivations, and are inextricably mixed; v. (2).

Godfrey de Lucey, 34 Hen. II: FF. x. 332.
Reginald de Lucy, co. Essex, Hen. III–Edw. I. K.
Gilbert de Lucie, co. Linc., 1273. A.
John de Luce, co. Norf., ibid.
Richard de Lucy, co. Essex, ibid.
Fulco de Lucy, co. Staff., 20 Edw. I. R.
Ancelina de Lucy. J.

(2) Bapt. 'the son of Lucy.'
Richard fil. Lucia. J.
Roger fil. Lucie, co. Norf., 1273. A.
Alice fil. Luce, co. Hertf., ibid.
Richard fil. Lucie, co. Hunts, 20 Edw. I. R.
Elena fil. Luce, co. York, ibid.
Charles Lucey, 1513: Reg. Univ. Oxf. i. 87.
1612. Bapt.—Ann, d. Robert Lucey: St. Antholin (London), p. 48.
London, 4, 3; Philadelphia, 10, 0.

Luddington.—Local, 'of Luddington,' (1) a parish in cos. Northampton and Hunts, six miles from Oundle; (2) a hamlet in the parish of Old Stratford, co. Warwick.

Henry de Ludinton, co. Soms., Hen. III–Edw. I. K.
William de Ludinton, co. Warwick, ibid.
Hamund de Lodingtone, co. Hunts, 1273. A.
Edelina de Lodinton, co. Northampt., ibid.
Walter de Lodyngton, co. Hunts, ibid.
1606. Bapt.—Eliz., d. Vallintonne Luddingtonne: St. Peter, Cornhill, i. 56.
1661-2. Stephen Lodington and Eliz. Neesham: Marriage Alleg. (Canterbury), p. 67.
1670. Married—James Tridway and Saray Ludington: St. Jas. Clerkenwell, iii. 172.
MDB. (co. Lincoln), 1; Philadelphia, 3.

Ludford.—Local, 'of Ludford,' a parish near Ludlow, partly in co. Hereford, partly in co. Salop. Also two parishes (Magna and Parva Ludford) in co. Lincoln.

John Lodeford, co. Soms., 1 Edw. III: Kirby's Quest, p. 215.
1450. John Lydford, or Ledford, or Ludford: Marriage Lic. (Faculty Office), p. 10.
1548. William Askeryck and Eliz. Ludford: Marriage Lic. (Faculty Office), p. 13.

1669. William Ludford and Vertue Roker: Marriage Alleg. (Canterbury), p. 23.
London, 3.

Ludgate.—Local, 'at the ludgate'; v. Lidgate and Lidgater.

London, 1; Boston (U.S.), 6.

Ludgater.—Local, 'the ludgater,' i.e. one who lived by the ludgate; v. Lidgate and Lidgater.

Crockford, 2; MDB. (co. Kent), 2.

Ludlam.—Local, 'of Ludlam,' seemingly some place in co. Derby. I have not found the locality.

1575. Robert Lodlam, co. Derby: Reg. Univ. Oxf. vol. ii. pt. ii. p. 68.
1707. Buried — James Ludlam: St. Michael, Cornhill, p. 279.
London, 3; MDB. (co. Derby), 4; Philadelphia, 4.

Ludlow.—Local, 'of Ludlow,' a market-town and parish in co. Salop. In the Hundred Rolls (1273) the name of the place is variously Ludelawe, Ludelawie, Ludelawye, Ludelowe.

Nicholas de Ludelawe, co. Glouc., 1273. A.
John de Ludloe, co. Glouc., 15 Edw. I: Atkyns' Hist. Glouc. p. 161.
1591. Henry Ludlowe, co. Wilts: Reg. Univ. Oxf. vol. ii. pt. ii. p. 185.
1610. Roger Ludlowe, co. Wilts: ibid. p. 311.
1695. Married—William Bracey and Mary Ludlow: St. Michael, Cornhill, p. 48.
1746. — William Ludlow and Eliz. Halbert: St. Geo. Han. Sq. i. 37.
London, 8; MDB. (co. Warwick), 3; New York, 19.

Luff.—Bapt. 'the son of Love.' whence Lovekin, q.v. Lufkin and Lufkins are corruptions of Lovekin; so no doubt Luff of Love.

William Luffe, co. Bucks, 1273. A.
Cf. the immediate entry above with
Walter Lufesone, co. Oxf., 1273. A.
which is manifestly 'the son of Love.'
1679. John Steward and Mary Luffe: Marriage Lic. (Faculty Office), p. 147.
1741. Bapt.—Mary, d. George Luff: St. Peter, Cornhill, i. 41.
London, 14; Philadelphia, 6.

Lufkin, Lufkins.—Bapt.; v. Lovekin.

Lugg.—? Local, 'at the lug' (?), from residence thereby. Lug, a

measure of land, anciently 20 ft. 'Lug, a pole in measure' (Kennett). Forty-nine square yards of coppice wood make a *lug* (Halliwell); cf. Hyde. 'Lugger, a strip of land, Glouc.' (ibid.)

Thomas Lugge, co. Kent, 1273. A.
Josep Lugge, co. Kent, ibid.
Richard Lug', co. Hunts, ibid.
1620. Toby Lugge, St. Mary Hall: Reg. Univ. Oxf. i. 405.
1638. Robert Lugge, St. John's College: ibid. p. 148.
1716. Married—Henry Harris and Rachael Lugg: St. Jas. Clerkenwell, iii. 239.
London, 8.

Luggar, Lugar.—? ——. A curious surname which I dare not attempt to classify. It is found in Norfolk three centuries ago, and probably came from the Low Countries. From Norfolk it crossed into Essex as Lugar. But v. Lugg.

1558. Philip Lewgar, co. Norf.: FF. viii. 120.
1573. Thomas Lewger, vicar of Windham, co. Norf.: ibid. ii. 508.
1809. Married—Marshall Lugar and Mary Mapes: St. Geo. Han. Sq. ii. 400.
London, 1, 0; MDB. (co. Essex), 0, 1; Philadelphia, 0, 10.

Luke, Lukes, Luks. — (1) Bapt. 'the son of Luke.' Lucas was the more popular form. Yet the diminutives seem formed from Luke; v. Luckett, Luckin, and Luccock. (2) Local, 'of Luke,' i.e. Liege. For further proof, v. Luck (2).

Lucas de Luk, London, 1273. A.
Lucas de Lukes, London, ibid.
Katerina Luke, co. Norf., ibid.
1669. Nicholas Luke and Martha Tibby: Marriage Alleg. (Canterbury), p. 22.
London, 9, 2, 1; New York, 6, 0, 0.

Lukeing, Luken (s; v. Luckin.

Luker; v. Looker.

Lumb, Lomb.—Local, 'at the lum,' from residence thereby, a North-English surname. '*Lum*, a woody valley, a deep pool. North England' (Halliwell). The final *b* is excrescent. There can be little doubt about the truth of this derivation, although I have no proofs; cf. Lumby and Lumley, North-English place-names.

1753. Married—Beaumont Bellamy and Eliz. Lum: St. Geo. Chap. Mayfair, p. 261.

1753. Married—Edward Clark and Mary Lumb: ibid. p. 262.
MDB. (co. Cumberland), 6, 0; West Rid. Court Dir., 13, 0; London, 2, 0; New York, 1, 3.

Lumbard; v. Lombard.

Lumby.—Local, 'of Lumby,' a township in the parish of Sherburn, W. Rid. Yorks; v. Lumb.

Robertus de Lumby, 1379: P. T. Yorks. p. 192.
1693-4. Zephaniah Lumby and Martha Wilson: Marriage Alleg. (Canterbury), p. 285.
London, 3; West Rid. Court Dir., 1; Sheffield, 2.

Lumley, Lumly.—Local, 'of Lumley,' a township in the parish of Chester-le-Street, co. Durham; v. Lumb.

Roger de Lumeleye, co. Leic., 1273. A.
Robert de Lumley, 1431: DDD. i. 74.
1620. Married—George Lumbly and Jone Tatnam: St. Antholin (London), p. 55.
1671. Bapt.—Richard, s. Francis Lumley: St. Jas. Clerkenwell, i. 252.
1703. Married—Stephen Anderson and Anne Lumley: St. Michael, Cornhill, p. 52.
London, 17, 0; New York, 2, 1; Boston (U.S.), 0, 1.

Lummis.—Local, a variant of Lomas, q.v.

1702. Bapt.—Eliz., d. Edward Lumis: St. Jas. Clerkenwell, ii. 18.
1796. Married—William Lummis and Margery Kneebone: St. Geo. Han. Sq. ii. 148.
Manchester, 1; East Rid. Court Dir., 1; New York, 2.

Lumpkin.—Bapt. 'the son of Lambert,' from the nick. Lamb and dim. Lambkin. No doubt a variant of Lambkin or Lampkin, q.v.

Philadelphia, 5.

Lumsden.—Local, 'of Lumsden,' an ancient manor in the parish of Coldingham, co. Berwick.

1616-7. John Lumisden, *Scotus*: Reg. Univ. Oxf. vol. ii. pt. ii. p. 358.
London, 6; Boston (U.S.), 1.

Lund, Lound, Lounds, Lowndes, Lownds, Lowne, Lond.—Local, 'at the laund' or 'lund,' i.e. lawn, which is a modern form, an open space in a wood, a glade. 'Lawnde of a wode, *saltus*': Prompt. Parv.

'At the hartes in these hye laundes.' Morte Arthur.

A property in my late parish (Ulverston) has been from time immemorial called 'The Lund.' A high piece of greensward, it once overlooked the forest of Furness. The final s in Lowndes, &c., is probably the patronymic, as in Williams, Jennings, &c. ; cf. Knowles, Styles, Brooks, Holmes, &c.

Richard de la Lund, co. Norf., 1273. A.
Henry del Lund, co. Linc., ibid.
Robert de la Laund, co. Essex, ibid.
Thomas de Lound, co. Linc., ibid.
William de la Londe, co. Devon, ibid.
John de la Lound, co. Bedf., 20 Edw. I. R.
Alice du Lund, C. R., 32 Edw. I.
Beatrice atte Lound, co. Norf., temp. Edw. III · FF.
Johannes del Lound, 1379 : P. T. Yorks. p. 24.

Lund is the commonest form of entry in early rolls.

1625-6. Thomas Madlocke and Catherine Lownes : Marriage Lic. (London), ii. 162.
1628. Thomas Lowndes and Eliz. Spenser : ibid. p. 193.
London, 10, 1, 1, 4, 2, 2, 1 ; Philadelphia, 9, 0, 0, 1, 0, 1, 0.

Lung. — Nick. 'the lung,' i.e. Long, q.v. A common variant in the Hundred Rolls ; cf. Lang.

Geoffrey le Lung, co. Norf., 1273. A.
Thomas le Lung, co. Glouc., ibid.
Walter le Lung, Fines Roll, 12 Edw. I.
John le Lung, de Doncaster, 4 Edw. II :
Freemen of York, i. 13.
London, 1 ; Boston (U.S.), 1.

Lungley. — Local, 'of Lungley,' a form of Langley or Longley, q.v. ; cf. Lung for Long or Lang.

Robert de Lungeleye, co. Essex, 1273. A.
Ralph de Lingeley, co. Suff., ibid.
London, 3 ; Oxford, 1.

Lunn. — (1) Bapt. 'the son of Lune.' But while there seems every reason to suppose that some of our Lunns are thus derived, there can be no doubt that (2) is the chief parent.

Lone le Lef, co. Hunts, 1273. A.
Reginald fil. Lune, co. Linc., ibid.
William Luneson, co. Oxf., ibid.
Bartelom' Lune, co. Suff., ibid.
Robert Lune, co. Camb., ibid.
Cf. Lunell Wodeward, co. Essex, ibid.

(2) Local, 'of the lund,' q.v. In this case the final d has been dropped.

1722. Bapt.—Richard, s. Richard and Anne Lund : St. Peter, Cornhill, i. 33.
1728. — Caroline, d. Richard and Anne Lunn : ibid. p. 35.
1581. Henry Lunde, or Lunne, co. Cumb. : Reg. Univ. Oxf. vol. ii. pt. ii. p. 109.
London, 10 ; Philadelphia, 8.

Lunt. — Local, 'of Lunt,' a township in the parish of Sephton, near Liverpool. Probably in some cases a sharpened form of Lund, q.v.

1568. Gilbert Lunt, of Litherland : Wills at Chester (1515-1620), p. 128.
1592. Humphrey Lunt, of Maghull, ibid.
1669. Richard Lunt, of the Lunt, co. Lancaster : ibid. (1660-80), p. 174.
1678. Robert Lunt, of Lunt : ibid.
1802. Married—John Lunt and Eliz. Bishop : St. Geo. Han. Sq. ii. 257.
Liverpool, 14 ; London, 2 ; Boston (U.S.), 37.

Lupson. — Bapt. 'the son of Love,' q.v. Loveson would readily corrupt to Lupson, and no other interpretation seems possible.

Walter Lufesone, co. Oxf., 1273. A.
Roger fil. Love, co. York, ibid.
London, 2.

Lupton. — Local, 'of Lupton,' a township in the parish of Kirkby Lonsdale, co. Westmoreland. The surname crossed the border into Yorkshire at an early period, and is much more familiar in the West Riding than in its native county.

Thomas de Lupton, 1379 : P. T. Yorks. p. 289.
Thomas Lupton, of Dalton, 1596 : Lancashire Wills at Richmond (1457-1680), p. 187.
John Lupton, of Tatham, 1640 : ibid.
1685. John Lupton and Alice Hall : Marriage Lic. (Faculty Office), p. 177.
— Bapt.—Thomas, s. Thomas Lupton : St. Jas. Clerkenwell, i. 314.
London, 11 ; West Rid. Court Dir., 19 ; Philadelphia, 9.

Lurryman, Loriman, Lorriman. — Occup. 'the servant of Lorry' or 'Lowry,' i.e. Lawrence ; cf. Matthewman, Addyman, &c. Naturally we find this surname in Yorkshire, where so many of this class abound ; v. Lowrie.

James Lurryman, 1662 : Preston Guild Rolls, p. 133.
Thomas Lurryman, 1662 : ibid.
Richard Lorriman, of Cansfield, 1687 : Lancashire Wills at Richmond (1681-1748), p. 169.

West Rid. Court Dir., o, o, 2 ; Lofthouse-cum-Carlton (West Rid. Yorks), o, 1, o.

Lusby. — Local, 'of Lusby,' a parish in co. Lincoln, near Spilsby.

1750. Married — Samuel Lusby and Grace Fitch : St. Geo. Chap. Mayfair, p. 178.
London, 3 ; MDB. (co. Lincoln), 1 ; Philadelphia, 1.

Luscious. — Nick. 'the luscious.' Professor Skeat says (v. luscious), ' It evidently arose (I think) from attaching the suffix -ous to the M.E. lusty, pleasant, delicious.' My instance below suggests rather that the suffix was -wise (way, mode) ; cf. righteous from M.E. rightwis. The two corruptions go hand in hand. My instance is 300 years earlier than those usually found in dictionaries, &c.

Thomas Lustwys, co. Oxf., 1273. A.

Luscombe, Luscomb. — Local. ' of Loscoombe,' (1) a locality in the parish of Illogan, co. Cornwall ; (2) ' of Loscombe,' a hamlet in the parish of Netherbury, co. Dorset ; (3) ' of Luscombe,' an estate near Dawlish, co. Devon, which belonged to the family, and was their residence temp. Henry V ; and probably much earlier, as the name of Hugh de Luscombe occurs in that county, 9 Edw. I ' (Lower, Patr. Brit. p. 203). No doubt the last is the true home of nine-tenths of the Luscombes or Luscombs of our directories.

1587. Henry Luscombe, co. Devon : Reg. Univ. Oxf. vol. ii. pt. ii. p. 160.
1798. Married—Robert Luscombe and Mary Ford : St. Geo. Han. Sq. ii. 179.
MDB. (co. Devon), 15, 0 ; London, 3, 0 ; Boston (U.S.), 6, 6.

Lush. — ? ——. I cannot offer any solution.

1671. Robert Lush (co. Berks) and Precilla Garrard : Marriage Lic. (Faculty Office), p. 120.
Richard Lush, 1722 : Reg. Broad Chalke, co. Wilts, p. 54.
Dorothy Lush, 1722 : ibid.
1751. Married—George Pawson and Rachael Lush : St. Geo. Chap. Mayfair, p. 192.
London, 5 ; Philadelphia, 10.

Lusher, Luscher. — ? ——. I cannot suggest a solution.

1546. George Bewmond and Eliz. Lusher: Marriage Lic. (Faculty Office), p. ⁸.
1600. Richard Lusher, co. Surrey: Reg. Univ. Oxf. vol. ii. pt. ii. p. 241.
London, 3, 1; Philadelphia, 1, 0.

Lushington.—Local, ' of Lushington.' I cannot find the place. Manifestly of Kentish extraction.

1606-7. Thomas Lushington, co. Kent: Reg. Univ. Oxf. vol. ii. pt. ii. p. 293.
1687. George Walker and Ann Lushington, co. Kent: Marriage Alleg. (Canterbury), p. 288.
1747. Married—Nathaniel Belsey and Ellen Lushington: Canterbury Cath. p. 89.
London, 3; MDB. (co. Kent), 5.

Lusty.—Nick. ' the lusty.' full of spirit, merry, jovial; cf. Merry, Gay, &c.

1746. Married—John Lusty and Eliz. Towne: St. Geo. Chap. Mayfair, p. 67.
1784. — William Lusty and Eliz. Brumhead: St. Geo. Han. Sq. i. 356.
London, 5; Bristol, 3.

Luter.—Occup. ' the luter,' a player on the lute. In some cases this surname may be but a variant of Luther, q.v.

German le Lutrere. T.
John de Leuter, London, 20 Edw. I. R.
1537-8. ' Item, given to Philip the Luter, 11s. 4d.': Privy Purse Expenses, Princess Mary, p. 60.
1542-3. ' Haunce the Luter, 2s. 6d.': ibid. p. 104.
1578. Buried — Christopher Lewter, clothworker: St. Michael, Cornhill, p. 195.
1584. Bapt.—Anne, d. John Luter: ibid. p. 93.
New York, 2.

Luther.—(1) Local; v. Lowther. (2) Bapt. 'the son of Lothar.' This German name never became popularized in England, except as Lothario. The French form was Lothaire. Martin Luther has made the cognomen immortal.

Luther Buchard, C. R., 3 Edw. I.
1593. Bapt.—Salomon, s. Arthur Luther, or Luter: St. Jas. Clerkenwell, i. 27.
1596. — Mary, d. Arthur Luther, or Lewter: ibid. p. 30.
1649. Thomas Luther (co. Essex) and Anne Jackson: Marriage Lic. (Faculty Office), p. 42.
Philadelphia, 9.

Lutley.—Local, 'of Luttley,' a hamlet in the parish of Hales Owen, co. Worc.

Philip de Lotteleg, co. Staff., Hen. III–Edw. I. K.
Thomas de Luttelegh, co. Staff., 20 Edw. I. R.
Crockford, 1.

Luttrell.—Local. A Norman surname found in England soon after the Conquest. Lower says, ' The name is probably derived from a diminutive form of the French *loutre*, an otter.' We may more safely conjecture that it is of local origin.

Geoffrey de Lutterell, 7 John: FF. vii. 152.
Robert Lutrel, co. Notts, Hen. III–Edw. I. K.
Margeria Luterel, co. Soms., 1273. A.
Andreas Loterel. L.
Robert Lutterell, or Lotterel, 1532: Reg. Univ. Oxf. i. 171.
Thomas Luterel, co. Soms., 1579: ibid. vol. ii. pt. ii. p. 88.
Thomas Lutterell, or Luttrell, co. Soms.: ibid. p. 223.
London, 1; MDB. (co. Somerset), 8; New York, 2.

Lutwyche, Lutwidge.— Local, 'of Lutwich,' an estate in the parish of Munslow, nine miles from Ludlow, co. Salop.

Henry de Lotwich, co. Salop, 1273. A.
William de Lotwich, co. Salop, ibid.
Thomas Lutwich, de Lutwich, co. Salop: Visitation of Shropshire (1623), ii. 346.
Richard Lutwiche, de Lutwiche Hall, in Mu'slowe in co. Salop: ibid.
1575. Thomas Luttwyche and Johanna Warde: Marriage Lic. (London), i. 67.
1588-9. Edward Lutwyche, co. Salop: Reg. Univ. Oxf. vol. ii. pt. ii. p. 168.
London, 1, 0; MDB. (co. Kent), 0, 1; (co. Salop), 1, 0.

Luxmoore, Luxmore, Luzmore, Loosemore, Losemore.— Local, 'of Luxmoor' or 'Luxmore.' A Devonshire surname. I cannot find the locality.

1661. Benjamin Donne and Anne Loosemore: Marriage Lic. (Faculty Office), p. 52.
London, 1, 1, 1, 2, 0; Devon Court Dir., 4, 3, 0, 2, 0; MDB. (co. Devon), 4, 6, 0, 7, 1.

Luxton.—Local, ' of Luxton.' I cannot find the spot, but if it is referred to in my first instance, then the surname hails from Lewston, an extra-parochial liberty in the hundred of Sherborne, co. Dorset.

Henry de Lewistone, co. Hants, 20 Edw. I. R.

1594. Bernard Luxton, co. Devon: Reg. Univ. Oxf. vol. ii. pt. ii. p. 202.
London, 3; MDB. (co. Devon), 24; New York, 2.

Lyall, Lyel, Lyell. — Bapt. ' the son of Lionel,' from the nick. Lyell. A great Scottish border name. Endless instances proving its past popularity might be adduced. Sir Charles Lyell, the geologist, was a Forfarshire man.

Lyell Robson, 1541: TTT. p. xlix.
Gowde Lyall, 1541: ibid.
Lyell Charltoun, 1541: ibid.
Liell Gray, 1542: QQQ. p. xx.
Lyell Fenwick, 1561: ibid. p. xxxii.
Lyonel Robson, 1663: KKK. vol. iv. p. 202.
Lyonell Lister, 1663: ibid. p. 203.
David Lyonell, 1670: QQQ. p. 160.
1752. Married—Thomas Hyett and Eliz. Lyell: St. Geo. Chap. Mayfair, p. 226.
1760. — David Lyall and Mary Geed: St. Geo. Han. Sq. i. 97.
London, 6, 1, 4; New York, 6, 0, 4.

Lyard, Liard. — Nick. ' the lyard,' one with iron-grey or dapple grey hair. Burns uses *liart* for locks of iron-grey; and Aubrey in his Lives describes Butler, author of Hudibras, as having ' a head of sorrell haire.'

Henry Lyard, co. Oxf., 1273. A.
William Liard, c. 1300. M.
Walter Lyhert. H.
1577. Married—William Burton, stationer, and Anne Lyard: St. Peter, Cornhill, i. 231.
New York, 0, 2.

Lycett.—?

1736. Caesar, s. William and Mary Lycett, lodgers: St. Peter, Cornhill, ii. 39.
London, 2; MDB. (co. Stafford), 5; New York, 3.

Lyde, Lyd.—Local, ' of Lyde,' a township in the parish of Pipe, co. Hereford.

1589. Allan Lyde, co. Devon: Reg. Univ. Oxf. vol. ii. pt. ii. p. 170.
1591. Bapt.—Sarai, d. John Lyde: St. Jas. Clerkenwell, i. 24.
1679. — Mary, d. Richard Lyde: ibid. p. 288.
London, 1, 0; MDB. (co. Hereford), 0, 1; Philadelphia, 3, 0.

Lydiate.—Local, ' of Lydiate,' a township in the parish of Halsall, co. Lancaster, near Ormskirk; v. Lidgate.

1555. Richard Lydiate, of Chester: Wills at Chester (1545-1620), p. 128.

1623. Richard Lydiate, of Weston: Wills at Chester (1621-50), p. 144.
1631. Thomas Lydiate, of Lydiate: ibid.
MDB. (co. Chester), 1.

Lye. — (1) Local, 'of Lye,' a chapelry in the parish of Swinford, co. Worc. (2) Upper Lye, a township. in the parish of Aymestrey, co. Hereford. Evidently this is the chief parent.

Jacobus de Lye, co. Wilts, Hen. III-Edw. I, K.
Philippus de Lye, co. Wilts, Ibid.
Ela de Lye, co. Wilts, 1273. A.
Hugh Lie, or Lye, co. Soms., 1575: Reg. Univ. Oxf. vol. ii. pt. ii. p. 66.

(3) Local, 'at the lye,' i.e. Lee, q.v.
Herebert de la Lye, co. Southampt., Hen. III-Edw. I. K.
Elyas de la Lye, co. Southampt., ibid.
William de la Lye, co. Notts, 1273. A.
1583-4. Robert Lye, yeoman, and Anne Williams : Marriage Lic. (London), i. 129.
1590. Barnaby Ligh, or Lyghe, co. Hants: Reg. Univ. Oxf. vol. ii. pt. ii. p. 180.
London, 4 ; New York, 1.

Lyel(1 ; v. Lyall.

Lyford, Lind, 'of Lyford,' a chapelry in the parish of West Hannay, near Wantage, co. Berks ; v. Lye and Ford.

John de Lyford, co. Oxf., 1273. A.
1615. William Lyford, co. Berks: Reg. Univ. Oxf. vol. ii. pt. ii. p. 336.
1661-2. John Morton and Mary Lyford: Marriage Alleg. (Canterbury), p. 19.
1742. Married—Henry Granger and Betty Lyford: St. Peter, Cornhill, ii. 84.
London, 1.

Lyle.—Local ; v. Lisle.

Lynch.—Local, 'at the linch,' from residence thereby. 'A.S. hlinc, a hill, but especially a balk or boundary, a sense still preserved in modern provincial English linch' (Skeat, y. link). ' Linch, a balk of land (Kent). Any bank or boundary for the division of land' (Halliwell). A large portion of the New York Lynches must be ascribed to an Irish parentage, as such prefixes as Michael, Patrick, and Terence abound (v. New York Directory).

Emma de Linches. J.
William de la Lynche, C.R., 55 Hen. III.
Roger Ate-lynch, Fines Roll, 12 Edw. I.
Simon de Lynche, co. Norf., 20 Edw. I. R.

John Uppelynch (i.e. John up the Lynch), co. Soms., 1 Edw. III : Kirby's Quest, p. 270.
1780. Married—William Lynch and Martha Richa : St. Geo. Han. Sq. i. 313.
London, 13 ; New York, 477.

Lyndall; v. Lindale.

Lynd(e ; v. Lind.

Lyne ; v. Line.

Lyner ; v. Liner.

Lynn. — Local, 'of Lynn.' There are several parishes of Lynn in co. Norfolk. In Devon there is Lynmouth.

Cecilia de Lynn, co. Devon, Hen. III-Edw. I. K.
Reginald de Lyn, co. Devon, 1273. A.
John de Lynne, bailiff of Norwich, 1396 : FF. iii. 116.
1546. John Dyneley and Margery Lyn : Marriage Lic. (Faculty Office), p. 8.
1680. Mathew Key and Eliz. Lynn : Marriage Alleg. (Canterbury), p. 26.
London, 18 ; New York, 17.

Lynton.—Local ; v. Linton.

Lyon, Lyons.—(1) Bapt. ' of Leonc.' Many Jews in modern times have taken the name of Lyon (the Lion of the tribe of Judah). This seems to have been an early custom, judging by my first reference. The London Directory will prove by its personal names how Jewish the surname is.

Lyoyne (alias Leoyn) Duningh, co. Camb., Hen. III-Edw. I. K.
Judaeus Leo, co. Linc., 1273. A.
Jacob fil. Leonis, co. Linc., ibid.
John Leon, co. Oxf., ibid.
Lyon Raithbye, C. R., 1-2 Philip and Mary, pt. viii.

(2) Local, ' of Lyons.'
Roger de Leonibus fil. Jeffrey de Lions, co. Norf., temp. Hen. III : FF. ix. 374.
John de Leonibus, co. Southampt., Hen. III-Edw. I. K.
Peter de Leonibus, co. Northampt., ibid.
Roger de Lyons, co. Wilts, 1273. A.
Richard de Lyons, co. Northampton, Edw. I. R.
John de Lyouns, co. Northampt., ibid.
Edmond de Lyons, co. Soms., 1 Edw. III : Kirby's Quest, p. 93.
London, 36, 29 ; New York, 118, 218.

Lysons, Licence. — ? Local. This name was 'spelt in the 16th century Lysans, Leyson, and Lison. Probably derived from Lison, a place in the department of Calvados, in Normandy' (Lower, Patr. Brit. p. 204). Of course Licence is an imitative variant.

1677-8.' Fergus Farrell and Ann Licence: MarriageAlleg.(Canterbury),p.275.
1739. Bapt.—Layer, d. Zebulon Licence: St. Jas. Clerkenwell, ii. 244.
London, 1, 1 ; MDB. (co. Glouc.), 1, o.

Lyster ; v. Lister.

Lyte, Lyteman.—Nick. ' the lyte,' i.e. the little ; A.S. lyt, little.

Agnes le Lit, co. Soms., 1 Edw. III : Kirby's Quest, p. 201.
Richard Liteman, co. Bedf., 1273. A.
William le Lyt, 1313. M.
John Lytman, temp. 1570. Z.

The following, no doubt, is an imitative variant :
1582. Humphrey Lighteman and Agnes Woode : Marriage Lic. (London), i. 108.
1729. Married—George Lyte and Eliz. Read: St. Geo. Chap. Mayfair, p. 303.
Crockford, 1, o.

Lyth, Lythe.—Nick. ' the lithe,' soft, tender, mild, hence pliant, flexible, supple.

' To maken lithe that erst was hard ' : Chaucer, House of Fame, l. 118.

' Lithe, calm, quiet' (Kennett).
Gonnilda le Lyth, co. Bucks, 1273. A.
Cf. Henry Lithfot, co. Oxf., ibid.
1540. Buried—John Lythe : St. Dionis Backchurch, p. 178.
London, 1, o ; Manchester, 2, 0 ; Beverley, 1, 1.

Lytham.—Local, 'of Lytham,' a parish in the union of Fylde, co. Lanc.

Prior de Lythom. K.
John Lythom, 1602 : Preston Guild Rolls, p. 62.
Liverpool, 1.

Lythgoe, Lithgoe, Lithgow. — Local, ' of Lythgoe.' I cannot find the spot. This is a South Lancashire surname ; but it has a Scotch look. Lower says, ' A contraction of Linlithgow, a well-known Scotch town': Patr. Brit. p. 196. He furnishes no proof. Eight persons named Lithgow appear in the County Directory of Scotland, 1882.

Robert Lythgoe, of Abram, husbandman, 1578: Wills at Chester (1545-1620), p. 129.
William Lythgoe, of Abram, 1592 : ibid.
Mathew Lythgoe, of Bedford, parish of Leigh, yeoman, 1633: ibid. (1621-50), p.145.
Robert Lythgoe, of Abram, parish of Wigan, husbandman, 1647 : ibid.
1721-2. Bapt.—Joseph, s. Joseph Lythgoe : St. Dionis Backchurch, p. 157.
London, 1, 0, 1, 0; Manchester, 4, 1, 0, 1 ; Philadelphia, 0, 0, 9, 0.

Lyttle ; v. Little.

M

Maas, Maass.—?——. An importation from the Low Countries, probably. The published and unpublished 'Household Expenses' of kings, queens, and wealthy nobles invariably show that the minstrels in attendance were foreigners.

Hanekin Almond, varlet of the Countess of Surrey: Household Book of Queen Isabella, 1358, Cot. MS. Galba, E. xiv.
Janin Maas, varlet of the Countess of Surrey: ibid.

The first of these two was evidently a German by descent.

1795. Married — John Sudlow and Hannah Gertrude Maass: St. Geo. Han. Sq. ii. 131.
London, 3, 0; Boston (U.S.), 3, 2; New York, 28, 11.

Mabb, Mabbs, Mobbs. — Bapt. 'the son of Mabel,' from nick. Mab (v. Mapp). Oddly enough, the modern form is generally Mobbs; cf. Maggs and Mogg.

Alicia Mab, 1379: P. T. Yorks. p. 154.
Agnes Mabbe, 1379: ibid. p. 209.
1616. Married — Frauncis Mydleton and Katherain Mabb, of Woodford, co. Essex: St. Michael, Cornhill, p. 21.
1626. — Daniell Mabbes and Hannah Crakell: ibid. p. 24.
1800. — John Mobbs and Susanna Ambler: St. Geo. Han. Sq. ii. 231.
London, 0, 0, 7; Liverpool, 0, 1, 0.

Mabbett, Mabbitt, Mabbott. —Bapt. 'the son of Mabel,' from nick. Mab, and dim. Mabb-ot or Mabb-et (v. Mappin); cf. Elliot, Tillotson, Emmott, &c.

Mabota Ryder, 1379: P. T. Yorks. p. 214.
Willelmus Mabotson, 1379: ibid. p. 280.
Willelmus Mabetson, 1379: ibid.
Richard Mabot, or Mabatt, 1509: Reg. Univ. Oxf. i. 65.
1646. Bapt. — William, s. William Mabbett, *pewterer*: St. Peter, Cornhill, ii. 91.
1648. Buried — William, s. William Mabbutt: ibid. p. 204.
1769. Married — Joseph Howel and Mary Mabbutt: St. Geo. Han. Sq. i. 191.
1807. Married — Joseph Bland and Martha Mabbatt: ibid. ii. 364.
London, 1, 1, 1; Philadelphia, 2, 0, 0.

Mabley, Maberley, Maberly. — Bapt. 'the son of Mabel,' familiarly Mabley. I can only furnish a few instances out of many. Not as a rule to be confounded with Moberley (q.v.), but confusion would easily arise. It is quite possible that Maberley is the same as the local Moberley, but I doubt it.

Andrew fil. Mabilie, co. Hunts, 1273. A.
Philip fil. Mabilie, co. Camb., ibid.
Nicholas Mabely, co. Oxf., ibid.
John Mably, co. Camb., ibid.
1603. Buried — Arthur Maberly: St. Antholin (London), p. 42.
1665. — John, s. Luke Mably: St. Michael, Cornhill, p. 254.
1692. — Thomas Mabley, St. John the Baptist, on Wallbrook, p. 190.
London, 1, 1, 2.

Mabon. — Bapt. 'the son of Mabel,' from the nick. Mab, and dim. Mab-on; cf. Marion from Mary, Guyon from Guy, &c.

Emanuelle Mabon, Patent Roll, 1 Eliz. pt. x.
1582. Richard Morecocke and Eliz. Mabone: Marriage Lic. (London), i. 110.
1806. Married — Andrew Mabon and Sarah Wright: St. Geo. Han. Sq. ii. 358.
London, 1.

Mabson. — Bapt. 'the son of Mab' (Mabel); cf. Mabotson (s.v. Mabbett). It will be seen that Mabel, with its nick. Mab, was popular in the hereditary surname period.

John Mabson, Patent Roll, 8 Ric. II. pt. ii.
Michael Mabson, York, 1494. W. 11.
1672. Bapt. — Steeven, s. William Mabson: St. Jas. Clerkenwell, i. 257.
Sheffield Dir., 4.

Mace.—Bapt. 'the son of Mace.' Lower says, 'Originally Macé, a French nurse-name of Matthew.' As with all other fontal names, this was turned into a feminine, as in the following instances:

Massia Billesby, C. R., 24 Hen. VI.
Macius le Teynturer, co. Devon, 1273. A.
Duce fil. Masse, co. Hunts, ibid.
Adam Mace, co. Oxf., ibid.
William Mace, co. Bucks, ibid.

The following, no doubt, refer to the same individual:

Macius de Besile, co. Oxf., 1273.
Macias de Betille, co. Oxf., ibid.
Matheus Besyl, co. Oxf., ibid.
1663. Philip Mace and Ann Right: Marriage Alleg. (Canterbury), p. 115.
1733. Bapt. — Stanfield, s. Thomas Mace: St. Jas. Clerkenwell, ii. 208.
London, 18; Philadelphia, 5.

Macey, Macy.—(1) Bapt. 'the son of Macy'; v. Mace. A fem. form is found.

Alan Macy, co. Suff., 1273. A.
Henry Macy, co. Suff., ibid.
Walter Masci, co. Hunts, ibid.
1391. Massia Newport: Cal. of Wills in the Court of Husting (2).

(2) Local, 'of Macei,' near Avranche, in Normandy (Lower).

Robert de Meysy, co. Wilts, 1273. A.
William de Macy, co. Wilts, ibid.
1581. Bapt.—Grace, d. Jeames Macey: St. Michael, Cornhill, p. 92.
1621. — Laurence, s. John Macye: St. Jas. Clerkenwell, i. 90.
London, 9, 0; New York, 0, 39.

Machell.—Nick.; originally 'le Machel' or Manchell, 'bad whelp.' Latinized as Malus-Catulus. A certain Roger Malus-Catulus was Vice-Chancellor of England; but I have lost my reference to this. The following occur in records of the Machells of Crackenthorpe:

Halthe le Machel, temp. Hen. I: Transactions of Cumb. and West. Ant. Arch. Soc. viii. 418-9.
Humfrey le Machel, temp. Henry II: ibid.
William Malus Catulus, 1179: ibid.
William Manchel, 1206: ibid.
1606. Buried—Eliz. Machell: St. Jas. Clerkenwell, iv. 95.
1619. John Machell, co. Surrey: Reg. Univ. Oxf. vol. ii. pt. ii. p. 377.
1798. William Machell and Eliz. Allen: St. Geo. Han. Sq. ii. 180.
London, 2.

Machen, Machin, Machan, Machon. — Bapt. 'the son of Matthew'; a familiar Yorkshire surname found in every district. The O.F. nick. of Matthew was Mace or Mache, and this, with the dim. -on or -in, became Machon and Machin. It is commonly found in the Poll Tax (1379). I only furnish a few instances. It has left an indelible mark upon Yorkshire nomenclature.

Thomas Mathen, 1379: P. T. Yorks. p. 186.
Eva Machon, 1379: ibid.
Ricardus Machon, 1379: ibid. p. 194.
Beatrice Machon, 1379: ibid.
Johannes Machon, 1379: ibid. p. 198.
Willelmus Mathon, 1379: ibid.

The first two entries lie in the same hamlet, so also the last three. Therefore Mathon may be looked upon as a more English form eventually settling down to Mattin, as in Mattinson; v. Mace, Masson (2), Mattin, and Maton.

1558. Married — John Rypleye and Margarett Machyn : St. Michael, Cornhill, p. 7.
1662. — Edward Machin and Cassandra Trendall: Marriage Alleg. (Canterbury), p. 58.
London, 1, 12, 0, 0 ; West Rid. Court Dir., 5, 2, 1, 0 ; Sheffield, 3, 6, 2, 2 ; New York, 1, 2, 0, 1 ; Philadelphia, 0, 0, 0, 2.

Mackareth, Mackreth, Mackeroth. —Local, ' of Mackareth,' a distinctly English Lake-district surname. It is still found in the neighbourhood of Windermere. I cannot discover the spot. Probably the suffix is -heath.

1591. George Macreth, of Hauxhead : Lancashire Wills at Richmond, i. 188.
1670. Brian Mackereth, of Skelwith, Hawkeshead : ibid.
Thomas Macareth, of Natland, 1602: Hist. West. and Cumb. i. 96.
Edward Maccareth, of Natland, 1602: ibid.
1622. Robert Willis and Eliz. Mackreth : Marriage Lic. (Westminster), p. 28.
1664. Buried—Johanna, wife of Roberd Mackereth : St. Jas. Clerkenwell, iv. 358.
1760. Married — Edward Mackereth and Jane Brockbank : Reg. St. Mary, Ulverston, p. 403.
Ulverston, 0, 0, 1 ; London, 0, 2, 0.

Mackarness. — Local, ' of Maukerness,' seemingly some spot on the East Coast ; cf. Holderness. There is no connexion with the Mac's or Mc's of Ireland or Scotland, as in Macdonald or McGrath.

William de Maukurneys, co. Linc., 1273. A.
Henry Maukurneys, 18 Edw. II : Freemen of York, i. 22.
Cecilia Maugurnays, 1379: P. T. Yorks. p. 273.
Robertus Magornays, 1379: ibid. p. 266.

1626. Bapt. — Thomas, s. Richard Makernes : St. Thomas the Apostle, London, p. 47.
1649. Buried — Ann, wife of William Mackernes : St. Jas. Clerkenwell, iv. 282.
John Mackerness, 1745 : Reg. Canterbury Cath. p. 87.
Crockford, 3.

Mackerell, Mackrell, Mackrill, Mackrille, Macrell. — Nick. ' the mackerel.' M.E. and O.F. *makeral*, a fish known by that name ; cf. Keeling, a Yorkshire surname, on whose coast the particular cod of that name was caught. The earlier instances below are from the Lincoln coast, although by 1273 one had reached Cambridge.

Hugh Makarel, co. Linc., Hen. III-Edw. I. K.
Walter Makarel, co. Linc., ibid.
William Makerell, co. Linc., 1273. A.
Richard Makarel, co. Camb., ibid.
Richard Makerell, Pat. Roll, o Edw. IV.
Richard Mackerell, 1513 : Reg. Univ. Oxf. i. 86.
1546. Buried — Jone Makarell : St. Dionis Backchurch, p. 181.
1593. — One Mackerell, out of the feildes : St. Jas. Clerkenwell, iv. 52.
London, 1, 3, 2, 0, 0 : Philadelphia, 3, 0, 0, 0, 0 ; New York (Macrell), 3 ; Boston (U.S.) (Mackrille), 1.

Mackeson.—Bapt. ' the son of Margaret,' from the nick. Magg or Maggy. The son of Magg or Maggy became Maggeson ; this, when sharpened, became Mackeson. In the same way Moggson became Mockson and Moxon, q.v. There is no difficulty about the derivation. The solution is very simple.

John Makkesone, Disley, co. Ches., 1333 : East Ches. ii. 85.
Agnes Makkesone, Disley, co. Ches., 1333 : ibid.
1765. Married — Henry Mackeson, of Deal, and Eliz. Hooper : Canterbury Cath. p. 96.
London, 3.

Macklin, Mackling.—? Bapt. Seemingly ' the son of Maculin.'

Maculin Cosin, canon of the ' free chaple of Berkynge,' temp. Ric. III : Hist. Allhallows, Barking, p. 140.
1797. Married—John Maclin and Eliz. Bonn : St. Geo. Han. Sq. ii. 175.
1808. — John Maklin and Mary Dunster : St. Geo. Han. Sq. ii. 392.
London, 6, 1 ; Philadelphia, 5, 0.

Mackman ; v. Makeman.

Mackness.—Local ; v. Mackarness.   London, 6.

Mackrell, Mackrill ; v. Mackerell.

Mackreth ; v. Mackareth.

Mackworth.—Local, ' of Mackworth,' a parish in co. Derby.

Robert de Makeworth, co. Derby, 1273. A.
1695. Married — Edmund Taylor and Ann Mackworth : St. Peter, Cornhill, ii. 61.
1761. — Herbert Mackworth and Eliz. Trefusis : St. Geo. Han. Sq. i. 103.

Macy ; v. Macey.

Mad. Nick. ' the mad.'

Jordan le Madde, co. Lanc., 20 Edw. I. R.

Maddick, Maddicks, Maddock, Maddocks, Maddox, Maddux. — Bapt. ' the son of Madoc.' An early Welsh personal name. For history, v. Yonge, ii. 29. With Maddox for Maddocks, cf. Rix, Dixon, Simcox, &c.

Kenwrec fil. Maddoc : Pipe Roll, 7 Hen. II.
Madoc de Sotton, co. Salop, Hen. III-Edw. I. K.
Tudor ab Madoc, co. Salop, 1273. A.
Walter fil. Madoc, co. Salop, ibid.
Maddoc le Estrange, co. Salop, ibid.
Madoc fil. Griffin. J.
1573. Buried — Judith Madox : Reg. Stourton, co. Wilts, p. 1.
1593. Robert Madox, co. Oxf. : Reg. Univ. Oxf. vol. ii. pt. ii. p. 198.
1602. George Maddockes, co. Glouc. : ibid. p. 262.
1604. John Madocke, co. Glouc. : ibid. p. 271.
London, 4, 1, 3, 1, 6, 0 ; Philadelphia, 0, 0, 9, 0, 6, 1 ; Boston (U.S.), 0, 0, 4, 1, 6, 0.

Maddison, Madison.—Bapt. ' the son of Maud,' i.e. Matilda, either from a pet form Maddy, or a mere corruption of Maudson (v. Maud).

1558. Bapt.—Annes Maddesonne : St. Peter, Cornhill, i. 8.
Henry Maddeson, of Melling, 1679 : Lancashire Wills at Richmond, p. 189.
Anne Maddesson of Whittington, 1680 : ibid.
' Here rest in Christian hope the bodies of Lionel Maddison, son of Rowland Maddison,' &c., 1624 : Epitaph, St. Nicholas, Newcastle-on-Tyne (Brand's Hist. of Newcastle, i. 291).
1704. Bapt.—David, s. John Maddison : St. Thomas the Apostle (London), p. 69.
London, 3, 0 ; Philadelphia, 0, 17 ; Boston (U.S.), 0, 7.

Maddock(s, -dox ; v. Maddick.

Maden.—Local, 'of Maden,' a small locality in the parish of Rochdale, co. Lanc., whence all the Madens have sprung.

Charles Holt, of Maden, in Spotland, 1595: Wills at Chester (1545-1620), p. 99.
John Maden, of Hopwood, *yeoman*, 1637: ibid. (1621-50), p. 145.
Manchester, 3 ; New York, 2.

Mader, Maderer, Maderman, Madder. — Occup. ' the maderer,' a collector and seller of madder; cf. Garlicker, Garlickmonger, &c. Just as Pepperer is now found as Pepper, so Maderer has been reduced to Mader and Madder.

Jacob le Madur, co. Linc., 1273. A.
John Maderman, temp. 1300. M.
Laurence Maderer. H.
Thomas Maderer. XX. 1.
1748. Married — James Madder and Christian Black : St. Geo. Chap. Mayfair, p. 120.
London, 1, 0, 0, 1; Philadelphia, 2, 0, 0, 0.

Madge. — Bapt. 'the son of Margaret'; v. Maggs.

Madgett, Matchet, Matchett.—(1) Bapt. 'the son of Margaret,' from nick. Madge, and dim. Madg-et ; cf. Maggot, a dim. of the harder nick. Magg. (2) Bapt. 'the son of Mache,' from Mache, the O. F. nick. for Matthew, and dim. Machet ; cf. Emmett (v. Emmott),Collett, &c. The evidence seems to confirm this view; v. Machen.

Willelmus Machet, 1379 : P. T. Yorks. p. 10.
1670. Married — Franses Pickerin and Mary Matchett : St. Jas. Clerkenwell, iii. 174.
1736. — Richard Saunders and Mary Matchitt : St. Geo. Han. Sq. i. 16.
London, 1, 0, 0; Doncaster, 0, 1, 0; Sheffield, 1, 0, 0; Boston (U.S.), 0, 0, 1; New York, 0, 0, 3.

Madin ; v. Maiden.

Madison ; v. Maddison.

Madswain.—Nick. 'the foolish swain'; cf. Goodswain, Littleswain.

Alan Madsweyn, co. Essex, 1273. A.

Mager ; v. Major.

Maggot, Maggotson.—Bapt. 'the son of Margaret,' from O.F. Margot, sharpened and abbreviated in England to Magot. This form was especially liked in northern

counties. In the 14th century it was enormously popular in Yorkshire. The mag-pie was equally familiar as the magot-pie. Shakespear says :

'Augurs, and understood relations, have.
By magot-pies, and choughs, and rooks brought forth
The secret'st man of blood.'
Macbeth, Act iii. sc. 4.

With this, cf. Magota Pye, 1379, P. T. Yorks. p. 45, an evident connexion of ideas. v. Madgett.

Maggot Fin, co. Hunts, 1273. A.
Richard Maggote, co. Camb., ibid.
Robert Maggot, co. Camb., ibid.
Thomas Magotson, 1379 : P. T. Yorks. p. 18.
Cecilia fil. Magote, 1379 : ibid. p. 190.
Magota Malet, 1379 : ibid. p. 59.
Johannes fil. Magote, 1379: ibid. p. 121.
Magota Merchalk, 1379 : ibid. p. 45.
Johannes Magotson, 1379 : ibid.
1644. Bapt.—Joan, d. Joseph Maggot, St. Jas. Clerkenwell, i. 159.
1591. Married — John Magett and Janne Richarsone: St. Dionis Backchurch, p. 12.

Maggs, Magson, Madge.—Bapt. 'the son of Margaret,' from the nick. Magg. The mag-pie still preserves the memory of this homely name.

Magge Flie, co. Camb., 1273. A.
John Magge, co. Hunts, ibid.
Ralph fil. Magg, co. Camb., ibid.
Isabella Mag-doghter, 1379: P. T. Yorks. p. 143.
Ricardus Magge, 1379 : ibid. p. 58.
Robertus Magson, 1379 : ibid. p. 280.
Rogerus Magson, 1379 : ibid. p. 138.

The next two occur together :

Johannes Megson, 1379 : P. T. Yorks. p. 131.
Robertus Magson, 1379 : ibid.
1751. Married — Eli Maggs and Jane Mason : St. Geo. Han. Sq. i. 45.
1760. — Richard Boyden and Mary Magson : ibid. p. 92.
London, 12, 0, 1; West Rid. Court Dir., 0, 1, 0; Manchester, 0, 1, 0; Leeds, 0, 0, 1; New York, 0, 0, 3 ; Philadelphia, 0, 1, 1.

Magill.—Local, ' of Maghull,' a manor in the parish of Halsall, co. Lanc.

William de Maghull, c. John : Baines' Lanc. ii. 424.
Richard Maghull, 21 Edw. I : ibid. p. 425.
Matthew Maghull, 27 Hen. VIII : ibid.
Richard Maghall, of Maghall, 1606: Lancashire Inquisitions, i. 66.
1646. Ellen Maghull, of Aintree, *widow* : Wills at Chester, ii. 145.
Liverpool, 2 ; Philadelphia, 32.

Magnus. — Bapt. 'the son of Magnus.' A North-British name. In Shetland, Magnus as a font-name is tenth in order of frequency, and eleventh as a surname in the form of Manson (Magnus-son). There are also seventeen Magnussons ; v. Scotsman, Oct. 16, 1886.

1780. Married—William Magnus and Alice Sherman : St. Geo. Han. Sq. i. 310.
London, 9 ; Boston (U.S.), 1 ; New York, 19.

Magson ; v. Maggs.

Mahenild.—Bapt. 'the son of Maginhild' (Yonge, ii. 415).

Mahenyld Brycth, co. Norf., 1273. A.
Alan Mahenyld, co. Norf., ibid.
Alan Maghenyld, co. Norf., ibid.

I do not see any of this name in modern registers.

Maiden, Madin.—Nick. 'the maiden.' Perhaps the bearer was somewhat effeminate ; cf. Milksop. But probably a servant, a female attendant ; v. Mann and Servant. This is practically settled by such an entry as :

Alicia Martynmayden, 1379 : P. T. Yorks. p. 157.
Matilda Marschalmaydyn, 1379 : ibid. p. 111.

An instance of Mayden as a surname from the same register will be found below.

Robert le Mayden : Fines Roll, 12 Edw. I.
Adam le Maiden, co. Camb., 1273. A.
Johanna Mayden, 1379 : P. T. Yorks. p. 105.
1730. Married — Thomas Hyett and Jane Maiden : St. Geo. Chap. Mayfair, p. 311.
1753. — George Madin and Ann Harris: St. Mary Aldermary, p. 52.
London, 1, 0 ; Sheffield, 0, 1 ; West Rid. Court Dir., 0, 1 ; Manchester, 2, 0 ; Philadelphia, 2, 0.

Maidment, Maidman.—Bapt. 'the son of Maymond'; v. Mayman. For corruption into *-ment*, cf. Rayment (Raymond) and Garment (Garmund) ; for *-man*, cf. Wyman (Wymond) and Osman (Osmund).

1744. Married — John Maidman and Eliz. Anderson : St. Geo. Chap. Mayfair, p. 38.
1749. — John Maidman and Ann Walker : St. Geo. Han. Sq. i. 43.
1802. — Moses Lavell and Ann Maidment : ibid. ii. 270.
London, 5, 1.

Maidstone.—Local, ' of Maidstone,' now as a surname more generally Mayston, q.v.

1690. Bapt. — Robert, s. Robert Maidstone: St. Antholin (London), p. 107.
1702. Buried — Charles, s. John Madston: ibid. p. 115.

Maidwell.—Local, 'of Maidwell,' a village in co. Northampton, ten miles from Northampton. Probably distinct from Meadwell, q.v.; cf. Maidenwell, a parish in co. Lincoln, five miles from Louth.

John Maydenwell.Pat.Roll,43 Edw.III.
1547. Bapt. — Annes Madewell: St. Peter, Cornhill, i. 3.
1687. Married — James Maydwell and Annabella Coningsbey: St. Mary Aldermary (London), p. 33.
London, 1.

Maile; v. Male.

Mailmaker, Maler.—Occup. ' the mail-maker.' A manufacturer of bags or wallets. M.E. *male*, a bag, whence mail-coach, &c.

John de Redinges, *maler*, 4 Edw. III: Freemen of York. i. 26.
Henry Malemaker. RR. 2.

Main, Maine.—(1) Bapt. ' the son of Main'; v. Mayne (1).

Ralph fil. Main, co. Northumb., 1166: KKK. v. 9.
Walter fil. Main, co. Northumb., 1168. KKK. vi. 11.

(2) Local, 'of Maine'; v. Mayne (2).

1798. Married — Thomas Main and Jane Dawson : St. Geo. Han. Sq. ii. 190.
1805. — William Dodson and Ann Maine: ibid. p. 331.
London, 14, 4 ; Boston (U.S.), 6, 4.

Mainprice, Mainprize, Mainprize, Mimpriss.— Offic. or nick. 'the mainprize,' i.e. (1) one who is security for another, or (2) *one who has found sureties for his appearance on the proper day : a prisoner at large. ' Mainprize, one who is bail-pledge, or security for another person' : Bailey's Dict., 1742 (v. Outlaw). Mimpriss was an inevitable modification or corruption. In another form it occurs as early as 1440, 'Maynprysed, menprisyd (maymprysyd or memprisyd), *manucaptus, fidejussus*' : Prompt. Parv. An entry below exactly corresponds to one of these forms.

1625. Buried — Roberte, s. Thomas Memprisse : St. Peter, Cornhill, i. 186.
1659. Married — Isaack Mempris and Mary Allen : St. Jas. Clerkenwell, iii. 103.
1663. — William Morgan and Elizabeth Mempris : St. Dionis Backchurch, p. 37.
London, 1, 0, 0, 1 ; Wirksworth, co. Derby, 0, 1, 0, 0 ; Derby, 0, 0, 3, 0.

Mainwaring, Mannering.— Local, from 'the manor of Warin.' This family, so long established in co. Cheshire, claim to have come with the Conqueror in the person of Ranulph de Meinilwarin, and is distinctly Norman, as its earlier forms, Menilwarin and Mesnilwarin, prove. The second half of the name is Warin or Guarin, a once common font-name, introduced by the Normans into England; v. Warren (2) and Wareing. It is said that this name can be found spelt in no less than 131 different ways.

Robert de Meynwareing, co. Derby, 1273. A.
Thomas de Meynnegaryn, co. Norf., ibid.
1663. Bapt. — Ann, d. Allen Manwaring : St. Jas. Clerkenwell, i. 218.
1669. Bapt. — Elisebeth, d. Doctor Manerring : ibid. p. 242.
London, 2, 2 ; Boston (U.S.), 2, 0 ; Philadelphia, 1, 0.

Mair, Maire. — Offic. ' the mayor,' the magistrate of the town. M.E. *maire*. v. Meyer.

'Saloman the sage
A sermon he made
For to amenden maires.'
Piers P. 1541-3.

Ricardus Mayre, 1379 : P. T. Yorks. p. 111.
Willelmus Mayre, 1379 : ibid.
1574-5. Richard Maior, co. Bucks : Reg. Univ. Oxf. vol. ii. pt. ii. p. 61.
1677. Thomas Mayor and Martha Puckerin : Marriage Alleg. (Canterbury), p. 207.
London, 2, 2 ; Philadelphia, 13, 3.

Major, Mager. — Bapt. ' the son of Malger ' or ' Mauger.' The modern form is imitative. The font-name was fairly popular in the 13th century. Mauger is found as a single personal name in the Hundred Rolls (ii. 609, and again ii. 797). For other instances, v. Mauger.

Hugh fil. Magri, co. Devon, 1273. A.
Thomas fil. Magri, co. Linc., ibid.
Walter Mauger, co. Camb., ibid.

Richard Malgor, co. Bucks, ibid.
Mauger de la Neuland, C. R., 31 Hen. VI.

I find no evidence to prove that Major as a surname is the Latin *major*, i.e. mayor, a town magistrate (v. Mair). The present military *major* is modern from a surname point of view.

1561. Bapt.—Robert, s. John Maygor : St. Mary Aldermary, p. 54.
1577. — Alice, d. William Mager : St. Peter, Cornhill, i. 19.
1742. Married — Robert Major and Eliz. Davis : St. Geo. Chap. Mayfair, p. 17.
London, 13, 2 ; Philadelphia, 22, 15.

Makebliss.—Nick.
Julian Makeblise, co. Oxf., 1273. A.

Makeblithe.—Nick. A pretty nickname ; cf. Makepeace and Makejoy. This surname does not seem to have descended to modern times, although found in three different parts of the country. Makepeace has fared better.

William Makeblithe, co. Oxf., 1273. A.
Radulphus Makblyth', *textor*, 1379 : P. T. Yorks. p. 290.
Robert Maykblythe, co. York, 1511 : W. 11, p. 174.
1597. William Makblythe, co. Warw.: Reg. Univ. Oxf. vol. ii. pt. ii. p. 224.

Makehate.—Nick. This seems to be the opposite of Makepeace, Makejoy, &c.

Alicia Makehayt, co. Bucks, 1273. A.
William Makehayt, co. Oxf., ibid.
John Makeheyt, co. Oxf., ibid.

Makejoy.—Nick. As pretty as Makepeace and Makeblithe. 'Make-joy,' Prompt. Parv.; 'joyū or make-joy, *gaudeo, exulto*' (ibid.).

Maud Makejoy, c. 1300. M.

Makeman, Mackman. — ? Bapt. ' the son of Maymond ' (?), i.e. Magin-mond. Probably the *k* and *ck* represent the original *g* sound. As a Lincolnshire form this is the more likely. Other forms of the surname are Mayman, Maidman, and Maidment, q.v.

MDB. (Lincoln), 1, 2 ; New York, 0, 1.

Makepeace.—Nick. A pretty and gracious sobriquet, always to be remembered as the second name of Thackeray. It occurs early in Yorkshire, and has always maintained its existence, though it must be included among the rarer surnames ; cf. Makebliss and Makejoy.

'Joan Makepeace was the name given to the daughter of Edward II, when the long war with the Bruces was partly pacified by her marriage' : Yonge, i. 112.
Thomas Makpays, 1379 : P. T. Yorks. p. 296.
Richard Makepeace, co. York. W. 20.
1601. Laurence Makepeace, co. Northampton : Reg. Univ. Oxf. vol. ii. pt. ii. p. 247.
1706. Bapt. — Sarah, d. of Margaret Makepeace : St. Thomas the Apostle (London), p. 70.
1712. John Makepeace, rector of Quedgley, co. Glouc.: Rudder's Hist. Glouc. p. 613.
1752. — Ann, d. Jonathan Makepeace : St. Mary Aldermary (London), p. 132.
1786. Married—John McKee and Eliz. Makepeace, of Waltham Cross, Herts : St. Geo. Han. Sq. i. 393.
London, 1.

Makin, Makinson, Makein, Making, Makings, Makins.—
Bapt. 'the son of Matthew' (Fr. Maheu), from nick. May (v. May, Maycock, &c.), and dim. May-kin ; cf. Wil-kin, Wat-kin. The *g* in Making and Makings is excrescent, and the *e* in Makein intrusive. The nick. May is distinguished from the nick. Mat as being the offspring of Maheu, and not Matthew.

Henry Maykin, co. Camb., 1273. A.
Mathew de Sutheworth, *dictus*, Maykyn, C. R., 20 Edw. III. pt. i.
Maykyn de Sythwrt (sic), 1379 : P. T. Yorks. p. 271.
Johannes Maykeson (i.e. Maykinson): ibid. p. 216.
Makin Lappyng, Pat. Roll, 1 Hen. VII. pt. i.
Maykina Parmunter. H.

This last is a feminine form.

1565. Married — Richard Makin and Alice Langden : St. Thomas the Apostle, p. 4.
1613. Married — Henry Jenkinson and Isabel Makinson : St. Jas. Clerkenwell, p. 39.
1753. — John Makings and Mary Scott : St. Geo. Chap. Mayfair, p. 248.

The Manchester Dir. contains fifteen Makins and nine Makinsons.

London, 3, 1, 2, 1, 1, 2 ; West Rid. Court Dir., 4, 0, 0, 1, 0, 1 ; New York, 5, 0, 0, 0, 0, 0 ; Philadelphia, 1, 5, 1, 0, 0, 1.

Malbon, Mallabone, Mallebone, Mallabund.—? Local, ' of Malbanc'(?). As Malbon undoubtedly arose in Cheshire, it probably represents the old de Malbancs of that county. Ellen de Malbanc was second wife of Sir Robert de Stokeport, who was living in 1268 (East Cheshire, i. 337–8). Otherwise I cannot explain it. The corruptions into Mallabone, Mallabund, &c., are not singular ; cf. Allibone for Alban. The *d* in Mallabund is excrescent, as in Simmonds, or the provincialism *gownd* for *gown*. The corruptions seem to have increased as the name extended into the further counties of Stafford and Warwick. A family named Malbon resided near Mottram, co. Cheshire, for many generations.

William Malbon, co. Ches., 1479 : East Cheshire, ii. 294 *n*.
Robert Malbon, co. Ches., 1479 : ibid.
William Malbon, of Great Budworth, *yeoman*, 1582 : Wills at Chester (1545-1620), p. 129.
1586. Bapt.—Thomas Malbon, of Mottram, co. Ches. : Reg. Prestbury Ch., p. 88.
1634. — George, s. Joseph Malbone : ibid. p. 292.
1651. Married — Henry Gouldsmith and Hanna Malbone : St. Jas. Clerkenwell, iii. 86.
1625. Buried—Robert Mallibone : St. Thomas the Apostle (London), p. 115.
London, 1, 0, 0, 0 ; MDB. (co. Warwick), 0, 1, 1, 1 ; (co. Stafford), 2, 0, 0, 0 ; Boston (U.S.), 1, 0, 0, 0.

Malcolm.—Bapt. ' the son of Malcolm.' 'The great St. Columba, who established the centre of his civilizing and christianizing efforts at Iona, had many a grateful disciple, as Gillecolumb, or Maelcolum' (Yonge, ii. 116) ; cf. Gilpatrick and Gilmichael.

Melcolinus de Inghou, co. Northumb., Hen. III-Edw. I. K.
Maucolumb' Com', co. Hunts, 1273. A.
London, 8 ; New York, 14 ; Boston (U.S.), 16.

Malcovenant. — Nick. ; cf. Manclarke, Malregard. Probably *n* for *l* in the instance below.
Robertus Mancowennant, co. Linc., 1273. A.

Male, Maile.— ?——. I can offer no satisfactory suggestion as to the derivation of this name.

Roger de la Male. [I have lost my reference to this.]
1607. John Mayle, London : Reg. Univ. Oxf. vol. ii. pt. ii. p. 296.
1616. Robert Mayle, London : ibid. p. 357.
1714. Married — George Male and Sarah Longworth : St. Peter, Cornhill, ii. 70.
1735. Bapt.—Sarah, d. Thomas Maile : St. Jas. Clerkenwell, ii. 221.
London, 3, 3 ; New York, 1, 0.

Malham, Maleham, Mallam, Malam.—Local, ' of Malham,' a township in the parish of Kirkby-in-Malham-Dale, W. Rid. Yorks.

John de Malghom, 1379 : P. T. Yorks. p. 269.
Stephen de Malgham, *draper*, 1379 : ibid. p. 265.
Thomas de Malgham,*cissor*, 1379 : ibid. p. 267.
Willelmus de Malghom, 1379 : ibid. p. 269.

The above instances occur in the immediate neighbourhood of Malham ; cf. also

Adam de Mallom, 1379 : P. T. Yorks. p. 254.
Thomas de Mallum, 1379 : ibid. p. 245.
1774. Married — William Barrett and Eliz. Mallam : St. Geo. Han. Sq. i. 243.
London, 2, 0, 4, 0 ; West Rid. Court Dir., 0, 2, 0, 0 ; Sheffield, 0, 4, 0, 0 ; Halifax (Malam), 1 ; Oxford (Mallam), 9 ; New York (Mallam), 1.

Malin.—Bapt. ' the son of Malin' ; v. Mallinson.

Malkin, Malkinson. — Bapt. ' the son of Matilda,' from dim. Malkin. ' Malkyne or Mawte, propyr name (Molt, K., Mawde, W.), Matildis (Matilda)' : Prompt. Parv. In the face of this clear statement it seems strange that Malkin should have been universally treated as the dim. of Mary. ' It was formerly a common diminutive of Mary' (Halliwell), I suspect Malkin represented Mary in the North of England, and Matilda in Norfolk and South-East England generally. At any rate, Maid Marian was also known as Malkin, and Marian, or more correctly Marion, is an unquestionable diminutive of Mary. Malkin is found early :

'Nor those prude yongemen
That loveth Malekyn.'
A Litul soth Sermun, E.E.T.S.

'And Malkin, with hire distaf in hire hond.' Chaucer, C. T. 15391.

Hence a kitchen wench. 'The kitchen malkin pins Her richest lockram': Coriolanus, ii. 1. Burton is still more unkind. 'A filthy knave, a deformed quean, a crooked carcass, a *maukin*, a witch': Anat. of Melancholy, part iii. sect. 2, mem. 2, subsect. 3. Hence, too, *malkin*, a baker's clout to clean ovens with, or a scarecrow (v. Halliwell), on the same principle by which implements taking Jack's place took Jack's name; cf. *bootjack*, or *jack*, a turnspit.

Thomas Malkynson, *webster*, 1379: P. T. Yorks. p. 287.
Johannes Malkynson, 1379: ibid. p. 12.
William Malkynson, 1379: ibid. p. 248.
Matilda Dikwyuemalkynson, *vidua*, i.e. Matilda, the wife of Dick, the son of Malkyn, *widow*: ibid. p. 42.
Willelmus Malkynson, ibid. p. 173.

Malkinson exists in Yorkshire, but it is rare; Malkin later on, as the name of a drab, having, like Parnall and Nan, lost caste. Nevertheless some of our Makinsons are doubtless thus originated; v. Makin.

1604. Bapt. — Joseph, s. Joshua Malkin: St. Jas. Clerkenwell, i. 358.
West Rid. Court Dir., 2, 0; Sheffield, 2, 0; MDB. (co. Linc.), 0, 2.

Mallabone,-bund; v. Malbon.

Mallalieu, Mallalue.—Nick. A corruption of Melladew; v. Merridew.

London, 2, 1; Manchester, 3, 0; Boston (U.S.), 3, 0.

Mallam; v. Malham.

Mallard.—Nick. 'the mallard,' i.e. the wild drake; cf. Wildgoose. 'Malarde, bryde, *anas*': Prompt. Parv. Probably absorbed in the course of generations by Mallet, q.v.

1580. John Malard, co. Hereford: Reg. Univ. Oxf. vol. ii. pt. ii. p. 94.
1638. Married — Ralph Beech and Marye Mallard: St. Jas. Clerkenwell, iii. 70.
1742. — Francis Mallard and Ann Hinderson: St. Geo. Chap. Mayfair, p. 17.
New York, 5; Boston (U.S.), 8.

Malledew.—Nick.; v. Merridew.

Liverpool, 1.

Malleson, Mallison.—Bapt. 'the son of Mallin,' from Mary; v. Mallinson, of which it is a modification; cf. Patteson for Pattinson. Sometimes more directly from Mally, the earlier form of Molly. It is still Mally in Furness, and Moll is still Mall.

Ricardus fil. Roberti Malleson, 1379: P. T. Yorks. p. 219.
1560. Bapt. — Fraunces Mallisonne: St. Peter, Cornhill, i. 9.
1777. Married — James Mallison and Mary Dickens: St. Geo. Han. Sq. i. 280.
London, 1, 1.

Mallet, Mallett.—Bapt. 'the son of Malet.'

Malet fil. Henry. C.
Baldwin Malet, co. Soms., 1273. A.
Sarra Malet, co. Camb., ibid.
Harvey Malet, co. Bucks, ibid.
Alan Malet, co. Derby, Hen. III–Edw. I. K.
Malet Molendinarius (Malet the Miller), Jersey: 20 Edw. I. R.
Magota Malet, 1379: P. T. Yorks. p. 59.
Johannes Malet, 1379: ibid. p. 167.
1586. Gawen Mallett, co. Soms.: Reg. Univ. Oxf. vol. ii. pt. ii. p. 151.
1619. Married — Anthony Mallet and Margaret Meredeth: St. Jas. Clerkenwell, iii. 47.
London, 3, 17; New York, 0, 1; Boston (U.S.), 2, 0.

Mallinson, Malin. — Bapt. 'the son of Mallin,' from Mary, nick. Mall, dim. Mall-in or Mal-in; cf. Rob-in, Col-in, Perr-in, Gibb-in. Molly is always Mally in the Ulverston parish registers to the close of last century; cf.

'Mall, or Maria Frears, of Ulverstone,' 1624: Lancashire Wills, Archdeaconry of Richmond, p. 116.
Malyna de Acstede, co. Kent, Hen. III–Edw. I. K.
Peter Maghlaynoone, C. R., 5 Edw. III. pt. i.
Malyn de Went, 1379: P. T. Yorks. p. 100.
Robertus Malyn, 1379: ibid. p. 163.
Johannes Malynson, 1379: ibid. p. 92.
Richard Malynson, 1379: ibid. p. 146.
Beatrix Malyn, doghter, 1379: ibid. p. 287.
Malin Gogun, co. Oxf., 1273. A.
Malin' ad Ecclesiam, co. Camb., ibid.

1655. Buried — Thomas Malin: St. Thomas the Apostle, p. 130.
London, 1, 4; Leeds, 5, 0; West Rid. Court Dir., 24, 0; Philadelphia, 4, 22; Boston (U.S.), 0, 2.

Mallory, Mallorie. — Local, 'de Malore' or 'Mallore' (three syllables). Evidently some Norman local surname.

Anketil de Malore, cos. Berks, Oxf., and York: Hen. III–Edw. I. K.
Robert Malhore, or Mallore, or Mallori, or Mallory, or Mallure, co. Northampton: ibid.
Anketil Malore, co. Salop, 1273. A.
Crisplane Malure, co. Leio., ibid.
Bertram Malore, co. Bedf., 20 Edw. I. R.
Johannes Malore, 1379: P. T. Yorks. p. 225.
Alicia fil. Johannes Maulore, 1379: ibid.
Peter Malure, co. Heref., ibid.
1578. Married—William Cotton, *gent*, and Elizabeth Mallare: St. Dionis Backchurch (London), p. 8.
1664. — Foulke Malober and Frances Mallory: St. Michael, Cornhill, p. 38.
1726. Bapt.—Mary, d. Stephen Malary: St. Jas. Clerkenwell, p. 165.
Crockford, 2, 0; West Rid. Court Dir., 0, 3; New York, 34, 0.

Malpas, Malpass.—Local, 'of Malpas,' a parish in the union of Wrexham, co. Ches.

William de Malpas, co. Ches., temp. 1230: East Ches. i. 264.
David del Malpas, co. Ches., 1391: ibid. p. 172 *n*.
1556. Married—Rycharde Wheler and Jone Mallipez: St. Michael, Cornhill, p. 7.
1737. — John Bendford and Mary Malpass: Canterbury Cath. p. 82.
1746. — Anthony Malpas and Jane Roberts: St. Michael, Cornhill, p. 71.
London, 2, 1; Philadelphia, 1, 6.

Malregard.—Nick. 'evil eye.' The English verbs *regard* and *reward* are doublets. F. *regarder*, to eye, to look.

William Malregard. T.
Geoffrey Malreward. J.
Walter Maureward, co. Linc., 1273. A.
Robert Maureward, co. Wilts, Hen. III–Edw. I. K.
Thomas Malreward, co. Wilts, 20 Edw. I. R.

Maltby.—Local, 'of Maltby,' parishes in the diocs. of York and Lincoln.

William de Malteby, co. Linc., 1273. A.
Walter de Malteby, co. Norf., ibid.
Robert de Malteby, co. Norf., 20 Edw. I. R.
Willelmus de Maltby, 1379: P. T. Yorks. p. 50.

Isabella de Maltby, 1379: P. T. Yorks. p. 53.

1706. Married — William Maltby and Mary Westly: St. Mary Aldermary (London), p. 38.

London, 9; MDB. (Lincoln), 12; Philadelphia, 3; Boston (U.S.), 3.

Malter.—Occup. ' the malter ' ; v. Maltmaker and Maltster.

Thomas Malter, C. R., 35 Hen. VI.

1677. Married — William Bell and Marvell Malter: St. Jas. Clerkenwell, iii. 184.

1795. — Antoine Rousseau and Marie Ann Malter: St. Geo. Han. Sq. ii. 126.

Malthouse, Malthus.—Local, ' at the malt-house,' found early as Malthus; cf. Loftus and Kirkus for Lofthouse and Kirkhouse.

Thomas de Malthous, 1379: P.T.Yorks. p. 238.

Beatrix Malthus, co. York. W. 16.

1570. William Malthus, co. York: Reg. Univ. Oxf. vol. ii. pt. ii. p. 80.

1615. Married — John Thomson and Ann Malthus, of Reading: St. Mary Aldermary (London), p. 13.

London, 2, 0; New York, 0, 1.

Maltmaker. — Occup. ' the maltmaker.' I suspect this surname did not last more than two or three generations.

Hugh le Maltmakere,co.Bucks,1273. A.

Rosa Carttwryth : *maltemaker*, 1379 : P. T. Yorks. p. 27.

Maltman.—Occup. ' the maltman,' a maltster, a dealer in malt. As a surname, scarce.

Liverpool, 1; Philadelphia, 1.

Malton.—Local, ' of Malton,' two parishes (New and Old) in N. Rid. Yorks. The surname does not seem to have made much impression upon our registers.

John de Malton, *mason*, 4 Edw. II : Freemen of York, i. 4.

Thomas de Malton, 1379 : P. T. Yorks. p. 159.

1603. William Malton and Alice Cooke: Marriage Lic. (London), i. 280.

London, 1; MDB.(East Rid. Yorks), 2.

Maltster.—Occup. ' the maltster.' The feminine terminative is common to these domestic employments; cf. Brewster, Baxter, Sempster or Simister, Kempster. ' Malstere or maltestere, *brasiatrix*, *brasiator* ': Prompt. Parv. When men more frequently took their part in some of these avocations the feminine term was still retained. There is no Maltster in the Hundred

Rolls (1273), but Maltmaker occurs. v. Malter.

Johannes de Pillay, 1379: P. T. Yorks. p. 87.

Dionicia ancilla ejus, *malster*, 1379: ibid.

Thomas Malster, 1379: ibid. p. 140.

Johannes Malster, 1379: ibid. p. 156.

Robertus Malster, 1379: ibid. p. 153.

John Malster. B.

Aleyn le Maltestere. H.

I dare not say that Maltster, as a surname, is extinct, but I believe such to be the case.

Manby.—Local, ' of Manby,' a parish in co. Lincoln. With the variant Manbee, infra, cf. Applebee for Appleby.

Robert de Manby, co. Linc., 1273. A.

Ricardus Maunby, 1379: P. T. Yorks. p. 245.

1581. Francis Manby, co. Linc.: Reg. Univ. Oxf. vol. ii. pt. ii. p. 113.

1583. William Manbee, co. Linc.: ibid. p. 127.

1788. Married — Joseph Manby and Hannah Littlewood: St. Geo. Han. Sq. ii. 8.

1804. — Thomas Pope and Maria Manbey: ibid. ii. 299.

London, 5; West Rid. Court Dir., 3; MDB. (co. Linc.), 1.

Mancell, Mansel, Mansell, Maunsell.—(1) ? Local. An inhabitant of Le Mans, the capital of Maine, a native of Maine—so says Lower. I suggested in English Surnames that it might be an abbreviation of Manciple, q.v. Probably Lower is right.

Thomas le Mansell, co. Bucks, 1273. A.

Sampson le Maunsel, co. Bedf., ibid.

John le Maunsel, 1313. M.

Robert le Mansel. J.

Johannes Mauncell, 1379: P. T. Yorks. p. 285.

Alicia Maunsell, 1379: ibid. p. 134.

(2) Bapt. ' the son of Mansel,' possibly a form of Marcel.

Frater Maunsel, co. Norf., 1273. A.

Maunsel (without surname), co. Hunts, ibid.

Thomas Maunsel, co. Camb., ibid.

Hence the dim. Mancel-ot or Maunsel-ot.

Henricus Maunselot, rector of Gateshead, 1322: Brand's Hist. Newcastle, i. 501.

Hugh Mancelot, co. Linc., 1273. A.

London, 2, 1, 13, 0 ; Oxford (Maunsell), 1 ; New York, 0, 0, 0, 7.

Manchester.—Local, ' of Manchester.' We do not often find

many representatives of our large cities. The tendency was to come to them, not to leave them. Hence many little spots are the fruitful parents of surnames.

John de Manchestre, 18 Edw. II : Freemen of York, i. 22.

John Manchester, C. R., 5 Hen. VI.

Richard Manchester, of Ratcliffe, 1671 : Wills at Chester (1660-80), p. 177.

Sarah Manchester, of Manchester, 1676: ibid.

1787. Married—David Allen and Mary Manchester : St. Geo. Han. Sq. i. 407.

1726. — Laurence Bath and Abigail Manchester : St. Jas. Clerkenwell, iii. 252.

London, 2; Liverpool, 2 ; New York, 13 ; Boston (U.S.), 11.

Manciple.—Offic. ' the manciple,' a caterer for a college, convent, &c.

' A gentil manciple was ther of a temple,
Of which achatours mighten take ensemple.'
Chaucer, C. T. 571.

The name is still officially used in several Oxford colleges. v. Mancell.

William Mannsipple : Pardon Roll, 6 Ric. II.

Thomas Mancipill, 1441 : Munim. Acad. Oxon. p. 525.

Manclarke.—Nick. Malclerk, the opposite of Beauclerk or Bonclerk, both of which existed side by side with it. Manclarke is not a modern corruption, only an early change from *l* to *n*; v. Malcovenant, and cf. *bannister* for *baluster*.

Walter Manclerc, co. Oxf., 1273. A.

Walter Malclerk. PP.

Godfrey Mauclerk. PP.

Colman Manclarke, mayor of Yarmouth, 1770 : FF. xi. 332.

' Aug. 28, 1888. Married—Amedée F. Mieville to Rose Manclark,of Rochester ': Times, Aug. 31, 1888.

Crockford, 1 ; MDB. (Norfolk), 1.

Mander; v. Maunder.

Manderson.—Bapt. ' the son of Magnus.' A corruption of Magnusson. This surname comes from Shetland, where Manderson and Magnusson run side by side ; v. Magnus. There need be no hesitation in accepting this solution. The corruption is of a most ordinary character.

1804. Married — William Manderson and Ann Maria Marsh : St. Geo. Han. Sq. ii. 310.

London, 1 ; Philadelphia, 17.

Mandeville, Manvell, Manville. — Local, 'of Mandeville.' I quote from Lower : 'Goisfrid de Mandeville was a Domesday chief-tenant in many counties. His descendants were the famous Earls of Essex, extinct in the 13th cent. From a younger branch probably sprang the famous traveller, Sir John M., in the 14th cent. In charters "de Magna Villa" and "de Mandaville." Magneville is near Valognes, in Normandy; and there are two places called Mandeville, one near Louviers, and another in the arrondissement of Bayeux.' Manvell is a manifest variant.

Nigel de Manderville, co. Berks, 1273. A
Ernald de Maundeville, co. Suff., ibid
Walter de Maundeville, co. Kent, 20 Edw. I. R.
John de Maundeville, 33 Edw. I. DBB. p. 696.
Ricardus Maunfill, 1379 : P. T. Yorks. p. 171.
1667. Married — Geo. Mandevell and Eliz. Clinch : St. Jas. Clerkenwell, iii. 138.
1751. — Peter Nott and Eliz. Mandeville : St. Geo. Chap. Mayfair, p. 201.
1757. Bapt. — Eliz. Maria, d. Robert Mandeville : St. Peter, Cornhill, ii. 47.
1766. Married—Richard Manvell and Ann Richbell : St. Geo. Han. Sq. i. 160.
London, 2, 3, 0 ; New York, 9, 0, 1.

Mandley.—Local; v. Manley.

Mandrell.—? Bapt. 'the son of Maundrell' (?).

Thomas Maundrell, et Elena uxor ejus, 1379 : P. T. Yorks. p. 129.
1605. Henry Mandrell, co. Wilts: Reg. Univ. Oxf. vol. ii. pt. ii. p. 284.
1614. Emme Maundrell, wife of Henry Mandrell (sic) : Marriage Lic. (London), ii. 30.
1663. John Bartlet and Grace Pitts, married by Mr. Mandrill, per licence : St. Peter, Cornhill, i. 263.
1696. Married—John Jacob and Mary Mandrill : St. Jas. Clerkenwell, iii. 217.
London, 2.

Manfred.—Bapt. 'the son of Manfred'; O. Ger. Maginfred (Yonge, ii. 415).

Bernardus Manifred, 1290-1325, Compotus of Bolton Abbey: Whitaker's Craven, p. 455.
Hugo Madefray, C. R., 11 Edw. III. pt. i.
London, 1.

Manger.—Bapt. 'the son of Mangar.' A common entry in the Hundred Rolls.

Manger, father of Thomas Manger, co. Oxf., 1273. A.
Manger (without surname), co. Oxf., ibid.
Richard Manger, co. Camb., ibid.
John Manger, co. Wilts, ibid.
Johannes Maungerson, 1379 : P. T. Yorks. p. 218.
1753. Buried — Thomas Manger : St. John the Baptist on Wallbrook, p. 215.
London, 4 ; New York, 1 ; Philadelphia, 4.

Manggolfe.—Bapt. 'the son of Meginulf,' mighty wolf ; v. Yonge, ii. 415, Meïnolf.

Willelmus Manggolfe, et Beatrix uxor ejus, 1379 : P. T. Yorks. p. 110.

Manifold.—Local, 'of the Manifold,' probably from residence by the river of that name in co. Derby.

Robert Manifold, 1595 : Wills at Chester (1545-1620), p. 130.
Thomas Manifold, of Great Aldersey, 1618 : ibid.
Manchester, 1 ; Liverpool, 4 ; Philadelphia, 3 ; New York, 1.

Manikin.—Bapt. 'the son of Main,' dim. Manekin ; v. Main.

Manekyn le Heaumer. H.
Stephen Manekin, co. Kent, Hen. III-Edw. I. K.
Robert Manekin, co. Suff., 1273. A.
Simon Monekin, co. Oxf., ibid.

In course of time the surname would probably be discontinued, when confused with *manikin*, a dwarf. Nevertheless, I find two instances across the Atlantic.

New York, 2.

Manley, Mandley, Manly, Mandly.—Local, 'of Manley,' a township in the parish of Frodsham, co. Chester. The South-English variant Manly is imitative. The *d* in Mandley is intrusive.

1577. Thomas Manley, co. Ches. : Reg. Univ. Oxf. vol. ii. pt. ii. p. 74.
Nicholas Manley, of Poulton, 1595 : Wills at Chester (1545-1620), p. 130.
Ann Manley, of Chester, *widow*, 1618 : ibid.
Thomas Manley, of Manley, *husbandman*, 1665 : ibid. (1660-80), p. 177.
1621. Married—Thomas Mandley and Mary Lambert. St. Jas. Clerkenwell, iii. 50.
1629. Bapt.—Eliz., d. Tobitha Manly, *widow* : St. Michael, Cornhill, p. 120.
Manchester, 5, 1, 0, 0 ; London, 19, 0, 1, 0 ; MDB. (co. Ches.), 3, 0, 0, 0 ; New York, 18, 0, 0, 1.

Mann, Man.—(1) Occup. 'the man,' i.e. the servant, in early use.

Henry le Man, co. Camb., 1273. A.
Bartholomew le Man, co. Suff., ibid.
Michael le Man, co. Oxf., ibid.
Henry le Man, co. Soms., 1 Edw. III :
Kirby's Quest, p. 108.
Richard le Man. E.

(2) Local, 'from Maine,' the French province. A common Yorkshire surname.

Patricius de Man, 1379 : P. T. Yorks. p. 151.
Johannes de Man, 1397 : ibid. p. 28.
Cecilia Manne, 1379 : ibid. p. 29.
Johannes de Manne, 1379 : ibid. p. 60.

For many other and conclusive instances, v. Mayne (2).

1586. Buried—Phillippe Colston, servant of Richard Man : St. Thomas the Apostle (London), p. 97.
1720. Bapt.—Anne, d. Daniel Mann : St. Jas. Clerkenwell, ii. 121.
London, 51, 0 ; Sheffield, 6, 0 ; Leeds, 14, 0 ; New York, 76, 7.

Mannering.—Local. Norman; v. Mainwaring.

Manning, Mannin. — Personal, 'the son of Manning,' an early personal name. Mr. Ferguson derives it from the Old Norse *manningi*, a valiant man. The name is preserved in such local terms as Manningford, Manningham, Mannington, and Manningtree, all parishes set down in Crockford. It occurs in Domesday as Mannig (co. Suffolk).

Henry Maninge, co. Camb., 1273. A.
Nicholas Mannyng, co. Kent, ibid.
Richard Mannyng, co. Hertf., 20 Edw. I. R.
Johannes Mannyng, 1379 : P. T. Yorks. p. 238.
Nora Mannyng, 1379 : ibid.
1757. Married—Thomas Renshaw and Jane Mannin : St. Geo. Han. Sq. i. 70.
London, 48, 0 ; New York, 120, 1.

Mansel(1 ; v. Mancell.

Manser.—Bapt. 'the son of Manser.'

Manser Arsik, co. Oxf., 1273. A.
Mancer de Pentelun, co. Bedf., ibid.
Fr. (frere?) Manserus, co. Norf., ibid.
Manser de Morton, co. Hunts, 20 Edw. I. R.
Leo fil. Manser, temp. Edw. III :
Kal. and Inv. (Palgrave), i. 79.
1670. William Saunders and Eliz. Manser : Marriage Alleg. (Canterbury), p. 44.
1791. Married — Edward Manser and Christiana Davis : St. Geo. Han. Sq. ii. 62.
London, 3 ; Philadelphia, 4.

Mansergh, Mansurgh.—
Local, 'of Mansergh,' a manor in the parish of Kirkby Lonsdale.

Thomas de Mansergh, 12 Edw. II : Nicolson's Hist. Westm. and Cumb., i. 252.
John de Mansergh, 7 Ric. II : ibid.
Thomas Manser, or Mansergh, of Burton, 1580 : Lancashire Wills at Richmond, p. 189.
George Mansergh, 1573 : ibid.
Elizabeth Manzer, of Barwicke, 1608 : ibid.
London, 1, 0 ; Manchester, 2, 0 ; Liverpool, 1, 1 ; Lancaster, 1, 0.

Mansfield, Mansfeld.— Local, 'of Mansfield,' a parish in co. Notts.

Robertus Mannsfeld', *carpenter*, 1379 : P. T. Yorks. p. 147.
1577. Richard Mannsfeilde and Susanna Selbie : Marriage Lic. (London), i. 76.
1581. Francis Mansfield, co. Derby : Reg. Univ. Oxf. vol. ii. pt. ii. p. 105.
1606. Thomas Mansfeild, co. Leic. : ibid. p. 289.
1745. Bapt.—Sarah, d. George Mansfield : St. Peter, Cornhill, ii. 43.
London, 39, 1 ; New York, 38, 0.

Manson.—(1) Bapt. 'the son of Magnus,' q.v. Manson is a common surname in Shetland. 'Manson is the contracted form of Magnusson': Scotsman, Oct. 16, 1886. (2) Bapt. 'the son of Main.' For instances, v. Main. So far as Manson is an English surname, this is the true derivation.

1592. Thomas Manson and Edith Connaway : Marriage Lic. (London), i. 201.
1794. Married — Daniel Manson and Ann Seewell : St. Geo. Han. Sq. ii. 111.
London, 1 ; Philadelphia, 10.

Mantell, Mantle, Mantel.—
? Nick. 'Turstinus Mantel occurs in the Domesday of co. Bucks as a tenant-in-chief. Probably a sobriquet from the French *mantelé*, cloak-wearer' (Lower). This is quite possible, for we have several familiar surnames still existing taken from the dress of the bearers; v. Chaperon. The variant Mantle is purely imitative.

Robert Mantel, co. Bucks, 1273. A.
Roger Mauntel, co. Essex, ibid.
John Mauntel, co. Oxf., ibid.
1596. Tristram Mantell and Helen Duplex : Marriage Lic. (London), i. 230.
1755. Buried—Eliz. Basset Mantle : St. Peter, Cornhill, ii. 142.
London, 3, 5, 0 ; MDB. (co. Oxf.), 1, 0, 0 ; New York, 1, 2, 7.

Manton.—Local, 'of Manton. Parishes in the diocs. of Lincoln and Peterborough.

William Manton, co. Camb., 1273. A.
Robert de Mantone, co. Notts, 20 Edw. I. R.
Willelmus de Manton, *smyth*, 1379 : P. T. Yorks. p. 58.
1603. Married — James Manton and Amey Thorlbey : St. Jas. Clerkenwell, iii. 27.
1667. Richard Cutts and Dorothy Manton : Marriage Lic. (London), p. 100.
London, 7 ; New York, 8.

Manuel, Manwell, Manuell.
—Bapt. ' the son of Emanuel,' nick. Manuel, corrupted to Manwell ; cf. Samwell for Samuel. A rare English surname, through lateness of its introduction into England.

Edward, son of Manuel Roger, 1542 : Reg. St. Columb Major, Cornwall, p. 2.
Humphrey, son of Emanuell Roger, 1545 : ibid. p. 3.
Manuell, son of John Tucker, 1602 : ibid. p. 21.
John, son of Emanuel Harvey, 1610 : ibid. p. 24.
1609. Buried — John Manuell : ibid. p. 204.
1778. Married—William Fielder and Sarah Manwell : St. Geo. Han. Sq. i. 287.
1806. — Anthony Manuel and Cecilia Salt : ibid. ii. 359.
London, 2, 2, 0 ; New York, 4, 2, 1.

Manvell, -ville ; v. Mandeville.

Mapledoore.—Local, 'at the mapledore,' i.e. the maple-tree ; cf. Appledore, and the local names, Mapledur-well and Maple-durham, where (in the latter instance) the hyphen seems to be in the wrong place.

1629. Married—Francis Ball and Eliz. Mapledoore : St. Dionis Backchurch, p.23.

Maples, Maiples, Marples, Mapples.—Local, 'at the maples,' from residence beside the maple-trees. Evidently some spot in W. Rid. Yorks ; cf. Mapplewell, a village near Barnsley. The modern Yorkshire form seems to be Marples.

Robert de Mapeles, co. York, 1273. A.
Willelmus de Mapples, 1379 : P. T. Yorks. p. 27.
Johannes de Mapples, 1379 : ibid.
1617. Bapt.—Thomasin, d. John Maples : St. Jas. Clerkenwell, i. 79.
London, 11, 0, 0, 0 ; West Riding Court Dir., 0, 1, 10, 0 ; MDB. (West Rid. Yorks), Mapples, 1 ; Philadelphia, 4, 0, 0, 0.

Maplesden. Mapelsden.—
Local, 'of Maplesden,' a locality to be found somewhere in co. Kent.

William de Mapplesden, co. Kent, 1273. A.
Stephen de Mapplisden, co. Kent, ibid.
1600. Gervase Maplesden, co. Kent : Reg. Univ. Oxf. vol. ii. pt. ii. p. 245.
1660. Walter Croxton and Mary Maplisden : Marriage Alleg. (Canterbury), p. 53.
1666. John Maplesden and Jane Cobham : ibid. p. 131.
1667. George Mapplesdon and Katharine Horsmonden : ibid. p. 137.
1687. Benjamin Fissenden and Eliz. Maplesden, of Maidstone : ibid. p. 51.
London, 1, 3 ; MDB. (co. Kent), 4, 0 ; New York, 0, 1.

Mapleson.—Bapt. 'the son of Mabel.' The *b* is sharpened into *p*, as in Mapps, Mappin, or Maplet, all from the same name. But while it seems so natural and easy of solution, it must not be forgotten that Mapleson may be a modification of Mapleston, and thus have a local origin ; cf. Kelson for Kelston, where the *t* is similarly elided.

London, 3 ; Liverpool, 1 ; New York, 1.

Mapleston, Maplestone.—
Local, 'of Mapleston,' probably for Mapleton.

1575. John Mapleston and Barsaba Newton : Marriage Lic. (London), i. 67.
1791. Married — Thomas Maplestone and Eliz. Davenport : St. Geo. Han. Sq. ii. 54.
London, 1, 2 ; Philadelphia, 1, 0.

Maplet.—Bapt. 'the son of Mabel,' from dim. Mabelot, sharpened to Mapelot, whence the shorter Maplet.

1619. Henry Maplet, or Mapelett, co. Cumb. : Reg. Univ. Oxf. vol. ii. pt. ii. p. 378.

Maplethorpe. — Local, ' of Maplethorpe,' some small spot in co. Lincoln that I cannot find.

MDB. (co. Linc.), 5.

Mapp, Mapps, Mapson.—
Bapt. 'the son of Mabel' (cf. Mapleson), from nick. Mab (sharpened to Map), whence dim. Mabbin (sharpened to Mappin). A Yorkshire surname, where Mabel was particularly popular ; v. Mabb and Mabson. Thus Nob, from Oliver, became Nopps and Nopson.

1585. John Mapes and Ann Cater: Marriage Lic. (London), i. 130.
1647. Married—Thomas Mapsonne to Elizabeth Border: St. Mary Aldermary (London), p. 20.
1722. Bapt.—Ann, d. Richard Mapp: St. Jas. Clerkenwell, ii. 137.
1737. — Mary, d. John Mapson : ibid. ii. 231.
London, 3, 0, 1 ; Philadelphia, 0, 1, 0.

Mappin.—Bapt. 'the son of Mabel,' from nick. Mab and dim Mab-in, sharpened to Mappin ; v. Mapp.

Hugh Mapping, C. R., 3 Edw. I.
Maude Mabyn, wyfe of Roger Mabyn, 1603: St. Columb Major (Cornwall), p. 201.
1729. Married—Joseph Mapping and Mary Long: St. Geo. Chap. Mayfair, p. 294.
London, 2 ; Sheffield, 12 ; New York, 1.

Mapplebeck, Maplebeck.— Local, 'of the maple-beck,' the beck or stream where the maples grew ; cf. Ellerbeck for the elder-beck. Yorkshire seems to have been a great place for maple-trees; cf. the local Mapplewell, and v. Marples.

Ricardus de Mapelbek', et Beatrix uxor ejus, webester, 1379: P. T. Yorks. p. 25.
Adam de Mappelbek', 1379 : ibid. p. 120.
Doncaster, 1, 0 ; MDB. (West Rid. Yorks), 2, 1.

Mapples.—Local ; v. Maples.

Mappleton, Mapleton. — Local, 'of Mappleton,' two parishes, one in co. Derby, the other in E. Rid. Yorks.

Robert de Mapelton, co. Derby, 1273. A.
Thomas de Mapelton, co. Derby, ibid.
1693. William Mappleton and Agnes Lowe: Marriage Alleg. (Canterbury), p. 268.
1803. Married — John Mapleton and Ann Evans: St. Geo. Han. Sq. ii. 281.
MDB. (co. Somerset), 0, 1 ; (co. Hants), 0, 1.

Marbiler, Marbrer.—Occup. 'the marbler' or 'marbrer,' a worker in marble, a sculptor, a marble-mason.

'Masones, malemakers, and merbelers.'
Cocke Lorelle's Bote.

From O.F. marbre, altered in England to marbel, marbil, and marble.

Geoffrey le Merberer. B.
John le Merbrer, London. X.
Walter le Marbiler, London. X.
Agnes Mabler, 1379: P. T. Yorks. p.141.
Johannes Marlebare (sic), 1379 : ibid.
Hugh Marbeler was Sheriff of London in 1424.

Marbury, Marberough. — Local, 'of Marbury,' a parish in co. Chester, three miles from Whitchurch.

1545. John Marbery and Alice Marbery : Marriage Lic. (Faculty Office), p. 5.
1610. William Marburie, co. Ches. : Reg. Univ. Oxf. vol. ii. pt. ii. p. 375.
1627. Bapt.—Rebecca, d. Lewes Marbury : St. Thomas the Apostle, p. 48.
London, 0, 1 ; New York, 2, 0.

March.—(1) Local, 'of March,' a market-town and chapelry in the parish of Doddington, co. Cambridge. As with several other local surnames, the early entries have le instead of de as prefix ; cf. Le Bruce for De Bruce.

Henry le March, co. Camb., 1273. A.
William le March, co. Camb., ibid.
Philip le March, co. Oxf., ibid.
Willelmus de Marche, 1379 : P. T. Yorks. p. 237.
Johannes de Marche, 1379 : ibid. p. 246.

(2) Local, 'at the march,' i.e. the border, limit, or boundary-line of a district.

Johannes de la Marche, 1379 : P. T. Yorks. p. 261.
Ricardus del Marche, 1379 : ibid. p. 245.
Agnes del Marche, 1379 : ibid. p. 171.
1584. Edward Marche, co. Kent : Reg. Univ. Oxf. vol. ii. pt. ii. p. 138.
London, 16 ; West Rid. Court Dir., 3 ; New York, 14.

Marcham.—Local, 'of Marcham,' a parish near Abingdon, co. Berks ; v. Markham and Marsham.

Robert de Marcham, co. Notts, 1273. A.
Peter de Marcham, 1379 : P. T. Yorks. p. 13.
1742. Married — John Marcham and Mary Towell : St. Geo. Chap. Mayfair, p. 19.
London, 1 ; Oxford, 1.

Marchant, Marchand. — Occup. 'the merchant'; M.E. marchant. 'Marchaunte, mercator': Prompt. Parv.

Thomas le Marchaunt, co. Hunts, 1273. A.
John le Marcaunt, co. Hunts, ibid.
Samson le Marchant, co. Suff., ibid.
William Marchand, co. Hunts, ibid.
Adam Mercator, co. Oxf., ibid.
Willelmus Castleforth, merchand, 1379 : P. T. Yorks. p. 159.
Isabella Marchaunt, 1379 : ibid. p. 110.
1615. John Picknett and Mary Markant : Marriage Lic. (London), ii. 35.
London, 29, 2 ; New York, 2, 2 ; Philadelphia, 8, 1.

Marchington. — Local, 'of Markington,' a village near Ripley and Ripon, co. York.

Johannes de Merkyngton, 1379 : P. T. Yorks. p. 259.
Alicia de Merkyngton, 1379 : ibid.
West Riding Court Dir., 2 ; Sheffield, 1 ; Boston (U.S.), 2.

Marcroft.—Local, 'of Marcroft,' probably a variant of Moorcroft, q.v. The instances below from the Chester Wills settle the origin of the Lancashire Marcrofts beyond dispute. Evidently it was some small farmstead between Rochdale and Middleton.

Thomas Hardman, of Marcroft, parish of Rochdale, 1594 : Wills at Chester (1545-1620), p. 82.
Thomas Marcroft, of Kersley, parish of Dean, 1607 : ibid. p. 130.
Robert Marcroft, of Middleton, 1613 : ibid. p. 131.
Liverpool, 2.

Marcus.—Bapt. 'the son of Mark'; cf. Lucas for Luke. 'Marke, propyr name, Marcus': Prompt. Parv.

John Marcus, co. Essex, 1273. A.
1508. Married—John Wright and Alice Marcus : St. Jas. Clerkenwell, iii. 4.
1752. Bapt.—Lewis, s. Lewis Marcus : ibid. ii. 301.
London, 5 ; Philadelphia, 14.

Margaret, Margretts.—Bapt. 'the son of Margaret.'

Henry fil. Margaret, co. Camb., 1273. A.
William fil. Margaret, co. Oxf., ibid.
Hugh Margarete, co. Bucks, ibid.
Johannes Margaret, 1379 : P. T. Yorks. p. 190.
1615. Married — Robert Jennison and Elizabeth Margrettes : St. Jas. Clerkenwell, iii. 42.
1642. Bapt.—Ann, d. Robert Margarets, fishmonger : St. Peter, Cornhill, i. 89.
1666. Buried — Elizabeth Margritts : St. Antholin (London), p. 92.

Margerison. Margesson. Marginson, Marjason. Marjerrison, Margisson, Margeson.—Bapt. 'the son of Margaret,' from the popular pet form Margery. Careless pronunciation has in course of time brought about the corrupted forms ; v. Margery.

Robert Marjorison, 1379 : P. T. Yorks. p. 243.
Richard Marjorison, 1379 : ibid.
Roger Margeryson, 1379 : ibid. p. 104.
1619. Griffin Margison and Anstis Hall : Marriage Lic. (Westminster), p. 28.

1716. Bapt.—Elenor, d. Richard Margeson : St. Peter, Cornhill, ii. 30.

The Blackburn Directory (co. Lanc.) has Margerison (3), Margerson (1), and Margeson (2).

London, 1, 0, 1, 1, 0, 0, 0; Crockford, 0, 1, 0, 0, 0, 0, 0; Manchester, 2, 0, 0, 0, 0, 0; Sheffield, 2, 0, 0, 0, 2, 0, 0; West Rid. Court Dir., 4, 0, 0, 0, 1, 0, 0; MDB. (co. Linc.), 0, 0, 0, 0, 1, 1, 0; Philadelphia, 5, 0, 0, 0, 0, 0, 0; Boston (U.S.), 0, 2, 0, 0, 0, 0, 10.

Margery, Margrie, Margries.—Bapt.'the son of Margaret,' from the popular pet form Margery or Marjory. ' Margery, propyr name, *Margeria* ': Prompt. Parv.

John Margerie, co. Suff., 1273. A.
Margeria (without surname), co. Oxf., ibid.
Margerie le Bercher. T.
Johannes Marjory, 1379 : P. T. Yorks. p. 197.
Marjoria Love, 1379 : p. 199.
Agnes Marjory-mayden, 1379 : ibid. p. 237.
Marjoria Norris, 1379 : ibid. p. 11.
London, 0, 4, 1.

Margetts, Margetson, Margot.—Bapt. 'the son of Margaret,' from the popular abbreviated Margot or Marget ; v. Maggot.

Margota Servant, co. York. W. 2.
Robert Margets, temp. Eliz. Z.
Francis Margetson, co. Norf. FF.
Joyce Margetson. PP.
1656. Bapt.—John, s. James Margetson, Dr. in Divinity : St. Jas. Clerkenwell, i. 196.
1709. Married—Philip Margot and Anne Dauborne : Canterbury Cath. p. 69.
London, 5, 5, 2 ; Boston (U.S.), 0, 0, 8.

Margrie.—Bapt. 'the son of Margaret,' popularly Margery, q.v.

Maries ; v. Marison.

Marigold, Marygold.—?Nick. This surname seems to have had Staffordshire for its home.

John Marigold, minister of Cartmel, 1643: Baines' Lanc. (Croston), p. 309.

Possibly the same clergyman is referred to in the following :

1643. 'Item, for charges and expenses uppon divers Ministers (to witt), Mr. Fornace, Mr. Mariegould . . . which bestowed their paines in preaching with us when wee had no constant minister ': Northenden Church, East Cheshire, i. 293.

This is confirmed by the fact that a John Marigold occurs as 'pastor of Waverton,' in Cheshire, in 1648. He seems to have died in 1662.

1662. John Margold, of Waverton, *clerk* : Wills at Chester (1660-80), p. 177.

London, 1, 0 ; MDB. (Worcester), 1, 0 ; (Stafford), 1, 0 ; Oxford, 0, 1 ; Philadelphia, 1, 0.

Mariner, Marner, Marriner.—Occup. 'the mariner,' a sailor, a shipman ; Fr. *marinier*. Marner is a natural abbreviation.

Jacobus le Mariner, co.'Camb., 1273. A.
Roger le Mariner, co. Hunts, ibid.
Henry le Mariner. H.
John Maryner, co. Soms., 1 Edw. III : Kirby's Quest, p. 267.
1689. Bapt.—Elinor, d. James Mariner: St. Dionis Backchurch (London), p. 129.
1795. Married—John Waller and Mary Marner : St. Geo. Han. Sq. ii. 123.
London, 2, 5, 1 ; West Rid. Court Dir., 0, 0, 5 ; Philadelphia, 20, 0, 2.

Marion, Maryon, Marrian.—Bapt. 'the son of Mary,' from the dim. Mari-on, 'little Mary'; cf. Gibbon from Gib, Alison from Alice, Diccon from Dick. Marion or Marian is now a separate name from Mary, as is Eliza from Elizabeth. The doublet Mary Ann helps to perpetuate the modern idea that Marian is a compound of Mary and Ann. It is ludicrous to read that ' Marian, more frequently written Marion, is not formed from Mary and Ann, as some French writers have supposed, but more probably from Mariamne, the wife of Herod, &c.': A Lytell Geste of Robin Hode, i. 342. This is 'out of the frying-pan into the fire.' Maid Marian was as often styled ' Malkin, the May Lady,' Malkin being the English dim. of Mary. Jamieson has unfortunately permitted the 'Mariamne' view a place in his dictionary.

Marion Lambert, 1379 : P. T. Yorks. p. 41.
Mariona fil. Henry, 1379 : ibid. p. 262.
Johannes Marion, 1379 : ibid. p. 104.
Johannes Marionson, 1379 : ibid. p. 111.
Robertus Marion, 1379 : ibid. p. 214.
1391. Gilbert Marion : Cal. of Wills in the Court of Husting (2).
1638. Married—Thomas Allamby and Averine Marrian : St. Jas. Clerkenwell, p. 69.
1688. Bapt. — Thomas, s. Thomas Maryan : St. Mary Aldermary (London), p. 109.
London, 2, 5, 1 ; West Rid. Court Dir., 0, 0, 2 ; Philadelphia, 16, 0, 0.

Marison, Maris, Maries.—Bapt. 'the son of Mary.' Mariot the dim. was almost universal,

Mary being rare ; v. Marriott. Maris might seem to be one of the many early forms of Marsh (q.v.), but it seems more natural to place it here. However, v. Marriss.

Hugh fil. Mary, co. Linc., 1273. A.
William fil. Marie, co. Linc., ibid.
Henry fil. Marie, co. Devon, 20 Edw. I. R.
1621. Jasper Maries, co. Worc. : Reg. Univ. Oxf. vol. ii. pt. ii. p. 393.
1806. Married—Isaac Fitch and Maria Maris : St. Geo. Han. Sq. ii. 349.
London, 1, 4, 2 ; Boston (U.S.), 2, 0, 0 ; Philadelphia, 0, 18, 0.

Mark, Marks, Marx.—Bapt. 'the son of Mark'; v. Marcus. 'Marke, propyr name': Prompt. Parv. In many cases Marks (and Marx) is a variant of March, q.v. Mark was a rare personal name in the 13th and 14th centuries. With Marx, cf. Dix, Rix, Cox, Wilcox, &c.

William Marke, co. Southampton, 1273. A.
Thomas Mark, co. Oxf., ibid.
Johannes Markson, 1379 : P. T. Yorks. p. 278.
1575. John Marks, co. Devon : Reg. Univ. Oxf. vol. ii. pt. ii. p. 64.
1593-4. George Marks, co. Cornwall : ibid. p. 200.
1749. Married—John Marks and Sarah Powell : St. Geo. Chap. Mayfair, p. 149.
London, 3, 49, 3 ; Philadelphia, 2, 83, 15.

Markby.—Local, ' of Markby,' a parish in the union of Spilsby, co. Lincoln.

Prior de Markeby, co. Linc., 1273. A.
1744. Married—Thomas Markby and Mary Skhellington : St. Geo. Chap. Mayfair, p. 36.
1805. — John Martin and Eliz. Markby : St. Geo. Han. Sq. ii. 334.
London, 2.

Markendale.—Local. A variant or corruption of Martindale (q.v.), a hamlet in the parish of Barton, co. Westmoreland ; v. Martindale.

1726. Married—James Markendle and Mary Thomas: St. Antholin (London), p. 141.
Manchester, 3.

Marketman. — Occup. 'the market-man.'

Nicholas Marketman. TT.
'Articles exhibited against Clement Marketman, executor of Clement Stuppeney': State Papers, July 25, 1623.

'Mr. William Markettman was appointed by the Committee of Plundered Ministers in 1650 to the rectory of Elstree': Clutterbuck's Hist. of Herts, i. 161.

Markham.—Local, 'of Markham,' a parish near Tuxford, co. Notts.

Johannes Marcam, Ibbota uxor ejus, 1379 : P. T. Yorks. p. 44.
Nicholaus Marcam, Isabella uxor ejus, 1379 : ibid.
Henricus de Markham, 1379 : ibid. p 154.
1573. Married—Christopher Markeham and Margerye Turke : St. Michael, Cornhill, p. 10.
1585. Henry Marcham or Markham : Reg. Univ. Oxf. vol. ii. pt. ii. p. 144.
Sheffield, 5 ; London, 10 ; MDB. (co. Linc.), 4 ; New York, 13.

Marking, Markin. — Bapt. 'the son of Mark,' from the dim. Mark-kin ; cf. Wil-kin, Tomp-kin, Jeff-kin, &c. The final g is excrescent, as in Jennings, &c. The name has always been rare, whether as personal name or surname ; but it has survived five centuries of neglect.

Johannes Markyn, 1379 : P. T. Yorks. p. 78.
1626. Bapt.—Milles, s. Milles Markine : St. Mary Aldermary (London), p. 79.
1659. Bapt.—Alise, d. Ann Markin : Kensington Church, p. 44.
London, 1, 0 ; New York, 0, 2.

Markland.—Local, 'of Markland.' Mr. Lower, quoting Jamieson, says, 'In Scotland a division of land.' If it be a North-British surname it migrated to South Lancashire a few centuries ago.

Matthew Markland, of Wigan, 1561 : Wills at Chester (1545-1620), p. 131.
John Markland, of Pemberton, 1611 : ibid.
Gerard Markland, temp. 1662 : East Cheshire, ii. 11 n.
1644. Married — Michael Markeland and Mary Perry : St. Dionis Backchurch (London), p. 24.
Manchester, 5 ; Philadelphia, 7.

Marland.— Local, 'of Marland,' an estate in the township of Castleton and parish of Rochdale.

'Marland, or Mereland (from its water), in this township (Castleton), is of high antiquity. Alan de Merland, Adam de Merland, and Andrew de Merland were living in the 13th century. . . .A branch of the family of Marland continued to reside and hold lands at Marland from the earliest period until the latter part of the 17th century — James Marland, of

Marland, gentleman, being buried within Trinity Chapel, in Rochdale Church, in 1675' : Baines' Lanc. i. 505.

The name is not extinct in South Lancashire.

James Marland, of Rochdale, 1584 : Wills at Chester (1545-1620), p. 131.
Alice Marland, of Bradley, 1589 : ibid.
John Marland, of Hartshead, Ashton-under-Lyne, 1610 : ibid.
1699. Married—James Mareland and Sarah Sanson : St. Peter, Cornhill, ii. 62.
Manchester, 2 ; Philadelphia, 2.

Marlborough. — Local, 'of Marlborough,' a well-known town in co. Wilts.

John de Marleberge, co. Oxf., 1273. A.
Thomas de Marleberge, co. Soms., 1 Edw. III : Kirby's Quest, p. 176.
1595. Bapt.—William, s. Mr. Marlborowe : St. Jas. Clerkenwell, i. 30.
1604. — Anne, d. Robert Marlboroe : ibid. i. 44.
1775. Married—Francis Marlborough and Eliz. Hall : St. Geo. Han. Sq. i. 259.
London, 3.

Marler.—Occup. 'the marler,' one who marled fields or who worked in a marl-pit ; M.E. marle, a rich earth used for manure.

'Til he was in a marle-pit yfalle.'
       Chaucer, C. T. 3460.
Alice le Marlere, co. Oxf., 1273. A.
Alan le Marler, C. R., 3 Edw. II.
Willelmus Marlar, 1379 : P. T. Yorks. p. 79.
Johannes Merler, 1379 : ibid. p. 7.
Stephen le Marlar, co. Soms., 1 Edw. III : Kirby's Quest, p. 106.
1566. Married — John Wattes and Johane Marler : St. Jas. Clerkenwell, iii. 3.
1790. — Robert Marler and Sarah Clinch : St. Geo. Han. Sq. ii. 45.
London, 3 ; New York, 1.

Marley.—Local, 'of Marley,' now Marley Hill, in the parish of Whickham, near Gateshead. A family of this name were early settled there.

'In 1380 Gilbert de Merley held the vill of Merley,' i.e. Marley : DDD. ii. 256.
Adam de Merley, 1201 : ibid.
William de Merley, 1339 : ibid.
Roger de Merlay, co. York, 1273. A.
Margareta de Marlay, 1379 : P. T. Yorks. p. 272.
Thomas de Marlay, 1379 : ibid. p. 153.

Marley is a well-established surname in co. Durham.

1746. Bapt.—Mary, d. Joseph Marley : St. Jas. Clerkenwell, ii. 278.
London, 3 ; MDB. (co. Durham), 4 ; Philadelphia, 35.

Marmaduke.—Bapt. 'the son of Marmaduke'; somewhat rare in the surname period. Nevertheless it was popular in Yorkshire, and made the pet nicks. Doket and Doke (now Duckett and Duke) favourites long enough for them to become surnames and attain immortality in our directories. Whether the full name ever reached surnominal honours so as to live into modern times I cannot say. I have not met with it.

Marmaduc' de Twenge, co. York, 1273. A.
John Marmaduc, co. Northumberland. 20 Edw. I. R.
John fil. Marmaduc, 1315 : DDD. p. 19.
Marmedoke (without surname), 1379 : P. T. Yorks. p. 269.
1569. Bapt.—Margaret, d. Marmaduke Servant : St. Jas. Clerkenwell, i. 5.
1619. Marmaduke Greathead and Katherine Dorrell : Marriage Lic. (London), p. 81.

Marner.—Occup. 'a mariner. sailor'; v. Mariner.

Marples. — Local, 'at the maples,' i.e. the maple-trees. This familiar Yorkshire surname has no connexion with Marple, the parish in East Cheshire. At some period an r seems to have intruded itself into Maples or Mapples, q.v.

Thomas de Mapples, 1379 : P. T. Yorks. p. 6.
Johannes de Mapples, 1379 : ibid. p. 27.
Willelmus de Mapples, 1379 : ibid.

The two latter dwelt in Rotherham.

Sheffield, 19 ; West Rid. Court Dir., 10 ; London, 0 ; New York, 2.

Marquis, Marquiss.—? Bapt. Probably a continental form of Marcus. Marquis, strange to say, is a common modern baptismal name in co. York, but it refers to the title of nobility, and is the outcome of eccentric fashion ; v. Duke. Earls, Dukes, Marquises, and Squires abound in some parts of the West Riding.

Markisa Galle, C. R., 11 Edw. II.
'Item, to Marques Loryden, mynstrelle, 66s. 8d' : Privy Purse Exp., Elizabeth of York, p. 100.
1797. Married—Archibald Marquisand Helen Scott : St. Geo. Han. Sq. ii. 162.
London, 1, 0 ; MDB. (co. Devon), 0, 3 ; Philadelphia, 9, 0 ; New York, 6, 0.

Marr.—Local, 'of Marr,' a small parish four miles from Doncaster. The Scotch Marrs are from the district of Marr, in Aberdeenshire.

Johannes de Merre, 1379 : P. T. Yorks. p. 52.
Henricus de Marre, 1379 : ibid. p. 61.
1748. Married—Joseph Meadows and Faith Marr : St. Geo. Chap. Mayfair, p. 111.
Sheffield, 1 ; London, 8 ; New York, 21.

Marrable.—Bapt. 'the son of Mirabell' (not in Yonge). Notice that in one instance the entry is *de* Mirabell, suggesting a local origin. Most of the other instances, however, are distinctly fontal.

Lucia Mirabile, co. Oxf., 1273. A.
Roger Mirabel, co. Devon, ibid.
William Mirabel, co. Essex, ibid.
Roger de Mirabell, co. Devon, Hen. III–Edw. I. K.
Mirabella Wal, co. York. W. 2.
Belina fil. Mirabilis. DD.
Mirabilla Judaeus, temp. 1300. M.
1604. James Gentleman, *tailor*, and Joane Marable : Marriage Lic. (London), i. 286.
London, 1 ; Crockford, 2.

Marriage.—? Local. The spelling is evidently imitative, and the suffix should probably be -*ridge*, as in Coleridge, Ridgway, Brownrigg, &c.

1616. Thomas Egerton and Alice Marriage (co. Warwick) : Marriage Lic. (London), ii. 41.
1626. Samuel Marredge (co. Middlesex) and Margaret Legge : ibid. ii. 180.
1709. Married—Stephen Marridge and Susanna Browning : St. Jas. Clerkenwell, iii. 231.
London, 3.

Marrian.—Bapt. 'the son of Mary,' from dim. Mary-on ; v. Marion.

Marrin.—Bapt. 'the son of Mary,' from the dim. Mari-on, corrupted to Marrin.

Walter Maryne, co. Soms., 1 Edw. III : Kirby's Quest, p. 249.
Thomas Marynson, 1379 : P. T. Yorks. p. 262.
Elizabeth, d. of James and Marrin Nettle, 1681 : Reg. St. Columb Major, p. 236.
1689. Peter Maligue and Mary Marrin : Marriage Alleg. (Canterbury), p. 126.
London, 1 ; New York, 13.

Marriott, Marryatt, Marratt, Marritt.—Bapt. 'the son of Mary,' from the dim. Mari-ot ; cf.

Philipot (fem.), Emmot (Emma), Tillot (Matilda). Another French dim., Marion, came about a century later ; v. Marion.

Nicholas Maryot, co. Suff., 1273. A.
John fil. Mariot, co. Hunts, ibid.
Mariota in le Lane, co. Camb., ibid.
Walter fil. Mariot, co. Wilts, ibid.
Ricardus Mariot, 1379 : P. T. Yorks. p. 44.
Thomas Haliday et Mariot uxor ejus, 1397 : ibid. p. 79.
Johannes Redebarne et Mariota uxor ejus, 1379 : ibid. p. 80.
1436. 'Received 10*s*. of Robert Atkynson, of Fenham, for the merchet of Mariot his daughter' : QQQ. p. 118.

In Cornwall, where diminutive forms lingered on later than in other counties, Mariot is found in the last century.

1677. Richard Marryott and Catherine Bradbourne : Marriage Alleg. (Canterbury), p. 267.
1725. Buried—Mariot Nettle, *widow* : Reg. St. Columb Major, p. 261.
London, 21, 1, 1, 1 ; New York, 4, 0, 1, 0.

Marris, Maris.—Local, 'at the marsh' (q.v.), from residence thereby. We naturally find this surname in the Fen country. Fr. *marais*, a marsh. But v. also Marison.

John de Mareys, co. Camb., 1273. A.
William du Mareys, co. Suff., ibid.
1745. Married—Henry Lane and Eliz. Marriss : St. Geo. Chap. Mayfair, p. 58.
1786. Married—William Marriss and Jane Ticklepenny : St. Geo. Han. Sq. i. 386.
MDB. (co. Linc.), 13, 0 ; (co. Camb.), 1, 2 ; London, 1, 0 ; Philadelphia, 3, 18.

Marryatt ; v. Marriott.

Marsden, Marsdin.—Local, 'of Marsden.' Parishes in the diocs. of Ripon, Durham, and Manchester. Lit. the marsh-valley, the dale in the swamp. A familiar surname in cos. Lanc. and York.

Robert de Marcheden, co. York, 1273. A.
Nicholaus Mercheden, 1379 : P. T. Yorks. p. 208.
Johanna de Mersseden, 1379 : ibid. p. 184.
1609. Richard Marsden, of the Castle, in Clitheroe : Wills at Chester, i. 131.
1677. William Gibbins and Catherine Marsden : Marriage Alleg. (Canterbury), p. 203.
London, 14, 0 ; West Rid. Court Dir., 38, 5 ; Manchester, 43, 0 ; Philadelphia, 42, 0.

Marsh.—Local, 'at the marsh' (from residence thereby), i.e.

swamp, bog. Low Latin, *mariscus* ; M.E. *mersche*.

Isabel ate Mershe, co. Oxf., 1273. A.
John in le Merse, co. Oxf., ibid.
Ricardus de Marisco, co. Suff., ibid.
Brian de Marisco, co. Wilts, ibid.
Katerina del Mersch,*huswyfe, webster*, 1379 : P. T. Yorks. p. 66.
1567. Married—Peter Foxe and Eliz. Marshe St. Michael, Cornhill, i. 9.
1567–8. William Woods and Isabel Marsh : Marriage Lic. (London), i. 38.
London, 70 ; New York, 98.

Marshall, Marshal.—Occup. 'the marshal,' i.e. farrier. Like the smith, the marshal was a necessity in every centre of population. Hence it is found in all counties.

William le Marechal, co. Camb., 1273. A.
Gunnilda le Marescall, co. Soms., ibid.
Robert Marescallus, co. Oxf., ibid.
'Ego Matilda, quae fuit uxor Willelmi Benetson, marschall, compos mentis,' &c., 1392 : Testamenta Ebor. pt. i. p. 180, Surt. Soc.
Thomas de Tiveryngton, *mareschal*, 28 Edw. I : Freemen of York, i. 8.
Willelmus de Scheplay, *marchall*, 1379 : P. T. Yorks. p. 171.
Johannes Mareschall, 1379 : ibid. p. 181.
1572. Christopher Marshall and Eliz. Byrde : Marriage Lic. (London), i. 54.

In the course of time, as marshal began to be associated solely with the military title, we find a kind of compromise in

Jacobus Laurence, *horsmarshall*, 7 Hen. VII : Freemen of York, i. 216.
Richard Henryson, *horsmarshall*, 7 Hen. VII : ibid.
London, 157, 1 ; New York, 116, 2 ; Philadelphia, 230, 0.

Marsham.—Local, 'of Marsham,' a parish in co. Norfolk, near Aylsham ; v. Marcham.

1619. John Marsham, co. Middlesex : Reg. Univ. Oxf. vol. ii. pt. ii. p. 378.
1754. Bapt.—Eliz., d. William Marsham : St. Antholin (London), p. 166.
London, 2.

Marshfield.—Local, 'of Marshfield,' a parish in co. Monmouth, five miles from Newport.

Peter de Marsfelde, co. Soms., 1 Edw. III : Kirby's Quest, p. 271.
London, 1 ; MDB. (co. Soms.), 1.

Marshman.—Local, 'the marshman,' from residence beside the marsh.

Richard Merischman, co. Soms., 1 Edw. III : Kirby's Quest, p. 188.

1711. Married—John Evile and Mary Marshman: Reg. Stourton,co.Wilts, p.54.
1766. — William Marshman and Ann Anderson: St. Geo. Han. Sq. i. 157.
London, 1; MDB. (co. Soms.), 1; (co. Wilts), 1; New York, 1; Philadelphia, 3.

Marsland.—Local, 'at the marsh land,' from residence thereby. I cannot find any particular spot bearing this name, but it seems to be North English.

Ricardus Mersland, 1379: P. T. Yorks. p. 180
Thomas Marsland, of Chester, 1609; Wills at Chester (1545-1620), p. 132.
John Marsland, of Stockport, 1603: ibid.
1742. Married — Joshua Kelly and Patience Marsland: St. Michael, Cornhill, p. 69.
West Rid. Court Dir., 3; London, 5; Manchester, 10; New York, 5.

Marson.—(1) Local, 'of Marston,' q.v. No doubt occasionally it is the case that Marson is a lazy abbreviation of Marston; cf. Kelson for Kelston. (2) Nick. 'the son of the mayor'; cf. Wrightson, Taylorson, Clerkson, &c. In any case, *not* 'the son of Mary.'

David fil. Meyr, co. Linc., 1273. A.
Robert Mayerson, of Wray, parish of Melling, 1589: Lancashire Wills at Richmond, i. 193.
1601. John Marson, co. Worc.: Reg. Univ. Oxf. vol. ii. pt. ii. p. 253.
1636. Married — Francis Parker and Ann Marson: St. Peter, Cornhill, i. 255.
1660. Bapt. — Eliz., d. George Marsoone: St. Jas. Clerkenwell, ii. 206.
London, 4; Boston (U.S.), 6.

Marston.—Local, 'of Marston.' There are at least twenty-five parishes of this name in England, including parishes in the diocs. of York, Lincoln, Hereford, and Oxford, of which instances are furnished below. The meaning is, 'the town on the marsh' (v. Town); M.E. *mersche*; A.S. *mersc*, a marsh.

Petronilla de Merston, co. Oxf., 1273. A.
Rither de Merston, co. Bedf., ibid.
Gilbert de Merston, co. Linc., Hen. III-Edw. I. K.
William de Merston, co. Heref., ibid.
Margeria de Merston, 1379: P. T. Yorks. p. 147.
Johannes de Merston, 1379: ibid. p. 257.
1591. John Marston, co. Warw.: Reg. Univ. Oxf. vol. ii. pt. ii. p. 187.
1690. Francis Marston and Eliz. Goold: Marriage Alleg. (Canterbury), p. 166.
London, 9; New York, 20; Boston (U.S.), 73.

Martel, Martell, Myrtle (?).—Bapt. 'the son of Martin,' otherwise 'Martel'; cf. Martle-mas for Martin-mas, common in North England. The dim. Martinet became Martnet and Martlet, hence the bird, the *martin*, which takes its name from the saint, is also known as the *martlet*. 'Martnet, byrd, *turdus*': Prompt. Parv. 'Martynet, a byrde, *martinet*': Palsg.

Johannes fil. Mertel, co. Norf., 1273. A.
Robert Martel, co. Norf., ibid.
Walter Martel, co. Norf., ibid.
William Martell, 20 Edw. I. R.
Ricardus Martyll, 1379: P. T. Yorks. p. 100.
1574-5. John Martill, Ireland: Reg. Univ. Oxf. vol. ii. pt. ii. p. 59.
1684-5. Henry Kelsey and Sarah Martel; Marriage Alleg. (Canterbury), p. 189.
London, 1, 2, 0; Manchester, 0, 0, 1; Philadelphia, 6, 0, 1; Boston (U.S.), 0, 13, 0.

Marten, Martens.—Bapt. 'the son of Martin,' q.v. Strictly speaking the Dutch form, but sometimes merely an English variation.

1541 Buried — Thomas Marten, *a priest*: St. Peter, Cornhill, i. 105
London, 6, 2; Philadelphia, 4, 1.

Marter.—Nick.; v. Martyr.

Martin, Martins, Martinson.—Bapt. 'the son of Martin'; v. Martel. This once popular font-name, coming as it did in the hereditary surname period, has swelled our 19th century directories enormously.

Martin de Littlebyr, C. R., 42 Hen. III.
William fil. Martin, co. Camb., 1273. A.
Mariota fil. Martini, co. Hunts, ibid.
Martin le Cordwaner, C. R., 9 Edw. II.
Johannes Martynson, 1379: P. T. Howdenshire, p. 32.

It is interesting to notice that Martinson still lives, although it does not now appear in the London Directory.

1797. Married — Thomas Martinson and Sarah Burrows: St. Geo. Han. Sq. ii. 169.
London, 243, 4, 0; MDB. (Lincoln), 34, 0, 2; (West Rid. Yorks), 8, 0, 1; New York, 600, 13, 0.

Martindale, Markendale, Martindell.—Local, 'of Martindale,' in co. Cumb. Markindale was an early corruption, as the reference below fully proves; v. Markendale.

1475. Katerina Martyngdale, co. York: W. 11, p. 98.
1476. John Markyngdale, co. York: ibid. p. 99.
Robert Martinndall, of the Grainge, in Cartmell, 1581: Lancashire Wills at Richmond, i. 191.
John Martyndall, 1590: ibid.
London, 3, 0, 0; Manchester, 2, 3, 0; Philadelphia, 10, 0, 5.

Martinet.—Bapt. 'the son of Martin,' from dim. Martin-et; v. Martel for further observations. Probably a somewhat modern importation from France.

1644. André Martinet and Mary Rosanpré: Marriage Alleg.(Canterbury), i. 289.
1670-1. John Taunay and Lucrece Martinett: ibid. ii. 50.
1775. Married—Claudy Martinet and Esther Thurston: St. Geo. Han. Sq. i. 253.
1782. — George Clarke and Priscilla Martinet: ibid. p. 338.
1845. Buried—Louis Martinet: Canterbury Cath. p. 158.
New York, 2.

Martland.—Local, 'of Markland,' a Lancashire variant of that county surname (v. Markland); cf. Martindale and Markendale.

Blackburn, 2; Manchester, 2.

Marton.—Local, 'of Marton.' Parishes in cos. Linc., Warwick, W. Rid. Yorks, and N. Rid. Yorks, besides several townships and chapelries in various counties. It is probable that Marton, as a surname, has gradually become lost in Martin, q.v.

Symon de Marton, 1379: P. T. Yorks. p. 268.
1799. Married — Geo. Rich. Marton and Ann Pocklington: St. Geo. Han. Sq. ii. 200.
MDB. (West Rid. Yorks), 1; (North Rid. Yorks), 1; Philadelphia, 2.

Martyn.—Bapt. 'the son of Martin,' q.v.

Henry Martyn, co. Hunts, 1273. A
John Martyn, co. Norf., ibid.
Elena Martyn, 1379: P. T. Yorks. p. 236.
1580. Married—Timothie Goose and Susan Martyn: St. Jas. Clerkenwell, iii. 8.
London, 5; Philadelphia, 2; Boston (U.S.), 3.

Martyr, Marter.—(1) Nick. 'the martyr,' one who had obtained that sobriquet by suffering of some sort for his faith's sake. M.E. *martir*; A.S. *martyr*. (2) Nick. 'the martre,' the marten, a weasel. F. *martre*, a martin, Cotg.; so spelt by Caxton in Reynard the Fox (Skeat). This is the more likely origin, nicknames from animals being so common.

William le Martre. J.
John le Martre. G.
1554. Married — Thomas Graye and Eliz. Martyr, co. Surrey: St. Dionis Backchurch (London), p. 3.
1603. — John Martir and Katherin Bromely: St. Peter, Cornhill, i. 243.
1644. Bapt. — Samuel, s. George Martin: St. Antholin (London), p. 77.
1726. Married — Robert Marter and Margaret Tomkins: St. Geo. Han. Sq. i. 2.
London, 2, 2; Philadelphia, 0, 14.

Marvell, Marvill.—Nick. 'the marvel.' M.E. *mervaile*; Fr. *merveille*, the wonder. Probably the name of some youthful prodigy in learning or physical prowess; cf. Marvellous. Andrew Marvell, born at Hull in 1620, made the name familiar, and it is in Yorkshire we find the surname still existing.

Warin Merveyl, co. Camb., 1273. A.
Richard Merveyle, co. Camb., ibid.
1702. Bapt. — William, s. William Marvel: St. Jas. Clerkenwell, ii. 8.
1724. Married—Richard Marvel and Elizabeth Walford: St. Mary Aldermary (London), p. 46.
Leeds, 3, 0; Philadelphia, 2, 8.

Marvellous.—Nick. 'the marvellous,' the wonderful. M.E. *mervaile*, a wonder.

Robert le Mervyllous, 'clericus de Kesteven,' co. Linc., 1273. A.

Marvin, Mervin, Mirfin, Mervyn, Murfin.—Bapt. 'the son of Merfin' or 'Mervyn' (Yonge, ii. 154-6). The Brittany form of this famous name was Merlin. Miss Yonge says Mervyn is still in use in Wales as a font-name. The story of 'Mervyn Clytheroe' has made the name familiar to modern ears; cf. Dolphin, Turpin, or Halpin, the suffix in all three cases being *-fin*. The Yorkshire form of the surname to-day is Murfin or Mirfin, practically the

same as Mirfyn in the 14th century.

Mervin (without surname), rector of Chester-le-Street, 1085: DDD. ii. 144.
Matilda Marwyn, co. Hunts, 1273. A.
Willelmus Mirfyne, *smyght*, 1379: P. T. Yorks. p. 69.
Johannes Myrfyn, 1379: ibid. p. 16.
Thomas Mirfyn, 1379: ibid. p. 50.
Edmund Marvyn, or Marwyn, 1537: Reg. Univ. Oxf. i. 189.
1564. Married—Danyell Ashpoole and Agnes Morfyn: St. Jas. Clerkenwell, iii. 2.
1635. James Marvyn and Eliz. Phillpott: Marriage Lic. (London), ii. 223.
1692. Bapt. — John, s. John Mirfin, *butcher*: St. Peter, Cornhill, ii. 16.
1699. Mervin Perry, vicar of Dyrham, co. Glouc.: Atkyns' Hist. Glouc. p. 216.
1710. Bapt.—Ann, d. Daniel Murfin: St. Peter, Cornhill, ii. 28.
London, 5, 0, 1, 0, 1; West Rid. Court Dir. (Murfin), 3; Sheffield (Mervine), 24; (Mirfin), 2; Philadelphia, 4, 1, 0, 0, 0.

Marwood.—Local, 'of Marwood,' a parish in co. Devon, four miles from Barnstaple. Also, a township in the parish of Gainford, co. Durham.

William Marwod, *pulter*, 6 Edw. II: Freemen of York, i. 14.
1538. William Marwode, or Merwodde: Reg. Univ. Oxf. i. 190.
1604. Thomas Marwoode, co. Devon: ibid. vol. ii. pt. ii. p. 278.
1674. Richard Covere and Jane Marrwood: Marriage Alleg. (Canterbury), p. 236.
1687. George Marwood and Constance Spencer: ibid. p. 296.
MDB. (co. Dorset), 1; (North Rid. Yorks), 2.

Marx.—Bapt.; v. Mark.

Marychurch. — Local, ' of Marychurch,' a parish in co. Devon, two miles from Torbay (St. Marychurch). A family sprung from this place seem to have settled some centuries ago in co. Pembroke, where they attained to a position of importance.

1520. Anne, daughter and heiress of Rudd (or Read), of Rock Castle, Esq., married John St. Marichurch.
1684. Bapt.—Morrish, s. Jenkin Marychurch: Reg. Haverfordwest Parish Ch.
1686. — Elizabeth, d. William Marychurch: ibid.

The above references have been supplied to me by Mr. Marychurch, of Oxford.

1613. Thomas Marichurch: Reg. Univ. Oxf. vol. ii. pt. ii. p. 330.
Oxford, 1; MDB. (West Rid. Yorks), 1; (co. Pemb.), 1.

Marygold; v. Marigold.

Maryon; v. Marion.

Mascall, Maskall, Maskell, Maskill.—Occup. 'the marshal' (q.v.). No doubt, as suggested by Mr. Lower, a corruption of Marscal. 'I believe that the Mascalls of Kent and Sussex were originally Marshalls. There is armorial evidence of this, and in a document of the 16th century I find the name written Marscal, which is about midway between Mareschal and Mascall': Patr. Brit. p. 218. There is no need to go back to Mareschal, as Marscal existed so early as the 13th century, and one of my instances belongs to co. Sussex.

Gilbert le Marscale, co. Sussex, 1273. A.
Thomas le Marsscal, co. Camb., ibid.
Peter Marscallus, co. Oxf., ibid.

The transition from Marscal to Mascall was inevitable.

1360. Simon Maschal, rector of St. Buttolph the Abbot, Norwich: FF. v. 442.
1550. Bapt.—Sara Mascall: St. Peter, Cornhill, i. 5.
1551. Buried — Joane Mascoll: ibid. p. 110.
1565. Married—Harrye Maskolle and Alyce Walker: St. Michael, Cornhill, p. 9.
London, 2, 3, 4, 0; Leeds (Maskill), 2; New York, 0, 1, 1, 1; Boston (U.S.), 1, 0, 4, 0.

Mash, Mashman.—These are mere provincialisms of Marsh and Marshman, q.v.

1625. Richard Mash and Lucretia Johnson: Marriage Lic. (London), ii. 156.
1692. Bapt.—John, s. John Mash: St. Jas. Clerkenwell, ii. 345.
1758. Married — Perfect Mash and Familiar Ford: St. Geo. Han. Sq. i. 77.
1764. — William Mash and Susanna Wright: ibid. p. 137.
London, 7, 1; New York, 2, 1.

Masham, Massam.—Local, 'of Masham,' a market-town and parish in N. Rid. Yorks.

Robert de Masseham, *faber*, 8 Edw. III: Freemen of York, i. 28.
1606-7. William Masham, London: Reg. Univ. Oxf. vol. ii. pt. ii. p. 293.
1660. Buried—John Masham: Kensington Ch. p. 130.
1685. Sir Francis Masham and Mrs. Damaris Cudworth: Marriage Alleg. (Canterbury), p. 205.
London, 2, 1; Philadelphia, 0, 3.

Mashmaker. — Occup. One who steeped malt, or perhaps a maker of mash-vats. In any case, connected with the brewing trade. This curious name is found in the Saint Edmund's Gild, Bishop's Lynn, the ordinances of which are signed by 'Johannes Mashemaker' (English Gilds, p. 96) ; v. *maschel* and *maschyn* in Prompt Parv.

Mashrudder. — Nick. for one who steeped malt, or maschscherel, *remulus*' : Prompt. Parv. Mr. Way adds in a note, 'This term evidently implies the implement used for mashing or mixing the malt, to which, from resemblance in form, the name *rudder* is also given.' In Withal's little Dictionary, enlarged by W. Clerk, among the instruments of the brewhouse is given 'a rudder, or instrument to stir the meash-fatte with, *motaculum*.'

1517. Robert Mashorudder, co. York : W. 11, p. 186.
1536. Laurence Maschrodder, co. York : ibid. p. 226.
1584. Peter Mashrether, of Chigwell, Essex, *yeoman*, and Judith Bacon : Marriage Lic. (London), i. 130.

Maskall, -kell; v. Mascall.

Maskelyne. — Bapt. 'the son of Masculin.'

Henry Maskelyn, co. Wilts, Hen. III-Edw. I. K.
Masculin de la More, co. Worc., 2 Hen. IV : v. Pedigree of Bishop, Visitation of London, 1633-5, vol. i. p. 74.
1655. Buried — Mrs. Sarah Masklin : St. Michael, Cornhill, p. 247.
London, 2.

Maskill ; v. Mascall.

Maslen, Maslin. — Bapt. 'the son of Mazelin,' probably for Marcelin, a dim. of Marcel ; v. Masson (2).

Mazelin de Rissebi, co. Suff., 1273. A.
John Mazelyn, co. Oxf., ibid.
1629. Bapt.—Rachell, d. John Maslin : St. Michael, Cornhill, p. 120.
1772. Married — Thomas More and Esther Maslin : St. Geo. Han. Sq. p. 219.
1780. — William Maslem and Ann Allaway : ibid. p. 311.
London, 6, 5 ; Philadelphia, 0, 1.

Mason. — (1) Occup. 'a stone-mason, a woodmason.' M.E. *mason*; O.F. *maçon, masson* (Skeat).

Gotte le Mazoun, co. Hunts, 1273. A.
Nicholas le Macun, co. Bucks, ibid.

Adam le Mazon, 1307. M.
Willelmus Mason, *mason*, 1379 : P. T. Yorks. p. 282.
(2) Bapt. 'the son of Matthew.' O.F. Mayheu, shortened into Maye; v. May (2) and Mayson (1).
Roger fil. Maye, co. Salop, 1273. A.
1579. Bapt. — Eliz., d. John Mason : Kensington Ch. p. 8.
London, 137 ; Boston (U.S.), 187.

Massam ; v. Masham.

Masser. — Occup. 'the mercer,' a Lanc. provincialism for mercer (Halliwell). In the registers of the Parish Church, Ulverston, N. Lanc., I have frequently seen in entries of the 17th and 18th centuries a man described as a 'marcer.'

1727. Bapt. — Susanna, d. Thomas Masser : St. Jas. Clerkenwell, ii. 169.
1744. Married — John Bowdery and Ann Massar : St. Geo. Han. Sq. i. 32.
West Rid. Court Dir., 2 ; Philadelphia, 1.

Massey, Massie. — Local, 'of Mascy.' A Norman surname that came over with William. Hamon Massie acquired Dunham, in co. Ches., and the patronymic spread rapidly. Mr. Lower points out several places in Normandy whence the name may have come, 'viz. Macé-sur-Orne, Macei in the arrondissement of Avranches, Marcei in that of Argentan, and Marcei, on the Broise, near the town of Avranches.

Robert de Mascy, of Tatton, co. Ches., 1353 : Hist. of East Ches. ii. 157 n.
Ameria de Mascy, 1353 : ibid.
1583. James Massye, co. Lanc. : Reg. Univ. Oxf. vol. ii. pt. ii. p. 131.
1588. Gerard Massye, co. Ches. : ibid. p. 167.
1592. John Massie, of Shocklach, *husbandman* : Wills at Chester, i. 132.
1609. Alice Massey, of Manchester : ibid. p. 133.
London, 20, 1 ; Oxford, 0, 1.

Massingberd, Massingbird. — ? —. I can discover nothing satisfactory with regard to this name. I suspect it came at some fairly early period from the Low Countries. As Massingham (q.v.), however, is a parish in co. Norf., it may be that Massingberd was originally some spot called Massingbergh in co. Linc. Indeed Massingberg is in MDB. (co.

Lincoln), only I fear it is a misprint.

1581. Thomas Massingberd, co. Linc. : Reg. Univ. Oxf. vol. ii. pt. ii. p. 114.
1681. Married—William Ash and Eliz. Massinbird, of Northampt.: St. Peter, Cornhill, ii. 55.
1701. Buried — Daniel, son of John Masingbard, *gent.* : FF. iv. 501.
1774. — Charles Burrell Massingberd and Ann Blackall : St. Geo. Han. Sq. i. 248.
Crockford, 1, 0 ; MDB. (co. Linc.), 0, 1.

Massinger. — Offic. ; for Messenger, q.v.

Massingham. — Local, 'of Massingham,' two parishes in co. Norfolk.

Walter de Massingham, co. Camb., 1273. A.
Adam de Messingham, co. Linc., ibid.
John de Messingham, London, ibid.
Thomas de Messyngham, 1379 : P. T. Yorks. p. 49.
1799. Married — Henry Ford and Harriot Massingham : St. Geo. Han. Sq. ii. 207.
London, 2 ; Oxford, 1.

Masson. — (1) Occup. 'the mason.' O.F. *maçon* or *masson* ; v. Mason.

Osbert le Masson, co. Oxf., 1273. A.
Richard le Massun, co. Salop, ibid.
John le Mascon, co. Southampt., ibid.
Ricardus de Brodesworth, *masson*, 1379 : P. T. Yorks. p. 73.

(2) Bapt. 'the son of Masse,' a nick. of Marcel. Massilia is found likewise for Marcilia (A. ii. 580).

Duce fil. Masse, co. Hunts, 1273. A.
1685. Peter Masson and Mary le Febvre : Marriage Alleg. (Canterbury), p. 282.
London, 3 ; Philadelphia, 7.

Master. — Offic. 'the master,' a superior, a teacher, 'Maystyr, *magister, pedagogus, didascolus*' : Prompt. Parv. v. Masters.

Agnes le Maistre, co. Camb., 1273. A.
Thomas Magister, co. Camb., ibid.
Hamund le Mester, co. Hunts, ibid.
Roger le Mestre, co. Hunts, ibid.
John Hume le Mestre, C. R., 2 Edw. I.
John Maistre, C. R., 17 Ric. II.
Thomas le Mayster, C. R., 1 Hen. IV. pt. i.
Johannes Mastere, 1379 : P. T. Yorks. p. 14.
1562. Buried—Anne, d. Thomas Master, *embroderer* : St. Mary Aldermary (London), p. 134.
1746. Married — Edward Raby and Mary Master : St. Jas. Clerkenwell, iii. 276.
Crockford, 6 ; Philadelphia, 5.

Masterman.—(1) Official, 'the master,' a superior, modern 'gaffer,' American 'boss,' with augmentative *man* as in merchantman. (2) Occup. 'the master's man,' a servant; cf. Vickerman, Matthewman, &c. This is the more probable derivation; v. Ladyman for convincing proof.

Richard Maysterman, co. Camb., Pardons Roll, 6 Ric. II.
Johannes Maysterman, 1379: P. T. Yorks. p. 224.
Willelmus Mausterman, 1379: ibid. p. 231.
1748. Married — Robert Eastee and Sarah Masterman: St. Jas. Clerkenwell, iii. 280.
1782. — William Springal and Ann Masterman: St. Geo. Han. Sq. i. 335.
London, 6; Ripon, 2; New York, 1.

Masters, Masterson.—Nick. 'the master's son' (v. Master); cf. Taylorson, Clerkson, Smithson, Millerson. Considering the large number of early and later entries relating to this surname, it is curious that Masterson should be so rarely met with in the present generation in England. It flourishes, I find, in New York. But nomenclature is full of surprises of this kind.

Hugh fil. Magistri, co. Devon, 1273. A.
Thomas fil. Magistri, co. Linc., ibid.
Henry fil. Robert Magistri, co. Camb., ibid.
John Maisterson, 17 Edw. II: Freemen of York, i. 21.
Roger le Maistressone. G.
Dorothy Masterson, temp. Eliz. Z.
Robert Maystrson. XX. 1.
John Maysterson, C. R., 3 Hen. VI.
1583. Married — John Kilbecke and Cecily Masterson: St. Jas. Clerkenwell, iii. 10.
1616. William Pym and Eliz. Masters: Marriage Lic. (London), ii. 43.
Thomas Maisterson, of Wich Malbank, co. Chester: Wills at Chester (1660–80), p. 177.
London, 29, 1; New York, 8, 66.

Matchet; v. Madgett.

Mather.—Of this surname, so well known in co. Lanc., there seem to be two origins, one occupative, the other baptismal. But there is distinctly more evidence on behalf of the first. (1) Occup. 'the mather,' i.e. the mower; cf. Mawer, q.v., probably a general term for a husbandman. We still use *math* or *after-math* in poetry. Mr. J.

Paul Rylands, F.S.A., supplies me with my first two and most important references.

'16 August, 5 Hen. V. (1417). Writ to the Sheriff of Lancashire, commanding him to attach . . . Mathew le Madour, of Culcheth, husbandman; Ric. le Madour, of Culcheth, husbandman': Risley Charters, in the possession of Mr. Ireland Blackburne, of Hale.
Johannes Madyr, 1379: P. T. Yorks. p. 202.
Thomas Madour, 1379: ibid. p. 204.
1582. Roger Mather, of Leigh, co. Lanc.: Wills at Chester, i. 134.
1616. Ellis Mather, of Liverpool: ibid. p. 133.

(2) Bapt. 'the son of Madur.' I have only one clear reference, and it concerns co. Hunts. The genitive of this would be Mathers; cf. Williams, Jones.

Emma fil. Madur, co. Hunts, 1273. A.
1635. Married — Roland Mather and Eliz. Gibson: St. Peter, Cornhill, i. 255.
London, 12, 2; Liverpool, 6, 0; New York, 19, 6.

Matheson, Mathison, Mathieson. — Bapt. 'the son of Mathew,' from the popular form Mathie. For further instances, v. Matthey.

John fil. Mathie, co. Wilts, 1273. A.
Henry fil. Mathie, co. Oxf., ibid.
Herbert fil. Mathey, co. Devon, ibid.
1601. Robert Mathison, co. York: Reg. Univ. Oxf. vol. ii. pt. ii. p. 251.
1802. Married—Gilbert Mathison and Catherine Farquhar: St. Geo. Han. Sq. ii. 257.
London, 3, 2, 3; Boston (U.S.), 7, 4, 4.

Mathew, Mathews, Mathewson, Matthew, Matthews, Matthewson, Mathewes.—Bapt. 'the son of Mathew.' Found in French and English forms in large quantities in the early registers. The nicks. and dims. also are numerous, as the pages of this dictionary will show. The two chief nicks. were Mat (English) and May (French). Mathew or Mayheu was exceedingly popular with our forefathers. As Miss Yonge reminds us, some form or other of

'Matthew, Mark, Luke, and John
Bless the bed I sleep upon'

has existed for centuries.

Matheu Robert, 1379: P. T. Yorks. p. 174.

Willelmus Matheu, 1379: ibid.
Agnes Mathewe, 1379: ibid. p. 47.
Ricardus fil. Mathei, 1379: ibid. p. 184.
1559. Married — Robert Mathewson and Joane Goringe: St. Thomas the Apostle (London), p. 3.
London, 8, 39, 4, 5, 143, 1, 1.

Mathias.—Bapt. 'the son of Mathias'; v. Mathew.

1807. Married—George Mathias and Mary Dennison: St. Geo. Han. Sq. ii. 373.
London, 6; New York, 6.

Matkin.—Bapt. 'the son of Mathew,' from nick. Mat, and dim. Mat-kin; cf. Watkin, Wilkin, &c.

Richard Matkyn, temp. Eliz. ZZ.
Jeremiah Matkyn, ibid.
1584. Richard Price and Martha Matkyns: Marriage Lic. (London), i. 132.
1614. Francis Matkin, New Coll. Oxf.: Reg. Univ. Oxf. vol. ii. pt. iii. p. 333.
1618. John Matking, co. Linc.: ibid. vol. ii. pt. ii. p. 370.
West Rid. Court Dir., 1; London, 3.

Matley.—Local, 'of Matley,' a township in the parish of Mottram, co. Ches.

William de Mattelegh, 1316: East Ches. ii. 157.
Hugh de Mattelegh, 1316: ibid. ii. 155.
Richard de Mattlegh, 1300: ibid. ii. 155.
1633. James Matley, of Rixton, *husbandman*: Wills at Chester, ii. 151.
1635. Alice Matley, of Bostock, co. Ches.: ibid.
1794. Married—Matthew Matley and Martha Bothamly: St. Geo. Han. Sq. ii. 111.
Manchester, 3; New-York, 1.

Maton.—Bapt. 'the son of Matthew,' from nick. Mat, dim. Mat-on. Alison is still the dim. of Alice in Scotland. For further instances, v. Mattin and Mattinson.

William Matun, co. Norf., 1273. A.
Robertus Mathon, 1379: ibid. p. 137.
Willelmus Mathon, 1379: ibid. p. 198.
1581. Edward Maton, co. Wilts: Reg. Univ. Oxf. vol. ii. pt. ii. p. 115.
1588. William Maton, co. Wilts: ibid. p. 167.
1683. John Maton and Mary Thompson: Marriage Alleg. (Canterbury), p. 3.
London, 3.

Matterson.—Bapt. 'the son of Matthew,' v. Mathew. A Yorkshire form of Matthewson or Mattinson; cf. Dickenson, Catterson, and

Patterson for Dickinson, Cattinson, and Pattinson :

London, 2 ; York, 6.

Matthew, &c. ; v. Mathew.

Matthewman.—Occup. ' the servant or labourer of Matthew'; cf. Perryman and Addyman. This is one of the most familiar representatives of this class of surname. Its origin as here deduced admits of no doubt. Perhaps the following instance will best exemplify the circumstances under which such a surname arose :

Matheus de Lofthous, *firmarius*, 1379: P. T. Yorks. p. 241.
Willelmus Mathewman, 1379 : ibid.
Magota Mathewoman, 1379 : ibid.

Here are Mathew himself, the farmer, William his hind, and Magot his kitchen wench. The two servants took their surname from the position they occupied to their master.

Cf. Willelmus Thomasman, 1379 : P. T. Yorks. p. 210.
Ricardus Watman, 1379 : ibid.
Thomas Robertman, 1379 : ibid. p. 293.
Hugo Mathewman, 1379 : ibid. p. 248.

The master's name almost immediately precedes in each case. Matthewman is still one of the leading indigenous surnames of Yorkshire.

1762. Married — Thomas Mathewman and Ann Colgate : St. Geo. Han. Sq. i. 111.
London, 3 ; West Rid. Court Dir., 10.

Matthey, Matthes. — Bapt. ' the son of Matthew,' popularly Matthey. The final s in Matthes is genitive, as in Matthews, Williams, Jones, &c.

Mathy del Jarty, co. Devon, 1273. A.
Hugh fil. Mathey, co. Oxf., ibid.
William Mathy, co. Wilts, ibid.
Henry Matthe, co. Camb., ibid.
Agnes uxor Mathie, 1379 : P. T. Yorks. p. 27.
1771. Married — Henry Matthey and Ann Aston : St. Geo. Han. Sq. i. 205.
1786. — Charles Mathis and Mary Dean : ibid. p. 385.
London, 3, 5 ; Boston (U.S.), 0, 1.

Mattin, Mattinson, Mattison.—Bapt. ' the son of Matthew,' from nick. Matt, dim. Matt-in or Maton (q.v.); cf. Colin, Robin, Alison, &c.

The first three following belonged to one village :

Robertus Maton, 1379 : P. T. Yorks. p. 137.
Adam Mathin, 1379 : ibid.
Johannes Mathin, 1379 : ibid.
Johannes Mathon, 1379 : ibid. p. 183.
Willelmus Mathon, 1379 : ibid. p. 198.
Thomas Mateson, 1379 : ibid. p. 195.
1672. Bapt. — Thomas, s. Thomas Mattison : St. Jas. Clerkenwell, p. 275.
1783. Married — John Crawford and Isabella Mattison : St. Geo. Han. Sq. p. 343.
London, 0, 2, 1 ; Philadelphia, 0, 0, 6.

Mattock, Mattocks, Mattick, Mattox.—Bapt. ' the son of Madoc ' ; v. Maddock, Maddox, and Maddick, of which these are sharpened forms.

1687. Oliver Mattox and Alice Westwood : Marriage Alleg. (Canterbury), p. 33.
1750. Married—George Mattocks and Eliz. Restell : St. Geo. Chap. Mayfair, p. 166.
1753. — Francis Stewart and Mary Mattax : ibid. p. 249.
1802. — Robert Teasdale and Sarah Mattock : St. Geo. Han. Sq, ii, 263.
London, 2, 5, 1, 0 ; Bristol, 0, 0, 1, 0 ;
Philadelphia, 1, 0, 0, 2.

Matts, Mattson, Matson.— Bapt. ' the son of Matthew,' from the nick. Mat; v. Mattin.

Adam Matte, co. Wilts, 1273. A.
Thomas Mateson, 1379 : P. T. Yorks. p. 195.
Marmaduke Matteson, co. York. W. 16.
Anne Mattson, co. York, ibid.
Roger Matson, of Cocken, Furness, 1605 : Lancashire Wills at Richmond, p. 193.
Robert Mattson, of Cockon, Furness, 1673 : ibid.
1729. Married—John Matts and Sarah Pickett : St. Antholin (London), p. 143.
Sheffield, 3, 0, 2 ; Sheffield, 0, 1, 0;
New York, 0, 1, 4 ; Boston (U.S.), 0, 6, 4.

Maud, Maude, Mawd, Maudson, Mawson.—Bapt. ' the son of Matilda,' of which a popular form was Maud. Fr. Mathilde, Mahaud (Yonge, ii. 415).

Maud Gladewyse, Close Roll, 7 Edw. II.
Geoffrey Maude, co. Hunts, 1273. A.
Robertus Maweson, 1379 : P. T. Yorks. p. 219.
Johannes Mawde, 1379 : ibid. p. 184.
Willelmus Mawde, 1379 : ibid. p. 198.
1646. Bapt. — Elizabeth, d. James Maude : St. Michael, Cornhill, p. 134.

1682. Married—Thomas Mawson and Elizabeth Holden : ibid. p. 43.
London, 3, 7, 0, 1, 4 ; Leeds, 4, 5, 0, 1, 7 ; Philadelphia, 1, 3, 0, 0, 17.

Maudling.—Bapt. ' the son of Magdalene.' M.E. Maudelein or Magdelaine. The final g is, of course, excrescent, as in Jennings, &c.

' His barge ycleped was the Magdelaine.'
     Chaucer, C. T. 412.
' And also Marie Maudeleyne.'
     Piers P. 10203.

Hence such phrases as 'maudlin sentiment.'

Simon Maudeleyn, co. Oxf., 1273. A.
Maudlin Hoby. V. 2.
Robert Maudelyn. O.
1562. Bapt. — Mawdelyn, d. John Champyon : St. Jas. Clerkenwell, i. 2.
1608. Married—William Marrett and Maudlyn Tatome : ibid. p. 34.
1669. Bapt.—John, s. Thomas Maudlin : ibid. ii. 239.
1674. — Mary, d. Richard and Avis Maudlin : ibid. p. 267.
1696. Married — John Lokwex and Maudlin Lernoult : St. Michael, Cornhill, p. 49.
London, 1.

Maudsley, Mawdsley, Maudslay, Mawdesley.—Local, ' of Mawdesley,' a village parish in the old mother parish of Croston, co. Lanc., eight miles from Chorley. The place originated a surname at an early period.

Adam de Moudesley, 35 Hen. III : Baines' Lanc. ii. 118.
William Mawdsley, of Mawdsley, 1584 : Wills at Chester (1545-1620), p. 134.
Robert Mawdsley, of Mawdsley, 1617 : ibid.
1605. Thomas Mawdisley, Bras. Coll. : Reg. Univ. Oxf. vol. ii. pt. ii. p. 283.
1671. Thomas Mawdesley and Ann Cary : Marriage Lic. (Faculty Office), p. 118.
Manchester, 2, 2, 0, 1 ; London, 3, 1, 0, 0.

Maudson.—Bapt. ' the son of Maud ' ; v. Maud and Mawson.

Sheffield, 1.

Mauger, Maugerson.—Bapt. ' the son of Malger ' or ' Mauger.' Malger, Archbishop of Rouen, opposed William's marriage (Freeman, Norm. Conq. iii. 94); v. Major. As a personal name Mauger lasted till the 18th century in the Vavasour family (v. Vavasseur).

Malger le Clerk, co. Bucks, 1273. A.
Thomas fil. Mauger, co. Norf., ibid.
Mauger (without surname), co. Oxf., ibid.
Mauger (without surname), co. Hunts, ibid.
Walter Mauger, co. Oxf., ibid.
Mauger fil. Elie, c. 1300. M.
Mauger le Vavasour. J.
Hugh Maugason. H.
William Maugerson. FF.
Margre Warner, 1379: P. T. Yorks. p. 38.
Robert Maugere, *smyth*, 1379: ibid. p. 70.
Morker Baynbrigg, 1379: ibid. p. 259.
1569. Bapt. — Margery, d. James Mawger, or Maugere: St. Jas. Clerkenwell, i. 5.
London, 1, 0; Philadelphia, 14, 0.

Maul, Maule, Maull, Mawle.
—Local, 'of Maule,' 'from the lordship of Maule, near Paris,' says Lower, and adds, 'According to Douglas's Peerage of Scotland, Guarin de Maule, a younger son of Arnold, lord of Maule, accompanied William to the Conquest of England. Robert de Maule, his son, accompanied David I into Scotland, and obtained from him a grant of lands in Lothian.'

Xp̃ia de Maulea, co. Essex, 1273. A.
Cristiana de Maule, co. Hertf., 20 Edw. I. R.
1587. Married — Thomas Maull and Anne Atkinsonne : St. Peter, Cornhill, i. 236.
1602. George Maull, co. Essex, and Suzanna Herdde: Marriage Lic. (London), i. 273.
1619. Thomas Maule, co. Salop: Reg. Univ. Oxf. vol. ii. pt. ii. p. 376.
1782. Married — Henry Maule and Hannah Rawson: St. Geo. Han. Sq. i. 339.
London, 1, 4, 1, 0; MDB.(co.Northampt.) (Mawle), 5; Philadelphia, 12, 18, 42, 0.

Maunder, Mander.—Occup.
(?) 'the maunder,' a maker of baskets called *maunds*. Lower says, 'Maunder, a beggar; O.E. *maund*, to beg.' I strongly suspect my own interpretation to be the true one, although I have no early instances. 'Mawnd, skype, *sportula*': Prompt. Parv. Mr. Way, commenting on this word, adds, 'Caxton says, in the Book for Travellers, "Ghyselin the mande maker (*corbillier*) hath sold his vannes, his mandes (*corbilles*) or corffes."' This is strong evidence. In Ulverston registers to this day

a maker of *swills* (i.e. baskets) is set down as a *swiller*, not a swill-maker.

1566. Richard Maunder, co. Herts, and Margery Graves : Marriage Lic. (London), i. 34.
1583. Robert Maunder, co. Devon : Reg. Univ. Oxf. vol. ii. pt. ii. p. 129.
1683. Buried—Sarah, wife of Michaill Maunder: St. Mary Aldermary, p. 195.

Of course Maunder and Mander are the same :

1664. Buried—Elisha, s. George and Barbara Mander : St. Antholin (London), p. 91.
1665. — Barbery Maunder : ibid. p. 92.

We may take for granted that Barbara and Barbery refer to the same woman.

London, 11, 9; MDB. (co. Devon), 9, 0; New York, 0, 4; Boston (U.S.), 1, 0.

Maunsell ; v. Mancell.

Maurice.—Bapt. 'the son of Maurice'; v. Morris.

William fil. Maurici, co. Hunts, 1273. A.
Richard fil. Maurycii, co. Camb., ibid.
Peter fil. Maurice, co. Linc., ibid.
1678. Robert Maurice and Frances King : Marriage Alleg. (Canterbury), p. 290.
1754. Married — Thomas Reeve and Margaret Maurice: St. Geo. Chap. Mayfair, p. 276.
London, 7 ; New York, 13.

Maw, Mawe.—Local, 'at the maw,' i.e. *mow*, a stack of hay or corn; cf. Mawer for Mower. We still sing of the 'barley-mow.' This surname is very strongly represented in co. Lincoln.

Alice de la Mawe, co. Suff., 1273. A.
William de la Mawe, co. Suff., ibid.
Sibill de la Mawe, co. Suff., ibid.
William de la Mawe, bailiff of Yarmouth, 1275 : FF. xi. 322.
William atte Mawe, bailiff of Yarmouth, 1354 : ibid. p. 323.
Willelmus Mawe, 1379 : P. T. Yorks. p. 217.
1663. Bapt.—Margarett, d. John Mawe: St. Jas. Clerkenwell, i. 217.
1674. Thomas Mawe and Mary Monke: Marriage Alleg. (Canterbury), p. 227.
London, 5, 1 ; MDB. (Suffolk), 1, 0 ; (Lincoln), 33, 0; Boston (U.S.), 1, 0.

Mawby, Mawbey.—Local, 'of Mautby,' a village and parish in co. Norfolk. The *t* has been omitted in modern spelling. In some instances Mawby will represent Maltby, q.v.

Walter de Mauteby, co. Norf., 1273. A.
Robert de Mauteby, co. Norf., ibid.

Simon de Maudeby, 10 Ric. I, co. Norf.: FF. xi. 226.
Robert de Mauteby, 4 Hen. III, co. Norf. : ibid.
1755. Married—Jeffray Edwards and Mary Mawby : St. Geo. Han. Sq. i. 55.
MDB. (Norfolk), 2, 0 ; (Lincoln), 5, 0 ; London, 2, 1 ; New York, 0, 5 ; Philadelphia, 2, 0.

Mawditt.—Local, ' de Mauduit,' a Domesday surname. At first sight this appears to be a dim. of Maud. This is not the case. It is well represented as a local surname in the Hundred Rolls (A.) and in many guises. Only one entry in the London Directory (a confectioner) preserves its memory, 'sic transit gloria mundi.' William Mauduith was chamberlain to William the Conqueror.

William de Maudut, co. Salop, 1273. A.
Flaundrina Mauduyt, co. Bedf., ibid.
John Maudeyt, co. Bucks, ibid.
Gilbert Maudit, co. Essex, ibid.
Johanna Mawduyt, 1379 : P. T. Yorks. p. 241.
Robertus Maudyt, 1379 : ibid. p. 60.
1616. John Everard and Elizabeth Mauditt : Marriage Lic. (London), ii. 46.
1635. William Bathurst and Eliz. Mawdett: ibid. p. 225.
Jasper Mauditt, 1687 : Lanc. and Ches. Rec. Soc. xi. 77.
1752. Buried—Elizabeth Mauduit: St. Dionis Backchurch (London), p. 318.
London, 1.

Mawdsley ; v. Maudsley.

Mawer.—Occup. 'the mower'; v. *mow* (Skeat). This formerly common surname seems to have become lost in Moore, which was a very natural result. It is found in its original form but rarely.

Rogerus Hamerton, *mawer*, 1379 : P. T. Howdenshire, p. 14.
Henricus Mawer, 1379 : P. T. Yorks. p. 127.
Johannes Rayner, *mawer*, 1379 : ibid. p. 31.
Robertus Mawer, 1379 : ibid. p. 32.
Robert Dymond, *mawer*, 1379 : ibid. p. 91.
1623. John Mawer, *haberdasher*, and Sarah Woollet : Marriage Lic. (Westminster), p. 29.
1676. Maurice Jarvis and Eliz. Mawer: Marriage Alleg. (Canterbury), p. 256.
London, 4 ; Oxford, 2.

Mawle ; v. Maul.

Mawley.—Local, ' de Mauley.' Mr. Lower says that Peter de Mauley, a squire of King John,

who was employed to murder Prince Arthur, was a native of Poitou. He received much land from the king in the West of England.

Peter de Maulley, co. Somerset, 1273. A.
Peter de Maulay, co. Sussex, Hen. III-Edw. I. K.
1717. Bapt.—Joyce, d. Thomas Mauley: St. Jas. Clerkenwell, ii. 101.
1787. Married—Thomas Oakley and Barbara Mawley: St. Geo. Han. Sq. i. 198.
London, 3; Philadelphia, 3.

Mawson, Mawsom.—Bapt. 'the son of Matilda' (v. Maud for instances). In Mawsom *m* takes the place of *n*, as in Ransom and Hansom for Ranson and Hanson; cf. also Sansom.

1692. Bapt. — Thomas, s. Samuel Mauson: St. Jas. Clerkenwell, p. 348.
Leeds, 7, 0; West Rid. Court Dir., 14, 1; Philadelphia, 17, 0.

Mawtus.—Local, 'of the malthouse.' This, of course, became Malthus (q.v.) and then Mawtus; cf. provincial *sawt* for salt.

Miniskip, near Ripon, 1.

Maxey, Maxcy, Maxcey.—Local, 'of Maxey,' a parish in co. Northampton. A member of this family seems to have settled early in London, whence occasional registrations in the City churches. I furnish a few instances out of many:

1575. Married—John Slatur and Eliz. Maxse: St. Antholin (London), p. 24.
1658. Bapt.—John, s. Ralph Maxee: St. Jas. Clerkenwell, i. 201.
1710. Bapt. — Charles, s. Arabella Maxey, *widow*: St. Dionis Backchurch (London), p. 279.
London, 1, 0, 0; New York, 3, 4, 1.

Maxfield.—Local, 'of Macclesfield,' a town in co. Cheshire. In the Index to Earwaker's East Cheshire the author has 'Maxfield; see Macclesfield.'

1539. Bapt—William, s. John Maxfeild: St. Antholin (London), p. 1.
1608. Buried—John Maxfeild, *brasier*, dwellinge in Cornhill: Reg. St. Peter, Cornhill, i. 163.
London, 2; West Rid. Court Dir., 2; Manchester, 2; New York, 4; Boston (U.S.), 6.

May.—(1) Nick. 'the may,' a young lad or girl.

'Thou glory of womanhed, thou faire may.' Chaucer, C. T. 5271.
Richard le Mey, co. Hunts, 1273. A.
Bateman le May, co. Bedf., ibid.
Cristin le May, co. Camb., ibid.
Emma le May, co. Oxf., ibid.

(2) Bapt. 'the son of Matthew.' Just as the English form Matthew took the nick. Mat, so the French form Maheu took the nick. May. This was augmented into Maycock and May-kin; v. Maycock and Makin.

Roger fil. Maye, co. Salop, 1273. A.
John fil. Maye, co. Linc., ibid.
Willelmus May, 1379: P. T. Yorks. p. 145.
May de Hindley, 1379: ibid. p. 278.
May Downe, 1370: ibid. p. 130.
London, 88; New York, 135.

Mayall, Mayhall, Mayell.—? Bapt. 'the son of Michael' (?); v. Miell.

1616. Bapt.—Ann, d. James Mayall: Kensington Ch. p. 18.
London, 1, 0, 5; Manchester, 5, 0, 0; Oldham, 7, 0, 0; Leeds, 0, 1, 0; New York, 0, 0, 1; Boston (U.S.), 8, 0, 0.

Maycock.—Bapt. 'the son of Mathew,' from the nick. May (v. May, 2), and with suffix May-cock; cf. Wil-cock, Dan-cock, Jeff-cock, &c. In some parts of Lancashire and Yorkshire the form was Mycock and Mocock; v. Mycock.

Hugh Maykoc, co. Bedf., 1273. A.
John Maykoc, co. Bedf., ibid.
Alicia Makok, 1379: P. T. Howdenshire, p. 15.
1578. William Macock, co. Warw.: Reg. Univ. Oxf. vol. ii. pt. ii. p. 82.
John Macocke, 1643: Reg. St. Dionis Backchurch (London), p. 107.
1680. Thomas Maycocke and Joane Payne: Marriage Alleg. (Canterbury), p. 38.
London, 4; Oxford, 3; New York, 1.

Mayer.—Offic. 'the mayor'; v. Meyer.

London, 19; New York, 258; Boston (U.S.), 18.

Mayes. — Bapt. 'the son of Matthew,' from the nick. May; v. May and Mays.

Mayger.—Bapt.; v. Major.

1568. Buried — Arthure, son of John Mayger, *clothworker*: St. Mary Aldermary, p. 137.
1570. — John, son of William Maygor: ibid. p. 138.
— — Thomas, son of John Maygor, *clothworker*: ibid.
London, 2; Philadelphia, 1.

Mayhew, Mayow, Mayo, Mayhow, Mayho.—Bapt. 'the son of Matthew,' from O.F.Mayheu. It was impossible to keep this surname from corrupted forms. There is probably no connexion with co. Mayo, Ireland, in any single instance.

Adam fil. Maheu, co. Camb., 1273. A.
Robert Maheu, co. Oxf., ibid.
Mayeu de Basingbourne, c. 1300. M.
Johannes Mahewe, 1379: P. T. Yorks. p. 125.
1537. Nicholas Mayowe, or Mayo, or Mayhewe: Reg. Univ. Oxf. i. 188.
1572. Elizabeth, d. of Nowell Mayhew: Reg. St. Columb Major, p. 8.
1580. James, s. of Nowell Mathew: ibid. p. 11.
1641. Married—John Mayhoe and Eliz. Beverley: Kensington Ch. p. 71.
London, 25, 0, 13, 0, 1; New York, 18, 0, 8, 0, 0.

Maykin.—Bapt. 'the son of Matthew'; v. Makin.

Leeds, 1.

Maylin.—Bapt. 'the son of Malin' (v. Mallinson). A variant.

1741. Married — Joseph Maylin and Sarah Leavesley: St. Antholin (London), p. 151.
London, 2; Philadelphia, 1.

Mayman.—Bapt. 'the son of Maymond.' From a forgotten name 'Maymond,' i.e. Magin or Main, *mighty*, and Mund or Mond, *protection*. For other forms, v. Maidment and Maidman; for corruption into -man, cf. Wyman for Wymond, or Osman for Osmond. Mr. Lower has unfortunately permitted himself to write, 'Mayman, probably the superintendent of the sports of May-day': Patr. Brit. p. 221.

Maimon, prior of Castleacre, co. Norf., temp. 1200: FF. viii. 375.
Lucia Meymund, co. Oxf., 1273. A.
Richard Meymund, co. Oxf., ibid.
Alice Maymund, co. Hunts, ibid.
Johannes Maymund, 1379: P. T. Yorks. p. 262.
Johannes Maymond, 1379: ibid. p. 266.
Willelmus Maymund, 1379: ibid. p. 257.

Two centuries later it is found in the last-named county as Mayman.

1541. Antony Mayman, co. York: W. 11, p. 228.
1616. Thomas Bond and Margaret Mayman, widow of John Mayman, *girdler*: Marriage Lic. (London), ii. 43.

Naturally this surname was imitated into Mammon.

1651. Married—John Billing and Margaret Mammon : St. Jas. Clerkenwell, i. 86.

London, 2 ; Dewsbury, 1 ; Philadelphia, 1.

Maynard.—Bapt. 'the son of Maynard' (Yonge, ii. 415).

Maynard de Abyngdon, vicar of Dersingham, co. Norf.: FF. viii. 399.
Maynard de Capella, co. Bucks, 1273. A.
Hugh Maynard, co. Oxf., ibid.
Robert Maignard, co. Wilts, ibid.
Henricus Manerd, 1379 : P. T. Yorks. p. 119.
Johannes Manerd, 1379 : ibid. p. 120.
1609. Married—Mathewe Staples and Alice Maynard : St. Thomas the Apostle (London), p. 11.
1647. — James White and Cathrine Mainard : St. Jas. Clerkenwell, iii. 81.
London, 23 ; Philadelphia, 9 ; Boston (U.S.), 76.

Mayne, Main, Maine, Mann, Manns, Manson.—(1) Bapt. 'the son of Mayne' (Yonge, ii. 415).

Radulphus fil. Main, Pipe Roll, 5 Hen. II.
Walterus fil. Main, ibid.
Matilda Meyn, co. Oxf., 1273. A.
1719. Bapt.—Mary, d. Thomas Manson: St. Jas. Clerkenwell, ii. 112.

(2) Local, 'from Maine,' the French province ; v. Mann (2).

Walter de Man, co. Camb., 1273. A.
Joel de Meyn, co. Devon, ibid.
Roger de Magen, co. Hereford, Hen. III–Edw. I. K.
Cristiana de Manne, co. Hertf., 20 Edw. I. R.
Peter de Manne, co. Suff., Hen. III–Edw. I. K.
Johannes de Manne, 1379: P. T. Yorks. p. 212.
Johannes de Man, 1379 : ibid. p. 233.

For another interpretation of Mann, v. Mann (1).

London, 5, 13, 4, 51, 1, 1 ; New York (Manne), 1 ; Philadelphia, 10, 10, 2, 0, 0, 0.

Mayo(w ; v. Mayhew.

Mayor.—Offic. 'the mayor'; v. Meyer.

Maypowder.—Local, ' of Maypowder,' a parish in co. Dorset.

John Maupudre, co. Soms., 1273. A.
Robert Maupudre, co. Camb., ibid.

Mays, Mayes, Mayse.—Bapt. ' the son of May'; v. May (2). This solution requires no proof. As William became, through its nick. Will, patronymically Wills and Wilson, so Matthew, through its nick. May, became patronymic-

ally Mays, or Mayes, or Mayse. The only difference is that Will is still a nick. of William, while May as a nick. of Matthew (through the O.F. Mayheu) is forgotten. v. Mayhew.

1542. Bapt. — Thomas, s. Richard Mays: St. Antholin (London), p. 3.
1619-20. Richard Mays and Ellen Richmond : Marriage Lic. (London), p. 83.
1655. Buried—Elizabeth Mayes : St. Antholin (London), p. 84.
1682. Married — John Clearke and Anne Mayes : St. Jas. Clerkenwell, p. 196.
London, 4, 11, 2 ; Philadelphia, 13, 1, 0.

Mayson.—(1) Bapt. 'the son of May'; v. May (2).

Cf. Willelmus Mayson, Wigglesworth, 1379 : P. T. Yorks. p. 278.
Maye de Hindley, 1379 : ibid.
Johannes Mayson, 1379 : ibid. p. 204.
William Mayesone, C. R., 7 Edw. II.

(2) Occup. ; for Mason (1), q.v.

Adam de Mortan, mayson, 1371 : P. T. Yorks. p. 37.
1745. Married — Henry Mayson and Mary Joynes : St. Geo. Chap. Mayfair, p. 53.

Mayston, Maidstone.—Local, ' of Maidstone.' There can be no doubt that Mayston is a modern variant of Maidstone, a surname taken from the important town of that name in co. Kent. It is not likely that such a once familiar surname should leave but one representative in the London Directory. Besides, the corruption is a perfectly natural one, and found where we should expect to meet with it, viz. in London and the neighbourhood ; v. Maidstone.

1666-7. John Tibbs and Margaret Maidstone : Marriage Lic. (Canterbury), ii. 96.
1696. Buried—Robert, s. Robert Maidston : St. Antholin (London), p. 111.
1733. Bapt.—Charlotte, d. Nathaniel Maidstone : St. Jas. Clerkenwell, ii. 211.
1745. Married—William Mayston and Easter Donfall : St. Geo. Chap. Mayfair, p. 55.
London, 4, 1.

Mazerer, Mazeliner.—Occup. 'the mazerer' or 'mazeliner,' a manufacturer of mazers or maslins, a bowl or cup maker ; so called because made of maple, which is a knotted wood. 'Masar of woode, masière, hanap': Palsgrave. 'Mazer, a broad standing-cup': New World

of Words. Maslin was a dim., a cup of smaller size.

'They fet him first the swete win, And mede eke in a maselin.'
Chaucer, C. T. 13781.

These bowls are frequently mentioned in early wills and inventories. In my old parish of Ulverston an ancestor of Chancellor Fell bequeathed (1542) 'A masser unto the saide Leonarde after the wedowheade or death of Ann, my wife' (v. my Chronicles of the Town and Church of Ulverston, p. 65). For general information, v. Way's note. Prompt. Parv. p. 328, and Skeat on mazer.

Adam le Mazerer, co. Northampt., 1273. A.
John le Mazerere. N.
William le Mazerer, London. X.
John le Mazelyner, c. 1300. M.
William le Mazeliner, London, 20 Edw. I. R.

Meacham, Mecham.—Local; v. Measham.

Meacock.—Bapt. 'the son of Matthew'; v. Maycock. Meacock is to Maycock as Meakin is to Makin.

1585. John Mecocke, co. Oxf.: Reg. Univ. Oxf. vol. ii. pt. ii. p. 144.
1670. Married—William Mecocke and Mary Fisher: St. Jas. Clerkenwell, iii. 174.
1788. — John Meacock and Amelia King : St. Geo. Han. Sq. ii. 12.
London, 5 ; New York, 1.

Mead, Meade, Meed, Meads.—Local, 'at the mead,' from residence thereby ; M.E. mede, a meadow; v. Meadows and Medd.

William at Mede, 1278. M.
Nicholas atte Mede, co. Soms., 1 Edw. III : Kirby's Quest, p. 236.
Henry del Myde, co. Lanc., 20 Edw. I. R.
Alan atte Mede, C. R., 14 Edw. III. pt. ii.
Willelmus del Mede, 1379 : P. T. Yorks. p. 214.
1552. Bapt.—Andrew Meade : St. Jas. Clerkenwell, i. 1.
1672. John Mede and Jane Wardour : Marriage Alleg. (Canterbury) p. 201.
London, 42, 2, 1, 2 ; Philadelphia, 46, 28, 0, 1.

Meadley.—Local ; v. Medley.

Meadowcroft, Meddowcroft.—Local, 'of Meadowcroft'; v. Metcalf. The Lancashire Meadowcrofts appear to have originated at Meadowcroft, a small estate in the parish of Middleton, near Manchester.

Ricardus de Meducroft, 1379: P. T. Yorks. p. 54.

Willelmus Miducroft, 1379: ibid. p. 67.
Isabella Birch, of Meadowcroft, Middleton, 1615: Wills at Chester (1545-1620), p. 19.

The surname is found in the immediate neighbourhood in the 16th and 17th centuries.

Richard Meadowcroft, of Smethurst, 1581: Wills at Chester (1545-1620), p. 134.
Francis Meadowcroft, of Ratcliffe, 1616: ibid.

The above solution is amply proved by the following entries:

Nicholas de Meducroft, co. Lanc., 20 Edw. I. R.
Roger de Middelton, co. Lanc., ibid.
Adam de Roddes, co. Lanc., ibid.

Rhodes is close by Middleton. The three surnames occur together. The place is again referred to:

'John, son and heir of John de Radclif, of Chaderton, deceased, was born at Medecroft, on Monday before the Purification of the Virgin, 16 Ric. II': Baines' Hist. of Lancashire (Croston's edit.), iii. 97.

Manchester, 9, 1; London, 1, 0; Rochdale, 4, 0; New York, 1, 0; Philadelphia, 10, 0.

Meadows, Meadow.—Local, 'at the meadow' or 'meadows.' The final s is probably not plural, but that so common in local names of a distinctive and specific character; cf. Brooks, Styles, Bridges, Dykes, Sykes, &c. Possibly a patronymic s, as in Williams, Jones, Collins, &c.

John atte Medowe, rector of Metton, co. Norf., 1429: FF. viii. 140.
William att the Meadow, rector of East Beckham, co. Norf.: ibid. p. 87.
1689. Bapt. — William, s. Ralph Meadowes: St. John Baptist on Wallbrook, p. 170.
1719. Married — Philip Lynall and Barbara Medowe: St. Dionis Backchurch, p. 59.
London, 25, 0; Philadelphia, 3, 0.

Meadwell, Medwell.—Local, 'of Meadwell,' which I do not find. But v. Maidwell, of which it may be a variant.

Agnes de Meydewell, co. Oxf., Hen. III-Edw. I. K.
Alanus de Meydewelle, co. Bucks, ibid.
1629. Married — John Hutchens and Margeritt Medwell: St. Michael, Cornhill, p. 26.

1694. Thomas Templer and Eliz. Medwell, co. Northampt.: Marriage Lic. (Faculty Office), p. 212.
London, 1, 0; New York, 0, 1.

Meagre, Meager (?), **Meagreman.**—Nick. 'the meagre,' i.e. the lean, the poor. A sufficiently common sobriquet in the 13th and 14th centuries to ensure its becoming an hereditary surname; cf. Fatt.

Robert le Megre, C. R., 48 Hen. III.
Robert le Megre, co. Leic., Hen. III-Edw. I. K.
William le Megre, co. Oxf., 1273. A.
Hugh le Megre, c. 1300. M.
John le Meaugre. O.
Basilia le Megre. T.
Martin Megreman, C. R., 35 Hen. VI.
1420. John Megre: Cal. of Wills in Court of Husting (2).
1796. Married—Thomas Meager and Amy Hooker: St. Geo. Han. Sq. ii. 143.
London, 0, 3, 0; New York, 0, 1, 0.

Meagresauce.—Nick. One who gave scanty allowance (?). *Meagre*, thin, scanty; *sauce*, salted condiments. v. Meagre.

Peter Meagresause, co. Linc. R.

Meakin, Meakins.—Bapt.'the son of Matthew'; v. Makin and Makins, of which these are but variations.

1729. Married—John Meakins, *Indian weaver*, and Rebecca Jones: St. Geo. Chap. Mayfair, p. 294.
1804. — Samuel Meakin and Mary Ann Kendal: St. Geo. Han. Sq. ii. 298.
London, 4, 1; Boston (U.S.), 0, 2.

Mealman, Mealmonger.—Occup. 'the meal-monger,' a dealer in meal; cf. Cornmonger.

William Meleman: Fines Roll, 8 Ric. II.
John le Melmongere. M.
1499. Geoffrey Meleman: Cal. of Wills in Court of Husting (2).

Meals.—Local, 'at the meols' (i.e. the sands or sand-banks), from residence thereby. On the Cumberland and Lancashire shores are several Meols—Eskmeols and Northmeols being instances. The word is styled Meales (temp. Jas. I; Lanc. and Ches. Records, pt. ii. p. 484) and Meeles (ibid. pt. i. p. 127).

Margery de Meoles, co. Soms., 1 Edw. III: Kirby's Quest, p. 207.
John de Meoles, co. Soms., 1 Edw. III: ibid. p. 208.
1605. Katherine Meoles, of Wallasey: Wills at Chester, i. 135.

1628. William Meoles, of Wallasey, *gent.*: ibid. ii. 152.
1636. John Meoles, of Newton, near Chester, *gent.*: ibid. Liverpool, 2.

Mearbeck, Marbeck.—Local, 'of Mearbeck,' a hamlet in the parish of Settle, W. Rid. Yorks.

Willelmus de Merebeke, 1379: P. T. Yorks. p. 284.
Robertus Merebek, 1379: ibid. p. 287.
Petronilla Merbeke, 1379: ibid. p. 236.
1581. Married — William Grosse and Barbery Marbeck: St. Antholin (London), p. 28.
West Rid. Court Dir., 2, 0.

Mears, Meares.—Local, 'at the mere,' from residence by a pool, with s as customary suffix in local surnames of one syllable; cf. Holmes, Brooks, Briggs, Styles, Sykes, Milnes. Perhaps it represents the patronymic, as in Williams, Jones, Wilkins, &c. Then Mears = Mear's son.

Stephen atte Mere, co. Soms., 1 Edw. III: Kirby's Quest, p. 91.
Gregory de la Mere, co. Wilts, 1273. A.
William ad le Mere, co. Camb., ibid.
Robert atte Meere, C. R., 4 Hen. VI.
Henricus del Mere, 1379: P. T. Yorks. p. 210.
Alex. Atte-mere, rector of Ashwell Thorp, co. Norf., 1337: FF. v. 162.
Henry Meare, of Hough, 1673: Wills at Chester (1660-80), p. 183.
William Meare, of Pott Shrigley, 1673: ibid.
London, 18, 1; Philadelphia, 6, 2.

Measham, Meacham, Meacham.—Local, 'of Measham,' a parish in co. Derby.

London, 0, 0, 5; MDB. (co. Derby), 2, 0, 0; Manchester, 2, 0, 0.

Meatyard. — ? Nick. Until proved local this must be set down in the nickname class. Possibly from the straight back of the original possessor, or his occupation as a draper. The 'meteyard' was the old measuring-stick. 'Ye shall do no unrighteousness in judgement, in meteyard, in weight, or in measure': Lev. xix. 35. A.S. *metgeard*, a measuring rod; M.E. *meten*, to measure; hence to mete out, to distribute impartially. Yard (M.E. *yerde*), a stick, a rod. 'Nothing take ye in the weye, neither yerde, ne scrippe, neither breed, ne money' (Wyclif, Luke ix. 3); v. Skeat, s.v. *mete*; cf. Shakespear, Wagstaff, &c.

1618. Married—John Meatyarde and Anne King : Reg. Broad Chalke, co. Wilts, p. 4.
London, 2.

Medcalf, -calfe, Medcraft.— ? Local; v. Metcalf.

Medd, Meed.—Local, 'at the mead,' i.e. meadow (v. Mead), from residence thereby.

Richard atte Med, co. Oxf., 1273. A.
Philip atte Medde, 1278. M.
Thomas atte Mede : Lay Roll, co. Soms., 1327.
1684. Joseph Mede and Eliz. Dede : Marriage Alleg. (Canterbury), p. 173.
1791. Married—Alexander Macintosh and Eliz. Meed : St. Geo. Han. Sq. ii. 66.
London, 0, 1 ; Crockford, 3, 0 ; Philadelphia, 1, 0.

Medland.—Local, 'of Medland' or 'at the medland,' from residence beside some particular meadowland ; v. Medd.

Walter de Medeland, co. Camb., 1273. A.
1768. Married—John Turner and Eliz. Medlond : St. Geo. Han. Sq. i. 172.
London, 3 ; Philadelphia, 1.

Medler, Medlar.—(1) ? Nick. An obtrusive person, a busybody.

Nicholas de Medler, co. Salop, 1273. A.

(2) Local, ' of Medlar,' a township in the parish of Kirkham, co. Lanc.

Richard de Medler, co. Salop, Hen. III-Edw. I. K.

Query : as both these instances (1) and (2) occur in co. Salop, is not instance (1) a misprint or misreading for *de* Medler? Probably such is the case.

1640. John Hicks and Anne Medler (or Needler ?) : Marriage Lic. (London), ii. 250.
London, 1, 0 ; Philadelphia, 0, 4.

Medley, Meadley. — Local, (1) 'at the mid-ley,' from residence by the middle field ; (2) 'at the mead-ley,' from residence by the meadow pasture.

Simon atte Middele, co. Soms., 1 Edw. I : Kirby's Quest, p. 258.
1578. John Medley : Reg. Univ. Oxf. i. 364.
1792. Married — George Medley and Eliz. Constance : St. Geo. Han. Sq. ii. 84.
London, 1, 1 ; Philadelphia, 2, 0.

Medlicott, Medlycott.— Local, 'of Middle-cote'; cf. Middle-

ditch, &c., and v. Coates and Cotes. I have not discovered this locality, which I doubt not lies in co. Devon, or some adjacent shire.

Richard de Middelcote,co.Dev.,1273. A.
Katherine Medlecoate, married, 1593 : Reg. St. Mary Aldermary (London), p. 9.
1586. Bapt. — Mary, d. Christopher Medlicott : St. Thomas the Apostle (London), p. 11.
London, 4, 1 ; MDB. (co. Soms.), 0, 2.

Medpleck.—Local, ' at the meadow pleck.' ' *Pleck*, a plot of ground, a small enclosure, a field. Co. Warw.' (Halliwell). ' *Plecks*, a term in hay-making applied to the square beds of dried grass. Co. Chester ' (ibid.). v. also *plack* and *plek* in Halliwell.

Jordanus atte Medpleck, co. Oxf., 1273. A.

Medwin.—Bapt. 'the son of Medwin.' One of the many personal names with suffix *-win* ; cf. Godwin, Unwin, Baldwin, and Goldwin. ' In the unreformed calendar the feast of St. Medwyn stands for Jan. 1 ' (Lower). 'St. Mawdwen (or Modwin) was one of St. Patrick's Irish nuns ; and another later Modwin, also Irish, came to England in 840, and educated Edith, daughter of King Ethelwolf, and founded an abbey at Polsworth ' (Yonge, ii. 135).
Modewine, wife of Clement Cotton, C. R., 3 Edw. IV.
1787. Married—John Morris and Patty Medwin : St. Geo. Han. Sq. i. 399.
London, 4.

Mee, Mees, Meeson, Meese. —? Bapt. 'the son of Matthew ' (?). This surname is quite beyond me. I can only suggest that as May, Makin, and Maycock (q.v.) represented Matthew, and as Makin and Maycock are generally found as Meakin and Meacock, so Mee may be also a variant of May. There is no doubt that Matthew, through the O.F. Mayheu, which was popularized in England, had many nick. forms, some of which are now obsolete. The favourite was May, and this would have variants. All this is corroborated by the existence of Mees and Meeson, corresponding to Mayes and Mayson. Circum-

stantial evidence, therefore, is entirely in favour of the above suggested solution.

1608. Robert Meese, co. Oxf. : Reg. Univ. Oxf. vol. ii. pt. ii. p. 302.
William Mee, of March Croft, co. Lancaster, 1613 : Wills at Chester (1545-1620), p. 135.
Hugh Mee, 1615: ibid.
1642. Henry Meese, of Brockhurst, in Pennington : St. Jas. Clerkenwell, ii. 152.
1691. Bapt.—Mary, d. Thomas Meeson : ibid. p. 339.
London, 6, 1, 2, 0 ; Manchester, 8, 0, 1, 0 ; Philadelphia, 2, 1, 0, 0 ; New York, 5, 0, 0, 2.

Meed.—Local ; v. Mead, Medd.

Meek.—Nick. ' the meek '; cf. Humble. ' Meke and mylde ' : Prompt. Parv.

Alicia Meke, *laborer*, 1379 : P. T. Yorks. p. 223.
1692. Married—John Martin and Jane Meek : St. Antholin (London), p. 107.
1697. Anthony Meek and Eliz. Cook : Marriage Lic. (London), ii. 322.
London, 16 ; Manchester, 3 ; New York, 9.

Meggett, Meggott. — Bapt. ' the son of Margaret,' from nick. Meg, and dim. Megg-ot or Megg-et ; v. Maggot.

Robertus Meggot-son, 1379 : P. T. Yorks. p. 119.
1677. Married—George Meggott and Mary Crosse : St. Jas. Clerkenwell, i. 185.
1705. Robert Megott and Patience Holt : Marriage Lic. (London), ii. 334.
London, 1, 0 ; Boston (U.S.), 1, 0.

Meggs, Meggeson, Megson, Meggy.—Bapt. ' the son of Margaret,' from nick. Megg, popularly Meggy ; v. Moxon.

John fil. Megge, co. Oxf., 1273. A.
Robert Megge, co. Bedf., ibid.
John Megge, co. Berks, ibid.
Adam Meggessone, c. 1300. M.
Johannes Mekson, 1379 : P. T. Yorks. p. 216.
Robertus Megson, 1379 : ibid. p. 157.
Johannes Megson, 1379 : ibid.
1578. William Megges and Alice Banckes : Marriage Lic. (London), i. 79.
1735. Married—John Megson and Ann Harrison : St. Jas. Clerkenwell, iii. 263.
London, 4, 1, 1, 2 ; Philadelphia (Meggs), 1 ; New York (Megson), 1.

Megucer.—Occup. 'a leather dresser '; Fr. *mégissier*, a tawer of leather ; v. Whittawer or Whittier. According to Strype, the London ' Company of Megusers ' dealt in the skins of dead horses, and flayed them. He mentions 'Walter le Whitawyer' in the same account (London, ii. 232).

John le Megucer: Munimenta Gildhallae Londoniensis.
Richard le Megucer : ibid.
1272. Norman le Meggecer : Cal. of Wills in Court of Husting.

Meiklejohn, Meiklejon. — Nick.'big John'; one of the Scottish Border names. M.E. *mikel.* Cf. Littlejohn.

Cf. 'To Mickle Willie, £2 0s. 0d., April 23, 1607': Nicolson and Burn, Hist. Westm. and Cumb., vol. i. p. cxx.
'Mekill Henry Nikson,' 1516: TTT. p. 207.
'Mekle Johne Burne in Branxhelm,' 1495 : ibid. p. 188.
London, 1, 0 ; Boston (U.S.), 0, 1.

Melhuish, Melluish, Mellish, Meluish.—Local, 'of Melhuish,' a place in co. Devon.

'Chagkford, xiiᵗ; Churiton, viᵗ; Eghbeare, xiiᵈ; Melehewis, xiiᵈ; Fuleford, viᵈ': Hundred Rolls, 1273, i. 84.
William de Melehywis, co. Devon, Hen. III-Edw. I. K.
John de Melewis, co. Devon, ibid.
Elinora de Melhywys, co. Devon, 1273. A.
1674. Married—Robert Mellish and Anne Smith : St. Michael, Cornhill, p. 40.

Driving through Dalton-in-Furness in Oct. 1887, I saw 'Mellish' over a small shop in the Market-place. I wondered how it had got there. The mystery was easily explained. The town is largely peopled with Cornishmen, who work at the iron-ore mines.

London, 8, 1, 8, 1 ; MDB. (co. Devon), 15, 0, 0, 0 ; Boston (U.S.), (Mellish), 5.

Melladew ; v. Merridew.

Melling.—Local, ' of Melling ': (1) an extensive parish in North Lancashire, six miles from Kirkby-Lonsdale ; (2) a chapelry in the parish of Halsall, six miles from Ormskirk. This has manifestly been the chief source.

Robertus Mellyng', 1379 : P. T. Yorks. p. 113.
Richard Mellinge, 1602 : Guild Rolls, Preston, p. 62.
Alexander Mellinge, fil. ejus, 1602 : ibid.
Reginald Melling, of Liverpool, 1572 : Wills at Chester (1545-1620), p. 135.
John Melling, of Chorley, 1614 : ibid.
John Melling, of Skelmersdale, parish of Ormskirk : ibid.

John Melling, of the parish of Mellinge, 1583 : Lancashire Wills at Richmond, p. 194.
Robert Melling, of Hallett, parish of Melling, 1622 : ibid.
Manchester, 3 ; Liverpool, 8 ; Preston, 10 ; Philadelphia, 7 ; Boston (U.S.), 2.

Mellody, Mellodey, Melody, Melledy.—(1) ? Nick. The same as Mellodew. All the forms are confined to cos. Lanc. and York, where ' Merydewe' existed in the 14th century ; v. Merridew.

'Margaret Mellodey took Bishop's prize for religious knowledge'; Manchester Courier, June 7, 1886.

(2) ? Nick. for a singer or minstrel; M.E. *melodie,* an air, a tune.
Richard Melodie, co. Oxf., 1273. A.
1550. Married—William Spencer and Margaret Melledy : St. Peter, Cornhill, i. 222.
Liverpool, 1, 0, 0, 0 ; Blackburn, 1, 0, 0, 0 ; New York, 0, 0, 1, 0 ; Boston (U.S.), 0, 0, 3, 5.

Mellor, Meller.—(1) Local, 'of Mellor,' a chapelry in the parish of Glossop, near Manchester. (2) Local, 'of Mellor,' a township in the parish of Blackburn, co. Lanc. (3) Occup. 'the miller,' q.v.

Hugo Bell, *meller,* 1379 : P. T. Yorks. p. 75.
Willelmus de Meller, 1379 : ibid. p. 177.
1588. Edward Mellor, of Oldham : Wills at Chester, i. 135.
1603. Eliz. Mellor, of Mottram : ibid.
1677. Charles Wynne and Eliz. Meller : Marriage Alleg. (Canterbury), p. 192.
London, 6, 3 ; Manchester, 40, 2 ; New York, 3, 7.

Melton.—Local. ' of Melton,' parishes in cos. Suffolk, Norfolk, W. Rid, Yorks, Leicester, and Lincoln.

John de Melton, co. Norf., 1273. A.
Nicholas de Melton, co. York, ibid.
Adam de Meltone, co. Suff., ibid.
Ricardus de Melton, *souter,* 1379 : P. T. Yorks. p. 301.
Henricus de Melton, 1379 : ibid. p. 74.
1593. Married—Geo. Melton and Ann Cannings : St. Antholin (London), p. 36.
1596. Buried — Alice, wife of Steven Melton : St. Jas. Clerkenwell, iv. 58.
London, 2 ; MDB. (co. Suff.), 1 ; Philadelphia, 2.

Memory.—Local. A variant of Mummery (q.v.), which is a variant of Mowbray. There can be no question as to the correctness of this solution; it is simply imitative.

1589. Christopher Membrey or Membrye, of Corpus : Reg. Univ. Oxf. ii. 93.

1730. Bapt.—Eliz., d. Samuel and Rachael Memory : St. Jas. Clerkenwell, ii. 192.
1756. Married — John Membery and Jane Bottomley : St. Geo. Han. Sq. i. 63.
1759. — Samuel Memory and Mary Taylor : ibid. p. 87.
1784. — John Brittain and Margery Memorey : ibid. p. 356.
New York, 1.

Mendfault.—Nick. A complimentary sobriquet that does not seem to have descended to many generations ; M.E. *faute,* a fault.
1416. Walter Mendfaute, co. York : W. 11, p 19.

Mercer, Mercier. — Occup. 'the mercer,' a dealer in clothes ; Fr. *mercier,* a draper.

Jordan de Mercer, co. Linc., 1273. A.
Adelard le Mercer, co. Oxf., ibid.
Ketel le Mercer, co. Camb., ibid.
Johannes Payge, *mercer,* 1379 : P. T. Yorks. p. 79.
Thomas Mercer, 1379 : ibid. p. 170.
1694. Bapt.—Success, son of Thomas Mercer : St. Michael, Cornhill, p. 157.
London, 19, 3 ; New York, 18, 2.

Merchant.—Occup. ' the merchant'; v. Marchant. From the rarity of this form it is clear that while as a dictionary word and in a commercial sense *merchant* has gained the superiority, as a surname Marchant has never lost its original hold ; cf. Clark, the surname, and *clerk,* the occupative term.

Benet Mercator, co. Camb., 1273. A.
1563. Buried—Roger Merchant : St. Thomas the Apostle (London), p. 86.
1697. Samuel Howard and Eliz. Merchant : Marriage Lic. (London), p. 322.
London, 2 ; New York, 9 ; Boston (U.S.), 9.

Meredith, Morodyth.—Bapt. ' the son of Meredith ' (Welsh); v. Merridew.

Meredydd, son of Bleddyn : Freeman's Norman Conquest, iv. 675.
Meredydd, son of Gruffydd : ibid. p. 183.
Meredydd, son of Owen : ibid. p. 503.
Meredith ap Eynon, 1322 (co. Glamorgan). M.
Meredith Walshman, 1431 : Toulmin-Smith, Old Birmingham, 1864, p. 80.
1575. Richard Meredith, co. Radnor : Reg. Univ. Oxf. vol. ii. pt. ii. p. 68.

I remember seeing a curious pun in an epitaph in Marshfield Church, recorded by Rudder in his Hist. Gloucestershire. The monument is to the memory of A. Meredeth. A rhyming epitaph ends thus:

'Judge, then, what he did lose who lost but breath,
Lived to die well, and dyed *A Meredeth.*'
London, 27, 0; MDB. (co. Ches.), 5, 1; New York, 10, 0; Philadelphia, 54, 0.

Merrall, Merrell, Merrill.— Bapt. 'the son of Muriel.' From an early period there was a disposition to pronounce this name Meriel or Merrell.

Muriel Manekyn, co. Norf., 1273. A.
Matilda Miriel, co. Camb., ibid.
Henry fil. Mirield, co. Linc., ibid.
Robert fil. Muriel, co. Hunts, ibid.
Thomas fil. Muriel, co. Salop, ibid.
Richard Miriel, co. Norf., ibid.
1550. Married—Jeames Meriall and Margaret Shingleton : St. Antholin (London), p. 8.
1593. Buried—Nicholas Meriall : St. Peter, Cornhill, i. 143.
Meryell. d. of Sir John Burton : Visit. Yorks. 1563, p. 116.
Meryell, d. of Sir Hugh Hastings : ibid. p. 113.
' Merriall Saltonstall, aged 22, and her daughter Merriall, aged nine months, embarked in the Suzan for New England in the year 1635': Hotten's Lists of Emigrants, p. 59.
London, 1, 6, 2 ; New York, 1, 1, 51.

Merrick, Meyrick. — Bapt. 'the son of Merick.' Probably a variant of Almerick; v. Amery. Miss Yonge connects Meyrick, Merrik, and Merich with Almeric (Hist. Christian Names, ii. 259, and v. Glossary).

Henry Meriche, 1379: P. T. Yorks. p. 237.
Johannes Miricheson, 1379: ibid. p. 241.
Meurik de Hope, Hen. III-Edw. I : K. p. 45.
1550. Bapt.—William Mericke : St. Peter, Cornhill, i. 5.
1563. Buried—Anthonye Meryck : St. Michael, Cornhill, p. 185.
1582. Maurice Merricke, or Mayrick, or Maericke, New Coll. : Reg. Univ. Oxf. vol. ii. pt. ii. p. 118.
1610. Richard Merrick and Martha Tither, alias Walker : Marriage Lic. (Westminster), p. 18.
London, 8, 3 ; New York, 12, 0.

Merridew, Melladew, Mellodew, Merriday.—? Bapt. 'the son of Meredith.' An early English corruption, also a well-recognized Irish form of the same. The corruptions of this North-English surname, besides those recorded above, are Malledew, Mallalieu, Mellody,

and Mellodey, q.v. The following entries concerning the same individual are interesting as bearing on the point :

1596. Bapt.—Sybell, d. John Meredithe : St. Michael, Cornhill, p. 100.
1598. — Phillipe, s. John Meredaye : ibid. p. 101.
1599. — John, s. John Meredaye : ibid.
Thomas Merydewe, 1379 : P. T. Yorks. p. 58.
Johannes Meridewe, 1379 : ibid. p. 57.

The two entries following are very decisive :

1680. Bapt.—George. s. George and Eliner Merideth : St. Jas. Clerkenwell, i. 291.
1682. — Mary, d. George and Eliner Meriday : ibid. p. 301.
1711. — John, son of John Merryday : ibid. ii. 60.
London, 1, 1, 0, 0 ; Oldham, 0, 0, 6, 0 ; Philadelphia (Mellodew), 1.

Merrifield, Merrefield, Merryfield.—(1) Local, 'of Merevale,' a parish near Atherstone, co. Leicester. A corruption; cf. Tubberfield for Tubberville; v. Merrifill, infra. (2) Local, 'of Merryfield' probably for Maryfield. Mr. Lower (Patr. Brit. p. 223) says, 'The site of Salisbury Cathedral is so called in mediaeval documents, being a corruption of St. Mary's Field.' Other spots might easily be so called.

John de Merefeld, co. Soms., 1273. A.
Lovecok de Murifield, co. Soms., 1 Edw. III : Kirby's Quest, p. 174.
1582. Married—Richard Merefeild and Sislie Skeles : St. Mary Aldermary (London), p. 7.
1584. — Edward Merefeeld and Annes Foden : St. Peter, Cornhill. i. 234.
1756. — William Merryfield and Maria Harpley : St. Geo. Han. Sq. p. 65.
1781. Nicholas Merrifill (co. Worc.) and Mary Wright : ibid. p. 325.
London, 2, 0, 0 ; Crockford, 0, 1, 0 ; New York, 4, 1, 0 ; Boston (U.S.), 13, 0, 0 ; Philadelphia (Merryfield), 1.

Merriman, Merryman. — Nick. 'the merry man,' one of a joyous, festive disposition. In proof of the familiarity of this sobriquet I may remind the reader of the dog's name in the Taming of the Shrew :

' Huntsman, I charge thee, tender well my hounds ;
Trash Merriman, the poor cur is embossed.'   Induction, Scene 1.

For an opposite characteristic, v. Muddeman.

Adam Myryman, 1379 : P. T. Yorks. p. 211.
William Merryman. F.
John Meryman, co. York. W. 15.
Gerard Merriman, co. York. W. 16.
1684. Married—John Merryman and Hester Poole : St. Michael, Cornhill, p. 44.
1778. — Thomas Jesson and Mary Merryman : St. Geo. Han. Sq. i. 285.
London, 12, 1 ; New York, 0, 1 ; Philadelphia, 1, 2 ; Boston (U.S.), 4, 0.

Merriott; v. Meryett.

Merritt, Merrett.—Local, 'of Merriott,' a parish in co. Somerset. As Merrett it still lives in that shire ; v. Meryett for early instances.

1753. Married—Robert Merritt and Jane Backhouse : St. Geo. Chap. Mayfair, p. 245.
1808. — Silas Merritt and Sarah Mansell : St. Geo. Han. Sq. ii. 382.
London, 9, 6 ; MDB. (co. Soms.), 0, 1.

Merry.—Nick. 'the merry'; v. Merriman. M.E. *merie, mirie,* and *murie* (Skeat).

John le Mirie, co. Oxf., 1273. A.
Geoffrey le Mirie, co. Kent, ibid.
John Merie, co. Norf., ibid.
William Merrye. Z.
1625. Bapt. — Sammuell, s. Audrian Merry : St. Antholin (London), p. 59.
1663. Thomas Clarke and Eliz. Merry : Marriage Alleg. (Canterbury), p. 97.
London, 12 ; New York, 8 ; Boston (U.S.), 9.

Merrycock. — Nick. 'merry fellow.' Cock, a pert, lively young lad ; v. Cock.

Richard Merricocke, rector of Flordon, co. Norf., 1555: FF. v. 73.

Merryman.—Nick. 'the merry man'; v. Merriman.

Merrymouth.—Nick. 'a ready laugher,' one given to merriment.

John Merrymouth. V.
Richard Merrymouth. X.

Merryweather, Merryweather, Merewether, Merewether.—Nick. 'merry weather'; a happy, genial, sunshiny fellow ; a colloquial expression. Nothing to do with a wether sheep. Cf. Fairweather, used in exactly a similar sense, and still existing as a surname. 'Fayre, mery wedur or tyme (fayir as wedyr, K.), *amenus*': Prompt. Parv. 'Myry weder, or softe weder, *malacia*' (ibid.). Merry is here used in the sense of pleasant. Way adds a quotation from Vegecius, attributed to Trevisa, Roy. MS. 18 A. xii, where it is observed that wise warriors in olden times used to 'occupie theire foot menne in dedes of armes in the felde in mery wedire,' i.e. fair weather (v. Way's edit. Prompt. Parv.). As a surname it occurs, among some other fictitious characters, in one of the Coventry Mysteries, where mention is made of

'Bontyng the Brewster, and Sybyly Slynge,
Megge Mery-wedyr, and Sabine Sprynge.'

Andrew Murlweder, co. Oxf., 1273. A.
Thomas Murweder, co. Camb., ibid.
Henry Muriweder. O.
1617. Married—Thomas Church and Francis Merryweather : St. Peter, Cornhill, i. 250.
1667. John Ferris and Jane Merrywether (co. Wilts): Marriage Alleg. (Canterbury), p. 134.
London, 8, 1, 2, 0; Crockford, 1, 0, 4, 1; Philadelphia (Merryweather), 1.

Merton.—Local, ' of Merton,' parishes in cos. Oxford, Devon, Norfolk, and Surrey. This surname is a proof how names rise and fall. There is but one solitary representative in the London Directory. It was familiar in its day, and one Oxford college will for ever preserve it from obscurity. The first two instances probably refer to Marton in the W. Rid. Yorks:

Aliela de Merton, 1379 : P. T. Yorks. p. 256.
Thomas de Merton, 1379 : ibid.
John de Merton, co. Oxf., 1273. A.
William de Merton, co. Wilts, ibid.
Walter de Merton, co. Norf., ibid.
Richard de Merton, co. Hertf., 20 Edw. I. R.
1759. Bapt.—Ann Theodosia, d. Luke Merton : St. Peter, Cornhill, ii. 48.
London, 1.

Mervin, Mervyn; v. Marvin.

Meryett, Merriott.—Local, ' of Merriott,' a parish in co. Somerset, in the union of Chard; v. Merritt.

John de Meriet, co. Linc., 1273. A.
Simon de Meriet, co. Soms., ibid.
Hugo de Meriet, co. Soms., Hen. III– Edw. I. K.

John de Meryet, co. Soms., 1 Edw. III : Kirby's Quest, p. 93.
George de Meriet, co. Soms., 1 Edw. III : ibid.
1799. Married — James Merriett and Mary Crick : St. Geo. Han. Sq. ii. 205.
1802. — Richard Meryett and Jane Dew : ibid. p. 267.
London, 1, 0 ; MDB. (co. Somerset), 0, 3.

Messenger, Massinger, Messinger.—Occup. ' the messenger '; M.E. *messager*; cf. *passenger* for *passager*, Pottinger for Potager, Clavinger for Claviger, &c.

'Item, to Owen Whitstones, messagier, xls.': 1503 (Privy Purse Exp. Eliz. of York. p. 100).
'Of April that is messager to May.'
         Chaucer, C. T. 4427.
Reginald le Messager, co. Norf., 1273. A.
Jacob le Messager, co. Soms., ibid.
Thomas le Messager, co. Camb., ibid.
Ricardus le Messager, 12 Edw. II : Freemen of York, i. 18.
Richard le Messager, co. Soms., 1 Edw. III : Kirby's Quest, p. 205.
William Messanger, 1379 : P. T. Yorks. p. 293.
Richard Messanger, C. R., 20 Hen. VI.
1636-7. Thomas Messenger and Jane Underwood : Marriage Lic. (London), p. 229.
1693. Bapt.—William, s. Eliz. Messinger : St. Jas. Clerkenwell, p. 351.
London, 13, 1, 0 ; Boston (U.S.), 22, 1, 13.

Messer.—Occup. ' the messer.' An old and very common entry for a mower (v. Mawer), harvester, or reaper.

John le Messer, co. Camb., 1273. A.
Adam le Messor, co. Oxf., ibid.
Milo le Messer, co. Bedf., ibid.
William le Messor, co. Suff., ibid.
1658. Married—Robert Boskitt and Mary Messer: St. Jas.Clerkenwell,iii.100.
1771. — Thomas Messer and Elizabeth Denn : St. Geo. Han. Sq. i. 215.
London,10 ; Oxford, 3 ; Philadelphia, 6.

Metcalf, Metcalfe, Medcalf, Medcalfe, Medcraft, Meadowcroft.—? Local. I feel assured this name is local, and that it is a modification of Medcroft or Medcraft (v. Craft and Croft, and cf. Calcraft and Calcroft), of which an instance still remains in the London Dir. Mead and meadow are double forms still exist. M.E. *mede*, a grassfield, so called because mowed (Skeat). Metcalf and Turnbull were great Yorkshire names. I have seen them side by side in

Yorkshire records of 500 years ago. Horace Smith still keeps them in company :
'Mr. Metcalf ran off on meeting a cow, With pale Mr. Turnbull behind him.'
Willelmus Miducroft, 1379 : P. T. Yorks. p. 67.
Ricardus de Meducroft, 1379 : ibid. p. 54.
Nicholas de Meducroft, C. R., 7 Edw. III. pt. ii.
Nicholas de Meducroft, co. Lanc. 20 Edw. I. R.
Miles Metkalff : Patent Roll, 1 Hen.VII.
James Medcalfe, 1570 : Reg. Univ. Oxf. i. 279.
Mark Meadcalfe, 1568 : ibid. p. 271.
It is a remarkable fact that I cannot find Metcalf in the Yorks. P. T. of 1379. But the Meducrofts are there. Probably the corruption had not yet taken place; cf. Duncalf and Duncuft, i.e. Duncroft (?), also Crostkalf infra.
Agnes de Crostkalf (i. e. Crosscroft ?), 1379 : P. T. Yorks. p. 127.
London, 5, 22, 14, 1, 1, 1 ; New York, 13, 7, 0, 2, 0, 1.

Meth, Methe.—Nick. ' the methe,' i. e. courteous. ' *Methe*, courteous ' (Halliwell). ' Thou was methe and meke' (ibid.).
'Alle that meyné mylde and meth Went hem into Nazareth.'
         Cursor Mundi, Halliwell.
Henry Methe, co. Suff., 1273. A.
John Methe, co. Salop, ibid.
1616. Bapt.—Anne, d. Thomas Mythe : St. Jas. Clerkenwell, i. 76.
New York, 2, 1.

Methley.—Local, ' of Methley,' a village situate between Leeds and Pontefract.
Ricardus de Methelay, *souter*, 1379 : P. T. Yorks. p. 80.
Emma de Methlay, 1379 : ibid. p. 94.
Johannes de Methlay, *tayllour*, 1379 : ibid. p. 95.
West Rid. Court Dir., 1 ; Sheffield, 1 ; London, 1.

Methven, Methuen, Methwin.—Local, ' of Methven,' a parish in co. Perth.
1618. Anthony Methwin, *cler*., co. Soms.: Reg. Univ. Oxf. vol. ii. pt. ii. p. 368.
1677. Paul Methwen and Deborah Hough : Marriage Lic. (London), ii. 301.
London, 3, 0, 0 ; Boston (U.S.), 2, 1, 0.

Meuse; v. Mewze.

Mew.—Nick. ' the mew,' a sea-mew, a gull; v. Seafowl.
John le Mew, C. R., 20 Edw. I.

William le Mewe, co. Soms., 1 Edw. III: Kirby's Quest, p. 192.

Johannes Mewe, et Agnes uxor ejus, 1379: P. T. Yorks. p. 118.

1625. Buried—Ellen Mew: Kensington Ch. p. 107.

1687-8. John Blanch and Hannah Mew: Marriage Alleg. (Canterbury), p. 42.

London, 4; Boston (U.S.), 1.

Mewett.—(1) Bapt. 'the son of Matthew,' from nick. Mew (i.e. Mahew), dim. Mewot. (2)? Nick.; perhaps a dim. of Mew ('the mew'), q.v.

Richard Mewot, co. Hunts, 1273. A.

1804. Married—Geo. Mewitt and Mary Sturt: St. Geo. Han. Sq. ii. 314.

London, 1.

Mewze, Meuse.—? Local, 'of Meux' (?), a township in the parish of Waghen, E. Rid. Yorks. The evidence below seems to confirm this view:

William de Mewse, 1379: P. T. Yorks. r. 146.

John de Mewhes, 1379: ibid. p. 147.

These individuals are found on the borders of the East Riding.

1685. Charles Hances and Ann Meux: Marriage Alleg. (Canterbury), p. 222.

1692. Rannulph Mewsse and Ann Lee: ibid. p. 226.

London, 0, 1; Philadelphia, 1, 0; New York, 5, 0.

Meyer, Mayer, Mayor.— Offic. 'the mayor'; M.E. *maire*, a mayor. Generally these names in the London Directory are of modern German importation. Germ. *meier*, a bailiff, steward, farmer, mayor; cf. Fr. Lemaire; Dutch Meyer. v. Mair.

David le Meir, co. Linc., 1273. A.

William Mair, co. Camb., ibid.

Willelmus Meyre, 1379: P. T. Yorks. p. 37.

Matilda Mayre, *laborer*, 1379: ibid. p. 219.

1586. Christopher Maier, co. Durh.: Reg. Univ. Oxf. vol. ii. pt. ii. p. 150.

London, 29, 19, 6; Sheffield, 1, 0, 4; New York, 560, 124, 0.

Meyler.—Bapt. 'the son of Meyler.' Found in the Welsh Principality and on the English border.

Meyler, canon of St. David's, 1202: Hist. and Ant. St. David's, p. 364.

Nicholas ap-Meyler, canon of St. David's, 1222: ibid.

Meyler de Stretton, co. Salop, 1273. A.

Henry Meyler, co. Salop, ibid.

Walter Meyler, co. Salop, ibid.

Robert fil. Meilir, co. Salop, ibid.

1764. Married—Richard Henessy and Margaret Meyler: St. Geo. Han. Sq. i. 131.

MDB. (co. Pembroke), 5; South Wales Court Dir., 3; Narberth, S.W., 2; New York, 1.

Meyrick; v. Merrick.

Miall.—Bapt. 'the son of Michael'; v. Miell.

1798. Married—Thomas Young and Hannah Miall: St. Geo. Han. Sq. ii. 182.

London, 4.

Michael, Michaels, Michaelson.—Bapt. 'the son of Michael,' more commonly Mitchell, q.v.

Hugh fil. Micahel, co. Linc., 1273. A.

Roger Michel, co. Norf., ibid.

Michael de Audewarp, 1379: P. T. Yorks. p. 73.

Sometimes, perhaps, a foundling name:

1657. Bapt. — Peregrinus Michael, a foundling in this parish: St. Michael, Cornhill, p. 141.

London, 5, 3, 2; New York (Michaelson), 7; Boston (U.S.), 4, 0, 1; Philadelphia, 37, 22, 0.

Michell.—Bapt. 'the son of Michael,' q.v. A variant, like Mitchell, q.v.

Robert Michel, co. Oxf., 1273. A.

Walter Michel, co. Camb., ibid.

Johannes Michell, 1379: P. T. Yorks. p. 253.

Johannes Michol', 1379: ibid. p. 43.

1578. Married—William Smyth and Margery Michell: St. Jas. Clerkenwell, i. 7.

1645. Bapt.—Eliz., d. William Michill: Kensington Ch. p. 35.

London, 15; New York, 1.

Michelthwaite, Mickelthwaite, Micklethwait, Micklethwaite.—Local, 'of Micklethwaite,' part of the township of Bingley, co. York; also 'of Micklethwaite,' a village in the same parish.

Adam de Mekkelhawayth, 1379: P. T. Yorks. p. 84.

Magota Mekkelwayth, 1379: ibid.

Johanna de Mickilwayte, 1379: p. 80.

William de Mickilwayte, 1379: ibid.

1615. Paul Muclethwait: Reg. Univ. Oxf. i. 359.

1690. Joseph Micklethwait and Frances Johnson: Marriage Alleg. (Canterbury), p. 162.

1691. Nathaniel Micklethwaite and Sarah Sutton: ibid. p. 191.

West Rid. Court Dir., 1, 1, 3, 5.

Micklewright. — Nick. 'the mickle wright,' i.e. the big wright.

Evidently a North-English or Border surname; cf. Meiklejohn.

1619. George Durye, *fletcher*, and Sibell Michaelwright: Marriage Lic. (London), p. 78.

1692. Married—Timothy Michelwright and Mary Brittaine: St. Jas. Clerkenwell, iii. 212.

Manchester, 1.

Midday; v. Midnight.

Middle.—(1) Local, 'of Middle,' a parish in co. Salop, eight miles from Shrewsbury.

Richard le (de?) Midel, co. Oxf., 1273. A.

(2) Local, 'at the middle,' i.e. the middle house, field, farm, &c.

Robert atte Midle, co. Soms., 1 Edw. III: Kirby's Quest, p. 80.

Henry atte Middel, co. Soms., 1 Edw. III: ibid. p. 108.

London, 2.

Middleditch.—Local, 'at the middle dike,' from residence thereby.

1590. Bapt. — Roberte, s. Richard Myddleditche: St. Michael, Cornhill, p. 96.

1646. Elizabeth Middleditch: St. Mary Aldermary (London), p. 20.

1808. Married—William Middleditch and Ann Mills: St. Geo. Han. Sq. ii. 394.

London, 1; New York, 2.

Middlehurst.—Local, 'at the middle hurst,' i.e. wood, from residence thereby; cf. Midwood. Both belong to the North.

1610. Alice Middlehurst, of Grappenhall: Wills at Chester, i. 135-6.

1615. John Middlehurst, of Latchford: ibid.

Liverpool, 2; Manchester, 1.

Middlemass, Middlemiss, Middlemist, Middlemost.—(1) Bapt. or nick. 'Michaelmas'; cf. Candlemas, Pentecost, Nowell, Saturday, Christmas, &c., from the day or season whereon or wherein the child was born. The evidence in favour of this origin is sufficiently strong, although I suggest another interpretation infra. For one thing we find one undoubted instance:

1547. Shorman Myglemas: Churchwarden's Accounts, Ludlow (Camd. Soc., v. Index).

Michaelmas was commonly so pronounced. In the Treatise of Fishing with an Angle, in the St.

Alban's Book, the following are given as baits for roach in July, 'the not worme, and mathewes, and maggotes tyll Myghelmas': Sign. i. ii (v. Prompt. Parv. p. 331, *n.*). For further proof v. Mighill. From Migglemas to Middlemas would be an easy transition. The final *t* in Middlemast and Middlemost would thus be excrescent.

(2) Nick. or local, 'the middlemost,' i.e. the middle one in the family, or the middle house in a row of cottages, 'at the middlemost.' We find this somewhat uncouth superlative in Ezek. xlii. 5, 'the middlemost of the building.' Still earlier, c. 1450, we find it in some curious nursery lines upon the fingers (v. *fingers*, Halliwell), wherein the little finger is styled 'litylman,' and the longest 'longman.' 'Longman hat the mydilmast, for longest fynger hit is.'

1694. Married—Moses Pearepoint and Mary Midlemass: St. Jas. Clerkenwell, iii. 214.
1700. — Searles Middlemas and Elizabeth Court: Canterbury Cathedral, p. 69.
London, 3, 2, 3, 0; West Riding Court Dir., 0, 2, 0, 3; New York, 1, 1, 0, 0.

Middleton.—Local, 'of Middleton,' i.e. the middle town, or farmstead; v. Town. There are several dozen places, larger or smaller, scattered up and down England of this name.

Richard de Midelton, co. Bucks, 1273. A.
Thomas de Middilton, co. Linc., ibid.
Gilbert de Middelton, co. York, ibid.
Johannes de Midillton, 1379: P. T. Yorks. p. 286.
Thomas de Midilton, 1379: ibid.
Ricardus de Midilton, 1379: ibid. p. 263.
1580. Christopher Middelton, co. Ches.: Reg. Univ. Oxf. vol. ii. pt. ii. p. 94.
London, 34; New York, 27.

Midgall.—Local, 'of Midghall,' some small spot near Preston, co. Lanc., which I have not as yet been able to identify.

Edward Midghall, of Goosnargh, 1662: Lancashire Wills at Richmond, i. 195.
Anne Midgehall, of Blackehale, *widow*, 1612: ibid.
Preston, 1.

Midgley, Midgely.—Local, 'of Midgley,' a village five miles from Halifax, W. Rid. Yorks. This sur-

name has ramified strongly in the surrounding district. Under heading of 'Migelay' (i.e. township) occurs:

Ricardus de Migeslay, 1379: P. T. Yorks. p. 188.
Johannes Migeslay, 1379: ibid.
1595. Richard Midgley, of Dinkerley: Wills at Chester, i. 136.
1788. Married—Thomas Midgley and Sarah Price: St. Geo. Han. Sq. ii. 10.
London, 1, 0; West Rid. Court Dir., 20, 0; New York, 1, 0; Worcester (U.S.), 14, 3.

Midnight.—Nick. It is curious to note that both Midday and Midnight were early surnames.

Elena Mydnyght, 1379: P. T. Yorks. p. 200.
Adam Midday, bailiff of Norwich, 1335: FF. iii. 98.
Roger Midday, bailiff of Norwich, 1348: ibid. p. 99.
Boston (U.S.), 1.

Midwinter.—Bapt. 'the son of Midwinter.' Christmas and Noel were in common use as names for children born at this season. Midwinter was a synonym. 'The sheriffs, by the custom of the city, do ride to several parts thereof every year, betwixt Michaelmas and Midwinter, that is Yoole' (Hist. and Ant. York, ii. 54). Robert of Gloucester says that the Conqueror purposed 'to midwinter at Gloucester, to Witesontid at Westminster, to Ester at Wincester.' Cf. Yool and Youle.

Gounilda Midewynter, co. Oxf., 1273. A.
John Midewynter, co. Soms., 1 Edw. III: Kirby's Quest, p. 220.
William Mydwynter, C. R., 14 Hen. IV.
John Mydwinter. H.
1688. Bapt. — Mary, d. Thomas Midwinter: St. Jas. Clerkenwell, ii. 329.
This surname occurs constantly in Kirby's Quest (co. Soms.), quoted above.
London, 3.

Midwood, Middlewood.—Local, 'at the middle wood,' from residence thereby; cf. Middlehurst.

Johannes de Middelwode, 1379: P. T. Yorks. p. 55.
Willelmus Midrewode, 1379: ibid. p. 161.
Manchester, 3, 1; Philadelphia, 2, 0.

Miell, Mihell, Myhill.—Bapt. 'the son of Michael.' Mihell was a common form of this popular

name, even when the proper orthography was preserved.
'At Michael's term had many a trial, Worse than the Dragon and St. Michael.'
Hudibras, pt. iii. canto 2.
1626. Married—Thomas Yearly, of Sant Mihills in Cornhill: Reg. St. Dionis Backchurch (London), p. 22.
A castaway called, no doubt, after the patron saint of the parish, is thus entered in the baptisms of St. Michael, Cornhill:
1585. Joane Myhell, a foundling: St. Antholin (London), p. 93.
1549. Bapt. — Richard, s. Mihill Cristen: ibid. p. 7.
— Married — Mihill Assherst and Christian Bowen: ibid.
1779. — James Kay and Priscilla Miell: St. Geo. Han. Sq. i. 301.
There are many corruptions of this surname, as for instance, Miall, Mayall, Mayell, q.v.
London, 3, 3, 1.

Mighill.—Bapt. 'the son of Michael,' popularly called Mighel, often softened to Miell, q.v. 'Mighell = Michael': Palsgrave. Mihill is very common in old writers.
'The sothfastenes and nothing hele, That thou herdest of seynt Myghele.'
Cursor Mundi, Halliwell.
1598. Married—Mighell Axendall and Marye Wall: St. Mary Aldermary (London), p. 9.
1626. Francis Bevis and Margaret Mighell: Marriage Lic. (London), i. 173.
1789. Married — Philip Mighell and Sarah Bolton: St. Geo. Han. Sq. ii. 21.
For further proof, v. Middlemass.
Worcester (U.S.), 1.

Milbank, Millbank.—Local, 'of the mill-bank,' one who resided on the slope by the mill; v. Mill and Miller. Perhaps in some cases the 'meol-bank,' i.e. the sandbank (?); v. Meals, and cf. the first entry following:
1621. Married — John Barker and Isabell Mealebanke: St. Jas. Clerkenwell, i. 49.
1685. John Milbanke and Margaret Lane: Marriage Alleg. (Canterbury), p. 209.
1804. Married — John Gardner and Eliz. Milbank: St. Geo. Han. Sq. ii. 304.
London, 3, 1; New York, 5, 2.

Milburn, Milborn, Milbourn, Milbourne.—Local, 'of Milburn,' a chapelry in the parish of Kirkby Thore, co. Westm.; also

M m 2

two townships in co. Northumberland, in the parish of Ponteland. It is evidently to the latter we owe the surname with its variants.

Margaret de Milleburn, co. Northumb., Hen. III–Edw. I. K.
1594. Robert Milborne: Reg. Univ. Oxf., i. 354.
1662. Thomas Milburne and Winifred Francis: Marriage Alleg. (Canterbury), p. 54.
1679. Edward Milbourne and Mary Kemp: ibid. p. 8.
1683. Alex. Milbourn and Eliz. Watson: ibid. p. 142.
London, 3, 1, 3, 4; MDB. (co. Northumberland), 7, 0, 0, 0; New York, 2, 0, 0, 0; Philadelphia, 7, 0, 0, 2.

Mildmay.—Nick. 'the mild-maiden'; M.E. *may*, maid; v. Sadmay and May. Mild-maiden was from the earliest times a title given to the Blessed Virgin.

1546. Walter Myldmay and Mary Walsyngham: Marriage Lic. (London), i. 7.
1548. Edward Mylmaye and Joanna Awparte, ibid. p. 13.
1616. Thomas Mildmay and Anne Savile: ibid. ii. 49.
1744. Carew Hervey Mildmay (co. Somerset) and Edith Phellips: St. Geo. Han. Sq. i. 32.
Crockford, 4.

Mildred.—Bapt. 'the son of Mildred,' a fairly popular fontal name in the 13th and 14th centuries.

Melred Forest', 1170: KKK. vi. 16.
Maldred de Glentendon, 1187: ibid. vi. 41.
Robert fil. Meldredi, 1196: ibid. vi. 56.
Robert fil. Mildred, 37 Hen. III. BBB. p. 54.
William Mildrede, C. R., 4 Hen. VI.
1611. Married — John Lowdell and Isabell Mildred: St. Dionis Backchurch, p. 17.
1686. Bapt.—Anne, d. John Mildred: St. Jas. Clerkenwell, ii. 316.
London, 2.

Miles, Myles.—Bapt. 'the son of Miles'; v. Mills (2). This is still a popular personal name in North England.

William fil. Milon', co. Bedf., 1273. A.
Milo le Messer, co. Bedf., ibid.
Peter Myles, co. Kent, ibid.
Wychard Miles, co. Linc., ibid.
1584. Alex. Miles, co. Northampton: Reg. Univ. Oxf. vol. ii. pt. ii. p. 135.
1694-5. Lewis Myles, co. Pembr.: ibid. p. 281.
London, 76, 1; New York, 59, 6.

Milestone.—Local, 'of Milston,' a parish two miles from Amesbury. co. Wilts. 'Milestone, from resi-

dence near one': Lower. History, I believe, has not recorded that milestones were in use in the 13th century.

Richard de Mildestane, co. Wilts, 1273. A.
London, 2.

Milford.—Local, 'of Milford,' parishes in diocs. Winchester, York, and Southwell; also Milford Haven, in dioc. St. David's, Wales; also Long Melford, in dioc. Ely. In all cases probably the mill-ford, the mill by the ford; cf. Mulford.

John de Milforde, co. York, 20 Edw. I. R.
William de Melford, co. Camb., ibid.
Ralph de Milford, co. York, 1273. A.
Adam de Milford, co. Suff., ibid.
Hugh de Meleford, co. Suff., ibid.
Johannes de Milforth, 1379: P. T. Yorks. p. 215.
Adam de Milforth, 1379: ibid.
1618. George Milforde, co. Wilts: Reg. Univ. Oxf. vol. ii. pt. ii. p. 367.
London, 8; New York, 3.

Milkandbread. — Nick.; cf. Milksop.

William Milkanbred, 11 Edw. I.
Walter, s. William Milk-and-bred, ibid.

Unfortunately, G. H. D., who communicated these and other curiosities in nomenclature to N. and Q. (Jan. 24, 1857), did not furnish his authorities.

Milker.—Occup. 'the milker,' a milkman.

Thomas le Milkar, co. Salop, 1273. A.
William Milkar, co. Oxf., ibid.
William le Milker, co. Soms., 1 Edw. III: Kirby's Quest, p. 183.
Henry Mylker, 1379: P. T. Yorks. p. 79.
1273. William le Melker: Cal. of Wills in Court of Husting.

Milksop, Milsop, Mellsop. —Nick. 'the milksop,' a soft, effeminate kind of fellow.

'To wed a milksop, or a coward ape.'
Chaucer, C. T. 13916.

Oddly enough this sobriquet continued as a surname till the middle of the last century, and as Milsop probably still lives.

Roger Melkesopp, co. Bucks, 1273. A.
Robert Mulksop, co. Oxf., ibid.
John Milesop, co. Oxf., ibid.
William Milksop, c. 1300. M.
William Milkesop. J.
Hugh Milkesop. RR. 1.

Exactly three centuries after the instances in A. we find the name in the same district:

1572. James Edwards, of Reading, and Dionise Milkesopp, *spinster*, of St. Albans, Herts: Marriage Lic. (London), i. 53.

Later we find representatives in the metropolis:

1620. Buried — John, s. Thomas Milksopp: St. Thomas the Apostle (London), p. 111.
1621. Bapt. — Thomas, s. Thomas Melksopp: ibid. p. 45.

In the last century the family had contrived to get rid of the *k*.

1736. Bapt.—Mary, d. Robert Milsop: St. Jas. Clerkenwell, p. 225.

This curious and interesting surname still thrives in the United States as Mellsop.

Worcester (U.S.), 0, 0, 2.

Mill —Local, 'at the mill,' from residence thereby (v. Miln, Milnes, and Mills, 1).

Roger atte Mille, co. Oxf., 1273. A.
John del Mill, c. 1300. M.
Hugh Atte-myll, rector of Gillingham, co. Norf., 1349: FF. viii. 12.
William Atte-Mylle, rector of Mundford, co. Norf., 1412: ibid. ii. 247.
1612. William Mill and Eliz. Greene: Marriage Lic. (London), ii. 16.
1633. Pointz Mill and Eliz. Wright: ibid. p. 213.

Mill is now an extremely scarce surname, Mills having become the accepted form. This final *s* is common in monosyllabic local surnames; cf. Holmes, Sykes, Brooks, Lowndes, Knowles, &c.

London, 1; Philadelphia, 4.

Millage, Milledge. — Local, 'of Milwich,' a parish in co. Stafford (Lower).

1666. Matthias Melledge and Mary Ryal: Marriage Alleg. (Cant.), p. 122.
1690. Bapt. — William, s. William Millage: St. Jas. Clerkenwell, ii. 336.
London, 1, 1.

Millard.—Offic.; v. Millward.

Millbank; v. Milbank.

Millen.—Local, 'de Millen,' probably of Dutch origin. The bearer settled in London in the 16th century.

1583. Buried — Alexsander de Millen, *stranger*: St. Dionis Backchurch, p. 198.
1584. — William, s. Alexsander Millen: ibid.
London, 5; New York, 13; Philadelphia, 6.

Miller.—Occup. 'the miller,' one who grinds corn, a 'milner' (q.v.), a surname found in the records of every county in England.

John le Mellere, c. 1300. M.
Adam le Molendinator, co. Oxf., 1273. A.
Achard Molendinarius, co. Hunts, ibid.
Wymund Molendinarius, co. Soms., 20 Edw. I. R.

Molendinarius is a very frequent entry in the Hundred Rolls (A.), but, oddly enough, no instance is given in English.

1572. George Miller, co. Warwick: Reg. Univ. Oxf. vol. ii. pt. ii. p. 54.
London, 198; New York, 1,100.

Millerson.—Nick. 'the miller's son'; cf. Taylorson, Smithson, Wrightson, Hindson, and Herdson, but this class of names is distinctly small. Possibly Milson and Millson are so originated. The surname was still in existence in the last century.

William fil. Molendinarii, co. Camb., 1273. A.
Henry fil. Molendinarii, co. Hunts, ibid.
Gilbert Millerson, co. York. W. 3.
Thomas Milnerson, 1379: P. T. Yorks. p. 279.
Ricardus Milnerson, 1379: ibid. p. 56.
John Milnerson, of Ulverston, 1589. Lancashire Wills at Richmond, i. 196.
William Milnerson, of Sowtergate, in Ulverston, 1605: ibid.

The variants in the Ulverston parish church registers are Milnerson, Millerson, Milnerson, and Mellerson. All the entries relate to one family. One of the latest references is:

1727. Married — Thomas Millerson and Dorothy Gibson: Reg. Ulverston, p. 373.

Millett, Millet, Millot. — Bapt. 'the son of Mille,' (1) i.e. Miles, from dim. Mill-ot, or Mil-ot, or (2) perhaps from Mille, the nick. of Millicent, a popular girl's name in the 13th and 14th centuries, especially in Yorkshire. This again would become as dim. Mill-ot, or Mil ot, just as in the same county Margaret gave us Magot and Magotson, and Matilda Tillot and Tillotson, the one from the nick. Magg, the other from the nick. Till. On the whole it is probable that Millicent is the parent.

Richard fil. Milot. MM.
Roger Millot, co. Notts, 1273. A.

John Milot, co. Hunts, 1273. A.
Willelmus Melot, 1379: P. T. Yorks. p. 23.
Johannes Millot, 1379: ibid.
Rogerus Millotson, 1379: ibid. p. 19.
Matilda Millot, 1379: ibid.

The last two instances are together.

Thomas Mylett, co. York. W. 9.

Members of the same family are found thus entered:

John Mylote, co. Durham, temp. 1380. QQQ. ii. 153.
William Melot, co. Durham, 1433: ibid.
Robert Millot, co. Durham, 1513: ibid.
1696. Married — William Millett and Beatre Vodell: St. Michael, Cornhill, p. 49.
London, 3, 0, 0; New York, 4, 6, 3.

Millhouse.—Local, 'at the mill-house,' the cottage where the miller lived, close beside the mill, or the body of the mill itself. 'Myllehowse, *molendina, molendinum*': Prompt. Parv.

John de Molendino, co. Oxf., 1273. A.
William de Molendino, co. Oxf., ibid.
1624. John Milnhouse, James Citty, Virginia: Hotten's Lists of Emigrants, p. 219.
London, 3; Philadelphia, 5.

Millicent, Millisent.—Bapt. 'the son of Millicent' (Yonge, ii. 257-8).

Joan fil. Milicente, co. Bucks, 1273. A.
Peter Milisent, co. Salop, ibid.
Millesenta Cruche, co. Norf., ibid.
William Millecent, C. R., 29 Edw. III.
Mylisant Wyte, 1379: P. T. Yorks. p. 88.
John Myllicent, bailiff of Yarmouth, 1549: FF. xi. 327.
'The story of Sir John Millicent that would have had a patent from King James for every man to have had leave to have given him a shilling': Pepys' Diary, Aug. 8, 1662.
1583. Married — Richard Davis and Millysent Leather: St. Jas. Clerkenwell, p. 9.
1717. Bapt.—Mary, d. John Millissent: St. Jas. Clerkenwell, iii. 99.
London, 1, 1.

Millichamp, Millichap. — Local, 'of Millichamp,' seemingly a Norman name, like Beauchamp. Millichap is one more instance of the tendency of a surname to corrupt when it passes the border of the county of its original settlement.

1620. William Millichap, or Millechappe, or Millichamp, co. Salop: Reg. Univ. Oxf. vol. ii. pt. ii. p. 383.

1774. Married — Richard King and Mary Milchup: St. Geo. Han. Sq. i. 244.
1795. — Henry Draper and Ann Millichamp: ibid. ii. 126.
MDB. (co. Salop), 3, 0; (co. Hereford), 0, 1.

Millikin, Milliken. — Bapt. 'the son of Milligan.' Looking at the large contingent of persons bearing this name in the States, it is safe to conclude that it is simply a sharpened form of the Irish Milligan. The only evidence of a personal name with the suffix -*hin* (as in Jenkin) is furnished below. But it is an isolated instance, and probably came from the Low Countries:

John Mulkyn, co. Suff., 1273. A.

The following entry, however, practically settles the question, being the halfway house between Milligan and Millikin:

1798. Married — John Chandler and Susanna Millican : St. Geo. Han. Sq. ii. 189.
London, 2, 1; New York, 2, 18; Philadelphia, 4, 20.

Millington.—Local, 'of Millington.' There is a parish in co. York of this name. Millington has been an East Cheshire surname for centuries. This name arose from Millington, an estate near Bowdon, co. Ches. It has always kept itself in view in South Lanc. and on the Cheshire border.

Hugh de Mulynton, 1400: East Ches., ii. 50.
Roger de Mulynton, 1401: ibid. p. 9.
'John Millington, of Millington, near Bowdon,' c. 1530: ibid. p. 256.
1606. Married — Robert Milligeton and Ann Wodd: Reg. Prestbury Ch., Ches., p. 172.
1608. James Millington, of Knutsford: Wills at Chester, i. 130.
1615. Margerie Millington, of Chelford, *widow*: ibid.
Manchester, 3; London, 7; New York, 2; Philadelphia, 4.

Millman; v. Milman.

Millmaster. — Offic. 'the manager of a mill'; v. Millward.
'Mr. Andrew Milmaster, of the Old Jewry, died Aug. 23, 1630': Smith's Obituary.

Mills.—(1) Local, 'at the mill,' from residence thereby. There is a column of Mills in the London Directory. A large number of these are local in origin. The final *s* (probably genitive) is common to all monosyllabic local surnames; cf. Brooks, Briggs, Styles, Dykes, Holmes, &c. For instances, v. Mill and Miln.

(2) Bapt. 'the son of Miles,' a once popular font-name, or 'the son of Millicent,' from the nick. Mille, or Milly; v. Milson.

Margery Mylys, co. Camb., 1273. A.
1645. Bapt. — Ann, d. Anthony Mills: St. Jas. Clerkenwell, i. 161.

The name is so universal that modern instances are needless.

West Rid. Court Dir., 16; London, 144; New York, 14.

Millward, Milward, Millard.—Official, 'the mill-ward,' the keeper of the mill; M.E. *melle*, *mulle*, and *mulne*. As with *miller* even now, so *mill* then meant always a place for grinding corn; cf. Milman, Millmaster, and Windmilward, q.v. Millard is a modified form.

'Manumissio Thomae Haale, alias dicti Mylleward de Hextone,' 1480: XX. 2, p. 210.
Richard Muleward, C. R., 12 Ric. II.
Walter le Meleward. N.
Robert le Milleward, co. Hunts, 1273. A.
William le Milward. G.
1662. John Milward (co. Derby), and Mary Corderoy: Marriage Alleg. (Canterbury), p. 80.
1677. Henry Plumtree and Joyce Millward: ibid. p. 272.
1696. Married — Richard Millard and Mary Rhymes: St. Dionis Backchurch (London), p. 45.
London, 4, 7, 29; New York, 1, 0, 15; Philadelphia, 9, 0, 20.

Milman, Millman.—Occup. 'a millward'; v. Millward.

William Meleman, Close Roll, 13 Ric. II. pt. i.
1563. Buried — Harry Milman: St. Antholin (London), p. 15.
1564. Married — Nicholas Bridgman and Als (Alice) Milmon: ibid. p. 17.
1791. Married—Thomas Andrews and Sarah Milman: St. Geo. Han. Sq. ii. 56.
London, 2, 1; New York, 1, 1; Philadelphia, 0, 9.

Miln, Milne, Milnes, Milns. —Local, 'at the mill'; A.S. *myln*, a mill; Latin *molina*; v. Milner. The final *s* is common in these local surnames; cf. Brooks, Holmes, Styles, Knowles, &c.

Thomas atte Milne. B.
Petrus atte Milne, 1379: P. T. Yorks. p. 41.
Johannes de Milne, 1379: ibid. p. 287.
Thomas atte Milne, 1379: ibid. p. 254.
Robertus del Milne, 1379: ibid. p. 169.
1766. Married — William Nicol and Eliz. Milne: St. Geo. Han. Sq. i. 150.
1785. — Robert Shore Milnes and Charlotte Frances Bentinck: ibid. i. 380.
London, 1, 23, 4, 1; West Rid. Court Dir., 0, 3, 18, 1; New York, 1, 12, 0, 0; Boston (U.S.), 1, 2, 2, 0.

Milner.—Occup. 'the milner,' the more correct form of miller, which has slipped the *n*; A.S. *myln*, a mill; Latin *molina*. Mulliner (London Directory) is probably a reminiscence of 'mulnere,' although it may be a corruption of Molineux.

Robert le Melner, co. Derby, 1273. A.
Alan le Milner. G.
William le Melner, c. 1300. M.
Emmot Mylner, co. Yorks. W. 9.
'William Bannester, *milner*, 1397': Preston Guild Rolls, p. 1.
Robertus Mylner, 1379: P. T. Yorks. p. 131.
Henricus Tele, *milner*, 1379: ibid p.265.
London, 16; New York, 4; Philadelphia, 15.

Milnes; v. Miln.

Milsom.—Bapt. (1) 'the son of Miles'; (2) 'the son of Millicent' (v. Milson, 3). The change from Milson to Milsom finds many parallels; cf. Ransom for Ranson, or Hansom for Hanson.

1763. Married — William Milsom and Sarah Staples: St. Geo. Han. Sq. i. 119.
1773. — John Saunders and Eliz. Millsum: ibid. p. 231.

The more correct form is found in the same register:

1777. Married — John Millson and Hanna Hyatt: ibid. p. 278.
London, 4; New York, 1.

Milson, Millson.—(1) Local, 'of Milson,' a parish in co. Salop, near Cleobury-Mortimer. (2) Bapt. 'the son of Miles,' a popular font-name in the surname period. (3) Bapt. 'the son of Millicent' (q.v.), early modified into Milson, or from the nick. Milly, whence Millison. Of these three (1) has had little influence. The real contest lies between (2) and (3), and doubtless both have contributed their due share.

Reginald fil. Militis, co. Hunts, 1273. A.
Robert fil. Militis, co. Hunts, ibid.

Amongst the inhabitants of Leeds were:

Thomas Milsson, 1379: P. T. Yorks. pp. 214-5.
Elisota Milesson, *mayden*, 1379: ibid.
1601. Henry Myleson, of Sutton: Wills at Chester, i. 140.
1606. William Myleson: ibid.

Of distinct connexion with Millicent, we have the following:

Iveta Milsent, co. Camb., 1273. A.
1577. Bapt.—Mylson, d. Henrie Gwynnowe: Reg. St. Columb Major, p. 10.
1584. — Mylson, child to young Cocker: ibid. p. 12.
1601. — Mellison, d. David Fyne: ibid. p. 20.

Further proof of Millicent's relationship to this name is seen from several registers:

Ann Millison, co. York. W. 16.
1689-90. Gabriell Million, of Greenwich, and Ruth Day: Marriage Alleg. (Canterbury), p. 137.
1701. Married — Thomas Millison and Sarah Bills: Canterbury Cathedral, p. 66.
London, 1, 1; Philadelphia, 3, 0; Boston (U.S.), 0, 1.

Milsted.—(1) Local, 'of Milstead,' a parish in co. Kent. (2) Local, 'of Minstead,' a parish in dioc. Winchester. The change from *n* to *l* is too common in the dictionary and directory to need illustration.

Richard de Minsted, co. Bucks, 1273. A.
1763. Married—Francis Milstead and Ann Holmes: St. Geo. Han. Sq. i. 116.
London, 3; New York, 1; Philadelphia, 1.

Milthorp, Milthorpe.—Local, (1) 'of Milnethorp,' a hamlet in the parish of Sandal Magna, near Wakefield, W. Rid. Yorks; cf. Mill and Miln; (2) a market-town in the parish of Heversham, co. Westm. The former seems to have been parent of the name.

Geoffrey de Milnethorp, co. Linc., 1273. A.
Robertus de Milnethorp, 1379: P. T. Yorks. p. 83.
Joanna Milnethorp, 1379: ibid.
West Rid. Court Dir., 1, 1.

Milton. — Local, 'of Milton.' About thirty parishes of this name occur in Crockford, representing England alone. Smaller spots bearing the same name must be common. The 'mill-town' would naturally be a frequent local sobriquet. Cf. Milford.

Alan de Miltone, co. Hunts, 1273. A.
Hugh de Miltone, co. Oxf., ibid.
Gregorius de Multon, co. Camb., ibid.
Agnes de Multon, co. Norf., ibid.
Thomas de Multon, 1379 : P. T. Yorks. p. 294.
Isabella de Melton, 1379 : ibid. p. 301.

It is unnecessary to furnish modern instances.

London, 15 ; New York, 5.

Milverton.—Local, ' of Milverton,' two parishes, one in co. Somerset, the other in co. Warw.

1751. Married—Thomas Bird and Eliz. Pitt Milverton : St. Geo. Han. Sq. i. 53.
MDB. (co. Dorset), 1.

Miner, Minor.—Occup. ' the miner,' an excavator. 'And therupon anon he bad His minours for to go and mine' : Gower, C. A. ii. 198 (Skeat).

Benedict le Mineur, C. R., 33 Hen. III.
1275. John le Minour : Cal. of Wills in Court of Husting.
Richard le Minnor, co. Soms., 1 Edw. III : Kirby's Quest, p. 205.
1690. Bapt. — Easter, d. Nathaniel Minor : St. Jas. Clerkenwell, i. 334.
1760. Married — James Mineur and Eliz. Barrow : St. Geo. Han. Sq. ii. 91.
Boston (U.S.), 30, 8.

Minett, Minnitt, Minet, Minnot.—? Bapt. Lower says, ' French Protestant refugees after the Rev. of the Edict of Nantes.' But the surname existed earlier.

John Mynot, cos. Warw. and Notts, 1273. A.
Nicholaus Mynyot, 1379 : P. T. Yorks. p. 91.
1579. —— Minet, co. Glouc. : Reg. Univ. Oxf. vol. ii. pt. ii. p. 87.
1749. Married—Benjamin Minnitt and Mary Veale : St. Geo. Han. Sq. i. 42.
1770. — Martin Manney and Margaret Minnett : ibid. p. 197.
London, 3, 1, 0, 0 ; New York, 1, 0, 1, 1.

Minister, Minster. — Local, ' at the minster,' i.e. monastery ; cf. Westminster. Not a minister, an attendant, as stated by Lower. Minister is imitative.

Thomas de Mynistre, Close Roll, 45 Hen. III.
Haldanus Minister, co. Norf., 1273. A.
1768. Married — Thomas Minster, co. Oxf., and Ellen Prichard : St. Geo. Han. Sq. i. 171.

London, 2, 0 ; MDB. (co. Norfolk), 1, 0 ; (co. Warwick), 0, 1 ; Philadelphia, 5, 10.

Minn, Minns.—Bapt. ' the son of Min.' There is some evidence in favour of an old personal name Min, which was probably a nick. Minnie is still used as a girl's pet name for Emmeline. The existence of Minson strongly favours this view. Further it must be remembered that Emmeline was a very popular girl-name in the hereditary surname period, and must have had a nick.

1541. Buried—John Myn, servant to Mr. Gammadge : St. Antholin (London), p. 3.
1595. Married — William Mynne and Anne Phenney : St. Jas. Clerkenwell, p. 19.
1748. — Joseph Gant, or Grant, and Ann Mins : ibid. p. 279.
1793. — Robert Minson and Ann Dakins : St. Geo. Han. Sq. ii. 98.
London, 2, 5 ; New York, 2, 0 ; Boston (U.S.), 0, 3.

Minshall, Minshull.—Local, ' of Minshull,' now Church Minshull, a parish five miles from Nantwich, co. Chester. Minshall is a South English variant, and seems to have arisen in the 18th century.

William Mynshull, co. Ches., 1359 : East Cheshire, ii. 160.
Thomas Minshull, of Eaton, Tarporley, 1580 : Wills at Chester (1545-1620), p. 137.
Ralph Minshull, of Minshull, 1602 : ibid. p. 137.
1746. Married — Richard Davies and Eliz. Minshull : St. Geo. Han. Sq. i. 37.
1765. — Nathan Minshall and Esther Clench : ibid. i. 144.
London, 2, 3 ; Manchester, 0, 6 ; New York, 1, 2.

Minskip.—Local, ' of Minskep,' a township in the parish of Aldborough, W. Rid. Yorks.

Sheffield 1.

Minster ; v. Minister.

Minstrel.—Occup. or offic. ' the minstrel.'

William le Menestral, Close Roll, 30 Edw. I.

Minter.—Occup. ' the minter,' a mint-master ; v. Monier, Moneymaker, Moneyman. The reason why these surnames are found scattered over the country lies in the fact that the greater lords, and more considerable cities, had power to issue coin.

Henry le Munetar, co. Salop, 1273. A.
Geoffrey Monetare, co. Salop, ibid.
William Monetarius, co. Salop, ibid.
Ralph le Myneter. N.
Theobald Monetarius, cos. Notts and Derby, Hen. III-Edw. I. K.
1723. Bapt. — Mary, d. Claudius Minter : St. Jas. Clerkenwell, ii. 140.
1781. Married—John Davis and Mary Minter : St. Geo. Han. Sq. i. 323.
London, 9 ; Boston (U.S.), 1.

Mintern, Minterne, Minturn.—Local, ' of Mintern,' two parishes (Magna and Parva) in co. Dorset. In the form of Minturn the name is fairly thriving in the U.S.

1575. John Mintorne, co. Dorset : Reg. Univ. Oxf. vol. ii. pt. ii. p. 66.
1610. Robert Minterne, co. Dorset, ibid. p. 314.
1672. Thomas Rosse and Mary Minterne, co. Soms. : Marriage Lic. (Faculty Office), p. 123.
1750. Married — John Mintern and Rebeckah Roden : St. Geo. Chap. Mayfair, p. 180.
1752. — Thomas Mintren and Sarah Watson : ibid. p. 212.
London, 1, 0, 0 ; MDB. (co. Dorset), 2, 2, 0 ; New York, 0, 0, 10.

Minting.—Local, ' of Minting,' a parish in co. Linc., about six miles from Horncastle.

(Prior) de Mintinge, co. Linc., 1273. A.
London, 1.

Minton.—Local, ' of Mindtown,' a parish five miles from Bishop's Castle, co. Salop. Probably also some smaller spot in co. Northumberland. But this family name has sprung from Shropshire.

Jordan de Minton, co. Northumberland, 1169. KKK. vi. 14.
Peter de Mineton, cos. Salop and Staff., Hen. III-Edw. I. K.
1744. Married — Samuel Minton and Ann Grimsley : St. Geo. Chap. Mayfair, p. 42.
1796. — Francis Minton and Lucy Coleman : St. Geo. Han. Sq. ii. 150.
London, 10 ; MDB. (co. Salop), 8 ; New York, 16.

Mintsmith.—? Occup. ' a maker of coin,' a minter ; v. Minter.

John le Mynsmuth, c. 1300. M.

Mirfield.—Local, ' of Mirfield,' a parish near Dewsbury, W. Rid. Yorks.

Thomas de Mirfield, et Alicia uxor ejus, 1379 : P. T. Yorks. p. 80.
Johannes de Mirfield', et Agnes uxor ejus, 1379 : ibid. p. 179.

Willelmus de Mirfeld, *chivaler*, of Mirfeld', 1379 : ibid. p. 180.
West Rid. Court Dir., 2.

Mirfin.—Bapt. ; v. Marvin.

Mirrorer.—Occup. 'the mirrorer,' a maker of looking-glasses. The manufacture seems to have been confined to London, where, as the centre of fashion, we should naturally expect to see it.
Crispian le Mirorer, London, 1273. A.
John le Mirorer. H.
Richard le Mirouror, London. X.

Misselbrook.—Local, ' of Misselbrook.' I cannot find the spot.
1575. Edward Miselbroke, New Coll. : Reg. Univ. Oxf. iii. 76.

Also found spelt as Missilbrooke, Mistilbrooke, Misselbroke, and Mislebrough.

1751. Married — Stephen Misslebrook and Mary Gough : St. Geo. Chap. Mayfair, p. 191.
London, 1.

Missenden.—Local, ' of Missenden.' Great and Little Missenden are parishes in co. Bucks; also Missenden, a hamlet in the parish of Hitchin, co. Hertford.
Roger de Messindene, co. Bucks, 1273. A.
Hugo de Messenden, co. Northampt., Hen. III–Edw. I. K.
Roger de Messingeden, co. Middlesex, ibid.
1727. Married — William Smith and Sarah Musseldine : St. Jas. Clerkenwell, iii. 254.
1783. Married—George Missildine and Eliz. Adams : St. Geo. Han. Sq. i. 348.
London, 1.

Misson, Mizen, Mizon, Musson.—Local, ' of Misson,' a parish near Bawtry, co. Notts; v. also Musson.
Hugo Mussun, co. Notts, Hen. III–Edw. I. K.
1697. Married — Jerimiah Myson and Susanna Darlow : St. Antholin (London), p. 111.
1753. Bapt.—George, s. Thomas Misen : St. Geo. Chap. Mayfair, p. 11.
1770. Married — Thomas Argill and Mary Misson : St. Geo. Han. Sq. i. 194.
1780. — George Musson and Ann Matthews : St. Geo. Chap. Mayfair, p. 320.
MDB. (co. Notts), (Musson), 3 ; New York (Musson), 2 ; London, 1, 4, 2, 6 ; Philadelphia, 1, 0, 0, 7.

Mister.—Nick. ' the master '; v. Master. It seems to be merely

spelt as ' master ' is colloquially pronounced. Possibly, however, an abbreviation of Minister, q.v.
London, 2 ; New York, 1.

Mitcham.—Local,' of Mitcham,' a parish in co. Surrey, nine miles from London.
Peter de Micham, London, 1273. A.
1754. Married — Daniel Thorp and Sarah Mitcham : St. Geo. Chap. Mayfair, p. 281.
1763. — Thomas Mitcham and Sarah Mash : St. Geo. Han. Sq. i. 126.
London, 3.

Mitchelboy.—Occup. ' Mitchell's boy,' i.e. his young servant ; cf. Matthewman, Addyman, &c. One of a large class.
William Michelboy, co. Suff., Edw. I. R.

Mitchell, Mitchelson.—Bapt. ' the son of Michael,' popularly Mitchell ; cf. *dike* and *ditch*, *kirk* and *church*, &c.
Hugh fil. Micahel, co. Linc., 1273. A.
Roger Michel, co. Norf., ibid.
Mikael de Brackele, London, ibid.
Johannes Michelson, 1379 : P. T. Yorks. p. 15.
Thomas Michilson, 1379 : ibid. p. 19.
Adam Michelson, 1379 : ibid. p. 190.
1563. Bapt.—John, s. Thomas Michell : St. Jas. Clerkenwell, i. 2.
1754. Married — William Mitchel and Eliz. Herring : St. Geo. Han. Sq. i. 53.
London, 168, 4 ; New York, 258, 0 ; Philadelphia, 450, 0.

Mitchinson, Mitcheson.—Bapt. Corruptions of Mitchelson, q.v. Mitchinson is well-known in co. Cumb. The change from *l* to *n* is not uncommon ; cf. *banister* for *baluster*. With the abbreviated Mitcheson cf. Patteson for Pattinson.
1749. Married—Edward L'Epine and Ann Mitchinson : St. Geo. Chap. Mayfair, p. 151.
London, 3, 2 ; MDB. (co. Cumberland), 11, 0 ; Philadelphia, 0, 6.

Mitford.—Local (1) ' of Mitford,' a parish in the union of Morpeth, co. Northumberland. William Mitford, the historian, often resided at Newton Park in the parish, and his ancestors were early lords of Mitford ; (2) ' of Mutford,' a parish in co. Suffolk, three miles from Beccles. Probably the two streams have mingled.

Adam de Mitford, co. Suff., 1273. A.
Peter de Mitford, co. Northumb., ibid.
Robert de Mitford, bailiff of Newcastle-on-Tyne, 1275 : PPP. ii. 12.
Hugh de Mutford, co. Suff., Hen. III–Edw. I. K..
John de Mutteford, co. Kent, 20 Edw. I. R.
1685–6. Lionel Mitford and Katherine Clinton : Marriage Lic. (Cant.), p. 179.
1761. Married—Booth Brathwaite and Ann Mitford : St. Geo. Han. Sq. i. 101.
Crockford, 2.

Mitton.—Local, ' of Mitton,' a parish in the union of Clitheroe, W. Rid. Yorks, but partly in co. Lanc.
John de Miton, 17 Edw. II : Freemen of York, i. 22.
Adam de Mytton, 1379 : P. T. Yorks. p. 268.
Johannes de Mytton, *sutor*, ibid. p. 266.
Robert Mitton, of Great Marsden, *clothier*, 1558 : Wills at Chester (1545–1620), p. 137.
William Mitton, of Burnley, 1570 : ibid.
Henry Mitton, of Colne, 1597 : ibid.
West Rid. Court Dir., 8 ; London, 3 ; Manchester, 6 ; Colne, 1 ; New York, 1 ; Philadelphia, 12.

Mizen, -zon ; v. Misson.

Mobbs ; v. Mabb.

Moberley, Moberly.—Local, ' of Mobberly,' a parish in co. Chester, two miles from Nether Knutsford.
Patrick Moberlegh, c. 1220 : East Cheshire, ii. 550.
William de Modburlegh, 1308 : ibid. p. 85.
1565. Bapt. — Margery Mobberleye : Reg. Prestbury, co. Ches., p. 15.
1568. — John Moberleye : ibid. p. 24.
1585. Edward Mobberley, of Norley, *yeoman* : Wills at Chester (1545–1620), p. 137.
1756. Married—Richard Moberly and Jane Adams : St. Geo. Han. Sq. i. 62.
Crockford, 1, 6 ; London, 0, 4 ; Boston (U.S.), 0, 1.

Mocker.—Nick. ' the mocker,' one who derided, a scoffer.
William le Mokare, Fines Roll, 11 Edw. I. Philadelphia, 2.

Mockridge ; v. Moggridge.

Moffat, Moffatt.—Local, ' of Moffatt,' a parish partly in Lanarkshire, and partly in Dumfriesshire.
1778. Married—John Curtis and Eliz. Moffatt : St. Geo. Han. Sq. i. 291.
1787. — Mathew Swan and Margaret Moffett : ibid. p. 406.
London, 2, 10 ; New York, 11, 7.

Mogford, Mugford.—Local, ' of Mogford ' or ' Mockford.' I cannot identify the spot. For similar changes in the spelling of the first syllable v. Moggridge.

1777. Married — Francis Resin and Eliz. Mugford : St. Geo. Han. Sq. i. 282.
— — John Mockford and Margaret Musgrove: ibid.
London, 5, 1 ; New York, 0, 1 ; Boston (U.S.), 0, 2.

Mogg, Mogge, Moggs.—Bapt. 'the son of Margaret,' from the nick. Mogg or Moggy ; v. Moxon. Margaret ran riot among the vowels with Mag, Meg, and Mog for nicks.

William Mogge, co. Soms., 1 Edw. III : Kirby's Quest, p. 269.
Peter Mog, co. Soms., 1 Edw. III: ibid.
1729. Married — Daniel Moggs and Grace Baker: St.Geo.Chap.Mayfair,p.295.
1798. — Robert Mogg and Mary Ann James : St. Geo. Han. Sq. ii. 186.
London, 3, 2, 0.

Moggridge, Mockridge, Muggeridge, Mogridge.— Local, ' of Moggridge.' I cannot discover the spot ; manifestly the suffix is -ridge. The curious tricks that can be played with the spelling of surnames is well exemplified by Lower, who states that he once saw Mugridge over a small shop in co. Sussex, while in the window 'Muggerages ginber-beer' was announced for sale.

1586. George Mogerege, co. Wilts, Balliol College: Reg. Univ. Oxf. vol. ii. pt. ii. p. 150.
1590. Married — Tristram Blaby and Joane Morgradge : St. Mary Aldermary (London), p. 8.
1760. — James Clarke and Ann Mugrige : St. Geo. Han. Sq. i. 97.
1773. Thomas Pring and Mary Mugridge : ibid. i. 227.
London, 10, 3, 10, 0 ; MDB. (co. Soms.), 1, 0, 0, 1 ; Philadelphia (Mogridge), 3.

Mohun.—Local, 'de Mohun' ; v. Moon, its modern representative.
Crockford, 1 ; Philadelphia, 1.

Mold.—Bapt. ; v. Mould.

Mole.—Local, ' of Mole.'
Willelmus Praepositus de Mole, co. Glouc., temp. Hen. III-Edw. I. K.
Nicholas de Mol, ibid.
London, 4 ; Oxford, 5 ; Philadelphia, 2.

Molehunt.—Occup. 'the mole-hunt,' one who hunted down moles for the farmers, receiving a stated price ; v. Hunt = Hunter.
William Molehunte, co. Suff., 1273. A.

Molesworth.—Local,' of Molesworth,' a parish in co. Hunts.

John de Molesworthe, co.Hunts, 1273. A.
Richard de Molesworth, co. Hunts, ibid.
Nicholas de Mulsewrthe, co. Hunts, ibid.
1624. Bapt. — Winkfeilde, s. William Molsworthe: St. Michael. Cornhill, p. 117.
1762. Married—John Molesworth and Barbara St.Aubyn: St.Geo.Han. Sq. i. 112.
London, 2 ; Crockford, 8 ; New York, 2.

Molineaux, Molineux, Mollineux, Molyneux, Mollyneux, Mullineaux, Mullineux.—Local, ' de Molineaux.' Probably, like the noble family who trace from William the Conqueror, from Molineaux-sur-Seine, near Rouen. This name has ramified very strongly in co. Lanc., and is found in all classes of society, from the highest to the lowest. Six centuries have brought their troubles upon younger branches of the family.

Adam de Mulyneus, alias Molynens, co. Lanc., Hen. III-Edw. I. K.
Richard de Molyneaus, co. Northumb., 20 Edw. I. R.
1578. John Molynex, co. Lanc.: Reg. Univ. Oxf. vol. ii. pt. ii. p. 79.
1608. James Mollineux, co. Lanc. : ibid. p. 300.
1583-4. John Hollande and Mary Mollenax : Marriage Lic. (London), i. 129.
1592. Thomas Molineux, of Garstang, co. Lanc. : Wills at Chester, i. 137.
1607. William Molineux, of Ormskirk: ibid.
1603. Buried — James Mullinax: St. Michael, Cornhill, p. 212.
1634. Bapt.—Henry, s. John Mollinox : St. Jas. Clerkenwell, i. 126.
London, 1, 1, 1, 6, 0, 0, 1 ; MDB. (co. Lanc.), 0, 0, 0, 9, 1, 1, 1 ; Manchester (Molyneux), 18 ; New York, 0, 2, 0, 1, 0, 1, 0 ; Philadelphia, 6, 0, 0, 0, 0, 16, 0.

Moll, Mollison, Mollinson, Molleson.—Bapt. ' the son of Mary,' from the nick. Mall, and dim. Mall-in; v. Malleson and Mallinson. Later on Mall and Mally became Moll and Molly ; cf. Magg and Mogg, the nicks. of Margaret.

Margaret Molleson, 1379 : P. T. Yorks. p. 89.
1550. Bapt. —— the son of Fraunces Molsonne : St. Peter, Cornhill, i. 5.
1741. Married — Francis Mollison and Eliz. Fletcher : St. Geo. Chap. Mayfair, p. 15.
1789. — John Molisone and Miriam Seal : St. Geo. Han. Sq. ii. 28.
Manchester, 1, 1, 1, 0 ; New York, 21, 0, 0, 5.

Molland.—Local, ' of Molland,' a parish in co. Devon.
Simon de Molland, co. Devon. K.
London, 2 ; MDB. (co. Devon), 1.

Mollett, Mollet.—Bapt. ' the son of Mary,' from the nick. Moll, and dim. Moll-et or Moll-ot ; cf. Emmott, Tillot, Bartlett, &c.

Alicia Molot, 1379 : P. T. Yorks. p. 89.
1685-6. James Mollet and Mary Langdon : Marriage Alleg. (Cant.), p. 222.
1766. Married — Amos Mollett and Eliz. Sauberre : St. Geo. Han. Sq. i. 157.
London, 2, 0 ; Manchester, 1, 0 ; New York, 2, 1.

Mollison ; v. Moll.

Molyneux ; v. Molineaux.

Mompesson.—Local, ' de Mont Pinson,' a castle on the river Scie, in Normandy (Lower),

Philip de Mumpinzun, co.York,1273. A.
Adam le Mūpincū, co. Norf., ibid.
Oliver de Mounpynson, vicar of Attleborough, co. Norf., 1320 : FF. i. 524.
John Mompesson, rector of Hasingham, co. Norf., 1717 : FF. vii. 234.
1693-4. Edward Momperson and Jane Gardner : Marriage Alleg. (Canterbury), p. 285.
1703. Charles Mompesson and Eliz. Longueville : Marriage Lic. (Faculty Office), p. 246.

Monday, Munday, Mundey, Mundy.—(1) Personal or baptismal, ' the son of Monday ' ; cf. Saturday, Friday.

Simon Moneday, co. Hunts, 1273. A.
Simon Mundi, co. Camb., ibid.
Henry Mundi, co. Camb., ibid.
Edmund Moneday,co. Soms.,1 Edw.III : Kirby's Quest, p. 245.

(2) Local, ' of Mondaye.' A correspondent writes : ' Mondaye, a hill in the parish of Juaye, about six miles from Bayeaux, is still extant, likewise the abbey. . . . The hill was originally called Mont d'Aë : in the langue d'oïl Aë signifies water.' It is highly probable that Monday is in some cases local, but I have not any early instances to bring forward in evidence.

1584. Married — Thomas Gibbyns and Agnes Munday : St. Jas. Clerkenwell, i. 11.
1657. — Richard Chase and Bridgett Monday : St. Michael, Cornhill, p. 37.
London, 3,15, 1, 13 ; New York, 5, 5, 0, 6.

Money, Monney.—(1) Local, ' de Monyé.' Probably ' Monnay, a place in Normandy, in the department of Orne ' (Lower).

John de Mony, co. Soms., 1273. A.
William de Monye,co.Glo.,20 Edw.I. R.
William de Money, co. Oxf., Hen. III-Edw. I. K.

(2) Official, 'the monk,' one of the endless forms of 'le Moyne' or 'le Moigne'; v. Munn.

Robert le Monhe, co. Norf., 1273. A.
William le Mone, co. Kent, ibid.
Robert Monay, co. Oxf., ibid.
Henry le Monie, co. Glouc., 20 Edw. I. R.
John le Monie, co. Glouc., ibid.
1785. Married — Joseph Money and Eliz. Withey : St. Geo. Han. Sq. i. 380.
London, 5, 0; Oxford, 7, 0; New York, 1, 0; Boston (U.S.), 3, 3.

Moneymaker, Moneyman. Occup.'a maker of coin'; v. Monier.

John Monemaker, co. York. W. 2.
' In the 38th of Henry VIII, Robert Moneyman conveyed two messuages, 40 acres of land,' &c.: Randworth, co. Norf., FF. xi. 113.

Moneypeny. — Local. One thing is very certain, this surname has nothing to do with *money* generally, nor a *penny* specifically. Although now a recognized Scotch surname, it is early found on English soil. Lower says, 'that it is local is proved by the prefix *de* with which it is found in early records.' Unfortunately my instances are without any prefix.

John Manipenyn, co. Bedf., 1273. A.
Herbert Manipeni, co. Hunts, ibid.
Henry Muddepenyng, C. R., 14 Edw. III. pt. ii.
John Manypany, C. R., 45 Edw. III.
Thomas Monipeni, co. York. W. 2.
Alex. Moneypenny. FF.
Crockford, 2 ; New York, 2.

Monier.—Occup. 'the moneyer,' a maker of coin, a mint-master; v. Minter. The name still exists, but it is hard to find modern instances.

Henry le Moneur, co. Salop, 1273. A.
Haco le Muner, co. Suff., ibid.
Henry le Moneur, C. R., 3 Edw. II.
Walter le Monner, London, 20 Edw. I. R.
John le Monnier. N.
Hamo le Monner. T.
Gilbert le Muner. G.
Philadelphia, 2.

Monk, Monke, Munk. — Official, 'the monk,' a recluse. A.S. *munec.*

William le Monek, 1273. A.
Peter le Monek, temp. 1300. M.
John le Monck. G.
Johannes Mounke et Agnes uxor ejus, 1379: P. T. Yorks. p. 23.
Willelmus Mounke et Alicia uxor ejus, 1379: ibid.

Agnes Moncke, 1379 : ibid. p. 38.
Johannes Moncke, 1379 : ibid.
1638. Married—William Worslye and Agnes Monke : St. Jas. Clerkenwell, iii. 70.
London, 28, 0, 1 ; New York, 7, 0, 3.

Monkey.—Local. 'of the monkhaw,' i. e. the monk's enclosure ; cf. Hay and Haw in Hayward or Haward, q.v.

John del Monkhagh, 1379 : P. T. Yorks. p. 147.

More than a century afterwards the tendency to imitation appears :

'Johannes Monkey, nuper de Laystoff in Com. Suffochire,' 2 Hen. VIII : HHH. p. 124.

I do not find the name in modern directories.

Monkhouse.—Local, 'at the monk-house,' i.e. the house where the monk or monks resided; cf. Chanonhouse (i. e. Canon-house). With such forms as Munkus, &c., cf. Loftus for Lofthouse, or Malthus for Malthouse.

Rogerus del Munkhous, 1379 : P. T. Yorks. p. 234.
Thomas Munkas, of Chorlton, Manchester, 1660: Wills at Chester (1660–80), p. 193.
1602. Married—Thomas Fulwode and Ales Munckus : St. Antholin (London), p. 41.
1762. Married — Peter Mounkhouse and Mary Booth : St. Geo. Han. Sq. i. 113.
London, 1 ; York, 3; Crockford, 4; MDB. (co. Cumberland), 13; Philadelphia, 7.

Monkman, Monckman, Monkmon.—Occup. 'the monk's man,' i. e. servant of the monk; v. Priestman. Almost all these names ending in man (=servant) belong to the county of York; v. Matthewman.

John Monkeman, co. York, 1273. A.
Henry Munkeman, co. York, ibid.
William Munkeman, co. York. W. 15.
Robertus Monckeman, 1379: P. T. Yorks. p. 118.
Johannes Munkman, *barker*, 1379: ibid. p. 98.

The surname still clings to Yorkshire. An action was tried at York to recover damages, in which one of this name appears, hailing from Malton (Manchester Evening News, March 12, 1886).

York, 2, 0, 0 ; Bradford, 0, 2, 1.

Monkton, Monckton.—Local, 'of Monkton,' i.e. the monk's stead or farm. Parishes in various diocs. are so called, viz. Ripon (2), York (1), Salisbury (2), Exeter (1), Canterbury (1), Bath and Wells (2), &c.

William de Moneketon, co. Wilts, 1273. A.
Peter de Munkton, *sutor*, 5 Edw. II : Freemen of York, i. 14.
Henricus de Monketon, 1379: P. T. Yorks. p. 299.
Johannes de Monkton,1359: ibid. p. 212.
William de Muncketon,1379: ibid. p. 47.
1774. Married — Charles Monckton and Betsey Edwards: St. Geo. Han. Sq. i. 246.
London, 3, 4 ; Crockford, 0, 1.

Montagu, Montague.—Local, 'of Montagu,' in Normandy. The Latinized form was 'de Monte Acuto,' whence the occasional Montacute. The 'Prior Montis Acuti' is mentioned in the Hundred Rolls (ii. 125). The parish of Montacute, co. Somerset, took its name from the family. 'Drogo de Monte-Acuto, the great Domesday tenant, came over in the retinue of Robert Earl of Mortain, the Conqueror's half-brother' : Collins, quoted by Lower.

William de Monte Acuto, co. Southampton, 1273. A.
William de Montagu, co. Bucks, ibid.
Symon de Monte Acuto, co. Devon, ibid.
1526. John Muntagew and Catherine Slene : Marriage Lic. (London), i. 5.
1628. Bapt. — Edward, s. Thomas Mountague : St. Jas. Clerkenwell, i. 109.
London, 2, 11 ; New York, 0, 19.

Montford ; v. Mountford.

Montgomery, Montgomerie, Montgomray.—Local, 'of Montgomerie,' near Lisieux, in Normandy. Of this great family, which gave name to the shire and town of Montgomery in Wales, Lower says, 'One of them, Roger de Montgomery, a kinsman of the Conqueror, accompanied him, and led the centre of his army at Hastings' (Patr. Brit. p. 228). It is more natural to refer back the surname to the Norman estate than to the county to which the family gave their name.

Fulco de Mongomery, co. Devon, 1273. A.
Lucia de Mongomery, co. Notts, ibid.

Gregory de Montgomery, co. Salop, 1273. A.
1530. John Dalton and Eliz. Mungumbery: Marriage Lic. (London), i. 7.
1745. Married—Hugh Fergusson and Margaret Montgomery: St. Geo. Han. Sq. i. 34.
1758.—George Montgomerie and Eliz. Lloyd: ibid. p. 77.
London, 11, 3, 1; New York, 90, 0, 0.

Monument, Mornement.— ? Local. Lower says, 'from residence at or near a monument.' I do not think this view satisfactory, and question its local application in the surname epoch. Perhaps it represents an early form (corrupted later on) of Monmouth. In this case the corruption would be, as usual, imitative.

John de Monemuta, co. Glouc., 1273. A.
1767. Married — Samuel Monument and Eliz. Holmes: St. Geo. Han. Sq. i. 182.
London, 0, 1.

Moody, Moodey, Moodie, Mudie.—Nick. 'the moody,' i.e. the brave, the bold, the resolute. A common sobriquet in the Hundred Rolls. Mudie is a Scottish form. Moody also frequently hails from over the Border.

'Aslaked was his mood,' i.e. anger.
Chaucer, C. T. 1762.
'Mody, Mwdy, adj., proud, brave. Moodie, Mudie, gallant, courageous' (Jamieson).

Adam Mody, co. Oxf., 1273. A.
Roger Mody, co. Salop, ibid.
Simon Modi, co. Camb., ibid.
Johannes Mody, husband, 1379: P. T. Howdenshire, p. 15.
Thomas Mody and Sibota uxor ejus, 1379: P. T. Yorks. p. 5.
Thomas Mody and Agnes uxor ejus: 1379: ibid. p. 101.
1544. Married—Henry Mody and Anne Laurence: Marriage Lic. (Canterbury), p. 3.
1605. — Henry Modye and Deborah Dunche: St. Mary Aldermary, p. 11.
1621. Thomas Moody and Margaret Scrivenor: Marriage Lic. (London), p. 108.
London, 22, 1, 1, 7; West Rid. Court Dir., 12, 0, 0, 0; New York, 34, 1, 1, 0.

Moon, Moone, Munn.—Local, 'de Mohun'; cf. Boon, and in some cases Bunn for 'de Bohun.' Lower says, 'Moon, a corruption of Mohun. The Itin. de la Normandie, speaking of the place from whence the Mohuns derived their name (Moyon), says, 'Masseville appelle ce bourg Moon.' (2) Offic. 'the monk'; v. Munn.

John de Mohun, co. Somerset, 1273. A.
Reginald de Mohun, co. Devon, Hen. III—Edw. I. K.
William de Mohun, co. Wilts, ibid.
1651. Married — Thomas Haynes and Dorothy Moone: St. Jas. Clerkenwell, iii. 87.
1661. — William Mohun and Mary Morgan: Marriage Lic. (Canterbury), p. 55.
1762.—William Moon and Mary Stuart: St. Geo. Han. Sq. i. 116.
London, 26, 1, 7; New York, 9, 0, 19.

Moor, Moore, More.—Local, 'at the moor' (A.S. mór, a heath), from residence thereby; v. Moorhouse.

John atte Mor, co. Norf., 1273. A.
Adam atte More, co. Oxf., ibid.
Fulco de la More, co. Hunts, ibid.
Pontius de la More, co. York, ibid.
Agatha atte More, co. Soms., 1327: Tax Roll.
Alicia del More, 1379: P. T. Yorks. p. 219.
Johannes atte More, 1379: ibid. p. 31.
1578. Married—Henrie More and Alice Simpson: St. Mary Aldermary (London), p. 6.
London, 2, 243, 6; New York, 3, 602, 21.

Moorcock, Morcock.—Bapt. 'the son of Maurice,' from the nick. Mor (v. Morin), with the suffix -cock (v. Cock) as in Wilcock, &c. It may possibly be a nickname = Moorcock, the red grouse, but the first definition is more natural and according to rule. The fact that Mor-kin also existed (cf. Jenkin, Wilkin, &c.) is additional evidence. On the other hand, Moorhen (q.v.) also existed as a nickname. It is hard, after all, to say which is the true definition.—Since writing the above I have lighted on an entry in Kirby's Quest which settles the matter:

Morecok Chepman, co. Soms., 1 Edw. III: Kirby's Quest, p. 264.
Nicholas Morcok, co. Soms., 1 Edw. III: ibid. p. 155.
Morekin de Vautham, London, 1273. A.
Morekin le Wolmongere, London, ibid.
Henricus Morekok, 1379: P. T. Yorks. p. 94.
Joan Morecocke, 1661: St. Peter, Cornhill, i. 103.
1625. Nicholas Morecocke and Anne Eate: Marriage Lic. (London), i. 163.
1773. Married — William Price and Sarah Moorcock: St. Geo. Han. Sq. i. 233.

Moorcraft, Moorcroft, Morecroft. — Local, 'at the moor-croft,' i.e. from residence at the enclosure, or croft, on the moor (v. Croft and Craft). With the variant Moorcraft, cf. Meadowcraft. Some small spot on the borders of Cheshire has given birth to a surname which still thrives in south Lancashire. But v. Marcroft.

Brian Morecroft, priest, 1524: East Ches. ii. 92.
Bryan Morecroft, of Ormskirk, 1589: Wills at Chester (1545-1620), p. 138.
Henry Morecroft, of Swanscough, co. Ches., 1567: ibid.
1594. Ferdinando Moorecroft, co. Lanc.: Reg. Univ. Oxf. vol. ii. pt. ii. p. 207.
1635. Bapt.—Phillip, d. Richard Moorcraft: St. Antholin (London), p. 69.
Liverpool, 0, 3, 3; London, 1, 1, 0.

Moorhen.—Nick. 'the moor-hen,' seemingly the feminine of Moorcock, q.v. It maintained its existence till the 17th century.

Magota Morehen, 1379: P. T. Yorks. p. 54.
1627. Buried—Widdow Moorehen, one of the pencioners: St. Peter, Cornhill, i. 189.
1752. Married—William Morehen and Mary Woolly. St. Geo. Chap. Mayfair, p. 207.

I suspect this name is either extinct or lost in Morin.

Moorhouse, Morehouse.—Local, 'at the moor-house,' the cottage situate on the moor, a local name common to many places. I had a Moorhouse in my parish (Ulverston), a farmstead still far separated from other abodes. It gave rise to a family of Moorhouses resident in the immediate district for centuries. Some of the many Yorkshire Moorhouses, or Morehouses, are doubtless sprung from Moorhouse, now increased to a hamlet in the parish of Hooton Pagnell, near Doncaster. Naturally we find this name predominant in the North.

Geoffrey atte Morhouse, co. Soms., 1 Edw. III: Kirby's Quest, p. 232.
Adam de Merehowse (sic), 1379: P. T. Yorks. p. 274.
Johannes de Morehowse, 1379: ibid. p. 275.
Thomas Morehowse, 1379: ibid.
Elias de Morehous, 1379: ibid. p. 245.

1558-9. Oliver Morehouse and Katherine Sprickeman: Marriage Lic. (Westminster), p. 1.
1621. John Morehouse, co. Cumb.: Reg. Univ. Oxf. vol. ii. pt. ii. p. 398.
London, 3, 0; West Rid. Court Dir., 14, 3; Manchester, 15, 0; New York, 1, 6; Philadelphia, 12, 2.

Moorman.—Local, 'the moorman,' one who dwelt on the moor; cf. Bridgeman, Houseman, &c.

Johannes Morman, 1379: P. T. Yorks. p. 173.
Adam Morman (sic), co. Soms., 1 Edw. III: Kirby's Quest, p. 177.
1752. Married—James Moorman and Jane Grey: St. Geo. Chap. Mayfair, p. 227.
1787. Married—James Moorman and Sarah Glover: St. Geo. Han. Sq. i. 403.
London, 1; Manchester, 1; Philadelphia, 1.

Moorsom, Morson. — Bapt. 'the son of Morris.' From Morrison to Morson was a natural transition; cf. Morse for Morris. The *m* in Moorsom presents no difficulty, as the final -*son* was often corrupted to -*som*; cf. Ransom, Hansom, Sansom. Nevertheless Mr. Lower's suggestion that it is for Moorsham, a township in the parish of Skelton, N. Rid. Yorks, must not be overlooked. I see the Modern Domesday Book has one instance in the North Riding. This confirms Mr. Lower's view.

1693. Richard Morson and Mary Nutt: Marriage Alleg. (Canterbury), p. 264.
1778. Married—William Morson and Catherine Coffering: St. Geo. Han. Sq. i. 291.
1784. — Richard Toms and Catherine Morsom: ibid. p. 364.
London, 3, 1; Leeds, 1, 0; MDB. (North Rid. Yorks), 1, 0; New York, 0, 3.

Moorward.—Offic. 'the moorward,' the guardian or keeper of a moor. Probably lost in the local Moorwood, q.v.

German le Morward, co. Southampton, 1273. A.
Henry le Morward. B.

Moorwood, Morewood. — Local, 'of Moorwood.' Seemingly a spot in co. Lincoln.

Ralph de Morwode, or Morewude, co. Linc., 1273. A.
Alicia de Morewod', 1379: P. T. Yorks. p. 40.

1740. Married — Andrew Moorwood and Eliz. Sherman: St. Jas. Clerkenwell, iii. 270.
London, 1, 4; New York, 0, 6.

Morby, Morbey, Murby.—Local, 'of Moorby,' a parish in co. Lincoln, near Horncastle.

Elena de Moreby, 1379: P. T. Yorks. p. 154.
1675. Joseph Moreby and Mary Wood: Marriage Alleg. (Canterbury), p. 153.
London, 3, 1, 1; Philadelphia, 1, 0, 0.

Mordan, Morden, Murden.—Local, (1) 'of Mordon,' a township in the parish of Sedgefield, co. Durham; (2) also 'of Morden,' a parish in co. Dorset, six miles from Wareham; (3) also 'of Morden,' a parish in co. Surrey, one mile from Mitcham; (4) also 'of Morden,' two parishes in co. Cambridge.

John de Mordon, co. Camb., 1273. A.
John de Mordene, co. Camb., ibid.
Ralph de Mordone, co. Camb., ibid.
Symon de Mordone, co. Camb., ibid.
Gilbert de Mordon, Lond., 20 Edw. I. R.
Robert de Moredone, co. Devon, Hen. III-Edw. I. K.
Peter de Mordon, co. Wilts, ibid.
1619. George Morden and Martha Harris: Marriage Lic. (Westminster), p. 26.
1763. Married—James Morden and Priscilla Holdman: St. Geo. Han. Sq. i 125.
1769. — George Mackmolt and Mary Mordin: ibid. p. 190.
London, 2, 1, 1; MDB. (Cambridge), 0, 3, 0; New York, 0, 1, 0.

Mordaunt, Mordan.—Nick. 'the biter.' The legend has ever been that this is the origin of this Norman name. Mr. Lower quotes that 'Osbert le Mordaunt possessed Radwell, co. Bedford, by gift of his brother, who had received it from the Conqueror for services rendered' (Patr. Brit. p. 229).

Robert le Mordaunt, co. Bedf., 1273. A.
William le Mordaunt, co. Bedf., ibid.
1575. Edmund Mordant, co. Bedf.: Reg. Univ. Oxf. vol. ii. pt. ii. p. 64.
1739. George Dixon and Mary Mordaunt: St. Geo. Han. Sq. i. 22.
London, 2, 2; New York, 2, 0.

More.—Local; v. Moor.

Morecroft; v. Moorcroft.

Morehouse; v. Moorhouse.

Morel, Morell, Morrall, Morrell, Morrill. — (1) Nick. 'the morel,' dark-complexioned.

A once common name for a horse. 'Morel, horse, *morellus*': Prompt. Parv. Mr. Way in a note quotes, 'Morel: noir, tanné, tirant sur le brun': Roquefort. In the Towneley Mysteries, p. 9, 'Morelle' occurs as one of the steeds yoked to Cain's plough; cf. *morel*, a species of dark cherry.

Hervens Morel, co. Norf., 1273. A.
Nicholas Morel, co. Norf., ibid.
Thomas Morel, co. Hunts, ibid.
Ralph Morell. J.

(2) Bapt. 'the son of Morel,' i. e. dark-complexioned. White, Black, and Brown (q.v.) were all employed as baptismal names.

Moral de Hulfton, 1171: KKK. vi. 19.
Morel (without surname), co. Camb., 1273. A.
The heirs of Morell, co. Camb., ibid.
1666. Stephen Brewer and Anne Morrell: Marriage Alleg. (Canterbury), p. 115.
London, 5, 3, 4, 19, 2; New York, 1, 2, 0, 26, 0.

Moreton.—Local, 'of Moreton,' i.e. the enclosure on the moor; cf. Morton. Of course there are wellnigh endless places styled by this name, some of which have originated surnames. Moreton, a township in the union of Congleton, co. Ches., seems to be the parent of the Lancashire and Cheshire Moretons.

Eustace de Moreton, co. Worc., Hen. III-Edw. I. K.
William de Moreton, co. Soms., ibid.
John Moreton, of Moreton, 1598: Wills at Chester (1545-1620), p. 138.
Brian Moreton, of Congleton, 1614: ibid.
1613. Married—James Battey and Eliz. Moreton, or Mooreton: St. Jas. Clerkenwell, p. 39.
London, 6; Manchester, 2; Liverpool, 6; New York, 1; MDB. (Cheshire), 10; Boston (U.S.), 1.

Morewood; v. Moorwood.

Morey.—Local, 'at the moorhey,' from residence by the enclosure on the moor (v. Hey or Hay). This suffix -*hay* or -*hey* frequently slips the *h* and becomes -*ey*.

William Morehay, C. R., 14 Ric. II.
1738. Bapt.—Mary, d. John Moorey: St. Mary Aldermary (London), p. 128.
1747. Married—William Coleman and Mary Morey: St. Geo. Chap. Mayfair, p. 101.

1775. Married — Thomas Eades and Barbara Jane Morey: St. Geo. Han. Sq. i. 255.
London, 8; New York, 12.

Morgan, Morgans. — Bapt. 'the son of Morgan' (Welsh`. Latterly in the place of Ap-Morgan, the true Welsh patronymic, an English form Morgans has arisen; cf. Williams for Ap-William.

Walter Morgan, co. Oxf., 1273. A.
'Item, geven to David ap Morgan, xxs': 1537: Privy Purse Exp., Princess Mary, p. 45.
Morgan Gough, C. R., 20 Hen. VI.
1610. Dapt. John, • Morgan Davies: St. Jas. Clerkenwell, i. 76.
Thomas Morgan. of Chester, 1602: Wills at Chester (1545-1620), p. 137.
London, 200, 0; MDB. (co. Glamorgan), 64, 3; New York, 250, 0.

Morin, Moring, Morrin. — Bapt. 'the son of Maurice,' from nick. More, and dim. Mor-in; cf. Col-in, Rob-in. The name is a common one (always without prefix) in the Hundred Rolls, and the origin need not be doubted. There was evidently a nick. Mor or More, and the usual dims. Morin, Morcock, and Morkin were formed from it; v. Moorcock. The g in Moring is excrescent, as in Jennings.

Isabella fil. Morini, co. Camb., 1273. A.
Geoffrey Morin, co. Camb., ibid.
Ralph Moryn, co. Bedf., ibid.
Simon Morin. co. Oxf., ibid.
Flandrina Moryn, co. Northampton, ibid.
William Moryn, co. Soms., 1 Edw. III: Kirby's Quest, p. 228.

Since writing the above, I have found entries that absolutely settle the question. The same individual is thus referred to:

Morinus de la Bare, co. Devon, 1273. A.
Morinus de Bare, co. Devon, ibid.
• Moritius de Bare, co. Devon, ibid.
1668-9. Thomas Morin and Susanna Barnardiston: Marriage Alleg. (Canterbury), p. 161.
1756. Married — Nicholas Perrin and Ann Morin: St. Geo. Han. Sq. i. 65.
London, 1, 3, 1; New York, 2, 1, 1.

Morley.—Local, 'of Morley.' Parishes in cos. Derby and Norfolk (2); also an ecclesiastical district in the parish of Batley, W. Rid. Yorks, besides many small localities. 'The pasture on the moor' would naturally be styled by this name.

Johannes de Morelay, 1379: P. T. Yorks. p. 56.
Adam de Morlay, 1319: ibid.
Margeria de Morlay, 1379: ibid. p. 142.
1569. Married—Richarde Morley and Avis Tucke: St. Mary Aldermary, p. 5.
London, 41; MDB. (West Rid. Yorks), 11; New York, 4; Boston (U.S.), 18.

Morling.—Bapt. 'the son of Maurice,' dim. Mor-ling; cf. Hewling, Hickling, and v. Morin.

Hugh Morlyng, co. Camb., 1273. A.
1626. William Parsonn and Anne Morlinge: Marriage Lic. (London), i. 165.
1745. Married—John Morling and Mary Musgrave: St. Dionis Backchurch, p. 69.
London, 3.

Morpeth.—Local, 'of Morpeth,' co. Northumberland.

Roger de Morpath, co. York, 1273. A.
William de Morpathe, co. York, ibid.
London, 2.

Morrall, Morrell, Morrill; v. Morel.

Morrin.—Bapt.; v. Morin.

Morris, Morrish, Morriss, Morrison.—(1) Bapt. 'the son of Maurice,' commonly spelt Morris; v. Maurice.

Mauricius fil. Mauricii, co. Northampton, 20 Edw. I. R.
Thomas Moriz', co. Bedf., ibid.
Ricardus Morrisson, 1379: P. T. Yorks. p. 185.
William Moreson, 1379: ibid. p. 265.
Elena Morys, 1379: ibid. p. 56.
Johannes Morys, 1379: ibid.
Morice ap Owen. XX.
Jevan ap Moris Kemys: Visit. Glouc. 1623, p. 98.

(2) Nick. 'the Moreys,' i.e. the Moorish, the Moor; cf. Norris.

Robert le Moreys, co. Soms., 1273. A.
William de (sic) Morreys, co. Suff., ibid.
1575. Married — Robert Wolfe and Johane Morrys: St. Jas. Clerkenwell, p. 6.
1602. — Israell Garrett and Alice Morrice: ibid. i. 26.
London, 174, 6, 4, 41; New York, 344, 1, 0, 8.

Morrow, Marrow. — Local, 'of the moor-row,' i.e. the cottages on the moor. Row is a common suffix to early local surnames. A.S. raw, a row (Skeat); cf. Townd-row. Lower says that Morrow is a corruption of Mac Murrough. This may be true in certain cases, but there is undoubtedly an English surname Morrow also which has

to be explained. Neither must it be forgotten that there is a hamlet Morrowe in the parish of Wisbeach, co. Cumb.

Willelmus de Morerawe, 1379: P. T. Yorks. p. 241.
Johannes Marowe, 1379: ibid. p. 22.
William Marrow, of Leighton Wood, 1591: Wills at Chester (1545-1620), p. 131.
1567. Married—Umphrey Marrowe and Ellyn Todd: St. Michael, Cornhill, p. 9.
London, 4, 0: Halifax, 1, 0; Liverpool, 4, 2; New York, 46, 1.

Morse, Morss. — Bapt. 'the son of Morris' (q.v.), modified into Morse.

1555. Silvester Steweley and Mary Mors: Marriage Lic. (London), i. 17.
1610. John Morse and Dorothy Burnap: ibid. p. 319.
1684. Buried—Mary, d. Eward Morss: St. Mary Aldermary, p. 196.
London, 18, 2; New York, 55, 3.

Morson. — Bapt.; v. Moorsom.

Mortan, Morten.—Local; v. Mortyn. Not to be confounded with Morton.

Mortiboy, Martiboy.—Local. This name has been placed in the roll of fame by Sir W. Besant and the late Mr. Rice in their story Readymoney Mortiboy. It is no fancy name, as the London Dir. proves. Manifestly its last syllable is Fr. bois (v. Boys or Boyce), a wood, as in Talboys. This is confirmed by the entry:

1700. Bapt.—Jane, d. John Morteboyes: St. Jas. Clerkenwell, i. 389.
1702. — Rebecca, d. John Morteboys: ibid. ii. 8.

As I have found no earlier reference, I presume it is of fairly modern French extraction. I wonder where Sir W. Besant or Mr. Rice met it? Many of Charles Dickens' characters will be met with in this dictionary.

London, 2, 0; MDB. (co. Staff.), 0, 1.

Mortimer, Mortimore. — Local, 'de Mortimer,' Latinized in old rolls into de Mortuo Mari, i.e. Dead Sea. Lower says it was for this reason that the surname was supposed to have sprung from Crusading times. 'The castle and barony of Mortemer lie in the arrondissement of Neufchâtel in Normandy': Patr. Brit. p. 230.

Ralph de Mortimer, co. Linc., 1273. A.
Hugh de Mortuomari, co. Heref., ibid.
Lucia de Mortuomari, co. Heref., ibid.
Sir Robert de Mortimer, co. Norf., 1381 : FF. i. 485.
Willelmus Mortimere, 1379 : P.T.Yorks. p. 184.
1581. William Mortimer, co. Wilts : Reg. Univ. Oxf. vol. ii. pt. ii. p. 109.
1601. James Mortimer, co. Cardigan : ibid. p. 252.
London, 19, 10 ; New York, 39, 3.

Mortlock.—Local, 'of Mortlake,' a parish in co. Surrey. There can be no doubt about this derivation.

Walter Mortlake, co. Camb., 1273. A.
1565. John Mortlake and Dorothy Chesell : Marriage Lic. (London), i. 31.
1581. John Moreclacke and Eliz Woode : ibid. p. 105.
1744. Married—Geo. Brisac and Mary Mortlock : St. Geo. Chap. Mayfair, p. 41.
1746. — Richard Gale, of Mortlock, co. Surrey, and Grace Hughes: ibid. p. 65.
London, 13 ; Philadelphia, 1.

Morton.—Local, 'of Morton,' i. e. the moor-ton, the farm or enclosure on the moor. This naturally has given birth to many place-names, and as a consequence surnames. There are places, large and small hamlets and parishes, styled Morton in cos. Derby, Lincoln (3), Nottingham. York (4), Worcester, Warwick, Durham (2), Hereford, Norfolk, Northampton, &c.

Robert de Morton, co. Notts, 1273. A.
Egidius de Morton, co. Northampton, ibid.
Richard de Morton, co. Oxf., ibid.
Felicia de Morton, co. Linc., ibid.
Alicia de Morton, co. York, Hen. III-Edw. I. K.
Michael de Morton, co. Salop, ibid.
Rogerus de Morton, 1379 : P. T. Yorks. p. 197.
Johannes de Morton, 1379 : ibid.
Manser de Morton, co. Hunts, 20 Edw. I. R.
1594. John Morton, co. Leic. : Reg. Univ. Oxf. vol. ii pt. ii. p. 206.
London, 48 ; New York, 76.

Mortyn, Morten, Mortan.—Local, 'of Morteyn.' I cannot find the place. No doubt the surname is now generally absorbed by Morton. But it must be regarded as totally distinct in origin.

William de Morteyn, co. Notts, 1273. A.
Eustace de Morteyn, co. Notts, ibid.
Hugh de Morteyn, co. Bedf., Hen. III-Edw. I. K.
John de Mortayne, co. Salop, 20 Edw. I. R.
Roger de Morteyn, co. Cornwall, ibid.
Custance de Morteyne, co. Hunts, ibid.
1663-4. William Brom and Isabel Morten : Marriage Alleg. (Canterbury), p. 124.
London, 3, 4, 1.

Moseley, Mosley, Mosely.—Local, 'of Mossley,' till recently a hamlet, but now a rising town in the parish of Saddleworth, W. Rid. Yorks. Probably other small localities would bear the name.

Willelmus de Moslay, 1379 : P. T. Yorks. p. 81.
Ricardus de Moslay, smyth, 1379 : ibid. p. 82.
Thomas de Mosseley, 1379 : ibid. p. 168.
1588. John Moseley, co. Middlesex : Reg. Univ. Oxf. vol. ii. pt. ii. p. 167.
1591. Ralph Mosley, of Great Sankey, husbandman : Wills at Chester, i. 139.
1617. Rowland Mosley, of the Hough, Manchester : ibid.
West Rid. Court Dir., 5, 4, 1 ; New York, 7, 3, 1.

Moser, Mosser.—Local, 'of Mosser,' a chapelry in the parish of Brigham, co. Cumberland. It seems almost certain that this is the parent, as the surname is familiar to that and the neighbouring counties.

1590. John Moser : Lancashire Wills at Richmond, i. 198.

The surname has ramified strongly in the United States.

London, 3, 0 ; MDB. (co. Westm.), 2, 0 ; New York, 39, 3.

Mosley ; v. Moseley.

Moss.—(1) Local, 'at the moss,' from residence thereby. The name is too general to necessitate extracts from modern registers.

Henry Mosse, co. Linc., 1273. A.
Henry del Mosse, C. R., 6 Edw. III.
Robertus de Mos, 1379 : P. T. Yorks. p. 247.
Johannes del Mosse, 1379 : ibid. p. 295.

(2) Bapt. 'the son of Moses,' from nick. Moyse or Mosse (for instances, v. Moyse). It is curious to find that the modern practice, whereby Jews settling in England change their surname Moses into Moss, is supported by the fact that

six centuries ago Moss was the English nick. of Moses.

London, 78 ; West Riding Court Dir., 14 ; New York, 46.

Mossman.—(1) Bapt. 'the servant of Moss,' i. e. Moses (v. Moss, 2) ; cf. Matthewman, Wilman, Bartleman, &c. It is curious to notice that Mossman, as a modern surname, is commonest in Yorkshire, the county that has given us the largest number of surnames of this particular class. Moses was a popular font-name in the 13th and 14th centuries. (2) Local, 'the mossman,' one who lived on or close by a moss. I am obliged to suggest this, but doubt not (1) is the correct interpretation.

1687. James Mosman and Rebecca Hampton : Marriage Alleg. (Canterbury), p. 276.
1748. Married — James Mosman and Damask Rose : St. Geo. Chap. Mayfair, p. 106.
London, 3 ; West Rid. Court Dir., 5 ; New York, 1 ; Boston (U.S.), 2.

Mote, Moth ; v. Mott.

Mothersole, Mothersill. — Local, 'of Mothersoul.' For the suffix, v. Sale. I cannot find any hall or hamlet bearing this name.

Ralph Modersoule, C. R., 6 Edw. II.
1602. Buried — Thomas Mothersowle : St. Dionis Backchurch (London), p. 206.
1635. Bapt.—Agnes, d. William Mothersoale : Reg. Deopham. co. Norfolk.
1793. Married — John Mothersall and Esther Williams : St. Geo. Han. Sq. ii. 105.
Manchester, 0, 4 ; Crockford, 1, 0 ; MDB. (co. Suffolk), 2, 0.

Motley.—Local, 'of Motley.' I cannot find the place. It must undoubtedly be sought for in co. Linc.

Thomas de Motlawe, 1379 : P. T. Yorks. p. 174.
1570. Robert Dodds and Barbara Mottley : Marriage Lic. (London), i. 46.
1660. Buried—John, s. Edward Motley : St. Jas. Clerkenwell, iv. 337.
London, 1 ; MDB. (co. Linc.), 13 ; New York, 4.

Mott, Motte, Mote, Moth.—(1) Local, 'at the moat.' M.E. mote, O.F. mote, a dike, an embankment ; the same as modern Fr. motte, a mound ; cf. also mothe, a little earthen fortresse, Cotg.

(v. Skeat, s. v. *moat*, for full history of the word). All the above forms are found, without prefix, in the Hundred Rolls (1273); cf. French 'Delamotte.'

Saundrina de la Mote: Wardrobe Account, 21-23 Edw. III. 38/2.

(2) Bapt. 'the son of Motte.' Undeniably some of our Motts, &c., are of fontal origin. Whether this Mott was a nick. of some familiar personal name or not I cannot at present say. I give instances of both (1) and (2) together, as I cannot separate them.

Motte (without surname), co. Bucks, 1273. A.
William Moth, co. Norf., ibid.
Basilia Motte, co. Camb., ibid.
Richard Mote, co. Oxf., ibid.
Elena Mott, 1379: P. T. Yorks. p. 208.
Hugo Mott, 1379: ibid. p. 209.

Since writing the above it has occurred to me that Motte was but one more attempt at Matilda. 'Malkyne, or Mawt, propyr name, *Matilda*': Prompt. Parv. v. Moulson.

1786. Married—John Pain and Mary Moth: St. Geo. Han. Sq. i. 393.
London, 14, 1, 5, 4; New York, 86, 0, 1, 2.

Mottershead, Mottershadd.
—Local, 'of Mottershead,' a spot in the township of Mottram St. Andrew, in the parish of Prestbury, co. Ches.

'A family of the name of Mottershead held lands in this township from an early period.... An ancient deed without date, and probably of the 12th or 13th century, says that " Edward, son of Gamyl, lord of Mottram, gave to William, his son and heir, all that land in Mottersheved, in the vill of Mottram, ... which John de Chellegh then held, from which place he was called William de Mottershead, and his descendants Mottershead of Mottram "': East Ches. ii. 355.
Richard de Mottershead, of Mottram, 1337: ibid.
John de Mottershead, of Mottram, 1415: ibid.
1565. Bapt.—Anne Mottershed: Reg. Prestbury, p. 15.
— Buried—Agnes Mottershedde: ibid. p. 17.
1612. Jeffry Mottershead, of Mottram Andrew: Wills at Chester, i. 140.
Manchester, 6, 1; Liverpool, 1, 0; Philadelphia, 2, 0.

Mottram, Motteram.—Local, 'of Mottram,' a parish in East Ches. Motteram occurs in the London Directory. The tendency

to variation increases as the name wanders further from its native home; cf. Barnum for Barnham.

John de Mottrum, 1310: East Ches. ii. 348.
Adam de Mottrum, 1376: ibid.
1564. Bapt.—Elizabeth Mottram: Reg. Prestbury (East Ches.), p. 13.
1565. — Agnes Mottram: ibid. p. 16.
Hugh Mottram, of Mottram, 1595: Wills at Chester (1545-1620), p. 140.
Mary Mottram, of Mottram Andrew, 1605: ibid.
London, 3, 1; Manchester, 14, 0; Philadelphia, 2, 0.

Mould, Moul, Moule, Mold.
—Bapt. ' the son of Matilda.' For further information, v. Moulson. The final *d* has been dropped in Moul; cf. Mowl.

1566-7. Robert Mowlde and Alice James: Marriage Lic. (London), i. 35.
1568. William Molde and Susanna Totnam: ibid. p. 39.
1584-5. John Moule, or Moulde, co. Worc.: Reg. Univ. Oxf. vol. ii. pt. ii. p. 140.
1686. William Mould and Alice Hester: Marriage Lic. (Faculty Office), p. 180.
Leeds, 3, 0, 0, 0; West Rid. Court Dir., 1, 0, 0, 0; London, 6, 2, 4, 2; Oxford, 0, 0, 0, 3; Philadelphia, 2, 0, 0, 0.

Mouldsworth. — Local, ' of Mouldsworth,' a township in the parish of Tarvin, nine miles from Chester; v. Molesworth, by which this name seems to have been absorbed.

Hamnet Booth, of Mouldsworth, *husbandman*, 1590: Wills at Chester (1545-1620), p. 23.
Humphrey Mouldsworth, of Warmingham, 1587: ibid. p. 140.
1584. Anthony Mowlsworthe and Cicely Hurlande: Marriage Lic. (London), i. 131.

Moule; v. Mould.

Moulson.—Bapt. 'the son of Matilda.' Fr. Mathilde, O.E. Molde or Maude (v. Yonge, ii. 415-6). Prof. Freeman says, ' In the mouths of Englishmen pronouncing French names, it (Matilda) became Mahtild, Mahault, Molde, Maud, and so forth ' (Norman Conquest, ii. 291). Yorkshire has preserved a memory of this in Moulson (the *d* being dropped).

Walter Moldesone, co. Soms., 1 Edw. III: Kirby's Quest, p. 240.
Ricardus Maldson, 1379: P. T. Yorks. p. 185.
Thomas Maltson, 1379: ibid. p. 76.
Roger Moldson, 1379: ibid. p. 22.
Alicia Moldson, 1379: ibid. p. 116.

Henricus Moldson, *webster*, 1379: ibid. p. 136.
Mauld Beeston, 31 Edw. I: Visitation of Cheshire, 1580, p. 84.
1550. Bapt.—Fraunces Molsonne: St. Peter, Cornhill, i. 5.
1565. Married—Rycharde Molson and Agnes Glazier: St. Michael, Cornhill, p. 9.
West Rid. Court Dir., 6; Sheffield, 7; New York, 1.

Moult. — Bapt. ' the son of Matilda '; v. Moulson, Mould, and Mowl.

1628. Laurence Moult, of Congleton: Wills at Chester, ii. 159.
1636. Margaret Moult, of Congleton, *widow*: ibid.
MDB (co. Ches.), 4; Philadelphia, 2.

Moulton.—Local, ' of Moulton,' a village and parish in co. Chester; also parishes in cos. Suffolk, Northampton, Norfolk, and Lincoln. Many of these seem to be represented.

Agnes de Multon, co. Norf., 1273. A.
Thomas de Multon, co. Linc., ibid.
Adam de Multon, co. Camb., ibid.
Alex. de Multon, co. Oxf., ibid.
John de Moltone, co. Soms., 1 Edw. III: Kirby's Quest, p. 188.
1591. Thomas Moulton, co. Wilts: Reg. Univ. Oxf. vol. ii. pt. ii. p. 186.
Randle Lowndes, of Moulton, 1617: Wills at Chester (1545-1620), p. 128.
John Moulton, of Middlewich, 1616: ibid. p. 140.
London, 6; Manchester, 2; MDB, (co. Suff.), 4; New York, 15.

Moultrie, Moutrie.—Local, ' of Moultrie.' As stated by Mr. Lower, 'A small river in Fifeshire, now called the Motray.'

1566-7. John Fell and Joanna Mowtrye: Marriage Lic. (London), i. 35.
1754. Married—James Moultrie and Cecilia Stanton: St. Geo. Chap. Mayfair, p. 279.
1784. — James Neubigging and Margaret Mutrie: St. Geo. Han. Sq. i. 366.
London, 2, 2.

Mounsey, Mouncey.—Local, ' de la Monceau,' i.e. at the hillock or mound (cf. Munt). O.F. Moncel or Muncel; later Monceau. More specifically perhaps from some Norman town or hamlet of the name of Monceau or Monceaux.

Robert de Muncella, co. Wilts, 1273. A.
Robert de Munceaux, co. Norf., ibid.
Ingelram de Munceaus, co. York, ibid.
Gilbert de Munceaus, co. Linc., 20 Edw. I R.
Ralph de Muncy, co. Suff., ibid.
1568. Married—James Munsey and Jone Hollylande: St. Michael, Cornhill, p. 10.

1724. Bapt.—Robert, s. John Mounsey : St. Michael, Cornhill, p. 71.
1747. Married—Anthony Monsey and Sarah Hines : ibid. p. 168.
London, 4, 1 ; Manchester, 4, 2 ; MDB. (co. Cumberland), 13, 0 ; New York, 0, 1 ; Boston (U.S.), 0, 3.

Mount.—Local, 'at the mount,' i.e. the rising ground, M.E. *munt.* v. Munt for further early instances.
Alan atte Mount, C. R., 12 Edw. III. pt. ii.
1569. Thomas Mounte and Mary Kyrkebye : Marriage Lic. (London), i. 44.
1626. Robert Mount and Joane Stanley : ibid. ii. 170.
London, 7 ; New York, 30.

Mountain, Mountan.—Local, ' at the mountain.' Not very common in England, as we have but few mountains to boast of. But Hill and Hills have made up for any deficiency, even if they sound more modest ; cf. Fr. ' de la Montaigne.' No doubt in some cases this has been Anglicized to Mountain. Mr. Lower (Patr. Brit. p. 231) furnishes an instance of ' de Montaigne ' settling as Mountain in co. Norfolk after the Edict of Nantes.
Hugh de Muntein, co. Salop, 1273. A.
William de Muntein, co. Oxf., ibid.
Hugh supra Montem, co. Oxf., ibid.
Matilda supra Montem, co. Oxf., ibid.
1618. John Dentithe, *goldweaver*, and Eliz. Mountaine : Marriage Lic.(London), ii. 62.
1767. Married—John Cooper and Eliz. Mountain : St. Geo. Han. Sq. i. 163.
London, 4, 0 ; New York, 4, 2 ; Philadelphia, 12, 0.

Mountainacre. — Local, ' at the mountain acre,' i.e. the arable land on the hillside. This somewhat curious and lengthy surname existed for a time.
1598. Bapt. — Susan, d. Richard Mountaynacre : St. Jas. Clerkenwell, i. 33.
1600. — William, s. Richard Mountaynaker : ibid. p. 36.
1601. — Margaret, d. Richard Mountaynaker : ibid. p. 39.

Mountford,   Montford, Mountfort. — (1) Local, ' de Montfort.' Lower, in his Patr. Brit. (p. 228), says that there are two places in Normandy called Montfort, one situated near Argentan, the other near Pont-Audemer. The latter is a fortified town. (2) Local, ' of Montford,' a parish five miles from Shrewsbury, co. Salop.

Simon de Monteforte, co. Notts, 1273. A.
Petronilla de Monteforti, co. Wilts, ibid.
Henry de Monteforti, co. Soms., ibid.
Henry Mounfort, co. Soms., 1 Edw. III : Kirby's Quest, p. 84.
Reginald de Monte Forti, co. Soms., 1 Edw. III : ibid. p. 85.
1586. John Mountford, co. Warw. : Reg. Univ. Oxf. vol. ii. pt. ii. p. 155.
1602. Buried — John Mounford : St. Antholin, p. 41.
1621. Married—Frederic Steward and Abigall Mondeford, of Mondeford, in Norfolk : St. Michael, Cornhill, p. 23.
London, 9, 1, 0 ; New York, 1, 1, 1 ; MDB. (co. Salop), 0, 2, 0.

Mountjoy.—Local, ' of Muntjoy.' Lower writes, ' Fr. Mont-joie, which Cotgrave defines as as "a barrow, a little hill, or heap of stones, layed in or neare a highway for the better discerning thereof, or in remembrance of some notable act performed, or accident befallen in that place." . . . According to Sir John Maundeville, an eminence near Jerusalem was formerly so called, because it "gevethe joy to pylgrymes hertes because that there men seen first Jerusalem "' : Patr. Brit. p. 231.
Ralph de Munjay, alias de Munjoie, alias de Munjau, cos. Derby and Notts, 1273. A.
Ralph de Muntjoye, co. Derby, 20 Edw. I. R.
Serl de Muntjoye, co. Derby, ibid.

Mention is made of the
Canonici et Fres de Monte Jovis, co. Essex, 1273. A.
1586. Edward Wilberfosse and Ann Monioye, alias Mountioye (co. Essex) : Marriage Lic. (London), i. 152.
1610. John Montjoy and Ann Blackwood : ibid. p. 325.
1699. Married — Edmund Mountjoy and Mary Mannaton : St. Jas. Clerkenwell, iii. 221.
London, 1 ; New York, 1 ; Philadelphia, 4.

Mountney,   Montanye. — Local, ' de Mounteny.' I cannot find the spot, but it looks thoroughly Norman.
Robert de Mounteny, co. Camb., A. 1273.
Allexander de Munteny, co. Essex, ibid.
Johannes Mountenay, *armiger*, 1379 : P. T. Yorks. p. 31.
Johan Mountenay, Edden sa femme, *fleshewer*, 1379 : ibid. p. 43.
1586. Roger Mowntney and Frances Chetham : Marriage Lic. (London), i. 153.
1676. Married—Richard Mounteney and Mary Irons : St. Michael, Cornhill, p. 41.

1745. Edward Mountency (Garlick Hith, London) and Catherine Capen : St. Antholin (London), p. 153.
New York, 0, 4 ; Philadelphia, 4, 2.

Mouse, Muss, Musse.—Nick. ' the mouse ' ; M.E. *mous* ; cf. Ratt.
Roger Mus, co. Essex, 1273. A.
Isabel Mus, co. Camb., ibid.
John le Mous, burgess, returned for Wilton, 1302. M.
Hugh le Mus. E.
Richard Mowse, c. 1550. Z.
Richard Mouse, C. R., 1 Mary, pt. ix.
1661. Jacob Bodenduch and Susan Mouse : Marriage Alleg. (Canterbury), p. 14.
1720. Married—William Harrison and Mary Mouse : St. Jas. Clerkenwell, p. 244.
1768. — Michael Mows and Mary Walter : St. Geo. Han. Sq. i. 178.
New York, 0, 1, 2 ; Boston (U.S.), 1, 0, 0.

Mouth.—Local.
Fulk de Mouthe, C. R., 14 Hen. VI.
New York, 1.

Moutrie ; v. Moultrie.

Mowbray,   Mumbray. — Local, ' of Mowbray,' or ' Monbrai,' an ancient barony in Normandy. Robert de Mowbray was Earl of Northumberland, but his estates passed to his cousin Nigel de Albini, whose son Roger, at the command of Henry I, assumed the name of Mowbray, and affixed it to one of his fiefs, now Melton Mowbray. v. Lower, Patr. Brit. p. 231.
Nigel de Mumbray, temp. Hen. III–Edw. I. K.
Nigel de Moubray, ibid.
Roger de Munbray, co. Bedf., 1273. A.
London, 5, 0 ; Manchester, 1, 1.

Mowe.—Local, ' at the mow ' (v. Maw) ; cf. Mower and Mawer.
Oliver de la Mowe, Fines Roll, 14 Edw. II.
New York, 1.

Mower.—Occup. ' the mower.' one who cuts grass, commonly found in the North of England as Mawer, q.v.
Roger le Mower, Pardons Roll, 6 Ric. II.
Thomas Mower, C. R., 31 Hen. VI.
1551. Buried — Cristaball Mowre : St. Jas. Clerkenwell, iv. 1.
1659. Married — Daniell Mower and Sarah Powle : St. Dionis Backchurch, p. 34.
London, 1 ; New York, 3 ; Philadelphia, 24.

Mowl, Mowll.—Bapt. 'the son of Matilda.' For further information v. Moulson. Mowl is Mould with the final *d* dropped. An instance is furnished under Mould, q.v.

1615. Thomas Moule, co. Worc.: Reg. Univ. Oxf. vol. ii. pt. ii. p. 338.
1646. Buried — Joane, wife of Richard Moule: St. Peter, Cornhill, i. 202.
London, 4, 1.

Moxon.—Bapt. 'the son of Margaret,' from the nick. Mogg or Moggy, sharpened to Mock ; cf. Jagge for Jack (Piers Plow.), also Slagg for Slack, and Higg for Hick. Thus Mogson became Mockson and, of course, Moxon; cf. Coxon for Cockson, Dixon for Dickson, &c. Moxon is a Yorkshire surname, and it is there we find the early instances.

Johannes Mokesson, 1379 : P. T. Yorks. p. 186.
Robertus Mokeson, 1379: ibid. p. 81.
Johannes Mokeson, 1379: ibid. p. 35.
Roger Mokson, 1379: ibid. p. 236.
1655. John Mokesone and Jane Wardsworth: Reg. Silkstone Church, co. Yorks.
1764. Martha, d. John Mokeson, died Nov. 14, 1764 : Monument, Silkstone, co. Yorks.

But Moxon is found in the 16th century :

1592. Married — Antony Moxon and Annes Allenson: St. Peter, Cornhill, i. 239.

Moxon is now, I believe, the universal form.

London, 13; Leeds, 4; West Riding Court Dir., 11; New York, 1; Boston (U.S.), 6.

Moyer.—Occup. 'the mower,' a corruption of Mawer, q.v.

1776. Married—John Charles England and Mary Mower or Moyer: St. Geo. Han. Sq. i. 260.
London, 1; Philadelphia, 98.

Moyse, Moyce, Moyes.— Bapt. 'the son of Moses.' M.E. Moyses (q.v.), whence the nick. Moyse or Mosse (v. Moss); cf. O.F. Moise, i.e. Moses. This probably suggested the English forms.

Mosse fil. Jacob the Jew, co. Oxf., 1273. A.
Hasting Moyse, co. Suff., ibid.
William Moyse, co. Essex, ibid.
Mosseus Judeus, co. Northampton, 20 Edw. I. R.
1604. Married — John Lambert and Katherine Moyes: St. Mary Aldermary (London), p. 10.
1643. — Edmund Moys and Clement Pincknye: St. Jas. Clerkenwell, iii. 76.

1797. Married — William Cowley and Ann Moyce: St. Geo. Han. Sq. ii. 160.
London, 1, 1, 3 ; Boston (U.S.), 0, 0, 3.

Moyses.—Bapt. 'the son of Moses,' always so spelt in the older records. Moyses in our directories represents an English as distinct from a Jewish descent, and stands to Moses as Salmon does to Solomon ; v. Moyse.

'Yond is Moyses, I dar warand.'
York Mystery Plays, p. 81.
'Save that he, Moises, and King Salomon.' Chaucer, The Squire's Tale.
Moyses le Batur, co. Hunts, 1273. A.
Moyses Capellanus, 10 Hen. II : Pipe Roll, p. 43.
Alicia Moyses, 1379: P. T. Yorks. p. 299.
1573. Bapt.—Moyses, s. William Wood: St. Jas. Clerkenwell, i. 7.
1590. — Moyses, s. Robert Stuard: St. Peter, Cornhill, i. 36.
1592. Eliz. Moysses, or Moses, of Yealand Conyers: Lancashire Wills at Richmond, p. 198.
1629. Bapt. — Marye, d. of Robert Moyses: St. Mary Aldermary, p. 81.
April 24, 1761, Hugh Moises, A.M., morning lecturer on the death of R. Swinburne, All Saints, Newcastle-upon-Tyne: Brand's Newcastle, i. 390.
New York, 1.

Muckleston ; v. Muggleston.

Muddeman, Muddiman, Muddyman.—Nick. 'the moody man,' probably with the earlier sense of being quick to anger, brave, courageous ; v. Moody, and cf. Merry and Merriman.

'O mony were the moodie men Lay gasping on the green.'
Ballad of Captain Carre (Jamieson).
London, 1, 2, 1 ; West Rid. Court Dir., 2, 0, 0; Sheffield, 1, 0, 0.

Mudie—Nick. ; v. Moody.

Muff.—Nick. 'the mauf' or 'maugh,' i.e. the brother-in-law, a curious surname found in the W. Rid. Yorks alongside its compound Watmuff, i.e. Walter's brother-in-law ; cf. the Lancashire Hickmough, Richard's brother-in-law. In compounds it is found as *maghe, moghe, mough,* and *mouth* ; v. Watmough.

West Rid. Court Dir., 5; Sheffield, 2; Philadelphia, 3.

Muffit.—Local, 'of Moffatt,' a town on the borders of Lanarkshire and Dumfriesshire. Muffitt

or Muffet seems to have been an old corruption.

1569. Married — John Buxton and Joane Muffet: St. Thomas the Apostle (London), p. 4.
1598. — John Hake and Brigett Muffet : ibid. p. 9.
1651. — Thomas Wallis and Susanna Muffett : St. Dionis Backchurch (London), p. 27.
1663. — William Moffett and Mary Borne : ibid. p. 37.

Only one letter differs in these last two entries.

London, 1.

Mugford.—Local ; v. Mogford.

Muggeridge.—Local; v. Moggridge.

Muggleton.—Local, 'of Muckleston' (?). Probably a variant ; v. Muggleston.

1618. Thomas Powell and Judith Muggleton : Marriage Lic. (London), ii. 67.
1637. Bapt. — Mary, d. Lodowicke Mugelltone : St. Mary Aldermary, p. 85.
London, 2.

Muggleston, Mugliston, Muckleston. — Local, (1) 'of Muckleston,' a hamlet in the parish of Shawbury, co. Salop ; (2) 'of Muckleston,' a parish in the union of Market Drayton, co. Salop. The ancient form still remains, but is now generally modified into Mugliston.

1592. Edward Mucleston, co. Salop : Reg. Univ. Oxf. vol. ii. pt. ii. p. 191.
1601. Richard Mucleston, or Muckellstone, co. Salop : ibid. p. 247.
1675. John Goldwell and Ann Muggleston : Marriage Lic. (Westminster), p. 46.
1677. William Mugglestone and Eliz. Bookham : Marriage Alleg. (Canterbury), p. 209.
London, 1, 2, 0; MDB. (co. Derby), 0, 2, 0 ; (co. Salop), 0, 0, 1.

Mulcaster, Muncaster.— Local, 'of Mulcaster,' now Muncaster, a parish in co. Cumb. ; cf. *baluster* and *banister.*

Robert de Molecastre, co. Cumb., 1279. M.
Walter de Mulecastre, co. Cumb., 1287. M.
1560. Married—Rycharde Monckestre and Katherine Ashleye : St. Michael, Cornhill, p. 8.
1662. Henry Hesketh and Sarah Mulcaster : Marriage Alleg. (Canterbury), p. 71.
Crockford, 1, 0 ; Ulverston, 0, 1 ; Philadelphia, 0, 2.

N n

Mule.—Nick. 'the mule'; A.S. *mul*, a sobriquet for an obstinate man.

Roger le Mul, co. Wilts, 1273. A.

Mulford.—Local, 'of Mulford.' Possibly, but not probably, the place now known as Mudford, a parish three miles from Yeovil, co. Soms. The earliest references are found in that district. Cf. Milford.

Gilbert de Mullford, co. Wilts, Hen. III–Edw. I. K.
Edmund de Muleford, co. Wilts, 1273. A.
Richard de Muleford, co. Wilts, ibid.
1655. Buried—Eliz., wife of William Mulford: St. Jas. Clerkenwell, iv. 305.
1675. Thomas Grice and Judith Mulford: Marriage Alleg. (Canterbury), p. 146.
London, 1; New York, 30.

Mullin, Mullen.—Local; v. Mullins (1 and 2).

1722.Buried—(blank) Mullin: St.Thomas the Apostle (London), p. 149.
New York, 44, 119.

Mulliner.—(1) Occup. 'a milner'; M.E. *mulnere*; v. Milner. (2) Local, a corruption of Molineaux, q.v., and cf. Mullins and Molines.

Sancheus Moliner, co. Linc., 1273. A.
1564. Thomas Mulliner, Corp. Christi Coll. : Reg. Univ. Oxf. vol. ii. pt. ii. p. 15.
1715. Buried—Charles Molineer : St. Antholin (London), p. 128.
London, 2; Philadelphia, 1.

Mullineux.—Local; v. Molineaux.

Mullins,Mullings.—(1)Local. An English dress of the French 'de Molines.' The *g* in Mullings is an excrescence; cf. Jennings for Jennins.

William de Molyns, co. Glouc., 1273. A.
1587-8. Barentyne Molens, co. Berks: Reg. Univ. Oxf. vol. ii. pt. ii. p. 162.

(2) Local, 'at the miln,' i.e. mill. M.E. *miln* and *mulne*. The final *s* is common to these local surnames; cf. Meadows, Brooks, Sykes, Mills, &c. Perhaps it is the patronymic *s*, as in Williams, Jones, &c.

Laurence atte Mulene, 1278. M.
Gilbert atte Mullane, co. Soms., 1 Edw. III : Kirby's Quest, p. 154.
1670. Francis Shepherd and Abigaell Mullins: Marriage Alleg. (Canterbury), p. 41.

1787. Married—John Mullens and Jane Rebecca Trevor: Canterbury Cath. p. 98.
London, 15, 3; New York, 38, 0.

Mullock, Mulock, Mulloch, Mullocks.—? Bapt. 'the son of Mulloc' (?). This seems to be the only natural conclusion. This view is confirmed by the fact of the existence of the genitive Mullocks, i.e. Mullock's son; cf. Williams, Jenkins, &c.

Reginald Mulloc, or Mulluc, co. Camb., 1273. A.
Thomas Mulloc, co. Camb., ibid.
Johannes Mullok, 1379: P. T. Howdenshire, p. 29.
1750. Married—John Bassil and Eliz. Mullocks: St. Geo. Chap. Mayfair, p. 179.
Crockford, 0, 1, 0, 0; New York, 0, 0, 1, 0; Philadelphia, 0, 5, 0, 0.

Mumbray.—Local; v. Mowbray.

Mumby, Munby.—Local, ' of Mumby,' a parish in the union of Spilsby, co. Lincoln. Mumby is found as early as the 13th century; v. infra.

Alicia de Mumby, co. Linc., 1273. A.
Cf. Hereð de Munby, co. Linc., ibid.
Alan de Mumby, co. Linc., Hen. III–Edw. I. K.
Beatrice de Mumby, co. Linc., ibid.
1669. Married—Robert Hodskines and Eliz. Mumbee : St. Jas. Clerkenwell, iii. 161.
1690. Bapt. — Eliz., d. Barthollomew Mumbey : ibid. ii. 337.
London, 3, 1; New York, 1, 0.

Mumford, Munford.—Local, ' of Mundford,' a parish in co. Norwich, found as early as the 13th century; in the variant form Mumford was inevitable; cf. Munby for Mumby.

Adam de Mundeford, co. Norf., 1273. A.
Richard de Mundefode, co. Camb., ibid.
John de Mundeford, co. Northampton, 20 Edw. I. R.
Lora de Mumford, co. Herts, ibid.
Osbert Mundeford, C. R., 21 Hen. VI.

The following is interesting evidence :

1729. Bapt.—Anne, d. John and Mary Munford : St. Jas. Clerkenwell, ii. 184.
1733. — John, s. John and Mary Mumford : ibid. p. 208.
London, 19, 2; New York, 7, 1.

Mummery,Momerie.—Local, ' of Munbray ' or 'Mumbray,' variants of Mowbray, the earliest forms of which include Mumbray,

Mombray, and Munbray; v. Mowbray.

Walter Mombray, Mayor of Bristol, 1221: YYY. p. 669.
Roger de Moubray, 1283. M.
Roger de Mounbray, 1297. M.

The above two entries refer to the same person.

Roger de Mumbrai, co. Kent, 1273. A.
Pagan de Mumbray, co. Oxf., ibid.
Roger de Munbray, alias Mumbray, co. Bedf., ibid.
Roger de Munbray, co. York, 20 Edw. I. R.

All these Rogers, no doubt, refer to the same individual, one of the Mowbrays. Of the etymology of Mummery, therefore, there can be no question.

1660. Buried — Elizabeth Mummery : Canterbury Cath. p. 121.
London, 8, 0; Crockford, 1, 1.

Munby; v. Mumby.

Muncaster.—Local; v. Mulcaster.

Muncey,Muncy; v. Mounsey.

1568. Married — James Munsey and Jone Hollylande : St. Michael, Cornhill, p. 10.
London, 5, 2; MDB. (co. Herts), 2, 0.

Munday, Mundy; v. Monday.

Munden.—Local, 'of Munden,' two parishes in co. Hertford, Great and Little Munden.

Henry de Mundene, co. Wilts, 1273. A.
Henry de Munden, co. Linc., Hen. III–Edw. I. K.
1565. John Munden, New Coll. : Reg. Univ. Oxf. vol. ii. pt. ii. p. 15.
1669. John Munden and Eliz. Usher : Marriage Alleg. (Canterbury), p. 15.
London, 2; Philadelphia, 3.

Munford; v. Mumford.

Munk.—Offic. 'the monk'; v. Monk. This variant has always been rare as a surname. A.S. *munec*.

Beatrix le Munk, co. Hunts, 1273. A.
Peter le Munk, co. Norf. FF.
1682. Married—Robert Harrison and Mary Munke : St. Jas.Clerkenwell, iii.196.
London,1; NewYork, 3; Philadelphia, 2.

Munn.—Offic. 'the monk,' one of the many variants of 'le Moigne'; v. Money (2). Probably Moon (q.v.) in some instances is a similar variant.

Robert le Moun, co. York, 1273. A.
Walter le Moun, co. Essex, ibid.
Thomas le Mun, co. Norf., ibid.

Ralph Mun, co. Camb., 1273. A.
John le Moune, co. Kent, 20 Edw.
I. R.
1665. Married — Gabriell Seuens and
Ann Munn : St. Jas. Clerkenwell, iii. 119.
1782. — William Spencer and Mary
Munn : St. Geo. Han. Sq. i. 337.
London, 6; New York, 19.

Munt.—Local, 'at the mount.'
M.E. *munt* ; A.S. *munt* (Skeat).
My first instance settles the matter
beyond dispute.
William atte Munte, co. Kent, 20 Edw.
I. R.
Walter Munte, co. Dorset, 1273. A.
Cf. Roger de Munt Feront, co. Suff.,
ibid.
1677–8. William Ediall and Eliz. Munt :
Marriage Alleg. (Canterbury), p. 276.
1692–3. Bapt.—Mary, d. John Munt,
tailor : St. Dionis Backchurch (London),
p. 132.
London, 5 ; Oxford, 2 ; New York, 1.

Murby.—Local ; v. Morby.

Murch.—Local, (1) 'at the
march,' from residence thereby,
i.e. the boundary line ; v. March.
(2) 'At the marsh,' from residence
thereby, i.e. the swamp ; v. Marsh.
This variant seems to be of West-
country parentage.
Robert in the Merche, co. Soms., 1
Edw. III : Kirby's Quest, p. 99.
1772. Married — William Murch and
Esther Mitchell : St. Geo. Han. Sq. i. 225.
London, 4 ; MDB. (co. Soms.), 4.

Murcott, Murcutt.—Local, (1)
' of Murcot,' a hamlet in the parish
of Charlton - upon - Otmoor, co.
Oxford ; (2) ' of Morcott,' a parish
in co. Rutland ; (3) ' of Murcott,'
a hamlet in the parishes of Long
Buckby and Watford, co. Northampton. But such a local name
as the Moorcot, i.e. the cottage on
the moor, no doubt arose in several
places ; cf. Moorhouse.
William de Morcote, co. Oxf., 1273. A.
Robert Morcote, co. Oxf., ibid.
Laurence de Morcok (sic), co. Bucks,
Hen. III-Edw. I. K.
Alan de Morkote, co. Leic., ibid.
Martin de Morkot, cos. Norf. and Suff.,
ibid.
Thomas de Morcote, co. Northampton,
20 Edw. I. R.
1671. James Prescott and Ann Staper,
with consent of her mother, now wife of
Job Murcott : Marriage Lic. (Faculty
Office), p. 120.
London, 3, 4.

Murden.—Local ; v. Mordan.
Stephen de Murdon, co. Norf., 1273. A.

Murdoch, Murdock.—Bapt.
'the son of Murdoch,' Celtic (Yonge,
ii. 158).
Murdac, dean of Appleby, 32 Hen. II :
Nicolson and Burn, Hist. Westm. and
Cumb., i. 428.
Murdac de Gunton, cos. Warw. and
Leic., Hen. III-Edw. I. K.
1680. Job Nutt and Sarah Murdock :
Marriage Alleg. (Canterbury), p. 34.
London, 11, 0; New York, 15, 20.

Murfin.—Bapt. 'the son of
Mervin ' ; v. Marvin.

Murgatroyd, Murgitroyde.
—Local, ' of Mergret's royd,' i.e.
Margaret's clearing ; v. Royd. So
we read of Tom-rode, Wilimotrode, Smyth-rode (Whitaker's
Craven, p. 199). The instance
quoted below sets all doubt at
rest as to the origin. This surname has ramified strongly in
Yorkshire, the county of its birth.
Gilbert and Sullivan have immortalized the name, if it needed
immortalizing ; but it was a strong
flight of fancy to place it so far
from its true home.
Johannes Mergretrode, 1379 : P. T.
Yorks. p. 187.
1726. Bapt. — Benjamin, s. William
Murgytroyd : St. Dionis Backchurch,
p. 160.
1739. Married — Joseph Foster and
Eliz. Murgatroyd : St. Geo. Han. Sq.
i. 23.
West Rid. Court Dir.,16,0 ; New York,
4, 0 ; Philadelphia, 7, 6.

Muriel, Murrell, Murrells.
—Bapt. 'the son of Muriel' ; v.
Merrall.
London, 0, 16, 2 ; Crockford, 3, 3, 0 ;
New York, 0, 6, 0.

Murthwaite.—Local, ' of Murthwaite,' a small hamlet in Ravenstonedale, co. Westm.
William Myrthwaite,1541 : W. Nicholls,
Hist. and Traditions of Ravenstonedale,
co. Westm., p. 114.
Rowland Myrthwaite, 1541 : ibid.
Lancelot Myrthwaite, 1541 : ibid.
1678. William Ivatt and Mary Murthwaite : Marriage Alleg. (Canterbury),
p. 283.
1802. Bapt. — Thomas, s. John Murthwaite, *waller* : Parish Ch., Ulverston,
p. 542.
Liverpool, 2 ; Ulverston, 3 ; MDB. (co.
Cumb.), 1.

Muschamp.—Local, ' of Mus-
champ.' The exact locality I do
not know, probably somewhere in
North France. A family of this
name were early settled in North-
umberland.
Robert de Muscans, 1195 : KKK. vi. 54.
Also, de Muschans, 1198, and de
Muschauns, 1228 : ibid. pp. 63, 151.
Matilda de Muscamp, co. Northumb.,
Hen. III-Edw. I. K.
Thomas de Muscham, cos. Notts and
Derby, ibid.
Ada Muschamp, cos. Notts and Derby,
ibid.
Robert de Mustchamp, co. Northumb.,
ibid.
1587–8. Aymondesham Muschampe, co.
Middlesex : Reg. Univ. Oxf. vol. ii. pt. ii.
p. 162.
1655. Married—John Roy and Dorothy
Muschampe : St. Jas. Clerkenwell, iii. 94.
London, 2.

Musgrave, Musgrove.—Local, ' of Musgrave,' a parish near
Brough, co.Westm. It is probable,
however, that some spot in the
West of England has given birth
to a similar surname.
Roger de Mussegrave, 1277. M.
1581. John Mosgrove, co. Devon : Reg.
Univ. Oxf. vol. ii. pt. ii. p. 113.
1603. Henry Musgrove, co. Soms.:
ibid. p. 264.
1708. Married— Thomas Tompkins and
Mary Musgrave : St. Antholin (London),
p. 121.
London, 7, 6 ; New York, 6, 5.

Mushet, Mussett, Mushett.
—Nick. 'the musket,' a sparrow-
hawk ; v. Muskett. O.F. *mouschet*
(v. Skeat on *musket*).
John Muschat, co. Oxf., 1273. A.
William Muschet : Close Roll, 17 Edw.
III. pt. ii.
1692. Married—Thomas Musset and
Ellen Rice : St. Jas. Clerkenwell, iii. 211.
1788. — Emery Mussett and Mary
Lillywhite : St. Geo. Han. Sq. ii. 12.
London, 1, 1, 0 ; Philadelphia, 1, 0, 2.

Muskett, Muskette.— Nick.
'the musket,' a sparrow-hawk,
afterwards a hand-gun, when the
names of birds of prey were given
to firearms ; v. Mushet ; cf. Spark,
Hawk.
Robert Musket, co. Camb., 1273. A.
Nicholas Musket, *latoner*, 3 Edw. II :
Freemen of York, i. 12.

That Muskett and Mushet are
the same may be seen by two
entries concerning one individual :
William Muschet, co. Camb., 1273. A.
William Musket, co. Camb., ibid.

John Musket, co. Soms., 1 Edw. III: Kirby's Quest, p. 224.
1604. Edward Myles and Agnes Muskett: Marriage Lic. (London), i. 292.
1745. Married—Septimus Musket and Mary Maynard: St. Geo. Chap. Mayfair, p. 53.
London, 3, 0; Philadelphia, 0, 1.

Mussard.—Nick. 'the musard,' the dreamy, meditative man (?). The name seems to have survived.

Malcolm le Musard, c. 1300. M. London, 1.

Muss (e; v. Mouse.

Musset; v. Mushet.

Musson.—Local, ' of Muston,' parishes in cos. York and Leicester. I can scarcely hesitate to accept this solution. The corruption was, it seems to me, inevitable. But v. Misson.

Andrew de Muston, co. Leic., Hen. III-Edw. I. K.
John de Muston, co. Linc., 1273. A.
1702. Married — Hugh Musson and Phillis Lowe: St. Dionis Backchurch, p. 51.
1766. — John Muston and Mary Merrywether : St. Geo. Han. Sq. i. 159.
London, 6; New York, 2; Philadelphia, 7.

Mustard.—Nick. (1) for one of a sharp, keen, biting tongue, or (2) for a seller of mustard ; v. next article. Cf. Pepper and the remarks appended.

Jordan Mustard, co. Hunts, 1273. A.
John Mustard, co. Camb., ibid.
Margaret Mustard, co. Norf., ibid.
London, 3.

Mustarder. — Occup. ' the mustarder,' a maker of and dealer in mustard, an important manufacture in a day of pungent sauces; cf. Pepper, Garlickmonger, &c.
' Wo was his coke, but if his sauce were Poinant and sharpe.'
    Chaucer, C. T. 352-3.
Richard le Mustarder, co. Northampt., 1273. A.
Robert le Mustarder. H.
Thomas le Mustarder, London. X.
David le Mustarder, 1305. M.
William Mustarder, rector of Baldeswell, Norfolk, 1467: FF. viii. 186.

Mustardman, **Mustard-maker.**—Occup.'makers or dealers in mustard '; v. Mustarder. These surnames were too cumbrous to last, and probably were abbreviated to Mustard for convenience sake ; cf. Pepper and Pepperman.

Peter le Mustardman, co. Norf., 1273. A.
Robertus Musterdman, 1379: P. T. Yorks. p. 41.
Johannes Mustardman, 1379: ibid. p. 99.
Alicia Musterdmaker, 1379: ibid. p. 97.
John Alan, *musterdemaker,* 1479, co. York : W. 11, p. 105.
Alicia Mustardmaker de Ripon, 1397: W. 2, pt. i. p. 222.

Muttlebury.—Local, ' of Muttlebury.' This name seems to hail from co. Somerset.

Robert de Motelbury, co. Soms., 1 Edw. III : Kirby's Quest, p. 174.
Mr. Muttlebury rowed for Cambridge in the inter-University race, 1891.

Mutton. — (1) Nick. O.F. *moton,* a sheep, whence our mutton, the carcass, the flesh of a sheep. (2) Local, ' of Mutton.' I do not see any locality bearing this name, but I find the following entry :
' Robert de Mutone', co. Soms., 1 Edw. III : Kirby's Quest, p. 280.

Perhaps *de* is a misprint for *le*.

Philip le Mutton. B.
Willelmus Moton, 1379: P. T. Yorks. p. 27.
1729. Married— Richard Brackston and Margaret Mutton : St. Geo. Chap. Mayfair, p. 292.
London, 1.

Mycock.—Bapt. ' the son of Matthew'; v. Maycock. The variant Mocock, afterwards Mycock, seems to have been popular in East Lancashire and over the border into W. Rid. Yorks. It still remains in Manchester and district.

Mokock de la Lowe : De Lacy Inquisition, 1311.
Mokock del Moreclough : ibid.
Dik, son of Mocock : ibid.

Johannes Mocok', 1379 : P. T. Yorks. p. 180.
Dionisia Mocok', 1379 : ibid. p. 8.
Sheffield, 2 ; Manchester, 6.

Myers, Mires.—Local, ' at the mire,' swampy, low-lying land, a bog, found in such compounds as Hollowmire, Longmire, Blamire. The final s is common to short local surnames; cf. Holmes, Greaves, Brooks, Styles. A large number of the Myers in the London Directory are of German-Jewish descent, and have no connexion with the North-English Myers. M.E. *mire* and *myre.*
' And lette his shepe acombred in the mire.' Chaucer, C. T., Prologue.
David in the Mire, C. R., 24 Edw. I.
Henricus del Myre, 1379 : P. T. Yorks. p. 169.
Johannes del Mire, 1379 : ibid. p. 182.
Willelmus del Mire, 1379 : ibid. p. 275.
Richard del Myre, 1379 : ibid. p. 268.
1609. Thomas Awsten and Katherine Myers : Marriage Lic. (London), p. 314.
Roger Mires, 1642 : Preston Guild Rolls, p. 101.
William Mires, 1642 : ibid.
Richard Myres, of Preston, 1670 : Lancashire Wills at Richmond, p. 199.
Hugh Myres, of Docker, 1540 : ibid.
Thomas Myers, of Preston, 1671 : ibid.
West Rid. Court Dir., 14, 2 ; London, 48, 0 ; New York, 152, 0.

Myerscough. — Local, ' of Myerscough,' a township in the old parish of Lancaster. For the various early spellings, Mireschoghe, Merscowe, Myreskoo, Mirescoghe, Myrescoghe, and Myerscoe, v. Baines' Lanc. ii. 540.
' The heir of Henry de Fetherby, and William de Whytyngham, John de Staunford, and the heir of Richard de Mirscowe hold the mediety of the manor of Claghton': Knights' Fees, 23 Edw. III, Baines' Lanc. ii. 693.
London, 1 ; Manchester, 4.

Myhill.—Bapt. ; v. Miell.

Myles.—Bapt. ; v. Miles.

Myrtle.—Bapt. ; v. Martel.

N

Nabb, Nabbs, Nabs.—(1) Bapt. 'the son of Abel,' from the nick. Nabb, gen. Nabbs; cf. Nibbs from Isabella or Noll for Oliver. In the Alchemist (1610) Abel the tobacco-man is familiarly Nab.

'Six o' thy legs more will not do it, Nab.'   Act. ii. sc. 1.

(2) Local, 'at the nab,' from residence on a spot so called. Here *nab* is a variant of *knap*, the crown of a hill; v. Knapp. The Lancashire surname Nabb or Nabbs is undoubtedly of local origin.

1572. Thomas Nabb, of Tottington: Wills at Chester, i. 140.
1576. Jane Nabb, of Bury: ibid.
1596. Ann Nabbs, of Bury: ibid.
1604. John Slater, of the Nabb in Billington: ibid. p. 176.
Manchester, 1, 0, 0; Bury, 1, 2, 0; Philadelphia, 2, 0, 1,

Nagle, Nagele, Nagel.—?Local. A corruption of Nangle (?); v. Burke's Landed Gentry. This surname seems to have made enormous strides in the United States. One cannot help thinking that there must be some second parentage. But v. Neagle.

1749. Married—James Nagle and Mary Rowson: St. Geo. Chap. Mayfair, p. 131.
1796. — James Nagle and Margaret Hughes: St. Geo. Han. Sq. ii. 155.
London, 3, 0, 0; Philadelphia, 72, 14, 27.

Nail(e; v. Nale.

Nailer, Nailor.—Occup. 'the nailer'; v. Naylar.

London, 1, 2; New York, 0, 1; Philadelphia, 0, 1.

Nairn, Nairne, Nern.—Local, 'of Nairn,' co. Nairn. A Scottish surname. Nern, as a variant, seems to be confined to the United States.

Peter Nerne, 1601: Cal. State Papers (Scotland), p. 804.
1752. Bapt.—Eliz., d. Edward Nairne: St. Michael, Cornhill, p. 175.
1806. Married — George Nairn and Mary Busby: St. Geo. Han. Sq. ii. 250.

London, 2, 3, 0; Philadelphia, 4, 0, 0; New York, 1, 1, 1; Boston (U.S.), Nern, 1.

Naish.—Local, 'atten ash'; v. Nash. Naish is simply a variant of Nash; cf. Aysh for Ash. All these forms belong to the West country, especially Devonshire and Somersetshire. In the Reg. Univ. Oxf. the name is spelt indifferently Nash, Naish, and Nasshe; v. Index.

1524. John Hurdman and Anne Naysshe: Marriage Lic. (London), i. 3.
1799. Married—Samuel Whatley and Ann Naish: St. Geo. Han. Sq. ii. 210.
1804. — Henry Naish and Jane Stiell: ibid. p. 299.
MDB. (co. Somerset), 13.

Nakerer.—Occup. 'the nakerer,' a player on the naker or kettledrum.

'Pipes, trompes, nakeres, and clariounes.'   Chaucer, C. T. 2513.
Lambekyn Taborer, *minstrel*: Wardrobe Account, 48 Edw. III 1 Ric. II. 41/10.
Janyn Nakerer, *minstrel*: ibid.
Nicholas Trumpour, *minstrel*: ibid.

This surname has not survived.

Nalder, Nelder.—Local, 'atten alder,' i.e. at the alder-tree; A.S. *alr*, an alder-tree; the *d* is excrescent. The initial N is the last letter of the prefix *atten* (= at the); cf. Noakes and Nangle.

Robertus de Alre, co. Devon, 1273. A. Alice Attenalre. J.
John Nelder. H.
1749. Married—Stephen Nalder and Sarah Pearson: St. Geo. Chap. Mayfair, p. 143.
1784. — Daniel Nelder and Mary Spundley: St. Geo. Han. Sq. i. 363.
London, 5, 0; Plymouth, 0, 2; Tiverton, 0, 1; Philadelphia, 1, 0.

Nale, Nail, Naile.—Local, 'atten ale,' i.e. at the ale-house, the final *n* of *atten* becoming the prefix of the name proper.

'And maken him gret festes at the nale.'   Chaucer, C. T. 6931.

Cf. Nelmes, Noakes, &c. Nail was a natural modern variant.

1562. Married—John Nale and Sisley Barlow: St. Antholin (London), p. 14.
1584. John Naile, of Liverpool: Wills at Chester, i. 141.
1791. Married — William Naile and Sarah Wild: St. Geo. Han Sq. ii. 66.
1798. — Robert Nale and Maria Jervaise: ibid. p. 183.
London, 0, 1, 0; Philadelphia, 0, 2, 1.

Nall.—Local, 'atten hall,' i.e. at the hall, from residence there as owner or servant. The final *n* in *atten* has become the prefix of the name proper.

1665-6. Bapt.—William, s. William Nall, servant to Sir Edmond Turner: St. Dionis Backchurch (London), p. 118.
1681. William Nall and Jane Biber: Marriage Alleg. (Canterbury), p. 60.
Manchester, 7; Liverpool, 4.

Nance.—Local, 'of Nance.' 'An estate in the parish of Illogan, co. Cornwall, which was, not many generations ago, in the possession of the family' (Lower). For the meaning of this local term, v. Nanfan, and cf. Nancy in Lorraine, Nantes in Brittany, and Trenance in Cornwall.

Crockford, 1; Cornwall Dir. (List of Farmers), 5.

Nanfan.—Local, 'of Nanfan.' 'A Cornish family of some distinction, which produced, among other worthies, John Nanfan, the first patron of Cardinal Wolsey, who had been his chaplain. The name is evidently local, probably from Nanfan in the parish of Cury' (Lower). Cf. such other Cornish names as Nancarrow, Nankivell, Nanjulian, Nankervis, Pennant, &c. The root is Celtic, *nant*, a valley; cf. Nantwich (co. Chester) and Nantglyn (co. Denbigh).

John Nanfane, C. R., 26 Hen. VI.
1660. Married—Bridgis Nanfan and Katherine Hastings: St. Dionis Backchurch (London), p. 37.

Nangle.—Local, 'atten angle,' i.e. at the angle, the bend or corner; v. Angle. In this case, as in Nale and Nall, the initial is borrowed from the prefix. The name is Latinized into 'de angulo,' or 'in angulo,' in the Hundred Rolls; cf. Nash, Nelmes, &c.

John de Angulo, co. Norf., 1273. A.
Symon in Angulo, co. Linc., ibid.
1571. Peter Nangle (Dublin) : Reg. Univ. Oxf. vol. ii. pt. ii. p. 49.
London, 2 ; Worcester, 1 ; Boston (U.S.), 4.

Nanson. — Bapt. 'the son of Ann,' from nick. Nan ; cf. Noll, Nabb, Nibb. Nan later on became Nanny and Nancy. The French turned it into the diminutives Nanette and Nanon. Even Ann Boleyn was ' Nan.' James Harrison, a priest, when the proclamation was read forbidding the people to call Catherine of Arragon Queen, was accused of saying, 'Queen Catherine was Queen, and Nan Boleyn was not Queen': v. Dict. Nat. Biog. ix. 299. Nan gave us *nan-pie* for *mag-pie*, the phrase 'As nice as a nanny-hen,' i.e. very affected, and ' Miss Nancy,' an effeminate man (v. Halliwell). But Nan and Nanny fell into disrepute, like Parnall and Jill. A nanny-house was well known to the dissolute of both sexes in the 16th century. In the ballad, ' The Two Angrie Women of Abington,' Nan Lawson is a wanton ; indeed, in the 17th century she generally appears in the roistering songs in anything but a virtuous light. Respectable people, still liking the name, changed it to Nancy, and in that form it still lives among the peasantry.

Robertus Nanson, 1379 : P. T. Yorks. p. 123.
Benedictus Nanson, 1379 : ibid. p. 232.
Nicholaus Nanson, 1379 : ibid. p. 272.

Our Nansons. of course, have no connexion with Nan in her degraded days. They belong to Nan in her early youth, before she became tainted with the world.

London, 1 ; Carlisle, 4 ; MDB. (co. Cumberland), 6.

Naper, Napier, Napper, Napery. — Offic. 'the naper,' 'napier,' or ' napper,' from O.F. *nape,* a cloth ; Fr. *nappe,* a table-

cloth. Dim. *nap-kin.* 'Napet or napekyn': Prompt. Parv. ' The over nape schall double be layde ': The Boke of Curtasye. Thus the naper or napier had charge of the table-linen ; whence also the form ' de la naperye,' corresponding to ' de la paneterie,' 'de le eurerie,' ' de le butterye,' &c. With the intrusive *i* in Napier, cf. the *y* in Sawyer (Sawer), Bowyer (Bower), or *lawyer* for *lawer.*

John le Naper, Close Roll, 43 Hen. III.
Jordan le Nappere, co. Oxf., 1273. A.
Thomas le Nappere, co. Oxf., ibid.
John le Naper. C.
Robert Napparius. E.
Walter de la Naperye. L.
Robert le Nappere, co. Soms., 1 Edw. III : Kirby's Quest, p. 259.
1546-7. Edward Napper and Anne Peytoo : Marriage Lic. (London), i. 9.
1784. Married — The Right Hon. Francis, Lord Napier, and Maria Margaret Clavering : St. Geo. Han. Sq. i. 358.
1794. — Henry Rycroft and Jane Naper : ibid. ii. 114.
London, 0, 6, 5, 0 ; New York, 0, 11, 0, 0.

Nappy. — (1) ? Nick. This name just barely survives in Yorkshire, where it arose. ' Nap, expert. Yorks' (Halliwell). ' Nappy, strong, as ale, &c. " Noppy as ale is, *vigoreaux* " : Palsgrave' (Halliwell). (2) ? Nick. Perhaps connected with nap, the rough surface of cloth. A likely nickname in Yorkshire ; v. *nap* (2) (Skeat).

Walterus Napy, *laborer,* 1379 : P. T. Howdenshire, p. 6.
Selby (co. York), 2.

Napton, Knapton. — Local, ' of Knapton': (1) a township in the parish of Acomb, near York; (2) a parish in co. Norfolk. 'The town or farmstead on the nap'; v. Knapp.

Estrilda de Cnapetone, co. Norf., 1273. A.
William de Knapeton, co. Norf., ibid.
Johannes de Knapton, 1379 : P. T. Yorks. p. 295.
Ricardus de Knapton, 1379 : ibid.
1752. Married—Thomas Napton and Ann Wright : St. Geo. Chap. Mayfair, p. 213.
1790. — Bartholomew Napton and Susanna Hine : St. Geo. Han. Sq. ii. 47.
London, 1, 0 ; Boston (U.S.), 0, 6.

Nash. — Local, 'atten ash' (at the ash), from residence beside an

ash-tree. The final *n* in the prefix became the initial of the name proper ; v. Noakes and Nalder for similar tree instances. M.E. *asch, esche.* 'Esche, tre, *fraxinus* ': Prompt. Parv. Esh is still popular for ash in Furness, North Lanc. This surname is familiar to all the English-speaking world.

Agnes ate Nasse, co. Oxf., 1273. A.
Sarra Atteneshe. B.
William atte Nasche, c. 1300. M.
Pagan atte Nash. B.
1524. John Hurdman and Anne Naysshe : Marriage Lic. (London), p. 3.
1629. Married — Fardinando Simones and Alece Nashe : St. Mary Aldermary (London), p. 16.
London, 103 ; New York, 80.

Nasmith, Neasmith, Nesmith. — Occup. ' the nail-smith.' So says Lower, but see my remarks upon Knifesmith.

James Nasmite, co. York. W. 9.
John Naysmith, co. York. W. 13.
James Nasmith, sheriff of Norwich, 1734 : FF. iii. 449.
1745. Married—James Nasmith and Mary Barthol : St. Geo. Chap. Mayfair, p. 53.
1751. Bapt.—Ann, d. Alexander Nacsmith : St. Jas. Clerkenwell, ii. 298.
London, 1, 1, 0 ; Philadelphia, 0, 0, 4.

Nave. — (1) Nick. ' the neve ' ; v. Neave. A variant. (2) Occup. ' the knave,' a lad, a servant. The older meaning of knave is not disreputable. The Yorkshire Poll Tax (1379) has many instances to prove its purely occupative character ; cf. Napton for Knapton.

Johannes Jakkesknave, 1379 : P. T. Yorks. p. 268.
Nicholas Gaytknave, 1379 : ibid. p. 271.
Thomas Wyllknave, 1379 : ibid. p. 269.
London, 1 ; New York, 1.

Naylar, Nayler, Naylor. — Occup. ' the nailer,' a maker of nails. In the North of England, where the occupation is early found, the surname has taken the almost universal form of Naylor, following on the lines of Taylor.

John le Naylere, co. Northumb., 20 Edw. I. R.
Stephen le Naylere, London. X.
Johannes Nayler, 1379 : P. T. Yorks. p. 17.
Willelmus Nayler, 1379 : ibid. p. 272.
Johannes Strenger, *nayler,* 1379 : ibid. p. 172.
Thomas Pope, *nayler,* 1379 : ibid. p. 17.

1565. Married—Robert Nayler and Margaret Larke: St. Jas. Clerkenwell, iii. 2.
1603. Bapt. — William, s. Wylfrecan Naylor: ibid. iv. 75.
1744. Married—John Hicks and Sarah Naylor: St. Geo. Han. Sq. i. 41.

But Naylor was the general form till the middle of the last century.

London, 1, 7, 25; West Rid. Court Dir., 0, 0, 37; Philadelphia, 0, 0, 32.

Nead, Neads, Need, Needes, Needs. Bapt. 'the son of Eade' or 'Eede' (v. Edes, Eades, and Ede); nick. Nead, Need; gen. Needs, or Neads, or Needes; cf. Neddy, Nibbs, Nopps, Nabbs, &c. Although I have no actual proof, I am confident that this is the derivation of the surname. Ede or Eade was one of the most popular font-names in the hereditary surname period. My first two instances are strongly confirmatory of this view:

1678. Bapt.—Mary, d. Richard Nede: St. Jas. Clerkenwell, i. 281.
1681. Married—William Smith and Barbara Nedes: ibid. iii. 189.
1729. — Charles Smith and Rachael Needs: St. Jas. Clerkenwell, ii. 300.
1747. Bapt. — Susannah, d. William Need: St. Jas. Clerkenwell, ii. 283.
1780. Married — William Need and Mary Long: St. Geo. Han. Sq. i. 311.
London, 0, 0, 1, 4, 1; Philadelphia, 1, 3, 0, 0, 2.

Neagle.—? Local, 'atten eagle,' i.e. at the eagle, a sign-name with initial N borrowed from the prefix (v. Roebuck for other instances of sign-names); cf. Nelmes, Nash, Nangle, &c.

1673-4. John Falkon and Susanna Neagell: Marriage Alleg. (Canterbury), p. 109.
1679. Martin Neagle, in the Rebecca, for Virginia: Hotten's Lists of Emigrants, p. 39.
1762. Married—George Holland and Eliz. Neagle: St. Geo. Han. Sq. i. 110. London, 2; Philadelphia, 3.

Neal, Neale, &c.; v. Neil.

Neame, Neames.—Nick. 'the uncle' (O.E. *neme*), gen. Neames; cf. Neaves, Watmough, Bairnfather, Cousin, &c. Names of relationship will be found scattered in considerable numbers over this dictionary. v. also Uncle.

'In eyvll tyme thou dedyst hym wronge, He ys my neme.' Halliwell.

'And angels did him gret honoure, Lo! childe, he seid, this is thy neme.' Ibid.

1584. Thomas Neame, co. Kent: Reg. Univ. Oxf. vol. ii. pt. ii. p. 135.
1587. William Neames and Margaret Burton: Marriage Lic. (London), i. 159.
1594-5. Buried—William Neame, *gent.*, in the Chauncell: St. Jas. Clerkenwell, iv. 55.
1893. Died—Richard Beale Neame, at Hastings: Daily Telegraph, Dec. 26. London, 5, 0.

Neap, Neep. — Nick. 'the grandson' or 'nephew'; cf. Cousin, &c.; v. Neave.

Henry le Nep, co. Bucks, 1273. A.
Peter le Nep, co. Bucks, ibid.
Emma Nep, co. Hunts, ibid.

Close beside the reference to Emma is set Adam Nepos, where the Latin form is used.

1752. Married—Thomas Mathews and Ann Neap: St. Geo. Chap. Mayfair, p. 207.
1753. — Simon Reddish and Ely Neep: ibid. p. 235.
London, 1, 2.

Neasmith. — Occup.; v. Nasmith.

London, 1.

Neat, Neate.—Nick. (1) 'the neat,' trim, tidy; Fr. *net*, clean, pure. (2) The 'neat' (Icel. *naut*), an ox, a cow (v. Neatherd); cf. Bull and Bullock.

John Net et Avice uxor ejus, co. Camb., 1273. A.
Robert le Neyt, co. Wilts, 20 Edw. I. R.
Henricus Naute, 1379: P. T. Yorks. p. 200.
Johannes Naute, 1379: ibid.
1592. Matthew Neate and Ursula Taylor: Marriage Lic. (London), i. 202.
1770. Married—John Bambridge and Sarah Neate: St. Geo. Han. Sq. ii. 158.
London, 2, 9; Boston (U.S.), 3, 0.

Neatherd, Nothard, Nutter (?).—Occup. 'the neat-herd,' a tender of cattle; cf. Coward, Oxnard, Shepherd, Calvert, the suffix of all of which is -*herd*. M.E. *neet*, Icel. *naut*, cattle. Every variety of form is found in Yorkshire records. I will simply quote the Poll Tax.

Johannes Nawtehird, 1379: P. T. Yorks. p. 158.
Willelmus Nouthird, 1379: ibid. p. 14.
Johannes Nedhard, 1379: ibid. p. 114.
Johannes Nawtard, 1379: ibid. p. 164.
Willelmus Netherd, 1379: ibid. p. 86.
Cecilia Neawterd, 1379: ibid. p. 160.
Adam Netehird, 1379: ibid. p. 301.

I cannot find any modern representatives of these forms, saving one Nothard in the London Directory. I doubt not the present dress is Nutter through an intermediate stage Nuttard or Nutterd. Then the final *d* was dropped, and thus as Nutter this interesting surname still maintains a respectable appearance in our larger directories.

London, 0, 1, 17; Boston (U.S.), 0, 0, 31.

Neave, Neaf, Neaves, Neeve, Neeves, Neef. — Nick. 'the nephew'; O.F. *le neve*. 'Neve, sonye sone, *nepos*.' 'Neve, broderys sone, *neptis*': Prompt. Parv. Neve also acquired a secondary meaning, of waster or self-indulgent man, exactly as *nepos* did in Latin. 'Neve, neverthryfte or wastour, *nepos*': Prompt. Parv.

Rayner le Neve, co. Norf., 1273. A.
Walter le Neve, co. Norf., ibid.
John Neven, co. Essex, ibid.
Hugh Nepos, co. Linc., ibid.
Robert Bernardsnef, co. Linc.: Pardons Roll, 6 Ric. II.

This means Robert, the nephew of Bernard. The final *s* in Neaves and Neeves is the genitive; cf. Williams, Jones, &c.

1662. Married—Richard Neave and Avery Mason: Reg. St. Antholin (London), p. 89.
1655. Buried—William Neeves: St. Jas. Clerkenwell, iv. 307.
1807. Married—Edward Neaves and Amy Fenton: St. Geo. Han. Sq. ii. 365. London, 8, 0, 1, 1, 2, 0; Philadelphia, 0, 0, 1, 0, 0, 6.

Neaverson; v. Nevin.

Need, Needs; v. Nead.

Needham. — Local, (1) 'of Needham,' a parish in co. Norfolk; (2) a market-town in co. Suffolk; (3) of Needham, an estate in co. Derby, from which place Earl Kilmorey's family took their name (Lower). The surname is familiar both in cos. Lanc. and Derby, especially the first, and in that portion which is adjacent to the Derbyshire border.

Thomas de Nedham, co. Norf., 1227: FF. vii. 372.
Albric de Nedham, co. Camb., 1273. A.
John de Nedham, co. Derby, ibid.
1578. Thomas Needham, co. Staff.: Reg. Univ. Oxf. vol. ii. pt. ii. p. 83.

1587. John Nedham, co. Leic. : Reg. Univ. Oxf. vol. ii. pt. ii. p. 160.

1596. Bapt.—Ann, d. Henry Needam : St. Peter, Cornhill, i. 44.

1631. James Needham, of Ringstones, co. Ches. : Wills at Chester, ii. 160.

1634. Grace Needham, of Ringstones, co. Ches. : ibid.

London, 13 ; Manchester, 26 ; MDB. (co. Derby), 12 ; Philadelphia, 15.

Needler, Needlemaker. — Occup. ' the needler,' a maker of needles ; M.E. *nedeler* and *nedler*.

'Hikke, the hakeney-man,
And Hugh the nedlere.'
Piers Plowman, 3111-2.

' Pavyers, bellemakers, and brasiers,
Pynners, nedelers, and glasyers.'
Cocke Lorelle's Bote.

Reginald le Nedlere, co. Hunts, 1273. A.

Lucas le Nedlere, co. Camb., ibid.

Ricardus Godwynn, *nedeler*, 25 Edw. I : Freemen of York (Surt. Soc.), i. 6.

Richard le Nedlere, 1313. M.

John Nedlemakyere, ibid.

1563. Simon Nedler and Margaret Harryson : Marriage Lic. (London), i. 27.

1616. Married—Ralph Needler and Agnes Rawlins : St. Jas. Clerkenwell, iii. 43.

1661. Buried—Frauncis Baker, *gent.*, from Mr. Needler's house : ibid. iv. 343.

1667. Bapt. — William, s. William Needler : ibid. i. 230.

There must be present instances, but oddly enough I cannot find any. There is, however, an American variant Kneedler (q.v.).

Neep ; v. Neap.

Neeve(s ; v. Neave.

Negus. — ? Local. Doubtless from some local name ending in -*house* ; cf. Kirkus, Loftus, Bacchus, &c. The beverage so named took its title from Colonel Francis Negus, who ' mixed' it in Queen Anne's reign ; v. Life of Dryden (Malone), p. 414. Notes and Queries, Second Series, v. 224, records several Neguses in the neighbourhood of Norwich ; v. Skeat.

1598. William Negose, of London : Reg. Univ. Oxf. vol. ii. pt. ii. p. 229.

1636. Buried—Thomas Neegoose : St. Jas. Clerkenwell, iv. 219.

1671. Bapt.—Mary, d. John Negus : ibid. i. 252.

1685. William Negus : St. Mary Aldermary (London), p. 107

1697. Bapt.—John, s. of Peter Nyhouse : St. Jas. Clerkenwell, i. 372.

1707. — Ursula, d. of John Negus, a barber on College Hill : St. Thomas the Apostle (London), p. 71.

London, 4 ; Philadelphia, 3 ; New York, 7.

Neighbour, Nabor. — Nick. ' the neighbour.' This surname has a pleasant ring in it, and nothing could be more natural than its creation.

John Neyghbour, C. R., 33 Hen. VI.

1585. Buried—Adam Neighbore : St. Dionis Backchurch (London), p. 199.

1599. — Samuell Neyghbor : ibid. p. 205.

1694. John Frith and Sarah Neighbours : Marriage Alleg. (Canterbury), ii. 288.

1772. Married—Charles August Cramer and Eliz. Neighbour : St. Geo. Han. Sq. p. 220.

1779. — Moses Nabour and Mary Rose : ibid. p. 297.

London, 4, 0 ; New York, 0, 2 ; Boston (U.S.), 0, 1.

Neil, Neild, Neill, Neal, Neale, Neall, Nell, Neilson, Neison, Nelson, Niell, Nielson.—Bapt. 'the son of Neil.' For a full history of this personal name, common to all Northern Europe, v. Yonge, ii. 60-62. It is found in every possible guise in English rolls, and although Nell and Nelson must in many cases spring from Ellen or Eleanor, there can be no doubt that in general they are descendants of Neil. For instance, we find in Settle the following householders :

Nell de Hege, Elias Neleson, and Robert Nellson, 1379 : P. T. Yorks. p. 273.

Probably all these were closely related. The excrescent *d* in Neild seems peculiar to the North of England. There is no Neild in the London, while ten appear in the Manchester, Directory.

Roger fil. Nigelli, co. Linc., 1273. A.

Alan fil. Nigelli, co. Norf., ibid.

Robert fil. Nele, co. Linc., ibid.

John fil. Nel, co. Camb., ibid.

Henry le fiz Neel, C. R., 31 Edw. I.

Thomas Fitz-neel, 1301. M.

Ricardus Nelleson, 1379 : P. T. Yorks. p. 78.

Dionisius Nelle, 1379 : ibid. p. 79.

Alicia, servant of Nele, 1379 : ibid. p. 288.

London, 7, 0, 7, 32, 26, 2, 4, 6, 1, 50, 1, 0 ; Philadelphia, 17, 12, 50, 36, 3, 16, 15, 26, 0, 150, 0, 1.

Nelder.—Local ; v. Nalder.

Nelmes, Nelms.—Local,'atten elms,' i.e. at the elms. For ex-

planation of the initial N, v. Nash or Noakes. The name is Latinized into De Ulmo in the Hundred Rolls.

Osbert atte Elme, co. Oxf., 1273. A.

William ad Ulmum, co. Oxf., ibid.

Richard de Ulmo, co. Oxf., ibid.

1604-5. Married—Christopher Foster and Cassandra Nelme : St. Dionis Backchurch (London), p. 15.

1639. Buried — Marye, d. Jesper Nellmes : St. Mary Aldermary (London), p. 170.

1714. Married—Charles Byne and Eliz. Nelms : St. Dionis Backchurch (London), p. 57.

1803. — Thomas Degory and Eleanor Nelms : St. Geo. Han. Sq. ii. 274.

London, 1, 1 ; Oxford, 0, 2 ; Philadelphia, 0, 13.

Nelson.—(1) Bapt. 'the son of Eleanor,' from nick. Nell. (2) Bapt. 'the son of Neil.' There can be no doubt that both Eleanor and Neil are parents of Nelson ; v. Neil. There are many instances in the Hundred Rolls.

Nel Fawkes, co. Camb., 1273. A.

John fil. Nel, co. Camb., ibid.

Adam Nel, co. Oxf., ibid.

William Nelson. H.

Thomas Nelson, or Nellson, co. York. W. 11.

Thomas Nellson, 1379 : P. T. Howdenshire, p. 29.

1554. Buried—Mother Nelson : Reg. Kensington Parish, p. 83.

1687. Henry Nelson (co. Herts) and Sarah Raby (co. Camb.) : Marriage Alleg. (Canterbury), ii. 20.

1740. Buried—James Nelson, in the Vault : St. Peter, Cornhill, ii. 137.

Although we now spell the nick. Nell, as in ' Little Nell,' nevertheless Nel has been the prevailing form through all the last six centuries.

London, 50 ; Philadelphia, 150.

Nend, Nind.—Local, ' atten end,' i.e. at the end, one who resided at the end of a row of cottages, or the end of the lane, or wood, or town ; v. Ind and Townsend. Nend or Nind is formed by taking as its initial the final *n* of the prefix *atten* ; v. Noakes or Nash.

John atte Nende. B.

Christopher Nend, co. York, 1443. W. 11.

1795. Married — William Nind and Sarah Preston : St. Geo. Han. Sq. ii. 129.

London, 0, 11 ; Philadelphia, 0, 2.

Nesbit, Nesbitt, Nisbet, Nisbett, Nesbett.—Local, ' of

Nesbit.' There are several townships so called in cos. Durham and Northumberland, not to speak of Nesbit in co. Berwick. Nearly all originated a surname.

William de Nesebit, C. R., 18 Edw. I.
Thomas de Nesbyt, temp. 1380: Hist. Dunelmensis (Surt. Soc.), xlii.
1716. Married—Thomas Garbrand and Anne Nisbett: St. Antholin (London), p. 129.
1789. — Colebrooke Nesbitt and Eliza Sneyd: St. Geo. Han. Sq. ii. 32.
London, 1, 3, 3, 3, 0; Newcastle, 5, 0, 3, 0, 0; New York, 7, 26, 3, 1, 2; Philadelphia, 4, 11, 5, 0, 0.

Nesmith; v. Nasmith.

Ness, Nesse.—Local, 'at the ness,' i.e. at the promontory or headland; cf. Holderness, Sheerness, Harkness, &c.

William del Ness, of Ness, co. Norf., 10 Ric. I: FF. xi. p. 200.
Roger atte Nesse, co. Kent, 1273. A.
Alicia del Nesse, 1379: P. T. Yorks. p. 141.
Johannes del Nesse, 1379: ibid.
Simon de Ness, of Ness, co. Norf., 20 Edw III; FF. xi. 200.
1807. Married—John Alex. Paul Mac-Gregor and James Ness: St. Geo. Han. Sq. ii. 366.
London, 3, 0; New York, 5, 1; Philadelphia, 2, 0.

Netherclift.—Local, ' at the nether cliff,' i.e. at the lower cliff. The final t is an excrescence.

1605. Bapt.—Samuell, s. John Nethercleve : Reg. Kensington Parish, p. 15.
1742. Married—John Netherclift and Jane Barnet: St. Geo. Chap. Mayfair, p. 17.
London, 2.

Nethercote, Nethercott, Nethicott.—Local, ' of Nethercote,' a village in co. Northampton. The American Nethicott is a manifest modification of the name. The original meaning was ' the nether cot' or cottage.

1574. Buried — Eliz. Nethercott: St. Jas. Clerkenwell, iv. 16.
1655. Married — Edward Nethercote and Eliz. Twichell : St. Michael, Cornhill, p. 35.
1747. — Charles Osborn Nethercott and Maria Constantia Rodney : St. Geo. Chap. Mayfair, p. 87.
Crockford, 0, 2, 0; MDB. (co. Northants), 2, 0, 0; New York, 0, 2, 1.

Nethermill.—Local, 'at the nether mill,' the lower as distinct from the upper mill.

Richard Nedyrmyl, 1533: Reg. Univ. Oxf. i. 174.
1546. John Nethermyll and Winifred Dod: Marriage Lic. (Faculty Office), p. 7.

Nethersole.—Local, 'at the nether sale,' from residence therein (v. Sale); =' nether hall '; cf. Netherwood.

1399. Edmund Nethersole: Cal. of Wills in Court of Husting (2).
1618. William Nethersole, co. Kent: Reg. Univ. Oxf. pt. ii. p. 368.
1717. Married—Jacob Sharpe and Eliz. Nethersole: Reg. Canterbury Cath. p. 73.
1748. — Abraham Portal and Eliz. Nethersole: St. Geo. Chap. Mayfair, p. 111.
London, 1; MDB. (co. Kent), 4.

Netherway.—Local, 'at the nether way,' i.e. the lower road; cf. Nethergate in the Hundred Rolls.

Gundewyn de Nethergate, co. Suff., 1273. A.
Wacelin de Nethergate, co. Suff., ibid.
1642. Buried — Charles Nethwaye, a poor servant: St. Jas. Clerkenwell, iv. 255.
1651. Bapt.—John, s. John Netherway: ibid. ii. 178.
1682. Jonathan Netheway and Mary Clarke: Marriage Alleg. (Canterbury), p. 118.
1796. Married—John Kelly and Susannah Netherway: St. Geo. Han. Sq. ii. 145.
London, 1.

Netherwood.—Local, 'at the nether wood,' i.e. the lower wood.

Thomas de Netherwode, co. Essex, 1273. A.
Adam Nethyrwode, 1379: P. T. Yorks. p. 261.
John de Netherwode, 1379: ibid. p. 264.
1708. Married—Joseph Netherwood and Jane Sharp: St. Michael, Cornhill, p. 54.
1751. — Thomas Walker and Eliz. Netherwood: St. Geo. Chap. Mayfair, p. 205.
1781. — Joseph Woolley and Ann Netherwood: St. Geo. Han. Sq. i. 323.
London, 1; Sheffield, 1; MDB. (West Rid. Yorks), 3; Philadelphia, 1.

Netmaker.—Occup. 'the matmaker'; not a maker of nets. Originally ' nat maker,' i.e. a maker of mats; Fr. natte. 'Natte or matte, matta, storium': Prompt. Parv. 'A natte maker, storiator': Cath. Ang. 'Nat maker, natier': Palsg. 'In the curious poem entitled "The Pilgrimage to Jerusalem," ... one of the characters introduced is the "natte makere," who holds long

discourse with the Pilgrim' (v. Way's note on natte, Prompt. Parv. p. 351). In spite of all this the surname may mean the net-maker.

Isabella Nettemaker, 1379: P. T. Yorks. p. 26.
1603. Married—Lawrence Netmaker and Elizabeth Rice: St. Mary Aldermary (London), p. 10.
1621. Buried—Robert Netmaker, an old man : St. Antholin (London), p. 56.
1625. — Ann Netmaker: ibid. p. 59.
1683. Married — Sackvill Nettmaker and Ann Harford: Marriage Alleg. (Canterbury), p. 148.

I have many more instances. It seems strange that I should not be able to light upon any in the directories of to-day.

Netter.—? Occup. 'the netter,' a maker of nets (?). Perhaps one who netted fish.

Johannes Netter, 1379: P. T. Yorks. p. 209.
London, 1; Philadelphia, 3; New York, 5.

Nettlefield, Nettelfield. — Local, ' of the nettle-field,' from residence thereby. I fail to identify the locality, but it would be a common local term.

1662-3. James Round and Eliz.Bishopp; alleged by Ric. Nettlefield. Marriage Alleg. (Canterbury), p. 65.
1666. William Wood and Susanne Nettlefeild, of Rigate: ibid. p. 187.
London, 1, 2; New York, 1, 0.

Nettlefold. — Local, 'at the nettle-fold,' from residence thereby. I cannot find the spot.

1633. Married — George Nelson and Ann Nettlefold: St. Antholin (London), p. 67.
1635. George Nettelfold sailed in the Globe to Virginia: Hotten's Lists of Emigrants, p. 119.
1752. Married—John Poynton and Eliz. Nettlefold: St. Geo. Chap. Mayfair, p. 228.
1790. — John Nettlefold and Eliz. Humphry : St. Geo. Han. Sq. ii. 49.
' Nettlefold. On the 23rd inst. at Hallfield, Edgbaston, Birmingham, Hugh, son of the late Edward John Nettlefold': Daily Telegraph, Dec. 27, 1893.
London, 3.

Nettleship.—Local, 'of Nettleshope' (?). There can be little doubt as to the accuracy of this definition. The suffix (v. Hope) is common to place-names in North England, and in some instances has become -ship, as applied to surnames which owe their parentage to them. I have seen Blenkinsopp spelt Blenkinship; cf. Winship. Nettleship is a Yorkshire name, and seems to have arisen in the neighbourhood of Tickhell, on the borders of Notts.

1583. William Netelshippe, co. Notts, St. Alban Hall: Reg. Univ. Oxf. vol. ii. pt. ii. p. 126.
1688. Edward Nettleshipp and Susanna Nynn: Marriage Alleg. (Canterbury), p. 88.
1752. Married — Lacey Roberts and Mary Nettleship: St. Geo. Chap. Mayfair, p. 222.
1778. — James Brittain and Sarah Nettelship: St. Geo. Han. Sq. i. 291.
London, 4; Sheffield, 2; MDB. (co. Notts), 5; New York, 1.

Nettleton.—Local, 'of Nettleton,' parishes in cos. Lincoln (one mile from Caistor) and Wilts (eight miles from Chippenham).

1616. Buried—Ann Nettleton, servant to Eliz. Osborne: St. Jas. Clerkenwell, iv. 135.
1617. Robert Nettleton, *gent*, co. York: Reg. Univ. Oxf. vol. ii. pt. ii. p. 364.
1665. Bapt.—Ann, d. Thomas Nettleton: Kensington Parish, p. 40.
1665-6. Anthony Tye and Mary Nettleton: Marriage Alleg. (Canterbury), p. 160.
London, 4; MDB. (West Rid. Yorks), 4; New York, 2; Philadelphia, 2.

Nevett, Nevitt.—Local, 'of Knyvet.' I cannot identify the spot, but the corruption to Nevett and Nevitt is perfectly clear, although it did not commonly occur till the 17th century.

Mathew de Knyvet, co. Notts, 1273. A.
Geoffrey Knifet, co. Camb., ibid.
Alex. de Knyft, co. Oxf., ibid.
Thomas de Knyvet, co. Essex, ibid.
1583. Married — Henry Knevit and Frances Elsin: St. Antholin (London), p. 30.
1634. Bapt.—Ann, d. Edward Nevit: ibid. p. 68.
1635. — Mary, d. Edward Nevet: ibid. p. 70.
1782. Married—John Nevitt and Mary Lovett: St. Geo. Han. Sq. i. 338.
London, 2, 0; Crockford, 0, 1.

Nevin, Nevins, Nevinson, Nevison, Niven, Nivens, Nivison, Neaverson.—Bapt. 'the son of Niven,' or Nevin. I find no clue in the 13th and 14th century records. 'This series points to an early but forgotten personal name' (Lower's Patr. Brit. p. 236).

But for the existence of Nevin and Nevens I should at once assume that Nevinson and Nevison were Neve-son (v. Neave), i.e. Nephewson, the intrusive *n* in the former being extremely common in such forms. Neaverson presents no difficulty. Nevinson was bound to become Neverson, and of this Neaverson is but a variant; cf. Pattinson and Patterson, or Cattinson and Catterson. The two following entries seem oddly enough to concern the same couple:

1635. Married — Robert Sharpe and Jane Nevisonn: St. Antholin (London), p. 69.
1637. — Robert Sharpe and Jone Nevinson: ibid. p. 70.

The following reference probably dates about the first year of Henry VI:

Jenetta fil. Nevans, ap Lyon, ap Jestin: Visitation of Gloucestershire, 1623, p. 98.
1602. Richard Nevinson, co. Kent: Reg. Univ. Oxf. vol. ii. pt. ii. p. 258.

My next entry denotes the change mentioned above as a natural one:

1728. Buried — John Neverson: St. Thomas the Apostle (London), p. 15.

Nevison as a variant was inevitable:

1757. Married—John Park and Susanna Nevison.

The same changes are rung upon the Yorkshire Pattinsons, Pattersons, and Pattisons from the once familiar North-English Patrick.

London, 1, 2, 0, 0, 2, 0, 0, 0; Crockford, 2, 2, 1, 0, 2, 0, 0, 0; MDB. (co. Cumb.), (Nevison), 1; (co. Northampton) (Neaverson), 1; New York, 18, 34, 0, 1, 1, 1, 4, 0.

New.—Nick. ' the new,' i.e. the new-comer, the stranger just settled in the district or village; v. Newman and Newcome.

Richard le Newe, co. Camb., 1273. A.
Robert le Newe, co. Wilts, ibid.
Simon le Neue, co. Bedf., ibid.
Richard le Nywe, co. Soms., 1 Edw. III: Kirby's Quest, p. 232.
1617. Bapt.—Thomas, s. William Newe: St. Jas. Clerkenwell, i. 77.
1683. Thomas New and Bersheba Roe: Marriage Alleg. (Canterbury), p. 130.
— Charles Booth and Sarah Newe, of Oxford: ibid. p. 141.
1718. Married—Charles Fox and Elizabeth New: St. Mary Aldermary (London), p. 44.
London, 14; Philadelphia, 16.

Newall, Newell, Newhall.—Local, 'of Newhall,' townships in cos. Chester, York, &c.; cf. Sewall and Sewell. The surname means 'at the new hall,' probably as distinct from the old hall. No doubt co. Chester has supplied most of our Newalls and Newells.

Thomas atte Nywehalle, co. Soms., 1 Edw. III: Kirby's Quest, p. 196.
John de Newhalle, co. Camb., Pardons Roll, 6 Ric. II.
Hugo de Neuhalle, *souter*, 1379: P. T. Yorks. p. 18.
1630. Richard Newall, of Chester: Wills at Chester, i. 161.
1686. George Hunter and Honor Newell, co. Herts: Marriage Alleg. (Canterbury), p. 252.
1755. Married—Matthew Newall and Mary Moore: St. Geo. Han. Sq. i. 57.
1764. — John Newell and Sarah Caudery: ibid. p. 139.
London, 3, 19, 0; MDB. (co. Ches.), 4, 0, 0; Philadelphia, 3, 32, 11.

Newbart, Newbert.—Local, 'of Newbold,' q.v. These variants seem to be peculiar to co. Notts.

MDB. (co. Notts), 2, 2.

Newberry,-bery; v. Newbury.

Newbiggin, Newbeggin, Newbegin.—Local, ' of Newbeggin.' Two parishes, one in the dioc. of Carlisle and one in the dioc. of Newcastle, &c., go by this name; = new building; cf. Lowland Scotch and North English *big*, to build; v. Halliwell. There is also a township called Newbiggin in the parish of Middleton-in-Teesdale, co. Durham; also a township in the parish of Shotley, co. Northumberland; also a township in N. Rid. Yorks.

Robert de Newbigging, 7 Edw. II: Nicolson and Burn, Hist. Westm. and Cumb., i. 305.
1745. Married—Peter Newbigging and Catherine Dowling: St. Geo. Chap. Mayfair, p. 155.
Philadelphia, 1, 1, 0; Boston (U.S.), 0, 0, 8.

Newbold, Newbald, Newbolt, Newbould, Newboult.—Local, 'of Newbold,' i.e. the new dwelling. A.S. *bold*, a house, a dwelling (v. *build*, Skeat). Naturally many places bear this name. There are parishes in cos. Warwick, Worcester, and Leicester, also hamlets in cos. Leicester, Derby.

Northants, and Warwick. New-bald represents Newbald, a parish in the E. Rid. of Yorks, near Market Weighton ; cf. Newbiggin.

John de Neubald, co. Salop, 1273. A.
Richard de Newebald, co. Oxf., ibid.
Robertus de Newbald, 1379 : P. T. Howdenshire, p. 11.
Willelmus Newbald, 1379 ; P. T. Yorks. p. 149.
1654. Bapt.—Joseph, s. John Newball : St. Jas. Clerkenwell, p. 186.
1693-4. William Glenister (co. Bucks) and Eliz. Newboult (co. Bucks): Marriage Alleg, (Canterbury), i. 284.
1726. Married — George Ernest Eller and Mary Newbolt : St. Geo. Han. Sq. p. 2.
MDB. (co. Notts), 1, 0, 0, 1, 2 ; West Rid. Court Dir., 2, 1, 2, 7, 3 ; London, 7, 0, 1, 0, 0 ; Philadelphia, 26, 0, 0, 0, 0.

Newbond, Newbon, New-bound.—Occup. ' the new bond ' (v. Bond), i.e. the new householder, the newly-settled peasant who held under the tenure of bondage.

Roger le Neubonde, co. Bucks, 1273. A.
Henry Neubonde, co. Bucks, ibid.
Richard le Newebonde, co. Hunts, ibid.
William le Newebonde, co. Hunts, ibid.
Johannes Neubond', 1379 : P. T. Yorks. p. 294.
1808. Married—John Newbound and Ann Burford : St. Geo. Han. Sq. ii. 383.
London, 0, 4, 0 ; West Rid. Court Dir., 0, 0, 1.

Newbury, Newberry, New-bery.—Local, ' of Newbury,' a town in co. Berks. Also ' of Newborough,'a parish in co. North-ants, five miles from Peterborough. Also a township in parish of Coxwold, N. Rid. Yorks. All these places no doubt contributed their share to swell the number of Newburys, Newberrys, and New-berys in our directories. For similar changes rung on the suffix, v. Oxberry.

Henry de Neubury, co. Bucks, 1273. A.
John de Neubury, co. Soms., 1 Edw. III : Kirby's Quest, p. 161.
1680. Bapt. — Anthony, s. Anthony Newbery : St. Jas. Clerkenwell, i. 380.
1688. Jeremiah Newbrough and Eliz. Conniers : Marriage Alleg. (Canterbury), p. 62.
1691. Thomas Newborough and Martha Atkins : ibid. p. 198.
1693. David Newbery and Ann Dale : ibid. p. 268.
— Thomas James and Susanna New-bury : ibid. p. 254.

The following variants are found in the Reg. Univ. Oxf. (Index) :

Neuburgh, Newberough, New-brough, Neuberrye, Newberey, Newbrye, Nubery, and Newberie.

London, 3, 3, 18 ; Philadelphia, 0, 13, 1.

Newby.—Local, ' of Newby,' a township in the union of Ripon, Yorks ; also a township in the parish of Clapham, near Settle, Yorks; also a hamlet in the parish of Harewood, near Leeds, Yorks. Also other small places.

Nicholas de Neuby, co. York, 1273. A.
Robert de Neuby, co. York, ibid.
William de Neuby, co. Cumb., 20 Edw. I. R.
Galfridus de Nuby, 1379 : P. T. Yorks. p. 258.
Radulphus de Neuby, 1379 : ibid. p. 253.
London, 9 ; New York, 4.

Newcome, Newcomen, Newcomb, Newcombe.—Nick. ' the new-comen,' a newly-settled stranger ; cf. Newman (q.v.). The b in Newcomb is excrescent. New-comen is the invariable form in early rolls. M.E. cumen, comen, to come, pp. cumen, comen, come (Skeat).

' But the fllemynges among these things dere
Incomen loven beste bacon and beer.'
Old Political Song.

' Newcomes, strangers newly arrived ; v. Hollinshed, Conq. Ireland, p. 55 ' (Halliwell).

Gilbert le Neucum, co. Linc., 1273. A.
Gilbert le Neucomen, co. Linc., ibid.
Robert Neucomen, co. Linc., ibid.
Robert le Newcomen, C. R., 9 Edw. I.
Ricardus Newcomen, 1379 : P. T. Yorks. p. 264.
1660. Robert Maddison and Eliz. Newcomen : Marriage Alleg. (Canterbury), p. 53.
London, 0, 1, 5, 5; Philadelphia, 2, 0, 24, 3.

Newdick.—Local, ' at the new dike,' i.e. from residence by or near the new trench, mound, or dike ; cf. Cobbledick, and v. Dyke.

1676. Henry Newdick and Mary Nicholls : Marriage Alleg. (Canterbury), p. 169.
1743. Bapt.—Joseph Baden, s. Henry Newdick : St. Michael, Cornhill, p. 173.
1744. — Henry, s. Henry Newdick : ibid. p. 174.
London, 2.

Newell, Newhall ; v. Newall.

Newham.—Local, ' of New-ham.' There is a township of this name in co. Northumberland. But doubtless, like Newton, it is common to many counties.

John de Neuham, co. Essex, 1273. A.
Ambrose de Neuham, co. Camb., ibid.
Walter de Neuham, co. Camb., ibid.
1680. John Wyne and Eliz. Newham : Marriage Alleg. (Canterbury), p. 49.
1684. Buried—Ralph Newham, haber-dasher : St. Mary Aldermary, p. 195.
1772. Married—George Newham and Anne Quinlan : St. Geo. Han. Sq. i. 125.
London, 6.

Newhouse.—Local, ' at the new house,' from residence at a house so called. Many small spots go by this name up and down the country ; cf. Newton, Newby, New biggin, and Newham, which are strictly parallel cases, only in most cases of older origin. The family of Newhouse, however, are evidently sprung from co. York.

Johannes Newehowse, 1379 : P. T. Yorks. p. 287.
Alicia Newhouse, 1379 : ibid. p. 284.
Ricardus de Newhese, 1379 : ibid. p. 282.
1686-7. William Waller and Eliz. New-house : Marriage Alleg. (Canterbury), p. 260.
1771. Married—James Newhouse and Isabel Thwaites : St. Geo. Han. Sq. p. 207.
Crockford, 11 MDB. (West Rid. Yorks), 5 ; New York, 8 ; Philadelphia, 14.

Newington.—Local, ' of New-ington,' parishes and places in cos. Kent, Oxford, Surrey, Middle-sex, &c.

Ralph de Newentone, co. Hunts, 1273. A.
Richard de Newentone, co. Sussex, ibid.
Peter de Newentone, co. Bucks, ibid.
1622. Bapt.—Amy, d. William Newing-ton : St. Jas. Clerkenwell, i. 94.
1681. Charles Bidell and Mary New-ington : Marriage Alleg. (Canterbury), p. 60.
London, 1.

Newland, Newlands.—(1) Local, ' of Newland,' parishes in co. Worc. and Glouc. ; also town-ships in the parish of Ulverston, co. Lanc., and of Drax, W. Rid. Yorks. (2) ' Of Newlands,' a township in the parish of Bywell St. Peter, co. Northumberland ; also a chapelry in the parish of Crosthwaite, co. Cumb. But from my first instances it is manifest that the chief parent-age must be allowed to land reclaimed from the great fen district.

Roger de la Neuelonde, co. Camb., 1273. A.
Richard le (de ?) Neulond, co. Camb., ibid.
Thomas de la Neulaund, co. Essex, ibid.
G. de Neuland, co. Linc., ibid.
William atte Niwelond, co. Soms., 1 Edw. III : Kirby's Quest, p. 227.
1573. John Newlande and Grace Sampson : Marriage Lic. (London), i. 58.
1670. Married—William Newland and Mary Spratt : St. Jas. Clerkenwell, iii. 169.
1748. — Peter Newland and Joyce Atkinson : St. Geo. Chap. Mayfair, p. 104.
London, 10, 0 ; Liverpool, 0, 1 ; Philadelphia, 6, 0 ; Boston (U.S.), 1, 1.

Newling, Newlin.—Local, ' of Newlyn,' a parish in co. Cornwall, eight miles from Truro. With the natural adoption of an excrescent *g*, cf. Jennings, Collins, Collings, &c.

1614. Robert Newlin or Newling : Reg. Univ. Oxf. vol. ii. pt. ii. p. 335.
1687. Thomas Jolly and Catharine Newling : Marriage Alleg. (Canterbury), p. 280.
1707. Buried — Hannah, d. Susannah Newling : St. Antholin (London), p. 120.
1779. Married—William Matthews and Eliz. Newlyn : St Geo. Han. Sq. p. 302.
1782. — William Fordham and Sarah Newling : ibid. p. 341.
London, 11, 0 ; Philadelphia, 0, 30 ; Boston (U.S.), 2, 1.

Newman.—Nick. ' the new man,' the newly-settled stranger ; v. New and Newcome. A.S. *niwe*. This is a common entry in the Hundred Rolls.

Robert Niweman, co. Camb., 1273. A.
Herbert le Niweman, co. Oxf., ibid.
Mathew le Neuman, co. Hunts, ibid.
John le Neuman, co. Bedf., ibid.
London, 116 ; New York, 146 ; Philadelphia, 65.

Newmarch, Newmark.—Local, ' of Newmarch.' The opposite of Newland (q.v.), for this seems to be land lost instead of reclaimed from the marshes ; v. Marsh. I suspect Newmark is German.

Adam de Neumarche, co. Linc., 1273. A.
1591. Buried — John, s. John Newmarch : St. Jas. Clerkenwell, iv. 44.
1785. Married — Matthias Newmarch and Mary Rouse : St. Geo. Han. Sq. ii 372.

London, 1, 1 ; New York, 0, 7 ; Boston (U.S.), 1, 0.

Newnham, Newnam.—Local, ' of Newnham,' parishes in cos. Glouc., Herts, Kent, Northants, Southants, Warwick, and Oxford. I have a fairly early English instance of the American way of spelling the name.

Ralph de Neunenham, co. Camb., 1273. A.
1576. Buried—William Newnam : St. Jas. Clerkenwell, iv. 18.
1743. Married — Thomas Newnham and Ann Smith : St. Geo. Han. Sq. i. 30.
1750. — Thomas Newenham and Susanna Wandesford : St. Geo. Chap. Mayfair, p. 170.
1806. — Patrick Newnham and Ann Trattell : St. Geo. Han. Sq. ii. 354.
London, 3, 0 ; Philadelphia, 0, 10.

Newport.—Local, ' of Newport,' a large hamlet in co. Devon, a parish in co. Essex, and the well-known seaport town in Monmouthshire. It would seem as if the Essex town was the chief parent.

William de Neuport, co. Bucks, 1273. A.
Gernega de Neuport, co. Linc., ibid.
Maurice de Neuport, co. Linc., ibid.
1574. Francis Newporte, co. Salop : Reg. Univ. Oxf. vol. ii. pt. ii. p. 60.
1589. Charles Newporte, co. Northants: ibid. p. 173.
1604. Richard Newport, co. Salop : ibid. p. 276.
1654-5. Buried — John, s. Samuell Newport : St. Jas. Clerkenwell, iv. 303.
1744. Married—John Fuller and Hannah Newport : St. Geo. Chap. Mayfair, p. 36.
London, 6 ; Oxford, 7 ; Philadelphia, 6.

Newsam, Newsom, Newsome, Newsman, Newsum, Newsholme.—Local, (1)' of Newsome,' a village near Huddersfield ; (2) ' of Newsholm,' a township in the parish of Gisburne, near Clitheroe, W. Rid. Yorks. Newsman is a curious modern corruption. It occurs in the Sheffield Directory. Alongside it is found the more correct Newsome. It is needless to say that Newsham, q.v., is inextricably mixed up with the above.

Willelmus de Newsom (dwelling at Newsholm), 1379 : P. T. Yorks. p. 272.
Alicia de Neusom, 1379 : ibid. p. 137.
Willelmus de Newsome, 1379 : ibid. p. 66.

Walter de Newsom, 4 Edw. III : Freemen of York, i. 26.
1618. Thomas Newsam, co. Warw. : Reg. Univ. Oxf. vol. ii. pt. ii. p. 371.
1694-5. John Newsum and Dorothy Summers: Marriage Lic. (Faculty Office), p. 214.
1744. Married—Richard Sare Newsome and Eliz. Greame : St. Jas. Clerkenwell, iii. 274.
London, 2, 2, 1, 0, 0, 0 ; West Rid. Court Dir., 3, 0, 4, 0, 4, 2 ; Manchester, 0, 1, 0, 0, 0, 0 ; Philadelphia, 0, 0, 4, 0, 1, 0.

Newsham.—Local, ' of Newsham.' Townships in the parishes of Wressel, E. Rid. Yorks ; Kirby Wisk, N. Rid. Yorks ; Kirby Ravensworth, N. Rid. Yorks ; Kirkham, co. Lanc.; and Eaglescliffe, co. Durham. Many of the surnames which owe their parentage to these places are mixed up with Newsam, q.v. In the Index to the Register of St. George, Mayfair, the compiler has placed these names under one heading, as ' Newsham or Newsome.' In reality they ought to have been separated.

1615. Robert Newsham, of Whalley : Wills at Chester, i. 142.
1752. Married—Henry Newsham and Frances Bromley : St. Geo. Chap. Mayfair, p. 214.
1805. — John Nicholls and Elen Newsham : St. Geo. Han. Sq. ii. 337.
Manchester, 3 ; Liverpool, 1 ; Philadelphia, 13.

Newsom(e ; v. Newsam.

Newson. — Local, ' of Newsome'; v. Newsam. This is the obvious origin ; v. Ransom for Ranson, or Sansom for Samson. It is a very natural corruption. The following entry is of considerable assistance :

1641. Married — Peter Newsan and Bridgett Jeffes : St. Jas. Clerkenwell, iii. 73.

This denotes the first change from Newsam to Newsan. Newson was then inevitable.

1682. Married—John Jones and Eliz. Newson : St. Jas. Clerkenwell, iii. 198.
1720. Buried—Dorothy Newson, from Mr. Lockyer's, *poulterer* : St. Dionis Backchurch (London), p. 290.
1745. Married — Samuel Hankinson and Margaret Newsom : St. Geo. Han. Sq. p. 35.
1777. — William Newson and Rachel Shaw : ibid. p. 273.
London, 11 ; Liverpool, 1 ; Philadelphia, 4.

Newstead.—Local, 'of Newstead,' co. Notts, where the famous abbey was founded. But there are also places in cos. Lincoln and Northumberland that bear this name. With Newstead, 'the new holding' (v. Stead), cf. Newham, Newhouse, Newton, &c.

1616. Christopher Newsteade, co. Linc.: Reg. Univ. Oxf. vol. ii. pt. ii. p. 356.
1753. Married—Thomas Newstead and Jane Graham : St. Geo. Chap. Mayfair, p. 243.
1758. — William Newstead and Ann Coleman : St. Geo. Han. Sq. i. 78.
London, 6 ; Leeds, 1 ; New York, 2.

Newton.—Local, 'of Newton.' Naturally found in every county in England; cf. Oldham, Newham, Newstead, &c. It would be easy to furnish instances from every early register of names.

Gunnora de Neutone, co. Suff., 1273. A.
Ralph de Neutone, co. Hunts, ibid.
Alan de Neuton, co. Linc., ibid.
Willelmus de Neweton, 1379 : P. T. Yorks. p. 32.
Johannes de Neuton, 1379 : ibid. p. 98.
1579. John Newton, co. Salop : Reg. Univ. Oxf. vol. ii. pt. ii. p. 86.
1683. Bapt.—Thomas, s, Thomas Newton : St. Peter, Cornhill, ii. 10.
London, 94 ; Philadelphia, 63.

Nibbs.—Bapt. 'the son of Isabel,' from nick. Ibb (v. Ibb and Ibbett). This Ibb became familiarly Nibb, just as Oliver became Noll; cf. Nobbs. Isabel had a great many nicks., the name being very popular in its day, which happened to be the hereditary surname period. v. Knibb.

John Nybbe, co. Soms., 1 Edw. III : Kirby's Quest, p. 257.
1677. Bapt.— Margarett Nibb, d. Thomas Nib : St. Jas. Clerkenwell, i. 276.
1746. Married — William Nibbs and Mary Betts : St. Geo. Chap. Mayfair, p. 75.
1787. — John Nibbs and Sarah Johnaway : St. Geo. Han. Sq. i. 398.
London, 2.

Niblott.—Bapt. 'the son of Isabel,' from nick. Nib (v. Nibbs), and dim. Nib-elot ; cf. Hewlett for Hew-elot, i.e. little Hugh or Hew; also Noblett for Nobelot, from Nob (= Hob = Robert) ; v. Nobbs.

1687. Married — Phillip Niblett and Anne Biddulfe : St. Jas. Clerkenwell, p. 204.

1740. Married — William Niblet and Mary Lambert : St. Geo. Han. Sq. i. 24.
1742. — Henry Niblett and Susanna Todd : St. Geo. Chap. Mayfair, p. 19.
1781. — James Marsh and Eliz. Niblett : St. Geo. Han. Sq. p. 319.
London, 2.

Niche.—Local, 'at the niche,' i.e. nook, the recess. This seems an early instance and worth recording.

Simon atte Nych, co. Soms., 1 Edw. III : Kirby's Quest, p. 105.

Nicholas.—Bapt. 'the son of Nicholas.' This once popular font-name is the parent of a very large family ; v. Cole, Collin, Nicklin, Nix, Nixon, &c. A large list of variants is given under Nicholes.

Nicholas le Hunte, co. York, 1273. A.
John fil. Nicholai, co. Salop, ibid.
1585. Humphrey Nicholas, co. Camarthen : Reg. Univ. Oxf. vol. ii. pt. ii. p. 143.
1703. Bapt.— Eliz., d. John Nickless : St. Jas. Clerkenwell, ii. 12.
1730. — Robert, s. Thomas Nicholas : ibid. p. 189.
London, 16 ; Philadelphia, 34.

Nicholes, Nicholl, Nicholls, Nichols, Nicholson, Nickalls, Nickels, Nickolds, Nickoll, Nickolls, Nickols, Nicol Nicole. Nicoll, Nicolle, Nicols, Nicolson, Nickoles.—Bapt. 'the son of Nicholas,' from Nichol or Nicol, the nick. ; v. Nicholas. Nichol always held a fair place in popular favour, as our directories of to-day amply prove. But Collin (q.v.) was probably the greater favourite.

William fil. Nicoll, co. Salop, 1273. A.
John Nicole, co. Oxf., ibid.
Stephen Nichole, co. Oxf., ibid.
Alicia Nicholmayden and Robertus Nichol-man (i.e. the servant of Nichol), 1379 : P. T. Yorks. pp. 158, 154.
Nichol Gurdelere, C. R., 21 Edw. III. pt. ii.
John Niccolson, temp. Eliz. ZZ.
1562. Bapt.— Joane Nichollsonne : St. Peter, Cornhill, i. 10.
1575. Thomas Nicolls, co. Middlesex : Reg. Univ. Oxf. vol. ii. pt, ii. p. 62.
Nycall Spyght, 1602: Nicolson and Burn, Hist. Westm. and Cumb., i. 96.
1687. James Nickleson and Ann Goodman : Marriage Alleg. (Canterbury), p. 25.
1707. Married—Robert Nicholls and Eliz. Moye : St. Antholin (London), p. 120.

London, 5, 10, 65, 55, 67, 1, 3, 1, 2, 1, 3, 7, 2, 12, 1, 1, 1, 0 ; Philadelphia, 44, 2, 24, 122, 88, 0, 8, 0, 0, 0, 0, 3, 0, 0, 3, 2, 0, 1.

Nicholetts, Nicholet.—Bapt. 'the son of Nicholas,' from dim. Nichol-et ; cf. Collett. There is no doubt that Collett was the favourite. Nicholet made little headway. Nicklet is an obvious modification, and has managed to cross the Atlantic.

1603. Gabriel Nicholetts, co. Hereford, *pleb.* : Reg. Univ. Oxf. vol. ii. pt. ii. p. 267.
1659. Buried—Jane Nicholett, *spinster*, in the chancel : St. Jas. Clerkenwell, iv. 330.
1661. — Samuell Nicholetts : ibid. p. 340.
1743. Married—Caleb Nicholetts and Sarah Darby : St. Antholin (London), p. 152.
New York, 0, 1.

Nicholl(s, &c. ; v. Nicholes.

Nickerson.—Bapt. 'the son of Nicholas,' a corruption of Nicholson (v. Nicholes) ; cf. Patterson, Catterson. The following entry shows the preliminary step towards the corruption :

1759. Married — John Nickelson and Mary Knapton : St. Geo. Han. Sq. i. 85.
London, 3 ; Philadelphia, 13.

Nickinson, Nickisson.—Bapt. 'the son of Nicholas.' Nicklinson is probably a corruption of Nicklinson (v. next article) and Nickisson an extension of Nickson (v. Nix).

London, 2, 1.

Nicklin, Nickling, Nicklinson.—Bapt. 'the son of Nicholas,' from nick. Nicol, dim. Nicolin. Thomas Nycklyn (also written Nyclys, i.e. Nicholls) was Mayor of Coventry in 1575 (Coventry Mysteries, p. 129). The *g* in Nickling is excrescent, as in Jennings and hundreds of other cases. With the dim. Nicol-in, cf. *violin*, a little viol.

1733. Married — Thomas Nicklin and Sarah Tomlinson : St. Jas. Clerkenwell, p. 261.
1746. — William Nicklin and Esther Pugh : St. Geo. Chap. Mayfair, p. 62.
1771. — John Nicklin and Eliz. Doubtfire : St. Geo. Han. Sq. i. 205.
London, 0, 0, 1 ; Manchester, 1, 1, 0 ; Derby, 0, 0, 5 ; Shrewsbury, 1, 0, 0 ; New York, 0, 2, 0.

Nickoll(s, &c. ; v. Nicholes.

Nicks, Nickson.—Bapt. 'the son of Nicholas,' from the nick. form Nick ; v. Nix and Nixon.

1621. Edward Nickson, co. Ches.: Reg. Univ. Oxf. vol. ii. pt. ii. p. 396.
1652. Buried—Mary, d. Richard Nicks : St. Jas. Clerkenwell, iv. 292.
1741. Bapt.—Margaret, d. Henry Nickson : St. Geo. Chap. Mayfair, p. 3.
London, 2, o ; Manchester, o, 5 ; New York, o, 3.

Nidson.—Bapt. 'the son of Idonia,' from the nick. Idd, changed into Nidd (v. Iddison) ; cf. Nell, Ned, Noll, Numph, Nabb, Nibb, &c.

William Niddson, C. R., 4 Hen. IV. pt. i.

Niell(son ; v. Neil.

Niger-oculus.—Nick. 'black eye.'

Robertus Niger-Oculus ' pro felonia suspensus.' L.
1752. Thomas Blackeyes and Elizabeth Bridge, by Lic.: Canterbury Cath. p. 92.

Nightingale, Nightingall.—Nick. 'the nightingale,' probably given on account of the sweet voice of the nominee. Jenny Lind was called the Swedish Nightingale. A.S. *nihtegale*.

Ralph Niktègale, co. Norf., 1273. A.
Robert Nitingal, co. Norf., ibid.
Ricardus Nyetgale, 1379: P. T. Howdenshire, p. 24.
Thomas Nightegale, co. Glouc., 20 Edw. I. R.
1572. James Nightingale, co. Yorks : Reg. Univ. Oxf. vol. ii pt. ii. p. 55.
1575. Married — Ralphe Nightingale and Eliz. Kiddar: St. Jas. Clerkenwell, iii. 6.
1787. — William Nuttall and Eliz. Nightinggall : St. Geo. Han. Sq. p. 404.
London, 14, 1 ; MDB. (co. Surrey), 4, 1 ; Boston (U.S.), 8, o.

Nihill.—Bapt. 'the son of Nigel,' or Niel, or Neil, q.v. Possibly the *h* is a memory of the *g* in Nigel.

1565. Buried—John Nihell : St. Peter, Cornhill, i 118.
1796. Married — Matthew Nihill and Mary Foard : St. Geo. Han. Sq. ii. 152.
Crockford, 2 ; Philadelphia, 2.

Nind.—Local, ' atten end ' ; v. Ind and Nend.

Ninepence. — Nick. ' Ninepence ' ; cf. Twelvepence, Fourpence, and Fivepence. Possibly the sobriquet of some banker or money-lender. Of Thomas à Becket we read : ' He was sent to the hall of

Richer of L'Aigle, his father's friend, to learn courtly behaviour, and to the office of the wealthy Osbert Eightpenny to be taught business ' : Hist. England, by F. York Powell (Rivington, 1885), p. 92. We still hear lawyers called ' old six-and-eightpenny.'

John Ninepennys, ordained priest, 1334: Hist. of Newcastle and Gateshead, i. 88.
Sir Adam Ninepennys, chaplain of the chantry in All Saints' Church, Newcastle, 1335 : ibid. p. 95.
John Ninepence, co. York. W. 9.

I need scarcely say the surname is extinct, but it is clear that it lasted for several generations.

Nisbet, Nisbett ; v. Nesbit.

Niven(s.—Bapt. ; v. Nevin.

Nix, Nixon.—Bapt. 'the son of Nicholas,' nick. Nick, with patronymic *s* Nicks, whence Nix. Nixon, of course, is Nickson ; cf. Dixon, Jaxon, Baxter.

Henry Nix, co. Oxf., 1273. A.
William Nix, co. Oxf., ibid.
Margareta Nikeson, 1379 : P. T. Yorks. p. 19.
William Nicson, 1379 : ibid. p. 117.
1527. Thomas Nyxson and Johanna Scochyn : Marriage Lic. (London), i. 6.
1586. Married—Benedict Nix, *bacheler*, and Eliz. Cathron, *a mayden* : St. Peter, Cornhill, i. 235.
1635. Buried—Susan, d. Thomas Nixon : St. Jas. Clerkenwell, iv. 217.
London, 8, 28 ; Oxford, 5, 1 ; Philadelphia, o, 82.

Noad ; v. Nodes.

Noakes. Noke, Nokes, Nock. Noack, Nocke.—Local, ' atten oak,' from residence beside the oak-tree. M.E. *oke*. As with Nalder and Nash, the final *n* in the prefix *atten* (=at the) becomes the initial of the name proper (v. Oak). Nokes and Noakes merely represent a cluster of oak-trees.

Philip attenoke, C. R., 3 Edw. I.
William atte Noke, London. X.
Richard Attenok. B.
Richard atte Noke. P.
Robertus Nok, 1379 : P. T. Yorks. p. 74.
1594. Bapt.—Anne, d. Robert Nocke : St. Jas. Clerkenwell, p. 29.

In the Reg. Univ. Oxf. (Index) this name is spelt indifferently Knokes, Nokes, and Nooke.

1637. Married—Nicholas Firman and Ann Nokes : St. Jas. Clerkenwell, iii. 69.
1649. — Richard Hope and Susan Noke : ibid. p. 83.
1664. — Richard Wood and Mary Noakes : ibid. p. 115.
1749. — George Nock and Eliz. Long : St. Geo. Chap. Mayfair, p. 146.
London, 15, 2, 4, 5, o, o ; Philadelphia, o, o, 1, 7, 1, 1.

Nobbs, Nopps, Nobbe. — Bapt. ' the son of Robert,' from nick. Hob, familiarly Nob. Names beginning with vowels or the aspirate *h* were commonly nicked with prefix N ; cf. Nab (Abel), Nib (Isabel), Numph (Humphry), Noll (Oliver) ; v. Curiosities of Puritan Nomenclature, pp. 89,90. As regards the change from Nobbs to Nopps, cf. Ropps for Robbs, Hopps for Hobbs, Hopkins for Hobkins, &c. To ' hob and nob,' to pledge a health by touching glasses. To 'hobnob,' to associate closely. Perhaps the explanation lies in the fact that both were recognized nicks. of the same name, Robert.

Geoffrey Nobbe, co. Norf., 1273. A.
Philip Noppe, co. Hunts, ibid.
Richard Noppe, co. Hunts, ibid.
1590. Buried—John Nobbes : St. Jas. Clerkenwell, iv. 42.
1617. John Nobes, co. Berks : Reg. Univ. Oxf. vol. ii. pt. ii. p. 363.
New York, o, o, 1.

Noble. — Nick. 'the noble,' excellent, illustrious. This complimentary sobriquet was not allowed to die out by the fortunate possessors, and they have bred a large progeny.

Amice le Noble, co. Hunts, 1273. A.
Hugh le Noble, co. Bedf., ibid.
Thomas le Noble, co. Oxf., ibid.
Robertus Nobill', 1379 : P. T. Yorks. p. 102.
1607. Michael Noble, co. Staff. : Reg. Univ. Oxf. vol. ii. pt. ii. p. 295.
1670. Bapt. — Catherine, d. Mark Noble : Kensington Parish Reg. p. 52.
London, 31 ; Philadelphia, 76.

Noblet, Noblett, Noblit.—Bapt. ' the son of Robert,' from nick. Hob, changed to Nob (v. Nobbs), and dim. Nob-elot. In the same way Hob took the diminutive *-elot* and became Hobelot. Nob would similarly become Nobelot ; cf. Niblett and Hewlett.

Constancia Hobelot, co. Camb., 1273. A.
Agnes Nobelot, co. Oxf., ibid.
Roger Nobelot, co. Hunts, ibid.
William Noblet, co. Salop, ibid.
Alicia Nobelot, co. Soms., 1 Edw. III:
Kirby's Quest, p. 216.
1578. Buried—Peter Noblott, a Dutch-
man : St. Michael, Cornhill, p. 195.
1750. Married—Nicholas Tayler and
Alice Noblet : St. Jas. Clerkenwell,
p. 282.
John Noblet, 1 Geo. I : List of Papists,
Baines' Lanc. ii. 608.
London, o, 1, o ; Crockford, 1, 1, o ; New
York, o, 1, o ; Philadelphia (Noblit), 12.

Nobody.—?——. This curious
surname occurs in the 17th century;
cf. Peabody, Truebody, &c.

1618. Bapt.—John and Joseph, sons of
Valentine Nobodye : St. Jas. Clerkenwell,
p. 82.

There is no evidence of these
being foundlings, although the date
of the baptism is February 4, which
is somewhat near St. Valentine's
day.

Nock(e.—Local, 'at the oak';
v. Noakes.

Nodder.—Nick. 'the sleepy.'
There seems to be no escape from
the conclusion that this well-known
Yorkshire patronymic was a nick
name for one of sleepy or apathetic
habits : one who nodded. I have
tried to find an occupative origin,
but have hitherto failed.

Hugh le Nodder, of Pontefract, 1295. M.
Thomas Nodder', 1379 : P. T. Yorks.
p. 262.
1668. Edward Nodder, of Wood Plumpton : Lancashire Wills at Richmond,
i. 204.
1669. Dorothy Nodder, of Wood
Plumpton : ibid.
Sheffield, 7 ; West Rid. Court Dir., 4 ;
London, 1.

Nodes, Nodson, Noad. —
Bapt. 'the son of Ode' or Oddy
(v. Oddy), nick. Node or Noddy
(cf. Nibbs, Nobbs, Nabbs, &c.),
genitive Nodes (cf. Jones, Williams,
&c.).

Willelmus Node, 1379 : P. T. Yorks.
p. 102.
Agnes Node, 1379 : ibid.
Elias Ode, 1379 : ibid.
Alicia Ode, 1379 : ibid.

All dwelling in Villata de Camp-
sale.

Thomas Noddessone, C. R., 12 Edw.
III. pt. i.

William Nodes, of Stevenedge, co.
Herts, 1533 : Visit. Bedfordshire, 1634,
p. 127.
1626. Married — George Nodes and
Eliz. Cooley : St. Jas. Clerkenwell, iii. 56.
1766. — John Whitnell and Eliz.
Noads : St. Geo. Han. Sq. i. 156.
1784. — John Taylor and Sarah Nodes :
ibid. p. 356.
London, 8, o, o ; Philadelphia, o, o, 3.

Noel.—Bapt. 'the son of Noel,'
i.e. Christmas Day, Dies Natalis,
reduced in French to Noël. Still
given occasionally to children born
on this great feast; cf. Christmas,
Tiffany, Pascal, Pentecost, Midwinter, &c. A famous old carol
still preserves the word, and Halliwell quotes :

'Therfore let us alle syng nowelle,
Nowelle ! Nowelle ! Nowelle ! Nowelle !
And Cryst save mery Ynglond.'

v. Nowell.

Ralph Noel, co. Hunts, 1273. A.
Noel de Aubianis, co. Suff., ibid.
Noel atte Wynde, co. Soms., 1 Edw.
III : Kirby's Quest, p. 177.
Richard Noel, 1313. M.
1667. Peter Trovell and Hannah Noell :
Marriage Alleg. (Canterbury), p. 222.
1706. Noell, son of Noell Whiting :
Reg. St. Dionis Backchurch (London).
1768. Married — Rev. Rowney Noel
and Maria Boothby Skrymsher : St. Geo.
Han. Sq. i. 178.
London, 12 ; Philadelphia, 6.

Noelson, Knowlson.—Bapt.
'the son of Noel' (q.v.). Alexander
Nouelson, co. Northumberland,
Pardons Roll, 6 Ric. II. The
surname evidently had a precarious existence. It might seem
that Nolson was 'the son of Noll'
(i. e. Oliver), but I do not find
traces of that nick. further back
than the 17th century.

1617. John Nalson, co. York : Reg.
Univ. Oxf. vol. ii. pt. ii. p. 363.
1660. Married — George Nolson and
Dorothy Rye : St. Jas. Clerkenwell,
iii. 103.
1752. — Abraham Gordon and Ann
Nolson : St. Geo. Chap. Mayfair, p. 221.
London, o, 1.

Noke, Nokes ; v. Noakes.

Noon, Noone.—? Occup. 'the
nun ' (?) ; v. Nunn.

1575. Andrew Noone, co. Northants :
Reg. Univ. Oxf. vol. ii. pt. ii. p. 67.
1635. Buried—George Noone, *householder* : St. Jas. Clerkenwell, iv. 216.
1664. — Charles, s. Daniell Noone :
ibid. p. 358.

Died at Stoneygate, Leicester, Lucy,
widow of the late C. Noon : Daily Telegraph, July 17th, 1893.
London, 2, 1 ; Philadelphia, 13, o.

Nopps.—Bapt. ; v. Nobbs.

**Norbury, Norbery, Nor-
berry.**—Local, 'of Norbury,' a
township in the parish of Stockport,
co. Ches. This surname has ramified somewhat strongly, but is still
best represented in the surrounding
district, as at Manchester, for instance.

Thomas de Norburie, c. 1190 : East
Cheshire, i. 456.
Robert de Northbury, c. 1260 : ibid.
ii. 102 n.
Lyulph de Norbury, c. 1260 : ibid.
John Narbery or Northbury, 1515 :
Reg. Univ. Oxf. p. 94.
1523. Henry Humfrey and Eliz. Nor-
borowe : Marriage Lic. (London), i. 3.
1573. Buried — Roberte Norburye :
Reg. Prestbury, co. Ches., p. 43.
1616. Thomas Norbury, co. Oxon :
Reg. Univ. Oxf. vol. ii. pt. ii. p. 350.
1617. Buried—Peares Norburie : Reg.
Prestbury, co. Ches., p. 216.
1671. Married — John Norberye and
Eliz. Ferres : St. Jas. Clerkenwell, iii. 175.
London, 3, o, o ; Manchester, 15, o, o ;
Philadelphia, 6, 1, 1.

Norcross. — Local, ' at the
North Cross,' from residence
thereby. Although not common
in England, this surname has
ramified strongly in America.
There can be little doubt that
the spot lies somewhere upon
the borders of Lanc., Westm., and
Yorks.

1636. Agnes Norcrosse, of Alston,
widow : Lancashire Wills at Richmond,
i. 204.
1662. George Norcross, of Hothersale :
ibid.
1670. Eliz. Norcross, of Rawclift : ibid.
1724. Married—Jonathan Norcross and
Eliz. Odell : St. Jas. Clerkenwell, iii. 250.
1729. — James Norcross (of Trowbridge, co. Wilts) and Martha Poulton :
St. Geo. Chap. Mayfair, p. 296.
Manchester, 1 ; Liverpool, 1 ; MDB.
(co. Ches.), 1 ; Boston (U.S.), 36 ; Philadelphia, 9.

Norcutt.—Local ; v. Northcot.

Norden, Nordon.—Local, ' of
Norden,' i.e. at the north dean
(v. Dean), from residence therein.
I do not know the locality.

1580. John Norden and Margaret
Lewes : Marriage Lic. (Westminster),
p. 7.

1591. Bapt.—Martha, d. John Norden: St. Peter, Cornhill, i. 37.
1647. John Norden and Eliz. Skinner: Marriage Lic. (Faculty Office), p. 34.
1687. George Westhrop and Amy Norden: Marriage Alleg. (Canterbury), p. 36.
London, 3, 4; Philadelphia, 5, 0.

Norfolk.—Local, ' of Norfolk.'; v. Suffolk; cf. Lancashire, Cornish, Kent, &c. County names were very popular.

Roger de Norfolk, London, 1273. A.
Willelmus de Northfolk, *souter*, 1379: P. T. Yorks. p. 97.
1543. William Northfolke or Norfolke: Reg. Univ. Oxf. vol. ii. pt. i. p. 285.
1666. Thomas Drake and Margaret Norfolk: Marriage Alleg. (Canterbury), p. 120.
1795. Married—Richard Norfolk and Ann Platt: St. Geo. Han. Sq. ii. 131.
London, 3; MDB. (West Rid. Yorks), 4; Boston (U.S.), 2.

Norgate.—Local, 'at the north gate' or road. The persons below (P. T. Yorks) lived in Pontefract, and among other burghers is one Diota de Bougate (p. 100).

Ralph de Northgate, co. Norf., 1273. A.
Lodewysus de Northegate, 1379: P. T. Yorks. p. 98.
Johanna de Northgate, 1379: ibid.
1615. Married — Henry Forrest and Jane Northgate: St. Jas. Clerkenwell, iii. 42.
1631. — John Norgate and Rebecka Bonnivall: ibid. p. 62.
London, 4; Oxford, 1.

Norgrave, Norgrove. — Local, ' of Norgrave,' i.e. at the North Grave (a wood); v. Grave or Grove.

1632. Buried — Eliz., d. Thomas Norgrove: St. Jas. Clerkenwell, iv. 205.
1633. Bapt.—Thomas, s. Thomas Norgrave: St. Mary Aldermary (London), p. 83.
1731. — Sarah, d. William Norgrove: St. Jas. Clerkenwell, ii. 195.
MDB. (co. Hereford), 0, 1; Oxford, 0, 0; Philadelphia, 3, 0.

Norie.—Local, 'at the north-ey'; v. Northey, and cf. Norton for Northton, or Norham for Northam. The first two following instances occur together :

John atte Northeye, co. Soms., 1 Edw. III: Kirby's Quest, p. 258.
William Norye, co. Soms., 1 Edw. III: ibid.
1806. Married — John Gilbert and Martha Norrie: St. Geo. Han. Sq. ii. 340.
London, 1.

Norman, Normand. — (1) Local, ' the Norman,' i.e. north man. O.F. Normand, Dan. Normand. The English surname may imply either a Norman from Normandy or from Norway.

William Northman, co. Sussex, 1273. A.
Robert Northman, co. Oxf., ibid.
Alex. le Normaunt, co. Linc., ibid.
Mathew le Norman, co. Oxf., ibid.
Lucas Normannus, co. Devon, ibid.

(2) Bapt. 'the son of Norman.' The root is the same. From a national the term became a personal name (cf. German). As such it became a component of many local names, such as Normanby, Normanton, Normanvill, Normancote, Normansell, &c., perpetuating the name of the original settler.

Alicia fil. Normanni, co. Camb., 1273. A.
Robert fil. Normanni, co. Notts, ibid.
Philip Norman, co. Camb., ibid.
Norman de Arcy, co. Linc., ibid.
Norman de Redeman, 34 Hen. II: Hist. West. and Cumb. i. 202.
Robertus Normand, 21 Ric. II: Furness Coucher Book, i. 40.
1583. Bapt. — Geoffraie, s. Anthonie Normand: St. Mary Aldermary (London), p. 61.
1585. — Anne, d. Anthonie Norman: ibid.
London, 65, 1; New York, 24, 2.

Normanby.—Local, ' of Normanby,' parishes in cos. Lincoln (2) and York. The meaning is the *by* or habitation of Norman (q.v.).

Jacobus de Normanby, co. Linc., 1273. A.
Ralph de Normanby, co. Linc., ibid.
Alan de Normaneby, co. Linc., Hen. III–Edw. I. K.

Normancote.—Local, ' of Normancote,' i.e. the cote or cottage of Norman; cf. Normanton, &c.; v. Norman.

Thomas de Normonekot, co. Salop, 1273. A.

Normansell.—Local, ' of Normansell.' There has long been a family of Normansell settled in East Cheshire. The name went out to Virginia, and is in the list of dead at ' James Cittie' :

1623. Edward Normansell: Hotten's Lists of Emigrants, p. 192.

1501. Robert Normansell, of Bollington: East Cheshire, ii. 333.
1562. Married — James Clercke and Agnes Normansell: Reg. Prestbury, co. Ches., p. 7.
1567. — Hugh Normansell and Sycely Dale : ibid. p. 22.
1763. — Thomas Normansell and Ann Povey: St. Geo. Han. Sq. p. 117.
London, 1.

Normanton, Norminton, Normington.—Local, ' of Normanton,' parishes in cos. Lincoln, York, Nottingham, Rutland, Derby, and Leicester. The meaning, like that of Normanby, is obvious, viz. the town of Norman, q.v.

Henry de Normaneton, co. York, 1273. A.
Richard de Normanton, co. Notts, ibid.
Ralph de Normanton, co. Linc., Hen. III–Edw. I. K.
Hugh de Normanton, co. Notts, 20 Edw. I. R.
Magota de Normanton, 1379: P. T. Yorks. p. 97.
Laurencius de Normanton, 1379: ibid. p. 281.
1748. Married — William Norminton and Anne Bull: St. Geo. Han. Sq. i. 40.
London, 0, 1, 1; West Rid. Court Dir., 2, 0, 3; Philadelphia, 0, 0, 2; New York, 0, 1, 0.

Normanville. — Local, ' of Normanville,' a name exactly corresponding to English Normanby and Normanton. Lower says, 'The Itinéraire de la Normandie shows two places so called, one near Yvetot, and the other in the arrondissement of Evreux' (Patr. Brit. p. 239).

Galiena de Northmanville, co. Kent, 1273. A.
Thomas de Normanville, co. Linc., ibid.
Ralph de Northmanvyle, co. Kent, ibid.
Richard de Normanvill, co. Notts, Hen. III–Edw. I. K.
Ralph Normauille, *armiger*, 1379: P. T. Yorks p. 62.
1607. Buried — William Normavell, lodger att the spred egle: St. Peter, Cornhill, i. 162.

Normin(g)ton; v. Normanton.

Norrington.—Local, ' of Northampton' (?). There can be little doubt that this is the true etymology. The early forms of the surname were Norhampton, Norhamton, and Norhanton, and this would soon become Norrington. There is no Northampton in our directories, and yet the surname was common in the 13th century. Therefore we must look for it in some corrupted form. Norrington meets every difficulty.

John de Northampton, London, 1273. A.
Michael de Northampton, co. Linc., ibid.
William de Norhamton, co. Linc., ibid.
(Prior) de Norhanton, co. Linc., ibid.
Geoffrey de Norhantone, co. Salop, ibid.

From Norhanton to Norrington is but an easy single step.

1601-2. Nathanael Norringtonne: Reg. Univ. Oxf. vol. ii. pt. ii. p. 300.
1686. ' John Broadhurst and Jane Norrington: Marriage Alleg. (Canterbury), p. 240.
1699. Bapt. — Thomas Northampton, a foundling in Wood's Close : St. Jas. Clerkenwell, p. 381.
London, 4 ; MDB. (co. Devon), 1.

Norris, Norrish, Norriss.— (1) Local, 'the Noreis,' the northern, the man from the North: sometimes meaning a Norwegian, but generally the 'north countree.' (2) Offic. 'the nurse.' M.E. *norice.* v. Nurse.

Thomas le Noreis, 1273. A.
Robert le Norys. B.
Walter le Noreis, 1313. M.
1579. Edward Norries, co. Lanc.: Reg. Univ. Oxf. vol. ii. pt. ii. p. 87.
1766 Married—John Norriss and Mary McClary : St. Geo. Han. Sq. i. 158.
London, 65, 2, 2; Philadelphia, 98, 0, 0.

Norse.—Local, 'the Noreis,' the Norseman (v. Norris); cf. Morse for Morris.

1562. Buried — William Norse, *embroderer*: St. Mary Aldermary, p. 134.
New York, 1.

Norsworthy.—Local; v. Nosworthy.

North.—Local, 'of the North,' a settler from the northern direction; cf. South, East, and West ; v. Northern.

John de North, London, 1273. A.
Robert North, co. Oxf., ibid.
Willelmus del North, 1379: P. T. Yorks. p. 195.
Johannes del North, 1379: ibid. p. 116.
Margareta del North, 1379: ibid. p. 170.
1558. James Northe, of Mellinge : Lancashire Wills at Richmond, i. 204.
1706. Married—Elias Philpin and Joan North : St. Antholin (London), p. 119.
London, 40 ; New York, 17.

Northam.—Local, 'of Northam,' a parish in co. Devon, near Bideford.

1806. Married — John Northam and Susan Greenwood: St. Geo. Han. Sq. ii. 348.
MDB. (co. Devon), 4 ; London, 1 ; New York, 3.

Northcot, Northcote, Northcott, Norcutt, Norcott.— (1) Local, ' of Northcote,' a hamlet and estate in the parish of East Downe, co. Devon ; (2) 'of Northcott,' a liberty in the parish of Stone, co. Staff. Originally 'at the north cot' or dwelling; cf. Westcott. Other small spots would bear this name. With the corrupted Norcutt, cf. Norbury or Norfolk.

Amyas de Northcote, co. Linc., 1273. A.
Amicia de Northcotes, co. Linc., ibid.
William de Northcote, co. Soms., 1 Edw. III : Kirby's Quest, p. 192.
1656. Buried — Dorothy Northcott, *spinster* : St. Thomas the Apostle (London), p. 131.
1674. John Norcott (co. Bucks) and Grace Rockoll: Marriage Alleg. (Canterbury), p. 234.
1681. William Northcote, of Exeter, and Alice Northcote, of the same : ibid. p. 67.
1752. Married — Thomas Norcut and Sarah Appleby : St. Geo. Chap. Mayfair, p. 209.
London, 1, 5, 1, 1, 0 ; Philadelphia, 0, 0, 0, 0, 2.

Northeast.—Local, 'from the north-east' (?); v. North. If this is not the real origin of the name, then its modern representatives are imitative.

Ralph Northest, co. Norf., 1273. A.
1593. Bapt. — Walter Northest: Reg. Stourton, Wilts, p. 3.
1658. — Jeramiah Northest : Reg. Broad Chalke, co. Wilts, p. 68.
London, 2 ; MDB. (co. Wilts), 1.

Northern, Northen.—Nick. 'the northern,' one who has come from the north country; cf. Southern and Western ; v. North.

Thomas le Northeryn, co. Linc.,1273. A.
Geoffrey le Northern, co. Norf., ibid.
Thomas le Northern. M.
Richard le Northerne, co. Soms., 1 Edw. III : Kirby's Quest, p. 171.
William Northern, C. R., 33 Hen. VI.
1666. Thomas Browne and Ann Northerne : Marriage Alleg. (Canterbury), i. 191.
1686. James Hall and Winifred Northern : ibid. ii. 230.
London, 1, 2.

Northey. — (1) Local, ' of Northey,' i. e. of the north islet. ' An extinct chapelry and " deserted village" near Pevensey, co. Sussex. It was anciently a member of the Cinque Ports ' (Lower). Other spots in rivers would be similarly called ; v. Norie. (2) Local, 'at the north hey,' i.e. the north edge or enclosure.

William de Northye, co. Sussex,1273. A.
William de Northie, co. Kent, ibid.
John atte Northeye, co. Soms., 1 Edw. III : Kirby's Quest, p. 258.
Roger de la Northawe de Ledes, co. York : Close Roll, 17 Hen. VI.
1529. William Northy and Johanna South : Marriage Lic. (London), i. 7.
1764. Married—Henry Rowe and Jane Northy : St. Geo. Han. Sq. i. 132.

There can be little doubt that North-hey (v. Hey) is the chief parent.

London, 2 ; Boston (U.S.), 1.

Northley.—Local,' of the north ley ' or 'leigh,' i. e. the north meadow.

1602. Robert Northleighe, or Northley, co. Devon : Reg. Univ. Oxf. vol. ii. pt. ii. p. 257.
1618. Buried—Robart Nortly, servaunt to Mr. Vowell, in ye East yeard : St. Peter, Cornhill, i. 174.
1662. Married—John Nortley, *comber of wooll*, and Ann Wheeler : St. Jas. Clerkenwell, iii. 110.
1676. Francis Alanson and Dorothy Northleigh : Marriage Alleg. (Canterbury), p. 252.
MDB. (co. Cornwall), 1.

Northover.—Local, ' of Northover,' a parish in the dioc. Bath and Wells, co. Somerset, close by Ilchester.

(Prior) de Northover, 1273. A. ii. 861.
(Homines) de Nordovere, or Northowere, 20 Edw. I : R. p. 774.
1607. James Northover, co. Soms.: Reg. Univ. Oxf. vol. ii. pt. ii. p. 294.
1664. Bapt.—George, s. William Northover : St. Jas. Clerkenwell, i. 221.
1669. — Andrew, s. Charles Northover : ibid. p. 240.
1787. Married—Robert Smith and Eliz. Northover : St. Geo. Han. Sq. i. 396.
London, 1 ; MDB. (co. Soms.), 2 ; Philadelphia, 1.

Northrup, Northorp, Northrop, Northup.—Local, 'of Northope,' a parish in co. Linc. (No doubt originally North-thorp.) The American Northup is found in

England as Northop at an early period; v. Thorp.

Stephen de Northorp, co. Linc., 1273. A.
John de Northorp. H.
Willelmus Northop', 1379: P. T. Yorks. p. 197.
1682. Henry Tyler and Ellen Northupp: Marriage Alleg. (Canterbury), ii. 106.
1744. Married—Thomas Wheeler and Mrs. Northorp: St. Geo. Chap. Mayfair, p. 45.
1773. — John Northorp and Betty Kitchen: St. Geo. Han. Sq. i. 229.
London, 2, 0, 0, 0; West Rid. Court Dir., 0, 1, 1, 0; Boston (U.S.), 0, 0, 1, 5; Philadelphia, 0, 0, 3, 1.

Northway.—Local, 'of Northway,' a township in the parish of Ashchurch, near Tewkesbury, co. Glouc.

London. 1; MDB. (co. Devon), 2; Boston (U.S.), 1.

Northwood; v. Norwood.

Norton.—Local, ' of Norton,' i.e. the north town as distinct from the west town (v. Weston) or the south town (v. Sutton). The places so called are too many to mention. They may be found in almost every county in England. The Hundred Rolls (1273) teem with them.

R. de Northton, co. Norf., 1273. A.
Ralph de Norton, co. York, ibid.
Baldwin de Norton, co. Northants, ibid.
Johannes de Norton, 1379: P. T. Yorks. p. 120.
Magota de Norton, 1379: ibid. p. 110.
Howisia de Norton, 1379: ibid. p. 111.

The last three entries concern Norton in the parish of Campsall, near Doncaster. Another hamlet in the same parish is Sutton.

1578. Adam Norton, co. Staff.: Reg. Univ. Oxf. vol. ii. pt. ii p. 83.
London, 58; West Rid. Court Dir., 6; New York, 112.

Norway.—Local, ' from Norway'; cf. France, Espin, Portingale, &c.; v. Norris.

Ricardus de Norway, 1379: P. T. Yorks. p. 253.
Richard de Noreweye, co. Soms., 1 Edw. III: Kirby's Quest, p. 206.
1718. Buried— Richard Norway, a lodger: St. Mary Aldermary (London), p. 215.
London, 1.

Norwood, Northwood. — Local, ' of Norwood,' parishes in cos. Middlesex and Surrey. Smaller places so called in various counties.

Also the fuller form Northwood, parishes in cos. Salop and Hampshire. In all these cases the meaning is ' the north wood '; cf. Eastwood.

Mauger de Northwode, co. Bedf., 1273. A.
William de Northwode, co. Suff., ibid.
John de Northwode, co. Southampton, Hen. III–Edw. I. K.
Tillot de Northwode, 1379: P.T.Yorks. p. 284.
Johannes Norwode, 1379: ibid. p. 171.
1592. Edmund Northwoode, co. Bucks: Reg. Univ. Oxf. vol. ii. pt. ii. p. 194.
1671. Buried — Thomas Norwood: Kensington Parish Reg. p. 142.
1789. Married—William Norwood and Eliz. Higgins: St. Geo. Han. Sq. ii. 24.
1791. — James Northwood and Penelope: ibid. p. 64.
London, 6, 1; Philadelphia, 7, 0.

Nosworthy, Norsworthy, Noseworthy.—Local, ' of Nosworthy.' Evidently some spot in co. Devon or Wilts. The suffix -worth (v. Worth) is commonly found as -worthy; cf. Langworthy, Kenworthy.

Walter Noswuth, co. Wilts, 1273. A.
1730. Married — Joseph Nosworthy, carpenter, and Eliz. Pomfett: St. Geo. Chap. Mayfair, p. 309.
1800. — William Norsworthy and Mary Bray: St. Geo. Han. Sq. ii. 213.
London, 2, 2, 0; MDB. (co. Devon), 12, 1, 0; New York, 1, 1, 0; Boston (U.S.), 0, 0, 1.

Notary.—Occup. ' the notary,' a scrivener. O.F. notaire. ' Notary, notarius ': Prompt. Parv. This surname does not seem to have survived.

Robert Notare, co. Oxf., 1273. A.
Johannes Notare, 1379: P. T. Yorks. p. 170.
Johannes Guneys, notarius, 1379: ibid. p. 16.

Nothard; v. Neatherd.

Notman, Nutman, Nuttman.—(1) Occup. ' the nutman,' a dealer in nuts. M.E. note and nut, a nut. (2) Occup. ' the servant of Note' (Cnut or Canute); v. Nott (2). This is the more probable origin, belonging as it does to a special class of surnames, of which Matthewman and Addyman (q.v.) are the most familiar examples. Thus Matthewman means Matthew's man - servant,

and Noteman means Note's man-servant. Nevertheless (1) and (2) are open for selection.

John Noteman, co. Camb., 1273. A.
Richard Noteman, co. Bucks, ibid.
William Nuteman, co. Linc., ibid.
London, 2, 1, 3; New York, 3, 0, 1.

Noton; v. Notton.

Notson. — Bapt. ' the son of Ote,' from the nick. Note; cf. Nobbs, Nabbs, Nodes, &c. v. Oat).

Johanne Noteson, co. Soms., 9 Edw. II: Kirby's Quest, p. 136.
London, 3.

Nott (1).—Nick. ' nott-headed.' with the hair cropped close; cf. nott, to shear ;

'I have a lamb, . . .
Of the right kind it is notted.'
Drayton.
' Thou nott-pated fool.'
1 Hen. IV, Act ii. sc. iv.

Not-wheat is smooth unbearded wheat.

Alicia le Notte, co. Camb., 1273. A.
Hugh le Notte, co. Bucks, ibid.
Robert le Notte, co. Northampt., Hen. III–Edw. I. K.
Henry le Notte, co. Leic., ibid.
Willelmus Notte, 1379: P. T. Yorks. p. 84.
1580. James Nott, co. Glouc.: Reg. Univ. Oxf. vol. ii. pt. ii. p. 92.
1751. Married—Peter Nott and Eliz. Mandeville: St.Geo.Chap.Mayfair, p 201.
London, 11; New York, 7.

Nott (2), **Notson, Notts, Nutt, Nutson, Nutts, Nute.**—Bapt. ' the son of Cnut' (Canute), found in the 13th century as Note. The diminutive Nutkins and the patronymic Notson clearly establish the fontal origin of this little batch of surnames. There are two Cnuts in Domesday, one in co. York, the other in co. Derby; cf. Knutsford, a village in co. Ches.

Note Attehel (at the hill), co. Camb., 1273. A.
Alice Note, co. Oxf., ibid.
John Note, co. Suff., ibid.
John Noteson, co. Soms., 1 Edw. III: Kirby's Quest, p. 136.
Johannes Nottson, 1379: P. T. Yorks. p. 266.
Magota Nutte, 1379: ibid. p. 271.
1581. George Nutt, co. Kent: Reg. Univ. Oxf. vol. ii. pt. ii. p. 100.
London, 11, 3, 0, 6, 0, 0, 0; West Rid. Court Dir. (Notts), 1, 0; Philadelphia, 0. 5, 0, 21, 0, 0, 0; Brixham (Nute),1; Oxford (Nutt), 11.

Nottage, Nottidge.—? Nick. 'the nut-hatch.' Halliwell quotes: 'Nothagge, a byrde, *jaye*,' Palsgrave ; ' *Fidecula*, a nuthage,' Vocab. Rawl. MS. ; 'The nuthake with her notes newe,' The Squire of Low Degree, 55. Cf. Jay, Nightingale, Sparrow, Pidgeon, Woodcock, &c. ' Nothak, byrde, *picus*' : Prompt. Parv. The meaning is nut-hack, i.e. a nut-cracker. Should this derivation be deemed unsatisfactory (although the corruption into Nottage is a natural one), a local origin must be sought for.

1788. Married — John Nottage and Mary Whitehouse: St. Geo. Han. Sq. ii. 4.
1793. — Josias Nottidge and Emily Pepys: ibid. p. 103.
London, 3, 2 ; Boston (U.S.), 6, 0.

Nottingham.—Local, ' of Nottingham.'

Hugh de Notingham, co. Bucks, 1273. A.
Ralph de Notingham, co. Oxf., ibid.
Robert de Notingham, co. Notts, ibid.
1552. Married—Fraunces Nottingham and Mary Halliwell : St. Peter, Cornhill, i. 222.
1718. Bapt.—John, s. John Nottingham : St. John Baptist on Wallbrook.
London, 2 , Philadelphia, 1,

Notton, Noton.—Local, ' of Notton,' a village near Barnsley, W. Rid. Yorks.

Robertus de Notton, 1379 : P. T. Yorks. p. 137.
Sheffield, 0, 1 ; London, 0, 1 ; Manchester, 0, 1.

Nourse ; v. Nurse.

Nowell, Nowill.—Bapt. ' the son of Noel,' q.v. The modern Nowill is a natural variant of Nowell.

'General pardon to Nowell Harper, late of Boyleston, co. Derby, gent,' 1486, July 16: Materials for a History of Henry VII, p. 503.
1580. Bapt.— James, son of Nowell Mathew : Reg. St. Columb Major, p. 11.
1578. John Nowell, co. Sussex, *gent.*: Reg. Univ. Oxf. vol. ii. pt. ii. p. 83.
1622. Bapt. — Adam, s. Marmaduke Nowell: St. Jas. Clerkenwell, i. 94.
Petition of Nowell Warner, 1627-8 : Cal. State Papers (Domestic).
London, 8, 2 ; New York, 1, 1.

Nugent.—Local, ' of Nogent.' Several places are so called in France. The Nugents are among those who ' came in with the Conqueror.' 'Nogent, or Nugent,

says Salverte, is the name of many towns or villages built on the banks of a river in a pleasant position, such as Nogent-sur-Seine, Nogent - sur - Marne, &c.' (Essai, ii. 284) ; v. Lower (Patr. Brit. p. 240).

Bertram de Nugun, co. Norf., 1273. A.
Nicholas de Nugun, co. Norf., ibid.
Nicholas de Nugun, co. Sussex, Hen. III-Edw. I. K.
1571. William Nugent, co. Meath : Reg. Univ. Oxf. vol. ii. pt. ii. p. 49.
1748. Married—Benjamin Sargant and Mary Nugent : St. Geo. Chap. Mayfair, p. 122.
London, 6 ; Philadelphia, 76,

Nunhouse. — Local, 'at the nun-house,' from residence there, probably as a servant ; cf. Monkhouse.

Willelmus Nunhouse, 1379 : P. T. Yorks. p. 112.

Nunn.—Occup. ' the nun' ; v. Nunns. Possibly sometimes a nickname for a man of demure and devout demeanour.

Alice le Nonne, co. Northampton, 1273. A.
Robert Nunne, co. Camb., ibid.
Margaret Nunne, co. Norf. FF.
1614. Married—Thomas Jenkins and Abigaell Nunn : St. Jas. Clerkenwell, p. 40.
1746. — Edmund Nunn and Mary Park : St. Geo. Chap. Mayfair, p. 70.
London, 33 ; Boston (U.S.), 5.

Nunneley, Nunnerley. — Local, seemingly ' at the nunne ley,' i.e. the nun's meadow ; v. Nunne. Nunnerley is probably a variant. I cannot find the spot.

1739. Bapt.—William, s. William Nunnerly : St. Jas. Clerkenwell, ii. 243.
1790. Married—John Lilley and Margaret Nunnerley : St. Geo. Han. Sq. ii. 38.
Manchester, 1, 0 ; Liverpool, 0, 1 ; MDB. (co. Linc.), 1, 0 ; (co. Ches.), 0, 2

Nunnery. — Local, ' at the nunnery' (?), from residence therein ; cf. Nunhouse.

1718. Bapt.—Anne, d. Anne Nunnery : St. Jas. Clerkenwell, ii. 106.
MDB. (co. Linc.), 2 ; New York, 3.

Nunns, Nunson.—Nick. ' the son of the nun,' i.e. the child of a lapsed vowess. M.E. *nonne* and *nunne*. Lower recalls an A.S. Nun, a personal name, but this was in 710, and there is no evidence

that it survived to the 13th century. On the other hand we have proof of the origin given above.

Alice la Nonne, et Robert filius ejus co. Northampton, 1273. A.
John Nunnes, co. Notts, 20 Edw. I. R.
Hugo Nunneson, 1379 : P. T. Yorks. p. 221.
1548. Robert Nonson : Reg. Univ. Oxf. vol. ii. pt. ii. p. xv.
1742. Buried — Hannah Nonson : St. Mary Aldermary (London), p. 225.
London, 1, 0 ; New York, 2, 0.

Nurse Nourse.—Occup. ' the nurse.' M.E. *norice*. v. Norris (2).

Robertus la (sic) Norice, co. Bedf., 1273. A.
Matilda Nutrix, co. Camb., ibid.
Maria le Nøreyse, co. Camb., ibid.
Alicia le Noryce. B.
Thomas Nurse. B.
Agnes Noryce, 1379 : P. T. Yorks. p. 256.
Johanna Nurys, 1379 : ibid. p. 110.
Robertus Horbery, *tayllour*, et Johanna uxor ejus : ibid. p. 96.
Nutrix ejus : ibid.
Magota le Nuris : ibid. p. 274.
1685-6. Robert Pitt and Martha Nourse : Marriage Lic. (London), p. 178.
1792. Married — John Nurse, *cordwainer*, and Mary King : St. Geo. Chap. Mayfair, p. 303.
London, 5, 0 ; New York, 3, 6.

Nussey, Nursey.—Local, ' of Nussey.' This surname is almost peculiar to Yorkshire even in the 19th century. The first two instances below are found in the township of Appletreewick, in the parish of Burnsall, near Skipton.

Robertus de Nusse, 1379 : P. T. Yorks, p. 264.
Johannes de Nussay, 1379 : ibid.
1688-9. Samuell Nussey, *vintner*, and Eliz. Herrington : Marriage Alleg. (Canterbury), p. 94.
1787. Married—William Nursey and Eliz. Bensted : St. Geo. Han. Sq. i. 402.
London, 0, 1 ; West Rid. Court Dir., 13, 0.

Nutbeam. — Local, ' at the notebem,' i.e. the hazel-tree. A.S. *hnut-beám.* From residence beside some prominent nut-tree. A.S. *beám,* a tree.

John atte Notebem, co. Oxf., 1273. A.
John apud Notebem, co. Oxf., ibid.
Jordan Notebem, co. Oxf., ibid.
'A charge against Henry Nutbeam of illegally interfering with the police in the Southampton strike was dismissed ' : Standard, Sept. 12, 1890.

I have also seen the surname in the Devon Directory, but cannot find my reference.

Southampton, 1.

Nutbrown. — Nick. 'nutbrown.' Probably from complexion of the hair; cf. 'nutbrown maid.' v. Brownnutt.

'George Nutbrowne was sworne the same daye, *pistler*, and Nathaniel Pownell, *gospeller*': Cheque Bk. Chapel Royal, p. 12, Camd. Soc.
Hugo Nuttebroune, 1379: P. T. Yorks. p. 190.
William Notbrone, 1441, co. York. W. 11.
William Nutbrowne, c. Eliz. Z.
1550. Anthony de Sancto Oelia and Eliz. Nutbrowne: Marriage Lic. (London), p. 13.
1576. Married — Thomas Nutbrowne and Jone Wright: St. Peter, Cornhill, i.230. York, 2.

Nuthall; v. Nuttall.

Nute; v. Nott (2).

Nutkins.—Bapt. 'the son of Cnut' (Canute), found in the 13th century as Note (v. Nott and Nutt). With the diminutive appended this became Notekin, now as a surname Nutkins. It is interesting to notice that the surname is found in co. Essex in 1273, and again turns up in 1666 in the same shire. The genitive suffix in Nutkins seems of recent origin.

Adam Notekyn, co. Essex, 1273. A.
1662. John Nutkin, of Stepney, and Sarah Kempton: Marriage Alleg. (Canterbury), i. 59.
1666. John Nutkin (co. Essex), *miller*, and Esther Spowse: ibid. p. 183.
1735. Married — John Nutkins and Ann Cock: St. Geo. Chap. Mayfair, p. 251.
London, 3.

Nutley.—Local, 'of Nutley,' parishes in diocs. Chichester and Winchester, also smaller places in co. Bucks, &c.

Henry de Nuttele, co. Camb., 1273. A.
John de Nottele, co. Oxf., ibid.
Agnes de Nottelye, co. Devon, Hen. III–Edw. I. K.
John de Nuttele, co. Southampton, 20 Edw. I. R.
1672. William Nutley and Catherine Fettiplace: Marriage Lic. (Westminster), p. 45.
1691-2. William Nuttley and Amy Hooper: Marriage Alleg. (Canterbury), p. 213.
London, —1; Boston (U.S.), 3; New York, 3.

Nutman.—Occup.; v. Notman.

Nutson, Nutt; v. Nott (2).

Nuttall, Nuttle, Nuthall, Nuttell.—Local, 'of Nuttall' or 'Nuthall,' a parish in co. Notts. Possibly smaller spots may have assisted in spreading the name. One certainly in Cheshire has originated the numerous Nuttalls of Lancashire and Cheshire. The variants are of a natural character, and call for no notice.

Agatha de Nuthal, co. Notts, Hen. III–Edw. I. K.
1579. John Nuthall, co. Chester: East Cheshire, ii. 178.
Thomas de Nuthill: Patent Roll, 1 Hen. IV. pt. v.
1616. Richard Nuttall, of Nuttall, *gent*: Wills at Chester, i. 144.
1744. Married—John Nuttall and Jane Ellis: St. Geo. Chap. Mayfair, p. 41.
1748. — John Nuthall and Mary Sykes: ibid. p. 102.
1775. Married—James Smithson and Mary Nuthall: St. Geo. Han. Sq. p. 253.
London, 3, 0, 0, 0; Liverpool, 10, 1, 1, 0; Philadelphia, 24, 0, 0, 1.

Nutter.—? Occup. 'the nutter' (?), a dealer in nuts. The surmise is quite a natural one, but I have not discovered any proof, which always makes a definition of this sort unsatisfactory. v. Neatherd for another explanation.

1611. William Nutter, co. York: Reg. Univ. Oxf. vol. ii. pt. ii. p. 324.
1617. George Nutter, co. Lanc.: ibid. p. 359.

1617. John Nutter, of Pendle: Wills at Chester, i. 144.
1620.—James Nutter, of Burnley: ibid.

The name was strongly represented in Pendle and the neighbourhood of Whalley Abbey, Lanc. The above are only two out of many of these will-names. One large branch of this name seems evidently to have sprung up in this district.

1747. Married—James Nutter and Eliz. Freeman: St. Geo. Chap. Mayfair, p. 100.
London, 7; Manchester, 3; Burnley, 4; Philadelphia, 8.

Nutting.—?——. I can suggest nothing satisfactory.

Willelmus Nutyng, 1379: P. T. Yorks. p. 209.
1660. Buried—Mary, wife of Edward Nutting: St. Jas. Clerkenwell, iv. 337.
1659. Married — Robert Nutting and Mary Sibley: ibid. iii. 101.
London, 4; New York, 8.

Nye.—Local, 'atten ey' (?), at the *ey*, from residence on some small islet or eyot. The suffix -*ey* is common; cf. Northey, Forty, Ely, &c. In this case the final *n* in *atten* has become the prefix of the name proper; v. Nash, Noakes, Nelmes, for similar instances. The following entry seems conclusive:

Thoma atte Nye, co. Soms., 1 Edw. III: Kirby's Quest, p. 205.

We find Rodney spelt the same way:

Lucia de Rodenye, co. Soms., 9 Edw. II: Kirby's Quest, p. 112.
1613. Married—James Nygh and Isabel Hilliard: Kensington Parish Reg. p. 66.
1670. Buried—Judith, d. Philip Nye: ibid. p. 140.
1672. — Philyp Nye, *minister*: St. Michael, Cornhill, p. 258.
1677. — Rupert Nye, *dr. of physick*: ibid. p. 262.
London, 12; New York, 5.

O

Oak, Oake, Oakes, Oaks.—
Local, 'at the oak' or 'at the oaks,' from residence thereby.

Adam at ye Ock, co. Salop, 1273. A.
Philip del Okes, co. Salop, ibid.
Henricus atte Ok', 1379: P. T. Yorks. p. 132.
Johannes del Okes, 1379: ibid. p. 188.
Richard atte Oke. B.
Walter atte Ok, C. R., 2 Edw. II.
Roger of the Okes, 1319. M.
Walter atte Oke, co. Soms., 1 Edw. III: Kirby's Quest, p. 150.
1604. Bapt. — William, s. George Oakes: St. Dionis Backchurch, p. 91.
1754. Married — Arthur Ayres and Mary Oake: St. Geo. Chap. Mayfair, p. 273.
London, 0, 2, 12, 1; Philadelphia, 1, 0, 0, 2; New York (Oake), 1.

Oakden.—Local; v. Ogden.

Oakenfull.—Local, 'of the oaken field.' *Oaken* is the adjective; cf. Linden, Birchen or Birken, as in Birkenhead, and v. Akenhead and Akenside; *-full* is a corruption of *-field* when a suffix; cf. Hatfull for Hatfield. Probably a Norfolk surname.

Adam de Oakefeld, co. Norf., 1273. A.
1733. Married—John Oakinful and Ann Saddleton: Canterbury Cathedral, p. 79.
1798. — John Penny and Eliz. Oakenfull: St. Geo. Han. Sq. ii. 178.
London, 1; New York, 1.

Oakes; v. Oak.

Oakey, Okey, Okie.—Local, 'at the oak-ey,' i.e. the island covered with oak-trees; cf. Northey, &c.

Jack' Oky, co. Norf., 1273. A.
Nicholas Oky, co. Berks, ibid.
John de Oky, co. Soms., 1 Edw. I: Kirby's Quest, p. 203.
John Oky, co. Norf., 20 Edw. I. R.
1707. Married—Paul Grout and Anne Oakey: St. Antholin (London), p. 120.
London, 4, 3, 0; New York, 6, 0, 5.

Oakford, Ockford.—Local, 'of Oakford,' a parish in co. Devon, three miles and a half from Bampton.

1746. Married — James Eager and Sarah Okeford: Canterbury Cath. p. 88.
London, 1, 0; Philadelphia, 12, 0.

Oakley, Oakly.—Local, 'of Oakley.' No less than eleven

parishes bear this name in diocs. Oxford, Norwich, Ely, Winchester, &c.

Walter de Oclee, co. Wilts, 1273. A.
Godwin de Ocle, co. Suff., ibid.
Robert de Ocle, co. Oxf., ibid.
Thomas Acle, or Ocle, sheriff of Norwich, 1415: FF. iii. 136.
Simon de Akelegh. E.
Robert de Oklegh, co. Soms., 1327: Tax Roll.
Agnes de Acle, co. Norf., 1362: FF. iv. 336.
William de Acle, prior of Hoxne, co. Norf., c. 1380: ibid. iii. 609.
1541. Married — William Smith and Elisabeth Okely: St. Antholin (London), p. 3.
1687. — Benjamin Oakeley and Grace Hardistey: St. Michael, Cornhill, p. 45.
London, 23, 1; Philadelphia, 4, 0; New York, 51, 0.

Oastler, Osler, Ostler.—Occup. 'the hosteler,' a keeper of a hostel, an inn-keeper. O.F. *hostelier.*

'Be thou not wroth, or we departen here,
Though that my tale be of an hostelere.'
Chaucer, The Coke's Prologue.

Wyclif has 'ostiler' in Luke x. 35. This is very like the early forms.

Godfrey le Hoselur, 1273. A.
Reginald le Osiler. T.
Richard le Hosteler, c. 1318. M.
William le Ostiller. J.
Walter le Oyselur. T.
Richard Hosteler, bailiff of Yarmouth, 1501: FF. xi. 326.
1694. Bapt.—Martha, d. Henry Ostler: St. Jas. Clerkenwell, i. 357.
1668. Married — Laurence Osler and Eliz. Buttler: ibid. p. 146.
London, 1, 4, 1; MDB. (co. Norfolk), 0, 7, 0.

Oat, Oates, Oats, Oatson.—
Bapt. 'the son of Odo' (v. Oddy), otherwise Otho, Oto, Otto, Othes, and Otes. Camden says, 'Othes, an old name in England drawn from Otho': Remains, p. 73.

Hotys de Parme, co. Linc., 1273. A.
Andreas Otes, co. Norf., ibid.
Oto de Bayley, circa 1300: Baines' Lanc. ii. 100.
Johannes Hotes, 1379: P. T. Yorks. p. 187.
Robertus Otesson', 1379: ibid.
Otes de Howorth, 1379: ibid. p. 188.
Johannes Oteson, 1379: ibid.

John Otes, *glover*, 1439: Rental of Halifax, Cotton MSS. Vespasian, F. 15, Brit. Mus.
Oto Sagar, secular chaplain, 1522: Reg. Univ. Oxf. p. 124.
Otes Redish, of Redish, co. Lanc., circa 1550: Earwaker's East Cheshire, i. 260.
Otes Holland, 1541, Pendleton, Manchester:·Lanc. and Ches. Rec. Soc., vol. xii. p. 141.
Otes Redyche, 1541, Radcliffe: ibid. p. 144.
Adam, s. Otus Jeffery, 1547: Reg. St Columb Major, p. 4.
Thomas, s. Otes Dyar, 1547: ibid.
1575. Thomas Otes, Lincoln College: Reg. Univ. Oxf. vol. ii. pt. iv. p. 67.
1743. Married — William Oates and Margaret Preston: St. Geo. Han. Sq. i. 29.

Oats and Oates are the present directory forms. The form Oats seems to be confined to America.

1679. Bapt.—Joseph, s. George Oats, St. Michael's, Barbadoes: Hotten's Lists of Emigrants, p. 424.
London, 0, 5, 0, 0; West Rid. Court Dir., 0, 26, 0, 0; Philadelphia, 19, 3, 2, 0.

Oatmonger.—Occup. 'a dealer in oats'; cf. Cornmonger.

Denis de Otemonger, London. X.
Thomas le Otemangere, co. Soms., 9 Edw. II: Kirby's Quest, p. 128.

Oats; v. Oat.

Obey, Obee. —? Local, 'of Oby' (?). Mr. Lower says, 'An extinct parish now joined with Ashby, co. Norfolk.' But probably the name is a personal one, for besides Obe without local prefix we find the pet form Obekin, i.e. little Obe, and such place-names as Obley and Obthorpe. With the variant Obee, cf. Applebee.

Robert Obe, co. Oxf., 1273. A.
Nicholas Obekyn, co. Camb., ibid.
1788. Married — William Obey and Mary Birkett: St. Geo. Han. Sq. ii. 9.
1795. — John Morris and Ann Obee: ibid. p. 134.
London, 1, 1.

Oborn, Oborne.—Local, 'of Oborne,' a parish in co. Dorset, one mile from Sherborne.

1605. Maurice Oborne, co. Soms.: Reg. Univ. Oxf. vol. ii. pt. ii. p. 287.

1613. William Oburn, vicar of Boulton: Lancashire Wills at Richmond, i. 205.
1803. Married — Edward Jenkins and Sarah Watts Oborne: St. Geo. Han. Sq. ii. 286.
London, 1, 7; Philadelphia, 1, 0; New York, 1, 0.

Occleston, Ockleston, Ocklestone.—Local, 'of Occlestone,' a township in the parish of Middlewich, co. Chester. The meaning seems clear, i.e. the town or farmstead of Ogle. For a similar instance v. Oglethorpe, where that surname is found as Okolstorp as early as 1273.

1603. William Occleston, of Mere: Wills at Chester, i. 144.
1691. Henry Ocklestone, Prestbury, co. Ches.: East Cheshire, ii. 522.
MDB. (co. Chester). 0, 5, 1; Manchester, 1, 2, 0; Liverpool, 0, 2, 0; Philadelphia, 2, 0, 0.

Ockenden.—Local, 'of Ockenden,' i.e. the *dean* where the oak-trees grew (v. Dean). 'An estate at Cuckfield, co. Sussex, to which county the name seems mainly to be limited' (Lower).

1806. Married — John Longley and Mary Oakenden: St. Geo. Han. Sq. ii. 345.
London, 2; Oxford,2; MDB.(co.Sus.),2.

Ockford.—Local; v. Oakford.

Ockleshaw.—Local, 'of Ockleshaw,' probably a spot near Occleston, q.v. The derivation seems to be the shaw or wood belonging to Ogle.

1651. Ralph Ocleshaw: East Cheshire, ii. 68.
Liverpool, 1.

Odam, Odem, Odium.—Local, 'of Odiham,' a parish in co. Hants, twenty-six miles from Winchester.

Roger de Odiam, co. Norf., 1273.
Richard de Odiham, co. Norf., ibid.

The following corruption looks somewhat odious:

1580. Married — Thomas Early and Agnes Odium: St. Jas. Clerkenwell, p. 8.
London, 2, 1, 0; Philadelphia, 0, 0, 1.

Odcock.—Bapt. 'the son of Odo,' from the popular Ode or Oddy, with suffix -*cock* (v. Cock and Oddy). One more proof of the great favour extended to this personal name. The suffix -*cock*

was only appended to the more familiar names; cf. Wilcock, Simcock, Jeffcock, &c.
Amicus Odecock, co. Norf., 1273. A.

Oddy, Oddie, Ody, Odey.—Bapt. 'the son of Odo' or 'Oddo,' still popular in Germany as Otto (v. Oat), a personal name, probably of Norman importation; v. Odling.

'For a bishop he sent at morn when it was day,
Sir Ode of Wynchestre.'
Robert of Brunne, N. and Q., 1857, p. 113.
John fil. Ode, co. Hunts, 1273. A.
Matilda Odde, co. Hunts, ibid.
Henry fil. Ode, co. York, ibid.
Odo et alii thaine': Domesday Book.
Odo Arbalister: ibid.
Richard fil. Odonis: Pipe Roll, 6 Hen. II. p. 17.
William fil. Ode, 1379: P. T. Yorks. p. 194.

As a personal name found late:

Ottie Sagar, of Colne, 1597: Wills at Chester, i. 59.
Robert Oth, or Odd, 1508: Reg. Univ. Oxf. i. 59.
1751. Married—John Oddy and Grace Holmes: St. Geo. Chap. Mayfair, p. 205.
West Rid. (Yorks) Court Dir., 12, 2, 0; New York, 1, 2, 0, 1.

Odell.—Local, 'of Odell,' a parish in co. Bedford. Lower writes, 'The seat of an ancient barony written Wodhull, and by Norman corruption Wahull. The great Domesday Baron known as Walter Flandrensis, from his being a Fleming, held it, and his posterity was called " de Wahull " ' (Patr. Brit. p. 243). Thus the derivation is wood-hill, the hill covered with trees; v. Hull (2).

Walter de Wahull, co. Oxf., 1273. A.
John de Warhulle, co. Bedf., ibid.
Walter de Wadhulle, co. Bedf., ibid.
1615. Married—Richard Guilyams and Ruth Odill: St. Michael, Cornhill, p. 21.
1791. Married—Pierce Odell and Mary Bunning: St. Geo. Han. Sq. ii. 64.
London, 10; New York, 86.

Odger, Odgers, Oger, Ogier.—Bapt. 'the son of Oger'; v. Auger. The London Directory (1872) seems to have no instances. With the variant Odger, cf. Rodger for Roger. Also cf. Hodge and Hodgson from Roger; similarly Dodge and Dodson from Roger.

Oger fil. Oger, Fines Roll, Richard I. GG.
Oger de Kernik, C. R., 54 Hen. III.
Alan fil Oger, Roger fil. Oger. E.
Peter fil. Oggery, co. Oxf., Hen. III-Edw. I. K.
1637. Bapt.—Jane,d. Abraham Ottgar: St. Antholin (London), p. 71.
1792. Married — James Smith and Catharine Oger: St. Geo. Han. Sq. ii. 75.
Oxford (Odgers), 2; Philadelphia, 0, 8, 0, 1.

Odinel.—Bapt. 'the son of Odinel,' a double dim. of Odo (v. Oddy). This name seems to have been all but wholly confined to co. Northumberland. It became popular through a local hero, Odinel de Umfrayville, lord of Prudhoe Castle.

'Odinel de Umfranvile relevad le suen cri': Chronique de Jordan Fantosme, circa 1180, Surtees Soc., l. 1778.
Odonel de Ford, rector of Meldon, temp. 1200: KKK. ii. 8.
Galfridus Odenel, 1233: KKK. vi. 163.
Odinellus de Albaniaco, temp. Hen. III: BBB. p. 61.
Geoffrey Odinel, co. York, 1273. A.
William fil. Otnil, co. Linc., ibid.
Otnel Joce, co. Oxf., ibid.
Odnell Carnaby, 1561: QQQ. p. xxxii.
Johannes Odinell, cos. Norf. and Suff., Hen. III–Edw. I. K.
Walter Odynel, co. Soms., 1 Edw. III: Kirby's Quest, p. 210.
Odonel Selby, of Tweedmouth, 1555: QQQ. p. 388.

Odlin, Odling.—Bapt. 'the son of Odo,' from dim. Odelin; v. Oddy. The excrescent *g* in Odling is common; cf. Jennings.

Richard fil. Odeline, co. Salop, 1273. A.
Henry Odelin, co. York, ibid.
Odelina uxor Elye de Bleynnaker, C. R., 36 Hen. III.
Johannes Otheline, 1379: P. T. Yorks. p. 235.
'Odelina, wife of Roger Male-doctus': Parker's Early Oxford, p. 273.
1786. Married — Joseph Odling and Hannah Spencer: St. Geo. Han. Sq. i. 388.
London, 2, 1; Oxford, 0, 1; Boston (U.S.), 1, 0.

Ody.—Bapt.; v. Oddy.

Offer, Offor, Aufrere, Orfeur.—Occup. 'le Orfevre.' O.F. Orfevre, the goldsmith. The present modification can be easily traced. Orfeur still exists in co. Norfolk.

Peter le Orfeure, co. Wilts, 1273. A.
John le Orfevre, co. Camb., ibid.
Nicholas Aurifaber, co. Camb., ibid.
William le Orfeure, co. Bucks, 20 Edw. I. R.

John Barri, *orfeuer*, 6 Edw. II : Freemen of York, i. 14.
Richard de Dorem, *orfeuer*, 11 Edw. II : Freemen of York, i. 17.
Roger le Orfevre, 1313. M.
Richard Orfer. F.
William Offer, 1507: Reg.Univ.Oxf.i.51.
1696. Married — Thomas Orfeur and Ann Llewellen : St. Jas. Clerkenwell, p. 217.
1787. William Dawson and Sophia Aufrere, of Hoveton St. Peter, co. Norf. : St. Geo. Han. Sq. 399.
London, 1, 3, 0, 0 ; MDB. (Norfolk), 0, 0, 1, 0 ; Yarmouth, 0, 0, 0, 2.

Offley.—Local, ' of Offley,' (1) a parish near Hitchin, co. Herts ; (2) ' of High Offley,' a parish near Eccleshall, co. Stafford.

1176. William de Offcleghe, East Cheshire, ii. 379.
1621. Thomas Offley, Hart Hall, London : Reg. Univ. Oxf. vol. ii. pt. ii. p. 389.
1638. John Offley, of Hulmehouse, co. Ches.,*gentleman* : Wills at Chester,ii.164.
1808. Married—William Offley, Esq., and Mary Everett : St. Geo. Han. Sq. ii. 380.
London, 4 ; Boston (U.S.), 1.

Offor ; v. Offer.

Offord.—Local, ' of Offord,' a parish in the dioc. of Ely, three miles from Huntingdon. With regard to the instance Offorth infra, v. Forth.

Edelina de Offord, co. Hunts, 1273. A.
John de Offord, co. Hunts, ibid.
Thomas de Offorth, co. Camb., ibid.
1797. Married — James Offord and Eliz. Pack : St. Geo. Han. Sq. ii. 161.
London, 11 ; New York, 1.

Offring.—Local, ' of Offring.' I cannot find any 19th century instances.

Richard de Offringe, co. Wilts, 1273. A.
1735. Married—Alexander Chatto and Mary Offring : St. Jas. Clerkenwell, p. 263.

Ofspring. — Local ; v. Oxpring.

Ogan.—Bapt. ' the son of Ogan ' or ' Wogan,' q.v. ; cf. Orm and Worm, Ulf and Wolf.

William fil. Ogyn, co. Salop, 1273. A.
Michael Wogan, or Ogan, 1513 : Reg. Univ. Oxf. i. 90.
London, 1.

Ogbourn, Ogborn. — Local, ' of Oxbourn,' two parishes in co. Wilts. No doubt compounded of *oc*, oak, and *burn*, a stream, the stream flowing by the oak-trees. For this lazy way of pronouncing

the word cf. Slagg and Slack. Both parishes are situated near Marlborough.

Walter de Okeburne, co.Wilts, 1273. A.
1764. Married — Jeremiah Ogbourn and Mary Timson : St. Geo. Han. Sq. i. 133.
1793. — Thomas Delboux and Ann Ogbourne : ibid. ii. 97.
1808. — William Ogborn and Sarah Green : ibid. p. 385.
London, 1, 0 ; Philadelphia, 0, 7.

Ogden, Oakden.—Local, ' of Oakden,' i.e. the oak-den ; v. Dean. This family name, so familiar to South Lancashire, sprang up in the neighbourhood of Crompton and parish of Rochdale.

' In the reign of Edw. I. lived Sir Baldwin de Tyas . . . who granted to Sir Robert de Holland, in free marriage with Joan, his daughter, all his lands in Butterworth, the Cleggs, Garthside, Akeden, Holynworth, &c., in Rochdale ': Baines' Lanc. i. 505.

This surname has widely extended in America, and on the map I see a town called Ogdenville.

John de Okedon, co. York, 1273. A.
Richard de Okeden, 6 Edw. III.
1794. Married — Richard Davis and Mary Ogden : St. Geo. Han. Sq. ii. 106.
1806. — Robert Oakden and Ann Hughes : ibid. p. 343.
London, 6, 0 ; Manchester, 50, 0 ; Philadelphia, 92, 0.

Ogilby ; v. Ogleby.

Ogle.—Bapt. ' the son of Ogle,' Icel. Ogvalld (Yonge, ii. 243). A northern name found as component in several local names ; v. Oglethorpe. A Northumberland family of Ogle sprang from Oggil in that county (v. Lower).

Robertus Ogill, 1379 : P. T. Yorks. p. 236.
1582. Cuthbert Ogle, co. Northumb. : Reg. Univ. Oxf. vol. ii. pt. ii. p. 123.
1637. Married—John Barnes and Eliz. Ogle : St. Jas. Clerkenwell, iii. 68.
1802. — Charles Ogle and Charlotte Martha Gage : St. Geo. Han. Sq. ii. 256.
London, 8 ; Philadelphia, 13.

Ogleby, Ogilby, Oglesby.—Local, ' of Ogleby.' I cannot find the spot. Of course the meaning is ' the *by* (or dwelling) of Ogle,' the first settler or owner ; v. Oglethorpe and Ogle.

1617. Thomas Oglebye, of Rochdale : Wills at Chester, i. 145.

1640. Bapt. — Robert, s. Thomas Oglebye : St. Jas. Clerkenwell, i. 146.
London, 2, 1, 1 ; Philadelphia, 0, 0, 4.

Oglethorpe.—Local, ' of Oglethorp.' Oglestorp and Oglestun, in Domesday Book, are two places in co. York, near together, and under the same possessor. That Ogle as a component was a personal name is clear ; also that the bearers were Scandinavians ; v. Ogle.

Nicholas de Okolstorp, co. York, 1273. A.
John de Okilsthorp, 1379 : P. T. Yorks. p. 146.
William Ogylthorp, *merchand*, 1379 : P. T. Howdenshire, p. 22.
1581. Robert Ogelthroppe, co. York : Reg. Univ. Oxf. vol. ii. pt. ii. p. 100.
— Edward Ogelthroppe, co. Oxf., *armiger* : ibid. p. 98.
1604. Bapt. — William, s. Thomas Oglethorpe : St. Jas. Clerkenwell, i. 44.
1663. Married — Robert Oglethorpe and Sarah Haddon : Marriage Alleg. (Vicar-General), i. 100.
Lancaster, 1.

Ointer.—Occup. ' the ointer,' possibly a seller of ointments. O.F. *oindre*, to anoint.

Michael le Hointer, London, 1273. A.
Michael le Oynter, London. X.

Okell, Okill.—? Bapt. ' the son of Ogle ' (!). Everything points to this derivation. That the great personal name Ogle was sharpened into Occle is evident, and the variants would follow ; v. Oglethorpe, Occleston, and Ockleshaw. The London Directory has also Ockeford. I find no traces of Oakhill, which would first strike one as the parent.

1572. Thomas Okell, of Preston : Wills at Chester, i. 145.
1598. Hugh Okell, of Withington : ibid.
1609. Robert Okell, of Sutton : ibid.
1792. Married — William Brads and Eliz. Okell : St. Geo. Han. Sq. ii. 72.
Manchester, 2, 0 ; London, 1, 0 ; Philadelphia, 2, 2.

Okeover.—Local, ' of Okeover,' co. Stafford. The family is an extremely old one.

Hugo de Okouere, co. Staff., 1316. M.
Roger de Okouere, co. Staff., 1325. M.
1583. Edward Phillipps and Eliz. Okeover : Marriage Lic. (London), i. 118.
1638. John Okeover, New College : Reg. Univ. Oxf. i. 148.
Houghton C. Okeover, of Okeover, 1874 : MDB. (co. Derby).
MDB. (co. Derby), 1.

Okey, Okie.—Local; v. Oakey.

Old, Ould, Oulds, Olds.—(1) Nick. 'the old'; cf. Young, Senior, Youngman, Younghusband, &c.

Thomas le Old, co. Soms., 1 Edw. III : Kirby's Quest, p. 189.
John le Olde, co. Glouc., 1311. M.
Henry Olde, C. R., 7 Ric. II.
John Olde, incumbent of Cubington, 1548 : Dugdale's Warwickshire, p. 203.

(2) Bapt. 'the son of Old,' whence the patronymic form Oulds.

William fil. Alde, co. Salop, 1273. A.
1750. Married — John Old and Mary Duncan : St. Geo. Chap. Mayfair, p. 159.
— — Joshua Oulds and Mary Garnett : ibid. p. 186.
London, 5, 1, 2, 0 ; New York, 12, 0, 0, 0.

Oldaker.—Local, 'at the old acre,' i. e. the old field, from residence therein or thereby ; cf. Oldfield.

1767. Married — Richard Eades and Sarah Oldaker : St. Geo. Han. Sq. i. 161.
1796. — Robert Oldaker and Ann Allen : ibid. ii. 149.
London, 2.

Oldbury.—Local, 'of Oldbury,' parishes and hamlets in cos. Salop (2), Warwick, and Gloucester (2).

Thomas de Oldebury, co. Salop, 1273. A.
1614–5. Bapt.—Mary, d. Thomas Oldbury : St. Dionis Backchurch, i. 96.

Oldershaw, Olorenshaw, Ollerenshaw, Ollernshaw.—Local,'at the alder-shaw'(v. Shaw), more correctly the 'aller-shaw,' the d being intrusive. Allern is adjectival, as in Linden, Beechen, Birken, Oaken. Thus Ollernshaw is the nearest to a correct form, wanting a change in the initial vowel only. I believe the spot 'Ollerenshaw' is in the parish of Taxal, co. Derby, close by Shallcross Hall, which has made Shawcross and Shallcross so familiar a surname in that district. The Rev. M. Ollerenshaw was minister of Mellor, co. Derby (adjacent), in 1810 (v. East Cheshire, ii. 132) ; cf. Ellershaw, the North-English equivalent. The following entries occur in the neighbouring church of Prestbury :

1632. Buried — George Owlrenshaw and John Owlrênshaw, twines : Reg. Prestbury, p. 285.
1633. — Ellen Oulrenshawe : ibid. p. 290.
1634. Bapt. — Anne Owlrenshawe : ibid. p. 292.
London, 4, 2, 0, 0 ; Manchester, 0, 0, 3, 1 ; Philadelphia, 1, 0, 0, 0.

Oldfield.—Local, (1) 'at the old field' ; (2) 'of Oldfield.' Naturally this is a surname that belongs to various districts. Even the earliest instances are found scattered in separate parts of the country. 'Adam' or 'William at the Old Field' would be common. There is a hamlet in the parish of Heswall, co. Cheshire, which has given birth to many of the name.

Philip de la Holdefelde, co. Salop, 1273. A.
Robert de la Aldefeld, co. Camb., ibid.
Ricardus de Oldefelde, co. Glouc., 1315. M.
Thomas de Aldefeld, 1379 : P. T. Yorks. p. 296.
Adam de Aldefeld, wright, 1379 : ibid.
John del Oldefeld, 1438 : East Cheshire, ii. 86.
1564. Married—John Oldefeilde and Ellen Swydells : Reg. Prestbury, co. Ches., p. 13.
Roger Oldfield, yeoman, Sutton, co. Ches., 1641 : Wills at Chester, ii. 165.
London, 10 ; Manchester, 10 ; Philadelphia, 13.

Oldfriend.—Nick. 'old friend'; cf. Bellamy, Belcher, &c.

William Oldfeend, C. R., 7 Hen. IV.

Oldgroom.—Nick. 'the old groom,' the aged servant ; cf. Goodgroom.

Henry Eldegrome. O.
John Eldgrom. O.

Oldham.—Local, 'of Oldham,' the large and flourishing metropolis of cotton-spinning near Manchester.

Agnes de Oldom, 1379 : P. T. Yorks. p. 104.
Robertus de Oldom, 1379 : ibid.

This spelling was preserved till the 17th century :

1633. Bapt. — Susann, d. Thomas Ouldome : St. Jas. Clerkenwell, i. 123.
1610. John Oldham, co. Notts : Reg. Univ. Oxf. vol. ii. pt. ii. p. 310.
1621. William Oldham, of Manchester : Wills at Chester, ii. 165.
1746. Married — Charles Oldham and Margaret Coho : St. Geo. Chap. Mayfair, p. 66.

London, 11 ; Manchester, 26 ; Philadelphia, 11.

Oldis, Oldys.—Bapt. 'the son of Aldus' ; v. Aldhouse and Aldis, of the latter of which it is but a variant.

1610. William Oldis, co. Dorset : Reg. Univ. Oxf. vol. ii. pt. ii. p. 320.
1751. Married—Anthony Olddiss and Eliz. Banks : St. Geo. Chap. Mayfair, p. 192.
1752. — William Biddle and Hannah Oldis : ibid. p. 218.
New York, 2, 0.

Oldman.—Nick. 'the old man'; cf. Youngman. I cannot but think that the Oldhams of co. Norfolk are a corruption of Oldman ; cf. Swetman for Swetenham, Putman for Puttenham, &c. Of course in this case the change is in the opposite direction.

Walran Oldman, co. Suff., 1273. A.
Robert Oldman, co. Norf., ibid.
Richard Oldeman, of Colchester, 1307. M.
Robert Oldman, rector of Rockland Tofts, co. Norf., 1418 : FF. i. 474.
London, 2 ; MDB. (Norfolk), 1 ; (Oldham), 1 ; New York, 1.

Oldmixon.—Local, 'of Oldmixen.' I cannot find the spot, and I think the surname is extinct. But one can never be sure about the extinction of surnames. I have been taught many a lesson in these matters.

Ralph de Holdmixon, co. Somerset, 1273. A.
Nicholas de Oldemexen, co. Southampton, 20 Edw. I. R.
Ralph de Oldemexene, co. Southampton : ibid.
Thomas Oldemexon, co. Soms., 1 Edw. I : Kirby's Quest, p. 267.
John Oldemexen, co. Soms., 1 Edw. I : ibid.
1628–9. Anthony Oldmixon and Francis Watson : Marriage Lic.(London), 195.

Oldridge.—Bapt. 'the son of Alderich' ; v. Aldridge. A local etymology seems to strike one at once, 'at the old ridge,' but the above interpretation is, so far as I can discover, the best.

? Thomas Ordrich, co. Kent, 1273. A.
1728. Bapt.—Thomas, s. Thomas Oldridge : St. Jas. Clerkenwell, ii. 174.
1735. Married — James Oldridge and Susanna Harrison : St. Dionis Backchurch, p. 66.

1807. Married—James Oldridge and Sarah Swodridge: St. Geo. Han. Sq. ii. 376.
London, 3.

Oldroyd.—Local, 'of the old royd,' from residence therein (v. Royd). Possibly Holroyd (q.v.) is the same. In the Reg. Univ. Oxf., I find Oldesworth, Holdsworth, Holsworth, and Ouldswolth, a parallel instance. Of course the signification may be 'the royd of Old,' the personal name of the original settler or owner (v. Old and Ould). One thing is certain, the surname arises in Yorkshire, probably the West Riding; v. Holroyd.

1741. Married—William Moore and Eliz. Oldroyd: St. Geo. Chap. Mayfair, p. 14.
1771. — John Lee and Rachael Oldroyd: St. Geo. Han. Sq. i. 207.
London, 1; Philadelphia, 10; MDB. (W. Rid. Yorks), 13.

Oliff, Olliff, Olliffe. — Bapt. 'the son of Olive'; v. Olive and Oliver. I have come across many forms, the most popular being Olliph, Olyffe, Olif, and Olyff.

Adam Olif, 1379: P. T. Yorks. p. 196.
1579. Bapt.—Olyffe, d. Olyff Tooker: Reg. St. Columb Major, p. 10.
1581. — Olyff, d. Degorie Stubbs: ibid. p. 11.
1757. Married—Joseph Olliff and Grace Craft: St. Geo. Han. Sq. i. 71.
London, 2, 2, 0; New York, 1, 0, 1.

Oliphant, Olivant, Ollivant, Olyphant.—Nick. 'the elephant,' no doubt a complimentary allusion to the big, burly physique of the bearer. M.E. *olivaunt.*

'Item, pro aula "Olefante," Magister Kyllynworth, 1438': Mun. Acad. Oxon., p. 522.

This hall or smaller college was so called from the sign over the door or gate. Skelton has both 'olyfant' and 'olyphante.' He describes a woman in Eleanor Rummyng as

'Necked lyke an olyfant.'

I believe this is a Scottish surname.

1729. Married — Christopher Olivent and Ann Lane: St. Geo. Chap. Mayfair, p. 294.
1749. — John Olivant and Eliz. Lester: ibid. p. 152.
1753. — George Oliphant and Mary Micheau: ibid. p. 250.

London, 3, 1, 1, 0; Philadelphia, 4, 0, 0, 0; New York (Olyphant), 3.

Olive, Ollive.—Bapt. 'the son of Olive'; v. Oliff for variants.

Thomas fil. Olive, co. Oxf., 1273. A. Margaret fil. Olive, co. Salop, ibid. Johanna fil. Olive, 1379: P. T. Yorks. p. 139.
1797. Married—John Hickman Olive and Alice Ann Hickes: St. Geo. Han. Sq. ii. 164.
1806. — Isaac Olive and Mary Kempester: ibid. p. 355.
London, 3, 2; New York, 4, 1.

Oliver, Ollier, Olver, Olliver.—Bapt. 'the son of Oliver.' Fr. Olivier, Breton, Olier. For 'a Rowland for an Oliver,' v. Yonge, i. 419. The paladin of Charlemagne made it popular, and gave it a knightly sound. After the Protector's days its popularity waned, and it has not yet recovered itself as a baptismal name. The Breton form Olier found friends in this country, and as a surname is fairly common.

Oliver le Quarreur, C. R., 33 Hen. III.
Oliver Crane, co. Hunts, 1273. A.
Peter fil. Oliver, co. Oxf, ibid.
Holiver Hankoc, *husbond,* 1379: P. T. Yorks. p. 163.
Walter Oliver, co. Soms., 1 Edw III: Kirby's Quest, p. 160.
Oliver le Hoge, co. Soms., 1 Edw. III: ibid. p. 200.
1582. Johana, d. Thomas Olver: Reg. St. Columb Major, Cornwall.
1750. Married—David Oliver and Sarah Cocks: St. Geo. Chap. Mayfair, p. 174.
1801. — Richard Ollier and Charlotte Hull: ibid. ii. 239.
London, 80, 2, 3, 2; New York, 66, 0, 0, 3.

Oliverson.—Bapt. 'the son of Oliver,' q.v. I believe this surname to be almost if not actually extinct. I have looked in vain in Manchester and the district for representatives.

1593. John Oliverson, of Heaton Norris: Wills at Chester, ii. 145.
1594. Hugh Oliverson, of Pendlebury: ibid.
1606. Thomas Oliverson, of Heaton Norris: ibid.

Olivet, Ollett, Olyett.—Bapt. 'the son of Olive,' dim. Oliv-et. As Olley was the usual nick., naturally a dim. Olliet or Olyett was formed from it; v. Olley (2). From my first instances it will be seen that this diminutive arose in

good time to become an aspirant for hereditary honours.

William Olivat, Liberate Roll, 17 Edw. II.
Agnes Olyot, 1370: P. T. Yorks. p. 163.
1625. Buried—Eliz. Ollett: St. Jas. Clerkenwell, iv. 179.
1783. Married—John Olyet and Ann Roberts: St. Geo. Han. Sq. i. 352.
London, 1, 1, 3; New York, 1, 0, 0.

Ollerhead.—Local, 'of Ollerhead,' from residence at the head of the alder-trees; cf. Birkett, Akenhead, Birkenhead; v. Oldershaw.

Richard Ollerhead, of Foulk Stapleford, 1629: Wills at Chester, ii. 165.
Eliz. Ollerhead, of Chester, 1644: ibid. Manchester, 1.

Oller(e)nshaw.—Local; v. Oldershaw.

Ollett; v. Olivet.

Olley.—(1) Local, 'de Oilli,' or 'Oyly,' or 'Oilgi.' Robert de Oilgi appears as a tenant-in-chief in many counties; also Wido de Oilgi in co. Oxford (Domesday). Probably one of the Oullis near Falaise (Lower). At any rate, our Olleys may say they 'came over with the Conqueror.' The surname ramified strongly, and is now represented in every grade of society. v. Doyle.

Matilda de Oyly, co. Dorset, 1273. A.
Thomas de Oylly, co. York, ibid.
Henry de Oilli, Pipe Roll, 11 Hen. II. p. 71.
Roger de Oilli: ibid. p. 72.
Henry de Olly, co. Staff., Hen. III–Edw. I. K.
John de Oyly, co. Staff., 20 Edw. I. R.
1637. Buried—Mary, d. William Oylie: St. Jas. Clerkenwell, iv. 231.

(2) Bapt. 'the son of Olive,' pet form Olly; v. Olive. This being, so far as evidence goes, of more modern origin, we must gave the local derivation the first position, although both must have contributed to the number of our present Olleys.

1554. John, s. Thomas Ollye: Reg. St. Columb Major, p. 7.
1591. Olly, d. Nicholas Vallis: ibid. p. 15.
1601. John, s. Ollye Moyses: ibid. p. 20.
1639. Thomas Olye: Reg. Univ. Oxf. i. 359.
1693. Bapt.—Eliz., d. Samuel Oley: St. Jas. Clerkenwell, ii. 352.
1803. Married — Thomas Olley and Eliz. Baylis: St. Geo. Han. Sq. ii. 283.
London, 15; Philadelphia, 2.

Ollier, Olliver; v. Oliver.

Olliff(e; v. Oliff.

Ollivant; v. Oliphant.

Olney.—Local, 'of Olney.' A parish in dioc. Oxford, co. Bucks.

Walter le Olnei, co. Oxf., 1273. A.
John de Olneye, co. Oxf., ibid.
William de Olneye, co. Bucks, 1322. M.
1729. Married—John Olney and Sarah Bubrick : St. Geo. Chap. Mayfair, p. 299.
1801. — Richard Ody and Jane Olney : St. Geo. Han. Sq. ii. 237.
London, 8 ; Boston (U.S.), 6.

Olver; v. Oliver.

Olyett; v. Olivet.

Ombler.—Occup. 'the ambler' (q.v.), an East Riding variant of the great Yorkshire surname.

Nafferton (E. Rid. Yorks), 1 ; Market Weighton (E. Rid. Yorks), 1.

Onehand.—Nick. for a one-handed man. This surname does not seem to have survived.

William Onhand. B.
John Onehand. D.
Richard Onhand, C. R., 23 Hen. VI.

Onion, Onions.—Bapt. 'the son of Enion,' a favourite personal name in old Welsh records. The modern directories abound with variants, &c. (v. Benyon, Pinnion, &c.). Mr. Lower says, 'In the register of East Grinstead, Sussex, in the first half of the 17th century, the name is written indifferently Ennion and Onion.' This quite tallies with my own observations.

1661. William Davies and Ann Onyon : Marriage Lic. (London), ii. 282.
1720. Married—Abraham Taylor and Margaret Onion : St. Dionis Backchurch, p. 60.
Liverpool, 0, 1 ; Manchester, 0, 1 ; New York, 2, 1 ; London, 1, 0 ; MDB. (co. Glouc.), 0, 1.

Onley, Only. — Local, ' of Onely,' a hamlet in the parish of Barby, co. Northants, seven miles from Daventry. Although I do not see any early instances, the first of my references settles the matter.

Edward Onley, or Onelie, co. Northampt., 1583 : Reg. Univ. Oxf. vol. ii. pt. ii. p. 128.

The following two quotations evidently refer to the same individual :

1655. Bapt.—Eliz., d. George Only, *vintner* : St. Peter, Cornhill, i. 97.

1655. Buried—George Onely, *vintner*, in the pit : ibid. p. 209.
1633. Buried—John Onelye, a poor child : St. Jas. Clerkenwell, iv. 210.
1686. Thomas Onely and Catharine Broderick : Reg. Vicar-General (Canterbury), p. 253.
1771. Married — Edward Only and Isabella Davies : St. Geo. Han. Sq. i. 214.
London, 1, 0 ; Philadelphia, 0, 1 ; Boston (U.S.), 3, 1.

Onslow.—Local, ' of Onslow,' a place within the Liberty of Shrewsbury, co. Salop (in Domesday Book spelt Ondeslow). A family of this name early arose here. 'The Onslows were seated at Onslow in Shropshire as far back as Ric. I, and probably earlier. The punning motto of this ancient house, 'Festina lente,' On Slow, is probably one of the happiest conceits of its kind ' (Lower).

1676. Married—Richard Onslowe and Eliz. Tulse : St. Dionis Backchurch, p. 38.
1800. — Emanuel Ducemetiere and Mary Onslow : St. Geo. Han. Sq. ii. 228.
London, 3 ; MDB. (co. Salop), 3 ; Philadelphia, 1.

Onthank.—Local, v. Unthank.

Onwhyn.—Bapt. ' the son of Unwin' (q.v.). A curious variant; cf. Goodwin, Baldwin, &c.

William Onwinne, co. Oxf., 1273. A.
1809. Married—Joseph Onwhyn and Fanny Thomas : St. Geo. Han. Sq. ii. 401. London, 2.

Openshaw.—Local, ' of Openshaw,' a parish and village about four miles from Manchester. The surname is strongly represented in South Lancashire.

Samuel Openshawe. ZZ.
1575. Robert Opinshawe, co. Suff. : Reg. Univ. Oxf. vol. ii. pt. ii. p. 66.
1607. Lambert Openshaw, of Aynsworth : Wills at Chester, i. 145.
1611. Buried—John, s. William Openshawe : St. Jas. Clerkenwell, iv. 118.
London, 1 ; Manchester, 14 ; New York, 1 ; Philadelphia, 5.

Opie, Oppey, Oppy.—?——. Lower says, 'Seems indigenous to Cornwall. Opye occurs there in the 15th century, and Oppie at a later date.' I have only met with it in the same county.

1590. Buried — Harrie Opie : St. Columb Major, p. 193.
1749. Married—John Opie and Sarah Burrows : St. Geo. Chap. Mayfair, p. 147.
Cornwall Dir. (Farmers' Lists), 3, 1, 5 ; Philadelphia, 1, 0, 0.

Orable, Orbell, Orbel. — Bapt. 'the son of Orable,' a variant of Arable, i.e. Arabella. The surname still clings to the neighbourhood of co. Cambridge, where the personal name was popular six centuries ago.

Orable de Hatele, co. Camb., 1273. A.
Orabilia Martin, co. Camb., ibid.
John Orable, co. Camb., ibid.
Arable de Meyhamme, co. Kent, Hen. III-Edw. I. : K. p. 209.
Orable de Meyhamme, co. Kent : ibid. p. 211.
Orabell de Caunsfeld, co. Lanc., 1332 : Lay Subsidy (Rylands), p. 96.
Alexander Orable, C. R., 23 Hen. VI.
1543. Buried—Nicholas Errable, Mr. May's servant : St. Antholin (London), p. 4.

This surname is now found in the guise of Orbell.

1750. Married—Ambrose Orbell and Ann Curtis : St. Geo. Han. Sq. i. 44.
MDB. (Suffolk), 3, 0, 0 ; Cavendish (Suffolk), 0, 1, 0 ; New York, 0, 0, 1.

Oram, Orem. — Local, ' of Oram ' (?). I cannot discover the spot. There are North and South Owram, two townships in the parish of Halifax. This is the probable origin.

1605. Bapt.—Henrie, s. Peter Orom : St. Jas. Clerkenwell, i. 46.
1609. Richard Oram : Reg. Univ. Oxf. vol. ii. pt. i. p. 327.
1778. Married—John Oram and Sarah Lamb : St. Geo. Han. Sq. i. 294.
Manchester, 2, 0 ; MDB. (N. R. Yorks), 1, 0 ; London, 11, 0 ; Philadelphia, 19, 6.

Orbater. — Occup. ' a gold-beater'; Fr. *or*, gold, and *batteur*, a beater, from *battre*, to beat.

Walter le Orbater, London, 1273. A.
John de Erkendene, *orebatur*, 28 Edw. I : Freemen of York, i. 8.

Orbell; v. Orable.

Orby.—Local, 'of Orby,' a parish in dioc. Lincoln.

Geoffrey de Orby, co. Hunts, 1273. A.
John de Orby, co. Hunts, ibid.
Fulco de Orreby, co. Linc., Hen. III-Edw. I. K.
Robert de Orreby, co. Notts, ibid.
John de Horreby, co. Linc., 1316. M.

Orchard, Orchart. — Local, ' at the orchard.' Many local terms took an initial *n*, which in reality was the final letter of the prefix -*atten* (=at the). Thus arose Noakes, Nash, Nalder, Nangle,

&c. Orchard was no exception. I find, for instance:

Robert atte Northcherd, co. Oxf., 20 Edw. I. R.

Which more correctly should be

Robert atten Orthcherd.

But in general the entries run thus:

John de la Orcharde, co. Soms., 1273. A.
Richard atte Orchard, co. Soms., 1 Edw. III: Kirby's Quest, p. 212.
John atte Orchard, C. R., 14 Edw. III. pt. i.
William de la Orchard, co. Dorset, 1316. M.
1683. Married—Robert Orchard and Elisebeth Goodlad: St. Jas. Clerkenwell, iii. 201.
London, 11, 1; Philadelphia, 5, 0.

Orchardson.—Bapt. A curious patronymic; perhaps a corruption of Richardson.

London, 1.

Ord, Orde.— Local, 'of Orde,' a township in North Durham.

Peter de Orde, 1201; Raine's North Durham, p. 147.
'John Orde for lands in Orde, £6 13s. 4d.,' 1631: ibid. p. 156.
John Owrde, 1542: ibid. p. xx.
Thomas Ord, of Ord, 1631: ibid. p. 156.
1585. Richard Orde, co. Northumb.: Reg. Univ. Oxf. vol. ii. pt. ii. p. 145.
Bartram Ord, of Fenwick, 1631: ibid.
'Mr. Lance Ord for the tyth, £10,' 1663: Hodgson's Northumberland, iv. 276.
1750. Married—John Buckland and Dorothy Ord: St. Geo. Chap. Mayfair, p. 162.
London, 3, 0; Crockford, 3, 5; New York, 5, 0.

Ordiner.—Offic. 'the ordinary,' a bishop or overseer. Fr. *ordinaire*. I see no signs of its present existence, but one cannot speak positively on this question. These surnames turn up when least expected.

Walter Ordinar', co. Camb., 1273. A.
Elena Ordiner, co. Camb., ibid.
Thomas Ordiner, co. Suff., ibid.
Isabel Ordiner, co. Camb., ibid.
John de Ordeiner, 1326. M.

Ordway.— ? Bapt. (?). Seemingly a personal name; v. Ottaway for a similar instance. Without doubt it belongs to the southeastern counties.

John Ordwy, co. Oxf., 1273. A.
Ralph Ordwey, co. Bedf., ibid.
Matilda Ordivy, co. Norf., ibid.

1613. William Ordway: Reg. Univ. Oxf. vol. ii. pt. ii. p. 331.
1658. Married—William Billington and Anne Ordway: St. Jas. Clerkenwell, p. 100.
1742.— Humfrey Maynwaring Howorth and Sarah Ordway: St. Geo. Chap. Mayfair, p. 28.
London, 3; Boston (U.S.), 30.

Orem; v. Oram.

Orfeur; v. Offer.

Orford.—Local, 'of Orford,' a parish in co. Suffolk. Also 'of Orford,' in the parish of Warrington, whence the Lancashire Orfords. Orford Hall still stands, and was the residence of John Blackburne, 'the Evelyn of his day.'

(Homines) de Oreford, co. Suff., 1273. A.
Robert Holbrooke, of Orford, in the parish of Warrington, 1594: Wills at Chester (1545-1620), p. 96.
John Orford, of Haydock in Makerfield, 1616: ibid. p. 145.
1778. Married—Mark Gibbs and Ann Orford: St. Geo. Han. Sq. i. 232.
London, 2; Manchester, 2; Philadelphia, 1

Organ.— Bapt. 'the son of Organ,' probably a form of Organ or Wogan, q.v.; cf. Orgar.

Organus Pipard, co. Oxf., Hen. III– Edw. I. K.
Simon Organ, C. R., 37 Edw. III.
John Organ, C. R., 7 Ric. II.
1397. William Organ: Cal. of Wills in Court of Husting (2).
Richard Orgen, 1589: Reg. Univ. Oxf. vol. ii. pt. ii. p. 169.
Edward Organ, *vintner*, 1616: Reg. St. Dionis Backchurch, p. 96.
1707. Bapt.—Edward, son of Maurice Organ: St. Jas. Clerkenwell, p. 37.
London, 1; Oxford, 3; New York, 3; Boston (U.S.), 2.

Organer.—Occup. 'the organist' or 'the organ-maker.' An interesting name which existed till the 18th century, and probably still lives, although I have found no instances.

Peter le Organer, co. Warw., 1318. M.
1761. Married—William Organer and Eliz. Fuller: St. Geo. Han. Sq. i. 111.
1764. — Robert Organer and Sarah Dickenson: ibid. p. 129.
1797. — Thomas Harington and Mary Orgainer: ibid. ii. 166.

Orgar, Orger.—Bapt. 'the son of Orgar.' In Domesday Orgar is found in cos. Somerset, North-

ampton, and Essex; cf. Orgarswick, a parish in co. Kent, i.e. the dwelling of Orgar, the first settler. v. Worger.

Geoffrey fil. Orgari, co. Camb., 1273. A.
Bernard Orgar, co. Camb., ibid.
Matilda Oregar, co. Oxf., ibid.
William Oregar, co. Oxf., ibid.
Roger Orger, co. Middlesex, 20 Edw. I. R.
1748. Married—Thomas Garner and Susannah Orgar: St. Geo. Chap. Mayfair, p. 327.
London, 2, 1.

Oriel, Oriol.—Local, 'at the oriel,' i.e. the gilded chamber; cf. Bower, and v. *oriel* (Skeat).

Nicholas de Oryel, co. Kent, 20 Edw. I. R.
Poncius Oriol, Bristol, 1320. M.
1788. Married—John Biss and Jane Oriell: St. Geo. Han. Sq. ii. 12.
1808. — George Keith and Sarah Oriell: ibid. p. 384.
London, 2, 0; New York, 0, 1.

Orlebar.—Local, 'of Orlingbury,' four miles from Wellingborough, co. Northampton, in which neighbourhood the surname has existed since Edw. III. This surname does not seem to have crossed the Atlantic.

Robert de Orlingbir', co. Northampt., 1273. A.
Ralph de Orlingbir', co. Northampt., ibid.
Hugh de Orlingbere, co. Northampt., 1316. M.
1679. Bapt.—Richard, s. Henry Orliber: St. Jas. Clerkenwell, i. 285.
1687. Cooper Orlebar, of Hinwicke, co. Bedf., and Eliz. Powney: Marriage Alleg. (Canterbury), p. 298.
Crockford, 3; MDB. (co. Northampt.), 1; (co. Bedford), 5.

Ormandy. — Local, 'of Osmotherly,' a township in the parish of Ulverston, co. Lanc. This surname is still almost entirely confined to the Furness district of N. Lanc. The former name of Osmotherly was Osmunderlaw, and Ormandy is found in the neighbourhood since the beginning of the 15th century. Everything points to prove the above origin; v. Osmotherly.

1552. Married—William Holme and Agnes Ormundie: Reg. St. Mary, Ulverston, p. 18.
1553. Bapt.—Ann Ormundie: ibid. p. 129.

1597. Richard Ormandie, of Ulverston : Lancashire Wills at Richmond, i. 205.
1663. Bapt.—Alice, d. John Ormandy : Reg. St. Mary, Ulverston, p. 17.
1673. John Ormondy, of Smiddy Greene, in Ulverston : Lancashire Wills at Richmond, i. 205.
Crockford, 1 ; Ulverston, 7 ; Preston, 1.

Orme, Ormes, Ormson,.
Orm.—Bapt. 'the son of Orme' (Orm, Domesday) ; cf. the local Urmston, Ormston, Ormsby, Ormskirk, Ormerod, and the Great Orme's Head. In this last the meaning Orm, the serpent (whence *worm*), comes out, i.e. 'the serpent's head.' Miss Yonge (ii. 290) says there are twenty-two Ormes in the Landnama-bok.

Alice fil. Orme, co. Camb., 1273. A.
William Orm, co. Notts, ibid.
Orme de Neville, co. Linc., 20 Edw. I. R.
Ormus Archebrgge, co. Westm., ibid.
John fil. Orme, co. York. W. 19.
Gospatric, son of Orme, 32 Hen. II : Nicolson and Burn, Westm. and Cumb., i. 428.

Very popular in the Cumb. and North Lancashire district.

Orm fil. Bernulfi, 21 Ric. II : Fùrness Coucher Book, i. 188.
Robert fil. Orm, 21 Ric. II : ibid.
Orm de Orgrave, 21 Ric. II : ibid.

Hence a common surname in the North.

1593. Buried—Thomas Scott, servant to John Orme : St. Jas. Clerkenwell, iv. 52.
1609. Bapt.—Edward Ormeson : Reg. Prestbury Ch., co. Ches., p. 181.
London, 16, 1, 1, 0 ; Manchester, 8, 0, 0, 0 ; Liverpool (Ormson), 1 ; Philadelphia, 5, 0, 0, 1.

Ormerod, Ormrod, Omrod.
—Local, 'of Ormerod,' i.e. Ormeroyd ; Orme's ridding or clearing ; v. Orme and Royd, and cf. Murgatroyd, i.e. Margaret's clearing. Ormerod is in the parish of Whalley, co. Lanc.

'Ormerod is a house of great antiquity, which remained in the family of that name from 1311 until 1793 ' : Baines' Hist. of Lanc. ii. 41.
1593. John Ormerod, of Gambleside : Wills at Chester, i. 146.
1600. George Ormerod, of Crawshaw Booth : ibid.
1732. Married — Peter Ormred and Isabel Davis : St. Geo. Han. Sq. i. 10.
1784. Laurence Ormerod, of Ormerod, co. Lanc., to Martha Anne Leghe : East Ches. ii. 301.

Manchester, 7, 12, 0 ; London, 2, 0, 0 ; West Rid. Court Dir., 6, 1, 0 ; MDB. (West Rid. Yorks), 8, 1, 1 ; Philadelphia, 1, 5, 0.

Ormesher,Ormshire.—Local, 'of Ormeshaw,' the shaw, coppice, or wood of Orme, the proprietor or first settler. The corruption is a very natural one. v. Orme.

Gilbert Ormeshaw, of Scarisbrick, 1590 : Wills at Chester, i. 146.
Roger Ormeshaw, of Burscough, 1620 : ibid.
1718. Married—Aaron Hawkins and Mary Ormishaw : St. Michael, Cornhill, i. 59.
Manchester, 1, 0 ; Liverpool, 1, 0 ; MDB. (co. Lanc.), 0, 1.

Ormiston, Ormston.—Local, 'of Ormiston,' the town or stead of Orme, the first settler (v. Orme), a parish in co. Haddington, also a locality in co. Roxburgh. The *i* is intrusive, just as *a* is intrusive in Greenaway, q.v.

1733. Married—John Slamaker and Eleanor Ormaston : St. Geo. Han. Sq. i. 12.
London, 1, 7 ; MDB. (co. Northumberland), 0, 1 ; Philadelphia, 2, 3.

Ormond.—Bapt. 'the son of Osmond ' (?), q.v.; a variant (?) ; cf. Ormandy for Osmunderly. But it is quite possible that Ormond in that form was a personal name so distinct from Osmond. The variant from Osmond to Ormand is not natural.

Thomas Ormu(n)de, 1379 : P. T. Yorks. p. 260.
1602. William Ormond, co. Pembroke : Reg. Univ. Oxf. vol. ii. pt. ii. p. 255.
1634. John Ormond, of Huncote, co. Lanc. : Wills at Chester, ii. 166.
London, 2 ; MDB. (co. Lancaster), 6 ; Boston (U.S.), 5.

Ormsby, Ornsby, Ormsbee.
—Local, 'of Ormsby,' parishes in diocs. of York, Lincoln, and Norwich. The meaning is manifestly the *by* or dwelling of Orme (v. Orme). It is now becoming recognized that a large proportion of our place-names are compounded with the personal name of the original settler. Ormsbee is a natural Americanism (cf. Applebee).

William de Ormesby, co. Norf., 1273. A.
Robert de Ormesby, co. Linc., ibid.

William de Ormesby, co. Camb., 20 Edw. I. R.
Thomas de Ormesby, co. Norf., 1324. M.
1685. John Ormsby and Eliz. Kingdon : Marriage Alleg. (Canterbury), p. 198.
1761. Married—Arthur Ormsby, Esq., and Eliz. Greene : St. Geo. Han. Sq. i. 102.
London, 0, 1, 0 ; Crockford, 7, 0, 0 ; Philadelphia, 14, 1, 1.

Ormshire ; v. Ormesher.

Ormson ; v. Orme.

Ormston ; v. Ormiston.

Orne, Ornsby.—Probably corruptions of Orme and Ormsby, q.v.

1602. John Orne, of Holt : Wills at Chester, i. 146.
London, 0, 1.

Orped, Orpedman. — Nick. 'the orped,' i.e. brave, daring. ' Orpud, *audax*, *bellipotens* ' : Prompt. Parv. ; v. Way's notes thereon.

'Doukes, kinges, and barouns,
Orped squiers, and garsouns.'
Arthour and Merlin, p. 81 (Halliwell).
Walter le Orpede, co. Bucks, 1273. A.
Sym Orpedeman, London, ibid.
Thomas Orpedeman, London, ibid.
Stephen le Horpede, co. Kent, ibid.
Peter Orpedeman. H.
John Orpood, co. Oxf., 1589 : Reg. Univ. Oxf. vol. ii. pt. ii. p. 174.

The present form is Orpwood, q.v. This surname is to be found in co. Bucks. It was there in the 13th century as 'le Orpede.'

Orpen, Orpin.—' The family of Orpen or Erpen is of remote antiquity, and is stated to be derived from Erpen, a French noble of royal descent.' Such is the statement in Burke's Landed Gentry, though the pedigree as there given does not go further back than the 16th century (v. Lower's Patr. Brit. p. 250).

1680. John Orpen and wife. List of the Inhabitants of St. Michael's, Barbadoes : Hotten's Lists of Emigrants, p. 438.
1806. Married—Charles Orpin and Sarah Watson : St. Geo. Han. Sq. ii. 339.
1861. Married—William Orpin and Esther Cooper : Reg. Canterbury Cath. p. 107.
Boston (U.S.), 2, 6.

Orpwood.—Nick. 'the orped ' ; v. Orped. ' Orpud (ornwode, s. sic pro orpwode?), *audax, bellipotens* ' : Prompt. Parv. p. 371.

1584. Christopher Orpudde, co. Oxf.: Reg. Univ. Oxf. vol. ii. pt. ii. p. 138.
1617. Paul Orpwood, co. Berks : ibid. p. 365.
1791. Married—William Benwell and Eliz. Orpwood : St. Geo. Han. Sq. p. 67. London, 2 ; Oxford, 1.

Orr.—Local, ' of Orr,' a parish in co. Kirkcudbright.

Egidius de Or, co. Kent, 1273. A.
Matilda Orre, 1379 : P. T. Yorks. p. 16.
Johannes Ore, 1479 : ibid. p. 164.
1744. Buried—Ann Orr : St. Michael, Cornhill, p. 297.
1789. Married—Samuel Dimeto and Eliz. Ore : St. Geo. Han. Sq. ii. 21.
London, 4 ; Philadelphia, 104.

Orred.—Local, ' of Orred.' A Cheshire surname ; probably, as suggested by Lower, a place-name whose suffix was originally -head ; cf. Birkenhead, &c.

1588. Eliz. Orred, of Manchester : Wills at Chester, i. 146.
1636. Gyles Orred, of Lower Hulton, Dean, blacksmith : ibid. ii. 166.
MDB. (co. Ches.), 1.

Orrell, Orrill.—Local, (1) ' of Orrell,' a township in the parish of Wigan, co. Lanc. The suffix, as will be seen below, is -hull, i.e. -hill.

' Richard de Horul in the reign of Richard I. held half a carucate in thanage ' : Baines' Lanc. ii. 186.
' In 32 Edw. I. Robert de Holand had a charter for free warren in Holand, Hale, Orhull, and Martlan ' : ibid.

(2) ' Of Orrell,' a township in the parish of Sephton, co. Lanc.

' In 13 Edw. III. Henry Blundell, of Crosby, gave to William, his son, all his property in Rainil, Orel, Downlitherland, Thornton, and Sephton ' : Baines' Lanc. ii. 398.

The surname passed over the border into co. Cheshire, and is well known there and in Lancashire.

1590. Peter Orrell, co. Lanc. : Reg. Univ. Oxf. vol. ii. pt. ii. p. 176.
1602. William Orrell, of Wigan : Wills at Chester, i. 146.
1610. Alexander Orrell, of Orrell, parish of Wigan : ibid.
1781. Married—Anthony Holmes and Ann Orrell : St. Geo. Han. Sq. i. 327.
Liverpool, 6, 0 ; Manchester, 4, 0 ; Philadelphia, 7, 0 ; Boston (U.S.), 1, 1.

Orton. — Local, ' of Orton,' parishes in diocs. Norwich, Peterborough, Ely, and Carlisle. All

these places seem to have contributed their share of surnames.

Robert de Orton, co. Oxf., Hen. III-Edw. I. K.
Henry de Orton, co. Suff., 1273. A.
Walter de Orton, co. Linc., ibid.
Alan de Orreton, co. Cumb., 20 Edw. I. R.
John de Orreton, co. Cumb., 1321. M.
1592. James Ortonne, co. Ches. : Reg. Univ. Oxf. vol. ii. pt. ii. p. 194.
1774. Married—William Orton and Ann Chandler : St. Geo. Han. Sq. i. 242.
London, 6 ; Philadelphia, 6.

Osbaldston, Osbaldeston, Osbaldiston. — Local, ' of Osbaldeston,' a township in the parish of Blackburn, co. Lanc. The Osbaldestons of Osbaldeston had a charity in Blackburn Parish Church (Baines' Lanc. ii. 66). The meaning is ' the town (i.e. settlement) of Osbald.' The i and e in Osbaldiston and Osbaldeston are intrusive ; cf. Greenaway for Greenway, where the a is equally intrusive.

Edward Osbaldeston, Esq., of Osbaldeston, 1590 : Wills at Chester, i. 146.
Matilda Osbaldeston, of Blackburn, 1592 : ibid.
Henry Osboston, 1595 : Reg. St. Dionis Backchurch (London), p. 13.
John Osbaldeston, Esq., of Osbaldeston, 1605 : ibid.
1786. Married—John Osbaldeston and Susanna Crook : St. Geo. Han. Sq. i. 387.
London, 1, 0, 0 ; Manchester, 0, 2, 1 ; Preston, 0, 2, 0.

Osbert. — Bapt. ' the son of Osbert.' This surname does not seem to have survived. I cannot find any modern instances. Strange that its rival Osborn should be so familiar to our directories to-day.

Robert fil. Osbert, co. Hunts, 1273. A.
Osbert le Ferrur, co. Camb., ibid.
Roger fil. Osbert, co. Suff., ibid.
Richard Osbert, co. Camb., ibid.
William fil. Osbert. C.
Osbert de Bellebeck, co. York, 20 Edw. I. R.
Osbert Houbard, co. Soms., 1 Edw. III : Kirby's Quest, p. 227.

Osborn, Osborne, Osbourn, Osbourne.—Bapt. ' the son of Osbern,' a favourite personal name in the hereditary surname period. It is scarcely ever used now at the font, but flourishes strongly as a surname.

Gerard fil. Oseberne, co. Hunts,1273. A.
Robert Oseberne, co. Oxf., ibid.

Osborne le Haukere. H.
Osbarn Dawson, 1379 : P. T. Yorks. p. 23.
Thomas Smithson and Osberne Walynton, servauntes of Sir Edward Wydevile,' 1489 : Wardrobe Accounts, Edw. IV. p. 164.

In the Register of the University of Oxford the following forms are found : Osborne, Osbern, Osberne, Osborn, Osbourne, and Osburne (v. Index). The following variants are found amongst the marriages of a single register :

1790. George Avius and Ann Osburn : St. Geo. Han. Sq. ii. 85.
— Richard Osborne and Ann Smith : ibid. p. 163.
1792. William Osbon and Mary Thackham : ibid. p. 43.
1797. Frances Phillips and Lucy Orsborn : ibid. p. 46.
1798. William Osburne and Eliz. Yates : ibid. p. 148.
London, 42, 41, 1, 2 ; Philadelphia, 34, 47, 5, 1.

Osborough.—Local, ' of Oxborough.' For this change of x for s, v. Oscroft. For variants of Osborough, v. Oxberry.

Philadelphia, 1.

Oscroft. — Local, ' at the oxcroft,' i.e. the enclosure for oxen. Naturally the surname would settle down into Oscroft. A parallel instance will be found in the case of Oxspring and Ofspring, q.v. Another example of the change is to be seen in the Philadelphia Directory, where Osborough takes the place of Oxborough.

Stephen de Oxcroft, co. Suff., 1273. A.
1746. Married—John Brand and Margaret Oscroft : St. Geo. Chapel, Mayfair, p. 64.

Oscroft was a familiar figure some years ago on the Notts county cricket-ground, and a young Oscroft played for the same county in the season of 1894.

MDB. (co. Notts), 1.

Osekin, Oskins.—Bapt. One of the many pet forms ending in -kin (cf. Wilkin). Oskin would be the familiar appellation of some Osmund, Osbern, Oswin, or Osbert. It is quite possible that Hoskins is its present representative. The aspirate presents no difficulty, and the final _s_ is of course genitive, as in Tompkins or Jones ; v. Hosken.

Osekin (without surname), London, 1273. A.
Robert Osekin, London, ibid.
Philadelphia, 0, 3.

Osgathorpe, Osgathorp. — Local, 'of Osgarthorpe,' i.e. the thorp of Osgod, the first settler ; a parish in co. Leicester, four miles from Ashby ; v. Osgerby and Osgood.

Sheffield, 2, 0 ; Oxford, 0, 1.

Osgerby. — Local, 'of Osgodby': (1) a township in the parish of Lavington, co. Linc. ; (2) also a parish in co. Linc., four miles from Market Rasen ; (3) also a township in the parish of Hemingbrough, near Selby, E. Rid. Yorks. The change of the surname to Osgerby was very natural. The origin is plain, 'the dwelling of Osgod,' from the name of the first settler or proprietor ; v. Osgood.

Eva de Osgoteby, co. York, 1273. A.
Hugh de Osgoteby, co. York, ibid.
Dionise de Osgotby, co. Linc., ibid.
1598. Buried — John, s. John Osgarbye : St. Michael, Cornhill, i. 208.
— Bapt. — John, s. John Osgerby : ibid. p. 101.
1609. Married — Edward Wilson and Jane Osgrobie : ibid. p. 19.
1614. Robert Osgoodby : Reg. Univ. Oxf. vol. ii. pt. ii. p. 372.
1668. William Osgodby, of Exeter House, Strand : Marriage Alleg. (Canterbury), p. 255.
1668-9. William Osgoodby, of Exeter House, Strand : ibid. p. 260.
MDB. (East Rid. Yorks), 1.

Osgood. — Bapt. 'the son of Osgod' (v. Yonge, ii. 181) ; v. Osgerby.

Tofig the Proud married Gytha, the daughter of Osgod Clapa : Freeman, Norm. Conq. i. 523.
Alveva fil. Osgod, Fines Roll, 7 Ric. I–16 John.
John Osegod, co. Oxf., 1273. A.
William Osegod, co. Oxf., ibid.
Gilbert Osegot, co. Camb., ibid.
John Osgode, co. Hertf., 20 Edw. I. R.
Ricardus Osgod, 1379 : P. T. Howdenshire, p. 23.
William Osegod, co. Soms., 1 Edw. III : Kirby's Quest, p. 232.
1605. Tristram Osgood, co. Cornw. : Reg. Univ. Oxf. vol. ii. pt. ii. p. 286.
1614. John Osgood : ibid. p. 334.
1789. Married — William Oakey and Sarah Osgood : St. Geo. Han. Sq. ii. 20.
London, 1 ; New York, 10.

Oskettle, Oskell. — Bapt. 'the son of Oskettle,' 'divine cauldron,' a compound of Kettle (q.v.). A Norman guise of the same name was Anskettle (q.v.) or Askettle. The Abbot of Croyland in 992 was Osketyl.

Oskell Somenour. AA. 3.
Osketil atte Mere, Fines Roll,57 Hen.III.

Oskins ; v. Osekin.

Osler. — Occup. ; v. Oastler.

Osman ; v. Osmond.

Osmar. — Bapt. 'the son of Osmar,' a personal name found in Domesday Book as Osmar and Osmer.

1790. Married — Charles Shoubridge and Ann Osmer : St. Geo. Han. Sq. ii. 35. London, 1.

Osmond, Osmund, Osman, Osment, Osmint, Osmon, Osmand, Osmun. — Bapt. 'the son of Osmond,' the Scandinavian Asmundr ; cf. Wyman for Wymond, and Mayman for Maymond. This personal name gave rise to several local names ; v. Osmotherly, and cf.

John de Osemundeston, co. Norf., 1273. A.
Geoffrey Osmund, co. Devon, ibid.
Nicholas Osemund, co. Suff., ibid.
Richard Osmund, co. Middlesex, 1313. M.
John Osmond, co. Hertf., 1315. M.
1603. Buried — Thomas Osmond : St. Thomas the Apostle (London), p. 104.
1649. Married — William Bannister and Margaret Osman : ibid. p. 18.
Edward, son of Edward Osman, 1658 : Reg. Broad Chalke, co. Wilts, p. 68.
John, son of Edward Osmand, 1660 : ibid.
Grace, d. of Edward Osmund, 1663 : ibid.
1788. Married — Charles Ballard and Sarah Osmon : St. Geo. Han. Sq. ii. 18.
London, 0, 17, 6, 1, 1, 1, 0, 0 ; Oxford, 1, 0, 2, 0, 0, 0, 0, 0 ; Philadelphia, 11, 0, 1, 0, 0, 1, 1, 1 ; Liverpool (Osmond), 1 ; Boston (U.S.) (Osman), 1.

Osmotherly. — Local, 'of Osmotherly,' a parish in N. Rid. Yorks, and a township in the parish of Ulverston, North Lancashire. It is found early in the Furness district as Asmunderlaw. It is curious that while the surname has long disappeared from the North, it should be found at Cliffe, near Rochester (but v. Ormandy). The derivation is simple,

i.e. 'the law of Osmund,' a _law_ meaning a rising ground ; v. Low.

Ywan de Asmunderlaw, 1440 : Coucher Book of Furness, ii. 351.
Walter de Osmunderlaw, c. 1300 : ibid. p. 383.
1598-9. John Osmotherley, B.A., Magd. Coll. : Reg. Univ. Oxf. vol. ii. pt. ii. p. 213.
Mr. E. Osmotherly, Gravesend : National Benevolent Institution Report, 1891.
1635. William Osmotherly embarked in ship the Globe for Virginia : Hotten's Lists of Emigrants, p. 119.
MDB. (co. Kent), 1.

Osney. — Local, 'of Oseney,' near the river on the west side of Oxford, the site of a famous monastery.

Richard de Oseney, co. Oxf., 1273. A.
Walter de Oseney, co. Oxf., ibid.
1682. Thomas Smally and Eliz. Osney : Marriage Alleg. (Canterbury), p. 101.

I cannot find any later instances.

Ostcliffe. — Local, 'of Oxcliffe,' a township in the parish of Lancaster. The surname therefrom has received many modifications. For a similar change from _x_ to _s_, v. Oscroft. For loss of _c_ in Osliff, cf. Antliff. The surname seems to have crossed the Morecambe Sands to Furness at an early period.

1591. Brian Osklef, of Winderin Cartmell : Lancashire Wills at Richmond, i. 205.
1626. John Oscliffe, of Pennington (Ulverston) : ibid.
1633. Henry Osliffe, of Pennington (Ulverston) : ibid.
1638. Bapt. — Margaret, d. Râphe Osliffe : St. Jas. Clerkenwell, iv. 235.
1639. — John, s. Raph Osliff : ibid. p. 237.
1686. Buried — Bryan Oslief, of Trinkalt : Reg. of Ulverston, i. 175.
1702. Thomas Osliffe, of Warton : ibid. ii. 186.
Bradford, 1.

Ostler. — Occup. 'a keeper of an hostelry' ; v. Oastler.

Ostringer, Astringer. — Offic. 'the ostricer,' a falconer. Dame Julyan Berners says, 'Ye shall understonde that they ben called Ostregeres that kepe goshawkes or tercelles' (edit. 1496, Bk. iii). I dare not hazard a guess at its origin, but the earliest form is Ostricer. This became Ostriger. 'John Woodde, one of the Ostregers of ower sovereygn Lord' (30 Henry VIII ; v. Notes and Queries, 1885, p. 306). This same individual is styled in a deed a fortnight earlier, ' Oistrynger' (ibid.). Shakespeare has it *astringer*. Astringer and Ostringer are natural corruptions (cf. Pottinger from Potager, *messenger* from *messager*, &c.). Ostringer occurs in Blount's Gloss, p. 459 (Halliwell).

Robert Ostriciator, co. Notts, 1173. A.
Alan Ostriciare, co. Hunts, ibid.
Robert le Ostricer, co. Norf., ibid.
Alan le Ostrizur. L.
William le Ostricer. T.
Sybil la Ostricer, Close Roll, 27 Edw. I.

Oswald, Oswell, Oswill, Oszwald, Oszwold, Oswalt.— Bapt. 'the son of Oswald,' corruptly Oswell or Oswill. A very early personal name ; cf. Oswald Kirk, a parish in co. York.

'Osewold the Reve': Chaucer, C. T. 3857.
Simon Aswald, co. Oxf., 1273. A.
John Oswald, co. Glouc, 1325. M.
Oswell Fairewather, 1540: Reg. St. Antholin (London), p. 2.
Oswall Mosley, 1620: Reg. St. Mary Aldermary (London), p. 14.
Ozwell Stephens, 1744: Reg. Canterbury Cath., p. 87.

All Manchester people are familiar with the name of Sir Oswald Mosley.

1570. Married—William Osewell and Marye Mills: St. Michael, Cornhill, p. 10.
1632 Bapt.—John, s. John Oswell: St. Jas. Clerkenwell, i. 120.

I need not furnish modern instances of Oswald.

London, 4, 3, 0, 0, 0, 1; Philadelphia, 20, 1, 1, 1, 1, 0.

Oswin.—Bapt. 'the son of Oswin' (v. Yonge, ii. 185).

Oswin Ogle, co. York. W. 9.
Oswin Sharparrow, co. York. W. 3.
1671. Bapt.—Eliz, d. Robert Oswin: St. Jas. Clerkenwell, i. 252.
1691.— James, s. James Oswine: ibid. p. 340.
London, 5.

Otley, Ottley.—Local, 'of Otley,' parishes in co. Suffolk and W. Rid. Yorks ; v. Uttley.

Richard de Otteleye, co. Suffolk, 1273. A.
Henry Otleghe, co. Soms., 1 Edw. III: Kirby's Quest, p. 83.

Henry Hotlay, 1379: P.T.Yorks. p. 161.
1405. John Oteleve: Cal. of Wills in Court of Husting (2).
1789. Married—John Otley and Mary Rivers: St. Geo. Han. Sq. ii. 29.
1808. — William Denley and Mary Ottley: ibid. p. 382.
Sheffield, 2, 0; West Riding (Yorks) Court Dir., 2, 2 ; Philadelphia, 3, 0 ; New York, 0, 2.

Ottaway, Ottway, Otway.— ? Local, ' of Ottway' (?). I cannot identify the spot. The \a will be intrusive, as in Greenaway for Greenway. Probably the way or road that belonged to Ote (v. Oat). I have not found any instances in the leading American Directories.

John Otewy, co. Suff., 1326. M.
Richard Otewy, co. Suff., ibid.

The two instances above, the earliest I can find, seem to suggest a personal rather than a local derivation.

1790. Married — Henry Otway and Sarah Cave: St. Geo. Han. Sq. ii. 37.
1797. — John Mann and Hannah Ottway: ibid. p. 162.
1806 — John Brown and Mary Ottaway: ibid. p. 339.
London, 3, 1, 1.

Otter.—(1) Bapt. 'the son of Ottur' (v. Yonge, ii. 305). (2) Nick. 'the otter.' M.E. *oter*. The former is evidently the chief parent of the surname, as will be seen below. Oter was a great Scandinavian personal name (v. Lower, p. 251).

Edward Oter, co. Camb., 1273. A.
Robert Oter, co. Suff., ibid.
Walter Oter, co. Oxf., ibid.
Otuer de Insula, Hen. III-Edw. I. K. p. 344.
Otverus de Insula, ibid. p. 382.
Johannes Otour, *spicer*, 1379: P. T. Yorks. p. 135.
1766. Married — Robert Otter and Sarah Henslow: St. Geo. Han. Sq. i. 150.
London, 3.

Ottiwell, Ottewell, Ottwell. —Bapt. 'the son of Otewel.' Halliwell under *larder* quotes :

'Thowas Otuwel fol of mood
And faught as he were wood.'
Romance of Otuel, p. 64.

A popular favourite in its time, but now, I fear, quite obsolete as a font-name, but found till the beginning of the last century. An

early legendary name (v. Yonge). As a surname it still survives the ravages of time. Ottiwell, natural son of Hugh Lupus, Earl of Chester, was tutor to the children of Henry I, who perished at sea in 1120 (Lower). Perhaps this may account for the popularity of the baptismal name in Cheshire. Ottiwell Higgynbotham gave evidence in 1522 as to the boundary of Marple (Earwaker's East Cheshire, ii. 52).

1549. Otewell Shallcrosse: Earwaker's East Cheshire, i. 276.
Ottiwell Worsley, temp. Henry VI: ibid. ii. 52 n.
Ottiwell Rowbotham : ibid. p. 276.
1564. Married—William Ottiwell and Margret Street: St. Mary Aldermary (London), p. 4.
1580. Bapt.—William, s. Otuell Rilance: Reg. Wigan, Lanc.
— Married—John Otwell and Joane Smith: St. Antholin (London), p. 28.
1587. Robert Rychardson and Magdalen Ottwell: Marriage Lic. (London), i. 163.
1588. Ottiwell Hodgkinson, of Manchester: Wills at Chester, i. 96.
1607. Buried—Ralph Ottewell, *clothworker*: St. Thomas the Apostle (London), p. 106.
1639. Othowell Mererell: Reg. Royal Coll. Phys.: N. & Q. 1857, p. 305.

I could give many other instances of the font-name as well as surname, but these will suffice.

London, 0, 1, 0; Derby, 0, 6, 0; New York, 4, 0, 0; Philadelphia, 0, 0, 3.

Ottley; v. Otley.

Ould, Oulds; v. Old.

Oulston, Ouston, Owston.— Local, ' of Oulston,' a township in the parish of Coxwold, N. Rid. Yorks. Ouston and Owston were inevitable variants of the surname, and it will be seen that the N. and E. Rid. of Yorks have most of these variants.

1674. Edward, s. Masster Oulton, hee being the Erle of Albery's butler: St. Jas. Clerkenwell, i. 265.
New York, 1, 0, 0; (Yorks, N. R.), 0, 4, 0 ; (Yorks, E. R.), 0, 0, 6.

Oulton.—Local, ' of Oulton.' Parishes, townships, &c., in cos. Norfolk, Suffolk, W. Rid. Yorks, Cheshire, and Cumberland. The family, however, seem to have sprung, so far as North England is concerned, from the township of Oulton, near Tarporley, co. Ches.

Thomas Olton, Mottram, co. Ches., 1455: Earwaker's East Ches. ii. 114.
Richard Olton, of Congleton, 1588: Wills at Chester, i. 145.
Blanch Oulton, of Bradley, *widow*, 1629: ibid. ii. 167.
Liverpool, 3; Manchester, 2; Boston (U.S.), 2.

Ousby.—Local, 'of Ousby,' a parish in co. Cumb., nine miles from Penrith.

1635. Buried—William Ousby or Ousbye, *householder*: St. Jas. Clerkenwell, iv. 635.
Manchester, 1.

Ouseley, Ousley.—Local, 'of Ouseley.' As Lower and others suggest, 'the meadow by the Ouse' is probably the correct derivation. I cannot find the spot. v. Houseley.

1684. Newdigate Owsley and Eliz. Jones: Marriage Alleg. (Cant.), i. 183.
1688. John Sheffield and Ann Ousley: ibid. ii. 58.
Crockford, 1, 0; Philadelphia, 0, 1.

Ouston; v. Oulston.

Outerbridge, Outbridge.—Local, 'at the outer bridge,' from residence thereby. I have not identified the spot.

1571. Married—Nicholas Outbridge and Eliz. Peccowe: St. Thomas the Apostle (London), p. 5.

I find an instance of one who died of the plague raging in London at the period:

1625. Buried — Helen Outerbridge, servant to Mr. Sanbroke, plague: St. Michael, Cornhill, p. 228.
Philadelphia, 6, 0; New York, 1, 0.

Outlaw.—Offic. 'one out of protection of the civil law'; perhaps, more spiritually, one excommunicated.

Richard Utlawe, co. Bedf., 1273. A.
John Outlagh, co. Camb., 1322. M.
Roger Outlawe, C. R., 16 Edw. III. pt. i.
William Outlawe. V. 9.
Richard Outlaw, rector of Necton, co. Norf., 1661: FF. vi. 53.

The Ulverston News of Dec. 4, 1886, announced the marriage of Florence J. Outlaw, of Birmingham.

MDB. (Norfolk), 1; Boston (U.S.), 1.

Outram, Outran, Owtram, Owttrim.—Local, 'of Outram,' probably for Outerham (cf. Outerbridge), i. e. the outer *ham* or dwelling. I cannot find the spot.

1806. Married — Joseph Outram and Ann Locke: St. Geo. Han. Sq. ii. 343.
London, 1, 1, 1, 2; Manchester, 0, 0, 2, 0; New York (Outram), 1.

Outred, Oughtred.— Bapt. 'the son of Ughtred.' Domesday Book, Uctred. One of the earliest priors of Hexham was 'Uthred erl Killer sune' (Priory of Hexham, Surt. Soc.). 'Uthred . . . gathered an army, rescued Durham, and gained a signal victory over the Scots.' This was a famous Earl of Northumberland. Hence we find the surname in that district (v. Freeman's Norman Conquest, i. 326).

Ughtred de Preston, C. R., 12 Edw. I: Hist. West. and Cumb. i. 202.
Ketel fil. Uchtred, 34 Hen. II: ibid.
Uhtred de Witingeham, 7 Hen. II: Pipe Roll, iv. 24.
John Vtreth, 1379: P. T. Yorks. p. 144.
1642. William Oughtred, prebend of Heathfield: Walker's Sufferings of the Clergy, edited by Whitaker, p. 26.

I once saw Oughtred over a public-house by the bridge at Newcastle. I also saw in the Visitors' book at Conishead Priory, Lanc., 'W. Oughtred, Didsbury, Manchester, Sept. 4, 1886.'

Ovenden.—Local, 'of Ovenden,' a township in the parish of Halifax, W. Rid. Yorks.

Ricardus de Ovenden, 1379: P. T. Yorks. p. 189.

This instance occurs in Halifax.

1601. Married—Robert Ovenden and Katherine Stevens: St. Peter, Cornhill, i. 242.
1775. — Rice James and Mary Ovenden: St. Geo. Han. Sq. i. 258.
London, 3; Philadelphia, 1.

Over.—Local, 'of Over,' parishes in diocs. Ely and Chester. The first seems to have been the parent of the surname. I do not find any traces of an old settled family in the county of Cheshire. 'Over, A.S. ófer, . . . a shore': Taylor, Words and Places (ed. 1885), p. 331. 'Ófer, the land bordering

on water, a river-bank, sea-shore, *over* in local names': Bosworth and Toller, A.S. Dict.

Richard de Overe, co. Hunts, 1273. A.
Nicholas Over, co. Oxf., ibid.
Sybil de Ouere, co. Camb., ibid.
John de Ouere, co. Camb., ibid.
Lucas de Overe, 1300. M.
1714. Bapt. — Letitia, d. Mathew Over: St. Jas. Clerkenwell, ii. 76.
1780. Married — William Over and Sarah Crissick: St. Geo. Han. Sq. i. 316.
London, 4; Philadelphia, 1.

Overall.—Local, 'of the Overhall.' The suffix is, of course, -*hall*, with the *h* dropped; cf. Blackall, &c. Overall, therefore, means the hall by the shore of the sea or near the bank of a river; v. Over.

Thomas del Ouerhalle, 1379: P. T. Yorks. p. 173.
1647. William Overall, of Bury: Wills at Chester, ii. 167.
1750. Married—John Morgan and Ann Overall: St. Geo. Chap. Mayfair, i. 180.
London, 4; Manchester, 1; New York, 1.

Overbury.—Local, 'of Overbury,' a parish in co. Worc., five miles from Tewkesbury; v. Over and Bury.

1606. Giles Overbury, co. Glouc.: Reg. Univ. Oxf. vol. ii. pt. ii. p. 292.
1610. Walter Overbury, co. Glouc.: ibid. p. 313.
1623-4. William Overbury and Gertrude Gee: Marriage Lic. (London), ii. 135.
1641. Married—William Watson and Eliz. Orwerbere: St. Michael, Cornhill, i. 29.
New York, 1.

Overdo.— ? Nick. The sobriquet of a kitchener or cook (?).

'Thing that is overdon . . . it is a vice.' Chaucer, C. T. 16113.
Henry Overdo, Close Roll, 14 Edw. IV.

Such nicknames were common and popular, but few survived.

Overend.—Local, 'at the Overend'; cf. Townsend, Woodend, Fieldsend, &c. (v. Over). With Overheynd, cf. Townshend. The letter *h* seems to have crept in easily. 'At the end of the shore' seems to be the derivation. All these compounds of *Over* go to prove that the affix implied a flat river-side as well as the sea-shore.

Michael de Overende, co. Bedf., 1273. A.
William de Overende, co. Bedf., ibid.
Robertus del Overheynd, 1379: P. T. Yorks. p. 276.

1694. John Overend, of Melling, *husbandman*: Wills at Chester, iv. 337. ·
1805. Married—Wilson Overend and Wilhelmina Eliz. Pringle: St. Geo. Han. Sq. ii. 329.
London, 3; Liverpool, 5; Philadelphia, 3.

Overman. — Offic. 'the overman,' a gaffer (?). William le Overer occurs (Close Roll, 2 Edw. I). Overman still lives, but seems to have found its latest home in America.

1647. Thomas Overman and Eliz. Ross: Marriage Lic. (London), ii. 278.
1650. Married—George Saunders and Alice Overman: St. Dionis Backchurch, i. 27.

In the London Directory occurs 'Overman's Alm Houses, Montague Close, Borough, S.E.'; probably an old endowment. This surname seems to have gone to America and taken the whole family with it.

New York, 1; Boston (U.S.), 2; Philadelphia, 2.

Overstone.—Local, ' of Overstone,' a parish in co. Northampton, five miles from the capital town.

MDB. (co. Warwick), 2.

Overton.—Local, ' of Overton,' parishes in diocs. of Winchester, Peterborough, Manchester, York, St. Alban's, and Sarum.

Adam de Overton, co. Oxf., 1273. A.
Ode de Overton, co. Hunts, ibid.
Geoffrey de Overton, co. Salop, ibid.
John de Overton, co. Hunts, 1324. M.
Sarra de Overtone, co. Soms., 1 Edw. III: Kirby's Quest, p. 261.
1624. Jane Overton, of Overton: Wills at Chester, ii. 167.
1788. Married—Francis Parish and Eliz. Overton: St. Geo. Han. Sq. ii. 7.
London, 10; Liverpool 1; New York, 17.

Overy, Ouvry.—Local, ' of Overy.' Mr. Lower says that this is an extinct parish in co. Oxf. If it be true that the Ouvrys came into England at the Revocation of the Edict of Nantes in 1685, a statement which seems to be well established, then Ouvry has a separate parentage.

Richard de Overe, co. Hunts, 1273. A.
Robert Overhe, co. Camb., ibid.
1683. Thomas Rodan and Catherine Ovrey: Marriage Alleg. (Canterbury), i. 145.

1711. Married — William Overy and Martha Scott: Reg. Canterbury Cath., p. 70.
1774. Married—William Musgrove and Mary Overy: St. Geo. Han. Sq. i. 241.
London, 5, 1; Philadelphia, 1, 0.

Owen, Owens.—Bapt. ' the son of Owen.' Owens is the genitive form; cf. Jones, Jennings, Williams, Simmonds, &c.

Hoel fil. Oeni, Pipe Roll, 7 Hen. II.
Oenus de Porchint', ibid.
Nicholas fil. Oweyn, co. Oxf., 1273. A.
Richard fil. Owen, co. Camb., ibid.
Matthew Owen, co. Wilts, 1316. M.
1742. Married—Cornelius Owen and Eliz. Rowell: St. Geo. Chap. Mayfair, p. 31.
1747. — Rowland Owens and Sarah Narboys: ibid. p. 96.
London, 76, 6; Philadelphia, 43, 56.

Owston; v. Oulston.

Owtram, -rim; v. Outram.

Ox, Oxx.—Nick. 'the ox'; cf. Bullock, Bull, Cow, &c. This surname has not made much way. Bull has done better; v. Oxnard.

Stephen Oxe, Pardons Roll, 6 Ric. II.
1745. Married—John Gedion Stone and Mary Oxx: St. Geo. Chap. Mayfair, p. 59.
New York, 0, 2; Philadelphia, 4, 0.

Oxberry, Oxborrow, Oxenbury, Oxbrow, Oxenberry.—Local, ' of Oxburgh' (or Oxborough), a parish in co. Norfolk, three miles from Stoke Ferry. All the variants are of an extremely natural character.

William de Oxeburgh, co. Norf., 1273. A.
Nicholas de Oxeburgh, co. Norf., 1316. M.
1669. Thomas Oxborow and Ellen Corker: Marriage Alleg. (Cant.), p. 17.
1796. Married—Stephen Dear and Eliz. Oxborough: St. Geo. Han. Sq. ii. 141.
London, 1, 3, 1, 0, 0; Exeter (Oxenberry), 2.

Oxenden.—Local, ' of Oxendon,' now Oxendon Magna, a parish in co. Northampton, two or three miles from Harborough.

John de Oxendon, co. Northampt., 1273. A.
Stephen de Oxindon, co. Bucks, ibid.
Adam de Oxindon, co. Northampt., Hen. III—Edw. I. K.
Ivo de Oxinden, co. Northampt., 1316. M.
1572. Henry Oxenden: Reg. Univ. Oxf. vol. ii. pt. ii. p. 38.
1661. William Dalton and Rebeccah Oxenden: Marriage Alleg. (Cant.), 18. Crockford, 1.

Oxenford, Oxford. — Local, ' of Oxford.' Oxenford is an old form of Oxford. Thus Bristow represents Bristol as Stopford represents Stockport.

'Whilom ther was dwelling in Oxenforde A riche gnof.' Chaucer, C. T. 3186.
William de Oxenford, *peller*, 7 Edw. II: Freemen of York, i. 15.
Johannes de Oxenford, 1379: P. T. Yorks. p. 23.
Cristiana de Oxenford, 1379; ibid.
John Oxeneford, co. Soms., 1 Edw. III: Kirby's Quest, p. 83.
1693. John Cux, or Cox, and Mary Oxenford: Marriage Alleg. (Canterbury), p. 266.
1764. Married — Thomas Oxford and Olle Woolldridge: St. Geo. Han. Sq. i. 118.
1779. — Thomas Oxford and Ann Thomas: ibid. p. 298.
London, 1, 4; Philadelphia, 1, 2.

Oxenham, Oxhenham. — Local, ' of Oxenham.' I cannot find the spot.

Richard Oxnam, 1590: Reg. St. Columb Major, co. Cornwall, p. 193.
Richard Oxenham, 1602: ibid. p. 200.
1778. Married—John Oxenham and Mary Mills: St. Geo. Han. Sq. i. 285.
London, 4, 1; Boston (U.S.), 2, 0.

Oxenhird.—Occup. 'a tender of oxen'; v. Oxnard.

Oxford; v. Oxenford.

Oxlade, Oxlid. — Local, ' of the oak-slade' (v. Slade). The modification of Ocslade into Oxlade was inevitable. Probably some spot in co. Oxon. Both cos. Berks and Bucks have instances still existing.

Michael de Ocslade, co. Oxf., 1273. A.
1621. Francis Oxladde: Reg. Univ. Oxf. i. 343.
1717. Bapt.—Ann, d. Robert Oxlade: St. Jas. Clerkenwell, p. 97.
1750. — Ann, d. Benjamin Oxlid: ibid. p. 295.
1783. Married — Thomas Frost and Mary Oxlade: St. Geo. Han. Sq. i. 349.
London, 1, 0; MDB. (co. Bucks), 1, 0; (co. Berks), 1, 0.

Oxley, Oxlee.—Local, ' of Oxley.' I cannot find the spot. A familiar Yorkshire surname, but probably known to other counties, as the 'ox-meadow' would readily become a local title.

1562. Robert Oxeley, *weaver*, and Eliz. Goodchild: Marriage Lic. (London), i. 24.
1731. Married—Daniel Oxlee and Mary Surman: St. Geo. Han. Sq. i. 8.

1780. Married — Richard Oxley and Mary Foster : St. Geo. Han. Sq. i. 314. London, 14, 2 ; New York, 4, 0.

Oxnard, Oxner.—Occup. 'the oxen-herd,' a keeper of oxen ; cf. Coward, Calvert, Shepherd, Gozzard. A North-English name, as are most of the compounds of *-herd*. Bullockherd is found in co. Somerset :

Adam Bollokhurd, 9 Edw. II : Kirby's Quest, p. 136.
Johannes Oxinhird, 1379 : P. T. Yorks. p. 216.
Thomas Oxenhyrde. W. 3.
John Oxenhyrde. W. 3.
Peter Oxhird. W. 2.
Alice Hoxherd, C. R., 4 Hen. IV. pt. i.

The abbreviation to Oxnard was inevitable :

1650. Christopher Oxnard and Faith Toulson : St. Dionis Backchurch (London).
1604. Christopher Oxnerd, *laborer*, recusant in Yorkshire : Dawson's Hist. of Skipton, p. 315.
— Stephen Oxnerd, *laborer*, recusant in Yorkshire : ibid.
1729. Henry Oxenard, *coachman*, and Jane Chillingworth : St. Geo. Chap. Mayfair, p. 308.
1793. Married—Jeremiah Oxnard and Mary Blakiston : St. Geo. Han. Sq. ii. 105.

For several years I thought Oxnard was extinct. I was much

pleased, therefore, on leaving Cullercoats Station, Newcastle, Aug. 29, 1886, to see the name over a shop in the immediate street to the left. Afterwards I found several instances in the Newcastle Directory.

Newcastle-on-Tyne, 2, 0 ; Boston (U.S.), 3, 0 ; New York, 0, 1.

Oxpring, Oxspring, Offspring.—Local, ' of Oxspring,' a village in the parish of Penistone, W. Rid. Yorks. There is good evidence that all who bear this name, wherever settled in later times, spring from this spot. Under the title ' Villata de Oxpryng' occur the names :

Richard de Oxpring co. York, 1273. A.
Matilda de Oxpring', 1379 : P. T. Yorks. p. 86.
William Oxpring, 1379 : ibid.
Gervase de Ospringe : Pipe Roll, 11 Hen. II. p. 103.

Ofspring is a manifest corruption, although a manor named Offspring is mentioned (A.D. 1273 ; v. A. i. 226) in the Hundred of Folkestone, co. Kent.

'Thomas Ofspringe, alias Oxspringe, of Kent, whoe came out of Yorkshire.'

His son Charles Ofspringe was rector of St. Antholin's, London, in 1634 : Visitation of London, 1635, ii. 129.

No doubt Offspring Blackall, Bishop of Exeter (1654-1716), born in London, was a connexion, as surnames turned into fontal names were becoming fashionable at that period.

1771. Married—Offspring Webb and Mary Withington : St. Geo. Han. Sq. i. 207.
Sheffield, 1, 4, 0 ; Philadelphia, 0, 1, 0.

Oxton. — Local, of ' Oxton,' parishes in diocs. Chester and Southwell, and spots elsewhere. One more instance in which the oak-trees figure in local names.

Richard de Okeston, co. Devon, 1273. A.
Alexander de Ockeston, co. Devon, ibid.
Johannes de Oxton, 1379 : P. T. Yorks. p. 145.
1663. Thomas Oxton and Ann Rutlish : Marriage Alleg. (Canterbury), p. 109.
1681. Married—Netor Oxston and Eliz. Gillford : St. Jas. Clerkenwell, iii. 190. London, 1, 1.

Oyler, Ollier.—? Occup. 'the oiler ' (?), i.e. an oilman. Far more likely to be a form of Oliver, q.v.

Roberte Deane, *oylman*, 1642 : Reg. St. Mary Aldermary, London, p. 88. London, 2, 2.

P

Pace, Pacey.—Bapt. 'the son of Pace,' pet Pacey. The variants of this Easter name are many ; v. Pash, Pask, Peace, &c. Easteregging in North Lancashire is still Pace-egging, and in my old parish (Ulverston) the sale of pace-eggs is large as the Easter comes round ; cf. Noel, Pentecost, &c.

Hugo Pacy, co. Notts, 1273. A.
William Pacy, co. Linc., ibid.
William Pace, co. Devon, Hen. III-Edw. I. K.
Alexander Pacye, 1564 : Reg. Univ. Oxf. vol. ii. pt. ii. p. 29.
1583. Edward Spendlowe and Eliz. Pace : Marriage Lic. (London), i. 117.
London, 4, 2 ; Boston (U.S.), 5, 0.

Pack, Pakes, Packe.—Bapt ' the son of Pack.' Probably it is

a harder form of Patch, q.v. Pakes is the genitive form ; cf. Jones, Williams, Collins, &c. (v. Paxon for further evidence).

John fil. Pake, co. Camb., 1273. A.
Alex. Pake, co. Camb., ibid.
William Pakke, co. Camb., ibid.
Agnes Pake, co. Bedf., ibid.
Edward Pake, co. Soms., 1 Edw. III : Kirby's Quest, p. 193.
1568-9. Humfrey Pakes and Martha Brittaine : Marriage Lic. (London), i. 41.
1590. Matthew Pake and Eliz. Rogers : ibid. p. 187.
1603-4. Edward Pack and Hester Blunt : p. 281.
London, 9, 1, 0 ; Philadelphia, 4, 0, 1.

Packard.—No doubt, as suggested by Mr. Lower, a corruption of Picard, q.v. This form is very

strongly represented in the United States.

1770. Married — Peter Packard and Jane Colebean : St. Geo. Han. Sq. i. 198. London, 2 ; Boston (U.S.), 76.

Packer.—Occup. 'the packer,' a packman. In Yorkshire a woolpacker. v. Packman (1).

Walter le Packere, co. Bedf., 1273. A.
' Richard, the son of William, the son of Orme, quit-claimed the whole of his land in Prestbury, to St. Werbergh and the Abbey. . . Similar grants were made by William, the son of Robert Pigot, Robert, the son of William le Paker, and others ': East Cheshire, ii. 180 n.
Mathew le Packere. D.
Adam le Packer. M.
William le Packere. J.
Robert de Lyndesay, *pakker*, 8 Edw. II : Freemen of York, i. 16.

1583-4. Edward Packer and Eliz.
Leonard: Marriage Lic. (London), i. 126.
1642. Bapt.—John, s. Andrew Packer,
dwelling in Bowe Lane: St. Mary
Aldermary, p. 88.
London, 21 ; Philadelphia, 28.

Packham, Peckham.—Local,
' of Peckham,' two parishes in co.
Kent. The variation was a natural
and easy one. For a second derivation of Packham, v. Pakenham.

1575. George Peckam, co. Bucks:
Reg. Univ. Onf. vol. ii. pt. ii. 64.
1588. Henry Peccam, co. Sussex:
ibid. p. 164.
1808. Married — William Hale and
Sarah Packham: St. Geo. Han. Sq.
ii. 383.
London, 3, 4 ; MDB. (co. Kent), 2, 1.

Packman.—(1) Occup. 'the
packman'; v. Packer. (2) Occup.
a variant of Pakeman, q.v.

1580. Arthur Gynne and Mary Packe-
man: Marriage Lic. (London), i. 96.
1669. Married—Richard Pacman and
Saray Pane: St. Jas. Clerkenwell, iii.
166.
London, 8 ; Philadelphia, 1.

Packwood.—Local, 'of Packwood,' a parish in co. Warwick,
near Henley-in-Arden.

1617. Josiah Packwood, co. Warwick:
Reg. Univ. Oxf. vol. ii. pt. ii. 361.
1640. Bapt. — Christofer, s. Thomas
Packwood: St. Jas. Clerkenwell, i. 145.
London, 2.

Pacy.—Bapt. 'the son of Pace,'
from the pet Pacey ; v. Pace.

London, 2.

Padbury.—Local, 'of Padbury,'
a parish in co. Bucks, three miles
from Buckingham.

Robert de Padeburi, co. Bucks, 1273. A.
Symon de Padeburi, co. Oxf., ibid.
1778. Married — Nathaniel Gardner
and Eliz. Padburey: St. Geo. Hanover
Sq. i. 287.
MDB. (co. Oxf.), 2 ; London, 4.

Paddey, Paddie, Paddy.—
Bapt. 'the son of Patrick,' from
the nick. Pat, and pet form Patty
or Paddy. All these forms are
purely English; v. Paddison or
Pattison, and Patey or Pate.

1560. John Borne and Margaret Pad-
dye, of Hadley, co. Essex: Marriage Lic.
(London), i. 20.
1585. John Paddie, co. Bucks: Reg.
Univ. Oxf. vol. ii. pt. ii. p. 144.
1770. Married — Joseph Paddy and
Eliz. Cope: St. Geo. Han. Sq. i. 203.
London, 1, 1, 1.

Paddison.—Bapt. ' the son of
Patrick '; v. Pattinson, of which
Paddison is a lazier form. Although
Paddy is Irish, Paddison is purely
of English descent. It must never
be forgotten that Patrick was a
most popular North-English personal name in the surname period.

1678. Bapt. — Bartholomew, s. John
Paddyson: St. Jas. Clerkenwell. i. 281.
1795. Married—Samuel Paddison and
Eliz. Vergette : St. Geo. Han. Sq. ii. 138.
MDB. (co. Linc.), 13 ; London, 2.

Padget, Padgett.—Official; v.
Paget.

Padley.—Local, ' of Padley,' a
hamlet in the parish of Hope, co.
Derby. The surname has crossed
the border into Nottinghamshire.

Nicholas de Paddeleye, co. Derby,
1273. A.
Henricus de Padelay, 1379: P. T.
Yorks. p. 30.
London, 3 ; MDB. (co. Notts), 3.

Pagan. — Bapt. 'the son of
Pagan.' A very familiar font-name
in the 13th century, and earlier,
leaving a large legacy to our
directories in the shape of Paine,
Payn, Payne, and their other forms
(q.v.). Edmundus filius Pagani
(Domesday). For a history of this
word, v. Gibbon's Decline and
Fall, ch. xxi. ad finem. For diminutives, v. Paynel and Pannett.

Paganus de Vilers, temp. 1109: Lincoln-
shire Survey, p. 9.
Geoffrey, s. Paganus: ibid. p. 2.
Pagan de Shenefeld : Pipe Roll, 11 Hen.
II, p. 18.
Pagan de Staning: ibid. p. 92.
Pagan a la Legh, co. Wilts, 1273. A.
Pagan de la Hale, co. Kent, ibid.
Roger fil. Pagan, co. Devon, ibid.

This surname has been gradually
shuffled off or changed into Paine,
Payne, &c., the bearers not caring
to be so entitled. Yet it is one of
the most interesting names in our
directories.

Cruckford, 1 ; Philadelphia, 3.

Page, Paige.—Official, 'the
page,' a young servitor, a personal
attendant in a noble's house.

Lambert Page, co. York, 1273. A.
Philip Page, co. Essex, Hen. III—Edw.
I. K.
John le Page, 1300. M.
William le Page. BB.

1584. Anthony Page and Eliz. Blounte:
Marriage Lic. (London), i. 131.
London, 128, 2 ; MDB. (co. Devon), 2.
11 ; Boston (U.S.), 57, 36.

**Paget, Pagett, Padget, Pad-
gett, Padgit.**—(1) Nick. ' the
page,' dim. Paget. Boy pages seem
to have been held in high esteem.
No instance, however, occurs in
the Hundred Rolls or other contemporary records so far as my
observation goes. I presume it is
a 14th or 15th century importation
from France, and corresponds
exactly to our Littlepage and
Smallpage, q.v.

Johannes Paget, taylour, 1379: P. T.
Yorks. p. 118.

(2) Bapt. 'the son of Pachet.'
If Paget be (occasionally) a corruption of Pachet, then early
instances abound in plenty ; v.
Patchett. Padget or Padgett would
also be natural corruptions.

1779. Married — John Briggs and
Mary Padget: St. Geo. Han. Sq. i. 207.
1807. — John Kellick and Eliz. Paggitt :
ibid. ii. 379.
London, 11, 0, 0, 5, 0; West Rid.
Court Dir., 2, 0, 2, 5, 0 ; New York, 0, 1,
0, 0, 1.

Pagnam.—Local, ' of Pakenham,' a parish in co. Suffolk, five
miles from Bury St. Edmunds.
The corruption to Pagnam is
according to recognized custom ;
cf. Slagg for Slack, and Debnam
for Debenham. An early instance
occurs below.

William de Pakenham, co. Norf.,
1273. A.
Henry de Pakenham, co. Norf., 1373:
FF. i. 480.
Ralph de Pagenham, co. Soms., 1 Edw.
III: Kirby's Quest, p. 154.
1574. Married — Robert Pagnam and
Curlellaw (sic) Chicheley: St. Jas. Clerk-
enwell, i. 6.
1626. Oswald Tilman and Eliz. Pack-
nam: Marriage Lic. (London), i. 179.
George Frederick Pagnam, butcher,
Eccles New Road, Salford: Manchester
Directory.
Manchester, 1.

Pagnel.—Bapt. ; v. Paynel.

Paice.—Bapt. 'the son of Pace';
v. Pash and Pace. One of many
variants of this Easter name ; cf.
Whitsunday, Christmas, Nowell,
Pentecost, &c.

1616. Barnard Paise and Eliz. Surbey: Marriage Lic. (London), ii. 41.
1765. Married — Samuel Lewington and Jemima Paice: St. Geo. Han. Sq. i. 139. London, 9.

Paige; v. Page.

Pailthorpe, Palethorp, Pale-thorpe.—Local, 'of Palethorpe,' a chapelry in co. Notts (Lower).

1753. Married—George Sylvester and Sarah Palthorpe: St. Geo. Han. Sq. i. 50.
1763. — William Pailthorpe and Eliz. Woolcott: ibid. p. 127.
MDB. (co. Lincoln), o. o, 3; (co. Notts), o, o, 2; London, 1, o, 1; Philadelphia, o, 5, o.

Pain, Paine, Payn, Payne.—Bapt. 'the son of Pagan,' popularly Pain and Payne. How great a favourite this font-name was in the 12th, 13th, and 14th centuries will be seen by a glance at the London and provincial directories. The softened form of pagan (a countryman) is found in Chaucer:

'The Constable, and Dame Hermegild,
    his wife,
Were payenes, and that country every-
    where.'   Man of Lawes Tale.

Pagan or Payn was of Norman introduction. It is curious that a great leader of atheistical principles should have borne this name.

' He never knew pleasure who never
    knew Payn,'

has been said of several jovial bearers of the cognomen.

Payn de Santon, co. Norf., 1273. A.
Robert fil. Payn, co. Hunts. ibid.
Gilbert Payn, co. Essex, ibid.
Elis le Fitz-Payn, 1297. M.
Pain del Ash, 1301. M.
Payne le Paumer, C. R., 35 Hen. III.
Payen le Doubber. M.
Thomas Payn, co. Soms., 1 Edw. III: Kirby's Quest, p. 110.

For diminutives, v. Pannett and Paynel. Also v. Penson. It would be useless to furnish modern instances. They abound in every church register and in every city directory.

London, 31, 37, 2, 120; Philadelphia, 1, 14, o, 50.

Painter, Paynter. — Occup. 'the painter,' one who depicted in colours. This surname has made a strong impression upon American directories.

John Peyntur, co. Camb., 1273. A.
Ric. le Paintur, C. R., 4 Edw. II.

William de Blida, *payntour*, 8 Edw. II: Freemen of York, i. 16.
Ricardus Peyntour, 1379: P. T. Yorks. p. 161.
Richard Peyntour, rector of Congham, co. Norf., 1439: FF. viii. 389.
1636. Married — Richard Painter and Katherine Witt: St. Jas. Clerkenwell, iii. 67.
London, 20, 2; Philadelphia, 45, 31.

Pairpoint. — Local; v. Pierpoint, of which it is a palpable variant.

Paisley.—Local, 'of Paisley.' Found chiefly in the North of England and near the Scottish border.

MDB. (co. Cumberland), 4.

Paitson.—Bapt. 'the son of Patrick,' from the nick. Pait or Patey; v. Patey and Pattinson. A North-English form.

Pate Stevinson, 1528: TTT. p. xxx.
Pait Tailyeour, 1541: ibid. p. xlix.
Pait Graham, 1544: ibid. p. liii.
Richard Pateson, of Wray, 1611: ibid.
Jenet Pateson, of Much Singleton, *widow*, 1623: Lancashire Wills at Richmond, i. 211.
Ulverston, 1; MDB. (co. Cumberland), 1; (co. Westm.), 1.

Pakeman.—Occup. 'the servant of Pake'; v. Pack; cf. Addyman, Matthewman, &c., one of a fairly large class.

John Pakeman, co. Oxf., 1273. A.
William Pakman, co. Derby, 20 Edw. I. R.
Simon Pakeman, C. R., 7 Hen. VI.
1714. Married—Jasper Roffe and Mary Pakeman: St. Jas. Clerkenwell, iii. 237.
London, 1.

Pakenham, Packham, Pack-enham, Packingham.— Local, 'of Pakenham,' a parish in co. Suffolk, near Bury St. Edmunds. Very early corrupted to Packham. Several variants of the name seem peculiar to the United States.

John de Pakeham, co. Norf., 1273. A.
William de Pakenham, co. Norf., ibid.
William de Pakeham, or Pakenham, co. Suff.: ibid.
Thomas de Pakeham, co. Norf.: FF. x. 449.
Edmund de Pakenham, co. Norf., 1388: ibid. i. 253.
1808. Married — William Hale and Sarah Packham: St. Geo. Han. Sq. ii. 383.
London, o, 3, o, o; Crockford, 1, o, o, o; New York, 2, o, 2, 4.

Pakes.—Bapt.; v. Pack.

Palcock.—Bapt. 'the son of Paul,' from the pet Paulcock; cf. Wilcock, Simcock, &c.; v. Cock.

Jordan Palecok, co. Bucks, 1273. A.
Johannes Palcock, et Beatrix, uxor ejus, 1379: P. T. Yorks. p. 52.

This surname, I believe, still exists, but I have not met with an instance.

Palethorp(e.—Local; v. Pailthorpe.

Paley.—Local, ' of Paley,' now Paley Green, in the parish of Giggleswick, W. Rid. Yorks, consisting of two farmsteads. Mr. Lower writes, 'This was borne as a personal name by a powerful Dane, mentioned in the Saxon Chronicle as Pallig, A.D. 1101' (Patr. Brit. p. 255). My derivation is manifestly the correct one, as all the Paleys come from Yorkshire.

Robertus de Palay, of Litton, in the parish of Arncliffe, 1379: P. T. Yorks. p. 278.
Adam de Palay, of Giggleswick, 1379: ibid. p. 279.
John Paley, of Melling, on the Yorkshire border, 1591: Wills at Chester, i. 147.
Richard Paley, of Clifton, 1673: Lancashire Wills at Richmond, i. 206.

These four references conclusively show that the Paleys are sprung from the spot indicated above.

London, 2; West Rid. Court Dir., 7; Philadelphia, 1.

Palfrey.—Nick. 'the palfrey,' a saddle-horse for a lady's use. M.E. *palfrei*; O.F. *palefrei*; v. Palfreyman.

'And to the paleis rode ther many a route
Of lordes, upon stedes and palfreis.'
        Chaucer, Knight's Tale, l. 2495.

Thomas Palfrei, co. Linc., 1273. A.
Richard Palefray, co. Salop, ibid.
Gilbert Palfrey, co. Norf., ibid.
John Palefrey, co. Norf., ibid.
1667. Thomas Palfrey and Margaret Maxham: Marriage Lic. (Faculty Office), p. 100.
1668. Married—Richard Pallfrey and Mary Halton: St. Jas. Clerkenwell, iii. 140.
London, 2; Philadelphia, 1.

Palfreyer.—Official, 'the palfreyer,' the keeper of 'my lady's' palfreys; v. Palfreyman.

Gile Palfreur, co. Camb., 1273. A.
Richard le Palefreyur, C. R., 3 Edw. I.
Roger le Palefrour, ibid.
Roger le Palefreyour, co. York. W. 2.
This surname seems to have become extinct.

Palfreyman,   Palframan, Palfreeman.—Official, 'the palfreyman,' the keeper of 'my lady's' palfreys.

'Item, the same daye to John Stormy for keping of twoo palfrayes of the Quenes after the decense of Richard Payne, palfreyman, xs.' 1502, May 1 Privy Purse Expenses, Elizabeth of York, p. 17.
'10 hobyes and palfreys the whiche the kinges highnesse yave unto my lady, Duchesse of Bourgoinge': Privy Purse Expenses, Edw. IV, 1480, p. 153. v. Hobman.
John le Palfreyman, co. Camb.,1273. A.
Robert Palfreyman, co. Bucks, ibid.
Thomas Palfrayman, 1379: P. T. Yorks. p. 300.
1553. Bapt. — Mary Pauefreman: St. Peter, Cornhill, i. 117.
1578. Buried — Anne Palphreman: ibid. p. 211.
1576. John Paphraman, or Palframan: Reg. Univ. Oxf. vol. ii. pt. iii. p. 57.
West Rid.Court Dir , 2, 1, 0; Sheffield, 5, 0, 0; Coneythorpe (Knaresboro'), 0, 0, 1; Boston (U.S.), 1, 0, 0; Philadelphia, 1, 0, 0.

Palgrave.—Local, ' of Palgrave,' a parish in co. Suffolk, one mile from Diss ; also a hamlet in the parish of Sporle, co. Norfolk. This surname has no connexion with the German Pfalzgraf, a Count-Palatine, as has been several times suggested. It is local, not official.

1311. Sir Ralph de Palegrave, rector of Bodney : FF. iii. 631.
1728. Bapt. — Susanna, d. Robert Paulgrave : St. Jas. Clerkenwell, ii. 181.
London, 2; MDB. (Norfolk), 1.

Paliser, Palliser, Palser, Palister, . Pallister. — Occup. 'the palliser,' or with feminine suffix 'the pallister,' a surname seemingly peculiar to Yorkshire, where it still flourishes. The Surtees Society records contain early references (unfortunately I have mislaid my notes) to such persons as 'Robert Redman, palayser.'

'Paid to James Foster, palycer, as a present for making the payle (i. e. fence) near the dwelling of the Lord Prior, near

the butgarth, 12d.' : Liber Bursarii. Eccles. Dunelmensis, Surt. Soc.
The *palliser* (Fr. *palis*, a pale, a stake) was a kind of parker, one who guarded or fenced enclosures. As regards *pallister*, it may be as well to say that the Poll Tax (1379) proves that the feminine suffix -*ster* was very popular in all occupative names (v. Slaster for Slater) ; cf. *palisade*.
Robertus Palycer, 1379: P. T. Yorks. p. 240.
John Pallyser, co. York. W. 9.
Thomas Palysar, co. York ; ibid.
William Pallyster, co. York : ibid.
John Palyster, co. York : ibid.
Robert Paylyster, co. York. W. 11.
'The Rev. Thomas Palaser, or Pallicer, born at Ellerton-upon-Swale, a Roman Catholic priest, was executed for his religion at Durham, Aug. 9, 1600' : Old Yorkshire, ii. 140.
1793. Married—Alex. Paul and Sarah Pallister : St. Geo. Han. Sq. ii. 92.
1794. — Thomas Haverly and Eliz. Palser : ibid. p. 110.
Leeds, 1, 1, 0, 0, 1 ; York, 1, 0, 0, 0, 2 ; Rawdon (W. Rid.), 0, 2, 0, 0, 0; New York, 0, 0, 0, 1, 1 ; London (Palser), 7.

Palismaker. — Occup. 'the palis maker,' a maker of fences ; v. Paliser or Pallister.

William Palycemaker, 1379: P. T. Yorks. p. 242.

Pallet, Pallett, Pallatt.—Local, ' of Pawlett,' q.v. I doubt not these are variants. Pellatt is well established in the United States. As will be seen below, the form Palet is early found in co. Soms.

John Palet, co. Soms., 1 Edw. III : Kirby's Quest, p. 208.
Robert Palet, co. Soms., 1 Edw. III : ibid.
1797. Married — Richard Brooks and Lucy Pallet : St. Geo. Han. Sq. ii. 168.
1798. — Joseph Pallett and Mary Youngman : ibid. p. 191.
London, 1, 6, 0 ; Philadelphia, 1, 1, 12.

Palmer.—Occup. ' the palmer,' a pilgrim to the Holy Land ; a common entry in the Hundred Rolls.

' The faded palm-branch in his hand, Showed pilgrim from the Holy Land.'
                                        Scott.
Alice le Palmere, co. Camb., 1273. A.
Ralph le Palmere, co. York, ibid.
Robert le Palmere, co. Linc., ibid.
Richard le Palmere, co. Soms., 1 Edw. III : Kirby's Quest, p. 219.

Roger le Palmere, co. Middlesex, 20 Edw. I. R.
Ricardus Palmer, *mason*, 1379 : P. T. Yorks. p. 25.
1565. Henry Palmer and Agnes Hayes, *widow* : Marriage Lic. (London), i. 31.
London, 225 ; Boston (U.S.), 153.

Palphramand. — Offic.   A curious corruption of Palfreyman. q.v. The York Directory has also Palfreeman and Palfreman.
York, 1.

Palser.—Occup. ' the palliser ' (q.v.). Palser is now the commoner form.

Pamphilon, Pamplin, Plampin, Pampling.—Local or nick. For meaning of the name ' Papillon,' of which these are corruptions, v. Papillon. The following in Halliwell's Dict. may, however, prove that a different application of the word gave them existence. 'Pampilion, a coat of different colours, formerly worn by servants. It occurs with this explanation in Hollyband's Dictionarie, 1593. There was a kind of fur so called.' If a cant name for a servitor attired in butterfly colours, then Pamphilon and Pamplin are nicknames. But the local origin seems the more probable, for which v. Papillon.

Miriel Pampilwn, co. Hunts, 1273. A.
Godfrey Paunphilon, C. R., 33 Edw. I.
Galfridus Pamphilun, 34 Edw. I : BBB. p. 728.
1603. Married — William Mandesford and Margaret Pamplyn : Marriage Lic. (London), i. 277.
Edward Pamphilon, 1710 : Reg. St. Mary Aldermary (London), p. 40.
1767. — Thomas Simmons and Esther Pamphilon : St. Geo. Han. Sq. i. 164.
London, 3, 2, 1, 0 ; Boston (U.S.) (Pampling), 1.

Pancefoot, Pauncefort. — Local, ' de Pauncevote,' probably of Norman extraction. ' In charters it is Latinized De Pede Planco, that is, " of the Splay Foot," but for this rendering there appears to be no authority. The first of the name on record is Bernard Pancevolt, a Domesday tenant-in-chief in Hampshire. Geoffrey de Pauncevote was steward to the household of King John ' : Lower, Patr. Brit. p. 255.

Isabel Pancefote, C.R., 51 Hen. III.
Lamual Pancevot, co. Hamp., Hen.
Edw. I. K.
Elena Pancefot, co. Heref., ibid.
Grimbald Pancefot, co. Hertf., 1273. A.
Walter Pancevot, co. Somerset, ibid.
Richard Pauncefot, co. Glouc., 20
Edw. I. R.
John Paucefot, co. Soms., 1 Edw. III:
Kirby's Quest, p. 208.
1544. Robert Barker and Margery
Pawnfott: Marriage Lic. (Faculty Office),
p. 3.
1676. Tracy Paunsforth and Jane Part-
ridge: ibid. p. 136.
1681. James Bourne and Eliz. Paunce-
fort: ibid. p. 156.
London, o, 1 ; Boston (U.S.), o, 1.

Panckridge.—Bapt. 'the son
of Pancras,' popularly styled Pan-
cridge.

' Whilst Pancradge Church, arm'd with a
samphier blade,
Began to reason of the businesse thus.'
Taylor's Workes, 1630, i. 120.
For meaning and history of
Pancras, v. Miss Yonge's History
of Christian Names, i. 211.

' Pancrace Grout sup. for B. Grammar,
June, 1532, has been teaching boys thirteen years in the county, &c.': Reg.
Univ. Oxf. i. 170.
1698. Married — Robert Panckridge
and Margaret Dolman: St. Jas. Clerkenwell, iii. 219.
Crockford, 1 ; MDB. (co. Oxf.), 1.

Pancoast.—Local; a corruption
of Pankhurst. This well-
established American surname
went out as Pancrust (obviously
for Pankhurst). By degrees it
settled down as Pancoast.

1635. Anus (Agnes) Pancrust, to New
England: Hotten's Lists of Emigrants,
p. 87.
1798. Married—Owen Evans and Eliz.
Pancoust: St. Geo. Han. Sq. ii. 192.
Philadelphia, 47.

Pangbourne, Pangborn.—
Local, ' of Pangbourne,' a parish in
co. Berks, six miles from Reading.

— Pangeburn (personal name not
given), co. Oxf., 1273. A.
London, 1, o ; Philadelphia, o, 2.

Pankhurst.—Local, ' of Penk-
hurst,' an estate in East Sussex
(Lower). For a curious corruption,
v. Pancoast.

1798. Married — Nicholas Pankhurst
and Eliz. Walter: St. Geo. Han. Sq.
ii. 183.
— — Owen Evans and Eliz. Pancoust:
ibid. p. 192.

MDB. (co. Kent), 3 ; (co. Sussex), 1 ;
London, 7.

Pannell.—Bapt. 'the son of
Paynel' (q.v.), a dim. of Payn or
Pain, q.v. ; v. Pannett for a parallel
instance. The same individual is
thus referred to :
Fukey Panel, co. Notts, Hen. III–Edw.
I. K.
Fulco Painel, co. Notts, ibid.

If any doubt existed as to the
origin of Pannell, the above quotation settles it.

1584. William Poore and Alice Panell:
Marriage Lic. (London), i. 33.
1658. Buried — Ann, wife of Edward
Pannell: St. Peter, Cornhill, i. 211.
London, 13.

Pannett.—Bapt. 'the son of
Paynot,' a dim. of Payn or Pain,
q.v. ; cf. Pannell for Paynel, q.v. In
the same way we get Emmett or
Emmott from Emma.

Henry Paynot, co. Hunts, 1273. A.
John Paynot, co. Hunts, ibid.
Walter Paynet, co. Soms., 1 Edw. III:
Kirby's Quest, p. 141.
Geoffrey Paynet, co. Soms., 1 Edw. III:
ibid. p. 230.
Emma Paynot, co. York. W. 2.
John Paynett, temp. Eliz. Z.
1690-1. Francis Milles and Mary
Pannot: Marriage Lic. (Faculty Office),
p. 198.
London, 2.

Pannier.—Occup.'the pannier,'
one who carried bread from house
to house for sale, or more officially
one who superintended the pantry
(v. Pantry) where the bread was
kept. v. next article.

Editha Panier, co. Camb., 1273. A.
Robert le Pannier, C. R., 3 Edw. I.
1680. Bapt.—Sarah, d. Daniel Panyer:
St. Michael, Cornhill, p. 155.
1690. Buried — Mary Panyer: ibid.
p. 272.

I do not suppose the name is
extinct, but I cannot find an
instance.

Panter, Panther, Pantler.—
Offic. 'the panter,' the steward
of the pantry, also the baker for
the household, a paniter; Fr.
pannetier.

Richard le Paneter. C.
Robert le Panter, co. Camb., 1273. A.
Geoffrey le Paneter. G.

The serjeant ' which is called the
Chief Pantrer of the kinges mouthe'

(Liber Niger domus Edw. IV,
Household Ord., p. 70, quoted by
Way in Prompt. Parv.). The
Prompt. Parv. has ' panthere,
panitarius.' Mr. Way reminds us
in a note that this form survives
in the surname ' Pantler.' John
Russell, in his Boke of Nurture,
directs :

'The furst yere, my son, thou shalt be
pantere, or buttilare,
Thou must have three knyffes kene in
pantry, I say thee, evermare.'

One duty of the monastery panter
was the distribution of loaves to
the poor (v. Lower, Patr. Brit.).
Panther is a somewhat ferocious-
looking corruption ; cf. Gunther
and Gunter.

1758. Married — Samuel Panter and
Mary Smith: St. Geo. Han. Sq. i. 76.
1768. — Daniel Hocknell and Eliz.
Panther : ibid. p. 182.
London, 4, 1, o ; Oxford, 4, o, o.

Panton, ? Pantin, ? Panting.
—Local, ' of Panton,' a parish in
co. Lincoln.

Hugh de Panton, co. Linc., 1273. A.
Jacop de Panton, co. Linc., ibid.
Baldwin de Panton, co. Linc., Hen.
III–Edw. I. K.
William de Panton, co. Linc., ibid.
1769. Married — Peter Morgan and
Emry Panton: St. Geo. Han. Sq. i. 189.
London, 2, 1, 1 ; Oxford, o, o, 3 ; Phila-
delphia, 1, 1, o.

Pantry.—Official, ' at the pantry,' the officer of the pantry ; v.
Panter, and cf. Wardrober and
de la Wardrobe, Spencer and de
la Spence, Kitchener and de la
Kitchen.

John de la Paneterie, London, 1273. A.
Henry de la Paneterie, 1307. M.
John atte Pantery, C. R., 6 Hen. IV.
1551. William Pantrie, citizen of Oxford: Reg. Univ. Oxf. pt. i. p. 297.
John Pantrey, M.A., sup. for B.D.,
1509, Provost of Queen's, but resigned in
1534 : ibid. p. 66.
1693. Bapt.—Eliz., d. William Pantry:
St. Jas. Clerkenwell, i. 353.

Panyerman. — Occup. 'the
panyerman,' a peddler, cheap jack.

Richard Panyerman, co. York, 1471.
W. 11.

Pape.—Nick. 'the pape,' i.e.
Pope. Fr. pape, Latin papa ; cf.
Cardinal, King, Emperor, &c. ; v.
Pope.

Hugo Pape, London, 1273. A.
Ricardus Pap, co. Camb., ibid.
Nicholas Pappe, co. Camb., ibid.
Hugh le Pape. J.
William le Pape, C. R., 39 Hen. III.
pt. i.
Robertus Pape, 1379: P. T. Yorks.
p. 261.
1785. Married — David James and
Betty Pape: St. Geo. Han. Sq. i. 375.
London, 4; MDB. (co. Cumberland),
7; Philadelphia, 7.

Papillon.—Local, 'of the pa-
vilion.' Fr. *pavillon*, 'a pavillion,
tent' (Cotg.). 'So called because
spread out like the wings of a
butterfly. Latin, *papilionem*, acc.
of *papilio*, (1) a butterfly, (2) a tent'
(Skeat). The word was in early
use, and is largely used in our
Authorized Version; cf. Pamphilon
and Pamplin, which are mere
corruptions, but are placed separately, as a different use of the
term *papillon* may have brought
them into the directory.

Toraldus de Papilloyn, co. Dorset, Hen.
III-Edw. I. K.
Nicholas Papalion, co. Linc., 1273. A.
John le Pavilloner (a maker of pavi-
lions), 16 Edw. II: Freemen of York,
i. 21.
Turaldus de Papileon: Hist. Dunelm-
ensis, Surt. Soc. v.
Turald de Papeleon: ibid. vii.
1686-7. Married—Thomas Weely and
Mary Papillon: St. Dionis Backchurch,
p. 41.
1791. Married—Thomas Papillon and
Anne Pelham: St. Geo. Han. Sq. ii. 61.
Crockford, 4.

Papworth.—Local, 'of Papworth,' a parish four miles from
Huntingdon, but on the Cambridgeshire border. This surname
has ramified strongly and extended
far beyond the limits within which
it arose. 'Benjamin Papworth,
shoemaker,' occurs in the Philadelphia Directory (U.S.A.).

John de Pappeworth, co. Camb., 1273.
A.
Aylboda de Papworth, co. Camb., ibid.
Walter de Pappewrth, co. Camb., ibid.
1547. Richard Papworth and Margery
Griffinge: Marriage Lic. (London), i. 11.
1732. Bapt.—Anne, d. Ralph Papworth:
St. Michael, Cornhill, p. 171.
London, 7; MDB. (co. Camb.), 20;
(co. Hunts), 6; Philadelphia, 1.

Paradice, Paradise, Paradis.
—Local, 'of Paradise.' It was
seemingly as common to call a

pretty spot 'a perfect Paradise'
six centuries ago as to-day. The
surname was taken from residence
in some spot familiarly known as
'Paradise.'

'Item, do et lego Willielmo filio meo
unum burgag in Sadlergate, et unum
gardinum in tenurâ Ricardi Arnald juxta
Paradys emptum de Johanne Cuthbert':
Will of Matilda Bowes, 1420 (DDD. i.
278).
John de Paradyshowe, C. R., 5 Ric. II.
Anthony Paradise, C. R., 1-2 Philip and
Mary, pt. ii.
1564. Married—Rychard Paradyse to
Elyzabeth Savage: St. Dionis Back-
church.
John Paradise, 1622: Reg. Broad
Chalke, co. Wilts, p. 16.
Thomas Paradice, vicar of All Saints,
Bristol, 1693: Barrett's Bristol, p. 441.
1791. Married—George Paradice and
Eliz. Guppy: St. Geo. Han. Sq. ii. 67.
London, 1, 0, 0; Boston (U.S.), 0, 3, 0;
New York, 0, 1, 2.

**Paramor, Paramore, Parra-
more.** — Nick. 'the paramour,'
a lover in an honest sense. But
Chaucer says:

'My fourthe husbonde was a revellour,
This is to sayn, he had a paramour.'
John Paramour, co. Linc., 1273. A.
Roger Paramour, 1301. M.
1581. Robert Paramour and Katherine
Warde: Marriage Lic. (London), i. 101.
1623. Bapt. — Mathew, s. Thomas
Parramour: St. Jas. Clerkenwell, i. 96.
'1635. April 18, Whitehall. Captain
Thomas Paramour, appointed to the
Adventure': State Papers, 1635 (Do-
mestic).
1701. John Paramour and Mary
Wallbanke, by banns: Canterbury
Cathedral.
MDB. (co. Devon), 0, 5, 0; Crockford,
0, 3, 0; London, 1, 0, 0; Philadelphia, 0,
7, 2.

Parcheminer. — Occup. 'le
parcheminer,' a maker of parchment, used for testamentary, legal,
and other literary purposes. Fr.
parchemin, parchment. 'Alle bedels,
...alle stacioners, alle bokebynders,
lympners, wryters, pergemeners':
Mun. Acad. Oxon. p. 346. 'The
Parchemyners and Bukbynders
marched together in the York
Pageant': York Mystery Plays,
p. xx.

John le Parchmyner. B.
Hamo le Parchemener. L.
Cristiana le Parchemyner. G.
Geoffrey le Parcheminer. J.
Helena Parchemener, 1379: P. T. Yorks.
p. 98.

Johannes Parmyner, 1379: P. T. Yorks.
p. 48.

The surname seems to have
become extinct.

Parchmenter. — Occup.; v.
Parcheminer. William Parch-
mentar was seized for holding
independent views of the Sacra-
ments (1389); v. Nicholl's Leicestershire Index.

Parchmentmaker.—Occup.;
v. Parcheminer.
William Parchmentmaker, Close Roll,
4 Hen. V.

Pardew, Purdoe.—Nick. 'par
dieu.' This is Lower's suggestion,
and may be true. The common
use of the oath might readily
inflict on the user the epithet.
Parde and *pardy* were the later
forms of the expletive. Nevertheless a local origin for the surname
may be forthcoming; v. Purday.
John Pardieu. H.
1808. Married — James Pardoe and
Sarah Birt: St. Geo. Han. Sq. ii. 397.
London, 0, 2.

Pardon. — Nick. Probably a
sobriquet for one who had received
the royal clemency; cf. Outlaw,
Mainprice, &c. Of course it may
be local, -*don* being a common
suffix in place-names.
Thomas Pardoun, C. R., 17 Edw. III.
pt. i.
1671. Bapt. — William, s. William
Pardon: St. Jas. Clerkenwell, i. 252.
London, 1.

Pardoner.—Offic. and eccles.
'the pardoner,' a licensed seller
of the Pope's indulgences.
'With him ther rode a gentil pardonere.
. . . .
His wallet lay beforne him in his lappe,
Bret-ful of pardon come from Rome al
hote.'
Canterbury Tales, Prologue.
Matthew le Pardouner, Close Roll,
1 Edw. III. pt. i.
Walter le Pardoner, c. 1300. M.
Thomas Pardoner. O.
Johannes Queldryk, *pardoner*, 1379:
P. T. Yorks. p. 99.
This surname does not seem to
have lasted long.

Parfett, Parfitt.—Nick. 'the
perfect.' M.E. *parfit, parfet*; O.F.
parfit.

'He was a veray parfit gentil knight.'
　　　　　Chaucer, C. T. 72.
'The Apostle St. Peter, like a perfit workman, . . . first layeth a sure foundation': Archbishop Sandys, Works, Parker Soc., p. 386.
Robert Parfyte. B.
Robert Parfite. H.
1620. Anthony Parfitt: Reg. Univ. Oxf. i. 405.
1717. Married — William Littlebury and Mary Parfitt: St. Jas. Clerkenwell, iii. 241.
1780. — John Parfit and Esther Vickers: St. Geo. Han. Sq. ii. 313.
London, 3, 9; New York, 0, 1.

Pargeter, Pargiter.—Occup. 'the pargeter,' a plasterer, one who rough-casted walls. ' Parget, or playster for wallys, *gipsum* ': Prompt. Parv. Way quotes (in a note to above), ' for lathing, pargetting, tiryng and white casting all the roves, walles, particyons, &c., for pargetments, and zelyng with mortre and here': Rokewode's Thingoe Hund. pp. 146, 148.

1533. James Pergetor, co. Norf.: FF. i. 46.
1617. Edmund Pargitur, co. Oxf.: Reg. Univ. Oxf. vol. ii. pt. ii. p. 366.
1644. Married—Thomas Pargiter and Tomsin Dickens: St. Peter, Cornhill, i. 257.
1761. — John Hooke and Mary Pargitter: St. Geo. Han. Sq. i. 106.
London, 3, 0; MDB. (co. Stafford), 2, 0.

Parham, Parram.—Local, 'of Parham,' parishes in cos. Sussex and Suffolk.

Richard de Parham, co. Camb., 1273. A.
John de Perham, co. Sussex, ibid.
Nicholas de Perham, co. Wilts, ibid.
Ralph de Parham, co. Norf. (no date): FF. vi. 170.
1594. Married — John Parham and Margaret Egerton: St. Dionis Backchurch, p. 13.
London, 0, 1; Oxford, 1, 0; Philadelphia, 7, 0.

Paris, Parriss, Parris, Pariss.—Local, 'of Paris.' A common entry in early registers. Of course Parish is inextricably mixed up with it.

Lotyn de Paris, co. Linc., 1273. A.
Robert de Paris, London, ibid.
Ralph de Paris, co. Kent, ibid.
Roger de Paris, London, 20 Edw. I. R.
Simon de Parys, London, 20 Edw. I. R.
Johannes de Parys, 1379: P. T. Yorks. p. 201.

John Parys, co. Soms., 1 Edw. III: Kirby's Quest, p. 142.
1526-7. John Paris and Elena Hevercroft: Marriage Lic. (London), i. 5.
1743. Married.— Thomas Paris and Ann Sommons: St. Geo. Han. Sq. i. 29.
London, 20, 3, 1, 0; Boston (U.S.), 5, 0, 4, 1.

Parish, Parrish.—Local, ' of the parish,' from residence within its limits. M.E.*parische*. 'Parysche, *parochia*': Prompt. Parv. p. 384. No doubt at times confounded with Paris, q.v.

Willelmus de Parysch, 1379: P. T. Yorks. p. 164.
Thomas de Parysch, 1379: ibid. p. 123.
Marjoria Parysch, co. York, 1455: W. 11.
1787. Married — Samuel Parrish and Eliz. Farrant: St. Geo. Han. Sq. i. 410.
London, 12, 4; MDB. (co. Linc.), 11, 5; Boston (U.S.), 3, 1.

Park, Parke, Parkes, Parks.
—Local, 'at the park,' from residence therein. It must not be forgotten that while Park may be pluralized into Parks and Parkes (cf. Bridges, Styles, Sykes, Dykes), it is just as likely that they are abbreviations of Parkins; cf. Perkins (v. Parkin).

John del Parc, co. Suff., 1273. A.
Roger atte Parke, 1301. M.
William atte Park, C. R., 29 Edw. III.
William Aparke was seized of the manor of Parke, co. Glouc.: Visitation of Glouc., p. 169 (Harl. Soc.).
1611. Bapt.—Eliz, d. Thomas Parkes: St. Jas. Clerkenwell, i. 61.
London, 12, 4, 19, 14; Philadelphia, 81, 19, 5. 37.

Parker.—Occup. ' the parker,' the guardian, keeper, or custodian of a park. Found in every early register all over the country. I furnish but a few instances; v. Park. 'Parcar, *verdier*': Palsgrave. 'Parkere, *indagator*': Prompt. Parv. This surname has almost become a rival of Smith, Wright, Green, Brown, Jones, and Robinson for numbers.

John Parcar, co. Dorset, 1273. A.
Adam le Parker, co. Norf., ibid.
Peter le Parker, co. York, ibid.
Martin le Parkar, co. Soms., 1 Edw. III : Kirby's Quest, p. 205.
Hamo le Parkere. B.
Robert le Parkere. G.
1570. Hugh Parker and Alice Bate-

man, *widow*: Marriage Lic. (London), i. 46.
London, 196; Boston (U.S.), 387.

Parkerson.—Bapt. 'the son of Peter' (v. Parkin); cf. Patterson for Pattinson, or Catterson for Cattinson. Of course, it may be 'the son of the parker' (v. Parker), and belong to a small class of which Smithson, Wrightson, Taylorson, or Hindson are prominent members. But the baptismal derivation is the more probable.

1737. Married — Richard Cook and Margaret Parkerson: St. Geo. Han. Sq. i. 19.
Philadelphia, 5.

Parkes; v. Park.

Parkhill.—Local, ' of the park hill,' i. e. from residence on the hill in the park. I do not know the spot.
Philadelphia, 9.

Parkhouse.—Local, 'at the park house,' the cottage where the parker lived. From residence therein.

Johannes del Parkhouse, 1379: P. T. Yorks. p. 127.
London, 4; New York, 4.

Parkhurst.—Local, 'at the park hurst,' i. e. the wood in the park; v. Hurst. I cannot discover the spot. Mr. Lower says, 'A place in the Isle of Wight.' Of course many places might be so styled.

1581. John Parkehurst, co. Surrey: Reg. Univ. Oxf. pt. ii. p. 95.
1619. Robert Parkhurst, co. Middlesex: ibid. p. 376.
1772. Married — Fleetwood Parkhurst and Ann Danforth: St. Geo. Han. Sq. i. 218.
London, 4; Boston (U.S.), 14.

Parkin, Parkins, Parkinson, Parkisson, Parkeson, Perkin, Perkins, Perkinson, Parkyn, Parkyns. — Bapt. ' the son of Peter,' from the pet Perkin or Parkin; cf. Wat-kin, Wil-kins, Wil-kinson, &c. There are no Perkins or Parkins in the Hundred Rolls, while the French diminutives Perrin and Perrott are common. What may be called the Flemish forms appeared in Yorkshire and the East counties about the beginning of the 14th century. With Perkins and Parkins, cf. Clerk and Clark, Derby and Darby, &c.

Johannes Perkynson, 1379 : P. T. Howdenshire, p. 5.
Johannes Parkynson, 1379: P. T. Yorks. p. 270.
John Perkyn, co. Soms., 1 Edw. III : Kirby's Quest, p. 171.
Robert Perkinson, or Parkinson, 1564 : Reg. Univ. Oxf. i. 254.

Of all the other forms it would be useless to furnish modern instances. Every register has them in abundance.

London, 12, 12, 26, 1, 0, 1, 66, 0, 2, 1 ; MDB. (co. Cornwall), Parkyn, 9 ; Philadelphia, 5, 1, 37, 0, 1, 0, 75, 2, 1, 0.

Parkman.—Occup. 'the park man.' The same as Parker, q.v. ; cf. Bridger and Bridgman.

1668. Married — Humfrey Parkman and Alice Hyon : St. Jas. Clerkenwell, iii. 151.
1790. — Edmund Smallman and Jane Parkeman : St. Geo. Han. Sq. ii. 37.
London, 2 ; New York, 1.

Parlebien, Parlby (?).—? Nick. This name was so generally established in the 13th and 14th centuries that it ought to have left some descendants. Probably Parlby is one of them.

Peter Parlebon, co. Linc., 1273. A.
William Parleben, co. Kent, ibid.
Walter Parleben, co. Linc., 20 Edw. I : R.
John Parlebien, 1336 : PPP. i. 95.
Ricardus Parlebene, 1379 : P. T. Yorks. p. 155.
Robertus Parlebeneson et uxor, 1379 : ibid.
Richard Parlben, vicar of Hemenhale, co. Norf., 1397 : FF. v. 181.
1806. Married—John Parlby and Eliz. Harper : St. Geo. Han. Sq. ii. 347.
London, 0, 2.

Parlour, Parlor.—Local, ' at the parlour,' the servant who attended the parlour, literally, ' the room for conversation,' a sitting-room ; cf. Kitchen, Pantry, Spence.

Richard ate Parlur, 1301. M.
Henry del Parlur. B.
William Parlour, co. York. W. 19.
Symon Parler, for the Barbadoes, 1635: Hotten's Lists of Emigrants, p. 73.
1619. David Parler and Anne Pullocke : Marriage Lic. (London), ii. 78.
London, 1, 0 ; MDB. (co. Hereford), 2, 1.

Parman.—Local, 'of Parnham.' Almost every local surname ending

in -nham becomes -man by corruption ; cf. Swetman for Swetenham, Deadman for Debenham, &c.

1759. Married—Thomas Parnham and Eliz. Ayscough : St. Geo. Han. Sq. i. 84.
1786. William Bennett and Ann Parnum : ibid. p. 385.
London, 2.

Parmelee, Parmele, Parmly, Parmalee.—Local, ' of Palmerley.' I cannot find the spot, though doubtless it exists somewhere in the south of England, nor can I discover any trace of the surname on English soil. It went out to America with the Pilgrim Fathers as Palmerley, i.e. ' the meadow that belonged to the palmer ' (v. Palmer) ; cf. Palmerston.

John Palmerley (aged 20), for New England, 1635, in the Elizabeth and Ann barque : Hotten's Lists of Emigrants, p. 58.

His descendants may be found in most of the cities in the United States in the various disguises enumerated above.

Boston (U.S.), 16, 0, 0, 0 ; New York, 3, 2, 6, 0 ; Philadelphia, 0, 0, 0, 7.

Parmenter, Parmiter, Parminter, Parmater.—Occup. ' le parmentier,' the tailor ; O.F. parmentier. ' Parmentier, a taylor ' (Cotgrave, quoted by Lower).

Ralph le Parmenter, co. Camb., 1273. A.
Robert Parmintre, co. Oxf., ibid.
Walter le Parmunter, co. Salop, ibid.
John Permonter, co. Soms., 1 Edw. III: Kirby's Quest, p. 153.
Roger Permonter, co. Soms., 1 Edw. III : ibid.
John le Permonter, co. Soms., 1 Edw. III : p. 220.
Roger le Parmenter : Close Roll, 51 Hen. III.
Saher le Parmentier. H.
Hamo le Parmenter. T.
Isabella Parmeter, 1379 : P. T. Yorks. p. 264.
Johannes Parmenter, 1379 : ibid. p. 64.
1530. John Parmynter and Margaret Dunnyngton : Marriage Lic. (London), i. 7.
London, 4, 1, 0, 0 ; Devon Court Dir., 0, 0, 4, 0 ; West Rid. Court Dir., 0, 0, 0, 1; Boston (U.S.), 13, 0, 0, 0.

Parnall, Parnell.—Bapt. ' the son of Petronilla.' This was abbreviated to Paronel, and then to Parnel or Pernel. One of our commonest girl-names, it lost character, like Nan and Nanny, by

becoming a cant term for women of ill repute. ' Parnel, a lascivious girl' (Bailey). Halliwell says, ' Pernel, the pimpernel, a flower that always shuts up its blossoms before rain.' Then he quotes, 'But these tender pernels must have one gown for the day, another for the night ': Pilkington's Works, p. 56. But is not the Puritan bishop referring to Pernel in the sense ascribed above ? Endless instances might be given of the name in its earlier and more honest popularity As usual, Cornwall kept to the name long after it had been given up by the rest of the world :

1706. Bapt. — Peternell Michell : Reg. St. Columb Major, Cornwall.
1714. — Petronell Peters : ibid.

St. Petronilla was besought for fevers. Barnby by Googe says :

'The quartane ague and the rest
Doth Pernell take away :
And John preserves his worshippers
From prison every day.'

Petronilla de le Le, co. Oxf., 1273. A.
Pernel Clere, co. Hunts, ibid.
William Peronel, co. Camb., ibid.
Alexander Pernel, co. Camb., ibid.
Johannes Peronele, Hen. III–Edw. I. K.
Ricardus Jannel et Paronel, uxor ejus, 1379 : P. T. Yorks. p. 44.
1528-9. John Thomplynson and Parnell Saunder : Marriage Lic. (London), i. 6.
1680. Bapt. — Robert, s. Arthur and Parnell Dogood : St. Mary Aldermary, p. 105.
1686-7. — William, s. Robert Parnell: St. Dionis Backchurch, p. 128.
London, 2, 12 ; Boston (U.S.), 0, 5.

Parnham.—Local, ' of Barnham ' (?). Probably a sharpened form of Barnham, in America found as Barnum ; cf. Peverley for Beverley ; v. Barnum.

1803. Married — William Hoad and Eliz. Parnum : St. Geo. Han. Sq. ii. 295.
1806. — Thomas Parnam and Ann Bearfoot : ibid. p. 358.
Boston (U.S.), 1.

Parnwell.—Bapt. 'the son of Petronilla,' from the popular Parnell (v. Parnall). This was corrupted into Parnwell ; cf. Samwell for Samuel.

Parnwell Graystocke, of Preston, 1670 : Lancashire Wills at Richmond, i. 126.

1801. Married — William Parnewell and Sarah Cockerton: St. Geo. Han. Sq. ii. 245.
London, 1.

Parr.—(1) Local, 'of Parr,' a township in the parish of Prescot, co. Lanc. 'Brian Parre died seised of the manor of Parre in 20 Henry VIII': Baines' Lanc. ii. 248. Catharine Parr, wife of Henry VIII, was sprung of the Parrs of Parr. (2) Bapt. 'the son of Peter,' from Pierre, commonly in England Parr; cf. Parratt and Parkin.

Alan de Par, co. Lanc., 46 Edw. III: Lanc. and Ches. Rec. Soc. vol. viii. p.370*n*.
Richard Parr, co. Lanc., 1637: ibid. vol. xi. p. 25.
1618. Alexander Parr, parish of Prescot, co. Lanc.: Wills at Chester, i. 148.
1649. Richard Parr, co. Surrey, and Eliz. Moyse: Marriage Lic. (Faculty Office), p. 42.
London, 22; Manchester, 9; Philadelphia, 17.

Parram; v. Parham.

Parramore.—Nick.; v. Paramor.

Parratt, Parrett, Parritt, Parrott, Perratt, Perrett, Perot, Perrot, Perrott, Porrett. — (1) Bapt. 'the son of Peter,' from Fr. Pierre, dim. Perrot or Parrot (little Peter). *Par* and *Per* are similarly found in Parkinson or Perkinson, Parkins or Perkins; v. Porrett. (2) Nick. 'the parrot,' i.e. the chatterer. The origin is exactly the same, the application only being different. In France *pierrot*, i.e. little Peter, is still the name for a sparrow, as Robin with us for the redbreast. The first instance below will prove how early the diminutive of Peter gave name to the tropical bird we are familiar with, and how popular the name of Peter was; cf. *mag-pie*, and v. Philipshank.

William le Perot, 1277. M.
Ralph Perot, 1277. M.
Simon Peret, 1290. M.
Perot Gruer. G.
Thomas Perret. H.
Perrot Loppes: see Index, Wars of English in France, Henry VI.
John Porrett, or Perott, or Parott, or Parrett, 1520: Reg. Univ. Oxf. i. 113.
Edward Parrett, or Perott, or Perrett, 1546: ibid. p. 212.

Parrott is the commonest form in the United States.

London, 1, 8, 1, 12, 2, 6, 9, 0, 0, 1; Oxford (Parrott), 5; Philadelphia, 1, 0, 0, 12, 0, 3, 1, 0, 16, 5.

Parrin.—Bapt. 'the son of Peter,' a variant of Perrin, q.v.; cf. Parkin and Perkin, or Parratt and Perrott, all from the same source.

Lawrence Parrin, of Manchester, *felt-maker*, 1647: Wills at Chester (1621-50), p. 169.
Adam Perrin, of Pendleton, Manchester, *yeoman*, 1666: ibid. (1660-80), p. 204.
Manchester, 1.

Parris, Parriss; v. Paris.

Parrish; v. Parish.

Parrock, Parrick. — Local, 'at the parrock,' i.e. park. 'Parrocke, a lytell parke, *parquet*' (Palsgrave). The modern form *paddock* is a corruption (v. Skeat, *paddock* 2); Halliwell, *parrick*; Prompt. Parv. *parrok*. A.S. *pearroc*, a small enclosure. The surname Parrick is a modern variant of Parrock.

Elwin de Parrok, co. Kent, 1273. A.
John de la Parocke, co. Sussex, ibid.
John de la Parroke, co. Sussex, 20 Edw. I. R.
1553. Philip Parrock, rector of Feltwell, co. Norf.: FF. ii. 198.
1791. Married—William Worster and Eliz. Parrock: St. Geo. Han. Sq. ii. 59.
1805. Samuel Croft and Hannah Parrick: ibid. p. 332.
London, 3, 0; Boston (U.S.), 0, 1.

Parrott; v. Parratt.

Parry.—(1) Bapt. 'Ap-Harry' (Welsh), i.e. 'the son of Harry'; cf. Pritchard, Bowen, Price, Bethell, &c.

Stephen ap-Parry: Cal. State Papers, Hen. VIII (see Index).
John Ap-harry, 1541: Reg. Univ. Oxf. i. 202.
1569-70. Hugh Apparrye and Elizabeth Pynner: Marriage Lic. (London), i. 44.
1584. Richard Jones and Dousam Apharrye: ibid. p. 134.

(2) Bapt. 'the son of Peter,' from Fr. Pierre. This was popularly Parr (v. Parr, 2). Hence Par-kin, Par-son, Par-att, q.v. Hence also the pet form Parry; cf. Charley, Teddie, Willy, &c.

John Pary, co. Camb., 1273. A.
Johannes Parrey, 1379: P. T. Yorks. p. 92.

For a similar double English and Welsh name, cf. Powell.

London, 36; Philadelphia, 31.

Parsley, Parslow.—Local, 'of Passelewe,' further corruptions of a once famous name; v. Pashley and Pashler.

1794. Married — Thomas Cropp and Jane Parsley: St. Geo. Han. Sq. ii. 121.
1802. — William Parsloe and Ann Raine: ibid. p. 262.
London, 4, 2; Oxford, 1, 2.

Parson. — (1) Official, 'the parson.' For further instances, v. Parsonson.

William Persona, co. Norf., 1273. A.
John Person, co. Soms., 1 Edw. III: Kirby's Quest, p. 206.
Walter le Persone. H.
1570. Married—John Bayes and Margaret Persone: St. Jas. Clerkenwell, p. 4.

(2) Bapt. 'the son of Peter,' from Fr. Pierre, popularly in England (among other forms) Parr.

John Parson, co. Soms., 1 Edw. III: Kirby's Quest, p. 142.
1425. John Paresson, rector of Yaxham, co. Norf.: FF. x. 283.
1581. Married — John Willson and Hellen Parson: St. Jas. Clerkenwell, iii. 9.
London, 5; Devon Court Dir., 5; Philadelphia, 7.

Parsonage. — Local, 'of the parsonage,' from residence therein as attendant on the minister; cf. Vickridge, Priestman.

John Parsonage, 1575: St. Dionis Backchurch (London), p. 194.
1789. Married — James Ackland and Phoebe Parsonage: St. Geo. Han. Sq. ii. 16.
London, 1; Manchester, 2; Sheffield, 1.

Parsonson, Parsons.—Nick. 'the parson's son'; cf. Taylorson, Hindson, Smithson, Clerkson, &c. A small but distinct class of surnames. Parsons is genitive; cf. Williams, Jones, &c.

Clemens fil. Persone, co. Norf., 1273. A.
William Parson, co. Soms., 1 Edw. III: Kirby's Quest, p. 104.
John Personson, Pardons Roll, 6 Ric. II.
Johannes Parsonson, 1379: P. T. Yorks. p. 18.
Isabel Parsones, co. Soms., 1 Edw. III: Kirby's Quest, p. 173.
1570. Married—Thomas Parsons and Agnes Smythe: St. Jas. Clerkenwell, iii. 4.

1775. Married — William Horrex and Ann Parsonson : St. Geo. Han. Sq. i. 258.
West Rid. Court Dir., 3, 3 ; Sheffield, 1, 1 ; Oxford, 0, 14 ; Philadelphia, 0, 52.

Part. — ? Bapt. 'the son of Peter' (?), an abbreviation of Parot; v. Parratt. I have no actual proof, but strongly suspect this is the derivation. v. Peart.

John Part, of Hale, 1590 : Wills at Chester, i. 148.
Robert Part, of Ditton, 1610 : ibid.
1618. James Part and Anne Hayward : Marriage Lic. (London), ii. 65.
London, 4.

Partington.—Local, ' of Partington,' a parish in co. Chester. This surname is well known in South Lancashire.

Adam Partington, Barton-on-Irwell, 1541 : Subsidy Roll, Salford Hundred, L. & C. R. S., p. 140.
1616. Married—John Partington and Ellen Foster : Prestbury Church, co. Ches., p. 210.
George Partington, of Partington, yeoman, 1646 : Wills at Chester, ii. 169.
Manchester, 15 ; London, 4 ; New York, 4.

Partree; v. Peartree, of which it is a variant.

Boston (U.S.), 1.

Partridge.— Nick. 'the partridge.' M.E. partriche, pertriche. Cf. Nightingale, Wildgoose, Sparrow, &c. Also cf. Aldridge for Aldrich.

Walter Purtrich, co. Camb., 1273. A.
Gilbert Partrich, co. Oxf., ibid.
Ancelm Partrich, co. 1300. M.
Hugh Pertrich, C. R., 3 Edw. I.
Adam Pertrich, co. Soms., 1 Edw. III : Kirby's Quest, p. 89.
Thomas le Partrich, co. Soms., 1 Edw. III : ibid. p. 91.
Robertus Pertryk, 1379 : P. T. Yorks. p. 201.
1719. Married—Wharton Partridge and Joanna Roberts : St. Michael, Cornhill, p. 61.
London, 46 ; Philadelphia, 17.

Pascall, Paskoll, Pascal.— Bapt. ' the son of Pascall'; v. Pash and Pask. This font-name lingered on in Cornwall long after the Reformation.

Pascowe, son of John Langdon, 1571 : Reg. St. Columb Major, p. 7.
Philep, d. of Paskell Langdon, 1606 : ibid. p. 22.
Richard, son of Paskell Langdon, 1608 : ibid. p. 24.

1585. William Pascoll and Agnes Urlyn : Marriage Lic. (London), i. 139.
1803. Married—Robert Brown and Eliz. Paskall : St. Geo. Han. Sq. ii. 288.
London, 3, 2, 0 ; Philadelphia, 0, 2, 1.

Paschall.—Bapt. ' the son of Pascall,' q.v., a variant ; cf. Pash and Pask.

John Paschall, Suffragan Bishop of Norwich, 1344 : FF. iv. 422.
1578. John Paschall (co. Essex) and Mary Bridges : Marriage Lic. (London), i. 83.
Philadelphia, 10.

Pascoe.— Bapt. ' the son of Pascall'; an English provincialism ; cf. Pentecost, Nowell, Christmas, Tiffany, &c. Pascoe still exists as a font-name in Cornwall, that last sanctuary of decayed English personal names.

Pascow, d. of Henrie Yolde, 1542 : Reg. St. Columb Major, p. 2.
John, son of Stephen Pascowe, 1549 : ibid. p. 5.
Pascawe, son of John Langdon, 1571 : ibid. p. 7.
James, son of Pauscow Anhey, 1551 : ibid. p. 6.
Paskow, son of Thomas Vivian, 1590 : ibid. p. 15.
1725. Married — William Pascoe and Mary Ridge, widow : St. Jas. Clerkenwell, p. 252.
1796. — Edward Pasco and Mary Phillips : St. Geo. Han. Sq. ii. 152.
London, 6 ; MDB. (co. Cornwall), 19 ; Philadelphia, 17.

Pash, Pashson.—Bapt. ' the son of Pasche' (i. e. Easter) ; v. Pask. ' Also, we command that no manner of men walk in the city, nor in the suburbs by night, without torch before him, from Pasche to Michaelmas after ten of the clock, and from Michaelmas to Pasche after nine of the clock': Hist. and Ant. York, ii. 54.

Hugh fil. Pasche, co. Camb., 1273. A.
Joseph Pach, co. Camb., ibid.
Felicia relicta Pasche, co. Camb., ibid.
Robertus Pache, 1379 : P. T. Yorks. p. 62.
Thomas Pasch, 1379 : ibid. p. 114.
Antony Pascheson, Norwich, 1571 : FF. ii. 288.
1770. Married—Edward Wild and Ann Pash : St. Geo. Han. Sq. i. 204.
London, 5, 0.

Pashler.—Local. Doubtless a variant of Passelewe (v. Pashley). It is found in the district wherein

the surname flourished for many centuries.

MDB. (co. Hunts), 5 ; (co. Suffolk), 1.

Pashley, Pasley.—Local, ' of Passelewe,' now Pashley or Pasley, a manor in the parish of Ticehurst, co. Sussex (Lower). I doubt whether this is correct. There is no trace of a Sussex parentage. I suspect it is of Norman extraction, although we need not accept Skinner's etymology : ' à Fr. passe l'eau, sc. a tranando vel transeundo aquam.' This is a meaningless guess. Possibly Lower is correct, and it may be that the name passed from Sussex to Norfolk at an early period. Nevertheless, without proof it is not satisfactory.

Robert Passelewe, co. Norf., 1273. A.
Ralph de Passelewe, co. Norf. (no date): FF. vii. 72.
1450. John Passelaw, canon of West Dereham, co. Norf. : ibid. vi. 93.
1622. Married — Robert Northam and Alice Paslew : St. Jas. Clerkenwell, iii. 51.
1809. — John Pasley and Maria Jackson : St. Geo. Han. Sq. ii. 408.
For further corruptions v. Parsley, Parslow, and Pashler.
London, 1, 1 ; MDB. (co. Norfolk), 1, 0 ; (co. Suffolk), 1, 0 ; Philadelphia, 1, 0.

Pask, Paske.—Bapt ' the son of Pask ' (i. e. Easter) ; cf. Pascall, Noel, Christmas, Pentecost, Whitsunday, &c. v. Pash. The harder Pask is found in Wyclif. ' Whanne Jhesus hadde endid all these words, he seide to his disciplis, ye weten that after tweyn days Paske schal be made': Matt. xxvi. 1.

'Witnesse in the Pask wyke
Whan he yede to Emaus.'
Piers P. 7027-8.

John Pask, co. Oxf., 1273. A.
1634. Thomas Paske, co. Norf. : FF. vi. 285.
1651. Married—Thomas strato (sic) and Paskey Prideaux : Reg. St. Peter, Cornhill, i. 258.
1702. — Samuel Boldwin and Martha Paske : St. Dionis Backchurch, p. 50.
London, 4, 1.

Paskell.—Bapt. ; v. Pascall.

Pasket. — Bapt. ' the son of Pask ' (q.v.), dim. Pask-et ; cf. the softer form, Patchett. No doubt Baskett (q.v.) is an imitative corruption.

William Pasket, co. Berks, 1273. A. New York, 1.

Paskin, Paskins.—Bapt. ' the son of Pask,' dim. Pask-in (v. Pask); cf. French and Italian Pasquina or Paschina.

Paskinus Mercator. C.
London, o, 1 ; West Rid. Court Dir., 1, o ; MDB. (co. Stafford), o, 1.

Pasmore.—Local, 'of Pasmore.' I cannot find the spot.

Adam Passmere, co. Soms., 1 Edw. III : Kirby's Quest, p. 234.
London, 7.

Pass.—Bapt. ' the son of Pash ' (q.v.). One more of the endless variants of this great Easter name.

Richard dict' Pas, co. Camb., 1273. A.
Robert Passe, co. Sussex, ibid.
Nigel Passe, co. Norf., ibid.
William Pas, 1379 : P. T. Yorks. p. 218.
Johanna Pas, 1379 : ibid.
London, 4 ; West Rid. Court Dir., 2.

Passage.—Local, ' of the passage,' from residence in an entry or narrow thoroughfare ; cf. Twitchen, Gore, Goreway, &c.

Adam de Passagio, co. Suff., 1273. A.
Agnes del Passage, co. Suff., ibid.
Walter Passage, co. Soms., 1 Edw. III : Kirby's Quest, p. 154.

Passavant.—Offic. ' a pursuivant,'a messenger,one who attended upon the herald in royal processions or journeys. This seems to be the meaning.

Adam Passevaunt, co. Wilts, 1273. A.
Walter Passavant, C. R., 33 Hen. III.
Roger Passavant. E.
William Passavaunt. H.
West Rid. Court Dir., 3.

Passenger, Passager.—Nick. ' the passenger,' a wayfarer, a traveller, from O.F. *passager,* with intrusive *n* ; cf. Messenger.

1771. Married — William Leutten and Rebecca Passenger : St. Geo. Han. Sq. i. 208.
London, 2, o ; Philadelphia, o, 1 ; MDB. (co. Kent), 1, o.

Passey.—Local, ' de Pasey.' Probably from some spot in Normandy.

Robert de Pascy, co. Linc., 1273. A.
1635. Bapt. — Richard, s. Valentine Passie : St. Jas. Clerkenwell, i. 130.
1798. Married — William Blain and Mary Passey : St. Geo. Han. Sq. ii. 176.
London, 1 ; Oxford, 1.

Passingham.—Local, 'of Passenham,' a parish in co. Northampton.

1762. Married—Robert Passingham and Eliz. Lloyd : St. Geo. Han. Sq. i. 115.
London, 2 ; MDB. (co. Bedford), 1 ; (co. Camb.), 1.

Paston.— Local, ' of Paston.' Parishes in cos. Norfolk and Northampton ; also a township in the parish of Kirk Newton, co. Northumberland.

Eustace de Paston, co. Norf., 1273. A.
Warin de Paston, co. Norf., ibid.
Alicia de Paston, 1379 : P. T. Yorks. p. 50.
1665. Buried--John Paston, servant to John Clerke, *stationer* : St. Peter, Cornhill, i. 219.

Patch.—(1) Bapt. ' the son of Pache' (i.e. Easter), one of almost endless variants of Pasche ; v. Pask, Pash, Pass, Pace, Peace, Pease, &c. For a dim., v. Patchett.

John Pacche, co. Bucks, 1273. A.
Richard Pacche, co. Oxf., ibid.
Robertus Pache, 1379 : P. T. Yorks. p. 62.

(2) Nick. ' Patch,' an old name for the official fool, a very honourable personage in his day. Wolsey had two fools, both occasionally called Patch (v. Douce, Illustrations of Shakespeare, i. 258). It is hard to say which, (1) or (2), is meant in the following :

' Item, the same day to Pache in rewarde for bringing a present,' 1502 : Privy Purse Exp., Eliz. of York, p. 74.
' Item, delivered to Pache, for a present of poyngarnettes oranges,' 1503 : ibid. p. 93.

The following is obvious :

' And ii payer (of hosen) for patche, the kinges fole (fool),' 1530 : Privy Purse Expenses, Henry VIII, p. 86.
1610. Married — Richard Patch and Catherine Major : St. Jas. Clerkenwell, iii. 36.
1614. John Blague and Anne Patche : Marriage Lic. (London), ii. 30.
London, 3 ; Boston (U.S.), 41.

Patchell.—(1) Bapt. ' the son of Pascal,' q.v. This became Paschall and Patchell ; v. Patch and Patchett. (2) Local, 'of Pattishall,' a parish in co. Northampton (v. Pateshall). It is possible this is the true derivation. From Pateshall

to Patchell is but a single and easy step.

1738. Martha Patchell, *pensioner,* died Aug. 15 : St. Dionis Backchurch, p. 306.
Boston (U.S.), 2 ; Philadelphia, 10.

Patchett.—Bapt. ' the son of Pache ' (i.e. Easter), from the dim. Pachet, one becoming popularly Patch (q.v.) and the other Patchet. There can be no doubt about this derivation (v. Pash, Pask, Pace, Peace, Pease, &c.). Patchett is still a well-known Yorkshire surname.

Gilbert Pachet, co. Suff., 1273. A.
Richard Pachet, co. Oxf., ibid.
John Pachet, co. Soms., 1 Edw. III : Kirby's Quest, p. 125.
Henry Pachet, co. Soms., 1 Edw. III : ibid. p. 186.
Cecilia Pachet, *souster*, 1379 : P. T. Yorks. p. 229.
Alicia Pachot, 1379 : ibid. p. 126.
1571. Richard Pachet, rector of Litcham, co. Norf. : FF. x. 14.
1766. Married—Thomas Robinson and Ann Patchitt : St. Geo. Han. Sq. i. 154.
1790. — George Patchett and Eleanor Vaughan : ibid. ii. 39.
London, 1 ; West Rid. Court Dir. 8; Boston (U.S.), 1 ; Oxford, 1.

Patching, Patchen. — (1) Bapt. ' the son of Pachin,' from Pach (Easter), dim. Pachin or Pachon ; cf. Patch (q.v.) for Pach. The *g* is, of course, excrescent, as in Jennings. Rob-in and Col-in are familiar examples of this dim. in England, and Alison (little Alice) in Scotland.

Johannes Pachon, co. Oxf., 1273. A.

(2) Local, ' of Patching,' a parish in co. Sussex, five miles from Arundel. As I find the surname is well known in co. Sussex, this must claim first place.

1422. Thomas Pacchyng : Cal. of Wills in Court of Husting (2).
1783. Married—William Watson and Ann Patching : St. Geo. Han. Sq. i. 342.
1809. — Payn Patching and Sarah Whitehouse : ibid. ii. 420.
London, 1, o ; MDB. (co. Sussex), 4, o ; New York, o, 4.

Pate, Pates.—Bapt. ' the son of Patrick,' from nick. Pate or Pait (Irish Pat). A great North-English name in its day ; v. Patey and Paitson.

Walter Patte, co. Camb., 1273. A.
Willelmus Payt, 1379 : P. T. Yorks. p. 59.

Cecilia Payt, 1379 : P. T. Yorks. p. 227.
Johannes Patte, 1379 : ibid.
1573. Henry Pate and Ann Stebberyncke : Marriage Lic. (London), i. 56.
1574. Robert Pates and Johanna Vynte, *widow* : ibid. p. 58.
1723. Bapt.—John, s. William Pate : St. Jas. Clerkenwell, ii. 140.
London, 1, 2 ; New York, 6, 0.

Pateman, Patman. — (1)
Occup. 'Pate-man,' i.e. the servant of Pate, i.e. Patrick ; cf. Addyman, Matthewman, Jackman, &c. ; a fairly large class. (2) Bapt. 'the son of Bateman' (q.v.), a sharpened form ; cf. Peverley for Beverley or Parnham for Barnham.

1652. Married — Francis Patman and Mary Graunt : St. Jas. Clerkenwell, iii. 88.
1786. — Thomas Harwood and Ann Patman : St. Geo. Han. Sq ii. 383.
London, 5, 4.

Paternoster. — Occup. 'the paternostrer,' a maker of paternosters, rosaries, chaplets, beads strung together for pattering aves. Paternoster Row may have been the Paternosters' Row.

'And thinne was it a pece of the paternoster,
Fiat voluntas tua.'
Piers Plowman's Vision, 9006.

1276. Robert Ornel, *paternoster* : Riley, Memorials of London, p. xxi.
William le Paternostrer, London. X.
Robert Paternoster, co. Camb., 1273. A.
John Paternoster, co. Camb., ibid.
Stephen Paternoster, co. Norf., ibid.
Roger Paternoster, C. R., 17 Ric. II.
1789. Married — George Paternoster and Sarah Collins : St.Geo. Han. Sq. i. 18.
London, 7.

Paterson ; v. Pattinson.

Pates ; v. Pate.

Pateshall.—Local, 'of Pattishall,' a parish in co. Northampton, four miles from Towcester ; cf. Patchell (2).

John de Pateshulle, co. Bedf., 1273. A.
Robert de Patheshulle, co. Oxf., ibid.
1583-4. George Tourner and Katherine Pattsell : Marriage Lic. (London), i. 129.
1596. William Patshall, co. Hereford ; Reg. Univ. Oxf. vol. ii. pt. ii. p. 213.
MDB. (co. Hereford), 3 ; London, 2.

Patey, Paty.—Bapt. 'the son of Patrick,' from nick. (North England and Border) Pait, Pate, or Patey ; v. Paitson. In the North this nick. lasted till modern times ; v. Pattie.

John Pati, co. Linc., 1273. A.
Hugh Paty, co. Notts, ibid.
Robert Paty, co. Soms., 1 Edw. III : Kirby's Quest, p. 120.
'Geordie of Calfhill, Patie of the Hairelowe, Willie Cany, &c.,' 1587 : Nicolson and Burn, Hist. Westm. and Cumb., vol. i. p. xxxv.
Patie Grannie, 1587 : ibid.
'Patie's Geordie's Johnie,' 1552 : ibid. p. lxxxii.
1581. Robert Patye or Patie ; Reg. Univ. Oxf. vol. ii. pt. iii. p. 97.
1706. Bapt.—John, s. Humphrey Paty : St. Jas. Clerkenwell, ii. 29.
London, 6, 0 ; Boston (U.S.), 0, 1.

Patman ; v. Pateman.

Patmore, Pattemore.—Local, 'of Patmer,' a hamlet in the parish of Albury, co. Hertford.

Philip de Patmere, co. Camb., 1273. A.
1802. Married—Edward Patmore and Hannah Isaac : St. Geo. Han. Sq. ii. 256.
MDB. (co. Essex), 7, 0; (co. Herts), 3, 0; (co. Somerset), 0, 2.

Paton. — Bapt. 'the son of Patrick,' from nick. Pate or Pat, and dim. Pat-on ; v. Patten. This was the favourite Border form, and remains a Scottish surname to-day ; cf. Alison for Alice, or Marion for Mary. It must be remembered that Patrick was one of the most popular of North-English fontnames in the surname period.

Agnes Paton-wyf, i.e. the wife of Paton, C. R., 18 Hen. VI.

The following is decidedly Scottish :

1774. Married—David Paton and Jane Blair : St. Geo. Han. Sq. i. 236.
London, 9 ; New York, 17.

Patrick, Patrickson.—Bapt. 'the son of Patrick.' A once great North-English font-name, leaving many descendants ; v. Pattinson, Patterson, Pate, Paitson, Patey, Pattie, &c. The Cumberland surname of Patrickson is almost extinct, but has a representative living in Furness, North Lancashire.

William Patric, co. Linc., 1273. A.
Ivo Patrik, co. Linc., ibid.
Ralph Paterik, co. Hertf., 20 Edw. I. R.
Patric de Culwen, 35 Edw. I : Westm. and Cumb. i. 91.
Willelmus Patrik, 1379 : P. T. Howdenshire, p. 25.
Johannes Patryk, 1379 : P. T. Yorks. p. 47.
John Paterik, 1379 : ibid. p. 141.

1566. William Patrickson, fellow of Queen's, 1569 : Reg. Univ. Oxf. i. 251.

Queen's is, by its endowments, the recognized Cumberland college.

1793. Married—John Patrick and Mary Ann Mills : St. Geo. Han. Sq. ii. 103.
London, 15, 0; Scales (Ulverston), 0, 1 ; Philadelphia, 17, 0.

Pattemore ; v. Patmore.

Patten, Patton.—Bapt. 'the son of Patrick,' from the nick. Pate, and dim. Patt-in or Patt-on ; v. Paton and Pattinson. Mr. Lower quotes Burke's Landed Gentry to the following effect :

'Richard Patten, son and heir of Richard Patten, was of Patine, or Patten, near Chelmsford, co. Essex, in 1119. From him the Pattens of Bank Hall, co. Lanc., claim lineal descent' : Patr. Brit. p. 258.

I do not assert that this is true or false. All I say is that the Scottish and North-English Pattens have no local derivation, but are the sons of Patrick.

1583. Edward Patten and Dorothy Wainforde : Marriage Lic. (London), i. 122.
1695. Bapt.—Martha, d. Thomas Patton : St. Jas. Clerkenwell, i. 361.
London, 10, 4 ; New York, 21, 22.

Pattenden.—Local, 'of Pattenden.' I do not know where the spot is located.

Henry Pattenden, or Battenden, B.A., 1582-3 : Reg. Univ. Oxf. vol. ii. pt. iii. p. 112.
1790. Married — George Fowle and Margaret Pattenden : St. Geo. Han. Sq. iii. 39.
London, 3.

Pattenmaker, Pattener.—Occup. 'the pattener,' i.e. a maker of pattens. 'Pateyne, of tymbyre or yron to walke with, *calopodium*' : Prompt. Parv. 'Calopifex, a maker of patens or styltes' : Ortus. 'Paten-maker, *patinier*' : Palsg. Mr. Way says : 'Used by ecclesiastics when treading the cold pavement of a church,' and quotes church accounts of St. Mary Hill, London, 1491, 'for ii pair of pattens for the priests.' But he adds that they were part of every gentleman's costume. In 1464 the Patynmakers of London alleged as a grievance that the 'fletchers alone could use aspen wood, the lightest tymbre to make of patyns and clogges': Rot. Parl. iv. 567.

'Alys easy a gay tale-teller,
Also Peter Patynmaker.'
Cocke Lorelle's Bote.

John Rykedon,*patynmaker*,1412:RR.1.
Robert Patener, et Mariona uxor ejus, co. York. W. 11.
James Patynmakere. S.
1641. John Pattener and Anne Rainer: Marriage Lic. (London), ii. 256.

Patterson; v. Pattinson.

Pattie, Patty.—Bapt. 'the son of Patrick,' from nick. Pate, dim. Patie and Pattie; v. Patey for instances. Chiefly found in Northumberland, as would be expected.

1795. Married — James Hannam and Martha Patty: St. Geo. Han. Sq. ii. 129.
1804. — Philip Hind and Lucy Pattey: ibid. p. 309.
London, 1, 0; Newcastle, 3, 0; New York, 0, 1.

Pattinson, Pattison, Patteson, Pattisson, Patterson, Paterson.—Bapt. 'the son of Patrick' (q.v.), from the nick. Pate and dim. Patt-in; cf. Colin, Robin. Patterson is a corruption of Pattinson; cf. Matterson, Dickerson, Catterson, for Mattinson, Dickinson, Catterson. Patrick was a great North-English font-name in the surname period. It would be useless furnishing many instances. Sufficient will be found under Pate, Patten, Paton, &c.

Patricius Syke, 1379: P. T. Yorks. p. 263.
Patricius Hyrd, 1379: ibid. p. 268.
Patricius et uxor, 1379: ibid.
Robert Pattensone, co. York. W. 15.
1598. Bapt. — Margaret, d. William Pattinson: St. Jas. Clerkenwell, i. 34.
1614. — Hector, s. Daniell Pattisonne: ibid. i. 69.
1697. Thomas Paterson, rector of Welborne, co. Norf.: FF. ii. 453.
London, 5, 15, 4, 3, 20, 20; New York, 0, 9, 3, 0, 151, 21.

Patton; v. Patten.

Paul, Paulson, Pawle.—Bapt. 'the son of Paul'; v. Pawson.

Stephen Paul, co. Notts, 1273. A.
1521. John Pawle: Reg. Univ. Oxf. i. 120.
1588. John Paule and Agnes Haywarde: Marriage Lic. (London), i. 174.
1702. Bapt.—Eliz., d. Richard Paulson: St. Jas. Clerkenwell, ii. 7.
Sheffield, 0, 1, 0; London, 32, 1, 2; Boston (U.S.), Paulson, 3.

Paulden, Paulding.—Local, 'of Paulden.' I cannot find the

spot. The *g* in Paulding is excrescent, as in Jennings. Evidently a Yorkshire or, at least, North-English local surname.

Johannes de Paldeyn, 1379: P. T. Yorks. p. 284.
1402. Richard Paldene, rector of Northenden: East Cheshire, i. 289.
1672. John Palden, of Bowdon: Wills at Chester (1660-80), p. 203.
1771. Married — William Woods and Ann Paulden: St. Geo. Han. Sq. i. 211.
1784. — William Broderick and Eliz. Paulding: ibid. p. 359.
Manchester, 2, 0; Boston (U.S.), 0, 6.

Paulett, Pawlett, Paulet.—Local, 'of Pawlett,' a parish in co. Somerset.

Isabel Pawlett. B.
Amys Pawlet. H.
John Paulett. H.
Agnes Poulet, co. Soms., 1 Edw. III: Kirby's Quest, p. 171.
1579. Anthony Paulet, co. Soms.: Reg. Univ. Oxf. vol. ii. pt. ii. p. 91.
1580. George Paulet, co. Soms.: ibid.
1742. Bapt. — John, s. Thomas Pawlet: St. Jas. Clerkenwell, ii. 258.
Crockford, 1, 0, 1.

Pauley, Pauly; v. Pawley.

Paulin, Pawlin, Paullin, Pauline, Pauling, Pawling.—Bapt. 'the son of Paul,' from the dim. Paul-in; cf. Colin, Rob-in. The *g* in Pauling is, of course, excrescent; cf. Jennings.

Paulinus de Bointon, co. Oxf., 1273. A.
Paulin de Basset, co. Oxf., ibid.
Augustin fil. Paulin, co. Hunts, ibid.
Roger Paulyn, co. Oxf., ibid.
Poleyn le Webbe, co. Soms., 1 Edw. III: Kirby's Quest, p. 125.
John Paulyn, co. Soms., 1 Edw. III: ibid. p. 18.
William Pawelyn, 1397: Preston Guild Rolls, p. 1.
1581-2. Thomas Pawlyn and Eliz. Hope: Marriage Lic. (London), i. 107.
1607. William Paulinge, co. Worc.: Reg. Univ. Oxf. vol. ii. pt. ii. p. 299.
1702. Bapt.—Adam, s. William Paulin: St. Jas. Clerkenwell, ii. 9.
London, 2, 0, 0, 0, 0, 0; Oxford (Pauling), 2; Philadelphia, 5, 0, 18, 4, 2, 3.

Paulson; v. Paul.

Pauncefort.—Local; v. Pancefoot.

Pauper.—Nick. 'the pauper'; v. Power.

Mathew le Pauper, London, 1273. A.
William le Pauper, co. Oxf., ibid.

Pavely.—Local, 'of Pavely.' I cannot find the place.

John de Pavely, co. Norf., 1273. A.
Robert de Pavely, co. Bucks, ibid.
Geoffrey de Pavely, co. Oxf., ibid.
Reginald de Pavely, co. Wilts, 20 Edw. I. R.
Walter de Pavely, co. Soms., 1 Edw. III: Kirby's Quest, p. 84.
1572-3. John Paveley and Eliz. Spryver: Marriage Lic. (London), i. 55.
1800. Married — Mark Scadding and Ann Pavely: St. Geo. Han. Sq. ii. 224. London, 6.

Pavett, Pavitt.—Bapt. 'the son of Pavia' (q.v.), popularly Pavey, dim. Pav-ette.

1591. Buried—Edward, s. John Pavet, *cuntryman*: St. Peter, Cornhill, i. 139.
1763. Married — Joseph Stafford and Jane Pavet: St. Geo. Han. Sq. i. 121.
1805. — Charles Pavitt and Ann Wykes: ibid. ii. 331.
London, 2, 7; Philadelphia, 0, 6.

Pavia, Pavey, Pavy, Pavie.—Bapt. 'the son of Pavia,' popularly Pavey. Probably closely related to Paulina (v. Yonge, i. 351). Lat. Parva. With the diminutives Pavin and Pavett (q.v.), cf. Paulin and Paulett, strengthening the view taken above.

Pavia, widow of Robert de Grinsdale, E. and F., co. Cumb., p. 155.
'In the 12th year of King Henry III, Radulph, the son of said William de Bochardby, entered to the seignory. His sisters Alice, Pavy, and Agnes were his heirs': ibid. p. 102.
1604. Richard Pavye, London: Reg. Univ. Oxf. pt. ii. p. 277.
1614. Buried — Martha, d. Thomas Pavie: St. Dionis Backchurch, p. 212.
1747. Married — William Pavey and Susanna Winch: St. Geo. Han. Sq. i. 38.
London, 2, 4, 2, 0; New York, 0, 0, 0, 2.

Pavier, Pavyer, Paver, Paviour.—Occup. 'the pavior,' more correctly paver (cf. *sawyer* and *lawyer* for *saw-er* and *law-er*), a maker of pavements.

Gerard le Pavier. E.
1621. Tristram Pavier, co. Soms.: Reg. Univ. Oxf. vol. ii. pt. ii. p. 309.
1648. Marlion Rithe and Sarah Paviour: Marriage Lic. (London), ii. 280.
1669. Married — William Paveer and Frances Tealor: St. Jas. Clerkenwell, iii. 162.
London, 1, 1, 1, 0; MDB. (co. Soms.), 0, 0, 0, 1; Oxford (Pavier), 4.

Pavin.—Bapt. 'the son of Pavia' (q.v.), popularly Pavey, dim. Pav-in. Lower says Pavin still exists, and is found in the 13th century.

Pavitt; v. Pavett.

Paw.—Nick. 'the peacock'; A.S. *pawe*, Lat. *pauo*. *Cock* is excrescent; cf. *peahen*; v. Pea, Pay, or Poe.

Alan Pawe, Close Roll, 5 Edw. II.

Pawle; v. Paul.

Pawlett; v. Paulett.

Pawley, Pauley, Pauly.—Bapt. 'the son of Paul,' from the pet form Pauley; cf. Charley, Teddie, &c. I cannot find any trace of a local origin. Paul was one of the favourite personal names in the 13th century. Thus I am driven to the above conclusion. Of course Pawley has a very local look.

Geoffrey Pauly, co. Camb., 1273. A.
William Pauly, co. Camb., ibid.
1574. Thomas Haynes and Eliz. Pawlye, *widow*: Marriage Lic. (London), i. 59.
1575. Thomas Pawlie, co. Cornwall: Reg. Univ. Oxf. pt. ii. p. 64.
London, 7, 2, 0; Boston (U.S.) o, o, 1; Philadelphia, 0, 6, 2.

Pawlin(g. —Bapt.; v. Paulin.

Pawson, Porson.—Bapt. 'the son of Paul,' a familiar Yorkshire surname. Dialectically, *all* frequently becomes *aw*. 'I'm going to t' haw' (i.e. to the hall). In Ulverston, Picthall (a common local surname) is only known as Pictaw.

Simon Paweson, 1379: P. T., Yorks. p. 220.
Ricardus Paweson, 1379: ibid.
Thomas Paweson, 1379: ibid.
Hugo Paweson, 1379: ibid. p. 269.
William Pawson, co. York. W. 13.
1564-5. John Pape and Marion Pawson: Marriage Lic. (London), i. 30.
West Rid. Court Dir., 6; London, 4.

Paxon, Paxson.—Bapt. 'the son of Pack' (i.e. Easter). One of very many variants of this once familiar personal name (v. Pack); cf. Dixon for Dickson. In some cases, no doubt, a corruption of Paxton, q v.

1608. William Stanborough and Catherine Paxen: Marriage Lic. (London), i. 307.
1678. Ann Packson, Christ Church, Barbadoes: Hotten's Lists of Emigrants, p. 489.
London, 2, 0; Philadelphia, 3, 48.

Paxton.—Local, 'of Paxton,' two parishes (Great and Little Paxton) near St. Neot's, co. Hunts.
Clemencia de Pacston,co.Hunts,1273. A.

Thomas de Paxton, co. Hunts, 1273. A.
1550. John Paxton and Gertrude Mylborn: Marriage Lic. (London), i. 12.
MDB. (co. Oxf.), 2; London, 8; Philadelphia, 5.

Pay, Paye.—Nick. 'the pay,' i.e. peacock; A.S. *pawe*; v. Poe and Pea.

Elias Paye, co. Devon, 1273. A.
William Pa, *zonarius*, 14 Edw. II: Freemen of York, i. 19.
Hugo Paye, et Cecilia uxor ejus, 1379: P. T. Yorks. p. 58.
Cf. Johannes Pakok, 1379: ibid. p. 218.
1800. Married—Thomas Pay and Sarah Young: St. Geo. Han. Sq. ii. 387.
London, 3, 0; New York, 0, 2; Philadelphia, 2, 0.

Payan. — Bapt. 'the son of Pagan' or Pain. q.v.
Worcester (U.S.), 1.

Paybody; v. Peabody.

Payn, Payne.—Bapt. 'the son of Pain,' q.v.

Paynel, Pagnel, Pennell, Pinnell, Pannell, Painell.—Bapt. 'the son of Paganel' or 'Paynel,' a dim. of Pagan or Pain, q.v. One of the chief tenants *in capite* in Domesday is a Ralph Paganel. The corruptions are many, but natural.

Katerina Paynel, co. Oxf., 1273. A.
John Painel, co. Wilts, ibid.
Hugo Paignel, Hen. III–Edw. I. K.
William Paganoll, ibid.
Fulco Painel, ibid.
Warin Pinel, ibid.
Paganel, or Pain, del Ash, 1301. M.
Robert Paynel, co. Soms., 1 Edw. III: Kirby's Quest, p. 100.
'John Pennel, or Penell, sup. for B.A., 1524: Reg. Univ. Oxf. i. 136.
1619-20. John Smeeth and Anne Paynell: Marriage Lic. (London), ii. 83.
1783. Married—Thomas Weldon and Rose Pagnell: St. Geo. Han. Sq. i. 347.
London, 0, 0, 4, 2, 13, 1; Philadelphia (Pennell), 12.

Paynter.—Occup.; v. Painter; cf. Payne for Paine.

Payton.—Local, 'of Payton,' a township in the parish of Leintwardine, co. Hereford. But v. Peyton.

1594. Edward Payton, co. Warwick: Reg. Univ. Oxf. pt. ii. p. 206.
1606-7. Samuel Payton, co. Kent: ibid. p. 292.
1779. Married — James Payton and Sally Watmer: St. Geo. Han. Sq. i. 304.
London, 3; Philadelphia, 5.

Pea.—Nick. 'the pea,' a peacock or peahen; v. Pay and Poe.
Richard le Pe, co. Berks, 1273. A.
1640. Married — Thomas Allen and Alice Pea: St. Jas. Clerkenwell, iii. 72. London, 1.

Peabody, Paybody.—? Nick. I find no early trace of this name. Paybody seems to have been the original form of the prefix, but what it means I cannot say; cf. Gentilcorps, Freebody, Goodbody, Baldbody, &c.

1615. Thomas Paybodie, co. Leic.: Reg. Univ. Oxf. vol. ii. pt. ii. p. 347.
— Married—Thomas Stubbs and Eliz. Pyebody: St. Jas. Clerkenwell, iii. 41.
1629. — Thomas Mason and Susan Payboddye: ibid. p. 42.
1635. Francis Peboddy sailed for New England: Hotten's Lists of Emigrants, p. 45.
London, 1, 0; MDB. (co. Bucks), 0, 1; Philadelphia, 10, 0.

Peace, Pease.—Bapt. 'the son of Pece,' a great Yorkshire surname. No doubt Pece was one of the many variants of Pace, i.e. Easter, so given because born or baptized on that day; v. Pask, Pace, Pass, Pacey, &c. In Lancashire Easter-egging is still Pace-egging or Peace-egging.

John Pese, co. Bedf., 1273. A.
Willelmus Pece, 1379: P.T.Yorks. p. 286.
Thomas Paas, 1379: ibid.
1566. John Pease and Margery Robertes: Marriage Lic. (London), i. 33.
1649. Bapt.—John, s. John Peace: St. Jas. Clerkenwell, i. 173.
London, 6, 1; Sheffield, 22, 0; New York, 0, 32.

Peach, Petch.—Local, 'de Peche,' probably a spot in Normandy. The same individual is thus referred to in the following three entries:

Almaric Pecche, co. Suff., 20 Edw. I. R.
Almaric Petche, co. Norf., ibid.
Almaric de Peche, co. Norf., 1 Edw. I: FF. xi. 118.
John de Pecche, co. Salop, 1273. A.
Reginald Peche, co. Hunts, ibid.
Bartholomew de Pecche, alias Bartholomew Peche, co. Berks, Hen. III– Edw. I. K.
John Petche, co. Warwick, 20 Edw. I. R.
1807. Married — Thomas Smith and Dorothy Petch: St. Geo. Han. Sq. ii. 377.
London, 7, 4; Boston (U.S.), 8, 2.

Peacock, Peacocke, Pocock, Pococke, Pycock.—Nick. 'the

peacock,' the gaudy, the proud. Probably the sobriquet would not be unacceptable to the bearer. At any rate the surname is common to-day. M.E. *pecok, pacok, pocok, pehen,* and *pohen*; v. Skeat.

Geoffrey Pokoc, co. Camb., 1273. A.
Hugh Pokok, co. Oxf., ibid.
Robert Pokoc, co. Linc., ibid.
Margaret Pakok, 2 Edw. II : Freemen of York, i. 24.
Adam Pacok, C. R., 19 Edw. II. pt. ii.
Walter Pokok, co. Soms., 1 Edw. III : Kirby's Quest, p. 107.
Roger Pokok, co. Soms., 1 Edw. III : ibid. p. 278.
John Pekok. H.
William Pecocke, sup. for B.C.L., 1510: Reg. Univ. Oxf. i. 73.
London, 51, 1, 19, 2, 0 ; Leeds (Pycock), 3 ; New York (Peacock), 13.

Peak, Peake, Peek, Peeke.— Local, 'at the peak,' i.e. the hilltop ; v. Peck and Pick (2).

William del Peke, *pistor,* 17 Edw. II : Freemen of York, i. 21.
Isabella del Pek,1379: P. T. Yorks. p. 76.
Martyn del Pek, 1379 : ibid. p. 77.
1557. Anthony Peake and Margaret Vippan: Marriage Lic. (London), i. 18.
1724–5. Buried—Mary Peak : St. Dionis Backchurch, p. 294.
1806. Married—John Peek and Sophia Pike : St. Geo. Han. Sq. ii. 345.
London, 3, 26, 6, 1 ; Philadelphia, 27, 4, 1, 0.

Pearce, Pearse. — Bapt. ; a variant of Piers, q.v.

Oxford, 12, 1.

Peard, ? Peart.—? Nick. 'the pear-headed,' from the shape of the head. This solution seems strange, but it is highly probable. The surname Pearhead occurs in the Hundred Rolls, as may be seen below :

Robert Perheved, co. Notts, 1273. A.
1581. Edward Peard, co. Devon : Reg. Univ. Oxf. vol. ii. pt. ii. p. 99.
1588. John Pearte and Eliz. Eyre : Marriage Lic. (London), i. 170.
1618. Hugh Peard, of Bristol : Reg. Univ. Oxf. vol. ii. pt. ii. p. 373.
MDB. (co. Notts), 0, 1 ; (co. Devon), 4, 0.

Pearl.—Nick. or personal name; M.E. *perle,* a precious gem.

Thomas Perle, C. R., 17 Edw. III. pt. ii.
1805. Married — Matthew Pearl and Sarah Ellen Morris: St. Geo. Han. Sq. ii. 317.
London, 6 ; Philadelphia, 5.

Pearman, Pearmain, Pearmine, Permain.—Local, ' de

Permond,' probably a spot in Normandy or the Low Countries. As with all other names ending in *mond,* the final *d* is dropped ; cf. Osman, Wayman, &c.

John de Permond, bailiff of Norwich, 1316 : FF. iii. 79.
John Pyrmund, bailiff of Norwich, 1336: ibid. iv. 356.
1675. Married—Thomas Permount and Jone Turner: St. Jas. Clerkenwell, iii. 178.
1738. — Richard Sound and Catherine Perman : ibid. p. 266.
1800. — Thomas Pearman and Mary Hitchcox: St. Geo. Han. Sq. ii. 220.
London, 7, 5, 1, 2.

Pears, Pearse.—Bapt. 'the son of Peter '; v. Pearson and Piers.

Robert Peres, co. Soms., 1 Edw. III : Kirby's Quest, p. 250.
Ralph Peyres, co. Soms., 1 Edw. III : ibid. p. 255.
Adam Pereys, co. Soms., 1 Edw. III : ibid. p. 276.
London, 4, 18 ; New York, 1, 6.

Pearsall, Pearsaul, Piersol, Persoll, Peirsol.—Local, ' of Pearshall ' or ' Pershall,' a township in the parish of Eccleshall, co. Stafford.

Thomas de Peshale, co. Stafford, Hen. III-Edw. I. K.
Edmund Pershall, of Over, 1676: Wills at Chester, iii. 208.
Thomas Peashall, of Checkley, co. Chester, 1634 : ibid. ii. 171.
London, 2, 0, 0, 0, 0 ; MDB. (co. Stafford), 0, 0, 0, 3, 0 ; Philadelphia, 8, 2, 11, 0, 7.

Pearson, Pierson, Peirson.— Bapt. 'the son of Piers,' i.e. Peter; Fr. Pierre, O.E. Pearse or Piers. I furnish examples only of the more peculiar spellings. The settled orthography is to all intents and purposes Pearson, and every register or directory has its instances.

Walter Peressone, co. Soms., 1 Edw. III : Kirby's Quest, p. 241.
Richard Peresone, co. Soms., 1 Edw. III : ibid.
Robertus Perisson, 1379 : P. T. Yorks. p. 152.
Johannes Pereson, 1379: ibid. p. 116.
Hugo Perison, 1379 : ibid. p. 131.
1510. John Peyrson, or Pereson, or Person : Reg. Univ. Oxf. i. 73.
1554. John Peerson and Dorothy Stoderd : Marriage Lic. (London), i. 15.
1629. Bapt.—Frances, d. John Peirson : St. Dionis Backchurch, p. 105.
London, 74, 2, 6; Philadelphia, 79, 37, 8.

Peart, Pert.—? Bapt. 'the son of Perot' (?) ; v. Perrott. A modification ; cf. Part for Parot.

Agnes Pert, 1379 : P. T. Yorks. p. 64.
Henricus Pert, 1379 : ibid. p. 265.
1593. Buried—Emlyn Pearte, of plague : St. Michael, Cornhill, p. 204.
1615. Bapt. — Richard, s. Richard Pearte : St. Jas. Clerkenwell, i. 72.
London, 8, 0 ; New York, 0, 1.

Peartree.—Local, 'at the peartree,' from residence beside some conspicuous tree ; cf. Crabtree, Plumptre, or Rowntree.

Emma ate Peretre, co. Hunts, 1273. A.
Nicholas Peretre, co. Hunts, ibid.
Hutchin Grame, of Peretree, 1587 : Nicolson and Burn, Hist. Westm. and Cumb., vol. i. p. xxxiv.
Mary Peartree, of Aston, 1671 : Wills at Chester (1660–80), p. 206.
1738. Married—John Ward and Ann Peartree : St. Geo. Han. Sq. i. 21.
London, 3.

Peascod, Peasegood, Peasgood.—Nick. ' Peas-cod,' a peapod. ' Pescodde, *siliqua* ': Prompt. Parv. ' Pescodes ': Lydgate's London Lickpenny. Probably, like Freshfish, a nick. from the street cry of ' hot peascods.' It still remains with us as a surname ; cf. Peppercorn and Barleycorn. Peasegood is a manifest corruption.

1502. 'Item, to wif of William Greneweye for bringing a present of peesecoddes to the Quene, 11s ': Privy Purse Exp., Elizabeth of York, p. 16.
1443. Godwin Pescod, of Norwich : FF. iv. 170.
1622. William Emerton and Mabell Peascodd : Marriage Lic. (London), ii. 119.
1664. Married—William Spencer and Katherine Peasgood: St. Jas. Clerkenwell, iii. 117.
1665. Nicholas Pescod, co. Norf. : FF. iv. 365.
London, 1, 0, 0 ; West Rid. Court Dir., 0, 1, 0 ; MDB. (co. Cumb.), 3, 0, 0 ; (co. Linc.), 0, 0, 7; Philadelphia, 0, 0, 3.

Pease.—Bapt.; v. Peace.

Peasnall, Peasnell.—Local, ' of Peasenhall,' a parish in co. Suffolk.

Ralph de Pesenhal, co. Suff., 1273. A.
William de Pessenhall, bailiff of Norwich, 1259 : FF. iii. 59.
1793. Married — John Commins and Martha Peasnell : St. Geo. Han. Sq. ii. 104.
MDB. (co. Northampton), 1, 2.

Peat, Peatt, Peet, Peete.— (1) Nick. A delicate person, a pampered pet ; the older form of *pet.*

'A pretty peat': Taming of the Shrew, Act i. sc. 1.

'I overtook the wench, the pretty peat': Donne's Poems, p. 90 (Halliwell). 'As sick as a peate': Notes and Queries, 1857, p. 382.

I can suggest no other derivation; cf. Sweetlove, Sweet, Leifchild, Leaf, &c.

(2) Local, 'at the peat,' from residence thereby.

Richard de Peyt, co. Soms., 1 Edw. III. Kirby's Quest, p. 80.
1655. Married — Enock Peate and Barbery Salter: St. Peter, Cornhill, i. 260.
1664. — John Peat and Isabel Rosse: St. Jas. Clerkenwell, iii. 117.
London, 10, 0, 4, 1; New York, 2, 1, 20, 0.

Peattie, Peaty. — Bapt.; for Beattie, q.v. One more instance of change from B to P; cf. Peverley for Beverley.

1802. Thomas Peatey and Jane Young: St. Geo. Han. Sq. ii. 254.
London, 1, 0; Oxford, 1, 1.

Peberdy, Pipperday. — Doubtless variants of Peabody, q.v.
London, 2, 0; MDB. (co. Leic.), 1, 1; Philadelphia, 15, 0.

Peck. — Local, 'at the peck,' i.e. the hilltop; v. Peak. M.E. pek, 'the hul of the pek,' i.e. the hill of the Peak, in Derbyshire, Rob. of Glouc. p. 7 (v. peak in Skeat's Dict.). v. Peak and Pick (2).

John del Pek, London, 1273. A.
Henry Pek, co. Soms., 1 Edw. III: Kirby's Quest, p. 162.
Ricardus del Pecke, 1379: P. T. Yorks. p. 17.
Magota del Pecke, 1379: ibid. p. 4.
1590. Buried—An, wife of John Peck: St. Antholin (London), p. 34.
1660. Bapt. — Katherine Pecke: St. Peter, Cornhill, i. 100.
London, 17; New York, 108.

Peckham; v. Packham.

Peddell, Peddle. — Offic. 'the beadle.' German, Pedell. If not of German descent, the name is English by change of b to p; cf. Peverley for Beverley, or Peattie for Beattie.

1801. Married—William Coe and Eliz. Piddle: St. Geo. Han. Sq. ii. 242.
1808. — William Peedle and Sarah Bolton: ibid. p. 384.
With Piddle, cf. Biddle (v. Beadle).
London, 1, 2.

Pedder, Pedlar, Pedler. — Occup. 'the pedder,' a chap-

man, a pedlar. 'Peddare, calatharius, piscarius' (Prompt. Parv.), i.e. one who makes baskets, or one who hawks fish, from ped, a pannier or basket. The market in Norwich was, or is, a ped-market, according to Way, from the fact that the wares were brought in from the country in peds, and thus exposed for sale. Hence in general a hawker or pedlar. Way has many references from the Paston Letters, Tusser, and others to the 'ped,' or wicker basket. Skeat explains pedlar from a diminutive peddle, a little ped, hence through peddle-er to pedler and pedlar.

Martin le Peddere, co. Norf., 1273. A.
Hugh le Pedder, c. 1300. M.
William Pedeleure, ibid.
Thomas le Pedeler. DD.
William Pedman, Pipe Roll, Ric. I.
Johannes Fox, pedder, 1379: P. T. Yorks. p. 13.
1616. Married — Richard Pedder and Ann Gayle: St. Jas. Clerkenwell, iii. 42.
1771. — James Evans and Mary Pedder: St. Geo. Han. Sq. i. 210.
London, 4, 1, 1; MDB. (co. Cornwall), 0, 2, 3; Boston (U.S.), 0, 2, 0.

Peek, Peeke; v. Peak.

Peel, Peal, Peall, Peale. — Local, 'at the peel,' from residence at a fortified house so termed. There can be no doubt about this derivation. 'Peel, a square tower, a fortress' (Halliwell).

Geoffrey atte Pele, co. Soms., 1 Edw. III: Kirby's Quest, p. 169.

Many old mansions still bear the name of 'the Peel' in the North of England. Peel Castle in Furness is well known, and no doubt 'John Peel' of Cumberland hunting celebrity got his name from that spot. The name is still well known in that county. 'Within my recollection almost every old house in the dales of Rede and Tyne was what is called a peel-house, built for securing the inhabitants and their cattle in moss-trooping times': Archaeologia Aeliana, i. 246. The surname still keeps to the North. For other variants, v. Peil and Piel.

1541. Roger Pele, parson of Dalton-in-Furness: Lancashire Wills at Richmond i. 213.

1577. Robert Peel, of Blackburn, co. Lanc.: Wills at Chester (1545-1620), p. 149.
London, 5, 1, 1, 2; MDB. (co. Cumb.), 0, 0, 0 0; Manchester, 15, 0, 0, 1; Boston (U.S.), 2, 0, 0, 2.

Peerless, Pearless. — ? Local. I cannot find the spot. No doubt this is an imitative corruption of some local surname with suffix -levs, the plural of -ley, a meadow. Mr. Lower says: 'Unequalled, referring to character '(Patr. Brit. p. 261). I cannot accept this derivation. It is altogether unsatisfactory.

1796. Married — William Wood and Patience Pearless: St. Geo. Han. Sq. ii. 145.
MDB. (co. Sussex), 4, 4.

Peet, Peete; v. Peat.

Pegg, Peggs. — Bapt. 'the son of Margaret,' from nick. Peg and Pog (v. Pogson). A much earlier nick. than is usually imagined.

Peter Peg, co. Oxf., 1273. A.
John Fegge, co. Oxf., ibid.
Martin Peggi, co. Oxf., ibid.
Bartholomew Peggi, co. Oxf., ibid.
Henry Pegge, co. Soms., 1 Edw. III: Kirby's Quest, p. 184.
Peter Pegge, co. Soms., 1 Edw. III: ibid. p. 262.
Johannes Pegge, 1379: P. T. Yorks. p. 14.
Magota Pegge, 1379: ibid. p. 7.
1680. Married—Joseph Harrison and Martha Pegg: St. Jas. Clerkenwell, iii. 187.
1739. Married — John Pegg and Eliz. Traunter: St. Geo. Han. Sq. i. 22.
London, 9, 2; Philadelphia, 1, 1.

Pegram, Pegrum, Peggram, Piggrem, Pigram. — Bapt. 'the son of Peregrine.' O.F. pelegrin, a pilgrim. The first two instances below strongly confirm this view; in fact, all but settle it. The change from n to m is common; cf. Ransome for Ranson. v. Peregrine.

William Pegrin, co. Camb., 1273. A.
Alicia Pegrin, co. Camb., ibid.
1604. Robert Pigrome (co. Essex) and Eliz. Butler: Marriage Lic. (London), i. 288.
1785. Married — Isaac Pegram and Martha Wyatt: St. Geo. Han. Sq. i. 325.
London, 3, 1, 1, 0, 2; MDB. (co. Essex), 0, 2, 0, 0, 0; Boston (U.S.), 1, 0, 0, 3, 0.

Peil, Peile, Peill. — Local, 'at the peel,' from residence therein; v. Peel.

Q q

1601. Edward Peele, or Peile, co. Cumb.: Reg. Univ. Oxf. pt. ii. 246.
1623. William Peile, of Netherlawton, Furness: Lancashire Wills at Richmond, i. 213.
London, 0, 1, 0; MDB. (co. Cumb.), 2, 2, 1.

Peirson; v. Pearson.

Pelham.—Local, 'of Pelham.' There are three Pelhams, parishes in co. Hertford, viz. Pelham Brent, Pelham Furneaux, and Pelham Stocking.
Geoffrey de Pelham, co. Suff., 1273. A.
Walter de Pelham, co. Camb., ibid.
Roger de Pelham, 13 Edw. II: Freemen of York, i. 19.
1791. Married—Thomas Papillon and Anne Pelham: St. Geo. Han. Sq. ii. 61.
London, 4; Boston (U.S.), 8.

Pelican.—Nick. 'the pelican'; cf. Nightingale, Sparrow, Goldspink, &c.
Robert Pellican, Close Roll, 6 Ric. II. pt. ii.

Pell, Pelle, Pells.—(1) Bapt. 'the son of Pell,' probably for Phil, i.e. Philip.
Walter fil. Pelle, co. Hunts, 1273. A.
William Pelle, co. Oxf., ibid.
1414. John Pelles, rector of Twyford, co. Norf.: FF. viii. 283.
(2) Local, 'at the pell.' 'Pell, a hole of water, generally very deep, beneath an abrupt waterfall' (Halliwell). The evidence is in favour of (1), especially as Pells exists; with the patronymic s cf. William and Williams, Simon and Simmonds, &c.
1724. Married — Robert Bates and Sarah Pells: St. Jas. Clerkenwell, iii. 249.
1757. — John Pell and Eliz. Hunt: St. Geo. Han. Sq. i. 73.
London, 1, 1, 5; MDB. (Lincoln), 7, 0, 9; (Suffolk), 0, 0, 2.

Pellegrin.—Bapt. 'the son of Peregrine' (q.v.); v. Pegram.
Philadelphia, 2.

Pelling.—Local, 'of Pilling,' a parish in co. Lanc. The variant was an early one; v. Pilling.
Wylelmus Pylyng, 1379: P. T. Yorks. p. 269.
Johannes Pellyng-man, i.e. *servant*, 1379: ibid.
1755. Married—John Pelling and Hannah Feild: St. Geo. Han. Sq. i. 56.
London, 4.

Pellipar.—Occup. 'a furrier,' a dealer in hairy skins, a pilch-

maker; v. Pelliter and Pilcher. 'A pylche-maker, *pelliparius*': Cath. Ang. '*Pelliparium*, a pylchery': Ortus (v. Way's note on *pylche* in Prompt. Parv.)..
Miles Pelliparius, co. Camb., 1273. A.
Ricardus Skynner, *pelliparius*, 1379: P. T. Yorks. p. 262.
Hugo Pelliperarius, co. Norf.: FF. vi. 2.
Ralph Pellipar, co. Norf.: ibid. xi. 246.

Pelliter, Pilter, Pelter. — Occup. 'the pilter,' a dealer in furs, a pilch-maker; v. Pilcher and Pellipar. Way (Prompt. Parv. p. 398) quotes Caxton's Book for Travellers: 'Wauberge the pylche-maker (*pelletière*) formaketh a pylche well.'
Richard de Peleter, co. Hunts, 1273. A.
John Pelletare, co. Camb., ibid.
Adam de Peleter, co. Norf., ibid.
John le Peleter. G.
Reyner le Peleter, co. 1300. M.
Johannes Pelter, *merchaunt*, 1379: P. T. Yorks. p. 155.
Geoffrey le Pelter, Close Roll, 50 Hen. III.
1608. Bapt. — John Pelliter, son of Matthew Pelliter: St. Michael, Cornhill.
A rare surname in the 19th century.
West Rid. Court Dir., 0, 1, 0; MDB. (co. Cumberland), 0, 0, 1.

Pells.—Bapt. 'the son of Pell,' possibly like Phil, a pet-name of Philip; v. Pell.

Pelly.—Local, 'of Pelly.' I cannot find the spot.
Elys de Peleye, co. Norf., 1273. A.
London, 4.

Pelton.—Local, 'of Pelton,' a township in the parish of Chester-le-Street, co. Durham.
1805. Married—John Pelton and Cecilia Beckett: St. Geo. Han. Sq. ii. 336.
London, 2; Philadelphia, 2.

Pemberton.—Local, 'of Pemberton,' a township in the parish of Wigan, co. Lanc.
Adam de Pemberton, c. Ric. I.
Alan de Pemberton, 3 John: Baines' Lanc. ii. 188.
Thomas Pemberton, of Whitley, 1595: Wills at Chester, i. 150.
William Pemberton, of Wigan, 1602: ibid.
1619. John Pemberton, of London, *goldsmith*, and Mary Lyndsey: Marriage Lic. (London), ii. 81.
Manchester, 10; London, 12; Philadelphia, 11.

Pembridge.—Local. 'of Pembridge,' a parish in co. Hereford.
John de Penbrigge, co. Glouc., 1273. A.
Reginald de Penbrugg', co. Glouc., ibid.
William de Pennebrigge, co. Glouc., 20 Edw. I. R.
1604. Anthony Pembridge or Penbridge, co. Hereford: Reg. Univ. Oxf. vol. ii. pt. ii. p. 276.
London, 1.

Pembroke.—Local, 'of Pembroke.'
1621. William Pembroocke, co. Berks: Reg. Univ. Oxf. vol. ii. pt. ii. p. 389.
1649. Buried—Katherine Pembrooke: St. Peter, Cornhill, i. 204.
1769. Married — Henry Tatchell and Jane Pembroke: St. Geo. Han. Sq. i. 183.
London, 2; Boston (U.S.), 1.

Pendegrass, Pendergast, Pendergrast, Pendergrass, Pendergest, Penderghest.— Local. Corruptions of Prendergast. These forms are largely represented in the leading cities of the United States. This is almost entirely due to Irish immigration. For history of the name, v. Prendergast.
1758. Married—James Pendergrass and Ann Williams: St. Geo. Han. Sq. i. 78.
1766. — Nicholas Pendergrass and Ann Blagrave: ibid. p. 156.
Liverpool, 2, 1, 1, 0, 0, 0; London, 0, 1, 0, 1, 0, 0; Boston (U.S.), 0, 49, 0, 1, 0, 0; Philadelphia, 1, 6, 2, 0, 1, 1,

Pender.—Offic. 'the pinder,' a keeper of a pound or penfold; v. Pinder.
Edmundus del Rodes, *pendder*, 1379: P. T. Yorks. p. 17.
William le Pendere. N.
1625. Buried—David Pendere, a *clothworker*, in Basing Lane: St. Mary Aldermary, p. 163.
Manchester, 2; Liverpool, 2; Philadelphia, 1.

Pendered, Pendred. Pendreth. — Bapt. 'Ap - Henrich' (Welsh). This has taken the forms given above; v. Pendrick, Pendry, and Penry.
Robert Pendred sailed for Barbadoes, 1635: Hotten's Lists of Emigrants, p. 52.
Lieutenant Pendred, co. Ches., 1644: Hist. East Cheshire, i. 431.
1704. Bapt.—William, s. William Pendred: St. Jas. Clerkenwell, ii. 19.
London, 1, 1, 1.

Pendergast, &c.; v. Pendegrass.

Pendlebury, Pendleberry. —Local, 'of Pendlebury,' a township in the parish of Eccles, near Manchester.

Margaret Pendlebury, of Bolton, 1584: Wills at Chester. i. 150.
James Pendlebury, of Westhoughton, 1618: ibid.
1602. Bapt. — Thomas, s. William Pendleburie: St. Jas. Clerkenwell, i. 41.
London, 2, 0; Manchester, 13, 0; Philadelphia, 9, 1.

Pendleton.—Local, 'of Pendleton,' formerly a chapelry in the parish of Eccles, near Manchester.

Thomas de Peneltou, 1379: P. T. Yorks. p. 284.
William Pendleton, of Pendleton, 1588: Wills at Chester, i. 150.
Isabella Pendleton, of Pendleton, *widow*, 1592: ibid.
Hugh Pendleton, of Manchester: ibid.
London, 1; Manchester, 3; Boston (U.S.), 20.

Pendred, -dreth; v. Pendered.

Pendrick, Appenrick. — Bapt. 'the son of Henry'; Welsh Ap-Henry, abbreviated to Pendry and Pendrick (*d* is intrusive). Henry, Hendry, and Henrick were all common forms in the Principality. Philip Henry, father of Matthew Henry, the commentator, went by the name of Hendry and Henrick in his own circle of friends. He was a Welshman by birth (v. Life of Philip Henry); cf. Parry for Ap-Harry, and v. Pendry.

1788. Married — John Pendrick and Ann Shepherd: St. Geo. Han. Sq. ii. 4.

Pendry.—Bapt. 'the son of Henry' (Welsh Ap-Henry), corruptly Pendry, *d* being intrusive as in Simmonds, Hammond, &c. (v. Hendry); cf. Bevan, Pritchard, Bowen, Bethell, Price, &c. v. Penry.

1605. Robert Jennings and Joane Pendrie, of Hereford: Marriage Lic. (London), i. 298.
1677. Bapt. — Saray, d. of Thomas Pendrey: St. Jas. Clerkenwell, i. 277.
London, 2; MDB. (co. Monmouth), 1.

Penfold, Pinfold.—Local, 'at the pinfold,' a pound for strayed cattle, from residence thereby. Probably the original 'at the pinfold' was the Pinder himself; v. Pinder and Pender.

Robert del Punfold, co. Suff., 1273. A.
Philip de la Pundfold, co. Sussex, ibid.
Roger de la Pundfaude. co. Oxf., ibid.
Philip atte-punfold, C. R., 3 Edw. I.

William Punfold, co. Soms., 1 Edw. III: Kirby's Quest, p. 201.
Richard Punfolde, 1513: Reg. Univ. Oxf. i. 88.
1706. Bapt. — John, s. John Pinfold: St. Jas. Clerkenwell, ii. 29.
1769. Married — John Collings and Mary Penfold: St. Geo. Han. Sq. i. 186.
London, 14, 2; New York, 5, 0.

Penistone, Penistan, Peniston.—Local, 'of Penistone,' a market-town and parish eight miles from Barnsley, W. Rid. Yorks.

Helewise de Penneston, co. Suff., 1273. A.
1793. Married—Samuel Penistone and Ann Barker: St. Geo. Han. Sq. 95.
1805. — Joseph Robinson and Mary Penniston: St. Geo. Han. Sq. p. 326.
West Rid. Court Dir., 1, 0, 3; MDB. (co. Derby), 3, 0, 0; London, 0, 1, 0; Philadelphia, 0, 0, 1.

Penketh.—Local, 'of Penketh,' a manor in the ancient parish of Prescot, co. Lanc.

1363. Jordan de Penket, 37 Edw. III: Baines' Lanc. ii. 255.
'Thomas Penketh, the famous Scottish doctor, was a monk of the Warrington monastery (1487) . . . who, writing with Dr. Shawe in support of Richard against Edward V, brought a stain upon his order in England. He is mentioned by Shakespeare :—
"Go, Lovel, with all speed to Doctor Shaw;
Go thou [*to Catesby*] to Friar Penker; bid them both
Meet me within this hour at Baynard's Castle": Ric. III, Act iii. sc. 5.'
ibid. p. 224.

The surname was found at Warrington nearly 150 years after.

Mary Penketh, of Warrington, 1621: Wills at Chester, ii. 172.
John Penketh, of Warrington, 1630: ibid.
1570. Robert Penkeathe and Anne Brisowe: Marriage Lic. (London), i. 48.
London, 1; Liverpool, 1.

Penkethman, Penkeyman. —Nick. 'the man of Penketh,' i.e. Penketh's servant. Of this somewhat large class of surnames Matthewman (q.v.) is one of the most familiar instances. In this particular case Penketh is a local surname. The spot Penketh is mentioned frequently in Lancashire and Cheshire Records, pt. ii. (v. index of *places*). It is quite possible Penkethman may mean exactly what it seems to represent, 'a Penketh man,' a man from Penketh;

but this class of surname is extremely rare. v. Penketh.

Cf. Robertus Wortleyman (i. e. from Wortley), 1379: P. T. Yorks. p. 170.
1581. Hammet Penketman and Isabell Browne: Marriage Lic. (London). i. 103.
Richard Penkethman, of Warrington, *husbandman*, 1593: Wills at Chester i. 150.
Thomas Penkethman, of Warrington, 1641: ibid. ii. 172.
Peter Penkethman, 1671: St. Mary Aldermary (London), p. 102.

The Penkeths were long settled at Warrington; v. Penketh.

Manchester, 4, 0; Liverpool, 0, 1.

Penn.—(1) Local, 'at the pen, i.e. the pound, fold, from residence thereby; cf. Penfold, Penner. As every village and town had its pound, the name was naturally common. I could furnish many more instances.

William de la Penne, co. Norf., 1273. A.
John de la Penne, co. Berks, ibid.
Adam de la Penne, co. Oxf., ibid.
William atte Penne, co. Soms., 1 Edw. III: Kirby's Quest, p. 134.
Richard atte Penne, co. Soms., 1 Edw. III: ibid.
Nicholas de la Penne, temp. Hen. III : BBB. p. 190.

(2) Local, 'of Penn,' parishes in dio. s. Lichfield and Oxford.

William de Penna, co. Oxf., 1273. A.
Hugh de Penna, co. Oxf., ibid.
Peter de Penna, co. Oxf., ibid.
Warin de Penne, co. Staff., 20 Edw. I. R.

Both parishes are represented in the above instances.

1667. Married—John Pen and Mary Chantree: St. Jas. Clerkenwell, iii. 130.
London, 15; Oxford, 6; Philadelphia, 39.

Pennant.—Local, 'of Pennant,' a parish in co. Montgomery. There may have been some other spot of that name.

Philip de Penant, cos. Norf. and Suff., Hen. III-Edw. I. K.
1504. Edward Pennant, otherwise Edward ap Rees, rector of Newton, co. Norf.: FF. v. 68.

This is strongly corroborative of the Welsh origin.

London Court Dir., 1.

Pennell.—(1) Bapt. 'the son of Petronilla,' which became Peternel, finally Pernel, Parnel, and Pennell; v. Parnall. (2) Bapt.

'the son of Painel' (v. Paynel). The three following are the children of one household :

Thomas, s. of Pethericke Pernell, 1580: Reg. St. Columb Major, p. 10.
John, s. of Pethericke Pennell, 1583: ibid. p. 12.
Zenobia, d. of Petherick Pennell, 1586: ibid. p. 13.
1671. Bapt. — Samuel, s. of Mathew Penell : St. Mary Aldermary, p. 102.
1797. Married — Richard Burroughes and Sarah Pennell : St. Geo. Han. Sq. ii. 164.
London, 4 ; Boston (U.S.), 6.

Penner.—Offic. ' the penner,' or pinder, one who impounded strayed cattle ; v. Pinner and Penfold.

John le Penner, co. Soms., 1 Edw. III : Kirby's Quest, p. 20'.
Willelmus Penner, 1379 : P. T. Howdenshire, p. 21.

Perhaps the two following entries concern the same occupation :

Eborard Penier, co. Linc., 1273. A.
Thomas le Peniur, co. Norf., ibid.

Cf. *lawyer* for *law-er*, or *sawyer* for *saw-er*.

1793. Married — Thomas Palmer and Eliz. Penner : St. Geo. Han. Sq. ii. 192.
London, 1.

Penniger, Pennigar, Pinnegar, Pinniger, Pinnijer, Pinnigar.—Offic. 'the pennager,' an ensign - bearer. In the York Mystery, *pennagers* walked between the various crafts in the procession (v. Hist. and Antiquities of City of York, ii. 119).

Thomas le Penniger. E.
William le Pennager. E.

The following is a curious corruption :

1803. Married — George Pindgar and Lucy Elmer : St. Geo. Han. Sq. ii. 277.
'Mr. Thomas Pinnegar, Calne, 1l. 1s. 0d.': List of subscribers to the Religious Tract Society, Report, 1887, p. 458.
MDB. (co. Wilts), 0, 0, 0, 7, 1, 0 ; (co. Glouc.), 0, 0, 0, 1, 0, 1 ; New York (Pinniger), 2.

Penniman.—(1) Occup. ' the servant of Penny' (q.v.) ; cf. Matthewman or Addyman. (2) Nick. equivalent to Pennyfather, q.v.

William Peniman, co. Camb., 1273. A.
1538. Nicholas Pennyman, *chaplain*, Norwich : FF. iv. 368.

1676. Married—John Faukingham and Catherine Pennyman : St. Michael, Cornhill, p. 41.
1706. Buried — John Pennyman : St. Dionis Backchurch, p. 275.
Boston (U.S.), 9.

Penny, Penney, Penson, Pensom. — Bapt. ' the son of Penny.' There can be no doubt, I think, about the derivation of this name. Pennyson is early found. With Pensom, cf. Ransom for Ranson, and Sampson for Sansom. If conclusive evidence were required for this derivation, we have it in the contemporaneous Penycock (cf. Wil-cock, Sim-cock, and v. Cock).

Hurtin Peni, co. Kent, 1273. A.
Alexander Peny, co. Camb., ibid.
Agatha Peny, co. Oxf., ibid.
Robert Peni, co. Kent, ibid.
Walter Peny, co. Soms., 1 Edw. III : Kirby's Quest, p. 128.
Johanne Peny, co. Soms., 1 Edw. III : ibid. p. 100.
John Pennesone, C. R., 17 Edw. III. pt. ii.
Johanna Penson, 1379 : P. T. Yorks. p. 162.
Mergareta Penycok, 1379 : ibid. p. 51.
Thomas Penycok, 1379 : ibid.
William Penson, sup. for B.A., 1561 : Reg. Univ. Oxf. i. 246.
London, 20, 10, 1, 1 ; New York, 12, 5, 0, 0.

Pennyfather, Pennefather.—Nick. ' the penyfather,' i.e. a miser, a niggardly man. 'Sordidus, a niggard, a penyfather' : Junius, Nomenc. 'Pinse-maille, a pinchpenny, scrape - good, niggard, penny-father' : Cotg. (v. Prompt. Parv. p. 400).

'The liberall doth spend his pelfc,
The pennyfather wastes himself.'
Cotg. (quoted by Lower).
Richard Penifadir, co. Oxf., 1273. A.
John Penifader, co. Bucks, ibid.
Robert Penifader, co. Sussex, 20 Edw. I. R.
Roger Penyfader, London. X.
John Penyfader, C. R., 35 Edw. III.
1795. Married—Thomas Marshall and Sarah Pennyfather : St. Geo. Han. Sq. i. 132.
London, 2, 0 ; Crockford, 0, 2.

Penrith.—Local, ' of Penrith,' a well-known town in co. Cumberland ; very rare.

Beatrice de Penreth, co. Cumb., 20 Edw. I. R.

William de Penryth, co. Cumb., ibid.
Robert de Penreth, 1 Edw. II : Freemen of York, i. 11.
MDB. (co. Westm.), 1.

Penrose.—Local, ' of Penrose,' a parish in co. Monmouth.

1611. Married — Alex. Penrose and Margaret Goldinge : St. Jas. Clerkenwell, iii. 36.
1619. — Rowland Pendrye and Alice Penrose : ibid. p. 47.
London, 5 ; Philadelphia, 38.

Penruddocke. — Local, ' of Penruddock,' a hamlet in the parish of Greystoke, co. Cumb.

Simon de Penredek, co. Cumb., 20 Edw. I. R.
1672. Thomas Penruddock (co. Wilts) and Frances Hanham : Marriage Lic. (Faculty Office), p. 123.
Crockford, 1 ; MDB. (co. Somerset), 2.

Penry. — Bapt. ' the son of Henry.' The Welsh patronymic of this was Ap-Henry or Ab-Henry, compounded into Penry, equivalent to our Henrison, just as Parry (Ap-Harry) corresponds to our Harrison (v. Pendry).

Cadogann Ab-Henry, 23 Edw. I : BBB. p. 507.
Philip ap-Henry : Cal. State Papers, Hen. VIII.
1748. Bapt. — Joseph Penry, *parish clerk* : St. Jas. Clerkenwell, ii. 288.
1796. Married — William Dockwray and Winifred Eleanor Penry : St. Geo. Han. Sq. ii. 126.
London, 1 ; MDB. (co. Glamorgan), 1.

Penson, Pinson.—Bapt. ' the son of Pain' (?) ; v. Pagan and Pain. Nevertheless, v. Penny, which I believe to be the more correct derivation.

Pentecost, Pentycross. — Bapt. ' the son of Pentecost.' Originally a name given at the font to children born on the festival ; cf. Whitsuntide, Nowell, Pascal, and Christmas. The name is found very early. It is almost certain that Pentycross is a corruption.

'—filius Pentecosti,' Pipe Roll, 11 Hen. II, p. 32.
William Pentecoste. co. Oxf., 1273. A.
1278. Pentecost le Gras : Cal. of Wills in Court of Husting.
Pentecost de London. E.
Pentecost Servius. E.
Pentecost de Morton, C. R., 4 Edw. III.
John Pantecost, C. R., 45 Edw. III.

In Cornwall, the home of decayed personal names, especially those that lost caste at, and after, the Reformation, the name was used at baptism till the close of the 17th century.

1610. Bapt.—Pentecost, d. of William Tremain: St. Columb Major.
1696. Bapt. — Pentecost, d. of Mr. Ezekiel and Pentecost Hall: St. Dionis Backchurch (London).
London, 2, 0; Crockford, 0, 1.

Pentlow, Pentelow, Pentelowe.—Local, 'ot Pentlow,' a parish in co. Essex, near Clare.

William de Pentelauwe, co. Essex, 1273. A.
London, 1, 0, 0; MDB. (co. Hunts), 0, 2, 1.

Pentney.—Local, 'of Pentney,' a parish in co. Norfolk, eight miles from Swaffham.

John de Penteneye, co. Norf., 3 Ric. II: FF. viii. 518.
Roger de Penteneye, co. Norf., 1290: ibid. iv. 336.
1805. Married — Joseph Wright and Ann Pentoney: St. Geo. Han. Sq. ii. 318.
London, 1.

Penyon.—Bapt.; v. Pinnion.

Pepin, Pippin, Pipping.— Bapt. 'the son of Pepin'; v. Peppiatt. This royal French name made but little impression in England, and was never properly naturalized. Among the early kings of France were Pepin l'Heristal and Pepin le Bref. The *g* in Pipping is an excrescence, as in Jennings. See, however, Pippin for another derivation of that name.

Richard Pepin, co. Hunts, 1273. A.
William Pepin, co. Hunts, ibid.
William Pippin, co. Bedf., ibid.
Hugh Pepin, C. R., 20 Edw. I.
1793. Married — Thomas Pippen and Mary Evans: St. Geo. Han. Sq. ii. 98.
London, 1, 0, 0; Boston (U.S.), 1, 0, 1.

Pepper. — Occup. 'the pepperer,' a spicer; cf. Salter, Mustarder, &c. Upholsterer has gained an *er*, Pepper has lost one; cf. Pewter for Pewterer.

Martin Peper, co. Hunts, 1273. A.
Ricard Pepir, co. Linc., ibid.
John le Peper. H.
Robertus Pepir, 1379: P. T. Yorks. p. 133.
Margareta Pepir, 1379: ibid.
1573. Robert Pepper and Agnes Lynecar: Marriage Lic. (London), i. 58.

1655. Bapt.—Mary, d. Allen Pepper: St. Michael, Cornhill, p. 140.
London, 16; West Rid. Court Dir., 9; Boston (U.S.), 18.

Pepperall, Pepperell, Pepperill; v. Peverall.

Peppercorn, Peppercorne.— Nick. Undoubtedly the sobriquet of a spicer or pepperer. The second instance below is valuable; v. Pepper, Peascod; cf. 'Old John Barleycorn.'

Geoffrey Peppercorn, co. Hunts, 1273. A.
Ricardus Peperourne, *spysar*, 1379: P. T. Yorks. p. 95.
1430. Robert Pepirkorne, co. York. W. 11.
London, 1, 2; MDB. (co. Bedford), 4, 0; Oxford, 1, 0; Philadelphia, 1, 0.

Pepperman.—Occup. 'a dealer in pepper'; cf. Mustardman. I suspect the surname is now obsolete.

1590. Buried—A son of Andrias Pepperman: St. Dionis Backchurch, p. 200.

Peppiatt, Peppiett, Peppiette, Pippet, Pippett, Pippitt.—Bapt. 'the son of Pepin,' dim. Peppictte. The personal name Pepin, common in France, made little mark on English nomenclature, and the diminutives are probably the result of later immigration; v. Pepin.

1627. Bapt.—Eliz., d. Robert Peppit: St. Mary Aldermary, p. 80.
1678-9. Thomas Holgate and Rebecca Peppyatt: Marriage Alleg. (Canterbury), p. 294.
1794. Married — George Peppett and Eliz. Brewer: St. Geo. Han. Sq. ii. 109.
1797. — Thomas Peppet and Hannah Coldwell: ibid. p. 163.
1800. — William Peppiatt and Grace Nicholls: ibid. p. 218.
1804. — John Fisher and Mary Peppitt: ibid. p. 306.
London, 4, 1, 1, 0, 1, 0; Philadelphia, 0, 0, 0, 1, 2, 2.

Pepys.—Bapt. (?). Like Mr. Lower, I give up this surname in despair. Probably it is of easy solution, but I cannot at present come to any safe conclusion. It is a Norfolk surname.

Richard Pepis, co. Camb., 1273. A.
John Pepes, co. Camb., ibid.
John Peppes, 1602: Reg. St. Dionis Backchurch (London), p. 14.
1526-7. Richard Walker and Johanna Peppis: Marriage Lic. (London), ii. 280.

1581. Fermer Pepys, co. Norf.: FF. vii. 83.
1647-8. Robert Faukoner and Temperance Pepes: Marriage Lic. (London), i. 5.
1660. Edward Pepes, co. Norf.: FF. viii. 144.
London, 2.

Perceval, Percival, Percivall.—Bapt. 'the son of Percival.' Instances in early registers are extremely rare. Probably the following entry concerns the name:

Robert Passingbal, co. Camb., 1273. A.
Maurice Perceval, co. Soms., 1 Edw. III: Kirby's Quest, p. 248.

The varieties of spelling in church registers are amusing reading. I furnish a few instances:

Percyvallus Pensax, 1379: P. T. Yorks. p. 247.
1666. Bapt.—Persefall, son of William Persefall: St. Jas. Clerkenwell, i. 230.
Parcevill Fell, 1720: Annals of Cartmel, p. 260.
1776. Married — Thomas Warburton and Sally Parsivell: St. Geo. Han. Sq. i. 260.
1793. — Joseph Caythorp and Ann Persifull: ibid. ii. 88.
London, 2, 18, 4; Philadelphia, 0, 11, 0.

Perch. — Nick. 'the perch,' from the fish of that name. M.E. *perche*.

Nicholas le Perche, Fines Roll, 11 Edw. I.
New York, 1.

Percival; v. Perceval.

Perckings.—Bapt. 'the son of Peter'; v. Parkin. The *g* is excrescent, as in Jennings.
Boston (U.S.), 1.

Percy.—Local, 'of Perci,' a parish and canton near St. Lo, Normandy. William de Perci is set down as a tenant *in capite* in Domesday in many counties, notably in York and Lincoln (Lower). Percy is one of the earliest examples of a local surname becoming a font-name. In modern times, of course, the practice has become familiar, as in the case of Sidney in England, and Chauncy and Washington in the United States.

William de Percy, co. York, 1273. A.
Peter de Percy, co. York, ibid.
John de Percy, co. Sussex, ibid.
Robert de Percy, 1277. M.

William Percehay, C. R., 7 Ric. II.
Edmund Percehay: Visitation of Yorks, 1563, p. 120.
William Percy, co. Soms., 1 Edw. III: Kirby's Quest, p. 128.
1668. Married—John Percey and Mary Willimes: St. Jas. Clerkenwell, iii. 151.
London, 14; Boston (U.S.), 8.

Peregrine.—Bapt. 'the son of Peregrine'; v. Pegram.

Peregrinus Bernard, co. Northampt., 20 Edw. I. R.
1781. Married — Owen Peregrine and Lettice Cane: St. Geo. Han. Sq. i. 326. London, 1.

Perfect.—Nick. 'the perfect,' very excellent. A modern form of O.E. *parfitt*; v. Parfett.

London, 4; MDB. (West Rid. Yorks), 3.

Perham.—Local, 'of Perham.' A West-country name. I cannot find the spot.

Johanna de Perham, co. Soms., 1 Edw. III: Kirby's Quest, p. 174.
John de Perham, co. Soms., 1 Edw. III: ibid. p. 202.
MDB. (co. Soms.), 2.

Perkin(s.—Bapt.; v. Parkin.

Perler.—Occup. 'the pearler,' seemingly a dealer in pearls. M.E. *perle*.

Thomas le Perler, London. X.
Margareta Perler, 1379: P. T. Yorks. p. 270.
Johannes Pyrler, 1379: ibid. p. 271.
William Pirler, co. York. W. 2.

Permain; v. Pearman.

Perot; v. Parratt, Perrott.

Perowne.—Bapt. 'the son of Peter,' from O.F. dim. Perron (v. Perrin). The form Perowne was introduced into England by a French family who settled at Norwich after the Revocation of the Edict of Nantes. Several members of this family now occupy high positions in the Anglican Church.
Crockford, 3.

Perrier; v. Perryer.

Perrin, Perrins, Perring, Perrings, Perren, Perin. — Bapt. 'the son of Peter,' from O.F. Pierre, dim. Per-in or Per-on.

Perina Clanvowe, Close Roll, 20 Ric. II. pt. i.
'The wife of Peryn.' Manor of Ashton-under-Lyne: Cheth. Soc. p. 97.

The list in the London Directory (of English descent, not counting foreigners) is conclusive proof of the popularity of this pet-form of Peter; v. Perowne. The *g* in Perring and Perrings, of course, is excrescent; cf. Jennings.

William Peron, co. Linc., 1273. A.
John Perin, co. Camb., ibid.
Perand serviens Johannes de Hyperon: 1379: P. T. Yorks. p. 96.

As might be expected, Perin lingered longest in Cornwall.

1524. John Peron and Alice Champyon: Marriage Lic. (London), p. 10.
1546. William Perynne and Eliz. Russell: ibid. p. 4.
1578. Married—James Nankevell and Peren Eves: Reg. St. Columb Major, p. 140.
1606. — Richard Jeninges and Jone Perrin: St. Mary Aldermary (London), p. 11.
London, 25, 1, 2, 1, 4, 0; Boston (U.S.), 14, 4, 0, 0, 0, 2.

Perrott, Perrot.—Bapt. 'the son of Peter,' from nick. Pierre, dim. Perr-ot; v. Parratt.

Ralph Perot, co. Bedf., 1273. A.
Robert Perot, co. Kent, ibid.
Perrot de Pyketon, co. York, ibid.
Adam Perottessone, 1340: KKK. vol. vi. p. xl.
Perot Tempest, 1379: P. T. Yorks. p. 285.
1625. Richard Perrott and Anne Tilly: Marriage Lic. (London), i. 154.
1662. Bapt.—Eliz., d. Adam Perrott: St. Jas. Clerkenwell, i. 215.
London, 9, 0; Philadelphia, 1, 5.

Perry.—(1) Local, 'at the pery,' i.e. the pear-tree; v. Pury.

'And thus I let him sitting in the pery, And January and May roming ful mery.' Chaucer, C. T. 10091.

Walter atte-pyrie, co. Oxf., 1273. A.
Roger de la Peyre, co. Camb., ibid.
Richard de la Pirie, co. Oxf., ibid.
Richard atte Pyrye, co. Soms., 1 Edw. III: Kirby's Quest, p. 106.
William atte Perye, C. R., 26 Edw. III.

(2) Bapt. 'the son of Perry,' i.e. Peter, from O.F. Pierre, rendered popular in England as Perry; v. Perryman.

John Pery, co. Oxf., 1273. A.
1619. Daniel Perry and Eliz. Pye: Marriage Lic. (London), ii. 72.
1644. Bapt. — Thomas, s. William Perry: St. Peter, Cornhill, i. 90.
London, 91; Philadelphia, 116.

Perryer, Perrier, Purrier.—Local, 'at the pear-tree.' F. *poirier*, a pear-tree; cf. Perry (1) and Pear-tree.

Robert del Perer, London, 1273. A.
Ernulph del Perer, co. Wilts, ibid.
Roger de la Perere, co. Salop, ibid.
1592. Henry Gourney and Margaret Perryer: Marriage Lic. (London), i. 199.
1610. Married — William Rivis and Mary Purryor: St.Jas.Clerkenwell, iii. 36.
London, 1, 4, 3; New York, 0, 1, 1.

Perryman.—(1) Occup. 'the servant of Perry,' i.e. Peter; v. Perry (2); cf. Matthewman and Addyman. No relation with the growth or sale of pears, or the making of perry. The following were members of one household:

Petrus Baylle, *taverner*, Johanna uxor ejus, 1379: P. T. Yorks. p. 100.
Johannes Perys-man, 1379: ibid.
Robertus Perys-man, 1379: ibid.
Alicia serviens dicti Petri, 1379: ibid.
Johannes serviens Petri,1379: ibid. p.215.

Perys here is Piers, but the favourite form was Perry (i.e. Pierre).

William Peryman, co. Camb., 1273. A.

(2) Occup. 'a man who looked after the pear orchard'; v. Pury.

Adam Puryman, co. Soms., 1 Edw. III: Kirby's Quest, p. 125.
1580-1. John Perryman and Rose Griffyn, *widow*: Marriage Lic. (London), i. 99.
1600. Married — Richard Perryman and Anne Stewardson: St. Jas. Clerkenwell, iii. 24.
London, 6.

Pershouse, Purshouse. — Local, 'of the purse-house' (?), a Staffordshire name. The suffix is, of course, -*house*. Like Counting-house (q.v.), it probably means the office where the purser received and paid accounts for his lord. Thus Thomas or William 'de la Purse-house' would easily originate a surname.

William Persehouse, co. Staff., 1589: Reg. Univ. Oxf. vol. ii. pt. ii. p. 169.
1806. Married—John Gray and Mary Pearcehouse: St. Geo. Han. Sq. ii. 344.
MDB. (co. Stafford), 6, 3.

Persoll.—Local; v. Pearsall.

Pescott, Peskett. — Nick. 'Peascod,' q.v.; a natural corruption.

London, 1, 2.

Pessoner. — Occup. 'le pessoner,' i.e. the fisher. The pessoners and mariners went together in the York Pageant (v. York Mystery Plays, p. xx).

Egeas Fisher, alias Pessoner,was Mayor of Gloucester in 1241 : Rudder's Glouc. p. 113.
Ralf le Pecimer was bailiff of Norwich in 1239 : Bromefield's Norfolk, iii. 58.

A similar corruption is furnished in one of the instances below:

William le Pessoner, or Pessimer, co. Northampt., 1273. A.
Robert Pessoner, London, 20 Edw. I. R.
Richard le Pessoner, 1303. M.
Henry le Pessoner. C.

Pester.—Occup. 'le pestour,' i.e. the baker, pastry-cook.

Herman le Pestur, co. Norf., 1273. A.
Richard le Pester, co. Bedf., ibid.
John le Pestour, co. Oxf., ibid.
1371. Walter le Pestour, Pistor, or Baker, Norwich : FF. iv. 109.
Reginald le Pesthur, co. Linc., 20 Edw. I. R.
1599. Bapt. — Marie, d. Alexander Pistore : St. Antholin (London), p. 40.
1736. Married—John Hayes and Eliz. Pistar : St. Geo. Han. Sq. i. 17.
London, 1 ; Philadelphia, 6.

Petch.—Local ; v. Peach.

Peter, Peters, Peterson.— Bapt. 'the son of Peter.' This personal name has naturally been the parent of many forms and variations; cf. Parkin, Parnall, Perkin, Perkinson, Parkinson, Peterman, &c.

Henry fil. Pet', co. Camb., 1273. A.
Simon fil. Pet', co. Camb., ibid.
William Petres, co. Soms., 1 Edw. III : Kirby's Quest, p. 126.
London, 5, 37, 2.

Peterkin, Peterken.—Bapt. 'the son of Peter,' dim. Peterkin ; cf. Wat-kin, Tomp-kin, Lamb-kin.

London, 0, 4 ; Manchester, 1, 0 ; Boston (U.S.), 1, 0 ; New York, 1, 0.

Peterman.—Occup. 'the servant of Peter'; cf. Perryman, Matthewman, or Addyman.

1691. Married—Robert Peaterman and Eliz. Ladam : St. Michael, Cornhill, p. 46.
Philadelphia, 42.

Peterson; v. Peter.

Pether. — Bapt. 'the son of Peter' ; v. Pither.

Petherick, Pethick.—Bapt. 'the son of Patrick.' The Cornish form, I presume, of Patrick, where it still exists as a font-name. There is a parish of Little Petherick in the dioc. of Truro, probably from the patron saint.

Pethroke, son of John Trevanan, 1547 : Reg. St. Columb Major, p. 4.
Pethericke, son of John Snell, 1579 : ibid. p. 10.
Pethericke, son of Richard Reynolds, 1580 : ibid. p. 11.
Thomas, son of Pethericke Pernell, 1580 : ibid.
Thomas, son of John Pathicke, 1592 : ibid. p. 16.
1789. Married — Lionel Pethick and Margaret Hanlson. St. Geo. Han. Sq. ii. 25.
London, 2, 3 ; MDB. (co. Cornwall), 2, 9.

Peticurteis. — Nick. for one scant of courtesy.

Walter Peticurteis, co. Oxf., 1273. A.
William Petitkorteys, co. Oxf., ibid.

Petipas, Petitpaw. — ? Nick. 'Little-step,' one who stepped shortly ; cf. Lightfoot, Golightly, Purchase, &c.

William Petipas, co. Camb., 1273. A.
John Petypase, co. York. W. 11.
Thomas Petitpas. MM.
Boston (U.S.), 4, 1.

Petit, Petitt, Pettet, Pettit, Pettitt.—Nick. 'le petit,' the little; cf. Little and Petty.

Roger Petyt, co. Norf., 1273. A.
Hamo le Petit, co. Suff., ibid.
Robert Petet, co. York, ibid.
William le Petit, C. R., 2 Edw. I.
Robert le Petit, co. Heref., 20 Edw. I. R.
1552-3. Richard Petytte and Philippa Turke : Marriage Lic. (London), i. 14.
1671. Married—Josiah Petit and Eliz. Petit : St. Michael, Cornhill, p. 40.
1712. Buried. — Thomas Pettit : St. Antholin (London), p. 124.
London, 4, 1, 6, 17, 7 ; Philadelphia, 2, 2, 0, 44, 0.

Pett.—Local, 'of Pett,' a parish in co. Sussex.

Carolus de Pette, co. Kent, 1273. A.
1562. Married — Nicholas Charnocke and Margery Pette : St. Jas. Clerkenwell, i. 2.
1681. Phineas Pett and Sarah Harden : Marriage Lic. (London), ii. 304.
1717. Bapt.—William, s. William Pett : St. Jas. Clerkenwell, i. 97.
London, 4.

Pettegell, Pettingell, Pettingill,Pettengill.—Local. From Portugal. 'Portingall, a Portuguese' (Halliwell) ; v. Pettingell ; cf. Spain and Espin.

1566. Buried—John Pettingale, *clothworker* : Reg. St. Mary Aldermary (London).
1568. Married—Elizabeth Pettingale : ibid.
London, 1, 0, 0, 0 ; Boston (U.S.), 0, 1, 6, 1.

Petter, Petters, Petterson.— Bapt. 'the son of Peter,' an old dialectic form.

1538-9. Married—Petter Skreven and Alys Langlee : St. Dionis Backchurch (London).
Petter Newton : Visit. Glouc. p. 116.
1775. Married—Robert Elliot and Ann Petters or Peters : St. Geo. Han. Sq. i. 251.
London, 2, 1, 0 ; Philadelphia, 0, 0, 2.

Pettifer, Petifer, Pettafer, Pettafor, Pettepher, Pettifor, Pettipher, Pettyfor,Puddifer.—Nick. O.F. Pedefer,'iron-footed'; cf. Dent-de-fer, 'iron-tooth'; also Brazdefer and Firebrace, 'iron-arm,' and M.E. Ironsides. Mr. Lower's 'petite-fere,' little wild beast, is very fanciful.

Patrick Pedefere, 7 Edw. III : Freemen of York, i. 27.
Robertus Pedefer, *gentil*, 1379 : P. T. Yorks. p. 277.
Bernard Pedefer. G.
Fulbert Pedefer. X
William Pedefer. E.

By the close of the 16th century many of the modern forms had come into vogue :

William Petifer, or Petefer, or Petipher, or Petyfre, 1548 : Reg. Univ. Oxf. I. 216.
Robert Pettifer, Sheriff of Gloucester, 1603 : Rudder's Glouc. p. 116

The most curious corruption of all is the imitative Pottiphar :

1777. Married—Moses Pottiphar and Jane Lee : St. Geo. Han. Sq. i. 283.

Pharaoh (q.v.) occurs as a surname in the same register.

1633. Married—John Pettiver and Eliz. —— : St. Jas. Clerkenwell, iii. 64.
1651. — Edward Petiver and Mary Keys : ibid. p. 86.
1668. — William Faukner and Mary Petifar : ibid. p. 147.
1703. — Samuel Pettifur and Ann Aslin : ibid. p. 226.
London, 5, 1, 1, 1, 1, 1, 1, 1, 0 ; Liverpool (Puddifer), 1.

Pettingell, Pettingle, Petingale, Pettengell. — Local, 'of Portugal,' 'a Portuguese'; v. Portingale, of which these are variants ; v. Pettengell.

1622. Bartholomew Pettingall : Reg. Univ. Oxf. vol. ii. pt. iii. p. 412.
1791. Married — Rev. S. Smith and Susanna Pettingel : St. Geo. Han. Sq. ii. 59.
1792. Married—Ward Pettingell and Ann Pettingell : ibid. p. 78.

MDB. (co. Cambridge), 2, 0, 0, 0; Great Yarmouth, 0, 1, 0, 0; New York, 0, 0, 1, 4.

Pettinger, Petinger.—Occup. A North-English form of Pottinger, q.v.

1805. Married — John Pettinger and Sarah Holmes Foster : St. Geo. Han. Sq. ii. 335.
Manchester, 4, 0; West Rid. Court Dir., 1, 1; MDB. (co. Linc.), 8, 0.

Pettit(t ; v. Petit.

Petty, Pettey, Pettee.— Nick. 'the petty,' i.e. small in stature; v. Petit. The people bearing this name in the United States have selected Pettee as a preferable form ; cf. Little, Littlejohn, Small, or Smallman.

Willelmus Pete, 1379 : P. T. Yorks. p. 286.
Robertus Petyson, 1379 : ibid. p. 287.
Richard Peteson, 1379 : ibid.
Robertus Pety, 1379 : ibid. p. 49.
1602. Married — Thomas Pettie and Joane Hanson : St. Jas. Clerkenwell, iii. 26.
London, 8, 0, 0 ; Boston (U.S.), 0, 1, 19.

Petyclerk.— ? Offc.

John Petitclerk, Close Roll, 32 Edw. I.
Richard Petyclerk, c. 1300. M.
William Peticlerk, ibid.
John Peticlerk, co. York. W. 2.

Perhaps not a nickname for small stature or meagre learning (though compare Beauclerk and Manclerk, q.v.), but rather ' an under clergyman,' a vicar. The frequency of the name in separated districts is against the nickname theory. Again, it is significant that the French Petyclerk is met by the seeming English translation, 'Smallwriter' (q.v.). A large number of such translations appear in this dictionary ; cf. Handsomebody, Fairchild, Fairbrother (q.v.).

Peverall, Peverell, Pepperall, Pepperell, Pepperill.—
—— ? 'William Peverel was a natural son of William the Conqueror, who entered England at the Conquest.' . . . 'In Domesday it is continually spelt Piperellus. Mr. Planché (Journal of Arch. Assoc. viii. 196) conjectures that it had a personal signification, and

that ' it is a corruption of Puerulus, which is almost identical with Peuerellus, as we find it written in the Anglo-Norman Pipe and Plea Rolls' (v. Lower's Patr. Brit. p. 265). This would make the meaning to be Littleboy. It does not seem satisfactory. In any case Pepperall, Pepperell, and Pepperill are variants of Peverall.

Pagan Peverel, co. Camb., 1273. A.
Richard Peverel, co. Hunts, ibid.
Sir Hugh le Peverel (sic), 1344 : FF. xi. 53.
1757. Married—Benjamin Pepperel and Mary Grange : St. Geo. Han. Sq. i. 72.
1806. — George Hillem and Margaret Peverell : ibid. ii. 355.
London, 1, 1, 1, 1, 1 ; Philadelphia, 1, 0, 0, 0, 0.

Peverley.—Local, a corruption of Beverley.

London, 1.

Pew.—Bapt. ' the son of Hugh,' a variant of Pugh, q.v. (In the same way Hugh is found as Hew ; cf. Hew or Hewson for Hugh or Hughson.) Thus we find Pewes for Pughs :

1607. Bapt. — Joan, d. John Pewes : St. Jas. Clerkenwell, i. 51.

For several instances, v. Pugh.

Hugh Pue, of Hoole, 1685 : Wills at Chester (1681-1700), p. 203.
Lewis Pew, of Wigland, yeoman, 1698 : ibid. p. 196.
1808. Married — Thomas Collins and Hannah Pew : St. Geo. Han. Sq. ii. 391.
London, 1 ; Boston (U.S.), 1.

Pewterer, Powter.— Occup. 'the pewterer,' a worker in lead and tin : 'Pewtyr, metalle' : Prompt. Parv. ' Pewtrere, electuarius, vel stannarius' : ibid. The Pewterers and Founders marched together in the York Pageant (York Mystery Plays. p. xx). The surname Pewterer has dropped the final er ; cf. Pepper for Pepperer.

Nicholas le Peuterer, C. R., 29 Edw. III.
Henry Pewterer, temp. Eliz. ZZ.
William Peuterere. S.
1795. Married — Luke Pewter and Mary Jackson : St. Geo. Han. Sq. ii. 125.
1798. — Abraham Pewter and Mary Darby : ibid. p. 182.
London, 0, 4.

Pewtress.—Occup. ' the pewteress,' a female worker in lead and

tin (v. Pewterer) ; cf. Huntress and Hunter.

1753. Married—Thomas Pewtress and Eliz. Barber : St. Geo. Han. Sq. i. 49.
London, 2.

Peyton.—Local, 'of Peyton,' a chapelry in the parish of Bampton, co. Devon. But v. Payton.

London, 4 ; Philadelphia, 7.

Pharaoh, Pharoah, Pharo.
— ? Local. A manifest imitative corruption of some local or other surname; cf. Pottiphar (v. Pettifer). The tendency to imitate Scripture names seems to have amounted to a fascination. Probably the local Farrow is the true parent ; cf. Physick for Fishwick. All the above corruptions have found their way across the Atlantic.

1655. Bapt. — Eliz., d. James Pharo : St. Jas. Clerkenwell, i. 192.
1702. — Eliz. Pharao : St. Jas. Piccadilly, p. 22.
1763. Married — Giles Pharaoh and Sarah Vincent : St. Geo. Han. Sq. i. 118.
1770. — William Clark and Mary Farrow : ibid. p. 197.
London, 2, 0, 0 ; MDB. (co. Surrey), 0, 1, 1 ; Oxford, 3, 1, 0 ; Philadelphia, 1, 2, 2.

Pheasant.—Nick. ' the pheasant' ; 'fesaunt' (Chaucer). O.F. faisan. The wilder birds were popular nicknames ; cf. Partridge, Hawk, Kite, Heron.

Robert Fesant, co. Oxf., 1273. A.
John ffesaunt, C. R., Edw. III. pt. ii.
Willelmus Faysand, 1379 : P. T. Yorks. p. 150.
William Fesaunt, rector of Wood Rysing, co. Norf., 1380 : FF. x. 280.
James Phesaunte, c. 1550. ZZ.
1767. Married—Morris Jones and Eliz. Pheasant : St. Geo. Han. Sq. i. 168.
London, 2 ; MDB. (co. Linc.), 2 ; Boston (U.S.), 1 ; Philadelphia, 1.

Phelps, Phelp, Phelips.—
Bapt. ' the son of Philip,' from the nick. Philp or Phelp, whence the genitive Phelps; cf. Jones, Coles, Williams. &c. Philip is early found as Phelip, and nearly all the surnames formed from it are Westcountry.

Richard Phelip, co. Soms., 1 Edw. III : Kirby's Quest, p. 218.
Simon Phelip, co. Soms., 1 Edw. III : ibid. p. 243.
John Phelpes, temp. 1570. Z.
Charles Felpes, 1603 : Reg. St. Dionis Backchurch (London), p. 14.

Margaret Felpes, 1590: Reg. Broad Chalke, co. Wilts, p. 2.
1583. Richard Phelpes, co. Somerset : Reg. Univ. Oxf. vol. ii. pt. ii. p. 129.
1611. Married — Thomas Woodcock and Philippa Phelps : St. Michael, Cornhill, p. 20.
London, 14, 0, 0 ; MDB. (co. Soms.), 26, 3, 2 ; Philadelphia, 16, 0, 0.

Phennemere ; v. Finnemore.
MDB. (co. Salop), 1.

Phethean ; v. Phythian.

Phetteplace. — An American corruption of Fettiplace, q.v. ; cf. Phillimore and Filmore.
Worcester (U.S.), 8.

Pheysey. — Local, 'de Vesci.' For proof absolute, v. Vesey.

1578. Buried—Sara Feseye, *a maiden*, plague : St. Michael, Cornhill, p. 195.
1788. Married — Edward Briscoe and Catherine Pheasey : St. Geo. Han. Sq. ii. 14.
1802. — Louis Humeau and Ann Phesay : ibid. p. 271.
— — Thomas Phesey and Mary Evans : ibid. p. 272.
London, 1.

Philbert. Bapt. ; v. Filbert.

Philbrick, Philbrook. — Local, 'of Felbrigg,' a parish in co. Norfolk, three miles from Cromer ; cf. Phillimore. The variants are easily proved by the evidence given below.

Matilda de Felbregge, co.Norf., 1273. A.
Roger de Felebregge, co. Norf., 20 Edw. I. R.
Robert de Fellbrigg, abbot of North Creak, co. Norf., 1412 : FF. vii. 77.
1577. Married—Harrye Felbricke and Susan Sowthwicke : St. Michael, Cornhill, p. 13.
1652. — John Langstone and Martha Filbrigg, *widow*, of Chelmsford, in Essex : ibid. p. 31.
1658. Walter Tooker and Abigail Filbricke : St. Jas. Clerkenwell, iii. 100.
1792. — William Smith and Mary Philbrook : St. Geo. Han. Sq. ii. 165.
1797. — George Philbrick and Eliz. Ballamy : ibid.
London, 3, 0 ; MDB. (co. Essex), 1, 0 ; Philadelphia, 1, 0 ; New York, 3, 3.

Philby. — Local, 'of Filby' (q.v.) ; cf. Phillimore and Philbrick.

1325. Richard de Phileby, rector of Stokesby, co. Norf. : FF. xi. 251.
1800. Married — Thomas Dennis Philbey and Jane Jones : St. Geo. Han. Sq. ii. 215.
London, 1.

Philcox. — Bapt. 'the son of Philip,' from nick. Phil, with suffix *-cock* (v. Cocks) ; cf. Philkin, and Wilcock or Wilcox.

Ricardus Filkok, 1379 : P. T. Yorks. p. 160.
1613. Bapt. — Peludia, d. Richard Filcockes : Canterbury Cathedral, p. 3.
1617. — Kathern, d. Richard Filcock : ibid. p. 4.
London, 1 ; MDB. (co. Sussex), 2.

Philibert. — Bapt. ; v. Filbert.

Philip, Philipp, Philipps, Philips, Phillipp, Phillipps, Phillips, Phillipson. — Bapt. 'the son of Philip.' There is little need of instances for this batch of familiar surnames. Philip ceased to be popular as a font-name after the reigns of Mary and Elizabeth for patriotic reasons. Nevertheless its earlier predominance has given it immortality in our directories.

Simon fil. Philippi, co. Kent, 1273. A.
Henry Phelipe, co. Norf., ibid.
Alicia Philippes, co. Hunts, ibid.
Ellis fil. Philip, co. Hunts, ibid.
Cecilia Philipp, 1379 : P. T. Yorks. p. 83.
1617. Hugh Fisher and Eliz. Philipson : Marriage Lic. (London), ii. 54.
London, 3, 2, 4, 1, 1, 6, 287, 3

Philipshank. — Nick. Sparrow-legged, from *shank* and Philip, the familiar name for the sparrow ; cf. Sheepshank.

Johannes Philipschank, 1379 : P. T. Yorks. p. 104.

Philkin. — Bapt. 'the son of Philip,' from the nick. Phill (v. Philson), and the dim. Philkin ; cf. Watkin from Walter, or Wilkin from William. For examples, v. Filkin, the modern form.

Robert Philkynn sailed for Barbadoes, 1635 : Hotten's Lists of Emigrants, p. 52.

Phillimore, Filmore. — Nick. of endearment, 'fin amour,' pure love (v. Douceamour and Plainamour). The change of *n* to *l* was common ; cf. Bannister for Ballister (v. Bannister), and *banister* for *baluster*. For instances, v. Finnemore. *Ph* and *f* interchange frequent civilities ; v. Fillpot for Philpot, Filbert and Philbert, Farrimond and Pharamond, &c.

1683. Married — Thomas Foster and Saray Phillmore : St. Jas. Clerkenwell, iii. 200.
1795. — William Phillimore and Eliz. Davis : St. Geo. Han. Sq. ii. 130.
London, 5, 2.

Phillipp(s ; v. Philip.

Phillis. — Bapt. 'the son of Phillis,' i.e. Felicia. The letters *f* and *ph* are commonly interchangeable in English nomenclature.
'And fecche Felice hom
Fro the wyuen pyne.'
Piers P. 2529-30.
Thomas Coline et Felisia uxor ejus, 1379 : P. T. Yorks. p. 67.
Emma Felis, 1379 : ibid. p. 104.
Johannes Fylysson, 1379 : ibid. p. 201.
Alan Nelleson et Filisia uxor ejus : 1379 : ibid. p. 17.
1436. John Phelysson, bailiff of Yarmouth : FF. xi. 325.
1564. Michael Philles, 'plumber to Merton College' : Reg. Univ. Oxf. vol. ii. pt. i. p. 288.
1569. Bapt.—Fillys, d. Robert Grymes : St. Jas. Clerkenwell, i. 5.
1666. — Elisabeth, d. Steven and Phillis Griffith : ibid. p. 230.
1603. Phillis, wife of Ralphe White : Reg. Broad Chalke, co. Wilts, p. 42.
1677. Bapt. — Thomas, s. Thomas Dam, and Fillis, his wife : St. Thomas the Apostle (London), p. 68.
London, 1.

Phillot, Phillots. — Bapt. 'the son of Philot,' from Philip, nick. Phil, dim. Philot. Phillots represents the full patronymic ; cf. William and Williams, Philpott and Philpotts.

Philota de Kender, co. Derby, 1273. A.
MDB. (co. Dorset), 0, 1.

Phillpot, Phillpott, Phillpotts, Philpot, Philpott. — Bapt. 'the son of Philip,' from the dim. Philip-ot, abbreviated to Philpot ; cf. Marri-ot or Emm-ot for Mary and Emma. The name was used for both sexes. v. Fillpot.

Thomas Phylypotte. B.
John Philpot. N.
Johannes Schikyn, Philipot uxor ejus, 1379 : P. T. Yorks. p. 75.
Nov. 1543. Item, geven to Fylpot, my lady of Suffolk's lackaye, viis. *vid.* : Privy Purse Expenses, Princess Mary.
William Phellpot, co. Hereford, 1587 : Reg. Univ. Oxf. vol. ii. pt. ii. p. 159.
1583. John Phillpott and Judith Thompson : Marriage Lic. (London), i. 121.
London, 1, 1, 2, 14, 7.

Philp, Philpp, Philps. — Bapt. 'the son of Philip,' from the nick. or abbreviated form Philip: cf. Peart for Perrot. A North-English and Border form ; v. Phelps.

Philp Gledstanes, 1541 : TTT. p. lxxxi.
Patrik Phylp, 1547 : ibid. p. lii.
John Philpe, c. Eliz. Z.
1714. Married — John Philip and Rebecca Snelgrove : St. Jas. Clerkenwell, iii. 237.
1790. — Sparks Philp and Martha Honnor : St. Geo. Han. Sq. ii. 42.
London, 15, 2, 3.

Philpot(t ; v. Phillpot.

Philson, Phill.—Bapt. 'the son of Philip,' from the nick. Phil.

1601. Edward Phill, co. Glouc. : Reg. Univ. Oxf. vol. ii. pt. ii. p. 253.
Philadelphia, 4, 0.

Phin, Phinn, Phinney.— Bapt. ; v. Finn.

Crockford, 1, 0, 0 ; Boston (U.S.), 0, 0, 42 ; New York (Phin), 1.

Phippen, Phippin. — Bapt. 'the son of Philip,' from nick. Phip, dim. Phip-in ; cf. Colin (Nicholas), Lambin (Lambert).

George Phippen, co. Dorset, 1606-7 : Reg. Univ. Oxf. vol. ii. pt. ii. p. 293.
Elizabeth Fippin, 1628 : St. Jas. Clerkenwell, i. 110.
1792. Married — William Phippen and Catherine Merrett : St. Geo. Han. Sq. ii. 80.
1799. William Phippin and Ann Willey : ibid. p. 205.
London, 3, 0 ; Manchester, 0, 1 ; MDB. (co. Somerset), 9, 4 ; Boston (U.S.), 11, 0.

Phipps, Phipson.—Bapt. 'the son of Philip,' from the nick. Phip. 'Phip, a sparrow. The noise made by a sparrow' : Halliwell. I think this is not the true derivation. The sparrow went by the name of Philip (v. Philipshank), as the red-breast by the name of Robin. Phip was merely the nick. of Philip, and applied familiarly to the sparrow.

1583. Roger Phippes, co. Glouc. : Reg. Univ. Oxf. vol. ii. pt. ii. p. 130.
1587. John Fipp, *saadler*, and Catherine Easterbye : Marriage Lic. (London), i. 160.
Christopher Phipp, of Bold, *yeoman*, 1592 : Wills at Chester, i. 151.
1765. Married — Henry Black and Mary Phips : St. Geo. Han. Sq. i. 147.
London, 19, 2 ; Oxford, 20, 0 ; Philadelphia, 17, 0.

Phizackerley. — Local ; v. Fazackerley.

Phoenix.—? Bapt. 'the son of Felix' (?), an imitative corruption ; cf. Phillis for Felicia, and *banister* for *baluster*.

MDB. (Lincoln), 4 ; Philadelphia, 3.

Physick.—Local, 'of Fishwick.' A natural and an inevitable imitative corruption of a well-known Lancashire name ; v. Fishwick.

1617. Nicholas Phisicke : Reg. Univ. Oxf. vol. ii. pt. iii. p. 362.
1620. Bapt. — John, s. Eliz. Fishick : St. Jas. Clerkenwell, i. 87.
London, 4.

Phythian, Phethean.—Bapt. 'the son of Fithion,' i.e. Vivian. When passing through Bolton, Lanc., on Sept. 27, 1886, I saw ' John Phethean, plumber and gasfitter,' over a window in a street leading to Halliwell.

Henry Fithion, co. Kent, 1273. A.
Richard Fithion, co. Kent, ibid.
Hugh Fifiane, co. Soms., 1 Edw. III : Kirby's Quest, p. 122.
Robertus Fethethyan, 1379 : P.T.Yorks. p. 262.
Hugh Phytheon, of Tetton, 1582 : Wills at Chester, i. 65.
John Fitheon, of Overton, 1613 : ibid. p. 151.
Richard Phytheon, of Moston, 1593 : Wills at Chester, i. 151.
'In the 6th Hen. VIII (1514-5), "William Byrtheles, son and heir of Fithian (or Vivian) Byrtheles," grants to trustees all his messuages,' &c. : East Cheshire, ii. 357.
1624. Married—Thomas Fytheone and Jane Smith : Reg. Prestbury, co. Ches., p. 246.
London, 2, 0 ; Bolton (Lanc.), 0, 1 ; Manchester, 1, 1.

Picard, Pickard, Pitcher.— Bapt. 'the son of Pichard' or ' Picard' ; cf. Richard and Ricard. The commonest form was Pichard, and of this Pitcher is doubtless an imitative corruption. Very common in Yorkshire records.

Roger fil. Pichard : Pipe Roll, 11 Hen. II, p. 41.
Alan Pichard, co. York, 1273. A.
Stephen Picard, co. Northumb., ibid.
Nicholas Pichard, co. Salop, ibid.
Roger Pichard, co. Camb., ibid.
Alan Piccard, co. Linc., 20 Edw. I. R.
Emma Picard, 1379 : P. T. Yorks. p. 207.
Ricardus Picard, 1379 : ibid.
1524. Anthony Sylver and Margaret Pykkarde : Marriage Lic. (London), p. 4.
1784. Married — Richard Pickard and Eliz. Reason : St. Geo. Han. Sq. ii. 366.
London, 4, 11, 8 ; Philadelphia, 8, 5, 5.

Pick.—(1) Nick. 'the woodpecker.' Fr. *pic*. v. Speck ; cf.

Goldfinch, Spark, Nightingale, Crow, Raven, &c.

Simon Pic, co. Suff., 1273. A.
Agnes Pick, co. Hunts, ibid.
Hugh Pick, co. Oxf., ibid.
Thomas Pik, co. Soms., 1 Edw. III : Kirby's Quest, p. 277.
Richard Pyk, co. Soms., 1 Edw. III : ibid. p. 131.

(2) Local, 'at the pike,' a peaked hill ; cf. Langdale Pikes in the Lake district. v. Peak and Pike.

Ralph del Pikke, co. Hertf., 20 Edw. I. R.
1590. Bapt.—Richard, s. Philip Pick : St. Antholin (London), p. 34.
1668. — Saray, d. Thomas Picke : St. Jas. Clerkenwell, i. 237.
1721. — Leonard, s. John Pick : ibid. p. 130.
London, 7 ; New York, 8.

Pickard ; v. Picard.

Pickavance, Pickavant, Pickvance, Pickance. — Nick. 'Prick-advance,' spur forward. We must not be tempted to refer these various forms to the pikedevant or piked beard. 'A young, pitti-vanted, trim-bearded fellow ' : Anatomy of Melancholy, Tegg's edit. p. 533. Found in the portraits of courtiers in the 16th and 17th centuries, it was not an early enough fashion to be immortalized by a patronymic. 'Tis true the following entry occurs :

1600. Married—John Gibbs and Joan Pickedevant : St. Jas. Clerkenwell, p. 24.

But the date itself would suffice to show that it was an imitation of the term or the then prevailing fashion. No doubt her real name was Pickavant. Prikeavant was, no doubt, the nickname of a harbinger, pursuivant, or herald, from *prick* ; M.E. *prike*, to put spur to horse (cf. 'kick against the pricks,' Auth. Vers.), and *avance*, forward, to the front. A herald was one who 'rode to the front.' The instances amply confirm this view :

William Prikeavant, co. Bedf., 1273. A.
1678. Buried—Simon Prickadvance : Reg. Peasmarsh, co. Sussex.

A similar surname is Sturtevant, q.v.

Edward Pickavance, of Much Woolton, *husbandman*, 1662 : Wills at Chester (1660-80), p. 209.

Manchester, o, o, 1, o ; Liverpool, o, o, o, 1 ; Southport, o, 1, o, o ; St. Helens, 3, o, o, o.

Picker, Pecker.—Occup. ' the picker.' Probably one engaged in fruit-picking or in the fields.

William le Pekkere, co. Hunts, 1273. A.
Roger le Peckere, co. Hunts, ibid.
Simon le Peckere, co. Hunts, ibid.
Paulin Peckere, co. Hunts, ibid.
1784. Married — Richard Angle and Mary Pecker : St. Geo. Han. Sq. ii. 356.
London, 1, o ; Boston (U.S.), o, 4.

Pickerdite. — Local. A corrupted form of Bickerdike, q.v. ; cf. Peverley for Beverley, &c.

London, 1.

Pickering.—Local, ' of Pickering,' a parish in the N. Rid. Yorks.

Hugh de Pikering, co. York, 1273. A.
William de Pikering, co. York, ibid.
Jacobus de Pikeryng, *pistor*, 1 Edw. I : Freemen of York (Surt. Soc.), i. 1.
John Pykeryng, co. Soms., 1 Edw. III : Kirby's Quest, p. 87.
Diota de Pykeryng, 1379 : P.T. Yorks. p. 143.
Johannes de Pykerryng, 1379 : ibid. p. 67.
1592. Anthony Pykerynge, co. Hants : Reg. Univ. Oxf. vol. ii. pt. ii. p. 192.
1705. Bapt.—Ann, d. William Pickering : St. Jas. Clerkenwell, ii. 27.
London, 22 ; Sheffield, 6 ; MDB. (North Riding Yorks), 14 ; Boston (U.S.), 44.

Pickernell. — Official, ' the spigurnel' (v. Spicknell), a curious corruption, but not without precedent ; cf. Sturgess for Thurges, Pichfat for Spichfat, or Pilsbury for Spilsbury. Thus may an ancient and honourable name be disguised.

1769. Married — John Tillier and Ann Pickernell : St. Geo. Han. Sq. i. 183.
1781. — Richard Pink and Eliz. Pickernell : ibid. p. 328.
London, 1.

Pickersgill.—Local, ' of Pickersgill.' Some spot in the N. Rid. of Yorks which I have failed to discover.

1679. Married—Henry Boyce and Eliz. Picersgill : St. Jas. Clerkenwell, iii. 186.
MDB. (W. R. Yorks), 31 (N. R. Yorks), 5 ; London, 2 ; Philadelphia, 1.

Pickett.—Bapt. ' the son of Picot.' Mr. Lower says, ' A well-known corruption of Pigott.' This is to reverse the true order. Pigott is a corruption of Pickett, or, more correctly, Picot or Pichot. It is

strange that while the name has ramified so strongly, so little can be gleaned of its history. Camden's derivation from O.F. *picote*, the small - pox, *picote*, pock - marked, freckled, is unkind ; but he gave no authority for the statement. That Picot was a personal name is clear, for Picot, a chief tenant in Hampshire, and Picot de Grentebrig', both occur in Domesday. It is curious, too, to observe that two families in Cheshire, the Pigots and Pichots, ran side by side for some generations, and Dr. Ormerod long ago surmised that both sprang from one common ancestor—Gilbert Pichot, lord of Broxton (Earwaker's East Cheshire, ii. 361). Radulphus Picot (Pipe Rolls, 6 Hen. II, pp. 53, 55). Also Picot and Picotus, as a personal name (ibid. pp. 32, 46).

Picotus de Laceles, temp. 1109 : Lincolnshire Survey, p. 12.
Picot de Tani, Pipe Roll, 7 Hen. II, p. 67.
Picot de Flexbergh, co. Wilts, 1273. A.
Elis Pyket, co. Bucks, ibid.
Walter Pycot, co. Camb., ibid.
Godfrey Piket, co Soms., 1 Edw. III : Kirby's Quest, p. 137.
London, 20 ; Boston (U.S.), 25.

Pickford, Pitchford.—Local, ' of Pitchford,' a parish in co. Salop. ' No doubt the same as Pitchford in Shropshire. In the Rotuli Hundredorum of the county the possessor of that estate, spelt Picheford, is styled Sir John de Picford ' (Lower).

John de Picford, or Picheford, co. Salop, 1273. A.
Ralph de Pickford, or Picheford, co. Salop, Hen. III–Edw. I. K.
John de Pycheford, 1277. M.
Galfridus de Picheford, 1296. M.
1591. Bapt. — Moyses Pickford : St. Jas. Clerkenwell, i. 25.
1599. — Theoder, s. John Pitsfort : ibid. p. 34.
London, 12, 1 ; Philadelphia, 3, o.

Pickin ; v. Piggins.

Pickles, Pighills.—Local, ' of Pickhill,' a parish in the N. Rid. Yorks. I suspect this is the origin, and that there was an irresistible tendency to imitate the dictionary word on the part of the bearers of the surname. Several

early entries, however, point to some small locality in the West Riding.

Ricardus de Pighkeleys, 1379 : P. T. Yorks. p. 182.
Stephanus de Pykedleghes, 1379 : ibid. p. 183.

These persons dwelt in the village of Haworth, in which district the two names are now so familiar. In this case the word means ' the meadows on the hilltop,' the owner taking his name from residence thereon ; v. Pick(2). The Directory for Wilsden, W. Rid. Yorks, contains the two following names, seemingly related :

Nathan Pickles, *beer-retailer*.
Nathan Pighills, *farmer*.

It is curious to note how little the name has wandered from its native county. Nevertheless, it has reached America.

MDB. (W. R. Yorks), 34, 4 ; London, 2, o ; Philadelphia, 4, o.

Pickman.—Occup. ' the pikeman,' a soldier, one who carried a pike ; cf. Spearman. With the form Pickman may be set *pick* and *pick-axe*.

Stephen Pykeman, London, 1273. A
Geoffrey Pykeman, London, ibid.
Thomas Pikeman, or Pikman, London, 20 Edw. I. R.
Giles Pykeman. X.
1587. Married—George Pickman and Gillmett Johnson : St. Jas. Clerkenwell, iii. 12.
1628. Bapt.—Eliz., d. Philip Pickman : ibid. i. 109.
London, 2 ; Boston (U.S.), 2.

Picknell.—Local, ' of Pikenhall.' I cannot find the spot.

Thomas de Pikenhale, co. Camb., 1273. A.
1680. Married — John Pecknell and Mary Thomas : St. Dionis Backchurch, p. 39.
MDB. (co. Linc.), 1 ; London, 1 ; Boston (U.S.), 5.

Picksley, Pixley.—Local ; v. Pikesley.

Pickston, Pickstone. — Corruptions of Pingston, q.v.

Pickup, Pickop.—Local, ' of Pickup.' A Lancashire surname from a township and village in the parish of Walley, now styled Yatecum-Pickup Bank. The name has ramified strongly, and can be easily traced back to the neighbourhood of Blackburn as its original home.

1584. Roger Piccop, of Over Whiteley: Wills at Chester, i. 152.
1592. James Piccop, of Nether Darwen: ibid.
1623. John Piccope, of Rawtenstall: ibid. ii. 173.
— John Piccopp, of Eccleshill: ibid.
Robert Holden, of Picope Bank, 1595: ibid. i. 97.
John Tattersall, of Piccope, 1581: ibid. p. 188.
Robert Tattersall, of Piccope, yeoman, 1587: ibid.
Manchester, 8, 1; Blackburn, 23, 3; Philadelphia, 15, 1.

Pickwell.—Local, 'of Pickwell,' a parish in co. Leicester, near Melton Mowbray.

MDB. (co. Lincoln), 7.

Pickwick.—Local, 'of Pickwick' or Bickwick, some spot in the West country; cf. Buckle and Puckle, Burser and Purser, Bickerdike and Pickerdike,&c. My earliest reference is from the county of Wilts. This is interesting. The Pall Mall Gazette (March 3, 1888) says: 'During the hearing of a case in the High Court of Justice yesterday, Mr. Dickens, a son of the famous novelist, and counsel for the defendant, said he should call as a witness a Mr. Pickwick (laughter). He added: It may interest your lordship (Baron Huddleston) to learn that this gentleman is a descendant of Mr. Moses Pickwick, who kept a coach at Bath, and I have very good reason to believe that it was from this Mr. Moses Pickwick that the name of the immortal Pickwick was taken.' Evidently the surname is a West-country one, and has existed there at least six centuries.

William de Pikewike, co. Wilts, 1273. A.
Thomas de Bykewyk, co. Soms., 1 Edw. III: Kirby's Quest, p. 103.
Ralph de Bykewyk, co. Soms., 1 Edw. III: ibid.
Walter de Bykewyk, co. Soms., 1 Edw. III: ibid.

The three last-named were all resident in Redlysch.

1647. Married — Charles Pikwik and Maria Potter: Reg. Darrington, co. York.

For this last entry I am indebted to Notes and Queries, Feb. 5, 1887, p. 112.

MDB. (co. Soms.), 1; Neath (South Wales), 1; Philadelphia, 1.

Pickworth.—Local, 'of Pickworth,' a parish in co. Lincoln, near Falkingham. The meaning is 'the farmstead on the sharp-pointed hill'; v. Pike and Worth.

Robert de Pickewurth, co. Linc., Hen. III–Edw. I. K.
Hugo de Pykewurth, co. Linc., ibid.
Richard de Pikeword, co. Linc., ibid.
William de Pikworth, co. Linc., ibid.
1739. Bapt. — Ann, d. Thomas Pickworth: St. Jas. Clerkenwell, ii. 247.
London, 5; MDB. (co. Lincoln), 6.

Picthall.—Local, 'of Pickthall,' an old house in the parish of Ulverston, Furness. The surname is well known in the district, and pronounced Picthaw.

1545. Bapt. — Esabell Picthawe: Reg. Ulverston Church, p. 1.
1547. Buried — Jenet Pickthowe: ibid. p. 5.
John Turner, of Pickthawe, 1644: Lancashire Wills at Richmond, i. 289.
James Picthowe, of Pickthowe Ground in Dunerdale, 1610: ibid. p. 216.
Thomas Picthall, of Sandscale, parish of Dalton, 1718: ibid. ii. 197.
James Picthall, of Picthall Ground in Durinerdale, 1734: ibid.
MDB. (co. Cumberland), 3; Ulverston, 1; Liverpool, 1; Boston (U.S.), 3.

Picton.—Local, (1) ' of Picton,' a place close by Haverfordwest. William de Picton came to Pembrokeshire (N. and Q., 1858, p. 329), whence the Pictons in that district. Nevertheless, my instances point to Picton nearer at hand, viz. (2) ' of Picton,' a township in the parish of Plemonstall, four miles from Chester.

Hugh Picton, canon of St. David's, Hist. and Ant. St. David's, p. 364.
Thomas Picton, prebendary of St. David's, 1399: ibid. p. 361.
Jane Taylor, of Picton, 1615: Wills at Chester (1545–1620), p. 189.
John Picton, of Newton, near Chester, 1593: ibid. p. 152.
Henry Picton, of Acton Grange, 1610: ibid.
London, 1; Liverpool, 1; New York, 1.

Pidcock, Piddocke. — Bapt. ' the son of Peter,' from Peter-cock, a corruption (v. Cocks); cf. Wilcock, Simcock, &c. Lower quotes from Burke's Landed Gentry, 'The surname is derived from the armorial bearing of the family, a pied cock!' Lower adds, 'The cock is not pied, but simply parted per fesse, Or and Argent.' This is setting the cart before the horse with a vengeance.

Gilbert Pittcok, co. Camb., 1273. A.
1738. Married — Thomas Piddock and Mary Gaudy: St. Geo. Han. Sq. i. 28.
1755. John Spencer and Ann Pidcock: ibid. p. 59.
Crockford, 5, 1; MDB. (co. Derby), 1, 2; Philadelphia, 2, 0.

Piddington.—Local, ' of Piddington,' parishes in cos. Northampton and Oxford.

Richard de Pidinton, co. Oxf., 1273. A.
William de Pidinton, co. Oxf., ibid.
Walter de Pidington, co. Oxf., ibid.
1802. Married—Peter Piddington and Anna Rapley: St. Geo. Han. Sq. ii. 269.
London, 4; MDB. (co. Hunts), 1.

Pidgeon, Pigeon, Pidgin.—Nick. ' the pidgeon'; cf. Dove, Woodcock, Pye, &c. Bird-names are among the most common of the nickname class of surnames. M.E. pygeon.

William Pigun, co. Norf., 1273. A.
Richard Pigun, co. Camb., ibid.
Walter Pygeon, C. R., 1 Hen. V.
Henricus Pygyn, 19 Edw. I: BBB. p. 431.
1757. Married—John Pidgin and Eliz. Collins: St. Geo. Han. Sq. i. 74.
London, 4, 1, 0; Boston (U.S.), 6, 3, 4.

Pidgley, Pidsley.—Local, ' of —— ?' The first entry is manifestly the parent of the name.

Walter de Pideneslegh, co. Devon, 1273. A.
1761. Married — Samuel Taunton and Martha Pidgley: St. Geo. Han. Sq. i. 105.
Devon Court Dir., 2, 7; London, 0, 2.

Piebaker.—Occup. ' the pie-baker,' a pastry-cook. ' Pye-baker, cereagius': Prompt. Parv. Way adds as a note, ' Cereagius, pistor qui ad modum cere deducit pastam': Cath. Ang.

' Drovers, cokes, and pulters,
Yermongers, pybakers, and waferers.'
　　　　　　Cocke Lorelle's Bote.
Andrew le Pyebakere, London. X.
Hugh Pybakere, C. R., 47 Edw. III.

Piel.—Local, 'at the peel,' from residence therein; v. Peel or Peil.

New York, 2.

Pierpoint, Pierpont, Pairpoint, Pearpoint, Pierrepont. —Local, ' of Pierrepont,' from the castle of that name on the southern borders of Picardy (Lower). The name is Latinized into ' de Petro-Ponte.' Godfrey de Perpont occurs in Domesday.

Henry de Perpunt, co. Linc., 1273. A.
Hugh de Perpunt, co. Notts, ibid.
John de Perpunt, co. Notts, Hun. III-Edw. I. K.
Simon de Perepont, co. Suff., 20 Edw. I. R.
Henry Perpunt, co. Linc., 20 Edw. I. R.
1575. George Perpount and Agnes Raynoldes: Marriage Lic. (London), i. 65.
London, 5, 1, 4, 1, 0; Boston (U.S.), 1, 3, 0, 0, 1.

Piers, Pierce, Pears, Pearse, Peers, Peirce, Pierse.—Bapt. ' the son of Peter,' from O.F. Pierre, O.E. Piers or Pierce. Although Peter, and with it Piers, lost much of its popularity after the Reformation, we cannot fail to see from our directories (Pearson, &c.) how extremely familiar the name was in all parts of England at the time surnames were becoming hereditary.

Richard Perys, co. Soms., 1 Edw. III : Kirby's Quest, p. 133.
Isolda Peer-doghter, co. York. W. 15.
Magota Peres-wyf, 1379 : P. T. Yorks. p. 117.
Peres Rothwell, 1541, Tottington, Lanc.: Lanc. and Ches. Rec. Soc. vol. xii. p. 144.
Peares Armerod, temp. Eliz. ZZ.
Pearse Edgcombe, temp. Eliz. Z.
Robert Pearce, temp. Eliz. Z.
Jane, d. of Pears Marten, 1541 : Reg. St. Columb Major, p. 1.
John, s. of Peirce Penhale, 1604 : ibid. p. 22.
William Pearce, or Perce, or Peirs, or Perse, or Peirce, or Peirse, or Pearse, adm. B.A. 1601 : Reg. Univ. Oxf. vol. ii. pt. iii. p. 221.
1692. Married — George Peares and Anna Padgett : St. Michael, Cornhill, p. 47.
1738. — Thomas Pearce and Eliz. Jones : ibid. p. 68.
London, 0, 13, 4, 18, 1, 10, 14.

Piersol.—Local ; v. Pearsall.

Pierson ; v. Pearson.

Pigg.—Nick.'the pig'; cf. Hogg, Wildbore, Purcell. Probably the epithet would be less offensive then than now. Two gentlemen named Pigg were about 1882 among our best county cricketers.

Goceline Pig, co. Norf., 1273. A.
Richard Pig, co. Berks. ibid.
Walter Pigge, co. Northampt., ibid.
John Pyg. H.
1626. John Pittman and Alice Pigge, widow : Marriage Lic. (London), ii. 179.
1787. Married — Richard Waite and Mary Pigg : St. Geo. Han. Sq. i. 399.
Manchester, 1.

Piggins, Piggin, Pickin, Picking. — Bapt. ' the son of Richard' (?). Probably popular variants of Higgins, Higgin, and Hickin, q.v. We still talk of higgledy-piggledy. The g in Picking is an excrescence, as in Jennings, &c.

1386. Roger Pickyn, rector of Billingford, co. Norf. : FF. viii. 194.
1574-5. Anthony Pickins, co. Worc. : Reg. Univ. Oxf. vol. ii. pt. ii. p. 59.
1614-5. Anthony Piggin and Sarah Ireland : Marriage Lic. (London), ii. 30.
1619. Thomas Hoggery and Joane Piggyn : ibid. p. 81.
1807. Married — Daniel Daniel and Alice Picking : St. Geo. Han. Sq. ii. 364.
London, 0, 1, 1, 1 ; MDB. (co. Linc.), 3, 0, 0, 0 ; (co. Notts), 1, 5, 2, 0.

Piggott, Pigot, Pigott.— Bapt. ' the son of Pigot' or 'Picot'; v. Pickett. The personal name Pigot without surname occurs in the Hundred Rolls ; no doubt a variant of Picot.

' De dono Pigoti et Reginaldi' : A. i. 336.
Astin Pigot, co. York, 1273. A.
Richard Pigot, co. Linc., ibid.
Robert Pigod, co. Salop, ibid.

The parish of Framlingham Pigot, co. Norfolk, is in Bromefield's History of Norfolk (v. 435) headed Framlingham Picot.

Thomas Pygot, or Picot, co. Norf., 1434 : FF. v. 435.

The popular form in co. Norfolk is Pickett, q.v.

1561. Richard Piggotte : Reg. Univ. Oxf. i. 245.
London, 16, 4, 4 ; Boston (U.S.), 1, 0, 9.

Pigherd.—Occup. ' the pigherd,' a tender of pigs ; v. Swinnart, Calvert, Herd, &c.

Walter Pyghurde, co. Soms., 1 Edw. III : Kirby's Quest, p. 112.

Pighills ; v. Pickles.

Pigram ; v. Pegram.

Pigsflesh. — Nick. Cf. Hogsflesh.

Reyner Piggesflessh, Close Roll, 13 Edw. II.

Pike.—Local ; v. Pick (2).

Walter Pik, co. Hunts, 1273. A.
Richard Pik, co. Wilts, ibid.
Baldewyn Pike, co. Soms., 1 Edw. III : Kirby's Quest, p. 114.
London, 53 ; Worcester (U.S.), 18.

Pikesley, Pixley, Picksley. —Local, ' of Pixley,' a parish in co. Hereford, three miles from Ledbury.

Hugo de Pikesley, co. Hereford, Hen. III-Edw. I. K.
1632. Married — Edmund Davy and Alice Pixly : St. Jas. Clerkenwell, iii. 63.
1682. — John Nero and Eliz. Pickesley : ibid. p. 198.
1764. — George Miller and Sarah Pixley : St. Geo. Han. Sq. i. 133.
London, 1, 2, 0 ; Manchester, 0, 0, 1 ; MDB. (co. Oxf.), 1, 0, 0 ; (co. Linc.), 0, 1, 3.

Pilbrow. — Local, 'of Pulborough,' a parish in co. Sussex ; cf. Plimpton for Plumpton.

1795. Married — George Pratt and Mary Pilbrough : St. Geo. Han. Sq. ii. 136.
1803. — Henry Pilbrough and Eliz. Swinton : ibid. p. 292.
MDB. (co. Bucks), 1 ; Philadelphia, 1.

Pilcher, Pilger.—Occup. ' the pilcher,' a pilch-maker. ' Pylche pellicium': Prompt. Parv. Mr. Way has a long and interesting note on the word (pp. 397-8). Properly a fur gown, a garment of skin, with the hairs on. Bishop Ridley in his letter of farewell, quoting Heb. xi. 37, says, ' Some wandered to and fro in sheep's pilches, in goats' pilches.' v. Pelliter and Pellipar.

' After great heat commeth cold ;
No man cast his pilche away.'
Chaucer, Proverbs.

Hugh le Pilecher, co. Camb., 1273. A.
Nicholas Pilchere, co. Camb., ibid.
Ralph Pilkere, co. Camb., ibid.
John Pilcher. G.
1625. Buried—John Pilcher, merchant : St. Dionis Backchurch, p. 217.
1761. Married — John Wise and Eliz. Pilcher : St. Geo. Han. Sq. i. 105.
London, 2, 0 ; MDB. (co. Kent), 22, 0 ; New York, 2, 8.

Pile.—Local ; v. Pill.

Pilgrim.—Occup. ' the pilgrim,' a wanderer, one who went long distances to visit a shrine. It is possible the name was sometimes given in baptism; v. Pegram and Peregrine. A good instance of the intermediate stage is found in the following :

Edmund Pylgrvne, rector of Sydistrond, co. Norf.: FF. viii. 170.
Henry Pelrim, co. Camb., 1273. A.
Robert Pelerin, co. Suff., ibid.
Leticia Pelrin, co. Camb., ibid.
John Pilegrim, co. Oxf., ibid.
Geoffry Pilegrim, co. Norf., ibid.
Richard Pilgrym, C. R., 2 Hen. V.
Willelmus Pylgrem, 1379: P. T. Yorks. p. 51.
1762. Married — James Ridley and Ann Green, with consent of Rev. John Pilgrim : St. Geo. Han. Sq. i. 110.
London, 8 ; MDB. (co. Essex), 5.

Pilkington.—Local, 'of Pilkington,' a manor in the parish of Prestwich, co. Lanc.

'Roger de Pilkington, for an oxgang of land in Pilkington, homage and service of 12d.,' 1311 : Baines' Lanc. i. 483.
Roger de Pilkinton, 19 Edw. I : ibid. p. 448.
Oliver Pilkington, of Bolton, co. Lanc., 1594 : Wills at Chester (1545-1620), p. 153.
Adam Pilkington, of Salford, *gentleman*, 1596 : ibid.
Manchester, 13 ; London, 4 ; Philadelphia, 10.

Pill, Pile.— Local, 'at the peel' or fortified house (v. Peel), from residence therein. 'Pile, a small tower' (Halliwell).

Richard de la Pile, co. Soms., 1273. A.
Benedict de la Pille, co. Devon, ibid.
Nicholas de Pille, co. Essex, ibid.
Walter atte Pyle, co. Soms., 1 Edw. III : Kirby's Quest, p. 98.
Richard atte Pile, co. Soms., 1 Edw. III: ibid. p. 140.
William atte Pyle, co. Soms., 1 Edw. III: ibid. p. 194.
Thomas del Pille, 1379 : P. T. Yorks. p. 155.
1789. Married — Benjamin Pile and Ann Meredeth : St. Geo. Han. Sq. ii. 32.
1804. George Tunks and Margaret Pill : ibid. p. 302.
London, 2, 12 ; Philadelphia, 0, 12.

Pillar, Piller.—Local, 'at the pillar,' from residence thereby. M.E. *piler*, a column, a support.

Walter atte-piler, C. R., 10 Edw. I.

The following instance is probably 'de le,' the *de* being omitted, as is so common in early rolls.

John le Piler, co. Soms., 1 Edw. III : Kirby's Quest, p. 219.

1666. Married — William Piller and Mary Leager : St. Jas. Clerkenwell, iii. 126.
1745. — Thomas Miles and Eliz. Piller: ibid. p. 275.
Philadelphia, 0, 1 : Boston (U.S.), 0, 2.

Pilley.—Local, 'of Pilley.' a manor, now the property of Lord Wharncliffe, in the parish of Tankersley, nine miles from Sheffield, W. Rid. Yorks.

Johannes de Pillay, of Tankersley, 1379 : P. T. Yorks. p. 87.
Magota de Pillay, of Tankersley, 1379 : ibid.
Gilbert de Pilleghe, co. Soms., 1 Edw. III : Kirby's Quest, p. 152.

This entry probably represents a different place in the West Country.

1780. Married—John Pilley and Mary Crush : St. Geo. Han. Sq. i. 308.
London, 2 ; Sheffield, 1 ; Philadelphia, 5.

Pilling. — Local, 'of Pilling,' a township in the parish of Garstang, co. Lanc. 'The township is characterized by its fence-dykes, mentioned in the ballad of Flodden Field :

"They wᵗʰ ye Standley howte forth went From Pemberton and Pillin Dikes."'
v. Baines' Lanc. ii. 537.
Rowland Pilyn, Bras. Coll. 1579 : Reg. Univ. Oxf. vol. ii. pt. i. p. 391.
Hugh Pilling, of Tunstead, 1579 : Wills at Chester, i. 152.
Edmund Pillinge, of Bacup, 1595 : ibid.
Edmund Pilling, of Baxtenden, 1592 : ibid.
1671. Married — Abraham Pillin and Jane Snosedale : St. Jas. Clerkenwell, p. 175.
London, 3 ; Manchester, 16 ; MDB. (co. Lanc.), 11 ; Philadelphia, 16.

Pillinger.—Offic.; v. Penniger; cf. *banister* for *baluster*, or *messenger* for *messager*.

London, 1 ; MDB. (co. Somerset), 1.

Pillington.—Local, ' of Billington' (q.v.), a sharpened form; cf. Pickerdite for Bickerdike, or Peverley for Beverley.

Johannes de Pyllyngton, 1579 : P. T. Yorks. p. 167.
1673. Married—Samuel Pillington and Anne Wright : St. Jas. Clerkenwell, iii. 177.
London, 1.

Pilsbury, Pillsbury.—Local, 'of Spelsbury,' a village in co. Oxford ; v. Spilsbury. These cor-

rupted forms are commonly found in the United States. I met with instances daily in the course of a tour through the States in May and June, 1888. But the correcter forms, Spilsbury and Spillsbury, are not unknown. The corruption into Pilsbury is a very natural one.

1792. Married — John Pilsbury and Ann Westmacott : St. Geo. Han. Sq. ii. 73.
— Richard Pilsbury and Anna Maynard : ibid. p. 76.
Philadelphia, 0, 1 ; Boston (U.S.), 2, 36.

Pilson.—Local, 'of Puleston.' This surname Puleston is found in the Reg. Univ. Oxon. (v. Index) as Pilston and Pillson ; cf. Paxon for Paxton.

1522. Hugh Pylstone : Reg. Univ. Oxf. i. 123.
1569. William Weston and Katherine Pylson : Marriage Lic. (London), i. 42.
1580. Edward Pilson, co. Denbigh : Reg. Univ. Oxf. vol. ii. pt. ii. p. 94.
1601. John Puleston, co. Oxf. : ibid. pt. ii. p. 249.
1675. Married—Robert Pulleston and Mildred Eastland : St. Jas. Clerkenwell, p. 181.
Edward Pilson, 1679, bound for New England : Hotten's Lists of Emigrants, p. 397.

I cannot find the place Puleston. Philadelphia, 3.

Pilsworth, Pillsworth. — Local, 'of Pilsworth,' a township in the parish of Middleton, near Manchester.

1548. Roger Pyllysworthe and Ellen Polkynhorne : Marriage Lic. (Faculty Office), p. 13.
1577. William Pilsworth, London: Reg. Univ. Oxf. vol. ii. pt. ii. p. 76.
Jane Pilsworth, of the parish of Eccles (Manchester), 1603 : Wills at Chester (1545-1620), p. 153.
1807. Married—Robert Pillsworth and Mary Hissey : St. Geo. Han. Sq. ii. 375.
Boston (U.S.), 1, 0 ; MDB, (co. Linc.), 1, 1.

Pilter.—Occup.; v. Pelliter.

Pilton.—Local, 'of Pilton,' a parish in co. Devon.

Richard de Pilton, co. Devon, 1273. A.
Adam de Pylton, co. Soms., 1 Edw. III: Kirby's Quest, p. 255.
1790. Married — William Pilton and Ann Oxley : St. Geo. Han. Sq. ii. 37.
London, 5.

Pim, Pimm, Pymm, Pym.— Bapt. 'the son of Pimme.' Considering that Eufemia is fairly common in the Hundred Rolls, that Pimme is feminine, and Phemie is still the nick., it is all but certain that we have here the solution of the name in question. Personally I have no doubt that this derivation is correct.

Eufemmia de Neville, co. Linc., 1273. A.
Katerina Eufemme, co. Norf., ibid.
Pimme, widow of Peter Seman, co. Cumb., ibid.
Bartholomew fil.Pimme, co. Hunts, ibid.
Chun Pimme, co. Camb., ibid.
Henry Pimme, co. Camb., ibid.
Roger Pym, co. Soms., 1 Edw. III : Kirby's Quest, p. 142.
Eufemia fil. Rogeri, co. Suff., 20 Edw. I. R.
Eufemmia Craker, 1379 : P. T. Yorks. p. 234.
Euphemia Forster, 1379 : ibid. p. 91.
Agnes Pyme, 1379 : ibid. p. 280.
Johannes Pymson, 1379 : ibid. p. 266.

Probably the following entries concern the same name :

1561. Bapt.—Effam Adlington : Reg. St. Peter, Cornhill, i. 11
1620. — Frauncis, son of Alexander Brounescome and Ellym, his wife : ibid. p. 68.
1635. Buried—Epham Vowell, widow : ibid. p. 195.
London, 6, 7, 3, 0 ; New York, 3, 0, 0, 1.

Pimlott, Pimblett, Pimblott, Pimblotte, Pimlock.—Bapt.'the son of Pim' (q.v.), dim. Pimelot ; cf. Hewlett for Huelot (Hugh), &c. I have no proof of this statement. It is a name of Cheshire parentage. Of course the *b* in Pimblett, &c., is intrusive. In America a corrupted form, Pimlock, has sprung up ; cf. Glasscott and Glasscock.

1561. Buried—Mergret Pymlot : Reg. Prestbury, Cheshire, p. 6.
1562. Bapt.—Robert Pymlot, ibid.
Richard Pimlott, of Buglawton, 1624 : Wills at Chester (1621-50), p. 174.
Isabell Pimlott, 1648 : East Cheshire, i. 25.
Manchester, 4, 1, 0, 0 ; MDB. (co. Chester), 3, 0, 1, 2, 0 ; Philadelphia, 1, 0, 0, 0, 1.

Pinchard.—Local; v. Punchard.

Pinchback, Pinchbeck. — Local, 'of Pinchbeck,' a parish near Spalding, co. Lincoln.

Gilbert de Pincebek, co. Linc., 1273. A.
Walran de Pincebek, co. Linc., ibid.
William de Pincebeck, co. Linc., ibid.

Thomas de Pincebeck, co. Linc., Hen. III-Edw. I. K.

The form Pinchback is found so early as the 16th century :

1551. Married — William Pyncheback and Jone Hamson : St. Michael, Cornhill, p. 6.

Pinchbeck is now a dictionary word, one Christopher Pinchbeck having given his name to an alloy of copper and zinc.

London, 1, 3 ; MDB. (co. Linc.), 0, 4 ; Philadelphia, 1, 0.

Pinchin(g ; v. Punshon.

Pinckard ; v. Punchard. A variant.

MDB. (co. Northampton), 3.

Pinckney ; v. Pinkney.

Pinder, Pindar, Pindard.—Offic. 'the pinder,' an impounder of strayed cattle ; v. Pinner. 'Pyndare of beestys, pynnar, *inclusor*': Prompt. Parv. 'A pyndor, *inclusor*': Cath. Ang. The final *d* in Pindard is excrescent.

Hugh le Pinder, co. Linc., 1273. A.
Walter le Pinder, co. Notts, ibid.
Henry le Pynder, c. 1300. M.
John le Pindere. T.
John le Pinder. E.
1661. William Pindar and Catherine Jorden : Marriage Lic. (Faculty Office), p. 55.
1749. Married — John Pinder and Mary Butterfield : St. Geo. Han. Sq. i. 42.
London, 9, 4, 2 ; Philadelphia, 10, 0, 0.

Pine.—Local; v. Pyne.

Pingeon ; v. Punshon.

Pinfold.—Local ; v. Penfold.

Pingston, Pinkstone, Pixton, Pickston, Pickstone.—Local, 'of Pinxton,' a parish in co. Derby. Over the border in Lancashire this surname has become popularized into Pixton, Pickston, &c.

1670. William Peckston, of Wrenbury : Wills at Chester (1660-80), p. 207.
1680. William Penkston, of Middlewich : ibid. p. 206.
1785. Married — William Dove and Mary Pinkstone : St. Geo. Han. Sq. i. 375.
London, 1, 0, 0, 0, 0 ; Manchester, 0, 0, 3, 2, 1.

Pink, Pinke.—Nick.'the pink,'

i.e. chaffinch ; cf. Finch, Goldfinch, Chaffinch, Goldspink, and Spink.

Adam Pink, co. Norf., 1273. A.
John Pynke, co. Soms., 1 Edw. III : Kirby's Quest, p. 267.
1665. Bapt. — Eliz., d. John Pincke : St. Jas. Clerkenwell, i. 226.
London, 13, 0 ; New York, 3, 2.

Pinkerton.—Local, 'of Punchardon.' Mr. Lower says, 'We search in vain the gazetteers of England and Scotland for any locality bearing the designation of Pinkerton.' He declares that it is a corruption of Punchardon, and asserts that Punchardon is found as Pynkerton in Ragman Roll, A.D. 1296 (Patr. Brit. p. 268). I doubt not he is right. It is believed that Punchardon is the place now called Pont-Chardon, in the arrondissement of Argentan, Normandy. In Domesday the surname is found as Ponte-Cardon. We may take it therefore that the family came into England at the Conquest (v. Patr. Brit. p. 279).

Olyver de Punchardon, co. Devon, 1273. A.
Eudo de Punchardon, co. York, ibid.
Robert de Punchardun, co. Devon, Hen. III-Edw. I. K.
1752. Married — William Lake and Susanna Pinkerton : St. Geo. Han. Sq. i. 48.
London, 2 ; Philadelphia, 20.

Pinkney, Pinckney.—Local, 'de Pincheni.' It is probable that the name came into England at the Conquest. Mr. Lower says that Giles de Pincheni (temp. Henry I) endowed the monks of St. Lucien, in France, with lands at Wedon, co. Northants (Patr. Brit. p. 268).

Hamon de Pinkeney, co. Norf., temp. Hen. III : FF. vii. 195.
Henry de Pinkeni, co. Bucks, 1273. A.
Roesia de Pinkeny, co. Norf., ibid.
1751. Married—Richard Pinkney and Susanna Leisnot : St. Geo. Han. Sq. i. 46.
1756. — Roger Pinckney and Susanna Parsons : ibid. p. 64.
London, 2, 5 ; New York, 41, 11.

Pinn.—Local; v. Pyne.

Pinnell.— ?——. I find no prefix ' de ' or ' de la ' to the early instances. Ralph Pinel was a tenant *in capite* in cos. Essex and Suffolk at the date of Domesday. Two centuries later, as will be seen below, the surname was still settled there. I cannot classify the name, but probably it is local in spite of the absence of local prefixes, and of Norman extraction.

John Pinel, co. Essex, 1273. A.
Henry Pinel, co. Hunts, ibid.
Roger Pinel, co. Oxf., ibid.
Mathew Pinel, co. Suff., ibid.
Warin Pinel, co. Oxf., Hen. III–Edw.
I. K.
1564. Robert Brown and Eliz. Pynell: Marriage Lic. (London), i. 27.
London, 2; MDB. (co. Oxf.), 3; New York, 2.

Pinner.—(1) Offic.'the pinner,' a pinder, an impounder of strayed cattle; v. Pinder. 'Pyndare of beestys, pynnar, *inclusor*': Prompt. Parv. Mr. Way in a note (p. 400) says, 'Amongst manorial or municipal officials the pounder of stray cattle is still in some places, as in Warwickshire, termed the pinner.' v. Penfold. (2) Occup. 'the pinner,' a pin-maker.

'Pynners, nedelers, and glasyers.'
    Cocke Lorelle's Bote.
Andrew le Pynner. G.
Walter le Pinner. X.
1569–70. Hugh Apparrye and Eliz. Pynner: Marriage Lic. (London), i. 44.
1788. Married — William Pinner and Eliz. Edwards: St. Geo. Han. Sq. ii. 8.
London, 5; New York, 15.

Pinnigar, -ger; v. Penniger.

Pinnington.—Local, 'of Pennington'; two parishes in co. Lanc. are so named.

1621. John Pinnington, of Horwich: Wills at Chester (1621–50), p. 175.
1639. Gilbert Pinnington, of Wigan: ibid.
Huyton (co. Lanc.), 2.

Pinnion, Pinyon, Penyon.—Bapt. 'Ap-Einion' (Welsh); v. Benyon, Baynham, or Bunyan.

MDB. (co. Kent), 0, 2, 1; London, 1, 1, 0.

Pinnock, Pinnick.—Local,'of Pinnock,'two parishes in cos. Cornwall and Gloucester.

William Pinnoc, co. Oxf., 1273. A.
Walter Pinnock, co. Wilts, ibid.
Roger Pynnock, co. Soms., 1 Edw. III:
Kirby's Quest, p. 236.
London, 10, 1; MDB. (co. Soms.), 2, 0.

Pinson; v. Penson.

Pipe.—(1) Bapt. 'the son of Pipe.' A personal name in Domesday (Lower). (2) Local, 'of Pipe,'

a parish in co. Hereford, about three miles from Hereford.

Alicia Pipe, co. Hunts, 1273. A.
Harvey Pippe, co. Camb., ibid.
Margery Pipe, co. Soms., 1 Edw. III:
Kirby's Quest, p. 130. *
John Pype, co. Soms., 1 Edw. III: ibid.
London, 8.

Piper.—Occup. 'the piper,' a player on the bagpipes.

'A baggepipe cowde he blowe and sowne.
    Chaucer, C. T. 567.
Henry le Pipere, co. Oxf., 1273. A.
Adam le Piper, co. Camb., ibid.
Arnald le Pyper. P.
Robert le Pipere. M.
Peter le Pipre, Close Roll, 4 Edw. I.

Whether this was the Peter Piper who originated the alliterative nursery rhyme, 'Peter Piper picked a peck of pickled peppercorns,' I cannot say.

John le Pipere, co. Soms., 1 Edw. III:
Kirby's Quest, p. 216.
Robert le Pipere, co. Soms., 1 Edw. III:
ibid. p. 276.
Ema Pipere, 1379: P. T. Yorks. p. 136.
1714. Married—Hugh Piper and Eliz.
Matthews: St. Geo. Han. Sq. i. 14.
London, 25; Philadelphia, 34.

Pipester.—Occup. 'a female piper'; v. Piper.

Alice Pipestre, Close Roll, 30 Edw. I.

Pippett, Pippitt, &c.; v. Peppiatt.

Pippin.—(1) Bapt. 'the son of Philip.' A variant of Phippen (q.v.), and found in co. Somerset, where Phippen is a familiar name. (2) Bapt. 'the son of Pepin,' q.v. Probably a variant in some cases.

William Pippin, co. Bedf., 1273. A.
Richard Pipping, co. Soms., 1 Edw.
III: Kirby's Quest, p. 217.
John Pippyng, co. Soms., 1 Edw. III:
ibid. p. 243.

In the last two references the *g* is excrescent, as in Jennings, &c.

William Pippin, co. Bedf., 1273. A.
MDB. (co. Somerset), 2.

Pirie.—Local, ' at the pirie,' i.e. the pear orchard; v. Pury.

Geoffrey de la Pirie, co. Camb., 1273. A.
Robert del Pirie, co. Oxf., ibid.
William de la Pirie, co. Salop, ibid.
London, 2.

Pitcairn.—Local, ' of Pitcairn,' a village in the parish of Redgorton, co. Perth.

London, 5; Philadelphia, 1.

Pitcher.—Local. Not an occupation, but an abbreviation of Pichard'(v. Picard). Many instances will be found in this dictionary with the final *d* dropped.

Alan Pichard, co. York, 1273. A.
Walter Pichard, co. York, ibid.
John Picher, co. Soms., 1 Edw. III:
Kirby's Quest, p. 182.
Gilbert Pycher, co. Soms., 1 Edw. III:
ibid. p. 243.
1759. Married — John Pitcher and Catherine Shannon: St. Geo. Han. Sq. i. 85.
London, 8; Philadelphia, 5.

Pitchford.—Local; v. Pickford.

Pitchfork.—Local, 'of Pitchford'; v. Pickford. An imitative corruption. The intermediate form is represened in the following :

John de Picford, or de Picheford, or de Pichefort, co. Salop, Hen. III–Edw.
I. K.
1601. Bapt.—Barnaby, s. John Pitchfort: St. Jas. Clerkenwell, i. 38.
1608–9. William Nocke and Eliz.
Pitchfork (co. Salop) : Marriage Lic.
(London), i. 310.
MDB. (co. Lincoln), 2.

Pither, Pether.—Bapt. 'the son of Peter.' Pither must be looked upon as a variant of Pether, and that seems undoubtedly to represent Peter.

Thomas Pither, co. Glouc., 20 Edw.
I. R.
John Peter, or Pether, B.A., 1526:
Reg. Univ. Oxf. i. 181.
1778. Married—Thomas Pether and Arabella Fancourt: St. Geo. Han. Sq. i. 286.
1780. — John Pithor and Ann Benham: ibid. p. 310.
1783. — James Dredge and Sarah Pither: ibid. p. 351.
MDB. (co. Berks), 6, 0; London, 3, 3; New York, 0, 1.

Pithouse.—Local, 'at the pithouse,' from residence in the house by the pit.

Thomas Bennett, of Pithouse, co.
Dorset, 1623: Visitation of Dorset, 1623.

The grandfather of the above was John Bennett of Pithouse. Oddly enough, his younger brother is styled in the same document Thomas Bennett, alias Pitt. And Bennett, alias Pite of Knockbillingsby, co. Limerick and co. Wilts, appears in Burke's General Armory, ed.1878. (Communicated by T. Paul Rylands.)

London, 1 ; Langley (co. Bucks), 1.

Pitkethly.—Local, 'of Pitcaithly.' 'A well-known locality in the parish of Dumbarnie, co. Perth' (Lower).

London, 1 ; Boston (U.S.), 1.

Pitkin. — Bapt. 'the son of Peter,' from dim. Peterkin, corrupted to Pitkin ; v. Peterkin.

1545. John Pitkyn and Margaret Forward : Marriage Lic. (London), i. 10.
Franses Pittkin, 1668 : Reg. St. Jas. Clerkenwell, i. 235.
1760. Married—William Pittkin and Martha Roseblade : St. Geo. Han. Sq. i. 93.
1762. John Redhead and Sarah Pitkin : ibid. p. 111.
London, 6 ; Boston (U.S.), 5.

Pitman, Pittman.—Local, 'the pitman,' one who dwelt beside a deep hollow or pit ; cf. Bridgman, Styleman, &c. ; v. Pitt.

John Piteman, co. Bucks, 1273. A.
1626. John Pittman and Alice Pigge : Marriage Lic. (London), ii. 179.
1643. Buried—Andrew Pitman : St. Dionis Backchurch, p. 224.
London, 12, 18 ; Philadelphia, 6, 3.

Pitney.—Local, ' of Pitney,' a parish in co. Somerset.

London, 2 ; MDB. (co. Somerset), 1.

Pitt, Pitts.—Local, 'at the pit' or 'pitts,' from residence beside a hole, natural or artificial, or precipitous hollow, so called ; cf. *coal-pit.* Pitts represents several such hollows : or the final *s* is the patronymic, as in Williams, Jones, Wilkins, &c. ; cf. Brooks, Styles, Knowles, Holmes, &c. v. Putt.

Simon de la Pitte de Shottebrok, C. R., 36 Hen. III.
Robert in the Pyt, c. 1300. M.
Simon atte-Pitte, C. R., 26 Edw. III.
Richard Attepitte, 4 Hen. IV, co. Norf. : FF. vii. 189.
1588. Married—Richard Pit and Mary Bates : St. Antholin (London), p. 33.
1630-1. Arthur Pittes and Anne Pennington : Marriage Lic. (London), ii. 201.
1655. Bapt.—Robert, s. John Pitt : St. Jas. Clerkenwell, i. 190.
London, 36, 15 ; Philadelphia, 19, 18.

Pittam, Pittom.—Local, ' of Petham,' a parish in co. Kent.

1575. John Pittam, co. Oxf. : Reg. Univ. Oxf. vol. ii. pt. ii. p. 69.
1671. Married—John Pittham and Anne Wilmote : St. Jas. Clerkenwell, iii. 175.
London, 1, 0 ; MDB. (co. Northampton), 2, 3.

Pitts.—Local ; v. Pitt.

Pittway, Pittaway.—Local, 'at the pit-way,' the way or path to the pit or hollow. Pittaway is formed like Ottaway, Greenaway, or Hathaway, from Ottway, Greenway, or Hathway.

1701. Bapt.—John, s. John Pitway, *milliner* : St. Dionis Backchurch, p. 143.
1757. Married — John Pittaway and Mary King : St. Geo. Han. Sq. i. 72.
London, 1, 0.

Pixley.—Local ; v. Pikesley.

Pixton ; v. Pingston.

Place, Plaice.—Local, 'at the place,' i.e. the stead, the farm, &c., any building or locality styled 'the Place'; Fr. *place.* 'A place, a room, a stead . . . a faire large court': Cotgrave. Hence *place* in the titles of mansions and villas. The surname arose from residence at such a spot.

William de la Place, co. Linc., 1273. A.
John atte Place, co. Soms., 1 Edw. III : Kirby's Quest, p. 258.
1592. Richard Preiste and Agnes Playce, *widow* : Marriage Lic. (London), i. 204.
1604-5. John Place, co. Yorks : Reg. Univ. Oxf. vol. ii. pt. ii. p. 280.
1627-8. Married—John Place and Eliz. Richardson : St. Dionis Backchurch, p. 22.
London, 5, 0 ; Philadelphia, 7, 0 ; Northumberland Court Dir., 1, 1.

Plackett.—Local. A sharpened form of Blackett, q.v.

1666. Married—William Placket and Eliz. Hutchinson : St. Jas. Clerkenwell, iii. 123.
London, 1.

Plaice.—Local ; v. Place.

Plain.—Local ; v. Plane.

Plaisted.—Local ; v Playsted.

Plaister, Plaster.—Occup. 'the plasterer.' The usual term was Dauber, q.v.

John le Cementarius. B.
Adam le Plastier. X.
Walterus Plasterar, 1379 : P. T. Yorks. p. 132.
Joanna Plaisterer, co. York. W. 13.
William Plaisterer, co. York, ibid.

1660-1. Married—Thomas Diason and Margrett Plasterer : St. Dionis Backchurch, p. 36.
1713. Bapt.—John, s. Abraham Plastrier : St. Jas. Clerkenwell, ii. 74.
1793. Married—Samuel Plaster and Eliz. Symes : St. Geo. Han. Sq. ii. 103.
London, 1, 1 ; Oxford, 4, 0.

Plaistow, Plaistowe, Plasto, Plastow.—Local, 'at the playstow,' i.e. playground, the place set apart for games and sports ; M.E. *stowe,* a place (cf. Chepstow, Stowmarket, &c.). There are several parishes called Plaistow (v. Crockford), all of similar origin.

Robert atte Pleistowe, co. Oxf., 1273. A.
Nicholas de la Pleystowe, co. Oxf., ibid.
John de la Playstowe, co. Wilts, ibid.
Gunilda Attepaleystowe, C. R., 6 Edw. I.
1760. Married—John Welch and Mary Plaistow : St. Geo. Han. Sq. i. 94.
1783. — Matthew Plestowe and Charlotte Houghton : ibid. p. 352.
London, 1, 1, 1, 1.

Plampin ; v. Pamphilon.

Plane, Playne, Plain.—Local, 'at the plane-tree,' from residence thereby ; cf. Box, Maple, Ash, Oak, Birch, Birk, &c.

Gilbert Plane, co. Camb., 1273. A.
1581. William Playne and Mary Lusher : Marriage Lic. (London), i. 102.
1797. Married — William Plane and Louise Middlecott : St. Geo. Han. Sq. ii. 159.
MDB. (co. Essex), 2, 0, 0 ; (co. Gloucester), 0, 10, 0 ; (co. Norf.), 4, 0, 2 ; London, 1, 2, 0.

Plank.—Local, 'at the plank,' from residence thereby ; M.E. *planke,* Fr. *planche.* The derivation seems curious, but cf. Pear-tree, Birch. Surnames taken from residence beside single trees were common.

William de la Plaunke, C. R., 46 Edw. III.
Matilda de la Plank, 17 Edw. I. BBB.
Jacobus de la Planche and Plaunche : 34 Edw. I. BBB.
1788. Married—Edward Plank and Susanna Willis : St. Geo. Han. Sq. ii. 13.
London, 4 ; Philadelphia, 5.

Plant, Plante.—? ——. I give this up. I can suggest no satisfactory solution.

Robert Plante, co. Camb., 1273. A.
Roger Plante, co. Camb., ibid.
1605. Married — Symon Plante and Catherine Weaver : St. Jas. Clerkenwell, iii. 30.

1809. Married — John Plant and Ann Stubbs : St. Geo. Han. Sq. ii. 417.
London, 11, 2 ; Philadelphia, 10, 0.

Planterose.—? ——. It seems impossible to offer any satisfactory solution of such a name as this ; cf. Pluckrose.

John Plaunterose, tenet 1 mes' et 1 croft', co. Camb., 1273. A.
London, 1.

Plaskett, Plasket, Plaskitt. —Local, ' of Plaskets,' a township in the parish of Falstone, co. Northumberland (Lower).

1683. Married—Robert Plaskett and Mary Ebsworth : St. Jas. Clerkenwell, iii. 201.
1761. — Abraham Plasket and Susanna Pocock : St. Geo. Han. Sq. i. 107.
London, 2, 1, 2.

Plaster ; v. Plaister.

Plasto, Plastow.—Local ; v. Plaistow.

Plater, Platter.—Occup. ' the plater,' i.e. a maker of metal plates, flat dishes, &c. ; v. Platesmith.

Walter Playtur, co. Hunts, 1273. A.
Anne Playter. V.
1435. Edmund Playter, co. Norf. : FF. ii. 454.
1767. Married—John Lane and Martha Playter : St. Geo. Han. Sq. iii. 168.
London, 3, 0 ; New York, 0, 2.

Platesmith.—Occup. 'the platesmith,' one who hammered metal into plates, flat dishes, &c. The surname is quite extinct.

Johannes Platesmyth, 1379 : P. T. Yorks. p. 70.
Johanna Platesmyth, 1379 : ibid. p. 80.

Platfoot.— Nick. 'splay-footed.' ' Plat-footed, splay-footed ' (Halliwell) ; cf. Barefoot, Proudfoot.

William Platfote, C. R., 1–2 Philip and Mary, pt. ii.

Platt, Platts.—Local, ' of the plat,' i.e. a small patch of ground, the same as plot ; v. Skeat, who adds that ' the spelling is probably due to M.E. plat, Fr. plat, flat,' whence our plate, a flat dish. Monosyllabic surnames often take an s at the end ; cf. Holmes, Lowndes, Bridges, Styles, &c. Hence Platts.

1349. James de Plat, rector of Trimingham, co. Norf. : FF. viii. 178.

Robertus del Platte, 1379 : P. T. Yorks. p. 190.
Johannes de Plattes : 1379 : ibid. p. 221.
1577. John Platt and Eliz. Longe : Marriage Lic. (London), i. 76.
1668. Bapt.—Eliz., d. John Plattes : St. Jas. Clerkenwell, i. 235.
London, 23, 3 ; West Rid. Court Dir., 5, 2 ; New York, 62, 0.

Player.—Occup. ' the player,' probably on a musical instrument, and therefore similar in origin to Piper, Tabor, Trumper, Fiddler, &c.

Arthur Player, temp. Eliz. Z.
1582. John Badsey and Edith Player : Marriage Lic. (London), i. 113.
1619. John Player : Reg. Univ. Oxf. vol. ii. pt. i. p. 361.
1755. Married—Michael Player and Eliz. Reeves : St. Geo. Han. Sq. i. 58.
London, 5 ; MDB. (co. Somerset), 7 ; Philadelphia, 1.

Playfair.—Nick. 'the playfere,' a playfellow. Now almost entirely a Scotch surname : the word occurs in Jamieson's Scottish Dictionary. ' Pleyfere, collusor ' : Prompt. Parv. (1440). ' And whanne sche hadde go with hir felowis and pleiferis ' (sodalibus, Vulg.) : Judges xi. 38 (Wyclif).

1596. Thomas Playfere : Reg. Univ. Oxf. vol. ii. pt. i. p. 347.
1608. Thomas Playfere, rector of Shipdam, co. Norf. : FF. x. 247.
1796. Married—Thomas Playfair and Sarah Boyer : St. Geo. Han. Sq. ii. 157.
London, 2.

Playne ; v. Plane.

Playsted, Playstead, Plested, Plaisted.—Local, ' at the playstead,' i.e. playground, from residence thereby ; cf. Plaistow.

Alex. atte Pleystude, co. Soms., 1 Edw. III : Kirby's Quest, p. 81.
John atte Pleystude, co. Soms., 1 Edw. III : ibid. p. 110.
Philip atte Pleystede, co. Soms., 1 Edw. III : ibid. p. 158.
1581. Edward Plaisteed, co. Sussex : Reg. Univ. Oxf. vol. ii. pt. ii. p. 99.
1652. Robert Plasteed : St. Mary Aldermary (London), p. 22.
1711. Married—James Plaisted and Lettitia Tayler : St. Dionis Backchurch, p. 56.
1794. Married — Samuel Cook and Mary Playsted : St. Geo. Han. Sq. ii. 106.
London, 1, 0, 1, 0 ; MDB. (co. Glouc.), 0, 2, 0, 0 ; Philadelphia, 0, 0, 0, 2.

Pleader.—Occup. ' the pleader,' i.e. a lawyer, one who pleaded a case before a judge. Fr. plaideur, a lawyer.

' Pledoures shulde peynen hem to plede ' : P. Plowman, B. vii. 42 (quoted by Skeat).

Henry le Pleidour, co. Salop, 1273. A.
Roger Pleadour, C. R., 15 Edw. III. pt. i.
Ralph Pledour, C. R., 31 Edw. III.

Pleasant, Pleasance. — (1) Bapt. ' the son of Pleasant,' or Pleasance ; cf. Clement and Clemence, Constant and Constance.

Pleysaunt Aylmar. H.
Plesencia Fromund, C. R., 29 Hen. III.

The font-name lingered on into the last century.

1612. Married — Pleasance Beales (fem.) : Reg. Burgh, Norfolk.
1681. Bapt.—Pleasance Tarlton (fem.) : Reg. St. Dionis Backchurch (London).
1757. Married—Pleasant Dadd (fem.) : Reg. Canterbury Cath.
Robert Pleasaunce, rector of Boldon, 1655 : DDD. ii. 62.

(2) Local, ' of Plesence.'

Reginald de Plesence, co. Linc., 1273. A.
Peter de Plesenc', co. York, ibid.
Astin de Plesenz, co. Linc., ibid.
London, 1, 1 ; MDB. (co. Camb.), 0, 1.

Pledger.—Occup. ' the pledger,' one who gave securities (?).

1805. Married—James Tarlton and Sarah Pledger : St. Geo. Han. Sq. ii. 324.
MDB. (co. Camb.), 1 ; (co. Essex), 5.

Plevin. — Bapt. ' the son of Blethyn,' a Welsh personal name. The usual patronymic is Blevin, but Plevin is not without representatives (v. Blevin and Blethyn) ; cf. Pinnion and Benyon, Pumphrey and Boumphrey, also Welsh surnames.

Alice Plethin, alias Mayo, of the city of Chester, 1670 : Wills at Chester (1660–80), p. 212.
William Plevin, of Kinnerton, 1685 : ibid. (1681–1700), p. 199.

The Manchester Courier, October 26, 1886, announces the marriage of ' George James, son of the late James Plevin, Nantwich, to Rhoda,' &c. Nantwich is near the Welsh border.

Manchester, 1.

Plews, Plues. — Bapt. Ap-Lewis (Welsh), whence Plewis, Plews, now found also as Plues. One of these latter tells me his great grandfather wrote it Plews; cf. Price, Pritchard, Ployd, &c. I lack absolute proof of the above derivation.

Griffin Lewys, or Lews, 1518 : Reg. Univ. Oxf. i. 108.
1702. Married—Thomas Plews and Charlotte Doyce: St. Geo. Han. Sq. ii. 80.
1802. — Michael Francis Plues and Mary Birley : ibid. p. 254.
London, 4, o; Philadelphia, 6, o; Kendal (Plues), 1.

Pleynamour.—Nick. 'full of love' (v. Fullalove); cf. Paramor, Douceamour, Phillimore.

'And geven me pleyne (full) poure and might
The kyngdom of heuene for to preche.'
York Mystery Plays, p. 160, ll. 103-4.
'Men speken of romaunces of pris,
Of Hornchild, and of Ipotis,
Of Bevis, and Sire Guy,
Of Sire Libeux, and Pleindamour,
But Sire Thopas, he bereth the flour
Of real chevalrie.'
Chaucer, C. T. 13825-30.
Andreas Pleynamur, co. Suff., 1273. A.
Cristiana Playnamur, co. Suff., ibid.
Philip Pleyndamour, C. R., 14 Edw. II.
Agnes Playnamour, 1379 : P. T. Yorks. p. 282.
Thomae Pleynamour, C. R., 4 Hen. IV. pt. i.

Plimley.—Local, 'of Plumley,' q.v., a variant ; cf. Plimpton for Plumpton.

1665. Bapt.—Ann, d. John Plimley : St. Jas. Clerkenwell, i. 226.
1796. Married—Rev. Henry Plimley and Thomasin Porter : St. Geo. Han. Sq. ii. 147.
London, 1.

Plimmer.—Occup. 'the plumber'; a variant of Plummer (q.v.). Cf. Plimpton for Plumpton, or Plimley for Plumley.

1780. Married—James Plimmer and Jane Talbot : St. Geo. Han. Sq. i. 313. Manchester, 2.

Plimpton, Plympton.—Local, ' of Plympton,' a parish in co. Devon. Sometimes, however, a variant of Plumpton, q.v.

Robert de Plimpton, co. York, 20 Edw. I. R.
Simon de Plymptone, co. Soms., 1 Edw. III : Kirby's Quest, p. 278.
London, 4, 0; Boston (U.S.), 16, 11.

Plimsaul, Plimsoll. — Local, ' of Plemonstall'(?), a parish about four miles from Chester. From Plimstall to Plimsoll would be an

easy stage. I have no certain proof of this.
London, 1, 1; MDB. (co. Norf.), 1, 0; Sheffield, 0, 1.

Plomer; v. Plummer.

Plowden. — Local, ' of Plowden,' an estate in co. Salop. The Plowdens of Plowden Hall in that county still exist.

Roger de Ploeden, co. Salop, 1273. A.
1618. Edward Ployden, co. Salop : Reg. Univ. Oxf. vol. ii. pt. ii. p. 374.
MDB. (co. Salop), 2 ; New York, 1.

Plowman. — Occup. ' the ploughman,' a farm labourer, one engaged in ploughing.

John le Ploghman, co. Rutland, 1273. A.
John le Plouman, co. Linc., ibid.
John le Ploman, co. Soms., 1 Edw. III : Kirby's Quest, p. 232.
Luke le Ploman, co. Soms., 1 Edw. III : ibid.
Willelmus Ploghman, 1379 : P. T. Yorks. p. 256.
Alicia Plughman, 1379 : ibid. p. 96.
1602-3. Humphrey Dovey and Juliana Plowman : Marriage Lic. (London), i. 275.
London, 8 ; Philadelphia, 11.

Plowright. — Occup. ' the ploughwright,' a maker of ploughs; cf. Plowsmith.

William le Plowritte, co. Camb., 1273. A.
William le Ploughwryte, 1307. M.
Thomas Hyneson, ploghwryght, 1379 : P. T. Yorks. p. 292.
Catherine Ploughwright, co. York. W. 2.
1778. Married — Thomas Lloyd and Mary Plowright : St. Geo. Han. Sq. i. 290.
Manchester, 1 ; New York, 1.

Plowsmith. — Occup. ' the plowsmith,' a maker of ploughs. Plowright was the usual name, but we have proof that Plowsmith existed.

' Until a smith, men callen Dan Gerveis, That in his forge smithed plow-harness.'
Chaucer, Milleres Tale, 3758-9.
William le Plousmith, Rot. Fin., 7 Edw. I.

Ployd. — Bapt. ' the son of Lloyd,' from the Welsh Ap-Lloyd. This is found in England generally as Bloyd (q.v.), in America as Ployd ; cf. Breese and Preece.
Philadelphia, 7.

Pluck. — I do not know the origin of this surname, and therefore simply confine myself to instances. Perhaps a French importation.

John Pluk, C. R., 3 Edw. IV.

1775. Married — Auguste François Plique and Jeanne Josephine Viulley : St. Geo. Han. Sq. i. 249.
London, 3.

Plucknett.—Local, ' of Plukenet'; v. Plunkett, of which it is a variant.

William de Plukenet, co. Berks, 1273. A.
Alanus de Plugenet, 50 Hen. III : BBB. p. 122.
Alanus de Plukenet, 28 Edw. I : ibid. p. 587.
Eliner Plucknete, 1652 : Reg. St. Mary Aldermary (London), p. 93.
John Plucknet, 1655 : ibid. p. 94.
1735. Married — John Austin and Susanna Plucknett : St. Geo. Han. Sq. i. 15.
London, 1.

Pluckrose.—Nick. This surname is as old as the 13th century. Lower suggests that it and Pullrose arose out of feudal custom. He finds them in Sussex in 1296, and in the same county knows property close to Ashdown Forest held of the Duchy of Lancaster by one red rose. The reeve of the manor comes periodically and plucks a rose from the tree (v. Patr. Brit. p. 271).

Alan Pluckerose, co. Suff., 1273. A.
Richard Pluckerose, co. Wilts, ibid.
London, 6.

Plues; v. Plews.

Plum, Plumb, Plumbe, Plume, Plumm.—Local, ' at the plum,' i.e. plum-tree (v. Plumptre): cf. Crabb and Crabtree. The b in Plumb and Plumbe is, of course, excrescent.

Richard Plumbe, co. Camb., 1273. A.
Symon Plumbe, co. Hunts, ibid.
Agnes Plombe, of Woodbank, spinster, 1590 : Wills at Chester, p. 153.
Robert Plumb, of Wavertree, 1618 : ibid.
London, 2, 6, 3, 2, 1.

Plumber; v. Plummer.

Plumbly; v. Plumley.

Plumbridge; v. Plumridge.

Plumer.—Occup. ' the plumber.' For early instances, v. Plummer.

1566. Ralph Plumer and Agnes Lendall : Marriage Lic. (London), i. 34.
1739. Married—Richard Plumer and Deborah Atkins : St. Geo. Han. Sq. i. 23.
1779. — John Plumer and Ann Finch : ibid. p. 305.
London, 1 ; New York, 9.

Plumley, Plumly, Plumbly, Plumbley.—Local, 'of Plumley,' a township in the parish of Great Budworth, co. Chester. The *b* in Plumbly is the usual excrescence. For a variant, v. Plimley. Of course many other small spots would be called Plum-ley, 'the meadow where the plum-trees grew.'

Henry Plomlegh, co. Soms., 1 Edw. III : Kirby's Quest, p. 108.
1552-3. Buried — Thomas Plumlye: St. Dionis Backchurch, p. 183.
1773. Married—George Plumley and Dorothy Avis: St. Geo. Han. Sq. i. 231.
London, 0, 0, 1, 0; Liverpool, 1, 0, 0, 1; Philadelphia, 6, 9, 0, 0.

Plummer, Plumber, Plomer.—Occup. 'the plumber.' Cotg. 'plummer.' Fr. *plomb*, lead. 'Plumber or plomere, *tlumbarius*' : Prompt. Parv. 'The Plummers and Patenmakers marched together in the York Pageant' (York Mystery Plays, p. xxii).

William le Plummer, C. R., 39 Hen. III. pt. i.
Henry le Plomere, London, 1273. A.
Andrew le Plumer, or Plummer, co Kent, ibid.
John le Plumer, co. Oxf., ibid.
Gilbert le Plomer, co. Camb., ibid.
Henry le Plomer, 25 Edw. I : Freemen of York (Surt. Soc.), i. 6.
Ricardus Plummer, 1379 : P. T. Yorks. p. 161
1631. Married—George Arnold and Eliz. Plummer : St. Jas. Clerkenwell, iii. 62.
1804. — Jarrard John Howard and Margery Plomer: St. Geo. Han. Sq. ii. 208.
MDB. (co. Kent), 4, 1, 6; London, 22, 0, 0; Boston (U.S.), 74, 0, 0; New York, 11, 2, 0.

Plumpton.—Local, 'of Plumpton': (1) a township in the parish of Kirkham, co. Lanc.; (2) a parish in co. Sussex; (3) a parish in co. Northumberland. Also other smaller spots in various counties; cf. Plimpton and Plympton.

William de Plumton, co. Northampton, 1273. A.
Robert de Plumpton, co. Northampton, ibid.
John Plumpton, of West Derby, co. Lanc., 1582: Wills at Chester, i. 153.
Thomas Plumpton, of West Derby, co. Lanc., 1619: ibid.
1576. Richard Plumpton and Johanna Husband: Marriage Lic. (London), i. 73.
London, 3.

Plumptre, Plumptree, Plumtre.—Local, (1) 'of Plumtree,' a parish in co. Nottingham, five miles from the capital; (2) 'at the plumtree,' from residence by some particular fruit-tree; cf. Peartree, Crabtree, Rowntree, &c.

John Plumtre, or Plumtree, 1538 : Reg. Univ. Oxf. i. 191.
Alban Plumtree, co. Bedford, 1585: ibid. vol. ii. pt. ii. p. 140.
1755. Married—Francis Plumptre and Dorothy Bury : St. Geo. Han. Sq. i. 56.
London, 2, 0, 0; MDB. (co. Notts), 0, 1, 1.

Plumridge, Plumbridge, Plummeridge.—Local, 'at the plum-ridge.' I cannot discover the precise locality. Plumbridge is a manifest variant, the *b* being intrusive ; cf. Plumb for Plum.

1784. Married—James Plumridge and Susanna Clarke: St. Geo. Han. Sq. i. 357.
London, 3, 4, 2; Oxford, 9, 1, 0; Boston (U.S.), 1, 0, 0.

Plumstead.—Local, 'of Plumstead,' a parish in co. Kent.

Simon de Plumpstede, co. Norf., 1205: FF. v. 461.
William de Plumstede, co. Norf., Hen. III–Edw. I. K.
1763. Married—Thomas Martin and Eliz. Plumstead : St. Geo. Han. Sq. i. 127.
1771. — John Lawrence Jones and Ursula Plumstead : ibid. p. 210.
Philadelphia, 1.

Plunkett, Plunket, Plunkitt.—(1) Local, 'of Plukenet.' The same as the once great name of Plucknett (q.v.), by transference of *n* from the second to the first syllable. There are many such instances in this dictionary.

Joceus de Plukenet, co. Berks, 1273. A.
Joceus de Plunkenet, co. Berks, ibid.

(2) Nick. (?) from the complexion : *blanchet*, *blanket*, white ; whence blanket and plunket for a coarse woollen cloth (v. *plunket*, Halliwell). A statute of Richard III calls it 'plonket.' The form in Prompt. Parv. is 'plunket.' Mr. Way quotes a line from Awntyrs of Arthure :

'Hir belte was of plonkete, with birdis fulle baulde.'

Nevertheless, although some of our Plunketts may owe their name

to (a), like Russell, Burnett, Blount, &c., the general derivation is undoubtedly (1).

1574-5. Edward Plunket, of Ireland : Reg. Univ. Oxf. vol. ii. pt. ii. p. 59.
1786. Married—Christopher Plunkett and Sarah Fimester : St. Geo. Han. Sq. i. 387.
London, 7, 0, 0 ; New York, 38, 5, 1.

Plympton; v. Plimpton.

Pobjay, -joy ; v. Popjay.

Pochin.—Bapt. 'the son of Pochin,' evidently the dim. of some personal name.

Adam Pochon, co. Soms., 1 Edw. III : Kirby's Quest, p. 83.
Manchester, 1.

Pocklington.—Local, 'of Pocklington,' a parish in E. Rid. Yorks. From the East Riding the surname crossed the river into co. Lincoln, where it is familiarly known to-day.

Remigius de Poclinton, co. York, 1273. A.
Adam de Poklyngton, *mercer*, 2 Edw. I : Freemen of York (Surt. Soc.), i. 1.
Ricardus Pokelyngton, 1379 : P. T. Howdenshire, p. 17.
1575. William Pocklington, co. Linc. : Reg. Univ. Oxf. vol. ii. pt. ii. p. 67.
1709. Married — Joseph Pocklington and Eliz. Roberts: St. Geo. Han. Sq. ii. 206.
London, 2 ; MDB. (co. Linc.), 10.

Pocock.—Nick. ; v. Peacock.

Podger.—A variant of Proger (q.v.), 'the son of Roger.'

1789. Married—William Baker and Ann Podger : St. Geo. Han. Sq. ii. 28.
London, 1 ; MDB. (co. Somerset), 4.

Podmore. — Local, 'of Podmore,' a township in the parish of Eccleshall, co. Stafford. The surname crossed over the border into Cheshire.

John Podmore, of Sandbach, 1626 : Wills at Chester, ii. 176.
Reginald Podmore, of Hassall, co. Ches., 1628 : ibid.
Richard Podmore, of Sandbach, c. 1650 : East Cheshire, ii. 405.
London, 4 ; MDB. (co. Staff.), 3 ; New York, 1.

Poe.—Nick. 'the peacock'; cf. Pocock for Peacock. '*Poe*, a turkey. North England ' (Halliwell). The name seems in this case to have been transferred from one fowl to another ; v. Pea and Pay.

1660. Thomas Jenner and Anne Poe (co. York): Marriage Lic. (Faculty Office), p. 48.
Leeds, 1; New York, 4.

Pogmore, Pogmoor.—Local, 'of Pogmore,' some spot in the W. Rid. Yorks.
Willelmus de Poggemore, 1379: P. T. Yorks. p. 17.
Thomas Pogemore, 1379: ibid.
Adam Pogemore, 1379: ibid.

The above lived in the township of Brampton Bierlow, in the parish of Wath-upon-Dearne, near Barnsley.
Sheffield, o, 1; MDB. (co. Ches.), 1, o.

Pogson, Pockson, Poxon, Pogge.—Bapt. 'the son of Margaret.' Pog was the earlier form of Peg, as Mog was of Meg. As Mogson became also Mockson (now Moxon), so Pogson became Pockson and Poxon. Why names in M should take P for their initial in the nick. form I cannot say; cf. Patty from Martha, and Polly from Mary, the intermediate form being Matty and Molly.
Margareta Pogge, 1379: P. T. Yorks. p. 141.
Adam Pogge, 1379: ibid. p. 106.
1577. Married — Robert Pogge and Agnes Camden: St. Antholin (London), p. 26.
1620. John Pogson, of Manchester, barber: Wills at Chester (1545-1620), p. 153.
1666. Married—Richard Scrooke and Eliz. Pog: St. Jas. Clerkenwell, p. 128.
1754. — John Pogson and Eliz. Mary Milward: St. Geo. Han. Sq. i. 52.
London, 3, 1, 0, 0; Linthwaite (Yorks), 1, 0, 0, 0; West Rid. Court Dir., 1, 0, 0; MDB. (co. Derby), 0, 0, 1, 0, New York, 0, 0, 0, 1.

Poignant.—Nick. One who was sharp, biting, stinging, in retort. There is no reason why the surname should not have lived, but I fear it has disappeared.
John Poignant, C. R., 15 Ric. II.
Gilbert Poygnant. J.
1700. Married—Albanis Beaumont and Louisa Poignand: St. Geo. Han. Sq. ii. 50.

Pointdexter, Poingdestre.—Nick. An heraldic term. One of the nine chief local points of an escutcheon. 'Point-dexter parted ten (in Heraldry), an abatement due to a Braggadochio': Bailey's Dictionary, 1742. John Poyndexter, Fellow of Exeter College, Oxford, was dispossessed of his living in 1642 (Walker's Sufferings of the Clergy). The name still exists. 'Poingdestre and Truman, Chemists, 187 Newington Butts': London Directory.
1767. Married — John Troulliet and Eliz. Poingdestre: St. Geo. Han. Sq. i. 170. London, o, 1.

Pointer, Poynter, Pointmaker. — Occup. 'the pointer,' a maker of points. A manufacturer of tagged lace, for fastening hose and doublet together, &c. Falstaff in the act of saying, 'Their points being broken,' is interrupted by the remark, 'Down fell their hose' (1 Henry IV). The name and occupation occur in the Privy Purse Expenses, Elizabeth of York (p. 120): 'John Poyntmaker, for pointing of XL dozen points of silk pointed with agelettes of laton.' An Act passed 1 Edw. IV mentions, among others, 'Keper of oure Armour in the Toure of London, maker of poyntes, constable of oure castell of Hadleigh, &c.': Rot. Parl. Edw. IV.
Vasse le Poynter, co. Camb., 1273. A.
John le Poyntour. B.
Robert le Poyntour. T.
William Poyntmakere. S.
Robert Ponyter (sic), co. Soms., 1 Edw. III: Kirby's Quest, p. 240.
1607. Bapt. — William, s. Andrew Poynter: St. Jas. Clerkenwell, i. 50.
1617. John Poynter, London: Reg. Univ. Oxf. vol. ii. pt. ii. p. 359.
London, 3, 4, 0; Philadelphia, 2, 9, 0.

Pointing, Pontin, Ponting, Poynton.—Local, 'of Pointon,' formerly a chapelry in the parish of Sempringham, co. Lincoln. But v. Poynton.
Emecina de Poynton, co. Linc., 1273. A.
Jordan de Poynton, co. Linc., ibid.
Thomas de Poynton, co. Linc., ibid.
1790. Married—Jonathan Poynton and Mary Wood: St. Geo. Han. Sq. ii. 36.
1795. — James Dewley and Esther Ponton: ibid. p. 140.
1809. William Pointing and Eliz. Wright: ibid. p. 419.
London, 4, 1, 4, 0; Philadelphia, 0, 0, 0, 2.

Pole, Poll. — Local, 'at the pool,' from residence beside a pond or small lake; v. Pool. In some cases the parent of this name is Poole, a seaport in co. Dorset. The etymology is the same.
Hugh de la Pole, co. Camb., 1273. A.
Peter de la Pole, co. Oxf., ibid.
Anthony de la Pole, co. Devon, Hen. III-Edw. I. K.
Griffin de la Pole, co. Salop, 20 Edw. I. R.
Richard de la Pole, co. Derby, ibid.
John atte Pole, co. Soms., 1 Edw. III: Kirby's Quest, p. 118.
Robert atte Pole, co. Soms., 1 Edw. III: ibid. p. 126.
Francis Pole, or Poole, co. Devon, 1609-10: Reg. Univ.Oxf.vol.ii.pt.ii.p.300.
David Pole, or Poole, Bishop of Peterborough, 1557: ibid. vol. i. p. 141.
1736. Married — John Marshall and Jane Pole: St. Jas. Clerkenwell, iii. 264.
London, 4, 0; Philadelphia, 12, 1.

Polecat.— ? Nick. 'the polecat' (?).
Bernard Pilechat, co. Hunts, 1273. A.

Polkin.—Bapt.'the son of Paul,' from the dim. Paulkin; cf. Watkin, Wilkin, &c.
John Polkyn, or Palkyn, sup. for B.A., 1526: Reg. Univ. Oxf. i. 142.

Polkinghorne, Polkinhorn, Puckinghorne.—Local. 'of Polkinhorne.' An estate in the parish of Guinear, co. Cornwall.
'From this place were denominated an old family of gentlemen, surnamed Polkinhorne': Gilbert's Cornwall, ii. 152 (quoted by Lower).
Robarte Pokenghorne, 1541: Reg. St. Dionis Backchurch (London), p. 71.
1808. Married—Henry Polkinghorne and Mary Hill: St. Geo. Han. Sq. ii. 394.
London, o, 1, o; MDB. (co. Cornwall), 5, 0, 2.

Pollard.—Nick. 'pollard,' one who had his hair cropped short, from poll, the head, and suffix -ard, Hence a pollard tree, a tree lopped at the top; cf. Ballard.
John Polhard, C. R., 56 Hen. III.
William Polard, co. Camb., 1273. A.
Stephen fil. Pollard, co. Kent, ibid.

In this last case the father is simply called by his nickname, not his personal name.
Henry Pollard, c. 1300. M.
1548. Ellis Pollard and Johanna Chapman: Marriage Lic. (London), i. 11.
1717. Bapt.—Eliz., d. Edward Pollard: St. Dionis Backchurch, p. 154.
London, 27; Philadelphia 25.

Pollett, Pollitt, Poulett, Powlett.—(1) Bapt. 'the son of Paul,' from the popular form Poll, and dim. Poll-ett. Another familiar form was Powl, whence the dim. Powl-ett. (2) Local, ' of Pawlett,' a parish in co. Somerset; v. Paulett.

Quintinus Poulet, Pat. R., 7 Hen. VII.
John Pawlet, or Poulett, or Pollett, sup. for B.A., March, 1530: Reg. Univ. Oxf. i. 159.
Robert Paulet, or Pollett, 1538: ibid. p. 190.
1661. Elias Hirons and Joane Pollett: Marriage Lic. (London), ii. 288.
1759. Married—Edmund Powlett and Frances Kelly: St. Geo. Han. Sq. i. 83.
London, 7, 1, 0, 0; Philadelphia, 1, 12, 0, 0.

Polley, Polly.—(1) Bapt., a variant of Pawley, q.v. (cf. Polson for Paulson). (2) Local, a variant of Pooley; v. Pulley. It is probable that both (1) and (2) have contributed to the existence of these surnames.

1574. Robert Polley and Grace Gooddaye: Marriage Lic. (London), i. 61.
1805. Married—William Polley and Eliz. Hodsdon: St. Geo. Han. Sq. ii. 319.
London, 4, 1; Boston (U.S.), 4, 0.

Pollinger, Bollinger.—Occup.; v. Bullinger and cf. Pullinger.

William Pallinger, c. Eliz. Z.
London, 1, 1.

Pollman; a variant of Pullman, q.v.

New York, 2.

Pollyblank, Polyblank.— Local. An undoubted local Cornwall name beginning with ' Poly,' so familiar to that county. Perhaps it is a corruption of Polyphant, a hamlet in the parish of Lewannick, near Launceston.

By Tre, Pol, and Pen
You may know Cornish men.'
London, 1, 3; Devon Court Dir., 0, 2.

Polson.— Bapt. 'the son of Paul,' from the popular form Pol; v. Powle.

1571. James Polson, New College: Reg. Univ. Oxf. vol. ii. pt. iii. p. 10.
Pol Withipol summoned to attend the Council: Proc. and Ord. Privy Council, vii. 156.
1796. Married — Thomas Polson and Hannah Solitzky: St. Geo. Han. Sq. ii. 157.
London, 2; Manchester, 1; Boston (U.S.), 5.

Pomeroy, Pomroy. — Local, ' de la pommeraye,' at the apple orchard, from residence thereby; cf. Pury, i.e. at the pear orchard.

Joan de la Pomeroy. H.
Henry de la Pomereye, or Pomeraye, co. Devon, 1273. A.
John Pomeray, co. Oxf., ibid.
Isota de la Pomerey, co. Devon, Hen. III–Edw. I. K.
Robert Pomeroy, co. Soms., 1 Edw. III: Kirby's Quest, p. 156.
1594. Andrew Pomeroy, or Pomroy, co. Devon: Reg. Univ. Oxf. vol. ii. pt. ii. p. 201.
1638–9. Pascoe Pomroy and Eliz. Wilson: Marriage Lic. (London), ii. 239.
MDB. (co. Devon), 5, 0; London, 2, 1; New York, 16, 3.

Pomfret, Pontefract, Pomfritt, Pomphrett.—Local, ' of Pontefract,' co. York. As everybody knows, Pomfret is the usual pronunciation, and has been for many centuries.

Robert Pumfret, co. Norf., 1273. A.
Thomas le Lang, de Pontefracto, 3 Edw. II: Freemen of York, i. 13.
Johannes de Poumefrgyte, 1370: P. T. Yorks. p. 108.
1579. Garrett Florence and Catherine Pomfrett: Marriage Lic. (London), i. 91.
1776. Married—William Pomfrett and Sarah Burton: St. Geo. Han. Sq. i. 265.
London, 1, 1, 0, 0; MDB. (co. Kent), 3, 0, 0, 0; Manchester, 0, 1, 1, 0; Boston (U.S.), 0, 0, 0, 1.

Pond. — Local, 'at the pond,' i.e. the pound, or enclosure for strayed cattle, from residence thereby; v. Ponder.

Geoffrey ad le Pond, co. Bedf., 1273. A.
Bartholomew de la Ponde, co. Bucks, Hen. III–Edw. I. K.
Sewal atte Ponde, c. 1300. M.
Henry Ponde, co. Soms., 1 Edw. III: Kirby's Quest, p. 223.
Roger atte Ponde, C. R., 17 Edw. III. pt. ii.
1626. 'Ellionem'. Pond and Mary Chamberlaine: Marriage Lic. (London), ii. 177.
1650. Married—Thomas Pond and Ann Hathaway: St. Jas. Clerkenwell, iii. 85.
London, 12; Philadelphia, 11.

Ponder.—Offic. 'the ponder,' the keeper of the pond or pound; v. Pond. Other forms are Pounder and Pinder.

William le Pondere, co. Camb., 1273. A.
Symon Pondere, co. Hunts, ibid.
1561. John Ponder (co. Essex) and Eliz. Wroughte: Marriage Lic. (London), i. 21.
1589. Married — Henry Ponder and Amy Fisher: St. Jas. Clerkenwell, iii. 14.
London, 9.

Ponsonby, Ponsaby.—Local, ' of Ponsonby,' a parish in co. Cumberland.

' The Ponsonbys of Hale were originally of Ponson, where they are to be traced before the reign of Edward II. At an earlier period the first of the family of whom we find any mention was called Ponson, and his son Fitz-Ponson ': Hist. of Allendale Ward, co. Cumb., by S. Jefferson, p. 56.

Thus Ponsonby means the *by* or dwelling of Ponson, a then familiar Norman personal name; v. Punshon.

1624–5. Simon Ponsonbey, *stationer*, and Eliz. Turner: Marriage Lic. (London), ii. 150.
1731. Married—William Punsonby and Jane Jenkinson: Reg. Parish Church, Ulverston, p. 375.
MDB. (co. Cumberland), 2, 0; Philadelphia, 0, 2.

Pontefract; v. Pomfret.

Pontifex.—Nick. ' the pontiff.' A Latinization like Faber; cf. Pope, Pape, Cardinal, Bishop.

Adam Pontif, co. Norf., 1273. A.
Richard Pontif, co. York, ibid.
London, 13.

Pook.—Nick. 'the puk,' from the complexion of the hair or dress, a colour between russet and black (v. Halliwell); cf. Russell and Black, or Borrell. But perhaps of Dutch parentage.

William le Puk, co. Soms., 1 Edw. III: Kirby's Quest, p. 102.
John Pouk, co. Soms., 1 Edw. III: ibid. p. 123.
Richard Pouk, co. Soms., 1 Edw. III: ibid. p. 195.
1667. Samuell Pooke, *weaver*: St. Peter, Cornhill, ii. 87.
1787. Married—James Albon and Ann Pook: St. Geo. Han. Sq. i. 401.
London, 6.

Pool, Poole.—Local, 'at the pool' (v. Pole), from residence thereby.

Walter atte Pulle, C. R., 39 Hen. III.
Walter de la Pulle, co. Oxf., 1273. A.
Boniface atte Poule, co. Soms., 1 Edw. III: Kirby's Quest, p. 192.
Stephen atte Poule, co. Soms., 1 Edw. III: ibid.
Philip atte Poule, co. Soms., 1 Edw. III: p. 223.
Johanna de Pulle, 1379: P. T. Yorks. p. 118.
1595. Bapt.—John, s. William Poole: St. Jas. Clerkenwell, i. 30.
London, 19, 71; Boston (U.S.), 26, 61.

Pooley.—Local, 'the islet in the pool'; v. Pulley.

Poore, Poor.—Nick. 'the poor'; v. Power and Pauper.

William le Poure, C. R., I Edw. I.
1580. Married—John Poore and Eliz. Budworth: St. Dionis Backchurch, p. 9.
1797. — Richard Poor and Jane Brook: St. Geo. Han. Sq. ii. 169.
London, 7, 0; Boston (U.S.), 7, 44.

Poorfish.—Nick.; cf. Rotten-herring, Hardfish.

John Pourfisshe, 1313. M.

Pope.—Nick. 'the popu'; cf. Bishop, &c. A sobriquet for one of an austere, ascetic, and ecclesiastical appearance.

Alan le Pope, co. Oxf., 1273. A.
Hugh le Pope, co. Suff., ibid.
Robert le Pope, co. Soms., I Edw. III: Kirby's Quest, p. 201.
London, 39.

Popham.—Local, ' of Popham,' a parish in co. Hants, seven miles from Basingstoke.

1620. Bapt.—Eliz., d. John Popham: St. Jas. Clerkenwell, i. 89.
1621. Alex. Popham, co. Wilts: Reg. Univ, Oxf. vol. ii. pt. ii. p. 393.
1763. Married—William Leyborn Leyborn and Ann Popham: St. Geo. Han. Sq. i. 121.
London, 3; MDB. (co. Berks), 2; (co. Hants), 2; Philadelphia, 3.

Popjay, Popjoy, Pobgee, Pobjoy, Pobjay. — Nick. 'the popinjay,' the talking jay, i. e. parrot; cf. Popinjay. M.E. *popingay*, O.F. *papegay*. The *n* is excrescent, as in Pottinger, Messenger, Clavinger. Mr. Lower has found Popjay and Popjoy still existing. The curious corruption Pobgee, however, is in the London Directory. The change from *p* to *b* seems to have occurred at the close of the 18th century.

1502. ' Item, for bringing of a popyngay to the Quene to Windesore, 13s. 4d.': Privy Purse Exp., Eliz. of York, p. 30.
Robert Papyngeye, C. R., 45 Edw. III.
Richard Popingay. TT.

Of the Popinjay Inn at Norwich, Blomefield writes:

'The middle messuage belonged to the prior and convent, and the other two messuages in 1330 to Roger Papinjay, in whose family it continued till Roger Papinjay, his grandson, turned the corner house into an inn, and in allusion to his own name made it the sign of the " popinjay, or great green parrot, from which time it hath been a publick-house to this day, it now being the Popinjay Tavern"': FF. iv. 117.

' Richard Popynjay, surveyor of the works at Portsmouth,' July 8, 1568: Rec. Office, Cal. State Papers (Domestic), i. 311.
1759. Married — William Popjoy and Mary Maynard: St. Geo. Han. Sq. i. 84.
1770. — John Francis Popejoy and Mary Freeman: ibid. p. 200.
1784. — James Pobjoy and Margaret Harris: ibid. p. 366.

From this latter the transition to the Pobgee of the London Directory is easy.

London, 0, 0, 1, 0, 0; MDB. (co. Somerset), 0, 0, 0, 1, 0; New York, 0, 0, 0, 0, 1.

Popkin, Popkins, Popkiss.—Bapt. ' the son of Robert,' from nick. Hob, and dim. Hobkin, sharpened to Hopkin, whence Welsh Ap - Hopkin = Popkin or Popkins, corrupted into the curious-looking Popkiss of the London Directory; cf. Perkins and Perkiss, or Hotchkins and Hotchkiss. Thus English Hopkinson, Welsh Popkins.

Hopkyn ap Popkyn, temp. Eliz. Z.
John ap Hopkin, temp. Eliz. ZZ.
Thomas Hopkis, 1602: Reg. St. Mary Aldermary, p. 10.
1759. Married—Thomas Popkins and Hannah Forrister: St. Geo. Han. Sq. i. 90.
1787. — John Popkin and Mary Long: ibid. p. 403.
London, 0, 0, 1; MDB. (co. Carmarthen), 1, 1, 0.

Poplar.—Local, ' at the poplar,' from residence thereby; cf. Plumptre, Rowntree, Crabtree, Birch, Oak, Ash. M.E. *poplere*, a poplar tree.

Thomas Popeler, 1379: P. T. Yorks. p. 150.
Johannes Popeler, 1379: ibid.
Willelmus Popler, 1379: ibid. p. 226.
1667. Bapt.—Ann, d. Richard Popler: St. Jas. Clerkenwell, i. 233.
1779. Married—Ralph Popler and Sarah Letsom: St. Geo. Han. Sq. i. 302.
London, 2.

Pople; v. Popple.

Poppinger.—Nick. 'the popinjay,' i.e. the talkative man; v. Popjay.

Boston (U.S.), 2.

Popple, Pople. — Local, ' at the popple-tree,' from residence thereby. Provincial English for a poplar-tree: ' Popple, a poplar-tree' (Halliwell); cf. Ash, Birch, Oak, &c.; v. Poplar.

1690. Bapt. — Frances, d. William Pople: St. Jas. Clerkenwell, i. 334.
1788. Married — Joseph Spinks and Mary Popell: St. Geo. Han. Sq. ii. 7.
1794. — James Pople and Ann Holmes: ibid. p. 112.
1797. — Richard Popple and Mary Ann Potter: ibid. p. 163.
London, 1, 0; MDB. (co. Linc.), 13, 0; (co. Soms.), 0, 11; New York, 1, 0.

Poppleton.—Local, 'of Poppleton,' a parish in W. Rid. Yorks.

Willelmus de Popilton, *sutor*, 12 Edw. I: Freemen of York (Surt. Soc.), i. 4.
Johannes de Popilton, 12 Edw. I: ibid. i. 5.
Johanna de Popelton, 1379: P. T. Yorks. p. 18.
London, 2; West Rid. Court Dir., 4; MDB. (co. Linc.), 2.

Popplewell, Poppwell. — Local, ' of Popplewell,' lit. ' the well by the poplar-tree.' Provincial English, ' popple, a poplar-tree' (Halliwell); cf. Poppleton. The spot Popplewell must be sought for in the immediate neighbourhood of Heckmondwike, W, Rid. Yorks.

Thomas Popilwell, of Cleckheaton, 1379: P. T. Yorks. p. 182.
Johannes de Popiwell, of Heckmondwike, 1379: ibid. p. 185.

Curious to note, there are two Popplewells in the Heckmondwike Directory of to-day.

1563. Buried—Betteris (Beatrice) Popplewell, servant to Robert Diconson: St. Antholin (London), p. 16.
1771. Married—Richardson Warburton and Ann Popplewell: St. Geo. Han. Sq. i. 209.
London, 4, 0; West Rid. Court Dir., 6, 0; Philadelphia, 1, 1.

Porch, Portch.—Local, ' at the porch.' M.E. *porche*, a covered entrance or portico. Probably a door-keeper, or doorward; v. Dorward.

Richard atte Porche, co. Soms., I Edw. III: Kirby's Quest, p. 218.
Stephen atte Porche, C. R., 43 Edw. III.

This surname seems to have become corrupted into Porridge:

1601. Bapt.—Anne, d. Simon Porridge: St. Antholin (London), p. 40.

1657. Married — Robert Porch and Elizabeth Barton : St. Mary Aldermary, p. 27.

It is interesting to notice that Mr. R. B. Porch played for Somerset v. Essex, and carried out his bat for 85, July 11, 1885.

London, 1, 5; MDB. (co. Soms.), 5, 1; Boston (U.S.), 1, 0; Philadelphia, 0, 1.

Porcher.—Occup. 'the porker,' a swineherd, lardiner, a feeder of pork. Fr. *porc*, a hog, pork.

John Porcarius, co. Essex, 1273. A.
Emma la Porcher, co. Oxf., ibid.
John le Porker, co. Camb., ibid.
Thomas le Porker, co. Oxf., ibid.
Nicholas Porker, co. Bucks, ibid.
Roger le Porcher. B.
Gilbert le Porcher. H.
London, 3 ; New York, 2.

Porrett, Porritt.—Bapt. 'the son of Peter,' from Pierre, dim. Perrot, Parrot, Porret, &c. ; v. Parratt.

John Porrett, or Perott, or Parott : Reg. Univ. Oxf. i. 13.
Robert Porrett, or Perrott : ibid. p. 98.
1775. Married — William Porrott and Margaret Thomas : St. Geo. Han. Sq. i. 257.
1780. — Thomas Porrett and Eliz. Haley : ibid. p. 316.
London, 1, 0 ; Manchester, 0, 2.

Port.—(1) Nick. (?). Perhaps an abbreviation of de la Porte ; v. (2).

John le Port, 1273. A.
Charles le Port. BB.
Oliva le Port. BB.

(2) Local, 'of the port.' Latin *portus*, a haven, as in Portsmouth ; or Latin *porta*, a gate, as in *portal*, *porter*, *portcullis*. The same as Porter (2), q.v. ; cf. Kitchen and Kitchener, Spence and Spencer.

Hugh de la Port gave land to the Church of St. Peter, at Gloucester, 1096 : Atkyns' Hist. Glouc. p. 75.
William de la Porte, Close Roll, 39 Hen. III. pt i.
Walter de la Porte, co. Soms., 1273. A.
Henricus del Port, co. Bucks, ibid.
Adam ad Portam, co. Camb., ibid.
Robert ad Portam, co. Hunts, ibid.
1601. Bapt.—Robert, s. Robert Porte : St. Jas. Clerkenwell, i. 39.
London, 5 ; New York, 7.

Portbury.—Local, 'of Portbury,' a parish in co. Somerset.

Adam Portbury, co. Soms., 1 Edw. III : Kirby's Quest, p. 154.
London, 4.

Portch.—Local ; v. Porch, a corruption.

Porteous, Porteus.—(1) Nick. 'port-horse,' i.e. a pack-horse ; cf. *porter*, a carrier, also *portfolio* and *portmanteau*. Just the sort of name that would be affixed to some hardworking, plodding man.

John Portehors, Close Roll, 54 Hen. III.
Robert Portehors, 1273. A.
John Portehors. V. 8.
Ralph Portehors. V. 8.
Ralph Portehors, 20 Edw. I. R.

(2) Local, ' at the porter-house,' i.e. a lodge-keeper, from residence at the lodge.

Robertus de Porterhouse, 1379 : P. T. Yorks. p. 202.
1667. Married—Timothy Weaver and Ann Portris : St. Jas. Clerkenwell, iii. 132.
1788. — William Porthouse and Eliz. Tinkler : St. Geo. Han. Sq. ii. 6.
London, 2, 1.

Porter. — (1) Occup. 'the porter,' a carrier. Fr. *porteur*. 'Portowre, *portator*' : Prompt. Parv. (2) Offic. a door-keeper. Fr. *portier*. ' Portere, *janitor*' : Prompt. Parv.

Francis le Porter, C. R., 45 Hen. III.
Robert le Porter, 1273. A.
Richard le Porter, 20 Edw. I. R.
William de Hodeles, *portour*, 21-2 Edw.I : Freemen of York (Surt. Soc.), i. 5.
Albin le Portour. N.
Adam Porter, co. Soms., 1 Edw. III : Kirby's Quest, p. 118.
Richard le Porter, co. Soms., 1 Edw. III : ibid. p. 130.
1674. Buried—Mr. John Portter : St. Antholin (London), p. 95.
London, 86 ; New York, 123.

Portingale, Portigall, Portugal, Puttergill. — Local, ' of Portugal.' An immigrant from Portugal ; v. Pettingell.

1543-4. Buried — Fransys Wallar, *a portyngall* : St. Dionis Backchurch, p. 180.
John Portingale, of Youghall, 1569 : Cal. State Papers (Domestic), i. 331.
1574. Bapt.—Jone Portingale : Prestbury Church, co. Chester, p. 43.
MDB. (co. Linc.), 0, 1, 1, 1.

Portingdon. Portington. — Local, ' of Portington,' a township in the parish of Eastrington, E. Rid. Yorks. Thence it has passed over the Humber into Lincolnshire.

Robert de Portington, co. Yorks, 1273. A.

1580. Robert Portington, co. Yorks : Reg. Univ. Oxf. vol. ii. pt. ii. p. 92.
1653. Bapt. — George, s. Hugh Portington : St. Jas. Clerkenwell, i. 183.
MDB. (co. Linc.), 1, 4.

Portman. — Offic. ' the portman,' equivalent to Portreve, q.v.

John Portman, co. Soms., 1 Edw. III : Kirby's Quest, p. 274.
Thomas Portman, co. Soms., 1 Edw. III : ibid.
Oxford, 1.

Portreve. — Offic. ' the portreeve,' the chief magistrate of a town ; see a brief dissertation on the origin of the portreeve of Gravesend in Lambard's Perambulation, 1596, p. 483 (Halliwell).

Augustin le Portereve, co. Hertf., 1273. A.
Henry Porterewe, co. Kent, ibid.
William le Portereve, co. Oxf., ibid.
Philip le Portereve, co. Soms., 1 Edw. III : Kirby's Quest, p. 138.
John Protereave, co. Soms., 1 Edw. III : ibid. p. 214.

Portsmouth.—Local,'of Portsmouth.'

MDB. (co. Berks), 1.

Portugal.—Local; v. Portingale.

Portway.—Local, ' at the portway,' i.e. gateway ; v. Port (2). Fr. *porte*, 'a port, or gate,' Cotg. The surname has not wandered much. Found in the 13th century in co. Hunts, it is familiar in the 19th to co. Essex.

Matilda de la Portweye, co. Hunts, 1273. A.
Richard de la Portweye, co. Hunts, ibid.
'The chair was occupied by Mr. G. R. Portway' : Liberal meeting at Leeds, Yorkshire Post, April 7, 1887.
West Rid. Court Dir., 2 ; MDB. (co. Essex), 4.

Portwine.—Local, ' le Poytevin,' from Poictou, a Poictevine. An imitative corruption.

Robert Pevtewin, co. Devon, 1273. A.
Robert le Peytevin, co. Glouc., ibid.
Preciosa Potewyne, co. Camb., ibid.
Peter le Pettevin. J.
Henry le Poytevin. J.
William Peytevyn, co. York, 20 Edw. I. R.
John Peytevyn, co. Soms., 1 Edw. III : Kirby's Quest, p. 217.
William Paitefyn, co. Soms., 1 Edw. III : ibid. p. 262.
Willelmus Paytfyn, 1379 : P. T. Yorks. p. 217.
London, 1.

Posnett. — Local, 'of Postle-thwaite.' This familiar Cumberland and Furness surname is abbreviated to Poslett in colloquial intercourse. It is frequently so registered. By the common change from *l* to *n*, Poslett has become Posnett; cf. *baluster* and *banister*. v. Postle-thwaite.

Gerard Postlet, of Dalton, 1596: Lanc. Wills at Richmond, i. 218.
William Postlet, of Marton, 1597: ibid.

In the Ulverston Church Registers it is found as Postlat.

Philadelphia, 2.

Posselwhite.—Local. A corruption of Postlethwaite, q.v.; cf. Applewhite for Applethwaite.

John Postelwaite, of Kirkbie, 1587: Lancashire Wills at Richmond, i. 218.
1766. Married — Richard Postlewhite and Ann Terry : St. Geo. Han. Sq. i. 154. London, 1.

Postill, Postel, Postol. — Nick. 'the Apostle'; cf. Bishop, Archbishop, &c. For lapse of initial vowel, cf. Potticary for *apothecary*. Halliwell (s.v. Postle) quotes :

'Like a postle I am,
For I preche to man.'
Armonye of Byrdes, p. 7.

'Posteles,' Piers Plowman, B. vi. 151 (Skeat). A.S. form *apostol* (ibid.).

Geoffrey Postel, London, 1273. A.
Hugh Postoyle, co. York, ibid.
William Postel, co. Sussex, Hen. III-Edw. I. K.
1560. William Yonge and Eliz. Postle : Marriage Lic. (London), i. 20.
1679. John Postle, of Lodmore Lane : Wills at Chester (1660-80), p. 214.

Probably the local Postlethwaite refers to the settlement or clearing of some early apostle or preacher, who had found his way into Cumberland. Cf.

Richard de Postelcumbe, co. Oxf., 1273. A.
William de Postlecumbe, co. Oxf., ibid.
London, 2, 0, 0 ; Philadelphia, 0, 2, 1.

Postlethwaite. — Local, 'of Postlethwaite.' I cannot discover the spot. There can be little doubt that the surname originally arose on the Cumberland side of the Duddon, and advanced eastward into Furness. To this day it is an established Furness name; v. Postill

for probable origin. For suffix, v. Thwaites.

1546. Buried—Richard Postlethwaite : Reg. Ulverston Church, p. 3.
1547. Married—William Postlethwait and Sebell Asburner : ibid. p. 5.
1587. John Postlethwayt, co. Westm. : Reg. Univ. Oxf. vol. ii. pt. ii. p. 161.
John Posteltwhett, of Ulverston (in Furness), 1622 : Lancashire Wills, i. 218.
William Postlewhat, of Kirkbie Ierleth (in Furness), 1592 : ibid. p. 219.
MDB. (co. Cumberland), 8 ; (co. Lanc.), 22 ; London, 4 ; Philadelphia, 1.

Potkin. — Bapt. 'the son of Philip,' from the dim. Philip-ot, whence the abbreviation Pot, and further dim. Pot-kin; cf. Watkin, Wilkin, &c. v. Potts.

Thomas Potekin, co. Camb., 1273. A.
Alice Potekyn, co. Camb., ibid.
Geoffrey Potekine, co. Camb., ibid.
Thomas Potkin. HH.
Peter Potkyn, 1506 : Reg. Univ. Oxf. i. 46.
1581. Christopher Pottkyn and Ann Heron : Marriage Lic. (London), i. 101.

Probably this name has become lost in Popkin, q.v.

Pott.—Bapt. 'the son of Philip'; v. Potts.

Pottor. Occup. 'the potter,' a maker of pots, vessels for cooking or drinking. A common entry in 13th century registers.

Michael de Potere, London, 1273. A.
John le Pottere, London, ibid.
Ranulph le Poter, co. Essex, ibid.
Nicholas le Potter, bailiff of Yarmouth, 1303 : FF. xi. 322.
1598. Robert Bruffe and Margaret Potter : Marriage Lic. (London), i. 258.
London, 96 ; Boston (U.S.), 97.

Potterton.—Local, 'of Potterton,' a township in the parish of Barwick-in-Elmett, W. Rid. Yorks.

1664. Bapt. — Mathew, s. Mathew Potterton : St. Jas. Clerkenwell, i. 224.
MDB. (co. Linc.), 1 ; London, 1 ; Philadelphia, 2.

Potticary, Pothecary. — Occup. 'the apothecary.' Originally one who kept a store for non-perishable goods, such as spices, drugs, and preserves. The spicer and apothecary sold between them what the grocer now sells, minus the modern tea, coffee, &c. (v. Groser).

William Apotecarius, co. Northampton, 1273. A.

1591. Christopher Potticary, co. Wilts : Reg. Univ. Oxf. vol. ii. pt. ii. p. 186.
William Clapham, London, *potticary*, 1633 : Visitation of London, 1634, p. 164.
Josias Barnard, *pottycary*, 1645 : Reg. St. Mary Aldermary (London), p. 89.
1788. Married—James Potticary and Ann Knight : St. Geo. Han. Sq. ii. 13.
1803. — Richard Hancock and Maria Pottecary : ibid. p. 291.
London, 0, 1 ; MDB. (co. Cambridge), 1, 0.

Pottin. — Bapt. 'the son of Potin,' i.e. Philip from Pot (the nick. of Philipot), dim. Pot-in (v. Pottle) ; cf. Cobbin (v. Coppin), the dim. of Cob, the nick. of Jacob.

John Potin, co. Kent, 1273. A.
Benedict Potin, co. Kent, ibid.
Simon Potin, co. Kent, ibid.

Pottinger.—Occup. 'the potager,' a maker of pottage, i.e. thick soup or broth, a favourite mess in older days. The intrusive *n* is regular ; cf. Messinger and *passenger*, for Messager and *passager*.

'Suppe not with grete sowndynge,
Neither potage ne other thynge.'
Boke of Curtasye.

Ralph Prestbury was sworn to keep the peace towards

'Thomam Halle, *potygare*, alias *chirurgicum*,' 1439 : Mun. Acad. Oxon. p. 523.

From his knowledge of herbs the potager gradually became looked upon as a 'medicine man,' or herbalist (v. English Surnames, 5th edit., p. 207).

Walter le Potager, 1303. M.
John le Potager, co. Soms., 1 Edw. III : Kirby's Quest, p. 272.
Simon de Wederhale, *potager*, 2 Edw. III : Freemen of York, i. 24.
Robert le Potager. G.
John Potenger. F.
1575. Simon Pottinger, co. Hants : Reg. Univ. Oxf. vol. ii. pt. ii. p. 64.
1762. Married — Benjamin Pottinger and Eliz. Dance : St. Geo. Han. Sq. i. 112.
1776. — John Bostock and Anne Potenger : ibid. p. 261.
Sheffield, 1 ; London, 4 ; Boston (U.S.), 3.

Pottiphar.—Nick. An imitative corruption of Pettifer. The half-way house was Pettipher ; v. Pettifer.

Gilbert Portefer, co. Soms., 1 Edw. III : Kirby's Quest, p. 106.

Pottle. — Bapt. 'the son of Potel,' i.e. Philip, from Pot (the nick. of Philipot), dim. Pot-el; v. Potts, Pottin, and Potkin. Once more in such a surname as this we see the early and widespread influence of the apostolic name of Philip.

Richard Potel, co. Bucks, 1273. A.
Nicholas Potelle, Pat. Roll, 1 Hen. VII. pt. i.
1779. Married — Thomas Pottle and Jane Simmons: St. Geo. Han. Sq. i. 297. London, 6.

Potton. — Local, 'of Potton,' a parish and market-town in co. Bedford.

Gilbert de Pottone, co. Bedf., 1273. A.
Simon de Pottone, co. Camb., ibid.
1805. Married — Timothy Potton and Eliz. Oldham: St. Geo. Han. Sq. ii. 337. London, 2.

Potts, Pott. — Bapt. 'the son of Philip,' dim. Philipot or Philpot, whence nick. Pot (v. Potkin). The frequency of Potts as a surname (see London Directory) is owing to the once great popularity of the apostolic name. The Spanish Armada and the marriage of Mary with Philip ruined the prospects of Philip at the font as much as the Gunpowder Plot ruined the name of Guy. Cf. the French importation Potelette in the London Directory, evidently a diminutive formed on the nick. Pot. The Hundred Rolls have 'John Potin, co. Kent,' another diminutive (cf. Col-in from Nicholas) which corresponds with Coppin (q.v.), a dim. of Cob, the last syllable of Jacob or Jacop.

Colin Pot, co. Linc., 1273. A.
Ricard Pot, co. Essex, ibid.
Reginald Pot, co. Hunts, ibid.
William Pote, co. Norf., ibid.
London, 22, 10.

Poucher. — Occup. 'the poucher,' a maker of pouches, pokes, or bags; v. Pouchmaker.

John Poucher, C. R., 19 Edw. II. pt. ii. MDB. (co. Lincoln), 2.

Pouchmaker. — Occup. 'the pouchmaker.' This surname, although well established, did not live. But it is represented by the shorter Poucher, q.v.

Nicholas Pouchemakere, C. R., 51 Edw. III.
William Pouchemaker. H.

Walter Pouchmaker, C. R., 24 Edw. III. pt. ii.
Nicholaus Pouchmaker, 1379: P. T. Yorks. p. 98.
Agnes Pouchemaker, co. York. W. 2.

Poulett; v. Pollett.

Poulson. — Bapt. 'the son of Paul,' from a provincial form Poul; v. Powle.

Poulter, Poulterer. — Occup. 'the poulter,' a poulterer. O.F. polete, a young hen, a pullet. 'Pulter, gallinarius,' Prompt. Parv.

'I have no peny,
Poletes to bugge (buy).'
Piers Plowman.

'Drovers, cokes, and pulters.'
Cocke Lorelle's Bote.

Osbert le Puleter, Close Roll, 52 Hen. III.
Osbert le Puleter, 1273. A.
Adam le Poleter, c. 1300. M.
Willelmus de Menthorp', pulter, 1379: P. T. Howdenshire, p. 16.
Elyas Pulter, husband, 1379: ibid. p. 17.
Ricardus Pulter, 1379: P. T. Yorks. p. 242.
1621. William Poulter and Alice Belley: Marriage Lic. (London), i. 106.
1781. Married — Robert Poulter and Mary Axtell: St. Geo. Han. Sq. i. 326. London, 10, 0; Philadelphia, 1, 9.

Poulton. — Local, 'of Poulton.' There are several parishes and townships of this name in cos. Lancaster and Chester; also a parish in co. Wilts, near Cirencester. 'The homestead by the pool' would naturally cause many Poultons to arise in different districts.

Henry de Pulton, co. Soms., 1 Edw. III: Kirby's Quest, p. 104.
Walter de Pulton, co. Soms., 1 Edw. III: ibid.
1627. John Rogers and Dorothy Poulton: Marriage Lic. (London), ii. 189.
Ellen Poulton, of Dalton, 1635: Lancashire Wills at Richmond, i. 217.
Richard Poolton, of Barton, 1670: ibid. i. 219.
London, 14; Manchester, 2; Philadelphia, 4.

Pound. — Local, 'at the pound,' the enclosure for strayed cattle, the pin-fold; v. Pond for early instances.

William atte Pounde, co. Soms., 1 Edw. III: Kirby's Quest, p. 105.
Adam atte Pounde, co. Soms., 1 Edw. III: ibid. p. 130.
Henry del Pount de Eldreford, C. R., 47 Hen. III.
1579. Ralph Proby and Alice Pounte: Marriage Lic. (London), i. 91.

1634. Bapt.—Marie, d. Thomas Pound: St. Jas. Clerkenwell, i. 128.
London, 11; Philadelphia, 6.

Pounder. — Offic. 'the pounder,' the keeper of the pinfold; v. Pinder and Ponder.

1601. John Cartwright and Amy Pownder: Marriage Lic. (London), i. 266.
1803. Married — Robert Pounder and Esther Mays: St. Geo. Han. Sq. ii. 284.
London, 1; Boston (U.S.), 3.

Poundsend. — Local, 'at the pound's-end'; v. Pound, and cf. Townsend.

John de Poundesend. D.

Pourtrayer. — Occup. 'the pourtrayer,' a drawer, one who depicts, a painter. O.F. portraire, to depict.

Richard le Pertriur, co. York. W. 4.
Geoffrey le Purtreour, London. X.

Povey, Povah. — Nick. 'the povey,' i.e. owl. Almost all birds are represented in our directories; cf. Nightingale, Sparrow, Goldfinch, &c. 'Povey, an owl. Gloucestershire' (Halliwell). It is in Shropshire and on the Welsh border that the surname is so familiarly known. In Ellesmere I saw (in 1886) Povah and Povey over shops within fifty yards one of the other.

Richard Povah, of Shocklach, 1581: Wills at Chester (1545-1620), p. 154.
David Povey, of Shocklach, 1593: ibid.
Edward Povey, of Shocklach, 1595: ibid. p. 155.
Randle Povah, of Shocklach, 1605: ibid. p. 154.

It is quite manifest that Povah and Povey are the same name under two guises.

London, 8, 0; Crockford, 0, 4; MDB. (co. Glouc.), 1, 0.

Powdrell, Powderhill. — Local, 'of Powderhill' (?).

Willelmus Powdrell, 1379: P. T. Yorks. p. 83.
1586. George Powderhill, co. Berks: Reg. Univ. Oxf. vol. ii. pt. i. p. 394.
1592. Martin Powdrill, co. Berks: ibid. p. 419.
1610. William Powdrell, co. Berks: ibid. p. 327.
1660. John Poudrell, of Great Peover, yeoman: Wills at Chester (1660-80), p. 214.
London, 1, 0; Philadelphia, 0, 1.

Powell. — (1) Bapt. Ap-hoel or Ap-howel (Welsh), 'the son of Hoel'; v. Howel.

Elizabeth Ap-Howell. B.
John Ap-Howell. D.
John Appowell. F.
1547. William Pypar and Jone Appowell : St. Dionis Backchurch (London).
John ap-Howell, prebendary of St. David's, 1554 : Hist. and Ant. St. David's, p. 361.
William ap John ap Howell : Visit. of Glouc., Harl. Soc., p. 179.

(2) Bapt. 'the son of Poul,' or Powl, or Powel, i. e. Paul (v. Powle). 'Powle, a propyr name, Paulus': Prompt. Parv. 'Powel' (i.e. Paul), Piers Plowman.

Henry Powel, London, 1273, A.
Geoffrey Powel, co. Camb., ibid.
Mazelina Powel, co. Suff., ibid.
Hugh Poul, co. Buck, ibid.
John Powell, or Powle, sup. for B.A., June, 1532 : Reg. Univ. Oxf. i. 170.

Probably half of our Powells are of pure English descent. That all Powells are Welsh is a great fallacy.
London, 139.

Power. — Nick. 'the poor.' Although a great name, there can, it seems to me, be no doubt as to the derivation of the name. All the early entries point to one and the same source. Probably the vow of poverty would give the devotee such a sobriquet among his friends, and the title would be proudly borne ; cf. Barefoot. v. Pauper and Poore. The instances are very numerous ; only a few can be given.

John le Poer, co. York, 1273. A.
Warin le Powre, co. Norf., ibid.
William le Povre, co. Devon, ibid.
Ralph le Pouwer, co. Bucks, ibid.
John Povere, co. Camb., ibid.
Emma le Pouere, co. Oxf., ibid.
1561-2. Robert Power and Eliz. Gilbert: Marriage Lic. (London), i. 23.
1667. Bapt.—Susanna, d. Richard Pore: St. Jas. Clerkenwell, i. 230.
London, 13 ; Philadelphia, 52.

Powle, Powles, Powlson, Poulson.—Bapt. 'the son of Paul,' from a provincial form Poul. Poulson has ramified strongly in the United States. 'Powle, propyr name, Paulus': Prompt. Parv.

'Poul, after his prechyng,
Paniers he made.'
Piers Plowman, 10195.
'Rob Peter, and pay Poule, thou sayst I do.
But thou rob'st and poul'st Peter and Poule too.' Heywood.

John Poul, co. Soms., 1 Edw. III : Kirby's Quest, p. 117.
1521. John Pawle, or Powle : Reg. Univ. Oxf. i. 120.
1529. Richard Pawll, or Powle : ibid. p. 158.
1593-4. Richard Powle, sadler, and Ann Hockley : Marriage Lic. (London), ii. 213.
1681. Alice Poulson, of Chipping : Lancashire Wills at Richmond, ii. 200.
1797. Married — Henry Poulson and Mary Short : St. Geo. Han. Sq. ii. 171.
London, 1, 5, 0, 3 ; Manchester, 0, 0, 2, 0 ; Philadelphia, 0, 0, 0, 24.

Powlesland, Powsland, Pousland. — Local, 'of Paulsland,' land belonging to Paul (v. Powle).
London, 3, 1, 0 ; Boston (U.S.), 0, 0, 5.

Powlett ; v. Pollett.

Powley.—A variant of Pawley, q.v. ; v. Powle.
1805. Married—James Rudd and Mary Powley : St. Geo. Han. Sq. ii. 320.
London, 2.

Powling.—Bapt. 'the son of Paul,' a variant of Paulin ; v. Powle.
London, 1.

Powlson ; v. Powle.

Pownall, Pownell. — Local, 'of Pownall,' a township in the parish of Wilmslow, co. Ches.
1561. Buried—Edmund Pownall : Wilmslow Church.
1592-3. Bapt.—Uryan Pownall : ibid.
Humphrey Pownall, of Bramhall, 1604 : Wills at Chester (1545-1620), p. 155.
John Pownall, of Styal, Wilmslow, 1614 : ibid.
London, 9, 0 ; Manchester, 16, 1 ; Philadelphia, 4.

Pownceby.—Local, 'of Ponsonby,' q.v. ; a corruption. This is Mr. Lower's suggestion, and it seems satisfactory. In the United States the corrupted form is Ponsaby.
London, 4.

Poxon ; v. Pogson.

Poynter.—Occup. ; v. Pointer.

Poynton, Pointon, Poynting. Pointing.—Local, 'of Poynton,' a chapelry in the parish of Prestbury, near Stockport, co. Ches. Poynting, &c., is a corruption, the

g being an excrescence, as in Jennings. For another local origin, v. Pointing. Both have become inextricably mixed.

John de Poynton, barber, 12 Edw. II : Freemen of York, i. 18.
William Poynton, parish of Bunbury, 1617 : Wills at Chester (1545-1620), p. 155.
Randal Poynton, of Congleton, 1620 : ibid.
Manchester, 4, 2, 1, 0 ; London, 0, 0, 0, 4 ; Philadelphia, 2, 0, 0, 0.

Poyntz. — Bapt. 'the son of Poynz.'

'Walter fil. Ponz, a tenant-in-chief at the time of the Norman survey, and Drogo, his brother, were sons of Walter Ponz, a noble Norman. From Drogo fil. Ponz descended the family of Clifford': Lower's Patr. Brit. p. 275.
Hugo Poynz, co. Kent, 1273. A.
Nicholas Poynz, co. Kent, ibid.
William Poynz, co. Devon, ibid.
1614. William Duncumbe, Esq., and Elizabeth Morris, daughter of Sir John Poyns, Kt. : Marriage Lic. (London), ii. 27.
Crockford, 2.

Poyser, Poysere. — Occup. 'the poiser,' i. e. the weigher, probably a maker of scales ; v. Balancer. M.E. poisen, peisen, to weigh ; O.F. pois, peis, a weight. Poyser is a common surname in Derbyshire. Hence George Eliot's use of the name in Adam Bede.

Joscens le Peisur. DD.
London, 2, 0 ; Manchester, 3, 0 ; MDB. (co. Derby), 4, 0 ; Philadelphia, 1, 1.

Prance. — ? Nick. One who pranced in his gait (?). Cf. Golightly, Lightfoot, &c.

Ricardus Praunce, 1379 : P. T. Yorks. p. 134.
Willelmus Prance, 1379 : ibid. p. 226.
1787. Married — William Prance and Mary Honnor : St. Geo. Han. Sq. i. 400.
London, 3.

Prankerd.—Bapt. 'the son of Prankard.' Perhaps a variant of Punchard, q.v.

William Praucard (sic), co. Soms., 1 Edw. III : Kirby's Quest, p. 199.

Probably a misprint for Prancard. Close by in the same roll occurs Agnes Punchard (p. 200).
MDB. (co. Soms.), 5.

Pratt.—Bapt. 'the son of Prat' (?). It seems strange that the origin of this surname should be in any doubt. No less than thirty Prats are mentioned in the Hundred Rolls (1273), proving a very early popularity. In no single case, however, is there any prefix *de*, or *de la*, or *atte*, pointing to a local derivation. I see no other conclusion than that it was a personal name. Sprat or Sprot was, we know, a familiar personal name at the same period. Mr. Lower suggests that as the surname Meadow is Latinized into 'de Prato' in early registers, Pratt is a 'contraction.' This is utterly beside the mark.

Norman Prat, co. Camb., 1273. A.
Thomas Prat, co. Glouc., ibid.
Osbert Prat, co. Hunts, ibid.
Eustace Prat, co. Camb., ibid.

So the name runs. Until proof to the contrary is advanced, I am driven to the conclusion that Prat was an old personal name.

Richard Pratt, co. Soms., 1 Edw. III: Kirby's Quest, p. 168.
1579-80. Henry Pratt, *collier*, and Avice Sharpe : Marriage Lic. (London), i. 95.
London, 70 ; Philadelphia, 55.

Preacher. — Official, ' the preacher,' one who was set apart to preach. Equivalent to Sermoner, q.v.

John le Precheur, co. Notts, 1273. A.
John le Prechur, C. R., 43 Hen. III.
Thomas le Prechur. T.
Jacob Preacher. W. 20.

After looking vainly for years in search of a modern instance, I concluded the surname was obsolete. I was therefore delighted to find it existing in Hampshire.

1750. Bapt.—Jane, d. William Preacher: St. Jas. Clerkenwell, ii. 297.
MDB. (co. Hants), 1.

Precious; v. Pretious.

Preece, Preese. — Bapt. ; v. Price.

Preferment.—? ——. A curious surname, manifestly a corruption.

MDB. (co. Hereford), 1.

Preist; v. Prest.

Prelate.—Nick. ' the prelate '; cf. Bishop, Pontifex, Pope, Cardinal.

William Prelate, C. R., 15 Hen. VI.

Prendergast.—Local, ' of or from Prendergast,' a parish in co. Pembroke. Hence went forth Maurice de Prendergast to assist Strongbow in the Conquest of Ireland. In the many corruptions of this name the first *r* has been dropped ; v. Pendegrass.

London, 2.

Prentice, Prentis, Prentiss. —Occup.'the apprentice,' familiarly 'prentice or 'prentis ; cf. Potticary for *apothecary*. These forms are often found in church registers.

Thomas Prentys, London, 20 Edw. I. R.
William Prentys, co. Soms., 1 Edw. III : Kirby's Quest, p. 134.
Ricardus Prentys, 1379 : P. T. Yorks. p. 237.
Johannes Prentys, 1379 : ibid. p. 14.
1563. Buried—Richarde Skott, prentice to Roger Beawe : St. Mary Aldermary, p. 135.
—— William Ashforde, prentis to Roger Beawe : ibid.
1737. Bapt. — Mary Ann, d. Anthony Prentice : St. Jas. Clerkenwell, ii. 235.
London, 15, 2, 0 ; Philadelphia, 4, 3, 2.

Prescott.—Local, ' of Prescott,' parishes in cos. Lancaster, Oxford, and Gloucester. This surname has ramified strongly in the United States. The meaning is Priesthouse, ' the house the priest lived in.' The Lancashire town gave rise to a family that still flourishes in its local directories.

(Heredes) de Prestecote, co. Oxf., 1273. A.
Adam le Prestecote, co. Soms., 1 Edw. III : Kirby's Quest, p. 247.
1580. Bapt.—Alice, d. Thomas Prescott : St. Jas. Clerkenwell, i. 12.
Robert Prescott, of Standish, *yeoman*, 1596: Wills at Chester (1545-1620), p. 155.
Thomas Prescott, of Burscough, 1619 : ibid.
Manchester, 11 ; London, 10 ; Boston (U.S.), 93.

Presow.—Local, ' of Preesall.' Hackersall and Preesall form a township in the parish of Lancaster. The surname as Presow has crossed the sands into Furness ; cf. Lindow for Lindall. How early the name was so pronounced we find from the following entries :

Rogerus de Presawe, 1379 : P. T. Yorks. p. 163.
' Richard de Hakenshawe holds the mauor of Hackinsawe cum Prisowe, . . .

by homage . . . and two cross-bows ' : Baines' Hist. Lancashire, ii. 541.
Alice Prisoe, *widow*, of Dalton, 1605 : Lancashire Wills at Richmond, i. 221.
James Priseye, of Dalton, 1600 : ibid.
Thomas Presoe, of the parish of Aldingham, 1593 : ibid. p. 200.
Agnes Presoo, of Stanke, 1615 : ibid.
John Presall, of Preston, 1668 : ibid. p. 220.
Ulverston, 1 ; MDB. (co. Lanc.), 3.

Press. — Bapt. Ap-Rees, the son of Rees. A Welsh surname, a variant of Preece, &c. ; cf. Pritchard, Prodger, Ployd, Price, &c.

1580. Simon Presse, co. Staff: Reg. Univ. Oxf. vol. ii. pt. ii. p. 92.
London, 6 ; Philadelphia, 17.

Pressland. — Local, ' at the priest-land,' the land belonging to the parson, from residence on land so styled.

William Prestlond, co. Chester, 1453 : East Cheshire, ii. 89.
John Prestland, of Sounde, *gent.*, 1580 : ibid. i. 252.
Margaret Priestland, of Prestland Greaves, co. Chester, *widow*, 1620 : Wills at Chester, i. 156.

Of course the *t* was bound to be dropped in social intercourse, and the name is now found as Pressland.

1800. Married — John Presland and Mary Combs : St. Geo. Han. Sq. ii. 228.
London, 2.

Presson; v. Priestson.

Prest, Priest, Preist.—Offic. ' the priest.'

John le Prest, co. Hunts, 1273. A.
Roger le Prest, co. Wilts, ibid.
John le Prest, co. Soms., 1 Edw. III : Kirby's Quest, p. 167.
Adam Prest, et Magota uxor ejus, 1379 : P. T. Yorks. p. 134.
1615. Richard Warne and Susan Preist : Marriage Lic. (London), ii. 37.
1799. Married —Thomas Priest and Charlotte Yerbury : St. Geo. Han. Sq. ii. 200.
London, 3, 11, 3 ; Philadelphia, 0, 24, 0.

Prestage.—Local. Mr. Lower says, ' A corruption of Prestwich,' which is possible. I would, however, suggest that as we have Vicar-age and Parson-age (the latter a surname), so our forefathers may have spoken of a Prest-age, ' the residence of the Priest '; v. Prest.

1791. Married — John Cox and Eliz. Prestage : St. Geo. Han. Sq. ii. 53.
1801. — Francis Woodley and Isabella Prestidge : ibid. p. 245.
London, 3 ; Manchester, 1.

Prester, Priester.—Official, 'the prester,' i.e. presbyter. O.F. *prestre* ; M.F. *prêtre* ; cf. Prester John, in Mandeville's Travels (Skeat).

Richard le Prestre, co. Norf., 1231 : FF. i. 481.
Thomas le Prestre, co. Essex, 1273. A.
Gervase le Prestre, co. Soms., 1 Edw. III : Kirby's Quest, p. 206.
1591. John Jesopp and Margaret Prestar : Marriage Lic. (London), i. 198
New York, 0, 2.

Preston.—Local, 'of Preston.' No less than twenty-four parishes, situated in every part of England, bear this name in the Index to Crockford. No wonder the surname is so familiar. I furnish a few early instances out of many.

Laurence de Preston, co. Linc., 1273. A.
Alice de Preston, co. Northampt., ibid.
Adam de Preston, co. Westm., 20 Edw. I. R.
Robert de Preston, co. Salop, ibid.
John de Prestone, of Preston, co. Soms., 1 Edw. III : Kirby's Quest, p. 212.
Johannes de Pryston, 1379 : P. T. Yorks. p. 281.
Isabella de Preston, 1379 : ibid. p. 285.
1562. Rowland Preston and Anne Mellowe : Marriage Lic. (London), i. 24.
London, 30 ; Boston (U.S.), 53.

Prestwich.—Local, 'of Prestwich,' a parish near Manchester, and now practically a suburb ; v. Prestage.

Adam de Prestwich, 1325 : Baines' Lanc. i. 446.
Henry de Prestwich, 1331 : ibid.
'In 12 Hen. VI, Ralph de Prestwych granted the manor house (Hulme Hall, Manchester) to Henry de Byron' : ibid. p. 400.
Laurence Prestwich, of Gorton, Manchester, 1587 : Wills at Chester (1545-1620), p. 156.
Ellis Prestwich, of Broughton, Manchester, 1611 : ibid.
Nicholas Prestwyk, co. Soms., 1 Edw. III : Kirby's Quest, p. 160.
Whitefield (a village in parish of Prestwich), 4 ; Manchester, 3 ; London, 1.

Pretious, Precious. — Bapt. 'the son of Precious' (i.e. dear). Mr. Lower writes of this Yorkshire surname, 'A correspondent sends me the following anecdote : "Walking through a town with

a friend, I noticed the name of Precious. My friend said to me, 'You knew John Priesthouse ; he was the father of this Precious.' Here the vulgar had corrupted the name, probably in ridicule of Priesthouse."' Whatever truth may attach to this story communicated to Mr. Lower, it does not alter the fact that the surname Pretious or Precious is descended of a personal name Precious or Preciosa, as it was sometimes found in formal documents.

Preciosa Potewyne, co. Camb., 1273. A.
Preciosa de Kirkeby : Pat. Roll, 13 Edw. III.
Preciosa Scherwynd, *webester*, 1379 : P. T. Yorks. p. 98.
Johannes Precyus, 1379 : ibid. p. 241.
Richard Pretiouse, co. York, 1471 : W. 11.
1730. Married — James Bickett and Mary Precious : St. Geo. Han. Sq. i. 24.
London, 1, 0 ; MDB. (co. Suffolk), 0, 2 ; (East Rid. Yorks.), 0, 5.

Prett ; v. Pritt.

Prettyjohn, Prettejohn. — Nick. 'Prettyjohn.' But possibly an English corruption of the French Petit-jean. John was so very common in the 13th and 14th centuries, that such nicknames as Littlejohn, Properjohn, or Micklejohn were given in order to secure identity.

1530. 'Item, . . . paied to petit-John and his fellawe in rewarde by the Kinges commandment' : Privy Purse Exp., Hen. VIII, p. 52.
London, 0, 1.

Prottyman, Pretyman. — ? Nick. 'the prettyman' (?), i.e. the comely or clever one (v. *pretty* in Skeat's Dict.). A surname of East Anglian parentage ; still found in co. Suffolk. The name has flourished across the Atlantic.

1631. Peter Prettiman, co. Norf. : FF. i. 362.
1635. William Prettiman, rector of Hilburgh, co. Norf. : ibid. vi. 115.
1669. Married — Thomas Prittman and Margaret Banes : St. Jas. Clerkenwell, iii. 168.
MDB. (co. Suffolk), 3, 0 ; London, 0, 1 ; Philadelphia, 22, 0.

Prevost, Provost, Provis, Provest.—Official, 'the provost,'

i.e. the prefect, the chief magistrate, or mayor of a town. Commonly entered as Prepositus in the Hundred Rolls. O.F. *provost*, or *prevost*.

Walter le Provost, co. Wilts, 1273. A.
Henry Prepositus, co. Bucks, ibid.
Alan Prepositus, co. Norf., ibid.
Nicholas le Proust : Close Roll, 39 Hen. III. pt. i.
Geoffrey le Provost. H.
Robert fil Provost. T.
John le Preost, co. Soms., 1 Edw. III : Kirby's Quest, p. 128.
1766. Married — Thomas Provis and Ann Robinson : St. Geo. Han. Sq. i. 160.
London, 5, 1, 1, 0 ; Boston, U.S. (Provest), 1 ; New York, 5, 7, 0, 0.

Prewett, Pruitt.—Nick. 'the proud,' the arrogant, the haughty. M.E. *prute*. The surname early assumed a disyllabic form ; v. Proud for further information.

Andrew Pruet, co. Camb., 1273. A.
William Pruet, co. Camb., ibid.
Thomas Pruwet, co. Soms., 1 Edw. III : Kirby's Quest, p. 124.
Walter Prowet, co. Soms., 1 Edw. III : ibid. p. 142.
Juliana Prouet, co. Soms., 1 Edw. III : ibid. p. 264.
1680. Buried—May Pruett, nurse at Mr. Parr's : St. Dionis Backchurch, p. 247.
1717. Married — John Pruet and Mary Pruit (sic) : ibid. p. 58.
London, 1, 0 ; Philadelphia, 1, 3.

Price, Preece, Preese.—Bapt. Welsh Ap-Rice or Ap-Rees = son of Rice (q.v.).

'Item, geven to Harry ap-Rice, xvis.', 1544 : Privy Purse Exp., Princess Mary, p. 158.
Philip ap Rys. C.
Lodovicus Apprise. F.
John Apryce. F.
Lewis ap-Rhys, prebendary of St. David's, 1502 : Hist. and Ant. St. David's, p. 361.
1563. Arnold Appryce and Elizabeth Andrewes : Marriage Lic. (London), i. 27.
1579. Thomas Aprees and Margaret Barker : ibid. p. 88.
London, 167,9,1 ; Boston (U.S.),44, 1, 0.

Prichard ; v. Pritchard.

Prichett.—Bapt. A variant of Prichard or Pritchard ; cf. Prickett for Prickard ; v. Pritchard. The form Prichett, without the *t*, seems peculiar to the United States.
Philadelphia, 10.

Prickard.—Bapt. Ap-Rickard, a variant of Pritchard, q.v. ; cf. Rickard and Richard (v. Prickett).
MDB. (co. Radnor), 3.

Prickett, Prickitt.—(1) Bapt. Ap-Richard (Welsh), i.e. the son of Richard. Just as Richard is met by the harder Rickard, so is the Welsh Prichard met by the harder Prickard (q.v.). And just as Pritchard or Prichard became corrupted into Pritchett and Prit-chitt, so also did Prickard become corrupted into Prickett and Prickitt. The origin is thus simple enough.

(2) Nick. 'the pricket,' a buck in his second year ; cf. Buck, Stagg, Roebuck, &c.

'Weele haunt the trembling prickets as they rome
About the fields, along the hauthorne bushes.'
The Affectionate Shepheard, 1594.
'And I say beside that 'twas a pricket that the princess killed': Love's Labour's Lost, Act iv. Sc. 2.

Mr. Lower says, 'The crest of the family is allusive, being "a pricket—tripping, proper"': Patr. Brit. p. 277.

Richard Priket, co. Derby, 1273. A.

The above, of course, represents (2), not (1).

1793. Married—William Prickett and Hannah Weston : St. Geo. Han. Sq. ii. 91.
London, 2, 1 ; MDB. (co. Pembroke), 1, 0 ; Philadelphia, 5, 7 ; New York, 0, 3.

Prickhorse. — Nick. 'prick-horse,' a sobriquet for a hot rider, equivalent to Hotspur ; cf. Touch-prick.

Johannes Prikehors, 1379: P. T. Yorks. p. 217.

Priddy, Pridee.—Local, 'of Priddy,' a parish in co. Somerset, four miles from Wells. The sur-name is familiar to the district. Not to be confounded with Prideaux.

1792. Married—Abraham Priddy and Mary Pain: St. Geo. Han. Sq. ii. 73.
1805. — Thomas Flint and Ann Priddey: ibid. p. 334.
London, 2, 0 ; MDB. (co. Somerset), 1, 0 ; (co. Wilts), 3, 0 ; Boston (U.S.), 0, 1.

Pride, Pryde.—(1) Local, 'of Pride.' Some spot seemingly in co. Devon. (2) Nick. 'Pride,' probably the sobriquet of one who took the part of Pride in an early Mystery Play. But it may have been a nickname affixed on one of a haughty demeanour.

Roger de Prid, co. Devon, 1273. A.
W. de Prid, co. Devon, ibid.
Roger Pride, London, ibid.
John Pride, co. Derby, Hen. III–Edw. I. K.
Stephen Pride, co. Soms., 1 Edw. III : Kirby's Quest, p. 122.
Richard Pryde, co. Staff., co. Derby, 20 Edw. III. R.
1760. Married — William Pride and Ann Rogers : St. Geo. Han. Sq. i. 93.
London, 3, 0 ; Boston (U.S.), 7, 1.

Prideaux. — Local, 'of Pri-deaux.' 'The ancient family of Prideaux trace their descent from Paganus, lord of Prideaux Castle, in Luxilion, co. Cornwall, in the time of William I': Shirley's Noble and Gentle Men (quoted by Lower). There is no doubt Prideaux gave name to the family of Prideaux. They are early found in the neighbouring county of Devon.

Roger de Prydeaus, or Prydyaus, or Prudeaus, co. Devon, 1273. A.
Thomas de Prideas, co. Cornwall, 20 Edw. I. R.
Geoffrey de Pridias, co. Devon, Hen. III–Edw. I. K.
London, 6 ; Devon Court Dir., 10.

Pridgeon. — Nick. 'Prujean,' valiant John, a corruption of a French name ; cf. Grosjean, Pretti-john, Littlejohn, Micklejohn, &c.

Philip Pridgeon, co. Linc., 1596: Reg. Univ. Oxf. vol. ii. pt. ii. p. 218.
Crockford, 1 ; MDB. (co. Linc.), 4.

Pridham.—Nick. A variant of Prudhomme, q.v.

Priest; v. Prest.

Priester; v. Prester.

Priestfather. — Nick. 'the father of the priest.'

Walter Prestfadre, Close Roll, 11 Edw. III. pt. ii.

Priestknave. — Occup. 'the priest's knave,' i.e. the servant of the priest.

1564. Bapt.—Elizabeth Presteknave : Reg. Prestbury, co. Ches., p. 13.
1565. Married—John Presteknave and Anne Duncalfe : ibid. p. 17.

Priestley, Priestlay, Priest-ly.—Local, 'of Priestley' (i.e the priest's meadow), some small estate in the near neighbourhood of Bradford, W. Rid. Yorkshire. The surname is familiar in all English-speaking countries. But other spots would bear the same name.

Walter Prestlegh, co. Soms., 1 Edw.III: Kirby's Quest, p. 132.

The two following lived in Hipperholme, near Bradford :

Elena de Presteley, 1379 : P. T. Yorks. p. 194.
Johannes de Presteley, 1379 : ibid.
1561. William Priestlye and Margaret Sorrowgold : Marriage Lic.(London), i. 22.
London, 13, 0, 0 ; Philadelphia, 18, 0, 0 ; West Rid. (Yorks) Court Dir. 24, 1, 2.

Priestman. — Occup. 'the priest's man,' i.e. the servant of the priest ; cf. Matthewman, Addyman, Priorman, Monkman. Nevertheless, it may be an augmentative as in Masterman, merchantman, husbandman, &c. The former is by far the most satisfactory derivation.

Roger Presteman, co. York, 1273. A.
Robert Prestman, co. York, ibid.
Robertus Prestman, 1379 : P. T. Yorks. p. 200.
Isabella Prest, servant, 1379 : ibid.
1574. John Prestman : Reg. Univ. Oxf. vol. ii. pt. iii. p. 46.
1590. Christopher Wright and Alice Presteman : Marriage Lic.(London). i. 187.
London, 3 ; West Rid. Court Dir., 5 ; Philadelphia, 1.

Priestnall, Priestner.—Local, 'of Priestnall,' probably some spot in co. Chester. Priestner is a corruption of Priestnow, which is the usual pronunciation in the north of names ending in -all ; cf. Preesow for Preesall, Shawcross for Shallcross, &c.

1566. Bapt.—Anne Prestenall : Reg. Prestbury, co. Chester, p. 18.
1581. Married—John Baret and Sibell Priestnowe : Cheadle Ch., East Cheshire, 231.
Richard Pristnall, of Styal, in Wilm-slow Parish, 1595 : Wills at Chester, i. 156.
1601. Buried — Geffrey Prestener : Reg. Prestbury, co. Chester, p. 152.
London, 1, 0 ; MDB. (co. Chester), 0, 2 : Liverpool, 1, 0.

Priestson, Presson. — Bapt. 'the son of the priest.' One of a small class of patronymics from office and occupation ; cf. Clarkson, Frearson, Taylorson.

John le Prest, et Ivo filius ejus : co. Hunts, 1273. A.
'Walter Prestfadre and Walter Prest-son': Close Roll, 11 Edw. III. pt. ii.
William le Prestessone. G.

Doubtless this became Preson and Presson; cf. Pressland for Prestland.

1564. Married—John Russell and Margery Presson: St. Dionis Backchurch, p. 5.
1621. John Preson and Jane Marsh: Marriage Lic. (London), ii. 99.
Boston (U.S.), 0, 2.

Priggen. — Nick. This is a modification of Prujean. There is a Prujean Square in Old Bailey, London.

London, 2.

Primate.—Nick. 'the primate'; v. Prelate, and cf. Prince.

1611. Richard Primmitt, co. Linc.: Reg. Univ. Oxf. pt. ii. p. 398.
1621. Stephen Primatt, co. Linc.: ibid. p. 323.
Richard Primate, of Chester, *innkeeper*, 1618: Wills at Chester, i. 156.
1729. William Primate, rector of West Walton, co. Norf.: FF. ix. 140.

Primmer. — Official (?), 'the primer.' Probably a priest whose duty it was to conduct 'prime'; cf. Sermoner, Preacher, Chanter.

Petrus le Primur, co. Camb., 1273. A.
1795. Married—Richard Primmer and Ann Edwards: St. Geo. Han. Sq. ii. 128.
1803. — John Hubbard and Mercy Primer: ibid. p. 292.
London, 1.

Primrose.—Local. 'of Primrose,' an estate in co. Fife (Lower's Patr. Brit. p. 277). The name is in general found on Scottish soil.

Henry Prymros: Pardons Roll, 12 Ric. II.
Johannes Primerose, 1379: P. T. Yorks. p. 180.
Thomas Primerose, C. R., 3 Hen. VI. pt. ii.
1438. Robert Primerose, vicar of Easton, co. Norf.: FF. ii. 394.
1618. Duncan Primrose and Nichola Primrose: Marriage Lic. (London), ii. 59.
New York, 4.

Prince.—Nick. 'the prince'; cf. King, Bishop, Primate, Prelate, &c.

Willelmus Prynce, 1379: P. T. Yorks. p. 272.
Isolda Prynce, 1379: ibid. p. 273.
John Prince, priest in St. Michael's Church, Norwich, 1418: FF. iv. 492.
1690. Bapt.—Eliz., d. Joseph Prince: St. Mary Aldermary, p. 109.
London, 29; Philadelphia, 28.

Pring.—Nick.(?). 'Pryne, chief, first? (A.N.). "Hym wyl he holde most pryne"': Halliwell. The final *g* in Pring is modern and excrescent; cf. Hewling for Hewlin, or Jennings from Jenin.

William Prin, co. Berks, 1273. A.
John Prynne, or Pryn, 1506: Reg. Univ. Oxf. p. 49.
Thomas Pryn, of Swanswicke, co. Somerset, 1618: Abstract of Somersetshire Wills, p. 19.
London, 6; MDB. (Somerset), 10.

Pringle.—Local (?). A Scottish surname, of which I can gather no satisfactory account.

Alanus Prynkayle, 1379: P. T. Yorks. p. 131.
1784. Married — Robert Pringle and Jane Balneavis: St. Geo. Han. Sq. i. 362.
London, 12; New York, 11.

Prior, Pryor.—Official, 'the prior,' the head of a convent.

Hugh le Priur, co. Suff., 1273. A.
Richard le Prior, co. Suff., ibid.
Hugh Priour, co. Hunts, ibid.
John Priour, co. Som., 1 Edw. III: Kirby's Quest, p. 80.
John Priour, London, 20 Edw. I. R.
1577. Anthony Prior and Eliz. Sharsey: Marriage Lic. (London), i. 75.
1610. Bapt. — Susan, d. Edward Pryor: St. Jas. Clerkenwell, i. 58.
London, 36, 8; Philadelphia, 4, 23.

Pritchard, Prichard, Pritcher, Pritchett, Pritchitt, Prichett.—Bapt. Ap-Richard (i.e. the son of Richard), a well-known Welsh surname with several variants.

'Item, geven to William ap-Richard vs.,' 1536: Privy Purse Exp., Princess Mary, p. 4.
David Aprycharde, 1521: Reg. Univ. Oxf. i. 123.
William Prichard, or Ap-Richard, 1547: ibid. p. 215.
Thomas Prichett, London, 1616: ibid. vol. ii. pt. ii. p. 356.
London, 61, 10, 1, 7, 7, 0; Philadelphia, 13, 8, 0, 5, 0, 10.

Pritt, Prett.—Local, 'of Pret' or Preet. I cannot find the spot.

Peter Pret, co. Worc., 1273. A.
Robert de Preet, co. Lanc., 20 Edw. I. R.
William de Preet, or Pret, co. Lanc., ibid.
Richard Prett, sup. for B.A., 1543: Reg. Univ. Oxf. i. 205.
1610. Married — Edward Prett and Alice Parks: St. Dionis Backchurch, p. 17.
MDB. (co. Cumberland), 2, 0; London, 1, 1; Philadelphia, 0, 1.

Privett.—Local, 'of Privett,' a parish in co. Hants, near Petersfield.

1702. Married — Joseph Hallson and Ann Privett: St. Geo. Han. Sq. ii. 75.
London, 2; MDB. (co. Hants), 1.

Probart, Probert.—Bapt. Ap-Robert (Welsh), equivalent to English Robertson; cf. Pritchard, Price, &c.

1540. Buried — Thomas Uprobarte, prentice with Toson: St. Antholin (London), p. 2.
Lloyd ap-Robert. ZZ.
Ellice ap-Robert. Z.
'Item, geven to oon Davyd ap-Robert, xviii,' 1544: Privy Purse Exp., Princess Mary, p. 159.
1792. Married — Joseph Probert and Sarah Owen: St. Geo. Han. Sq. ii. 71.
London, 1, 3; MDB. (co. Hereford), 0, 11; (co. Radnor), 0, 2.

Probyn.—Bapt. Ap-Robin (the son of Robin = Robinson); cf. Probert = Ap-Robert. This surname crept across the borders of the Principality into Cheshire, and acquired a solid footing there.

William Ap-Robyn. H.
William Ap-Robyn. XX. 1.
William Probin, of Oldcastle, parish of Malpas, 1576: Wills at Chester (1545-1620), p. 156.
Bryan Probin, of Newton, 1578: ibid.
Hugh Probyn, of Newton, 1616: ibid.
William Probyn, archdeacon of Caermarthen, 1789: Hist. and Ant. St. David's, p. 360.
London, 3; MDB. (co. Monmouth), 3; (co. Gloucester), 5.

Proctor, Prockter, Procktor, Procter.—Offic. 'the proctor,' an attorney in a spiritual court. 'Proketowre, *procurator*': Prompt. Parv.

Thomas le Procurator, co. Linc., 1273. A.
John le Procuratour. D.
William le Procuratur, co. Linc., 20 Edw. I. R.
Willelmus Proktour, 1379: P. T. Yorks. p. 292.
1579. Edward Proctor and Effie Shewte: Marriage Lic. (London), i. 87.
1625. Bapt. — Ann, d. John Procter: St. Jas. Clerkenwell, i. 101.
London, 7, 8, 2, 14; Philadelphia, 22, 0, 0, 10.

Proffitt, Profit; v. Prophet.

Oxford, 2, 1.

Proger, Prodger. — Bapt. (Welsh) Ap-Roger = Prodger; cf. Price, Pumphrey, Powell, Pritchard, Prothero, &c. The *d* in Prodger is, of course, intrusive, as in Rodger.

John ap-Roger ap. Gilliant : Visit. Glouc. 1623, p. 104.
Roger Aproger. ZZ.
1607. Charles Proger, Jesus Coll., co. Monmouth : Reg. Univ. Oxf. vol. ii. pt. ii. p. 299.
London, 1, 0.

Prophet, Proffitt, Prophett. —Nick. 'the prophet,' one who was credited with a forecasting faculty. Thus 'Prophet, Priest, and King' are all English surnames.

Ricardus Profet, 1379 : P. T. Yorks. p. 283.
Willelmus Profet, 1379 : ibid.
1673. Ann Prophett, of Kingsley : Wills at Chester (1660–80), p. 216.
1764. Married—William Bricknell and Winifred Profit : St. Geo. Han. Sq. i. 139.
1771. William Proffett and Susanna Richardson : ibid. p. 214.
Manchester, 3, 1, 0; London, 0, 1, 0; MDB. (co. Chester), 0, 0, 1.

Prosser, Prossor.—Bapt. Ap-Rosser (Welsh) = the son of Rosser.

Thomas ap-Rosser. H.
John Approsser. Z.
David ap-Rosser. F.
Howell ap-Rosser : Visit. London, 1634, ii. 359.
1659. Married—John Currey and Ann Prosser : St. Dionis Backchurch, p. 35.
Henry Prosser, 1694 : Reg. St. Mary Aldermary (London), p. 111.
London, 9, 1 ; Philadelphia, 9, 0.

Prothero, Protheroe, Prothroe, Prytherch, Prytherat, Prythuch.—Bapt. Ap-Rhydderc, Welsh. The English form would be Roderickson. Some remarks on this name will be found in Miss Yonge's History of Christian Names (ii. 370).

Evan Prhydderch, co. Carnarvon, 1617: Reg. Univ. Oxf. vol. ii. pt. ii. p. 366.

A note is appended by the editor to say that he was the son of Roderic Evans, of Llanor, co. Carnarvon. Thus after the Welsh custom he became Evan Ap-Roderic or Prhydderch ; v. Rhydderch.

William Prythergh, or Protherugh, or Protherough, Jesus Coll., B.C.L., 1580–1: Reg. Univ. Oxf. vol. ii. pt. iii. p. 99.

The above entry supplies the stages by which Prothero or Protheroe was reached. The fact that the individual concerned was at Jesus College practically settles his nationality.

Walter ap-Riderch, 1384 : Hist. and Ant. St. David's, p. 374.
Rhydderch, bishop of St. David's, 961: ibid. p. 357.

The following is very Welsh :
Rhys Caradoc Pytherch, *chemist*: South Wales Dir. (Llanwrtyd).
1575. Roderohe Powell, co. Merioneth: Reg. Univ. Oxf. vol. ii. pt. i. p. 390.
1784. Married—William Pearson and Eliz. Prothero : St. Geo. Han. Sq. i. 355.
1797. — Thomas Prythergch and Ann Phillips: ibid. ii. 161.
London, 3, 4, 0, 0, 0, 0 ; MDB. (co. Carmarthen), 2, 3, 2, 7, 1, 1.

Proud.—Nick. 'the proud,' an arrogant man. M.E. *prud, proud, prut,* or *prout,* arrogant, haughty (v. Skeat). v. Prout.

Hugh le Proude, co. Bedf., 1273. A.
Robert le Proud, co. Bedf., ibid.
John Prude, co. Bucks, ibid.
Cristina le Prute, co. Oxf., ibid.
Herbert le Prute, co. Wilts, ibid.
1740. Married—John Bannister and Mary Proud : St. Geo. Han. Sq. i. 25.
1802. — John Skinner and Eliz. Prout : ibid. ii. 270.
London, 2 ; Philadelphia, 5.

Proudfellow. — Nick. 'the proud fellow'; cf. Longfellow, also a Yorkshire surname, and Goodfellow.

Rogerus Proudefelawe, 1379: P. T. Howdenshire, p. 6.

Proudfoot, Proudfit.—Nick. One who walked with a haughty step.

Thomas Proudfot, co. Hunts, 1273. A.
John Protfot, co. Oxf., ibid.
Robert Prudefot, co. York, ibid.

A common entry in the Hundred Rolls—evidently a familiar and colloquial term for a haughty man.
William Proudfot. H.
Richard Prudfot : Close Roll, 27 Hen. III. pt. i.
Agnes Proudefote, 1379 : P. T. Howdenshire, p. 17.
1801. Married—John Proudfoot and Eliz. Sparks : St. Geo. Han. Sq. ii. 244.

In the United States this surname is occasionally found in the corrupted form of Proudfit.
London, 4, 0 ; New York, 2, 2.

Proudlove.—Nick. ; cf. Phillimore, Sweetlove, &c. This surname seems to have had South Lancashire and East Cheshire as its chief habitat.

Wyllyam Proudlove, Manchester, 1541: Lanc. and Ches. Rec. Soc. vol. xii. p. 139.
Georgius Prowdlove de Manchester, 1600 : ibid. p. 250.
Eliz. Proudlove of Manchester, 1608 : ibid.
Richard Proudlove, of Sandbach, 1614 : ibid.
West Rid. Court Dir., 1 ; MDB. (co. Chester), 4.

Proudman.—Nick. 'the proud man'; v. Proud, Proudfellow, &c. Cf. Prudhomme.

1792. Married — John Proudman and Ann Chapman : St. Geo. Han. Sq. ii. 82.
London, 2 ; Boston (U.S.), 3.

Prout. — Nick. 'the prout,' haughty, proud (*prut*, Ancren Riwle; *prout*, Layamon; v. Skeat, *proud*). v. Proud.

Cristina le Prute, co. Oxf., 1273. A.
Herbert le Prute, co. Wilts, ibid.
John le Prute. H.
John le Proute, co. Soms., 1 Edw. III : Kirby's Quest, p. 138.
Cristina le Prout, co. Soms., 1 Edw. III: ibid. p. 216.
1609-10. Henry Lloyd and Mary Prout: Marriage Lic. (London), i. 318.
1802. Married — John Skinner and Eliz. Prout: St. Geo. Han. Sq. ii. 270.
London, 8 ; Philadelphia, 3.

Provis, Provost; v. Prevost.

Prowse, Prouse, Pruce.—Local (?), 'of Pruce,' i.e. of Prussia. If this be the origin, then the prefix *le* should be *de* in the Hundred Roll instances furnished below—a common error.

'And som wol have a Pruce sheld or a targe.' Chaucer, C. T. 2124.
Richard le Prouz, co. Devon, 1273. A.
William le Prouz, co. Devon, ibid.
William Prous, co. Oxf., ibid.
1758. Married—Edward McLean and Mary Prowse : St. Geo. Han. Sq. i. 79.
London, 6, 2, 1 ; MDB. (Devon), 3, 2, 0.

Prudhomme, Pridham, Proudman(?), Prudame, Pruden(?).—Nick. 'Prudhomme.' An old name for a superior craftsman ; 'a good and true man, a man well versed in any art or trade': Sadler. Green (Hist. Eng. People, i. 223), speaking of the conflict between the Merchant Guilds and the Crafts Guilds, says : 'It is this struggle, to use the technical terms of the time, of the 'greater folk' against the 'lesser folk,' or of the 'commune,' the general mass of the inhabitants, against the 'prud-hommes,' or 'wiser' few, which brought about . . . the great civic revolution of the 13th and 14th centuries.' The surname was common at the same period.

John Prodhome, co. Devon, 1273. A.
Richard Prodham, co. Bucks, ibid.
Geoffrey Prudhomme, or Prodomme, co. Bucks, ibid.

Many other early instances might be given, but these are sufficient. Pruden doubtless is a corruption. Pridham is found as Prudham in the 13th century.

Symon Prudham, co. Norf., 1277 : FF. x. 244.
1789. Married — Richard Bunn and Eliz. Prudden : St. Geo. Han. Sq. ii. 27.
London, 0, 3, 2, 0, 1 ; Philadelphia, 0, 1, 1, 0, 3.

Pruitt.—Nick. 'the proud'; v. Prewett.

Prust. — Offic. 'the prust.' Doubtless a form of Priest. A.S. preóst. v. Prest.

Thomas le Prust, co. Oxf., 1273. A.
Henry Prust, co. Oxf., ibid.
Robert Prust, co. Oxf., ibid.
1804. Married — Stephen Prust (co. Glouc.) and Sarah Summers : St. Geo. Han. Sq. ii. 304.
London, 4 ; MDB. (Devon), 7.

Pryor.—Offic. ; v. Prior.

Prytherat, Prytherch. — Bapt. ; v. Prothero.

Puckridge.—Local, 'of Pucke-ridge,' a hamlet in the parish of Standon, co. Hertford.

1709. Bapt.—James, s. Richard Pucke-ridge : St. Jas. Clerkenwell, ii. 48.
1775. Married—Robert Anderson and Susanna Puckridge : St. Geo. Han. Sq. i. 256.
London, 7.

Puddephatt, Puddefoot, Puddifoot.—Nick. (?). The sur-name is first found in co. Bucks. It is well known there to-day.

Walter Podefat, co. Bucks, 1273. A.
1755. Married — John Puddephatt, of Berkhamsted, co. Herts, and Mary Bed-ford : St. Geo. Han. Sq. i. 59.
1785.— John Breech and Mary Pudde-phatt : ibid. p. 376.
London, 1, 1, 1 ; MDB. (co. Bucks), 3, 0, 0.

Puddifer.—Nick. ; v. Pettifer.

Puddle.—Local, 'at the puddle,' from residence thereby. M.E. podel, a muddy pond.

John Podel, co. Soms., 1 Edw. III : Kirby's Quest, p. 106.
Thomas Podel, co. Soms., 1 Edw. III : ibid.
Johanna del Podell', 1379 · P. T. Yorks. p. 23.
Robertus del Podell', 1379 : ibid.
1574. Bapt. — Joan Puddell : St. Jas. Clerkenwell, i. 8.
London, 1.

Pudsey.—Local, 'of Pudsey,' a parish in W. Rid. Yorks, six miles from Leeds.

Willelmus de Puddesay, 1379 : P. T. Yorks. p. 268.
Johannes de Puddesay, 1379 : ibid. p. 51.
Nicholas de Pudesay, of Pudesay, 1379 : ibid. p. 192.
1667-8. Bapt.—Elizabeth, d. Nathaniel Pudsey : St. Jas. Clerkenwell, i. 233.
MDB. (North Riding Yorks), 1.

Pugh. — Bapt. 'Ap - Hugh' (Welsh), i.e. 'the son of Hugh,' of which an early form was Hew. The better class Welsh seemingly began to adopt the English style in the 17th century. William Ap-Hugh, of the parish of Llanegfan, co. Anglesey, gentleman, by will dated May 18, 1665, bequeathed legacies to his brother Edmund Ap-Hugh, and to his sons Hugh Hughes, and Henry Hughes. The will is printed in N. and Q., Sept. 3, 1887 (p. 186). For a variant, v. Pew.

1610. John Ap Hugh and Katherine Whitfield : Marriage Lic. (Westminster), p. 18.
1614-5. Richard Ap-Hugh, alias Hughes, and Anne Knight : ibid. p. 22.
John Apew, 1642 : Peacock's Army List of Roundheads and Cavaliers, p. 29.
John Pew, 1642 : ibid.
London, 23 ; Boston (U.S.), 6.

Puleston.—Local, 'of Puleston'; v. Pilson. Perhaps the following represents the place :

Roger de Pynelesdon, co. Salop, 1273. A.
MDB. (co. Salop), 1.

Pulford.—Local, ' of Pulford,' a parish in co. Chester, five miles from Chester.

1590. Randall Pulford, co. Denbigh : Reg. Univ. Oxf. vol. ii. pt. ii. p. 181.

Bryan Pulford, of Barton, 1593 : Wills at Chester, i. 156.
Griffith Pulford, of Pulford, 1612 : ibid.
MDB. (co. Chester), 1 ; Manchester, 2 ; London, 3.

Pulham.—Local, ' of Pulham,' a parish in co. Norfolk.

Nicholas de Pulham, co. Norf., 1273. A.
Richard de Pulham, vicar of Tofts, co. Norf., 1348 : FF. vii. 205.
William de Pulham, co. Norf., 1372 : ibid. iv. 100.
1607. Richard Chambers and Alice Pulham, widow, relict of Robert Pulham, of Garbledisham, co. Norf. : Marriage Lic. (London), i. 301.
London, 4 ; MDB. (Suffolk), 1 ; New York, 1.

Pullen, Pullan, Pullein, Pulleng, Pulleyn, Pullin, Pulling.—Nick. 'le Pullen.' If pullen was used in the singular as well as plural sense, the origin of this not uncommon surname is very obvious, and takes its place in the class of poultry and bird nicknames ; cf. Duck, Drake, Jay, Nightingale, &c. In a note to pullavly (Prompt. Parv. p. 416) Mr. Way quotes the use of pullen for poultry by Tusser ; also pullayne by Palsgrave. He adds, 'Gerarde observes that in Cheshire they sow buck-wheat for "their cattell, pullen, and such like."'

Nicholas le Pullen, co. Salop, 1273. A.
John Puleyn, co. Wilts, ibid.
Thomas Pulein, co. York, ibid.
Richard Puleyn, co. Dorset, ibid.
John Polayn, co. Soms., 1 Edw. III : Kirby's Quest, p. 124.
Nicholas Polayn, co. Soms., 1 Edw. III : ibid. p. 319.

The g in Pulleng and Pulling is, of course, excrescent, as in Jen-nings and a hundred other names. The forms Pullan (8), Pullein (1), Pullen (2), Pullin (1), Pullon (3), and Pullyen (1) occur in the W. Rid. Court Directory. As Paulin (or Powlin) was so common a font-name in co. York and elsewhere, it is probable that many of the above are of baptismal origin. If so, v. Paulin.

London, 33, 1, 1, 1, 1, 4, 6.

Pulley, Pooley. Polley, Poley.—Local, 'of Pooley,' i.e. the islet in the pool ; cf. Pooley

Bridge on Ulleswater. M.E. *pol* or *pole*, a pool. The forms Polhey and Polhay, however, suggest a different origin, i.e. the enclosed pool. But it is impossible to separate the two. They have become as surnames inextricably mixed.

Peter de Poleye, co. Herts, 1273. A.
William de Poleye, co. Bucks, ibid.
Ralph de Polhay, or Poley, co. Essex, ibid.
Elyas de Polhey, or Poleye, co. Essex, ibid.
George Polley, or Pooley, vicar of Attleborough, co. Norf., 1516 : FF. i. 524.
London, 5, 9, 4, 2 ; Philadelphia, 3, 5, 0, 6.

Pullin(g ; v. Pullen.

Pullinger. — Occup. A corruption of Bullinger, q.v. ; cf. Peverley for Beverley, &c. This form has ramified strongly in the United States.

1769. Married — John Twidd and Rebecca Pullinger : St. Geo. Han. Sq. ii. 186.
London, 1 ; Philadelphia, 18.

Pullman, Pulman. — Occup. 'the pool-man,' a resident by the pool ; cf. Bridgman, Stileman.

1617. Bapt.—William, s. John Pulman : St. Jas. Clerkenwell, i. 77.
1803. Married—John Gill and Sarah Poullman : St. Geo. Han. Sq. ii. 292.
1805. — John Pulman and Ann Evans : ibid. p. 323.
London, 1, 5 ; Philadelphia, 4, 0.

Pumphrey, Pumfrey.—Bapt. 'the son of Humphrey.' Welsh Ap-Humphrey ; cf. Price, Probert, Prodger, &c.

1563. John Graye and Annable Pumfrey : Marriage Lic. (London), i. 27.
1633. Whitlocke Pumfrey and Magdalen Gray : ibid. ii. 210.
London, 1, 0 ; MDB. (co. Berks), 0, 3 ; Oxford, 0, 1.

Punch.—Nick. (?). I cannot explain this name. Halliwell has '*punch*,' short, fat' ; and Little, Short, Fatt, &c., are well-known surnames. Punch may belong to this class of sobriquets.

Robert Punche, co. Oxf., 1273. A.
Philip Punche, co. Suff., ibid.
Roger Punch, temp. Hen. III. T.
John Punche, yeoman of the crown. H.
1809. Married — Benjamin Punch and Mary Norris : St. Geo. Han. Sq. ii. 408.
London, 1 ; Boston (U.S.), 9.

Punchard, Puncher, Pinchard.—Local, 'de Ponte-cardon' (Domesday). Probably from Pont-Chardon, in the arrondissement of Argentan, Normandy, as suggested by Lower. The family gave the suffix to Heanton Punchardon, co. Devon. We may fairly surmise that Punchard is a contraction, Puncher and Pinchard being corruptions of the second stage. v. Pinkerton.

Robert de Punchard, co. Southampton, Hen. III-Edw. I. K.
Richard de Punchardon,co.Southampt., ibid.

The above pair are placed together as if members of the same family.

Robert de Punchardun, co. Devon, Hen. III-Edw. I. K.
Nicholas de Punchardon, 1323 : Hodgson's Northumberland, v. 303.
1681. Married — Robert Reeves and Mary Puncher : St. Jas. Clerkenwell, iii. 192.
1785. — John Hulse and Jane Punchard : St. Geo. Han. Sq. i. 370.
London, 2, 1, 1 ; Boston (U.S.), 2, 0, 0.

Puncheon ; v. Punshon.

Punderson.—Nick. ' the son of the pounder' (v. Pounder) ; cf. Taylorson, Clerkson, Herdson.

MDB. (North Riding Yorks), 1.

Punshon, Pinchin, Pinching, Pingeon, Puncheon. — Bapt. 'the son of Puncun,' or 'Pincun,' a Norman personal name, not a corruption of Punchardon, as suggested by Lower. Representatives are found in every 13th century register.

'Ranulf, Bishop of Durham, two carucates which Pinceon Dapifer holds,' 1109 : Lincolnshire Survey, p. 13.
Oliva Pingun, co. Suff., 1273. A.
Robert Pinchun, co. Hunts, ibid.
John fil. Punzun, 1180 : RRR. p. 25.
Hugo fil. Pincun : Pipe Roll, 5 Hen. II.
William Puncyn, 1313. M.
Robertus Pynchon, 1379 : P. T. Yorks. p. 51.
Thomas Pynchon, 1379 : ibid. p. 50.
William Pownshon, 1539 : Hist. Newcastle and Gateshead, p. 11.
Henry Poynschon, 1539 : ibid. p. 174.
John Punsion, 1548 : Reg. Univ. Oxf. i. 215.
John Punchon, 1663 : Hodgson's Northumberland, iv. 252.
London, 0, 2, 1, 1, 0 ; MDB. (co. Middlesex), Puncheon, 1.

Punt.—Local, 'at the punt,' from residence beside the punt, a kind of boat ; cf. Shipp. The word was in early use.

Martin del Punt, Fines Roll, 11 Edw. I.
1579. George Punte and Margery Goslinge : Marriage Lic. (London), i. 92.
London, 1 ; Philadelphia, 1.

Punter.—Occup. 'the punter,' one who worked a punt ; v. Punt. The only other possible derivation is Punder (i.e. Pounder, q.v.), sharpened into Punter. Punder for Pounder is found below, and this might easily become Punter. Perhaps this is the true solution.

William Punter, C. R., 3 Hen. IV. pt. ii.
1557. William Puntare : Reg. Univ. Oxf. pt. ii. p. 17.
1586. Married — George Pounter and Alice Manning : St. Peter, Cornhill, i. 235.
1592. Bapt.—Golde, d. Henry Punder, St. Jas. Clerkenwell, i. 26.
1730. Married — Daniel Punter and Anne Kirby : ibid. iii. 258.
1795. — John Punter and Ann Morris : St. Geo. Han. Sq. ii. 125.
London, 2.

Purcell, Purssell, Pursell.— Nick. 'the porcel.' M.E. *pork*, O.F. *porc*, a pork, a hog ; dim. *porcell*, a young pig. 'Porcellys, young pigs' (Halliwell). Ital. *porcella*, 'a sow-pig, a porkelin' (Florio). Cf. Pigg, Grice, Hogg, Bacon ; also the dim. Porchet (O.F. *porquet* ; Eng. *porket*).

Reyner Porchet, co. Salop, 1273. A.
Edward Porcel, co. Bucks, ibid.
Roger Porcel, co. Salop, ibid.
Agnes Purcel, co. Oxf., ibid.
John Purcel, 1313. M.
1633. Bapt.—Sara, d. Joseph Purcell : St. Jas. Clerkenwell, i. 123.
1634. Anne, d. Joseph Pursell : ibid. p. 127.

This name with its variants is very familiar to the United States. It went out with the Pilgrim Fathers.

1635. William Pursell, for Virginia (aged 26) : Hotten's Lists of Emigrants, p. 136.
London, 4, 0, 0 ; Crockford, 6, 0, 0 ; MDB. (co. Bucks), 0, 2, 0 ; Boston (U.S.), 33, 1, 1.

Purchas, Purchase, Purches, Purchese. — Nick. Purchase (= eager pursuit). One of a class of names given to pursuivants, messengers, heralds, couriers, &c. (v. Swift, Lightfoot) ; cf.

Bonaventure, also a pursuivant title.

Geoffrey Purchaz, co. Devon, Hen. III–Edw. I. K.
John Purkace, co. Linc., 1273. A.
'Adam Purcas, servant of the (late) Black Prince'; C. R., 14 Ric. II.
Roger Purcheiz, co. Som., 1 Edw. III: Kirby's Quest, p. 159.
'Purchace the Pursuivant': Wars of England in France, Hen. VI, (v. index).
1620. Bapt. — Henry, s. William Purchase: St. Jas. Clerkenwell, i. 88.
1763. Married—Thomas Warner and Susanna Purches: St. Geo. Han. Sq. i. 126.
London, 1, 7, 1, 5; Philadelphia, 0, 2, 0, 0.

Purchaser.—Offic. A pursuivant, courier. O.F. *purchacer*, to pursue intently.

Thomas Purchassour or Purchaceour, C. R., 15 and 29 Edw. III.
John Purchasour, Pardons Roll, 6 Ric. II.

Purday, Purdey. Purdie, Purdy, Purdue.—? Nick. Probably corruptions of Pardew, q.v. The instances suggest early corrupted forms.

Cf. Thomas Dampurday, rector of Wood Rysing, co. Norf., 1383: FF. x. 280.

Also cf. Flowerday.

John Purdeu, co. Camb., 1273. A.
William Purdeu, co. Camb., ibid.
John Purde, co. Camb., ibid.
1667. Married — William Pen and Grace Purdey: St. Jas. Clerkenwell, iii. 131.
1713. — John Penny and Eliz. Purdue: ibid. p. 236.

In the United States the surname has settled down to one form, that of Purdy.

London, 1, 1, 4, 7, 1; Philadelphia, 0, 0, 0, 16, 0.

Purdon, Purdom.—Local, 'of Purdon' or Purden. For suffix, v. Downe or Dean.

John Purden, co. Camb., 1273. A.
Adam Purdone, co. Som., 1 Edw. III: Kirby's Quest, p. 114.
London, 1, 2.

Purefoy. — Nick. (?). O. F. *pure-foy* (?), pure faith, i.e. staunch and true. The family were seated at Misterton, co. Leic., in 1277. The motto borne by one branch is 'Pure foy est ma joie' (Lower, p. 279).

1546–7. William Fawnte and Jane Pureffey or Purfrey: Marriage Lic. (Faculty Office), p. 9.
1581. Francis Purefei, 1569: Reg. Univ. Oxf. vol. i. p. 275.
1581. Francis Purferey (co. Essex) and Johanna Berington: Marriage Lic. (London), i. 101.
Richard Purifey, co. Bucks, 1585: Reg. Univ. Oxf. vol. ii. pt. ii. p. 139.
Arthur Purefaye, co. Norf., 1585: FF. v. 360.
Crockford, 2.

Purey; v. Pury.

Purrier.—Local, 'at the pear-tree'; v. Perryer.

Purser.—Offic. 'the purser,' a purse-bearer, one who paid the expenses, a treasurer, though possibly a purse-maker sometimes; v. Burser.

'And by hire gildel heng a purse of lether.' Chaucer, C. T. 3251.
John le Pussar (sic), co. Som., 1 Edw. III: Kirby's Quest, p. 139.
John Haunsy, *purser*, 11 Edw. III: Freemen of York, i. 32.
Robert le Pursere. G.
William Purser. D.
Johanna Pursar, 1379: P. T. Yorks. p. 98.
1805. Married — William Purser and Ann Bailes: St. Geo. Han. Sq. ii. 320.
London, 10; New York, 2.

Pursell; v. Purcell.

Purshouse; v. Pershouse.

Purslow,? Pursglove, Purseglove. — Local, 'of Purslow,' a hundred in the county of Salop. Mr. Lower, with some show of reason, declares that Pursglove is a corrupted form.

1587. Thomas Purslowe, co. Salop; Reg. Univ. Oxf. vol. ii. pt. ii. p. 162.
1595. Thomas Barrowe and Eliz. Purslowe: Marriage Lic. (London), i. 226.
MDB. (co. Derby), 0, 2, 0; (co. Salop), 1, 0, 0; (co. Notts), 0, 0, 1; London, 1, 0, 0.

Purton.—Local, (1) 'of Puriton,' a parish in co. Somerset, near Bridgewater; (2) 'of Purton,' a parish in co. Wilts, near Wootton Bassett.

Adam de Piriton, co. Oxf., 1273. A.
Robert de Puriton, co. Som., ibid.
Simon de Purytone, co. Som., 1 Edw. III: Kirby's Quest, p. 245.
Gilbert de Puritone, co. Som., 1 Edw. III: ibid.

From these entries it seems obvious that the meaning is 'the

farmstead with the pear-orchard'; v. Pury and Town. Alongside my last two instances is 'Walter atte Purye' (p. 246).

London, 1.

Pury, Purey.—Local, 'at the perry,' i.e. the pear-tree or pear-orchard; v. Perry, and cf. Purrier for Perrier.

Ralph de la Purye, co. Somerset, 1273. A.
Nicholas de la Purie, co. Oxf., ibid.
Andrew de Purie, co. Oxf., ibid.
Lucia atte Purye, co. Soms., 1 Edw. III: Kirby's Quest, p. 86.
William atte Purye, co. Soms., 1 Edw. III: ibid. p. 127.
Robert atte Purye, co. Soms., 1 Edw. III: ibid. p. 231.

Thus we find such entries as 'at the pury bridge':

William atte Purybrigge, co. Soms., 1 Edw. III: Kirby's Quest, p. 252.
London, 2, 0; Crockford, 0, 2.

Puryer.—Local, 'at the pear-tree'; v. Perryer.

London, 2.

Pusey, Puzey. — Local, ' of Pusey,' a parish in co. Berks. There is also Pewsey, a parish in co. Wilts, near Marlborough. The two surnames are inextricably mixed.

Henry de Pusey, co. Berks, 1273. A.
John Pusey, co. Bucks, 1579: Reg. Univ. Oxf. vol. ii. pt. ii. p. 87.
1626. Married — Robert Pewsye and Judith Atkins: St. Jas. Clerkenwell, iii. 57.
1659. — Edward Alder and Mary Pusey: St. Dionis Backchurch, p. 35.
London, 0, 12; Crockford, 1, 0; Philadelphia, 22, 2.

Putman, Putnam. — Local, 'of Puttenham,' parishes in cos. Hertford and Surrey. Putman was an inevitable corruption (cf. Deadman for Debenham, or Swetman for Swettenham); not to be connected with Pitman, I think, which, nevertheless, see.

Richard de Puteham, co. Bucks, 1273. A.
1621. Edward Putman or Putnam (v. Index): Reg. Univ Oxf. vol. ii. pt. ii. p. 403.
1774. Married — John Putnam and Catharine Hust: St. Geo. Han. Sq. i. 240.
London, 4, 4; Philadelphia, 1, 4.

Putney. — Local, 'of Putney,' a parish in co. Surrey, four miles from London.

1795. Married — Thomas Putney and Ann Shephard : St. Geo. Han. Sq. ii. 127. London, 1 ; Boston (U.S.), 7.

Putt.—Local, 'at the pit,' from residence thereby ; v. Pitt.

Nicholas de la Putte, co. Oxf., 1273. A.
John de la Putte, co. Oxf., ibid.
John atte Putte, co. Soms., 1 Edw. III : Kirby's Quest, p. 92.
William atte Putte, co. Soms., 1 Edw. III : ibid. p. 101.
Ostin atte Putte, co. Soms., 1 Edw. III : ibid. p. 185.
London, 8 ; Oxford, 4.

Puttergill.—Local ; v. Portingale.

Puttock, Puttick.—Nick. 'the puttock,' i.e. the kite ; 'metaphorically applied to a greedy, ravenous fellow' (Halliwell) ; cf. Kite, Hawk, Sparrow, Sparrowhawk.

'Some bileve that yf the kite or the puttock fle ovir the way afore them that they should fare wel that daye' : Brand, iii. 113.
Richard Puttac, co. Kent, 1273. A.
Walter Puttok, co. Hunts, ibid.
Leticia Puttoc, co. Camb., ibid.
1601. William Puttocke, co. Sussex : Reg. Univ. Oxf. vol. ii. pt. ii. p. 251.
1755. Married — Emery Puttick and Mary Elvin : St. Geo. Han. Sq. i. 59.
London, 5, 3 ; Boston (U.S.), 0, 1.

Puxon.—Local, ' of Puxton,' a parish in co. Somerset.

London, 2.

Puzey ; v. Pusey.

Pyatt.—Nick. ; v. Pyett.

Pybus.—Local, 'of the pykebusk' (?), i.e. the bush on the pike, that is, the hill. Until absolutely conclusive evidence is shown to the contrary, I cannot doubt my conclusion. The surname is a Yorkshire one, and with the entry

below no other interpretation can be accepted.

Elena Pykebusk, 1379 : P. T. Yorks. p. 12.
HumphreyPybus, merchant adventurer, April, 1691, St. Nicholas', Newcastle-on-Tyne : v. Brand's Hist. Newcastle, i. 290.
1787. Married—Benjamin Davies and Sarah Pybus : St. Geo. Han. Sq. i. 402.
MDB. (North Rid. Yorks), 8 ; London, 1.

Pycock ; v. Peacock.

Pye, Py.—Nick. 'the pie,' i.e. magpie ; cf. Nightingale, Lark, Finch, Goldfinch. A common entry in early registers.

Agnes relicta Pye, co. Oxf., 1273. A.
John Pye, co. Norf., ibid.
Walter Pye, co. Norf., ibid.
Willelmus Py, 1379 : P. T. Yorks. p. 202.
Robertus Pye, 1379 : ibid.
1607. Bapt.—Thomas, a. Robert Pye : St. Jas. Clerkenwell, i. 49.
1615. Otwell Pye, co. Cornwall : Reg. Univ. Oxf. vol. ii. pt. ii. p. 345.
London, 15, 0 ; New York, 9, 5.

Pyecroft.—Local, 'at the pyecroft,' the enclosure frequented by magpies ; v. Croft and Pye. From residence beside an enclosure so called.

John Pycroft, of Manchester, *linen webster*, 1590 : Wills at Chester, i. 156.
Edward Pycroft, of Manchester, 1614 : ibid.
MDB. (co. Linc.), 2.

Pyefinch.—Nick. ' a piefinch' ; cf. Goldfinch and Finch, and v. Pye.

1785. Married — William Cross and Margaret Pyefinch : St. Geo. Han. Sq. i. 372.
MDB. (co. Hereford), 1 ; Hull, 1.

Pyeshank.—Nick. ; cf. Cruikshank, Sheepshank, Philipshank, &c.

John Pyeschanke, Close Roll, 15 Edw. I.

Pyett, Pyott, Pyette, Pyatt.
—Nick. 'the piot,' i.e. magpie ; a dim. of pie (v. Pye).

William Pyatt, co. Soms., 1 Edw. III : Kirby's Quest, p. 105.
1584. Richard Pyott and Margery Roberts : Marriage Lic. (London), i. 131.
1744. Married — Richard Pyott and Eliz. Grout : St. Geo. Han. Sq. i. 32.
1778. — George Pyott and Eliz. Norris : ibid. p. 292.
London, 1, 0, 0, 2 ; MDB. (co. Derby), 0, 1, 0, 0 ; New York, 0, 1, 1, 5.

Pyke.—Local, ' at the pike,' or peaked hill ; v. Pick (2).

William Pyk, Hen. III-Edw. I. K. Oxford, 3.

Pym.—Bapt. 'the son of Pimme.' v. Pim.

Pyne, Pine, Pinn.—Local, 'at the pine,' i.e. the pine-tree, from residence thereby ; cf. Lind, Crabb, Birch, Box, Oak, &c. A well-known Devonshire name, though not confined to that county. All the forms are common to Devon directories. Pinn is a hamlet in the parish of Otterton, co. Devon, probably derived from the pines that grew there.

Thomas de Pyn, co. Devon, 127?. A.
Herbert de Pyn, co. Devon, ibid.
Radulphus del Pyn, co. Devon, Hen. III-Edw. I. K.
Richard atte Pynne, co. Soms., 1 Edw. III : Kirby's Quest, p. 180.
Hercules Pine, 1563 : Reg. Univ. Oxf. p. 252.
1585-6. Tertullian Pyne and Mary Charles : Marriage Lic. (London), i. 145.
London, 11, 3, 9 ; Topsham (Devon), 0, 2, 0 ; Devon Court Dir., 6, 2, 5 ; New York, 10, 22, 0.

Pyser.—Occup. ; v. Poyser, of which it is a variant.

New York, 1.

Q

Quadling; v. Quodling.

Quaife.— ? ——? Mr. Lower, knowing cos. Kent and Sussex well, says that this name was spelt 'Coyt and Coyfe, 150 years ago, both in East Sussex and West Kent.' I suppose it is a nickname from the dress of one of the mediaeval ecclesiastical or monastical orders ; v. Capron or Chapron for an exactly similar instance.

1701. Bapt.—Catherine, d. John Quoif, of ye Padocke : Canterbury Cathedral, p. 22.
1761. Married—David Coyfe (co. Middlesex) and Ann Fry : St. Geo. Han. Sq. i. 107.
1789. — William Quaife and Eliz. Whittington : ibid. ii. 24.
MDB. (co. Kent), 2.

Quail, Quaile, Quayle.—(1) Nick. ; a bird, the quail.

John Quaille, C. R., 30 Edw. III.

(2) Bapt. A Manx surname. It has crossed into Lancashire, 'contracted from Mac-Phail, Paul's son. This is one of the most widely distributed names in the Island. Early forms are Mac Quayle, Quayle, 1540 ; Quale, 1602 ; Quaille, 1604 ; Quail, 1656.' v. The Manx Note Book, i. 134 ; cf. Quirk.

1793. Married—Edward Hickmott and Jane Quayle : St. Geo. Han. Sq. ii. 93.
London, 5, 0, 0 ; Liverpool, 0, 2, 18 ; Philadelphia, 6, 0, 0, 3.

Quaint, Quant.—Nick. 'the Quaint,' that is, neat or spruce. O.F. *coint*, 'quaint, ... spruce, brisk, trim' : Cotg.

'And of Achilles for his queinte spere.'
Chaucer, C. T. 10553.
Michael le Queynt. M.
John le Quent, C. R., 14 Edw. II.
Margaret le Coynte. B.
1664. Bapt. — William, s. Thomas Quaint : St. Jas. Clerkenwell, i. 222.
1692. — John, s. William Quint (sic) : ibid. p. 345.
1707. Married — Dows Quant and Frances Johnson : ibid. iii. 229.
MDB. (co. Linc.), 0, 1.

Quaintance. — ? Nick. 'the acquaintance' ; cf. Friend, Neighbour, &c. This is Mr. Lower's suggestion, and I see no difficulty in accepting his view. I cannot find any English instance, although he writes of it as an English surname. It has crossed the Atlantic

Philadelphia, 1.

Quaintrell,   Quantrell, Queintrell.—Nick. ; v. Cantrell, of which these are variants.

Richard Queynterel, co. Camb., 1273. A.
Robertus Quintrell, 1379 : P. T. Yorks. p. 86.
Johannes Quayntorell, 1379 : ibid. p. 28.
1446. Gregory Queyntrill, of Norwich : FF. iv. 443.
1473. John Queyntrell, vicar of Ormsby, co. Norf. : ibid. xi. 239.
London, 2, 1, 1 ; Philadelphia, 0, 3, 0.

Qualter,   Qualters.—Bapt. 'the son of Walter.' From Gualter, sharpened to Qualter. v. Quilliam and Quelch.

Liverpool, 1, 0 ; Boston (U.S.), 3, 2.

Quant; v. Quaint.

Quantock, Quantick.—Local, 'of Quantock,' probably some spot in co. Somerset ; cf. East and West Quantoxhead, two parishes in that county.

MDB. (co. Somerset), 3, 0 ; London, 1, 0 ; Cardiff, 0, 1.

Quarell, Quarrell. — Local, 'at the quarel,' from residence beside a quarry. 'Quarel, a stone quarry.' '*Saxifragium*, a quaryle,' Nominale MS. (Halliwell).

Ivo de Quarel, co. Camb., Hen. III-Edw. I. K.
John Quarel, C. R., 16 Edw. III. pt. i.
Johannes Qwarell, 1379 : P. T. Yorks. p. 190.
1620. George Quarrell and Eliz. Webling : Marriage Lic. (London), ii. 88.
1779. Married — Edward Charlwood and Betty Quarrell : St. Geo. Han. Sq. i. 305.
London, 1, 0 ; MDB. (co. Worc.), 0, 7.

Quarles.—Local, ' of Quarles.' 'An extra-parochial district in the Hundred of North Greenhoe, co. Norfolk ' : Lower.

'Richard Quarles, *husbandman* nuper de Weveton in Com. Norfolk,' 17 Hen. VII : HHH. p. 135.

The above named was at this time settled at Beverley, co. York.

Francis Quarles, the sacred poet, was born in 1592 at Romford in Essex, a distance from Quarles not far for a surname to travel. There need be no hesitation in deciding that this is the original home of the family.

'Half a fee formerly held by Robert de Quarles, in Quarles, but now by Edmund de Baconesthorp' : FF. v. 146.
1505. Bennett Quarles, New College : Reg. Univ. Oxf. vol. ii. pt. ii. p. 22
1622. Bapt.—Jonas, s. Jonas Quarles : St. Jas. Clerkenwell, i. 93.
Philadelphia, 1.

Quarmby, Quarnby.—Local, ' of Querenby,' now Quarmby, in the parish of Huddersfield, co. York. I need not say that Quarmby is a variant of Quarnby.

Willelmus de Querenby, 1379 : P. T. Yorks. p. 134.
Alexander de Quarnby, 1437 : East Cheshire, i. 349.
1589. Married—John Warren and Margery Quarmeby : Reg. Prestbury, co. Ches., p. 102.
MDB. (West Rid. Yorks), 9, 1 ; London, 1, 0.

Quarrell; v. Quarell.

Quarrier.—(1) Occup. 'the quarrier,' one who worked in a stone quarry.

Hugh le Quareur, co. Oxf., 1273. A.
Thomas le Quareur, co. Oxf., ibid.

(2) Local, 'at the quarry,' from residence thereby. M.E. *quarrere*, a quarry.

Henry de la Quarrere, co. Oxf., 1273. A.
Isabella ad Quarere, co. Camb., ibid.
William atte Quarrer, co. Soms., 1 Edw. III : Kirby's Quest, p. 158.
Richard atte Quarrer, co. Soms., 1 Edw. III : ibid. p. 226.
1635. James Quarrier embarked for Virginia : Hotten's Lists of Emigrants, p. 94.
Andrew Querrier, of Nether Alderley, 1698 : Wills at Chester (1681-1700), p. 204.

Quarrington.—Local, (1) 'of Quarrington,' a township in the parish of Kelloe, near Durham; (2) a parish in co. Lincoln, near Sleaford.

1726. Married—Joseph Patterson and Ann Quarrington: St. Geo. Han. Sq. i. 2. London, 1; Crockford, 1.

Quartermain, Quartermaine, Quarterman. — Nick. 'four hands.' It is possible the name is local, but I find no trace of such an origin.

Clare Quatremayns, co. Oxf.,1273. A.
William Quatremeyns, co. Oxf., ibid.
Thomas Quatermains, 1313. M.
Guy Quatreman. B.
Richard Catermayn. H.
1622. Roger Quatermaine and Emeria Nicholls: Marriage Lic. (London), ii. 116.
1711. Married—John Quatermayne and Catherine Barnes: St. Mary Aldermary, p. 40.
1798. — Richard Quarterman and Ann Reed: St. Geo. Han. Sq. ii. 192.
London, 1, 1, 9; Oxford, 0, 0, 6.

Quarton.—Local, 'of Wharton' (q.v.); cf. Quixley for Whixley, or Quickfall for Wigfall, or *wick*, a provincialism for *quick*.

William de Querton, co. Notts, Hen. III-Edw. I. K.
Gilbert Querton, co. Westm., 20 Edw. I. R.
Francis Quarton, of Lancaster, 1707: Lancashire Wills at Richmond, ii. 203.

Thus we find instead of Whitehead:

Henry Quytheved, 20 Edw. I. R.
William Qwythed, 1557: Lancashire Wills at Richmond. i. 224.

Or, in place of Whiteside:

Merget Quitesyd, or Whytsyd, 1562: Lancashire Wills at Richmond, i. 224.
MDB. (East Rid. Yorks), 3; (West Rid. Yorks), 1.

Quatermass. — Local, 'de Quatremars.' Some spot across the Channel that I have not identified.

Colin de Quatremars, co. York, Hen. III-Edw. I. K.
Adam de Quatremars, co. Kent, ibid.
William Quatremeys, co. Oxf., 1273. A.
Simon de Quatremarch, co. Norf.: FF. ix. 159.
1809. Married—Thomas Quartermass and Sophia Anderson: St. Geo. Han. Sq. ii. 402.
Thomas Quatermass, *bootmaker*, 94 Aldersgate St., E.C.: London Directory. London, 1.

Quayle; v. Quail.

Queen.—(1) Nick. 'the Queen'; cf. King, &c. (2) Bapt. A variant in America of Quinn; cf. McQueen for McQuinn. In the Philadelphia Directory I find seven McQueens and two McQuinns. With (2) this dictionary has nothing to do. The following references relate to (1), the nickname.

Matilda le Quen, co. Oxf., 1273. A.
Simon Quene, co. Camb., ibid.
Alicia Qwene, 1379: P. T. Yorks. p. 272.
Richard Qwene, or Quene, 1511: Reg. Univ. Oxf. i. 78.

The following entries are interesting:

Johannes Queneson, 1379: P. T. Yorks. p. 55.
Alicia Queneson, 1379: ibid.

This is good evidence that Queen was a nickname for one who acted as Queen of the May, &c. The sobriquet stuck and became the surname. Kingson arose in a similar way, only that survives and Queenson is gone.

Boston (U.S.), 4; Philadelphia, 12.

Queenborough. — (1) Local, 'of Queniborough,' a parish in co. Leicester; (2) 'of Queenborough,' a parish in co. Kent.

Nicholas Quenbure, co. Leic., Hen. III-Edw. I. K.
Osceline de Quinbergh, co. Norf., 4 Edw. III: FF. x. 272.
MDB. (co. Leicester), 1; (co. Kent), 1.

Queintrell; v. Quaintrell.

Quelch.—Local, ' the Welsh,' i.e. the Welshman. Cf. Gwyllim for William, Quilliams for Williams, and Quhitelaw for Whitelaw, and v. Whitehead. In the instances below an intermediate form Gwelch is given:

1612. Thomas Quilche and Mary Wellam: Marriage Lic. (London), i. 12.
William Quelch, 1613: St. Mary Aldermary, p. 13.
1655. Married—Henry Quelch and Jane Collins: St. Peter, Cornhill, i. 259.
Margaret Gwelch, 1686: St. Jas. Clerkenwell, i. 315.
Margaret Quelch, 1688: ibid. p. 327.

These last two entries refer to the same person.

London, 3; Oxford, 8; Boston (U.S.), 1.

Quennell, Quinnell. — (1) Bapt. 'the son of Quenilda' or 'Quenild,' the Norman form of Gunnilda, already resident in England before the Conquest. Miss Yonge has an interesting account of Gunhild or Gunnilda (ii. 316), but she is mistaken in saying, 'After the Conquest Gunhild died away in England.' It was fairly popular for three centuries in both the Danish as well as the Norman dress; v. Gunnell.

Richard fil. Qwinild. FFF.
Thomas Qwinild. W. 4.
Thomas Quenild, co. Norf., 1273. A.
Alicia Quenild, co. Bucks, ibid.
Quenilda Dewicar, co. Lanc., 1332: Lay Subsidy, Rylands, p. 112.

There are eight Gonnilds to one Quenild in one single township in 1273; v. Hundred Rolls, vol. ii. pp. 354-5. It is needless to say that Quenild would be sure to become Quennell.

(2) Local. Mr. Lower suggests that Quennell is the French Quesnel, equivalent to our English Oak or Oakes. In some instances this may be quite possible. Nevertheless (1) must be considered the general parent.

1602. Robert Quennell, or Quennyl, co. Surrey: Reg. Univ. Oxf. vol. ii. pt. ii. p. 262.
1621. Peter Quennell, co. Surrey: ibid. p. 403.
London, 2, 2; Boston (U.S.), 3, 0.

Quentin; v. Quintin.

Quested.—Local, ' of Quested.' I cannot find the spot. The suffix seems to be *-stead*, as in Playsted, Hampstead, &c.

1622. Mark Quested and Eliz. Halsall, *widow*: Marriage Lic. (London), ii. 110.
1692. Bapt.—John, s. Samuel Quested: St. John Baptist on Wallbrook, p. 171. London, 1.

Quick, Quicke.—Nick. ' the quick'; v. Quickman. One of active and lively disposition.

Robert Quic, co. Camb., 1273. A.
William Quykke, C. R., 14 Hen. VI.
John Quicke, C. R., 3 Edw. IV.
1602. Bapt.—John, s. John Quicke: St. Michael, Cornhill, p. 103.
1613. Philip Quicke: Reg. Univ. Oxf. vol. ii. pt. ii. p. 330.
London, 25, 1; Philadelphia, 24, 0.

Quickfall.—Local. A corruption of Wigfall, q.v.; cf. Quixley for Whixley; v. Quarton.

1794. Married—John Quickfall and Ann Wyatt: St. Geo. Han. Sq. ii. 111. West Rid. Court Dir., 1; MDB. (co. Lincoln), 3.

Quickley, Quigley. —? ——. Seemingly an Irish name. In the Boston Directory there are eight Michael and ten Patrick Quigleys. Evidently Quickley is a sharpened variant.

1793. Married—John Quickly and Susanna Butt: St Geo. Han. Sq. ii. 99. Manchester, 1, 2; Boston (U.S.), 0, 96.

Quickman. — Nick. 'the quick man,' lively, energetic; v. Quick, and cf. such double forms as Merry and Merriman, Long and Longman, &c.

Adam Quikeman, co. Kent, 1273. A. Thomas Quikman, 1303. M. Denis Quicman, C. R., 17 Ric. II.

Quickman as a surname may still exist, but I cannot find any instances.

Quiddington. — Local, 'of Quiddington.' I cannot find the spot. But evidently it must first be looked for in co. Surrey

1594-5. Married—Stockdall Quedington and Frances Ismangale, of Rigate in Surrey: St. Dionis Backchurch, p. 13. 1764. Married—Henry Quittenton, of Titsey, co. Surrey, and Eleanor Hincklen: St. Geo. Han. Sq. i. 137.

A note appended by the editor says:

'Son of John Quiddington, baptized at Titsey, Nov. 26, 1743.' London, 1.

Quigley; v. Quickley.

Quilliam.—Bapt. 'the son of William' (Welsh), a sharpened form of Gwilliam (q.v.); cf. Quelch for Welch.

Liverpool, 5.

Quilter.—Occup. 'the quilter,' a manufacturer of quilts. 'Quylte, of a bedde, *culcitra*': Prompt. Parv.

Richard le Quilter, co. Oxf., 1273. A. Thomas le Queylter. T. Egidius le Quylter. J. Robert le Quilter, Fines Roll, 12 Edw. I. John Quylter, B.A., 1507: Reg. Univ. Oxf. i. 55. London, 8.

Quiltmaker. — Occup.; v. Quilter.

John Quyltemaker. H.

Quin, Quinn.—Bapt. 'the son of Quin,' an ancient Celtic personal name found commonly as McQuinn or McQueen; v. Queen (2).

London, 6, 3; Boston (U.S.), 2, 269.

Quinby, Quimby. Quenby, Quemby.—Local, 'of Quenby,' a hamlet in the parish of Hungerton, co. Leic.

Ralph de Quenebi, co. Hunts, 1273. A. 1791. Married — William Beech and Jane Quenby: St. Geo. Han. Sq. ii. 59. Liverpool, 2, 1, 0, 0; London (Quemby), 1; Oxford, 0, 1, 1, 0; Boston (U.S.), 12, 23, 0, 0.

Quince.—? ——. Mr. Lower says 'the same as Quincey,' but furnishes no evidence. I cannot arrive at any satisfactory conclusion. The original form seems to have been Quinch.

1454. Jeffery Quinch, sheriff of Norwich: FF. iii. 165. 1620. Married — Edward Kennyman and Mary Quince: St. Dionis Backchurch, p. 20. 1622. Married — Edward Sayve and Margaret Quince: Marriage Lic. (London), ii. 116. MDB. (co. Camb.), 2; (co. Hunts), 1.

Quincy, Quinsey.—Local, 'de Quency.' Probably a Norman local surname. Saier de Quency was a favourite of Henry II, and his son was created Earl of Winchester by King John.

Robert de Quency, co. Essex, 1273. A. Hawyse de Quency, co. Bedf., ibid. 1670. Richard Cumberland and Anne Quinsey (co. Linc.): Marriage Lic. (London), ii. 207. 1730. Married—William Quincey and Mary Seager: St. Geo. Han. Sq. i. 8. 1742. Buried—William Quincy: St. Mary Aldermary, p. 226. London Court Dir., 2, 0; Birmingham, 0, 1; Liverpool, 0, 1; Boston (U.S.), 13, 0.

Quiney.—I can furnish no history of this surname, but I append instances.

1619-20. George Quiney, or Quinney, co. Warw.: Reg. Univ. Oxf. vol. ii. pt. ii. p. 382. 1788. Married—Thomas Quinney and Ann Towler: St. Geo. Han. Sq. ii. 10. London, 4.

Quinland.—Not a variant of Queenland, but the Irish Quinlan (so familiar to the United States) with an excrescent *d*; cf. Jolland for Jollan, or Simmonds for Simmons.

Boston (U.S.), 1.

Quinn; v. Quin.

Quinnell; v. Quennell.

Quinsey; v. Quincy.

Quintin, Quentin.—(1) Bapt. 'the son of Quentin.' Quentin became a somewhat popular personal name in Scotland, and has been immortalized by Walter Scott. It was still familiar in the 17th and 18th centuries, but is gradually losing ground.

Quintinus Poulet, Patent Roll, 7 Hen. VII. Quintine Routledge, 1617: VVV. p. 440. Quintine Foster, 1618: ibid. p. 443.

(2) Local, 'of St. Quentin,' on the Somme, called after the missionary martyred there in 287. It was he who caused the Quentin mentioned above to be a popular baptismal name. Probably the 'St.' was occasionally dropped, as seems to have been the case in several instances below.

Richard Quintine, co. Wilts, 1273. A. John de St. Quintino, co. Wilts, ibid. Adam Quintin, co. Hunts, ibid. Robert Quintyn, co. Norf., ibid. Willelmus de Qwyntyn, 1379: P. T. Yorks. p. 128. 1647. Married—Thomas Quintin and Ann Tunstall: St. Jas. Clerkenwell, iii. 81.

It is clear that (1) rather than (2) is in general the chief parent. But both are now practically lost in Quinton, q.v.

Philadelphia, 4, 2.

Quinton.—Local, 'of Quinton.' Parishes in cos. Northampton and Gloucester.

Richard de Quenton, co. Northampt., 1273. A. Thomas de Quenton, co. Oxford, ibid. 1665. Married—Richard Quinton and Marg. Midletich: St. Jas. Clerkenwell, iii. 121. 1713. John Quinton, rector of Thwayt, co. Norf.: FF. x. 184. 1729-30. Married—John Quinton and Eliz. Walker: St. Dionis Backchurch, p. 63. London, 7; Philadelphia, 8.

Quirk.—Bapt. A Manx surname, being a contraction of Mac Cuirc, i.e. Corc's son. McQuyrke, Quyrke, 1511; Queerke. 1601; Quirk, 1641 (Manx Note Book, ii. 60). v. Quail.

1590. Married—Richard Querck and Jane Palnes: St. Antholin (London), p.34.

1623. William Querke, living in Virginia: Hotten's Lists of Emigrants, p. 188.
Crockford, 4; Liverpool, 9; Philadelphia, 33.

Quixley.—Local, 'of Quixley,' now Whixley, a parish in the dioc. of Ripon, called Quixley in P. T. Yorks. 1379; v. Quarton.

Johannes de Quixley, 1379: P. T. Yorks. p. 227.
London, 2.

Quodling, Quadling, Codling.—Nick. 'Cœur-de-lion,' lionhearted.

Robert Querdelioun, C. R., 2 Edw. III. pt. i.

Ralph Querdelyun. T.
William Querdelion, London. X.

By the middle of the 15th century the form assumed was Querdling. In 1433 John Querdling occupied a magisterial position in Norwich. Of him or an immediate descendant a rhyme is quoted:

'Whoso hath any quarrel or ple,
If he but withstand John Hankey,
John Qwerdlyng, Nic. Waleys, John
    Belagh, John Meg,
Sore shall him rewe,
For they rule all the Court with their
    lawes newe.'
                              FF. iii. 145.

Later on it became Codling or Codlin (q.v.), but even to this day

in Norfolk and Suffolk Quodling or Quadling exists as a surname. No doubt Richard I made the sobriquet popular. I had the pleasure of pointing out in Notes and Queries (1888) that *codling*, an apple, is the same word as *cœur-de-lion* (sound to the core), the same intermediate stages having been gone through. 'Querdlynge, appulle, *duricenum*': Prompt. Parv.

'In July come . . . plummes in fruit, ginnitings, quadlins': Bacon, Essay 46 (Of Gardens).
1436. Simon Codlyng, rector of Bittering, co. Norf.: FF. ix. 460.
London, 1, 1, 2; MDB. (co. Norfolk), 0, 1, 0; (co. Suffolk), 0, 1, 1.

R

Raban.—(1) Bapt. 'the son of Raban,' i.e. Raven, a popular personal name in the 12th century (v. Raven). O.H.G. *hraban*, a raven (v. Skeat's Dict.). It is curious to note that the only modern instances of the surname I have seen are in Somersetshire and Gloucestershire, in which latter county we find Raban a personal name as long as eight centuries ago. This must be ranked amongst the curiosities of nomenclature.

'Raban the Englishman gave land to the Church of St. Peter, Gloucester, c. 1150': Atkyns' Hist. Glouc. p. 73.

(2) Local, ' de Raban.'

Elias de Raban, or Rabeyn, co. Linc., 1273. A.

I cannot discover the spot.

MDB. (Somerset), 1; (Gloucester), 1.

Raby.—Local, 'of Raby,' a township in the parish of Neston, co. Chester.

Thomas Penkett, of Raby, 1670: Wills at Chester (1660-80), p. 207.
Nicholas Raby, of Cuerden, 1674: ibid. p. 217.
Manchester, 4.

Rackstraw, Rexstrew. — ? Local. This surname is still familiar to Lancashire and Yorkshire, where it has flourished for

centuries. I suggested in my English Surnames, 2nd edit., p. 483, that it was a nickname for a scavenger or dust-heap searcher, quoting Piers Plowman's 'ratoner and rakyer of Cheape,' i.e. ratcatcher and scavenger of Cheapside. I have grown more careful as I have proceeded in my studies, and feel sure it is a local surname, but I cannot find the spot.

William Rakestraw, co. York. W. 11.
George Raikestray, of Ulverston, 1603: Lancashire Wills at Richmond, i. 225.
Thomas Rakestrawe, of Heysham, 1618: ibid.
1628. Bapt.—Eliz., d. Edward Rakestraw: St. Jas. Clerkenwell, i. 110.
1632. Married — Arthur Swann and Mary Rakestrawe: ibid. p. 64.

The name may be a nickname after all. I have seen Rackstraw as one of the dramatis personæ in a 17th-century play, but I cannot lay my hand on it, having lost the reference. In any case the name is of North-English origin.

London, 3, 1; Sheffield, 2, 0.

Radbone.—Local; v. Rathbone.

Radborne, Radburn, Radbron.—Local, (1) 'of Radbourne,' parishes in cos. Derby and Warwick; (2) 'of Redbourne,' parishes

in cos. Herts and Lincoln. The modern pronunciation is Rad-, not Red-.

Robert de Redeborne, co. Hunts, 1273. A.
William de Redeburn, alias Redborn, co. Linc., ibid.
John de Reddeburn, co. Linc., ibid.
1797. Married—William Williams and Eliz. Redburn: St. Geo. Han. Sq. ii. 172.
1805. — Nathaniel Rogers and Sarah Redborn: ibid. p. 338.
London, 1, 3, 1.

Radcliff, Radcliffe, Radclyffe, Ratcliff, Ratcliffe. — Local, ' of Radcliffe,' a parish in co. Lanc., one of four only places in the Salford Hundred mentioned in Domesday. Radcliffe is two miles from Bury, and it is in this district that the surname is especially common.

William de Radeclive, 6 Edw. I: Baines' Lanc. i. 528.
'John de Radclif holds the tenth part of one Knight's fee in Rissheton': Knight's Fees, 23 Edw. III, ibid. ii. 694.
Willelmus de Radclif, 1379: P. T. Yorks. p. 201.
1608. Richard Radcliffe, co. Lanc., St. Mary Hall: Reg. Univ. Oxf. vol. ii. pt. ii. p. 301.
Alys Radcliffe, of Wymersley, 1554: Wills at Chester (1545-1620), p. 157.
Robert Ratcliffe, of Manchester, 1616: ibid. p. 158.
1708. Married—William English and Ann Radleff: St. Geo. Han. Sq. ii. 189.

With this corruption, cf. Cunliffe for Cuntcliffe.

London, 1, 8, 6, 13, 10; Manchester, 0, 12, 0, 6, 8; MDB. (co. Lanc.), 0, 23, 0, 0, 8; Philadelphia, 9, 25, 0, 4, 1.

Radford, Radforth.—Local, ' of Radford,' 'villages and hamlets in cos. Notts, Oxford, and Warwick' (Lower). For suffix, v. Ford and Forth. Radford in co. Notts originated a surname which spread over the border into Derbyshire, and thence to Cheshire and Lancashire. In fact, it is the chief parent.

Ralph de Radeford, co. Oxf., 1273. A.
Adam de Radeford, co. Oxf., ibid.
Serlo de Radeford, co. Notts, ibid.
William de Radeford, co. Notts, ibid.
Thomas de Ratford, co. Soms., 1 Edw. III: Kirby's Quest, p. 133.
John de Raddeford, co. Soms. 1 Edw. III: ibid. p. 229.
Katherine Radforth, *widow*, 1584: Wills at Chester, i. 157.
Ralph Radford, of Chester, *tanner*, 1595: ibid.

Radford, a parish in co. Dorset, has manifestly been a parent of some of the Radfords.

London, 13, 0; Liverpool, 2, 1; Manchester, 10, 0; MDB. (co. Notts), 9, 0; (co. Derby), 19, 0; Philadelphia, 8, 0.

Radley, Redley.—Local, ' of Radley,' a parish in co. Berks.

Roger de Redlee, co. Essex, 1273. A.
Warin de Redleye, co. Essex, ibid.
Richard de Redlege, co. Essex, ibid.
1671-2. Charles Radley and Bridgett Cracroft: Marriage Lic.(London), ii. 199.
1781. Married—George Radley and Betty Cooke: St. Geo. Han. Sq. ii. 322.
London, 10, 1; Philadelphia, 3, 0.

Radmall, Radmell.—Local, ' of Rodmill,' co. Sussex, formerly written Radmell. 'It had owners of its own name, called de Rademylde, in the 14th century' (Lower, Patr. Brit. p. 283). But Redmall is a parish in co. Norwich; and Redmile, a parish in co. Leicester; and Rathmell, a parish in dioc. Ripon. Probably all have one and the same root origin as local names.

1305. William de Rademelde, vicar of West Rudham, co. Norf.: FF. vii. 161.
London, 3, 0.

Radmond, Radmon; v. Redmond, of which they are variants.

Manchester, 1, 0; Philadelphia, 1, 1.

Radnall.—Local, ' of Redenhall,' a parish in dioc. Norwich. But some spot in North England of the same name may have originated the surname in that part of the country. One of my instances lies in co. Northumberland.

Warin de Redenhale, co. Norf., Hen. III-Edw. I. K.
Thomas de Redinhale, co. Northumb., ibid.
John de Radenhale, co. Bedf., 20 Edw. I. R.
1414. Stephen de Redenhall, Rector of Holveston, co. Norf., FF. v 488. Ulverston, 1.

Radway.—Local, ' of Radway,' a parish in co. Warwick, and dioc. of Worcester. For further information, v. Rodway, the commoner modern form.

Geoffrey de Radeweye, co. Devon, Hen. III-Edw. I. K.
Thomas de Radeweye, co. Devon, ibid.
London, 1.

Rae.—Nick. 'the roe,' a Scottish form. North English *ra*; A.S. *ráh*; v. Ray and Roebuck.

London, 10 ; Philadelphia, 5.

Raeburn, Reyburn.—Local, ' of Raeburn,' a stream in the parish of Eskdalemuir, co. Dumfries.

1803. Married—Allan Raeburn and Mary Saunders: St. Geo. Han. Sq. ii. 291.
Newcastle, 1, 0; Philadelphia, 0, 4.

Raffe. — Bapt. 'the son of Ralph,' popularly Raff. ' Raaf, propyr name, Radulphus': Prompt. Parv. Cf. Ruff, Roof, Rofe, &c., for Rolf, from Rudolph.

Amice Raffe, co. Camb., 1273. A.
Thomas Rauf, co. Hunts, ibid.
Adam Rauf, co. Soms., 1 Edw. III: Kirby's Quest, p. 252.
Margerie, d. of Raff Mirkett, 1548: Reg. St. Columb Major, p. 5.
Raff Aslakeby, temp. 1550: Visitation of Yorkshire, p. 4.
Mawde, d. to Raff Grey, temp. 1550: ibid.
1668. Bapt.—Mary, d. Thomas Rafe: St. Jas. Clerkenwell, i. 237.
London, 1; Philadelphia, 7.

Raffles.—Local, ' of Raffles.' Lower says, ' A place in the parish of Mouswald, in Dumfriesshire. That parish contains five old border fortresses ; the least dilapidated is that of Raffles' (Patr. Brit. p. 283).

Crockford, 1 ; Liverpool, 1.

Raffman.—Occup. 'a dealer in raff' (cf. *riff-raff*). So far as I can find, both surname and occupation (so termed) are peculiar to co. Norfolk. The Prompt. Parv. has ' Raaf, ware.' Raff meant refuse, shearings of cloth, wool—any rubbish in fact that was saleable. In the Guild of St. George, Norwich, 1385, occurs the name of John Raffman, also Robert Smith, raffman, and John Smith, raffman (Early Eng. Text Soc., English Gilds). Nevertheless Blomefield (FF. iii. 207), enumerating the companies in the procession of Corpus Christi Day, mentions the 'grocers and raffmen,' and explains in a note, 'i.e. raftermen, those that deal in rafts or timber pieces.' I do not think this will bear investigation.

1406. Henry Rufman, bailiff of Yarmouth: FF. xi. 324.
1506. Richard Hill, *rafeman*, gave a suit of vestments : ibid. iv. 249.

Ragg, Ragge.—Bapt. ' the son of Ragg,' a nick. of Ragner (Reyner) or Raginhold (Reynold), both very familiar personal names in the surname period. The instances adduced are from Yorkshire, where Ragg, Ragge, and Wragg (q.v.) are well-known surnames, and where Reyner (Ragner) was at the same time one of the favourite fontnames. Wragg is the favourite modern Yorkshire form ; cf. Wray and Ray (2).

Johannes Reyg', 1379 : P. T. Yorks. p. 43.
Johannes Rage, 1379 : ibid. p. 39.
Isabella Rage, 1379 : ibid. p. 20.
Johanna Rage, 1379 : ibid.
1743. Married—William Rhodes and Ann Ragg' : St. Geo. Han. Sq. i. 30.
1747. — Richard Hunter and Ann Ragg: St. Jas. Clerkenwell, iii. 277.
London, 1, 1; West Rid. Court Dir., 4, 0; Sheffield, 4, 1; Philadelphia, 1, 0.

Raggett, Ragget.—Nick. ' the ragged,' i.e. the shaggy, the rough-haired. Lower says, ' Reigate, in Surrey, locally so pronounced.' It may be so. But a familiar entry in mediaeval records is 'le Ragged,' and that seems the more natural elucidation. 'Raggyd (or torne, P.), *laciniosus, lacinosus*': Prompt. Parv. v. Ragman.

Thomas le Ragged, co. York, 1273. A.
Richard le Raggide, co. Derby, ibid.
Robert le Raggidde, co. Derby, ibid.
1795.Married—GeorgeRaggett andAnn Grimwood: St. Geo. Han. Sq. ii. 127.
London, 4, 0; Boston (U.S.), 0, 1.

Ragman.—Nick.'onewho went ragged.' 'Ragmann, or he that goythe wythe jaggyd clothys, *pannicius, vel pannicia*': Prompt. Parv. It is, once more, interesting to notice that Prompt. Parv. was written in Norfolk, the county whence my instance comes.

Richard Ragman, co. Norf., 1273. A.

Rain, Raine, Raines, Rains, Rayne, Raynes.—(1) Bapt. 'the son of Reine.' Fr. Reine (Queen).

Reine Bacun, co. Camb., 1273. A.
Alice Reine, co. Camb., ibid.
John Reyn, co. Linc., ibid.
Nicholas Reyn, co. Linc., ibid.

(2) Bapt. 'the son of Rayne,' seemingly a nick. of Reyner or Reynold, common in N. England, where Reyner was extremely popular.

Robert Rayne, 1379: P. T. Yorks. p. 65.
Johannes Rayne, ibid.
Richard Rayneson, ibid. p. 39.
William Rayne, ibid. p. 118.

(3) Local, 'of Rennes.'

Robert de Rennes, co. Oxf., 1273. A.
Richard de Rennes. R.
William de Rainis. E.
Ricardus de Raines, Pipe Roll, 11 Hen. II, p. 20.
London, 2, 6, 3, 7, 2, 1.

Rainbird, Raynbird.—Bapt. 'the son of Reynebaud.' A manifest corruption, and found in the district where Reynebaud or Reynebold was an early and familiar personal name (v. Rumball for instances). The corruption is, as usual, imitative. My instances are decisive.

'Witnesses, Roger, sub-prior, Rainbird, the sacrist, and William, the deacon,' temp. 12th cent., co. Norf.: FF. ii. 207.
1483. Thomas Reynberd, of Thetford, co. Norf.: ibid. ii. 62.
1549. Robert Raynbald, of Norwich: ibid. iv. 232 n.
London, 2, 1; MDB. (Suffolk), 0, 1; Norwich, 1, 0; Ipswich, 1, 0.

Rainbow.—Bapt. 'the son of Reynebaud'(v. Rainbird). Doubtless an imitative corruption as found in co. Norfolk, the habitat of the Rainbirds. I have no doubt in my own mind as to the truth of this derivation.

1524. Stephen Rainbow, sheriff of Norwich: FF. iii. 219.
London, 3; Oxford, 1; Philadelphia, 1.

Rainford, Rainforth.—Local, 'of Rainford,' a chapelry in the parish of Prescot, co. Lancaster. For suffix, v. Ford and Forth.

Margaret Rainforth, of Winstanley, 1612: Wills at Chester, i. 157.
Robert Rainforth, of Pemberton, 1613: ibid.
John Rainford, of Rainford, 1673: ibid. iii. 218.
William Rainford, of Weetton, 1705: Lancashire Wills at Richmond, ii. 204.
Thomas Rainforth, of Weeton, 1717: ibid.
Manchester, 2, 1; Liverpool, 1, 0; Preston, 4, 0.

Rainger, Ranger. — Occup. 'the ranger,' a forester. Lower quotes Nelson's Laws of Game, where the ranger's specific duties are described.

1615. Adam Ranger, co. Wilts: Reg. Univ. Oxf. vol. ii. pt. ii. p. 338.
1801. Married—William Rainger and Esther Hardy: St. Geo. Han. Sq. ii. 237.
London, 4, 1; MDB. (co. Sussex), 0, 2.

Rainscroft; v. Ravenscroft.

Raistrick.—Local; v. Rastrick.

Raively; v. Reveley. An American variant.

Raleigh, Rawley, Ralley.—Local, 'of Raleigh.' Some spot (I cannot find it) in co. Devon where the family were settled so long ago as six centuries. Sir Walter Raleigh's father lived at Fardel in that county, and he was born at Hayes on the coast. Rawley seems to have been the pronunciation (the present orthography), hence the point of the many epigrams on Sir Walter.
The following spellings occur in the Index to Reg. Univ. Oxf.: Ralegh, Raleighe, Rallegh, Raughley, Raughlie, Raughly, Raugleigh, Rauleigh, Rauly, Rawlie, Rawleigh, Rawley, Rawleygh, Rawlei, Rawlighe, Rawlye, and Raylye.

William de Raleigh, or Ralee, or Rayley, or Radley, or Rawleigh, bishop of Norwich, formerly 'treasurer of the church at Exeter,' 1239: FF. iii. 484.
Hugh de Ralegh, co. Devon, 1273. A.
Warin de Raleghe, co. Soms., ibid.
Peter de Ralegh, co. Cornwall, 20 Edw. I. R.
Wymund de Ralegh, co. Devon, Hen. III-Edw. I. K.
Simon de Raleghe, co. Soms., 1 Edw. III: Kirby's Quest, p. 167.
John de Raleghe, co. Soms., 1 Edw. III: ibid.
London, 0, 5, 0; Philadelphia, 5, 6, 1.

Ralf, Ralph.—Bapt. 'the son of Ralph'; v. Randolph.

John Radulphus, 1273. A.
Ralph le Gras. B.
Ralph fil Ivo. T.
London, 0, 9; Boston (U.S), 0, 6.

Ram, Ramm.—(1) Nick. 'the ram'; cf. Bull, Bullock, &c.

Geoffrey le Ram, co. Essex, 1273. A.
John le Ram,' co. Bucks, ibid.
Nicholas le Ram, Fines Roll, 11 Edw. I.
Robert le Ram, C. R., 30 Edw. I.
Robert le Ram, co. Soms., 1 Edw. III: Kirby's Quest, p. 94.

(2) Local, 'at the Ram,' an innsign; cf. Roebuck and Roe (2).

William atte Ramme, Fines Roll, 14 Edw. II.
1809. Married—Thomas Hamilton Miller and Mary Ann Ram: St. Geo. Han. Sq. ii. 405.
London, 3, 1; MDB. (co. Norf.), 0, 3.

Ramage, Ramadge.—Nick. 'the ramage,' i.e. the wild. 'The term was very often applied to an untaught hawk' (Halliwell); cf. Wild, Wildgoose, Hawk, &c.

'No more than is a gote ramage.'
Chaucer, R. R. 5384.

Perhaps allied to *rammish*, ramlike, strong-scented:

'For all the world they stinken as a gote:
Hir savour is so rammish.'
Chaucer, C. T. 16355.

William le Rameys, co. Soms., 1273. A.
William Ramage. B.
London, 5, 1; Philadelphia, 14, 0.

Rambart, Rambaut, Rambeau.—Bapt.'the son of Rambald'; v. Rimbault.

Johannes fil. Rambaldi, co. Berks, 1273. A.
1773. Married—James Poirier and Marie Rambault: St. Geo. Han. Sq. i. 232.
London, 1, 0, 1; Crockford, 1, 2, 0.

Rampton.—Local, 'of Rampton,' a parish in co. Camb., dioc. Ely.

Simon de Rampton, co. Camb., 1273; A.
Eustace de Rampton, co. Camb., ibid.
1660. Married—James Rampton and
Fraunces Williams: St. Jas. Clerkenwell,
iii. 104.
1662. — John Baker and Dorothy
Rampton: ibid. p. 109.
London, 1.

Ramsbotham, Ramsbottom, Ramsbotton.—Local, 'of Ramsbottom,' a populous village in the township of Tottington-Lower-End, and in the ancient parish of Bury, co. Lanc. Nearly all the surnames with suffix *-bottom* or *-botham* hail from S.E. Lancashire or the Cheshire border ; v. Higginbotham, Shufflebotham, Sidebotham, &c.

Adam Romsbotham, Rossendale, co. Lanc., 1556 : Wills at Chester, i. 164.
Ellis Romsbotham, *husbandman*, co. Lanc., 1587: ibid.
William Romesbotham, 1602: Preston Guild Rolls, p. 63.
John Romsbottom, of Romsbottom, 1614: Wills at Chester, ii. 165.
John Ramsbothom, of Elton, parish of Bury, 1693 : ibid. iv. 205.
London, 1, 1, 0; Bury (co. Lanc.), 0, 6, 0 ; Manchester, 1, 7, 1 ; Philadelphia, 1, 4, 0.

Ramsden.—Local, ' of Ramsden,' i.e. the ram's den or dean. A.S. *ram, rom + den*, a dell, glen, or dingle. Some small spot, probably in the W. Rid. of Yorkshire, has given birth to a large contingent of Ramsdens resident in that county ; cf. the places Ramsbotham, co. Lanc., and Ramsgill, W. Rid. Yorks ; cf. also Ramsden, a parish in dioc. Oxford.

Thomas de Rammesden, co. Essex, 1273. A.
Mathæus de Romsdeyn, 1379 : P. T. Yorks. p. 174.
1562. Married—Humfraye Ramsdon and Alys Skepens : St. Dionis Backchurch, p. 4.
1607. Hugh Ramsden, co. York, Magd. Hall : Reg. Univ. Oxf. vol. ii. pt. ii. p. 298.
1801. Married—John Ramsden and Mary Salter : St. Geo. Han. Sq. ii. 232.
London, 10 ; West Rid. Court Dir., 40.

Ramshire ; v. Ravenshear.

Ramskill.—Local, ' of Ramsgill,' now a parish in the valley of the Nidd, not far from Pateley Bridge, W. Rid. Yorks ; v. Gaskell for a similar sharpening of pronunciation of *gill*, a ravine, dell. Cf. Ramsden.

Leeds, 1 ; Crockford, 1 ; West Rid. Court Dir., 4.

Ranacre ; v. Runacres.

Rance ; v. Rand.

Rancock.—Bapt. ' the son of Randolph,' from the nick. Ran or Rand, with suffix *-cock* (v. Cock) ; cf. Rankin, Wilcock, Simcock, &c.

Isabel Rancok, 1510. W. 11, p. 171.

Rand, Rands, Rance, Randson.—Bapt. ' the son of Randolph,' from the nick. Rand. ' Rande, or Randolf, propyr name: *Ranulphus, non Radulphus, Raaf*' : Prompt. Parv. Rand was a Yorkshire favourite, and the surnames founded on it survive there (v. Rankin). For other forms, v. Ranson.

Thomas Randson, co. York. W. 3.
Janet Rande, co. York : ibid.
Thomas Ranson, co. York. W. 20.
Adam serviens Ran Wiles, 5 Edw. II : Freemen of York, i. 14.
Alicia Randoghter, 1379 : P. T. Yorks. p. 203.
Johannes Randson, 1379 : ibid. p. 200.
Ricardus Randes, 1379 : ibid. p. 65.
Agnes Randewyf, 1379 : ibid. p. 65.
Robert Randson, 1379 : ibid. p. 220.

Rance for Rands is natural ; cf. Evance for Evans.

1735. Bapt. — William, s. William and Rebecca Rants : St. Jas. Clerkenwell, ii.221.
1736. — Mary, d. William and Rebecca Rance : ibid. p. 227.

Here Rands has become Rants, then Rance.

1742. Bapt.—John, s. John Rands : ibid. p. 262.
London, 7, 2, 3, 0 ; West Rid. Court Dir., 4, 0, 0, 0 ; MDB. (Norfolk), 0, 1, 0, 0 ; (Suffolk), 2, 4, 0, 0 ; Boston (U.S.), 89, 0, 1, 0.

Randall, Randell, Randle, Randal. — Bapt. ' the son of Randolph,' from the nick. Randle. For the popularity of Randle in Cheshire, v. Randolph.

Randle de Arclet, co. Ches., temp. 1290 : East Cheshire, ii. 375.
Randle Poole, co. Ches., 1600 : ibid. p. 383 *n*.
1571. Randall Smythe and Mary Lightfoot, *widow*: Marriage Lic. (London), i. 49.
1637. Bapt.—Alexander, s. Cristofer Randall : St. Jas. Clerkenwell, i. 137.
1640. Bapt. — William, s. Richard Randall : St. Michael, Cornhill, p. 130.
1652-3. Buried—Randle Newton : Wilmslow Ch., Cheshire.
1664. Bapt.—Jone, d. Randall Lawson : St. Jas. Clerkenwell, i. 222.
London, 59, 8, 4, 0 ; Philadelphia, 61, 1, 3, 1.

Randolph.—Bapt. 'the son of Randolph.' The Lond. Dir. owes many entries to this once famous name. Randle was the favourite nick. form, and for centuries held its own as a font-name in Cheshire on account of the popularity of Randle, Earl of Chester, the Crusader. On the same page of the Index to Earwaker's East Cheshire I find Rander Borowes, Randle Blackshaw, and Randle Blundeville. The directory forms are Randle, Randall, and Randell. Rand was another abbreviation, and to it we owe Rand, Rands, and Ranson. With the diminutive *kin* added we get Rankin, Ranken, and Ranking. Ralph was, however, the most generally favoured corruption of Randolph. Primary stages will be found below :

Robert fil. Ranulf, co. Linc., 1273. A.
Peter Randulf, co. Bedf., ibid.
Ranulph fil. Ranulph, co. Suff., ibid.
Engilard fil. Radulf, co. Salop, ibid.
William fil. Radulf, co. Hunts, ibid.
Richard Randolf, bailiff of Yarmouth, 1290 : FF. xi. 322.
William Randolf, co. Soms., 1 Edw. III : Kirby's Quest, p. 96.
Henricus Randolf, *osteler*, 1379 : P. T. Yorks. p. 161.
London, 3 ; Crockford, 9 ; Philadelphia, 32.

Ranford ; v. Rainford ; a corruption. In the same way Ravensford became Rainsford and Ransford, q.v.

Liverpool, 2.

Ranger.—Occup. ; v. Rainger.

Ranigar ; v. Runacres.

Ranken ; v. Rankin.

Rankill.—Bapt. ' the son of Ravenchil,' an old personal name, very early reduced to Rankil. I am confirmed in my view by the fact that all my instances belong to one locality.

Rauenchil, co. York : Domesday.
Ranchil, co. York : ibid.
Rankil, the Miller (Molendiuarius), 1176 : RRR. p. 162.
Robertus Rankell, 1379 : P. T. Yorks. p. 43.
Robert Ravenchil, Yorks, temp. 1390 : FFF. p. 106.
Robert Ravenkil, Yorks, temp. 1390: ibid.
Stephen Ravenchil, Yorks, temp. 1390 : ibid. p. 47.

Stephen Ramchel, Yorks, temp. 1390: FFF. p. 106.

Thus it is clear that the Yorkshire personal name Ravenchil or Ranchil became a surname in the guise of Rankil or Rankill. I believe Ravenhill (q.v.) is the present descendant. It is incredible that the surname should have entirely died out. Query: Is Rankin (a Yorkshire surname) sometimes a corruption of Rankil?

Rankin, Ranken, Ranking. —Bapt. 'the son of Randolph,' from nick. Ran or Rand, and dim. Rand-kin or Ran-kin. The first two instances below, however, rather point to Reyner or Reynold as the parent source. Cf. Rancock.

Gilbert Reynkyn, co. Kent, 1273. A.
Richard Reynkyn. H.
John Rankyn, co. Soms., 1 Edw. III: Kirby's Quest, p. 124.
Elena Rankyn, 1379: P. T. Yorks. p. 96.
1612. Giles Rankin, of London: Reg. Univ. Oxf. vol. ii. pt. ii. p. 328.
London, 3, 3, 1.

Ransdale.—Local, 'of Ravensdale.' There is a Ravendale, a hamlet, in the parish of Muggington, co. Derby. But probably several places of this name exist. With the corrupted Ransdale, cf. Rainscroft for Ravenscroft, or Ransley for Ravensley. v. Raven.
London, 1.

Ransford.—Local, 'of Ravensford.' I do not know where the spot is. The meaning is 'the ford which belonged to Raven'; v. Raven and Ransdale, or Rawnsley.

1670. Married—Robert Ransford and Katharin Willson: St. Jas. Clerkenwell, iii. 171.
1695-6. Dominick Melochling and Mary Ransford: Marriage Lic. (London), ii. 318.
London, 6; Philadelphia, 5.

Ransley.—Local; v. Rawnsley.

Ranson, Ransom, Ransome. —Bapt. 'the son of Randolph,' from the nick. Rand, and patr. Randson. This became Ranson, and then Ransom or Ransome; cf. Hansom for Hanson (q.v.), or Sansom for Sanson (v. Sampson),

or Milsom (q.v.) for Milson. The Ransons and Ransoms run side by side in cos. Norfolk and Suffolk. For further particulars, v. Rand. Mr. Lower says, 'I should judge this name was originally Ransham, though I find no place so called' (!!). Mr. Ferguson finds the etymon in the O. Norse *ransamr*, praedabundus, piratical. 'What curious changes,' says he, 'the whirligig of time brings round! We take our money to the descendant of the old sea-robber to take care of for us— Ransom & Co., bankers, Pall Mall. Another Ransome has turned his sword into a ploughsnare, and become famed as a maker of agricultural implements at Ipswich' (!!!). All this is purely imaginary.

1601. Bapt.—Margaret, d. Anthony Rannson, or Rannsom: St. Jas. Clerkenwell, i. 38.
1788. Married—John Ransom and Jane Jones: St. Geo. Han. Sq. ii. 1.
1796. — Robert Ranson and Mary Ann Stanton: ibid. p. 156.
London, 8, 9, 9; MDB. (Norfolk), 0, 2, 3; (Suffolk), 3, 3, 4; Boston (U.S.), 1, 24, 0.

Rant.—Bapt. 'the son of Rand,' q.v., a sharpened form; cf. Brand and Brandt. As Rand is almost peculiar to Yorkshire, so is Rant to Norfolk and Suffolk.

Henry Rant, co. Norf., 1444: FF. v. 491.
1598. Buried—Robert Rant, St. Stephen's, Norwich: ibid. iv. 152.
William Rant, of Yelverton, co. Norf., died 1687: ibid. v. 492.
1635. William Rant and Jane Dingley: Marriage Lic. (London), ii. 222.
MDB. (Suffolk), 2.

Raper.—Occup. 'the roper,' a ropemaker. N. England *raper*; v. Roper.

Alan de Postoill, *raper*, 10 Edw. III: Freemen of York, i. 30.
Willelmus Raper, *raper*, 1379: P. T. Yorks. p. 222.
Johannes Raper, 1379: ibid. p. 241.
1715. Bapt.—Hellen, d. Edward Rapier (sic), St. Jas. Clerkenwell, ii. 85.
1736. Married—William Raper and Ruth Grosvenor: St. Michael, Cornhill, p. 67.
London, 6; West Rid. Court Dir., 3.

Rapkin, Rapkins.—Bapt. 'the son of Ralph,' from the nick Rap (one of the many nicks. of a fontname that has made such a mark

on our directories), and dim. Rapkin; cf. Wilkin, Jefkin, &c.
London, 2, 1.

Rapson.—Bapt. 'the son of Ralph,' from the nick. Rap; v. Rapkin.

John Rapson, temp. Eliz. Z.
1581. Thomas Rapshion, co. Soms.: Reg. Univ. Oxf. vol. ii. pt. ii. p. 111.
1804. Married—William Oak and Mary Rapson: St. Geo. Han. Sq. ii. 309.
London, 1; Philadelphia, 5.

Rascal.—Nick. 'the rascal,' a lean ragged deer, afterwards applied to the rabble (v. my English Surnames, 3rd edit., p. 488, for several instances); cf. Hart, Stagg, Ray, &c. As the term rascal grew more opprobrious, the surname seems to have been silently changed into Rastall, q.v.

John Raskele. H.
Robert Rascal was persecuted for his religion in 1517: Foxe.
'Received for a pewe in the lower end of the churche set to Richard Rascalle, vi°:' Ludlow Churchwarden's Accounts, Camden Soc.
Thomas Rascall, 1578: Reg. Univ. Oxf. vol. ii. pt. ii. p. 81.
Thomas Rascall, or Rastall, M.A., of Balliol Coll., 1584: ibid. vol. ii. pt. iii. p. 93.
John Raskell, Poulton-le-Fylde, 1672: Lancashire Wills at Richmond, i. 225.

Rashleigh, Rassleigh. — Local, 'of Rasleigh.' 'Rashleigh, in the parish of Wemworthy, in Devonshire, gave name to this ancient family, the elder line of which became extinct in the reign of Henry VII': Shirley's Noble and Gentle Men (quoted by Lower).

1576. John Rashlighe, co. Cornwall: Reg. Univ. Oxf. vol. ii. pt. ii. p. 71.
1592. Thomas Rashley, co. Devon: ibid. p. 191.
1643. Walter Blurton and Mary Rashleigh: Marriage Lic. (London), ii. 271.
London, 3, 0; Boston (U.S.), 0, 1.

Rastall, Restall, Restell. —?——. I can offer no suggestion as to the derivation of this name. Cf. Rascal.

Nicholas Rastel, co. Hants, Hen. III-Edw. I. K.
Roger Rastell, co. Notts, ibid.
Ralph Rastel, or Rastal, co. Hunts, 1273. A.
1574. Roger Rastall and Dionise Mayre: Marriage Lic. (London), i. 37.
1621. Roger Rastell and Joane Lewson: ibid. ii. 104.
'William Rastall, of Wisbeach, hanged

on the charge of helping in an insurrection in favour of Charles II, 1650': FF. iii. 400.

London, 2, 2, 4; Oxford, 0, 2, 0; Philadelphia, 1, 1, 0.

Rastrick, Raistrick.—Local, 'of Rastrick,' formerly a chapelry in W. Rid. Yorks, three miles from Huddersfield.

Katerina Rastrike, 1379: P. T. Yorks. p. 221.

1803. Married—William Reid Rastrick and Elizabeth Emery: St. Geo. Han. Sq. ii. 287.

London, 1, 0; MDB. (co. Surrey), 2, 0; (W. Rid. Yorks), 0, 7; Philadelphia, 0, 1.

Rat.—Nick. 'the rat,' possibly intended as a complimentary sobriquet.

Jordan le Rat, co. Linc., Hen. III-Edw. I. K.
Robert le Rat, co. Linc., ibid.
Nicholas le Rat, co. Oxf., 1273. A.
Walter le Rat. J.
William le Rat, co. Soms., 1 Edw. III: Kirby's Quest, p. 213.

Ratcliff, Ratcliffe. — Local, 'of Radcliff,' q.v. Simply a sharpened pronunciation.

Rathbone, Rawbone, Rawbon, Rathborne, Radbone.— ? Local, 'of Ruabon' (?). There seems little doubt that these surnames hail from co. Ches., also that Ruabon is the parent. The change to Rathbone is peculiar, but perhaps the place-name Ruabon has undergone a change. I furnish an instance of Rawbone from the Prestbury registers (co. Ches.) dated 1603. A Thomas Rathbone was living there in 1695. His name occurs in a document; v. East Cheshire, ii. 226. This is corroborative. I see Lower says, 'Rawbone, a corruption of Rathbone.' It may be the other way about.

1547. Robert Radbone and Eliz. Smyth: Marriage Lic. (London), p. 11.
1592. Peter Rathbone, of Brereton: Wills at Chester (1545-1620), p. 158.
1605. Ann Rathbone, of Moreton, *widow*: ibid.
1664. Married—Thomas Rawbone and Alice Okes: Reg. Prestbury Ch. (co. Ches.), p. 163.

London, 7, 2, 1, 1, 0; MDB. (co. Ches.), 3, 0, 0, 0, 0; Liverpool, 8, 0, 0, 0, 0; Oxford (Radbone), 4.

Rathmell.—Local, 'of Rathmell,' a village three miles from Settle, co. York.

Willelmus de Rauthmell, 1379: P. T. Yorks. p. 286.

Ricardus Rauthemell, 1379: ibid.
John Rathmell, of Poulton, 1587: Lancashire Wills at Richmond, i. 225.
Richard Rathmell, of Garstang, 1621: ibid.
MDB. (West Rid. Yorks), 2; Hawkswick (Arncliffe, Yorks), 1.

Rattray.—Local, 'of Rattray,' a parish in co. Perth. Lower says, 'Derived from a barony of the same name in Perthshire. The first of the name on record is Alan de Ratheriff, who lived in the reigns of William the Lion and Alexander III. The family still reside at Craighall, in the parish of Rattray': Patr. Brit. p. 285.

London, 1.

Raveley.—Local, 'of Raveley,' two parishes (Great and Little Raveley) in co. Hunts.

Emma de Ravele, co. Hunts, 1273. A.
Richard de Ravele, co. Hunts, ibid.
Philadelphia, 1.

Raven. — Bapt. 'the son of Raven.' In Domesday the name existed both in Derbyshire and Cheshire; cf. Sparrowhawk, also a personal name at the same period. In place-names like Ravenscroft, Rawnsley, &c., the probability is that the spot took its name from Raven, the proprietor, rather than from the fact that ravens abounded there.

Raven de Slinghawe, 1155: DDD. i. 2.
Gospatric fil. Raven, 1177: Hodgson's Northumberland, vi. 26.
William Raven, 1190: ibid. p. 49.
Raven de Riding, 1233: ibid. p. 163.
Henry Raven, co. Camb, 1273. A.
1618. John Raven and Leah Cotton: Marriage Lic. (London), ii. 61.
1791. Married—Robert Hoodless and Eliz. Raven: St. Geo. Han. Sq. ii. 55.
London, 11; Philadelphia, 1.

Ravenhill.—?——. Mr. Lower says, 'Local, "the hill frequented by ravens."' This is easy enough to write, and, of course, it is well-nigh impossible to contradict the statement. At the same time I cannot discover a hill so called, nor any entry with a local prefix. Yet the surname is a familiar one, there being eight in the London Dir. alone. May it not be the once great personal name of Ravenchil? 'Rauenchil, co. Yorks' (Domesday). In the same county we find later on:

Roger fil. Ravenkelli, 21 Ric. II: Furness Coucher Book, i. 188.
William fil. Robert Ravenchil: FFF. p. 47.
Stephen Ravenchil: ibid. p. 106.

Ravenhill is now found in the West Riding; cf. also

Mariota Ravenild, co. Kent, 1273. A.
Robertus Ravenild, co. Kent, ibid.

a manifest font-name, which would easily corrupt to Ravenhill; v. Rankill for many instances.

1700. Bapt.—Anna Maria, d. John Ravenell: St. Mary Aldermary, London, p. 114.
1787. Married—John Ravenhill and Mary Patrick: St. Geo. Han. Sq. i. 400.
London, 8; Sheffield, 1.

Ravenscroft, Rainscroft.—Local, 'of Ravenscroft,' a township in the parish of Middlewich, co. Chester.

1565. Martin Raynscrofte, Ch. Ch.: Reg. Univ. Oxf. vol. ii. pt. ii. p. 12.
1574. Richard Ravenscrofte, of Occleston: Wills at Chester, i. 158.
1618. John Ravenscroft, of Wettenhall, co. Ches.: ibid.
1757. Married—John Ravenscroft and Eliz. Colman: St. Geo. Han. Sq. i. 68.
London, 7, 0; MDB. (co. Chester), 5, 0; Boston (U.S.), 1, 0.

Ravenshear, Ramshire.—(1) Bapt. 'the son of Ravenswar,' a Domesday personal name (v. Yonge, ii. 286). I have no instances, but the origin seems unimpeachable, being one of the many compounds of Raven. (2) Local, 'of Ravenshaw'; v. Renshaw.

1606 Robert Ravenshaw, of Bromall, *yeoman*: Wills at Chester, i. 158.
1617. Robert Ramshaw, of Bridgemere: ibid.

The modern general form is Renshaw, q.v. In proof we may point out that one of the Bridgemere family is thus recorded:

1613. Randle Renshaw, of Bridgemere: Wills at Chester, i. 159.
1802. Married—William Ramshaw and Eliz. Maria Hall: St. Geo. Han. Sq. ii. 251.
London, 2, 1.

Raw, Rawe.—(1) Bapt. 'the son of Ralph,' from the nick. Raw, whence such surnames as Raw-son or Raw-kins, q.v. (2) Local, 'at the Row,' for the row of cottages. N.E. *raw*, from residence therein or thereby. Probably the latter is in general the true parent, being a North-English surname.

1574. Married—William Rawe and Dorothy Tanner : St. Jas. Clerkenwell, iii. 6.
1591. — Robert Rawe and Ann Filkes : ibid. p. 16.
Katherine Raw, of Barrow, 1613 : Lancashire Wills at Richmond, i. 225.
Richard Raw, of Bispham, 1631 : ibid.
William Raw, of Poulton, 1660 : ibid.
London, 2, 1 ; Manchester, 3, 0.

Rawbon, Rawbone ; v. Rathbone.

Rawcliffe ; v. Rowcliffe.

Rawdon.—Local, 'of Rawdon,' a chapelry in the parish of Guisely, W. Rid. Yorks.

John de Rawdon, 1379 : P. T. Yorks. p. xv.
West Rid. Court Dir., 1.

Rawkins.—Bapt. 'the son of Ralph,' from the nick. Raw, dim. Raw-kin ; with patronymic s, Rawkins. Cf. Wil-kin and Wilkins, &c., and v. Rawson.

Joane Rawkyns, temp. Eliz. Z.
Walter Rawkyns, temp. Eliz. Z.
1579. Married—Edward Rawkyns and Eliz. Robartes : St. Dionis Backchurch, p. 9.
1672. John Rawkins and Mary Thornborough : Marriage Alleg. (Canterbury), p. 201.
London, 1 ; Preston, 1.

Rawle, Rawles.—Bapt. ' the son of Raoul,' i. e. Ralph ; Fr. Raoul. Hence Rawle and Rawles are equivalent to Rowle, Rolle, Rolls, and Rowles. v. Rawkins.

Thomas Raules, co. Soms., 1 Edw. III : Kirby's Quest, p. 188.
John Raweles, co. Soms., 1 Edw. III : ibid.
1612. Stephen Rawle and Alice Greenley : Marriage Lic. (London), ii. 14.
1726. Bapt.—Mary, d. Noah Raoul : St. Michael, Cornhill, p. 168.
London, 3, 1 ; Philadelphia, 10, 0.

Rawlence.—Local ; v. Rylands.

Rawley.—Local ; v. Raleigh.

Rawlin, Rawling, Rawlings, Rawlins, Rawlinson. — (1) Bapt. ' the son of Ralph,' i. e. Randolph, dim. Rawlin and Rollin ; through French Raoul-in, the dim. of Raoul ; cf.

Raoul Partrer : v. Index, Wars of English in France in reign of Henry VI.
Raoulin Reynault : ibid.
Raoulin Meriel : ibid.
Raoul de Saige : ibid.

Miss Yonge says Raoul is the French Rodolphe, not Randolph. In any case, I am sure the dim. Raoulin in England represented Randolph, i. e. Ralph.

Raulyn de la Fermerie, 1306. M.
Anabella Raulyn, 1379 : P. T. Yorks. p. 139.
Raulinus Bassett. E.
Raulina de Briston. FF.
Robert Rawlyngson. ZZ.
John Rawlynson. F.

(2) Bapt. ' the son of Rowland,' pronounced Rawland and Rolland in Furness and co. Cumb., where a large family of Rawlinsons has sprung up, undoubtedly descendants of Rowland through Rawlandson.

London, 2, 5, 24, 18, 11.

Rawnsley, Ransley.—Local, ' of Ravensley,' i. e. the meadow that belonged to Raven, the original settler (v. Raven). I cannot find the spot.

Ralph de Ravenleg, co. Bedf., 1273. A.
Margareta de Rauenslawe, 1379 : P. T. Yorks. p. 189.
1749. Buried—Mary Ransley, widow : St. Michael, Cornhill, p. 299.
1789. Married—Robert Ransley and Eliz. Nichols : St. Geo. Han. Sq. ii. 31.
London, 1, 4 ; West Rid. Court Dir., 3, 1 ; Philadelphia, 6, 9.

Rawson, Raws.—Bapt. ' the son of Ralph' or ' Rauf,' nick. Raw. Rawson has been a familiar Yorkshire surname for the last five hundred years.

Willelmus Raufson, 1379 : P. T. Yorks. p. 134.
Johannes Rauson, 1379 : ibid. p. 135.
Ricardus Raweson, 1379 : ibid. p. 136.
1570. Buried—Edmonde Rawson : St. Michael, Cornhill, p. 191.
London, 8, 0 ; West Rid. Court Dir., 21, 0 ; Philadelphia, 9, 5.

Rawsthorne, Rawstorne, Rawstion, Rawstron, Rostron, Roston, Rosthern.—Local, ' of Rostherne,' a parish and village in co. Ches. A family of Rosthernes seem early to have removed into the neighbouring county of Lancashire, and settled in the district around Bury, thence distributing themselves over the county. A representative family named Rawsthorne still holds a good position

in co. Lancashire. The corrupted forms are many, the favourite being Roston. Five Rostons are still found in the Bury Directory.

Roger de Venables, parson of Roustorn, 1399 : Hist. East Ches. i. 48.
James Legh, rector of the church of Rosthorn, 1484 : ibid. ii. 426.
William Rawstorne, gentleman, of co. Lancaster, 1580 : Wills at Chester (1545-1620), p. 165.
Agnes Rawstorne, widow, of the parish of Bury, 1594 : ibid. p. 165.
Jane Rosthern, widow, of Ainsworth : 1613 : ibid.
John Rawstorne, co. Ches. 1610 : Reg. Univ. Oxf. vol. ii. pt. ii. p. 311.
Laurence Rowsterne (? Warrington), 1684-5 : Exchequer Depositions (co. Lanc.), p. 66.
Thomas Stubbs, parish of Rawsthorne, 1638 : Wills at Chester (1621-50), p. 210.

This last entry sets all doubt at rest.

MDB. (co. Lanc.), 7, 4, 2, 7, 13, 0, 0 ; Manchester, 0, 1, 0, 1, 8, 1, 0.

Ray.—(1) Nick. ' the roe ' ; cf. Stagg, Buck, Roebuck, and Scottish Rae, q.v. North English, ra ; A.S. ráh. Such sobriquets were highly popular and gladly retained, being of a complimentary character.

Reginald le Raye, co. Oxf., 1273. A.
Nicholas le Ray, co. Suff., ibid.
Richard le Ray, co. Camb., ibid.
William le Ray, co. Soms., 1 Edw. III : Kirby's Quest, p. 239.
John le Ray, co. Soms., 1 Edw. III : ibid.
Etheldreda le Ray, C. R., 17 Edw. III, pt. i.

(2) Local, ' of the Wray ' ; v. Wray. This would inevitably be stripped of the initial w in many cases.

1790. Married—Robert Ray and Eliz. Adlington : St. Geo. Han. Sq. ii. 45.
London, 32 ; Philadelphia, 59.

Raybold, Reybold, Raybould.—Bapt. ' the son of Reinbold,' a corruption ; v. Rimbault and Rumball.

1600. Edward Raybould : Reg. Univ. Oxf. vol. ii. pt. iii. p. 219.
London, 0, 0, 1 ; Philadelphia, 4, 7, 0.

Rayment, Raymond.—Bapt. ' the son of Raymond ' ; cf. Garment for Garmond, Osment for Osmond.

Reimond de Luka, C. R., 29 Hen. III.
Richard fil. Reimund, co. Camb., 1273. A.

Robert fil. Reimund, co. Camb., 1273. A.
Philip Remond, co. Soms., 1 Edw. III :
Kirby's Quest, p. 91.
1582. Bapt.—Margery, d. John Rayment, *poulter*: St. Mary Aldermary, p. 24.

Among Drake's companions in the Golden Hind in 1580 was Gregory Raymon (World Encompassed, pp. 168-170). In the State Papers (Domestic) Elizabeth he is set down as Gregory Raymente; v. N. and Q., Sept. 3, 1887, p. 187.
A curious Christian name is found in the following entry :

1717. Bapt.—Bargeriljah, son of Bargeriljah Raymond : St. Antholin (London), p. 129.
London, 22, 9 ; Philadelphia, 0, 36.

Raynbird; v. Rainbird.

Rayne, Raynes; v. Rain.

Rayner, Raynor, Reyner.—Bapt. 'the son of Reyner' (v. Yonge, ii. 378). In Domesday Raynar, a common font-name in the 13th and 14th centuries, especially in Yorkshire and on the East Coast generally.

Rayner le Blake, co. Norf., 1273. A.
Reyner Custance, co. Norf., ibid.
Reyner Piggesflessh, C. R., 13 Edw. II.
Reyner, son of Reyner Fleming, temp. Edw. II : Visitation of Yorks, 1563, p. 103.
Anabilla Rayner, 1379 : P. T. Yorks. p. 196.
Thomas Rayner, 1379 : ibid. p. 137.
1601. Edward Reyner, or Reinar, co. Yorks : Reg. Univ. Oxf. vol. ii. pt. ii. p. 248.
1740. Married—John Rayner and Priscilla Elliot : St. Jas. Clerkenwell, iii. 269.
London, 41, 0, 0 ; West Rid. Court Dir. 23, 1, 0 ; Philadelphia, 8, 16, 0.

Rayson.—(1) Bapt.; v. Reason. (2) Local, ' of Rasen,' now three parishes, Middle, West, and Market Rasen, co. Lincoln. This will probably represent the Cambridge and York instances given under Reason, q.v. In a word, Rayson is almost certainly local, and Reason and Reeson may be the same.

Robert de Rasen, co. Linc., 1273. A.
Thomas de Rasne, co. Linc., Hen. III-Edw. I. K.
William de Rasne, co. Linc., ibid.
Robert de Rason, co. Linc., 20 Edw. I. R.
William Ryson, co. Soms., 1 Edw. III : Kirby's Quest, p. 95.
1790. Married—Symonds Rayson and Mary Hiley : St. Geo. Han. Sq. ii. 225.

1800. Married—Edward Rayson and Mary Creick : ibid. p. 39.
London, 2 ; Philadelphia, 4.

Read, Reade, Reed, Reid.—Nick. ' the red,' a sobriquet given on account of the ruddy face or the sanguine red complexion of the hair ; cf. Black, White, Russell, Blunt, &c. M.E. *reed* or *rede*, red. Reid is a Scottish and N. English variant. Our directories teem with the name in all its forms, as is the case with all nicknames taken from the complexion of hair or face.

Godwin la Rede, co. Norf., 1273. A.
Roger le Rede, co. Hereford, ibid.
Robert le Rede, co. Surrey, Hen. III-Edw. I. K.
Martin le Rede, et Jacoba uxor ejus, Fines Roll, 1 Edw. III.
William Red, co. Soms., 1 Edw. III : Kirby's Quest, p. 118.
Robert le Rede, co. Soms., 1 Edw. III : ibid. p. 202.
1568. Married—George Warde and Denys Reade : St. Michael, Cornhill, p. 9.
1592-3. Richard Read, co. Bedf. : Reg. Univ. Oxf. vol. ii. pt. ii. p. 195.
1788. Married—Edward Reed and Eliz. Mellon : St. Geo. Han. Sq. ii. 8.
— — Alex. Reid and Nancy Lewer : ibid. p. 14.
London, 95, 3, 72, 56 ; Philadelphia, 9, 0, 1, 59.

Reader, Reeder.—Occup. 'the reeder,' i. e. a thatcher. ' Redare of howsys, *calamator* ': Prompt. Parv. Naturally we find a ' Robertus Brown, redere,' in the Guild of St. George, Norwich.

Emma le Redere, 1273. A.
Adam le Redere, ibid.
John de Redere, ibid.
William Redere, rector of Baldswell, co. Norf., 1420 : FF. viii. 186.
' In 1512 John King, *reder*, was buried in the churchyard, and gave 20s. towards building St. Vaste's new porch ': FF. iv. 105.
' The Reders, Thaxters, Rede-sellers,' Corpus Christi Guild Procession, Norwich, 1533 : ibid. ii. 148.
William le Redere, London. X.
1661. Richard Eaton and Eliz. Reader : Marriage Lic. (London), ii. 285.
London, 7, 3 ; Boston (U.S.), 2, 1 ; Philadelphia, 9, 27.

Readford.—Probably for Retford. But v. Redford.

London, 2.

Reading, Redding.—Local, ' of Reading,' an important market-town in co. Berks.

1305. Henry de Reding, rector of Matlask, co. Norf. : FF. viii. 137.
1328. John de Reding, rector of Aldeburgh, co. Norf. : ibid. v. 352.
1621. Bapt.—Eliz., d. Symond Reading : St. Jas. Clerkenwell, i. 91.
1714. Henry Redding and Mary Tomlinson : St. Michael, Cornhill, p. 57.
London, 11, 7 ; MDB. (co. Warwick), 10, 0 ; Philadelphia, 16, 12.

Readwin.—Bapt. ' the son of Redwin,' one of the endless compounds of *-win*. Some surnames linger on curiously. There is but one entry in the Hundred Rolls, yet it is represented in the London Directory also by one ; cf. Goldwin, Unwin, Baldwin, &c.

Simon Redwin, co. Kent, 1273. A.
1722. Peter Redwin, of Norwich : FF. iv. 470.
London, 1.

Reams.—Local, ' of Rheims.' The surname has crossed over from Norfolk to Lincoln. The spelling is much corrupted.

Hugo de Reymes, co. Norf., 1273. A.
Richer de Reymes, co. Norf., 34 Hen. III : FF. viii. 143.
William de Reymes, co. Suff., 20 Edw. I. R.
1653-4. Married—William Reymes and Dorothy Fowke : St. Dionis Backchurch, p. 30.
MDB. (co. Lincoln), 1.

Reason, Reeson, Rayson.—(1) Bapt. ' the son of—— ' (?). (2) Local, ' of Rasen ' (?). Several instances below suggest that the suffix is not *-son*, but the dim. *-on* or *-in*, as in Mari-on, Rob-in, &c. Possibly it is the dim. of the once popular Rose (q.v.), of which the German dim. was Roschen, the French Rosine, and the later English Rosanne. All is conjecture, but I feel nearly positive that *-son* is not the terminative. The entries in the Hundred Rolls (A.) would be John fil. Ray, not John Raysun, as below. But v. Rayson, which will explain much.

Henry Reson, co. Oxf., 1273. A.
Richard Reson, co. Oxf., ibid.
Geoffrey Resun, co. Suff., ibid.
Betricia Raysun, co. Camb., ibid.
John Raysun, co. Camb., ibid.
Albray Rayson, 1379 : P. T. Yorks. p. 41.
Willelmus Reyson, 1379 : ibid.
1792. Married—John Lennon and Susanna Reason : St. Geo. Han. Sq. ii. 84.
London, 4, 2, 2 ; Philadelphia, 5, 0, 4.

Rebbeck. — ? Bapt. 'the son of Rebecca (?); Fr. Rebecque. It has nothing to do with *rebeck*, an old name for a violin, as suggested by Lower. The dim. Ribek-on is early found. Abraham, Sarah, Jacob, and Isaac were very popular at the same time.

Gilbert Ribekon, co. Camb., 1273. A.
1804. Married—Isaac Rawlings and Sarah Rebbeck: St. Geo. Han. Sq. ii. 299.
London, 1.

Record. — (?) Local. Lower says, 'Record, a known corruption of Rickword. A Sussex family in the 18th century wrote themselves Record, alias Rickword.' This is confirmed by the registers of St. Mary Aldermary, London, where Record, Rikecord, and Rikeworth are entries that seem to belong to one and the same family.

1595. Buried—Anne, d. John Record, &c.: St. Mary Aldermary, p. 144.
1599. — A still-born childe of John Rikecord, sonne of Malliard Rikecord, stranger, in Mr. Hassald's house, &c.: ibid. p. 148.
1601. — John Rikeworth, stranger, out of Mr. Hassald's house, &c.: ibid. p. 151.
1794. Married—James Record and Jane Evans: St. Geo. Han. Sq. ii. 118.
London, 5; Boston (U.S.), 4.

Redbeard. — Nick. 'with the red beard'; v. Beard, Brownbeard, Blackbeard. M.E. *berd* and *berde*.

Richard Redberd, co. Soms., 1 Edw. III: Kirby's Quest, p. 188.
Thomas Redberd, bailiff of Yarmouth, 1407: FF. xi. 324.

A contributor to Notes and Queries, Jan. 14, 1860, quotes an old Ipswich record, in which is mentioned an 'Alexander Redberd' dwelling there in the early part of the 16th century.

Reddall, Reddell. — Local: (1) 'at the red hall' or red hill, from residence therein or thereby; cf. Blackall, &c. (2) v. Riddell.

Richard atte Redehulle, co. Soms., 1 Edw. III: Kirby's Quest, p. 108.
London, 3, 1.

Reddick; v. Ruddock.

Redding.—Local; a variant of Reading, q.v.

Reddish.—Local, 'of Reddish,' a village near Stockport, co. Ches.

Mathew de Redish, 1260: East Ches. ii. 102 *n.*

John Reddish, of Reddish, 1557: Wills at Chester, i. 159.
George Reddish, of Reddish, 1588: ibid.
1571. Married—John Reddiche and Dorothe Shrigleye: Reg. Prestbury Ch., co. Ches., p. 35.
1572. Buried—Jone Redyche: ibid. p. 39.
1578. Alexander Redyche, co. Lanc.: Reg. Univ. Oxf. vol. ii. pt. ii. p. 80.
1603. Married—Roger Reddiche and Ellyn Haigh: Reg. Mottram-in-Longendale, co. Ches.
London, 3; Manchester, 4; Boston (U.S.), 5.

Reddock; v. Ruddock.

Redfern, Redfearn, Redferne.—Local, 'of Redfern,' a well-known Lancashire surname. I cannot identify the spot. Probably it will be found near Rochdale. The name has spread into Lancashire and travelled to London, not to say the United States. Probably it was the name of some small estate or homestead.

James Redfearn, of Redfern, 1604: Wills at Chester, i. 159.
Edmund Redfearn, of the parish of Rochdale, 1616: ibid.
Thomas Redferne, Rochdale, 1610: Baines' Lanc. i. 489.
1661. Married—Thomas Redferne and Mary Tomkins: St. Jas. Clerkenwell, iii. 108.
London, 10, 4, 0; MDB. (co. Derby), 17, 6, 0; Manchester, 11, 0, 0; Philadelphia, 17, 4, 1.

Redford.—Local, 'of Radford,' q.v. A variant. It must be remembered, however, that East Retford in co. Notts was spelt Redeford (v. R. p. 162).

William de Redford, co. Northumb., 20 Edw. I. R.
1804. Married—Thomas Fowler and Ann Redford: St. Geo. Han. Sq. ii. 315.
London, 3; MDB. (co. Lincoln), 2; Philadelphia, 3.

Redgrave, Redgrove.—Local, 'of Redgrave,' a parish in co. Suffolk. In meaning equivalent to Redwood, q.v. (v. Grave and Grove.)

1344. Robert de Redgrave, of Norwich: FF. iv. 172.
1477. Adam de Redgrave, co. Norf.: ibid. v. 115.
1801. Married—William Redgrave and Mary Reynard: St. Geo. Han. Sq. ii. 249.
London, 6, 1; Philadelphia, 2, 0.

Redhead.—Nick. 'with the red head'; cf. Whitehead, Silverlock, Brownbeard, &c. It is quite possible the name is local, from some red-coloured headland of rock or soil. There are such spots so called in Forfarshire and Orkney. But one thing is certain, Yorkshire is the source of the family of Redheads that have drifted westwards into the Furness district of North Lancashire. No prefix is found, pointing distinctly to a nickname origin.

William Redhed, co. York, 1273. A.
John Redheved, co. Camb., ibid.
John Redeheued, C. R., 25 Edw. III.
Thomas Redhed, 1379: P. T. Yorks. p. 153.
Johannes Redhed, 1379: ibid. p. 254.
1547. Buried—Isabell Redhead: Reg. Ulverston Ch. p. 5.
Richard Redhead, of Water-end in Blawith, Furness, 1627: Lancashire Wills at Richmond, i. 227.
Marian Readhead, of Nibthwaite, Furness, 1641: ibid.
London, 3; MDB. (co. Lanc.), 3; New York, 3.

Redhouse. — Local, 'of Redhouse,' or 'at the red house,' from residence at a dwelling so called. Cf. Reddall.

William de Redhus, co. Southampton, Hen. III-Edw. I. K.
London, 2; Fulbourn (co. Camb.), 2; Boston (U.S.), 2.

Redley; v. Radley.

Redmakere. — Occup. Probably a cutter of rushes or reeds for the candlemaker or thatcher; v. Reader.

John Redmakere, C. R., 45 Edw. III.

Redman; v. Redmond.

Redmile.—Local, 'of Redmile,' a parish in co. Leicester, nine miles from Grantham.

MDB. (co. Lincoln), 3.

Redmond, Redman, Redmayne.—(1) Bapt. 'the son of Redmond' (v. Yonge, ii. 371). Of course Redmond was occasionally corrupted into Redman; cf. Wyman for Wymond, or Mayman for Maymond. (2) Local, 'of Redmain,' a township in the parish of Isell, co. Cumb.

Norman de Redman, 34 Hen. II: Hist. Westm. and Cumb. i. 202.
Matthew de Redman, temp. Edw. I: ibid. p. 89.

Thomas de Redeman, 49 Edw. III:
Hist. Westm. and Cumb. i. 37.

Mathew de Redeman, co. Lanc., Hen.
III-Edw. I. K.

Henry de Rydeman, co. Westm., 20
Edw. I. R.

John Redman, or Redmand, 1537:
Reg. Univ. Oxf. i. 188.

There can be no doubt that (2)
is the true parent of the vast
majority of Redmans, Redmaynes,
and Redmonds. But the two
streams now flow in one common
channel; cf. Simonds for Simons.

London, 4, 16, 1; MDB, (co. Lanc.),
0, 0, 5; Philadelphia, 41, 15, 0.

Redpath, Ridpath.—Local,
'of Redpath,' a village in co. Berwick.

1801. Married—James Cooper and Jane
Redpith: St. Geo. Han. Sq. ii. 239.
1805. — George Redpath and Charlotte
Whisker: ibid. p. 335.
London, 2, 3.

Redshaw.—Local, 'at the redshaw,' from residence beside the
shaw or wood of a red soil (v.
Shaw). I cannot find the spot; cf.
Redgrave and Ridley.

1575. Richard Redshawe, co. Oxf.:
Reg. Univ. Oxf. vol. ii, pt. ii. p. 67.
1712. Married—Christopher Redshaw
and Eleanor Kirby: St. Michael, Cornhill, p. 56.
1746. Bapt.—Ann, d. William Redshaw: St. Jas. Clerkenwell, ii. 270.
London, 1; MDB. (co. Lincoln), 4;
Philadelphia, 1.

Redsmith.—Occup. 'the redsmith,' a goldsmith (?); cf. Whitesmith (tin), Blacksmith (iron),
Greensmith (lead or laten), Brownsmith (copper or brass).

John Rodesmithe (?). D.

Redwood. — Local, ' of Redwood'; cf. Redshaw and Redgrave.

John de Redewode, co. Northumb.:
Hen. III-Edw. I. K.
1767. Married—William Redwood and
Ann Newton: St. Geo. Han. Sq. i. 171.
London, 2; Philadelphia, 2.

Ree.—Local, 'at the ree.' I
do not know what Ree means. One
of my entries refers manifestly to
Rye, a town in Sussex. Lower
says, 'La Rie, meaning a bank, is a
very common name of localities in
Normandy' (Patr. Brit. p. 298).
It is not to be confounded with the
Cumberland Reay, or Scotch Rae,
q.v.

Philip ad Ree, co. Bedf., 1273. A.
Robert de Ree, co. Sussex, ibid.
Ralph de Ree, co. Salop, ibid.
John atte Ree, C. R., 3 Edw. IV.
1646. Bapt.—Robart, s. Robart Re:
St. Michael, Cornhill, p. 134.
London, 1.

Reed; v. Read.

Reeder; v. Reader.

Rees, Reese, Reece.—Bapt.
'the son of Rhys' (Welsh). Other
variants and derivations are Rice,
Price, Preece, q.v.

Edward Reece, co. Hereford, 1601:
Reg. Univ. Oxf. vol. ii. pt. ii. p. 250.
Reese Myricke (co. Glamorgan), Jesus
Coll., 1607: ibid. p. 298.
Thomas ap-Reese, 1606: Wills at
Chester, i. 159.
Thomas Rees, of Tybroughton, 1647:
ibid. ii. 182.
Giles Reece, combmaker, of Chester:
ibid. iii. 221.
London, 36, 1, 7; MDB. (co. Glamor-
gan), 42, 0, 0; Philadelphia, 59, 93, 3.

Reeson; v. Rayson, Reason.

Reeve, Reeves. — Offic. 'the
reeve,' a bailiff, a steward.

'His lordes shepe, his nete, and his
deirie,
His swine, his hors, his store, and his
pultrie,
Were holly in this reves governing.'
Chaucer's C. T., Prologue.

Hence *borough-reeve, port-reeve*,
&c.

Sampson le Reve, co. Suff., 1273. A.
John le Reve, co. Camb., ibid.
William le Reve, co. Soms., 1 Edw.
III: Kirby's Quest, p. 92.
John le Reveson, co. Soms., 1 Edw.
III: ibid. p. 163.
William le Reveson, co. Soms., 1 Edw.
III: ibid. p. 103.
Sager le Reve. H.
1611. William Reve and Joyce Head-
ley: Marriage Lic. (London), ii. 7.
1638-9. John Trott and Eliz. Reeve:
Marriage Lic. (Westminster), p. 37.

Reeves is a genitive form (= 'the
son of the reeve'), just as Williams
is the genitive of William.

1686. James Petre and Eliz. Reves:
Marriage Lic. (London), ii. 307.
1729. Bapt.—Ann, d. William Reeves:
St. Dionis Backchurch, p. 162.
London, 40, 58; Philadelphia, 16, 112.

Reginald. Bapt. 'the son of
Reginald'; v. Reynold.

Roysia fil. Reginaldi, co. Camb., 1273. A.
Reginald le Porter. J.
Philadelphia, 1.

Register, Regester. — Offic.
'the registrar,' a recorder. M.E.
registrere; cf. Breviter. Lower says,

'A corruption of Rochester.' This
is not probable.

MDB. (co. Norfolk), 2, 0; Lynn (co.
Norfolk), 0, 2.

Reid; v. Read.

Remblant; v. Remnant.

Remfry.—Bapt. 'the son of
Reinfreid' (Remfrid, Yonge, ii.
378). In Cornwall, where the
font-name has lingered on for
many centuries, this surname is not
unfamiliar.

Gilbert fil. Reinfridi, alias Reymfrey,
co. Notts, Hen. III-Edw. I. K.
Reynfrey de la Bruere, co. Camb.,
1273. A.
Luke, son of Remfrey Carter, 1542:
Reg. St. Columb Major, p. 2.
Remfrey, son of Harrie Phluyesie,
1551: ibid. p. 6.
Rempfrey, son of John Rowse, 1591:
ibid. p. 15.
Elizabeth Renfrey, *widow*, 1603: ibid.
p. 200.
Renfreid, son of John Moyle, 1604:
ibid. p. 21.
1729. Married—Gilbert Remphrey and
Eliz. Ullithorn: St. Geo. Han. Sq. i. 7.
London, 1; Crockford, 1; MDB. (Corn-
wall), 4.

Remington, Riminton. —
Local, 'of Rimmington,' a township
in the parish of Gisburn, W. Rid.
Yorks. This surname crossed over
the border and settled in North
Lancashire several centuries ago.

Alan de Rymyngton, 8 Edw. III: Free-
men of York, i. 28.
Matilda de Remyngton, 1379: P. T.
Yorks. p. 264.
Robertus de Rymyngton, 1379: ibid.
p. 283.
1551. Matthew Remyngton, of Melling:
Lancashire Wills at Richmond, i. 228.
1599. Reginald Remington, of Melling:
ibid.
1733. Married—Abraham Harris and
Eliz. Rimington: St. Geo. Han. Sq. i. 11.
London, 2, 1; MDB. (co. Lanc.), 7, 0;
Boston (U.S.), 6, 0.

Remnant, Remblant.—Bapt.
'the son of Rembrandt'; cf. the
name of the artist Rembrandt.
This was really his baptismal name:
probably he was Rembrandt Her-
manszoon (Hermanson), or Rembrandt van Rhyn of Leyden. He
was buried as 'Rembrant van
Rign,' Oct. 8, 1669 (v. Chambers'
Encyclop. viii. 180). I suspect
Remnant (an imitative corruption)
is an immigrant from the Low

Countries. Remblant is an intermediate stage.

1619. Robert Remnant and Margaret Collyer: Marriage Lic. (London), ii. 78.
1620. Married—Anthonye Remnante and Catherin Drewe: St. Mary Aldermary, p. 250.
1800. Married—Edward Remnant and Eliz. Maskall: St. Geo. Han. Sq. ii. 218.
London, 3, 0; MDB. (co. Surrey), 2, 0; Bungay (co. Suffolk), 0, 2.

Renaud, Renáut, Rennard. —Bapt. 'the son of Reynold,' i.e. Reynard, not always of French extraction. The form has existed in England for six centuries; cf. Arnaud for Arnold; v. Reginald and Reynolds.

Richard fil. Renaut, co. Salop, Hen. III-Edw. I. K.
John Reynaud, co. Norf., 1273. A.
Sampson Reynaud, co. Norf., ibid.
William fil. Reynaud, co. Camb., ibid.
Robert Reynaud, co. Suff., ibid.
John Renand, co. Soms., 1 Edw. III: Kirby's Quest, p. 92.
1780. Married—Jonathan Rennard and Mary Stephenson: St. Geo. Han. Sq. ii. 18.
1798. — David Renand and Jane Probeart: ibid. p. 190.
London, 2, 1, 0; Crockford, 3, 1, 0; West Rid. Court Dir., 0, 0, 1.

Rendall, Rendel, Rendell, Rendle.—Bapt. Probably mere changes rung upon Randle or Randal, the nick. of Randolph (v. Randall). Perhaps, however, it would be more natural to refer them to Rennell (q.v.), a popular form of Reynold. Then the d would be merely intrusive, as is common after n; cf. Simmonds, Hammond, riband, and the vulgar gownd.

Solomon Rendoll, 1678: Reg. Canterbury Cath. p. 61.
1757. Married—James Rendall and Rachel Witcomb: St. Geo. Han. Sq. i. 68.
London, 12, 3, 8, 1.

Render, Rinder.—Occup. or official, 'the renderer,' one who paid rent, one who held by an annual payment; v. redditus (i.e. rent) capitalis, redditus mobilis, redditus servicii, redditus assisus, &c. (Introduction to Pipe Roll, p. 90). v. Rinder. This surname still exists in Yorkshire, where it is found five centuries ago.

Willelmus Rendrour, 1379: P. T. Yorks. p. 155.
Johannes Rendrour, 1379: ibid. p. 155.
Matilda Rendurer, 1379: ibid. p. 200.
Johannes Rendour, 1379: ibid. p. 293.

1667. Thomas St. George and Damaris Render: Marriage Alleg. (Canterbury), p. 139.
Harrogate, 2, 0; Leeds, 1, 0; Liverpool, 2, 0; West Rid. Court Dir., 0, 6; Philadelphia, 1, 0.

Rendfrey.—Bapt. 'the son of Reinfred'; v. Remfry. The d is intrusive.

Philadelphia, 1.

Rennard; v. Renaud.

Rennell, Rennels.—Bapt. 'the son of Reynold,' popularly Rennel; v. Reynell and Reynold. The first instance below is very conclusive:

1769. Married—Robert Rennelds and Eliz. Bond: St. Geo. Han. Sq. i. 188.

Later on the d is omitted.

1788. Married—John Rennels and Sally Fenn: St. Geo. Han. Sq. ii. 5.
1809. — John Tremayne Rodd and Jane Rennell: ibid. p. 416.
London, 1, 1; Philadelphia, 0, 2.

Rennick; v. Renwick.

Rennison, Renison. — (1) Bapt. 'the son of Reynold,' a corruption of Reynoldson. (2) Bapt. 'the son of Reyner' (v. Rayner), a corruption of Reynerson. No doubt both (1) and (2) have contributed. But as Reyner was a great Yorkshire font-name in the 13th and 14th centuries, (2) must be looked upon as the chief parent.

Anne Rennison, co. York. W. 14.
John Reynerson, co. York. W. 10.
Thomas Rennison, co. York. W. 20.
John Rennison, of Tunstall, 1695: Lancashire Wills at Richmond, ii. 207.
1739. Married—Lancelot Rennyson and Mary Billington: St. Geo. Han. Sq. i. 23.
1753. — Richard Renneson and Mary Robinson: St. Jas. Clerkenwell, iii. 285.
Farmers' Dir. (North and East Rid. of Yorks), 5, 0; Boston (U.S.), 1, 4; Philadelphia, 1, 0.

Renshaw.—Local, 'of Ravenshaw,' some small but, I fear, lost spot in East Cheshire. The surname has ramified very strongly. The suffix is found alike as -shall or -shaw; cf. Henshall and Henshaw, Shallcross and Shawcross, in the same district. Ravenshaw means the shaw or wood belonging to Raven, an early personal name of much popularity (v. Rawnsley and Raven, and cf. Ravenscroft, a surname found in East Cheshire

also). The full form ran alongside the abbreviated for a time.

John Ravenshaw, of Walkerton, 1673: Wills at Chester (1660-80), p. 220.

The first step towards the modern form was Rainshaw (cf. Rainow, formerly Ravenowe, a township in the parish of Priestbury).

1570. Bapt.—Alice Raynshawe: Prestbury Ch. (Cheshire), p. 33.
Sir Ralphe Raynshaw, vicar of Potte, 1548: East Cheshire, ii. 330.

This same Ralph was buried at Prestbury:

1561. Buried—Sir Rauffe Renshae, preste: Prestbury Ch. (Cheshire), p. 6.

Thus in two entries concerning the same individual we see the last stage practically reached.

John Rainshaw, of Sale, 1647: Wills at Chester (1621-50), p. 180.
John Renshaw, yeoman, of Mobberley, 1661: ibid. (1660-80), p. 221.
John Renshall, of Sale, 1679: ibid.
Ralph Renshall, of Mobberley, 1680: ibid.
London, 10; Manchester, 28; MDB. (Cheshire), 4; Philadelphia, 14.

Renton.—Local, 'of Renton.' Lower says, 'Renton, a small town in Dumbartonshire.' Probably some of our English-seeming Rentons hail from this place, but evidently, from the large number, not all.

Mathew de Renedon, or Reneton, co. Devon, 1273. A.
Robert de Reyndon, co. Warw., ibid.
1802. Married—Robert Downham and Margaret Renton: St. Geo. Han. Sq. ii. 257.
London, 10; Boston (U.S.), 2.

Renwick, Rennick.—Local, 'of Renwick,' a parish in co. Cumb., eleven miles from Penrith. With Rennick, cf. Physic for Fishwick.

1726. Married—John Elliot and Ann Rennick: St. Geo. Han. Sq. i. 2.
London, 1, 0; MDB. (co. Northumberland), 4, 0; (co. Cumb.), 1, 0.

Repington, Rippington. — Local, 'of Repton,' a parish in co. Derby, 'otherwise written Repinton,' says Mr. Lower (Patr. Brit. p. 288). This is borne out by the Hundred Rolls:

Prior de Repindon, co. Derby, 1273. A.
Also cf.
Prior de Reppendon, or Reppedon, co. Derby, Hen. III-Edw. I. K.

Later on we find the *d* sharpened into *t* :

John Reapington, co. Warw., 1574 : Reg. Univ. Oxf. vol. ii. pt. ii. p. 57.
Humphrey Repington, co. Warw., 1590 : ibid. p. 180.
Edward Repington, or Rippington, 1598 : ibid. p. 227.

It is quite manifest that Rippington and Repington originally hail from Repton in Derbyshire.

London, o, 2 ; MDB. (co. Suffolk), 1, o ; Oxford, o, 3.

Reskimer.—Local, ' of Reskymer.' Seemingly an old Cornish font-name. The instances are before the period when surnames were (saving in exceptional cases) turned into Christian names. Nevertheless Lower, quoting Gilbert's Hist. of Cornwall, says, ' The family (Reskymer) became extinct in the 17th century. They had resided for fourteen generations on their estate of Reskymer, in the parish of St. Mawgan, near Helston.' Doubtless therefore the name is local. The surname still exists in the form of Reskimer, as I have personally met with a gentleman of that name.

Reskimer, son of Henrie Sprey, 1605 : Reg. St. Columb Major.
Reskimer, son of John Pearse, 1606 : ibid.

Restall ; v. Rastall.

Reston.—(1) Local, ' of Reston,' two parishes (North and South Reston) in co. Lincoln. (2) Local, ' of Riston,' a parish in E. Rid. Yorks.

Richard de Riston, co. Notts, Hen. III–Edw. I. K.
Ralph de Riston, co. Linc., 1273. A.
Gomer de Riston, co. Norf., ibid.
1603. Bapt.—John, s. William Reston : St. Jas. Clerkenwell, i. 41.
1634. Daniel Eyres and Eliz. Reston : Marriage Lic. (London), ii. 219.
London, 1 ; Philadelphia, 2.

Reuter.—Occup. ; v. Rutter.

Reveley, Raively.—Local, ' of Reaveley,' a township in the parish of Ingram, co. Northumberland. Lower says, ' The Reveleys, who trace their pedigree to the reign of Edward II, were originally seated at the manor-house of Reveley, on the northern bank of the river Breamish, at the south-

eastern foot of Cheviot.' The surname is thus distinctly Northumbrian.

1801. Married—John Gregory and Isabel Revely : St. Geo. Han. Sq. ii. 244.
1808. — John Stevenson and Hannah Reaveley : ibid. p. 380.
MDB. (co. Northumberland), 1, o ; (North Rid.Yorks), 1, o ; Philadelphia, o, 3.

Revell, Revill.—Bapt. ' the son of Revel,' a forgotten personal name. Mr. Lower says, ' Two places in Normandy bear the name of Réville, one near Bernai, the other in the arrondissement of Valognes. The surname still exists in Normandy.' The objection to this is that there is no prefix *de* in our instances, not even in the Testa de Neville, and it is found familiarly in different places widely scattered. The matter is practically settled by the occurrence of Revel as a personal name, without surname, in the Hundred Rolls. It is a common surname in present Yorkshire directories.

Richard Revel, co. Soms., Hen. III–Edw. I. K.
William Revel, co. Berks, ibid.
Revel (without surname), co. Soms., 1273. A.
Alan Revel, co. Camb., ibid.
Thomas Revel, co. Wilts, ibid.
Thomas Ryuell, 1379 : P. T. Yorks. p. 36.
Roger Ryuell, 1379 : ibid.
Adam Reuell, 1379 : ibid. p. 45.
Ricardus Ryuyll, 1379 : ibid. p. 35.
London, 7, 1 ; Sheffield, 2, 12 ; Philadelphia, 1, o.

Reveter.—Occup. ' the revetor,' a man who made rivets for armour. ' Ryvet, revet,' Palsgrave (v. Skeat).

Richard le Reveter, 7 Edw. II : Freemen of York, i. 15.
' William Revetor, a chantry priest' : v. York Plays (L. Toulmin Smith), Introduction, p. xxx.

Rew.—Local, ' at the rew,' a row, from residence therein. ' The shadyside of a street. Devon' (Halliwell) ; v. Raw and Row (2).

' And lete anon commande to hacke and hewe
The okes old, and lay hem on a rew.'
    Chaucer, C. T. 2868.

John atte Rewe, co. Soms., 1 Edw. III : Kirby's Quest, p. 258.
Richard atte Rewe, co. Soms., 1 Edw. III : ibid.
William in the rew, co. Soms., 1 Edw. III : ibid. p. 106.

Adam atte Rewe, co. Soms., 1 Edw. III : ibid. p. 99.
1603. John Rewe : Reg. Univ. Oxf. i. 316.
1677. Bapt.—Anne, d. John Rewe : St. Jas. Clerkenwell, i. 279.
1789. Married—Alex. Rew and Eliz. Wright : St. Geo. Han. Sq. ii. 18.
London, 6 ; MDB. (co. Devon), 3.

Rex.—(1) Nick. ' the king.' Latinized into Rex. This is quite possible ; cf. Faber for Wright ; v. King.

Adam Rex, co. Camb., 1273. A.
John Rex, co. Camb., ibid.

(2) Bapt. ' the son of Richard,' from the nick. Rick (cf. Dick and Hick), whence the genitive Ricks, (cf. Williams for William) modified to Rix (cf. Dix for Dicks), and lastly to Rex. Nine-tenths of our Rexes must be thus derived. For instances, v. Rix and Rixon. The change from Rix to Rex is modern, and, of course, imitative of the Latin.

1718. Bapt.—Rebecca, d. Ann Rex : St. Jas. Clerkenwell, ii. 104.
London, 1 ; Philadelphia, 1.

Rexstrew.—Nick. ; v. Rackstraw.

Raybold ; v. Raybold.

Reyburn ; v. Raeburn.

Reynell.—Bapt. ' the son of Reynold,' popularly Reynell ; v. Rennell.

1778. Married—James Doran and Mary Reynell : St. Geo. Han. Sq. i. 292.
1803. — George Reynell and Frances Linney Hutchinson : ibid. ii. 281.
London, 4.

Reyner ; v. Rayner.

Reynold, Reynolds, Reynoldson. — Bapt. ' the son of Reynold,' i.e. Reginald. Fr. Regnauld and Renaud. One of the most popular font-names of the surname period ; v. Reginald and Renaud.

John Reynold, co. Camb., 1273. A.
Roger fil. Reynald, co. Oxf., ibid.
William fil. Reynaud, co. Camb., ibid.
Rainaldus fil. Willelmi, 1379 : P. T. Yorks. p. 191.
Ricardus Raynoldson, 1379 : ibid. p. 91.
Reginald, or Reynold Reading, 1566 : Reg. Univ. Oxf. vol. ii. pt. i. p. 420.
1617. Robert Reyghnoldes and Jane Watts : Marriage Lic. (London), ii. 51.
London, 1, 122, o ; Boston (U.S.), o, 127, o.

Rhind, Rind.—Local, 'of Rhynd,' a parish in co. Perth. There is also a place called Rhind in co. Fife. The name occurs in the Chartulary of Moray early in the 13th century, and it has been variously spelt Rhynd, Rhind, Rynd, and Rind (v. Lower's Patr. Brit. p. 288).

1728. Married—John Rind and Edith Barwell : St. Michael, Cornhill, p. 64.
1789. — Robert Rhind and Mary Atkinson : St. Geo. Han. Sq. ii. 17.
London, 4, 1 ; Manchester, 4, 0 ; Boston (U.S.), 1, 0.

Rhodes, Rhoads.—(1) Local, 'of Rhodes.' Many of the Manchester Rhodes hail from Rhodes, two estates, one between Prestwich and Ringley, and the other near Middleton. Probably both local terms are equivalent to *royds* and imply an earlier *ridding*. (2) Local, 'at the roads,' i.e. cross-roads. Here the *h* is intrusive. This was a common Yorkshire entry, and explains the large number of Rhodes in the West Riding Dir. For instances, v. Roades.

London, 30, 2 ; West Rid. Court Dir., 84, 0 ; Manchester, 19, 0.

Rhydderch.—Bapt. 'the son of Rhydderch,' the Welsh accepted form of Roderic ; v. Prothero for fuller statement.

MDB. (co. Carmarthen), 1.

Rhys.—Bapt. 'the son of Rhys' (Welsh) ; v. Rice, Rees, Reece, or Price for further information.

1790. Married—John Rhys and Mary Williams : St. Geo. Han. Sq. ii. 49.
MDB. (co. Glamorgan), 3.

Ribble.—(1) Nick. 'a ribald,' a low fellow. M.E. *ribaud.*

William le Ribote. J.
Philip Riband, co. York. W. 15.

(2) Bapt. 'the son of Ribald,' probably a curtailment of Rimbault, q.v.

Ralph fil. Ribaldi, Pipe Roll, 11 Hen. II, p. 9.
Folco Ribald, ibid. p. 36.
Ribald de Middleham, co. Norf., temp. 1200 : FF. iii. 483.
Ribaldus (without surname), co. Norf., 1273. A.
Philadelphia, 5.

Ribchester.—Local, 'of Ribchester,' near Preston, co. Lanc.

Richard Ribchester, of Ribchester, 1662 : Lanc. Wills at Richmond, i. 228.
Robert Ribchester, of Dutton, 1676 : ibid. Preston, 3.

Ribston.—Local, 'of Ribston,' townships in the parishes of Hunsingore and Spofforth, in W. Rid. Yorks.

Robert de Ribstan, co. York, 1273. A.
Margareta de Ribstane, 1379 : P. T. Yorks. p. 298.

Ricard, Ricards, Riccard, Ricart.—Bapt. 'the son of Ricard,' i.e. Richard (v. Rickard). Probably the earlier form. For change from *c* to *ch* see Skeat, s.v. *rich* (Etym. Dict.).

Hamo fil. Ricardi, co. Norf., 1273. A.
Alice Ricardiswyf, C. R., 8 Edw. I.
Adam Ricard, co. Soms., 1 Edw. III : Kirby's Quest, p. 92.
Walter Rykard, 1379 : P. T. Yorks. p. 109.
Johannes Ricard, 1379 : ibid. p. 71.
Thomas Ricards and Joane Lovelacke : Marriage Lic. (London), ii. 10.
Philadelphia, 0, 2, 2, 1.

Rice.—Bapt. 'the son of Rhys' (Welsh) ; v. Price, Reece, Rees, or Rhys. As with these other variants, Rice is strongly represented in the United States, and proves that the Welsh are great wanderers.

Rice, or Rise Powell, 1570 : Reg. Univ. Oxf. vol. i. 276.
Thomas Rice, of Great Saughall, 1605 : Wills at Chester, i. 159.
Henry Rice (co. Carmarthen), 1607, Jesus Coll. : Reg. Univ. Oxf. vol. ii. pt. ii. p. 299.
Rice Evans, of Hawarden, 1693 : Exchequer Depositions (Cheshire), p. 161.
1697. Bapt.—Francis, s. Rice Winn : St. Mary Aldermary, p. 112.
London, 33 ; Philadelphia, 159.

Rich, Riches.—(1) Bapt. 'the son of Richard,' nicked occasionally into Rich, whence with patronymic *s* Riches ; cf. Ricks, Rix, and Rixon. Also cf. Hitch (q.v.), another nick. of Richard.

Johannes Riche, 1379 : P. T. Yorks. p. 258.
Matilda Ryche, 1379 : ibid.
These paid the peasants' tax of 4*d.*
(2) Nick. Nevertheless Rich is also a nickname, denoting a man of fortune. Riches in this case has no connexion, being strictly of the baptismal class.

Reimbal le Riche. C.
Gervase le Riche. H.

Henry le Ryche, co. Oxf., 1273. A.
Hugo le Ryche, co. Oxf., ibid.
Bruman le Riche, co. Oxf., ibid.
William le Riche, co. Soms., 1 Edw. III : Kirby's Quest, p. 249.
John le Riche, co. Soms., 1 Edw. III : ibid. p. 113.
London, 17, 35.

Richard, Richards, Richardson. — Bapt. 'the son of Richard' ; v. Ricard.

London, 7, 158, 188 ; Philadelphia, 19, 216, 240.

Richart, Richert.—Bapt. 'the son of Richard,' q.v. These American variants are closely allied to the German Reichart.

Philadelphia, 12, 4.

Richbell.—Bapt. 'the son of Richbell' ; cf. Richard.

Richebelle Pirse, Fines Roll, 10 Edw. I.
John Richebele, C. R., 4 Edw. IV.
1674. Bapt. — Rebecca, d. William Richbell : St. Jas. Clerkenwell, i. 264.
1766. Married—Richard Manvell and Ann Richbell : St. Geo. Han. Sq. i. 160.
1767. — John Richbell and Eliz. Moore : ibid. p. 161.
London, 1 ; MDB. (co. Surrey), 1.

Richelot.—Bapt. 'the son of Richard,' from the dim. Richelot. Rikelot is the dim. of the harder form Ricard ; cf. Hewlett for Hughelot, or Hamlet for Hamelot.

Richard Rikelot, co. Hunts, 1273. A.
Rikelot. CC. 1.
Robert Richelot, co. York. W. 15.
Robert Richelot. RR.

Richer. — Bapt. 'the son of Richer' (Yonge, ii. 381). To be distinguished from Richard, but absorbed by it so far as English surnames are concerned. It was very common in its day.

Cuthbert Ricerson, co. York. W. 3.
John Rycerson, co. York. W. 3.
Henry fil. Richer, co. Norf., 1273. A.
Ranulf Richer, co. Glouc., ibid.
Geoffrey fil. Richer, co. Camb., ibid.
1665-6. John Richer and Mary Gerrard : Marriage Lic. (London), ii. 294.
1668. Married—Antony Richer and Cristian Robinson : St. Jas. Clerkenwell, iii. 150.
London, 1 ; Boston (U.S.), 1 ; Philadelphia, 2.

Riches.—(1) Bapt. 'the son of Richer' (q.v.), from the genitive Richers, imitated into Riches. (2) Bapt. 'the son of Richard,' from the nick. Rich, genitive Riches, as in the case of Watts, Williams, Jones, &c. But the first derivation is the correct one in most instances. The following doubtless refer to one individual :

Henry Richers, co. Norf., 1572 : FF. ii. 492.

Henry Riches, co. Norf., 1573 : ibid. p. 484.

John Richers (of Walpole), co. Norf., 1707 : ibid. ix. 113.

Edmund Riches, of Norwich, 1740 : ibid. iv. 161.

1769. Married—Thomas Newton and Martha Riches : St. Geo. Han. Sq. i. 185.

London, 34 ; MDB. (co. Norfolk), 29 ; Philadelphia, 1.

Richey, Richie.—Bapt. ' the son of Richard ' ; v. Ritchie.

Riching, Richings.— Bapt. ' the son of Richard,' from nick. Rich, and dim. Richin ; the g is intrusive, the s in Richings, patronymic.

Oxford, 0, 5 ; Philadelphia, 1, 0.

Richman, Rickman.—Bapt. ' the son of Richman ' or Rickman ; cf. Richard and Rickard. The local Rickmansworth in the diocese of St. Alban's is thus explained. Richman le Savener, with his daughters Alvena, Mabilia, and Matilda, sold soap to the undergraduates of Cambridge in 1273 (A. ii. 382). v. Richmond.

John fil. Rikeman, co. Hunts, 1273. A. Richeman fil. John, co. Hunts, ibid.

Lucia Richeman, co. Camb., ibid.

William Richeman, co. Soms., 1 Edw. III : Kirby's Quest, p. 88.

John Rycheman, C. R., 15 Ric. II.

1577. Buried—Lawrence Rickman : St. Michael, Cornhill, p. 195.

1672-3. John Kirk and Anne Richman : Marriage Alleg. (Canterbury), p. 211.

London, 3, 2 ; Philadelphia, 10, 1.

Richmond.—Local, ' of Richmond,' a parish in co. York (N. Rid.). No doubt sometimes confounded with Richman, q.v.

Roald de Richemond, co. York, 20 Edw. I. R.

Geoffrey de Richemond, 26 Edw. I : Freemen of York, i. 7.

Nicholas Richemonde, co. Soms., 1 Edw. III : Kirby's Quest, p. 183.

Adam Rikemound, co. Soms., 1 Edw. III : ibid.

Nicholas Richeman, co. Soms., 1 Edw. III : ibid.

Agnes de Richemond, 1379 : P. T. Yorks. p. 250.

Johannes de Rychmond, 1379 : ibid.

Thomas Rychmond, Cistercian : Reg. Univ. Oxf. i. 158.

1581. John Richman or Richmonde : ibid. vol. ii. pt. ii p. 107.

1624. Bapt.—John, s. Robart Richmond, or Richman : St. Jas. Clerkenwell, i. 98.

London, 19 ; West Rid. Court Dir., 7 ; Philadelphia, 44.

Rick, Ricks.—Bapt. ' the son of Richard,' from the nick. Rick ; like Dick, taken from the harder form Ricard. The modern dress of Ricks in England is Rix (q.v.) ; cf. Dix for Dicks.

London, 0, 1 ; Philadelphia, 9, 7.

Rickaby ; v. Rickerby.

Rickard, Rickards.—Bapt. ' the son of Richard ' ; v. Ricard.

1602. Bapt.—Henry, s. George Rickardes : St. Jas. Clerkenwell, i. 40.

1625-6. Nathaniel Rickard and Grace Wosted : Marriage Lic. (London), ii. 163.

London, 7, 18 ; Philadelphia, 19, 19.

Rickart, Rickarts. — Bapt. ' the son of Richard ' ; v. Ricard and Rickard.

Philadelphia, 3, 2.

Rickatson, Ricketson. — Bapt. ' the son of Ricard ' (i. e. Richard), from the nick. Rick, and dim. Rick-et (cf. Emmett from Emma, nick. Emm), whence the patronymic Ricketson ; v. Ricket.

London, 1, 0 ; Boston (U.S.), 0, 0.

Rickerby, Rickaby.—Local, ' of Rickerby,' a township in the parish of Stanwix, co. Cumberland. Rickaby is a corrupted form. The original name of the place was Ricardby, i. e. the dwelling of Ricard (Richard), the proprietor.

(Homines) de Ricardeby, co. Cumb., 20 Edw. I. R.

1563. Buried—Jenet Rickobye : Reg. St. Mary Ulverston, p. 42.

1758. Married—William Baker and Catherine Rickerby : St. Geo. Han. Sq. i. 82.

1773. — George Brown and Rachel Rickerby : ibid. p. 234.

1785. — William Parkins and Rachel Rickaby : ibid. p. 369.

London, 3, 2 ; Sunderland, 0, 5 ; MDB. (co. Cumb.), 5, 0 ; Philadelphia, 1, 0.

Rickerson.—Bapt. ' the son of Richard,' a variant of Ricardson ; v. Ricard.

Philadelphia, 1.

Rickert, Rickerts. — Bapt. ' the son of Richard ' ; v. Ricard and Richart.

Philadelphia, 7, 3.

Ricket, Rickets, Rickett, Ricketts. — Bapt. ' the son of Ricard,' from the nick. Rick, and dim. Rick-et. Ricketts is the genitive ; cf. Williams, Jones, &c. v. Rickson.

1606. Married—John Scarbroughe and Hester Rickett : St. Mary Aldermary, p. 11.

1659. Bapt.—Eliz., d. Ralph Ricketts : St. Jas. Clerkenwell, i. 206.

1664. Married—Samuel Ricketts and Hannah Hughes : St. Michael, Cornhill, p. 48.

London, 2, 1, 4, 12 ; Philadelphia, 2, 0, 3, 21.

Rickman.—Bapt. ; v. Richman.

Rickon.—Bapt. ' the son of Richard,' from nick. Rick, dim. Rick-on ; cf. the corresponding forms Dick and Dickon or Diccon (v. Dicconson, s.v. Dickens).

Thomas fil. Ricun, co. Hunts, 1273. A. London, 1 ; MDB. (co. Kent), 2.

Rickson.—Bapt. ' the son of Ricard,' from the nick. Rick, whence the patronymic Rick-son. The usual modern dress is Rixon, q.v.

1551. Anthony Ricson, of Bleasdale : Lanc. Wills at Richmond, i. 230.

1791. Married—Francis Rickson and Eliz. Wood : St. Geo. Han. Sq. ii. 54.

Boston (U.S.), 3.

Riddell, Riddall, Riddel, Riddal, Riddle, Ridel.—(1) Local, ' of Riddell,' in the parish of Lilliesleaf, co. Roxburgh. A clan name of great antiquity. (2) Local ; v. Reddall (1).

1761. Married—William Ridell and Mary Simpson : St. Geo. Han. Sq. i. 106.

1768. — James Riddle and Mary Humphry : ibid. p. 172.

1770. — Samuel Harper and Helen Riddell : ibid. p. 194.

London, 8, 2, 0, 0, 0, 0 ; Philadelphia, 17, 0, 1, 1, 29, 1.

Ridding.—Local ; a variant of Reading, q.v.

Crockford, 3.

Riddington. — Local, ' of Wrightington,' a township in the parish of Eccleston, co. Lancaster. Wrightington first became Rightington, then Riddington ; cf. Ridlington.

Mary Wrightington, of Wrightington, 1580 : Wills at Chester, i. 219.

1713. Bapt.—John, s. John and Eliza Rightington : St. Jas. Clerkenwell, ii. 73.

1716. — Eliz., d. John and Eliz. Wrightington : ibid. p. 93.

In the next generation we find the following:

1736. Bapt.—Mary, d. John and Mary Ridington: St. Jas. Clerkenwell, ii. 229.
1738. Bapt.—Eliz., d. John and Mary Rightington: ibid. p. 241.

Thus Riddington is conclusively proved to be a corruption of Wrightington.

MDB. (co. Lincoln), 3.

Riddle; v. Reddall and Riddell.

London, 4.

Riddlesworth. — Local, ' of Riddlesworth,' a parish in co. Norfolk. This place gave birth to a local surname at a very early period; v. FF. i. 279 for an account of the family of Riddlesworth of Riddlesworth.

Gunner of Ridlesworth, co. Norf., temp. 1100: FF. i. 285.
Peter de Redelesworth, co. Norf., 1289: ibid. p. 279.
Roger de Redelesworth, co. Norf., 1335: ibid.
MDB. (co. Norf.), 1.

Ridehalgh, Riddeough, Redihalgh, Redihough. — Local, ' of the riddyhough.' The suffix -hough is generally found as -halgh in co. Lanc.; cf. Whitehalgh and Greenhalgh (pronounced halsh). Ridehalgh lay in the neighbourhood of Preston without doubt.

Robt. del Riddyough, 1397: Preston Guild Rolls, p. 1.
Edw. Riddihough, 1682: ibid. p. 174.
Edw. Riddihalgh, 1682: ibid. p. 201.
James Riddihough, of Preston, 1678: Lanc. Wills at Richmond, i. 230.
John Riddihalgh, Skipton-in-Craven, 1697: Exchequer Depositions (co. Lanc.), p. 93.
Manchester, 2, 1, 0, 0; West Rid. Court Dir., 0, 0, 1, 1.

Rideout, Ridout, Ridoutt. —? Local, ' of the redoubt' (?). Of this surname and its variants I can find no satisfactory derivation. Mr. Lower says, ' Possibly from redoubt, a military fortification. Fr. reduit; Ital. ridotto; Span. reduto. The Hundred Rolls' Ridhut will, however, hardly bend to this etymology': Patr. Brit. p. 289. v. Skeat's Dict. on redoubt.

Elyas Ridhut, co. Soms., 1273. A.
Willelmus Rydhowt, 1379: P. T. Yorks. p. 272.

1718. Bapt.—Maria, d. Giles Ridout: St. Jas. Clerkenwell, ii. 107.
1730. Married—Theophilus Ridout and Love Barnes: St. Geo. Han. Sq. i. 7.
London, 0, 2, 1; Crockford, 2, 0, 0; Leeds, 0, 1,0; Boston (U.S.), 11, 0, 0.

Rider, Ryder.—Occup. ' the rider,' i. e. trooper; v. Ritter or Rutter.

Roger le Ridere, co. Camb., 1273. A.
Stephen le Ridere, co. Hunts, ibid.
Adam le Rydere, co. Hunts, ibid.
John le Ridere, C. R., 9 Edw. II.
Nicholas le Ridere, co. Soms., 1 Edw. III: Kirby's Quest, p. 146.
John le Rider, 2 Edw. III: Freemen of York, i. 24.
Ricardus Rydere, textor, 1379: P. T. Yorks. p. 261.
1789. Married—William Minchin and Mary Rider: St. Geo. Han. Sq. ii. 24.
— — Robert Ryder and Sarah Gore: ibid. p. 28.
London, 21, 14; Leeds, 10, 1; Boston (U.S.), 3, 88.

Ridge, Rigg.—Local, ' at the ridge,' from residence on the rig or back of a hill; cf. Bridge and Brigg. In North Lancashire and Cumberland Rigg is a very familiar surname, almost as common as Fell; v. Riggs.

Thomas de la Rigge, co. Hants, 1273. A.
John de Legh del Rigge, 1437: Earwaker's East Cheshire, ii. 527.
Edward Rigge, of Hawkshead, 1586: Lanc. Wills at Richmond, i. 231.
Clement Rigg, of Hawkshead, 1590: ibid.
Robert Rig, of Hawkshead, 1611: ibid.
William Rigg, of Satterthwaite, 1611: Wills at Chester, i. 161.
1620. Thomas Ridge and Jane Waters: Marriage Lic. (London), ii. 89.
London, 13, 6; MDB. (co. Cumberland), 0, 14; Philadelphia, 13, 11.

Ridgway, Ridgeway.—Local, ' at the ridge-way,' i. e. the road over the back of the hill. A Cheshire family so called ramified strongly.

Lucia atte Rugewey, co. Soms., 1 Edw. III: Kirby's Quest, p. 105.
Johannes de Rygeway, 1379: P. T. Yorks. p. 5.
John del Ruggeway, co. Ches., 1355: East Cheshire, i. 464.
Hugh Ridgeway, co. Ches., 1577: ibid. p. 350.
1560. Buried—Katerine Ridgeway: Reg. Prestbury Ch., co. Ches., p. 2.
1572. Married—Roger Rydgewaye and Ellen Getscare: ibid. p. 38.
James Ridgway, of Offerton, 1594: Wills at Chester, i. 160.
London, 14, 0; Manchester, 10, 0; Boston (U.S.), 7, 1.

Riding, Ridding, Ryding.— Local, ' of the ridding,' from residence beside the clearing in the woods, called a ridding.

Isolda de Riddyng, 1379: P. T. Yorks. p. 244.
Willelmus de Ryddyng, 1379: ibid. p. 288.
Henry Ryding, husbandman, of Preston, 1590: Lanc. Wills at Richmond, i. 239.
William Rydeinge, of Preston, 1668: ibid.
London, 1, 0, 0; Preston, 4, 0, 3; Manchester, 3, 0, 0.

Ridler.—Occup. ' the riddler,' a maker of riddles. M.E. ridil; cf. Sivier.

Thomas le Ridelar, co. Soms., 1 Edw. III: Kirby's Quest, p. 226.
Walter le Ridelare, co. Soms., 1 Edw. III : ibid. p. 232.
John Ridler, temp. Eliz. Z.
William Rydler, ibid.
1618. Walter Ridler, co. Glouc. : Reg. Univ. Oxf. vol. ii. pt. ii. p. 368.
1792. Married—Anthony Ridler and Mary Fielder: St. Geo. Han. Sq. ii. 71.
London, 5; MDB. (co. Somerset), 5; Philadelphia, 2.

Ridley.—Local, ' of Ridley,' i.e. the red ley, or meadow, from the complexion of the soil. Many small spots would be so entitled. One Ridley is now a parish in co. Kent. Another Ridley is a township in the parish of Bunbury, co. Ches. Again, a third Ridley is a township in the parish of Haltwhistle, co. Northumberland. Cf. Redshaw.

Ricardus de Redleye, or Redlege, co. Essex, 1273. A.
Roger de Redlee, co. Essex, ibid.
Robert de Ridley, co. Lanc., 20 Edw. I. R.
John Ridley, of Chester, 1608: Wills at Chester, i. 161.
1678. Married—Jonathan Ridley and Eliz. Bawyer: St. Michael, Cornhill, p. 42.
London, 29; Philadelphia, 3.

Ridlington.—Local, ' of Ridlington': (1) a parish in co. Norfolk; (2) a parish in co. Rutland.

Adam de Wrydlington, co. Camb., 1273. A.
Ralph de Wridlingtone, co. Camb., ibid.
1383. John de Ridlington, rector of Ridlington, co. Norf.: FF. xi. 63.
1384. Roger de Ridlington, bailiff of Norwich: ibid. iii. 116.
London, 1; MDB. (co. Lincoln), 3.

Ridout(t; v. Rideout.

Ridpath; v. Redpath.

Ridsdale, Riddelsdell. — Local, 'of Redesdale,' co. Northumberland.

1782. Married—William Harwood and Mary Ridsdale: St. Geo. Han. Sq. i. 337.
1803. — James Riddelsdell and Sarah Morton: ibid. ii. 287.
London, 5, 1 ; Newcastle, 3, 0.

Rigby, Rigsby.—Local. ' of Rigsby,' a parish in co. Lincoln, near Alford ; found in early records as Rigby also.

Thomas de Ryggesby, co. Linc., Hen. III-Edw. I. K.
John de Ryggeby, or Ryggesby, co. Linc., 1273. A.
Willelmus de Rygby, 1379 : P. T. Yorks. p. 270.
Johannes de Riggeby, 1379 : ibid. p. 26.
1623. William Simon and Martha Riggesby : Marriage Lic. (London), ii. 133.
1627. John Rigby and Margery Deacon : ibid. p. 188.
London, 11, 0 ; MDB. (co. Lincoln), 0, 1 ; Boston (U.S.), 4, 0.

Rigden.—Local, ' of Rigden.' Mr. Lower, quoting Hasted, says, ' That this name originated among the dens of Kent is quite certain, though I cannot find the locality. The family have long been connected, by landed possessions, with various parishes in that county' : Patr. Brit. p. 290.

London, 2 ; MDB. (co. Kent), 11.

Rigg ; v. Ridge.

Riggs.—Local, ' of the ridge ' (q.v.), a variant. Practically a compromise between Rigg and Ridge.

1591. Bapt.—Frauncis, s. Cuthbert Rigges : St. Jas. Clerkenwell, i. 25.
1601-2. Thomas Riggs, co. Hants : Reg. Univ. Oxf. vol. ii. pt. ii. p. 254.
1612-3. Robert Nedler and Ellen Riggs : Marriage Lic. (London), ii. 19.
London, 3 ; Philadelphia, 22.

Righteous.—Nick. ' the righteous.'

James Rightwys, Fines Roll, 14 Edw. II.
John Ryghtwyse, co. Soms., 1 Edw. III : Kirby's Quest, p. 88.
John Rightwyse. H.
John Rightwys, London. X.
John Rightwise, sheriff of Norwich, 492 : FF. iii. 191.

Rigmaiden.—Local, ' of Rigmaden,' an estate near Kendal, co. Westm. Guessing is dangerous. Lower suggests that it is a nickname, and means ' the romping girl' (!). Trollop, also local, has been assigned to the same class and origin !

John de Rigmarden, 16 Edw. II (1322-3) : Baines' Lanc. ii. 529.
1593. Buried—Frauncis Rygmayden : St. Michael, Cornhill, p. 205.
1654. Bapt.—Jane, d. John Riggemayden : Annals of Cartmel, p. 558.
Susannah Rigmaiden, of Holker (Furness), 1689 : Lanc. Wills at Richmond, p. 210.
Thomas Rigmaiden, of Lancaster, 1735 : ibid.
Liverpool, 1.

Riley.—Local, ' of Riley,' i.e. High Riley, in the parish of Altham, co. Lanc. Probably several places bear the name. The frequency of Riley in the United States is owing to the fact that the Irish O'Reilly, or Reilly, is there generally rendered in that form.

Johannes de Rylay, 1379 : P. T. Yorks. p. 89.
Robert Riley, of Chorley, 1595 : Wills at Chester (1545-1620), p. 162.
Reynold Riley, of High Reiley, 1605 : ibid.
London, 34 ; Manchester, 46.

Rimbault.—Bapt. ' the son of Rembald ' or Reinbold (Yonge, ii. 378) ; v. Rumball.

Willelmus fil. Erembaldi, Pipe Roll, 5 Hen. II.
Reimbald le Riche. C.
John fil. Rambaldi, 1273. A.
Renebaud le Palmer, ibid.
1549. ' An yron gonne, call'd a slyng, which gonne Robert Raynbald found in the barley without St. Austen's gates ' (Norwich) : FF. iv. 232 n.
1675. Henry Townsend and Mildred Rumbould : Marriage Alleg. (Canterbury), p. 243.
London, 1.

Riminton ; v. Remington.

Rimmer, Rymer, Rimer.— Occup. ' the rhymer,' poet, versifier, singer. M.E. rime or ryme. In South-west Lancashire Rimmer has ramified very strongly ; but it was spelt Rymer in the 16th century.

Roger Rymer, of Walton, 1579 : Wills at Chester (1545-1620), p. 168.
Peter Rymer, of North Meols, 1591 : ibid.
William Rymer, of Formby, 1614 : ibid. p. 162.
John Rimmer, of Formby, 1615 : ibid.
Gilbert Rimmer, of North Meols, 1617 : ibid.
Liverpool, 31, 0, 0 ; Manchester, 1, 1, 1 ; London, 0, 6, 3 ; MDB. (co. Lanc.), 19, 1, 0.

Rind ; v. Rhind.

Rinder. — Occup. ' the rendour ' ; v. Render.

Ringbell. — Nick. ; probably the sobriquet of a bellringer ; v. Bellman.

Henry Ringebell, co. Suff., 1273. A.
Richard Ringebelle, co. Suff., ibid.
Matilda Riggebelle, co. Suff., ibid.

Ringland.—Local, ' of Ringland,' a parish in co. Norwich.

1330. William de Ringland, rector of Felthorp : FF. x. 415.
London, 1 ; Philadelphia, 5.

Ringrose.— ? —. I have no satisfactory derivation to offer regarding this surname. It is clearly sprung from East Yorkshire.

Robert Ryngrose, 1544, York : W. 11, p. 233.
1615. John Ringrose, co. Northants : Reg. Univ. Oxf. vol. ii. pt. ii. p. 342.
1744. Married—John Thirlwall and Hannah Ringrose : St. Geo. Han. Sq. i. 33.
London, 3 ; MDB. (East Rid. Yorks), 9 ; Philadelphia, 1.

Ripley.—Local, ' of Ripley,' a parish north of the Nidd, near Ripon, co. York.

John de Riplay, 3 Edw. III ; Freemen of York, i. 25.
Matilda de Riplay, 1379 : P. T. Yorks. p. 279.
1572. Bapt.—Eliz., d. Thomas Ripley : St. Jas. Clerkenwell, i. 25.
1758. Married—Richard Ripley and Sybell Morel : St. Geo. Han. Sq. i. 83.
London, 7 ; West Rid. Court Dir., 8 ; Philadelphia, 13.

Riplingham.—Local, ' of Riplingham,' a township in the parish of Rowley, E. Rid. Yorks.

1628. Sir Henry Appleton and Alice Riplingham : Marriage Lic. (London), ii. 194.
MDB. (East Rid. Yorks), 1.

Ripon, Rippon.—Local, ' of Ripon,' a cathedral city in W. Rid. Yorks.

William de Ripon, co. York, 1273. A.
William de Ripon, 1319-20 : Freemen of York, i. 19.
Johanna de Ripoñ, 1379 : P. T. Yorks. p. 167.
1601. Married — James Rippen and Joane Smithe : St. Mary Aldermary, London, p. 10.
1623. Bapt.—Thomas, s. John Rippon : St. Jas. Clerkenwell, i. 98.
London, 1, 1 ; Middlesbrough (North Rid. Yorks), 0, 1.

Rippingale, Rippingall.—
Local, 'of Rippingale,' a parish in
co. Lincoln, four miles from Falkingham.

John de Repinghal, co. Linc., 1273. A.
Hugh de Repinghale, co. Linc., ibid.
John de Repinghale, co. Linc., 20 Edw.
I. R.
1587. John Reppingall, *tailor*, and Eliz.
Catlyn : Marriage Lic. (London), i. 164.
1733. John Rippinghall, rector of. Boy-
ton, co. Norf. : FF. xi. 100.
MDB. (co. Norfolk), 1, 4 ; London, 1, 0.

Rippington ; v. Repington.

Risbrough, Riseborough.—
Local, 'of Risborough,' two parishes
in co. Bucks.

Thomas de Riseberghe, co. Bucks, 20
Edw. I. R.
1698. Elizabeth Riseborow, of Aylesham, co. Norf. : FF. vi. 280.
1704. John Riseborough, or Risebrow,
or Riseborow, sheriff of Norwich : ibid.
iii. 436 ; iv. 222, 204.
1729. Bapt.—John, s. Timothy Rise-
burer (sic) : St. Jas. Clerkenwell, ii. 187.
Long Stratton (co. Norf.), 0, 1 ; Philadelphia, 4, 0.

Riseley.—Local, 'of Riseley,'
a parish in co. Bedford. This is
sometimes spelt Risley, q.v.

Harvey de Risle, co. Bedf., 1273. A.
Geoffrey de Risle, co. Bedf., ibid.
Richard de Riseale, co. Norf., 8 Edw. II :
FF. ii. 156.
1602. Nicholas Ryselye, rector of
Harpham, co. Norf. : ibid. i. 418.
1725. Bapt.—Sarah, d. James Risely :
St. Jas. Clerkenwell, i. 153.
MDB. (co. Lincoln), 1.

Rishton ; v. Rushton.

Rishworth, Rushworth.—
Local, (1) 'of Rishworth,' a township in the parish of Halifax, W. Rid.
Yorks ; (2) of Rushworth, co. Norfolk, styled in Domesday Rus-
ceuuorda (v. FF. i. 284). M.E.
rusche, rische, a rush. v. Worth.

Domina de Ruseworthe, co. Norf.,
1273. A.
John de Russeworthe, co. Norf., ibid.
1368. William de Rusheworth, rector
of Santon, co. Norf. : FF. ii. 157.
1594. Thomas Rishworth, co. Lincoln :
Reg. Univ. Oxf. vol. ii. pt. ii. p. 204.
1702. Married—John Rose and Alice
Rushworth : St. Michael, Cornhill, p. 51.
MDB. (West Rid. Yorks), 9, 9 ; Boston
(U.S.), 0, 1.

Rising.—Local, 'of Rising,'
now Woodrising, a parish in co.
Norfolk, two miles from Hingham.

Roger de Rysing, co. Norf., 12 Hen. III.
Simon de Rising, co. Norf., 1273. A.
Roger de Wode Rising, co. Norf., 14
Edw. I : FF. x. 274.
1323. Eustace de Rising, rector of
Thurgartòn, co. Norf. : ibid. viii. 177.
1654. John Riseing, of Fouldon, co.
Norf. : ibid. vi. 35.

The surname has ramified strongly in Norfolk, and has wandered
little. Nevertheless, it has its
representatives in the United
States.

London, 1 ; Yarmouth, 6 ; MDB. (co.
Norfolk), 10 ; New York, 3.

Risley. — Local, 'of Risley' :
(1) a parish in co. Bedford, near
Kimbolton ; (2) a chapelry in
the parish of Sawley, co. Derby ;
(3) an estate in the parish of
Winwick, co. Lanc., where a
family of the same name dwelt
for centuries. For other references
to (1) v. Riseley. All three places
have become the parents of surnames.

John de Risley, co. Norf., 44 Hen. III :
FF. vii. 353.
Nigel de Risleye, co. Norf., Hen. III-
Edw. I. K.
William de Riseleg, co. Derby, ibid.
Thomas de Rysshelegh, 1379 : P. T.
Yorks. p. 91.
John Risley, of Risley, co. Lanc., 1617 :
Wills at Chester (1545-1620), p. 162.
London, 2 ; MDB. (co. Oxf.), 6.

Ritch.—A variant of Rich, q.v. ;
cf. Pritchard and Prichard.

Philadelphia, 3.

Ritchie, Richey, Richie.—
Bapt. 'the son of Richard,' from
the North-English and Border nick.
Richie. In the United States
Richie and Richey still live. These
forms seem to be extinct in England, a *t* having crept in, as in the
case of Pritchard.

Richie of the Moat, 1581-7 : Nicolson and Burn, Hist. Westm. and Cumb.,
vol. i. pp. xxxiii-xxxv.
Richie Bell, 1581-7 : ibid.
Richie Maxwell, 1581-7 : ibid.
Richie Blakeburne, 1602 : ibid. p. cxiv.
1793. Married—William Ritchie and
Letitia Robertson : St. Geo. Han. Sq.
ii. 96.
London, 21, 0, 0 ; Philadelphia, 87,
3, 16.

Ritson.--Bapt. 'the son of
Richard,' from the North-English
nick. Rich or Ritchie, whence the
patronymic Richson, or Richison,
corrupted to Ritson. This is a
familiar Cumberland surname. v.
Ritchie.

1801. Married—Richard Walker and
Margaret Ritson : St. Geo. Han. Sq. ii.
240.
1806. — William Gibbs and Sarah Ritt-
son : ibid. p. 357.
MDB. (co. Cumb.), 8 ; Philadelphia, 3.

Ritter.—Occup. ; v. Rutter.

Rively.—Local ; a variant of
Reveley, q.v.

Philadelphia, 5.

River.—Local, 'at the river,'
from residence on its bank. I do
not find River now existing as a
surname. Probably it has taken
an *s* to it, like Brooks, and is lost in
Rivers, q.v.

Richard de la River, co. Bedf., Hen.
III-Edw. I. K.
Andreas de la River, co. Notts, 1273. A.
Richard de la Rivere, co. Wilts, ibid.
1709. Bapt.—George River, a foundling,
by the New River : St. Jas. Clerkenwell,
ii. 47.

Rivers.—(1) Local, 'de Rivers' ;
probably a Norman local surname,
representing a family of importance.
(2) Local, 'at the river' ; v. River.

Margaret de Rivers, co. Essex, Hen.
III-Edw. I. K.
Richard de Rivers, co. Devon, 1273. A.
Simon de Rivers, co. Suff., ibid.
Robert de Riveres, co. Worc., ibid.
1794. Married—William Rivers and
Ann Gilbert : St. Geo. Han. Sq. ii. 107.
London, 8 ; Philadelphia, 13.

Rivington.—Local, 'of Rivington,' an old chapelry in the parish
of Bolton, co. Lanc. This surname
is now extremely rare in the county,
and has gone to the south.

John Rivington, of Wigan, co. Lanc.,
1587 : Wills at Chester (1545-1620), p. 162.
Thomas Rivington, of Chester, *gent.*
1616 : ibid.
1642. Roger Rivington, *taylor* : Preston
Guild Rolls, p. 102.
London, 5.

Rix.—(1) Bapt. 'the son of
Ricard' or Rickard, i.e. Richard ;
nicked to Rick, whence Rix and
Ricks ; cf. Dix for Dicks, and v.
Rickard.

1701. Married—Richard Instance and
Eliz. Rix : St. Jas. Clerkenwell, iii. 224.
1789. — Cecil Rix and Grace Bennett :
St. Geo. Han. Sq. ii. 18.

(2) Local, 'at the rix.' Rix is sometimes local. '*Rix*, a reed. Exmoor' (Halliwell). This seems to have existed since the 13th century. 'At the reeds' would seem to be meant by

John de la Rixe, co. Soms., 1273. A.
Osbert de la Rixe, co. Soms., ibid.

unless 'ricks' (i.e. small stacks) is meant.

London, 11; Philadelphia, 1.

Rixon.—Bapt. 'the son of Ricard,' from the nick. Rick, whence the patronymic Rickson, spelt Rixon (v. Rix and Rickson); cf. Dixon for Dickson.

1731. Married—Thomas Rixon and Eliz. Smith: St. Jas. Clerkenwell, iii. 259.
1805. — Joseph Cooper and Sarah Rixon: St. Geo. Han. Sq. ii. 317.
London, 8; Philadelphia, 3.

Roach.—Local, 'at the rock'; v. Roche.

Roades, Roads, Road.—(1) Local, 'at the roads,' i.e. the cross-roads, the point where the roads meet. Also simply, 'at the road,' one who lived by the road-side. It was natural for people to live at the conjunction of roads, hence the plural form. (2) Local, 'at the rode' or rodes; v. Royd.

Simon de la Rode, co. Suff., 1273. A.
William del Rode, co. Norf., ibid.
William atte Rode, co. Soms., 1 Edw. III: Kirby's Quest, p. 98.
Robert atte Rode, co. Soms., ibid. p. 139.
Edmundus del Rodes, 1379: P. T. Yorks. p. 17.
Agnes del Rodes, 1379: ibid. p. 207.
Alicia del Rodes, 1379: ibid. p. 201.
Henry del Rodes, 1379: ibid.

There are eighty-four Rhodes in the West Rid. Court Dir. alone, manifestly the descendants of such persons as are named above; v. Rhodes (2).

1621. Margery Rodes, of Ribchester, *widdow*: Lancashire Wills at Richmond, i. 236.
1706. Edward Roads, or Rhodes, of Thornley: ibid. ii. 211.
London, 1, 3, 0.

Roadhouse.—Local; v. Roydhouse.

Roadnight, Redknight, Rodnight.—Offic. 'the road-knight,' a riding servitor or attendant on horseback. In feudal times rod-knights were 'certain servitors who held their lands by serving their lords on horseback' (Lower, Patr. Brit.). 'Rodknightes': Spelman's Gloss. The name still exists, though not in Lond. Dir. I met the name in my own parish (Oct. 1885) at Conishead Priory Hydropathic Establishment among the list of visitors.

1586. Elizabeth Redknighte, relict of Thomas Redknighte, *wax-chandler*: Marriage Lic. (London), i. 156.
Liverpool, 1, 0, 0; Atherstone (co. Warwick), 2, 0, 0; MDB. (co. Bucks), 1, 0, 0; (co. Northants), 0, 0, 1.

Roads; v. Roades.

Roafe. — Bapt. 'the son of Ralph'; v. Rolf.

London, 1.

Roan.—(1) Local, 'of Rouen,' the capital of Normandy; a mediaeval spelling. An old poet, speaking of Richard I, says:

'Thy bowels only Carceol keeps;
Thy corse Font Everard;
But Roan hath keeping of thy heart,
O puissant Richard.'
    (v. Lower's Patr. Brit. p. 290.)

(2) Local, 'at the rowan,' from residence beside a rowan-tree; cf. Roantree for Rowantree (v. Rowntree). So also we have Crabb and Crabtree, Plumb and Plumptre. Of (1) and (2) the second is probably the true derivation in most cases.

1774. Married—John Keats and Eleanor Roan: St. Geo. Han. Sq. i. 246.
London, 6, 0; Philadelphia, 7, 3.

Roanson.— Bapt. 'the son of Rowland,' an abbreviation of Rowlandson; v. Rownson and Ronson.

Roantree.—Local; v. Rowntree, a manifest variant.

Rob, Robb.—Bapt. 'the son of Robert,' from the nick. Rob. The favourite nicks. were Hob and Dob. The patronymics of the three are Robson, Hobson, and Dobson.

Manchester, 0, 2; MDB. (North Rid. Yorks), 2, 1.

Robberds.— Bapt. 'the son of Robert.' A variation of Roberts, q.v.

1622. Edmund Robardes and Jane Nicholson: Marriage Lic.(London), ii.116.
1676. William Roberds, of Blackdyke: Wills at Chester, iii. 225.
Norfolk Court Dir., 3.

Robbey, Robbie.—Bapt. 'the son of Robert,' from the pet Robbie; cf. Charlie or Charley, Teddie, &c.

MDB. (co. Cumb.), 1, 0; Liverpool, 0, 1.

Robbins; v. Robin.

Roberson.—Bapt. 'the son of Robert,' a corruption of Robertson (v. Robert).

1788. Married—William Roberson and Grace Say: St. Geo. Han. Sq. ii. 2.
1789. — Christopher Roberson and Mary Oliver: ibid. p. 22.
London, 3; Deepham (co. Norf.), 1; Swaffham (co. Norf.), 1; Philadelphia, 4.

Robert, Roberts, Robertson.—Bapt. 'the son of Robert.' The influence of this name was enormous, as our directories prove. Its chief nicks. were Hob and Dob, whence with dims. Hobkin, Hopkin, Dobinson, &c., q.v. But the most famous dim. was Robin. Hence our Robinsons, &c. (v. Robin).

Adam fil. Roberti, co. Oxf., 1273. A.
Agatha fil. Roberti, co. Oxf., ibid.
Thomas fil. Roberti, co. Soms., 1 Edw. III: Kirby's Quest, p. 145.

It is useless giving other illustrations. It ran a fine race with Richard and Roger, one giving us the nicks. Hick and Dick, the other Hodge and Dodge, all of which see.

London, 4, 273, 96.

Robertshaw, Robishaw.—Local, 'of Robertshaw,' i.e. the wood that belonged to Robert. This is a West Riding (Yorks) surname, but I cannot find the precise spot. v. Robert and Shaw.

Laurence Robteshay, of Clayton-in-the-Moors, co. Lanc., 1610: Wills at Chester (1545-1620), p. 164.
1794. Married—William Robertshaw and Ann Mason: St. Geo. Han. Sq. ii. 122.
MDB. (West Rid. Yorks), 9, 0; Oldham, 0, 1; Boston (U.S.), 0, 1.

Robeson; v. Robison.

Robilard.—Bapt. 'the son of Robilard.'

Robelard (without surname), co. Sussex, 1273. A.

Robilard de Boteleria (i. e. the Cellar), co. Glouc., 1290: Household Exp., Ric. de Swinfield, Cam. Soc., p. 170.

Robin, Robins, Robbins, Robinson.

—Bapt. 'the son of Robert,' from nick. Rob, and dim. Rob-in; cf. Col-in from Nicholas. The number of entries in the London Directory is sufficient proof of the early popularity of Robin. Birds, flowers, and weeds soon took possession of the name, the ruddock giving way to robin-redbreast so completely as to cause the earlier name to be forgotten.

'Now am I Robert, now Robin.'
            Chaucer, R. R. 6337.
Dera Robins, co. Camb., 1273. A.
John Robin, co. Oxf., ibid.
Robin le Gentyle, C. R., 4 Edw. I.
Robin le Herberjer. E.
William Robyn, co. Soms., 1 Edw. III : Kirby's Quest, p. 117.
Roger Robynsoun, 1379 : P. T. Yorks. p. 220.
Roger Robyn-man (the servant of Robin), 1379 : ibid. p. 248.
Adam Robyn-man (the servant of Robin), 1379 : ibid.
1606. Bapt.—William, s. Arthur Robinsonne : St. Peter, Cornhill, i. 56.
London, 3, 28, 20, 258 ↑ Philadelphia, 1, 15, 108, 578.

Robinet, Robinett.

— Bapt. 'the son of Robert,' from nick. Rob, and double dim. Rob-in-et ; cf. Colinet from Nicholas ; cf. also '*robinet*, the cock of a cistern' (Halliwell).

Robinet de Bocland, co. Glouc., 1290 : Household Exp., Ric. de Swinfield, Cam. Soc., p. 189.
Richard Robynet. H.
Robinet of the Hill. Y.
1694. Married—Robert Hallywell and Susanna Robinett, of Saffron Walden, co. Essex : St. Dionis Backchurch (London).
1804. — Henry Standford and Lucy Rabnett : St. Geo. Han. Sq. ii. 306.
1806. — Edward Humphreys Robnet and Bertie Maria Kleboe : ibid. p. 359.
London, 0, 1 ; Foulmire (co. Camb.), 0, 1 ; Liverpool, 2, 0 ; Philadelphia, 0, 2.

Robishaw ; v. Robertshaw.

Robison, Robeson.

— Bapt. 'the son of Robert,' from the pet Robbie, whence the patronymic Robison.

Thomas Robyson, *faber*, 1379 : P. T. Yorks. p. 266.
1567. James Robyson, of Wray : Lancashire Wills at Richmond, i. 236.
1801. Married — Francis MacGowran

and Eliz. Robeson : St. Geo. Han. Sq. ii. 248.
London, 2, 2 ; Philadelphia, 4, 6.

Robkin, Ropkins.

—Bapt. 'the son of Rbbert,' from the nick. Rob, and dim. Rob-kin ; cf. Wil-kin and Tom-p-kin (with intrusive *p*). I fear the surname is nearly extinct. Robin took all the honours. Ropkins is a sharpened form ; cf. Wilkin and Wilkins, &c.

Adam Robekin, co. Oxf., 1273. A.
Stephen Robekin, c. 1300. M.
1558. Thomas Robkin, co. Norf. : FF. xi. 80.
1562. Thomas Robkins : Reg. Univ. Oxf. i. 248.
1609. Buried—William Robkin, *minister*, Reg. Pulham, co. Norf. : FF. v. 391.
London, 0, 1.

Roblet.

— Bapt. 'the son of Robert,' from nick. Rob, and dim. Robelot ; cf.'*roblet*, a large chicken. East' (Halliwell). The instances below are from the Eastern counties, agreeing with Halliwell's statement.

Henry Robelot, co. Suff., 1273. A.
Richard Robelot, co. Hunts, ibid.
Rus Robalot, co. Camb., ibid.
William Robelot, co. Soms., 1 Edw. III : Kirby's Quest, p. 120.
John Robolot, vicar of Lillington, 1397 : Dugdale's Warwickshire, p. 204.

Roblin.

—Bapt. 'the son of Robert,' from nick. Rob, and dim. Rob-elin ; cf. Hewling (with excrescent *g*) for Hew-elin.

Simon Roblyn, co. Bedf., 1273. A.
Henry Roblyn (co. Pembroke), Jesus Coll., 1607 : Reg. Univ. Oxf. vol. ii. pt. ii. p. 299.
London, 1.

Robotham ; v. Rowbotham.

Robson.

—Bapt. 'the son of Robert,' from the nick. Rob or Robbie ; cf. the other nick. Hob, and Hobson. v. Robison.

Ricardus Robson, 1379 : P. T. Yorks. p. 202.
1565. Bapt.—Thomas, s. Richard Robson : St. Jas. Clerkenwell, i. 3.
1598. John Robson, co. Westm. : Reg. Univ. Oxf. vol. ii. pt. ii. p. 230.
1625. Francis Robson and Wilseam (sic) Harbert : Marriage Lic. (London), ii. 153.
London, 33 ; West Rid. Court Dir., 17 ; Philadelphia, 25.

Roche, Roach.

—Local, 'at the rock' (O.F. *roche*, a rock), from residence beside some prominent rock ; v. Rock.

Alice de la Roche, co. Camb., 1273. A.
Gilbert de la Roche, co. Wilts, ibid.
William de la Roch, co. Soms., ibid.
Agnes de la Roche, co. Camb., 20 Edw. I. R.
1660. Bapt. — Seenehouse, s. John Roche : St. Jas. Clerkenwell, i. 208.
1675-6. — Eliz., d. Thomas Roach : St. Dionis Backchurch, p. 121.
London, 11, 12 ; Philadelphia, 38, 78.

Rochester.

—Local,' of Rochester,' a cathedral city in co. Kent ; v. Rossiter, probably a variant.

Avicia de Rofa, co. Kent, 1273. A.
Ralph de Roff', co. Hertf., ibid.
Salamon de Roff', co. Berks, 20 Edw. I. R.
1549. Married—Thomas Rochester and Eliz. Starkey : St. Michael, Cornhill, p. 5.
1748. — John Harrison and Hannah Rochester : St. Dionis Backchurch, p. 69.
London, 2 ; Philadelphia, 1.

Rochford, Rochfort.

—Local, ' of Rochford.' Lower says, ' The Irish family settled in that country at, or soon after, the Anglo-Norman invasion. Their name was Latinized " de Rupe Forti," of the strong rock, which is doubtless its true meaning ' : Patr. Brit. p. 292. This is not satisfactory. The name has sprung from two towns in England, Rochford in co. Essex, and Rochford in co. Hereford. The meaning is the *ford* on the river Roche, so far as the Essex town is concerned, the Latinization being a mere play on the name.

Guido de Rocheford, London, 1273. A.
Eustace de Rocheford, co. Essex, ibid.
Walter de Rocheford, co. Norf., 20 Edw. I. R.
Ralph de Rocheford, co. Soms., ibid.
1601. Bapt.—Michael, s. George Rochforde : St. Jas. Clerkenwell, i. 39.
1777. Married—John Cable and Sarah Rochford : St. Geo. Han. Sq. i. 276.
1788. — William Rochfort and Eliz. Sperling : ibid. ii. 6.
London, 0, 1 ; Philadelphia, 2, 2.

Rock, Rocke.

—Local, ' at the rock,' from residence beside some prominent boulder ; v. Roche.

Geof. de la Roke, co. Oxf., 1273. A.
Eudo de la Roche, co. Hunts, ibid.
Jordan de la Roche, co. Devon, ibid.
Alicia atte Roch, co. Soms., 1 Edw. III : Kirby's Quest, p. 235.
1576. Bapt.—Francis, s. Robert Rocke : St. Jas. Clerkenwell, i. 9.
1711. Married—Thomas Wanless and Mary Rock : St. Michael, Cornhill, p. 56.
London, 9, 1 ; Philadelphia, 23. 0.

Rockley.—Local, ' of the rockley,' i.e. the meadow by the rocks, from residence beside such a spot. Several places seem to have been so termed.

Roisa de la Rokele, co. Oxf., Hen. III-Edw. I. K.
Robert de la Rokele, co. Bucks, ibid.
Richard de la Rokele, co. Essex, 1273. A.
William de la Rokele, co. Norf., ibid.
Johannes Roklay, 1379: P. T. Yorks. p. 165.
1700. Married—Charles Rockley and Alice Clerke: St. Dionis Backchurch, p. 49.
London, 3; Philadelphia, 1.

Rockliffe, Rockliff, Roccliffe.—Local, ' of Rockcliff,' a parish in co. Cumb., four miles from Carlisle. No doubt, in some cases, variants of the Yorkshire Rawcliffe or Rowcliffe, q.v.

MDB. (West Rid. Yorks), 1, 1, 1; Liverpool, 0, 3, 0.

Rodbard, Rodbeard.—Bapt. ' the son of Radberd,' an early personal name; v. Yonge, ii. 372.

Thomas Radbird, 1677: St. Mary Aldermary (London), p. 104.
1792. Married—John Rodbard and Sarah Price: St. Geo. Han. Sq. ii. 79.
London, 1, 0, MDD. (co. Somerset), 6, 1; Philadelphia, 3, 0.

Rodd.—Local: (1) 'at the rod,' probably at the *rod* of land, so called from its size, measuring a rod; cf. Hyde. (2) Lower says, 'Rodd, a place near Leominster, co. Hereford, formerly the residence of the family.' (3) The most probable derivation is Rudd or Rood, q.v.

Nicholas de la Rodde, co. Devon, 1273. A.
Johannes Rodde, 1379: P. T. Yorks. p. 255.
1685. William Wardour and Anna Sophia Rodd: Marriage Lic. (London), ii. 307.
1801. Married—John Rodd and Eliz. Shaw: St. Geo. Han. Sq. ii. 248.
London, 3; Philadelphia, 2.

Roddam.—Local, 'of Roddam,' a township in the parish of Ilderton, co. Northumberland.

MDB. (co. Northumberland), 4.

Roderick, Rodrick.—Bapt. ' the son of Roderick.'

London, 0, 1; Crockford, 4, 0.

Rodger, Rodgers.—Bapt. 'the son of Roger,' q.v. The *d* is, of course, intrusive.

Rodman. — Occup. Probably the *radmannus* of Domesday: one who held by some tenure similar to that of the *radcniht*; v. Roadnight.

William Rodman, co. Northampt., Hen. III-Edw. I. K.
1783. Married—Henry Marden and Sarah Rodman: St. Geo. Han. Sq. i. 353.
London, 2; Philadelphia, 10.

Rodney.—Local, ' of Rodney,' i.e. Rodney Stoke, a parish in co. Somerset, but traced back earlier to Rodney, a small moss island in the parish of Wedmore in the same county.

Richard de Rodeneye, 32 Edw. I : BBB. p. 670.
Walter de Rodeneye, co. Soms., 1 Edw. III : Kirby's Quest, p. 87.
Thomas de Rodeneye, co. Soms., 1 Edw. III : ibid. p. 228.
Ralph de Rodeneye, co. Soms., 1 Edw. III : ibid. p. 249.
'The vicar of Wedmore has been publishing some interesting notes upon the field names of that parish in the Wedmore Chronicle. In the number for March, 1887, p. 287, he states that Rodney "is the name of a little hump, or island, rising out of Mark Moor," and he traces the Rodney family back from Rodney Stoke to Mark': N. and Q., Oct. 29, 1887, p. 350.
1665. Charles Howard and Eliz. Rodney (of Pilton, co. Soms.): Marriage Alleg. (Canterbury), p. 107.
London, 1; Philadelphia, 16.

Rodnight; v. Roadnight.

Rodway, Radway. — Local, ' of Radway,' a parish in co. Warwick, four miles from Kington; cf. Rodwell (2) for Radwell.

John de Radewaye, co. Soms., 1 Edw. III : Kirby's Quest, p. 112.
Henry de Radewaye, co. Soms., 1 Edw. III : ibid.
Stephen Rodweye, or Radwaye, London, 1581: Reg. Univ. Oxf. vol. ii. pt. ii. p. 103.
1585. William Rodway and Eliz. Sawnders: St. Mary Aldermary, p. 7.
1642. Bapt.—Thomas and Francis, sons of John Rodway: Reg. Stourton, Wilts.
London, 7, 1.

Rodwell.—Local, (1) ' of Rodwell,' a parish in dioc. of Rochester; (2) ' of Radwell,' a hamlet in the parish of Felmersham, co. Bedford.

Robert de Radewell, co. Bedf., 1273. A.
John de Radewell, co. Bedf., ibid.
Alan de Rodewell, co. Leic., ibid.
1598. Married—Thomas Arundell and Honora Radwell: St. Jas. Clerkenwell, i. 21.
1789. — William Rodwell and Eliz. Smirthwaite: St. Geo. Han. Sq. ii. 30.
London, 10; Oxford, 2.

Roe.—(1) Nick. 'the roe'; cf. Buck, Hart, Roebuck, &c. M.E. *ro*, the female deer.

Geoffrey le Ro, co. Hunts, 1273. A.
John le Ro, co. Norf., ibid.
Alicia le Ro, co. Hunts, ibid.
John le Ro, co. Soms., 1 Edw. III : Kirby's Quest, p. 95.
John le Roo, co. Soms., 1 Edw. III : ibid. p. 195.

This must be looked upon as the parent of nine-tenths of our Roes. The following combination of names was a happy one :

1630. Married—Robert Roe and Eliz. Hart: St. Jas. Clerkenwell, iii. 61.

(2) Local, ' at the roe,' i.e. at the sign of the Roe; cf. Roebuck (2).

John de la Roe. O.

(3) Local, 'at the row' (v. Row).
London, 18; Philadelphia, 20.

Roebuck.—(1) Nick. 'the roebuck' (v. Roe). Found in co. Yorks for many centuries.

Thomas Rabuk, co. Linc., 1273. A.
Ricardus Rabuk, 1379: P. T. Yorks. p. 293.
Robertus Rabuk, 1379: ibid. p. 294.

(2) Local, 'at the Roebuck,' a sign-name.

William atte Robuck, 1313. M.
1795. Married—Ebenezer Roebuck and Zipporah Tickell: St. Geo. Han. Sq. ii. 138.
London, 3; Sheffield, 4; Leeds, 3; West Rid. Court Dir., 10; Philadelphia, 4.

Rofe, Roff.—Bapt. ' the son of Rudolph,' through the popular form Rolf, q.v.

1570. Bapt.—Anthony, s. Thomas Roffe: St. Jas. Clerkenwell, i. 6.
1788. Married—Thomas Jennings and Amy Rofe: St. Geo. Han. Sq. ii. 8.
London, 2, 3; Philadelphia, 0, 3.

Roffey.—Local. Probably ' of Roughwray,' a township in the parish of Wrotham, co. Kent. The surname Roffey is still familiar to that and the adjacent counties.

Amfr' de la Rogheye, co. Kent, 1273. A.
1678. Aldricke Roffey and Mary Grove:
Marriage Lic. (London), ii. 282.
1775. Married—James Masdon and Ann
Roffee: St. Geo. Han. Sq. i. 256.
London, 9; MDB. (co. Surrey), 6; (co.
Sussex), 1.

Rogecock.—Bapt. 'the son of
Roger.' An attempt was made to
add *cock* to Roger (or Rodge) as
with Wilcock, Jeffcock, Mycock,
&c., but it was cumbrous and did
not lilt, so was evidently soon
dropped. But it proves the popularity of the font-name.

Stephen Rogekoc, co. Camb., 1273. A.
Ranulf Rogekoc, co. Camb., ibid.

**Roger, Rogers, Rogerson,
Rodger, Rodgers.**—Bapt. 'the
son of Roger.' In Domesday
Rogerus, co. Norf. Exceedingly
common in the 13th century all over
the country, giving us the nicks.
Hodge and Dodge, and through
them Hodgson, Hodgkins, Hodgkinson, &c., q.v. Roger vied with
Robert, John, and William for
popularity for several centuries.
In France, too, the name was a
favourite, the French proverb for
'There's a good time coming'
being 'Roger Bon Temps.'
Hodge is now an English synonym
for a peasant or agricultural
labourer. Once a knightly name,
Roger has fallen from his high
estate, and is, as Joan, ever among
the poor. Early registers teem with
the name. I furnish one or two instances for form's sake:

Adam fil. Rogeri, co. Linc., 1273. A.
Robert fil. Rogeri, co. Norf., ibid.
Eufemia fil. Rogeri. co. Suff., 20 Edw.
I. R.
Waltero Rogero, co. Soms., 1 Edw.
III: Kirby's Quest, p. 88.
Willelmus Rogerson, 1379: P. T. Yorks.
p. 135.
Rogerus Smyth, 1379: ibid.
1788. Married—John Cooper and Eliz.
Rogerson: St. Geo. Han. Sq. ii. 2.
1808. — James Rodgers and Mary
Spencer: ibid. p. 396.
London, 2, 189, 7, 2, 6; Boston (U.S.),
0, 336, 3, 0, 12.

Rokster.—Occup. 'the rokster,'
a woman who worked the distaff.
The terminative is the feminine
-ster, as in *spinster*, a synonymous
term.

'Sir, for Jack nor for Gille
Wille I turne my face,
Tille I have on this hille
Spun a space upon my rok.'
Towneley Mysteries.

'Rokke, of spynnynge': Prompt.
Parv.

Juliana Rokster, 1388. RR. 2.
Agnes Rockestre, C. R., 6 Hen. IV.

Perhaps now lost in the local
Rochester.

Roland.— Bapt.; v. Rowland.

1802. Married—Alex. Roland and Ann
Austin: St. Geo. Han. Sq. ii. 251.
London, 2; Philadelphia, 12.

Rolf, Rolfe, Rolfes, Rolph.
—Bapt. ' the son of Rudolph,' from
the nick. Rolf or Rolph. As
Ralph represented Randolph, so
Rolph or Rolf stood for Rudolph.
Lower says it is the same as Ralph,
and adds, 'The great landowner
Goisfrid de Bec, son of Rollo, and
grandson of Crispinus, baron of
Bec, is styled in Domesday "filius
Rolf"': Patr. Brit. p. 292.

Allan Rolfe, co. Camb., 1273. A.
Roger Rolf, co. Hunts, ibid.
John Rolf, co. Oxf., ibid.
1614. Robert Rolfe and Cicely Pratt:
Marriage Lic. (London), ii. 29.
1654. Married—Jasper Devenish and
Eliz. Rolph: St. Michael, Cornhill, p. 33.
1721. — Thomas Rolph and Ann Bates:
St. Mary Aldermary, p. 45.
London, 0, 24, 1, 5; Philadelphia, 2, 2,
0, 2.

Roll, Rolls, Rolles, Rowles.
—Bapt. 'the son of Ralph,' i. e.
Randolph or Radulph, from the
Norman-Fr. Raoul, the dim. of
which was Raoul-in, whence our
Rawlins and Rawlinsons, also in
some cases our Rollins and Rollin-
sons; v. Rawlin.

Raoul Partrer: v. Index, Wars of
English in France in the reign of Henry
VI.
Raoul le Saige: ibid.

Rolls, Rolles, or Rowles, are
genitive forms; cf. Williams for
William, or Jenkins for Jenkin.

1589. John Rolles, or Rowle, co. Devon:
Reg. Univ. Oxf. vol. ii. pt. ii. p. 170.
1594. Henry Rolle, or Rowles, co.
Devon: ibid. p. 202.
1611-2. Giles Rowles and Mary Stapley:
Marriage Lic. (London), ii. 10.
1647. Thomas Rolles (co. Devon) and
Florence Rolles: ibid. p. 280.

1648. Thomas Rolls and Eliz. Jenkins:
ibid. p. 281.
London, 2, 8, 1, 1; Philadelphia, 3, 1,
1, 0.

Roller.—? Occup.

Philip le Roulour, co. Soms., 1 Edw.
III: Kirby's Quest, p. 200.
London, 1.

Rolleston, Rollston, Rolston.
—Local, ' of Rolleston,' a parish in
co. Stafford. Cf. Roulston.

1609-10. William Rollstone, co. Soms.:
Reg. Univ. Oxf. vol. ii. pt. ii. p. 309.
1619-20. Thomas Rolleston, co. Devon:
ibid. p. 382.
1675. Bapt.—Frances, d. John Roules-
ton: St. Jas. Clerkenwell, i. 271.
Crockford, 4, 0, 1; Philadelphia, 1,
1, 1.

**Rollin, Rollins, Rollings,
Rollinson, Rolling.**—Bapt. ' the
son of Ralph,' from the dim. Rawlin or Rowlin, of which Rollin
was a popular variant (v. Rawlin).
The *g* in Rolling and Rollings is
an excrescence, as in Rawling or
Rawlings.

John Rolyns, co. Soms., 1 Edw. III:
Kirby's Quest, p. 125.
1701. Married—George Evelyn and
Rebecca Rollinson: Marriage Lic. (London), ii. 327.
1809. — Thomas Rollings and Harriet
Bishop: St. Geo. Han. Sq. ii. 408.
London, 1, 1, 2, 2, 0; Philadelphia, 3,
6, 1, 0, 3.

Rollinson.—Bapt. ' the son of
Rowland.' Many of the North-
English Rollinsons are thus descended. (For origin of the South-
English Rollinsons, v. preceding
article.) In the Furness district of
North Lancashire many changes
have been rung on Rowlandson,
the following being the chief, viz.
Rollandson and Rollingson. Such
entries as the following were
common:

William Rollandson, of Cartmell, 1596:
Lancashire Wills at Richmond, i. 237.
John Rollingson, of Cartmell, 1596:
ibid.
London, 2.

Rollison.—Bapt. A variant of
Rollinson, q.v.

1720. Married—Nicholas Adams and
Mary Rollison: St. Jas. Clerkenwell, i.
244.
1805. — William Simmonds and Sarah
Rollisson: St. Geo. Han. Sq. ii. 322.
Manchester, 1; Philadelphia, 3.

Rolph; v. Rolf.

Rolt.—Bapt. 'the son of Roald.' A common personal name in the 13th and 14th centuries. As to the truth of this derivation there cannot be the shadow of a doubt. Roald, which owing to its popularity was bound to leave descendants, was gradually sharpened into Roalt, and then became Rolt.

Ricardus fil. Roaldi: Pipe Roll, 11 Hen. II, p. 15.
Roaldus de Eston, cos. Oxon and Berks, Hen. III–Edw. I. K.
Rowald de Eston, cos. Oxon and Berks, ibid.
Alanus fil. Roaldi, co. Oxon, 34 Hen. III: BBB. p. 28.
Alanus fil. Rowaldi, co. Oxon, 1273. A.
1618. Walter Rolte and Frances Dixey: Marriage Lic. (London), ii. 66.
1745. Married — John Hillam and Eleanor Rolt: St. Geo. Han. Sq. i. 35.
London, 5; Philadelphia, 2.

Romain, Romaine, Roman.
—Local, 'the Roman,' i.e. from Rome; cf. Janaway, Gascoigne, Portwine, Lubbock, &c.

John Romanus, co. Linc., 1273. A.
Reginald le Romayn, co. Linc., ibid.
Thomas Romeyn, London, 20 Edw. I. R.
John le Romayn. L.
Richard Romeyn, co. Soms., 1 Edw.
III: Kirby's Quest, p. 96.
1789. Married—John Roman and Grace Kennell: St. Geo. Han. Sq. ii. 20.
1790. — John Goff and Ann Romaine: ibid. p. 51.
1796. — John Romain and Ann Jones: ibid. p. 156.
London, 0, 1, 0; Philadelphia, 2, 3, 7.

Romans; v. Rummans.

Rome.—Local, 'of Rome'; cf. Romaine, Janaway, &c.

Johannes de Rome, *hostiler*, 1379: P.T. Yorks. p. 148.
Ricardus de Rome, 1379: P. T. Howdenshire, p. 21.
1616. John Hudson and Isabell Rome: Marriage Lic. (London), ii. 45.
London, 3; Philadelphia, 1.

Romer.—Occup. 'the romer,' i.e. the pilgrim to Rome, a pilgrim.

'And religiouse romeris': Piers P. iv. 2321.
'And alle Rome renneres': ibid. 2337.

Cf. Pilgrim and Palmer.

Cristiana la Romere, co. Suff., 1273. A.
1675. Married — Crisstopher Romor and Martha Browne: St. Jas. Clerkenwell, i. 181.

1772. — Andrew Romer and Diana Shaw: St. Geo. Han. Sq. i. 222.
London, 6; Philadelphia, 3.

Romilly.—Local, 'of Romilly'; probably Romilly, a town in Savoy, near Geneva (Lower). The present Romillys are descendants of a French Protestant who settled in England at the beginning of the last century (v. Memoirs of Sir Samuel Romilly, i. 2). Romeley existed six hundred years ago, but is evidently of English origin. It either died out or became incorporated with Romeny, now Romney and Rumney.

Robert de Romeley, co. Camb., 1273. A.
Baldwin de Romeli, co. Camb., ibid.
Lucia de Romely, co. Camb., ibid.
Avice de Romelli, co. York, 20 Edw. I. R.
London, 2.

Romney; v. Rumney.

Ronald, Ronaldson.—Bapt. 'the son of Ronald.' The Scottish form of English Reynold, q.v.

London, 1, 7.

Ronson.—Bapt. 'the son of Rowland,' a North Lancashire abbreviation of Rowlandson; v. Roanson and Rownson.

Rood; v. Rudd.

Roodhouse.—Local; v. Roydhouse.

West Rid. Court Dir., 2.

Roof, Roofe, Rooff.—Bapt. 'the son of Rudolph'; v. Rolf, of which these are variants, like Rofe and Roff.

1791. Married — John Grounds and Mary Roofe: St. Geo. Han. Sq. ii. 68.
1792. — John Westley and Sarah Roof: ibid. p. 85.
London, 1, 1, 2; MDB. (co. Norfolk), 0, 5, 0.

Rook, Rooke. — Nick. 'the rook,' a nickname given probably to one with black hair or dark complexion. A.S. *hróc*, a rook; cf. Sparrowhawk, Hawk, Crow, &c.

Geoffrey le Roke, co. Oxf., 1273. A.
William le Roc, co. Oxf., ibid.
Adam le Roc, co. Oxf., ibid.
Hugh le Rook, co. Soms., 1 Edw. III: Kirby's Quest, p. 113.
Hugh le Rook, co. Soms., 1 Edw. III: ibid. p. 147.
Richard Rook, C. R., 45 Edw. III.
1623. Richard Stacie and Frances Rooke: Marriage Lic. (London), ii. 129.

1665. Married — George Baker and Hannah Rooke: St. Jas. Clerkenwell, iii. 122.
London, 7, 13; Boston (U.S.), 0, 2.

Rooker.—Occup. 'the rocker,' i.e. the spinner; v. Rokster, and cf. Weaver and Webster.

Richard le Rockare, co. Oxf., 1273. A.
Ralph le Roker, co. Hunts, ibid.
1697. Married—Richard Rooker and Mary Slemaker: St. Jas. Clerkenwell, i. 218.
1751. — Francis Rooker and Eliz. Hatfield: ibid. p. 283.
London, 2.

Rookherd.—Occup. 'the rookherd,' a tender or keeper of rooks; cf. Gozzard, Swanherd, Coward, &c.

Henry le Rocherde, co. Oxf., 1273. A.

Rookledge.—Local; v. Routledge. A manifest corruption.

Root, Roote, Roots.—Bapt. 'the son of Root.' There is no prefix to early examples denoting a local derivation. No doubt Root was a personal name, Roots being the genitive form; cf. William and Williams, Jenkin and Jenkins.

Simon Rote, co. Hunts, 1273. A.
Peter Rote, co. Camb., ibid.
1623-4. William Roote (co. Essex) and Eliz. Dagnet: Marriage Lic. (London), ii. 136.
1745. Bapt.—Thomas, s. Robert Rootes: St. Jas. Clerkenwell, ii. 273.
1798. Married—James Root and Eliz. Camplin: St. Geo. Han. Sq. i. 175.
London, 5, 2, 7; Philadelphia, 42, 0, 0.

Roper.—Occup. 'the roper,' a manufacturer of ropes; cf. N.F. Raper.

Peter le Roper, co. Notts, 1273. A.
Walter le Ropere, co. Camb., ibid.
Gerald Roppere, co. Suff., ibid.
John le Roper, co. Soms., 1 Edw. III: Kirby's Quest, p. 152.
1347. Thomas le Roper, rector of Eccles, co. Norf.: FF. ix. 296.
Rogerus Roper, *roper*, 1379: P. T. Yorks. p. 267.
1613. Bapt.—Richard, s. William Roper: St. Jas. Clerkenwell, i. 68.
London, 27; West Rid. Court Dir., 12; Philadelphia, 15.

Ropkins.—Bapt. 'the son of Robert,' from nick. Rob and suffix -kin (v. kin, Introd. p. 25). Ropkins is the genitive of Robkin with the b sharpened to p; cf. Hopkins for Hobkins. v. Robkin.

Rosamund; v. Roseaman.

Roscoe, Roscow.—Local (?). Mr. Lower says, 'Possibly a corruption of Roscrowe. It is certainly a Cornish name' (Patr. Brit. p. 293). I take leave to doubt this statement. I feel sure it is a Lancashire local surname, although I cannot find the spot.

Gilbert Roscoe, of Euxton (co. Lanc.), 1293: Wills at Chester, i. 165.
James Roscoe, of Farnworth (co. Lanc.), 1594: ibid.
John Roscow, of Leigh (co. Lanc.), 1594: ibid.
London, 6, 0; Crockford, 0, 1; Manchester, 4, 1; MDB. (co. Lanc.), 2, 4; Philadelphia, 7, 0.

Rose.—(1) Bapt. 'the son of Rose.' Latin *rosa*, a rose. Very popular at the period surnames were becoming hereditary; hence strongly represented in all our directories.

Thomas fil. Rose, co. Camb., 1273. A.
Richard fil. Rose, co. Notts, ibid.
Adam Costenoght et Rosa uxor ejus, 1379: P. T. Yorks. p. 6.
Johannes Rose, 1379: ibid. p. 9.
Rosa Held, 1379: ibid. p. 18.

Or, again from the same period:
Johanna Rose-doghter, 1379: P. T. Yorks. p. 33.
Isabella filia Rose, 1379: ibid.
Rosa de Berlowe, 1379: ibid.

(2) Local, 'of the rose,' i.e. at the rose-tree, or at the sign of the Rose.

John de la Rose, co. Oxf., 1273. A.
Robert de la Rose, co. Oxf., ibid.
Elena de la Ros, co. Oxf., ibid.
London, 86; Boston (U.S.), 49.

Roseaman, Rosoman, Rosemond, Rosamund.—Bapt. 'the son of Rosamund.' A common girl's name at the surname period. The suffix -*mond* or -*mund* became by corruption -*man*; cf. Osman, Wyman, or Redman.

Rosamunda (without surname), co. Oxf., 1273. A.
Rosamond Udelin, Fines Roll, 10 Edw. I.
1469. Edith Rosamond: Cal. of Wills in Court of Husting (2).

The following occur in early Yorkshire pedigrees:
Rosamund Monford: Index, Visitation of York, 1563-4 (Harl. Soc.).
Rosamond Mallet: ibid.
Rosamond Clapham: ibid.

1665. Married—Thomas Chaplin and Rozeman Gowen: 'St. Jas. Clerkenwell, iii. 120.
1669. — James Bell and Rosaman Davis: ibid. p. 158.
1797. — Thomas Roseman and Eliz. Jupe: St. Geo. Han. Sq. ii. 167.
London, 1, 1, 0, 0; West Rid. Court Dir., 0, 1, 0, 0; Philadelphia, 0, 0, 0, 1; Boston (U.S.), 0, 0, 3, 0.

Rosewarne, Rosewarn. — Local, 'of Roswarne,' an estate in the parish of Camborne, co. Cornwall (Lower's Patr. Brit. p. 285).

London, 1, 0; Cornwall Court Dir., 1, 0; Philadelphia, 3, 0.

Rosewell; v. Roswell.

Roskell.—Local, 'of Rossgill.' Some small spot on the borders of North Lancashire and the West Riding that I have not discovered; cf. Gaskell from Gasgill.

Hugh de Rasegille, co. York, 1273. A.
Walter de Rasegille, co. York, ibid.
Crystyan Rossegyll, 1563: Visitation of Yorkshire (Harl. Soc.), p. 271.
Robert Rossegyll, 1563: ibid.
John Roskell, of the Black poole, yeoman, 1628: Lancashire Wills at Richmond, i. 237.
John Roskell, of the Greene, parish of Cartmel, 1664: ibid.
London, 1; Manchester, 1.

Roskilly, Roskelly.—Local, 'of Roskilly,' an estate in St. Keverne, co. Cornwall, anciently the residence of the family (v. Lower's Patr. Brit. p. 294).

London, 3, 0; Cornwall Court Dir., 1, 0; Boston (U.S.), 0, 1.

Roskruge, Rosekroge. — Local, 'of Roscruge,' an estate in the parish of St. Anthony, co. Cornwall. It gave 'name and original,' says Hals, 'to a family of gentlemen now or lately in possession thereof' (Lower, quoting Gilbert's Cornwall).

Cornwall Court Dir., 1, 1.

Rosling, Rusling.—Bapt. 'the son of Rocelin.' This was at an early period popular in co. Lincoln as a personal name. As a result it is to that county we now look for representatives of the surname. Lower says, 'Rosling: a corruption of Roslyn, a village in co. Edinburgh.' He does not furnish a tittle of evidence. The final *g* is,

of course, an excrescence, as in Jennings.

'Three carucates which the sons of Rocelin hold,' temp. 1109: The Lincolnshire Survey, p. 21.
Rocelinus de Bracton, co. Wilts, Hen. III-Edw. I. K.
Rocelin le Bunne, co. Wilts, 1273. A.
Roscelin de Bratton, co. Wilts, ibid.
Johanna Roscelin, co. Linc., ibid.
Thomas Roscelin, co. Norf., ibid.
Johannes Rosselyn, 1379: P. T. Yorks. p. 178.
Emma Roscelyn, 1379: P. T. Howdenshire, p. 1.
Robertus Roscelyne, 1379: ibid. p. 4.
Richard Roscelyn, rector of Patesley, 1408: FF. x. 28.
1628. Married—Samewell Randall and Frances Ruslinge: St. Mary Aldermary, p. 16.
London, 1, 0; MDB. (co. Lincoln), 4, 3; Philadelphia, 0, 5.

Rosoman; v. Roseaman.

Rossall, Rossell.—(1) Local, 'of Rossall,' near Fleetwood, co. Lanc. It was formerly a grange belonging to the abbey of Deulacres, co. Stafford. In Domesday it is styled Rushale. The following dwelt close by Rossall:

Margrett Rossall, of Bispham, *widdow*, 1578: Lancashire Wills at Richmond, i. 237.
John Rossall, of Warbrecke, *yeoman*, 1618: ibid.
Thomas Rossall, of Norbrecke, 1667: ibid.
Richard Rossell, of Bispham, 1730: ibid. ii. 216.

(2) Nick.; v. Russell.

John Rossel, co. Soms., 1 Edw. III: Kirby's Quest, p. 86.
Preston, 1, 0; Manchester, 0, 1; Fleetwood (co. Lanc.), 1, 0; MDB. (co. Lanc.), 7, 0.

Rosser. — Bapt. 'the son of Rosser' (Welsh), whence Prosser (=ap-Rosser), q.v. Mr. Lower says, 'A dweller upon a heath, or upon a promontory.' This is quite untenable. He connects it with the Scottish Ross. It is a purely Welsh surname.

Rosser Morres. Z.
Robert ap-Rosser. H.
John Roser, co. Soms., 1 Edw. III: Kirby's Quest, p. 88.
William Roser, co. Soms., 1 Edw. III: ibid. p. 250.
1685. Bapt.—Anne, d. Thomas Rosser: St. Jas. Clerkenwell, i. 313.
1700. — Gload, s. Lewis Rossear: ibid. p. 386.
London, 4; Philadelphia, 1.

Rossiter. — (1) Local, 'of Wroxeter,' a parish in co. Salop. So says Mr. Lower, and I see no reason to doubt the statement (v. Patr. Brit. p. 294). (2) Local, 'of Rochester.' This derivation is probably in most cases the correct one. From Roucester to Rossiter would be an inevitable step.

William de Roucester, co. Norf., 33 Hen. III : FF. vii. 276.
Eustace de Roucestre, co. Essex, Hen. III–Edw. I. K.
Peter de Roucestre, co. Suff., 1273. A.
1581. John Rociter, co. Soms.: Reg. Univ. Oxf. vol. ii. pt. ii. p. 109.
1601. Married—John Pratt and Joane Rosseter: St. Jas. Clerkenwell, i. 25.
1641. — Dudleye Rositer and Sara Wilson : ibid. p. 74.
1709. — Mathew Rossiter and Frances Richmond : St. Geo. Han. Sq. ii. 198.
London, 4 ; Philadelphia, 19.

Rosthern, Roston, Rostron. —Local ; v. Rawsthorne.

Roswell, Rosewell.— ? Local, ' de Rosseville ' (?). Mr. Lower writes, 'Said to be a corruption of the French Rosseville. It is therefore local, but I know not the place. Kent, in his Grammar of Heraldry, speaks of the Rev. S. Rosewell, of London, M.A., as descended from the Rosewells of Somersetshire, Wiltshire, and Devon, who came in with the Conqueror ' : Patr. Brit. p. 295. I do not think there is any ground for this. I believe the West-country Rosewells, Ruswells, Rowsells, and Rousells are all mere variants of Russell (v. Rowsell). I cannot find any early Rossevilles in English registers.

1519. Adam Russell, or Ruswell, or Rossewell : Reg. Univ. Oxf. i. 112.
1580. Alex. Ruswell, co. Soms.: ibid. ii. 92.
1599. John Roswell, co. Soms.: ibid. p. 237.
1606-7. Henry Rosewell, co. Devon : ibid. p. 293.

Rowsell seems to be the modern Somersetshire form.

London, 3, 1.

Rotherham.—Local, ' of Rotherham,' a parish in the W. Rid. of Yorks.

Robertus de Roderham, 1379 : P. T. Yorks. p. 27.

1591-2. Edmund Rotheram, co. Bedf. : Reg. Univ. Oxf. vol. ii. pt. ii. p. 188.
1709. Buried—Sara, d. William Rotheram : St. Dionis Backchurch, p. 278.
1711. — Richard, s. William Rodderam : ibid. p. 150.
London, 3 ; MDB. (West Rid. Yorks), 2.

Rothero.—Bapt. ; v. Prothero. Shrewsbury, 1.

Rothwell.—Local, ' of Rothwell,' parishes in cos. Lincoln and Northants, and also a parish in the W. Rid. Yorks.

Robert de Rothewelle, co. Linc., 1273. A.
John de Rothewell, cotoler, 7 Edw. II : Freemen of York, i. 15.
Johanna de Rothewell, 1379 : P. T. Yorks. p. 103.
Johannes de Rothewell, 1379 : ibid. p. 183.
1598. Married—Thomas Olyver and Joane Rothewelle : St. Michael, Cornhill, p. 16.
London, 9 ; Philadelphia, 9.

Rottenherring. — Nick. ; cf. Poorfish and Goodherring. ' This name occurs in the archives of Hull in the 14th century ': Lower, Patr. Brit. p. 295.

John Rotenherring, 5 Edw. III : Freemen of York, i. 26.

Rough.—Nick. ' the rough,' the harsh, the uncouth.

Henry le Rogh, co. Soms., 1 Edw. III : Kirby's Quest, p. 132.
London, 1 ; Oxford, 1.

Roughley.—Local, ' of Roughley,' i.e. Roughlee Booth, a township in the parish of Whalley, co. Lanc.

1592. Richard Roughley, of Windle : Wills at Chester, i. 165.
1613. Thomas Roughley, of Sutton : ibid.
1664. Richard Roughley, of Sutton, co. Lanc.: ibid. iii. 229.
Liverpool, 2.

Roughton.—Local, ' of Roughton,' two parishes, one in co. Lincoln, the other in co. Norfolk.

1378. John de Roughton, dean of the rural deanery of Ingworth, co. Norf.: FF. vi. 370.
1418. Thomas Roughton, Norwich : ibid. iii. 603.
1797. Married—William Roughton and Susanna Irvin : St. Geo. Han. Sq. ii. 159.
Manchester, 1 ; MDB. (co. Leicester), 1.

Roulston.—Local, ' of Roulston,' a parish in co. Lincoln ;

occasionally, no doubt, confounded with Rolleston, q.v.
MDB. (co. Leicester), 2.

Round, Rowand.—Local, ' at the rowan,' from residence beside a rowan-tree ; cf. Ash and Nash, Oak and Oakes, Birch, &c. The excrescent d is natural ; cf. Simmonds and Hammond, and also ribbon and riband. Thus we find Rowntree entered :

Christopher Roundtree, 1687: St. Jas. Clerkenwell, i. 322.

There may be a second derivation, but I have not hit upon it, supposing it exists.

1626. Bapt. — Dorothy, d. William Round: St. Jas. Clerkenwell, i. 103.
1799. Married—Thomas Round and Mary Wallis : St. Geo. Han. Sq. ii. 201.
London, 8, 0 ; Crake Valley (Ulverston), 0, 1 ; Philadelphia, 4, 0.

Rous, Rouse, Rowse, Ruse, Russ.—Nick. ' le rous,' from the reddish complexion of hair or face ; v. Russell.

Alexander le Rous, co. Camb., 1273. A.
Juliana la Rouse, co. Oxf., ibid.
Alicia Rouze, co. Camb., ibid.
John le Rus, co. Linc., ibid.
Gilbert Russ, co. Linc., ibid.
Lucia la Russe, co. Oxf., ibid.
Robert le Ruus, co. Soms., 1 Edw. III : Kirby's Quest, p. 102.
1643-4. Thomas Salter and Philippa Rous : Marriage Lic. (London), ii. 273.
1659. Buried—George Ruse : St. Peter, Cornhill, i. 212.
1666. Thomas Rowse and Mary Norwood : Marriage Lic. (Faculty Office), p. 94.
1668. Married — Nicolas Rouse and Jone Woodmus : St. Jas. Clerkenwell, iii. 140.
1767. — Samuel Russ and Mary Jones : St. Geo. Han. Sq. i. 161.
London, 2, 21, 2, 3, 7.

Rousby.—Local, ' of Roxby ' (?), a parish in co. Lincoln, nine miles from Barton-on-Humber.

Geoffrey de Rauceby, co. Linc., Hen. III–Edw. I. K.
Adam de Rouceby, co. York, 1273. A.
Iseware de Rouceby, co. Linc., ibid.
Ranulf de Rouceby, co. Linc., ibid.
Crockford, 1.

Rousell ; v. Rowsell.

Routledge, Rookledge, Rucklidge.—Local, ' of Routledge.' I cannot find the spot. It has representatives in every part of the world. It is a great Border name, and whether it be Scotch or

English, it must live for ever. The suffix *-ledge* is *-lake*; v. Depledge. For other variants, v. Rutlidge.

1781. Married—John Routledge and Ann Jones: St. Geo. Han. Sq. i. 327.
1789. — Robert Routledge and Phœbe Sherol: ibid. ii. 27.
London, 8, 0, 0; York, 1, 1, 1; MDB. (co. Cumberland), 15, 0, 0.

Row, Rowe, Roe.—(1) Bapt. 'the son of Rowland,' from the nick. Rowe. A once familiar personal name on the Scottish border and in North England generally.

Rowe Elwald, 1515: TTT. p. 205.
Rowe Crosier, 1586: QQQ. p. xxxvi.

(2) Local, ' of the row,' i.e. the row of cottages. M.E. *rowe*, A.S. *raw* and *rawe*; North Eng. *raw*. v. Roe (3) and Raw.

William del Rawe, 1350: DDD. vol. ii. p. 340.

The following names occur in the list of the mayors of Macclesfield :

Richard del Rowe, 1368.
Stephen del Rowe, 1426.
Roger del Rowe, 1441.
Hugh Rowe, 1477.
Roger Rowe, 1581, &c., &c., &c.
Charles Roe, 1747.

Evidently all were of the same family (v. East Cheshire, ii. 464-8).
London, 11, 44, 18.

Rowan.—Local, 'at the rowan,' from residence beside some prominent rowan-tree; v. Roan, Round, and Rowntree. A North-English and Scottish surname.

1714. Married—Edmund Roune and Anne Nash: St. Mary Aldermary, p. 42.
1805. — Charles Maclaren and Sarah Rowan: St. Geo. Han. Sq. ii. 336.
London, 2; Philadelphia, 69.

Rowand ; v. Round.

Rowbotham, Rowbottom, Robotham, Robottom.—Local, ' at the roe-bottom,' from residence in the depressed ground frequented by the deer. I cannot find the spot, but the name sprung up in the same district as Shufflebotham, Winterbottom, and Ramsbotham (q.v.), somewhere in the southeast corner of Lancashire. The surname is strongly represented across the Atlantic.

1546. Married — Robert Rowe and Dorythye Robotom: St. Michael, Cornhill, p. 5.

1592. Oliver Robotham, co. Bucks: Reg. Univ. Oxf. vol. ii. pt. ii. p. 192.
1613. Thomas Rowbotham, of Winwick, co. Lanc.: Wills at Chester, i. 165.
1626. William Rowbotham and Sarah Owen: Marriage Lic. (London), ii. 169.
Sheffield, 6, 1, 0, 0; Manchester, 11, 2, 1, 0; MDB. (co. Lincoln), 3, 5, 1, 1; Philadelphia, 17, 5, 1, 0.

Rowcliffe, Rawcliffe.—Local, ' of Rawcliff,' a parish in the W. Rid. Yorks, eleven miles from Selby; also a township in the parish of Snaith, W. Rid. Yorks.

Ricardus de Rouclyff, 1379: P. T. Yorks. p. 127.
Henricus de Rouclyffe, 1379: ibid. p. 299.
John Rawcliffe, of Chipping, 1682: Lancashire Wills at Richmond, ii. 204.
George Rawcliffe, of Ribchester, 1729: ibid.
London, 8, 0; Leeds, 0, 1; Philadelphia, 0, 1.

Rowcroft ; v. Rycroft.

Rowe ; v. Row.

Rowell.—Local, ' of Rowell,' an extra-parochial hamlet in the union of Winchcomb, co. Glouc.

Letitia de Rowelle, co. Bedf., 1273. A.
1621. Bapt.—Ann, d. Thomas Rowell: St. Jas. Clerkenwell, i. 91.
London, 11; MDB. (co. Devon), 6; Oxford, 6; Boston (U.S.), 37.

Rowland, Rowlands, Rowlandson.—Bapt. ' the son of Roland.' Roland or Orlando was the nephew of the great Charles, who fell at Roncesvalles.

'Before the Duke the minstrel sprung,
And loud of Charles and Roland sung.'
Walter Scott.
Rouland de Flamville, Hen. III-Edw. I. K.
Robert Rouland, co. Wilts, 1273. A.
William Roulond, co. Worc., ibid.
Roulandus Bloet. C.
Roulandus fil. Roulandi. C.
1683. Bapt.—Saray, d. William Rowland: St. Jas. Clerkenwell, i. 303.
1790. Married—Thomas Rowlandson and Anne Waters: St. Geo. Han. Sq. ii. 43.
1803. — Samuel Richardson and Eliz. Rowlands: ibid. p. 284.
London, 28, 11, 2; Philadelphia, 86, 1, 0.

Rowlatt, Rowlett.—Bapt. 'the son of Ralph,' from the Fr. Raoul, dim. Raoulin (whence our Rawlin and Rowling) and second dim. Raoulet, whence Rowlett and Rowlatt ; cf. Emmett from Emm (Emma) or Hewlett from Hew (Hugh).

'June 25, 1679. Mr. John Rawlett appointed to Lectureship' (of St. Nicholas, Newcastle-on-Tyne). He married a daughter of a Mr. Butler. 'They had been some time in love together, but he falling sick (at her request, and that she might bear his name) married her upon his deathbed, and left her both a maid, a wife, and widow ': Brand's Newcastle, i. 315.
1710. Married—Edmund Reade and Elisabeth Rowlett: St. Mary Aldermary (London), p. 39.
London, 2, 1; Philadelphia, 0, 3.

Rowles. — Bapt. Probably ' the son of Rowland,' from a nick. Rowl ; v. Roll and Rowlinson.

John Roules, co. Soms., 1 Edw. III: Kirby's Quest, p. 139.
London, 1; Oxford, 8.

Rowley.—Local, ' of Rowley,' a parish in the E. Rid. Yorks ; also a parish in co. Stafford. Both places have furnished surnames.

Adam de Roulay, co. York, 1273. A.
Gervase Rolegh, co. Soms., 1 Edw. III: Kirby's Quest, p. 105.
John Roley, co. Soms., 1 Edw. III: ibid. p. 106.
William Roleghe, co. Soms., 1 Edw. III: ibid. p. 205.
Johannes de Rouley, 1379: P. T. Yorks. p. 169.
1607. Richard Rowley, co. York: Reg. Univ. Oxf. vol. ii. pt. ii. p. 295.
1613. Benjamin Rowley, co. Salop: ibid. p. 332.
Ralph Rowley, of Over Peover, 1631 : Wills at Chester, i. 188.
London, 27; Philadelphia, 27.

Rowling, Rowlings.—Bapt. ' the son of Rowland,' from the dim. Rawlin. Of course the *g* is an excrescence, as in Rawling or Rawlings. For further instances v. Rawlin.

1768. Married — James Soleirol and Mary Rowlings: St. Geo. Han. Sq. i. 173.
London, 3, 0; West Rid. Court Dir., 2, 0.

Rowlinson.—Bapt. ' the son of Rowland,' a corrupted form. It is found commonly in the wills of the great Rowlandson family of Furness, North Lancashire. v. Rollinson.

John Rowlinson, of Haverthwaite, 1608: Lancashire Wills at Richmond, i. 218.
Robert Rowlinson, of Knott in Ulverston, 1630: ibid.
Philadelphia, 1.

Rownson, Ronson, Roanson.—Bapt. ' the son of Rowland.' All these are abbreviated and corrupted forms of Rowlandson, and are peculiar to North Lancashire; cf. in the same district Townson for Tomlinson (pronounced Toneson).

1607. Richard Rowlandson, or Rownesonn: Lancashire Wills at Richmond, i. 237-8.
1614. Michael Rowanson, of Cartmell: ibid.
1639. John Rowanson, or Rownson, of Warton: ibid.
1715. John Rowlandson, or Rownson: ibid. ii. 216.

Many more instances might be furnished.

London, 2, 0, 0; Preston, 0, 1, 1; Preesall (co. Lanc.), 0, 1, 0; MDB. (co. Cumb.), 0, 1, 0.

Rowntree, Rountree, Roantree.—Local, 'at the rowan-tree' (the mountain ash), from residence beside such a tree. A well-known North-English surname; cf. Crabtree, Plumptre, Peartree.

William Rowentree, co. York. W. 16.
Ralph Roentree, co. York. W. 20.
1639. Bapt.—Eliz., d. John Roundtree: St. Jas. Clerkenwell, i. 204.
1683. Mary, d. John Rantree: ibid. p. 301.
1809. Married—John Sweeting and Jean Rontree: St. Geo. Han. Sq. ii. 417.
London, 4, 0, 0; Crockford, 2, 2, 0; MDB. (North Rid. Yorks), 0, 4, 0; (East Rid. Yorks), 6, 0, 1; Philadelphia, 0, 3, 3.

Rowse.—Nick.; v. Rous, a variant.

1547. Buried—Anne Rowse: St. Peter, Cornhill, i. 108.
1618. Henry Rowse and Eliz. Matthewes: Marriage Lic. (London), ii. 65.
London, 2.

Rowsell, Rowsel, Rousell.—Nick.; variants of Russell, q.v.

London, 10, 0, 0; Crockford, 6, 0, 0; MDB. (co. Somerset), 11, 1, 3.

Rowson.—Bapt. 'the son of Ralph,' a variant of Rawson, q.v.

Reginald Rowson, of Lyme, 1611: Wills at Chester, i. 166.
Thurstan Rowson, of Stockport, 1620: ibid.
London, 2; Liverpool, 5; Manchester, 1; Philadelphia, 1.

Rowton.—Local, 'of Rowton,' a chapelry in the parish of Adderbury, co. Salop.

Richard de Routon', co. Salop, 1273. A.
Ivo de Roweton, co. Salop, ibid.
London, 3; Oxford, 1.

Roxbrough, Roxburgh. — Local, 'of Roxburgh,' capital of the Scottish county of that name.

London, 1, 2; Oxford, 1, 0.

Roxby.—Local, 'of Roxby': (1) a parish in co. Lincoln; (2) a township in the parish of Pickhill, N. Rid. Yorks; (3) a chapelry in the parish of Hinderwell, N. Rid. Yorks.

1776. Married—George Creick and Mary Roxbee: St. Geo. Han. Sq. i. 260.
Crockford, 3; MDB. (East Rid. Yorks), 2.

Roy. — Nick. 'le roi,' the king; v. King and Rex.

Simon Roy, co. Camb., 1273. A.
Edonia Roy, 1379: P. T. Yorks. p. 31.
Galfridus Roye, 1379: ibid.
1614. Thomas Downton and Anne Roye: Marriage Lic. (London), ii. 27.
London, 7; Boston (U.S.), 4.

Royce, Royse.—Bapt. 'the son of Royse'; v. Yonge. i. 420, where Rohais, wife of Gilbert de Gaunt (1156), is mentioned; also Roese de Lucy, wife of Fulbert de Dover (temp. Hen. II). The name seems to have been always feminine.

Royaia Avered, 1273. A.
Henry fil. Royse, ibid.
William fil. Royse, ibid.
Radulph fil. Roysie, ibid.
Roys le Bon'e (fem.), ibid.
Roger Roys, co. Northampt., 20 Edw. I. R.

In the registers of St. Mary Aldermary the name is spelled Roise (1639), Royce (1634), Royse (1639), Roys (1636).

1720. Richard Roys and Mary Marsh: Marriage Lic. (London), ii. 341.
London, 2, 0; Doncaster, 0, 1; Philadelphia, 2, 1.

Roycraft, -croft; v. Rycroft.

Royd, Royds.—Local, 'at the rode' (so always spelt in early records), an old term implying a ridding, or clearing. Compounded with the Christian name of the proprietor or settler we get Murgatroyd (Mergret = Margaret) or Ormerod (Orme). Whitaker, in his Hist. and Ant. of Craven, has such spots as Tomrode and Wilimotrode (Wilmot = William): p. 199. Sometimes 'royd' is compounded with the names of the hills cleared, as in Holroyd or Acroyd; sometimes with the profession of the

resident, as Monkroyd or Smithroyd (Whitaker, p. 199); sometimes with a word descriptive of the locality, as in Huntroyd. The glossary to Hulton's Coucher Book of Whalley Abbey says: 'Roda, an assart or clearing. Rode land is used in this sense in modern German, in which the verb roden means to clear. The combination of the syllable rod, rode, or royd with some other term, or with the name of an original settler, has, no doubt, given to particular localities such designations as Huntroyd, Ormerod, &c.' See Notes and Queries, 1st Ser., vol. v. p. 571, for further authorities. Dr. Whitaker styles it 'a participial substantive of the provisional verb rid, to clear or grub up': see Hist. Whalley, 3rd edit., p. 364. v. Roades for further instances.

Johannes del Rode, 1379: P. T. Yorks. p. 154.
Adam de Roides, 1379: ibid. p. 161.
Johannes del Rodes, 1379: ibid. p. 292.
Crockford, 0, 9; Philadelphia, 0, 3.

Roydhouse, Roodhouse, Roadhouse. — Local, 'at the royd-house,' i.e. from residence in the house on the royd, or clearing; v. Royd, Ormerod, Murgatroyd, &c.

Henricus del Rodehouse, 1379: P. T. Yorks. p. 194.
1786. Married—Edward Cox and Eliz. Rodhouse: St. Geo. Han. Sq. i. 393.
London, 1, 0, 0; Leeds, 0, 2, 0; Rotherham, 0, 0, 1; West Rid. Court Dir., 0, 0, 1; Philadelphia, 2, 0, 0.

Roylance.—Local; v. Rylands.

Royle.—Local; v. Ryle.

Royse.—Bapt.; v. Royce.

Royston.—Local, 'of Royston': (1) a parish in W. Rid. Yorks, near Barnsley; (2) a parish partly in co. Camb. and partly in co. Hertford.

1632. Married—William Styll and Eliz. Royston: St. Jas. Clerkenwell, i. 63.
London, 4; MDB. (West Rid. Yorks), 4.

Rubbatham.—Local. A curious corruption of Rowbotham, q.v.

Southport, 1.

Rubery.—Local, 'of Rowberrow,' a parish in co. Somerset, four miles from Axbridge. The references I furnish are amply sufficient to prove my statement.

1585. Anthony Rouborow, co. Soms. : Reg. Univ. Oxf. vol. ii. pt. ii. p. 145.
1750. Married—Charles Ruberry and Eliz. Clarke : St. Geo. Han. Sq. i. 43.
1765. — Benjamin Morris and Mary Rubery : ibid. p. 150.
London, 2 ; Philadelphia, 1.

Rucklidge ; v. Routledge. A manifest corruption.

Rudd, Rood.—Local, ' at the rood,' i. e. cross, from residence thereby ; cf. Cross, Crouch, Crossman, Crotchman, &c. v. Rodd.

Margaret atte Rude. J.
William de la Rude, co. Southampt., 1273. A.
Walter Rud, co. Derby, ibid.
Agnes Rudde, co. Camb., ibid.
Ralph Rudde, co. Linc., ibid.
Richard atte Reode, co. Soms., 1 Edw. III : Kirby's Quest, p. 254.
John atte Rude, C. R., 30 Edw. III.
1554. George Rudd, or Roode : Reg. Univ. Oxf. i. 224.
1620-1. Thomas Rudd and Eliz. Greene : Marriage Lic. (London), ii. 95.
1779. Married—John Rood and Susanna Sturton : St. Geo. Han. Sq. i. 297.
London, 16, 1 ; Philadelphia, 4, 1.

Ruddiman ; v. Rudman.

Ruddock, Ruddick, Reddock, Rudduck, Reddick.—Nick. ' the ruddock,' i.e. the robin redbreast ; cf. Sparrow, Nightingale, &c. Reddock is a variant.

'The tame ruddocke, and the coward kite.'
Chaucer, Assembly of Fowls, l. 349.
Edward Ruddock, co. York. W. 16.
Ralph Ruddoc, co. Herts, 1273. A.
1604. Married—William Redock and Anne Squier : St. Mary Aldermary, p. 10.
1799. — Robert Hewison and Barbara Ruddock : St. Geo. Han. Sq. ii. 209.
1803. — Thomas Reddock and Mary Blake : ibid. p. 278.
1807. — Edward Long and Amelia Rudduck : ibid. p. 369.
London, 5, 3, 1, 0, 0 ; Philadelphia, 0, 0, 0, 5, 3.

Rudge.—(1) Local, ' of Rudge,' a township in the parish of Pattingham, co. Salop. (2) Local, ' at the ridge ' ; v. Rugg and Ridge. (3) Nick. ' le rouge.' Fr. *rouge*, red ; taken from the ruddy complexion ; cf. Rufus and Russell. I have no evidence for (1), and therefore must suppose (2) and (3) to be the true parents.

John le Rug, co. Oxf., 1273. A.
Mariot Ruge, co. Oxf., ibid.
Richard le Ruge, co. Essex, ibid.
Osbert le Rugge, co. Kent, ibid.
1686. Married—Thomas Rudge and Martha Hernshaw : St. Mary Aldermary, p. 33.
London, 3 ; Oxford, 3 ; Philadelphia, 3.

Rudkin, Rudkins.—(1) Bapt. ' the son of Rudolph ' (?), dim. Rudkin ; cf. Watkin, Wilkin, &c. As Rudolph, saving in the form of Rolf, was not common in England, it is probable Rudkin and Rudkins are of Dutch extraction and modern immigration. I find no early instances. (2) Nick. ' the Rutterkin.' Since writing the above it has occurred to me that this is but the Dutch Rutterkin (v. Rutter). It would naturally be found on the East coast.

London, 6, 1 ; MDB. (co. Lincoln), 2, 0.

Rudman, Ruddiman.—? Nick. ' the roodman,' i.e. the man who lived by the rood or cross ; v. Rudd. An exactly analogous case is that of Cross and Crossman. The *i* in Ruddiman is euphonic ; cf. Ottaway and Greenaway for Ottway and Greenway. Perhaps both Rudman and Ruddiman represent the German Rudmann. I have no proof of the derivation I have given above.

1682. Bapt.—Ann, d. Christopher Rudman : St. Jas. Clerkenwell, i. 297.
1760. Married—James Taylor and Eliz. Ruddiman : St. Geo. Han. Sq. i. 94.
1780.— George Rudman and Mercy Brice : ibid. p. 315.
London, 1, 2.

Ruff.—Bapt. ' the son of Rudolph,' through the popular form Rolf, whence such variants as Rofe, Roff, Roof, and Ruff ; cf. Raffe for Ralph, from Randolph. The following entries will be sufficient to show that Roff and Ruff are the same :

1696. Bapt.—Susan, d. John and Eliz. Roffe : St. Jas. Clerkenwell, i. 366.
1697.— William, s. John and Eliz. Ruffe : ibid. p. 372.
1698.— Sarah, d. John and Eliz. Roffe : ibid. p. 377.
London, 5 ; Philadelphia, 16.

Rufus.—Nick. ' the red.' Latin *rufus*, red. A common entry in the Hundred Rolls ; cf. Faber for Wright.

Martin Ruffus, co. Oxf., 1273. A.
Walter Rufus, co. Oxf., ibid.
William Ruffus, co. Northumb., 20 Edw. I. R.
London, 1 ; Philadelphia, 1.

Rugg.—Local, ' at the rigg,' from residence on the rigg or rugg of the hill (v. Ridge). That Rugg is a variant of Rigg is certain. The surname Ridgway (i.e. the way over the ridge) is occasionally found as Rudgway. In the Index to Reg. Univ. Oxf. it is spelt Ridgeway, Rydgewaye and Rudgwaye.

John Rigge, or Ryge, or Rugge, 1506 : Reg. Univ. Oxf. i. 45.
1700. Bapt.—William, s. William Rugg : St. Jas. Clerkenwell, i. 390.
London, 5 ; Boston (U.S.), 11.

Rumball, Rumble, Rumbles, Rumbol, Rumbold, Rumboll.—Bapt. ' the son of Reinbold ' (Yonge, ii. 378) ; v. Rimbault. In Domesday there are recorded Reinbald, co. Worc., and Reinbold, co. Soms. Lower adds Rumbaldus. Cf. the local Rumboldswyke, a parish in dioc. Chichester. The surname has run riot in corrupted forms. The following is a curious proof of this statement :—

'After the Dissolution, King Henry VIII, in the year 1545, granted the impropriate rectory (of Keteringham, co. Norf.) to Robert Rumbold, alias Reynbald, and his heirs, to be held *in capite* by knight's service ; and in 1558, Anne wife of Benjamin Reynbald...had livery of it ' : FF. v. 90.

To this day Rumball is a popular surname in cos. Norfolk and Suffolk. For a curious imitative corruption, v. Rainbird.

Roger Rumbold, co. Camb., 1273. A.
Adam Rumbold, co. Bucks, ibid.
Reynebaud le Paumer, co. Norf., ibid.
Rombald Cosin, co. Oxf., ibid.
1665. John Rumboll and Joane Jether : Marriage Alleg. (Canterbury), p. 111.
1688. Married—Thomas Watts and Anne Rumball : St. Mary Aldermary, London, p. 34.
1785.— Daniel Prale and Mary Rumble : St. Geo. Han. Sq. i. 370.
London, 4, 5, 1, 2, 3, 1 ; MDB. (co. Norfolk) (Rumball), 2 ; (Suffolk), 3.

Rumbelow. — Nick. ' Rumbelow,' a sobriquet for a sailor. Rumbelow was the sailor's 'Heave-ho' of later days, and the burden of all early sea-songs. In 'The Squire of Low Degree' it is said—

'Your mariners shall synge arow, Heyhow, and rumbylow.'

Halliwell says, 'The burden of the Cornwall furry-day song is, "With halantow rumbelow."' As seen below, Rumbelow is found as a Cornish surname. 'Well, old Rumbelow, how are you?' would be the kind of way in which the sobriquet arose. The Constable of Nottingham Castle in 1369 was one Stephen Rumbilowe (v. my English Surnames, 2nd edit. p. 512).

John Rumbelow: Reg. St. Columb Major, p. 248.
Mary Rumbelow: ibid.
John Rumbelowe, or Rumblowe, B.A., 1615: Reg. Univ. Oxf. vol. ii. pt. iii. p. 339.
1803. Married—William Rumbelow and Charlotte Bush: St. Geo. Han. Sq. ii. 286.
MDB. (co. Suffolk), 4.

Rumble(s, Rumbol(l, Rumbold ; v. Rumball.

Rumfitt, Rumford.—Local, 'of Romford,' a parish in co. Essex. The corruption is a natural one ; cf. Brumfitt for Broomfield.

1796. Married—John Johnson and Mary Rumford: St. Geo. Han. Sq. ii. 114.
London, 2, 2; York, 1, 0; Philadelphia, 0, 7.

Rumley ; v. Rumney.

Rummans, Rummens, Rumens, Rummons, Romans. — ? Bapt. 'the son of Rumin' (?). Lower, quoting Ferguson, says, 'Rumun, an Old Norse personal name.' This view seems confirmed by the fact that it is found early on the East coast.

John Rumin, co. Linc., 1273. A.

But v. Romaine, of which it may be but a vulgar corruption. Romans is found in the London Dir. side by side with Romaine. Rummen in the first of the following instances seems to be a corrupted form of Romaine :

1767. Married—William Rummen and Mary Hine: St. Geo. Han. Sq. i. 168.
1774. — John Rummins and Ann Faulkner: ibid. p. 247.
1802. — John Rumens and Marg. Catley: ibid. ii. 282.
London, 1, 2, 1, 0, 1; Middlesbrough, 0, 0, 0, 1, 0.

Rumminger. — Occup. 'the rummager,' a sailor who stowed away luggage in the hold of vessels. 'The master must prouide a perfect mariner called a *romager*, to raunge and bestow all merchandize in such place as is conuenient' (Hackluyt's Voyages, iii. 862) ; v. *rummage* in Skeat's Dict.

'Robert Rommongoure, alias Robert Copehed de Branketre, Rommongoure, alias Robert Copehed de Nestede, Rommongoure': Pardons Rolls, 5–21 Ric. II, Anno 8, 1384-5.
Honorius le Rumongour. N

For 'ing,' cf. Messinger for Messager, Pottinger for Potager, &c.

1589. Married—William Rumenger and Joane Robinson: St. Jas. Clerkenwell, i. 14.
1594. Bapt. — Elizabeth, d. William Rummenger: ibid. p. 28.

Rumney, Romney, Rumley. —(1) Local, 'of Romney,' two parishes in co. Kent. (2) Local, 'of Romilly' (q.v.), by change of *l* to *n* (cf. *baluster* and *banister*). There can be no doubt that nearly all our Romneys, Rumneys, and Rumleys are so derived. Rumney, a parish in co. Monmouth, does not seem to have given birth to any surname.

Baldwin de Rumeny, co. Worc., Hen. III-Edw. I. K.
Baldwin de Rumely, co. Worc., ibid.
Baldwin de Romeny, co. Oxf., 1273. A.
Baldwin de Romely, co. Camb., ibid.
John de Romeny, co. Oxf., ibid.
John de Romely, co. Camb., ibid.
1409. John Romley, rector of Brandeston, co. Norf.: FF. viii. 200.
1413. William Rumley, rector of Brandeston, co. Norf.: ibid.
1607. Richard Rumney, co. Cumb., Queen's Coll.: Reg. Univ. Oxf. vol. ii. pt. ii. p. 296.
MDB. (co. Cumb.), 4, 0, 0; Philadelphia, 3, 1, 0; Boston (U.S.), 9, 1, 1.

Rump. — Bapt. 'the son of Rumpe,' probably a nick. of Humphrey, the initials R and H being interchangeable in the nicks. of personal names; cf. Hodge for Roger, Hick for Richard, or Hob for Robert. The surname still lives in the counties where it is found six centuries ago.

Geoffrey fil. Rumphar', co. York, 1273. A.

The above looks like Humphrey in full with R for H.

Casse Rumpe, co. Cumb., 1273. A.
Robert Rumpe, of Cawston, co. Norf., 1521: FF. vi. 266.

Although this derivation is satisfactory to a certain degree, it must not be forgotten that there is a well-known German surname Rumpp. The two may have a common parent. Should that be the case, the above solution would have to be given up.

Norwich, 5; MDB. (co. Norfolk), 5.

Rumsey — Local, 'of Romsey,' a parish in co. Hants, near Southampton ; cf. Rumney for Romney.

Walter de Romesy, co. Soms., 1 Edw. III : Kirby's Quest, p. 91.
John de Romesy, co. Soms., 1 Edw. III : ibid. p. 143.
John Rumsey, 1536: Reg. Univ. Oxf. i. 186.
Walter Rumzey, 1600: ibid. vol. ii. pt. ii. p. 241.
1670-1. John Rumsey and Eliz. Fisher : Marriage Lic. (Faculty Office), p. 116.
London, 10; MDB. (co. Hants), 1; Philadelphia, 7.

Runacres, Ranacre, Ranigar.—Local, 'of Ranacre.' I cannot find this Lancashire spot, but it is the parent of these three surnames; cf. Greenacre or Greenacres, Whittaker, &c. The suffix is -*acre*, a field. At first the place would be styled Ravenacre, i.e. the field of Raven, the first proprietor; v. Raven, Rawnsley, Ransford, &c.

1592. Thomas Ranicars, of Prescot : Wills at Chester, i. 158.
1623. George Ranicar, of Pinnington : ibid. ii. 180.
1641. Richard Ranikers, of Pinnington: ibid.
1665. Piers Ranakers, of Pennington : ibid. iii. 218.
1666. John Renicar, or Renicars, of Atherton : ibid. p. 221.
1672. Richard Ranikars, of Leigh : ibid. p. 218.
1807. Married—Anthony Runacres and Mary Rowley: St. Geo. Han. Sq. ii. 379.
London, 1, 0, 0; Manchester, 0, 1, 1.

Runciman, Runchman.—Occup. 'the runcyman,' one who dealt in *runces*, or hackney horses : cf. Palfreyman.

'Rex igitur cum persecutus esset imperatorem fugientem lucratus est *runcinum* vel jumentum sacculo retro sellam

collocato, &c.': Itinerarium of Ric. I, p. 191.
'Magistro Willelmo de Apperle, pro restauro unius runcini favi appreciati pro Roberto de Burton, valletto suo, &c., £8': Wardrobe Accounts, Edw. I, p 17.
'He rode upon a rouncie, as he couthe.'
Chaucer, C. T. 392.
1696-7. Adam Runciman and Jane Waugh: Marriage Lic. (London), ii. 820.
1797. Married—James Runcieman and Mary Burton: St. Geo. Han. Sq. ii. 170.
London, 3, 2; Boston (U.S.), 2, 0.

Runcy.—Nick. 'the runcy,' a somewhat uncomplimentary sobriquet for a porter or carrier, who was a 'beast of burden,' like a runcy or rouncy, i.e. a hackney horse; v. Runciman.

Thomas Runcy, co. Oxf., 1273. A.
Laurence Runci, or Runcy, or Rouncy, co. Oxf., ibid.
Roger Runcy. V. 8.

It seems to occur as a signname :

Ralph de la Runce, co. Notts, Hen. III-Edw. I. K.

Cf. Whitehorse, Roebuck, &c.

Rupell.—Local, 'at the rupel,' or coppice, from residence thereby. 'Ripple, a small coppice, co. Hereford' (Halliwell).

Philip atte Ruple, co. Soms., 1 Edw. III : Kirby's Quest, p. 135.

Ruse; v. Rous.

Rush.—Nick.; v. Rous. There can be little doubt that Rush is a variant of Russ, as that is unquestionably of Rous. In the Index to Reg. Univ. Oxf., Rush and Russe are placed under one heading.

1554. Anthony Rushe, B.A.: Reg. Univ. Oxf. i. 224.
1600. Married—Thomas Rushe and Eliz. Smyth: St. Jas. Clerkenwell, i. 24.
1638. Hugh Massie and Thomasine Rush: Marriage Lic. (London), ii. 235.
London, 6; Philadelphia, 69.

Rushall.—Local, 'of Rushall,' parishes in cos. Norfolk, Stafford, and Wilts.

Henry de Ryveshale, co. Norf., 1273. A.
Peter de Ryveshale, (?) co. Norf., ibid.
London, 1.

Rushbrook, Rushbrooke.—Local, 'of Rushbrooke,' a parish in co. Suffolk, three miles from Bury St. Edmunds.

William de Rushbroke, co. Norf., 1362: FF. v. 47.
Robert Rushbrooke, Norwich, 1730: ibid. iii. 452.
1789. Married—Joseph Rushbrook and Ann Deirinckx : St. Geo. Han. Sq. ii. 19.
London, 7, 1; MDB. (co. Norfolk), 2, 2; (co. Suffolk), 0, 3.

Rusher.—Occup. 'the rusher,' a thatcher, or perhaps a candlewick maker.

Johannes Ryscher, 1379: P. T. Yorks. p. 125.
London, 1 ; Oxford, 1.

Rushford, Rushforth. — Local, 'of Rushford.' There is a parish so called in co. Norfolk, but I do not find the surname in the vicinity. Various fords where rushes grew may have contributed to our directories.

London, 0, 2; Oxford, 0, 1.

Rushmere, Rushmer, Rushmore.—Local, ' of Rushmere,' two parishes in co. Suffolk.

William de Rusmara, co. Linc., Hen. III-Edw. I. K.
1799. Married—Thomas Hickey and Mary Rushmore: St. Geo. Han. Sq. ii. 205.
1803.— Samuel Pearson and Sarah Rushmer: ibid. p. 277.
Yarmouth, 1, 3, 0; MDB. (co. Norfolk), 2, 1, 1.

Rushton, Rishton. — Local, 'of Rishton,' an ancient manor in the parish of Blackburn, co. Lanc. For the double prefix Rish and Rush, v. Rishworth.

'Henry, the grandson of Henry de Blackburn, took the name of Rishton, or Rushton, both orthographies being found in ancient authentic documents': Baines' Lanc. ii. 85.
1602. James Rishton, of Rishton : Wills at Chester, i. 162.
— Geoffrey Rishton, of Blackburn : ibid.
1662. Edmund Rushton, of Farnworth: ibid. iii. 225.
1668. Christopher Rishton, of Farnworth: ibid. p. 231.
London, 9, 0; Manchester, 10, 1; Philadelphia, 16, 0.

Rushworth; v. Rishworth.

Rusling; v. Rosling.

Russ; v. Rous and Russell.

1634. Buried — William Russe : St. Mary Aldermary, p. 168.
London, 7.

Russell, Russel, Rowsell, Rousell.—Nick.'Russell,'the dim. of Rous, a sobriquet for one with hair or complexion of a reddish-brown. Just as O.F. *brun*, brown, took two dims. *burnett* and *burnell*, so *rous*, reddish brown, took two dims. *russet* and *russell*. From nicknames these became hereditary surnames, and are all in existence to-day except Russet. The fox from his colour was called Russel.

'Dan Burnel the asse.'
Chaucer, C. T. 15319.
'Dan Russel the fox.'
ibid. 15341.
Miriel Russell, co. Hunts, 1273. A.
Simon Russel, co. Camb., ibid.
Elyas Russell, London, ibid.
Johannes Russell, 1379: P. T. Yorks. p. 234.
Robertus Russell, 1379: ibid.

Endless instances might be furnished of this familiar nickname; v. Rous.

London, 154, 1, 10, 0; MDB. (co. Somerset), 13, 0, 11, 3.

Rust. — ? Bapt. 'the son of Rust' (?). Probably a Scandinavian personal name. It still flourishes in co. Norfolk, where it is found in the 13th century.

Robert Rust, co. Hunts, 1273. A.
Thomas Rust, co. Camb., ibid.
Peter Rust, co. Norf., ibid.
1492. Thomas Rust, rector of Congham, co. Norf.: FF. viii. 389.
1610. Nicholas Ruste, rector of Bixley, co. Norf.: ibid. v. 450.
1712. Married—Thomas Levett and Ann Rust: St. Dionis Backchurch, p. 56.
London, 11; Norwich, 3; Philadelphia, 11.

Ruston.—Local, 'of Ruston,' two parishes in co. Norf.

Walter de Ruston, co. Camb., 1273. A.
John de Rustone, co. Camb., ibid.

The surname passed early into the county of Cambridge and is still found there.

1666-7. Robert King and Anne Ruston: Marriage Lic. (Westminster), p. 43.
1751. Married—Benjamin Ruston and Dorothy Beech: St. Geo. Han. Sq. i. 45.
London, 5; Chatteris (co. Camb.), 6; Boston (U.S.), 4.

Rutland.—Local, 'of Rutland'; cf. Darbyshire, Cornish, Cumberland, &c.

Richard de Roteland, co. Oxf., 1273. A.
1584. William Rutland, co. Surrey:
Reg. Univ. Oxf. vol. ii. pt. ii. p. 137.
1728. Married—Barnes Rutland and
Eliz. Norman : St. Geo. Han. Sq. i. 5.
London, 9 ; Philadelphia, 2.

**Rutlidge, Ruttledge, Rutt-
lidge.** — Local ; v. Routledge ;
manifest variants.

1637. Bapt.—George, s. George Rut-
lige : St. Jas. Clerkenwell, i. 137.
1766. Married—John Burton and Mary
Rutlidge : St. Geo. Han. Sq. i. 155.
1788. — John Rutledge and Ann Rich-
urds : ibid, ii, 12.
London, 0, 1, 0 ; Liverpool, 0, 0, 1 ;
MDB. (East Rid. Yorks), 1, 0, 0.

Rutter, Ritter, Reuter.—
Occup. German *ritter*, a rider, i.e.
a trooper ; ' *rutter*, a rider, a
trooper, from the German' (Halliwell) ; a name given to mercenary
soldiers engaged from Brabant, &c.
(v. my English Surnames, 3rd edit.,
p. 201). An old song begins :

' Rutterkyn is come into owre towne
In a cloke withoute cote or gowne,
Save a ragged hood to kover his crowne
Like a rutter hoyda.'
        (ibid. p. 201.)

John le Rotour, co. Somn., 1 Edw. III :
Kirby's Quest, p. 87.
Thomas le Reuter. H.
Ranulph le Ruter. J.
Adam le Ruter. E.
Thomas le Roitour. C. R., 9 Edw. III.
1618. Ferriman Rutter, co. Glouc. :
Reg. Univ. Oxf. vol. ii. pt. ii. p. 372.
1627. Bapt.—Mary, d. John Rutter,
tayler : St. Peter, Cornhill, i. 77.
London, 21, 5, 2 ; Boston (U.S.), 2, 3, 6.

**Rycroft, Roycroft, Row-
croft, Roycraft.**—(1) Local, ' of
Ryecroft,' a hamlet in the township
of Tong, and parish of Birstall, co.
Yorks. There are several smaller
localities bearing this name.

Margareta de Rycroft, 1379 : P. T.
Yorks. p. 181.
Ricardus Rycroft, 1379 : ibid.
Margaret Rycroft, of Haigh, *widow*,
1582 : Wills at Chester (1545-1620),
p. 167.
George Minshull, of Rycroft, *yeoman*,
1586 : ibid. p. 137.
Richard Ricroft, of Groppenhall, co.
Ches., 1638 : East Cheshire, i. 179.
1779. Married—James Ryecroft and
Eliz. Diana Abbiss : St. Geo. Han. Sq.
i. 303.

London, 1, 0, 0, 1 ; West Rid. Court
Dir. (Rycroft), 7 ; MDB. (Cheshire), 2, 3,
0, 0 ; Manchester, 2, 1, 2, 0.

Ryder.—Occup. ; v. Rider.

Ryding; v. Riding.

Rydon.—Local, ' of Rydon.'
Alan de Rydon, co. Norf., 1273. A.
Thomas de Ridone, co. Soms., 1 Edw.
III : Kirby's Quest, p. 187.
London, 3.

Rye.—Local, (1) ' of Rye,' a
town in co. Sussex ; (2) ' de la
Rie,' Mr. Lower says, 'la Rie,'
meaning a bank, is a very common
name of localities in Normandy.
There can be little doubt that this
is one, if not the chief, parent of the
surname.

Hubert de Rie, castellan of Norwich
Castle, c. 1100 : FF. x. 54.
Philip de Rye, co. Linc., Hen. III-Edw.
I. K.
Robert de Rye, co. Linc., ibid.
John de Rye, co. Linc., 1273. A.
John de la Rye, co. Kent, ibid.
1791. Married—George Rye and Su-
sanna Owen : St. Geo. Han. Sq. ii. 58.
London, 5 ; New York, 3.

Rygate.—Local, ' of Reigate,'
a town in co. Surrey.
John de Reygate, London, 1273. A.
Stephen de Reygate, co. Wilts, ibid.
London, 1.

**Rylands, Roylance, Rylance,
Rawlence, Ryland.**—Local, ' of
the Rylands.' There are two places
that have originated surnames bearing this title. Mr. J. Paul Rylands,
F.S.A., says the name ' Ryelands is
derived from the Anglo-Saxon *rye*
or *rhee*, a water-course or stream,
and *lands*, the lands adjoining or
above the stream.' (1) Rylands,
a spot situated in the township
of Westhoughton, and parish of
Deane, co. Lanc.

Robert del Ruylondes, of West Halgh-
ton, 1 Edw. III : ' The Rylands of the
Rylands, within Westhoughton, co. Lan-
caster,' by J. Paul Rylands, F.S.A.
William de Rylondes, of Halghton, 6
Edw. III : ibid.
Nicholas del Rylondes, 1436 : ibid.

(2) Rylands, a spot within the
parish of Wilmslow, co. Ches.

' The hamlets of Styhale, Curbichelegh,
and Northcliffe, Rylondis, Stanilondis,
and Harethorn ' : Earwaker's East Ches.,
i. 42.
Thomas de Ruylonds, of Wilmslow,
c. 1300 : ibid. p. 138.

Roylance, although it has a
chivalrous aspect, is purely imitative. If any doubt rested on this,
it would be dispelled by the following entry concerning a farmer
who was twice sued for tithe by
his vicar :

Thomas Rylands, or Thomas Rylance,
Warmincham, co. Chester, 1686 : Ex-
chequer Depositions, pp. 148-9, L. and C.
R. S. vol. xl.

From Rylance to Roylance was
as easy as it was an inevitable
change. With Rylance cf. Sandilance for Sandilands.

Henry Sandilance, of Cotton, 1609 :
Wills at Chester (1545-1620), p. 169.
London, 2, 1, 0, 1, 0 ; Manchester, 4,
4, 4, 0, 0 ; Philadelphia, 0, 1, 0, 0, 3.

Ryle, Royle.—Local, ' of Ryle.'
in the manor of Etchells, in the
parish of Northendon, co. Ches.

' Sir Nicholas de Eton . . . concedes to
Sir William de Baggylegh, knt. . . . one
hamlet . . . in the vill of Echeles, which
is called Ruyhul . . . which Richard de
Ruyhul held . . . &c.' 1318 : East Ches.
i. 327.

Most of the Cheshire and Lancashire Royles and Ryles are sprung
from this spot, including the late
Bishop of Liverpool. In the form
of Royle the surname has ramified
very strongly.

1574. Married—Edward Royle and
Eliz. Booth : Reg. Prestbury, co. Ches.,
p. 45.
Ellen Ryle, of Etchells, 1603 : Wills at
Chester, i. 166.
Reginald Royle, of Etchells, 1609 :
ibid. p. 167.
Nathaniel Royle, of Cross Acres, 1661 :
Reg. Prestbury, co. Ches., iii. 231.
Ellen Ryle, of Cross Acres, 1669 : ibid.
p. 232.
Manchester, 0, 50 ; MDB. (co. Chester),
1, 14 ; Philadelphia, 1, 8.

Rymer.—Occup. ; v. Rimmer.

Rynd.—Local ; v. Rhind.
Oxford, 1.

S

Saar.—Bapt. 'the son of Sayer,' q.v., one of over twenty variants of this once popular personal name.

1643. Married — Edmund Saare and Anne Hukin : Canterbury Cath. p. 56.
1746. — William Greenaway and Mary Saar : St. Geo. Chap. Mayfair, p. 69. Philadelphia, 2.

Sabbe.—Bapt. 'the son of Sabin,' from the nick. Sab and pet Sab-ey (cf. Charley, Teddie, &c.) ; v. Sabin.

Alicia uxor Sabson (i. e. Alice, the wife of the son of Sab), 1379 : P. T. Yorks. p. 110.
1583. Thomas Coles and Audrey Sabb : Marriage Lic. (London), i. 124.
1716. Married — Robert Saxby and Lydia Sabb, of Maidstone : St. Mary Aldermary, p. 43.

Mr. Lower says this surname is still existing. I have not come across it in modern directories.

Sabben, Saben ; v. Sabin.

Sabey, Saby.—Bapt. 'the son of Sabine,' popularly Sabey. Sabine was a favourite font-name in the sur-name period ; v. Sabbe and Sabin.

1641. Bapt.—James, sonne of William Saby, *blacksmith* : St. Peter, Cornhill, i. 89.
1655. Buried—Maudlin, wife of William Sabie, *blacksmith* : ibid. p. 208.
1668-9. James Sabey and Jane Lucock : Marriage Alleg. (Canterbury), p. 259.
1782. Married — John Saby and Ann Burgan : St. Geo. Han. Sq. i. 339.
London, 5, 0 ; Philadelphia, 0, 1.

Sabin, Sabine, Sabins, Sab-ben, Saben.—Bapt. 'the son of Sabine.' St. Sabina was martyred in Hadrian's persecution. The name was in much favour for a time in England. In one of the Coventry Mysteries occurs :

'Bontyng the Brewster, and Sybyly Slynge,
Megge Mery-wedyr, and Sabyn Sprynge.'

Also there was St. Sabinus, the martyr bishop of Assisium.

Sabyn Hubert, co. Camb., 1273. A.
Alexander Sabine, co. Essex, ibid.

Sabina Gaylard. H.
Sabinus Chambre. V. 4.
Sabyna Vesy, co. Soms., 1 Edw. III : Kirby's Quest, p. 143.
William Sabin, co. Soms., 1 Edw. III : ibid. p. 155.
Robert Sabynson, 1379 : P. T. Yorks. p. 162.
1758. Married — William Saben and Susanna Wright : St. Geo. Han. Sq. i. 78.
1791. — James Mans and Susanna Sabben : Canterbury Cath. p. 99.
Crockford, 1, 1, 0, 1, 1 ; London, 4, 7, 0, 0, 0 ; Philadelphia, 5, 1, 6, 0, 0 ; Boston (Saben), 5.

Sacheverell.— ? Local. I can-not suggest any derivation of this surname. 'Sacheverel, the iron door, or blower to the mouth of a stove' (Halliwell). This great name is represented, so far as I can see, in the 19th century by only one person, viz. : William Henry Sacheverell, clogger, Oldfield Road, Salford, Lancs.

Nicholas Saucheverel, alias Sauzcheve-rel, alias Saunz Cheverel, co. Camb., 1273. A.
Patricia Saucheverel, cos. Notts and Derby, Hen. III–Edw. I. K.
Patricia Sauchevel, cos. Notts and Derby, ibid.
1581. Ambrose Sacheverall, co. Leic. : Reg. Univ. Oxf. vol. ii. pt. ii. p. 109.
1590. Buried—Frances Sacheverell, *a maid*, d. of John Sacheverell : St. Peter, Cornhill, i. 138.
1776. Married — William Sacheverell and Jane Secker : St. Geo. Han. Sq. i. 260.
Manchester, 1.

Sack.—Bapt. 'the son of Sagge' ; cf. Jagge for Jack, and endless instances where *g* becomes *ck*— Hick for Higg, Hickin for Higgin, &c.

Avice fil. Sage (*g* hard), co. Camb., 1273. A.
Alan Sage, or Sagge, co. Norf., ibid.
Thomas Sagge, co. Norf., ibid.
1798. Married—Joseph Sack and Sarah Biddle : St. Geo. Han. Sq. ii. 188.
London, 7 ; Philadelphia, 4.

Sacker.—Occup. 'the sacker,' a maker of sacks. M. E. *sak,* Chaucer, C. T. 4019. v. Secker (2).

Adam the Sakker, Fines Roll, 14 Edw. II.
Adam le Sakkere, London. X.
John Sakkere. H.

Cf. Canvaser, q.v. The occupa-tive name *sack-weaver* existed, but did not live :

Jurdan Sakwebbe, co. Soms., 1 Edw. III : Kirby's Quest, p. 276.
1576. Married — Richard Saker and Anne Spilberrie : St. Mary Aldermary, p. 6.
1630. Buried — Eliz. Saker : St. Jas. Clerkenwell, iv. 198.
1661-2. Richard Atkinson and Mary Sacker : Marriage Lic. (London), ii. 290.
London, 3 ; Boston (U.S.), 1.

Sackerson, Sackrison.—Bapt. 'the son of Sagger,' i.e. Sagar (v. Sayer). No doubt Sackerson is the form that went out to America, as it is found in that dress in the Puritan period. The English form is Saggerson (v. Saggers).

1610. Married — Miles Crakel and Margaret Sackerson : St. Michael, Corn-hill, p. 17.
1717. Bapt.—John, son of John Seger-son : St. Jas. Clerkenwell, ii. 100.
1721. — William, son of John Sagesson, or Saggeson : ibid. ii. 127.
1739. — Ann, d. John Sadgerson : ibid. ii. 248.
New York, 1, 0 ; Boston (U.S.), 0, 1.

Sackville.—Local. 'A place in Normandy now called Sanque-ville, about seven miles from Dieppe' (Lower) ; v. long article in Lower's Patr. Brit. p. 299. The family seem to have come in with the Conqueror, or immediately after, and were highly placed.

John de Sakewyle, co. Suff., 1273. A.
Jordan de Sakeville, co. Suff., ibid.
Gwydo de Sakevill, co. Sussex, Hen. III–Edw. I. K.
Robert de Saccavill, co. Devon, ibid.
Andrew de Sakevile, co. Norf., 20 Edw. I. R.

Like Harcourt, Sackville has not become the property of the com-monalty. There is no representa-tive in the London Directory. There is none, also, in Crockford.

Philadelphia, 1 ; New York, 1.

Sadd.—Nick. 'the sad,' i.e. the sober, the discreet, the serious. 'A sad man in whom is no pride' : MS. Rawl. C. 86 (Halliwell).

Margaret Sad, co. Suff., 1273. A.
Seman Sad, co. Suff., ibid.
William Sad, co. Hunts, 20 Edw. I. R.
1429. John Sadd, prebend of Norwich : FF. iv. 173.
1600. Married — Henrie Sadd and Parnell Eaden : St. Jas. Clerkenwell, iii. 24.
1667. Thomas Cornwall and Hannah Sadd : Marriage Alleg. (Canterbury), p. 208.
London, 1.

Saddington.—Local, ' of Saddington,' a parish in co. Leicester.

Nicholas de Sadingden, co. Berks, 1273. A.
Robert de Sadyngton, *chancellor* : FF. iii. 89.
Thomas de Sadyngton, 1379 : P. T. Howdenshire, p. 20.
1797. Married—Joseph Saddington and Eliz. Brown : St. Geo. Han. Sq. 163.
London, 3 ; MDB. (co. Kent), 1 ; (co. Leic.), 4 ; New York, 1.

Saddlebow.—Nick., probably affixed to a saddler.

John Sadelbowe, co. Camb , 1273, A.
Richard Sadelbowe, co. Camb., ibid.

Saddler, Sadler, Sadtler.— Occup. 'the saddler,' a maker of saddles. An important craft in its day. v. Fewster.

John le Sadeler, co. Soms., 1 Edw. III : Kirby's Quest, p. 104.
Thomas Sadeler, 1379 : P. T. Yorks. p. 47.
Willelmus Sadeler, 1379 : ibid.
Nicholaus Sadiler, 1379 : ibid. p. 41.
Willelmus Sadeller, 1379 : ibid. p. 131.
1612. John Sadler and Jane Hogge : Marriage Lic. (London), ii. 16.
London, 1, 39, 0 ; Philadelphia, 3, 24, 2.

Saffery.—Bapt. ; v. Savory.

Sagar, Sager.—(1) Occup. 'a sawyer.' A.S. *saga*, a saw. Yorkshire dialect *sager*, a sawyer. (2) Bapt. 'the son of Sagar' (v. Seager). This must be looked upon as the chief parent.

Richard le Saghiere, C. R., 21 Edw. III, pt. ii.
Simon Sagher, 1379 : P. T. Yorks. p. 59.
Johannes Saghher, 1379 : ibid. p. 16.
1621. Buried—Temperance, d. Mathew Sager : St. Jas. Clerkenwell, iv. 153.
Robert Sagar, of Billington, 1632 : Wills at Chester, ii. 191.
Richard Sagar, of Padiham, 1648 : ibid.
West Rid. Court Dir., 2, 2 ; Leeds, 3, 2 ; Philadelphia, 3, 16.

Sage. — Nick. 'the sage,' the wise, the sagacious. Naturally an acceptable sobriquet, and likely to be handed down.

Bernard le Sage, co. Norf., temp. Ric. I : FF. xi. 117.
Richard le Sage, co. Oxf., 1273. A.
William le Sage, C. R., 1 Edw. I.
1618-9. John Sage and Joane Vesey : Marriage Lic. (London), ii. 69.
1802. Married—James Sage and Isabella Walker : St. Geo. Han. Sq. ii. 293.
London, 12 ; Philadelphia, 17.

Saggers, Saggerson.—Bapt. 'the son of Sagar'; v. Seager. Sagar and Saggerson are common surnames in West Lancashire. For examples, v. Sackerson.

London, 4, 0 ; Prescot (co. Lanc.), 0, 5.

Saies.—Nick. ; v. Sayce.

Sailer, Sailor. — Occup. ; v. Saylor.

Sailes.—Local ; v. Sayles.

Saint.—Nick. 'the saint,' a man of holy character, perhaps, however, given cynically for one who affected to be better than his neighbours.

John le Seynt, C. R., 39 Hen. III, pt. i.
1559. Married—Reignhold Salnct and Margarett Meridith : St. Thomas the Apostle (London), 3.
1700. —Richard Saint and Ann Bright : St. Mary Aldermary, p. 36.
1745. — John Saint and Ann Townsend : St. Geo. Han. Sq. i. 44.
London, 3 ; Philadelphia, 1.

Saise.—Nick. ; v. Sayce.

Salamon, Salaman, Saleman, Saloman, Salomans.— Bapt. 'the son of Solomon,' found variously as Saloman, Salaman, and Saleman ; v. Salman and Sloman.

Salomon Judaeus. C.
Salomon fil. Ivo. C.

The three following entries relate to the same individual :

Richard Salaman, co. Oxf., 1273. A.
Richard Saleman, co. Oxf., ibid.
Richard Saloman, co. Oxf., ibid.
Alicia Saleman, co. Camb., ibid.
Salemande Grecton, co. Camb., ibid.
Saleman pater Johannis Seliman, co. Camb., ibid.
Christian Saleman, Wardrobe Account, 1 Edw. III, 33/2.
William Saleman, co. Soms., 1 Edw. III : Kirby's Quest, p. 264.

Thomas Salman, 1379 : P. T. Yorks. p. 146.
1588. Bapt.—Anne, d. Thomas Sallomon : St. Peter, Cornhill, i. 33.
London, 1, 5, 0, 5, 6 ; New York, 3, 0, 0, 56, 50.

Sale, Sales.—Local, ' of the sale,' i.e. the hall ; cf. Fr. *salle-à-manger*, a dining-hall. Halliwell quotes :

'Some thay sembled in sale
Bathe Kynges and Cardenale.'

Instances of the surname are found in every important 13th century roll.

Robert a la Sale, 1273. A.
Nicholas de la Sale, 20 Edw. I. R.
William de la Sale, ibid.
Robert de la Sale, bailiff of Norwich, 1327 : FF. iii. 98.
Ralph de la Sale, C. R., 56 Hen. III.
John de la Sale. T.

With excrescent s in Sales, cf. Briggs, Brooks, Sykes, Styles, &c., a common adjunct of one-syllabled local surnames, possibly genitive.

1598. Henry Sales and Abigail Brabye : Marriage Lic. (London), i. 255.
1745. Buried—John Sale : St. John the Baptist (Wallbrook), p. 213.
London, 7, 6 ; Philadelphia, 4, 0 ; New York, 3, 1.

Sales ; v. Sayles.

Salisbury, Salisberry.—(1) Local, ' of Salisbury,' a city in co. Wilts.

Robert de Salisbyr', co. Wilts, 1273. A.
1547. Married—Henry Salisburye and Jone Mathewe : St. Michael, Cornhill, p. 5.

(2) Local, ' of Salesbury.' The Lancashire Salisburys hail from Salesbury, a village-parish between Blackburn and Ribchester. The corruption is a very slight one, and simply imitative of the name of the southern cathedral city.

Ralph Salisbury, of Hindley, 1670 : Wills at Chester (1660-80), p. 234.
Ann Salisbury, of Hindley, 1674 : ibid.
Thomas Salisbury, of Chipping, 1669 : Lancashire Wills at Richmond, p. 240.
Richard Sailsbury, of Chipping, 1663 : ibid.
Henry Sailsbury, of Chepin, 1626 ibid.

The last three entries place my statement of a local Lancashire origin beyond the range of controversy.

London, 13, 0 ; Liverpool, 5, 0 ; Blackburn, 4, 0 ; Manchester, 2, 0 ; West Rid. Court Dir., 0, 1 ; New York, 12, 0.

Salkeld.—Local, 'of Salkeld,' a parish (called Great Salkeld) in co. Cumb., three miles from Kirk-Oswald. Little Salkeld is a township in the neighbouring parish of Addingham.

John de Salkild, co. Cumb., 20 Edw. I. R.
Thomas de Salkeld, co. Cumb., ibid.
1593. Thomas Salkell and Matilda Hickopp : Marriage Lic. (London), i. 207.
1610. Richard Salkeld, co. Cumb. : Reg. Univ. Oxf. vol. ii. pt. ii. p. 317.
1804. Married — James Reynolds and Mary Salkeld : St. Geo. Han. Sq. ii. 311.
London, 3 ; MDB. (co. Cumb.), 16 ; Boston (U.S.), 4.

Salman, Salmon, Salmond. —Bapt. 'the son of Solomon,' popularly in M.E. Salamon, and with excrescent *d* Salamond (cf. Simmonds and Hammond for Simmons and Hamon). These forms represent families of English descent, Solomon representing modern Jewish immigrations. Of course the London Directory has several Salamons, undoubtedly Jewish, but, speaking generally, our Salomans, Salamans, Salemans, Salmons, Salmans, Salmonds, Sammons, and Sammonds, are of English extraction, just as much as our Davies and Davidsons are (excepting when these are Welsh or Scottish).

William Salman, 1379 : P. T. Yorks. p. 108.
1574. Buried—Alexander Sawllmond : St. Peter, Cornhill, i. 122.
1620. John Salmon and Constance Fallwell : Marriage Lic. (London), ii. 93.
1797. Married—William Salmond and Eliz. Corns : St. Geo. Han. Sq. ii. 165.
London, 1, 48, 0 ; New York, 1, 22, 0 ; Boston, U.S. (Salmond), 1.

Salomon(s ; v. Salamon.

Salsbery, Salsbury, Salsburry.—Local ; v. Salisbury.

1601. John Salsbury, or Salisbury, co. Devon : Reg. Univ. Oxf. vol. ii. pt. ii. p. 247.
— Bapt.—Marie, d. John Salsburie : St. Jas. Clerkenwell, i. 39.

The following is a still briefer form :

1670. Bapt.—Eliz., d. Robert Salsbee : St. Jas. Clerkenwell, i. 244.
1630. Married—Edward Lloyde and Ursley Salsberye : St. Mary Aldermary, p. 17.

London, 0, 4, 0 ; Philadelphia, 1, 2, 0 ; New York, 0, 1, 1.

Salt.—Local, 'of Salt,' a township in the parish of St. Mary and St. Chad, four miles from Stafford. This is the parent of all the Salts. It is a very familiar surname in the county of Stafford.

'In the reign of Hen. III, Ivo de Saut held one Knight's fee in Saut of the Barony of Stafford' : Lower's Patr. Brit. p. 302.
Ranulph de Saut, co. Camb., 1273. A.
Ivo de Saut, co. Stafford, Hen. III– Edw. I. K.
1597. Buried — Margery Sawlte : St. Jas. Clerkenwell, iv. 61.
1599. — Alyce Salte : ibid. iv. 66.
1621. Ann Salt, of Chester : Wills at Chester, ii. 191.
London, 6 ; MDB. (co. Stafford), 33 ; Philadelphia, 3.

Salter.—(1) Occup. 'the salter,' a manufacturer or dealer in salt ; cf. Salthouse. The Salters' Company was early among the London Guilds.

John le Saltere, co. Camb., 1273. A.
Nygel le Salter, co. Wilts, ibid.
Ralph le Salter, C. R., 20 Edw. I.
Thomas le Saltar, co. Soms., 1 Edw. III : Kirby's Quest, p. 272.
Willelmus Salter, 1379 : P. T. Yorks. p. 177.
Thomas de Wollay, *salter*, 1379 : ibid. p. 92.

(2) Occup. 'the sautreour,' a player on the psaltery, or 'gay sawtrye,' as Chaucer styles it. A stringed instrument of the harp class.

William le Sautreour. X.
Janetto la Sautreour, minstrel of Queen Isabelle, Close Roll, 2 Edw. III.

This would easily get corrupted to Salter, as the form *psalterie* was in use in the 12th century.

1597. Married — William Prior and Margaret Salter : St. Mary Aldermary, p. 9.
1618. Edmund Rolfe and Dorothy Salter : Marriage Lic. (London), ii. 65.
London, 33 ; Philadelphia, 14.

Salters.—Local, 'of the salt-house,' a manifest corruption ; v. instances in Salthouse.

Philadelphia, 2.

Salthouse, Southouse. — Local, 'of the salthouse,' the place where salt was made from sea-water

---

by evaporation. M.E. *salt*, Dutch *zout.* v. Southouse. In the first instance below I suspect the occupation of souter (shoemaker) is accidental. But, if not, Southouse in London Directories is an abbreviation of Souter-house, the shoemaker's house. I had a Southgate in my late parish (Ulverston), i.e. the shoemaker's road. But this abbreviation would scarcely occur in a formal record in 1379. It is far more natural to make Southouse, the surname, a variant of Salthouse. Two small places, a Salthouse in Lytham, and a Salthouse in Furness, where salt was obtained from sea-water, have originated two families of Salthouse in North Lancashire.

Simon del Southouse, *souter*, 1379 : P. T. Yorks. p. 254.
Adam de Salthus, co. Norf., 1273. A.
(This is the parish of Salthouse, co. Norfolk.)
Janet Saltehowse, of Pulton, 1562 : Lancashire Wills at Richmond, p. 240.
Agnes Saltus, of Ulverston, 1596 : ibid. 241.
John Salthouse, of Saltcoathouses, 1661 : ibid.
William Saltus, of Banke, 1662 : ibid. Manchester, 3, 0 ; London, 0, 1 ; Blackpool (near Lytham, co. Lanc.), 3, 0 ; Philadelphia, 3, 0.

Saltmarsh.—Local, 'of Saltmarsh,' a township in the parish of Howden, E. Rid. Yorks.

Robert Saltmerssh, C. R., 25 Edw. III.
Nicholaus de Saltmerssh', 1379 : P. T. Howdenshire, co. York, p. 19.
Philippus de Saltmerssh', 1379 : ibid. p. 20.
Johannes Saltemerche, 1379 : P. T. Yorks. p. 151.
1618. Lawrence Saltmarsh and Margaret Jarrett : Marriage Lic. (London), ii. 65.
1650-1. Married—Jeremy Saultmarsh and Susan Thorn : St. Dionis Backchurch, p. 27.
London, 2 ; MDB. (co. Essex), 4 ; (East Rid. Yorks), 3 ; Boston (U.S.), 3.

Saltonstall.—Local, 'of Saltonstall.' I cannot find the spot. But it must probably be looked for in co. Essex and neighbourhood. The name of the daughter of Sir Peter Saltonstall is thus entered :

1642. Edward Chester and Anne Salthingston (co. Herts): Marriage Lic. (London), ii. 265.
1610. Richard Saltonstall, co. Essex: Reg. Univ. Oxf. vol. ii. pt. ii. p. 314.
1615. John Saltonstall, co. Essex: ibid. p. 343.
1805. Married—Robert Bradley and Ellen Saltonstall: St. Geo. Han. Sq. ii. 338.
Boston (U.S.), 5.

Salusbury.—Local; v. Salisbury, a manifest variant.

1742. Bapt.—Sarah, d. John Salusbury: St. Geo. Chap. Mayfair, p. 5.
1760. Married—Gilbert Atkinson and Esther Salusbury: St. Geo. Han. 8q. i. 92.
Crockford, 6.

Sambourne.—Local, 'of Sambourn,' a hamlet in the parish of Coughton, co. Warwick.

Peter de Samborne, co. Soms., 1 Edw. III: Kirby's Quest, p. 254.
1577. Barnabas Samborne, co. Soms.: Reg. Univ. Oxf. vol. ii. pt. ii. p. 77.
1592. James Samborn, co. Hants: ibid. p. 193.
MDB. (co. Devon), 1.

Sambrook, Shambrook. — Local, 'of Sambrook,' a parish in the dioc. of Lichfield. If the instances below refer to this town, the terminal was originally *bridge* and not *brook*.

John de Samebrugg, co. Oxf., 1273. A
Henry de Samebrugg, co. Oxf., ibid.
Simon de Sambrigg, co. Surrey, 20 Edw. I. R.
1645. Buried—A female, stillborn, of William and Elizabeth Shambrooke: St. Thomas the Apostle (London), p. 125.
1677-8. John English and Eliz. Sambrooke: Marriage Alleg. (Canterbury), p. 275.
1742. Married—George Sambrooke and Hannah Purkes: St. Geo. Chap. Mayfair, p. 26.
London, 4, 1.

Sammon, Sammonds, Sammons, Samons, Samon.—Bapt.; v. Salman.

London, 1, 0, 0, 1, 0; Oxford (Sammons), 4; Philadelphia, 5, 2, 0, 1, 4.

Samms, Sams.—Bapt. 'the son of Sampson,' from nick. Sam or Samp, genitive Sams (cf. William and Williams). This name was so popular, and Samuel so rare, that we must needs give it the preference; v. Sampson.

Samme Parvus (the little), co. Linc., 1273. A.

Samme (without surname), co. Salop, ibid.
Hugelin Samp, or Sampe, co. York, ibid.
Samme (without surname), co. Linc., ibid.
Alan Samme, 1379: P. T. Yorks. p. 209.
1643-4. Henry Sams and Anne Wren: Marriage Lic. (London), ii. 273.
1664. Bapt.—Dorothy, d. Aylott Sammes: St. Jas. Clerkenwell, i. 224.
London, 0, 10; MDB. (co. Hertford), 0, 3; Philadelphia, 0, 1.

Samper, Semper, Sampier. —Local, 'de St. Pierre,' from some Norman chapelry of that name; cf. St. John, Semple, Sinclair, &c. 'In an Inquisition post mortem taken at Chester, 1428, Urian le (de?) Seint pierre took oath': Earwaker's East Cheshire, ii. 292.

Agnes Seynpere. B.
Robert de Seyntpere, c. 1300. M.
Brian de St. Petro, co. Salop, 1273. A.
John Seynpere. G.
London, 1, 0, 0; Philadelphia, 0, 1, 0; New York, 0, 0, 1.

Sampford.—Local, 'of Sampford,' parishes in cos. Somerset, Devon, and Essex.

Roger de Samford, co. Oxf., 1273. A.
Thomas de Samford, co. Camb., ibid.
Alicia de Samford, co. Oxf., Hen III–Edw. I. K.
1574. Married—Robert Wright and Alice Samforte: St. Michael, Cornhill p. 6.
1614-5. John Burton and Marg. Sampford: Marriage Lic. (London), ii. 31.
1626. John Tapsell and Theodora Samford: ibid. p. 182.
London, 1.

Sample.—Local, 'de St. Paul'; cf. Samper, Simbarb, Sinclair, &c. The usual form is Semple, q.v.

1579. Peter Buckley and Julian Sample: Marriage Lic. (London), i. 90.
1748. Married—George Sample and Sarah Coney: St. Geo. Chap. Mayfair, p. 123.
1782. — Ephraim Sampell and Cath. Griggs: St. Geo. Han. Sq. i. 334.
New York, 4; Philadelphia, 13.

Sampson, Samson, Sansom, Sansome, Sanson, Sansum.—Bapt. 'the son of Samson.' O.E. Sampson; O.F. Sanson. With the forms Sansom, &c., cf. Ransome for Ranson, or the dictionary word *random* for *randon*. It has been stated that Sansom stands for some local St. Anselm (cf. Semple for St. Paul, Sampier for St. Pierre). This is without foundation. As a personal name Samson was in very

early use. Mr. Freeman has three instances in Index to vol. iv (Hist. Norm. Conquest). One was Bishop of Worcester; a second, chaplain to William I; a third, messenger to Matilda. The following entries concern one individual:

Sampson Foliot, Hen. III–Edw. I. K. p. 104.
Sanson Foliot, ibid. p. 105.
Saunsum Foliot, ibid. p. 106.
Sansum le Rus, co. Camb., 1273. A.
Samson de Baterford, co. Bedf., ibid.
Sampson de Boxe, co. Wilts, ibid.
'Item, the vi. day of Aprylle, my mastyr made a covenaunt wyth Saunsam, the tylere, that he schalle perget,' &c.: Accounts of Sir John Howard (A.D. 1467), p. 395; v. Prompt. Parv. p. 383, ed. Way.

A well-known monastery near Rouen was built by the Archbishop of Dol, known as St. Sansone or St. Sampson. The personal name lingered long in Cornwall, where so many pre-Reformation favourites died hard.

1559. Married — John Sampson and Eliz. Clarke, *widow*: St. Michael, Cornhill, p. 7.
1582. Bapt.—Warne, son of Sampson Morcambe: Reg. St. Columb Major, Cornwall, p. 11.
1736. Married — Abraham Sampson and Ann Lawton: St. Geo. Han. Sq. i. 16.
1756. — Thomas Younger and Ann Sansum: ibid. i. 67.
1769. — John Sansom and Eliz. Bellton: ibid. i. 183.
1777. — Moses Samson and Mary Best: ibid. i. 279.
London, 26, 16, 14, 1, 2, 2; Philadelphia, 22, 4, 5, 0, 12, 0.

Sams; v. Samms.

Samuel, Samuels, Samuelson.—Bapt. 'the son of Samuel.' Not always Jewish. There are many Samuels of English descent; v. Samwell.

Matilda Samuel, co. Soms., 1 Edw. III: Kirby's Quest, p. 139.
Geoffrey Samuel, co. Essex, 1273. A.
John Samuel, co. Hunts, ibid.
Seman fil. Samuel, co. Hunts, ibid.

All these baptismal names establish the fact above stated, that Samuel and Samuels were not confined to Jews; v. Salman.

1626. Buried — Xpian, wife of John Samuell: St. Jas. Clerkenwell, iv. 188.
London, 30, 12, 2; New York, 25, 34, 3.

Samwell.—Bapt. 'the son of Samuel,' an early corruption.

William Samwel, co. Oxf., 1273. A.
1612. Bapt.—Alice, d. William Samwell : St. Mary Aldermary, p. 172.
1628. Married—Samewell Randall and Frances Ruslinge : ibid. p. 16.
1708. Buried—Mary Sammiwell : St. Antholin (London), p. 121.
Crockford, 1.

Sanborn.—Local, a corruption of Sambourne, q.v.; cf. Sandbrook for Sambrook.

1799. Married—John Crick and Rebecca Sanburn : St. Geo. Han. Sq. ii. 197. Philadelphia, 4.

Sancton.—Local, 'of Sancton,' a parish in E. Rid. Yorks.

John de Sancton, co. Linc., 1273. A. MDB. (co. Cumb.), 2.

Sanctuary. — Local, 'at the sanctuary,' from residence beside a shrine. 'Several monasteries had an ambit or surrounding space, where criminals might take refuge from immediate or impending danger, as the Sanctuary at Westminster. A person resident in a place so privileged, though no criminal, would readily acquire the name of Thomas or John at the Sanctuary' (Lower's Patr. Brit. p. 302). For a parallel instance, v. Galilee. Although I have no references at hand, there can be no doubt about this derivation.

MDB. (co. Dorset), 2; Crockford (1891), 1.

Sanday, Sandy.—Local, ' of Sandy,' a parish in co. Bedford.

Nicholas de Sandye, co. Hunts, 1273. A. London, 0, 2 ; Oxford, 1, 0 ; New York, 2 2.

Sandbach, Sanbach.—Local, ' of Sandbach,' a market-town and parish in co. Ches.

1578. Buried — Eliz. Sanbacke : St. Thomas the Apostle (London), p. 94.
1624. Mathew Sandbach, of Eaton : Wills at Chester, ii. 192.
1636. John Sandbadge, of the Nunns, parish of St. Mary's, Chester : ibid.
1749. Married—Aaron Haynes and Rebecca Sandbach : St. Geo. Chap. Mayfair, p. 143.
MDB. (co. Ches.), 9, 0 ; Manchester, 5, 1 ; Philadelphia, 1, 0.

Sandborn. — Local. A corruption of Sambourne, q.v.; cf. Sandbrook for Sambrook.

Philadelphia, 1.

Sandbrook.—Local. A corruption of Sambrook, q.v.

1613. William Farmer and Marg. Sandbrooke (of Shrewsbury): Marriage Lic. (London), ii. 20.
London, 2 ; Oxford, 1.

Sandell, Sandall.—Local, ' of Sandal,' a parish, now Sandal Magna, near Wakefield, co. Yorks. Also Long Sandall, a parish four miles from Doncaster.

Johannes de Sandall', 1379 : P. T. Yorks. p. 161.
Isabella de Sandale, 1379 : ibid. p. 135.
1615. Peter Letten and Anne Sandell : Marriage Lic. (London), ii. 33.
1803. Married—Thomas Sandall and Jane Chapman : St. Geo. Han. Sq. ii. 286.
London, 6, 0 ; New York, 0, 1.

Sandeman, Sanderman. — Occup. 'the servant of Sandy' or Saunder, i.e. Alexander ; cf. Addyman, Matthewman, Jackman, Ladyman, Vickerman, &c. One of a large class. Robert Sandeman, the founder of the sect styled Sandemanians, was a native of Perth. The first five of my instances occur together, settling the origin beyond dispute:

Alexander de Rokeby, marchaunt des bestes, 1379 : P. T. Yorks. p. 22.
Mergeria serviens dicti Alexandri, 1379 : ibid.
Matilda Saunder-wyf, 1379 : ibid.
Johannes Saundirman, et 'uxor ejus, 1379 : ibid.
Johannes Saundirman, senior, 1379 : ibid.
Robertus Alexsanderman, 1379 : ibid. p. 33.
Marmaduke Sandimanne, hirde, 1634. VVV. p. 322.
1682-3. John Archer and Bridgett Sandyman : Marriage Alleg. (Canterbury), p. 119.
New York, 0, 3 ; Philadelphia, 3, 0.

Sander, Sanders, Sanderson.—Bapt. 'the son of Alexander,' from nick. Sander ; v. Saunder.

London, 7, 75, 38 ; New York, 20, 60, 20.

Sandercock.—Bapt. 'the son of Alexander,' from the nick. Saunder and suffix -cock ; cf. Wilcock, Simcock, Watcock, &c., from William, Simon, and Walter (v. cock, Introd. pp. 25-6).

MDB. (co. Devon), 1.

Sandford, Sandiford, Sanford, Sandyfirth.—Local, ' of Sandford,' parishes in cos. Devon

and Oxford (2), townships in cos. Berks and Salop, and hamlets in cos. Westmoreland and Berks. For suffix, v. Ford and Forth.

Richard de Sanford, co. Oxf., 1273. A.
William de Sanforth, co. Oxf., ibid.
Ralph de Sandford, co. Oxf., ibid.
Johannes de Sandeforthe, 1379 : P. T. Yorks. p. 112.
Willelmus de Sandeforthe, 1379 : ibid.
1616. Married—John Cooke and Eliz. Sandiford : St. Jas. Clerkenwell, i. 43.
1651. — Edward Sanderford and Ann Heydon : St. Mary Aldermary, p. 22.
1684. Buried—Joseph, s. Joseph Sandford : ibid. p. 195.
1725. Bapt.—Mary, d. Samuel Sandeforth : St. John Baptist, Wallbrook, p. 181.
London, 3, 1, 7, 0 ; West Rid. Court Dir., 2, 0, 0, 0 ; Philadelphia, 2, 1, 19, 1.

Sands, Sandys, Sondes. — Local, 'at the sands,' from residence thereby. M.E. sand or sond.

Walter atte Sond, bailiff of Yarmouth, 1335 : FF. xi. 323.

Earl Sondes owns a large estate in co. Norfolk.

Johannes del Sandes, 1379 : P. T. Yorks. p. 235.
Thomas del Sandes, 16 Ric. II : E. and F., co. Cumb., p. 174.
Paulina atte Sonde, C. R., 12 Hen. IV.
Richard atte Sonde, C. R., 8 Hen. V.
1589. Henry Sandes, London : Reg. Univ. Oxf. vol. ii. pt. ii. p. 174.
1633. William Sandys and Cicily Steed : Marriage Lic. (Faculty Office), p. 31.
London, 19, 3, 0 ; Philadelphia, 46, 0, 0.

Sandy ; v. Sanday.

Sanger, Sangster, Sanxter, Songster, Songer.—Occup. 'the singer' or songster. A.S. sangere, fem. sangystre.

Willametta Cantatrix. E.
Adam le Sangere. T.
Robert le Sangar, co. Soms., 1 Edw. III : Kirby's Quest, p. 112.
Thomas le Sanggere, co. Soms., 1 Edw. III : ibid. p. 244.
1640. Bapt. — Arthur, s. of Arthur Sangar : Reg. Stourton, Wilts, p. 9.
1714. Married—William Wilkins and Susanna Sangar : Reg. St. Dionis Backchurch, p. 57.
Manchester, 0, 1, 0, 0, 0 ; London, 7, 10, 0, 0, 0 ; MDB. (Wilts), 5, 0, 0, 0, 0 ; Foxton (co. Camb.), 0, 0, 1, 0, 0 ; Philadelphia, 3, 1, 0, 3, 1.

Sankey.—Local, ' of Sankey,' a township in the parish of Prescot, co. Lanc.

Gerard de Sanki, co. Lanc., Hen. III—Edw I. K.
William de Sonkey, 25 Edw. I : Baines' Lanc. ii. 211.

Roger de Sonky, 27 Edw. I : Baines'
Lanc. ii. 254.
Roger Sanckey, 11 Jas. I : ibid.
Edward Sankey, of Little Sankey,
1602 : Wills at Chester, i. 169.
Thomas Sankie, of Little Sankey,
1623 : ibid. ii. 192.
Manchester, 4 ; London, 4 ; Boston
(U.S.), 2.

Sansom, Sanson, Sansum.—
Bapt. ; v. Sampson.

Santer.—Nick. 'sans-terre,' i.e.
Lackland. The instance below
seems very conclusive. One is
almost in danger of suggesting the
old origin of the verb to *saunter*
(v. *saunter*, Skeat). The same
individual is thus referred to :

John Sansterre, co. Linc., 1273. A.
John Sanzterre, co. Linc., ibid.
John Sauntere, co. Linc., ibid.
London, 2 ; Crockford, 1.

Santon.—Local, 'of Santon,'
parishes in the diocs. of Norwich
and Ely.

Payn de Santon, co. Norf., 1273. A.
Thomas de Santon, co. Linc., ibid.
1315. Harvey de Santone, patron of
living of Santon, co. Norf.: FF. ii. 157.
1628. Bapt. — Margrett, d. Thomas
Santon : St. Jas. Clerkenwell, i. 108.
1640. Buried—Philip Santon : ibid.
iv. 246.

Santony.—Local, 'of St. Antony,' some chapelry in Normandy,
no doubt ; cf. Sinclair, Simbarb,
St. John, &c.

Dominus St. Antonis, co. Suff., 1273. A.
1782. Married — Robert Stacey and
Mary Santany : St. Geo. Han. Sq. i. 329.
New York, 1.

Sanxter. — A variant of Sangster ; v. Sanger.

Sare.—Bapt. 'the son of Sayer'
(q.v.). The intermediate form was
Saer, then Sare. This is one more
of the endless descendants of Sagar
(q.v.). The truth of this derivation
is absolutely certain.

William Sare, co. Glouc., 1273. A.
1605. John Sare, or Sayer, of Nantwich : Wills at Chester, i. 169.
1642. Richard Sare, of Wych Malbank,
ostler : ibid. ii. 192.
1675. Thomas Sare, of Warrington :
ibid. iii. 235.
1789. Married—Taylor Sare and Eliz.
Fountain : St. Geo. Han. Sq. ii. 25.
London, 1 ; South Lopham (Norfolk), 1.

Sargeant, &c. ; v. Serjeant.

Sargood.— ? Bapt. 'the son of
Sigurd' (?). (Yonge, ii. 306.)

1781. Married — Charles Ball and
Susanna Sargood : St. Geo. Han. Sq.
i. 328.
London, 4 ; Oxford, 1 ; New York, 2.

Sarjeant, &c. ; v. Serjeant.

Sarkins. — Bapt. 'the son of
Sarah' ; cf. Wilkins, Hopkins,
&c. I find the dim. Saralin also.

William Saralyn, co. Soms., 1 Edw.
III : Kirby's Quest, p. 197.

Cf. this with Hewling or Embelin, q.v.

London, 1.

Sarl, Sarle, Sarll.—Bapt. 'the
son of Sarle,' i.e. Serle, q.v. It is
interesting to note that the form Sarl,
found as a personal name in co.
Cambridge in 1273, still flourishes
there as a surname.

Sarle Tinctor, co. Hunts, 1273. A.
Matilda Sarle, co. Camb., ibid.

Sometimes Sarl is registered as
Sarel (cf. Serrell for Serle).

1788. Married — Edward Sarel and
Mary Philcox : St. Geo. Han. Sq. ii. 15.
London, 1, 1, 1 ; Gamlingay (co.
Camb.), 0, 0, 6.

Sarson.—(1) Bapt. 'the son of
Sara,' i.e. Sarah, a favourite name
in the 13th and 14th centuries.

Sara de Clayton, 1379 : P. T. Yorks.
p. 12.
Johannes Sareson, 1379 : ibid. p. 63.
Alicia fil. Sarr', co. Hunts, 1273. A.
Laurence fil. Sarre, co. Camb., ibid.
Richard fil. Sarre, co. Bucks, ibid.

(2) Local, 'the Saracen.'

'Amonges Sarzens and Jewes' : Piers
P. 6312.
Nicholas le Sarazyn, C. R., 42 Hen. III.
Peter Sarracen. C.
Henry Sarrasin. J.
William Sarrazein. C.
1742. Buried—Catherine Sarazan : St.
Michael, Cornhill, p. 296.
London, 3 ; New York, 1.

Sarvent, Sarvant. — Occup.
'the servant' ; v. Servant ; cf.
Perkin and Parkin, Clerk and Clark,
person and *parson*.

London, 1, 0 ; New York, 0, 1.

Sass, Sasse.—Local, 'at the
sasse.' 'Sasse, a look in a river'
(Halliwell). 'Sasse, from sass
(Belgic), a sluice or lock, especially
in a river that is cut with floodgates,
to shut up or let out water for the
better passage of boats and barges,
as in Misterton Sasse' (The Isle

of Axholme, its place-names and
river-names, John K. Johnstone,
p. 59).

1617. John Sas and Jane Delabarr :
Marriage Lic. (London), ii. 51.
London, 2, 1 ; New York, 9, 5.

Satchell.—? Bapt. 'the son of
Sachel.' Lower says : 'Satchell,
a small sack or bag. Probably an
ancient trader's sign' (Patr. Brit.
p. 303). This is very unlikely.
Probably one of the many personal
names ending in -*el*.

Thomas Sachel, co. Soms., 1 Edw. III :
Kirby's Quest, p. 190.
1715. Bapt.—Prtity William, s. William
Satchell : St. Jas. Clerkenwell, ii. 86.
London, 6 ; Philadelphia, 4.

**Satterlee, Satterley, Satterly,
Saturley.**—Local, 'of Satterley'
or Satterleigh, a parish in co.
Devon, near South Molton.

London, 0, 0, 0, 1 ; New York, 16, 1, 4, 0.

Satterthwaite, Satterthwait.
—Local, 'of Satterthwaite,' an
ancient chapelry in High Furness,
near Hawkshead. Small and secluded as is the spot, it has originated
a surname that has spread far and
wide. It seems to have reached
London about the 16th century.
But it is still familiar in the
immediate district, as I can testify.

Robert Saterthwaite, of Coutehouse in
Hawkshead, 1596 : Lancashire Wills at
Richmond, i. 243.
William Satewhait, of Saterthwaite,
1604 : ibid.
George Saterwhat, of Hauxhead, 1613 :
ibid. p. 244.
1642. Bapt.—Robert, s. Maylin Setter-
thwayte : St. Jas. Clerkenwell, i. 152.
1649. Married — John Satterthwaite,
stationer, and Marye Peele : St. Michael,
Cornhill, p. 30.
1668. Buried — Isabella, d. William
Saterthwayte, of Arrad : Ulverston
Parish Ch. i. 134.
London, 2, 0 ; Manchester, 2, 0 ; Ulverston, 2, 0 ; Philadelphia, 1, 5.

Saturday.—Nick. or personal ;
cf. Monday, Pentecost, Whitsunday,
Pask, &c.

Willelmus Ceterday, 1379 : P. T. Yorks.
p. 119.

Saturley ; v. Satterlee.

Saucemaker.—Occup. 'a maker
of sauces' ; v. Saucer.

Joan Sausemaker, co. York. W. 11.

Saucer.—Occup. 'the saucer,' i.e. a maker of sauces, a most important avocation in the 13th, 14th, and 15th centuries, when some seasoning, like salt-pickle, for a relish was deemed a vital necessity. Hence *saucer*, a deep-rimmed plate, or shallow vessel, to hold sauce in. v. Saucemaker.

' Wo was his cook, but if his sauce were
Poinant, and sharpe, and redy all his
gere.' Chaucer, C. T. 352.

The early registers teem with entries.

William le Sauser, co. Devon, Hen. III–Edw. I. K.
Geoffry le Sauser, co. Oxf., 1273. A.
Robert le Sauser, co. Camb., ibid.
John de Weteley, *sauser*, 25 Edw. I:
Freemen of York, i. 6.
Roger le Sauser. N.
Matilda le Sausere. B.

Curiously enough, I cannot find any present representatives of the name. The latest are:

1662. Bapt.—Alexander, son of Laurance Sawcer: St. Michael, Cornhill, p. 143.
1670. Buried—Robert, son of Laurance Sawcer: ibid. p. 257.
1735. Married—Thomas Edwards and Keturah Sawcer: St. Geo. Han. Sq. i. 15.

Saucery.—Local, 'of the saucery,' practically official; an officer of the household who had charge of the sauces; cf. de la Pantrie, de la Spence. v. Saucer.

Robert de la Saucee, co. Northants, 1273. A.
William de la Saucery, 44 Edw. III. P.
Johannes de Sausre, 1379: P.T.Yorks. p. 192.
Gilbert de la Saucerie, C. R., 15 Ric. II.
William Walsingham, alias William of Saucerie, C. R., 9 Hen. IV.

Saul, Saull.—(1) Bapt. 'the son of Saul'; cf. Paul. This personal name was somewhat uncommon. (2) Local, 'at the saule' (i.e. Sale, q.v.), from residence therein as owner or servitor. O.E. *sel*, a hall; Fr. *salle*. The surname of the famous knight commemorated by Froissart (1332–48) is variously written de la Sale, de la Saule, de Aula, or de Halle (Notes and Queries, 1st S. v. 291). No doubt both (1) and (2) have contributed to our directories.

Johannes Saule,1379: P.T.Yorks. p. 136.
Cecilia Saule, 1379: ibid. p. 42.

Johannes Saule, 1379 : ibid. p. 58.
1582–3. Arnold Saule, co. Glouc.: Reg. Univ. Oxf. vol. ii. pt. ii. p. 124.
1602. Bapt.—Mary, d. Edward Saule: St. Michael, Cornhill, p. 103.
London, 8, 1; MDB. (co. Cumb.), 15, 1; New York, 18, 0.

Saulsbury, Saulsberry; v. Salisbury, a variant.

Manchester, 1, 0; Philadelphia, 2, 1.

Saunder, Saunders, Saunderson.—Bapt. 'the son of Alexander,' from the nick. Saunder. In early use. v. Sander.

Alisandre, or Sandre de Leycestre, London, 1273. A.
Richard frater Sander, co. Salop, ibid.
Thomas fil. Saundre, co. Northampton, ibid.
Saunder de M're, co. Salop, ibid.
William Saundres, co. Soms., 1 Edw. III : Kirby's Quest, p. 157.
Cristiana Sawndir, 1379: P. T. Yorks. p. 141.
Ricardus Sawndirson, 1379: ibid.
Matilda Saunder-wyf, 1379: ibid. p. 22.
Johannes Saundirman, 1379: ibid.
Sawnder Manggo, 1379: ibid. p. 109.
Johannes Saundirson (son of above), 1379: ibid.
Saundir Saryaunte, 1379: ibid.
London, 1, 136, 1 ; New York, 1, 41, 1.

Savage.—Nick. 'the savage' (cf. Wild). It is curious that Wild and Savage should be so popular as sobriquets, but fierceness was fascinating. The invariable forms are Salvage, Sauvage, and Savage.

Geoffrey le Sauvage, co. Leic., Hen. III–Edw. I. K.
Walter Salvage, co. Oxf., 1273. A.
Robert le Savage, co. Suff., ibid.
Beatrix Sawage, 1379: P. T. Yorks. p. 19.
Robertus Sawfage, 1379: ibid. p. 213.
Adelmya le Sauvage. J.
John le Savage. H.
William le Salvage. B.
1734. Married—Andrew Savage and Mary Gill: St. Geo. Han. Sq. i. 13.
London, 48; New York, 60.

Savill, Saville, Savile, Seville, Sevill.—Local. An old surname of the East Riding, which has penetrated into Lanc. as Saville and Seville. It looks like a surname of Norman local extraction.

Robertus Sayuill, 1379: P. T. Yorks. p. 134.
Johannes Seyuyll', 1379: ibid. p. 183.
Johannes Sayuyll', 1379: ibid. p. 184.
1611. John Payne and Fridiswith Savill (co. York): Marriage Lic. (London), ii. 1.

1616–7. Sir Thomas Mildmay and Anne Savile (parish of Wakefield, co. York): ibid. ii. 49.
Oldham (Seville), 5, (Sevill), 1; London, 10, 4, 1, 0, 0; West Rid. Court Dir., 0, 4, 0, 0, 0; Philadelphia, 0, 9, 0, 4, 0.

Savoner.—Occup. 'the soaper'; v. Soper.

Nicholas le Sauoner, Close Roll, 2 Edw. I.
Agneta la Savoner. A.
Adam la Savonier. E.

Savory, Savery, Saffery, Savary. — Bapt. 'the son of Savary.' Latinized as Savaricus. The Hundred Rolls form is sometimes Saffrey, almost unaltered in the present Saffery.

Savaric de Maulcon, 1224: Davies' Hist. of Southampton, p. 24.
Richard Saveri, co. Camb., 1273. A.
Robert Saffrei, co. Camb., ibid.
Richard Saffrey, co. Camb., ibid.
Savaricus de Penlieze, co. Wilts, ibid.
Saufray de Som'y, co. Sussex, ibid.
Savar' de Claville, co. Bucks, ibid.
John Sauvary, co. Wilts, Hen. III–Edw. I. K.
Savericus de Bohun, 12 Edw. I. BBB. p. 345.
Saffredus de Hawkswell, 16 Edw. I, ibid. p. 388.

Savericus de Bohun is called Savary by Dugdale.

William Savery, 1605: Reg. Broad Chalke, co. Wilts, p. 3.
1708. Bapt.—Elizabeth, d. of John and Abigail Saveory, lodging at Mr. Pitman's: St. Thomas the Apostle (London), p. 71.
1805. Bapt.—Eliz., d. James Saffery: Canterbury Cath. p. 42.
London, 8, 1, 2, 0; Philadelphia, 0, 6, 0, 0; Boston (U.S.), 8, 1, 0, 4.

Saward.—Bapt. 'the son of Siward,' one of many variants. For many instances, v. Seward (2).

Hugh Saward, co. Norf., 1273. A.
1590. Robert Boothe and Agnes Sawarde: Marriage Lic. (London), i. 187.
1736. Married—John Saward and Bridget Forsbrook: St. Geo. Han. Sq. i. 18.
1741. Bapt. — Susanna, d. William Saward: St. Antholin (London), p. 163.
London, 4 ; MDB. (co. Essex), 4 ; New York, 2.

Sawer; v. Sawyer.

Sawkins, Sawkings.—Bapt. 'the son of Saer,' dim. Saykin, modified to Sawkin (v. Sayer). If we were sure that Saunderkin existed from Alexander, then naturally Sawkin would be the corruption. But *-kin* as a suffix was almost invariably added to a nick. monosyllable; and we have a clear case of the once great name of Saer becoming Saykin. The *g* in Sawkings is, of course, excrescent; cf. Jennings. The same individual is thus described:

Saer Bude, co. Essex, 1273. A. p. 146.
Saykinus Bude, co. Essex, ibid. p. 159.
1661. Buried—Grace Greeton, mayd servant to John Sawkins: St. Jas. Clerkenwell, iv. 338.
1720. Married—Thomas Sawkins and Sarah Wilmott: St. Dionis Backchurch, p. 60.
London, 1, 1.

Sawman.—Bapt. 'the son of Salmon,' i.e. Solomon. It is tempting to derive the name from O.F. *saumon*, English *salmon*, the fish, and make it a nickname, but this origin is improbable; v. Salman.

William Saumon, co. Hunts, 1273. A.
Adam Sauman, co. Linc., ibid.
1551. Bapt.—Robert Sawmon: St. Jas. Clerkenwell, i. 1.
1616. — John, s. George Sawman: ibid. p. 75.
London, 1.

Sawrey.—Local, 'of Sawrey,' a hamlet on the west shore of Windermere, near Hawkshead, North Lanc. A branch of the family settled in Ulverston parish as early as the reign of Henry VI (v. West's Antiquities of Furness).

1545. Buried—John Sowraie: St. Mary Ulverston, p. 1.
1551. Bapt.—William Sowraie: ibid. p. 19.
John Saurey, of Hauxhead, 1583: Lancashire Wills at Richmond, i. 245.
William Sawrey, of Sawrey, 1593: ibid.
1619-20. Anthony Sawrey, co. Bucks: Reg. Univ. Oxf. vol. ii. pt. ii. p. 382.
MDB. (co. Cumb.), 3; Ulverston, 2.

Sawyer, Sawer.—Occup. 'the sawyer,' one who saws wood, &c.; *y* as in *law-yer* and *bow-yer* is intrusive.

Ralph le Sawiere, co. Hunts, 1273. A.
Geoffrey le Sawere, London, ibid.
Henry le Sawer, C. R., 9 Edw. I.
William Saweyer, co. Soms., 1 Edw. III: Kirby's Quest, p. 101.
Richard le Saghiere, Close Roll, 21 Edw. III. pt. ii.
Henry le Saghier. M.
Walter le Sawyere. G.
Hugo Sawer, 1379: P. T. Yorks. p. 156.
Thomas Sawer, 1379: ibid.

1767. Married—Richard Sawyer and Jane Jessatt: St. Geo. Han. Sq. i. 168.
— — Richard Meares and Frances Sawer: ibid. p. 171.
London, 30, 1; Philadelphia, 20, 0.

Saxby. — Local, 'of Saxby,' parishes in cos. Lincoln (2) and Leicester.

1577. Bapt.—Robert, son of — Sacksbye: St. Jas. Clerkenwell, i. 10.
1661. Buried—Richard Saxbee, a poore old man: ibid. iv. 343.
1808. Married—John Saxby and Mary Elkins: St. Geo. Han. Sq. ii. 394.
London, 10; MDB. (co. Kent), 5.

Saxelby, Saxelbye. — Local, 'of Saxelby,' parishes in cos. Lincoln and Leicester.

William de Saxelby, co. Linc., Hen. III—Edw. I. K.
Geoffrey de Saxelby, co. Linc., 1273. A.
1768. Married — William Evans and Eliz. Saxelby: St. Geo. Han. Sq. i. 178.
MDB. (co. Worc.), 1, 0; (East Rid. Yorks), 0, 1.

Saxon. — Local, 'of Saxton,' q.v. (2). I doubt not this is the true origin. That it means a Saxon by race and blood is chronologically absurd.

1669. Bapt.—John, s. Audery Saxson: St. Jas. Clerkenwell, i. 239.
1742. Married — Thomas Saxon and Mary Bullock: St. Geo. Chap. Mayfair, p. 24.
1791. — John Saxon and Eliz. Wilson: St. Geo. Han. Sq. ii. 54.
London, 2; Philadelphia, 2.

Saxton, Sexton, Sextone.—(1) Offic. 'the sacristan,' now sexton or verger of a church. This, without doubt, has added to the modern directories. Although my instances are few, I suspect it is the parent of many of our Saxtons and Sextons.

Hugh Sacristan, co. Kent, 1273. A.
John Sexteyn, C. R., 7 Edw. IV.

(2) Local, 'of Saxton,' a parish in the dioc. of York.

Johannes de Saxton, 1379: P. T. Yorks. p. 99.
Robertus de Saxton, 1379: ibid. p. 125.
1771. Married — Charles Saxton and Mary Bush: St. Geo. Han. Sq. i. 211.
1782. — George Sexton and Mary Liddell: ibid. p. 338.
London, 6, 14, 1; Philadelphia, 13, 30, 0.

Say.—Local, 'at the sea,' i.e. by the seaside, from residence thereby; cf. Sands, Sandys, and

Shore. The family of Say are found entered as Attsee (i. e. at the sea) and De la See in the Yorkshire Visitation, 1563; as for instance:

Sir Thomas Say, p. 168.
Johanes de Say, p. 277.
Say (otherwise Attsee, and De la See), p. 277.
John le (? de) Say, co. Soms., 1 Edw. III: Kirby's Quest, p. 243.
Henery Attsee, of Herne: Visitation of Bedfordshire, 1566, p. 167.
1619. Edward Say, co. Kent: Reg. Univ. Oxf. vol. ii. pt. ii. p. 379.
— William Say, co. Kent: ibid.
1623. Edward Say and Margaret Tooting: Marriage Lic. (London), ii. 131.
London, 6; Philadelphia, 1.

Sayce, Sayse, Saies, Seys, Saise.—Nick. 'the foreigner,' the stranger, the Englishman. A Welsh surname; cf. Inglis, Walsh, Irish.

Anian Seys, 1309, Bishop of Bangor.
William Sys, co. Soms., 1 Edw. III: Kirby's Quest, p. 121.
Rogerus Seys, 1384: Hist. and Ant. St. David's, p. 371.
1619. Henry Sayse and Margaret Warren: Marriage Lic. (London), ii. 80.
Ilyke de Ivon Seys: Visitation Glouc. (1623), p. 98.
Joane Howell ap Evan Sais: ibid. p. 180.
'At the Chepstow police-court on Saturday, before Messrs. G. Gwyn and H. Lowe,' &c.: South Wales Daily News, Aug. 26, 1889.
MDB. (co. Monmouth), 1, 0, 0, 2, 0; Bristol (Saise), 3, (Sayce), 3; Tenby (Saies), 2; Pembroke (Sayse), 1; New York (Sayce), 1.

Sayer, Sayers.—Bapt.' the son of Sayer,' also found as Sagar, Sigar, and Seger. A forgotten personal name that has left an indelible mark on our directories. From twenty to twenty-five surnames separately spelt are the offspring, and many have a large number of representatives. The name was popular so early as Domesday as Segar and Sigar, and Latinized as Sigarus. Siger de Frivile is found in the Hundred Rolls as Siger, Saer, Sayer, and Seer (ii. 152, 514, 153, 523). The following surnames (amongst others) will be found in their proper place, unquestionable descendants of Siger or Sayer, viz. Seager, Seeger, Seaker, Sugar, Sugars, Siggers, Saggers, Sagar, Sager, Secker, Sear, Sears, Searson, Seare, Seares, Seear, Syer, and Syers. Also a dim. Saykin.

John Sayer, co. Norf., 1273. A.
Saer Batayle, co. Essex, ibid.
John fil. Saeri, London, ibid.
Sayer Herberd, London, ibid.
Saher de Braban. E.
Saher Clerk. C.
Saher le King. H.
Agnes Sayer. N.
London, 24, 9; Philadelphia, 7, 12.

Sayles, Saile, Sales, Sayle. — Local, 'at the sayles,' i.e. the hurdles (cf. Paliser, also a great Yorkshire surname). 'Sales, the upright stakes of a hurdle' (Halliwell). The only instances I can find, ancient or modern, are in co. York. The name has remained there at least 500 years. But as an alternative, v. Sale.

Agnes del Sayles, 1379: P. T. Yorks. p. 66.
William Salys, 1379: ibid. p. 95.
Alanus Sayle, 1379: ibid. p. 102.
Robertus Schayle, 1379: ibid. p. 106.
Willelmus Saylles, 1379: ibid. p. 124.
Margeria del Saylle, 1379: ibid. p. 141.
John Sale, co. York, 1577: Reg. Univ. Oxf. vol. ii. pt. ii. p. 79.
West Rid. Court Dir., 2, 1, 3, 0; Sheffield, 6, 0, 1, 0; New York, 9, 3, 1, 1.

Saylor, Sailer, Sailor. — Occup. 'the sailour,' a dancer, a hopper. 'Saille, to leap (A.N.), hence sailours, leapers, dancers' (Halliwell).

'There was many a timbestere,
And sailours that I dare well swere
Couthe hir craft full perfitly.'
Chaucer, R. of R. 769-71.

Sailor is a comparatively modern term for one who sails on the sea. Mariner (q.v.) was the term in general use. Dancer and Hopper are familiar surnames. Doubtless the surname concerns the dancer. Oddly enough, I cannot find the surname on English soil. It is a common name in the United States.

John le Saillur, 1273. A.
William le Saylliur, ibid.
Nicholas le Saler, ibid.
1790. Married — John Maddocks and Frances Sayler: St. Geo. Han. Sq. ii. 45.
Philadelphia, 40, 35, 18.

Saynor.—Nick.; v. Senior.

Sayse.—Nick.; v. Sayce.

Scadlock; v. Scathlock.

Scaife.—Nick.; v. Skaife.

Scales.—Local, 'at the scales.' Norse scale, a shepherd's hut; cf. Scottish shealing (Taylor, p. 486). Hence Winterscale and Summerscales (q.v.). A hamlet in the parish of Aldingham, Furness, is called Scales. A farmstead in Ulverston parish is named Cockinskale, which gave rise to a surname corrupted to Cockinshell; cf. Portingscale, near Keswick. See, however, shale (Skeat's Dict.).

Isolda del Scales, 1379: P. T. Yorks. p. 219.
Johannes del Scales, 1379: ibid. p. 250.
Willelmus de la Scale, 1379: ibid. p. 261.
Robert Scales, of Hauxhead, 1591: Lancashire Wills at Richmond, i. 245.
George Skales, of Ulverston, 1670: ibid. p. 256.
London, 6; West Rid. Court Dir., 5; New York, 1; Boston (U.S.), 7.

Scambler. — (1) Occup. 'a scambler'(?), i.e. one who kept a stall; v. Scamell. (2) Nick. 'a scambler'(?), one who sprawled in his walk, a shambler (of which word scambler is the stronger form). Probably this is the true derivation.

Edmund Scambler, or Schambler, bishop of Peterborough, 1560: Cal. State Papers, i. 164, 374, &c.
1580. Robert Scamler, of Hornby: Lancashire Wills at Richmond, i. 245.
1588. Agnes Skamler, of Wraye: ibid. p. 256.
1793. Married — John Shambler and Hannah Coats: St. Geo. Han. Sq. ii. 96.
1794. — Joshua Thurston and Ann Scambler: ibid. p. 119.
Manchester, 1; MDB. (co. Essex), 1; (co. Lancaster), 4.

Scamell, Scammell.—Local, 'at the shamble,' i.e. the stall. M.E. schamel, a bench; A.S. scamel, a stool (v. shambles, in Skeat's Dict.). A surname for one who kept a stall or bench for meat, &c., in the street or market.

Simon de la Scamele, co. Essex, 1273. A.
Simon de la Schamele, co. Essex, ibid.
Walter Schamel, co. Dorset, ibid.
Symon del Scameles, 31 Edw. I: Freemen of York, i. 9.
Richard Skammell, co. Dorset, 1316. M.
William Scammell, 1563: Reg. Broad Chalke, Wilts, p. 1.
Mary Scammell, 1592: ibid. p. 2.

1790. Married—William Scammell and Eliz. Searle: St. Geo. Han. Sq. ii. 46.
London, 2, 4; Boston (U.S.), 1, 0; New York, 0, 5.

Scamp.— ? ——. A curious name. Of course it has no connexion with the dictionary scamp. No doubt local.

Ilfracombe, 5.

Scampton.—Local, 'of Scampton,' a parish in co. Lincoln.

1705. Bapt.—Eliz., d. Francis Scampton: St. Michael, Cornhill, p. 65.
1732. Married—John Leeson and Eliz. Scampton: ibid. p. 161.
MDB. (co. Leic.), 1; Philadelphia, 3.

Scarborough, Scarbrow, Scarboro.—Local, 'of Scarborough,' co. York.

Henry de Scardeburgh, co. Linc., 20 Edw. I. R.
Johannes de Scardeburgh, 1379: P. T. Yorks. p. 265.
Nicholas de Scardburgh, 1379: ibid. p. 218.
1571. Married — Stephen Scarborough and Eliz. Eaton: St. Antholin (London), p. 21.
1606. — John Scarboroughe and Hester Rickett: St. Mary Aldermary, p. 11.
1646. Bapt. — Dennis, s. Matthew Scarburrow: St. Dionis Backchurch, p. 108.
London, 2, 1, 0; West Rid. Court Dir., 7, 0, 0; MDB. (co. Leic.), 2, 0, 1; Philadelphia, 7, 0, 0.

Scarf(e; v. Scarth.

Scargill, Scargle.—Local, 'of Scargill,' a township in the parish of Barningham, N. Rid. Yorks. The surname has ramified strongly, and in America has assumed the guise of Scargle.

William de Scargill, co. York, 16 Edw. II: FF. x. 129.
Willelmus de Scargill, chivaler, 1379: P. T. Yorks. p. 119.
Johannes de Schargill, 1379: ibid. p. 216.
1674. Thomas Cranmer and Dorothy Scargill: Marriage Alleg. (Canterbury), p. 228.
Sheffield, 2, 0; Philadelphia, 0, 10.

Scarisbrick, Scarsbrick, Scarsbrook, Scarasbrick, Scarrisbrick.—Local, 'of Scarisbrick,' a township in the parish of Ormskirk, co. Lancashire. In London the name settled down to Scarsbrook.

1508. Thomas Scarysbrig, D.D.: Reg. Univ. Oxf. i. 56.

Edward Scarisbrick, of Scarisbrick, 1599: Wills at Chester, i. 169.
Henry Scarisbrick, of Scarisbrick, 1608: ibid.
1615. Anthony Scarsbricke, *mercer*, of London, and Jane Glascocke: Marriage Lic. (London), ii. 35.
1768. Married—Joseph Whitmore and Mary Scasbrook: St. Geo. Han. Sq. i. 177.
Liverpool, 3, 2, 0, 1, 1; MDB. (co. Ches.), 1, 0, 0, 0, 0; London, 0, 3, 0, 0, 0.

Scarlett.—Nick. ' the scarlet,' of bright red complexion in dress or person; cf. Russell, Rous, Blunt, Blundell, &c.
Henry Scarlath, alias Henry Scarlet, co. Bucks, 1273. A
Peter Scarlet, co. Camb., ibid.
Hugh Skarlet. D.
John Scarlet, co. Soms., 1 Edw. III: Kirby's Quest, p. 83.
Robert Skerlet, 1379: P. T. Yorks. p. 46.
Thomas de Scarlett (?), 1379: ibid. p. 219.
Gregory Skarlett, 1506: Reg. Univ. Oxf. vol. ii. pt. i. 49.
1650. Married—Guy Scarlet and Ann Whitton: St. Jas. Clerkenwell, iii. 85.
London, 12; West Rid. Court Dir., 1; New York, 3.

Scarsbrick, -brook; v. Scarisbrick.

Scarth, Scarf, Scarfe, Soarff, Scarffe. Local, ' of Scarth.' I cannot find the spot. The surname is clearly of Yorkshire parentage.
Henry Scharf, co. Linc., 1273. A.
John de Scharth, 1379: P. T. Yorks. p. 265.
1615. John Scarth, co. York: Reg. Univ. Oxf. vol. ii. pt. ii. p. 340.
1662. Married — John Milborne and Margery Scarfe: St. Jas. Clerkenwell, iii. 111.
1723. — James Wightman and Eliz. Scarfe: St. Mary Aldermary, p. 46.
London, 0, 1, 6, 2, 1; West Rid. (Yorks) Court Dir., 2, 1, 1, 0, 0; MDB. (North Rid. Yorks) Scarth, 10; Philadelphia (Scarf), 1.

Scatchard,   Scatcherd, Scratcherd. — ? Occup. ' the scatch-herd '(?). I cannot find the term in the dictionaries. Yorkshire, where the surname is chiefly found, has given us a large number of this class; cf. Calvert, Shepard, Oxenhird, Coward, Geldard, Stodart, Swinnart, Coulthard, all compounds of *herd*. Of course they were not all confined to that county. Scatchard is probably of this class, Scratcherd being a manifest corruption.

1753. Married—James Finch and Esther Scatchard: St. Dionis Backchurch, p. 70.
West Rid. Court Dir., 6, 2, 1; London, 1, 0, 0; Philadelphia, 8, 0, 0.

Scathlock, Scadlock.—Bapt. ' the son of Scathlock.' Found in the district of Sherwood Forest, where we should expect to find it.
> ' Readily Little John went forth,
> And Scathelock went before.'
>   Robin Hood, i. 233.

Cf. Tuck, Littlejohn, and Hood.
Geoffrey Scatheloc, co. Notts, 1273. A. York, 0, 1; London, 0, 1.

Scatliff.—Local, ' of Scaitliff,' in the parish of Rochdale, co. Lanc. Of course the suffix is -*cliff*; cf. Topliff for Topcliff, and Cunliffe for Cuncliffe.
1637. John Scatleffe and Mary Shakespeare: Marriage Lic. (London), ii. 233. London, 1.

Scattergood.—Personal, ' the son of Schatregod.' In my book on the Sources and Signification of English Surnames I placed this in the nickname class, and said that it implied a spendthrift. There can be no doubt that it was an old personal name, one of the very many that terminate in -*god*, -*gode*, -*gaud*, or -*good*. The surname has ramified strongly in the United States; cf. Osgood, Goodwin, &c.
Wimcot Schatregod, co. Bedf., 1273. A.
Thomas Skatergode. F.
Mathew Scatergude, co. York. W. 2.
Richard Scatergood, Patent Roll, 3 Edw. VI, pt. v.
1703. Married—Henry Edwards and Eliz. Scattergood: St. Jas. Clerkenwell, iii. 226.
London, 2; West Rid. (Yorks) Court Dir., 2; Philadelphia, 49.

Scholar, Scholer, Schollard. —Occup. ' a scholar,' one belonging to a school, a learned man.
(Magister) Scholasticus, Jersey, 20 Edw. I. R.
1619. Edward Smith and Sarah Scoller: Marriage Lic. (London), ii. 82.
1751. Married — Joseph Schollar and Grace Burgess: St. Geo. Chap. Mayfair, p. 198.
1769. — William Scholar and Mary Roberts: St. Geo. Han. Sq. i. 189.
New York, 1, 1, 0; Worcester (U.S.), 0, 0, 3.

Scholefield, Schofield. Scholfield, Schoolfield.—Local, ' at the school-field.' A Lancashire

surname, which has spread far and wide; cf. Scowcroft and Schoolcraft. Probably this *field* or *croft* was used as a playground. But I dare not pronounce definitely on this point. The plural form in Scholes (q.v.) is difficult to explain. The precise spot so termed seems to have been within the ancient parish of Rochdale, co. Lanc.
1596. Edmund Scholfield, of Middleton: Wills at Chester, i. 170.
1613. Alex. Scholfield, of Scholfield: ibid.
1623. Edmund Scholefield, of Saddleworth, ibid. ii. 193.
1664. Married — John Scofeild and Jone Hudson: St. Jas. Clerkenwell, iii. 112.
London, 2, 19, 3, 0; West Rid. Court Dir., 27, 9, 5, 0; Manchester, 2, 42, 3, 0; Philadelphia, 0, 125, 0, 0; New York (Schoolfield), 2.

Scholes, Schoales.—Local, (1) ' at the school' or schools, from residence therein or thereby; cf. Scholefield, Schoolcraft, Scowcroft, &c.; v. Scholefield. Schoales is an American variant. (2) ' of Scholes,' a township in the parish of Barwick-in-Elmett, nine miles from Leeds, W. Rid. Yorks.
Johannes del Scholes, 1379: P. T. Yorks. p. 181.
Ricardus del Scholes, 1379: ibid. p. 195.
Ricardus del Scoles, 1379: ibid. p. 67.
On page 195 of the same register is found the name of Hugh Alderscholes, a manifest local surname.
Edmund Scholes of Prestwich (Manchester), 1587: Wills at Chester, i. 170.
Francis Scholes, of Chadderton, 1596: ibid.
London, 1, 0; West Rid. Court Dir., 7, 0; Manchester, 11, 0; Philadelphia, 9, 10.

Scholey, Schooley. — Local, ' of Scoley,' some small spot in W. Rid. Yorks.
Johannes de Scolay, 1379: P. T. Yorks. p. 91.
Robertus de Scolay, 1379: ibid.
Ricardus de Scolay, 1379: ibid. p. 103.
1581-2. Richard Scholey, co. Yorks.: Reg. Univ. Oxf. vol. ii. pt. ii. p. 116.
1735. Married — Beale Scholey and Mary Carr: St. Jas. Clerkenwell, iii. 263.
1784. — John Butler and Eliz. Schoolly: St. Geo. Han. Sq. i. 361.
London, 2, 2; West Rid. Court Dir., 4, 0; Sheffield, 4, 0; Philadelphia, 11, 0.

Schoolcraft.—Local, ' at the school-croft,' from residence in the school enclosure; v. Scowcroft.

A distinguished American, Henry Rowe Schoolcraft, both ethnologist and geologist (1793–1864), bore this name ; v. Craft and Croft.

1681. John Schoulcroft and Judith Bythell: Marriage Alleg. (Canterbury), p. 80.
Worcester (U.S.), 2.

Schoolfield ; v. Scholefield, an American variant.

Schoolhouse.—Local, 'at the school-house,' from residence therein. This surname lingered on for several centuries, and may still exist.—Since writing this I find it has crossed the Atlantic.

Ralph atte Skolehus, co. Norf., 1273. A.
1534. Henry Scolehouse, alderman of Norwich: FF. iii. 208.
1615. Alice Scolows, Norwich: ibid. iv. 496.
New York, 1.

Schoolmaster.—Occup. 'the schoolmaster.'

Ralph the Scolemaistre, C. R., 32 Edw. I.
Thomas Skolmayster. B.
John Scolemastre, C. R., 3 Hen. V.
New York, 1.

Scissons.—Bapt. ; v. Sisson.
London, 1.

Sclaster.—Occup. 'the slater' or 'sclater,' with feminine suffix Scla-ster ; cf. Brewster and Baxter. This form did not live, but as an occupative term *maltster* does, which is quite as uncouth in sound.

Willelmus Carter, *slaster*, 1379 : P. T. Yorks. p. 61.
Robertus Clerkson, *sclaster*, 1379: ibid. p. 111.
Agnes Sclaster, 1379 : ibid. p. 3.
Hugo Sclaster, 1379 : ibid. p. 34.
Elena Slaster, 1379 : ibid. p. 23.

Sclater ; v. Slater.

Scobell, Scoble ; v. Scovell.

Scoffer.—Nick. ' the scoffer.'

Matilda le Scoffar, co. Soms., 1 Edw. III : Kirby's Quest, p. 113.

Scoggins, Scoging. — Bapt. ' the son of Scogan.' Scoggins is the genitive ; cf. Williams. The final *g* in Scoging is an excrescence ; cf. Jennings. The surname still lives in cos. Norfolk and Suffolk.

Robert Scogan, co. Norf., 1357 : FF. vii. 144.
Henry Scogan, co. Norf., 1407: ibid.

Robert Scoggan, co. Norf., 45 Edw. III : ibid. x. 83.
Thomas Scoggan, co. Norf., 1420: ibid. vii. 142.
London, 3, 0 ; MDB. (co. Suffolk), 3, 1 ; Ipswich, 1, 0 ; Philadelphia, 2, 0.

Scolding, Skoulding.—?Local, ' of Shouldham ' (?). These two variants seem more or less imitative of the dictionary word *scolding*.

Rein de Sculdeham, co. Norf., temp. Hen. II : FF. vii. 514.
William de Sculdham, co. Norf., temp. Rich. I : ibid. ix. 178.

The next stage of corruption was Scoulden :

Robert Scoulden, *common-councilman*, Norwich, 1687 : FF. iii. 423.

The last step was the imitative Scolding :

1654. Mr. Scolding, *ensign*, Norwich : FF. iii. 400.
London, 1, 0 ; MDB. (co. Suffolk), 1, 1.

Scorer, Scorrar.—Occup. (1) ' the scorer,' a military spy, a scourer of the country. 'The Kinge, beinge at Notyngham, and or he came there, sent the scorers al abowte the contries adjoynynge to aspie and serche yf any gaderyngs in any place were agaynst hym' : Arrival of King Edward IVth (Halliwell). (2) 'The scorer,' one who scores or counts by notches, a tally-man, one who kept accounts.

Thomas le Scorur, C. R., 4 Edw. II.
Willelmus Skorer, 1379 : P. T. Yorks. p. 80.
Johannes Skorer, 1379 : ibid.
1667. John Scorror, of Disley Stanley : Wills at Chester (1660–80), p. 237.
1695. William Scorer, of Disley : ibid. (1681–1700), p. 221.
1800. Married—John Steel and Ann Scorer : St. Geo. Han. Sq. ii. 213.
London, 2, 1.

Scoresby, Sorsby, Soresby.—Local, ' of Scawsby,' a hamlet in the parish of Brodsworth, near Doncaster, co. York.

William de Schauceby, co. Northumb., Hen. III–Edw. I. K.
Johannes de Scausceby, 1379 : P. T. Yorks. p. 46.
Ricardus de Scausceby, 1379 : ibid. p. 47.
Johannes de Scausby, 1379: ibid. p. 120.

William Scoresby, the great Arctic explorer, was son of William Scoresby, a whale-fisher, and

born at Cropton, co. York, Oct. 5, 1789.

1686. Robert Mosse and Ann Scoresby : Marriage Lic. (Faculty Office), p. 183.
West Rid. Court Dir., 0, 2, 0 ; MDB. (co. Derby), 0, 0, 3.

Scotland.—Local, 'of Scotland'; cf. Britton, Ireland, Cornwall, Burgoyne, &c.

Simon Scotland, co. Norf., temp. Hen. IV : FF. viii. 504.
1801. Married—William Spencer and Ann Scotland : St. Geo. Han. Sq. ii. 247.
Boston (U.S.), 2.

Scotney.—Local, ' of Scotney.' An estate, with castle, in East Sussex, which belonged to the family in the 13th and 14th centuries. The first of the name on record is Walter de Scotney, steward of the Earl of Gloucester, temp. Henry III, who was hanged on a charge of attempting the life of his master (Blaauw's Barons' War, p. 61, quoted by Lower).

Lambert de Scoteni, co. Linc., 1273. A.
Thomas de Scoteney, co. Linc., ibid.
Peter de Scotenye, co. Linc., ibid.
1772. Married—Stephen Scotney and Dorothy Gibson : St. Geo. Han. Sq. i. 226.
London, 2 ; MDB. (co. Camb.), 2.

Scotson.—Nick. 'the son of the Scot,' one of an extremely rare class ; cf. Taylorson, Hindson, Clerkson. It is natural to find it at first in such counties as Durham and York.

Alexander Scotteson, 1379 : P. T. Yorks. p. 206.
Gilbert Scotessun, of Durham. W. 15.
1798. Married — Abraham Bass and Margaret Scotson: St. Geo. Han. Sq. ii. 177.
Ulverston, 1 ; Manchester, 1 ; Liverpool, 4.

Scott.—Local, ' the Scot,' one who came from Scotland, q.v. This is probably the most flourishing of local surnames.

Roger le Scot, London, 1273. A.
Elias le Scot, co. Salop, ibid.
Walter Scot, co. York, ibid.
Johannes Scot, 1379 : P. T. Yorks. p. 8.
Adam Skotte, 1379 : ibid. p. 27.
1638. Robert Scott and Anne Payne : Marriage Lic. (London), ii. 37.

The double *t* in Scott is now universal.

London, 248 ; Philadelphia, 558.

Scotto.—Local; v. Skottowe.

Scotton, Scotten.—Local, ' of Scotton,' a parish in co. Lincoln. Also two townships in co. York, one in the parish of Catterick, N. Rid., the other in the parish of Farnham, W. Rid. The Lincolnshire parish seems to be the chief parent.

Robert de Scotton, co. Linc., 1273. A.
Thomas de Skotton, 13 Edw. 1: Freemen of York, i. 4.
John de Scottone, co. Linc., 20 Edw. I. R.
1663. Edward Scotton and Margaret Archer: Marriage Lic. (Faculty Office), p. 71.
1750. Married — James Bracey Perry and Ann Scotton: St. Geo. Chap. Mayfair, p. 185.
London, 1, 1; Philadelphia, 0, 1.

Scovell, Scobell, Scoble, Scovil, Scovill, Scoville.—Local, ' of Scoville.' Lower says, ' From Escoville, now Ecoville, in the arrondissement of Caen, in Normandy.' There can be little doubt that Scobell and Scoble are variants.

Roger de Schovill, co. Norf., Hen. III-Edw. I. K.
Matilda de Scowile, co. Norf., 1273. A.
1610. Charles Skovell, co. Dorset: Reg. Univ. Oxf. vol. ii. pt. ii. p. 311.
1615. William Scoble, co. Devon: ibid. p. 339.
1663. Sir Richard Braham and Jane Scobell: Marriage Alleg. (Canterbury), p. 86.
1805. Married — Charles Andrew Scovell and Editha Slocombe: St. Geo. Han. Sq. ii. 331.
MDB. (co. Devon), 0, 2, 2, 0, 0, 0;
London, 3, 1, 0, 0, 0, 0; Crockford, 0, 3, 0, 0, 0; New York, 1, 1, 3, 1, 2, 5;
Philadelphia, 0, 0, 0, 1, 0, 0.

Scowcroft.—Local, ' of the school-croft,' i.e. the school enclosure (v. Croft); cf. Scholefield. In a copy of one of the Oldham papers several years ago, dealing with local matters, I noted the following:

Adam de Scolecroft, 6 Edw. III.

I have lost all other references, but it is clear that the estate from which the name was taken lay in the ancient parish of Oldham.

Thomas Taylor, of Scolecroft, parish of Oldham, 1588: Wills at Chester (1545-1620), p. 191.
Richard Scholecroft, of Farnworth, 1589: ibid. p. 170.

Richard Scowcroft, of Haugh, co. Lanc., *husbandman*, 1689: ibid. (1681-1700), p. 347.
Eliz. Scolecroft, of Haulgh (Bolton-le-Moors), 1690, ibid.

These last two belonged to the same family. It may be taken for granted that the change to Scowcroft became established orthographically about the year 1700. The pronunciation would be much older.

1609. Married—Stephen Scocrofte and Grace Creycall: St. Mary Aldermary, p. 11.
Manchester, 2; Bolton, 6; Philadelphia, 1.

Scraggs; v. Scroggs.

Scratcherd. — Occup. (?) A corruption of Scatchard, q.v.

Scrimgeour, Scrymgeour, Scrimiger, Scrymigar.—Offic. ' the scrimmager'; v. Skirmisher.

1681. George Jones and Eliz. Skrymsher: Marriage Lic. (Faculty Office), p. 158.
1802. Married — William Scrimgeour and Eliz. Hawkins: St. Geo. Han. Sq. ii. 261.
New York, 3, 2, 0, 2.

Scripps.—Bapt. ' the son of Crispin,' a corruption of Cripps, q.v. Crispin took two nicks., Crisp and Crips. Both as surnames are found with an initial S in the Hundred Rolls. In one case the same individual bears both names; cf. *crawl* and *scrawl*; also v. Sturgess (s.v. Sturge).

Alanus Scrips, co. Camb., 1273. A.
Jacobus Scrips, co. Camb., ibid.
Geoffrey Scrisp, co. Camb., ibid.
Jacobus Scrisp, co. Camb., ibid.
London, 1.

Scripture. — Occup. ' the writer'; cf. Faber.

William Scriptor, co. Oxf., 1273. A.
1686. Bapt.—Mary, d. John Scripture: St. Jas. Clerkenwell, i. 317.
1694. — John, son of John Scripture: ibid. p. 357.
New York, 1 ; Boston (U.S.), 3.

Scriven, Screven.—(1) Occup. ' the scriven,' i.e. copyist, notary. O.F. *escrivain*, a scrivener: Cotgrave.

' But if scryveynes lie.'
Piers P. 6278.

(2) Local, ' of Scriven,' a township in the parish of Knaresborough,

W. Rid. Yorks. But (1) must be looked upon as the chief parent.

William le Scriueyn, C. R., 42 Hen. III.
Margaret Scrivein, co. Camb., 1273. A.
Henry le Escriveyn, co. Oxf., ibid.
Robert le Schrevein, co. Wilts, ibid.
William de Skrevyn, *tannator*, 3 Edw. II : Freemen of York, i. 12.
Johannes Schryuen, 1379: P. T. Yorks. p. 198.
1539. Married — Petter Skreven and Alys Langlee: Reg. St. Dionis Backchurch, p. 1.
London, 9, 0; West Rid. Court Dir., 1, 0; Philadelphia, 1, 1.

Scrivener. — Occup. ' the scrivener,' a later form of Scriven, q.v.

Johannes Scryuener, 1379: P. T. Yorks. p. 251.
Johannes Screuyner, 1379: ibid. p. 40.
Custancia Skryvener, 1379: ibid. p. 148.
1562. Married—Thomas Browne, *skrivener*, and Wenefrid Skot: St. Mary Aldermary, p. 3.
1767. — John Scrivener and Eliz. Wargon: St. Geo. Han. Sq. i. 160.
MDB. (co. Bedf.), 2; Abingdon, 2; New York, 1.

Scroggs, Scraggs.—Local, ' of Scroggs,' a village in co. Dumfries (Lower).

1576. William Scrogges and Alice Marten: Marriage Lic. (London), i. 69.
1753. Married—William Scraggs and Mary Stevens: St. Geo. Chap. Mayfair, p. 26.
MDB. (co. Bedf.), 3, 1; Oxford, 3, 0.

Scrogie, Scroggie, Scroggy.—Local, ' of Scrogie,' a village in co. Perth (Lower).

1802. Married — Charles Scrogie and Eliz. Bywater: St. Geo. Han. Sq. ii. 250.
London, 0, 3, 0; Philadelphia, 0, 0, 2.

Scruby.—Local, ' of Scrooby,' a parish in co. Notts.

Richard de Scrobby, co. Linc., 1273. A.
1686. John Camden and Eliz. Scrooby: Marriage Alleg. (Canterbury), p. 252.
1795. Married — William Scruby and Charlotte Newling: St. Geo. Han. Sq. ii. 137.
London, 3; MDB. (co. Camb.), 3; (co. Essex), 6.

Scruton, Scrutton. — Local, ' of Scruton,' a parish in the N. Rid. Yorks.

Johanna de Scruton, 1379: P. T. Yorks. p. 254.
1740. Married—Matthew Pearson and Ann Scruton: St. Geo. Chap. Mayfair. p. 147.
1804. — William Moffatt and Hariot Scruton: St. Geo. Han. Sq. ii. 315.
London, 3, 6; West Rid. Court Dir., 3, 0; New York, 2, 0.

Scrymigar, Scrymser; v. Skirmisher.

Scudamore, Skidmore. — Local, 'of Scudamore.' I cannot trace the exact spot, but probably it will be found in the south-west of England. 'Walter de Scudamore was lord of Upton, co. Wilts, in the reign of Stephen' (Lower). Skidmore was an early variant, as the following spellings of the name of one and the same individual will show:

Walter de Scudamore, 1316. M.
Walter de Skydemor, 1319. M.
Wauter de Skidemore, 1321. M.

Petrus de Skidemore, co. Wilts, 1273. A.
Godfrey de Skidemor, co. Wilts, ibid.

The family motto is imitative, 'Scuto Amoris Divini,' but to derive on this account the name from O.F. *escu d'amour* is out of the question. The origin is manifestly local. Mottoes are made to fit names, not names mottoes. Surnames precede mottoes.

1596. Henry Scudamore and Joane Howe: Marriage Lic. (London), i. 231.
1657. Bapt.—Mary, d. Thomas Skidmore: St. Jas. Clerkenwell, i. 198.
London, 6, 7; New York, 0, 28.

Scudder; v. Skudder.

Sculthorpe.—Local, 'of Sculthorpe,' a parish in co. Norfolk.

1325. John de Sculthorp, rector of Testerton, co. Norf.: FF. vii. 197.
1752. Buried — Mary Sculthorp: St. Michael, Cornhill, p. 206.
1798. Married — John Sculthorpe and Esther Millward: St. Geo. Han. Sq. ii. 181.

MDB. (co. Warwick), 2; London, 1.

Scurry, Skurray.—? Local, 'of Scurry' (?). Seemingly some spot in co. Somerset.

Seman Scury, co. Soms., 1 Edw. III: Kirby's Quest, p. 205.
John Scurye, co. Soms., 1 Edw. III: ibid. p. 206.
London, 1, 0; Abingdon, 0, 1.

Scutt.—Nick. 'the Scot.' The temptation is strong to make Scut a variation of Schet or Sket (v. Skeate), especially as the counties referred to below comprise the district in which that name was familiar. But 'le Scut' forbids the idea.

William le Scut, co. Kent, 1273. A.
Hugh le Skut, co. Wilts, ibid.
Griminilda Scut, co. Camb., ibid.
John Scut, co. Norf., ibid.
1807. Married — Thomas Scutt and Mary White: St. Geo. Han. Sq. ii. 366.
London, 3.

Seaber.—Bapt. 'the son of Sigborg,' modulated to Siber and Seber (v. Yonge's Christian Names, ii. 310). The surname is still familiar to co. Cambridge, where it is found six centuries ago; cf. the local Sebergham, a parish in co. Cumb., i.e. the *ham* or home of Seberg.

John Seber, co. Camb., 1273. A.
Agnes Siber, co. Oxf., ibid.
1749. Married — Philip Pamplin and Mary Seaber: St. Geo. Chap. Mayfair, p. 153.
MDB. (co. Camb.), 5; London, 1; Boston (U.S.), 3.

Seaborn, Seaborne, Seabourne.—Bapt. 'the son of Sebern.' Icelandic Sigbjorn; cf. Osborne. Sebern did not impress itself strongly on English nomenclature.

Alexander Sebern, co. Hunts, 1273. A.
William Seberne, co. Oxf., ibid.
Geoffrey Sebern, co. Camb., ibid.
1581. William Seiborne, co. Ches.: Reg. Univ. Oxf. vol. ii. pt. ii. p. 100.
1789. Married — Robert Seaborn and Mary Banting: St. Geo. Han. Sq. ii. 21.
1797. — William Arnett and Ann Seaborne: ibid. p. 161.
1805. — Thomas Preece and Mary Seabourn: ibid. p. 327.
London, 4, 2, 1; MDB. (co. Essex), 5, 1, 0; Philadelphia, 0, 0, 2.

Seabright, Siebert, Sebright, Seabert.—(1) Bapt. 'the son of Sigbert,' the English form of which was Seabert (Yonge, ii. 309) or Seabright. (2) Local, 'of Sebright.' 'William Sebright, of Sebright, in Much Baddow, co. Essex, living in the reign of Henry II, was the ancestor of this ancient family, who removed into Worcestershire at an early period': Lower, quoting Shirley's Noble and Gentle Men.

Sybryth fil. Roberti, co. Suff., 1273. A.
Richard Sebriht, co. Oxf., ibid.
Simon Sebright, C. R., 18 Edw. I.
1601. Edward Sebright, co. Worc.: Reg. Univ. Oxf. vol. ii. pt. ii. p. 254.
1604. Married — John Sebright and Wynnifride Whitehead: St. Dionis Backchurch, p. 15.

The above is interesting, as the spelling in the licence varies:

1604. John Seabright and Winifred Whitehead: Marriage Lic. (London), i. 289.
London, 1, 4, 0; New York, 0, 50, 0; Philadelphia (Seabert), 3.

Seabrook, Seabrooke.—Local, 'of Seabrook,' a hamlet in the parish of Ivinghoe, co. Bucks.

1613. Gilbert Seabrooke: Reg. Univ. Oxf. vol. ii. pt. ii. p. 330.
1688. John Seabrook, mayor of Thetford, co. Norf.: FF. ii. 144.
1708. Bapt. — James, s. Jonas Seabrooke: St. Jas. Clerkenwell, i. 42.
MDB. (co. Bedf.), 3, 0; (co. Essex), 14, 4; London, 10, 0; Philadelphia, 2, 0.

Seacombe, Secombe, Seccombe.—Local, 'of Seacombe,' a part-township in the parish of Wallasey, co. Ches. It is manifest, however, that another place in co. Devon or Cornwall is the parent of many of these names.

1630. John Seacome, of Everton: Wills at Chester, ii. 194.
1642. Ralph Seacome, of Liverpool, *alderman* : ibid.
1687. Thomas Seccombe and Eliz. Bolwell: Marriage Alleg. (Canterbury), p. 22.
London, 2, 1, 0; MDB. (co. Cornwall), 0, 5, 4; (co. Devon), 0, 0, 4.

Seafowl.—Nick. 'the sea-fowl.'

Robert Sefoul, co. Oxf., 1273. A.
Ralph Sefughel, C. R., 24 Edw. I.
Alan Sefoul, C. R., 2 Edw. II.
John Sefoughel, Fines Roll, 14 Edw. II.
John Sefoghel, co. Soms., 1 Edw. III: Kirby's Quest, p. 250.
George Sefoul, C. R., 12 Ric. II.
Thomas Sefoule, co. Norf., 1564: FF. vii. 206.

Seager, Seeger, Seaker.—Bapt. 'the son of Sigar'; v. Sayer and Segar.

Henry fil. Sigar, co. Camb., 1273. A.
John Seger, co. Norf., ibid.
William Siger, co. Norf., ibid.
Hillarius Sigar, 25 Edw. I: BBB. p. 542.
John Seger, co. Soms., 1 Edw. III: Kirby's Quest, p. 100.
Eudo fil. Sygar. C.
Eudo fil. Seger. E.
1730. Married—William Quincey and Mary Seager: St. Geo. Han. Sq. i. 8.
London, 19, 4, 1; Boston (U.S.), 3, 0, 0.

Seagrave. — Local, 'of Seagrave,' a parish in the dioc. Peterborough and co. Leicester.

Gilbert de Segrave, co. Camb., 1273. A.
Nicholas de Segrave, co. Hunts, ibid.
John de Segrave, co. Kent, 20 Edw. I. R.

Stephen de Segrave, co. Kent, 20 Edw. I. R.

1700. Buried—John Seagrave, son of John Seagrave, haberdasher of hats: St. Dionis Backchurch, p. 268.

1733. Bapt.—Robert, s. William Seagrave: St. Antholin (London), p. 160.

London, 4; Boston (U.S.), 4.

Seal, Seale, Seel, Seals.—(1) Local, 'at the sele,' i.e. Sale, q.v. A variant. Just as Sale is found as Sales, so Seal has become Seals. (2) Local, 'of Seal,' parishes in cos. Leicester, Surrey, and Kent.

John atte Sele, C. R., 20 Edw. III, pt. i.

1571. Richard Seale, co. Warwick: Reg. Univ. Oxf. vol. ii. pt. ii. p. 57.

1689. Buried—Jane Seale: St. Mary Aldermary, p. 200.

1789. Married—William Seels and Ann Teeboe: St. Geo. Han. Sq. ii. 32.

London, 14, 6, 0, 0; Philadelphia, 22, 0, 9, 7.

Sealey, Sealy; v. Seeley.

Seaman, Semon, Seman, Seamons, Seamans, Seamen. —Bapt. 'the son of Seman,' whence Seaman, genitive Seamans; cf. William and Williams.

John fil. Semanni, 1169: KKK. vi. 14.
Seman de Reston, co. Suff., 1273. A.
Seman le Carpenter, co. Suff., ibid.
Seman Eche, co. Suff., ibid.
Herveus Seman, co. Camb., ibid.
Robert fil. Seman, co. Suff., ibid.
Seaman le Baylif. J.
Seaman Champayne. B.
Seman le Coliar, co. Soms., 1 Edw. III: Kirby's Quest, p. 204.
Robertus Saymon, 1379: P. T. Yorks. p. 206.
Semannus Joye: Pardons Roll, Ric. II. Anno 11, 1387-8.

1795. Married — Charles Button and Susan Seaman: St. Geo. Han. Sq. ii. 127.

London, 7, 2, 0, 1, 0, 0; MDB. (co. Bucks), 0, 0, 0, 3, 0, 0; Philadelphia, 12, 3, 0, 1, 1, 1.

Seamer.—Local, (1)'of Seamer,' a parish in the N. Rid. Yorks; (2) a variant of Seymour, q.v. It is almost certain that (2) is the true parent.

Thomas Semer, co. Soms., 1 Edw. III: Kirby's Quest, p. 204.
Thomas de Semer, 25 Edw. III: Freemen of York (Surt. Soc.), i. 47.

1657. Married — Richard Seamer, barber-chirurgion, and Martha Greenhill: St. Geo. Han. Sq. p. 37.

1744. — William Wyatt and Eliz. Seamour: St. Geo. Han. Sq. i. 34.

1780. — William Seamer and Eliz. Goode: ibid. p. 309.

London, 2.

Seanor.—Nick. 'the senior,' a corruption of a great Yorkshire surname; v. Senior.

West Rid. Court Dir., 2.

Sear, Sears, Searson, Seare, Seares, Serson.—Bapt. 'the son of Sayer,' q.v. All unmistakable descendants of the great Northern personal name that has made such an impression on English nomenclature. Sears is the genitive of Sear as Williams is the genitive of William. Sears = Searson.

Walter fil. Sere, co. Notts, 1273. A.
Seur lu Faber, co. Camb., ibid.
Seer de Freville, co. Camb., ibid.
Godwin Seer, co. Camb., ibid.
Thomas Seer, co. Camb., ibid.

1611. Married—William Searson and Alice Mason: St. Mary Aldermary (London), p. 12.

1790. — John Sears and Sarah Elliott: St. Geo. Han. Sq. ii. 45.

1795. — Edward Martindale and Mary Seare: ibid. p. 139.

1807. — Thomas Willshire and Eliz. Searson: ibid. p. 369.

London, 8, 6, 1, 4, 3, 0; Crockford (Serson), 1; Philadelphia (Sears), 23.

Seargeant. — Offic. ' the sergeant'; v. Serjeant, one of many variants.

1754. Thomas Jackson and Katherine Seargeant: St. Geo. Han. Sq. i. 52.

London, 1.

Searl(e, Searles; v. Serle.

Seaton.—Local, ' of Seaton,' parishes and townships in cos. Cumberland, Devon, Durham, Rutland, Yorks (E. Rid.), and Northumberland.

Richard de Seton, or Setoune, co. Devon, 1273. A.
Elena de Seton, co. York, ibid.
John de Seton, co. Cumb., 20 Edw. I. R.
John de Seton, co. Northumb., ibid.
Isabella de Sayton', webester, 1379: P. T. Yorks. p. 221.
Johannes de Sayton', marchant, 1379: ibid.

1626. Bapt.—Ann, d. Joseph Seaton: St. Jas. Clerkenwell, i. 103.

London, 11; West Rid. Court Dir., 6; New York, 2.

Seaward; v. Seward (2).

Sebley.—Bapt. ' the son of Sybil '; v. Sibley.

1806. Married—Edward Taylor and Jane Sebley: St. Geo. Han. Sq. ii. 343.

London, 2.

Seburgham. — Local, 'of Sebergham'; v. Seaber.

Henry de Seburgham, co. Cumb. R.

Secker.—(1) Bapt. 'the son of Seger' or Segger; v. Seager; cf. Slagg and Slack. No doubt it is a sharpened pronunciation of Segger. (2) Occup. ' the sacker,' a maker of sacks; v. Sacker.

John le Sekker, 9 Edw. III: Freemen of York, i. 29.

Icelandic sekkr (Skeat).

Gilbert Segger, co. Devon, 1273. A.

1754. Married—John Secker and Jane Baxter: St. Geo. Chap. Mayfair, p. 273.

1776. — William Sacheverell and Jane Secker: St. Geo. Han. Sq. i. 260.

London, 5; Philadelphia, 3.

Secombe; v. Seacombe.

Secular.—Offic. ' the secular,' one unbound by monastic rules; the opposite to religious.

'Religious folke ben full covert,
Secular folke ben more apert.'

Walter le Seculer, co. Salop, 1273. A.
Alice la Seculere, fil. and coh. Henrici le Seculer, Close Roll, 6 Edw. I.
Alexander le Seculer. L.
Nicholas le Secular. B.

Seddon.—Local, ' of Seddon,' some spot in south-west Lancashire, which I cannot find. The surname is well distributed over Lancashire, and has found its way into distant parts of the world.

1615. Laurence Seddon, co. Lanc.: Reg. Univ. Oxf. vol. ii. pt. ii. p. 348.

1627. John Seddon, of Liverpool: Wills at Chester, i. 194.

1638. Michael Seddon, of Pilkington, yeoman: ibid.

— Margaret Seddon, of Winwick: ibid.

Manchester, 17; MDB. (co. Ches.), 4; London, 1; Philadelphia, 8.

Sedgwick, Sidgwick.—Local, ' of Sedgwick,' a township in the parish of Heversham, four miles from Kendal, co. Westm. The surname has ramified strongly. The prefix is evidently the personal name of the first settler in the wick (v. Wike) and a compound of sig; cf. Sigismund, Sigmund, Sigward, Sigwald (v. Miss Yonge, i. cxxiii); cf. also Segar and Sayer.

Johannes de Segheswyk, 1379: P. T. Yorks. p. 288.
Willelmus de Seglewyk, 1379: ibid.
Robertus de Seglewyk, 1379: ibid.

The above are from Dent, near Sedgwick.

Thomas de Sigeswik, 1379: ibid. p. 237.
Elizabeth Sigeswicke, of Botton, 1580:
Lancashire Wills at Richmond, i. 251.
George Sigeswicke, of Tatham, 1584:
Lancashire Wills at Richmond, i. 251.
Thomas Sigswicke, of Lancaster, 1624:
ibid.
London, 13, 2; West Rid. Court Dir.,
9, 5; Philadelphia, 6, 0.

Seear.—Bapt. 'the son of
Sayer'; v. Sear. This is quite a
modern variant—one more surname
that owns the famous Segar for its
parent.

1805. Married — Thomas Seear and
Kezia Ivory: St. Geo. Han. Sq. ii. 328.
London, 8.

Seeger; v. Seager.

Seekins, Seekings.—Bapt.'the
son of Segin.' This personal name,
in early records almost peculiar to
Cambridgeshire, seems to have
settled down into Seekins, the
final *s* being patronymic as in
Williams, the *g* in Seekings being
an excrescence as in Jennings.

Richard Segin, co. Linc., 1273. A.
Alan Segin, co. Camb., ibid.
John Segyn, co. Camb., ibid.

Also spelt Segeyn. It is interesting to note that the surname is
still well-nigh confined to co.
Cambridge.

1757. Married—Thomas Seekins and
Mary Wilkins: St. Geo. Han. Sq. i. 74.
Cambridge, 1, 0; MDB. (co. Cam-
bridge), 1, 1; London, 1, 0.

**Seeley, Seelie, Seely, Sealey,
Sealy, Seelye.**—(1) Nick. 'the
seely,' the simple, the innocent,
the harmless; cf. Simple. 'Seely
= simple, silly' (Halliwell).

'This sely carpenter beginneth quake.'
Chaucer, C. T. 3601.

William Sely, co. Oxf., 1273. A.
Egidius Sely, co. Norf., ibid.
John Sely, co. Glouc., ibid.
Thomas Sely, London, 20 Edw. I. R.

(2) Bapt. 'the son of Cecil,' from
the nick. Sill and pet Sillie; cf.
Willie, Charlie, &c. (v. Silcock).
There can scarcely be the shadow
of a doubt as to this being a chief
parent of the surname.

Sely atte Bergh, co. Soms., 1 Edw. III:
Kirby's Quest, p. 266.
Sely Percy, co. Soms., 1 Edw. III:
ibid.
Sely Scury, co. Soms., 1 Edw. III:
ibid. p. 205.

William Sely, co. Soms., 1 Edw. III:
ibid. p. 268.
1618-9. John Symonds and Anne
Seley: Marriage Lic. (London), ii. 69.
1621-2. William Stanmore and Margaret Seely: ibid. p. 109.
1760. Bapt.—William Jeffrey, son of
W. Jeffrey Sealy: St. Peter, Cornhill, i. 48.
London, 9, 1, 1, 3, 7, 0; Philadelphia,
20, 0, 5, 5, 2, 2.

Sefton.—Local; v. Sephton.

Segar, Seger.—Bapt. 'the son
of Sigar'; for instances, v. Seager.

Penketh, near Warrington, 1, 0;
Southport, 1, 0; Boston (U.S.), 1, 1.

Selby.—Local, 'of Selby,' a
parish and market-town in E. Rid.
Yorks.

William de Seleby, co. York, 1273. A.
Robert de Selby, *barber*, 34 Edw. I:
Freemen of York, i. 11.
Johannes de Selby, 1379: P. T. Yorks.
p. 100.
Willelmus de Selby, 1379: ibid. p. 136.
1618. Bapt. — Edward, s. George
Selbye: St. Jas. Clerkenwell, i. 81.
London, 23; West Rid. Court Dir., 2;
Philadelphia, 14.

Selden, Seldon.—Local, 'of
Selden.' I cannot find the spot.

Ansell de Seleden, cos. Warw. and
Leic., Hen. III-Edw. I. K.
1600. John Selden, co. Sussex: Reg.
Univ. Oxf. vol. ii. pt. ii. p. 242.
1789. Married — Daniel Selden and
Mary Gray: St. Geo. Han. Sq. ii. 32.
London, 2, 1; Philadelphia, 5, 1.

Self, Selfe.—(1) Local, 'of
Shelf' (?), a village in the union
of Halifax. The third entry is
strongly confirmatory of this
origin. (2) Bapt. 'the son of
Seleth' (v. Selth). I suspect this
is the true parent of the great
majority of our Selfs, &c.

Cristiana del Schelf, 1379: P. T. Yorks.
p. 181.
Johannes de Schelf, 1379: ibid.
Ricardus Scelue (*u* for *v*), 1379: ibid.
p. 278.
1639. Married — Randdall Selfe and
Alice Reaman: St. Michael, Cornhill,
p. 28.
London, 9, 3; Boston (U.S.), 2, 2.

Selkirk.—Local, 'of Selkirk,'
the county town of Selkirkshire.

London, 1; Philadelphia, 5.

Sellar(s; v. Seller(s.

Selleck, Sellick.—Local, 'of
Sellack,' a parish in co. Hereford,
near Ross. The following entries

are quite sufficient to prove the
derivation:

1603. John Sellak, co. Somerset: Reg.
Univ. Oxf. vol. ii. pt. ii. p. 265.

A note appended says: 'Sellack.
There was a family of Selleckes
at Lydiard St. Lawrence, Somerset.'

1595. Nicholas Sellecke, or Sellick, co.
Somerset: Reg. Univ. Oxf. vol. ii. pt. ii.
p. 209.
1676-7. Thomas Wyne and Theophila
Selleck, of Wells, co. Somerset: Marriage Alleg. (Canterbury), p. 264.
1795. Married — William Sellick and
Sarah Saville: St. Geo. Han. Sq. ii. 139.
MDB. (co. Devon), 2, 1; (co. Somerset),
0, 6; London, 0, 2; Philadelphia, 0, 4.

Seller, Sellar.—Occup. 'the
seller,' a saddler. M.E. *selle*, a
seat. O.F. '*selle*, a stool, a seat,
also a saddle': Cotg. '*Sele*, horsys
harneys': Prompt. Parv. '*Seale*,
horse harnesse': Palsgrave. The
'Sellers ("sadellers", written over),
Verrours, and Fuystours' (v.
Fewster) went together in the
York Pageant (York Mystery Plays,
ed. Toulmin Smith, p. xxvi).

Bartholomew Sellarius, co. Kent, 1273. A.
Henry Sellarius, co. Warw., ibid.
Richard Sellarius, London, ibid.
Warin le Seler, temp. 1300. M.
John le Seler. G.
Hugh le Seler. O.
1615. Bapt.—George, s. Thomas Sellor:
St. Jas. Clerkenwell, i. 72.
1809. Married — Joshua Hartley and
Harriet Sellar: St. Geo. Han. Sq. ii. 409.
London, 3, 2; Philadelphia, 3, 0.

Sellers, Sellars.—Local, 'of
the cellar.' Practically official =
the cellarer, the same as Butler
or Buttery, q.v. This has become
one of the most familiar of Yorkshire surnames, with an *s* at the
end; cf. Briggs, Styles, and Brooks.
Attached no doubt to one of the
monasteries or feudal houses.

Adam de Celer, co. York, 1273. A.
Roger del Celer, co. York, ibid.
Alicia del Seler, 1379: P. T. Yorks.
p. 157.
Adam del Seler', 1379: ibid. p. 238.
Juliana del Seler', 1379: ibid.
Agnes del Seler', 1379: ibid. p. 296.
1617. Bapt. — Robert, s. Thomas
Sellers: St. Jas. Clerkenwell, i. 79.
London, 2, 1; Sheffield, 4, 7; West
Rid. Court Dir., 7, 1; Philadelphia, 73, 0.

Sellick; v. Selleck.

Sellinger.—Local, 'of St. Leger,'
a chapelry in Normandy (?). Cf.
St. John, Sinclair, Simple, &c.

Geoffrey de St. Leodegare, co. Sussex, 1273. A.
1386. Isabel de St. Legar: FF. vii. 220.
Thomas Sentlegar, Norwich, temp. Ric. III: ibid. iii. 173.
1630. Buried—The lady Thornix, wife of Mr. Anthony Sellinger: Canterbury Cath. p. 118.
Philadelphia, 1; New York, 1.

Sellman, Sellmon, Selman, Seelman, Selmond.—(1) Bapt. 'the son of Seliman,' i.e. Solomon; v. Salamon and Salman. No connexion with *sale*, a hall, as suggested by Lower. The *d* in Selmond is an excrescence; cf. Simmonds for Simmons, or Salmond for Salmon.

Cecilia fil. Selmon, co. Hunts, 1273. A.
Simon Seliman, co. Bucks, ibid.
William Seliman, co. Wilts, ibid.
Thomas Selman, co. Camb., ibid.

(2) ? Nick. 'the silly man,' i.e. the innocent, quiet man (v. Seeley, 1); or 'the servant of Silly,' a well-known personal name in the West country; cf. Matthewman, Addyman, &c.; v. Seeley(2).

Gregory Selyman, co. Soms., 1 Edw. III : Kirby's Quest, p. 79.
Walter Selyman, co. Soms., 1 Edw. III : ibid. p. 143.
1569. Bapt. — Robarte Selman, s. Robert Sellman (sic): St. Dionis Backchurch, p. 81.
1693. — Daniel, s. Robert Sellman : St. Jas. Clerkenwell, i. 353.
London, 1, 1, 1, 1, 0; Philadelphia, 0, 0, 1, 0, 1.

Selmes.—Local, 'at the selm' (?), from residence thereby (?). ' *Selms*, gate-rails. Northumberland' (Halliwell).

John atte Selme, co. Soms., 1 Edw. III : Kirby's Quest, p. 87.
London, 2; New York, 2.

Selth, Self, Selfe.—Bapt. 'the son of Seleth.' The order of corruption was very simple, as follows: Seleth, Selth, and Self or Selfe. But for a second derivation, v. Self. Nevertheless, Seleth was so popular that it must have made its mark on our permanent nomenclature, and I doubt not Selth, Self, and Selfe are its offspring.

Selade (without surname), co. Bedf., 1273. A.
Selede (without surname), co. Camb., ibid.
Herveus fil. Selede, co. Camb., ibid.
Selithe de Wenham, co. Suff., ibid.
Robert Seled, co. Oxf., ibid.

Eustace Selede, co. Camb., 1273. A.
1775. Married—William Goodall and Mary Selfe: St. Geo. Han. Sq. i. 251.
1775. Married — John Self and Eliz. Larner: ibid. p. 253.

Selth lingered on as a surname in the district in which as a personal name it arose.

1722. William Selth, rector of Folsham, co. Norf.: FF. viii. 209.
London, 2, 9, 3; Boston (U.S.), 0, 2, 2.

Selwyn, Selwin.—Bapt. 'the son of Selwin,' one of the almost endless compounds in *-win*; cf. Sherwin, Unwin, Godwin, Baldwin, &c.

Hugo Salveyn, co. Linc., Hen. III-Edw. I. K.
Osbert Selveyn, co. Linc., ibid.
Geoffrey Selveyn, co. Linc., ibid.
Willelmus Shilwyn, 1379 : P. T. Yorks. p. 163.
Agnes Saluayne, 1379 : ibid. p. 52.
Nicholas Selewyne, Pat. Roll, 8 Ric. II, pt. ii.
1622. Bapt. — William, s. William Selwin : St. Jas. Clerkenwell, i. 93.
London, 1, 0; Philadelphia, 0, 1.

Seman, Semon; v. Seaman.

Semper.—Local, 'of St. Pierre,' probably a chapelry in Normandy; cf. Sinclair, Simple, Sellinger, &c.

Urian de St. Petro, co. Salop, 1273. A.
Nicholas de Seyntpiere, C. R., 19 Edw. II, pt. ii.
Thomas le (? de) Seintepier, co. Ches., 1383 : East Cheshire, ii. 234.
David le (? de) Seintepier, co. Ches., 1383 : ibid.
Richard Semper, alias Sentpyer, C. R., 1-2 Philip and Mary, pt. v.
1613. Buried — Owen Sempeer : St. Antholin (London), p. 50.
1628. Married — John Samues and Margret Simper : St. Mary Aldermary (London), p. 16.
Crockford, 1; Philadelphia, 1.

Semple, Sempill.—Local, 'of St. Paul,' probably some chapelry in Normandy. Not to be confounded with Simple (q.v.), although, no doubt, now inextricably mixed; cf. Sinclair, Semper, Sellinger, &c.

William de Sainpol, Hen. III-Edw. I. K
Gunilda de St. Paul, co. Linc., 1273. A.
John de St. Paull', co. Oxf., ibid.
Emulda de St. Paul, co. Linc., ibid.
Willelmus Sayndepaule, 1379 : P. T. Yorks. p. 20.
Johannes Seynpoule, 1379 : ibid. p. 21.
Johanna Sayntpaule, 1379 : ibid. p. 117.
1626. William Mackphell and Barbara Semple : Marriage Lic. (London), ii. 167.

London, 5, 1; West Rid. Court Dir., 1, 0; Philadelphia, 19, 0.

Sempster, Simister, Semister.—Occup. 'the sempster,' i.e. sempstress, a common entry for women. Without doubt some of the North-English Simisters (perhaps all) are thus derived. But v. Simister.

Cristiana de Belthorp', *semster*, 1379 : P. T. Yorks. p. 231.
Elizabetha Semster, 1379 : ibid. p. 197.
Sissot Seymster, 1379 : ibid. p. 100.
Isabella Semester, 1379 : ibid. p. 249.
Margareta Semester, 1379 : ibid. p. 235.
Elen Semster, co. York. W. 2.
Emma Semister, co. York. W. 9.
Hellen Semster, co. York. W. 16.
Isabella Maw, *semster*, in Fosgate, York, 1433. W. 11.
Manchester, 0, 12, 0; West Rid. (Yorks) Court Dir., 0, 1, 0; Philadelphia, 0, 0, 1.

Senecal. — Bapt. 'the son of Senicle.'

Senecle (without surname), co. Bucks, 1273. A.
Stephen Sinckel, co. Suff., ibid.
Senicula le Wright, Pat. Roll, 6 Edw. III.
Thomas Senycle, C. R., 18 Ric. II.
Thomas Synykill, Pat. Roll, 1 Hen. IV, pt. v.
1509. Thomas Senycle, official to the Archdeacon of Norwich: FF. iii. 660.
1775. Married — George Senegal and Sarah Womack: St. Geo. Han. Sq. i. 253.
London, 1.

Senhouse.—Local, ' of Sevenhouse' or Senhouse, in the parish of Cross Canonby, co. Cumb. Still found in the neighbourhood of Maryport. A well-known Cumberland family.

Walter de Sevenhouse, temp. Edw. III : Hutchinson's Cumberland, ii. 268.
Thomas de Senhous, C. R., 9 Ric. II.
John Senhouse, vicar of Trimdon, 1501 : DDD. i. 108.
Thomas Senowys: Visit. Yorks., 1563, p. 181.
1617. John Senhouse, co. Cumb. Reg. Univ. Oxf. vol. ii. pt. ii. p. 365.
1635. Richard Senhouse, rector of Claughton : Lancashire Wills at Richmond, i. 247.
MDB. (co. Cumb.), 3.

Senior, Senier, Seanor, Saynor, Synyer.—Nick. 'the senior,' i.e. the older of two or more persons, generally of the same personal name. This mode of expression is as early as the 13th and 14th centuries, and is very commonly found in the Yorkshire Poll Tax, 1379. The cause is simple. John was so popular that not only father and son, but two and three brothers would often bear the name. For instances, v. my Curiosities of Puritan Nomenclature, pp. 4, 5.

Johannes Holynghege, senior, 1379: P. T. Yorks. p. 172.
Johannes Holynghege, junior, 1379: ibid.
Johannes Bullok, senior, 1379: ibid. p. 2.
Johannes Bullok, junior, 1379: ibid.
Cf. Ricardus ye Elder, 1379: ibid. p. 214 (v. Elder).

Hence such an entry as:
Willelmus Synyer, 1379: P. T. Yorks. p. 233.

Johannes Seygnour, 1379: ibid. p. 9.
Michael le Seigneur. E.
William le Seignour, 1302. M.
Edmund Seignyowr, co. York. W. 2.
Thomas Senior, co. York. W. 16.
'Mr. H. Synyer, of Nottingham, came first in the Two-mile Bicycle Race': Manchester Courier, Sept. 19, 1887.
West Riding Court Dir., 21, 0, 2, 0, 0; London, 10, 1, 0, 0, 0; Sheffield (Saynor), 5; Philadelphia, 14, 0, 0, 0, 0.

Sennett, Sennitt, Synnot, Sunnett, Sennott, Sinnott, Sinnett, Synett, Synnott, Synnet, Sennet. — Bapt. 'the son of Senot' or Sunot. A girl's name, but it is not mentioned in Miss Yonge's book, and I can glean no more of its history than what is recorded below. Its place as a feminine baptismal name is well marked, and that it has obtained permanent surnominal honours our directories fully prove.

Stephen Sinot, co. Suff., 1273. A.
Richard fil. Sunod, co. Hunts, ibid.
Sunod Silvestre, co. Hunts, ibid.
Sunnota fil. Jakelini, 3 Edw. I: BBB. p. 219.
Johanna fil. Sunnotoe, 3 Edw. I: ibid.
Helias stori et Senota uxor ejus, 1379: P. T. Yorks. p. 120.
Johannes Sinhit, 1379: ibid.
1673. John Sinnott (co. Kent) and Barbara White: Marriage Alleg. (Canterbury), p. 214.
MDB. (co. Camb.), 2, 5, 0, 0, 0, 0, 0, 0, 0, 0, 0; Manchester, 0, 0, 0, 1, 0, 0, 0, 0, 0, 0; New York, 1, 0, 0, 0, 0, 20, 1, 0, 0, 1, 1; Boston (U.S.), 0, 0, 0, 0, 0, 16, 17, 4, 3, 1, 0.

Senskell, Sensecal. — Offic. 'the seneschal,' a steward.

Alexander le Seneschal. B.
William le Seneschal. H.
Ivo Seneschallus. T.
1693. Married — John Henry Beckman and Sarah Senskell: St. Mary Aldermary (London), p. 35.
1793. — Richard Dearlove and Mary Senescall: St. Geo. Han. Sq. ii. 95.
1805. — Joseph Augustus Seneschal and Ann Dicker: ibid. p. 333.
MDB. (co. Oxford), 0, 1.

Sephton, Sefton.—Local, 'of Sephton,' a parish in co. Lanc., seven miles from Liverpool.

Thomas Sefton, of Skelmersdale, 1593: Wills at Chester, i. 171.
Robert Sephton, of Mollington, 1602: ibid.
1754. Married—Richard Etherington and Mary Sefton: St. Geo. Chap. Mayfair, p. 282.
1806. — Robert Page and Mary Sefton: St. Geo. Han. Sq. ii. 349.
London, 0, 2; Liverpool, 2, 4; Philadelphia, 1, 0.

Serf.—Occup. 'the serf' (?).
Emma le Cerf: Fines Roll, 17 Edw. II.

Sergeantston. — Local. Not to be confounded with Sergeantson.
Ricardus de Sergerstane, 1379: P. T. Yorks. p. 58.
West Riding Court Dir., 1.

Serjeant, Sergeant, Sergent, Sargant, Sargeant, Sargeaunt, Sargent, Sarjant, Sarjeant, Sarjent, Seargeant.—Offic. 'the sergeant' or serjeant, an officer of the law, a policeman. Few surnames have undergone more varieties of spelling than this. Even in our latest dictionaries two forms are recognized. Agreeing with O.F. sergant and serjant, Serjaunt is the commonest form in early rolls.

John le Serjaunt, co. Bucks, 1273. A.
Walter le Serjaunt, co. Camb., ibid.
John le Serjant, co. Salop, ibid.
Robert Sergant, co. Camb., ibid.
Roger le Serjaunt, co. Norf., ibid.
Nicholas le Serjaunt, co. Linc., 20 Edw. I. R.
Thomas Elys, serjaunt, 1379: P. T. Yorks. p. 97.
London, 3, 3, 1, 4, 8, 1, 16, 2, 1, 1, 1; Philadelphia, 0, 8, 0, 0, 5, 0, 26, 0, 0, 0, 0.

Serjeantson, Sergeantson, Serginson, Sarginson, Sergerson, Sergeson, Sergison, Sergason.—Nick. 'the son of the serjeant,' q.v.; cf. Taylorson, Wrightson, and Smithson. This class of names (a very small one) seems almost peculiar to Yorkshire (v. Taylorson). There can be no doubt that that county is the home of the family.

Willelmus Sergantson, 1379: P. T. Yorks. p. 299.
Johannes Serigantson, 1379: ibid. p. 12.
Thomas Sergeauntson. H.
Thomas Sargandson, co. York. W. 11.
Henry Serchauntson, co. York, ibid.
Mary Sergison, co. York. W. 16.
William Surgisson embarked for Virginia, 1634: Hotten's Lists of Emigrants, p. 36.

This early emigrant was twenty-five years old. Probably the American Sergersons, Sergesons, and Sergisons are his descendants.

Exeter (Sergason), 1; Manchester (Serginson), 1, (Sarginson), 1; Crockford (Sergeantson), 2; West Riding Court Dir., 1, 1, 0, 0, 0, 0, 0, 0; Philadelphia, 0, 0, 0, 0, 1, 11, 3, 0.

Serle, Searle, Serrell, Serlson, Searles, Serrill, Serrills, Searl.—Bapt. 'the son of Serle.' Searle is the common present surnominal form. Serle is the old baptismal form. Searles or Serrills is the genitive of Searl; cf. William and Williams.

Serle Gotokirke, co. Camb., 1273. A.
Osbert fil. Serlonis, co. Hunts, ibid.
Richard Serle, co. Camb., ibid.
Hugh Serlson, temp. 1300. M.
Richard Serelson, temp. 1300. M.
William Serleson, co. York. W. 2.
Thomas Serlson, 1379: P. T. Yorks. p. 213.
John Serlson, 1379: ibid.
Serill Pynder, 1379: ibid. p. 254.
Serell de Westwik, 1379: ibid. p. 260.
Robert Serlys, 1512: Reg. Univ. Oxf. i. 220.
John Seryll, or Serell, 1553: ibid. i. 79.
1732. Married — Humphry Searls and Hester Bayley: St. Jas. Clerkenwell, i. 259.
London, 1, 40, 2, 0, 3, 0, 0, 0; Sheffield (Searls), 2; Philadelphia, 0, 11, 0, 0, 13, 8, 4, 5.

Sermoner.—Offic. 'the sermoner,' one who preached sermons. 'Sermonen, to preach': O.E. Homilies, i. 81, l. 14. In the North they still talk of 'listning to th' sarmon.'

'Quen He sendes his messageres,
That es at say, thir sarmonneres.'
English Metrical Homilies, p. 147, John Small, Edinb. 1862.

Richard le Sarmuner. E.
William le Sarmoner, Hen. III. T

Richard Sarmoner, co. Soms., 1 Edw. III : Kirby's Quest, p. 118.
'I find the name John le Sarmoner occurring in a deed dated 1316 ': E. H. in N. and Q., March 12, 1887.

Serrill(s ; v. Serle.

Serson ; v. Sear.

Servant, Servent. — Occup. 'the servant.' A Yorkshire surname, found so early as the 14th century.

Seman Serviens, co. Norf., 1273. A.
Sewall Serviens, co. Norf., ibid.
Robertus Westrin, 1379 : P, T. Yorks. p. 39.
Ricardus serviens dicti Roberti, 1379 : ibid.
Johannes Cowper, *glover*, 1379 : ibid. p. 41.
Johannes serviens ejus, 1379 : ibid.
Emma Seruantman, 1379 : ibid. p. 56.
Willelmus Seruantman, 1379 : ibid.p.63.
1699. Bapt. — Frances, d. John Servant : St. Jas. Clerkenwell, i. 383.
Leeds, 2, 1 ; West Rid. Court Dir., 2, o.

Servelady.—Nick. for a lady's maid.
Avice Serueladi, Close Roll, 1 Edw. II.
In the Yorkshire Poll Tax (1379) there are many such entries for the bower-maiden ; v Ladyman.

Setchell.—? Bapt.; v. Satchell.
Oxford, 1.

Setter.—Occup. ' the setter,' supposed to be the same as *tipper*, one who fixed arrow-heads to the shaft.
'Sponers, torners, and hatters, Lyne-webbers, setters, with lyne-drapers.'
　　　　　Cocke Lorelle's Bote.
Clement le Settere. N.
Alexander le Settere, London. X.
John de Belegame, *setter*, 18 Edw. III : Freemen of York, i. 37.
Robertus Cetter, 1379 : P. T. Yorks. p. 261.
Walter Setter, C. R., 9 Hen. IV.
1685. Thomas Harford and Barbary Setter : Marriage Alleg. (Canterbury), p. 196.
London, 1.

Setterington. — Local, ' of Settrington,' a parish in E. Rid. Yorks.
Robert de Seterinton, co.York, 1273. A.
William de Seteringron, *wayder*, 4 Edw. II : Freemen of York, i. 13.
For the occupative term *wayder*, v. Wader.
1804. Married—John Watson and Jane Setterington : St. Geo. Han. Sq. ii. 308.
MDB. (E. Rid. Yorks), 3.

Settle.—Local, ' of Settle,' a parish in W. Rid. Yorks.
Alicia de Settle, 1379 : P. T. Yorks. p. 273.
Johannes de Setle, 1379 : ibid. p. 272.
Johannes de Setill', 1379 : ibid. p. 145.
Hugh Settle, of Cartmell, 1594 : Lancashire Wills at Richmond, i. 247.
James Settle, of Tatham, 1671 : ibid.
1689. Richard Benson and Eliz. Settle (co. Lincoln) : Marriage Alleg. (Canterbury), p. 195.
London, 2 ; West Rid. Court Dir., 3 ; Philadelphia, 11.

Sevenpence.—Nick. ; cf. Ninepence and Twelvepence.
Robert Seuchepens (*u* for *v*), Pardons Roll, 5 Ric. II (Suffolk).

Severe, Sever, Seaver. — Nick. ' the severe,' i.e. the grave, the austere in manner and demeanour.
John le Severe, co. Hunts, 1273. A.
Henry Sever, co. Norf., 1441 : FF. iii. 535.
John Seaver, co. Berks, 1616 : Reg. Univ. Oxf. vol. ii. pt. ii. p. 356.
Manchester, o, 1, o ; Philadelphia, o, o, 7.

Seville ; v. Savill.

Seward (1).—Occup. ' a sowherd ' ; cf. Calvert, Coward, Stoddard, &c. But v. Seward (2).
Alicia Sueherd, 1379 : P. T. Yorks. p. 158.

Seward (2), **Seaward, Sewards, Suart.** — Bapt. ' the son of Siward ' (Yonge, ii. 308).
Syward Godwin. J.
Siward Oldcorn. L.
Siward, Earl of the Northumbrians, Freeman, Norm. Conq. i. 515.
Siward, Abbot of Abingdon, ibid. ii. 67.
Cf. Sewardstone, co. Essex, and Sewardesley, co. Northampton.
Siward de Liment', ipe Roll, 5 Hen. II.
Sygwat Kat'bode, co. Norf., 1273. A.
Syward (without surname), co. Oxf., ibid.
Sywardus (without surname), co. Oxf., ibid.
Thomas Sywat, co. Suff., ibid.
Richard Syward, co. Bucks, ibid.
Hugo Syward, 1379 : P. T. Yorks. p. 52.
Johanna Syward, 1379 : ibid. p. 70.
1728. Bapt.—Ann, d. John Suertt : St. Jas. Clerkenwell, ii. 176.
London, 7, 8, 1, 2 ; Philadelphia, 7, 0, o, o.

Sewell, Sewill, Sewelson, Sewall, Sewalt.—Bapt. ' the son of Sewal ' (v. Sigwald in Miss Yonge's History of Christian Names, ii. 310).
Sewallus de Cleton, co. Hertf., 1273. A.
Sewale de Retcote, co. Oxf., ibid.
Robert fil. Sew', co. Northants, ibid.
Thomas Sewald, co. Oxf., ibid.
Godard Sewale, co. Camb., ibid.
Sewal atte Ponde, temp. 1300. M.
Sewall Dapifer. J.
As a personal name Sewal lingered on into the 16th century :
Sewall Worth, of Titherington, co. Ches., 1520 : East Cheshire, ii. 290.
The modern English form is Sewell. The United States have preserved Sewall from oblivion.
1586. Francis Hodges and Joanna Sewell : Marriage Lic. (Westminster), p. 9.
1664. Robert Sewell and Jane Ryves : Marriage Alleg. (Canterbury), p. 82.
London, 52, 2, 0, 0, 0 ; Manchester, 8, 0, 1, 0, 0 ; Philadelphia, 11, 0, 0, 2, 1 ; Boston (U.S.) (Sewall), 13.

Sewer.—Offic. ' the sewer,' an officer who brought in and took away the dishes, one who superintended the ' courses' at table, from O.F. *sevre, suir*, to follow. A substantive ' sewes,' dishes, is found in Chaucer, who, describing the rich feasts of Cambuscan, King of Tartary, says time would fail him to tell
' Of their strange sewes,'
which may be from the same root. But see Skeat, *sewer* (2), and Wedgwood. ' Seware, at mete, *dapifer* ': Prompt. Parv. ' Sewyn, at mete, or sette mete, *ferculo, sepulo* ': ibid.
Robert le Suur, 1273. A.
Nicholas le Suur, ibid.
Henry le Suur. G.
Geoffrey le Suur, Close Roll, 50 Hen. III.
All these references seem to point to O.F. *sevre*, and connect themselves naturally with such words as *sue, ensue, pursue*, &c.
1637. Richard Sewer and Eliz. Poulter : Marriage Lic. (Westminster), p. 37.
1675. Richard Vokins and Eliz. Sewer : Marriage Alleg. (Canterbury), p. 145.

Sewster.—Occup. ' the sewster,' one who sewed ; cf. Simister. The suffix is the feminine -*ster*. Cf. Brewster, Webster, and Kempster.
1383. Robert Sewstere, vicar of Gateley, co. Norf. : FF. ix. 506.

1548. Nicholas Sewester and Juliana Cave: Marriage Lic. (Canterbury), p. 14.
1802. Married — John Seuster and Martha Cull : St. Geo. Han. Sq. ii. 266.

Sexsmith ; v. Shoesmith, an American variant.

Philadelphia, 1.

Sexton ; v. Saxton.

Seymour, Seymer, Seamer.
—Local, (1) 'of St. Maur,' some forgotten chapelry in Normandy. Local, (2) 'of Semer,' a parish in co. Suffolk. Bapt. (3) 'the son of Semar' (i.e. Sigmar ; v. Yonge, ii. 311). All these various names must inevitably be mixed now, the tendency being towards the aristocratic Seymour; v. Seamer for a further derivation.

Laurence de Sancto Mauro, co. Derby, 1273. A.
Henry de Sancto Mauro, co. Oxf., ibid.
Richard de Semare, co. Bucks, ibid.
Henry de St. Maur, c. 1300. M.
Richard de Semere, vicar of Hindringham, co. Norf., 1349 : FF. ix. 230.
Elizabeth Seyntmaur. B.
Adam Semar, co. Hunts, 1273. A.
Hewerad Samar, co. Camb., ibid.
William Samar, co. Hunts, ibid.
Johannes Semer, 1379 : P. T. Yorks. p. 100.
Richardus Semar, 1379 : ibid. p. 133.

These last five references evidently concern (3), the personal name. Many of our Seymours are descendants of this Scandinavian personal name, having assumed the form of Seymour in later times.

London, 39, 1, 2 ; Philadelphia, 31, 0, 0.

Seys.—Nick. ; a variant of the Welsh Sayce, q.v.

Shackel, Shackell, Shackells, Shakel, Shakell, Shackle. —
Bapt. 'the son of Shakell' ; cf. the local Shackleton, i.e. the settlement of Shakell, also Shackleford and Shackerley, the latter probably standing for Shackle-ley.

Willelmus Shakelle, 1379 : P. T. Yorks. p. 160.
The Vicarage of Corpesty, co. Norf., 'was sold by Heydon to Thomas Jecks and John Shakle, and by them to the Bacons,' 1611 : FF. vi. 365.

This form still remains in Norfolk, Shackle being found in the Modern Domesday Book for that county.

1597. Married—William Shackle and Jane Durham : St. Mary Aldermary, p. 9.
1761. — Thomas Shackle and Mary Cox : St. Geo. Han. Sq. i. 101.

London, 1, 5, 1, 3, 1, 0 ; MDB. (co. Norf.) (Shackle), 1.

Shackelton, Shackleton.—
Local ; v. Shackel.

London, 1, 3 ; Boston (U.S.), 0, 4.

Shacklady.—? Local, 'of Shackerley' (?) ; v. Shakerley. 'Known in Lancashire as a corruption of the ancient local surname of Shackerley' (Lower). I believe this solution to be the true one. The two surnames have run side by side for many generations. Probably Shackerley was originally Shackel-ley, i.e. the field that belonged to Shackel, the first settler (v. Shackel). This would readily corrupt into Shacklady.

1521. John Stokys and Eliz. Shaklady : Marriage Lic. (London), p. 2.
Hugh Shakerley, of Liverpool, 1623 : Wills at Chester, ii. 194.
Peter Shakerley, 1624 : ibid.
Robert Shakelady, of Wrightington, 1630 : ibid.

MDB. (co. Lanc.), 3 ; Liverpool, 1.

Shackleford, Shackelford.—
Local ; v. Shackel.

Philadelphia, 0, 2.

Shacklock. — (1) Nick. 'a gaoler,' one who fetters his charge :

'And bids his man bring out the five-fold twist,
His shackles, shacklocks, hampers, gyves, and chains.'
Browne's Britannia's Pastorals, i. 129 (Halliwell).

Or perhaps, like Shakespear, Shakelance, and Shakeshaft, from his rattling the keys of incarceration. (2) Bapt. 'the son of Scathlock,' q.v., probably a variant, as found in co. Derby, on the borders of co. Notts.

Hamo Shakeloc, co. Camb., 1273. A.
Simon Shakelok, 1313. M.
1342. John Shakelok, rector of Ashby, co. Norf. : FF. x. 95.
Willelmus Schakelok, 1379 : P. T. Yorks. p. 192.
Johannes Shakelok', 1379 : ibid. p. 65.
Isolda Schakelok', 1379 : ibid. p. 222.
1568. Married—John Skott and Grace Shacklocke : St. Jas. Clerkenwell, i. 4.

London, 2 ; MDB. (co. Derby), 6.

Shadbolt, Shotbolt. —? Nick. 'Shootbolt' (?). A cross-bowman, one who shot bolts from a catapult ; cf. Drawsword, Shakespear, Wagstaff, and a hundred others, all sobriquets of employment, from the weapon or wand carried. Now found as Shadbolt.

Thomas Shotbolt, C. R., 35 Hen. VI.
John Shotbolt : Index to Clutterbuck's Hertfordshire.
Thomas Shotbolte, temp. 1570 : Cal. of Proceedings in Chancery (Elizabeth).

Shadbolt is modern, and clearly a corruption of Shotbolt.

1775. Married—William Shadbolt and Lydia Bratt : St. Geo. Han. Sq. i. 249.

London, 3, 0.

Shadd.—Personal, 'the son of Shad'; cf. the local terms Shadwell, Shadforth, and Shadworth, i.e. the well, or ford, or worth where Shad lived. Probably same as Chad, q.v.

Nicholas Schadd, co. Wilts, 1273. A.
1587. Married — Thomas Woolfe and Cecilia Shadd : Marriage Lic. (London), i. 164.
1693. — Thomas Shadd and Mary Henfrey : St. Jas. Clerkenwell, iii. 213.

Philadelphia, 5.

Shadforth.—Local, 'of Shadforth,' a township in the parish of Pittington, co. Durham. v. Ford and Forth.

1618-9. Thomas Shadford and Amy Rotherie : Marriage Lic. (London), ii. 70.

MDB. (co. Durham), 2.

Shadrack, Shadrake, Shadrick. — Nick. ; an imitative corruption of Sheldrake, q.v.

MDB. (co. Essex), 2, 0, 0 ; London, 0, 1, 0 ; Philadelphia, 0, 0, 1.

Shadwell.—Local, 'of Shadwell,' a parish in co. Middlesex, London, E.

William de Schadwell, 13 Edw. I : Freemen of York, i. 4.
1334. Robert de Shadwell, rector of Intwood, co. Norf. : FF. v. 42.
1620. Married—Whorwood Shadwell and Eliz. Halsey : Marriage Lic. (London), ii. 91.
1667.—John Shadwell and Alice Hickman : St. Jas. Clerkenwell, i. 130.

MDB. (co. Bucks), 1 ; London, 2 ; Boston (U.S.), 1.

Shafto.—Local, 'of Shafto,' a township in the parish of Hartburn, co. Northumberland.

John de Schafthou, co. Northumb., 1273. A.
William de Shafthou, 5 Edw. I : KKK. ii. 4.
Thomas de Shafthow, 1340 : ibid. p. 6.
William de Shafthowe, 1367 : ibid.
1794. Married — William Terry and Ann Shafto : St. Geo. Han. Sq. ii. 121.
London, 1 ; Crockford, 1.

Shakel ; v. Shackel.

Shakelance. — Nick. ; cf. Bruselance, and v. Shakespear and Shakeshaft.

Henry Shakelaunce, co. Northampt., 1273. A.

Shakerley.—Local, ' of Shackerley,' a hamlet in the parish of Leigh, co. Lancashire, 'formerly almost exclusively the property of the Shakerleys of Somerford in Cheshire. . . . The site of the hall is marked by a moat, and continued to be the residence of the Shakerleys till the middle of the last century' (Baines' Lanc. ii. 201). For probable derivation, v. Shackel and Shacklady.

1592. Geoffrey Shakerley, of Hulme : Wills at Chester (1545-1620), p. 172.
1596. Buried—John Shawkerley, gent : Reg. Northenden Church, East Cheshire, i. 301.
1652. Peter Shakerley, of Shakerley, co. Lanc. : ibid. ii. 505.
MDB. (Cheshire), 3.

Shakeshaft.—Nick. equivalent to Shakelance and Shakespear, q.v.

Nicholas Shakeshaft, 1542 : Preston Guild, p. 17.
Johannes Shakeshafft, 1542 : ibid. p. 22.
Henry Shakeshaft, of Warrington, 1617 : Wills at Chester, i. 172.
1744. Bapt. — Anne, d. of Hugh Shakeshaft : St. Ann, Manchester.
George Shakeshaft, 1748 : St. Peter, Cornhill, ii. 85.
1778. Married—Thomas Mort and Ann Shakeshaft : St. Geo. Han. Sq. i. 284.
Manchester, 1 ; Preston, 2 ; Boston (U.S.), 1.

Shakespear, Shakespeare.—
Nick. ' a spearman.' William Shakespere (V. 1) ; cf. Simon Shakelok (M.), i.e. Shake-lock, Henry Shakelaunce, 1273 (A.), i.e. Shake-lance. Hugh Shakeshaft (Eng. Sur., 2nd edit., p. 461), i.e. Shake-shaft. It is impossible to retail all the nonsense that has been written about this name. Silly guessing has run riot on the

subject. Never a name in English nomenclature so simple or so certain in its origin. It is exactly what it looks—Shakespear ; one of a class of nicknames, nearly all of which have come down to to-day because that which was derisive in them had been soon forgotten, and they had become almost accepted as official. ' Catch-poll ' (q.v.) actually attained the honours of an authorized and official title. A serjeant who cleared the way was equally well known as ' Drawsword ' (q.v.), a bailiff as ' Wagstaff,' a huntsman as ' Wag-horn,' a jailer as ' Shake-lock,' a pikeman or spearman as ' Shake-lance ' and ' Shake-spear,' and a well-known bird, from its customary habit, as a ' Wag-tail.' *Wag* and *shake* were the chief elements in these vigorous sobriquets ; v. names under Wag- and Shake-, and for others, not in our nomenclature, v. Halliwell.

Robertus Schaksper, *couper*, 1379 : P. T. Yorks. p. 96.
1730. Married — William Fellows and Margaret Shakespear : St. Geo. Han. Sq. i. 7.
1758. — William Guy and Rebecca Shakspar : ibid. p. 76.
MDB. (co. Warwick), 2, 3 ; Philadelphia, 0, 3.

Shallcross ; v. Shawcross.

Shallis, Shalless, Shalles.—
Local, ' de Schalis.' I cannot identify the spot, but probably Calais is meant. Challis, q.v., is still a Suffolk surname ; cf. Shannon and Canon.

Robert de Schalis, co. Suff., 1273. A.
London, 2, 2, 0 ; Crockford, 1, 0, 0 ; Philadelphia, 0, 0, 1.

Shambrook ; v. Sambrook, a variant.

Shann, Shand. — Local, ' of Shande.' Mr. Lower says, ' Philibert de Shaunde was created Earl of Dath in 1485 ' ; Patr. Brit. p. 310.

Johannes Schaune, *webster*, 1379 : P. T. Yorks. p. 118.
Thomas Shan, 1379 : ibid. p. 236.
1742. Married — Thomas Shand and Frances London : St. Geo. Chap. Mayfair, p. 20.
1750. — Robert Hogg and Margaret Shann : ibid. p. 175.

West Riding Court Dir., 6, 0 ; London, 0, 10 ; New York, 1.

Shannon.—Offic. ' the canon M.E. *chanon* ; v. Channon.
' Monk or frere, Preest or Chanon.'
Chaucer, C. T. 16307.

The canon-house near Ulverston, once attached to Conishead Priory, is now a farmstead called ' Shannon - house,' but styled ' Chanon - house ' in the Church registers of last century (v. my Chronicles of Ulverston, p. 38).

1750. Married — John Shannon and Ann Smith : St. Geo. Chap. Mayfair, p. 165.
1789. — John Pitcher and Catherine Shannon : St. Geo. Han. Sq. i. 83.
London, 8 ; Philadelphia, 76.

Shaper.—Occup. ' the shaper,' a cutter-out of cloth ; v. Shapster. Sheffield, 1.

Shapster, Shepster, Shipster.—Occup. ' the shapster,' a female shaper or cutter-out of cloth garments.

' As a shepsteres shere.'
Piers Plowman, 8683.
' To Alice Shapster for making and washing of xxiii sherts and xxiiii stomachers ': Privy Purse Expenses, Eliz. of York, p. 122.
N. and Q. (1886, p. 68) has an indenture of apprenticeship dated 1552, which describes the master and mistress as ' Rogero Myners civi et cloth - worker, Lond', et Johanna uxor ejus shepstre.'
Matilda Shapistre, co. Suff., 1273. A.
Cristiana la Schippestere, C. R., 2 Edw. II.

Shard ; v. Shird.

Shardlow.—Local, ' of Shardlow,' a township in the parish of Aston-upon-Trent, co. Derby.

Edmund de Scardelowe, co. Camb., 1273. A.
1684. Joseph Collins and Eliz. Shardlow : Marriage Lic. (Canterbury), p. 168.
London, 1 ; New York, 2.

Sharman.—Occup. ' a clothshearman ' ; v. Shearman.

1717. Married — John Sharman and Mary Mason : St. Geo. Chap. Mayfair, p. 80.
New York, 2.

Sharp, Sharpe.—Nick. ' the sharp,' the quick, keen, cutting. Naturally this was a sobriquet likely to be handed down as being complimentary. Several instances have lately cropped up where the child has received the baptismal name Luke, which looks as if a little humour were intended.

Alexander Scharp, co. Bucks, 1273. A.
John Scharp, co. Sussex, ibid.
William Scharpe, co. Linc., ibid.
Adam Scharpe, 1379 : P. T. Yorks. p. 92.
Leticia Scharppe, 1379 : ibid. p. 133.
1589. Bapt.—Anne, d. Edward Sharpe: St. Jas. Clerkenwell, i. 22.
London, 73, 48 ; New York, 62, 15.

Sharparrow.—Nick. ' Sharparrow,' a good bowman, a complimentary sobriquet.

John Sharparrow, co. York. W. 2.
William Sharparrow, co. York. W. 11.
Oswin Sharparrow, co. York. W. 3.
John Sharpearrowe, Patent Roll, 19 Eliz. pt. iii.
' Orate pro anima dom. Johannis Sharparrowe. quondam parsone in Eccles. Cath. Ebor., qui obiit xxv. die Oct. an. 1411 ': York Minster, Drake's Eboracum, i. 498.
Robertus Sharparowe, 1379 : P. T. Yorks. p. 228.
Adam Sharparowe, 1379 : ibid.
John Sharparrow, vicar of Shernbourn, co. Norf., 1603 : FF. x. 361.

Complimentary as this Yorkshire surname was, it died out. I can find no descendants. Cf. Benbow and Sharpspear.

Sharples, Sharpless.—Local, ' of Sharples,' a township in the parish of Bolton, co. Lanc. The surname is familiar enough in South Lancashire, but does not seem to have spread far. Baines, in his History of Lancashire (i. 475), says a family of Sharples early arose there and occupied the Hall.

1602. Thomas Sharpples : Preston Guild Rolls, p. 64.
Laurence Rigby, of Sharples, 1617 : Wills at Chester, i. 161.
Richard Sharples, of Sharples, 1618 : p. 172.
1762. Married — Henry Penry and Mary Sharpless : St. Geo. Han. Sq. i. 108.
London, 1, 0 ; Manchester, 13, 1 ; Bolton, 6, 0.

Sharplin.—? Bapt. The suffix is clearly a diminutive ; cf. Embelin, Tomlin, &c.

Alicia Sarpeline, co. Oxf., 1273. A.
1622. Buried — John Sharpling : St. Jas. Clerkenwell, iv. 157.
1801. Married — John Robinson and Eliz. Sharplin : St. Geo. Han. Sq. ii. 235.
London, 1.

Sharpspear.—Nick. ' Sharpspear.' Cf. Sharparrow, a Yorkshire surname that lasted some centuries.

William Sharpspere, Close Roll, 6 Edw. I.

Sharrow.—Local, ' of Sharow ' ; v. Skirrow.

Robert de Scharhow, 28 Edw. I : Freemen of York, i. 8.
Johannes de Sharowe, 1379 : P. T. Yorks. p. 300.
Ricardus Sharrowe, 1379 : ibid.
London, 2.

Shavenhead. — Nick. ' the Shavenhead ' ; cf. Whitehead, Redhead, &c.

Robert Shevenehod, co. Camb., 1273. A.

Shaw.—Local, ' at the shaw,' from residence beside a small wood or shaw.

John atte Schaghe, co. Soms., 1 Edw. III : Kirby's Quest, p. 190.
John atte Schawe. H. (Index.)
Johannes del Schagh', 1379 : P. T. Yorks. p. 25.
Radulph del Schagh', 1379 : ibid. p. 104.
Alicia Shaghe, 1379 : ibid. p. 131.
Robertus del Schaghe, 1379 : ibid. p. 166.
1608. Bapt. — Anthonie, s. Anthonie Shawe : St. Jas. Clerkenwell, i. 55.
London, 118 ; New York, 172.

Shawcross, Shallcross, Shalcross. — Local, ' of Shallcross.' Shallcross Hall lies in the parish of Taxal, Derbyshire, on the confines of Cheshire. The Shallcross's of Shallcross were considerable people in the 17th and 18th centuries. The name is still strong in the immediate district, as the Manchester Directory shows. The modern form of the surname is generally Shawcross.

James Shalcrosse, 1537 : Reg. Univ. Oxf. i. 189.
1605. William Shallcross, of Stockport : Wills at Chester, i. 172.
1806. Married—Charles Fernley and Mary Shallcross : St. Geo. Han. Sq. ii. 350.
London, 2, 0, 1 ; Manchester, 14, 1, 0 ; Philadelphia, 5, 36, 0.

Shayler, Shaylor, Shailer.—Nick. One who shailed, one who walked crookedly, a cripple. 'Esgrailler, to shale or straddle with the feet or legs' (Cotgrave). 'I shayle with the feet' (Palsgrave). 'Shailer, a cripple' (Halliwell, v. shail and shale 4).

Johannes Scayler, 1379 : P. T. Yorks. p. 12.
1680. Bapt. — James, s. Thomas Shayler : St. Mary Aldermary (London), p. 105.
1734. Married — Roger Evans and Anna-Maria Shaler : St. Peter, Cornhill, ii. 81.
London, 5, 0, 0 ; Boston (U.S.), 0, 0, 2.

Sheard.—Occup. ; v. Shepard, a corruption. Cf. Shearson.

1671. Bapt. — William, s. Edward Sheard : St. Jas. Clerkenwell, i. 250.
1788. Married — Matthew Cook and Hannah Barracluf Sheard : St. Geo. Han. Sq. ii. 11.
London, 5 ; Oxford, 3 ; Philadelphia, 9.

Shearer.—Occup. ' the shearer,' i. e. a cloth shearman ; v. Shearman.

Matilda le Scherher, co. Linc., 1273. A.
Richard le Sherere, temp. 1300. M.
Reginald le Scherere, temp. 1300. M.
1809. Married — James Shearer and Margaret Ritchie : St. Geo. Han. Sq. ii. 402.
London, 3 ; Boston (U.S.), 3.

Shearman, Sharman, Sherman.—Occup. ' the shearman,' a cloth-shearer, one who sheared the nap ; v. Liber Albus, p. 630. The Shermen formed a company in the York Guild (York Mystery Plays, p. lxxvii and p. 337). The Shermen and Fullers appeared in the Norwich Play (Blomefield, ii. 148).

John le Sheremon, c. 1300. M.
Robert le Sherman, c. 1300. M.
William le Sherman. R.
Oliver Sherman, 1379 : P. T. Yorks. p. 100.
Johannes Wykir, shereman, 1379 : ibid. p. 25.
1638. Bapt.—Eliz., d. John Sherman : St. Jas. Clerkenwell, i. 139.
1792. Married — Edward Sharman and Sarah Barlow : St. Geo. Han. Sq. ii. 81.
London, 14, 24, 10 ; Boston (U.S.), 1, 1, 105.

Shearsmith. — Occup. ' the shearsmith,' a maker of shears.

Walter le Scheresmythe, c. 1300. M.
Thomas Schersmyth, co. York, 1440 : W. 11.

1736. Bapt. — William, s. William Sharesmith : St. Jas. Clerkenwell, ii. 226.
1753. Married — Benjamin Ward and Ann Shearsmith : St. Geo. Chap. Mayfair, p. 249.
1759. Married — Samuel Shearsmith and Sarah Marshall : St. Geo. Han. Sq. i. 65.

Shearson.—Nick. A corruption of Shepherdson, q.v. A North-English corruption ; cf. Sheard for Shepherd.

Robert Shearson, of Ellel, 1675 : Lancashire Wills at Richmond, i. 249.
Edmund Sheirson, of Ellel, 1672 : ibid.
Richard Shearson, of Cockerham, 1687: ibid. ii. 226.
Margaret Shierson, of Marton, 1716 : ibid. p. 227.
Thomas Sherson, of Lancaster, 1725: ibid. p. 228.
Liverpool, 3.

Sheat, Sheate.—Bapt. 'the son of Schet' ; v. Skeate.

Walter Scheat, co. Camb., 1273. A.
1724. Bapt.—Eliz., d. John Sheat : St. Jas. Clerkenwell, ii. 149.
London, 1, 1.

Sheath.—Local, 'at the Sheath.' Possibly a bubbling spring of salt water. ' *Sheath*, a fountain of salt water' (Halliwell). But more probably the name attached to some chasm in the rocks resembling the scabbard, or sheath of a knife or sword.

Humfrey de la Shethe, co. Devon, Hen. III-Edw. I. K.
1747. Married — Thomas Carpenter and Esther Sheath : St. Geo. Chap. Mayfair, p. 99.
1785. John Taylor and Sarah Sheath : St. Geo. Han. Sq. i. 372.
London, 5.

Sheather.—Occup. 'the sheather,' a maker of sword-slips ; v. Swordslipper, also a Yorkshire name. 'Schedare or schethare, *vaginarius*' : Prompt. Parv. p. 444.

Henry le Schether, 31 Edw. I : Freemen of York, i. 9.
John Schether, co. Soms., 1 Edw. III : Kirby's Quest, p. 168.
Johannes de Breres, *shether*, 1379: P. T. Yorks. p. 136.
Johannes Schether, 1379 : ibid. p. 249
Johanna Shether, 1379 : ibid. p. 59.
Thomas Schether, 1379 : ibid. p. 252.
London, 2.

Sheepdriver. — Occup. 'the sheep-driver,' a tender of sheep.

Michael le Sheepdriuere, Rot. Fin., 4 Edw. II.

Sheepshank. — Nick. 'with the sheep-shanks.' Though not complimentary, it has lived till to-day, and is respected, in one instance at least. by the whole country ; cf. Philipshank, Longshank, &c. I believe the word *leg* did not commonly exist in the popular English language at the early period of hereditary surnames. This surname sprang up in co. York. Cf. Shortshank.

Alicia Shepshank', *chapman*, 1379 : P. T. Yorks. p. 3.
Willelmus Schepschank, 1379 : ibid. p. 99.
1802. Married — John Sheepshanks, M.A., of Leeds, co. York, and Mary Anderson : St. Geo. Han. Sq. ii. 260.
West Riding Yorks Court Dir., 4 ; Harrogate, 1.

Sheepshead. — Local, 'of Sheepshed,' co. Leic.

Baldwin Shepesheued, Close Roll, 2 Hen. IV. pt. i.
John Schepishead, co. Leic. PP.
William Schepishead, co. Leic. PP.
James Hall, of Sheepshed, co. Leic. MDB.

Sheepway.—Local ; v. Shipway.

Sheffield. — Local, 'of Sheffield,' the well-known town in co. York.

Johannes de Schefeld, 1379 : P. T. Yorks. p. 74.
Johannes de Schefell', 1379 : ibid. p. 79.
Agnes Shefeld, 1564 : Lancashire Wills at Richmond, i. 249.
1601. Bapt.—Matthew, s. of Nathaniell Sheffeild : St. Michael, Cornhill, p. 103.
London, 16 ; West Rid. Court Dir., 1 ; New York, 8.

Sheldon.—Local, 'of Sheldon,' a chapelry in the parish of Bakewell, co. Derby; also parishes in cos. Devon and Warwick. Worcestershire has for many centuries been the habitat of a family of this name.

1584-5. Francis Sheldon, co. Worc. : Reg. Univ. Oxf. vol. ii. pt. ii. p. 141.
1621. Edward Sheldon, co. Worc. : ibid. p. 401.
1737. Married — Francis Sheldon and Ann Read : St. Geo. Han. Sq. i. 19.
MDB. (co. Derby), 18 ; London, 13 ; Manchester, 6 ; New York, 42.

Sheldrake, Sheldrick, Shildrick. — Nick. 'the sheldrake,'

a kind of drake. M.E. *scheldrak* ; v. Shadrack for a modification.

Adam Sceyldrake, co. Suff., 1273. A.
John Sheldrake. D.
1662. Adam Sheldrake and Mary Pittman : Marriage Alleg. (Canterbury), p. 26.
1802. Married — William Sheldrick and Eliz. Coates : St. Geo. Han. Sq. ii. 302.
London, 2, 4, 1 ; Philadelphia, 17, 0, 0.

Shelmerdine. — Local, ' of Shermanden,' gradually corrupted to Shelmerdine. I cannot find the spot ; cf. Haseltine for Haselden. The habitat must be sought for in South Lanc. or East Ches.

1632. John Shelmerdine, of Lower Ardwick : Wills at Chester, i. 196.
1639. Ralph Shelmerdine, of Gorton : ibid.
1636. Married—Francis Shelmerdyne and Dorothy Cotterell : Reg. Prestbury Ch., East Cheshire, p. 302.
1643. ' Item, for charges and expenses uppon divers ministers (to witt), Mr. Furness, Mr. Mariegould, Mr. Worsley, Mr. Hall, Mr. Bate, Mr. Shelmerdyne,' &c. : East Cheshire, i. 293.
1647. Mary Shermantine : Cal. of Wills in Court of Husting (2).
London, 1 ; Manchester, 13 ; Philadelphia, 7.

Shelton.—Local, ' of Shelton,' a parish in co. Norfolk, near Long Stratton ; also a parish in co. Notts, six miles from Newark ; also a parish in co. Bedford, four miles from Kimbolton. Cf. Skelton.

1561. Richard Shelton and Jane Hollingworth : Marriage Lic. (London), i. 21.
1700. Bapt.—Eliz., d. Henry Shelton : St. Jas. Clerkenwell, i. 386.
MDB. (co. Camb.), 1 ; London, 12 ; Boston (U.S.), 10.

Shemeld, Shimeld.— ? Bapt. ' the son of Schwanhilde' or Svanhild, a favourite Scandinavian personal name. There can scarcely be a doubt that this is a modified form.

Adam Schemylde, 1379 : P. T. Yorks. p. 45.
Robertus Schemylde, *smyth*, 1379 : ibid.
1771. Married—Hugh Ellis and Sarah Shimeld : St. Geo. Han. Sq. i. 214.
Sheffield, 1, 3 ; West Rid. Court Dir., 1, 0 ; Philadelphia, 2, 0.

Shenston, Shenstone. — Local, ' of Shenstone,' a parish

in co. Stafford, three miles from Lichfield.

1792. Married — William Shenston and Eliz. Smith: St. Geo. Han. Sq. ii. 85. London, 1, 0; MDB. (co. Stafford), 0, 1.

Shenton.—Local, ' of Shenton,' a chapelry in the parish of Market Bosworth, in co. Leicester. Also some spot seemingly in co. Ches.

John Shenton, 1577, co. Ches.: Reg. Univ. Oxf. vol. ii. pt. ii. p. 76.
John Shenton, of Church Coppenhull, 1607: ibid.
Thomas Shenton, of Stoke, 1611: Wills at Chester, i. 174.
1778. Married—William Shenton and Mary Penn: St. Geo. Han. Sq. i. 286. London, 4; MDB. (co. Camb.), 1; Philadelphia, 3.

Shepard, Shephard, Shepheard, Sheppard, Shepperd, Shepherd, Shepherd.—Occup. ' the shepherd.' With the many variants of this surname, cf. Calvert for Calve-herd, Coward for Cow-herd, Stoddard for Stot-herd, &c.

Josse le Sephurde, co. Oxf., 1273. A.
Margaret le Sephirde, co. Hunts, ibid.
Walter le Schepherde, co. Camb., ibid.
John le Shepherde, c. 1300. M.
William Shephirde, 1379: P. T. Yorks. p. 299.
Johannes Schephirde, 1379: ibid. p. 195.
James Sheppard, of Eccles, *butcher*, 1614: Wills at Chester, i. 174.
London, 7, 19, 10, 68, 43, 6, 1; Philadelphia, 7, 8, 1, 72, 8, 0, 60.

Shepherdson, Shephardson.—Nick. ' the shepherd's son'; cf. Taylorson, Wrightson, Smithson. Taylorson is peculiar to co. Yorks, as is Shepherdson. Wrightson is also familiar to that county.

John Shepherdson, 1423: DDD. ii. 370.
Alice Shipperdon, co. York. W. 9.
William Shipperdson, co. Durham. SS.
1738. Married—William Curling and Ann Shephardson: Canterbury Cath. p. 83.
1798. — William Shepperson and Sabina Strong: St. Geo. Han. Sq. ii. 191.
West Rid. Court Dir., 1, 0; Sheffield, 1, 0; Boston (U.S.), 0, 4.

Shepley, Shipley.—(1) Local, ' of Shepley,' a township in the parish of Kirk Burton, W. Rid. Yorks. (2) Local, ' of Shipley,' a parish in W. Rid. Yorks, three miles from Bradford. Both places seem to have been originally spelt Scheplay, so both Shepley and

Shipley as surnames are now inextricably mixed.

Katerine de Scheplay, 1379: P. T. Yorks. p. 194.
Joanna de Scheplay, 1379: ibid.
Adam de Scheplay, 1379: ibid. p. 155.
1698. Bapt. — Hannah, d. Henry Shepley: St. Jas. Clerkenwell, i. 376.
1714. Buried — Samuel Shipley: St. Mary Aldermary, p. 213.
London, 0, 3; MDB. (co. Ches.), 4, 0; Manchester, 3, 0; Boston (U.S.), 7, 17.

Sherar, Sherer, Sherrer.—Occup.; v. Shearer.

London, 1, 1, 0; Boston (U.S.), 0, 0, 1.

Sherard, Sherrard, Sherratt.—Local. Probably a corruption of Sherwood, q.v. The first stage would be Sher'ood, then Sherad, then Sherratt. That this is no idle guess is proved by the fact that in the Index to the Reg. Univ. Oxf. to the name Sherwood is added, ' or Sherewood, or Sherrat.'

William Sherratt, of Moss Side, Manchester, 1588: Wills at Chester, i. 174.
John Sherratt, of Church Lawton, 1604: ibid.
1665-6. George Sherard and Mary Deakins: Marriage Alleg. (Canterbury), p. 164.
London, 0, 8, 2; Manchester, 0, 0, 6; Boston (U.S.), 0, 4, 0; New York, 1, 2, 0.

Sheraton,? Sheridan.—Local, ' of Sheraton,' a village south of Castle Eden, anciently Shurveton. The name is still found in the neighbourhood of Newcastle. It is very probable that Sheridan is the modern form. The corruption was all but inevitable.

Stephen de Shurveton, 1318: DDD. i. 54.
Robert de Shirveton, 1398: ibid. p. 55.
London, 0, 4; Liverpool, 1, 4; Manchester, 0, 4; New York, 0, 160.

Sherborne, Sherborn, Sherburn, Sherburne.—Local, ' of Sherburne.' There are parishes and hamlets of the name of Sherborne, or Sherburne, in cos. Dorset, Warwick, Gloucester, Hants, Durham, and York.

Adam de Schirburn, *couraour*, 31 Edw. I: Freemen of York, i. 9.
John de Schireburne, co. Soms., 1 Edw. III: Kirby's Quest, p. 178.
William Schurebourne, co. Soms., 1 Edw. III ibid. p. 262.
William de Shirborn, co. Soms., 1 Edw. III: ibid. p. 278.
Ricardus de Schyrburn, 1379: P. T. Yorks. p. 237.

Johannes de Shirburn', of Schyrburne, 1379: ibid. p. 147.
1585. Augustine Sherborne, co. Oxf.: Reg. Univ. Oxf. vol. ii. pt. ii. p. 143.
1598-9. Richard Sherborne, co. Lanc., ibid. p. 232.
London, 2, 2, 0, 0; Philadelphia, 5, 0, 0, 0; New York, 0, 0, 1, 0; Boston (U.S.) (Sherburne), 30.

Shergold.—Bapt. ' the son of Shergold.' Probably a form of Sargood, q.v. Found in co. Wilts as Shergoll.

William Shergall, co. Wilts, 1552: Reg. Broad Chalke, p. 7.
Ricard Shergoll, 1603: ibid.
1661. Buried — Percival Shergould: St. Jas. Clerkenwell, iv. 342.
1669. Bapt. — John, s. Alexander Shurgall: ibid. p. 239.
1775. Married — William Hill and Mary Shergold: St. Geo. Han. Sq. i. 256. London, 1.

Sheridan.—Local; v. Sheraton.

Sheriff, Sherriff.—Offic. ' the Sheriff '; v. Shreeve.

Robert le Shirreve, co. Suff., 1273. A
Lena le Shireve, co. Suff., ibid.
John Schiref, co. Northumberland, ibid.
Thomas Shurreve, co. Soms., 1 Edw. III: Kirby's Quest, p. 122.
Johannes Schyref, 1379: P. T. Yorks. p. 91.
Thomas le Shirreve. B.
1786. Married — Alex. Sherriff and Mary Chilcott: St. Geo. Han. Sq. i. 394. London, 2, 0; Boston (U.S.), 0, 4.

Sheringham.—Local, ' of Sheringham,' a parish in co. Norfolk, three miles from Cromer.

1793. Married — Samuel Hallaway and Mary Ann Sheringham: St. Geo. Han. Sq. ii. 105.
MDB. (co. Glouc.), 1.

Sherlock.—(1) Nick. (?), ' with shorn locks.' A.S. *sceran, sciran*, to cut, to shear; cf. Blacklock, Whitelock, Silverlock, Lovelock, &c., a large class. (2) Probably, however, Sherlock was a personal name.

Beatrice Schyrlok, co. Bedf., 1273. A.
Philip Schyrlok, co. Soms., 1 Edw. II: Kirby's Quest, p. 94.
Johannes Shirlok', 1379: P. T. Yorks. p. 228.
1568-9. William Shirlocke and Aveline Stubbes: Marriage Lic. (London), i. 41.
1669. Thomas Freeman and Eliz. Shurlock: Marriage Alleg. (Canterbury), p. 11.
London, 5; Manchester, 3; Philadelphia, 25.

Sherman.—Occup. 'the shearman,' a cloth shearman; v. Shearman.

Sherrard, -ratt; v. Sherard.

Sherrin, Sherring. — Bapt. 'the son of Sherwin,' q.v. Many of the names ending in -*win* are now -*in* or -*ing*; cf. Boddin for Baldwin, Gunning for Gundwin, Golding for Goldwin. The *g* in Sherring is therefore an excrescence, as in Jennings.

Sciring (without surname), co. Camb., 1273. A.
1629. Buried—Mary Sherryn; St. Jas. Clerkenwell, iv. 197.
London, 4, 7; MDB. (co. Somerset), 13, 4.

Sherrington. — Local, 'of Sherrington,' parishes in the diocs. of Oxford and Salisbury; cf. Cherrington, Charrington, and Carrington.

1567-8. Alex. Sherington and Edith Horne : Marriage Lic. (London), i. 38.
1642. Bapt. — John, s. William Sherrington : St. Jas. Clerkenwell, i. 152.
1662. Buried — Eliz., d. William Sherington : St. Peter, Cornhill, i. 214.
London, 4.

Shorston, Sherson. — Local, 'of Sherston,' two parishes in co. Wilts.

Thomas Scherston, co. Soms., 1 Edw. III: Kirby's Quest, p. 231.
1560. Married — Thomas Sherson and Ellen Vintner : St. Peter, Cornhill, i. 225.

With this entry, cf. Kelson for Kelston, &c. These modified forms are as natural as they are common.

London, 1, 1.

Sherwell, Sherwill, Shervill. — Local, 'of Sherwill,' a parish in co. Devon, four miles from Barnstaple.

1789. Married — Ralph Shervill and Mary Clarke : St. Geo. Han. Sq. ii. 29.
MDB. (co. Devon), 3, 0, 1 ; London, 3, 0, 2.

Sherwin.—Bapt. 'the son of Sherwin.' One of the many personal names ending in -*win*; cf. Unwin, Baldwin, Godwin. The *d* in my instances is, no doubt, excrescent, as in Simmonds or Hammond; v. Sherrin.

John Surewyne, co. Oxf., 1273. A.
William Surewyne, co. Oxf., ibid.

Robert Serewynd, co. Camb., 1273. A.
Geoffrey Scherewynd, co. Camb., ibid
Peter Scherewynd, co. Camb., ibid.
Robert Shirwynd, C. R., 16 Ric. II.
William Sherwynd, C. R., 2 Hen. IV. pt. i.
Hugo Scherwynd, 1379: P. T. Yorks. p. 99.
Preciosa Scherwynd', *webster*, 1379 : ibid. p. 98.
Thomas Schiruen, 1379 : ibid. p. 192.
London, 6 ; New York, 2.

Sherwood.—Local, ' of Sherwood,' i.e. Sherwood Forest.

Ralph de Scirewode, co. Linc., 1273. A.
Margareta de Shyrwode, 1379 : P. T. Yorks. p. 128.
Alexander de Shyrwode, 1379 : ibid. p. 74.
Willelmus de Schiwode, 1379 : ibid. p. 129.
1577. William Sherwood and Dionise Butler : Marriage Lic. (London), i. 75.
1610. Henry Sherwood, co. Oxf. : Reg. Univ. Oxf. vol. ii. pt. ii. p. 317.
1661. Married — John Sherwood and Judith Cooke : St. Thomas the Apostle (London), p. 21.
London, 13 ; West Rid. Court Dir., 2 ; Boston (U.S.), 9.

Sheward.—Bapt. 'the son of Seward' (q.v.), a variant. In the Index to Reg. Univ. Oxf., added to Seward is ' or Sheward, or Shewarde ' ; vol. ii. pt. iv. p. 376.

Henry Shewarde, co. Hereford, 1504 : Reg. Univ. Oxf. vol. ii. pt. iv. p. 204.
1612. Married—Richard Sheward and Elizabeth Ashe : St. Mary Aldermary (London), p. 12.
1645. Bapt.—Jane, d. Martin Sheward : St. Thomas the Apostle (London), p. 56.
London, 2.

Shields.—Local, ' of Shields,' i.e. North Shields, a seaport and market-town, co. Northumberland.

Willelmus de Scheles 1379: P. T. Yorks. p. 193.
1736. Married — William Shields and Martha Sedley : St. Geo. Han. Sq. i. 17.
1785. Thomas Pocknell and Margaret Shiells : ibid. p. 371.
London, 5 ; Boston (U.S.), 48.

Shilcock, Schilcock, Shillcock.—Nick. ' the shilcock' ; cf. Sheldrake, and v. Skeat on *sheldrake.*

Johannes Schalkok', 1379: P. T. Yorks. p. 200.
London, 3, 0, 0 ; Sheffield, 0, 1, 0 ; MDB. (co. Leic.), 9, 0, 1 ; Philadelphia, 1, 0, 0.

Shildrick.—Nick. ; v. Sheldrake.

Shilito, Shillito, Shillitoe, Shilleto, Shillitto.—? Local, ' of Selito ' (?). This great Yorkshire name completely baffles me. Probably, like Sholto (co. Northumberland), the suffix is -*how* (v. How, 2), in which case, of course, the name is local. But I cannot identify the spot, and there is no prefix *de* to the instances. No entry is found in any of the great rolls, like the Testa de Neville, the Hundred Rolls, or the Placita quo Warranto.

Adam Selito (Houghton Grass), 1379 : P. T. Yorks. p. 133.
Johannes Selito (Houghton Grass), 1379: ibid.
Jurdanus Selito (Whitwood), 1379 : ibid. p. 167.
Johannes Selito (Whitwood), 1379 : ibid.
Cf. Ricardus Ruscheto, 1379 : ibid. p. 249.
1721. Bapt.—John, s. Peter Selleto : St. Mary Aldermary (London), p. 122.
London, 0, 2, 3, 1, 0 ; West Rid. Court Dir., 1, 2, 0, 1, 1 ; Sheffield (Shillito), 4.

Shilling.—(1) Bapt. ' the son of Shilwin ' or Schilling. Lower says, ' Schelin, Schelinus, a Domesday personal name.' Probably most of our Shillings descend from an old personal name Shilwin, one of the endless names with suffix *win*; cf. Sherwin and Sherring, or Goldwin and Golding. (2) Local, ' of Schilling.' I cannot find the spot.

Henry de Scilling, co. Norf., 1273. A.
William Schilling, co. Norf., ibid.
John Schelling, co. Wilts, ibid.
Cecilia Schyllyng, 1379 : P. T. Yorks. p. 140.
Willelmus Shilwyn, 1379 : ibid. p. 161.
1565. Bapt.—William Shilling and Mary Rider : St. Jas. Clerkenwell, i. 3.
1796. Married—John Shilling and Mary Rider : St. Geo. Han. Sq. ii. 143.
London, 4 ; Philadelphia, 9.

Shillingford. — Local, ' of Shillingford,' parishes in co. Berks and Devon. Probably originally Killingford; v. Killingsworth, where such variants as Chillingworth and Shillingsworth are mentioned.

1663. Charles Shillingford, alias Izard, and Mary Pryor : Marriage Alleg. (Canterbury), p. 99.
London, 1 ; Oxford, 1 ; Philadelphia, 6.

Shillingsworth. — Local ; v. Killingsworth.

1753. Married—George Smedley and Elizabeth Shillingsworth.

Shillito, &c.; v. Shilito.

Shilston, Shillson. — Local, 'of Shillingston,' a parish in co. Dorset. It is almost certain that these are variants. With Shillson, cf. Kelson for Kelston.

1689. John Chilston (or Shilston) and Ann Brady : Marriage Alleg. (Cant.), p. 111.
1801. Married—James Cormick and Sarah Shilstone : St. Geo. Han. Sq. ii. 236.
MDB. (co. Devon), 2, 1 ; London, 1, 0.

Shimeld; v. Shemeld.

Shingler.—Occup. 'the shingler,' a tyler. Shingles were square-shaped wooden tiles for the roofs of houses. Langland speaks of Noah's ark as the 'shyngled ship.'

'Flouren cakes beth the schingles alle
Of cherche, cloister, boure, and halle.'
Halliwell.

In a statute (1563) relating to the apprenticeship of children, reference is made to the occupations of ' Tyler, Slater, Healyer, Tile-maker, Thatcher or Shingler' (5 Eliz. c. 4, 23). All these represent different modes of roofing houses, and are familiar surnames to-day. v. Hillier.

1747. Bapt.—Anne, d. Thomas Shingler : St. Mary Aldermary (London), p. 130.
1767. Married—Thomas Shinglar and Ann Selby : St. Geo. Han. Sq. i. 170.
London, 1 ; MDB. (co. Ches.), 1.

Shinn.—Local. This is clearly a variant of Chinn (v. Ching). Both hail from co. Cambridge.

1629. Buried—Mary Shinn : St. Jas. Clerkenwell, iv. 194.
1803. Married — Benjamin Hardwick Shinn and Eliz. Knight Ayres : St. Geo. Han. Sq. ii. 287.
1809. — William Shinn and Mary Nichols : ibid. p. 402.
MDB. (co. Camb.), 3 ; Philadelphia, 62.

Shipley; v. Shepley.

Boston (U.S.), 2.

Shipman.—Occup. 'the ship-man,' a sailor, one who worked aboard a ship. ' Schypmanne, nauta' : Prompt. Parv. I cannot find Sailor in our nomenclature ; Mariner and Shipman were the usual terms.

'A shipman was ther woned fer by West, ..
He knew wel alle the havens as they were,
Fro' Gotland to the Cape de Finisterre.'
Chaucer's C. T., Prologue.

Hugh le Schipman, C. R., 36 Hen. III.

William Schippeman, co. Linc., 1273. A.
Alexander Schipman. H.
Willelmus de Seyton, schypmane, 1379 : P. T. Yorks. p. 127.
Robertus Shypman, 1379 : ibid.
Richard Harman, shippeman, 1379 : ibid. p. 50.
Willelmus Shipman, 1379 : ibid. p. 30.
1602. William Shipman, of Bristol : Reg. Univ. Oxf. vol. ii. pt. ii. p. 257.
1756. Married — John Shipman and Mary Tillie : St. Geo. Han. Sq. i. 64.
London, 4 ; Sheffield, 10 ; New York, 18.

Shipp.—Local, 'at the ship,' one who was living on a ship or boat ; cf. Barge.

Ralph At Ship, Prepositor of Bristol, 1230 : YYY. p. 669.
Isolda del Shippe, 1379 : P. T. Yorks. p. 297.
1762. Married—James Hobbs and Ann Ship : St. Geo. Han. Sq. i. 115.
1789. — Robert Ship and Eliz. Jarvis : ibid. ii. 17.
London, 5 ; Boston (U.S.), 3.

Shippard, Shipperd.—Occup. 'the shepherd ' ; a corruption. Nevertheless another origin is quite possible, viz. Shipward, the guardian of a ship ; cf. Millard for Millward.

John Shipward, mayor of Bristol, 1477 : Barrett's Hist. of Bristol.
George Shippherd, of Fell End, Kirby, 1666 : Lancashire Wills at Richmond, i. 250.
Cuthbert Shipperd, 1599 : ibid.
1677. Jonathan Shippard and Eliz. Beale : Marriage Alleg. (Cant.), p. 194.
London, 2, 0 ; Philadelphia, 0, 1.

Shipton.—Local, ' of Shipton,' parishes in cos. Salop, Devon, Dorset, &c. Also a chapelry in parish of Market Weighton, E. Rid. Yorks ; also a township in parish of Overton, E. Rid. Yorks.

Baldwin de Schipton, co. York, 1273. A.
Simon de Shupton, firmarius, 1379 : P. T. Yorks. p. 234.
1590-1. Edward Shipton, London : Reg. Univ. Oxf. vol. ii. pt. ii. p. 182.
1753. Married—Mark Hipworth and Anna Shipton : St. Geo. Han. Sq. i. 50.
London, 5 ; MDB. (co. Derby), 7.

Shipwash. — Local, 'at the sheepwash.' There is a spot called Sheepwash near Waterhead, Old-ham, co. Lanc. Probably many small localities would obtain this name, being favourite places for sheep-washing. Any one living beside such a running pool would readily be termed ' Robert at the sheepwash.'

1657. Bapt.—Joseph, s. Adrey Sheep-wash : St. Mary Aldermary (London), p. 96.
John Shipwash, 1725 : Reg. Canterbury Cath. p. 76.
1800. Married—Robert Shipwash and Mary Barlow : St. Geo. Han. Sq. ii. 217.
London, 1.

Shipway, Sheepway. — (1) Local, ' of Shepway,' one of the lathes, or great divisions of the county of Kent (Lower). This is confirmed by the following entry :

Ballivus (the bailiff) de Shipweye, co. Kent, 1273. A.

(2) Local, 'at the sheep-way,' from residence along the track trod by the sheep ; cf. Greenway, Hathway, Otway, &c.

Richard Shippway, co. Ches., 1603 : Reg. Univ. Oxf. vol. ii. pt. ii. p. 265.
1608-9. Christopher Shipway and Margaret Drake : Marriage Lic. (Westminster), p. 17.
London, 7, 0 ; MDB. (co. Glouc.), 2, 2 ; New York, 1.

Shipwright. — Occup. 'the shipwright,' a boat - builder. ' Schypwryte, naupicus' : Prompt. Parv.

Hugh le Schypwryte, co. Camb., 1273. A.
Richard Schypwryte, co. Camb., ibid.
Robert Schypwryte, co. Camb., ibid.

Perhaps made boats for the ' torpids ' in the 'Varsity races of the period !

Willelmus Schypwright, 1379 : P. T. Yorks. p. 157.
Thomas Shypwryght, 1379 : ibid. p. 127.
Johannes Boteler, shippewryght, 1379 : ibid. p. 51.
1805. Married—Martin Skelt and Mary Shipwright : St. Geo. Han. Sq. ii. 324.
London, 3.

Shird, Shirt, Shard.—Local, ' of the Sherd,' a place in Disley, in the parish of Stockport. Sherds of Sherd existed at an early period, and the junior branches spread into Lancashire, Derbyshire, and beyond. As for the meaning of Sherd, cf. ' shard, an opening in a wood. Yorkshire ' (Halliwell). ' Shard, a gap in a fence. Var. dial.' (ibid.) That Shirt is the modern imitative corruption of the surname is manifest.

Richard del Sherd, 1369 : v. East Cheshire, ii. 86.

William del Sherd, an archer of the Crown, 1398 : East Ches. ii. p. 87.

Hugh del Sherd, of Sherd, 1473 : ibid.

William Sherd, of Sherd, 1475 : ibid.

Jeffery Shirt, of Staley, 1593 : Wills at Chester, i. 174.

Thomas Shirt, co. Chester, *preacher*, 1618 : ibid.

Richard Sherte, co. Ches. : Reg. Univ. Oxf. vol. ii. pt. ii. p. 254. Manchester, 1, 2, 1.

Shire, Shires.—Local, 'at the shire,' a division of territory, from residence therein ; genitive Shires ; cf. Brooks, Holmes, Knowles, &c. Also cf. Hallamshire.

1397. Gregory atte Shire : Cal. of Wills in Court of Husting (2).

1668. George Shyres and Sarah Rogers : Marriage Alleg. (Canterbury), p. 151.

1777. Married — William Shires and Ann Pocock : St. Geo. Han. Sq. i. 282. London, 0, 3 ; Philadelphia, 1, 0.

Shirley.—Local, ' of Shirley,' parishes in cos. Derby, Hants, &c.

Johannes de Scherlay, 1379 : P. T. Yorks. p. 130.

Willelmus de Scherlay, 1379 : ibid. p. 120.

1573. George Shyrlye, co. Leic. : Reg. Univ. Oxf. vol i. pt. ii. p. 56.

1579. Anthony Sherlye, co. Sussex : ibid. p. 90.

1582. John Shurley, co. Sussex : ibid. p. 461.

West Rid. Court Dir., 3 ; London, 14 ; Boston (U.S.), 5.

Shirt ; v. Shird.

Shirtcliff, Shirtcliffe. — Local, 'of Shircliff.' I cannot find the spot. It is one of the many Yorkshire surnames with suffix *-cliff* ; cf. Topliff, Wickliffe, &c.

Johannes de Shirclyf', 1379 : P. T. Yorks. p. 8.

Robertus de Shirclyf', 1379 : ibid.

1621. Nicholas Sheircliffe, or Sherclyff, co. York : Reg. Univ. Oxf. vol. ii. pt. ii. p. 389.

West Rid. Court Dir., 1, 6 ; Sheffield, 0, 4 ; Philadelphia, 1, 0.

Shmith.—Occup. ' the smith,' q.v. Perhaps englished out of the German Schmidt.

London, 2.

Shobbrook, Shoebrook, Shubrick, Shubrook, Shuebruk. —Local, ' of Shobrooke,' a parish in co. Devon, two miles from Crediton.

MDB. (co. Devon), 2, 1, 0, 0, 0 ; London, 0, 0, 1, 3, 0 ; Boston (Shuebruk), 1.

Shoebeggar.—Nick. ' a beggar of old shoes.' The occupation is not extinct.

Simon le Shobegg'e, co. Camb., 1273. A.

Shoebotham.—Local. Almost all our surnames in *-botham* come from East Cheshire ; v. Shufflebotham and Higginbotham ; v. also Botham.

1605. Married — Thomas Potter and Margerie Showbothom : Reg. Prestbury, co. Ches., p. 167.

Manchester, 2.

Shoemaker. — Occup. ' the shoemaker ' ; rare, the general trade-names were Souter and Cordwaner. Christopher Shoomaker was burnt at Newbury (1518), according to Foxe. Harry Shomaker was an attendant upon the Princess Mary (1542) ; v. Privy Purse Expenses, p. 2. In the Chester Mystery the 'Corvesters and Shoemakers' marched together (Ormerod's Cheshire, p. 301).

1581. Married — Thomas Shomaker : Reg. St. Columb Major, p. 141.

Richard Shomaker. V. 3.

1591. Yeocum Shoemaker and Catharine Britten : Marriage Lic. (London), i. 225.

The name lingered on till the close of the 18th century :

1781. Buried — Mary, wife of John Showmaker : Reg. St. Ann's, Manchester.

Almost all the American Shoemakers are of German extraction.

Philadelphia, 178.

Shoesmith, Shoosmith, Shuxsmith, Sucksmith, Sixsmith, Shucksmith. — Occup. ' the shoesmith,' a maker of horseshoes, a farrier. Sixsmith may be a corruption of *sickle-smith* (v. Sucksmith) ; but it is probable, however strange it may appear, that all the above names are changes rung upon Shoesmith. Having once reached Sucksmith, the final step to Sixsmith was easy.

William le Shosmyth, C. R., 16 Edw. I.

Henry Shughsmythe, co. York. W. 2.

Margerie Shughsmythe. AA. 1.

Bryan Sukesmythe, temp. Eliz. ZZ.

1577. Bapt. — Mary, d. John Shewsmith : St. Thomas the Apostle, London, p. 27.

1576. Bryan Shusmith, of Winwick : Wills at Chester (1545-1620), p. 175.

1602. Thomas Sixsmith, of Atherton : ibid. p. 176.

1608. John Sixsmith, of Wigan : ibid.

1617. Thomas Sixesmith, or Sicksmith, co. Lanc. : Reg. Univ. Oxf. vol. ii. pt. ii. p. 359.

London, 2, 1, 0, 0, 0, 0 ; (Shoesmith), Halifax, 7 ; (Sixsmith), Manchester, 1, Liverpool, 1 ; (Sucksmith), Lightcliffe, near Halifax, 1.; Philadelphia, 0, 0, 0, 0, 8, 1.

Shooter, Shuter.—Occup. ' the shooter,' one who got his living by shooting birds ; cf. Hunter, Todhunter, Fowler, &c.

Johannes Shoter, 1379 : P. T. Yorks. p. 9 .

Willelmus Shoter, 1379 : ibid.

Johanna Schoter, 1379 : ibid. p. 41.

Johannes Schewter, 1379 : ibid. p. 165.

1784. Married — John Shuter and Ann Seller : St. Geo. Han. Sq. i. 355.

Sheffield, 1, 0 ; London, 0, 6.

Shop, Shopp.—Local, ' at the shop,' one who dwelt at a stall, or house, for sale. Cf. Shipp.

Margery atte Shoppe : Wardrobe Roll, 7 Edw. III, 35/26.

New York, 0, 3.

Shore.—Local, ' at the shore,' from residence beside the sea ; cf. Sands or Sandys.

Adam de Schore, 1379 : P. T. Yorks. p. 189.

Johannes de Schore, 1379 : ibid.

1659. Bapt.—John, s. John Shore : St. Jas. Clerkenwell, i. 204.

1768. Married — Joseph Shore and Deborah Lebarre : St. Geo. Han. Sq. i. 180.

London, 4 ; MDB. (co. Ches.), 2 ; New York, 2.

Shorland, Sherland.— Local, ' of Shorland ' (?). I cannot. find the spot.

Robert de Schirlaunde, co. Kent, 20 Edw. I. R.

Richard de Scholand, co. Kent, ibid.

Richard de Scholound, co. Kent, ibid.

1607. Christopher Shorland, co. Northants : Reg. Univ. Oxf. vol. ii. pt. ii. p. 294.

1774. Married — William Lawrence and Sarah Shorland : St. Geo. Han. Sq. i. 245.

London, 2, 0.

Short, Shortt.—Nick. ' the short,' of low stature ; cf. Long and Lang, Little, &c.

William Short, co. Suff., 1273. A.

Richard le Shorte, c. 1300. M.

Simon Schort, co. Soms., 1 Edw. III : Kirby's Quest, p. 176.

Johannes Short, 1379 : P. T. Yorks. p. 226.

Willelmus Short, 1379 : ibid. p. 115.

Willelmus Schort, 1379 : ibid.

Alice Short, of Ashton, 1672 : Lancashire Wills at Richmond, i. 251.
London, 36, 1 ; Boston (U.S.), 20, 0.

Shorter, Shotter.—Nick. 'the shorter,' to distinguish between two brothers, &c., of the same Christian name, especially in families where two or three boys were all Johns (v. my Curiosities of Puritan Nomenclature, Chatto and Windus, p. 4). Cf. Younger, Senior, Elder, &c.
John Shorter : Patent Roll, 15 Edw. IV. pt. ii.
John Shorter. H.
Anna Shawter, co. York. W. 20.
1771. Married—John Shorter and Jane Bishop : St. Geo. Han. Sq. i. 207.
London, 8, 2 ; Boston, 2, 0.

Shortfriend.—Nick. 'the short friend,' one who changed his intimacies frequently and soon forgot old acquaintances.
Hugo Schortfrend, co. Oxf., 1273. A.
Robertus Shortfrende, 1379 : P. T. Yorks. p. 259.

Shorthose, Shorthouse.—Nick. 'with the short hose.' Still found in Derbyshire. This was the nickname of Sir Thomas Woodcock, Lord Mayor, 1405 :
'Hic jacet Tom Shorthose,
Sine tomb, sine sheets, sine riches.'
William Shorthose, Close Roll, 17 Ric. II.
1585. Robert Shortus, co. Linc. : Reg. Univ. Oxf. vol. ii. pt. ii. p. 144.
John Shorthose, rector of Edlington, 1667 : Hunter's South Yorks. i. 95.
1631. Married—Franses Mosse and Margery Shorthose : St. Michael, Cornhill, p. 27.
Sheffield, 1, 0 ; MDB. (co. Derby), 1, 1.

Shortshank. — Nick. 'shortshank,' with short legs; cf. Sheepshank, Longshank, Philipshank. Sheepshank has survived, not so the others. Yorkshire seems to have been the district of these sobriquets.
Johannes Shortshank, 1379 : P. T. Yorks. p. 54.

Shott, Shot.—(1) Nick. 'the Scot'; cf. Shutt and Scutt. The two entries following are placed together :
Johannes Schote, et Matilda uxor ejus, 1379 : P. T. Yorks. p. 109.
Sissot Scote, 1379 : ibid.

(2) Local ; v. Shutt and Shute.
West Rid. Court Dir., 1, 0 ; Philadelphia, 4, 1.

Shotter.—Nick. ; v. Shorter, of which it is probably a variant.
1765. Married — James Shotter and Mary Anderson : St. Geo. Han. Sq. i. 157.
London, 2 ; New York, 1.

Shoulding; v. Shuldham.

Shoveller, Showler, Shouler. —Occup. 'the shoveler,' one who shovels with a spade ; cf. Dicker. *Showl* is dialectic for shovel :
'Who'll dig his grave?
I says the owl;
With my spade and showl
I'll dig his grave.'
Cock Robin.
1609. Nicholas Shoveler and Mary Daye : Marriage Lic. (London), i. 313.
1703. Married—Daniel Shoveler and Mary Ferris : Canterbury Cath., p. 66.
1777. — Edward Crouch and Martha Shouler : St. Geo. Han. Sq. i. 274.
London, 2, 2, 0 ; MDB. (co. Bucks), 0, 1, 1 ; (Showler), Boston, 1.

Shreeve, Shreve.—Offic. 'the sheriff,' early corrupted to Shreeve ; v. Sheriff. 'Schyreve, schreve, *vicecomes*': Prompt. Parv. p. 447.
'Cuthbert Conyers, shreve of the Bishopryke, 1564 ': Visit. Yorks. p. 71. Harl. Soc.
1580. Bapt.—Joyce, d. John Shreve : St. Jas. Clerkenwell, i. 12.
1665. William Panchast and Sarah Shreeve : Marriage Alleg. (Canterbury), p. 157.
1798. Married—John Shreve and Ann Stewart : St. Geo. Han. Sq. ii. 184.
London, 5, 0 ; New York, 0, 2.

Shrewsbury. — Local, 'of Shrewsbury,' the capital town of Shropshire.
Agnes de Sewesebyry, 1379 : P. T. Yorks. p. 174.
1582. Henry Shrewsbury and Eliz. Turtle : Marriage Lic. (London), i. 108.
1590. Thomas Shrewesbury, co. Northants : Reg. Univ. Oxf. vol. ii. pt. ii. p. 179.
London, 2 ; Sheffield, 1 ; MDB. (co. Camb.), 3.

Shrubsole, Shrubshall. — Local, 'of Shrubsole.' I cannot find any locality of this name. The suffix will be -*sole* or -*sale*, a hall ; v. Sale.
John de Sobesole, co. Kent, 1273. A.
1683. Edward Mecum and Ann Shrubsholl : Marriage Alleg. (Canterbury), p. 154.
London, 3, 1 ; Sheffield, 1, 0.

Shubrick, Shubrook.—Local; v. Shobbrook.

Shufflebotham, Shufflebottom. — Local, 'of Shippalbothom,' evidently some small spot in the ancient parish of Bury, co. Lanc., or the near neighbourhood. Like Higginbottom, Sidebotham, and several other local surnames with the suffix -*bottom* (v. Botham), Shufflebotham has East Cheshire or South-east Lancashire for its native home. The several stages of corruption after Shippobotham are Shifabottom and the imitative Shufflebotham. In the light of the subjoined entries, the assertion that the origin is Shaw-field-bottom (Lower) falls to the ground.
1582. Married — John Shippobotham and Anne Wilkynson : Reg. Prestbury (East Ches.), p. 74.
1587. Bapt.—Edwarde Shippobothom : ibid. p. 92.
1626. Married—Charles Shifabothom and Jone Horderne : ibid. p. 256.
Evidently the place is referred to in the following list of 'messuages, lands and rents' in 'Walton, Lancaster, Wigan, Haughton, Skelmersdale, . . . Bury, Cheetham, Cheetwood, Tottington, Undesworth, Salford, Shuttleworth, Shippalbothan, Middleton,' &c.: (1485) Baines' Lanc. i. 516.—Since writing the above I find the following references to this family, conclusively proving my points:
James Shepobotham, of Heap, Bury, 1579 : Wills at Chester (1545-1620), p. 174.
Francis Shippowbotham, Tottington, 1602 : ibid.
George Shupplebotham, of the parish of Bury, 1621 : ibid. (1621-50), p. 198.
James Shipplebotham, of Heap, Bury, 1642 : ibid.
Richard Shufflebotham, of Betchton, 1674 : ibid. (1651-80), p. 243.
The place itself also acquired the same form :
Roger Kay, of Shufflebotham, 1614 : Wills at Chester (1545-1620), p. 112.
Manchester, 2, 4 ; London, 3, 0 ; MDB. (co. Ches.), 11, 0 ; Philadelphia, 0, 2.

Shuldham, Shuldam, Shoulding.—Local, 'of Shuldham,' a parish in dioc. Norwich. The prior of Shuldham, co. Norfolk, is several times referred to in the Hundred Rolls (1273) ; v. Index. Shoulding is a natural and ordinary corruption.

Thomas Shouldham, co. Norf., 1467: FF. vii. 9.

Thomas Shuldham, co. Norf., temp. 1580: ibid. i. 478.

John Shouldham, lord of Marham and Shouldham, 1551: ibid. vii. 113.

MDB. (Suffolk), I, 0, 1; (Norfolk), 0, 1, 0.

Shute, Shutt, Shott.—(1) Local, 'of Shute,' a parish in co. Devon, two miles from Colyton.

1610. John Shute, of London: Reg. Univ. Oxf. vol. ii. pt. ii. p. 315.

1621. John Shute, co. Devon: ibid. p. 386.

1764. Married — Richard Shute and Ann Nightingale: St. Geo. Han. Sq. i, 139.

(2) Local, 'at the Shut' or Shoot, a West-country surname. ' Shut, a narrow street. West' (Halliwell). ' Shott, a nook, an angle, a field, a plot of land; v. Carlisle's Account of Charities, p. 305 ' (Halliwell). Hence Aldershot, Cockshott.

Robert atte Shoete, co. Soms., I Edw. III: Kirby's Quest, p. 79.

Simon atte Sheote, co. Soms., I Edw. III: ibid. p. 83.

William atte Shote, co. Soms., I Edw. III : ibid. p. 98.

Walter atte Shotte, co. Soms., I Edw. III: ibid. p. 228.

London, 7, 1, 0; West Rid Court Dir. (Shott), 1; Philadelphia, 10, 1, 13.

Shuter.—Occup. ; v. Shooter.

Shutt, Shut.—(1) Nick. 'the Scot' (?), probably a form of that term; v. Scutt and Shott. (2) Local; v. Shute.

Alicia Schutte, 1379: P. T. Yorks. p. 244.

William Schutt, 1379: ibid. p. 245.

Henry Schutte, 1379: ibid. p. 35.

1794. Married — Thomas Shutt and Hannah Gregory: St. Geo. Han. Sq. ii. 115.

Sheffield, 2, 0; West Rid. Court Dir., 1, 0; New York, 0, 1.

Shuttleworth.—(1) Local, 'of Shuttleworth,' a township in the parish of Bury, co. Lanc. (2) Local. The Shuttleworths of Shuttleworth Hall, in the parish of Whalley, co. Lanc., were in residence there as early as 3 Edw. III (1329), when Henry de Shuttleworth died seised of it and eight oxgangs (Baines' Lanc. ii. 60).

Thomas Schytylworth, co. York, 1477. W. 11.

Richard de Shuttleworth, co. Lanc., 20 Edw. I. R.

1605. Utred Shuttleworthe, co. Lanc.: Reg. Univ. Oxf. vol. ii. pt. ii. p. 283.

1619. Richard Shuttleworth, of Bedford, co. Lanc. : Wills at Chester, i. 175.

Manchester, 3; New York, 5.

Shuxsmith ; v. Sucksmith.

Shylock.—?——. This American representative of Shylock may be an imitative corruption of Sherlock (q.v.); but like Dickens, Shakespeare often took names from real life.

William Sylock, co. Soms., I Edw. III : Kirby's Quest, p. 244.

Philadelphia, 2.

Sibary, Sibray, Sibery, Sybry.—Bapt. 'the son of Sibry,' probably, and almost positively, a corruption of Sibley, the recognized popular form of Sybil; v. Sibley. Sybil was one of the greatest favourites in co. Yorks at the surname era, and it flourished there in every possible form. The corruption is a perfectly natural one.

Alan Sibri, co. York, 1273. A.

Stephen Sibry, co. York, ibid.

Thomas Sybry, 1379: P. T. Yorks. p. 132.

1687 John Masters and Katherine Sibrey : Marriage Alleg. (Canterbury), p. 207.

West Rid. Court Dir., 1, 4, 0, 1, London, 0, 0, 1, 0; Sheffield (Sybry), 1

Sibbet, Sibbett, Sibbitt.—Bapt. 'the son of Sybil,' from the nick. Sib, dim. Sibbot or Sibbet ; v. Sibbs. A family of Sibbitt lived for centuries at Ancroft, North Durham.

1664. Matthew Sibbitt: QQQ. p. 219.

1737. Adam Sibbitt : ibid.

1811. Isabella Sibbitt : ibid.

Sibota serviens ejus, 1379: P. T. Yorks. p. 110.

Sybota Tournour, 1379: ibid. p. 162.

Thomas Sibbotson, 1379: ibid. p. 156.

Sybil was exceedingly common. Hence are four on one page :

Sibilia Toged, 1379: P. T. Yorks. p. 74.

Sibilla de Kerre, 1379: ibid.

Sibilla de Melton, 1379: ibid.

Sibilla Schepherd, 1379: ibid.

Newcastle, 1, 0, 0; London (1886), 3, 0, 0; New York, 0, 0, 1; Philadelphia, 3, 1, 1.

Sibbs, Sibson.—Bapt. 'the son of Sybil,' from the nick. Sib ; cf. Ciss and Siss, q.v.

' Neat Nancy, jolly Joan, nimble Nell, kissing Kate, tall Tib, slender Sib, will quickly lose their grace': Anatomy of Melancholy, p. 598.

' Sybby Sole, mylke wyfe of Islynton.'   Cocke Lorelle's Bote.

Willelmus Sibilson, 1379: P. T. Yorks. p. 206.

Thomas Sibson, 1379 : ibid. p. 40.

Agnes Sybson, webster, 1379: P. T. Howdenshire, p. 17.

Magota Jonwif Cybson (i. e. Magot, wife of John, the son of Sib), 1379: P. T. Yorks. p. 86.

Thomas Sibson, 1379: ibid. p. 40.

Robert Sibbs, of Counston, co. Suff., 1524: FF i. 481.

Richard Sibson (co. Cumb.), Queen's Coll. : Reg. Univ. Oxf. vol. ii. pt. ii. p. 123.

London, 0, 2; MDB. (co. Cumb.), 0, 13; Philadelphia, 3, 9.

Sibley.—Bapt. 'the son of Sybil' (v. Sibbs), popularly Sibley. ' Sybyle, propyr name (Sibbe, K. Sybbly, P.). Sibilla ': Prompt. Parv.

Geoffrey Sibilie, co. Suff., 1273. A.

Robert Sibili, co. Oxf., ibid.

Thomas Sibely, co. Camb., ibid.

Isabel Sibeli, co. Hunts, ibid.

John Sibely, co. Soms., I Edw. III: Kirby's Quest, p. 79.

1604. Henry Sibly, co. Soms. : Reg. Univ. Oxf. vol. ii. pt. ii. p. 273.

1732. Bapt.—Mary, d. George Sibley : St. Peter, Cornhill, ii. 37.

London, 16 ; New York, 7.

Sibson ; v. Sibbs.

Sibthorpe. — Local, ' of Sibthorpe,' a parish in co. Notts.

William de Sibbethorp, co. Notts. Hen. III–Edw. I. K.

Theobald de Sybethorp, co. Hunts, 1273. A.

1613. Robert Fovell and Anne Sibthorpe (co. Essex) : Marriage Lic. (London), ii. 23.

— Robert Sibthorp, co. Soms. : Reg. Univ. Oxf. vol. ii. pt. ii. p. 332.

London, 1.

Sickerson.—A sharpened form of Siggerson; v. Siggers, and cf. Sackerson with Saggerson, all descended from the same parentname ; v. Sayer.

New York, 1.

Sicklemore, Sickelmore, Syckelmoore.—Local, 'at the sycamore'; cf. Oak, Birch, Ash, Nash, &c. I cannot of course be positive that Sicklemore is a corruption of Sycamore, but it is highly probable.

1557-8. Richard Wade and Agnes Silkelmare : Marriage Lic. (London), i. 18.

1662-3. Edmund Sicklemore and Mary Clarke: Marriage Alleg. (Canterbury), p. 68.

Umfrid' Sicomer, 1578, incumbent of North Gosforth Chapel, Newcastle-on-Tyne: Brand's Newcastle, i. 322.
1786. Married—Johan Christian Koenig and Sally Anne Sickelmore: St. Geo. Han. Sq. i. 387.
London, 1, 2, 0; Philadelphia, 0, 0, 3.

Sickman.—Bapt. 'the son of Sigmund.' The suffix -*mund* becomes -*man*; cf. Osman, Wyman, &c. The form Sickman exists or existed both in New York and Philadelphia (Bowditch's Suffolk Surnames, pp. 388-9). It once existed in England.

Richard Sukemund, co. Wilts, 1273. A.
Ricardus Sykman, *smyth*, 1379: P. T. Yorks. p. 79.

Siddall, Siddell, Syddall.—Local, (1) 'of Siddall,' a hamlet in the parish of Halifax, co. York; (2) 'of Siddall,' some small estate in the parish of Middleton, co. Lanc.

Thomas Sydall', 1379: P. T. Yorks. p. 194.
1503. Janet Sydell, of Fullwood: Lancashire Wills at Richmond, i. 267.
John Jones, of Sidal, parish of Middleton, 1611: Wills at Chester, i. 111.
Giles Siddall, of Whitefield, in Pilkington, 1614: ibid. p. 175.
Richard Siddall, of Stockport, 1616: ibid.
1749. Married—Isaac Siddal and Ann Triggs: St. Geo. Han. Sq. i. 42.
Manchester, 9, 0, 3; West Rid. Court Dir., 5, 2, 0; Sheffield, 19, 0, 0; Philadelphia, 20, 4, 0; New York, 0, 3, 0.

Sidebotham, Sidebottom.—Local, 'of the Side-bottom,' probably the side of the hollow, or bottom, as was the term in cos. Yorks, Lanc., and Cheshire, where most of the Ramsbottoms, Higginbothams, &c., spring from; v. Botham. Like Higginbotham, Sidebotham springs from the immediate neighbourhood of Stockport.

Thomas de Sidebotham, 2 Hen. IV, 1400: Earwaker's East Cheshire, ii. 50.
Robert Sidbothom, 1445 (knights, gentlemen, and freeholders in Macclesfield Hundred): ibid. i. 17.
1576. Married—William Sydebotham and Margaret Andrewe: Reg. Prestbury, p. 53.
1581. Thomas Sidebotham, of Romiley: Wills at Chester, i. 175.
Elizabeth Sydebothome, 1675, Stockport: Exchequer Depositions (co. Lanc.), p. 140.
John Sydbotham, 1680, Manchester: ibid. p. 57.
Manchester, 11, 6; London, 1, 1; Philadelphia, 7, 7.

Sidgreaves.—Local, 'of the Sidgreaves'; v. Greaves.

Richard del Sydgreues, made member of the Guild, 1397: Preston Guild, p. 5.
'Mr. T. T. Sidgreaves has been placed on the Commission of the Peace for the Borough of Preston': Manchester Evening Mail, Sept. 17, 1887.

Five centuries of interval between the two incidents.

Manchester, 1; Preston, 1; Boston (U.S.), 1.

Sidgwick; v. Sedgwick.

Sidney, Sydney.—Local, 'de St. Denis' (?). This is the generally accepted derivation, and I doubt not it is the true one. Lower says, 'The founder of this family in England was Sir William Sydney, Chamberlain of Henry II, who came from Anjou with that monarch, and was buried at Lewes Priory in 1188': Patr. Brit. p. 337. Like Chauncy and Washington in the United States, Sidney and Percy have been turned into baptismal names in England. Sydney has also given title to one of the great cities of Australia.

Richard de Sanct' Deonise, co. Norf., 1273. A.
Robert de Sanct' Deonisio, co. Devon, ibid.
John de Sanct' Dene, co. Sussex, 20 Edw. I. R.
(Prior) de Sanct Dionisio, co. Wilts, ibid.
1627. Bapt. — Humfrie, s. Thomas Sydney: St. Jas. Clerkenwell, i. 105.
1798. Married—John Sidney and Eliz. Gumby: St. Geo. Han. Sq. ii. 182.
London, 7, 8; Philadelphia, 3, 1.

Siebert; v. Seabright.

Siggers, Sigers.—Bapt. 'the son of Seger' or Sagar; v. Sayer and Seager.

1792. Married—William Siggers and Sarah Cripps: St. Geo. Han. Sq. ii. 74.
London, 3, 0; Philadelphia, 0, 1.

Siggins.—Bapt. 'the son of Segin,' probably a later English form of Segrim, one of the many compounds of Sigg (v. Siggs); genitive Siggins; cf. William and Williams.

Richard Segrym, co. Oxf., 1273. A.
Alan Segeyn, co. Camb., ibid.
Hugh Segin, co. Oxf., ibid.
John Segyn, co. Camb., ibid.

Robert Segym, co. Camb., 1273. A.
1617. Married—William Siggins and Olive Brown: St. Jas. Clerkenwell, iii. 44.
1669. — Edmun Glover and Martha Siggines: ibid. p. 168.
London, 3; New York, 1; Philadelphia, 1.

Siggs.—Bapt. 'the son of Sigg,' found in such compounds as Sigismund, Sigfrid, Sigward, Sigwald, Sigurd, &c. The genitive of Sigg is Siggs; cf. William and Williams.

Sigge de Anemere, co. Norf., 1273. A.
1791. Married—Moses Siggs and Sarah Wood: St. Geo. Han. Sq. ii. 66.
London, 1.

Sikes.—Local; v. Sykes.

Silcock, Silcocks, Silcox.—Bapt. 'the son of Cecil,' nick. Sill (less commonly Cill), with terminative -*cock* (v. Introd. p. 25). It would appear that to preserve a distinction between the popular fem. Cecilia and masc. Cecil, the nick. of the former was Siss (v. Sisson and Sissot), and of the latter, Sil or Sill; v. Silson.

Cf. Johannes Cyllson, 1379: P. T. Yorks. p. 269.

I have not yet found a single Silas in mediaeval records. Mr. Lower's suggested origination from this Apostolic name, which I carelessly accepted in my English Surnames, is out of the question. The name was unknown. Of course Silcocks or Silcox is the genitive form; cf. William and Williams, or Wilcock and Wilcocks, or Wilcox.

Silcokkus de Altrichelun, C. R., 11 Edw. I.
Adam Silkok, 1379: P. T. Yorks. p. 20.
Johannes Silcok, 1379: ibid.
Matilda Sylkok, 1379: ibid. p. 79.
William Selecok, 1379: ibid. p. 79.
III: Kirby's Quest, p. 210.
John Selcok, co. Soms., 1 Edw. III: ibid. p. 275.

In some cases very likely absorbed by Simcock or Simcox, q.v.

1785. Married—Nathan Silcock and Frances Cadney: St. Geo. Han. Sq. i. 374.
London Dir., 6, 1, 2; Philadelphia, 0, 0, 9.

Silk.—Local, 'of Silk,' a parish in co. Lincoln, now styled Silk-Willoughby.

1615. Bapt.—William, s. John Sylke: St. Jas. Clerkenwell, i. 72.
1748. Married—Samuel Silk and Sarah Mann : St. Geo. Chap. Mayfair, p. 121.
1769. — William Sick and Ann Clethers : St. Geo. Han. Sq. i. 193.
London, 7 ; MDB. (co. Camb.), 10 ; Philadelphia, 5.

Silkin.—Bapt. 'the son of Cecil,' from the nick. Sill or Sil, and dim. Sil-kin ; v. Silcock.

John Silkyn, 1531, Tattenhall, co. Ches. : Earwaker's East Cheshire, i. 56.

Silkman.—Occup. 'the silk-man,' a dealer in silk.

Thomas Silkman, Close Roll, 51 Edw. III.
'Sylke-women, pursers, and gar-nysshers.'   Cocke Lorelle's Bote.
New York, 3.

Silktippet.—Nick.

Roger Sylketypet : R. Pat., 4 Edw. III. pt. ii.

Sillifant.— Bapt. 'the son of Sullivan.' 'This Devonshire family, originally written Sullivan, were derived from the Sullivans of Ire-land, and settled in England in the year 1641 ' : Patr. Brit. p. 315.

MDB. (co. Devon), 3 ; London, 1.

Sillito, &c. ; v. Shilito.

Silson, Sills.—Bapt. 'the son of Cecil,' from the nick. Cill or Sill (v. Silcock) ; genitive Sills ; cf. William and Williams.

Johannes Cyllson, 1379 : P. T. Yorks. p. 269.
1746. Married—Samuel Sills and Eliz. Sharp : St. Geo. Chap. Mayfair, p. 80.
1750. — Richard Sills and Mary Stonnill : St. Geo. Han. Sq. i. 43.
London, 0, 5 ; Boston (U.S.), 0, 2.

Silverlock. — Nick. 'silver-grey,' from the complexion of a particular tress of the hair ; cf. Blacklock, Whitlock, Lovelock, &c.

Peter Siluerlok, C. R., 43 Edw. III.
Richard Selverlok, 1313. M.
James Silverlock. HH.
Alex. Silverlock. V. 5.
1622. Gilbert Seabrooke and Eliz. Sil-verlocke : Marriage Lic. (London), ii. 117.
1634. Married — James Sylverlocke and Ann Robinson : St. Thomas the Apostle (London), p. 15.
1682. Hugh Nurse and Eliz. Silver-lock : Marriage Alleg. (Canterbury), p. 94.
London, 4.

Silverside, Silversides. — Local, ' of Silverside,' some small locality in co. Lanc. which I have

not discovered. Probably near Sil-verdale, perhaps on the slope of it.

John de Syluersyd, *sadeler*, 1397 : Preston Guild Rolls, p. 5.
1744. Married—George Silverside and Susanna Price : St. Geo. Chap. Mayfair, p. 36.
1800. — William Silversides and Bar-bara Hunt : St. Geo. Han. Sq. ii. 212.
London, 3, 1 ; Manchester, 0, 1.

Silverthorn, Silverthorne.—Local, 'at the silver-thorn,' from residence thereby ; cf. Thorn and Hawthorn.

Roger Selverthorn, co. Soms., 1 Edw. III : Kirby's Quest, p. 159.
Richard Selverthorn, co. Soms., 1 Edw. III : ibid.
1693. Thomas Denkin and Amy Silver-thorne : Marriage Alleg. (Canterbury), p. 261.
1765. Married—Thomas Cockett and Sarah Silverthorne : St. Geo. Han. Sq. i. 150.
London, 1, 1 ; Philadelphia, 12, 0.

Silvester, Sylvester.—Bapt. 'the son of Silvester,' a fairly popu-lar font-name in the surname era.

Robert fil. Silvestre, co. Camb., 1273. A.
Thomas Silvestre, co. Oxf., ibid.
Silvestre le Euncyse, co. Hunts, ibid.
Thomas fil. Silvestre, co. Norf., ibid.
Ganfrid fil. Silvester. C.
Silvester le Carpenter, C. R., 33 Hen. III.
Willelmus Siluestre, 1379 : P. T. Yorks. p. 141.
Robertus Siluester, 1379 : ibid. p. 128.
1642. Bapt.—John, s. Walter Siluester : St. Jas. Clerkenwell, i. 151.
London, 15, 2 ; Philadelphia, 0, 34 ; New York, 3, 16.

Sim, Simes, Simms, Sims, Simpson, Simson.—Bapt. 'the son of Simon,' from the nick. Sim, whence Simpson, with intrusive *p*, as in Thompson, Hampson, &c. Sims or Simms is the genitive of Sim ; cf. William and Williams.

Robertus Symmes, 1379 : P. T. Yorks. p. 15.
Johannes Symson', 1379 : ibid. p. 288.
Thomas Symme, 1379 : ibid. p. 11.
Johannes Symmeson', 1379 : ibid.
Johannes Symnson, 1379 : ibid. p. 136.
Christopher Sims, co. Berks, 1594 : Reg. Univ. Oxf. vol. ii. pt. ii. p. 204.
Ellen Simms, of Warrington, 1593 : Wills at Chester, i. 175.
1800. Married — Louis Baumes and Margaret Sim : St. Geo. Han. Sq. ii. 227.
London, 5, 6, 8, 39, 149, 9 ; New York, 2, 2, 28, 13, 152, 4.

Simbarb. — Local, 'of St. Barbe,' a Norman surname intro-

duced into England. Formed after the fashion of Sinclair, &c. Even in the Pipe Rolls (Henry II) ' de Sancta Barbara ' is sometimes written Senbarb or Simbarb (Introduction to Pipe Rolls, P. R. Soc. p. 5). Barbe was the Norman Fr. form of our Barbara (v. Babb, Barbot, and Barbe).

Prior de Sancta Barba, co. Linc., 1273. A.
Thomas Seymt-barbe. B.
Jordan de St. Barbe. M.
William Sembarbe. V. 3.
'Commission of rebellion to Edward Saintbarbe (co. Somerset), Feb. 12, 1592' : Cal. State Papers (Domestic), iii. 182.
1546. William Simbarbe and Mary Litell, of the King's Household : Marriage Lic. (Faculty Office), p. 7.
1572. William Saintbarbe, or Simberbe : Reg. Univ. Oxf. vol. ii. pt. iii. p. 56.

Simcock, Simcox, Sim-cockes, Symcox.—Bapt. 'the son of Simon,' from the nick. Sim, with popular suffix -*cock* (v. Introd. p. 25). Simcocks (varied into Sim-cox) is the genitive ; cf. Wilcock and Wilcox.

Robert Symcot (? Simcock), co. Camb., 1273. A.
Vide Glasscock for change from *cock* to *cott*, and vice versa.
Gregory Symekok, co. Soms , 1 Edw. III : Kirby's Quest, p. 95.
Simon Simcok, co. Soms., 1 Edw. III : ibid. p. 131.
James Sympcock, co. York. W. 9.
Thomas Symcoxe : Coventry Mysteries, p. 65.
1586. Dier Simcockes, co. Soms. : Reg. Univ. Oxf. vol. ii. pt. ii. p. 150.
1616. Thomas Simcock, of Samlesbury : Wills at Chester, i. 175.
1669. Bapt.—Eliz., d. Robert Cim-cockes : St. Jas. Clerkenwell, i. 241.
Crockford, 0, 3, 1, 0 ; London (Sym-cox), 1 ; New York (Simcox), 2 ; Phila-delphia (Simcock), 2.

Simeon.—Bapt. 'the son of Simeon' ; kept distinct from Simon in early records.

Ralph fil. Simeon, co. Camb., 1273. A.
Stephen Symeon, co. Oxf., ibid.
Jacobus Simeon, co. Oxf., ibid.
Roger Simeon, co. Soms., 1 Edw. III : Kirby's Quest, p. 164.
1734. Married—Thomas Morrice and Sarah Simeon : St. Geo. Han. Sq. i. 13.
Crockford, 3 ; Oxford, 2.

Simes ; v. Sim.

Simister.—(1) Official (?), ' the summaster.' I will first furnish instances.

William Sumaster. Z.
William Summayster. B.
John Somayster. F.
William Summaster. Z.

Query (1), a summaster, i.e. chamberlain or clerk of expenses; (2) a summister, one who summarizes, abridges writings, &c. This is most probable, as the word occurs twice at least: 'Over this, if the historian be long, he is accompted a trifler; if he be short, he is taken for a summister' (Holinshed, Chron. Ireland, p. 80). 'And thus, though rudely, have I plaied the summister' (The Meane in Spending, 1598): both quoted by Halliwell. The name occurs in Mun. Acad. Oxon. (1462) as head of 'Sykyll Halle' (v. English Surnames, 5th edit., p. 206). Simister is a well-known North-English surname.

Samuel Summaster, co. Devon, 1607: Reg. Univ. Oxf. vol. ii. pt. ii. p. 297.
George Summaster, 1569: ibid. i. 274.

(2) Occup.; v. Sempster. As all the directories point to North England as the source, it is certain that some of our Simistres derive their name from the old form of Sempstress; v. instances under Sempster, which practically prove the case.

Manchester, 12; Liverpool, 2.

Simkin, Simkins, Simpkin, Simpkins, Simkinson.—Bapt. 'the son of Simon,' from the nick. Sim, dim. Sim-kin, as in Wilkin, Wilkinson, Tomkin, Tomkinson, &c. The *p* in Simpkin is, of course, intrusive, as in Simpson, Thompson, &c. For a variant of Simkins, v. Sinkins.

Simmerquin or Symchine Waller: Wars of England in France, Henry VI (v. Index).
Ralph Sympkynn: Hotten's Lists of Emigrants (v. Index).
1667. Christopher Symkinson, of Thurnham: Lancashire Wills at Richmond, i. 268.
1790. Married—Francis Simkins and Mary Edgar: St. Geo. Han. Sq. ii. 36.
1805. — James Gibson and Mary Simkin: ibid. p. 326.
London, 7, 10, 2, 3, 0; Philadelphia, 0, 8, 0, 19, 0; (Simpkin) Boston (U.S.), 1.

Simmance; v. Simmonds, of which it is a variant; cf. Evance for Evans.

1806. Married—Thomas Simmans and Sally King: St. Geo. Han. Sq. ii. 352.
MDB. (co. Essex), 1; (co. Hertford), 1.

Simmonds, &c.; v. Simon.

Simms; v. Sim.

Simnit, Simmonite, Simonett, Simnett.—Bapt. 'the son of Simon,' from the dim. Simonet.

Simonettus Mercator. E.
Symonet Villain. CC. 4.
London, 1, 0, 1, 0; Oldham Dir. (Simmonite), 1; Rotherham, 2; Derby (Simnett), 1; (Simonet) Boston (U.S.), 1.

Simon, Simmonds, Simmons, Simonds, Simons, Simonson.—Bapt. 'the son of Simon,' or Simond with excrescent *d*. 'Cym, propyr name (Cymund, H. P.), Simon': Prompt. Parv. p. 77 (cf. *gownd*, provincial for gown, *ribband* and *ribbon*, Hammond for Hamon, v. Hammon). One of the most popular font-names of the surname period (v. Sim, Simkin, Simcock). Our directories teem with examples. So do the early rolls. No connexion with Sigismund.

'He sit neither with Seint Johan, Symond, ne Jude.'
　　　　Piers Plowman, i. 240.
'Awake, Simond, the fend is on me fall.'
　　　　Chaucer, C. T. 4283.
John Simond, co. Oxf., 1273. A.
Nicholas Simond, co. Soms., 1 Edw. III: Kirby's Quest, p. 189.
John Symondes, co. Soms., 1 Edw. III: ibid. p. 218.
'Johannes that was seruant of Symond Godewyne of Salthous': Patent Roll, 17 Ric. II. pt. ii.
Robert Symondson. W. 8.
Marquis Symondesson. H.
Alicia relicta Symonys, 1379: P. T. Yorks. p. 118.
Johanna Symond, 1379: ibid. p. 193.
Sir Simond Musgrave, 1582: Nicolson and Burn, Hist. Westm. and Cumb., vol. i. p. xxxi.
Symond Puthperker, of Muncke-Coniston, 1640: Lancashire Wills at Richmond, i. 223.
Simond Battie, of Burrow, 1623: ibid. p. 25.
London, 10, 48, 79, 8, 16, 1; Philadelphia, 152, 1, 70, 0, 70, 1.

Simpkin; v. Simkin.

Simple.—Nick. 'the simple.' A guileless, easily deceived fellow, originally more complimentary than as at present understood.

William le Simple, Close Roll, 52 Hen. III.

Jordan le Simple, co. Oxf., 1273. A.
Richard le Simple, co. Oxf., ibid.
Henry le Simple, 1307. M.

No doubt now confused with the local Semple, q.v.

1558. Buried—Margaret Simple: St. Antholin (London), p. 12.
1625. — James Simple: St. Dionis Backchurch, p. 218.
London, 1; Philadelphia, 1.

Simpson, Simson; v. Sim.

Sinclair, Sinclaire. — Local, 'of St. Clair,' some chapelry in Normandy; cf. Simbarb, St. John, &c.

John de Sancto Claro, co. Suff., 1273. A.
Robert de Sancto Claro, co. Soms., ibid.
William de Sancto Claro, co. Kent, ibid.
Richard Seinteclere, co. Soms., 1 Edw. III: Kirby's Quest, p. 122.
William Seyncler, co. Soms., 1 Edw. III: ibid. p. 192.
1611. Bapt. — Helene, d. Nicholas Sayntcleare: St. Jas. Clerkenwell, i. 62.
1618. James Sinclar: Reg. Univ. Oxf. vol. ii. pt. ii. p. 369.
1777. Married—John Sinclaire and Ann Holborn: St. Geo. Han. Sq. i. 277.
London, 19, 0; New York, 43, 4.

Sincox.—Bapt. A corruption of Simcox, q.v.; cf. Sinkinson for Simkinson. The variants of Simcocks are placed under one heading in Index to Reg. Univ. Oxf. They include Simcox, Sincocks, and Symcockes; vol. ii. pt. iv. p. 382.

MDB. (co. Essex), 1.

Singer.—Occup. 'the singer'; v. Sanger and Sangster; cf. Dancer, Hopper, &c.

1583. John Synger and Joane Burton: St. Dionis Backchurch, p. 10.
1768. Married—John Singer and Mary Reilly: St. Geo. Han. Sq. i. 173.
London, 4; Philadelphia, 34.

Single.—Nick. 'the single,' i.e. the separate, one who lived alone.

Richard le Sengle, co. Worc., 1273. A.
London, 1; Philadelphia, 2.

Singleton.—Local, 'of Singleton,' a parish in co. Sussex, six miles from Midhurst. Also a chapelry in the parish of Kirkham, co. Lanc. Doubtless other and smaller spots are so termed.

Adam de Syngleton, 1379: P. T. Yorks. p. 276.
Thomas Singleton, of Shrigley, 1616: Wills at Chester, i. 176.
1597. Isaac Singleton, London: Reg. Univ. Oxf. vol. ii. pt. ii. p. 222.

1615. John Singleton, co. Cumb.: Reg. Univ. Oxf. vol. ii. pt. ii. p. 336.
Sheffield, 4; West Rid. Court Dir., 4; New York, 10.

Singular.—Nick. 'the singular,' the peculiar.

Robert le Senguler, C. R., 55 Hen. III.
1776. Married — Richard Parry and Ellen Singler: St. Geo. Han. Sq. i. 265.

Sinkins, Sinkinson.—Bapt. ' the son of Simon.' Sinkinson is a corruption of Simkinson; v. Simkin. Cf. Ransom for Ranson, and Milsom for Milson, an opposite tendency.

Synkyn-dogter (i. e. the daughter of Simkin), 1379: P. T. Yorks. p. 162.
1639. Bapt.—Samuel, s. Simon Sinkinson: St. Jas. Clerkenwell, i. 144.
Cf. 1736. — Thomas, s. John Sinson: ibid. ii. 226.
1794. Married — James Evans and Susanna Sinkinson: St. Geo. Han. Sq. ii. 113.
London, 2, 0; Ulverston, 0, 1; MDB. (co. Lanc.), 0, 1; (co. Somerset), 4, 0; Philadelphia, 0, 4.

Sinnett, -nott; v. Sennett.

Sire, Syre.—Nick. ' the sire,' i.e. the master.

John le Sire, co. Hunts, 1273. A.
Alexander le Sire, co. Hunts, ibid.
Walter le Sire, co. Bucks, ibid.
Simon le Sire, Fines Roll, 17 Edw. II.
Cecilia Syre, 1379: P. T. Yorks. p. 154.
Ricardus Syre, 1379: ibid. p. 196.
1796. Married—John Syer and Catherine Green: St. Geo. Han. Sq. ii. 157.
New York, 4, 0.

Sired, Siret, Sirett, Syrett, Syratt.—Bapt. 'the son of Sigrid.' Sired (Domesday): Yonge, ii. 310. Sigrid, mother of Cnut (Canute) and Olaf of Sweden: Freeman's Norm. Conq. i. 410.

Roger Syrad, co. Oxf., 1273. A.
John Syred, co. Hunts, ibid.
Martin Sired, co. Kent, ibid.
Sigreda de Urmeston, Close Roll, 9 Edw. III.
Sigreda de Skelton, 1346: Accounts of the Exchequer, 19-20 Edw. III.
Cyred Tone, 1379: P. T. Yorks. p. 240.
1722. Married — John Syrett and Susanna Hippeth: St. Mary Aldermary (London), p. 45.
1769. — John Green and Eliz. Siret: St. Geo. Han. Sq. i. 189.
London, 0, 1, 4, 5, 1.

Sirrell.—A variant of Serrill; v. Serle.

MDB. (co. Hereford), 5

Siss.—Bapt. 'the son of Cecilia,' from the nick. Ciss, Cess, and Siss. This form lasted till the 17th century, and still exists as Sissy in the nursery. Such rhymes as the following will be commonly met with in D'Urfey:

' Long have I lived a bachelor's life,
  And had no mind to marry ;
But now I would fain have a wife,
  Edith, Doll, Kate, Sis, or Mary.'

'Cesse the souteresse' (v. Sisson for quotation). Almost all the instances of names founded on Siss given below come from Yorkshire and its border. A great impetus was given to it there on account of Cicely Neville, the Rose of Raby, 'proud Ciss,' 'the Duchess of York' (v. Yonge, i. 310). The Conqueror's daughter, Cecily, Abbess of Caen, gave it favour still earlier to the country at large.

Alicia Sisse-doghter, *webster*, 1379: P. T. Howdenshire, p. 19.

Sisselot. — Bapt. ' the son of Cecilia,' from the dim. Cecilot (cf. Hewlett from Hugh).

Alicia fil. Sisselot, 1273. A.
Bella Cesselot, co. Oxon, ibid.

Sisselson.—Bapt. ' the son of Cecil.'

Richard Sisselson. H.

Sisson, Sison, Sissons. — Bapt. ' the son of Cecilia,' from the nick. Siss or Cess ; v. Siss.

' Cesse the souteresse
  Sat on the benche.'
       Piers Plowman, l. 3105.
Johannes Sisson, 1379: P. T. Howdenshire, p. 21.
Robertus Cisson, 1379: ibid. p. 19.
Henricus Sisson, 1379: P. T. Yorks. p. 226.
Thomas Cysson, 1379: ibid. p. 269.
William Cisson, 1379: ibid.
Henry Sysson, co. York. W. 9.

Staying at the Bull Hotel, Sedbergh (W. Rid. Yorks), in June, 1886, Sisson stared me in the face over a shop across the road. Sisson has taken a curious genitive form, Sissons ; cf. William and Williams.

MDB. (co. Cumb.) Sisson, 7 ; West Rid. (Yorks) Court Dir. (Sissons), 4 ; London (Sissons), 5 ; Crockford (Sisson), 5 ; Philadelphia, 2, 4, 0.

Sissot, Sissotson, Sississon, Sisserson.—Bapt. ' the son of Cecilia,' from the nick. Cess or Siss (v. Siss), dim. Sissot or Cessot.

'Willelmus Crake and Cissot sa femme.' W.D.S.
Cissota West, co. York. W. 2.
Syssot, wife of Diccon Wilson. AA. 2.
Syssot, wife of Jak of Barsley, ibid.
John Sissotson, co. York. W. 2.
Agnes Sissotson, co. York. W. 11.
Robert Syssottysone, rector of Lecceworthe, 1478. XX. 2, p. 187.

The nearest modern approach to the original is Sississon, found, as might be expected, in Yorkshire. Nevertheless, I am surprised that more descendants of this once common pet-name are not in existence as surnames in the 19th century. v. Sisterson.

Hull, 0, 0, 1, 0; New York (Sisserson), 2.

Sisterson.—Bapt. 'the son of Cecilia,' from the nick. Siss, dim. Sissot. Thus Sissotson became by imitation Sisterson. There can be no doubt about this origin. It is found in the very district where Sissotson arose and became familiar (v. Sissotson and Sissot). Any idea that it means a nephew, i.e. sister's son, must be discarded. The form is simply imitative ; cf. Ibberson for Ibbotson from Isabella.

Corbridge-on-Tyne, 2.

Sivewright, Sievewright.—Occup. ' the sievewright,' a maker of sieves (v. Sivier). M.E. *sive.*

' And all this mullok in a sive ythrowe.'
      Chaucer, C. T. 16408.

Cf. Arkwright, Wainwright, &c.

Boston (U.S.), 1, 1.

Sivier.—Occup. ' the sievyer,' a sieve - maker ('siveyer, seve makere, *cribrarius*': Prompt. Parv.). v. Sivewright.

Ralph le Siviere, co. Camb. A.
Peter Syvyere. B.
1615. Bapt.—Susanna, d. John Sevier: St. Jas. Clerkenwell, ii. 92.
1793. Married — John Sievier and Frances Waud: St. Geo. Han. Sq. ii. 102.
1798. — Richard Sivier and Frances Mattingley: ibid. p. 175.
London, 1.

Sixsmith; v. Shoesmith and Sucksmith.

Sizer.—Offic. 'the sizar,' probably an 'assizer,' one who jotted down the rations of bread, otherwise a poor University scholar who got his bread cheap at the buttery; v. Panter.

Willelmus Sisar, 1379: P. T. Yorks. p. 158.
1715. Buried—Samuel Siser: St. Peter, Cornhill, ii. 122.
1774. Married — Leonard Sizer and Eliz. Northorp: St. Geo. Han. Sq. i. 247.
London, 3; MDB. (co. Essex), 3; Philadelphia, 1; New York, 3.

Skaife, Scaife, Scafe, Scaif.—Nick. or personal name. 'Skafe, awkward. Lincolnshire' (Halliwell). Mr. Lower says, 'Scaif, a northern provincialism for timid or fearful.'

Henry Skayf, co. York, 1273. A.
Hugh Skave, co. Norf., ibid.
Willelmus Skayf, 1379: P. T. Yorks. p. 206.
Robertus Scayff, 1379: ibid. p. 259.
Simon Sca'f', 1379: ibid. p. 232.
Alicia Scayf', 1379: ibid.
1605-6. Married—Francis Scaff, of Richmond, co. York, *carrier*, and Christian Fossett: St. Dionis Backchurch, p. 15.
1759. — John Channer and Eliz. Skaife: St. Geo. Han. Sq. i. 91.
London, 5, 2, 0, 0; West Rid. Court Dir., 0, 2, 1, 1; Philadelphia (Scaife), 1.

Skalls; v. Skeels.

Skeate, Skeats, Skeet.—Bapt. 'the son of Sket.' In Domesday described as Schett and Scheit, co. Norfolk. Found frequently as Sket in Norfolk and neighbouring county of Suffolk in the Hundred Rolls. Also once as a single personal name in the form of Sketh:

Sketh, co. Norf., 1273. A.
Alan Sket, co. Suff., ibid.
Nicholas Sket, co. Suff., ibid.
John Sket, co. Norf., ibid.
Warinus Sket, burgess in Parl. for Dunwich, 1311. M.
Adam Skete, 1379: P. T. Yorks. p. 157.
1616. John Skeat, co. Wilts: Reg. Univ. Oxf. vol. ii. pt. ii. p. 357.
1631. Married—Edward Skeite and Mary Lozeyer: St. Thomas the Apostle (London), p. 15.
1743. Bapt.—Mary, d. of John Skett: St. Michael, Cornhill, p. 173.

Skeats is the genitive form; cf. Williams with William.

1797. Married — Isaac Skeates and Harriet Mayriss: St. Geo. Han. Sq. ii. 160.
London, 1, 2, 5; New York, 0, 1, 0.

Skeels, Skalls, Skeeles, Skeel.—Bapt. 'the son of Schayl,' genitive Schayls, now Skalls or Skeels; cf. William and Williams. It will be seen that the surname still flourishes in the district where it is first found six centuries ago.

Dionise Schayl, co. Camb., 1273. A.
Philip Schayl, co. Hunts, ibid.
Walter Schayl, co. Oxf., ibid.
Richard Skeeles, co. Norf., 1723: FF. iv. 501.
1796. Married—Benjamin Skeel and Lucy Lambert: St. Geo. Han. Sq. ii. 152.
London, 3, 0, 1, 2; MDB. (co. Camb.), 7, 2, 0, 0; New York, 3, 0, 0, 5.

Skeffington, Skevington, Skeavington, Skivington, Skiffington.—Local, 'of Skeffington,' a parish in co. Leicester.

David de Scheftinton, co. Leic., Hen. III-Edw. I. K.
Baldewinus de Scheftinton, co. Leic., ibid.
1575-6. William Skevington, co. Staff.: Reg. Univ. Oxf. vol. ii. pt. ii. p. 70.
1611-2. Married, s. William Skevington: St. Dionis Backchurch, p.94.
London, 5, 0, 0, 0, 0; MDB. (co. Bedf.), 0, 1, 0, 0, 0; (co. Derby), 0, 1, 1, 1, 0; Philadelphia, 9, 0, 0, 0, 8.

Skegg, Skeggs.—? Bapt. 'the son of Skeg' (?). A Scandinavian personal name, probably (found in such local names as Skegness and Skegby). Genitive, Skeggs; cf. Williams with William.

Thomas Skegge, *laborer*, 1376: P. T. Howdenshire, p. 5.
Thomas Skegges, of Chelfield, Kent, 1714: Reg. St. Peter, Cornhill, ii. 70.
1715. Bapt.—John, s. James Skegg: St. Jas. Clerkenwell, ii. 86.
1790. Married—Anthony Sprigmore and Sarah Skeggs: St. Geo. Han. Sq. ii. 48.
London, 2, 5; New York, 0, 1.

Skelding.—Local, 'of Skelding,' a township in the parish of Ripon, co. Yorks.

1620. Rowland Skeldinge, of Cartmell: Lancashire Wills at Richmond, i. 256.
1678. Thomas Skelding, of Newbarnes (Dalton-in-Furness): ibid.
1640. Bapt. — Hester, d. Edmund Skeldinge: St. Jas. Clerkenwell, i. 144.
London, 3; New York, 3.

Skelton, Skeleton. — Local: (1) 'of Skelton,' a village near Ripon, co. York. Skeleton is not a happy corruption, but it is imitative, like a hundred other corrupted

spellings; cf. Deadman, Physick. (2) 'of Skelton,' a parish in co. Cumberland.

Willelmus de Skelton, 1379: P. T. Yorks. p. 242.
Thomas de Skelton, 1379: ibid.
1617. John Skelton, co. Cumb.: Reg. Univ. Oxf. vol. ii. pt. ii. p. 359.
1632-3. John Skelton and Prudence Summers: Marriage Lic. (Faculty Office), p. 26.
MDB. (co. Cumb.), 21, 0; West Rid. Court Dir., 13, 0; Newcastle, 1, 2; New York, 2, 0; Boston (U.S.), 5, 0.

Sketchley.—Local, 'of Sketchley,' a hamlet in the parish of Aston Framville, co. Leicester.

1678. John Skechley and Eliz. Crosfeild: Marriage Alleg. (Canterbury), p. 229.
1742. Married—Lewis Sketchley and Hannah Dew: St. Geo. Chap. Mayfair, p. 23.
1757. — Richard Sketchley and Susanna Stockley: St. Geo. Han. Sq. i. 74.
London, 4; MDB. (co. Leic.), 5; Philadelphia, 2.

Skidmore.—Local; v. Scudamore, of which it is a variant.

Philadelphia, 2; Oxford, 1.

Skiftling.—Nick. 'the skiftling,' one who moved from one place to another. *Skift* is used for *shift* in the Furness dialect. Dan. *skifte*, to remove.

Johannes Skyfftlyng, 1379: P. T. Yorks. p. 127.
Willelmus Skyftlyng, 1379: ibid. p. 128.
1566. John Skiffling, or Skiftlinge: Reg. Univ. Oxf. vol. ii. pt. ii. p. xvi.

Skillman.—? Nick. 'Skillman,' a man of reason, craft, knowledge.

Henry Skileman, co. Camb., 1273. A.
John Skyleman, co. Norf., ibid.
Richard Skyleman, co. Norf., ibid.
1802. Married—William Smith and Mary Skillmon: St. Geo. Han. Sq. ii. 267.
London, 1; New York, 5.

Skinner.—Occup. 'the skinner,' a dealer in skins.

Henry le Skyniar', co. Oxf., 1273. A.
Richard le Skynnere. B.
Robert le Skynnere, 1302. M.
Robert le Skynnar, co. Soms., 1 Edw. III: Kirby's Quest, p. 105.
Johannes Sckynner', 1379: P. T. Yorks. p. 96.
Willelmus de Parlyngton, *skynnar*, 1379: ibid. p. 106.
Robertus Skynner, *skynner*, 1379: St. Jas. Clerkenwell, i. 108.
1618. Bapt.—Richard, s. John Skinner: ibid. p. 82.
London, 65; Boston (U.S.), 76.

Skipp.—Local, 'at the skip,' from residence in or beside a ship; A.S. *scip.* v. Shipp.

1273. John Skyp : Cal. of Wills in Court of Husting.
1682. Bapt.—Thomas, s. Thomas Skip: St. Jas. Clerkenwell, i. 296.
1701. Robert Yeomans and Eliz. Skipp: Marriage Lic. (Faculty Office), p. 241.
1746. Married—Henry Skipp and Mary Parker: St. Geo. Chap. Mayfair, p. 65.
London, 1.

Skipper.—Occup. 'the skipper,' a captain of a ship.

Herman le Skippere, C. R., 12 Edw. II.
1646. Married—Thomas Skipper and Ann Cornwell : St. Peter, Cornhill, i. 257.
1657. John Skipper to Elizabeth Kelke : St. Michael, Cornhill, p. 37.
James Skipper, 1738, Norwich : FF. iv. 207.
London, 6; MDB. (co. Essex), 3; Philadelphia, 1.

Skipworth.—Local, ' of Skipwith,' a parish in the E. Rid. Yorks, near Selby.

1596. Charles Skipwith, Magd. Hall : Reg. Univ. Oxf. vol. ii. pt. iii. p. 198.
1671. Bapt.—Mary, d. John Scipworth : St. Jas. Clerkenwell, i. 249.
1690. — Susanna, d. John Skipwith : ibid. p. 336.
MDB. (co. Stafford), 1.

Skirmisher, Skrimshire, Scrimshaw, Scrimgeoure, Scrymgeour, Scrimiger, Scrymser, Scrymigar. — Offic. 'the skirmisher,' a fencer. O.F. *eskirmir,* to fence. O.F. *escarmouche,* a skirmish, hence English scrimmage, and the form scrimgeour, i. e. scrimmager, one who mingled in a scrimmage.

' Qe nul teigne Escole de Eskermerye, ne de Bokeler deins la citee.'
Liber Albus.

Scrimmage was in early use, and is not in any true sense provincial. Lower quotes Crawford's Scottish Peerage as follows : ' Alexander I, by special grant, appointed a member of the Carron family, to whom he gave the name of Scrimgeour, for his valour in a sharp fight, to the office of hereditary standard-bearer.' This settles any doubt, if any doubt existed; v. Patr. Brit. p. 307.

Henry le Eskirmessur, co. York, 1273. A.

William le Shyrmisur, co. Salop, 1273. A.
Peter le Eskurmesur. E.
Abraham le Skirmisur, C. R., 34 Hen. III.
Elizebetha Skrymsher. EE.
Alexander Schirmissure. SS.
Roger le Skirmisour, London. ⊙X.
John le Eskirmesour, co. Berks, Hen. III-Edw. I. K.
London, 0, 1, 0, 6, 0, 0, 0, 0 ; Crockford, 0, 4, 0, 1, 0, 0, 0, 0; Sheffield, 0, 0, 4, 0, 0, 0, 0, 0 ; Liverpool (Scrimiger), 1 ; New York, 0, 0, 0, 0, 3, 0, 6, 2.

Skirrow.—Local, ' of Sharow ' (?), a village, a mile from Ripon. Possibly some spot nearer the Lancashire border of the West Riding. v. Sharrow.

Thomas de Skyrhow, 1379 : P. T. Yorks. p. 290.
1570. William Skerowe, of Wray, in Melling : Lancashire Wills at Richmond, i. 256.
1611. Bapt. — Margaret, d. Henry Skerrow : St. Antholin (London), p. 48.
1620-1. Harman Curital and Frances Skerro : Marriage Lic. (London), ii. 95.
1634. Thomas Skirow, of Wray : Lancashire Wills at Richmond, i. 256.
1638. Christopher Skirroe, of Wray : ibid.
West Rid. Court Dir., 1 ; London, 1 ; Leeds (Scurrah), 2 ; Liverpool (Scurry), 1 ; Boston (U.S.) (Scurrah), 1.

Skottowe, Scotto, Scottowe. —Local, ' of Scottow,' a parish in co. Norfolk.

Jeffry de Scothowe, co. Norf., 1120 : FF. vi. 341.
John de Scothowe, co. Norf., 1279 : ibid.
William de Skothow, rector of Hethill, co. Norf., 1329 : ibid. v. 109.
Richard Skottowe, alderman, of Norwich, 1616 : ibid. iv. 292.
John Scotto, co. Norf., 1631 : ibid. i. 383. MDB. (co. Berks), 1, 0, 0 ; (co. Ches.), 0, 0, 1 ; London, 0, 1, 0.

Skoulding; v. Scolding.

Skudder, Scudder.—Occup. Probably an immigrant from Holland, equivalent to English Shooter, q.v.

1604. Married—Robert Skutter and Goodwith White : St. Mary Aldermary (London), p. 10.
1690. Bapt.—Anne, d. Robert Scudder : Canterbury Cath., p. 19.
London, 2, 1 ; Philadelphia, 0, 2.

Skull. — ? Bapt. 'the son of Scowle' (?).

William Scowle, co. Linc., 1273. A.
1579. Ralph Skull and Margery Turnor : Marriage Lic. (London), i. 87.

1808. Married—William Adcock and Winifred Skull : St. Geo. Han. Sq. ii. 389.
London, 1 ; MDB. (co. Bucks), 1.

Skurray; v. Scurry.

Slack, Slagg.—Local, ' at the Slack' or Slagg, from residence thereby, a place where the road becomes less steep, a gap in the hills (slacken, to ease off). John del Slak, Pardons Roll, 6 Ric. II. With the lazier Slagg, cf. Jagg and Jack (Jagg, Piers Plowman). Probably both *slack* and *slag* refer to that point of the hilltop where the stones and earth began to dribble down the slope (hence slag, *scoria*) ; v. Skeate.

Johannes del Slak', 1379 : P. T. Yorks. p. 180.
Thomas de Slake, 1379 : ibid. p. 192.
Johannes Sclake, 1379 : ibid.
1579. Thomas Lane and Eliz. Slegge : Marriage Lic. (London), i. 88.
1587. Buried—John Slake, a rogue : St. Peter, Cornhill, i. 134.
London, 9, 0 ; Manchester, 8, 1 ; MDB. (co. Cumb.), 13, 0 ; Philadelphia, 45, 0.

Slade.—Local, 'at the slade,' from residence thereby, a small strip of green in a woodland.

'It had been better of William a Trent
To have been abed with sorrowe,
Than to be that day in the greenwood slade
To meet with Little John's arrowe.'

In compounds *slade* is found in such local surnames as Greenslade, Moorslade, Whiteslade, Oakslade, Waldslade, and Sladen (q.v.).

Nicholas de la Slade, c. 1300. M.
Henry atte Slade, co. Soms., 1 Edw. III : Kirby's Quest, p. 178.
John atte Slade, C.R., 20 Edw. III. pt. i.
Richard atte Slade, C. R., 21 Edw. III. pt. ii.
1596. Bapt.—Mary, d. John Slade : Kensington Ch., p. 12.
1615. Ammiel Slade, co. Devon : Reg. Univ. Oxf. vol. ii. pt. ii. p. 346.
— Francis Slade, co. Berks : ibid. p. 336.
1645. Bapt.—Grace, d. George Slayd : Kensington Ch., p. 35.
London, 24 ; New York, 12.

Sladen.—Local, ' of Sladen,' a hamlet in the parish of Littleborough, co. Lanc. Probably other small spots are so termed (v. Slade and Dean).

Johannes Sladen, 1379 : P. T. Yorks. p. 187.
Jennet Hill, of Sladen, *widow*, 1599 : Wills at Chester (1545-1620), p. 93.

1767. Bapt.—Isaac, s. Isaac Sladden : Canterbury Cath., p. 33.
1806. Married—Benjamin King and Mary Sladen : St. Geo. Han. Sq. ii. 344.
London, 3; West Rid. Court Dir., 1; Philadelphia, 2.

Slagg; v. Slack.

Slape.—Local, 'at the slape' (i.e. a shelving declivity), from residence thereby. A slope, a slape, or a slipe seem all to express the same meaning. In Oxfordshire the shelving bank between the base of a fortification and the moat below is a slipe. In Cumberland a farmer will say of the roads in frosty weather, 'They're terrible slape to-day,' i.e. slippery.

Matilda de Slape, co. Oxf., 1273. A.
Randulph atte Slape, co. Soms., 1 Edw. III : Kirby's Quest, p. 153.
Nicholas atte Sclape, co. Soms., 1 Edw. III : ibid. p. 240.
William atte Sclape, co. Soms., 1 Edw. III : ibid.
1604. Married—Roche Slape and Eliz. Gloover : St. Jas. Clerkenwell, iii. 29.
1610. Richard Slape, co. Soms. : Reg. Univ. Oxf. vol. ii. pt. ii. p. 316.
1696. Bapt.—Ann, d. William Slape : St. Jas. Clerkenwell, i. 368.
1749. Married—Thomas Slape and Ann Green : St. Geo. Chap. Mayfair, p. 130.

It is abundantly clear that co. Somerset was the chief habitat of the name.

London, 1; MDB. (co. Somerset), 1.

Slater, Sclater, Slatter. — Occup. 'the slater.' M. E. *sclat*; v. Wyclif, Luke v. 19 (Skeat). There is no modern affectation in the forms of Sclater and Slatter. They are the unbroken use of centuries; cf. Reader, Tyler, Thacker, Thackster, &c.

Adam le Sclattere, co. Oxf., 1273. A.
Richard le Sclattere, co. Oxf., ibid.
Walter Sclatter, co. Bucks, ibid.

Slatter is still familiar to co. Oxford.

1684. Bapt.—Eliz., d. John Sclator : St. Jas. Clerkenwell, i. 306.
1807. Married—Thomas Slatter and Esther Bael : St. Geo. Han. Sq. ii. 361.
London, 46, 1, 10 ; Oxford, 2, 0, 3 ; Philadelphia, 44, 0, 1.

Slaughter.—Local, 'of Slaughter,' two parishes in co. Glouc., viz. Upper and Lower Slaughter.

Ballivus de Sloutre, co. Glouc., 1273. A.
John de Sloghtre, C. R., 26 Edw. III.
Paris Slaughter. V. 2.

1783. Married—William Hill and Eliz. Slaughter : Canterbury Cath., p. 98.
1791. — Thomas Slaughter and Eliz. Davies : St. Geo. Han. Sq. ii. 55.
1803. — Joseph Wood and Eliz. Slafter : ibid. p. 286.
London, 6; Philadelphia, 18.

Slay.—Nick. 'the sly' (q.v.). Oxford, 7.

Slaymaker. — Occup. 'the slaymaker,' a maker of slays (v. Slaywright). ' "*Slay*, an instrument belonging to a weaver's loom that has teeth like a comb": Phillips. "*Slay*, a wever's tole." Palsgrave' (Skeat). The weaver's reed. A petition to Parliament in 1467 from the worsted manufacturers complains that in the county of Norfolk there are 'divers persones that make untrue ware of all manner of worstedes, not being of the assises in length or brede . . . and that the *slayes* and yern thereto belonging are untruly made and wrought' (Rot. Parl. Edw. IV).

1594. Henry Slaymaker, or Slymaker, Trin. Coll. : Reg. Univ. Oxf. vol. ii. pt. iii. p. 180.
Johannes Slaymaker, 1379 : . P. T. Yorks. p. 51.
1705. Elizabeth Slaymaker : St. Peter, Cornhill, ii. 65.
1715. Bapt.—Mary, d. John Slaymaker : St. Jas. Clerkenwell, ii. 92.
London, 2 ; Oxford, 1 ; Philadelphia, 4.

Slaywright. — Occup. 'the slaywright,' one who manufactured slays ; v. Slaymaker.

Reginald Slaywright, co. Soms., 1 Edw. III : Kirby's Quest, p. 185.
Thomas Slawryghte, co. York. W. 11.
The Prior of the Hermit Friars, Warrington, in 1520 was one Slaywright : Baines' Lanc. ii. 224.
William Slywright, C. R., 1 Mary, pt. iii.
1576. John Brockett and Margery Slewright : Marriage Lic. (London), i. 70.
1589. Thomas Sliwright, or Slywright, co. Kent : Reg. Univ. Oxf. vol. ii. pt. ii. p. 173.

I cannot find any modern representatives of this name, but it would be dangerous on that account to assert that it did not exist.

Sleddall. — Local, ' of Long Sleddale,' a chapelry in the parish of Kendal, co. Westmoreland.

Thomas Sleddall, 1586 : Lancashire Wills at Richmond, i. 256.
Richard Sleddell, of Lancaster, 1686 : ibid. ii. 234.

Maria Sleddall, of Goosenargh, 1692 : ibid.
1690. Henry Sleddall and Prudence Lucas : Marriage Alleg. (Canterbury), p. 142.
Kirkby Stephen, 1 ; Ulverston, 1.

Slee, Sleigh; v. Sly.

Sleeman.—Bapt. ; v. Slyman.

Sleep, Sleap. — (1) Local. Lower says : ' Sleep, a hamlet in the parish of St. Peter, in the liberty of St. Alban's, co. Hertford' (Patr. Brit. p. 318). The evidence below suggests another locality. (2) 'of Sleap,' a township in the parish of Wem, co. Salop. No doubt this is one of the chief parents.

Coc de Slepe, co. Salop, 1273. A.
Hugh de Slepe, co. Salop, ibid.
Richard de Slepe, co. Salop, ibid.
1574. Buried—Ursula Slepe : St. Jas. Clerkenwell, iv. 16.
1600. Married — Thomas Sleepe and Jone Lee : St. Peter, Cornhill, i. 242.
1729. — John Sleap and Parnell Buckinham : St. Geo. Chap. Mayfair, p. 288.
1749. — Charles Burney and Esther Sleep : ibid. p. 137.
London, 4, 5 ; Boston (U.S.), 2, 0.

Slemmon, Slimmon, &c.; v. Slyman.

Slinger.—Occup. 'the slinger,' one who used the sling in warfare.

Henricus Slenger, 1379 : P. T. Yorks. p. 265.
Alicia Slynger, 1379 : ibid.
1674. Bapt. — Robert, s. Richard Slinger : St. Dionis Backchurch, p. 120.
1674-5. Buried — Eliz., d. Richard Slinger : ibid. p. 241.
Manchester, 3 ; Leeds, 1 ; West Rid. Court Dir., 3 ; New York, 2.

Slingsby.—Local, 'of Slingsby,' a parish in the N. Rid. Yorks, six miles from New Malton.

John de Slengesby, *wayder* (v. Wader), 33 Edw. I : Freemen of York, i. 10.
Henricus de Slyngesby, 1379 : P. T. Yorks. p. 245.
Ricardus de Slyngesby, 1379 : ibid.
Willelmus de Slenggesby, 1379 : P. T. Howdenshire, p. 8.
Charles Slingesbey, co. York, 1577 : Reg. Univ. Oxf. vol. ii. pt. ii. p. 78.
1787. Married—Thomas Ashley and Hannah Slingsby ; St. Geo. Han. Sq. i. 407.
London, 2 ; West Rid. Court Dir., 1.

Slipper, Sleeper.—(1) Occup. 'the slipper,' i. e. a maker of sword-slips (v. Swordslipper), an important craft in its day. (2) Nick. 'the sleeper,' a dull, heavy, sleepy sort of a fellow.

Simon le Slepar', co. Oxf., 1273. A.
Johannes Slipar, 1379: P. T. Yorks. p. 109.
London, 4, 0; New York, 2, 30; Philadelphia, 0, 9.

Slocombe, Slocum, Slocumb, Slocomb, Slocom.—Local, ' of Slocombe,' some place in the south-west of England that I have not discovered. The suffix -comb is very common in Devonshire placenames; v. Combe.

1564. Henry Slocum, or Sloocume: Reg. Univ. Oxf. i. 255.
1596. Gilbert Slocumbe, co. Soms.: ibid. vol. ii. pt. ii. p. 216.

A curious variant is found in the following entries:

1730. Married—Thomas Slokam and Isabella Brown: St. Jas. Clerkenwell, ii. 257.
1808. — Joseph Thompson and Ann Slockham: St. Geo. Han. Sq. ii. 386.
London, 7, 0, 0, 0, 0; MDB. (co. Devon), 2, 0, 0, 0; Boston (U.S.), 0, 18, 0, 3, 1; New York, 0, 8, 1, 0, 0; Philadelphia, 0, 13, 0, 5, 0.

Sloley, Slowley, Slowly.— Local, ' of Sloley,' a parish in co. Norfolk.

Peter de Sloleye, co. Norf., 1273. A.
John de Sloley, of Norwich, 1420: FF. iv. 91.
1577. Robert Slowghleigh, co. Soms.: Reg. Univ. Oxf. vol. ii. pt. ii. p. 75.
MDB. (co. Devon), 5, 0, 0; London, 0, 2, 1.

Sloman, Slowman, Slomon. —Bapt. ' the son of Solomon,' one of the many variants of this once popular font-name; v. Salman.

1571. Married—George Sloweman and Agnes Humfreye: St. Dionis Backchurch, p. 7.
1601. Robert Slowman, co. Devon: Reg. Univ. Oxf. vol. ii. pt. ii. p. 250.
1663. George Boraston and Eliz. Slowman: Marriage Alleg. (Canterbury), p. 86.
1678. Antony Sloman and Rachell Smith: ibid. p. 287.
London, 6, 0, 0; Philadelphia, 4, 0, 1.

Sloper, Slopier.—Occup. ' the sloper,' a maker of slops. Sometimes a loose overcoat or garment, more generally large loose trousers.

' His overest sloppe is not worth a mite.'
Chaucer, Chanon Yemannes Tale.
' Item, the xxii daye paied to Cicyll for a payer of sloppes, for the Kinges Grace, vis. 8d.': Privy Purse Expenses, Henry VIII, 1532.
Agatha le Slopere, co. Hunts, 1273. A.
1610. John Sloper, co. Wilts: Reg. Univ. Oxf. vol. ii. pt. ii. p. 313.
1615. Simon Sloper, co. Wilts: ibid. p. 341.
1792. Married—William Sloper and Eliz. North: St. Geo. Han. Sq. ii. 85.

' Ally Sloper' has immortalized this name.
London, 0, 1; New York, 1, 0.

Slott.—Local, ' at the slot,' from residence therein.

' Slot, a castle, a fort.

" Thou paydst for building of a slot
That wrought thine owne decay."
Riche's Allarme to England, 1578' (Halliwell).

Cf. slot, a bolt or bar, the fastener of a door. ' Slot, sloot, schytyl of a dore': Prompt. Parv.
Walter de la Slot, co. Norf., 1273. A.
William de Sloth, co. Norf., ibid.
Simon de la Slode, co. Oxf., ibid.
John Slodde, co. Oxf., ibid.

In the New York Directory are Sloat, 11; Sloate, 1; and Slote, 9. Perhaps variants.
New York, 2.

Slough, Slow, Slowe.—Local, ' of the slough,' a hollow, miry place, from residence thereby. The 'Slough of Despond' is familiar to all readers of the Pilgrim's Progress.

Stephen de la Slou, co. Bucks, 1273. A.
Matilda ad le Slow, co. Camb., ibid.
Hugh de la Slo, co. Wilts, ibid.
Adam del Slo. L.
William atte Slo', co. Soms., 1 Edw. III: Kirby's Quest, p. 110.
Nicholas atte Sloo, co. Soms., 1 Edw. III: ibid. p. 116.
1648. Married—Edward Hopkins and Mary Slow: St. Jas. Clerkenwell, iii. 83.
1806. — William Slow and Mary Brown: St. Geo. Han. Sq. ii. 340.
London, 1, 1, 0; Philadelphia, 13, 5, 1.

Slowley, Slowly; v. Sloley.

Sly, Slee, Sleigh. — Nick. ' the sly,' the cunning. M.E. sly and sley.

Ralph Sly, co. Hunts, 1273. A.
John Sley, co. Camb., ibid.
John le Slege, co. Oxf., ibid.

John le Slegh, 8 Edw. III: Freemen of York, i. 28.
Juliana Slegh, co. Soms., 1 Edw. III: Kirby's Quest, p. 81.
1533-4. Henry Rowgholt and Matilda Slye: Marriage Lic. (London), i. 8.
1610-11. William Slee, co. Devon: Reg. Univ. Oxf. vol. ii. pt. ii. p. 321.
1658. Married—Thomas Sly and Sarah Drake: St. Thomas the Apostle (London), p. 20.
1662. Edward Nelthorpe and Mary Sleigh: Marriage Alleg. (Canterbury), p. 76.
1667. Henry Temple and Margaret Sligh: ibid. p. 136.
London, 8, 8, 5; Philadelphia, 0, 1, 4.

Slyman, Slemmon, Sleeman, Slimmon, Sleman.—Bapt. ' the son of Seliman,' i.e. Solomon; cf. Sloman. I see no evidence in favour of 'slyman,' i.e. cunning man. The middle stage between these forms and the original Seliman was Selman or Sellman, q.v., where many instances will be found.

1588. Henry Sliman, co. Oxf.: Reg. Univ. Oxf. vol. ii. pt. ii. p. 167.
1741. Buried — Mary Slyman: St. Dionis Backchurch, p. 169.
London, 1, 1, 2, 0, 0; New York, 0, 0, 1, 2, 1.

Smale, Small. — Nick. ' the small '; cf. Large, Bigg, Little, &c.

Robert le Small, co. Hunts, 1273. A.
Henry le Smale, co. Soms., ibid.
Richard le Smale, C. R., 9 Edw. II.
Adam le Smale, co. Soms., 1 Edw. III: Kirby's Quest, p. 117.
Willelmus Smale, 1379: P. T. Yorks. p. 220.
Thomas Smale, rector of Lerling, co. Norf., 1468: FF. i. 431.
1508. Nicholas Smale or Small: Reg. Univ. Oxf. i. 63.
1621. Bapt.—Eliz., d. John Small: St. Jas. Clerkenwell, i. 89.
1731. Married—John Smale and Ann Collett: St. Geo. Han. Sq. i. 9.
London, 12, 14; New York, 1, 44.

Smallbone, Smallbones. — ? Nick. Seemingly a sobriquet affixed on one of small and delicate frame. But this is just a case where such a guess is tempting, and evidence of a local or other origin might at any moment upset the conclusion.

1593. Buried—William Smalbone: St. Michael, Cornhill, p. 205.
1691. Bapt.—Joseph, s. Joseph Smallbones: St. Jas. Clerkenwell, i. 341.

1740. Married—William Taylor and Mary Smallbones: St. Geo. Han. Sq. i. 25.
1787. — Frances D. Weissense and Judith Smallbone: ibid. p. 407.
London, 3, 0; MDB. (co. Bucks), 0, 3.

Smallcombe.—Local, 'at the small combe,' from residence thereby; v. Smale and Combe. Of course it is a West-country surname.

John Smalecome, co. Soms., 1 Edw. III: Kirby's Quest, p. 163.
1806. Married—Thomas Smallcomb and Ann Griffiths: St. Geo. Han. Sq. ii. 340.
London, 1.

Smalley.—Local, 'of Smalley,' a chapelry in the parish of Morley, co. Derby, seven miles from Derby.

Alicia Smalhaghe, 1379: P. T. Yorks. p. 99.
1682. James Smalley, of Liverpool: Wills at Chester, iii. 228.
1689. Edward Smalley, of Blackburn: ibid.
Sheffield, 3; MDB. (co. Camb.), 3; New York, 16.

Smallman.—Nick. 'the small man,' small of stature; cf. Small, Bigg, Little, Longfellow, Longman, &c.

Richard Smaleman, co. Suff., 1273. A.
Alan Smalman, Pardons R., 6 Ric. II.
1590. Francis Smalman, co. Salop: Reg. Univ. Oxf. vol. ii. pt. ii. p. 181.
1605. Bapt. — William, s. William Smalman: St. Jas. Clerkenwell, i. 47.
— Married—John Smalmanne to Elizabeth Tenche: St. Peter, Cornhill, i. 244.
1790. Married — Edmund Smallman and Jane Parkeman: St. Geo. Han. Sq. ii. 37.
London, 2; Manchester, 3; Boston (U.S.), 3.

Smallpage, Smalpage. — Official, a page or servitor. The small 'tiger' of former days; cf. Littlepage.

'To Percivall Smallpage, for his expenses, xxs.': Household Accounts, Princess Eliz., Camd. Soc.
'Robert Smallpage for cupboard, William Page for cellar, Thomas Drax cupbearer': Arrangements for wedding of Roger Rockley and Elizabeth Nevill, Jan. 14, 1526; Whitaker's Craven, p. 380.
Thomas Smallpage, co. York. W. 2.
Ralph Smallpage. V. 3.
1535. Ralph Smalpage: Reg. Univ. Oxf. i. 184.
1564. Thomas Smallpage, manciple of Ex. Coll.: ibid. vol. ii. pt. i. p. 288.

1607. Percival Smalpage, co. Sussex: ibid. pt. ii. p. 296.
London, 0, 1; Manchester, 2, 0; Leeds, 2, 1.

Smallpiece.— ? ——. I am not able to suggest any satisfactory derivation of this surname.

Francis Smallpece, mayor of Norwich, 1622: FF. iv. 469.
1663. Jeremy Washford and Eliz. Smallpiece: Marriage Alleg. (Canterbury), i. 120.
1675-6. Thomas Smallpeice and Ann Field: ibid. p. 160.
1676. Thomas Battin and Eliz. Smallpiece: ibid. p. 166.
MDB. (Surrey), 10.

Smallpride. — Nick. 'Small pride,' one without arrogance; cf. Littleproud.

Richard Smalprout, co. Oxf., 1273. A.
Robert Smalprout, co. Oxf., ibid.

Smallshanks. — Nick. 'with the small shanks'; cf. Sheepshanks, Longshanks, &c.

1573. Buried—Margrett Smaleshankes: St. Michael, Cornhill, p. 192.
1803. Married — Luke Smallshankes and Isabella Forbes: St. Geo. Han. Sq. ii. 295.

Smallwood.—Local, 'of Smallwood,' a township in the parish of Astbury, co. Ches.

Robert Smallwod, C. R., 51 Hen. III.
Elizabetha Smallwode, 1379: P. T. Yorks. p. 125.
John Turner, of Smallwood, 1675: Wills at Chester (1660-80), p. 272.
William Smallwood, of Peover, 1674: ibid. p. 246.
Randle Smallwood, of Lower Withington, 1673: ibid.

Still earlier we find the entries:

James Smallwood, of Smallwood, 1617: Wills at Chester (1545-1620), p. 176.
Randle Smallwood, of Middlewich, 1592: ibid.
1559. Married—Thomas Pedley and Ales Smalewodde: Prestbury Ch. (Cheshire), p. 2.
Thomas Smallwood, of Chelford, 1662: Earwaker's East Cheshire, ii. 366.
1748. Married—John Smallwood and Mary Turner: St. Geo. Han. Sq. i. 40.
Manchester, 2; Liverpool, 3; London, 3; MDB. (Cheshire), 2; Philadelphia, 9.

Smart.—Nick. 'the smart,' i.e. the brisk; cf. Snell.

Simon Smert, co. Northumb., 1273. A.
Adam Smart, co. Oxf., ibid.
Martin Smart, co. Camb., ibid.
John Smert, co. Soms., 1 Edw. III: Kirby's Quest, p. 188.
Richard Smert, C. R., 8 Ric. II.

1651. Bapt.—John, s. John Smart: St. Jas. Clerkenwell, i. 178.
London, 54; New York, 25.

Smertknave. — Nick. 'the smart knave,' i.e. the brisk, active servant; cf. Goodknave or Goodgroom.

Cristiana Smartknave, co. Oxf., 1273. A.

Smeathman.—Probably a variant of Smitheman, q.v.

MDB. (co. Bucks), 1; (North Rid. Yorks), 1.

Smeaton, Smeeton. — Local, 'of Smeaton,' now Kirk Smeaton, near Womersley, co. York.

Johannes Smeton, 1379: P. T. Yorks. p. 161.
1620-1. John Mason and Rosamond Smeton: Marriage Lic. (London), ii. 95.
1756. Married — John Smeaton and Ann Jenkinson: St. Geo. Han. Sq. i. 64.
1769. — James Smeeton and Jane Sherwood: ibid. p. 192.
London, 3, 6; West Rid. Court Dir., 0, 4; Philadelphia, 0, 3.

Smedley.—Local, 'of Smythley.' I cannot identify the spot.

Willelmus de Smythlay, 1379: P. T. Yorks. p. 4.
Magota de Smythlay, 1379: ibid.
1693. Bapt.—Mary, d. Thomas Smedley: St. Jas. Clerkenwell, i. 351.
MDB. (co. Derby), 25; Sheffield, 6; London, 1; Philadelphia, 48.

Smee.— ? ——. Lower says, 'a mispronunciation of Smeeth' (q.v.). He advances no evidence. I cannot suggest a satisfactory solution.

1573. Bapt.—Thomas, s. John Smye: St. Jas. Clerkenwell, i. 7.
1574-5. John Smy (or Sury), co. Berks: Reg. Univ. Oxf. vol. ii. pt. ii. p. 59.
London, 9; MDB. (co. Essex), 3; Philadelphia, 1.

Smeeth, Smeed.—(1) Local, 'at the smethe,' a smooth place. 'A large open level' (Halliwell); an open, level, smooth turf.

Johannes del Smethe, Isolda uxor ejus, 1379: P. T. Yorks. p. 162.

(2) Local, 'of Smeeth,' a parish in co. Kent. No doubt the origin is identical with (1).

Laurence de Smethe, co. Kent, 1273. A.
1746. Married—Thomas Smeed and Mary Booker: Canterbury Cath., p. 88.
1757. — John Smethe and Rose Broughton: St. Geo. Han. Sq. i. 72.
London, 1, 3; MDB. (Kent), 1, 3.

Smelt. — Nick. or personal. Either (1) 'the Smelt,' which would be a nickname, or (2) 'the son of Smelt,' which would be personal or baptismal. This appears to be one of the very few names really taken from the finny tribe (v. Salman, Turbot, or Chubb). A.S. *smelt*, Danish *smelt*.

William Smelt, co. Kent, 1273. A.
William Smelte, co. Norf., ibid.
Richard Smelt, C. R., 19 Edw. III. pt. i. 1666. Married — Edward Hews and Jane Smelt · St. Jas. Clerkenwell. iii. 123.
1743. Bapt. — Martha, d. William Smalt : ibid. ii. 226.
London, 1 ; Crockford, 3.

Smelter, Smilter. — Occup. 'the smelter,' one who smelted, or melted iron ore; cf. Bloomer, Ashburner, and Collier.

Henricus Smelter, 1379: P. T. Yorks. p. 265.
1762. Married — James Wigman and Hannah Smilter: St. Geo. Han. Sq. i. 116.
West Rid. Court Dir., 0, 1.

Smerdon, Smerden. — Local, 'of Smarden,' a parish in co. Kent, nine miles from Cranbrook.

MDB. (co. Devon), 8, 6; London, 3, 0; New York, 0, 1.

Smethurst. — Local, 'of Smethurst,' some small spot in the neighbourhood of Rochdale or Bury, co. Lanc. I have not discovered its exact position.

Richard Meadowcroft, of Smethurst, 1581 : Wills at Chester (1545-1620), p. 134.
John Smethurst, of Blakeley, 1582 : ibid. p. 177.
Richard Smethurst, of Bury, 1618: ibid. 1591-2. Richard Smethurst, co. Ches. : Reg. Univ. Oxf. vol. ii. pt. ii. p. 187.
1604. Buried—Martha Smythurst : St. Thomas the Apostle (London), p. 104.
Manchester, 18 ; Philadelphia, 8.

Smilter; v. Smelter.

Smirthwaite; v. Smurthwaite.

Smith, Smyth, Smythe. — Occup. 'the smith.' Common to every village in England, north, south, east, and west. The *y* in Smyth is the almost invariable spelling in early rolls, so that it cannot exactly be styled a modern affectation. There are 300,000 Smiths in England ; very different from the state of Israel, when

'there was no smith found throughout all the land of Israel' (1 Sam. xiii. 19). This always seems to me the hardest verse in the Bible to read in Church without smiling ; the most difficult, with regard to proper emphasis, being Luke xxiv. 25.

Philip le Smethe, co. Hunts, 1273. A.
William le Smeth, co. Oxf., ibid.
William le Smyth, co. Sussex, ibid.

The following occur on one single page, representing the village of Kimberworth :

Johannes Tagge, *smyght*, 1379: P. T. Yorks. p. 67.
Willelmus Smyght, 1379: ibid.
Johannes Trogne, *smyght*, 1379: ibid.
Ricardus Sawdre, *smyght*, 1379: ibid.
Robertus Smyght, 1379: ibid.
Johannes Losseland, *smyght*, 1379: ibid.
London, 1194, 23, 3 ; Philadelphia, 2971, 84, 9.

Smitheman, Smitherman, Smithman.—Occup. 'the smithman' or smithyman, one who worked at a smithy, the smith's assistant; cf. Priestman, Vickerman, Matthewman, Ladyman, &c.

Robert Smythyman, C. R., 2 Edw. II.
Henry Smytman, C. R., 7 Ric. II.
Henricus Smythman, 1379: P. T. Yorks. p. 209.
Johannes Smythman, 1379: ibid. p. 214.
Alanus Foxe, *smethyman*, 1379: ibid. p. 219.
Robertus Smytheman, 1379: ibid. p. 279.
1624. Francis Ketelby and Mary Smitheyman : Marriage Lic. (Westminster), p. 30.
1717. Married—John Smithyman and Anne Austen : St. Michael, Cornhill, p. 59.
London, 1, 0, 0 ; MDB. (co. Essex), 0, 2, 0 ; Philadelphia, 11, 1, 1.

Smithett.—Local, 'of Smurthwaite,' one of the many localities in cos. Cumberland, Westmoreland, and North Lancashire whose suffix is *-thwaite* (v. Thwaite). The first stage of corruption was Smurthwaite, the second Smithwaite. This became Smithett just as Smithwick became Smithick ; v. Smorfitt, Smithwaite, Smurthwaite. In my late parish (Ulverston) Poslet represents Postlethwaite.

1798. Married — Thomas Smuthwaite and Eliz. Maxfield : St. Geo. Han. Sq. ii. 188.
1805. Married—George Smithwaite and Mary Hancock : ibid. p. 333.
London, 3.

Smithies, Smithers, Smithyes, Smither, Smythers, Smythies, Smithee.—(1) Local, 'at the smithy,' with suffix (perhaps patronymic) *s*, as in Brooks, Styles, &c. Smithers is a vulgar corruption. (2) Local, 'of Smethurst.' It seems almost certain that Smithers is more generally a corruption of Smethurst (v. Reg. Univ. Oxf. vol. ii. pt. iv. p. 384). No doubt the two are mixed.

Johannes del Smethe, 1379: P. T. Yorks. p. 162.
Margareta del Smethes, 1379: ibid. p. 21.
Johannes de Smethe, *smyth*, 1379: ibid. p. 42.
Cecilia de Smethe, 1379: ibid.
Margeria del Smythe, 1379: ibid.
Willelmus del Smithi, 1379: ibid. p. 225.
Osbert le (de ?) Smythes, co. Soms., 1 Edw. III : Kirby's Quest, p. 134.
1607. Buried — Catherine Smithyes : St. Mary Aldermary (London), p. 204.
London, 3, 14, 3, 5, 1, 1, 0 ; West Rid. Court Dir., 2, 2, 0, 0, 0, 0, 0 ; MDB. (co. Norf.), Smithee, 3 ; Philadelphia, 0, 18, 0, 1, 0, 0, 0.

Smithson.—Nick. 'the smith's son'; cf. Clarkson, Wrightson, Taylorson, Serjeantson, and Shepherdson.

Johannes Smytheson', 1379: P. T. Yorks. p. 177.
Johannes Smyth' et Alicia uxor ejus, 1379: ibid.
Johannes Smyth et uxor, 1379: ibid. p. 214.
Johannes Smythson, 1379: ibid.
Cf. Agnes Smythwyf, 1379: ibid. p. 194.
1573. Married—Robert Watteson and Margaret Smethson : Reg. St. Dionis Backchurch, p. 7.
1579. William Smythson and Margaret Pryce : Marriage Lic. (London), i. 88.
London, 7 ; York, 4 ; Philadelphia, 9.

Smithwaite.—Local, a corruption of Smurthwaite ; v. Smithett.

MDB. (West Rid. Yorks), 1.

Smithwick, Smedick. — Local, 'of Smethwick,' a township in the parish of Brereton, co. Ches., four miles from Sandbach ; also a hamlet in the parish of Harborne, co. Stafford. Of course the popular pronunciation was Smithick (cf. Physick for Fishwick). This was further corrupted to Smedick.

1311. Ralph de Smethwyk, rector of Beteley, co. Norf. : FF. ix. 467.
1621. Bapt.—Ellyn, d. Thomas Smithicke : St. Peter Cornhill, i. 70.

1663. Married—Roger Chiswicke and Jane Smethicke: St. Jas. Clerkenwell, i. 111.

1680. Thomas Smethwick, of Smethwick: Wills at Chester, i. 247.

Liverpool, 1, 0; New York, 2, 1; Boston (U.S.), 1, 0.

Smoker.—Occup. 'the smoker,' probably a maker of smocks, meaning shifts, &c.

Robert le Smoker, co. Soms., 1 Edw. III: Kirby's Quest, p. 136.
William Smoker, co. Soms., 1 Edw. III: ibid. p. 159.
John Smoker, co. Soms., 1 Edw. III: ibid.

Philadelphia, 5.

Smorfitt.—Local, a corruption of Smurthwaite; v. Smithett. It is found in a London register as Smurfoote, a kind of halfway stage in the corruption.

1661. Bapt.—Bridget, d. Robert Smurfoote: St. Jas. Clerkenwell, i. 212.
1753. Married — John Smurfit and Catherine Gainer: St. Geo. Han. Sq. p. 258.
MDB. (West Rid. Yorks), 1.

Smurthwaite, Smirthwaite. —Local, 'of Smurthwaite'; v. Smithett, Smorfitt, &c.

1733. Married—John Russell and Edith Smurthwate: St. Geo. Han. Sq. i. 12.
1779. — Christopher Smirthwaite and Eliz. Brooksbank: ibid. p. 300.
MDB. (North Rid. Yorks), 2, 0; Manchester, 1, 0; Philadelphia, 1, 3.

Smyth(e; v. Smith.

Snaith; v. Sneath.—Local, 'of Snaith,' a village and parish a few miles from Goole, co. York.

Henry de Snayth, *tannator*, 2 Edw. I: Freemen of York, i. 1.
Ricardus de Snayth, 1379: P. T. Yorks. p. 125.
Thomas de Snayth, 1379: ibid.
Alicia de Snayth, 1379: ibid.
1751. Married—Nathaniel Snaith and Anna Maria Davis: St. Geo. Han. Sq. i. 206.
1798. — John Moulden and Catherine Sneath: ibid. ii. 189.

Liverpool, 1, 0; Philadelphia, 0, 2.

Snape. — (1) Local, 'at the snape,' from residence thereby. Most probably a piece of land with soil starved and pinched; from *snape*, to pine or wither. (2) Local, 'at the snape,' from residence thereby; a spring in arable ground. (3) Nick. 'the snape,' i. e. the woodcock; v. Halliwell's Dict.

Henry de la Snape, co. Sussex, 1273. A. Ralph de Snape, co. Norf., ibid.

This last entry will be connected with Snape, a parish in co. Norfolk. An estate in the parish of Scarisbrook, co. Lanc., has helped to foster the name in the co. Palatinate.

Adam del Snape, co. Lanc., 1332: Lay Subsidy Roll, co. Lanc. (Rylands), p. 6.
William Snaype, 1379: P. T. Yorks. p. 216.
1594. John Edwardson, of Snape, within Scarisbrook, *husbandman*: Wills at Chester, i. 60.
1600. John Lawton, of Snape: East Ches. ii. 383.

London, 4; Crockford, 3; Manchester, 7; Philadelphia, 6.

Snazle, Snazel, Snazell. — Local, (1) 'of Kneesall,' a parish in the dioc. of Lincoln; (2) 'of Knettishall,' a parish in the dioc. of Norwich. There was evidently a difficulty in pronouncing the last local term. It would readily corrupt. It is quite possible that the Lincolnshire surname Snushall is a corruption of (1); cf. Sturges for Thurgis, and v. Spurdance.

John de Gnadeshall, or Knateshall, or Knetsall, bailiff of Norwich, 1366: FF. iii. 100.
William de Knateshall, bailiff of Norwich, 1635: ibid.
William de Knateshale, or Gnatishale, burgess in Parl. for Norwich, 42 Edw. III: ibid. p. 101.
1656. Buried—Francis Snawsell: St. Jas. Clerkenwell, iv. 314.
London, 1, 1, 0; MDB. (Suffolk), 0, 1, 0; (co. Camb.), 0, 0, 1.

Snead, Sneed, Sneyd. — (1) Local, 'of Sneyd,' a township in the parish of Burslem, co. Stafford. (2) Local, 'of Snead,' a hamlet in the parish of Rock, co. Worc.

1574. William Stokes and Eliz. Snede: Marriage Lic. (London), i. 63.
1581. William Sneade and Eliz. Snede: Stafford: Reg. Univ. Oxf. vol. ii. pt. ii. p. 100.
1590. John Sneade, co. Worc.: ibid. p. 178.
1739. Married — John Parsons and Margaret Sneed: St. Geo. Chap. Mayfair, p. 13.
1745. — Erasmus Carter and Eliz. Snead: ibid. p. 53.

London, 4, 1, 0; Philadelphia, 2, 1, 10.

Sneegum.—? Local. Probably a corruption of Snettisham, a parish in co. Norwich. I find, after writing this, that Mr. Lower is of

the same opinion (v. Patr. Brit. p. 322); cf. Barnum for Barnham.

Richard de Snetisham, co. Norf., 1273. A.
Roger de Snetesham, prebend. Norwich Cathedral, 1306: FF. iv. 173.
London, 2; MDB. (co. Essex), 1.

Snell.—Bapt. 'the son of Snel.' This name is found in the Hundred Rolls as a single personal name, a strong argument in favour of a fontal origin. If not so, it must be a nickname. 'Snell, sharp, keen, piercing. Cumberland.

"Teche hem alle to be war and snel"'
(Halliwell).

As a personal name Snel is found as a compound in such local words as Snelston, Snelland, or Snelsmore.

Snel, co. Derby, 1273. A.
William Snell, co. Oxf., ibid.
Johannes Snell', 1379: P. T. Yorks. p. 116.
Willelmus Snell, 1379: ibid. p. 37.
Ricardus Snell, 1379: ibid. p. 215.
London, 31; New York, 10.

Snelling.—Bapt. 'the son of Snelling'; cf. Browning and Harding. Mr. Lower says Snelling is found in Domesday as a previous tenant (Patr. Brit. p. 322). Of course this implies a personal name.

Walter Snellyng, co. Soms., 1 Edw. III: Kirby's Quest, p. 118.
Michael Snellyng, co. Soms., 1 Edw. III: ibid. p. 119.
John Snellyng, co. Soms., 1 Edw. III: ibid. p. 132.
1582-3. Robert Snellinge and Eliz. Bull: Marriage Lic. (London), i. 114.
1790. Married—William Snelling and Sarah Jennings: St. Geo. Han. Sq. ii. 41.
London, 14; New York, 8; Philadelphia, 2; Boston (U.S.), 15.

Snelson.—Local, 'of Snelson,' a township in the parish of Rostherne, co. Ches.; in Domesday Senelestune. A family sprang up here called alike Snelson or Snelston. Both surname and local name have modernly dropped the *t*. Occasionally it may be 'the son of Snell'; v. Snell.

William de Snelleston, 1369: Hist. East Ches. ii. 643.
Thomas de Snelleston, 1379: ibid. p. 551.
Benedict Snelson, of Little Budworth, *yeoman*, 1606: Wills at Chester (1545-1620), p. 180.

1596. Richard Snellson and Katherine Mustyan: Marriage Lic. (London), i. 233. 1774. Married—David Hartley and Sarah Snellson: St. Geo. Han. Sq. i. 243. MDB. (co. Ches.), 4; Liverpool, 1.

Sneyd; v. Snead.

Snibson.—Local, ' of Snibston,' a chapelry in the parish of Packington, co. Leic. A palpable modification ; cf. Kelson for Kelston.

Liverpool, 1.

Snidall, Snidle, Snittle. — Local, 'of Snydale,' a village a mile east of Normanton, co. York.

Johanna de Snydal, 1379: P. T. Yorks. p. 159.
Johannes Snydale, 1379: ibid.
Johannes Snytall, 1379: ibid. p. 146.
Sheffield, 2, 0, 0; West Rid. Court Dir., 0, 1, 0.

Snoad.—? Bapt. 'the son of Snod.' Snod is found as a single personal name in the Hundred Rolls ; cf. the local Snodgrass, where the prefix is probably the original settler's personal name.

Snod serviens Ricard Giffard, co. Suff., 1273. A.
1349. John Snod, vicar of Attlebridge, co. Norf. : FF. x. 402.
1602. Theodore Snode: Reg. Univ. Oxf. vol. ii. pt. ii. p. 259.
1657. Bapt.—Eliz., d. Charles Snode: St. Jas. Clerkenwell, i. 265.
London, 3.

Snodgrass. — Local, 'at the snodgrass,' from residence thereby. ' *Snod*, smooth, demure ' (Halliwell). But v. Snoad for another derivation of the prefix. The surname is far more commonly found in the United States than in England.

1730. Married—Andrew Snottgrass and Ann Cressum: St. Geo. Chap. Mayfair, p. 321.

The name of Snodgrass occurs in the Cheltenham register, Aug. 1863 (N. and Q., Dec. 4, 1886).

New York, 1; Philadelphia, 23.

Snodin.—Local, 'of Snowdon'; v. Snowden. The following seems a very conclusive instance. It is clearly the half-stage of the corrupted form :

1795. Married—William Snowdin and Frances Blakes: St. Geo. Han. Sq. ii. 129.

1573. John Snodon : Reg. Univ. Oxf. vol. ii. pt. iii. p. 25.
London, 3.

Snook, Snooke, Snooks. — Local, ' of Sevenoaks ' (?), a market-town and parish in co. Kent. Mr. Lower says, 'The Kentish town is usually pronounced Se'noaks.' ' The further contraction, coupled with the phonetic spelling of former days, easily passed into Snooks. Messrs. Sharp and Harrison, solicitors of Southampton, had in their possession a series of deeds in which all the modes of spelling occur, from Sevenoakes down to S'nokes, in connection with a family now known as Snooks ' (Notes and Queries, 1st S. v. p. 438, quoted by Lower). ' A Sussex family in the early part of the last century bore the name of Snooke. Sevenoke, the early orthography of the town, has also been modified into Sinnock and Cennick ' (Lower).

Stephen Sevenac', co. Linc., 1273. A.
Simon Senenok, co. Soms., 1 Edw. III : Kirby's Quest, p. 147.
Robert Snouk, co. Soms., 1 Edw. III : ibid. p. 218.
1617. Richard Snook, co. Dorset: Reg. Univ. Oxf. vol. ii. pt. ii. p. 366.
1642. Bapt. — Margery, d. Daniel Snoaks: Kensington Ch., p. 33.
1766. Married — Thomas Snook and Ann Autrick : St. Geo. Han. Sq. i. 266.
London, 9, 2, 2; Philadelphia, 1, 0, 0; New York, 5, 0, 0.

Snow. — Personal or, as we should now say, baptismal, ' the son of Snow'; cf. Winter, Frost, and such ecclesiastical seasons (as distinct from the natural) as Pentecost, Nowell, Pask, Whitsunday, or Midwinter. A name given originally to a child born in the time of snow. The practice is repeated to-day. A clergyman wrote to me some time ago to say he had just baptized a child by the name of Sou'-wester. This turned out to be the father's Christian name, who was born on board ship in a sou'-westerly gale.

Henry Snou, co. Bucks, 1273. A.
William Snou, co. Oxf., ibid.
Roger Snow, C. R., 14 Edw. I.
Willelmus Snawe, 1379 : P. T. Yorks. p. 239.
Ricardus Snaw, 1379 : ibid. p. 122.

1569. James Jobson and Saban Snowe : Marriage Lic. (London), i. 43.
London, 31 ; Philadelphia, 19.

Snowball.— ? Nick. I cannot suggest any satisfactory derivation. It is possible that it was a nickname for one with snow-white hair and a round head ; cf. Whitehead and Snowwhite.

1546-7. William Stacye and Katherine Snowball : Marriage Lic. (Faculty Office), p. 9.
1745. Married—George Snowball and Mary Winn : St. Geo. Han. Sq. i. 34.
1746. — Richard Clingo and Jane Snowball : St. Geo. Chap. Mayfair, p. 61.
MDB. (co. Ches.), 2 ; (co. Durham), 6 ; London, 1, Manchester, 1 ; Philadelphia, 1 ; New York, 1.

Snowden, Snowdon.—Local, 'of Snowdon.' Possibly the Welsh mountain, but more probably some smaller spot in the West country. Not one in a hundred Welsh surnames is local. The parent must be sought for elsewhere.

John Snowdone, co. Soms., 1 Edw. III : Kirby's Quest, p. 93.
1558. Thomas Snowdon and Alice Heritage: Marriage Lic. (London), i. 18.
1744. Married—Patrick Hevy and Eliz. Snowden: St. Geo. Chap. Mayfair, p. 36.
London, 12, 6; Philadelphia, 22, 11.

Snowwhite. — Nick. ' with snow-white hair.' Cf. Snowball.

John Snowhite, Close Roll, 3 Hen. V.

Snushall.—Local, ' of Knesall ' (?), a parish in the dioc. of Lincoln ; v. Snazle.

1580. Married—Edward Snowsell and Sisley Wilson: St. Mary Aldermary, p. 6.
MDB. (Lincoln), 4.

Soanes; v. Sones.

Soapers-lane. — Local, ' of Soapers' Lane,' a street in London where soap was manufactured.

Thomas de Sopereslane, London, 1273. A.

Soar; v. Sor.

Soden.—Local; v. Sowden.

Oxford, 4.

Sojourner. — Nick. or occup. ' the sojourner.' This surname I have only met with in North Lancashire, between Preston and the Duddon Sands. For centuries it appears in the Ulverston and Dalton registers as Suggener, and in that form a charity was left to the poor of the latter parish. In the Preston Guild Rolls occurs 'John Sojorner, butter - maker,' 1622 (p. 89). Possibly the Sojourner was, like Tasker, a worker by the day or job, a day-labourer, as we now say. If we take it in its accepted sense it will denote a new-comer, who from a passing visitor has become a settler. It is suggested in N. and Q. (Sept. 17, 1887) that the French Sigourney, or Sigournai, is of the same origin.

1547. Married—Thomas Asburner and Elisabeth Suggener: Reg. Parish Ch., Ulverston, p. 4.
1549. Buried—John Suggener: ibid. p. 10.

Sokerel.—Nick. 'the sokerel.' 'Sokerel, a child not weaned' (Halliwell). A very likely sobriquet for a simple and silly fellow. Cf. Suckling.

Richard Sokerel, co. Soms., 1 Edw. III: Kirby's Quest, p. 155.

Sole, Soles. — Local, 'at the sole,' i.e. pond. 'Sole, a pond. Co. Kent' (Halliwell). This solution is proved by the instances furnished below :

Peter de la Sole, co. Kent, 1273. A.
Richard atte Sole, co. Kent, ibid.
John de Soles, co. Kent, ibid.
Hamo de Soles, co. Kent, Hen. III-Edw. I. K.
1665. Married — John Knowler and Susanna Sole: Canterbury Cath. p. 60.
1690. — John Swaine and Margaret Sole: ibid. p. 64.
London, 4, 0; MDB. (Kent), 1, 0; New York, 0, 2.

Soleyndeamur.—Nick. 'seriously in love' (?).

Hugh Soleyndeamur, Close Roll, 55 Hen. III.

Cf. Finnemore, Paramor, Pleynamour, Douceamour.

Soller.—Local, 'at the soler,' an upper room, a garret, a loft. L. Lat. solarium. 'Solarium, an upper room, chamber, or garret, which in some parts of England is still called a sollar': Kennett, p. 134.

'In a soler was in that town
A childe cast another down.'
Cursor Mundi (Halliwell).

Gilbert de Solario, co. Linc., 1273. A.
Adam ad Solarium, co. Oxf., ibid.

Agnes de Solar', co. Linc., 1273. A.
Walter atte Solere, co. Soms., 1 Edw. III: Kirby's Quest, p. 123.
1607. John Soller and Mary Grammett: Marriage Lic. (Westminster), p. 16.
1711. Married — William Sollars and Eliz. Thackitt: St. Jas. Clerkenwell, iii. 234.
London, 1; New York, 1; Philadelphia, 1.

Solloway, Solway. — Local, 'at the sale-way.' This surname, so familiar to Oxford citizens, hails from co. Somerset. Its derivation is very simple. The original bearer of the name lived on the *way* that led to the *sale*, or hall (v. Sale). For change to o, cf. Salomon and Solomon. For the change into three syllables (for euphony), cf. Ottaway, Greenaway, Hathaway, in place of Ottway, Greenway, and Hathway.

Robert Saleway, co. Soms., 1 Edw. III : Kirby's Quest, p. 129.
John Selewey, co. Soms., 1 Edw. III : ibid. p. 133.
Richard Salweye, co. Soms., 1 Edw. III : ibid. p. 279.
1669. Married — Hercules Hale and Mary Soloway: St. Jas. Clerkenwell, iii. 158.
1752. — William Solway and Mary Mackey: St. Geo. Chap. Mayfair, p. 219.
Oxford, 2, 0; MDB. (co. Soms.), 0, 2; New York, 3, 0.

Solman, Soloman, Solomans, Solomon, Solomons. — Bapt. 'the son of Solomon.' The first o is very rare in early records. The spelling is almost invariably Saloman. A large proportion of the Solomons in the London Directory represents the modern Jewish invasion, as the personal names attached to them will sufficiently prove, not to mention the occupations ; v. Salman for the old English representatives of a once popular fontal name.

John Solyman, co. Wilts, 1273. A.
Walter Solyman, co. Wilts, ibid.
1705. Married — Mathew Wayne and Barbery Solman: St. Antholin (London), p. 118.
London, 1, 2, 1, 63, 13 ; New York, 0, 9, 0, 125, 7.

Solway ; v. Solloway.

Somerby.—Local,'of Somerby,' two parishes in co. Lincoln, anciently called Somerdeby.

Robertde Somerdeby, co. Linc.,1273. A.

Hugh de Somerdeby, alias Somerteby, co. Linc., 20 Edw. I. R.
Ralph de Somertheby, co. Linc., Hen. III-Edw. I. K.
Thomas de Somerdeby, co. Linc., ibid. Boston (U.S.), 9.

Somers ; v. Summer.

Somersall, Summershall.—Local, 'of Somersall,' a parish in the co. of Derby, four miles from Uttoxeter.

1730. Married—John Springfield and Ann Somersale: Canterbury Cath. p. 78.
1737-8. John Summersol and Alice Potten: ibid. p. 82.
London, 1, 0; Heywood (co. Lanc.), 0, 1.

Somerset, Somersett, Summerset. — Local, 'of Somerset.' one who had left the county and received his surname as an emigrant from that particular shire; cf. Lancashire, Wiltshire, Cornish, Kentish, &c.

William de Somersete, co. Salop, 1273. A.
Roger de Somersete, co. Soms., 1 Edw. III: Kirby's Quest, p. 204.
1591. Henry Somerset, co. Hereford : Reg. Univ. Oxf. vol. ii. pt. ii. p. 183.
1804. Married—Hugh Henry Mitchell and Harriet Isabella Somerset : St. Geo. Han. Sq. ii. 307.
MDB. (co. Derby), 2, 9, 0; Manchester, 2, 0, 0; Philadelphia, 10, 0, 0; New York, 0, 0, 1.

Somerton, Sommerton. — Local, 'of Somerton,' parishes in cos. Oxford, Somerset, Norfolk, and Suffolk ; v. Summer.

William de Somerton, co. Oxf., 1273. A.
Richard de Somerton, co. Norf., ibid.
Bartholomew de Somerton, co. Norf., 20 Edw. I. R.
Constancia de Somerton, co. Norf., ibid.
Robert Somerton, co. Soms., 1 Edw. III : Kirby's Quest, p. 123.
John de Somerton, co. Soms., 1 Edw. III: ibid. p. 237.
1669. Married — John Somerton and Eliz. Robertes: St. Jas. Clerkenwell, i. 158.
1766. — Thomas Hawkins and Hannah Sumerton : St. Geo. Han. Sq. i. 152.
London, 1, 0 ; Oxford, 0, 1.

Somerville, Sommerville, Somervail, Somervell, Somerwill. — Local, 'de Somerville.' Lower says, 'The progenitor of the noble family was Walter de Somerville, lord of Wicknor, &c., in Staffordshire, and of Aston Somerville, in co. Gloucester, who came into England with William the Conqueror, and left two sons, who became ancestors respectively of the English and of the Scottish Somervilles. This name has been anglicized to Somerfield': Patr. Brit. p. 323.

Jacobus de Somerwill, co. Devon, 1273. A.
Robert de Somervile, co. Staff., 20 Edw. I. R.
Roger de Somerville, co. Staff., ibid.
1639-40. Christopher Grainger and Mary Somervell: Marriage Lic. (Westminster), p. 38.
1669. Edward Sommervill and Mary Beaufoy: Marriage Alleg. (Canterbury), p. 162.
London, 4, 1, 1, 1, 2; New York, 8, 2, 0, 0, 0.

Sommer(s; v. Summer.

Sommerlad, Sommerlat. — Bapt. 'the son of Sumalide' (Yonge, ii. 432). 1086, Summerled (Domesday). A curious instance of the survival of a probably rare personal name. Mr. Lower says Somerlad, Thane of Argyle, living in the 12th century, was founder of the Clan Macdonald (Patr. Brit. p. 323).

London, 1, 1

Sommerton; v. Somerton.

Sommerville; v. Somerville.

Sondes; v. Sands.

Sones, Soanes, Sounes. — ? Local, 'at the sands,' from residence thereby (v. Sands). Probably a modified form of Sondes, the early form. Sounes is unmistakably a variant.

1681. Bapt.—George, s. George and Jane Sones: St. Jas. Clerkenwell, i. 309.
1684. — Peter, s. George and Jane Sounds: ibid. p. 295.
1689. — William, s. George and Jane Soanes: ibid. p. 330.
1795. Married — John Cumberpatch and Eliz. Sones: St. Geo. Han. Sq. ii. 140.
1805. — John Souness and Ann Hamlin: ibid. p. 331.
London, 3, 4, 3; Oxford, 0, 7, 0; Boston (U.S.), 1, 0, 0.

Songer, Songster. — Occup. American variants of Sanger and Sangster, q.v.
Philadelphia, 1, 3.

Soper.—Occup. 'the soaper,' a maker of soap. M.E. *sope*, soap. Cf. Savoner.

Julian le Sopere, co. Dorset, 1273. A.
Nicholas le Sopere, co. Glouc., ibid.
John le Sopere, co. Soms., 1 Edw. III:
Kirby's Quest, p. 80.
1795. Married—Joseph Soper and Eliz. Powell: St. Geo. Han. Sq. ii. 135.
London, 12; Philadelphia, 4; Boston (U.S.), 5.

Sor, Sore, Soar.—? Nick. 'the sor,' the sore, the susceptible to wounded feelings, the sensitive. But much more probably one of the endless nicknames from the complexion of the hair, from O.F. *sor*, the dim. of which was Sorel, a reddish-brown, hence a favourite name for a horse; v. Sorrel.

Elena la Sore, co. Somerset, 1273. A.
Matheu le Sore, C. R., 26 Edw. III.
Philip le Soor, co. Soms., 1 Edw. III:
Kirby's Quest, p. 170.
Roger le Sor, co. Soms., 1 Edw. III:
ibid. p. 238.
John le Sor. H.
Philip le Sor. T.
1605. John Soare, Trin. Coll. Oxf.:
Reg. Univ. Oxf. vol. ii. pt. iii. p. 256.
1807. Married — William Sore and Lillies Staig: St. Geo. Han. Sq. ii. 375.
London, 0, 0, 2; New York, 0, 0, 1.

Sorby, Sorbey. — Local, 'of Sowerby,' a parish in W. Rid. Yorks.

Julianna de Saureby, 1379: P. T. Yorks. p. 89.
Thomas de Sawrebe, 1379: ibid. p. 87.
Thomas de Saureby, 1379: ibid. p. 13.
Paulinus de Saureby, 1379: ibid. p. 80.
Thomas de Schorby, 1379: ibid. p. 155.
1597. Thomas Sowerbye, co. Cumb.,
Reg. Univ. Oxf. vol. ii. pt. ii. p. 221.
1609. Francis Sowerby, co. Durham:
ibid. p. 221.

The variants of these surnames in the Index to Reg. Univ. Oxf. (p. 391) are Sourbie, Sourby, Surby.
West Rid. Court Dir., 6, 0; Sheffield, 7, 0; New York, 1, 1.

Soresby.—Local; v. Scoresby.

Sorrel, Sorrell.—Nick. 'the sorel,' a nickname of complexion, of a reddish-brown colour. O.F. *sor*, dim. sorel; cf. Blondel, Burnell, Russell; v. Sor.

John Ourel, co. Oxf., 1273. A.
Robert Sorel. J.
Richard Sorel, c. 1300. M.
'Sorrell Tempest, Whit Tempest, Baye Tempest,' names of three horses, 1526, belonging to Tempest family: Whitaker's Craven, p. 403.
1684. Bapt. — Timothy, s. Timothy Sorrell: St. Jas. Clerkenwell, i. 310.

1797. Married — John Sorrill and Rachel Haslewood: St. Geo. Han. Sq. ii. 160.
London, 1, 9; MDB. (co. Essex), 0, 6; Philadelphia, 1, 2.

Sorsby.—Local; v. Scoresby.

Sotham; v. Southam.

Sotheran; v. Southern.

Sotherton, Southerton. — Local, 'of Sotherton,' a parish in co. Suffolk.

1581. John Sotherton or Southerton, co. Middlesex: Reg. Univ. Oxf. vol. ii. pt. ii. p. 103.
1601. Bapt. — Alexander, s. George Sotherton; St. Jas. Clerkenwell, i. 38.
1607. Nowel Sotherton, Norwich: FF. iv. 317.
London, 0, 1; New York, 0, 1.

Soulby. — Local, 'of Soulby,' a township in the parish of Dacre, co. Cumberland; also a chapelry in the parish of Kirkby Stephen, co. Westmoreland.

1795. Married—John Soulby and Alice Houghton: St. Mary Ulverston, p. 440.
Liverpool, 2; Ulverston, 1; London, 1.

Sounes; v. Sones.

Sour. — Nick. 'the sour,' i.e. sour-visaged or sour-tempered.

Gilbert le Sour, co. Camb., 1273. A.
New York, 1

Sourbutts; v. Sowerbutts.

Sourmilk. — Nick. 'a sour-tempered girl'; cf. Milksop.

Alicia Sowremilke, 1379: P. T. Yorks. p. 197.

Souster.—Occup. 'the souster,' a female shoemaker, fem. suffix -ster (v. Soutar); cf. Yorkshire Spenster (for Spenser) and Slaster (for Slater). 'Sewstare or Sowstare, *sutrix*': Prompt. Parv. Not an englished form of German Schuster, but of independent English origin.

Emma le Sowester, C. R., 35 Edw. I.
William Sewster, temp. Hen. VIII. F.
Alicia Seuster, 1379: P. T. Yorks. p. 63.
1796. Married—Thomas Souster and Eliz. Coleman: St. Geo. Han. Sq. ii. 142.
London, 3.

Soutar, Souter, Soutter.—Occup. 'the souter,' i.e. shoemaker. Till lately in use in North England; cf. Souter-gate in

Ulverston, North Lanc. (i. e. the shoemaker's road). 'Sowtare or cordewaner': Prompt. Parv.

'Sowters and shepherdes.'
Piers Plowman.
'Cesse (Cecilia), the souteresse.'
ibid.
'Also, everych sowtere that maketh shon of newe rothes lether,' &c.: Usages of Winchester (English Gilds), p. 359.

John le Suter, co. Camb., 1273. A.
William le Sutere, co. Camb., ibid.
Johannes de Morton, *souter*, 1379: P. T. Yorks. p. 249.
Johannes Schether, *souter*, 1379: ibid.
Johannes Sowter, *sutor*, 1379: ibid. p. 301.
Adam Souterson, *souter*, 1379: ibid. p. 239.
Robert le Souter, c. 1300. M.
David le Souter, ibid.
London, 1, 6, 6; New York, 0, 1, 3.

South.—Local, ' of the south'; cf. West, North, Southern, Western, &c.

William de la Sothe, co. Devon, 1273. A.
Maurice bi Suthe, co. Oxf., ibid.
Willelmus del South, 1379: P. T. Yorks. p. 37.
Thomas de Sowth, 1379: ibid. p. 269.
1664. Bapt. — Richard, s. Richard South: St. Jas. Clerkenwell, i. 223.
London, 16; Philadelphia, 15.

Southall, Southal. — Local, ' of Southall,' a chapelry in the parish of Hayes, co. Middlesex.

Nicholas de Suthalle, co. Norf., 1273. A.
1563. Eliz. Southall, co. Norf.: FF. v. 370.
1799. Married — John Southall and Mary Clark: St. Geo. Han. Sq. ii. 209.
London, 5, 0; New York, 0, 1.

Southam, Sotham.—Local, ' of Southam,' a parish and market-town in co. Warwick; also a hamlet in the parish of Bishop's Cleeve, co. Glouc.

Thomas de Sutham, co. Oxf., 1273. A.
1388. John de Southam, rector of West Walton, co. Norf.: FF. ix. 141.
1666. Bapt. — Nicolas, s. Nicolas Southam: St. Jas. Clerkenwell, i. 229.
London, 2, 0; Philadelphia, 0, 1.

Southcott, Southcote. — Local, ' of Southcote.' Lower says, 'A tithing near Reading, co. Berks' (Patr. Brit. p. 324). There is also Southcoates, a township in the parish of Drypool, E. Rid. Yorks. In spite of this it is

probable that the surname is of Devonshire descent, and represents some estate in that county bearing this name, -*cote* (an enclosure) being a common West-England suffix.

Richard de Suthcote, co. Wilts, 1273. A.
Walter Sowthcott, *chaplain*, 1513: Reg. Univ. Oxf. i. 86.
1586. Richard Southcott, co. Devon: ibid. vol. ii. pt. ii. p. 155.
1595. John Southcote, co. Devon: ibid. p. 210.
London, 4, 0; MDB. (co. Devon), 2, 1; Philadelphia, 4, 0.

Southern, Sotheran, Southerne, Southren.—Local, ' the southern,' from the south. M.E. *sothern.*

'But trusteth wel, I am a sothern man.'
Chaucer, C. T. 17342.

Naturally the surname is found in the North and not the South; v. Western.

Willelmus Sothorn, 1379: P. T. Yorks. p. 285.
Willelmus Sotheran, 1379: ibid. p. 118.
Johannes Sotheron, 1379: ibid. p. 13.
Ricardus Sothryn, 1379: ibid. p. 25.
1586. Bapt.—Anne, d. John Sothernne: St. Dionis Backchurch, p. 86.
1587. — Mary Sotherne, d. William Southerne (sic): ibid. p. 87.
John Southerine, 1588: Reg. St. Dionis Backchurch (London), p. 87.
London, 4, 1, 0, 0; West Rid. Court Dir., 2, 0, 1, 1; Boston (U.S.), 3, 0, 0, 0.

Southerton; v. Sotherton.

Southerwood, Southernwood.—Local, ' at the southernwood,' from residence thereby; cf. Norwood and Eastwood; cf. also Southwood, a parish in co. Norfolk, four miles and a half from Acle.

1547. William Southerwood and Eliz. Whyskerd: Marriage Lic. (London), i. 10.
1663. John Southearnwood and Elinor Hickson: Marriage Alleg. (Canterbury), p. 110.
1803. Married—Thomas Harrison and Ann Southernwood: St. Geo. Han. Sq. ii. 274.
London, 1, 0; MDB. (co. Bucks), 0, 1.

Southey.—Local, ' of Southea,' a parish in the dioc. of Ely, co. Hunts.

Beatrice de Suthae, co. Norf., 1273. A.
Geoffrey de Suthae, co. Norf., ibid.
John de Southeye, co. Soms., 1 Edw. III: Kirby's Quest, p. 255.

1746. Married — Henry Southey and Dorcas Southey: St. Geo. Han. Sq. i. 36.
London, 12; MDB. (co. Devon), 7.

Southgate.—Local, ' of Southgate,' a parish in co. Middlesex, near London.

1349. Roger de Southgate, rector of Swainsthorp, co. Norf.: FF. v. 61.
1353. John de Southgate, rector of Barmere, co. Norf.: ibid. vii. 4.
Thomas de Southgate, 1379: P. T. Yorks. p. 119.
1790. Married—Christopher Southgate and Ann Mason: St. Geo. Han. Sq. ii. 47.
London, 14; MDB. (co. Suffolk), 4; Philadelphia, 1; Boston (U.S.), 2.

Southouse. — Local, ' of the salthouse'; v. Salthouse. *Saut* is still a Northern provincialism for salt; cf. Dutch *zout*, salt.

1345. John de Southouse, co. Norf.: FF. ii. 365.
Simon del Southouse, 1379: P. T. Yorks. p. 254.
William Sauthowse, 1512: HHH. p. 61.
1658. Martin Southouse, co. Norf.: FF. vi. 232.
1742. Married—Henry Southouse and Jane Munden: Canterbury Cath. p. 85.
London, 1; MDB. (co. Hants), 1.

Southrey.—Local, ' of Southery,' a parish in co. Norfolk.

Robert de Suthereye, co. Wilts, 1273. A.
Henry de Suthereye, co. Norf., ibid.
William de Suthery, co. Norf., 15 Edw. II: FF. ii. 183.
Philadelphia, 2.

Southward; v. Southworth.

Southwell.—Local, ' of Southwell,' a market-town and parish in co. Notts.

1474. Richard de Southewell, co. Norf.: FF. viii. 57.
1592. Bapt.—Henry, s. Richard Sowthwell: St. Jas. Clerkenwell, i. 25.
1664. Married—Robert Southwell and Eliz. Dering: Kensington Ch. p. 77.
London, 8; Philadelphia, 8.

Southwick.—Local, ' of Southwick,' parishes in cos. Northants, Southants, and Sussex; also a chapelry in the parish of North Bradley, co. Wilts; also a township in the parish of Monkwearmouth, co. Durham.

William de Suthewyk, co. Hunts, 1273. A.
1617. Buried—Eliz. Southwaike: St. Jas. Clerkenwell, iv. 139.
1690. Married — Daniell Southwicke and Eliz. Taylor: St. Peter, Cornhill, ii. 62.
Philadelphia, 8.

Southwood.—Local, 'of South-wold,' a seaport and parish in co. Suffolk, in mediaeval times frequently described as Southwood. In the Hundred Rolls (1273) the following varieties of the name of the town occur: Suthwald, Suthwaud, Suthwode, Suthwold, Sutwaud (v. Index Locorum, vol. ii. p. 899).

Roger de Suthwode, London, 1273. A. 1443. Thomas Southwood, co. Norf.: FF. ii. 320.
1520. John Southwood, rector of Witchingham, co. Norf.: ibid. viii. 311.
1790. Married — Augustus Caesar Manning and Jane Southwood: St. Geo. Han. Sq. ii. 50.
London, 1.

Southworth, Southward.—Local, 'of Southworth,' a township in the parish of Winwick, co. Lanc.

1587. Thomas Southworth, of Winwick, co. Lanc.: Wills at Chester, i. 180.
1591-2. John Sothworth, co. Lanc.: Reg. Univ. Oxf. vol. ii. pt. ii. p. 189.
1599. Henry Southworth, of Witton, yeoman: Wills at Chester, i. 180.
1607. Robert Southworth, of Warrington: ibid
1615. Edmund Sowthworth, co. Yorks: Reg. Univ. Oxf. vol. ii. pt. ii. p. 337.
MDB. (co. Ches.), 1, 1; London, 2, 0; Liverpool, 2, 2; Philadelphia, 6, 0; Boston (U.S.), 18, 6.

Soutter; v. Soutar.

Sowden, Sowdon, Soudon.—Local, 'of Suddon,' i.e. the south down; cf. Sudlow, &c., a well-known West-country name.

Walter de Suddon, co. Soms., 1 Edw. III: Kirby's Quest, p. 115.
London, 2, 1, 0; Philadelphia, 12, 0, 0.

Sowerbutts, Sourbutts. — ? Local. This looks very like a nickname. A brewer of bad beer would easily acquire the title. Nevertheless, it may be but a compound of *butt*, a mark to shoot at, and represent some long-forgotten spot. It is a Lancashire surname, and is still familiar to that county. It sprang up in the neighbourhood of Preston.

Robert Sowerbutts, 1682: Preston Guild Rolls, p. 177.
James Sowerbutts, 1682: ibid.

The earlier form is found in the following:

William Sowerbutt, of Cadate Field (Preston), 1559.
Cecilia Sorbutt, of Chepyn, 1562.

In the same record a hundred years later appears:

Arthur Sowerbutts, of Ribchester (near Preston), 1676: Lancashire Wills at Richmond, i. 260.
Preston, 3, 0; London, 3, 0; Manchester, 4, 0; Liverpool, 1, 1.

Sowerby.—Local, 'of Sowerby.' Chapelries in parishes of Thirsk and Halifax (2), townships in cos. Westmoreland and Lancaster.

Stephen de Soureby, co. York, 1273. A.
Thomas de Sawreby, 1379: P. T. Yorks. p. 87.
Johannes de Saureby, 1379: ibid. p. 89.
1597. Thomas Sowerbye, co. Cumb.: Reg. Univ. Oxf. vol. ii. pt. ii. p. 221.
1609. Francis Sowerby, co. Durham: ibid. p. 307.
London, 8; MDB. (co. Durham), 4; Philadelphia, 6.

Sowter. — Occup. 'the shoemaker'; v. Soutar.

London, 3.

Spackman; v. Speakman.

Spafford. — Local; v. Spofforth.

Manchester, 1; Philadelphia, 1; New York, 3.

Spain. — Local, 'of Spain.' A very early incomer; cf. Portingale.

Michael de Ispania, co. Oxf., 1273. A.
John de Ispania, co. Hunts, ibid.
William de Spayne, co. Salop, ibid.
Henricus de Ispania, Pipe Roll, 11 Hen. II. p. 47.
Willelmus del Spayn, 1379: P. T. Yorks. p. 25.
John de Spayn, 1379: ibid.
1652. Married—John Fillpott and Mary Spaine: Canterbury Cath. p. 58.
London, 5; Philadelphia, 7.

Spalding, Spaulding.—Local, 'of Spalding,' a parish in co. Linc.

Ralph de Spaldinge, co. Hunts, 1273. A.
Ida de Spaldingge, co. Camb., ibid.
Robertus de Spaldyng, 1379: P. T. Yorks. p. 48.
Margareta de Spaldyng, 1379: ibid. p. 101.
1808. Married — William Williams, otherwise Spalding, and Maria Davis: St. Geo. Han. Sq. ii. 379.
London, 3, 0; Philadelphia, 6, 1; New York, 5, 20.

Spanald.—Local. Spanish, a Spaniard; cf. *spaniel*, a dog.

O. F. *espqgneul*, a spaniel. v. Spain.

Willelmus Spanald, Isabella uxor ejus, 1379: P. T. Yorks. p. 166.

Spaniard.—Local, from Spain, q. v.

William Spanyard, Close Roll, 6 Ric. II. pt. ii.

Sparham.—Local, 'of Sparham,' a parish in co. Norfolk, three miles from Reepham.

Geoffrey de Sparham, co. Norf., 1273. A.
William de Sparham, of Sparham, temp. Ric. I: FF. viii. 258.
1754. Married—William Sparham and Catherine Williams: St. Geo. Chap. Mayfair, p. 275.
London, 1.

Sparhawk; v. Spark, where references will be found.

1694-5. Mark Anthony and Mary Sparhauke: Marriage Lic. (Faculty Office), p. 214.
Philadelphia, 6.

Spark, Sparke, Sparks, Sparkes.—(1) Bapt. 'the son of Sparrowhawk'; found as early as Domesday in the forms Sperhauoc (co. Notts), Sparhauoc (co. Suffolk). (2) Nick. 'the sparrow-hawk.' M.E. *sperhauke* (Piers Plowman).

Sparheuk Sutor, co. Suff., 1273. A.
Thomas Sperheuk, co. Linc., ibid.
Nicholas Sparke, co. Norf., ibid.
Bartholomew fil. Sparhavec, co. Norf., temp. Hen. II: FF. ix. 206.
Gilbert Sperhauk, co. Soms., 1 Edw. III: Kirby's Quest, p. 125.
John Sparhauk, rector of St. Buttolph the Abbot, Norwich, 1351: FF. iv. 442.
Magota Spark, 1379: P. T. Yorks. p. 154.
Robertus Spark, 1379: ibid. p. 14.
Olive Sparrehawke, temp. Eliz. 2.
Richard Sparhawke, rector of Fincham, 1534: FF. vii. 358.
1632-3. Married — Johan Sparrowhawke: St. Dionis Backchurch (London).
'The learned Dr. Fuller, being in company of one Mr. Sparrowhawk, unwittingly asked him, "What is the difference between an owl and a sparrowhawk?" and it is said that he received the unexpected reply, "An owl is *fuller* in the head, *fuller* in the face, and FULLER all over"': T. E. Bailey's Life of Thomas Fuller, p. 3.
1777. Married—Thomas Sparrowhawke and Susannah Hampton: St. Geo. Han. Sq. i. 279.
London, 4, 1, 26, 3; West Rid. Court Dir., 2, 1, 0, 0; Philadelphia, 1, 0, 51, 0.

Sparrow. — Nick. 'the sparrow.' A common sobriquet in

mediaeval registers. A homely, chirpy disposition would readily give rise to the surname.

John Sparuwe, co. Oxf., 1273. A.
Laurence Sparwe, co. Camb., ibid.
Hugh Sparewe, co. Camb., ibid.
Rogerus Sparowe, 1379: P. T. Yorks. p. 25.
Adam Sparowe, 1379: ibid. p. 51.
1529-30. Robert Sparrow and Eliz. Fest: Marriage Lic. (London), i. 7.
1572. Married—Francys Sparrowe and Jone Mahewe: Reg. St. Dionis Backchurch, p. 7.
London, 20; New York, 6.

Sparrowhawk, Sparhawk.
—(1) Nick.; (2) Bapt.; v. Spark.
'Charles Sparrowhawk, dealer, was charged with the unlawful possession of two ponies': Standard, Aug. 27, 1888, p. 2.
Philadelphia, 0, 6.

Sparshott.—Local, ' of Sparsholt,' parishes in cos. Berks and Hants. -holt (q.v.) as a suffix sometimes becomes -hott; cf. Aldershot. But v. Shute (2).
1744. Married — Thomas Sparshott and Jane Brathwait: St. Geo. Chap. Mayfair, p. 38.
1794. — Charles Bowden and Elizabeth Sparshatt: St. Geo. Han. Sq. ii. 120.
London, 1; Boston (U.S.), 1.

Spaulding; v. Spalding.

Spawforth.—Local; v. Spofforth.
London, 2.

Speakman, Spackman, Speckman.—Bapt. 'the son of Speakman.' There is not the slightest trace of an occupative or official origin. It must be set in the same class as Bateman and Tiddiman, all used as personal or baptismal names. It is, and has been for centuries, a familiar surname in co. Lanc.
Henry Spakeman, co. Kent, 1273. A.
Isolda Spekeman, co. Oxf., ibid.
Richard Spekeman, co. Oxf., ibid.
John Speakman, of Astley, husbandman, 1578: Wills at Chester (1545-1620), p. 181.
1717. Buried—John Godman, lodger at Mr. Spackman's: St. Dionis Backchurch, p. 287.
London, 2, 3, 0; Manchester, 8, 0, 0; Philadelphia, 15, 9, 2.

Spear; v. Spyer.

Speck.—Nick. 'le spec' or 'le speke,' the woodpecker; v. Speke

(2), and v. glossary to Geraldus Cambrensis, vi. 125, 'dicitur autem picus avicula lingua gallica "spec" dicta.'
William le Spek, co. Devon, 1273. A.
1642. Buried—Joane, wife of Zachary Speck: St. Peter, Cornhill, i. 199.
1750. Married—Joseph Speck and Eliz. Leathwait: St. Michael, Cornhill, p. 72.
London, 3; Philadelphia, 18.

Speckman; v. Speakman.

Speechley, Speechly.—Local, ' of Spetchley,' a parish in co. Worcester, near Worcester.
1770. Married—William Speechly and Mary Chell: St. Geo. Han. Sq. i. 209.
London, 2, 3; MDB. (co. Camb.), 1, 2.

Speed, Speedy. — ? Bapt. Probably a font-name, wishing prosperity or good-speed to the child. The original meaning of speed is 'success.' If not this, it must be a nickname, significant of the quick, hasty movements of the first ancestor. If baptismal, Speedy is but a pet-form, as in the case of Charlie, Tommy, Willy, &c.
Johannes Sped, co. Suff., 1273. A.
Margaret Sped, co. Camb., ibid.
Roger Sped, co. Oxf., ibid.
1555-6. John Speede and Eliz. Cheynye: Marriage Lic. (London), i. 17.
Cicilie Speed, of Tattenhall, widow, 1578: Wills at Chester (1545-1620), p. 181.
London, 7, 3; Manchester, 3, 0; Philadelphia, 5, 1.

Speer; v. Spyer.

Speight, Speaight. — Nick. 'the speight' or specht, an old English name for the woodpecker.
Matilda Speght, 1379: P. T. Yorks. p. 185.
Hugo Speght, 1376: ibid.
Johanna Spite, 1379: ibid. p. 191.
John Spight, co. York. W. 16.
Richard Speight, co. York. W. 16.
1540. Buried — Richard Speite: St. Antholin (London), p. 1.
West Rid. Court Dir., 9, 0; London, 4, 2; Philadelphia, 2, 0; New York, 2, 2.

Speke, Speak, Speake.—(1) Local, ' of Speke,' a township in the parish of Childwall, co. Lanc.
Hugh Pilkington, of Speke, 1603: Wills at Chester (1545-1620), p. 153.
Ellen Speake, of Dinckley, widow, 1614: ibid. p. 181.
Charles Speak, of Goldshawe, 1670: ibid. (1660-80), p. 252.

(2) Nick. Lower says, 'The Spekes of Somersetshire descend from Richard le Espek, who lived in the reign of Henry II. Wemworthy and Brampton, in Devonshire, were the original seats; but temp. Hen. VI Sir John Speke married the heiress of Beauchamp, and so obtained Whitelackington, co. Somerset': Patr. Brit. p. 325. This surname has a distinct origin. It stands for ' le speke,' the woodpecker, and is a nickname of the same class as Nightingale, Lark, Sparrowhawk, &c. (v. Geraldus Cambrensis, vi. 125). For an early instance v. Speck, which is but a variant of the same name.
1701. Bapt. — Samuel, s. Richard Speake: St. Jas. Clerkenwell, ii. 1.
1725. Married—John Farrey and Mary Speake: St. Antholin (London), p. 140.
London, 1, 0, 0; Manchester, 0, 1, 0; Liverpool, 1, 0, 0; MDB. (co. Somerset), 2, 0, 0; Philadelphia, 0, 1, 1; Boston (U.S.), 0, 2, 0.

Speller, Spellar.—Occup. 'the speller.' Probably refers to the teacher, not the taught. One who spells the letters for the child to learn (v. Grammer). 'Spellare, sillabicator': Prompt. Parv. If the earlier sense of spell, a discourse, a story, originated the name, then the speller would be a professional story-teller. The surnames Speller and Spelman, q.v., are now well established.
Ralph le Speoler, co. Soms., 1 Edw. III: Kirby's Quest, p. 256.
Gerard le Speller. H.
Miles le Speller, C. R., 35 Edw. I.
Thomas Spellere, C. R., 19 Ric. II.
Thomas Speller, 1379: P. T. Yorks. p. 300.
Johannes Speller, 1379: ibid.
London, 5, 1; New York, 1, 0.

Spelman, Spellman.—Bapt. 'the son of Spileman.' I am much tempted to set the name beside Speller, but saving in one or two cases all the entries have it Spileman, without prefix le. I think it must go as a personal name with Bateman, Tiddiman, &c. Cf. the German Spielmann; v. Speakman.
John Speleman, co. Notts, 1273. A.
William Spelesman, co. Wilts, ibid.
Eustace Spileman, co. Oxf., ibid.

There are nine entries of Spile-man in the Hundred Rolls, repre-senting five counties.

Richard Spileman, co. Wilts, Hen. III-Edw. I. K.
Nicholas Spilman, co. Wilts, ibid.
Thomas Spyleman, C. R., 44 Hen. III. pt. i.
John Speleman, co. Soms., 1 Edw. III: Kirby's Quest, p. 133.
Roger Spileman, co. Soms., 1 Edw. III: ibid. p. 219.
London, 1, 0; Philadelphia, 0, 4.

Spence, Spens.—Local, 'at the upence.' The custodian of the store-room. A store-room, a store-closet, in small farms a cupboard. v. Spencer.

West Rid. Court Dir., 10, 0; Crockford, 5, 1; London, 20, 0; Philadelphia, 55, 0.

Spencer, Spenser.—Offic. A house-steward, one who, strictly speaking, had charge of the buttery or spence. In the Sumner's Tale the glutton is well described as:

'All vinolent as botel in the spence.'

while Mr. Halliwell quotes:

'Yet had I lever she and I
Were both together secretly
In some corner in the spence.'

In an inventory of household goods, dated 1574, I find the furniture of the hall first described, and this begins: 'A cupboard and a spence, 20s.' (Richmondshire Wills, p. 248). The office of 'la despencer' or 'la spencer' was amongst the highest in the king's household, and proportionately great among the barons. Practically such a name as 'Thomas de la Spence' was as official as 'Thomas la Spencer,' but, as in similar in-stances elsewhere, I have set it down as local.

John le Spencer, co. Southampton, 1273. A.
Henry le Spenser, co. Camb., ibid.
Henry del Spens, 1292: KKK. p. xli.
Thomas del Spens: Patent Rolls, 4 Edw. III. pt. ii.
Nicholas de la Despense, C. R., 4 Edw. III.
Thomas Spenser, 1379: P. T. Yorks. p. 56.
Agnes Spenser, 1379: ibid. p. 25.
West Rid. Court Dir., 25, 2; Crockford, 41, 0; London, 92, 1; Philadelphia, 86, 0.

Spender. — Official, 'one who spends money'; cf. Spenser or Spencer. 'Dispensier, a spender,

also a cater, or clarke of a kitchen' (Cotgrave, quoted by Skeat).

Johannes Spender, husband, et Anabilla uxor ejus, 1379: P. T. Howdenshire, p. 14.
1577-8. James Spender and Johanna Godfrey: Marriage Lic. (London), i. 79.
London, 2.

Spendlove,   Spendlow,
Spindelow.—Nick. or personal, 'the son of Spenlof.' No doubt of Scandinavian origin; cf. spend-thrift, a 'spend-all.'

Alicia Spendelove, co. Camb., 1273. A.
William Spendelove, co. Oxf., ibid.
Thomas Spenloff, 1379: P. T. Yorks. p. 291.
Robertus Spenlof, 1379: ibid.
Johannes Spendlove, 1379: ibid. p. 258.
'The heir of Robert Spendelufe holds half a bovate of land,' 23 Edw. III, Knight's Fees of Blakeburnshire: Baines' Lanc. ii. 693.

With the corrupted Spendlow, cf. Waddilove and Waddilow.

1593. Bapt.—Susan, d. William Spende-lowe: St. Jas. Clerkenwell, i. 27.
1598. — Mary, d. William Spendeloe: ibid. p. 33.
1602. — Joseph, s. William Spendlove: ibid. p. 40.
London, 2, 0, 2; MDB. (co. Derby), 6, 0, 0.

Spens(er; v. Spence(r.

Spenster.—Offic. 'the spencer,' with fem. suffix -ster; cf. Yorkshire Slaster for Slater, also spinster for spinner.

Thomas Spenster, 1379: P. T. Yorks. p. 136.

Sperling, Sperlings, Spil-
ling, Spillings, Spurling,
Spillin.—Bapt. 'the son of Spirling,' one of the endless suffixes in -ing; cf. Browning, Harding, &c. The s in Sperlings and Spil-lings is the genitive, as in Williams, Jones, Simmonds, &c. The only other possible origin is a nickname; German sperling, a sparrow.

Geoffrey Spirling, co. Norf., 1273. A.
Henry Sperling, co. Soms., 1 Edw. III: Kirby's Quest, p. 221.
1631. Bapt. — Dennys, d. Abraham Spillinge: St. Jas. Clerkenwell, i. 118.
MDB. (Suffolk), 0, 2, 1, 1, 1, 0; London, 1, 0, 0, 4, 0; Philadelphia, 2, 0, 0, 0, 1, 0.

Sperring.—Bapt.; v. Spiring.

Spicer.—Occup. 'the spicer,' the earlier term for the modern grocer. Thus spices meant various kinds. Latin, species.

'Spycers speken with hym.'
Piers P. 1332.
'Many a dyvers spyse
In bagges about thy bear.'
An old Song, written against the Mendicant Friars.
Simon le Spicere, co. Camb., 1273. A.
William le Spicere, co. Oxf., ibid.
William Speciar, co. Linc., ibid.
Sacr le Spicer. N.
Amphelisa le Spicer. O.
Richard le Spycer, co. Soms., 1 Edw. III: Kirby's Quest, p. 254.
Ricardus Chapman, spicer, 1379: P. T. Yorks. p. 25.
Adam Spisar, spicer, 1379: ibid. p. 27.
Giliaum Spyser, 1379: ibid. p. 89.
London, 21; Philadelphia, 26.

Spichfat, Pichfatt.— ? Nick. 'Bacon-fat' (?). This derisive sobri-quet seems to have died out, but many instances occur:

William Spichefat, Close Roll, 7 Edw. II.
Benedict Spichfat, C. R., 6 Edw. III.
Robert Spichfat. X.
William Spichfat. W. 11.

These represent separate dis-tricts, north and south. 'Spyk, or set flesche (spike of fleshe), popa': Prompt. Parv. 'A spycke of a bacon flycke': Skelton, quoted by Halliwell; cf. Hogsflesh and Pigsflesh (q.v.). Found as Pichfatt.

1684. Married — Richard Kirby and Mary Pichfatt: St. Michael, Cornhill (Harl. Soc.).
1735. — Charles Pickfatt and Jane Corr: St. Jas. Clerkenwell, iii. 263.

Spicknell, Spickernell.—Offic. 'the spigurnel,' a sealer of writs. Geoffrey Spigurnell pos-sessed this office in the reign of Henry III (Bailey's Dict. 1742).

Edmund Spigurnel, co. Notts, 1273. A.
Nicholas Spigurnel, co. Suff., ibid.
Nicholas Spikernel, co. Norf., ibid.
Henry Spigurnel, co. Kent, 20 Edw. I. R.
Matilda Sprygonell, 1379: P. T. Yorks. p. 151.
Roger Spygurnel, co. Soms., 1 Edw. III: Kirby's Quest, p. 124.
London, 1, 0; MDB. (co. Hants), 0, 3.

Spier, Spiers; v. Spyer.

Spillin, Spilling, Spillings; v. Sperling.

Spillman.—Bapt. 'the son of Spileman'; v. Spellman.
London, 3.

Spilsbury.—Local, 'of Spels-bury,' a parish in co. Oxford, near Chipping Norton.

1621. John Spilsbury, co. Worc.: Reg. Univ. Oxf. vol. ii. pt. ii. p. 389.

1633. Bapt.—Thomas, s. Thomas Spils-
burie: St. Geo. Han. Sq. ii. 232.
1801. Married—Edgar Ashe Spilsbury
and Emma Gybbon: ibid.
London, 1.

Spindelow; v. Spendlove.

Spink, Spinks.—Nick. 'the
spink,' i.e. the chaffinch or goldfinch; cf. Goldspink. A.S. *finc*,
a finch; Ger. *fink*; Prov. Eng.
spink. Spinks is a genitive form
(cf. Williams, Styles, Brooks, &c.).

Nicholas Spinc, co. Bedf., 1273. A.
Emma Spink, co. Norf., ibid.
Johannes Spink, 1379: P. T. Yorks. p.
100 (common in this Roll).
Hugo Spynk, 1379: ibid. p. 208.
Willelmus Spynk, 1379: ibid.

Pye, Cock, and Fox occur alongside these two entries.

1620. Bapt.—John, s. Edward Spinck:
St. Jas. Clerkenwell, i. 89.
1788. Married — Joseph Spinks and
Mary Popell: St. Geo. Hanover Sq. ii. 7.
London, 11, 9; West Rid. Court Dir.,
5, 0; Sheffield, 2, 0; Philadelphia, 6, 0.

Spinner.—Occup.'thespinner';
v. Wheelspinner.

Michael le Spinner, co. Soms., 1 Edw.
III: Kirby's Quest, p. 177.
Cristiana Spyner, 1379: P. T. Yorks.
p. 93.
Alicia Spynner, 1379: ibid. p. 124.
New York, 7; Philadelphia, 1.

Spire; v. Spyer.

Spirett, Spurrett.—Bapt. 'the
son of Spirhard.'

Leticia Spirold, co. Suff., 1273. A.
Philip Spirhard, co. Norf., ibid.
Ricardus Spyrad, 1379: P. T. Yorks.
p. 140.
Johannes Spirard, 1379: ibid.
Magota Spirard, 1379: ibid. p. 151.
Willelmus Spyrad, 1379: ibid. p. 203.
1338. Robert Spirhard, rector of Ful-
modeston, co. Norf.: FF. vii. 90.
1349. Peter Spirhead, co. Norf.: ibid.
v. 445.
1802. Married — Richard Dyas and
Mary Spurrett: St. Geo. Han. Sq. ii. 270.
West Rid. Court Dir., 3, 0; London,
0, 1.

Spiring, Sperring. — Bapt.
'the son of Spiring'; cf. Browning, Harding, &c.

Reginald Spiring, co. Soms., 1 Edw.
III: Kirby's Quest, p. 190.
1665-6. Roger Spering and Helen Skinner: Marriage Alleg. (Canterbury), p. 161.
London, 1, 2.

Spittle, Spittal, Spittall.—
Local, 'at the spittle,' i.e. hospital.
Spittleman.—Offic. ' the spittle-

man,' a guardian or attendant at a
hospital. **Spittlehouse.**—Local,
'at the spittle-house,' from residence
at the lodge of the hospital. This
little batch of names is connected
with the hospitals of mediaeval
times; cf. the local Spitalfields,
London. 'A spittle, hospitall, or
lazar-house': Baret, 1580 (quoted
by Skeat, v. *spittle*).

Gilbert de Hospitall, co. Oxf., 1273. A.
William Spitelman, co. Norf., Hen. III-
Edw. I. K.
Richard atte Spitale, 1301. M.
Adam del Hospital, Fines Roll, 12
Edw. I.
Robert Spitelman, Close Roll, 39 Hen.
III. pt. i.
Robert del Spitelle, C. R., 3 Hen. V.
Thomas atte Spytell, C. R., 11 Hen. VI.
Johannes del Spitilhous', 1379: P. T.
Yorks. p. 55.
Robertus de Spitell', 1379: ibid. p. 157.

It is interesting to notice that
Spittlehouse, occurring as we have
just seen in Yorkshire, is still found
in that county five hundred years
after.

'Esau Spittlehouse, beer-retailer,
Brookhouse, Laughton-en-le-Morthen':
West Rid. Yorkshire Directory.
1578. Buried—Antony Spittell: Reg.
St. Dionis Backchurch, p. 195.
London, 2, 0, 0, 0, 0; MDB. (Yorks,
West Rid), 0, 0, 0, 0, 1; (co. Leic.), 0, 0,
0, 0, 1; Philadelphia, 0, 0, 7, 0, 0; New
York (Spittle), 1.

Splatt.—Local, 'at the splott'
or splatt, from residence thereby.
'*Splat*, a row of pins as they are
set upon the paper. Co. Somerset'
(Halliwell). Thus *splatt* may have
implied a row of cottages.

William atte Splotte, co. Soms., 1 Edw.
III: Kirby's Quest, p. 216.
Hugh atte Splotte, 1379, co. Soms., 1
Edw. III: ibid. p. 246.

With the form Splot, cf. Sprott
and Spratt.

London, 1; Philadelphia, 1.

Spofforth, Spofford.—Local,
'of Spofforth,' a parish near
Knaresborough, co. Yorks. It has
taken in surnames the forms of
Spawforth and Spafford, q.v. (ford
= forth). Thus in the P. T. Yorks.
1379, Clifford is found as Clifforth;
v. Forth.

Robert de Spofford, *seler*, 3 Edw. II:
Freemen of York, i. 13.
Johannes de Spofford, 1379: P. T.
Yorks. p. 222.

Willelmus de Spoford, 1379: ibid. p. 88.
Robertus de Spofford, 1379: ibid. p.
301.
London, 3, 1; Philadelphia, 0, 1;
Boston (U.S.), 0, 17.

Spon, Spong.—Local, 'at the
spong,' from residence thereby.
'*Spong*, an irregular, narrow,
projecting part of a field, whether
planted or in grass': Moor
(Halliwell's Dict.). 'A boggy wet
place. Norfolk' (Halliwell's Dict.).

Ricardus del Spon, 1376: P. T. Yorks.
p. 193.
1741. Bapt. — George, s. George
Spong: St. Geo. Chap. Mayfair, p. 3.
1749. Married — John Sponge and
Martha Hatt: ibid. 143.
1802. — Thomas Spong and Jane
Mary Ann Brooks: St. Geo. Han. Sq. ii.
266.
London, 1, 7.

Spooner.—Occup. 'the spooner,'
a maker of spoons; an important
manufacture when no forks were
used, and so many messes, stews,
soups, &c., were popular; cf.
Cutler and Nasmith.

Robertus Sponer, 1379: P.T.Yorks. p. 82.
Willelmus Sponer, 1379: ibid. p. 127.
Henricus Spuner, 1379: ibid. p. 266.
'1585. Buried—John Sponer (Spooner)'
—thus entered: St. Jas. Clerkenwell,
iv. 33.
1625. John Spooner and Florence
Fryer: Marriage Lic. (London), ii. 160.
1728. Married — Henry Spooner and
Mary Taylor: St. Mary Aldermary, p. 41.
London, 24; Philadelphia, 8.

**Spottiswood, Spottiswoode,
Spottswood.**—Local, 'of Spottiswoode.' 'The name is derived from
the barony of Spottiswoode. The
family were benefactors to the
abbeys of Melrose and Kelso in
early times. The ancestor . . . was
Robert de Spottiswood, who was
born in the reign of King Alexander
III, and died in that of Robert
Bruce' (Lower, quoting Burke's
Landed Gentry). Spottiswood is
in the parish of Gordon, co.
Berwick. The American form
existed in England at one time.

1613. Robert Spotswood, Exeter Coll.:
Reg. Univ. Oxf. i. 275.
MDB. (co. Cumb.), 2, 0, 0; London, 0,
2, 0; Philadelphia, 0, 0, 3.

**Spracklin, Spratling, Sprack-
len.**—? Bapt. 'the son of Sparkling';
cf. Harding, Browning, &c.

SPRADBROW

Robertus Esprakelin, co. Cornwall, Hen. III-Edw. I. K.
Geoffrey Sparkelyng, co. Soms., 1 Edw. III: Kirby's Quest, p. 230.
1645. Bapt. — Robert, s. Mr. Robert Spratling: Canterbury Cath. p. 10.
1652. — Eliz., d. Thomas Spraklin: St. Jas. Clerkenwell, i. 182.
1653. — Adam, s. Mr. Robert Sprackling: Canterbury Cath. p. 10.
London, 1, 1, 0; Philadelphia, 0, 0, 1.

Spradbrow, Spradbery. — Local, 'of Sprotborough,' a parish in W. Rid. Yorks, near Doncaster, a curious corruption; v. Spratt and Spratley for the derivation of the name; lit. the borough of Sprot, the first settler.

Thomas Sprotburghe, co. York, 20 Edw. I. R.
Johannes de Sprotburghe, of Sprotburghe, 1379: P. T. Yorks. p. 53.
1632. Bapt. — Robert, s. Edward Spradbrowe: St. Michael, Cornhill, i. 122.
1656. — Henry, s. William Sprattberry: St. Jas. Clerkenwell, i. 195.
1670. Married—Robert Spredborough and Bridget Cutberd: ibid. p. 170.
London, 0, 2; Liverpool, 1, 0.

Spragg, Sprague.—Nick. 'the spragg,' the quick, the nimble; v. Sprake.

Ralph Spragg, of Knutsford, co. Ches., 1632: East Cheshire, ii. 343.
Thomas Spragg, of Great Budworth, 1664: Wills at Chester (1660–1680), p. 253.
London, 0, 7; MDB. (co. Chester), 1, 0; Manchester, 2, 0; Philadelphia, 0, 11.

Sprake, Spragg, Sprague.—Nick. 'the sprack,' i.e. the quick, the lively, the active; *sprack* and *sprag* (West), Halliwell. The surname still lives in co. Somerset. With Sprake and Spragg, cf. Slack and Slagg. The dim. Spraket is also found.

William Spraket, co. Soms., 1 Edw. III: Kirby's Quest, p. 252.
William Sprak, co. Soms., 1 Edw. III: ibid. 253.
1682. Samuell Spragg and Mary Randall: Marriage Alleg. (Canterbury), ii. 116.
1690. Bapt.—Mary, d. Robert Spragg: St. Jas. Clerkenwell, i. 326.
1807. Married — Charles Spragg and Sarah Stevens: St. Geo. Han. Sq. ii. 378.
London, 2, 0, 7; MDB. (co. Soms.), 1, 1, 0.

Spratley.—Local, 'of Sproatley,' a parish in E. Rid. Yorks, seven miles from Hull, lit. the field that belonged to Sprot; v. Spratt.

1612. Edward Spratley, *cook*, and Ellen Moorton: Marriage Lic. (London), ii. 14.
1795. Married — Thomas Porter and Mary Spratley: St. Geo. Han. Sq. ii. 124.
London, 3; MDB. (co. Berks), 2; New York, 2.

Spratling; v. Spracklin.

Spratt, Sproat, Sprott, Sprout, Sproutt.—Bapt. 'the son of Sprot,' Domesday (co. Derby). For further instances, v. Sproat.

Henry Sprot, co. Camb., 1273. A.
Richard Sprot, co. Oxf., ibid.
Simon Sprot, co. Bedf., ibid.
John Sprot, co. Soms., 1 Edw. III: Kirby's Quest, p. 149.
Agnes Sprote, 1379: P. T. Yorks. p. 112.
1449. John Sprott de Surlingham, co. Norf.: FF. v. 467.
1582. John Spratte and Eliz. Wheatlye: Marriage Lic. (London), i. 108.
1594. Edward Sprott of Spratt, co. Staff.: Reg. Univ. Oxf. vol. ii. pt. ii. p. 207.
MDB. (co. Soms.), Sprott, 2; London, 13, 4, 0, 0, 0; Philadelphia, 17, 0, 0, 0, 0; New York, 5, 1, 2, 1, 1.

Sprigg, Spriggs.—Bapt. 'the son of Sprig,' very probably a nick. of the personal name, Sprigin (v. Spriggin). This is the more likely as Sprigg and the genitive Spriggs are found chiefly in the neighbourhood of co. Norfolk, where Spriggins and Spurgeon, &c., arose.

1607. Married — William Sprig, *blacksmith*, and Grace Percye: St. Michael, Cornhill, p. 18.
1632. Buried—Mary Spriggs: St. Jas. Clerkenwell, iv. 205.
1655. — Lidia, wife of John Sprigg: ibid. p. 306.
MDB. (co. Bucks), 1, 1, ; London, 0, 3; Philadelphia, 1, 4.

Spriggin, Spriggen, Spriggins, Sprigens.—Bapt. 'the son of Sprigin,' a variant of the old Norfolk personal name, now immortalized as Spurgeon, q.v. The genitive of Spriggin is Spriggins; cf. Williams, Jones, Tompkins, &c.

William Sprigin, co. Norf., 1273. A.
Spriginus (without surname), co. Norf., c. 12th cent.: FF. vi. 457.
Roger Spriggens, co. Norf.: ibid. vii. 350.

SPROSTON

1559. Buried—Roger Sprigen, servant with John Hawley, draper: St. Michael, Cornhill.
1620. Married—Robert Spriggins and Ann Linnell: St. Jas. Clerkenwell, iii. 48.
1664. — Timothy Spriggin and Edith Lee: ibid. p. 115.

Spurgeon and Spurgin (q.v.) are the modern Norfolk forms of the surname.

London, 0, 0, 0, 1; New York, 0, 0, 1, 0.

Springall, Springhall, Springett, Springle.—Nick. or personal. Either 'the springald,' i.e. an active, alert young man (spring), or 'the son of Springald.' The latter is the more probable.

Julian Springald, co. Oxf., 1273. A.
Walter Springaud, co. Oxf., ibid.
Alan Springold, co. Camb., ibid.
Geoffrey Spurnegold, Fines Roll, 11 Edw. I.
William Spryngold, co. Soms., 1 Edw. III: Kirby's Quest, p. 80.
Alice Spryngot, Pat. Rolls, 4 Edw. III. pt. ii.
1662. Married—Francis Springall and Rhode Padnall: St. Dionis Backchurch, p. 37.

The Manchester Evening News, Dec. 8, 1885, records the murder of an old man named Springhall at Hingham in Norfolk.

London, 2, 1, 2, 1; Crockford, 0, 0, 1, 0; New York (Springett), 1; Boston (U.S.), 4, 0, 0, 0.

Sproat. — Bapt. 'the son of Sprot,' a Domesday personal name; v. Spratt, which is a variant.

1628. William Sproate, of Hornby: Lancashire Wills at Richmond, i. 260.
1666. Henry Sprote, of Hornby, ibid.
1616. Christopher Sprote, of Tatham: ibid.
1623. Margaret Sprotte: ibid.

These last two are manifestly of one family. Their descendants are now found invariably as Sproat in co. Lanc.

1733. Christopher Sproat, of Tatham: ibid. ii. 238.
— Susan Sproat, of Tatham: ibid.
Preston, 2; New York, 1; Boston (U.S.), 2.

Sproston, Sprosson, Sproson. — Local, 'of Sproston,' a township in the parish of Middlewich, co. Chester. With Sproston and Sprosson, cf. Snelston and Snelson in the same district.

Thomas Cranage, of Sproston, 1618 : Wills at Chester (1505-1620), p. 46.
Ralph Sproston, of Middlewich : ibid. p. 181.
Robert Sproston, of the city of Chester, alderman, 1663 : ibid. (1660-80), p. 253.
1789. Married — John Sproson and Susanna Walker : St. Geo. Han. Sq. ii. 25.
1797. — Samuel Sproston and Eliz. Kendall : ibid. p. 171.
London, 1, 1, 0 ; MDB. (co. Chester), 6, 0, 0 ; New York, 0, 0, 2.

Sprott, Sprout(t ; v. Spratt.

Spurdance, Spurdens. — ? Nick. I cannot trace the origin of this surname. Sometimes the initial *s* is omitted ; cf. Turges and Sturges. The surname is still found in co. Norfolk.

Richard Purdance, bailiff of Norwich, 1403 : FF. iii. 123.
Richard Spurdaunce, mayor of Norwich, 1420 : ibid. p. 136.
Richard Purdaunce, alderman of Norwich, 1424 : ibid. p. 138.
Richard, Spurdaunce, mayor of Norwich, 1433 : ibid. p. 163.
MDB. (Norfolk), 0, 1.

Spurgeon, Spurgin.—Bapt. 'the son of Sprigin.' There can be little doubt about this. It is evidently an old and long-forgotten Scandinavian personal name. Norfolk is the home. It occurs there so early as 1273. The spelling of the surname is imitative, a copy of *surgeon*, v. Spriggin.

William Sprigin, co. Norf., 1273. A.
Simon Sp'ugin, co. Camb., ibid.
Ralph Spraging, 1622 : Marriage Lic. (London), p. 28.
1566. Robert Spurgynne, vicar of Fouldon, co. Norf. : FF. vi. 35.
John Spurgeon, mayor of Yarmouth, 1712 : ibid. xi. 331.
1764. Bapt. — Daniel, s. Daniel Spurgeon : St. Peter, Cornhill, ii. 49.
London, 6, 1 ; MDB. (Norfolk), 6, 2 ; (Suffolk), 1, 1 ; New York, 1, 0 ; Boston (U.S.), 3, 0.

Spurling.—Bapt. ; v. Sperling.

Spurrett.—Bapt. ; v. Spirett.

Spurrier.—Occup. 'the spurrier,' a maker of spurs. I see no instance in the Hundred Rolls of 1273.

Robert de Gisburgh, *sporier*, 26 Edw. I : Freemen of York (Surt. Soc.), i. 7.
Nicholas Sporiare,co. Soms., 1 Edw.III: Kirby's Quest, p. 239.
Nicholas le Sporiere, C. R., 29 Edw. III.
Benedict le Sporier. J.

Nicholas le Sporiere, London. X.
1579. John Spurier, co. Somerset : Reg. Univ. Oxf. vol. ii. pt. ii. p. 88.
1798. Married—John Smith and Eliz. Spurrier : St. Geo. Han. Sq. ii. 186.
London, 3 ; Philadelphia, 1.

Spyer, Speer, Spier, Spire, Spear, Spiers. — Occup. 'the spier,' i.e. watchman ; v. Scorer. The final *s* in Spiers is genitive.

Robertus Spyer, 1379 : P. T. Yorks. p. 142.
Richard Spyre, 1515 : Reg. Univ. Oxf. i. 95.
1662-3. John Spier, co. Oxf., and Jane Price : Marriage Lic. (Faculty Office), p. 68.
1802. Married — Robert Spear and Maria Baker : St. Geo. Han. Sq. ii. 256.
London, 4, 6, 2, 1, 4, 1 ; Oxford, 0, 0, 0, 0, 1, 4 ; Philadelphia, 0, 20, 2, 1, 30, 0.

Squatfoot.—Nick. 'with the squat foot' ; cf. Lightfoot, Barfoot, &c.

Anabilla Squatfoot, C. R., 35 Edw. III.

Squibb. — Nick. ; a term of disdain, a poor kind of fellow ; v. Spenser's Mother Hubbard's Tale, 371 ; v. Skeat, from whom I got the reference.

John Squybbe, 1536 : Reg. Univ. Oxf. i. 187.
1693. Bapt.—Eliz., d. Thomas Squibb: St. Jas. Clerkenwell, i. 353.
London, 2 ; Philadelphia, 1.

Squiller, Skiller. — Occup. 'the squiller.' A washer of dishes, &c. 'Sqwyllare, dysche-wescheare, *lixa*' : Prompt. Parv.

John le Squylier. H.
Geoffrey le Squeller. O.
Geoffrey le Squeler : Close Roll, 52 Hen. III.
John de la Squillerye. H.

The word seems closely related to the O.F. *escuelle*, a dish, but Professor Skeat (Etym. Dict., *scullery*) says the original form was *swiller*, from *swill*, to wash, passing from *swiller* to *squiller*, and as a habitat from *squillery* to *scullery*. 'The squyler of the kechyn' is mentioned by Robert of Brunne.

'The eleven messes to the children of the kechyn, squillery, and pastrey, with porters, scowerers, and turn broches, &c.' : Ord. Henry VIII at Eltham.

We may add 'Roger de Norhamptone, squyler,' in Mr. Riley's Memorials of London. The

French *escuelle*, a dish, if not radically connected, must have influenced the changes that have passed over the word. Amongst other gifts from the City of London to the Black Prince, in 1371, were '48 esqueles and 24 salt-cellars, weighing by goldsmith's weight, 76lb. 5oz. o dwt.'(Riley's Memorials of London, p. 350). 'Sergeant, squylloure' (Halliwell).

'Hugh Skeller, alias Dalton, was abbot of Furness, 13 Edw. III : West's Ant. of Furness, p. 84.

Squire, Squires, Squier, Squiers. — Offic. 'the esquire,' an attendant upon a knight, a shield-bearer. Squires is the genitive form ; cf. Brooks, Williams, Tompkins, &c.

John le Squier, co. Camb., 1273. A.
William Squier, co. Hunts, ibid.
Thomas le Esquier, C. R., 33 Hen. III.
Thomas Squier, 1379 : P. T. Yorks. p. 50
Agnes Squier, 1379 : ibid. p. 139.
Walter le Squier, c. 1300. M.

Squire, like Marquis, Duke, Earl, &c., has become a favourite fontname among the 'lower orders' in Yorkshire ; v. Duke for an explanation.

London, 36, 15, 0, 0 ; Philadelphia, 4. 7, 0, 0 ; New York, 13, 14, 9, 1.

Squirrel, Squirrell. — Nick. 'the squirrel,' a sobriquet referring to physical agility or prudent thrift. O.F. *escurel*.

Geoffrey le Esqurel, co. Essex, 1273. A.
Thomas Squyrrelle. N. (v. Index).
Henry Squyrel, co. Soms., 1 Edw. III : Kirby's Quest, p. 217.
1279. Married — Benjamin Ruffe and Sarah Squirrell : St. Geo. Chap. Mayfair, p. 297.
London, 1, 3 ; MDB. (co. Suffolk), 0, 3 ; Philadelphia, 0, 1.

Stable, Stables.—Local, 'at the stable,' from residence thereby. Stables has the suffix *s*, as in Brooks, Styles, &c. (perhaps patronymic). Possibly it is really plural, implying the stables, as distinct from a stable.

Wido de Stabulo, co. Bucks, 1273. A.
John de Stabulo, co. Hunts, ibid.
William de la Stable, Fines Roll, 11 Edw. I.
William del Stabell, C. R., 1 Hen. V.
Radulphus del Stabill, 1379 : P. T. Yorks. p. 53.

Agnes del Stabill', 1379 : P. T. Yorks. p. 196.

Johannes del Stable, 1379 : ibid. p. 242.

1628. Bapt.—John, s. John Stables : St. Jas. Clerkenwell, i. 110.

London, 1, 3 ; West Rid. Court Dir., 0, 3 ; New York, 1, 0.

Stableford.—Local ; v. Stapleford.

Stabler.—Occup. 'the stabler,' a stableman, an ostler ; the keeper of an inn where horses were kept for hire.

Alan le Stabler, co. Camb., 1273. A. William le Stabler, co. Hunts, ibid. Thomas le Stabeler, co. Linc., ibid. William le Stabler. R. Anne Stabler. W. 16. John Stabler, C. R., 20 Ric. II. pt. i. Willelmus Stabeler, 1379 : P. T. Yorks. p. 262.

1793. Married — James Whitnell and Ann Stabler : St. Geo. Han. Sq. ii. 92.

London, 1 ; Philadelphia, 2.

Stables ; v. Stable.

Stace, Stacey, Stacy, Stacye. —Bapt. 'the son of Eustace,' from the nicks. Stace and Stacey, dim. Stacekin.

Roger Stace, co. Hunts, 1273. A. Stacius Warewnar, co. Linc., ibid. William Stacy, co. Devon, ibid. Stacius le Boloneis. C. Thomas Stacy, co. Soms., 1 Edw. III : Kirby's Quest, p. 148. Stacy Hernowe, co. Soms.,1 Edw. III : ibid. p. 270. Robertus Stasy, 1379 : P. T. Yorks. p. 44. Ricardus Stase, 1379 : ibid. Johannes Stase, 1379 : ibid. Robert Stace, sup. for B.C.L., 1552 : Reg. Univ. Oxf. i. 79.

An early dim. and masculine Stacekin is met with, proving that Eustace and not Anastasia is the parent of the above; also Latinized as Stacius.

Stacekinus de Burnes, co. Kent, Hen. III–Edw. I. K.

West Rid. Court Dir., 0, 15, 0, 1 ; London, 3, 17, 8, 0 ; Sheffield, 0, 19, 0, 1 ; Philadelphia, 0, 6, 0, 0.

Stafford.—Local, 'of Stafford,' the capital of co. Stafford. The surname is now far more familiar to the United States than to England.

Martin de Stafford, co. Suff., 1273. A. Ranulf de Stafford, co. Salop, ibid. Cf. John de Staffordsire (Staffordshire), ibid.

1562. Bapt.—Edward, sonne unto Sir Robert Stafford, knight : St. Jas. Clerkenwell, i. 2.

1576. Anthony Stafforde, co. Oxford : Reg. Univ. Oxf. vol. ii. pt. ii. p. 71.

MDB. (co. Derby), 2 ; London, 2 ; Oxford, 2 ; Philadelphia, 55.

Stagg.—Nick. 'the stag' ; cf. Buck, Hart, Doe, &c.

Thomas Stagge, C. R., 17 Edw. III. pt. ii.

Adam Stagge, 1379 : P.T. Yorks. p. 169. 1579-80. William Stagge, co. Dorset : Reg. Univ. Oxf. vol. ii. pt. ii. p. 91 1586. Married—William Hudson and Margaret Stagg: St. Dionis Backchurch, p. 11.

London, 13 ; Sheffield, 3 ; Philadelphia, 8.

Stalley ; v. Staley

Stainer.—Occup. 'the stainer'; cf. Painter. Mr. Lower says, 'The London Painters and Stainers were united into one company in 1502 ' (Patr. Brit. p. 327). But v. Stanier.

John Stynour, co. Soms., 1 Edw. III : Kirby's Quest, p. 269. 1705. Buried—John Staner : St. Thomas the Apostle (London), p. 144. 1791. Married—Benjamin Stainer and Ann Davis : St. Geo. Han. Sq. ii. 67.

London, 3 ; Philadelphia, 1.

Staines, Stains, Stanes.— Local, ' of Staines,' a market-town and parish in co. Middlesex.

Richard de Stanes, co. Kent, 1273. A. William de Staines, co. Kent, Hen. III– Edw. I. K. 1328. William de Stanes, rector of Welborne, co. Norf. : FF. ii. 453. 1677. Bapt.—John, s. Richard Stanes : St. Jas. Clerkenwell, i. 277.

London, 8, 1, 5 ; Philadelphia, 1, 2, 0.

Stainforth.—Local, ' of Stainforth,' a township in the parish of Giggleswick, W. Rid. Yorks.

1749. Married — Luke Stainforth and Judith Nutt : St. Geo. Chap. Mayfair, p. 135.

West Rid. (Yorks) Court Dir., 1 ; MDB. (co. Derby), 2.

Stainsby ; v. Stanesby.

Stainton.—Local, ' of Stainton,' townships in the parishes of Stanwix (co. Cumb.), Dacre (co. Cumb.), Gainford (co. Durham), Urswick (co. Lanc.), and Downholme (W. Rid. Yorks) ; also parishes in cos. York (N. Rid. and W. Rid.), Lincoln, and Durham. v. Stanton.

Herbert de Staynton, co. Linc., 1273. A. Robert de Staynton, co. Linc., ibid. Thomas de Staynton, 1379 : P.T. Yorks. p. 88.

Juliana de Staynton, 1379 : ibid. 1804. Married — Robert Fernyhough and Ann Stainton : St. Geo. Han. Sq. ii. 302.

London, 6 ; West Riding Court Dir., 1 ; Ulverston, 1 ; New York, 2.

Staley, Stailey.—Local, ' of Staley,' now a parish called Staleybridge, near Ashton-under-Lyne, formerly Staveley, a common local name ; v. Staveley.

Robert de Stavelegh, or Staley, 1389 : East Ches. ii. 155. Thomas de Staveley, 1400 : ibid. p. 167. Ralph Staveley, or Staley : ibid. i. 79. 1608. Bapt.—John, s. Richard Staley : St. Jas. Clerkenwell, i. 52.

MDB. (co. Derby), 19, 0 ; Manchester, 3, 0 ; London, 1, 0 ; Philadelphia, 24, 5.

Stalker.—Occup. 'the stalker,' a huntsman, a fowler. 'Stalk, to use a stalking-horse for obtaining wild-fowl and game ' (Halliwell).

Amabil le Stalker, co. Hunts, 1273. A. 1802. Married—John Alison and Ann Stalker : St. Geo. Han. Sq. ii. 270. 1806. — John Grear and Jane Stalker : ibid. p. 340.

London, 1 ; Liverpool, 2 ; Boston (U.S.), 6.

Stallard, Stollard. — ? Bapt. Probably ' the son of Stannard ' or Stonard, a once popular fontname. The change from n to l is extremely common in English nomenclature ; cf. banister for baluster, and v. Phillimore or Banister. There is no trace of a name Stallard or Stollard in the Hundred Rolls. The double variants, too, run side by side with the more correct ones ; v. Stannard. Nevertheless cf. Icelandic personal name ' Stal-hardr,' hard as steel (v. Icel. Dict. stal, where the name and derivation are given).

1648. Buried — Sarah, d. Thomas Stollard : St. Peter, Cornhill, i. 203. 1740. Married—Edmund Stallard and Catherine Cox : St. Dionis Backchurch, p. 67.

London, 3, 2 ; New York, 1, 0.

Stallebrass, Stallibrass, Stallybrass.— ? ——. I cannot suggest any satisfactory solution.

1652. Married — Joseph Sumner and Joyce Stallowbrace, of Waltham, co. Essex : Reg. St. Peter, Cornhill, i. 259.

London, 1, 2, 0 ; MDB. (co. Essex), 0, 3, 1.

Stallon.—Local, 'of Stalham,' a parish in co. Norfolk. The corruption took place at an early period.

Nicholas de Stalham, co. Norf., 1273. A.
Ralph Stalum, co. Norf., ibid.
Herbert Stalun, co. Norf., ibid.
1336. Jeffrey de Stalham, bailiff of Yarmouth : FF. xi. 323.
1367. William de Stallon, bailiff of Norwich : ibid. iii. 100.
1370. John de Stalham : ibid. xi. 323.
1626. Married — Anthony Griffin and Eliz. Stallonn : St. Antholin (London), 61.
1694. Christopher Stallon or Stalham, mayor of Norwich : FF. iii. 426.
MDB. (Norfolk), 2.

Stalman, Stallman.—(1) Local, 'of Stalmine,' a parish in dioc. Manchester. (2) Occup. 'the stallman.' Mr. Lower says, 'The keeper of a stall in any fair or market who paid the impost known in municipal law as stallage' (Patr. Brit. p. 327).

Adam de Stalmyn, co. Lanc., 20 Edw. I. R.
John de Stalmyn, co. Lanc., ibid.
London, 2, 0 ; Philadelphia, 0, 17.

Stalwart, Stalwartman, Stallworthy.—Nick. 'the stalwart.' M.E. *stalworth* (Pricke of Conscience, 689). For the suggested curious origin of this word, 'good at stealing,' hence brave, strong, v. Skeat. With Stallworthy, cf. the local Kenworthy and Langworthy for Kenworth and Langworth.

John le Stalewrthe, co. Oxf., 1273. A.
Henry Stalewrth, co. Camb., ibid.
Thomas Stalwrygh', 1379 : P. T. Yorks. p. 156.
John Staleworthman, C. R., 12 Ric. II.
1685. Bapt. — Mathew, s. Edward Stolwortman : St. Antholin (London), p. 102.
1794. Married — Charles Hyde and Sarah Stalworth : St. Geo. Han. Sq. ii. 108.
London, 0, 0, 1 ; MDB. (co. Bucks), 0, 0, 1.

Stamford.—Local, 'of Stamford,' a market-town in co. Lincoln. It appears that the original name of the place was Stanford (the stony ford), q.v.

Richard de Stanfordia, co. Linc., 1273. A.
Clemens de Stanford, co. Norf., ibid.

The following three references clearly attach to the same individual :

Alban de Stanford, co. Norf. : FF. x. 387.
Albon de Stamford, co. Norf. : ibid. viii. 460.
Albin de Standford, co. Norf. : ibid. p. 199.
1626. John Greene and Mary Stamford, widow of Edward Stamford (sic) : Marriage Lic. (London), i. 168.
London, 6 ; Philadelphia, 1.

Stamper.—Occup. 'the stamper,' probably a stamper of coins, a mint-man.

John Stamper, co. Camb., 1273. A.
Robert Stamper, co. York. W. 16.
1658. Married—John James and Anne Stamper : St. Thomas the Apostle (London), p. 20.
1699-1700. Robert Stamper and Ann Man : Marriage Lic. (Faculty Office), p. 235.
London, 1 ; MDB. (co. Cumb.), 9 ; Philadelphia, 1.

Stanborough, Stanbrough, Stanbury, Stanbery, Stanberry.—Local, 'of Stainbrough,' a township in the parish of Silkstone, W. Rid. Yorks. Mr. Lower says, ' A hundred in the county of Devon.' Both may have contributed, but looking at the directories it is clear that Devonshire holds the first place as parent.

Thomas de Staynburghe, 1379 : P. T. Yorks. p. 52.
1686. Married—Francis Nicholls and Jane Stanburrow : St. Dionis Backchurch, p. 41.
MDB. (co. Devon), 0, 0, 13, 0, 0 ; Plymouth, 0, 0, 9, 0, 0 ; London, 2, 1, 3, 0, 0 ; Devon Court Dir., 0, 0, 5, 0, 0 ; New York, 0, 3, 2, 1, 1 ; Philadelphia, 0, 0, 2, 0, 0.

Stanbridge.—Local, (1) 'of Stanbridge,' a chapelry in the parish of Leighton Buzzard, co. Bedford ; (2) 'of Stanbridge,' a parish in co. Dorset. This seems to be the chief parent.

Robert de Stanbrugge, co. Soms. 1 Edw. III : Kirby's Quest, p. 234.
Stephen Stenbrugge, co. Soms., 1 Edw. III : ibid. p. 243.
Walter Stenbrigge, co. Soms., 1 Edw. III : ibid.
1760. Married — Thomas Haines and Ann Stanbridge : St. Geo. Han. Sq. i. 92.
London, 3 ; MDB. (co. Bedf.), 1 ; Philadelphia, 3.

Stanbury ; v. Stanborough.

Stancliff.—Local, 'of Stancliff.' Stayncliff, a locality in co. Yorks, is mentioned in the Hundred Rolls,

1273 (vol. ii. pt. iii). No doubt the surname takes its rise from Staincliff, a hundred in the W. Rid. Yorks.

1565. Richard Stankelefe : Reg. Univ. Oxf. vol. ii. pt. ii. p. 17.
1572. James Stancleif : ibid. p. 30.
1580. Richard Stancliffe, of Atherton, *yeoman* : Wills at Chester, i. 181.
1617. Richard Stancliffe, of Atherton : ibid.
1674. Samuel Stancliffe and Eliz. Ash : Marriage Lic. (Faculty Office), p. 130.
London, 2 ; Philadelphia, 2.

Standering, Standring.—Local, 'of Stannering.' This spot in South Lancashire I have not been able to discover. It will be found in the neighbourhood of Middleton. The *d* is intrusive, as in Simmonds.

1631. John Stannering, of Hopwood : Wills at Chester, ii. 207.
1633. Eliz. Stannering, of Sidhall, parish of Middleton : ibid.
1763. Married—Samuel Standring and Sarah Storer : St. Geo. Han. Sq. i. 122.
Manchester, 0, 8 ; West Rid. Court Dir., 2, 3 ; Philadelphia, 0, 3.

Standerwick. — Local, 'o Standerwick,' a parish in co. Somerset, four miles from Frome.

1746. Married — Richard Shipley and Eliz. Standerwick : St. Geo. Chap. Mayfair, p. 77.
MDB. (co. Devon), 1 ; (co. Somerset), 2 ; New York, 1.

Standfast.—Nick. 'the firm, the steady, the resolute, the steadfast in purpose.'

Thomas Stanfast, co. Oxf., 1273. A.
John Standfast, of Lynn, co. Norf., 2 Edw. 6 : FF. vi. 507.
1765. Married — Edward Brooke and Eliz. Standfast : St. Geo. Han. Sq. i. 150.
London, 3 ; Philadelphia, 1.

Standfield ; v. Stanfield.

Standish, Standage.—Local, 'of Standish,' a parish in co. Lanc., near Wigan. With the corrupted Standage, cf. Aldridge for Aldrich.

William de Standisch, 1311 : Baines' Lanc. ii. 164.
Hugh de Standisch, 1311 : ibid.
1614. Eliz. Standish, of Standish, *widow* : Wills at Chester, i. 182.
1605. John Standish, of Wigan, *carpenter* : ibid. p. 183.
Manchester, 1, 1 ; Liverpool, 2, 0 ; Philadelphia, 6, 0.

Standring ; v. Standering.

Stanes ; v. Staines.

Stanesby, Stainsby.—Local, 'of Stainsby,' a hamlet in the parish of Ashby Puerorum, co. Lincoln; also a township in the parish of Ault Hucknall, co. Derby. Other places would be so called.

1598. John Stanesby or Stainsby, co. Wilts: Reg. Univ. Oxf. vol. ii. pt. ii. p. 227.
1663. Buried—Alice, wife of Richard Stansby: St. Jas. Clerkenwell, iv. 350.
1665. — John Stansbee: ibid. p. 365.
London, 4, 0; Philadelphia, 0, 1.

Stanfield, Standfield.—Local, 'of Stanfield.' There is a parish so called in co. Norfolk, six miles from East Dereham; but other and smaller spots would naturally bear this name, i. e. the stony field.

Geoffrey atte Stondfeld, co. Soms., 1 Edw. III: Kirby's Quest, p. 108.
The *d* here is intrusive, as in Symonds; cf. the provincial *gownd* for *gown.*
1587. Buried—Wenefrede Standfeild: St. Jas. Clerkenwell, iv. 36.
1683. John Stanfeild and Mary Tray: Marriage Alleg. (Canterbury), p. 141.
London, 2, 1; MDB. (co. Soms.), 1, 2; Philadelphia, 2, 0.

Stanford, Staniford.—Local, 'of Stanford.' There are no less than ten parishes in the south of England of this name. The North-English form was Stanforth, and there Staniford is met by Staniforth, q.v.; v. Stamford also.

Adam de Stanford, co. Oxf., 1273.
Symon de Stanford, co. Hunts, ibid.
Florentia de Stanforde, co. Soms., 2 Edw. III: Kirby's Quest, p. 238.
1622. Thomas Stanniford, Ball. Coll.: Reg. Univ. Oxf. vol. ii. pt. iii. 408.
1630. Bapt. — George, s. Thomas Stanford: St. Jas. Clerkenwell, i. 116.
London, 13, 2; Philadelphia, 11, 0.

Stanger.—Occup. 'the stanger.' Lower says it is a North-English term for a thatcher (v. Patr. Brit. p. 327). But there may be a local origin.

Jordan de Stangar, co. Soms., 1 Edw. III: Kirby's Quest, p. 179.
The following represents a still existing Cumberland baptismal name:
Gawen Stangar, Christ Ch., Oxford, 1568: Reg. Univ. Oxf. i. 259.
1784. Married—Thomas Stanger and Charlotte Jones: St. Geo. Han. Sq. i. 360.
London, 1; MDB. (co. Cumb.), 7; Philadelphia, 13.

Stanier, Stanyer, Stoner.—Occup. 'the stanyer' or stone-hewer, a hewer of stones, a quarryman. Sometimes simply 'stonier.' With the intrusive *i* or *y*, cf. *lawyer*, Sawyer, Bowyer, &c.

Richard Stenere, 1379: P. T. Yorks. p. 18.
Richard Stonhewer. SS.
John Stonchewer. AA. 4.
Thomas Hirst, *stenyhour*, co. York, 1433. W. 11.
1689. Nathaniell Stanyar and Catherine Bryan: Marriage Alleg. (Canterbury), p. 101.
Robert Stoner, rector of Clenchwarton, co. Norf., 1736. FF. viii 382.
London, 1, 0, 3; Philadelphia, 0, 0, 8.

Staniforth, Stainforth, Stanford, Staniford. — Local, 'of Stainforth,' a township in the parish of Giggleswick; also a township in the parish of Hatfield, 'near the navigable river Don' (West Riding Dir., 1867, p. 389). This phrase reminds us of the origin of the name, viz. the stony ford, *forth* being an early English form of *ford*; v. Forth, and cf. Sandforth and Spofforth; v. Stanford and Stamford. For suffix, v. Ford and Forth.

Henricus de Staynford, 1379: P. T. Yorks. p. 10.
Johannes de Staynford, 1379: ibid.
Thomas Stenford, 1379: ibid. p. 19.
Willelmus de Staynforth, 1379: ibid. p. 51.
1567. Vincent Pidcocke and Dorothy Stannefoorde: Marriage Lic. (London), i. 36.
1747. Married — Richard Winkworth and Hester Staneforth: St. Geo. Chap. Mayfair, p. 86.
West Rid. Court Dir., 8, 1, 0, 0; Boston (U.S.), 0, 0, 12, 8.

Stanley.—Local, 'of Stanley.' There are at least ten ecclesiastical parishes of this name in England ('the stony meadow'). For suffix, v. Legh, Lee, or Lees.

William de Stanlegh, co. Wilts, 1273. A.
John de Stanleye, co. Oxf., ibid.
Johannes de Staynlay, 1379: P. T. Yorks. p. 252.
Robertus de Stanelay, 1379: ibid. p. 135.
Robertus de Stanelegh, 1379: ibid. p. 174.
1578-9. Edward Stanley, co. Lanc.: Reg. Univ. Oxf. vol. ii. pt. ii. p. 85.
London, 39; Philadelphia, 39.

Stannard, Stonard, Stannart.—Bapt. 'the son of Stanard' or Stanhard; v. Freeman, Norm. Conq. v. 817. A well-known Norfolk and Suffolk surname. There are two Stanards in Domesday (Stanardus, co. Essex; Stanart, co. Suffolk). Stonhard is found as a single personal name, co. Essex (Hundred Rolls, 1273, i. 154). The form Stonhard was common.

Stannard de Corton, co. Suff., 1273. A.
Stanardus Cobbe, co. Kent, ibid.
Stannard Dilker, co. Norf., ibid.
Sella Stonhard, co. Camb., ibid.
Richard Stonhard, co. Camb., ibid.
Richard Stonehard, co. Soms., 1 Edw. III: Kirby's Quest, p. 158.
John Stonard, co. Soms., 1 Edw. III: ibid. p. 179.
Richard, s. of Stannard, co. Norf.: FF. xi. 175.
William Stanard, rector of Stockton, co. Norf., 1634: ibid. viii. 44.
1607. William Stonnard, Ch. Ch., Oxf.: Reg. Univ. Oxf. i. 147.
London, 11, 1, 0; MDB. (Norfolk), 5, 10, 0; (Suffolk), 9, 0, 0; Philadelphia, 1, 0, 3.

Stannus.—Local, 'of the stonehouse'; cf. Loftus for Lofthouse, or Kirkus for Kirkhouse; v. Stonehouse.

Robert de Stanghouse, co. Northumb., 1273. A.
Tuel de Stanhuse, co. Devon, Hen. III-Edw. I. K.
London, 2.

Stanton.—Local, 'of Stanton,' townships in cos. Derby, Stafford, and Northumberland; also parishes in cos. Gloucester, Suffolk, Wilts, Bucks, Derby, Somerset, Dorset, and Oxford; v. Stainton.

Alice de Stanton, co. Camb., 1273. A.
Walter de Stanton, co. Oxf., ibid.
Edmund de Stanton, co. Wilts, ibid.
1615. Francis Stanton, co. Bedf.: Reg. Univ. Oxf. vol. ii. pt. ii. p. 339.
1619. Henry Stanton or Staunton, co. Cornwall: ibid. p. 380.
1624-5. Married—Arthur Stanten and Eliz. Clapen: St. Dionis Backchurch, p. 21.
London, 23; MDB. (co. Glouc.), 10; Boston (U.S.), 49.

Stanway.—Local, 'of Stanway,' parishes in cos. Essex and Gloucester.

Hervey de Stanweye, co. Norf., 1273. A.
Hawise de Stanwey, co. Camb., ibid.
Alicia Stanwey, co. Soms., 1 Edw. III: Kirby's Quest, p. 174.

1511. William Stanwey, vicar of Besthorp, co. Norf.: FF. i. 492.
1807. Married — John Stanway and Sarah Spencer: St. Geo. Han. Sq. ii. 370. London, 3.

Stanwix.—Local, 'of Stanwix,' a parish within a mile of Carlisle, co. Cumberland.

Hugh Skot, de Staynwikes, 18 Edw. II: Freemen of York, i. 22.
MDB. (co. Cumb.), 2.

Staple, Staples, Stapler.—Local, 'at the staple,' a staple (O.F. *estaple*), a mart, a general centre of merchandise. Originally the place was the staple, not the commodity. Stapler is the occupative form, and Staples the genitive form; cf. Styles, Brooks, Holmes, &c.

Robert de Stapel, co. Kent, 1273. A.

The above entry no doubt refers to Staple-next-Wingham, a parish in co. Kent.

Robert atte-Staple, C. R., 5 Edw. I.
Robertus Staple, *mercer*, 1379: P. T. Yorks. p. 280.
Willelmus Staple, 1379: ibid. p. 281.
1623. Thomas Winson and Joan Stapler: Marriage Lic. (London), ii. 124.
1666. Married — Jacob Staple and Susan Goodman: St. Jas. Clerkenwell, iii. 125.
London, 1, 22, 1; Philadelphia, 1, 8, 1.

Stapleford, Stableford.—Local, 'of Stapleford,' parishes in cos. Cambridge, Hertford, Leicester, Lincoln, Notts, Wilts, and Essex; v. Staple and Ford.

Gilbert de Stapelford, co. Linc., 1273. A.
Hugh de Stapelford, co. Bedf., ibid.
Simon de Stapilford, co. Linc., Hen. III–Edw. I. K.
Robert de Stapelford, co. Linc., 20 Edw. I. R.
1572–3. William Stapleforde and Alice Wales: Marriage Lic. (London), i. 55.
1596. George Hancocke and Eliz. Stapleford: ibid. p. 232.
London, 1, 1; Manchester, 0, 2; Philadelphia, 3, 0.

Stapler; v. Staple. But possibly for Stabler, q.v.; and cf. Stapleford.

Stapleton.—Local, 'of Stapleton,' a village in the parish of Darrington, near Pontefract, co. York; also parishes in cos. Cumberland, Gloucester, and Salop.

William de Stapelton, co. Oxf., 1273. A.
Nicholas de Stapelton, co. York, ibid.

Milo de Stapelton, co. York, 20 Edw. I. R.
Richard de Stapiltone, co. Soms., 1 Edw. III: Kirby's Quest, p. 144.
Mergareta de Stapilton, 1379: P. T. Yorks. p. 117.
Robertus de Stapulton, 1379: ibid. p. 113.
Bryan de Stapilton, 1379: ibid. p. 296.
1585–6. John Stapleton and Jane Kele: Marriage Lic. (London), i. 147.
London, 15; Philadelphia, 13.

Stapley.—Local, ' of Stapeley,' a township in the parish of Wybunbury, co. Chester; also a tithing in the parish of Odiham, co. Hants.

Roger de Stapelye, co. Sussex, 1273. A.
Gilbert de Stapelyge, co. Kent, ibid.
1604. John Stapley, co. Sussex: Reg. Univ. Oxf. vol. ii. pt. ii. p. 277.
1799. Married—Richard Stapley and Jane Maitland: St. Geo. Han. Sq. ii. 194.
London, 4; MDB. (co. Sussex), 2.

Starbuck.—Local, ' of Starbeck,' a hamlet between Ripon and Knaresborough. Mr. Lower writes, partly quoting Mr. Ferguson, ' In O. Norse *bokki* means " vir grandis, corpore et animo." Hence *Storbocki*, from *stór*, great, " vir imperiosus." ' This may be true, but I take it that Starbuck is simply the local Starbeck. The surname still remains in the West Riding.

Robertus Starbok', 1379: P. T. Yorks. p. 4.
1772. Married — John Lambeld and Sarah Starbuck: St. Geo. Han. Sq. i. 223.
London, 2; West Riding Court Dir., 1; Sheffield, 1; New York, 2.

Starcher.—Occup. ' the starcher,' i.e. a cloth stiffener, a starcher of linen; from *stark*, strong, stiff, weakened to starch. The occupation is referred to in Cocke Lorelle's Bote:

' Butlers, sterchers, and mustard-makers,
Hardeware men, mole seekers, and
ratte-takers.'
Ralph le Starkere, co. Hunts, 1273. A.

Stare.—Nick. ' the stare,' i.e. the starling (v. Starling); cf. Sparrow, Nightingale, &c.

Robert Stare, co. Oxf., 1273. A.
Richard le Staar, co. Soms., 1 Edw. III: Kirby's Quest, p. 259.
Ricardus Stare, 1379: P. T. Yorks. p. 80.
1796. Married—Philip Stare and Margaret Tooley: St. Geo. Han. Sq. ii. 146. Philadelphia, 1.

Stark, Starke, Starkman.—Nick. ' the stark,' i.e. the strong, the stiff.

' He had a pike-staff in his hand
That was both stark and strang.'
Robin Hood, i. 98.

William Starckeman or Starcman, co. Camb., 1273. A.
Geoffrey Starckman. T.
1745. Married — Francis Stark and Martha Orom: St. Geo. Chap. Mayfair, p. 52.
1757. John Starke and Honour Paterson: St. Geo. Han. Sq. i. 70.
London, 8, 1, 0; Philadelphia, 32, 5, 0.

Starkbone.—Nick. ' stiff,' or strong-boned.

Robertus Starkbane, 1379: P. T. Yorks. p. 224.
Johannes Starkbayn, 1379: ibid.

Starkey, Starkie.—Nick. ' the stark,' i.e. the strong, the stiff; cf. Strong, &c. (v. Stark). Starkey seems undoubtedly to be a dialectic variant of Stark (cf. Teddy or Teddie for Edward). ' Starky, stiff, dry. Westmoreland' (Halliwell).

1579. Francis Starkey, co. Derby: Reg. Univ. Oxf. vol. ii. pt. ii. p. 87.
1592. George Starkie, of Pennington: Wills at Chester, i. 182.
1609. Ellen Starkey, of Pennington: ibid.
London, 13, 2; Philadelphia, 16, 0.

Starling.—(1) Nick. ' the starling'; formed from *stare*, a bird, with dim. *ling*.

' The false lapwing, full of trecherie,
The stare, that the counsaile can bewrie.'
Chaucer, Assembly of Fowls.

(2) Nick. ' the starling,' i.e. sterling, true, from starling, a coin or true weight.

' So that ye offre nobles or starlings.'
Chaucer, C. T. 12841.

Symon Starlyng, co. Herts, 1273. A.
William Starling, co. Norf., ibid.
Geoffrey Starlyng, C. R., 17 Ric. II.

It is probable that (1) is the true parent of the surname.

1622. Bapt. — Christopher, s. Thomas Starling: St. Jas. Clerkenwell, i. 93.
London, 17; Philadelphia, 3.

Starr.—(1) Nick. ' the star'; M.E. *sterre*, or perhaps 'the steer,' i.e. the young ox (v. Steer). (2) Personal, 'the son of Star.' Probably Star was a personal or baptismal name as Stella is to-day.

Johannes le Ster, co. Oxf., 1273. A.
Robert le Ster, co. Sussex, ibid.

William Ster, co. Camb., 1273. A.
1416. Richard Sterre, vicar of Happesburgh, co. Norf. : FF. ix. 300.
1465. John Sterre, vicar of Quidenham, co. Norf. : ibid. i. 334.
1705. William Pynsent and Mary Starr, *widow* : Marriage Lic. (London), ii. 334.
London, 10 ; Philadelphia, 41.

Startup.—Local, ' of Startup,' a portion of the township of Twizle, co. Northumberland.

1592. Arthur Startupp and Margaret Lixlade : Marriage Lic. (London), i. 199.
1603. John Startuppe and Susan Tyte: ibid. p. 276.
1737. Andrew Startup rented Startup: KKK. ii. 467.
London, 1 ; New York, 2.

Starziker ; v. Stirzaker.

Statham.—Local, ' of Statham.' I cannot find any place of this name. Possibly it stands for a parish styled Statherne, in co. Leicester. But this is pure conjecture on my part.

John de Statham, co. Camb., 1273. A.
1562. Bapt.—John, s. Thomas Statham: St. Jas. Clerkenwell, i. 2.
1689. Thomas Statham and Mary Goweth : Marriage Alleg. (Canterbury), p. 106.
Manchester, 6 ; MDB. (co. Derby), 8 ; London, 8 ; Philadelphia, 1.

Staunton.—Local, ' of Staunton,' parishes in cos. Worcester, Notts, Monmouth, and Hereford. v. Stanton and Stainton.

Avice de Staunton, co. Linc., 1273. A.
Nicholas de Staunton, co. Essex, ibid.
William de Staunton, co. Oxf., ibid.
Robert de Staunton, co. Derby, 20 Edw. I. R.
Harvey de Staunton, co. Camb., ibid.
John de Stauntone, co. Soms., 1 Edw. III : Kirby's Quest, p. 92.
1798. Married — William Hadnutt and Esther Staunton : St. Geo. Han. Sq. ii. 191.
London, 2 ; Boston (U.S.), 2.

Staveley, Stavley, Stavely. —Local, ' of Staveley.' There are parishes of this name in cos. Derby and York ; a chapelry nine miles from Ulverston, co. Lanc. ; and both a township and chapelry in the parish of Kendal, co. Westmoreland.

Adam de Stavell, co. Notts, 1273. A.
Adam de Staveleia, co. Cumb. K.
Adam de Staveley, co. York. R.
1560. Married — Peter Staveley and Edith Hams: Marriage Lic.(London),i.21.
1621. Miles Stavly, of Killington (Westm.) : Wills at Richmond, i. 261.

1809. Bapt. — Jane, d. John Stavely : St. Mary, Ulverston, p. 569.
London, 0, 1, 0 ; Oxford, 1, 0, 0 ; Liverpool, 1, 0, 1 ; Philadelphia, 0, 0, 2.

St. Clair ; v. Sinclair.
Philadelphia, 20.

Stead, Steade.—Local, ' at the stead,' a place, a station, a settlement ; cf. homestead, market-stead (= market-place). A great Yorkshire surname. The Market-place, Manchester, was the Market-stead till the close of the last century. The Market-stead, Ulverston, is commonly so set down in the parish registers till 1790.

John Stede, co. Suff., 1273. A.
Robertus del Stede, 1379 : P. T. Yorks. p. 208.
Ricardus del Stede, 1379 : ibid.
Petrus del Stede, 1379 : ibid.
Laurence del Stede, 1379 : ibid.
1589. Bapt. — Katherine, d. John Steade : St. Jas. Clerkenwell, i. 21.
West Riding Court Dir., 31, 1 ; London, 9, 0 ; Philadelphia, 32, 0.

Steadman, Stedman, Steedman.—Occup. ' the steadman,' one who occupied a stead, a farmer ; v. Stead.

Richard Stedeman, co. Camb., 1273. A.
Gilbert de Stedman, co. Oxf., ibid.
Simon le Stedman, 35 Edw. I. BBB. p. 739.
John le Stedman, 1306. M.
Johannes Stedeman, 1379 : P. T. Yorks. p. 49.
Johannes Stedeman, 1379 : ibid. p. 220.
1553. Married — Wyllyam Nevell and Jone Steedman : St. Michael,Cornhill, p. 6.
London, 4, 13, 3 ; Philadelphia, 2, 5, 0.

Stean, Steane, Steanes.—Local, ' of Steane,' a parish in co. Northants.
London, 3, 2, 0 ; MDB. (co. Northants.), 0, 0, 1.

Steavenson ; var. of Stephenson and Stevenson (v. Stephen and Steven).

1613. Married — John Lydgold and Fayth Steavenson : Kensington Ch. p. 66. London, 2.

Stebbing, Stebbings, Stebbens, Stebbins.—(1) Local, ' of Stebbing,' a parish in co. Essex. Stebbings, &c., are genitive forms; cf. Brooks, Styles, Williams, Jones, &c.

Richard de Stebing, co. Essex, 1273. A.
Thomas Stebin, co. Camb., ibid.
1581. Bapt.—Isabel, d. George Stebbyn : St. Jas. Clerkenwell, i. 12.

1615. Martin Stebbyn, Norwich : FF. iv. 354.
1807. Married—John Burton Marshall and Sarah Stebbings: St. Geo. Han. Sq. ii. 374.
London, 9, 4, 1, 0 ; Philadelphia, 4, 0, 0, 4.

Sted-, Steedman.—Occup. ; v. Steadman.

Steel, Steele, Stell, Stelle.— Bapt. ' the son of Steel " (?). The old Danish Staal (v. Yonge, ii. 293); Icel. Stál. Lower says, 'A northern pronunciation of *stile*.' This is quite inadmissible. All early instances are without prefix. Besides, as ' atte style ' became Styles, so ' atte steel ' would have become Steels. It will be noticeable that all my examples are from the EastCoast. The Scandinavian origin is manifest. Iron and steel are components of many of these early northern personal names ; v. Stallard.

Robert Stele, co. Linc., 1273. A.
John Stel, co. Suff., ibid.
Johannes Stele, 1379 : P. T. Yorks. p. 255.
Willelmus Steel, 1379 : ibid. p. 250.
Willelmus Steel, 1379 : ibid. p. 154.
1651. Married—John Steele, *batchler*, and Abigell Hannkok : St. Mary Aldermary, p. 21.
London, 25, 21, 0, 0 ; West Rid. Court Dir., 6, 6, 0, 0 ; Philadelphia, 115, 66, 2, 2 ; Manchester (Stell), 1.

Steel., Steenson ; v. Stenson.

Steeple.—Local, ' of Steeple,' parishes in cos. Dorset and Essex. Of course the origin may be derived from residence beside any steeple attached to a church in the country, especially in such cases where the steeple was actually detached from the body of the church.

Morecambe, near Lancaster, 3 ; Philadelphia, 2.

Steer, Steere, Steers.—Nick. ' the steer,' the young ox ; cf. Bull, Stott, &c. But v. Sterry, Storr, and Storey.

Willelmus Stere, 1379 : P. T. Yorks. p. 106.
Johannes Stere, 1379 : ibid.
1572. William Steere and Margery Pallemer : Reg. St. Dionis Backchurch, p. 7.
1580. Nicholas Steer, rector of Burnham Norton, co. Norf. : FF. vii. 18.
1697. Bapt. — Randall, s. Randall Steeres : St. Mary Aldermary, p. 112.

1748. Buried—John Steer : St. Mary Aldermary, p. 228.

Sheffield, 3, 0, 0 ; London, 20, 1, 3.

Steinkettle.—Bapt. 'the son of Steinketel,' i.e. 'stone cauldron.' Steinchetel is the form in Domesday, a compound of Kettle (v. Kettle and Chettle). It is found later as Stinkel ; cf. Arkettle.

Richard Stinkel, co. Bedf., 1273. A.

Stelfox.—Nick. ; v. Colfox.

Thomas Stelfox, of High Leigh, 1602 : Wills at Chester, i. 183.

William Stilefox, of Goosnergh, 1672 : Lancashire Wills at Richmond, i. 262.

London, 1 ; MDB. (co. Ches.), 4.

Stella.—(1) Bapt. 'the son of Stella.' (2) Local, 'of Stella,' a township in the parish of Ryton, co. Durham.

Stella de Thornholme, 1379 : P. T. Yorks. p. 120.

London, 1 ; Philadelphia, 2.

Stemson ; v. Stenson and Stimpson.

Stennett.—Bapt. 'the son of Steven' or Stephen, dim. Stevenet, modified into Stennett ; v. Stephen.

1726. Bapt. — William, s. Rowland Stennet : St. Jas. Clerkenwell, ii. 163.

London, 1.

Stenning, Stennings.—Bapt. 'the son of Stening'; cf. Browning, Harding, &c. Stennings is the genitive ; v. Jennings.

John Stenyng, co. Soms., 1 Edw. III : Kirby's Quest, p. 142.

1665. Richard Gardiner and Margaret Stenning : Marriage Alleg. (Canterbury), p. 104.

1750. Married — Richard Vezey and Mary Stenning : St. Geo. Chap. Mayfair, p. 159.

London, 3, 1.

Stenson, Steenson, Stemson.
—(1) Bapt. 'the son of Stephen,' from the nick. Steen ; v. Stimpson and Stephen. (2) Local,'of Stenson,' a township in the parish of Barrow, co. Derby. As Stenson is a Derbyshire surname it is manifest that (2) is the more probable derivation. On the contrary it is almost certain that Steenson must be referred to (1).

Francis Steanson, co. York. W. 16.

John Steanson, co. York, ibid.

1747. Married — John Francis and Charlotte Stenson : St. Geo. Chap. Mayfair, p. 81.

1763. Married — Joseph Stenson and Ann Fareham : St. Geo. Han. Sq. i. 126.

MDB. (co. Derby), 3, 0, 0 ; Oxford, 0, 0, 1 ; Philadelphia, 5, 3, 0.

Stephen, Stephens, Stephenson, Stephan.—Bapt. 'the son of Stephen.' There is no instance of Stephen in Domesday Book. But like John and Peter, it gained popularity with great rapidity ; and Stephen of Blois, of course, exercised an influence in its favour. It was enormously popular in the hereditary surname period, and, as a consequence, has endless representatives of nick. and pet forms in the directories of to-day (v. Steven, Stevens, Stevenson, Stimpson, &c.).

Gilbert fil. Stephani, co. Linc., 1273. A.

Jordan fil. Stephani, co. Essex, ibid.

Richard Stephen, co. Oxf., ibid.

Richard Stephenes, co. Soms., 1 Edw III : Kirby's Quest. p. 101.

1585. Bapt. — Dorothy, d. William Stephens : St. Jas. Clerkenwell, i. 16.

1739. Married — James Stephen and Flora Young : St. Geo. Han. Sq. i. 22.

London, 1, 83, 35, 0 ; Philadelphia, 11, 81, 46, 7.

Stephings.—Bapt. 'the son of Stephen,' a corruption of Stephens, q.v. (cf. Jennings or Hewlings).

London, 1.

Stepkin.—Bapt. 'the son of Stephen,' from nick. Step, and suffix -kin ; cf. Wilkin.

Lieutenant Charles Stepkin served under the Duke of Northumberland in 1640 : v. Peacock's army list of Roundheads and Cavaliers, p. 78.

Theodosia Stepkin. V. 10.

1558. John Stepkyn and Alice Dades : Marriage Lic. (London), i. 18.

1628. Bapt.—Eadye, d. Roger Stepkin : St. Jas. Clerkenwell, i. 108.

Stepney, Stephany (?). — Local, 'of Stepney,' an important parish in co. Middlesex, now part of London.

1600. Robert Stepneth or Stepney, co. Herts : Reg. Univ. Oxf. vol. ii. pt. ii. p. 243.

1753. Married—William Hopkins and Eliz. Stepheny : St. Geo. Han. Sq. i. 49.

1760. — Daniel Holland and Jane Stepney : ibid. p. 95.

MDB. (co. Sussex), 2, 0 ; London, 0, 1 ; New York, 1, 4.

Steptoe, Stepto, Steptow.—Local. I cannot find the spot. The suffix is probably -how (v. How), as we find it in Shafto or

Shillito, &c. Mr. Lower says, 'Probably refers to gait.' This may be so, but the local derivation must be looked for first.

1751. Married—John Woodward and Eliz. Steptoo : St. Geo. Chap. Mayfair, p. 191.

1753. — Francis Fosset and Sarah Steptoe : ibid. p. 257.

1788. — Andrew Duncanson and Ruth Knight : St. Geo. Han. Sq. ii. 6.

1802. — William Steptoe and Martha Knight : ibid. p. 255.

London, 1, 3, 1 ; MDB. (co. Berks), 1, 0, 0 ; Oxford, 2, 0, 0.

Stern, Sterne. — Nick. 'the stern,' i. e. austere.

Henry Sterne, co. Camb., 1273. A.

Aubri Steryn, co. Camb., ibid.

William Sterne or Steryn, co. Camb., ibid.

1460. Henry Sterne, co. Norf. : FF. ii. 475.

1587. Bapt. — Anne, d. John Sterne : St. Jas. Clerkenwell, i. 19.

London, 4, 1 ; Philadelphia, 62, 4.

Sterry. — Bapt. 'the son of Sterre' (?) ; v. Starr.

Henricus Sterre, 1379 : P.T. Yorks. p. 57.

Thomas Stere, 1379 : ibid.

Henricus Sterre, 1379 : ibid. p. 109.

1765. Married—Christian Sterry and Mary Frazier : St. Geo. Han. Sq. i. 147.

London, 5 ; Boston (U.S.), 2.

Steven, Stevens, Stevenson.—Bapt. 'the son of Stephen,' an early form ; v. Stephen.

Philip Stevene, co. Soms., 1 Edw. III : Kirby's Quest, p. 240.

William Stevene, co. Soms., 1 Edw. III : ibid.

Magota Steuen-doghter (u for v), 1379 : P. T. Yorks. p. 46.

Thomas Steuenson, 1379 : ibid. p. 43.

Robert Steuen, 1379 : ibid.

1423. Laurence Stevene, rector of Wickhampton, co. Norf. : FF. xi. 136.

1600. Anthony Stephenes or Stevens, co. Wilts : Reg. Univ. Oxf. vol. ii. pt. ii. p. 242.

London, 1, 212, 54 ; Philadelphia, 2, 159, 251.

Steventon.—Local, 'of Steventon,' parishes in cos. Berks and Hants.

Edmund de Stewincton, co. Camb., 1273. A.

1321. Robert de Stevington, rector of Knapton, co. Norf. : FF. viii. 135.

1754. Married—James Steventon and Hannah Haynes : St. Geo. Han. Sq. i. 53.

MDB. (co. Salop), 2 ; London, 2.

Steverson.—Bapt. 'the son of Stephen,' a corruption of Stephenson ; cf. Patterson for Pattinson, or Catterson for Cattinson.

1656. Married — Robart Warner and Katherin Steverson : St. Peter, Cornhill, i. 260.
London, 4 ; New York, 1.

Steveson.—Bapt. 'the son of Stephen,' a corruption of Stephenson ; cf. Pattison for Pattinson.

Philadelphia, 2.

Steward, Stewardson, Stewards, Stuard.—(1) Bapt. 'the son of Steuhard' or Stuard, genitive Stewards.

Stuard Cachellus, co. Norf., 1273. A.
Martin Steuhard, co. Norf., ibid.
Nicholas Stuward, co. Soms., 1 Edw. III : Kirby's Quest, p. 275.
Adam Staward, co. Soms., 1 Edw. III : ibid.
Willelmus Stuard, 1379 : P. T. Yorks. p. 126.
1581. John Steward or Stuarde, co. Northampt. : Reg. Univ. Oxf. vol. ii. pt. ii. p. 101.
1710. Richard Stewardson, appointed under-usher of Grammar School attached to St. Mary's Hospital, Newcastle-on-Tyne : Brand's Newcastle, i. 95.
1800. Married — Joseph Stewardson and Eliz. Bland : St. Geo. Han. Sq. ii. 214.

(2) Offic. 'the steward.'

Adam fe Stiuuard, co. Glouc., 1273. A.
Hugh le Stiward, co. Norf., ibid.
London, 26, 1, 1, 0, Philadelphia, 10, 4, 0, 16.

Stewart, Stuart.—Sharpened forms of Steward and Stuard, q.v. The following entries manifestly refer to the same parents :

1723. Bapt.—John, s. Robert and Edy Steward : St. Jas. Clerkenwell, i. 144.
1725. — Jane, d. Robert and Ede Stewart : ibid. p. 152.
London, 82, 44 ; Philadelphia, 561, 89.

Stibbard.—Local,'of Stibbard,' a parish in co. Norfolk, four miles from Fakenham.

Alice de Stiberd, co. Norf., 1273. A.
Richard de Stibarde, co. Norf., ibid.
1806. Married — Giles Stibbert and Jane Slatter : St. Geo. Han. Sq. ii. 348.
London, 2.

Sticker.—Occup. 'the sticker,' probably a pig-sticker. Wiltshire and the adjacent district are still famous for their bacon.

John le Stikkere, co. Soms., 1 Edw. III : Kirby's Quest, p. 190.
1686. Buried — Lucilla Sticher : St. Michael, Cornhill, p. 269.

The preceding entry is quoted, but it is doubtful whether or no it concerns Sticker.

New York, 1 ; Philadelphia, 4.

Stickley.—Local, 'at the Stickley,' from residence thereby ; probably some meadow of a sticky soil.

William atte Sticlegh, co. Soms., 1 Edw. III : Kirby's Quest, p. 113.
Simon Sticcle, co. Soms., 1 Edw. III : ibid. p. 194.
1606. Married — John Stickley and Rose Powell : St. Mary Aldermary, p. 11.
1752. — William Stickly and Sarah Bonus : St. Geo. Chap. Mayfair, p. 224.
London, 2 ; Oxford, 1 ; Philadelphia, 5.

Stickney.—Local, 'of Stickney,' a parish in co. Lincoln, nine miles from Boston.

1582. William Stickney and Dorothy Clenche : Marriage Lic. (London), i. 108.
Philadelphia, 9.

Stiff.—Nick. 'the stiff,' rigid in feature or obstinate in temper. 'The vowel was once long' (Skeat). Hence the form of entry immediately below :

John Stife, co. Wilts, 1273. A.
Robert Stife, co. Wilts, ibid.
1682. Married — Thomas Stiffe and Margaret Pane : St. Jas. Clerkenwell, i. 196.
1782. Bapt.—William, s. Joseph Stiffe : ibid. ii. 8.
London, 9 ; Philadelphia, 1.

Stiffbow.—Nick. The opposite of Benbow, q.v.

John Stiffbowe : Patent Roll, 3 Edw. VI. pt. v.

Stiggins.—Bapt. 'the son of Stigand,' the name of the arch-bishop who crowned Harold ; more recently immortalized by Charles Dickens in ' Pickwick.'

Bartholomew Stegin, co. Camb., 1273. A.
Gervase fil. Stigandi, Pipe Rolls, 6 Hen. II.
1706. Married—John Carrier and Anne Stigans : St. Peter, Cornhill, ii. 66.
1747. — John Harris and Mary Stiggins : St. Geo. Han. Sq. i. 38.
Boston (U.S.), 1.

Stileman. — Local ; v. Styleman.

Stile(s.—Local ; v. Style.

Still. — Nick. 'the still,' the quiet ; cf. the opposite Snell or Quick, the active. While this seems perfectly satisfactory, v. Style and Styleman for another parentage. But Mr. Lower says that Stille was a tenant prior to Domesday. Therefore the name may be personal.

Walter Stille, co. Oxf., 1273. A.
Robert Stille, co. Soms., 1 Edw. III : Kirby's Quest, p. 196.
1610. Nathaniel Still and Jane Whitmore : Marriage Lic. (London), i. 319.
1639. Married—John Caille and Eliz. Stille : St. Mary Aldermary, p. 18.
London, 10 ; Philadelphia, 1.

Stillingfleet.—Local, ' of Stillingfleet,' a parish in E. Rid. Yorks, seven miles from York.

Henricus de Stilyngflete, 1379 : P. T. Yorks. p. 29.
Johannes de Stilyngflete, 1379 : ibid.
Willelmus de Styllyngflete, 1379 : P. T. Howdenshire, p. 20.
1587. Married—Robert Lockson and Alice Stullingflet : St. Peter, Cornhill, i. 236.
1783. — Rev. James Stillingfleet and Eliz. Hale : St. Geo. Han. Sq. i. 346.
Crockford, 1.

Stillman.—Local ; v. Styleman, a variant.

Stimpson, Stimson, Stinson. —Bapt. 'the son of Stephen' or Steven, patr. Steven-son, corrupted to Stinson or Stimson. The p in Stimpson is intrusive and follows m, as in Simpson, Thompson, or Hampson ; cf. Sinkinson for Simkinson.

Joseph Stinson, co. York. W. 11.
1624. Bapt.—Hugh, son of John Stimpson : Reg. St. Jas. Clerkenwell, i. 98.
John Stimpson, Norwich : FF. iv. 448.
1793. Married—Thomas Edbrook and Mary Stempson : St. Geo. Han. Sq. ii. 90.

In a muster-roll of able-bodied men at Newcastle-on-Tyne in 1539 occur the names of

Edward Stynson : PPP. ii. 174-94.
Stewyn Sotheron : ibid.
Allen Stewenson : ibid.
John Stewynsone : ibid.
Stewne Smythe : ibid.
1705. Bapt.—Thomas, s. Thomas Stimson : St. Jas. Clerkenwell, i. 27.
London, 6, 4, 2 ; MDB. (co. Leic.), 0, 0, 3 ; Philadelphia, 0, 0, 55.

Stirk, Stirke. — Nick. ' the Stirk ' (v. Stirkherd) ; cf. Bull, Stott, Steer, &c.

Juliana Sterk, co. Soms., 1 Edw. III : Kirby's Quest, p. 126.

Maurice Sterk, co. Soms., 1 Edw. III: Kirby's Quest, p. 127.
John le Sterk, co. Soms., 1 Edw. III: ibid. p. 226.
William le Sterk, co. Soms., 1 Edw. III: ibid.
Thomas Styrke, 1379: P. T. Yorks. p. 277.
Robertus Styrke, 1379: ibid.
1742. Bapt.—Ann, d. Robert Stirke: St. Jas. Clerkenwell, ii. 260.
1746. Married — Benjamin Stirk and Ann Gorsuch : St. Geo. Chap. Mayfair, p. 65.
London, 1, 1; Philadelphia, 7, 0.

Stirkherd.—Occup. ' the stirk-herd,' a tender of stirks ; v. Hird and Herd. Cf. Stoddart, Calvert, Coward, Oxnard, &c.

Gilbert Stirkhirde: Pardons Roll, 6 Ric. II.
Johannes Styrkhyrd-smith, 1379: P. T. Yorks p. 268.

Stirling.—Local, ' of Stirling,' the capital of the shire of that name in Scotland.

1770. Married—John Stirling and Ann Bunyard : St. Geo. Han. Sq. i. 195.
London, 7; Philadelphia, 18.

Stirrup, Stirrip.—Local, ' of Styrrup,' a township in the parishes of Blyth, Harworth, and Houghton, co. Notts.

Ingeram de Stirap, co. Notts, 1273. A.
Norman de Stirap, co. Notts, ibid.
Margery de Styrop, 44 Edw. III. P.
William de Styrapp, Close Roll, 18 Ric. II.
Willelmus Styrape, 1379: P. T. Yorks. p. 73.
Agnes que fuit uxor Willelmi Sterappe, osteler, 1379 : ibid. p. 72.
1751. Bapt.—Mary, d. Thomas Stirrup: St. Dionis Backchurch, p. 175.
London 0, 1; New York, 2, 0.

Stirziker, Starziker, Stirzacker.—Local, ' of Steresaker,' some spot not far from Preston, co. Lanc., which I have not identified. The suffix, of course, is -acre, as in Whittaker, Linaker, &c.—Since writing the above I find the spot is in Garstang parish.

Johannes de Steresaker, 1379: P. T. Yorks. p. 262.
William Steresaker, York, 1477 : W. 11, p. 101.
1620. Thomas Styrsaker, co. Leic. (? Lanc.): Reg. Univ. Oxf. vol. ii. pt. ii. p. 384.
John Mawdesley de Sturzaker. 1622: Preston Guild Rolls, p. 85.

Robert Sturzaker, 1664, Garstang : Exchequer Depositions, co. Lanc., p. 38.
John Sturzaker, 1664, Garstang : ibid. p. 39.
Evan Pilkinton, of Sturzaker, in Garstang, 1668 : Lancashire Wills at Richmond, i. 216.
1738. Bapt.—James, s. George Sterzaker : St. Jas. Clerkenwell, ii. 240.
Liverpool, 4, 0, 0; Croston (co. Lanc.), 0, 1, 0; MDB. (co. Lanc.), 4, 0, 1; Lancaster, 3, 0, 0.

St. John.—Local, ' of St. John.' Several parishes in Normandy bear this title. It is found in England soon after the Conquest.

William de St. John, co. Bedf., 1273. A.
Robert de St. John, co. Hants, ibid.
Hugh de St. John, co. Hants, 20 Edw. I. R.
1530. Alexander Seynt John and Jane Leventhorpe : Marriage Lic. (London), i. 7.
1785. Married — Philip Hingston and Ann Saint John : St. Geo. Han. Sq. i. 376.
London, 7; Philadelphia, 9.

Stobbs.—Local, ' at the stobbs,' from residence thereby. A variant of Stubbs, q.v.

MDB. (co. Durham), 5; Philadelphia, 1.

Stock, Stocks.—Local, ' at the stock,' the stump, the trunk of a tree, post, &c., from residence thereby; cf. Stubbs. A big, exposed tree-trunk, or clump of tree-trunks, would readily give a surname to one who lived close by. But v. Stoke.

Reginald de la Stocke, co. Oxf., 1273. A.
William de la Stocke, co. Oxf., ibid.
Jordan atte Stokk, co. Soms., 1 Edw. III : Kirby's Quest, p. 110.
William atte Stock, co. Soms., 1 Edw. III : ibid. p. 178.
Reginald atte Stocke, Close Roll, 4 Edw. III.
Johanna del Stok, 1409: W. 11, p. 239.
1788. Married—Richard Vaughan and Mary Stocks: St. Geo. Han. Sq. ii. 2.
1790. — Thomas Stock and Eliz. Beake: ibid. p. 52.
London, 27, 4; Philadelphia, 28, 3.

Stockbridge.—Local, ' of Stockbridge,' a parish in co. Hants.

Cristina de Stocbrugg', co. Oxf., 1273. A.
Richard de Stokebrigg', co. Hants, 20 Edw. I. R.
Sibilla de Stokbrig', 1379: P. T. Yorks. p. 49.
1790. Married — Robert Sharpe and Mary Stockbridge : St. Geo. Han. Sq. ii. 52.
London, 1; MDB. (co. Camb.), 6; Boston (U.S.), 8.

Stockdale.—Local, ' of Stockdale,' one of the dales in North England. I have failed to identify it. The surname is fairly familiar in the northern counties, and has crossed the Atlantic. Probably the locality will be found in Yorkshire, on the borders of Westmoreland.

Willelmus de Stokdale, 1379: P. T. Yorks. p. 282.
Johannes de Stokdele, 1379: ibid.
1593. Gregory Stocdaile or Stockdale, co. York : Reg. Univ. Oxf. vol. ii. pt. ii. p. 197.
1624. Francis Stockdale, of Aynsome: Lancashire Wills at Richmond, i. 263.
1695. Margaret Stockdall, of Warton : ibid. ii. 240.
1731. Married—Thomas Stockdale and Eliz. Colly: St. Geo. Han. Sq. i. 9.
1773. — Edward Stockdell and Sarah Gooch : ibid. p. 236.
London, 1; Lancaster, 2; MDB. (co. Cumb.), 5; Philadelphia, 9.

Stocker, Stoker.—Occup. 'the stocker,' possibly one who lived by a stub, stock, or stump. But more probably occupative. 'Stockers, persons employed to fell or grub up trees. West England' (Halliwell). With this rendering, cf. Grubber.

1260. Walter le Stockere: Cal. of Wills in Court of Husting.
Elena le Stocker, co. Bucks, 1273. A.
Cf. Alan Stayker, co. Linc., ibid.
John Stokker, C. R., 28 Hen. VI.
1740. Buried—Mary Stocker: St. Mary Aldermary (London), p. 225.
1794. Married — Alex. Stoker and Mary Maria Cook : St. Geo. Han. Sq. ii. 118.
London, 13, 5; Philadelphia, 24, 12.

Stockham, Stockum.—Local, ' of Stockham,' a township in the parish of Runcorn, co. Ches. Stockum is an American variant ; cf. Barnum for Barnham. As I have said of Stockwell, probably other small spots were called Stockham; v. Stock and Ham.

William de Stockham, co. Somerset, 1273. A.
Crockford, 1, 0; Philadelphia, 6, 3.

Stocking, Stocken, Stockin.—Local, ' at the stocking,' i.e. the little stock, a dim. of Stock, q.v. Curiously enough, the article of dress so called is a dim. of the same word (v. stocking. Skeat's Dict.).

Edmund del Stocking, co. Bucks, 1273. A.
1759. Married — John Stocking (co. Norf.) and Eliz. Wright : St. Geo. Han. Sq. i. 88.
London, 1, 6, o ; MDB. (co. Camb.), 1, o, o ; Boston (U.S.), 1, o, 3.

Stockley, Stokley, Stokely. —Local, ' of Stockley.' Two parishes in co. Devon, and a township in the parish of Brancepeth, in co. Durham, bear this name. Other smaller spots would probably bear it ; v. Stock and Ley.

Ralph de Stockleye, co. Suffolk, 1273. A.
Pagan de Stockleye, co. Oxf., ibid.
1791. Married — Phillip Stone and Temperance Stockley : St. Geo. Han. Sq. ii. 63.
London, 2, o, o ; Philadelphia, 8, 14, 3.

Stockman.—Occup. ' the stockman,' the man who lived at the stock ; v. Stock and Stoke ; cf. Stead and Steadman, Bridge and Bridgman, Style and Styleman.

Emma Stokeman, co. Oxf., 1273. A.
Johannes Stokman, 1379 : P. T. Yorks. p. 115.
1548. Buried—Mabell Stockman : St. Michael, Cornhill, p. 75.
William Stockman, Sarum, 1609 : Reg. Univ. Oxf. ii. pt. ii. p. 307.
London, 6 ; Philadelphia, 15.

Stockport.—Local, ' of Stockport' ; very rare, Stopford (q.v.) being the accepted form.
MDB. (co. Lanc.), 2.

Stockton.—Local, ' of Stockton-on-Tees.' But many small spots would naturally bear this name ; v. Stock and Town.

Geoffrey de Stockton,co.Worc., 1273. A.
John de Stokton, zonarius, 1 Edw. II : Freemen of York, i. 11.
Johannes de Stokton, 1379 : P. T. Yorks. p. 294.
1605-6. Jonas Stockton, co. Warwick : Reg. Univ. Oxf. vol. ii. pt. ii. p. 288.
1627. Thomas Stockton, of Wiglands : Wills at Chester, ii. 209.
1650. Margaret Stockton, of Durham : ibid.
West Rid. Court Dir., 1 ; Manchester, 1 ; Philadelphia, 40.

Stockwell.—Local, ' of Stockwell,' formerly a chapelry in the parish of Lambeth, co. Surrey. Probably other and smaller spots were so called ; v. Stock and Well.

Egidius de Stokwelle, co. Oxf., 1273. A.
Alicia de Stokwell, co. Oxf., ibid.
Elias de Stokwell, 1379 : P. T. Yorks. p. 7.
1581-2. William Stockwell, co. Warwick : Reg. Univ. Oxf. vol. ii. pt. ii. p. 117.
1587. Buried—Eliz., wife of William Stockwell : St. Jas. Clerkenwell, iv. 36.
West Rid. Court Dir., 3 ; London, 3 ; Philadelphia, 7.

Stodart, Stoddard,Stoddart, Stodard.—Occup. (1) ' the studherd' ; v. Studdard.

' A false stodmere,' i.e. studmare : York Mystery Plays, p. 193, l. 13.

(2) Possibly the same as Stotherd, q v. With the sharpened forms Stodart and Stoddart, cf. Calvert for Calveherd.

1765. Married—George Stoddart and Esther Tallents : St. Geo. Han. Sq. i. 140.
1789. — Swinton Stodart and Jane Whinham : ibid. ii. 16.
1803 — John Jenkins and Mary Stoddard : ibid. p. 287.
London, 2, 1, 7, o ; West Rid. Court Dir., o, o, 2, o ; New York, 1, 18, 10, 1.

Stogdon, Stogden. — Local, ' of Stockton' (?). Probably a variant of Stockton, q.v. ; cf. Slagg and Slack, &c.

1753. Married — John Stogdon and Mary Britton : St. Geo. Chap. Mayfair, p. 239.
Crockford, 2, o ; Philadelphia, o, 1.

Stoke, Stokes. — Local, ' of Stoke.' There are sixty-six parishes in Crockford either simply Stoke or compounded, as in such cases as Stoke Bishop, Stoke Canon, Stoke Ash, Stoke Courcy. It is to be noticed that all the entries of Stoke (with one exception) are prefixed with de, those of Stock with de la or atte ; ' de Stoke ' implies a town or village, ' de la Stock ' or ' atte Stock,' some single stump of a tree, &c., where the nominee dwelt. Etymologically, Stoke is a much older form than Stock. Monosyllabic local surnames commonly add the genitive s, as in Williams, Jones, &c. ; cf. Holmes, Brooks, Styles. Hence Stoke is now almost unknown.

Baldewin de Stoke, co. Suff., 1273. A.
Mariota de Stoke, co. Hunts, ibid.
Robert de Stokes, co. Oxf., ibid.
Seman de Stokes, co. Northampt., ibid.
Adam del Stoke, 1379 : P. T. Yorks. p. 270.

Walter de Stoke, co. Soms., 1 Edw. III : Kirby's Quest, p. 137.
London, o, 49 ; Philadelphia, o, 125.

Stokely, Stokley ; v. Stockley. The variants are American.
Philadelphia, 3, 14.

Stoker.—Occup. ; v. Stocker.

Stollard ; v. Stallard.

Stonard ; v. Stannard.

Stone, Stones.—Local, ' at the stone ' or stones (cf. Styles, Stubbs, Stocks, &c.), from residence beside some remarkable roadside stone or rock.

Warin de la Stane, co. Devon, 1273 A.
Reginald ad Ston', co. Bedf., ibid.
John de la Stone, co. Sussex, ibid.
Johannes del Stone, 1379 : P. T. Yorks. p. 53.
Robertus del Stones, 1379 : ibid. p. 180.
Elena de Stons, 1379 : ibid. p. 42.
Robert atte Stone, C. R., 31 Edw. I.
John atte Stone, co. Soms., 1 Edw. III : Kirby's Quest, p. 139.
1609. Bapt.—John, s. Francis Stone : St. Jas. Clerkenwell, i. 57.
London, 119, 3 ; West Rid. Court Dir., 4, 9 ; Philadelphia, 91, 2.

Stoneham.—Local, ' of Stoneham.' North and South Stoneham are parishes in co. Hants, near Southampton. Smaller localities bearing the name doubtless exist, and have furnished representatives.

William de Stonham, co. Camb., 1273. A.
Stephen de Stonham, co. Linc., ibid.
1603. John Stoneham : Reg. Univ. Oxf. i. 356.
1790. Married — Thomas Stoneham and Rebecca Markwick : St. Geo. Han. Sq. ii. 42.
London, 6 ; Philadelphia, 1.

Stonehewer, Stonier. — Occup. ' the stone-hewer,' a stonemason or quarryman. Similarly we find Woodhewer, Fleshhewer (q.v.), Blockhewer, and Blocker ; cf. ' hewers of wood ' (Authorized Version). My first instance is no doubt a misreading :

Thomas Stonehewaa, co. Oxf., 1273. A.
Richard Stonehewer. SS.
1605. John Stonehewer or Stonier, of Barleyford, co. Ches. : Wills at Chester, i. 184.
1638. George Stonier, of Odd Rode : ibid. ii. 209.
1792. Married—Charles Edward Pigon and Charlotte Rycroft ; witness, Richard Stonehewer : St. Geo. Han. Sq. ii. 81.

Manchester, o, 6; MDB. (co. Ches.), 1, o; (co. Essex), 1, o.

Stonehill, Stonhill. — Local, 'at the stone-hall' (?), from residence therein. The evidence is, so far as I can discover, in favour of this derivation, viz. the hall or mansion built of stone, not the stony hill, which is a modern and natural corruption.

Michael de Stonehale, co. Salop, 1273. A. William de la Stonhall, co. Camb., ibid.

I cannot hesitate to say that this is the origin of the name; cf. these two entries:

1693. Buried—Richard Stonehall: St. Michael, Cornhill, p. 273.
1694. — Mary Stonell: ibid. p. 274.

The following are manifest corruptions:

1703. Married — Richard Stonell and Eliz. Spakeman: St. Jas. Clerkenwell, i. 226.
1750. — Richard Sills and Mary Stonnill: St. Geo. Han. Sq. i. 43.
1797. '— Nathaniel Stonhill and Catherine Anderton: ibid. ii. 171.
London, o, 1; Oxford, 1, o; Philadelphia, 2, o.

Stonehouse, Stonhouse. — Local (1), 'at the stone-house' (v. Stannus), from residence therein; cf. Woodhouse, Moorhouse, Parkhouse, &c. Many dwellings would be so termed.

John del Stonhuse, C. R., 47 Hen. III.

(2) Local, 'of Stonehouse,' a parish in co. Gloucester.

John de Stonhus, co. Glouc., 1273. A.
1581. Walter Stonehouse or Stonhowse, co. Middlesex: Reg. Univ. Oxf. vol. ii. pt. ii. p. 111.
1618. Bapt. — Thomas, s. Cristofer Stonhowse: St. Dionis Backchurch, p. 97.
1773. Married—William Stonehouse and Rebecca Kerby: St. Geo. Han. Sq. i. 228.
London, 2, o; Crockford, 1, 1; Boston (U.S.), 3, o.

Stoneman.—Local, ' the stoneman,' the man who dwelt at the stone; v. Stone; cf. Bridgman, Stockman, Steadman, Styleman, &c.

1572. —— Stoneman: Reg. Univ. Oxf. vol. ii. pt. ii. p. 31.
1751. Married — John Stoneman and Hannah Clifford: St. Geo. Chap. Mayfair, p. 204.
1753. — Richard Stoneman and Mary Chipperfield: ibid. p. 236.
London, 4; Philadelphia, 2.

Stoner. — Local or occup.; v. Stanier.

Stonestreet.—Local, 'at the stone street,' i.e. the paved road, from residence therein. Mr. Lower suggests that as this name sprang up in the neighbourhood of Sussex, it may represent the old Roman road from Chichester to London, anciently called Stanistreet (Patr. Brit. p. 331).

Salomon de Stonstrete, co. Kent, 1273. A.
1616. John Coppin and Sarah Stonistreet: Marriage Lic. (London), ii. 47.
1754. Married—William Box and Mary Stonestreet: St. Geo. Han. Sq. i. 54.
MDB. (co. Sussex), 1; Worcester, (U.S.), 1.

Stoney.—Local, ' of Stoney.' Several places, Stoney Middleton (Derbyshire) and Stony Stratford (Bucks), for instance, bear this name as a prefix. But I can supply no further information.

Agnes Stany, 1379: P. T. Yorks. p. 139.
Peter Stoney, C. R., 6 Edw. II.
1803. Married — Elijah Stoney and Sarah Weaver: St. Geo. Han. Sq. ii. 295.
London, 1; West Rid. Court Dir., 1; Philadelphia, 3.

Stonhill; v. Stonehill.

Stonier; v. Stonehewer.

Stonor.—Local, ' of Stonor,' an estate in co. Oxford, thus described by Leland: ' Stonor is three miles out of Henley. Ther is a fayre parke and a warren of Connes and fayre woods. . . . Sir Walter Stonor, now possessor of it, hathe augmentyd and strengthed the howse. The Stonors hath longe had it in possessyon' (v. Lower's Patr. Brit. p. 331).

Richard de Stonore, co. Oxf., 1273. A.
1545. Roger Tidder, of the household of our Lord the King, and Margery Stonar, of Dioc. Oxon, *widow*: Marriage Lic. (Faculty Office), p. 4.
1621-2. William Stonor, Esq., and Eliz. Lake: Marriage Lic. (London), ii. 108.
London Court Dir., 2.

Stoodley; v. Studley.

Stopford, Stopforth.—Local, ' of Stockport.' The old name for Stockport, an important town and parish in co. Cheshire, near Manchester.

Thomas Stoppforth, 1379: P. T. Yorks. p. 43.
Roger de Stokeport, 17 Edw. I: East Cheshire, ii. 338.

1549. Oliver Stokport, mayor of Stockport: ibid. p. 347.
1574. Married — Robert Stopforthe and Ellen Osbalston: Prestbury Ch., co. Ches., p. 45.
1594. James Stopforth, of Latham: Wills at Chester, i. 184.
1601. Married—Ralph Stockport and Margaret Collier: East Cheshire, ii. 405.
1616. William Stopford, of Melling: Wills at Chester, i. 184.
1674. William Stopford, of Macclesfield: East Cheshire, i. 457.
London, 2, o; MDB. (co. Lanc.), 2, 2.

Stoppard.—Local, ' of Stockport,' a corruption of Stopford, an old name for Stockport; v. Stopford. There need be no hesitation in accepting this derivation.

1625. Married — Edward Mottershed and Joane Stopport: Prestbury Ch., East Ches., p. 251.
1635. — John Delves and Margaret Stoppard: ibid. p. 297.
1659. 'Mr. Stoppard, a minister in Lancashyre': East Cheshire, i. 228.

Of this solution there cannot be the shadow of a doubt. From Stopford the popular pronunciation became Stoppard.

Manchester, 1.

Stops, Stopps, Stopp.—Local, ' at the stopps' (?), i.e. stoup or gatepost: the usual term in Ulverston, or Furness generally, for any tall stone post. Probably, however, the instance below is an early variant of Stobb or Stubb (v. Stubbs); cf. Hopps for Hobbs.

William del Stopp, 1379: P. T. Yorks. p. 177.
1759. Married—John Paine and Mary Stopps: St. Geo. Han. Sq. i. 87.
London, 1, o, o; West Riding Court Dir., o, 1, o; New York, o, o, 2.

Storer.—Occup. and offic. ' the storer,' one who stored goods, probably an officer in the feudal household; v. Storey. But more probably a wool-storer, a warehouseman. The name is frequently met with in the Yorks. Poll Tax, 1379.

Johannes Storour, 1379: P. T. Yorks. p. 256.
Hugo Storrour, 1379: ibid. p. 257.
Thomas Storour, 1379: ibid. p. 21.
Henricus Storour, 1379: ibid.
1771. Married — Joseph Storer and Mary Kightley: St. Geo. Han. Sq. i. 216.
London, 8; West Rid. Court Dir., 1; Sheffield, 2; Philadelphia, 7.

Storey, Story, Storry, Storie, Storrie, Storrey.—Personal, 'the son of Storr' (q.v.), popularly Storry.

Thomas Storre, 1379: P. T. Yorks. p. 109.
Johannes Storre, 1379: ibid. p. 43.
Roger Storre, 1379: ibid.

Storey is still among the most familiar of Yorkshire names, but it has become, of necessity, mixed with Storer, which also is well established in that county.

Johannes Staury, 1379: P. T. Yorks. p. 40.
1554. John Williams and Agnes Storry: Marriage Lic. (London), i. 15.
1576. Bapt.—Christopher Storey: St. Jas. Clerkenwell, i. 9.
West Rid. Court Dir., 6, 5, 1, 0, 0, 0; London, 23, 11, 1, 1, 0, 0; Philadelphia, 22, 24, 3, 0, 3, 1.

Stork, Storck.—Nick. 'the stork,' the bird so called; cf. Nightingale, Hawk, Sparrow, &c.

Thomas Storck, co. Suff., 1273. A.
John Stork, C. R., 16 Hen. VI.
Simon Storke, 1535: Reg. Univ. Oxf. i. 184.
1580-1. Edward Graves and Eliz. Storke: Marriage Lic. (London), i. 100.
1784. Married — James Round and Mary Storck: St. Geo. Han. Sq. i. 355.
Sheffield, 5, 0; Philadelphia, 9, 2.

Storm, Sturm.—? Bapt. 'the son of Storm.' No doubt a personal name; cf. Frost, Winter, Snow, and, in later epoch, Christmas, Midwinter, &c.

Edmund Storm, co. Norf., 1273. A.
Hugo Storm, co. Norf., ibid.
Agnes Storme, 1379: P. T. Yorks. p. 157.
1643. Bapt.—Oliver, s. Henrye Storme: St. Jas. Clerkenwell, i. 156.
Sheffield, 1, 0; London, 0, 1; Philadelphia, 10, 14.

Storr, Storrs.—Personal, 'the son of Storr.' A.S. *stor*, large, big; Danish *stor*, large, great. Genitive Storrs; cf. Williams, Jenkins, &c.; v. Storey.

1751. Married—Holland Cooksey and Eliz. Storrs: St. Geo. Chap. Mayfair, p. 203.
1784. — John Hewett and Norris Storr: St. Geo. Han. Sq. i. 356.
London, 5, 1; West Rid. Court Dir., 2, 1; New York, 0, 11; Philadelphia, 2, 0.

Stotherd, Stodart, Stoddart, Stoddard, Stodhart, Stothard,

Stothert.—Occup. 'the stot-herd,' one who tended stots, i.e. bullocks, the bullock-herd; v. Stott. All these forms are North English, and must be distinguished from Studdard and Stuttard (q.v.), with their other corruptions, although no doubt all are now inextricably mixed; cf. Calvert, Coward, Oxnard, Shepard, &c.

Willelmus Stothyrd, 1379: P. T. Yorks. p. 278.
Willelmus Stautohird, 1379: ibid. p. 165.
1778. Married—William Stothart and Mary Heath: St. Geo. Han. Sq. i. 294.
1788. — Swinton Stodart and Jane Winhamm: ibid. ii. 16.
1802. — Benjamin Wray and Mary Stothard: ibid. p. 266.

The West Rid. Court Directory has also the form Stothert.

London, 0, 2, 7, 1, 0, 1, 0; New York, 0, 1, 10, 18, 0, 1, 0.

Stott.—Nick.; v. Stotherd. A familiar North-English surname. 'Stot, a bullock. Scandinavian' (Skeat). 'Stot, a young ox. North' (Halliwell). 'Stotte, *boveau*' (Palsgrave). Cf. *stot-plough* (Halliwell).

The live stock at Bolton Abbey (1526) included 'xx oxen, xii wedders, ix tuppes, xxvi stotts': Whitaker's Craven, p. 403.
1634. Charles Stott, of the parish of Rochdale: Wills at Chester, ii. 209.
1649. James Stott, of Heywood, parish of Bury: ibid.
1651. Bapt.—Eliz., d. Richard Stot: St. Jas. Clerkenwell, i. 178.
London, 4; West Rid. Court Dir., 18; MDB. (co. Lanc.), 30; Philadelphia, 35.

Stoughton.—Local, 'of Stoughton,' a parish in co. Sussex; also a chapelry in the parish of Thurnby, co. Leic.

Eborard de Stouton, co. Hunts, 1273. A.
1577. Thomas Whitehorne and Eliz. Stoughton: Marriage Lic. (London), i. 75.
1687. Bapt.—Mary, d. Philip Stoughton: St. Jas. Clerkenwell, i. 324.
London, 1; MDB. (co. Glouc.), 1; Philadelphia, 6.

Stout, Stoute. — Nick. 'the Stout'; cf. Bigg, Little, &c. Stout was once a familiar surname in cos. Lancaster and York. It is now somewhat rare in England, but flourishes in America.

Willelmus Stoute, 1379: P. T. Yorks. p. 300.
Johannes Stoute, 1379: ibid. p. 142.

Robert Stout, of Lowd Scales, 1692: Lancashire Wills at Richmond, ii. 241.
Jenet Stoute, of Borwick, parish of Warton, 1720: ibid.
London, 2, 0; Liverpool, 3, 0; Philadelphia, 103, 2.

Stovel, Stovell.—Local, 'of Stovile.' I do not know the place. It looks what is usually termed 'of Norman extraction.'

Agnes de Stovile, co. Camb., 1273. A.
Humfrey de Stovil, co. Bucks, ibid.
1765. Married—Robert Fortescue and Mary Stovell: St. Geo. Han. Sq. i. 141.
London, 1, 5; Philadelphia, 0, 5.

Stovin. — Local, 'of Stoven,' a parish in co. Suffolk. This surname seems to have passed through co. Lincoln into Yorkshire, and thence into North Lancashire.

1612. Edmund Stovine, of Caton: Lancashire Wills at Richmond, i. 263.
1627. William Stovin, of Caton: ibid.
1628. Geoffrey Stovyne, of Caton: ibid.
1720. Richard Stoving, of Heysham: ibid. ii. 241.
MDB. (co. Lincoln), 3.

Stow, Stowe. — Local, 'of Stow.' A.S. and M.E. *stów*, a place; cf. Chepstow, i.e. the market-place, and Plaistow, the play-place, the open space for games, &c. There are six parishes of Stow and five of Stowe in England (v. Crockford). The parishes in cos. Lincoln and Cambridge seem to have been the chief parents.

Baldwin de Stow, co. Camb., 1273. A.
Warin de Stowe, co. Camb., ibid.
Fulk de Stow, co. Linc., ibid.
Oda de Stow, co. Linc., ibid.
Ricardus de Stowe, 1379: P. T. Yorks. p. 250.
1765. Married — Samuel Stow and Hannah Needham: St. Geo. Han. Sq. i. 141.
London, 5, 2; Philadelphia, 12, 2.

Stowell.—Local, 'of Stowell,' parishes in cos. Gloucester and Somerset; also a tithing in the parish of Overton, co. Wilts.

Richard de Stawell, co. Wilts, 1273. A.
Lecia Stowelle, co. Camb., ibid.
Geoffrey de Stawelle, co. Soms., 1 Edw. III: Kirby's Quest, p. 118.
Adam de Stawell, co. Somerset, Hen. III–Edw. I. K.
Urmfrey de Stoville, co. Wilts, ibid.
1591. John Stowell, co. Somerset: Reg. Univ. Oxf. vol. ii. pt. ii. p. 183.

3 A

1754. Married—John Stowell and Margaret Traley : St. Geo. Han. Sq. i. 54. London, 3 ; Philadelphia, 1.

Strafford, Stratford.—Local : (1) ' of Strafforth,' in the W. Rid. Yorks ; v. Ford and Forth. (2) ' of Stratford,' parishes in cos. Bucks, Warwick, Wilts, Suffolk, &c.

Roger de Stratforthe, co. Bucks, 1273. A.
William de Stratford, co. Oxf., ibid.
Hugh de Stratford, co. Bucks, ibid.
Walter de Stratforde, co. Soms., 1 Edw. III : Kirby's Quest, p. 112.
Thomas Strafforth, 1379 : P. T. Yorks. p. 160.
Anthony Stratford, co. Glouc., 1589 : Reg. Univ. Oxf. vol. ii. pt. ii. p. 174.
George Stratford, co. Glouc., 1589 : ibid.
1620. Bapt.—Roger, s. Edmond Stratforde : St. Jas. Clerkenwell, i. 87.
1803. Married—Edmund Norton and Mary Strafford : St. Geo. Han. Sq. ii. 273.
Leeds, 1, 11 ; Sheffield, 3, 0 ; Philadelphia, 3, 1.

Strainbow.—Nick. Cf. Stiffbow, Benbow, &c. Sobriquets from archery taking off moral qualities were of likely occurrence.

John Straynbowe, Pardons Roll, 6 Ric. II.

Strang.—Nick. 'the strang,' i.e. the strong, vigorous. A.S. *strang* ; cf. Lang and Long. The surname is Scottish and North English, but generally the former.

Adam Strang, 1379 : P. T. Yorks. p. 159.
1767. Married—William Strang and Eliz. Connell : St. Geo. Han. Sq. i. 169. London, 1 ; Philadelphia, 17.

Strange.—Nick. ' the strange,' i.e. the new-comer, the stranger ; cf. Newman.

Stephen le Straunge, co. York, 1273. A.
John le Straunge, co. Camb., ibid.
Hamond le Straunge, co. Berks, ibid.
John le Strange, co. Soms., 1 Edw. III : Kirby's Quest, p. 172.
Willelmus Strange, 1379 : P. T. Yorks. p. 104.
1578. Bapt.—John, s. William Straunge : St. Michael, Cornhill, i. 89.
1780. Married—Thomas Strange and Eliz. Woods : St. Geo. Han. Sq. i. 318. London, 27 ; Philadelphia, 7.

Strangeman. — Nick. ' the strange man ' ; v. Strange.

John Strangeman, C. R., 1 Hen. IV. pt. i.

Strangeways. — Local, ' of Strangeways,' an estate now occupied by the Assize Court on the Bury New Road, Manchester. The Strangeways family occupied the hall for centuries (v. Baines' Lancashire, i. 400-1).

1546. John Strangwayes and Gertrude Cutson : Marriage Lic. (London), i. 9.
Giles Strangyuyshe, C. R., 1 Eliz. pt. i.
1589. Giles Strangwaies, co. Dorset : Reg. Univ. Oxf. vol. ii. pt. ii. p. 173.
1601. John Strangewayes, co. Dorset : ibid. p. 253.
MDB. (N. Rid. Yorks), 4 ; London, 3.

Strangman, Strongman. — Nick. 'the strong man ' ; cf. Strang and Strong.

Idone Strangman, co. Soms., 1 Edw. III : Kirby's Quest, p. 159.
William Strangman, co. Soms., 1 Edw. III : ibid.
Nicholas Strangman, C. R., 7 Edw. IV. Harrie, son of John Strongman, 1551 : Reg. St. Columb Major, p. 6.
Michell, son of Martin Strangman, 1603 : ibid. p. 21.
Katherine, d. of William Strangman, 1604 : ibid. p. 22.
London, 1, 0 ; Boston (U.S.), 4, 2.

Stratford ; v. Strafford.

Stratton, Stratten, Strattan. —Local, ' of Stratton,' parishes in cos. Cornwall, Dorset, Gloucester, Norfolk, Wilts, Buckingham, Hants, and Somerset, besides several hamlets, &c.

William de Straton, co. Oxf., 1273. A.
John de Stratton, co. Suff., ibid.
Nicholas de Stratton, co. Norf., ibid.
Ralph de Strattone, co. Bucks, ibid.
1564-5. Robert Stratton and Joanna Harryson, *widow* : Marriage Lic. (London), i. 30.
1795. Married—William Stratton and Martha Dean : St. Geo. Han. Sq. ii. 128. London, 12, 1, 0 ; Philadelphia, 63, 0, 1.

Stream.—Local, 'at the stream,' from residence thereby. This as a surname seems never to have caught the popular fancy like Beck and Brook.

William atte Streme, co. Soms., 1 Edw. III : Kirby's Quest, p. 270.
1582. Edward Marsh and Ann Streame : Marriage Lic. (London), i. 109.
1613. Married—Thomas Streame and Frances Savidge : St. Antholin (London), p. 49.
New York, 1 ; Boston (U.S.), 1.

Streat ; v. Street.

Streater ; v. Streeter.

Streatfeild.—Local, ' of Streatfeild.' Mr. Lower says, 'There may be several places of this name. I only know of one, which is a "borough" of the manor of Robertsbridge, in East Sussex, called in a document before me, of temp. Eliz., Stretfelde ; and this locality is within a few miles of that which has been, for three centuries and a half, the chief habitat of the name' (Patr. Brit. p. 332). The Streatfeilds of Chiddingstone, co. Kent, still maintain this old-fashioned spelling of *field*.

1591. Robert Streatfeild and Eliz. Harris : Marriage Lic. (London), i. 194.
1678. James Adams and Hannah Kellett, at her own disposal : alleged by John Streatfeild, cabinet-maker : Marriage Lic. (Faculty Office), p. 143.
MDB. (co. Kent), 4.

Street, Streat.—Local, ' at the street,' i.e. the paved road, from residence therein.

Alice de la Strete, co. Oxf., 1273. A.
Alexander de la Strete, co. Kent, ibid.
Adam of the Strete, Fines Roll, 11 Edw. I.
William atte Strete, c. 1300. M.
John atte Strete, co. Soms., 1 Edw. III : Kirby's Quest, p. 259.
Thomas del Strete, C. R., 28 Edw. III.
Elyas del Strete, 1379 : P. T. Yorks. p. 93.
Alicia del Strete, 1379 : ibid. p. 55.
1572. Bapt.—Thomas, s. Robert Streete : St. Jas. Clerkenwell, i. 7.
1803. Married—John Streat and Rose Preedy : St. Geo. Han. Sq. ii. 280.
London, 27, 1 ; Boston (U.S.), 8, 1.

Streetend, Streeten (?), Streeton (?).—Local, ' at the street end ' ; cf. Woodend and Townsend. Although Streeten and Streeton would seem to be variants of Stretton, q.v., it seems likely that they are but popular variants of Streeten. This was a common mediaeval surname, and yet it has no modern representatives, unless my view be accepted.

Adam de Stretende, co. Kent, 1273. A.
Ralph de Strethende, co. Kent, ibid.
John atte Stretesend, co. Norf. FF.
William Stretende, C. R., 26 Hen. VI.

Of course I may be wrong ; if so, Streeten and Streeton are

unquestionable variants of Stretton, q. v.

London, o, 2, 6 ; Philadelphia, o, o, 10.

Streeter, Streater. — Local, 'the streeter,' he who dwelt in the street ; cf. Bridger, Brooker, &c. With Streater, cf. Streat for Street.

1593-4. William Streeter, co. Sussex : Reg. Univ. Oxf. vol. ii. pt. ii. p. 199.
1659. Buried—Jone Streeter : St. Jas. Clerkenwell, iv. 332.
1729. Married — David Streeter and Eliz. Reed, both of Waltham Abbey : St. Geo. Chap. Mayfair, p. 297.
1746. — Robert Streater and Ann Duke : ibid. p. 70.

London, 4, 1 ; Philadelphia, 8, o.

Strelley, Striley.—Local, 'of Strelly,' a parish in co. Notts, four miles from Nottingham. Lower, quoting Burke's Landed Gentry, says, 'Strelly, anciently Strellegh, co. Notts, gave name and residence to the knightly family of the Strelleys, one of the oldest and most famous in the county.'

1578. Francis Strellye, co. Notts : Reg. Univ. Oxf. vol. ii. pt. ii. p. 83.
— George Strellye, co. Notts : ibid.
1664. George Strelley and Eliz. Reading : Marriage Lic. (London), ll. 217.
1676. Bapt.—Eliz., d. George Strilley : St. Jas. Clerkenwell, i. 274.
MDB. (co. Leic.), 1, o ; Boston (U.S.), o, 1.

Stretch. — ? Local. I cannot suggest any satisfactory origin of this surname, except the foreign Stretz. The Philadelphia Directory has three Stretzes and twenty-two Stretches. Nevertheless, seeing that Stretch was a familiar name in co. Ches. so early as the 16th century, it is almost certain that it is of English local origin.

1596. William Stretch, of Gorstich : Wills at Chester, i. 184.
1606. John Stretch, of Chester, innholder : ibid.
1763. Married—John Potter and Hannah Stretch : St. Geo. Han. Sq. i. 125.
MDB. (co. Ches.), 5 ; London, 3 ; Philadelphia, 22.

Strettell, Strettle.—Local, 'of Strettell.' The suffix is doubtless -hill ; cf. Windle for Windhill, &c. The spot that has originated the surname will probably have to be sought for in co. Chester.

1572. James Strettell and Margaret Braythwa : Marriage Lic. (London), i. 52.
1593. Thomas Strettell, of Marthall : Wills at Chester, i. 184.
1603. Ellen Strettell, of Mobberley, co. Ches.: ibid.
1672. Robert Strethill, of Snelson, in the parish of Rostherne, co. Ches. : East Ches. ii. 643.
Liverpool, 3, o ; Crockford, 1, o ; London, 1, o ; New York, o, 1.

Stretton.—Local, 'of Stretton,' parishes and places in cos. Chester, Derby, Rutland, Stafford, Warwick, Salop, Hereford, and Leicester. It is quite possible that Streeten and Streeton are variants. But v. Streetend. Of course the derivation lies between one or the other.

Meyler de Stretton, co. Salop, 1273. A.
William de Stretton, co. Notts, ibid.
Roger de Strettun, co. Linc., ibid.
1610. Henry Stretton, of Grappenhall : Wills at Chester, i. 184.
1640. John Stretton, of Marton, Prestbury, co. Ches.: ibid. ii. 210.
1768. Married—Thomas Stretton and Eliz. King : St. Geo. Han. Sq. i. 175.
MDB. (co. Derby), 5 ; London, 6 ; Philadelphia, 2.

Strickland.—Local, 'of Strickland,' originally Stirkland, four townships in co. Westmoreland, viz. Great and Little Strickland in the parish of Morland, and Strickland Kettle and Strickland Roger in the parish of Kendal. The surname is now familiar over the English-speaking world.

William de Stirkland, 20 Edw. I : Nicolson and Burn, Hist. Westm. and Cumb. i. 90.
Walter de Stirkeland, 35 Edw. I : ibid. i. 91.
William de Stirkelaunde, co. Westm., 20 Edw. I. R.
1588. Roger Strickland, of Cartmellfell : Lancashire Wills at Richmond, i. 264.
1618. John Strickland, co. Westm. : Reg. Univ. Oxf. vol. ii. pt. ii. p. 368.
1662. James Strickland, of Satterthwaite : Lancashire Wills at Richmond, i. 264.
London, 16 ; MDB. (co. Lanc.), 9 ; Philadelphia, 18.

Stringer.—Occup. 'the stringer,' a manufacturer of cord or twine ; cf. Stringfellow, Corder, Roper, or Raper. No doubt the Stringer made the special cord for bows. It is a common Yorkshire entry in the 14th century.

Godwynd Strenger, co. Soms., 1 Edw. III : Kirby's Quest, p. 100.
Willelmus Strynger, 1379 : P. T. Yorks. p. 101.
Johannes Strenger, 1379 : ibid. p. 172.
Ricardus Stryngar, 1379 : ibid. p. 66.
1574. Married — Richard Collie and Bettres Stringer : St. Mary Aldermary (London), p. 5.
1575. George Stringar, co. Staff. : Reg. Univ. Oxf. vol. ii. pt. ii. p. 66.
1646. John Stringer, of Nantwich, victualler : Wills at Chester, ii. 210.
West Rid. Court Dir., 2 ; London, 13 ; Philadelphia, 21.

Stringfellow. — Occup. 'the stringer,' a maker of bow-strings. All surnames with suffix -fellow seem to have sprung from the North of England, especially from co. York ; v. Longfellow.

Laurencius Stryngfelagh, 1379 : P. T. Yorks. p. 11.
John Strengfellow, of Openshaw, 1616 : Wills at Chester, i. 184.
Richard Strengfellow, of Rochdale, 1617 : ibid.
1713. Buried — Rebeckah, d. John Stringfellow : St. Mary Aldermary (London), p. 213.
London, 2 ; Manchester, 4 ; West Rid. Court Dir., 2 ; Philadelphia, 6.

Stringlayer. — Occup. 'the stringlayer,' a roper, one who worked on a rope-walk (?).

William le Strenglayer, C. R., 13 Edw. II.

Strode, Strude.—Local, (1) 'of Stroud,' a parish in co. Glouc. ; (2) 'of Strood,' a parish in co. Kent (v. Stroud). Both seem to have been anciently styled Strode. Mr. Lower, quoting Shirley's Noble and Gentle Men, says that 'the name is derived from Strode, in the parish of Ermington, co. Devon, which was in the possession of Adam de Strode in the reign of Henry III' (Patr. Brit. p. 333). However true this may be, it is obvious that the towns of Stroud and Strood have also their representatives in our directories in the form of Strode.

William de Strode, co. Oxf., 1273. A.
William de la Strode, co. Surrey, Hen. III-Edw. I. K.
John de Strode, co. Wilts, ibid.
1571. Swithin Strowde, co. Soms. : Reg. Univ. Oxf. vol. ii. pt. ii. p. 52.
1607. Francis Strode, co. Devon : ibid. p. 297.
1617. William Strodd or Strowde, co. Devon : ibid. p. 361.

1767. Married—William Strode and Ann Fozard : St. Geo. Han. Sq. i. 163. London, 1, 1 ; Philadelphia, 9, 0.

Strong.—Nick. ' the strong ' ; cf. Strongfellow and Strongman, and also Long, Longman, and Longfellow. Naturally this has taken a firm hold upon our directories, the sobriquet being a popular one. There is no need for many instances.

Simon Strong, co. Camb., 1273. A.
Joscelin le Strong. H.
William le Strong. T.
1539. Bapt.—Peter, s. Martyn Strong, a straunger : St. Dionis Backchurch, p. 71.
London, 29 ; Philadelphia, 31.

Strongbow.—Nick. ; cf. Hotspur, Sharparrow, Stiffbow, or Benbow, a decidedly complimentary sobriquet.

Ranulf Strongbowe, co. Essex, 1273. A.
Simon Strongebowe. H.
Izabell Strongboo, d. of Richard Earl of Pembroke : Visitation of Yorks, Harl. Sdc., p. 282.

Strongfellow. — Nick. ' the strong fellow ' ; cf. Longfellow. But possibly an imitative corruption of Stringfellow (q.v.) after the origin of this occupative name had become obscured through the variant Strengfellow.

Robert Strongfellowe, temp. Eliz. Z.
Frances Strongfellowe, ibid.

Strongitharm.—Nick. ' strong-in-the-arm ' ; cf. Armstrong, Brasdefer, &c. This name is still found in co. Cheshire, but is always rare.

1570. Married—Thomas Davenporte and Ellen Strongethearme : Reg. Prestbury, co. Ches., p. 30.
1581. Roger Strongeitharme and Ales Hollynshed : ibid. p. 69.
1597. Richard Stronge in Arme and Margaret Wyatt : Marriage Lic. (London), i. 243.
1621. — William Burghill and Marie Strongitharme : ibid. p. 232.
William Strongitharm, of Swettenham, 1598 : Wills at Chester (1545-1620), p. 184.
George Strongitharm, of Allostock, 1617 : ibid. p. 185.
Barrow-in-Furness, 1.

Strongman. — Nick. ' the strong man ' ; v. Strangman.

John Strongman, rector of Brunstead, co. Norf., 1389 : FF. ix. 289.
Boston (U.S.), 2.

Strother. — Local, ' of the strother,' i.e. marsh, from residence there beside. ' Strother, a marsh. North Engl.' (Halliwell). This surname has its home in Northumberland. In Newcastle and the district it is commonly met with. It is interesting to note that Chaucer places his Strother in the far North, where Allen, too, was the favourite name. v. Langstroth.

' John highte that on, and Alein highte
that other,
Of o toun were they born, that highte
Strother,
Fer in the North, I can not tellen where.'
Chaucer, C. T. 4010-11.
Edward Elliot, of The Strother, 1763 : Brand's Hist. of Newcastle, i. 560.
Alan del Strother, bailiff of Tindall, 1358 : Hodgson, Hist. Northumberland, ii. 542.
William Strother, mayor of Newcastle, 1360 : Hist. Newcastle, Gateshead, i. 160.
Henry del Strother, temp. Henry III : Hodgson, Hist. Northumberland, v. 327.
1706. Bapt. — George, s. William Strother : St. Jas. Clerkenwell, p. 29.
MDB. (co. Northumberland), 2 ; London, 3 ; Philadelphia, 1.

Stroud.—Local : (1) 'of Stroud,' a parish in co. Glouc. ; v. Strode. (2) 'of Strood,' a parish in co. Kent. For further instances, v. Strode.

Edytha atte Stroude, co. Soms., 1 Edw. III : Kirby's Quest, p. 95.
Matilda atte Strode, co. Soms., 1 Edw. III : ibid. p. 202.
Thomas atte Strode, co. Soms., 1 Edw. III : ibid. p. 268.
1641. Buried—Ann, d. Nicholas Stroude : St. Jas. Clerkenwell, iv. 240.
1652. Married—Thomas Harlackenden and Eliz. Stroude : St. Dionis Backchurch, p. 28.
London, 18 ; Philadelphia, 29.

Strude ; v. Strode.

Strutt.—? Nick. ' one who strutted ' (?). Sobriquets from gait or peculiarities of walking are endless. The reason is obvious ; they gave individuality, readily seized upon when it became manifest that surnames were necessary to eke out identity.

Simon Strut, C. R., 48 Hen. III.
John le Strut (also John Strutt), co. Wilts, 1273. A.
Robert Strut, co. Camb., ibid.
William Strut, co. Hunts, ibid.
1762. Married—John McDonald and Esther Strutt : St. Geo. Han. Sq. i. 113.
London, 3 ; Philadelphia, 1.

Stuard ; v. Steward.

Stuart ; v. Stewart.

Stubbing, Stubbings, Stubbins, Stubbin.—Local, ' of the stubbings,' from residence beside a number of stumps or stocks of trees ; v. Stubbs (2).

Nicholas de Stubbings, co. Salop, 1273. A.
Henricus de Stubbyng, 1379 : P. T. Yorks. p. 211.
1632. Edmond Stubbing and Jone Wolley : Marriage Lic. (Faculty Office), p. 22.
1674. Bapt. — William, s. William Stubbins : St. Jas. Clerkenwell, i. 264.
London, 1, 4, 2, 0 ; MDB. (co. Camb.), 0, 3, 0, 0 ; Philadelphia (Stubbins), 4 ; (co. Essex), 2, 1, 0, 1.

Stubbs, Stobbs.—Local (1), ' of Stubbs,' a township in the parish of Adwick-le-Street, W. Rid. Yorks, near Doncaster ; (2) 'at the stubbs,' one who lived by some stump of a tree or stumps of trees. Cf. Styles, Briggs, Stocks, &c.

George Stobbis, le pownder, per annum 6s. 8d. : Liber Bursarii, Eccles. Dunelmensis, Surtees Soc.
' Old stocks, and stubs of trees.'
Spenser, F. Q. i. 9. 34.
' Item, una acra et una roda terroe jacent aput Stob-tres,' 1367 : Ext. from grant of John de Clynt, chaplain to David de Wolloure, at Ripon, GGG. i. 194.
Henry de Stubbes, co. York, 1273. A.
Richard de Stubbes, co. York, ibid.
Henricus de Stubbys, 1379 : P. T. Yorks. p. 210.
Alicia de Stubbes, 1379 : ibid. p. 125.
Johannes Stubbe, 1379 : ibid. p. 41.
Johannes de Stubbes, 1379 : ibid. p. 123.
John Stubbe, co. Soms., 1 Edw. III : Kirby's Quest, p. 80.

It is probable that most of our many North-English Stubbs hail from (1), but (2) must have many representatives in our directories. The actual derivation of both (1) and (2) will be the same.

Elizabeth Stobbs, coffee rooms, Pateley Bridge, West Riding Dir.
London, 20, 0 ; Sheffield, 5, 0 ; MDB. (co. Durham), 2, 5 ; New York, 7, 0.

Studdard, Stuttard, Studdert, Stutard. — Occup. ' the stud-herd,' one who kept a stud of horses ; v. Stodart, and cf. Stotherd. One of a large class of North-English surnames with suffix -herd, as in Shepherd ; cf. Calvert,

Coward, Geldard, or Oxnard. The variant Stuttard is, of course, a mere sharpening of the more correct form, as in the case of Calvert for Calve-herd. Studdard evidently represented the old stud-herd, a breeder of horses or mares (v. Skeat on *stud*).

Robertus Studhyrd, 1379 : P. T. Yorks. p. 279.
Johannes Studhyrd, 1379 : ibid. p. 277.
Petrus Studehird, 1379 : ibid. p. 211.
Thomas Studhird, 1379 : ibid. p. 292.
1745. John Studdart, of Hawkshead : Lancashire Wills at Richmond, ii. 242.
1783 Married—Joseph Levermore and Helen Stuttard : St. Geo. Han. Sq. i. 351.
London, 1, 1, 0, 0 ; Crockford, 0, 0, 2, 0 ; Manchester, 0, 3, 0, 1.

Studley, Stoodley. — Local, (1) 'of Studley,' parishes and places in cos. Bucks, Warwick, and W. Rid. Yorks (2) ; (2) 'of Stoodleigh,' a parish in co. Devon, five miles from Bampton. There can be no doubt that the Dorset and Devon Studleys in general represent the last-named place.

William de Stodley, co. Leic., 1273. A.
Thomas de Studle, co. Bedf., 20 Edw. I. R.
Walter de Stodleghe, co. Soms., 1 Edw. III : Kirby's Quest, p. 252.
1584. Nathaniel Studley, co. Dorset : Reg. Univ. Oxf. vol. ii. pt. ii. p. 134.
1586. Thomas Stoodlie, co. Dorset : ibid. p. 153.
1610. Peter Studley, co. Salop : ibid. p. 321.
1644. Bapt. — Ellenor, d. Thomas Studley : St. Dionis Backchurch, p. 108.
London, 1, 0 ; MDB. (co. Devon), 4, 0 ; (co. Dorset), 3, 2 ; New York, 12, 0.

Sturdee, Sturdy.—Nick. 'the sturdy,' the strongly rash or inconsiderate (v. Skeat on *sturdy*, showing how the meaning of the word has changed). M.E. *sturdi*.

Hamond Sturdi, co. Hunts, 1273. A.
Walter Sturdi, co. Oxf., ibid.
Robertus Sturdy, 1379 : P. T. Yorks. p. 227.
1618. Buried — Dyana, wife of James Sturdy : St. Peter, Cornhill, i. 174.
1787. Married — Thomas Atkinson Sturdy and Ann Wood : St. Geo. Han. Sq. i. 410.
London, 2, 3 ; New York, 0, 2.

Sturdevant; v. Sturtevant.

Sturge, Sturges, Sturgess, Sturgis. — Bapt. 'the son of Thurgis or Turgis,' with prefixed *s*. The surname, like the early fontal name, is common to all parts of England.

Turgis (without surname), co. Linc., 10 Hen. II : Pipe Roll, p. 22.
Thurgis le Caldecote, co. Norf., temp. King John : FF. vi. 57.
Thurgis (without surname), co. Linc., 1273. A.
Turgis (without surname), co. Linc., ibid.
Turgeus de Corton, co. Suff., ibid.
Turgisius de Heredefeld, co. Kent, ibid.
William Thurgys, co. Wilts, ibid.
Adam Thurgis, co. Bedf., ibid.
Richard Turgis, co. Wilts, ibid.

A century later *s* had stolen to the front :

Johannes Sturgys, 1379 : P. T. Yorks. p. 248.
Johannes Sturgys, junior, 1379 : ibid.
1626. Bapt. — John, son of Sturges Sturgis : St. Dionis Backchurch, p. 100.

The earlier and more correct form lingered on for several centuries.

1629. Buried — John Turges, son of Thomas Turges : St. Dionis Backchurch, p. 220.
1646. Married—Thomas Langham and Sarah Turgis : ibid. p. 25.
1666. Paul Bowes and Bridgett Sturges : Marriage Lic. (Faculty Office), p. 94.
1785. Married—Thomas Sturgis and Sarah Whitmee : St. Geo. Han. Sq. i. 374.
London, 2, 8, 1, 3 ; Oxford, 0, 3, 2, 0 ; Philadelphia, 0, 14, 0, 13.

Sturgeon.—? Nick. 'the sturgeon,' but perhaps a personal name ; cf. Dolphin and Herring, undoubted personal names.

Willelmus Sturgeon, 1379 : P. T. Yorks. p. 299.
John Sturgeon, C. R., 22 Hen. VI.
John Sturgeon, Rot.Pat., 2 Ric.III.pt.i.
1559. Buried—Margery Sturgion : St. Peter, Cornhill, i. 114.
1647. Married — John Scudder and Eliz. Sturgeon : St. Dionis Backchurch, p. 25.
London, 6 ; MDB. (co. Suffolk), 5 ; Philadelphia, 5.

Sturgess, -gis ; v. Sturge.

Sturm ; v. Storm.

Sturman.—(1) ? Occup. 'the steerman' (?) ; cf.Cowman, Bullman, &c., and v. Steer. (2) Occup. 'the steerman,' navigator.

Robert le Steresman, co.Camb., 1273. A.
Roger le Steresman, co. Camb., ibid.

Two early ' 'Varsity coxes '! Mr. Lower says, ' Stirman or Stirmannus occurs in Domesday as the

designation of an official. Edric Stirman was, t. Edward Confessor, commander of the land and sea forces of the bishop of Worcester for the King's service (Stermannus navis episcopi, et ductor exercitus ejusdem episcopi, ad servicium regis) ' : Heming Chartul., quoted in Ellis's Introd. ii. 89.

1548. William Sturman and Eliz. Norryce : Marriage Lic. (London), i. 12.
1553. Bapt.— Mary Sturmanne : St. Peter, Cornhill, i. 114.
1619. Buried—John Styrman: ibid.p.175.
London, 6 ; Oxford, 2 ; New York, 5.

Sturmy.—Local, 'of Sturmy.' I cannot find the place.

John de Sturmi, co. Heref., Hen. III– Edw. I. K.
Richard de Sturmy, co. York, 1273. A.
William de Sturmy, co. Norf., ibid.
1671. Thomas Sturmy and Eliz. Maddison : Marriage Alleg. (Canterbury), p. 192.
1677. Married — John Sturmey and Elizabeth Clarke : St. Mary Aldermary (London), p. 32.
London, 1.

Sturt. — Local, 'of Stert,' a parish in co. Wilts, near Devizes. As suggested by Mr. Lower, this seems the probable origin. The evidence I furnish below confirms this view :

William de la Sturte, co. Devon, 1273. A.
Thomas atte Sturt, co. Soms., 1 Edw. III : Kirby's Quest, p. 178.
1600. Bapt.—William, s. John Sturte : St. Jas. Clerkenwell, i. 36.
1615. Waymond Stert or Sturt, co. Devon : Reg. Univ. Oxf. vol. ii. pt. ii. p. 343 (see Index).
London, 7 ; MDB. (co. Devon), 3.

Sturtevant, Sturtivant, Sturdevant, Sturdivant. — Nick. At first sight this sobriquet would seem to be a compound of *sturdy*, rash, inconsiderate ; and *avaunt*, a boast, a vaunt, and also an old French sobriquet for some reckless boaster. But I have no doubt it is one of the early nicknames given to pursuivants, harbingers, or heralds, of which this dictionary has so many instances. Thus it means ' go-before,' from *start* (M.E. *stirt* and *stert*), and *avaunt*, forward, to the front. We are still familiar with the *avant-courier*. An exact parallel will be found in the case of Prickadvance (spur-forward) ; v. Pickavance, Purchas, Golightly, Lightfoot, &c.

Willelmus Styrtauant, 1379: P. T. Yorks. p. 273.

Cf. also

Willelmus Stirciuant, 1379: ibid. p. 60.
Robertus Stircyuant, 1379: ibid.
John Sturdyvaunte, 1570: Reg. St. Dionis Backchurch, p. 6.
1604. Buried — Mathew Sturdyvant, Old Buckenham, co. Norf.: FF. i. 392.

A well-known firm of solicitors existed in Preston about 1830 styled Buck and Startifant.

1685. Buried — Elizabeth, wife of Thomas Stertevant: St. Mary Aldermary (London), p. 196.
London, 1, 1, 0, 0 ; Philadelphia, 2, 0, 3, 0 ; New York, 8, 0, 0, 0 ; Boston (U.S.), 34, 0, 0, 6.

Sturton.—Local, 'of Sturton.' Several parishes and townships bear this name in cos. Lincoln, Notts, and W. Rid. Yorks.

Nicholas de Sturton, co. Wilts: Hen. III–Edw. I. K.
1594. David Barnard, *embroiderer*, and Margery Sturton: Marriage Lic. (London), i. 215.
1779. Married — John Rood and Susannah Sturton: St. Geo. Han. Sq. i. 297.
MDB. (co. Lincoln), 4.

Stuttard.—Occup. 'the studherd'; v. Studdard.

Stydolph.— ? Bapt. 'the son of Stydulf' (?), one of the endless compounds of Ulf or Wolf, as in Randolph. But Lower says a corruption of St. Edolph, which would make it local, from some chapelry of that name ; cf. Sinclair.

Adam Stydulff and Katherine Kingsleye: Dioc. of Chichester.
John Stydulff and Constance Kingsleye: ibid.

I have lost the reference to the above.

1610. Thomas Stydolfe, co. Surrey: Reg. Univ. Oxf. vol. ii. pt. ii. p. 314.
1624-5. William Stydolffe and Mary Lupie: Marriage Lic. (London), ii. 150.

Still existing, I am told, but I cannot find it.

Style, Styles, Stiles, ?Stile.— Local, 'at the stile,' from residence thereby. The seeming plural form Stiles or Styles is really the genitive ; cf. Williams for William (=William's son). So Styles = Style's son ; cf. Holmes, Briggs, Brooks. The genitive form in local surnames is almost entirely confined to monosyllabic surnames.

'For som tyme I served
Symme atte-Style.'
Piers P. 2874.

See also the suggestions with regard to Still.

Alina de la Stigela, C. R., 54 Hen. III.
Richard de la Style, co. Bedf., 1273. A.
John Atte Stile, co. Oxf., ibid.
Robert ate Stiele, co. Oxf., ibid.
Roger atte Styhill, 1379: P. T. Yorks. p. 120.
1575. Nicholas Style and Gertrude Bright: Marriage Lic. (London), i. 67.
1761. Married—Henry Styles and Eliz. Reader : St. Geo. Han. Sq. i. 107.
London, 1, 13, 10, 0 ; Philadelphia, 0, 7, 68, 1.

Styleman, Stileman, Stillman.—Local, 'the stileman,' i.e. the man who lived at the stile ; v. Style, and cf. Bridgman, Stockman, Steadman, &c.

1586. John Stileman and Alice Hill: Marriage Lic. (London), i. 152.
1661. Bapt. — Elizabeth, d. Nicholas Stillman : St. Jas. Clerkenwell, i. 212.
1701. Married — Andrew Cooper and Sarah Stileman: Reg. St. Dionis Backchurch, p. 50.
London, 0, 2, 2 ; Philadelphia, 0, 0, 14.

Suart.—(1) Occup. 'the sowherd,' i.e. a keeper of sows ; cf. Swinnart, Hoggard, Calvert, Oxnard, Coward. With the sharpened form, cf. Stuttard. (2) Perhaps sometimes personal for Seward (2), q.v.

Cecilia Sueherd, 1379 : P. T. Yorks. p. 158.
William Suart, 1379: ibid. p. 298.
1777. Married — James Shuttelworth and Mary Suart : St. Geo. Han. Sq. i. 273.
London, 2 ; Crockford, 1.

Such, Suche, Sutch.—Local, an old form of 'de la Zouch.' I cannot give any satisfactory derivation of this local term. Lower says, 'The baronial family who gave the suffix to Ashby-de-la-Zouch, co. Leic., were a branch of the Earls of Brittany. . . . The founder of the race in England was William le Zusche, who died in the first year of King John. In a charter he calls Roger la Zusche his father, and Alan, Earl of Brittany, his grandfather.' . . . Lower adds that Camden asserts that 'Zouch signifieth the stocke of a tree in the French tongue.' If this be true, Zouch and its variants, such as Souch, Such, Sutch, are but equivalent to the English Stubbs, Stock, Stubbings, &c.

Alan de la Souche, co. Devon, 1273. A.
Roger de la Soche, ibid.
William de la Soche, co. Devon., ibid.
Walter Such, co. Soms., 1 Edw. III : Kirby's Quest, p. 118.
1584-5. Henry Sutche, *yeoman*, and Anne Prentice : Marriage Lic. (London), i. 137.
1602. Francis Souch, London : Reg. Univ. Oxf. vol. ii. pt. ii. p. 260.
1610. Silvester Such, of Ormskirk : Wills at Chester, i. 185.
1615. Thomas Sutch, of Burscough : ibid.
1637. Bapt.—Ann, d. Samuel Sutch : St. Jas. Clerkenwell, i. 137.
London, 6, 1, 3 ; Philadelphia, 0, 0, 9.

Suckbitch. — Local, ' of Soghespich.' Mr. Lower writes : 'This name, borne by more than one respectable family in the West of England, might be supposed to be derived from some legend analogous to that of Romulus and Remus. The earliest form of it, Sokespic, however, excludes such an origin. See Notes and Queries, 1st S. v. 425.' The name is local, and has been turned into an imitative form.

Jordan de Soghespich, co. Devon, 1273. A.

Close beside this entry is the mention of a place Spichwick, no doubt closely connected.

Suckling. — Nick. 'the suckling.' This, at least, seems to be the origin. Mr. Lower thinks it is a local surname, but furnishes no evidence ; cf. Child, Ayre, Eyre.

Adam Sucklin, co. Oxf., 1273. A.
Robert Sucling, co. Oxf., ibid.
Walter Sucling, co. Suff., ibid.
1432. John Sokelyng : Cal. of Wills in Court of Husting (2).
1551. Buried—Richard Sucklyne: St. Peter, Cornhill, i. 110.
1801. Married—Charles Suckling and Eliz. Bartlett : St. Geo. Han. Sq. ii. 246.
London, 2 ; Crockford, 3.

Sucksmith.—Occup.; v. Shoesmith. I may, however, suggest that Sucksmith and Sixsmith may be corruptions of *scythe-smith* or *sickle-smith*, one who manufactured scythes. In Tobacco Tortured (London: Richard Field, 1616) several characters appear whose names are 'Cocke-on-hoope the Cobbler,' 'Martin the Mariner,' 'Thin-gut the Thatcher,' and 'Simkin the Sithe-smith' (v. Notes and Queries, 1885, p. 126).

1754. Married —Charles Dowley and Ann Sucksmith: St. Geo. Chap. Mayfair, p. 276.

Sudbury.—Local, 'of Sudbury,' a parish in co. Suffolk.

Robert de Sudbyr, co. Norf., 1273. A.
Ralph de Sudebyre, co. Essex, ibid.
John de Sudbury, co. Bedf., 20 Edw. I. R.
1551. Richard Sudbury, Christ Church: Reg. Univ. Oxf. i. 97.
1580. Benjamin Gilbert, or Bury, of Alta Rothinge, co. Essex, and Eliz. Sudbury: Marriage Lic. (London), i. 97.
MDB. (co. Essex), 2; London, 1; Boston (U.S.), 1.

Sudlow.—Local, 'of Sudlow,' evidently some small spot in the parish of Over Tabley, co. Ches., or the neighbouring parish of Rostherne.

Thomas Stubbs, of Sudloe, parish of Rawsthorne, 1638: Wills at Chester, ii. 210.
William Sudlow, of Witton, 1593: ibid. i. 185.
Richard Newall, of Sudlow, in Over Tabley, *carpenter*, 1663: ibid. iii. 194.
William Sudlow, of Great Budworth, *husbandman*, 1638: ibid. ii. 211.
1763. Married — Robert Sudlow and Catherine Worsdall: St. Geo. Han. Sq. i. 127.
Manchester, 4; London, 2; New York, 4.

Suffolk.—Local, 'of Suffolk'; cf. Kent, Cheshire, Cornwall, &c. These surnames easily arose from migration from one county to another.

Thomas Suffauk, London, 1273. A.
Thomas de Suffolk, London, 20 Edw. I. R.
1733. Married — Manvel Oliver and Mary Suffolk: St. Geo. Han. Sq. ii. 11.
1750. — Francis Hughes and Deborah Suffolk: St. Geo. Chap. Mayfair, p. 170. London, 1.

Sugar, Sugars.—Bapt. 'the son of Sigher'; v. Sayer and Seager.

Robert Sulgar, 1379: P. T. Yorks. p. 160.
Johannes Sulgar, 1379: ibid.
Jone wyf to Sugero, filio Hemoney Copledale: Visitation of Yorks, p. 40.
Hugh Sugar, Patent Roll, 1 Hen. VII.
1609-10. Gregory Sugar, or Suger, co. Dorset: Reg. Univ. Oxf. vol. ii. pt. ii. p. 309. (v. Index.)
1650. Married—John Sugar and Mary Holten: St. Dionis Backchurch, p. 27.
London, 3, 0; Manchester, 0, 1; New York, 2, 0.

Sugden.—Local, 'of Sugden,' some small spot in W. Rid. Yorks, which I have failed to identify.

Robertus de Sugden, 1379: P. T. Yorks. p. 183.
Willelmus Sugden, 1379: ibid. p. 211.
Robertus de Sugdeyn, 1379: ibid. p. 263.
1555. William Sugden and Catherine Lenyall: Marriage Lic. (London), i. 16.
London, 3; West Riding Court Dir., 30; Philadelphia, 10.

Sully. — Local, 'of Sudeley,' now Sudeley Manor, a parish in co. Gloucester, often written Sully in old records. A family of Sudeleys resided here for centuries.

Bartholomew de Sulley, or Sudeley, co. Glouc., 1273. A.
Henry de Sully, co. Devon, ibid.
Walter de Sully, co. Devon, ibid.
Reymond de Suleye, co. Devon, Hen. III-Edw. I. K.
Mabillia de Suly, co. Glouc., 20 Edw. I. R.
Ralph de Sudlegh, or Sule, or Suley, co. Glouc., Hen. III-Edw. I. K.
Adam Sulleygh, co. Soms., 1 Edw. III: Kirby's Quest, p. 265.
1762. Married —Thomas Leigh and Joan Sully: St. Geo. Han. Sq. i. 109.
London, 8; Philadelphia, 1.

Summer, Summers, Somers, Sommers, Sommer.—Bapt. 'the son of Summer.' Just as ecclesiastical seasons gave us such personal names as Noel, Pentecost, Pask, Christmas, &c., so several centuries earlier popular names for children were descriptive of the natural season in which the child was born, or even the state of the weather. Hence such personal names as Snow, Storm, Winter, Summer, Spring, &c. Several years ago a child was baptized Sou'-wester because born on shipboard in a south-westerly gale. This case I can vouch for.

M.E. *somer,* summer. Cf. such local names as Somerby, Somercoates, Somerford, Somersby, Somersham, Somerton, all implying that the first settler bore the name of Somer (now Summer); v. Winter for further information. Summers, Somers, &c., are the genitive form; cf. Williams and William.

John Somer, co. Soms., 1 Edw. III: Kirby's Quest, p. 133.
1600. Bapt.—Joan, d. Peter Somers: St. Jas. Clerkenwell, i. 37.
1687. — John, s. John Sumer: ibid. p. 322.
1755. Married—Charles Summers and Sarah Mason: St. Geo. Han. Sq. i. 58.
London, 1, 25, 8, 5, 0; Philadelphia, 4, 69, 32, 31, 35.

Summersby.—Local, 'of Somersby,' a parish in co. Lincoln, seven miles from Spilsby.

? Robert de Somerdeby, co. Linc., 1273. A.
London, 1.

Summerscales, Summersgill. — Local, 'of Somerscales.' Summersgill may be of independent origin, but is more probably a corruption of Somerscale; cf. Winterscale and Wintergill. For prefix v. Summer; for suffix v. Scales.

Johannes de Somerscales, 1379: P. T. Yorks. p. 287.
Johannes de Somerscale, junior, 1379: ibid. p. 288.
Thomas Prockter, of Somerscall, in Botton, 1606: Lancashire Wills at Richmond, p. 222.
1803. Married—John Summersgill and Mary Phillips: St. Geo. Han. Sq. ii. 292.
West Rid. Court Dir., 3, 1.

Summerset; v. Somerset.

New York, 1.

Summersford, Summerford.—Local, 'of Somerford,' three parishes in co. Wilts.

William de Sumeford, co. Bucks, 1273. A.
Alexander de Somerford, co. Wilts, ibid.
Richard de Somerford, co. Wilts, ibid.
Nicholas de Somerford, co. Hunts, ibid.
1591. Robert Glover and Anne Somerford: Marriage Lic. (London), i. 193.
1603. Edward Somerford, co. Middlesex: Reg. Univ. Oxf. vol. ii. pt. ii. p. 265.
Crockford, 1, 0; London, 0, 1; Oxford, 3, 1.

Summershall; v. Somersall.

Summerson.—Nick. 'the son of the Sumner' (q.v.), one of several

Yorkshire surnames of a particular class ; cf. Taylorson, Herdson, Clarkson, Wrightson, &c.

1752. Married — Thomas Summerson and Ann Hall: St. Geo. Chap. Mayfair, p. 212.

MDB. (co. Durham), 1 ; New York, 1 ; Market Weighton (East Rid. Yorks), 1.

Sumner, Sumpner. — Offic. 'the summoner,' a legal officer, the sheriff's messenger. In the Coventry Mysteries it is said :

Sim Somnor, in haste wend thou thi way,
Byd Joseph, and his wyff by name,
At the coorte to apper this day,
Him to purge of her defame.'

The *p* in Sumpner is intrusive, as in Thompson, or Simpson, or Hampton.

Hugh le Sumenor, co. Camb., 1273. A.
Sarra le Sumenur, co. Oxf., ibid.
John le Sumenur, C. R., 20 Edw. I.
Henry le Sumenour. B.
Ralph le Somenur. T.
Adam Somendour, 1379 : P. T. Yorks. p. 62.
Henry le Somnor, 1397 : Preston Guild Roll, p. 1 (Lanc. and Ches. Rec. Soc.).
1573. Reginald Sumner and Ellinor Sagell : Marriage Lic. (London), i. 57.
1627. Married—Nicholas Sumpner and Dorothy Banes : St. Dionis Backchurch, p. 22.
London, 17, 1 ; Philadelphia, 3, 0.

Sumpter, Sumter, Sumterman, Sunter. — Offic. ' the sumpter.' O.F. *sommetier*, a packhorseman, one who carried baggage on horseback ; in modern English applied to the horse, not the driver, a sumpter-horse being really a sumpter's horse (v. Skeat, *sumpter*); cf. Palfreyman, q.v.

' Willelmo Mone Sometario ad unum somerum pro armis Regis ': Wardrobe of Edward I. p. 77.
Gilbert del Bed prays a reward for long services as ' King's Sumeter': H. i. 156 b.
William le Sumeter, 1273. A.
William le Somter, c. 1300. M.
John le Somyter, co. Soms., 1 Edw. III : Kirby's Quest, p. 114.
Simon le Sometier, varlet of the king's stable : Wardrobe Roll, 19 Edw. II.
Geoffrey le Someter, C. R., 54 Hen. III.
Richard Somterman. RR. 2.
Willelmus Sumpter, 1379 : P. T. Yorks. p. 235.

Sunter is, no doubt, a corruption ; cf. Sinkinson for Simkinson, &c.

1782. Married—Henry Sumpter and Catherine Davies : St. Geo. Han. Sq. i. 336.
1794. — Henry Sunter and Ann Mills : ibid. ii. 110.
London, 2, 0, 0, 3 ; Philadelphia, 1, 0, 0, 0.

Sumption, Sumpton.—?——.
Mr. Lower writes, ' This very remarkable name (Sumption) appears to be a contraction of " Assumption " (i.e. of the Virgin Mary), the church festival, and to be cognate with Pentecost, Christmas, Easter, &c.' (Patr. Brit. p. 334). This is quite possible, as nearly all the church festivals are recorded in our directories ; but it is more probable, for want of evidence, that both Sumption and Sumpton are variants of Somerton, the *p* being intrusive, as in Thompson or Simpson.

MDB. (co. Glouc.), 2, 0 ; London, 1, 1.

Sunderland.—Local, ' of Sunderland,' a seaport parish in co. Durham ; a great Yorkshire surname that seems early to have passed the borders of the more northern county.

Adam de Sunderland, co. Lanc., 20 Edw. I. R.
Thomas de Sundirland, 1379 : P. T. Yorks. p. 184.
1779. Married—John Sunderland and Dina Dickson : St. Geo. Han. Sq. i. 295.
MDB. (West Rid. Yorks), 31 ; Philadelphia, 11.

Sunman.—Bapt. ' the son of Soneman.' This name occurs as a personal name without surname in the Hundred Rolls (co. Camb.), i. 545.

Soneman ad Cap' Ville, co. Camb., 1273. A.
Sunemanne del Fen, co. Suffolk, ibid.
Soneman de Pote, co. Camb., ibid.
Charles Soneman, co. Camb., ibid.
Roger Soneman, co. Camb., ibid.
William Soneman, co. Suff., ibid.
1887. Married — Henry Sunman, L.R.A.M., of Oxford, to Margaret Elizabeth Noddings : Standard, July 6.
London, 4 ; Oxford, 1.

Sunnett.—Bapt. ; v. Sennett.

Sunter.—Occup. ; v. Sumpter. This corruption still occurs in the district where it has existed at least three centuries. Several entries concerning the family of

Sumpter are thus found in the Prestbury registers, East Cheshire:

1560. Buried—Jees Sunter. xxx. Sept., p. 3.
— — Richard Sunter. xviii. Nov., ibid.
I have accidentally omitted to name the register.

Manchester, 3 ; Boston (U.S.), 1.

Surfleet.—Local, ' of Surfleet,' a parish in co. Lincoln, four miles from Spalding.

(Persona) de Surflet, co. Linc., 1273. A.
1673-4. William Surflett and Mary Gibbs : Marriage Alleg. (Canterbury), p. 108.
MDB. (co. Lincoln), 7.

Surgeon. — Occup. ' the surgeon,' i. e. a chirurgeon. The following entries represent the transition period :

William le Suriegien, co. Northampton, 1273. A.
Robert le Surgien, co. Camb., ibid.
1678. William Holding and Eliz. Surgion : Marriage Alleg. (Canterbury), p. 229.
1719. Bapt.—Abigal, d. Hugh Surgen : St. Jas. Clerkenwell, ii. 115.
MDB. (co. Cumb.), 1 ; Philadelphia, 2.

Surman, Surmon, Sermon. — Occup. ' the shearman.' A.S. *sciran*, to clip (Skeat) ; v. Shearman.

Bartholomew Scireman, co. Camb., 1273. A.
Hugh Scireman, co. Camb., ibid.
Mabil Scireman, co. Camb., ibid.
1661. Married—Thomas Knowlls and Elizabeth Surman : St. Dionis Backchurch, p. 37.
1756. — Daniel Sirman and Ann Ross : St. Geo. Han. Sq. i. 62.
London, 3, 2, 0 ; MDB. (co. Glouc.), 7, 0, 0 ; New York, 2, 0, 0.

Surr, Surre.—Bapt. ' the son of Sayer,' one of the endless forms of this once popular font-name ; v. Sayer.

Ser Manneisin, co. Salop, 1273. A.
Walter fil. Sere, co. Notts, ibid.
1730. Married — John Surr and Eliz. Booth : St. Geo. Chap. Mayfair, p. 161.
1785. — George Surr and Margaret Wilkinson : St. Geo. Han. Sq. i. 376.
London, 3, 0 ; New York, 0, 2.

Surrage ; v. Surridge.

Surrey.—Local, ' of Surrey ' ; cf. Wiltshire, Darbyshire, Lancaster, Devonish, Cornwall, Kent, &c.

John de Surreye, co. Oxf., 1273. A.
1746. Married—Peter Walker and Eliz. Surry : St. Geo. Chap. Mayfair, p. 66.

1798. Married — Joseph (or John) Metcalf and Tamar Surrey: St. Geo. Han. Sq. ii. 183.
London, 1; Philadelphia, 1.

Surreys.—Local, 'the Surreys,' a Surrey man, a man who hailed from that county; cf. Cornish, Cornwallis, Kentish, &c.
Roger le Surreys, co. Suff., 1273. A.
Seman le Sureys, co. Salop, ibid.
Robert Surreys, co. York, ibid.

Surridge, Surrage. — (1) Local, ' of Surridge,' seemingly some spot in co. Somerset.
Adam de Schirrugge, co. Soms., 1 Edw. III: Kirby's Quest, p. 137.
Edith de Schirugge, co. Soms., 1 Edw. III: ibid.
Thomas de Shirigge, co. Soms., 1 Edw. III: ibid. p. 146.
(2) Bapt. 'the son of Sirich.' This seems the more probable origin; cf. Aldridge for Aldrich. But as Surrage and Surridge are familiar to co. Somerset, (1) must be looked upon as having a large share in the parentage.
John Soriche, co. Soms., 1 Edw. III: Kirby's Quest, p. 199.
Eylmer fil. Sirich, co. Suff., 1273. A.
Aubert Syrik, co. Linc., ibid.
Robert Syrik, co. Linc., ibid.
1753. Married—John Surridge and Ann Price: St. Geo. Chap. Mayfair, p. 255.
1754. — Thomas Surridge and Sarah Clayton: St. Geo. Han. Sq. i. 55.
London, 7, 0; MDB. (co. Essex), 9, 0; (co. Soms.), 1, 4; New York, 1, 0.

Surtees. — Local, ' Super Teisam' or ' Sur Tees,' from residence upon the bank of the Tees; an ancient family, co. Durham. Practically of the same class as Tindal, Tweddle, and Teasdale.
Richard super Teisam, 1198. KKK. vi. 63.
John de Surties, bailiff of Newcastle, 1295. PPP.
1787. Married — John Horford and Margaret Surtess: St. Geo. Han. Sq. i. 403.
1802. — Aubone Surtees and Frances Eliz. Honeywood: ibid. ii. 272.
London, 1; Newcastle, 2; MDB. (co. Durham) 12; Philadelphia, 1.

Sutch; v. Such.

Sutcliff, Sutcliffe, Sutliff, Sutlieff. — Local, ' of Sutcliffe,' i.e. the South Cliff, a surname that has made a deep impression upon Yorkshire nomenclature. With Sutliff, cf. Topliff for Topcliff.
Willelmus Sothclyff, of Stanley, 1379: P. T. Yorks. p. 163.

Willelmus de Southclif', of South Owram, 1379: ibid. p. 187.
Adam Southclif', of Wadsworth, 1379: ibid. p. 188.
1588. John Sutcliffe, of Dyneley: Wills at Chester, i. 185.
1746. Married— John Currer and Mary Suttliff: St. Geo. Chap. Mayfair, p. 86.
1794. — Joseph Sutliffe and Mary Richardson: St. Geo. Han. Sq. ii. 106.
MDB. (West Rid. Yorks), 0, 67, 1, 0; Manchester, 2, 31, 0, 0; London, 1, 8, 0, 1; West Rid. Court Dir., 1, 46, 1, 0; Philadelphia, 1, 21, 1, 0.

Suter, Sutter, Sutor.—Occup. 'the souter,' i.e. the shoemaker; v. Soutar.
Cf. Adam Wild, *sutter*, 1379: P. T. Yorks. p. 17.
Jordan Sutor, co. Hunts, 1273. A.
Adam Sutor, co. Camb., ibid.
Matilda Sutor, co. Hunts, ibid.
Isabel la Sutare, co. Camb., ibid.
1803. Married — William Suter and Ann Williams: St. Geo. Han. Sq. ii. 288.
London, 12, 0, 1; Philadelphia, 10, 23, 0.

Suthery, Sutthery. — Local, ' of Southery,' a parish in co. Norfolk.
William de Souther', co. Camb., 1273. A.
Robert de Suthereye, co. Wilts, ibid.
MDB. (co. Bucks), 4, 3; Philadelphia, 1, 0.

Sutliff; v. Sutcliff.

Sutterle, Sutterley, Suttley. —Local, possibly sometimes a variant ' of Southery' (v. Suthery), of which the following seems to be an intermediate form:
Roger de Soterle, co. Suff., 20 Edw. I. R.
This closely resembles the American form Sutterle; but more probably Sutterley is a distinct name from Suthery, the one being the Souther-ley, the other the Souther-hey (v. Lee and Hey).
London (Suttley), 1; Philadelphia, 3, 3, 0.

Suttle, Suttill. — (1) Local, ' of Soothill,' a township in the parish of Dewsbury, W. Rid. Yorks, in the neighbourhood of which the surname is chiefly found.
Ricardus de Sutill', 1379: P. T. Yorks. p. 182.
(2) Nick. ' the subtle,' the artful. O.F. *sutil.* No doubt this is also represented in our modern directories.

Adam le Sutel, London, 1273. A.
Robert le Sotele, co. Bedf., ibid.
1606. Buried—Thomas Sutle: St. Peter, Cornhill, i. 162.
London, 2, 0; Philadelphia, 2, 1; Otley (West Rid. Yorks), 3, 0.

Sutton. — Local, ' of Sutton,' i.e. the south town, the south enclosure. The places so called are too numerous to mention. Lower says there are over sixty ecclesiastically marked districts, chapelries, and parishes in England of this name. Of course this does not include small manors and farms; cf. Norton, Weston, Eaton, or Easton.
Johannes de Soutton, 1379: P. T. Yorks. p. 173.
Johannes de Sutton, 1379: ibid. p. 100.
Symon de Sutton, 1379: ibid. p. 98.
Geoffrey de Suttone, co. Hunts, 1273. A.
Saer de Sutton, co. York, ibid.
Albinus de Sutton, co. Notts, 20 Edw. I. R.
1593. Married—Jeames Sutton and Margaret Bonnor: St. Dionis Backchurch, p. 12.
London, 72; Philadelphia, 75.

Swabey, Swaby.—Local, ' of Swaby,' a parish in co. Lincoln, near Louth.
Roger de Swaby, co. Linc., 1273. A.
1707. Married— John Sadler and Eliz. Swaby: St. Geo. Han. Sq. i. 164.
1791. — John Miller and Mary Swaby: ibid. ii. 68.
London, 4, 0; Crockford, 3, 2; MDB. (co. Bucks), 1, 0; Philadelphia, 0, 1.

Swaffield. — Local, ' of Swafield,' a parish in co. Norfolk.
William de Swafeld, co. Bedf., 20 Edw. I. R.
1750. Married—George Swaffield and Kezia Overly: St. Geo. Chap. Mayfair, p. 174.
London, 3; MDB. (co. Derby), 2.

Swain, Swaine, Swainson. —(1) Bapt. 'the son of Swain,' literally a young lad; cf. Brownswain, Boatswain. Swainson is a well-known surname in cos. Lancaster and York.
Alicia Swayneson, 1379: P. T. Yorks. p. 171.
Robertus Swaynne, 1379: ibid. p. 135.
Thomas Swaynesson, 1379: ibid. p. 193.
Sweyn de Canewyk, co. Linc., Hen. III-Edw. I. K.
Adam fil. Suani, co. Linc., 1273. A.
William Svein, co. Suff., ibid.
(2) Occup. 'the swain,' i.e. the peasant, the servant.

John le Swein, co. Oxf., 1273. A.
Robert le Swein, co. Oxf., ibid.
Geoffrey le Sueyn, co. Norf., ibid.
1583. James Swaneson, of Ulverston:
Lancashire Wills at Richmond, i. 266.
London, 21, 4, 4 ; Philadelphia, 39, 0, 0.

Swainston, Swanston. —
Bapt. 'the son of Swain.' A corruption of Swainson and Swanson ; cf. Johnston and Johnstone, strongly represented in the London Directory, and not always local. Also cf. Snelston and Snelson.

1754. Married—Thomas Swanston and Anne Butler : St. Geo. Chap. Mayfair, p. 274.
1787. — John Brown and Eliz. Swanston : St. Geo. Han. Sq. i. 408.
London, 3, 2.

Swale, Swales.—Local : (1) 'of Swallow Hill,' a hamlet near Barnsley, co. Yorks. At least there is evidence in favour of this view. (2) 'At the Swale,' from residence beside the river of that name, whence Swaledale. Doubtless this will be deemed the more satisfactory solution. Swales is the genitive form ; cf. Williams, Jones, Brooks, Styles, &c. The first reference is in Darton, the parish in which Swallow Hill lies.

Isabella de Swahill, 1379 : P. T. Yorks. p. 88.
Robertus de Swaloughill, 1379 : ibid. p. 51.
Ricardus Swale, 1379 : ibid. p. 70.
Thomas de Swale, 1379 : ibid. p. 252.
1754. Married — Matthew Swales and Dorothy Johnson : St. Geo. Chap. Mayfair, p. 273.
MDB. (West Rid. Yorks), 15, 7 ; West Riding Court Dir., 6, 2.

Swallow. — (1) Nick. 'the swallow' ; cf. Nightingale, Sparrow, Goldfinch, &c. Fr. *hirondelle.* (2) Local, 'of Swallow,' a parish in co. Lincoln, four miles from Caistor.

Helevisa Swalwe, co. Hunts, 1273. A.
Ralph de Swallwe, co. Linc., Hen. III-Edw. I. K.
John Swalewe, co. Soms., 1 Edw. III : Kirby's Quest, p. 127.
Thomas Swalowe, 1379 : P. T. Yorks. p. 219.
Ricardus Swalough, 1379 : ibid. p. 30.
John Swalowe. H.
1624. Married—Samuell Swallow and Francis Denyson : St. Jas. Clerkenwell, iii. 54.
London, 7 ; Philadelphia, 7.

Swalwell.—Local, 'of Swalwell,' a township in the parish of Whickham, near Gateshead, co. Durham.

MDB. (co. Durham), 2.

Swan, Swann, Swanne, Swanson.—(1) Bapt. 'the son of Swan,' i.e. Swain, q.v.

Hamo fil. Swañ, C. R., 30 Hen. III.
Swan le Riche, co. Linc., 1273. A.
Alexander Swan, co. Camb., ibid.
Agnes Swanson, temp. Eliz. ZZ.
Magota Swan, 1379 : P. T. Yorks. p. 24.
Matilda Swanson, 1379 : ibid. p. 171.

(2) Nick. 'the swan' ; cf. our modern 'swanlike.'

Geoffrey Svan, co. Camb., 1273. A.
Simon le Swon, 1307. M.
Henry le Swan. H.
Nicholas le Swon, C. R., 2 Hen. V.

(3) Local, 'at the Swan,' an early sign-name.

Thomas atte Swan, C. R., 2 Hen. IV. pt. ii.
London, 16, 19, 1, 5 ; West Rid. Court Dir. (Swann), 5 ; Philadelphia, 19, 9, 0, 8.

Swancock, Swanncott. — (1) Bapt. 'the son of Swan' (?), q.v., with suffix -*cock* ; v. Cocks, and cf. Willcock, Simcock, &c. (2) Local, 'at the swan-cote' (?), from residence beside the cote wherein the swans were kept. Cf. Glasscock and Glasscott for a similar confusion of suffix.

1548. Buried—Thomas Swancock : St. Michael, Cornhill, p. 178.
1759. Married—John Bye and Mary Swancoat : St. Geo. Han. Sq. i. 85.
London, 0, 1.

Swanherd.—Occup. 'the swanherd,' a keeper of swans, an important calling when this bird was a favourite roast ; cf. Rookherd and Gozzard.

William le Swonherde, c. 1300. M.

Swanson.—A variant of Swanson ; v. Swain and Swan.

London, 5 ; Philadelphia, 8.

Swanston.—Bapt. ; v. Swainston.

Swanton. — Local, 'of Swanton,' three parishes in co. Norfolk, viz. Swanton Abbott, Swanton Morley, and Swanton Novers.

Nicholas de Swanton, co. Kent, 1273. A.
Thomas de Swanton or Swantun, co. Norf., ibid.
William de Swanton, co. Wilts, 20 Edw. I. R.
1685. Married—Thomas Swanton and Christian Roll : St. Dionis Backchurch, p. 40.
1782. — James Simpson and Ann Swanton : St. Geo. Han. Sq. i. 336.
MDB. (co. Hereford), 1 ; Boston (U.S.), 6 ; Philadelphia, 2.

Swanwick.—Local, 'of Swanwick,' a hamlet in the parish of Alfreton, co. Derby. The meaning is 'the *wick* or dwelling of Swan,' the original settler ; v. Swan and Wick.

1604. Margaret Swanwick, of Worswall : Wills at Chester, i. 186.
1619. Hugh Swanwick, of Swanwick Green : ibid.
1668. John Swanwick and Mary Winspeare : Marriage Alleg. (Canterbury), p. 247.
1711. Married — Thomas Parish and Hannah Swanwick : St. Mary Aldermary, p. 41.
MDB. (co. Ches.), 3 ; (co. Derby), 2 ; Manchester, 1.

Swarbrick, Swarbrigg. — Local, 'of Swarbrick' or Swartbrick, some small spot in the neighbourhood of Winmarleigh, co. Lanc. Probably the suffix is -*brigg* =bridge ; cf. Philbrick.

1581. John Swartbrecke, of Rossaker : Lancashire Wills at Richmond, i. 267.
1622. Edward Swarthbrecke, of Much Singleton : ibid.
1669. Margaret Swartbreck, of Winmerleigh : ibid.
1680. Joanna Swarbrick, of Winmerleigh : ibid.
MDB. (co. Lanc.), 4, 0 ; Manchester, 6, 0 ; Philadelphia, 0, 2.

Swatman ; v. Sweetman.

Swayne.—Bapt. ; v. Swain, of which it is a variant.

1600-1. Ellis Swayne or Swaine, co. Dorset : Reg. Univ. Oxf. vol. ii. pt. ii. p. 246.
1738. Married — Joseph Swayne and Mary Jason : St. Geo. Han. Sq. i. 21.
Crockford, 2 ; Philadelphia, 22.

Sweatinbed.—Nick.

Alan Swet in bedde, Close Roll, 3 Edw. I.

Sweatman.—(1) Bapt. 'the son of Swetman' ; v. Sweetman. (2) Local, 'of Swetenham' ; v. Swetnam.

Crockford (1891), 1.

Sweepstake. — Local. The suffix is -*stake*, as in Copestake, &c.

I simply record it because it so nearly approaches in appearance our modern ' sweepstake.'

Robertus Swepstak, 1379 : P. T. Yorks. p. 208.

Sweet.—(1) Bapt. ' the son of Sweet,' analogous to the early introduced French ' Douce '; v. Dowse. (2) Nick. ' the sweet '; cf. Good.

Swet' le Bone, co. Norf., 1273. A.
Adam Swet, co. Oxf., ibid.
Roger Swet, co. Camb., ibid.
Roger Swet, Fines Roll, 11 Edw. I.
Walter Swete, co. Soms., 1 Edw. III : Kirby's Quest, p. 130.
Johannes Suete, 1379 : P. T. Yorks. p. 89.
Johannes Swete, 1379 : ibid. p. 295.
1578. Robert Sweete and Johanna Sweete : Marriage Lic. (London), i. 80.
1700. Bapt. — Ann, d. James Sweet : St. Jas. Clerkenwell, i. 389.
London, 14 ; Philadelphia, 10.

Sweetapple. — (1) Nick. (?), ' sweet apple '; v. Sweet. (2) Local, ' at the sweet-apple,' from residence beside a particular sweet apple-tree. This is the more probable origin ; cf. Crabb, Crabtree, Appletree, Plumptre, Ash, Nash, Birch, &c. It is evidently a West-country surname.

Edward Swetapple. RR. 1.
Roger Sweetappull, C. R., 4 Hen. V.
1585-6. Henry Gatcombe and Alice Sweethable (co. Middlesex) : Marriage Lic. (London), i. 147.
1613. Married — Edmund Sweetaple and Sibille Bennet : Reg. Broad Chalke, co. Wilts, p. 4.
1614. — Thomas Bennet and Margrett Sweetaple : ibid.
1687. Married — John Sweetaple and Elizabeth Brett : St. Michael, Cornhill, p. 45.
MDB. (co. Soms.), 1.

Sweetcock.—Bapt. ' the son of Sweetcock.' The name occurs as a single personal name in the Hundred Rolls. Of course the term is one of endearment originally. ' Nice young fellow' is our modern equivalent (v. Cocks). The feminine form given below is ' confusion worse confounded.' v. Sweet, and cf. Lovecock, frequently found as a baptismal name at the same period.

Adam Swetcoc, co. Camb., 1273. A.
Swetecoka de Hornden, C. R., 16 Edw. I.

Sweetgood.—Bapt. 'the son of Sweetgood.' One of the many surnames with prefix *-sweet* or suffix *-good* ; cf. Scattergood and Sweetlove.

Alicia Swytegode, 1379 : P. T. Yorks. p. 71.
Agnes Swythgode, 1379 : ibid.

Sweeting, Sweeten. — (1) Bapt. ' the son of Sweeting '; v. Sweet. Lower says, ' Sweeting, an old A.S. personal name. In Domesday, Sueting, Suetingus.' The Testa de Neville gives one instance betokening a local origin. But all the East-coast Sweetings are of fontal origin ; v. Browning or Harding.

Richard Swetyne, co. Norf., 1273. A.
Thomas Swetyene, co. Norf., ibid.
Willelmus Swyting, 1379 : P. T. Yorks. p. 221.
Isabella Swyting, 1379 : ibid.
Robert Swyting, 1379 : ibid.

(2) Local, ' of Sweeting.'

John de Sweting, co. Wilts, Hen. III-Edw. I. K.
Robert Swetynge, co. Soms., 1 Edw. III : Kirby's Quest, p. 265.
London, 7, 0 ; Philadelphia, 5, 9.

Sweetlove.—Nick. 'Sweetlove,' a term of endearment. Probably a translation of Douceamour.

Cf. Robert Douceamour, Close Roll, 8 Hen. IV.

It may be a baptismal name, judging by the first reference below ; v. Sweet.

Swetelove (without surname), co. Camb., 1273. A.
Margery Swetelove, co. Camb., ibid.
Peter Swetlove, co. Camb., ibid.
1572. Alexander Sweetlove, of Sharples : Wills at Chester, i. 186.
1614. Jane Sweetlove, of Great Lever : ibid.
1633. Margaret Sweetlove, of Sharples : ibid. ii. 212.
MDB. (co. Kent), 1.

Sweetman, Swetman, Swatman. — (1) Bapt. ' the son of Sweetman,' the same as Sweet, with the augmentative *-man* appended ; cf. Bateman and Tiddiman ; v. Sweet.

Osmund fil. Swetman, co. Berks, Hen. III-Edw. I. K.
Swetman (without surname), co. Oxf., 1273. A.
Swetman fil. Edith, co. Oxf., ibid.
Swetman de Heligham, co. Norf., ibid.
Sweteman Textor, co. Bucks, ibid.

Adam Swetman, co. Oxf., 1273. A.
John Swetemon, C. R., 51 Edw. III.
1757. Married—William Sweetman and Penelope Dunn : St. Geo. Han. Sq. i. 74.

(2) Local ; v. Swetenham and Swetnam.

London, 3, 0, 2 ; Philadelphia, 5, 0, 0.

Sweetmouth. — Nick. ' with the sweet mouth '; v. Sweet.

Robert Swetemouth. D.
William Swetmouth. Q.
John Swetemouthe, C. R., 35 Hen. VI.

Sweetpintle.—Nick.

John Swetpintel, co. Norf., 1273. A.

Sweetser, Sweitzer, Sweetzer, Sweetsir, Switzer.—? Local. Lower suggests ' Switzer,' a Swiss, a native of Switzerland. The surname is no doubt foreign, but was early settled in England, and has acquired an English appearance. At the time of writing there is being advertised ' Schweitzer's Cocoatina.' Cotgrave quotes :

' A Switzer's bellie and a drunkard's face
Are no true signes of penetentiall grace.'
' Leading three thousand must'red men in pay,
Of French, Scots, Alman, Swisser, and the Dutch.'
Drayton's Poems, p. 84.

Richard Swetesire, C. R., 29 Edw. III.
1584. Richard Sweetser and Cecily Harrys : Marriage Lic. (London), i. 131.
1778. Married—John Godfrey Sweetser and Jane Mottea : St. Geo. Han. Sq. i. 283.
London, 2, 0, 0, 0, 0 ; Philadelphia, 1, 13, 0, 0, 11 ; Boston (U.S.) (Sweetsir), 1 ; New York, 7, 5, 2, 0, 14.

Swetenham, Swettenham, Sweetenham, Sweetnam. — Local, ' of Swettenham,' a parish in co. Chester, five miles from Congleton ; v. Swetnam for modifications.

Richard Swetinam, co. Bucks, 1273. A.
William de Swetenham, co. Ches., 1297 : East Cheshire, ii. 644.
Roger de Swetenham, co. Ches., 1366 : ibid.
1561. Married — William Swettenam and Agnes Plante : Reg. Prestbury Ch., co. Chester, p. 5.
1584. William Swettnam, co. Ches. : Reg. Univ. Oxf. vol. ii. pt. ii. p. 135.
1597. Laurence Swettenham of Somerford : Wills at Chester, i. 186.
1611. Thomas Swettenham, of Swettenham : ibid.
MDB. (co. Ches.), 2, 1, 0, 0 ; Manchester, 0, 0, 1, 1.

Swetnam, Swetman. — (1)

Local, 'of Swetenham,' q.v. ; cf. Debnam and Deadman for Debenham, Putnam and Putman for Puttenham, &c.

1649. Bapt.—Edmund, s. of Edmund and Jone Swetnam : Reg. Stourton, co. Wilts, p. 11.
1650. — Manuell, s. of Edmund and Jone Swetnam : ibid.
1652. — John, s. of Edmund and Jone Swetman : ibid.
1655. — Abraham, s. of Edmund and Jone Swetnam : ibid. p. 12.
1664. — John, s. of John and Deborah Swetnam : St. Jas. Clerkenwell, i. 124.
1666. — Dorothy, d. John and Deborah Swetman : ibid. p. 129.

Afterwards invariably Swetman, the real local origin thus becoming lost. (2) For baptismal origin of Swetman, v. Sweetman.

Swift.—Nick. 'the swift.'

One of a class of names implying speed, comprehending Purchas, Shearwind, Lightfoot, Golightly, Bullet, &c., given to pursuivants and couriers. Purchas was the favourite.

Matilda Swyft, co. Camb., 1273. A.
Roger Swyft, co. Bucks, ibid.
Arnulph Swyft, co. Norf., ibid.
Ralph Swyft, courier to Edward III: Issues of the Exchequer, edited by Frederick Devon.
Henricus Swyft, 1379 : P. T. Yorks. p. 16.
1754. Married — Godfrey Swift and Christiana Williams : St. Geo. Han. Sq. i. 55.
London, 24 ; Philadelphia, 51.

Swinbank.—Local, 'of Swinbank,'

probably the bank where the swine fed. The spot is somewhere in or near the parish of Ravenstonedale, co. Westm.

Reynold Sywnebank, 1541 : Hist. and Traditions of Ravenstonedale, co. Westm., W. Nicholls, p. 113.
Cuthbert Swynebank, 1541 : ibid.
Liverpool, 1 ; MDB. (co. Durham), 2.

Swinburn, Swinburne, Swinborn, Swinborne, Swynburne. — Local, ' of Swinburn,'

a township in the parish of Chollerton, co. Northumberland.

William de Swinburne, 1278, co. Northumb. : Lower's Patr. Brit. p. 336.
John de Swynburne, co. Northumb., 20 Edw. I. R.
Nicholas de Swynburne, co. Northumb.: ibid.
William de Swyneburne, co. Northumb.: ibid.

1576. Henry Swynburn, co. Yorks : Reg. Univ. Oxf. vol. ii. pt. ii. p. 71.
1793. Married—Paul Binfield and Mary Frances Swinburne : St. Geo. Han. Sq. ii. 101.
London, 1, 2, 1, 1, 0 ; MDB. (co. Northumberland), 1, 1, 0, 0, 0 ; (co. Hereford), 0, 0, 0, 0, 1.

Swindell, Swindle. — Local,

' of Swindale,' a chapelry in the parish of Shap, co. Westmoreland.

1540. Buried — Alys Swyndelle : St. Dionis Backchurch, p. 178.
1608. Richard Westrawe and Agnes Swindell : Marriage Lic. (London), i. 308.
1790. Married — John Swindell and Lydia Mullins : St. Geo. Han. Sq. ii. 36.
London, 4, 0 ; Boston (U.S.), 1, 1.

Swindells, Swindles.—Local,

' of Swindells,' most probably the spot referred to in the following :

'A branch of the family of Howford held a small estate here (Bosden) in the 14th century, called "Swyndelves" ' : East Cheshire, i. 264.

This was in the parish of Cheadle, in which immediate district all our Swindells have sprung (for the suffix, v. Delf).

Roger Swyndels, of Marple, 1522 : East Cheshire, ii. 52 n.
1561. Married—Humfry Swyndells and Isabell Woorthe : Prestbury Ch. (co. Ches.), p. 5.
William Swindells, of Stockport : Wills at Chester (1545-1620), p. 186.
John Swindells, of Northenden, 1620 : ibid.
1656. Bapt. — Ursula, d. John Swendalls : St. Jas. Clerkenwell, i. 195.
London, 2, 0 ; Manchester, 10, 0 ; MDB. (co. Ches.), 7, 0 ; Boston (U.S.), 1, 0 ; Philadelphia, 1, 1.

Swinden, Swindin. — Local,

' of Swinden,' a township in the parish of Gisburne, W. Rid. Yorks ; also a township in the parish of Kirkby Overblow, W. Rid. Yorks. Only two entries separate the following :

Johannes de Swyndeyn, 1379 : P. T. Yorks. p. 285.
Thomas Swynhyrd, 1379 : ibid.
Adam de Swynden', 1379 : ibid. p. 93.
Johannes de Swyndene, 1379 : ibid.
1790. Married—George Bateman and Martha Swinden : St. Geo. Han. Sq. ii. 46.
Sheffield, 1, 2 ; West Rid. Court Dir., 2, 1 ; Philadelphia, 1, 0.

Swindlehurst, Swinglehurst.—Local, ' of Swindlehurst.'

This is a North-English surname, but I cannot find the precise locality. It is quite clear that

Swinglehurst is a corruption of Swindlehurst ; v. Swindell and Hurst. The meaning would seem to be 'the wood in the swine-dale.'

1576. John Swinlehurst, of Chepin : Lancashire Wills at Richmond, i. 267.
1594. William Swindlehurst, of Clitheroe : Wills at Chester, i. 186.
1623. Bapt. — Richard, s. Roger Swinglehurst : St. Jas. Clerkenwell, i. 96.
1635. William Swinglehurst, of Chepin : Lancashire Wills at Richmond, i. 267.
Manchester, 0, 1 ; MDB. (West Rid. Yorks), 4, 0 ; Boston (U.S.), Philadelphia, 0, 1.

Swinfen.—Local, ' of Swinfen,'

a hamlet in the parish of Wreford, co. Stafford. An old family bearing this name resided here.

1659. Married—Stephen Casingale and Eliza Swinffon : St. Jas. Clerkenwell, i. 103.
1672. Ralph Swynfen and Eliz. Moreton : Marriage Alleg. (Canterbury), p. 203.
1795. Married—Samuel Swinfen and Susanna Durrant : St. Geo. Han. Sq. ii. 130.
London, 2.

Swinford.—Local, ' of Swinford,'

parishes in cos. Leicester and Stafford ; also a tithing in the parish of Cumnor, co. Berks.

William de Swyneford, co. Suff., 1273. A.
William de Swynneford, co. Hunts, ibid.
1626. Bapt.—Marye, d. Peeter Swinford : Reg. Canterbury Cath., p. 6.
1633. — Eliz., d. Peter Swinforde : ibid. p. 7.
MDB. (co. Kent), 5.

Swingler.—Occup. 'the swingler,' i.e. a flax-beater, possibly a

wool-beater, hence ' swinglingstick, a stick used for beating or opening wool or flax. Lanc.' (Halliwell). ' Fleyhe, swyngyl, tribulum' : Prompt. Parv. 'Swingle, a staff for beating flax ' (Skeat, and see his article).

Nicholas Swingler, 1682 : St. Peter, Cornhill, p. 9.
London, 3 ; Derby, 5.

Swinhoe.—Local, 'of Swinhoe,'

a township in Northumberland.

Newcastle, 1 ; Oxford, 2.

Swinnart, Swinyard, Swinehart.—Occup. 'the swine-herd ';

cf. Calvert, Coward, Stoddart, &c. Swinyard is almost certainly a corruption of swine-herd. No traces of the local term ; cf. y in Sawyer, Bowyer, &c. 'Swinyard, a keeper of swine. "Chandlers, herdsmen, or swinyards, coopers, blacksmiths," &c. (Bishop's Marrow of Astrology, p. 36)': Halliwell.

Walter le Swynhurde, co. Soms., 1 Edw. III: Kirby's Quest, p. 200.
Thomas le Swenhurde, co. Soms., 1 Edw. III: ibid. p. 207.
Robert Swynherd, C. R., 7 Edw. III. pt. ii.
John Swynhird, co. York. W. 2.
Clement Swynhird, 1379: P. T. Howdenshire, p. 9.
Nicholas Swynard, 1379: P. T. Yorks. p. 150.
Johannes Swyndherd, 1379: ibid. p. 59.
Wylymot Swynhirde, 1379: ibid. p. 256.
1668. Nicholas Swinnarde and Susanne Andrews: Marriage Alleg. (Canterbury), p. 233.
London, o, 3, o; Philadelphia, o, o, 1; New York, o, 2, o.

Swinnerton, Swinerton. — Local, 'of Swinnerton,' a parish in co. Stafford, three miles from Stone.

Robert de Swinnerton, co. Staff.: Hen. III-Edw. I. K.
John de Swynnerton, co. Derby, 20 Edw. I. R.
1563. John Swynerton and May Fawnte: Marriage Lic. (London), i. 27.
1609. Henry Swinarton, London: Reg. Univ. Oxf, vol. ii. pt. ii. p. 305.
1617. Randle Swinnerton, of Church Lawton: Wills at Chester, i. 186.
1802. Married—William Utterston and Henrietta Swinerton: St. Geo. Han. Sq. ii. 258.
MDB. (co. Stafford), 1, o; London, 1, o; New York, 1, o; Boston (U.S.), o, 2.

Swinstead.—Local, 'of Swinstead,' a parish in co. Lincoln.

Gocelin de Swynested, co. Linc., 1273. A.
1583. Richard Swinsted, *farrier*, of Cheshunt, co. Herts, and Judith Hammond: Marriage Lic. (London), i. 119.
MDB. (co. Bedford), 3; London, 2; Oxford, 1.

Swinyard; v. Swinnart.

Swire, Swyer. — Offic. 'the squire,' early corrupted to Swyer or Swire.

Ricardus Sqwyer, 1379: P. T. Yorks. p. 268.
Thomas Swyer, 1379: ibid. p. 266.
Willelmus Swyer, 1379: ibid.
1618. Bapt.—Anna, d. of Julin Squire, *vulgaritur*, John Swyer, of Skipton: Reg. Skipton Ch.

In the same church is a mural tablet to John Swire, 1760.

1807. Married—William Coates and Mary Swyer: St. Geo. Han. Sq. ii. 362.
London, 3, 3; West Rid. Court Dir., 2, o; Philadelphia, 4, o.

Swithenbank, Swithinbank. —Local, 'of Swithenbank,' i. e. the bank on which Swithen, the first proprietor, had settled; v. Swithin. I cannot find the spot. It is a North-English surname; cf. Gillbanks, Windebank, &c.

Manchester, 1, o; MDB. (West Rid. Yorks), 2, o; London, o, 1; New York, 1, o.

Swithin.—Bapt. 'the son of Swithin'; cf. local Swithinbank.

Thomas Swethyne, co. Norf., 1273. A.
1609. Bapt. — Anne, d. William Gwythen: St. Jas. Clerkenwell, i. 57.
1751. Married—John Tuckman and Margaret Swithin: St. Geo. Chap. Mayfair, p. 203.
Tynemouth, 1.

Switzer; v. Sweetser.

Sworder.—Occup. 'the sworder,' a bladesmith, a maker of swords. M.E. *swerd*.

John le Serdere, c. 1300. M.
John Swerder. Z.
Henry Swerder. H.
William Serdier, Close Roll, 16 Edw. III. pt. ii.
London, 1.

Swordslipper. — Occup. 'a sheather,' one who made swordslips; v. Sheather.

Johannes Swerdslyper, 1379: P. T. Yorks. p. 251.
Johanna Swerdsliper, 1379: ibid. p. 25.

This name as a specific occupation occurs in the registers of St. Nicholas, Newcastle, till the close of the 16th century.

William Browne, *sword-slipper*, 1576: Brand's Newcastle, ii. 360.
Robert Heslop, *sword-slipper*, 1586: ibid.

Swyer; v. Swire.

Sybry; v. Sibary.

Syddall; v. Siddall.

Sydenham.—Local, 'of Sydenham,' a parish in co. Kent, near Blackheath.

John de Sydenham, co. Soms., 1 Edw. III: Kirby's Quest, p. 182.
Simon de Sidenham, co. Soms., 1 Edw. III: ibid. p. 192.
1586-7. Roger Raston and Rachael Sydnam: Marriage Lic. (London), i. 159.
1674. Humphey Sydenham and Eliz. St. Johns, *widow*: Marriage Alleg. (Canterbury), p. 231.
1803. Married—Thomas Sydenham and Frances Bunbury: St. Geo. Han. Sq. ii. 295.
London, 4.

Sydney; v. Sidney.

Syer, Syers.—Bapt. 'the son of Saier,' one of the many forms of Sayer, q.v. The fuller form was Sigher or Sighar.

Saier Perkesgate, C. R., 17 Ric. II.
1637. Married—Roberte Syers and Ann Washington: St. Jas. Clerkenwell, i. 69.
1768. — Robert Syer and Ann Brown: St. Geo. Han. Sq. i. 173.
1796. — John Syer and Catherine Greene: ibid. ii. 157.
London, 3, 2; Philadelphia, o, 5.

Sykes, Sikes.—Local, 'at the syke,' from residence beside a sike, i.e. a stream. One of the greatest of Yorkshire surnames. It has ramified in a marvellous manner. '*Sike*, a gutter, a stream. North England' (Halliwell). Sykes is almost the invariable dress; cf. Dykes for Dikes. The suffix -s is the genitive form, as in Jones, Brooks, Holmes, Williams, &c., meaning Sykes' son. Sometimes it may mean residence beside two streams, as in one of my references below; then Sykes is plural. Cf. Beck, Brook, Brooks, Gott, &c.

Robertus del Syke, 1379: P. T. Yorks. p. 190.
Rogerus del Sykes, 1379: ibid.
Johannes del Cyke, 1379: ibid. p. 211.
Agnes del Syke, 1379: ibid. p. 212.
Henricus del Syke, 1379: ibid. p. 178.
1794. Married—Samuel Weeden Sykes and Jemima Jones: St. Geo. Han. Sq. ii. 115.
1804. — James Sikes and Eleanor Adie: ibid. p. 300.
West Rid. Court Dir., 87, 3; Philadelphia, 58, 3.

Sylvester; v. Silvester.

Symcox; v. Simcock.

Symes, Syms, Symmes. — Bapt. 'the son of Simon,' from the nick. Sim or Sime; v. Sim.

Margret Symes, died in Virginia, 1624: Hotten's Lists of Emigrants, p. 243.
Alexander Symes, bound for Virginia, 1635: ibid. p. 138.
1788. Married — William Syms and Mary Griffiths: St. Geo. Han. Sq. ii. 2.
1794. — Joseph Symes and Amelia Lock: ibid. p. 108.
1802. — John Greenwood and Mary Ann Symmes: ibid. p. 266.
London, 13, 3, o; Philadelphia, o, o, 3.

Symonds, Symmons, Symondson, Symons. —Bapt. 'the son of Simon.' The *d* is excrescent, as fully shown under Simon, q.v. I cannot find any traces of Sigismund, otherwise it might easily be the parent of some of our Symmonds, &c.

Thomas Symond, co. Suff., 1273. A. Alice fil. Symon, co. Oxf., ibid. Maurice fil. Symon, co. Oxf., ibid. 1587. Married—Thomas Holland and Christabell Symondes: St. Dionis Backchurch, p. 11. 1664. Buried—Goodwife Symmons, of this parish: ibid. p. 235. 1722. Bapt. — Symmonds Symmonds, the mother a lodger at Mr. Kempton's, *porter*: ibid. p. 158.

London, 1, 8, 20, 2, 29; Philadelphia, 0, 3, 3, 0, 0.

Sympson.—Bapt. 'the son of Simon,' q.v. The *p* is intrusive, as in Thompson, Hampson, &c.

Willelmus Symmeson', 1397: P. T. Yorks. p. 7. Johannes Symmeson', 1379: ibid. p. 10. 1554-5. Married — Dominick Croope and Jone Symson: St. Dionis Backchurch, p. 3. 1763. — John Sympson and Ann Blower: St. Geo. Han. Sq. i. 118. London, 5; Philadelphia, 1.

Syms.—Bapt.'the son of Simon'; v. Symes and Sim.

Synnett, Synnot, Synnott.—Bapt.; v. Sennett.

Syratt, Syrett; v. Sired.

Syre; v. Sire.

Syson. — Bapt. 'the son of Sybil'; v. Sisson.

1759. Married—Peter Syson and Mary Dawson: St. Geo. Han. Sq. i. 89. 1772. — Jasper Syson and Jane Watkin: ibid. p. 223. West Rid. (Yorks) Court Dir., 1.

T

Tabberer, Taberer, Tabor, Tabrar, Taber. — Occup. 'the taborer,' a player on the tabor or tabour (cf. tambourine), a small drum. There are many entries of this vocation. With the shortened Taber or Tabor, cf. Pepper for Pepperer.

John le Taburer, co. Northants, 1273. A. Peter le Taburer, Close Roll, 17 Edw. I. William le Tabourer. B. Edmund Tabour. V. Robert Tabur, co. Soms., 1 Edw. III : Kirby's Quest, p. 188. 1616. Humphrey Tabor, co. Somerset: Reg. Univ. Oxf. vol. ii. pt. ii. p. 357. 1775. Married — David Yetman and Eliz. Tabor: St. Geo. Han. Sq. i. 258. 1780. Robert Taber and Ann Atterbury: ibid. p. 314. London, 1, 2, 4, 1, 0; Boston (U.S.), 1, 0, 4, 0, 18.

Taberner.—Occup. 'the taberner,' i.e. innkeeper; v. Taverner. '*Tabern*, a cellar (North); see Ray's EnglishWords,1674,p. 48. *Taberna*, a tabyrn, a tavern, or inn, Nominale MS. Hence Taberner, a tavernkeeper' (Halliwell). Probably this form still exists as a surname, although I have not met with it in registers of the present century.

William Tabernator,co. Berks,1273. A. Benedict Taberner, co. Devon, ibid. Eustace Tabnar', co. Oxf., ibid. Willelmus Taburner, 1379: P. T. Yorks. p. 12. 1764. Married — Henry Taberner and Ann Perry: St. Geo. Han. Sq. i. 135.

Tabler, Tableter. — Occup. 'the tabler' or 'the tableter,' a maker of tables or tablets for putting down daily expenses, &c., of slate, wax, &c.

'A pair of tables all of ivory, And a pointel, ypolished fetisly, And wrote alway the names as he stood.' Chaucer, C. T. 7323-5.

Also tables for backgammon or chess.

1530. 'Item, the same daye paied to John the hardewarman for . . . 2 coffers, a payer (pair) of tabulles and chesses, . . . etc.': Privy Purse Expenses, Henry VIII, p. 51. Roger Tablour, c. 1300. M. Bartholomew le Tabler, ibid. Richard le Tableter, ibid. Geoffrey le Tableter, C. R., 19 Edw. II. pt. ii. Bartholomew le Tableter, London. X.

Tabor, Tabrar; v. Tabberer.

Tackley.—Local (1), 'of Tackley,' a parish in co. Oxford; (2) 'of Takeley,' a parish in co. Essex. These two surnames, Tackley and Takeley, are no doubt inextricably mixed.

William de Takeleye,co. Essex, 1273. A. Agnes de Takele, co. Oxf., ibid. Robert de Takkele, co. Oxf., ibid. (Villani) de Tackeleg', co. Essex, 20 Edw. I. R. 1800. Married — Robert Starling and Ann Tackley: St. Geo. Han. Sq. ii. 225. London, 4.

Tacon. — Bapt. 'the son of Tacoln.' This is a Norfolk and Suffolk surname. Hence the name

of Tacolneston, a parish in co. Norfolk, i.e. the town of Tacoln.

Eustace de Tacolnestun, co. Norf., 1273. A. MDB. (co. Suffolk), 6.

Tadhunter, Tadman (?). — Occup. 'a fox-hunter'; v. Todhunter.

1798. Married—Francis Tadman and Mary Young: St. Geo. Han. Sq. ii. 184. London, 1, 5.

Tadley. — Local, 'of Tadley,' a parish in co. Hants. Possibly, however, this surname is a modification of Tadlow; v. Tadloo.

Philadelphia, 3.

Tadloo.—Local, 'of Tadlow,' a parish in co. Camb.

Roysia de Tadelowe, co. Camb., 1273. A. London, 1.

Tadman; v. Tadhunter.

Tagg, Tag.—Bapt. 'the son of Agnes,' a great favourite in the 13th and 14th centuries. Nick. Tagg and Taggy. The latter continues to be used in Furness, where Agnes is still almost first favourite. I had a Taggy in my kitchen at Ulverston. We find the French dim. as a suffix in Taggon; cf. Marion from Mary, Alison from Alice, Gibbon from Gib = Gilbert. v. Agate (2).

Richard Tagg, co. Oxf., 1273. A. Thomas Tagge, et Sissota uxor ejus, 1379: P. T. Howdenshire, p. 8. Thomas Tagon, 1379: P. T. Yorks. p. 82.

Johannes Tagge, 1379 : P.T.Yorks. p. 67.
Robertus Tag, 1379 : ibid. p. 8.
1637. Buried — Tagi Witt, co. Wilts :
Reg. Broad Chalke, p. 45.
1771. Married—James Tagg and Bett
Miles : St. Geo. Han. Sq. i. 209.
London, 6, 0 ; Sheffield, 1, 0 ; Oxford,
2, 0 ; Philadelphia, 4, 7.

Tagget, Taggett, Taggitt.—
Bapt. 'the son of Agnes,' from
nick. Tagg, q.v., with dim. Taggett.
New York, 1, 1, 1.

Tailer, Tailor ; v. Taylor.

Taillefer.—Bapt. ; v. Telfer.
New York, 1.

Taintor, Tainturer, Tainter.
—Occup. ' the teinturer,' or ' teyn-
tour,' a dyer. 'Lystare, or Lytaster
of cloth dyynge, *Tinctor*' : Prompt.
Parv. Cf. *taint, tint, tinge, tincture.*
For a longer statement, v. my
English Surnames, pp. 322-3 (5th
edit.).
Fulk le Taynturor, C. R., 36 Hen. III.
Robert le Teynturer, co. Linc., 1273. A.
Stephen le Teynterer, co. Kent, ibid.
Alexander Wauteresman, le teynturer
(i. e. Alex. the servant of Walter the
teynturer) : C. R., 25 Edw. I.
Warin le Teyntour. T.
John le Teyntour. II.
Philip le Tentier. H.
1702. Married—William Tainter and
Mary Cleiney : St. Jas. Clerkenwell, i.
224.
New York, 7, 0, 0 ; Boston (U.S.), 0,
0, 8.

Tait, Taite, Taitt.—A Scottish
surname, concerning which I have
not gathered any information.
Mr. Lower says, ' Teit was a personal name in Norway in the 11th
century. See the Heimskringla '
(Patr. Brit. p. 338).
London, 9, 2, 0 ; Philadelphia, 35, 6, 7.

Talbot, Talbott, Talbut. —
Bapt. ' the son of Talbot.'
Richard Talbot, Domesday.
Ricardus Talbot, Pipe Roll, 5 Hen. II.
Talebot de Hadfeld, ibid.
Talebotus Talebot, Fines Roll, 12
Edw. I.
Talebotus de Hintlesham, 34 Edw. I :
BBB. p. 727.
The vexed question of the origin
of this name is absolutely settled
by my last references. It is a per-
sonal name. It was not local, for
it is never found in conjunction
with ' de.' Many surnames may
be seen in Domesday, and Talebot

would simply be Richard's patronymic. This explains to a certain
extent the early use of Talbot as
a dog's name, personal names being
freely used in this manner. Gilbert
as Gib became the recognized name
for a cat, Cuddy (Cuthbert) for a
donkey.
' Ran Colie our dogge, and Talbot, and
Gerlond.'   Chaucer, C. T. 15386.
Willelmus Talbot, 1379 : P. T. Yorks.
p. 146.
Willelmus Talbot-man, 1379 : ibid.
1580-1. John Hedlea and Susanna Talbott : Marriage Lic. (Westminster), p. 7.
London, 27, 2, 1 ; Philadelphia, 31, 0, 0.

Talboys.—Local, ' of the underwood.' Two great Anglican Church
musicians, Tallis and Boyce (q.v.),
represent the separate constituents
of Talboys. Tallboy (q.v.) is an imitative corruption.
Isabella Taylbous, co. York, 1477 : W.
11, p. 101.
William Taylbus, co. York, 1512 : ibid.
p. 178.
Walter Talebois. B.
William Tailboys. H.
Thomas Taylebushe, *merchant-taylor*,
1570 : Reg. St. Mary Aldermary, p. 57.
1768. Married — James Nelson and
Hannah Talboys : St. Geo. Han. Sq. i. 173.
Oxford, 9.

Talintyre.—Local, ' of Tallen-
tire,' a township in the parish of
Bridekirk, co. Cumb.
Alexander de Talentir, 1212 : RRR.
p. 144.
Alexander de Tarentir, 1214 : ibid.
p. 154.
Richard Talentire, 1559 : Reg. Univ.
Oxf. i. 239.
' To Thomas Tallentire, ultra x shill-
ings,' 1619 : VVV. p. 129.
London, 1.

Tallboy.—Local. An imitative
corruption of Talboys, q.v.
1610. Bapt.—William, son of William
Talboy : St. Jas. Clerkenwell, i. 61.
London, 2.

Tallemach ; v. Talmadge and
Tollemache.
London, 2.

Tallis. — Local, ' de la taillis,'
from residence beside a small
copse. O. F. *taillis*, ' a copse,'
grove, underwood, such wood as
is felled or lopped every seven or
eight years ' (Cotgrave).
Richard Tailles', co. Cornwall, 1273. A.
Aaron Tallis, 1698 : Reg. St. Mary
Aldermary, p. 36.

1887. Buried—Mary Jane Tallis : Manchester Courier, June 18, 1887.
Manchester, 1 ; Boston (U.S.), 2.

Tallman, Talman.—Nick. ' the
tall man ' ; cf. Smallman, Bigg,
Little, &c.
Walter Talman, co. Soms., 1 Edw. III :
Kirby's Quest, p. 186.
1658. Married—Richard Tallman and
Ann Meller : St.Mary Aldermary, p. 28.
1693-4. Married—James Tallman and
Eliz. Millington : St. Dionis Backchurch
(London), p. 43.
Boston (U.S.), 4, 0 ; Philadelphia, 15, 3.

**Talmadge, Talmage, Tall-
madge. —** ? Local. Variants of
Tollemache, q.v.
Willelmus Talemasche, 7 Hen. II, Pipe
Roll, iv. 4.
John Talmach, 1677 : Reg. St. Mary
Aldermary, p. 104.
London, 2, 1, 0 ; Philadelphia, 0, 7, 2.

Tamblyn, Tamlin, Tamlyn.
—Bapt. ' the son of Thomas,' from
the nick. Tom (commonly Tam)
and dim. Tomlin (commonly Tamlin). The *b* in Tamblyn is the
usual excrescence; cf. Hamblin for
Hamlin, and v. Tomblin, Tamplin,
and Tomlin. It is interesting to
notice how determinately the *o* in
Tom became *a*. Even Tomlinson
is found as Taminson.
1689. Bapt.—Thomas, son of Thomas
Taminson : St. Jas. Clerkenwell, i. 332.
London, 1, 1, 1.

Tame, Thame. — Local, ' of
Tame,' from residence beside the
river Thame ; an early Oxfordshire
surname.
Claricia de Tame, co. Oxf., 1273. A.
John de Tame, co. Oxf., ibid.
Robert de Tame, co. Bucks, ibid.
Edmund Tame, C. R., 27 Hen. VIII.
pt. ii.
1653. Married—Anthonye Robins and
Sarah Tame : St. Michael, Cornhill, p. 31.
London, 3, 0 ; MDB. (co. Oxford), 1, 1.

Tamlin, -lyn ; v. Tamblyn.

Tammadge ; a corruption of
Talmadge, q.v.
London, 2.

Tamplin.—Bapt. ' the son of
Thomas.' The order is Thomas,
nick. Tom, dim. Thomelin or Tomlin, North or South-West English
Tamlin, then with intrusive but
inevitable *p*, Tamplin ; cf. Thompson
and Thomson from same root. v.
Tomlin, Tamblyn, and Taplin.

William Tamlen, 1572 : Reg. St. Columb Major, p. 8.

Constance Tamblyn, 1743 : ibid. p. 272.

The fem. Thomasine is invariably Tamson in the same register.

Tamson, d. of Joane Jenken, 1573 : ibid. p. 8.

Tamson, d. of John Adam, 1574 : ibid. p. 9.

1785. Married — James Mitchell and Sarah Tamplin : St. Geo. Han. Sq. i. 379. London, 3 ; Philadelphia, 1.

Tamson, Tams.—Bapt. ' the son of Thomas,' from the nick. Tom (commonly Tam) and patronymic Tams or Tamson ; v. Tamblyn, Tamplin, &c.

1753. Married — Moses Waddop and Ann Tams : St. Geo. Chap. Mayfair, p. 263. Philadelphia, 1, 5 ; Oxford, 0, 1.

Tancock.—Bapt. ' the son of Daniel,' from nick. Dan, pet Dancock, sharpened to Tancock (cf. Tennyson, Dennison, &c.). For suffix, v. *cock*, Introd. p. 25.

London, 1 ; Penzance, 1.

Tancred ; v. Tankard.

Tandy. — Bapt. ' the son of Andrew,' from nick. (Scottish) Dandy, then Tandy ; cf. Dennison and Tennyson, Dannett and Tannett, &c.

1582. John, s. of Homfrey Dandy : Reg. St. Dionis Backchurch (London), p. 85.

1584. Joane, d. of Homfric Tandy : ibid.

1638. Married — Elias Clark and Sarah Tandy : St. Peter, Cornhill, i. 256. London, 2 ; Oxford, 1 ; Boston (U.S.), 2.

Tanett ; v. Tannett.

Taney ; v. Tawney.

Tanfield.—Local, ' of Tanfield' : (1) a chapelry in the parish of Chester-le-Street, co. Durham; (2) a parish in the N. Rid. Yorks, six miles from Ripon.

Ricardus de Tanfeld, 1379 : P. T. Yorks. p. 240.

1544. Robert Tanfyld and Wilgeforda Fitzherbert : Marriage Lic. (Faculty Office), p. 2.

1551. Married—Thomas Tanfelde and Margaret Colman : St. Michael, Cornhill, p. 6.

1610. — Thomas Drayton and Marie Tanfeild : ibid. p. 19.

Sheffield, 2 ; London, 1 ; New York, 1.

Tangye. — Bapt. ' the son of Tengy,' a common name in the Hundred Rolls.

Tengy ad Fontem, co. Camb., 1273. A.

Allan Tengy, co. Camb., 1273. A.

Nel Tengy, co. Camb., ibid.

London, 1.

Tankard, Tancred. — Bapt. ' the son of Tancred,' very early written Tankard. It is interesting to note that there are no Tankards in the London Directory, and that they are found chiefly in Yorkshire, where the family of Tancred was originally settled.

Robert Tankard, co. Soms., 1 Edw. III : Kirby's Quest, p. 280.

Emma Tankard, 1379 : P. T. Yorks. p. 220.

Johannes Tankerd, 1379 : ibid.

Edmund Tankard, Patent Roll, 14 Edw. IV. pt. i.

Ricardus Tankart, 1427, Ripon : GGG. p. 329.

William Tankerd, 1571, Ripon : ibid. p. 308.

1678. Richard Wood and Ursula Tanckred (co. York) : Marriage Alleg. (Canterbury), p. 285.

Liverpool (Tancred), 1 ; West Riding Court Dir., 4, 0 ; Bradford, 5, 0 ; Boston (U.S.), 0, 4.

Tann.—(1) Bapt. (?), ' the son of Daniel,' from the nick. Dan, sharpened to Tan ; cf. Tancock for Dancock, and Tannett for Dannett. (2) Local, ' of Tan.' I cannot find the spot.

Geoffrey de Tan, co. Camb., 1273. A.

William de Tan, co. Camb., ibid.

Adam Tan, et Ydonia uxor ejus, 1379 : P. T. Yorks. p. 114.

London, 4 ; Oxford, 1.

Tanner.—Occup. ' the tanner,' one who tanned leather. Fr. *tan*, ' the bark of a young oak, wherewith leather is tanned ' : Cotgrave (v. *tan*, Skeat). Hence Barker, q.v.

Ansketill le Tanur, 1189 : RRR. p. 52.

Elfer Tannator, co. Sussex, 1273. A.

John Tannarius, co. Oxf., ibid.

Philip le Tannour, co. Hunts, ibid.

Henry le Tanur, co. Notts, ibid.

Henry le Tanner, co. Soms., 1 Edw. III : Kirby's Quest, p. 177.

1613. Bapt.—Mary, d. James Tanner : St. Jas. Clerkenwell, i. 69.

1699. Married — Stephen Tanner and Alice Adams : St. Peter, Cornhill, ii. 62. London, 30 ; Philadelphia, 8.

Tannett, Tanett.—Bapt. ' the son of Daniel,' from the nick. Dan, and dim. Danet, sharpened to Tanet (v. Dannett) ; cf. Tennyson for Dennison, or Tancock for Dancock. The Cheshire Wills contain many references to the

family of Danat, or Dannat, or Dannett. In two instances the initial letter is T, not D.

1670. Thomas Tanat, of Broxton : Wills at Chester, iii. 262.

1674. Ann Tannat, of Broxton : ibid.

1768. Married—Thomas Tannatt and Sarah Jones : St. Geo. Han. Sq. i. 176. West Rid. Court Dir., 2, 1 ; Philadelphia, 1, 0.

Tanshelf.—Local, ' of Tanshelf,' a township in the parish of Pontefract, W. Rid. Yorks.

MDB. (East Rid. Yorks.), 1.

Tansley.—Local, ' of Tansley,' a hamlet in the parish of Crich, co. Derby, near Matlock.

1788. Married — Thomas Pooley and Catherine Tansley : St. Geo. Han. Sq. ii. 15.

1806. — James Tansley and Charlotte Ablett : ibid. p. 352. London, 2 ; Philadelphia, 2.

Tanton, Taunton.—Local, ' of Taunton' ; also ' of Taynton,' parishes in diocs. Oxford, Glouc., and Bristol ; v. Taunton.

Guido de Tanton, co. Somerset, 1273. A.

William de Tantun, co. Norf., ibid.

Archid de Tanton, co. Soms., 1 Edw. III : Kirby's Quest, p. 262. London, 1, 3 ; Philadelphia, 0, 2 ; New York, 1, 1.

Tantum.—Local, ' of Taunton '; v. Tanton. This corruption is a very natural one ; cf. Ransom for Ranson, or Sansom for Sanson. Also cf. the dictionary word *random* for *randon*.

1753. Married — William Tantum and Mary Ward : St. Geo. Chap. Mayfair, p. 265.

Philadelphia, 1.

Tapiser, Tapner, Tapster(?). — Occup. ' the tapecer ' or tapener, a worker of tapestry for decorating walls, &c. ' Tappet, a clothe, *tappis*' : Palsgrave. ' Tapecer, *tapetarius*' : Prompt. Parv. The Ordinances for the Guild of St. Katharine, Lynn, are signed by ' Peter Tapeser' (English Gilds, p. 68, E. E. Text Soc.). Simon Tapser (H.). The Couchers and Tapisers went together in the York Corpus Christi Pageant (York Mystery Plays, p. xxiii, Toulmin Smith). Spelt also Tapiters. In the old usages of Winchester, the trade is called Tapener (English

Gilds, Toulmin Smith, p. 350). As Tapner it is in the London Directory.

1783. Married — Thomas Hall and Eliz. Tapner : St. Geo. Han. Sq. i. 354.
Marmaduk Myddulton, *tapitour* : Freemen of York, i. 265 (Surt. Soc.).
Robertus Vessy, *tapitour* : ibid.
London, o, 1, 1.

Taplay, Tapley.—Local, (1) ' of Tapley,' some small place in co. Devon which I have not succeeded in finding ; (2) ' of Taplow,' a parish in co. Bucks, one mile from Maidenhead, a natural modification of the name.

Adam de Tapplegh, co. Devon, Hen. III–Edw. I. K.
Robert de Tapplegh, co. Devon, ibid.
' Robertus and Adam de Tapplegh, tenent in Tappelegh unum feodum,' etc. : K. p. 175.
1744–5. Married—Thomas Tapley and Mary Keet : Canterbury Cath. p. 87.
London, 2, 1 ; Boston (U.S.), o, 7.

Taplin, Tapling.—Bapt. ' the son of Thomas,' from 'nick. Tam, and dim. Tamlin, which became Tamplin (q.v.), corrupted to Taplin. Thus the *p* is intrusive as in Tompson, and the *g* excrescent as in Röbling or Hawking ; cf. Thruson for Tampson.

1754. Married — William Powell and Mary Taplin : St. Geo. Chap. Mayfair, p. 276.
1801. — Press Bell and Hannah Taplin : St. Geo. Han. Sq. ii. 244.
London, 9, 2 ; Boston (U.S.), 3, o.

Tapner.—Occup. ; v. Tapiser.
Toluredus le Tapmer. C.
It is almost a certainty that this is a misprint for Tapiner (v. York Plays, p. lxxvii).
London, 1.

Tappenden.—Local, ' of Tappenden,' an ancient Kentish family, long resident at Sittingbourne, but originally of Tappenden, otherwise Toppenden, in the parish of Smarden (v. Hasted's Kent, vii. 479), quoted by Lower.

1748. Married—John Clare and Mary Tappenden, of Feversham, co. Kent : St. Dionis Backchurch, p. 69.
1799. — James Scartchin and Mary Tappenden : St. Geo. Han. Sq. ii. 210.
MDB. (co. Kent), 1 ; London, 3.

Tapper.—Occup. ' the tapper,' one who tapped the barrel, i.e. the

tapster ; the feminine suffix gained ground, as females gradually monopolized the place.
' And every hosteler and gay tapstere.'
    Chaucer, C. T. 241.

' Tapper, an inn-keeper. North England ' (Halliwell).
John le Tapper, co. Camb., 1273. A.
Robert le Tappere, c. 1300. M.
1614. Richard Tapper : Reg. Univ. Oxf. vol. ii. pt. ii. p. 333.
1635. Thomas Tapper, aged 18 years, embarked to St. Christopher : Hotten's Lists of Emigrants, p. 128.
1750. Married — William Tapper and Phebe Davies : St. Geo. Chap. Mayfair, p. 177.
Crockford, 1 ; Philadelphia, 8.

Tappin, Tapping.—Bapt. ' the son of Thomas,' a corruption of Tamplin, q.v.

1646. Bapt. — Thomas, s. Walter Tappin, *vintner* : St. Peter, Cornhill, i. 90.
1647. — John, sonn of Richard Tapping : *vintner* : ibid. p. 91.
1651. — Martha, d. William Tapping, *vintner* : ibid. p. 93.
London, 4, 4 ; New York, 9, 1.

Tapson. — Bapt. ' the son of Thomas,' a corruption of Tampson (v. Tamplin and Tamblyn), just as Taplin is a corruption of Tamplin (i.e. Tamlin, or Tomlin).
London, 4 ; Devon Court Dir., 2.

Tapster.—Occup. ' the tapster ' ; v. Tapper. Cf. Tapiser.
1548. Bapt. — William Tapster : St. Peter, Cornhill, i. 4.
1749. Married — Robert Tapster and Mary Adams : St. Geo. Chap. Mayfair, p. 143.
London, 1.

Tarbuck.—Local, ' of Tarbuck,' a township in the parish of Huyton, co. Lanc. (Torboc, Domesday). An early family of Tarbocks was settled here.

Henry Tarbock, of Tarbok, 20 Hen. VII : Baines' Lanc. ii. 271.
Bryan Soothworth, of Tarbocke, 1646 : Baines' Lanc. (Croston), p. 308.
Adam Tarbocke, 1622 : Preston Guild Roll, p. 79.
1580. Edward Torbock, co. Lanc. : Reg. Univ. Oxf. vol. ii. pt. ii. p. 95.
— Thomas Torbock, co. Lanc. : ibid.
Manchester, 1 ; Liverpool, 5 ; London, 1.

Targett.—Local, ' at the target,' from residence thereby, a dim. of *targe*, a shield, something to aim

at. The archer practised at the targe or target, hence the local surname for one who lived by the spot.

Richard Targe, co. Linc., 1273. A.
1695. Bapt. — Samuel, s. Christopher Targett : Reg. Stourton, Wilts, p. 19.
1759. Married — Richard Collins and Lucy Targett : St. Geo. Han. Sq. i. 87.
London, 4 ; Philadelphia, 2.

Tarleton.—Local, ' of Tarleton,' a parish in West Lancashire, eight miles from Ormskirk.

Adam de Tarleton, 10 Ric. II : Baines' Lanc. ii. 131.
Magota de Tarlton, 1379 : P. T. Yorks. p. 184.
1580. James Tarleton, of West Derby : Wills at Chester, i. 187.
1588. Katherine Tarleton, of Halewood : ibid.
1618. Thomas Tarleton of Liverpool : ibid.
1779. Married — Richard Myers and Eliz. Tarlton : St. Geo. Han. Sq. i. 305.
Liverpool, 4 ; Philadelphia, 2.

Tarrant, Tarratt, Tarrett.—Local, ' of Tarrant,' the name of several parishes in the county of Dorset. Tarratt and Tarrett are doubtless corruptions.

(Abbatissa) de Tarento, co. Dorset, 1273. A.
(Abbatissa) de Tarente, co. Dorset, Hen. III–Edw. I. A.
1621. George Tarrant, co. Hants : Reg. Univ. Oxf. vol. ii. pt. ii. p. 394.
1784. Married — William Tarrant, of Redbridge, co. Southampton, and Mary Sharp : St. Geo. Han. Sq. i. 361.
London, 12, 1, 1 ; Philadelphia, 1, o, o.

Tarry, Tarrie. — Bapt. ; v. Terry ; cf. Darby and Derby, Clark and Clerk, Parkin and Perkin.
1786. Married — James Tarry and Sarah Killick : St. Geo. Han. Sq. i. 394.
London, 7, o ; Philadelphia, o, 1.

Tasker.—Occup. ' the tasker,' one with some fixed work to do, possibly one paid by the job. ' *Triturator*, a tasker, Nominale MS., 15th century ' (Halliwell). Hence a thresher or reaper in some places is called a tasker. I met the word in Burton's Anatomy of Melancholy (Introduction) · ' Many poor country vicars, for want of other means, are driven to their shifts . . . as Paul did, at last turn taskers, maltsters, costermongers, graziers.'

3 B

Benedict le Taskur, co. Hunts, 1273. A.
Gilbert Tasker, co. Bucks, ibid.
Roger le Tasker, C. R., 7 Edw. I.
Alexander Tasker, 1307. M.
Radulphus Tasker, 1329 : P. T. Yorks. p. 106.
Willelmus Tasker, 1379: ibid. p. 205.
1677. Bapt.—Eliz., d. William Tasker: St. Dionis Backchurch, p. 122.
1773. Married — Peter Tasker and Mary Bowers: St. Geo. Han. Sq. i. 229.
London, 10; West Rid. Court Dir., 6; Sheffield, 6; Philadelphia, 18.

Tasseler. — Occup. 'the tasseler,' one who scratched cloth, to make a nap, with teasels, a prickly plant known as the Fuller's Thistle.

'Cloth that cometh fro' the wevyng
Is nought comely to wear
Til it be fulled under foot,
. . . . . .
And with taseles cracched.'
Piers Plowman.

'Item, that every fuller, from the said feast of St. Peter, in his craft and occupation of fuller, rower, or tayseler of cloth, shall exercise and use taysels, and no cards, deceitfully impairing the same cloth' (4 Edw. IV, c. 1),—'en sa arte et occupacion de fuller et scalpier ou tezeiler de drap, exercise et use teizels, &c.' 'Tasyl, carduus, cardo fullonis': Prompt. Parv. 'Tazills, 5s. 8d. more in tazills, 2s.' (Richmondshire Wills, Surt. Soc. p. 274. Inventory of property of Edward Kyrkelands, of Kendall, 1578).

Gilbert le Tasselere. H.
Matilda la Tasselere. H.
Edward Taylzer. W. 9.

This last name occurs (1568) in the will of Walter Strykland (Richmondshire Wills, p. 224). It is manifestly connected with tazill, instanced above. Thus Taylor in the Kendal district may have absorbed Taziller.

1610. Edward Tesler, or Teasler: Reg. Univ. Oxf. vol. ii. pt. i. 402.

Tatchell.—Bapt. 'the son of Tachel,' one of the numerous personal names ending in -el. The surname is still found in co. Somerset.

Gilbert Tachel, co. Oxf., 1273. A.
William Tachel, co. Soms., 1 Edw. III : Kirby's Quest, p. 198.
London, 1; MDB. (co. Soms.), 2.

Tate.—Bapt. 'the son of Tate' (Yonge, ii. 428). Probably in some cases a modern variant of the Scotch Tait.

Nicholas Tate, co. Camb., 1273. A.
1635. Married — William Tate and Joane Lewis: St. Dionis Backchurch, p. 23.
London, 11; Philadelphia, 27.

Tatham, Tattam, Tatum, Tateham, Tatem.—Local, 'of Tatham,' a parish in North Lancashire, which early gave rise to a surname.

'King John, when Earl of Moreton, gave the services of William of Tatham, in Tatham . . . to Robert de Monte Begon': Baines' Lanc. ii. 625.
Thomas de Tatham, 1379 : P. T. Yorks. p. 289.
Johannes de Tatam, 1379: ibid.
John Tatam, 1564 : Reg. Univ. Oxf. i. 253.
1576. Nicholas Colpotts and Katherine Tatham : Marriage Lic. (London), p. 74.
1604. Robert Tatum and Dorothy Bisley : ibid. p. 290.
1666. Buried—Boniface Tatam, vintner : St. Peter, Cornhill, i. 162.
Edwarde Tathame, of Overlocke, parish of Turnstill, 1597: Lancashire Wills at Richmond, pp. 269-270.
James Tatam, of Warton, 1620 : ibid.
Edmund Tatham, of Tunstall, 1627 : ibid.
1744. Married — Nathaniell Still and Sarah Tatum : Reg. Stourton, Wilts, p. 56.
1765. Married — Richard Tattam and Caroline Smart : St. Geo. Han. Sq. i. 141.
London, 27, 2, 6, 0, 0; West Rid. Court Dir. (Tateham), 2; Philadelphia, 12, 0, 12, 0, 21.

Tatler. — Nick. 'the tattler,' one who prated much, a prattler; v. Totiller.

Christopher Tatler, de Mapelthorne, yoman, 7 Hen. VII: HHH. p. 149.
1766. Married — John Tattler and Anna Maria Norgrave : St. Geo. Han. Sq. i. 150.
London, 2.

Tatlock.—Local, 'of Tatlock,' some spot in South Lancashire or co. Chester.

1593. Richard Tatlock, of Simonswood: Wills at Chester, i. 188.
1607. Catherine Tatlock, of Cunscough: ibid.
London, 3; Manchester, 3; Boston (U.S.), 1.

Tatlow. — Local. Probably a sharpened form of Tadlow; v. Tadloo.

1807. Married — Joseph Tatlow and Sarah Farmer : St. Geo. Han. Sq. ii. 361.
London, 1; Philadelphia, 5.

Tatnall, Tatnell.—Local, 'of Tattenhall,' a parish in co. Chester.

Thomas Tatnall, co. Chester, 1459 : Earwaker's East Cheshire, i. 174 n.
Robert Tatnall, of Saighton, 1612 : Wills at Chester, i. 188.
1748. Married — John Tattnall and Abigail Kent : St. Geo. Chap. Mayfair, p. 105.
London, 1, 2; Philadelphia, 1, 0.

Tattam; v. Tatham.

Tattersall, Tattershall, Tattersill.—Local, 'of Tattershall,' a parish in co. Lincoln, nine miles from Horncastle, corrupted by imitation into Tortoiseshell (q.v.).

Robert de Tateshale, or Tatteshall, or Tatersale, 26 Edw. I : BBB. p. 557.
Robert Tatersall, C. R., 9 Hen. IV.
1585. Bapt. — Edwarde, s. James Tattersall : St. Michael, Cornhill, p. 93.
1803. Married — Thomas Ridgway and Sarah Tattershall : St. Geo. Han. Sq. ii. 277.
London, 6, 3, 1; Philadelphia, 1, 0, 0.

Tatton.—Local, 'of Tatton,' a township in the parish of Rostherne, co. Chester.

Andrewe de Tattone, co. Southampton, 1273. A.
Robert de Tatton, co. Chester, 1290 : East Cheshire, ii. 308.
Robert de Tatton, of Wythenshawe, 1396: ibid.
Nicholas de Tatton, co. Chester, 1451 : ibid.
1579. Robert Tatton, of Wythenshawe : Wills at Chester, i. 188.
1600. Dorothy Tatton, of the Peele, co. Chester : ibid.
1601. William Tatton, co. Chester : Reg. Univ. Oxf. vol. ii. pt. ii. p. 247.
1776. Married — James Tatton and Sarah Strange : St. Geo. Han. Sq. i. 261.
London, 4; Manchester, 2; Philadelphia, 2.

Tatum; v. Tatham.

Taunton.—Local, 'of Taunton,' a well-known market-town in co. Somerset.

Gilbert de Tauntone, co. Somerset, 1273. A.
Gwydo de Tauntone, co. Somerset, ibid.
John Taunton, abbot of Cirencester, 1440 : Atkyn's Hist. Glouc. p. 178.
1761. Married — Samuel Taunton and Martha Pidgley : St. Geo. Han. Sq. i. 105.
1780. — John Taunton and Sarah Thompson : ibid. p. 317.
MDB. (Wilts), 5; (Somerset), 4; London, 3; Philadelphia, 2.

Taverner, Tavner, Tavener, Tavernor, Taviner, Tavinor, Tavnor.—Occup. 'the taverner,' a keeper of a tavern. 'Tavernere, *tabernarius*': Prompt. Parv. v. Taberner.

'Of which the taverner had spoke beforn.'
Chaucer, C. T. 12619.

Richard le Taverner, co. Camb., 1273. A.
Armvin le Taverner, London, ibid.
Falco le Taverner, London, ibid.
Robert le Taverner, co. Soms., 1 Edw. III : Kirby's Quest, p. 104.
Walter le Taverner. B.
John le Tevernour. C.
1553-4. Robert Taverner and Joanna Blakemoi : Marriage Lic. (London), i. 15.
1615. Bapt. — Wyborrowe, d. John Taverner : St. Jas. Clerkenwell, i. 73.
London, 5, 2, 2, 0, 0, 0, 0; MDB. (co. Somerset), 0, 0, 0, 1, 1, 1, 0 ; Boston (U.S.) (Tavener), 6 ; New York (Tavnor), 1.

Tawer, Tawyer.—Occup. 'the tawyer' (lit. tawer, the *y* is intrusive as in Sawyer), one who dressed skins. 'Tewynge of lethyr': Prompt. Parv. Professor Skeat (s.v. *taw, tew*) quotes Wyclif's use of *tawer* for a leather-dresser, where a later version has 'curriour,' i.e. currier. A.S. *tawian*, to prepare, v. Tower (2) and Whittear.

'Item, to John Massy, tawyer, for tawing of a tymbre of hole sables, iiiis.': Wardrobe Accounts of Edw. IV, p. 121.
John le Tawrare, co. Wilts, 1273. A.
Ralph le Tawyere, co. Wilts, ibid.
William le Tawyare, Close Roll, 2 Edw. I.
John le Tawyere, co. Wilts, 20 Edw. I. R.
Cf. 1585. Thomas Castle, *white-tawer*, and Ellen Broke : Marriage Lic. (London), i. 141.
Hugh Tawyer, aged 18 years, 'imbarqued in the Ann and Elizabeth' for Barbadoes, 1635 : Hotten's Lists of Emigrants, p. 71.

Tawny, Tawney, Taney.—Nick. 'the tawny,' i.e. of a tanned complexion ; cf. Black, White, Blount, Russell, &c.

Ida le Tauny, co. Norf., 1273. A.
1645. Married — Adam Buddell and Margret Tauny : St. Mary Aldermary, p. 19.
1742. — William Tawney and Frances Jacobs : St. Geo. Chap. Mayfair, p. 26.
— — Thomas Tawney and Sarah Dobney : ibid. p. 28.
MDB. (co. Norf.), 0, 0, 1 ; Philadelphia, 0, 2, 0.

Taylor, Tayler, Tailer, Tailor.—Occup. 'the taylor,' a cutter-out of cloth, a maker of clothes. M.E.

tailor, taylor; O.F. *tailleur*, a cutter. It is now understood that *tailor* shall be the trade-name, and Taylor and Tayler the surname. The early rolls are full of instances, and as a result Taylor is the fourth commonest patronymic in England, giving precedence only to Smith, Jones, and Williams. The Hundred Rolls (1273) have the following variations: Taillar, Taillour, Taillur, Tailur, Taliur, Tallur, Tallyur, Talur, Talyur, Tayler, Tayllour, Tayllur, Taylour, and Taylur.

Henry le Taliur, co. Norf., 1273. A.
Cecil le Tayllour, co. Camb., ibid.
Roger le Taylur, co. Linc., ibid.
Richard le Taylor, co. Northampt., ibid.
1593. Bapt. — Abel, s. John Tailor : St. Peter, Cornhill, i. 39.
1790. Witnesses to marriage, Eliz. Taylar, Richard Tayler : St. Geo. Han. Sq. ii. 38.
1802. Married — Robert Julian and Mary Taylar : ibid. p. 260.
London, 531, 21, 0, 0 ; Philadelphia, 597, 0, 1, 1.

Tayloress.—Occup. 'the tailoress,' a female cutter-out ; v. Taylor.

Alicia la Tayluresse, co. Hunts, 1273. A.

Taylorson, Taylerson.—Nick. 'the taylor's son'; v. Taylor. Still found in the county of York, where the earliest instances are to be met with ; cf. Smithson, Wrightson, Cooperson. Nevertheless, -son as a suffix to a trade-name is rare.

Willelmus Talliorson, 1379 : P. T. Yorks. p. 265.
Robertus Taylorson, 1379 : ibid. p. 33.
Agnes Taylour-doghter, 1379 : ibid.
1776. Married — Richard Taylorson and Sarah Brotherton : St. Geo. Han. Sq. ii. 266.
Ripon, 0, 1 ; MDB. (co. Durham), 1, 1.

Taynton.—Local, 'of Taynton,' parishes in cos. Oxford and Gloucester.

Henry de Teynton, co. Oxf., 1273. A.
John de Teynton, co. Oxf., ibid.
1605. Richard Taynton, co. Worc. : Reg. Univ. Oxf. vol. ii. pt. ii. p. 287.
London, 2.

Teal, Teall, Teel.—Nick. 'the teal,' a small duck ; M.E. *tele*; cf. Duck, Drake. The names of John and Thomas Telcock, co. Oxford, occur in the Hundred Rolls (1273) ; probably a masculine form, equivalent to Drake.

Matilda Tele, co. Camb., 1273. A.
Martin Tele, co. Camb., ibid.
John Teel, co. Soms., 1 Edw. III : Kirby's Quest, p. 169.
1749. Married — Richard Teale and Mary Haselwood : St. Geo. Chap. Mayfair, p. 157.
1790. — William Teal and Eliz. Wardman : St. Geo. Han. Sq. ii. 38.
London, 1, 1, 0 ; Philadelphia, 16, 0, 1.

Teape.—? Bapt. I can furnish no information about this surname.

Johannes Tepe, co. Devon, 1273. A.
1579. Buried — Richarde Teape, servant to Mathew Joyner : St. Dionis Backchurch, p. 196.
London, 3.

Teas, Teaz ; v. Tees.

Teasdale, Teesdale.—Local, 'of Teesdale,' i.e. the valley of the river Tees ; cf. Tweedale, Tyndale, &c.

William de Tesedal, co. York, 1273. A.
Alan de Teysedale, co. Northumb., 20 Edw. I. R.
Henry de Tesdale, Prior of Finchale, 1295 : The Priory of Finchale, Surt. Soc., p. xxvi.
Hugh de Tesedale, 1350 : DDD. i. 63.
Johannes de Tesedale, 1379 : P. T. Yorks. p. 245.
1613. Thomas Tisdale and Barbara Draper : Marriage Lic. (London), ii. 26.
1646. Buried — A young child of Mr. William Teusdall (sic) and Rose his wife' : St. Peter, Cornhill, i. 241.
Manchester, 5, 1 ; London, 3, 0 ; Philadelphia, 3, 1.

Tebay, Teebay, Tibby, Tebby. — Local, 'of Tebay,' a township in the parish of Orton, co. Westmoreland.

Thomas de Tybay, co. Cumb., 20 Edw. I. R.
Walter de Tybay, co. Westm. : ibid.
Johannes Tybey, of Sedburgh, near Tebay, 1379 : P. T. Yorks. p. 289.
1784. Married — John Tebay and Catherine Patience Pritchard : St. Geo. Han. Sq. i. 361.
1801. — John Tibbey and Susanna Woollerton : ibid. ii. 233.
Ulverston, 1, 0, 0, 0 ; Liverpool, 0, 2, 0, 0 ; London, 0, 0, 1, 0 ; Oxford (Tebby), 1.

Tebb, Tebbs, Tibbs. — (1) Bapt. 'the son of Theobald,' from the nick. Tebb or Tibb. (2) Bapt. 'the son of Isabella,' from the nick. Tib ; cf. the Yorkshire Till for Matilda and Tagg for Agnes. This solution is important as helping to the origination of Tib, the once familiar name for a female cat, Gib (Gilbert) standing for the male ; v. Gibb. Tibby is still the pet-name of Isabella in the North of England; and a *tib-cat* still means a female cat in Yorkshire, where Isabella was once so popular as a girl's name. But while all this is true, there can be no doubt that Tib, for a cat's name, was originally masculine and ran side by side with Gib, without particular reference to sex. In Reynard the Fox, Tibald is pussy's name (cf. Tibert, a cat: Halliwell); and the nick. of Tibald (i.e. Theobald) was in England Tib. This is clear from Gower's lines on Tyler's insurrection:

> '*Hudde* ferit, quem *Judd* terit, dum *Tibbe* juvatur,
> *Jacke* domosque viros vellit, en ense necat,'

where only masculine names are introduced. Originally, then, Tib for a cat was the nick. of Theobald. By degrees, however, Tib for Isabella ousted the popularity of Tib for Theobald. Besides, Theobald itself was becoming forgotten as a font-name. Hence the idea slowly crept in that Tib stood for the female cat, and had always done so. Of course the convenience of having a female name to correspond with Gib was obvious. In the Elizabethan and Stuart period Isabella was universally Tib (Tib for Theobald having disappeared), and Tib was still the lady cat. In Gammer Gurton's Needle Hodge says:

> 'And while her staff she took
> At Tyb her cat to fling.'

Burton in his Anatomy of Melancholy, in a list of names, includes ' tall Tib, slender Sib'; while the 'Psalm of Mercie,' a Commonwealth squib, says:

> '" So, so," quoth my sister Bab;
> And " kill 'um," quoth Margerie:
> "Spare none," cries old Tib;" no quarter," says Sib,
> " And hey for our monarchie." '

No doubt there is an occult connexion between Tib and *tabby*.

Tebbe Molend', i.e. the miller, co. Camb., 1273. A.
John Tybbesone, co. Soms., 1 Edw. III : Kirby's Quest, p. 251.
Walter Tybbe, co. Soms., 1 Edw. III: ibid. p. 116.
Richard Tybbe, co. Soms., 1 Edw. III : ibid. p. 193.
Tebb fil. William. J.

Margery Tebbe, co. York. W. 11.
Thomas Tebbe, co. York. W. 12.
John Tibbs, temp. Eliz. Z.
1606. Thomas Tibbes: Reg. Univ. Oxf. vol. ii. pt. ii. p. 290.
1665. Buried — John, son of John Tebbe: St. Michael, Cornhill, p. 255.
1707. John Cranidge and Eliz. Tibbis: Marriage Lic. (London), ii. 336.
London, 3, 7, 4 ; Philadelphia, 1, 2, 0.

Tebbitt, Tebboth, Tebbott, Tebbut, Tebbutt, Tebbets, Tebbetts.—(1) Bapt. 'the son of Theobald.' These are not diminutives formed from the nick. Tebb, q.v., though practically they became so. They are corrupted forms of the shorter Tebald. (2) Bapt. 'the son of Isabella,' nick. Tib, dim. Tibot ; v. Tebb. Tibet Talkapace is one of the heroines in Udall's Ralph Roister Doister (circa 1550). ' Work, Tibet ; work, Annot ; work, Margery ;

> Sew, Tibet ; knit, Annot ; spin, Margery;
> Let us see who will win the victory.'

The surnames descended from the above two names are now inextricably mixed.

Tibota Foliot, co. Oxf., 1273. A.
Robert Tebaud, co. Norf., ibid.
Margery Tebbolt, co. Camb., ibid.
Thomas Tedbald, co. Camb., ibid.
Ralph Tebaud, or Tebald, or Tebawd, co. Hunts, ibid.
Robert Tebaud-man, i.e. the servant of Teboud, 1379 : P. T. Yorks. p. 148.
Adam Thebaud, *hostiler*, occurs above.
Tibaud de Russell. PP.
Tibot Fitz-Piers. Y.
Tybota Hendre, C. R., 14 Hen. VI.
Roger Tebbott, temp. Elizabeth. Z.
Tybott Creffe, 1592: Cal. State Papers (Domestic), iii. 170.
Lease to Stephen Tebold, alias Theobold, 1591: ibid. p. 17.
London, 1, 1, 2, 2, 1, 0, 0 ; Boston (U.S.), 0, 0, 0, 0, 0, 3, 7.

Tebby ; v. Tebay.

Tedd. — Bapt. 'the son of Edward,' from the nick. Ted.

London, 3 ; Oxford, 1.

Tedman.—? Local, ' of St. Edmund's ' (?) ; cf. Toomer (2). The suffix *-mond* or *-mund* always corrupts to *-man* ; cf. Osman, Wayman, &c.

John de St. Edmund, London, 1273. A.
Godfrey de St. Edmund, co. Norf., ibid.
These refer, of course, to Bury St. Edmund.
1632. Buried — Edmond Tedmond, a nurse-child at Goodwife Toppen's, came

out of St. Edmund's parish : St. Michael, Cornhill, p. 232.
London, 1.

Tees, Teese, Teas, Teaz.— Local, ' of the Tees,' from residence beside the river of that name. With Tees and Teesdale, cf. Tweed and Tweedale. With the form Teas, cf. Teasdale. This surname with its variants has spread extensively in the United States. Teaz is very American. v. Surtees.

1608. Valentine Penson and Anne Tees, *widow* : Marriage Lic. (London), ii. 62.
London, 1, 0, 0, 0 ; Philadelphia, 36, 10, 2, 2.

Teesdale ; v. Teasdale.

Tegg, Tigg, Tegge. — Nick. ' the teg,' a sheep in the second year ; still in common use in Oxfordshire and the West country. ' A teg or sheep with a little head, and wooll under its belly': Florio, p. 32 (Halliwell) ; cf. Lamb, and v. Twentyman.

Thomas Tege, co. Soms., 1 Edw. III: Kirby's Quest, p. 95.
William Tegge, co. Soms., 1 Edw. III: ibid. p. 139.
Thomas Tigge, co. Soms., 1 Edw. III : ibid. p. 149.
William Tyg, co. Soms., 1 Edw. III: ibid. p. 189.
London, 1, 1, 0 ; Philadelphia, 0, 0, 1.

Teleress.—Occup. ; v. Teller.

Ida le Teleresse. T.

Telfer, Telford, Telfour.— Bapt. ' the son of Taillefer,' i.e. cut-iron. This surname seems to have originally flourished in the Lowlands, and to have worked its way across the border into Northumberland. The corruption into Telford must not lead us astray, although it looks distinctly local. ' Thomas Telford, the great engineer, used to say, " When I was ignorant of Latin, I did not suspect that Telfor, my true name, might be translated, ' I bear arms' (*tela fero*), and, thinking it unmeaning, adopted Telford"' (Lower). In the neighbourhood of Newcastle the two forms are common, and in recent generations either form was used by people of the same stock. John Taylfar, in 1558, obtained a grant from the Bishop of Durham of the reversion of the office of seneschal in the cities and boroughs of Gateshead, Durham, &c., expectant on the death of Christopher Browne (PPP. ii. 334). This is the earliest instance I can find in the district.

On Nov. 1, 1696, twenty-eight people were drowned at Canoubie, after attending church. Reference is made to one in an inscription in the churchyard: 'Here lyes George Tealer, who died in the water, Nov. the 1, 1696, being the Lord's day, as they were going home from the Kirk': Trans. Cumb. and Westm. Ant. and Arch. Soc., vol. viii. p. 287.

The famous Taillefer of the battle of Hastings will be familiar to the reader. Lower says that Tailzefer was the Scotch form in the 16th century. Cf. Gulliver and Gulliford.

William Tailefer, co. Kent, 1273. A.
Taylfre de Wyncestre, co. Hertf., 20 Edw. I. R.
London, 8, 3, 0 ; Newcastle, 3, 7, 1 ; Philadelphia, 0, 4, 0.

Teller, Tellier.—Occup. ' the teller,' i.e. the weaver. O.F. *telier,* a linen-weaver.

Lithulph le Teler, 1257 : KKK. vi. 236.
Henry le Telere, temp. 1310. M.
Johannes Teller, 1379 : P. T. Yorks. p. 235.
Symon Telar', 1379 : ibid. p. 121.
John le Teler. E.
Robert le Teler. J.
1610. William Teler and Mary Holborne : Marriage Lic.(Westminster), p.18.
London, 1, 1 ; Philadelphia, 14, 0.

Telwright, Tellwright, Tilewright.—Occup. ' the tilewright,' a maker of tiles ; later, and more generally, a potter, one who bakes and moulds clay. Tilewright seems to be the true form, *tigel-wyrhta* (Matt. xxvii. 7) occurring in an Anglo-Saxon Gospel (v. Skeat, s.v. *tile*). In the York Mystery Plays (Toulmin Smith : Clarendon Press) they are styled Tielmakers or Tillethekkers (i.e. tile-thatchers). In a statute of 1563 they are Tilemakers (5 Eliz. c. 4-23). In the Potteries the term *tilewright* is still used, and it is there the surname Tellwright or Telwright has existed for centuries.

MDB.(co. Stafford),0, 2, 0; Manchester, 0, 1, 0.

Temberli, Temperley ; v. Timperley. The first is an American corruption.

Tempany, Temperly.—Local. Obvious corruptions of Timperley, q.v., the second marking the ' first step from the right path.'

1800. Married — Edmund Tempany and Susanna Tomlin : St. Geo. Han. Sq. ii. 224.
London, 3, 4 ; New York, 0, 1.

Tempest.—? ——. I dare not hazard a conjecture as to the class to which this surname belongs. Mr. Lower says, ' This family, who are doubtless of Norman origin, are traced to Roger Tempest (temp. Henry I), who held three carucates and two oxgangs of land in the Shipton Fee, co. York ' (Patr. Brit. p. 340).

Isabella Tempest, 1379 : P. T. Yorks. p. 257.
1579. John Tempest, co. York : Reg. Univ. Oxf. vol. ii. pt. ii. p. 89.
1758. Married — Henry Tempest, of Broughton, co. York, and Eleanor Jones : St. Geo. Han. Sq. i. 76.
MDB. (West Rid. Yorks), 9 ; Philadelphia, 4.

Templar, Templer. — Offic. (1) One of the great religious body vowed to protect the Temple and Holy Sepulchre, a Crusader ; (2) the custodian of a temple or church in England ; cf. Churcher, and v. Temple.

William le Templyr et Alicia uxor : C. R., 43 Hen. III.
William le Templer, co. Linc., 1273. A.
Agnes le Templer, co. Oxf., ibid.
Adam le Templer, 1307. M.
John Templer, co. Soms., 1 Edw. III : Kirby's Quest, p. 118.
William le Templer. J.
1641. Thomas Hutchinson and Lettice Templar : Marriage Lic. (London), ii. 257.
1766. Married — William Templer and Eliz. Dunn : St. Geo. Han. Sq. i. 155.
London, 1, 2 ; MDB. (co. Devon), 0, 4 ; Philadelphia, 2, 0.

Temple.—Local,' of the temple,' any sacred enclosure. A.S. *tempel*; M.E. *temple,* from residence thereby.

Matilda du Temple, co. Oxf., 1273. A.
Petrus del Templi, 1379 : P. T. Yorks. p. 294.
Matilda de Tempell, 1379 : ibid.
1576. Leonard Temple, co. Oxon : Reg. Univ. Oxf. vol. ii. pt. ii. p. 69.
1634. William Chapman and Joane Temple : Marriage Lic. (London), ii. 220.
London, 31 ; Philadelphia, 29.

Templeman.—Local or occup. ' the temple-man,' one who lived

at or had charge of a temple ; v. Temple, and cf. Churchman and Kirkman.

Ambrose le Templeman, co. Camb., 1273. A.
Robert Templeman, co. Camb., ibid.
Willelmus Tempulman, 1379 : P. T. Yorks. p. 109.
1696. Married—Mark Warkman and Anne Templeman: St. DionisBackchurch, p. 45.
1780. Married — Thomas Templeman and Eliz.Coulton : St. Geo. Han.Sq. i. 316.
London, 9 ; Boston (U.S.), 5.

Templeton.—Local, ' of Templeton,' a parish in co. Devon, five miles from Tiverton.

1764. Married—James Templeton and Eliz. Lobb : St. Geo. Han. Sq. i. 134.
London, 3 ; Philadelphia, 15.

Tench.—? Nick. ' the tench,' the fish of that name. There are so few fish-names that I hesitate much in suggesting this solution. Salman, Chubb, Spratt, Gudgeon, &c., have no connexion with the finny tribe.

John Tenche, co. Linc., 1273. A.
1599-1600. Married—Willyam Tenche and Joane Eaton : St. Dionis Backchurch, p. 14.
1618. James Tench and Mary Eyres : Marriage Lic. (London), ii. 67
1640. Married — John Gouldwell and Mabell Tench : St.Mary, Aldermary, p. 18.

Tenison, &c. ; v. Tennyson.

Tennant, Tennent.—Occup. ' the tenant,' one who holds land under another.

Willelmus Tenaunt, 1379 : P. T. Yorks. p. 279.
Johannes Tenant, 1379 : ibid.
Ricardus Tenaunt, 1379 : ibid.
1563-4. Married—Philip Swalowe and Eliz. Tennante : St. Dionis Backchurch, p. 5.
1564-5. Silvester Tenante, Ch. Ch. : Reg. Univ. Oxf. vol. ii. pt. ii. p. 13.
1748. Bapt.—Ann, d. William Tenant: St. Michael, Cornhill, p. 175.
London, 15, 3 ; Philadelphia, 2, 5.

Tenniswood, Tinniswood.—Local, ' of Tenniswood,' some small spot in co. York. There can be no doubt that this is a sharpened form of Denniswood, i.e. the wood that belonged to Denis ; v. Tennyson.

MDB. (North Rid. Yorks), 2, 0 ; Manchester, 0, 1 ; York, 1, 0.

Tenny, Tenney.—Bapt. ' the son of Dennis,' from the pet Denny sharpened into Tenny; v. Tennyson.

Boston (U.S.), 1, 46.

Tennyson, Tenison, Tenison, Tenneson.—Bapt. 'the son of Dennis.' O.E. Dionys, Denis, whence Denison, sharpened to Tenison; cf. Haseltine for Hazeldean, Tancock for Dancock, Tanett and Tannett for Danett and Dannett; cf. Tenniswood (i.e. Denniswood), York Dir. 1. Also note that the surname Toket is referred to as Doket in Index of Visitation of Yorkshire (Harl. Soc.). Yorkshire and the Lincolnshire border strongly affected Denis in the surname period. We also find Dandridge for Tandridge, and Tandy for Dandy. Dogood in the old registers is manifestly Toogood.

Arthur Doegood, 1680: Reg. St. Mary Aldermary (London), p. 105.
1711. Bapt. — Dorothy, d. Edward Tennison: Canterbury Cath., p. 23.
London, 0, 0, 1, 1; MDB. (East Rid. Yorks), 0, 0, 4, 0; Boston (U.S.), 0, 0, 1, 0.

Tenter, Teinter, Teinturer.—(1) Occup. 'the tenterer' or tenter, one who looked after the tenter-hooks and the cloth he stretched on the frame thereby. The *tenter* was the frame. 'Tenture, tentowre, for cloth; *extensorium*': Prompt. Parv. By Statute 1 Ric. III, c. 8, *tentors* must be set in open places, not in houses.

'Item, tenture posts and woodde. 6*d*., 2 tentures, 20*s*.,' 1562, Kendal: Richmondshire Wills, p. 156.

(2) Occup. 'the teinturer,' i.e. dyer. 'Lystare, or lytaster, of cloth dyynge; *tinctor*': Prompt. Parv.

Warin le Teyntour. T.
John le Teynter. H.
William le Teinturer. E.
Richard le Tenter. H.
Philip le Tenter. H.
Thomas le Teynturer, co. Oxf., 1273. A.
Sarra le Teynturere, co. Oxf., ibid.
William le Teynturer, co. Hunts, ibid.
Berenger Tinctor, co. Hunts, ibid.
Sarle Tinctor, co. Hunts, ibid.

Tepper.—Occup.; v. Tipper.

Termday.—? Nick. With probably some reference to the University Terms.

Margaret Termeday, co. Oxf., 1273. A.
William Termeday, co. Oxf., ibid.

Terrell, Tyrrell, Tirrell, Terrill, Turrell, Turrill.—Bapt. 'the son of Turold,' popularly Tirrell. There can be no doubt as to the personal or baptismal origin of the surname. And it will account for the name of Walter Tyrrel, as a reference to the Index of Freeman's Hist. Norman Conquest will conclusively prove the popularity of Turold in the 11th century.

Henry Tyrel, co. Devon, 1273. A.
Walter Tyrel, co. Norf., ibid.
Roger Tirel, co. Hereford, Hen. III-Edw. I. K.
William Torel, co. Soms., 20 Edw. I. R.
John Tyrell, co. Kent, ibid.
Hugh Tyrel, co. Southampton, ibid.
Thomas Torel, co. Soms., 1 Edw. III: Kirby's Quest, p. 116.
Katerina Terell, 1379: P. T. Yorks. p. 28.
1623. John Tirell and Jane Stokes: Marriage Lic. (London), ii. 123.
1624. Peter Drapier and Barbara Tirrill: ibid. p. 141.
1641. George Tyrell and Anne Thurlow: ibid. p. 258.
London, 3, 15, 1, 0, 3, 1; Boston (U.S.), 46, 5, 2, 1, 1, 3.

Terry, Terrey.—Bapt. 'the son of Theodoric' (Tedric, Domesday), from the nick. Terry, probably from the French nick. Thierry.

David fil. Tirry, E. and F., co. Cumb., p. 140.
Terry (without surname), co. York, 1273. A.
Richard Terry, co. Hunts, ibid.
Terricus le Alemaunde, co. Bucks, ibid.
Geoffrey Terri, co. Oxf., ibid.
Terricus Baril, co. Soms., Hen. III-Edw. I. K.
Johannes Tyrry, 1379: P. T. Yorks. p. 275.
Petrus Terre, 1379: ibid. p. 241.
1613. James Browne and Bridget Terry: Marriage Lic. (London), ii. 23.
Terye Robsort, 1629: Reg. St. Mary Aldermary, p. 166.
Thomas Terrick, 1694, co. Ches.: Earwaker's East Ches. i. 407.
London, 49, 7; Boston (U.S.), 16, 0.

Tesseyman, Tyzemon, Tissiman.—Bapt. 'the son of Trasemond.' No doubt the Trasemundus and Trasmundus of Domesday, found in cos. Wilts and Dorset. As a surname, I can only discover instances in Norfolk and the North of England. It has existed four centuries at least in York. The terminative -*mund* or -*mond* becomes -*man*; v. Osman, Wyman, &c.

Richard Tacyman, 1340, Alnwick. KKK. vi. 40.
John Theysman, 1487. W. 11.
Briand Tossemund, 1523: W. 11, p. 200.
Bryan Tesymon, 1537: ibid.
Jac. Tesymond, 1545: ibid. p. 234.
Richard Thesymon, 1546: ibid. p. 236.

The last four names above occur among members of the Corpus Christi Guild, York.

Thomas Tesmond, sheriff of Norwich, 1559: FF. iii. 358.
John Tesmond, mayor of Norwich, 1601: ibid. p. 359.
1614. William Tessamond and Rebecca Gushe: Marriage Lic. (London), ii. 28.
Mr. Burleigh Tesseman sung at the concert at St. Paul's School, London, July 20, 1887: Standard, July 21.
York, 3, 0, 0; Moor Monkton, near York, 2, 0, 0; Sunderland, 1, 0, 0; Leeds, 2, 0, 0; Scarborough, 0, 0, 2; South Shields (Tyzemon), 1.

Tester, Testard.—Bapt. 'the son of Testard,' an early baptismal name; cf. Fr. Tetard.

Henry Testard, co. Hunts, 1273. A.
Robert Testard, co. Suff., ibid.
Ralph Testard, co. York, ibid.
Richard Testard, co. Surrey, Hen. III-Edw. I. K.
Willelmus Testard, 1379: P. T. Yorks. p. 145.
Johannes Testard, 1379: ibid.
1606. Married—Anthony Testard and Martha Cominglby (sic): St. Dionis Backchurch, p. 45.
London, 4, 0; Manchester, 2, 0; Philadelphia, 1, 0.

Testimony.—? Nick.

Adam Testimonie, co. Oxf., 1273. A.
Ralph Testimonie, co. Oxf., ibid.

Tetley, Tetlow, Titley, Titlow.—Local, 'of Tetlow' or Tetley, some spot in East Cheshire or South-east Lancashire. The name ramified strongly. Also 'of Titley,' a parish in co. Hereford.

Thomas Tyttelegh, 1539: Earwaker's East Cheshire, p. 160.
Edmund Tetlowe, 1554: ibid. p. 127 *n*.
Reginald Tetlawe, of Godley, *husbandman*, 1649: ibid.
Reginald Tetlaw, 1663: ibid.
Laurence Hulme, of Tetlow, 1599: Wills at Chester (1545-1620), p. 103.
Henry Tetlow, of Oldham, 1611: ibid. p. 191.
John Tetlow, of Coldhurst, Oldham, 1597: ibid.
London, 5, 0, 2, 2; Manchester, 3, 8, 1, 0; Philadelphia, 1, 6, 0, 9; MDB. (co Hereford), 0, 0, 1, 0.

Teversham.—Local, 'of Teversham,' a parish in co. Cambridge, near Cambridge.

William de Teweresham, co. Camb., 1273. A.
London Court Dir., 2.

Tew.—Local, 'of Tew,' two parishes in co. Oxf., Great and Little Tew.
MDB. (co. Oxf.), 1; Crockford, 1; Boston (U.S.), 3.

Tewer, Tuer.—Occup. 'the 'tewer,' i.e. the tawyer, one who prepared or dressed skins. To tew, to toil hard (Furness dialect, North Lanc.). 'Tew, or tewynge oflethyr': Prompt. Parv. 'A Tewer of skynnes': Cath. Angl. v. Tawer and Tuer.
1394. 'Item, pro tewyng 14 pellium laporum, 1s. 9d.': FFF. p. 623.
Richard de Bulmer, *tewer*, 1310-2: Freemen of York, Surt. Soc., i. 14.
Elyas Tewar, *souter*, 1379: P. T. Yorks. p. 99.
Robertus Tewer, 1379: ibid. p. 161.
1584. John Tuer, London: Reg. Univ. Oxf. vol. ii. pt. ii. p. 135.
1594. Daniel Tuer, co. Middlesex: ibid. p. 203.
London, 0, 1.

Tewksbury, Tuxbury.—Local, 'of Tewkesbury,' a parish and market-town in co. Gloucester, ten miles from Gloucester. Oddly enough, I am altogether without English instances.
Mabel de Teuksbury, co. Glouc., 1273. A.
Boston (U.S.), 29, 1.

Thacher; v. Thatcher.

Thacker.—Occup. 'the thacker,' a thatcher; cf. Kirk and Church. Among the craftsmen who went in procession in the performance of the York Mystery were the 'Tillethekers,' i.e. Tile-thatchers' (The York Mystery Plays, p. 112).
William le Thekere, co. Norf., 1273. A.
William Thecker, 1301. M.
Johannes Theker, *tector*, 1379: P. T. Yorks. p. 296.
Ricardus Theker, 1379: ibid.
Stephanus Theker, 1379: ibid. p. 293.
1565. Married—Robert Thacker and Agnes Blage: St. Jas. Clerkenwell, i. 3.
1748. Married—Edward Thacker and Eliz. Peartree: St. Geo. Chap. Mayfair, p. 116.
London, 6.

Thackeray, Thackery, Thackrah, Thackray, Thackwray, Thackara, Thackaray.—Local, 'at the thack-wray,' i.e. the corner or place set apart for storing thack, or thatch; v. Wray.

Not Thackery for Thacker, as Vicary for Vicar. Wray is found in many compounds in Yorkshire place-words.
William de la Thekere, co. Norf., 1273. A.
Johannes de Thakwra, 1379: P. T. Yorks. p. 238.
Robertus de Thakwra, 1379: ibid.
Thomas Thackwray, co. York. W. 16.
1748. Married—Joseph Thackeray and Martha Houldroide: St. Geo. Chap. Mayfair, p. 122.
1806. — William Thackray and Hannah Blake: St. Geo. Han. Sq. ii. 352.
West Rid. Court Dir., 1, 2, 5, 10, 1, 0, 0; London, 1, 3, 1, 1, 1, 0, 0; Philadelphia, 2, 0, 0, 4, 0, 13, 5.

Thackster, Thaxter.—Occup. 'the thacker' (fem. suffix -*ster*); v. Thacker, and cf. Baxter and Baker. Thakstare, *sartitector*: Prompt. Parv.
'The Reders, Thaxters, Rede-sellers,' &c., Norwich Pageant: FF. ii. 148.
Thomas Thackstere. H.
John Thackster, co. Norf. FF.
Johannes Thekester, 1379: P. T. Yorks. p. 244.
Robert Thakster, rector of Carlton, co. Norf., 1541: FF. v. 98.
John Thaxter, 1567, Coll. Reg.: Hist. C.C.C., Cambridge.
Edmund Thaxter, bailiff of Yarmouth, 1675: FF. xi. 330.
I am afraid this surname is obsolete in England, but I dare not speak positively. It is well represented across the Atlantic.
Boston (U.S.), 0, 31.

Thain, Thaine, Thane.—Offic. 'the thane,' equivalent to Earl (q.v.), a man who occupied the high position of a thane.
John le Theyn, co. Wilts, 1273. A.
Adam Theyn, co. Norf., ibid.
Roger le Theyn. T.
Nicholas le Then. T.
Cecilia la Theyn, co. Soms., 1 Edw. III : Kirby's Quest, p. 233.
1640. Married—Alex. Thayne and Ann Fisher: St. Antholin (London), p. 7.
1779. — David Brodie Thain and Sarah Luntley: St. Geo. Han. Sq. i. 295.
London, 1, 1, 2; Boston (U.S.), 4, 0, 0.

Thame.—Local; v. Tame.

Tharp.—Local, 'at the thorp,' from residence therein. A manifest corruption of Thorp, q.v.
1743. Married—Thomas Tharp and Frances Wheelock: St. Geo. Han. Sq. i. 31.
1760. — Alexander Tharp and Mary Moss: ibid. p. 96.
London, 4; Philadelphia, 4.

Thatcher, Thacher.—Occup. 'the thatcher.' For other variants, v. Thacker, Thackster, and Thaxter.
Reginald le Thechare, co. Oxf., 1273. A.
Reginald le Theccher. L.
John le Thacher, c. 1300. M.
1591-2. Robert Thatcher, co. Oxf.: Reg. Univ. Oxf. vol. ii. pt. ii. p. 189.
1593-4. William Thatcher, co. Sussex: ibid. p. 199.
London, 11, 0; Philadelphia, 25, 9.

Thaxter; v. Thackster.

Thayer.—? Bapt. 'the son of Theodoric' (?), from the O.F. popular nick. Thierry or Thierre (v. Terry). Thayer is, I presume, a modern English modification of the surname. But while it barely exists in England, it is a familiar entry in American directories. I have no actual proof for my conjecture, but I strongly believe I shall be found correct.
1605. Anthony Thayer and Martha Bourman: Marriage Lic. (London), i. 297.
1753. Married — Bartholomew Penny and Ann Thayer: St. Geo. Chap. Mayfair, p. 236.
1756. — John Huggins and Hannah There: St. Geo. Han. Sq. i. 66.
London Court Dir., 1; Philadelphia, 27.

Theakston, Theakstone, Thexton, 'of Theakstone,' a township in the parish of Burneston, N. Rid. Yorks.
1619. William Thekeston, co. Northts.: Reg. Univ. Oxf. vol. ii. pt. ii. p. 377.
1773. Married—John Willis and Mary Theakstion (sic): St. Geo. Han. Sq. i. 230.
London, 1, 1, 1; MDB. (North Rid. Yorks), 2, 2, 0; (West Rid. Yorks), 1, 2, 2.

Theed. — Bapt. 'the son of Theodoric' (?), spelt Thedric in the Hundred Rolls. It is almost certain that Theed is a nick. of Thedric. The name was very popular. v. Terry.
Nicholas Thede, co. Camb., 1273. A.
William Thede, co. Camb., ibid.
1611. Richard Theede, co. Bucks: Reg. Univ. Oxf. vol. ii. pt. ii. p. 325.
1748. Married—Christopher Theed and Eliz. Carterledge: St. Geo. Chap. Mayfair, p. 111.
London, 2; Crockford, 4.

Thelen.—Bapt. 'the son of Llewelyn,' through the difficulty of pronunciation; cf. Floyd for Lloyd. This derivation is, of course, beyond dispute.

Richard Thwellin, of Holt, 1618 : Wills at Chester (1545-1620), p. 192.

1607. Married — Edwarde Thwellinge and Jane Cotterill : Reg. Prestbury Ch. (Cheshire), p. 175.

— Bapt. — Margarett Thelline : ibid. p. 173.

1633. Buried — Anne Thewllen : ibid. p. 289.

Edward Twallen, co. Chester, 1695 : Farwaker's East Cheshire, ii. 226.

Manchester, 1 ; London, 1 ; Philadelphia, 1.

Thelwall.—Local, 'of Thelwall,' formerly a chapelry in the parish of Runcorn, near Warrington, co. Chester.

1617. Buried—Edward Thelwall, servant to Mr. Craven, *upholster*: St. Michael, Cornhill, p. 221.

1622. John Thelwall, of Bold : Wills at Chester, ii. 216.

1630. Marian Thelwall, of Acton Grange : ibid.

Manchester, 1.

Theobald, Theobalds.—Bapt. 'the son of Theobald.'

Theobald Laver, co. Camb., 1273. A.

Walter Theobald, co. Camb., ibid.

1620. Married—John Castell and Grisogond Theobalde : St. Jas. Clerkenwell, i. 49.

1746. — Richard Theobalds and Sarah Penson : St. Geo. Chapel, Mayfair, p. 73.

1791. Married—Daniel Theobald and Ann Bishop : St. Geo. Han. Sq. ii. 69.

1792. — Jesse Theobald and Sarah Young : ibid. p. 70.

London, 9, 0 ; Liverpool, 0, 1 ; Philadelphia, 12, 0.

Thetford.—Local, 'of Thetford,' a market-town in co. Suffolk, thirty miles from Norwich.

1721. Bapt.—Susanna, d. Arthur Thetford : St. Jas. Clerkenwell, ii. 129.

New York, 2.

Thewlis.—? Local, 'of Thewleys.' This Yorkshire surname, I doubt not, is local, the suffix being the plural of *ley*, a meadow. But I cannot find the spot in question.

Thomas Thewelesse, 1379 : P. T. Yorks. p. 177.

West Rid. Court Dir., 2 ; Philadelphia, 2.

Thexton.—Local, a variant of Theakston, q.v.

Thick, Thicke.—Nick. 'the thick,' plump, fat, compact.

'The grete tour that was so thikke and strong.'

   Chaucer, C. T. 1058.

Goscelin Thikke, Pardons Roll, 2 Ric. II.

William le Thikke, co. Soms., 1 Edw. III : Kirby's Quest, p. 101.

John le Thikke, co. Soms., 1 Edw. III : ibid. p. 126.

London, 3, 3 ; Oxford, 3, 1.

Thickbroom.—Local, 'at the thick broom,' from residence thereby.

William de Tikebrom, co. Suff., 1273. A.

Cf. William Thikthorn, co. Soms., 1 Edw. III : Kirby's Quest, p. 109.

London, 1.

Thickness, Thicknesse. — Local, 'of Thickness,' some headland on the English coast that I have not been able to identify ; cf. Holderness, Furness, &c. The suffix is -*ness*, a nose of land. Mr. Lower cruelly writes, 'Thicknesse, *nese* or *nesse*, is O.E. for nose, from A.S. *nese*, and this surname therefore probably refers to the thick nose of the original bearer' (Patr. Brit. p. 341).

William Thyknes, C. R., 14 Ric. II.

1643. Buried — Mary Thikneys : St. Peter, Cornhill, i. 200.

1675. Ralph Thicknes, of Maldon, Essex, and Mary Pulley : Marriage Alleg. (Canterbury), p. 243.

Crockford, 0, 2.

Thickpenny.— ? ——. I can offer no satisfactory solution of this surname.

1590. Buried — Leonard Thickpenny, minister of Enfeld, brought from the Kinges Bench in a coffen with a flap to open, with a writing one it in verse, laid at Ledenhall gate by night : St. Peter, Cornhill, i. 137.

1748. Married—Christopher Wass and Margaret Thickpenny : St. Geo. Chap. Mayfair, p. 326.

London, 1 ; Philadelphia, 1.

Thimbleby.—Local, 'of Thimbleby,' a parish in co. Lincoln, near Horncastle ; also a township in the parish of Osmotherley, N. Rid. Yorks.

Alice de Thumbleby, co. Linc., Hen. III-Edw. I. K.

1586. George Thymblebie, co. Linc. : Reg. Univ. Oxf. vol. ii. pt. ii. p. 152.

London, 1 ; MDB. (North Rid. Yorks), 1 ; (co. Lincoln), 2.

Thin.—Nick. 'the thin' ; v. Thynne.

London, 1.

Thirgood ; v. Thurgood.

Thirkell, Thirkettle.—Bapt. ; v. Thurkettle.

Thirlwall, Thirlwell.—Local, 'of Thirlwall,' a chapelry in the parish of Haltwhistle, co. Northumberland ; the Roman wall is in the neighbourhood of Gilsland and Thirlwall Castle. v. Thirlway.

Richard de Thurlewall, temp. Hen. III : KKK. v. 311.

Brice de Thirlwall (no date, but early).

John de Thirlewall, 1386 : KKK. iii. 145.

Rouland de Thirwall, 1460 : KKK. iv. 27.

1744. Married — John Thirlwall and Hannah Ringrose : St. Geo. Han. Sq. i. 33.

Liverpool, 1, 0 ; West Rid. Court Dir., 1, 1 ; Crockford, 1, 0.

Thirlway, Thirlaway.—Local, 'at the thirlway,' i.e. the road leading through the breach or gateway in the Roman wall. With Thirlaway, cf. Greenaway or Ottaway for Greenway and Ottway ; v. Thirlwall.

MDB. (co. Durham), 0, 2 ; (West Rid. Yorks), 1, 0 ; Newcastle, 0, 1.

Thirst. — Local. Probably a corruption of Thirsk, co. Yorks.

John de Tresk, *sutor*, 28 Edw. I : Freemen of York, i. 8.

Johannes de Thresk, 1379 : P. T. Yorks. p. 241.

1575. Married—John Lambe and Eliz. Thurske : St. Peter, Cornhill, i. 230.

London, 1.

Thirston.—A variant of Thurston (v. Thurstan).

Boston (U.S.), 1.

Thirticle.—Bapt. 'the son of Thurkettle,' q.v., a curious variant. I have not found any 19th century instances. v. Thirtle.

1675. Bapt. — William, s. Thomas Thirticle : St. Mary Aldermary (London), p. 103.

1677. — Eliz., d. Thomas Thirticle : ibid. p. 104.

Thirtle.—Bapt. 'the son of Thurkettle,' a variant of Thirkell or Thurkle (v. Thurkettle) ; cf. Thurtle. This corruption was seemingly an early one, for a township in the parish of Swine, E. Rid. Yorks, bears the name of Thirtleby, i.e. the dwelling of

Thurkell, the first settler. No doubt it was originally Thurkellby.

MDB. (Norfolk), 2.

Thiselton, Thistleton.—Local, ' of Thistleton,' a parish in co. Rutland, eight miles from Oakham. Other places probably existed of this name. It is interesting to notice that my first entry is from a Lincolnshire document. The name still exists in that county.

Adam de Thiselton, co. Linc., 1273. A.
1622. John Thistleton, of Woodplumpton, *husbandman* : Lancashire Wills at Richmond, i. 274.
1662. Thomas Thistleton, of Kellamargh : ibid. p. 275.
Crockford, 2, 0 ; MDB. (co. Lincoln), 2, 1.

Thistlethwaite. — Local, ' of Thistlethwaite,' one of the many local names with suffix -*thwaite*, so common to the North of England (v. Thwaite). I cannot find the exact spot.

1577. Alexander Thistlethwaighte and Mary Lisley : Marriage Lic. (London), i. 78.
1682. Thomas Thistlethwaite and Mary Sturmy : Marriage Lic. (Faculty Office), p. 162.
1784. Married—Arthur Stanhope and Eliz. Thistlethwaite : St. Geo. Han. Sq. i. 355.
MDB. (West Rid. Yorks), 2 ; London, 1.

Thistlewood. — Local, ' of Thistlewood.' Probably some spot in co. Lincoln.

MDB. (co. Lincoln), 5 ; Philadelphia, 1.

Thom, Thoms, Thomes.—Bapt. ' the son of Thomas,' from the nick. Thome or Tom, Thome being the earlier form ; v. Thomson.

Robert fil. Thome, co. Linc., 1273. A.
William Thome, co. York, 20 Edw. I. R.
Richard fil. Thome, co. York, ibid.
Alicia relicta Thome, 1379 : P. T. Yorks. p. 138.
Alicia uxor Thome, 1379 : ibid. p. 119.
Petrus Thome-son, 1379 : ibid. p. 115.
1698. Buried—John Tom, of Gaverigan : Reg. St. Columb Major, p. 245.

The earliest instances of Tom (without the *h*) I can find are :

Johanna Tom-doutter, the daughter of Tom, 1379 : P. T. Yorks. p. 88.
Johannes Tom-son, 1379 : ibid.
1791. Married—Samuel Ford and Mary Thoms : St. Geo. Han. Sq. ii. 69.
London, 5, 6, 0 ; Boston (U.S.), 2, 4, 1.

Thomas, Thomason, Thomasson, Thomassin, Thomeson.
—(1) Bapt. ' the son of Thomas.' Thomas or Thome (whence Tom) was a universal favourite. The 13th and 14th century registers teem with it ; v. Tomlin, Tomlinson, Thomson, Thompson, Tomkins, Tomkinson, Tombs, &c.
(2) Bapt. ' the son of Thomasin ' (q.v.). The two have become mixed.

Roger fil. Thomas, co. Camb., 1273. A.
Richard Thomas, co. Suff., ibid.
Walter Thomas, co. Wilts, ibid.
William Thomas, co. Soms., 1 Edw. III : Kirby's Quest, p. 101.
Adam Thomasson, 1379 : P. T. Yorks. p. 174.
Johannes Thomasson, 1379 : ibid. p. 138.
1582. Married — Thomas Bryse and Alyce Thomas : St. Michael, Cornhill, p. 12.
— John Thorne and Anne Thomasyne, *widow* : Marriage Lic. (London), i. 111.
1801. Married — Thomas Wyatt and Nancy Thomason : St. Geo. Han. Sq. ii. 239.
1806. — John Baptiste Thomesin and Jane Prin : ibid. p. 355.
London, 219, 5, 1, 0, 0 ; Boston (U.S.), 220, 0, 0, 1, 0 ; Philadelphia, 693, 12, 3, 0, 1.

Thomasin.—Bapt. ' the son of Thomas,' from the dim. Thomasin. A feminine Thomasina or Thomasine arose about the year 1350, and was popular as a font-name over the whole country till the 18th century. It is found in every register in every conceivable form, including Tamzen and Tomson. No doubt Thomasin, as a surname, has long been lost in Thomason or Thomson.

' Thomasinus, varlet of Nicholas le Herier, C. R., 4 Edw. I.
1538. Married — Edward Bashe and Thomeson Agar : St. Dionis Backchurch (London), p. 1.
1622. Buried—Tomson, d. John Moyer : St. Columb Major, p. 210.
1623. — Tomson Simon, *widow* : ibid.
1640. Buried—Thomasing, filia William Sympson : Wirksworth, co. Derby.
1657. Married — John Galley and Thomison Harte : St. Dionis Backchurch (London), p. 33.

For other instances, v. Thomas.

Thomasset, Tompsett, Thomsett, Tomsett. — Bapt. ' the son of Thomas,' from the dim. Thomas-et. The *p* in Tomp-

sett is intrusive, as in Thompson. Although there cannot be the shadow of a doubt about the origin of this surname, I have not come upon any early instances.

1792. Married—Nicholas Peter Thomasset and Sarah Morgan : St. Geo. Han. Sq. ii. 72.
1801. Bapt.—Frederic John, s. Charlotte Thomsett : Canterbury Cath., p. 41.
1809. Married—Charles Norley and Ann Tomsett : ibid. p. 102.
London, 1, 4, 1, 0 ; MDB. (co. Sussex), 0, 6, 0, 1.

Thomerson. — Bapt. A corruption of Thomasson (v. Thomas).

London, 1

Thomlinson, Thomlin.—Bapt. ' the son of Thomas,' from the nick. Thom, and the dim. Thom-lin ; v. Tomlin for early instances.

1528-9. John Thomplynson and Parnell Saunder : Marriage Lic. (London), i. 6.
1572. Bapt.—Alice, d. Thomas Thomlinson : St. Peter, Cornhill, i. 15.
1730. Married—John Thomlin and Jane Golde : St. Geo. Chap. Mayfair, p. 320.
1742. — Richard Thomlinson and Catherine Ferrer : ibid. p. 17.
London, 2, 0 ; Liverpool, 1, 0.

Thoms. — Bapt. ' the son of Thomas,' from the nick. Thom (later on Tom), and genitive Thoms. Hence Thomson. v. Thom.

John Thoms, co. Soms., 1 Edw. III : Kirby's Quest, p. 233.
London, 7 ; Philadelphia, 4 ; Boston (U.S.), 4.

Thomson, Thompson.—Bapt. ' the son of Thome,' i.e. Thomas (v. Thom). The *p* in Thompson is, of course, intrusive ; cf. Simpson for Simson.

Eborard fil. Thome, co. Camb., 1273. A.
Abraham fil. Thome, co. Bedf., 20 Edw. I. R.
1602. Married—Thomas Thomson and Mawdelen Langson : St. Jas. Clerkenwell, iii. 26.
1630. — Robert Thompson and Elline Lettice : ibid. p. 62.
London, 78, 245 ; Philadelphia, 91, 781.

Thor, Thore.—(1) Bapt. ' the son of Thor.'

Orm fil. Thore, 1179 : RRR. p. 167.

(2) Local, ' of Thore,' i.e. Kirkby Thure or Thore, a parish in co. Westmoreland. Nevertheless

(1) seems to be the true derivation.

London, 1, 0 ; Boston (U.S.), 0, 4.

Thorald; v. Thorold.

Thorburn, Thurburn. —
Bapt. 'the son of Thurbern'
(Thorbjorn occurs fifty-one times
in Iceland Roll, Yonge, ii. 205).
Torbern and Thurbern, Domesday ; cf. Osbern.

William Thorebern, co. Oxf., 1273. A.
Richard Thorbarn, co. Oxf., ibid.
Dominus Thurbern, co. Suff., ibid.
Nicholas Thurbern, co. Wilts, ibid.
Philip Thorbarn, co. Soms., 1 Edw.
III : Kirby's Quest, p. 113.
1574. Miles Case and Agnes Thurbarne:
Marriage Lic. (London), i. 61.
1808. Married—John Thorburn and
Ann Atkins, or Atkinson : St. Geo. Han.
Sq. ii. 380.
London, 4, 2 ; Boston (U.S.), 2, 0.

Thoreby; v. Thurlby.

Thorley.—Local, 'of Thorley,' a
parish in co. Hertford ; cf. Thurley.

Robert de Torly, co. Sussex, 1273. A.
Thomas de Torlaye, or Thorlay, or
Thorley, co. Linc., ibid.
William de Torleye, co. Hertf., 20
Edw. I. R.
Adam de Thorle, co. Norf., 1337 : FF.
ix. 476.
Theobald de Thorlee, co. Norf., temp.
Hen. V : ibid. ii. 276.
1654. Buried—Anthony Thorley, smallpox : St. Michael, Cornhill, p. 247.
London, 2 ; Manchester, 6 ; MDB.
(Norfolk), 1 ; Boston (U.S.), 1.

Thorman, Thurman, Thormund, Thurmond.—Bapt. 'the
son of Thormond'; cf. Wyman from
Wimond, Osman from Osmund, &c.

Henry Thurmond, co. Oxf., 1273. A.
Walter Thurmond, co. Oxf., ibid.
Alan Thurmod, co. Norf., ibid.
Henry Thurmund, co. Hants, 20
Edw. I. R.
1653. Buried—Edward Thurman : St.
Peter, Cornhill, p. 207.
'Messrs. Thurmond and Wilson,
woollen manufacturers ': West Riding
Dir., Batley.
London, 3, 1, 0, 0 ; Soothill, near
Dewsbury, 0, 0, 1, 0 ; Philadelphia, 3, 9, 0, 0.

**Thorn, Thorne, Thornes,
Thorns.**—Local, 'at the thorn'
or thorns, i. e. thorn-bush, or
clump of thorns. There is a parish
of Thorne in dioc. York, and
Thornes in dioc. Ripon.

William ad Spinam, co. Camb., 1273. A.
Hugh Thorne, co. Camb., ibid.
John de Thorn, co. Devon, ibid.

Walter de la Thorne, Fines Roll, 11
Edw. I.
Adam atte Thorne, co. Soms., 1 Edw.
III : Kirby's Quest, p. 177.
William de Thorn, co. Soms., 1 Edw.
III : ibid. p. 105.
Roger atte Thorn, C. R., 3 Hen. VI.
Robert atte Thornes, ibid., 25 Edw. III.
1579. Philip Thorne and Eliz. Hammond, *widow* : Marriage Lic. (London),
i. 87.
1746. Married—Thomas Thornes and
Sarah Truelove : St. Geo. Chap. Mayfair,
p. 71.
London, 33, 28, 1, 2 ; Philadelphia, 46,
26, 0, 0.

**Thornbarrow, Thornbery,
Thornbury, Thornberry,
Thornber.**—Local, ' of Thornborough,' co. Oxford, or Thornbury,
cos. Exeter, Hereford, &c. ; also
Thonborough in Allerton Mauleverer, near Knaresborough, co.
York. With the Yorkshire variant
Thornber, cf. the pronunciation
Sedber for Sedbergh, in the same
county.

Ricardus de Thornbargh, 1379 : P. T.
Yorks. p. 273.
Robert Thornbrughe, 1541 : Hist. and
Traditions of Ravenstonedale, co. West.,
W. Nicholls, p. 114.
Robert Thorneboroughe, 1541 : ibid.
1575. Edward Thorneboroughe, co.
Hants : Reg. Univ. Oxf. vol. ii. pt. ii. p. 62.
MDB. (West Rid. York), 0, 0, 0, 0, 3 ;
London, 0, 1, 1, 0, 0 ; Philadelphia, 0, 0, 0,
1, 0.

Thorncroft; v. Thornycroft.

Thorndyke, Thorndike. —
Local, 'at the thorn-dike,' from
residence thereby. I cannot find
the spot ; v. Thorn and Dyke.

1620. Edward Thorndicke : Reg. Univ.
Oxf. vol. ii. pt. i. p. 361.
1696. Bapt. — William, s. Herbert
Thorndicke : St. Jas. Clerkenwell, i. 369.
1806. Married—John Thorndyke and
Eliz. Nunn : St. Geo. Han. Sq. ii. 355.
London, 3, 0 ; Philadelphia, 0, 1 ;
Boston (U.S.), 0, 28.

Thorne(s; v. Thorn.

Thornhill, Thornell, Thornill.—Local, ' of Thornhill,' an
extensive parish six miles from
Wakefield, co. York. Thornell is
a manifest variant. There is also
Thornhill, a tithing in the parish
of Stalbridge, co. Dorset.

Walter de Thornhulle, co. Soms., 1
Edw. III : Kirby's Quest, p. 254.
Willelmus Thornyll, 1379 : P. T. Yorks.
p. 120.
Leticia de Thornhyll, 1379 : ibid. p. 126.

1580. Robert Curtys and Katherine
Thornell : Marriage Lic. (London), i. 99.
1661. Married—William Thornhill and
Jane Terrill : St. Jas. Clerkenwell, i. 108.
London, 7, 1, 0 ; Boston (U.S.), 1, 1, 0 ;
MDB. (co. Lincoln), 2, 1, 1.

**Thornley, Thorneley,
Thorniley, Thornalley,
Thornally, Thornlay.**—Local,
' of Thornley,' a township in the
parish of Kelloe, co. Durham ;
also a township in the parish of
Chipping, co. Lancaster. Probably
many small spots bore this name.

1581. John Thornelie, co. Ches. : Reg.
Univ. Oxf. vol. ii. pt. ii. p. 97.
1588-9. Thomas Thorneley and
Johanna Longe : Marriage Lic. (London), i. 176.
1662. Richard Thornley, of Chipping :
Lancashire Wills at Richmond, i. 276.
1675. Thomas Thornley, of Chipping :
ibid.
London, 1, 1, 1, 0, 0, 0 ; Philadelphia,
13, 0, 0, 0, 0, 0 ; MDB. (co. Lincoln), 0,
0, 0, 1, 1, 1.

Thorns; v. Thorn.

Thornthwaite. — Local, ' of
Thornthwaite,' a chapelry in the
parish of Hampsthwaite, W. Rid.
Yorks.

1724. Peter Thornthwaite, of Stock-in-Furness Fells : Lancashire Wills at
Richmond, ii. 253.
London, 1.

Thornton.—Local, ' of Thornton,' near Bradford, co. York ; also
parishes in diocs. Lincoln, Oxford,
Chester, Peterborough, Canterbury, &c. The explanation of so
many Thorntons in the Yorkshire
directories lies in the fact that
there are at least three Thorntons
in that county—the Thornton above
mentioned, Thornton-in-Craven,
and Thornton-in-Lonsdale.

Roger de Thorntone, co. Camb., 1273. A.
Hugh de Thorneton, co. York, ibid.
Richard de Thorneton, co. York, ibid.
1549. Buried — John Thornetone : St.
Michael, Cornhill, p. 179.
1570. George Thorneton and Johanna
Alondon : Marriage Lic. (London), i. 46.
London, 35 ; West Rid. Court Dir.
41 ; Philadelphia, 98.

**Thornycroft, Thorneycroft,
Thornicroft, Thorncroft,
Thornecroft.**—Local, 'of Thornycroft,' in the township of Siddington, in the parish of Prestbury,
East Cheshire. The family that

rose here has spread its roots all over England.

'Richard, lord of Siddington, confirms and quit claims to Richard, the son of Hamo de Thornicroft, all his right, &c., in certain lands and tenements in a certain place called Thornicroft, in Sydyngton, &c.': Harl. MSS. 2131.

Richard de Thornicroft, 1361: Earwaker's East Ches. ii. 400.

Hugh Thornicroft, of Thornicroft, 1436: ibid. p. 401.

1631. Edward Thonicroft, of Thornicroft: Wills at Chester, ii. 218.

1692-3. Bapt.—Thomas, s. John Thornycroft: St. Dionis Backchurch, p. 132.

London, 1, 2, 1, 2, 0; Manchester, 0, 1, 0, 0, 1.

Thorogood; v. Thurgood.

Thorold, Thorald.—Bapt.'the son of Thorald,' a favourite early and even Middle-English personal name. The surname still clings to co. Lincoln, where it was evidently popular as a personal name six centuries ago. v. Terrell and Turrell.

Turold, Domesday.

Thorold the Sheriff: Freeman, Norm. Conq. iii. 778.

Ralph fil. Thorald, co. Linc., 1273. A.

Torold Camerarius, co. Essex, ibid.

Symon Thorald, co. Norf., ibid.

Martin Torald, co. Oxf., ibid.

William Torel, or Thorel, London, ibid.

Richard Torel, co. Oxf., ibid.

Ralph Turold, co. Suff., ibid.

Turald de Papileon: Hist. Dunelmensis, Surtees Soc., vii. temp. 1400.

1638. Married—Robert Chesham and Phebe Thorold: St. Michael, Cornhill, p. 28.

1649. — Richard Thorrold and Mabella Gay: St. Jas. Clerkenwell, i. 84.

MDB. (co. Lincoln), 16, 1.

Thoroughgood; v. Thurgod.

Thorp, Thorpe, Thripp, Thrupp, Throop, Throup.—(1) Local, 'at the thorp,' i.e. the village. (2) Local, 'of Thorpe.' Many parishes, hamlets, &c., are so named in England.

Adam de la Throppe, co. Wilts, 1272. A.

Augustinus de Thorpe, co. Suff., ibid.

Warin de Thorpe, co. Camb., ibid.

1728. Married — Henry Chamner and Barbara Thorp: St. Geo. Han. Sq. i. 5.

1729. — William Thorpe and Frances Fox: ibid. p. 6.

1745. — John Throp and Mary Lunt: ibid. p. 34.

1770. — John Throop and Mary Burgin: ibid. p. 196.

1778. — Joseph Thrupp and Mary Burgon: ibid. p. 290.

London, 16, 30, 1, 4, 0, 0; Boston (U.S.), 4, 22, 0, 0, 1, 1.

Thorrington.—Local, 'of Thorrington,' a parish in co. Essex, seven miles from Colchester.

Roger de Thorington, co. Camb., 1273. A.

William de Thorinton, co. Devon, Hen. III-Edw. I. K.

Robert de Thorinton, co. Lanc., ibid.

1749. Married — Joseph Thorrington and Eleanor Thorp: St. Geo. Chap. Mayfair, p. 155.

London, 1.

Thousandpound. — Nick. 'Thousand-pound'; cf. Hundredpound, Centlivre, Ninepence, Twentymark, Twelvepence, Fourpence, &c. Thus in the present day a rich colonial is often nicknamed 'the Nugget.'

'Thomas Thousandpound' appears in the Wardrobe Accounts of Edward I. v. Index.

Thrasher; v. Thresher.

Threadgold, Thridgould, Tredgold.—? Nick. 'Threadgold,' a sobriquet of an embroiderer, or tapiser, or coucher. But far more probably a personal name, one of the many names ending in *good*, *gaud*, *got*, or *gold*; v. Scattergood, which is probably a personal and not a nickname.

Walterus Tredegold, co. Kent, 1273. A.

William Tredegold, co. Warw., ibid.

Robert Dredegold, co. Soms., 1 Edw. III: Kirby's Quest, p. 148.

1746. Married—John Thridgould and Ann Hilder: St. Geo. Chap. Mayfair, p. 68.

1765. Married—Benjamin Growcock and Frances Thridgould: St. Geo. Han. Sq. i. 140.

Adlingfleet, co. Yorks, 1, 0, 0; Sykehouse, co. Yorks, 1, 0, 0; London, 2, 1, 0.

Thredder. — Occup. 'the threader,' a maker of thread.

Willelmus Treder, 1379: P. T. Yorks. p. 15.

Christopher Threder, 1555, rector of Wissingset: FF. x. 86.

1574. Ezekiel Threader and Ellen Cumminge: Marriage Lic. (London), i. 60.

1741. Married—William Pening and Ann Threader: St. Geo. Han. Sq. i. 27.

1797. — John Dobbs and Sarah Thredder: ibid. ii. 167.

London, 2.

Threlfall.—Local, 'of Threlfall,' an estate in the parish of Kirkham, co. Lancaster. This surname has ramified very strongly, and is extremely familiar in the Palatinate. The family was 'ori-

ginally seated at Threlfall in the Fylde, of which were John and Henry Threlfall in the time of Edward VI, and Edmund Threlfall in 19 Jas. I, who died seised of lands in Threlfall, Goosnargh, and Hothersall': Baines' Lancashire, ii. 605.

Edmund Threlfall, of Threlfall, *yeoman*, 1591: Lancashire Wills at Richmond, p. 278.

William Threlfall, of Goosnargh, 1662: ibid. p. 279.

George Threlfall, of Goosnargh, *husbandman*, 1630: ibid. p. 278.

1747. Married—James Threlfa (sic) and Mary Pryor: St. Geo. Chap. Mayfair, p. 100.

Manchester, 8; Goosnargh, 2; MDB. (Lancashire), 13; Philadelphia, 3.

Threlkeld.—Local, 'of Threlkeld,' a chapelry in the parish of Greystock, co. Cumb., four miles from Keswick.

Henry de Threlkeld, co. Cumb., 14 Edw. II: Nicolson and Burn's Hist. of Cumb. ii. 373.

William de Threlkeld, co. Cumb., 13 Ric. II: ibid.

Richard Thrilkelde, Queen's College, 1565: Reg. Univ. Oxf. vol. ii. pt. ii. p. 23.

1567. Edward Threlkeld, rector of Great Salkeld: Jefferson's History of Leath Ward (co. Cumb.), p. 265.

1793. Thomas Threlkeld left £20 to his executors, the interest of which was to be paid to the poor of the parish of Croglin: ibid. p. 103.

MDB. (co. Cumb.), 2; Boston (U.S.), 1.

Thresher, Thrasher.—Occup. 'the thresher,' a grain thresher.

Robert le Thressher, co. Soms., 1 Edw. III: Kirby's Quest, p. 244.

Ricardus Trescher, 1379: P. T. Yorks. p. 111.

Thomas Thresshere, C. R., 7 Hen. IV.

1696. Married—Samuel Taylor and Hannah Thresher: St. Dionis Backchurch, p. 45.

1752. Married—Edward Bennett and Eliz. Thrasher: St. Geo. Chap. Mayfair, p. 215.

London, 5, 0; MDB. (co. Worcester), 0, 1; Philadelphia, 1, 3.

Thring, Tring. — Local, 'of Tring,' a parish and market-town in co. Hertford.

Robert de Thring, co. Kent, 1273. A.

Edgar Thring, 1606: Reg. Broad Chalke, co. Wilts, p. 42.

Annis Thring, 1606: ibid.

1743. Married—Daniel Thring and Eliz. Stork: St. Geo. Han. Sq. i. 31.

1766. — William Tring and Susanna Norris: ibid. p. 154.

London, 3, 1.

Thripp ; v. Fripp and Thorp.

Throckmorton. — Local, ' of Throckmorton,' a chapelry in the parish of Fladbury, co. Worc. Mr. Lower (quoting Shirley's Noble and Gentle Men) says, 'John de Trockemerton was dwelling there about the year 1200' (Patr. Brit. p. 344).

1571. Arthur Throckmorton, London : Reg. Univ. Oxf. vol. ii. pt. ii. p. 52.
1572. Francis Throckmorton,co.Worc.: ibid. p. 53.
1584. Clement Throckmorton, co. Warwick : ibid. p. 84.
1623. John Throgmorton settled in Virginia : Hotten's Lists of Emigrants, p. 189.
London Court Dir., 1 ; Philadelphia, 1.

Throop, Throup ; v. Thorp.

Thrower. — Occup. ' the thrower,' a thread or silk winder, one who throws thread. It is almost certain that Trower is a corrupted form of Thrower ; cf. Thring and Tring (v. Thunder for a reverse corruption).

John Thrower, rector of Flordon, co. Norf., 1418 : FF. v. 73.
Clemens Thrower, C. R., 28 Henry VII. pt. ii.
1774. Married—Thomas Thrower and Eliz. Philby : St. Geo. Han. Sq. i. 237.
London, 4 ; MDB. (Norfolk), 7.

Thrupp ; v. Thorp.

Thunder.—Occup. ' the tunder,' an American imitative corruption ; cf. Thring with Tring and Thrower with Trower. Nevertheless, this same corruption is found in English registers ; v. Tunder and Tunneler.

1669. Bapt.—Honour, d. Pattnoe (sic) Thunder : St. Jas. Clerkenwell, i. 239.
1800. Married—Valentine Riviere and Henrietta Thunder (co. Bucks) : St. Geo. Han. Sq. ii. 230.
1801. — Gregory Staples and Mary Thunder : ibid. p. 248.
Philadelphia, 3.

Thurburn ; v. Thorburn.

Thurgaland.—Local, 'of Thurgoland,' a township in the parish of Silkstone, W. Rid. Yorks.

1620. John Hill and Eliz. Thurguland : Marriage Lic. (Westminster), p. 27.
1621. Avery Thurgoland, co. Yorks : Reg. Univ. Oxf. vol. ii. pt. ii. p. 389.
Philadelphia, 4.

Thurgall.—Bapt. ' the son of Thorkettle ' ; v. Thurkettle. This Norfolk surname is easily proved to be thus descended. It is only a variant of Thurkle ; cf. Thurkleby, a local surname (i.e. the *by* or dwelling of Thorkettle).

'In the priory church (Langley, co. Norf.) was buried Sir Robert Thurgelby': FF. x. 149.
'Sir Roger de Thurkelby had a grant of free warrant in the 29th of Hen. III ': ibid. viii. 22.

In the same way Thurkle or Thurkell became Thurgall, and is so found to this day in co. Norfolk, where Thirkettle, or Thurkettle, or Thurkell are still familiar. It is simply a variant. In compounds the suffix *-kettle* almost invariably became *-kell* or *-kle* ; v. Arkettle, Oskettle, Thurkettle, &c.

MDB. (Norfolk), 1.

Thurgar, Thurgur. — Bapt. ' the son of Turgar ' or Thurgar (Yonge, ii. 206).

Thurger del Childhus, co. Suff., 1273. A.
Pagan Thurgar, co. Bedf., ibid.
John Thurgar, co. Camb., ibid.
Hugh Thurgar, co. Camb., ibid.
1801. Married — Christopher Thurgar and Charlotte King : St. Geo. Han. Sq. ii. 240.
London, 0, 1.

Thurgood, Thirgood, Thorogood, Thoroughgood, Thorowgood, Toogood, Towgood.—Bapt. ' the son of Thurgod ' (Turgod, Domesday ; cf. Tur-ulf for Thur-ulf, and Tor-ald for Thor-ald). ' William Togod, alias Thogod ' (L.). This is an important entry, proving, if proof were wanting, that our Toogoods and Towgoods are the same. That Thurgood should be euphemized to Thoroughgood was as natural as inevitable.

Alicia Thurgod, co. Bedf., 1273. A.
Geoffrey Togod, co. Hunts, ibid.
Isolda Togod, co. Hunts, ibid.
William Togod, co. Soms., 1 Edw. III : Kirby's Quest, p. 174.
Hugo Togod, 1379 : P. T. Yorks. p. 74.
' Edward Togoode, sup. for B.A., Jan. 1525-6 ': Reg. Univ. Oxf. i. 141.
1557. Bapt.—Dority Througood : St. Antholin (London), p. 12.
1650. Bapt. — William, s. Richard Thoroughgood, *fishmonger* : St. Peter, Cornhill, i. 93.

1651. Bapt.—Joseph, s. Richard Thorogood, *fishmonger* : ibid.
London, 4, 2, 8, 1, 1, 10, 2 ; Oxford, 1, 0, 1, 0, 0, 1, 0; Philadelphia, 0, 0, 1, 1, 0, 0, 0.

Thurkettle, Thurkell, Thurkle, Thurkill, Thirkettle, Thirkell.—Bapt. ' the son of Thurkettle,' a compound of Kettle, q.v. *Kettle* as a suffix became *-kell*, *-kill*, or *-kle*. v. Thirticle, Thirtle, Thurtle, Thurtell, all variants.

Turketyl, abbot of Croyland, 946-55.
Thurkill the Sacrist : Freeman, Norm. Conq. iii.432.
Thurcytel Marehead : ibid. i. 344.
Walter fil. Turchilli, temp. 1250: FFF. p. 221.
Thurkeld le Seneschal, co. Linc., 20 Edw. I. R.
William Thurkel, temp. 1300. M.
Nicholas Thirkle, vicar of Wiggenhall, co. Norf., 1541 : FF. ix. 182.
Robert Thirkettle, vicar of Aldeburgh, co. Norf., 1554 : ibid. v. 353.
Margaret Thurketel, co. Norf., temp. 1580 : ibid. v. 401.
Francis Thirkell, co. Norf., 24 Hen. VIII : ibid. x. 159.

Just as Thurgood (q.v.) became Thoroughgood, so Thurkettle became Thoroughkettle.

1700. Bapt. — Mary Thoroughkettle : St. James, Piccadilly.
London, 0, 0, 2, 0, 2, 2; MDB. (Suffolk), Thurkettle, 3 ; (Norfolk), Thirkettle, 3.

Thurlby, Thoreby. — Local, ' of Thurlby.' Two parishes and a hamlet bear this name in co. Lincoln. Also a township named Thoralby, in the parish of Aysgarth, N. Rid. Yorks. This readily suggests the derivation, viz. the *by* or dwelling of Thorald.

Nicholas de Thurleby, co. Linc., 1273. A.
Roger de Thurleby, co. Linc., ibid.
1576. Henry Thyrlibe, co. Norf. : Reg. Univ. Oxf. vol. ii. pt. ii. p. 71.
London, 1, 0 ; MDB. (Lincoln), 7, 2.

Thurley.—Local, ' of Thurleigh,' a parish in co. Bedford ; cf. Thorley.

1569-70. Robert Thurley and Eliz. Smithe : Marriage Lic. (London), i. 45.
1794. Married—William Jackson and Eliz. Thurley : St. Geo. Han. Sq. ii. 117.
London, 5.

Thurlow.—Local,'of Thurlow.' Great and Little Thurlow are parishes in co. Suffolk.

Matilda de Threlowe, co. Camb., 1273. A.
John de Thrillowe, co. Camb., ibid.

1795. Married — Samuel Thurlow and Eliz. Lowe : St. Geo. Han. Sq. ii. 125. London, 6 ; Philadelphia, 3.

Thurman.—Bapt. ; v. Thorman.

Thurnam.—Local, ' of Thurnham,' a township in the parish of Lancaster.

Carlisle, 2.

Thursby.— Local, ' of Thoresby.' North and South Thoresby are parishes in co. Lincoln.

Gilbert de Thoresby, co. Linc., 1273. A.
John de Thoresby, co. Linc., 20 Edw. I, R.
Robertus de Thoresby, 1379 ; P. T. Yorks. p. 278.
1628. Married — Samuel Robins and Katherine Thursby : St. Jas. Clerkenwell, i. 58.
1800. — George Augustus Thursby and Frances Pelham : St. Geo. Han. Sq. ii. 220.
Crockford, 3 ; MDB. (co. Lanc.), 2.

Thursfield.—Local, ' of Thursfield,' a chapelry in the parish of Wolstanton, co. Stafford.

1804. Married—Joseph Thursfield and Eliza Quelch : St. Geo. Han. Sq. ii. 307. London, 2.

Thurstan, Thurston, Tustin, Tustian.—(1) Bapt. ' the son of Thurstan.' Danish Thorstein, i e Thorstone.

Turstanus Machinator : Domesday.
Thurstan, abbot of Ely : Freeman, Norm. Conq. iii. 68.
Thurstan Goz : ibid. ii. 203.
Thurstan, housecarl of Eadward : ibid. i. 737.
Robert fil. Thurstani, co. Kent, 1273. A.
Thurstan de Torp, co. Hunts, ibid.
Thurstan de Holland, 1313. M.
Thurstayn de Cruce, co. Soms., 1 Edw. III : Kirby's Quest, p. 144.
Johannes Thurstan, 1379 : P. T. Yorks. p. 15.
Thryston Hodgkin, 1544 : Reg. St. Dionis Backchurch.

The omission of *h* was an early one.
Turstan de Bricetwell, co. Oxf., 1273. A.

(2) Local, ' of Thurston,' a parish in co. Suffolk.

Hervey de Thurstan, co. Norf., 1273. A.
William de Thurston, co. Norf., ibid.
London, 0, 16, 1, 2 ; New York, 0, 19, 0, 0.

Thurtle, Thurtell. — Bapt. ' the son of Thurkettle,' variants of Thurkle and Thurkell (v. Thurkettle) ; cf. Thirtle. These surnames are found in Norfolk and Suffolk, where, of course, we

expect to see them, as Thurkettle has been established as a surname there for six centuries.

1802. Married — Samuel Thurtle and Susanna Lucas : St. Geo. Han. Sq. ii. 256. MDB. (co. Norfolk), 1, 1 ; London, 1, 0.

Thurwood.—Bapt. ' the son of Thurgard,' i.e. Thor's guard.

Agnes Thoreward, co. Oxf., 1273. A.
Richard Thoreward, co. Oxf., ibid.
William Thoreward, co. Oxf., ibid.
London, 1.

Thwaite, Thwaites, Thwaits.—Local, ' of the thwaites ' or thwaite, i.e. the meadows, the clearings or clearing, frequently found in such compounds as Thistlethwaite, Cooperthwaite, Thornthwaite, Haverthwaite, or Postlethwaite, which are all North English in origin. Probably connected with *whittle*, a knife. M.E. *thwitel*, a knife. Hence *thwaite*, a woodland clearing.

John del Thwaites, c. 1300. M.
Thomas de Thwaytes. B.
Robertus del Twaytes, 1379 : P. T. Yorks. p. 273.
1607. Samuel Thwaytes, of London : Reg. Univ. Oxf. vol. ii. pt. ii. p. 299.
1718. Buried—John Thwaits, in the new vault : St. Michael, Cornhill, p. 285.
London, 0, 17, 3 ; MDB. (West Rid. Yorks), 4, 3, 0.

Thynne.—Nick. ' the thin,' i.e. lean, slender. M.E. *thinne* and *thynne*.

' My tale is don, for my wit is but thinne.'   Chaucer, C. T. 9556.

Cf. Thick, Large, Small, Bigg, Little, Fatt, &c. The old orthography has been maintained in this name. For a strange but unconfirmed story of a local origin, viz. ' John of th' Inne,' one of the Inns of Court, v. Lower's Patr. Brit. p. 345. Until better proof is shown we may be content with the satisfactory derivation given above.

Thomas Thynne, co. Northampton, 1273. A.
1577. Francis Thynne, co. Wilts : Reg. Univ. Oxf. vol. ii. pt. ii. p. 76.
1583. Henry Thynne, co. Wilts : ibid. p. 120.
1758. Married—John Thinn and Sarah Gee : St. Geo. Han. Sq. i. 82.
London, 4.

Tibbalds, Tibbard, Tibbles, Tibbals.—Bapt. ' the son of Theobald ' ; v. Tebbitt.

' For thus sings the divine Mr. Tibbalds, or Theobalds, in one of his birthday poems :
" I am no scollard, but I am polite ;
Therefore be sure I'm no Jacobite."
Polite Conversation, p. 339, Dean Swift's Works (Chatto and Windus, 1876).
1533-4. John Bastall and Tiballe Schryvener : Marriage Lic. (London), i. 9.
1574. Bapt.—Jesper, s. William Tibbold : St. Peter, Cornhill, i. 16.
1598. John Tibbolls and Eliz. Claye : Marriage Lic. (London), i. 253.
London, 1, 1, 1, 0 ; Boston (U.S.), 0, 0, 0, 1 ; Philadelphia, 0, 0, 0, 4.

Tibbatts, Tibbitts, Tibbutt, Tibbits, Tibbetts, Tibbet, Tibbett, Tibbitt, Tibbott.—Bapt. (1) ' the son of Theobald ' ; (2) ' the son of Isabel ' (v. Tebbitt). The variations are almost innumerable. They have run riot through the vowels.

1568. Richard Tybbott and Alice Haselam : Marriage Lic. (London), i. 39.
1729. Married—Roger Persons and Sarah Tibbets : St. Geo. Han. Sq. i. 6.
1744. — William Tibbitt and Eliz. Cammack : ibid. p. 33.
1802. — John Tibbatts and Martha May : ibid. ii. 257.
1805. — John Cock and Catherine Tibbatt : ibid. p. 333.
London, 1, 5, 1, 0, 0, 0, 0, 0, 0 ; Boston (U.S.), 0, 0, 0, 1, 5, 1, 0, 0, 0 ; Philadelphia, 0, 0, 0, 0, 2, 1, 2, 2, 1.

Tibbenham, Tibenham. — Local, ' of Tibbenham,' a parish in co. Norfolk.

MDB. (co. Suffolk), 2, 1.

Tibbetts, &c. ; v. Tibbatts.

Tibbles ; v. Tibbalds.

Tibbs.—Bapt. ; v. Tebb.

Tibby.—Local ; v. Tebay.

Tibbyson.—Bapt. ' the son of Tib ' ; v. Tebb.

Johannes Tibbeson, 1379 : P. T. Yorks. p. 219.
1788. Married — George Breffitt and Caroline Tibson : St. Geo. Han. Sq. ii. 10.

Ticehurst.—Local, ' of Ticehurst,' a parish in co. Sussex, ten miles from Tonbridge Wells.

MDB. (co. Kent), 1.

Tichborne.—Local, ' of Tichbourne,' in co. Hants.

Richard de Ticheburn, co. Bucks, 1273. A.
Walter de Tycheburn, co. Wilts, Hen. III-Edw. I. K.
1581. Roger Tutcheborne, co. Hants : Reg. Univ. Oxf. vol. ii. pt. ii. p. 98.
1602. Henry Ticheborne, co. Hants : ibid. p. 256.

1617. John Tychborne, co. Hants: Reg. Univ. Oxf. vol. ii. pt. ii. p. 365.
1783. Married — William Tichborne and Sarah Worthington : St. Geo. Han. Sq. i. 345.
London Court Dir., 1 ; New York, 1.

Tickell, Tickle, Tickel. — Local, ' of Tickhill,' a parish in the Union of Doncaster, co. York. By removal of a branch of this family into Lancashire, the surname is now more familiar in that county than in the county of its parentage.

Jordan de Tykehull, co. Notts, 20 Edw. I. R.
Richard de Tikhill, 28 Edw. I : Freemen of York, i. 8.
Henricus de Tikhill, 1379 : P. T. Yorks. p. 114.
Arthur Tickle, of Ormskirk, 1590 : Wills at Chester (1545-1620), p. 192.
Edward Tickle, of Manchester, *apothecary*, 1616 : ibid.
Alice Tickhill, of Manchester, 1618 : ibid.
1795. Married—Ebenezer Roebuck and Zipporah Tickell : St. Geo. Han. Sq. ii. 138.
London, 2, 2, 0 ; Manchester, 1, 3, 0 ; Liverpool, 0, 3, 0 ; Philadelphia, 0, 0, 1.

Ticklepenny, Tickelpenny. — Local, ' of Ticklepenny,' a place near Grimsby, co. Lincoln ; v. Lower's Patr. Brit. p. 346.

1786. Married—William Marriss and Jane Ticklepenny : St. Geo. Han. Sq. i. 386.
MDB. (co. Lincoln), 1, 0 ; Hull, 0, 1.

Tickner.—?Occup. Mr. Lower, quoting Mr. Ferguson, says, ' Dutch *teekenaar*, a drawer or designer ' (Patr. Brit. p. 346). This seems the more probable as the surname is modern in England, and may be the result of immigration.

1575. Henry Tycknor and Agnes Anderson, *widow* : Marriage Lic. (London), i. 67.
1630. Bapt.—Michaell, s. Lawrence Ticknor : St. Peter, Cornhill, i. 81.
1649. — Thomas, s. Thomas Tickner, *grocer* : ibid. p. 92.
1771. Married—Benjamin Tickner and Ann Coles : St. Geo. Han. Sq. i. 212.
London, 6 ; Philadelphia, 9.

Tidball.—Bapt. ' the son of Theobald ' ; v. Tudball.

London, 1 ; MDB. (co. Somerset), 5 ; New York, 1.

Tidd.—(1) Bapt. ' the son of Tiddeman,' from the nick. Tidd ; v. Tiddeman. But possibly a

nick. of Tiffany, q.v., the old name for Epiphany (i.e. Theophania).

   ' Tid, Mid, and Miseray,
   Carlin, Pome, and Pace-egg Day,'

is a North-English rhyme by which children still learn the chief Sundays from Epiphany to Easter. (2) Local, ' of Tydd,' parishes in cos. Cambridge and Lincoln. Probably these are the chief parents.

Thomas de Tid, co. Camb., 1273. A.
Johannes Tydde, 1379 : P. T. Yorks. p. 134.
John de Tydd, co. Norf., 27 Edw. III : FF. viii. 133.
1795. Married — Samuel Martin and Eliz. Tidd : St. Geo. Han. Sq. ii. 136.
London, 4 ; Philadelphia, 1 ; Boston (U.S.), 8.

Tiddeman, Tiddiman, Tidyman, Tidman, Titman, Tideman.—Bapt. ' the son of Tiddeman.' I cannot explain its origin, but it seems to have come from the Low Countries.

Tethingman le Auste, co. Glouc., 1273. A.
Tiddeman Boker. H.
Tydyman le Swarte. N.
Robert Tethingman, co. Soms., 1 Edw. III : Kirby's Quest, p. 189.
Tideman de Winchcomb, 1394, bishop of Llandaff : Crockford, p. xl.

Cf. Bateman, Coleman, Sweetman, all baptismal names.

1772. Married — Richard Tiddeman and Sarah Frost : St. Geo. Han. Sq. i. 226.
1788. — William Tidman and Margaret Davison : ibid. ii. 11.
London, 0, 0, 1, 1, 10, 1, 0 ; Philadelphia, 0, 0, 0, 1, 1, 1.

Tidmarsh.—Local, ' of Tidmarsh,' a parish in co. Berks.

1602. John Tidmershe, co. Worc. : Reg. Univ. Oxf. vol. ii. pt. ii. p. 258.
1749. Married — Richard Tidmarsh and Sarah Moythen : St. Geo. Chap. Mayfair, p. 142.
London, 4 ; MDB. (co. Wilts), 2 ; Oxford, 3 ; Philadelphia, 1.

Tidswell, Tidgewell.—Local, ' of Tideswell,' a parish in co. Derby.

Henry de Tideswell, co. Derby, 1273. A.
Ricardus de Tyddeswelle, 1379 : P. T. Yorks. p. 54.
1545. William Coplande and Joanne Tyddeswell : Marriage Lic. (London), i. 10.

1770. Richard Tidswell and Mary Thorley : St. Geo. Han. Sq. i. 203.
London, 2, 0 ; Boston (U.S.), 1, 1.

Tidy, Tidey. — (1) ? Bapt. ' the son of Tiffany ' (?), from the nick. Tidd, and the pet form Tiddy or Tidy ; v. Tiffany. (2) Nick. ' the tidy,' the neat in personal appearance and habit.

Stephen Tydy, C. R., 26 Edw. III.
1788. Married—Joseph Piggon and Henrietta Tidy : St. Geo. Han. Sq. ii. 4.
London, 6, 0 ; Boston (U.S.), 0, 1.

Tidyman.—Bapt. ; v. Tiddeman. Nothing to do with tidiness or orderliness. Not a nickname.

London, 1.

Tierney, Tiernay.—Bapt. ' the son of Tierney.' St. Tigernath or Tierney was an Irish saint of the 6th century, and third bishop of Clogher. In the Philadelphia Directory are six Patricks Tierney, two Michaels, and one Terence. This will sufficiently demonstrate the Irish parentage of the surname.

London, 1, 0 ; Philadelphia, 53, 4.

Tiffany, Tiffen, Tiffin.—Bapt. ' the son of Theophania ' (i.e. Epiphany), popularly Tiffany, the pet form being Tiffen and Tiffin. Of course the thin gauzy fabric known as *tiffany* has the same origination. One of our old mysteries include :

   ' Megge   Merrywedyr,   and   Sabyn Sprynge,
   Tiffany Twynkeler fayle for no thynge.'

The font-name is found in Cornwall in the 17th century :

1600. Bapt. — Tiffeny, d. of Harry Hake : St. Columb Major.
1695. — Epipheney, d. of Humfry Oxnam : ibid.

A curious entry meets us in the Testa de Neville (Hen. III-Edw. I), p. 317 :

   ' Thephanya Hugo de Harington, prior de Giseburn.'

It reads strangely like a double font-name, a custom supposed to be unknown then. It is a man's name, too. All my instances are feminine. Possibly it was his spiritual name.

Tiffonia de Karduil, Hen. III-Edw.
I : K. p. 289.
Theofania de Bolebek, C. R., 46
Hen. III.
Thifania Simme, co. Camb., 1273. A.
Cristina Typhayn, co. Soms., 1 Edw.
III : Kirby's Quest, p. 102.
Johannes Holand et Tiffan uxor ejus,
1379 : P. T. Yorks. p. 134.
Teffan Danyll, 1379 : ibid. p. 148.
Nicholas fil. Tiffaniae. T.
Tyffanie Seamor, temp. Ellz. Z.
Teffania de Wildeker. E.
John Tyffyn, 1536: Reg. Univ. Oxf. i. 185.
1540. Married—Robert Yerson and
Isabell Tyffenne : St. Peter, Cornhill, i. 221.
1632. — Edward Somes and Mary
Tiffin : St. Antholin (London), p. 66.
1750. —. Whitelock More and Ann
Tiphaine : St. Geo. Han. Sq. i. 45.
London, 2, 0, 0; Boston (U.S.). Court
Dir., 2, 0, 0; Boston (U.S.), 9, 0, 1.

Tigg.—Nick. ; v. Tegg.

Tigh, Tighe.—Local ; v. Tye.

Tilbrook.—Local, 'of Tilbrook,'
a parish in co. Bedford.
William de Tilbroc, co. Linc., 1273. A.
MDB. (co. Suffolk), 2 ; (co. Camb.), 3 ;
Philadelphia, 1.

Tilbury.—Local, ' of Tilbury,'
three parishes in co. Essex.
Richard de Tillebyr', co. Essex, 1273. A.
1740. Bapt — Elizabeth, d. Edward
Tilbury : St. Dionis Backchurch, p. 170
1753. Married—Thomas Tilbury and
Eliz. Head : St. Geo. Chap. Mayfair, p. 240.
London, 8 ; Oxford, 1.

Tilden. — Local, ' of Tilden,'
seemingly some spot in co. Kent.
Perhaps a variant of Tilton, q.v.
But this is improbable. I doubt
not that the place must be sought
in the above-named county.
Henry de Tildenne, co. Kent, 20 Edw.
I. R.
1573. Richard Tylden and Mabell
Lamb : Marriage Lic. (London), i. 56.
1610. Theophilus Tylden, co. Kent:
Reg. Univ. Oxf. vol. ii. pt. ii. p. 313.
Philadelphia, 11.

Tildesley, Tildsley, Tyldsley.
—Local, ' of Tyldesley,' a parish in
South Lancashire. The surname
passed on at some period to London,
and is commoner there than in
Lancashire.
Hugo de Tyldesley, co. Linc., 20 Edw.
I. R.
Henry de Tyldesley, co. Linc., ibid.
Thurstan Tyldesley, co. Lanc., 1563:
Wills at Chester (1545-1620), p. 279.
Richard Tildesley, of Preston, co.
Lanc. : ibid. p. 290.

1593. Thurstan Tyldslay : Lancashire
Wills at Richmond, i. 290.
1624. Married — Philip Tillsley and
Ann Daniell : St. Mary Aldermary, p. 15.
London, 5, 0, 0 ; Manchester, 2, 2, 0 ;
Philadelphia, 0, 0, 1.

Tileston ; v. Tilston.

Tilewright ; v. Telwright.

Tilford, Tillford.—Local, ' of
Tilford,' a tithing in the parish of
Farnham, co. Surrey.
1808. Married — William Gurr May-
mott and Ann Tilford : St. Geo. Han.
Sq. ii. 394.
Philadelphia, 2, 0 ; New York, 7, 1.

Till, Tillson.—Bapt. ' the son
of Matilda,' from the nick. Till ; v.
Tilson.

Tillcock.—? Nick. ' the teal-
cock ' (?), the male teal. M.E. tele ;
cf. Peacock, Moorcock, &c. If not
a nickname, then baptismal from
some nick. Till, with suffix -cock ;
cf. Wilcock, Jeffcock, Simcock.
This surname was settled in Oxfordshire for centuries.
John Telcok, co. Oxf., 1273. A.
Thomas Telcok, co. Oxf., ibid.
1548. William Tylcokks, bailiff of
Oxford : Reg. Univ. Oxf. vol. ii. pt. i. p.
261.
1556. William Tilkoke, mayor of
Oxford : ibid. p. 7.
1789. Married—Thomas Coggin and
Eliz. Tillcock : St. Geo. Han. Sq. ii. 24.
London, 1.

Tilleard.—? Bapt. ' the son of
Teyllard.'
John Teyllard, co. Soms., 1 Edw. III :
Kirby's Quest, p. 162.
London, 3.

Tiller ; v. Tillyer.

Tillett. — Bapt. ' the son of
Matilda,' from the nick. Till, and
dim. Till-ett (v. Tillotson).
1593. Married—Richard Tyllett and
Johan Tene : St. Dionis Backchurch,
p. 12.
1798. — William Tillet and Martha
Martin : St. Geo. Han. Sq. ii. 190.
London, 13 ; Philadelphia, 1.

Tilley, Tillie, Tilly. — (1)
Local, ' from Tilly,' a village in
' the department of Calvados in
Normandy,' as described by Lower.
He adds, ' There is a second place
so called in the department of
Eure.'

Phillipa de Tylly, or Tilli, 33 Hen. III :
BBB. p. 21.
Ralph de Tilly, 14 Edw. I : ibid. p. 373.
The latter had property in Nor-
mandy.
John Tylye, co. Soms., 1 Edw. III :
Kirby's Quest, p. 103.
Philip de Tylly, co. Dorset, Hen. III-
Edw. I. K.
Henry de Tilli, co. Devon, ibid.
Johannes Tilly, 1379 : P. T. Yorks.
p. 173.

(2) Bapt. (?). A pet form of Matilda ; v. Till, Tilson, and Tillotson.
This second probable origin will
help to explain the large number
of Tilleys and Tillys in our directories.
1756. Married — John Shipman and
Mary Tillie : St. Geo. Han. Sq. i. 65.
1761. — Thomas Tilley and Susanna
Turnedge : ibid. p. 102.
1774. — Henry Tilly and Susanna
Whittington : ibid. p. 246.
London, 21, 1, 10 ; Boston (U.S.),
6, 0, 1.

Tilling. — Bapt. ' the son of
Matilda,' from nick. Till, dim.
Till-in, more generally dim. Tillot
(v. Tillotson). The g in Tilling is
excrescent, as in Jenning (v. Jennings). Cornwall, the last home of
many a decayed font-name and pet
form, retained Tillin till modern
times.
Stephanus Tyllyng, 1379 : P. T. Yorks.
p. 79.
1691. Married — John Tilling and
Margaret Joy : St. Jas. Clerkenwell,
i. 209.
1779. Bapt. — Tillane, daughter of
William Hewett : Reg. St. Columb
Major (Cornwall), p. 135.

Colin is spelt Colane in the
same register.
London, 9.

Tillison.—A corruption of Tillotson, q.v. In the same way
Ibbison is often a corruption of
Ibbotson, and Sissison of Sissotson,
all being Yorkshire surnames derived from feminine personal
names, viz. Matilda, Isabel, and
Cecilia.
1677. Married — George Smith and
Hannah Taylor, by Dr. Tillison (i, e,
Tillotson): St. Michael, Cornhill, p. 41.
1748. — Richard Tillison and Margaret Stone : St. Geo. Chap. Mayfair,
p. 121.
Boston (U.S.), 2.

Tillman, Tillmon.—(1)Occup. 'the tileman,' i.e. the tiler, one who covered roofs with tiles; v. Tyler. The tendency would be to the modern spelling and pronunciation. (2) Occup. 'the tillman,' i.e. a husbandman. 'Because there were so fewe tylmen, the erde (earth) lay untilled': Capgrave's Chron.. sub. A. D. 1349. (Lower's Patr. Brit. p. 346.)

Geoffrey Tileman, co. Hunts, 1273. A.
Walter Tileman. N.
1572. Isaac Tylman, Magdalen Hall: Reg. Univ. Oxf. vol. ii. pt. ii. p. 38.
1661. Buried A child of Mr. Tilman's, the chirurgion: St. Dionis Backchurch, p. 233.
London, 6, 0; Boston (U.S.), 8, 2.

Tillotson, Tillott, Tillottson. —Bapt. 'the son of Matilda,' from the nick. Till, and dim. Till-ot. This was and is a familiar Yorkshire surname. The archbishop sprang from a Yorkshire family.

Cecilia Tillote, co. Oxf., 1273. A.
Tyllot Thompson, co. York. W. 9.
Magota Tillosson (sic), 1379: P. T. Howdenshire, p. 16.
Tillot Punte, 1379: P. T. Yorks. p. 269.
Tillot Hobwyfe, 1379: ibid. p. 271.
Tillot Clynch, 1379: ibid. p. 273.
Tillot de Carr, 1379: ibid. p. 272.
Tillot de Northwod, 1379: ibid. p. 284.
Willelmus Tillotson, 1379: ibid.
Johannes Tillotson, 1379: ibid.
1777. Married — Thomas Rice and Sarah Tillott: St. Geo. Han. Sq. i. 272.
1800. — George Richardson and Caroline Catherine Tillotson: ibid. ii. 246.
London, 1, 0, 0; West Rid. Court Dir., 5, 0, 0; Philadelphia, 2, 0, 1.

Tilly; v. Tilley.

Tillyer, Tiller.—Occup. 'the tiller,' a tiller of the soil. With Tillyer, cf. Sawyer for Sawer, or lawyer for lawer.

1769. Married—John Tillier and Ann Pickernell: St. Geo. Han. Sq. i. 183.
1780. — Thomas Roberts and Eleanor Tiller: ibid. p. 317.
London, 0, 1; Philadelphia, 6, 1.

Tilney. — Local, 'of Tilney,' two parishes in co. Norfolk.

Robert de Tilney, co. Norf., 1273. A.
Nicholas de Tilneye, co. Norf., ibid.
1564. Edward Chafforne and Ursula Tylney: Marriage Lic. (London), i. 28.
1583. Married—Edmund Tylney, Esq., and the Lady Bray: St. Jas. Clerkenwell, i. 9.
London, 7; Philadelphia, 1.

Tilson, Till, Tillson, Tills, Tilles.—Bapt. 'the son of Matilda,' from nick. Till. Chiefly found in Yorkshire, where Matilda was extremely popular (v. Tillotson).

Alexander fil. Tylle. DD.
John Tilson, co. York. W. 2.
Robert Tilleson, 1397: Preston Guild Rolls, p. 1.
Agnes Tylleson, 1379: P. T. Howdenshire, p. 16.
Robertus Tilleson, 1379: P. T. Yorks. p. 244.
Willelmus Tyllson, 1379: ibid. p. 273.
John Tills, or Tillis, sheriff of Norwich, 1485: FF. iii. 173.
1690. Bapt. — Benjamin, s. Nathan Tillson: St. Jas. Clerkenwell, i. 339.
1742. Married—James Tilson and Jane Tilson: St. Geo. Han. Sq. i. 28.
1748. — John Bell and Eliz. Till: ibid. p. 40.
London, 0, 16, 1, 1, 0; Boston (U.S.), 2, 3, 8, 0, 1.

Tilston, Tileston.—Local, 'of Tilston,' a parish in co. Chester. Not to be confounded with Tilson or Tillotson, q.v.

1586. Thomas Tylston, co. Salop: Reg. Univ. Oxf. vol. ii. pt. ii. p. 153.
1663. Mary Tilston, of Huxley, widow: Wills at Chester, ii. 269.
1672. Peter Tilston, of Tattenhall: ibid.
Liverpool, 2, 0; Boston (U.S.), 0, 18.

Tilton, ? Tilden. — Local, 'of Tilton,' a parish in the dioc. of Peterborough. Tilden may possibly be a corruption of Tilton; but v. Tilden.

John de Tylton, co. Linc., 1273. A.
London, 1, 0; Boston, 47, 34.

Tim.—Bapt. ; v. Timm.

Philadelphia, 1.

Timbrell.— ?——.

Robert Tymbrel, co. Soms., 1 Edw. III: Kirby's Quest, p. 174.
London, 2,

Timbs. — Bapt. 'the son of Timothy,' from the nick. Tim, patr. Timbs, with excrescent b; cf. Tombs for Toms. Similarly the b is excrescent in timber.

1752. Married—Edward Tymbs and Heneretta Maria Smith: St. Antholin (London), p. 156.
London, 1; Oxford, 2.

Timbury.—Local, 'of Timsbury': (1) a parish in co. Somerset;

(2) a parish in co. Hants. Possibly a corruption of Timperley, q.v.

1771. Married — John Timbury and Ennis Francis: St. Geo. Han. Sq. i. 209.
1782. — William Jones and Mary Timbery: ibid. p. 333.
London, 1.

Timcock.—Bapt. 'the son of Timothy,' from nick. Tim, and suffix -cock (v. Introd. p. 25); cf. Wilcock, Simcock, Jeffcock, &c.

John Tymcock. HH.
John Timcock. V. 5.

Timm, Timms, Tims, Times, Timson, Timmis.—Bapt. 'the son of Timothy,' from the nick. Tim; v. Timbs.

1564-5. Richard Tyms, New Coll.: Reg. Univ. Oxf. vol. ii. pt. ii. p. 22.
1752. Married— Dennis Tims and Mary Edwards: St. Geo. Han. Sq. i. 52.
1764. — Jeremiah Ogbourn and Mary Timson: ibid. p. 133.
1771. — Richard Timms and Mary Hughes: ibid. p. 206.
1785. — Matthew Times and Mary Hall: ibid. p. 376.
London, 0, 1, 3, 2, 3, 0; Manchester (Times), 1; Philadelphia, 4, 1, 1, 0, 1, 0.

Timmins, Timmons, Timins. —Bapt. 'the son of Timothy,' from the nick. Tim, and dim. Tim-in; cf. viol and viol-in, Rob and Rob-in, Col and Col-in, &c. Hence Robins, Collins, &c.

Gilbert Timin, co. Camb., 1273. A.
Agnes Tymandson, co. York, 1477. W. 11.
1603. Buried—John Timmens, servant to George Timmens: St. Michael, Cornhill, p. 212.
1756. Married—Samuel Timings and Mary Overton: St. Geo. Han. Sq. i. 61.
1784. — Robert Smith and Ann Timmins: ibid. p. 361.
London, 1, 0, 0; Philadelphia, 17, 9, 0; MDB. (co. Kent), 0, 0, 2.

Timothy.—Bapt. 'the son of Timothy.' I find few traces of this name in early records.

'John Timothy was, with a hundred other men, transported from Taunton, co. Somerset, to the West Indies, in 1685': Hotten's Lists of Emigrants, p. 316.
London, 3; Philadelphia, 4.

Timperley, Temberli, Temperley.—Local, 'of Timperley,' a parish in co. Chester.

1611. Thomas Timperley, of Hale: Wills at Chester, i. 192.
1623. Married — Thomas Tymperley and Anne Haygh: Reg. Prestbury Ch., co. Ches., p. 241.

1761. Married—William Timperley and Mary Hone : St. Geo. Han. Sq. i. 105.
London, o, o, 4 ; Manchester, 4, o, 2 ; Philadelphia, 2, 1, o.

Timpson, Timson. — Bapt. 'the son of Timothy,' from the nick. Tim. The *p* is intrusive, as in Thompson, Simpson, &c. ; v. Timmins.

1742. Bapt.—Maria, d. Robert Timson : St. Geo. Chap. Mayfair, p. 6.
1764. Married — Jeremiah Ogbourn and Mary Timson : St. Geo. Han. Sq. i. 133.
London, o, 2 ; Boston (U.S.), o, 6 ; Philadelphia, 1, 1.

Tims, Timson ; v. Timm.

Tinckler ; v. Tinkler, of which it is a variant.

Tindal, Tindall, Tindale, Tindell, Tindle, Tindill, Tindel. —Local, 'of Tynedale,' from residence by the first bearer on the banks of the river Tyne; cf. Coverdale, Tweedale, Lonsdale, Teasdale, &c. v. Tyndale.

William de Tyndale, co. Northumb., 20 Edw. I. R.
Thomas deo Tyndale, 1317 : DDD. i. 34.
William de Tyndale, 1457 ; ibid p. 35.
Robertus de Tyndale, 1379 : P. T. Yorks. p. 213.
1575. John Tindall, co. York : Reg. Univ. Oxf. vol. ii. pt. ii. p. 64.
1580. Bapt.—Robert, s. Robert Tyndall : St. Jas Clerkenwell, i. 12.
1729. Married—John Tindle and Anne Powell : St. Geo. Chap. Mayfair, p. 291.
1788. — William Bishop and Mary Tindell : St. Geo. Han. Sq. ii. 6.
London, 2, 3, 8, 2, o, o, o; MDB. (East Rid. Yorks), o, 9, 1, o, 3, 2, o; Philadelphia, o, 13, o, 1, o, o, 2.

Tingay, Tingey.—Local, 'of Tingay (?). I do not know of such a place, but as it belongs to the fen district it may be 'of Tingrith,' a village parish in co. Bedford, four miles from Woburn. This place is styled Tyngri in the Hundred Rolls (i. 546), and the surname is similarly spelt :

Petrus de Tyngrye, co. Bedf., 1273. A.

The change from Tyngrye to Tingay or Tingey is not at all a surprising one in English nomenclature.

1619. Married—Richard Tingey and Isabell Flyng : St. Jas Clerkenwell, i. 46.
1774. — Edward Tingey and Mary Murrow : St. Geo. Han. Sq. i. 240.

London, o, 5 ; MDB. (Bedford), 2, 2 ; (Cambridge), o, 2.

Tingle.—(1) Local, 'of Tinghill' (?). Apparently some small spot in co. Yorks.

Ricardus Tynghill, 1379 : P. T. Yorks. p. 199.
Elene Tyngyl, 1424, co. York : W. 11, p. 25.

(2) Local, 'of Tynedale,' a variant of Tindal, q.v. The following entries seem to prove this :

1779. Married—Laurence Tingdall and Margaret Carr : St. Geo. Han. Sq. i. 302.
1784. — John Tingle and Ann Chamberlain : ibid. p. 361.

In spite of (2) it must be manifest that (1) is the chief parent.

London, 2 ; Sheffield, 2 ; West Rid. Court Dir., 1 ; Philadelphia, 6.

Tining.—Local, 'at the tining,' from residence thereby. '*Tining*, a newly enclosed piece of ground. Co. Wilts' (Halliwell).

Thomas atte Tynyng, co. Soms., 1 Edw. III : Kirby's Quest, p. 116.
William atte Tunyng, co. Soms., 1 Edw. III : ibid.

Tinker.—Occup. 'the tinker.' All the early instances are South English ; v Tinkler for North-English form. Travelling pedlars were so called because they made their approach known by tinking, i.e. ringing, or making a tinkling noise. The mending of pots and pans does not seem to have been the particular pursuit of the mediaeval tinker. He was a general pedlar.

' No person, or persons commonly called Pedler, Tynker, or Pety Chapman, shall wander or go from one towne to another ...and sell pynnes, poyntes laces, gloves, knyves, glasses, tapes, or any suche kynde of wares whatsoever, or gather connye skynnes ' : 5 & 6 Edw. VI, c. 21.
Thomas le Tyneker, co. Bucks, 1273. A.
Angin' Tineker, co. Hunts, ibid.
Peter le Teneker, co. Soms., ibid.
Richard le Tinekere. T.
William le Tynekar, co. Soms., 1 Edw. III : Kirby's Quest, p. 142.
1574. Buried—John Tynker, of Adlyngton : Reg. Prestbury Ch., co. Ches., p. 47.
1777. Married—John Tinker and Eliz. Durrant : St. Geo. Han. Sq. i. 279.
London, 1 ; Philadelphia, 4.

Tinkerson.—Nick. 'the tinker's son ' ; cf. Taylorson, Smithson, Wrightson, &c.

1588. Married—John Tinkerson and Sibell Lee : St. Antholin (London), p. 33.

Tinkler, Tinckler. — Occup. 'the tinkler,' i.e. Tinker, q.v. The term being North English, so is the surname. 'A tincker or tinkeler ' : Baret's Alvearie, 1580 (Halliwell).

' Hey ! sirs ! what cairds and tinklers,
And ne'er-do-weel horse-coupers.'
            v. Jamieson on *Caird.*

Tinkle is merely the frequentative of *tink*. Hence both Tinker and Tinkler.

William de Westerdale, *tynkler*, 12 Edw. III : Freemen of York, i. 32.
Roger Tynkeler, C. R., 20 Edw. III. pt. i.
Rogerus Tynkler, 1379 : P. T. Yorks. p. 204.
Ricardus Tyncler, 1379 : ibid. p. 35.
Alice Tynkeller, co. York. W. 9.
Richard Tynkler, co. York. W. 8.
1726. Married—George Fawcett and Ann Tenkler : St. Geo. Han. Sq. i. 2.
1746. — Joseph Tinkler and Elinor Smallwood : St. Geo. Chap. Mayfair, p. 77.
London, 2, 1 ; Newcastle, 2, o ; New York, 2, o.

Tinniswood ; v. Tenniswood.

Tinsley, Tinslay.—Local, 'of Tinsley,' a chapelry in the parish of Rotherham, W. Rid. Yorks.

Lecia de Tyneslawe, 1379 : P. T. Yorks. p. 40.
1648. Married—William Scriven and Amye Tinsly : St. Jas. Clerkenwell, i. 83.
1675. — Edward Burton and Mary Tinsley : ibid. p. 180.
London, 4, 2 ; Philadelphia, 2, o.

Tipkins.—Bapt. 'the son of Theobald,' from nick. Tib, and pet *kin* ; v. Tebb.

1537. 'Item, payed to Typkyn for cherys, xxd.' : Privy Purse Expenses, Princess Mary.

Tiplady.—Local ; v. Toplady.

Tipler ; v. Tippler.

Tipper, Tepper.—Occup. 'the tipper,' one who mounted mazers, drinking horns, or cups with metals. ' To tip, to put on tips at the ends of horns, brims of drinking vessels, &c.' (Bailey). Possibly he was an arrow-header also, a clumsy term for an important occupation, and sure to have a shorter equivalent.

'Arowe-heders, maltemen, and corne-mongers.'
Cocke Lorelle's Bote (1510).
'Arowe-hede, *barbellum*': Cath. Ang. (1483).

Tipper is still strongly represented in the directory.

William le Tipper, co. Suff., 1273. A.
Henry le Tipper, co. Bedf, ibid.
Alice Tippere, co. Camb., ibid.
John le Tipper, 1313. M.
1563. Married — Thomas Beane and Jone Typper: St. Peter, Cornhill, i. 226. London, 11, 5; Philadelphia, 1, 0.

Tippett, Tippetts, Tippitt, Tippets.—Bapt. (1) 'the son of Theobald,' (2) 'the son of Isabella, sharpened forms of Tibbett, Tibbetts, and Tibbitt (v. Tibbatts). The change from *b* to *p* is exceedingly common; cf. Hobbs and Hopps, Hobson and Hopson. In the registers of St. Columb Major, co. Cornwall, the well-known family of Tippett are also occasionally entered as Tibbett:

1599. Bapt. — Nicholas, son of John Tibbett: Reg. St. Columb Major, p. 19.
1603. — Hughe, son of William Tippett, p. 21.
John Typpet, 1568: Reg. Univ. Oxf. i. 272.
1788. Married — John Burgess and Priscilla Tippett: St. Geo. Han. Sq. ii. 2.
London, 6, 1, 2, 0; Devon Court Dir., 1, 1, 1, 0; Philadelphia, 0, 0, 0, 1.

Tipping, Tippin.—Bapt. 'the son of Thorphin'; a variant of Topping. Turpin (q.v.) was the Yorkshire form; Toppin, later Topping, with excrescent *g*, the Lancashire form. Tipping seems to have arisen in the neighbourhood of Preston, and is unquestionably a variant of Topping, as the Preston Guild Rolls fully demonstrate.

John fil. William Toppyng, 1397: Preston Guild Rolls, p. 3.
John Toppynge, 1415: ibid. p. 7.
Ewan Typpynge, 1542: ibid. p. 15.
John Typynge, 1622: ibid. p. 69.
Thomas Typpyng, of Ribchester, 1563: Wills at Chester (1545-1620), p. 290.
Jenet Typpynge, of Preston, 1572: ibid.
William Tipping, of Shaw, *husbandman*, 1634: ibid. p. 279.
1566. Buried—Margaret Typynge, of Pointon: Reg. Prestbury Ch., co. Ches., p. 20.
London, 2, 0; Preston, 4, 0; Liverpool, 9, 0; Manchester, 3, 0; Philadelphia, 3, 1.

Tipple. — Bapt. 'the son of Theobald,' popularly Tibble sharpened to Tipple; v. Tebbitt (1) and the entries there recorded. For change from *b* to *p*, v. Tippett.

Tipel (without surname), co. Norf., 1273. A.
Alicia Typpell, 1379: P. T. Yorks. p. 21.
1762. Married—James Price and Mary Tibball: St. Geo. Han. Sq. i. 113.
'Bedford Chapel, Bloomsbury. Rev. S. A. Tipple will preach to-morrow at 11 a.m. and 7 p.m.': Standard, Feb. 19, 1887. London, 2.

Tippler, Tipler.—Occup. 'the tippler'; not one who habitually goes in for small potations, as now understood by the term, but a seller of drink, an alehouse keeper. Mr. Lower quotes two 'communes tipulatores' in the records of the Corporation of Seaford, co. Sussex, 36th Elizabeth, who had broken the assize of bread and beer, and were fined 2s. 6d. The same year one Symon Collingham, of Seaford, is licensed as a tipler, and is to abstain from the use of unlawful games 'duringe the time of his tiplinge' (v. Lower's Patr. Brit. p. 347).

William Tipeler, co. Linc., 1273. A.
1806. Married—Francis Tipler and Sarah Bayley: St. Geo. Han. Sq. ii. 354. MDB. (co. Linc.), 0, 1; (co. Essex), 1, 1.

Tipton. — Local, 'of Tipton,' a parish in co. Stafford, near Dudley. The family bearing this name seems to have settled somewhat early in the neighbouring county of Salop.

1585-6. John Typton, or Tipton, co. Salop: Reg. Univ. Oxf. vol. ii. pt. ii. p. 149.
1616. Edmund Tipton, co. Salop: ibid. p. 350.
1808. Married—Thomas Copland and Margaret Tipton: St. Geo. Han. Sq. ii. 389.
MDB. (co. Salop), 2; Philadelphia, 7.

Tirebuck.—Local,'of Tarbock,' a township in the parish of Huyton, seven miles from Liverpool; v. Tarbuck, of which it is a variant.
Liverpool, 1; London, 1.

Tirrell; v. Terrell.

Tisbury.—Local, 'of Tisbury,' a parish in co. Wilts, three miles and a half from Hindon.
London, 1.

Tisdall Tisdale. Local, 'of Teesdale,' from residence in the valley of the river Tees; v. Teasdale for early instances.

1585. Edward Tayler and Johanna Tysdalle, *widow*: Marriage Lic. (London), i. 141.
1632. Roger Tisdale and Eliz. Gyles: Marriage Lic. Faculty Office), p. 18.
London, 5, 0; Boston (U.S.), 0, 11; Philadelphia, 5, 2.

Tissiman; v. Tesseyman.

Tissington.—Local,'of Tissington,' a parish in co. Derby, four miles from Ashbourn.

1768. Married—George Tissington and Margaret Barker: St. Geo. Han. Sq. i. 179.
London, 1; Crockford, 1; New York, 1.

Titchmarsh.—Local, 'of Titchmarsh,' a parish in the dioc. of Peterborough, co. Northants. To be distinguished from Tidmarsh, q.v.

John de Tichemershe, co. Northampt., 20 Edw. I. R.
Henry de Tichemersh, co. Northampt., ibid.
1756. Married—Philip Foley, *clerk*, M.A., and Ann Titchmarsh: St. Geo. Han. Sq. i. 65.
London, 1.

Titford.—Local, 'of Tetford,' a parish in co. Lincoln, six miles from Horncastle.
London, 4.

Titherington, Titterington, Titrington.—Local, 'of Titherington,' a township in the parish of Prestbury, co. Ches.

Jordan de Tyderinton, 19 Edw. I: East Cheshire, i. 264.
William de Tyveryngton, *furbour*, 11 Edw. II: Freemen of York, i. 17.
John de Tyderynton, vicar of Sandback, 1356: ibid. ii. 334 *n*.
1561. Married—John Burey and Ales Tyderinton (of Tytherington): Reg. Prestbury, co. Ches., p. 5.
1614. Buried—Thomas Tydderingeton (of Tydderinton): ibid. p. 204.
1723. Married—Hewitt Tittrington and Rachel Britton: St. Jas. Clerkenwell, i. 248.
MDB. (West Rid. Yorks), 0, 5, 0; Manchester, 1, 1, 0; Philadelphia, 1, 0, 0; New York, 0, 2, 1.

Tithinglamb.—Nick.
William Tythinglomb, Close Roll, 15 Edw. III. pt. ii.

Titley, Titlow. — Local, 'of Titley,' a parish in co. Hereford. Also v. Tetley and Tetlow, of which in some instances probably these are variants.

1750. Married—Thomas Tittley and Martha Maria Ballord : St. Geo. Chap. Mayfair, p. 183.

1790. — John Titley and Eliz. Newell : St. Geo. Han. Sq. ii. 46.

1798. — Isaac Titlow and Eleanor Cornforth : ibid. p. 181.

Philadelphia, 0, 9.

Titman ; v. Tiddeman.

Titmas, Titmus, Titmuss.— Nick. 'the titmouse.' Not to be confounded with Titchmarsh, q.v. 'Tytemose, bryd, _frondator_' : Prompt. Parv. 'The mouse a titti-mouse-was no doubt' (Halliwell).

1651. Married—William Titimouse and Anne Pertus, of Ingerston, co. Essex : Reg. St. Peter, Cornhill, i. 258.

In a list of recusants, 1580, presented by the Vicar of Kirkham, co. Lanc., appears :

'Also Diev. Tytmouse, conversant in the company of two widows, viz. mistress Alice Clyfton and mistress Jane Clyfton' : Croston's edit. of Baines' Lanc. p. 240.

London, 1, 4, 1.

Titsworth.—Local, 'of Tittisworth,' a township in the parish of Leek, co. Stafford.

Philadelphia, 1.

Titterington ; v. Titherington.

Tobias. — Bapt. 'the son of Tobias.'

1774. Married—Joseph Beal and Ann Tobias : St. Geo. Han. Sq. i. 239.

1788. — John Tobias and Eliz. Jacks : ibid. ii. 2.

London, 3 ; Philadelphia, 9.

Tobin, Tobyn.— Bapt. 'the son of Tobias,' from the dim. Tob-in ; cf. Col-in, Rob-in, &c. I suspect that Tobin is a French importation of somewhat recent date.

1737. Buried — John Tobin : St. Antholin (London), p. 209.

1794. Married—John Harriman and Eliz. Tobin : St. Geo. Han. Sq. ii. 118.

London, 4, 0 ; Philadelphia, 80, 2.

Tobitt, Tobbutt.—Bapt. 'the son of Theobald '; v. Tebbitt.

London, 1, 3 ; New York, 1, 0.

Toby, Tobey.— Bapt. 'the son of Tobias,' from the nick. Toby.

'And kan telle of Tobye,
And of twelve Apostles.'
Piers P. 5667-8.

William Toby, co. Linc., 1273. A.
Thomas Toby, co. Soms., 1 Edw. III : Kirby's Quest, p. 221.

1584. Bapt.—Elizabeth Tobye : Reg. Stourton, Wilts, p. 2.

1801. Married — Thomas Jinks and Lovey Tobey : St. Geo. Han. Sq. ii. 240.

London, 7, 0 ; Philadelphia, 1, 7.

Tod, Todd.—Nick. 'the tod,' i.e. the fox, q.v. ; cf. Todhunter, a North-English surname. Halliwell says, 'Tod, a fox, still in use '; v. also Jamieson's Dict. Cf. Lowrie.

John le Tod, c. 1300. M.

1575. Abraham Todde, of Newcastle : Reg. Univ. Oxf. vol. ii. pt. ii. p. 66.

1597. Robert Baker and Jane Todd, _widow_ : Marriage Lic. (London), i. 240.

London, 7, 42 ; Boston (U.S.), 0, 53.

Todhunter.—Occup. 'the tod-hunter,' from North-English _tod_, a fox. The surname is still found in Cumberland and the Lake District, and the local nomenclature (cf. Todbusk, Todbank, &c.) still proves a past familiarity with the word. The tod-hunter would obtain a livelihood by keeping down the number of these farmyard burglars. Afterwards, under a statute of Henry VIII, he got twelvepence per fox-head from the parish warden. Todhunter is a great name within the old limits of the parish of Greystock, co. Cumb.

1585. Thomas Todhunter, co. Cumb. : Reg. Univ. Oxf. vol. ii. pt. ii. p. 147.

1591. Married—Fraunces Hocken and Margret Todhunter : St. Mary Aldermary, p. 8.

MDB. (co. Cumb.), 10 ; London, 3 ; Ulverston, 1 ; New York, 1.

Todman.—Local, 'of Todden-ham,' a parish in co. Glouc., near Moreton-in-the-Marsh. The modifications are quite regular, first Toddenham, then Todnam, finally Todman. This is one of a fairly large class ; cf. Tottman for Tottenham, Swetman for Swetenham, Deadman for Debenham. All local surnames ending in _-enham_ seem by some natural law to become modified into _-man_.

Muriel de Todenham, co. Soms., 1 Edw. III : Kirby's Quest, p. 202.

London, 1.

Tofield, Tuffield, Tuffill. — Local, 'at the to-fall ' (?), probably from residence beside or inside a pent-house, once called a 'to-fall.' The _d_ in Tofield would thus be

excrescent, and imitative of the word _field_. 'To-falle, schudde, _appendicium_' : Prompt. Parv. p. 495. 'Teefall, a mode of building in the pent-house form, common in Northumberland ' (Halliwell) ; and v. Brockett's North Country Glossary and Jamieson's Dict.

1632. Married—Edward Sneller and Audry Tofeild : St. Jas. Clerkenwell, i. 64.

1729. — William Murril and Abigal Tofell : St. Geo. Chap. Mayfair, p. 296.

1802. — James Tofield and Emily Wiltshire : St. Geo. Han. Sq. ii. 271.

London, 3, 1, 1 ; West Rid. Court Dir., 4, 0, 0.

Tofts, Toft.—Local, (1) 'of Tofts,' a parish in co. Norf ; (2) 'at the tofts ' or toft. A homestead seemingly amid trees, as it is frequently compounded with tree-names ; cf. the old proverb, 'He hath neither toft nor croft,' i.e. without house or land. Tofts implies an aggregation of such dwellings.

Johannes Atte toftes et uxor, 1379 : P. T. Yorks. p. 185.

(3) Toft, a township in the parish of Knutsford, co. Chester, is the parent of the Cheshire Tofts.

Gundreda de Toftes, co. Norf., 1273. A.
Eborard de Toft', co. Norf., ibid.
Alan de Toft, co. Camb., ibid.
Robert de Toft, co. Bedf., ibid.
1394. Hugh de Toft, co. Ches. : East Cheshire, ii. 355.
1580. Married—John Hatton and Ales Toft : Reg. Prestbury Ch., co. Ches., p. 66.
1585. William Toft, of Buglawton, _yeoman_ : Wills at Chester, i. 193.
Manchester, 0, 5 ; London, 1, 0 ; Philadelphia, 0, 1 ; New York, 1, 1.

Toke ; v. Tuck.

Tokelin.— Bapt. 'the son of Toke,' from dim. Tokelin. This is interesting as showing the popularity of Toke ; v. Tuck.

Richard Tokelyn, co. Soms., 1 Edw. III : Kirby's Quest, p. 96.
Margery Toklyne, co. Soms., 1 Edw. III : ibid. p. 107.
John Tuckling, co. Soms., 1 Edw. III : ibid. p. 159.

Toleman, Tollman, Tolman. — (1) Occup. 'the tollman,' one who took tolls and taxes ; v. Toller.

Thomas Tolman. B.

1752. Married—John Dyer and Susanna Tollman : St. Geo. Chap. Mayfair, p. 229.

1791. Married — Thomas Young and Patty Tollman : St. Geo. Han. Sq. ii. 56. London, 5, 1, 5 ; Boston (U.S.), 1, 0, 6 ; Philadelphia, 0, 0, 46.

Tolfree, Tolfrey.—Bapt. 'the son of Thorfrey' (?) ; v. Fray. I strongly suspect that Tolfree and Tolfrey are modifications of this name.

John Torfray, co. Oxf., 1273. A.
1599. Married—Augustin Clarke and Katherine Tolefree : St. Jas. Clerkenwell, i. 22.
London, 1, 1.

Tollemache, Talmage, Talmage, Tammadge, Tallemach, Tallmadge.—? Local. I can offer no satisfactory solution of this surname. The county of Suffolk seems to have been its original home.

William Talemasche, 7 Hen. II : Pipe Roll, iv. 4.
Hugo Talemasch, alias Talmach, co. Suff., 1273. A.
Alice Talemache, co. Camb., ibid.
Peter Talemache, co. Oxf., ibid.
Hugo Talemache, co. Norf., Hen. III—Edw. I. K.
William Talemache, co. Hants, ibid.
1568. Buried—Fraunces Talmach : St. Peter, Cornhill, i. 119.
London, 0, 2, 1, 2, 2, 0 ; (Tallmadge), Boston, 1 ; (Tollemache), Crockford, 5 ; Philadelphia, 0, 0, 8, 0, 0, 2.

Toller, Toler. — Offic. 'the toller,' a toll-taker by road or in market ; v. Toleman.

'Taillours and tynkers
And tollers in markettes.'
Piers Plowman, Prologue, 438-9.
'Tollers' office it is ill,
For they take toll oft against skill,'
i.e. often contrary to reason (v. Halliwell).

Ralph le Toller. B.
Bartholomew le Toller, c. 1300. M.
John le Toller, 28 Edw. I : Freemen of York, i. 8.
Willelmus Toller, 1379 : P. T. Yorks. p. 273.
Robertus Toller, 1379 : ibid. p. 272.
1602. Married—Francis Toler and Bridgitt Rafton : St. Jas. Clerkenwell, i. 26.
1761. — Samuel Toller and Eliz. Haggett : St. Geo. Han. Sq. i. 107.
London, 2, 1 ; Philadelphia, 2, 0.

Tolley, Tolly.—Bapt. 'the son of Bartholomew,' from the nick. Tholy. The following seems to prove a diminutive existed :

'Godus Tholyn-wyf,' i.e. Godus, the wife of Tholyn, 1379 : P T. Yorks. p. 21.

Toly Museye, co. Linc., 1273. A.
Douce Toly, co. Camb., ibid.
Tholy Oldcorn, co. Camb., ibid.
Stephen Toli, co. Camb., ibid.
Johanna fil. Tholy, 39 Hen. III : BBB. p. 65.
William fil. Tholy. E.
William, the son of Tole : English Gilds, p. 150.
1795. Married — William Jude and Mary Tolley : St. Geo. Han. Sq. ii. 127.
London, 10, 1 ; Oxford, 8, 0 ; Philadelphia, 7, 0.

Tollman, Tolman. — Occup. 'the toll-man' ; v. Toleman.

Tolmin, Tolming, Toulmin. —Bapt. 'the son of Thomas,' a curious inversion of Tomlin. I have no absolute proof of this, but I cannot doubt it. If I am wrong, then these names are variants of Toleman, q.v. In Furness and the neighbouring districts, where Tomlin and Tomlinson (now often Townson,q.v.) were very familiar,we find Tolming settled for generations.

John Tolmin, of Bolton juxta Arenas, 1641 : Lancashire Wills at Richmond, i. 280.
Richard Towlmyn, of Bolton-by-the-Sands, 1607 : ibid.
Ellen Tolman, of Bolton-le-Sands, 1699 : ibid. ii. 285.
Thomas Tolming, of Bolton Holms, parish of Bolton, 1728 : ibid.
London, 0, 0, 5 ; Liverpool, 0, 0, 3 ; Boston (U.S.), 0, 0, 1.

Tolson, Toulson, Towlson, Towlsion.—(1) Bapt. 'the son of Thomas.' Odd as it may seem, these are but corruptions of Tomlinson, and in the Lake District and other parts of North England they have gone through the stages of Towlinson and Towlnson to Towlson. Townson (q.v.) is the popular modern form.

1551. John Towlyngson, of the parish of Mellynge : Lancashire Wills at Richmond, i. 285.
1587. Richard Towlson, or Tounsoun, of Dalton : ibid.
1672. George Toulson, of Poulton : ibid. p. 283.
1673. George Towlnson, of Pilling : ibid.

That this is the true derivation there cannot be the shadow of a doubt.

1650. Married — Christopher Oxnard and Faith Toulson : St. Dionis Backchurch, p. 26.
1713. — John Tolson and Barbara Wanley : St. Michael, Cornhill, p. 57.

Manchester, 0, 3, 0, 0 ; West Rid. Court Dir., 8, 0, 0, 0 ; London, 2, 1, 0, 0 ; Sheffield, 0, 0, 2, 0 ; Leeds, 1, 2, 0, 0 ; Boston (U.S.), 0, 0, 0, 1.

Tom.—Bapt.'the son of Thomas,' from the nick. Tom ; v. Toms.

MDB. (co. Cornwall), 8 ; Philadelphia, 1 ; Boston (U.S.), 1.

Tomalin.—Bapt. ; v. Tomlin, of which it is a corruption ; cf. Ottaway for Ottway, Greenaway for Greenway, Hathaway for Hathway.

London, 4.

Tombleson.—Bapt. 'the son of Thomas,' a corruption of Tomblinson ; v. Tomblin.

MDB. (co. Camb.), 1 ; (co. Norfolk), 1 ; London, 1.

Tomblin, Tomblinson. — Bapt. 'the son of Thomas,' from the nick. Tom, dim. Tom-lin, with usual excrescent b after m ; cf. Timbs and Tombs, and v. Tomlin. The two following names are contained in the list of high sheriffs of Rutland :

1756. Robert Tomblin,of Edithweston, Esq. : Notes and Queries, 1886, Sept. 18, p. 224.
1796. Robert Tomlin, of Edithweston, Esq. : ibid.
1666. Bapt. — Robert, son of John Tomberlin : St. Jas. Clerkenwell, i. 230.
Cf. Thomas Tomblinson, of Kirkham, 1708 : Lancashire Wills at Richmond, p. 256.
1664. Buried — John Tomblans (Tomlins), servant to one Bateman, taylor : St. Michael, Cornhill, p. 253.
1706. Married — Peter Tombling and Frances Godden : Canterbury Cath., p. 68.
Crockford, 1, 0 ; Philadelphia, 0, 1.

Tombs, Toombs.—Bapt. 'the son of Thomas,'from the nick. Tom, patr. Toms, with intrusive b after m ; cf. Tomblin.

1632. Roger Newcourt and Alice Tomes : Marriage Lic. (Faculty Office), p. 19.
1683. Married — Edward Tomes and Dorothy Collier : St. Jas. Clerkenwell, i. 194.
1701. — Thomas Tombes and Mary Broffe : ibid. p. 223.
1702. — Abraham Russell and Rebeccah Tombs : St. Michael, Cornhill, p. 52.
London, 4, 1 ; MDB. (co. Hereford), 4, 0 ; Oxford, 6, 1 ; Boston (U.S.), 6, 2.

Tomes ; v. Toms, of which it is a variant. Cf. Times, a variant of Tims or Timms ; v. Timm.

Tomkin, Tomkins, Tomkinson, Tomkies.—Bapt. 'the son of Thomas,' from the nick. Thom, by-and-by reduced to Tom, dim. Tom-kin (v. *kin*, Introd. p. 25). Tomkies, of course, is a corruption of Tomkins, as Perkiss or Purkiss is of Perkins.

Robertus Thomkyn, 1379 : P. T. Yorks. p. 221.
1586. Married — John Tomkyns and Joane Freeman : St. Jas. Clerkenwell, i. 12.
1621. — John Tomkins and Margery Hill : ibid. p. 49.
1632. — William Tomkin and Mary Trapps : ibid. p. 63.
1738. — William Bacon and Martha Tomkinson : ibid. p. 266.
London, 1, 26, 3, 2 ; Boston (U.S.), 0, 1, 3, 0.

Tomlin, Tomlins, Tomlinson, Tomlyn.—Bapt. 'the son of Thomas,' from the nick. Tom, and dim. Tom-lin ; v. Thomlinson.

John Tomelyn : co. Soms., 1 Edw. III : Kirby's Quest, p. 129.
John Thomelyn, co. Soms., 1 Edw. III : ibid. p. 191.
Robert Thomelynsone : Pardons Roll, 16 Ric. II.
Henricus Thomlynson, 1379 : P. T. Yorks, p. 172.
Alicia Tomlyn-wyff, 1379 : P. T. Howdenshire, p. 30.
Recardus Tomlynson, 1379 : ibid.
Matilda Tomelyn-doghter, 1379 : P. T. Yorks. p. 12.
1752. Married — Alex. Tomlyn and Ann Knight : St. Geo. Chap. Mayfair, p. 219.
1763. — Thomas Tomlins and Eliz. Blake : St. Geo. Han. Sq. i. 121.
London, 13, 3, 25, 1 ; Philadelphia, 30, 0, 84, 0.

Tompkin, Tompkins.—Bapt. 'the son of Thomas,' from the nick. Tom, and dim. Tom-kin. The *p* is intrusive, as in Thompson ; cf. Wilkin, Watkin, Simpkin, &c. v. Tomkin.

1566. Richard Tompkyn and Margaret Stevens : Marriage Lic. (London), i. 33.
1580. John Tompkyns and Ellen Stanner : ibid. p. 98.
London, 2, 12 ; Philadelphia, 0, 35.

Tompsett ; v. Thomasset.

Tompson.—Bapt. 'the son of Thomas,' from the nick. Tom. The *p* is intrusive, as in Tompkins, Simpkins, &c. ; v. Thomson.

1552. Married — Rycharde Glascock and Hellen Tompson : St. Michael, Cornhill, p. 6.
1574. John Tompson and Emma Frenche, *widow* : Marriage Lic. (London), i. 61.
1744. Married — John Tompson and Laetitia Bliss : St. Geo. Chap. Mayfair, p. 40.
London, 6 ; Boston (U.S.), 4.

Toms, Tomes, Tomson. — Bapt. 'the son of Thomas,' from the nick. Tom ; v. Thom and Tombs.

1736. Buried — Rachiel Toms : St. Antholin (London), p. 209.
1746. Married — Robert Peverel and Mary Tomes : St. Geo. Chap. Mayfair, p. 73.
1749. — Clifton Tomson and Anne Hoggor : ibid. p. 139.
1768. — Richard Tomes and Mary Bingham : St. Geo. Han. Sq. i. 176.
London, 2, 19, 1 ; Philadelphia, 11, 4, 9.

Tomsett ; v. Thomasset.

Tong, Tonge, Tongue. — Local, 'of Tonge' or Tong, parishes in cos. Salop, Kent, Lancaster (2), and W. Rid. York. Tongue, of course, is merely imitative. Probably all these places are so termed from the shape of the land (like a tongue). M.E. *tonge* or *tunge*, a tongue. Of Tong in co. Salop it is said, 'The river Werf commences from the union of two brooks at the western extremity of the parish' (Lewis's Topographical Dictionary of England, iv. 357). The tongue of land in this case might lie between the two streams.

John de Tonghe, co. Salop, 1273. A.
Nicholas Tonge, co. Bucks, ibid.
Simon de Tonge, co. Kent, ibid.
Roger Tunge, co. York, ibid.
Willelmus de Tonge, 1379 : P. T. Yorks. p. 186.

The township of Tongue is mentioned on the same page.

Peter Tonge, of Chester, *shoemaker*, 1572 : Wills at Chester (1543–1620), p. 193.
William Tonge, of Farnworth, co. Lanc., 1583 : ibid.
1659 60. Married—Charles Tonge and Mary Hancocke : St. Dionis Backchurch, p. 35.
1770. — John Tongue and Eliz. Griffiths : St. Geo. Han. Sq. i. 204.
London, 1, 1, 2 ; West Rid. Court Dir., 1, 2, 2 ; Manchester, 1, 6, 1 ; Philadelphia, 6, 1, 6.

Tonkinson, Tonkins, Tonks, Tunks, Tonkin, Tonkyn. — (1) Bapt. 'the son of Antony,' from the nick. Ton-kin, and with dim. suffix Ton-kin. *Kins* becomes *ks* ; cf. Perks from Perkins, Dawks from Dawkins, &c. (The order of corruption is Perkins, Perkiss, Perkes, Perks.) (2) Bapt. A corruption of Tomkinson and Tomkins ; cf. Sinkinson and Sinkins for Simkinson and Simkins.

1569. Bapt. — The daughter of James Tonkinson : St. Antholin (London), p. 20.
1603. Buried—Thomas Tunckes : ibid. p. 151.
1789. Married—John Tonks and Mary Dardwell : St. Geo. Han. Sq. ii. 18.
London, 2, 0, 0, 2, 0, 0 ; MDD. (co. Cornwall), 0, 0, 0, 0, 8, 2 ; Philadelphia, 0, 0, 0, 0, 2, 0.

Tonson.—Bapt. (1) 'the son of Anthony,' from the nick. Tony ; (2) a corruption of Tomson, v. Toms.

London, 1 ; New York, 1.

Toogood ; v. Thurgood.

Took, Tooke ; v. Tuck.

Tooker.—Occup. 'the tucker,' q.v. The Somersetshire form was almost invariably Touker.

Alex. le Toukere, co. Soms., 1 Edw. III : Kirby's Quest, p. 218.
Matilda Toukere, co. Soms., 1 Edw. III : ibid. p. 252.
MDB. (co. Soms.), 1 ; New York, 24.

Tookey.—Bapt. ; v. Tuckey.

Tooley. — Bapt. 'the son of Toly,' probably a nick. of the immense favourite Bartholomew. Lower writes, 'Tooley, a crasis of St. Olave. Tooley Street in Southwark is so called from its proximity to the church of St. Olave.' This is true enough so far as the street is concerned, but it is no help to the elucidation of the surname, which probably existed before Tooley Street was dreamt of. The absence of all prefixes in early registers seems to prove a baptismal origin ; v. Tolley. In some instances Tooley may be local ; cf.

Richard Tulegh, co. Soms., 1 Edw. III : Kirby's Quest, p. 133.

Tooley is a hamlet in the parish of Peckleton, co. Leic.

Robert Toly, co. Camb., 1273. A.
William Toly, co. Essex, ibid.
William Toli, co. Oxf., ibid.
John Toly, co. Soms., 1 Edw. III:
Kirby's Quest, p. 92.
1631. Married — David Toolye and
Jane Bayle: St. Michael, Cornhill, p. 26.
1649-50. — Edmund Tooley and
Martha Harford: St. Dionis Backchurch,
p. 26.
London, 7; Philadelphia, 1.

Toombs; v. Tombs.

Toomer. — (1) ? Occup. 'the
toomer' (?). 'Toom, to take wool
off the cards' (Halliwell). (2)
? Local, 'of St. Omer' (?).

William de St. Omero, co. Wilts, 1273.
A.
Petronilla de St. Omero, co. Camb.,
ibid.

A common entry in the Hundred Rolls; probably this is the
origin:

Richard de Tomere, co. Soms., 1 Edw.
III: Kirby's Quest, p. 218.
Thomas de Thomere, co. Soms., 1 Edw.
III: ibid.

These are strongly in favour of
the St. Omer theory.

1698. Married — Tobias Humber and
Sarah Toomer: St. Jas. Clerkenwell,
i. 219.
London, 6.

Toon, Toone; v. Town.

Toop, Topp, Toope.—? Local.
I dare not hazard a guess at
the derivation of this name. Probably Mr. Lower is right in supposing it to be 'at the top,' from
residence on some summit of a
small hill, corresponding with
Bottom, from residence in some
hollow.

Robert Top, co. Soms., 1 Edw. III:
Kirby's Quest, p. 123.
William Toppe, co. Soms., 1 Edw. III:
ibid. p. 281.
1606-7. Henry Topp, co. Dorset:
Reg. Univ. Oxf. vol. ii. pt. ii. p. 294.
1612. John Toppe, co. Wilts: ibid. p. 328.
1580. Bapt.—John Tooppe: Reg. Stourton, Wilts, p. 2.
1639. — David, s. Robert Toope: ibid.
p. 9.

Found also as Top in the same
register.

1669. Married — Edward Top and
Ann Lavington: St. Jas. Clerkenwell, iii.
167.
London, 5, 2, 0; New York, 0, 3, 2.

Tootal, Tootle. — Local; v.
Toothill. It is related of a Mr.

Tootle, who went rather late to
an evening party with wife and
daughters, that much tittering was
caused by the flunkey's loud an-
nouncement of 'Mr. Tootle, Mrs.
Tootle, and the Misses Tootle, too!'
London, 1, 2; New York, 0, 2.

Tooth. — ?——. Lower says,
'This name probably has reference
to some peculiarity in the teeth of
the original bearer' (Patr. Brit.
p. 350). Certainly there is some
foundation for this. M.E. toth,
a tooth.

Thomas Toth, co. Northampton, 1273.
A.
William Tothe, rector of Outwell, co.
Norf., 1334: FF. vii. 474.
Richard Tooth, co. Norf., 40 Edw. III:
ibid. p. 504.
1765. Married—Seth Tooth and Mary
Beck: St. Geo. Han. Sq. i. 142.
London, 1; Crockford, 4; New York, 1.

Toothacher, Toothaker. —
Local, 'German Todtenacker, field
of the dead, a burying ground;
analogous to our indigenous name
Churchyard' (Lower, Patr. Brit.
p. 350).

Richard Toothaker, 1641: St. Jas.
Clerkenwell, p. 150.
Nicholas Toothacher, 1642: ibid. p. 154.
1675. Married — Thomas Goldington
and Margarett Toothacre: St. Michael,
Cornhill, p. 41.
1774. — William Salter and Isabella
Toothaker: St. Geo. Han. Sq. i. 242.
Philadelphia, 0, 2; Boston (U.S.), 0, 3.

**Toothill, Tootle, Tothill,
Tootal, Tottle, Tootell, Tootill,
Tuthill, Tuttle, Toutill.**—Local,
'of Totehill,' i.e. the look-out hill.
Many spots are so called in all
parts of England. A hill with
a good outlook against an enemy's
approach. There are two Tottle
Banks in the old parish of Ulverston,
each with a good outlook. 'Tote-
hyll, montaignette': Palsgrave.
'A tote-hill is an eminence from
whence there is a good outlook':
Ches. Archaeol. xix. 37.

'Item, the same daye paied for a great
bote ... to wayte upon the Kinges grace
fro Yorke place to Brydewell, and fro
thence to Totehill,' 1531: Privy Purse
Expenses, Hen. VIII, p. 118.

'Totehylle, specula': Prompt.
Parv. 'Totehylle, or hey place of
lokynge': ibid. In Way's notes

thereon he quotes Wyclif's
translation of 2 Kings v. 7: 'For-
sothe David toke the tote hil Syon,
that is, the citee of David.' For
various instances of the word, v.
Way's note. We still use the
verb to 'tout' or 'toot,' spy about,
and the substantive 'touter'; v.
Skeat on tout.

'On Tootle Height, in the township of
Dilworth (Ribchester), there is a valuable
stone quarry': Baines' Lanc. ii. 111.
'Near the Forest Chapel is a small
quadrangular Roman camp, situate on
a hill called Toot-hill': Earwaker's
East Ches. ii. 437, Macclesfield Forest
Township.

The Romans had used the hill
for the same purpose seemingly.

Custance Totel, co. Camb., 1273. A.
Roger Tothull, co. Oxf., ibid.
Johannes de Totehill, 1379: P. T. Yorks.
p. 66.
Willelmus de Totehill, 1379: ibid.
p. 64.
Johannes de Tutill, 1379: ibid. p. 189.
Agnes fil. Thome de Totehill, 1379: ibid.
p. 61.
John de Totehill, 1379: ibid. p. xiv.
Alice Tootell, of Bardsea, 1693: Lan-
cashire Wills at Richmond, p. 257.
William Tootle, of Atherton, 1587:
Wills at Chester, p. 193.
Manchester, 1, 0, 0, 1, 0, 6, 1, 0, 0, 0;
West Rid. Court Dir., 3, 0, 0, 4, 0, 0, 0,
0, 0, 2; London, 0, 2, 3, 1, 1, 0, 0, 0, 2,
0; MDB. (co. Norfolk), (Tuthill), 2;
(Tuttle), 2; New York, 1, 2, 0, 0, 0, 0, 0,
18, 39, 0.

Toovey, Tovey. — (1) Bapt.
'the son of Tofig' or Tovi.
Tofig the Proud was Harold's forerunner in the foundation of
Waltham. He appears in Florence
as 'Danicus et praepotens vir
Tovius, Pruda cognomento.' He
signs himself in 1033 as 'Tovi
Pruda.' His surname was needed
to distinguish him from two name-
sakes: 'Tovi hwita' and 'Tovi
reada' (Freeman, Hist. Norm.
Conq. i. 769). The name is found
in Domesday as Tovi or Tovius.
The personal name lingered on
long enough to become hereditary
as a surname. (2) Local (?).
Evidently a Norman surname.

Berenger de Tovi, co. Linc., Hen. III-
Edw. I. K.
1583. William Tovye, co. Wilts: Reg.
Univ. Oxf. vol. ii. pt. ii. p. 131.
1771. Married — Samuel Toovey and
Mary Torr: St. Geo. Han. Sq. i. 213.
London, 6, 5; Crockford, 2, 6.

Toplady, Tiplady.—? Local. Tiplady seems the original form. It is almost certain that the parentage of this surname must be sought for in co. Yorks.

John Typlady, co. York, 1477. W. 11.
1664. Bapt.—Sarah, d. of Robert Toplady, *gent* : St. Jas. Clerkenwell.
Benjamin Tiplady, 1691 : St. Peter, Cornhill, ii. 59
Hull, o, 2 ; West Rid. Court Dir., o, 1; London, o, 2 ; Philadelphia, o, 2.

Topliff.—Local, 'of Topcliffe,' a parish in N. Rid. Yorks., near Thirsk ; cf. Cunliffe for Cuncliff.

Alan de Topclyf, co. Linc., 1273. A.
Richard de Toppeclyve, vicar of Great-ham, 1308 : DDD. iii. 140.
Alicia Topcliffe, 1379 : P. T. Howdenshire, p. 27.
Boston (U.S.), 3.

Topp ; v. Toop.

Toppin, Topping.— Bapt. ; variants of Turpin, q.v.

Topple.—(1 Bapt. 'the son of Theobald' ; v Tebbitt (1). The corruptions of Theobald are almost astounding. (2) Local. The instance below, however, seems to point to a local derivation.

1769. Married = Philip Tophill and Ann Smith : St. Geo. Han. Sq. i. 126.
London, 3.

Tordoff. — Bapt. 'the son of Thjodulf' (v. Yonge. ii. 338). This name has ramified somewhat strongly in Yorkshire.

Simon Thudolf, co. Oxf., 1273. A.
Geoffrey Thedolf, co. Bucks, ibid.
London, 1 ; Allerton, Yorks, 1 ; Liversedge, Yorks, 2 ; North Bierley, Yorks, 6.

Torkington, Talkington, Turkington—Local, 'of Torkington,' a township in the parish of Stockport, a surname familiar to South Lanc. and the Cheshire border.

Simon de Torkinton, 1225 : East Ches. ii. 105.
Robert de Torkinton, 1225 : ibid.
Thomas de Torkinton, 1357 : ibid. 106.
1605. Buried — Alexander Torkinton, of Stockport : Reg. Parish Church, Stockport.
1617. — Ales Torkinton : Reg. Prestbury, Ches., p. 218.
1774. Married — Peter Lefargue and Eliz. Torkington : St. Geo. Han. Sq. i. 244.
Manchester, 3, 1, o ; London, 1, o, o; Philadelphia, 3, o, 9.

Torpin. — Bapt. ; v. Turpin, a variant.
Philadelphia, 1.

Torr, Torre.—Local, (1) 'of the tower.' O.F. *tur*, later *tour*, 'a tower' (Skeat). (2) 'Of the Torr.' Gaelic *torr*, a hill or mound, specially one of conical form.

Hugh de la Tour. B.
Henry atte Torre. T.
John de la Torre, 31 Edw. I : BBB. p. 645.
Hugh atte Torre, co. Soms., 1 Edw. III : Kirby's Quest, p. 152.
Edith atte Torre, co. Soms., 1 Edw. III : ibid. p 155.
1804. Married — James Torre and Rosellen Eliza Whitwell : St. Geo. Han. Sq. ii. 316.
London, 6, 2 ; Philadelphia, 9, o.

Torrance, Torrence, Torrens. — ?——. I can supply no satisfactory information in regard to this well-established surname.

1750. Married — John Torrence and Mary Cheldrey : St. Geo. Chap. Mayfair, p. 184.
1769. — George Torrans and Fanny Wilkinson : St. Geo. Han. Sq. i. 191.
1804. — William Manners and Ann Torrance : ibid. ii. 303.
London, 2, o, o ; Philadelphia, 2, 9, 11.

Tortoiseshell. — Local. An imitative corruption of Tattersall, found in Manchester Directory in 1861 and onwards (v. Tattersall).

Tosland ; v. Tozeland.

Tothill.—Local ; v. Toothill.

Totiller.—Nick. 'the totiller,' the whisperer ; *title*, *tattle*, and *tottle* seem all to have been in use. A totiller was a whisperer of secrets, an idle and rather mischievous chatterbox. v. Tatler.

'For in your court is many a losengeour, And many a queinte totoler accusour.' Chaucer, Legend of Good Women, l. 353.

'Totelare, *susurro*. Totelynge, *susurrium*. Totelon Talys, totylyn tale in onys ere, *susurro*' (Prompt. Parv. p. 498). The form *tittler* (*titelere*) was also in use. Has the child's game, 'Tom Tiddler's ground,' any connexion ?

Richard le Titteler, co. Suff., 1273. A.
Simon le Tuteler, co. Suff., ibid.
John Totiller. H.
1766. Married—John Tattler and Anna Maria Norgrave : St. Geo. Han. Sq. i. 150.

Totman, Tottenham.—Local ; v. Tottman.
Crockford, o, 4.

Tottie, Totty.—Bapt. 'the son of Otto.' But possibly the Danish Thjod (v. Yonge, ii. 338). But far more probably the nick. of Otty or Oddy (q.v.), one of the most popular names of the time. Several Yorkshire font-names took an initial T as their nick. before a vowel ; cf. Tagg and Taggy for Agg and Aggy. Nevertheless, the instance recorded below, Robertus Thotte, looks very like the Danish Thjod.

Beatrix Totty, 1379 : P. T. Yorks. p. 200.
Willelmus Totty, 1379 : ibid.

The following pair are registered together :

Johannes Totty, 1379 : P. T. Yorks. p. 215.
Robertus Thotte, 1379 : ibid.
Robert Totty, co. York, 1519. W. 11, p. 194.
1577. George Tottie and Eliz. Periman, *widow* : Marriage Lic. (London), i. 77.
1789. Married—John Byrne and Mary Tottey : St. Geo. Han. Sq. ii. 25.
West Rid. Court Dir., 1, o ; London, 1, o ; Barnsley, o, 1 ; Boston (U.S.), o, 2.

Tottman, Totman — Local, 'of Tottenham,' a parish in Middlesex, a corruption ; cf. Deadman, Buckman, Putman, Swetman, &c. This corruption is one of a large class.

In 1632 John Totman was shipped to New England : v. Hotten's Lists of Emigrants, p. 150.

Probably he was the ancestor of the Boston Totmans.

1568. William Moulde and Susanna Totnam : Marriage Lic. (London), i. 39.
1753. Married—Thomas Tattnem and Ann Fat : St. Geo. Chap. Mayfair, p. 243.
1796. — John Tottenham and Mary Eaton : St. Geo. Han. Sq. ii. 155.
London, 1, o ; Boston (U.S.), o, 12.

Touchprick. — Nick. 'a hot rider,' one who spurred his horse.

Robertus Touchepryk, et Alicia uxor ejus, 1379 : P. T. Howdenshire, p. 4.

Toulmin.—Bapt. 'the son of Thomas,' a corruption of Tomlin (q.v.). No connexion, as I take it, with Tollman, a tax-gatherer (v. Toleman). The fact is that Toulmin is a North Lancashire surname, where Tomlinson and Tomlin were almost a clan (v. Townson, Towerson, &c.). Toulmin simply reverses the two letters *m* and *l* (cf. Grundy for Gundry, and v. Broderick).

1607. Richard Towlmyn, of Bolton-le-Sands: Lancashire Wills at Richmond, i. 285.
1623. Richard Towlmyne, of Boulton-by-the-Sands: ibid.
1650. Robert Toulmin, of Bolton-le-Sands: ibid. p. 283.
1664. Edmund Touleming, of Harlocks, Bolton-le-Sands: ibid.
1804. Married — Joseph Toulmin and Maria Sampson: St. Geo. Han. Sq. ii. 301.

Whether I be right or wrong in my solution, one thing is certain, the derivation must be sought for in North Lancashire.

London, 5; Preston, 7; Boston (U.S.),1.

Toulson; v. Tolson.

Tournay.—Local; v. Turney.

Tout. — ? Nick. 'the stout,' a modification of *tort*. '*Tort*, large, fat. Co. Glouc.' (Halliwell). It will be observed that my first instance is from Sómerset, and that Tout is unquestionably a Western counties surname.

Robert le Tort, co. Soms., 1 Edw. III: Kirby's Quest, p. 156.
Laurence le Tort, co. Soms., 1 Edw. III: ibid. p. 245.
London, 5; MDB. (co. Soms.), 5; Philadelphia, 3.

Tovey; v. Toovey.

Tower. — (1) Local, 'of the tower'; v. Torr.

John de la Tour de Shrowesbury, C. R., 21 Edw. III. pt. i.

(2) Occup. 'the tower,' i.e. tawyer, a dresser of skins. To tew, to taw, and to tow seem all to be forms of one verb, and to signify the same thing, viz. to work or operate upon an article; v. Tewer, Tawer, and Whittear. Also v. *tow* (2) in Skeat's Dictionary.

Gilbert le Tower, 1273. A.
Thomas le Toure, ibid.
Juliana la Touestre, ibid.
London, 2; Boston (U.S.), 62.

Towerson.—Bapt. 'the son of Thomas,' one of endless corruptions

of Tomlinson (v. Tolson and Townson). The stages of corruption were first Towlnson, then Towenson, then Towerson; cf. Catterson for Cattinson, or Patterson for Pattinson.

1559. Married—William Towreson and Margery Hawes: St. Michael, Cornhill, p. 7.
1590. Agnes Towenson, of Kirkby Ireleth: Lancashire Wills at Richmond, i. 283.
1591. John Toweson, of Channon-house, in Pennington: ibid. p. 285.
1635. Thomas Towenson, or Tomlinson, of Channon-house, Pennington: ibid. p. 283.
1616. William Towerson, co. Hunts: Reg. Univ. Oxf. vol. ii. pt. ii. p. 352.
1681. Married—John Poole and Mary Towerson: St. Jas. Clerkenwell, i. 193.
MDB. (co. Cumb.), 3.

Towgood. — Bapt. ; v. Thurgood.

Towler.—Occup. ; v. Toller, of which it is a variant ; cf. Coulson for Colson or Coulthurst for Colthurst.

Thomas Towler, co. York. W. 16.
1595. Edward Towler (co. Herts) and Mary Howe: Marriage Lic. (London), i. 221.
1788. Married—Thomas Quinney and Ann Towler: St. Geo. Han. Sq. ii. 10.
— — Thomas Drewett and Mary Towlear: ibid. p. 12.
London, 3; Rathmell, near Settle, Yorks, 2; Boston (U.S.), 3.

Towlson; v. Tolson.

Town, Towne, Toon, Toone. —Local, 'of the town,' from residence therein; originally an enclosure, a farmstead, a farm with all its outbuildings. Lowland Scotch *toon*; v. Skeat's Dict.

Geoffrey de la Tune, co. Sussex, 1273. A.
Robert de Tune, co. Norf., ibid.
Ralph de la Tune. B.
Thomas atte Toune, co. Soms., 1 Edw. III: Kirby's Quest, p. 105.
1602. Thurstan Toone, co. Leic.: Reg. Univ. Oxf. vol. ii. pt. ii. p. 260.
1793. Married — William Green and Ann Towne: St. Geo. Han. Sq. ii. 102.
1801. — Thomas Mockett and Anna Town: ibid. p. 232.
London, 4, 5, 3, 1; Philadelphia, 20, 3, 4, 1.

Towndrow,Townroe,Townrow.—Local, 'at the town-row,' the one continuous line of town or farm buildings. Many places would bear this name; cf. Town-

end and Townsend. The *d* is, of course, intrusive; cf. *riband, gownd,* &c. 'Town-raw is used to denote the privileges of a township. To "thraw one's self out o' a townraw," to forfeit the privileges enjoyed in a small community. Roxb. ; *q.* a row of houses' (Jamieson's Dict.). For the suffix, v. Row (2).

Richard Mercer, of Townrowe, in West Derby (Liverpool), 1628 : Wills at Chester (1621–50), p. 152.
Henry Townerow, or Townroe, 1557 : Reg. Univ. Oxf. i. 234.
1562. Thomas Townraye: ibid. vol. ii. pt. ii. p. 7.
1615. Bapt.—John, s. William Townerawe : St. Michael, Cornhill, p. 111.
London, 3, 0, 0; Sheffield, 4, 4, 0; Manchester, 0, 0, 1.

Townend ; v. Townsend.

Towner.—Occup. 'the towner,' probably equivalent to Farmer, one who kept or laboured on a town or farm; v. Townman and Town. A well-known auctioneer in Eastbourne bears this name.

1786. Married — Robert Towner and Eliz. Wordsworth : St. Geo. Han. Sq. i. 390.
1806. — Thomas Towner and Ann Pinock : ibid. ii. 356.
Eastbourne (Sussex), 1; Boston (U.S.), 2.

Townherd, Tunnard. — Occup. 'the town-herd,' i. e. the man who guarded the town cattle; v. Town and Herd, and cf. Coward (Cowherd), Calvert (Calveherd), &c. Lower says, 'Tunnard, an ancient Lincolnshire family. In 1333 the name occurs as Tonnehyrd, and in 1381 as Tunherd. . . . The name may signify the "town-herd," one to whom was entrusted the care of the common herd of a town or village, a well-known office in the Middle Ages' (Patr. Brit. p. 358).

Augustin Tunherd, co. Camb., 1273. A.
Adam Tonhurde, co. Soms., 1 Edw. III : Kirby's Quest, p. 96.

Townley.—Local, 'of Townley,' an ancient manor in Habergham Eaves, Burnley, co. Lanc. The place gave rise to a family of distinction in very early times. Richard de Townley was sheriff of Lancashire, 1376-1379. The surname is now scattered over the county, either through younger branches of the representative family or humbler stocks. Townley is simply a reversal of the syllables in Layton, or Leyton, or Leighton. Townley emphasizes the relation of the meadow to the farm, the others the relation of the farm to the meadow. Townley means the farm - meadow, the others the meadow-farm. v. Town and Ley.

Cecilia de Tonley, 1330: v. Baines' Hist. Lanc, ii. 36.
Johannes de Townlay, 1379: P. T. Yorks. p. 284.
1588. Bernard Townley, co. Lanc.: Reg. Univ. Oxf. vol. ii. pt. ii. p. 166.
1618. Zouch Townley, co. Lanc.: ibid. p. 373.
London, 6; Manchester, 12; Philadelphia, 5.

Townman. — Occup. 'the townman,' a labourer in or occupier of a town; v. Town.

John Tuneman, co. Bedf., 1273. A.
Ralph Tuneman, co. Bedf., ibid.
John Tounman, co. Soms., 1 Edw. III: Kirby's Quest, p. 96.
1598. Richard Tunman, of Dalton-in-Furness: Lancashire Wills at Richmond, i. 288.
1672. Robert Tunman, of Ireleth-in-Furness: ibid.

I fear the name is extinct, but, of course, cannot be positive.

Townroe, -row; v. Towndrow.

Townsend, Townshend, Townend.—Local, 'at the town-end' or town's-end, from residence thereby. The *h* in Townshend was an early intrusion. Bridge-end, Pounds-end, Greaves-end, Woods-end, Streets-end, and Wick-end are all found with the same intrusive *h* in mediaeval registers (v. my English Surnames, 3rd edit., p. 114, for a long list). 'At the town-end' is still a familiar phrase in the North of England.

Geoffrey de la Tuneshende, co. Norf., 1273. A.
Henry atte Tunesende, co. Oxf., ibid.
Alice atte Tunishende, co. Bucks, ibid.
Richard de la Tuneshend, Close Roll, 2 Edw. I.
Ricardus atte ye Thounhende, 1379: P. T. Yorks. p. 171.
Johannes atte Tonehende, 1379: ibid. p. 134.
1628. Married — Thomas Townesend

and Anne Bradeshawe: St. Dionis Back-church, p. 22.
1760. Married — Thomas Townshend, Esq., and Elizabeth Powys: St. Geo. Han. Sq. i. 94.
London, 46, 3, 11; West Rid. Court Dir., 13, 0, 14; Philadelphia, 145, 1, 0.

Townson.—Bapt. 'the son of Thomas.' However odd this may seem to be, it is unmistakably true. Townson is a North Lancashire corruption of the great Furness surname Tomlinson through the stage Towenson. Of this there cannot be the shadow of a doubt. Even now Townson is pronounced Tone-son in the district.

1571. Edmund Tollenson, or Townson, of Catton: Lancashire Wills at Richmond, i. 280.
1587. Richard Towlson, or Tounsonn, of Dalton: ibid. p. 283.
1588. Jenet Towenson, or Tomlinson, of Ulverston: ibid.
1594. Thomas Toulnson, or Townson, of Gressingham: ibid.
1620. Thomas Tolnson, or Townson, of Catton: ibid. p. 280.
1635. Thomas Towenson, or Tomlinson, of Pennington: ibid. p. 283.
1683. Eliz. Toulnson, of Pilling: ibid. ii. 257.

The present form in Furness, where Tomlinson has predominated for centuries, is Townson; cf. Rawson for Rawlinson in the same record, viz. Lanc. Wills at Richmond, i. 227.

1730. Married—William Townson and Mary Blackwell: St. Geo. Chap. Mayfair, p. 320.
London, 2; Crockford, 4; Ulverston, 2; Philadelphia, 1.

Towson. — Bapt. 'the son of Thomas,' an abbreviated form of Townson, q.v. This corruption is early found in North Lancashire, where Townson and Towson, &c., arose. Towson is thus but a modification of Towenson as that is of Tomlinson.

Cf. 1591. John Toweson, of Channon-house, Pennington: Lancashire Wills at Richmond, i. 280.
1669. John Tomlinson, of Channon-house, Pennington: ibid. p. 285.
1695. Richard Towson, of Priest Hutton: ibid. ii. 260.
1570. Roger Wildynge and Christian Towson: Marriage Lic. (London), i. 46.
1595. Bapt. — Alice, d. John Towson, or Tyson: St. Jas. Clerkenwell, i. 30.
Philadelphia, 2.

Towster.—Occup., a feminine form of Tower (2), q.v.

Juliana la Touestre, co. Oxf., 1273. A.

Toy, Toye.—? Bapt. 'the son of Toy' (?). This seems to be the only reasonable derivation. Further than that it is an old personal name I cannot go.

Warin Toy, co. Camb., 1273. A.
Wydo Toye, co. Suff., ibid.
Johannes Toye, 1379: P. T. Howden-shire, p. 6.
Willelmus Toye, 1379: ibid.
1600. Griffith Toy, co. Pembroke: Reg. Univ. Oxf. vol. ii. pt. ii. p. 244.
1748. Married — Thomas Toy and Anne Bird: St. Geo. Chap. Mayfair, p. 121.
London, 1, 6; Boston (U.S.), 10, 1.

Tozeland, Tosland. — Local, 'of Toseland,' a parish in co. Hunts, four miles from St. Neots.

1750. Married — Simon Tosland and Margaret Hill: St. Geo. Han. Sq. i. 44.
1780. — Samuel Towesland and Mary Toseland (sic): St. Geo. Han. Sq. p. 308.
London, 1, 1.

Tozer, Towzer, Tozar. — Occup. 'the tozer' or teaser (v. Tasseler), one who tosed or teased cloth, one who carded wool, or raised the nap on cloth.

'What schepe that is full of wulle
Upon his backe they tose and pulle.'
   Gower's Confessio Amantis.

A recipe from an old Harleian MS. thus begins, 'Recipe brawne of capons, or of hennys, and dry them well, and towse them small.' 'Toze, the same as touse' (Halliwell). 'Touse, to tug or pull about' (ibid.). Hence 'dog Towzer.' 'Tosynge of wulle' (Prompt. Parv.). 'Tosare of wulle, *carptrix*' (ibid.).

Johannes Tesur, 1379: P. T. Yorks. p. 157.
John Toser, co. Norf. F.
1665-6. Thomas Sowersby and Mary Tozer: Marriage Alleg. (Canterbury), p. 113.
1748. Married — Samuel Touzer and Jane Town: St. Geo. Chap. Mayfair, p. 109.
London, 20, 0, 0; MDB. (co. Devon), 21, 0, 0.

Tracy, Tracey — Local, 'of Traci-Boccage,' in the arrondissement of Caen. Settled in Barn-staple, co. Devon, the parishes, manors, &c., of Woolcombe-Tracy, Bovey-Tracy, Minet-Tracy, and

Bradford-Tracy bear witness to their local ascendency; v. Fuller's Worthies, i. 558.

Henry de Tracy, co. Devon, 1273. A.
Richard de Tracy, co. Devon, ibid.
William de Tracy, co. Sussex, ibid.
Henry Tracy, co. Soms., 1 Edw. III: Kirby's Quest, p. 145.
1597. Richard Tracy, co. Glouc.: Reg. Univ. Oxf. vol. ii. pt. ii. p. 223.
1601. Samuel Tracy, co. Glouc. : ibid. p. 253.
London, 10, 3 ; Boston (U.S.), 70, 0.

Trader.—Occup. 'the trader' (?). I find no early references to such a name, and am inclined to think it a corruption of Thredder, q.v.

London, 2 ; Philadelphia, 4.

Trafford, Traford. — Local, ' of Trafford,' a property in the suburbs of Manchester, whence the baronetage of ' de Trafford ' gets its title.

Stephen de Trafford, co. Lanc., 20 Edw. I. R.
Henry de Trafford, co. Lanc., ibid.
1572. George Trafford, of Manchester, *gentleman* : Wills at Chester, i. 194.
1591. Henry Trafford, rector of Wilmslow : ibid.
1589. William Trafforde, co. Ches. : Reg. Univ. Oxf. vol. ii. pt. ii. p. 171.
1610. John Trafforde, co. Ches. : ibid. p. 317.
London, 3, 1 ; Oxford, 7, 0; Manchester, 2, 0 ; Philadelphia, 2, 0.

Tragetour.—Occupative, ' the tragetour,' a master of legerdemain, a juggler.

' Swiche as thise subtil tregetoures play.'
Chaucer, C. T. 11451.

My first instance seems to imply a misreading of the text :

Richard le Tregheler : Kirby's Quest, p. 136.
Symon le Tregetor, co. Camb. 1273. A.
William le Tregetur, co. Camb., ibid.
Simon Tregetour, *webster*, 1379 : P. T. Howdenshire, p. 4.

The last instance proves that the merely occupative title had settled down into an ordinary surname, but I fear it has not survived.

Trainer, Tranner ; v. Trayner.

Tranter, Traunter.—Occup. ' the tranter,' i. e. a pedlar, a hawker. D. *tranten*, to walk slowly (Annandale). ' Tranter, a carrier. Various dialects' (Halliwell).

'And had some traunting chapman for his sire.' Bishop Hall, Satires.
Agnes Traunter : Churchwardens' Accounts, Ludlow, 1547 : Camden Soc.
Annes Tranter : ibid.
1622. Married—William Tranton and Martha Laine : St. Jas. Clerkenwell, i. 51.
1739. — John Pegg and Eliz. Traunter: St. Geo. Han. Sq. i. 22.
London, 4, 0 ; Derby, 4, 0 ; MDB. (co. Lanc.), 0, 1 ; Boston (U.S.), 1, 0 ; Philadelphia, 0, 1.

Trantom, Trantum ; v. Trentham.

Trapnell.—Bapt. ' the son of Tropinel,' a West-country name, one of the many personal names ending in -*el*.

Walter Tropinel, co. Wilts, 1273. A.
Walter Tropinel, co. Norf., ibid.
John Tropenel, co. Soms., 1 Edw. III: Kirby's Quest, p. 99.
MDB. (co. Soms.), 1.

Trapp.—Local, ' de Trap.' I cannot discover the spot.

John Trappe, co. Hunts, 1273. A.
Richard Trappe, co. Hunts, ibid.
Hanelyn de Trap. H.
Elena Trap, co. Soms., 1 Edw. III : Kirby's Quest, p. 128.
1619. John Trappe, co. Worc. : Reg. Univ. Oxf. vol. ii. pt. ii. p. 376.
1702. Married—Benjamin Trapp and Ann Hale : St. Jas. Clerkenwell, i. 225.
London, 4 ; Philadelphia, 5.

Traverse, Travers, Travis, Traviss. — Local, Fr. ' de la traverse,' from residence beside a crossway, a point where roads met. Oddly enough, I have no early instance to show, but the origin is unmistakable. The full form Traverse is found at Rainhill, Liverpool. The intermediate stage between Traverse and Travis is seen in such an entry as this :

1640. Bapt.—Cordwell Traverse, son of Phillip Travesse : St. Dionis Backchurch (London).
Walter de Travers, 1219 : KKK. vi. 117.
Hugh Travers, co. Linc., 1273. A.
Nigel Travers, co. Bucks, ibid.
Robertus Trauers, 1379 : P. T. Yorks. p. 152.
1578. Ann Travis, or Travers, of Burtonwood : Wills at Chester, i. 194.
1614. James Travis, of Burtonwood : ibid.
1609. Elizabeth Travers, of Bold : ibid.
1614. Elizabeth Travis, of Bold, *widow*: ibid.

This is proof beyond question that Travis or Traviss is a corruption of Travers or Traverse.

London, 1, 9, 3, 0 ; Rainhill, 2, 0, 0, 0; Liverpool (Traviss), 1 ; Boston (U.S.), 0, 31, 13, 0.

Travis(s.—Local ; v. Traverse.

Trawin ; v. Trown.

Trayner, Traynor, Trainor, Tranner, Trainer.—Occup. ' the trainer,' probably of horses ; v. Ambler. It seems very natural that this surname should be first found in Yorkshire.

Robertus Trainer, 1379 : P. T. Yorks. p. 132.
1746. Married—Edward Trayner (co. Linc.) and Jane Webb : St. Geo. Han. Sq. i. 36.
1807. — Owen Traynor and Sarah Harvey : ibid. ii. 364.
London, 2, 1, 0, 0, 0 ; Hull, 0, 2, 1, 1, 0 ; Philadelphia, 0, 7, 53, 0, 34 ; Boston (U.S.), 0, 0, 5, 0, 33.

Treadhard.—Nick. ' a heavy-footed man '; cf. Golightly and Lightfoot, q.v.

Symon Tredhard, 1379 : P. T. Yorks. p. 141.

Treasure.—?——. O.E. *tresor*, treasure, a hoard. It is manifest that the Somersetshire Treasures are descended from Nicholas Tresor mentioned below. The only difficulty is to account for the sobriquet. Possibly it is a local surname meaning 'at the Treasure,' a treasurer, one in care of his lord's money-bags ; v. Treasurer, Countinghouse, Chamberlain, &c.

Nicholas Tresor, co. Wilts, 1273. A.
1596. Edmund Tressur and Margaret Eastfield : Marriage Lic. (London), i. 232.
1803. Married — David Treasur and Janet Forfar : St. Geo. Han. Sq. ii. 274.
MDB. (Somerset), 4 ; London, 1.

Treasurer.—Offic. ' the treasurer.'

Gillam Treasorer, C. R., 1-2 Philip and Mary, pt. iv.
1643. Buried—Gilbert Treasurer, servant to Mr. Stile : St. Dionis Backchurch, p. 224.

Treble.—Bapt. (?). Probably a form of Theobald, q.v. In the Philadelphia Directory is found Treebold, which is eminently suggestive.

Relicta Tyreball, co. Bucks, 1273. A.
Robert Trepel, co. Soms., 1 Edw. III :
Kirby's Quest, p. 158.
1687. Married — Joseph Trebell and
Grace Winstanly : St. Dionis Backchurch,
p. 41.
1797. — John Treble and Emma
Silvester : St. Geo. Han. Sq. ii. 158.
London, 3.

Treblecock, Trebilcock. —
Local. A Cornish surname, one
of the many local surnames beginning with *Tre* and ending with
-*cott*, corrupted to *cock*; cf. Glasscock
for Glascott.
1742. Married — John Trebilcock, of
Gt. Column Major, co. Cornwall, and
Frances Sargent : St. Geo. Han. Sq. i. 29.
1777. — Samuel Freake and Jane Tre-
blecook : ibid. p. 278.
MDB. (co. Cornwall), 0, 5 ; Cornish
Court Dir., 0, 1 ; Truro, 0, 1.

Tree, Trees.—Local, 'at the
tree' or trees, from residence
thereby ; cf. Oak, Birch, Box, &c.
Johannes del Trees, 1379 : P. T. Yorks.
p. 258.
1583. William Leevers and Eliz. Tree :
Marriage Lic. (London), i. 119.
1665. Married — John Tree and Jane
Baily : St. Jas. Clerkenwell, i. 117.
1756. — John Barnaby and Eliz. Tree :
St. Geo. Han. Sq. i, 66.
London, 5, 0 ; Darley (co. York),
Trees, 1 ; Philadelphia, 1, 0.

Treffry, Trefry.—Local, ' of
Treffry.' Mr. Lower says, 'This
name is derived from the manor of
Treffry, in the parish of Lanhydrock,
where it is traced to a very early
period' (v. for fuller account his
Patr. Brit. p. 353).
MDB. (co. Cornwall), 7, 0 ; Boston
(U.S.), 0, 7.

Trefusis, Trefuses. — Local,
' of Trefusis,' an estate in the parish
of Milor, co. Cornwall, where the
family bearing the name have
resided for many centuries.
1578. John Trefusis, co. Cornwall :
Reg. Univ. Oxf. vol. ii. pt. ii. p. 82.
1589. Nicholas Trefusis, co. Cornwall:
ibid. p. 176.
1605. John Trefusis, co. Cornwall :
ibid. p. 282.
Crockford, 1, 0 ; London, 0, 1.

Tregarthen, Tregarthian.—
Local, ' of Tregarthian.' ' A place
in the parish of Gorran, co. Cornwall, where the family were seated
temp. Edw. I, or earlier' : Lower,
quoting Gilbert's Cornwall.
London, 1, 0 ; Oxford, 0, 1.

Tregear.— Local, 'of Tregeare.'
' A place in the parish of Crowan,
co. Cornwall. The family were
resident there so lately as 1732.
Richard Tregeare, of Tregeare, was
sheriff of the county in 1704' :
Lower, quoting Gilbert's Cornwall.
London, 2.

**Treherne, Trehearne, Tre-
harne.**—Bapt.'the son of Trahern.'
' An ancient Welsh personal name,
as Trahern ap Caradoc, Prince of
North Wales, 1073' : Lower's Patr.
Brit. p. 354.
1578. Bapt. — Marie, d. William Treherne, cloth-worker : St Mary Aldermary, p. 59.
1802. Married — William Laker and
Susanna Treherne : St. Geo. Han. Sq. ii.
264.
London, 3, 1, 0 ; Boston (U.S.), 0, 0, 1.

Trelawny. — Local, ' of Trelawny.' Two manors of this name
exist in co. Cornwall, one in the
parish of Alternon, the other in
that of Pelynt. The former was
the original seat of the Trelawnys,
afterwards the latter, which is still
the seat of the family' : Shirley's
Noble and Gentle Men (Lower).

**Tremain, Tremayne, Tre-
maine.**— Local, 'of Tremayne.'
' An estate in the parish of St.
Martin, co. Cornwall. The pedigree
is traced to Perys de Tremayne of
Tremayne, in the reign of Edward
III' : Lower, quoting Shirley's
Noble and Gentle Men (Patr. Brit.
p. 354).
1704-5. Married — John Forster and
Jane Tremaine : St. Dionis Backchurch,
p. 53.
London, 3, 0, 0 ; Crockford, 0, 1, 0 ;
Boston (U.S.), 0, 0, 1.

Tremble, Trimble.—Variants
of the border name of Turnbull
(q.v.), found in co. Cumberland.
MDB. (co. Cumberland), 5, 3 ; Philadelphia, 0, 43.

Tremellen.— ? ——.
William Tremillin, co. Staff., 1273. A.
London, 1.

Tremenheere. — Local, ' of
Tremenheere.' ' The family name
of Tremenheere is derived from
lands so named in the parish of
Ludgvan, of which Nicholas de
Tremenheere was seised before

the reign' of Edward I' : Gilbert's
Cornwall, quoted by Lower, Patr.
Brit. p. 354.
Crockford, 2.

Tremeer, -mor ; v. Trimmer.

Trenchard. — Nick. ' the
trenchant.' Fr. *trenchant*, cutting ;
doubtless a sobriquet conferred on
some skilled swordsman ; cf. Sharparrow, Bruselance, &c.
William Trenchaunt, co. Oxf., 1273. A.
London, 1 ; Philadelphia, 1 ; New
York, 2.

Trendell.—Local, 'of Trendle';
v. Trundle.

Trent.—Local, ' of Trent,' a
parish in co. Somerset, near
Sherborne.
Gibert de Trent, co. Soms., 1 Edw. III :
Kirby's Quest, p. 216.
London, 1 ; MDB. (co. Soms.), 2 ;
Boston (U.S.), 1.

**Trentham, Trantum, Tran-
tom.**—Local, ' of Trentham,' a
parish in co. Stafford, four miles
from Newcastle.
John, Prior de Trentham, co. Staff., 20
Edw. I. R.
The American form is almost
identical with that of an early
emigrant's name.
1635. ' Imbarqued in the Blessing' for
New England, Thomas Trentum, aged
14 years : Hotten's Lists of Emigrants,
p. 108.
1747. Married — James Trentam (co.
Notts) and Patience Damnall : St. Geo.
Chap. Mayfair, p. 100.
London, 1, 0, 0 ; Liverpool, 0, 0, 1 ;
Philadelphia, 0, 2, 0.

Tresillian.—Local, ' of Tresillian.' ' Two places in Cornwall
are so designated, one in the parish
of Newlyn, and the other in
Merther. The distinguished Sir
Robert Tresillian . . . who fell a
victim to the resentment of the
barons at Tyburn in 1388, was of
this family' : Lower, quoting Gilbert's Cornwall.

Trespass.—Nick.
Thomas Trespas, co. Hunts, 1273. A.
John Trepas, London, ibid.

Trevarthen.—Local, ' of Tre-
varthian.' ' The manor of Trevar-
thian, in the parish of Newlyn,
near Truro, is undoubtedly the
spot that gave origin to this family,

who in former times ranked among the most distinguished names that have been known in the county of Cornwall ': Lower, quoting Gilbert's Cornwall (Patr. Brit. p. 355).
London, 1.

Trevelion, Trevelyan, Trevilian, Trevillion.—Local, ' of Trevelyan,' an estate in the parish of St. Veep, near Fowey, co. Cornwall, where dwelt in the reign of Edw. I Nicholas de Trevelyan, whose ancestors had possessed the property from a still earlier period (Shirley's Noble and Gentle Men, quoted by Lower, Patr. Brit. p. 355).

1734. Married—George Trevillion and Mary Allen : St. Michael, Cornhill, p. 66.
London, 1, 1, 1, 2.

Trevitt, Trevett.—Bapt. ' the son of Trivet,' possibly a variant of Troite ; v. Trott.

John Trivet, co. Soms., 1 Edw. III : Kirby's Quest, p. 253.
Edmund Trivet, co. Soms., 1 Edw. III : ibid.
Nicholas Trivet, co. Soms., 1 Edw. III : ibid.

There are a fair number of Trivets in this Exchequer Roll.

Philadelphia, 1, 0 ; Boston (U.S.), 0, 1.

Trew ; v. True.

Trewhitt.—Bapt. ' the son of Troite' ; v. Trott. But it must not be forgotten that there is High and Low Trewhitt, a township in the parish of Rothbury, co. Northumberland.

Nicholas Tryut, co. Soms., 1 Edw. III : Kirby's Quest, p. 272.
London, 1.

Trewinnard. — Local, ' of Trewinnard.' ' An estate in the parish of St. Erth, co. Cornwall. The earliest recorded ancestor seems to be William de Trewinnard, a knight of the shire, 28 Edw. III ' : Lower, quoting Gilbert's Cornwall.
London, 2.

Tricker.—Bapt. ' the son of Troggar,' whence Trigger (q.v.), and the sharpened Tricker ; cf. Trickett for Triggett, and cf. also Slagg and Slack.
London, 2 ; Philadelphia, 6.

Trickett, Triggett. — Bapt. ' the son of Trigot,' possibly a dim. of Trig ; but v. Traugott (Yonge, ii. 491). It had an unquestioned footing for a time in North, if not South England. Cf. German Traugott, still in use as a font-name.

' But Traugott Waldteufel, for so he was called, profited by his crime hardly at all ' : Westall's Two Pinches of Snuff, iii. 230.

Baldewin Triket, co. Bedf., 1273. A.
Thomas Triket, co. Norf., ibid.
Ida Triket, co. Middlesex, Hen. III-Edw. I. K.
Simon Triket, cos. Essex and Herts : ibid.
Emma Trigot, 1379 : P. T. Yorks. p. 123.
Sibilla Trigot, 1379 : ibid. p. 103.
1706. Married—Jonathan Trickett and Mary Williamson : St. Michael, Cornhill, p. 53.
London, 6, 0 ; Philadelphia, 7, 0.

Trigg, Triggs. — Bapt. ' the son of Trig,' a favourite old Northern name (Yonge, ii. 414), genitive Triggs ; v. Trickett.

' No clown would be considered worth his salt if he could not vault over six horses like King Teutobach, or play with three missiles at the same time like Olaf Trygesson ' : Standard, March 31, 1887.
Robert Trig, co. Camb., 1273. A.
William Triggs, co. Camb., ibid.
Alan Trig, co. Linc., ibid.
William Tryg, co. Soms., 1 Edw. III : Kirby's Quest, p. 271.
Johannes Tryg, 1379 : P. T. Yorks. p. 78.
1549. Henry Nelson and Agnes Triggs : Marriage Lic. (London), i. 12.
1597. Buried — Edward Trygge : St. Michael, Cornhill, p. 208.
1657. Married—Hugh Coles, *confecksonor*, and Ann Trigg : St. Mary Aldermary, p. 27.
London, 8, 7 ; Boston (U.S.), 0, 3.

Trigger.—Bapt. ' the son of Troggar ' ; v. Tricker.

Hugh Troggar, co. Soms., 1 Edw. III : Kirby's Quest, p. 264.
London, 1.

Trimbell, Trimble ; v. Tremble.

Philadelphia, 1, 43.

Trimbey, Trimby, Trymby.—Local, ' of Thrimby,' a chapelry in the parish of Morland, co. Westmoreland. Probably some other spot was so called in co. Wilts. As a surname Trimby was certain

to become the popular lazy variant for Thrimby ; cf. Trower for Thrower.

1615. Bapt. — Mary, d. Cuthbert Tremby : Reg. Stourton, co. Wilts, p. 6.
1624. — Andrew, s. Cutbert Trimbey : ibid. p. 7.
1713. — John, s. John Trimby : ibid. p. 22.

Found also in the same register as Thrimboy (v. Index).

London, 2, 1, 0 ; Philadelphia, 0, 0, 3.

Trimmer, Tremeer, Tremer.—(1) Occup. (?) ' the trimmer,' probably some kind of embroiderer. But I have no proof. (2) Local, ' of Tremere.' Lower suggests 'Tremere,' an estate in Lanivet parish, co. Cornwall. The elder line failed in the 14th century ; v. Gilbert's Cornwall.

1658. Bapt. — Robert, s. Edmund Trimmer : St. Jas. Clerkenwell, i. 202.
1792. Married—Edward Trimmer and Mary Hewitt : St. Geo. Han. Sq. ii. 87.
London, 4, 0, 0 ; MDB. (co. Surrey), 1, 0, 0 ; (co. Cornwall), 0, 1, 0 ; Philadelphia, 4, 0, 2.

Trinder.—Occup. ' the trinder.' Probably a wheeler, a maker of trindles. ' *Trindles*, the felloes of a wheel' (Halliwell) ; cf. ' Trendelyn, as with a rownd thynge ; *volvo, trocleo.*' ' Trendyl, *troclea* ' : Prompt. Parv. p. 502. The instance below is from co. Norf., agreeing with the locale of the two last quotations.

Hugh le Trinder, co. Norf., 1273. A.
1615. Martin Trender, co. Wilts : Reg. Univ. Oxf. vol. ii. pt. ii. p. 342.
— Thomas Trender, co. Wilts : ibid.
1791. Married—Benjamin Trinder and Catharine Barnwell : St. Geo. Han. Sq. ii. 55.
London, 4 ; Oxford, 9 ; Philadelphia, 1.

Tring ; v. Thring.

Trinity.— ? —.

1700. Married — Robert Butler and Sarah Trinity : St. Michael, Cornhill, p. 55.

Tripcony.—Local, ' of Tripcony,' a Cornish name.

' Presentment of James Trypconye, deputy for the haven of Haylerford or Helford, touching piracies ' on coast of Cornwall, April 30, 1579 : Cal. State Papers (Domestic), i. 473.
John Dyer, of Tripcony, 1619 : Reg. St. Columb Major, p. 208.
London, 1.

Tripp, Trippet.—Bapt. 'the son of Tripp,' an early personal name.

William Trip, co. Camb., 1273. A.
Robert Trippe, co. Bedf., ibid.
Gilbert Trip, co. Wilts, ibid.
John Tryp, co. Soms., 1 Edw. III: Kirby's Quest, p. 107.
Johannes Trypet, 1379: P.T.Yorks.p.44.
Simon Trippe, 1564: Reg. Univ. Oxf. i. 253.
1580. Married — Reinald Trip, *goldsmith*, and Christian Feelding : St. Mary Aldermary, p. 6.
1629. Buried—Prudence Trippit, a *servant* : ibid. p. 166.
London, 13, 0 ; West Rid. Court Dir., 2, 0 ; Sheffield, 1, 0 ; Boston (U.S.), 37, 0.

Tripper, Trippier.—Occup. 'a tripherd,' a goatherd, cos. York and Lanc. ' *Trip*, a flock of sheep, a herd of swine or goats' (Halliwell).

' Item, in pane pro triphyrdes sarculant metent,' 1305: Whitaker's Craven, p. 460, compotus de Bolton.
'Item pro geldherds, pro tripherds,' 1317: ibid. p. 465.

The editor adds, 'Trip is a herd of goats, and has given origin to the surname yet remaining in Lancashire, Tripver'; cf. Tupper for Tupherd.

Walter Tripper, 1379: P.T.Yorks. p. 49.
Willelmus Tripper, 1379: ibid.

A Mrs. Trippier let lodgings at Seascale, co. Cumberland (1887).

Penrith, 0, 1 ; Liverpool, 0, 1 ; Treales (near Kirkham, co. Lanc.), 0, 1 ; Wharles (ibid.), 0, 1.

Trist.—Local, 'at the tryst,' the place of meeting. M.E. *trist*, 'a tryst, meeting-place ; station in hunting' (Mayhew and Skeat). Lower says, ' Fr. *triste*, sad, pensive.' It may be so, but I find no evidence.

Peter atte Treste, co. Bucks, 1273. A.
1589. Richard Tryst or Trist, co. Northants : Reg. Univ. Oxf. vol. ii. pt. ii. p. 172.
1679. Buried—Mrs. Sarah Tryst : St. Antholin (London), p. 98.
London, 2 ; Philadelphia, 3.

Triston.—Bapt. 'the son of Tristram,' familiarly known as Tristam. Once popular in Cornwall.

1622. Buried—Grace Tresteene, *widow*: Reg. St. Columb Major, p. 210.
Adam Trestean, 1629: ibid. p. 212.
1784. Married—Thomas Heseltine and Katherine Triston : St.Geo.Han. Sq. i. 358.
London, 2.

Tristram.—Bapt. 'the son of Tristram.'

Tristram de Haule, co. Suff., 1273. A.
John Tristian, co. Soms., 1 Edw. III : Kirby's Quest, p. 130.
Cecilia uxor Trystrem, 1379: P. T. Yorks. p. 265.
Isolda Trestrem, 1379 : ibid.
1585. John Tristrum and Eliz. Emley: Marriage Lic. (London), i. 139.
Tristram Blaby, 1590 : Reg. St. Mary Aldermary (London), p. 8.
London, 1 ; Crockford, 2 ; New York, 1.

Troate.—Bapt. ; v. Trott.

Trodd.—Bapt. ; v. Trott.

Trollope—Local, 'of Trollop.' Probably ' hope' is the suffix (v. Hope). Northumberland seems to be the home of the family, but the spot I have failed to identify. They are also early found in co. Lincoln.

William de Trollop, 1383 : Prior of Holy Island : QQQ. p. 61.
John Trolop, 1401 : DDD. vol. i. p. 85.
1612. Buried—Grace, w. Roger Trowlupp (Reg. Crossgate) : DDD. i. 91.
1744. Married — John Trollop and Sarah Munvell : St. Geo. Han. Sq. i. 32.
London, 7.

Trood.—Bapt. ; v. Trott.

Trotman, Trottman.—Occup. ' Trotisman,' i.e. the servant of Trot or Trote (v. Trott) ; cf. Matthewman, Addiman, Harriman, &c. One of a somewhat large class of names. No relationship with Trotter.

Bartholomew Troteman, 34 Edw. I : BBB. p. 728.
Samuel Trotman. HH.
1628. Married—Richard Archer and Eliz. Trotman : St. Jas. Clerkenwell, i. 59.
Throgmorton Trotman, a native of Cam, co. Glouc., a London merchant, 1663 : Rudder's Hist. Glouc. p. 318.
1783. Married — Richard White and Mary Trotman : St. Geo. Han. Sq. p. 342.
London, 15, 0 ; MDB. (co. Glouc.), 7, 0 ; Philadelphia, 2, 1 ; Boston (U.S.), 3, 0.

Trott, Troate, Trood, Trout, Trodd.—Bapt. ' the son of Troit ' or Trote or Troyt. One of the forms of Trude, found in such compounds as Ger-trude, Hil-trude; formerly a name of itself. Hence ' Dame Trott' in the nursery rhyme (v. Yonge, ii. 235-6). The name is frequently found in the Exchequer Lay Subsidies, co. Soms.,

1 Edw. III, and in various forms is still familiar to that county. Speaking generally, the surname has steadily settled down into Trott.

Robertus fil. Troite, 7 Hen. II, Pipe Roll, iv. 40.
Robert fil. Trote, 1165: RRR. p. 7.
Richard fil. Truite, 1179 : ibid. p. 20.

The first two probably represent the same individual. I furnish both instances because of the twofold spelling. It will be well to furnish some early variants :

Nicholas Truhyt, co. Soms., 1 Edw. III ; Kirby's Quest, p. 151.
Thomas Truht, co. Soms., 1 Edw. III : ibid. p. 153.
Robert Trote, co. Soms., 1 Edw. III : ibid. p. 156.
Thomas Trut, co. Soms., 1 Edw. III : ibid. p. 159.
Robert Tryut, co. Soms., 1 Edw. III : ibid. p. 146.
John Trout, co. Soms., 1 Edw. III : ibid. p. 224.
Simon Trot, co. Hunts, 1273. A.
Godwin Trote, co. Norf., ibid.
Philip Troyt, co. Norf., ibid.
Jeffry Trote, bailiff of Yarmouth, 1340 : FF. xi. 323.
1661. Married — William Fitter and Jane Trott : St. Michael, Cornhill, p. 38.
London, 8, 0, 1, 0, 1 ; MDB. (co. Soms.), 8, 1, 4, 1, 0 ; Boston (U.S.), 10, 0, 0, 7, 0.

Trotter, Trottier. — Official, 'the trotter,' a messenger, one who trotted. Skeat says (v. *trot*): ' Fr. *trotter*, "to trot" : Cotg. O.F. *troter*, 13th century : Littré. We also find O.F. *trotier*, a trotter, a messenger, Low Lat. *trotarius*, = Lat. *tolutarius*, going at a trot.' It is possible that in some cases it is a nickname from the gait of the progenitor, as ' trotter' for a horse was in use. ' Trottare, horse, *succursarius*' : Prompt. Parv. The first, of course, is the natural origin. 'Leon Trottier, French confectioner,' in the London Directory, reminds us of the French equivalent.

Johannes Trotter, 1379: P. T. Yorks. p. 300.
Thomas Trotter. W. 13.
Richard Trotter. C.
1596-7. Married—Walter Trotter and Eliz. Golding : St. Dionis Backchurch, p. 13.
1581. Edward Mott and Isabel Trotter : Marriage Lic. (London), i. 101.
London, 6, 1 ; Philadelphia, 27, 0.

Troughton. — Local, 'of Troughton,' a small estate, now Troughton Hall, in Woodlands, near Ulverston, North Lancashire. The surname is very familiar in the district.

1547. Bapt.—William Troghton : St. Mary, Ulverston, p. 4.
— Buried—Anne Troghton : ibid. p. 5.
1549. Bapt.—Elizabeth Troghton : ibid. p. 8.
1584. Ann Troughton, of Ulverston : Lancashire Wills at Richmond, i. 287.
1599. Barnard Troughton, of Riddinge, parish of Ulverston : ibid.
1660. Miles Troughton, of Ulverston : ibid.
1747. Married — James Throughton and Miss Middleton : St. Geo. Chap. Mayfair, p. 98.
London,4 ; Liverpool,5 ; Philadelphia,3.

Trounce ; v. Trown.

Trousdale, Trowsdale, Truesdale, Trowsdall.—Local, ' of Troutsdale,' a township in the parish of Brompton, near Scarborough, N. Rid. Yorks.

1635. Phines Trusedell (aged 18 years) embarked for the Barbadoes : Hotten's Lists of Emigrants, p. 142.
1679. Buried — Ann Trowsdale, St. Michael's, Barbadoes : ibid. p. 433.

Probably Phineas was the parent of the American Trowsdales, Trousdales, or Truesdales. The different forms are still chiefly found, so far as England is concerned, in the N. Rid. Yorks, in the neighbourhood of Troutsdale.

MDB. (N. Rid. Yorks), 1, 1, 0, 1 ; Scarborough, 0, 1, 0, 0 ; Boston (U.S.), 1, 1, 3, 0 ; Philadelphia, 0, 0, 2, 0.

Trout.—(1) Nick. (?) 'the trout,' the fish so named. The earliest instance I can find is in co. York. It is there we find the surname Bucktrout, q.v. (2) Bapt. 'the son of Trote.' This must undoubtedly be considered the parent. For an account of the name, v. Trott. Scarcely a single seeming fish-name like Salmon, Turbot, Chubb, &c., represents the finny tribe.

Thomas Trout, 1379: P.T.Yorks. p. 121.
1601-2. John Rae and Susan Trowte, *widow* : Marriage Lic. (London), i. 267.
1602-3. John Trout, co. Somerset : Reg. Univ. Oxf. vol. ii. pt. ii p. 263.
1776. Married—Jacob Trout and Eliz. Evans : St. Geo. Han. Sq. i. 266.
Philadelphia, 61.

Troutbeck.—Local, ' of Troutbeck,' a parish in co. Westmoreland, five miles from Ambleside.

1568. Edward Troutebecke, or Trutbecke : Reg Univ. Oxf. i. 270.
1591. Robert Trowtebecke, co. Cumb.: Reg. Univ. Oxf. vol. ii. pt. ii. p. 186.
1593. Robert Troutbeck, vicar of Newton-Regny : Jefferson's Hist. of Leath Ward, co. Cumb., p. 151.
1621. Anthony Troutbecke, co. Cumb.: Reg. Univ. Oxf. vol. ii. pt. ii. p. 398.
Crockford, 1 ; MDB. (co. Cumb.), 5.

Trover.—Occup. Probably a shortened form of Troubadour (v. *troubadour*, Skeat's Etym. Dict.).

Simon le Trovur, temp. Hen. III.
William le Trovur, temp. Hen. III.

I have lost my reference to these entries.

London, 1.

Trow.—Local, 'at the trow,' i.e. trough. ' *Trow*, a trough': Halliwell. Mr. Lower quotes Mr. Ferguson as saying, ' Trow, Troy, and Try are different forms of True, as Old Frieslandic *trowe*. *troiwe*, German *treu*.' It may be so. The evidence is altogether against it as regards Trow. Residence by an artifical trough, or a natural trough in a stream, seems the inevitable solution, judging by my first and earliest instances.

William atte Trowe, co. Wilts, 1273. A.
Thomas atte Trowe, co. Soms., 1 Edw. III : Kirby's Quest, p. 243.
Roger atte Trowe : co. Soms., 1 Edw. III : ibid.
1624-5. Philip Gardner and Anne Trow : Marriage Lic. (London), ii. 148.
1694. Bapt. — Gilbert, s. Thomas Trowe : St. Jas. Clerkenwell, i. 358.
1774. Married — Richard Trow and Jane Harper : St. Geo. Han. Sq. i. 242.
London, 1 ; Boston (U.S.), 4.

Trowbridge.—Local, ' of Trowbridge,' a market-town and parish in co. Wilts.

Richard Trowbrigge, co. Soms., 1 Edw. III : Kirby's Quest, p. 104.
John de Trowbrugge, co. Soms., 1 Edw. III : ibid. p. 179.
William de Trowbrugge, co. Soms., 1 Edw. III : ibid.
1583. George Trobrydgecco. Devon : Reg. Univ. Oxf. vol. ii. pt. ii. p. 125.
1731. Bapt.—John, s. John Trowbridge : Reg. Stourton, co. Wilts.
1809. Married — Charles Bulkeley Egerton and Charlotte Troubridge, co. Sussex : St. Geo. Han. Sq. ii. 419.
London, 3 ; Philadelphia, 4.

Trowell.—Local, (1) 'of Trowell,' a parish in co. Notts, near Nottingham ; (2) 'of Trowle,' a tithing in the parish of Great Bradford, co. Wilts. Both seem to be parents.

Richard de Truwell, co. Linc., 1273. A.
Batin de Trowell, co. Wilts, 1 Edw. III : Kirby's Quest, p. 168.
London, 3 ; Philadelphia, 1.

Trower.—Probably a corruption of Thrower, q.v.

London, 9 ; Boston (U.S.), 2.

Trown, Trawin, Trounce, Trounson.—Bapt. 'the son of Trogne.' Peculiar to co. York, so far as I can discover. Trounce, more correctly Trowns (the *s* as in Jones, Jennings, Williams, &c.), may be compared with Ellice for Ellis, or Pierce for Piers.—Since writing the above I find Trounson in co. Devon. I have still more recently met with it in Southport, co. Lanc.

Magota Trogune, 1379, Kimberworth : P. T. Yorks. p. 67.
Willelmus Trogñe, 1379, Kimberworth : ibid.
Johannes Trogñe, 1379, Kimberworth : ibid.
Rogerus Tron, 1379, Hooton Pagnell : ibid. p. 29.
Stephanus Troune, 1379, Hooton Pagnell : ibid.
Johannes Troune, 1379, Hooton Pagnell : ibid. p. 15.
1582. William Trawnson, *myller*, and Eliz. Johnson : Marriage Lic. (London), i. 112.
1791. Married — Charles Cutter and Mary Eliz. Trounce : St. Geo. Han. Sq. ii. 56.
London, 0, 2, 2, 0 ; West Rid. Court Dir., 1, 0, 0, 0 ; Sheffield, 2, 0, 0, 0 ; Leeds, 0, 1, 0, 0 ; (Trounson) North Lew, co. Devon, 1 ; Plymouth, 1 ; New York, 4, 0, 0, 0.

Trowsdale, &c. ; v. Trousdale.

Trowse.—Local, ' of Trowse,' co. Norfolk. This surname still exists in co. Norfolk, where it existed at least five centuries ago. The parish of Trowse-Newton is in co. Norfolk, one mile from Norwich, and it seems to have been the home of the family. Originally the village must have been called Trowse, and the Newton has been added later.

John de Trowse, bailiff of Norwich, 1387: FF. iii. 116.
Nicholas de Trowes, co. Norf., 20 Edw. I: ibid. x. 66.
1371. Buried—Thomas de Trows, of Norwich: ibid iv. 137.
Thomas Troys, co. Norf., 1517: ibid. v. 248.
London, 1; MDB. (Norfolk), 1.

Troy.—Local, 'de Troyes,' the French town of that name. It is almost certain that this is the origin. In fact, the following entries concerning one and the same individual may be said to prove it. Copin, let it be noticed, was the pet name for Jacob; v. Coppin.

Copin' de Troye (London citizen), 1273. A.
Jacobus de Troye (London citizen), ibid.
Jacobus de Troys (London citizen), ibid.
James de Troys (London citizen), ibid.
1793. Married — William Troy and Eleanor Fitzgerald: St. Geo. Han. Sq. ii. 95.
1809. — John Troy and Maria Moore: ibid. p. 416.
London, 1; Boston (U.S.), 24.

Trubridge.—Local, a variant of Trowbridge, q.v. A similar form is found in an English register.

1761. Married — Samuel Sitchell and Jane Truebridge: St. Geo. Han. Sq. i. 100.
New York, 1.

True, Trew.—Nick. 'the true,' a faithful and trustworthy man. M.E. *trewe.*

Henry Trewe, co. Bedford, 1273. A.
1595. Bapt.—Eliz., d. John True: St. Dionis Backchurch, p. 89.
1596. Buried—Eliz. Trew: ibid. p. 204.
1807. Married—Charles Walker and Ruth Trew: St. Geo. Han. Sq. ii. 372.
London, 0, 5; Philadelphia, 2, 0; Boston (U.S.), 17, 0.

Truebody.—Nick. 'truebody,' faithful, loyal (cf. Trueman and Truefellow). In the Countess of Leicester's service (18 Edw. I) were several messengers, all bearing names allusive to their office, viz. Slingaway, Bolett (= Bullet), and Treubodie (v. Household Expenses of Ric. de Swinfield, A.D. 1289-90, Camden Soc., p. 143 *n*).

Stephen Trewbody. H.
1630. Buried—Annes Truboddy: Reg. St. Columb Major, p. 213.

Truecock. — Nick. 'faithful fellow'; v. Cocks.

John Truccok, co. Derby, 1273. A.

Truefellow. — Nick. 'truefellow,' an honest companion, a loyal partner; cf. Goodfellow and Trueman.

Johannes Trewfelagh, 1379: P. T. Yorks. p. 147.

Truelove.—Nick. 'betrothed' or 'bound,' from the Scandinavian *troe lof,* bound in law, a bondsman (Lower, quoting Ulst. Jour. Arch. No. 2). The late Dr. Littledale suggested to me 'betrothed, from Norse *at trulofa,* to pledge one's faith, to betroth.' Hence the meaning of the paradoxical line in the old song:

'So my true love was false to me.'

The Hundred Rolls form of the surname is Trewelove.

Richard Trewlove. G.
Stephen Truelove. H.
John Truvelove, co. Soms., 1 Edw. III: Kirby's Quest, D. 120.
Willelmus Trewluf, 1379: P. T. Yorks. p. 146.
Ricardus Trewluff, 1379: ibid. p. 292.
1597. Rowland Trewlove and Winifred Paynter: Marriage Lic. (London), i. 443.
1802. Married — Robert Ireland and Mary Truelove: St. Geo. Han. Sq. ii. 258.
London, 3.

Trueman, Truman. — Nick. 'the true man,' a true, trustworthy, or faithful man. M.E. *trewe.* Probably the sobriquet of some herald or messenger; v. Truebody.

Agnes Treueman, co. Camb., 1273. A.
Thomas Treweman, co. Worc., ibid.
Richard Treweman, Rot. Claus., 22 Ric. II. pt. ii.
1621. Married — Rychard Trewman and Eliz. Somner: St. Dionis Backchurch, p. 4.
1792. — William Stukeley Burns and Ann Truman: St. Geo. Han. Sq. ii. 82.
London, 3, 11; Philadelphia, 4, 14.

Trumper.—Occup. 'the trumper,' a blower on the trump.

'The trompoures with the loud min stralcie.' Chaucer, C. T. 2673.
William le Trompour, c. 1300. M.
John le Trompour, c. 1300. M.
John Skot, *trumper,* 19 Edw. II: Freemen of York, i. 23.
John Trompour, co. Soms., 1 Edw. III: Kirby's Quest, p. 210.

Walterus Tromper, 1379: P. T. Yorks. p. 133.
1644. Clare Trumper: Cal. of Wills in Court of Husting (2).
1789. Married — George Elliott and Diana Trumper: St. Geo. Han. Sq. ii. 25.
London, 2; MDB. (co. Hereford), 6; New York, 2.

Trundle, Trendell.—Local, 'of Trendle,' a tithing in the parish of Pitminster, co. Somerset. The Norfolk Trundles are clearly descended from the Trendle family in that county, found there so early as 1360 (v. infra). Whether they hailed from Trendle in Somersetshire, or from some spot so called in Norfolk, I cannot say. Undoubtedly the Trendells of Abingdon, near Oxford, came from the Somersetshire tithing.

1360. Thomas Trendyl, vicar of Witton, co. Norf.: FF. xi. 84.
1569. John Tryndell, rector of Wimbotsham, co. Norf.: ibid. vii. 519.

The last-named is probably referred to in the following:

1565. John Trundell, rector of Bexwell, co. Norf.: FF. vii. 310.
1631. Thomas Trendle, vicar of Mendham, co. Norf.: ibid. v. 385.
1639. William Trundell, of Hetherset, co. Norf.: ibid. p. 28.
1733. Married—Laurence Allison and Judith Trundle: St. Geo. Han Sq. i. 12.
London, 0, 1; MDB. (Norfolk), 5, 6; Crockford, 1, 1; Abingdon, 0, 1.

Trussharness.—Nick. for an ostler or stableman.

Agnes Trusseharneys, C. R., 8 Edw. III.

Trustram, Trustrum.—Bapt. 'the son of Tristram,' q.v.

1601. John Tristram or Trustram, co. Devon: Reg.Univ.Oxf. vol. ii. pt. ii. p. 250.
1656-7. Married — John Heath and Bridgett Trustram: St. Dionis Backchurch, p. 32.
London, 1, 1.

Tubb, Tubbs, Tubby.—Bapt. 'the son of Theobald.' There can be no reasonable doubt that this is the case. Theobald and its forms have run riot among the vowels; v. Tebb. Tubby is the pet form; cf. Charley and Sibley. Tubbs is, of course, the genitive or patronymic form; cf. Jones or Williams.

Thomas Tubb', *souter,* 1379: P. T. Yorks. p. 26.

Matilda Tubb', 1379: P.T.Yorks. p. 26.
1745. Married—Antony Paul Tubb and Eliz. Bushell: St. Geo. Chap. Mayfair, p. 59.
1748. — John Tubbs and Maria Evers: ibid. p. 119.
London, 8, 7, 2 ; Boston (U.S.), 0, 4, 0.

Tubman. — (1) Occup. 'the tubman,' i.e. the cooper. (2) Occup. 'the man of Tub,' i.e. the servant of Tub ; cf. Addyman, Matthewman, Harriman, &c.; v. Tubb. The first derivation is the most probable. The name is found in Furness, North Lancashire, always noted for cooperage.

Henry Tubman, co. York. W. 16.
John Tubman, co. Norf. F.
1549. Married—Robert Tubman and Jelian Schales: St. Mary, Ulverston, p. 9.
1661. Nicholas Tubman, of Barrowhead, Furness : Lancashire Wills at Richmond, i. 288.
1737. Buried—Thomas, son of Thomas Tubman : St. Mary, Ulverston, p. 260.
1745. William Tubman, of Barrow Head : Lancashire Wills at Richmond, ii. 261.
Philadelphia, 2.

Tuck, Took, Tooke, Tuke, Toke, Tuckson.—Bapt. 'the son of Toke.' The Domesday form was Toka, 'liber homo Stigandi Toka Francigine' (? Toka the Frenchman) ; v. Freeman, Norm. Conq. v. 768. Mr. Lower enumerates among the Domesday forms of this familiar personal name Toc, Tocho, Tochi, and Toka, also the patronymic Godric Tokeson (Godric fil. Toke). Tycho Brahe represented the Danish form (v. Yonge, ii. 410). Friar Tuck, whether an historic or legendary personage, bears unmistakably the same name. For a diminutive v. Tokelin. Of many instances I furnish a few.

Toke Dando, co. Somerset, 1273. A.
Toke Lanarius (i.e. the woolmonger), co. Linc., ibid.
Tokus Bobyning, C. R., 3 Edw. I.
Peter Tuck, C. R., 6 Edw. I.
Thomas Tuke, 1379 : P. T. Yorks. p. 295.
Johannes Tokson, 1379 : ibid. p. 150.
1526. Nicholas Toke, or Tocke, or Tuke : Reg. Univ. Oxf. i. 142.
1571. John Tuke and Margaret Willyams : Marriage Lic. (London), i. 48.
1675. Bapt.—James, s. Henry Tucke : St. Jas. Clerkenwell, i. 269.
1676-7. Thomas Tooke (co. Herts) and Eliz. Atkins: Marriage Lic. (London), ii. 300.

1708. William Toke (co. Kent) and Eliz. Hilton : ibid. p. 337.
1753. Married—Roger Took (co. Norfolk) and Eliz. Grandee : St. Geo. Chap. Mayfair, p. 263.
London, 23, 1, 2, 2, 0, 0 ; Crockford (Toke), 1 ; West Rid. Court Dir., 1, 0, 0, 4, 0, 0 ; Boston (U.S.), 13, 0, 0, 0, 0, 0 ; Philadelphia (Tuckson), 1.

Tucker.—Occup. 'the tucker,' a fuller, or walker of cloth. 'Wollen-weaver, weaving housewiefes, or householde clothe . . . clothe-fuller, otherwise called tucker or walker' (5 Eliz. c. 4, 23). Tucker is still a great Westcountry surname, being very strongly represented in cos. Devon, Wilts, and Dorset. As is Lister or Walker (q.v.) to Yorkshire, so is Tucker to these said parts. v.Tooker.

Roger le Tukere, co. Dorset, 1273. A.
Percival le Toukere, 1301. M.
Robert le Tuckere, C. R., 13 Edw. II.
William le Touker. G.
1582-3. Charles Tooker or Tucker, co. Wilts : Reg. Univ.Oxf. vol. ii. pt. ii. p. 124.
1583. Edmund Gylman and Florence Tucker (of Exeter) : Marriage Lic. (London), i. 126.
London, 92 ; MDB. (co. Devon), 75 ; Philadelphia, 73.

Tuckerman. — Occup. 'the tuckerman,' a tucker, a walker, a dyer; cf. Merchantman, Husbandman, &c. v. Tucker.

Barbara Tuckerman, 1660 : Reg. Canterbury Cath. p. 121.
1689. John Tuckerman and Mary Bartlett : Marriage Alleg. (Canterbury), p. 101.
MDB. (co. Devon), 1 ; Philadelphia, 2 ; Boston (U.S.), 13.

Tuckett.—? Bapt. 'the son of Tuket' or Touchet, probably a dim. of Tuke or Tuck, q.v.

Nicholas Tochet, co. Linc., 1273. A.
Simon Tochet, co. Linc., ibid.
Thomas Touchet, co. Derby, ibid.
Nicholas Tuchet, co. Linc., 20 Edw. I. R.
Thomas Tuchet, co. Rutl., ibid.
Robert Touschet, co. Derby, ibid.
Willelmus Tuket, 1379 : P. T. Yorks. p. 127.
Tochet Beston, 7 Hen. VIII : East Cheshire, ii. 86.
1809. Married—Nicholas Tuckett and Martha Hole : St. Geo. Han. Sq. ii. 416.
London, 4 ; Boston (U.S.), 4.

Tuckey, Tuckie, Tookey.—Bapt. 'the son of Tochi,' a variant of Tuck, q.v., where Domesday instances will be found. This

derivation is absolutely certain, as proved by the Hundred Roll references below.

Richard Toky, co. Wilts, 1273. A.
John Toky, co. Oxf., ibid.
Thomas Toky, co. Oxf., ibid.
William Toky, co. Oxf., ibid.
1599. Thomas Tookye, co. Leic.: Reg. Univ. Oxf. vol. ii. pt. ii. p. 236.
1604. Job Tookye, co. Leic. : ibid. p. 273.
William Toky, co. Soms., 1 Edw. III : Kirby's Quest, p. 151.
Adam Toky, co. Soms., 1 Edw. III : ibid. p. 205.
1624. William Elliott and Joane Tuckey : Marriage Lic. (London), ii. 142.
1779. Married — Henry Tookey and Ann Beardshaw : St. Geo. Han. Sq. i. 300.
1782. — Francis Tookie and Eliz. Elborn : ibid. p. 340.
London, 8, 1, 2.

Tuckson.—Bapt. 'the son of Tuck.' It is curious that I should have to go to America for the only modern instance I can find of this very early English surname. Instances of Tuckson will be found under Tuck, q.v.

Philadelphia, 1.

Tudball.—Bapt. 'the son of Theobald,' one more of the many variants of Theobald.

Thomas Tedball, co. Camb., 1273. A.
1578. William Kimloughe and Cicely Tudball : Marriage Lic. (London), i. 80.
MDB. (co. Somerset), 5.

Tudor, Tuder.—Bapt. 'the son of Tudor.' Miss Yonge has an interesting paragraph showing the probability that Tudor was a Welsh form of Theodore (Hist. Christian Names, i. 232).

Tuder fil. Griffini ab Mereduk, 12 Edw. I : BBB. p. 348.
Margaret Holl ap Rees ap Tewdor : Visit. Glouc., Harl. Soc., p. 114.
Rys ap Madoc ap Tudir : Visit. London, 1633, i. 220.
1707. Buried — Albinia, wife of Mr. John Tudor, scrivener : St. Mary Aldermary, p. 210.
1751. Married — Francis Tudor and Eliz. Higgs : St. Geo. Chap. Mayfair, p. 187.
London, 7, 0 ; Philadelphia, 6, 3.

Tuer.—Occup. 'the tewer,' a dresser of leather, a currier (v. Tewer). 'Teware, corridiator' : Prompt. Parv. p. 490. 'Tewyn lethyr, corrodio,' ibid. Possibly Twyer is the same.

Willelmus Twyer, 1379: P. T. Yorks. p. 72.
Robertus Twyer, 1379: ibid. London, 1.

Tuffield, Tuffill; v. Tofield.

Tuke; v. Tuck.

Tulloch.—Local, 'at the tulloch,' from residence there beside. A Scotch name. Lower writes, 'Tulloch, Gael. *tulach*, a hillock. There are places specifically so called in the shires of Perth, Ross, and Aberdeen': Patr. Brit. p. 358.
London, 3; Philadelphia, 4.

Tumber.—Occup. 'the tumber,' i.e. the tumbler. 'Saltator, *tumbere*': Wright's Voc. i. 39, col. 2 (v. Skeat on *tumble*). Cf. fem. 'tombesteres Fetis and smale' (Chaucer, The Pardoner's Tale).
William le Tumber, c. 1300. M.

Tummon, Tummond, Tummons.—Occup. 'tom-man,' i.e. the servant of Tom. A curious but natural corruption. Tummon is one more instance of the many Yorkshire surnames of this class; cf. Matthewman, Addyman, Jackman, Ladyman, Bartleman, Sandeman, &c. The *d* in Tummond is excrescent, as in Simmonds or Hammond for Simon or Hamon.
Robert Thomasman, Fines Roll, 11 Edw I.
William Thomasman. V. 13.
Willelmus Thomasman, 1379: P. T. Yorks. p. 210.
Hugo serviens Thome, 1379: ibid. p. 157.
Alicia serviens Thome, 1379: ibid. p. 207.
The following two entries placed side by side settle the matter:
Johannes Tomman Cisson (i.e. John, the servant of Tom Cisson), 1379: P. T. Yorks. p. 269.
Thomas serviens Thome Cisson, 1379: ibid.
Also notice:
Willelmus Thomeman, 1379: P. T. Yorks. p. 213.
Thomas Tonman, 1379: ibid.
Sheffield, 4, 0, 0; West Rid. Court Dir., 0, 1, 1.

Tunbridge.—Local, 'of Tunbridge' or Tonbridge, a parish in co. Kent, fourteen miles from Maidstone.

Salomon de Tonebregg, co. Essex, 1273. A.
Robert de Tonebrugge, London, ibid.
London, 2; MDB. (co. Essex), 2.

Tunder, Thunder. — Occup. 'the tunder,' i.e. a vintner, a wine-tunner, one who poured wine into barrels or tuns. Hence such terms as 'tunnel' or 'tun-dish,' the vessel used for transferring the wine from cask to bottle (v. my English Surnames, p. 381). For further information, v. Tunneler and Aletunner.
Edmund le Tunder, bailiff of Norwich, 1271: FF. iii 58.
Hugh le Tundur, 1273. A.
Richard le Tundur. T.
John de Northfolk, *tounder*, 8 Edw. III: Freemen of York, i. 28.

It was inevitable that an imitative variant in the shape of Thunder should arise after the meaning of the surname Tunder had become forgotten. Indeed, it is only in this form that the name has survived. For modern instances, v. Thunder. Lower's and Ferguson's suggestion that Thunder is a personal name and that it is an alias of Thor, the Jupiter-tonans of Northern mythology, cannot be upheld.
Philadelphia, 0, 3.

Tunks.—Bapt.; v. Tonkinson.

Tunnard; v. Townherd.

Tunneler. — Occup. 'the tunneler,' one who fills casks with wine, &c., from *tunne*, a barrel (v. Skeat on *ton*). The tunneler used the tunnel, or funnel, or tunner to expedite his work. 'Fonel, or tonowre, *fusorium, infusorium*': Prompt. Parv. 'Tonell, to fylle wyne with': Palsgrave. v. Tunder.
William le Toneleur. H.
Ralph le Toneler (I have lost my reference to this).
John de Tikhill, *toundour*, 4 Edw. II: Freemen of York, i. 19.
Geoffrey le Thuneler, 9 Edw. III: ibid. p. 29.

Tunnicliffe, Tunnacliffe.—Local, 'of Tunnicliff,' in the parish of Rochdale, co. Lanc. For an American variant, v. Dunnicliff.
James Scholfield, of Tunnicliffe, par Rochdale, *husbandman*, 1663: Wills at Chester (1545-1620), p. 237.

1724-5. Married—John Tunnecliff and Eliz. Capp: St. Dionis Backchurch, p. 61.
1753. — Thomas Gould and Eliz. Tunnecliff: St. Geo. Chap. Mayfair, p. 236.
Joseph Tunnicliff, mayor of Macclesfield, 1818: Earwaker's East Cheshire, ii. 467.
Manchester, 2, 1; Rochdale, 1, 0; New York, 1, 0.

Tunnock.—Bapt. 'the son of Tunnoc,' an interesting name, found in co. Northumberland so early as the 12th century, and remains as Tunnock in that district still. I strongly suspect that some of the many Tullochs in the Newcastle Directory are not so Scotch as they look, but are an assimilation. Besides, there is a tendency to this interchange; cf. Bannister for Balister, or *banister* for *baluster*.
John fil. Tunnoc, 1196: KKK. vi. 59.
William fil. Tunnok, 1250: ibid. vi. 220.
Roger Tunnok, 1313: PPP. i. 29.
Robert Tunnokman and Richard Tunnokson were witnesses to the will of Henry of Wallsend, *clerk*, 1319: ibid. p. 149.
William Tunnok, *mariner*, 1335: ibid. p. 92.
In Mr. Welford's Hist. of Newcastle and Gateshead is recorded a benefaction to the Virgin Mary Hospital by
'Robert Tunnikysiman and Matilda his wife in 1305': PPP. i. 9.
This, of course, is Robert Tunnockman, literally Robert Tunnock's servant; cf. Matthewman, Bartleman, Jackman, &c.
Sunderland, 1.

Tunstall, Tunstill. — Local, 'of Tunstall,' parishes in diocs. Canterbury, Lichfield, York, Manchester, and Norwich; also as Townstall in dioc. Exeter. Tunstall, thirteen miles from Lancaster, is the parent of the Lancashire Tunstalls.
Hugh de Tonstalle, co. Kent, 1273. A.
Henry de Tunstal, co. Lanc., 17 Edw. II: Baines' Lanc. ii. 621.
William Tunstal, co. Lanc., 47 Edw. III: ibid.
1547. Married—Thomas Hurthelstone and Alyce Tonstale: St. Michael, Cornhill, p. 5.

3 D

Brian Tunstall, of Tunstall, Lancashire, 1609: Lancashire Wills at Richmond, p. 288.

Edmund Tunstall, of Netherburrow, parish of Tunstall, 1636: ibid.

London, 6, 1; Manchester, 1, 2; Lancaster, 1, 0; Philadelphia, 1, 0.

Tunwright. — Occup. 'the tun-wright,' a maker of tuns or casks, a cooper; cf. Arkwright, Sivewright, Cartwright, &c.; v. Tunder and Tunneler.

Johannes Tunwryght, 1379: P. T. Yorks. p. 217.

Tup.—Nick. 'the tup,' i.e. the ram; cf. Buck, Roebuck, Ram, &c.

John Tupp, *carnifex*, 10 Edw. II: Freemen of York, i. 17.

Margareta Tup, 1379: P. T. Yorks. p. 91.

Robertus Tup, 1379: ibid.

1756. Married — George Wilson and Ann Tupp: St. Geo. Han. Sq. i. 61. London, 1.

Tuphead.—Nick. Not a complimentary one.

Robert Tuppeheued, Pardons Roll, 6 Ric. II.

Tupman. — Occup. 'the tupman,' a tup-herd (v. Tupper); cf. Cowman, Steerman, Bullman. 'Tupman, a breeder of tups or rams': Halliwell. For other Pickwickian names, v. Pickwick and Snodgrass.

1756. Married—William Tupman and Sarah Abbott: St. Geo. Han. Sq. i. 64. London, 1; Philadelphia, 2.

Tupper, Tupherd. — Occup. 'the tup-herd'; cf. Coward, Gelderd, Calvert, Stoddard, &c. The final *d* is also lost in Tripherd (v. Tripper) and sometimes in Gelderd (v. Geldard).

Willelmus Tuphird, 1379: P. T. Yorks. p. 217.

1746. Married — George Tupper and Eliz. Drury: St. Geo. Chap. Mayfair, p. 79.

1792. — Richard Davis and Maria Tupper: St. Geo. Han. Sq. i. 84. London, 6, 0; Boston (U.S.), 11, 0.

Turbefield, Turbyfield, Turburville.—Local, 'of Turberville.' The locality in Normandy (?) cannot be found. The suffix *-ville* frequently becomes *-field* by corruption.

John de Turbervile, co. Berks, 1273. A. Robert de Turbervill, co. Glouc., ibid. Galiena de Turbevile, co. Wilts, ibid.

1566. Bapt.—Basil, s. William Trublefelde: Kensington Parish, i. 5.

1635. Married — Philip Colby and Rebecca Trubellvile: ibid. p. 71.

1639. — Thomas Wilkenson and Mary Turbervile: St. Dionis Backchurch, p. 24. London, 1, 1, 1.

Turbot, Turbat, Turbit, Turbett. — Bapt. 'the son of Turbert,' inevitably corrupted, almost as soon as it arose, into Turbot. In Domesday found as Turbert, a personal name. Not to be confounded with Tebbutt (v. Tebbitt), though it may have become absorbed in it.

Emonus Turberd, co. Yorks, 1273. A. Eymes Turbert, co. Notts, ibid. Andreas Turbut, co. Oxf., ibid. Turbert de Wescot, Pipe Roll, 11 Hen. II, p. 74.

Henry Turbot, C. R., 32 Hen. III. Adam Turbut, 1379: P. T. Yorks. p. 81. Daniel Turbot, co. York. W. 20.

Few of the supposed fish-names are what they seem; v. Salman.

1748. Married—John Turbot and Mary Clark: St. Michael, Cornhill, p. 74.

1753. — William Turbitt and Mary Kennedy: St. Geo. Chap. Mayfair, p. 241.

— — William Millington and Margaret Turbutt: ibid. p. 243.

1791. — William Turbett and Eliz. King: St. Geo. Han. Sq. ii. 65. Liverpool, 0, 1, 0, 0; Boston (U.S.), 0, 0, 1, 0; Philadelphia, 0, 0, 0, 1.

Turk.—Local, 'the Turk,' a Mohammedan; 'all Jews, Turks, Infidels, and Heretics': The Book of Common Prayer. Cf. Sarson.

William le Turc, co. Essex, 1273. A. John Turk, co. Kent, ibid. Philip Turk, co. Soms., 1 Edw. III: Kirby's Quest, p. 83. Jacob le Turk. DD.

1552-3. Richard Petytte and Phillipa Turke: Marriage Lic. (London), i. 14. 1613. Bapt.—Jone, d. Robert Turke: St. Michael, Cornhill, p 111. 1751. Married—Thomas Turk and Eliz. Jones: St. Geo Chap. Mayfair, p. 202. London, 3; Philadelphia, 4.

Turkington.—Local, 'of Torkington,' q.v., an American variant.

Turle.—An abbreviated form of Turrell, q.v.

1641. George Tyrell and Anne Thurlow: Marriage Lic. (London), ii. 258. 1760. Married — Thomas Berry and Mary Tyrrl: St. Geo. Han. Sq. i. 96. London, 2; New York, 1.

Turnbuck.—Nick. This is a name that helps to elucidate the origin of Turnbull, q.v.

Alicia Turnebuk, 1379: P. T. Yorks. p. 66.

Turnbull, Trumble, Trumbull. – ? Nick. 'turn-bull' (?). There can be little doubt about the origin of this name. Two great clan nicknames grew up in Liddesdale and the 'Debateable Land,' the Armstrongs and Turnbulls, both significant of that prowess which was so necessary in the times of Scotch and English raids across the border. To turn the bull at the baiting would be an exploit worthy a sobriquet in those rude times, and the possessor would be proud to bear it. The idea that this name is local must be given up. Trumble is a corruption of Turnbull, not Turnbull of Trumble. The earliest form is Turnebull.

Johannes Turnebull, 1379: P. T. Yorks. p. 268.

In the same record we find a similar nickname, that of Turnbuck.

Alicia Turnebuk, 1379: P. T. Yorks. p. 66.

The New York form Trumbull is met with in the 15th century:

David Trumbull or Turnbull, 1494-5: TTT. p. 187.

George Trumbull or Turnbull, 1494-5: ibid. p 188.

Jock Trumble, 1544: ibid. p. lii. Wat Trombull, 1562: ibid. p. ciii.

1707 Bapt. — James, son of William Trumbal: St. Thomas the Apostle (London), p. 71.

For other variants, v. Tremble and Trimble.

London, 26, 1, 0; West Rid. Court Dir., 5, 1, 0; New York, 20, 2, 5.

Turnell.— ? Local. Probably a corruption of the Yorkshire name of Thornhill, which is early found in the form of Thornell (v. Thornhill).

Hugo Turnell', et uxor, 1379: P. T. Yorks. p. 151.

West Rid. Court Dir., 5; London, 3; Philadelphia, 1.

Turner, Turnour. — Occup. 'the turner,' one who worked with a lathe. Lower quotes Mr. Ferguson as saying, ' Out of all proportion to the number of persons engaged in the trade '; also as suggesting that the name was in many cases baptismal and of Norman introduction. In a day that knew little of ornamental fictile vessels the turner would be busy enough, and the only wonder is that it is not, as a surname, as common as Smith. A glance at early registers will show how familiar the occupation was. Chaucer's Miller of Trumpington could ' turn cuppes.'

' There dwelled also turners of beads ': Stow, iii. 174.
' Sponers, torners, and hatters.'
Cocke Lorelle's Bote.

To assert that Turnour is local from ' de Tour Noire,' the Black Castle (in Normandy, of course), is childish ; and little better is Tourneour, a tilter. There is no evidence.

Aylbricht le Turnur, London, 1273. A.
Geoffrey le Turner, co. Camb., ibid.
William le Turnor, co. Oxf., ibid.
Johannes Turnour, *turnour*, 1379: P. T. Yorks. p. 218.
William le Tournour. G.
Henry le Turnour, co. Soms., 1 Edw. III: Kirby's Quest, p. 91.
1791. Married — George Turnor and Ann Eleanor Hanmer : St. Geo. Han. Sq. ii. 63.
London, 338, 0 ; Crockford, 62, 1 ; Philadelphia, 329, 0.

Turney, Tournay.—Local, ' of Tournay,' in Artois. Gosfrid Tornai occurs in the Domesday of Lincolnshire.

Geoffrey de Turnai, co. Linc., 1273. A.
Richard de Turney, co. Bucks, ibid.
William Turney, co. Notts, ibid.
1692. — Nathaniell Peacock and Mary Turney : St. Michael, Cornhill, p. 47.
London, 8, 0 ; MDB. (co. Kent), 0, 3 ; Philadelphia, 8, 0.

Turnham.—Local, ' of Turnham.' Turnham Green, formerly a hamlet, now a parish, in co. Middlesex, five miles from London. Perhaps some other spot in North England bore the same name.

Johannes de Turneham, 1379: P. T. Yorks. p. 117.
1790. Married—Thomas Turnham and Martha Emerton : St. Geo. Han. Sq. ii. 44. London, 7.

Turnour.—Occup. ; v. Turner.

Turnpenny. — ? Local, ' of Turnepeny ' (?). I cannot find the spot. I suspect, after all, that Twopeny or Twopenny may be one of the modern forms of this name (v. Twopenny). From Turnpenny to Turpeny was inevitable, and the step from this to the imitative Twopeny is easy. The assertion that it hails from Tupigny in Flanders is only a guess. I have 'Abbas de Turpenay (C.)' in my notebook. A London firm, Gamble and Turnpenny, were known for many years familiarly as ' Pitch and Toss.'

Matilda Tornepeni, co. Oxf., 1273. A.
Nicholas Turnepeny, co. Oxf., ibid.
William Turnepenny, C. R., 9 Edw. I.
John Tournepeny, co. Soms., 1 Edw. III: Kirby's Quest, p. 207.
Robert Turnepeny. G.
John Turnpeny. D.
1727. Married—Arthur Tawke and Eliz. Turnpenny : St. Michael, Cornhill, p. 64.
London, 3 ; Stanningley, co. York, 1 ; Philadelphia, 2.

Turpin, Toppin, Topping. —Bapt. ' the son of Thorfin,' a popular name among the Danes, which originated some of our place-names ; e g Thorpanstye, otherwise Thorfinstye Hall, in the parish of Cartmel, co. Lanc., was so named from the owner Thorfin or Torpin, a great landowner (of twelve manors) at the time of the Doomsday Survey ; v. Annals of Cartmel (Stockdale, pp. 510, 592). Sty, A.S. *stig, stigo* ; M.E. *stie, stye.* Meaning (1) a path, as in ' Sty Head Pass ' ; (2) an enclosure for swine.

' He groneth as our bore, lith in our stie.'
Chaucer, C. T. 7411.

(3) part of a house, probably what we call ' a dais ' (v. *sty*, Skeat). v. Tipping.

John Turpin, co. Oxf., 1273. A.
William Turpyn, 1379 : P. T. Yorks.
London, 12, 1, 3 ; Oldham (Lanc.), 0, 1, 0 ; Boston (U.S.), 3, 0, 1.

Turrell, Turrill. Bapt ' the son of Turold ' (v. Thorold). The final *d* seems to have been dropped through laziness ; v. Terrell.

Ralph Turold, co. Suff., 1273. A.
Thomas Torel, co. Soms., 1 Edw. III : Kirby's Quest, p. 116.

Willelmus Turyell, 1379: P. T. Yorks.
p. 301.
1596-7. John Pluckwell and Audrey Turrall: Marriage Lic. (London), i. 236.
1673. Married — George Martur and Mary Turrell : St. Jas. Clerkenwell, i. 177.
London, 3, 3 ; Boston (U.S.), 1, 3.

Turtle, Turtill, Turtille.— Bapt. ' the son of Thurkle '; v. Thurkettle. This is Mr. Lower's explanation, and I doubt not it is the correct one.

Reginald Turtel, co. Camb., 1273. A.
John Turkyl, co. Camb., ibid.
Roger Turtle. D.
1627. Married — Henry Turtle and Hanna Greene : St. Dionis Backchurch, p. 22.
1750. = Richard Turtle and Lydia Thorn : St. Geo. Chap. Mayfair, p. 177.
London, 5, 1, 0 ; West Rid. Court Dir., 2, 0, 0 ; Sheffield, 4, 0, 0 ; New York, 0, 0, 1.

Turton. — Local, ' of Turton,' a township in the parish of Bolton, co. Lancaster. The surname has crossed the borders into Yorkshire and ramified strongly there.

1523. Sir Henry Turton, *priest*, fellow of Christ's College, Manchester : Wills at Chester, i. 198.
1563. Married — Rodger Turton and Eliz. Shrigleye : Prestbury Church (co. Chester), p. 11.
1601-2. Constantine Turton, co. Hants : Reg. Univ. Oxf. vol. ii. pt. ii. p. 254.
Manchester, 3 ; London 4 ; Sheffield, 17 ; Philadelphia, 2.

Turvey, Turvy.—Local, ' of Turvey,' a parish in co. Bedford, four miles from Olney.

1621. Richard Turvy, co. Worc. : Reg. Univ. Oxf. vol. ii. pt. ii. p. 393.
1799. Married — William Turvey and Sarah Dean : St. Geo. Han. Sq. ii. 200.
London, 4, 1 ; Philadelphia, 2.

Tusler.— Occup. ' the touseler '; v. Tasseler, of which it is but a variant. Also v. Tozer.

1793. Married—James Tusler and Mary Denyer : St. Geo. Han. Sq. ii. 96.
London, 1.

Tustian, Tustin. — Bapt. Thurstan, q.v.

Tuthill, Tuttle.—Local ; v. Toothill.

Tuxbury.—Local, ' of Tewkesbury,' q.v.

Tuxford.—Local, ' of Tuxford,' a parish in co. Notts, thirty miles from Nottingham.

1753. Married—James Entwesle and Eliz. Tuxford : St. Geo. Chap. Mayfair, p. 259.

London, 4.

Twaddle, Tweddell, Tweddle, Twaddell. — Local, 'of Tweeddale,' from residence in the valley of the Tweed. Cf. Teasdale, Tindal, Lonsdale, &c.

John Tweddel, 1587, accused of raiding over the Border : Nicolson and Burn, Hist. Westm. and Cumb. i. p. xxxi.
Willie Tweddel, 1587 : ibid.
John Twedall, of Strines, 1670 : Wills at Chester (1660–80), p. 273.
Edmund Twaddell, of Mierscough, 1666 : Lancashire Wills at Richmond, p. 290.
1787. Married—Richard Badham and Grace Tweeddale : St. Geo. Han. Sq. i. 397.

Mr. H. J. Twaddle announced the change of his name to Tweeddale in the Times, Jan. 4, 1890.

London, 1, 1, 1, 0 ; Philadelphia, 0, 0, 4, 24.

Twamley ; v. Twemlow.

Tweed. — Local, 'from the Tweed,' i.e. from the valley of the Tweed ; v. Twaddle.

Adam Twede, 1379 : P. T. Yorks. p. 196.
London, 2 ; Philadelphia, 9.

Tweedale, Tweedle. — Local, 'of Tweeddale' ; v. Twaddle.

Philadelphia, 10, 3.

Tweedie, Tweedy. — Local, 'of Tweeddale.' Probably a corruption of Tweedale (v. Twaddle).

1624. Married — William Lake and Eliz. Twedy : St. Peter, Cornhill, i. 252.
1745. — Francisco Sisco and Mary Tweedy : St. Geo. Chap. Mayfair, p. 54.
London, 5, 3 ; Philadelphia, 3, 2.

Twelfthman. — ? Official, 'the twelfthman' (?) ; cf. Hundred. Twentyman (q.v.) is not of this class ; it is occupative.

Johannes Twelfemen, 1379 : P. T. Yorks. p. 276.

Twell, Twells, Twelves. — Local, 'at the well,' from residence thereby. In this case Atte-well (v. Attwell) has become Twell ; cf. Nash for 'Atten-ash.' Twell, Twells, and Twelves are all found in co. Lincoln, the last being an imitative corruption. The final s in Twells and Twelves is the genitive form ; cf. Jennings, Jones, Williams, &c.

1661. Married—George Twell and Ann Bateman : St. Jas. Clerkenwell, i. 107.
1703-4. Walter Wells and Dorothy Twells : Marriage Lic. (London), ii. 331.
1747. Married—John Astrie and Eliz. Twelves : St. Geo. Chap. Mayfair, p. 81.
MDB. (Lincoln), 7, 1, 3 ; Philadelphia, 0, 4, 3.

Twelvepence.—Nick. 'Twelvepence' ; cf. Fourpence and Ninepence. The latter, as will be seen by reference, survived several generations ; v. Thousandpound.

Fulco Twelpenes, co. Camb., 1273. A.

Twemlow, Twombley, Twomeley, Twamley.—Local, 'of Twemlow,' co. Chester.

Lyulph de Twemlowe, 1208 : East Ches. ii. 42.
William de Twemlowe, 1376 : ibid. p. 50 n.
1578. Married—Rauffe Brodehurst and Margery Twamlowe : Reg. Prestbury, Ches., p. 59.
1587. Thomas Beeche and Jone Twamlowe : ibid. p. 93.
William Kenedy, of Twemlow, 1591 : Wills at Chester (1545-1620), p. 113.
John Twemlow, of Mere, co. Chester, husbandman, 1649 : ibid. (1621-50), p. 222.
Manchester, 3, 0, 0, 0 ; Philadelphia, 0, 1, 1, 0 ; Crockford (Twamley), 4.

Twentyman. — Occup. 'the twinterman,' North English, one who tended twinters, i.e. two-year-old beasts. A.S. twy-winter. Mr. Lower says, 'The officer who commanded twenty armed men was called a vintenarius ; and of this word I take Twentyman to be a translation' (Patr. Brit. p. 359). There is no evidence in support of this. The corruption to Twentyman is imitative.

'At Fenham, 20 stirks and twynters,' 1428 : QQQ. p. 118, Accounts of Monastery on Holy Island.
'20 oxen, 26 stotts, 12 wedders and twints, 9 tupps,' Stock at Bolton Abbey, 1526 : Whitaker's Craven, p. 403.
'6 oxen, 18 steres, 11 heifers, 21 twenters, 23 stirks,' 1556 : Richmondshire Wills, Surt. Soc., p. 93.

Cf. Cowman, Steerman or Stierman, Bullman. The surname is still familiar in co. Cumberland.

Henry Twentyman. TT.
1618. Buried — Joseph XXman, of Woodhouses : Reg. Great Orton Church, Carlisle.
1748. Married — Henry Twentyman and Ann Martin : St. Geo. Han. Sq. i. 41.

1787. — John Spinks and Mary Twentyman : ibid. p. 401.
London, 5 ; Crockford, 2.

Twentymark. — Nick. ; cf. Twentypence. The old English mark was a coin valued at 13s. 4d. Possibly a sobriquet affixed to one whose salary was set down at that sum.

Geoffrey Tventimarc, co. Camb., 1273. A.
'1342. June 21. Ralph changed with John Twentimark for Warsop in Yorkshire': The Rectory of Brisingham, co. Norf. : FF. i. 64.

Twentypence.—Nick.

Roger Twentipens, Close Roll, 39 Hen. III.

Cf. Fivepence, Sevenpence, Ninepence, Twelvepence. Probably a translation ; cf.

Roger Vint-deners, co. Berks, 1273. A.

Twiceaday, Twisaday. — ? ——. This curious name has existed for centuries in the district of Furness, North Lancashire. Probably it is a form of Tuesday, as other day-names exist, or existed (v. Saturday, Friday, Monday). Perhaps, like Christmas, Pentecost, &c., it was a personal name given to the child because born or baptized on that day.

Thomas Twysday. H.
Thomas Twisaday, Patent Roll, 1 Hen. VII. pt. iii.
1548. Married—Harry Twisedaie and Katherine Naila : St. Mary, Ulverston, i. 7.
1551. Buried—Harry Twisedaie : ibid. i. 15.
1618. Henry Twisaday, of Ulverston : Lancashire Wills at Richmond, i. 290.
1661. Edward Twiceaday, of Ulverston : ibid.
1664. George Twiseaday, of Ulverston : ibid.
'The account of Henry Twiceaday, collector of the window tax for the year ended March 25, 1725': Annals of Cartmel, p. 262.

The name still exists in Furness in both the above forms.

MDB. (co. Lanc.), 1, 2.

Twichell ; v. Twitchell.

Twidale.—Local, 'of Tweeddale' ; v. Twaddle.

Manchester, 1.

Twiddy, Twidy.—Local. A variant of Tweedie, q.v.; cf. Twidale for Tweedale.

London, 3, 0 ; New York, 0, 1.

Twin, Twinn, Twine. — Nick. 'the twin,' one of twin brothers or sisters, a natural sobriquet.

Edmund Twyn, C. R., 8 Hen. IV.
Thomas Twyne, 1564 : Reg. Univ. Oxf. i. 254.
Laurence Twine, 1564 : ibid. p. 255.
1612-3. Stephen Newson and Avice Twine : Marriage Lic. (London), i. 19.
1624. William Clarke and Anne Twynn : ibid. p. 145.
1698. Married — Francis Palmer and Catharine Twine : St. Dionis Backchurch, p. 47.
1750. — Henry Twin and Mary Johns : St. Geo. Chap. Mayfair, p. 185.
London, 1, 1, 1 ; New York, 0, 1, 2.

Twineham, Twyman, Twynam, Twynham, Twinem. — Local, 'of Twineham,' a parish in the dioc. of Chichester, co. Sussex ; cf. Deadman and Putman for Debenham and Puttenham ; also Swetman for Swettenham.

1565. Edward Preston and Anne Twynam : Marriage Lic. (London), i. 30.
1611. Married — Thomas Fidge and Hester Twyman : Canterbury Cath., p. 61

Mr. G. Twyman played for Kent v. Essex in a cricket match, Aug. 15, 1887 ; v. Standard.

London, 1, 3, 1, 0, 0 ; Manchester, 0, 0, 0, 1, 0 ; Liverpool, 0, 0, 0, 0, 1 ; Philadelphia (Twyman), 1 ; Boston (U.S.) (Twynam), 1.

Twining.—Local, 'of Twining,' a parish in co. Gloucester, two miles from Tewkesbury.

1804. Married — Martin Kelly and Hester Twining : St. Geo. Han. Sq. ii. 298.
London, 5 ; Philadelphia, 21.

Twisaday ; v. Twiceaday.

Twisden.—Local, 'of Twysden.' Mr. Lower, quoting Shirley's Noble and Gentle Men, writes, 'This surname is derived from Twysden, or Twysenden-Brough, an estate in the parish of Goudhurst, co. Kent . . . where Adam de Twysden resided in the reign of Edw. I. His descendants sold it in the reign of Henry VI.' Mr. Lower adds that 'at Sandhurst in the same county there is another Twysden,

also said to have been a seat of the family, temp. Edw. I' (Patr. Brit. p. 359).

1591. Charles Tuisden, co. Kent : Reg. Univ. Oxf. vol. ii. pt. ii. p. 186.
— Roger Tuisden, co. Kent : ibid.
1609. Thomas Dalyson and Eliz. Twisden, of East Malling, co. Kent : Marriage Alleg. (Canterbury), p. 175.
London, 1 ; MDB. (co. Kent), 2.

Twiss, Twisse, Twist. — Local, 'of Twiss.' The spot is undoubtedly either the hamlet styled Twiss Green, in the parish of Newchurch-Kenyon, co. Lanc., or a place so called in the immediate vicinity. All the earlier instances hail from that district. With Twist, cf. Gorst for Gorse in the same neighbourhood.

Richard Twiss, of Kenion, 1619 : Wills at Chester (1545-1620), p. 196.
Randle Twisse, of Coppenhall, 1585 : ibid.
Thomas Twist, of Kenyon, 1593 : ibid.
1787. Married — Thomas Twist and Ann Gray : St. Geo. Han. Sq. i. 402.
1805. Married—Rev. Robert Twiss and Fanny Walker : ibid. ii. 320.
Manchester, 3, 1, 3 ; Liverpool, 3, 0, 3 ; London, 3, 0, 1 ; Philadelphia, 4, 0, 4.

Twitchell, Twichell. Local, 'at the twitchel,' a passage, an alley, from residence thereby. For further information, v. Twitchin.

1655. Married — Edward Nethercoate and Eliz. Twichell : St. Michael, Cornhill, p. 35.
1665. Andrew Atkins and Eliz. Twitchell : Marriage Alleg. (Canterbury), p. 129.
1806. Married—Josiah Spencer Twitchell and Eliz. Watson : St. Geo. Han. Sq. ii. 341.
Crockford, 1, 0 ; New York, 1, 0 ; Philadelphia, 3, 0 ; Boston (U.S.), 22, 4.

Twitchin, Twitching, Twitchings, Twitchen.—Local, 'at the twitchen,' an alley that led from one parish to another, or between two main thoroughfares. 'Twitchel, a narrow passage, an alley. North' (Halliwell). In the South it was Twitchen. The *g* in Twitching and Twitchings is an excrescence, the final *s* being genitive (cf. Jennings from Jenin). In Wood's City of Oxford, edited by Mr. Clark, I find, 'A messuage in " Kibald's twychen," that is, I sup-

pose, " Kibaldi bivium," a double way, or a way having two parts, and common to tow parishes, as that was without doubt to St. Maries and St. Johns' (i. 187). Further on I find mention of 'Kepeharme's Twychen' (p. 199) ; and again, 'Sewey's Twychen' (p. 223). That the word was familiar in the hereditary surname period is clear from the following entries :

Richard Twychenweye, co. Soms., 1 Edw. III : Kirby's Quest, p. 238.
Henry Twychenweye, co. Soms., 1 Edw. III : ibid. p. 234.
Nicholas Twycheenweye, co. Soms., 1 Edw. III : ibid.

i.e. 'at the Twychen way,' the way that led to the twitchen, or more probably the passage or alley itself. The surname still lingers in the neighbourhood of Oxford.

Richard de la Twichena, co. Devon, 1273. A.
1604. Andrew Twitchin, co. Hants : Reg. Univ. Oxf. vol. ii. pt. ii. p. 278
1744. Married—James Twickten (sic) and Mary Benson : St. Geo. Han. Sq. i. 33.
London, 1, 1, 1, 0 ; MDB. (co. Berks),0, 0, 0, 1 ; New York, 2, 0, 1, 0.

Twombley, Twomeley ; v. Twemlow.

Twopenny, Twopeny.—Said to be from Tupigny in Flanders (Edin. Review, April, 1855), presumably because there happens to be a place so called. The twopenny piece was an early coin in England; v. topens (Halliwell). Both Fourpence and Fourpenny (q.v.) were English surnames. I suspect Twopenny is a nickname, if it be not a corruption of Turnpenny, q.v.

Twoyearold.—Nickname ; cf. Twentyman.

Thomas Twoyearolde, co. Lanc. AA. 1.
William Twoyearold, of Wich Malbank, Nantwich, 1660 : Wills at Chester (1660-80), p. 273.

Twycross.—Local, 'of Twycross,' a parish in co. Leicester, six miles from Atherstone. The place probably took its name from some spot on which was fixed a double cross ; v. Twyford.

1586. William Twycross, or Tuicrosse : Reg. Univ. Oxf. iii. 134.

1689. John Blisse, of Oxford, *grocer*, and Dorothye Twycrosse, of the same : Marriage Alleg. (Canterbury), p. 114. London, 1 ; Boston (U.S.), 1.

Twydell.—Local, ' of Tweeddale ' ; v. Twaddle.

London, 1.

Twyford, Twiford. — Local, ' of Twyford,' parishes in cos. Bucks, Leicester, Norfolk, and Hants. Also chapelries in cos. Wilts and Derby. Probably the place-name arose from the fact that there was a double ford there. Hence the commonness of the place-name ; cf. Twycross. Of Tiverton, in Devonshire, Lewis writes, ' This place, formerly called Twyford, Twyfordton, or Twofordton, derives its name from its situation between two rivers, the Exe and the Lowman ' : Top. Dict. iv. 349.

(Dominus) de Twyford, co. Bucks, 20 Edw. I. R.
1642. Thomas Twyford and Mary Henwood : Marriage Lic. (Westminster), p. 40.
1770. Married — Henry Twiford and Martha Wheeler : St. Geo. Han. Sq. i. 202.
London, 3, 0 ; Philadelphia, 0, 1 ; New York, 1, 0.

Twyman, Twynam, Twynham.—Local ; v. Twineham.

Tyas, Tyers, Tyars.— ?——. I can furnish no satisfactory solution of this surname.

Walerand le Tyeis, co. Soms., 1273. A.
Henry le Tyeys, co. Oxf., ibid.
Franco le Tyeys, co. York, ibid.
Terric le Tyes, cos. Essex and Hereford, Hen. III-Edw. I. K.
1770. Married — Richard Tyas and Eliz. White : St. Geo. Han. Sq. i. 199.
1783. — Jonathan Thompson and Mary Tyers : ibid. p. 350.
London, 2, 2, 2 ; Philadelphia, 0, 2, 0.

Tydd.—Bapt. ; v. Tidd.

Oxford, 1.

Tye, Tighe, Tygh, Tyghe, Tigh.—Local, ' at the Tye.' ' *Tye*, an extensive common pasture ' : Halliwell. ' *Tye* : it generally means a small piece of common land close to a village, as Telscombe Tye, a few miles from Brighton ' : Lower, Patr. Brit. p. 359.

Hugh de la Tye, co. Sussex, 1273. A.
Peter atte-Tye, co. Norf., 10 Edw. III : FF. vi. 114.

Peter de Ty, co. Norf., 1342 : ibid. vii. 395.
John Tye, co. Norf., 3 Hen. IV : FF. x. 67.
1574. Married—Bartholomew Milborn and Parnell Tye : St. Thomas the Apostle (London), p. 5.
1608. — Thomas Tye and Marie Collins : St. Michael, Cornhill, p. 19.
1703. — Richard Bridgman and Eliz. Tigh : St. Mary Aldermary (London), p. 37.
1784. — James Tye and Sarah Lord : St. Geo. Han. Sq. i. 357.
London, 4, 3, 0, 0, 0 ; MDB. (Norfolk), 4, 0, 0, 0, 0 ; Philadelphia, 0, 0, 3, 2, 0 ; Boston (U.S.), 2, 4, 0, 0, 2.

Tyerman.—Occup. ' the tireman,' ' a dealer in dresses and all other kinds of ornamental clothing ' (Halliwell).

John Tyerman, temp. Eliz. Z.
John Tireman, co. Norf. FF.
1638. Buried — John Tyreman : Kensington Parish Church, p. 114.
1663. Married — John Tyreman and Eliz. Wood : St. Jas. Clerkenwell, i. 111.
London, 3.

Tyers ; v. Tyas.

Tygh, Tyghe.—Local ; v. Tye.

Tyldsley.—Local, ' of Tyldesley ' ; v. Tildesley.

Tyler, Tylor. — Occup. ' the tiler,' one who bakes clay into tiles, a tiler. A.S. *tigele*, Latin *tegula*, a tile, from *tegere*, to cover.

Geoffrey le Tylere, co. Hunts, 1273. A.
Ralph le Tilere, co. Hunts, ibid.
Hugh le Tygheler. H.
Adam le Tyghelere, c. 1300. M.
Robert le Tiegheler, co. Soms., 1 Edw. III : Kirby's Quest, p. 187.
1611. Robert Tyler and Alice Callis : Marriage Lic. (London), ii. 7.
1658. Married — Thomas Nash and Mary Tiler : St. Jas. Clerkenwell, i. 99.
London, 58, 3 ; Philadelphia, 40, 0.

Tyndale, Tyndall. — Local, ' of Tynedale,' from residence in the valley of the Tyne ; cf. Tweedale and Tweedall ; for early references v. Tindal.

1643-4. Francis Butler and Amphillis Tyndall : Marriage Lic. (London), ii. 273.
1798. Married — Samuel Phelps and Anne Catherine Tyndale : St. Geo. Han. Sq. ii. 177.
London, 2, 2 ; Philadelphia, 12, 1.

Tyrrell ; v. Terrell.

Tyson. — Bapt. ' the son of Dionise,' from the nick. Dy, whence Dyson, sharpened to Tyson. In spite of adverse criticism I still cleave to this as the true solution ; cf. Tennyson (q.v.) for Dennison from the same once popular North-English personal name. The name Tyson has almost assumed the dimensions of a Scottish clan in Furness and South Cumberland. Of the truth of this derivation I have not a doubt ; v. Denny, Dennis, Dyson, &c.

1553. Married — William Tyson and Esabell Cowhird : St. Mary, Ulverston, p. 20.
1557. Buried — Esabell Tyson : ibid. p. 28.
1567. Bapt. — Mathewe Tyson : ibid. p. 49.
1577. Leonard Tyson, of Broughton-in-Furness : Lancashire Wills at Richmond, i. 291.
1593. William Tyson, of Dalton-in-Furness : ibid.
1598. John Tyson, of parish of Aldingham : ibid.
London, 5 ; MDB. (co. Cumb.), 22 ; Philadelphia, 82.

Tytherleigh. — Local, ' of Tytherley.' East and West Tytherley are two parishes in co. Hants, near Stockbridge.

1790. Married—Jacob Bown and Mary Tytherleigh : St. Geo. Han. Sq. ii. 39.
London, 3 ; MDB. (co. Devon), 1.

Tyzack.—? Local. This curious-looking name perplexed me for years, being well established in Yorkshire, yet without representatives in the Yorkshire Poll Tax, 1379. Several allusions in Brand's History of Newcastle, published in 1789, explain its history. In 1619 Sir Robert Mansell built some glass-works at Newcastle, bringing several skilled artisans, with their families, from France. Of these there were two brothers, married, called Teswicke.

1619. Bapt.—John Teswicke, sonne of Tymothie Teswicke, *glasse-maker*, a Frenchman (Reg. St. Nicholas) : Brand, Hist. Newcastle, ii. 43.
1620. Samuel Tizick, *glasmaker* (ibid.) : ibid. p. 43.
1647. Robert Tizzick, *broadglasmaker* (ibid.) : ibid.
1679. William Tizacke obtained a lease of the ' Western glass-houses ' : ibid. p. 45.
1684. Peregrine Tizack obtained a lease of the ' Eastern glass-houses ' : ibid. p. 46.

1679. Buried — Abigail, d. of John Tizacke: Brand, Hist. Newcastle, i. 340.

The surname spread with surprising rapidity, all the branches being prolific. Henzell and Tittery were two other French families introduced into Newcastle with the glass-works. The three names monopolized glassmaking in the district for generations. I feel deeply indebted to the clerk of St. Nicholas for adding that one magic word 'Frenchman' to the first entry, occurring as it does in the very year that glass-works were set up.

West Rid. Court Dir., 7; Sheffield, 9; Leeds, 1.

Tyzemon; v. Tesseyman.

U

Ubank.—Local, 'of the yew bank,' from residence on the bank or slope where the yew-trees grew. For further instances of U for Yew, v. Udall (= Yewdale).

1541. Thomas Ubanke: Reg. St. Peter, Cornhill, i. 105.
1573. Henry Ewbanke, London: Reg. Univ. Oxf. vol. ii. pt. ii. p. 56.
1600. Bapt.—Marie, d. Henry Vbancke: St. Jas. Clerkenwell, i. 37.
1604-5. Toby Ewbanke, co. Durham: Reg. Univ. Oxf. vol. ii. pt. ii. p. 280.
1754. Married—William Ubank and Eliz. Fox: St. Geo. Chapel, Mayfair, p. 270.
Crockford, 1.

Udall, Udell, Udale.—Local, 'of or from Yewdale,' a valley at the north end of Coniston Lake; cf. Ubank for Yewbank.

1586. Thomas Arneway and Margaret Udall: Marriage Lic. (Westminster), p. 9.
Agnes Udall, widow of Yewdale, Furness, 1613: Lancashire Wills at Richmond, i. 291.
1747. Married—Benjamin Capon and Mary Vdall: St. Geo. Chap. Mayfair, p. 98.
London, 3, 0, 0; Manchester, 3, 1, 0; MDB. (co. Derby), 0, 0, 1; (co. Stafford), 0, 0, 2; Oxford, 0, 1, 0; Philadelphia, 1, 2, 0.

Udy.—Bapt. 'the son of Udie,' seemingly peculiar to Cornwall and parts of Devon.

1544. Married — Richard Udie and Alse Nanskevell: Reg. St. Columb Major, p. 137.
1545. Bapt. — Richard, son of Udie Myll: ibid. p. 3.
1546. — John, son of Udie Geyne: ibid. p. 4.
1548. — Dorothie, son of Udie Typpett: ibid. p. 5.
1550. — Robert, son of Udie Hodge: ibid. p. 6.
1553. — Thomas, son of Robert Udie: ibid. p. 7.
Cornwall Dir. (Farmers' List), 5; MDB. (Cornwall), 3.

Uff — Local, 'of Ulph,' q.v.; a corruption.

MDB. (co. Hertford), 1; (co. Bucks), 1.

Ufford. — Local, 'of Ufford,' parishes in cos. Suffolk and Northants.

Robert de Ufford, co. Suffolk, 1273. A.
1635. Bapt.—Diana, d. Joseph Vfforde: St. Jas. Clerkenwell, i. 129.

Uglow.—? Local. The derivation of this name must be sought for in co. Cornwall.

1750. Married — James Dudding and Sarah Uglow: St. Geo. Chap. Mayfair, p. 184.
MDB. (co. Cornwall), 1?

Ulfkettle.—Bapt. 'Ulf-ketel' or 'Wulf-ketel,' i.e.' Ulf's cauldron.' The Domesday form is 'Ulchetel,' one more of many compounds of *kettle*; v. Chettle and Kettle. This form is again reduced to Ulkell and Ulchel (v. Kell and Chell) in Hist. Dunelm., Surtees Soc., pp. 19, 20.

Ulfcytel of East Anglia marries a daughter of Æthelred: Freeman, Norm. Conq. i. 412.

Ulger.—Bapt. 'the son of Ulger,' no doubt a form of Algar, q.v.

William Ulgar, co. Oxf., 1273. A.
Cristina Ulger, co. Oxf., ibid.
1667. Thomas Atkins and Susanne Ulgar: Marriage Alleg. (Canterbury), p. 134.

Ullathorne.—Local. Probably a variant of the North-English Ellithorne, q.v.

1596. Roger Ullathorne, of Netherburrow, parish of Tunstall: Lancashire Wills at Richmond, i. 291.
1633. Richard Vllathornes, of Dalton: ibid. p. 292.

1729. Married—Gilbert Remphrey and Eliz. Ullithorn; St. Geo. Han. Sq. i. 7. London, 3.

Ullmer, Ulmer, Ulmar.—Bapt. 'the son of Ulmar' or Wulmar; v. Woolmer for early English instances of this personal name.

1578. Johann Rodolph Ulmerus (Zurich): Reg. Univ. Oxf. vol. ii. pt. ii. p. 82.
1768. Married — Matthew Frederick Ullmer and Susanna Collins: St. Geo. Han. Sq. i. 175.
London, 6, 0, 0; Boston (U.S.), 0, 3, 3.

Ullock, Hullock.—Local, 'of Ullock,' a part-township in the parish of Dean, near Cockermouth, co. Cumb.

1611. Jenet Vllocke: Lancashire Wills at Richmond, i. 292.
1667. Married — Henry Ullock and Margaret Johnson: Parish Church, Kensington, p. 78.
1680. William Vllock: Lancashire Will at Richmond, i. 292.
1800. Bapt. — Eleanor, d. George Ullock: Parish Church, Ulverston, p. 539.
MDB. (co. Cumb.), 1, 2; (co. Westmoreland), 1, 1.

Ulph.—(1) Bapt. 'the son of Ulf,' a favourite personal name at the time of the Conquest and for a century onward; v. Wolff (v. Yonge, ii. 267). (2) Local, 'of Ulph,' a parish in the dioc. of Norwich.

London, 2; MDB. (Norfolk), 3.

Ulyat, Ulyatt, Ulyeat.—Local. The suffix is doubtless -*yate* (i.e. *gate*); v. Yate. I cannot discover any spot of this name. (2) Bapt. Possibly a corruption of Elliot, q.v.; cf. Ulgar for Elgar and Algar.

1742. Married — John Ulyat and Ann Clasan: St. Geo. Chap. Mayfair, p. 24.
MDB. (co. Cambridge), Ulyatt, 6; London, 0. 1, 1; Crockford, 2, 0, 0; West Rid. Court Dir., 0, 1, 0.

Umfreville, Umfrewill, Umphreville.—Local, 'de Umframvile,' evidently of Norman descent.

Gilbert de Umfraunville, co. Northumberland, 1273. A.
John de Umfravile, co. Devon, ibid.
Ingram de Umframville, co. Northumberland, 20 Edw. I. R.
Gilbert de Umframville, co. Northumberland, ibid.

I find only one representative of this great old name in the London Directory.

Samuel Umfrewill, boot and shoe maker.
London, 0, 1, 0; MDB. (Essex), 0, 0, 1; (co. Kent), 1, 0, 0.

Umpleby, Umphelby.—Local, 'of Umpleby.' This is another local surname of whose history I can find no trace. It evidently represents some locality in co. York.

MDB. (West Rid. Yorks), 11, 0; London, 0, 1.

Unchaste.—Nick. 'the unchaste.'

Symon Incaste, co. Wilts, 1273. A.

Uncle, Uncles, Unkles.—Nick. 'the uncle'; cf. Cousin and Neave. Uncles doubtless represents the patronymic or genitive s, as in Williams, Jones, Neaves, &c.

John le Uncle, co. Essex, 1273. A.
Walter Unkle, co. Linc., ibid.
Robert Unkle. H.
'Lease to Thomas Unkle of a wood within the Manor of Bolynbroke, Nov. 30, 1485': Materials for Hist. Henry VII, p. 593.
1551. Married—John Lucas and Jone Unkulles: St. Dionis Backchurch, p. 3.
1557. — John Clyffe and Jone Unckell: ibid.
1607. John Uncle, co. Sussex: Reg. Univ. Oxf. vol. ii. pt. ii. p. 295.
1670. Bapt.—Margarett, d. John Uncle: St. Jas. Clerkenwell, i. 247.
1792. Married — Thomas Uncle and Louisa Maria Noble: St. Geo. Han. Sq. ii. 79.
London, 0, 2, 0; New York, 0, 0, 4.

Uncleson. — Nick. (?). Eliza Uncleson occurs in the Philadelphia Directory. Probably it is a corruption of some other surname.

Underdown.—Local, 'of the under-down,' i.e. below the down or hill. Synonymous with Underhill; v. Downe.

Richard Underdoune, co. Devon, Hen. III-Edw. I. K.
1580. Married—Raphaell Hearne and Allice Underdowne: St. Dionis Backchurch, p. 9.
London, 3; Philadelphia, 6.

Underhay. — Local, 'under the hay,' i.e. hedge; v. Hay, one who lived below the hedge.

Cf. William Underwalle, co. Oxf., 1273. A.
1752. Married—Edward Underhay and Eleanor Asher: St. Geo. Chap. Mayfair, p. 230.
London, 5.

Underhill.—Local, 'under the hill,' one who resided below the hill.

William Underhill, co. Bedf., 1273. A.
John Underhelde, co. Camb., ibid.
1751. Married — John Carruthers and Betty Underhill: St. Dionis Backchurch, p. 70.
1752. — George Manley and Catherine Underhill: St. Geo. Chap. Mayfair, p. 219.
London, 11; Oxford, 8; Philadelphia, 5.

Underwood.—Local, 'of the under-wood,' living at the foot of the wood.

Robert Underwode, C. R., 33 Hen. III.
John Underwode, co. Oxf., 1273. A.
Hugh Underwod, co. Camb., ibid.
Alexander de Sub-bosco, co. Camb., ibid.
Robertus Vndrewode, 1379: P. T. Howdenshire, p. 27.
1650. Married—Benjamin Underwood and Margrett Buxton: St. Dionis Backchurch, p. 27.
London, 38; Philadelphia, 14.

Undrell. — Local, 'under the hill,' one who resided below the hill; a corruption of Underhill, q.v. This solution is easily proved.

1625. Francis Lee and Sarah Underell: Marriage Lic. (Westminster), p. 31.
1646. Bapt.—Elissabeath, d. Humphrey and Elissabeathe Undrill: Parish Church, Kensington, p. 36.
1656. — Rebeckea, d. Humphray Undrell: ibid. p. 42.
1659. Buried—Thomas Underell: ibid. p. 129.
London, 1.

Unett.—?——. I cannot suggest any derivation of this surname at all satisfactory to myself.

1598-9. Richard Unet, co. Hereford: Reg. Univ. Oxf. vol. ii. pt. ii. p. 233.

1612. John Unett, son of Walter Unett: St. Dionis Backchurch (London), p. 95.
1753. Married — Robert Miller and Frances Unett: St. Geo. Chap. Mayfair, p. 248.
London, 3; MDB. (co. Hereford), 2.

Unsworth, Hunsworth. — (1) Local, 'of Unsworth,' a parish, once a chapelry in the ancient parish of Oldham, three miles from Bury, co. Lancaster. (2) Local, 'of Hunsworth,' a township in the parish of Birstall, three miles from Bradford, W. Rid. Yorks. No doubt these two surnames have become inextricably mixed.

David de Honneswrth, co. Staff., 1273. A.
Robertus Hunsworth, 1379: P. T. Yorks. p. 73.
John Unsworth, of Golborne (co. Lanc.), 1590: Wills at Chester (1545-1620), p. 196.
Richard Unsworth, of Bury (co. Lanc.), 1590: ibid.
James Unsworth, of Bolton (co. Lanc.), 1608: ibid.
Henry Unsworth, 1682: Preston Guild Rolls, p. 196.
London, 4, 0; Manchester, 13, 0; Philadelphia, 0, 8.

Unthank, Onthank.—Local, 'of Unthank.' There are two townships of this name, one in Cumberland, the other in Northumberland.

'To George Clementson for xvi. bushells of wheat to sow at Unthanke, £vi. ivs.' 1623: VVV. p. 217.
William de Unthanc, 1233: KKK. vi. 163.
John de Unthanc, 18 Edw. I: KKK. iv. 218.
Richard de Unthank, co. Cumb., 20 Edw. I. R.
Edmond Unthank, 1539: PPP. pp. 174-194.
John Unthanke, 1561: QQQ. p. xxxii.
1577. Henry Onthancke and Margery Maye: Marriage Lic. (London), i. 76.
'James Unthank, in 1732, gave by will £20 to the poor of the township of Culgarth': Jefferson's Hist. and Ant. of Leath Ward, co. Cumberland, p 452.
MDB. (co. Cumb.), 1, 0; (co. Durham), 1, 0; Worcester (U.S.), 0, 2.

Unwin.—Bapt. 'the son of Unwin.' This surname has ramified in a most extraordinary manner. Lower records an Onwen, a manumitted slave (Cod. Dipl. 971). One of the many personal names with -win as suffix; cf. Baldwin, Aylwin, Goodwin.

Unwona, bishop of Dorchester: Parker, Early Hist. of Oxford, p. 138.
Philip Unwyne, co. Hunts, 1273. A.
William Unwine, co. Camb., ibid.
William Onwinne, co. Oxf., ibid.
Reginald Hunwyn, co. Camb., ibid.
Simon Unnewyn, co. Linc., ibid.
1617. Bapt. — Katharine, d. George Unwen: St. Jas. Clerkenwell, i. 80.
1794. Married — Samuel Unwin and Hannah Hawkridge: St. Geo. Han. Sq. ii. 123.
London, 16; West Rid. Court Dir., 12.

Upcher, Upsher.—(1) Local, 'of Upshire,' a hamlet in the parish of Waltham Abbey, co. Essex. (2) Local, 'of Upchurch,' a parish in co. Kent. Possibly occasionally a corruption. But (1) must be considered the true parent.

1620-1. Thomas Upcher (of Colchester, co. Essex) and Anne Ayre: Marriage Lic. (London), i. 96.
1639. Buried—Roger, s. William Upchurch: St. Thomas the Apostle (London), p. 122.
Crockford, 7, 0; London, 0, 1; MDB. (Huntingdon), 0, 1.

Upcott.—Local, 'of Upcott.' There are four hamlets of this name in co. Devon, in the parishes of Culmstock, Dowland, North Molton, and Rockbeare.

Robert de Uppecote, co. Soms., 1273. A.
Joel de Uppecote, co. Devon, ibid.
John de Uppecot, co. Devon, ibid.
Reginald de Uppecot, co. Devon, Hen. III–Edw. I. K.
1600. John Upcott, co. Devon: Reg. Univ. Oxf. vol. ii. pt. ii. p. 243.
1789. Married—John Tucker and Ann Upcott: St. Geo. Han. Sq. ii. 18.
London, 1; Crockford, 1; MDB. (Devon), 4.

Upcraft.—Local, 'at the upcroft,' i. e. the upper enclosure (v. Craft), from residence therein or thereby.

1643. Married — John Upcraft and Eustace Warren: St. Jas. Clerkenwell, iii. 178.
1774. — James Upcroft and Mary Pearson: St. Geo. Han. Sq. i. 246.
London, 1; New York, 1.

Upfold, Upfill.—Local, 'at the up-fold,' i.e. the upper pen or enclosure, from residence thereby. Upfill represents a common corruption of -fold or -field as a suffix.

1713. William Upfold and Anna Maria Cockayne: Marriage Lic. (London), ii. 339.
London, 1, 1; MDB. (Sussex), 1, 0; (co. Hereford), 0, 2.

Upham.—Local, 'of Upham,' a parish in Hampshire. This surname has ramified in an extraordinary manner in the United States.

Nicholas de Upham, co. Wilts, 1273. A.
1749. Married — Joseph Upham and Anne Holt: St. Geo. Chap. Mayfair, p. 130.
1753. — Edward Upham and Mary Empson: ibid. p. 249.
London, 1; MDB. (Soms.), 3; Boston (U.S.), 51.

Uphill.—Local, 'of Uphill,' a parish in co. Somerset.

Henry Uppenhull, co. Wilts, 1273. A.
Robert Uppehull, co. Oxf., ibid.
Geldanus Uppenhill, co. Devon, Hen. III–Edw. I. K.
John Uppehulle, co. Soms., 1 Edw. III: Kirby's Quest, p. 89.
1629. Bapt.—Ann, d. Robert Uphill: St. Jas. Clerkenwell, i. 112.
1675. Richard Uphill and Ellinor Leigh: Marriage Alleg. (Canterbury), p. 239.
Boston (U.S.), 1.

Upholster.—Occup. 'the upholsterer,' obsolete as a surname.

1397. Alice Upholdesterr: Cal. of Wills in Court of Husting (2).

Upjohn.—Bapt. 'the son of John,' a corrupted form of the Welsh patr. Ap-john (= English Johnson). Such corruptions seem to have been common, as the following entries will testify:

Nycholas up-Thomas, 1557: St. Dionis Backchurch (London), p. 77.
1563. Buried—John Upharrye, prentice with John Cooke: ibid. p. 187.
1571. — Hughe Uprice, servant with William Poole: St. Michael, Cornhill, p. 192.
1585. Married — John Peycocke and Margarete Updavi: St. Dionis Backchurch, p. 10.
Robert Upprichard, 1637: St. Mary Aldermary (London), p. 18.
Roger ap-John, of Worthenbury, 1638: Wills at Chester (1621–50), p. 124.
Ellis ap-John, of Allington, 1641: ibid.
1750. Bapt.—Francis, — of James and Mary Upjohn: St. Jas. Clerkenwell, ii. 293.
Of all the above specimens I have only found two, Upjohn and Uprichard, in modern directories.
London, 4.

Upperton.—Local, 'of Uppington.' Probably a corruption; cf. Catterson for Cattinson, or Patterson for Pattinson. Uppington is a parish in co. Salop.

(Dominus) de Uppiton, co. Salop, 1273. A.

1578. Thomas Upperton, co. Berks: Reg. Univ. Oxf. vol. ii. pt. ii. p. 82.
1619. John Uppington, co. Soms.: ibid. p. 377.
1789. Married—Joseph York and Eliz. Upperton: St. Geo. Han. Sq. ii. 23.
London, 2; Boston (U.S.), 1.

Uprichard.—Bapt. 'the son of Richard'; v. Upjohn.

Philadelphia, 1; New York, 1.

Upright.—Nick. 'the upright.'

Symon Upriht, co. Camb., 1273. A.

Five centuries later this surname turns up in co. Sussex:

1787. Married—John Upright, of Heatfield, Sussex, and Ann Holgate: St. Geo. Han. Sq. i 397.
Philadelphia, 1; New York, 2.

Upsall.—Local, 'of Upsall,' two townships in the parishes of South Kilvington and Ormsby, N. Rid. Yorks.

Geoffrey de Upsal, co. York, 1273. A.
Richard de Upsale, co. York, ibid.
Robertus de Vpsale, 1379: P. T. Yorks. p. 67.
Cecilia de Vpsale, 1379: ibid.
1727. Married — Joseph Upstale (sic) and Mary Poulton: St. Geo. Han. Sq. i. 3.
London, 2.

Upshire, Upsher.—Local, 'of Upshire,' a hamlet in co. Essex.

London, 0, 1; New York, 1, 0.

Upton.—Local, 'of Upton,' parishes in cos. Bucks, Glouc., Chester, Lincoln, Norfolk, Somerset, &c., besides many townships scattered over the whole country.

John de Upton, co. Berks, Hen. III–Edw. I. K.
Henry de Upton, co. Hunts, 1273. A.
Richard de Upton, co. Wilts, ibid.
Thomas de Upton, co. Salop, ibid.
Walter de Upton, co. Bucks, 20 Edw. I. R.
1662. Buried — Ralfe, son of Allice Upton, widow: St. Dionis Backchurch, p. 233.
London, 23; Philadelphia, 10.

Upwood, Upward. — Local, 'of Upwood,' a parish in the dioc. of Ely. Upward is an imitative corruption.

Thomas de Upwode, co. Hunts, 1273. A.
Alice de Upwode, co. Hunts, ibid.
1697. Thorowgood Upwood (co. Norfolk) and Eliz. Cockayne: Marriage Lic. (Faculty-Office), p. 227.
1776. Married—William Upward and Maria Gretton: St. Geo. Han. Sq. i. 264.

1789. Bapt.—Eliz., d. Henry Upward: Reg. Stourton, co. Wilts, p. 43.
London, 4, 1.

Urban.—Bapt. 'the son of Urban,' i.e. polished, city-mannered, a name common to Western Europe, the opposite of Pagan, rustic, simple (v. Pain). Pope Urbanus gave it an impetus. Lat. *urbs*, a city. Cf. Italian Urbani in London Directory.

Urbanus de Lecheworth, Hen. III-Edw. I. K.
William Urban, co. Hereford, 1273. A.
William Urbane, 1519: Reg. Univ. Oxf. i. 3.
London, 1; Philadelphia, 12.

Urcy, Hearsey, Hersee, Hersey.—Bapt. 'the son of Ursey,' the popular form of Urse or Ursel, i.e. Ursula. The aspirate is found invariably in names beginning with a vowel; cf. German Herschell for Urschel = Ursula. Fitz-Urse was one of the assassins of Thomas à Becket.

Ralph fil. Urcy, co. Wilts, Hen. III-Edw. I. R.
Henry Urs', co. Berks, 1273. A.
Walter Urs', co. Essex, ibid.
Cok' fil. Ursell', co. Worc., ibid.
Ursellus (without surname), co. Linc., ibid.
Hursel (without surname), co. Linc., ibid.
Henry Hurs, co. Norf., ibid.
London,0,2,3,3; Boston (U.S.),0,3,2,10.

Urian, Urion, Uren, Urin, Uran.—Bapt. 'the son of Urian.' Both the masculine Uranius and feminine Urania were in use as personal names. On a Welsh variant Urien, v. Yonge, i. 172. A surname founded on this name seems to have crept into Staffordshire and Cheshire, and thence into Lancashire.

John fil. Urian, co. Hunts, 1273. A.
Uryene (without surname), co. Camb., ibid.
1633. Bapt.—Henry, s. Finsby Vrin: St. Jas. Clerkenwell, i. 123.
1635.—Joan, d. Finlye Eurin: ibid. p.131.
1671. John Urran, of Everton: Wills at Chester, iii. 275.
1680. Alice Urian, of Christleton: ibid. iii. 274.
Manchester, 1, 0, 0, 0, 0; Liverpool, 0, 0, 0, 0, 1; London, 0, 0, 1, 0, 0; MDB. (co. Stafford), 0, 2, 0, 0, 0; Philadelphia, 17, 0, 0, 1, 0.

Uridge.—Local, 'de Eweregge'; cf. Udall for Yewdale. Lower says, 'An East Sussex name.'

It is found in that district, temp. Edw. II, in the form of de Eweregge (Sussex Arch. Coll. xii. 25).'
London, 1; MDB. (co. Sussex), 3.

Urlwin, Urling.—Bapt. 'the son of Urlwin,' one of the endless compounds in *-win*; cf. Baldwin and Unwin. *-win* invariably becomes *-ing* as the surname descends to modern times. Hence the form Urling; cf. Golden, and v. Herlwin.

Richard Urlewyn, co. Oxf., 1273. A.
1581. Roger Urlen, co. Middlesex: Reg. Univ. Oxf. vol. ii. pt. ii. p. 102.
1665. Thomas Urlin and Rebecca Mills: Marriage Alleg. (Canterbury), p. 110.
1666. Bapt. — Margaret, d. Richard Urlwin: Kensington Parish Ch. p. 49.
1671. Simon Urlin, of Ampthill, co. Bedf., and Anne Robinson: Marriage Alleg. (Canterbury), p. 197.
1764. Married — Richard Payne and Mary Urlwin: St. Geo. Han. Sq. i. 131.
London, 1, 1.

Urmson.—Local, 'of Urmston,' a township in the parish of Flixton, on the Cheshire border; an early corruption, *not* a form of Ormson (v. Orme). The family of Urmston have many entries in the Prestbury Church registers. Two early ones are given below:

1570. Married—Raffe Urmeson and Isabell Manyfold: Reg. Prestbury, co. Ches., p. 31.
1572. Bapt. — Ellen Urmeston: ibid. p. 37.
Richard Urmston, of Horwich, 1598: Wills at Chester (1545-1620), p. 197.
John Urmson, of Wheelton, 1677: ibid. (1660-80), p. 274.
Liverpool, 4; MDB. (co. Chester), 1.

Urquhart.—Local, 'of Urquhart.' There are places called Urquhart in the shires of Moray, Inverness, and Ross. The family are traced to Galleroch de Urchart, who lived temp. Alex. II. His descendants were hereditary sheriffs of Cromarty (Lower's Patr. Brit. p. 362). Not being an English surname I proceed no further.

London, 7; Boston (U.S.), 6.

Urry, Urie, Hurry.—? Bapt. 'the son of Urry' (?). Possibly the popular form of Urian, q.v. More probably it is local, but I have no proof.

John Hurri, co. Oxf., 1273. A.
Simon Urri, co. Oxf., ibid.

Ricardus Urry, co. Norf., 20 Edw. I. R.
1677. Roger Barton and Anne Drew, with consent of her mother, Dulsabella Urry: Marriage Alleg. (Canterbury), p. 271.
1748. Bapt.—Betty, d. James Hurry: Reg. Stourton, co. Wilts, p. 31.
1777. Married—John Lewis and Elizabeth Urry: ibid. p. 60.
London, 4, 1, 6.

Urwen.—Local; v. Irving.

Urwick.—Local, 'of Urwick.' Mr. Lower suggests that it is a variant of Urswick, a parish in Furness, North Lancashire. This is very improbable, as Urswick does not appear to have become the parent of an hereditary surname. Besides, Urwick as a surname is almost entirely confined to South, and especially Southwest, England. I suspect it will be found to represent some small spot in the neighbourhood of co. Somerset.

MDB. (co. Soms.), 5; London, 5.

Urwin.—Local; v. Irving.

Usborn, Usborne.—Bapt. 'the son of Osbern,' a variant. We find Osebern in the Hundred Rolls, and this would readily become Usbern; v. Osborn.

Gerard fil. Osebern, co. Hunts, 1273. A.
1521. Christopher Usborne and Katharine Grene: Marriage Lic. (London), i. 2.
1700. Married—William Usbourne and Eliz. Edwards: St. Peter, Cornhill, ii. 63.
MDB. (co. Kent), 1, 4; (co. Hereford), 0, 1.

Usher.—Offic. 'the usher,' 'a door-keeper, one who introduced strangers. M.E. *vschere*' (Skeat).

Peter le Usser, co. Berks, 1273. A.
London, 13; Boston (U.S.), 8.

Usherwood. — Local, 'of Usherwood.' I cannot find the spot, but I doubt not it is in co. Lancaster, where in the modern form of Isherwood it is a familiar surname; v. Isherwood.

1668. Married—Cornelius Thorogood and Jane Usserwood: St. Jas. Clerkenwell, i. 141.
1682. Bapt.—Thomas, s. Thomas Userwood: ibid. p. 296.
1683. — Thomas, s. Thomas Usherwood: ibid. p. 305.
MDB. (co. Kent), 2.

Utley.—Local; v. Uttley.

Uttermare, Uttermere. — Local. Mr. Lower says from the French 'D'outre mer, from beyond the sea; a foreigner—foreign, that is, in regard to France, from which country the name seems to have been imported. It appears to be almost entirely limited to the county of Somerset.' I must still believe that it is a native of Somerset till further evidence is produced, and that it is sprung from some small locality in that county. No doubt it is of local origin.

MDB. (co. Soms.), 5, 1.

Utterson.—Bapt. 'the son of Oughtred' or Utred. Found early in Northumberland as a patronymic in the form of Utrickson. From Utrickson to Utterson was an inevitable descent. Naturally we find this name in the county where Oughtred was once so popular. v. Outred.

Thomas Utrickson, 1349 : PPP. p. 134.
1792. Married—John Outherson and Eliz. Fountain : St. Geo. Han. Sq. ii. 165.

Utrick as a font-name survived till the 18th century.

'Here lieth interred the body of Utrick Reay, son and heir of Henry Reay, Esq., alderman of Newcastle-upon-Tyne': Brand's Newcastle, ii. 120.

Newcastle, 5.

Utting, Outing.—Bapt. 'the son of Utting,' a long-forgotten personal name. As a surname Utting has strongly ramified in co. Norfolk. 'Utting de Cresswell was witness to a deed temp. King John. Gent. Mag., Oct. 1832': Lower.

Hutting de Schipdon, co. York, 1273. A.
Richard Uttying, co. Hunts, ibid.
Adam fil. Utting, 1379 : FFF. p. 270.
Amicia Vttyng-wyf (i. e. the wife of Utting), 1379 : P. T. Yorks. p. 191.
Petrus Vttyng', 1379 : ibid. p. 116.
Johannes Vttyng', 1379 : ibid. p. 234.
Nicholaus Vttyng', 1379 : ibid.
John Uttyng, rector of Bridgham St. Mary, co. Norfolk, 1448 : FF. i. 439.
1794. Married—James Utting and Ann Callingham : St. Geo. Han. Sq. ii. 113.
London, 5, 1 ; MDB. (Norfolk), 13, 0.

Uttley, Utley.—Local. Probably 'of Otley,' two parishes, one in co. Suffolk, the other in W. Rid. York ; v. Otley.

London, 0, 2 ; MDB. (co. Lanc.), 3, 2 ; Philadelphia, 4, 0.

V

Vacher.—Occup. 'the vacher,' a cow-keeper, a dairyman. Hence in old records the 'vacherie,' a cowhouse. 'Vaccary, a cow-pasture. Lanc. "Vachery, a dairy": Prompt. Parv.' (Halliwell).

Alice la Vacher (probably a dairymaid), co. Camb., 1273. A.
Robert le Vacher, co. Oxf., ibid.
Simon le Vacher, co. Bedf., ibid.
Cf. also Richard de la Vache (probably the cow-shed or dairy), co. Derby, ibid.

The Daily Telegraph (March 22, 1898) records the death of Fred. S. Vacher.

London, 3.

Vaizey.—Local ; v. Vesey.

Vale, Vail, Vaile.—Local, 'of the vale' (M.E. val, F. val), from residence therein ; cf. French Duval.

Eustace del Val, co. Northumberland, 1273. A.
Hugh de la Val, co. Northumb., ibid.
John del Vale, armorer, 18 Edw. I : Freemen of York, i. 22.
Robert de la Vale, co. Northumb., 20 Edw. I. R.
Hugh de la Vale, Northumb., ibid.
Ralph du Val, Guernsey, ibid.

1655. Bapt.—George, son of Godfrey Vale : St. Jas. Clerkenwell, i. 192.
1792. Married—John Vale and Mary Fielder : St. Geo. Han. Sq. ii. 79.
London, 8, 3, 3 ; Philadelphia, 0, 9, 0.

Valentine, Vallentine, Valentin, Vallentin.—(1) Nick. 'a valentine, a sweetheart' ; v. Skeat's Dict.

Hugh le Valentyne, Close Roll, 8 Edw. III.

(2) Bapt. 'the son of Valentine.' St. Valentine's day is February 14, the season when birds begin to pair. In either case the saint has originated the name.

Valentine Fairwether, Close Roll, 1-2 Philip and Mary, pt. viii.
1578. Matthew Nicholson and Alice Valentine : Marriage Lic. (London), i. 82.
1803. Married — James Valentin and Ann Halfacer : St. Geo. Han. Sq. ii. 275.

The Italian Valentini is englished into Valentiny in the London Directory.

London, 8, 2, 3, 2 ; New York, 101, 1, 3, 0.

Vallet. — Occup. 'the valet,' a young groom, a young attendant (v. Skeat's Dict.), now valet.

Adam le Vallet, C. R., 5 Edw. II.
Walter Vallet, co. Soms., 1 Edw. III : Kirby's Quest, p. 185.

Valls.—Local, 'of Valois.'

John, son of James Valloyes, 1601 : Reg. St. Columb Major, p. 198.
Elizabeth, d. of John Vallyes, 1573 : ibid. p. 8.
Olly, d. of Nicholas Vallis, 1591 : ibid. p. 15.
Elizabeth, d. of James Valleys, 1602 : ibid. p. 21.
1765. Married—John Wise and Joanna Valless : St. Geo. Han. Sq. i. 142.
London, 3.

Vann, Van.—Local, 'at the van,' i.e. the threshing-floor, from residence thereby. Fr. van, a fan, a threshing instrument ; v. Vanner.

Robert atte Vanne, co. Westm., 20 Edw. I. R.
Richard atte Vanne, co. Wilts, ibid.
1677. Bapt.—Susan, d. Leonard Van : St. Jas. Clerkenwell, i. 279.
1746. Married — Samuel Vann and Hannah Jenkins : St. Geo. Chap. Mayfair, i. 77.
London, 1, 0 ; New York, 0, 2.

Vanner.—Occup. 'the fanner.' Fr. vanneur, a winnower ; v. Fanner and Vann.

Walter le Vanner, co. Oxf., 1273. A.
John le Vannere, co. Oxf., ibid.
Ralph le Vannere, co. Bucks, ibid.
Henry Vannere, City of London. X.
London, 4.

Varley. — Local, 'of Verley,' a parish in Essex ; cf. Derby and Darby, Clerk and Clark.

Hugo de Verli, 1184. RRR. p. 168.
William Vyrly, co. Soms., 1 Edw. III : Kirby's Quest, p. 259.
Roger de Virlie, or Verly, bailiff of Norwich, 1335 : FF. iii. 99.

This Roger was bailiff several times. He is entered Verley in 1343, and Verli in 1344 (FF. iii. 99).

1596. William Varleigh, or Varly : Reg. Univ. Oxf. vol. ii. pt. iii. p. 194.
1801. Married—John Varley and Ann Silvester : St. Geo. Han. Sq. ii. 246.
London, 6 ; Philadelphia, 4.

Varney.—Local, a variant of Verney, q.v. ; cf. Clerk and Clark, Parkin and Perkin, &c.

Varnham, Varnum, Varnam.—Local, 'of Vernham Dean,' a parish in co. Southampton. As usual, the American form is Varnum ; cf. Barnum for Barnham. An early instance occurs in the Hundred Rolls, so our friends across the Atlantic have a long precedent in their favour.

Ralph de Vernum, co. Glouc., 1273. A.
1585. James Varnam, or Vernam, London : Reg.Univ.Oxf.vol.ii.pt. ii. p.148.
1600. Bapt., s. Ralph Varnam, *merchaunt tailor* : St. Peter, Cornhill, i. 50.
1624. John Varnham and Eliz. Holcrofte : Marriage Lic. (London), i. 143.
1802. Married—Charles Varnham and Maria Harris : St. Geo. Han. Sq. ii. 267.
London, 1, 0, 1 ; Philadelphia, 0, 1, 0 ; Boston (U.S.), 0, 5, 1.

Vass.—Bapt. 'the son of Vass.' Of this early personal name I can supply no history.

Vasse le Poynur, co. Camb., 1273. A.
1601. Buried — Jone Vasse : Reg. Prestbury, Ches., p. 152.
1784. Married — Henry Martin and Susan Vass : St. Geo. Han. Sq. i. 356.
1800. — Thomas Vass and Mary Plain : ibid. iii. 213.
London, 3 ; Philadelphia, 1.

Vassar, Vasser.—Offic. 'the Vavasseur' (q.v.), seemingly an early modification.

Nicholas Vausour, 1379 : P. T. Yorks. p. 150.

1743. Married — Henry Vawser and Ann Bullen : St. Geo. Chap. Mayfair, p. 32.
1749. — James Vassar and Ann Johnson : St. Geo. Han. Sq. i. 41.
London, 1, 1 ; Boston (U.S.), 1, 0.

Vaughan, Vaughn. — Nick. Welsh, 'the little' ; cf. English Little, Bigg, &c. Lower says, 'Vaughan, Welsh *vychan*, little in stature, a personal name of great antiquity' : Patr. Brit. p. 364. Vaughn seems to be a modern Americanism.

William Vachan, co. Salop, 1273. A.
Adam ap-Thewely Vachan, co. Cardigan, 20 Edw. I. R.
Owen Vaghan, co. Salop, ibid.
Davey Watkynge Vaghan : Visit. Gloucester, 1623, p. 104.
1601. Evan Vaughan, co. Salop : Reg. Univ. Oxf. vol. ii. pt. ii. p. 254.
Jenkin Vaughan, prebendary of St. David's, 1621 : Hist. and Ant. St. David's, p. 361.
Jerworth Vachan : Visit. London, 1633, i. 220.
London, 40, 0 ; Philadelphia, 47, 14.

Vavasseur, Vavazor, Vavasour. — Offic. 'the vavasour,' a principal vassal, holding of a great lord, a man of second rank, one of the inferior nobility. ' *Vavasour,* antiently a Nobleman, next in dignity to a Baron' : Bailey's Dict. (1742).

' Bothe Knightes and vavasour,
This damisels love paramour.'
Arthour and Merlin, p. 320 (Halliwell).
Reginald le Vavassur, co. Berks, Hen. III–Edw. I. K.
Adam le Vavasour, co. Bucks, 1273. A.
Mauger le Vavasur, co. York, 20 Edw. I. K.

This latter personal name was evidently handed down in the family, as the following entry, four hundred years later, fully demonstrates :

1696. Maugre Vavasour, of St. Ann's, Holborn, *gent.,* and Mary Moor : Marriage Lic. (London), ii. 318.
London, 3, 1, 0 ; Crockford, 0, 0, 1.

Veal, Veale, Veall. — Nick. 'the veal,' i.e. the calf. M.E. *veel,* O.F. *veel,* 'a calfe or veale,' Cotgrave (v. Skeat) ; cf. Bacon.

Thomas le Veyle, co. Norf., 1273. A.
Roger le Vel, co. Hunts, ibid.
John le Vele, co. Soms., 1 Edw. III : Kirby's Quest, p. 205.
Robert le Veel, C. R., 25 Edw. I.
Hubert le Veyll. B.

1576. Edward Veele, co. Glouc. : Reg. Univ. Oxf. vol. ii. pt. ii. p. 71.
1576. Thomas Veale, co Linc. : ibid. p.72.
1673. Bapt. — Margaret, d. Thomas Veale : St. Jas. Clerkenwell, i. 260.
1790. Married — James Hall and Martha Veall : St. Geo. Han. Sq. ii. 37.
London, 6, 3, 1 ; Philadelphia, 2, 3, 0.

Vear, Veare.—Local ; v. Vere.

Veasey.—Local ; v. Vesey.

Venables, Venable, Vennable. — Local, 'from Venables, a parish in the arrondissement of Louviers, in Normandy' (Lower). One of this family was tenant under Hugh Lupus, temp. William I, so we may say he 'came over with the Conqueror.'

William de Venables, co.Salop, 1273. A.
1616. Thomas Venables, co. Bucks : Reg. Univ. Oxf. vol. ii. pt. ii. p. 356.
1621. Richard Venables, co. Southampton : ibid. p. 389.
1690. Married — Ann Venables : St. Antholin, Budge Row, London, p. 106.
1754. — John Venable : ibid. p. 157.
1791. Married — John Venables and Eliz. Norman : St. Geo. Han. Sq. ii. 61.
London, 12, 1, 0 ; Philadelphia, 2, 5, 2.

Vender.—Occup. 'the vender,' a seller, a dealer.

William le Vendour. D.
Agnes Vendir, co. York. W. 11.
Thomas le Vyndre, C. R., 7 Ric. II.

I fear this surname is obsolete.

Veness, Venes, Venis, Venus. — Local, 'of Venice' ; an early importation ; cf. Jannaway and Lombard. Lower quotes, 'Stephen de Venuse, *miles,*' but gives no reference.

John de Venuz, co. Essex, 1273. A.
Leonard de Venetia. E.

It is interesting to note that all the above forms exist in co. Sussex, where the surname has long been established.

1623. Married—Henry Venus and Anne Starte : St. Jas. Clerkenwell, p. 53.
1787. — Thomas Venes and Eliz. Grocal : St. Geo. Han. Sq. i. 404.
John Venus, 1745 : Blair's Hist. of Alnwick, p. 457.

It may be added that Venus, representing the goddess of love, became a baptismal name ; but far too late to have any influence upon surnames.

1631. Married — John Cotton and Venus Levat : St. Peter, Cornhill, i. 253.

1756. Buried—Love Venus Rivers : St. Peter, Cornhill, ii. 142.

By Archbishop Peckham's law the minister could have refused to baptize either of the above. ' The minister shall take care not to permit wanton names, which being pronounced do sound to lasciviousness, to be given to children baptized, especially of the female sex ; and if otherwise it be done, the same shall be changed by the bishop at confirmation.'

London, 1, 0, 0, 0 ; Crockford, 1, 0, 0, 0 ; MDB. (Sussex), 3, 1, 1, 1 ; New York (Venus), 1.

Venimore.—Nick. ' fin-amour ' (v. Finnemore) : cf.Venn and Fenn, Vidler and Fidler, Vanner and Fanner.

London, 1.

Venn. — Local, ' at the fen,' from residence beside a bog or fen (v. Fenn) ; cf. Vanner and Fanner.

John atte Venne, co. Soms., 1 Edw. III : Kirby's Quest, p. 94.
Simon Ven, alias Fen, temp. 1580 : Visit. London, 1633, ii. 308.
John Ven, alias Fen, 1634 : ibid.
1594. John Ven, *draper* (London), and Ellinor Clerke : Marriage Lic. (London), i. 217.
1619. Richard Venne, co. Devon : Reg. Univ. Oxf. vol ii. pt. ii. p. 374.
1657. Married—Ambrose Venn and Ellinor Nottingham : St Jas. Clerkenwell,i.99.
London, 10 ; New York, 1.

Vennell, Vennall, Venel, Fennell.—Local, ' at the vennel,' i.e. a small street or passage ; cf. 'vennel, a gutter, a sink. North' (Halliwell). Cf. Fr. 'Enfiler la venelle,' to run away. Still in use in Scotland for a small lane or passage. From a large number of entries in the Hundred Rolls a few instances may be given.

Geoffrey de la Venele, Fines Roll, 11 Edw. I.
Alexander in Venella, co. Hunts, 1273. A.
Thomas in Venello, co. Hunts, ibid.
Isabel de la Venele, co. Hunts, ibid.
Richard en le Venel, co. Bedf., ibid.
Matilda de Venella, co. Oxf., ibid.

Also in cos. Rutland and Cambridge.

' Simon Venell, alias Fennell, *priest*,' 1592 : Cal. State Papers (Domestic), iii. 176, 452, &c.
' London,2,1,0,10 ; Philadelphia,0,0,1,10.

Venner, Fenner.—Occup. ' le veneur,' a huntsman.   Lower's explanation is unsatisfactory (Patr. Brit. p. 111). Besides, there is no difficulty in the solution of the name.   The early instances are conclusive.   Venner must be carefully distinguished from Vanner, q.v. As regards the initial F in Fenner, cf. Fanner, Venn, Vowell, Fennell, &c.

Robert le Venur, co. Linc., 1273. A.
William Venator, co. York, ibid.
Geoffrey le Venour, co. Salop, ibid.
Robert le Veneur, co. Linc., 20 Edw. I. R.
John le Venour. B.
Thomas le Veneur. T.
Robert Hunter, alias Venour : London Visit. 1633, i. 405.
1691-2. Buried—Alce (Alice) Venner, *widow* : St. Dionis Backchurch, p. 250.
1707. Married — Nathaniel Walker and Margaret Fenner : St. Michael, Cornhill, p. 54.
London, 3, 16 ; Boston (U.S.), 5, 3.

Ventris, Ventriss, Venters. —Local (?). I find no trace of this surname in the early rolls. Probably it is of later and foreign importation. Lower suggests La Ventrouse in the arrondissement of Montagne, Normandy, as the home of the family.

1586-7. Married — Thomas Ventris and Annes Lynge : St. Dionis Backchurch, p. 11.
1614. Bapt. — George, son of Robert Ventresse : St. Michael, Cornhill, p. 111.
1650. Married — John Ventris and Eliz. Gillett : St. Thomas the Apostle (London), p. 19.
London, 1, 1, 1, 2.

Venus.—Local ; v. Veness.

Verdin, Verdon. —Local, ' of Verdun,' a town in the department of Meuse, N.E. France.

Rosa de Verdon, co. Linc., 1273. A.
Wydo de Verdum, co. Norf., ibid.
Bertram de Verdun, 7 Hen. II : Pipe Roll, iv. 41.
1796. Married — Robert Whitton and Sarah Verdon : St. Geo. Han. Sq. ii. 151.
1802. — George Verdin and Ann Aikman : ibid. p. 255.
London, 2, 3 ; New York, 0, 4.

Vere, Vear, Veare. — Local, ' of Ver,' ' a parish and château in the canton of Guvray, in La Manche, Normandy' (Lower). Clutterbuck, in his Hist. of Hertfordshire, says, ' de Veer,' from a town so called

in the island of Walcheren in Holland. All the early entries by their spelling confirm the former view, save the instance with Baldwin for a Christian name. One single Vere in the London Directory saves the name from complete extinction, save in the variant Vear or Veare.

Albric' de Ver, co. Camb., 1273. A.
Baldewin de Ver, co. Oxf., ibid.
Henry de Ver, co. Suff., ibid.
1581. Robert Vere, co. Essex : Reg. Univ. Oxf. vol. ii. pt. ii. p. 113.
1605. Henry de Vere : ibid. i. 236.
1780. Married—William Sercome and Jane Vear : St. Geo. Han. Sq. ii. 23.
London, 1, 0, 1 ; Boston (U.S.), 1,0, 0.

Verey, Veary.—? Bapt. ; v. Verry.   Oxford, 1, 1.

Verge.—Local, ' at the verge,' from residence therein. Probably for *verger* (Chaucer), a garden ; F. *vergier*. Chaucer has the form *verge* :
' Ne had Idlenesse thee convaid
In the verge where Mirth him pleid.'
Rom. of Rose.
Richard de la Verge, C. R., 3 Edw. I.

Oddly enough, I cannot light on any instances in modern church registers.   But the one quotation above is worth a hundred such entries, as it at once settles the origin of the surname.

London, 2 ; Boston (U.S.), 4.

Verity. — ? ——. I cannot classify this surname. The earliest form found in Yorkshire is Verty.

Agnes Verty, *vidua*, 1379 : P. T. Yorks. p. 252.
1745. Married—Christopher Verity and Ann Clarke : St. Geo. Chap. Mayfair,p. 56.
1751. — Timothy Cahill and Eleanor Verty : ibid. p. 204.
London, 5 ; Pudsey (Yorks), 4.

Verney, Varney.—Local, ' of Vernai,' ' a parish in the arrondissement of Bayeux' (Lower). The variant Varney seems to be the most popular modern form ; cf. Parkin and Perkin, Clark and Clerk, Darby and Derby, &c.

Lucya de Vernai, co. Oxf., 1273. A.
Simon deVernay,co. Northampton, ibid.
Ralph de Verney, co. Oxf., ibid.
1600. Francis Verney, London : Reg. Univ. Oxf. vol. ii. pt. ii. p. 241.
1563. Buried — Jeames Verney : St. Peter, Cornhill, i. 117.
1637. Bapt.—Francis, s. John Varney : St. Jas. Clerkenwell, i. 137.

London, 0, 6; Oxford, 1, 4; Crockford, 1, 0; Boston (U.S.), 3, 27.

Verrall, Verrill. — ? Local. Mr. Lower says, 'This name, abundant in East Sussex and seldom found out of it, may be a corruption of Firle, a parish near Lewis—sometimes in old documents written Ferle, and usually pronounced as a dissyllable' (Patr. Brit. p. 367).

1575. Edmund Wyllson and Johanna Ferrall: Marriage Lic. (London), i. 67.
MDB. (Sussex), 7, 0; Philadelphia, 1, 3.

Verrer, Verrier.—Occup. 'the verrour' or verrer, a glazier.

'In alle the erthe y-halowed and y-holde,
In a closet more clere than verre or glas.'
Lydgate (v. *verre*, Halliwell).

The Verrours walked in the York Pageant (York Mystery Plays, p. xxvi, ed. Toulmin Smith).

Edward le Verrer, Close Roll, 39 Hen. III. pt. i.
John le Verrer, Close Roll, 54 Hen. III.
Thomas le Verer, co. Oxf., 1273. A.
Simon le Verrour, co. Northampton, ibid.
Walter le Verrour : Freemen of York, i. 15.
Laurence de Stok, *verrour* : 7 Edw. II : ibid.

1750. Married — William Willis and Ann Verrier : St. Michael, Cornhill, p. 72.
London, 0, 1; MDB. (co. Kent), 0, 2; (Somerset), 0, 1.

Verry, Very. — ? Bapt. 'the son of Everard' (?), from a supposed nick. Very. This is Mr. Lower's suggestion, and there is much to be said in its favour. Everard, being so popular a personal name in the surname period, was bound to have a nick., and Very seems the natural one; v. Everson.

1600. Married — William Very and Margerie Knight : St. Jas. Clerkenwell, i. 24.
1613. Robert Verey : Reg. Univ. Oxf. vol. ii. pt. ii. p. 331.
1795. Married — Samuel Verry and Susanna Edgley : St. Geo. Han. Sq. ii. 135.
London, 2, 0; Boston (U.S.), 5, 7.

Vertue ; v. Virtue.

Vesey, Vezey, Pheysey, Voisey, Vaizey, Veasey. — Local, 'de Veci' or Vesci. Lower says, ' Robert de Veci assisted William I to conquer England, and was rewarded with great estates in the counties of Northampton, Leicester, Warwick, and Lincoln. Ivo or John de Veschi

was his near kinsman, and from him in the female line descended Lord Vesey' (Kelham's Domesday) ; v. Patr. Brit. p. 366.

Willelmus de Vesci, 7 Hen. II : Pipe Roll, iv. 23.
Eustace de Vescy, co. Linc., 1273. A.
Richard de Vescy, co. York, ibid.
1512. John Veys-y, or Vesey, or Voysye, or Pheysy : Reg. Univ. Oxf. i. 81.
1603. Walter Veysey, co. Devon : ibid. vol. ii. pt. ii. p. 266.
1603-4. James Voyzey, co. Devon : ibid. p. 269.

Other spellings of the names of the two students last mentioned are Voysey, Vesey, and Veisey (v. Index). For other instances, v. Pheysy.

London, 1, 1, 1, 1, 1, 0; Philadelphia, 2, 2, 0, 0, 0, 1.

Vestmentmaker. — Occup. 'the vestment maker,' a maker of robes, especially embroidered ones.

' To Thomas Cheiner, of London, in discharge of £140 lately due to him, for a vest of velvet embroidered with divers work,' July 15, 24 Edw. III : Issues of the Exchequer.

Vestment-makers (York Pageant); v. York Mystery Plays, ed. Toulmin Smith, p. xxiii. In a note the editor says, ' Old-fashioned people in Yorkshire still remember the vests made of well-dressed skins, often handsomely embroidered.' It is in Yorkshire I find the surname.

Robert Vestmentmaker : Testimente Ebor., Surt. Soc., v. Index.

Coke Lorelle's Bote has it ' vestyment-swoers' (sewers).

Viall(s ; v. Viel.

Vicary, Vickery, Vicarey, Vittery.—Offic. ' the vicar.' The absence of ' Vicar ' or ' Vicker,' and the great frequency of Vicary and Vickery, prove these to be official and not local.

'Sire preest, quod he, art thou a Vicary? Or art thou a Person? say soth by thy fay.
Chaucer, The Persones Prologue.
Richard Vicary. B.
1574-5. Stephen Vyccarye and Margaret Johnson : Marriage Lic. (London), i. 63.
1585. John Vicary, co. Devon : Reg. Univ. Oxf. vol. ii. pt. ii. p. 144.
1749. Married — Thomas Platt and Anne Vickery : St. Geo. Han. Sq. i. 133.
1749. Married—James Brown and Jane Vickery : ibid.

Vittery seems to be a West-country corruption.
London, 5, 10, 1, 0; MDB. (co. Devon), 10, 4, 0, 2; Philadelphia, 1, 16, 0, 0.

Vickerage, -idge ; v. Vickridge.

Vickerman. — Occup. ' the vicar's man,' the servant of the vicar; cf. Priestman, Matthewman, Bartleman, Addiman, &c. Found early in co. York, where the surname is still common.

Willelmus Vikarman, 1379 : P. T. Yorks. p. 100.
Willelmus serviens Vicarii, 1379 : ibid. p. 201.
Beatrix serviens Vicarii, 1379 : ibid.
Cf. Adam Parsonman : ibid. p. 241.
Emma Parsonwoman, 1379 : ibid.
Isabella Vikerwoman, 1379 : ibid. p. 50.

In South England it is found as Vicars-man.

Richard le Wycarisman, co. Camb., 1273. A.
London, 3; West Rid. Court Dir., 6; New York, 1; Philadelphia, 1.

Vickers.—(1 Nick. · the vicar's son ' (v. Vickerson) ; cf. Williams, the genitive of William. (2) Local, ' at the vicar's,' i.e. at the vicar's house, from residence therein. The first is the chief parent.

Peter atte Vicars, 1379 : P. T. Howdenshire (co. York), p. 19.
1581. John Vicears, London : Reg. Univ. Oxf. vol. ii. pt. ii. p. 106.
1618. Edward Wilkinson and Sarah Vicars, *widow* : Marriage Lic. (London), ii. 60.
1655. Bapt. — Parnell, d. Rowland Vickars : St. Jas. Clerkenwell, i. 191.
1689. Married — Francis Vickers and Eliz. Lamden : St. Peter, Cornhill, ii. 59.
London, 22; Philadelphia, 16.

Vickerson.—Nick. ' the son of the vicar' ; v. Vickers and Vickress. I can find but one modern instance, and it is in the United States.

William Vickereson, C. R., 14 Ric. II. Boston (U.S.), 1.

Vickery ; v. Vicary.

Vickress.—Nick. ' the son of the vicar,' from the old popular Vicary, a vicar, genitive Vicarys, corrupted to Vickress (v. Vicary). Thus Vickress is equivalent to Vicars or Vickers, q.v. (cf. Williams, the genitive of William = William's son).

1614-5. William Collins and Margaret Vicares : Marriage Lic. London), ii. 30.
1617-8. John Wells and Joan Viccaries : ibid. p. 57.

1765. Married—William Vickress and Sarah Oliver : St. Geo. Han. Sq. i. 149.
1795. — Edward Godsall and Rebecca Vickress : ibid. ii. 130.
London, 3.

Vickridge, Vickerage, Vickeridge —Local, ' of the vicarage,' from residence thereat (cf. Parsonage); probably the housekeeper for the vicar. I can produce no early instance, but the origin needs no explanation.

1547. John Vicarish and Margery Gerard : Marriage Lic. (Faculty Office), p. 11.
1665. John Hatton and Alice Vicaridge : Marriage Alleg. (Canterbury), p. 111.
Thomas Vicaridge, 1703 : Reg. St. Mary Aldermary (London), p. 37.
1710. Married — Richard Eycott and Eliz. Vicaridge : St. Jas. Clerkenwell, iii. 232.
1770. — William Harwich and Kezia Vickredge : St. Geo. Han. Sq. i. 195.
London, 1, 0, 0 ; MDB. (co. Somerset), 0, 1, 0 ; (co. Glouc.), 0, 0, 1.

Vidler.—Occup. ' the fiddler,' a player on the fiddle (v. Fidler). The *V* here is a connecting link between *viol* and *fiddle*; cf. Vowler for Fowler, Venn for Fenn, Vanner for Fanner, and probably the Devonshire Vivash for Fiveash. For further instances, v. Vowler.

Reginald le Vielur, co. Oxf., 1273. A.
Robert Vidulator, co. Oxf., ibid.
1786. Married — Matthew Vidler and Frances Barnes : St. Geo. Han. Sq. i. 393.
1808. Edmund Vidler and Ann Meager : ibid. ii. 370.
London, 5 ; MDB. (co. Sussex), 2 ; Boston (U.S.), 1.

Viel, Vial, Vialls, Vialle, Viall.—Bapt. ' the son of Viel.' Probably a French form of Vitalis. I have furnished but few of the Hundred Roll entries, which prove Viel to have been a fairly familiar font-name. Vialls is the genitive ; cf. Williams, Jones, &c.

Vitalis de Engayne, co. Essex, Hen. III-Edw. I. K.
Viel Engayne, co. Northampton, ibid.
William fil. Viel, co. Hunts, 1273. A.
Julliana Vyal, co. Essex, ibid.
Agnes Vial, co. Oxf., ibid.
1731. Married – Daniel Vial and Sarah Larching : St. Geo. Han. Sq. i. 12.
1775. — John Viall and Sarah Colquhoun : ibid. p. 251.
1780. — Walter Mason and Eliz. Vialls : ibid. 316.
London, 0, 1, 2, 0, 0 ; Boston (U.S.), 1, 0, 0, 10, 5.

Vigers, Vigurs, Viguers.— ? Official. Probably a modern corruption of Vicars or Vickers (q.v.) through defective and lazy pronunciation ; cf. Hicks and Higgs, Hickson and Higson, and endless instances throughout this dictionary. This view is confirmed by the fact that these forms are found in co. Devon and the surrounding districts, where Vowler for Fowler, and Vivash for Fiveash, &c., are, or were, familiar.

1598. Lewis Vigures, co. Devon : Reg. Univ. Oxf. vol. ii. pt. ii. p. 227.
1609. Christopher Vigures, co. Devon ; ibid. p. 304.
1642. Married — Walter Vigures and Eliz. Raminge : St. Jas. Clerkenwell, i. 75.
1746. — Samuel Vigars and Grace Bridam : St. Geo. Chap. Mayfair, p. 66.
1801. — William Vigers and Anne Hitchen : St. Geo. Han. Sq. ii. 238.
London, 4, 1, 0 ; Philadelphia, 0, 0, 7.

Vigourous.—Nick. ' the vigorous,' i.e. the strong. O.F. *vigoureux*; cf. Strong, Strongitharm, &c.

William Vigerus, co. Oxf., 1273. A.
Nicholas Vigerous, co. Northumb., 20 Edw. I. R.
John Viggorus, 1396 ; FFF. p. 584.
Richard Vigerous, rector of Downham, co. Norf., 1449 ; FF. vii. 343.
1585. Robert Vigerous and Mary Roberts : Marriage Lic. (London), i. 142.
London, 1.

Villain, Vilain.—Occup. ' the villain,' i.e. the small farmer, the bondman, servant. The surname, though common, gradually got dropped as the term became de graded to its later sense.

William le Vileyn, co. Hunts, 1273. A.
Hugh le Vilein, co. Salop, ibid.
Richard le Vilein, co. Oxf., ibid.
John Vyleyn, C. R., 20 Edw. I.
New York, 0, 1.

Vinall, Vinal. — Local, ' of Vine-hall,' an estate in the parish of Watlington, co. Sussex, which was possessed by the family in the 14th century. The estate gave name to the Vynehalls, afterwards of Kingston, near Lewes, who, as Vinalls, in 1657, obtained a grant of arms (Sussex Arch. Coll. ix. 75, and v. Lower's Patr. Brit. p. 367. The variant Vinal has ramified strongly in the United States of America.

1579. Buried — Ales Fletewood, servant to George Vynoll : St. Mary Aldermary, p. 141.
1752. Married—John Mierr and Mary Vinall : St. Geo. Chap. Mayfair, p. 225.
1780. — William Taylor and Hannah Vinall : St. Geo. Han. Sq. i. 314.
London, 7, 0 ; Boston (U.S.), 2, 37.

Vince. — Bapt. ' the son of Vincent,' from the nick. Vince (v. Vincent).

1794. Married — William Vince and Grace Salter : St. Geo. Han. Sq. ii. 116.
1809. — John Vince and Sarah Larkin : ibid. p. 413.
London, 11.

Vincent, Vincett.—Bapt. ' the son of Vincent.' Vincett must be looked on not as a dim., but a corruption. It might naturally be deemed a dim. of Vince, the nick. of Vincent, just as Emmett is of Emma, or Hewett of Hugh, but there is no evidence of such a dim. being in use, and no doubt it is a modern corruption of the full name Vincent.

Roger Vincent, co. Berks, 1273. A.
Richard fil. Vincent, co. Hunts, ibid.
Vincent atte More, co. Soms., 1 Edw. III : Kirby's Quest, p. 220.
Johannes Vynsand, 1379 : P. T. Yorks. p. 102.
1581. Married — Richard Hart and Judith Vincent : St. Thomas the Apostle (London), p. 6.
1582. Francis Vincent, co. Surrey : Reg. Univ. Oxf. vol. ii. pt ii. p. 121.
1583. James Vincente and Lucy Batchellor : Marriage Lic. (London), i. 121.
London, 42, 1 ; New York, 37, 0.

Vine.—Local, ' at the vine,' i.e. the vine-tree, from residence there beside ; cf. Box, Birch, Plumptre, Crabb, Crabtree, Oak, &c.

Matilda la (? de la) Vine, co. Oxf., 1273. A.
Richard Vygn, co. Soms., 1 Edw. III : Kirby's Quest, p. 271.
1554. Henry Vyne and Jane Dowdyng : Marriage Lic. (London), p. 15.
1689. Buried — Ann Vyne : St. Mary Aldermary, p. 199.
1740. Married — Edward Fidler and Hannah Vine : St. Geo. Han. Sq. i. 24.
London, 14.

Viner, Vyner.—Occup. ' the viner,' probably a vine-grower—not a taverner, but one who superintended a vineyard.

Adam de Viner, C. R., 2 Edw. I.
William le Vinyour, co. Hunts, 1273. A.
Reginald le Vinour, co. Bedf., ibid.
John le Vynor, co. Oxf., ibid.

1577. Henry Vyner, co. Salop: Reg. Univ. Oxf. vol. ii. pt. ii. p. 75.

1655. Married — William Joyner and Mary Chillingsworth, by Alderman Thomas Vyner: St. Michael, Cornhill, p. 34.

1756. Married — Benjamin Viner and Susanna Spearing: St. Geo. Han. Sq. i. 63.

London, 1, 1 ; Boston (U.S.), 1, 0.

Vinson, Vinsun.—(1) Bapt. 'the son of Vincent' (q.v.), manifest corruptions. (2) Bapt. 'the son of Vincent,' from the nick. Vince (q.v.) and patr. Vince-son. The first is probably the true parent.

1582. Bapt. — Lucrece, d. Humfrey Vincent or Vinson: St. Jas. Clerkenwell, i. 15.

1611. Married — Francis Vinson and Frances Ewers: ibid. p. 38.

1776. — Thomas Vincen and Ann Lee: St. Geo. Han. Sq. i. 271.

London, 1, 1 ; Boston (U.S.), 8, 0.

Vinter.—Occup. 'the vinter.' Fr. *vinetier*, a tavern keeper, a wine-seller.

Juliana la Vynetar, C. R., 45 Hen. III. Abellus Vinetar, co. Bedf., 1273. A. Richard le Viniter, co. Oxf., ibid. William le Vineter, co. Northampton, ibid.

Robert Vyneter, co. Soms., 1 Edw. III : Kirby's Quest, p. 250.

William le Vyneter, co. Soms., 1 Edw. III : ibid.

1582-3. John Farrante, *husbandman,* and Mary Vinter : Marriage Lic. (London), i. 115.

1772. Married — William Vinter and Harriott Row : St. Geo. Han. Sq. i. 225.

London, 3.

Vintner.—Occup. 'the vintner,' a taverner, a wine-seller. The second *n* is intrusive; v. Vinter, which is the older and more correct form. 'Vyntenere, *vinarius*': Prompt. Parv.

, Thomas Vyntener, 1379 : P. T. Yorks. p. 150.

1560. Married—Thomas Sherson and Ellen Vintener : St. Peter, Cornhill, i. 255.

1605. John Vintener : Reg. Univ. Oxf. vol. ii. pt. i. p. 356.

1631. John Gerard and Mary Vintner : Marriage Lic. (London), ii. 203.

I find no instances in the modern directories, but probably the surname still exists.

Violett.—(1) Nick.; from the light purple attire of the wearer ; cf. Borrell, Burnell, &c. In Some

Extracts from Somerset Wills, by A. J. Monday, occurs a bequest (1565) of a 'violett coate,' p. 157, Somerset. Arch. Soc. (2) Bapt. 'the son of Violet,' probably in use early enough to become a surname.

Nicholas Vyolet, Close Roll, 9 Edw. IV.

1526. Robert Fabyan and Marion Violett : Marriage Lic. (London), i. 5.

1581. Nicholas Violett, London : Reg. Univ. Oxf. vol. ii. pt. ii. p. 104.

Violat Mumford, 1637 : Reg. St. Mary Aldermary (London), p. 85.

Francis Violet, 1698 : Reg. St. Peter, Cornhill, i. 61.

London, 2.

Vipan, Vipon, Vipond. — ? Local, 'of Vipont.' Lower says : 'v. pont, v. pon, latinized "de Veteri Ponte," of the Old Bridge. There are several places in Normandy called Vieupont, and the great Anglo-Norman family so designated (i. e. Vipont) came from Vipont, near Lisieux' ; v. Sussex Arch. Coll. ii. 77.

Robert de Veteri Ponte, co. Oxf., 1273. A.

Richard de Veteri Ponte, co. Devon, Hen. III-Edw. I. K.

John de Veteri Ponte, co. Notts and Derby, ibid.

Ivo de Veteri Ponte, co. York, 20 Edw. I. R.

1662. Bapt. — Catherine, d. Thomas and Rosamond Vipin : St. Jas. Clerkenwell, i. 216.

1761. Married — Thomas Lasey and Mary Vipoint : St. Geo. Han. Sq. i. 107.

1772. — Thomas Vipond and Mary Eagle : ibid. p. 222.

London, 1, 0, 0 ; MDB. (co. Camb.), 13, 0, 0; (co. Norfolk), 5, 0, 2 ; Crockford, 2, 0, 0 ; Boston (U.S.), 0, 0, 1 ; Philadelphia, 0, 1, 0.

Virgin.—Nick. (?) 'the virgin,' probably given to some one who had taken the part of the Virgin Mary in one of the Mirarcle Plays; cf. King and Virtue.

1581. William Virgyn (co. Essex) and Lettice Sheppie : Marriage Lic. (London), i. 105.

1587. John Virgin, co. Somerset : Reg. Univ. Oxf. vol. ii. pt. ii. p. 158.

1610. Married — John Vergine and Margaret Barrowes : St. Jas. Clerkenwell, i. 36.

1637. — John Virgin and Lenia Harrington : ibid. p. 68.

1800. — George Wellen and Mary Virgin : St. Geo. Han. Sq. ii. 217.

Oxford (1895), 1 ; Boston (U.S.), 5.

Virtue, Vertue. — Nick. (?). Probably a sobriquet affixed to one who had represented Virtue in one of the early Miracle Plays ; cf. King, and v. Virgin. M.E. *vertu,* F. *vertu,* virtue.

1510. Simeon Vertu, Benedictine : Reg. Univ. Oxf. i. 69.

1579. Nathaniel Vertwe, or Virtu, co. Berks: ibid. vol. ii. pt. ii. p. 89.

1617-8. Married—Christopher Vertue and Ann Saull : St. Dionis Backchurch, p. 19.

1682. — Nicolas White and Mary Vertue : St. Jas. Clerkenwell, i. 195.

1792. — Samuel Vertue and Elenor Rowles : St. Geo. Han. Sq. ii. 88.

London, 2, 2 ; Philadelphia, 10, 0.

Viscount. — Offic. 'a vice-count,' one who supplied the place of a count ; cf. vice-gerent, vice - chancellor, &c. This surname, unlike many others of same official class, does not seem to have lasted long. I find no modern instances.

John le Viscont, C. R., 29 Hen. III. Eustace le Vechounte, 1273. A. John le Viscounte. B.

Visick.—Local, a corruption of Fishwick, q.v. A more imitative corruption is found in Physick, q.v.

'Visick and Norman, ladies' boarding school, 82, Carlton Hill, London, N.W.': London Dir. 1870.

London, 1 ; Devon Court Dir., 1.

Vittery; v. Vicary, of which it is a corruption.

Vivash.—? Local, 'at the Five-ash-trees.' 'A name still of some distinction in the neighbourhood of Devizes, betraying the Western pronunciation of Five-Ashes'; so says a correspondent of Mr. Lower, who adds, 'I should prefer deducing it from the Fr. *vivace,* which Cotgrave defines as "livelie, lustie . . . full of life, mettall, spirit"'; v. Fiveash, and cf. Vowler for Fowler or Venn for Fenn.

1771. Married — Joshua Jackson and Betty Vivesh : St. Geo. Han. Sq. i. 215.

1774. — Thomas Mills and Mary Vivish : ibid. p. 243.

1784. — Thomas Vivaish and Betty Croom : ibid. p. 356.

The Daily Telegraph, May 16, 1894, records the marriage of Simeon Viveash.

Vivian, Vyvyan.—Bapt. 'the son of Vyvyan' or Viviana, the name of the enchantress of King Arthur's Court (v. Yonge, i. 407–8); cf. Phythian.

Vivianus Gernet, co. Lanc., 30 Hen. III : BBB. p. 11.
Isabel fil. Viviani, co. Camb., 1273. A.
John Vivian, or Vivien, or Vivyan, London, 20 Edw. I. R.
Viviana fil. Clementi le Bonde, Close Roll, 10 Edw. II.
Vivian, son of John Browne, 1544 : Reg. St. Columb Major, Cornwall, p. 3.
Vivian, son of Luke Pollard, 1544 : ibid.
Vivian, son of Edward Merifield, 1544 : ibid.
Emblen, d. of Thomas Vivian, 1544 : ibid. p. 10.
1586. Humphrey Vivian, co. Merioneth: Reg. Univ. Oxf. vol. ii. pt. ii. p. 153.
1593-4. Michael Vivian, co. Cornwall : ibid. p. 200.
London, 11, 1 ; MDB. (co. Cornwall), 17, 4 ; Boston (U.S.), 3, 0.

Vizard.—Bapt. ; v. Whiskard. An early use of *v* for *w*, the name gradually assuming an imitative form.

Warin Vischard, co. Bucks, 1273. A. London, 3.

Vizer. — Occup. ? Perhaps a maker of vizors or vizards. The more correct form, however, would be Vizerer, and this does not correspond with the first instance below.

John le Visur, co. Worc., 1273. A.
1616. Robert Vizer, co. Somerset: Reg. Univ. Oxf. vol. ii. pt. ii. p. 354.

1805. Married — William Vizer and Mary Henrahan: St. Geo. Han. Sq. ii. 331.
London, 2 ; New York, 2.

Voisey ; v. Vesey, of which it is an undoubted variant.

Voller ; a variant of Vowler, q.v.

Oxford, 1.

Voss, Vos.—Nick. Vos, a Dutch and Low German form of Fox, q.v. (Lower's Patr. Brit. p. 367). Its importation into England is comparatively modern.

1692. Bapt. — John, s. David Voss : St. Jas. Clerkenwell, i. 316.
1694. — Eliz., d. David Voss : ibid. p. 356.
London, 8, 2 ; New York, 37, 1.

Vowell, Vowle, Vowles, Voules.—(1) Nick. 'the fowl.' A West-country form of Fowell and Fowle, a fowl, a bird ; cf. Vivash and Visick for Fiveash and Fishwick. Especially cf. Vowler for Fowler. The genitive of Vowle is Vowles ; cf. Brooks for Brook, or Williams for William. (2) Bapt. 'the son of Voel,' an ancient Welsh personal name. Just as Hoel became Howell, so Voel has become Vowell. It is probable that, so far as Vowell is concerned, (2) is the chief parent.

Walter le Fowel, co. Oxf., 1273. A.
Matthew le Fowel, co. Oxf., ibid.
John le Fouel, co. Oxf., ibid.
Nicholas le Foghele, c. 1300. M.
1578. William Vouell, co. Pembroke : Reg. Univ. Oxf. vol. ii. pt. ii. p. 83.

1586. George Voyell, co. Pembroke : ibid. p. 153.
1609. William Voile, co. Hereford : ibid. p. 308.
1608. Buried — Thomas Vowell, the father of John Vowell, *poulter*, dwelling in Gratious (Gracechurch) streete : St. Peter, Cornhill, i. 163.
1620. Frauncis, the sonne of Allexander Brounescome and Effym his wife, brought a bead at Mr. Vowelles howse : ibid. p. 68.
London, 0, 0, 2, 0 ; MDB. (co. Somerset), 0, 0, 29, 2.

Vowler, Voller.—Occup. 'the fowler.' A West-country surname, just where we should expect to find it ; cf. Vidler for Fidler. v. Vidler for other instances of *v* for *f* ; but some from a Somersetshire Roll may be quoted :

John Vox (Fox), co. Soms., 1 Edw. III : Kirby's Quest, p. 93.
Stephen le Vryc (Fry), co. Soms., 1 Edw. III : ibid. p. 171.
John le Vreynch (French), co. Soms., 1 Edw. III : ibid. p. 230.
Raph Vouler, co. Bucks, 1273. A.
John le Voulere, C. R., 20 Edw. II. pt. ii.
Edward le Vowelar, co. Soms., 1 Edw. III : Kirby's Quest, p. 256.

The variant Voller occurs in the Oxford Directory (1896). It is found in church registers.

1761. Married — John Voller and Dorothy Hanson : St. Geo. Han. Sq. i. 104.
MDB. (co. Devon), 4, 0 ; Oxford, 0, 1.

Vyner.—Occup. ; v. Viner.

Vyvyan ; v. Vivian.

W

Wace. — Bapt. 'the son of Wace,' a long-forgotten personal name, found at first in the Eastern counties, on the sea border.

Wacius fil. Robert, co. Linc., 1273. A.
Geoffrey Wace, co. Norf., ibid.
Philip Wase, co. Norf., ibid.
Wacius fil. Huberti, co. Linc., ibid.
John Wason, co. Soms., 1 Edw. III : Kirby's Quest, p. 239.
Johannes Wase, 1379 : P.T. Yorks. p. 145.
1568. Leonard Waice, or Wace : Reg. Univ. Oxf. vol. ii. pt. ii. p. 29.
London, 2 ; Crockford, 4.

Wackett, Waggett, Weggett.—? Bapt. 'the son of Waket' (?). Whatever be the origin, Waggett and Weggett must be considered as simple variants ; cf. Slagg and Slack.

Henry Waket, co. Linc., 1273. A.
Hugh Waket, co. Berks, ibid.
Ralph Waket, co. Linc., ibid.
1581. John Waggatt, or Waggotte (co. Surrey) : Reg. Univ. Oxf. vol. ii. pt. ii. p. 110.
In 1635 Thomas Waggitt, aged 17, sailed in the Thomas and John, for Vir-

---

ginia : Hotten's Lists of Emigrants, p. 85.
1731. Married — Thomas Pepper and Mary Wackkett : St. Geo. Chap. Mayfair, p. 322.
1742. Bapt.—William Thomas Wagget : ibid. p. 4.
London, 3, 6, 0 ; Boston (U.S.), 0, 1, 1.

Waddecar, Waddacor, Waddicar.—Local, 'of Wedacre,' in the parish of Garstang, co. Lanc.

'Wedicer Hall, commonly called Wood-acre, belonged to the family of Rigmaden, and in a charter concerning Cockersand Abbey, in 37 Edw. III. (1363), Thomas de Rigmayden is styled lord of the manor of Wedacre': Baines' Hist. of Lanc. ii. 534.

Willelmus ffyfe de Waddicar, 1642: Preston Guild Rolls, p. 122.
Willelmus ffyfe de Waddaker, 1662: ibid. p. 144.
Ralph Wediker, of Goosnargh, 1672: Lancashire Wills at Richmond, ii. 304.
Ann Wadiker, of Longton, 1675: Wills at Chester (1660-80), p. 276.
Manchester, 0, 1, 0; Preston, 1, 0, 0; Ramsbotham, 0, 0, 1.

Waddell, Waddle. — Local, 'of Odell,' a parish in co. Bedford. For proof, v. Odell. Waddle is a natural variant, but seems confined to America.

Robert de Wadhulle, co. Bedf., 1273. A.
1658. Married — John Waddell and Mary Saint: Reg. Canterbury Cathedral, p. 59.
1706. Married—William Waddell and Alice Ball: St. Jas. Clerkenwell, iii. 28.
1764. — Adam Waddell and Helen Elliot: St. Geo. Han. Sq. i. 131.
London, 4, 0; Philadelphia, 9, 2; Boston (U.S.), 4, 0.

Waddilove, Waddilow, Wadlow. — Personal or bapt. ' the son of Wadelief,' one of several personal names ending in -lief, dear; cf. Spendlove, Leifchild, &c.

John Wadeinlove, co. Hunts, 1273. A.
Henry Wadeinlove, co. Hunts, ibid.
Agnes Wadyloue, 1379: P. T. Yorks. p. 30.
Henricus Wadyloef, 1379: ibid. p. 241.
Robertus Wadyloef, 1379: ibid.
Adam Wadinlof, 1379: ibid. p. 120.
1564. Thomas Wadloffe admitted to be a parchment-seller: Reg. Univ. Oxf. vol. ii. pt. ii. p. 322.
1683-4. Francis Lund and Susanna Wadlow: Marriage Alleg. (Canterbury), p. 157.
1686. Thomas Halton and Eliz. Wadloe: ibid. p. 252.
London, 2, 0, 0; MDB. (West Rid. Yorks), 2, 0, 0; Philadelphia, 0, 0, 3.

Waddington. — Local, ' of Waddington,' a village and parish near Clitheroe, co. York. It is natural to find the name crossing the border into Lancashire. This surname has ramified very strongly in the Northern counties.

Laurencius de Wadyngton, 1379: P. T. Yorks. p. 284.
Johannes de Wadyngton, 1379: ibid. p. 273.

1588. George Waddington, of Leyland: Wills at Chester, i. 198.
1610. Matthew Waddington, co. York: Reg. Univ. Oxf. vol. ii. pt. ii. p. 315.
— Nicholas Waddington, co. York: ibid.
1616. Margaret Waddington, of Over Darwen: Wills at Chester, i. 198.
London, 3; Manchester, 9; Sheffield, 4; West Rid. Court Dir., 11; Boston (U.S.), 1; New York, 2.

Waddle; v. Waddell.

Waddster.—Occup. ' a wadster,' one who used woad (A.S. wád) in dyeing cloth (v. woad, Skeat). As a Yorkshire entry it may be the parent of Walster and Waltster (q.v.), found in the Sheffield Directory. The corruption would easily arise.

Thomas Waddester, 1379: P. T. Yorks. p. 285.

Waddup.—Offic. 'of the Wardrobe,' q.v. In Heyford, co. Oxf., and the surrounding districts the variants are Waddrupp, Wadrup, Wadrop, Wardrup, and Waddup. Like wardrober, one who looked after the wardrobe, a somewhat high official position.

Wade.—(1) Local, ' at the wade.' 'Wath, a ford. N.E.' (Halliwell). This surname has made such a deep impression upon our registers that there is no need to furnish modern instances. With Wade and Waythe, cf. Ford and Forth.

Henry de la Wade, co. Oxf., 1273. A.
Johannes atte Waythe, 1379: P. T. Yorks. p. 71.
Alicia de Wath', 1379: ibid.
Hekyn of Wath', 1379: ibid. p. 70.

(2) Bapt. ' the son of Wade'; v. Wadeson. But (1) is probably the source of most of our Wades.

Andrew Wade, co. Camb., 1273. A.
Rosa Wade, co. Camb., ibid.
Roger Wade. H.
Johannes Wade, 1379: P. T. Yorks. p. 162.
London, 54; Philadelphia, 40; Boston (U.S.), 67.

Wader.—Occup. ' the wader,' one who waded in the Ouse, and probably netted fish.

William de Adle, wayder, 25 Edw. I: Freemen of York, i. 6.

John le Waider, 21 Edw. I: ibid. p. 5.
Robert de Walcheford, wayder: ibid. p. 2.

This occupative term occurs frequently in the above-quoted work. Possibly the following entry may refer to the surname:

1545. William Lyghtfot and Agnes Wadder: Marriage Lic. (Faculty Office), p. 5.

Wadeson.—Bapt. ' the son of Wade'; v. Wade (2). In Domesday found as a personal name in the form of Wada (co. Dorset), Wade (co. Dorset), Wado (co. Wilts).

Nicholas Wodeson. H.
1614. Married—Tobias Waideson and Alice Graye: St. Peter, Cornhill, i. 248.
Thomas Wadeson, of Dalton, 1697: Lancashire Wills at Richmond, ii. 264.
Jenetta Waideson, of Burton, 1718: ibid.
London, 4.

Wadham.—Local, ' of Woodham,' q.v., a natural corruption.

William de Wodham, co. Norf., 1273. A.
1522. John Waddeham, or Waddam: Reg. Univ. Oxf. ii. 126.
1764. Married—John Bull and Mary Wadham: St. Geo. Han. Sq. i. 130.
London, 4; Boston (U.S.), 1.

Wadley, Wadleigh.—Local, ' of Wadley,' a tithing in the parish of Great Farringdon, co. Berks. Seemingly meaning ' the ford by the meadow'; v. Wade (1).

Hugh de Wadele, co. Norf., 1273. A.
1652. Bapt. — Ann, d. Thomas Wadly: Reg. Stourton, co. Wilts, p. 11.
1776. Married—Lewis Price and Eliz. Wadeley: St. Geo. Han. Sq. i. 267.
London, 3, 0; Boston (U.S.), 1, 28; Philadelphia, 0, 2; New York, 2, 2.

Wadlow; v. Waddilove.

Wadsworth, Wordsworth. —Local, ' of Wadsworth,' a large township in the parish of Halifax, co. York. In the parish church of Silkstone the name is variously found as Waddysworth (1556), Wardsworth (1656), Wadsworth (1666), and Wordsworth (1668, and forward). Longfellow had for his second name Wadsworth, and was on both father and mother's side of Yorkshire lineage. Query, was the poetic fire of Wordsworth and Wadsworth Longfellow kindled on the same original hearth ? The poet's family must have journeyed by degrees from the Yorkshire border, across Westmoreland, into Cumberland, where, at Cockermouth, John Wordsworth, attorney, was agent for the estates of the first Earl of Lonsdale. His son, the poet, was born there in 1770.

Peter de Waddeworth, *sellarius*, 4 Edw. II : Freemen of York, i. 13.

Alicia de Waddesworth, 1379 : P. T. Yorks. p. 57.

1592. Married — Thomas Hudde and Dorothie Wadsworth : St. Jas. Clerkenwell, iii. 16.

1791. Married — John Hockley and Ann Wordsworth : St. Geo. Han. Sq. ii. 54.

London, 6, 3; West Rid. Court Dir., 16, 5; Philadelphia, 10, 0; Boston (U.S.), 15, 0; New York, 0, 1.

Waferer, Wafer. — Occup. 'the waferer,' a wafer-baker, also a wafer-seller. Wafer, a small thin sweet or spiced cake, 'a thin leaf of paste' (Skeat).

'Singers with harpes, baudes, wafereres, Which ben the veray devils officeres.'
Chaucer, C. T. 12413.
' Than Haukyns wif the wafrer.'
Piers Plowman, Vision, 8956.
' Yermongers, pybakers, and waferers.'
Cocke Lorelle's Bote.
'Pay to Ralph Crast, the waferer, 40s. of our gift': Issues of Exchequer, 26 Hen. II.
'Cakes of fine flour mingled with oil, or unleavened wafers': Lev. ii. 4.

Simon le Waffrer, co. Hereford, Hen. III–Edw. I. K.

Robert le Wafre, co. Salop, 1273. A.

William le Wayfre. J.

John the Wafferer, co. Glouc., 1290 : Household Exp., Bishop Swinfield, Cam. Soc., p. 149.

Lambert le Wafrer, Close Roll, 10 Edw. II.

Theobald Wayferer, co. York. W. 2.

1618. Married — William Lovitt and Ann Wafer : St. Jas. Clerkenwell, iii. 46.

1638. Buried—Mr. Edward Wayferrer : St. Michael, Cornhill, p. 235.

1667. Myrth Waferer, of Winchester, D.D., and Mrs. Eliz. Wroth, of Blenden Hall, Bexley, Kent : Marriage Lic. (Canterbury), p. 141.

I do not find any existing examples in England, but I doubt not they exist. Perhaps Weaver has absorbed this surname.

Philadelphia, 0, 5.

Wager.—Occup. 'the wager,' one who paid or was paid by fixed wages (?); cf. Tasker.

Willelmus Wagur et Cecilia, uxor, *smyth*, 1379: P. T. Yorks. p. 116.

Margareta Wagur, 1379 : ibid.

1603. Buried—John Wager, *a poor man* : St. Jas. Clerkenwell, iv. 76.

1614. Married — Edward Wager to Margret Congrie: St. Peter, Cornhill, i. 248.

London, 3; Philadelphia, 6; New York, 4.

Wagg. — (1) ? Nick. probably connected with *wag*, to move from side to side, as in wag-tail; v. Wagstaff, Wagspear, &c. (2) Local, 'at the wagg,' probably a wall (v. *waghe*, Halliwell) ; cf. Wall.

John Wagge, co. York, 1273. A.

Robert Wagge, co. Linc., ibid.

Robert le Wag, co. Oxf., ibid.

William Wag, co. Oxf., ibid.

Robert atte Wagge, co. Soms., 1 Edw. III : Kirby's Quest, p. 195.

Henry atte Wagge, co. Soms., 1 Edw. III : ibid.

1607. Buried — Thomasen, d. David Wagg : St. Jas. Clerkenwell, iv. 99.

1720. Bapt.—Mary, d. Edward Wagg : ibid. ii. 122.

London, 3; New York, 1; Boston (U.S.), 1.

Waggett ; v. Wackett.

Waghorn, Waghorne.—Nick. 'Waghorn'; v. Shakespear; cf. Wagspear and Wagstaff.

John Waghorne, C. R., 17 Ric. II.

John Waghorne, C. R., 9 Hen. IV.

1736. Married — William Lane and Mary Waghorne : St. Michael, Cornhill, p. 67.

1795. Married—Daniel Waghorn and Mercy Wait : St. Geo. Han. Sq. ii. 137.

London, 6, 2.

Wagner, Waggener, Waggoner, Wagoner, Wagener.—Occup. 'the wagoner,' a wainman, a carter. Wagon, wain (Dutch), a cart for carriage of goods. Probably as 'Wainman' (q.v.) was the common English term, Wagner is generally of German importation. The following entry confirms this ;

James Waggoner, son of James Waggoner, christened at the Dutch Church, 1610 : Reg. St. Dionis Backchurch (London), p. 94.

Godemar le Waghener. DD.

John Wiggoner, co. York. W. 16.

1808. Married—Anthony Wagner and Sarah Harby : St. Geo. Han. Sq. ii. 381.

London, 14, 0, 0, 0, 1; Philadelphia, 384, 2, 1, 6, 0; Boston (U.S.), 34, 1, 0, 0, 0.

Wagspear.—Nick. *Wag* and *shake* were the two invariable verbs that went to the formation of those vigorous sobriquets by which all officious officials were nicknamed by the railing crowd. Hence Wag-spear, Wag-tail, Wag-staff, Wag-horn (for others not in nomenclature, v. Halliwell). Shakespeare having immortalized this class of names, my chief remarks will be found under that name.

Mabill Wagsper, co. York : W 1 (Index).

'Elias Gile gave all his land in Haverbrec, which William Knipe and William Wagspear held': Revenues of the Priory of Conishead, v. West's Ant. of Furness, p. 191.

Wagstaff, Wagstaffe.—Nick. 'Wagstaff,' an official who was officious ; v. Shakespear ; v. also the statement under Wagspear.

Walter Waggestaf, co. Norf., 1273. A.

Robert Waggestaff, co. Oxf., ibid.

Edward Wagstaffe. PP.

1585. Thomas Wagstaffe, co. Warw. : Reg. Univ. Oxf. vol. ii. pt. ii. p. 144.

1696. Bapt.—Ellen, d. Thomas Wagstafe : St. Jas. Clerkenwell, i. 368.

1737. Married—John Wagstaffe and Alice Littler: St. Michael, Cornhill, i. 67.

London, 21, 3; Philadelphia, 6, 0; Boston (U.S.), 2, 0.

Wagtail.—Nick. 'wagtail'; v. Shakespear and Wagspear.

Richard Wagetail. Y.

Waight. — Offic. 'the wait' (q.v.), a natural corruption. This variant led on to the imitative Weight, q.v.

1595. Bapt.—Alice, d. Richard Waight, *poulter*: St. Peter, Cornhill, i. 45.

1610. Rondulph Waight, co. Ches. : Reg. Univ. Oxf. vol. ii. pt. ii. p. 311.

1665. Buried — Mary Waight died of the plague: St. Jas. Clerkenwell, iv. 367.

1795. Married — John Waight and Charlotte Griffith: St. Geo. Han. Sq. ii. 135.

London, 6.

Wailes.—Local, 'of Wales'; v. Wales. That Wailes is a corrupted spelling can easily be proved. The family of Wales, long connected with Furness and North

Lancashire, are found described indiscriminately as Wales and Wailes.

John Wailes, of Kirkby Ireleth, 1587: Lancashire Wills at Richmond, p. 292.
James Wales, of Kirkby Ireleth, 1612: ibid. p. 293.
Edmond Wales, of Boulton-by-the-Sands, 1623: ibid.
Ellen Wailes, of Bolton-juxta-Arenas: 1635: ibid. p. 292.
London, 1; Philadelphia, 3.

Wainman, Wenman. — Occup. 'the wainman,' a wagoner, a carter. Clemens Hall, wayneman (Liber Bursarii, Eccles. Dunelmensis, Sur. Soc.). Wainmen, wagoners (Halliwell).

Henry Wayneman. F.
Hugh Wayneman. W. 3.
Thomas Wenman. Z.

Evidently a common term in its day. Wagon = wain, the earlier form; cf. Charles's Wain, Wainwright.

Johannes Wayneman, 1379: P. T. Yorks. p. 135.
Johannes Wayneman, 1379: ibid. p. 255.
1583. Thomas Wenman, co. Glouc.: Reg. Univ. Oxf. vol. ii. pt. ii. p. 132.
1587. Ferdinand Wainman, or Waynman, co. Bucks: ibid. p. 161.
1604. Bapt.—Elizabeth, d. Syr Ferdinando Wenman: St. Peter, Cornhill, i. 55.
1802. Married—Mark Wainman and Harriott Potts: St. Geo. Han. Sq. ii. 266.
Manchester, 1, 0; London, 0, 4; New York, 3, 4.

Wainwright, Wainewright. — Occup. 'the wainwright,' a wagon-maker, a cartwright. With the instance Wenwright infra, cf. Wenman for Wainman.

1568. Edward Waynwright, Magd. Coll.: Reg. Univ. Oxf. i. 323.
1577. Bapt.—Annes, d. Thomas Wenwright: St. Peter, Cornhill, i. 19.
1678. — Hanna, d. John Waneright: St. Jas. Clerkenwell, i. 283.
London, 14, 2; Philadelphia, 27, 0; New York, 8, 1.

Wait, Waite, Waitt, Wayte, Wayt. — Offic. 'the wait,' i. e. watchman (v. Wayt for a longer notice); also musicians in general.

'The waytis blew lowde.'
'Grete lordys were at the assent,
Waytys blewe, to mete they wente.'
Halliwell.
Robert le Weyte, co. Oxf., 1273. A.
Sarra le Weyte, co. Oxf., ibid.

Ralph le Weyte, or Wayte, co. Essex, ibid.
Henry le Weyte. D.
Robert le Wayte. H.
Johannes Wayte, 1379: P. T. Yorks. p. 74.
Willelmus Wayte, 1379: ibid. p. 42.
1636. Buried—Barbara, wife of Tho. Waite: St. Jas. Clerkenwell, iv. 227.

Further instances are needless.

London, 5, 20, 1, 2, 1; Philadelphia, 1, 20, 3, 1, 0; Boston (U.S.), 13, 24, 40, 0, 0.

Waithman, Wayman, Weyman. — Occup. 'the waithman,' a hunter, Scotch and North Eng. M.E. *waith*, to hunt, fish. Jamieson says: '*Waithman, waythman*, a hunter.

"Lytil John and Robyne Hude,
Waythmen ware commendyd gude."
Wyntown, vii. 10. 432.
"About this tyme was the waithman Robert Hode with his fallow litil Johne."
Bellend. Cron. B. xiii. c. 19.'

This surname was for several centuries settled in the neighbourhood of Lancaster. From this district it seems now to have disappeared.

Richard Waitheman, of Newtoun, 1566: Lancashire Wills at Richmond, i. 292.
Jean Wayman, or Waithman, of Warton, 1612: ibid. p. 303.
Thomas Wayman, or Waithman, of Warton, 1613: ibid.
Jarvis Waythman, of Carnforth, 1625: ibid.
James Waythman, chantry-priest at Cheadle, co. Ches.: Hist. East Cheshire, i. 202.
1777. Married—Richard Waithman, of Lancaster, and Jane Law: Reg. Ulverston Ch., p. 421.
1778. Bapt.—Mary, d. Capt. Waithman: ibid. p. 494.
London, 0, 2, 0; West Rid. Court Dir., 2, 1, 0; Philadelphia, 0, 4, 10; Boston (U.S.), 0, 0, 1.

Wake.—Nick. 'the wake' (?), i. e. the vigilant, the watchful (?). Hereward the Wake is said to have acquired his surname thus.

Isaac Wake was University orator in 1607. Dr. Sleep was the foremost preacher in Cambridge at the same time. James I, who dearly loved a pun, said 'he always felt inclined to wake when he heard Sleep, and to sleep when he heard Wake': Brooke's Puritans, ii. 180.

John Wake, co. Linc., 1273. A.
Nicholas Wake, co. Derby, ibid.
Thomas le Wake, co. Derby, 20 Edw. I. R.
Baldwin de (le?) Wake, co. Northampton, ibid.

1687. Married — George Wake and Eliz. Sherman: St. Jas. Clerkenwell, p. 204.
London, 16; New York, 4.

Wakefield.—Local, 'of Wakefield,' co. York.

Thomas de Wakefeld, co. Derby, 20 Edw. I. R.
Johannes de Wakfeld', 1379: P. T. Yorks. p. 222.
Willelmus Waykfeld, *barker*, 1379: ibid. p. 95.
Thomas Wakefeld, *lyster*, 1379: ibid.
1563. Married—John Cocklowe and Alice Wakefild: St. Thomas the Apostle, (London), p. 3.
1714. Married — George Roberts and Mary Wakefeld: St. Mary Aldermary, p. 44.
London, 16; Philadelphia, 9; Boston (U.S.), 25.

Wakeling, Wakelin.—Bapt.; v. Wanklyn. In addition to the earlier instances given under Wanklyn, I add the following:

1763. Married — John Wakeling and Eliz. Harrison: St. Geo. Han. Sq. i. 127.
1775. — John Wakelin and Martha Phillips: ibid. p. 252.
London, 6, 6; Oxford, 0, 12.

Wakeman.—Offic. 'the wakeman,' i.e. watchman. In Ripon Cathedral, if I remember rightly, there is a mural monument commemorating the social and official virtues of the City Wakeman. '*Wakmen*, watchmen': Halliwell.

Johannes Wakeman, 1379: P. T. Yorks. p. 203.
Jacob Waykman, co. Norf. F.
Joan Wakeman. H.
John Wakeman, bailiff of Yarmouth, 1586: FF. xi. 328.
1809. Married—James Wakeman and Ann Pirkiss: St. Geo. Han. Sq. ii. 415.
London, 2; Boston (U.S.), 1; Philadelphia, 1.

Walborn; v. Whalebone.

Walcock.—Bapt. 'the son of Walter,' from nick. Wal, and suffix -*cock*, as in Wilcock, Simcock, &c. (v. Cocks). The probable reason why this surname can scarcely be found now is because it has become absorbed into Walcott (q.v.). For a parallel case, v. Glasscock.

Edith, relict of Walekoc, co. Camb., 1273. A.
Thomas Walkoc, 1379: P. T. Yorks. p. 138.
Willelmus Walcok, 1379: ibid.
1611. Buried — William Walcock, *a poor man*: St. Jas. Clerkenwell, iv. 117.

Walcot, Walcott.—Local, 'of Walcott': (1) a parish, co. Lincoln ; (2) a hamlet in the parish of Misterton, co. Leic. ; (3) a chapelry in the parish of Billinghay, co. Linc. ; (4) a parish in co. Norfolk, a parish in co. Somerset, a hamlet in the parish of Holy Cross, co. Worc.

Savaric de Walecote, co. Oxf., Hen. III-Edw. I. K.
Symon de Walcote, co. Linc., ibid.
Roger de Walecote, co. Salop, 1273. A.
Thomas de Walecote, co. Norf., ibid.
Nicholas de Walecote, co. Linc., ibid.
Emma de Walcote, co. Linc., 20 Edw. I. R.
Walter de Walecot, co. Norf., ibid.
1625. Buried—Francis Walcott: St. Jas. Clerkenwell, iv. 166.
1639. — Mary Peplow, servant to Richard Walcott: St. Thomas the Apostle (London), p. 121.
London, 2, 0 ; Crockford, 1, 2 ; Philadelphia, 1, 4 ; Boston (U.S.), 0, 19.

Walden. — (1) Local, ' of Walden,' a well - known and ancient town in co. Essex, now Saffron Walden. A monastery at Walden gave impetus to the surname. This I have found to be commonly the case. Two parishes, also in co. Herts, have helped, no doubt, to swell the total.

Alice de Waledene, co. Camb., 1273. A.
Richard de Waledene, co. Camb., ibid.
John de Waledene, co. Bucks, 20 Edw. I. R.

(2) Bapt. ' the son of Waldron.' Naturally and easily corrupted to Waldin and Walding, now Walden.

Walden fil. Gospatrick, co. Cumb., Hen. III-Edw. I. K.
Thomas Waldyng', 1379: P. T. Yorks. p. 143.
Johannes Waldyng', 1379: ibid.
1573. Thomas Walden, Ch. Ch.: Reg. Univ. Oxf. iii. 40.
London, 14 ; Philadelphia, 8 ; Boston (U.S.), 15.

Waldie, Waldo ; v. Waldy.

Waldron.—Bapt. ' the son of Waleran ' (?). The d is intrusive. For other forms, v. Walrand. The name seems to have been fairly popular in the hereditary surname period.

Walarinus de Cartone, 1273. A.
1522. John Walronde or Walderon : Reg. Univ. Oxf. i. 25.
1600. John Walrond, co. Devon : ibid. vol. ii. pt. ii. p. 245.
1603. Francis Waldron, co. Soms.: ibid. p. 265.

1730. Bapt.—Sarah, d. William Waldron: St. Mary Aldermary (London), p. 125.
London, 6 ; Philadelphia, 24 ; Boston (U.S.), 40.

Waldy, Waldie, Waldo, Wilthew.—Bapt. ' the son of Waldeve.' No doubt an abbreviation, or nick. of Waldeve or Waltheof, an early English personal name. This was early corrupted to Waldew, and the present forms were inevitable. The name was common (I have many more instances) and must have left descendants. As Waltho or Waldie the name crept northwards into co. Roxburgh, and there the surname has flourished for centuries.

Waldief de Haulton, 7 Hen. II : Pipe Roll, iv. 24.
Willelmus fil. Waldief, 7 Hen. II : ibid.
Waldeve fil. Gamel, temp. Hen. II : Hist. Westm. and Cumb. i. 345.
Waldeof, or Waltheof, or Waldew, fil. Gospatric : E. and F., co. Cumb., v. Index.
Waldeof, fil. Dolphin, Hen. II : ibid. p. 42.
Waldeof de Langthwait, Hen. II : ibid.

Almost all the instances are confined to North England.

Waldive Lagoe, 1661, Manchester : Exchequer Depositions, co. Lanc., p. 35.

Wilthew, a surname found in Newcastle and the neighbourhood, must be looked upon as an unquestionable descendant of some Walthew or Waldew.

Adam Walthawe, *spicer*, 1379 : P. T. Yorks. p. 281.
London, 0, 1, 1, 0 ; Crockford, 3, 1, 1, 0 ; Philadelphia, 0, 3, 0, 0 ; Boston (U.S.), 0, 0, 4, 0.

Wale.—(1) Nick. ' the whale ' ; v. Whale. (2)—— ? —— ? Perhaps local, as the ' Prior de Wale ' is mentioned in R. p. 828, in relation to some land in Guernsey.

William Wale, co. Linc., 1273. A.
Adam Wale, co. Oxf., ibid.
Walter Wale, co. Camb., ibid.
Thomas Wale, co. Northampt., Hen. III-Edw. I. K.
Prior de Wale, Guernsey, 20 Edw. I. R.
1655. Buried—Jone, d. William Wale : St. Jas. Clerkenwell, iv. 306.
1808. Married—Richard Wale and Ann Tringham : St. Geo. Han. Sq. ii. 387.
London, 7 ; Oxford, 2 ; New York, 1.

Wales.—Local, ' of Wales,' a parish ten miles from Sheffield, W. Rid. York. A family of this

name must have settled early on the Yorkshire border of North Lancashire. In the course of time they penetrated into Furness, and spelt their name Wales and Wailes (q.v.).

Cecilia de Wales, 1379 : P. T. Yorks. p. 118.
William Wales, of Over Kellett, 1587 : Lancashire Wills at Richmond, p. 293.
John Wales, of Cockin (Dalton-in-Furness), 1661 : ibid.
London, 3 ; Philadelphia, 2 ; Boston (U.S.), 39.

Walesby, Walsby. — Local, ' of Walesby ': (1) a parish near Market Rasen, co. Linc. ; (2) a parish near Ollerton, co. Notts.

Osbert de Walesby, co. Linc., 1273. A.
William de Walesby, co. Notts, ibid.
1764. Married—Edward Mortimer and Ann Walesby : St. Geo. Han. Sq. i. 132.
1793. — Edward Walsby, D.D., and Henrietta Bisset : ibid. ii. 98.
1815. Buried—Edward Walsby, D.D.: Canterbury Cath., p. 94.
London, 1, 1.

Walford.—Local, ' of Walford ': (1) a parish near Ross, co. Hereford ; (2) a township in the parish of Leintwardine, co. Hereford.

1572. Clement Walforde, St. Alban Hall : Reg. Univ. Oxf. vol. ii. pt. ii. p. 41.
1663. Thomas Houghton and Hannah Walford : Marriage Alleg. (Canterbury), p. 91.
1672. Thomas Francke and Eliz. Walford : Marriage Lic. (Westminster), p. 201.
1787. Married—Thomas Walford and Mary Coleback : St. Geo. Han. Sq. i. 408.
London, 15 ; Philadelphia, 3 ; New York, 2.

Walkden.—Local, ' of Walkden,' now a parish called Walkden Moor, in the ancient parish of Eccles, near Manchester.

John de Walkedene, 1408 : East Ches. ii. 335 n.
1610. Robert Walkden, Rochdale : Baines' Lanc. i. 489.
1619-20. Francis Walkeden, co. Lanc. : Reg. Univ. Oxf. vol. ii. pt. ii. p. 381.
1661-2. Simon Harker and Mary Walkadine : Marriage Alleg. (Canterbury), p. 25.
1622. Hugh Walkden, of Bolton : Wills at Chester, ii. 224.
1640. Alexander Walkden, of Charples : ibid.
Manchester, 6 ; London, 3.

Walker.—Occup. ' the walker,' i.e. fuller : ' a term applied to a fuller of cloth (from his stamping on or pressing it). A.S. *wealcere* (Skeat). For a curious fem. suffix, v. Walkster.

'Cloth that cometh fro the wevyng
Is nought comely to wear
Til it be fulled under foot.'
Piers Plowman.

An Elizabethan statute speaks of 'cloth-fuller, otherwise called Tucker, or Walker' (5 Eliz. c. 4. 23).

'Of William Reynolds, *walker*, for half a pewe with Edward Doughtie,3s.4d.: Churchwardens' Expenses, Ludlow,p.154.

In the Chester Play, 1339, the weavers and walkers marched together (Ormerod's Hist. Cheshire, i. 300).

Geoffrey le Walkare, London, 1273. A.
Peter le Walkar, co. Glouc., 20 Edw. I. R.
Ralph le Walkere. T.
Johanna Walkar, 1379: P. T. Yorks. p. 159.
Robertus Megson, *walkare*, 1379: P. T. Yorks. p. 159.
Robertus Welos, *walkare*, 1379: ibid.
Willelmus Walkere, *fullo*, 1379: ibid. p. 267.

No modern instances are needed. Their name is legion.

London, 307; Philadelphia, 512; Boston (U.S.), 299.

Walkington. — Local, 'of Walkington,' a parish in the union of Beverley, E. Rid. Yorks.

Thomas de Walkynton, 1379: P. T. Howdenshire, p. 9.
1795. Married—James Crump and Eliz. Walkington: St. Geo. Han. Sq. ii. 125.
London, 1.

Walklate, Walklett.—? Local. Seemingly some small spot on the borders of Cheshire and Derbyshire.

1637. William Walklate, of Charlesworth, co. Derby: Wills at Chester, ii. 226.
1653. Married—Ralph Britall and Elizabeth Walklate, Reg. Mottram, co. Ches.: East Ches. i. 135.
1796. — Richard Gallsworthy and Ann Walklate: St. Geo. Han. Sq. ii. 150.
1803. — George Walklett and Elenor Hodgson: ibid. p. 295.
London, 2, 0; Manchester, 0, 1; Oxford, 0, 5.

Walkling.—Bapt.; v. Wanklyn.

Walkmill.—Local, 'of Walkmill,' a township in the parish of Warkworth, co. Northumberland, originally the place where the cloth was thickened by the walker (v. Walker).

1394. 'Item, pro 3 bands ad walkmylne, 20d.': FFF. p. 617.
1609. Richard Wharffe for ye Walk-Mylne . . . one barne, and one little croft, £5 6s. 8d.: Dawson's Hist. of Skipton, p. 275.
Johannes de Walkmylne, 1379: P. T. Yorks. p. 41.

Walkster.—Occup. 'a walker,' a fuller, with fem. *-ster*. Probably the Walster and Waltster (q.v.) of the Sheffield Directory. Yorkshire was famous for its love of the fem. suffix; v. Slaster, &c.

Johannes Walkester, *fullo*, 1379: P. T. Yorks. p. 186.

Wall, Walle.—Local, 'at the wall,' from residence thereby. One of the walls that defended towns and cities; cf. Barr and Wagge (2).

Godfrey atte Wall, co. Essex, 1273. A.
Walter de la Walle, co. Devon, ibid.
Lecia Atte-wal, C. R., 18 Edw. I.
John of the Wall (Hereford), Pardons Roll, 6 Ric. II.
Thomas atte Walle, co. Soms., 9 Edw. II : Kirby's Quest, p. 113.
Adam del Wall, 14 Edw. III : Freemen of York, i. 34.
Willelmus atte Wall', 1379: P. T. Yorks. p. 242.
1630. John Wall, of Helsby: Wills at Chester, ii. 226.
1682. Bapt.—Richard, s. George Wall: Reg. Canterbury Cath., p. 17.
London, 34, 0; Philadelphia, 88, 0; Boston (U.S.), 91, 0; (Walle), New York, 1.

Wallace, Wallis, Walsh, Welch, Welsh. — Local, 'the Welsh,' from Wales, i. e. the Welshman. Many of the instances in the directories must be looked upon as of Scottish descent; v. Gales.

'And Rose the dyssheres;
Godefray of Garlekhithe,
And Griffyn the Walshe.'
Piers Plowman, 3124.

A regulation of Edw. III concerning wool speaks of 'merchandises en Engleterre, Gales (i. e. Wales), ou Irlande'; also of 'merchantz Engleis, Galeis (i. e. Waleis), ou Irreis' (Stat. of Realm, i. 334). Henry le Galeys (i. e. Welsh) was Lord Mayor in 1298.

Henry le Waleis, co. Wilts, 1273. A.
Roger le Waleis, co. Oxf., ibid.
Adam le Waleys, co. Oxf., ibid.
Iggelram le Waleys, co. Wilts, ibid.
William le Wales, co. Sussex, ibid.
Howell le Walsshe. J.
John le Waleis. B.
Ingleram le Waleys. B.
Mabil le Walleys. J.
'Richard Walensis, a name afterwards called le Walays and Walsh,' c. Hen. III : Baines' Lanc. ii. 400.
'Richard le Walais, lord of Litherland,' c. Hen. III : ibid.
'Richard le Walays, 15 Edw. II': ibid.
Roger Walsche, 1379: P. T. Yorks. p. 74.
Richard Walays, 1379: ibid. p. 280.
William Wallays, 1379: ibid.
Alicia Walas, 1379: ibid. p. 162.
London, 21, 65, 19, 61, 4; Philadelphia, 328, 11, 199, 58, 377; Boston (U.S.), 121, 23, 317, 428, 43.

Wallen, Walling, Wallin, Wallon. — Bapt. 'the son of Walter,' from the nick. Wal, dim. Wal-in or Wal-on. The *g* in Walling is excrescent; cf. Jennings, Wareing, &c. v. Walcock for a similar proof of the use of this nick. But it did not make much headway, as Wat soon became the popular abbreviation of Walter. The same individual is thus described:

Walter Scalpyn, co. Berks, 1273. A.
Walton Scalpyn, co. Berks, ibid.
1615. Married—John Tucker and Jane Wallin : St. Jas. Clerkenwell, iii. 42.
1622. Buried—John Wallen : St. Peter, Cornhill, i. 179.
London, 2, 2, 0, 0; Philadelphia, 8, 7, 4, 0; Boston (U.S.), 0, 2, 0, 2.

Waller.—Occup. 'the waller,' one who builds walls, a mason. A mason is still a 'waller' in Furness, N. Lanc. I constantly entered the occupation in my church registers at Ulverston. M.E. *wal*. 'Wallare, that werkythe wythe stone and morter, *cementarius*': Prompt. Parv.

William le Waller, bailiff of Norwich, 1232 : FF. iii. 58.
Robert le Walur, co. Norf., 1273. A.
Peter le Walur, co. Oxf., ibid.
Thomas Dyekok, *waller*, 1379: P. T. Yorks. p. 110.
Willelmus Goderd, *waller*, 1379: ibid. p. 31.
1608. Edmund Waller, co. Bucks : Reg. Univ. Oxf. vol. ii. pt. ii. p. 301.
1731. Married—William Waller and Honour Spicer : St. Mary Aldermary, p. 49.

London, 53; MDB. (Norfolk), 7; Philadelphia, 7; New York, 23.

Walley.—Local; v. Whalley.

Wallin, Walling; v. Wallen.

Wallingford. — Local, ' of Wallingford,' a borough and market-town in co. Berks. Oddly enough, I find no intervening references, although the surname still exists, and has crossed 'to the other side.'

Wygod de Walingford, co. Berks, Hen. III–Edw. I. K.
Symon de Wallingford, co. Oxf., 1273. A.
Bryan de Walingeford, co. Bucks, ibid.
London, 1, Boston (U.S.), 19.

Wallington. — Local, ' of Wallington.' Parishes in cos. Hertford and Norfolk, also a hamlet near Croydon, Surrey.

Ralph de Walington, co. Devon, 1273. A.
1635. Joseph Walkington sailed for the Barbadoes, in the Ann and Elizabeth, aged 19 : Hotten's Lists of Emigrants, p. 70.
— William Wallington sailed for Virginia in the Transport, aged 32 : ibid. p. 101.
1668. Married—Peeter Grin and Margarett Wallington : St. Jas. Clerkenwell, p. 149.
1743. Buried—T. Wallington : St. Mary Aldermary, p. 226.
1749. Married—John Smith and Mary Wallington : St. Geo. Chap. Mayfair, p. 154.
London, 10 ; Philadelphia, 8.

Wallis; v. Wallace.

Wallraven, Walraven, Walravin. — Bapt. ' the son of Walraven.' In Domesday, 'Walrauen,' co. Lincoln. It does not seem to have obtained a strong footing in England, and possibly some of our Wallravens are later immigrants from Scandinavia ; cf. Raven and Wolfraven.

Walrafnus de Muirteus, co. Camb., 1273. A.
1679. Buried — Prudence Wallraven, related to Mr. Loverow : St. Dionis Backchurch, p. 246.
1687–8. Married—Lancelott Copleston and Hakell Wallraven : ibid. p. 41.
1702. — Matthias Wallraven and Mercy Waymarke : ibid. p. 51.
Philadelphia, 0, 6, 1.

Wallwork, Wallworth, Walworth.— Local, ' of Wallworth.' A well-known Lancashire local surname, although I cannot

identify the spot. No doubt Wallworth is the proper orthography, the suffix -*worth* (v. Worth) being common in the local nomenclature of South Lancashire ; cf. Whitworth, Butterworth, Wardleworth, all places and surnames in the same district where Wallwork or Wallworth is found. Probably the first two following entries concern relatives, as they hail within a mile from one another :

1605. Margaret Walworth, of Prestwich : Wills at Chester, i. 201.
1618. Lawrence Walwork, of Crumpsall : ibid. p. 201.
1748. Married — Thomas Davis and Hannah Wallwork : St. Geo. Chap May fair, p. 122.
1777. — Stephen Wallworth and Eliz. Scurfield : St. Geo. Han. Sq. i. 279.
Manchester, 11, 3, 0 ; London, 0, 2, 0; Philadelphia, 5, 0, 1 ; Boston (U.S.), 0, 0, 8.

Walmsley, Walmesley, Walmisley. — Local, ' of Walmersley,' a township in the parish of Bury, co. Lanc. This surname is very familiar to the southern portion of the County Palatine.

1600. Married—John Walmsley and Luce Dunster : St. Jas. Clerkenwell, iii. 24.
— Alice Walmesley, *widow* : Wills at Chester, i. 200.
1608. Henry Walmsley, of Accrington : ibid.
1620. Richard Walmisley, co. Lanc. : Reg. Univ. Oxf. vol. ii. pt. ii. p. 384.
1639. Robert Walmsley, of Walmsley : Wills at Chester, ii. 227.
1746. Married—John Walmesley and Mrs. Warrington : St. Geo. Chap. Mayfair, p. 73.
Manchester, 23, 1, 0 ; London, 7, 1, 3 ; Philadelphia, 24, 0, 0 ; Boston (U.S.), 1, 0, 0.

Walpole.—Local, 'of Walpole.' 'Walpole in Mershland, co. Norfolk, gave name to this historical family, and here Joceline de Walpole was living in the reign of Stephen' : Shirley's Noble and Gentle Men (quoted by Lower).

Alexander de Walepol, 34 Edw. I : BBB. p. 722.
Henry de Walpol, Rot. Fin., 4 Edw. II.
Walter de Walepole, co. Suff., 1273. A.
William de Walepole, co. Suff., ibid.
1579. Married—Roberte Kenigame and Alice Waullpoole : St. Michael, Cornhill, p. 12.
1662. George Bromley and Margaret Walepoole : Marriage Alleg. (Canterbury), p. 32.

1666–7. William Walpool and Luce Draper : ibid. p. 203.
London, 4 ; MDB. (Norfolk), 9 ; Boston (U.S.), 3 ; New York, 3.

Walrand, Walrond. — Bapt. ' the son of Walrand.' Probably, as suggested by Miss Yonge, founded upon Valerian (v. Christian Names, i. 327). The excrescent *d* is common after *n* ; cf. Simond or Simmonds and Hammond, and the provincial *gownd* for *gown*. v. Waldron.

Waleran Venator, Domesday. B.
Walrand Clerke, 1273. A.
Walran Oldman, co. Suff., ibid.
Walerand le Tyes, co. Cornwall, ibid.
Robert Wallerond. G.
1621. William Dormur and Ann Walrond : Marriage Lic. (London), ii. 105.
1662. Buried — Eliz., d. Humphry Walrond: St. Jas. Clerkenwell, iv. 347.
Crockford, 0, 3.

Walraven, Walravin ; v. Wallraven.

Walsby.—Local ; v. Walesby.

Walsh ; v. Wallace.

Walsham. — Local, ' of Walsham,' parishes in cos. Norfolk and Suffolk.

Roger de Walesham, co. Camb., 1273. A.
Nicholas de Walsham, co. Norf., ibid.
Gilbert de Walsham, co. Norf., Hen. III–Edw. I. K.
Roger de Walsham, co. Camb., 20 Edw. I. R.
1630. Buried—William Wallsham : St. Mary Aldermary, p. 166.
1677–8. Maximilian Walsham and Ann Marryott : Marriage Alleg. (Canterbury), p. 198.
London, 2.

Walsingham. — Local, ' of Walsingham.' Great and Little Walsingham are parishes in co. Norfolk.

Reginald de Walsyngham, co. Norf., 1273. A.
1546. Walter Myldmay and Mary Walsyngham : Marriage Lic. (Faculty Office), p. 7.
1584. Francis Walsingham : Reg. Univ. Oxf. i. 369.
1614. Clement Terry and Catherine Walsingham : Marriage Lic. (Westminster), p. 21.
London, 1 ; MDB. (co. Suff.), 1.

Walster, Waltster.—Occup. (1) ' the waller ' (q.v.), with fem. suffix -*ster*. Almost all occupative names in Yorkshire took this suffix ; cf. Walkster for Walker, Slaster for Slater, Wimplester for Wimpler, and endless others. A waller was a mason, a builder. (2) Probably sometimes a corruption of Waddster, q.v.

Sheffield, 1, 1.

Walter, Walther, Walters.
—Bapt. 'the son of Walter.' This once popular font-name has left an indelible mark upon our nomenclature; v. Watt, Watkin, Wallen, Waters, and Waterson.

Baruntinus Walter, C. R., 20 Edw. I.
Edmund fil. Walter, co. Camb., 1273. A.
Walter Walrond, co. Oxf., ibid.
1598. Charles Walter, co. Monm. : Reg. Univ. Oxf. vol. ii. pt. ii. p. 227.
1663. John Walters and Grace Plumer : Marriage Alleg. (Canterbury), p. 101.
London, 43, 3, 29 ; Philadelphia, 158, 13, 126 ; Boston (U.S.), 23, 9, 24.

Waltham. — Local, 'of Waltham,' parishes in cos. Kent, Lincoln, Essex, Hants, Berks, Sussex, Hertford, and Leicester. From the instances furnished below it will be seen that several of the localities mentioned above may claim the honour of originating the surname.

Matilda de Waltham, co. Norf., 1273. A.
Maurice de Waltham, London, ibid.
William de Waltham, co. Linc., ibid.
Henry de Waltham, co. Leic., Hen. III-Edw. I. K.
Thomas de Waltham, co. Sussex, 20 Edw. I. R.
Roger de Waltham, co. Bedf., ibid.
1604. David Waltham, co. Devon : Reg. Univ. Oxf. vol. ii. pt. ii. p. 272.
1663. William Waltham and Anne Winch : Marriage Alleg. (Canterbury), p. 97.
London, 6.

Walton.—Local, 'of Walton.' There are twenty-five parishes of Walton in England. It would seem to suggest a stead or dwelling built of stone in place of wood ; v. Wall and Town.

Alicia de Walton, 1379 : P. T. Yorks. p. 302.
William de Walton, 1415 : Preston Guild Rolls, p. 8.
John de Walton, 1415 : ibid.'

The last two extracts will represent Walton-le-dale, near Preston.

1578. Married — Hugh Walton and Margaret Woulerrye : St. Thomas the Apostle, p. 4.
London, 50 ; Philadelphia, 192 ; Boston (U.S.), 29.

Walworth ; v. Wallwork.

Wanklyn, Wakeling, Walkling, Wakelin, Wanklin. — Bapt. 'the son of Walkelin.' A Domesday personal name. The *l* was gradually lost, but in the effort to preserve it, it was resolved into *n*, and Wanklyn became the later English form. Where the *l* was entirely lost, the name took the forms of Wakelin and Wakeling, which now figure more largely in our directories. In Wakeling the *g* is excrescent, as in Wareing or Jennings.

Walchelin the Moneyer, Pipe Roll, 5 Hen. II.
William fil. Wakelin, cos. Notts and Derby, Hen. III-Edw. I. K.
Walkelinus fil. Walkelini, co. Linc., 1273. A.
Andrew Wakelyn, co. Norf., ibid.
Ywud Walklin, co. Oxf., ibid.
Thomas Walkelyn, co. Northampt, 20 Edw. I. R.
Isabella Walkelyn, 1379 : P. T. Yorks. p. 8.
'Walkelyn Dennis, of Rosington, co. Derby' (living circa 1550) : Earwaker's East Cheshire, ii. 647.
Mrs. Walkling, mother of the landlord of the Hop Pole, Swanley Junction, Kent, died Jan. 13, 1887, aged 103 years : Standard, Jan. 14, 1887.
London, 1, 6, 0, 6, 0 ; Crockford, 0, 2, 0, 0, 0 ; Manchester, 2, 0, 0, 0, 0 ; Tiverton, 0, 0, 1, 0, 0 ; Philadelphia, 0, 3, 0, 0, 0 ; New York, 0, 4, 0, 0, 0 ; Boston (U.S.), (Wakeling), 2.

Want.—Nick. 'the want,' i. e. the mole (Halliwell).

John Wante, co. Norf., 1273. A.
Walter le Wante. J.
London (Court Dir.), 1 ; Philadelphia, 2.

Waple.—Local, 'of Walpole,' q.v. A somewhat curious though natural corruption.

1557. Married — Hillary Wapolle to Joane Garret : St. Peter, Cornhill, i. 223.
London, 3.

Warbleton.—Local, 'of Warbleton,' a parish in co. Sussex. Doubtless lost in Warburton ; cf. Hamilton and Hamerton.

Osbert de Warbeltone, co. Sussex, 1273. A.
Amice de Warbilton, co. Camb., ibid.
William de Warbilton, co. Camb., ibid.
1555. Married — James Caterall and Elyne Warbillton : St. Dionis Backchurch, p. 3.

Warboys, Warboise, Worboys, Worboyse. — Local, 'of Warboys,' a parish in the dioc. of Ely, seven miles from Huntingdon. The favourite and natural variant seems to be Worboys.

Alan de Wardeboys, co. Hunts, 1273. A.
Richard de Wardeboys, co. Hunts, ibid.
Persona de Wardeboys, i. e. the Vicar of W., co. Hunts, ibid.
William Wardeboys, C. R., 1 Hen. IV. pt. i.
1510. John Warboys, abbot of Ramsey : Reg. Univ. Oxf. i. 112.
1741. Married — William Nixon and Ann Worbiss : St. Jas. Clerkenwell, iii. 270.
1804. — Thomas Worboyes and Mary Ann Poskett : St. Geo. Han. Sq. ii. 314.
London, 1, 0, 7, 2.

Warbrick.—Local, ' of Warbrick,' a township in the parish of Bispham, co. Lancaster.

1566. John Warbricke, Bras. Coll. : Reg. Univ. Oxf. vol. ii. pt. ii. p. 27.

His college almost claims him as of Lancashire extraction.

Richard Warbreck, of Warbreck, 1671 : Lancashire Wills at Richmond, i. 300.
Henry Warbrecke, of Laton, 1580 : ibid. p. 301.
Robert Warbrick, of Goosnargh, 1666 : ibid.

Layton and Goosnargh are in the immediate neighbourhood of Warbrick.

1628. Richard Warbreck, of Orendall (?) : Wills at Chester, ii. 228.
Liverpool, 1 ; Bolton, 2 ; Philadelphia, 3 ; New York, 2.

Warburton, Warburtan.— Local, ' of Warburton,' a village six miles from Warrington, co. Chester. The surname sprung from this place has ramified in a remarkable manner.

1412. Richard de Warberton : East Cheshire, ii. 488.
1593. Hamlet Warburton, of Carrington : Wills at Chester (1545-1620), p. 202.
1594. Edward Warburton, co. Ches., *pleb.* : Reg. Univ. Oxf. vol. ii. pt. ii. p. 205.
1596. Married — Richard Warburton and Joane Blagrove : St. Jas. Clerkenwell, iii. 20.
1597. Thomas Warburton, of Warburton, *clerk* : Wills at Chester (1545-1620), p. 201.
1693. Buried—Thomas Warbaton : St. Antholin (London), p. 191.
MDB. (Cheshire), 24, 0 ; Manchester, 41, 0 ; London, 3, 0 ; Boston (U.S.), 0, 1 ; Philadelphia, 11, 0 ; New York, 5, 0.

Warcup.—Local, ' of Warcop,' a parish in co. Westm., three miles from Brough. Query, 'the fortified hill ' (v. Cope).

William de Warthecop, 23 Hen. III : Hist. West. and Cumb. i. 89.

1588. Thomas Warcoppe, co. Westm., *pleb.* : Reg. Univ. Oxf. vol. ii. pt. ii. p. 164.

1608. Buried—Awdry, d. Alex. Warcope : St. Jas. Clerkenwell, iv. 105.

1613. — Alex. Warcopp : ibid. p. 123.

1641. Joseph Littlewood and Ann Warcupp : Marriage Lic. (London), ii. 260.

1689. Joseph Leech and Margarett Warcap : Marriage Alleg. (Canterbury), p. 100.

London, 2.

Ward, Warde.—(1) Offic. 'the ward,' a guard, a watchman. This surname has naturally grown to great dimensions in our modern directories, and recent registers need not be quoted.

Robert le Warde, co. Oxf., 1273. A.
Simon le Ward, co. Bucks, ibid.
John le Warde, co. Hunts, ibid.
Warin Warde, co. Camb., ibid.
Willelmus Warde, 1379 : P. T. Yorks. p. 279 (a common entry in this register).

(2) Local, 'of the ward,' at the place of guard.

Walter de la Warde, co. Suff., 1273. A.
1541. Bapt. — Andrew Warde : St. Peter, Cornhill, i. 56.
1606. Buried—Peter, sonne of Thomas Ward, *upholster*, who loged att the Blacke Bull in Leadenhall Streete : ibid. p. 106.

London, 677, 0 ; West Rid. Court Dir., 64, 0 ; Philadelphia, 416, 1 ; Boston (U.S.), 227, 1.

Wardale, Wardell. — Local ; variants of Wardle, q.v.

Oxford, 1, 0.

Warden. — (1) Offic. ' the warden '; cf. *churchwarden, waywarden.* (2) Local, 'of Warden,' parishes in cos. Kent, Northumberland, Northants, and Bedford.

William de Wardon, co. Oxf., 1273. A.
Elyas Wardeden, co. Bucks, ibid.
Walter Wardein, co. Oxf., ibid.
1595. Buried—Annes, wife of Robert Warden, *poulter* : St. Peter, Cornhill, i. 144.
1684. Buried — Edward, s. Thomas Warden : St. Mary Aldermary, p. 114.
1700. Bapt.—John, s. John Wardin : ibid. p. 195.

London, 8 ; Philadelphia, 14 ; Boston (U.S.), 3.

Warder.—Offic. 'the warder,' the guard. With my first two instances, cf. *ward* and *guard* (v. Ward). A warder was generally a doorkeeper ; cf. Durward.

Robert le Gardur, co. Hunts, 1273. A.
Robert le Garder, co. Oxf., ibid.

1594. Edward Wardoure, co. Middlesex : Reg. Univ. Oxf. vol. ii. pt. ii. p. 202.

1629. Walter Wardour and Margaret Thrower : Marriage Lic.(London), ii. 196.

1685. William Wardour and Anna Sophia Rodd : ibid. p. 307.

London, 1 ; Philadelphia, 4.

Wardle, Wardell, Wardill.
—Local, (1) 'of Wardle,' a township in the parish of Bunbury, co. Chester ; (2) a township in the parish of Rochdale, co. Lanc. The suffix is clearly -*hill.*

Richard de Wardle, co. Linc., 1273. A.
Nicholas de Werdhyl, co. Lanc., 20 Edw. I. R.
Johannes de Wardale, 1379 : P. T. Yorks. p. 298.
1602. John Wardell, of Liverpool, *gent.* : Wills at Chester, i. 202.
1649. Humphrey Wardle, of Wardle, *yeoman* : ibid. ii. 228.
1649-50. Timothy Osborne and Arbella Wardell : Marriage Lic. (Faculty Office), p. 44.
1770. Married—Richard Wardle and Susan Porter : St. Geo. Han. Sq. i. 202.

London, 3, 3, 2 ; Manchester, 6, 0, 0 ; Philadelphia,13,11,0 ; Boston(U.S.),0,2,0.

Wardman.—Offic. ' the wardman,' a guardian, a warder (v. Ward and Warden). This surname seems to have found its final home in America.

1617. Eliz. Wardman, of [Tatham], *widow* : Wills at Chester, i. 202.
1750. Married—Henry Wardman and Eliz. Mulinex : St. Antholin (London), p. 155.
1779. — Jonathan Gaven and Jane Wardman : St. Geo. Han. Sq. i. 302.

New York, 1.

Wardrobe, Wardrop, Wardroper, Wardropper, Wardrupp.—Offic. ' the wardrober,' or in local form ' de la wardrobe '; the keeper of the wardrobe. O.F. *warderobe, garderobe.* The Book of Curtasye says :

' The usshere shalle bydde the ward-
    ropere
Make redy for alle, night before they
    fere.'

' *Wardrope*, a dressing-room. Yorkshire' (Halliwell). It will thus be seen that the *b* was early changed into *p*.

Thomas de la Wardrobe, co. Camb., 1273. A.
John atte Warderobe, C. R., 8 Edw. III.
Adam de la Garderobe. B.
Thomas de la Wardrobe. R.
Elizabeth Wardraper. Z.
Robert Wardropper, co. York. W. 17.

Wardrupp is found in co. Oxf. in the neighbourhood of Lower Heyford.

1570. Buried — Thomas Wardroppe : St. Thomas the Apostle (London), p. 90.
1574-5. Walter Wardroper, co. York : Reg. Univ. Oxf. vol. ii. pt. ii. p. 62.

London, 0, 1, 0, 0 ; Crockford, 0, 0, 3, 0, 0 ; Sheffield, 4, 0, 0, 0, 0 ; New York, 1, 3, 0, 0, 0 ; Philadelphia, 0, 2, 0, 0, 0 ; Boston (U.S.), 0, 2, 0, 0, 0 ; (Wardrope), 1.

Ware, Warr, Warre. — (1) Local, 'at the weir,' from residence thereby, i. e. the weir or wear. '*Ware*, a weir or dam' (Halliwell).

Ralph de la Ware, co. Essex, 1273. A.
William atte Ware, co. Kent, ibid.
Maurice de la War, co. Devon, Hen. III-Edw. I. K.
Jordan de la Ware, co. Wilts, ibid.
Henry atte Warr, co. Soms., 1 Edw. III : Kirby's Quest, p. 134.

(2) Local, 'of Ware,' a parish in dioc. of St. Albans.

Jordan de Ware, co. Norf., 1273. A.
Henry de Ware, London, ibid.
1585. Humphrey Weare, co. Devon : Reg. Univ. Oxf. vol. ii. pt. ii. p. 147.
1635. William Warr sailed to the Barbadoes in the Expedition : Hotten's Lists of Emigrants, p. 141.

London, 25, 11, 2 ; Philadelphia, 51, 9, 0 ; Boston (U.S.), 64, 3, 0.

Wareham, Warham, Waream.—Local, (1) 'of Wareham,' a town in co. Dorset ; (2) 'of Warham,' a parish in co. Norfolk.

Henry de Warham, co. Norf., 1273. A.
1583. Edward Warum (Waram), co. Dorset : Reg. Univ. Oxf. vol. ii. pt. ii. p. 130.

London, 4, 0, 0 ; Philadelphia, 4, 0, 2.

Wareing, Waring, Warin.—Bapt. ' the son of Warin.' O.F. Guarin. For excrescent *g* in Wareing, cf. Jenning for Jennin. This was one of the most popular of the Norman-introduced names, and though now obsolete, it has left many memorials. The diminutives Guarinot and Warinot remain in Garnett and Warnett, the full patronymic in Garrison and Warison, while simple Waring, Wareing, and Warren (v. Warren, 2) fill columns of the London Directory.

Fulco fil. Warin, co. Salop, 1273. A.
Symon fil. Warin, co. Hunts, ibid.
Warin de la Stane, co. York, ibid.
Guarinus de Chancy. E.
Ivo fil. Guarin. C.

1591-2. Edward Wareinge, co. Staff.:
Reg. Univ. Oxf. vol. ii. pt. ii. p. 189.
1615. William Waring, of Chorley:
Wills at Chester, i. 202.
free sadler: St. Peter, Cornhill, i. 99.
1659. Bapt.—John, s. Robert Wareing,
1661. John Waryn and Catherine
Twist : Marriage Lic. (London). ii. 41.
London, 0, 9, 2 ; Crockford (Wareing),
2 ; Philadelphia, 0, 5, 0 ; Boston (U.S.),
0, 1, 0.

Warham; v. Wareham.

Warin(g; v. Wareing.

Warinot, Warnett. — Bapt.
'the son of Waren' (O.F. Guarin),
from dim. Warin-ot ; cf. Philipot,
Mariot, Wilmot (Philip, Mary,
William). The present form is
Warnett. I had a modern instance,
but have lost it.

Robert Warinot, co. Hunts, 1273. A.
William Warinot, co. Kent, 20 Edw. I. R.

Warison.—Bapt. 'the son of
Warin' (v. Wareing). This surname is quite enough to prove the
early popularity of the Norman
font-name of Guarin. The abbreviation of Warinson to Warison
presents no difficulty ; cf. Pattison
for Pattinson.

Warinus fil. Warin. B.
John Warison. B.
Mabil Warison. G.

Wark.—Local, 'of Wark,' a
parish in co. Northumberland.

1349. Richard de Werk : Freemen of
York, i. 42.
London, 2 ; Philadelphia, 17.

Warman.—Bapt. 'the son of
Warmund' (Yonge, ii. 412) ; *-mond*
or *-mund* becomes *-man* by corruption ; cf. Osman, Wayman, &c.

Wormundus de Portu, Hen. III-Edw.
I. K.
Wormund de Bremore, co. Devon,
1273. A.
Wormund de Porremore, co. Devon, ibid.
John Waremund, co. Berks, ibid.
1602. Bapt. — Bennet (Benedicta), d.
William Warman : St. Peter, Cornhill, p.51.
London, 8 ; Boston (U.S.), 1.

Warmington. — Local, 'of
Warmington': (1) a parish near
Oundle, co. Northampton ; (2)
a parish in co. Warwick, near
Banbury.

Robert de Wermington, co. Hunts,
1273. A.
William de Wermingtone, co. Hunts,
ibid.
Henry de Wermyngton, co. Hunts, ibid.

1577. William Warmyngton, co. Dorset : Reg. Univ. Oxf. vol. ii. pt. ii. p. 75.
1779. Married — Thomas James and
Mary Warmington : St. Geo. Han. Sq.
i. 297.
London, 3.

Warn, Warne. — Local, 'at
the warn,' from residence thereby.
What this local term means I cannot say ; it belongs to the West
country. Possibly 'Warren' (q.v.);
cf. Warner for Warrener.

Jervase de Werne, co. Soms., 1273. A.
John de Werne, co. Soms., ibid.
Alex. atte Werne, co. Soms., ibid.
Roger Warne, co. Norf., ibid.
Gervase de Werne, 1 Edw. III : Kirby's
Quest, p. 280.
1607. Edward Warne, co. Glouc. :
Reg. Univ. Oxf. vol. ii. pt. ii. p. 296.
1661. Robert Browne and Mary Warne :
Marriage Alleg. (Canterbury), p. 13.
1702. Bapt.—William, son of Stephen
Warne : Reg. St. Columb Major, Corn-
wall.
1707. — John, son of Stephen Warne :
ibid.
London, 4, 22 ; MDB. (co. Cornwall)
4, 14 ; Philadelphia, 0, 10 ; Boston (U.S.),
0, 1.

Warner.—Two distinct origins,
accounting for its large numbers in
the present day—one official, one
baptismal. (1) Offic. 'the warrener.' '*Warrener*, a keeper of a
warren': Bailey's Dict. 'Warnere,
warinarius': Prompt. Parv. Warren, preserved ground or water
for rabbits, hares, fish, &c. O.F.
warrene (v. Skeat, *warren*).

Robert le Warner, C. R., 1 Edw. I.
Richard le Warner, co. Camb., 1273. A.
Jacke le Warner, co. Norf., ibid.
Eustace le Warner. T.

Langland speaks familiarly of
'Watte the Warner' as frequenter
of a tavern. '*Warren*, a place
privileged for the keeping of conies,
hares, partridges, and pheasants'
(Bailey's Dict.).

'The warriner knows
There are rabbits in breeding.'
Cobbe's Prophecies, 1614.

(2) Bapt. Warner. O.F. Garnier.
Warnerus and Warnerius (Domesday).

'Warnerus avunculus Radulfi fil.
Rogeri': Pipe Roll, 5 Hen. II.
Warnerus de Lisoriis, ibid.
Warner Buckston, co. Hunts, 1273. A.
Wariner le Botiler, co. Hunts, ibid.
Henricus Warner, 1379 : P. T. Yorks.
p. 21.

Modern instances are needless.
The directories teem with them.
I simply supply one or two quaint
spellings.

1572. Bapt.—Richard Warinor : Reg.
Stourton, co. Wilts, p. 1.
1621. — John, s. Ann Warrenner :
Kensington Parish Church, p. 20.
London, 53 ; Philadelphia, 184 ; Boston
(U.S.), 63.

Warnett; v. Warinot.

Warr(e.—Local ; v. Ware.

Warren, Warrin.—(1) Local,
'at the warren,' from residence by
or in the privileged inclosure for
rabbits, hares, partridges, &c. v.
Warner.

Richard de Warenne, co. Norf., 1273. A.
John de Warenne, co. York, ibid.
William de Warren, co. York, ibid.

(2) Bapt. 'the son of Warin'
(v. Wareing). O.F. Guarin. Very
early Warren became the popularized form.

Warren le Latiner. H.
'Agnes, the widow of Warren de Men-
yngwarin (Mainwaring, i. e. the manor
of Warin), and William Trussell, junior,
and Matilda, his wife,' 1307 : Earwaker's
East Cheshire, ii. 425.
Sir John Borlase Warren, of Stapleford, co. Notts, is great great-great
grandson of Sir Arnold Waring, knighted
March 4, 1632-3, who was son of William
Waring : ibid. p. 281.

One and the same individual is
thus described :

Warinus de Engayne : Hen. III-Edw.
I. K. p. 302.
Warrenus de Engayne, ibid. p. 309.
John Warren, alias Waryng, sup. for
B.A., 1512 : Reg. Univ. Oxf. i. 80.
1583. Bapt.—Mary, d. Rafe Warren :
Kensington Parish Ch., p. 9.
London, 117, 0 ; Philadelphia, 110, 3 ;
Boston (U.S.), 100, 2.

**Warrener, Warrender,
Warriner.**—Offic. 'the warrener.'
His duties were similar to those
of the parker, forester, or woodward, all custodians of the forest,
chase, park, or warren. The *d* in
Warrender is, of course, intrusive.

Robert le Warenner, co. Somerset,
1273. A.
Thomas le Wariner, London, ibid.
William le Warenner, co. Glouc., ibid.
'John Theerles, waryner' (the Earl's
warrener): C. R., 15 Edw. III. pt. i.
For modern and other instances,
v. Warner.
London, 0, 1, 0 ; Philadelphia, 0, 0, 1 ;
Boston (U.S.), 1, 0, 2.

Warrick; v. Warwick.

Warring.—Bapt. 'the son of Warin' or Waring. O.F. Guarin (v. Wareing and Warren). The *g* is excrescent, as in Jennings.

William Waryn or Warryng: Reg. Univ. Oxf. i. 90.
1653. Bapt. — Robert, s. Robert Warrin: St. Peter, Cornhill, i. 94.
London, 1; Philadelphia, 1; Boston (U.S.), 2.

Warrington.—Local, 'of Warrington,' co. Lancaster. It were idle to furnish more than two or three examples of this familiar place and name.

Roger de Warinton, co. Derby, 1273. A.
1587. Hugh Warrington, of Whalley: Wills at Chester (1545-1620), p. 203.
1619. Robert Warrington, of Lawton: ibid.
1743. Married—John Warrington and Eliz. Lightfoot: St. Antholin (London), p. 152.
London, 7; Manchester, 7; Philadelphia, 26; New York, 1.

Warwick, Warwicke, Warrick.—Local, 'of Warwick,' the chief town of the county of that name.

John de Warrewyc, co. York, 1273. A.
Matilda de Warewyok, co. Camb., ibid.
John de Warewyk, co. Oxf., ibid.
1601. Married—Richard Warwick and Hester Thruxton: St. Mary Aldermary, p. 10.
1619. — John Baker and Joane Warricke: St. Jas. Clerkenwell, p. 47.
London, 25, 1, 1; Philadelphia, 26, 0, 7; Boston (U.S.), 6, 0, 0.

Washington, Washburn, Washburne.—Local, 'of Washbourn,' a parish in co. Gloucester; also a chapelry in the parish of Overbury, co. Worcester. According to Lower the latter place gave rise to a patronymic at an early period. As with all surnames ending in the local -*bourn*, the variants are many.

William de Wassebourn, co. Hunts, 1273. A.
Walter de Wasseburne, co. Devon, ibid.
1593. Anthony Washbourne, co. Worc.: Reg. Univ. Oxf. vol. ii. pt. ii. p. 198.
1598. Norman Washeborne and Margaret Midnall: Marriage Lic. (London), i. 254.
1599. Daniel Washbourne, or Washburne, of London: Reg. Univ. Oxf. vol. ii. pt. ii. p. 237.
1616. Bapt. — Sammuell, s. Robert Washborne: St. Antholin (London), p. 51.

London, 3, 1, 0; Philadelphia, 0, 4, 2; Boston (U.S.), 0, 54, 4; New York (Washbourne), 1.

Washington. — Local, 'of Washington': (1) a parish in co. Durham, five miles from Gateshead; (2) a parish in co. Sussex, ten miles from Shoreham.

Laurence Wasshington, 1567: Reg. Univ. Oxf. i. 266.
1588. Christopher Washington, co. Northants: ibid. vol. ii. pt. ii. p. 167.
1594. Laurence Washington, co.Herts, *gent*: ibid. p. 203.
1605. Philip Washington, co. York: ibid. pt. iii. p. 288.
1780. Married — Thomas Read and Mary Washington: St. Geo. Han. Sq. p. 312.
London, 5; Philadelphia, 47; Boston (U.S.), 18.

Wass, Wasse. — Local, 'of Wass,' a township in the parish of Kilburn, near Helmsley, N. Rid. Yorks. This is an established Yorkshire name. Probably the two following entries do not concern this name:

Nicholas Waz, co. Wilts, 1273. A.
William Waz, co. Oxf., ibid.
1748. Married—Christopher Wass and Margaret Thickpenny: St. Geo. Chap. Mayfair, p. 326.
1765. — Samuel Lane and Rose Wass: St. Geo. Han. Sq. i. 145.
Manchester, 0, 1; London, 2, 0; MDB. (North Rid. Yorks), 1, 0; (West Rid. Yorks), 2, 0; Philadelphia, 2, 0; Boston (U.S.), 7, 0.

Wasselin.—Bapt. 'the son of Wace,' from dim. Wacelin; cf. Hewlin for Hewelin, little Hew, i.e. Hugh. Wasselin still struggles on for a place in the directory.

Richard Wacelyn, 1273. A.
Andrew Wasselyn, ibid.
Walter Wacelin, ibid.
Nicholas Wascelyn, co. Suff., 1 Edw. II. R.
Andrew Wascelin, co. Norf., ibid.
1662. Samuel Wasling and Eliz. Ayling: Marriage Alleg. (Canterbury), p. 35.
1742. Married — William Hyde and Eliz. Waslyn: St. Geo. Chap. Mayfair, p. 24.
London, 1.

Watcher.—Offic. 'the watcher,' a watchman. M.E. *wacche*, a watch, a keeping guard. With the third instance (Waker), cf. Wakeman.

Ellis le Wacher, co. Camb., 1273. A.
William le Wacher, co. Camb., ibid.

Roger Waker, co. Bedf., ibid.
Peter Waker, co. Dorset, ibid.

Waterbailiff. — Official. 'Water-bailiffs (in port towns) were certain officers formerly appointed for certain ships': Bailey's Dict.

Henry Waterbailiff de Cales: Close Roll, 13 Ric. II. pt. ii.

Waterbearer. — Occup. 'the water-bearer'; v. Waterman (2), Waterleader.

Richard Waterbearer. H.
1648. Buried — Richard Randall, *water-bearer*: St.Michael,Cornhill, p. 242.

Waterfall. — Local, 'at the waterfall,' from residence thereby.

Richard de Watterfall, co. Devon, 1273. A.
Johanna Waterfall', 1379: P.T. Yorks. p. 58.
1692. Married—Robert Mathews and Rachell Waterfall: St. Jas. Clerkenwell, iii. 212.
1750. — William Waterfall and Margaret Eglestone: St. Geo. Chap. Mayfair, p. 162.
London, 1.

Waterfield.—Local, 'at the water-field,'from residence thereby. I cannot find a spot so named.

1600-1. John Waterfield: Reg. Univ. Oxf. vol. ii. pt. ii. p. 245.
1636. Buried—Joseph Waterfeild: St. Jas. Clerkenwell, iv. 225.
1798. Married — William Waterfield and Eliz. Weeke Patey: St. Geo. Han. Sq. ii. 185.
London, 2; Philadelphia, 2.

Waterhouse.—Local, 'at the water-house,' from residence thereby. Evidently many small localities were so called in various districts.

1585. Henry Waterhouse, co. Herts: Reg. Univ. Oxf. vol. ii. pt. ii. p. 146.
1591. Edward Waterhowse, co. Sussex: ibid. p. 182.
1567. Married—Thomas Waterhowse and Marie Kirbie: St. Mary Aldermary, p. 4.
1666. Stephen Waterhowse and Eliz. Cod: Marriage Alleg. (Canterbury), p. 194.
London, 10; Philadelphia, 26; Boston (U.S.), 36.

Waterleader. — Occup. 'the water-leader,' a water-carrier. Farmers still *lead* hay (i.e. carry) in Furness, N. Lanc., and in the North generally. v. Waterbearer.

William Waterleader. D.
Rogerus Devonys Waterleder, 19 Edw.
III : Freemen of York, i. 38 (Surt. Soc.).

Waterman.—(1) Occup. 'the servant of Water,' i.e. Walter ; cf. Matthewman, Addiman, &c. ; v. Waters and Waterson.

Geoffrey Walterman, co. Sussex, 1273. A.

The following occur in the roll of a small hamlet, but the nick. Wat is used instead of the fuller Water :

Walterus Nelesthorp, 1379 : P. T. Yorks. p. 210.
Robertus Watman, 1379 : ibid.
Ricardus Watman, 1379 : ibid.
Johannes Watson, 1379 : ibid.
Thomas Watman, 1379 : ibid. p. 145.

(2) Occup. 'the waterman,' i.e. the water-carrier, water-bearer, water-leader.

William le Waterman, co. Oxf., 1273. A.
Adam le Waterman, co. Oxf., ibid.
Robert le Waterman, co. Oxf., ibid.
Julian Waterman, Pat. R., 3 Edw. VI. pt. iii.
1613. Peter Weterman : Reg. Univ. Oxf. vol. ii. pt. ii. p. 330.
1655. Buried — Ann, wife of Hugh Waterman : St. Jas.Clerkenwell, iv. 304.
1729. Married — Joseph Bull to Anne Waterman : St. Mary (London), p. 48.
London, 6 ; West Rid. Court Dir., 2 ; Sheffield, 2 ; Philadelphia, 26 ; New York, 38.

Watermill.—Local, 'at the water-mill,' from residence thereby.

Reginald de Watermill,co. Northampt., 20 Edw. I. R.
1692. Married — John Monke and Sarah Watermill : St. Jas. Clerkenwell, iii. 212.

Waters, Waterson. — Bapt. the son of Walter.' M.E. Water, O.F. Wauter and Watier.

' My name is Walter Whitmore.
How now ! why start'st thou ? what ! doth death affright ?
Suffolk. Thy name affrights me, in whose sound is death.
A cunning man did calculate my birth,
And told me that by *Water* I should die.'
2 Henry VI, Act iv. sc. 1, ll. 31-5.

' The account of Wattare Taylor and Wyllyam Partrynge, benge churchewardens ' : Churchwardens' Accounts, Ludlow, 1541, Cam. Soc., p, 6.
Wauter de Cornwaille, 1313. M.
Alicia Wartson, 1379 : P. T. Yorks. p. 160.
Johannes Wauterson, 1379 : ibid. p. 226.
William Watterson, 1495, co. York. W. 11.

John Waterson, co. York. W. 16.
1579. Judith, d. of Water Arksone, *stranger* : St. Dionis Backchurch (London), p. 84.
1563. Bapt. — William, son of Water Lancaster : St. Antholin (London), p. 15.
— Buried — Water Right, servant to Ric. Clarke : ibid.
1588. Margaret Watterson, of Cartmell : Lancashire Wills at Richmond, i. 303.
1607. Married — Edward Waterson and Jane Harrison : St. Michael, Cornhill, p. 18.
London, 39, 0 ; Philadelphia, 93, 3 ; Boston (U.S.), 75, 2.

Watford.—Local, 'of Watford' : (1) a parish in co. Hertford ; (2) a parish in co. Northampton, near Daventry.

Eustace de Watforde, co. Northampt., 1273. A.
Walter de Wateford, London, ibid.
1621. Robert Watford and Ellen Ruddeford : Marriage Lic. (London), ii. 100.
1748. Married — Thomas Hains and Martha Watford : St. Geo. Chap. Mayfair, p. 104.
London, 3 ; Philadelphia, 1.

Watkin, Watkins, Watkinson, Watkiss.—Bapt. 'the son of Walter,' nick. Wat, dim. Watkin. Watkiss is a corruption of Watkins, as Perkiss is of Perkins ; cf. the curious Popkiss for Hopkins. Watkin, which is still familiar in Wales, was a general favourite throughout England in the hereditary surname period.

Watkin, son of Henry Balistarius : Wardrobe Account, 36 Hen. III. 1/5.
Thomas ap-Watkin. B.
Watkynge Llooyde : Visit. Gloucester, 1623, p. 104.
1547. Bapt. — Jane Watkinnes : St. Peter, Cornhill, i. 4.
1580. Edward Watkinson, co. York : Reg. Univ. Oxf. vol. ii. pt. ii. p. 92.
1594. Edward Watkine, co. York : ibid. p. 204.
1662. Thomas Watkys : Preston Guild Rolls, p. 155.
1700. Married — Henry Watkinson and Mary Clarke : St. Peter, Cornhill, ii. 63.
London, 0, 91, 5, 3 ; Philadelphia, 10, 46, 3, 0 ; Boston (U.S.), 1, 30, 0, 0.

Watling.—(1) Bapt. 'the son of Watelin,' from Walter, nick. Wat, dim. Watelin, and with excrescent *g* Watling ; cf. Hewling for Hew-elin. (2) Local, ' of Wateling,' some locality. probably in co. Suffolk.

Geoffrey Wateling, co. Norf., 1273. A.
John de Wateling, co. Suff., ibid.
1639-40. Abraham Watling and Katherine Clances : Marriage Lic. (London), ii. 249.
1689. Bapt. — Robert Wattlin : St. Mary Aldermary (London), p. 109.
London, 13 ; New York, 1.

Watmough, Watmuff, Whatmore, Whatmough. — Nick. 'Wat's brother-in-law,' i.e. the brother-in-law of Walter, familiarly Wat. A very interesting North-English surname of a small but distinct class (v. Muff and Hitchmough) compounded of the Christian name and *maghe* or *mauf*, probably in general a brother-in-law, though other relationships are included. ' Maug, a brother-in-law. North E.' (Halliwell). ' Mauf, Maugh, or Meaugh, a brother-in-law' (Brockett). 'Mow, husbondys syster, or wyfys systyr, or syster-in-lawe' (Prompt. Parv.). ' Mauf denotes a brother-in-law. N. of E.' (Grose). 'A.S. *mæg* or *mag*, the guttural sound being changed into that of *f*, as in laugh' (Jamieson). Only a few of these compounds have come down to us in the form of surnames, Watmough and its variants being the prominent instance. The Yorkshire Poll Tax, however, has several others, which although now obsolete are uncontrovertible evidence of the former familiarity of such titles.

William Barnmawe, the child's brother-in-law, co. York, 1273. A.

With the above we must cf. the Yorkshire Barnfather (the child's father).

Cf. also Robert Susannemagh, Fines Roll, 10 Edw. I.
Johannes Elysmagh (Ellis's brother-in-law) : P. T. Yorks. p. 272.
Willelmus Hudmagh (Richard's brother-in-law) : ibid. p. 251.
Ricardus Gepmouth (Geoffrey's brother-in-law) : ibid. p. 114.
Johannes Tailliourmoghe (the tailor's brother-in-law), ibid. p. 283.

Coming to Watmough we find :

Robertus Watmaghe (Walter's brother-in-law) : ibid. p. 287.

Later we find it as Watmouth (now Watmuff) :

Myles Watmough, vicar of Medomsley, 1582 : DDD. ii. 287.

Hugo Watmouth, rector of Thornton-in-Craven,1599 : Whitaker's Craven, p.120.

The modern variant Whatmough is imitative. With this class of surname cf.

William Gamelstepsone (the stepson of Gamel), 25 Edw. I : BBB. p. 544.

Henricus Parson-cosyn, 1379 : P. T. Yorks. p. 91.

Thomas Viker-cosyn, 1379 : P. T. Yorks. p. 226.

1581. Hugh Watmoughe, co. York : Reg. Univ. Oxf. vol. ii. pt. ii. p. 114.

I am glad to find that this most interesting North-country name has reached America.

West Rid. Court Dir., 2, 2, 1, 0 ; Huddersfield, 4, 0, 0, 0 ; Manchester, 2, 0, 0, 3 ; Philadelphia, 6, 0, 1, 0.

Watt, Watts, Watson, Wattson.—Bapt. 'the son of Walter,' from nick. Wat. Walter being one of the great fontal names of the 13th and 14th centuries, and Wat being the popular nick., it can scarcely be a matter for surprise that Watts and Watson are two of our most familiar surnames. They are confined to no particular district. There is no need to quote from modern registers. Everybody has a friend or acquaintance bearing one or other of the above forms.

William Wattes, co. Oxf., 1273. A.

John Wattessone, C. R., 12 Edw. III. pt. iii.

Johannes Watson, 1379 : P. T. Yorks. p. 144.

Alicia Wat-wyf, 1379 : ibid. p. 92.

Johannes Wattson', 1379 : ibid. p. 279.

Johannes Watte, 1379 : ibid. p. 159.

1598. Married—Thomas Chamberlaine and Jane Wattes : St. Mary Aldermary, p. 9.

London, 13, 107, 212, 1 ; Philadelphia, 57, 61, 339, 7 ; Boston (U.S.), 15, 59, 207, 0.

Watters.—Bapt. A variant of Waters, q.v. Similarly Watterson was a variant of Waterson.

1791. Married — Joseph Watters and Deborah Perry : St. Geo. Han. Sq. ii. 60.

London, 3 ; Philadelphia, 6 ; Boston (U.S.), 5.

Waud.—Local, 'of the wood.'

Thomas de la Waude, co. Bucks, 1273. A.

1793. Married — John Sievier and Francis Waud : St. Geo. Han. Sq. ii. 102. London, 8.

Waugh.—?——. This name is occasionally found in co. Cumb., especially in the neighbourhood of Wigton. Probably it is of Scotch descent, having crossed the Border. Mr. Lower says (Patr. Brit. p. 374), 'The Waughs of Help, co. Roxburgh,held these lands from the 13th to the 17th century.' In this case the name does not come within the scope of this dictionary.

Willelmus Wahh, 1379 : P. T. Yorks. p. 26.

1696-7 Adam Runciman and Jane Waugh : Marriage Lic. (London), ii. 320.

1699. Dr. John Waugh and Eliz. Fiddes: ibid. p. 325.

London, 11 ; Philadelphia, 13 ; Boston (U.S.), 18.

Way, Waye.—Local, 'at the way' (M.E. wey), from residence by the wayside ; cf. Lane, and v. Ridgway.

John ate Wey, co. Camb., 1273. A.

Robert de le Weye, co. Devon, ibid.

Thomas de la Weye, co. Kent, ibid.

1584. John Weaye, co. Somerset : Reg. Univ. Oxf. vol. ii. pt. ii. p. 134.

1605. Henry Waie, or Waye, co. Dorset : ibid. p. 280.

1637. Married — William Way and Eliz. Harris : St. Jas. Clerkenwell, iii. 68.

London, 16, 1 ; Philadelphia, 32, 0 ; Boston (U.S.), 13, 0.

Waygood.—Bapt. 'the son of Wigod' ; v. Wiggett, and cf. Wayman for Wyman, and Waymark for Wymark.

1623. Buried—Thomas Waygood, free of the Cookes (buried by night) : St. Peter, Cornhill, i. 181. London, 1.

Wayland, Waylen, Weyland.—Local, 'of Wayland,' a hundred in the county of Norfolk. There is no evidence in favour of a personal origin, although Wayland was familiar to legendary history. But v. Welland.

(Ballivus Hundred) de Wayland, co. Norf., 1273. A. i. 439.

Thomas de Weyland, or Waylaunde, co. Suff., 1273. A.

Richard de Weylaund, co. Suff., ibid.

Nicholas Weylond, co. Norf., ibid.

Rither de Wayland, co. York, 20 Edw. I. R.

Hubert de Weylaund, co. Suff., ibid.

1622. William Flookes and Eliz. Wayland : Marriage Lic. (London), ii. 112.

1660. Married — Mark Weyland and Mary Underwood : St. Jas. Clerkenwell, iii. 158.

1741. Bapt. — John, s. Frederic and Susanna Weiland : ibid. ii. 257.

1770. Married — Swithin Waylen and Maria Jeanetta Alt : St. Geo. Han. Sq. i. 203.

London, 3, 2, 0 ; MDB. (co. Suff.), 2, 0, 0 ; (co. Norfolk) 1, 0, 0 ; Philadelphia, 2, 1, 3 ; Boston (U.S.), 5, 0, 0.

Wayman.—(1) Bapt. ; v. Wyman. (2) Occup. ; v. Waithman.

Waymark ; v. Wymark.

Wayt, Wayte.—Official, 'the wait,' i.e. the watchman. O.F. waite, a sentinel, a guard. 'Wayte, a spye. Wayte, waker' : Prompt. Parv. Still survives in the Christmas waits. For further instances than recorded below, v. Wait.

Adam le Wayte, co. Camb., 1273. A.

Robert le Wayte, co. Hunts, ibid.

Ralph le Wayte. B.

Stephen le Wayte. T.

Johannes Wayt, 1379 : P. T. Yorks. p. 242.

Willelmus Wayt, 1379 : ibid.

1643. Buried—John Wayt, Esq., in the Chauncel : St. Jas. Clerkenwell, iv. 257.

London, 1, 2 ; Philadelphia, 0, 1.

Weakley, Weekley, Weekly.—Local, 'of Weekley,' a village near Kettering, co. Northampton.

1647. Timothy Reyner and Anne Weekely (co. Bedf.): Marriage Lic. (London), ii. 279.

1676. Thomas Weekely and Anne Bishop : Marriage Alleg. (Cant.), p. 252.

1792. Married—Thomas Weekly and Jane Brown : St. Geo. Han. Sq. ii. 73.

London, 1, 0, 0 ; Philadelphia, 7, 2, 4 ; New York, 2, 0, 0.

Weakling, Weaklin.—Bapt. ; v. Wakeling and Wanklyn.

London, 0, 1.

Weakspear.—Nick. for a poor spearman ; cf. Shakespear, Wagspear, Breakspear, &c.

William Hudde, alias Weykspere : Pat. R., 14 Hen. VII.

Weald ; v. Weld.

Weale, Weall.—Local, 'of the wele' or weld ; v. Weld.

Simon del Wele, 17 Edw. II : Freemen of York, i. 22.

1609. John Boomer and Mary Weale : Marriage Lic. (London), i. 316.

1749. Married — Lancelot Weale and Tabitha Lucas : St. Geo. Chap. Mayfair, p. 136.

London, 2, 1 ; Philadelphia, 2, 0 ; Boston (U.S.), 2, 0.

Wear, Weare, Weir.—Local, 'at the wear.' A.S. wer, a dam, a fence, a wear or weir ; v. Ware.

John de la Were, co. Oxf., 1273. A.

Robert de la Were, co. Glouc., ibid.

1665. Married — Thomas Weare and Isabella Wilkinson : St. Jas. Clerkenwell, p. 120.
1805. — Charles Weir and Mary Harding : St. Geo. Han. Sq. ii. 333.
London, 2, 2, 13 ; Philadelphia, 8, 2, 60 ; Boston (U.S.), 2, 4, 27.

Wearing.—Bapt. ; v. Wareing.
Ulverston, 1 ; New York, 1.

Weatherby, Wetherby, Weatherbee, Wetherbee. — Local, ' of Wetherby,' a market-town in the parish of Spofforth, W. Rid. Yorks. This surname has thriven better in the United States than in England. Wetherbee is an Americanism, but not entirely unknown in this country ; cf. Applebee.
Robertus de Wethirby, 1379 : P. T. Yorks. p. 249.
London, 1, 0, 0, 0 ; Philadelphia, 5, 4, 0, 2 ; Boston (U.S.), 0, 0, 6, 48.

Weatherhead, Wetherherd, Weathered, Wethered. — Occup. ' the wether-herd ' ; v. Herd, and cf. Coward, Stoddart, Oxnard, Calvert, &c. The wether-herd was a tender of rams. The change of the suffix -herd into -head was a natural one, and is now all but universal.
John le Wetherhurde, co. Soms., 1 Edw. III : Kirby's Quest, p. 218.
John Wetherhird. O.
Johannes Wetherhyrd, faber, 1379 : P. T. Yorks. p. 290.
Thomas Jonson Wetherhird (i.e. Thomas, the son of John Wetherherd), 1379 : ibid.
Agnes Wederhead, of Hornby, 1580 : Lancashire Wills at Richmond, i. 304.
1583-4. William Smithe, yeoman, and Joan Wetherhedd : Marriage Lic. (London), i. 128.
1618. Edward Wethered, co. Oxf. : Reg. Univ. Oxf. vol. ii. pt. ii. p. 372.
1633. Bapt. — Mary, d. Nicholas Wetherhead : St. Michael, Cornhill, p. 123.
London, 3, 0, 0, 0 ; Philadelphia, 0, 1, 0, 0 ; New York, 1, 0, 1, 1.

Weatherhog, Weatherhogg. —Nick. ' the wether-hog.' ' A male, or heder-hog. Also a surname in the county. Linc.' (Halliwell) ; cf. Hoglamb, an early Lincolnshire surname.
MDB. (co. Lincoln), 1, 6 ; London, 0, 1.

Weaver.—Occup. ' the weaver.' Webster, with the fem. suffix -ster as in spinster, was so much more popular that Weaver has not pushed its way into the directories so successfully as might have been expected. But in America it has prospered wonderfully. The simple Webb (q.v.) also took from the success of this name.
1522. George Wever : Reg. Univ. Oxf. i. 129.
1585. Thomas Weaver, of Wettenhall, gent. : Wills at Chester, i. 204.
1610. Married — Henrie Planncon, Dutchman, and Margrett Weaver : St. Peter, Cornhill, i. 247.
1646. Cecilia Weever, of Warrington, widow : Wills at Chester, ii. 230.
Nicholas Weever, of Goosnargh, 1670 : Lancashire Wills at Richmond, ii. 305.
London, 21 ; Philadelphia, 112 ; Boston (U.S.), 22.

Webb, Webbe.—Occup. ' the webbe,' i.e. a weaver. M.E. webbe ; A.S. webba.

' My wife was a webbe,
And woolen cloth made.'
Piers Plowman.
' An haberdasher, and a carpenter,
A webbe, a deyer, and a tapiser.'
Chaucer, C. T. 363-4.

This surname does not require any modern instances. The directories teem with representatives. v. Weaver and Webster.
Adam le Webbe, co. Essex, 1273. A.
Elyas le Webbe, co. Bucks, ibid.
Roger le Webbe. B.
Simon le Webbe. N.
Robert le Webbe, co. Soms., 1327 : Tax Roll.
Johannes Wybbe, 1379 : P. T. Yorks. p. 67.
1603. Nicholas Webbe, of Chester : Wills at Chester, i. 204.
1623. William Webb, of Chester : ibid. ii. 230.
London, 210, 3 ; Oxford, 33, 0 ; Philadelphia, 125, 0 ; Boston (U.S.), 61, 0.

Webber.—Occup. ' the webster,' a webb, a webster, a weaver.
' Coryers, cordwayners, and cobelers, Gyrdelers, forborers, and webbers.'
Cocke Lorelle's Bote.
The popular form webster ousted webber to a certain extent at an early date.
Robert le Webber. B.
Clarice le Webbere. B.
1524. John Webber and Eliz. Letyll : Marriage Lic. (London), i. 4.
1577. Matthew Webber, co. Cornwall : Reg. Univ. Oxf. vol. ii. pt. ii. p. 75.
1603. Buried — Freze Webber, a poor woman : St. Jas. Clerkenwell, iv. 69.

1658. Buried — Thomas Webber : St. Michael, Cornhill, p. 250.
London, 45 ; Philadelphia, 10 ; Boston (U.S.), 91.

Webster.—Occup. ' the webster,' a cloth weaver, lit. feminine of Webb or Webber, a weaver.
John le Webestere, co. Norf., 1273. A.
Alicia Wryght, huswyfe, webster, 1379 : P. T. Yorks. p. 66.
Robertus Webester, webster, 1379 : ibid. p. 99.
Willelmus Webester, webster, 1379 : ibid.
John le Webstere. G.
1575. Buried — Eliz. Webster : Kensington Parish, p. 88.
London, 68 ; MDB. (West Rid. Yorks), 26 ; Philadelphia, 86 ; Boston (U.S.), 124.

Weddell, Weddle, Wedell. —Local, ' of Wedhill.' I cannot find the spot. Weddle is the usual variant in these cases ; cf. Windle for Windhill, or Pickles for Pickhills.
Walter de Wedhulle, co. Wilts, 1273. A.
1680. John Weddell and Jane Jones : Marriage Lic. (London), ii. 302.
1745. Married — George Weddel and Mary Gibson : St. Geo. Chap. Mayfair, p. 48.
1778. Married—William Weddle and Betty Windmill : St. Geo. Han. Sq. i. 286.
London, 1, 1, 0 ; Philadelphia, 2, 0, 3 ; New York, 0, 3, 0.

Weddicombe ; v. Widdicombe.

Wedge ; v. Wegg.

Wedgwood, Wedgewood.— Local, ' of Wedgewood,' a township in the parish of Wolstanton, three miles from Burslem, co. Staff. The surname is still familiar to the county, and has become historic.
1592. William Wedgwood, co. Warw. : Reg. Univ. Oxf. vol. ii. pt. ii. p. 191.
1621. John Wegewood, co. Staff. : ibid. p. 395.
1658. Buried — Leonard Wedgwood : St. Jas. Clerkenwell, iv. 323.
1753. Married — Robert Goodall and Mary Wedgewood : St. Geo. Chap. Mayfair, p. 263.
1795. — Richard Wedgewood and Jane Evans : St. Geo. Han. Sq. ii. 127.
London, 2, 0 ; MDB. (co. Stafford), 4, 0 ; Boston (U.S.), 0, 5.

Wedlake, Wedlock.—? Local. Lower, quoting Ferguson, says, ' from an old German personal name Widolaic'(Patr. Brit. p. 375). I find no trace of this name on

English soil. Wedlock is evidently imitative.

1593. John Widlocke, vicar of Acton, co. Glouc. : Atkyns' Hist. Glouc., p. 105.
1690. Married—Richard Bedford and Alice Wedlock : St. Jas. Clerkenwell, iii. 207.
1740. Buried — Joseph Wedlock, a German : St. Dionis Backchurch, p. 308.
1744. Married — Richard Warburton and Eliz. Wedlock : St. Geo. Chap. Mayfair, p. 34.
London, 4, 0 ; MDB. (co. Devon), 0, 1 ; Philadelphia, 0, 1 ; New York, 0, 2.

Wedmore.—Local, ' of Wedmore,' a parish six miles from Axbridge, co. Somerset.

Egidius de Wedmor, co. Soms., 1 Edw. II : Kirby's Quest, p. 173.
MDB. (co. Somerset), 5.

Weeden, Weedon. — Local, ' of Weedon' : (1) a hamlet in the parish of Hardwicke, co. Bucks ; (2) a parish near Daventry, co. Northampton.

John de Wedon', co. Bucks, 1273. A.
Ralph de Wedone, co. Bedf., ibid.
Nicholas de Wedon, co. Notts, Hen. III-Edw. I. K.
Henry de Wedon, co. Bucks, 20 Edw. I. R.
1582. Robert Weedon, or Weeden, co. Bucks : Reg. Univ. Oxf. vol ii. pt. ii. p. 121.
— William Weedon, co. Bucks : ibid. p. 122.

The three following entries evidently relate to the same individual :

1606. Buried — Mary, wife of Robert Weedon : St. Jas. Clerkenwell, iv. 94.
1608. — Sisley, wife of Robert Weedone : ibid. p. 102.
1611-2. — Fayth, d. of Robert Weeden : ibid. p. 118.
London, 12, 17 ; Philadelphia, 2, 2 ; Boston (U.S.), 3, 0.

Weekley, Weekly ; v. Weakley.

Weeks, Weekes.—Local, ' at the wyke,' a corruption of Wykes, q.v.

1571. Married — John Weekes and Isabell Parkin : St. Thomas the Apostle, London, p. 5.
1581-2. Anthony Weekes, or Wikes, co. Wilts : Reg. Univ. Oxf. vol. ii. pt. ii. p. 115.
1618. Thomas Weekes, co. Sussex : ibid. p. 373.
1603. Bapt.—Jane, d. Thomas Weekes : St. Jas. Clerkenwell, i. 41.
1747. Married — Richard Weeks and Ann Additer : St. Geo. Chap. Mayfair, p. 99.

London, 22, 11 ; Philadelphia, 51, 0 ; Boston (U.S.), 88, 1.

Weeper.—Nick. ' the weeper,' an emotional fellow. I am afraid the surname has not survived.

John le Wepere, co. Oxf., 1273. A.
Henry le Wepere, co. Oxf., ibid.
Robert le Weper, C. R., 25 Edw. I.

Wegg, Wegge, Wege, Wedge.
—Bapt. ' the son of Wig' ; v. full statement under Wigg. There can be little doubt that Wedge is a softened form of Wegg.

John Wegge, co. Soms., 1 Edw. III : Kirby's Quest, p. 92.
Willelmus Wege, 1379 ; P. T. Yorks. p. 75.
1625. George Peirse and Joyce Wedge : Marriage Lic. (London), ii. 152.
1646. Buried — Grace, d. Robert Wedge : St. Jas. Clerkenwell, iv. 267.
1719. Bapt.—John, s. George Wegge : St. Peter, Cornhill, ii. 31.
1785. Married — Edmund Rush Wegg and Ann Manwaring : St. Geo. Han. Sq. i. 371.
London, 2, 0, 0, 2 ; MDB. (co. Soms.), Wedge, 1 ; New York, 0, 1, 1, 0 ; Boston (U.S.), 0, 0, 0, 3.

Weggett ; v. Wackett.

Weigall, Weigel, Weigell.
—Local, ' of Wighall.' I cannot find the spot, but the derivation is clear, ' the hall of Wiga,' a Domesday personal name. v. Wigg.

Katerina de Wyghehale, 1379 : P. T. Yorks. p. 269.
London, 1, 1, 0 ; New York, 0, 8, 2.

Weight.—Official, ' the wait,' i.e. the watchman (v. Wayt and Wait). This, of course, is an imitative form. Weight conveyed a meaning when the original sense of Wait was forgotten.

1610. Buried — Richard Weight, free of the Poulterer : St. Peter, Cornhill, i. 165.
1805. Married — Samuel Weight and Joyce Smith : St. Geo. Han. Sq. ii. 326.
London, 3 ; Philadelphia, 1 ; New York, 2.

Weightman. — Nick. ' the wightman,' i.e. the brave strong man. Although *weightman*, ' a weigher,' seems the natural derivation, we are on much safer ground in referring it to Wightman (q.v.), as being a variant of that name.

1613. Bapt. — Eliz., d. Peter Weightman : St. Peter, Cornhill, i. 62.

1796. Married—John Weightman and Matilda Hardum : St. Geo. Han. Sq. ii. 146.
London, 6 ; West Rid. Court Dir., 1 ; Philadelphia, 20 ; Boston (U.S.), 1.

Weir ; v. Wear.

Welbourn, Welbourne, Wellborne, Welburn, Wellburn.—(1) Local, ' of Welborne' : a parish in co. Norf. ; (2) ' of Welbourn,' a parish in co. Lincoln ; (3) ' of Welburn,' a township in the parish of Bulmer, N. Rid. Yorks.

Hugh de Welleburn, co. Linc., 1273. A.
1680. John Glyn and Robert Welbourne : Marriage Lic. (Faculty Office), p. 151.
1706. Married — Rowland Welborne and Eliz. Douthwaite : St. Dionis Backchurch (London), p. 53.
1749. — Francoise Polus le Caan and Mary Wellborn : St. Geo. Han. Sq. i. 42.
London, 1, 0, 3, 0, 0 ; MDB. (co. Linc.), 8, 1, 0, 0, 0 ; (North Rid. Yorks), 1, 0, 0, 2, 6.

Welby.—Local, ' of Welby' : (1) a parish five miles from Grantham, co. Lincoln ; (2) a chapelry in the parish of Melton Mowbray, co. Leicester.

Richard de Wellebie, co. Linc., 1273. A.
Richard de Welbe, co. Middlesex, temp. Edw. I. R.
1544-5. John Welby and Eliz Mannyng : Marriage Lic. (Faculty Office), p. 3.
1574-5. Thomas Welbie, co. Linc., *gent.* : Reg. Univ. Oxf. vol. ii. pt. ii. p. 59.
1637. Married—Toby Welbe and Margret Evans : Kensington Parish, p. 71.
1791. — John Welby and Mary Ashly : St. Geo. Han. Sq. ii. 61.
MDB. (co. Linc.), 4 ; London, 1 ; Boston (U.S.), 1.

Welch.—Local ; v. Wallace.

Welchman.—Nick.' the Welshman' ; v. Wallace.

Willelmus Walesman, 1379 : P.T. Yorks. p. 272.
1564. John Welsheman and Ann Pallydaye : Marriage Lic. (London), i. 29.
1621. Thomas Welchman, of Samlesbury : Wills at Chester, ii. 231.
1627. William Welshman, of Mollington : ibid.
1638. Thomas Walchman, of Blackburn, *woollen-webster* : ibid. p. 225.
Edward Welchman, Archdeacon of Cardigan, 1727 : Hist. and Ant. St. David's, p. 360.
London, 6.

Welcome, Wellicome, Willicombe.—(1) Nick. ' the welcome.' M.E. *wilkome.* (2) Local, ' of

Wellcombe,' a parish in co. Devon, five miles from Hartland.

Picotus Wilicom, co. Camb., 1273. A. Robert de Welcombe, co. Somerset, 1 Edw. III : Kirby's Quest, p. 235.
1584. Thomas Welcom, or Welcombe, co. Linc. : Reg. Univ. Oxf. vol. ii. pt. ii. p. 137.
1609. Married— John Willicome and Jone Lemman : St. Michael, Cornhill, p. 19.
1631. Thomas Welcome, of Dalton (Furness): Lancashire Wills at Richmond, i. 305.
London, 0, 1, 2 ; Philadelphia, 1, 0, 0 ; Boston (U.S.), 3, 0, 0.

Weld, Weald, Welde, Wold.— Local, 'at the weld,' from residence thereby. A woody or stubbly waste, a wold ; cf. Fenn ; v. also **Weale.**

Walter de la Wolde, Fines Roll, 11 Edw. I.
John atte Welde, Rot. Pat.,4 Edw. III. pt. ii.
Willelmus del Weld, 1379 : P. T. Yorks. p. 33.
1614. James Welde : Reg. Univ. Oxf. vol. ii. pt. ii. p. 334.
1632. Sir John Cutts and Anne Weld: Marriage Lic. (Faculty Office), p. 21.
1656. Married—William Kery, *kalinder*, and Roes Weld : St. Mary Aldermary, p. 26.
London, 0, 1, 0, 0 ; Crockford, 1, 0, 0, 0 ; Philadelphia, 5, 0, 5, 0 ; Boston (U.S.), 48, 0, 0, 1.

Weldon.—Local, ' of Weldon,' two parishes in dioc. of Peterborough, co. Northants.

Geoffrey de Weldone, co. Hunts, 1273. A.
Lucas de Weldon, co. Linc., ibid.
Hugh de Weledon, co. Linc., ibid.
1545-6. George Duke and Philippa Weldon : Marriage Lic. (Faculty Office), p. 6.
1596. William Weldon, co. Northants: Reg. Univ. Oxf. vol. ii. pt. ii. p. 216.
1600. Francis Weldon, co. Berks : ibid. p. 241.
London, 5 ; MDB. (Northants), 2.

Welfare, Welfear. — ! Nick. ' well fare,' an expression of good will (?). I see no reason to doubt this origin. Nevertheless, Lower writes, ' Probably from Wifare, or rather Wulpher, a personal name, occurring in Domesday' : Patr. Brit. p. 376. This, of course, was the old personal name Ulfr, coming in such local names as Ulverston, **W**olverhampton, &c. My instance is so early in its unaltered form

that I prefer my own view ; cf. **Welcome.**

Simon Welfare, co. Norf., 1273. A.
1654. Buried—Alse Welfare: Kensington Church, p. 124.
London, 1, 1 ; MDB. (co. Sussex), 2, 0.

Welford. — Local, ' of Welford,' parishes in cos. Berks, Northants, and Warwick.

Richard de Welleford, London, temp. Edw. II. R.
1606. Andrew Welford, Magd. Coll. : Reg. Univ. Oxf. vol. ii. pt. iii. 265.
1650. Married—Clement Welford and Mary Haines : St. Jas. Clerkenwell, iii. 85.
London, 6 ; Oxford, 3.

Welham.—Local, 'of Welham,' a parish in co. Leic., four miles from Harborough ; also a township in the parish of Norton, E. Rid. York. The variant Wellum looks like an Americanism (cf. Barnum for Barnham). But it is not found now either in England or the States.

Walter de Welham, co. Soms., 1 Edw. III : Kirby's Quest, p. 224.
1612. Thomas Quilche and Mary Wellam (co. Essex): Marriage Lic. (London), ii. 12.
1665. — John Wellum and Ann Warrener : St. Jas. Clerkenwell, iii. 118.
1696. Married—Mark Sayer and Anne Welham : St. Mary Aldermary (London), p. 35.
1790. — Samuel Wellum and Eliz. Butler : St. Geo. Han. Sq. ii. 47.
London, 4.

Welk, Welkshorn. — Nick. ' the whelk.' The *h* is intrusive ; cf. Winkle.

Matilda le Welke, co. Camb., 1273. A.
William Welkeshorn, co. Suff., ibid.
Philadelphia, 2, 0 ; New York, 1, 0.

Well, Wells.—Local, ' at the well.' Of course Wells, saving in particular cases, has nothing to do with the city of Wells in the West country. The final *s* is added in common with other monosyllabic local surnames ; cf. Styles, Brooks, Bridges, &c. There is also a parish Wells-by-the-Sea, in dioc. Norwich.

Gilbert de Welles, co. Norf., 1273. A.
William de Welles, co. Linc., ibid.
Hervy del Welle, vicar of Mendham, co. Norf., 1320 : FF. v. 385.
Johannes del Well, 1379 : P. T. Yorks. p. 139.
1583. Anthony Welles, co. Sussex : Reg. Univ. Oxf. vol. ii. pt. ii. p. 130.

1617-8. John Wells and Joane Vicaries: Marriage Lic. (London), ii. 57.
London, 0, 141 ; Philadelphia, 1, 144 ; Boston (U.S.), 0, 137 ; New York (Well), 3.

Welland.—(1) Bapt. ' the son of Welland.' In Domesday Welland (co. Devon). (2) Local, ' of Welland,' a parish in co. Worc.

William de Welond, co. Glouc., 1273. A.
Thomas Welond, co. Oxf., ibid.
Richard Welond, co. Suff., ibid.
1787. Married—Thomas Welland and Alice Peach : St. Geo. Han. Sq. i. 405. London, 3.

Wellard ; v. Willard.

Wellbeloved. — Nick. ' the well-beloved.' A common mode of address by prince or ecclesiastic in formal declarations. The Rev. C. Wellbeloved published a translation of the Bible in 1838, printed by Smallfield & Co., London.

Thomas Welebeloved, C. R., 2 Edw.IV.
William Welbilove. O.
1527-8. John Welbelovyd, of Feltham, and Johanna Farr of Ashford : Marriage Lic. (London), i. 6.
1596. Hugh Welbeloved, *yeoman*, and Anne Hyne, of Feltham, co. Middlesex : ibid. p. 232.
1634. Richard Wellbeloved and Helen Galfield : ibid. ii. 217.
1729. Married—Charles Welbeloved, of Thorpe, co. Surrey, and Margaret Chapman : St. Antholin (London), p. 143.
1766. — Joseph Copeland and Jane Wellbeloved : St. Geo. Han. Sq. i. 157.
London, 2 ; Leeds, 2 ; West Rid. Court Dir., 2.

Wellborne, -burn ; v. Welbourn.

Weller.—Occup. ' the weller,' one who resided by a well, and probably plied the occupation of a Wellman, Waterman, or Waterleader, q.v. (cf. Crossweller, Fielder, Crofter, Bridger, &c. Probably the last took toll for crossing the bridge).

1683. Bapt. — Cornelius, s. Thomas Weller : St. Jas. Clerkenwell, i. 303.
1756. Married—Christian Weller and Ann Poll : St. Geo. Han. Sq. i. 90.
London, 19 ; Oxford, 11 ; New York, 12 ; Boston (U.S.), 5.

Wellesley.—Local, ' of Welesley.' Mr. Lower says, ' a locality in Somersetshire.' A standard-bearer of this name served under Hen. II. The name soon became corrupted to Wesley, and only at the beginning of the 18th century a branch of the family resumed the original form. Patr. Brit. p. 376. v. Wesley and Wolsey.

Wellicome; v. Welcome.

Welling, Wellen.—Local, 'of Welling,' a village, partly in the parish of Bexley and partly in that of East Wickham, co. Kent.

William de Wellynge, co. Norf., 1273. A.
1578. Richard Welling, co. Lanc.: Reg. Univ. Oxf. vol. ii. pt. ii. p. 81.
1619. George Horwood and Anne Wellinge: Marriage Lic. (London), ii. 73.
1654-5. Buried — Eliz., wife of Nathaniell Wellen, a stranger: St. Dionis Backchurch (London), p. 229.
1787. Married — John Welling and Eliz. Wainwright: St. Geo. Han. Sq. i. 71.
MDB. (co. Sussex), 1, 1; (co. Glouc.), 0, 1; Boston (U.S.) 1, 0; Philadelphia, 1, 0.

Wellington.—Local, 'of Wellington,' parishes in cos. Hereford, Salop, and Somerset.

Robert de Welinton, co. Salop, 1273. A.
Johannes de Welington, co. Devon, 20 Edw. I. R.
William de Welynton, co. Somerset, ibid.
Johannes de Welinton, 30 Edw. I: BBB. p. 621.
1581. James Wellington, co. Heref.: Reg. Univ. Oxf. vol. ii. pt. ii. p. 104.
1583. Peter Wellington, co. Devon: ibid. p. 132.
1661. Married Richard Wellington and Eliz. Marriott: St. Jas. Clerkenwell, iii. 106.
London, 6; Philadelphia, 5; Boston (U.S.), 17.

Well-liking.—Nick. 'the well-liking,' i.e. of comely appearance; cf. Wellbeloved.

'Well-liking lips they have.'
Love's Labour's Lost, act v. sc. 2.
Alice Welikeing, co. Oxf., 1273. A.

Wellman.—Occup. 'the well-man,' one who resided by a well as water-carrier; v. Weller.

1752. Married — Thomas Rayner and Mary Welman: St. Geo. Chap. Mayfair, p. 223.
1730. — Richard Wellman and Jone Cox: ibid. p. 316.
London, 4; New York, 10.

Wellock; v. Wheelock.

Wells.—Local; v. Well.

Wellspring.—Local, 'at the well - spring,' from residence thereby. This surname has held a precarious existence for six centuries.

Walter Wilspryng, C. R., 14 Edw. III. pt. ii.
1780. Married — Thomas Wellspring and Lucy Nutt: St. Geo. Han. Sq. i. 316. London, 1.

Wellstead, Wellsted, Wellsteed, Welstead, Welsted, Wellstood.—Local, 'at the wellstead,' i.e. the dwelling or homestead by the well. I cannot find the spot. It is clear, however, that it is a West-country name. The variants are somewhat numerous. Wellstod, entered below, shows the way to Wellstood.

1585. Robert Welsted, co. Somerset: Reg. Univ. Oxf. vol. ii. pt. ii. p. 144.
1606. Henry Welsteed, co. Dorset: ibid. 291.
1608. Married — Henrie Welstod and Katharine Clarke: St. Jas. Clerkenwell, iii. 33.
1741. Bapt. — Richard, s. Richard Wellstead: ibid. ii. 255.
London, 1, 1, 1, 0, 0, 0; Oxford (Wellstood), 4; New York, 1, 0, 0, 2, 1, 6.

Welsh.—Local; v. Wallace.

Welshman, Welchman, Welsman.—Local, 'the Welshman'; v. Wallace.

Alan Walseman. R.
William Walssheman, London. X.
Lewis Welsheman. XX. 1.
Johannes Walseman, 1379: P. T. Yorks. p. 143.
1544. Buried—Davye Welchman: St. Dionis Backchurch, p. 180.
1564. John Welsheman and Ann Pallydaye: Marriage Lic. (London), i. 29.
1623. John Welshman, of Newton: Wills at Chester, ii. 231.
London, 2, 6, 2.

Welstead; v. Wellstead.

Welton.—Local, 'of Welton,' parishes in cos. Lincoln, Northants, E. Rid. Yorks.

Roger de Weltone, co. Bedf., 1273. A.
Stephen de Weltone, co. Bedf., ibid.
Hugh de Weltone, co. Oxf., ibid.
1574-5. Basil Smithe and Johanna Welton, widow: Marriage Lic. (London), i. 63.
1638. Edmund Welton and Hester Everard: ibid. ii. 235.
1796. Married—William Welton and Eliz. Sleet: St. Geo. Han. Sq. ii. 141.
London, 5; New York, 6; Philadelphia, 2.

Wend, Wende; v. Went.

Wenden, Wendon. — Local, 'of Wenden,' or Wendon. I cannot find the locality. It will

have to be sought for in the Fen country.

Peter de Wendon, co. Linc., 1273. A.
Alex. de Wenden, co. Camb., ibid.
1626-7. Isaac Downham and Sarah Wendon: Marriage Lic. (London), ii. 186.
1652. Reginald Wendon and Sicely Dennys: ibid. i. 24.
1798. Married—Samuel Sanderson and Ann Wendon: St. Geo. Han. Sq. ii. 180.
London, 6, 0; Philadelphia, 0, 1.

Wendling, Wendlin.—Local, 'of Wendling,' a parish near East Dereham, co. Norf.

William de Wendling, co. Norf., 1273. A.
London, 1, 0; Philadelphia, 3, 0; New York, 6, 1.

Wenham.—Local, 'of Wenham.' There are two parishes of this name in co. Suffolk.

Selithe de Wenham, co. Suff., 1273. A.
Hawisa de Wenham, co. Soms., 9 Edw. II: Kirby's Quest, p. 103.
1682-3. Thomas Wenham and Eliz. Upshaw: Marriage Alleg. (Canterbury), p. 119.
1788. Married — Francis Wenham, of Nevis, West Indies, and Anne Williams: St. Geo. Han. Sq. ii. 14.
London, 3.

Wenman.—Occup. 'the wainman,' a wagoner; v. Wainman.

London, 4; New York, 4.

Wenn.—Local, 'at the wen,' from residence on a fen; a variant of the Somerset Venn (v. Fenn and Venn).

Johannes atte Wenne, co. Soms., 9 Edw. II: Kirby's Quest, p. 71.
1742. Married — James Wenn and Sarah Merris: St. Geo. Chap. Mayfair, p. 29.
1803. — William Day and Mary French (witness R. Wenn): St. Geo. Han. Sq. ii. 286.
London, 1.

Wensley.—Local, 'of Wensley,' a parish in N. Rid. Yorks. Also Wensley-Fold, a township in the parish of Blackburn, co. Lanc.

1609. Bapt.—Jane, d. John Wendesley: St. Mary Aldermary, p. 70.
1625. Buried—Danniell, s. John Wendesle: ibid. p. 163.
1707. Married — Peter Wensley and Eleanor Parker: St. Antholin (London), p. 121.
London, 1; Crockford, 1; New York, 1; West Rid. Yorks, 1.

Went, Wend, Wende, Wente.—Local, 'at the went.' M.E. went, a passage. There are one or two wents, still so called, in my late parish (Ulverston). '*Went*, a crossway, a passage' (Halliwell). Literally, a small passage leading from one main street to another.

Henry de la Wente, co. Suff., 1273. A.
Stephen ad le Wente, co. Camb., ibid.
William atte Wend, rector of Scoulton, co. Norf., 1368: FF. ii. 344.
Hugo de Went, 1379: P. T. Yorks. p. 135.
Ricardus de Went, 1379: ibid. p. 134.
John atte Wend, of Great Ellingham, co. Norf., 1381: FF. i. 485.
1664. Buried — Moses Went, a youth that belonged to my Lord Bishop of London's house: St. Jas. Clerkenwell, iv. 355.
1807. Married — William Went and Sarah Brown: St. Geo. Han. Sq. ii. 371.
London, 1, 0, 0, 0; New York, 0, 1, 1, 1.

Wentworth. — Local, ' of Wentworth,' a chapelry in the parish of Wath-upon-Dearne, W. Rid. Yorks. This surname has ramified strongly both in England and America. There is also a parish of this name in co. Camb., four miles from Ely. There is clear evidence that this place has helped to swell the total.

Willelmus de Wynteworth, 1379: P. T. Yorks. p. 10.
Johannes de Wynteworth, 1379: ibid. p. 25.
Johannes Wyntworth, 1379: ibid. p. 73.
1586. Paul Wentworthe, co. Bucks: Reg. Univ. Oxf. vol. ii. pt. ii. p. 151.
1593-4. George Wentworth, co. York: ibid. p. 199.
1610. Peter Wentworth, co. Northants: ibid. p. 313.
1622. John Welbore and Anne Wenthworth (co. Bedf.): Marriage Lic. (London), ii. 112.
1677. Buried—Mary Wentworth: Reg. St. Antholin (London), p. 97.
London, 6; Philadelphia, 3; Boston (U.S.), 118.

Werry, Gery, Gerry.—Bapt. ' the son of Werry' or Gerry; cf. Warin and Guarin, Warner and Garner, &c. The surname seems to have settled down as Gery at an early period.

Thomas Gery, co. Oxf., 1273. A.
Gerri de Planastre, co. Oxf., ibid.
Warin Gery, co. Camb., ibid.
Werry de Cadamo, co. Camb., ibid.
Henry Werri, co. Camb., ibid.
Peter Werri, co. Camb., ibid.
1598. James Gery, co. Heref.: Reg. Univ. Oxf. vol. ii. pt. ii. p. 230.
1601. John Gery, co. Camb.: ibid. p. 247.

1642-3. George Gery and Eliz. Stoner: Marriage Lic. (London), ii. 269.
1808. Married — Edward Gearry and Mary Button: St. Geo. Han. Sq. ii. 389.
London, 0, 1, 0; Philadelphia, 0, 4, 2; Boston (U.S.), 0, 0, 36.

Wesker; v. Whiskard.

Weslake; v. Westlake.

Wesley.—Local, ' of Westley': (1) a parish in co. Suffolk, near Bury St. Edmunds; (2) a parish in co. Cambridge, near Newmarket. (The *t* was naturally elided; cf. Weslake for Westlake, q.v.); (3) a variant of Wellesley; v. Wolsey. Other small spots would easily acquire the name.

William de Westle, co. Camb., 1273. A.
Walter de Westleghe, co. Soms., 1 Edw. III: Kirby's Quest, p. 232.
1581. Bapt. — Margaret, d. Robert Wesley: St. Michael, Cornhill, p. 91.
1600. Thomas Westley, co. Warw.: Reg. Univ. Oxf. vol. ii. pt. ii. p. 240.
1602-3. John Westley, co. Warw.: ibid. p. 263.
1749. Married — William Williamson and Ann Wesly: St. Geo. Chap. Mayfair, p. 153.
London, 4; Philadelphia, 20.

West.—Local, 'from the West.' One who had settled eastwards; cf. Western, Westerman, and Westray. This surname is so universal that to furnish modern instances were idle.

Algar West, co. Oxf., 1273. A.
Albricius West, co. Camb., ibid.
Robert del West, 1379: P. T. Yorks. p. 208.
Ricardus del West, 1379: ibid. p. 210.
Magota del West, 1379: ibid. p. 119.
1575. Richard Weste, co. Devon: Reg. Univ. Oxf. vol. ii. pt. ii. p. 65.
1615. Buried — Joane, d. Michaell Weste: St. Jas. Clerkenwell, iv. 132.
London, 142; West Rid. Court Dir., 9; Philadelphia, 211; Boston (U.S.), 136.

Westacott; v. Westcott.

Westall.—Local, 'of the Westhall,' from residence thereby or therein.

Richard atte Westhalle, alias Westalle de Amcotes (co. Linc.), 30 Edw. I: BBB. p. 619.
1564-5. Owen Westall, New Coll.: Reg. Univ. Oxf. vol. ii. pt. ii. p. 21.
1569-70. Jerome Westall and Margaret Lewes: Marriage Lic. (Westminster), p. 2.
1703. Married — James Flintoft and Martha Westall: St. Geo. Han. Sq. ii. 92.
London, 10; New York, 3.

Westbrook.—Local, 'of Westbrook,' a tithing in the parish of Boxford, co. Berks. No doubt other and smaller localities bear the same name; cf. Easterbrook.

Richard de Westbrek, co. Surrey, temp. Edw. I. R.
1584. Mark Westbrooke, co. Surrey: Reg. Univ. Oxf. vol. ii. pt. ii. p. 139.
1628. Thomas Westbrook, of Hockley, co. Essex, and Joane Aylet: Marriage Lic. (London), ii. 194.
1741. Bapt.—Mary, d. William Westbrook: St. Geo. Chap. Mayfair, p. 3.
1747. Married — William Westbrooke and Ann Rosewell: ibid. p. 94.
London, 8; Philadelphia, 7; New York, 9.

Westbury.—Local, ' of Westbury,' parishes in diocs. Bath and Wells, Hereford, Oxford, Salisbury.

Agnes de Westbnri, co. Bucks, 1273. A.
William de Westburi, co. Bucks, ibid.
John de Westbyr, co. Southampt., Hen. III-Edw. I. K.
1649. Buried — William, s. William Westberry: St. Jas. Clerkenwell, iv. 282.
1651. — Eliz., d. Thomas Westbury: ibid. p. 290.
1748. Married—Thomas Croucher and Sarah Westbury: St. Geo. Chap. Mayfair, p. 112.
London, 3; Oxford, 1.

Westby, Westerby, Westoby, Westbay. — Local, ' of Westby,' a parish in co. Lincoln. With Westerby and Westoby, cf. Westaway and Greenaway for Westway and Greenway. The surname still flourishes in co. Lincoln as Westerby.

Johannes de Westeby, 1379: P. T. Yorks. p. 38.
1542. Buried — Robert Westerbe: St. Peter, Cornhill, i. 106.
1595. Married — John Slawter and Margaret Westabie: St. Jas. Clerkenwell, iii. 19.
London, 2, 3, 4, 0; MDB. (co. Linc.), 0, 4, 0, 0; New York, 0, 0, 0, 1.

Westcott, Westcoatt, Wesscott, Westacott. — Local, ' of Westcott,' parishes and hamlets in cos. Gloucester, Bucks, Berks, &c. *West*, and *cot*, a hut, a small dwelling, situated westward of some other dwelling or dwellings; cf. Northcot.

Ricardus de Westkote, co. Bucks, 1273. A.
Nicholas de Westcote, co. Oxf., ibid.
William de Westcote, co. Somerset, ibid.

Richard de Wescote, co. Soms., 1 Edw. III: Kirby's Quest, p. 182.

Dennys Wescott, 1593: Reg. St. Columb Major, p. 16.

1611. Bapt. — Margrett, d. Thomas Westcott, *baker*, of Cornhill: St. Peter, Cornhill, i. 60.

1689. John Seager and Ann Westcote: Marriage Alleg. (Canterbury), ii. 130.

London, 8, 1, 0, 2; Philadelphia, 32, 0, 3, 1; Boston (U.S.), 9, 0, 15, 1.

Westend. — Local, 'at the West-end' of the town, still a familiar phrase with a somewhat altered sense; cf. Townsend, Wood-end, &c.

Matilda atte Westende, co. Oxf., 1273. A.

Westerby; v. Westby.

Westerman, Westman. — Local, 'the western-man,' one from the West. Found in Yorkshire, where surnames from the points of the compass were common (v. Western and Westray). The following entries lie close together:

Johannes Westeman et Peronilla uxor ejus, 1379: P. T. Yorks. p. 115.

Thomas Westman, 1379: ibid. p. 116.

Johanna del West, 1379: ibid.

Among the householders of Wakefield in the same register are:

Willelmus de West, 1379: P. T. Yorks. p. 159.

Willelmus Westrynneman, i.e. Westerman, 1379: ibid. p. 160.

'George Westerman, blacksmith,' may be seen in my Wakefield Directory (1868).

1628. Married—John Smith and Francesse Westerman: St. Dionis Backchurch, p. 22.

London, 1, 0; West Rid. Court Dir., 2, 0; Leeds, 1, 0; Thorpe Audlin, near Pontefract, 1, 0; Philadelphia, 12, 1; Boston (U.S.), 0, 4.

Western, Westren, Westron. — Local, 'the western,' a man from the West; cf. Southern, and v. Westerman.

Henricus Westryn, 1379: P. T. Yorks. p. 124.

Johannes Westryn, 1379: ibid.

1690. Samuel Western and Anna Maria Finch: Marriage Lic. (London), ii. 312.

1735. Married—James Dolliffe and Anne Western: St. Geo. Chap. Mayfair, p. 12.

1749. — Joseph Westron and Martha Palmer: ibid. p. 149.

London, 11, 0, 0; Sheffield, 0, 1, 0; Leeds, 1, 0, 0; Philadelphia, 3, 0, 0; Boston (U.S.), 0, 0, 1.

Westgarth.—Local, 'of the west garth'; v. Garth.

London, 1; Ulverston, 1.

Westgate. — Local, 'at the west gate,' from residence thereby, probably as warder.

'And at the west gate of the toun, quod he,
A carte ful of donge ther shalt thou see.'
           Chaucer, C. T. 15023-4.

William de Westgate, co. Norf., 1273. A.

Berthona de Westgate, co. Kent, ibid.

John de Westgate, 20 Edw. I. R.

William atte Westgate, Fines Roll, 16 Edw. II.

I find no Westgates in our English directories, the name having gradually assimilated itself to Westcott, Wescott, and Westacott, q.v. The true form, however, is preserved in America.

Philadelphia, 1; Boston (U.S.), 6.

Westhead.—Local, 'of Westhead,' a hamlet in the parish of Ormskirk, co. Lanc. This local surname is still chiefly confined to the county Palatine.

Gilbert Westhead, of Ormskirk, 1590: Wills at Chester (1545-1620), p. 205.

Hugh Houghton, of Westhead, parish of Ormskirk, 1610: ibid. p. 102.

Peter Westhead, of Westhead, in Lathom, 1613: ibid. p. 205.

Thomas Westhead, of Lathom, 1619: ibid.

Lathom in the above entries means Lathom, a township in the parish of Ormskirk.

1658. Married—William Clayton and Eliza Westead: St. Jas. Clerkenwell, p. 100.

Manchester, 2; Liverpool, 5; MDB. (co. Lanc.), 4.

Westlake, Weslake.—Local, 'at the west lake,' or pool, from residence thereby. I cannot find the spot. It seems to be a West-country name. For the omission of *t* in Weslake, cf. Wesscott or Wesley.

1566. Raymond Westlake, Ex. Coll.: Reg. Univ. Oxf. i. 244.

1729. Married — Richard Perry and Sarah Westlake: St. Geo. Chap. Mayfair, p. 303.

1805. — John Nankivell and Jane Westlake: St. Geo. Han. Sq. ii. 325.

London, 15, 2; MDB. (co. Soms.), 13, 0; New York, 5, 0.

Westley.—Local; v. Wesley.

London, 5.

Westmarland, Westmoreland, Westmorland. — Local, 'of Westmoreland,' a native of that county who has gone to reside outside its borders; cf. Wiltshire, Darbyshire, &c.

Johannes Westmarland, 1379: P. T. Yorks. p. 141.

1600. Married—Mathyas Westmarland and Elyzabeth Pecke: St. Antholin (London), p. 40.

1791. — Robert Westmorland and Mary Keen.

London, 1, 1, 0; West Rid. Court Dir., 0, 0, 2; MDB. (co. Cumb.), 0, 0, 6.

Westoby; v. Westby.

Westover.—Local, 'of Westover' (v. Over and West); cf. Northover. Westover is a tithing in the parish of Wherwell, near Andover, co. Hants.

William Weshovere (sic), co. Soms., 1 Edw. III: Kirby's Quest, p. 236.

The next entry to this is:

Ivone Esthovere, i. e. East-over.

1572. William Westofer and Alice Younge: Marriage Lic. (Faculty Office), p. 16.

1602. James Westover, co. Devon: Reg. Univ. Oxf. vol. ii. pt. ii. p. 256.

1732. William Westover and Amy Ranes: St. Geo. Han. Sq. i. 10.

MDB. (co. Somerset), 3; Boston (U S), 2.

Westray.—Local, 'at the west wray,' i.e. at the west corner, from residence therein. Alike singly and in compound local place-names *wray* plays an important part in North England; v. Wray, Thackeray, Dockreay, &c.

1549. Buried — Joane Westra: St. Peter, Cornhill, i. 110.

1552. Married—Richard Westray and Joane Fullor: St. Antholin (London), p. 9.

1582-3. Edward Hill and Ellen Westwraye: Marriage Lic. (London), i. 15.

1604-5. John Westwray, co. Essex, *gent.*: Reg. Univ. Oxf. vol. ii. pt. ii. p. 279.

1666. Married — Ralph Sauidge and Eliz. Westraie: St. Jas. Clerkenwell, iii. 124.

London, 1; MDB. (co. Cumb.), 2; New York, 1; Boston (U.S.), 1.

Westren, -ron; v. Western.

Westrop, Westrup, Westropp. — Local, 'of Westrop,' a tithing in the parish of Highworth, co. Wilts, i. e. West-thorp; cf. Winthrop, Northrup; v. Thorp.

1656-7. Buried — John, s. John Westropp: St. Jas. Clerkenwell, iv. 314.
1687. Francis Westthorpe and Ann Griffin: Marriage Alleg. (Canterbury), p. 14.
— George Westthrop and Amy Norden: ibid. p. 36.
1693-4. Samuel Westthropp and Sarah Booth: ibid. p. 280.
1746. Married — John Pettit and Dorothy Westrop: St. Geo. Chap. Mayfair, p. 64.
London, 1, 3, 0; New York, 0, 0, 1.

Westwick.—Local, 'of Westwick': (1) a hamlet in the parish of Oakington, co. Camb.; (2) a township in the parish of Gainford, co. Durham; (3) a parish in the county of Norfolk; (4) a township in the parish of Ripon, co. York.

John de Westwik, co. Camb., 1273. A.
Katerina de Westwyc, co. Camb., ibid.
Isabella de Westwyk, co. Camb., ibid.
London, 3.

Westwood.—Local, 'of Westwood,' parishes in diocs. Exeter, Worcester, Lincoln, and Salisbury. Many small localities would, no doubt, be similarly called.

Richard de Westwode, co. Kent, 1273. A.
Henry de Westwode, co. Camb., ibid.
Henry de Westewode, co. Devon, Hen. III—Edw. I. K.
Willelmus de Westwod', 1379: P. T. Yorks. p. 268.
1579. William Westwood, co. Glouc.: Reg. Univ. Oxf. vol. ii. pt. ii. p. 91.
1608. Rowland Westwood, London: ibid. p. 302.
1746. Married — John Westwood and Eliz. Edwards: St. Geo. Chap. Mayfair, p. 78.
London, 9; Philadelphia, 6; Boston (U.S.), 1.

Wetherall, Wetherell, Wetherill.—Local, 'of Wetheral,' a parish near Carlisle. This North-English surname has made a fair impression upon our directories on both sides of the water.

Adam de Wederhale, *horner*, 3 Edw. II: Freemen of York, i. 12.
Hugh de Wederhale, co. Cumb., 20 Edw. I. R.
Humfrey de Wederhall: E. and F., co. Cumb., p. 164.
1617. Thomas Wethereld, co. Cumb.: Reg. Univ. Oxf. vol. ii. pt. ii. p. 362.
1618. Rowland Wetherall and Margaret More: Marriage Lic. (London), ii. 64.
1628. Nicholas Searle and Eliz. Wetherill: ibid. p. 193.
1744. Married—Peter Scott and Eliz.

Weatherell: St. Geo. Chap. Mayfair, p. 37.
London, 1, 4, 0; New York, 0, 3, 3; Philadelphia, 0, 4, 42; Boston (U.S.), 0, 14, 0.

Wetherby, Wetherbee; v. Weatherby.

Wethered; v. Weatherhead.

Wetherfield.—Local, 'of Wethersfield,' a parish in co. Essex.

Roger de Wetheresfeld, co. Camb., 1273. A.
Geoffrey de Wethirisfeld, co. Camb., ibid.
London, 2.

Wetherherd; v. Weatherhead.

Wetherill.—Local; v. Wetherall.

Philadelphia, 42; New York, 3.

Wethey.—Local; v. Withey.

Wetweather. — Nick. One who threw a damper on things in general; cf. Fairweather.

Thomas Wetwedder: Charters, Davies.

Wewer; v. Wooer.

Weyland; v. Wayland.

Weyman; v. Waithman.

Weymouth.—Local, 'of Weymouth,' a seaport and market-town in co. Dorset.

1572. Hugh Weymouthe, St. Alban's Hall: Reg. Univ. Oxf. vol. ii. pt. ii. p. 40.
1749. Married—Alex. Chatto and Mary Weymouth: St. Geo. Chap. Mayfair, p. 130.
London, 3; Boston (U.S.), 19; New York, 3.

Whale, Whal. — Nick. 'the whale,' probably affixed like Oliphant, i. e. the elephant, on account of the ponderous and ungainly build of the bearer.

Thomas Wal, co. Oxf., 1273. A.
Ralph le Wal, co. Oxf., ibid.
Thomas le Whal, 31 Edw. I: BBB. p. 651.
Philemon Whale, Pat. Roll, 19 Eliz. pt. iii.
1613. Richard Whale (co. Essex) and Mary Drywood: Marriage Lic. (London), ii. 19.
1642. Bapt.—Marye, d. William Whale: St. Jas. Clerkenwell, i. 151.
— Buried — Alice, wife of William Whale: ibid. iv. 254.
1795. Married — William Whale and Ann Lamb: St. Geo. Han. Sq. ii. 123.
London, 18, 0; New York, 0, 1.

Whalebelly. — ? Local. An imitative corruption of some such local surname as Walbury. This name is borne by a respectable family in south-east England.

Robert Whalebelly, Saham Toney, co. Norfolk: MDB. (1875).

Whalebone, Walborn. — ? Local. A manifest corruption, possibly a variation of Wellborne.

George Whalebone, *coach painter*: London Dir., 1870.
Philadelphia, 0, 4.

Whalley, Walley, Whally.—Local, 'of Whalley,' a parish in co. Lanc., famous for its abbey. Walley is a comparatively modern rendering of the surname.

'Robert de Whalley, who died before 1193, was rector of Rochdale': Baines' Lanc. i. 485.
1415. Geoffrey Whalley: Preston Guild Rolls, p. 8.
1590. Thomas Whalley, of Blackburn, *carpenter*: Wills at Chester (1545-1620), p. 200.
1592. Edmund Walley, of Blackburn: ibid. p. 205.
1604. Raffe Walley, Middlewich: Exchequer Depositions (co. Chester), p. 113.
Manchester, 12, 8, 0; London, 1, 0, 0; Preston, 4, 1, 0; Philadelphia, 8, 1, 14; Boston (U.S.), 3, 7, 0.

Wharmby.—Local, 'of Wharmby,' some small spot, seemingly in East Cheshire, in the vicinity of Stockport.

1578. Thomas Wharmeby: East Cheshire, ii. 61 *n*.
1580. Henry Wharmby, of Offerton, *husbandman*: Wills at Chester, i. 205.
1592. Robert Wharmby, of Manchester, *butcher*: ibid.
1603. William Wharmby, of Bredbury: ibid.
Manchester, 4; MDB. (co. Ches.), 1; New York, 1.

Whately, Whatley, Wheatley, Wheatly.—Local, (1) 'of Whatley,' a parish in dioc. of Bath and Wells; (2) 'of Wheatley,' parishes in diocs. Oxford and Southwell; (3) 'of Wheatley,' three separate hamlets in co. York, one a township in the parish of Doncaster, one a hamlet in the parish of Ilkley, and one a hamlet in the parish of Ovenden.

Peter de Watele, co. Oxf., 1273. A.
Henry de Watele, co. Oxf., ibid.

Alexander de Whately, or Watteleye, London, ibid.
John de Whateleghe, co. Dorset, ibid.
John de Watelegh, co. Wilts, ibid.
Robert de Whateleg, co. Wilts, Hen. III-Edw. I. K.
Mathew de Wateley, co. Oxf., ibid.
John de Weteley, *sauser*, 25 Edw. I : Freemen of York, i. 6.
Johannes de Whetlay, 1379 : P. T. Yorks. p. 99.
Henricus de Wytlay, 1379: ibid. p. 91.
London, 2, 7, 22, 3 ; West Rid. Court Dir. (Wheatley), 6 ; Philadelphia, 0, 2, 16, 0 ; Boston (U.S.), 0, 0, 1, 0 ; New York, 2, 1, 4, 2.

Whatman.—Occup. 'the servant of Wat,' i.e. Walter. If this be so, the *h* is intrusive ; cf. Addlman, Matthewman, Wilman, &c.

Richard Whatteman, co. Soms., 9 Edw. II : Kirby's Quest, p. 129.
1557. Christning of Richard Whatman : St. Peter, Cornhill, p. 7.
1565. Bapt.—Sara, d. John Whattman : St. Dionis Backchurch, p. 79
1591. Francis Whatman, co. Sussex, *pleb.*: Reg. Univ. Oxf. vol. ii. pt. ii. p. 186.
1794. Married—Roger Whatman and Jane Webb : St. Geo. Han. Sq. ii. 111. London, 2.

Whatmore, -mough ; v. Watmough.

Wheatcroft.—Local, 'at the wheat croft,' from residence thereby ; cf. Rycroft ; v. Croft or Craft.

Seman de Wetecroft, co. Suff., 1273. A.
Matilda de Wetecroft, co. Suff., ibid.
Robert de Wetecroft, co. Linc., Hen. III-Edw. I. K.
Thomas Whitecroft, C. R., 27 Edw. III.
1604. Married — Cutbert Crackplace and Anne Whitcraft : St. Peter, Cornhill, i. 244.
1703. William Legg and Eliz. Whitcroft : Marriage Lic. (Faculty Office), p. 245.
London, 1 ; Manchester, 3 ; Philadelphia, 2 ; New York, 1.

Wheatley, -ly ; v. Whately.

Wheatman.—Bapt. ; v. Wightman.

Wheeler, Wheeller.—Occup. the wheeler,' a maker of wheels, a wheelwright. This surname, representing an occupation of so much importance, is naturally found in large numbers. Modern references are needless.

Hugh le Welere, co. Camb., 1273. A.
Richard le Whelere, C. R., 21 Edw. III. pt. i.

Robert le Whelere. G.
William Wheler, co. Soms., 1 Edw. III : Kirby's Quest, p. 186.
1591. Married — Arthure Mayo and Ann Wheler : St. Michael, Cornhill, p. 15.
1593-4. Gilbert Wheeler, or Wheler, co. Worc. : Reg. Univ. Oxf. vol. ii. pt. ii. p. 200.
1691. Married—Thomas Wheeler and Judith Hiliard : St. Mary Aldermary, p. 34.
London, 76, 2 ; Philadelphia, 73, 0 ; Boston (U.S.), 220, 0.

Wheelhouse.—Local, 'of the wheel-house,' from residence thereby, the place where wheels were made or stored ; cf. Wheeler and Wheelwright. This surname is distinctly indigenous to W. Rid. Yorks.

Willelmus de Whelehous, 1379 : P. T. Yorks. p. 253.
Willelmus de Welchous, *carpenter*, 1379 : ibid. p. 221.
1747. Married—Robert Wheelhous and Ann Bethell : St. Geo. Chap. Mayfair, p. 91.
1795. Married — Samuel Wheelhouse and Lucy White : St. Geo. Han. Sq. ii. 133.
London, 3 ; West Riding Court Dir., 4.

Wheelock, Wellock, Whillock, Whellock. — Local, ' of Wheelock,' a parish in co. Chester.

John de Whelok, co. Ches., 2 Hen. IV (1400). East Cheshire, i. 240.
1657. Married — William Beuer and Jane Wheellocks : St. Mary Aldermary, p. 28.
Randle Wheelock, of Wheelock, 1661 : Wills at Chester (1660-80), p. 287.
Hugh Wheelock, of Wheelock, 1677 : ibid.
1743. — Thomas Tharp and Francis Wheclock : St. Geo. Han. Sq. i. 31.
Manchester, 1, 1, 0, 0 ; MDB. (Cheshire), 0, 0, 1, 0 ; London, 1, 0, 0, 2 ; Philadelphia, 3, 1, 0, 0 ; Boston (U.S.), 52, 6, 0, 0.

Wheelspinner.—Occup. ' the wheelspinner ' ; v. Spinner.

Isabella Whelespynner, 1379: P. T. Yorks. p. 296.

Wheelwright. — Occup. 'the wheelwright ' ; v. Wheeler, and cf. Cartwright and Wainwright. This is still a familiar surname in W. Rid. York.

Walter Welwryhte, co. Essex, 1273. A.
Willelmus Whelewryght, 1379 : P. T. Yorks. p. 125.
Robertus Whelewryght, 1379 : ibid. p. 242.
1778. Married—William Wheelwright and Eliz. Gibbs : St. Geo. Han. Sq. ii. 291.

1785. — John Smith and Rachel Wheelwright : ibid. p. 368.
West Rid. Court Dir., 9 ; Philadelphia, 1 ; Boston (U.S.), 22.

Wheen. — Nick. ' the wheen,' i. e. the queen (q.v.) ; cf. *wheencat*, a female cat (Halliwell). Also *wheene*, a queen ; North England (Halliwell). ' That es called the wheene of the Amazonnes,' Hampole MS. Bowes, p. 136, quoted by Halliwell ; cf. *wick* or *whick* for *quick* (Lancashire dialect).

Nicholas le Whene, Close Roll, 23 Edw. III. pt. ii.
New York, 2.

Whelp. — Nick. ' the whelp (cf. Kenn) ; M.E. *whelp.*

Richard le Whelp, C. R., 6 Edw. I.
Thomas Whelp, co. Soms., 1 Edw. III : Kirby's Quest, p. 223.
New York, 1.

Whenman.—Occup. ; a curious corruption of Wenman, q.v. ; cf. Whyman for Wyman, or Whatman for Watman.
London, 4.

Whetstone.—Local, ' of Whetstone,' a parish in co. Leicester, five miles from the capital. Also a hamlet, partly in co. Herts and partly in co. Middlesex.

1615. Edward Whytestone, or Whetstone, co. Bedf. : Reg. Univ. Oxf. vol. ii. pt. ii. p. 337.
1719. Married — John Whetstone and Jane Price : St. Antholin (London), p. 132.
1750. — Nicholas Wetstone and Mary Bowman : St. Geo. Chap. Mayfair, p. 158.
1752. — Edward Whetstone and Margt. Watkins : ibid. p. 202.
London, 2 ; MDB. (co. Leic.), 2 ; Philadelphia, 10.

Whichcord.—Bapt. A corruption of Guichard (?), q.v.

Whillock ; v. Wheelock.

Whimple, Whipple, Whippell.—Local, ' of Whimple,' a parish in co. Devon, four miles from Ottery St. Mary. The surname, however, has apparently been modified into Whipple, &c. Nevertheless, v. Whipple for another origin.

Hugo de Curteney habet . . . apud Wympell : A., co. Devon, i. 92 (1273).
Richard Bysothewympel (i.e. by South Wympel) : ibid. p. 67.
1657. Married—Richard Simons and

Mary Whimple : St. Thomas the Apostle (London), p. 20.
London, 1, 2, 0 ; MDB. (co. Devon), 0, 1, 2 ; Philadelphia, 0, 4, 0 ; Boston (U.S.), 0, 24, 0.

Whineray, Whinnerah, Winrow, Whinery, Whinnery, Winroe.—Local, 'at the whin-wray,' i.e. the corner where the whin was stored for bedding cattle, or the corner of the field where the whin grew. Whin is still used for bedding purposes in Furness and Cumberland ; cf. Thackeray (i.e. the thack-wray), and v. Wray.

1584. John Whinwray, of Tatham : Lancashire Wills (Richmond), i. 307.
1595. John Whinrow, of Dalton-in-Furness : ibid. p. 306.
1597. Margaret Whinerawe, of Dalton : ibid.
1631. Robert Whinwrey, of Dalton : Lancashire Wills at Richmond, i. 307.
Barrow-in-Furness, 1, 1, 0, 0, 0, 0 ; Ulverston, 1, 0, 0, 0, 0, 0 ; Manchester, 0, 1, 0, 0, 0, 0 ; London, 1, 0, 0, 0, 0, 0 ; Philadelphia, 0, 0, 1, 5, 1, 0 ; New York, 0, 0, 2, 0, 0, 2.

Whipp, Whipps, Whip.— ? Bapt. ' the son of Whip ' (?). Although I have put a query to this statement, there can be little doubt of its accuracy. There are no local prefixes to the early entries, and the surname is found in widely separated districts.

Nicholas Wipe, co. Norf., 1273. A.
Allan Wyppe, co. Camb., ibid.
Henry Whippe, Fines Roll, 4 Edw. III.
Johannes Wippe, 1379 : P. T. Yorks. p. 6.
Johannes Whyppe, 1379 : ibid. p. 91.
James Whippe, of Twiston, 1677 : Wills at Chester (1660-80), p. 287.
Richard Whipp, of Castleton, Rochdale, 1678 : ibid. p. 375.
1687. Richard Whipp, *goldsmith*, and Eliz. Morse : Marriage Alleg. (Canterbury), ii. 11.
London, 2, 1, 0 ; Manchester, 1, 0, 1 ; Philadelphia, 2, 0, 0 ; New York, 1, 0, 0.

Whipple.—Local, ' of Whiphill.' I cannot find the spot. The suffix is *-hill*, as proved below ; cf. Tickle or Tickell for Tickhill, &c. But v. Whimple.

Richard Wiphulle, co. Wilts, 1273. A.
William de Whiphulle, co. Soms., 1 Edw. III : Kirby's Quest, p. 192.
Richard de Whyphull, co. Soms., 1 Edw. III : ibid. p. 174.
London, 2 ; Boston (U.S.), 24.

Whiskard, Whisker, Wiscar, Wesker, Wisker.—Bapt. ' the son of Wisgar,' or Wiscar. In Domesday described thus : ' Wiscar,' co. Suffolk ; ' Wisgar,' co. Suffolk ; ' Wisgarus,' co. Essex. The long article on ' Whiskers ' appended to this name in Lower is quite out of place. The solution has nothing to do with ' facial ornaments.' The modern form Whisker is simply imitative.

Nicholas Wiscard, co. Salop, 1273. A.
Wiscard Litel, co. Hunts, ibid.
Whischard de Charrum, 1269 : KKK. vi. 275.
Wiscard, or Wyschardus Ledet, Hen. III–Edw. I. K.
1805. Married—George Redpath and Charlotte Whisker : St. Geo. Han. Sq. ii. 335.
London, 1, 3, 2, 0, 0 ; Sheffield (Wesker), 1 ; Manchester (Whisker), 1 ; New York, 0, 2, 0, 0, 2.

Whistler, Whisler, Wisler, Wissler.— Nick. ' the whistler,' one who was constantly whistling. The sobriquet would readily fasten itself upon the bearer, and as it denoted a cheery spirit would not be unacceptable to the nominee.

Thomas le Whistlar, co. Soms., 9 Edw. II : Kirby's Quest, p. 138.
Johannes Whisteler, 1379 : P. T. Yorks. p. 13.
1607-8. Hugh Whistler (co. Oxford), Trinity Coll. : Reg. Univ. Oxf. vol. ii. pt. ii. p. 300.
1626-7. Philip Hinslow and Eleanor Whistler : Marriage Lic. (London), ii. 184.
1678. Bapt.—Ann, d. Thomas Whistler : St. Mary Aldermary, p. 105.
1800. Married—Webster Whistler (co. Sussex) and Jane Mackay : St. Geo. Han. Sq. ii. 228.
London, 5, 0, 0, 0 ; MDB. (co. Sussex), 1, 0, 0, 0 ; Philadelphia, 0, 1, 15, 4 ; New York, 0, 0, 4, 2.

Whiston, Wiston.—(1) Local, ' of Whiston,' parishes, hamlets, &c., in cos. Lancaster, Stafford, Yorkshire, Worcester, and Northampton.

Arnald de Wiston, co. Notts, 1273. A.
William de Whiston, co. Northampt., 20 Edw. I. R.

(2) Bapt. 'the son of Wistan,' an early form of Wulstan.

William Wlefstan, co. Norf., 1273. A.
Wystan, or Wolstan de Paston, co. Norf., temp. Ric. I : FF. vi. 481.
1742. Buried—Elizabeth Whiston : St. Mary Aldermary, p. 226.

London, 1, 0 ; Crockford, 2, 0 ; Boston (U.S.), 5, 1.

Whitacre,-aker ; v. Whittaker.

Whitbourne. — Local, ' of Whitbourne,' a parish in co. Hereford, six miles from Bromyard.

Thomas de Wytebourne, co. Soms., 1 Edw. III : Kirby's Quest, p. 275.
1794. Married—Francis Whitburn and Sarah Mildred : St. Geo. Han. Sq. ii. 112.
1796. — John Whitburn and Catherine Earl : ibid. p. 143.
London, 1.

Whitbread, Whitebread.— Nick. (?). (1) A direct translation of the earlier Blanchpain (?), (q.v.). (2) But perhaps a corruption of Whitebeard, of which an early instance seems to be found below ; cf. Blackbeard, Brownbeard. The first derivation is feasible as translations of the French were common.

William Wytebred, co. Linc., 1273. A.
John Witbred, London, ibid.
Nicholas Wytberd, co. Glouc., ibid.
Henry Whitebread. H.
1589. Married—Nicholas Wiblen and Katherine Whytebread : St. Dionis Backchurch, p. 11.
1661. — Thomas Whitebread and Debora Boden : St. Mary Aldermary, p. 29.
1750. Buried—Benjamin Whitebread, *parish clerk* : St. Michael, Cornhill, p. 299.
London, 10, 0 ; New York, 1, 0.

Whitby, Witby.—Local, ' of Whitby,' a seaport, borough, and market-town in N. Rid. Yorks.

Ricardus de Whiteby, 21-2 Edw. I : Freemen of York, i. 5.
Robertus de Whytby, *smyth*, 1379 : P. T. Yorks. p. 99.
1585. Thomas Whitbey, co. Warw. : Reg. Univ. Oxf. vol. ii. pt. ii. p. 145.
1619. Oliver Whitbie, co. Bedf. : ibid. p. 377.
— Married — Mathew Whitby and Prudence Spencer : St. Dionis Backchurch, p. 19.
London, 7, 0 ; Philadelphia, 13, 1 ; Boston (U.S.), 2, 0.

Whitchurch ; v. Whitechurch.

White, Whyte.—Nick. ' the white,' of fair complexion ; cf. Black, Brown, Read, Russell, Blunt, &c. There is no need to furnish modern illustrations.

Geoffrey le Whyte, co. Camb., 1273. A.
Roger le Whyte, co. Sussex, ibid.
William the White, C. R., 13 Edw. III. pt. iii.

Thomas White, *souter*, 1379: P. T. Yorks. p. 98.

Magota Whyt, 1379: ibid. p. 72.

London, 402, 10; Boston (U.S.), 619, 9; Philadelphia, 724, 6.

Whitebeard.— ? Nick. 'with the white beard' (?). But v. Wiberd; if an offshoot of this, then the surname is baptismal.

Philip Wytberd. T.

William Witberd, co. Glouc., 20 Edw. I. R.

Cf. Johannes Blakberd, 1379: P. T. Yorks. p. 197.

Alicia Wytberd, 1379: ibid. p. 270.

Whitebelt.—Nick. 'with the white belt'; cf. Broadgirdle.

Johannes Whitebelt, 1379: P. T. Yorks. p. 160.

Cecilia Whytebelt, 1379: ibid. p. 167.

Whitebreast. — Nick. ' with the white breast '; cf. *robin redbreast*.

John Whitebrest, Pat. Roll, 15 Ric. II. pt. i.

Whitebull.—Nick. 'the white bull.'

Johannes Whytebull, 1379: P. T. Yorks. p. 98.

Johannes Whyttebull, 1379: ibid. p. 101.

Whitechild.—Nick. 'the white child.'

John Whitechild, C. R., 17 Hen. VI.

Whitechurch, Whitchurch. —Local, (1) 'at the White Church'; (2) 'of Whitchurch,' parishes in diocs. Lichfield, Exeter, Hereford, Oxford, Winchester, &c.

William de la Wytechirch, C. R., 33 Hen. III.

William de Witchirch, co. Oxf., 1273. A.

Nicholas de Withchurch, co. Bucks, ibid.

John del Whitechirche, C. R., 5 Edw. I.

1706. Bapt. — John, s. James Whitchurch : St. Dionis Backchurch, p. 145.

London, 2, 3; Philadelphia, 1, 0; Boston (U.S.), 3, 1.

Whitefield; v. Whitfield.

Whitefoot.— ? Local. But v. Whitehand and Barefoot. It is likely enough to be a nickname. As a rule, however, *-foot* is a local suffix; v. Foot (1).

Roger Wytfot, co. Devon, Hen. III-Edw. I. K.

John Whitefot, C. R., 9 Edw. III.

1634. Married — Edmond Whitefoot

and Martha Walker : St. Antholin (London), p. 68.

London, 1.

Whitehalgh.—Local, ' of the white halgh '; cf. Ridehalgh or Greenhalgh. v. Halgh.

Gilbert del Whithalgh, 1397: Preston Guild, p. 4.

William de Whitehalgh, 1397: ibid. p. 8.

Whitehand.—Nick. 'with the white hand.' Oddly enough, a fairly common sobriquet in the 13th and 14th centuries. Perhaps a translation of Blanchmains; cf. Humbert Blanchmains (Nicholls, Hist. Leicestershire, Index). The surname still lives. Cf. Whitehead.

Robert Whithond, C. R., 13 Edw. I.

Alexander Whitehand, 3 Edw. III : Freemen of York, i. 25.

Adam Whythand, 1379: P. T. Yorks. p. 95.

Gilbert Whithand. T.

Humbert Whitehand. PP.

Bartholomew Whitehande, of London, Oriel Coll., 1578: Reg. Univ. Oxf. vol. ii. pt. ii. p. 83.

1583. Buried—Alyce Breese, who dyed in bow lane in ye house of John Whitehande: St. Michael, Cornhill, p. 198.

William Whitehand, 1665: Hist. C. C. Coll., Camb.

London, 1.

Whitehead.—Nick. 'with the white head,' a common sobriquet, as our records prove, especially in North England; cf. Hoar. There is no evidence of a local origin, although Redhead and Blackett (Blackhead) are, like Greenhead, local occasionally. Modern instances are needless. The name exists wherever Englishmen settle.

Roger Witheved, co. Hunts, 1273. A.

William Witheved, co. Camb., ibid.

Adam Whiteheued, 1379: P. T. Yorks. p. 240.

Johannes Whitehed, 1379: ibid. p. 149.

Robertus Qwytheued, 1379: ibid. p. 266.

John Qhwiteheved, co. York. W. 9.

Rauf Whytehed, co. York. W. 2.

1745. Married — Owen Whitehead to Mary Russel: St. Michael, Cornhill, p. 70.

London, 60; Manchester, 50; Philadelphia, 60; Boston (U.S.), 12.

Whitehorse.—(1) Local, ' at the White Horse,' a sign-name; cf. Whitelam, Grayhorse, and Roebuck.

William del Whithors, Fines Roll, 2 Edw. I.

Mary Whithors: Household Book of Queen Isabella, 1358; Cott. MS. Galba, E. xiv.

Walter Whitehors. O.

(2) Possibly in some cases a translation of French Blaunchival; cf. Whitbread for Blanchpain.

Henry Blaunchival, co. Somerset, 1273. A.

1651. Buried—Robert Whitehorse: St. Peter, Cornhill, i. 205.

1714. Married — Hugh Rance and Sarah Whitehorse: St. Jas. Clerkenwell, iii. 238.

Whitehouse.—Local, ' at the white house,' from residence therein ; cf. Wodehouse, Parkhouse, Moorhouse, &c. I cannot light upon the precise spot.

Stephen atte Whitehous, co. Soms., 1 Edw. III : Kirby's Quest, p. 138.

1720. Married—Gualtero Bernard and Mary Whitehouse : St. Michael, Cornhill, p. 61.

1788. — John Nottage and Mary Whitehouse : St. Geo. Han. Sq. ii. 4.

London, 22 ; Philadelphia, 12 ; Boston (U.S.), 22.

Whiteknave. — Nick. ' the white knave,' i.e. the white servant; v. Goodknave.

Acelin Wyteknave, co. Hunts, 1273. A.

Thomas Whitteknave, 1379 : P. T. Yorks. p. 206.

Johannes Whiteknafe, 1379: ibid.

Whiteknight. — Nick. ' the white knight'; cf. Halfknight, and v. Knight.

Maurice Whiteknyght, Pat. Roll, 2 Hen. IV. pt. ii.

Whitelam, Whitlam.—Nick. ' the white lamb,' possibly a signname, 'at the White Lamb'; cf. Whitehorse.

Isabel Whitlamb, co. York. W. 14.

Alicia Whitlambe, 1379 : P. T. Yorks. p. 230.

Richard Whitelomb, Inc. of Long Ichington, 1428: Dugdale's Warwickshire, p. 230.

1769. Married—Cotton Whitelamb and Eliz. Stone: St. Geo. Han. Sq. i. 188.

1804. — Thomas Whitelam and Ann Field : ibid. ii. 302.

London, 1, 0; Swinton, near Rotherham, 0, 1; Philadelphia, 1, 1.

Whitelegge, Whitelegg. — Local, ' of the white legh ' (v. Lee). The same as Whiteley or Whitley; v. Whately for a similar form.

1584. Married—William Hudson and Agnes Whytlegge : St. Jas. Clerkenwell, iii. 11.

Mary Whitlegg, of Gatley, 1672 : Wills at Chester (1660-80), p. 288.

James Whitelegg, of Northendon, 1680 : ibid.

'Thomas Whitelegg was the next witness.' Inquest at Coroner's Court, Salford, July 22, 1887 : Manchester Courier, July 23, 1887.

Crockford, 2, 0 ; Manchester, 2, 6 ; New York, 1, 0.

Whiteley, Whitley, Whitely. — Local, 'of Whiteley' (the white meadow) ; v. preceding article. There are many places naturally bearing this name. Whitley is a tithing in the parish of Cumnor, co. Oxf. ; a hamlet in the parish of St. Giles, Reading ; a chapelry in the parish of Tynemouth, co. Northumb. ; also townships in W. Rid. Yorks, &c.

William de Witeleye, co. York, 1273. A. Simon de Whitleghe, co. Soms., 1 Edw. III : Kirby's Quest, p. 187.

1582. William Whitleaye, or Whyteley, co. Linc. : Reg. Univ. Oxf. vol. ii. pt. ii. p. 119.

1688. Thomas Whitlee, *lighterman*, and Mary Ambros : Marriage Alleg. (Canterbury), ii. 55.

London, 3, 7, 0 ; Philadelphia, 31, 6, 6.

Whitelock, Whitlock. — (1) Nick. 'white-lock,' from the complexion of the hair or a particular tress ; cf. Blacklock, Silverlock, Lovelock. This is quite satisfactory. But it may be an imitative form of Witlac, a Scandinavian personal name ; cf. Goodlake. (2) Local, 'at the white lake,' from residence thereby.

Emma fil. Witlok, co. Hunts, 1273. A. William Witlohc, co. Oxf., ibid. William atte Whytelak, co. Soms., 1 Edw. III : Kirby's Quest, p. 178. Walter Whytelock, co. Soms., 1 Edw. III : ibid. p. 105. John Wytlock, C. R., 29 Edw. III. 1581. William Whitlock, co. Berks : Reg. Univ. Oxf. vol. ii. pt. ii. p. 103. 1601. Married—John Baber and Jane Whitlocke : St. Michael, Cornhill, p. 17. 1799. — Edward Whitelock and Mary Ann Mullard : St. Geo. Han. Sq. ii. 208. London, 8, 15 ; Philadelphia, 7, 11 ; Boston (U.S.), 0, 2.

Whiteman, Whitman.—(1) Bapt. ; v. Wightman. (2) Nick. 'the white man,' from the pallid 'appearance of the bearer ; cf. Blackman and Greenman.

Agnes Wyteman, co. Oxf., 1273. A. John Wyteman, co. Camb., ibid. Thomas Wyteman, co. Oxf., ibid. William Wytman, co. Hunts, ibid. 1607. Buried—John, s. Peter Whitman, *vintner* : St. Peter, Cornhill, i. 163. 1637-8. Christopher Whiteman and Alice Aldrington : Marriage Lic. (Westminster), p. 37. London, 10, 1 ; Philadelphia, 64, 33 ; Boston (U.S.), 0, 51.

Whiteoak, Whittock, Whittick.—Local, 'at the white oak,' from residence thereby. The variants here given were inevitable.

1702. Bapt.—Sarah, d. Samuel Whittock : St. Jas. Clerkenwell, ii. 11. 1726. — Eliz., d. Peter Whittick : ibid. p. 159. London, 0, 0, 4 ; Keighley (West Rid. Yorks), 1, 1, 0 ; New York, 0, 0, 1.

Whiter ; v. Whittear.

Whiteside. — Local, 'at the white side,' i.e. from residence at the white side of some wood, orchard, hill, &c. ; cf. Garside, i.e. the side of the garth or orchard ; or Akenside, i.e. the side of the clump of oak-trees.

Richard Whitside, co. Camb., 1273. A. Willelmus Whitesyde, 1379 : P. T. Yorks. p. 253. 1575. Buried—Agnes Whiteside : St. Jas. Clerkenwell, iv. 7. 1752. Married — James Clough and Frances Whiteside : St. Geo. Chap. Mayfair, p. 212. London, 2 ; Manchester, 1 ; New York, 7.

Whiteskirts.—Nick.

Henry Whiteskyrtes, Close Roll, 12 Edw. I.

Whitesmith. — Occup. 'the whitesmith,' a worker in tin-plate. I think the surname is obsolete ; cf. Brownsmith, Blacksmith, Greensmith, and Redsmith. Whitesmith and Blacksmith are still occupative terms.

William le Wyteswyth (sic), co. Camb., 1273. A. Robert le Withsmyth, co. Camb., ibid. Richard le Wytesmith, C. R., 45 Hen. III. William le Wytesmyth, 1313. M.

Whitey, Whitty, Wittey, Witty, Wittie.—Local, 'at the white hay,' i.e. hedge, from residence thereby ; v. Hay.

Thomas ate Wytheg', co. Oxf., 1273. A. William ate Wytheg', co. Oxf., ibid. Nicholas de la Wytheg', co. Oxf., ibid.

Walter de la Wythege, co. Southampt., ibid. 1574-5. — Whitty, Ireland, *gent.* : Reg. Univ. Oxf. vol. ii. pt. ii. p. 59. 1632. Walter Williams and Jane Witty : Marriage Lic. (Faculty Office), p. 18. 1676. George Withey and Alice Cotton : Marriage Alleg. (Canterbury), p. 174. London, 1, 3, 1, 1, 0 ; Philadelphia, 1, 7, 0, 2, 2 ; Boston (U.S.), 0, 3, 0, 0, 0.

Whitfield, Whitefield. — Local, 'of Whitfield,' parishes in diocs. Canterbury, Newcastle, Southwell, and Peterborough.

Margery de Wytefeld, co. Oxf., 1273. A. Peter de Whytefeld, co. Norf., ibid. Walter de Wytefeld, co. Salop, Hen. III–Edw. I. K. Elyas de Wytefeld, co. Oxf., ibid. 1610. Henry Whitfeld, co. Kent : Reg. Univ. Oxf. vol. ii. pt. ii. p. 314. 1610. Jevan ap-Hugh and Katherine Whitfield : Marriage Lic. (Westminster), p. 18. 1675. Guy Miege and Mary Whitefeild : Marriage Alleg. (Canterbury), p. 146. London, 19, 5 ; Philadelphia, 9, 7 ; Boston (U.S.), 0, 2.

Whitgift.—Local, 'of Whitgift,' a parish in the W. Rid. Yorks. I fear this name is extinct.

Johannes Thomson de Whidgift, 1379 : P. T. Yorks. p. 112.

'John Whitgift, Archbishop of Canterbury, was born 1530, at Great Grimsby, Lincolnshire ' : Lemprière's Universal Biography.

Witham.—Local ; v. Witham.

Whiting, Whitting. — (1) ? Bapt. I think there can be no question of two separate origins, but the first I cannot exactly elucidate ; cf. the many hamlets called Whittington and Whittingham, where the A.S. family suffix comes in.

Adelina Wyting, co. Hunts, 1273. A. John Witting, co. Oxf., ibid. Felicia Wyting, co. Camb., ibid. Gerin Wyting, co. Bedf., ibid.

(2) Local.

Thomas de Wytin, co. Notts, 1273. A. John de Wyten, co. Hereford, Hen. III–Edw. I. K. Robert de Whyten, co. Notts, 20 Edw. I. R. 1689-90. Samuel Starkey and Eliz. Whiting : Marriage Alleg. (Canterbury), p. 136. 1706. Bapt.—Noell, son of Noell Whiting : St. Dionis Backchurch, p. 145. London, 25, 4 ; Philadelphia, 12, 2 ; Boston (U.S.), 87, 0.

Whitlam ; v. Whitelam.

Whitley; v. Whiteley.

Whitlock; v. Whitelock.

Whitman; v. Whiteman.

Whitmore, Witmore.—Local, 'of Whitmore,' a parish in dioc. of Lichfield, co. Stafford, formerly Whittimere.

William de Witimere, co. Salop, 1273. A.
Johannes Whittemore, 1379: P. T. Yorks. p. 157.
1581. Peter Whitmore, co. Staff., *gent.*: Reg. Univ. Oxf. vol. ii. pt. ii. p. 98.
1612. Bapt.—John, s. Humphrey Whitmoore: St. Michael, Cornhill, p. 110.
1616. Thomas Whitmore, co. Salop, *pleb.*: Reg. Univ. Oxf. vol. ii. pt. ii. p. 357.
London, 13, 0; Philadelphia, 8, 1; Boston (U.S.), 18, 0.

Whitnell, Whitnall.—Local, 'of Whitenhull.' I cannot find the exact locality. Evidently it must be sought for in the West country.

Ralph de Whitenhull, co. Soms., 9 Edw. II: Kirby's Quest, p. 140.
Stephen de Whitenhull, co. Soms., 9 Edw. II: ibid. p. 142.
1793. Married — James Whitnell and Ann Stabler: St. Geo. Han. Sq. ii. 92.
MDB. (co. Soms.), 1, 0; London, 0, 1.

Whitney. — Local, 'of Whitcy,' a parish in co. Hereford. It is quite clear that co. Hereford is the chief home of this family. Nevertheless Witney, the formerly well-known town in co. Oxford, must have swelled the total.

John de Witteneye, co. Suff., 1273. A.
Thomas de Whytene, co. Notts, ibid.
Robert de Wyttenye, co. Hereford, Hen. III-Edw. I. K.
1604. Henry Whitney, co. Heref.: Reg. Univ. Oxf. vol. ii. pt. ii. p. 275.
1605. Thomas Whitney, co. Heref.: ibid. p. 285.
1676. George Whitney and Sarah Todd: Marriage Alleg. (Canterbury), ii. 169.
London, 8; MDB. (co. Hereford), 1; Philadelphia, 28; Boston (U.S.), 216.

Whitsunday.—? Bapt. Pentecost was once a familiar fontname; cf. Nowell, Pask, and Christmas. As confirmations were general on Whitsunday, and it was a common circumstance to change the baptismal name then, it was natural that Pentecost, or 'Whitsunday,' should sometimes become the new name. The candidates were addressed by

name till 1552. For the rule concerning the exchange of names—under exceptional circumstances—laid down by Archbishop Peckham, v. my Curiosities of Puritan Nomenclature, p. 75.

William Wytesoneday, co. Somerset, 1273. A.

Whittaker, Whitacre, Whitaker, Whittiker. — Local, 'of the white acre.' No doubt many small localities scattered over the country bearing this name have helped to swell the large total of Whitakers found in our modern directories. Over and Nether Whitacre are parishes in co. Warwick.

Simon de Withacre, co. Leic., Hen. III-Edw. I. K.
Alan Witacur, co. Oxf., 1273. A.
Richard de Whitacre, co. Northampton, ibid.
Jordan de Whitacre, co. Northampton, 20 Edw. I. R.
Henricus Wyteacre, 1379: P. T. Yorks. p. 194.
Willelmus de Wetaker, 1379: ibid. p. 195.
Rogerus Whitteacres, 1379: ibid. p. 271.
1618. Married — John Whitaker and Mary Storey: St. Dionis Backchurch, p. 19.
London, 10, 0, 41, 0; West Rid. Court Dir., 4, 1, 35, 0; New York, 11, 0, 9, 1; Philadelphia, 32, 0, 72, 0.

Whittam, &c.; v. Witham.

Whittear, Whittier, Whityer, Whiter.—Occup. 'the white tawer' or tower, one who dressed the lighter kid skins for the glover; v. Tawer and Tower (2).

Eustace le Wittowere, co. Hunts, 1273. A.
Thomas le Wytewere, co. Hunts, ibid.
Geoffrey le Whitetawier. N.
1634. William Lilley and Grace Whityer: Marriage Alleg. (Westminster), p. 34.
1674-5. Edward Ap-Price and Mary Whitter: ibid. p. 237.
1782. Married — Thomas Short and Eliz. Whitear: St. Geo. Han. Sq. i. 241.
London, 0, 0, 0, 5; Philadelphia, 0, 2, 0, 0; Boston (U.S.), 0, 47, 0, 0.

Whitteridge, Whittredge.— Local, 'of Whitrigg,' co. Cumb.; 'a long white rigg upon the banks of the Wathinpool' (E. and F., co. Cumb. p. 75).

William Wyterik, co. Camb., 1273. A.
Robert de Whyterigg, or Whyterik, or Whyteryk, co. Cumb., 20 Edw. I. R.
Walter de Whyteryk, co. Cumb., ibid.

Thomas de Whitrigg: E. and F., co. Cumb. p. 26.
London, 1, 0; Boston (U.S.), 0, 8.

Whittick; v. Whiteoak.

Whittier; v. Whittear.

Whitting; v. Whiting.

Whittingham. — Local, 'of Whittingham,' a parish in co. Northumberland, eight miles from Alnwick; also a township in the parish of Kirkham, co. Lanc.

1608. William Whittingham, co. Ches.: Reg. Univ. Oxf. vol. ii. pt. ii. p. 301.
1608-9. Thomas Whittingham, co. Ches.: ibid. p. 304.
1669. George Whittingham and Susanne Seagood: Marriage Alleg. (Canterbury), p. 15.
1766. Married—Thomas Whittingham and Sarah Hudson: St. Geo. Han. Sq. i. 152.
London, 11; New York, 5.

Whittington. — Local, 'of Whittington,' parishes in cos. Glouc. and Bristol, Southwell, Lichfield, Norwich, Manchester, and Worcester.

Johannes de Whityngton, 1379: P. T. Yorks. p. 259.
Isabella de Wetyngton, 1379: ibid. p. 61.
1590-1. Thomas Whittington, co. Heref.: Reg. Univ. Oxf. vol. ii. pt. ii. p. 182.
1617. Henry Whittington, co. Glouc.: ibid. p. 358.
1713. Bapt.—Richard, s. John Wittington: St. Peter, Cornhill, ii. 29.
— Buried — Richard Whittington, under the gallery: ibid. p. 121.
London, 4; Philadelphia, 24; Boston (U.S.), 3.

Whittle.—Local, (1) 'of Whittle,' generally called Whittle-in-the-Woods, a township in the parish of Leyland, co. Lanc.; (2) also hamlets and townships in cos. Northumberland and Derby. All the Lancashire Whittles, a numerous progeny, hail from (1). This name is commonly found in the Chorley and Preston district. It reached London in, or earlier than, the 17th century.

1581. John Whittle, of Chorley, co. Lanc.: Wills at Chester (1545-1620), p. 208.
1617. Robert Whittle, of Leyland, co. Lanc.: ibid.
1662. Gulielmus Whittle: Preston Guild Rolls, p. 139.

1667. Sackvill Whittle, *barber-chirurgeon*, and Margaret Fox: Marriage Alleg. (Canterbury), p. 141.
London, 8; Manchester, 8; Chorley, 5; Preston, 8; Philadelphia, 9; Boston (U.S.), 20.

Whittock, Whittuck. — ? Nick. 'the white cock'(?). What may be the origin of this name I dare not say, but one thing is absolutely certain, Wytcok below is the parent. But v. Whiteoak.

Robert Wytcok, co. Wilts, 1273. A.
1690. Bapt.—William, s. Samuel Whittock: St. Jas. Clerkenwell, i. 338.
1696. — Joseph, s. Samuel Whittock: ibid. i. 365.
MDB. (co. Soms.), 2, 2.

Whitty; v. Whitey.

Whitwell.—Local, 'of Whitwell,' a hamlet in the parish of Tinsley, near Sheffield; also parishes in cos. Derby, Norfolk, and Rutland; also townships in cos. Westm. and York (N. Rid.). It is manifest that several of these places, north and south, have originated the surname.
Eborard de Wytewelle, co. Camb., 1273. A.
Walter de Wytewelle, co. Camb., ibid.
Johannes de Whitwell, 1379: P. T. Yorks. p. 292.
Thomas de Whitewell, 1379: ibid. p. 250.
1608. Miles Whitwell, Kendall: Wills at Chester, i. 208.
1630. Edmund Whitwell, of Burton: Lancashire Wills at Richmond, i. 309.
1701. Bapt. — Richard, s. Anthony Whittwel: St. Jas. Clerkenwell, ii. 2.
1713. — Eleanor, d. Anthony Whitwel: ibid. p. 70.
London, 4; Boston (U.S.), 16.

Whitworth.—Local, 'of Whitworth,' a chapelry in the parish of Rochdale, co. Lanc. This surname has a vigorous existence in the county Palatine.
1615. Susanna Whitworth, of Castleton, parish of Rochdale: Wills at Chester, i. 208.
1619. James Whitworth, of Brandwood, parish of Rochdale: ibid.
1635. Married—Jeremy Whitworth and Mary Pecke: St. Mary Aldermary, p. 18.
1646. Edmund Whitworth, of Prestwich, *husbandman*: Wills at Chester, ii. 235.
Manchester, 19; Philadelphia, 6; Boston (U.S.), 2.

Wholesworth; v. Holdsworth.

Whyatt; v. Wyatt.

Whybreu, Whybrow, Wybroo, Wybrow.—(1) Bapt. 'the son of Werburgha.' A nun of this name is said to have been patron saint of the ancient abbey of St. Werbergh, Chester; v. Chambers' Book of Days, i. 215. (2) Local; v. Wybroo.
1560. Buried—Whitburga, d. Robert Soham, Beetley, Norfolk: St. Mary, Beetley.
1564. Married—Rycharde Johnson and Wyboroe Wylson: St. Michael, Cornhill, p. 8.
London, 3, 5, 1, 3; New York (Whybrew), 1.

Whyman.—Bapt. 'the son of Wymond'; v. Wyman.
London, 2; New York, 2.

Whyte.—Nick.; v. White.

Wiberd, Wiber, Wybert.—Bapt. 'the son of Wiberd,' i.e. Wigbert (Yonge, ii. 409). Found in Domesday as Wiber and Wibert (co. York).
Wibert fil. Hacun, 1188: RRR. p. 50.
Wybert, rector de Gynynton, 1273. A.
Thomas Wyberd, co. Suff., ibid.
Adam Wyberd, co. Kent, ibid.
Robert Wyberd, co. Norf., ibid.
William Wyberd, co. Glouc., Hen. III–Edw. I. K.
William fil. Wiberti, Pipe Roll, 5 Hen. II.
Wybert de Littelton, Pat. R., 4 Edw. III. pt. ii.
Hugo Wyberd, 1379: P. T. Yorks. p. 30.
1579. Married — Christopher Dodson and Agnes Wyberde: St. Michael, Cornhill, p. 12.
1611–2. Walter Wyberd (co. Essex) and Eliz. Swifte: Marriage Lic. (London), i. 9.
1718. Married—Thomas Johnson and Eliz. Wibard: St. Mary Aldermary, p. 44.
London, 0, 1, 0; New York, 0, 0, 1.

Wick, Wicks, Wickes, Wicke.—(1) Local, 'at the wyke'; v. Wike and Wykes. (2) Bapt. 'the son of William'; v. Wilkerson and Wilkes.
London, 0, 20, 2, 0; Philadelphia, 18, 5, 1, 4; Boston (U.S.), 0, 4, 0, 0.

Wicken(s; v. Wickin.

Wicker, Wickers, Whicker, Whickers.—Bapt. 'the son of Wyger.' But v. Wilkerson and Wilkes.
Thomas Wyger', co. Camb., 1273. A.
Henry Wyger, co. Devon, ibid.
William Wyger, co. Hunts, ibid.
Johannes Wykir, *shereman*, 1379: P.T. Yorks. p. 25.

Robertus Wyker, 1379: ibid. p. 26.
1581. Thomas Whicker, co. Devon: Reg. Univ. Oxf. vol. ii. pt. ii. p. 105.
1798. Married—Thomas Middleton and Ann Wickers: St. Geo. Han. Sq. ii. 179.
1807. — William Wicker and Eliz. Vining: ibid. p. 378.
London, 3, 2, 1, 0; Philadelphia, 3, 0, 0, 0; New York, 3, 1, 0, 0.

Wickerson; v. Wilkerson.

Wickett.—(1) Local, 'at the wicket,' a small gate, from residence thereby; cf. Barr.
Robert atte Wychit, Close Roll, 14 Edw. II.
Walter Wyket, Close Roll, 2 Edw. I.
(2) Bapt. A sharpened form of Wiggett, q.v.
1541. Bapt.—Jane Wicket: St. Peter, Cornhill, i. 2.
1717. Married — George Wickett and Ann Cotes: St. Michael, Cornhill, i. 59.
1750. — William Grace and Mary Wickett: St. Geo. Chap. Mayfair, p. 169.
Sheffield, 2; New York, 2.

Wickham.—Local, 'of Wickham.' There are many spots and parishes of this name in cos. Kent, Glouc., Essex, Suffolk, Hants, Berks, Lincoln, Oxford, Camb., &c. Its meaning seems to be exactly equivalent to our 'homestead'; v. Wickstead and Wykes.
William de Wykham, co. Oxf., 1273. A.
1572. Married—John Wyckham and Mary Ovenden: St. Dionis Backchurch (London), 7.
1577. Edward Wickam, co. Oxf.: Reg. Univ. Oxf. vol. ii. pt. ii. p. 74.
1594. Richard Wickham, co. Kent: ibid. p. 205.
1762. Buried—Susanna Wickham: St. Peter, Cornhill, i. 144.
London, 14; Philadelphia, 1; Boston (U.S.), 4.

Wickin, Wicken, Wickins, Wickens, Wicking.—(1) Bapt. 'the son of William,' corruptions of Wilkin and Wilkins (q.v.). (2) Bapt. 'the son of Wiggin,' sharpened to Wickin. This is a more probable derivation. The *g* in Wicking is excrescent, as in Jennings.
'Thomas Wykynsone holds lands, and tenements, 5s. 3d.': Rental of Halifax, 1439, Cotton MS. Vespasian, F. 15, Brit. Mus.
'John Wykynsone holds lands, and tenements, 8d.': ibid.
Willelmus Wykyn, 1379: P. T. Yorks. p. 25.
Johanna Wykyn, 1379: ibid. p. 35.

For corroborative evidence of (a), v. Wiggin, where the popularity of the personal name is conclusively shown.

1667. Bapt. — Thomas, s. Samuell Wickins: St. Peter, Cornhill, i. 88.
1669. Buried—Eliz., servant to Samuel Wickens: ibid.
1678. Married — John Wicken and Isabel Mellen: St. Jas. Clerkenwell, iii. 185.
1808. Married—Edward Radclyff and Harriot Wicking: St. Geo. Han. Sq. ii. 385.
London, 0, 1, 0, 8, 3; Boston (U.S.), 0, 0, 0, 4, 0.

Wickliffe; v. Wycliffe.

Wicks; v. Wykes.

Wickstead, Wicksted, Wicksteed.—Local, 'at the wick-stead,' from residence therein; v. Wykes, and cf. *homestead.* Lower says the name hails from a manor called Wicksted in co. Ches. That this is true is evident. Any number of references can be quoted from that county.

1602. John Whicksteed, or Weecksteede, London: Reg. Univ. Oxf. vol. ii. pt. ii. p. 257.
1611. Henry Wicksted, of Wick Malbank: Wills at Chester, i. 209.
1648. Thomas Wickstead, of Wickstead, co. Chester: ibid. ii. 235.
1649. Hugh Wickstead, of Chester, *glover*: ibid.
1796. Married — William Boles and Eliz. Wicksted: St. Geo. Han.Sq. ii. 158.
1799. Married — John Wickstead and Honoria Tichborne: St. Geo. Han. Sq. ii. 203.
London, 0, 1, 4; MDB. (co. Ches.), 1, 0, 1; New York, 0, 0, 4.

Widder(s; v. Widow.

Widdicombe, Widicombe, Weddicombe, Withecomb, Widdicomb.—Local, 'of Widecombe-in-the-Moor,' a parish in co. Devon, six miles from Ashburton; also Widcombe, a parish in co. Somerset. These probably share the parentage.

Robertus Wythecumbe, co. Soms., 9 Edw. II: Kirby's Quest, p. 76.
Walter de Wydecu'be, co. Soms., 9 Edw. II: ibid. p. 95.
Ammyra de Wydecombe, co. Soms., 9 Edw. II: ibid. p. 119.
Elena de Wydecombe, co. Soms., 9 Edw. II: ibid. p. 131.
London, 3, 0, 0, 0, 0; Devon Court Dir., 0, 1, 1, 0, 0; New York, 0, 0, 0, 0, 1; Manchester, 0, 0, 0, 1, 0

Widdows; v. Widow.

Widdowson; v. Widowson.

Widger.—? Bapt. 'the son of Wicher' (?). Widger seems to be quite a modern, even recent, variant; cf. Wickersley (the meadow of Wicker), a parish in W. Rid. Yorks. This represents the harder N.E. pronunciation.

John Wycher, co. Camb., 1273. A.
Juliana Wycher, co. Camb., ibid.
William Wycher, co. Hunts, ibid.
Robert Wiger, co. Suff., ibid.
1753. Married — John Dawkins and Abigail Whitcher: St. Geo. Chap. Mayfair, p. 235.
1754. — Thomas Whitchar and Hannah Snow: ibid. p. 269.
London, 1; Philadelphia, 2; Boston (U.S.), 2.

Widgington; v. Wigginton.

Widmer.—Local, 'of Widmerpool,' a parish in co. Notts, nine miles from the capital.

Durand de Wydmerpol, London, temp. Edw. II. R.
Walter de Wythmer, co. Soms., 1 Edw. III: Kirby's Quest, p. 260.
Stephen Wedmer, co. Soms., 1 Edw. III: ibid. p. 272.
1581. Thomas Widmerpooll, co. Notts: Reg. Univ. Oxf. vol. ii. pt. ii. p. 110.
1586. Nicholas Wydmer, or Widmore, co. Bucks: ibid. p. 151.
1789. Married — Thomas Shotter and Eliz. Widmer: St. Geo. Han. Sq. ii. 22.
1806. — William Bowles and Maria Widmor: ibid. p. 340.
London, 1; Boston (U.S.), 3; New York, 2.

Widow, Widders, Widows, Widder, Wider, Widdos, Widdoes, Widows.—Bapt. 'the son of Wydo,' English for Guido (Guy) (v. Widowson, 2); cf. Warin for Guarin, &c.

William fil. Wydo, co. Norf., 1273. A.
Reg. fil. Wydonis, co. Hunts, ibid.
Thomas Wydowe, C. R., 20 Ric. II. pt. ii.
Annabella Wydow, 1379: P. T. Yorks. p. 146.

Widders is a natural corruption of Widows with the patronymic *s.* 'Beware of widders' does not apply in this case, but points to a similar corruption.

London, 0, 1, 4, 0, 0, 0, 0, 1; Philadelphia, 0, 0, 2, 0, 0, 1, 2, 0; New York, 0, 0, 0, 3, 10, 0, 0, 0.

Widowhood.—Nick.

Reginald Widewohod, Close Roll, 49 Hen. III.

Widowson, Widdowson, Widows, Widdison. — (1) Nick. 'the widow's son.' (2) Bapt. 'the son of Wydo'; v. Widow. Doubtless (1) is the chief parent.

Andrew fil. Vidue, co. Camb., 1273. A.
Symon fil. Vidue, co. Oxf., ibid.
Edmund fil. Vidue, co. Soms., 1 Edw. III: Kirby's Quest, p. 101.
Willelmus Wydowson, 1379: P. T. Yorks. p. 215.
Ricardus Widowson, 1379: ibid.
Adam Wydouson, 1379: P. T. Howdenshire, p. 25.
1571. Richard Widoson, co. Notts: Reg. Univ. Oxf. vol. ii. pt. ii. p. 50.
1583. Garrett Florence and Ann Wyddowson, relict of Robert Wyddowson: Marriage Lic. (London), i. 118.
1666. Married—Adam Wydeson and Alice Rauen: St. Jas. Clerkenwell, iii. 124.
London, 0, 0, 1, 4, 0; West Rid. Court Dir. (Widdison), 2; Sheffield (Widdowson), 8; New York, 0, 1, 0, 0.

Wigan.—(1) Local, 'of Wigan,' an important town in South Lanc. (2) Bapt. 'the son of Wigan'; v. Wiggin. Although it is certain that our Cheshire and Lancashire Wigans hail from the town, it is equally certain that the surname, generally speaking, belongs to (2).

Willelmus de Wygan, *ffranklayn*, 1379: P. T. Yorks. p. 127.
1592. William Wigan, of Great Harwood: Wills at Chester, i. 209.
1617. John Wigan, of Heap: ibid.
1638. Benjamin Wigan, of Atherton: ibid. ii. 236.
1801. Married—James Lambley and Grace Wigan: St. Geo. Han. Sq. ii. 243.
London, 3; Liverpool, 1; Philadelphia, 1; Crockford, 3.

Wigand, Wigans; v. Wiggin.

Wigfall, Wigfull.—Local, 'of Wigfall,' some small spot in co. York.

Henricus de Wigfall, *webester*, 1379: P. T. Yorks. p. 82.
Ibota de Wigfall, 1379: ibid.
Johannes Wigfall, 1379: ibid. p. 81.
1654. Buried—Henry Wigfall, servant with Mr. Thomas Chewning: St. Michael, Cornhill, p. 246.
1701. Married — Richard Wigfall and Alice Hull: St. Jas. Clerkenwell, iii. 223.
West Rid. Court Dir., 5, 4; Sheffield, 4, 3; Philadelphia, 5, 8; Boston (U.S.), 1, 0.

Wigg, Wiggs, Wigson.— Bapt. 'the son of Wig' (v. Lower, Patr. Brit. 'Wigg,' and Yonge,

Christian Names, ii. 409). As a personal name the forms in Domesday are Wiga (cos. York and Bucks), Wige (co. York), and Wig (co. Bedford). Another early form of Wig was Vig (Yonge, ii. 409), whence possibly Figg, Figgs, and Figgin (q.v.). Another form, Wigel, was once common in Holland, and is found in Wigglesworth, co. York.

Thomas Wigge, Close Roll, 3 Edw. I.
Robert Wygge, co. Kent, 20 Edw. I. R.
William Wygge, Pardons Roll, 5 Ric. II.
1586. Bapt.—Agnes Wigges, daughter of William Wigs : St. Peter, Cornhill, i. 30.
1715. Married — Charles Trinquand and Mary Wigg : St. Michael, Cornhill, p. 58.
1804. — William Wigson and Sarah St. John : St. Geo. Han. Sq. ii. 314.
London, 6, 4, 0 ; New York, 1, 0, 0 ; Boston (U.S.), 1, 0, 0.

Wiggett.—Bapt. 'the son of Wigod' or Wigot. In Domesday Wigod is found in co. Devon, and Wigot in cos. Sussex, Bedford, and Berks. As a font-name Wigot or Wigod lasted till the 14th century.

Tokig, son of Wiggod (Freeman, Hist. Norm. Conq. iv. 47), called Wiggod, of Wallingford (ibid. iv. 45, 728).
'Walter de Ganto, 3 carucates, which Wigotus holds': Lincolnshire Survey, p. 18, temp. 1109.
Adam Wigod, co. Hunts, 1273. A.
Thomas Wigod, co. Camb., ibid.
Margaret fil. Wyggotti, co. Linc., ibid.
John Wygot, co. Oxf., 20 Edw. I. R.
Robertus Wygot, co. Linc., ibid.
Robertus Wygott, 1379: P. T. Howdenshire, p. 32.
Constance Wygood, C. R., 1 Hen. IV. pt. i.
London, 3 ; Philadelphia, 1.

Wiggin, Wiggins, Wigan, Wigans, Wiggan, Wiggans, Wigand. — Bapt. 'the son of Wigand' (v. Yonge, ii. 409). This personal name has made a deep impression upon English nomenclature, and just as Stigand became Stiggin and Stiggins, so Wigand became Wiggin and Wiggins. As regards Wigan, this has in some cases a local parentage (v. Wigan). The final s in Wiggins, &c., is genitive; cf. Williams, Jones, &c.

Wyganus Marescall, Hen. III-Edw. I : K. p. 88.
Wuganus de Wyleby, ibid. p. 89.
William Wygeyn, co. Norf., 1273. A.
Wygan le Bretun, co. Essex, ibid.

Eva Wigeyn, co. Oxf., 1273. A.
Thomas Wygan, 1379: P. T. Howdenshire, p. 7.
Robert Wyghene, 1379: P. T. Yorks. p. 81.
1705. Married—Daniel Wiggen and Mary Bridge: St. Mary Aldermary (London), p. 38.
1760. — John Wigans and Mary Spong : St. Geo. Han. Sq. i. 98.
1789. — George Neves and Mary Wiggin : ibid. ii. 22.
1790. — Thomas Wiggins and Anna Maria Adcock : ibid. p. 50.
1793. — Thomas Wiggens and Eliz. Beakley : ibid. p. 93.
London, 2, 17, 3, 1, 0, 0, 0 ; West Rid. Court Dir., 2, 1, 0, 0, 0, 0, 0 ; Philadelphia, 1, 38, 1, 0, 2, 0, 7 ; Boston (U.S.), 65, 3, 0, 0, 0, 0.

Wigginton, Wiginton, Widgington.—Local, 'of Wigginton,' parishes in cos. York, Hertford, Oxford, and Stafford. Lit. 'the town of Wiggin'; v. Wiggin, and cf. the local Wiggenhall, Wigginthorpe, Wiggonby, and Wiggonholt. Several of the local Wiggintons are represented in the instances below :

Guido de Wygynton, co. Oxf., 1273. A.
Roger de Wygynton, co. Oxf., ibid.
John de Widington, co. Linc., ibid.
Samuel de Wygenton, co. Hertf., Hen. III-Edw. I. K.
1682. Edward Wiggington and Hanna Jackson : Marriage Alleg. (Canterbury), p. 118.
1785. Married—Richard Pim and Eliz. Widginton : St. Geo. Han. Sq. i. 375.
London, 3, 2, 2 ; New York, 1, 0, 0.

Wigglesworth. — Local, ' of Wigglesworth,' a township of Long Preston, W. Rid. Yorks.

Johannes de Wykelsworth, 1379 : P. T. Yorks. p. 255.
Willelmus de Wyglesworth, 1379 : ibid. p. 257.
Matthias Wiglesworth, co. Yorks : Reg. Univ. Oxf. vol. ii. pt. ii. p. 114.
1795. Married—Benjamin Wiglesworth and Hanna Johnson : St. Geo. Han. Sq. ii. 125.
London, 2 ; West Riding Court Dir., 8 ; Boston (U.S.), 5.

Wight.—Nick. 'the wight,' i.e. the active, strong ; v. Wightman.

'Y schalle gyf the two greyhowndys,
As wyghte as any roo.' Halliwell.
William le Wyhte, co. Sussex, 1273. A.
John le Wighte, co. Soms., 1 Edw. III : Kirby's Quest, p. 90.
1729. Married—Joseph Wight and Mary Hart : St. Geo. Chap. Mayfair, p. 289.
1792. — Nicolas Joseph Henrij and Margt. Wight : St. Geo. Han. Sq. ii. 80.
London, 3 ; New York, 19.

Wightman, Weightman, Whiteman, Wheatman.—(1) Nick. 'the wightman.' A.S. wight, active, brave, strong.
'A wightman of strengthe.'
Piers P. 5195.

(2) Bapt. 'the son of Wigmann' (Yonge, ii. 410). It is clear from the evidence that there was some difficulty in pronouncing this early personal name :

Alexander Wigman, co. Northampton 1273. A.
Geoffrey Wygeman, or Wygman, or Wigeman, co. York, ibid.
Johannes Wygh'man, 1379 : P. T. Yorks. p. 63.
Willelmus Wyghman, 1379 : ibid.
Johannes Wyghman, 1379 : ibid.
Richard Wightman, co. York. W. 15.
William Whytman. B.
Audrey Whiteman, temp. Eliz. Z.

I strongly suspect the baptismal origin (2) is the correct one. I believe also that all the four modern directory forms given above are varieties of one name. If there were evidence enough (1) would be a tempting solution.

Sheffield, 4, 0, 0, 2 ; London, 7, 6, 10, 0 ; Philadelphia, 8, 20, 64, 0 ; Boston, 6, 1, 2, 0.

Wigley.—Local, ' of Wigley,' i.e. the meadow that belonged to Wigg (q.v.). I cannot find the spot, but it is manifest that it must first be looked for in co. Derby.

John de Wyggeley, co. Derby, 20 Edw. I. R.
1601. Edmund Wigley, co. Derby, pleb. : Reg. Univ. Oxf. vol. ii. pt. ii. p. 251.
1793. Married — Joseph Wigley and Mary Heath : St. Geo. Han. Sq. ii. 95.
London, 6 ; Philadelphia, 1 ; Boston (U.S.), 5.

Wigman ; v. Wikman.

Wigmore.—Local, 'of Wigmore,' a parish in co. Hereford, ten miles from Leominster.

Richard de Wigmore gave land to the Church of St. Peter, Gloucester, in 1239 : Atkyns' Hist. Gloucestershire, p. 75.
1596. Warnecombe Wigmor, co. Heref. : Reg. Univ. Oxf. vol. ii. pt. ii. p. 216.
1602. Michael Wigmor, co. Soms. : ibid. p. 262.
1688. Henry Wigmore, or Wigmor, and Sarah Croke : Marriage Alleg. (Canterbury), p. 55.
1771. Married—Richard Wigmore and Mary Weston : St. Geo. Han. Sq. i. 208.
London, 5 ; MDB. (co. Gloucester), 2 ; Philadelphia, 6 ; Boston (U.S.), 1.

Wignall.—Local, 'of Wiggen-hall.' There are several parishes so named in co. Norfolk.

William de Wigenhale, co. Norf., temp. Hen. III : FF. vii. 352.
Richard de Wigenhale, co. Norf., 1273. A.
1588. Buried — Anne, wife of William Wignell : St. Mary Aldermary, p. 144.
1604. Elizabeth Wignall, of Chester : Wills at Chester (1545-1620), p. 209.
1605. Thomas Wignall, of Tarleton : ibid.
London, 2 ; MDB. (Norfolk), 1 ; Philadelphia, 6 ; Boston (U.S.), 1.

Wigzell.—Local, ' of Wigsell,' 'anciently Wigsale, an estate in the parish of Salehurst, co. Sussex ' (Lower).

London, 1.

Wike.—Local, ' at the wike,' from residence therein. ' *Wike,* a home, a dwelling' (Halliwell) ; v. Wykes.

William del Wik, or Wike, co. Kent, Hen. III-Edw. I. K.
Walter de la Wike, co. Bucks, 1273. A.
Henry de la Wyke, co. Oxf., ibid.
1777. Married—Robert Betterton and Mary Wike : St. Geo. Han. Sq. i. 273.
London, 1 ; Philadelphia, 1.

Wikman, Wigman, Wich-man, Wickman.—Bapt. 'the son of Wigman' (v. Yonge, ii. 410).

'Haec nomina sunt eorum, et hic census per annum, Johannes xii denarios, Osbernus 18d., Gualterus presbyter 8d., ... Wikemanus, 10d.'(Norwich) : FF. iv. p. 430 n.
William Wygeman, co. Soms., 1 Edw. III : Kirby's Quest, p. 93.
Alex. Wigman, co. Northampton, 1273. A.
Alan Wichman, co. Suff., ibid.
Geoffry Wygeman, co. York, ibid.
1565. John Wickman, Ch. Ch. : Reg. Univ. Oxf. vol. ii. pt. ii. p. 12.
London, 1, 0, 0, 0 ; Philadelphia, 0, 1, 1, 0, New York, 0, 0, 2, 1.

Wilberforce.—Local, ' of Wilberfoss,' a parish in E. Rid. Yorks, five miles from Pocklington.

Robert de Wylberfosse, co. York, 1273. A.
Peter de Wilberfoss, *potter,* 4 Edw. II : Freemen of York, i. 13.
John de Wilberfosse, *potter,* 4 Ric. II : ibid. i. 78.
1586. Edward Wilberfosse and Ann Monioye, alias Mountioye : Marriage Lic. (London), i. 152.
London, 1 ; Crockford, 3.

Wilbraham.—Local, ' of Wilbraham,' a manor in co. Ches.

Richard de Wilburgham, of Wilburgham, 43 Hen. III : Shirley's Noble and Gentle Men, quoted by Lower.
William de Wilburgham, 1286 : Cal. of Patent Rolls, i. 239.
Randle de Wylberham, co. Ches. : East Ches. ii. 397.
1508. William Wylbram : Reg. Univ. Oxf. i. 59.
1572. Richard Wilbraham, of Worleston : Wills at Chester, i. 209.
1611. Thomas Wilbraham, of Woodhey : ibid.
1622. Married — Randoll Wilbraham and Martha Markham : St. Michael's, Cornhill, p. 23.
London, 3 ; Philadelphia, 13.

Wilby.—Local, ' of Wilby,' villages in cos. Norfolk, Suffolk, and Northampton.

Robert de Wylcby, co. Northampton, Hen. III-Edw. I. K.
Wigan de Wyleby, co. Leicester, ibid.
Juliana de Wylleby, co. Notts, 1273. A.
1577-8. Richard Wilbie and Emma Tailor : Marriage Lic. (London), i. 79.
1603. Thomas Wilbe, or Wilbee, or Wilbie, co. York : Reg. Univ. Oxf. vol. ii. pt. ii. p. 264.
1687. John Wilby (co. Kent) and Mary Putnume : Marriage Alleg.(Canterbury), ii. 41.
London, 1 ; Philadelphia, 7 ; Boston (U.S.), 2.

Wilcock, Wilcocke, Wilcocks, Wilcockson, Wilcox, Wilcoxon, Wilcoxen. — Bapt. 'the son of William,' from nick. Will, and suffix *-cock* (v. Cocks) ; cf. Jeffcock, Simcock, &c.

Wilecoc Rossel, co. Devon, 1273. A.
Ricardus Wilkokson, 1379 : P. T. Yorks. p. 266.
Adam Wylkokson, 1379 : ibid.
Radulfus Wylcok', 1379 : ibid. p. 145.
Willelmus Wilkocson, 1379 : ibid. p. 174.
1526-7. Lawrence Hillis and Wynefred Wylcoks : Marriage Lic. (London), i. 5.
1576. Bapt.—John, s. Robert Wylecockes : St. Michael, Cornhill, p. 89.
1617. William Wilcock, of Flixton : Wills at Chester, i. 209.
1666. Richard Wilcoxen (co. Ches.) and Eleanor Starkey : Marriage Lic. (Faculty Office), p. 93.
London, 3, 3, 2, 2, 24, 1, 0 ; Philadelphia, 4, 0, 0, 0, 53, 0, 0 ; New York, 1, 0, 0, 0, 39, 1, 1.

Wild, Wilde, Wyld, Wylde. —Nick. 'wild, violent, untamed.' It was a popular sobriquet in Yorkshire, judging by the 1379 Poll Tax and the present county directory.

Emma la Willde, co. Oxf., 1273. A.
Walter le Wilde, co. Suff., ibid.
William le Wilde, co. Hunts, ibid.
William le Wild, 1313. M.

Johannes Wylde, 1379 : P. T. Yorks. p. 119 (common in this roll).
1660. Married—John Wray and Rachell Wylde : St. Dionis Backchurch, p. 36.
London, 30, 12, 3, 10 ; Sheffield, 28, 4, 0, 0 ; Philadelphia, 36, 38, 2, 0 ; Boston (U.S.), 29, 33, 0, 0.

Wildash, Wildish. — Local, ' at the wild ash,' from residence thereby ; cf. Ash, Nash, Birch, Rowntree, &c. The above seems to be the natural solution, but I have no proof.

1799. Married—Thomas Wildish and Mary Beale : St. Geo. Han. Sq. ii. 202.
1893. — Thomas Wildash and Hannah Beatson : Daily Telegraph, June 28, 1893.
London, 1, 4.

Wildblood.—Nick.'an untamed spirit.' The earliest instance I can discover is met with in Yorkshire. The surname still remains there.

Richard Wyldeblode, co. Yorks. W. 9.
Leonard Wildblood, 1607 : St. Mary Aldermary, p. 11.
1607. Bapt.—Edward, s. Richard Wildbloud : St. Jas. Clerkenwell, i. 48.
1626. James Carr and Mary Wildbloud : Marriage Lic. (London), ii. 164.
1633. George Johnson and Susanna Sturt, with consent of mother, Susanna Wildbloud : ibid. p. 216.
West Rid. Court Dir., 1.

Wildbore.—Nick. ' the wild boar'; cf. Wildgoose, Pigg, Hogg, Weatherhog, &c.

Willelmus Wyldebore, 1379 : P. T. Yorks. p. 193.
Johannes Wildebore, 1379 : ibid. p. 15.
Richard Wildbore, C. R., 35 Hen. VI.
1630. Married—Tobit Wildebore and Prissila Jonsonn : St. Antholin (London), p. 64.
1792. — Geo. Augustus Wildbore and Caroline Matilda Meadows : St. Geo. Han. Sq. ii. 76.
London, 2 ; West Rid. Court Dir., 1 ; Boston (U.S.), 1.

Wildern.—Local, ' at the wildern,' from residence in a wild, desert place, a wilderness ; v. Skeat on *wilderness.*

John atte-Wilderne, Fines Roll, 11 Edw. I.

Wilderspin ; v. Witherspoon.

Wildgoose.—Nick. 'the wildgoose,' from some characteristic resemblance to the habits of the bird.

Alicia Wyldguse, 1379 : P. T. Yorks. p. 172.
Robertus Wyldgose, *souter,* 1379 : ibid.

Simon Wildegose, C. R., 2 Ric. II.
1582-3. John Wylgose, co. Sussex:
Reg. Univ. Oxf. vol. ii. pt. ii. p. 126.
1603. Buried — William Wildgoose,
servant to William Pickering: St. Dionis
Backchurch, p. 207.
1774. Married — John Wildgoose and
Catherine Garvie: St. Geo. Han. Sq.
i. 240.
Sheffield, 1.

Wildish; v. Wildash.

Wildman.—Nick. 'wild man.'
In this case it is merely the familiar
nickname Wild, with an augmentative -*man*; cf. Merry and Merriman.

John Wildeman, C. R., 18 Ric. II.
Willelmus Wyldman, 1379: P. T.
Yorks. p. 286.
1748. Married—Thomas Wissett and
Ann Wildman: St. Michael, Cornhill,
p. 71.
London, 1; West Riding Court Dir.,
1; Leeds, 3; Philadelphia, 8; New
York, 1.

Wildsmith, Wyldsmith. —
Occup. I cannot discover an early
instance. I do not know the
origin. My first example is Wool-
smith, but that seems as hard of
solution as the rest. Nevertheless,
as the surname is almost entirely
confined to Yorkshire, the centre
of the woollen trade, some connexion may exist.

John Wollesmyth, C. R., 32 Hen. VI.
1659. Married—Afery Welsmith, Canterbury Cath. p. 59.
1787. Married—Joshua Jones and Anne
Wilesmith: St. Geo. Han. Sq. i. 398.
London, 1, 0; West Rid. Court Dir.,
3, 0; Sheffield, 1, 1; Leeds, 1, 0.

Wileman; v. Willman.

Wiley; v. Wylie.

Wilford.—Local, ' of Wilford,'
alias 'Wilfrid's-Ford,' a parish in
co. Notts.

Henry de Wylleford, co. Notts, 1273. A.
Gervase de Wyleford, co. Notts, Hen.
III–Edw. I. K.
Thomas de Wilford, co. Notts, 20 Edw.
I. R.
1555. Christopher Wilford and Frances
Jackes: Marriage Lic. (London), i. 16.
1559. Married—Thomas Wylforde and
Eliz. Hawes: St. Michael, Cornhill, p. 7.
1584. Robert Wylforde, co. Kent:
Reg. Univ. Oxf. vol. ii. pt. ii. p. 134.
London, 1; Philadelphia, 2; New
York, 6.

Wilful.—Nick. 'the wilful,' the
obstinate.

William le Wilfulle, co. Wilts, 1273. A.

Wilkerson, Wickerson.—
Bapt. 'the son of William,' corruptions of Wilkinson (v. Wilkin);
cf. Dickerson for Dickinson, Catterson for Cattinson, &c.

1782. Married — Robert Girling and
Ann Wilkerson: St. Geo. Han. Sq. i. 341.
London, 1, 0; New York, 1, 0; Boston
(U.S.), 1, 0.

Wilkes, Wilks.—Bapt. 'the
son of William,' from nick. Will,
and dim. Wil-kin (v. Wilkin); a
corruption of Wilkins through
Wilkiss or Wilkess. Cf. Perks and
Perkes for Perkins, Dawks and
Dawkes for Dawkins, &c. So early
as the 14th century we find Wilkson
for Wilkinson.

Thomas Wylkson, 1379: P. T. Yorks.
p. 144.
Johannes Wylkson, 1379: ibid.
1574. Robert Wylkes, co. Northampt.:
Reg. Univ. Oxf. vol. ii. pt. ii. p. 58.
1632. Bapt. — Dennys, d. Richard
Wilkes: St. Jas. Clerkenwell, p. 121.
1737. Married—Henry Wilks and Mary
Crafts: St. Geo. Han. Sq. i. 18.
London, 19, 16; Philadelphia, 2, 7;
New York, 3, 5.

Wilkey, Wilkie.—Bapt. 'the
son of William,' a pet form of
Wilkin, q.v. We also find Wilkison for Wilkinson.

1663-4. Buried—Susanna, wife of James
Wilkey: St. Dionis Backchurch
(London), p. 234.
1756. Married—Alex. Wylkie and Mary
Francis: St. Geo. Han. Sq. i. 62.
1788. Married — James Forward and
Sarah Wilkison: ibid. ii. 15.
London, 1, 12; Philadelphia, 3, 9;
New York, 2, 7.

**Wilkin, Wilkins, Wilkin-
son.**—Bapt. 'the son of William,'
from nick. Will, and dim. *kin*
(v. *kin*, Introd. p. 25); cf. Wat-kin,
Tomp-kin.

Wilechin fil.Monetarii,1167:KKK.vi.11.
Wilkelin de Laurecost,1196: RRR.p.78.
Ralph Wylekin, co. Norf., Hen. III–
Edw. I. K.
Amice Wylekun, co. Sussex, ibid.
Wilekin fil. Austen. C.
Wilkin le Furmager. O.
Thomas Wylkynson, 1379: P. T. Yorks.
p. 145.
Adam Wylkynson, 1379: ibid. p. 89.
Matilda Wylkyn, *doghter*, 1379: P. T.
Yorks. p. 175.
London, 11, 64, 122; Philadelphia, 0,
86, 157; Boston (U.S.), 1, 64, 55.

Wilks; v. Wilkes.

Wilkshire.—Local, a corruption of Wiltshire, q.v.

Boston (U.S.), 2.

Will.—(1) Local, 'at the well,'
from residence thereby. This form
occurs with fair frequency in
Kirby's Quest. (2) Bapt. 'the son
of Will,' gen. Wills; v. Willis.

William atte Wille, co. Soms., 1 Edw.
III: Kirby's Quest. p. 261.
1743. Married—John Will and Patience
Gardener: St. Geo. Han. Sq. i. 30.
London, 3; Philadelphia, 18; Boston
(U.S.), 3.

Willan, Willans.—Bapt. 'the
son of William,' from nick. Will,
and dim. Will-in, corrupted in the
North to the familiar Willan (v.
Willin); cf. *violin*, a little viol, or
Colin, little Cole (Nicholas).

1584. William Willeyne, co. Westm.:
Reg. Univ. Oxf. vol. ii. pt. ii. p. 137.
Rychard Willen, 1602, Hackthorp:
Hist. Westm. and Cumb. i. 97.
Christopher Wyllen, 1602, Hackthorp:
ibid.
1678. Married — Geffrey Willan and
Judeth Fawcett: St. Dionis Backchurch,
p. 39.
London, 3, 3; West Rid. Court Dir.,
3, 3; Philadelphia, 0, 5; New York, 0, 1.

Willard, Wellard.—Bapt. 'the
son of Willihard' (Yonge, ii. 227).
Although not confined to Kent,
that is the district in which the
surname is chiefly found.

Wihelardus de Trophil, 1168: KKK.
vi. 302.
Wilard de Pikeden, 1227: ibid. vi. 150.
Emayn Wylard, 1379: P. T. Yorks.
p. 294.
1602. William Willarde, co. Kent:
Reg. Univ. Oxf. vol. ii. pt. ii. p. 258.
1690-1. Nicholas Willard (co. Sussex)
and Jane Coumber: Marriage Alleg.
(Canterbury), ii. 175.
1750. Married—Sarah Willard: Reg.
Canterbury Cath.
London, 2, 2; Philadelphia, 42, 0;
Boston (U.S.), 63, 0.

**Willets, Willett, Willetts,
Willet.** — Bapt. 'the son of
William,' from the nick. Will, and
dim. Will-et or Will-ot; v. Gillott.

Richard Wylyot, co. Norf., 1273. A.
John Wylot, c. 1300. M.
Thomas Wiliot. J.
Thomas Wylott. F.
John Wilot, co. Soms., 1 Edw. III:
Kirby's Quest. p. 264.
1586. Buried, the wife of John Willet:
St. Thomas the Apostle (London), p. 97.
1764. Married—George Avery and
Eliz. Willett: St. Geo. Han. Sq. i. 138.

London, 1, 20, 2, 0; Manchester, 0, 6, 0, 0; Philadelphia, 5, 8, 5, 2; New York, 24, 17, 1, 3.

Willey.—(1) Local; v. Wylie. (2) Bapt.; v. Willy.

Willgoose.—A corruption of Wildgoose, q.v.

'Her bridesmaids, Miss Willgoose, Miss Leatherbarrow, . . . wore pretty costumes of cream colour': The Southport Visitor, Aug. 4, 1888.

Williams, Williamson, Willyams, William.—Bapt. 'the son of William.' For nearly eight centuries William and John have raced for first place in popularity. Legion is the name of their offspring, and to furnish instances would be absurd.

Johannes fil. Willelmi, 1379: P. T. Yorks. p. 144.
Hugo Williamson, 1379: ibid.
London, 464, 58, 1, 0; Philadelphia, 944, 154, 0, 8.

Willicombe; v. Welcome.

Willie; v. Willy.

Willimott; v. Wilmot.

Willin, Willing, Willings, Willinson, Willins, Wyling.—Bapt. 'the son of William,' from nick. Will, dim. Will-in (v. Willan). The g in Willing, &c., is excrescent, as in Jennings or Wareing.

Cecilia Wylyn, 1379: P. T.Yorks. p. 266.
Ricardus Wylyn, 1379: ibid.
Johannes Willion, 1379: ibid. p. 268.
1578-9. John Willins, co. Cardigan: Reg. Univ. Oxf. vol. ii. pt. ii. p. 86.
1704. Henry Willinson, of Docker: Lancashire Wills at Richmond, p. 283.
1750. Married—Frederic Willing and Eliz. Franklin: St. Geo. Chap. Mayfair, p. 161.
London, 1, 3, 2, 0, 0, 0; Philadelphia, 0, 8, 2, 0, 0, 1; New York, 0, 5, 1, 0, 1, 0.

Willis, Willison, Wills, Willies, Williss. — Bapt. 'the son of William,' from the nick. Will, Willy, or Willie. The final s represents the patronymic, as in the case of Williams, Jones, &c.

Johannes Willeson, 1379: P. T. Yorks. p. 231.
Willelmus Willeson, 1379: ibid. p. 62.
Adam Wylis, 1379: ibid. p. 174.
Robert Wylis, F.
Henry Wyllys, or Wylles, 1508: Reg. Univ. Oxf. i. 65.
1579. Bapt.—William, s. Henrie Willison: St. Mary Aldermary, p. 59.

1795. Married—Henry Willis and Sarah Linden: St. Geo. Han. Sq. ii. 140.
London, 82, 1, 36, 1, 0; West Rid. Court Dir., 11, 0, 1, 0, 2; Philadelphia, 59, 1, 61, 0, 0; New York, 68, 0, 13, 0, 0.

Willmer, Willmore, Wilmer, Wilmore, Willmire.—Bapt. 'the son of Wilmar' (Yonge, ii. 227).

Roger fil. Wilmer, co. Notts, 1273. A.
Nicholas Wilmar, co. Hunts, ibid.
Peter Wlmar, co. Camb., ibid.
1689. Bapt. — Edward Wilmore: St. John Bapt. on Wallbrook.
1730. Buried—John Willmore: St. Mary Aldermary (London), p. 221.
1806. Married—Matthew Willmer and Ann Warner: St. Geo. Han. Sq. ii. 357.
London, 3, 3, 0, 0, 0; Philadelphia, 0, 1, 20, 1, 1; New York, 2, 0, 4, 2, 0.

Willoughby.—Local, 'of Willoughby,' parishes in cos. Lincoln, Warwick, Notts, and Leicester.

Robert de Wylugheby, co. Linc., Hen. III-Edw. I. K.
Henry de Wiluby, co. Bucks, 1273. A.
William de Wilughby, co. Northampt., 20 Edw I. R.
Richard de Willughby, co. Notts, ibid.
Robert de Willughby, co. Derby, ibid.
1582. Edward Willoughbey, co. Linc.: Reg. Univ. Oxf. vol. ii. pt. ii. p. 119.
1501. Henry Willughby, or Willabie, co. Wilts: ibid. p. 187.
1620. Bapt. — Ann, d. John Willobie: St. Michael, Cornhill, p. 115.
London, 15; Philadelphia, 7; Boston (U.S.), 10.

Willows—Local, 'at the willows,' one who lived by a clump or stretch of willow trees.

Johannes atte Wylowes, 1379: P. T. Howdenshire, p. 16.
1579. William Willowes and Mary Westwoode: Marriage Lic. (London), i. 93.
1803. Married—Charles Willows and Eliz. Alderson: St. Geo. Han. Sq. ii. 281. London, 2.

Wills; v. Willis.

Willsher, Willshire.—Local. From Wiltshire, q.v.

London, 5, 1.

Willson; v. Wilson.

Willy, Willie, Willey.—(1) Bapt. 'the son of William,' from nick. Will, popularly Willy (v. Willis).

Thomas Wyly, 1379: P. T. Yorks. p. 150.

(2) Local; v. Wylie.

1586. Bapt.—Mary Willy, daughter of Richard Willye: St. Peter, Cornhill, i. 30.
1614. Thomas Williams and Eliz.

Willey: Marriage Lic. (Westminster), p. 22.
London, 6, 1, 11; West Rid. Court Dir., 0, 0, 7; Philadelphia, 0, 4, 0; New York, 0, 2, 8.

Wilman, Wileman, Willman.—Occup. 'Will-man,' i.e. the servant of Will; cf. Matthewman, Addiman, Harriman, Ladyman, Vickerman, &c. Nearly all this class of surnames hails from Yorkshire.

Adam Willeman, 1379: P. T. Yorks. p. 171.

The first three following dwelt in the village of Harewood.

Willelmus Thome-man, 1379: P T Yorks. p. 213.
Thomas Jon-man, 1379: ibid.
Walterus Wilman, 1379: ibid.
Simon Willeman, co. Camb., 1273. A.
1563. Married—Harry Willman and Alis Worship: St. Antholin (London), p.15.
1753. Married—William Willman and Eliz. Jackson: St. Geo. Chap. Mayfair, p. 266.
London, 0, 2, 1; West Rid. Court Dir., 4, 0, 0; Philadelphia, 2, 0, 1; New York, 0, 2, 0.

Wilmer v. Willmer.

Wilmington.—Local, 'of Wilmington,' parishes in cos. Kent and Sussex.

Stephen de Wilminton, co. Kent, Hen. III-Edw. I. K.
Robert de Wilmiton, co. Kent, ibid.
Jacob de Wylmingtun, co. Kent, 1273. A.
1599. John Willmington, co. Soms.: Reg. Univ. Oxf. vol. ii. pt. ii. p. 234.
London, 1; Philadelphia, 2; Boston (U.S.), 1.

Wilmot, Wilmott, Willimott.—Bapt. 'the son of William,' from dim. William-ot, used for both sexes. It existed in Cornwall as a girl's name till the close of the last century.

Williametta Cantatrix. E.
Gwillimett (without surname). E.
Gilemota Carrecke, co. York. W. 2.
Henry Wilmot, co. Camb., 1273. A.
Wylmot Swynhird, 1379: P. T. Yorks. p. 256.
Matilda Wylymot, 1379: ibid. p. 116.
1579. Hugh Wyllymott, of Knutsford, co. Ches.: East Cheshire, i, 309.
1603. Bapt. — John, son of Wyllmott Scobeld: Reg. St. Columb Major, p. 12.
1592. — Willmott, daughter of Robert Edwardes: St. Jas. Clerkenwell, p. 26.
1613. — Symon, s. Symon Willimott, *vintner*: St. Peter, Cornhill, i. 62.

1631. Bapt. — Wilmote, d. Patient Wilmote : Reg. St. Columb Major, p. 213.
London, 11, 3, 1 ; Philadelphia, 4, 1, 0 ; Boston (U.S.), 7, 0, 0.

Wilsher.—Local. From Wiltshire, q.v.

1653. Married—John Cane and Marye Wilshire : St. Michael, Cornhill, p. 31.
London, 5.

Wilson, Willson.—Bapt. 'the son of William,' from nick. Will. This surname rivals, in the multitude of its representatives, the famous patronymics Johnson, Jackson, Robinson, and Dickson or Dixon ; v. Willis.

Adam Wyllson, 1379 : P. T. Yorks. p. 279.
Thomas Wyllson, 1379 : ibid.
1604. Edw. Willson, or Wilson, co. Lanc. : Reg. Univ. Oxf. vol. ii. pt. ii. p.272.
London, 321, 32 ; Philadelphia, 930, 6.

Wilthew.—Bapt. ; v. Waldy, an undoubted descendant of Walthew or Waldew.

Newcastle-on-Tyne, 2.

Wilton.—Local, 'of Wilton,' a parish and borough in co. Wilts, on the river Wily, whence its name.

Margery de Wiliton, co. Berks, 1273. A.
Ralph de Wylyton, co. Wilts, ibid.
Ralph de Wyliton, co. Glouc., Hen. III-Edw. I. K.
Simon de Wiltone, co. Soms., 1 Edw. III : Kirby's Quest, p. 194.
1591. Bapt.—Mary, d. George Wilton : St. Jas. Clerkenwell, i. 25.
1751. Married—William Wilton and Mary Pearson : St. Geo. Han. Sq. i. 46.
London, 9 ; MDB. (co. Soms.), 10 ; Boston (U.S.), 10.

Wiltshire, Wiltsheare, Wiltsher, Wiltshier, Wiltshear.—Local, 'from Wiltshire.' This surname has now many forms ; v. Willsher, Wilsher, &c.; cf. Darbyshire, Cheshire, Kentish, Cornish, &c.

Hunfridus de Wilechier, 7 Hen. II : Pipe Roll. iv. 13.
Michael de Wyltesire, co. Camb., 1273. A.
William de Wyltesyre, co. Soms., ibid.
Roger de Wilteschire, co. Salop, ibid.
Almaric de Wilteshire, 1313. M.
Richard Wilteshire. B.
John Wiltsheere, 1680 : Reg. St. Mary Aldermary (London), p. 105.
1794. Married—William Wiltshire and Ann Hazell : St. Geo. Han. Sq. ii. 109.
1798. — Isaac Wiltshear and Sarah Dalloway : ibid. p. 184.

London, 19, 1, 1, 1, 0 ; MDB. (co. Oxford), 0, 0, 0, 0, 1 ; Philadelphia, 4, 0, 0, 0, 0 ; New York, 3, 0, 0, 0, 0.

Wimble.—Local. 'of Wymbhull.' I cannot find the spot. The suffix is *-hill* (v. Hull). It is quite natural to find the surname drop into the form of Wimble. Such modifications are common ; cf. Cockle, Windle, &c.

Roger de Wymbhull, co. Bedf., Hen. III-Edw. I. K.

Probably Wimple is a variant. It is found in the same district as the above.

1690. Thomas Foster and Mary Wimple (co. Essex) : Marriage Alleg. (Canterbury), ii. 163.
1789. Married—James Wimble and Martha Challand : St. Geo. Han. Sq. ii. 34.
London, 4.

Wimbush, Winbush.—Local, ' of Wimbush,' a parish in dioc. of St. Alban's, co. Essex.

Thomas de Winebise, co. Leic., Hen. III-Edw. I. K.
John de Wymbisse, co. Camb., 1273. A.
John Wimbis, co. Essex, ibid.
Simon de Wymbisse, co. Essex, ibid.

The modern corruption was early anticipated in the following entry :

John Wymbusch, Patent Roll, 1 Hen. VI. pt. v.
London, 1, 1 ; Philadelphia, 0, 1.

Wimer ; v. Wymer.

Wimpler. — Occupative, ' the wimpler,' a maker of wimples.

'Full seemly her wimple pinched was.'
Chaucer, C. T. 151.

Of Shame :

' Humble of her port, and made it simple,
Wearing a vaile, instede of wimple,
As nuns done in their abbey.'
id. R. Rose, 3863-5.

Alan le Wympler : Wardrobe Account, 49 Hen. III. 1/31.
Henry le Wimpler, co. Hunts, 1273. A.
William le Wimpler, C. R., 34 Hen. III.
William le Wympler. N.

Wimplester. — Occup. ' the wimplester,' a curious feminine of Wimpler. The only instance I have met with is that below ; cf. Slaster for Slater, or Walkster for Walker in the same county.

Crystiana Wympylster, 1379 : P. T. Howdenshire, p. 3.

Wimpory ; v. Winpenny.

Winbolt.—Bapt. ' the son of Winibald ' (v. Yonge, ii. 224).

Hence such place-names as Wimbledon, anciently written Wymbaldon, i.e. the *dune* or *down* of Wimbald, or Wimbald ; or Wimbotsham, a parish in co. Norf., i.e. the *ham* of Wimbot ; cf.

1618. Ellen Whishall, *widow*, of Wimbolsley (i. e. the meadow of Wimbald) : Wills at Chester, i. 205.

William Wernbald, co. Camb., 1273. A.
Matilda Weribold, co. Camb., ibid.
Wynebold de Balon gave half a hide to St. Peter of Glouc. in 1126 : Atkyns' Hist. of Glouc. p. 71.
1628. Married—Steeven Winnibote and Alis Eshbeach : St. Antholin (London), p. 62.
1795. — John Marscott and Rebekah Winboult : St. Geo. Han. Sq. ii. 132.
1746. — Edward Stallard and Eliz. Winbolt : St. Dionis Backchurch, p. 69.

Winbolt is now the accepted form. With this variant cf. Newbolt for Newbold.

London, 1.

Winbush ; v. Wimbush.

Winch.—(1) Local, 'of Winch.' There are two parishes in Norfolk of this name, viz. East and West Winch.

Peter de Winch, vicar of Ameringhall, co. Norf., 1382 : FF. v. 419.

(2) Local, 'at the winch,' from residence beside some particular windlass for drawing water from a deep well, &c.

Thomas atte Wynch, 19 Edw. I : BBB. p. 434.
1628. Bapt.—Nathaniell, d. William Winch, *grocer* : St. Peter, Cornhill, i. 78.
1752. Buried—Ann Winch, in the churchyard : St. Michael, Cornhill, p. 300.

It is probable that (1) has furnished us with most of our Winches.

London, 16 ; MDB. (Norfolk), 2 ; Philadelphia, 6 ; Boston (U.S.), 14.

Winchester.—Local, ' of Winchester,' a city in co. Hants.

Ralph de Wincestre, co. Norf., 1273. A.
Nicholas Winchestre, co. Suff., ibid.
John de Wynchester, *piscarius*, 7 Edw. II : Freemen of York, i. 15.
Robertus Wynchester, 1379 : P. T. Yorks. p. 91.
1724. Bapt.—John, son of John Winchester : St. Jas. Clerkenwell, p. 151.
1804. Married—James Winchester and Eliz. Edge : St. Geo. Han. Sq. ii. 312.
London, 5 ; Oxford, 4 ; Philadelphia, 18 ; Boston (U.S.), 21.

Winckle ; v. Winkle.

Wincott, Winnicott.—? Bapt. 'the son of Wingod.' The name looks local, but I find no spot of that shape or form, while Wynegod was early turned into a surname, and its inevitable corruption would be Wincot. Nevertheless, on the face of it the origin would seem to be local.

Robert Wynegod, co. Oxf., 1273. A.
William Wynegod, co. Soms., ibid.
1582-3. Charles Wincote, co. Warw.: Reg. Univ. Oxf. vol. ii. pt. ii. p. 125.
1590. William Wyncotte, co. Warw.. ibid. p. 180.
1761. Married—John Dipple and Sarah Wincote: St. Geo. Han. Sq. i. 102.
London, 2, 1.

Windebank. — Local, 'of Windebank,' probably from residence 'at the windy bank.' Many small spots would naturally bear this name; cf. Swithenbank, Brooksbank, &c.

Nan of Windebank, 1422, Ashton-under-Lyne: Custom Roll and Rental, Cheth. Soc.
1599. Francis Windebank, or Wyndebancke, London: Reg. Univ. Oxf. vol. ii. pt. ii. p. 234.
1686. Sir Francis Windebanke, Bart., and Eliz. Parkhurst: Marriage Lic. (Faculty Office), p. 179.
1792. Married—Ottewell Timmess and Sarah Windebank: St. Geo. Han. Sq. ii. 85. London, 1.

Windel (1; v. Windle.

Winder.—Local, (1) 'of Winder,' a township in parish of Lamplugh, co. Cumb. ; (2) Low Winder, a township in parish of Barton, co. Westm. ; (3) High Winder, near Carnforth, North Lanc. There can be no doubt as to the local origin of the Cumberland and North Lancashire Winders. The home of the latter is High Winder.

Thomas Winder, of Hygh Winder, 1616: Lancashire Wills at Richmond, p. 318.
Christopher Winder, of Hye Winder, 1618: ibid. p. 317.
Elizabeth Winder, of High Winder, 1676: ibid.
1604. Samuel Winder, co. Berks: Reg. Univ. Oxf. vol. ii. pt. ii. p. 278.
1736. Bapt.—Sarah, d. Michael Winder: St. Jas. Clerkenwell, ii. 230.
London, 7; Lancaster, 1; Ulverston, 1; Philadelphia, 5; New York, 3.

Windhouse; v. Windus.

Windle, Windell, Windel.— Local, 'of Windhill,' a hamlet in the township of Idle, co. York. The tendency of the suffix -hill is to become -le ; cf. Cockle, Wimble, &c. Also 'of Windle,' a township in the parish of Prescot, co. Lanc.

Willelmus de Wyndhill, 1379 : P. T. Yorks. p. 55.
Johannes de Wyndhill, 1379 : ibid.
1577. Christopher Windle, co. York : Reg. Univ. Oxf. vol. ii. pt. ii. p. 79.
1607. George Rowley and Margaret Windle : Marriage Lic. (London), i. 301.
1684. William Cooper and Isabel Windell : Marriage Alleg. (Canterbury), p. 166.
1726. Bapt.—Mary, d. George Windall : St. Jas. Clerkenwell, ii. 159.
London, 6, 2, 0 ; Philadelphia, 12, 2, 0 ; New York, 0, 0, 1.

Windmill. — Local, 'at the windmill,' from residence thereby, a miller.

1683. Buried—Richard Windmill : St. Mary Aldermary, p. 195.
1779. Married—William Windmill and Mary Elsley : St. Geo. Han. Sq. i. 299.
MDB. (co. Soms.), 4.

Windmiller, Winemiller.—Occup. 'the wind-miller.' I do not think this is English. I find no traces of it. But v. Windmillward.

Philadelphia, 1, 0 ; Boston (U.S.), 0, 1.

Windmillward.—Offic. 'the custodian of a windmill'; v. Millward.

William Wyndmilward. D.

Windows.—Local ; v. Windus. Oxford, 2.

Windross.—Local, 'of Winderhouse.' The local term winder is common in North Lancashire; v. Winder.

Nicholas Winderhouse, of Tarniker, 1672 : Lancashire Wills at Richmond, i. 318.
George Windresse, of Bispham, 1661 : ibid.
William Windress, of Lower Wyersdales, 1678 : ibid.
Robert Windrass, of Lytham, 1707 : ibid. ii. 287.
Manchester, 1.

Windsor.—Local, 'of Windsor,' a parish, borough, and market-town, co. Berks, anciently Windleshora, said to have arisen from the winding course of the Thames.

Hugh de Windelsor, London, 1273. A.
John de Wyndesoure, co. Oxf., ibid.
1564-5. Miles Wyndser, Corp. Christi Coll. : Reg. Univ. Oxf. vol. ii. pt. ii. p. 15.

1620. Buried — Dorothy, d. Henry Windsore : St. Jas. Clerkenwell, iv. 149.
1734. Married— — Windsor and Eliz. Perkins : St. Geo. Han. Sq. i. 14.
London, 10 ; Philadelphia, 2 ; Boston (U.S.), 3.

Windus, Windhouse.—Local, 'of the wind-house,' probably a place for winding threads ; v. Windross. With the suffix -us for house, cf. Loftus, Kirkus, Bacchus.

Willelmus de Wyndhows, 1379 : P. T. Yorks. p. 275.
1674. Robert Dowling and Frances Windowes : Marriage Alleg. (Canterbury), p. 120.
1692. Married—Arthur Windus and Mary Soloman : St. Jas. Clerkenwell, iii. 211.
London, 2, 0 ; New York, 0, 1.

Winfarthing. — Local, 'of Winfarthing,' a parish in Norfolk.

Thomas de Wynneferthyn, co. Camb., 1273. A.
Walter de Wynneferthing, Close Roll, 5 Edw. I.
Robert de Winfarthing, rector of Bergh-Apton, 1342 : FF. x. 99.

Winfield. — Local, 'of Winfield,' a township in the parish of Wrotham, co. Kent. Occasionally this surname represents Wingfield, q.v.

Richard de Winfeld, co. Northumb., 1273. A.
1778. Married Joseph Winfield and Mary Nickolls : St. Geo. Han. Sq. i. 220.
1788. — James Wynfield and Eliz. Adams : ibid. ii. 12.
MDB. (co. Kent), 1; (co. Derby), 3; London, 3; New York, 4; Boston (U.S.), 6.

Wing. — Local, 'of Wing,' parishes in cos. Rutland and Bucks. It is found at an early period in the district.

Geoffrey Wenge, co. Hunts, 1273. A.
William Wenge, co. Hunts, ibid.
1599. John Wynge, co. Oxf. : Reg. Univ. Oxf. vol. ii. pt. ii. p. 235.
1621. Matthew Wynge, co. Oxf., ibid. p. 402.
1626. Married — Richard Gwynn and Dyonis Winge : St. Jas. Clerkenwell, iii. 56.
London, 11 ; MDB. (co. Oxf.), 3 ; (co. Bedford), 3 ; Philadelphia, 5 ; New York, 23.

Wingate, Winget.—(1) ? Bapt. 'the son of Wingod' (?). This might be easily corrupted to Wingate. Both prefix and suffix are common ingredients in early personal names ; cf. Baldwin, Selwin, Oswin, Un-

3 G

win, and Osgood, Thoroughgood, &c. Wingod is simply Godwin reversed.

John Wynegod, co. Oxf., 1273. A.
Robert Wynegod, co. Oxf., ibid.
William Wynegod, co. Soms., ibid.
1776. Married — Charles Nevill and Mary Wingod: St. Geo. Han. Sq. i. 269.

(2) Local, 'of Wingate,' a township in the parish of Kelloe, co. Durham.

John de Wyngate, co. Kent, Hen. III–Edw. I. K.
1672. Married—Sir Francis Wingate, Kt., and Ann Fish: St. Mary Aldermary, p. 31.

(1) needs more confirmatory evidence before it can be accepted.
London, 2, 1; Philadelphia, 11, 0; Boston (U.S.), 4, 0.

Wingfield.—Local, 'of Wingfield,' parishes in cos. Suffolk and Derby (2). Winfield is the present form in Derbyshire of this local surname; v. Winfield.

1674. Buried — Edward Wingfeild, Esq., under the gallery: Kensington Parish Church, p. 146.
1703. Married—Henry Wingfeild and Mary Bunby: St. Mary Aldermary, p. 37. London, 14; New York, 1.

Wingham.—Local, 'of Wingham,' a parish nine miles from Canterbury, co. Kent. From the evidence below it would seem that other spots were so called.

Henry de Wyngeham, co. Kent, 1273. A.
Henry de Wingham, co. Linc., ibid.
Walter de Wingham, co. Som., ibid.
William de Wingham, co. Wilts, ibid.
William de Wingham, co. Surrey, 20 Edw. I. K.
Hugh de Wyngeham, co. Soms., Hen. III–Edw. I. K.
1616. Arthur Wingham, London: Reg. Univ. Oxf. vol. ii. pt. ii. p. 356.
1618. Roger Bragg and Mary Wingham: Marriage Lic. (London), ii. 66. London, 3; New York, 1.

Winkfield.—Local, 'of Winkfield,' parishes in co. Berks and co. Wilts.

1558. Bapt. — Ellen Winckefeeld, *daughter*: St. Peter, Cornhill, i. 8. London, 2; Manchester, 2.

Winkle, Winckle, Winkel. —(1) Local, 'of Wincle,' a township near Macclesfield, on the extreme border of Cheshire, only separated from Staffordshire by the river Dane. It is called 'Winchul,'

c. 1200 (East Cheshire, ii. 432), so we may presume that *-hill* is the suffix; cf. Windle, Cockle, &c.

1565. Richard Winkle: Reg. Univ. Oxf. i. 424.
Jane Winckle, of Leyland, *husbandman*, 1635: Wills at Chester (1621-50), p. 239.
1675. James Clowse and Mary Winckle: Marriage Alleg. (Canterbury), ii. 143.
1779. Married — John Grange and Mary Winkell: St. Geo. Han. Sq, i. 298.

(2) Nick. 'the winkle,' the periwinkle. I do not suppose this bears any relation to our present Winkles, but it is worth while recording the following entry:

John le Wenchel, co. Bucks, 1273. A.
Manchester, 1, 0, 0; Liverpool, 0, 1, 0; New York, 5, 2, 0; Philadelphia, 2, 3, 0.

Winkley. — Local, (1) 'of Winkley,' or Winckleigh, a parish in co. Devon; (2) 'of Winckley,' a hall and estate in the township of Aighton, and parish of Mitton, co. Lanc. Hence the Lancashire surname. 'In the Coucher Book of the neighbouring abbey of Whalley, the name of Robert de Wynkedelegh occurs in 4 Edw. I' (Lower's Patr. Brit. p. 385).

Michael de Wynklegh, co. Devon, 1273. A.
Richard de Wynklegh, co. Devon, ibid.
Michael de Wynkeleg, co. Devon, Hen. III–Edw. I. K.
1677-8. William Winckley and Magdalen Taylor: Marriage Alleg. (Canterbury), ii. 215.
Francis Winckley, of Preston, 1746: Lancashire Wills at Richmond (1681-1748), p. 286.
Thomas Winckley, of Preston, 1714: ibid.
1807. Married—Thomas Winkley and Eliz. Watson: St. Geo. Han. Sq. ii. 375. London, 3; Manchester, 1; Boston (U.S.), 12.

Winks, Wink.—? Bapt. 'the son of Wink' (?). This surname is firmly established in co. York; cf. Winkfield and Winkley.

Ricardus Wynk', 1379: P. T. Yorks. p.4.
Alexander Wynk, 1379: ibid. p. 163.
Robertus Wynk, 1379: ibid.
1587. Richard Wyncke and Johanna Bonner: Marriage Lic. (London), i. 161.
1727. Married—Robert Kyll and Margaret Wincks: St. Jas. Clerkenwell, iii. 254.
West Rid. Court Dir., 3, 0; Sheffield, 3, 0; London, 3, 0.

Winn(e.—Nick.; v. Wynn.

Winnicott; v. Wincott.

Winpenny, Wimpeny, Wimpery, Wimpory.—? Nick. 'Winpenny' (cf. Pennyfather). Perhaps what it looks, 'Win-penny,' a sobriquet for one of 'acquisitive habits.' But the entry

John Vympany: Pat. Roll, 3 Edw. VI. pt. iii.

which manifestly is the same name, seems a somewhat early contradiction of this view. In any case, Wimpory appears to be a corruption.

Henry Winpenny, bailiff of Bristol, 1316: Barrett's Hist. Bristol.
William Wynpeny, co. York, 1468. W. 11.
1794. Married — William Cross and Sarah Winpenny: St. Geo. Han. Sq. ii. 6.
Manchester, 2, 0, 0, 2; Philadelphia, 6, 0, 0, 0; New York, 1, 0, 0, 0.

Winrow.—Local; v. Whineray.

Winscombe.—Local, 'of Winscombe,' a parish in co. Somerset, two miles from Axbridge.

William Wynscombe, co. Soms., 9 Edw. II: Kirby's Quest, p. 134.
MDB. (co. Soms.), 2.

Winser, Winsor.—Local, 'of Windsor,' a natural modification; v. Windsor.

1605. Married — Griffith Evan and Ann Winsor: St. Mary Aldermary (London), p. 11.
Robert Masone, of Winsore, 1626: ibid. p. 16.
1794. — Joseph Winsor and Mary Miller: St. Geo. Han. Sq. ii. 106.
London, 5, 6; Philadelphia, 0, 4; Boston (U.S.), 0, 25.

Winsome. — Nick. 'the winsome,' attractive, lovely. M.E. *winsom.*

Matilda Wensom, co. Hunts, 1273. A.

Winstanley.—Local, 'of Winstanley,' a township in the parish of Wigan, co. Lanc.

Roger de Winstanleg', temp. John: Baines' Lanc. ii. 189.
1555. James Winstanley, of Winstanley: Wills at Chester (1545-1620), p. 212.
1603. Edward Winstanley, of Woodhouses, Wigan: ibid.
1575. Married — Thomas Porte and Margaret Wynstanley: St. Michael, Cornhill, p. 11.
Manchester, 8; London, 6; Philadelphia, 2.

Winston, Winstone, Winson.—Local, 'of Winston': (1)

a hamlet near Barnard Castle, co. Durham; (2) a hamlet near Debenham, co. Suffolk; (3) a hamlet near Cirencester, co. Gloucester. The variant Winson is fairly familiar. In a similar way Kelson is a modification of Kelston.

John de Wynston, co. Kent, 1273. A.
William de Wynestone, co. Suff., ibid.
Adam de Wynestone, co. Hunts, ibid.
Thomas Wynston, 1379: P. T. Howdenshire, p. 27.
1651. Married — William Smith and Anne Winston: St. Dionis Backchurch, p. 27.
1657. Buried — Francis, wife of Edmond Browne, from Mr. Winstons: St. Mary Aldermary, p. 180.
1790. — John Winson and Maria Allison: St. Geo. Han. Sq. ii. 41.
London, 0, 5, 0; Philadelphia, 7, 0, 3; Boston (U.S.), 10, 0, 0.

Winter, Wynter.—Bapt. 'the son of Winter.' The ecclesiastical seasons all made their mark on the font; cf. Pentecost, Whitsunday, Noel, Nowell, Christmas, Middlemass (Michaelmas). The natural seasons gave personal names in the same way. 'Summer and Winter are both ancient names; in the *Cod. Dip. Alamannioe* there are two brothers called respectively Sumar and Winter, A. D. 858.' Winter was also the name of one of the companions of Hereward the Saxon' (Ferguson, Surnames as a Science, p. 182). Although a pre - Norman personal name, Winter survived the Conquest, and attained hereditary honours as a surname in the 13th cent. We may observe here that Winter is compounded with several local surnames, such as Wintersgill, Winterbotham, Winterburn, or Winterflood. Professor Skeat shows that *winter* means literally the wet season. In these placewords we recognize low-lying hollows or streams liable to be flooded by winter rains, although dry in the summer.

Philip Winter, C. R., 48 Hen. III.
John Winter. H.
Wynter Mariot, co. Norf., 1273. A.
Colle Winter, co. Camb., ibid.
Emma Wynter, 1379: P. T. Yorks. p. 300.
London, 47, 0; Crockford, 18, 2; Philadelphia, 51, 0; Boston (U.S.), 18, 0.

Winterborn, Winterburn, Winterbourn.—Local, ' of Winterburn,' a township in the parish of Gargrave, near Skipton, co. York. There are also twenty parishes called Winterbourne in England. For suggested origin, v. Winter and Burn.

Walter de Winterburne, co. Oxf., 1273. A.
Thomas de Wynterburn, 1379: P. T. Yorks. p. 258.
1672. Bapt. — Warrdell, s. William Winterborne: St. Jas. Clerkenwell, p. 253.
London, 2, 1, 2; Oxford (Winterborne), 2; Philadelphia, 0, 1, 0; New York, 0, 3, 0.

Winterbottom, Winterbotham. — Local, ' of Winterbottom'; for origin, v. Winter. Like most of the surnames whose suffix is the local -*bottom*, Winterbottom arose in the south-east corner of Lancashire, on the Cheshire and Yorkshire borders. It is believed that Saddleworth is its precise and original habitat; v. Higginbotham, Shufflebottom, and Botham.

1564. Married — John Dowleye and Agnes Wintrebothom: Reg. Prestbury Ch. (Cheshire), p. 14.
1590. Orme Winterbottom, parish of Ashton-under-Lyne: Wills at Chester (1545–1620), p. 213.
1593. Jarvis Winterbottom, of Mosley, Ashton-under-Lyne: ibid.
1618. Richard Winterbotham, of Hartshead, Ashton-under-Lyne: ibid.
1644. Buried—George Winterbothom, stewarde of Stockport: Reg. Stockport Parish Ch. (vide East Cheshire, i. 408).
1653. Robert Winterbothom, mayor of Stockport: ibid. p. 347.
Manchester, 7, 2; London, 3, 3; Philadelphia, 27, 1; New York, 8, 0.

Winterflood. — Local, ' of Winterflood'; v. Winter for origin. I do not find the spot.

Walter de Winterflod, co. Essex, 1273. A.
Ralph de Wynterfled, co. Essex, ibid.
1567. Thomas Sedgewyke and Grace Winterfloode, co. Norf.: Marriage Lic. (Faculty Office), p. 14.
1808. Married—John Ellison and Eliz. Winterflood: St. Geo. Han. Sq. ii. 383. London, 4.

Winterscale, Wintersgill.—Local, ' of Winterscale,' i. e. the winter cot or hut; v. Scales. Wintersgill is a corruption, though -*gill* is a local suffix; cf. Summerscales and Summersgill. The spot

whence the surname arose lies in the parish of Ingleton, W. Rid. Yorks.

William Proctor, of Winterscall, parish of Ingleston (sic), 1611: Wills at Chester (1545–1620), p. 156.
Magota de Wynterscale, 1379: P. T. Yorks. p. 290.
Johannes Wynterscalle, 1379: ibid. p. 288.

Of these two, Magota lived in Ingleton, and John in Dent, in the immediate district. No further evidence is needed as regards the precise spot.

1638. Married—William Winterscale and Jane Hurd: St. Jas. Clerkenwell, iii. 20.
1769. — Thomas Loomes and Ann Wintersgill: St. Geo. Han. Sq. i. 189.
West Rid. Court Dir., 0, 1; Leeds, 0, 1; Manchester, 0, 1.

Winterton.—Local, ' of Winterton,' two parishes, one in co. Norf., the other in that of Lincoln.

Richard de Winterton, co. Norf., 1273. A.
Walter de Winterton, co. Warw., ibid.
Henry de Wyntreton, co. Staff., Edw. I. R.
1626. Robert Winterton and Mary Bateman: Marriage Lic. (London), i. 181.
1636. Buried — A still-born child of Thomas Winterton: St. Jas. Clerkenwell, iv. 219.
London, 3, New York, 2; Boston (U.S.), 4.

Winthrop.—Local, ' of Winthorpe,' parishes in cos. Lincoln and Notts. v. Thorp.

1539. Bapt.—Alice, d. Ade Wintrop: St. Peter, Cornhill, i. 1.
1543. — Bridget Wintrope: ibid. p. 3.
1652. — Margiat, the dafter (sic) of Stephen Winthrop: Kensington Parish Church, p. 39.
1714. Married — Peter Wentrup and Jane Archer: St. Jas. Clerkenwell, iii. 237.
Crockford, 1; New York, 13.

Winton.—Local, ' of Winton': (1) a township in parish of Kirkby-Sigston, N. Rid. Yorks; (2) a township in parish of Kirkby-Stephen, co. Westmorland.

Thomas de Wineton, co. Kent, 1273. A.
John de Wintun, co. Kent, ibid.
1576. Roger Robynson and Alice Wynton: Marriage Lic. (London), i. 72.
1645. Scudamor Winton and Faith Scott: ibid. ii. 276.
London, 3; Philadelphia, 2; Boston (U.S.), 1.

3 G 2

Winyard.—Local, 'at the wine-yard,' from residence thereby. A.S. *win-geard*, vineyard.

William atte Wyneard, co. Soms., 1 Edw. III : Kirby's Quest, p. 138.
1506. William Wynnyarde : Reg. Univ. Oxf. i. 49.
1577. Richard Wynyard, Merton Coll.: ibid. vol. ii. pt. ii. p. 456.
1665. Married — Edward Winniyard and Mary Banister : St. Jas. Clerkenwell, iii. 118.
1729. — Thomas Whinyard and Eliz. Larcomb : St. Antholin (London), p. 143. London, 4.

Wiredrawer. — Occup. ' the wire-drawer.'

'Cappers, wyerdrawers, pynners,' Chester Play, 1339: Ormerod's Hist. Cheshire, i. 300.
'Bedmakers, fedbedmakers, and wyre-drawers' : Cocke Lorelle's Bote.
Robert le Wyrdraere: Wardrobe Account, 49 Hen. III, 1/31.
Will. de Pontefracto, *wyrdragher*, 42 Edw. III : Freemen of York, i. 65.
William de Wirdrawere, London. X.
Rauf le Wyrdrawere, ibid.

This surname I believe to be extinct.

Wisbey, Wisby.—Local, ' of Whisby,' a chapelry in the parish of Doddington, co. Linc.

1758. Married — Thomas Wisbey and Margaret Ryan: St. Geo. Han. Sq. i. 77. London, 1, 2.

Wiscar.—Bapt. ; v. Whiskard.

Wisdom.—Local, ' of Wisdom,' a place or estate in the parish of Cornwood, co. Devon. v. Lower's Patr. Brit. p. 386. All my instances prove the surname to be West Anglian.

Wymund Wysdom, co. Somerset, 1273. A.
Hugh Wysdam, co. Somerset, ibid.
Richard Wysdem, co. Somerset, 20 Edw. I. R.
Robert Wisdom, co. Soms., 1 Edw. III: Kirby's Quest, p. 206.
Thomas Wisdom, M.P. for Wilton, C. R., 51 Edw. III.
Elizabeth Wisedome, 1542 : Reg. Broad Chalke, co. Wilts, p. 6.
Dorothy Wisedom, 1551 : ibid.
1653. Married—Henry Wisdome and Alyce Haward : St. Jas. Clerkenwell, iii. 89.
1756. — John Wisdom and Lydia Beedal : St. Geo. Han. Sq. i. 67. London, 4; Philadelphia, 4; Boston (U.S.), 1.

Wise, Wyse.—Nick. 'the wise,' the learned ; v. Wiseman. Of the nine instances of Wise in the Hundred Rolls (vol. ii), eight resided either in Oxfordshire or Cambridgeshire. No doubt all were University men !

Elias le Wyse, co. Oxf., 1273. A.
Henry le Wyse, co. Hunts, ibid.
William le Wyse, C. R., 4 Edw. II.
Thomas le Wys, Pat. Roll, 3 Edw. VI. pt. iii.
1668-9. Stephen Dring and Patience Wyse, d. John Wise: Marriage Alleg. (Canterbury), ii. 262.
London, 30, 0; Philadelphia, 92, 0; New York, 36, 1.

Wisehead.—Nick. ' the wise-head '; cf. Wise and Wiseman.

Johannes Wysehede, 1379: P. T. Yorks. p. 158.

Wiseman. — Nick. ' the wise man,' the clever, the learned man ; v. Wise. It is curious and interesting to note that the instances of Wise and Wiseman in the Hundred Rolls are nearly all from the two University counties.

Roger Wyseman, co. Oxf., 1273. A.
Alan Wysman, co. Camb., ibid.
John Wysman, co. Oxf., ibid.
Johannes Wysman, 1379 : P. T. Yorks. p. 152.
Petrus Wysman, 1379 : ibid. p. 145.
1656. Married — Thomas Duncombe and Margaret Wiseman: St. Michael, Cornhill, p. 37.
London, 17; Philadelphia, 15; Boston (U.S.), 9.

Wisker ; v. Whiskard.

Wisler, Wissler ; v. Whistler.

Wiston ; v. Whiston.

Witby; v. Whitby.

Witcomb.—Local, 'of Witcomb Magna,' a parish in co. Glouc., near Painswick.

1757. Married — James Rendall and Rachael Witcomb: St. Geo. Han. Sq. i. 68.
London, 1 ; Oxford, 2 ; New York, 1.

Witham, Whitham, Whittome, Whittum, Whittam, Whittem.—Local, ' of Witham,' parishes in cos. Essex, Somerset, and Lincoln (3). The variant Whittum is American; cf. Barnum for Barnham.

John de Wytham, 'the king's chaplain,' 1286: Cal. of Patent Rolls, i. 240.
1583-4. John Cramp and Thomasine Wyttham: Marriage Lic. (London), i. 127.

1625. Buried — A childe of William Wittam's: St. Jas. Clerkenwell, iv. 184.
1752. Bapt. — Thomas, s. John Whittam : ibid. ii. 302.
1777. Married—Philip Paine and Mary Witham : St. Geo. Han. Sq. i. 278.
London, 6, 1, 3, 0, 1, 0; MDB. (co. Camb.), Whittome, 3; Philadelphia, 0, 3, 0, 0, 0, 1 ; Boston (U.S.), 20, 0, 0, 2, 0, 1.

Withecomb ; v. Widdicombe and Withycomb.

Withers.—Bapt. ' the son of Wither.' Lower writes : ' Wither occurs in Domesday as a tenant prior to that census.' The surname constantly appears in the Hundred Rolls, but always without prefix, suggesting that its origin is personal; cf. Witherslack, Withersfield, Withersdale, Witherley, all parishes set down in Crockford.

Agnes Wyther, co. Camb., 1273. A.
Richard Wyther, co. Oxf., ibid.
Simon Wyther, co. Hunts, ibid.
Walter Wythor, co. Camb., ibid.
1590. Married — Jeames Wythers and Ann Graye : St. Michael, Cornhill, p. 15.
London, 28 ; Oxford, 3 ; Philadelphia, 11 ; Boston (U.S.), 4.

Witherspoon, Wodder-spoon, Wilderspin, Wother-spoon. —? ——. I can make nothing out of this surname, and leave it to the consideration of more enlightened students. I can furnish them with materials, but that is all. My Yorkshire references clearly represent some of its ancestors.

Adam Wytherpyn, co. Norf., 1273. A.
Adam Wyerpin, co. Norf., ibid.
Johannes Withspone, 1379: P. T. Yorks. p. 36.
Willelmus Wythspone, 1379 : ibid.
John Wetherpyn, vicar of Thrickby, co. Norf., 1419 : FF. xi. 254.
Liverpool Court Dir., 1, 0, 0, 0 ; London, 1, 1, 1, 4 ; Philadelphia, 0, 0, 0, 3; Boston (U.S.), 4, 0, 0, 0.

Withey, Wethey, Withy, Withye. — Local, ' at the white hay,' i.e. the white hedge (v. Hay), from residence thereby ; cf. Whitfield, Whitworth, &c., and v. Whitey.

William ate Wythege, co. Oxf., 1273. A.
Nicholas de la Wythege, co. Oxf., ibid.
Walter de la Wythege, co. Hants, ibid.
Richard Whitheye, co. Linc., ibid.
Thomas atte Withigh, co. Soms., 9 Edw. II : Kirby's Quest, p. 154.
1564. William Withie, Ch. Ch. : Reg. Univ. Oxf. vol. ii. pt. ii. p. 12.

1799. Married — Thomas Withy and Mary Pratt : St. Geo. Han. Sq. ii. 202. London, 9, 2, 0, 0 ; MDB. (co. Soms.), 0, 0, 4, 1 ; New York, 2, 0, 0, 0 ; Boston (U.S.), 3, 0, 0, 0.

Withipoll.—Local, 'of Withypoole,' a parish in dioc. Bath and Wells. Blomefield seems to speak of another place :

The manor of West Bradenham, co. Norf., came by marriage to Sir William Wythypole, of Whythypole, in Shropshire : FF. vi. 143.
Poule Withipoule, *taillour* : Rutland Papers, Camden Soc.
1599. Buried — Edmund, s. Edmund Withypoole, Esq. : St. Jas. Clerkenwell, iv. 64.

Withthebeard.—Nick. Either to distinguish from another man of the same Christian name, or because the beard was rarely worn at the period.

William Withtheberd, Close Roll, 23 Edw. III. pt. ii.
John Wytheberd. RR. 1.
Peter Wi-the-berd. D.
Cf. Brownbeard and Blackbeard, q.v. ; also cf. Hugh Barbatus (Domesday).

Withy ; v. Withey.

Withycomb, Withecomb.—Local, 'of Withycombe,' a parish in co. Somerset. Cf. Widdicombe.

Walter de Wydecombe, co. Soms., 1327 : Tax Poll.
1665. Buried — William Withecom : St. Jas. Clerkenwell, iv. 368.
1793. Married — John Mortimer and Martha Withycombe : St. Geo. Han. Sq. ii. 105.
MDB. (co. Somerset), 3, 0 ; Manchester, 0, 1.

Witmore ; v. Whitmore.

Witney, Withney. — Local, 'of Witney,' a parish in co. Oxford ; v. Whitney.

John de Witteneye, co. Suff., 1273. A.
1619. Buried — Helline Witney : St. Jas. Clerkenwell, iv. 144.
1806. Married — Wright Witney and Amelia Worrall : St. Geo. Han. Sq. ii. 350.
London, 2, 0 ; New York, 0, 1.

Witton.—Local, 'of Witton'; parishes in cos. Lanc., Yorkshire, and Durham.

Johannes de Wytton, 1379 : P. T. Yorks. p. 206.
1681. Married — Mathew Wytton and Eliz. Harden : St. Jas. Clerkenwell, iii. 192.

1740. Buried — Eliz. Witton : St. Dionis Backchurch, p. 308.
London, 4 ; Philadelphia, 1.

Witty, Wittey.—Local, 'at the white hay,' from residence thereby ; v. Withey for early instances.

1697. Married — Griffith Roberts and Eliz. Wittie : St. Dionis Backchurch, p. 46.
1767. — James Wittey and Eliz. French: St. Geo. Han. Sq. ii. 170.
London, 1, 1.

Wix.—Local ; v. Wykes, and cf. Dix for Dicks, Rix for Ricks, or Nix for Nicks. All these variants are more or less modern.

1756. Bapt.—Sarah, d. Edward Wix : St. Peter, Cornhill, ii. 46.
1809. Married — Joseph Wix and Amy Minall : St. Geo. Han. Sq. ii. 273.

The death of Jemima Wix, Peckham, was announced in the Standard, Nov. 10, 1886.
London, 1 ; Philadelphia, 1.

Wodderspoon ; v. Witherspoon.
London, 1.

Wode ; v. Wood.

Wodehouse, Woodhouse.—Local, 'at the wood-house,' probably the woodward's residence.

Richard del Wodehus, co. Hunts, 1273. A.
Robert de Wodehous, co. Notts, 20 Edw. I. R.
William de la Wodehouse, Close Roll, 12 Edw. I.
John atte Wodehouse. X.
Petronil de la Wodehouse. B.
Johannes de Wodhous, 1379 : P. T. Yorks. p. 99.
1624. Married — William Wodhowse and Mary Ship : St. Peter, Cornhill, i. 252.
London, 0, 22 ; Crockford, 7, 19 ; Philadelphia, 0, 13 ; New York, 0, 7.

Wogan.—? Bapt. 'the son of Wogan' (?).

John Wogan, co. Cumb., 21 Edw. I. R.
John Wogan, 14 Edw. III : Furness Coucher Book, i. 132.
Rogerus Wargan, 1379 : P. T. Yorks. p. 32.
Richard Wogan, prebendary of St. David's, 1426 : Hist. and Ant. St. David's, p. 362.
David Wogan, prebendary of St. David's, 1487 : ibid.
1741. Married—William Worgan and Elizabeth Hide : St. Antholin (London), p. 151.
Philadelphia, 3 ; Boston (U.S.), 3.

Wold.—Local, 'at the wold,' from residence thereon ; v. Weald or Weld.

John atte Wold, C. R., 6 Edw. III. pt. ii.
Stephanus del Wold, 21-2 Edw. I. Freemen of York (Surt. Soc.), i. 5.
Boston (U.S.), 1.

Wolf(e ; v. Wolff.

Wolfenden, Woolfenden, Wolfendine, Wolffinden, Woofenden. — Local, 'of Wolfenden,' a district, once a hamlet, in Rossendale, co. Lanc. There are many variants of this surname.

George Hey, of Wolfenden, forest of Rossendale, 1620 : Wills at Chester (1545-1620), p. 91.
James Wolfenden, of Rochdale, 1614 : ibid. p. 214.
1620. Bapt. — Marie, d. Robert Wolfendene : St. Thomas the Apostle (London), p. 44.
1792. Married — Thomas Francis and Eliz. Wolfinden : St. Geo. Han. Sq. ii. 80.
Manchester, 6, 3, 0, 0, 0 ; MDB. (West Rid. Yorks) Woofenden, 1 ; Philadelphia, 9, 2, 1, 1, 1.

Wolferstan.—Local, 'of Woolverstone,' a village near Ipswich, co. Suff.

Hamo de Wolfreston, co. Suff., 20 Edw. I. R.
1621. Edmund Wolterston and Mary Preston : Marriage Alleg. (Westminster), p. 27.
1791. Married—James Wolferstan and Mary Langford : St. Geo. Han. Sq. ii. 68.
London, 2 ; Plymouth, 1.

Wolff, Wolf, Wolfe, Woolf, Woolfe, Wulff, Wulf, Wulfe.—(1) Nick. 'the wolf;' concerning the extermination of wolves in England, see Wolfhunt.

John le Wlf, co. Sussex, 1273. A.
Agnes le Wolf, co. Hunts, ibid.
Emma le Wolf, co. Bedf., ibid.
Adam le Wolf. H.
Philip le Wolf, 1306. M.
(2) Bapt. 'the son of Wolf,' or Ulf, a personal name, once so familiar that our local nomenclature could not escape its influence, as in Ulverston, Wolverton, Wolvesey, Wolvercote, Wolverley, Wolverhampton, Wolferton, &c. The Index to Freeman's Norm. Conq. will show that Ulf or Wolf was almost as common a personal name in England as in Iceland or Den-

mark. See also Miss Yonge, ii. 267. Ulf, son of Tur-ulf, witnessed the foundation charter of St. Mary's Priory, Lancaster (Baines' Lanc. ii. 654). Another Ulf married Canute's sister; yet a third was Bishop of Dorchester.

Ulf de Appelbi, 1163 : RRR. p. 5.
Ulf Stodhyrda, 1196 : RRR. p. 78.
Roger Ulfe, temp. 1250 : FFF. pp. 444–6.
William fil. Ulfe, temp. 1250 : ibid.
Peter Ulfe, temp. 1250 : ibid.
Magota Wlfe, 1379 : P. T. Yorks. p. 157.
Thomas Wolphe, or Wulph, co. Wilts, 1586 : Reg. Univ. Oxf. vol. ii. pt. ii. p. 150.
London, 17, 5, 6, 26, 4, 3, 0, 0; Philadelphia, 10, 255, 35, 3, 0, 1, 2, 3; Boston (U.S.), 18, 24, 13, 7, 0, 0, 1, 0.

Wolfhound.—Nick. 'the wolf-hound'; one more incidental proof of the existence of wolves at the period.

Robert Wolfhound, Fines Roll, 12 Edw. I.

Wolfhunt. — Occup. 'the wolf-hunt,' a hunter of wolves, from *wolf*, and Middle English *hunte*, a hunter, the latter being a later form (v. Hunt). Wolves were found in England longer than is supposed. A writ of Edward I (1281) commissions Peter Corbet to kill wolves in Gloucester, Worcester, Hereford, Shropshire, and Stafford (Rymer, i. 591). A family of this name held lands in Derbyshire by service of keeping down the wolves in Peak Forest (Arch. Assoc. Journal, vii. 197). John Engayne held lands (1273) in Huntingdonshire by tenure of maintaining dogs for the king's wolf-hunting (Hundred Rolls, ii. 627, quoted by Lower). An entry still later, relating to the district about Whitby, co. York, is interesting :

'Item, pro tewynge 14 pellium luporum, 1s. 9d.,' 1394 : FFF. p. 623.
Richard le Wulfhunt, co. Kent, 1273. A.
Walter le Wolfhunt. B.
John Wolfehunt. B.
Robert Wolfhunte, co. Notts, Pardons Roll, 6 Ric. II.

Wolfnoth, Woolnough. — Bapt. 'the son of Wolfnoth.' A.S. Ulnoth. 'An ancient baptismal

name, common in Domesday' (Lower).

Wolnotus Hostiarius, 1154 : GGG. p. 259.
Robert Welnoth, co. Norf., 1273. A.
The name occurs two centuries earlier (v. quotation from Freeman on 'Hacon').
1799. Married — Simon Woolnough and Eliz. Tagg : St. Geo. Han. Sq. ii. 196.
London, 0, 8.

Wolford ; v. Woolford.

Wolfraven.—Bapt. 'the son of Wolfraven'; cf. Wallraven and Raven.

Thomas Wlfraven, co. Oxf., 1273. A.
William Wlfraven, co. Oxf., ibid.

Wolfson, Woolfson, Wulfson.—Bapt. 'the son of Wolf,' or Ulf; v. Wolf (2). Wolfsohn is in the London Directory, a German immigrant of the same origin.

William fil. Ulfe, temp. 1200: FFF. p. 444.
Uctred Ulfson, temp. 1200: ibid. p. 93 n.
London, 0, 1, 1 ; Philadelphia, 2, 0, 0; Boston (U.S.), 9, 0, 0.

Wollaston.—Local, 'of Wollaston': (1) a parish in co. Glouc., near Chepstow ; (2) a parish in co. Northampton, near Wellingborough ; (3) a chapelry in co. Salop, nine miles from Shrewsbury; (4) a manor in the parish of Old Swinford, co. Stafford, which early gave rise to a surname (v. Lower's Patr. Brit. p. 388).

Ivo de Wolastone, co. Staff., 1273. A.
William de Wolastone, co. Salop, ibid.
Saer de Wolaveston, co. Northampt., ibid.
John de Wolaston, co. Bedf., 20 Edw. I. R.
William de Wolaston, co. Northampt., ibid.
1661. Buried — Margaret, d. John Woollaston : St. Jas. Clerkenwell, iv. 342.
1611–2. Samuel Wollerston, co. Northants : Reg. Univ. Oxf. vol. ii. pt. ii. p. 325.
London, 3 ; Philadelphia, 2.

Woller ; v. Wooler.

Wollmer; v. Woolmer.

Wolman, Wollman; v. Woolman.

Wolrige ; v. Woolrich.

Wolsdenholme ; v. Wolstenholme.

Wolseley.—Local, ' of Wolseley,' a hamlet in the parish of Colwich, co. Stafford.

Robert de Wolsley, vicar of Addingham in Craven, 1353 : Whitaker, p. 292.
1674. John Berry and Ann Wolseley, of Wolseley, co. Staff. : Marriage Alleg. (Canterbury), p. 233.
Crockford, 3.

Wolsey, Woolsey. — Bapt. 'the son of Wulsi.' At first sight the name seems local, and an abbreviation of Wolseley, q.v. A parallel is found in the case of the famous founder of Wesleyanism, whose latest biographer shows that his progenitors were Wellesleys. But no doubt can exist on the subject. Wolsey is a modern form of the personal name Wolsi or Wulsi, Lower (Patr. Brit. p. 388), quoting from Fuller's Worthies, reminds me that St. Wulsy was first abbot of Westminster.

William Wulsi, co. Camb., 1273. A.
1605. Bapt.—Israell,'s. Israell Wolsey: St. Dionis Backchurch, p. 92.
1613. Richard Letten and Mary Wolsey: Marriage Lic. (London), ii. 21.
1680. William Greene and Cassandra Wolsey: Marriage Alleg. (Canterbury), p. 30.
Philadelphia, 1, 2.

Wolstencroft, Wolsoncroft, Woolstencroft, Wozencroft, Worsencroft.—Local, ' of Wolstancroft,' i.e. the field or enclosure of Wulstan, the first settler or owner; cf. Wolstenholme, found in the same district of South Lanc. The corrupted Wozencroft looks queer. It is merely a variant of the already modified Wolsoncroft.

1584. Buried — Joane, d. James Wolsoncroft ; St. Thomas the Apostle (London), p. 96.
1610. Bapt.—Francis, s. Thomas Worsencroft : St. Jas. Clerkenwell, i. 58.
1613. William Woolstencroft, of Manchester : Wills at Chester, i. 217.
1635. John Wossencroft, of Poulton, co. Lanc. : ibid. ii. 244.
1637. Jeremy Wolstencroft, of Middleton, Manchester : ibid. p. 240.
1640. Robert Wolsoncroft, of Failsworth, Manchester : ibid.
1703. Married—Samuel Woosencrafte and Thomasine Blake : ibid. iii. 226.
1732. — Thomas Wosancroft and Eliz. Wilkes : ibid. p. 258.
Manchester, 3, 0, 3, 1, 1 ; Philadelphia, 7, 1, 0, 0, 0.

Wolstenholme, Woolstenholme, Wolsdenholme, Wolstenholmes.—Local, 'of Wolstenholme,' an ancient manor in Spotland, in the parish of Rochdale, co. Lanc.; literally, 'the holm of Wolfstan'; v. Holm, and cf. Wolstencroft.

Andrew de Wolstenholme, 1180: Baines' Lanc. i. 512.
1604. Margaret Wolstenholme, of Wolstenholme: Wills at Chester (1545-1620), p. 214.
1608. Robert Wolstenholme, of Stansfield, parish of Rochdale: ibid.
Manchester, 13, 3, 1, 1; Sheffield, 13, 0, 0, 0; London, 2, 0, 0, 0; Philadelphia, 8, 0, 0, 0; Boston (U.S.), 3, 0, 0, 0.

Wolston; v. Woolston.

Wolton.—Local, 'of Wolton.' I cannot find the place, and probably now the surname is lost in that of Walton, q.v.

Jordan de Wolton, co. Oxf., Hen. III-Edw. I. K.
Odo de Wolton, co. Worc., ibid.
Robert de Wolton, co. Kent, 1273. A.
1809. Married—Matthew Wolton and Jane Ludgater: St. Geo. Han. Sq. ii. 408.
London, 2.

Wolverton, Woolverton.—Local, 'of Wolverton,' i.e. the stead or dwelling of Wolf, the first settler (v. Wolff). Parishes in cos. Bucks, Norf., Hants, and Warwick are so named.

London, 1, 2; New York, 2, 0; Philadelphia, 0, 3.

Womack.—?——. Evidently a south-eastern counties' name, probably local.

Henry Womock, vicar of Great Ellingham, co. Norf., 1601: FF. i. 486.
1779. Married—James Womack and Ann Summers: St. Geo. Han. Sq. i. 295.
MDB. (co. Suffolk), 5; London, 5.

Wombwell, Wombell, Wombill.—Local, 'of Wombwell,' a village in the parish of Darfield, co. York. Wombill is a natural modification, but is probably somewhat modern.

Hugo de Wambewell, zonarius, 1277: Freemen of York (Surt Soc.), i. 3.
Isabella de Wombewell, 1379: P. T. Yorks. p. 102.
Avicia de Womwell, 1379: ibid. p. 74.
1558. Married—Thomas Wambwell, Knt., and Annie Perye: St. Michael, Cornhill, p. 7.
1632. William Wombwell and Frances Veale: Marriage Lic. (London), ii. 105.

1806. Married—William Wombill and Honor Triptree: St. Geo. Han. Sq. ii. 349.
London, 1, 0, 0; Sheffield, 2, 1, 0; Crockford (Wombill), 1.

Womersley.—Local, ' of Womersley,' a parish near Pontefract, co. York.

1789. Married — Edward Bunn and Hannah Womersley: St. Geo. Han. Sq. ii. 24.
London, 3; Halifax, 2.

Wonter, Wontner.—Occup. 'the wonter,' the mole-catcher. A.S. want, wont, a mole.

Henry le Wantur, co. Salop, 1273. A.
London, 0, 2; New York, 1, 0.

Wood, Wode.—Local, 'at the wood,' from residence thereby. Common to every mediaeval register all over the country. With Wode, cf. Wodehouse.

Andrew ate Wode, co. Oxf., 1273. A.
Richard de la Wode, co. Oxf., ibid.
Elias in le Wode, co. Camb., ibid.
Walter de la Wode, co. Heref., Hen. III-Edw. I. K.
Robertus del Wodde, webster, 1379: P. T. Yorks. p. 133.
Thomas del Wode, smythe, 1379: ibid. p. 91.
Robertus del Wode, 1379: ibid. p. 218.

Modern instances are needless.

London, 317, 0; Philadelphia, 450, 0; New York (Wode), 2.

Woodall.—Local, 'at the woodhall,' from residence therein or thereby. Doubtless several places would bear this title, and each might originate a surname; cf. Wodehouse.

Adam de Wodhall, 1379: P. T. Yorks. p. 25.
Matilda atte Wodhall, 1379: P. T. Howdenshire, p. 32.
1600. William Woodhall, co. Essex, Reg. Univ. Oxf. vol. ii. pt. ii. p. 242.
1613. Thomas Woodall (co. Herts) and Alice Jefferys: Marriage Lic. (London), ii. 20.
London, 9; Philadelphia, 3; Boston (U.S.), 1.

Woodard.—(1) Bapt. 'the son of Odard,' or Wodard.

Wadard 'homo episcopi' held lands of Bishop Odo: Freeman, Norm. Conq. iii. 571.
John fil. Wudardi, 1168: KKK. vi. 13.
John fil. Odard, 1161: ibid. p. 6.

The last two entries concern, I believe, the same individual.

Cristiana fil. Odard, temp. Hen. III. T.
Alan Wodard, 1273. A.
Wodard atte Barre, C. R., 3 Edw. I.

I furnish two other possible sources of the name, but the above is the undoubted parent of nine-tenths of the bearers of this patronymic. (2) Official. An abbreviation of Woodward, q.v. (3) Occup. 'the wood-herd,' probably a hog-tender; v. Herd. Cf. Coward for Cowherd.

Richard le Wodeherd, co. Norf., 20 Edw. I. R.
Richard ie Wodehirde, co. Norf., 1273. A.
1682. Married — Thomas Woodard and Alice Dobbey: St. Jas. Clerkenwell, iii. 197.
London, 7; Philadelphia, 1; Boston (U.S.), 4.

Woodberry, borough, v. Woodbury.

Woodbridge. — Local, ' of Woodbridge,' a parish in the county of Suffolk, seven miles from Ipswich.

John de Wudebrege, co. Camb., 1273. A.
Thomas de Wudebrige, co. Wilts, ibid.
1596. John Woodbridge, co. Oxf.: Reg. Univ. Oxf. vol. ii. pt. ii. p. 215.
1668. Married—Thomas Woodbridge and Ellin Davis: St. Jas. Clerkenwell, iii. 145.
London, 10; Philadelphia, 1; Boston (U.S.), 11.

Woodburn, Woodburne.—Local, 'at the wood-burn,' i. e. the woodland stream; v. Burn. Not in London Directory; a well-known surname in Furness, North Lanc. The register of the parish church of Ulverston teems with this patronymic.

1591. Gillian Woodburn, of Kirkbie Ireleth: Lancashire Wills at Richmond, i. 319.
1617. Richard Woodborne, of Kirkbie Ireleth: ibid.
1654. Bapt.—Jane, d. Rodger Woodburne, tourney: St. Mary, Ulverston, i. 127.
1656. — John, s. William Woodburne, marcer: ibid. p. 128.
1700. Married — Christopher Woodborne and Bridget Dawson: St. Jas. Clerkenwell, iii. 222.
Ulverston, N. Lanc., 5, 2; Philadelphia, 8, 1; Boston (U.S.), 4, 0.

Woodbury, Woodberry, Woodborough. — Local, ' of Woodbury,' or Woodborough: (1) of Woodborough, a parish in co. Notts; (2) of Woodbury, a parish in co. Devon. Both places are parents of the name.

David de Wodebir, co. Devon, 1273. A.
Edmund de Wodeburg', co. Suff., ibid.
Henry de Wodeburg', co. Notts, ibid.
Ralph de Wodeburg', co. Notts, ibid.
London, 3, 0, 1; Philadelphia, 6, 0, 0; Boston (U.S.), 74, 10, 0.

Woodcock.—Nick. 'the woodcock'; cf. Nightingale, Pidgeon, Jay, Dove, &c.

Adam Wodecok, co. Linc., 1273. A.
Wydo Wodcok, co. Suff., ibid.
Willelmus Wodcok, 1379: P. T. Yorks. p. 40.
Johannes Wodecok, ibid. p. 233.
1516. Lawrence Wudcocke, or Wodecocke: Reg. Univ. Oxf. i. 103.
1554. Thomas Cable and Emma Woddecokk: Marriage Lic. (London), i. 15.
1611. Married — Thomas Woodcock and Phillip (= Philippa) Phelps: St. Michael, Cornhill, p. 20.
London, 21; Philadelphia, 17; Boston (U.S.), 2.

Woodcroft. — Local, 'at the wood-croft,' i.e. the enclosure by the wood, from residence thereby; v. Croft or Craft.

1584-5. Geoffrey Woodcrofte, weaver, and Margaret Smithe: Marriage Lic. (London), i. 138.
1615. Bapt. — Anthony, s. Nicholas Woodcrofte: St. Dionis Backchurch, p. 22.
1626. Married—John Parey and Eliz. Woodcraft: ibid. p. 96.
London, 1.

Woodend. — Local, 'at the wood-end,' one who lived at the end of the wood; cf. Fieldsend, Townsend, and the place-name Gravesend. This surname still exists in Furness, North Lancashire. My instances prove it to have been there for 300 years at least. No doubt it has existed there for six centuries.

Adam de Wodeshende, co. Dorset, 1273. A.

With this, cf. Townend and Townshend. The h is, of course, intrusive.

1601. Bapt. — Richard, s. Nicholas Woodend: St. Mary, Ulverston, i. 91.
Nicholas Woodend, of Ulverston, 1624: Lancashire Wills at Richmond, i. 320.
James Woodend, of Lowick, 1662: ibid.
Blawith-in-Furness, 2; Boston (U.S.), 3.

Wooder; v. Woodger.

Wooderson, Woodson. — Bapt. 'the son of Wodard' (?); v.

Woodard. The only other etymology is 'Widowson,' q.v. But this seems somewhat forced. Upon careful consideration I see no reasonable doubt in accepting Woodard as the parent. It must be remembered that that baptismal name was popular in the hereditary surname period.

1565. Alex. Woodson, Ch. Ch.: Reg. Univ. Oxf. vol. ii. pt. ii. p. 13.
1604-5. John Woodsonne, Bristol: ibid. p. 280.

In this register the name is also spelt Wooddeson, Woddeson, and Wodison. It is manifest, therefore, that Wooderson is a member of the family; cf. Patterson for Pattison.

1634. Buried — Richard Woodison, servant to Mr. Darrell: St. Jas. Clerkenwell, iv. 214.
1674. George Wooddeson and Mary Balston: Marriage Alleg. (Canterbury), p. 230.
1803. Married—John Wooderson and Ann Oliver: St. Geo. Han. Sq. ii. 282.
London, 2, 0; Philadelphia, 0, 5; New York, 0, 1.

Woodford, Woodforde. — Local, 'of Woodford': (1) a parish in co. Wilts, four miles from Salisbury; (2) a parish in co. Essex, eight miles from London. Both places seem to have had a share in the origination of the surname.

Geoffrey de Wodeford, co. Wilts, 1273. A.
Symon Wodeford, co. Bucks, ibid.
Nicholas de Wodeford, co. Glouc., ibid.
Geoffrey de Wodeford, co. Soms., 1 Edw. I: Kirby's Quest, p. 180.
1577. Bapt.—Thomas Wodford, son of Gamaliel Woodford: St. Peter, Cornhill, i. 19.
1581. Robert Wodforde, co. Bucks: Reg. Univ. Oxf. vol. ii. pt. ii. p. 96.
1620. — Adryan, s. Emanuel Woodford: St. Jas. Clerkenwell, i. 87.
London, 6, 3; New York, 7, 0; Boston (U.S.), 3, 0.

Woodgate, Woodgates. — Local, 'at the wood-gate,' from residence beside the entrance into the wood. Such a spot would naturally lend itself to a surname.

Robert atte Wodgate, C. R., 2 Edw. I.
1585-6. Peter Woodgate, or Wodgate, co. Kent: Reg. Univ. Oxf. vol. ii. pt. ii. p. 149.
1618. Francis Quarles and Ursely Woodgate: Marriage Lic. (London), ii. 60.

1651. Buried — Eliz. Woodgate: St. Peter, Cornhill, i. 206.
London, 9, 1; New York, 2, 0.

Woodger, Woodyer, Woodyeare, Wooder. — Occup. (1) 'the wooder,' i.e. the woodman; (2) 'the wood-hewer,' i.e. a woodchopper. Both these names have resolved themselves into Woodger and Woodyer; cf. Sawyer for Sawer, or lawyer for lawer, or pavier for paver. With the corrupted Woodger for Woodyer, cf. Goodger for Goodier. As regards Woodhewer, that would naturally and inevitably become Woodyer.

Matthew le Woder, C. R., 35 Edw. I.
Robert le Wodehyewere. H.
John Wodhewher, 1379: P. T. Yorks. p. 209.
Robert Wodhewer, 1379: ibid. p. 267.
William Wodhewer, 1379: ibid. p. 223.
1605. Richard Woodyere: Reg. Univ. Oxf. i. 356.
1663. John Woodger and Mary Hudsdon: Marriage Alleg. (Canterbury), ii. 98.
1790. Married — John Woodrow and Ann Woodyer: St. Geo. Han. Sq. ii. 37.
1799. — William Woodyer and Catherine Wood: ibid. p. 210.

The present form of the name is now all but universally Woodyer.

London, 9, 0, 0, 1; West Rid. Court Dir. (Woodyeare), 1.

Woodhacker.—(1) Occup. 'a woodcutter.'

William le Wodehagger, Close Roll, 10 Edw. II.

Jack is Jagge in Piers Plowman, and Hick is Higg (v. Higg and Hick). (2) Nick.; the above applied to a bird, woodpecker, &c. 'Wodehake, or reyne fowle,-picus': Prompt. Parv.; v. woodwale, in Skeat.

Woodham.—Local, 'of Woodham,' three parishes in co. Essex; v. Wadham.

Peter de Wodeham, co. Northampton, 1273. A.
Egidius de Wodeham, London, ibid.
Reginald de Wodeham, co. Gloucester, ibid.
Thomas de Wodeham, co. Essex, ibid.
1613. John Woddam: Reg. Univ. Oxf. vol. ii. pt. ii. p. 330.
1625. Thomas Woodham (co. Middlesex) and Eliz. Mussage: Marriage Lic. (London), ii. 157.

1789. Married—James Woodham and Mary Rodam (or Rodman) : St. Geo. Han. Sq. ii. 31. London, 9.

Woodhay. -- Local, 'at the wood-hay' (v. Hay), from residence thereby.

Richard de la Wodehaye, co. Linc., 20 Edw. I. R.

Thomas de la Wodehaye, co. Linc., ibid.

1654. Married—Charles Woodey and Ann Hayle : St. Jas. Clerkenwell, iii. 92.

1668. — Philip Lancedowne and Mary Wooddey : ibid. p. 143.

Woodhead.—Local, 'of Wood-head,' a great Yorkshire surname. Literally, 'at the wood-head,' at the top of the wood; cf. Akenhead, Birkenhead, i,e. the head of the oaks or birches. The great tunnel between Lanc. and Yorkshire is called the Woodhead tunnel from the name of the locality; cf. Wood-end, q.v.

Rogerus de Wodehed, 1379 : P. T. Yorks. p. 199.

1686. William Woodhead and Margarett Birkhead : Marriage Alleg. (Canterbury), p. 245.

1789. Joseph Woodhead and Eliz. Parker : St. Geo. Han. Sq. ii. 28.

London, 8 ; West Rid. Court Dir., 30 ; Philadelphia, 8 ; Boston (U.S.), 3.

Woodhouse; v. Wodchouse.

Woodhull, Woodill,—Local, 'at the wood-hill,' from residence thereby; v. Hull. In Woodill the *h* is elided. The surname seems to have been closely confined to co. Northampton. Its present refuge is the United States.

1545. John Leveson and Ann Woodhull : Marriage Lic. (Faculty Office), p. 5.

1581. Anthony Wodhill, co. Warw. : Reg. Univ. Oxf. vol. ii. pt. ii. p. 98.

— Laurence Wodhill, co. Northampt. : ibid.

1598. Fulcke Wodhull, or Woodhull, co. Northampt. : ibid. p. 231.

— Giles Wodhull, co. Northampt. : ibid.

Philadelphia, 6, 2 ; New York, 11, 0.

Woodland, Woodlands. — Local, 'at the wood-laund' (cf. Buckland, Lund), a grassy space or glade in the heart of a wood.

Cicely de la Wodeland, Close Roll, 34 Hen. III.

Peter de Wodelonde, co. Soms., 9 Edw. II : Kirby's Quest, p. 75.

John de Wodelond, co. Soms., 9 Edw. II : ibid. p. 194.

1561. John Woodland and Joanna Darby : Marriage Lic. (London), i. 22.

1793. Married—James Woodland and Hannah Shadbolt : St.Geo.Han. Sq. ii.105.

London, 5, 1 ; Philadelphia, 14, 0 ; Boston (U.S.), 1, 0.

Woodlark.—Nick. 'the wood-lark'; cf. Lark.

Robert Wodlarke, C. R., 29 Hen. VI.

Woodley.—Local, (1) 'of Wood-ley,' a parish in co. Berks ; (2) 'of Woodleigh,' in co. Devon.

London, 9 ; Oxford, 1 ; Philadelphia, 2.

Woodman.—(1) Occup. 'the woodman,' generally one who resided in a wood, a woodcutter. (2) Bapt. 'the son of Wodemund'; cf. Osman for Osmund, or Wyman for Wymund, &c.

Thomas Wodemund, co. Oxf., 1273. A.

Thomas Wodeman, co. Oxf., ibid.

William Wudeman, co. Kent, ibid.

Eudo Wudeman, co. Linc., ibid.

Johannes Wodman, *laborer*, 1379 : P.T. Howdenshire, p. 15.

1621. Bapt.—Mary, d. Robert Woddman : St. Michael, Cornhill, p. 115.

1659. Married—Thomas Woodman and Jane Humphrey : St. Thomas the Apostle (London), p. 20.

London, 29 ; Philadelphia, 7 ; Boston (U.S.), 56.

Woodmansey, Woodmancy, Woodmansee. — Local, 'of Woodmansey,' a township in the parish of St. John, Beverley, E. Rid. Yorks.

MDB. (East Rid. Yorks), 2, 0, 0 ; Philadelphia, 0, 1, 1 ; Boston (U.S.), 0, 2, 0 ; New York, 0, 0, 2.

Woodmason. — Occup. 'the wood-mason.'

1773. Bapt. — James, s. James Woodmason : St. Peter, Cornhill, ii. 54.

1774. — Mary Magdalen, d. James Woodmason : ibid.

1798. Married — James Woodmason and Ann Bursey : St. Geo. Han. Sq. ii.185. London, 1 ; Bigbury (Devon), 1 ; MDB. (co. Cumb.), 1.

Woodmonger.—Occup. 'the woodmonger,' a seller of wood for firing purposes, &c.

Robert Wudemongere, London, 1273. A.

Woodnott, Woodnutt. — Bapt. 'the son of Godinot,' dim. of Godin, i.e. Godwin (v. Godinot); cf. Guyat and Wyatt, Gillott and Willott, Guillaume and William.

Ralph Wodenot, R. Pat., 4 Edw. III. pt. ii.

William Wodenotte. L.

Thomas Woodnotte, *grome* : Privy Purse Exp., Eliz. of York, p. 98.

1510. Richard Wodnet, or Wotnet : Reg. Univ. Oxf. i. 67.

1703. Bapt.—Winifred Woodnot : St. Jas. Piccadilly.

1729. Married—Thomas Williams and Ann Woodnutt : St. Geo. Chap. Mayfair, p. 300.

1745. — Richard Pulford and Rebecca Woodnott : ibid. p. 58.

London, 0, 2 ; Philadelphia, 0, 4.

Woodroffe, Woodroof, Woodrooffe, Woodrough, Woodruff.—Offic. 'the wood-reeve' or wood-bailiff, but I cannot find the term in official use ; from A S. * róf*, active (v. *reeve*, Skeat) ; cf. *sheriff*, *port-reeve*, *borough-reeve*. v. Woodward.

John Woderove, co. Oxf., 1273. A.

Robert Woderove, co. Hunts, ibid.

Henry Woderoue, co. Linc., ibid.

Thomas Woderoue, 1379 : P. T. Yorks. p. 88.

1524. William Woddrof, or Woderof : Reg. Univ. Oxf. i. 133.

George Woodruffe, temp. Eliz. Z.

1733. Married—Daniel Woodrooffe to Jemima Archer : St. Mary Aldermary (London), p. 49.

London, 9, 2, 1, 2, 6 ; Philadelphia, 6, 0, 0, 0, 47 ; Boston (U.S.), 2, 0, 0, 3, 12.

Woodside.—Local, 'of Wood-side,' townships in the parishes of Westward, co. Cumb., Shinnall, co. Salop; and Wigton, co. Cumb. Cf. Woodend and Woodhead.

Philadelphia, 16 ; Boston (U.S.), 18.

Woodson.—Bapt.; v. Wooderson.

Woodstock.—Local, 'of Wood-stock,' a borough and market-town, co. Oxford.

Hudde de Wodestok, co. Oxf., 1273. A.

John de Wodestok, co. Oxf., ibid.

1546. John Wodstocke and Eliz. Taylor: Marriage Lic. (Faculty Office), p. 8.

1635. Robert Woodstock, aged 40, sailed for St. Christopher's, in the Matthew, from London : Hotten's Lists of Emigrants, p. 81.

1653. Buried—Agnes, d. Jeremy Woodstocke : St. Jas. Clerkenwell, iv. 298.

1801. Married—William Bridgland and Ann Woodstock : St. Geo. Han. Sq.ii. 245.

London, 2 ; New York, 1.

Woodward, Woolwards.—Offic. 'the woodward,' a forest officer who looked after wood and vert. 'Wodewarde, or walkare in a wode for kepynge, *lucarius*' : Prompt. Parv. p. 531.

'John Keeper, or Woodward, of Buckholt-wood,' 31 Hen. VIII : Rudder's Gloucestershire, pp. 140-1.
Roger le Wodeward, Hen. III–Edw. I. K.
Aylward le Wodeward, co. Essex, 1273. A.
Adam le Wodeward, co. Oxf., ibid.
William le Wodewarde, co. Soms., 1 Edw. III : Kirby's Quest, p. 220.
Richard le Wodeward, co. Sussex, 20 Edw. I. R.
Johannes Woddeword, 1379 : P. T. Yorks. p. 86.

Modern instances are needless.

London, 44, 2 ; Philadelphia, 70, 0 ; Boston (U.S.), 67, 0.

Wooer, Wewer.—Nick. 'the wooer,' i.e. lover.

Geoffrey le Wowere, co. Suff., 1273. A.
Nicholas le Wowere, co. Suff., ibid.
John le Wower, co. Camb., ibid.
Hugo le Wewer, co. Wilts, 20 Edw. I. R.
Philadelphia, 0, 2.

Wooeress.—Nick. 'a female wooer' ; v. Wooer.

Emma le Woweres, co. Oxf., 1273. A.

Woofenden ; v. Wolfenden.

Wookey.—Local, 'of Wookey,' a parish in co. Somerset, near Wells.

1620-1. Nicholas Wookey, co. Soms.: Reg. Univ. Oxf. vol. ii. pt. ii. p. 386.
1690. Bapt.—John, s. John Wookey : St. Jas. Clerkenwell, i. 338.
1808. Married—William Wookey and Alice Pritchard : St. Geo. Han. Sq. ii. 382. MDB. (co. Soms.), 8.

Woolard.—Bapt. ; v. Woollard.
London, 1.

Woolchapman. — Occup. 'a chapman who dealt in wool.'

Robertus Wulchapman, 1379 : P. T. Yorks. p. 159.

Wooldridge, Wooldredge.— Bapt. 'the son of Wulfric' ; v. Woolrich. The *d* is intrusive.

Wooler, Wooller, Woller.— Local, 'of Wooler,' a parish in co. Northumberland. The surname having settled in Yorkshire has led to the impression that it meant a wool-merchant. There is, I believe, no evidence of this. The above is the natural solution.

Issabel Woller, 1487, co. York. W. 11.
1694. Married—Thomas Wooller and Abigail Dawson : St. Jas. Clerkenwell, iii. 213.
1710. Bapt. — Richard, s. Richard Woller : ibid. ii. 53.
1728. Married — William Wooller and Mary Morgan : ibid. iii. 254.
London, 0, 1, 0 ; Bierley, 3, 0, 0 ; Bradford, 2, 0, 0 ; Philadelphia, 2, 0, 1 ; New York, 0, 0, 1.

Wooley ; v. Woolley.

Woolf(e ; v. Wolff.

Woolfenden ; v. Wolfenden.

Woolford, Woollford, Wolford.—Local, 'of Wolford,' a parish in co. Warwick, near Shipston.

1669. Married — Samson Hisscockes and Ane Woolford : St. Jas. Clerkenwell, iii. 162.
1801. — Matthew Woolford and Eliz. Clayton : St. Geo. Han. Sq. ii. 241.
London, 2, 2, 0 ; Philadelphia, 6, 0, 8 ; Boston (U.S.), 2, 0, 1.

Woolfson ; v. Wolfson.

Woolgar, Woolger. — Bapt. 'the son of Wulgar.' In Domesday the form is Wlgar, co. Warwick, and Vlgar, co. Cheshire.

William fil. Wolgar, 1164 : KKK. vi. 7.
1678. Bapt.—Anne, d. William Wolgar : St. Michael, Cornhill, p. 150.
1683. Buried — William, s. William Woolgar : ibid. p. 268.
1685. William Woolger and Eliz. Forth : Marriage Alleg. (Canterbury), ii. 213.
London, 3, 1.

Woolhouse. — Local, 'at the wool-house,' the store-house for wool, from residence thereby. The stock at Bolton Abbey (1526) included : 'Item, Wolle in the Woolhouses, £45 4s. 0d.' (Whitaker's Craven, p. 403). Naturally we expect this to be a Yorkshire surname.

Sibota del Wolhouse, 1379 : P. T. Yorks. p. 198.
Robertus del Wolhouse, 1379 : ibid.
William Woolhouse, bailiff of Yarmouth, 1545 : FF. xi. 327.
1687-8. John Woolhouse, B.A., admitted fellow of Magd. Coll. Oxf. : Reg. Univ. Oxf. vol. ii. pt. i. p. 238.
1697. John Bush and Margaret Woolhouse : Marriage Lic. (Faculty Office), p. 223.
Sheffield, 8 ; West Rid. York (Court Dir.), 4.

Woollard, Woollett, Woollatt.—Bapt. From some long-

forgotten Wolfgard or Wolfhard. With Woollard, cf. Millard for Millward. The following first two entries occur on same page and in close proximity :

Wlward Hutlawe, co. Kent, 1273. A. ii. 544.
Reymund Wlward, co. Kent, ibid.
Wulward(without surname), co. Camb., 1273. A.
Thomas Wulward, co. Camb., ibid.
Geoffrey Wlvard, co. Suff., ibid.
Michael Woleward, co. Camb., ibid.
Walter Woleward, co. Soms., 1 Edw. III : Kirby's Quest, p. 216.
William Woleward, co. Soms., 1. Edw. III : ibid.
1629. Married—Thomas Woollard and Collat Hargrave : St. Peter, Cornhill, i. 253.
1750. — John Woollett and Anne Holmes : St. Geo. Chap. Mayfair, p. 180.
London, 9, 6, 2 ; Boston (U.S.), 4, 0, 0 ; New York, 0, 1, 0.

Wooller ; v. Wooler.

Woolley, Wooley.—Local, 'of Wooley,' a parish in dioc. Bath and Wells ; also 'of Woolley,' parishes in diocs. Ely and York. The North-English Woolleys hail from Yorkshire. The references will show that the origin is Wolfley, 'the meadow of Ulf,' or Wolf, a common personal name.

Johannes de Wulley, 1379 : P. T. Yorks. p. 159.
Elena de Wolley, 1379 : ibid.
Thomas de Wolley, 1379 : ibid. p. 92.
Adam de Wolueley, 1379 : ibid. p. 90.
Robert de Woluelay, 1379 : ibid.
1594. John Wooly, London : Reg. Univ. Oxf. vol. ii. pt. ii. p. 203.
1601. Thomas Woolley, co. Warw. : ibid. p. 248.
1682-3. John Bright and Ann Woolley : Marriage Alleg. (Canterbury), ii. 125.
London, 21, 2 ; Philadelphia, 16, 2 ; Boston (U.S.), 8, 0.

Woollford ; v. Woolford.

Woollven, Woolven, Woolvine, Wolven.—Bapt. 'the son of Wulwin.' In Domesday found as Wluuen.

Wulfwine the Reeve : Parker, Early Hist. of Oxford, p. 179.
Wulwinus Monetarius, 10 Hen. II : Pipe Roll, p. 3.
1730. Married—Thomas Woolven and Mary Haycraft : St. Mary Aldermary (London), p. 49.
1747. Married—Henry Whitaker and Ann Woolvan : St. Geo. Chap. Mayfair, p. 99.
London, 1, 1, 1, 0 ; New York (Wolven), 1.

Woolman, Wolman, Wollman.—Occup. 'the woolman,' a wool-buyer. This surname crossed the Atlantic, and has 'increased and multiplied' there. The original emigrant must have started early in the 17th century. If he had several boys, who lived, married, and had large families, the large number of Woolmans in America is easily accounted for. For opposite reasons Woolman is in danger of extinction in England.

John Gammwell, *wolman* (Beverley, co. York), 16 Hen. VI: HHH. p. 137.
1523. Richard Wulman: Reg. Univ. Oxf. i. 132.
1584. Bapt.—Griffith, s. John Woollman: St. Jas. Clerkenwell, p. 16.
1635. Richard Wollman, aged 22, sailed to Virginia in the Globe, of London: Hotten's Lists of Emigrants, p. 120.
1761. Married—John Woollman and Susanna Field: St. Geo. Han. Sq. p. 103.
London, 1, 0, 0; Philadelphia, 17, 1, 0; New York, 1, 0, 2.

Woolmer, Wollmer.—Bapt. 'the son of Wulmar,' or Ulmar. Wlmar, co. Linc., Wlmaer, co. Yorks; Wlmarus Presbyter, co. Bucks (Domesday). v. Ullmer.

Wulmar Bradfot, 1171 : RRR. p. 14.
Wolmer le Essex (London citizen), 1273. A.
Wlmerus de Neuton, co. Suff., ibid.
Wolmar de Estchep, London, ibid.
Ralph Wolmer, co. Norf., ibid.
John Wolmere, co. Soms., 1 Edw. III : Kirby's Quest, p. 86.
1579-80. Anthony Wollmer and Agnes Vincente : Marriage Lic. (London), i. 93.
1588. Bapt.—Cecily, d. Edwarde Woolmer : St. Jas. Clerkenwell, i. 20.
London, 5, 0 ; Philadelphia, 0, 1 ; New York, 0, 2.

Woolmonger. — Occup. 'the woolmonger,' a merchant in wool, often Flemings. Hence Morkin in the first instance. Cf. Woolman.

Morekinus le Wolmongere, London, 1273. A.
Walter le Wollemongere, co. Hunts, ibid.
Henry Wollemongere, co. Hunts, ibid.
Roger le Wolemongere, C. R., 9 Edw. II.

A curious corruption is found in the following entry :

1759. Married — Thomas Whitehead and Mary Willomanger : St. Geo. Han. Sq. i. 88.

Woolnough.—Bapt. ; v. Wolfnoth.

Woolrich, Woolrych, Wolrige, Woollright, Wooldridge, Woolridge, Wooldredge. — Bapt. 'the son of Wulfric' (v. Ulfric, Yonge, ii. 269), one of the many compounds of Ulf or Wolf; cf. Orme and Worm, Ulph and Wolff (2). Adam Wulfric was admitted to the Roll of Guild Merchants of Shrewsbury in 1231. He is the ancestor of the Shropshire Wolryches (Shirley's Noble and Gentle Men, quoted by Lower). With regard to the forms Woollright and Wooldridge, cf. the analogous Allwright and Aldridge from Aldrich.

William Wulurich, co. Wilts, 1273. A.
Robert Wolurich, co. Oxf., ibid.
Adam fil. Wlfric, co. Salop, ibid.
Astill fil. Wlfriche, co. Oxf., ibid.
Thomas Wlfrich, co. Bucks, ibid.
1658. Bapt. — Sarah, d. John Woolldrig : St. Mary Aldermary (London), p. 97.
1659. — Ann, d. Edward Wollrich : ibid.
1763. Married—Thomas Oxford and Olley Woolldridge : St. Geo. Han. Sq. i. 118.
London, 1, 1, 1, 1, 10, 0, 0 ; MDB. (co. Glouc.), Woolwright, 1 ; Boston (U.S.), 0, 0, 0, 0, 1, 1, 1.

Woolsey ; v. Wolsey.

Woolstencroft, -holme ; v. Wolstencroft, -holme.

Woolston, Woolson, Wolston, Wolson.—(1) Local, (a) 'of Wolstan,' a parish in co. Warw., near Rugby ; (b) ' of Woolstone,' two parishes near Newport Pagnell, co. Bucks ; (c) ' of Woolston,' a hamlet in the parish of North Cadbury, co. Somerset ; and (d) ' of Woolstone,' a tithing in the parish of Hound, co. Devon. With the corrupted Woolson, cf. Kelson for Kelston (q.v.). There can be little doubt that in some instances Wollaston and Wolston have become mixed up. (2) Bapt. ' the son of Wolfstan ' (v. Yonge, ii. 269). The probability is that (1) is the correct derivation.

William de Wolstone, co. Bucks, 1273. A.

1567. Christopher Gyll and Emma Woolson : Marriage Lic. (Faculty Office) p. 14.
1573. Buried — Richard Wolston : St. Thomas the Apostle, p. 91.
1581. Edward Woolson and Mary Tirrey : Marriage Lic. (London), i. 101.
1601. James Woolston, or Wolston, co. Devon : Reg. Univ. Oxf. vol. ii. pt. ii. p. 249.
1787. Married — William Woolstone and Eliz. White : St. Geo. Han. Sq. i. 377.
London, 1, 0, 0, 0 ; New York, 0, 2, 0, 0 ; Boston (U.S.), 0, 3, 1, 1 ; Philadelphia, 12, 3, 0, 0.

Woolven, -vine ; v. Woollven.

Woolverton ; v. Wolverton.

Woolvel, Woolvett. — Bapt. ' the son of Wulvard.' For strong corroborative evidence, v. instances under Woollard.

1590. Buried—William Wollfett : St. Jas. Clerkenwell, iv. 41.
1799. William Woolfett and Mary Sutton : St. Geo. Han. Sq. ii. 195.
London, 1, 1.

Wooster.—Local, ' of Worcester,' a corruption ; v. Worcester.

1567. Buried—Abraham, son of Reynold Woster : St. Antholin (London), p. 19.
1625. — Henry, s. John Woster : St. Jas. Clerkenwell, iv. 170.
1658. Married—John Watson and Alice Wooster : ibid. iii. 100.
1726. Bapt.—John, s. Robert Wooster : ibid. ii. 164.
London, 3 ; Philadelphia, 5 ; Boston (U.S.), 3.

Wootton, Wootten, Wooton, Wotton, Wooten.—Local, ' of Wootton ' : (1) a parish in co. Bedford ; (2) a parish in co. Berks, near Abingdon ; also parishes in cos. Kent, Lincoln, Northampton, Oxford, Southampton, Stafford, &c., besides many hamlets and manors scattered over the country ; also Wotton, a parish in co. Surrey. No doubt the origin is Wood-town, ' the enclosure in the wood.' This would at once explain the frequency of its occurrence as a place-name.

Robert de Wottone, co. Devon, Hen. III—Edw. I. K.
Fredeshet de Wottone, co. Bucks, 1273. A.
John atte Wodeton, London, ibid.
Thomas de Wodeton, co. Devon, ibid.

John de Wodeton or John de Wutton, co. Oxf., 1273. A.

1670. John Hill and Mary Wootton: Marriage Lic. (Westminster), p. 45.

1667. George Wotton and Eliz. Bagshaw: Marriage Alleg. (Canterbury), p. 141.

London, 14, 1, 1, 3, 0; Oxford, 2, 3, 0, 0, 0; Philadelphia, 1, 11, 0, 0, 1; New York, 1, 0, 0, 2, 0.

Worboy(s; v. Warboys.

Worcester, Wurster.—Local, 'of Worcester,' the capital of the county of that name, anciently Wigornaceastre.

Richard de Wygorn', co. Wilts, 1273. A.

Henry de Wygornia, co. Wilts, ibid.

1596. Thomas Worcester, or Worcettor: Reg. Univ. Oxf. vol. ii. pt. ii. p. 216.

1619. Arthur Blunt and Ann Worster: Marriage Lic. (London), ii. 72.

1663. Richard Worcester and Mary Gardner: Marriage Alleg. (Canterbury), p. 80.

1796. Married — Thomas Worcester and Sarah Hammond: St. Geo. Han. Sq. ii. 150.

Philadelphia, 1, 18; Boston (U.S.), 23, 1.

Wordsworth. — Local, 'of Wadsworth,' q.v.

Worger.—Bapt. 'the son of Orgar' (q.v.); cf. Ulf and Wulf, Orme and Worm, Oddard and Woodard, &c.

1674. Bapt.—Eliz., d. John Worgar: St. Jas. Clerkenwell, i. 263.

1677. — John Worgar, s. John Worger: ibid. p. 279.

London, 2.

Work.—Local, 'at the work,' the construction, i.e. the place where the work of defence is being carried on, from A.S. (ge)weorc, a fortification; cf. modern 'works,' a place where manufactures are carried on.

Robertus del Werk, 1379: P.T. Yorks. p. 161.

Philadelphia, 22; Boston (U.S.), 4.

Workman.—Occup. 'the workman,' a labourer, artisan. Cf. preceding article.

Gilbert le Worcman, co. Oxf., 1273. A.

Nicholas Workman, Close Roll, 35 Edw. I.

Johannes Werkman, 1379: P.T. Yorks. p. 243.

Robertus Warkman, 1379: ibid. p. 95.

1665. Giles Workman, vicar of Alderley, co. Glouc.: Atkyns' Hist. Glouc. p. 107.

This surname has ramified strongly in the county of Gloucester.

1696. Married—Mark Warkman and Anne Templeman: St. Dionis Backchurch, p. 45.

London, 3; West Rid. Court Dir., 1; MDB. (co. Glouc.), 12; Philadelphia, 13; Boston (U.S.), 3.

Worm.—Bapt. 'the son of Worm,' i.e. Orme, q.v. *W* precedes *o* and *u* in many names; cf. Ulf and Wolf, Oddard and Woodard, &c.

John Worme, Close Roll, 1 Hen. IV. pt. ii.

Thomas Worme, 1379: P.T. Yorks. p. 81.

William Worme, 1519: GGG. p. 315.

1569. Married — John Worme and Bridgett Vaughan: St. Jas. Clerkenwell, iii. 4.

1612. Cordwell Hamond and Margaret Worme: Marriage Lic. (London), ii. 16.

New York, 2; Philadelphia, 1.

Wormald.—Bapt. 'the son of Wormbald.' Wormald was an inevitable variant. It will be seen that the surname has its chief habitat in W. Rid. Yorks, where I find the personal name at an early period.

Wormboldus Harlam, 1429, co. York: W. ii. 245.

1797. Married — Edward Wolley and Ann Wormald: St. Geo. Han. Sq. ii. 170.

London, 6; West Rid. Court Dir., 11; Leeds, 9.

Wormall, Wormull, Wormell, Wormelle.—Local, (1) 'of Wormhill,' a chapelry in the parish of Tideswell, co. Derby.

Roger de Wormhyll, C. R., 3 Hen. V.

(2) 'Of Wormwall.'

Alex. de Wormwall, 1379: P.T. Yorks. p. 188.

As the Lancashire Aspinwall became Aspinall, so Wormwall would become Wormall, &c.

1730. Married—William Batt and Grace Wormell: St. Geo. Han. Sq. i. 7.

London, 0, 3, 0, 0; Boston (U.S.), 0, 0, 1, 1.

Wormet.—Bapt. 'the son of Worm' (Orme), dim. Wormet. If not this, it must be a corruption of Wormald.

Wormet Orfeour, Close Roll 6 Hen. IV.

Worrall, Worrell, Worrill.—(1) Local, 'of Wirral.' The district of Wirral, co. Ches., has originated most of the Worralls, &c., of Lancashire and Cheshire. The surname seems to have reached London at a somewhat early period. (2) Local, 'of Worrall,' a hamlet four miles from Sheffield.

John Wirrall, of ——, co. Chester, 1576: Wills at Chester (1545-1620), p. 213.

Thomasin Worrall, of Whiston, *widow*, 1590: ibid. p. 217.

Margaret Worrall, of Comberbach, 1611: ibid.

Hugh Wirrall, co. Ches., 1630: East Cheshire, ii. 12.

William Wyrhall, co. Ches., 1664: ibid. i. 22.

1586. Married — Robert Worrell and Joane Childe: St. Mary Aldermary (London), p. 7.

1590. Thomas Worrall, co. Ches.: Reg. Univ. Oxf. vol. ii. pt. ii. p. 176.

1797. Married — William Richardson and Susanna Worrell: St. Geo. Han. Sq. ii. 167.

Manchester, 11, 1, 0; London, 9, 2, 1; Sheffield, 4, 1, 0; Philadelphia, 18, 56, 0; Boston (U.S.), 1, 1, 0.

Worsdale, Worsdell.—Local, 'of Wyresdale,' a manor in the parish of Garstang, North Lancashire, situated on the river Wyre; also the valley itself, which is still beautifully wooded.

Johannes de Wyresdale, 1379: P.T. Yorks. p. 78.

William de Wiresdall', 1379: ibid.

1667. Married—John Woodeson and Ane Worsdall: St. Jas. Clerkenwell, iii. 137.

1793. — John Worsdale and Mary Chamberlain: St. Geo. Han. Sq. ii. 92.

London, 2, 0; Ulverston, 0, 1.

Worsencroft; v. Wolstencroft.

Worship. — Nick. a title of respect, short for *worth-ship*, honour. We say 'your Worship' or 'your Honour.'

Thomas Worthshipp, Close Roll, 16 Edw. III. pt. i.

Thomas Worthship. G.

Hugh Worshipp, temp. Eliz. Z.

1561. Bapt. — Elizabeth, d. William Worship: St. Antholin (London), p. 14.

1615. William Worship, D.D., and Eliz. Beale: Marriage Lic. (London), ii. 34.

Worsley, Worseley.—Local, 'of Worsley,' a parish near Manchester. But the instances below seem to suggest other small localities in South England. The Lancashire and Cheshire Worsleys, however, hail from the above, and have strongly ramified.

John de Wereslle, co. Hunts, 1273. A.
Alan de Weresle, co. Camb., ibid.
Robert de Weresl', co. Suff., ibid.
1571. James Worselye, co. Dorset:
Reg. Univ. Oxf. vol. ii. pt. ii. p. 49.
1593. Ottiwell Worsley, of Barton,
Manchester: Wills at Chester, i. 217.
1618. Ellen Worsley, of Pendleton,
Manchester: ibid.
1622. William Stane and Bridget
Worsley: Marriage Lic. (London), ii. 113.
1639. Thomas Worseley and Eliz.
Bosvile: ibid. p. 241.
London, 2, o; Manchester, 15, o; Philadelphia, 5, o; Boston (U.S.), o, 1.

Worsted.—Local, 'of Worsted' or Worstead, a village in co. Norfolk, whence came the thread so called. Flemish weavers, no doubt, settled there early.

Eustace de Wurstede, co. Norf.,
1273. A.
Robert de Wurstede, co. Norf., ibid.
Simon Worsted, C. R., 6 Ric. II. pt. ii.
1625-6. Nathaniel Rickard and Grace
Wosted: Marriage Lic. (London), ii. 163.

Worswick.—Local, 'of Urswick,' a parish in Furness, North Lanc. This place is popularly called Ursick, but in the past it was evidently Worswick or Worsick (cf. Physic for Fishwick). There is no difficulty about the initial w; cf. Worm and Orme, &c.

1670. Anne Worswick, of Plumpton:
Lancashire Wills at Richmond, i. 321.
1673. Thomas Worswick, of Catforth:
ibid.
1731. Alex. Worsick, of Great Singleton; ibid. ii. 289.
1735. Robert Worsick, of Poulton:
ibid.

The surname seems to have crossed the Morecambe Sands into the Fylde district of the county.

Manchester, 2; Boston (U.S.), 1.

Worth.—Local, 'at the worth,' from A.S. *worth*, an enclosed homestead, a habitation with surrounding land (Bosworth and Toller); hence an estate or manor, as in Whitworth, Rickmansworth, &c.

William de la Worthe, co. Soms.,
1273. A.
Richard de la Worthe, co. Devon, 20
Edw. I. R.
Reginald de la Wurth. E.

Philip atte Worthe, co. Soms., 1 Edw.
III: Kirby's Quest, p. 134.
1581. Anthony Worthe, co. Warw.:
Reg. Univ. Oxf. vol. ii. pt. ii. p. 97.
1672. William Worth and Eliz. Dalling:
Marriage Lic. (Faculty Office), p. 123.
London, 8; Oxford, 5; Philadelphia, 16;
Boston (U.S.), 15.

Worthington. — Local, 'of Worthington,' a township in the parish of Standish, co. Lanc.

'Hugh de Worthyngton and John de Heton hold of the said John half of one knight's fee in Worthyngton,' &c.:
Knights' Fees, 23 Edw. III: Baines'
Lanc. ii. 695.
Johannes de Worthyngton, *bocher*,
1379: P. T. Yorks. p. 160.
1598. John Worthington, of Warrington: Wills at Chester, i. 218.
1613. Edward Worthington, of Worthington: ibid.
1616-7. Married—John Hollywell and
Joyce Worthington: St. Dionis Backchurch, p. 19.
Manchester, 33; London, 7; Philadelphia, 57; Boston (U.S.), 11.

Worthy. — Local, 'at the worthy,' i.e. the worth, q.v.; cf. Kenworthy, Langworthy, &c.

1730. Bapt.—John, s. John Worthy:
St. Jas. Clerkenwell, ii. 187.
1806. Married—William Worthy and
Ann Griffiths: St. Geo. Han. Sq. ii. 352.
New York, 1.

Wortley.—Local, 'of Wortley,' two villages, near Leeds and Sheffield.

John de Wortlay, *taillour*, 8 Edw. III:
Freemen of York, i. 28.
Johannes de Wortelay, 1379: P. T.
Yorks. p. 89.
1608-9. Francis Wortley, co. York:
Reg. Univ. Oxf. vol. ii. pt. ii. p. 304.
1621. Thomas Wortlye, co. York: ibid.
p. 395.
1746. Married—Joseph Wortley and
Eliz. Ryall: St. Dionis Backchurch, p. 69.
Sheffield, 4; West Rid. Court Dir., 5;
London, 3; New York, 2.

Worton.—Local, 'of Worton,' several villages so called in co. Oxford.

Adam de Worton, co. Oxf., 1273. A.
Nicholas de Worton, co. Oxf., ibid.
1669. Married—Richard Worton and
Mary Pace: St. Jas. Clerkenwell, p. 167.
London, 2; Philadelphia, 2; Boston
(U.S.), 3.

Wostenholm, Wostinholm, Wostenholme. — Local; v. Wolstenholm. Variants peculiar to Yorkshire.

Sheffield, 7, 1, o; Philadelphia, 5, o, 2.

Wotherspoon; v. Witherspoon.

Wotton; v. Wootton.

Wozencroft; v. Wolstencroft.

Wragg, Wragge, Wraggs.— Bapt. 'the son of Ragg,' q.v. The early form is Ragg, clearly allied to Ragn, 'judgement' (Yonge, ii. 374), the chief element of such names as Ragner, Reginald, Raginbald, Raginmund (Raymond), and once a familiar nick. of Ragner, or Ragnar. For w, cf. Wray and Ray. Wragg has almost ousted Ragg, but the reason is obvious. The name seems peculiar to Yorkshire.

Peter Ragge, co. York, 1273. A.
William Ragge, co. York, ibid.
Johannes Ragge, 1379: P. T. Yorks.
p. 124.
1620. Thomas Wragg and Jane Smith:
Marriage Lic. (London), ii. 91.
1695. Thomas Wragge and Eliz. Houblon: ibid. ii. 316.
West Rid. Court Dir., 12, o, o; London,
11, 1, 1; Philadelphia, 3, o, o; New
York, o, 1, o.

Wray, Ray.—Local, 'at the wray,' i.e. in the corner, from residence therein (v. Wroe). Ray in North Lanc. represents Wray as a surname, although surrounded with numberless spots called Wray, or of which Wray is an element. This word means a corner (as of a field or yard) or secluded place. Mr. Atkinson (N. and Q. 1885, p. 252) finds a case of 'in le Wra' or 'del Wra' translated into 'in angulo' and 'in le herne' (v. Hearn and Nangle), and quotes 'Roger in le Wra' in Whorlton, 'Walter del Wra,' in Marske, and 'Robert in le Wra' in Thorgenby (1301). (Taxatio quindecimoe D'no Regi concessor in Com. Ebor. in parte de Northridinge.) Among the compounded place-names are Dockwray, Whin-wray, Capon-wray, and Thack-wray, all self-explanatory; cf.

Isabel Dockraya, 1569: Lancashire
Wills at Richmond, i. 95.
John Whinwray, of Dalton, 1591: ibid.
i. 307.
Also cf.

Antony Sawraye, of Plumpton, 1623 : ibid. p. 245.
John Blackburne, of Caponwray, 1636 : ibid. p. 36.

In fact, the compounds are many; cf.

Johannes de Somerscalewra, et uxor, 1379 : P. T. Yorks. p. 286.
Johannes de Somerscale, junior, et uxor, 1379 : ibid.

Amongst many instances I select the following :

Thomas de Ireby, in le Wra, in Villa de Bolton : E. & F., co. Cumb., p. 175.
Thomas del Wra, 1379 : P. T. Yorks. p. 242.
1598. Married—Thomas Johnson and Jane Wraie : St. Jas. Clerkenwell, iii. 21.
1616. — Richard Phelke and Eliz. Raye : ibid. iii. 42.
1640. — Edward Wraye and Eliz. How : ibid. p. 72.
London, 19, 32 ; Philadelphia, 51, 59 ; Boston (U.S.), 5, 58.

Wreaks.—Local, 'of Wreaks.' I cannot find the spot. Wreaksend (i. e. the end of the Wreak or Wreaks) is the name of an estate near Broughton-in-Furness.

Alicia de Wrekes, 1379 : P. T. Yorks. p. 236.
1730. Bapt. — Leonard, s. Leonard Wreaks : St. Jas. Clerkenwell, ii. 186.
West Rid. Court Dir., 1 ; Sheffield, 2 ; New York, 2.

Wren, Wrenn.—Nick. 'the wren.' M.E. *wrenne.* Cf. Sparrow, Nightingale, Woodcock, &c.

Alice Wrenn, co. Camb., 1273. A.
William Wrenne, co. Camb., ibid.
Wulfy Wrenne, co. Norf., ibid.
Adam Wrenne, 1379 : P. T. Yorks. p. 235.
1630. Married — Thomas Wrenn to Agnis Merceye : St. Mary Aldermary, p. 17.
1661. Buried—Isaac, s. of Margarett Wrenn : St. Michael, Cornhill, p. 251.
London, 11, 1 ; Philadelphia, 6, 0 ; New York, 8, 3.

Wrench.—? Bapt. 'the son of Wrench' (?). Found without prefix in the Hundred Rolls. It is a common entry, and scattered over many counties. The conclusion that it is baptismal is almost irresistible. One entry below seems to decide the question.

John Wrenche, co. Wilts, 1273. A.
Robert Wrench, co. Oxf., ibid.
Peter Wrench, co. Suff., ibid.
Warin Wrench, co., Bedf. ibid.

Wrennoc fil. Maurice, co. Salop, Hen. III-Edw. I. K.
1572. Buried — Joan, wife of John Wrenche : St. Peter, Cornhill, i. 121.
1577. Bapt. — Fraunces, s. Simon Wrenche : St. Mary Aldermary(London), p. 59.
London, 6 ; Philadelphia, 4 ; New York, 3.

Wright, Wrightson.—Occup. 'the wright,' often latinized in mediaeval rolls into *faber*, a skilled workman in various materials.

'He was a well good wright, a carpenter.' Chaucer, C. T. 616.

v. Cheesewright, Glasswright, Cartwright, Wheelwright, Arkwright, &c.

Robert le Wricte, co. Camb., 1273. A.
Roger le Wricte, co. Camb., ibid.
Margery le Wrytte, co. Camb., ibid.
Adam Wrygson, 1379 : P. T. Yorks. p. 84.
Johannes Redebarn, *wryght*, 1379 : ibid. p. 80.
Robert Wreghtson, 1379 : P. T. Yorks. p. 281.
Ann Wrighteson, co. York. W. 9.
1741. Bapt.—James, s. James Wrightson : St. Geo. Chap. Mayfair, p. 2.
1742. Married—Alex. Wright and Mary Harwood : ibid. p. 22.

Wrightson belongs to an extremely small but interesting class ; cf. Smithson, Hinson, Taylorson, and Herdson.

London, 380, 3 ; Philadelphia, 586, 4.

Wrigley.—Local, 'of Wrigley.' This name seems to have passed over the borders from the W. Rid. Yorks. into South-East Lanc. *via* Saddleworth, in which district it still possesses a strong foothold.

Willelmus Wryglegh, 1379 : P. T. Yorks. p. 173.
John Wrigley, of Millington, 1576 : Wills at Chester, i. 219.
John Wrigley, of Saddleworth, 1620 : ibid.
1635. Margaret Wrigley, of Saddleworth : ibid. ii. 246.
1747. Married—John Spatcher and Eliz. Wrigley : St. Geo. Chap. Mayfair, p. 100.
London, 1 ; Manchester, 18 ; Oldham, 13 ; Philadelphia, 36 ; Boston (U.S.), 2.

Wringrose ; v. Ringrose.

Wringrose : Church Defence Report, 1890-91.
Rugby, 1.

Wroe.—Local, 'at the wroe,' i.e. in the corner, a shelter for cattle, &c. ; v. Wray, Nangle, and Hearn.

'Nere Sendyforth ther is a wroo,
And nere that wro is a welle.'
True Thomas, Jamieson's Pop. Ball. ii. 39.
Thomas del Wro, co. Suff., 1273. A.
Adam del Wroo, 6 Edw. III : Old Homesteads, Crompton (Oldham Guardian).
John del Wroo, 6 Edw. III : ibid.
Johannes del Wroo, 1379 : P. T. Yorks. p. 78.
Matilda in ye Wro, 1379 : ibid. p. 200.
Eva in ye Wro, 1379 : ibid.
Thomas del Wro, 1379 : ibid. p. 138.
1742. John Ellis and Mary Wroe : St. Geo. Chap. Mayfair, p. 28.
1759. Married — John Wroe and Eliz. West : St. Geo. Han. Sq. i. 84.
London, 1 ; Manchester, 9 ; Oldham, 2 ; Philadelphia, 2.

Wulf(e, Wulff ; v. Wolff.

Wulfkettle, Wulfkill.—Bapt. 'the son of Wolf-kettle' (v. Ulfkettle). The abbot of Croyland, 1062-86, was Ulfcytel or Wulfketyl. His predecessors were Osketyl in 992, and Turketyl in 941. All compounds of Kettle (q.v.).

Wulfkill of Lincoln : Freeman's Norman Conq. iv. 217.

Wulfson ; v. Wolfson.

Wurster ; v. Worcester.

Wyard, Wyart.—Bapt. 'the son of Wygard' (Yonge, ii. 410). Now almost entirely lost in Wyatt, q.v.

Lena Wyard, co. Suff., 1273. A.
Adam Wyard, co. Camb., ibid.
Robert Wyard. D.
John Wyard. D.
John Wyhard, co. Worc., Hen. III-Edw. I. K.
Wiard le Corner, Wardrobe Accounts, 3 Edw. III.

The following may be placed here, but probably is a variant of Wyatt, q.v. :

1788. Married—Samuel Jesse and Mary Wyett : St. Geo. Han. Sq. ii. 10.
London, 1, 0 ; New York, 0, 1.

Wyatt, Whyatt, Wiatt.—Bapt. 'the son of Guy,' from dim. Guy-ot, in England Wyot (cf. Warin for Guarin, Warner for Garnier, Wilmot for Guillemot) ; v. Guion.

'Adam, son of Wyot, held an oxgang of land' : De Lacy Inquisition.
Ayote uxor Wyot, co. Salop, 1273. A.
Henry Wyot, co. Camb., ibid.
Wyott le Carpenter, co. Bucks, ibid.
Wyot de Dudelebury, co. Salop, ibid.

Wyot fil. Helias. DD.
Wyot Balistarius. E.
Wiotus de Colebrok, C. R., 8
Edw. II.
Margaret Wyotte, 1379: P. T. Yorks.
p. 66.
Mergeria Wyot, 1379: ibid. p. 134.
1575. John Wyot, co. Devon: Reg.
Univ. Oxf. vol. ii. pt. ii. p. 65.
1576. William Wyatt, co. Devon: ibid.
p. 73.
1581. John Wyatt, or Wiat, co. Worc.:
ibid. p. 103.
1603. Francis Wiat, co. Kent: ibid.
p. 267.

It is clear from the above that
the present form Wyatt is of fairly
recent growth, and will now remain
the recognized orthography for the
coming ages.

London, 55, 0, 0; Philadelphia, 12, 1,
1; Boston (U.S.), 9, 0, 0.

Wybert; v. Wiberd.

Wybroo, Wybrow.—(1)Local,
'of Wigborough.' Great and Little
Wigborough, parishes about seven
miles from Colchester, in co. Essex.
As will be seen from this dictionary,
the suffix -bury or -borough frequently becomes modified into
-brow; cf. Hembrow for Hembury. (2) Bapt.; v. Whybreu.

Richard de Wygebere, co. Soms., 1
Edw. III: Kirby's Quest, p. 242.
Richard de Wigebergh, co. Soms.,
Hen. III–Edw. I. R.
1760. Married—Frederick Wybrow and
Mary Munden: St. Geo. Han. Sq. i. 98.
1802. — George Wybrow and Hannah
Hockley: ibid. ii. 269.
London, 1, 3.

Wyburn.—Bapt. 'the son of
Wyborn.' This surname looks
wonderfully local, but, as suggested
by Mr. Lower (Patr. Brit. p. 391),
the probability is that it is an early
personal name. There is no local
prefix to it in the Hundred Roll
records; cf. Osborne.

Robert Wyborn, co. Oxf., 1273. A.
1575. — Wyburne, co. Kent: Reg.
Univ. Oxf. vol. ii. p. 69.
1805. Married—William Fred Parkes
and Maria Wyborn: St. Geo. Han. Sq.
ii. 338.
London, 2.

Wycliffe, Wickliffe.—Local,
'of Wycliffe,' the parish so called
in North Yorks, 'the white cliff.'
Any one who has seen it will readily

see the origin of the name in the
dull, whitey-grey cliff by which it
stands.

John Whitclive, co. Soms., 1 Edw. III:
Kirby's Quest, p. 138.
Johanna de Wyclayf, 1379: P. T.
Yorks. p. 122.
Willelmus Whyttloffe, 1379: ibid. p. 42.
Johannes Wytloffe, 1379: ibid.

These will probably be immediate
relatives of the Reformer.

Geoffrey Whiteclef, M.P. for Suth-
werk, Close Roll, 4 Ric. II.
1578. Bapt.—Bridget, d. John Wicklif:
St. Mary Aldermary, p. 59.
New York, 0, 1.

**Wykes, Wicks, Wickes,
Wix.**—Local, 'at the wyke,' i.e.
the home, the dwelling; v. Wike.
The suffix s is common to all local
surnames of one syllable; cf. Sykes,
Dykes, Brooks, Styles, &c. '*Wick*,
Anglo-Saxon *wic*, an abode, related
to the Latin *vicus*' (Isaac Taylor,
Words and Places, p. 484). v.
Wix.

William atte Wyk, co. Oxf., 1273. A.
Henry de la Wyke, co. Oxf., ibid.
Roger de la Wyke, co. Sussex, ibid.
William de la Wyk, co. Soms., ibid.

Cf. John de la Wykhend, co.
Bedf., in the same record (A.).
This is analogous to Townend or
Townshend, i.e. 'at the wyke-
end.' The h is intrusive.

Agneta atte Wykes, co. Soms., 1 Edw.
III: Kirby's Quest, p. 82.
1675. Richard Wykes and Mary West:
Marriage Alleg. (Canterbury), p. 242.
1691. Married—Benjamin Tiplady and
Ann Wicks: St. Peter, Cornhill, ii. 59.
London, 7, 20, 2, 1; Oxford (Wicks), 5;
Boston (U.S.), (Wyke), 2; Philadelphia,
1, 5, 1, 1.

Wyld; v. Wild.

Wyldsmith; v. Wildsmith.

**Wylie, Wyllie, Willey,
Wiley.**—(1) Local, 'of Willey,'
parishes in the diocs. of Hereford
and Worc.; (2) 'of Wylye' or
Wyly, a parish in the dioc. of
Salisbury, co. Wilts.

Nicholas de Wyly, co. Wilts, Hen. III–
Edw. I. K.
Richard de Wileye, co. Camb., 1273. A.
Roger de Wylye, co. Bedf., ibid.
Hugh de Wyly, co. Wilts, 20 Edw.
I. R.
1595. Edmund Willie, co. Soms.: Reg.
Univ. Oxf. vol. ii. pt. ii. p. 209.

1614. Thomas Williams and Eliz.
Wylley: Marriage Lic. (Westminster),
p. 22.
1621. Francis Willy, co. Herts: Reg.
Univ. Oxf. vol. ii. pt. ii. p. 402.
1746. Married—William Rogers and
Eliz. Wily: St. Geo. Chap. Mayfair, p. 63.
London, 7, 5, 11, 4; Boston (U.S.), 6,
2, 40, 49; Philadelphia, 29, 0, 2, 116.

**Wyman, Wayman, Way-
men.**—Bapt. 'the son of Wimond.'
The baptismal name lasted till the
Reformation:

Wimond Cary, Patent Roll, 2 Eliz.
pt. xiv.

The London Directory proves its
common use in the past. With
Wyman cf. Osman for Osmund, and
with Wayman cf. Waymark (v.
Wymark).

Reginald fil. Wymundi, Hen. III–Edw.
I. K.
Wymundus de Ralegh, ibid.
Wymund le Lyngedraper, 1273. A.
Wymond Brother, Close Roll, 13
Edw. II.
John Wyman, sup. for B.A., Jan. 27,
1527-8: Reg. Univ. Oxf. i. 150.

Wymond is the name of the
third soldier in the Shearmen's
Play:

'We, howe! Sir Wymond, howe?'
York Mystery Plays, p. 339.

'Goffridus, 1 carucate, which Widmun-
dus holds': Lincolnshire Survey, temp.
1109, p. 14.
Johannes Wymond, 1379: P. T. Yorks.
p. 134.
1582. Married—Peter Wayman and
Ann Bondde: St. Mary Aldermary
(London), p. 7.
1753. — James Wyman and Jane
McAulay: St. Geo. Chap. Mayfair, p. 225.
London, 8, 2, 1; Philadelphia, 14, 4, 0;
Boston (U.S.), 82, 0, 0.

Wymark, Waymark.—Bapt.
'the son of Wymarc.' 'On either
side of his bed stood the two great
chiefs of his realm, Harold the
Earl, and Stigand the Archbishop.
At the bed's head stood the Staller,
Robert the son of Wymarc, a man
of Norman birth'(Death of Eadward,
Freeman, iii. 9). Several Wymarcs
occur in Domesday. 'Wymarck
Piggesteyl, inhabitant of Win-
cholsea, as Edw. I' (Lower, Patr.
Brit.).

Wymarc Mercatrix, co. Hunts, 1273. A.
Wymarc Brown, co. Bedf., ibid.
Wymarca fil. Roberti, Henry III. T.

Wymarca Fraunceys, Henry III. T. Johannes Wymarkson, 1379: P. T. Yorks. p. 271.
Wymerk de Bland, 1379: ibid. p. 246.
John Wymerk, fellow of Merton, 1451: Reg. Univ. Oxf. i. 16.
1551. Buried — Ellis Wimarke: St. Antholin (London), p. 8.
1702. Married—Matthias Wallraven and Mercy Waymarke: St. Dionis Backchurch, p. 51.

With the variant Waymark, cf. Wayman for Wyman, q.v.

London, 2, 1.

Wymer, Wimer.—Bapt. 'the son of Wigmar' (Yonge, ii. 410). In England popularly Wymer or Wimer. Once decidedly a favourite, and incorporated with many local terms. Lord Winmarleigh takes his title from Winmarleigh in co. Lanc., formerly Winnerlie or Wimerlegh; cf. Wymersley in

the same county (v. Baines' Lanc. ii. 535).
Wimer de Eppeworth, Hen. III–Edw. I. K.
Wymer atte Grene, 1273. A.
John Wymer, co. Camb., ibid.
Peter Wymere, co. Camb., ibid.
Wimerus Dapifer, temp. Edw. I: Blomefield's Norfolk (edit. 1805), vol. x. p. 52.
Wymer de Alesham, 1364: ibid. p. 121.
Wyhomarus de Aske: Visitation of Yorkshire, p. 365.
London, 3, 0; Philadelphia, 0, 18.

Wynn, Wynne, Winn, Winne.—Nick. 'Gwynn' (Welsh), white, fair (v. Gwinn); cf. Gwalter and Gwilliam for Walter and William, both Welsh forms.

Oto Gwyn, or Hwyn, 1513: Reg. Univ. Oxf. i. 84.
Robert Wynne, or Gwinne, 1568: ibid. p. 271.
1593-4. Ellis Wynn, or Win, co. Carnarvon: ibid. vol. ii. pt. ii. p. 200.
1605. John Wynn, co. Carnarvon: ibid. p. 286.

1605. Morgan Wynne, or Winn, co. Denbigh: ibid. p. 285.
1719. Buried — Hugh Winn, in the middle isle: St. Peter, Cornhill, ii. 125.
London, 5, 9, 15, 0; Philadelphia, 19, 12, 20, 2; Boston (U.S.), 1, 4, 36, 2.

Wynter; v. Winter.

Wyon.—Bapt. 'the son of Guy,' from the dim. Guion. Just as another dim. Guiot became Wyot and Wyatt, so Guion became Wyon. No connexion with Wynn, q.v.

William Wyonn, co. Soms., 9 Edw. II: Kirby's Quest, p. 174.
1629. Married — Simon Wyan and Joane Charnocke: St. Thomas the Apostle (London), p. 14.
1632. — Robert Wyan and Mary Wentworth: St. Jas. Clerkenwell, iii. 64.
1670. — Oliver Beecher and Sarah Wyan: St. Michael, Cornhill, i. 39.
London, 3.

Wyse; v. Wise.

Y

Yalden.—Local, 'of Yalding,' a parish in co. Kent, near Maidstone. This seems to be the most satisfactory solution.
London, 2.

Yalland; v. Yelland.

Yapp.—? Local, 'at the gap'; v. Gapp; cf. Yates for Gates.
1620. Christopher Baylie and Eliz. Yapp: Marriage Lic. (London), ii. 91.
Richard Yapp, *haberdasher*, 1655: Reg. St. Peter, Cornhill, i. 259.
1792. Married — Francis Yapp and Lydia Shorland: St. Geo. Han. Sq. ii. 71.
London, 3; Philadelphia, 2; Boston (U.S.), 2.

Yarborough, Yarbrough, Yerburgh, Yarboro.—Local, (1) 'of Yarborough' or Yarburgh, a parish in the union of Louth, co. Lincoln; (2) also a hamlet in the parish of Croxton, co. Lincoln.
Gilbert de Yerdeburc, co. Linc., 1273. A.
Robert de Yerdeburch, co. Linc., ibid.

John de Yerbury, co. Soms., 1 Edw. III: Kirby's Quest, p. 227.
1635. Richard Yerbergh and Frances Proctor: Marriage Lic. (London), ii. 223.
1635-6. Rowland Hacker and Eliz. Yerborowe: ibid. p. 225.
1660-1. William Gilbert and Katherine Yarborough: Marriage Alleg. (Canterbury), p. 54.
Crockford, 1, 0, 2, 0; MDB. (Lincoln), 2, 2, 1, 1.

Yard, Yarde.—Local, 'at the yard' (M.E. *yerd*, an enclosure), from residence therein.
John de la Yhurde, co. Southampton, Hen. III–Edw. I. K.
William de la Yerd, C. R., 2 Edw. I.
William atte Yurd, C. R., 17 Edw. III. pt. i.
Hugh atte Yeurd, co. Soms., 1 Edw. III: Kirby's Quest, p. 167.
Walter atte Yurd, co. Soms., 1 Edw. III: ibid. p. 180.
1676. Buried—Mary, d. Thomas Yard: St. Thomas the Apostle (London), p. 141.
1807. Married—William Shergold and Mary Yard: St. Geo. Han. Sq. ii. 366.
London, 0, 2; Crockford, 1, 2; Philadelphia, 16, 0.

Yardley.—Local, 'of Yardley': (1) a parish in co. Hertford; (2) a parish near Birmingham, co. Worcester; (3) two parishes, Yardley - Gobion and Yardley - Hastings, in co. Northampton.
Richard de Yardele, co. Linc., 1273. A.
1592. Bapt.—Eliz., d. William Yardley: St. Jas. Clerkenwell, i. 26.
1612. Married — Richard Hinde and Anne Yardlye: St. Michael, Cornhill, p. 20.
London, 6; Philadelphia, 13.

Yarker.—? Offic. 'a whipperin' (?); v. *yark* in Halliwell.
Johannes Yarkar, 1379: P. T. Yorks. p. 211.
Johannes Yarker, 1379: ibid. p. 199
Manchester, 1; Pennington, near Ulverston, 1.

Yarnold, Yarnall. — Bapt. 'the son of Arnold.' The corruption was an early one. With Yarnall, cf. Arnall for Arnold.

Richard fil. Yarnord, co. Salop, 1273. A. 1783. Married—John Brill and Sarah Yarnould : St. Geo. Han. Sq. i. 351. London, 2, 0 ; Philadelphia, 0, 44.

Yarnton, Yarranton, Yarrington.—Local, ' of Yarington ' or Yarnton, a parish in co. Oxford. The London Directory form is manifestly a corruption of Yarrington as found below:

1626. John Ward and Eliz. Yarrington : Marriage Lic. (London), ii. 168.
— Arthur Croome and Dorothy Yarrington : ibid. p. 178.
London, 0, 1, 0 ; MDB. (co. Worc.), 0, 2, 0 ; Oxford, 1, 0, 0 ; Philadelphia, 0, 0, 1 ; Boston (U.S.), 0, 0, 7.

Yarrow.—Local, ' of Yarrow,' a parish in co. Selkirk.

1573. Buried — Sare Yarrowe, d. of Marques Yarrow, *a stranger* : St. Dionis Backchurch, p. 193.
1766. Married — John Yarrow and Susanna Merredith : St. Geo. Han. Sq. i. 151.
London, 10 ; Philadelphia, 7.

Yate, Yates.—Local, ' at the gate.' M.E. *gate, yate*. Monosyllabic local surnames frequently take a final *s*, perhaps the patronymic, as in Williams, Jennings, &c. ; cf. Stubbs, Styles, Stones, Bridges, Brooks. Hence Yates for Yate. 'Gate (or yate), *porta, foris*' : Prompt. Parv. Other forms of this surname are Yeatts, Yeates, and Yeats, q.v. Evidently the two following names were closely related :

1606. Laurence Yate, of Nether Darwen : Wills at Chester, i. 221.
1608. Laurence Yates, of Blackburn : ibid.

No doubt the family were known indifferently as Yate or Yates.

William atte Yete, co. Soms., 1 Edw. III : Kirby's Quest, p. 91.
Batin atte Yete, co. Soms., 1 Edw. III : ibid. p. 92.
Richard atte Yate, co. Soms., 1 Edw. III : ibid. p. 94.
Johannes atte Yate, 1379 : P. T. Yorks. p. 134.
Adam atte Yate, 1379 : ibid. p. 184.
1725. Married—Thomas Yate and Eliz. Collyer : St. Dionis Backchurch, p. 61.
London, 0, 37 ; Crockford, 2, 8 ; Philadelphia, 0, 47 ; Boston (U.S.), 0, 13.

Yate-, Yatman ; v. Yeatman.

Yaxley.—Local, ' of Yaxley,' parishes in cos. Hunts and Suffolk.
London, 3.

Yea ; v. Yeo.

Yeadon.—Local, ' of Yeadon,' a township in the parish of Guisley, near Leeds, W. Rid. Yorks.

John de Yedon, co. York, 1273. A.
Robert de Yedona, co. York, ibid.
MDB. (West Rid. Yorks), 2.

Yeaman ; v. Yeman.

Yeamans ; v. Yeoman.

Yearling. — Nick. ' the yearling ' ; cf. Tegg and Weatherhog.

John Yerling, co. Soms. 1 Edw. III : Kirby's Quest, p. 238.

Yeates ; v. Yeats.

Yeatman, Yatman.—Occup. ' the gate-man,' one who had care of a road or gate, or more simply one who lived on the road by the gate. *Yate* for gate is still in common use in the North. A farm in Ulverston is called Bowstead Yeats. v. Yates and Yeats.

1603. Bapt.—John, s. John Yateman : St. Jas. Clerkenwell, i. 41.
1758. Married — Thomas Wight and Ann Yeatman : St. Geo. Han. Sq. i. 77.
1775. — David Yetman and Eliz. Tabor : ibid. p. 258.
London, 6, 0 ; Crockford, 3, 1 ; Oxford (Yateman), 1 ; Philadelphia, 6, 0 ; Boston (U.S.), 0, 1.

Yeats, Yeates, Yeatts ; v. Yate and Yeatman.

1753. Married—John Yeats and Ann Davis : St. Geo. Han. Sq. i. 50.
1760. — John Baynom and Ann Yeates : ibid. p. 94.
London, 6, 6, 0 ; Philadelphia, 0, 0, 4.

Yeilding, Yelden.—Local, ' of Yielding,' otherwise ' Yelden,' a parish in co. Bedford, near Higham Ferrers.

1615. James Yeldinge, co. Hants : Reg. Univ. Oxf. vol. ii. pt. ii. p. 344.
London, 1, 1.

Yeldham. — Local, ' of Yeldham,' two parishes (Great and Little Yeldham) near Halsted, co. Essex.

1796. Married—John Smith and Lucy Yeldham : St. Geo. Han. Sq. ii. 148.
1801. — Joseph Yeldom and Letitia Lawrence : ibid. p. 242.
London, 2.

Yelland, Yeolond, Yolland, Yalland. — Local, ' of Yealand.' Yealand Conyers and Yealand

Redmayne are two townships in the parish of Warton, co. Lanc. Yealand Hall still remains ; v. Baines' Hist. Lanc. ii. 604.

John de la Yaldelonde, co. Devon, 1273. A.
William de Yelaund, co. Northumberland : ibid.
Adam de Yelland, warden of the Honor of Lancaster, 13 Hen. III : Baines' Hist. Lanc. ii. 604.
Willelmus de Yeland, 1379 : P. T. Howdenshire, p. 4.
MDB. (co. Devon), 7, 0, 3, 2 ; London, 1, 0, 0, 0 ; Sheffield, 0, 1, 0, 0 ; Philadelphia, 3, 0, 0, 0 ; Boston (U.S.), 1, 0, 0, 0.

Yellowley, Yellowly, Yellowlee.—Local, ' of Yellowley.' I cannot find the spot. It seems to be a North-English surname. Its meaning is simple, viz. ' the golden meadow,' whether from its yellow flowers or yellow clayey soil, I cannot say.

Northumberland Court Dir., 3, 1, 0 ; Crockford, 0, 1, 0 ; New York, 0, 0, 1.

Yelverton. — Local, ' of Yelverton,' a parish in co. Norfolk, about six miles from Norwich.

MDB. (co. Devon), 4 ; London Court Dir., 2 ; New York, 1.

Yeman, Yeaman. — Occup. ' the yeoman ' ; v. Yeoman.

William Yeaman, temp. Eliz. Z.
1805. Married — Thomas Shields and Frances Yeaman : St. Geo. Han. Sq. ii. 319.
London, 2, 0 ; New York, 0, 2.

Yeo, Yea, Yoe, Yohe.—Local, ' at the yew,' from residence thereby, a West-country name' ; cf. Box, Ash, Birch, Plumptre, &c. Lower says, ' An ancient Devonshire family. The Yeo is a small river of that county, a tributary of the Cready, into which it falls near the town of Crediton. C. S. Gilbert derives the name from Tre-yeo, in the parish of Lancells, near Stratton, co. Cornwall.—Hist. Cornw. ii. 335.' In some cases this is probably true.

Geoffrey de la Ya, co. Devon, Hen. III—Edw. I. K.
Nicholas de la Ya, co. Devon, ibid.
William atte Yoo, co. Soms., 1 Edw. III : Kirby's Quest, p. 89.
John atte Yo, co. Soms., 1 Edw. III : ibid. p. 182.

3 H

John atte Yoo, co. Soms., 1 Edw. III : Kirby's Quest, p. 251.

1547. William Yeo and Anne Turton : Marriage Lic. (London), i. 10.

1683. Bapt.—William, son of Richard Yeo : St. Jas. Clerkenwell, i. 302.

1722. Married—Arthur Yeo and Mary Dowling : St. Antholin (London), p. 137.

1739. — George Sikes and Mary Yoe : St. Dionis Backchurch, p. 67.

MDB. (Somerset), 2, 4, 0, 0 ; (Devon), 10, 0, 0, 0 ; London, 6, 0, 0, 0 ; New York, 0, 0, 1, 0 ; Philadelphia, 2, 0, 0, 5 ; Boston (U.S.), 4, 0, 0, 0.

Yeoland ; v. Yelland.

Yeoman, Yeomans, Yeomanson, Yeamans. — Occup. 'the yeoman,' one of some small position or estate. The s in Yeomans is the patronymic ; cf. Jones for Johnson, Roberts for Robertson, &c.

Henricus Yhoman, 1379 : P. T. Yorks. p. 106.

Johannes Yomanne, 1379 : ibid. p. 250. Robert Yomanson. F.

1539-40. Married—John Trevisam and Agnes Yemerson : St. Dionis Backchurch, p. 1.

1582. — Nicholas Speringe and Ellyn Yeomans : St. Michael, Cornhill, p. 13.

Fraunce Yeoman, 1596 : Reg. St. Columb Major, p. 17.

1781. Married—Thomas Yeoman and Hannah Neale : St. Geo. Han. Sq. i. 319.

London, 4, 10, 1, 0 ; Philadelphia, 0, 3, 3, 3 ; New York, 4, 0, 0, 1.

Yeowart ; v. Youard.

Yerburgh. — Local ; v. Yarborough.

Yetts. — Local ; v. Yate.

London, 3.

Yew, Yews ; v. Ewes.

Yewdall, Yeudall, Youdale. —Local, 'of Yewdale.' Probably the Yorkshire Yewdalls are sprung from some small dale of that name in the West or North Riding. There is a Yewdale at the northern end of Coniston Lake, which seems to have originated a surname. As the first instance below is found in the immediate neighbourhood of Skipton, it may be that the Coniston vale is the true parent of all the Yewdalls.

Alicia de Yowdall', 1379 : P. T. Yorks. p. 266.

1600. Geoffrey Yeodell, of Dalton in Furness : Lancashire Wills at Richmond, i. 324.

1616. William Yeodall, or Yewdell, of Cartmel, Furness : ibid.

1727. Bapt.—Timothy, s. of Eliz. Youdall : Reg. St. Mary, Ulverston, p. 315.

1788. Married—Joseph Ambrose and Mary Yewdall : St. Geo. Han. Sq. ii. 1.

West Rid. Court Dir., 7, 0, 0 ; Boston (U.S.), 1, 0, 0 ; Philadelphia, 0, 0, 3 ; New York, 0, 0, 1.

Yewen. — Bapt. 'the son of Jevan' ; v. Jevon.

Yevan de Yhtefelt, co. Salop, 1273. A. Heine fil. Yevan, co. Salop, ibid. London, 2.

Yoe, Yohe ; v. Yeo.

Yohman ; v. Yeoman.

New York, 1.

Yolland.—Local ; v. Yelland.

Yonge, Yung. — Nick. 'the Young,' q. v. M. E. *yong* and *yung*.

John le Yonge, co. Wilts, 1273. A. London, 2, 0 ; Philadelphia, 1, 3 ; Boston (U.S.), 1, 0.

Yool, Youle, Youll, Youell. —Bapt. 'the son of Yule,' a name given to children born on Christmas Day ; cf. Noel, Nowell, Christmas, Midwinter, Pentecost, Pace, Pascal, &c. From Yorkshire the surname seems to have gone northwards, as Youll is fairly familiar to the present directories of Durham and Northumberland.

William Yole, *peiter*, 8 Edw. III : Freemen of York, i. 29.

Isabella Yoll', 1379 : P. T. Yorks. p. 123. Johannes Yoll', 1379 : ibid. Robertus Youle, 1379 : ibid. p. 6. Willelmus Youle, 1379 : ibid.

1620. Thomas Youll and Eliz. Moseley : Marriage Lic. (London), ii. 97.

1778. Married—James Youell and Jane Franks : St. Geo. Han. Sq. i. 288.

London, 2, 3, 0, 0 ; Northumberland Court Dir., 0, 0, 2, 0 ; Philadelphia, 0, 0, 0, 3 ; New York, 0, 2, 0, 0.

Yorath. — Bapt. 'the son of Yerworth,' a Welsh personal name found at an early period.

Iorwerth, alias Gervase, bishop of St. David's, 1215 : Hist. and Ant. St. David's, p. 357.

John Yerworthe, co. Ches., 1581 : Reg. Univ. Oxf. vol. ii. pt. ii. p. 97.

Edward Yerworth, or Yearewarth, co. Ches., 1602 : ibid. p. 256.

1610. Samuel Yaroth, co. Dorset : ibid. p. 319.

1626. John Coles and Catherine Yarath, *widow* : Marriage Lic. (London), ii. 181.

'W. L. Yorath, who followed, was dis-

missed without scoring' ; Glamorganshire v. M.C.C. and ground : South Wales Daily News, Aug. 23, 1889. Swansea, 2 ; Cardiff, 3.

York, Yorke. — Local, ' of York.' Naturally, a name likely to become familiar to our directories.

Gilbert de Ebor', co. York, 1273. A. William de Ebor', co. York, ibid. Agnes de York, 1379 : P. T. Yorks. p. 155.

1557. Married—Guylberte Yorke and Amye Bonde : St. Michael, Cornhill, p. 7.

1659. Buried — Rebecca, d. Richard Yorke, *hosier* : St. Dionis Backchurch, p. 231.

London, 8, 2 ; West Rid. Court Dir., 3, 5 ; Philadelphia, 15, 2 ; Boston (U.S.), 44, 0.

Youard, Youart, Yeowart, Youatt.—Occup. 'the ewe-herd,' recorded as 'yowhird' (v. Ewart); cf. Calvert for Calveherd, Swinnart for Swineherd, &c.

'A ring for my cozen, Mrs. Ellen Yoward' . . . Will of Ric. Tempest, of Bracewell, 1657 : Whitaker's Craven, p. 97.

The live stock at Bolton Abbey (1526) included 'xx oxen, xxvi stotts, ix tuppers, x yowes' : ibid. p. 403.

Matilda Yowhyrd, 1379 : P. T. Yorks. p. 266.

Thomas Yowhyrd, 1379 : ibid. p. 264. Willelmus Euerhyrd, 1379 : ibid. p. 271. Johannes Euerhyrd, 1379 : ibid.

1611. Married—Richard Yeowart and Penelope Parker : Marriage Lic. (London), ii. 6.

1787. — William Jones and Martha Yourd, or Youd : St. Geo. Han. Sq. i. 401.

London, 0, 0, 0, 2 ; MDB. (North Rid. Yorks), 1, 0, 0, 0 ; Liverpool, 0, 0, 1, 0.

Youdale ; v. Yewdall.

Youell, Youll ; v. Yool.

Youmans ; v. Yeomans.

New York, 8.

Young, Younge.—Nick. ' the Young.' M. E. *yong* and *yung*. Probably in many cases the nickname was applied in the sense of *junior*, to distinguish father and son when both bore the same personal name (v. Senior) ; cf. Younger. Over a thousand people bear this name in London alone.

Hugh le Yunge, co. Oxf., 1273. A. Ralph le Younge, co. Staff., ibid. William le Yunge, co. Northumb., 20 Edw. I. R.

1561. Bapt. — John, son of Gregory Yong, *grocer* : St. Peter, Cornhill, i. 10. London, 240, 1 ; Philadelphia, 762, 0 ; Boston (U.S.), 396, 0 ; New York (Younge), 1.

Youngcock. — Nick. ' young cock,' a familiar term of address ; cf. the modern ' Well, old cock, how are you ? ' v. Cocks and Cox.

Willelmus Yongcok, 1379 : P. T. Yorks. p. 29.

Younger, Yunger. — Nick. ' the younger,' i. e. the younger of two bearing the same name ; cf. Elder and Senior.

Edmundus Yonger, 1379 : P. T. Yorks. p. 279.
Walter Yonger, C. R., 1 Hen. V.
1788. Married — John Younger and Eliz. Russell : St. Geo. Han. Sq. ii. 3.
London, 4, 0 ; Philadelphia, 8, 6 ; Boston (U.S.), 1, 0.

Youngerman, Yungerman. —Nick. ' the younger man,' to distinguish the original bearer of the name from the elder man ; v. Elder and Younger.

Boston (U.S.), 2, 0 ; Philadelphia, 0, 1.

Younghusband.—Nick. ' the young husband,' the young householder ; v. Husband ; cf. Youngsmith.

Roger le Younghusband. G.
Thomas le Yonghusband, temp. 1300. M.

Radulphus Yong' Hosband et Agnes uxor ejus, 1379 : P. T. Yorks. p. 164.
Bertram Younghusband : PPP. p. 19.

The following is a natural and yet curious corruption :

Richard Youngsband, vicar of Thorpmarket, co. Norf., 1608 : FF. viii. 174.
1806. Married—William Younghusband and Anne Younghusband : St. Geo. Han. Sq. ii. 341.
London, 4 ; Boston (U.S.), 1.

Youngling, Yungling. — Nick. ' the youngling,' a young man (v. Wyclif, Mark xvi. 5). I cannot find any instances in modern English directories. It seems to be one of many names which have died out in the old country and survived in the United States.

John Yonglyng, C. R., 9 Hen. IV.
Richard Yonglyng, C. R., 1 Hen. V.
New York, 1, 1 ; Philadelphia, 0, 1.

Youngman, Yungman. — Nick. ' the young man ' ; cf. Younghusband. An East Anglian surname, common in Norfolk and Suffolk.

William Yungman, co. Linc., 20 Edw. I. R.
Nicholas Youngman, 1365, co. Norf. : FF. i. 298.
1787. Married—John Youngman and Sarah Vanryne : St. Geo. Han. Sq. i. 401.

London, 8, 0 ; MDB. (Norfolk), 8, 0 ; (Suffolk), 13, 0 ; Philadelphia, 0, 1 ; New York, 0, 1 ; Boston (U.S.), 1, 0.

Youngmay.—Nickname, ' the young may,' i. e. the growing boy ; v. May (1).

Martin le Yungemey, co. Sussex, 1273. A.

Youngsmith. — Nick. ' the young smith,' as distinguished from the old. The surname ought to be extant, judging by the number of early entries, but I have not discovered it. It is found in the sixteenth century.

Johannes Yong', *smyth*, 1379 : P. T. Yorks. p. 165.
Johannes Yongsmyth, 1379. Ibid. p. 24.
John Yongsmith, temp. Eliz. F.
Bartholomew Youngsmithe, co. York. W. 16.
Bertram Youngsmith, 1502 : PPP. p. 10.

Youngson.—Nick. ' the son of Young ' (q.v.), or probably the younger as distinguished from the elder son ; v. Younger.

MDB. (East Rid. Yorks), 1.

Yung ; v. Younge.

Yunger ; v. Younger.

Yungerman ; v. Youngerman.

Yungling ; v. Youngling.

Yungman ; Youngman.

Z

Zachary.—Bapt. ' the son of Zachary,' the English form of Zachariah (v. Yonge, i. 124).

1586. Bapt.—Isabell, d. Thomas Zachary : St. Jas. Clerkenwell, i. 18.
London, 1 ; Crockford, 1.

Zeal, Zeall. — Local. Mr. Lower says, ' of Zeal, a parish in Devonshire, usually called Zeal-Monachorum.' There is also South Zeal in the same county, and Zeals is a tithing in co. Wilts. I find no

early instance of this surname, and think it is more probably a variant of Seal, q.v. ; and cf. Zouch and Such.

London, 0, 1.

Zealey.—? Nick. I find no traces of this name in early records, so conclude that it is a corruption of Seeley, q.v.

1749. Married — Simon Zealey and Abigail Churchill : St. Geo. Chap. Mayfair, p. 129.
London, 1.

Zouch.—Local, ' de la Zouch.' ' Zuches = stumps of trees ' : Halliwell. v. Such.

Ivo de la Zusch, co. Devon, 1273. A.
Ivo de la Zoche, ibid.
Alan de la Zouche, co. Wilts, Hen. III–Edw. I. K.
Guy de la Zouch, co. Sutherland, 20 Edw. I. R.
Olive de la Zouche, co. Hants, ibid.
1580. Married — Robert Arras and Elizabeth Zouche : St. Jas. Clerkenwell, iii. 8.
1641. William Zouch and Anne Bowling : Marriage Lic. (London), ii. 261.

ADDENDA ET CORRIGENDA

Abbey, Abbee, Abbe.—v. p. 37. The two local instances from Freemen of York were added after the publication of that work in 1897. The article remains as originally written, when the Author had only found the local instance in the Lay Subsidy (Rylands).

Bannerman.—Offic. 'the bannerman,'the ensign bearer. Though this name, being Scotch, has no place of right in this dictionary, it is interesting as being the equivalent of Penniger, q.v. ; also v. Mr. Lower's article in Patr. Brit. p. 17.

Manchester, 1 ; Philadelphia, 1.

Bramble.—Local, 'of Bramble.' I cannot find the place. It is probably some small spot in co. Kent.

Thomas de Bremble, co. Kent, 1273. A.
Helena Bramble, co. Kent, 13 Edw. IV, pt. ii.
1606-7. Richard Bramble (Dorset): Reg. Univ. Oxf. vol. ii. pt. ii. p. 293.
1623. John Bramble, 'Maior of Poole,' co. Dorset : Visitation of Dorsetshire, p. 1.
London, 3 ; Penzance, 1 ; Philadelphia, 10.

Brearley, Brierley, Brierly.—Local, 'of Brierley,' a township in the parish of Felkirk, West Riding, co. York ; v. Brear.

John de Brerelay, 13 Ric. II : Freemen of York, i. 89.
1782. Married—John Croker and Mary Brearley : St. Geo. Chap. Mayfair, p. 234.
London, 0, 4, 2 ; West Rid. Court Dir., 4, 8, 1.

Brooker, Brucker. — Local, 'the brooker,' one who lived by the brook (M.E. *brok* and *broke*, Mayhew and Skeat). Cf. Bridger, and v. next article. For instances, v. Broker, to which this should be added as an additional meaning.

Oxford, 3, 2.

Brookman.—Local,'the brookman,' one who lived by the brook ; cf. Bridgman, Pullman, &c.

John Brokeman. C.
1592. Francis Mason and Anne Brokeman : Marriage Lic. (London), i. 205.
1601. Edward Cooke and Katherine Brookeman : ibid. p. 264.
London, 2 ; Philadelphia, 1.

Butts.—Local, 'at the butts,' from residence thereby. Mr. Lower says,'Butts, the marks for archery. In old times all corporate towns, and most parishes, had a provision for this sport, and numerous fields and closes where the long bow was exercised are still called 'The Butts'(Patr. Brit. p. 48). v. Sowerbutts.

1563. Edmund Buttes and Thomasine Bedell : Marriage Lic. (London), i. 26.
1619. Richard Butts, co. Hereford : Reg. Univ. Oxf. vol. ii. pt. ii. p. 379.
London, 3 ; Boston (U.S.), 13.

Cambden, Camden.—Local, 'of Campden': (1) Chipping Campden ; (2) Broad Campden, a parish and a hamlet in co. Glouc.

Hugh de Campeden, co. Glouc., 1273. A.
John de Campeden, co. Northampt., ibid.
1570. William Camden : Reg. Univ. Oxf. i. 279.
1573. William Campden : ibid. vol. ii. pt. iii. p. 40.
London, 4, 1 ; Philadelphia, 0, 10.

Crawley.—Local, 'of Crawley.' Parishes and townships bear this name in cos. Northumb., Hants, and Sussex. There is also Crawley, a hamlet in co. Oxf., and North Crawley in co. Bedford.

Hugh de Craule, co. Bedford, 1273. A.
Margaret de Craule, co. Oxf., ibid.
Alan de Craule, co. Oxf., 20 Edw. I. R.
1659. Married—Thomas Crawley and Amye powell (sic) : St. Peter, Cornhill, p. 261.
London, 24 ; Boston (U.S.), 11.

Glanfield, Glanvill, Glanville.—Local, 'de Glanville.' Mr. Lower says, 'A place in the arrondissement of Pont l'Evéque in Normandy.' The change to Glanfield was natural ; cf. Merrifield for

Merivale. Mr. Lower, quoting Shirley's Noble and Gentle Men, says, 'Ranulf de Glanville entered England with the Conqueror'(Patr. Brit. p. 130).

Ranulf de Glanvile, co. Camb., 1273. A.
Reginald de Glanvil, co. Oxf., ibid.
1724. Bapt. — Mary, d. Samuel and Mary Glanvil : Reg. St. Columb Major, p. 97.
1727. — Eliz., d. Samuell and Mary Glanfield : ibid.

Evidently the parents were the same in the last two entries.

London, 4, 4, 8 ; Oxford, 1, 0, 3 ; Philadelphia, 0, 0, 1.

Lovegrove. — Local, 'of the grove,' or collection of trees, belonging to Love. v. Love and Grove.

1616. Buried — John, s. John Lovegrove : St. Jas. Clerkenwell, iv. 136.
1621. John Lovegroave and Agnes Whitmill : Marriage Lic. London, ii. 102.
London, 10 ; Oxford, 4 ; Philadelphia, 4.

Lyman, Lynam.—Local, (1) 'of Lyneham,' a chapelry near Burford, co. Oxf.; (2) 'of Lineham,' a parish in co. Wilts. The interchange of letters is common ; cf. Adnam and Adman for Addingham ; Swetnam and Swetman for Swetenham ; Debnam and Deadman for Debenham, &c.

William de Linham, co. Oxf., 1273. A.
William de Linham, co. Notts, ibid.

The following entries refer to the same individual :

1613. Richard Lynam (Queen's): Reg. Univ. Oxf. vol. ii. pt. ii. p. 331.
1616-7. Richard Lyman (Liman, Lynam) (Queen's): ibid. pt. iii. p. 353.
London, 1, 0 ; Oxford, 0, 3 ; Philadelphia, 13, 8.

Lyndhurst.—Local, 'of Lyndhurst,' a parish in the New Forest, co. Hants.

Henry de Lindherste, co. Hants, 1273. A.

Maydwell.—Local, 'of Maidwell,' a parish in co. Northampton. v. Maidwell.

Simon de Maydewell, co. Northampt., 1273. A.
Henry de Maydewelle, co. Oxf., ibid.
London, 2.

Ovenell, Overnell. — Local, 'of Ovenell.' I cannot find the spot, but the following entry seems to refer to this name :

Hugh de Ovonill, co. Salop, 20 Edw. I. R.
London, 0, 1 ; Oxford, 3, 0.

Penington, Pennington. — Local, 'of Pennington,' (1) a parish in the union of Ulverston, in the North Division of co. Lanc. ; (2) a township in the parish of Leigh, in the South Division of the same county ; (3) a hamlet in co. Hants. v. Pinnington. The name seems to have arisen in the northern county.

Alan de Penyngton, co. Lanc., 20 Edw. I. R.
Mabel Penington, of Ulverston, 1588 : Lancashire Wills at Richmond, i. 213.
John Pennington, of Ulverston : ibid. p. 214.
Myles Penyngton, of Hauxhead, 1611 : ibid.
1548. Bapt.—John Pennington : Reg. St. Mary, Ulverston, i. 6.
—— elin pennington (sic), ibid.
1803. Bapt. — William, s. George Pennington : ibid. ii. 628.

London, 0, 7 ; Ulverston, 0, 5 ; Philadelphia, 2, 47.

Salvage.—Nick. ; v. Savage, of which it is a variant.

London, 1.

Twelvetrees.—Local, 'at the twelve trees,' from residence by a clump of trees ; cf. Fiveash and Snook.

London, 1.

Watmough. — I have come across an interesting entry corroborative of the article on Watmough, q.v. ; also v. Barnmaw and *cock*, p. 25.

Cok ffenwick, the Maugh of Willy Charleton : Patent Roll, 14 Hen. VII.